# The Annals of the World

## James Ussher

# The Annals of the World

Revised and updated by
Larry and Marion Pierce

PAPERBACK
First printing: November 2006
Second printing: August 2007

CASEBOUND
First printing: October 2003; Second printing: December 2003; Third printing: February 2004; Fourth printing: December 2004; Fifth printing: August 2005; Sixth printing: November 2006; Seventh printing: August 2007

ISBN-13: 978-0-89051-510-5
ISBN-10: 089051-510-7
Library of Congress Number: 2006937549

All British spellings are based upon information from the *Oxford English Dictionary*, second edition, 1994, on CD-ROM.

Special thanks to Monica Cook, Glen Averil, Mike Matthews, and Brigitte Stoll for their contribution in proofreading the final manuscript.

**Printed in the United States of America**

For information regarding interviews, please contact
the publicity department at (870) 438-5288.

*This revised work is dedicated to Robert Huschka who enthusiastically taught me
ancient history, and Walter Eifert who taught me Latin for many years with a twinkle in his eye.*

Master
Books

# Contents

# Editor's Preface

Historian, Literary Critic, Theologian,
Among saints — most scholarly.
Among scholars — most saintly,

— extract from Ussher's epitaph (translated)

You hold in your hands the first major English revision that has been done of Rev. Archbishop Ussher's *Annals of the World* since it was published in 1658—two years after his death. In January of 1997, Answers in Genesis obtained photocopies of the 1650–1654 Latin copy and the 1658 English copy for us to examine. Ussher is ridiculed by *sciolists*. {*OED—Sci' olist: superficial pretender to knowledge. The first "i" is long.*} and we suggested it might be good to republish this old classic since very few people have actually seen what he wrote.

We set to work. My wife, Marion, typed in the whole English document—it was impossible to scan—and I started to edit it. An early review prompted the classic comment, *I cannot understand this old English!* The horrible thought crossed my mind that the whole document would have to be extensively revised. That was done. We updated the English and checked and updated over ten thousand footnotes against the Loeb Classical Library. We carefully checked the text against the most ancient sources and Ussher's Latin copy to verify the accuracy of what was being said. My wife read it aloud three times while we both amended the English. Over four years later, we finished the task and turned the work over to the publisher for the final proof-reading.

The format used for the footnoting is explained in the bibliography at the end of this work. In most history books, it is very difficult to tell where the material came from. Separating the editorials from the facts would challenge even Solomon. This is not true of Ussher's work. It contains more than twelve thousand footnotes from secular sources and over two thousand quotes from the Bible or the Apocrypha. There is very little editorialising and most editorial comments come from the original writers themselves. We were able to verify about 85 percent of the footnotes pertaining to secular history. The documents for the remaining footnotes are so rare, we did not pursue them.

Julian dates are used throughout the document. Julian dates are not necessarily the same as dates on the Gregorian calendar that we use today. The Julian calendar does not drop three days every four hundred years, so the seasons drift. This explains why Ussher has the autumnal equinox for 4004 BC on October 23, not September 21. Using the Julian calendar, October 23 was the correct date. However, on the Gregorian calendar the date was September 21, as we would normally expect. As we get closer to January 1, 45 BC when Julius Caesar reformed the calendar, the Julian and Gregorian dates converge. Astronomers use Julian dates today for dating astronomical events. They cite the actual number of the day from the start of the Julian Period (JP) in 4713 BC. The start of the millennium, January 1, 2001, would be day 2452142 or January 1, 6714 JP. Historians date all pre-Christian events using the Julian scale extended backward theoretically, as if it had been in use throughout.

We have added paragraph numbers to make it easier to cite references from this work. The original index was done by year and we changed it to use paragraph numbers instead. Some years, like 44 BC, are quite voluminous and we are sure you would rather have the paragraph number.

We have included the page numbers from the original 1654 Latin document. The start of page 34 in the Latin edition would be indicated as *[L34]*. Page numbers for the second Latin volume are prefixed with a "K." Likewise, the start of page 29 in the original 1658 English edition would be indicated as *[E29]*. Many of the older writers referred to the page numbers of Ussher's work and we thought it best to include them. We placed these markers as discretely as possible at the end of a sentence or a paragraph. They should be accurate to within one or two sentences of the actual page break.

Some may question the importance of including what we might deem as fables today in the early historical portions of the document. This is to document the approximate dates for the original events that spawned the legends and that these events are well within the biblical time frame. There is likely a kernel of truth in them just as there are in the aborigines' dream-time stories. Ussher dispassionately reports what others have written— usually without editorial comment. This is a totally different approach to history than is customary today.

The Greek and Hebrew fonts in the original documents were almost impossible to read. We did the best we could but there are definitely some errors in the Greek and Hebrew texts.

The following summarises the major changes made to the original work.

1) The language was updated to conform to modern usage.

2) Paragraph numbers were added to the main body of the document.

3) A bibliography of most of the authors Ussher referred to was compiled. Where possible, references were made to the Loeb Classical Library.

4) The Loeb Classical Library was used to update over ten thousand footnotes. The text of the original was compared with the Loeb text for accuracy. The modern critical text of the ancient writers was used to amend the original document.

5) Occasionally, editorial notes are inserted in the document. These usually denote textual problems between the current Loeb text and the text Ussher used. Such notes are usually in round brackets and are denoted "Editor." Wherever you find the pronouns *I* or *we* in the document, it is Ussher's direct comments to the reader. He does this over four hundred times in this book.

6) The index was totally reworked to use paragraph numbers and many new entries were added to the index.

7) Any obvious errors in the 1658 English edition or the 1654 Latin edition were corrected. These were mainly arithmetical errors.

8) Several articles on chronology were included as appendices. These were things that we gleaned as we did the work.

9) Historical maps were added to the document.

10) The headings at the top of each page were added throughout.

A special thanks to my wife, Marion, who typed the original document and helped proof-read and rewrite the document. Bruce Szwast has done an absolutely superb job on the Ussher CD that accompanies this book.

The works of the original historians contained many human interest stories and even some humour to keep your interest. Enjoy reading ancient history as you never have before. Let Ussher, known by his contemporaries as the *Leviathan of Learning*, be your expert guide!

— Larry Pierce

*Larry and Marion Pierce have lived in the village of Winterbourne in Ontario, Canada, since 1975 when they were married. Larry did his undergraduate and graduate work at the University of Waterloo, where he received his degrees in mathematics. He retired in 1991 to devote more time to his work with the Online Bible program, which he developed and manages. Having a good helpmate plus his experience in Latin, digitizing old biblical commentaries, and in computer programming helped make this republication of Ussher's greatest work possible.*

# The Epistle to the Reader

"For who does not know history's first law to be that an author must not dare to tell anything but the truth? And its second that he must be bold to tell the whole truth? That there must be no suggestion of partiality anywhere in his writings? Nor of malice?" {*Cicero, De Oratore, l. 2. c. 15. 3:243,254}

Censorinus dedicated the book, *De Die Natali*, to Quintus Caerellius on his birthday in 238 AD. The first part dealt with human life and its origins and the second part dealt with time and its divisions. In his preface he wrote:

"If the origin of the world had been known to man, I would have started there." {Censorinus, De Die Natali, l. 1. c. 20.}

A little later, speaking of this time:

"Whether time had a beginning or whether it always was, the exact number of years cannot be known." {Censorinus, De Die Natali, l. 1. c. 21.}

Therefore Ptolemy, from his book *Astronomical Calculations*, concerning the creation and history of the world, stated that this is beyond the knowledge of man:

"To find the details of the history of the whole world or such an immense period of time, I think is beyond us who desire to learn and know the truth." {Ptolemy, Great Syntaxis, l. 3.}

Julius Maternus Firmicus, in his discourse on birthdays, stated concerning the creation of the world (as received from Aesculapius and Anubis):

"That was not the creation of the world. Nor, indeed, did the world have any certain day for its beginning. Nor was there anything existing at the time when the world was formed by the wisdom of the divine understanding and provident deity. Nor could man in his human frailty so far extend himself, that he could easily conceive or unfold the world's origin." {Julius Maternus Firmicus, l. 3. c. 2.}

It is not strange that the heathen, who are totally ignorant of the Holy Bible, should despair of ever attaining to the knowledge of the world's beginnings. Even among Christians, that most renowned chronographer Dionysius Petavius, when asked his opinion concerning the creation of the world and the number of years from creation down to us, made this disclaimer:

"The number of years from the beginning of the world to our time cannot be known, nor in any way found out, without divine revelation." {Petavius, De Doctrina Temporum, l. 9. c. 2.}

Philastrius Brixiensis agreed with him and called it heresy:—

"To know the number of the years from the creation of the world is uncertain and men do not know the time of it." {Philastrius, De Heres., c. 6. p. 63.}

Lactantius Firmianus made this bold assertion:

"We who are trained by the Holy Scriptures in the knowledge of truth, do know both the beginning and the end of the world." {*Lactantius, Divine Institutions, l. 7. c. 14. 7:211}

Bold, because whatever may have happened in the past {Ac 1:7 Mt 24:36}, we are taught that the Father has reserved the knowledge of things future to himself. Nor is there any mortal to whom the whole period of time is known. Even the son of Sirach is thought to say:

"Who can number the sands of the sea, and the drops of rain and the days of eternity?" {Apc Sir 1:2}

When Nicolaus Lyranus was thought to have been speaking of history (as others interpret it here and in his book {*Lyranus, Days of Eternity, c. 18. s. 11.*}), he drew this erroneous conclusion: he thought that from the beginning of the world, time was never determined *certainly* and *precisely* by any man.

The first Christian writer (that I have known of) who attempted to calculate the age of the world from the Holy Bible was Theophilus, Bishop of Antioch. Concerning this whole account, he stated:

"All times and years are made known to those who are willing to obey the truth." {*Theophilus, Ad Autolycum, l. 3. c. 26. 2:119*}

But concerning the exactness of this calculation he later stated:

"And haply we may not be able to give an exact account of every year, because in the Holy Scriptures there is no mention of the precise number of months and days."

The Scriptures normally note only entire years and not the days and months in each instance. Hence, summing the years may give an inaccurate total because the partial years were not included.

Grant this one thing (and this is a most reasonable assumption), that the holy writers had this very purpose in mind when recording the years of the world in their various places with such diligence. They sought to reveal to us the history of the world that otherwise no one could know. This, I say, being granted, we affirm that the Holy Spirit has anticipated this doubt. He has started and ended each of the periods on which a chronological reckoning of time depends, and added the very month and day. For example, the Israelites left Egypt on the fifteenth day of the first month. {*Nu 33:3*} In the 480th year after their exodus, in the second month on the second day, Solomon began to build the temple. {*1Ki 6:1*} The months and days given for the start and end of the period show that eleven months and fourteen days are to be taken away. The period is not 480 whole years, but only 479 years and 16 days. {*2Ch 3:2*}

David Paraeus stated:

"Those who promise to give us an exact astronomical table of time, from the creation to Christ, seem to me more worthy of encouragement than praise, in that they attempt a thing beyond human capacity."

He was among the most recent of our writers who calculated the number of the years to Christ's time from the Holy Scriptures. Therefore, he abandoned astronomical calculations and used the civil time of the Hebrews, Egyptians and Persians as the only way to do this accurately.

But if I have any understanding in this matter, it does not matter what rule we use to measure the passing of time, as long as it starts and ends with a certain number of days. Anyone could, with David Paraeus, by some equal measure of years, define the time between the foundation of the world and Christ's time. Also it would be very easy without the help of any astronomical table, to set down how many years happened during that interval. The passing of time in any civil year from a season to the same season again is simply a natural astronomical or tropical year.

Anyone can do this who is well versed in the knowledge of sacred and secular history, of astronomical calculations and of the old Hebrew calendar. If he should apply himself to these difficult studies, it is not impossible for him to determine not only the number of years but even the days from the creation of the world. Using backward calculations, Basil the Great told us we may determine the first day of the world:

"You may indeed learn the very time when the foundation of the world was laid. If you return from this present time to former ages, you may endeavour studiously to determine the day of the world's origin. Hence you will find when time began." {*Basil, Hexaemeron, Homily 1. c. 6. 8:55*}

Historically, various countries have used different methods of calculating time and years. It is necessary that some common and known standard be used to which these may be reconciled. The Julian years and months are most suitable to the common collation of times. These start on midnight, January 1, AD. Using three cycles, every year is uniquely identified. These cycles are:

a) the Roman indiction[1] of fifteen years,

b) the cycle of the moon,[2] or golden number of nineteen years

c) the solar cycle[3] (the index of Sunday or Pascal days) of twenty-eight years.

It is known that the year 1650 AD is identified with the numbers of three in the Roman indiction, seventeen in the lunar cycle and seven in the solar cycle. (I do not say that of the year of the birth of Christ, which is still disputed among the learned.)

Since our Christian period comes long after the creation of the world, counting years backwards is difficult and error prone. There is a better way. Modern chronologers have extrapolated these three cycles backwards to the year when all the cycles would start at one on the 1st of January. This creates an artificial epoch 7980 years long based on the product of the three cycles multiplied together. *{The 19 year lunar cycle times 28 year solar cycle times 15 year indiction cycle equals 7980 years}*

I think this was first noted by Robert Lotharing, Bishop of Hereford, in England. Five hundred years later Joseph Scaliger adapted this to chronological use and called it by the name of the Julian Period (after his father), because it extended the cycle of Julian years back in time and forward. The cycle started at noon, January 1, 4713 BC, which is a leap year. Here the lunar cycle is one, the solar cycle is one and the indiction cycle is also one. Hence 1 AD is the year 4714 of the Julian period and is identified by the Roman indiction of four, lunar cycle of two and the solar cycle of ten.

Moreover, we find that the years of our forefathers, the years of the ancient Egyptians and Hebrews, were the same length as the Julian year. It consisted of twelve months containing thirty days each. (It cannot be proven that the Hebrews used lunar months before the Babylonian captivity.) Five days were added after the twelfth month each year. Every four years, six days were added after the twelfth month. *{*Diod. Sic., l. 1. c. 50. s. 2. 1:177}* *{*Strabo, l. 17. c. 1. s. 46. 8:125}* *{*Strabo, l. 17. c. 1. s. 29. 8:85}* *{*Herodotus, l. 2. c. 4. 1:279}* *{Ge 7:11,24 8:3-5,13,14}* I have noted the continual passing of these years as recorded in the Bible. Hence the end of Nebuchadnezzar's reign and the beginning of his son Evilmerodach's reign was in the 3442nd year of the world. (3442 AM) By collation of Chaldean history and the astronomical cannon it was in the 185th year of Nabonassar. This was 562 BC or 4152 JP (Julian Period). From this I deduced that the creation of the world happened in the beginning of the autumn of 710 JP or 4004 BC.[4] Using astronomical tables, I determined the first Sunday after the autumnal equinox for the year 710 JP or 4004 BC was October 23 of that year. I ignored the stopping of the sun in the days of Joshua and the going back of it in the days of Hezekiah. *{See note on 2553c AM. <<319>>}* *{See note on 3291c AM. <<644>>}* From thence I concluded that the preceding evening of October 23 marks the first day of creation and the start of time.

I ignored the difficulties raised by chronologers, who are occupied by the love of contention, as Basil noted. Hence, I deduce that the time from the creation until midnight, January 1, 1 AD was 4003 years, seventy days and six hours. Also, based on the death of Herod the Great, I concluded that the birth of our Saviour was four full years before January 1, 1 AD. According to our calculations, the building of Solomon's temple was finished in the 3000th year of the world. In the 4000th year of the world, Mary gave birth to Christ *{Lu 2:6}* (of whom the temple was a type). *{Joh 2:21}* Hence, Christ was born in the fall of 5 BC not 1 AD.[5]

But these things (which I note at the present), God willing, shall be more fully explained in our *Sacred Chronology*. This I intend to write with a *Treatise of the Primitive Years* and the *Calendar of the Ancient Hebrews*. In the meantime I thought it best to publish the *Annals of the Old Testament*. Based on this foundation, I included a chronicle of all the foreign affairs that happened in Asia and Egypt. These include events before the beginning of the Olympiads and matters relating to Greece and Rome and other areas.

In doing the sacred history, I have followed the translation of Janius and Tremellius, using their Hebraisms and the information from their work. In doing the secular history, I have noted the writings of their ancient authors or the best translation of their works from the Greek. In particular I used James Dalechamp's translation of Athenaeus. Although in noting the chapters, I followed the edition of Natalis Comitis. (The modern edition of

Athenaeus has deleted the chapters. Editor.) From these I have written this history, using material from Codomanes, Capellus, Emmias, Pezelius, Eberus, Salianus or any other chronologer which I had. However, I always referred to the original authors and did most of my work directly from their writings and not from second-hand sources. Since my purpose was to create an accurate chronology, I may not have followed the exact wording of these writers in every case, but I have preserved the intent of their writings.

Of the many historians who lived before Julius Caesar, the passing of time leaves only four of note—Herodotus, Thucydides, Xenophon and Polybius. The last one is poor and inaccurate in many places. These I esteemed the most authentic for their antiquity. I used them to correct the frequent errors in the chronology of Diodorus Siculus. However, in the matters that related to Alexander the Great, they are silent. For this period, I also followed not only Diodorus but Curtius and Arrian to try to determine the history of that period.

I used the following abbreviations:

AD - Years from the start of the Christian era.

AM - Years of the world from creation.

BC - Years before the Christian era.

JP - Julian Year starting at January 1, 4713 BC.

NK - Northern Kingdom of Israel.

SK - Southern Kingdom of Israel.

After the year denoted by AM, one of four letters may be affixed.

a - Autumn

b - Winter

c - Spring

d - Summer

Other things the prudent reader will figure out for himself. I wish you the enjoyment of these endeavours and bid you farewell. *London, the 13th of the Calends of July (June 19), according to the Julian period, in the 1650th year of the Christian era, from the true nativity of our Lord and Saviour, the 1654th year.*

# Explanatory Notes by the Editor

**1) Dictionary Definition of the *Roman Indiction.***

In chronology, a cycle of fifteen years instituted by Constantine the Great; originally, a period of taxation. Constantine, having reduced the time which the Romans were obliged to serve in the army to fifteen years, imposed a tax or tribute at the end of the term to pay the troops who were discharged. This practice introduced the keeping of accounts by this period. However as it is said, in honour of the great victory of Constantine over Mezentius, Sept. 24, 312 AD, by which Christianity was more firmly established, the council of Nice ordained that accounts of years should no more be kept by Olympiads, but that the *indiction* should be used as the point from which to reckon the date of the years. This was begun January 1, 313 AD. *Johnson Encyclopaedia*

> Taken from the definition of *Indiction* in *Noah Webster's First Edition of an American Dictionary of the English Language*, Republished 1989, by the *Foundation for American Christian Education*, California. (The dictionary was first published in 1828.)

**2) Lunar Cycle**

The lunar cycle consists of nineteen years or 235 complete orbits of the moon around the earth. This differs from nineteen years of 365.25 days each, by approximately one and a half hours. On the first year of the next cycle of nineteen years, the new moon would again be on the first of January.

**3) Solar Cycle**

The solar cycle consists of twenty-eight years. At the start of each new cycle every day and month of the year would correspond exactly to the days and months of the first year of the previous cycle.

**4) Time of Creation**

Since the Jews used to start their year in the autumn, this is not an unreasonable assumption. Also the biblical pattern of *evening and morning* seems to apply to years as well as days. First the dark months of autumn and winter and then the bright months of spring and summer.

**5) The Christian Era**

The following is quoted from *The Wonders of Bible Chronology.*

> The Christian Era should properly begin with the year Christ was born; and in devising it, the intention was to have it begin with that year. By the *Christian Era* is meant the system upon which calendars are constructed and by which historical events are now dated in practically all the civilised world. But the originator of the system made a miscalculation as to the year (in the calendar then in use) in which Christ was born, as the result of which the year 1 AD was fixed four years too late. In other words, the Lord Jesus was four years old in the year 1 AD.

> The mistake came about in this way: The Christian Era (that is the scheme of dates beginning 1 AD) was not devised until 532 AD. Its inventor, or contriver, was a monk named Dionysius Exiguus. At that time the system of dates in common use began from the era of the Emperor Diocletian, 284 AD. Exiguus was not willing to connect his system of dates with the name of that infamous tyrant and persecutor. Therefore, he conceived the idea of connecting his system with and dating all its events from the Incarnation of Jesus Christ. His reason for wishing to do this was, as he wrote to Bishop Petronius, *to the end that the commencement of our hope might be better known to us and that the cause of man's restoration, namely, our Redeemer's passion, might appear with clearer evidence.*

> (Taken from: *The Wonders of Bible Chronology*, Page 84, 85, Philip Mauro, first published 1922, Reprinted by Reiner Publications, Swengel, Pennsylvania.)

The rest of the explanation given in this book just cited is incorrect. Since we do not have the data Dionysius used in his calculations, we do not know how he made his mistake. Some have conjectured that Tiberius was made a partner in the empire four years before Augustus died. However, from Ussher's description of the year 12 AD we know Tiberius was a partner only two years (not four years) before the death of Augustus. (See paragraph 6198 of this work.) We know for certain that Jesus must have been born before the death of Herod. We can calculate the year of the death of Herod in two ways: from the events that occurred before he died and from the events that happened after he died. Using the events that happened before Herod died is the most accurate way to do it and is confirmed by the events that happened after his death.

According to paragraph 6082 in this work, Herod held the kingdom for thirty-four years after having killed Antigonus and thirty-seven years from the time that he was declared king by the Romans. {*Josephus, Antiq., l. 17. c. 8. s. 1. (191) 8:459} He started to reign after the death of Antigonus in 37 BC because 31 BC was the seventh year of his reign in which the battle of Actium was fought. {*Josephus, War, l. 1. c. 19. s. 2. (370) 2:173,175} Hence, 4 BC would be the last year of his thirty-four year reign.

This is partially confirmed astronomically, since Josephus records that a total eclipse of the moon happened before the Passover in the year that Herod died. There was an eclipse on March 13, 4 BC. Interestingly, this is the only eclipse recorded in all of Josephus' writings.

### Philip Melanchthon: His Account Concerning Philip Prince Palatine, to Rhenus.

I have often heard Capino relate the following when Dalburgius, the Bishop of the Vangions, Rudolphus Agricola and myself were with Philip Prince Palatine Elector. Not only in ordinary conversation but also in serious discussions about the affairs of the state, they would often bring notable examples from the Persian or Greek or Roman history. The Prince was very zealous to know more of history and he noted that the distinction of the times, nations and empires was necessary for this. Therefore, he wished them to make a chronology of the kingdoms of ancient history based on all available Hebrew, Greek and Latin authors. At that time, in 1480 AD, there were no books about the ancient empires in the German language. Nor had the Latins anything of that nature, save Justin's confused Epitome, which also lacked a detailed chronology. Those learned men were delighted to compile this work. Therefore, they compiled a chronology from Hebrew, Greek and Latin works of the various monarchies. To this they added all the most important events in the proper places and created a chronology of the nations and times. The grateful prince read these works most earnestly and delighted in them. Also, he was thankful that the times and the memory of the most important events were preserved by Divine Providence, since they showed him that the record of the history of the world was continuous, in that Herodotus began his writings a little before the end of the prophetic history. For even before the end of the Persian monarchy, of which we have a very clear account from Daniel, Ezra and Nehemiah, some of the names of the kings of Assyria and Egypt are the same in the prophets and Herodotus. Jeremiah foretold their destruction to Apries, which Herodotus also described. After Apries killed Jeremiah, Amasis strangled the proud king after he had captured him. The Palatine prince said he saw the witness of the divine presence in the ordering of empires. For these empires could neither be acquired nor retained by mere human power. It follows, therefore, that they were created in order that they might be the upholders of human society, unite many countries, restore law, justice and peace and indeed, that they might teach men concerning God. For this reason, he often repeated those words of Daniel, that God changes and confirms empires. {Da 2:21} He said, likewise, that by the changes and punishments of tyrants, the just judgment of the Almighty was most conspicuous. By these illustrious examples, all mankind was admonished to acknowledge God and was to understand that he wills and ordains justice, and is truly offended with those who transgress his ordination. Such were the remarks of that prince, concerning the rise and fall of empires.

# Key to References

## EACH SECTION is precisely dated.

**AM**    [Anno Mundi] Years of the world from creation, (a=Autumn, b = Winter, c=Spring, d= Summer)

**JP**    [Julian Period] Year, starting from January 1, 4713 B.C.

**BC or AD**    [Before Christ] Years before the Christian era or

     [Anno Domini] Years from the start of the Christian era

## EACH PAGE
### shows reference points.

**3 SK**    Year 3 of the king of the Southern Kingdom of Israel

Standard date (B.C./A.D.) covered in the spread

General subject covered in the spread

**6 NK**    Year 6 of the king of the Northern Kingdom of Israel

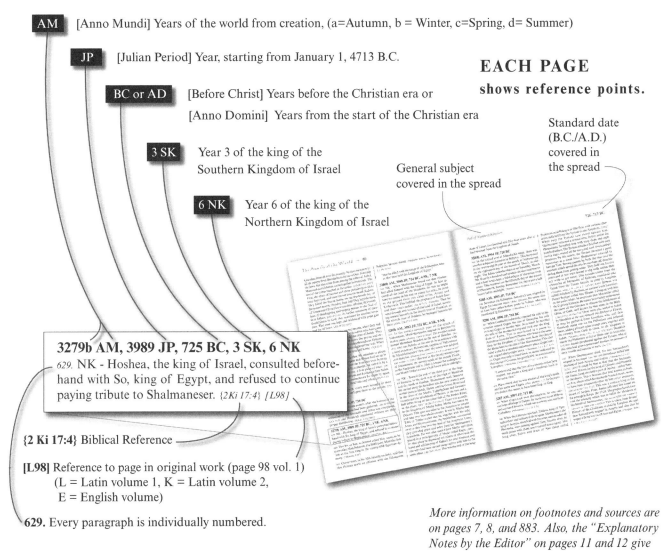

**3279b AM, 3989 JP, 725 BC, 3 SK, 6 NK**
*629.* NK - Hoshea, the king of Israel, consulted beforehand with So, king of Egypt, and refused to continue paying tribute to Shalmaneser. *{2Ki 17:4} [L98]*

**{2 Ki 17:4}** Biblical Reference

**[L98]** Reference to page in original work (page 98 vol. 1)
     (L = Latin volume 1, K = Latin volume 2,
     E = English volume)

**629.** Every paragraph is individually numbered.

*More information on footnotes and sources are on pages 7, 8, and 883. Also, the "Explanatory Notes by the Editor" on pages 11 and 12 give an overview of years, dates, etc.*

## EACH PARAGRAPH is carefully referenced.

---

**FOOTNOTES in the text are delimited by {...}.**

\* — reference verified. (No "\*" means unable to locate reference)

? — not sure of footnote reference

**Pliny** — name of author

**Natural History** — title of book

**l. 9.** — Book 9 in original author's series

**c. 23.** — chapter 23 in original author's series

**(56)** — Modern reference number in the original text. Not all writers are so indexed, e.g., Herodotus

**3:201** — Loeb Series, book 3, page 201

*{\*Pliny, Natural History, l. 9. c. 23. (56) 3:201}*

*{see note on 2560a AM <<3347>>}*

means see note under year 2560a AM paragraph 3347.

# VOLUME I

The
Annals of the
World *Deduced from*
the Origin of Time and continued to the
beginning of the Emperor *Vespasian's*
Reign and the Total Destruction and
Abolition of the Temple and
Commonwealth of the *Jews.*
Containing the
History
of the Old and New
Testament
With that of the
Maccabees.
Also all the most Memorable Affairs
of *Asia* and *Egypt*, and the Rise of
the Empire of the Roman Caesars, under
*Gaius Julius Caesar* and *Octavius Caesar*
Collected
From all History, as well as Sacred,
as Profane and Methodically Organized;

By the most *Reverend James Ussher*,
Archbishop of Armagh and Primate of
Ireland.
London,
Printed by E. Tyler, for J. Crook,
at the Sign of the Ship in St. Paul's
Churchyard and for G. Bedell, at the
*Middle-Temple-Gate, in Fleet-Street,*
MDCLVIII.

*(From the original Title Page)*

# The Annals of the Old Testament from the Beginning of the World

"The world's history is a divine poem of which the history of every nation is a canto and every man a word. Its strains have been pealing along down the centuries, and though there have been mingled discords of warring cannon and dying men, yet to the Christian philosopher and historian—the humble listener—there has been a divine melody running through the song which speaks of hope and halcyon days to come." {*James A. Garfield, Klopsch - Many Thoughts of Many Minds, 1:131}

## 1a AM, 710 JP, 4004 BC

*1.* In the beginning God created the heaven and the earth. {*Ge 1:1*} The beginning of time, according to our chronology, happened at the start of the evening preceding the 23rd day of October (on the Julian calendar), 4004 BC or 710 JP. (This day was the first Sunday past the autumnal equinox for that year and would have been September 21 on the Gregorian calendar. Historians routinely use the Julian calendar for all BC dates. Editor.)

*2.* On the first day {*Ge 1:1-5*} of the world (Sunday, October 23), God created the highest heaven and the angels. When he finished, as it were, the roof of this building, he started with the foundation of this wonderful fabric of the world. He fashioned this lower-most globe, consisting of the deep and of the earth. Therefore, all the choir of angels sang together and magnified his name. {*Job 38:7*} When the earth was without form and void and darkness covered the face of the deep, God created light on the very middle of the first day. God divided this from the darkness and called the one *Day* and the other *Night*.

*3.* On the second day {*Ge 1:6-8*} (Monday, October 24) after the firmament or heaven was finished, the waters above were separated from the waters here below, enclosing the earth.

*4.* On the third day {*Ge 1:9-13*} (Tuesday, October 25), when these waters below ran together into one place, the dry land appeared. From this collection of the waters God made a sea, sending out from here the rivers, which were to return there again. {*Ec 1:7*} He caused the earth to bud and bring forth all kinds of herbs and plants with seeds and fruits. Most importantly, he enriched the Garden of Eden with plants, for among them grew the tree of life and the tree of the knowledge of good and evil. {*Ge 2:8,9*}

*5.* On the fourth day (Wednesday, October 26), the sun, the moon and the rest of the stars were created. {*Ge 1:14-19*} (According to the astronomical calculations, if the moon had existed on the first day of creation then it would have been a new moon. Editor.)

*6.* On the fifth day (Thursday, October 27), fish and flying birds were created and commanded to multiply and fill the sea and the earth. {*Ge 1:20-23*}

*7.* On the sixth day (Friday, October 28), the living creatures of the earth were created as well as the creeping creatures. {*Ge 1:24-27*} Last of all, man was created in the image of God, which consisted in the capacity of the mind to have a knowledge of the divine, {*Col 3:10*} and in the natural and proper sanctity of his will. {*Eph 4:24*} When, by divine power, all living creatures were brought before him, Adam gave them their names. Among all of these, he found no one to help him who was like himself. *[L2]* Lest he should be destitute of a suitable companion, God took a rib out of his side while he slept and fashioned it into a woman. (Men and women both have the same number of ribs. Removal of a rib would not cause one's son to have one less rib any more than if one lost a leg, he would expect his son to be born with only one leg. The rib is the only bone in the human body that regenerates itself if it is removed. Editor.) He gave her to him for a wife, establishing by it the law of marriage between them. He blessed them and bade them to be fruitful and multiply. God gave them dominion over all living creatures. God provided a large portion of food and sustenance for them to live on. To conclude, because sin had not yet entered into the world:

> "God saw every thing that he had made, and, behold, it was *very good*. And the evening and the morning were the sixth day." {*Ge 1:31*}

*8.* Now on the seventh day (Saturday, October 29), when God had finished his work which he intended, he then rested from all labour. *[E2]* He blessed the seventh day and ordained and consecrated the Sabbath {*Ge 2:2,3*} because he rested on it {*Ex 31:17*} and refreshed himself. Nor as yet had sin entered into the world for none is cited. Nor was there any punishment given by God, either upon mankind, or upon angels. Hence it was that this day was set forth both for our sanctification in this world {*Ex 31:13*}, as well as for a sign of that eternal Sabbath to be enjoyed in the world to come. In it we expect a full deliverance from sin and its dregs and all its punishments. {*Heb 4:4,9,10*}

*9.* After the first week of the world ended, it seems that God brought the newly married couple into the Garden of Eden. He charged them not to eat of the tree of the knowledge of good and evil but left them free to eat of every other plant.

*10.* The Devil envied God's honour and man's obedience. He tempted the woman to sin by the serpent. By this, he obtained the name and title of *the old serpent.* {*Re 12:9 20:2*} The woman was beguiled by the serpent into eating the fruit, but the man deliberately ate the fruit. {*1Ti 2:14*} They broke the command of God concerning the forbidden fruit. Accordingly, when they were sought for by God and convicted of this crime, each had their punishments imposed on them. At this point, the promise was also given that the seed of the woman should one day bruise the serpent's head. Christ, in the fulness of time, should undo the works of the Devil. {*1Jo 3:8 Ro 16:20*} Adam first called his wife Eve, because she was then ordained to be the mother, not only of all that should live this natural life, {*Ge 3:20*} but of those also who should live by faith in her seed. This was the promised Messiah, as Sarah also later was called the *mother of the faithful.* {*1Pe 3:6 Ga 4:31*}.

*11.* After this, our first parents were clothed by God with clothing of skins. They were expelled from Eden and a fiery flaming sword was set to guard the way leading to the tree of life, so that they could never eat of that fruit which they had not yet touched. {*Ge 3:21,22*} It is very probable that Adam was turned out of paradise the same day that he was brought into it. This seems to have been on the tenth day of the world (November 1). On this day also, in remembrance of so remarkable an event, the day of atonement was appointed {*Le 23:27*} and the yearly fast on that day, that was mentioned by Paul. {*Ac 27:9*} On that day all strangers, as well as native Israelites, were commanded to afflict their souls, so that:

> "every soul which should not afflict itself on that day, should be cut off from among his people." {*Le 16:29 23:29*}

*12.* After the fall of Adam, Cain was the first of all mortal men that was born of a woman. {*Ge 4:1*}

## 130d AM, 840 JP, 3874 BC

*13.* When Cain, the firstborn of all mankind, murdered Abel, God gave Eve another son called Seth. {*Ge 4:25*} *[L3]* Adam had now lived a hundred and thirty years. {*Ge 5:3*} From which it may be gathered that, between the death of Abel and the birth of Seth, there was no other son born to Eve. For then, he should have been recorded to have been given her instead of Seth. (Since man had been on the earth a hundred and twenty-eight years and Adam and Eve had other sons and daughters, {*Ge 5:4*} the number of people on the earth at the time of this murder could have been as many as several hundred

thousand. Editor.) Cain might justly fear, through the awareness of the guilt of his crime, that every man that met him would also try to kill him. {*Ge 4:14,15*}

## 235d AM, 945 JP, 3769 BC

*14.* When Seth was a hundred and five years old, he had his son Enos. The fact that the worship of God was even then wretchedly corrupted by the descendants of Cain, indicates the lamentable condition of all mankind. Hence it came about that even then the distinction was made, that those who continued in the true worship of God were known by the name of the *children of God,* whereas those who forsook him, were termed the *children of men.* {*Ge 4:26 6:1,2*}

## 325d AM, 1035 JP, 3679 BC

*15.* Cainan, the son of Enos, was born when his father was ninety years old. {*Ge 5:10*}

## 395d AM, 1105 JP, 3609 BC

*16.* Mahalaleel was born when Cainan, his father, was seventy years old. {*Ge 5:12*}

## 460d AM, 1170 JP, 3544 BC

*17.* Jared was born when his father Mahalaleel was sixty-five years old. {*Ge 5:15*}

## 622d AM, 1332 JP, 3382 BC

*18.* Enoch was born when his father Jared was a hundred and sixty-two years old. {*Ge 5:18*}

## 687d AM, 1397 JP, 3317 BC

*19.* Methuselah was born when Enoch, his father, was sixty-five years old. {*Ge 5:21*}

## 874d AM, 1584 JP, 3130 BC

*20.* Lamech was born when his father Methuselah was a hundred and eighty-seven years old. {*Ge 5:25*}

## 930d AM, 1640 JP, 3074 BC

*21.* Adam, the father of all mankind, died at the age of nine hundred and thirty years. {*Ge 5:5*}

## 987d AM, 1697 JP, 3017 BC

*22.* Enoch, the seventh from Adam at the age of three hundred and sixty-five years, was translated by God in an instant, while he was walking with him, that he should not see death. {*Ge 5:23,24 Heb 11:5*} *[E3]*

## 1042d AM, 1752 JP, 2962 BC

*23.* Seth, the son of Adam, died when he was nine hundred and twelve years old. {*Ge 5:8*}

## 1056d AM, 1766 JP, 2948 BC

*24.* Noah, the tenth from Adam, was born when his father Lamech was a hundred and eighty-two years old. {*Ge 5:29*}

### 1140d AM, 1850 JP, 2864 BC

*25.* Enos, the third from Adam, died when he was nine hundred and five years old. {*Ge 5:11*}

### 1235d AM, 1945 JP, 2769 BC

*26.* Cainan, the fourth from Adam, died when he was nine hundred and ten years old. {*Ge 5:14*}

### 1290d AM, 2000 JP, 2714 BC

*27.* Mahalaleel, the fifth from Adam, died when he was eight hundred and ninety-two years old. {*Ge 5:17*}

### 1422d AM, 2132 JP, 2582 BC

*28.* Jared, the sixth from Adam, died when he was nine hundred and sixty-two years old. {*Ge 5:20*}

### 1536a AM, 2245 JP, 2469 BC

*29.* Before the deluge of waters over the whole wicked world, God sent Noah, a preacher of righteousness, to them, giving them a hundred and twenty years to repent from their evil ways. {*1Pe 3:20 2Pe 2:5 Ge 6:3*}

### 1556d AM, 2266 JP, 2448 BC

*30.* Noah was five hundred years old when his first son, Japheth, was born. {*Ge 5:32 10:21*} *[L4]*

### 1558d AM, 2268 JP, 2446 BC

*31.* Noah's second son, Shem, was born two years later because two years after the flood, Shem was a hundred years old. {*Ge 11:10*}

### 1651d AM, 2361 JP, 2353 BC

*32.* Lamech, the ninth from Adam, died when he was seven hundred and seventy-seven years old. {*Ge 5:31*}

### 1656a AM, 2365 JP, 2349 BC

*33.* Methuselah, the eighth from Adam, died when he was nine hundred and sixty-nine years old. He was the oldest man that ever lived. (Riddle: Who lived the longest of all men, yet died before his father? Editor.) {*Ge 5:24,27*}

*34.* On the tenth day of the second month of this year (Sunday, November 30), God commanded Noah that in that week he should prepare to enter the ark. Meanwhile the world, totally devoid of all fear, sat eating and drinking, and marrying and giving in marriage. {*Ge 7:1,4,10 Mt 24:38*}

*35.* In the 600th year of the life of Noah, on the seventeenth day of the second month (Sunday, December 7), he, together with his children and living creatures of all kinds, had entered into the ark. God sent a rain on the earth for forty days and forty nights. The waters flooded the earth for a hundred and fifty days. {*Ge 7:4,6,11-13,17,24*}

*36.* The waters abated until the seventeenth day of the seventh month (Wednesday, May 6), when the ark came to rest upon one of the mountains of Ararat. {*Ge 8:3,4*}

*37.* The waters continued receding until, on the first day of the tenth month (Sunday, July 19), the tops of the mountains were seen. {*Ge 8:5*}

*38.* After forty days, that is, on the eleventh day of the eleventh month (Friday, August 28), Noah opened the window of the ark and sent forth a raven. {*Ge 8:6,7*}

*39.* Seven days later, on the eighteenth day of the eleventh month (Friday, September 4), as may be deduced from the other seven days mentioned {*Ge 8:10*}, Noah sent out a dove. She returned after seven days, on the twenty-fifth day of the eleventh month (Friday, September 11). He sent her out again and towards evening she returned, bringing the leaf of an olive tree in her beak. After waiting seven more days, on the second day of the twelfth month (Friday, September 18), he sent the same dove out again, but this time she never returned. {*Ge 8:8-12*}

# The Second Age of the World

## 1657a AM, 2366 JP, 2348 BC

*40.* When Noah was six hundred and one years old, on the first day of the first month (Friday, October 23), and the first day of the new post-flood world, the surface of the earth was now all dry. Noah removed the covering of the ark. {*Ge 8:13*}

*41.* On the 27th day of the second month (Thursday, December 18), the earth was entirely dry. By the command of God, Noah left the ark with all that were with him in the ark. {*Ge 8:14-19*}

*42.* After he left the ark, Noah offered sacrifices to God for his blessed preservation. God restored the nature of things destroyed by the flood. He now permitted men to eat meat for their food, and he gave the rainbow for a sign of the covenant which he made with man at this point. {*Ge 8:15-9:17*}

*43. Man's lifespan was now half of what it had previously been.*

## 1658d AM, 2368 JP, 2346 BC

*44.* Arphaxad was born to Shem when he was a hundred years old, two years after the flood. {*Ge 11:10*}

(The Septuagint incorrectly inserted the name of Cainan in the genealogy. John Gill [c. 1760 AD] wrote: {*See Gill on "Lu 3:36"*}

"Ver. 36. Which was the son of Cainan....] This Cainan is not mentioned by Moses in Ge 11:12 nor has he ever appeared in any Hebrew copy of the Old Testament, nor in the Samaritan version, nor in the Targum; nor is he mentioned by Josephus, nor in 1Ch 1:24 where the genealogy is repeated; nor is it in Beza's most ancient Greek copy of Luke: it indeed stands in the present copies of the Septuagint, but was not originally there; and therefore could not be taken by Luke from there, but seems to be owing to some early negligent transcriber of Luke's Gospel, and since put into the Septuagint to give it authority: I say *early*, because it is in many Greek copies, and in the Vulgate Latin, and all the Oriental versions, even in the Syriac, the oldest of them; but ought not to stand neither in the text, nor in any version: for certain it is, there never was such a Cainan, the son of Arphaxad, for Salah was his son; and with him the next words should be connected...."

Since this was written, the oldest manuscript we have of Luke, the P75, was found. It dates to the late second century AD and does not include Cainan in the genealogy. This verse in Luke should not be used to prove the genealogies in Genesis have gaps because it has poor textual authority. Editor.)

## 1693d AM, 2403 JP, 2311 BC

*45.* Salah was born when his father Arphaxad was thirty-five years old. {*Ge 11:12*}

## 1723d AM, 2433 JP, 2281 BC

*46.* Eber was born when Salah, his father, was thirty years old. {*Ge 11:14*} *[L5]*

## 1757d AM, 2467 JP, 2247 BC

*47.* When Eber was thirty-four years old, Peleg, his son, was born. {*Ge 11:16*} He called him Peleg, for in his days the earth was divided. {*Ge 10:25 1Ch 1:19*} If this happened at the day of his birth, then it seems that when Peleg was born, Noah, who formerly knew all the places which were now covered with bushes and thorns, divided the land among his grandchildren. When this was done, they then went from those eastern parts (where they first went from the mountains of Ararat) into the valley of Shinar. {*Ge 11:2*} *[E4]* Here the people impiously conspired, as we find in the Apocrypha, {*Apc Wis 10:5*} to hinder their dispersion, which had been commanded by God and begun by Noah (this can be seen by comparing the following verses: Ge 11:4, 6, 8, 9). They co-operated together to build the city and tower of Babylon. God frustrated this project by the confusion of languages he sent among them. (Hence it took the name of Babel. {*Ge 11:9*}) The dispersion of nations followed. Many companies and colonies settled down in various places according to their languages. The thirteen sons of Joktan, the brother of Peleg, as recorded in Ge 10:26-30 were among the captains and heads of the various companies. These brothers were not yet born when Peleg was born. Eber was only thirty-four years old when Peleg was born to him. Even if we suppose that Joktan was born when Eber was only twenty years of age, and that Joktan's oldest son was born to him when he was likewise twenty years old, yet still it appears that the oldest son of Joktan must be six years younger than Peleg. So that at least the youngest of those thirteen sons of Joktan, namely, Jobab and three other brothers of his who are mentioned before him, must be younger still. The countries in which they settled, and which were rich in gold: Sheba, {*Ps 72:15*} Ophir {*1Ki 9:28*} and Havilah, {*Ge 2:11*} were named after these men. Because of their youth, these brothers could not have been capable of such an expedition of leading colonies until some years after Reu was born to Peleg.

48. *Man's lifespan was now a quarter of the length it was before the flood.*

### 1762d AM, 2472 JP, 2242 BC

49. The Tower of Babel happened five years after the birth of Peleg, according to Georgius Syncellus' translation of the Book of Sothis. {*Manetho, Book of Sothis, l. 1. 1:239}

### 1771a AM, 2480 JP, 2234 BC

50. Nineteen hundred and three years elapsed from this time to the capture of Babylon by Alexander the Great. This calculation was made according to the astronomical observations by Porphyry and the number of years is as we find recorded in Simplicius. {Simplicius, De Caelo, l. 2} He affirmed that these observations were taken to Greece from Babylon by Callisthenes at Aristotle's request. From these writings it appeared that the Babylonians devoted themselves to the study of astronomy, even from the very days of Nimrod, from whom all that region took the name of the land of Nimrod. {Mic 5:6} Nimrod built Babylon and was the instigator of the building of the Tower of Babel according to Josephus. {*Josephus, Antiq., l. 1. c. 4. s. 3. (118) 4:57} Moses affirmed that the royal seat of that kingdom was here. {Ge 10:10} Nimrod made Babylon famous in those days. {Jer 5:15} {See note on 3674a AM. <<1891>>}

### 1787d AM, 2497 JP, 2217 BC

51. Reu was born when Peleg, his father, was thirty years old. {Ge 11:18}

### 1816d AM, 2526 JP, 2188 BC

52. Constantinus Manasses stated that the Egyptian state lasted sixteen hundred and sixty-three years. Counting backward from the time that Cambyses, king of Persia, conquered Egypt, leads us to this date. About this time Mizraim, the son of Ham, led his colony into Egypt. Hence, Egypt was sometimes called the land of Mizraim, sometimes of Ham. {Ps 105:23,27 106:21,22} It was from this that the Pharisees later boasted that they were the sons of ancient kings. {Isa 19:11} {See note on 3479b AM. <<981>>}

### 1819d AM, 2529 JP, 2185 BC

53. Serug, or Saruch, was born when Reu was thirty-two years old. {Ge 11:20} [L6]

### 1849d AM, 2559 JP, 2155 BC

54. Nachor was born when Serug, his father, was thirty years old. {Ge 11:22}

### 1878d AM, 2588 JP, 2126 BC

55. Terah was born when Nachor, his father, was twenty-nine years old. {Ge 11:24}

### 1915c AM, 2625 JP, 2089 BC

56. At this time Egialeus, king of the city of Sicyon west of Corinth in Peloponnesus, began his reign thirteen hundred and thirteen years before the first Olympiad. {*Eusebius, Chronicles, l. 1. 1:17}

### 1920c AM, 2630 JP, 2084 BC

57. A people from Arabia bordering upon Egypt, called by the Egyptians Hyksos, meaning *Shepherd Kings*, invaded Egypt. They took Memphis and took over all of lower Egypt bordering on the Mediterranean Sea. Salatis, their first king, reigned nineteen years. {*Manetho, 1:81} {*Josephus, Apion, l. 1. c. 14. (77) 1:193}

### 1939c AM, 2649 JP, 2065 BC

58. Bnon, their second king, reigned for forty-four years. {*Manetho, 1:83} {*Josephus, Apion, l. 1. c. 14. (80) 1:195}

### 1948d AM, 2658 JP, 2056 BC

59. When Terah was seventy years old, Haran, the oldest of his three sons, was born. {Ge 11:26} Abram was not born for another sixty years, as we shall see later. Haran was later the father-in-law of the third brother Nachor. Haran died before his father, Terah, left Ur of the Chaldeans. Haran had a daughter, named Milcah, who was married to Abram's brother Nachor. {Ge 11:28,29}

### 1983c AM, 2693 JP, 2021 BC

60. At this time Apachnan reigned in Egypt for thirty-six years and seven months. {*Manetho, 1:83} {*Josephus, Apion, l. 1. c. 14. (80) 1:195}

### 1996d AM, 2706 JP, 2008 BC

61. Peleg, the sixth from Noah, died two hundred and nine years after the birth of Reu. {Ge 11:19}

### 1997d AM, 2707 JP, 2007 BC

62. Nachor, the ninth from Noah, died a hundred and nineteen years after the birth of his son Terah. {Ge 11:25}

### 2006d AM, 2716 JP, 1998 BC

63. Noah died when he had lived nine hundred and fifty years, three hundred and fifty years after the deluge. {Ge 9:28,29}

### 2008c AM, 2718 JP, 1996 BC

64. Abram was born. He was seventy-five years old when Terah his father died at the age of two hundred and five years. {Ge 11:32 12:1,4 Ac 7:4}

### 2018c AM, 2728 JP, 1986 BC

65. Sarai, who is also called Iscah the daughter of Haran, {Ge 11:29,30}, was born and was ten years younger than her husband Abraham. {Ge 17:17}

### 2020b AM, 2730 JP, 1984 BC

66. Apophis reigned in Egypt for sixty-one years. {*Manetho, 1:83} {*Josephus, Apion, l. 1. c. 14. (80) 1:195}

### 2026d AM, 2736 JP, 1978 BC

67. Reu, the seventh from Noah, died two hundred and seven years after the birth of Serug. {Ge 11:21} [E5]

### 2049d AM, 2759 JP, 1955 BC

68. Serug, the eighth from Noah, died two hundred years after the death of Nachor. {Ge 11:23}

### 2079b AM, 2789 JP, 1925 BC

69. About this time, Chedorlaomer king of Elam, or Elimais, situated between Persia and Babylon, conquered the kings of Pentapolis—Sodom, Gomorrah, Admah, Zeboiim and Bela, or Zoar. These served him for twelve years. {Ge 14:1,2,4}

### 2081b AM, 2791 JP, 1923 BC

70. Jannas reigned in Egypt for fifty years and one month. {*Manetho, 1:83} {*Josephus, Apion, l. 1. c. 14. (80) 1:195}

### 2083a AM, 2792 JP, 1922 BC

71. God called Abraham out of Ur of the Chaldeans, to go into the land that he would show him. {Ge 15:7 Jos 24:2,3 Ne 9:7 Ac 7:2-4} [L7] Ur was located in Mesopotamia according to Stephen, the first martyr. The historian Abarbenel noted on the passage in Genesis {Ge 11:28-32} that Ur was the city of those priests and mathematicians who, from their art, were called by the name of Chaldeans. By this name, even in Chaldea itself, those *Genethliaci*, or recorders of genealogies, were distinguished and singled out from the rest of the magi or wise men of that country, as we find in Daniel. {Da 2:2,10 4:7 5:11} They taught Terah and his sons idolatry. {Jos 24:2} Terah therefore took Abram his son, and Lot, Abram's nephew and the son of Haran, and Sarai, Terah's daughter-in-law and Abram's wife, and started their journey together from Ur of the Chaldeans to go into the land of Canaan. They came to Haran, still in that same country of Mesopotamia, where they remained because of the great infirmity and sickness of Terah. Terah lived for two hundred and five years and died in Haran. {Ge 11:31,32}

# The Third Age of the World

## 2083c AM, 2793 JP, 1921 BC

*72.* After Abram's father Terah died, God again called Abram from his own country, kindred and his father's house. A further promise and evangelical covenant of blessing was given to him. That is, in his blessed seed, our Lord Jesus Christ, all the nations of the earth would be blessed. {*Ge 12:1,2 Ac 7:4*} From the time of the giving of this promise and Abram's immediate departure, we mark the start of those four hundred and thirty years which Abram and his posterity spent in foreign lands. {*Ex 12:40,41 Ga 3:17*} The first and last day of this pilgrimage was on the 15th of the month of Abib, which in this year was Thursday, May 5, according to the Julian Calendar by our calculations.

*73.* Therefore, on this day, Abram, when he was seventy-five years old, obeyed the call of God. He took his wife Sarai, his nephew Lot, the son of Haran, with all the substance he had acquired and the souls which God had given him in Haran. He set out on his journey and at length came into the land of Canaan, through which he passed until he came to a place called Sichem, to the oak of Moreh, {*Ge 12:4-6*} which is mentioned later. {*Ge 35:4 Jos 24:25,26 Jud 9:6*} Here God promised Abram that he would give this land to his seed, and Abram built an altar to the Lord who had appeared to him there. Departing from there, he went toward the east into the hill country called Luz, later known by the name of Bethel. {*Ge 28:19*} There he again built an altar and called on the name of the Lord. From there he continued his journey and came into the south part of that country, which borders Egypt. {*Ge 12:7-9*}

## 2084a AM, 2793 JP, 1921 BC

*74.* A famine caused Abram to leave there and go down into Egypt. To avoid danger, Sarai his wife said she was his sister. She was taken into Pharaoh's house, but was returned unharmed not long after that, with many gifts and presents. They were given safe passage and allowed to depart from Egypt. {*Ge 12:10-20*} [L8]

## 2084c AM, 2794 JP, 1920 BC

*75.* Abram and Lot returned to Canaan. The country which they chose was not able to feed both men's herds of cattle. Therefore they parted company, and Lot went into the country of Sodom. After Lot's departure, the Lord renewed to Abram the promise of the possession of the land of Canaan and of Abram's numberless posterity. Abram left that place between Bethel and Hai, where he had formerly built an altar, and lived in the plain of Mamre near Hebron. There he built an altar to the Lord. {*Ge 13*}

## 2091 AM, 2801 JP, 1913 BC

*76.* Bera, king of Sodom, with the rest of the petty kings of Pentapolis, rebelled and shook off the yoke of Chedorlaomer, king of Elam, in the thirteenth year of their subjection to him. {*Ge 14:4*}

## 2092 AM, 2802 JP, 1912 BC

*77.* In the fourteenth year, Chedorlaomer, with other confederate princes, Amraphel of Shinar, Arioch of Ellasar and Tidal, king of the nations, combined their forces against those petty kings who had revolted against him. They first destroyed the Rephaims, the Zuzims, the Emims and the Horites, who inhabited all that region, which later was possessed by the Amalekites and the Ammonites. After that, they routed the kings of Pentapolis in the valley of Siddim and carried away Lot as prisoner with all the plunder of Sodom and Gomorrah. When tidings came to Abram, he armed three hundred and eighteen of his own servants. With his confederates, Aner, Eshcol and Mamre, they overtook Chedorlaomer and his army at Dan with the prey they had taken. There they defeated and killed many of them, pursuing the remainder to Hobah, to the west of Damascus. They rescued Lot and the other prisoners from the enemies' hands, and brought them back again with all that they had lost. When Abram returned from the slaughter of Chedorlaomer and the other kings, Melchizedek the king of Salem met him and blessed him. He was a priest of the Most High God. Abram, in return, offered him the tithe of the spoil which he had taken. He kept nothing of the spoil for himself but restored to every man his own possessions again. What was not owned he left to his troops for their service. {*Ge 14:1-24*} [E6]

*78.* Abram was grieved because he had no heir. Hence, God promised him a posterity equal to the stars of heaven in number. God said that after his descendants had spent four hundred years of sojourning and affliction in a land that was not theirs, he would bring them into the land promised to Abram, and bound his word with a covenant to perform it. {*Ge 15:1-21*}

## 2093c AM, 2803 JP, 1911 BC

*79.* Sarai was longing for that blessed seed. After ten years had passed since they came into the land of Canaan, she gave Hagar, her Egyptian servant, to Abram for a wife. Hagar conceived a child by her master Abram. She was badly treated by Sarai for her insolence. She fled from Sarai, but when she was warned by God through his angel, she returned and submitted herself to Sarai. {Ge 16:1,13,14}

### 2094b AM, 2804 JP, 1910 BC

*80.* When Abram was eighty-six years old, Hagar bore him Ishmael. {Ge 16:15,16 17:24,25}

### 2096d AM, 2806 JP, 1908 BC

*81.* Arphaxad, the third from Noah, died four hundred and three years after the birth of Salem. {Ge 11:13}

### 2107c AM, 2817 JP, 1897 BC

*82.* God made a covenant with Abram when he was now ninety-nine years old, concerning the seed of Isaac. He was to be born of Sarai about the same time—twelve months later. God gave him the sign of circumcision (changing both their names, Abram into Abraham and Sarai into Sarah) for a sure pledge and testimony of his promise. He promised also to favour Ishmael, the first-born, for his father's sake. These promises Abraham received and embraced with a genuine faith. Hence in true obedience, he circumcised himself when he was ninety-nine years of age, along with his son Ishmael, who was then thirteen years old, and all his household. He did this on the same day it had been commanded. {Ge 17:21-26}

*83.* Abraham invited angels, who looked like travelling men, into his house, and gave them a feast. *[L9]* These angels reiterated the promise of the birth of Isaac for Sarah's sake. They foretold the judgment of utter destruction which God intended to bring upon the five cities of the plain. Abraham, fearing what would become of Lot and his family in Sodom, made intercession to God for the sparing of that place. {Ge 18:23-33 19:29} Sodom, Gomorrah, Adamah and Zeboiim, for their horrible sins, perished by fire and brimstone that rained down upon them from heaven. {Ge 19:1-29} These cities were to be an example to all wicked men in times to come, of the pains of that everlasting fire to be inflicted on them in the lake of fire and brimstone, which is the second death. {2Pe 2:6,7 Jude 1:7 Re 19:20 20:10 21:8} The monument of this remains to this day, even the Dead Sea. The valley of Siddim, where these five cities stood in former times, was full of brimstone and salt pits. This has since grown into a vast lake which, because of the brimstone still floating in it, is called *Laces Asphaltitis* or *Lake of Brimstone* and because of the salt, *Mare Salsum* or the *Salt Sea*. {Ge 14:3,10 De 3:17 29:23 Zep 2:9} {Apc Wis 10:6,7} Concerning this, Solinus wrote: {Alexander Polyhistor, Chronography, l. 1. c. 35.}

"A long way off from Jerusalem, there lies a woeful spectacle, of a country to be seen, which was blasted from heaven and appeared by the blackness of the earth falling all to cinders. There were in that place before this, two cities, one called Sodom, the other Gomorrah, where if an apple grew, though it appeared to be ripe, yet it was not at all edible. Its outer skin contained nothing within it except a stinking smell, mingled with ashes and if ever so lightly touched, sent forth a smoke and the rest fell into a light dust of powder."

*84.* Lot was hurried from Sodom by the angels and avoided its destruction by fleeing to a little city called Bela, also called Zoar. His wife was turned into a pillar of salt. Lot was afraid to continue at Zoar and left the plain country. He went into the hills, as he had been commanded, taking his two daughters with him. {Ge 19:30-38}

*85.* Abraham left the plain of Mamre and went toward the south to dwell in a place which was later called Beersheba. He was entertained at Gerar by Abimelech, king of the Philistines. Sarah once again was presented as Abraham's sister and so was taken from him. After he was reproved and punished by God, Abimelech the king restored her untouched to her husband and presented him with generous gifts and presents. By Abraham's prayers, Abimelech and all his house were healed of their infirmities. {Ge 20:1-18}

### 2108c AM, 2818 JP, 1896 BC

*86.* When Abraham was now one hundred years old and Sarah ninety years old, their promised son Isaac was born to them. {Ge 17:17,21 21:1-7 Ro 4:19} Not long after this, Moab and Benammi were born to Lot, who was both father and grandfather to them. {Ge 19:36-38}

### 2113c AM, 2823 JP, 1891 BC

*87.* After Isaac was weaned, Abraham made a great feast. Sarah saw Ishmael, the son of Hagar the Egyptian, jesting with her son or rather *mocking* (as that word is translated in Genesis {Ge 39:14}) or even *persecuting* (as the apostle expounds it {Ga 4:29}). Ishmael, who was the older, claimed the right of inheritance to his father's estate. Sarah asked Abraham to cast out Ishmael, *for the son of this handmaid shall not be heir with my son Isaac.* Though he took this very grievously at first, yet he did it, for God had said to him, *in Isaac shall thy seed be called.* {Ge 21:8-12 Ro 9:7,8 Heb 11:17,18} Hence, we observe that Isaac is called his only begotten son. It was four hundred and thirty years from the time Abraham left Haran {Ga 3:17 Ex 12:41} until the exodus. Abraham was told his seed would be persecuted for four hundred years. Based on these verses (Ga 4:29, Ge 15:13 Ac 7:6), we conclude that this persecution started at this time when Isaac was five years old and Abraham made this feast. This was thirty years after Abraham left Haran. When writing on the traditions of the Jews on Genesis, Jerome stated:

> "Among the Hebrews there is a difference of opinions. Some hold that this was done in the fifth year after Isaac's weaning, others in the twelfth. *[L10]* We, choosing a shorter time of age, reckon that Ishmael was cast out with his mother, when he was eighteen years old."

*88.* This declaration of the elect seed and persecution (as the apostle terms it) of Isaac by Hagar's son, is taken by many of the Jews referred to above as the start of the four hundred year period during which the seed of Abraham was to be a stranger and sojourner and afflicted in a foreign land, as God had foretold him. {*Ge 15:13 Ac 7:6*} For those four hundred years were to be completed at the same time as the departure of the children of Israel from Egypt, as deduced from the following verses. {*Ge 15:14 Ex 12:35,36,41*} Although the ordinary reading from Augustine referred this to the very birth of Isaac as the start of the period. If this is so, then it would imply that scripture called the number of four hundred and five by the round number of four hundred years. *[E7]*

### 2126d AM, 2836 JP, 1878 BC

*89.* Salah, the fourth from Noah, died four hundred and three years after the birth of Heber. {*Ge 11:15*}

### 2131b AM, 2841 JP, 1873 BC

*90.* Assis reigned in Egypt for forty-nine years and two months. {*\*Manetho, 1:83*} {*\*Josephus, Apion, l. 1. c. 14. (80) 1:195*}

### 2133 AM, 2843 JP, 1871 BC

*91.* By faith Abraham, when he was tested, offered up his son Isaac. He knew that by his power God was able to raise him again from the dead, from where he also received him back, in a manner of speaking. {*Ge 22:1-19 Heb 11:17,19*}

*92.* Josephus said that at this time Isaac was twenty-five years old. {*\*Josephus, Antiq., l. 1. c. 13. s. 3. (227) 4:113*} He was at that time in the years of his prime. This may be deduced from the fact that he was able to carry the large quantity of wood required for the burning and consuming of such a burnt offering as Abraham intended to make. {*Ge 22:6*}

### 2145c AM, 2855 JP, 1859 BC

*93.* Sarah died in Hebron at the age of a hundred and twenty-seven. Abraham bought the cave for her burial in the field of Machpelah from Ephron the Hittite, for a sum of money. This was the first possession that he had in the land of Canaan. {*Ge 23:1,2,19,20*} As Abraham is known to us as the *father of the faithful,* {*Ro 4:11,12*} so is Sarah called the *mother of the faithful.* {*1Pe 3:6*} She is the only woman whose age at death is mentioned in the scripture.

### 2148b AM, 2858 JP, 1856 BC

*94.* Abraham was very careful about getting a wife for his son Isaac. He sent his chief servant, Eliezer of Damascus {*Ge 15:2*} (after first taking an oath from him), to find a wife for his son. Eliezer, under the guidance of God, went into Mesopotamia and there obtained for him Rebekah the daughter of Bethuel, sister to Laban, the Syrian. Isaac received her for his wife and brought her into the tent of his mother Sarah. By the solace and contentment which he found in her, he dispelled the sadness and grief which he had had since the death of his mother, three years earlier. {*Ge 24:1-67*} He was forty years old when he married Rebekah. {*Ge 25:20*}

*95.* About this time the reign of the Argives in Peloponnesus began, one thousand and eighty years before the first Olympiad, according to Eusebius {*\*Eusebius, Chronicles, l. 1. 1:31*} as derived from Castor of Rhodes.

*96.* The first king that reigned there was Inachus, who reigned fifty years. It was to him that Erasmus mentioned in the proverb *Inacho Antiquior.* Whom also I refer to that most learned Varro {*Varro, Human Antiquities, l. 17.*} (cited by Gellius {*\*Aulus Gellius, Attic Nights, l. 1. c. 16. s. 3,4. 1:81*} and Macrobius, {*Macrobius, Saturnalia, l. 1.*}), who said that to the beginning of Romulus are reckoned more than eleven hundred years. For from the beginning of Inachus' reign, according to the calculations of Castor, there mentioned, to the Palilia, or solemn festivals of Pales (the country goddess among the Romans) mentioned by Varro, are reckoned eleven hundred and two years.

### 2158d AM, 2868 JP, 1846 BC

*97.* Shem, the son of Noah, died five hundred years after the birth of Arphaxad. {*Ge 11:11*} *[L11]*

### 2167d AM, 2877 JP, 1837 BC

*98.* When Rebekah had been barren for nineteen years after her marriage, Isaac, in great devotion, prayed to God on her behalf and she conceived twins. {*Ge 25:21*}

### 2168c AM, 2878 JP, 1836 BC

*99.* When the twins strove in the womb, Rebekah asked counsel of God. God said that two differing and opposing nations should come from her in that birth, of which the one should be stronger than the other, and that the older would serve the younger. But at the time of her travail, the first that came forth was ruddy and hairy all over and he was named *Esau*. Then the other came forth, holding the former by the heel, as a result of which he was called *Jacob*. Isaac, their father, at the time of their birth, was sixty years old. {*Ge 25:22-26 Ho 12:3*}

### 2179 AM, 2889 JP, 1825 BC

*100.* Manetho wrote {*\*Manetho, 1:101*} {*\*Josephus, Apion, l. 1. c. 15. (94) 1:201*} that Tethmosis, king of Thebes or upper Egypt, besieged the Hyksos or Shepherd Kings, in a place called Auaris (containing ten thousand Egyptian *arourae* of ground or about eight square miles) with an army of four hundred and eighty thousand men. When he found no possibility of taking them, he agreed with them that they should leave Egypt and go freely wherever they wished. They, with all their substance and goods, and in number no fewer than two hundred and twenty-four thousand entire households, passed through Egypt and went by way of the wilderness into Syria. Because of the fear they had of the Assyrians, who then controlled all Asia, they built themselves a city in what is now called the land of Judah. This city was large enough to hold the entire number of inhabitants, and was called Hierosolyma or Jerusalem. Manetho stated this in Josephus. {*\*Manetho, 1:87*} {*\*Josephus, Apion, l. 1. c. 14. (85) 1:197*} Apion called this king Amosis. {*Apion, Egyptian Affairs, l. 4.*} He proved from the annals of Ptolemy of Mendes, an Egyptian priest, that he was contemporary with Inachus, mentioned previously, king of the Argives. {*\*Tatian, Address to the Greeks, l. 1. c. 39. 2:80*} Justin Martyr, {*\*Justin Martyr, Exhortation to the Greeks, l. 1. c. 9. 1:277*} Clement of Alexandria {*\*Clement, Stromateis, l. 1. c. 21. 2:324*} and others also stated this. All followed Josephus' and Justus Tiberiensis' account and understood it to have meant the Israelites, because they were primarily shepherds. {*Ge 46:33,34 47:3*} These writers deduced this because this people went from Egypt into Canaan and they imagined that Moses was contemporary with Inachus and was the man that conducted them on that journey. However, those things seem rather to refer to the Phoenicians, whom Herodotus {*\*Herodotus, l. 7. c. 89. 3:395*} reported as having come from the Red Sea and settled in Palestine. The departure of the Israelites from Egypt happened many years after Inachus, as the course of this chronology undoubtedly shows. *[E8]*

### 2180c AM, 2890 JP, 1824 BC

*101.* When Tethmosis or Amosis drove out these shepherds, he reigned in lower Egypt for twenty-five years and four months. {*\*Manetho, 1:101*} {*\*Josephus, Apion, l. 1. c. 15. (94) 1:201*}

### 2183c AM, 2893 JP, 1821 BC

*102.* Abraham died when he was a hundred and seventy five years old and a hundred years after entering Canaan. He was buried by his two sons, Isaac and Ishmael, in his cave at Machpelah, with Sarah his wife. {*Ge 25:7-10*} He lived fifteen years after the birth of Jacob, with whom he is said also to have lived in tents. {*Heb 11:9*}

### 2187d AM, 2897 JP, 1817 BC

*103.* Heber, the fifth from Noah, died four hundred and thirty years after the birth of his son Peleg. {*Ge 11:17*} This man lived the longest of any who were born after the flood. He outlived Abraham and from him Abraham came first to be surnamed the Hebrew. {*Ge 14:13*} In later times, all the posterity of his grandchild Jacob were known by the same name. {*Ge 40:15*} Canaan was called the land of the Hebrews while the Canaanites were still living there.

### 2200 AM, 2910 JP, 1804 BC

*104.* About this time, the promises previously made to Abraham, so it seemed, were starting to be fulfilled in his son Isaac. To wit:

  a) I will multiply thy seed, as the stars of heaven. *[L12]*
  b) To thy seed will I give this land.
  c) In thy seed shall all the nations of the earth be blessed. {*Ge 26:4*}

### 2205d AM, 2915 JP, 1799 BC

*105.* Chebron reigned in Egypt for thirteen years. {*\*Manetho, 1:101*} {*\*Josephus, Apion, l. 1. c. 15. (94) 1:201*}

### 2208c AM, 2918 JP, 1796 BC

*106.* When Esau was forty years old, he took two wives from the land of the Hittites. One was Judith, the daughter of Beeri, and the other was Bashemath, the daughter of Elon. These two wives were very troublesome and a grief to Rebekah. {*Ge 26:34,35 27:46 28:8*}

*107.* At this time the Ogygian Deluge occurred in the country of Attica one thousand and twenty years before the first Olympiad. This was noted by Hellanicus, Castor, Thallus, Diodorus Siculus, Alexander Polyhistor and by Julius Africanus, as we find it recorded in Eusebius. {*Alexander Polyhistor, Chronography, l. 3.*} {*\*Eusebius, Gospel, l. 10. c. 10. (488d) 1:524*} {*\*Julius Africanus, l. 1. c. 13. s. 3. 6:133*} Varro said this flood happened three hundred years earlier.

### 2218d AM, 2928 JP, 1786 BC

*108.* Amenophis reigned in Egypt for twenty years and seven months. {*\*Manetho, 1:101*} {*\*Josephus, Apion, l. 1. c. 15. (94) 1:201*}

### 2231b AM, 2941 JP, 1773 BC

*109.* Abraham's son, Ishmael, died at the age of a hundred and thirty-seven years. {*Ge 25:17*}

### 2239b AM, 2949 JP, 1765 BC

*110.* Amessis, the sister of Amenophis, reigned in Egypt for twenty-one years and nine months. {*\*Manetho, 1:101*} {*\*Josephus, Apion, l. 1. c. 15. (95) 1:201*}

### 2242 AM, 2952 JP, 1762 BC

*111.* Euechous began to reign in Chaldea two hundred and twenty-four years before the Arabians. {*Julius Africanus, Chronographies*} He seems to have been the same as Belus of Babylon, or Jupiter Belus, who was worshipped later by the Chaldeans as a god. {*Isa 46:1 Jer 50:2 51:44*}

### 2245a AM, 2954 JP, 1760 BC

*112.* Forty-four years before his death, Isaac had grown old and blind. He sent his oldest son Esau to hunt some venison for him. Isaac planned to bless him when he returned. However, Jacob his younger son, by the subtle advice of his mother, came disguised in Esau's clothing, bringing Isaac's favourite meat. Thus he stole away the blessing, unknown to his father. In time, the blessing seemed to have been forgotten, but God confirmed it to Jacob for ever. By so doing, Jacob incurred his brother's hatred. Jacob journeyed to Mesopotamia, to his uncle Laban, both to avoid his brother's plan to kill him, {*Ge 27:41*} and to find a wife from his own kindred. {*Ge 28:1*} Before he left, he asked for his father's blessing on the trip.

### 2245c AM, 2955 JP, 1759 BC

*113.* On his journey he saw a vision of a ladder. In this vision God confirmed to him all the blessings formerly given to his father. God assured him of his grace and favour for the future. In remembrance of this experience, Jacob set up a pillar. He changed the name of the place from Luz to Bethel and made a vow to God there. When he came to Haran he stayed with Laban for a month. He fell in love with Rachel, his daughter, and agreed to serve Laban seven years for her. {*Ge 27:1 29:20 Ho 12:12*} Jacob was seventy-seven years old this year.

*114.* When Esau knew Isaac had blessed Jacob and sent him away into Mesopotamia to find a wife there, and that Jacob did not like the daughters of Canaan, he tried to pacify his father's mind. Isaac was offended with him for marrying his first wife from Canaan. Therefore, he took a second wife, Mahalath, the daughter of Ishmael, the son of Abraham. {*Ge 28:6-9*}

*115.* Esau had now been a married man for thirty-seven years and was seventy-seven years old. Jacob, who was as old as he, had all this while lived as a bachelor. Remembering his father's command, he asked Rachel to be given to him for his wife because he had served the allotted time for her. {*Ge 29:21*} *[L13]* He was now of an age suitable for marriage, as Tremellius explained it. Tho. Lidyate understood this to have happened after the first month he was with Laban. However, Laban intended from the beginning to make full use of Jacob's industry and his managerial skills before he would give his daughter to Jacob. This no doubt was mentioned when Jacob first arrived, since this was the main purpose for his coming. {*See note on 2259 AM. <<122>>*}

*116.* However, by Laban's fraud, Leah, the older daughter, was put into Jacob's bed on the marriage night instead of Rachel. Nevertheless, at the end of the marriage week, {*Jud 14:12,17*} Rachel was also espoused to him, on the condition that Jacob would serve seven more years for her. *[E9]* Laban gave his maid-servant Zilpah to Leah for a handmaid, and to Rachel he gave Bilhah.

*117.* When Leah was not so favoured by Jacob as Rachel was, God made Rachel barren and Leah was made a mother of four children in four successive years. {*Ge 29:21-30:24*}

### 2246 AM, 2956 JP, 1758 BC

*118.* Leah bore Reuben, Jacob's firstborn. {*Ge 29:32*} Reuben later lost his birthright for his incest committed with Bilhah, his father's concubine. {*Ge 35:22 49:3,4 1 Ch 5:1*}

### 2247 AM, 2957 JP, 1757 BC

*119.* Simeon was born.

### 2248 AM, 2958 JP, 1756 BC

*120.* Levi was born. {*Ge 29:34*}

### 2249c AM, 2959 JP, 1755 BC

*121.* Judah was born, from whom the Jews took their name. {*Ge 29:35*}

### 2259c AM, 2969 JP, 1745 BC

*122.* God blessed Rachel and she bore Joseph to Jacob at the end of his fourteen years of service. Jacob asked permission from Laban to return to his own country. But he remained there six more years on another condition made between him and his father-in-law Laban for a certain part of his flock. {*Ge 30:22,25,31 31:41*} Jacob was ninety-one years old when Joseph was born and consequently, seventy-seven years old when he first began to serve Laban. This may be deduced, for Jacob was a hundred and thirty years old when he first stood before Pharaoh at the time when the seven years of plenty were past and two years of the famine were over. {*Ge 45:6 47:9*} Joseph was then thirty-nine years old. He was thirty years old when he first came before Pharaoh, just before the seven years of plenty. {*Ge 41:32,46*}

## 2261a AM, 2970 JP, 1744 BC

*123.* Mephres reigned in Egypt for twelve years and nine months. {*Manetho, 1:101} {*Josephus, Apion, l. 1. c. 15. (95) 1:201}

## 2265c AM, 2975 JP, 1739 BC

*124.* As the jealousy and malice grew between Laban and his sons against Jacob, God warned him to return to his own country. Jacob told his wives of this. When Laban was shearing his sheep at the latter end of the spring, {see note on 2974c AM. <<438>>} Jacob secretly fled from Laban, after twenty years of service. He took all his goods, wives and family, and crossed over the Euphrates River. {Ge 31:1,3,19,21,38,41} It is said that Jacob had twelve sons born to him in Mesopotamia. {Ge 35:22-26} Benjamin is not to be counted among them, because he was born later in the land of Canaan near Bethlehem. {Ge 35:18,19} In a similar manner, the twelve apostles are counted to make up that number, even though Judas was dead. {Joh 20:24 1Co 15:1} Concerning this matter, see Augustine in his 117th question on Genesis.

*125.* Three days later, Laban (for he was three days' journey from the place where Jacob kept his sheep) heard that his son-in-law was gone, so he pursued him with some of his friends and kindred. After travelling seven days, he caught up with him at Mount Gilead, the mountain which was named from this meeting. After many arguments, they were finally reconciled. As a testimony and monument to their covenant and agreement, Jacob erected a pillar from a heap of stones. [L14] Laban, the Syrian, called it *Jegar Sahadutha*, but Jacob, the Hebrew, called it *Galeed*, meaning *the heap of a testimony*, or *witness* between the two. {Ge 31:22-48}

*126.* After Jacob left Laban in peace, he was frightened by the news of his brother Esau's coming with a band of men. He divided his company into two groups and called on God. He sent messengers ahead of him with presents for his brother Esau. After wrestling with the angel, he was given the name of Israel by God. Jacob matured spiritually by depending more on the help of God than on man. {Ge 32:1-32 Ho 12:3,4}

*127.* Esau entertained his brother courteously. After much entreaty he accepted Jacob's presents, and offered to escort him on his way. When Jacob refused, Esau left. Then Jacob went on to Succoth. He called the place Succoth because he built a house there, and folds for his sheep. After passing over the Jordan River, he came into Canaan and pitched his tent in Shechem, a city of the Shechemites. He bought a parcel of ground from the sons of Hamor the Shechemite for a hundred pieces of silver. There he built an altar, which he called by the name of *El-Elohe-Israel* or *The mighty God, the God of Israel.* {Ge 33:1-20} It was in this same place that Abraham had built his first altar before {Ge 12:6,7} and where Jacob's well was, near Mount Gerizim. When the woman of Samaria spoke to our Saviour, she said that her fathers worshipped in this mountain. {Joh 4:5,6,12,20} This mountain was located in the country of the Shechemites. {Jud 9:7}

## 2273d AM, 2983 JP, 1731 BC

*128.* Mephramuthosis reigned in Egypt for twenty-five years and ten months. {*Manetho, 1:101} {*Josephus, Apion, l. 1. c. 15. (95) 1:201}

## 2276c AM, 2986 JP, 1728 BC

*129.* When Joseph was seventeen years old, he told his father of his brothers' wickedness and was told by God that he would one day be the head of all his father's family. For this his brothers hated him so much that they plotted his death. At length they agreed to sell him as a slave into a far country. When they drew him from the pit that they had cast him into, they sold him for twenty pieces of silver to the Ishmaelite and Midianite merchants. Both of these peoples were descended from their grandfather, Abraham. [E10] Joseph was carried away by them to Egypt. There they sold him to be a slave to Potiphar, the captain of Pharaoh's guard. {Ge 37:2-36} Justin mentioned Joseph and said: {Justin, Trogus, l. 36. c. 2.}

> "His brothers envied the excellency of his wisdom. After getting him privately into their hands, they sold him to foreign merchants who carried him into Egypt."

## 2287c AM, 2997 JP, 1717 BC

*130.* When Joseph was thrown into prison, he interpreted the dreams of two officers of Pharaoh's court. This was two years before he was brought before Pharaoh. {Ge 40:1-41:1}

## 2288c AM, 2998 JP, 1716 BC

*131.* Isaac died at the age of a hundred and eighty years and was buried by his two sons, Esau and Jacob. {Ge 35:28,29}

## 2289b AM, 2999 JP, 1715 BC

*132.* When Pharaoh could not have his dreams interpreted by his own wise men, and after hearing of Joseph's skill in expounding dreams, he sent for Joseph, who was thirty years old when he explained the king's dreams. The first dream was that of the seven years of plenty followed by seven years of famine. Moreover, he advised Pharaoh how to provide from the abundance of the first seven years of plenty, for the famine of the next seven years of scarcity. Thereupon Pharaoh, by the general agreement of all his nobles, made him governor of the whole kingdom. He gave him a wife, Asenath, the daughter of

Potiphar, governor of On or Heliopolis in Egypt. {*Ge 41:1-46*} Justin stated that he was very important to Pharaoh. For he said: {*Justin, Trogus, l. 36. c. 2.*}

> "Joseph was most skilled in explaining dreams or signs and was the first that found out and taught the art of the interpretation of dreams. Neither was there any part of divine or human intention, which seemed to be unknown to him in that he foretold a famine many years before it happened. *[L15]* All Egypt would have perished unless the king, by his advice, had ordered grain to be stored many years before the famine came."

133. From the harvest of this year started the seven years of plenty. In these years Joseph laid up an enormous supply of grain. Asenath, his wife, bore him two sons, Manasseh and Ephraim. {*Ge 41:47-53*}

## 2296c AM, 3006 JP, 1708 BC

134. The seven years of the famine began from the harvest of this year as predicted. Joseph's wisdom in laying up supplies not only sustained Egypt, but also helped relieve the famine in the neighbouring countries. {*Ge 41:54-57*}

## 2297d AM, 3007 JP, 1707 BC

135. Jacob sent ten of his sons into Egypt to buy grain. Joseph pretended not to know them and took them for spies. They were held and not released until Simeon, who was the instigator and the the oldest of those who consented to sell Joseph, was cast into prison. He was held to ensure that the rest should bring to Joseph Benjamin, their youngest brother, who was born of Rachel, Joseph's own mother. When they were sent away, they carried their grain and the money they had paid for it. This money was placed into each of their sacks by the secret orders of Joseph. They told their father Jacob all that had happened to them. They also told him it was necessary that their youngest brother Benjamin return with them to Egypt. They were not able to convince Jacob to allow this to happen. {*Ge 42:1-38*}

## 2298b AM, 3008 JP, 1706 BC

136. When Jacob was hard pressed by the famine, he sent his sons again and with them Benjamin, their brother. He sent twice the amount of money needed to buy grain, as well as other gifts for Joseph. When they arrived, they were courteously entertained and feasted by Joseph. Simeon was released and returned to them. {*Ge 43:1-34*}

137. When they were on their way home, Joseph arrested them for stealing his cup. This he had secretly caused to be hidden in Benjamin's sack. When they were confronted with their crime, they tried to show their honesty by the fact that they returned the money they found in their sacks when they came into Egypt the second time. They offered to die, or to be his slaves, if any such thing could be proven against them. But in the end the cup was found with Benjamin. They returned to Joseph and yielded themselves to him to be his slaves. When Joseph refused and said he would have no one but him with whom the cup was found, Judah then humbly offered himself to serve him in Benjamin's stead. {*Ge 44:1-34*}

138. When Joseph heard Judah make this offer, he revealed himself to his brothers. The brothers were all terrified at the remembrance of the sin which they had committed against Joseph. He comforted them by showing how that deed of theirs was an act of God's providence. From the king's supplies, Joseph ordered wagons and provisions for their journey. They were to go back and to return with all speed, bringing their father and their families with them. When they told their father, he did not believe them, until he saw the wagons and other supplies necessary for them to move to Egypt. {*Ge 45:1-28*}

139. After Jacob offered sacrifices and was encouraged by God, he and all his family went down into Egypt. This was in the beginning of the third year of the famine when Jacob was a hundred and thirty years old. {*Ge 45:6 46:1-27 47:9 De 26:5*}

140. After Joseph had told Pharaoh of the arrival of his family in Egypt, he brought his father and five of his brothers to Pharaoh. When Pharaoh had communed with them, he assigned them a suitable place in the land of Goshen, where Joseph took care of all their needs. {*Ge 47:1-12*} *[E11]*

## 2299d AM, 3009 JP, 1705 BC

141. Mephramuthosis died and Thmosis reigned in Egypt for nine years eight months. {*Manetho, 1:101*} {*Josephus, Apion, l. 1. c. 15. (96) 1:201*}

## 2300 AM, 3010 JP, 1704 BC

142. Joseph received all the money in Egypt and Canaan in return for the grain that he had sold to them. {*Ge 47:14*} *[L16]*

## 2301 AM, 3011 JP, 1703 BC

143. When all the money of both these countries had been used up, the Egyptians sold all their flocks and herds of cattle to Joseph in exchange for food to live on for that year. {*Ge 47:15-17*}

## 2302 AM, 3012 JP, 1702 BC

144. At the end of this year, when they had no money or cattle left, the Egyptians sold both their lands and

freedom to Joseph. In return he supplied them with grain for food and seed for planting in this seventh and final year of the famine. He was to be repaid in the following year, when the famine was over. So that Pharaoh would have a clear title and full possession of the lands he purchased, Joseph moved everyone from one side of the country to the other away from their original habitations according to the Targums of Jonathan and Jerusalem. {*See Gill on "Ge 47:21"} He assigned land to every man to till and work. A law was made giving Pharaoh a fifth part of the increase, or yield. Only the lands of the chief governors and the priests were not bought up by Pharaoh. These individuals lived on an allowance from the king and had no need to sell their lands for food as did everyone else. {Ge 47:18-26}

## 2309b AM, 3019 JP, 1695 BC

145. Amenophis reigned in Egypt for thirty years and ten months. {*Manetho, 1:103} {*Josephus, Apion, l. 1. c. 15. (96) 1:201}

## 2315c AM, 3025 JP, 1689 BC

146. When Jacob was about to die, he adopted Ephraim and Manasseh, the sons of Joseph. He blessed them by revelation from God and set the younger ahead of the older. {Ge 48:1-22 Heb 11:21} Calling his sons together, he blessed them all and foretold what should befall them in the future, including in his blessing that memorable prophesy of the Messiah. Then he gave orders to them concerning his burial. He died at a hundred and forty-seven years of age, the last seventeen years of which were spent in the land of Egypt. {Ge 49:1-33 47:25}

## 2315d AM, 3025 JP, 1689 BC

147. Joseph had the body of Jacob embalmed, a process taking forty days, while all the Egyptians mourned him for seventy days. With Pharaoh's permission, the body was conveyed into the land of Canaan by Joseph and his brothers, accompanied by a large number of the principal men of Pharaoh's court. {Ge 50:1-13} Here, lamentation was again made over him for seven days, after which he was buried with his kindred in the cave at Machpelah according to his wishes. {Ge 50:15-21}

## 2340b AM, 3050 JP, 1664 BC

148. Orus reigned in Egypt for thirty-six years and five months. {*Manetho, 1:103} {*Josephus, Apion, l. 1. c. 15. (96) 1:201}

## 2369c AM, 3079 JP, 1635 BC

149. By faith, Joseph on his death bed spoke of the departure of the children of Israel from Egypt. He asked that his bones might be carried with them. He was a hundred and ten years old when he died, having seen his children to the third generation. {Ge 50:22-26 Heb 11:22} The sons of Ephriam were Shuthelah, Becher and Tahan. The son of Shuthelah was Eran or Taran. {Nu 26:35,36} The sons of Manasseh were Macher and Gilead. {Nu 26:29} From here it is that the Greek expositors, speaking of the families of Jacob and Joseph, which were said to consist of seventy souls, {Ge 46:27 De 10:22} added to the total these five who were born to Joseph in Egypt {1Ch 7:20-29} to make up a number of seventy-five persons in all. It appears that Joseph ruled and governed the state of Egypt for eighty years under several Pharaohs. Eusebius correctly noted and summarised it thus: {*Eusebius, Chronicles, l. 1. 1:40}

"Joseph was made governor of Egypt when he was thirty years old and when his father Jacob was a hundred and twenty-two years old. He headed the government for eighty years. After he died, the Hebrews were held in bondage by the Egyptians for a hundred and forty-four years. {Ge 15:13 Ex 12:40 Ac 7:7 Ga 3:17} [L17] Therefore, the whole time which the Hebrews spent in Egypt was two hundred and fifteen years, starting from the time that Jacob and his sons went down into Egypt."

150. On this supposed problem of the number of people in Jacob's family, {Ge 46:27 De 10:22 Ac 7:14} Gill stated: {See Gill on "Ac 7:14"}

"and called his father Jacob to him, and all his kindred, threescore and fifteen souls; which seems to disagree with the account of Moses, who says that "all the souls of the house of Jacob, which came into Egypt, were threescore and ten," {Ge 46:27} But there is no contradiction; Moses and Stephen are speaking of different things; Moses speaks of the seed of Jacob, which came out of his loins, who came into Egypt, and so excludes his sons' wives; Stephen speaks of Jacob and all his kindred, among whom his sons' wives must be reckoned, whom Joseph called to him: according to Moses' account, the persons that came with Jacob into Egypt, who came out of his loins, and so exclusive of his sons' wives, were sixty-six; to which if we add Jacob himself, and Joseph who was before in Egypt, and who might be truly said to come into it, and his two sons that were born there, who came from his loins, as others in the account may be said to do, who were not yet born when Jacob went down, the total number is seventy, {Ge 46:26,27} out of which take the six following persons, Jacob, who was called by Joseph into Egypt, besides the seventy-five souls, and Joseph and his two sons then in Egypt, who could not be said to be called by him, and Hezron and Hamul, the sons of Pharez not yet born, and this will reduce Moses' number to sixty-four; to which sixty-four, if you add the eleven wives of Jacob's sons, who were certainly part of the kindred called and invited into Egypt, {Ge 45:10,19 45:5} it will make up completely seventy-five persons: or the persons called by Joseph may be reckoned thus: his eleven brethren and sister Dinah, fifty-two brother's children, to which add his brethren's eleven wives, and the amount is seventy-five: so that the Jew {R. Isaac Chizzuk Emuna, par. 2. c. 63. p. 450.} has no reason to charge Stephen with an error, as he does; nor was there any need to alter and corrupt the Septuagint version of Genesis {Ge 45:27} to make it agree with Stephen's account; or to add five names in it, in Acts {Ac 7:20} as Machir, Galaad, Sutalaam, Taam, and Edom, to make up the number seventy-five; and it may be observed, that the number is not altered in the version of Deuteronomy {De 10:22} which agrees with the Hebrew for seventy persons."

151. The book of Genesis ends with the death of Joseph and contains the history of the first twenty-three hundred and sixty-nine years of the world. This book was written by Moses. This is the opinion of the Talmudists and so it is generally believed by all the Hebrews. {Talmudists, Baba-bathra, l. 1.} Job likely lived toward the end of the period of history that was recorded in Genesis. The following account of Job was given by Severus Sulpicius: {*Sulpicius Severus, Sacred History, l. 1. c. 13. 11:76}

"At this time lived Job, a man embracing the law of nature, and the knowledge of the true God and very righteous and rich in goods. He was renowned for the fact that neither the enjoyment of those riches corrupted him, nor the loss of them depraved him in any way. When he was plundered of all his goods by Satan, bereft of his children and at last tormented with grievous botches and sores in his body, he did not sin. Having first been commended by God himself, he was later restored to his former health and had double of what he possessed before."

### 2376c AM, 3086 JP, 1628 BC

152. Acencheres, the daughter of Orus, reigned in Egypt for twelve years and one month. {*Manetho, 1:103} {*Josephus, Apion, l. 1. c. 15. (96) 1:201}

### 2385 AM, 3095 JP, 1619 BC

153. Levi died in Egypt when he was a hundred and thirty-seven years old. {Ex 6:16} He was the grandfather on the mother's side to Moses and Aaron and great grandfather on the father's side. Levi had begotten Kohath in Canaan, who died at the age of a hundred and thirty-three years, and a daughter called Jochebed in Egypt. Amram, the son of Kohath, married Jochebed, the daughter of Levi, his own aunt. From that marriage

(expressly forbidden later {Le 18:12 20:19}), Moses, Aaron and their sister Miriam were born. Amram lived a hundred and thirty-seven years, just as long as his grandfather and father-in-law, Levi. [E12] He died shortly before the Israelites left Egypt. {Ex 2:1 6:18,20 Nu 26:59} {See Perer. in chapter 2 of Exodus disputations 1.}

### 2388d AM, 3098 JP, 1616 BC

154. Rathotis, the brother of Acencheres, reigned in Egypt for nine years. {*Manetho, 1:103} {*Josephus, Apion, l. 1. c. 15. (96) 1:201}

### 2389 AM, 3099 JP, 1615 BC

155. When the Ethiopians came from as far as the Indus River, they settled on the borders of Egypt. {*Eusebius, Chronicles, l. 1. 1:53} This was that place to which the Panegyrist referred, when he said: (This may be an allusion to the work of Isocrates. Editor.)

"Let the victories of Egypt give place to this: under which the Ethiopian and Indus both did tremble"

156. J. Potken, in his Ethiopian Psalter printed at Rome in 1513 AD, wrote that Ethiopia, which is to the south of Egypt, was called the Greater India.

### 2397d AM, 3107 JP, 1607 BC

157. Acencheres I, the son of Rathotis, reigned in Egypt for twelve years and five months. (Josephus does not say this was Acencheres II, although there was a queen who reigned earlier with the same name. {See note on 2376c AM. <<152>>} Editor.) {*Manetho, 1:103} {*Josephus, Apion, l. 1. c. 15. (97) 1:201}

### 2410a AM, 3119 JP, 1595 BC

158. Acencheres II reigned in Egypt for twelve years and three months. {*Manetho, 1:103} {*Josephus, Apion, l. 1. c. 15. (97) 1:201}

### 2422b AM, 3132 JP, 1582 BC

159. Harmais reigned in Egypt for four years and one month. {*Manetho, 1:103} {*Josephus, Apion, l. 1. c. 15. (97) 1:201}

### 2426c AM, 3136 JP, 1578 BC

160. Ramesses reigned in Egypt for one year and four months. {*Manetho, 1:103} {*Josephus, Apion, l. 1. c. 15. (97) 1:201}

### 2427d AM, 3137 JP, 1577 BC

161. Ramesses Miamun reigned in Egypt for sixty-six years and two months. {*Manetho, 1:103} {*Josephus, Apion, l. 1. c. 15. (94) 1:201} The latter part of the surname seems to have been derived from the first part of the name Amenophis. His son after him as well as several of his predecessors were called by this name. The former part was from the word *Mou* which with the Egyptians signifies *water*, [L18] as Josephus {*Josephus, Apion, l. 1. c. 32.

(286) 1:279} and Clement {*Clement, Stromateis, l. 1. c. 23. 2:335} and Suidas (in Μωυ) affirmed. The school of writers called mythologists, who relate everything in the form of fables, gave him the name of Neptune, the feigned god of the waters. {See note on 2533 AM. <<261>>} This is that new king, who did not know Joseph. He was born after Joseph's death and had no recollection of the great benefits Egypt had received through him. By his policy the Egyptians, frightened at the number and strength of the Israelites in the land, subjected them to heavy and cruel bondage. In addition to tilling the ground, they forced them to also build the king's citadels and storehouses and the treasure cities of Pithom and Raamses or Ramesis. {Ex 1:8-14 Ac 7:18,19} The latter took its name, as Mercator thinks, from Ramesses, the founder of it, and the other perhaps from his queen.

## 2430b AM, 3140 JP, 1574 BC

162. Aaron was born three years before his brother Moses, eighty-three years before the departure of the Israelites from Egypt. {Ex 7:7}

## 2431b AM, 3141 JP, 1573 BC

163. The ungodly king could not prevail with Shiphrah and Pua, the two principal midwives of the Hebrew women, to force them to kill all the male children of the Hebrews. Therefore he proclaimed a barbarous edict to destroy them all by drowning them in the river. {Ex 1:15-22 Ac 7:19,20} This edict was made sometime between the birth of Aaron and the birth of Moses.

## 2433 AM, 3143 JP, 1571 BC

164. Forty-eight years after the death of her father Levi, Jochebed bore Moses to Amram, her nephew and husband. Moses was eighty years old when he first spoke to Pharaoh to let the children of Israel go. {Ex 7:7} Forty years later Moses died in the twelfth month when he was one hundred and twenty years old. {De 31:2 34:7}

165. Because Moses was an attractive child, as Justin mentioned him to have been, his parents hid him three months in their house. {Justin, Trogus, l. 36. c. 2.} They disregarded the king's edict. {Ex 2:2 Ac 7:20 Heb 11:23}

166. He was discovered through the diligent inquiry made by the king's searchers and their bad neighbours, the Egyptians. The parents put him in a basket of bulrushes, daubed over with slime and pitch, and placed this in the reeds by the side of the river. His sister Miriam or Mary {Nu 26:59 1Ch 6:3} stood nearby to see what would become of him. He was found there by Pharaoh's daughter. (Josephus called her Thermutis, as did Epiphanius, and others. {*Josephus, Antiq., l. 2. c. 9. s. 5. (224) 4:261} {Epiphanius, Panarion}) She gave him to be nursed, as it happened, to his own mother Jochebed! Afterward she adopted him

as her son and had him brought up and instructed in all the science and learning of the Egyptians. {Ex 2:5-10 Ac 7:21,22}

## 2448 AM, 3158 JP, 1556 BC

167. Cecrops, an Egyptian, transported a colony of the Sais into Attica {*Diod. Sic., l. 1. c. 28. s. 4. 1:91} and there set up the kingdom of the Athenians. This was seven hundred and eighty years before the first Olympiad, according to Eusebius, {*Eusebius, Chronicles, l. 1. 1:58} as derived from Castor. The chronology of the Isle of Pharos, published by that most learned J. Selden as part of his *Marmora Arundelliana*, deduced the history or antiquities of Greece from the time of Cecrops. After the time of Cecrops and Moses, who was his contemporary, many notable things happened in Greece. The accounts of these items may have been exaggerated with time and became encrusted as myths. Eusebius stated:

> "Now the history of the events so celebrated among the Greeks is later than the time of Cecrops. For after Cecrops comes the deluge in the time of Deucalion, and the conflagration in the time of Phaeton, and the birth of Ericthonius, and the rape of Proserpina, and the mysteries of Demeter, and the establishment of the Eleusinian mysteries, the husbandry of Triptolemus, the abduction of Europa by Zeus, the birth of Apollo, the arrival of Cadmus at Thebes, and still later than these, Dionysus, Minos, Perseus, Asclepius, the Dioscuri, and Hercules."
> {*Eusebius, Gospel, l. 10. c. 9. (484c) 1:518} [L19]

## 2465 AM, 3175 JP, 1539 BC

168. In the eighteenth year of Cecrops, the Chaldeans went to war against the Phoenicians. {*Eusebius, Chronicles, l. 1. 1:61}

## 2466 AM, 3176 JP, 1538 BC

169. In this war the Chaldeans were defeated, and the Arabians reigned in the country of Babylon for two hundred and sixteen years before Belus the Assyrian came to reign there. The first king of the Arabians was Mardocentes, who reigned there forty-five years, {Julius Africanus} and seems to have been the man that is called Merodach. He was later reputed by the Babylonians to be a god. {Jer 50:2} Succeeding kings copied their names from him as Merodoch, Baladan and Evil-merodach.

## 2473b AM, 3183 JP, 1531 BC

170. When Moses was forty years old, he visited his brethren, the Israelites. When he saw their sad plight and observed an Egyptian smiting a man of the Hebrews, he killed the Egyptian and buried him in the sand. [E13] This became known not only to his brethren but also to Pharaoh, who sought to kill him. Moses fled from there

into the land of Midian. He married Zipporah, the daughter of Jethro, and stayed there forty years. {*Ac 7:23-30 Ex 2:11-22 3:1 18:1,2 Nu 10:29 Jud 4:11*}

## 2474 AM, 3184 JP, 1530 BC

*171.* Caleb, the son of Jephunneh, was born forty years before he was sent by Moses to spy out the land of Canaan. {*Jos 14:7,10*}

## 2494a AM, 3203 JP, 1511 BC

*172.* Ramesses Miamun died in the sixty-seventh year of his reign about 1511 BC or 3203 JP. The length of his tyrannical reign seems to be noted in these words:

> "And it came to pass in process of time, that the king of Egypt died: and the children of Israel sighed by reason of the bondage, and they cried...." {*Ex 2:23*}

*173.* This was the cruel bondage which, even after Ramesses was dead, they endured for about a further nineteen years and six months under his son Amenophis, who succeeded him. For Manetho in his writings assigns so long a time and no longer to his reign. {*Manetho, 1:103*} {*Josephus, Apion, l. 1. c. 15. (97) 1:201*} Although Manetho is filled with a multitude of old wives' tales, all of which were abundantly refuted by Josephus in his first book *Against Apion*, yet there are two truths in Manetho's work:

a) Amenophis was the father of Sethosis or Ramesses who was the first king of the following dynasty, or successive principality, which Manetho makes to be the nineteenth dynasty. (This was not under the other Amenophis who was the third king in the eighteenth dynasty as Josephus vainly surmised.) It was the time of the second Amenophis in the eighteenth dynasty that the Israelites left Egypt, under the conduct of Moses, according to Manetho's account. {*Diod. Sic., l. 1. c. 28. s. 2,3. 1:91*}

b) The Egyptians called him Amenophis, the father of Sethosis and Harmais. The Greeks called Amenophis by the name of Belus, the father of Egyptus and Danaus. Thallus, the historian (as he was cited by Theophilus {*Theophilus, Ad Autolycum, l. 3. c. 20. 2:117*} and Lactantius), confirmed that the time of Belus agreed with the time of this Amenophis. However, the fable writers confounded this Belus of Egypt with Belus the Assyrian, the father of Ninus. They stated that certain colonies were transported by this Belus (who was drowned in the Red Sea) into the country of Babylon. {*Diod. Sic., l. 1. c. 28. s. 1. 1:91*}

## 2513b AM, 3223 JP, 1491 BC

*174.* God appeared to Moses in a burning bush that was not consumed by fire, while he was keeping his father-in-law Jethro's sheep on the mountain of Horeb. He called him to deliver His people Israel from their slavery and bondage in Egypt. Moses sought with many excuses to avoid doing this. At length however, he undertook the work, being persuaded partly by miracles and partly by assurance given him of the help of God. His brother Aaron was to be his assistant. {*Ac 7:30-35 Ex 3:1-4:18*}

*175.* Moses left Jether or Jethro, his father-in-law, and with his family journeyed toward Egypt. *[L20]* Because he had neglected to circumcise his son Eliezer, he was stopped by God along the way and not allowed to continue until he had done this. He sent back his wife Zipporah and his two sons, Gershom and Eliezer, to her father Jethro. Now freed from all encumbrance, he returned to Mount Horeb and met his brother Aaron. He went on and performed his duty, confirmed by miracles in the public sight of the children of Israel. {*Ex 4:18-31 18:1-6*}

*176.* Moses and Aaron declared God's message to Pharaoh, who charged them with being leaders in a rebellion and angrily sent them away. He increased the burden of the Israelites more than ever. Their overseers were beaten because the people could not do all the work. In vain they complained to Pharaoh. They complained to Moses and Aaron, and Moses complained to God. God graciously heard him and told him to finish the work he had begun. {*Ex 5:1-22*}

*177.* Moses returned to the Israelites with renewed promises of deliverance from God, but because of their oppression they did not heed him. Whereupon God commanded him to go again to Pharaoh. {*Ex 6:1-30*}

*178.* Moses was eighty years old and Aaron eighty-three when they were commanded by God to return again to Pharaoh. When the magicians by their sorcery imitated the miracles of Aaron's rod becoming a serpent, Pharaoh became more obstinate than ever. {*Ex 7:1-13*} The leaders of these magicians who opposed Moses were Jannes and Jambres, as named by the apostle Paul. {*2Ti 3:8*} These names are noted not only by the Jews in their Talmudical treatise of מנחות (that is, Oblations, c. 9.) where they are called by the names of יוחני and וממרא, that is Jochanne and Mamre. They are mentioned also in the Chaldee Paraphrase, where they are attributed to Jonathan, {*Ex 1:15 7:11*} as well as among some heathen writers, for Numenius Apamea, a Pythagorean philosopher, in his third book περι τ αγαθου cited by Eusebius. He related this account: {*Eusebius, Gospel, l. 9. c. 8. (411d) 1:443*}

> "Jannes and Jambres, interpreters of the mysteries of Egypt, were in great repute at the time when the

Jews were sent out of Egypt. It was the opinion of all men that these were inferior to none in the art of magic. For by the common opinion of the Egyptians, these two were chosen to oppose Moses, the ring leader of the Jews. Moses' prayers were most prevalent with God and they alone were able to undo and end all those most grievous calamities that God brought upon all the Egyptians."

179. Pliny in reference to this stated: {*Pliny, l. 30. c. 2. (11) 8:285}

"There is also another sect of magicians, derived from Moses, Jannes, Lotapes and the Jews."

180. Pliny is, however, incorrect on two counts:

a) In reckoning Moses among the magicians.
b) In making Jannes and Lotapes to be Jews.

181. But when Pharaoh's magicians could do no more, God through Moses sent his ten plagues upon the Egyptians. These are summarised in the Psalms. {Ps 78:1-72 105:1-45}. According to the Jews, these plagues lasted a year, but in fact they were all sent within one month, in the following order. [E14]

182. About the eighteenth day of the sixth month of the year (which later became the twelfth month {Ex 12:2}), God sent the first plague of the waters turning into blood. {Ex 7:17-24} After seven days, {Ex 7:25} about the twenty-fifth day, came the second plague of the frogs which were removed the next day. {Ex 8:1-15} On about the twenty-seventh day, the third plague of lice was brought upon them. {Ex 8:16-19}

183. About the twenty-eighth day, Moses threatened them with a fourth plague of flies. These came on the twenty-ninth day and were all taken away on the thirtieth day. {Ex 8:20-32} [L21]

## 2513c AM, 3223 JP, 1491 BC

184. About the first day of the seventh month (which shortly after was made the first month of the year {Ex 12:2}), Moses warned them of a fifth plague, which he brought upon them the following day. This was the plague of murrain in cattle. {Ex 9:1-7} About the third day, the sixth plague of boils and botches came upon man and beast. This plague came on the magicians as well. {Ex 9:8-11} Concerning this, Justin wrote: {Justin, Trogus, l. 36.}

"The Egyptians were afflicted with scabs and sores. When they were warned by an oracle, all that were infected with that disease expelled Moses out of Egypt, lest the plague should spread further among the people."

185. Note here also the sayings collected from Diodorus {*Diod. Sic., l. 40. c. 3. s. 3. 12:281} as recorded by Photius. {Photius, Bibliotheca, p. 620}

186. About the fourth day, Moses warned them of a seventh plague which came upon them on the fifth day of the same month. It was a plague of thunder and rain and grievous hail, mixed with fire, which ruined their flax and barley, because the barley was then in the ear and the flax bolled. But the wheat and the rye were not harmed, because they were not yet out of the ground. {Ex 9:12-35} Hence Nicolaus Fullerus correctly noted that this plague happened in the month of Abib. {Fullerus, Miscellany, l. 3. p. 389}

187. About the seventh day Moses threatened them with an eighth plague. The next day the plague of locusts came and devoured all the green plants. He removed the plague about the ninth day. {Ex 10:1-19}

188. The month of Abib, which was the seventh month, was from this time on made the first month of the year. {Ex 12:2 13:4} This was for a memorial of their departure from the land of Egypt. From the beginning of this month we deduce the epochs of the Jewish calendar. {Nu 9:1,2 Ex 40:17}

189. On the tenth day of this month (which was Thursday, April 30 according to the Julian Calendar), the feast of the Passover and Unleavened Bread was instituted. The Pascal lamb was chosen and killed four days later. {Ex 13:3,6}

190. Meanwhile Moses brought upon them the ninth plague of three days of darkness. It was so dark during that time, that none of the Egyptians left the place where they were while the darkness lasted. The Israelites, however, had light in their dwellings throughout that time. {Ex 10:22,23}

191. On the fourteenth day (Monday, May 4), Moses spoke with Pharaoh for the last time. Moses told him of the tenth plague which was to come upon him. This was the death of all the firstborn of Egypt, which came to pass on the following night at midnight. In a rage, Pharaoh ordered Moses to get out of his sight and never come back again. {Ex 10:24-29 11:1,4-8} That evening they celebrated the Passover. {Ex 12:11,12}

# The Fourth Age of the World

## 2513c AM, 3223 JP, 1491 BC

*192.* On the fifteenth day of the first month (Tuesday, May 5), at midnight, the firstborn of all Egypt were killed. Pharaoh and his servants quickly sent away the Israelites with all their goods and the plunder which they had received from the Egyptians. {*Ex 12:33,35,36*} It was exactly four hundred and thirty years from the first pilgrimage of Abraham's departure from Canaan to the day they were set free from bondage. The day after the Passover they journeyed toward Ramesses with about six hundred thousand men, besides women and children. {*Ex 12:29-31,37,41,51 Nu 33:3*} [*L22*] From there on, the camps are recorded by Moses. {*Nu 33*} In writing to Fabiola, Jerome expounded symbolically the Hebrew meaning of the words in his treatise of their forty-two camps. I assume the first camp to be at Ramesses. Thus then:

1) At Ramesses, where the Israelites had been placed by Joseph, {*Ge 47:11*}, they all met those who now either lived among the Egyptians {*Ex 3:22*} or who at that time were scattered over all Egypt to gather stubble. {*Ex 5:12*}

2) At Succoth, Moses first declared to them the commandments of God for the yearly keeping of the Passover and the sanctifying of the firstborn. {*Ex 13:1-22*}

3) At Etham, on the border of the wilderness, the Lord led them with a pillar of cloud by day and a pillar of fire by night. {*Ex 13:20,21*}

4) At Pihahiroth, between Migdol and the sea, opposite Baalzephon, Pharaoh overtook them with his army. There Moses divided the waters with his rod and they passed through the midst of the Trythraean or Red Sea, into the desert of Etham. When Pharaoh and his army tried to follow, they were all drowned when the waters came together again. [*E15*] At dawn, the Israelites were completely freed from the bondage of the Egyptians, whose bodies they saw floating all over the sea and washed up on the shore. {*Ex 14:26-30*} They sang a song of praise and thanksgiving to God for their deliverance. {*Ex 15:22*} This song is called the song of Moses and is the first song of deliverance sung by the Hebrews. {*Re 15:3*}

This happened on the twenty-first day of the first month on the last day of the feast of Unleavened Bread, as appointed by God. This is the general opinion of the Jews and is in accordance with known facts. {*Ex 12:16*}

From there they marched three whole days through the wilderness of Etham, from Tuesday the 22nd to Thursday the 24th and they found no water anywhere along the way. {*Ex 15:22 Nu 33:8*}

5) At Marah, named after its bitter waters, the people who had gone without water three whole days began to murmur. Moses threw a piece of wood into the water and made the waters drinkable. This taught the people over time to come to put their trust in God. {*Ex 15:23-26*}

6) At Elim were twelve springs of water and seventy palm trees. They camped near those springs. {*Ex 15:27 Nu 33:9*}

7) This camp was by the Red Sea. {*Nu 33:10*}

*193.* Now we come to the second month.

8) On the fifteenth day (Thursday, June 4), the Israelites came to the place of their eighth camp in the wilderness of Zin, between Elyma and Sinai. Because they were hungry, they murmured against God and their leaders. Towards evening God sent them quails and the next morning rained manna from heaven down on them. They lived on manna for forty years until they entered the land of promise. {*Ex 16:1-35*}

9) They camped at Dophkah.

10) They camped at Alush.

11) At Rephidim the people murmured again because of thirst. [*L23*] (This place was called Meribah and Massa.) Moses gave them water by striking the hard rock with his rod. {*Ex 17:1-7*} This *Rock* followed them throughout the wilderness. {*Ps 78:16,20 105:41 1Co 10:4 De 8:15*}

The Amalekites attacked the rear of the Israelites, who were all weary and tired from their long journey in the wilderness. They killed some of the stragglers and weakest among them. Moses sent out his servant Jehoshua or Joshua, the son of Nun, to fight against them. {*Ex 33:11*} His proper name was Hosea, but Moses changed it to Joshua, {*Nu 13:16*} or Jesus in the Greek. {*Ne 8:17 Ac 7:45 Heb 4:8*}

Joshua fought and defeated the Amalekites in Rephidim while Moses prayed on the top of the hill. The people were commanded by God to utterly destroy and root out that whole nation. As a memorial of this battle they built an altar there. {De 25:17-19 Ex 17:8-16}

*194.* The third month.

12) In the desert of Sinai, the Israelites camped opposite Horeb and stayed there almost a whole year. They left the wilderness of Sinai on the second day of the second month, of the second year after coming out of the land of Egypt. {Nu 10:11,12} They arrived there on the same day of the third month of the first year, after coming out of Egypt. This was on the third day of the third month (Monday, June 22), according to Fr. Ribera. {Ribera, De Temple, l. 5. c. 7.} {Ex 19:1}

*195.* When Moses went up into the mount, God declared to him that he would renew his covenant with the Israelites. He declared that he would bind them to himself by a law and that he would favour and love all those who would observe and keep that law. This they readily agreed to. God gave them two days to prepare and sanctify themselves to receive that law. He forbade everyone except Moses and Aaron to approach the mount. Afterward God came down to the mount in great majesty as they all watched and trembled at the sight. {Ex 19:1-25}

*196.* With a terrifying voice, God proclaimed his law as contained in the ten commandments. {Ex 20:1-26 De 5:1-33} This did not make void the promise of grace made to Abraham four hundred and thirty years earlier. {Ga 3:17}

*197.* The people were terrified as God gave them many other laws. {Ex 20:21-23 De 4:13,14} These were written in the book of the covenant Moses gave to the people. After this, Moses rose early in the morning and built an altar at the foot of the mountain. He set up twelve pillars corresponding to the twelve tribes of Israel. He sent twelve young men of the firstborn (as the Chaldee paraphrase has it) whom the Lord had consecrated to himself {Ex 13.2 Nu 3:13 8:16,17} to be ministers of the holy things. {Ex 19:22} This was before the Levitical priesthood was ordained. [E16] These men offered sacrifices, first for sin and then as a thanksgiving to the Lord. Moses read to the people the book of the covenant which contained the commandments found in Exodus. {Ex 20:1-23:33}. He then took the blood of the calves and goats that were offered, and with water, scarlet wool and hyssop he sprinkled the book as well as the twelve pillars representing the twelve tribes of Israel. This ratified that solemn covenant between God and his people. {Ex 24:3-8 Heb 9:19,20}

*198.* Moses and Aaron, Nadab and Abihu and seventy men of the elders of Israel went up into the mount and there beheld the glory of God. [L24] When the remainder returned, Moses, with his servant Joshua, stayed there for a further six days. On the seventh day God spoke to Moses and he continued there forty days and forty nights. {Ex 24:9-18} This time includes those six days which he spent waiting for the Lord. During this time, he ate no food nor drank water. {De 9:9} He received God's commands concerning the construction of the tabernacle, the priests' garments, their consecration, sacrifices and other things as related in Exodus. {Ex 25:1-Ex 31:18}

## 2513d AM, 3223 JP, 1491 BC

*199.* The fourth month.

*200.* When those forty days and forty nights were over, God gave Moses the two tables of the law written in stone by God's own finger. {Ex 31:18 De 9:10,11} God ordered him to go down quickly, for the people had already made a molten calf to worship. Moses, in prayer, pleaded with God on their behalf, and having prevailed, he went down from the mount. When he saw the people in the camp keeping a festival in honour of their idol, he broke the tables of the law at the foot of the mount. {Ex 32:1-19} Ever since this event, to this day the Jews have kept a solemn fast on the fourteenth day of the fourth month. This has led some men into the error that the forty days of Moses in the mount were to be started from the day immediately following the giving of the ten commandments, thus omitting altogether the intermediate time spent in writing and reading the book of the covenant and sanctifying the covenant made between God and his people with solemn rites and ceremonies. {Ex 24:1-18}

*201.* Moses burned and defaced the idol and the Levites killed three thousand of the people. {Ex 32:20-29 De 9:21 33:9}

*202.* The next day Moses returned again to the mount and there again entreated the Lord for the people. {Ex 32:30-32}

*203.* He commanded them to lay aside their gorgeous apparel and to set up the tent of the congregation outside the camp. This tent was used until the tabernacle was built by Bezaleel. The people, from a deep sense of God's wrath, repented of their sins. Moses prayed that God himself should be their guide and leader on their way, and not an angel as God had threatened. This prayer was heard. {Ex 33:1-23}

*204.* God commanded Moses to get new tables of stone and to bring them with him into the mount the next day. Moses brought them the next morning. When Moses stood in the cleft of a rock, God passed by and showed him a glimpse of his glory. {Ex 34:1-35}

205. Again Moses stayed another forty days and forty nights in the mount without food or water and prayed for the people. {De 9:18 10:10} God was appeased and renewed his covenant with the people, with certain conditions. He gave his laws again and told Moses to write them down. God himself rewrote the ten commandments on the tables which Moses brought to him. {Ex 34:10-28}

206. The sixth month.

207. After forty days, Moses returned from the mount with the tables in his hand. Because his face shone, he covered it with a veil. He proclaimed the laws of God to the people, ordering the observance of the Sabbath. He asked for a free will offering to be made toward the building of the tabernacle. {Ex 34:1-35:35}

208. So that this offering could be done in an orderly manner, all males were numbered from twenty years old and upward and there were found to be 603,550. According to the law prescribed by God, {Ex 30:12,13} each contributed half a shekel. The total sum amounted to a hundred talents of silver and seventeen hundred and seventy-five shekels. {Ex 38:25,26} [L25] From this we gather that among the Jews each talent amounted to three thousand shekels—every pound containing sixty shekels. {Eze 45:12}. In addition to this poll tax from the voluntary offering was the sum of twenty-nine talents and seven hundred and thirty shekels of gold; and seventy talents and twenty-four hundred shekels of brass. {Ex 38:24,29} As for other materials needed for the tabernacle, there came in more than enough, and the people were commanded to stop giving! {Ex 36:5-7}

209. Bezaleel and Aholiab were appointed by God as the chief workmen of the tabernacle. {Ex 31:2-6 35:30-35}

## 2514a AM, 3223 JP, 1491 BC

210. In the last six months of this year the tabernacle, the ark of the covenant, the altar, the table of showbread, the priests' garments, the holy ointments, the lampstands and other utensils and vessels belonging to the sacrifices were finished in the desert at Mount Sinai and were brought to Moses. {Ex 36:1-39:43} [E17]

## 2514b AM, 3224 JP, 1490 BC

211. God commanded Moses, that:

a) On the first day of the first month he should set up the tabernacle and furnish it with all the items belonging to it. {Ex 40:2-8}

b) He should anoint them with holy oil and should consecrate Aaron and his sons for the priesthood. {Ex 40:9-15}

212. He did this, but not both activities at the same time. {Ex 40:16} For on the very day God appointed, he erected the tabernacle with everything belonging to it. {Ex 40:17-33} The second command he performed later, at a time appointed by God. {Le 8:1-13} It took seven days for the consecration of the priests and altar. {Ex 29:35-37}

## 2514c AM, 3224 JP, 1490 BC

213. On the first day of the first month (Wednesday, April 21) of the second year after they left Egypt, the tabernacle of the covenant was set up and was filled with the glory of God. {Ex 40:2,17,34} From it God uttered his will and commandments to Moses. These are recorded in Leviticus. {Le 1:1-7:38} In the same year and this same first month, the Israelites, as commanded by God, celebrated the passover on the evening of the fourteenth day (Tuesday, May 4). On this day some of the people complained to Moses and Aaron that they could not keep the passover with the rest of the congregation on the appointed day, because they were unclean from touching a dead body. God made a law that all such persons should keep their passover on the fourteenth day of the second month if they could not keep it on the day first appointed. {Nu 9:1-14}

214. On the first day of the second month (Friday, May 21), God commanded Moses to count the number of all the males of the children of Israel from twenty years old to sixty by their tribes, except the Levites. He appointed the Levites to the service of the tabernacle and assigned to them the various responsibilities for setting it up, taking it down and moving and carrying it from place to place. {Nu 1:1 26:64}

215. The census came to 603,550, {Nu 1:1,46} the same number as seven months earlier, when they were taxed for a contribution toward the building of the tabernacle. {Ex 38:26} [L26]

216. Moses, according to God's command, {Ex 29:1-37 30:22-30 40:9-15} anointed the tabernacle and the altar and all the other things in it with the holy oil, consecrating them to the Lord. He also consecrated Aaron and his four sons with the same oil and with rites and ceremonies necessary for the execution of the priestly office. He commanded them not to leave the tabernacle for seven days. {Le 8:1-36} This was the time required for the consecration of themselves and the altar. {Ex 29:35-37 Le 8:33}

217. Moses outlined the order and position of the tribes in their march and encampments. {Nu 2:1-34}

218. The number of Levites from one month old and upward was found to be twenty-two thousand and three hundred. {Nu 3:15-35} The twenty-two hundred firstborn of the Levites managed the service of God in lieu of the

firstborn of Israel. {Nu 3:11-13} The number of the first-born of the children of Israel exceeded the entire number of the Levites (their firstborn deducted) by two hundred and seventy-three. Therefore, these were taxed redemption money—five shekels for every additional person. {Nu 3:39-50}

219. The Levites were set apart and consecrated to God for his service. Every man was appointed a certain time when he was to perform his ministry. {Nu 8:5-26}

220. Eighty-five hundred and eighty Levites were between thirty and fifty years old. Their offices and services were assigned among them according to their families. {Nu 4:1-49}

221. All leprous and unclean persons were put out of the camp. The laws for restoring of damages and of jealousy were ordained. {Nu 5:1-31}

222. The vow, the consecration and manner of the Nazarites was instituted. {Nu 6:1-27}

223. On the eighth day following the completion of the consecration, Aaron offered sacrifices and oblations, first for himself and then for all the people. All these offerings were consumed by fire that fell from heaven upon the altar. This sign ensured that the people accepted that the priestly office among them was ordained by God himself. {Le 9:1-24}

224. All the tabernacle was completely set up and anointed all over, together with the utensils and things belonging to it. The altar which had been consecrated for seven days was now dedicated by Aaron in making his first oblation of sacrifices on it. The seven previous days had been ordained for expiation and for the hallowing of the altar. {Ex 29:36,37}

225. The heads of the tribes brought six covered wagons and twelve oxen, and jointly offered them before the tabernacle. All this was given to the Levites, the sons of Gershon and Merari, for their duties. Every day leaders of the tribes brought their various sacrifices and things required for the ministry of the tabernacle and offered them toward its dedication. This took twelve days. {Nu 7:1-11,84,88} [E18]

226. On this first day, Nahshon (from whom David descended and according to the flesh, Jesus Christ himself) came and made his offering for the tribes of Judah. Then the rest also made offerings, every one for his tribe, according to the order in which they were ranked in their camps. {Nu 7:11-83}

227. Nadab and Abihu were Aaron's two oldest sons who had gone with their father up into Mount Sinai and had seen the glory of God there. {Ex 24:1,9,10} They went into the sanctuary with strange or common fire. This was not that fire which fell from heaven, {Le 9:24} and which was perpetually to be kept alive and continued for the burning of the sacrifices and incense in times to come. {Le 6:12,13} They were struck dead on the spot by fire sent from heaven. {Le 10:1,9 Nu 3:2-4 26:60,61} [L27] The priests were forbidden to make lamentation for them. Moreover, because some priests' neglect of duty, all the priests were ordered to abstain from wine and strong drink before they were to go into the tabernacle. A law was also made that what was left of the sacrifices should be eaten by the priests. Aaron's excuse for not doing this was accepted by Moses. {Le 10:6-20}

228. Upon this occasion the law was made (about the tenth day of this month, as it seems) that only the high priest should enter into the sanctuary and only once in each year. This was to be on the day of atonement and the general fast, which was to be kept on the tenth day of the seventh month. {Le 16:1-34}

229. On the fourteenth day of this month (Thursday, June 3), at evening, the passover was to be celebrated by those who were unable to keep it a month earlier because of their uncleanness. {Nu 9:1-23}

230. By God's command, the blasphemous son of an Israelite woman was carried outside the camp and stoned to death. {Le 24:10-12,23}

231. All the laws contained in the last seventeen chapters of Leviticus seem to have been made in this month.

232. God commanded two silver trumpets to be made to call the congregation together for the times of their moving and marching and sacrificing. {Nu 10:1-18}

233. Jethro, who was also called Hobab, brought his daughter Zipporah, with her two sons Gershom and Eliezer who were left with him, to Moses, his son-in-law. He congratulated him and the people for their deliverance from Egyptian bondage. He publicly declared, both by word and deed, his faith and devotion toward the true God. In accordance with his advice, Moses delegated the government of the people to various others and ordained magistrates for the deciding of lesser issues. {Ex 18:1-27 De 1:9-18 Nu 10:29}

234. The nineteenth day of this month seems to have been the last day that the twelve leaders of the tribes made their oblations for the dedication of the altar. This day, Ahira made his offering for the tribe of Naphtali. {Nu 7:78,88}

235. On the twentieth day of the second month (Wednesday, June 9), God commanded the Israelites to break

camp and to start their journey to take possession of the promised land. {Nu 10:11,12 De 1:6,7} Moses asked Jethro to go along with him but he refused and returned home. {Nu 10:29,30 Ex 18:27}

236. The cloud rose from the tabernacle and they arranged themselves into four squadrons, or battalions, and marched from Sinai. They had been there almost a year. After three days' journey they came to the wilderness of Paran, {Nu 10:12,33} where they stayed and rested for twenty-three days.

13) At their thirteenth camp, at a place called Kibrothhattaavah, {Nu 33:16} some who murmured were struck with fire from heaven. Hence that place was called Tabor. They were saved by the intercession of Moses. However, they again murmured and provoked God by their loathing of manna and desiring of flesh to eat. {Nu 11:1-10 Ps 78:19-21}

237. Moses complained to God of the great burden of this government and desired to be relieved from it. God chose seventy elders to help him. Two of these, Eldad and Medad, prophesied in the camp. {Nu 11:10-17,24-30}

238. God gave the people quails for a whole month, not just for a day as he did the year before. {Ex 16:12,13} He sent a most grievous plague among them. That place was called Kibrothhattaavah, after the graves of those who lusted after meat. {Nu 11:31-34 Ps 78:26-31 Ps 106:15}

14) The fourteenth camp was at Hazeroth. {Nu 11:35 33:17} Miriam and Aaron spoke evil of Moses, their brother, because he had married a woman from Ethiopia. [L28] Zipporah, his wife, was from Midian, which was a part of Eastern Ethiopia, otherwise called Arabia. They made themselves equal in all points with him. [E19] God honoured Moses over them and struck Miriam with leprosy. She was sent outside the camp, but at the prayer of Moses she was healed after seven days. {Nu 12:1-15 De 24:9}

## 2514d AM, 3224 JP, 1490 BC

239. Miriam was cleansed some time during the fourth month. Upon her return to camp, the Israelites left that place.

15) They camped in Hazeroth, in the desert of Paran, {Nu 12:6 33:18} near Kadeshbarnea. {Nu 13:26}

240. This was in the fifth month.

241. From the wilderness of Paran, {Nu 13:3} or Kadeshbarnea, {Nu 32:8 De 1:19,22 9:23 Jos 14:7} at the time of the ripe grapes, God commanded Moses to send twelve spies, one from every tribe, {De 1:22,23} to thoroughly spy out the land. Moses and the people were agreeable to this plan. {Nu 13:1,2,20} Among these men were the forty-year-old Caleb, the son of Jephunneh (of the tribe of Judah), {Jos 14:7} and Oshea the son of Nun, whom Moses called Joshua, from the tribe of Ephraim. These men entered the land from the south by the desert of Zin, passing through to Rehob in the very northern part. {Nu 13:2-22 De 1:23,24}

242. The sixth month.

243. The spies spent forty days in searching out the land before returning to Kadesh in the wilderness of Paran. They brought back with them the branch of a vine with a cluster of grapes on it gathered from the valley of Eshcol. This valley was named for its pomegranates and figs. {Nu 13:23-27 De 1:24,25} It is likely that this happened prior to the seventh month, before the feast of tabernacles. This feast was kept on the fifteenth day of that month, when the fruits of the barn and winepress were always harvested. {Ex 23:16 Le 23:39 De 16:13} Ten of the twelve men spoke ill of the country and its barrenness, magnifying the cities' strength and the giants living in the land. This discouraged the people from marching any further toward it. Caleb, however, did all he could to persuade the people to go on. {Nu 13:28-33 32:9}

244. The people were terrified by the report given by the ten spies and threatened to return to Egypt. They were ready to stone Caleb and Joshua for their conflicting report. When God threatened the people with sudden destruction, Moses again prayed and their lives were spared. However, God declared that all those who were over twenty years old would die in the wilderness and would never see the promised land, but wander in the wilderness for forty years. {Nu 14:1-35 26:64,65 32:10-13 De 1:26-36 9:23} {Jos 5:6 Ps 95:8-11 106:24-26} Their children entered the promised land in the thirty-ninth year. {Nu 32:13 De 2:14}

245. God destroyed the ten rebellious spies by a plague. {Nu 14:36,37} In memory of this event, the Jews keep a fast on the seventh day of the sixth month, called Elul.

246. God now commanded them to break camp and return back into the desert near the Red Sea. [L29] Instead, they disobeyed him by going forward into the mountain to begin taking the land by fighting the Amalekites and Canaanites who dwelt there. They were defeated and pursued all the way to Hormah. Therefore, they sat down and wept before the Lord, but he would not hear them. {Nu 14:40-45 De 1:40-45}

247. After this incident, as the Israelites continued to die in the wilderness, Moses composed the Psalm {Ps 90} *Lord thou hast been our refuge....* He also showed that the

normal age of men was reduced to seventy or eighty years. Therefore,

248. *The age of man was shortened by a third of what it was before.*

## 2515a AM, 3224 JP, 1490 BC

249. The Israelites remained in Kadesh for many days. {*De 1:46*} Because whether it was for a day, a month, or a year: as long as the cloud continued over the tabernacle, the camp did not move. {*Nu 9:22*} In some places the camp stayed for many years, since there were only seventeen camps mentioned in the thirty-seven years. After leaving Kadesh, they returned into the wilderness toward the Red Sea and camped around the hill country of Seir for many days. {*De 2:1 Jud 11:16*} The seventeen camps during this time in the wilderness of Seir are mentioned in the thirty-third chapter of Numbers in this order:

16th at Rimmonparez
17th at Libnah
18th at Rissah
19th at Kehelathah
20th at Mount Shapher
21st at Haradah
22nd at Makheloth
23rd at Thahash
24th at Thara
25th at Mithcah
26th at Hashmonah
27th at Moseroth
28th at Benehaajan, or Beeroth Bene Jaakan, the well of the sons of Jaakan {*De 10:6*}
29th at Horhagidgad, or Gudgodah {*De 10:7*} *[E20]*
30th at Jotbathah, a place of many springs of water {*De 10:7*}
31st at Ebronah
32nd at Eziongeber, which is near Elath and by the shore of the Red Sea, in the land of Edom {*1Ki 9:26*}

## 2515 AM, 3225 JP, 1489 BC

250. The only mention of these camps are the laws and historical events as recorded in Numbers. {*Nu 15:1-19:22*}

a) {*Nu 15:1-41*} A man was stoned by God's command for gathering sticks on the Sabbath. Although the sacrifices were omitted in the wilderness, the Sabbath was kept.

b) {*Nu 16:1-50*} Korah, Dathan and Abiram rebelled against Moses and Aaron. They were swallowed alive into the earth. Their two hundred and fifty associates who offered incense were destroyed by God through fire. God commanded their censors to be taken and used for a covering for the altar.

This was to be as a sign to the children of Israel. The people murmured against Moses and Aaron for this calamity and God killed fourteen thousand and seven hundred of them.

c) {*Nu 17:1-13*} The twelve rods were brought by the twelve leaders of the tribes and placed before the Lord in the sanctuary. Aaron's rod was the only one that budded and brought forth almonds. It was set before the ark as a warning against any future rebellions.

251. All these events are thought to have happened in the latter half of the second year after they left the land of Egypt. Moses wrote only what happened in the first two years and the last year of their travels in the wilderness. For the intervening events of those thirty-seven years see Abulensis. {*Abulensis, Numbers, c. 1. q. 3.*}

252. The scriptures also show that, after they moved from their thirty-second camp, the Israelites spent half a year in travelling from Kadeshbarnea until they passed the valley, or brook, of Zered. Another half year elapsed before they crossed the Jordan River, so making up the full thirty-eight years. *[L30]* During this time, all those who had rebelled against God perished. {*De 2:14-16*}

253. For the first nine years that the Israelites spent in the wilderness, Harmais governed in Egypt and Sethosis invaded the east. These two were brothers, and the sons of Amenophis who drowned in the Red Sea, as noted before. {*See note on 2494 AM. <<173>>*} Manetho {*\*Manetho, 1:103*} as quoted by Josephus {*\*Josephus, Apion, l. 1. c. 15. (98) 1:201ff.*} stated:

"Sethosis was well equipped with cavalry and ships, and made his brother Harmais ruler over all Egypt. He let Harmais use all power and authority there, except he was not to wear the crown and he charged him not to dishonour his wife, the queen and mother of his children. Harmais was also told to abstain from all other concubines of the king. Sethosis himself, however, made war in Cyprus and Phoenicia and against the Assyrians and the Medes. Some of these he subdued by his powerful army and others he overcame merely by the terror of his reputation. Puffed up with this great success near home, he went on with greater confidence to ravage and spoil all the kingdoms and countries of the east. A few years after he was gone, Harmais, whom he left in Egypt, recklessly did everything the king commanded him not to do. First, he violated the queen and lay repeatedly with the king's concubines. Later, he followed the advice of his friends and wore the crown, plainly rebelling against his brother."

*254.* Manetho added: {*Manetho, 1:105*} {*Josephus, Apion, l. 1. c. 15. (102) 1:205*}

> "Harmais was called Danaus and Sethosis was also called Egyptus."

*255.* Egypt was named after him. Ramesses was named after his grandfather. These similarities in names and events reveal that Tacitus called him *Rhamses* and Herodotus in the following accounts. *Sesostris.* {*Herodotus, l. 2. c. 102. 1:389*} Tacitus said: {*Tacitus, Annals, l. 2. c. 60. 3:491*}

> "A king called Rhamses conquered all Libya, Ethiopia, the Medes and Persians, Bactria, Scythia and all the lands which the Syrians and Armenians and the Cappadocians held, along with Bithynia and Lycia, by the Mediterranean Sea."

*256.* Tacitus also recorded him under the name of Sesosis. {*Tacitus, Annals, l. 6. c. 28. 4:201*} Regarding Sesostris, Herodotus wrote that their Egyptian priests said: {*Herodotus, l. 2. c. 102-107. 1:389-397*}

> "He was the first to bring all countries bordering the Red Sea under his subjection, sailing by way of the Arabian Gulf. He came back the same way and gathered a mighty army. Marching into the continent of Asia, he subdued all the countries which stood in his way. Leaving Asia, he crossed into Europe and conquered the Scythians and Thracians. It seemed he went no further, because the marks and monuments of his name and victories are found in Syria Palestina. Two monuments are in Ionia, one at Ephesus as you go into Phocaea, another one is on the way leading from Sardis to Smyrna."

*257.* A similar report came from Diodorus Siculus about Sesostris, {*Diod. Sic., l. 1. c. 53-58. 1:185ff.*} but he made him far more ancient than this. The time of his brother Danaus proves that he was a contemporary with Moses. *[E21]* Manetho and Diodorus recorded the timing of these events almost identically. They noted that when all foreigners were expelled from Egypt, Danaus and Cadmus, with their companies, came into Greece, and Moses, with his company, went into Judea. {*Diod. Sic., l. 1. c. 28. s. 2,3. 1:91*} {*Herodotus, l. 2. c. 104. 1:393*} This we find in the selections of Photius. For the better understanding of this thirty-seven year period, we include events from Eusebius as follows: {*Eusebius, Chronicles, l. 1. 1:62-69*} *[L31]*

## 2520 AM, 3230 JP, 1484 BC

*258.* Egypt (which was formerly called Aeria) was named after Egyptus or Aegyptus who was there made king after the expulsion of his brother, Danaus. Our account varies only two years from that of Eusebius. {*Eusebius, Chronicles, l. 1. 1:67*}

## 2522 AM, 3232 JP, 1482 BC

*259.* Egypt was also called Ramesses or Sesostris or Sethosis or Sesoosis. After spending nine years on many voyages and foreign wars, he returned to Pelusium. {*Diod. Sic., l. 1. c. 55. s. 10. 1:195*} During this time Harmais, who was also called Danaus, ruled over Egypt. He first attempted to kill his brother Egyptus, after a banquet held in the latter's honour, but failed in the attempt, as stated by both Herodotus and Diodorus. {*Herodotus, l. 2. c. 107. 1:395*} {*Diod. Sic., l. 1. c. 57. s. 8. 1:201*} Whereupon he fled for fear of his brother from the kingdom which he had ruled in Egypt and sailed by ship to Greece. This is according to Georgius Syncellus, based on Scaliger's account. {*Eusebius, Scaliger's Greek Eusebius, p. 26,27.*} {*Pliny, l. 7. c. 56. 2:645*}

## 2530 AM, 3240 JP, 1474 BC

*260.* According to Eusebius, Diodorus and Herodotus, when Danaus came into Greece, he made himself ruler of Argos and made it abound with waters. Danaus, through his fifty daughters, sought to destroy the fifty sons of his brother Egyptus, but one son, Lynceus, was spared, who reigned after him at Argos.

## 2533 AM, 3243 JP, 1471 BC

*261.* According to Eusebius, Diodorus and Herodotus, Busiris, the son of Neptunus, and Libya, the daughter of Epaphus, were joint tyrants in the area next to the Nile River. He barbarously murdered all strangers who passed that way and fell into his hands. Ovid asked, *who was more cruel than Busiris?* {*Ovid, Tristia, l. 3. c. 1. (60) 6:105*} Virgil asked who had not heard of Eurystheus' hard heart? {*Virgil, Georgics, l. 3. (5) 1:155*} Gellius stated the same thing. {*Aulus Gellius, Attic Nights, l. 2. c. 6. s. 3. 1:135*} The altars built by the unworthy Busiris were indeed unworthy to be defended. He himself was even less worthy of being commended by any man, which, according to Socrates the orator, in his *Busiridis' Encomium*, was yet to be his lot. Socrates and Eusebius stated that Busiris was the son of Libya, the daughter of Epaphus, and Neptunus. Note that this Ramesses, surnamed Miamun, {*See note on 2427 AM. <<161>>*} was surnamed Neptunus by the mythological writers, and was the man who commanded the newly born infants of the Hebrews to be drowned. He had two sons, Busiris and Amenophis or Belus of Egypt, the father of Egyptus and Danaus. Amenophis was that Pharaoh, the enemy of the Almighty God, who was drowned in the Red Sea with his army. Neptunus' son, Busiris, succeeded him and was infamous for butchering strangers—a fitting offspring for such a father. Based on this, Gellius stated that the poets were inclined to call men who were barbarous, cruel and devoid of humanity, the sons of Neptunus who was born of that merciless element, the sea. {*Aulus Gellius, Attic Nights, l. 15. c. 21. s. 1. 3:109*}

## 2543 AM, 3253 JP, 1461 BC

*262.* In these times lived Tat, the son of Hermes Trismegistos. {*Eusebius, Chronicles*} The Egyptians say that Sesostris learned his wisdom from this Hermes. {*Aelian, Historical Miscellany, l. 12. c. 4. 1:359*}

## 2549 AM, 3259 JP, 1455 BC

*263.* Cadmus and Phoenix went from Thebes in Egypt into Syria and founded the kingdoms of Tyre and Sidon. {*Eusebius, Chronicles, l. 1. 1:69*} (Both Moses and Joshua mention these places as existing in their time. {*Ge 10:19 Jos 19:29*} Hence they must have been founded no later than the date given by Eusebius and likely much earlier. Editor.)

## 2552b AM, 3262 JP, 1452 BC

*264.* After the Israelites had wandered around the hill country of Seir and Edom for thirty-seven years, they went from Kadeshbarnea to Eziongeber in Edom. As they were travelling south toward the shore of the Red Sea, God commanded them to turn northward and march straight for the land of promise. When the land of Edom lay directly in their way, he ordered them not to fight with the Edomites because they were their brothers. God reminded them of how great his providence and care toward them had been, in preserving them for forty years in the wilderness. {*De 2:1-8*} He used the round number of forty for the actual time of thirty-nine years. The exact time in the wilderness was just five days short of a forty full years.

## 2552c AM, 3262 JP, 1452 BC

*265.* In the first month of the fortieth year after they had left Egypt, the Israelites came into the wilderness of Zin and camped there.

> 33) They camped at Kadesh {*Nu 20:1 33:36-38 Jud 11:17*} *[L32]* on the edge of the wilderness of Zin, near the border of Edom, {*Nu 20:14,15*} towards Eziongeber and the Red Sea. {*Nu 33:36 De 2:8*} This was not at Kadeshbarnea, where they made their fifteenth camp and which lay near the border of Canaan, toward the south. {*Nu 34:4 Jos 15:3*}

*266.* Miriam died there four months before her brother Aaron and eleven months before her brother Moses. {*Nu 20:1*} She was the oldest of the three and lived a hundred and thirty years so that she was a rather mature maiden when Moses was born. {*Ex 2:4-7*} {*See note on 2433 AM. <<166>>*} The Jews to this very day keep the memory of her death upon the tenth day of their first month.

*267.* Again the people complained to Moses and Aaron about the lack of water. God commanded them to call water out of the hard rock simply by speaking to it. *[E22]* Through impatience and diffidence in God's command, Moses said something ill-advised and struck the rock twice with Aaron's rod. This was the rod that budded and blossomed. Moses drew water from the rock, as he had done from another rock thirty-seven years earlier. {*Ex 17:7*} Because of this incident the place was called Meribah, or waters of strife. {*Nu 20:2-13*}. (For it is most likely that the former water, which Tertullian called *Aquam Comtiem,* or *the water that followed them* as mentioned in the eleventh encampment, was lost in the Red Sea.) In this second instance of lack of water, the children complained just like their fathers had done, many years before.

*268.* Moses and Aaron, because of their diffidence and unbelief in executing the commandment of God, were not allowed to enter into the land of Canaan. {*Nu 20:23,24 27:14 Ps 106:32,33*}

## 2552d AM, 3262 JP, 1452 BC

*269.* The Israelites sent messengers to the Edomites and Moabites asking to pass through their land. They refused to let them pass through their countries, {*Nu 20:14-21 Jud 11:17*} but allowed them to pass along their borders. {*De 2:4,6,29*} On this occasion, they stayed a while at Kadesh, {*Jud 11:17*} then went forward again.

> 34) The thirty-fourth camp was in mount Hor, on the borders of Edom, {*Nu 20:22,23 33:37*} or Mosera {*De 10:6*}. The Israelites are said to have come to this place when they left Beeroth Bene Jaakan, or the wells of the sons of Jaakan, their twenty-eighth camp. They camped in Gudgodah, or Horhagidgad, Jotbathah and other places. For it is said {*De 10:7*} that from there they came to Gudgodah, and from Gudgodah to Jotbathah. These words *from there* are not to be understood of Mosera, but of Beeroth, as has been the view of many learned men on this passage over a long time.

*270.* On the first day of the fifth month (Tuesday, August 18), Aaron died at the age of one hundred and twenty-three years and was buried on the top of Mount Horeb. His son Eleazar succeeded him as the high priest. {*Nu 20:23-28 33:38,39 De 10:6*} The Israelites mourned thirty days for Aaron. {*Nu 20:29*} This was for the whole month in which he died.

*271.* In the sixth month, the king of Arad who lived on the southern part of Canaan, after hearing of the Israelites' approach, went out and fought against them, taking many of them prisoners. As a result the Israelites made a vow to God, and upon defeating them, they destroyed both them and their cities. *[L33]* For that reason, the place was called Hormah, that is: the place where the vow was made of utterly destroying the Canaanites. {Nu 31:1-3 33:40}

272. They left mount Hor and avoiding the plain country that led from Elath, and Eziongeber and the Red Sea, went straight to Edom. They went around Edom and came to the east side of it {Nu 21:4 De 2:8} and there made another camp.

35) They camped at Zalmonah, {Nu 33:41} named for the brazen serpent set up there. The people complained because of the fierce serpents sent among them by God. (Not a little worm, breeding in their flesh, as Fortunius Licetus imagined. {Licetus, de spontanco Viventium ortu, l. 3. c. 51}) These poisoned them with their bite, and they could only be healed by looking up to the image of a brazen serpent which God appointed to be set up on a pole. {Nu 21:5-9 Joh 3:14 1Co 10:9}

36) They camped at Punon. {Nu 33:42}

37) They camped at Oboth. {Nu 21:10 33:43}

38) They camped at Ijeabarim on the borders of Moab {Nu 33:44} in the desert lying to its east {Nu 21:11} and which is called the desert of Moab. {De 2:8} They had continued their march through that wilderness and so had come to the east of Moab. {Jud 11:18}

273. When they left there to pass by the valley or brook of Zared, God forbade them to make war on Moab. {Nu 21:12 De 2:8,13}

274. They passed over Zared, thirty-eight years after they sent their spies from Kadeshbarnea.

275. All those over twenty years old who had rebelled against God there had now died. {De 2:13-16}

39) They camped at Dibongad. {Nu 33:45}

40) They camped at Almondiblathaim, {Nu 33:46} also called Bethdiblathaim, in the wilderness of Moab. {Jer 48:22 Eze 6:14}

## 2553a AM, 3262 JP, 1452 BC

276. When the Israelites were passing the borders of Moab at Ar, and approaching the country of the Ammonites, God forbade them to make any war upon the Ammonites. {De 2:18,19,37} He commanded them to pass over the Arnon River which at that time was the boundary between Moab and Ammon. {De 2:24 Nu 21:13} They camped at Arnon and never entered the territory of Moab. {De 2:24 Nu 21:13 Jud 11:18}

277. Next they arrived at Beer, where the well was dug by the princes, nobles of the people and Moses with their staffs. They came to Matthan, Nahaliel, Bamoth and the valley which is in the country of the Moabites near the approach to the hill overlooking the wilderness {Nu 21:16-20} of Kedemoth. {De 2:26} There they camped. [E23]

41) They camped at Abarim opposite Nebo. {Nu 33:47} As for Maanah and the other places, these were not camps, as Tremellius observed in Numbers, {Nu 21:12} but only places through which they passed on their march before Moses sent messengers to the Amorites. The Chaldee paraphrase does not take them to be proper place names, but merely titles. [L34] They interpret them as the waters of that well (as the Rock {1Co 10:4}) which followed the Israelites to the brooks and from the brooks to the mountains and from the mountains to the valley of the Moabites.

278. From the wilderness of Kedemoth, Moses sent messengers to Sihon the Amorite, king of Heshbon. He asked permission to pass peacefully through his borders (as the Edomites and Moabites had done) because that was a short cut to the fords of Jordan. When he denied them passage and made war upon them, the Israelites killed Sihon and possessed all his cities and lived in them. {De 2:24-36 Nu 21:21-31 Jud 11:19-22}

279. Moses sent his spies to Jazer which they conquered with the towns associated with it. {Nu 21:32} They expelled the Amorites from there, all the land from the Arnon River, which is the boundary of Moab, {Nu 21:13 22:36} to the brook of Jabbok which divided it from Ammon. {De 3:16 Jos 12:2 13:10} They did not meddle with the country lying next to the Jabbok River, neither with any of the lands belonging at that time to the children of Ammon or Moab, as God had commanded them. {De 2:9,19,37} Therefore, two hundred and sixty-four years later when the Ammonites complained that the Israelites had taken their land from Jabbok to the Arnon River and even to the brooks of the Jordan River, Jephthah correctly answered them that this was not true. They had not touched the lands of either the Moabites or the Ammonites. When they had killed Sihon, they had taken all the lands belonging to the Amorites from the Arnon River to Jabbok and possessed it as their own inheritance. {Jud 11:13,15,22,23} It was also true that Sihon, king of the Amorites, had formerly taken from Vaheb, king of the Moabites, Heshbon and all that country of his to Arnon. {Nu 21:14,26,28} He had also taken from the Ammonites half their country, as far as to the Arnon River which lay opposite Rabbah. {De 3:11} All that land belonged formerly to the Ammonites and was later taken from the Amorites and assigned to the tribe of Gad to settle in. {Jos 13:25}

280. When the children of Israel marched on their way to Bashan, Og, king of Bashan, one of the giants, met and fought with them at Edrei. He and all his people were utterly destroyed. The Israelites possessed all his country which included sixty cities and all the land as far as Argob. {De 3:1-11 Nu 21:33-35 Am 2:9}

281. Jair, the son of Manasseh, seized all the country of Argob, stretching to the borders of the Geshurites and Maachathites and called them Havothjair, after his own name. {Nu 32:41 De 3:14} This Manasseh was the son of Segub, of the tribe of Judah. However, he was counted among the Manassites both in respect to the inheritance he had among them and also in reference to his grandmother. She was the daughter of Machir of the tribe of Manasseh. He was the father of Gilead who bore Segub, the father of this Jair, to Hezron when he was sixty years old. {1Ch 2:21,22} This passage stated that this Jair possessed twenty-three cities in the land of Gilead. He took Geshur and Aram (according to the best expositors) with the villages of Jair and Kenath with its villages, sixty cities in all. Nobah, who was under him, took Kenath with its villages and called it Nobah after his own name. {Nu 32:42}

282. After these victories the Israelites left the mountains of Abarim. They camped in the plain of Moab on this side of the ford of Jordan, which led to Jericho from Beth Jeshimoth to Abelshittim. {Nu 22:1 33:48,49}

> 42) They camped at Shittim, {Nu 25:1} or Abelshittim. {Nu 33:49} Here they stayed until Joshua led them to the bank of the Jordan River. {Jos 3:1}

283. Balak, the son of Zippor, was the king of Moab. When he saw what the Israelites had done to the Amorites, he was afraid lest they would also take his kingdom from him, under the pretence of passing through his country. Therefore, after taking counsel with the princes of the Midianites who were his neighbours, he sent for Balaam, the son of Beor. Balaam was a soothsayer from Mesopotamia. Balak asked him to come and curse the Israelites and promised him a large reward for his labour. Balak intended afterward to make war upon the Israelites. {Nu 22:1-6 De 33:4 Jos 24:9}

284. Balaam was warned by God and at first refused to come. When he was summoned a second time, he pleaded with God to let him go and went with the intention of cursing Israel. God was offended by his intentions and caused the dumb ass on which he was riding to speak with a man's voice, to reprove his folly. {Nu 22:7-35 2Pe 2:15,16}

285. Balaam twice offered sacrifices and attempted to curse Israel to gratify Balak but forced by the Spirit of God, he instead ended up blessing them. He foretold what good fortune was with them and what calamities would befall their enemies. {Nu 23:1-24:25 De 23:5 Jos 24:10} [E24]

286. By Balaam's advice, the women of Moab and Midian were sent to turn the Israelites away and to make them commit idolatry with them. {Nu 25:1-3 31:16 De 4:3 Ps 106:28 Re 2:14} Therefore, God commanded Moses first to hang all the leaders of this rebellion and then to give orders to the judges to put to death all who had joined themselves to Baalpeor. Finally, God sent a plague upon the people, in which twenty-three thousand men died in one day. {1Co 10:8} This number, plus those who were hung and killed with the sword, came to twenty-four thousand. {Nu 25:4,5,9}

287. Phinehas, the son of Eleazar, killed Zimri, the son of Salu, chief of his father's family of the tribe of Simeon. He also killed Cozbi, the daughter of Sur, a prince of the Midianites. This appeased the wrath of God and the plague was ended. {Nu 25:1-18 Ps 106:30} Therefore, God assigned the high priesthood to the house of Phinehas for ever. He then commanded the Israelites to make war against the Midianites. {Nu 25:12,13,17,18}

288. God commanded Moses and Eleazar to count the people twenty years of age and over. This was done in the plain of Moab, near the Jordan River, opposite Jericho. The number of men was 601,730 in addition to the Levites. Twenty-three thousand Levites were counted who were at least a month or more old. Moses received God's command for the division of the land of promise among the Israelites. {Nu 26:1-63}

289. The daughters of Zelophehad had their father's land divided among them because there was no male heir. Because of this situation, the law of inheritances was made. {Nu 27:1-11}

290. God told Moses that he was about to die and that Joshua was to be his successor. Moses laid his hands upon Joshua and gave him instructions. {Nu 27:12-23 De 3:26-28} [L35] Various laws were then made. {De 28:29,30}

291. Twelve thousand of the Israelites, led by Phinehas, defeated the Midianites and killed all their males including their five princes and Sur, the father of Cozbi. All were under the subjection of Sihon the Amorite while he lived. Balaam the soothsayer was killed because, when he should have returned to his country of Mesopotamia, {Nu 24:25} he had stayed instead, and so he died with the Midianites. {Nu 31:1-8 Jos 13:21,22} Of the females, only the virgins were spared. {Nu 31:9-54}

## 2553b AM, 3263 JP, 1451 BC

292. Moses divided the lands, which belonged to Sihon and Og, among the tribes of Reuben and Gad and the

half tribe of Manasseh. {*Nu 32:1-42 De 3:12-20 29:8 Jos 13:8-12 22:4*} This was from the Arnon River to Mount Hermon (which is also called Shenir and Sirion, and Sion), and is bounded by Anti-Lebanon. *[L36]* {*De 3:8,9 4:48 Jos 12:1 13:9,11*}

293. When the Israelites were about to enter the land of Canaan, God commanded them to drive out the Canaanites and destroy their idols. {*Nu 33:50-56*} They were to divide the land west of Jordan among the nine remaining tribes and the other half tribe of Manasseh. {*Nu 34:1-29*} Of the forty-eight cities of the Levites and the six cities of refuge, {*Nu 35:1-34*}, three were assigned by Moses on the east of Jordan. {*De 4:41-43*}

294. Moses addressed Israel in the plain of Moab on the fifth day of the eleventh month (Saturday, February 20) in the fortieth year after their departure from Egypt, as recorded in Deuteronomy. {*De 1:1,3,6 4:1-27:26*}.

295. Moses, with the elders of Israel, commanded the people to set up large stones after they had crossed the Jordan River. These were to be plastered and the ten commandments written on them. They were to speak the blessings from Mount Gerizim and the curses from Mount Ebal. {*De 27:1-26*} He exhorted them to observe the law of God by setting before them the benefits of obedience and the miseries that would happen to them for their disobedience. {*De 28:1-68*}

296. God commanded Moses to renew the covenant between God and them and their children in Mount Horeb. Moses again attempted to persuade them to keep that covenant which was hedged in by all the blessings and curses which would accrue to the keepers or breakers of it. {*De 29:1-29*} He gave a promise of pardon and deliverance if at any time, when they broke it, they should repent. He stated that God had declared his will to them so that no one who broke the law could plead ignorance of the law. {*De 30:1-20*}

297. When Moses had written this law, he gave it to the priests, the sons of Levi and the elders of the people, to be observed. When he finished the book of the law, he ordered it to be put in the ark. {*De 31:1-30*} The same day he wrote his song and taught it to the children of Israel. {*De 32:1-52*} *[E25]*

298. Just before Moses died, he blessed every tribe with a prophecy, except the tribe of Simeon. His last will and testament is contained in Deuteronomy. {*De 32:1-52*}

299. In the twelfth month of this year, Moses left the plain of Moab and climbed up Mount Nebo which was a part of the country of Abarim. From the top of it facing Jericho, he beheld all the land of promise and

then died at the age of a hundred and twenty years. {*Nu 27:12,13 De 3:23-29 32:49,50 34:1-5 31:2-4,7*} *[L37]* Of this time he spent forty years minus one month in governing the people of Israel. This is confirmed by Josephus. {*\*Josephus, Antiq., l. 4. c. 5. s. 49. (327) 4:633*} He stated that Moses died on the first day of the last month of the year. The Macedonians called this month, *Dystros*, but the Hebrews called it, *Adar*. This fits better with the account of historians who wrote shortly thereafter, than with the tradition of the Jews of later times. These historians say that he died upon the seventh of Adar, as in Seder Olam Rabba in his פטירה of book of the death of Moses in chapter ten. In the preface of Maimonides to the book called Misnaioth, this is also mentioned. It appears as well in the calendars of the Jews of this time. They still celebrate the memorial of his death by a solemn fast on this day.

300. God moved the body of Moses from the place where he died to a valley in the land of Moab opposite Bethpeor and buried him there. To this day, no one knows where the grave of Moses is. {*De 34:6*} This valley was in the land of Sihon, king of the Amorites, which the Israelites took from him. {*De 4:46*} Bethpeor was given to the Reubenites. {*Jos 13:20*} Therefore, Moses is said to have been buried in the land of Moab. Likewise, the covenant is said to have been renewed in the land of Moab. {*De 29:1*} It is to be understood that this land did formerly belong to the Moabites, but it had recently been taken from them by Sihon king of the Amorites, {*Nu 21:26*} and now the Israelites possessed it.

301. The archangel Michael disputed with the Devil over the body of Moses. {*Jude 1:9*} The Devil wanted to expose the body that it might become an object of idolatry to the people of Israel. Chrysostom {*Chrysostom, Commentary on Matthew, Homily 1.*} and Thodores {*Thodores, Deuteronomy, Question. 43.*} and Procopius Gazan and others stated this, though there is no evidence that the Jews ever gave themselves to the worshipping of relics. This dispute between Michael and the Devil about the body of Moses is found in the apocryphal book called *The Assumption of Moses*. We read this in Origen {*Origen, πσι αρχων, l. 3. c. 2.*} and in Gelasius Cyzicenus, {*Cyzicenus, Acts of the Council of Nice, part. 2. c. 20.*} and similar stories are found in אבות by Rabbi Nathan.

302. The Israelites mourned for Moses in the land of Moab for thirty days, or the entire twelfth month. {*De 34:8*}

303. Here ends the Pentateuch or the five books of Moses, containing the history of twenty-five hundred and fifty-two and a half years from the beginning of the world. The book of Joshua begins with the forty-first year after the departure of the children of Israel from Egypt.

**2553c AM, 3263 JP, 1451 BC**

*304.* The first month.

*305.* God confirmed the leadership of Joshua. {Jos 1:1-9} The latter sent spies from Shittim to the city of Jericho, and these were hidden by Rahab in an inn. They were secretly sent away when a search was conducted for them. They hid three days in the mountain and then returned to Joshua. {Jos 2:1-24}

*306.* Joshua commanded the people that, in addition to the manna which had not yet ceased, they should take other provisions with them. In three days they were to pass over the Jordan River. {Jos 1:10,11}

*307.* The next morning they left Shittim and came to the Jordan River, where they camped that night. {Jos 3:1}

*308.* Three days later they were instructed to provide food for their journey. [L38] The people were commanded to sanctify and prepare themselves to pass over the Jordan River on the following day. {Jos 3:2-5}

*309.* On the tenth day of the first month (Friday, April 30), the same day that the Pascal lamb was to be chosen from the flock, Joshua (a type of Christ) led the Israelites through the Jordan River into the promised land of Canaan, which was a type of that heavenly country. God divided the waters and they passed through the river dryshod. Normally in that season, the waters would overflow the banks. As a memorial of this miraculous passage, Joshua set up twelve stones in the very channel of the Jordan River. They took another twelve stones from out of the middle of the river and set them up at Gilgal where they next camped. {Jos 3:1-4:24}

*310.* The next day in Gilgal, Joshua renewed the practice of circumcision, which had been neglected for forty years. There the people rested and stayed until they were well again. {Jos 5:2-9} [E26]

*311.* On the fourteenth day of the first month (Tuesday, May 4), in the evening, the Israelites celebrated their first passover in the land of Canaan. {Jos 5:10}

*312.* The next day was the passover (Wednesday, May 5). They ate of the produce of the land of Canaan—unleavened bread and roasted grain. The manna stopped the very day after they began to live on the produce of the land. Never again did the children of Israel see manna. That year they lived on the fruits of the land of Canaan. {Jos 5:11,12}

*313.* Our Lord Jesus, the captain of his Father's host, appeared to Joshua (the type of Jesus) before Jericho, with a drawn sword in his hand. Jesus there promised to defend his people. {Jos 5:13-15}

*314.* The ark of God was carried around Jericho for seven days. On the seventh day, the walls of Jericho fell down flat when the priests blew their trumpets. The city was taken and utterly destroyed. All were killed except for Rahab and her family. {Jos 6:1-27} Later she married Salmon of the tribe of Judah and they had a son called Boaz. {Mt 1:5}

*315.* For the sacrilege of Achan, God abandoned Israel and they were defeated at Ai. Achan's sin was determined by the casting of lots and he was found guilty. God was appeased when he and his family and cattle were stoned and burned with fire. {Jos 7:1-26} Thereupon Ai was taken by an ambush and utterly destroyed. Twelve thousand men of Ai were killed in the battle. {Jos 8:1-29}

*316.* In accordance with the law, an altar was erected for sacrifices on Mount Ebal. The ten commandments were engraved on it. The blessings and cursings were repeated on Mount Ebal and Mount Gerizim. The book of the law was read to all the people. {Jos 8:30-35}

**2553d AM, 3263 JP, 1451 BC**

*317.* The kings of Canaan were stirred by this great success of the Israelites. They all united against Israel except the Gibeonites. These craftily found a way to save their own lives by making a pact with Israel. However, later they were assigned to do the menial work associated with the house of God. {Jos 9:1-27}

*318.* When Adonizedek, king of Jerusalem, with the kings of Hebron, Jarmuth, Lachish and Debir heard that Gibeon allied themselves with Israel, they united their forces and besieged Gibeon.

*319.* When Joshua raised the siege, he pursued those five kings and slaughtered their troops as far as Azekah and Makkedah. At this time the sun stood still over Gibeon and the moon over the valley of Ajalon for almost a whole day until the Israelites were fully avenged of their enemies. {Jos 10:1-14} On this account Laurentius Codomanus observed two things:

a) Since Ajalon was less than a mile west of Gibeon, it is very likely that the moon was then past the full and very close to a new moon. [L39]

b) Since both those great lights stopped and started together, the astronomical account of this is not invalidated by this event. Even as in music, the harmony is not broken, nor do the voices clash if they all rest at the same time and then begin again, each man playing his part until the end of the piece.

*320.* The five kings hid themselves in a cave at Makkedah, and Joshua commanded the entrance to be blocked with stones and a guard set up until the enemies were defeated. After the enemies fled into fortified cities, and when all the army was safely returned to Joshua at Makkedah, the stones were removed. The five kings were taken from the cave and each of the captains of the Israelite army was bidden to put his foot upon their necks. The kings were hung on five trees until evening and then their bodies were thrown into the same cave and the mouth of the cave blocked with stones. {Jos 10:16-27}

321. Thus ended that very busy year, 2553 AM. In the first six months Moses conquered all that land east of the Jordan. In the remainder of the year Joshua conquered most of the land west of the Jordan. In the middle of the year the manna ceased, and the people of Israel began to live off the food in the land of Canaan.

## 2554a AM, 3263 JP, 1451 BC

322. From the autumn of this year, after the manna stopped, the Israelites began to till the ground and sow it. This was to be reckoned the first year of their tillage. The sabbatical years are reckoned from this year. {Ex 23:10,11 Le 25:2-7 De 15:1-9 31:10}

## 2554b AM, 3264 JP, 1450 BC

323. When the five kings were defeated, all the rest of the kings united and fought against the Israelites. Joshua fought against them for six years. {Jos 11:1-18}

## 2559c AM, 3269 JP, 1445 BC

324. Joshua had now grown old. He was commanded by God to divide all the land west of the Jordan River among the nine remaining tribes and the other half tribe of Manasseh. {Jos 13:1-7} He first divided the land of Gilgal (where the tabernacle of God and the army were stationed at the time) among the tribes of Judah and Ephraim and the half tribe of Manasseh. {Jos 14:6 15:1-17:18} [E27]

## 2559d AM, 3269 JP, 1445 BC

325. At this time Caleb, the son of Jephunneh, forty-five years after the time that he was sent by Moses to spy out the land, desired to have Hebron, together with the mountain country of Judah. This was assigned to him for his part in undertaking to expel the Anakims from there. {Jos 14:5,10,13} Tremellius observed correctly that Joshua did not permit Caleb and his company to take Hebron alone but he went with the army to take it. When Hebron was conquered, Joshua gave Caleb the adjoining lands and villages. Joshua set apart the city with its common lands for a city of refuge and for the priests. {Jos 21:11-13 1Ch 6:55-57} Neither Hebron nor Debir had yet been taken by the Israelites, though both were within the inheritance assigned to Caleb. The Anakims were not expelled from there. {Jos 14:1-15:63} Hence the pas-

sages in Joshua and Judges seem to refer to this place, because the subject matter is the same. {Jos 10:28-11:23 Jud 1:9-15}

326. When the children of Judah and Joseph were settled in their possessions according to their tribes, a large part of the land of Canaan still remained in the hands of the Canaanites. Before dividing up more land, Joshua took the army from Gilgal [L40] and attacked Makkedah and Libnah and utterly destroyed the kings and people of both these cities. {Jos 10:28-30}

327. From there he marched with his army to Lachish and took it, after a two day battle. All the inhabitants were killed. When Horam, king of Gezer, came to help Lachish, Joshua defeated him and killed all his people. Joshua then marched to Eglon and took it that same day, killing all its inhabitants. {Jos 10:31-35}

328. After this Joshua, with all of Israel, went up from Eglon to Hebron and took it. He killed its new king, for the previous one had been hung six years before. The inhabitants of Hebron with all its cities were killed. {Jos 10:36,37} Caleb also expelled the three giants, Sheshai, Ahiman and Talmai, the sons of Anak. {Jos 15:14} These giants were among the reasons Israel had refused to enter the land forty-five years earlier. {Nu 13:22,23 Jos 15:14}

329. Joshua, with the army, marched from the south of Canaan to Debir, {Jos 10:38} which was formerly called Kirjathsepher. There Caleb had proclaimed that whoever took it should have his daughter for a wife. His first cousin, Othniel, the son of Kenaz, took it and married Caleb's daughter Achsah. Her dowry was a piece of land with its springs. {Jos 15:15-19 Jud 1:11-15} When Othniel took the city, he killed the inhabitants and their new king. The previous king had been hung with the rest, six years earlier. {Jos 10:39}

330. Joshua destroyed all the hill country, all the south parts, both plain and valley and all their kings, from Kadeshbarnea to Gaza, as well as all the country of Goshen (which was part of the land allotted to the tribe of Judah {Jos 15:51}) as far as Gibeon. Joshua took all these kings and all their lands (in one single operation), for God himself fought for Israel. When this had been accomplished, he and the host of Israel returned to Gilgal. {Jos 10:40-43}

331. The rest of the kings united their forces and came to the waters of Merom to fight against Israel. Joshua, in a surprise attack, defeated and killed them. He took all their lands, {Jos 11:1-16} from Mount Halak which rises toward Seir (which was the frontier of Edom), to Baalgad in the valley of Lebanon beside Mount Hermon. {Jos 11:17 12:7}

*332.* Then Joshua expelled the giants, the Anakims, from their cities, from the hill country of Hebron, Debir, and Anab and generally from the mountains of Judah and all Israel. Hebron was taken by the tribe of Judah. {*Jos 11:21,23 Jud 1:10*}

*333.* When the whole land had been conquered, Joshua in the following year divided it among the children of Israel according to their tribes. The land rested from war. {*Jos 11:23 14:15*} [*L41*]

## 2560a AM, 3269 JP, 1445 BC

*334.* The first sabbatical year they observed was the seventh year from the first year when they began tilling the ground in Canaan. Joshua, a type of Jesus, had brought them into this place of rest, it being a type of that Sabbath and rest which the true Jesus was to give to God's people. {*Heb 4:9*} From this time are reckoned the years of Jubilee, which were every fiftieth year. {*Le 25:8-13*}

*335.* On the fifteenth day of the seventh month (Saturday, November 5), according to the law, the Levites kept the feast of tabernacles in booths made from boughs of trees. {*Le 23:39,40*} This was done more solemnly than in the later times of the judges and kings {*Ne 8:17*}

*336.* God was now about to give the Israelites rest from all their enemies around them so that they could live there securely. It was necessary that a place should be chosen which God himself would select to place his name there. {*De 12:10,11*} After the whole land was subdued, they came together at Shiloh and set up the tabernacle of the congregation. {*Jos 18:1*} [*E28*] The tabernacle with the ark of the covenant stayed there for three hundred and twenty-eight years. The meaning of the name and the city called Shiloh seems to be the same place as Salem, for, as שלם signifies *Peace* or *Rest* {*Ge 34:21 Na 1:12*} so also does שלה. {*Da 4:1*} Also the Messiah is thought to have been called Shiloh, {*Ge 49:10*} because not only was he to be peaceable and quiet, but he was also the author of our eternal rest and peace. As well, Melchizedek, the king of Salem, the *king of peace* {*Heb 7:2*} lived there, according to Jerome in his 126th Epistle to Enagrius. In Jerome's time, the city was near the place where John baptized. {*Joh 3:23 Ge 33:18*} According to Jerome's account and the Septuagint translation, Shiloh was called Sichem because it was located in the country of Sichem. {*Jos 24:25,26 18:1 Ge 35:4 Jud 9:6 21:8-19*}

*337.* The remaining land was divided among the other seven tribes for their inheritance and the boundaries were recorded in a book. {*Jos 18:1-19:51*} After the seven nations of the Canaanites were destroyed, their lands were all distributed among the Israelites.

*338.* From the year after God's choosing Isaac until now, the period elapsed was about four hundred and fifty years, {*Ac 13:17,19,20*} because from the birth of the promised seed Isaac to this time is four hundred and fifty-two years, and from the rejection of Ishmael, four hundred and forty-seven. Hence the time was approximately four hundred and fifty years.

## 2560d AM, 3270 JP, 1444 BC

*339.* Forty-eight cities were selected out of the land from both sides of the Jordan for the inheritance of the Levites. Six of these were made cities of refuge. Sanctuaries were established there, where those who had not committed wilful murder might flee for protection. {*Jos 20:1-21:45*} The Israelites now possessed the land promised to their fathers. God gave them rest and peace on every side according to all that he had sworn to their fathers. {*Jos 21:43,44*} The companies of the Reubenites, Gadites and the half tribe of Manasseh, who came over the Jordan to help their brethren conquer the land, returned to their possessions on the other side of the Jordan. {*Jos 22:4 1:12,15 Nu 32:21,22*}

*340.* On their return journey they came to Gilead at the passage of the Jordan River, in the borders of the land of Canaan. There they built a large altar. The other tribes thought they intended to revolt, so they resolved to make war against these two tribes. They sent Phinehas, the son of Eleazar, the high priest, with ten other princes of the people, to find out why the altar had been built. When they understood that the altar had not been built to offer sacrifices, but only as a memorial and as a token of the fellowship which they had with the rest of the tribes of Israel, they changed their minds and did not fight with them. {*Jos 22:1-34*}

## 2561 AM, 3271 JP, 1443 BC

*341.* Joshua built the city of Timnathserah in Mount Ephraim, where he lived for many years after God had given rest to Israel. [*L42*] He was buried in Timnathserah and like Joseph, he lived to the age of a hundred and ten years. {*Ge 50:26 Jos 23:1 24:29,30*}

## 2591d AM, 3301 JP, 1413 BC

*342.* After the death of Joshua and the elders who had outlived him, the disorders happened that are recorded in Judges. {*Jud 17:1-21:25*} These were the idolatry of Micah and the children of Dan, and the war of the Benjamites and its causes. This was a time of anarchy, every man doing what seemed right in his own eyes. The elders who died were less than twenty years old when they came out of Egypt. They were eye-witnesses to all that God had done. However, the next generation forgot God and inter-married with the Canaanites, worshipping their idols. God was angry and gave them into the hands of Cushan, king of Mesopotamia. This was their first calamity, and it lasted eight years. {*Jud 2:7,10 3:6-8*}

## 2599d AM, 3309 JP, 1405 BC

*343.* Othniel, the son of Kenaz and son-in-law to Joshua, {*Jos 15:17 Jud 1:31*} of the tribe of Judah, was raised up by God to judge and avenge his people. He defeated Cushan and delivered the Israelites from their bondage. *And the land had rest forty years* subsequent to the first rest which Joshua procured for them. {*Jud 3:9-11*}

## 2609a AM, 3318 JP, 1396 BC

*344.* The first Jubilee was celebrated in the land of Canaan in the fiftieth year.

(Note, a Jubilee year fell on the seventh sabbatical year and occurred every forty-nine years. In Leviticus {*Le 25:8-10*} it states the Jubilee was in the fiftieth year. Also a Jubilee and sabbatical year started in the autumn. {*Le 25:9*} If a Jubilee occurred every fifty years, the text would have to say in the fifty-first year. If a child is one year old, he is in his second year. Likewise if a man is forty-nine years old, he is in his fiftieth year. In the Apocrypha it said that certain events happened in a sabbatical year. {*Apc 1 Ma 6:49*} From the associated text we know that year was 163 BC. If the sabbatical and Jubilee cycle was fifty years long, 163 BC would not be a sabbatical year. Likewise Josephus stated that 37 BC was a sabbatical year when Herod captured Jerusalem. This would not have been the case if the cycle was fifty years long and not forty-nine. This confirms the accuracy of Ussher's work. {*See note on 3841d AM. <<3474>>*} {*See note on 3967b AM. <<5473>>*} Editor.)

## 2658a AM, 3367 JP, 1347 BC

*345.* The second Jubilee.

## 2661d AM, 3371 JP, 1343 BC

*346.* After Othniel died, the Israelites again sinned against God and were delivered into the hands of Eglon, king of Moab. *[E29]* He, along with the Ammonites and Amalekites, defeated the Israelites and took Jericho. This was their second oppression and it lasted for eighteen years. {*Jud 3:12-14*}

## 2679d AM, 3389 JP, 1325 BC

*347.* After the tribe of Benjamin was almost entirely wiped out, God raised up Ehud the son of Gera, a Benjamite, to avenge his people. While feigning a message to Eglon from God, he stabbed him in the belly with his dagger and left him dead in his own dining room. After he escaped he gathered all Israel together in Mount Ephraim and killed ten thousand valiant men

of Moab. *And the land had rest forty years* after the former rest and deliverance by Othniel. {*Jud 3:15-30*}

*348.* Later, Shamgar the son of Anath also avenged Israel by killing six hundred Philistines with an ox goad. {*Jud 3:31*}

## 2682 AM, 3392 JP, 1322 BC

*349.* Belus the Assyrian reigned over the Assyrians in Babylon for fifty-five years, according to Julius Africanus.

## 2699d AM, 3409 JP, 1305 BC

*350.* After the death of Ehud, the Israelites sinned again. God gave them up into the hand of Jabin of Canaan who reigned in Hazor. Jabin had nine hundred chariots of iron and oppressed Israel for twenty years. {*Jud 4:1-3*}

## 2707a AM, 3416 JP, 1298 BC

*351.* The third Jubilee.

## 2719d AM, 3429 JP, 1285 BC

*352.* Deborah, the wife of Lapidoth, a prophetess, judged Israel at that time in Mount Ephraim. Barak of the tribe of Naphtali, son of Abinoam, was made captain of the host of Israel. In a battle at Megiddo, they defeated Sisera, who was the captain of Jabin's army. Sisera was killed by Jael, the wife of Heber the Kenite. She did this in her own tent by hammering a nail into the temples of Sisera's head. Deborah wrote a song in memorial of that victory, *and the land rested forty years* after the former rest restored by Ehud. {*Jud 4:1-5:31*} *[L43]*

## 2737 AM, 3447 JP, 1267 BC

*353.* Ninus, the son of Belus, founded the Assyrian Empire. This empire continued in Asia for five hundred and twenty years. {**Herodotus, l. 1. c. 95. 1:126*} Appian of Alexandria, in the beginning of his work, followed the same account. {**Appian, l. 1. c. 0. s. 9. 1:15*} However, Dionysius Halicarnassus, who is known for diligent research into such matters, said that the Assyrians had a very small part of Asia under their command. {**Dionysius Halicarnassus, Roman Antiquities, l. 1. c. 2. s. 2. 1:7*} Diodorus Siculus stated that Ninus joined with Ariaeus, the king of Arabia, and occupied all Asia and ruled India and Bactria for seventeen years. Finally, he subdued the Bactrians with their king Zoroastres. {**Diod. Sic., l. 2. c. 1-7. 1:351-371*} Justin wrote: {*Justin, Trogus, l. 1.*}

"When Ninus had conquered his adjacent neighbours, he added their forces to his own. By this he became stronger still to conquer the next enemy. Every victory was a step to another, and by this means he subdued all the people of the east. His last war was with Zoroastres, the king of Bactria.

This king is said to have been the first to find out the art of magic, and to have most diligently looked into the nature of the world and the motion of the stars. Ninus killed him and died some time later."

354. Julius Africanus and Eusebius said that Ninus reigned fifty-two years. {*Eusebius, Chronicles*}

## 2752d AM, 3462 JP, 1252 BC

355. The Israelites sinned again and were delivered into the hands of the Midianites. This fourth oppression lasted seven years. {*Jud 6:1*}

## 2756a AM, 3465 JP, 1249 BC

356. The fourth Jubilee.

## 2759d AM, 3469 JP, 1245 BC

357. When the Israelites fell into this fourth bondage, they cried to God for help and were reproved by a prophet. Then Gideon of Manasseh, son of Joash, the Abiezrite, was chosen to deliver them by an angel sent from God. At God's command, he overturned the altar of Baal and burned its grove. As a result of the strife between him and the people, he was called Jerubbaal or Jerubbesheth. {*Jud 6:32 2Sa 11:21*}. From thirty-two thousand volunteers he selected three hundred men according to God's criteria. Gideon and these men, equipped with their trumpets, pitchers and torches, so frightened the Midianites that they put to flight all their host. The Ephraimites then pursued them and killed their princes, Oreb and Zeeb. Gideon pacified the Ephraimites, who complained that they were not called to the battle at first. Then he crossed the Jordan River and defeated the remainder of the Midianite army. He also chastised the men of Succoth and Penuel, who had refused him provisions for his journey. He killed the two kings of the Moabites, Zebah and Zalmunna. After these great victories, he refused the Israelites' offer to make him and his posterity king. Using the enemies' golden earrings, a part of the plunder (which was taken as spoil in the battle), he made an ephod. This later caused them to fall into idolatry. After the Midianites were conquered, *the land had rest forty years*; this was after the former rest restored to them by Deborah and Barak {*Jud 6:1-8:28*}

## 2768d AM, 3478 JP, 1236 BC

358. As soon as Gideon was dead, the Israelites fell into idolatry and worshipped Baalberith as their god. {*Jud 8:33*} Abimelech, the son of Gideon (born by his concubine from Sichem), planned to be king and killed seventy of his brothers, all on the one stone. {*Jud 9:1-5,18,24,56*} [E30]

## 2769a AM, 3478 JP, 1236 BC

359. When Abimelech was made king with the Sichemites' help, Jotham the youngest son of Gideon, having es-caped Abimelech's clutches, challenged them from the top of Mount Gerizim about the wrong they had done to his father's house. [L44] Using a parable, he prophesied their ruin and then fled from there and lived quietly in Beeroth. {*Jud 9:1-57*}

## 2771d AM, 3481 JP, 1233 BC

360. After Abimelech reigned over the Israelites three years, Gaal, a man of Sichem, made a conspiracy against him. When Zebul discovered this, the city of Sichem was utterly destroyed and sowed with salt. The inhabitants were all killed and the temple of their god Beeroth was burned with fire. From there, Abimelech went to besiege Thebes. There he was hit on the head with the upper part of a millstone thrown by a woman and he was killed by his own armour bearer. {*Jud 9:22-54 2Sa 11:21*}

## 2772a AM, 3481 JP, 1233 BC

361. After Abimelech's time, Israel was judged for twenty-three years by Tola, the son of Puah, of the tribe of Issachar. {*Jud 10:1,2*}

## 2781 AM, 3491 JP, 1223 BC

362. After the Atyadans first reigned in Sardis, it was ruled by Argon, the son of Ninus. His posterity held the kingdom of Lydia for five hundred and five years, or twenty-two generations. Each son succeeded his father to the throne, until the time of Candaules, the son of Myrsus. {*Herodotus, l. 1. c. 7. 1:11*}

## 2789 AM, 3499 JP, 1215 BC

363. Semiramis, the daughter of Dercetidis, was the wife, first of Menon and later, of Ninus. Diodorus Siculus stated that she reigned for forty-two years over all Asia, with the exception of India, and lived sixty-two years. {*Diod. Sic., l. 2. c. 20. s. 2. 1:417*} Ctesias Cnidos described her noble acts at length, especially those against Strabrobates king of India. We find this also recorded in Strabo, quoting from Megasthenes, who wrote expressly of the Indian affairs. {*Strabo, l. 15. c. 2. s. 5. 7:135*} Arrian said that she died before she ever came into India. {*Arrian, Indica, l. 1. c. 5. s. 7. 2:319*} Herodotus stated that she constructed very large works around Babylon, whereas formerly the Euphrates River had overflowed all the lower parts of it. {*Herodotus, l. 1. c. 184. 1:229*} Justin also mentioned Semiramis and stated that: {*Justin, Trogus, l. 1.*}

"She built Babylon and walled it round with bricks, laying the stones with brimstone, instead of sand. This brimstone erupted naturally from the earth everywhere in that area. This queen did many other very memorable acts. Not content to keep her husband's conquests, she added Ethiopia to her dominions and she also made war on India. She was the first to enter India and Alexander the Great was the next."

*364.* All other writers agree that Dionysus or Bacchus conquered all of India. It was Diodorus and Trogus who falsely reported that this queen enclosed Babylon with a wall of brick. {*Diod. Sic., l. 2. c. 7. s. 2. 1:371,373} Strabo also {*Strabo, l. 2. c. 1. s. 26. 1:305} {*Strabo, l. 16. c. 1. s. 2. 7:195} is refuted by the sacred history of Genesis {Ge 11:1-32} and by Eupolemus. It was Nebuchadnezzar and his daughter-in-law, Nectoris, who built the wall of Babylon many years later. Eupolemus stated in his book, *Concerning the Jews of Assyria*: {*Eusebius, Gospel, l. 9. c. 17. (418c) 1:450}

"It was first built by those who escaped the deluge."

*365.* Erranius, mentioned by Stephanus Byzantinus in his book, *de Urbibus,* under the word *Babylon* and Eustathius in Dionysius Periegetes, {Dionysius Periegetes, Geography, p. 126.} noted that Babylon was built one thousand and two years before Semiramis was born. If he had said one thousand and twenty-two years, this date would very nearly agree with the Babylonian calendar sent from there by Callisthenes, as reported by Porphyry. {See note on 1771 AM. <<50>>} Porphyry {Porphyry, Against Christians, l. 4.} was cited by Eusebius. {*Eusebius, Gospel, l. 1. c. 9. (30ab) 1:35} {*Eusebius, Gospel, l. 10. c. 9. (485bc) 1:519} Eusebius spoke about the beginning of the Phoenicians, quoting Sanchuniathon of Berytus, a most ancient writer, who said he took his argument from Hierombalus or Jerubbaal. {See note on 2759d AM. <<357>>} [L45] This Jerubbaal (Gideon) was a priest of Jevo, that is Jehovah, the God of the Jews. Sanchuniathon dedicated his history to Abibalus, king of the Berytians. Eusebius stated further that this Sanchuniathon lived in the days of Semiramis, Queen of the Assyrians, who is said to have lived before the Trojan wars at that time. This agreed with my account of having her live after the war of Troy by eleven years after reigning for forty-two years.

## 2790d AM, 3500 JP, 1214 BC

*366.* Eli, the priest, was born, for he died at the age of ninety-eight years, in 1116 BC or 3598 JP. {1Sa 4:15}

## 2795a AM, 3504 JP, 1210 BC

*367.* After Tola died, he was buried at Shamir, in mount Ephraim. He was succeeded by Jair, a Gileadite from the tribe of Manasseh beyond the Jordan River, who judged Israel for twenty-two years. {Jud 10:1-3} He was descended from that Jair who took the cities of Argob and called them Bashan-Havothjair. {Nu 32:41 De 3:14} Following his example, the thirty sons of this second Jair (who, to distinguish him from the first Jair {1Sa 12:11

1Ch 7:17} and who seemed to have been surnamed Bedan) called the thirty cities which they possessed by the name of Havothjair. {Jud 10:4} [E31]

## 2799a AM, 3508 JP, 1206 BC

*368.* Because the Israelites forsook God and worshipped the gods of other nations, God gave them up into the hands of the Philistines and the Ammonites. This was their fifth oppression, lasting eighteen years. {Jud 10:8} The bondage ended in the victory over the Ammonites when Jephthah began his rule over Israel.

## 2805a AM, 3514 JP, 1200 BC

*369.* The fifth Jubilee.

## 2816d AM, 3526 JP, 1188 BC

*370.* During the nineteenth year of their slavery, the enemies defeated the Israelites who lived beyond the Jordan River. The Ammonites crossed over the river and attacked Judah, Benjamin and Ephraim, whom the Philistines had already crushed. The Israelites called on God and were grievously rebuked by him. However, they showed their repentance by abandoning their idols and obtained mercy. {Jud 10:8}

## 2817a AM, 3526 JP, 1188 BC

*371.* Jair died and was buried at Camon. {Jud 10:5}

*372.* That same year the Ammonites camped in Gilead. The Israelites camped in Mizpah, which is also in Gilead. {Jud 10:17 11:11} Jephthah the Gileadite was called by the men of Gilead to be captain of the host of Israel. He made war upon the Ammonites and subdued them. He vowed to God that if God would give him the victory, he would offer as a burnt offering whatever came from his house to meet him. His daughter was unaware of the vow and greeted him first. She was offered as a burnt offering to God. Jephthah also killed forty-two thousand Ephraimites, who behaved themselves insolently toward him. He judged Israel for six years. {Jud 11:1-12:7}

## 2820c AM, 3530 JP, 1184 BC

*373.* Troy was destroyed by the Greeks four hundred and eight years before the first Olympiad. {*Eusebius, Chronicles, l. 1. 1:148} (The Latin copy states it was four hundred and five years. Editor.) Eratosthenes, Apollodorus and Diodorus Siculus concur with this time. {See note on 3919b AM. <<4002>>} {*Diod. Sic., l. 1. c. 4. s. 5. 1:21,32}

## 2823a AM, 3532 JP, 1182 BC

*374.* When Jephthah died, he was buried in Gilead, and Ibzan the Bethlehemite judged Israel for seven years. {Jud 12:7-9}

## 2830a AM, 3539 JP, 1175 BC

*375.* Ibzan died and was buried at Bethlehem. Elon the Zebulunite succeeded him and judged Israel for ten years. {*Jud 12:10,11*}

## 2831 AM, 3541 JP, 1173 BC

*376.* When Semiramis tried to commit incest with her son, he killed her. She had ruled for forty-two years after her husband Ninus. {*Justin, Trogus, l. 1. c. 2.*} *[L46]* Although it seems incredible that a woman of sixty-two years of age would commit such an act of incest, Augustine seems to have believed it. {*Augustine, City of God, l. 18. c. 2. 2:362*} Diodorus stated more details about Semiramis and her death. {*Diod. Sic., l. 2. c. 20. s. 2. 1:417*} Semiramis' son, Ninus or Ninyus, was content with the empire which his parents had, and laid aside all cares of military affairs. Ninus was very effeminate in that he seldom kept company with men. He spent most of his years in the company of women and eunuchs. {*Justin, Trogus, l. 1. c. 2.*} {*Diod. Sic., l. 2. c. 21. s. 2. 1:419*} {*Athenaeus, l. 12. (528f) 5:387*} {*Ctesias, History of Persia, l. 3.*}

## 2840a AM, 3549 JP, 1165 BC

*377.* Elon died and was buried at Ajalon in the tribe of Zebulun. Abdon the Ephraimite, the son of Hillel the Pirathonite, succeeded him. He judged Israel for eight years. {*Jud 12:12-14*}

## 2848a AM, 3557 JP, 1157 BC

*378.* When Abdon died, he was buried at Pirathon in mount Ephraim. {*Jud 12:15*} After him came Eli, who judged Israel for forty years. {*1Sa 4:18*} He was also the high priest. This high priesthood was transferred from the descendants of Eleazar to Ithamar.

## 2848c AM, 3558 JP, 1156 BC

*379.* When Israel sinned again, God delivered them into the hands of the Philistines for the next forty years. {*Jud 13:1*} This was the Israelites' sixth oppression, which we think ended seven months after the death of Eli, when the ark was brought back again. Hence, it was about the beginning of the third month, called Sivan, when Eli began to judge Israel.

## 2848d AM, 3558 JP, 1156 BC

*380.* An angel appeared to the wife of Manoah of the tribe of Dan at Zorah. He told her that she, though barren, would conceive and bear a son. This child would be a Nazarite who would begin to deliver Israel out of the hands of the Philistines. {*Jud 13:5*}

## 2849b AM, 3559 JP, 1155 BC

*381.* As foretold by the angel, Samson the Nazarite was born at Zorah. {*Jud 13:24,25*} It seems he was conceived after the forty years of oppression by the Philistines had begun. {*Jud 13:1-5*} He avenged the Israelites against the Philistines for twenty years. {*Jud 15:20*} Obviously, Samson's birth could not have happened later unless he was judging Israel before he was eighteen years old, which seems unlikely.

## 2854a AM, 3563 JP, 1151 BC

*382.* The sixth Jubilee.

## 2867d AM, 3577 JP, 1137 BC

*383.* While Eli was executing the office of a judge in civil causes at the time of the Philistines, Samson picked a quarrel against him because he was engaged to marry a woman of Timnah. Samson had begun to judge the Israelites at the age of twenty-two. {*Jud 14:4*} On the day of his betrothal, he had killed a lion with his bare hands. He made a bet at the wedding feast and propounded a riddle to the guests. When he had lost, because his wife had told them the meaning of the riddle, he went off in a rage and killed thirty men of Askelon. He gave these wedding guests the suits of clothing which he had stripped off his victims' bodies to fulfil the terms of the wager, and returned home to his father. *[E32]*

## 2868c AM, 3578 JP, 1136 BC

*384.* At harvest time, Samson went to present his wife with a kid at her father's house, but found that she had been given away in marriage to another man. He then sought revenge by catching three hundred foxes and tying fire brands to their tails. He turned them all loose in the Philistines' grain fields, vineyards and olive gardens, setting these all ablaze. The Philistines were very angry, so they took Samson's wife and father-in-law and burned them to death. In revenge, Samson killed a large number of them and sat down upon the rock of Etam. *[L47]* From there, three thousand Jews arrested him and delivered him to the Philistines. He then killed one thousand of these Philistine men with the jawbone of an ass. When Samson prayed in that place called Lehi, God opened a hole in the jawbone and from it came a fountain of water. This fountain was called Enhakkore, meaning the fountain of him who called upon God. He refreshed himself with the water from this fountain, because he was thirsty and ready to faint. {*Jud 15:1-20*}

## 2887c AM, 3597 JP, 1117 BC

*385.* Delilah, Samson's concubine, betrayed him by having his hair cut, the symbol of his Nazarite vow, and delivered him to the Philistines. They plucked out his eyes and carried him away prisoner to Gaza. They put him in prison and bound him with chains of brass.

## 2887d AM, 3597 JP, 1117 BC

*385a.* In prison, his hair grew again and his strength was renewed. He pulled down the temple of Dagon while the princes of the Philistines and a large number of the people were in it. More men were killed when the temple fell, including Samson himself, than he had killed in all his lifetime. He was buried with his father between Zorah and Eshtaol. He had judged Israel for twenty years. {*Jud 16:30,31*}

## 2888a AM, 3597 JP, 1117 BC

*386.* The Israelites took courage from this great loss of the Philistines, and gathered together to a camp near Ebenezer (named by the prophet Samuel when, twenty-one years later, the Philistines were overthrown by him in the very same place). {*1Sa 4:1 7:12*} There the Israelites lost four thousand men. When they sent for the ark of the covenant from Shiloh to be brought into the camp, the Philistines saw all that was at stake. During that battle the Philistines encouraged one another to be strong and fight lest, they said:

> "we be forced hereafter to live in slavery under the Hebrews as they have been under us."

*387.* In that second battle, thirty thousand Israelites were killed. The ark of God was taken by the Philistines and Hophni and Phinehas, the two priests and sons of Eli, were killed there. When Eli heard the news, he fell off his chair backward and broke his neck for he was very fat. Furthermore, his daughter-in-law, the wife of his son Phinehas, went into labour because she was pregnant, and she delivered a son called Ichabod, and died. {*1Sa 4:1-22*} When the Philistines took the ark of God, they carried it to Ashdod and placed it in the temple of their god, Dagon.

*388.* Twice, Dagon was found lying prostrate and broken before the ark on the ground. Some of the inhabitants of the place died of the plague, and some were struck with filthy tumours in their private parts. {*1Sa 5:9 Ps 78:66*} They moved the ark from there, first to the Gittites and later to the Ekronites. However, the same plagues occurred wherever it went. After seven months, on the advice of their priests, the Philistines sent the ark home again with gifts into the land of the Israelites. Around the beginning of the third month, during wheat harvest time, fifty thousand and seventy men of Bethshemesh were killed for looking inside the ark. {*1Sa 5:1-6:1,13-19*} From there, the ark was moved and carried to the house of Aminadab in Gibeah, on the hill of the city of Kirjathjearim. {*1Sa 7:1,2, 2Sa 6:3,4*} This place was inhabited by the tribe of Judah and was also called Baalah and Kirjathbaal. {*1Ch 13:6 Jos 15:9,60*} However, all this time the tabernacle where God was worshipped remained at Shiloh in the tribe of Ephraim. {*Jud 18:31 1Sa 14:3*}

## 2891c AM, 3601 JP, 1113 BC

*389.* Barzillai the Gileadite was born, for he was eighty years of age when Absalom rebelled against David. {*2Sa 19:35*}

## 2903a AM, 3612 JP, 1102 BC

*390.* The seventh Jubilee.

## 2908c AM, 3618 JP, 1096 BC

*391.* For twenty years after the ark had come to Kirjathjearim, {*1Sa 7:2*} the Israelites were grievously oppressed by the Philistines. *[L48]* Finally, having been persuaded by Samuel, they returned to the Lord after abandoning all their idols. They came together at Mizpah, where they were said to have *drawn water*, that is, to have drawn tears from the bottom of their hearts and to have poured them out before the Lord. {*1Sa 7:6*} This perhaps symbolised some external effusion or pouring forth of water to signify their inward repentance and mourning for their sins. {*2Sa 14:14*} Some would understand this as speaking of the penitents themselves. {*Ge 35:2 Ex 19:14*} After their repentance, God immediately delivered the people of the Israelites from the invasion of the Philistines. {*1Sa 7:10,12 Jos 10:10,11*} God sent a terrible thunder that terrified the Philistines. *[E33]* They abandoned all the cities of the Israelites which they had formerly held. {*1Sa 7:14*} Several small garrisons were left in only a few places. {*1Sa 10:5*} No more did they come to invade their borders, because they saw that the hand of the Lord was against them all the days of Samuel until Saul became king. {*1Sa 7:12*} However, after Saul became king they returned again and oppressed Israel. When Samuel was old, he appointed his two sons to be judges over Israel at Beersheba. They did not serve the Lord like their father, but perverted judgment for rewards and bribes. {*1Sa 8:1-3*} He did not retire completely, for from the passage {*1Sa 7:15-17*} it appears that he continued judging the people by himself to his dying day.

## 2909c AM, 3619 JP, 1095 BC

*392.* Because Samuel's sons were taking bribes and perverting justice, the Israelites began to make light of Samuel's leadership, which troubled him and offended God. {*1Sa 8:6-8*} The Israelites were disgusted by the excessive behaviour of Samuel's sons and requested that they should have a king, as other countries had. {*1Sa 8:4,5*} In addition to this, the Philistines still had some garrisons in their land. Furthermore, Nahash, king of the Ammonites, had assembled men in preparation for war against them. This caused them great fear, so that they resolved no longer to rely on Samuel's wisdom or on the power of God, who had up to that time been their king and avenger. In spite of the fact that they had expelled the Philistines out of their land, they still expressed their desire to have a king. {1Sa 12:12,17,19} Though God was angered by their request, he gave them a king {Ho 13:10,11} whose name was Saul, the son of Kish, of the tribe of Benjamin. Saul reigned for forty years. {Ac 13:21} Saul's son Ishbosheth was forty years old when he succeeded his father to the kingdom. {2Sa 2:10} Ishbosheth is said to have been born when Saul was anointed king. Saul was first anointed privately, and afterward publicly before all the people at Mizpah, by Samuel. It was twenty-one years since the death of Eli {1Sa 7:2} and since Samuel had begun to judge Israel. {1Sa 10:1,24,25} About one month later {1Sa 12:12,16} (as the Septuagint and Josephus, {*Josephus, Antiq., l. 6. c. 5. s. 1. (68) 5:201} stated), Jabeshgilead was besieged by Nahash king of the Ammonites. This siege was lifted by Saul when he defeated the Ammonites. The whole congregation of Israel came together at Gilgal and Saul was again proclaimed king there. {1Sa 11:14,15} [L49] Samuel, however, questioned Saul's sincerity in fulfilling his royal position and complained of the wrong that had been done to him. Samuel called upon God to send thunder and rain, which terrified the people. Then he comforted them with the promises of God's mercies. {1Sa 12:17} This appears to have happened during their wheat harvest season, around the time of the feast of Pentecost in the beginning of the third month, twenty-one years after the ark arrived from the country of the Philistines. {1Sam 6:13} It seems that a full twenty years passed between the return of the ark and the subduing of the Philistines. {1Sa 7:2,13} One year had passed between the expelling of the Philistines from Israel and Saul's anointing as king, as is stated in the Hebrew: {1Sa 13:1}

> "Saul was the son of one year when he reigned; and he reigned two years over Israel."

393. Hence, Saul reigned for two years free from the subjection of the Philistines.

## 2911c AM, 3621 JP, 1093 BC

394. The Philistines attacked Israel and took them captive, but Saul shook off their yoke and recovered his kingdom again from their hands. {1Sa 14:47} War with the Philistines continued for many years during Saul's reign. Since the war began eight years before David was born, it was before it ended that Samuel prophesied of David succeeding to the throne after Saul. *The Lord hath sought him a man according to his own heart, and God hath commanded him to be ruler over his people.* {1Sa 13:14} The Philistines took from them all their smiths so they would have no weapons to fight with and no one to make any. Hence, when the day of battle came, only Saul and his son Jonathan had weapons. {1Sa 13:19,22} [E34]

## 2919c AM, 3629 JP, 1085 BC

395. David was born to Jesse the Ephrathite in his old age. {1Sa 17:12} This was thirty years before David succeeded Saul to the kingdom. {2Sa 5:4 1Sa 16:1} David was the youngest of eight sons born to Jesse and Bethlehem was later called the city of David as was Jerusalem. {1Sa 20:6 Lu 2:4 2Sa 5:7,9}

## 2941c AM, 3651 JP, 1063 BC

396. God had rejected Saul and his family from the kingdom. After mourning a long time about this, Samuel was sent by God to Bethlehem to anoint David as king. This occurred forty years before the rebellion of Absalom. {1Sa 16:1 2Sa 15:7} David was a handsome-looking lad who was called away from shepherding his father's sheep. {1Sa 16:11,12,18 2Sa 7:3 Ps 78:70,71} Because David was preferred over his older brothers and was being anointed in their presence, {1Sa 16:13} they were envious of him. {1Sa 17:28} David's brothers were as envious of him as Joseph's brothers were of him. David was also made king over Judah at the same age that Joseph was made ruler over Egypt. {Ge 41:46 2Sa 5:4} From the day of his anointing, the Spirit of God came upon him, giving him his courage and wisdom. {1Sa 16:13,18 18:5,13,14,30 2Sa 5:2} As a result of this, while Saul lived, he was made general over all Israel and became a great warrior to fight the Lord's battles. {1Sa 25:28} He became known as a prophet and *the sweet Singer of Israel* who, by his divine Psalms, would teach and instruct the people of God. {Ac 2:30 2Sa 23:1,2} [L50]

## 2944 AM, 3654 JP, 1060 BC

397. Mephibosheth (or Meribbaal), {1Ch 8:34 9:40} the son of Jonathan, was born five years before the death of his father. {2Sa 4:4}

## 2944c AM, 3654 JP, 1060 BC

398. David feared that he might at last fall into Saul's hands, so he fled to King Achish in Gath, where he previously had fled {1Sa 21:10}, taking six hundred men with him. Achish gave him the town of Ziklag to dwell in, and he lived there for one year and four months in the land of the Philistines.

## 2948a AM, 3657 JP, 1057 BC

399. From there he attacked and killed all the Geshurites, Gezrites and the Amalekites, leaving no one alive to carry news of the slaughter to King Achish. {1Sa 27:1-12}

## 2948c AM, 3658 JP, 1056 BC

400. While David was at Ziklag, many who were relatives of Saul came to join themselves with him. Also many valiant men of the tribe of Benjamin, the tribe of Gad and various good soldiers came across the Jordan River to join him, in the first month when it overflowed

all its banks. They were accompanied by many other captains and commanders of the tribes of Benjamin and Judah. {1Ch 12:1,15,18}

## 2949c AM, 3659 JP, 1055 BC

401. King Achish planned to invade the Israelites with his Philistine army. He took David along with him. {1Sa 28:1,2} While David was on the march with his six hundred men, he gathered a number of others from the tribe of Manasseh who joined him. {1Ch 12:19} The Philistines were then encamped at Shunem and the Israelites were in Gilboa. {1Sa 28:4}

402. When Saul saw the army of the Philistines, he became afraid and sought counsel from the Lord. Receiving no answer in a dream, or by Urim, or through his prophets, he went to Endor by night to consult with a witch. When she conjured up a vision of Samuel, Saul received the dreadful message:

> "God shall deliver Israel, together with thyself, into the hands of the Philistines; and tomorrow, thou and thy children shalt be with me." {1Sa 28:5,6,19 1Ch 10:13,14}

403. While David was away on his march, the Amalekites took Ziklag, plundered it and burned it. They carried away David's two wives, Ahinoam of Jezreel and Abigail, the widow of Nabal, along with all the wives and children of his men. {1Sa 30:1-31}

404. When Saul returned that same night from the witch, the Israelites moved to the fountain of Jezreel and the Philistines went to Aphek. The princes of the Philistines became jealous of David, so he and his men left the Philistine army early the next morning and returned to Ziklag. The Philistines in the interim marched up to Jezreel to fight with the Israelites. {1Sa 28:25 29:1,3,10,11} It seems that Saul and his sons were not killed on the day immediately following his communication with the apparition of Samuel (since all that day David was with the army of the Philistines), but Saul's death occurred some while after David's departure from them.

405. When David was returning to Ziklag, seven captains of the Manassites came to meet him. {1Ch 12:20,21} David arrived on the third day of his journey at Ziklag and found the town plundered and consumed by fire. Two hundred of his company were weary from marching and rested at the brook Besor, while David followed after the Amalekites and overtook them with the remaining four hundred men. The battle lasted from the twilight of the first day to the evening of the next. They recovered all that was lost and returned home with joy. {1Sa 30:1-31} [L51]

406. The host of Israel were soundly trounced. The three sons of Saul, Jonathan, Abinadab and Melchishua, were also killed. Saul and his armourbearer fell on their own swords. The following day the Philistines took off the head of Saul and hung up his armour in the temple of their idol Ashtaroth. His body and the bodies of his three sons were also left to hang on the walls of Bethshemesh. [E35] However, the men of Jabeshgilead remembered the deed of valour which Saul had done for them at the beginning of his reign. They stole away their bodies from there and burned them. They buried their bones under an oak at Jabesh and fasted for them for seven days. {1Sa 31:1-13 1Ch 10:1-14}

407. Mephibosheth was the son of Jonathan, who was now dead. When his nurse heard the news of his death she ran away with Mephibosheth. Because she was very afraid and in a great haste, he fell out of her arms and became lame in his feet for the rest of his life. {2Sa 4:4}

408. Three days after David's return from the slaughter of the Amalekites, he heard of the defeat of the Israelite army. A boy of the Amalekites who had been in the battle brought him the news, together with Saul's crown and bracelet, which he had removed from Saul's body. {2Sa 1:1-16} From this news, though quickly brought to David, it is inferred that the defeat in Gilboa happened a number of days after David left the Philistine army. It was not unusual for the battle to be so delayed. Much later, when the Syrians camped against the Israelites at the same place at Aphek, Israel waited seven days before fighting with them. {1Ki 20:26,29}

409. David executed the Amalekite who claimed to have killed Saul. In a funeral song he praised Saul, Jonathan and God's people. {2Sa 1:13-27} Daily, more companies of the Israelites' army flocked to him. {1Ch 12:22} He asked counsel of God before he went up to Hebron with his men and their families. There he was anointed king by the men of his own tribe at the age of thirty. He reigned over Judah for seven years and six months. {2Sa 2:1-4,11 5:4,5}

410. Abner, the former captain of Saul's army, took Ishbosheth, Saul's son, to Mahanaim and there he made him king over the rest of Israel. Ishbosheth was forty years old and reigned two years over Israel. {2Sa 2:8-10} He had two years of peace with the house of David, just as his father's two years of reign {1Sa 13:1} referred to two years of peace with the Philistines. {See note on 2909c AM. <<392>>}

411. David sent messengers to the men of Jabeshgilead and thanked them for the kindness which they had shown to King Saul. He informed them that he was now king over Judah. {2Sa 2:5-7} To strengthen his position, he made an alliance with Talmai, king of Geshur and

secured it by marrying his daughter, Maacah. She bore him Absalom and Tamar. {2Sa 3:3 13:1}

## 2951c AM, 3661 JP, 1053 BC

*412.* After the two years of peace with Ishbosheth, there was a long war between his people and the people of David. Joab, the son of Zeruiah, David's sister, headed up David's side and Abner commanded the other side. Many battles and skirmishes took place. David's side grew stronger and stronger, while Ishbosheth's side became weaker. {2Sa 2:26-3:1}

## 2952a AM, 3661 JP, 1053 BC

*413.* The eighth Jubilee. *[L52]*

## 2956d AM, 3666 JP, 1048 BC

*414.* When Abner was disgracefully used by Ishbosheth, he defected to David. He arranged with the chief men and heads of Israel to transfer the whole kingdom to David. {2Sa 3:6-21}

*415.* When David had fled from Saul, {1Sa 19:12} his wife Michal had been given by Saul in marriage to Phaltiel. David demanded that Ishbosheth send her back. {1Sa 25:44 2Sa 3:14,15}

*416.* When Abner came with twenty men to David, he was well received and given a feast. When he returned from David in peace, he was treacherously killed by Joab. David made a great mourning and lamentation over Abner, and he was buried at Hebron. {2Sa 3:17-39}

*417.* All Israel was troubled by the death of Abner. Baanah and Rechab, of the tribe of Benjamin, murdered Ishbosheth when he was resting on his bed in the heat of the day. They brought his head to David and he had them executed. {2Sa 4:1-12}

*418.* The captains and elders of all the tribes came to Hebron and anointed David king over Israel for the third time. {1Ch 12:23-40 11:1-3 2Sa 5:1-3}

## 2957a AM, 3666 JP, 1048 BC

*419.* David, with all Israel, marched to Jerusalem against the Jebusites. By Joab's valiant actions they captured the citadel of Zion. Henceforth, it was called the *City of David*, just as Bethlehem, his birthplace, was called. He made Jerusalem the capital of the kingdom and reigned over all Israel for thirty-three years. {2Sa 5:5-7,9 1Ch 11:4-7}

## 2957c AM, 3667 JP, 1047 BC

*420.* When the Philistines heard that David was made king over all Israel by every tribe, they twice led their army against him at the valley of Rephaim, and were defeated both times. {2Sa 5:22-25 1Ch 14:1-17} *[E36]* It was at

this place that David, in the time of harvest, desired a drink of water from the well at Bethlehem. To please him, three of the most valiant captains broke through the host of the enemy to get it. When they brought it to him, he would not drink it. {2Sa 23:13 1Ch 11:15}

## 2958b AM, 3668 JP, 1046 BC

*421.* David built up the city of Zion and strengthened its fortifications. Joab repaired the rest of the city. {2Sa 5:9 1Ch 11:8}

*422.* Hiram sent messengers to David. Hiram also sent cedar wood, and carpenters and masons, to build David's house. {2Sa 5:11 1Ch 14:1}

## 2959 AM, 3669 JP, 1045 BC

*423.* The ark of the covenant, which in the first sabbatical year had been brought from Gilgal to Shiloh, was now brought from Kirjathjearim in this sabbatical year. It had been moved from Shiloh seventy years earlier, from the house of Abinadab. Thirty thousand choice men from all Israel accompanied the move of the ark by David. He composed the sixty-eighth psalm for the occasion, as may be deduced from the psalm's title. {Ps 68:1} This verse appears to have been taken from a prayer which was appointed by Moses to be used and sung every time the ark was moved. {Nu 10:35} The ark was first carried to the house of Obededom. After three months, it was moved into the city of David, or the citadel of Zion. David himself rejoiced before it, and sang a psalm. {Ps 132:8} Solomon his son repeated this verse {2Ch 6:41} in the next Jubilee year, when he brought the ark into the Holy of Holies in the temple.

> "Arise oh Lord unto thy resting place, thou and the ark of thy strength"

*424.* See also this passage. {Ps 132:6,7} From the Hebrew:

> "Behold we (that is the men of Bethlehem dwelling there) have heard of it at Ephratah (our own country) and found it in the fields of Jair, or the wood; (that is in the hill of Kirjathjearim, for that signifies a city, bordering upon woods)"

*425.* From another psalm we have: *[L53]*

> "The Lord hath chosen Zion, for a habitation for himself; saying, This is my rest for ever here will I dwell, for I have a delight therein." {Ps 132:13,14}

*426.* The ark *came to rest there* at Zion {1Ch 6:31} and was moved into the new tabernacle which David had prepared for it at Jerusalem. {2Sa 6:17 1Ch 16:1 2Ch 1:4}

*427.* The tabernacle of the congregation, built by Moses, together with the brazen altar used for the daily sacrifices, remained at Gibeon, in the tribe of Judah, until the temple of Solomon was built. It was no longer in Shiloh in the tribe of Ephraim. {1Ch 6:32,48,49 16:39,40 21:29 2Ch 1:3,5,6 1Ki 3:2,4}

428. The ark was moved from the house of Joseph, of which the tribe of Ephraim was a part, into the tribe of Judah. After this, Shiloh played no part in Israel's worship. {Ps 78:67,68 Jer 7:12,14 26:6}

## 2960d AM, 3670 JP, 1044 BC

429. David now lived in the house of cedar which he had built, and enjoyed peace on every side. He told Nathan, the prophet, that he planned to build a house for God. God replied that this was a task that should be done by a man of peace, not war, and that his son Solomon would build the house, not David. {2Sa 7:1,2,11,13 1Ch 17:1-27 22:8-10 28:3,6 2Ch 6:8,9 1Ki 8:18,19} From now until the birth of Solomon, the time was spent in wars. David subdued the Philistines, the Edomites, the Amalekites, the Moabites, the Ammonites and the Syrians. {2Sa 8:3 1Ch 18:1-17} The borders of Israel stretched not only from Shihor in Egypt to Hamath, {1Ch 13:5} but even from there to the Euphrates River as far as the borders of Syria Zobah. {2Sa 8:3} This was the extreme boundary of all that land which had formerly been promised to the seed of Abraham. {Ge 15:18 De 11:24 Jos 1:3,4} It was never possessed by any of them, except by David and his son Solomon. {1Ki 4:21,24 2Ch 9:28}

430. At this time Hadadezer, also called Hadarezer (the ר and the ד look very similar in Hebrew), the son of Rehob, was king of Syria Zobah. He united his forces from Damascus with the forces of Rezon, the son of Eliadah. They prepared to fight against David not far from the Euphrates River. However, after David routed Hadadezer's army, he killed twenty-two thousand of the Syrians from Damascus and put garrisons in all that country. When Rezon saw that David had prevailed, he rebelled against Hadadezer and made himself captain over the forces he had recently raised. He marched with them to Damascus and there set up a kingdom for himself and his posterity. He was a very bitter enemy to Solomon, as was his kingdom to the rest of the kings of Israel. {2Sa 8:5,6 1Ch 17:5,6 1Ki 11:23-25} Concerning this battle fought by David near the Euphrates River, Nicolaus Damascene, quoted in Josephus, {*Josephus, Antiq., l. 7. c. 5. s. 2. (101) 5:413} mentioned this battle of David's and called this Rezon, Adad. He added that his name was passed on to his successors to the tenth generation, as Ptolemy did to his in Egypt.

## 2967a AM, 3676 JP, 1038 BC

431. After Nahash, king of the Ammonites, died, his son Hanun reigned in his place. He badly abused the mes-

sengers that David, out of kindness, had sent to comfort him over the death of his father. {2Sa 10:1-5} [E37] [L54]

## 2967c AM, 3677 JP, 1037 BC

432. Therefore, David sent out Joab, who defeated a large army of the Ammonites and Syrian mercenaries. David and Joab returned victorious to Jerusalem. {2Sa 10:1-19 1Ch 19:1-19}

## 2968b AM, 3678 JP, 1036 BC

433. David crossed the Jordan River with his army and slaughtered a vast number of the Syrians who were led by Shophach, the general of the army of Hadadezer, king of Syria Zobah. A time of peace followed between David and the petty kings of Syria, so that they sent no more aid to the Ammonites, but served David. {2Sa 10:1-19 1Ch 19:1-19}

## 2969b AM, 3679 JP, 1035 BC

434. At the end of the year, when kings went to battle, Joab, with his army, fought against the Ammonites and besieged Rabbah, the capital city of Ammon. In the meantime, David took his ease at Jerusalem. {2Sa 11:1 1Ch 20:1} There, he defiled himself in an adulterous relationship with Bathsheba, the wife of Uriah the Hittite. Uriah was in the army at that time. Consequently, David arranged to have Uriah killed at the hands of the Ammonites. {2Sa 11:1-27}

## 2970b AM, 3680 JP, 1034 BC

435. When David's child by adultery was born, David was convicted of his sin by Nathan, the prophet, whereupon he repented. David composed the 51st psalm {Ps 51:1-19} as a sad memorial of his sin with Bathsheba, but the child died. {2Sa 12:1-31}

## 2971a AM, 3680 JP, 1034 BC

436. Bathsheba, who was now David's wife, bore David another son called Solomon, whose name was given to him by God. This child proved to be a man of peace. {1Ch 22:9} His name means one beloved of God, the name of Jedidiah. {2Sa 12:25}

## 2972c AM, 3682 JP, 1032 BC

437. Amnon, David's oldest son, raped his sister Tamar. {2Sa 13:1-39}

## 2974c AM, 3684 JP, 1030 BC

438. Two years after he had raped his sister, Amnon was killed by his brother Absalom at the time of sheep shearing, before grain harvest. {2Sa 13:23} This occurred at the end of the spring, shortly after the middle of the first month and during the second mowing of the grass. Codomanus noted this from these passages. {Am 7:1 Jos 3:15 4:19 5:10-12}

439. After Absalom had killed Amnon, he fled to Geshur in Syria. He stayed three years with king Talmai, his grandfather on his mother's side. {2Sa 13:37,38 15:8}

## 2977c AM, 3687 JP, 1027 BC

440. After three years of exile, Absalom returned to Jerusalem. His father was pacified toward him by the speech of the woman of Tekoa, who was employed by Joab. {2Sa 13:38 14:1,23}

## 2979b AM, 3689 JP, 1025 BC

441. Absalom set Joab's barley on fire just before harvest time that year (for the following year was a sabbatical year, when there was no harvest in Judah). By this means he was admitted to his father's presence, whom he had not seen in the two years since his return from exile. {2Sa 14:28,30,33}

## 2980 AM, 3690 JP, 1024 BC

442. This sabbatical year came between the burning of Joab's grain field and the rebellion of Absalom against his father. In his rebellion, Absalom obtained chariots and horses and gathered a band of ruffians around him, while insinuating himself into the favour of the people. He stole away their hearts from his father David. {2Sa 15:1-6}

## 2981c AM, 3691 JP, 1023 BC

443. Forty years after the anointing of David by Samuel, Absalom followed the advice of his chief counsellor Ahithophel and took possession of his father's kingdom. {2Sa 15:7} This happened between the Passover and the Feast of Pentecost. Codomanus assumed this to be the season, from what Barzillai provided for David when he fled with new fruits and roasted grain. {2Sa 17:28}

444. David composed the third and fifty-fifth psalms against the practices of Absalom and Ahithophel. {Ps 3:1-8 55:1-23} Shimei, of the tribe of Benjamin, railed against David as he fled. {2Sa 16:5} [L55]

445. When Ahithophel saw that his counsel had not been followed by Absalom, he went and hanged himself. {2Sa 17:23}

446. In the battle with David, Absalom lost twenty thousand men and fled. A bough of a thick oak caught hold of his long hair, so he hung there until Joab came and thrust him through with darts, killing him. {2Sa 18:9-14}

447. After this victory, David was brought home again by the men of Judah and one half of the people of Israel. The other Israelites rebelled because they had not participated in that work. This rebellion was soon over when the head of Sheba, the son of Gera, was thrown over the walls to Joab by the people of Abel. {2Sa 19:1-20:22}

## 2983c AM, 3693 JP, 1021 BC

448. The harvest of this year failed and there was a famine which afflicted the land for three years. This famine was sent because the innocent blood of the Gibeonites had been shed by Saul and his family. {2Sa 21:1,2}

## 2986c AM, 3696 JP, 1018 BC

449. The famine still continued, so the Gibeonites hanged two of Saul's sons and five of his grandchildren at the beginning of the barley harvest. Rizpah, Saul's concubine, watched over their bodies and kept them from being devoured by ravenous birds or beasts, until water dropped from heaven upon them. {2Sa 21:8-10}

450. David took the bones of Saul and Jonathan his son and moved them from Jabeshgilead, along with the bones of the seven that had been hanged. They were buried at Zelah in the sepulchre of Kish, the father of Saul. {2Sa 21:12-14}

451. Many battles were fought with the Philistines and their giants. In one battle, David, who was now old, fainted in the battle and could have been killed by the giant Ishbibenob, but he narrowly escaped. [E38] This was the last battle that David took part in. {2Sa 21:16-22 1Ch 20:4-8}

## 2987d AM, 3697 JP, 1017 BC

452. Either Satan or David's pride motivated David to have a census taken, thereby kindling God's wrath against the Israelites. {1Ch 21:6 27:24} For this census, all the men over twenty years of age in every tribe (except the tribes of Levi and Benjamin) were counted. {1Ch 27:23}. This census took nine months and twenty days to complete. {2Sa 24:8} God sent the prophet Gad to David and gave him the choice of one of three punishments. He was to choose famine, sword or pestilence. {2Sa 24:11-14} This famine was to last three years, {1Ch 21:12} but for seven years according to the passage in Samuel. {2Sa 24:13}. The famine would have included the three years of the previous famine {2Sa 21:1} together with this present sabbatical year, in which no sowing would take place to compensate for the losses of the previous years, bringing a fourth year of dearth. Three years of famine for the slaughter of the Gibeonites were already past, and after this there would have been a poor harvest for lack of seed. This harvest would not have been able to supply the needs of the next two years, which the intervening sabbatical year would require. So the famine would still have continued in the land, especially among the poor. Now in addition to these past four years of famine, God proposed to David a choice of three more years of famine. To reconcile these two different passages, {2Sa 24:13 1Ch 21:12} I placed the

account of David's numbering the people in this sabbatical year.

453. Now of the three choices, David chose the plague. In one day, seventy thousand men died. When the angel was about to destroy Jerusalem, God in his mercy bade him withhold his hand. He commanded David to offer whole burnt offerings and peace offerings on the threshing floor of Araunah or Ornan, the Jebusite. {2Sa 24:1-25 1Ch 21:1-30} [L56]

## 2988a AM, 3697 JP, 1017 BC

454. David foresaw that the house of God would be built on the threshing floor of Araunah. {1Ch 22:1 2Ch 3:1} He began to prepare the materials necessary for so great a work. He exhorted his son Solomon and all the heads of Israel to carry the project through to a successful completion. {1Ch 22:1-19}

## 2988c AM, 3698 JP, 1016 BC

455. He took the number of the Levites, first from thirty, and then from twenty years old and upwards. He divided them into many ranks and assigned to each one his office. He established a set form both for ecclesiastical and civil government in the fortieth year of his reign. {1Ch 23:1-27:34} This was the beginning of the year, a year and a half before his death.

456. Rehoboam was born to Solomon by Naaman, an Ammonite woman. He was forty-one years old when he began his reign, and hence was born to Solomon a year before Solomon started to reign. {1Ki 14:21 1Ch 12:13} For although Solomon called himself a little child when he began to reign, {1Ki 3:7} and David his father said he was *a child, young and tender*, {1Ch 22:5 29:1} yet in another place he called him a man of wisdom. {1Ki 2:9} This was even before God granted him extraordinary knowledge and wisdom. These three things—tender years, a son born and perfect wisdom—were not unique to Solomon at eighteen. For the same things were attributed to king Josiah when he was only sixteen—{2Ch 34:1-3 2Ch 36:2,5} since Jehoiakim was born when Josiah was only fourteen years old and Jehoahaz was born when Josiah was sixteen.

## 2989b AM, 3699 JP, 1015 BC

457. David was now seventy years old. Broken with continual cares and wars, he was so weak and feeble that wearing extra clothes could hardly keep him warm. So Abishag, a young Shunammite maiden, was sent for to keep him warm. {1Ki 1:1-4}

## 2989c AM, 3699 JP, 1015 BC

458. When Adonijah saw his father's decline, he took counsel and advice from Joab and Abiathar, the high priest, and made himself king. When Bathsheba and Nathan told David of this, he ordered his son Solomon to be anointed king in Gihon by Zadok the priest, Nathan the prophet and Benaiah, the son of Jehoiada. As soon as Adonijah heard this, he fled to the sanctuary and took hold of the horns of the altar. He was pardoned by the grace and favour of Solomon and set at liberty. {1Ki 1:1-53}

459. David assembled all the governors, captains and commanders of Israel with his sons and servants. He exhorted them all to the fear and worship of God, especially Solomon his son. He ordered them to proceed with the building of the temple. He gave them the plans for the temple and consigned into Solomon's hands the gold and silver by weight for making every vessel and implement to be used in the temple. {1Ch 28:1-21} After this, because of David's example and exhortation, every man was moved to give gold, silver, brass, iron and stones, all in great abundance, toward the building of God's house. They gave thanks to God, and on the following day they offered a thousand young bullocks, a thousand rams and a thousand lambs, with the meat offerings. Solomon was anointed as king the second time, and Zadok was confirmed as the high priest. {1Ch 29:1-23} [E39]

## 2990a AM, 3699 JP, 1015 BC

460. After David had given his instructions to his son Solomon, he died. {1Ki 2:1-10}. He had reigned in Hebron for seven years and six months, and thirty-three years in Jerusalem over all of Israel. {2Sa 5:5} Concerning the forty years which the scripture attributes to his reign, we must take the term of his reign before he made Solomon king in his place, and consider that he lived for six more months after that. [L57] So that the years of Solomon's reign as mentioned in the scriptures are to be reckoned from the first month, a full half year before David's death.

## 2990b AM, 3700 JP, 1014 BC

461. Adonijah used Bathsheba to ask Solomon to give him Abishag, the Shunammite, as his wife. Therefore Solomon had him executed, as one still aspiring to be king. Abiathar, of the family of Eli, was put out of the high priesthood and Zadok, a descendent of Phinehas, replaced him. This had been foretold earlier by God to Eli. {1Sa 2:33,35} So the high priesthood reverted from the family of Ithamar to the family of Eleazar and continued there. Joab fled to the tabernacle in fear and took hold of the horns of the altar. He was executed by Benaiah, the son of Jehoiada, who was made captain of the host in his place by the king. Shimei, who had before railed upon David, was merely confined to his

house, yet with this condition, that if at any time he passed over the brook Kidron, he would be executed. {1Ki 2:1-46}

462. When Hadad, the Edomite, heard that Joab was dead, he returned from Egypt to his own country. When Solomon later began to follow after vanities, God used Hadad as an enemy against Solomon. {1Ki 11:14,21}

## 2991a AM, 3700 JP, 1014 BC

463. Pharaoh, king of Egypt, gave his daughter in marriage to Solomon. He gave her the city of Gezer located in the tribe of Ephraim. {Jos 21:21} Pharaoh had taken it from the Canaanites and killed all its inhabitants. {1Ki 9:16} Solomon brought her into Zion, the palace of David. {1Ki 3:1 2Ch 8:11}

## 2991c AM, 3701 JP, 1013 BC

464. Solomon offered a thousand whole burnt offerings at Gibeon where the tabernacle was situated. God appeared to him in his sleep and asked him to choose anything he wanted. Solomon chose wisdom to be given to him. Therefore, God gave him wisdom from above, as well as all other blessings over and above this. The first test of his wisdom was the deciding of the controversy between the two women about one of their children. This gave him a reputation and the respect of the people. {1Ki 3:1-28}

## 2992a AM, 3701 JP, 1013 BC

465. Solomon was visited by messengers sent from Hiram, king of Tyre, who wanted to help him with timber for the building of the temple. When Solomon met Hiram's terms, Hiram co-operated in the venture. Solomon supplied the workmen, over whom he set pay masters and other officers to oversee the work. {1Ki 5:1-18}

# The Fifth Age of the World

## 2992c AM, 3702 JP, 1012 BC

*466.* The foundation of the temple was laid in the four hundred and eightieth year after Israel's exodus from Egypt. This was in King Solomon's fourth year of reign, on the second day of the second month (called Zif, Monday May 21). {1Ki 6:1,37 2Ch 3:2}

## 2993b AM, 3703 JP, 1011 BC

*467.* Three years after he was commanded not to cross the brook Kidron, Shimei returned from Gath to bring back two runaway servants. Solomon had him executed. {1Ki 2:39-46}

## 3000a AM, 3709 JP, 1005 BC

*468.* In the eleventh year of Solomon's reign, in the eighth month, called Bul, the temple and its furnishings were completed. [L58] It had taken seven years and six months to build. {1Ki 6:38} The dedication of the temple was postponed until the autumn of the next year, because that was the beginning of the Jubilee year.

## 3001a AM, 3710 JP, 1004 BC

*469.* This was the ninth Jubilee, which opened the fourth millennium of the world. King Solomon celebrated the dedication of the temple with great pomp and splendour. All Israel was assembled together in the seventh month, called Ethanim. The ark was brought from Zion into the Holy of Holies. The tabernacle and holy vessels from Gibeon went into the temple treasury. God gave a visible and wonderful token of his presence. Solomon was standing on a scaffold made of brass, and knelt down to pray to God. After this he blessed the people. He then offered twenty-two thousand oxen and a hundred and twenty thousand sheep. They celebrated the feast of the dedication of the altar for seven days, and the feast of tabernacles another seven days. On the fifteenth day, the celebrations were completed and the people were dismissed to their homes. This was the twenty-third day of the seventh month. {1Ki 8:1-66 2Ch 5:3-5 6:1-42 8:1-11} [E40]

*470.* The eighth day of the seventh month (that is, Friday, October 30) was the first of the seven days of the dedication. According to Levitical law, the feast of atonement was held on the tenth day (Sunday, November 1). {Lev 25:9} At the sound of the trumpet, the Jubilee was proclaimed.

*471.* The feast of tabernacles was held on the fifteenth day (Friday, November 6). The last day of this feast was always very solemnly kept. This occurred on the twenty-second of the month (Friday, November 13). {2Ch 7:9 Le

23:36 Joh 7:37} The following day (Saturday, November 14), at the conclusion of the Sabbath, the people went home.

## 3012c AM, 3722 JP, 992 BC

*472.* In the thirteenth year after the temple had been built, Solomon finished building his own house. He spent twenty years on both of them: seven years and six months on the temple, and thirteen years on his own house. {1Ki 7:1 9:10 2Ch 8:1}

*473.* As a reward for Hiram's good will in helping to construct these houses, Solomon offered Hiram, king of Tyre, twenty cities of Galilee or Cabul, which were located within the tribe of Asher. Solomon purchased these cities himself. When Hiram refused to take them, Solomon reconstructed them all himself, planting colonies of Israelites in them. {1Ki 9:10-13 2Ch 8:1,2}

*474.* When Solomon had finished both houses and the wall of Jerusalem, he moved his wife, the daughter of Pharaoh, out of the city of David, into a house which he had built for her. {1Ki 3:1 7:8 9:24 2Ch 8:11} He also rebuilt Gezer, which Pharaoh, his father-in-law, had taken from the Canaanites and given to Solomon. {1Ki 9:15-17} Gezer was located within the tribe of Ephraim.

## 3026c AM, 3736 JP, 978 BC

*475.* Shishak, also called Sefonchis (according to Egyptian Chronology), began to reign in Egypt. Jeroboam, the son of Nebat, fled to him and continued with him until after Solomon died. {1Ki 11:40 12:2}

## 3029b AM, 3739 JP, 975 BC

*476.* Toward the end of his life, Solomon forsook the lusts and vanities to which he was addicted in his latter years. He testified of his deep repentance in his book called *The Preacher* (Ecclesiastes) and made his peace with God. {2Ch 11:17} Solomon died when he had reigned forty years. {1Ki 11:42 2Ch 9:30} [L59]

*477.* Rehoboam, Solomon's son, was made king by all Israel in Shechem. By his harsh approach to his rule, he alienated the hearts of the ten tribes. (Solomon died before the Jewish New Year otherwise he would have been said to have reigned forty-one years. Rehoboam would have reigned for sixteen not seventeen years unless he was anointed king on or before that Jewish New Year.) These tribes sent to Egypt for Jeroboam, the son of Nebat, to be their king. Under his leadership they rebelled against the house of David. They killed Adoram, whom Rehoboam had sent to them, and abandoned the true worship of God. {1Ki 12:1-33} In memory of this sad disaster, the Jews kept a solemn yearly fast on the twenty-third of the third month, called Sivan. {*Josephus, Antiq., l. 14. c. 4. s. 3. note (a) in Whiston's translation}

478. After this sad division of the kingdom, Rehoboam reigned over Judah and Benjamin for seventeen years, {1Ki 14:21 2Ch 12:1,2} and Jeroboam over Israel, that is, over the other ten tribes, for twenty-two years. {1Ki 14:20}

479. Rehoboam returned to Jerusalem and conscripted one hundred men and eighty thousand to fight against the ten tribes. Through the prophet Shemaiah, he was instructed by God to abandon this plan. {1Ki 12:1-33} There was continual wars between the kings for the rest of their days. {1Ki 14:30}

480. In the beginning of his reign, Jeroboam fortified Shechem where he was chosen king by the people. This place had been destroyed by King Abimelech, two hundred and fifty-eight years earlier. {Jud 9:45} Jeroboam lived there until he went over the Jordan and built Penuel. {1Ki 12:25} Finally, he built Tirzah and made that city the capital of his kingdom. {1Ki 14:17} He feared that his new subjects would revolt against him if they continued to worship at Jerusalem, so he devised a new religion. He set up two golden calves for the people to worship, the one at Bethel and the other at Dan. {1Ki 12:25-31}

### 3030a AM, 3739 JP, 975 BC, 1 SK, 1 NK

481. NK - On the fifteenth day of the eighth month (Monday, December 6), Jeroboam held a feast of his own creation similar to the feast of tabernacles among the Jews. On an idolatrous altar which he had built at Bethel, he offered sacrifices to his calf. {1Ki 12:32,33} [E41] At that time, God sent an unnamed prophet from Judah who foretold what judgment God, through Josiah, would execute on this altar and the priests that served it. This prophecy was confirmed by signs which appeared on the altar and on the very body of the king himself. {1Ki 13:1-34 2Ki 23:15-20} From the beginning of this idolatrous worship and public demonstration of God's judgment in that place, we are to reckon the three hundred and ninety years of the iniquity of Israel, as spoken of by Ezekiel. {Eze 4:5} {See note on 3420 AM. <<867>>} [L60]

482. This prophet was deceived by another prophet of Bethel, who lied about a message from God. Contrary to the express commandment of God, the former ate food at Bethel. Therefore, on his return home, he was intercepted and killed by a lion. When news of this reached the prophet who had deceived him, he fetched the body and gave it an honourable burial. He assured his sons that what had been foretold by this other prophet would undoubtedly come to pass. {1Ki 13:1-34 2Ki 23:17,18}

### 3030b AM, 3740 JP, 974 BC, 1 SK, 1 NK

483. SK - The priests, Levites and other Israelites who feared God, did not follow Jeroboam, but worshipped with Rehoboam in Jerusalem, which helped maintain the kingdom of Judah for three years. This was the time they walked in the ways of David and Solomon. {2Ch 11:17}

484. NK - Jeroboam continued in his revolt and excluded the priests, who were of the lineage of Aaron, and the Levites, from his worship. He appointed priests for the high places from among men of the common people. {1Ki 13:33,34 2Ch 11:14,15 13:9} Hence many of the priests and Levites abandoned their possessions in those tribes and settled in Judah. They were followed there by those of every tribe who wanted to worship the true God. They came to Jerusalem to worship and sacrifice to the God of their forefathers. {2Ch 11:13,14,16}

### 3032d AM, 3742 JP, 972 BC, 3 SK, 3 NK

485. SK - Rehoboam was now settled in his kingdom and forsook the law of the Lord, and all Israel and Judah with him. {2Ch 12:1} The Jews of Judah, who should have stirred up their Israelite brothers to repentance, provoked the Lord with their own sins. They behaved worse than their forefathers. They established high places, images and groves for themselves on every high hill and under every tree. [L61] They did all the wicked things the heathen did in their barbarous worship, including those nations whom God had cast out before them. {1Ki 14:22-24} [E42]

### 3033c AM, 3743 JP, 971 BC, 5 SK, 5 NK

486. SK - In Rehoboam's fifth year, Shishak, king of Egypt, invited perhaps by Jeroboam (who had formerly lived with him {See note on 3026 AM. <<475>>}), led out an army of a hundred and twenty chariots, sixty thousand horses and innumerable footmen from Egypt. The men were from the Lubims, Sukkiims and Cushites who entered the land of Judah. They had already captured all its other fortified cities when they finally came to Jerusalem. The king and his princes were brought to repentance by the preaching of Shemaiah, the prophet. The king received a gracious promise of their deliverance, but at a high cost. They were to give to the Egyptians all the treasure of the temple and of the king's house. Rehoboam replaced with brass all the shields of gold which Solomon had made. {1Ki 14:26,27 2Ch 12:2-12}

### 3046 AM, 3756 JP, 958 BC, 1 SK, 18 NK

487. SK - Abijah, the son of Rehoboam, succeeded his father, who died in the beginning of the eighteenth year of Jeroboam's reign. He reigned three years. {1Ki 15:1,2 2Ch 13:1,2} [L62]

**3047c AM, 3757 JP, 957 BC, 2 SK, 19 NK**

*488.* SK - Abijah and his army of four hundred thousand men fought with Jeroboam and his army of eight hundred thousand men. Because Abijah trusted in God, he was victorious against Jeroboam. He killed half a million of Jeroboam's soldiers. This was the highest casualty rate of any battle recorded in the Bible. Abijah captured the following cities: Bethel, where one of the calves was set up, Jeshanah and Ephrain, along with their associated towns. {2Ch 13:1-22}

**3049c AM, 3759 JP, 955 BC, 1 SK, 21 NK**

*489.* SK - After Abijah's death, and at the very end of the twentieth year of Jeroboam's reign in Israel, Asa succeeded his father Abijah and reigned forty-one years. {1Ki 15:8-10}

**3050a AM, 3759 JP, 955 BC, 2 SK, 22 NK**

*490.* This was the tenth Jubilee.

**3050d AM, 3760 JP, 954 BC, 2 SK, 1 NK**

*491.* NK - Nadab, in the second year of Asa, succeeded his deceased father Jeroboam to his kingdom, but reigned only two years. {1Ki 15:25} [E43]

**3051d AM, 3761 JP, 953 BC, 3 SK, 1, 2 NK**

*492.* NK - At the siege of Gibbethon of the Philistines, Nadab was killed by Baasha, a man from the tribe of Issachar, in the third year of the reign of Asa. In the same year that Baasha made himself king over Israel, he utterly destroyed all the family of Jeroboam. He reigned for twenty-four years. {1Ki 15:27-29,33}

**3053c AM, 3763 JP, 951 BC, 5 SK, 3 NK**

*493.* SK - God now gave ten consecutive years of peace to the land, {2Ch 14:1,6} even to the fifteenth year of King Asa's reign, or to the thirty-fifth year from the rebellion of the northern kingdom. {2Ch 15:10,19} In that year, this godly King Asa abolished all public idolatry, reformed his kingdom and fortified the cities of Judah against the invasion of his enemies. {2Ch 14:6} [L63]

**3055d AM, 3765 JP, 949 BC, 7 SK, 5 NK**

*494.* Jehoshaphat was born to Asa and Azubah was his mother. Later, at the age of thirty-five, he succeeded Asa to his kingdom. {1Ki 22:42 2Ch 20:31}

**3063c AM, 3773 JP, 941 BC, 15 SK, 13 NK**

*495.* In the beginning of Asa's reign, Zerah, the Ethiopian, mobilised an innumerable army to invade the land of Judah. This force had a million foot soldiers from the Cushites who, it seems, came from Arabia Petra and the desert and the Lubims, as well as those who fought aloft from the chariots. Asa met this army with three hundred thousand men from the tribe of Judah and two hundred and eighty thousand from the tribe of Benjamin. He called on the name of the Lord and routed and killed that vast army, taking much spoil from them. Following this, he was encouraged by Azariah the prophet. He assembled all his subjects together with a large number of the Israelites who were loyal to him. They met at Jerusalem in the third month in which the feast of Pentecost fell. From the spoil which they had taken, they sacrificed to God seven hundred oxen and seven thousand cattle, solemnly renewing their covenant with God. [E44] Asa continued reformation of his kingdom and removed Maachah, his grandmother, a great patroness of idolatry, from the honour of queen mother. He brought into the temple the things which he and his father had consecrated to God. {2Ch 14:8,9 15:1,10,11,13,16 16:8} [L64]

**3064c AM, 3774 JP, 940 BC, 16 SK, 14 NK**

*496.* NK - Baasha saw Asa actively restoring religion to Judah and observed that many of his subjects were defecting to Asa, so that they might be partakers in God's covenant blessings. {2Ch 15:9} For the rest of his life, he did not cease from making war against Asa. {1Ki 15:16,32} In Asa's sixteenth year and the thirty-sixth year since the division of the kingdom, Baasha began to fortify Ramah, to prevent more of his subjects from defecting to Asa. {2Ch 16:1}

**3064d AM, 3774 JP, 940 BC, 16 SK, 14 NK**

*497.* SK - Asa hired Benhadad, king of Syria, to come and hinder the building up of Ramah, which he did. Using the stones and timber from the city of Ramah, Asa built Geba and Mizpah. When Hanan the prophet reproved him for getting help from the king of Syria, he cast him into prison and at the same time Asa oppressed some of the people. {2Ch 16:1-14}

*498.* NK - At the same time, Benhadad, king of Syria, marched against the cities of Israel. He destroyed Ijon in the tribe of Asher and Dan in Dan, Abelbethmaachah in the tribe of Manasseh and all the borders of Chinnereth, with all the land of Naphtali. This forced Baasha to stop fortifying Ramah and retire to Tirzah. {1Ki 15:20,21 2Ch 16:4,5 Isa 9:1} Benhadad was the son of Tabrimon, who was himself the son of Hezion, {1Ki 15:18} or Rezon, the first king of Damascus of Syria. It was from him that the name of Hadad was passed on to his posterity in the kingdom. This is noted by Nicolaus Damascene, as recorded by Josephus, {*Josephus, Antiq., l. 7. c. 5. s. 2. (103) 5:415} where Nicolaus stated:

> "The third king of that name, who sought to wipe away the blot of the defeat that happened in his grandfather's days, marched into Judah and destroyed Samaria."

*499.* Josephus understood this to be the invasion made upon Samaria by Benhadad, in the time of Ahab. {*See note on 2960 AM.* <<430>>} {*See note on 3103c AM.* <<513>>} [L65]

### 3074d AM, 3784 JP, 930 BC, 26 SK, 24 NK

*500.* NK - When Baasha died and was buried at Tirzah, his son Elah succeeded him. {*1Ki 16:8-10*}

### 3075d AM, 3785 JP, 929 BC, 27 SK, 1 NK

*501.* NK - In the second year of Elah and the twenty-seventh of Asa, Zimri killed Elah and his entire family. [E45] He then reigned in Tirzah for seven days. But the soldiers at Gibbethon, a town of the Philistines, made Omri, the general of the army, king. He came to besiege Tirzah, and Zimri set fire to the king's palace, destroying both it and himself. {*1Ki 16:15-18*}

*502.* The people of Israel split into two factions, the one following Tibni, the son of Ginath, while the other followed Omri. Omri's side prevailed, and Omri became king. {*1Ki 16:8,21,22*}

### 3077d AM, 3787 JP, 927 BC, 29 SK, 3 NK

*503.* NK - Athaliah, the daughter of Ahab the son of Omri, was, so it seems, born forty-two years before her son, Ahaziah, reigned over Judah. {*2Ch 21:6 22:2*} {*See Gill on "2Ch 22:2"*}

### 3079d AM, 3789 JP, 925 BC, 31 SK, 5 NK

*504.* NK - Omri began to reign over all Israel in Tirzah by himself, in the thirty-first year of King Asa. {*1Ki 16:23*} [L66]

### 3080d AM, 3790 JP, 924 BC, 32 SK, 6 NK

*505.* SK - Jehoram was born to Jehoshaphat, thirty-two years before his father appointed him as viceroy of his kingdom. {*2Ki 8:17 2Ch 21:20*}

*506.* NK - At this point Omri had reigned six years in Tirzah, but he now moved the capital of his kingdom from Tirzah to Samaria. He established Samaria on the hill of Samaria, a place which he had purchased from Shemer. {*1Ki 16:23,24*}

### 3086d AM, 3796 JP, 918 BC, 38 SK, 1 NK

*507.* Omri died and was buried at Samaria. He was a poor father, but Ahab, the son who succeeded him, was much worse. Ahab reigned twenty-two years. {*1Ki 16:28,29*}

### 3087d AM, 3797 JP, 917 BC, 39 SK, 2 NK

*508.* SK - In the thirty-ninth year of his reign, Asa was diseased in his feet. He sought help from the physicians and not from God. {*2Ch 16:12*}

### 3090c AM, 3800 JP, 914 BC, 1 SK, 5 NK

*509.* SK - At the end of the forty-first year of his reign, Asa died and was buried in a sepulchre which he had prepared in the city of David. The tomb was filled with sweet odours and spices. {*2Ch 16:13,14*} He had been a good father, and an even better son succeeded him, called Jehoshaphat. At the very latter end of the fourth year of Ahab's reign, Jehoshaphat started to reign over Judah and ruled for twenty-five years. {*1Ki 22:41,42 2Ch 20:31*}

### 3092c AM, 3802 JP, 912 BC, 3 SK, 7 NK

*510.* SK - When Jehoshaphat was established in his kingdom, he began removing the high places and the groves. In the third year of his reign, he sent out the Levites and other chief men into all the cities to instruct the people. [E46] Jehoshaphat attacked some of his enemies to prevent them from invading him. God gave him peace. {*2Ch 17:7-10*}

### 3097d AM, 3807 JP, 907 BC, 8 SK, 12 NK

*511.* SK - Athaliah, the daughter of Ahab, king of Israel, married Jehoram, the son of Jehoshaphat, king of Judah. This union resulted from the marriage alliance Jehoshaphat made with Ahab. {*2Ch 18:1*} [L67] She had a son named Ahaziah who at the age of twenty-two succeeded Jehoram to the kingdom. {*2Ki 8:18,26,27 2Ch 21:6 22:2*}

### 3099a AM, 3808 JP, 906 BC, 9 SK, 13 NK

*512.* The eleventh Jubilee.

### 3103c AM, 3813 JP, 901 BC, 14 SK, 18 NK

*513.* NK - Benhadad, king of Syria, assembled his army together and with the assistance of thirty-two petty kings, besieged Samaria. He was defeated by Ahab and fled. {*1Ki 20:1-43*}

### 3104d AM, 3814 JP, 900 BC, 15 SK, 19 NK

*514.* NK - About a year later, Benhadad came up a second time as far as Aphek to fight against Israel. He was badly defeated and surrendered to Ahab. Ahab received him with all courtesy and honour, and after a while let him go in peace. Ahab made a pact of friendship with him, for which act God, through his prophet, pronounced judgment upon Ahab. {*1Ki 20:1-43*} However, as a result of this league, there were three years of peace between the two nations. {*1Ki 22:1*}

### 3105 AM, 3815 JP, 899 BC, 16 SK, 20 NK

*515.* NK - When Ahab could not persuade Naboth to sell him his vineyard, he was depressed. His wife Jezebel engaged false witnesses and had Naboth condemned to death and stoned. Thus Ahab got possession of the vineyard. The prophet Elijah told him of the destruction which was to befall him, Jezebel and all his posterity, on account of this wicked deed. Ahab trembled at this, and because of his timely repentance, he obtained a respite from this judgment. {*1Ki 21:1-29*} [E47]

### 3106d AM, 3816 JP, 898 BC, 17 SK, 21 NK

*516.* SK - As Ahab had done, Jehoshaphat made his son, also called Jehoram, viceroy of the kingdom. Jehoram, the other son of Ahab, later succeeded his brother Ahaziah as king over the Israelites in the eighteenth year of Jehoshaphat, king of Judah. {*2Ki 3:1*} This Jehoram is said to have begun his reign in the second year of his brother-in-law Jehoram, the son of Jehoshaphat. {*2Ki 1:17*}

*517.* NK - Ahab, in the seventeenth year of the reign of Jehoshaphat, made his son Ahaziah viceroy in the kingdom. {*1Ki 22:51*} [*L68*]

### 3107d AM, 3817 JP, 897 BC, 18 SK, 22,2 NK

*518.* SK - Jehoshaphat visited Ahab at the very end of the third year of the peace which Ahab had made with the Syrians. He was invited by Ahab to go with him to the siege of Ramothgilead. After being entreated, he agreed to join him, and barely escaped from there with his life. {*1Ki 22:1-53 2Ch 18:1-34*} When he returned home, the prophet Jehu, the son of Hanani, reproved him for helping such a wicked king. {*2Ch 19:1,2*}

*519.* NK - After Ahab had convinced Jehoshaphat to go with him, he set out to besiege Ramothgilead. Before he went, he asked four hundred false prophets, as well as Micaiah, the true prophet of God, what the outcome of the war would be. They all told him he would do well, except Micaiah, who foretold his defeat. Ahab disguised himself, but was killed in the battle. He was buried in Samaria. {*1Ki 22:1-53 2Ch 18:1-34*}

*520.* After his death, Moab revolted from the Israelites. {*2Ki 1:1 3:5*} They had been in subjection to them ever since King David's days. {*2Sa 8:2*}

### 3108a AM, 3817 JP, 897 BC, 18 SK, 2 NK

*521.* SK - When Jehoshaphat had built a fleet, he sent it to Ophir for gold. Ahaziah, the wicked son of Ahab, went into partnership with him in this venture. At first Jehoshaphat refused the joint venture, but later agreed to it. {*1Ki 22:49*} For so doing, God destroyed the fleet and reproved him through his prophet Eliezer, the son of Dodavah. {*2Ch 20:35-37*}

### 3108b AM, 3818 JP, 896 BC, 18 SK, 2 NK

*522.* NK - Ahaziah, king of Israel, was injured when he fell through a lattice of his dining room in Samaria. He asked Baalzebub, the god of the Ekronites, if he would recover. The prophet Elijah, with fire from heaven, destroyed two captains and their companies of fifty who were sent to capture him and bring him to the king. At last, he went voluntarily with the third captain who came for him. He told the king plainly that he would die. {*2Ki*

*1:1-18*} The king did die. He had reigned two years—partly with his father, partly by himself. {*1Ki 22:51*} [*L69*]

### 3108c AM, 3818 JP, 896 BC, 19 SK, 1 NK

*523.* NK - When Ahaziah was dead, his brother Jehoram, the other son of Ahab, succeeded him in the latter end of the eighteenth year of Jehoshaphat, and reigned twelve years. {*2Ki 3:1*}

*524.* Elijah was taken up into heaven in a fiery chariot. {*2Ki 2:1-25*}

### 3109c AM, 3819 JP, 895 BC, 20 SK, 2 NK

*525.* When Edom was still under the control of Judah, the three kings of Israel, Judah and Edom united to subdue the rebellious Moabites. [*E48*] In this war, the prophet Elisha miraculously furnished the army with water and assured them of the victory over their enemies. Mesha, king of the Moabites, was besieged in Kirhareseth and tried unsuccessfully to break out with the small forces he had left. He captured the firstborn son of the king of Edom, who was referred to as king of the Edomites by the prophet Amos. {*Am 2:1*} He offered him as a whole burnt offering on the wall of the city. {*2Ki 3:1-27*}

### 3112c AM, 3822 JP, 892 BC, 23,1 SK, 5 NK

*526.* SK - When Jehoshaphat was old, he desired to settle his estate. He gave the rest of his sons many gifts, along with fortified cities in Judah. His oldest son, Jehoram (whom he had formerly employed as his vice-regent), was made viceroy with him in the kingdom. He reigned for eight years. This was in the fifth year of Jehoram, king of Israel. {*2Ch 21:2,3,5,20 2Ki 8:16,17*} [*L70*]

### 3115c AM, 3825 JP, 889 BC, 4 SK, 8 NK

*527.* SK - Jehoshaphat died and was buried in the city of David. {*1Ki 22:50 2Ch 21:1*} This good king's wicked son Jehoram ruled alone for four years. When he was established in his kingdom, he killed all his brothers and many of the other princes in Judah. {*2Ch 21:1-20*} The Edomites revolted, having been under the control of Judah since King David's time. {*2Sa 8:14*} They had been smitten by Jehoram, but in accordance with the prophecy of Isaac, {*Ge 27:40*} they shook off Judah's yoke for ever. Libnah, a city of the priests in the tribe of Judah, {*Jos 21:13*} also revolted at this time. {*2Ki 8:20-22 2Ch 21:8-10*}

### 3116a AM, 3825 JP, 889 BC, 4 SK, 8 NK

*528.* SK - Jehoram followed the counsel of his wicked wife Athaliah and set up the idolatrous worship of Baal in Judah and Jerusalem, just as Ahab, his father-in-law, had done in Israel. He forced his subjects to worship Baal. [*E49*] God reproved him in a letter written by the prophet Elijah, who foretold what calamities and punishments would happen to him. {2Ch 21:11-15} These events occurred as predicted. {2Ch 21:16-20}

### 3116c AM, 3826 JP, 888 BC, 5 SK, 9 NK

*529.* SK - First, God stirred up the Philistines and Arabians against him. These attacked Judah and took away whatever they found in the king's house, together with his sons and wives. [L71] Since all his other sons had been killed, he had only Jehoahaz left. {2Ch 21:1-20} This Jehoahaz was also called Ahaziah and Azariah, and he succeeded his father to the kingdom. {2Ch 22:1,6}

### 3117c AM, 3827 JP, 887 BC, 6 SK, 10 NK

*530.* SK - After this, God struck Jehoram with an incurable disease in the bowels, which tormented him for two whole years. {2Ch 21:15,18,19}

### 3118d AM, 3828 JP, 886 BC, 7 SK, 11 NK

*531.* SK - When Jehoram was afflicted with this sickness, he made his son, Ahaziah, his viceroy in the eleventh year of Joram (also called Jehoram), the son of Ahab. {2Ki 9:29}

### 3119c AM, 3829 JP, 885 BC, 8,1 SK, 12 NK

*532.* When Jehoram's bowels fell out, he died a miserable death and was buried in the city of David, but without any pomp and not among the kings. {2Ch 25:19,20} After this, in the twelfth year of Joram, the son of Ahab, Ahaziah, Jehoram's son, succeeded him, reigning one year in Jerusalem. He followed in the steps of his wicked mother Athaliah and the whole house of Ahab, by setting up and maintaining the worship of Baal. {2Ki 8:25,27 2Ch 22:1-4}

*533.* Ahaziah had a son by Zibia of Beersheba, whose name was Joash or Jehoash. He was proclaimed king at the age of seven. {2Ki 11:21 2Ch 24:1}

### 3120b AM, 3830 JP, 884 BC, 1 SK, 12 NK

*534.* NK - Jehoram, king of Israel, and Ahaziah, king of Judah, went out together with their armies to Ramothgilead against Hazael, who had recently succeeded Benhadad to the kingdom of Syria, as Elisha the prophet had foretold him. In that battle, Jehoram was grievously wounded by the Syrians and retired to Jezreel to be healed of his wounds. {2Ki 8:1-29} Meanwhile, a certain son of the prophets was sent by Elisha and came to Ramoth. He anointed Jehu, the son of Jehoshaphat the son of Nimshi, king over Israel. [L72] He told him the will of God concerning the wiping out of the house of Ahab. As soon as Jehu had been proclaimed king by the captains and officers of the army, he marched to Jezreel. There he killed both Jehoram and Jezebel. {2Ki 9:1-37} Jehu sent letters to Samaria which were responsible for the death of the seventy sons of

Ahab, as foretold by Elisha. He took Jehonadab, the son of Rechab, with him to Samaria. There he destroyed all the family of Ahab with all the priests of Baal. Although he destroyed Baal worship, he still maintained the worship of Jeroboam's golden calves, and the associated idolatry by the Israelites, for the duration of his twenty-eight year reign. {2Ki 10:28,29,36}

### 3120c AM, 3830 JP, 884 BC, 1 SK, 1 NK

*535.* SK - Ahaziah returned from the battle at Ramothgilead against Hazael. Later he went to Jezreel to see Jehoram, the king of Israel, who was recovering from his wounds. When Jehu found many of Ahab's family attending him there, together with various princes of Judah, he killed them all. Then he searched for Ahaziah himself, who had escaped and fled to Megiddo. [E50] When he caught up with him on the way to Gur, which is in Ibleam, in the tribe of Manasseh, he killed him in his chariot. Ahaziah was carried from there by his servants, and was buried with his fathers in the city of David. {2Ki 9:1-37 2Ch 22:1-9} On his way back to Samaria, Jehu met forty-two men of Ahaziah's relatives heading to Jezreel with the intention of there greeting the king's children, but Jehu had them all killed. {2Ki 10:13,14}

*536.* When Athaliah, the daughter of Ahab, saw that her own son Ahaziah was dead, she killed all the royal family of the house of Judah and took control of the kingdom. Jehosheba, the daughter of king Joram and wife to Jehoiada, the high priest, took the infant Joash, who was the son of her brother Ahaziah. Joash and his nurse were hidden for six years in the temple while Athaliah ruled. Thus, his aunt spared him from the slaughter of the rest of the royal family. {2Ki 11:1-3 2Ch 22:10-12} [L73]

### 3126c AM, 3836 JP, 878 BC, 1 SK, 7 NK

*537.* Jehoiada, the high priest, brought out Joash at the age of seven and anointed him king. After he had Athaliah killed, Joash restored the worship of the true God, destroyed the house of Baal and commanded Baal's high priest Mattan to be killed before his altars. {2Ki 11:4-21 2Ch 23:1-21} Joash began his reign in the seventh year of Jehu and reigned forty years in Jerusalem. {2Ki 12:1 2Ch 24:1}

### 3140c AM, 3850 JP, 864 BC, 15 SK, 21 NK

*538.* Amaziah, the son of Joash and Jehoaddan, was born in Jerusalem. [E51] He was twenty-five years old when he began to reign. {2Ki 14:2 2Ch 25:1}

### 3147d AM, 3857 JP, 857 BC, 22 SK, 28 NK

*539.* Joash commanded the priests to repair the temple of God, using the poll tax that had been gathered for that purpose. {2Ki 12:4-16 2Ch 24:4-14}

**3148a AM, 3857 JP, 857 BC**

*540.* The twelfth Jubilee. *[L74]*

**3148c AM, 3858 JP, 856 BC, 23 SK, 1 NK**

*541.* SK - In the twenty-third year of his reign, Joash saw that the priests were quite slow in repairing the temple. Therefore, he assigned the task to Jehoiada, the chief priest, and others, to complete that work. *{2Ki 12:6,7 2Ch 24:5,6}*

*542.* NK - Jehoahaz succeeded his father Jehu as king over Israel in the twenty-third year of Joash, the son of Ahaziah. He reigned seventeen years *{2Ki 13:1}* and during that entire time Hazael, the king of Syria, cruelly oppressed the Israelites, *{2Ki 13:3,7,22}* as foretold by Elisha. *{2Ki 8:12}*

**3163c AM, 3873 JP, 841 BC 38 SK, 16 NK**

*543.* SK - Joash or Jehoash, the son of Jehoahaz, was made viceroy with his father toward the end of the thirty-seventh year of Joash, king of Judah. He reigned sixteen years. *{2Ki 13:10}*

**3164c AM, 3874 JP, 840 BC, 39 SK, 17,2 NK**

*544.* SK - After Jehoiada died, his son Zechariah, the priest, was stoned to death for reproving Judah for backsliding into idolatry. This was done at the king's command in the court of God's house. *{2Ch 24:17-22}*

**3165c AM, 3875 JP, 839 BC, 40,1 SK, 3 NK**

*545.* SK - The next year some small bands of men belonging to Hazael, king of Syria, attacked Judah and Jerusalem and killed all the chiefs of the people. They took all their spoil back to their king. When they were gone, Joash was left very sick. *[E52] [L75]* In revenge for Jehoiada's son Zechariah's death, his servants conspired against him and killed him in his bed at the beginning of the fortieth year of his reign. *{2Ch 24:1,23-27 2Ki 12:1,17-21}* His successor, Amaziah, began his reign of twenty-nine years toward the end of the second year of Joash, king of Israel. *{2Ki 14:1,2}* When he was established in his kingdom, he killed the servants who had murdered his father. He spared their children, however, according to the law of God as delivered by Moses. *{2Ki 14:5,6 2Ch 25:3,4}*

*546.* NK - When Jehoahaz, the son of Jehu, had reigned seventeen years, he died and was buried in Samaria. *{2Ki 13:1,9}* Shortly after his father's funeral, Joash visited Elisha, the prophet, who was lying on his death bed. Tearfully, he asked counsel of him concerning the state of the kingdom. Elisha foretold that he would have three victories over the Syrians. *{2Ki 13:14-20}*

**3168c AM, 3878 JP, 836 BC, 4 SK, 6 NK**

*547.* NK - Jeroboam II seems to have been made viceroy of the kingdom by his father Joash. He went to war and in each of three battles overthrew Benhadad, who had succeeded his father Hazael in the kingdom of Syria. From Benhadad he recovered those cities which Jehoahaz his father had lost. *{2Ki 13:25}* Hence, we may gather that Azariah, king of Judah, began his reign in the twenty-seventh year of Jeroboam II. *{2Ki 15:1} [L76]*

**3178 AM, 3888 JP, 826 BC 14 SK, 16 NK**

*548.* SK - Uzziah was born to Amaziah by Jecholiah of Jerusalem. He was also called Azariah, and was sixteen years old when he succeeded his father to the kingdom. *{2Ki 15:2 2Ch 26:2}*

*549.* Amaziah became proud of his recent victory over the Edomites. In the fourteenth year of his reign, Josephus stated that he provoked Joash, king of the Israelites, to battle. *{*Josephus, Antiq., l. 9. c. 9. s. 3. (199) 6:105}* In the battle at Bethshemesh, he was defeated and taken prisoner. He was released on payment of a large ransom, including hostages. *{2Ki 14:8-14 2Ch 25:17-24}*

*550.* NK - Joash defeated Amaziah, king of Judah, and took him prisoner. He broke down six hundred feet of the wall of Jerusalem from the gate of Ephraim to the corner gate. When he had taken all the treasure from both the temple and the king's house, he returned to Samaria. *{2Ki 14:13,14 2Ch 25:23,24}*

**3179c AM, 3889 JP, 825 BC, 15 SK, 1 NK**

*551.* Joash died fifteen years before the death of Amaziah. Jeroboam II, his son, succeeded him and reigned in Samaria for forty-one years. *{2Ki 14:23}*

*552.* God used Jeroboam II to deliver Israel. He recaptured Damascus and Hamath, which rightly belonged to the tribe of Judah. *{2Sa 8:6 2Ch 8:3} [E53]* He restored the former borders *{Nu 13:21}* from the entrance into Hamath to the sea of the plain. This fulfilled the prophecy of the Lord spoken by Jonah, the prophet, the son of Amittai. *{2Ki 14:25,27,28} [L77]*

**3194c AM, 3904 JP, 810 BC, 29 SK, 15 NK**

*553.* SK - When Amaziah discovered a conspiracy against him at Jerusalem, he fled to Lachish, where he was murdered. From there he was carried to the city of David and buried. *{2Ki 14:19,20 2Ch 25:27,28}* Uzziah, or Azariah, succeeded him in the twenty-seventh year of Jeroboam II, king of Israel, as reckoned from the time that he began to reign as co-regent with his father. *{See note on 3168 AM. <<547>>}* He reigned fifty-two years in Jerusalem *{2Ki 15:1,2}* and under him the kingdom of Judah prospered as much as Israel did under Jeroboam II. While he followed the advice of the prophet Zechariah, he applied his heart to religious matters. God prospered him and he subdued the Philistines and his neighbouring enemies. He became mighty in his kingdom. *{2Ch 26:2-16}*

**3197a AM, 3906 JP, 808 BC, 4 SK, 19 NK**

*554.* SK - This was the thirteenth Jubilee and it was held under two most prosperous kings, under whom there also lived several great prophets in both kingdoms. In Judah lived that evangelical prophet, Isaiah, the son of Amoz, {*Isa 1:1*} as well as Joel, the son of Pethuel. Joel prophesied prior to Amos, as Codomanus observed, because in the book of Joel he predicted a coming drought, which Amos in the book of Amos said had happened. {*Joe 1:20 Am 4:1-13*} [E54] [L78] Amos, who lived in Judah among the herdsmen of Tekoa, was called to be a prophet to the kingdom of Israel two years prior to the earthquake that occurred in the days of these two kings, Uzziah and Jeroboam II. {*Am 1:1 Zec 11:5*}

*555.* NK - During this same time, Jonah the son of Amittai and Hosea the son of Beeri prophesied in Israel.

*556.* Jonah was from Gathhepher, {*2Ki 14:25*} a town of the tribe of Zebulun, {*Jos 21:13*} in Galilee of the Gentiles. {*Isa 9:1*} This is referred to by the Pharisees when speaking with Nicodemus: *Search and know that out of Galilee never arose any prophet.* {*Joh 7:52*} It seems that at the time, the Syrians were oppressing Israel, and all were vulnerable to their invasions. They took great spoil and no one was able to oppose them. He foretold that Joash's son, Jeroboam II, would deliver Israel out of their hands and avenge them of the wrong they had endured. {*2Ki 14:25,26*} Jonah was later sent to Nineveh, the capital city of Assyria, where both the king and the people were brought to repentance through his preaching. {*Jon 3:1-10 Mt 12:41*}

*557.* When Jeroboam II was successfully ruling Israel, Hosea foretold its ruin and desolation. He also lived to see its ruin, since he continued as a prophet to the time of Hezekiah. {*Ho 1:1*} In the sixth year of Hezekiah's reign, Assyria conquered Israel. {*2Ki 18:10*}

*558.* Amos, while keeping his flocks, became the third prophet to be taken from Judah. He was sent to prophesy to the people of Israel. {*Am 1:1 7:14,15*} He was accused by Amaziah, the priest at Bethel, before Jeroboam II, who commanded him to return to Judah. Amos pronounced judgment against Amaziah, saying:

> "Thy wife shall play the harlot in the city, and thy sons and thy daughters shall fall by the sword. Thy land shall be divided by line, and thou shalt die in a polluted land (that is, in Assyria)."

*559.* This happened when Israel was carried away from her own land into captivity. {*Am 7:10,12,13,17*} [L79]

**3207 AM, 3917 JP, 797 BC, 14 SK, 29 NK**

*560.* In Lydia, Ardysus, of the clan of the Heraclidae, reigned thirty-six years. {*\*Eusebius, Chronicles, l. 1. 1:147*}

**3210 AM, 3920 JP, 794 BC, 17 SK, 32 NK**

*561.* The kingdom of Macedonia was set up by Caranus, a man of the clan of the Heraclidae. He ruled for twenty-eight years. {*\*Eusebius, Chronicles, l. 1. 1:143*} [E55]

**3213 AM, 3923 JP, 791 BC, 20 SK, 35 NK**

*562.* SK - There was an eclipse of the sun of about ten digits that year on the 24th day of June, on the Feast of Pentecost. (Twelve digits indicated a total eclipse, eleven digits would mean that eleven twelfths of the sun's disk was covered. Editor.) Another eclipse occurred of almost twelve digits, twenty years later, on November 8, 771 BC, during the Feast of Tabernacles. A third eclipse of over eleven digits happened the next year on May 5, 770 BC during the Feast of Unleavened Bread. It was to these events that the following prophecy of Amos referred, as he stated: {*Am 8:8-10*}

> "The sun shall set at noonday and I will bring darkness upon the earth in a clear day. I will turn your festivals into mourning and all your solemn songs into lamentations."

*563.* The early church fathers took this prophecy to refer to that darkness which came during the Feast of the Passover at the passion of our Saviour. [L80] It is thought that this prophecy was literally fulfilled by the three almost total eclipses which occurred during these three feasts, at a time when all the males were to be in Jerusalem before the Lord. Among the Greeks, Thales, by his knowledge of astronomy, was the first to predict solar eclipses. {*See note on 3403 AM. <<788>>*} So too among the Hebrews, Amos, by divine revelation and inspiration, was the first that ever foretold solar eclipses.

> (June 24, 791 BC, JD=1432685.1171, middle of the eclipse in Jerusalem - 18.89 hours UCT (for Babylon - 19.13), maximum - 0.92 Babylon - 0.63. Data taken from *Solar and Lunar Eclipses of the Ancient Near East from 3000 BC to 0 with Maps* by Manfred Kudlek and Erich Mickler, published in Neukirchen in 1971. Editor.)

**3220 AM, 3930 JP, 784 BC, 26 SK, 41 NK**

*564.* NK - When Jeroboam II died, the kingdom seriously declined. Tumults arose which headed the Israelites toward their ultimate destruction, beginning first with Jeroboam's own family and then affecting the whole kingdom. This was foretold by Amos. {*Am 7:1-8:14*} All was reduced to anarchy among the Israelites for eleven and a half years, and there was no king during this time. [E56] This can be deduced by comparing the times of these two kingdoms. We understand that in Israel the six-month-long reign of Zachariah, the son of Jeroboam II, occurred in the last six months of the thirty-eighth year of Uzziah. The one month that Shallum reigned was the first month of the thirty-ninth year of Uzziah. {*2Ki 15:8,13*} [L81]

## 3221c AM, 3931 JP, 783 BC, 42 SK, 1 NK

*565.* SK - Uzziah, king of Judah, and his wife Jerusha, the daughter of Zadok, had a son named Jotham. When Uzziah was quarantined because of his leprosy, Jotham ruled in the king's house and judged the people, but it was only when Uzziah died that Jotham succeeded him as king, at the age of twenty-five. {*2Ki 15:5,33 2Ch 26:21 27:1,8*} From this event we can deduce that, a short time after this when Menahem took over the kingdom of Israel, Uzziah was an old man. It was at this time, when he aspired to take the office of a priest, that he was stricken with leprosy. This is contrary to what the Jews and Procopius Gaseus affirm from their understanding of Isaiah {*Isa 7:1-25*}, namely that this overtook him in about the twenty-fifth year of his reign. The earthquake occurred in the days of Uzziah and Jeroboam II. {*Am 1:1 Zec 11:5*} It is clear that when Jeroboam II died, Jotham had not yet been born.

## 3228c AM, 3938 JP, 776 BC, 35 SK, 9 NK

*566.* In the summer of the year 776 BC or 3938 JP, the first Olympiad took place (according to Greek chronologers). Choroebus of Elis won the race according to the Iphitean account number 28. This was quoted by Julius Africanus from the writings of Aristodemus Aelius, and by Polybius in Eusebius. {*\*Julius Africanus, l. 1. c. 15. 6:134*} {*Eusebius, Scaliger's Greek Eusebius, p. 37,216.*} [L82] Here ended the period in history which the learned Varro termed mythological, because many mythological things are said to have happened. It is at this point that true Greek history begins. {*Censorinus, De Die Natali*} [E57]

## 3232a AM, 3941 JP, 773 BC, 38 SK, 1 NK

*567.* NK - Zachariah, the son of Jeroboam II, began his reign in the thirty-eighth year of Uzziah, king of Judah. He was the fourth and last of the family of Jehu, as was foretold by God. He reigned for six months. {*2Ki 15:8,12 10:30*}

*568.* At the end of those six months, he was murdered by Shallum the son of Jabesh, before all the people. {*2Ki 15:10*} It was at this time that the calamities foretold by Amos the prophet took place: {*Am 7:9*}

> "The high places of Isaac shall be desolate and the sanctuaries of Israel made a wilderness, when I shall arise with a sword against the house of Jeroboam."

*569.* Shallum, the son of Jabesh, reigned one month in the thirty-ninth year of Uzziah, king of Judah. {*2Ki 15:13*}

*570.* When Menahem, the son of Gad, was going from Tirzah to Samaria, he killed Shallum and destroyed Tiphsah with its borders. He also violently slaughtered all the pregnant women. {*2Ki 15:14,16*}

*571.* Sulpicius called Menahem by the name of *Mane.* {*\*Sulpicius Severus, Sacred History, l. 1. c. 49. 11:94*} This is the same name as referred to Manichaus, who lived later and was a heretic. The name means *comforter*.

## 3233c AM, 3943 JP, 771 BC, 39 SK, 1 NK

*572.* Boccaris Saites reigned in Egypt for forty years. {*Julius Africanus*}

*573.* NK - While Menahem spent eleven months fighting to take over the kingdom, God stirred up Pul, king of Assyria, to invade the land of Israel. {*1Ch 5:26 2Ki 15:19*} [L83]

*574.* Pul seems to have been the father of Sardanapalus. Sardanapalus was named after his father and called Sardan-Pul just as Merodach, king of Babylon, was called Merodach Baladan from Baladan his father. {*Isa 39:1*} The following chronologers agreed that he was the same person, but called him by different names: Julius Africanus called him *Acracarnes*, Eusebius called him *Ocrazapes*, Stephanus Byzantinus called him *Cindaraxes*, and Strabo, Arrian and Suidas called him *Anacyndaraxes* or *Anakyndaraxes*. {*\*Strabo, l. 14. c. 5. s. 9. 6:341*} {*\*Arrian, Anabasis, l. 2. c. 5. s. 2. 1:137*} By others again he was called *Anabaxares*. {*\*Athenaeus, l. 12. (528f) 5:387*} Furthermore, I considered the number of years assigned by Africanus and Eusebius to the reigns of Pul and his son. I then counted the years backward from the beginning of Nabonassar to the end of Sardanapalus' reign. I believe both lived at the same time. [E58] This man named Pul seems to have been the same man who was converted and brought to repentance by the preaching of the prophet Jonah. This means that the men of Nineveh may have risen in judgment against this nation. God here raised up a repentant, heathen man to take vengeance on unrepentant Israel.

*575.* Menahem gave Pul a thousand talents of silver to help settle and confirm him in his kingdom. {*2Ki 15:19,20*} Some see the following passage in Hosea as referring to this event: {*Ho 5:13*}

> "When Ephraim saw his sickness and Judah saw his wound, then Ephraim went to the Assyrian and sent to King Jareb, who should defend or uphold him." [L84]

*576.* When Menahem was thus confirmed in the kingdom, he was established as king toward the end of the thirty-ninth year of the reign of Uzziah. He held the kingdom for ten years. {*2Ki 15:17*}

## 3234a AM, 3943 JP, 771 BC, 39 SK, 1 NK

*577.* SK - There was an almost total eclipse of the sun at Jerusalem, on the third day of the Feast of Tabernacles on November 8. {*See note on 3213 AM. <<562>>*}

**3234c AM, 3944 JP, 770 BC, 40 SK, 2 NK**

*578.* SK - There was an almost total eclipse of the sun at Jerusalem, on the first day of the Feast of Unleavened Bread on May 5. {*See note on 3213 AM.* <<562>>}

**3237 AM, 3947 JP, 767 BC, 44 SK, 5 NK**

*579.* Sardanapalus held the kingdom of the Assyrians for twenty years according to Julius Africanus and Eusebius. In his epitaph (which is contained in Athenaeus from Clirarchus {*\*Athenaeus, l. 12. (529e) 5:391*} and in Strabo, {*\*Strabo, l. 14. c. 5. s. 9. 6:341*} and in Arrian {*\*Arrian, Anabasis, l. 2. c. 5. s. 4. 1:137*}), he is said to have built the cities of Anchialus and Tarsus in Cilicia within one day.

**3242 AM, 3952 JP, 762 BC, 49 SK, 10 NK**

*580.* SK - Ahaz, the son of Jotham, was born in this year. He was twenty years old when he began to reign {*2Ki 16:2 2Ch 28:1*} and he reigned for sixteen years. His son Hezekiah was twenty-five years old when he began to reign after Ahaz's death. {*2Ki 18:2*} Therefore, Ahaz would only be eleven years old when his son Hezekiah was born. Hence, Tremellius thought that Ahaz was twenty years old not when he himself reigned, but when his father Jotham began his reign.

**3243c AM, 3953 JP, 761 BC, 50 SK, 1 NK**

*581.* NK - Pekahiah succeeded his father Menahem, who died in the fiftieth year of Uzziah, king of Judah, and he reigned for two years. {*2Ki 15:23*}

**3245c AM, 3955 JP, 759 BC, 51 SK, 2 NK**

*582.* Alyattes, the elder, reigned in Lydia for fourteen years. {*\*Eusebius, Chronicles, l. 1. 1:155*} [L85]

*583.* NK - Pekah, the son of Remaliah, killed Pekahiah in his own palace in Samaria. He then reigned in Pekahiah's place for twenty years reckoned from the fifty-second year of Uzziah king of Judah. {*2Ki 15:25,27*} [E59]

**3246a AM, 3955 JP, 759 BC, 51 SK, 2 NK**

*584.* SK - The fourteenth Jubilee occurred. It was during this year that Isaiah saw the glory of the Lord sitting on his throne: God was surrounded with a guard of angels singing, *Holy, Holy, Holy, Lord God of Sabaoth.* The Jewish people grew more and more obstinate and blind every day, lest they should understand the words of the prophets who were being sent to them, and be converted and healed. {*Isa 6:1-13 Joh 12:40,41*}

*585.* Isaiah's vision came in the last year of king Uzziah. {*Isa 6:1*} He was buried in the city of David in the burying place of the kings, but separate from the rest because of his leprosy. Jotham, his son, succeeded him in the second year of Pekah, king of Israel. He reigned sixteen years in Jerusalem. {*2Ki 15:7,32,33 2Ch 26:23 27:1,8*}

*586.* Jotham fought a battle against the Ammonites and overthrew them. They became his tributaries for three years. {*2Ch 27:5*} Micah the Morasthite, Isaiah and Hosea executed the prophetic office in the reign of Jotham and his next two successors. {*Mic 1:1*} Josephus affirmed that Nahum, the prophet, foretold the defeat of the Assyrians and of Nineveh in his time. This came to pass a hundred and fifteen years later. By that reckoning, Josephus understood Nahum to have prophesied in the time of Ahaz, the son of Jotham. {*\*Josephus, Antiq., l. 9. c. 11. s. 3. (239-242) 6:127*} [L86]

**3252c AM, 3962 JP, 752 BC, 7 SK, 7 NK**

*587.* In this year, Hezekiah, the son of Ahaz, was born to his mother, Abijah, the daughter of Zachariah. He was twenty-five years old when he began to reign. {*2Ki 18:2 2Ch 29:1*}

**3254c AM, 3964 JP, 750 BC, 9 SK, 10 NK**

*588.* Two towns were built in this year, Ardus being one of them. It was constructed on a very small island, as Pomponius Mela noted. {*Pomponius Mela, De Chorographia*} The whole circumference of this island was taken up with this one town. Cyzicum, the second town, was located in Propontis. {*\*Eusebius, Chronicles, l. 1. 1:151,153.*}

*589.* Arbaces, the governor of Media, scorned the effeminate ways of Sardanapalus. {*\*Athenaeus, l. 12. (528f) 5:387*} He conspired with Belesis, the governor of Babylon, to send an army of four hundred thousand men, made up of Medes, Persians, Babylonians and Arabians, against Sardanapalus. [E60] He was overthrown in three battles, but in the fourth the Bactrian soldiers defected over to him. He surprised his enemies, attacking them by night and driving them from their camp. When Sardanapalus put the command of the entire army into the hands of Salaemenus, his wife's brother, he too was defeated twice by the conspirators. As a result he was almost killed and lost most of his army. When Nineveh was besieged, Sardanapalus sent three of his sons and two daughters into Paphlagonia with a great treasure. They gave it to Cotta, governor of that province. With this treasure Cotta dispatched messengers and commissioners throughout the land to conscript soldiers and provide all the necessities needed to endure a siege. {*\*Diod. Sic., l. 2. c. 24-26. 1:431-439*} [L87]

**3256c AM, 3966 JP, 748 BC, 11 SK, 12 NK**

*590.* SK - Rome was founded by Romulus according to the reckoning of Fabius Pictor, the most ancient of all Roman writers. This date is confirmed by the account of the secular games held most religiously by the ancient Romans. This happened shortly before the beginning of the 8th Olympiad, on the feast of their goddess, Pales, on the 10th day of April. However, according to Varro's account, the feast of Pales was a full five years earlier than it was according to Fabius. The poet Ovid said of this day: {*Ovid, Fasti, l. 4. c. 11. (855) 5:253}

*Urbs oritur (quis tunc hoc ulli credere posset?) Victorem terris impositura pedem.*

591. That is:

A city is born (which who then would have thought?) That since, the world has in subjection brought.

### 3257 AM, 3967 JP, 747 BC, 12 SK, 13 NK

592. In the third year of the siege of Nineveh the river overflowed with continual rains. It flooded a part of the city and undermined two and one half miles of the wall. When Sardanapalus realised this, he made a large pile of wood in his palace court and set it on fire, burning himself, his concubines, his eunuchs and all his riches. The palace itself was also burned to ashes.

593. The conspirators entered by the breach in the wall made by the river and took the city. They proclaimed Arbaces as their king. {*Diod. Sic., l. 2. c. 27. s. 1-3. 1:441} {*Athenaeus, l. 12. (529bc) 5:389} In this way, the kingdom of the Assyrians was destroyed. From the beginning of the reign of Ninus, the Assyrians had held all of upper Asia for five hundred and twenty years. {*Herodotus, l. 1. c. 95. 1:127}

594. After the kingdom fell, it was divided. Arbaces freed his countrymen the Medes from the Assyrian yoke and allowed them to live according to their own laws. Strabo called him *Orbacus* and Velleius Paterculus called him *Pharnaces*. {*Strabo, l. 16. c. 1. s. 2. 7:195} {*Velleius Paterculus, l. 1. c. 6. s. 2. 1:15} (Loeb copy does not have either of these spelling variations. Editor.) {*Herodotus, l. 1. c. 95. 1:127} [E61] [L88] Belesis was called Baladan in the scriptures, {Isa 39:1 2Ki 20:12} whereas Agathias {Agathias, Histories, l. 2.} and Alexander Polyhistor called him *Belessas* or *Beleussus*. Nicolaus Damascene, in his eclogues as recorded by Henry Valesius, called him *Naminybrus*. By Hipparchus, Ptolemy, and Censorinus, he is called *Nabonassarus*. He held the kingdom of Babylon for fourteen years.

595. From twelve o'clock on the first day of the Egyptian month of Thoth, that is, from the evening of Wednesday, February 26, in the year 747 BC, all astronomers unanimously start the calendar of Nabonassar.

596. Meles in Lydia reigned twelve years, {*Eusebius, Chronicles, l. 1. 1:157} and more may be read about him in Herodotus. {*Herodotus, l. 1. c. 84. 1:107}

597. Ninus, the younger, now held the kingdom of the Assyrians reduced now to its old boundaries. The empire had quite diminished in Sardanapalus' nineteen years. Eusebius reported this in his chronology based on the more extensive work of Castor, the Rhodian, who corrected many errors in the historical records. This Ninus seems to have assumed, for good luck, the name of the first founder of the Assyrian kingdom. His own original name was Thilgamus. {*Aelian, History of Animals, l. 12. c. 21. 3:39} (Loeb edition has different names. Editor.) In the scriptures he is known as *Tilgathpilneser* {1Ch 5:6,26 2Ch 28:20} or *Tiglathpileser*. {2Ki 15:29 16:7,10}

### 3262c AM, 3972 JP, 742 BC, 17 SK, 18 NK

598. Ahaz succeeded his father Jotham at the very end of the seventeenth year of Pekah, the son of Remaliah, and reigned for sixteen years in Jerusalem. {2Ki 16:1,2 2Ch 28:1} [L89]

599. Toward the end of the reign of Jotham, God began to stir up Rezin, the king of Syria, and Pekah, the son of Remaliah, against Judah. {2Ki 15:37} Judah was terrified at the approach of these enemies and expected a quick defeat at their hands. God sent a gracious message to Ahaz by Isaiah the prophet, promising deliverance for him and the destruction of his enemies. [E62] For a sign of his deliverance (when the incredulous king was asked what sign he wanted, he said none), God made him a promise that a virgin would bear Immanuel. He would be both God and man, or God with us, or dwelling in a human body. With regard to his office, he is the only Mediator between God and man. {1Ti 2:5} He would bring to pass that God would *be with us,* {Isa 8:10} both gracious and propitious to us and a very present help in trouble. {Ps 46:1,2,7 Ro 8:31,32} This message was most befitting the present situation in that all promises of God in Christ are *Yea and Amen,* {2Co 1:20} to be fulfilled generally in him and by him. Besides this, the land of Judah was to be privileged to be Immanuel's land. {Isa 8:8} Pertaining to his human lineage, he was to be born not merely of the Jews {Ro 9:5} but of the very house of David. According to the prophecy of Jacob, {Ge 49:10} [L90] this would happen before the sceptre would depart from Judah, that is, before Judah would cease to be a nation ruled by kings. Therefore, at that time Judah did not need to fear the destruction of the house of David or of the country of the Jews, the Southern Kingdom. However, sixty-five years later this happened to the Northern Kingdom, as predicted by Isaiah. {Isa 7:8}

600. For a sign of the destruction of those kings who came against Ahaz, the prophet was commanded to bring out Ahaz's son, Shearjashub. He told Ahaz that his son would eat butter and honey until he was old enough to know right from wrong. [L91] Before this

happened, both these kings would be dead. {*Isa 7:3,15,16*} At that time too, Isaiah's wife, a prophetess, bore him another son. God named him Mahershalalhashbaz signifying that the Assyrians would hurry and take away the spoil. *[E63]* They would plunder both Syrians and Israelites before the child would be able clearly to say: *My father*, or *My mother*. So the sons of the prophets were used by God to serve as signs from him to the Israelites. {*Isa 8:3,4,18*} After these prophecies, Rezin and Pekah together came up to besiege Jerusalem where Ahaz was. They could not take it, as had been predicted by Isaiah. {*Isa 7:1,7 2Ki 16:5*} But this wicked Ahaz had no sooner been delivered from the imminent danger than he forsook God his deliverer and walked in the ways of the kings of Israel. He set up the idolatrous worship of Baal and offered incense in the valley of Benhanan. He caused his own son to pass through the fire, and offered sacrifices in the high places, upon the hills and under every green tree. {*2Ch 28:2-4 2Ki 16,3,4*}

## 3263c AM, 3973 JP, 741 BC, 2 SK, 19 NK

601. SK - When Ahaz forsook God, God also forsook him. When Rezin and Pekah divided their forces, they overcame him. This they had not been able to do when their forces were united. God delivered him into the hands of the Syrians, who defeated him and carried away a large number of his people to Damascus as captives. As well as this, the king of Israel defeated him and slaughtered a large number of his people. {*2Ch 28:5*}

602. At this same time, Rezin conquered Elath, which Uzziah had recovered for Judah. Rezin rebuilt it and repopulated it with Syrians. {*2Ki 14:22 2Ch 26:2 2Ki 16:2*}

603. NK - Pekah killed a hundred and twenty thousand valiant men of Judah in one day. Zichri, a mighty man of the tribe of Ephraim, killed Maaseiah, the king's son, as well as Azrikam, the steward of the king's house, and Elkanah, who was next to the king in authority. The Israelites also carried away captive from Judah and Jerusalem two hundred thousand women, boys and maids. They plundered their goods and carried everything away to Samaria. When warned by Hadlai, a prophet of God, they released all of the prisoners and restored their goods to them in the presence of their princes and the whole congregation of Samaria. They treated them kindly and escorted them safely to Jericho. {*2Ch 28:6-15*}

## 3264c AM, 3974 JP, 740 BC, 3 SK, 20 NK

604. SK - The Edomites invaded Judah and carried away many captives. The Philistines, whom King Uzziah had conquered, {*2Ch 26:6,7*} *[L92]* now attacked the cities of Judah in the low countries and southern parts and settled there. God gave Judah over to their enemies because of

Ahaz's sin and because he had led Judah into sin. {*2Ch 28:17-19*}

605. Ahaz took all the gold and silver that was found in the Lord's house and in the treasury of the king's house. He sent it as a gift to Tiglathpileser, king of Assyria, desiring him to come and deliver him from the kings of Syria and Israel. *[E64]* He came and took Damascus, carrying away all its inhabitants to Kir and killing Rezin the king of Syria. {*2Ki 16:7-9*} This fulfilled the prophecy of Isaiah, {*Isa 7:16 8:4 9:11*} as well as that of Amos, who long before had foretold the ruin of the king of Damascus in these words:

> "I will send a fire upon the house of Hazael which shall consume the palaces of Benhadad, and I will break in pieces the bars of Damascus and root out the inhabitants of the valley of Aven, and him that beareth the sceptre out of the house of Eden and the people of Syria shall be carried away into Assyria, saith the Lord." {*Am 1:4,5*}

606. So the flourishing kingdom of Damascus of Hamath came to an end. {*Am 6:2 Jer 49:23 Isa 10:9 36:19 37:12,13*} This kingdom began with a man called Rezon {*1Ki 11:23,24*} and ended with one of the same name. It lasted for ten generations according to Nicolaus Damascene, as cited by Josephus. {**Josephus, Antiq., l. 7. c. 5. s. 2. (102) 5:413*} {*See note on 2960 AM. <<430>>*} *[L93]*

607. When Ahaz went to meet Tiglathpileser at Damascus, he congratulated him on his great victory. There he saw an altar, the pattern of which he sent to Uriah the priest, so that he might make one like it in Jerusalem. When he returned, he and the people offered their sacrifices on it. He moved the brazen altar far away from the front of the temple so that it would not stand between his altar and the house of the Lord. {*2Ki 16:1-20*}

608. NK - When Ahaz implored the aid of the kings of Assyria (as it says in Chronicles {*2Ch 28:16*} *kings* in the plural, by a usual analogy as in these verses: {*Ps 105:30 Jer 19:3 25:22*} {*Apc 1Es 1:52*}) against Pekah, Tiglathpileser came. He led away the people of Gilead or Peraea, that is, the Reubenites and the Gadites and the half tribe of Manasseh, to Habor and Hara and the Gozan River. When he then crossed over the Jordan River, he occupied Galilee and carried away into Assyria all the inhabitants of Naphtali whom Benhadad had left, together with the men of Galilee. {*1Ch 5:26 2Ki 15:29 1Ki 15:20 Isa 9:1*}

## 3265c AM, 3975 JP, 739 BC, 4 SK, 1 NK

609. SK - Ahaz, having now made himself a servant to the king of Assyria, {*2Ki 16:7 18:7*} found out that he had received more harm than help from him. {*2Ch 28:20,21*}

Isaiah had previously intimated this to him using the allegory:

"The Lord shall shave off the hair of thy head and feet with a hired razor, from beyond the river, even the king of Assyria, and it shall also consume the beard." {*Isa 7:20*}

610. Therefore, Ahaz built a secret passage from the king's house to the house of the Lord, because he feared the king of Assyria. {*2Ki 16:18*} Tremellius understood this to mean that he did this out of fear that the king of Assyria would assault him from the direction of the temple and break into his palace. {*E65*} In the midst of all of his afflictions, he sinned still more and more against the Lord. {*2Ch 28:22*}

611. NK - When Hoshea, the son of Elah, murdered Pekah, the son of Remaliah, he took over the kingdom twenty years after Jotham started to reign over Judah, {*2Ki 15:30*} or in the fourth year of the reign of Ahaz. {*See Gill on "2Ki 15:30"*} However, the kingdom was in civil disorder and anarchy for nine years. {*L94*}

### 3269 AM, 3979 JP, 735 BC, 8 SK, 5 NK

612. Candaules, whom the Greek authors, according to Herodotus, call Myrsylus, {*\*Herodotus, l. 1. c. 7. 1:11*} the son of Myrsus, was the last of the family of the Heraclidae. He reigned in Lydia for seventeen years. {*\*Eusebius, Chronicles, l. 1. 1:157*}

### 3271 AM, 3981 JP, 733 BC, 10 SK, 7 NK

613. Nadius or Nabius reigned over the Babylonians for two years. {*Ptolemy, Canon of Kings*}

### 3273c AM, 3983 JP, 731 BC, 12 SK, 9 NK

614. Chinziros and Poros reigned over the Babylonians for five years. {*Ptolemy, Canon of Kings*}

### 3274c AM, 3984 JP, 730 BC, 13 SK, 1 NK

615. NK - When Hoshea had restored order in Israel, he began a peaceful reign toward the end of the twelfth year of Ahaz, king of Judah. {*2Ki 17:1*}

### 3276b AM, 3986 JP, 728 BC, 14 SK, 2 NK

616. NK - Tiglathpileser, or Ninus the younger, reigned for nineteen years, according to Castor, and died. After him came Shalmaneser, also called Enemessar, as in the Greek copy of Tobias. {*Apc Tob 1:2*} This man seems to be that Shalman who, in the prophesy of Hosea, is said to have laid waste to Betharbel. {*Ho 10:14*} The place was famous later for the defeat of Darius the Persian. This is the country of Arbela, in the land of Assyria, south of Arpad. Shalmaneser came up in battle against Hoshea, king of Israel, who was forced to serve him and pay him tribute. {*2Ki 17:3*}

### 3277c AM, 3987 JP, 727 BC, 1,16 SK, 4 NK

617. After Sabacon, an Ethiopian, had taken Boccaris king of Egypt alive, he burned him to death and reigned in his stead for eight years. {*Julius Africanus*}

618. SK - In the last year of his reign, Ahaz made his son Hezekiah viceroy with him in the kingdom. This was toward the end of the third year of Hoshea, king of Israel. Hezekiah reigned for twenty-nine years in Jerusalem. {*2Ki 18:1,2*} {*L95*}

### 3278a AM, 3987 JP, 727 BC, 1, 16 SK, 4 NK

619. Jugaeus or Julaeus or Iloulaios reigned over the Babylonians for five years. {*Ptolemy, Canon of Kings*}

### 3278b AM, 3988 JP, 726 BC, 1, 16 SK, 4 NK

620. SK - Ahaz died in this year. The prophet Isaiah foretold the destruction of the Philistines (who at that time, unjustly held a part of Judah). {*See note on 3264c AM. <<604>>*} {*Isa 14:28-32*} {*E66*} Likewise, he predicted that a great disaster was to befall the Moabites within three years. {*Isa 15:1-16:14*} The fulfilments of these prophecies are recorded later. {*See note on 3280b AM. <<632>>*} {*See note on 3283 AM. <<634>>*}

### 3278c AM, 3988 JP, 726 BC, 1 SK, 6 NK

621. SK - After Ahaz died, Hezekiah, toward the end of the first year of his reign, in the first month called Abib, opened the doors of the Lord's house which his father had shut up. {*2Ch 28:24*} He commanded the priests and Levites to sanctify themselves and then to clean up the temple. {*2Ch 29:3,4*}

622. They were encouraged by Hezekiah and on the first day of the first month (Sunday, April 21), they sanctified themselves according to the king's command and came to cleanse the house of the Lord. On the eighth day of the same month (Sunday, April 28), they entered into the porch of the temple and sanctified the house of the Lord for a further eight days. On the sixteenth day of the first month (Sunday, May 6), they completed that task. {*2Ch 29:15,17*} {*L96*}

623. Early the next morning (Monday, May 6), King Hezekiah called together all the rulers of the city. Together with the people, he went up into the house of the Lord. Through the ministry of the priests and Levites, he offered many sacrifices on the altar of the Lord with great joy and gladness. {*2Ch 29:20-36*}

624. In accordance with the law in Numbers, {*Nu 9:10,11*} the Passover was delayed until the second month for the following reasons: The Passover could not be kept at the same time as the meeting and the cleansing of the temple was being done; the number of sanctified priests was not enough; all the people were not gathered together in

Jerusalem from all over the country. Notices were sent to all the people from Beersheba as far as to Dan. Not only the Jews, but also some from among the tribes of Asher, Manasseh and Zebulun, came together in Jerusalem. The rest of the tribes laughed at the notice. {2Ch 30:1-12} [E67] First, the altars of incense and those pertaining to idols were destroyed, and then thrown into the brook Kidron. They killed the Pascal lambs on the fourteenth day of the second month (Sunday, June 3). They kept the feast of Unleavened Bread for seven days, offering their sacrifices of thanksgiving and singing praises to the God of their fathers. {2Ch 30:13-22} As further testimony of their thankfulness to God, they continued for another seven days. This time was kept and celebrated with great glee and joy of heart. {2Ch 30:23} [L97]

625. About the end of the second month, when they had finished these activities, all the Israelites who had come together there, went out into all the cities of Judah. They broke down the images, cut down the groves and destroyed the high places and altars throughout Ephraim and Manasseh until they had completed the task. When this was done, the Israelites returned home. {2Ch 31:1}

626. Hezekiah went even further. He smashed to pieces that very same brazen serpent that Moses had set up in the wilderness, because now the Israelites were burning incense to it. {Nu 21:9} With contempt, he called it by a diminutive term, *Nehushtan, a little piece of brass.* {2Ki 18:4} He appointed the priests and Levites to their duties. He provided food and maintenance for them by again establishing the law of firstfruits and tithes. {2Ch 31:1-21}

627. In the third month, every man brought in their firstfruits and tithes and gave them to the priests. {2Ch 31:5-7}

### 3279a AM, 3988 JP, 726 BC, 3 SK, 6 NK

628. SK - In the seventh month, after the harvest of the whole year's produce had been gathered, {Ex 29:16} the collection of the firstfruits and tithes was completed, {2Ch 31:7} and Hezekiah appointed officers for their proper distribution. {2Ch 31:1-21} [E68]

### 3279b AM, 3989 JP, 725 BC, 3 SK, 6 NK

629. NK - Hoshea, the king of Israel, consulted beforehand with So, king of Egypt, and refused to continue paying tribute to Shalmaneser. {2Ki 17:4} [L98]

630. This So, or Sua, as Jerome called him, seems to be none other than Sabacon, the Ethiopian. Manetho lists him as the first king in the twenty-fifth Egyptian dynasty. {*Manetho, 1:167}

631. Chrysostom, in his 30th Homily on John, said that this Hoshea made an alliance with the Ethiopians.

Sulpicius Severus stated: {*Sulpicius Severus, Sacred History, l. 1. c. 49. 11:94}

"that he allied with the kings of the Ethiopians, who at that time held the kingdom of Egypt."

### 3280b AM, 3990 JP, 724 BC, 4 SK, 7 NK

632. NK - When Shalmaneser found out that Hoshea had allied himself with the king of Egypt, he first secured all the land of the Moabites. So that he might have no enemy at his rear to annoy his army, he razed to the ground their two chief cities, Arnon and Kirhareseth. This fulfilled the prophecy of Isaiah foretold three years earlier. {Isa 16:7-11} {Tremellius} Then he went through and wasted all the land of Israel, marching toward Samaria in the fourth year of Hezekiah. In the seventh year of Hoshea, he besieged Samaria for three years. {2Ki 17:4,5 18:9}

### 3283b AM, 3993 JP, 721 BC, 6 SK, 9 NK

633. In the twenty-seventh year of the epoch of Nabonassar, Mardokempados reigned in Babylon for twelve years. {Ptolemy, Canon of Kings} The prophet Isaiah named Merodach Baladan as the son of Baladan, {Isa 39:1} who was Belesis, or the son or, in accordance with a most customary Hebrewism, nephew of Nabonassar. In Mardokempados' first year, the moon was eclipsed over Babylon. {Ptolemy, Great Syntaxis, l. 4. c. 6.} {See note on 3257 AM. <<594>>} [L99] This was in the twenty-seventh year of Nabonassar, the twenty-ninth of the month Thoth, as the Egyptians call it (that is toward the midnight of our March 19), two and a half hours before midnight.

634. NK - Toward the end of the third year of the siege of Samaria, in the sixth year of the reign of Hezekiah and the ninth of Hoshea, Shalmaneser took Samaria. He carried away the Israelites into his own country and settled them in Halah, Habor and the Gozan River and in the cities of the Medes. Tiglathpileser had formerly transported the inhabitants of Peraea, or the two and a half tribes living on the other side of the Jordan River, to this place. {1Ch 5:26 2Ki 17:6 8:10,11} There was anarchy in the kingdom of Media before Media was taken by Dejoces. This gave occasion to the Assyrians to invade and take over that whole country. It was to Media that Tobit or Tobias stated that he, together with his wife, Anna, and his countrymen, the Nepthalites, was carried away at this time into the land of the Assyrians. Later, they provided grain and other food for Shalmaneser's household. He was also carried into Media and there placed in a principal city of Media called Rages. [E69] At that place he deposited ten talents of silver into the hand and safekeeping of Gabael, his near kinsman and one who had been carried away captive with him to the same place. {Apc Tob 1:10,14} This was the end of the king-

dom of Israel, two hundred and fifty-four years after it had revolted from the kingdom of Judah.

## 3284b AM, 3994 JP, 720 BC

*635.* In the second year of Merodach's reign, there was another eclipse of the moon in Babylon. This happened in the twenty-eighth year of the epoch of Nabonassar, on the eighteenth day of the month of Thoth, at midnight. The Julian calendar dates it on Saturday, March 9. Exactly a hundred and seventy-six days and twenty and a half hours later, a third eclipse of the moon took place. This occurred on the fifteenth day of the month of Phamenoth, Sunday, September 1, three and a half hours before midnight. {*Ptolemy, Great Syntaxis, l. 4. c. 6,7.*}

## 3285 AM, 3995 JP, 719 BC

*636.* Seuechus the Ethiopian, Sabacon's son, reigned in Egypt for fourteen years. {*Julius Africanus*} He seems also to have been called Sethos, priest to Vulcan, who was mentioned by Herodotus. {*\*Herodotus, l. 2. c. 141. 1:447*}

## 3286 AM, 3996 JP, 718 BC

*637.* When Candaules indecently exposed his wife to his courtier named Gyges, the son of Dascylus, his wife ordered Gyges to murder him. As a result he married the wife of the murdered king and took over the kingdom of Lydia. This is mentioned in a poem by Archilocus from the Isle of Pharos, who lived at the same time. So the kingdom of Lydia went from the clan of the Heraclidae to the clan of the Mermnadae. This clan ruled Lydia for a hundred and seventy years. Gyges himself reigned thirty-eight years. {*\*Herodotus, l. 1. c. 8-15. 1:11-19*} Gyges was only a freed slave, as seems indicated by that saying of Croesus, his grandchild, as mentioned by Xenophon: {*\*Xenophon, Cyropaedia, l. 7. c. 2. s. 24. 6:241*}

> "I understand that the first of my ancestors that here reigned, was made a king and a freedman both at the same time."

*638.* Plato stated that he was master of the king's cattle and his name was Gyges. {*Plato, Republic, l. 2.*} In the eastern dialect this seems to have been Gug, or Gog.

## 3287 AM, 3997 JP, 717 BC

*639.* When Gyges took over the kingdom, he sent various large offerings to Delphi. He made war upon Miletus and captured Smyrna, which was a colony sent out from Colophon. {*\*Herodotus, l. 1. c. 15. 1:19*}

*640.* When the Gitteans revolted, Eluleus, king of Tyre, sailed there and subjected them again. Shalmaneser, the king of Assyria, marched with his army and invaded all Phoenicia, also coming against Tyre. Shortly after, he made peace with them and returned home again. Not long after, Sidon and Acco or Ake (later called Ptolemais) and Poletyre or Old Tyre, with various other cities, defected from the Tyrians to the Assyrians. *[L100]* When only the Tyrians now stood against him, Shalmaneser returned a second time. In this action the Phoenicians furnished him with sixty ships and eight hundred sailors. The Tyrians attacked this fleet with only twelve ships, routed all the navy and took five hundred prisoners. By this action, the Tyrians obtained a good reputation as a naval force. Shalmaneser returned to besiege Tyre. Setting guards by both the river and the conduits which served the city, he cut them off, thus hindering them from getting water. They held out for five years and at last were forced to dig wells within their city walls to get water. This account comes from the chronicles of Menander of Ephesus, translated into Greek from the Tyrian Annals, as cited by Josephus. {*\*Josephus, Antiq., l. 9. c. 14. s. 2. (283-287) 6:151*} Eluleus was called Ayluleus by Rufinus, an ancient Latin historian. Hence Scaliger called him Eliseus. I disagree with him on the point where he maintains that Menander called the Cypriots Kitteans. However, he certainly understood the name of the Gitteans to denote the inhabitants of Gitta, or Gath, well known by that name in the Bible. {*2Sa 15:18 21:19 1Sa 17:4*} These were also added to Judah by Hezekiah at the very time of this Eluleus or Eliseus, as may be gathered from Josephus, who said that Hezekiah made war on the Philistines and defeated them, adding all their cities (except one), together with the country from Gath to Gaza, to the kingdom of Judah. {*\*Josephus, Antiq., l. 9. c. 13. s. 3. (275) 6:145*} Hezekiah smote the Philistines as far as Gaza and its territories. {*2Ki 18:8*} Isaiah prophesied against the Tyrians, who at this time had grown proud and insolent on account of their wealth and success in wars. {*Isa 23:1*}

*641.* When Shalmaneser died, his son Sennacherib reigned in his stead. {*Apc Tob 1:18*} Herodotus called him the king of both Assyria and Arabia. {*\*Herodotus, l. 2. c. 17. 1:295*} *[E70]* It could be that at that time the Assyrians ruled over Peraea (or the land of Gilead), and Hamath (or Iturea), and also held a part of Arabia—either Petra or the desert. This is because that land known as Ivah, or Ava, about which Sennacherib boasted much, seems to have been conquered either by him or his ancestors. {*2Ki 18:34 19:13 Isa 37:13*} This was a country lying in the desert of Arabia. Franc. Junius affirmed this based on the passage in Kings. {*2Ki 17:24*} The prophet Isaiah foretold the calamity which was to befall the Moabites at the hands of Shalmaneser. {*See note on 3278b AM. <<620>>*} {*See note on 3280b AM. <<632>>*} This is taken from Bersus' History of the Chaldeans as cited by Josephus. He said that Sennacherib reigned in Assyria and also that he waged a fierce war on all Asia and Egypt. {*\*Josephus, Antiq., l. 10. c. 1. s. 1. (4) 6:157*}

## 3291c AM, 4001 JP, 713 BC

*642.* This war of his on Egypt lasted three whole years, and Syria Palestina also joined with him in the war. This is deduced from Isaiah. {*Isa 20:1-6*} Isaiah was told to take off his coat of hairy cloth (belonging to his prophetic function, as in Zechariah {*Zec 13:4*}) as well as his shoes. He was commanded to walk up and down naked and barefoot for three years, as a sign to the Egyptians and Ethiopians. This intimated that when that time expired, they likewise would be stripped of their clothes by the king of Assyria and go barefoot into captivity and bondage. The prophet is said to have received this command in the year when Tartan was sent by Sargon, king of Assyria, besieging Ashdod and taking it. {*Isa 20:1*} Sargon is also called Sennacherib, and Tartan was one of his commanders. {*2Ki 18:17*} [*L101*] That famous city Azotus, a city of the Philistines near Ashdod, was conquered by King Hezekiah according to Josephus. {*See note on 3287 AM. <<640>>*} {*2Ki 18:8*}

*643.* Hezekiah had shaken off the king of Assyria's yoke (which his father Ahaz had taken) and would no longer serve him. {*2Ki 17:7*} Toward the end of the fourteenth year of his reign, Sennacherib came to make war against the kingdom of Judah. He besieged their fortified cities and took many of them. {*Isa 36:1 2Ki 18:13 2Ch 32:1*} When Hezekiah perceived that he intended to attack Jerusalem also, he consulted with his princes. He plugged up all the fountains that were around the city and diverted the brook Kidron which ran through the region. Then he built up all that part of the wall which Joash, the king of Israel, had demolished in the time of Amaziah. He fortified Millo in the city of David and provided arrows and shields in great abundance, setting captains and colonels over the people. He called them together and made a very short speech to them, persuading them to be of good courage and not to have any fear of the king of Assyria or of his army. {*2Ch 32:2-8,30*}

*644.* In those days when Hezekiah was very sick, he was told by Isaiah that he would die. He poured out his tears and prayers to God and was healed, another fifteen years being added to his life. {*Isa 38:1-5,21 2Ki 20:1-7 2Ch 32:24*} He composed a song. First he showed the seriousness of his illness and the anxiety he had had. He told of his prayer to God and then acknowledged the great benefit of his recovery received from God. Lastly he testified of his faith in God, and promised to be everlastingly thankful to him. {*Isa 38:9-20*}

*645.* It is true that in the scripture this is recorded after the story of the slaughter of Sennacherib and his army. However, the time was not precisely given but only with a general annotation: *In those days.* For that this slaugh-

ter happened after his sickness, is plainly shown by these scriptures:

> "I will add unto thy days fifteen years and will deliver thee and this city out of the hand of the king of Assyria and I will defend this city." {*Isa 38:5,6 2Ki 20:6*}

*646.* Now if we subtract these fifteen years from the twenty-nine years which Hezekiah reigned, we shall find that the slaughter of Sennacherib and his army happened toward the end of the fourteenth year of his reign.

*647.* The sign confirming the promise of Hezekiah's recovery, which God at his request gave to him, was that miraculous going back of the shadow of the sun on the sundial of Ahaz, as recorded in the book of Isaiah:

> "Behold I will bring again the shadow of the degrees, which is gone down in the sundial of Ahaz, ten degrees backward, so the sun returned ten degrees, by which degrees it was gone down." {*Isa 38:8*}

*648.* For Jerome renders the word מעלות (which Jonathan, in the Chaldee Paraphrase, translated שעראבך *the stone of the hours*) as *the hours of the clock.* Yet in his commentary on this passage, Jerome observed that the Hebrew word signifies *degrees.* Also Isaiah stated:

> "wilt thou that the shadow ascend ten degrees, or that it return back ten degrees?" {*2Ki 20:9*}

*649.* Nor may we ignore the Greek LXX interpretation of this passage, since it is more ancient than any of these writings. It stated that by the words used here, nothing other is meant in this history than the degrees of those scales or stairs which were made by Ahaz. It cannot be shown that until after their return from the captivity of Babylon there was any observation or use of hours whatsoever among the Jews. Others also attribute the invention of the sundial among the Greeks to men of a later date such as Anaximander or Anaximener. {*See note on 3457 AM. <<924>>*} [*L102*] [*E71*] However, it seems that they received it originally from the Babylonians as noted by Herodotus, when he said: {*\*Herodotus, l. 2. c. 109. 1:399*}

> "The sun-clock and the sundial and the dividing of the day into twelve hours, all these the Greeks learned from the Babylonians."

*650.* Concerning the retrograde motion of the sun mentioned in these passages {*Isa 38:8 Apc Sir 48:23*}, when the sun stood still at the prayer of Joshua, the moon also stood still at the same time. {*Jos 10:12,13*} It is apparent that the moon also, and all the frame of heaven, went backward with the sun, and that there was as much subtracted from the night as there was added to the day. There was a miraculous alteration in the parts of the normal day. By divine providence things were so ordered that no harm or disturbance happened to the predictable motion and harmony of the heavenly bodies. This is evidenced by those three solar eclipses of which I spoke earlier, from Ptolemy. Concerning the timing of these events, if calculated backward from our time, the calculations yield the same results in the times as was previously observed by the Chaldeans, and in the same manner as if no such retrogradation or going back of the sun had ever happened!

*651.* In the beginning of the fifteenth year of Hezekiah's reign, Merodach, or Berodach Baladan, the son of Baladan, the king of Babylon, sent messengers with presents to him. They wanted to know the reason for the miraculous retrogradation of the sun which happened in the world. Hezekiah, out of pride and vain ostentation, showed them all his treasures and the extent of his wealth. As a result, God immediately foretold the captivity of Babylon which was to happen:

"Behold the days come, that all that is in thine house and that which thy fathers have laid up in store until this day, shall be carried away into Babylon; nothing shall be left, saith the Lord." {Isa 39:6}

*652.* He added further that his sons who were not yet born should also be carried into captivity:

"Thy sons also, that shall issue from thee and which thou shalt beget, shall they take away and they shall be eunuchs in the palace of the king of Babylon." {Isa 39:1-8 2Ki 20:12-19}

*653.* Nevertheless, when Hezekiah, with the inhabitants of Jerusalem, had turned in humility from his former pride, the fierce wrath of the Lord did not fall on them in Hezekiah's lifetime. {2Ch 32:25,26,31}

*654.* Micah the Morasthite also prophesied to the people in Hezekiah's days:

"That Zion should be plowed and Jerusalem laid in heaps and the mountain itself of the house of the Lord, as the high places in a forest." {Mic 3:12 Jer 26:18,19}

(The important thing to note is that the earlier eclipse data was not disturbed by the events in Hezekiah's day. Whatever happened affected at the very least the sun, earth and moon system. God caused time to go backward, he did not simply have the earth rotate backward. Otherwise the eclipse data would have been inaccurate for those eclipses that had occurred before Hezekiah's event happened. An apparently insignificant detail in the scriptures verifies their authority. Of all the people in the world, it is recorded that only the Chaldeans visited Hezekiah. They were very careful in noting astronomical events and even as far away as in Babylon they had noticed something strange. They had no doubt heard that Hezekiah had something to do with it and hence came to him to learn more of this event. Editor.)

### 3292 AM, 4002 JP, 712 BC

*655.* Memnon wrote that Astacus in Bithynia was built by the Megarians, at the beginning of the 17th Olympiad. {Photius, Bibliotheca, p. 374.}

*656.* Herodotus stated that Sennacherib invaded Egypt with a vast army and made war upon Sethon, the priest of Vulcan. {*Herodotus, l. 2. c. 141. 1:447} This man was a weak king and famous for nothing except for being devoutly, or rather superstitiously, addicted to the worship of his petty god, Vulcan. Herodotus also added that even in his time, there still existed a stone image of Sethon holding a mouse in his hand. The following words were engraved on the statue:

Let every man that looks on me,
Learn godly and devout to be.

*657.* For the sake of his honour, as well as that of their country and their priesthood, the priests of that area offer the following explanation: Sethon, who was both king and priest, had, by virtue of his piety and prayers to his god Vulcan, prevailed with the god. *[L103]* Because when Pelusium, which stands at the very entrance to Egypt, was besieged by the enemy, their horse bridles and the buckles of their bucklers were so gnawn to pieces by mice that the next day they fled with the loss of many of their men. However, whatever the story was at Pelusium, the undoubted word of the prophet assures us that the Assyrians marched far into the very heart of Egypt and led away a large number of captives.

*658.* It is likely that Nahum's prophecy against the city of No was fulfilled by this expedition of Sennacherib's. No was a large and strong city in Egypt. The prophecy was:

"yet was she carried away; she went into captivity, her young children also were dashed in pieces in the top of every street, and they cast lots for their honourable men and all her great men were bound in chains." {Na 3:10}

### 3294c AM, 4004 JP, 710 BC

*659.* The prophecy made by Isaiah three years earlier concerning the rest of Egypt was fulfilled at this time.

"The king of Assyria shall carry away a large number of the Egyptians captive; and of the Ethiopians young and old prisoners, naked and barefoot." {Isa 20:4}

660. I do not see why the next two verses should not refer to the Jews:

> "And they shall be ashamed of Ethiopia their expectation and of Egypt their glory: and the inhabitants of this country shall say in that day: Behold such is our expectation, where can we flee for help to be delivered from the king of Assyria and how shall we escape?" {Isa 20:5,6} [E72]

661. The Assyrian messenger had a good reason for reminding them of Egypt when he said:

> "Now behold, you trust in the staff of this bruised reed Egypt, on which if a man lean, it will go into his hand and pierce it; for even so is Pharaoh, to all such as trust upon him." {2Ki 18:27}

662. For in Ezekiel and Isaiah we find the same simile used by God with reference to the Egyptians and Israelites. {Eze 29:6,7 Isa 30:1-31:9} Here many things were spoken against the vain hope which the Jews had of getting help from Egypt.

> "Therefore, saith he, shall the strength of Pharaoh be your shame, and your trust in the shadow of Egypt your confusion, for the Egyptians shall help in vain and to no purpose: therefore have I cried concerning this, "Their strength is to stay at home."
> {Isa 30:3,7}

663. When Sennacherib returned from Egypt into Palestine, he besieged Lachish with all his forces. {2Ch 32:9} Hezekiah sent to him at Lachish to buy his peace and made a pact with him for peace at a certain price. Therefore he drained all his own treasure, of which he had formerly been so proud, as well as the treasury of the temple. He paid him three hundred talents of silver and thirty talents of gold. When he had taken the money, Sennacherib broke his agreement and sent Tartan, who had now taken Azotus, and Rabsaris and Rabshakeh with a large army from Lachish to Jerusalem. {2Ki 18:14-17}

664. When these all arrived at Jerusalem, they stood at the conduit of the upper pool by the highway of the fuller's field. When they called out demanding to speak with the king, Eliakim the son of Hilkiah, and Shebna, the recorder, went out to meet with them. Because they refused to surrender the city, Rabshakeh cried out that Hezekiah vainly relied on God for help and that he himself had been sent by God. After he had reviled the God of Israel and his servant Hezekiah with many reproachful sayings, he tried to make the people rebel and defect to the king of Assyria. [L104] The Assyrians spoke loudly in the Hebrew language, so that the people who stood on the wall might hear and understand what they said.

This they did to frighten them and cause anxiety, so that in the resulting tumult they might easily assault and take the city. {Isa 36:1-22 2Ki 18:17-37 2Ch 32:9-18}

665. When Hezekiah heard of this, he tore his clothes, put on sackcloth and went into the house of the Lord. He sent Eliakim, Shebna and the elders of the priests, all likewise dressed in sackcloth, to Isaiah the prophet. They asked him to seek counsel from God about this sad situation and to pray to God for help. The prophet encouraged them, saying that the king of Assyria would hear a rumour, whereupon he would lift his siege and return to his country, where he would be murdered. This all came to pass. {Isa 37:1-7 2Ki 19:1-7}

666. When Rabshakeh could not take Jerusalem, he returned to Sennacherib. He left Lachish and besieged Libnah. {Isa 37:8 2Ki 19:8}

667. Tirhakah, king of Ethiopia, did not invade Egypt and Syria, as Scaliger groundlessly asserted in his notes on Eusebius (page 72) and in his Isagogical Canons (page 311). Rather, he sent forces to assist and help the Egyptians and Jews. For the Bible is clear that he came to fight against Sennacherib. {Isa 37:9 2Ki 19:9} Strabo referred to this Tirhakah as Tearco, or Tearko, the Ethiopian, and he also noted from Megasthenes, a writer of the history of India, that he passed over into Europe and went as far as the Pillars of Hercules. {*Strabo, l. 1. c. 3. s. 21. 1:227} {*Strabo, l. 15. c. 1. s. 6. 7:7,9}

668. When Sennacherib at Libnah heard a report that Tirhakah was coming, he sent his commander to Hezekiah with railing letters. He spoke of the God of Israel as if he were like one of the gods of the nations, mere works of men's hands. Hezekiah took it before the Lord in his temple and with many tears sought help and deliverance from God against the Assyrians. God answered him through Isaiah the prophet, who said that God would defend the city and that the king of Assyria would not even come by that way, but would return by the same way he had come. {Isa 37:9-35 2Ki 19:9-34 2Ch 32:17,19,20}

669. The very same night after these things had happened at Jerusalem, and a few days after his victory over the Ethiopians, which happened about this time as some gathered from Isaiah, God sent his angel to their camp. {Isa 18:1-7 20:1-6} He destroyed every man of valour, every commander and leader in the Assyrian army. The next morning a hundred and eighty-five thousand dead men were discovered. After this, Sennacherib broke camp in shame and returned to his own land to rest at Nineveh. It came to pass that as he was worshipping before his god Nisroch, Adrammelech and Sharezer killed him

with the sword. They fled at once into the land of Ararat or Armenia, and Esarhaddon his son reigned in his stead. {*Isa 37:36-38 2Ki 19:35-37 2Ch 32:21*} All this had been foretold by the prophet. {*Isa 37:1-38 31:8,9*} *[E73]*

670. The first chapter of the book of Tobit contains the following incidents which belong to this story. When Sennacherib fled from Judah, he killed many of the Jews because of the hatred he had toward the Israelites. Tobit, or Tobias the elder, stole away the dead bodies and gave them a proper burial. When he was accused of this before the king of Nineveh, he fled into hiding for a time. *[L105]* They plundered and spoiled all his goods, leaving him only Anne, his wife, and Tobias, his son. After forty-five days or, as the Greek copy has it, before fifty-five days, Sennacherib was murdered by his sons. When these fled into the mountains of Ararat, Esarhaddon, his son, reigned in his stead. Some copies incorrectly call him Achirdon or Sarchedon. The new king set Achiacarus, the son of Hananeel, Tobit's brother, over all his father's and his own affairs. He was his steward and keeper of his accounts, as well as the cupbearer having the privy seal, and so his position was that of second man to the king. {*Apc Tob 1:17-22*}

671. Hezekiah had his son Manasseh, by Hephzibah, three years after his life was lengthened and twelve years before his death. {*2Ki 21:1 2Ch 33:1*}

672. The Medes had up until now lived without a king. After Dejoces refused to judge their causes and controversies any longer, civil disorder ensued. The Assyrians used this occasion to take possession of many cities and places in Media. {*See note on 3283 AM. <<634>>*} The people did not like the resulting anarchy and submitted unanimously to Dejoces. This was a hundred and fifty years before Cyrus began his reign, according to Ctesias as cited by Herodotus. {*\*Herodotus, l. 1. c. 96-98. 1:127,129*} Both Dionysius {*\*Dionysius Halicarnassus, Roman Antiquities, l. 1. c. 2. s. 2. 1:7*} and Appian, in the beginning of his Roman Histories, agree. {*\*Appian, l. 1. c. 0. s. 9. 1:15*} Although Diodorus Siculus, whether through faulty memory or poor copying, wrote Cyaxares for Dejoces. He is said to have been elected king over the Medes in about the second year of the 17th Olympiad, according to Herodotus, {*\*Diod. Sic., l. 2. c. 32. s. 2-3. 1:457,459*} and for this reason: subtracting a hundred and fifty years from the beginning of the reign of Cyrus, which he supposed happened in the beginning of the 55th Olympiad, brings you to the middle of the year 560 BC or 4154 JP. It follows that the first year of Dejoces the first king of the Medes must be in the third year of the 17th Olympiad, in the middle of the year 710 BC or 4004 JP. This allowed the end period of the second year of the same Olympiad to have been spent

in the transaction of this business and election of the new king. This marks the beginning or the first epoch of this new kingdom of the Medes. Herodotus correctly determined and recorded this fact. The precise times of every king's reign can be determined in relation to the eclipse of the sun which happened in the reign of Cyaxares, as described later. {*See note on 3403 AM. <<788>>*}

### 3295a AM, 4004 JP, 710 BC

673. The fifteenth Jubilee, which was the half-way point of all the Jubilees observed, was the most joyful, apart from the one at Solomon's dedication of the temple. The fresh memory of so great a deliverance and of the prosperity that followed made this one of the best Jubilees ever. Many brought offerings and gifts to the Lord at Jerusalem and rich presents for the king. He was magnified later among all the nations and prospered in whatever he undertook. {*2Ch 32:23,27,30*}

674. After this great deliverance, God prospered Judah greatly. {*2Ch 32:22 Isa 37:31,32*} To realise that this was a Jubilee, it is necessary to understand the sign of God's mercy given the previous year to Hezekiah:

> "You shall eat, saith God, this year, that which groweth of itself; the second year, that which springeth of the same; and in the third year, sow ye and reap ye and plant vineyards and eat of the fruit thereof." {*Isa 37:30 2Ki 19:29*} *[L106]*

675. The previous year's harvest had either been gathered by the enemy as they roved all over the country (as God had declared in judgment {*Le 26:16 De 28:33 Jer 5:17*}) or been spoiled and trodden underfoot by them. It would be necessary that year for the people to live on whatever grew by itself, since it was not lawful either to sow or reap, because this year was a Jubilee. Otherwise, if no Sabbatical year had intervened, they would have been free to do this. Since the Assyrian army had been destroyed by the angel, there was nothing to hinder them from planting a crop. But the following year, when there was neither enemy to frighten them nor Sabbatical year to prevent them, they could lawfully resume farming as at other times.

### 3295b AM, 4005 JP, 709 BC

676. After Mardokempados, or Merodach Baladan, had reigned twelve years in Babylon, he was succeeded by Arkeanos in the thirty-ninth year of Nabonassar, and reigned five years. {*Ptolemy, Canon of Kings*}

677. According to Eusebius, Parium, on the coast of the Hellespont near Lampsacus, was built or rather re-established by the Milesians and Erythreans, who sent a colony there at this time. {*\*Eusebius, Chronicles, l. 1. 1:159*}

## 3296 AM, 4006 JP, 708 BC

*678.* Dejoces, king of the Medes, built Ecbatana this year in the first year of the 18th Olympiad according to Eusebius. {*Eusebius, Chronicles, l. 1. 1:158*} [E74] This city is called Achmetha in the book of Ezra, {*Ezr 6:2*} but Ctesias {*Ctesias, History of Persia*} like Stephanus Byzantinus, called it Agbatam. A fuller description of the construction of it is in Judith, {*Apc Jud 1:1-16*} where it is said that it was built by Arphaxad, the king of the Medes. Herodotus and other writers attributed it to Dejoces. {*Herodotus, l. 1. c. 98. 1:129*} It appears that the same man was called by both names. More will be said of this later. {*See note on 3448 AM. <<908>>*}

## 3299 AM, 4009 JP, 705 BC

*679.* Taracas or Tirhakah, the Ethiopian, reigned in Egypt for eighteen years. {*See note on 3294 AM. <<667>>*} {*Julius Africanus*}

## 3300 AM, 4010 JP, 704 BC

*680.* After Arkeanos, there was no king in Babylon for two years. {*Ptolemy, Canon of Kings*}

## 3302 AM, 4012 JP, 702 BC

*681.* Belibos, or Belithus or Belelus, held the kingdom of Babylon for three years. {*Ptolemy, Canon of Kings*}

## 3305 AM, 4015 JP, 699 BC

*682.* Apranadius reigned in Babylon for six years. {*Ptolemy, Canon of Kings*}

## 3306c AM, 4016 JP, 698 BC

*683.* Hezekiah was buried in the upper part of the sepulchres of the family of David. All Judah and the inhabitants of Jerusalem paid him every honour possible. {*2Ch 32:33*} After Hezekiah, Manasseh his son reigned for fifty-five years. {*2Ki 21:1 2Ch 33:1*} He again set up the high places which his father Hezekiah had pulled down. He built altars to all the host of heaven in the two courts of the house of the Lord. He made his son pass through the fire in the valley of the son of Hinnom. He used divinations, sorceries and soothsayings, and set up a molten image in the house of the Lord. He caused Judah and the inhabitants of Jerusalem to sin and do worse than all the nations whom God had driven out before the Israelites. {*2Ki 21:2-11 2Ch 33:2-9*} He also shed much innocent blood, to the extent that he filled Jerusalem with it. In addition to his own sin, he made Judah sin and do what was evil in the sight of the Lord. {*2Ki 21:16 24:4*} Manasseh is thought to have sawn the prophet Isaiah in half with a wooden saw. The Babylonian Talmud in their treatise, Justin Martyr {*Justin Martyr, Tryphon*} and Jerome, speaking of the passage in Isaiah, {*Isa 20:1-6 57:1-21*} and others of our men, explain the phrase *were sawn in pieces*

as referring to the passage in Hebrews and relate it to Manasseh and Isaiah. {*Heb 11:37*} [L107]

*684.* They considered the following words to refer to Isaiah's prophecies for God threatened that:

> "And I will stretch over Jerusalem the line of Samaria, and the plummet of the house of Ahab: and I will wipe Jerusalem as *a man* wipeth a dish, wiping *it*, and turning *it* upside down." {*2Ki 21:13*}

## 3311 AM, 4021 JP, 693 BC

*685.* Regebelos reigned over the Babylonians for one year. {*Ptolemy, Canon of Kings*}

## 3312 AM, 4022 JP, 692 BC

*686.* Mesisimordakos reigned over the Babylonians for four years. {*Ptolemy, Canon of Kings*}

## 3316 AM, 4026 JP, 688 BC

*687.* There was no king in Babylon for eight years. {*Ptolemy, Canon of Kings*}

*688.* According to Herodotus, Dejoces extended the kingdom of the Medes as far as the Halys River a hundred and twenty-eight years before the end of the reign of Astyages. {*Herodotus, l. 1. c. 130. 1:169*}

*689.* In the 23rd Olympiad, Herostratus of Naucratis, a merchant of Egypt, went to Paphos on the island of Cyprus. There he bought a little image of Venus about nine inches high and of very ancient workmanship. By its power, he was miraculously delivered from a storm at sea. He consecrated the image at Naucratis in the temple of Venus with great solemnity. This was according to Athenaeus who was born in the same place. However, according to Strabo there was no such town as Naucratis in Egypt at that time or for a time after, as it was only later built by the Milesians. This was in the time of Cyaxares, king of the Medes, and of Psammetichus, king of Egypt, who both lived at the same time. {*Athenaeus, l. 15. (676a) 7:119*} {*Strabo, l. 17. c. 1. s. 18. 8:67*}

## 3317 AM, 4027 JP, 687 BC

*690.* Civil disorder increased in Egypt, because there was no king for two years. {*Diod. Sic., l. 1. c. 66. 1:227*}

## 3319 AM, 4029 JP, 685 BC

*691.* After this, Egypt was ruled by an aristocracy of twelve men who governed the kingdom by a common council. This government lasted fifteen years. {*Herodotus, l. 2. c. 147. 1:455*} {*Diod. Sic., l. 1. c. 66. 1:227*} Tremellius thought that the burden of Egypt, spoken of by the prophet Isaiah, referred to the drying up of the Nile River as foretold in Isaiah:

"They shall want of their waters, to run into the sea, so that their river shall be dried up and turning away their waters, they shall empty and dry up their channels fenced with banks." {*Isa 19:5,6*}

692. Tremellius stated, based on Herodotus: {*Herodotus, l. 2. c. 147-149. 1:455-459*}

"The twelve petty kings using the labour of this poor people, shall strive to overrule the very works of nature and shall turn away the waters of the Nile River. Even to make its channels dry. They did this so that they might finish their pyramids and labyrinth beyond the Lake of Moeris solely for their lust and pleasure's sake."

693. However, Scaliger understood this to mean that so great a drought was to occur, that in summer the Nile River would not rise, nor flow, nor water Egypt, as it normally did. He connected this prophesy to the earlier times of Soij or Sabacon. {*Scaliger, Isagogical Canons, p. 311.*} [L108] [E75]

### 3324 AM, 4034 JP, 680 BC

694. When the family of the Babylonian kings died out, there were eight years of no kings before Esarhaddon, the king of Assyria, conquered Babylon and held that kingdom for twelve years. {*Bone, Chronology of the Hebrew Divided Kingdom, l. 1. 1:28,29.*} {*Grayson, Assyrian and Babylonian Chronicles*} Asaridinos appears to have been the same person as Esarhaddon. This is from the similarity in the names and the word of the Holy Scripture, which intimates that he was king both of Assyria and Babylon at the same time. {*2Ki 17:24 19:37*} {*See note on 3327 AM. <<697>>*} (Ptolemy stated Esarhaddon reigned for thirteen, not twelve years. {*Ptolemy, Canon of Kings*} This would make all the dates for the Babylonian kings one year later and create a contradiction between the secular dates for Nebuchadnezzar and the dates derived from the Bible. If you followed Ptolemy's Canon, the fall of Jerusalem would be later than 588 BC. Ussher was aware of the problem and assumed the interregnum was not a full eight years, but only seven years and a few months. He placed the starting date for Esarhaddon's reign at one year earlier in 3323c AM, which is 681 BC or 4033 JP. Editor.)

695. Ardys, the son of Gyges, reigned in Lydia for forty-nine years. He captured Priene and invaded Miletus. {*Herodotus, l. 1. c. 15,16. 1:19*}

### 3327 AM, 4037 JP, 677 BC

696. Two brothers, Antiphemus and Lacius, built the city of Gela in Sicily and Phaselis in Pamphylia. {*Eusebius, Chronicles, l. 1. 1:163*} They consulted the oracle at Delphi concerning a place to live. It answered that the one brother should sail westward and the other eastward, as Stephanus Byzantinus on the word *Gela* stated from Aristenetus in his first commentary of Phaselis. Heropythus, in his book the *Borders of the Colophonians*, spoke about the building of Phaselis, and said that Lacius, who was transporting a colony to that place, there met Cylabra, a shepherd with his flock. He paid for the ground on which he built his city by giving the shepherd the equivalent of the price in salted meat. Philostephanus gave a more detailed account about Lacius who was a man from Argos. {*Philostephanus, Cities of Asia*} One of them went with Mopsus (the founder of the city of Colophos), whom some call Lindius, brother to Antiphemus, the builder of Gela. (Lindius is said by Herodotus to have been from Rhodes. {*Herodotus, l. 7. c. 153. 3:463*} {*Thucydides, l. 6. c. 4. s. 3. 3:189*}) Lacius and other men were commissioned by Mopsus, the oracle and Mantus who was Mopsus' mother. Because the decks of Lacius' ships were wrecked in a storm around the Chelidonian Isles, he could not arrive till late at night. There he bought the plot of ground on which he built his city, as Mantus had foretold. In exchange for this land he gave certain salted meats to Cylabra, its owner, since this was what he desired most when given his choice from all their ship's provisions. {*Athenaeus, l. 7. (314f) 3:413*}

697. In this year the prophecy was fulfilled that was spoken by Isaiah. {*Isa 7:8*} Within sixty-five years from the beginning of the reign of Ahaz, Ephraim would be conquered and never be a country again. For although most of them were carried away by Shalmaneser forty-four years earlier and the kingdom was utterly destroyed, yet among those who were left there was some form of government. But they now ceased to be a distinct people because of the many foreigners who came to live there. Compared to the total population, the small number of the Ephraimites was insignificant. A few remained in their country, as appears from the story of Josiah. {*2Ch 34:6,7,33 35:18 2Ki 23:19,20*} Every now and then there were new colonies of people sent from Babel, Cush, Halvah and Sepharvaim, to live in Samaria and its cities. {*2Ki 17:24*} This was done by Esarhaddon, king of Assyria (who was also called Asnappar the Great and Magnificent). This is evident from the confession of the Cushites in Ezra. {*Ezr 4:2,10*}

698. At the same time as Israel was conquered, Judah was attacked by the same Assyrian army. They captured Manasseh, the king, as he was hiding in a thicket. They bound him with chains of brass and carried him captive into Babylon. {*2Ch 33:11*} Some think this calamity was foretold by the prophet Isaiah, when he said:

"within sixty-five years Ephraim shall be so broken in pieces, that it shall be no more a people. And the head of Ephraim is Samaria, and the head of Samaria is the son of Remaliah: And if you will not believe, you shall not be established." {Isa 7:8,9}

699. Jacobus Capellus noted in his history that they (the Jews) themselves would be broken in pieces as well. Furthermore, he added that the Jews in Seder Olam's Rabba, and the Talmudists cited by Rabbi Kimchi in his comment on Ezekiel, also stated this. {Eze 4:1-17}

700. In the twenty-second year of Manasseh's reign he was carried away captive into Babylon. [L109] After he repented of his sin, God restored him again to his kingdom, thirty-three years before his death. {2Ch 33:12,13} It is likely that his captivity did not last very long, since no mention is made of it in Kings. {2Ki 21:1-18} It is recorded that he reigned fifty-five years in Jerusalem. {2Ki 21:1 2Ch 33:1}

701. When the new inhabitants of Samaria did not serve the God of Israel, some were killed by lions. When the king of Assyria was told this, he ordered that one of the priests, who had been brought from there in the captivity, be sent back. When the priest returned, he made his residence at Bethel. There he taught them how to worship God, but according to Jeroboam's religion. They worshipped the calf at Bethel as well as their old idols. They are said to have feared God and not to have feared him. There is little difference between worshipping many gods and no God at all. {2Ki 17:25,33,41} [E76] This was the beginning of the animosity which grew later between the Samaritans and the Jews. {Ezr 4:1 Ne 4:2 Joh 4:9}

## 3329 AM, 4039 JP, 675 BC

702. According to Eusebius, {*Eusebius, Chronicles, l. 1. 1:163} Chalcedon, or Calcedon (as it is found on some old coins), was built by the Megarians, at the mouth of the Black Sea, among the Thracians who had possession of Bithynia in Asia. {*Thucydides, l. 4. c. 75. 2:341} {*Strabo, l. 12. c. 4. s. 1. 5:455} {*Strabo, l. 12. c. 3. s. 2. 5:375}

## 3334 AM, 4044 JP, 670 BC

703. Psammetichus Sais succeeded his father Pharaohnecho who was murdered by Sabacos, the Ethiopian, who was one of those twelve tyrants of Egypt. Psammetichus took over the kingdom and reigned there fifty-four years. {*Herodotus, l. 2. c. 152-157. 1:463-471} Isaiah seems to allude to this when he says:

"And the Egyptians will I give up into the hands of lords, which shall lord it cruelly over them, till a fierce king shall come to rule them." {Isa 19:4}

704. Psammetichus was driven out of his kingdom and confined to the low country near the sea. He hired sol-diers from Arabia and a number of pirates from Ionia and Caria, who roved about that shore. He assembled together all the Egyptians who sided with him. In the main battle fought near Memphis, he overthrew the rest of those domineering lords. For their good service, the Ionians and Carians had land assigned to them to live in. This land was around the cities of Bubastus and Pelusium, which stood on the mouth of the Nile River. From that time on, the Greeks and other foreigners were always welcome in Egypt. {*Diod. Sic., l. 1. c. 67. s. 7-12. 1:231} {*Herodotus, l. 2. c. 152. 1:463} Herodotus also reported that after a twenty-nine year siege, this same Psammetichus took by force a large city in Syria called Azotus. {*Herodotus, l. 2. c. 157. 1:469} That is the city of Ashdod. {See note on 3291c AM. <<642>>} In that note we showed that it was taken by Tartan, the commander of the king of Assyria, and his army, in one year. It was so destroyed by Psammetichus, that the prophet Jeremiah could say there was merely a remnant of its people left in his day. {Jer 25:20}

## 3336 AM, 4046 JP, 668 BC

705. After Asaridinos or Esarhaddon, Saosduchinos ruled both the empires of Assyria and Babylon for twenty years. {Ptolemy, Canon of Kings} In the book of Judith that was written in the Chaldee language by a Jew living in Babylon, he is called Nabuchodonosor, a name common to all kings of Babylon. However, he was called the king of Assyria and is said to have reigned in the great city of Nineveh. {Apc Jud 1:1} The learned Franc. Junius thought that Saosduchinos is the same person as Merodach Baladan of the Bible, the grandfather of that Nebucadnetzar and great-grandfather of Nebuchadnezzar. [L110] Hence, he thinks it was Merodach Baladan who took King Manasseh prisoner to Babylon and released him later. For he stated:

"this man was the first king of Babylon and was later made king of Assyria, succeeding in that kingdom after Esarhaddon the Great. When his brothers were found guilty of murdering their father, they were deemed unworthy of the kingdom. After this, all Asia was in a tumult from a war which lasted a long time after."

706. The succession of Asar-Adon, Merodach, Ben-Merodach and Nebuchadnezzar, first and second, is only based on Anianus who was that false Metasthenus. For indeed, Merodach was not the grandfather of Nabopolassar who was the father of Nebuchadnezzar the Great. Junius noted that Merodach was not at first merely a trustee of the king of Assyria only later becoming the king of both Assyria and Babylon. {2Ki 20:12} Merodach never succeeded Esarhaddon the Great in any

kingdom of his since this Mardokempados or Merodach died eleven years before Manasseh became king. Also forty-two years after Merodach's death, Aassaradinus, or Esarchaddon, left Saosduchinos to succeed him in both the Assyrian and the Babylonian kingdoms, as we noted from Ptolemy. {*Ptolemy, Canon of Kings*} If Junius, a man of no less modesty than learning, had seen this, no doubt he would have altered his opinion on this point. Therefore, I thought it good here to have the reader note that he should not seek, from an event that never happened, to interpret the prophecy of Ezekiel according to the manner in which Junius interprets the periods of these kings in Ezekiel. {*Eze 31:11,18*} Junius wrote of these two kings:

> "Esarhaddon the Assyrian was put down, or thrust out of his kingdom, by Merodach Baladan. Therefore, all defected from him and many of them fled to the king of Babylon."

707. He interprets this as a fulfilment of this verse:

> "So that now the land of Assyria was most shamefully trodden under foot and brought into contempt of all men." {*Isa 7:20*}

### 3339c AM, 4049 JP, 665 BC
708. Meshullemeth, the daughter of Haruz of Jotbah, bore a son Amon to Manasseh. He was twenty-two years old when he began to reign. {*2Ki 21:19*}

### 3344a AM, 4053 JP, 661 BC
709. This was the sixteenth Jubilee.

### 3347c AM, 4057 JP, 657 BC
710. Nabuchodonosor, king of Assyria, in the twelfth year of his reign, overcame Arphaxad, the king of the Medes, the founder of the city of Ecbatana. {*Apc Jdt 1:1-16*} This battle was in the great plain of Ragau, near the Euphrates and Tigris Rivers, and Jadason in the plain of the country of Erioch, king of the Elicians. {*Apc Jdt 1:1,5,6*} (We read this in the first chapter of the book of Judith which Jerome, at the request of Paula and Eustochiam, translated into Latin.) However, whoever first published that book in Greek with many alterations and additions of his own, told us that Nabuchodonosor in the twelfth year of his reign fought a battle with King Arphaxad. This battle was in a large plain near Ragau. [E77] Arphaxad was aided in the battle by all the peoples who inhabited the hill countries, all who bordered on the Euphrates, Tigris and Hydaspes Rivers and who lived in the plain of Arioch, king of the Elymeans. {*Apc Jdt 1:5-6*}. After reviewing the battles mentioned before, the writer stated that Nabuchodonosor fought this battle against Arphaxad in the seventeenth year. He conquered

all of Ecbatana and in the hill country of Ragan, thrust Arphaxad through with his own spear. When he had accomplished his aim in the war, he returned to Nineveh to feast and celebrate with his army for a hundred and twenty days. According to Herodotus, Dejoces' death occurred in the twelfth year of Saosduchinos' reign. [L111] One would argue that Saosduchinos and Dejoces are named Nabuchodonosor and Arphaxad in the book of Judith. In trying to determine an accurate succession of kings in Media using the inaccurate accounts of Ctesias, Franc. Junius would need to divide the Median empire into two parts. However, Herodotus, known as *the father of histories*, saw no division of the kingdoms at all. Franc. Junius gives one of the kingdoms to Dejoces (also called Arioch). {*Jer 49:34*} {*Apc Jud 1:6*} The other part of Media he assigned to Artecarmins (whom Ctesias called *Articam*, and who is here called *Arphaxad*). This King Arphaxad established his kingdom at Ecbatana for this reason. He thought this to be a strong place in which he could best withstand the assault of Dejoces and all other enemies. Since no division of Media ever occurred, both the name of Arphaxad and the Ecbatana kingdom should have been ascribed to Dejoces and not to Arioch or Atticarmes. The book of Judith stated that Arphaxad was the founder of Ecbatana. Herodotus and others affirmed that Dejoces (also called Arphaxad) was indeed the founder. {*Herodotus, l. 1. c. 98. 1:129*} No one ever wrote that Arioch or Atticarmes built it.

711. After Dejoces died, Phraortes, his son, succeeded him and reigned for twenty-two years. {*Herodotus, l. 1. c. 102. 1:133*}

### 3348c AM, 4058 JP, 656 BC
712. According to the Chaldee copy of Judith, Arphaxad (or Dejoces) is said to have been the thirteenth king of Ecbatana, but in the Greek copy, the eighteenth. {*Apc Jdt 2:1*} One year after Dejoces was overthrown, on the twenty-second day of the first month, Nabuchodonosor made plans to subdue nations and add countries to his dominion. He made Holophernes general of all his armies. Holophernes besieged Bethhoglah, also called Bethulia, a city of Judah. During this siege, he was beheaded by Judith, a woman of the tribe of Simeon. After the death of her husband Manasseh, who died at the time of the barley harvest, she spent three years of widowhood in that city. The Greek copy said she was a widow for four years. {*Apc Jdt 2:1-28 8:1-36 13:1-20*}

### 3349 AM, 4059 JP, 655 BC
713. In this year, the cities of Isthemus and Borysthenes were built in the country of Pontus. Lampsacus in the Hellespont, and Abdera in Thrace, were also built then,

according to Eusebius. {*Eusebius, Chronicles, l. 1. 1:167} In fact, Borysthenes was built by the Milesians of Ionia, Lampsacus by the Phocaeans and Abdera by the citizens of Clazomene. Solinus explained that the sister of Diomedes first built Abdera. {Solinus, c. 10} After it fell into ruin it was rebuilt and enlarged by the Clazomenians. This took place in the 31st Olympiad, which ended a year prior to this date. The leader of the Clazomenian colony was Timesius, a citizen of Clazomene. {*Herodotus, l. 1. c. 168. 1:211} Herodotus also added that Timesius was not able to complete the work because he was attacked by the Thracians.

## 3355c AM, 4065 JP, 649 BC

714. Amon and Jedidah, the daughter of Adaiah, had a son in Boscath, called Josiah who was eight years old when he began to reign. {2Ki 22:1}

## 3356c AM, 4066 JP, 648 BC

715. Kineladanos succeeded Saosduchinos to both the Assyrian and Babylonian kingdoms. He reigned for twenty-two years. {Ptolemy, Canon of Kings} Alexander Polyhistor called him Saracus or Saracen, which means *robber* or *spoiler*.

716. The oracle of Delphi ordered Grinnus, the son of Aesanius, king of the island of Thera, to go rebuild a city in Libya. This city had been in ruins because at that time no one knew where Libya was. It is said that there was no rain on that island for seven years, and that all the trees except one died in that drought. {*Herodotus, l. 4. c. 150,151. 2:351-355}

## 3361c AM, 4071 JP, 643 BC

717. In this year king Manasseh died who had previously returned from his captivity. He had partly restored the true worship of God, which he had formerly discredited. When he died he was buried in the garden of his own house. {2Ch 33:1-16 2Ki 21:18} [L112] According to his last will or testament, as if repenting for his former evil doings, he deemed himself unworthy to lie among his own royal ancestors. {Tremellius}

## 3363c AM, 4073 JP, 641 BC

718. After Manasseh died, his son Amon reigned for two years. Amon forsook the Lord God and offered sacrifices to all the graven images which his father had set up, and worshipped them. He never repented of this, as his father had done, but sinned more than his father ever had. {2Ki 21:19-21 2Ch 33:21-23}

719. This wicked Amon was murdered in his house by his own servants. He was buried with Manasseh, his father, in the garden of Uzzah. The people killed all who had conspired against him. {2Ki 21:23,24,26 2Ch 33:24,25} [E78]

720. Josiah, his son, succeeded him when he was eight years old and reigned thirty-one years. {2Ki 22:1 2Ch 34:1}

## 3364 AM, 4074 JP, 640 BC

721. The inhabitants of the isle of Thera, wearied by their seven years of drought, hired Corobius, a merchant in purple, from the city of Itanus on the isle of Crete; because he had at one time been driven by a storm into a place called Plataea, an isle of Libya, they sent him with some of their own countrymen to find that isle a second time. When they found it, they left Corobius there with provisions for some months. They returned home quickly to let their countrymen know what they had found. When they did not return to Plataea at the appointed time, it happened that a ship of Samos, whose captain was Colaeus, sailed from Egypt. It put in there and left Corobius and his men with provisions for another year. When it put out to sea again, it was caught by a strong wind and driven beyond the Pillars of Hercules into the main ocean, and finally came to Tartessus in Spain. {*Herodotus, l. 4. c. 151,152. 2:353}

722. The Thereans chose people by lot from their seven regions to establish a new colony. They sent them away to Plataea in two ships under the command of Battus, otherwise called Aristoteles, or Aristeus. {*Herodotus, l. 4. c. 153. 2:355} {*Herodotus, l. 4. c. 156. 2:359,361}

723. Thales, the son of Examius, was born in this year at Miletus in Ionia. This was the first year of the 35th Olympiad. {*Diogenes Laertius, Thales, l. 1. c. 1. (38) 1:39}

724. After the Cimmerians were driven from their dwellings by the Scythian Shepherds (called Nomads), they left Europe and went into Asia. Following the coast to Sardis, they captured the entire city, with the exception of the citadel. This was the time when Ardys, the son of Gyges, reigned there. {*Herodotus, l. 1. c. 15. 1:19} {*Herodotus, l. 1. c. 130. 1:169} {*Herodotus, l. 4. c. 1. 2:199} {*Herodotus, l. 4. c. 12. 2:213}

## 3366 AM, 4076 JP, 638 BC

725. When the Thereans had lived in Plataea for two years, they left one of their company behind and all sailed to Delphi. There they enquired of the oracle why things were no better since they came into Libya. The oracle answered that they had not yet come to the city in Libya where they were told to go, so they returned to Plataea. They took with them the one they had left there, and established a colony in a spot in the land of Libya, opposite the isle of Plataea, called Aziris. This place was surrounded with most scenic hills and a river running around it on either side. {*Herodotus, l. 4. c. 157. 2:361}

726. In that place near the gardens of the Hesperides and the greater Syrtes or quicksand, the earth was covered with a shower which rained down pitch, or sul-

phur. Presently there grew up a herb called *silphium*, or laserwort, and its juice was called *laser*, that is, *Benjamin*, as the Cyrenians said. This occurred seven years before the building of their city. {*Theophrastus, Plants, l. 6.*} {*Pliny, l. 19. c. 15. (38) 5:445*}

## 3369 AM, 4079 JP, 635 BC

727. Phraortes, king of the Medes, perished in the siege of Nineveh with a large number of his army. His son Cyaxares reigned for forty years after him. In the beginning of his reign, he wished to avenge his father's death. [L113] He compelled all Asia as far as the Halys River to join with him in his war against the Assyrians. {*Herodotus, l. 1. c. 103. 1:133*}

## 3370a AM, 4079 JP, 635 BC

728. When Josiah was sixteen years old, he had a son called Jehoiakim by Zebudah, the daughter of Pedaiah, of Rumah. Jehoiakim was twenty-five years old when he started his reign. {2Ki 23:36}

## 3370c AM, 4080 JP, 634 BC

729. The same year his son was born, he began to seek the God of his father David. {2Ch 34:3}

730. Cyaxares defeated the Assyrians in battle, but as he went to besiege Nineveh, a vast army of the Scythians attacked him. These were those Scythians who drove the Cimmerians from Europe. Pressing their advantage, they departed from Lake Maeotis (Sea of Azov) and left the Caucasus Mountains on their left hand. They entered Media under the command of their king, Madyes, the son of Protothyes. {*Herodotus, l. 1. c. 104. 1:135*} {*Herodotus, l. 4. c. 1. 2:199*} {*Herodotus, l. 7. c. 20. 3:335*} {*Strabo, l. 1. c. 3. s. 21. 1:227*} Madyes was also called Idanthyrsus, the Scythian, who, storming out of Scythia, crossed all of Asia until he came into Egypt. Arrian cited Megasthenes when he stated that Madyes was called Idanthyrsus. {*Arrian, Indica, l. 1. c. 5. s. 6. 2:319*} Madyes was the same man as Idanthyrsus, against whom Darius, the son of Hystaspes, later undertook such an unlucky expedition. {*Herodotus, l. 4. c. 76. 2:275*} {*Herodotus, l. 4. c. 125-127. 2:325-329*} When the Medes were defeated by the Scythians, they lost control of Asia. The Scythians then held Asia for the next twenty-eight years. {*Herodotus, l. 1. c. 104. 1:135*} {*Herodotus, l. 4. c. 1. 2:199*} Tremellius and Junius connect this with the following prophecy:

> "He (that is, Cyaxares, besieging Nineveh) shall reckon up his great men; but they shall fall in their journey (that is, in the journey of the Scythians)." {Na 2:5}

731. Their coming to Asia at this time is better called a journey through Asia, rather than an established government or kingdom in Asia. In twenty-eight years they overran, possessed and lost Media, Assyria and all Asia.

> "They shall hasten to his wall, as if they would be his protector (that is, they shall come hastily to Nineveh, as if they had delivered it out of the hand of Cyaxares and would deliver it)." {Na 2:5}

## 3371c AM, 4081 JP, 633 BC

732. In this year, Josiah had a son called Shallum or Jehoahaz by Hamutal, the daughter of Jeremiah of Libnah. He was made king after his father at the age of twenty-three years. The people chose him as king, passing over his older brothers. {2Ki 23:30,31} [E79] It seems the name of Shallum was changed to Jehoahaz for good luck, as the other Shallum, the son of Jabesh, only ruled one month before he was murdered by Menahem. {2Ki 15:13,14} Of the four sons that Josiah had who are mentioned in Chronicles, {1Ch 3:15} this Shallum was named last, not Johanan the firstborn, as some have thought. {Jer 22:11,12 2Ki 23:33,34 2Ch 36:3,4} It is easily deduced that Jehoahaz was not the firstborn, since it is said that he was anointed by the people. {2Ki 23:30} However, the firstborn of kings were not normally so anointed, because the kingdom was theirs by common right. Also, Jehoahaz was twenty-three years old when he was anointed king. However, three months earlier his brother, Eliakim, was made king at the age of twenty-five. Hence he was older by two years than Jehoahaz. This is confirmed by Josephus. {*Josephus, Antiq., l. 10. c. 6. s. 3. (98) 6:211*} {*Josephus, Antiq., l. 10. c. 7. s. 2. (102) 6:213*}

## 3373 AM, 4083 JP, 631 BC

733. Sadyattes, the son of Ardys, reigned in Lydia for twelve years. {*Herodotus, l. 1. c. 16. 1:19*} [L114]

734. When the Scythians had subjected all of upper Asia, they went straight into Egypt. When they came as far as Syria Palestina, Psammetichus, the king of Egypt, met them in person. He persuaded them by gifts and presents not to go any farther. {*Herodotus, l. 1. c. 105. 1:137*}

735. On their return they came to Askelon, which is in Syria. The greater part of the army passed through the area without doing any damage. However, some stragglers at the rear robbed the temple of Venus Urania. For this, all their posterity were smitten with *female* sickness or loss of virility. {*Herodotus, l. 1. c. 105. 1:137*} In this year, which was the second of the 37th Olympiad, the Scythians invaded Syria Palestina. {*Eusebius, Chronicles, l. 1. 1:169*} Also in this year, Sinope was built by the Milesians. It was the chief city in all the kingdom of Pontus. {*Strabo, l. 12. c. 3. s. 11. 5:387*} Phlegon (cited by Stephanus de Tribibus,) said that Sinope was built by Macritius, of the isle of Cos. It is certain that when the

Cimmerians came to Asia after having fled from the Scythians, they built in the Chersonesus, in the same place where Sinope, a city of the Greeks, now stands. {*Herodotus, l. 4. c. 12. 2:213} After having settled in Aziris for seven years, the people of Thera were persuaded by the Libyans to leave. They moved to a place called Irasa and settled there, near a fountain named after Apollo. {*Herodotus, l. 4. c. 1. s. 58. 2:363}

736. There Battus built the city of Cyrene, in the second year of the 37th Olympiad. He reigned for forty years, and after him his son Arcesilaus for sixteen years, but only over those of the first colony. Later in the reign of Arcesilaus, his son Battus went to live in that city with a large number of other Greeks who were inspired by the oracle of Delphi. The city of Cyrene was built during the time when Apries reigned over the Egyptians. This is a better account of events than others have given. {*Herodotus, l. 4. c. 159. 2:363}

### 3374c AM, 4084 JP, 630 BC

737. In the twelfth year of Josiah's reign, he began to cleanse Judah and Jerusalem from idolatry. He destroyed the high places, groves, and altars of Baal with their images. He burned the bones of their priests upon their own altars. He even went as far afield as the cities in Manasseh, Ephraim, Simeon and Naphtali, destroying all the altars, groves and carved images he found. {2Ch 34:3-7}

### 3375c AM, 4085 JP, 629 BC

738. In the thirteenth year of king Josiah, Jeremiah was called by God to be a prophet, but he refused. God called him again and encouraged him with promises and signs belonging to the office and function of a prophet. He was bidden to prophesy to the Jews of the calamity which was to befall Jerusalem at the hands of the king of Babylon. {Jer 1:2-17 25:3} At the same time, Zephaniah and others warned the rebellious people to repent, but they did not. {Zep 1:1 Jer 25:3-5}

739. Prusias or Prusa was built in Bithynia. {*Eusebius, Chronicles, l. 1. 1:171}

### 3378 AM, 4088 JP, 626 BC

740. Nabopolassar of Babylon (who was made general of the army by Saraco, who was also called Kineladanos, king of Assyria and Chaldea) and Astyages (who was made governor of Media by his father Cyaxares) made an alliance together. Astyages gave his daughter Amyitis in marriage to Nebuchadnezzar, the son of Nabopolassar. The two men joined their forces and took the city of Nineveh with its king Saraco. (We gather this from a fragment of the writings of Alexander Polyhistor that was misunderstood by Georgius Syncellus, whom Scaliger cited. [L115] {Eusebius, Scaliger's Greek Eusebius, p. 38,39.}) We find in the end of the book of the Greek copy of Tobit that Nabuchodonosor is called Nabopolassar, and Assuerus is Astyages and is also called Ahasuerus. {Da 9:1} Nineveh was taken while Tobit, the younger, was still living. When Shalmaneser took Samaria, he took Tobit and his father captive to Assyria. Tobit is said to have lived a hundred and twenty-seven years. Since only ninety-five years passed from the captivity of Israel to this time, Tobit must still have been alive. When Josiah was reigning (as Jerome in his commentaries on the prophet Jonah affirms), Nineveh was destroyed. Thus the prophecies of both Nahum and Isaiah concerning the destruction of Nineveh were fulfilled. This is also described in Ezekiel. {Eze 31:1-18} [E80]

741. When Saraco was killed, Nabopolassar ruled the kingdom of Chaldea for twenty-one years, according to Polyhistor. {Berosus, Chaldean History, l. 3} {Ptolemy, Canon of Kings}

### 3379 AM, 4089 JP, 625 BC

742. Sadyattes, king of Lydia, invaded the territory of the Milesians and started a war that lasted for six years. {*Herodotus, l. 1. c. 18. 1:21}

### 3380c AM, 4090 JP, 624 BC

743. In the eighteenth year of Josiah's reign, he charged Hilkiah, the high priest, to use the money which had been collected to repair the house of the Lord. While doing this, he found the original book of the law which had at first been stored in the side of the ark of the covenant. {De 31:26} This book seems to have disappeared at the beginning of Manasseh's reign. When he found it, he sent it to the king by Shaphan, the scribe. After Josiah had heard the entire book read to him, he asked counsel of Huldah, the prophetess. She prophesied to him that his kingdom should certainly be destroyed, but not in his lifetime. {2Ki 22:3-20 2Ch 34:8-28} The king called together the elders of Judah and Jerusalem, with the priests and prophets. He had the book of the law read to all the people and renewed the covenant between God and the people. Again, he cleansed the city from idolatry, and thoroughly restored the worship of God. {2Ki 23:1-14 2Ch 34:29,33} He demolished the altar and high place which Jeroboam the son of Nebat had set up. He burned the bones of the dead upon the altar as had been foretold three hundred and fifty years earlier. {2Ki 13:2} When he had destroyed the altars which the kings of Israel had built in the cities of Samaria, killed all their priests and burned dead men's bones upon them, he then returned to Jerusalem. {2Ki 23:15-20} Even with this renewing of the covenant and general reformation of religion, the inevitable decree of desolation to follow because of the people's sins still stood. This

time of renewing begins both the thirty years spoken of in the first chapter of the prophecy of Ezekiel, and also the forty years of the iniquity of Judah. {*Eze 4:6*} {*See note on 3416d AM <<867>>*}

744. Josiah kept the Passover in the same eighteenth year of his reign (toward the beginning of it), on the fourteenth day of the first month (Monday, May 4), in the presence of all Judah and Israel and the inhabitants of Jerusalem. He kept this with more solemnity than had ever been done by any of the kings of Israel or Judah in former times. {*2Ki 23:21-23 2Ch 35:1-19*} He abolished all witches and soothsayers, all images and gods, and all the abominations which were found in the land of Judah and in Jerusalem. He obeyed everything written in the book of the law which had been found by Hilkiah. {*2Ki 23:24 De 18:9-11*} [L116] (Ussher assigned this paragraph to the next year, 623 BC. We see no reason for that and included these events in that year. No chronological entry by Ussher is invalidated by so doing. Editor.)

### 3383c AM, 4093 JP, 621 BC

745. Toward the end of the fifth year of Nabopolassar (which is the 127th year from the epoch of Nabonassar), on the 27th day of the Egyptian month of Athyr, toward the 28th of the month, the moon was eclipsed at Babylon, beginning five measured hours after midnight. {*Ptolemy, Great Syntaxis, p. 125. Greek edition*} This was on Saturday, April 22, or the 27th of the month Athyr, as the day drew to a close. This was what Ptolemy meant when he said that it was from the 27th to the 28th, lasting in all six measured hours starting after midnight of the 27th day to the sunrising when the 28th day was to begin.

### 3384d AM, 4094 JP, 620 BC

746. Hamutal bore another son, Mattaniah, to Josiah, after Shallum, or Jehoahaz. He was later called Zedekiah and was twenty-one years old when he began to reign. {*Jer 51:1 2Ki 24:17,18*}

747. Xenophanes of Colophon, founder of the sect of the Eleatic discipline in philosophy, was born in the 40th Olympiad. {*Elius Empiricus, Contra Mathematicos, l. 1. c. 12.*} (More correctly reported by Apollodorus, as cited by Clement of Alexandria. {*\*Clement, Stromateis, l. 1. c. 14. 2:314*})

### 3385 AM, 4095 JP, 619 BC

748. The son of Sadyattes, called Alyattes the younger, reigned in Lydia for fifty-seven years. He spent the first five years fighting the war against Miletus that his father had started. {*\*Herodotus, l. 1. c. 18,25. 1:21,25*}

### 3387c AM, 4097 JP, 617 BC

749. Jehoiakim, son of Josiah, had a son by Nehushta, the daughter of Elnathan of Jerusalem, called Jehoiakim

or Jeconiah. He was eighteen years old when he began to reign. {*2Ki 24:8*}

### 3388 AM, 4098 JP, 616 BC

750. Necho, the son of Psammetichus, reigned in Egypt for sixteen years. {*\*Herodotus, l. 2. c. 159. 1:473*} The Bible called him Necho or Pharaohnecho. {*2Ch 35:20 2Ki 23:29 Jer 46:2*} This man began a channel from the Nile to the Gulf of Arabia, a work which cost the lives of a hundred and twenty thousand Egyptians. He abandoned the work when it was half done. He sent certain Phoenicians to sail around Africa. They set sail from the Gulf of Arabia, or the Red Sea, entering the southern sea and sailing around the coast. They finally came to the Pillars of Hercules and returned to Egypt, three years after they had started out. {*\*Herodotus, l. 2. c. 158. 1:471*} {*\*Herodotus, l. 4. c. 42. 2:239*}

### 3390 AM, 4100 JP, 614 BC

751. In the twelfth year of the war between the Lydians and the Milesians, the Lydian army burned the harvest of the Milesians, as they normally did each year. It so happened that the wind caught the flames and set the temple of Athena in Assesos on fire, burning it to the ground. After the army returned to Sardis, Alyattes became sick for a long time. [E81] Finally, he sent to consult the oracle at Delphi. The prophetess refused to entertain his request until the temple which his men had destroyed was rebuilt. Periander, the son of Cyphelus, ruler of Corinth, found out the reply of the oracle and passed it on to his good friend Thrasybulus, king of the Milesians. He cleverly ordered that when Alyattes and his envoys came to see about rebuilding the temple, the Milesians should be feasting and revelling, using all the remaining grain and supplies in the city. Alyattes expected to find that the Milesians would be starving from the long war. However, when he saw that they appeared to have plenty to eat, he made peace and a league of friendship with the Milesians. Alyattes built two temples of Athena at Assesos to replace the one he had destroyed. When he got well, he sent costly presents and offerings to Delphi. {*\*Herodotus, l. 1. c. 19-25. 1:22-29*} {*Polyaenus, Strategemata, l. 6.*}

### 3393a AM, 4102 JP, 612 BC

752. The seventeenth Jubilee.

### 3393c AM, 4103 JP, 611 BC

753. Anaximander of Miletus, the son of Praxidemus, was born in Ionia. {*See note on 3457 AM. <<954>>*} [L117]

### 3394c AM, 4104 JP, 610 BC

754. By God's command, Pharaohnecho, king of Egypt, set out to go into battle against the king of Assyria, who was at war with him at the time, and was planning

to besiege Carchemish on the Euphrates River. {2Ki 23:29 2Ch 35:20-22} Josephus stated that he went to fight against the Medes and Babylonians, who had overthrown the empire of the Assyrians. {*Josephus, Antiq., l. 10. c. 6. s. 1. (84) 6:205} Carchemish, at the time of Sennacherib, belonged to and was occupied by the Assyrians. {Isa 10:9} However, when that kingdom was destroyed, it returned into the hands of the Babylonians. Just as at the time when the king of Persia defeated Babylon and Assyria, {Ezr 6:22} he was called king of the Assyrians, so when the king of Babylon defeated Assyria, he was called king of Assyria. In addition, the secular authors also stated that Babylon was formerly part of Assyria, while the Holy Scriptures state that the kingdom of Chaldea was founded by the king of Assyria. {Isa 23:13 Nu 24:22 Isa 52:4 Ne 9:32}

755. When Josiah unadvisedly entered into this war, he was killed. {2Ki 23:29,30 2Ch 32:22,23} This took place in the valley of Megiddo which belonged to the tribe of Manasseh. {Jos 17:11 Jud 1:17} Herodotus, in referring to this story, said that Necho attacked the Syrians with an army and overthrew them in Magdolus. After the battle he took a large city of Syria named Cadytis. {*Herodotus, l. 2. c. 159. 1:473} Scaliger noted that this Cadytis was actually Kadesh which is mentioned in Numbers. {Nu 20:16} Scaliger also believed that Magdolus and Megiddo were located near each other. {Jer 46:14} Because Magdolus was the more noted place of the two, the battle was said to have taken place there. In the same way it is commonly understood that the battle between Alexander and Darius at Gaugamela is said to have been fought at Arbela, since Gaugamela was an obscure place. It may be that Magdolus and Megiddo were the same place, since that is the place from which the other Mary obtained her surname of Magdalene. In Matthew we see the name given as Magdala. {Mt 15:39} The Syrian renders it *Mageda* and the old Latin translates it *Magedan*, which appears to be similar to *Megiddo*. {*Herodotus, l. 2. c. 159. 1:473}

756. Since the good king was killed in this way and his being alive had postponed the Babylonian captivity from being visited on the nation, {2Ki 22:20} the previous year's Jubilee was turned into a year of lamentation. It almost became a common proverb, *The lamentation of Hadadrimmon in the valley of Megiddo*. {Zec 12:11} Not only did all the people of that time bewail the death of Josiah, but even later, a public mourning for him was voluntarily kept. The prophet Jeremiah also wrote a song of remembrance called the *Song of Threnes* or *Lamentations*. {2Ch 35:24,25} In this song he bewailed the calamities which were shortly to befall his people. Jeremiah wrote:

"The breath of our nostrils, the anointed of the Lord, is taken in their pits: of whom we said, under the shadow of his wings we shall live among the heathen." {La 4:20}

757. Hence, we may very justly question the first verse, or poem of that book which we find in the Greek and common Latin translations of Jeremiah, which disagreed with Jerome's translation from the Hebrew. This verse is prefixed before the *Threnes* or *Lamentations of Jeremiah:* [L118]

"And it came to pass, after Israel was taken captive, and Jerusalem made desolate, Jeremiah sat weeping, and lamented *with* this lamentation over Jerusalem and said:"

758. Whoever added this should have noted the verse:

"Add thou not unto his words, lest he reprove thee, and thou be found a liar." {Pr 30:6}

759. There was also a second Song of Lamentations for the miserable condition of the kingdom of the Jews after the death of Josiah. It was composed by the prophet Ezekiel and was intended to be sung. {Eze 19:1-14}

760. After the death of Josiah, the people feared that the king of Egypt would invade them in the absence of a king in the land, so they anointed his youngest son Shallum, or Jehoahaz, as king. He soon did all that was evil in the sight of the Lord, just as his forefathers had done. {2Ki 23:30-32 2Ch 36:1} {See note on 3371c AM. <<732>>} [E82]

## 3394d AM, 4104 JP, 610 BC

761. When Necho returned from Assyria, he deposed Shallum from the throne after he had only reigned three months. He made Eliakim, his older brother, king in the place of his father Josiah and changed his name to Jehoiakim. {2Ki 23:29-35 2Ch 36:2-4} This was a public witness that Jeremiah attributed the victory Necho had over the Assyrians to the Lord God only. Jeremiah had previously prophesied that it was God who sent him against the Assyrians. {2Ch 35:21,22} He imposed a tribute of one hundred talents of silver and one talent of gold on the land of Judah. He put Shallum or Jehoahaz in fetters at Riblah and carried him away prisoner into Egypt, where he eventually died. {2Ki 23:33-35 2Ch 36:3,4 Eze 19:3,4}

762. At God's behest, the prophet Jeremiah called on the new king Shallum in his palace. He earnestly entreated the king, his courtiers and all the people with promises and threats from Almighty God. He foretold that Shallum or Jehoahaz would be carried away captive into Egypt.

"Weep not for him that is departed (meaning Josiah) nor make lamentation for him; but weep for him that is to depart (that is, Shallum): because he shall return no more to see his native soil." {*Jer 22:1,2,10-12*}

### 3395a AM, 4104 JP, 610 BC

763. In the beginning of the reign of Jehoiakim, Jeremiah was commanded by God to stand in the court of the temple. He exhorted the people who were assembled from all the cities of Judah to humble themselves before the Lord. It was the feast of tabernacles, when all the males from the cities were required to appear at Jerusalem. {*De 15:16*} He told them to repent and when they would not, he pronounced the judgment of God against them, saying that the house would become as Shiloh: and that city should be accursed among all the nations of the earth. {*Jer 26:6*}

764. This resulted in his arrest by the priests and prophets and all the people who were in the court at the time. They accused him of being a man worthy of death, but he was acquitted and set at liberty by the public judgment of the princes and elders. {*Jer 26:1-19*}

### 3395b AM, 4105 JP, 609 BC

765. Like Jeremiah, Uriah, who was the son of Shemariah from Kirjathjearim, also prophesied against Jerusalem and the land of Judah. When Jehoiakim, the king, sought to put him to death, he fled into Egypt. The king sent Elnathan, the son of Achor, and others, after him. They overtook him and brought him back to the king, who had him killed and threw his carcass among the vilest sepulchres of the common people. However, Ahikam, the son of Shaphan, who had formerly been a man of great authority with king Josiah, was a friend of Jeremiah. {*2Ki 22:12 2Ch 34:20*} Ahikam prevented Jeremiah from being turned over to the people to be killed. {*Jer 26:20-24*} [*L119*]

766. To these I might add the prophet Habakkuk. When he complained of the stubbornness of the Jews, God replied that he would shortly send the Chaldeans into Judah. {*Hab 1:6*}

767. God further declared his purpose concerning the judgment of Judah with the words:

> "I will do a work in your days, which you will not believe when it shall be told unto you: For behold I will stir up the Chaldeans, a fierce nation and a swift: which shall walk through the breadth of the land, to possess a land which is none of theirs as their own inheritance." {*Hab 1:5,6*}

768. In the beginning of the reign of Jehoiakim, Jeremiah foretold that Zedekiah would be king of Judah, and that Nebuchadnezzar would be king of Babylon and would conquer his neighbouring countries. {*Jer 27:1-11*}

### 3397b AM, 4107 JP, 607 BC

769. The governor of Coelosyria and Phoenicia revolted against Nabopolassar king of Babylon. After Carchemish was taken, Nabopolassar sent a large army against the governor under the command of his son Nebuchadnezzar (whom he first made viceroy in the kingdom). This took place toward the end of the third and the beginning of the fourth year of Jehoiakim, king of Judah. {*Da 1:1 Jer 25:1*}.

770. When Nebuchadnezzar was made viceroy in the kingdom, God revealed several things to Jeremiah. Firstly, the Egyptians would be defeated at the Euphrates River, then later in their own country, and then Nebuchadnezzar would make himself master of Egypt. {*Jer 46:1-28*} The first came to pass almost immediately. Pharaohnecho's forces at Carchemish were cut off by Nebuchadnezzar, king of Babylon, in the fourth year of Jehoiakim. {*Jer 46:2*} The second happened after the taking of Tyre in the twenty-seventh year of the captivity of Jeconiah. {*Eze 29:17-19*}

771. In the fourth year of Jehoiakim, which was the first of Nebuchadnezzar, king of Babylon, the prophet Jeremiah reproved the Jews for not obeying the word of the Lord. He had proclaimed this word from the thirteenth year of king Josiah right up to that present fourth year of Jehoiakim, that is for twenty-three years in all. Throughout that time they had remained stubborn and disobedient, both to his admonitions and to those of all the other prophets whom the Lord had sent. [*E83*] Again he told them of the coming of Nebuchadnezzar against them and of their forthcoming captivity in Babylon, which was to last seventy years. He stated that Judah and the other nations would have to serve the king of Babylon.

### 3397c AM, 4107 JP, 607 BC

772. Lastly, the kingdom of Babylon itself would be destroyed and the land of Chaldea would be desolate. {*Jer 25:1,3,11,12*} Many years earlier, this seventy years had been mentioned by Isaiah in more obscure terms, when he spoke of the destruction of Tyre. {*Isa 23:15,17*}

### 3398a AM, 4107 JP, 607 BC

773. In the fourth year of Jehoiakim, Baruch, the son of Neriah, recorded on a scroll all that Jeremiah dictated. It contained all the words of the Lord concerning Israel and Judah, from the time of Josiah until Jeremiah's day. He read them in the house of the Lord, in the hearing of the men of Jerusalem and of all the Jews who were assembled there from all their cities on the day of

the fast, {*Jer 36:1-8*} that solemn fast which was kept yearly on the tenth day of the seventh month, {*Le 16:29 23:27 Nu 29:7*} five days before the Feast of Tabernacles. All the males from all the cities of Judah were to appear at Jerusalem. {*See note on 3395a AM. <<763>>*} [L120] Baruch was extremely amazed and afflicted in his soul at the horror of these dreadful judgments which he had recorded. Jeremiah comforted him with the word of the Lord, assuring him of his own life in the midst of all these troubles which God was revealing concerning the calamity which would be brought upon all the land by the Babylonians. {*Jer 45:1-5*} The other passage in Jeremiah may allude to this as well as to the promises made concerning the restoration of the church. {*Jer 30:1-31:40*}

774. When Nebuchadnezzar, king of Babylon, came to Judah, the Rechabites, or the descendants of Jonadab, the son of Rechab, {*2Ki 10:15*} left their tents and came into Jerusalem, for fear of the army of the Chaldeans and Syrians. They had lived in tents in accordance with the ruling of their forefather Jonadab. {*Jer 35:8-11*} Since material in this chapter of Jeremiah is written in the present tense, we gather that the time of the Rechabites refusing to drink wine occurred when the city was besieged by Nebuchadnezzar. {*Da 1:1*}

775. God gave Jehoiakim, the king of Judah, into the hands of Nebuchadnezzar, the king of Babylon, with part of the furnishings of the house of the Lord. {*Da 1:2*} This was in the ninth month called Chisleu, as may be gathered from the anniversary of the fast which was kept as a tradition of the Jews in remembrance of this calamity. {*Zec 7:3,5 8:19*} It was kept in this month. {*Jer 36:9*}

776. Nebuchadnezzar chained Jehoiakim to carry him away to Babylon. {*2Ch 36:6*} Later, upon his submission and promises of subjection, he let him stay in his own house, where he lived as his servant for three years. {*2Ki 24:1*} It was from the time of this event, when the king and people of the Jews were carried off into bondage by Nebuchadnezzar, that the seventy years of the captivity of Babylon which was foretold by the prophet Jeremiah began. {*Jer 25:11 29:10*}

777. Nebuchadnezzar ordered Ashpenaz, the overseer of the eunuchs, to carry off the best of the children of Israel, both from those of royal blood and from among the princes. {*Da 1:3*} This had been predicted to Hezekiah by Isaiah, the prophet. {*Isa 39:7*} They would be under Ashpenaz's care and were to be educated for three years in the language and sciences of the Chaldeans. The best of them were to be selected to stand before the king and serve in his palace. Among those taken from the tribe of Judah were Daniel, who was Belshazzar, Hananiah, who was Shadrach, Mishael, who was Meshach and Azariah,

who was Abednego. Each had his name changed at the discretion of the prince of the eunuchs. {*Da 1:3-7*}

778. After those Scythians (mentioned earlier {*See note on 3370c AM. <<730>>*}) had done as they pleased in Asia for twenty-eight years, Cyaxares and the Medes gave them a large feast. When they were all drunk on one particular day, he had most of their throats cut. {*\*Herodotus, l. 1. c. 106. 1:137*} As well as what happened to these Scythians, certain other Scythians of the nomads or shepherds were expelled from their own country by an opposing faction. They had been entertained by Cyaxares and employed by him, partly in hunting, partly in the education of children. But after this massacre, in which the other group of Scythians had been so poorly treated by him, they killed one of the boys whom they had taken to educate. They dressed his flesh like venison and set it before Cyaxares and his guests to eat. After this they quickly fled away to Alyattes, the king at Sardis, for protection. When Cyaxares demanded Alyattes surrender them to him, Alyattes refused, which started a five year war between the Medes and Lydians. {*\*Herodotus, l. 1. c. 73,74. 1:89,91*} As far as the Cimmerians are concerned, Alyattes drove them from all Asia. {*\*Herodotus, l. 1. c. 16. 1:19*} {*See note on 3370c AM. <<730>>*} [L121] [E84]

## 3399a AM, 4108 JP, 606 BC

779. In the ninth month of the fifth year of Jehoiakim, a solemn fast was proclaimed before the Lord to all the people at Jerusalem. This was in remembrance, it seems, of the taking of the city by the Chaldeans in the same month of the previous year. Baruch stood at the gate of the house of the Lord and read all the words of the Lord. These words were dictated to him by Jeremiah and recorded in a scroll. All the people who were assembled at Jerusalem from all the cities of Judah heard Baruch read the scroll. When the princes were told of this by Micah the son of Gemariah, they called Baruch to them. They heard him read the same scroll and fearing the king, advised him and Jeremiah to hide. When the king heard part of the scroll read, he first cut the scroll through with a pen-knife and then hurled it into the fire that was in the hearth and burned it. {*Jer 36:9-25*} In memory of this detestable act of the king, the Jews to this day keep a fast on the seventh day of the ninth month called Chisleu.

## 3399b AM, 4109 JP, 605 BC

780. When Jehoiakim had burned the scroll, he ordered Jerahmeel, the son of Hammelech, Seraiah, the son of Azriel, and Shelemiah, the son of Abdiel, to apprehend Baruch the writer and Jeremiah the prophet. God hid them and pronounced this sentence against that impious king and his kingdom:

"...Thou hast burned this roll, saying, Why hast thou written therein, saying, The king of Babylon shall certainly come and destroy this land and shall cause to cease from thence man and beast? Therefore, thus saith the LORD of Jehoiakim king of Judah; He shall have none to sit upon the throne of David: and his dead body shall be cast out in the day to the heat and in the night to the frost. And I will punish him and his seed and his servants for their iniquity; and I will bring upon them and upon the inhabitants of Jerusalem and upon the men of Judah, all the evil that I have pronounced against them...." {*Jer 36:29-32*}

781. Later, at God's command, Baruch again recorded the same words of Jeremiah which he had recorded before, as well as much additional material. {*Jer 36:26-32*}

782. Nebuchadnezzar capitalised on his victory over Necho and took all the lands which the Egyptians had possessed between Egypt and the Euphrates River. From that time on, Necho did not venture out of Egypt. {*2Ki 24:7*} Meanwhile Nabopolassar, Nebuchadnezzar's father, died in the land of Babylon, after having reigned twenty-one years. {*Ptolemy, Canon of Kings*}

783. When Nebuchadnezzar heard this, he ordered the deportation to Babylon of the captives of the Jews, Syrians, Phoenicians and Egyptians. His army and equipment were sent there also. He posted a small company at the nearest route through the desert and returned to Babylon ahead of his troops. He was made king over all his father's large dominions. When the captives were brought to Babylon, he distributed them into various colonies as he saw fit. {*Berosus, Chaldean History, l. 3.*} The vessels and other furnishings of the temple, which Nebuchadnezzar had taken with him to Babylon, were put in the temple of his god Belus. {*Da 1:2 2Ch 36:7*} His son was named after this god. According to Abydenus, in his *Assyrian History*, and Berosus, he greatly enriched and adorned that temple with the spoil which he had taken in that war. *[L122]*

784. The rest of the Scythians, who had escaped the slaughter of the Medes, returned home and were met by a large army of lusty young men. These had been born to their own wives, having been fathered by their slaves during the long absence of the Scythians. With these they fought many a sharp battle, but at length they laid aside their swords. Each man took a whip in his hand, as is more fitting for the correction of slaves, and thereby caused them all to flee. {*Herodotus, l. 4. c. 3,4. 2:201,203*}

### 3401a AM, 4110 JP, 604 BC

785. When Jehoiakim had lived in subjection to the king of Babylon for three years, he rebelled against him. {*2Ki 24:1*}

786. Daniel and his three followers refused the diet provided for them from the king's allowance. They dined only on vegetables and water. However, they were found to look better and to be of fairer complexion than the rest, who ate of the king's food. After three years, they were brought into court to attend the king. They greatly excelled in all matters of knowledge, wisdom and science, which the king chose to ask them. Their knowledge surpassed that of all the Magi and astronomers who were in his kingdom. {*Da 1:5-20*}

787. In the second year of his kingdom, Nebuchadnezzar dreamed of the great image made of various metals. When he forgot his dream, he asked his Magi and astronomers what his dream had been and what it meant. Because they could not satisfy him in so unreasonable a demand, he commanded them all to be put to death. When Daniel saw the execution being prepared and understood the reason for it, he asked the king to delay for a while. Daniel and his companions prayed to God, and God revealed both the dream and its interpretation to Daniel. He declared to the king what his dream had been, and also the four monarchies which were to come, because this was the meaning of the image which he had seen in his dream. *[E85]* As a result, the king enriched him with great gifts and made him governor of all the province of Babylon, and chief over all its wise men. Moreover, at Daniel's request, he made his three companions, Shadrach, Meshach and Abednego, principal officers in all that province. {*Da 2:1-49*}

### 3403d AM, 4113 JP, 601 BC

788. In the beginning of the sixth year of the war between the Medes and the Lydians, the war was stalemated. Thales, the philosopher of Miletus, had predicted to the Ionians that an eclipse of the sun would happen. When both the armies saw the day grow as dark as the night, they stopped fighting. Later they made peace with each other through the mediation of Syennesis of Cilicia and Labynetus, the Babylonian (who was Nebuchadnezzar). Alyattes gave his daughter Aryenis to Astyages, the son of Cyaxares, in marriage. {*Herodotus, l. 1. c. 74. 1:91,93*} This eclipse, as predicted by Thales, happened exactly when Cyaxares, the father of Astyages and king of the Medes, and Alyattes, Croesus' father and king of the Lydians, were fighting together. This is confirmed by Endemus in his *Astronomical History*. Pliny also spoke of it and noted the following: {*Pliny, l. 2. c. 9. (53) 1:203*}

> "Among the Greeks, the first one that found out how to predict the eclipses was Thales, the Milesian. He foretold the eclipse of the sun, in the fourth year of the 48th Olympiad, which was in the reign of Alyattes."

*789.* (For this is how the old copy reads, not in the reign of Astyages, as the common edition had it.) Pliny stated this happened in the one hundred and seventieth year after the building of Rome. Clement of Alexandria {*Clement, Stromateis, l. 1. c. 14. 2:315*} placed this battle of Cyaxares and the eclipse of the sun at about the 50th Olympiad. He differed greatly from the opinion of Endemus, whom he cited for it. For the time assigned by both Endemus and Pliny does not agree with the time of Cyaxares, but with the reign of Astyages. It also appears clear from Ptolemy's tables, {*Ptolemy, Great Syntaxis*} which agree with those of Hipparchus, that the sun was eclipsed in the fourth year of the 44th Olympiad. *[L123]* That is in the 147th year of Nabonassar, on the fourth day of the Egyptian month of Pachon (or Sunday, September 20, according to the Julian Calendar), three hours twenty-five minutes before noon. This eclipse was of nine digits (twelve digits is a total eclipse) and lasted almost two hours.

## 3404c AM, 4114 JP, 600 BC

*790.* Psammis, the son of Necho, reigned in Egypt for six years. {*Herodotus, l. 2. c. 161. 1:475*}

*791.* The people from Phocaea set sail from Ionia and built Massilia, or Marseilles as it is known today, on the coast of Liguria in Italy a hundred and twenty years before the naval battle at Salamis. (This is according to Marcianus in his Periegesis, as reported from Timaeus.) This was in the first year of the 45th Olympiad, according to both Eusebius and Solinus in Polyhistor. {*Eusebius, Chronicles, l. 1. 1:175*} However, Solinus confounded this first colony of the Phocaeans established in the days of Tarquinius Priscus with their later one under Servius Tullius. {*See note on 3461 AM. <<931>>*} The story of the wedding, which was the occasion for the building of this city, is described in detail by Athenaeus, based on Aristotle's account. {*Athenaeus, l. 13. (576) 6:109,111*} He spoke of the commonwealth of the Marseillians. Justin had a similar account and related the same thing, though differing in the names of the persons concerned. {*Justin, Trogus, l. 43.*}

*792.* Nebuchadnezzar's army of Syrians, Chaldeans, Moabites and Ammonites attacked Jehoiakim and destroyed all of Judah. {*2Ki 24:2*} They took three thousand and twenty-three prisoners from there in the seventh year of Nebuchadnezzar. {*Jer 52:28*}

*793.* Astyages or Ahasuerus, {*Da 9:1*} who had married Aryenis the year before, had a son called Cyaxares or Darius, the Mede. He was sixty-two years old when he succeeded Belshazzar, who was killed in the kingdom of the Chaldeans. {*Da 5:30,31*} Astyages, in the lifetime of his father, gave in marriage his daughter Mandane, who was born by his former wife, to Cambyses, son of Achemenes, king of Persia. {*Xenophon, Cyropaedia, l. 1. c. 2. s. 1. 5:9*} Cambyses derived his family pedigree from Perseus. From this union, Cyrus was born the next year. Hence, we do not believe Ctesias who, contrary to Herodotus and Xenophon and others, stated that Astyages was not related to Cyrus in any way.

## 3405c AM, 4115 JP, 599 BC

*794.* After Jehoiakim was taken prisoner by the Chaldeans, he was killed and his body was thrown out without a proper burial. He was given the burial of an ass, in that his body was dragged out of the gate of Jerusalem, as had been foretold by the prophet. {*Jer 22:18,19 36:30*} Though in a different sense from the usual, he also may be said to have slept with his fathers. {*2Ki 24:6*}

*795.* After him, his son Jehoiachin, who was also called Coniah and Jeconiah, reigned three months and ten days in Jerusalem. He did what was evil in the sight of the Lord, as his father Jehoiakim had done before him. {*2Ki 24:8,9 2Ch 36:8,9*} God pronounced this most dreadful decree against him:

> "Write this man childless, a man which shall not prosper in his days; for none of his seed shall prosper to sit in the throne of David, nor reign any more in Judah" {*Jer 22:30*}

*796.* Concerning this matter, refer to Christophorus Helvicus' book of the Genealogy of Christ. At this time, the prophecy contained in the next chapter of Jeremiah seems to have been uttered. {*Jer 23:1-40*} *[L124] [E86]*

## 3405d AM, 4115 JP, 599 BC

*797.* In the same year in which the earlier army had been sent, the servants of Nebuchadnezzar, the king of Babylon, came to besiege Jerusalem. When Nebuchadnezzar himself came to the city while his servants besieged it, Jehoiachin the king, together with his mother Nehushta, a woman of Jerusalem, his servants and officers, and with all his courtiers, came out to meet the king of Babylon. This happened in the eighth year of Nebuchadnezzar's reign over Babylon. Nebuchadnezzar took all the treasure, both of the temple and of the king's house, away with him. He broke in pieces all the golden vessels and furnishings which Solomon had made for the temple of the Lord, just as the Lord had foretold. {*Isa 39:6*} He carried away king Jehoiachin to Babylon, together with his mother, his wives and his courtiers. From among all the citizens of Jerusalem, he took ten thousand men: the magistrates, every man of strength, all the carpenters and skilled craftsmen. He left behind in Jerusalem only the poorer and weaker of the people. From the remainder of the land, he carried away seven thousand able-bodied men and a thousand of the smiths and carpenters. These were all strong men and fit for war, who were carried off as prisoners into Babylon. {*2Ki 24:8-16 2Ch 36:10 Jer 24:1 29:1,2 Eze 17:12*} Among the captives was Mordecai of the tribe of Benjamin, the son of Jair, {*Es 2:5,6*} and Ezekiel the priest, the son of Buzi. This is why, in his prophecy, Ezekiel started the captivity from this point, {*Eze 1:2,3*} which he also called his own banishment. {*Eze 40:1*} A letter, said to be Jeremiah's, was sent to those who were appointed to be carried away to Babylon. It warned them to beware of the idolatry which they would see practised in Babylon. {*Apc Bar 6:1-73*}

798. While the king of Babylon ravaged in Judah, God prepared a worm which in due time would eat out this spreading tree, {*Da 4:19-27*} for the cry of these suffering people reached the Lord:

> "Oh daughter of Babylon, wasted with misery, happy shall he be that shall reward thee, as thou hast served us, who shall take thy children and dash them against the stones." {*Ps 137:8*}

799. For in this very year, Cyrus, the Media-Persian, was born, whose father was a Persian and his mother a Mede, as I have shown before. Nebuchadnezzar himself, at the hour of his death, as Abydenus had it, uttered this prophecy:

> "There shall come a Persian Mule, who shall make use of your devils, as his fellow-soldiers, to bring you into bondage."

800. This was also foretold by that oracle given to Croesus:

> "When a mule king shall be born to the Medes...."

801. The Pythian Priests interpreted this to refer to Cyrus, who was to be born of a father and a mother of two different nations, a Persian and a Mede. {*\*Herodotus, l. 1. c. 55,91. 1:63,119*} However, Isaiah foretold, most plainly and truly, {*Isa 13:1,2*} that the Babylonians also should have a time in which they were to endure their own hell of slavery. Their children would one day be dashed against the stones before their eyes, {*Isa 13:16*} while these miserable, captive Jews would one day be restored to their liberty. Many years before the time of these events, Isaiah called their deliverer by his proper name of Cyrus. {*Isa 44:28 45:1*} God gave him the reason for this unusual revelation:

> "For my servant Jacob and for Israel my chosen's sake, have I called thee by thy name and given thee a surname, though thou hast not known me." {*Isa 45:4*}

802. As for the age of this Cyrus, Cicero cited it from Dionysius, a Persian writer, as follows: {*\*Cicero, De Divinatione, l. 1. c. 23. 20:275*} [*L125*]

> "The sun appeared to Cyrus in his sleep, standing at his feet. When Cyrus endeavoured to take the sun in his hands three times, the sun turned aside and went away. The Magi, who are counted as wise and learned men among the Persians, said that his three attempts to take hold of the sun meant that he should reign thirty years. This came to pass accordingly, for he started to reign at the age of forty and lived to the age of seventy."

803. From which dream perhaps, expounded in this way by the magicians, Cyrus took his name, for, as Ctesias correctly said:

> "*Cyrus*, in the Persian language, means *the sun.*"

804. Plutarch said the same thing. {*\*Plutarch, Artaxerxes, l. 1. c. 1. (1012) 11:129*} Likewise, Chur and Churshid, in the Persian poets, agreed. When the work of Cicero is compared with Daniel, it appears that Darius, the Mede, or Cyaxares, the son of Astyages, who was Cyrus' uncle, was born before Cyrus. Therefore, Xenophon mentioned Darius saying: {*Da 5:31*} {*\*Xenophon, Cyropaedia, l. 6. c. 1. s. 6. 6:123*}

> "seeing I am here present and am older than Cyrus, it is fitting that I speak first."

805. The same author stated that when Cyrus wrote to Cyaxares he used the following words: {*\*Xenophon, Cyropaedia, l. 4. c. 5. s. 27. 5:377*}

> "I advise you, though I be the younger of the two."

806. Nebuchadnezzar made Mattaniah, the son of Josiah, king in place of his nephew Jeconiah and changed his name to Zedekiah, meaning *the justice of the Lord.* {*Jer 37:1 2Ki 24:17*} Nebuchadnezzar had made a covenant with Zedekiah, requiring an oath of allegiance from him, and Zedekiah had sworn an oath by God to comply. {*2Ch 36:13 Eze 17:13,14,18*} By giving him this new name, he intended to remind Zedekiah of the just judgment of God, if Zedekiah would break the oath.

807. Zedekiah reigned a full eleven years in Jerusalem and did evil in the sight of the Lord his God. [*E87*] He did not humble himself before Jeremiah, the prophet, who spoke to him in the name of the Lord, but stiffened his neck and hardened his heart, so that he would not return to the Lord God of Israel. {*Jer 1:3 32:1,2 2Ki 24:18,19 2Ch 36:11-13*} Indeed, all the leaders of the priests, and the people of the whole land, transgressed the law and polluted the house of the Lord which God had sanctified

in Jerusalem. Nor would they listen to the word of the Lord, which came to them by the mouth of his prophet Jeremiah and other prophets. Instead, they despised them and mocked the messengers which God sent to them, until the fire of God's fury burst upon his people. {Jer 37:2 2Ch 36:14-16}.

808. After Jeconiah was carried away, God, in a vision of two baskets of figs, revealed to Jeremiah the captivity of the new king Zedekiah and the remainder of the people. {Jer 24:1,2,8,9,}

809. In the beginning of Zedekiah's reign, Jeremiah prophesied the captivity and restoration of the Elamites. {Jer 49:34,39} For Nebuchadnezzar had taken from Astyages the whole province of Elam, including the city of Susa on the Ulai River, and annexed it to his kingdom. {Jer 25:25 Da 8:1,2} Later, these Elamites combined with the Medes against the Babylonians. {Isa 21:2} When Belshazzar was overthrown, they recovered their state again under Cyrus, who appointed their chief city of Susa to be the capital of the Persian kingdom. {*Strabo, l. 15. c. 3. s. 2. 7:157} [L126]

810. When the envoys from the various kings of Edom, Moab, Ammon, Tyre and Sidon came to Jerusalem to visit the new king Zedekiah, God told Jeremiah to give each of them chains and whips, to be presented to their masters. He commanded them all to submit to Nebuchadnezzar and stop listening to their soothsayers and stargazers, who advised them not to submit. He advised Zedekiah to remain loyal to the king of Babylon and to beware of the false prophets. By threats and promises he persuaded many of the people to submit to and obey the king of Babylon. {Jer 39:1-18}

811. When Jeconiah was carried away with the other captives, Zedekiah sent Elasah, the son of Shaphan and Gemariah the son of Hilkiah, to Nebuchadnezzar in Babylon. Jeremiah sent with them a letter which he had written to the elders, the priests and prophets, and the rest of the people who had been carried from Jerusalem by Nebuchadnezzar, king of Babylon. In the letter, the prophet instructed them how to behave themselves in captivity, and comforted them with a gracious promise of deliverance at the end of the seventy years. He predicted the great calamities which were to befall those whom they had left behind in Jerusalem. He foretold the miserable end which would come to the two false prophets, Ahab, the son of Kolaiah, and Zedekiah, the son of Maaseiah. {Jer 29:1-23}

### 3406 AM, 4116 JP, 598 BC

812. Seraiah sent letters back with Zedekiah's messengers, when they returned from Babylon. They delivered

these to Zephaniah (who was the second chief priest) and to the rest of the priests at Jerusalem. {2Ki 25:18} Seraiah denounced what the prophet Jeremiah had written to them. When this was read to Jeremiah, he pronounced a heavy judgment from God upon him. {Jer 29:24-32} It seems that it was at this time, also, that he made those notable prophecies concerning the kingdom of Christ and restoration of the church in Jeremiah. {See note on 3395b AM. <<766>>} {Jer 30:1-31:40}

### 3407 AM, 4117 JP, 597 BC

813. Croesus was born. He was the son of Alyattes, king of Lydia, and his mother was a woman of Caria. He was thirty-five years of age when he began to reign. {*Herodotus, l. 1. c. 26,92. 1:29,121}

### 3408d AM, 4118 JP, 596 BC

814. In the fifth month of the fourth year of Zedekiah, Hananiah, a false prophet, made a false prophesy. He said that at the end of two years all the vessels and furnishings of the house of the Lord, together with Jeconiah and all the people who had been carried away to Babylon, would return and be brought home again. When Jeremiah mocked him, he took a wooden yoke from about Jeremiah's neck and broke it. He said that the Lord would break the yoke of Nebuchadnezzar, within two years precisely, from off the neck of all the nations.

815. Jeremiah replied that God, instead of that wooden yoke, would lay an iron one upon the neck of all these nations, under which they should bow, and serve the king of Babylon. {Jer 28:1-14}

### 3409a AM, 4118 JP, 596 BC

816. Hananiah, the false prophet, died in the seventh month of this year, in accordance with the word of Jeremiah. {Jer 28:16,17} Astyages, after the death of his father Cyaxares, reigned over the Medes for thirty-five years. {*Herodotus, l. 1. c. 130. 1:169} He is also called Ahasuerus, {Da 9:1} or Assuerus. {Apc Tob 14:15}

### 3409c AM, 4119 JP, 595 BC

817. God, through his prophet Jeremiah, foretold that Babylon and the land of Chaldea would be overrun and laid waste by the Medes and Persians. At the same time he comforted his people with the sweet promises of their deliverance. {Jer 50:1-51:64} [E88]

818. Zedekiah, in the fourth year of his reign, sent Seraiah, the son of Neriah, who was the son of Maaseiah, to Babylon. It was to him that Jeremiah had delivered the prophecies of the destruction of Babylon, which were written in a scroll. [L127] He read the scroll to the people and threw it into the Euphrates River.

{*Jer 51:59-64*} His brother Baruch, also the son of Neriah, the son of Maaseiah, {*Jer 32:12 51:59*} {*Apc Bar 1:1*} and who was Jeremiah's scribe, is thought to have gone to Babylon with Seraiah.

## 3409d AM, 4119 JP, 595 BC

*819.* Baruch is said to have read all the words of his own scroll to Jeconiah, the son of Jehoiakim, and to all the captives that were dwelling with him at that time in Babylon. This was in the fifth year (that is after Jeconiah was carried away to Babylon) in the seventh month, at the time when the Chaldeans took Jerusalem and set it on fire. {*Apc Bar 1:2-4*} Some think that this was the same month in which Jeconiah gave himself up to the king of Babylon, and Jerusalem was taken and perhaps partially set on fire by the Chaldeans. I cannot agree with Sulpicius Severus, who, perhaps taking it from that text in the Apocrypha, stated that at this very time: {*Sulpicius Severus, Sacred History, l. 1. c. 53. 11:96*}

> "Nebuchadnezzar entered Jerusalem with his army and laid both city and walls, temple and all, level with the ground."

*820.* Yet the guess of Franc. Junius concerning the quenching of the fire, and the taking of the city, was somewhat more plausible than that of our seminary priests of Downay, when they said that the whole time of the taking of Jerusalem lasted eleven years before it was wholly burned.

*821.* This refers to the time from when it was taken under Jeconiah until the time it was taken under Zedekiah. This scroll was written in the fifth year of that interval of time. Hugo Grotius thought that the original author meant here that the fifth year was after the deportation of Jeconiah. The phrase *the rest of the burning of Jerusalem*, was added later by someone else who was of the opinion that Baruch never went to Babylon until after the burning of Jerusalem, which happened in the reign of Zedekiah.

*822.* Ezekiel had his first vision from God in the beginning of the thirtieth year from the restoration of the worship of God in the eighteenth year of Josiah's reign, or the fifth year of the captivity of Jehoiachin or Jeconiah, on the fifth day of the fourth month (on Saturday, July 24). He was among the rest of the company that were carried away to Babylon on the Chebar or Chaborra River, according to Strabo and Ptolemy. {*Eze 1:1-28*} From here he was sent to be a prophet among the Jews of the captivity. When he came to those who lived at Telabib near the Chebar River, he sat down in a state of distress for seven days. After this, God reminded him of his call, with promises if he obeyed and with threats if he refused. He confirmed him with a new sign and gave him courage and boldness through his word. {*Eze 2:1-3:27*}

*823.* The prophet was commanded to make a drawing of the siege of Jerusalem, and to lie on his side for a very long time, for three hundred and ninety days. This was to symbolise how many days the siege of the city of Jerusalem would last and the number of years of the iniquity of the house of Israel from the time of Jeroboam. {*Eze 4:1-17*} {*See note on 3030a AM. <<481>>*}

## 3410b AM, 4120 JP, 594 BC

*824.* Shortly after Psammis, king of Egypt, returned from a journey he had made into Ethiopia, he died. His son Apries succeeded him, and reigned for twenty-five years. {**Herodotus, l. 2. c. 161. 1:475*} The Bible calls him Pharaohhophra. {*Jer 44:30*} With a well-equipped army he made an incursion into the isle of Cyprus and upon Phoenicia. He took Sidon by force, and the rest of that country by the very dread and terror which his name evoked. After a major victory at sea over both the Cypriots and Phoenicians, he returned to Egypt with much spoil taken from them. {**Diod. Sic., l. 1. c. 68. s. 1. 1:237*} [L128] It is reported of him that he said that no god was able to put him out of his kingdom, because he believed he had made his kingdom very secure. {**Herodotus, l. 2. c. 169. 1:483*} In Ezekiel (as Tremellius has noted), it is most elegantly expressed in that allegorical personification:

> "The river is mine own, for I have made it for myself." {*Eze 29:3*}

## 3410c AM, 4120 JP, 594 BC

*825.* When Ezekiel had lain on his left side for the three hundred and fifty days, he turned onto his right side and lay there for a further forty days. (Eze 4:9 seems to imply that the period of forty days overlapped the three hundred and ninety days so Ezekiel lay on his side for a total of three hundred and ninety days not four hundred and thirty days. However, Eze 4:5,6 seems to imply two separate periods are in view. Editor.) The former symbolised the three hundred and ninety years of Israel's iniquity and the latter the forty of years of Judah's iniquity, each day representing one year. {*Eze 4:5,6*} See also {*Eze 5:1-7:27*}

## 3410d AM, 4120 JP, 594 BC

*826.* On the fifth day of the sixth month of the sixth year of Jeremiah's captivity (which was Wednesday, September 22), God carried Ezekiel away by the Spirit to Jerusalem. There, in a vision, he showed him the infinite idolatry that was being practised there, and the plagues which were to befall the city for this, as well as a vision of the Spirit leaving the city. {*Eze 8:1 9:1-11:25*}

827. According to Ezekiel's prediction, Pelatia, the son of Benaiah, died. God comforted the godly during their captivity in Babylon by the sanctification of his presence, and with his evangelical promises for the time to come. When the vision was over, the prophet was brought back by the Spirit to his people in Chaldea and there declared to them all that God had shown him. {Eze 11:13-25} [E89]

### 3411a AM, 4120 JP, 594 BC

828. God, by signs and verbally, predicted Zedekiah's flight by night, the putting out of his eyes, his going into captivity and his dying in Babylon. He also foretold the captivity of the Jews and the calamities which they were to endure before this captivity. {Eze 12:1-28} In this same year, the next seven chapters of Ezekiel were written. From his writings we understand that Daniel's name was at that time very famous for his continual prayers on behalf of the people of the captivity. {Eze 14:14,20} Zedekiah had no regard for the covenant he had made and the oath which he had sworn, and rebelled against Nebuchadnezzar. {Eze 17:15,17}

### 3411d AM, 4121 JP, 593 BC

829. In the seventh year of Jeconiah's captivity, on the tenth day of the fifth month (Sunday, August 27), Ezekiel reproved the elders for their gross hypocrisy in coming to ask counsel of God. He prophesied regarding the calamity that was to befall all the nations. He pronounced God's judgment on the idolaters and his comfort to the godly. {Eze 20:1-23:49}

### 3413 AM, 4123 JP, 591 BC

830. After Battus had founded the kingdom of Cyrene, he was succeeded by his son Arcesilaus, who reigned for sixteen years. {*Herodotus, l. 4. c. 159. 2:363}

### 3414a AM, 4123 JP, 591 BC

831. This was a sabbatical year, in which the men of Jerusalem set their servants at liberty, according to the law. {Ex 21:2 De 15:1,2,12 Jer 34:8-10} The men of Jerusalem also heard that Nebuchadnezzar was approaching with his army. Nebuchadnezzar marched against Zedekiah and ravaged all the country. He took their strongholds and came right up to the walls of Jerusalem. {*Josephus, Antiq., l. 10. c. 7. s. 3. (109) 6:217} With his entire forces he had already besieged and taken all the cities of Judah except for Lachish, Azekah and Jerusalem. {Jer 34:1,7}

### 3414b AM, 4124 JP, 590 BC

832. The siege of Jerusalem did not begin until the middle of winter. In the ninth year of the reign of Zedekiah, on the tenth day (Thursday, January 30), Nebuchadnezzar came up to Jerusalem with all his army, and built citadels all around the city. {2Ki 25:1 Jer 39:1 52:4} In memory of this event, a yearly fast is kept among the Jews which began at the time of the captivity, and continues to this day. {Zec 8:19} [L129]

833. On the very day of the siege of Jerusalem, God revealed its complete destruction to Ezekiel, who was in Chaldea. This was represented to him in symbolic form by a seething pot. His wife died that day in the evening, but he was told not to mourn her death. In this way he was to signify the grievous calamity that would befall the Jews, which would surpass all expressions of grief by mourning. {Eze 24:1-27}

### 3414d AM, 4124 JP, 590 BC

834. God told the prophet Jeremiah to tell Zedekiah of the complete destruction and burning of Jerusalem at the hands of the king of Babylon. Zedekiah himself was to be carried away prisoner to Babylon, but he would die in peace and have an honourable burial. {Jer 34:1-7}

835. For this prophecy, Zedekiah imprisoned Jeremiah in the king's prison house. This happened in the tenth year of Zedekiah and the beginning of the eighteenth year of Nebuchadnezzar. Jeremiah recovered the land of Hanameel by right of redemption. {Jer 32:1-16} Then everything came to pass which Jeremiah had foretold and which is contained in his book. {Jer 32:1-33:26}

836. Pharaohhophra, also called Vaphris, came with his army from Egypt to help Zedekiah. The Chaldeans then raised the siege of Jerusalem. Jeremiah had been allowed to go free during the siege and was not thrown into the dungeon until later. Zedekiah sent messengers to Jeremiah to ask him to make intercession to God for the deliverance of the people. Jeremiah told him that the Egyptians would return to their own land, and the Chaldeans would come back to Jerusalem and destroy the city by fire. {Jer 37:3-10}

837. When the siege was raised, the people took back the Hebrew servants whom they had previously set free, because they no longer feared the enemy. They forced them back into their service, which was contrary to the law and covenant. Jeremiah reproved them for this barbarous act, telling them that if they released their servants, they would escape the sword, famine and pestilence of the returning Chaldeans. He told them the Chaldeans would be returning to make war again, and would take their city and burn it to the ground. {Jer 34:11-22}

838. While the Chaldeans withdrew to fight the Egyptian army, Jeremiah planned to escape, but was stopped at the gate by the princes. He was taken and scourged, and cast into the dungeon in the house of

Jonathan the scribe, where he was left for a long time. {Jer 37:11-16} At this time, when Nebuchadnezzar was pursuing the Egyptians, in the eighteenth year of his reign, he took eight hundred and thirty-two prisoners from Jerusalem and sent them all back to Babylon as a safeguard. {Jer 52:29}

839. Pittacus of Mitylene was one of the *Seven Wise Men* of ancient Greece. He was sent with a navy against Phrynon, who was surnamed the Pancratiast, which means *a man excellent in all feats of chivalry.* Phrynon was an Olympian, who won the bell in the games at Olympus. At that time, Phrynon was serving as the general of the Athenian army, and he had taken two towns, Sigeum and Achillium, from the Lesbians. In the ensuing battle with Pittacus, the Athenians were victorious. They took the shield of Alcaeus, since the poet of Mitylene had thrown it away in his efforts to escape. *[E90]* They hung it up in the temple of Athena in Sigeum. After this, Phrynon challenged any man that dared, to encounter him in single combat. Pittacus accepted the challenge and with a little net which he hid under the hollow of his shield, he caught him by the head and killed him with his three-forked spear. The Mitylenians offered him a large portion of land for killing Phrynon. He only accepted as much land as he could throw his spear across. On this land he built a temple and called it Pittacium. *[L130]* This story seems to be garbled and is less than correct in Herodotus. {*Herodotus, l. 5. c. 95. 3:117} However, the defects in his account are compensated for by taking the account of Plutarch together with Strabo. {*Plutarch, Malice of Herodotus, l. 1. c. 15. 11:29} {*Strabo, l. 13. c. 1. s. 38. 6:77} {Polyaenus, Strategmata, l. 1.} Festus stated that the word *Retiarius* meant a fighter with a net. Diogenes Laertius stated that the Mitylenians twenty years before his death, voluntarily made him their sovereign in return for that service. {*Diogenes Laertius, Pittacus, l. 1. c. 4. (75) 1:81} He said that this took place in the third year of the 52nd Olympiad. {*Diogenes Laertius, Pittacus, l. 1. c. 4. (79) 1:81} In carefully calculating it, I chose to place it in the third year of the forty-seventh, though Eusebius placed it in the second year of the 43rd Olympiad. This seemed to agree more closely, because in the *Catalogue of the Victorious Runners* who won prizes, Phrynon is said to have won the bell in the 36th Olympiad. The war did not end with this duel, but their quarrel was referred by both parties to Periander of Corinth, who was considered to be another of the *Seven Wise Men* of the world. As an impartial arbitrator, he ordered that each party should hold on to what they had in their possession. The Mitylenians were to keep the town of Achillium and the Athenians, Sigeum. {*Herodotus, l. 5. c. 94,95. 3:115,117} {*Strabo, l. 13. c. 1. s. 38. 6:77} Sosicates' account states that

Periander died six years after this and just before the 49th Olympiad. {*Diogenes Laertius, Periander, l. 1. c. 1. (95) 1:99} This reveals Herodotus' error in his chronology, in which he claimed this peace between the Athenians and Mitylenians to have been made toward the latter end of the life of Peisistratus or his successors in the Athenian government.

## 3415b AM, 4125 JP, 589 BC

840. In the tenth year of the captivity of Jeconiah and on the twelfth day of the tenth month (on Sunday, February 1), Ezekiel prophesied against Pharaoh and all Egypt. Ezekiel foretold that Pharaoh would prove to be only a staff or reed to the house of Israel. Pharaoh's attempts to relieve Israel would all be in vain. He predicted that Pharaoh himself would be defeated in the desert of Libya by the Cyrenians. {See note on 3430c AM. <<875>>} Egypt was to be miserably wasted by the Babylonians, and the Egyptian desolation would last for forty years. {Eze 29:1-16}

## 3415c AM, 4125 JP, 589 BC

841. When Nebuchadnezzar had routed the Egyptian army, he promptly returned to the siege of Jerusalem about the fifteenth day of the third month, three hundred and ninety days before he took Jerusalem. This is a similitude to the total length in years of the kingdom of Judah. {Eze 4:5,8} Jeremiah told Zedekiah that he would be given into the hands of Nebuchadnezzar. Zedekiah then commanded him to be transferred from the dungeon of the prison in Jonathan's house to the court of the prison. He was to be given a roll of bread each day as long as there was any bread left in the city. {Jer 37:17-21}

## 3415d AM, 4125 JP, 589 BC

842. As the siege continued, Zedekiah again inquired of Jeremiah, but he still sent him the same answer: both the king and people must fall into Nebuchadnezzar's hands. He said if any stayed in the city they would perish by the sword, or from famine or pestilence. However, any who would go out and submit to the king of Babylon would have their lives spared. {Jer 21:1-14}

843. The princes cast Jeremiah into Malchiah's dungeon, which was in the court of the prison, for answering the king in this way. He was delivered with the help of Ebedmelech, one of the king's eunuchs, and was again consulted by the king. When he still persisted in pronouncing judgment against the land of Judah, he was kept in the court of the prison until the city was taken. {Jer 38:1-28} He assured Ebedmelech, in the name of the Lord, that he would be kept free from all harm and danger during that calamity. {Jer 39:15-18}

**3416c AM, 4126 JP, 588 BC**

*844.* Tyre rejoiced to see the wretched treatment Jerusalem experienced at Nebuchadnezzar's hand. However, in the eleventh year of Jeconiah's captivity, on the first day of the first month, Ezekiel prophesied that Tyre would also perish in like manner at the same hand, and that all who had known of her former wealth and bravery would be amazed. *[L131]* Tremellius and Pradus placed this prophecy in the fifth month. This would put it in the twelfth year of Jeconiah's captivity in Babylon. Ezekiel also foretold the same misery for the Sidonians, Tyre's neighbours. {*Eze 26:1-28:26*} At that time the fame of Daniel's wisdom was so great, even in foreign nations, that they spoke proverbially of people being *as wise as Daniel*. God upbraided Ithobolus, king of Tyre, for his pride and arrogance in his mind: *[E91]*

> "behold, thou art wiser than Daniel; no secret can be hid from thee." {*Eze 28:3*}

*845.* In the same year, on the seventh day of the first month (Tuesday, April 26), God revealed to Ezekiel his intention of sending Nebuchadnezzar and his army against Pharaoh, to the ruin of Egypt. {*Eze 30:20-26*}

*846.* In the same year, on the first day of the third month (Sunday, June 19), God declared that the Egyptians could no more avoid this judicial sentence than the Assyrians could. {*Eze 31:1-18*}

**3416d AM, 4126 JP, 588 BC**

*847.* Near the end of the eleventh year of Zedekiah, {*Jer 1:3*} on the ninth day of the fourth month (Wednesday, July 27), the famine became quite severe in Jerusalem. The city wall was broken through and the Chaldeans entered. {*2Ki 25:2-4 Jer 39:2,3 52:5-7*}

*848.* When the city was taken, Zedekiah and all the men of war fled by night.

*849.* The Chaldeans pursued them and took Zedekiah, bringing him as a prisoner to Riblah, where Nebuchadnezzar was. He saw his children slaughtered, and then he had his eyes put out. He was chained with bronze shackles and taken away from there to Babylon. {*2Ki 25:4-7 Jer 39:4-7 52:7-11*} The prophecies were fulfilled which said that he would see the king of Babylon, {*Jer 32:4 34:3*} but he would not see Babylon, although he would die there. {*Eze 12:13*}

*850.* On the seventh day of the fifth month (Wednesday, August 24), Nebuzaradan, captain of the guard, was ordered by Nebuchadnezzar to enter the city. {*2Ki 25:8*} He spent two days preparing provisions. On the tenth day of that month (Saturday, August 27), he carried out his orders. He set fire to the temple and to the king's palace. He also burned all the noblemen's houses to the ground, with all the rest of the houses in Jerusalem. {*Jer 52:13 39:8*} Our countryman Tho. Lydiate thought that the fire was started on the seventh day but not fully burned down until the tenth. In remembrance of this calamity, the fast of the fifth month was ordained to be kept. {*Zec 7:3,5 8:19*} This fast is observed by the Jews to this day. However, it is kept by them on the ninth day, and not the tenth, of the month of Ab. The temple was destroyed toward the end of the nineteenth year of Nebuchadnezzar's reign. {*Jer 52:12 2Ki 25:9*} This was in the beginning of the first year of the 48th Olympiad, in the one hundred and sixtieth year of Nabonassar's account and four hundred and twenty-four years, three months and eight days from the time that Solomon laid the first stone for the temple.

*851.* In the same fifth month, {*Jer 1:3*} all the walls of Jerusalem were levelled to the ground. Nebuchadnezzar carried back to Babylon all the remaining people in the city, all those who had formerly defected to him, all the common people of the city, all the treasure of the king and of his nobles, and the furnishings of the temple. {*Jer 39:8,9 52:14-23 2Ki 25:10-17 2Ch 36:18-20*} *[L132]* Hence, the people of Judah were carried away out of their own land, four hundred and sixty-eight years after David began to reign over it. {*Jer 52:27 2Ki 25:21*} These events have been recorded as happening three hundred and eighty-eight years after the separation of the ten tribes from the tribe of Judah, and one hundred and thirty-four years after the destruction of the kingdom of Israel.

# The Sixth Age of the World

## The Babylonian Empire

### 3416d AM, 4126 JP, 588 BC

*852.* Nebuzaradan left the simplest of the people in the land of Judah to dress the vineyards and to till the ground. The king appointed Gedaliah, the son of Ahikam, a man of the same country, as governor, but without any kingly title. {*Jer 39:10 40:5,7 42:16 2Ki 25:11,22,23*} The reason for this is, as Sulpicius Severus noted: {*\*Sulpicius Severus, Sacred History, l. 1. c. 53. 11:96*}

> "To have some preeminence over a few miserable persons was not reckoned to be any dignity at all."

*853.* Nebuchadnezzar was at Riblah when Nebuzaradan brought him Seraiah, the chief priest, and Zephaniah, the second priest, as well as the three keepers of the gate of the temple and other principal men. There they were put to death. {*Jer 52:24-27 2Ki 25:18-21*} Jehozadak, the son of Seraiah and his successor as high priest, was carried away captive to Babylon. {*1Ch 6:15*}

*854.* Jeremiah was bound with chains and was carried off with the rest as far as Ramah on the way to Babylon. There his irons were removed and he was set free. He was given his choice of either going to Babylon and being honourably treated there, or staying in the country with the miserable wretches who had been left behind. He decided to stay, and was sent back with money in his purse to Gedaliah, the governor, at Mizpah in the tribe of Benjamin. {*Jer 39:11-14 40:1-6*} [E92]

*855.* The captains and companies who had fled by night when the city was first taken, were scattered all over the country. {*2Ki 25:4 Jer 52:7*} After a while, they and all the Jews who had fled to the Moabites and Ammonites and other nearby nations, returned to live under Gedalia in their own country. They were given a good provision of wine and oil and other summer fruits to live on. {*Jer 40:7-12 2Ki 25:23,24*}

*856.* Ishmael, the son of Nethaniah, of the family of the kings of Judah, was bribed by Baalis, king of the Ammonites, to kill Gedaliah. He came to him at Mizpah with ten resolute fellows. They were graciously entertained by Gedaliah, who gave no credence to those who told him of Ishmael's treachery, and who died as a result. {*Jer 40:13-16*}

### 3417a AM, 4126 JP, 588 BC

*857.* In the seventh month, Ishmael, with his ten companions, murdered Gedaliah as well as any Jews, Chaldeans and soldiers they found in Mizpah. {*Jer 41:1-3*}

*2Ki 25:25*} In remembrance of this, the Jews keep a fast to this day, on the third day of this month of Tishri. A day or two later, this same Ishmael killed some more men who were clad in mourning apparel, bringing offerings and frankincense from Sichem, Shiloh and Samaria to the house of the Lord that now lay in ruins. These had been tricked by him into going to Mizpah, where they were murdered in the open streets. Their bodies were cast into the pit made by King Asa. {*Jer 41:4-9*}

*858.* Ishmael returned to the king of Ammon, having taken the king of Judah's daughters and the rest of the people who were left at Mizpah as his prisoners. [L133] Johanan, the son of Kareah, met him with army officers and took away all his prisoners, setting them free. Ishmael, with only eight men in his company, fled to the Ammonites. {*Jer 41:10-15*}

*859.* Johanan and all his captains, with the rest of the people they had freed, remained near Bethlehem. For fear of the Chaldeans, they intended to flee into Egypt. {*Jer 41:16-18*} Many of them went to Jeremiah and asked him for an answer from God about this plan. After ten days, he told them God's message. He exhorted them not to leave their country. He assured them that if they stayed, God would protect them there and no harm would come to them from the Babylonians. If, however, they went into Egypt, every one of them would perish by sword, by famine or by other kinds of death. The majority went into Egypt according to their old custom of never obeying good counsel, or God's commands. They took Jeremiah and Baruch, the son of Neriah, with them to Tahpanhes. There, Jeremiah declared to them by means of symbolism, the destruction of Egypt by Nebuchadnezzar. {*Jer 42:1-43:13*} {*\*Sulpicius Severus, Sacred History, l. 2. c. 4. 11:98*}

### 3417b AM, 4127 JP, 587 BC

*860.* In the twelfth year of Jeconiah's captivity, on the fifth day of the tenth month (Wednesday, January 25), when news of the taking of Jerusalem reached Ezekiel, the prophet foretold of the utter destruction of the remaining Israelites. This was after the others had fled to Egypt. {*Eze 33:21-29*}

*861.* In the same twelfth year, in the first day of the twelfth month (Wednesday, March 22). Ezekiel prophesied of the grievous plague and affliction which Nebuchadnezzar would bring on the land of Egypt. {*Eze 32:1-16*}

*862.* On the fifteenth day, the same prophet predicted of Pharaoh and all the people of Egypt that they would be brought down to destruction, along with the rest of the uncircumcised nations. {*Eze 32:17-32*}

863. Jeremiah prophesied of the destruction which would follow the Israelites at Migdol not far from the Red Sea, {*Ex 14:2*} at Tahpanhes (or Daphne-Pelusium), at Noph, at Memphis and in Pathros, a country in Egypt. As a certain sign of their own impending misery, he gave them the sign of Pharaoh, or Apries, king of Egypt, whom they would see brought low before their eyes. {*Jer 44:1-30*}

864. Obadiah the prophet uttered a prophecy against Edom, which shamefully gloated over the calamity of the Jews when Jerusalem was destroyed. Jeremiah and the authors of the Psalms, who wrote about the same time, also made a similar prophecy. {*Jer 49:7 Eze 25:12 Ps 79:1-13 137:1-9*}

## 3418 AM, 4128 JP, 586 BC

865. When Cyrus had lived twelve years or more with his father in Persia, his grandfather Astyages sent for him. He and his mother Mandane went to him in Media. {*Xenophon, Cyropaedia, l. 1. c. 3. s. 1. 5:27*}

## 3419 AM, 4129 JP, 585 BC

866. When Ithobal was reigning in Tyre, it was besieged for thirteen years by Nebuchadnezzar. Josephus reported this from Philostratus and others who recorded the affairs of Phoenicia. {*Josephus, Antiq., l. 10. c. 11. s. 1. (228) 6:285*} {*Josephus, Apion, l. 1. c. 21. (156) 1:225*} It seems that during these thirteen years the neighbouring countries of the Moabites, the Ammonites and Edomites were also subdued by Nebuchadnezzar, in accordance with the predictions of the prophets. {*Jer 27:1-22 48:1-49:39 Eze 25:1-17*} [*E93*]

## 3420 AM, 4130 JP, 584 BC

867. In the twenty-third year of his reign, while Nebuchadnezzar besieged Tyre, which borders the land of Israel, {*Jos 19:29*} [*L134*] Nebuzaradan, captain of his guard, took away together seven hundred and forty-five remaining Jews and Israelites into Babylon. {*Jer 52:30*} This extreme depopulation was foretold by Ezekiel when he referred to the iniquity of Israel lasting three hundred and ninety years, which was distinct from Judah's iniquity, lasting forty years until its end. {*Eze 4:5,6*} {*See note on 3380d AM. <<743>>*}

## 3421 AM, 4131 JP, 583 BC

868. Cyrus was now almost sixteen years of age. Evilmerodach, the king of Assyria's son, was about to marry a wife called Nitocris. He went with a large army of cavalry and foot soldiers to the borders of Media. There he did as he pleased while hunting in the country. Astyages, with his grandson Cyrus and with

Cyaxares, marched out and engaged him in a battle with the cavalry. Cyrus was just old enough to bear arms. They defeated the Assyrians and drove them from their borders of Media. {*Xenophon, Cyropaedia, l. 1. c. 4. s. 18-23. 5:61-69*}

869. After this, Cyrus was called home by his father Cambyses. He had one year left of schooling. {*Xenophon, Cyropaedia, l. 1. c. 4. s. 25. 5:69*} {*Xenophon, Cyropaedia, l. 1. c. 5. s. 1. 5:75*} It is also mentioned in Athenaeus, based on Dinon's account, that Cyrus, who served Astyages as the holder of his battle-axe and later as one of his armour bearers, returned into Persia. It was at this time, while Astyages feasted his friends, that Angares, who was a musician, sang a song in which he said: {*Athenaeus, l. 14. (633e) 6:419*}

> "A fierce wild beast, more fierce than any boar, was let go, and sent into a sunny country and he should reign over all these provinces and should, with a handful of men, maintain war against large armies...."

870. Astyages tried to call Cyrus back again, but could not get him.

## 3422 AM, 4132 JP, 582 BC

871. Cyrus spent seventeen years among boys, and then he spent ten more years among the youths. {*Xenophon, Cyropaedia, l. 1. c. 5. s. 4. 5:79*}

## 3424 AM, 4134 JP, 580 BC

872. In the 50th Olympiad, Epitelides, the Lacedemonian, won the race in running. Certain men from Cnidos and Rhodes hoped to avoid the hostility of the kings of Asia by agreeing to make a colony elsewhere. They chose Pentathlus as their leader. He was a Cnidian, who was of the family of Hippotas, the son of Hercules. They sailed to Sicily when Egesta and Selinus were at war with each other. Pentathlus was killed while fighting for the side of Selinus. The rest planned to return home and made Gorgus, Thestor and Epethersides their captains. These men were all relatives of Pentathlus. They set sail from there and were persuaded to settle in the isle of Lipara. {*Diod. Sic., l. 5. c. 9. 3:121*}

## 3429 AM, 4139 JP, 575 BC

873. Arcesilaus reigned sixteen years in Cyrene and was succeeded by his son Battus who was surnamed *The Fortunate*. A large number of Greeks were advised by the oracle at Delphi to go to Battus in Cyrene. They ravaged the lands of the bordering Libyans and divided it among themselves. Before this, the colony in Cyrene had for fifty-six years consisted only of those who had come from the isle of Thera, whose founder had also been called Battus. {*Herodotus, l. 4. c. 159. 2:363*}

## 3429c AM, 4139 JP, 575 BC

*874.* On the tenth day of the first month (as Jonathan stated in the Chaldee Paraphrase) of the twenty-fifth year of the captivity of Jeconiah (Monday, April 30), and in the fourteenth year after the destruction of Jerusalem, Ezekiel had a vision. In this vision the temple, the city and the kingdom of the Israelites were restored. This also foreshadowed the restoration of the church by Christ with its greatness, honour and excellence. {*Eze 40:1-48:35*} (Ussher incorrectly listed this in the following year, as one can tell from the year of the captivity of Jeconiah. {*See note on 3431c AM. <<877>>*} Editor.)

## 3430c AM, 4140 JP, 574 BC

*875.* The Libyans, who were driven out from their lands and country by the inhabitants of Cyrene, put themselves under the protection of Apries, king of Egypt. He gathered a large army together and sent it against the Cyrenians, who were camped at a place called Irasa near the fountain called Thestes. These routed the army of the Egyptians so that only a few of them were left to return into Egypt. *[L135]* The Egyptians grew angry with Apries and revolted from him. They thought that he had deliberately sent them on a suicide mission to be rid of them. They reasoned that he did this so that he might more easily dominate the rest who were left. {*\*Herodotus, l. 4. c. 159. 2:365*} {*\*Herodotus, l. 2. c. 161. 1:475*} {*\*Diod. Sic., l. 1. c. 68. s. 2. 1:237*}

## 3431b AM, 4141 JP, 573 BC

*876.* Amasis, also called Sais (who was frequently spoken of by Plato {*Plato, Timaeus*}), was sent by his father to stop this rebellion of the people. However, they made him king instead of his father. Apries sent Paterbames, a person of nobility, to call Amasis back. When Paterbames returned, they cut off his nose and ears because he did not bring Amasis back with him. After this unworthy act took place, all the people defected from him to Amasis. {*\*Herodotus, l. 2. c. 162. 1:477*}

## 3431c AM, 4141 JP, 573 BC

*877.* On the first day of the first month of the twenty-seventh year of the captivity of Jeconiah (Tuesday, April 21,) God promised to give all Egypt to Nebuchadnezzar as spoil, to reward his long labour in defeating Tyre. {*Eze 29:17-20*} (Ussher incorrectly placed this item in the following year, as one can determine from the day, Tuesday, on the date of April 21. If it were the following year, the day would be Wednesday. Also, the year given for the captivity of Jeconiah indicates this year, not the next one. Editor.)

## 3432b AM, 4142 JP, 572 BC

*878.* Finally, Tyre surrendered to Nebuchadnezzar. It was now taken by force and was ransacked by the soldiers.

{*Eze 29:18,19*} Nebuchadnezzar replaced King Ithobal with Baal, a man of the same country, to be a petty king there, who governed them for ten years, as Josephus affirmed from the annals of the Phoenicians. {*\*Josephus, Apion, l. 1. c. 21. (157) 1:225*} *[E94]*

## 3432c AM, 4142 JP, 572 BC

*879.* When Cyrus was twenty-seven years old, he was taken from the rank of striplings and was numbered among the men, according to the discipline and custom of the Persians. {*\*Xenophon, Cyropaedia, l. 1. c. 5. s. 4. 5:79*}

*880.* Taking advantage of the rebellion in Egypt, Nebuchadnezzar invaded Egypt with his army after he was solicited by Amasis to help him against his father Apries.

## 3433 AM, 4143 JP, 571 BC

*881.* After Nebuchadnezzar conquered Egypt from Syene to the very ends of the land, he made havock of the Egyptians and of the Jews who lived there. Some he killed and the rest he led away into captivity, in accordance with Jeremiah's prophecies. {*Jer 43:1-44:30 46:1-28 Eze 29:1-31:18*} Pharaohhophra, or Apries, was forced to retreat into the country of Thebes. It seems that Nebuchadnezzar made Amasis his viceroy over all Egypt. Though Herodotus did not know of this, Scaliger observed in his notes, *Ad Fragmenta*:

> "The priests of Egypt told Herodotus of such things as he desired to know. They spoke only of things that glorified their country, but concealed the rest. This showed their cowardice and slavery, by concealing the payment of tribute they made to the Chaldeans."

## 3434 AM, 4144 JP, 570 BC

*882.* When Nebuchadnezzar finished his conquests, he returned to Babylon. While at ease in his own palace, he had that remarkable dream of the large tree whose destiny it was to be cut down. This tree represented him. The meaning of the dream was explained by Daniel, when he could not learn it from any of his wise men of Chaldea. {*Da 4:1-37*}

*883.* Nebuchadnezzar now built up Babylon in wonderful magnificence and beauty. He built a whole new city outside the old one, and enclosed all of it with a triple wall made of brick. As a favour to his Median wife called Amyitis, King Astyages' daughter, {*See note on 3378 AM. <<740>>*} he made that famous and so much renowned garden borne on pillars, of which Berosus wrote:

> "He built that garden, called the Hanging Gardens, because his wife desired the pleasure of the hills, since she was brought up in Media."

884. Curtius said: {*Curtius, l. 5. c. 1. s. 35. 1:339}

"It is said that a king of Syria, reigning in Babylon, built this great work at the importunity of his wife, whom he dearly loved. *[L136]* She desired to enjoy the pleasure of hills and woods in that low country of Babylon, and set her husband to the task of imitating the genius or spirit of nature itself, by the amenity and pleasantness of this work."

885. Those who want to know more of the infinite magnificence and sumptuousness of this work should read the fragments which are left from Berosus and Abydenus. The former blamed the Greek writers who attributed this work to Semiramis where indeed this and those other vast and magnificent structures were the works of this Nebuchadnezzar. So stated Josephus. {*Josephus, Apion, l. 1. c. 20. (142) 1:219} Josephus said plainly that those vast walls with their brazen gates were reckoned among the wonders of the world and remained to the times of Alexander the Great. Eusebius also attributed this work to Nebuchadnezzar. {*Eusebius, Gospel, l. 9. c. 41. (457c) 1:485} Cleitarchus and others, who accompanied Alexander on that journey, stated that the circumference of that wall was three hundred and sixty-five stadia (about forty-six miles), according to the number of the days of the year. {*Diod. Sic., l. 2. c. 7. s. 3. 1:373} They also stated that every stadia's length (about 200 yards) of it was built and completed in one day. {*Curtius, l. 5. c. 1. s. 26. 1:335}

886. Twelve whole months had no sooner elapsed, than Nebuchadnezzar grew proud and boastful of the magnificence of his buildings, lost his mind and was put out of his palace. He spent seven years in the woods and fields among the beasts. {Da 4:32,33}

887. Apries gathered an army of thirty thousand mercenaries from Ionia and Caria to help him fight against his son Amasis at Memphis, but the army was routed and he was taken prisoner. He was kept for a while in the city of Sais. Not long after this he was strangled, as had been prophesied by Jeremiah. {Jer 44:30} {*Herodotus, l. 2. c. 163,169. 1:479,483} {*Diod. Sic., l. 1. c. 68. 1:235,237}

888. After his death, Amasis reigned for forty-four years, paying tribute all that time to the king of Babylon. {*Herodotus, l. 3. c. 10. 2:13} The priests did not make that known to Herodotus.

### 3442a AM, 4151 JP, 563 BC

889. The Eighteenth Jubilee.

890. At the end of seven years, Nebuchadnezzar humbly acknowledged the power of God. He was restored both to his right mind and his kingdom. He publicly proclaimed

God's great grace and mercy shown toward him, and God's power over all nations. {Da 4:34-37}

### 3442b AM, 4152 JP, 562 BC

891. Nebuchadnezzar died after he had foretold that Cyrus would capture Babylon. So stated Abydenus (cited by Eusebius {*Eusebius, Gospel, l. 9. c. 39. (457a) 1:485}), based on the account from the Chaldeans. *[E95]* He died after he had reigned about twenty months as viceroy in the kingdom with his father, and forty-three years by himself.

892. After Nebuchadnezzar, his son Evilmerodach, or Illaoroudamos, reigned. In the thirty-seventh year of the captivity of Jehoiachin, or Jeconiah, about the twenty-fifth day of the twelfth month (Tuesday, April 15), Evilmerodach ordered Jeconiah to be promoted. {Jer 52:31} Two days later he took him from prison, changed his prison clothes and seated him ahead of all the princes in his court. He counted him among the king's friends and for the rest of his life, Jeconiah ate at the king's table. {2Ki 25:27-29}

893. In Lydia, after the death of Alyattes, his son Croesus reigned for fourteen years. {*Herodotus, l. 1. c. 86. 1:109}

894. After King Baal, the king of Babylon used judges to govern Tyre. The first one was Ecnibal, the son of Baslac, whom Scaliger called עכני-בעל בן מעלח. He ruled three months. Next came Chelbes, the son of Abdeus, whom Scaliger also called חלבש בן אברי. He ruled there for ten months, according to Josephus, who obtained this from the Phoenician Annals. {*Josephus, Apion, l. 1. c. 21. (156) 1:225} *[L137]*

### 3443 AM, 4153 JP, 561 BC

895. Abhar, the high priest, judged Tyre for three months. After him, Mitgonus and Gerastratus governed Tyre for six years. {*Josephus, Apion, l. 1. c. 21. (157) 1:225}

896. When Croesus was living at Sardis, all the wise and learned men of Greece came to him, including Solon, the law maker. Solon had that famous discussion with Croesus about the uncertainty of man's life and of all human happiness in it. {*Herodotus, l. 1. c. 28-33.1:33-41} According to Laertius, there exists a short letter of Solon's, written to Croesus when Solon was near the end of his life. In it he said that he visited Croesus at the time when Peisistratus governed Athens. {*Diogenes Laertius, Solon, l. 1. c. 2. (67) 1:69} At the same time Aesop, a Phrygian who composed those famous fables, was sent for by Croesus to come to him at Sardis. Croesus held Aesop in great esteem. Croesus was upset with Solon and dismissed Solon in an uncivil manner, because Solon spoke quite candidly to him. He sent Solon a letter, stating that kings must have either very few or very pleasing words spoken

to them. Solon wrote back that kings must have either very few or very honest things spoken to them. {*Plutarch, Solon, l. 1. c. 28. 1:483,485}

897. Aesop went from Sardis to Delphi and was most unjustly sentenced to die for no valid reason. He was thrown off the rock called Phoedrias, near Delphi, in about the 54th Olympiad, according to Suidas. That is near the end of the fourth year of that Olympiad, if the times were correctly calculated. The revenge for this murder was often threatened by the oracle there. It was later executed by Jadmon, grandson to that Jadmon of the isle of Samos. Aesop had been his slave for some time along with Rhodopis of Thrace, that famous strumpet. {*Herodotus, l. 2. c. 134. 1:437}

898. After Solon left Croesus, he went into Cilicia and there built a city called Solos, named after himself. He settled a number of Athenians there. In the course of time, they corrupted the native language and were said to commit *solecisms* in their speech. {*Diogenes Laertius, Solon, l. 1. c. 2. (51) 1:53} This place, and what is said of it, is more properly connected with the Solians in Cyprus than with the Solenses in Cilicia. This was shown by Solon, in his eulogies written to King Philocyprus, as recorded by Plutarch. Here, Plutarch also stated that this petty king of Cyprus employed Solon's wit and counsel in some of his own affairs. He moved a little town, formerly called Aipeia, to lower ground which was more fit and useful for habitation, and called it Solos, in honour of Solon. {*Plutarch, Solon, l. 1. c. 26. s. 4. 1:479}

899. After Solon departed, Croesus, who deemed himself the happiest man alive, found out through sad experience that everything Solon had told him about the uncertainty of man's life and his happiness in it, was true, for shortly thereafter he had a dream in which he saw his son Atys thrust through with a spear. This was a portent of the violent death which was soon to happen to him. Croesus sought diligently to prevent this, and was prepared to marry him off. Adrastus of Phrygia, a member of the king's family there, had accidently killed his own brother. He was banished against his will by his father Midas, the son of Gordias (not that old Midas, the son of Gordias king of Phrygia, whose epitaph was written by Homer and set upon his tomb, as Herodotus recounted in his account of the life of Homer). He came to Sardis, and Croesus pardoned him for this accidental death. When Croesus had done this, he committed to him the care and safe-keeping of his son Atys. At that time, the Mysians requested that Adrastus come and help kill a large boar which was destroying the grain and other crops growing around Mount Olympus. It had over time also killed many of the farmers. When Adrastus aimed at the boar with the point of his spear, he accidently

gored Atys and killed him. After Croesus had pardoned him for this, Adrastus killed himself on the tomb of Atys. When Croesus lost his son, he spent two whole years mourning for him. [L138] He broke off his mourning for fear of Cyrus' growing power, by whom he was also later conquered. {*Herodotus, l. 1. c. 34-46.'1:41-51} {*Diod. Sic., l. 9. c. 29. s. 1,2. 4:39} {*Valerius Maximus, l. 1. c. 7. ext. 4. 1:93,95} [E96]

### 3444c AM, 4154 JP, 560 BC

900. Evilmerodach, the king of Babylon, was a wicked man. He had many attempts made on his life and was eventually murdered by Neriglissoros, his sister's husband, when he had reigned little more than two years. {Berosus, Chaldean History, l. 3.} {*Josephus, Apion, l. 1. c. 20. (147) 1:223} Because we read that Jeconiah, king of Judah, had a daily food allowance given to him until he died, {Jer 52:34 2Ki 25:30} it is therefore most probable that Jeconiah himself died about the same time that Evilmerodach died.

### 3444d AM, 4154 JP, 560 BC

901. After Neriglassaros murdered Evilmerodach, he reigned for four years. {Berosus, Chaldean History, l. 3.} {*Josephus, Apion, l. 1. c. 20. (147) 1:223}

902. In the kingdom of Media, when Astyages or Assuerus died, {Apc Tob 14:15} he was succeeded by his son Cyaxares, Cyrus' mother's brother. {*Xenophon, Cyropaedia, l. 1. c. 5. s. 2. 5:77} This was in the beginning of the first year of the 55th Olympiad, thirty-one years before the death of Cyrus. Daniel called Cyaxares Darius the Mede, the son of Assuerus.

### 3445 AM, 4155 JP, 559 BC

903. The king of Babylon conscripted troops from his own subjects and sought the help of Croesus, the king of Lydia, together with the kings of Cappadocia, Phrygia, Caria, Paphlagonia and Cilicia, to the west. On the east he approached the Indians also, to join with him in battle against the Medes and Persians. He told them that they were two great nations who were now allied together. If they were not checked, they would eventually overrun and bring into subjection all countries near and far. Cyrus was made general of the Persian army by his father Cambyses and all the council of the kingdom. He was sent to Media with thirty thousand soldiers and a thousand commanders all of equal authority under his command. {*Xenophon, Cyropaedia, l. 1. c. 5. s. 2. 5:77} When he came, he was made general of the Median forces by his uncle Cyaxares, who had sent for him, and was placed solely in charge of the war against the Babylonians.

### 3445c AM, 4155 JP, 559 BC

904. The thirty years of Cyrus' reign started from this time, from the end of the first year of the 55th Olympiad. {Julius

*Africanus, l. 3.*} {*\*Diod. Sic., l. 9. c. 21. 4:31*} Thallus, Castor, Polybius, Phlegon, and other chronologers also count this as the beginning of the reign of Cyrus, as cited by Eusebius. {*\*Eusebius, Gospel, l. 10. c. 10. (488c) 1:523*} In the spring of that year, at the close of the same year of the same Olympiad, Solon left Philocyprus, the king, and the Solians. He was thought to have returned to Athens, as we find in his eulogies, mentioned before from Plutarch. However, he suddenly became sick and died in Cyprus at the age of eighty years. This happened in the year when Hegestratus was the archon of Athens, in the second year of Peisistratus ruling there, according to Phanias, the Ephesian, as cited by Plutarch. {*\*Diogenes Laertius, Solon, l. 1. c. 2. (62) 1:63*} {*\*Plutarch, Solon, l. 1. c. 32. s. 3. 1:497*}

## 3446b AM, 4156 JP, 558 BC

905. In the thirtieth year after the desolation of Jerusalem, the unknown author of second Esdras claimed to have had a conference with the angel Uriel. This is recorded in the Apocrypha at the time Salathiel was captain of the people, because Jeconiah was dead. {*Apc 2Es 3:1 4:1 5:16*}

906. When Croesus was preparing to fight against Cyrus, he sent generous presents to Delphi and consulted the oracle there on the matter of this war. The oracle told him that if he attacked the Persians, he would destroy a great empire. He did destroy a great empire, but it was his own empire, not Cyrus' empire! This was three years before Sardis was taken. {*\*Herodotus, l. 1. c. 53-55. 1:59-63*} {*\*Herodotus, l. 1. c. 91. 1:117,119*} {*\*Diod. Sic., l. 9. c. 31. 4:41*} [L139] Cicero mentioned the oracle as saying: {*\*Cicero, De Divinatione, l. 2. c. 56. 20:501*}

> When Croesus o'er the river Halys goes
> He will a mighty kingdom overthrow.

## 3447 AM, 4157 JP, 557 BC

907. When the king of Armenia saw that the Babylonians were making preparations against Cyaxares, he would neither send him aid nor pay him tribute any longer, in spite of the agreement he had made when Astyages, or Cyaxares, had overcome and subjected him. Therefore Cyaxares, under the pretence of a hunting trip, attacked Armenia and defeated both the king and his son, Tigranes, in a battle, putting them under his control again. He also conquered the mountains which lie between Armenia and Chaldea, and there built a strong citadel. He made peace on certain agreed conditions between the two nations. {*\*Xenophon, Cyropaedia, l. 2. c. 4. s. 16. - l. 3. c. 2. s. 11. 1:203-255*}

## 3448c AM, 4158 JP, 556 BC

908. Cyaxares and Cyrus marched against the Babylonian king, Croesus and the rest of the confederates, and gained a major victory over them. The king of Babylon fell in the battle and Croesus, with those who were left, broke his camp by night and fled. Cyrus, who had made a league with the Hyrcanians who had defected to him from the Babylonians, used their help and guidance along the route to pursue the fleeing enemy. He overtook them and defeated them after another battle. After Croesus sent away his women by night because the days were so hot, he left his camp with all his horses. The Hyrcanians attacked the companies of the Cappadocians and Arabians, killing both their kings. Cyrus spared the lives of those who were taken by force or had yielded to mercy. He divided the spoil of the battle among his soldiers. {*\*Xenophon, Cyropaedia, l. 3. c. 2. s. 1. - l. 4. c. 2. s. 33. 5:249-339*} [E97]

909. Laborosoarchodus, who was the son of Nerigasolassaros and a mere boy, was much more wicked than his father. He reigned after his father for nine months in Babylon according to Berosus. {*\*Josephus, Apion, l. 1. c. 20. (148) 1:223*}

910. Balatorus reigned in Tyre for one year according to the Phoenician records. {*\*Josephus, Apion, l. 1. c. 21. (157) 1:225*}

911. Gobryas had an only son who was killed by this new king of Babylon in a hunting match. He and his friends defected to Cyrus. {*\*Xenophon, Cyropaedia, l. 4. c. 6. s. 1-10. 5:391-397*}

912. Cyrus came to invade the country of Babylon. He stood outside the walls of the city and challenged the new king to a duel. Gadatas was a noble man of whom this new king was jealous, because the king's wife admired him, so he defected to Cyrus. The Babylonians sought revenge for this and spoiled Gadatas' lands. Cyrus pursued them and routed their forces. Unknown to Cyrus, the Cadusians, whom he had appointed as the rear guards of his army, had laid siege to a section of the countryside near the city. They were cut off by the king of Babylon and many were killed or wounded. When Cyrus first avenged the death of these men, he came to an agreement with the king to allow only the soldiers to fight, permitting the peasants on both sides to hold a truce. He passed beyond the city and captured three of their citadels, before returning to the confines of Assyria and Media, from where he had set out. He invited his uncle Cyaxares to come to him, and when he arrived there, Cyrus honourably received and entertained him in the pavilion of Neriglissoros, the king of Assyria. Since winter was approaching, they consulted together about the things necessary to maintain the siege of Babylon should it last that long. {*\*Xenophon, Cyropaedia, l. 5,6. 6:3-199*}

**3449b AM, 4159 JP, 555 BC**

*913.* After Laborosoarchodus, who was Nebuchadnezzar's grandson by his daughter, was disposed of by his subjects for his acts of villainy, Nebuchadnezzar's grandson by Evilmerodach succeeded Laborosoarchodus. Berosus called him *Nabonidus*, but Herodotus called him *Labynetus*, while Abydenus referred to him as *Nabannidochus* and Daniel as *Belshazzar* or *Baltazar*. (Some historians think Belshazzar was the son of Evilmerodach based on Daniel {*Da 5:7*}, where Belshazzar stated he would make anyone who interpreted the handwriting on the wall the third ruler in the kingdom. This implied that he was only the second ruler under his father. However, since this king had so many names, we will never know for sure. He reigned seventeen years, according to the third book of the Chaldean History by Berosus. {*Josephus, Apion, l. 1. c. 20. (150) 1:223*} {*Ptolemy, Canon of Kings*} [L140]

*914.* In the first year of this king's reign, Daniel had a vision of four beasts, which signified the four empires of the world. He also saw God overcoming all earthly powers, and the sovereignty of the Son of Man in all things. {*Da 7:1-28*}

*915.* When Balatorus, the petty king of Tyre, died, Merbalus was sent from Babylon to replace him and reigned for four years, according to the Phoenician records. {*Josephus, Apion, l. 1. c. 21. (157) 1:225*}

**3451 AM, 4161 JP, 553 BC**

*916.* In the third year of Belshazzar, Daniel had a vision of a ram and a he-goat, which foreshadowed the destruction of the Persian Empire by Alexander the Great and the great misery which Antiochus would bring upon the people of God. Daniel was living at Susa in the province of Elam, on the bank of the Ulai River. {*Da 8:1,2*} This river surrounded the citadel of Susa and separated the provinces of Susa from Elimais, that is, the Susachaeans from the Elamites, as the inhabitants of those two provinces are identified by Ezra and according to Pliny. {*Ezr 4:9*} {*Pliny, l. 6. c. 31. (135) 2:441*} From this we know that the province of Susa was not in the hands of the Medes or Persians at this time. It was controlled by the Babylonians, under whom Daniel then lived. {*See note on 3405c AM. <<809>>*}

*917.* Berosus stated ({*Berosus, Chaldean History, l. 3.*} as cited by Josephus, {*Josephus, Apion, l. 1. c. 20. (149) 1:223*}) that those walls about the river of the city of Babylon (which had been started by Nebuchadnezzar) were fully lined with baked brick and bitumen. This was because Belshazzar's wife Nitocris, an astute woman, saw the gathering storm about to break upon Babylon. She had turned the Euphrates River, which normally ran swiftly in a straight course. After drawing it through many winding channels, which she had cut for that purpose, she caused it to run more slowly than it did before. Then she raised a large dam on each side of the river. Upstream from the city, she constructed a large lake into which she diverted the river. In this way she left the channel of the river dry. She then lined the banks of the river inside the city with brick walls. She installed watergates in the walls around the city. She also built a stone bridge in the middle of the city. When this was done, she diverted the river from the lake back to its original channel. {*Herodotus, l. 1. c. 185,186,188. 1:229-235*} The magnificence of this stone bridge, which connected the king's houses that stood on each side of the river, was described by Philostratus. {*Philostratus, Apollonius, l. 1. c. 25. 1:75*} He said that it was built by a queen that came out of Media. Hence we gather that as Nebuchadnezzar married Amyitis, likewise his son Evilmerodach married this Nitocris from Media.

**3453 AM, 4163 JP, 551 BC**

*918.* When Merbalus died, the king of Babylon sent Hirom, his brother, in his place. He reigned in Tyre for twenty years, according to the Phoenician records. {*Josephus, Apion, l. 1. c. 21. (158) 1:225,227*}

**3455 AM, 4165 JP, 549 BC**

*919.* Darius, the son of Hystaspes, was born. He was almost twenty years old shortly before Cyrus died. {*Herodotus, l. 1. c. 209. 1:263*} [E98]

**3456c AM, 4166 JP, 548 BC**

*920.* When Croesus was made general of the army of the Babylonians and others, he crossed over the Halys River which divided the lands of Media and Lydia. Using the skill of Thales, the philosopher of Miletus, he crossed the river without a bridge and came into Cappadocia. There he took the city of Pteria (near Sinope) and all the surrounding cities. He utterly destroyed the Syrians, who had done him no wrong. {*Herodotus, l. 1. c. 75,76. 1:93,95*} Herodotus stated that the Cappadocians were called Syrians by the Greeks. {*Herodotus, l. 1. c. 72. 1:87*}

**3456d AM, 4166 JP, 548 BC**

*921.* After Cyrus had sent to the Ionians to see if they would join him or remain loyal to Croesus, he fought an indecisive battle with Croesus. The next day, Croesus returned to Sardis because Cyrus did not attack him again. [L141] He intended not to fight that winter, but to wait for the next spring to march against the Persians. In the meantime, he sent all his auxiliaries to their homes and sent envoys to those who were loyal to him, as were the Lacedemonians. He ordered them all to come together at Sardis in five months. When Croesus had disbanded his army, Cyrus attacked him with all his forces. When this surprise attack was made, Croesus, though greatly troubled, still went out to fight with him with as many of his Lydians as he had left. He trusted mainly in his cavalry. Cyrus thwarted his design by placing his camels in front of his troops, knowing that horses cannot tolerate the smell of camels. Therefore, all the horses of Croesus turned tail and carried their riders away with them. However, the Lydians left their horses and set themselves in battle array. But at last, after many had been killed on each side, they fled. The Persians followed up on this victory and attacked Sardis, which they took in fourteen days. Croesus was condemned to be burned. When he came to the place of execution, he cried out *Oh Solon, Solon*, whose wise counsel concerning the instability of human affairs he had formerly so much despised. On hearing this, Cyrus not only spared his life but also took him into his privy council. Cyrus arranged the funeral of Abradatas, the king of Susa (who had defected to him from the king of Babylon and had been killed in the battle). He also arranged the funeral of Panthea, Abradatas' queen, who killed herself after seeing her dead husband. He made a large and magnificent monument for them. {*Herodotus, l. 1. c. 75-90.'1:93-115} {*Xenophon, Cyropaedia, l. 7. c. 1-3. 6:203-251} {*Diod. Sic., l. 9. c. 31-34. 4:41-46} {*Plutarch, Solon, l. 1. c. 28. 1:483} {Polyaenus, Strategmata, l. 7. Cyrus and Croesus} {Alexander Polyhistor, Chronography (Ad Solinus), l. 1.} Eusebius stated that Cyrus attacked Sardis in the first year of the 58th Olympiad. {*Eusebius, Chronicles, l. 1. 1:183}

922. Croesus sent his shackles to Delphi as a present, complaining in vain that he had been misled by the oracle. {*Herodotus, l. 1. c. 90,91. 1:115-119} When the men of Ionia and Aeolia wanted to submit to Cyrus under the same conditions that they had formerly lived by under Croesus, Cyrus declined. He granted those terms only to the Milesians, who had feared what might happen to them and so had previously made peace with him. {*Herodotus, l. 1. c. 141,143,169. 1:181,183,211} The rest of the Greek city states were fortified. They sent Pythermos of Phocaea with other envoys to the Lacedemonians to seek help from them, which they refused to give. However, the Lacedemonians sent their envoy Lacrines to Cyrus to warn him not to touch any of the Greeks in Asia. He sent back word to them that he would shortly make them stop caring for the Ionians and the rest of the Greeks in Asia, and attend to their own affairs at home. Thales, the Milesian, advised them to hold a council at Teos, a city in the centre of Ionia. {*Herodotus, l. 1. c. 170. 1:213} {*Herodotus, l. 1. c. 141,152,153. 1:181,193}

## 3457 AM, 4167 JP, 547 BC

923. Cyrus remained at Sardis and built battering rams and other equipment with the intention of razing the walls of all that stood against him. The Carians sent and asked for his help to settle their civil war. He sent Adusius, a Persian, with an army. The Cilicians and Cypriots willingly joined this force. Adusius put an end to their differences, but not without leaving sufficient garrisons of his own in the cities of either party. {*Xenophon, Cyropaedia, l. 7. c. 4. 6:251-261}

924. At the end of the first year of the 58th Olympiad, Thales, the Milesian philosopher, died. {*Diogenes Laertius, Thales, l. 1. c. 1. (38) 1:39} Anaximander, his countryman was the first to observe the obliquity of the stars in the zodiac, according to Pliny. {*Pliny, l. 2. c. 6. (31) 1:189} However, Plutarch more correctly stated that this point of astronomy was known to Thales, the Milesian, Anaximander's teacher. {Plutarch, De Placitis Philosophorum, l. 2. c. 12} [L142] Anaximander died at the age of sixty-four in the second year of this Olympiad. {*Diogenes Laertius, Anaximander, l. 2. c. 1. (2) 1:131,133} We learn more from Phavorinus, who, in his *Varia Historia*, listed Anaximander's scientific inventions. He was the first to invent the sundial, which he installed in Sparta. He also invented the horoscopes for finding out the equinoxes and solstices for the dial, to determine the hour of the day. The horoscope or instrument is used to observe the equinoxes and the tropics, or the summer and winter solstice. [E99] Pliny attributed the invention of the sundial and clock to Anaximander's student and fellow citizen, Anaximenes. {*Pliny, l. 2. c. 79. (187) 1:319} {See note on 3291 AM. <<649>>}

> "This theory of shadows and the science called gnomonics, or dial work, was first discovered by Anaximenes of Miletus, Anaximander's student. He was the first that set up a *Hunt-the-Shadow*, which is a sundial to show what is the time in Sparta."

925. Anaximenes, the son of Eurystratus, succeeded Anaximander in his school at Miletus. {*Clement, Stromateis, l. 1. c. 14. 2:314} Following the advice of Thales, Pythagoras went into Egypt when both his teachers Anaximander and Anaximenes were dead. Polycrates of Samos sent him to Amasis, king of Egypt, with a letter of commendation. {*Diogenes Laertius, Pythagoras, l. 8. c. 1. (3) 1:323} It seems Amasis was surnamed Psemetnepserphreus by the Egyptians. Pliny stated that Pythagoras came into Egypt during his reign. {*Pliny, l. 36. c. 14. 10:57} (Loeb footnote on Pliny thought the name should be Sesothis. Editor.) Pythagoras stayed there for twenty-two years and conversed with the priests. From them he learned his knowledge of astronomy and geometry. He was initiated into all their rites

and ceremonies, according to Jamblichus, {*Jamblichus, Pythagoras, c. 3, 4.} therefore also being circumcised by them. He was admitted into the secrets of their religion so that he might more freely partake of the mystical philosophy of the Egyptians. For attaining this, he was mainly indebted to Sonches, the chief prophet among them. {*Clement, Stromateis, l. 1. c. 15. 2:315} I think this Sonchis was from Sais. He talked much with Solon, according to Plutarch. {*Plutarch, Solon, l. 1. c. 26. 1:477} They taught Pythagoras about Metempsuchosis or transmigration of souls from one body into another. {*Diod. Sic., l. 10. c. 5. s. 6. 4:61} He was quite familiar with their books and writings about history. {*Valerius Maximus, l. 8. c. 7. ext. 2. 2:229}

### 3458 AM, 4168 JP, 546 BC

926. Hystaspes and Adusius united forces and conquered all Phrygia bordering on the Hellespont. They captured the Phrygian king and brought him as a prisoner to Cyrus. {*Xenophon, Cyropaedia, l. 7. c. 4. s. 8-12. 6:255,257}

927. Cyrus committed Sardis to the keeping of Tabulus, a Persian. He committed the treasure of Croesus and the rest of the Lydians to Pactyes of Lydia. He made his way back to Ecbatana and took Croesus along with him. He paid little attention to the affairs of Ionia. No sooner had Cyrus left Sardis, than Pactyes immediately persuaded the Lydians to revolt from Cyrus and his governor Tabulus. Using the king's treasure to hire soldiers from other parts, he drove Tabulus into the citadel and besieged him there. When Cyrus was told about this on his way, he took the advice of Croesus. He sent back Mazares, a Median, with a part of his army. He defeated the Lydians and forced them to submit to the rule of Cyrus. {*Herodotus, l. 1. c. 153-157. 1:193-199} [L143] So the Lydians, a people who were famous for hard work, power and chivalry, grew soft from luxury and lost their courage and virtue. {Justin, Trogus, l. 1. c. 7.}

### 3459 AM, 4169 JP, 545 BC

928. Mazares demanded that Pactyes be returned by the Cymeans, with whom he had sought refuge. The Cymeans consulted the oracle at Branchidae who said that they should deliver him up. Aristodicus, the son of Heraclides, persuaded them not to give him up to be killed by the Persians. Since they did not want him to stay lest Cyrus come and destroy their city, they sent him away safely to Mitylene. When the Mitylenians were ready to surrender him, the Cymeans sent a ship to Lesbos and from there took him to Chios, but the men of Chios dragged him by force from the temple of Athena and delivered him to Mazares. Lesbos was rewarded by being given Atarneus, a place in Mysia opposite Lesbos. {*Herodotus, l. 1. c. 157-160. 1:197-201} Plutarch sought to justify both the Mitylenians and the men of Chios in this

matter using the more ancient historian, Caron of Lampsacus. {*Plutarch, Malice of Herodotus, l. 1. c. 20. 11:37} He stated the matter in this way:

> "When Pactyes heard of the approach of the Persian's army, he fled first to Mitylene and then to Chios and there Cyrus took him."

929. When Mazares had captured Pactyes, he marched against those who with Pactyes had attacked Tabulus. He conquered the inhabitants of Priene and partly ravaged the country lying on the Meander River. He gave both it and the city of Magnesia to his soldiers as a reward. {*Herodotus, l. 1. c. 161. 1:203}

### 3461 AM, 4171 JP, 543 BC

930. Harpagus, who was a chief general under Cyrus, marched with his army against Ionia. He fought with them, as Eusebius noted, in the second year of the 59th Olympiad, for Mazares was dying of a disease. {*Eusebius, Chronicles, l. 1. 1:183} Harpagus (whom some erroneously call Harpalus) was made general in the place of Mazares. When Harpagus came into Ionia, he immediately besieged whatever city he came to. He took Phocaea, the capital city of all Ionia. {*Herodotus, l. 1. c. 162,163. 1:203,205}

931. The Phocaeans abandoned the city when they saw that they could not hold it. With their wives and children they escaped by ship to Chios. [E100] Seeking revenge for the loss of Phocaea, they returned and killed the garrison which Harpagus had left behind to hold Phocaea. From there, they sailed to the isles of Oenussae and then to the isle of Cyrnus or Corsica where, twenty years earlier, they had established a colony and built a city called Alalia. When they had been there five years and wearied all the neighbouring countries by their robbing and plundering, the Italians and Carthaginians sent a navy of sixty ships against them. After several naval battles, the Phocaeans won, but at the cost of many lives and the loss of forty ships. They then moved to Rhegium in Italy and there built the city of Hyele, later called Velia or Elea, in the territory of Oenotria. {*Herodotus, l. 1. c. 164-167. 1:207} Thucydides also confirms that the Phocaeans, who built Marseilles, defeated the Carthaginians at sea. {*Thucydides, l. 1. c. 13. s. 6. 1:27} One group built Velia and another Marseilles in the time of Servius Tullius, the sixth king of the Romans. This was more than six hundred years after the coming of Aeneas into Italy, as was testified by Hyginus, who is quoted by Gellius. {*Aulus Gellius, Attic Nights, l. 10. c. 16. s. 9,10. 2:257} This colony of Marseilles is mentioned by Isocrates. {*Isocrates, Archidamus, l. 1. (87) 1:397} {See note on 3404c AM. <<791>>}

932. When Harpagus besieged the city of the Teians, they abandoned their city and sailed into Thrace. There they

built a city called Abdera. This city was begun earlier and unsuccessfully by Timesius, a man of the Clazomenians. {*See note on 3349 AM. <<713>>} [L144] Except for the Milesians, who had previously made a league with Cyrus, the rest of the Ionian territories were conquered one by one by Harpagus. He allowed them to stay in their own country, and they paid what was imposed upon them. {*Herodotus, l. 1. c. 168,169. 1:211} When they were afflicted in this way, they assembled in their old common council of Ionia, called Panionium. Bias of Priene, chief of all the wise men of Greece, counselled that they should build a common navy and sail to Sardinia, there to build a common city for all Ionians to live in happily and be free from this slavery. {*Herodotus, l. 1. c. 170. 1:211}

### 3464c AM, 4174 JP, 540 BC

933. As soon as Cyrus had subdued Asia Minor, he at once made war on the Assyrians. He marched with his army against Labynetus or Nabonidus their king. {*Herodotus, l. 1. c. 178,188. 1:221,233} The news of this reached Babylon two full years before the city was besieged {Jer 51:46} because Cyrus, while marching toward Babylon, was delayed at the Gyndes River, which flowed into the Tigris River. He was unable to cross over because he had no boats. While he was staying there, one of the white horses, which were consecrated to the sun, went into the river and drowned in its swift current. Cyrus was furious about this event and halted his march to Babylon. That summer he had the river divided into three hundred and sixty channels, with the intention of making it so shallow that a woman could pass through it and not get her knees wet. {*Herodotus, l. 1. c. 189,190,202. 1:237,255} {*Herodotus, l. 5. c. 52. 3:59}

### 3465b AM, 4175 JP, 539 BC

934. The next year Cyrus marched to Babylon. Here Cyrus defeated Belshazzar, or Nabonidus. The Chaldeans retreated into the city and resolved to endure the siege, which they took lightly for two reasons. {*Herodotus, l. 1. c. 190. 1:237} {Jer 51:27,28,30} First, they had more than twenty years of provisions in Babylon. Secondly, they thought there were many in Cyrus' army who favoured the Chaldeans more than the Persians. {*Herodotus, l. 1. c. 190. 1:237} {*Xenophon, Cyropaedia, l. 7. c. 5. s. 13,14. 6:267}

935. Cyrus made a vast trench around the wall of the city. He cast up the earth toward his own army and made bulwarks along the walls. He placed guards on these and divided his whole army into twelve parts. He ordered that each part should in turn stand watch for a month. {*Xenophon, Cyropaedia, l. 7. c. 5. s. 10-13. 6:267}

### 3466b AM, 4176 JP, 538 BC

936. When Cyrus had spent much time in this work with little to show for it, he finally made a ditch from the river to that vast lake, about forty to fifty miles wide, which Belshazzar's mother, Nitocris, had ordered to be dug. Then he opened the mouths of this and another of various ditches which he had recently built about the city, and let the river flow into them. In this way he made the channel, which was not more than four hundred yards wide, passable for his men to enter into the city. {*Herodotus, l. 1. c. 190,191. 1:237,239} {*Xenophon, Cyropaedia, l. 7. c. 5. s. 15-17. 6:267,269} {Jer 50:38 51:32,36}

937. Cyrus, with his army, went through the water gates in the wall and got into the city on a festival day, while all the men were banqueting. {*Herodotus, l. 1. c. 190,191. 1:237239} {*Xenophon, Cyropaedia, l. 7. c. 5. s. 26. 6:271} {Jer 51:39,57} So vast was that city that, as the inhabitants reported, when the people on its outskirts were surprised and taken by the enemy, those who lived in the heart of the city never heard of it. {*Herodotus, l. 1. c. 191. 1:239} [L145] Jeremiah alluded to this when he said:

> "post upon post and messenger upon messenger shall run to tell the king of Babylon that all the outskirts of the city were possessed by the enemies." {Jer 51:31} [E101]

938. When Belshazzar and all his nobles were feasting, he ordered his servants to bring all the vessels of the house of the Lord, which Nebuchadnezzar his father, or grandfather (for he was his son's son or his son. We do not know which. {Jer 27:7}) had brought away from Jerusalem. When they glorified the king's idols and reproached the true God, God sent a hand to write on the wall of the room where Belshazzar sat drinking. It wrote the number of years which the Babylonian empire was to last and that it had now been weighed in the balance and was found wanting, for which reason it was to be transferred to the Medes. This hand of God also declared what was to happen to Belshazzar. When his wise men of Chaldea could not read the writing, his queen advised him to send for Daniel, who came and read the writing and interpreted it for him. For his efforts, he was publicly proclaimed the third ruler in the kingdom. {Da 5:1-31} Since the king's wives are said to have been present at the banquet, {Da 5:2,3} and the queen to have come in afterward, {Da 5:10} this must be understood to be speaking of the queen mother, Nitocris. She was the mother of this last king of Babylon, as we have already shown from Herodotus.

939. In the very same night of this banquet, Belshazzar, the king of the Chaldeans, was killed by the soldiers of

Gobryas and Gadneas, {*Da 5:30} {*Xenophon, Cyropaedia, l. 7. c. 5. s. 30. 6:273} and so the Babylonian kingdom came to an end, just as it had been predicted, {Isa 13:1-14:32 21:1-17 43:1-28 46:1-13 Hab 2:1-20 Jer 25:1-38 50:1-51:64} and the empire was transferred to the Medes and Persians. {Da 5:21 6:8,12,15}

## The Persian Empire

*940.* Darius the Mede, son of Ahasuerus (or Cyaxares, the son of Hystages), took over the kingdom which Cyrus had conquered and given to him. {Da 5:31 9:1} Cyrus had set apart for himself the king's house and all his palaces in Babylon, so that if he should come to Babylon, he would have a palace of his own to stay in. {*Xenophon, Cyropaedia, l. 8. c. 5. s. 17. 6:403} In this first year of Darius' reign, the angel Michael was said to have confirmed and strengthened him in his kingdom. {Da 10:21,11:1} After this he is said to have reigned for two more years.

*941.* When Cyrus had set everything in order at Babylon, he returned through Media into Persia to his father Cambyses, and Mandane, his mother, who were still living. From there, he returned into Media and married the only daughter and heir of Cyaxares. As a dowry, he was given the whole kingdom of Media. After the marriage, he left for Babylon, taking his new wife with him. From Babylon, he sent governors into all his dominions: Megabyzus went into Arabia, Artabatas to Cappadocia, Artacamas into Greater Phrygia, Chrysantas into Lydia and Ionia, Adusius went into Caria, while Pharnuchus went into Aeolia and Phrygia on the Hellespont. He sent no Persian governors to Cilicia, Cyprus and Paphlagonia, because they had submitted to him and had voluntarily helped him against the king of Babylon. They were, however, required to pay tribute. {*Xenophon, Cyropaedia, l. 8. c. 5. s. 28. 6:409} {*Xenophon, Cyropaedia, l. 8. c. 6. s. 7. 6:413}

*942.* All the countries which Cyrus subdued in his role of general of the forces of Media, he added to the dominions of Cyaxares. {?Xenophon, Cyropaedia, l. 5.} [L146] Therefore it is most likely that, at a previous meeting in council, he made that distribution of the governments at the advice of Cyaxares. Xenophon {*Xenophon, Cyropaedia, l. 8. c. 6. s. 1. 6:409} stated about Cyrus:

> "It seemed good unto him, to set governors over all the countries which he had subdued."

*943.* Daniel, at this time, it seems, went with Cyrus from Babylon to Media. Cyrus had given control of the kingdom to Cyaxares who then appointed governors to manage the new kingdom. Daniel said of this Cyaxares:

> "It seemed good to Darius, to set over the kingdoms, one hundred and twenty governors, that they should be over all the kingdoms." {Da 6:1}

*944.* Over all these governors he set three overseers, the principal one being Daniel. As a result, the rest were envious of him and had the king make a decree that:

> "for thirty days, no petition should be made to any god or man, but to himself only." {Da 6:7}

*945.* Daniel, having broken this decree by praying to God, was cast into the lion's den, from which he was eventually delivered unharmed. Then Darius cast those who had plotted against Daniel into the same lion's den, publishing through all his dominions that famous decree, that every man should reverence and fear Daniel's God. {Da 6:1-28}

## 3467a AM, 4176 JP, 538 BC

*946.* From the year of the Babylonian captivity of the Jews, which began when Jehoiakim was defeated in the first year of Nebuchadnezzar, until the end of the first year of the reign of Darius the Mede, was almost seventy years. According to Jeremiah the captivity was almost over:

> "Thus saith the Lord, when the seventy years shall begin to be finished with Babylon, then will I visit you and perform my good word unto you and will bring you again to this place ... and when you shall call upon me to depart from thence and when you shall pray unto me, then will I hear you." {Jer 29:10,12}

*947.* Knowing the time of the captivity was almost up, Daniel prayed fervently for the remission of his own sins as well as those of his people, and for their release from captivity. The angel Gabriel brought him an answer which applied not only to this immediate matter, but also intimated the spiritual deliverance of the church, to be finally effected by the death of the Messiah. [E102] As a part of this, he gave that famous prophecy of the seventy weeks. {Da 9:12-27}

*948.* When Cyrus had spent one whole year with his wife in Babylon, he assembled his entire army. It was said to be made up of a hundred and twenty thousand cavalry, two thousand scythe-bearing chariots and six hundred thousand foot soldiers. When he had outfitted his troops, he undertook that campaign in which he was said to have subdued all the countries from Syria to the Red Sea. {*Xenophon, Cyropaedia, l. 8. c. 6. s. 19. 6:419,421}

## 3468a AM, 4177 JP, 537 BC

*949.* After Cyrus' father Cambyses died in Persia, Cyaxares in Media held all the empire of the east. It was from this year that Xenophon {*Xenophon, Cyropaedia, l. 8. c. 7. s. 1. 6:423} reckoned the beginning of the seven years of Cyrus' reign. Based on the records of the Medes and Persians, the Bible reckoned this as the first year, and stated that it was in this year that Cyrus, king of Persia, made that famous edict of his:

"Into my hand hath God given all the kingdoms of the earth...." {Ezr 1:2}

950. This was the year which marked the end of the seventy years of the Babylonian captivity, just as had been foretold by Jeremiah and in line with the prophecy of Isaiah, who had mentioned Cyrus by name. {Isa 44:28 45:13} He gave permission for all the Jews living anywhere in his empire to return to their own country. He ordered those who returned to rebuild the temple of God, leaving them free to build it as large as they wished. {Hag 2:3} They could use the resources from the king's treasury, and Cyrus restored all the vessels of the house of God which Nebuchadnezzar had removed from there. {2Ch 36:22,23 Ezr 1:1,2,7 5:13,14 6:2-5} [L147]

951. Cyrus made Sheshbazzar captain of the Jews who were returning to Jerusalem. In line with Cyrus' orders, Mithredath, the treasurer, gave to Sheshbazzar all the vessels belonging to the temple, for the purpose of returning them to Jerusalem. {Ezr 1:7-11 5:14,15} Sheshbazzar was his Chaldean name, but his Hebrew name was Zerubbabel. {Ezr 3:8,10 5:16}

### 3468c AM, 4178 JP, 536 BC

952. The Jews were preparing to return to their country, and the poor were given an allowance to help with the costs. {Ezr 1:5,6} There were 42,360 of the children of the province, or poor people of the Hebrews born in Chaldea, who returned. Their captain was Zerubbabel, the son of Shealtiel, or Salathiel, and their high priest, Jehu, or Jeshua, the son of Jozadak. In addition there were 7337 proselytes, and manservants and maidservants, who also returned. {Ezr 2:1-70 Ne 7:6-67 12:1-9} However, the total sum given in Ezra is only 29,818. In Nehemiah, the sum is 31,031. Neither of these add up to 42,360 but at the end of each list the total of 42,360 was given as the number of the whole congregation. {Ezr 2:64 Ne 7:66} To tally to 42,360, the Hebrews (in their great Chronicle, chapter 29) stated that we must include in this number those of the other tribes of Israel who came back from the captivity with the Jews. For even at the time of the end of the Jewish state there still existed a remnant of the other ten tribes, {Ac 26:7} made up not only of some from the dispersion, {Jas 1:1} and some still at Jerusalem {2Ch 9:3 Lu 2:36} and in other cities of Judah, {2Ch 11:16 31:6} but also of those who still lived on their lands, for Shalmaneser had not taken away everyone

belonging to the tribes. {See note on 3327 AM <<697>>} He had left a remnant of them in their own country who, together with the Jews and Benjamites and Levites, were later carried away to Babylon by Nebuchadnezzar. They were now being given their liberty and sent back again by Cyrus. After this first year of Cyrus, all the Israelites are said to have lived in their own cities. {Ezr 2:70} In the sixth year of Darius, they are said to have been present at the dedication of the temple, and there to have offered twelve male goats for the sin of all Israel. {Ezr 6:16,17} When Christ preached the gospel in Galilee, {Mt 14:14} he fulfilled the prophecy of Isaiah, that the people of Zebulun and Naphtali would see a bright light. {Isa 9:1,2} The chief men of their fathers' families came to Jerusalem and brought offerings, according to their ability, toward the rebuilding of the temple, a total of sixty-one thousand drachmas of gold, five thousand pounds of silver and a hundred priests' robes. The priests, the Levites and the rest of the people all settled again in their own cities. {Ezr 2:68-70}

### 3469a AM, 4178 JP, 536 BC

953. On the first day of the seventh month, during the Feast of Trumpets, the Israelites all came from their cities to Jerusalem and there built the altar. Every morning and every evening they offered the required daily sacrifice to God, and on the fifteenth day of the same month they kept the Feast of Tabernacles. They also provided materials and workmen for the building of the temple, for which Cyrus had given them permission. {Ezr 3:1-7} [E103]

### 3469c AM, 4179 JP, 535 BC

954. In the second year after their return from Babylon, in the second month, called Jair, they appointed Levites to oversee the work of the house of God. When they laid the foundation of the temple, the old men, who had seen the former temple as it had stood fifty-three years earlier, wept, while the young men greatly rejoiced to see the new temple going up. {Ezr 3:8-13} [L148]

955. The men of Cuth, old enemies of the Jews, who had previously been settled in Samaria by Esarhaddon, cunningly offered to join them in building the temple. When the Jews refused their help, they hindered the Jews in their work as much as they could and discouraged the people from completing the task. {Ezr 4:1-4}

### 3470a AM, 4179 JP, 535 BC

956. This was the first sabbatical year kept by the Jews, after their return from the captivity of Babylon.

### 3470c AM, 4180 JP, 534 BC

957. The Samaritans, by bribing certain courtiers of Cyrus, disrupted the Jews in their work of building the

temple. {*Ezr 4:5*} This was the reason for the three weeks of mourning by the prophet Daniel. He continued his fast, which he had begun about the third day of the first month in the third year of Cyrus, throughout the whole time of the Feast of the Passover. {*Da 10:1-4*} After this, on the twenty-fourth day of the first month, while he stood on the bank of Hiddekel or the Tigris River, he had the vision of the kings of Persia, of Alexander the Great and his successors and their kingdoms. This is recorded in Daniel and was the last vision that he had, shortly before his death. {*Da 10:1-12:13*}

## 3473 AM, 4183 JP, 531 BC

*958.* Amasis, it seems, defected from Cyrus. The people of Egypt, who had previously been carried away by Nebuchadnezzar, were now being sent back again by Cyrus into their own country, after forty years in exile. They returned to their old kingdom toward the end of the life of Amasis. Egypt was once again a kingdom, very old and ancient, it is true, but the least significant of all of them and no longer of much use to any other country. {*Eze 29:11-16 Jer 46:26*} {*Xenophon, Cyropaedia, l. 8. c. 8. s. 1. 6:439*} Xenophon, in the prologue to his whole work, stated that Cyrus had Egypt in his possession, {*Xenophon, Cyropaedia, l. 1. c. 1. s. 4. 5:7*} while all authors agree that it was later subdued by his son Cambyses. Hence, we conclude that in the intervening time they enjoyed their freedom.

*959.* It is possible that when Amasis revolted from Cyrus, Hirom was overthrown. He had been king of Tyre for a full twenty years and he was the last king mentioned by Josephus in his catalogue of the kings of Tyre. In his place, they had governors set over them by other countries, instead of being governed by men of their own country. The very Punic names of those kings and governors show that they were all native to the country of Tyre. This situation was similar to that of the Egyptians who had been ruled by Amasis who was an Egyptian.

## 3475b AM, 4185 JP, 529 BC

*960.* Cyrus died at the age of seventy years. He had first been made general of the Median and Persian armies a full thirty years earlier. He took Babylon nine years before his death and reigned for seven years, plus a month or so.

*961.* Authors differ as to how he died. Some say that he was killed in a battle against the Massagetae or Scythians. Others say he was decapitated by Tomyris, the queen of the Scythians, and she threw his dead body into a tub full of blood. She told him to satiate himself with blood, since he had so thirsted after it in his lifetime. {*Herodotus, l. 1. c. 214. 1:269*} {*Justin, Trogus, l. 1. c. 8.*}

{*Valerius Maximus, l. 9. c. 10. ext. 1. 2:357*} However, Diodorus stated that when she had taken him prisoner, she crucified him. {*Diod. Sic., l. 2. c. 44. s. 2. 2:31*} Ctesias related that, having been wounded in the thigh by a certain Indian in a battle against the Derbicans, the country bordering on Hyrcania, he killed Amorraeus, their king, and his two sons, whereupon he himself died, three days later. {*Ctesias, l. 11.*} Johannes Malela of Antioch, quoting a forged book attributed to Pythagoras of Samos, stated that he was killed in a naval battle against the Samians. Xenophon reported that he died a natural death in his own country of Persia. {*Xenophon, Cyropaedia, l. 8. c. 7. s. 25-28. 6:437-439*} He ordered his sons to wrap his body neither in gold nor silver but in plain cloth and bury him in an out-of-the-way place. [L149] They were to call together all his friends, Persians and others, to his grave, and dismiss them after having there presented them with whatever was fit to be given them at the funeral of a fortunate man. His tomb was made at Pasargada. This is stated by those who recorded the noble acts of Alexander the Great, such as Curtius, Plutarch and Arrian. {*Plutarch, Alexander, l. 1. c. 69. 7:417*} {*Curtius, l. 10. c. 1. s. 30-35. 2:477*} {*Arrian, Anabasis, l. 6. c. 29. s. 4-11. 2:193-197*} According to Strabo, Aristobulus was sent by Alexander to see the tomb. He also recounted this inscription found on his tomb: {*Strabo, l. 15. c. 3. s. 7. 7:167,169*}

> "Oh man, I am Cyrus, who founded the Persian monarchy and was king of Asia; and therefore envy me not that I have a monument."

*962.* Strabo, quoting from Onesicritus, cited a Greek epitaph written for Cyrus (if such a thing can be believed) in Persian letters. It was:

> Here Cyrus I do lie,
> Who king of kings was high.

*963.* It is of the same dubious nature as that one cited by Lucian, with the same Onesicritus as its source, namely that Cyrus, who missed his friends whom his son Cambyses had killed, died of grief at the age of one hundred. {*Lucian, Octogenarians, l. 1. (13) 1:233*} [E104]

*964.* Cyrus left his kingdom to his eldest son Cambyses and to his younger son, Tanaoxares or Tanyoxarcas, whom Herodotus called Smerdis. {*Herodotus, l. 3. c. 30. 2:39*} Justin called him Mergis. {*Justin, Trogus*} Ctesias claimed that Cyrus left Tanaoxares the governments of Bactria, Choromnea, Parthia and Carmania. Xenophon, however, stated that he received the governments of the Medes, the Armenians and Cadusians. {*Xenophon, Cyropaedia, l. 8. c. 7. s. 11-13. 6:429*}

*965.* In the beginning of the kingdom of Ahasuerus (for it is by that name that Cambyses is known in the Scriptures) the Samaritans, who before had secretly fought to undermine the Israelites, now openly sent a letter to the king against the inhabitants of Judah and Jerusalem. {*Ezr 4:6*} They knew very well what difference there was between the natures and dispositions of the father and the son. Cyrus was naturally kind and loving to those who were under him, while his son was uncontrollable by nature and impulsive in his resolutions. {*Diod. Sic., l. 10. c. 12. s. 14. 4:75*} {*Herodotus, l. 3. c. 89. 2:117*}

### 3477a AM, 4186 JP, 528 BC

966. This was the second Sabbatical year held by the Jews after their return from Babylon.

### 3478 AM, 4188 JP, 526 BC

967. Just as Cambapheus, a eunuch, controlled the king of Egypt, so also did his first cousin, Isabat, a eunuch, control Cambyses, king of Persia. Cambapheus betrayed the bridges, passages and other things important to Egypt to the Persians, when they promised him the government of Egypt for his trouble. {*Ctesias, History of Persia, l. 3.*}

968. Following up on this information, Cambyses gathered both an army and a navy. His army consisted of men from various other countries in his empire and of Greeks from Ionia and Aeolia in Asia. His naval forces came mainly from the Sidonians and Cypriots. Polycrates, the king or tyrant of Samos, furnished him with forty warships, using as sailors all he suspected as enemies at home. He hoped they would die in Cambyses' service and never return home to bother him again. {*Herodotus, l. 3. c. 1,19,44. 2:3,27,59*}

969. Phanes of Halicarnassus was a chief man in the Egyptian army and well versed in their affairs. He hated Amasis and when he saw that Cambyses was preparing to fight against Egypt, he defected to him. He told Cambyses many secrets of the land of Egypt. When Cambyses was greatly perplexed as to how to cross the desert without proper water supplies, he advised him to send to the king of Arabia to obtain permission to pass through his country, because without his consent no one could get into Egypt. {*Herodotus, l. 3. c. 4,7. 2:7,9*} {*Herodotus, l. 3. c. 88. 2:115*} [L150]

### 3479b AM, 4189 JP, 525 BC

970. The king of Arabia made a league with Cambyses through the messengers that were sent to him. He sent all his camels laden with leather bags full of water to the places where Cambyses and his army were to pass. {*Herodotus, l. 3. c. 9. 2:11*}

971. When Cambyses and his army arrived in Egypt, they found Amasis had recently died, after having reigned for forty-four years. {*Herodotus, l. 3. c. 9,10. 2:11,13*} Diodorus

stated that he died when Cambyses began his war in Egypt, toward the end of the third year of the 63rd Olympiad. {*Diod. Sic., l. 1. c. 68. s. 6. 1:237*} His son, Psammenitus (whom Ctesias called Amyrtaeus), reigned six months. {*Herodotus, l. 3. c. 14. 2:17*} During this time, it rained at Thebes in upper Egypt, which was considered a sign of good luck. {*Herodotus, l. 3. c. 10. 2:13*}

972. When the Persians had crossed the dry sandy deserts of Arabia, they came to the edge of Egypt. {*Herodotus, l. 3. c. 11. 2:13*}

973. When Cambyses came to besiege Pelusium, he placed ahead of his army cats, dogs, sheep, birds known as ibis, and all kinds of living creatures which were being worshipped as gods by the Egyptians. Hence the Egyptians did not shoot at the enemy, lest they hurt their own gods, and so Cambyses took Pelusium and got a toe-hold in Egypt. {*Polyaenus, Strategmata, l. 7.*}

974. The Greek and Carian mercenaries who came to help the Egyptians hated Phanes, who had been instrumental in bringing this foreign army to Egypt. They killed his sons before his eyes and after drinking their blood, started fighting with him. {*Herodotus, l. 3. c. 11. 2:15*}

975. After a sharp encounter, many were killed on both sides and the Egyptians were routed. {*Herodotus, l. 3. c. 11. 2:15*}

976. Cambyses sent a Persian herald up the river in a ship of Mitylene to Memphis, where the Egyptians had fled in great disorder and confusion.

977. The herald exhorted them to surrender, but the men of the city sallied out against the ship, captured it and destroyed it, tearing everyone on board limb from limb. They retired into the city and later endured the siege by Cambyses for a short time. {*Herodotus, l. 3. c. 13. 2:17*}

978. Arcesilaus, son of Battus the lame, and of Pheretime his wife, surrendered Cyrene to Cambyses and agreed to pay him tribute. {*Herodotus, l. 4. c. 165. 2:371*} The inhabitants of Cyrene, the men of Barce and the Libyans, all of whom bordered on Egypt, were terrified by Cambyses' success against their Egyptian neighbours. [E105] They submitted to him and sent him their presents. Cambyses graciously accepted what came from the Libyans. Because the Cyrenians' gift was so small, since they sent him only five hundred minas of silver, he took it and threw it among the soldiers. {*Herodotus, l. 3. c. 13,91. 2:17,119*}

979. Ten days after Cambyses had taken Memphis, he tried to humiliate Psammenitus, whom he had imprisoned with other Egyptians in the suburbs of the city. To show his contempt for Psammenitus, he sent his daughter with

other maidens of the Egyptian nobility to fetch him water from the river in pitchers. He sent the young son of Psammenitus, with two thousand more of the same age and all the principal noblemen's sons, with ropes about their necks and bridles in their mouths, to be shamefully put to death. He did this to revenge himself upon those men of Memphis who had destroyed the ship and murdered the Mitylenians he had sent to them. He ordered that for every Mitylenian who had been killed, ten of the leaders of the Egyptians should be put to death. The first to die was the son of Psammenitus. Cambyses intended to spare him, but he acted too late to do so. *[L151]* However, Psammenitus later lived at peace with Cambyses. Finally, when Psammenitus was convicted of stirring up the people to a new rebellion, he killed himself by drinking bull's blood. {*Herodotus, l. 3. c. 14,15. 2:17-23} Ctesias, however, stated that he was sent away as a prisoner to live in Susa.

*980.* Cambyses marched from Memphis and came with his army to the city of Sais. When he came to the palace of Amasis, against whom he had actually undertaken this war, he had his body hauled from its vault and brought before him. He had the corpse whipped with scourges and all kinds of reproach and contumely directed at it. Then he had it burned. {*Herodotus, l. 3. c. 16. 2:23} {*Diod. Sic., l. 10. c. 14. s. 2. 4:75,77}

*981.* Cambyses conquered Egypt in the fifth year of his reign. He ruled there for three years. {Julius Africanus} {*Eusebius, Chronicles, l. 1. 1:185} He killed fifty thousand Egyptians in battle and sent away seven thousand as prisoners to Susa. {Ctesias}

*982.* Jamblichus reported that Pythagoras was among those taken to Babylon, where he conversed with their wise men. {Jamblichus, Pythagoras} Another writer of his life, namely Malchus, or Paphyrius (may be Malalus, Editor.) said that at Babylon he not only conversed with the wise men among the Chaldeans, but also spent time with Zabratus, a Jew, who purified and cleansed him from the sins of his former life. This Zabratus was thought by some to have been that Nazaratus of Assyria of whom Alexander (Polyhistor I think), in his book of Pythagorical Opinions, inferred that he was Pythagoras' teacher. Others mistakenly thought him to have been the prophet Ezekiel. {*Clement, Stromateis, l. 1. c. 15. 2:316} All this merely showed that he did also converse with the wise men among the Jews in Babylon. He later made use of many of their opinions in the writing of his philosophy. These writers are of that opinion: Hermippus, in his first book of Pythagoras, {*Josephus, Apion, l. 1. c. 22. (164) 1:229} and in his first book of Law Makers, cited by Origen, {Origen, Against Celsus, l. 1.} and Aristobulus the Jew,

a Peripatetic philosopher, in his first book to Philometor. Others, who were mistaken, assumed he was the prophet Ezekiel. {*Clement, Stromateis, l. 1. c. 15. 2:316} Eusebius believed that the books of Moses were translated into Greek before the Persian empire began. {*Eusebius, Gospel, l. 13. c. 12. (664a) 1:718} However, it is far more likely that he got that part of his learning by talking with the Jews in Babylon. Pythagoras was familiar with Jewish writings, according to Porphyry who drew his information from Diogenes' work, *Of the incredible relation made of Thule.* {Porphyry, Pythagoras} {*Diogenes Laertius, Lives of Eminent Philosophers, l. 8. (3) 2:323}

### 3480 AM, 4190 JP, 524 BC

*983.* Cambyses wanted to prepare a navy to go against the Carthaginians, but gave it up when the Sidonians, upon whom he relied for naval service, refused to go against their own colony and kindred. Meanwhile, he sent for some of the *Fish Eaters* from the city of Elephantine, who were well versed in the Ethiopian language. He sent them as spies to the Ethiopians, who were known as the *Long Lived*. These are a generally very long-lived people who dwell in the parts of Africa south of Egypt, bordering on the Indian Ocean and Red Sea. The spies went under the pretence of bearing gifts for their king, and wanting to see what truth there was in the story of a *Table of the Sun* in that country. In their presence, the king of Ethiopia took his bow and bent it, and then straightened it again. He handed it to them to carry to Cambyses, and asked them to tell him that when his Persians were able to bend such bows as these with ease, then and not before, would he be able to gather a large army and fight against the long-lived Ethiopians. {*Herodotus, l. 3. c. 17-25. 2:25-35}

*984.* Cambyses' full brother, Smerdis or Tanyoxarces, tried to bend this bow and came within two fingers' breadth of the notch, but none of the other Persians came that close. Out of envy, Cambyses dismissed him and sent him to Persia. {*Herodotus, l. 3. c. 30. 2:39} *[L152] [E106]*

*985.* In a rage, Cambyses ordered an expedition against Ethiopia, without making any provisions for grain or food. Like a mad man, as soon as he had heard what his Fish Eaters had said, he immediately marched off with all his own foot soldiers, ordering the Greeks to stay behind. {*Herodotus, l. 3. c. 25. 2:33}

*986.* When he came as far as Thebes in Egypt, he selected about fifty thousand of his army and sent them to rob the land first, and then to burn the temple of Jupiter Ammon, making slaves of all the inhabitants of the place as they did so. Then he marched on toward Ethiopia. {*Herodotus, l. 3. c. 25. 2:33} {*Diod. Sic., l. 10. c. 14. s. 3. 4:77}

987. On that journey, Cambyses subdued those Ethiopians who bordered on the lower parts of Egypt, and who lived in the city of Nysa and kept the holy days to Dionysus. {*Herodotus, l. 3. c. 97. 2:125} Cambyses renamed Saba, the capital of the Ethiopians, and the island on which it stood, Meroes in honour of Meroe, who was his wife and his sister. {*Strabo, l. 17. c. 1. s. 5. (790) 8:19} {*Josephus, Antiq., l. 2. c. 10. s. 2. (249) 4:273} She had accompanied him into Egypt and later died there. No other king of Persia before him had married his sister. Shortly after this, he married his older sister Atossa. {*Herodotus, l. 3. c. 31. 2:41} After his death, she married Magus, and after him she married Darius Hystasphes. {*Herodotus, l. 3. c. 68,88. 2:89,115}

988. The army, which set out from Thebes against the Ammonians, travelled seven days across the sands before coming to the city of Oasis. (This city was inhabited by those Samians who were of the Aeschrionian tribe.) From there they came to a country called *The Isle of the Blest.*

989. As they marched from there across the sandy plains and were midway between Oasis and Ammonia, it is said that while they were eating, a very strong wind arose out of the south. It brought those shifting sands upon them and overwhelmed them all. {*Herodotus, l. 3. c. 26. 2:35,37} {Justin, Trogus, l. 1. c. 9.} Fifty thousand men died in that sand storm. {*Plutarch, Alexander, l. 1. c. 26. s. 6. 7:303}

990. The army which was going with him against the Ethiopians ran out of provisions after five days. When they had lost hope of any food, they cast lots and started to eat one another. When Cambyses saw this, he returned to Thebes, having lost most of his army. {*Herodotus, l. 3. c. 25. 2:35} {*Seneca, Natural Questions, l. 2. c. 30. s. 2. 7:147,149} Lucan stated: {*Lucan, l. 10. (280) 1:611}

> And mad Cambyses, marching toward the east,
> Came to the long-lived Ethiopians:
> And wanting food, his own men up did eat;
> And yet the head of the Nile never found.

991. When Cambyses returned to Memphis, he discharged his Greeks and shipped them home. {*Herodotus, l. 3. c. 25. 2:35} He saw the Egyptians keeping a holy day because their god Apis had appeared to them. Apis was a sacred bull worshipped in the temple of Ptah in Memphis. {*OCD, Apis, 1:121} Cambyses thought they had celebrated for joy at his disastrous journey. He sent for Apis and killed the animal with his sword. He commanded all his priests to be scourged with whips, and the rest of the Egyptians who were found keeping the holy day were to be killed by his soldiers. [L153] Apis was wounded by him and died in the temple. The priests took the body of the beast and secretly buried it. {*Herodotus, l. 3. c. 27-29. 2:37,39}

992. The Egyptians said that Cambyses, who was mentally unstable, now went stark raving mad. This first manifested itself when he killed his own brother. After he had sent him to Persia (as was said before), Cambyses dreamed that a messenger arrived from there to tell him that Smerdis, his brother, was sitting on the regal throne and touching the heavens with his head. He was astonished by this dream and immediately sent Prexaspes, his most trusted friend, to kill his brother Smerdis. When he came to Susa, he had him murdered. Some say he took him on a hunting trip, others report that he lured him along as far as the Persian Gulf and drowned him in it. {*Herodotus, l. 3. c. 30. 2:39} {*Herodotus, l. 3. c. 65. 2:83-87} Justin stated that this charge was committed to Cometes, one of the Magi, and that he did not murder Smerdis or Merges until after Cambyses was dead. {Justin, Trogus, l. 1. c. 9.} Ctesias disagreed with Herodotus. He said that Spendahates, one of the Magi, was scourged by Tanyaxares, who was a commander of Smerdis. Spendahates therefore accused him to Cambyses of seeking to make himself king. [E107] On the advice of Spendahates, Smerdis was ordered to come from from Bactria to Egypt. He was forced to kill himself by drinking bull's blood. Spendahates was sent back into Bactria, and because he looked like Tanyoxarces or Smerdis, he ruled there in his place.

## 3481 AM, 4191 JP, 523 BC

993. Cyrus had previously appointed Oroetes, a Persian, to replace Harpagus as governor of Sardis and of all the provinces of Lydia, Ionia and Phrygia. He is said to have sent a messenger to Polycrates of Samos to consult him on a certain matter. When the messenger arrived, Polycrates was lying on his bed in his chamber, with Anacreon of Teos sitting by him. He was that excellent lyrical poet of Ionia who, according to Clement of Alexandria, was the first inventor of love songs. Polycrates totally ignored the messenger. Oroetes resolved to avenge this insult. He sent Myrtus, a Lydian, the son of Gyges, with another message to Polycrates, saying that for fear of Cambyses he would defect to him with all his treasure. Polycrates heeded the message and quickly went to Oroetes in person, accompanied by Democedes, a noted physician of Croton in Italy. When he came as far as Magnesia, Oroetes captured and crucified him. He let the Samians who came with him go free. The rest of them, including Democedes, were made his slaves. {*Herodotus, l. 3. c. 120-127. 2:149-155} Valerius stated that Polycrates was crucified by Oroetes (which is what both he, and Cicero, called him, {*Cicero, De Finibus, l. 5. c. 30. 17:497}), who was governor under king Darius on the highest peak of Mount Mycale, {*Valerius Maximus, l. 6. c. 9. ext. 5. 2:97} that is, in that foreland of Ionia which looked toward Samos. At that time, Darius was one of the bodyguards to Cambyses

and held no high office in the Persian empire. Herodotus stated that during Cambyses' expedition into Egypt, Syloson, the brother of Polycrates, presented Cambyses with a most luxuriant robe publicly at Memphis. Hence the saying: *Syloson's robe.* {*Herodotus, l. 3. c. 139,140. 2:173}* He also said that Polycrates came to a foul end and that this happened while Cambyses was in Egypt. {*Herodotus, l. 3. c. 120. 2:149}* [L154] Pliny confirmed this in saying that it happened in the 230th year after the building of Rome, which, according to Varro, was in the 64th Olympiad. {*Pliny, l. 33. c. 6. (28) 9:25}*

994. When Cambyses saw his wife Meroe grieving for her brother Smerdis, he killed her too. {*Herodotus, l. 3. c. 31,32. 2:41,43}*

995. In the seventh year of Cambyses, the 225th year of Nabonassar's epoch, on the seventeenth day of the Egyptian month of Phamenoth (July 16), one hour before midnight, the moon was eclipsed at Babylon. {*Ptolemy, Great Syntaxis, l. 5. c. 14.}*

996. Cambyses killed Prexaspes' son, who was his cup bearer, with an arrow. The next day he had twelve principal men of the Persians buried alive with their heads downward, though they had done him no harm. He ordered that Croesus, who had for some time been king of Lydia, be executed because he had admonished him, in a fair and friendly manner, not to do such things. He changed his mind before the execution, but killed those whom he had appointed to kill Croesus. He played many similar mad pranks on the Persians and on his friends while he stayed at Memphis. He opened many of their sepulchres to see the bodies of those who lay buried there. He went into the temple of Vulcan, where he laughed exceedingly and mocked his image. Another time he went into the temple of the Cabeiri, where only the priests were to go. After jeering their images, he had them all burned. {*Herodotus, l. 3. c. 34-38. 2:45-51}* He either burned down, pulled down, defaced or destroyed the remainder of their temples and did the same to their obelisks. {*Strabo, l. 17. c. 1. s. 25. 8:79}*

### 3482 AM, 4192 JP, 522 BC

997. Patizithes, one of the Magi whom Cambyses had left to oversee his private estate at home, found out about the death of Smerdis. This was a closely guarded secret known only to a few Persians. He placed on the throne his own brother, who was also called Smerdis, and who had very similar features to the dead man. He immediately sent messengers to all parts of the empire and to the rest of the army in Egypt, that from now on they should obey only Smerdis, the son of Cyrus, and not Cambyses. {*Herodotus, l. 3. c. 61. 2:79}* Justin stated that Cometes, one of the Magi, who killed Merges or Smerdis

(to whom the kingdom rightfully belonged after Cambyses), set up his own brother Oropastes, who also closely resembled Smerdis. {*Justin, Trogus, l. 1. c. 9.}* However, Ctesias wrote that Bagabates, the eunuch, and Artasyras, a Hyrcanian, who were with Cambyses in Egypt and of great authority under him, took counsel while Cambyses was still living. They planned to set up as king Spendahates, one of the Magi who also looked very much like Smerdis, when Cambyses died.

998. Cambyses sent to the oracle of Butis. When it answered that he would die at Ecbatana, Cambyses assumed this to be the Ecbatana in Media, where all his treasure was. [E108]

999. While he was staying at Ecbatana in Syria, a messenger brought him word of what Patizithes had commanded. When he heard of the conspiracy against him, he leaped on his horse, intending to march quickly with his army to Susa against the conspirators. As he was leaping, his sword fell out of its scabbard and ran into his thigh. On the twentieth day after the accident, he sent for the nobles of Persia to come to him. He told them of the death of his brother and the treason of the Magi against himself. He charged them that they were by no means to allow the kingdom to return to the Medes, for Magus, the brother of Patizithes, was a Median. {*Herodotus, l. 3. c. 73. 2:97}* {*Herodotus, l. 3. c. 126. 2:155}* Soon after this, his wound festered and he died after having reigned only seven years and five months. {*Herodotus, l. 3. c. 62-66. 2:79-87}* [L155] Josephus stated that on his return from Egypt, he died at Damascus, {*Josephus, Antiq., l. 11. c. 2. s. 2. (30) 6:329}* thus writing Damascus for Ecbatana in Syria, as Herodotus had. Ctesias stated that he came as far as Babylon and that it was there that he was wounded and died. He wrote of his death and the signs leading up to it: {*Ctesias*}

> "When Cambyses was offering sacrifices, the beasts' throats were cut and no blood came out. He was much amazed. Roxane bore him a boy without a head and that amazed him more. The Magi told him that this portended that he should leave no successor of his own. His mother also appeared to him in a dream and seemed to threaten him with destruction, for his brother's death. This troubled him yet more than all the other signs. When he came to Babylon, he sat there whittling a little stick with a knife to pass the time. By chance he hurt a muscle in his thigh and died eleven days later."

When he left Egypt, he left Aryander to govern it in his place. {*Herodotus, l. 4. c. 166. 2:371}*

1000. After Cambyses died, the Persians did not know that they had Magus for their king. They thought

Cambyses' brother had indeed succeeded him in the kingdom. Prexaspes vouched for this and denied that he had killed him, nor was it in truth now safe for him to confess that he had killed a son of Cyrus. {*Herodotus, l. 3. c. 66. 2:87} The ruse was easy to conceal, for among the Persians it was proper that the king be rarely seen in public. {Justin, Trogus, l. 1. c. 9.} So it came to pass that this Magus or Smerdis, who impersonated Smerdis, the son of Cyrus, peacefully held the kingdom for seven whole months, thus making up the eighth year of Cambyses' reign. During that time he spared no cost to show all kinds of bounty and goodwill toward the subjects in all the empire. As soon as he took the title of king, he sent couriers throughout the empire and proclaimed three years of freedom from paying taxes and military service. After he died, Asia and all the other countries except the Persians, mourned for him. {*Herodotus, l. 3. c. 67. 2:87} He also took Atossa, the daughter of Cyrus, and all the rest of the wives of Cambyses. {*Herodotus, l. 3. c. 68,88. 2:89,115}

1001. Ammianus Marcellinus, citing ancient books, reported that after Cambyses' death seven Magi took over the management of the kingdom of Persia. {*Ammianus Marcellinus, l. 23. c. 6. s. 36. 2:369} Valerius Maximus agreed with this also. {*Valerius Maximus, l. 9. c. 2. ext. 6. 2:317} Of the seven men, two were chiefs, named by Herodotus: Patizithes, whom Trogus called Cometes, and his brother, who was king in name only by impersonating the son of Cyrus. He was called Smerdis by Herodotus, Mardus by Eschylus, Spendahates by Ctesias, and Oropastes by Trogus, while the scriptures identify him as Artaxerxes. {*Herodotus, l. 3. c. 61. 2:79} {*Herodotus, l. 3. c. 78. 2:101,102}

1002. The Samaritans sent letters to this Artaxerxes asking him to forbid the further building of Jerusalem. They claimed it was a rebellious and wicked place which, if it were rebuilt, would never pay tribute to the kings of Persia. {Ezr 4:7-16}

## 3483a AM, 4192 JP, 522 BC

1003. Artaxerxes sent a letter forbidding the rebuilding of Jerusalem until he should so order. The Samaritans, encouraged by this reply, came swiftly to Jerusalem and forced the Jews to stop building both the city and the temple, although Cyrus had expressly ordered them to finish the temple. [L156] They stopped all work until the second year of the reign of Darius. {Ezr 4:17-24}

1004. During the time that Artaxerxes held the kingdom, Oroetes the Persian ruled at Sardis. He was reproached by Mitrobates, governor of Dascylium in Asia Minor, for not having taken and annexed to his government the isle of Samos. In the lifetime of Polycrates, Oroetes took and killed Mitrobates and Mitrobates' son, Cranaspes, both men of good esteem among the Per-

sians. He committed other outrages also, such as murdering a messenger sent from Darius because he told him something displeasing. {*Herodotus, l. 3. c. 126. 2:155}

## 3483b AM, 4193 JP, 521 BC

1005. Ctesias stated that Isabates, the eunuch, who had been charged to carry the body of Cambyses into Persia, disclosed the plot of the Magi to the army. When he was pursued by them, he fled for safety into a temple, where they decapitated him. Herodotus, however, said that the matter was first brought to light eight months after Cambyses' death, by the cunning of Otanes, the son of Pharnaspes, and was later more fully explained by Prexaspes. [E109] When Prexaspes was in a certain tower, he called the people to him and from there declared to them that Cambyses ordered him to murder his brother Smerdis, the son of Cyrus, and that they were being ruled by the Magi. When he had said this, he threw himself down headlong among them. {*Herodotus, l. 3. c. 68,75. 2:89,99} Justin, from Herodotus and Trogus Pompeius, recorded Otanes' disclosure and the destruction of the Magi as follows: {Justin, Trogus, l. 1. c. 9.}

"Ostanes (who is that Otanes) sent a messenger to his daughter, who was one of the concubines of the king, and inquired whether it was a son of Cyrus who was king. She replied that she did not know, nor could she ask the other concubines, because they were kept in seclusion from each other. Then he advised her that when her turn came to lie with him, she was to feel his head as he lay asleep. For Cambyses, or (as Herodotus has it) Cyrus, had Magus' ears cut off. Later she assured him that the king had no ears. He told the princes of Persia, swearing an oath with them, and together they conspired against the impostor king. There were seven of them involved in this. Lest the matter be discovered, they hid a dagger in their coats and immediately went to the place where the king was, killing those who stood in their way. At last they came to where the Magi were assembled. The Magi killed two of the conspirators. Herodotus, however, maintained they stated they were only wounded. They were all apprehended by the Magi, who outnumbered them. Gobryas held one of them about the middle. When his companions could not get close enough to Magus to kill him, for fear of hurting Gobryas, he bade them kill Magus through his body. Fortunately, they killed Magus, and did not harm Gobryas."

1006. According to Ctesias, the names of these seven Persians (whom Jerome, writing on Daniel, {Da 11:2} called the Magi) were as follows: Onophas, Iderues, Naradobates, Mardonius, Barises, Artaphernes and

Darius, the son of Hystaspes. Herodotus called them Otanes, Hydarves, Megabyzus, Gobryas, Aspathines, Intaphernes and Darius. Darius had recently arrived there from Susa, where his father Hystaspes was governor. Ctesias and Herodotus stated that the Persians always kept a yearly festival upon the day when the Magi were overthrown. {*Herodotus, l. 3. c. 70,79. 2:91,105}

1007. Six days after the Magi were overthrown, those seven Persians met to decide what form of government suited Persia best. [L157] Otanes advised an aristocracy, Megabyzus an oligarchy, but Darius persuaded them to adopt a monarchy. Darius' opinion prevailed and was carried by majority vote. Otanes resigned all his rights to the other six on the condition that neither he himself, nor any of his descendants, should ever be subject to any of them or their posterity. Of all the Persians, only his family were left free and not subject to the king's command, provided that they broke no law of the Persians. Since he had been the first to act and organize the conspiracy, they thought it fit to heap all kinds of magnificence and honour upon him and his posterity. Each year he was presented with a Median Robe. For the election of a new king, they agreed on the following method. Each of them should get on horseback a little before sunrise and the rider of whichever horse happened to neigh first after the sun was up would become king in Cambyses' place. The horse of Darius, the son of Hystaspes, by the craft and cunning of his groom Oebares, neighed first. All the rest leaped off their horses and adored Darius, crying, *God save the king.* {*Herodotus, l. 3. c. 80-88. 2:105-117}

1008. Each of the seven had the following privileges: First, they could come to court whenever they pleased and have free access to the king (unless he was in bed with the queen) without any notice. {*Herodotus, l. 3. c. 84,118. 2:113,145} Secondly, they had the right to wear their turbans differently from all other men. Only the king and his heir wore their turbans upright. {*Seneca, On Benefits, l. 6. c. 31. s. 12. 3:431} {*Plutarch, Themistocles, l. 1. c. 29. s. 5. 2:81} {*Plutarch, Artaxerxes, l. 1. c. 26. s. 2. 11:191} The rest of the nobility wore them hanging backward; but it was granted to these men and their posterity that they should wear them pointing forward, because when they had gone to kill the Magi, they had used this as a sign among themselves. {*Plutarch, Precepts of Statecraft, l. 1. c. 27. 10:273} Darius had given this as a sign for each to know one another by in the dark. They were to turn around the buckle that fastened their turbans at the back, and wear it on the front. {Polyaenus, Strategmata, l. 7.}

1009. The greatest privilege granted to them was that, although the king had a perpetual dictatorship over them, each man in turn would have a tribunal power with him. [E110] I deduce this from the following: First,

these conspirators foresaw that they would prove burdensome (and, I ask, how more so than in this way?) to Darius, so they bound him with an oath, which was most religiously observed among the Persians. Darius swore that he would never put any of them to death, either by poison, or sword, or by any violent way, or by starving them. {*Valerius Maximus, l. 9. c. 2. ext. 6. 2:317,319} Secondly, because Eschylus (who was in the battle against the Persians at Marathon) named two kings successively between the slaughter of the Magi and the reign of Darius, namely Maraphis and Artaphernes. The first seems to be the one whom Ctesias called Mardonius and the other Artaphernes. Lastly, in Ezra, in the edict of Darius, we find Artaxerxes, also referred to as the *King of Persia,* {Ezr 6:14} to have given his consent for the rebuilding of the temple in the second year of his reign. It is hard to understand this to mean any other than Artaphernes.

1010. In the beginning of his reign, Darius took Atossa, the daughter of Cyrus, who had formerly been married to her own brother, Cambyses, and afterward to Magus, who had married her. [L158] He planned to establish his kingdom more firmly by marrying into royalty, so that the kingdom might not appear to have moved to another family, but rather to have remained in the family of Cyrus. {*Herodotus, l. 3. c. 88. 2:115} {*Herodotus, l. 7. c. 2. 3:303} {Justin, Trogus, l. 1. c. 10.} He was first called Ochus, {*Valerius Maximus, l. 9. c. 2. ext. 6. 2:317} yet later, when he took over the kingdom of Cambyses, he took his surname also. So I conceive that he was Achash-veroth or Ahasuerus, who in the story of Esther is said to have reigned from India to Ethiopia, over one hundred and twenty-seven provinces. His chief wife Atossa was none other than Vashti, as mentioned in the book of Esther.

1011. Oroetes still continued as governor at Sardis and kept a thousand Persians about him as his personal guards. Darius sent his royal letters by Bagaeus, the son of Artontes, to the soldiers there. When the soldiers read the letters, they killed Oroetes. His goods were confiscated and brought to Susa. Democedes, a physician of Croton, whom he had made his slave, was also taken to Susa. {*Herodotus, l. 3. c. 127-129. 2:157,159}

1012. It happened later that Darius fell from his horse while hunting and wrenched his foot badly. The Egyptian surgeons sought to straighten it, but their methods were so violent that he could not sleep for seven days. On the eighth day, Democedes was brought to him in shackles, in a poor and ragged condition. With gentleness he applied the Greek remedies, so that the king quickly went to sleep again and in a short time recovered. He was rewarded with rich gifts by the king and his wives. He lived in a good house in Susa and sat at the table with the king. He had everything that his heart could wish for, except that he was forbidden to go to Greece again. When Darius would have hung his Egyptian physicians because a Greek could do more to cure him than they all could, Democedes obtained their pardon from the king. There was a certain fortune teller of Elean, who had travelled in his company, having followed Polycrates to Magnesia and been brought to Susa with the rest of Oroetes' slaves. Democedes also obtained his freedom. {*Herodotus, l. 3. c. 129,130,132. 2:159-163}

1013. It happened later that Atossa, the daughter of Cyrus and wife of Darius, had an ulcer in her breast. After it was lanced, it spread further and further. When Democedes had cured her of that sore, he prevailed upon her to have the king make war on Greece. Darius at once called fifteen choice men, all Persians. He commanded them to follow Democedes and at his directions to spy out all the maritime places of Greece, and on their return to bring Democedes back again to him. They went into Phoenicia and from there to Sidon, where they outfitted themselves with ships and other provisions and sailed to Greece. They viewed all the sea coasts of Greece and drew maps. They were the first Persian spies that ever came to Greece. When they had viewed the most famous cities and places in the heart of Greece, they moved on from there to Tarentum in Italy. From there, Democedes stole away to Croton, where his own home was, and there married the daughter of that famous wrestler, Milon of Croton. He never returned to Darius. {*Herodotus, l. 3. c. 133-138. 2:163-173} {*Athenaeus, l. 12. (522bc) 5:358} {*Aelian, Historical Miscellany, l. 8. c. 17. 1:277}

### 3484a AM, 4193 JP, 521 BC

1014. This was the third sabbatical year held by the Jews, after their return from Babylon.

### 3484c AM, 4194 JP, 520 BC

1015. Mordecai, the Jew, in the Greek edition of Esther {Apc Est 11:1-12}, is said to have had a dream on the first day of the month of Nisan, in the second year of the reign of Artaxerxes the Great (or Ahasuerus or Darius, the son of Hystaspes), concerning a river signifying Esther and two dragons portending himself and Haman. {Apc Est 10:4-13} [L159] [E111]

### 3484d AM, 4194 JP, 520 BC

1016. In the second year of king Darius, which was in the 65th Olympiad, Haggai the prophet reproved the Jews for their idleness in not rebuilding the temple. Their neglect in this matter was the cause of crop failures and other plagues that continually happened to them between the first and third Sabbatical years. He earnestly persuaded them to change their ways. Then Zerubbabel, the governor of the Jews and Joshua, the high priest, and all

the people earnestly began to rebuild the temple on the twenty-fourth day of the same month. {Hag 1:1-15}

### 3485a AM, 4194 JP, 520 BC

1017. On the twenty-first day of the seventh month in the same year, Haggai encouraged the Jews to persevere in the work with a promise of God's presence and blessing on them. The beginnings of this present structure did not compare with the glory of the former temple of sixty-nine years earlier. However, he told them that the Messiah, who was born five hundred and sixteen years later, as it turned out, would be first shown in this temple, and that on account of this, peace would flow to all nations. If they considered that fact, then they would have to acknowledge that the glory of this temple would excel the beauty of the former. {Hag 2:1-9}

1018. In the eighth month of the second year of Darius, the people were exhorted to repentance by Zechariah, the son of Berachiah. {Zec 1:1-6}

1019. On the twenty-fourth day of the ninth month of this same second year, about halfway between seedtime (which immediately followed the end of the sabbatical year) and the harvest, the temple began to be built on its old foundations by Zerubbabel and Joshua, the high priest, with the assistance of the prophets Haggai and Zechariah. {Ezr 5:1,2 Hag 2:10,18,19}

1020. On the same twenty-fourth day, the two last prophecies of Haggai were revealed to him. One vision concerned the end of the plagues which they were experiencing. The other was about the overthrow of various kingdoms and the exaltation of Zerubbabel. {Hag 2:10-23}

### 3485b AM, 4195 JP, 519 BC

1021. Tatnai, governor of the countries on the west side of the Euphrates River, together with Shetharboznai and the Apharsachites, their associates, came to Jerusalem to hinder the work on the temple. They asked the elders of the Jews by whose command they were doing it. The elders replied that they were doing it by the authority of the edict of Cyrus, and continued with their work. {Ezr 5:3-5,13,16} The laws of the Medes and Persians were perpetual and unalterable. {Da 6:8,12 Es 1:19 8:8} Therefore, it was lawful for the Jews to proceed in the work without expecting any new order about it.

1022. Their enemies sent a letter to Darius containing the Jews' answer and desiring that a search might be made of the records at Babylon. They wanted to see whether or not any such grant had been made by Cyrus, and desired to know the king's further pleasure concerning this. {Ezr 5:5-17}

*1023.* The work was thus interrupted, and the famine continued in Judah because the grain was not yet ripe. On the twenty-fourth day of the eleventh month of Shebat, in the second year of Darius, the prophet Zechariah had a vision of horsemen galloping up and down over the face of the whole earth, which was at rest and quiet. *[L160]* When in the vision the prophet asked what this meant, God graciously answered with many comforting words to the angel who was entreating God to cease his anger and fury against the Jews, Jerusalem and the cities of Judah. These seventy years mentioned in the vision are to be reckoned from the coming of the Babylonians and their last siege laid to Jerusalem. {*See note on 3415c AM. <<841>>*} {*Jer 34:1 Eze 5:12,13 Zec 1:7-13*} This exhortation, which is recorded in Zechariah, {*Zec 2:6,7*} was sent to the Jews still remaining in Babylon. They were told to get out as fast as possible, to avoid that calamity which Darius brought upon Babylon a while later, when he took it.

*1024.* The edict of Cyrus for the rebuilding of the temple was found at Achmetha or Ecbatana, in the province of the Medes. Darius sent this and a second command in favour of the Jews to Tatnai and his companions. They were ordered not to hinder the work of the Lord's house but help it along. The costs of the project were to be taken from the king's tribute. Tatnai and his companions were to pay the costs for the daily sacrifices that were to be offered by the priests at Jerusalem. With this new command, and the encouragement of Haggai and Zechariah, they enthusiastically completed the work. {*Ezr 6:1-14*}

*1025.* I think that at this time Artaxerxes, who signed with Darius in this edict {*Ezr 6:14*} and shared power with him in ruling the kingdom, was one of the seven princes of Persia who killed Magus. This is the one whom Eschylus (in Persis) called Artaphernes Hellanicus, or (as his scholiast termed him), Dapherns. According to Ctesias, he was Artaphernes, and Herodotus called him Intaphernes. *[E112]* Therefore, as one of these seven princes, according to the privilege granted by Darius of having access to him without notice, he was detained by the doorkeepers of the bedchamber. They told him that the king was asleep with the queen. He thought they lied to him, so he drew his scimitar and cut off both their ears and noses, tied the reigns of a horse about both their necks and sent them running. When they came to the king they showed him what they had suffered and why. The king sent for the rest of the seven princes individually, fearing that this might have been done by their common consent. When he found this not to be the case, he executed Intaphernes and all his sons except the eldest, whom he spared at his mother's peti-

tion. Herodotus related this matter as having occurred shortly after the execution of the Magi. {*Herodotus, l. 3. c. 118,119. 2:145-149*} Valerius, however, who followed other authors, stated that Darius found himself checked by these princes and put them all to death by a newly devised type of punishment. {*Valerius Maximus, l. 9. c. 2. ext. 6. 2:319*} He said that Darius made a lower room which he filled with cinders, and supported the room over it with only one post. When he had feasted and filled them with food and drink, he put them all into that upper room. When they were all fast asleep, he had the post that supported the room removed and they all fell into the cinders in the lower room and died.

*1026.* Now, although it is not very likely that they perished in this manner, it is nonetheless very credible that he put them out of the government of the kingdom, and hence eased himself of their heavy yoke.

## 3485c AM, 4195 JP, 519 BC

*1027.* From that time on, Darius, who was called Ahasuerus in the Scriptures, was an absolute monarch. Therefore, Ahasuerus made a feast in the third year, reckoned from the beginning of his reign in his palace at Susa. He wanted to show the glory of his kingdom and magnificence of his state. He invited all the governors and great men of his dominions to the feast, which lasted a hundred and eighty days. {*Es 1:2-4*} *[L161]* Pliny stated that Susa was built by this Darius. {*Pliny, l. 6. c. 31. (133) 2:439*} Aelian stated rather that Susa was embellished with magnificent palaces by Darius, while Herodotus stated that he made this his home, and kept all his treasure there. {*Herodotus, l. 5. c. 49. 3:53*}

## 3486 AM, 4196 JP, 518 BC

*1028.* After this half-year long banquet was over, there followed another one lasting seven days. Everyone in Susa was invited. The men were sitting with the king in the court of the garden of the king's house, and the women were within the palace itself with Vashti, the queen, who was Atossa, the daughter of Cyrus. {*Es 1:5-9*}

*1029.* On the last day of this feast, the king, being somewhat drunk, wanted to show off the beauty of his queen to the men, and sent for her to come to him. She refused, and Darius divorced her on the advice of Memucan, one of the seven wise men of the Medes and Persians, who knew the laws and statutes of those countries. For these were the king's judges, who judged in all matters arising among the Persians and revealed all cases in point of law. {*Herodotus, l. 3. c. 14. 2:17-21*} {*Herodotus, l. 3. c. 31. 2:41*} {*Plutarch, Artaxerxes, l. 1. c. 29. s. 4. 11:199*} After this, they made a law that every man should be master in his own house. {*Es 1:10-22*}

1030. Consequently, a search was made for all the fair damsels that were to be found in the empire, to find a new queen for the king, to replace Vashti. Among the ones selected was Hadassah, a damsel of the Jews, who was also called Esther, a woman of Benjamin. {Es 2:1-8}

### 3487a AM, 4196 JP, 518 BC

1031. In the fourth year of Darius, on the fourth day of the ninth month, called Chisleu, the Jews, through Sharezer and Regemmelech, consulted with the priests and prophets concerning the appointed fast to be held to commemorate the day of the destruction of the city of Jerusalem and the temple. God replied that those fasts of the fifth and seventh months, which they had observed for seventy years, displeased him, and reminded him of their obstinacy and sins, which had caused that terrible desolation in the first place. {Zec 7:1-14} From the time of this destruction, and the death of Gedaliah two months later (which was the reason for the fast in the seventh month), to the very time of this prophecy, we, in our chronology, count seventy years.

1032. In the book of Zechariah, God told them that he would restore Jerusalem and put an end to all their former miseries, and that he would change their fasts into mirth and gladness. {Zec 8:1-23} These fasts were:

a) Fourth month, ninth day when the city was taken
b) Fifth month, tenth day when the temple was burned
c) Seventh month, when Gedaliah was murdered and they were scattered among the nations
d) Tenth month, tenth day when Nebuchadnezzar besieged the city under Zedekiah. [E113]

### 3489b AM, 4199 JP, 515 BC

1033. Toward the end of the sixth year of Darius on the third day of the twelfth month, called Adar, the temple was completed. At its dedication, the Israelites who had returned from the captivity celebrated with great joy and many sacrifices, and the priests and Levites once again performed their offices and duties in the temple. {Ezr 6:15-18}

1034. On the fourteenth day of the first month, they joyfully celebrated the first Passover in the second temple, and kept the Feast of Unleavened Bread for seven days, for God had favourably inclined the heart of Darius, king of Assyria, toward them. {Ezr 6:19,22} After a twenty-month siege, he took Babylon with the help of Zopyrus. [L162] He could now rightly be called king of the Assyrians as well as of the Persians. {*Herodotus, l. 3. c. 153. 2:187} {Justin, Trogus, l. 1. fin.}

### 3490a AM, 4199 JP, 515 BC

1035. When Esther's turn came to be brought before king Ahasuerus, she was brought from the house of the women to the king's chamber by Hegai, the eunuch. {Es 2:12,15} {*Herodotus, l. 3. c. 69. 2:91}

"The women in Persia come round in their turns, to their husbands' beds."

1036. In the seventh year of Ahasuerus' reign, in the tenth month called Tebeth, when Esther came to the king, she found grace and won his favour and approval more than all the other maidens. He put the crown of the kingdom upon her head and made her queen in Vashti's stead. {Es 2:16,17} From this I gather that as Vashti was Atossa, so Esther was the one Herodotus called the virgin, Artystone. He said that Darius loved her more than all his wives, and made a solid gold statue of her. {*Herodotus, l. 3. c. 88. 2:117} {*Herodotus, l. 7. c. 69. 3:383} Hadassah was another name given to Esther and sounds much like Atossa. Herodotus makes Artystone to have been Cyrus' daughter and Atossa's sister. We do not know whether Herodotus was not so well skilled in the Persian genealogies, or whether the Persians themselves, out of sheer envy, concealed the name of Esther.

### 3490b AM, 4200 JP, 514 BC

1037. In honour of his new marriage, Ahasuerus made a most sumptuous feast for all his princes and servants and called it Esther's feast. He relieved the provinces of many taxes and distributed gifts commensurate with the wealth of so great a king. {Es 2:18}

### 3491a AM, 4200 JP, 514 BC

1038. The Nineteenth Jubilee.

### 3491b AM, 4201 JP, 513 BC

1038a. Hippias, in the fourth year before his banishment from Athens, gave his daughter Archedice in marriage to Aeantides, the son of Hippocles, the tyrant of Lampsacus, because he saw that that family had great influence with King Darius. He foresaw that some misfortune might befall him and began to look for support abroad. {*Thucydides, l. 6. c. 59. 3:287}

### 3494b AM, 4204 JP, 510 BC

1039. Haman, the son of Hammedatha the Agagite, of the tribe of the Amalekites, hated the Jew Mordecai because he would not fall down and adore him as others did. He resolved on his account to take revenge on all the Jewish nation (which had always been at odds with his country {De 25:19}) and to destroy it. To establish a good time to do this, he cast pur that is, lots, before him on the first month called Nisan, in the twelfth year of King Ahasuerus. The lot fell on the twelfth month of Adar. {Es 3:1-7}

1040. For vacuous reasons, he offered Ahasuerus ten thousand talents of silver (which the king would not accept), and obtained a grant from him to destroy the Jews. {*Es 3:7-11*}

*1041.* On the thirteenth day of the first month, the king's edict was proclaimed in Susa, and copies of it were dispatched by couriers into all the provinces of the empire. On the thirteenth day of the twelfth month of Adar, all Jews without regard to sex or age were to be killed. {*Es 3:12-15*} When it was announced, Mordecai, Esther and all the Jews humbled themselves before the Lord in fasting and prayer. {*Es 4:1-17*} To this day, their posterity, in memory of this, observe a solemn fast on the thirteenth day of the month of Adar, which they call Esther's fast.

*1042.* Esther went to the king in gorgeous apparel and was graciously received by him. She invited the king to a banquet. Meanwhile, Haman was busy having a gallows made for Mordecai. {*Es 5:1-14*}

*1043.* One night, when Ahasuerus could not sleep, he had the records read to him. It was found that two of his servants, Bigthan and Teresh his doorkeepers, had plotted his death and that Mordecai had revealed this conspiracy to him. Thereupon, he ordered that Mordecai should be highly honoured publicly by none other than Haman himself. {*Es 6:1-14*} *[E114]*

*1044.* Shortly after this, Haman was hung on the gallows he had made for Mordecai. {*Es 7:1-10*} Haman's house was given to the queen. Mordecai, her uncle, who had raised her, had great honours bestowed upon him. {*Es 8:1,2,15-17*}

*1045.* On the twenty-third day of the month of Sivan there was an edict proclaimed at Susa, and copies of it were sent away speedily by couriers into the hundred and twenty-seven provinces. It stated that the Jews, on the thirteenth day of the month of Adar, which was the day appointed for their massacre, could defend themselves and could kill any who had wanted to kill them. They could keep the spoil of any man killed. In Susa and in all the provinces there was great rejoicing among the Jews, and people in various countries became Jews. {*Es 8:9-17*}

### 3494d AM, 4204 JP, 510 BC

*1046.* In the fourth year of his rule, Hippias was expelled from Athens by the Lacedemonians and the faction of the Alcmaeonidae. He left the Athenians and went first to Sigeum, from where he sailed to Lampsacus to his son-in-law Aeantides, and from there he went to Darius. Twenty years later, as a very old man, he went with the Persians on the expedition to Marathon. {*Thucydides, l. 6. c. 59. 3:287*} Peisistratus, Hippias' father, had committed Sigeum in Troas to Hegesistratus' son. This was a place to which Hippias, and later others of the family of Peisistratus, could escape when in trouble. {*Herodotus, l. 5. c. 65,91,94. 3:71,101,103,115*}

### 3495b AM, 4205 JP, 509 BC

*1047.* On the thirteenth day of the twelfth month of Adar, the Jews killed all those who intended to kill them according to Haman's decree. In Susa and the palace, they killed five hundred men together with Haman's ten sons. In the rest of the provinces, they killed seventy-five thousand men, but did not touch one penny of their goods. {*Es 9:1-16*} *[L163]*

*1048.* On the fourteenth day of the same month, the Jews in the provinces stopped killing their enemies and had a feast, but at Susa the Jews were granted one more day of vengeance by the king. They killed a further three hundred of their enemies and hung the bodies of Haman's ten sons on the gallows. {*Es 9:13-19*}

*1049.* On the fifteenth day, the Jews who lived in Susa made merry and feasted. {*Es 9:18*}

*1050.* Mordecai began the custom of keeping a holiday in remembrance of Purim on the fourteenth and fifteenth days of the month of Adar. This was established by Esther, {*Es 9:23-30*} and is now the Jewish Shrovetide, when they read the history of Esther. As often as the name of Haman is read, they rap and make a noise with their hands or mallets on the desks in their synagogues.

### 3500 AM, 4210 JP, 504 BC

*1051.* On the isle of Naxos, some of the rich were expelled by the poor and sought refuge with Aristagoras, son of Molpagoras and son-in-law and first cousin on the mother's side, to Histiaeus, the tyrant of Miletus. Histiaeus had left Aristagoras governor there on Naxos in his place, when Darius had honoured him by taking him to Susa. Aristagoras related the matter to Artaphernes, who was the son of Hystaspes and brother to Darius, governor of Ionia, who lived at Sardis. *[L164]* He persuaded him to annex for the king, the islands of Naxos, Paros and Andros and the rest of the Cyclades, all dependencies of Naxos. Darius at Susa liked the idea, and in the following spring he furnished two hundred ships for that war. {*Herodotus, l. 5. c. 30-31. 3:31-33*}

### 3501c AM, 4211 JP, 503 BC

*1052.* Artaphernes made Megabates, a Persian and a close cousin to himself and Darius, commander-in-chief of the Persian army. He ordered him to go to Miletus with his fleet of two hundred ships, where he was to join forces with Aristagoras and the Ionian army, which he did. They sailed from there to Chios, but when they had spent four months in the siege of Naxos, a disagreement occurred between Aristagoras and Artaphernes and nothing came of the siege, each returning home again having accomplished nothing. {*Herodotus, l. 5. c. 32-34. 3:33-37}

## 3502b AM, 4212 JP, 502 BC

1053. Seventy years had elapsed from the taking of Tyre by Nebuchadnezzar. This was the number of years of the bondage of that city. {Isa 23:15,17} After this time, it seems they lived in freedom from any foreign subjection, until the time it was again taken by Alexander the Great.

1054. Aristagoras feared what might happen to him because he had not been able to take Naxos. Because he had no money to pay his army, he began to think of revolting from the Persians. It so happened that at exactly that time a messenger came from Histiaeus in Babylon. His message was written in letters made with hot irons upon the flesh of his head and now overgrown with hair. He advised Aristagoras to defect from Darius and cause all Ionia to revolt, if he could. {*Herodotus, l. 5. c. 35. 3:37,39} {Polyaenus, Strategmata, l. 1.}

1055. Aristagoras told his friends of this, and persuaded them to side with him. Hecataeus, the historian, tried in vain to prevent them from rebelling against the king of Persia. The conspirators sent Iatrogoras to the army at Miletus. [E115] On their return from Naxos, they remained at Miletus and by a stratagem won over all the principal commanders of their fleet.

1056. Aristagoras now publicly revolted from Darius. He made a fair show of giving liberty to the Milesians, by taking away the rulers that were in some cities of Ionia. He then went to the Lacedemonians to ask for their help, but they flatly refused. {*Herodotus, l. 5. c. 36-38. 3:39-43} {*Herodotus, l. 5. c. 49-51. 3:51-57}

## 3503a AM, 4212 JP, 502 BC

1057. In the twentieth year of the reign of Darius, the 245th year of Nabonassar's era, on the twenty-eighth day of the month of Epeiph, according to the Egyptian calendar (November 19), there was an eclipse of the moon at Babylon, ending about midnight. {Ptolemy, Great Syntaxis, l. 4. c. 9.}

## 3503b AM, 4213 JP, 501 BC

1058. The Lacedemonians sent to Sigeum for Hippias, the son of Peisistratus. He went to Athens in the hope, which they had given him, that he might be restored to power, but this was all in vain and he returned to Asia. He accused the Athenians of many things to Artaphernes, hoping to bring Athens under the subjection of Darius. {*Herodotus, l. 5. c. 91,96. 3:101,102,117}

1059. When the Athenians understood that Hippias had defamed them to Artaphernes, they sent their messengers to Sardis to persuade the Persians not to give credence to those banished from among the Athenians. However, Artaphernes advised them that if they loved themselves and their own safety, they should call Hippias back home and welcome him again. They refused any such conditions. It happened that Aristagoras, the Milesian, returned empty-handed from Sparta. He came to Athens and there obtained twenty ships to aid the Ionians in their war against the Persians. They made Melanthius, an eminent man in Athens, commander of this fleet, which, as Herodotus has well noted, was the beginning of all the trouble between the Greeks and Persians. This was the beginning of all the wars which occurred between the Greeks and the Persians and which ended in the ruin of the Persian Empire. {*Herodotus, l. 3. c. 96,97. 3:117-121} [L165]

1060. When Aristagoras returned to Miletus, he persuaded the Paeonians to return to their own country. Megabazus, the governor of Thrace, had carried them away into Phrygia from their own country on the banks of the Strymon River and on the authority of Darius, had settled them there. They now took with them their wives and children and travelled to the sea coast. Some settled there for fear of going any farther. The rest went to Chios, and from there sailed to Lesbos and to Doriscus, from where they went overland into their own country. {*Herodotus, l. 5. c. 98. 3:119,121}

## 3504 AM, 4214 JP, 500 BC

1061. The Athenian fleet arrived at Miletus. Five triremes of the Eretrians came with them to help the Athenians. Aristagoras remained there, sending his own brother Charopinus, commander over the Milesians, together with Helmophantus, who commanded the rest of the Ionians, to fight against Sardis. The Ionians, with the Athenians and Eretrians, sailed to Ephesus. They left their ships at Coresus, a port of the Ephesians, and marched to Sardis. They took and burned it all, except for the citadel, which Artaphernes kept for himself. They even destroyed the temple of Cybele. When the Lydians and Persians united forces, they defended and held the market place, through which the Pactolus River ran. The fearful Ionians retired to the hill Tmolus next to the market and fled to their ships by night. The Persians who lived on that side of the Halys River gathered their forces and pursued them. They overtook them near Ephesus, where they fought and routed them. Many were killed, including Evalcides, captain of the Eretrians. He had won many garlands in many of their games and was highly commended in the poetry of Simonides. Those who escaped from the battle scattered into their various cities. The Athenians abandoned the Ionian cause from that time on, although they were earnestly entreated by Aristagoras to help the Ionians. {*Herodotus, l. 5. c. 99-103. 3:121-125}

1062. Onesilus deposed his older brother Gorgus, king of the Salaminians, and forced him to flee over to the Medes for help. Onesilus caused the whole island of Cyprus to defect from Darius, with the exception of the people of Amathus. When he was besieging that city, Darius received news of the burning of Sardis by the Athenians. He was very angry with the Athenians and ordered one of his attendants to remind him of it three times, whenever he sat eating, by saying, *Master, remember the Athenians.* He unwisely sent away Histiaeus, the brother of Aristagoras, from Susa to Miletus and Histiaeus later became the ringleader of the Ionian rebellion against him. {*Herodotus, l. 5. c. 104-106. 3:125-129}

1063. The Ionians sailed into the Hellespont and took Byzantium, along with other cities in those parts. Sailing from there, they caused many of the cities of Caria to join with them in this war against the Persians. When the city of Caunus heard of the burning of Sardis, they decided to join them, even though before this they had refused to do so. {*Herodotus, l. 5. c. 103. 3:125}

1064. At Clazomene, which was originally an island but later artificially joined to the continent of Ionia by a neck of land, {*Strabo, l. 1. c. 3. s. 17. 1:217} [E116] Anaxagoras the philosopher, the son of Hegesibulus, was born in the 70th Olympiad, according to Apollodorus. {*Diogenes Laertius, Anaxgoras, l. 2. c. 3. (7) 1:137}

1065. While Onesilus and his army were besieging Amathus, he received news that Artybius, a captain of the Persians, was heading to Cyprus with a very large army. Onesilus sent to the Ionians for help and they immediately sailed to Cyprus with a large fleet. The Persians left Cilicia and landed in Cyprus. They marched to the city of Salamis and sent the Phoenicians with their ships to take the point of a promontory in the island called the Keys of Cyprus. A naval and land battle ensued. [L166] At sea that day, the Ionians, especially the Samians, behaved valiantly and defeated the Phoenicians. On land, while the rest were busy fighting, first Stesenor, tyrant of Curium, betrayed his companions, and then presently the men of Salamis, who fought in chariots, did the same. The whole army of the Cypriots was routed and many were killed. Among the dead was Onesilus, the author of this war, and Aristocyprus, son of Philocyprus and king of the Solians, whom Solon, while he was at Cyprus, had greatly extolled in his poetry, more than all the other tyrants. When the Ionians heard that Onesilus was dead, that the rest of the cities of Cyprus were besieged, and that Salamis had welcomed back Gorgus their old king, they quickly returned

to Ionia. Of all the cities of Cyprus, Soli held out the longest, but after four months, the Persians undermined the wall around the city and took it. Hence, the Cypriots paid dearly for their one year of liberty and were again reduced to slavery. {*Herodotus, l. 5. c. 108-116. 3:131-139}

## 3505 AM, 4215 JP, 499 BC

1066. The Persian leaders, Daurises, Hymaees and Otanes at Sardis, who had married the daughters of Darius, pursued the Ionians who had helped in the attack against Sardis. After they had routed them near Ephesus and driven them aboard their ships, they divided the rest of the cities among themselves, so they could conquer them. {*Herodotus, l. 5. c. 116. 3:139} Daurises subdued the lands adjoining the Hellespont and in five days took the five cities, Dardanus, Abydus, Percote, Lampsacus and Paesus. He was on his way from there to the city of Parium when he received news that all Caria had revolted from the king and joined with the Ionians. He abandoned his plan to take Parium and marched with all his army to Caria. {*Herodotus, l. 5. c. 117. 3:139} Hymaees subdued the lands about Propontis and took the city of Cius in Mysia. When he heard that Daurises was marching from the Hellespont to Caria, he left Propontis and marched into the Hellespont. {*Herodotus, l. 5. c. 122. 3:143} Artaphernes, the governor of Sardis, and Otanes, the third commander, attacked Ionia and part of Aeolia. In Ionia, they took the city of Clazomene and in Aeolia, the city of Cyme. {*Herodotus, l. 5. c. 123. 3:143} After this, Anaxagoras met together with his men, to decide on a place to flee to. In this meeting, Hecataeus, the historian, advised them to move to the isle of Leros and fortify it, and to stay there until it was safe to return to Miletus. Aristagoras advised them to sail to a place called Myrcinus, a city of Edonia. These people lived on the bank of the Strymon River which his own brother Histiaeus had formerly built. Aristagoras committed the government of Miletus to Pythagoras and with a group of volunteers he sailed from there into Thrace and took control of the area he had planned to take over. {*Herodotus, l. 5. c. 124-126. 3:143-146}

1067. When Histiaeus, the tyrant of Miletus, was sent away from Susa by Darius, he went to Sardis, where Artaphernes charged him with being the author of all the unrest and rebellion in Ionia. He escaped by night to the coast and sailed over to Chios. The people thought that he had been sent there by Darius to enlist their support against the Greeks, and so they put him in irons. When they understood that he had come to help the Greeks, they quickly set him free. He immediately sent a message to Sardis, through Hermippus of Atarneus, to persuade certain of the Persians to revolt. Artaphernes got wind of this when he captured the messenger, and killed the Persians involved. When this plot failed, Histiaeus had the men of Chios escort him back to Miletus. [L167] The Milesians were glad to be rid of Aristagoras and did not want another tyrant in his place, so when Histiaeus tried to get into the city secretly by night, the men of Miletus wounded him in the thigh. Because he was expelled from there, he returned again to Chios. {*Herodotus, l. 6. c. 1-5. 3:149-151}

### 3506 AM, 4216 JP, 498 BC

1068. Daurises, the Persian, led his army against the Carians. They met at a place called the White Pillars near the Marsyas River. Pixodarus, the son of Mausolus, a man of Cindya, who had married the daughter of Sienoses, the king of Cilicia, advised the Carians to cross the Meander River, where they would have the river behind them and await the enemy there and fight from this good position. [E117] However, the opposite opinion prevailed, that the Persians should fight the Carians with the river at their backs. This would cut off all retreat and force the Persians to fight harder. When the Carians and Persians fought near the Marsyas River, the battle was fierce and long. The Persians lost two thousand men and the Carians ten thousand. The Carians fled to Labraunda to the temple of Zeus and there decided what to do. Should they submit to the Persians or abandon Asia? At this point, the Milesians with their allies came to help them. Thus encouraged, they fought again with the Persians who had invaded them. After a longer battle than the previous one, they fled again. They and the Milesians lost very many men. After these great losses, the Carians received more help, and fought with the Persians a third time. When they heard that the Persians were sacking their cities, they lay in ambush for them as they were marching to Mylasa. This was planned by Heraclides of Mylasa, the son of Ibanollis. They attacked the Persians at night and slaughtered them. The Persian commanders Daurises, Amorges, Sismaces and Myrsus, the son of Gyges, were killed. {*Herodotus, l. 5. c. 118-121. 3:139-143}

1069. Hymaees, the Persian, who led his army into the country of the Hellespont, defeated all the Aeolians who lived in the region of old Troy. He also subdued the Gergithes, the rest of the ancient Teucrians. After this he became sick and died at Troas. {*Herodotus, l. 5. c. 122. 3:143}

1070. When Histiaeus, the Milesian, could not get ships from Chios, he went to Mitylene. Here the Lesbians let him have eight triremes and sailed with him to Byzantium, where they intercepted certain ships of the Ionians who had come from Pontus. These submitted to the leadership of Histiaeus. {*Herodotus, l. 6. c. 5,26. 3:151,153,173}

1071. Aristagoras, Histiaeus' brother, was with his army at the siege of Myrcinus, a city of Edonia. He and his men were killed by the Thracians, who lied to him about granting him safe passage from the place. {*Herodotus, l. 5. c. 126. 1:145} Thucydides reckoned that it was sixty-one years from this time to the starting of a colony of the Athenians by Agnon, the son of Nicias, at Amphipolis. {*Thucydides, l. 4. c. 102. s. 2. 2:387} Diodorus stated that this took place in the 85th Olympiad. {*Diod. Sic., l. 12. c. 68. 5:71,73} We followed Diodordus and ended the six year rebellion of the Ionians against the Persians in the following year.

### 3507 AM, 4217 JP, 497 BC

1072. All the Persian commanders united in one large naval and land force to take the city of Miletus. In the navy, the Phoenicians were the best sailors. They were helped by the Cypriots (who had recently been subdued by the Persians), the Cilicians and the Egyptians. {*Herodotus, l. 6. c. 6. 3:153} This threat seems to be mentioned by Diogenes Laertius in letters which were attributed to Anaximenes, the Milesian, written to Pythagoras, who was living at Croton. {*Diogenes Laertius, Anaximenes, l. 2. c. 2. (5) 1:135} [L168] Pythagoras lived there for twenty years and then went to Metapontus, where he lived out the rest of his days. {Justin, Trogus, l. 20. c. 4.} This was the fourth year of the 70th Olympiad, which took up part of this year and part of the next year. {*Eusebius, Chronicles, l. 1. 1:189}

1073. The Ionian fleet had three hundred and fifty-three ships and the Persians had six hundred. Aeaces, the son of Syloson, the tyrant of Samos, was now in the Persian army, together with other tyrants of Ionia, who had been expelled by Aristagoras. They tried to draw as many of their countrymen as they could from the Ionian to the Persian side. The naval battle between the Phoenicians and the Ionians happened at Lade, a little island lying opposite Miletus. Of the sixty ships that came from the isle of Samos, fifty ships fled home from the battle in a cowardly manner. Likewise, seventy more of the Lesbian ships and others of the Ionians fled. There were a hundred ships of the isle of Chios which fought valiantly, until at length, having taken many of the enemy's ships and lost many of their own, they returned home with what they had left. Some were closely pursued by the enemy and were run aground at the promontory of Mycale. They escaped to shore and after travelling all night on foot, came safely to Ephesus. Here, the women were celebrating their feast and sacrifices, called Thesmophoria, in honour of their goddess, Ceres. The men of the city thought that the Chians were thieves who had come to plunder them at that time. They attacked them suddenly and killed them. Dionysius, captain of three ships of the Phocaeans, captured three ships of the enemies. He did not sail to Phocaea, which he knew was about to fall to the enemy with the rest of the Ionian territories, but sailed directly to Phoenicia. Here he sank a number of cargo ships and robbed them of their valuable cargo. He then set sail for Sicily. {*Herodotus, l. 6. c. 7-17. 3:153-165} [E118]

1074. When the Persians had defeated the Ionians at sea, they attacked the beleaguered city of Miletus, both by sea and land. They undermined its walls with all types of engines of war and utterly overthrew and razed it to the ground in the sixth year after Aristagoras began his rebellion against the king of Persia. {*Herodotus, l. 6. c. 18. 3:165} Some of the Milesians, who escaped with certain of the Samians, started a colony in Sicily. {*Herodotus, l. 6. c. 22. 3:169} The rest were carried away to Susa. Darius inflicted no further punishment on them and settled them in the city of Ampa on the Persian Gulf, near the mouth of the Tigris River. The Persians took the plain and low grounds lying near the city of Miletus and gave the mountainous parts to the Carians from Pedasa. {*Herodotus, l. 6. c. 20. 3:167}

1075. After the taking of Miletus, the Carians were all quickly captured. Some surrendered willingly and others by compulsion. {*Herodotus, l. 6. c. 25. 3:171} When Histiaeus, the Milesian, heard what had happened to his city of Miletus, he sailed to Chios with the Lesbians who were with him. He easily subdued the people of Chios because they were greatly weakened by their heavy losses at Lade. He went from there with a strong party of Ionians and Aeolians to Thasos. While he was besieging Thasos, he heard that the Persians were attacking the rest of Ionia. He lifted his siege from Thasos and immediately sailed to Lesbos with all his forces. When he saw that his men were short of food, he sailed to the province of Atarneus with the intention of foraging for food both there and in the countryside around the Caicus River in the province of Mysia. Harpagus, the Persian, was in those parts with a very large army. He attacked Histiaeus as he came from his ships at a place called Malene and took him alive, but killed most of his men. After Histiaeus was brought to Sardis as a prisoner, Artaphernes crucified him and sent his head to Darius at Susa. [L169] Darius criticised them for not bringing him alive to him, and ordered that his head should be interred, as a man respected by him and the Persian nation. {*Herodotus, l. 6. c. 27-29. 3:173-177}

**3508 AM, 4218 JP, 496 BC**

1076. The Persian navy wintered near Miletus. They captured the islands bordering on the continent and in less than two years had captured Chios, Lesbos, Tenedos and the rest. {*Herodotus, l. 6. c. 31. 3:177}

1077. The islands having been taken, the Persian captains went on to capture the cities of Ionia. When these were subdued, they selected the most beautiful boys and girls from among them and sent them to Darius. They burned the cities and their temples. Hence, the Ionians were brought into bondage three times, once by the Lydians and now twice by the Persians. {*Herodotus, l. 6. c. 31,32. 3:177,179}

1078. Before the Phoenician fleet came, the inhabitants of Byzantium and of Chalcedon, which lay opposite it, abandoned their cities and fled to the remotest parts of the Black Sea. Here they built a city called Mesembria. {*Herodotus, l. 6. c. 33. 3:179}

**3509 AM, 4219 JP, 495 BC**

1079. The Phoenician fleet sailed from Ionia and subdued all that lay on their left hand as you go into the Hellespont. What lay on the right hand in Asia had already been subdued by the Persians. The fleet took the Chersonesus and its cities, except the city of Cardia where Miltiades, the son of Cimon, had until then been tyrant. {*Herodotus, l. 6. c. 33,34. 3:179} When Miltiades sailed from Cardia with five triremes for Athens, the Phoenicians pursued him and took one of his ships containing his son Metiochus. He was sent prisoner to Darius, by whom he was honourably received and given both house and lands and a Persian woman for a wife. She bore him many children. {*Herodotus, l. 6. c. 41. 3:187}

1080. When Artaphernes, the governor of Sardis, found the Ionians fighting among themselves, he sent for some from each side to come to him. He made peace with them on certain conditions. He caused them to settle their differences by arbitration rather than by killing each other and ruining their country. {*Herodotus, l. 6. c. 42. 3:187,189}

1081. When Artaphernes made peace, he surveyed their country in parasangs (a Persian measure of length containing thirty furlongs or almost four miles) and formed divisions. On each division he imposed a tribute which was paid yearly to the king. The rate remained constant until at least the time of Herodotus. {*Herodotus, l. 6. c. 42. 3:189} That rate was first levied when Darius became king and he imposed it on all his empire. {*Herodotus, l. 3. c. 89,90. 2:117,119} This was before Darius was master of the islands. {*Herodotus, l. 3. c. 96. 2:123} According to Herodotus, we note that, to facilitate taxing, Darius now reduced the one hundred and twenty-seven provinces mentioned in Esther down to twenty, yet the bounds of that empire were still the same, stretching from India to Ethiopia. One side had been conquered by Cambyses and the other by Darius. Concerning the revenue from India, Herodotus stated: {*Herodotus, l. 3. c. 94. 2:123}

"Since the Indians were the most populous nation, more than all other men living that we know, they paid far more tribute than any other nation did, that is three hundred and sixty talents of gold dust and this was the twentieth province." [E119]

1082. Since we find that when Darius was made king he did not control India, as is evident even from Herodotus himself {*Herodotus, l. 4. c. 44. 2:245}, it is therefore likely that when the tax rate was set by Artaphernes in Ionia, a similar tax was imposed all over the kingdom by the governors of each of the provinces. [L170]

1083. It should therefore be considered whether this refers to the time which was spoken of in Esther: {Es 10:1-3}

"After this, the king Ahasuerus imposed a tribute upon the land and isles of the sea."

1084. That is, this refers to the very time when King Ahasuerus made all the earth and all the islands of the sea pay tribute. For, as Thucydides stated (and Plato confirmed this {Plato, Menexenus}), Darius subdued all the islands lying in the Aegean Sea by means of his Phoenician fleet. {*Thucydides, l. 1. c. 16. 1:31} Diodorus Siculus stated that they were all lost again by his son Xerxes immediately after his defeat in Greece. {*Diod. Sic., l. 11. c. 36,37. 4:221,223} {*Diod. Sic., l. 12. c. 1. 4:375} It was after the twelfth year of his reign that the scriptures stated that Ahasuerus imposed this tribute upon the isles. {Es 3:7 10:1} For in the war of Xerxes against Greece, all the islands which lay between the Cyanean Isles and the two forelands of Triopium in Cnidos and of Sumium in Attica sent him ships. Diodorus Siculus stated that his successors held none of these isles at all except for Cyprus and Clazomene, which was at that time a small and poor island. {*Diod. Sic., l. 12. c. 3,4. 4:379-383} {*Thucydides, l. 8. c. 14. 4:213} {*Thucydides, l. 8. c. 31. 4:243} {*Plutarch, Cimon, l. 1. c. 13. s. 4. 2:445} {*Livy, l. 33. c. 20. 9:331} This is demonstrated by the tenor of Antalcidas' peace, as recorded by Xenophon. {*Xenophon, Hellenica, l. 5. c. 1. s. 31. 2:21} This seems to me to be a good argument for believing that the Ahasuerus mentioned in Esther is none other than Darius. For this and other similar impositions laid upon the people, the Persians used to call him a crafty merchant or huckster, as Herodotus noted of him. Under Cyrus and Cambyses, his two predecessors, there was no mention of any tribute charged upon the subjects but that they only brought the king presents. {*Herodotus, l. 3. c. 89. 2:117} Strabo stated: {*Strabo, l. 15. c. 3. s. 21. 7:185}

"The first that ever brought up paying of tribute was Darius the Long-armed."

1085. Strabo mistook the surname of Artaxerxes, the grandchild, and gave it to the grandfather. He also said:

"for before him, men paid their kings from what every country yielded, as grain, horses...."

1086. Polyaenus stated: {Polyaenus, Strategmata, l. 7.}

"Darius was the first that ever imposed a tribute upon the people. Nevertheless, to make it more palatable to them, he had his officers set the rate first. When they imposed a very heavy tax, he took off one half of it which they willingly paid and took it for a great favour, too, from the king's hand."

1087. This story is also mentioned by Plutarch. {*Plutarch, Sayings of Kings and Commanders (172f) 3:13}

### 3510 AM, 4220 JP, 494 BC

1088. In the beginning of this spring, the king relieved all the commanders and sent away the young gentleman Mardonius, the son of Gobryas, who had recently married the king's daughter Arotozostra. Mardonius came to the coast of Cilicia with a vast, well equipped army and navy. He sent his army overland to the Hellespont while he took the navy to parts of Ionia. He deposed the tyrants in each of the cities and restored their elected governments. Shortly after this, he subdued the men of Thasos with his fleet and the Macedonians with his army. His navy sailed from Thasos to Acanthus. While they tried to round the cape of Mount Athos, a violent storm destroyed three hundred of his ships and over twenty thousand men. While Mardonius stayed in Macedonia with his army, the Thracians, known as the Brygi, attacked his camp at night. They killed many of his men and wounded Mardonius. When he had subdued Macedonia, he left and returned into Asia. {*Herodotus, l. 6. c. 43-45. 3:47,49}

### 3511 AM, 4221 JP, 493 BC

1089. The next year, Darius ordered the inhabitants of Thasos, who had been accused of intending to rebel against him, to demolish the walls of their city and to send away all their shipping to Abdera. He then determined to see whether the Greeks would fight, or submit to him. He sent envoys into Greece with the order to demand a gift of earth and water from them. [L171] (This gift would signify their submission to the Persian king.) He ordered his towns on the sea coast to send fighting ships and other towns to send horses to him. Therefore, many in Greece and in the adjacent isles gave him earth and water. The Aeginetans were the first to do this. {*Herodotus, l. 6. c. 46,48,49. 3:193,195}

### 3512 AM, 4222 JP, 492 BC

1090. The Aeginetans, who were traitors to Greece, were now attacked by Cleomenes, king of the Spartans. Demaratus, the other Spartan king, was expelled from

Sparta when a disagreement arose between him and Cleomenes. He fled into Asia to Darius, who entertained him magnificently and gave him cities and lands to rule. {*Herodotus, l. 6. c. 49,50,61,67,70. 3:195,207,215,219}

## 3513 AM, 4223 JP, 491 BC

1091. There was an eclipse of the moon at Babylon in the thirty-first year of Darius, the 257th year of Nabonassar's epoch, on the third day of the month of Tybi (April 25), half an hour before midnight. {Ptolemy, Great Syntaxis, l. 4. c. 9.} Darius removed Mardonius from his command because of his poor handling of the navy and sent others to take charge of the war against Eretria and Athens. [E120] These were Datis, a Median, and Artaphernes (whom the Scholiast of Aristophanes called Artabaxus), commander of the cavalry, the son of Darius' brother, Artaphernes. While they were camped in a plain of Cilicia near the sea, they repaired all the naval forces and prepared their ships for transporting the horses which the tributary cities had provided. With the army and horses on board, they sailed for Ionia with a fleet of six hundred ships. {*Herodotus, l. 6. c. 94,95. 3:245,247} However, Plato {Plato, Menexenus} stated they had only three hundred ships and half a million soldiers. Lysias also confirmed this number. {Lysias, Corinthian Auxiliaries} But Emilius Probus stated the fleet had five hundred ships, two hundred thousand soldiers and ten thousand horses. {Emilius Probus, Miltiades}

## 3514c AM, 4224 JP, 490 BC

1092. The Persians sailed from Samos to Naxos and burned all its houses and temples. They spared Delos and went to the other islands. From there they took men captive to serve them, as well as taking their children as hostages. When the men of Casrystos refused to cooperate, they were besieged until at last they too were forced to surrender their city and themselves to the enemy. {*Herodotus, l. 6. c. 95,96,99. 3:247-251}

## 3514d AM, 4224 JP, 490 BC

1093. The Persians took Eretria after a seven day long siege. After spending a few days in settling things there, they sailed to the land of Attica and destroyed a great part of it. At last, with the guidance of Hippias, the son of Peisistratus, they came to the plain of Marathon. There they were defeated by the men of Athens and of Plataea, under the command of Miltiades. He had the government of the Chersonesus in Thrace. The Greeks lost a hundred and ninety-two men, while the Persians lost sixty-four hundred. {*Herodotus, l. 6. c. 101,102,112,117. 3:253,255,267,271}

1094. The Persians fled to their ships, many of which were subsequently sunk or captured. In these two battles the Persians lost two hundred thousand men. Hippias,

the author of this war and a former tyrant of Athens, died there. {Justin, Trogus, l. 2. c. 9.} The entire army of the Persians in this battle consisted of three hundred thousand men. {*Valerius Maximus, l. 5. c. 3. ext. 3c. 1:489} Plutarch thought the number was at least this large. {*Plutarch, Parallel Stories, l. 1. c. 1. 4:257} Justin and Orosius followed his account and said there were six hundred thousand men in all. Emilius Probus stated that there were a hundred thousand soldiers and twenty thousand cavalry. {Emilius Probus, Miltiades} On the Athenian side there were ten thousand men, as well as a thousand of their auxiliaries from Plataea, according to Justin and Orosius. Probus stated that the Athenians, together with the men of Plataea, totalled only ten thousand. This significant victory happened on the sixth day of the month of Boedromion, the third month in the Attic calendar after the summer solstice, {*Plutarch, Camillus, l. 1. c. 19. s. 3. 2:139} when Phanippus was in charge of Athens. [L172] Plutarch stated that this happened in the third year of the 72nd Olympiad, four years before the death of Darius. {*Plutarch, Aristides, l. 1. c. 5. s. 7. 2:227?} Sulpicius, likewise, said the same thing. {*Sulpicius Severus, Sacred History, l. 2. c. 9. 11:101} This was in the tenth year before Xerxes entered into Greece, {*Thucydides, l. 1. c. 18. s. 1,2. 1:33} {Lysias, Corinthian Auxiliaries} and ten full years before the naval battle at Salamis, in the same month of Boedromion. {Plato, De Legibus, l. 3.}

1095. Datis and Artaphernes returned into Asia, taking with them to Susa their captives from Eretria. {*Herodotus, l. 6. c. 119. 3:273} But according to Ctesias, Datis was killed in the battle at Marathon and the Athenians refused to give the Persians his body.

## 3515 AM, 4225 JP, 489 BC

1096. When the Eretrian captives were brought to Darius, he had them settled in a part of the Cissian country called Ardericca, about twenty-six miles from Susa. {*Herodotus, l. 6. c. 119. 3:273} This is described in more detail by Philostratus. {*Philostratus, Apollonius, l. 1. c. 24. 1:69}

## 3517d AM, 4227 JP, 487 BC

1097. After Darius had spent three years in making greater preparations against Greece than before, the Egyptians revolted in the fourth year. {*Herodotus, l. 7. c. 1. 3:301}

## 3519 AM, 4229 JP, 485 BC

1098. When Darius was now ready to begin his war against the Egyptians and Athenians, he was required by the laws of the Persians to name his successor in the kingdom.

1099. Artobazanes, whom others call Artemenes, or Ariamenes, was his son by Gobryas' daughter. He was born to him before he came to be king, and claimed the succession by right of the firstborn. Xerxes was born after Darius became king. Xerxes' mother was Atossa, the daughter of Cyrus, who had founded the Persian Empire. {*Herodotus, l. 7. c. 2,3. 3:301,303} There was friendly rivalry between the two brothers. For more on this, see Justin and Plutarch. {Justin, Trogus, l. 2. c. 10.} {*Plutarch, Artaxerxes, l. 1. c. 2. 11:131} {*Plutarch, Sayings of Kings and Commanders (173c) 3:15} {*Plutarch, On Brotherly Love, l. 1. c. 18. 6:303-307}

### 3519c AM, 4229 JP, 485 BC

1100. When Darius had declared Xerxes to be the next king, he was now ready to take his journey. According to Diodorus {*Diod. Sic., l. 11. c. 2. s. 2. 4:123} he was on his way into Greece in the year following the revolt of the Egyptians. Toward the latter half of that year he died, having reigned for a full thirty-six years. {*Herodotus, l. 7. c. 4. 3:305} [E121]

1101. After him came Xerxes, the fourth king of Persia after Cyrus. He trusted in his riches (which were indeed exceedingly great) and stirred up his own subjects, together with all his allies and friends, to make war on the Greeks, as had been prophesied by Daniel. {Da 11:2} This was not originally his intention but he was put up to it by Mardonius, his first cousin, and by the Aleuadae who were the princes of Thessaly, as well as by the family of Peisistratus and by Onomacritus, a sorcerer of Athens. {*Herodotus, l. 7. c. 5,6. 3:305,307}

### 3520 AM, 4230 JP, 484 BC

1102. At the beginning of the second year of his reign after the death of Darius, Xerxes undertook an expedition against the rebellious Egyptians. After he had subdued them, he brought them into a harder state of bondage than they had ever experienced under his predecessors. He made his brother Achemenes, the son of Darius, ruler over them. {*Herodotus, l. 7. c. 7. 3:309}

1103. In this year, Herodotus, the historian, the son of Lyxus and Eryone, was born at Halicarnassus in the province of Caria. He was fifty-three years old when the Peloponnesian War began. {*Aulus Gellius, Attic Nights, l. 15. c. 23. s. 1,2. 3:113} At that time Artemisia, the daughter of Lygdamis of Halicarnassus, following the death of her husband, obtained the government he had held. This occurred during the schooling of her young son, whose name was Psindelis, as may be gathered from Suidas in Herodotus. [L173] She ruled over Halicarnassus, Cos, Nisyros and Calydnos. Some time later she came into Greece with five good fighting ships to help Xerxes in his war. {*Herodotus, l. 7. c. 99. 3:401}

### 3523 AM, 4233 JP, 481 BC

1104. Xerxes gathered together from all of his empire of Egypt, Phoenicia, Cyprus, Cilicia, Pamphylia, Pisidia, Lycia, Caria, Mysia, Troas, the Hellespont, Bithynia and Pontus, twelve hundred ships to meet him at Cyme and Phocaea in Ionia. He set out from Susa with all the troops and cavalry he could muster in the beginning of the fourth year of the 74th Olympiad. However, Diodorus merged the events of these two years into one by stating this took place in the first year of the same Olympiad. {*Diod. Sic., l. 11. c. 1-2. 4:121-125} Herodotus said that the above preparation took place three whole years before this year, but with a note on the previous chapter which cannot be consistent with the chronological record. He said: {*Herodotus, l. 7. c. 20. 3:335}

> "From the subduing of Egypt, he took four years in gathering an army and in making his preparations. In the beginning of the fifth year, he began to march with a large army."

1105. He left Susa in the beginning of his fifth year, not from the subduing of Egypt but from his becoming king. Hence, both Justin and Orosius follow Herodotus and incorrectly assign five years to this period. {Justin, Trogus, l. 2. c. 10.} {Orsius, l. 2. c. 9.} Julian, in his first oration of the praises of Constantius, incorrectly said that Xerxes spent ten years preparing. More ingenuous than all of these (though his account was not very carefully researched) was Labianus, who claimed that between Darius and Xerxes ten years were spent in the preparation against Greece. We say this because we have previously shown from Plato that only ten years elapsed from the battle at Marathon to the battle at Salamis, which was fought in the first year of the 75th Olympiad (almost a full year after Xerxes left Susa).

1106. All Xerxes' forces came together at Critalla in Cappadocia. From there he passed over the Halys River and came to Celaenae, a city in Phrygia. Here Pythius, a Lydian (Pliny stated that he was from Bithynia {*Pliny, l. 33. c. 47. (137) 9:103}), the son of Atys, entertained him and his whole army in a most magnificent and sumptuous manner. From here they passed by Anaua, a city of Phrygia, and Lough, where salt was made, and came to Colosse in Phrygia. It was here that the Lycus River disappeared underground. Moving on from there he came to a town called Cyndrara in Phrygia, then on to Lydia, after which he passed by the Meander River. He passed the city called Callatebus and finally arrived at Sardis. From here he dispatched his messengers into Greece to demand earth and water from them, in other words, he required them to surrender to him. {*Herodotus, l. 7. c. 26-32. 3:341-347}

1107. In the meantime, the navy was at Elaeus in the Chersonesus. From here, part of the army dug through the neck of Mount Athos for about one and a half miles.

They and the Bastinadoes were forced to do this work, and the neighbouring inhabitants were compelled to help. Bubares, the son of Megabyzus, and Artachaees, the son of Artaeus, who were both Persians, were appointed to oversee the work. When that neck of land was cut through and the sea let in, the channel was wide enough for two large ships, with their oars extended, to pass each other without touching. {*Herodotus, l. 7. c. 22-24. 3:337,339} [L174] Another part of the army built a bridge of ships over the Hellespont, where the sea from Abydus to the shore on the other side is a little less than a mile wide. When the bridge was completed, a fierce storm arose and destroyed it. In a rage, Xerxes caused three hundred stripes to be given to the Hellespont, and a pair of shackles to be thrown into the sea to bind and fetter it with. [E122] He decapitated those who had made the bridge and then employed others to work at making the bridge stronger. {*Herodotus, l. 7. c. 33-36. 3:347,351}

### 3524b AM, 4234 JP, 480 BC

*1108.* At the beginning of the spring, Xerxes and his whole army left Sardis, where they had spent the winter, and marched toward Abydus. As he was starting his journey, the sun stopped shining. There were no clouds and the air was clear, but the day was turned into night. At this incredible sign, Pythius, the Lydian, was terrified (for it was no natural eclipse, as the astronomical tables easily show), and besought the king that of his five sons who were in his army he would leave his oldest out to be a comfort to him in his old age. In a rage, Xerxes had his oldest son cut in two, and the whole army marched between the halves of his dead body. {*Herodotus, l. 7. c. 37-39. 3:351-355}

*1109.* Hermotimus of Halicarnassus was the most influential of all the eunuchs with Xerxes. When he came into the country of Atarneus, in the province of Mysia, he sent for Panionius and his family from the isle of Chios. Panionius, who was a slave trader, came with his wife and children. Hermotimus made the father castrate his sons and then had them do the same to their father. In this way, Hermotimus was avenged of the wrong done to him by Panionius, who had castrated him and sold him into slavery as a eunuch to the Persians. {*Herodotus, l. 8. c. 105,106. 3:105,107}

*1110.* Xerxes and his army went from Lydia to the Caicus River and the country of Mysia. From there they came into the country where old Troy or Illium had stood. That night, as he slept at the foot of the hill Ida, a very violent thunderstorm arose which killed many in his army. After this, they came to the Scamander River, which they drained dry, in their quest to satisfy the men and animals with water. When Xerxes arrived there, he went up to see the old citadel of King Priam. There he sacrificed a thousand oxen to Athena of Troy. The Magi that attended him offered cakes to the nobles. At night, a panic fell on his army and he left there in the morning as soon as it was light, and came to Abydus. {*Herodotus, l. 7. c. 42,43. 3:357,359}

*1111.* Here Xerxes took a fancy to survey all his army at once. So he had a luxurious hall built of fair white stone, and he sat in the hall, from where he could see his navy at sea and all his army. He also wanted to see a naval battle. At the conclusion of that battle, the Phoenicians won the prize. The king took great pleasure in the battle and in the number of his men. He looked across all the sea of the Hellespont covered with his ships, and all the shores and plains about Abydus that were covered with his soldiers. When he considered the brevity of man's life, and that none of all these men would be alive after a hundred years, he wept. {*Herodotus, l. 7. c. 44,46. 3:359,361} {*Valerius Maximus, l. 9. c. 13. ext. 1. 2:383}

*1112.* Xerxes sent his uncle Arcabanus to be viceroy at Susa, and there to take care of his house and the kingdom, while he prepared to enter Europe. As soon as the sun was up, he held a golden vial in his hand over the sea. He prayed to the sun that nothing might hinder him in the conquest of Europe, till he had reached its utmost bounds. Having said this, he flung the vial, as well as a golden goblet and a Persian scimitar, into the Hellespont. [L175] When this was done, he sent his cavalry and foot soldiers to pass over the bridge on the right hand side, which was on the side of the Pontus. He ordered all the bags and baggage, servants and carriages to pass over on the left hand side, which was on the side of the Aegean Sea. It took them a whole week to cross over. When all this was done, the navy sailed west from the Hellespont to a place called Sarpedon's Cape. His army passed through the Chersonesus to Agora and turned aside to a place called the Black Bay, at the mouth of the Black River. This river was not able to supply enough water for all his army to drink. When they had passed this river, the army marched west to Doriscus, which is the name of a sea coast and of a spacious field in the country of Thrace through which the large Hebrus River flows. Here they camped. {*Herodotus, l. 7. c. 52-59. 3:367-375}

### 3524c AM, 4234 JP, 480 BC

*1113.* When the navy came to this place, they were ordered ashore, as Xerxes wanted to count all his navy and army. According to Herodotus, his foot soldiers numbered one million and seven hundred thousand men. {*Herodotus, l. 7. c. 60. 3:375} His horses, besides camels and chariots, numbered eighty thousand horses. {*Herodotus, l. 7. c. 87. 3:393} Among the commanders of his army, Herodotus mentioned two of Darius' sons born by his queen Artystone. (I think she was Esther, because Herodotus stated Darius loved her more than all his wives.) The son he called Arsames was commander of the Ethiopians from the south of Egypt. {*Herodotus, l. 7. c. 69. 3:383} The other, whom he called Gobryas, was leader of the Ligyes, Matieni, Mariandyni and the Syrians. {*Herodotus, l. 7. c. 72. 3:383,385} Diodorus Siculus tallied his foot soldiers at eight hundred thousand men, less than half of what Herodotus maintained. {*Diod. Sic., l. 11. c. 3. s. 7. 4:129} [E123] Yet the number which Diodorus attributed to the foot soldiers, was assigned by Ctesias to the army as a whole, eight hundred thousand besides the chariots. Isocrates stated that there were seven hundred thousand men in his armies of foot soldiers. {*Isocrates, Panathenaicus, l. 1. (49) 2:408} Aelian assigned the number of seven hundred thousand to the whole army. {*Aelian, Historical Miscellany, l. 13. c. 3. 1:421} Pliny numbered the army at seven hundred and eighty-eight thousand men and called Xerxes, Darius. {*Pliny, l. 33. c. 47. (127) 9:103} Justin and Orosius stated that Xerxes had seven hundred thousand men of his own subjects, and three hundred thousand auxiliaries from his allies. {Justin, Trogus} {Orosius, l. 1. c. 10.} Emilius Probus stated that his foot soldiers were seven hundred thousand men and his cavalry four hundred thousand. {Emilius Probus, Themistocles}

1114. His naval force consisted of twelve hundred and seven ships, of which the Phoenicians had supplied him with three hundred, including the ones sent by the Syrians in Palestine. {*Herodotus, l. 7. c. 89. 3:395} By Palestine Herodotus meant all the sea coast of Syria as far as Egypt. In another place he said that it had formerly been called Syria Palestina, and that its inhabitants were all circumcised. {*Herodotus, l. 3. c. 91. 2:2:119} {*Herodotus, l. 2. c. 104. 1:393} The Jews were also part of the Persian Empire. Josephus stated that some of his countrymen were in this army against the Greeks. To prove this, he cited those verses of the poet Choeilus: {*Josephus, Apion, l. 1. c. 22. (173) 1:233}

> His camp a nation strange to see, did follow,
> Who spoke the language of Phoenicia;
> And did the Solymian hills inhabit,
> Near to a broad lake which on them doth border:
> Whose heads were rounded and on their bald crowns,
> Of a horse head the dried skin did wear.

1115. [L176] The learned Salmasius thought that the Jews were meant by this, {Salmasius, Linguae Hellenistacae Ossilegio} although Scaliger, Cunaeus and that most learned Bochartus took it to be speaking of the Soylmi in Pisidia. {Eusebius, Scaliger's Greek Eusebius (Ad Fragmenta)} {Cunaeus, De Republic Hebra., l. 2. c. 18.} {Bochartus, Sacred Geography, Part 2. l. 1. c. 6.}

1116. Besides these warships, Herodotus stated that Xerxes had cargo ships, some of thirty oars, others of fifty oars apiece, besides smaller vessels and ships to carry horses, adding up to a total of three thousand. {*Herodotus, l. 7. c. 97. 3:401} Diodorus stated there were eight hundred and fifty ships for carrying horses and three thousand cargo ships of thirty oars apiece. {*Diod. Sic., l. 11. c. 3. s. 8. 4:131} The poet Eschyius in Persia in the writing his poem introduced a messenger to report the number of the ships in this way:

> I know that Xerxes' ships a thousand were;
> But full two hundred and seven ships he had,
> Exceeding swift ones. So the fame doth go.

1117. He could have meant that the total sum of them was a thousand, and so the two hundred and seven swift ships were part of the total, or both sums added together to give twelve hundred and seven. If so, this latter number agreed best with the particular catalogue of the ships which every country contributed to this expedition, as mentioned by Herodotus. It is not clear from the poetry what the exact total should be. Ctesias seemed to favour the former opinion and so did Cicero. {*Cicero, Against Verres II, l. 1. c. 18. 7:173} Isocrates agreed with the latter. {*Isocrates, Panegyricus, l. 1. (93) 1:177} {*Isocrates, Panathenaicus (49) 2:403} Lysias, in his epitaph, said there were about twelve hundred war ships, plus three thousand cargo ships. Justin must have been wrong when he said there were a million ships. Herodotus determined that about two hundred and forty-one thousand troops were in the twelve hundred and seven ships which came from Asia as follows. He had two hundred men in every hold, plus troops from the Persians, the Medes and the Sacae, for a total of 36,210 passengers. In the three thousand cargo ships he placed two hundred and forty thousand men, an average of about eighty per ship. So the whole navy consisted of 517,610 men. The number of the army was one million seven hundred thousand foot soldiers and eighty thousand cavalry. The Arabians who had charge of the camels, and the Libyans who tended the wagons, totalled about twenty thousand. The total number in Xerxes' forces would have been 2,317,610 plus horses, boys and other servants, and not including those who supplied the camp with food. {*Herodotus, l. 7. c. 184. 3:501}

1118. Xerxes marched from Doriscus into Greece. As he came to any country, he conscripted all who were fit for fighting. {*Herodotus, l. 7. c. 108. 3:413} He added a hundred and twenty ships to his navy and added two hundred more troops per ship, so increasing the naval forces by a total of twenty-four thousand men in all. Herodotus thought that his army increased by three hundred thousand. Diodorus thought the increase was less than two hundred thousand. {*Diod. Sic., l. 11. c. 4. s. 5. 4:135} [E124] So the total of Xerxes' army in European and Asiatic soldiers amounted to 2,641,610 men. [L177] Diodorus believed that the number of boys keeping the horses, the servants and sailors in the cargo ships and others, was larger than the number of soldiers. This means that even if that former sum were only doubled, the number of those which Xerxes carried by sea to Sepias and by land to Thermopylae would come to 5,283,220 men. This did not include the women cooks and the eunuchs, for no man can tell the exact number of them. Neither could he give the exact number of the horses and other beasts of burden, and the Indian dogs with their keepers, that followed the nobles in the camp for their pleasure. Hence, it was no wonder that so many rivers were exhausted from the thirst of so many people. {*Herodotus, l. 7. c. 185-187. 3:501-505} Juvenal stated: {Juvenal, Satire, 10.}

> We now believe that many rivers deep,
> Did fail the Persian army, at a dinner.

1119. Therefore, it was less of a wonder that both Isocrates and Plutarch claimed that Xerxes took over five million men into Greece. {*Isocrates, Panathenaicus, l. 1. (49) 2:403} {*Plutarch, Parallel Stories, l. 1. c. 2. 4:259}

1120. Yet in this large host, there was not a man as handsome as Xerxes or one that might seem more worthy of that great empire than he. {*Herodotus, l. 7. c. 187. 3:505} Like Saul among the children of Israel, so Xerxes might well seem to have been worthy of a crown. {1Sa 10:23,24} Yet, stated Justin, when you spoke of this king, you would find cause to commend his wealth, mentioned before in Daniel, {Da 11:2} rather than his character, of which he said: {Justin, Trogus}

> "There was such infinite abundance in his kingdom, that when whole rivers failed the multitude of his army, yet his wealth could never be exhausted. As for himself, he was always seen last in the fight and first in the flight. He was fearful when any danger was, but puffed up with pride when there was none."

1121. Leonidas, king of Sparta, with an army of four thousand Greeks, interposed himself against him and his whole army of three hundred thousand troops at the pass of Thermopylae in Thessaly. It was called this after the hot springs which were there. In this epitaph by Herodotus, we read: {*Herodotus, l. 7. c. 228. 3:545}

> Here against three hundred thousand Persians,
> Four thousand Spartans fought it out and died.

1122. Thirty myriads is three hundred thousand, which was the total given by Theodoret as the size of the whole army. {Theodoret, l. 10.} Diodorus in the Greek and Latin

edition of his work when commenting on this epitaph in Herodotus, wrote twenty myriads, which was two hundred thousand, instead of thirty myriads. {*Diod. Sic., l. 11. c. 4. s. 5. 4:135} Yet in another place he said that the whole army consisted of a little less than a hundred myriads, or a million troops. In referring to this battle at Thermopylae, he said that five hundred men held off a hundred myriads, or a million troops. {*Diod. Sic., l. 11. c. 11. s. 2. 4:151} Justin related the same story, and stated that six hundred men broke into the camp of half a million or, as in Orosius, six hundred thousand men. {Justin, Trogus, l. 2. c. 11.} Isocrates said that a thousand of them went against seven hundred thousand Persians. {*Isocrates, Archidamus, l. 1. (99,100) 1:405,407} Instead of the thousand mentioned by Isocrates, Justin and Orosius said it was six hundred, while Diodorus said five hundred. These were those men who were left when the rest of the Greeks were sent away. [L178] They held out against the Persians to the last man, including their Spartan king, Leonidas. Of this number, three hundred were Spartans, the rest were Thespians and Thebans. {*Herodotus, l. 7. c. 222,224. 3:539,541} They killed twenty thousand of the enemy. {*Herodotus, l. 8. c. 24. 4:25}

1123. While these things were happening at Thermopylae, various naval battles occurred about Artemisium, a cape of Euboea. {*Herodotus, l. 8. c. 15. 4:17} Eurybiades, a Lacedemonian, was admiral of the Greek fleet of two hundred and seventy-one ships, besides nine others of fifty oars a piece. One hundred and twenty-seven were sent by the Athenians and Plataeans. {*Herodotus, l. 8. c. 1. 4:3} However, Isocrates stated that the Athenians supplied only sixty ships. {*Isocrates, Panegyricus, l. 1. (90) 1:175} Emilius Probus stated that the whole Greek fleet had three hundred ships and that two hundred were from the Athenians. Themistocles, Herodotus, Diodorus and Probus all say this battle was a draw, with neither side winning. Isocrates and Aelian stated that the Persians were decisively defeated. {*Isocrates, Panegyricus, l. 1. (92) 1:175} {*Aelian, Historical Miscellany, l. 2. c. 25. 1:97} The day this battle was fought was said by Aelian to have been the sixth of the month of Thargelion, which was the second month of spring by the Athenian reckoning. [E125] This does not agree with Herodotus, who said that this took place in midsummer, after the end of the spring, when the Olympic games were held in spite of all the trouble in Greece. {*Herodotus, l. 8. c. 12. 4:13} {*Herodotus, l. 8. c. 26. 4:27} This was in the 75th Olympiad, according to Dionysius Halicarnassus when Xerxes made war upon the Greeks. {*Dionysius Halicarnassus, Roman Antiquities, l. 9. c. 1. 5:287}

### 3524d AM, 4234 JP, 480 BC

1124. Four months after crossing the Hellespont with his army, Xerxes came to Athens and found it abandoned by all its inhabitants. Callias was the ruler of Athens at this time. {*Herodotus, l. 8. c. 51. 4:47} In this year, Anaxagoras of Clazomene, a scholar of Anaximenes the Milesian, was made public reader of philosophy in Athens at the age of twenty, according to Laertius, as from Demetrius of Phalerum in his catalogue of the fifty archons of Athens. {*Diogenes Laertius, Anaxagoras, l. 2. c. 3. (7) 1:137} This was the time that philosophy was first brought from Ionia and established in Athens, according to Clement, who stated: {*Clement, Stromateis, l. 1. c. 14. 2:314} {*Aulus Gellius, Attic Nights, l. 7. c. 17. s. 1,2. 2:139}

> "When Xerxes had taken Athens, he also took a multitude of books, which Peisistratus and the Athenians had stored there. He sent them to Persia. The rest of the city, except the Acropolis, he burned, according to Aulus Gellius."

1125. I do not agree with him, for Herodotus stated plainly that all the Acropolis was burned. {*Herodotus, l. 8. c. 53. 4:51} Ctesias also stated likewise. Diodorus further affirmed that the temple of Athena, which was undoubtedly in the Acropolis, was destroyed. {*Diod. Sic., l. 11. c. 14. s. 5. 4:163}

1126. The farther Xerxes marched into Greece, the more countries joined him. The Melians, Dorians, Locrians, Boeotians, Carystians, Andrians, Tenians and various others sent troops. Hence his army and navy were fewer in number at Salamis and Athens than when he first landed at Sepias and came to Thermopylae. {*Herodotus, l. 8. c. 66. 4:63} The verses of Eschylus mentioned earlier also seemed to imply this, where he told us that there were a thousand or twelve hundred and seven of Xerxes' ships at the battle at Salamis. Ctesias stated that the Persians had a thousand ships in that battle. Plutarch stated that the victory of Themistocles at Salamis destroyed a thousand enemy ships. {*Plutarch, Glory of the Athenians, l. 1. c. 7. 4:517} At the naval battle before Salamis, the Greek fleet was far larger than when they fought at Artemisium. They had three hundred and eighty warships, of which Sparta had sent sixteen. [L179] The Athenians had sent their one hundred and eighty ships. {*Herodotus, l. 8. c. 42-44,48,82. 4:41,45,81} Plutarch agreed with Herodotus about the number of the Athenian ships. {*Plutarch, Themistocles, l. 1. c. 14. s. 2. 2:41} However, Herodotus, in another place, as well as Diodorus, said of the Athenians that they had two hundred ships in their navy. {*Herodotus, l. 8. c. 61. 4:57} {*Diod. Sic., l. 15. c. 92. s. 3. 7:211} Aeschylus said that the total number of Greek ships in the battle before Salamis was only three hundred, not including ten others of an extraordinary size. Ctesias, however, wrote that there were seven hundred in the Greek fleet, and that they lost forty ships while the Persians lost two hundred apart from those which were taken together with their men. {*Diod. Sic., l. 11. c. 19. s. 3. 4:173} Ctesias reported that the Persians lost five hundred ships during that battle. Artemisia, the queen of Halicarnassus, who came to aid Xerxes, was praised by him for her heroic courage. {Justin, Trogus, l. 2. c. 12.} Xerxes on this occasion was heard to say: {*Herodotus, l. 8. c. 88. 4:87}

> "That his men had behaved like women and the women like the men in that battle."

1127. Under the leadership of Eurybiades the Lacedemonian, and by the wise and prudent counsel and great prowess of Themistocles the Athenian, the Greeks won as great a victory at Salamis as they had done at Marathon. Plutarch contradicted himself as to the time when the battle at Salamis was fought. He stated it was the sixteenth day of the month of Mounychion, which is the first of the months of spring with the Athenians. {*Plutarch, Lysander, l. 1. c. 15. 4:273} However, in another place he stated it was on the twentieth day of the month of Boedromion, which was their third month in summer. {*Plutarch, Camillus, l. 1. c. 19. s. 4. 2:139} It is true that in the Bay of Saron, also called the Bay of Salamis {*Strabo, l. 8. c. 6. s. 16. (375) 4:179} between the two islands of Salamis and Aegina, there was a night naval battle between ten Lacedemonian ships commanded by Gorgopas and thirteen Athenian ships commanded by Eunomus. This was near Zoster, a cape of the isthmus of Attica. In the days of Artaxerxes king of Persia, Xenophon mentioned: {*Xenophon, Hellenica, l. 5. c. 1. s. 9. 2:7}

> "In a naval battle fought by moonlight, Gorgopas took four warships and drew them after him, carrying them away to Aegina. The rest of the Athenian fleet fled home to their port of Piraeus."

1128. It was the sixteenth day of that lunar month in Athenian reckoning when Gorgopas attacked that small fleet of the Athenians. It happened to be a full moon, which helped the Athenian fleet sail to safety with the loss of only four ships. Therefore, the Athenians consecrated that day to Diana and kept it as a holy day in her honour. This is the reason why Plutarch confounded this later naval battle fought at Salamis with that other battle fought in the same place against Xerxes. {*Plutarch, Glory of the Athenians, l. 1. c. 7. 4:519} [E126] He was mistaken when he wrote of it in this manner:

> "They consecrated the sixteenth day of the month of Mounychion to Diana, because upon that day after the victory won by the Greeks, the goddess appeared full that night."

1129. The victory of the Greeks against Xerxes happened about the twentieth day of the month of Boedromion, as Plutarch observed. {*Plutarch, Camillus, l. 1. c. 19. s. 3. 2:139}

It plainly appeared in Herodotus that the main day of that holy solemnity was the twentieth of the month of Boedromion. {*Herodotus, l. 8. c. 65. 4:61} [L180] On this day, accordingly, the mysterious *Pomp of Iacchus* was publicly shown to the people. {*Plutarch, Camillus, l. 1. c. 19. s. 6,7. 2:141} Themistocles prevented his countrymen from pursuing the enemies after their defeat at Salamis, which had put them to flight. He said this: {*Herodotus, l. 8. c. 109. 4:111}

> "Now, let us stay in Greece and take care of ourselves and our families and look to the tillage and sowing of our land, since the enemy is expelled from it. When the spring comes, then will we take time to sail into the Hellespont and Ionia."

1130. Hence concludes the argument that the Persians were vanquished at Salamis, not in the beginning of the spring, but near the end of summer.

1131. After the naval battle, Xerxes executed certain Phoenicians who had been the first to flee, and threatened the rest with punishments corresponding to to their conduct. Out of fear, the Phoenicians returned that very day to Africa. The following night, they sailed to Asia in the first year of the 75th Olympiad. {*Diod. Sic., l. 11. c. 19. s. 4. 4:173} Many other ships, fearing the rage of the king more than the fury of the enemy, slunk away to their homes. {Justin, Trogus, l. 2. c. 12.} Xerxes was terrified by this disaster at sea and committed his sons to Artemisia, the queen. She transported them to Ephesus to be with Hermotimus, their guardian. {*Herodotus, l. 8. c. 103,107. 4:103,105}

1132. Cleombrotus of Sparta, the brother of Leonidas who died at Thermopylae, built a wall across the neck of land which is called the Isthmus of Corinth. This was to stop Xerxes from coming by land into Peloponnesus. {*Herodotus, l. 8. c. 71. 4:69} While he was offering a sacrifice against the Persians, the sun was eclipsed. When this happened, he withdrew his army which was building this fortification, and shortly after this he died. He was succeeded by his son Pausanias, who was first cousin and guardian of Pleistarchus, who was the young son of the dead Leonidas. {*Herodotus, l. 9. c. 10. 4:169} The Prutenian account stated there was an eclipse of the sun of eight digits (2/3 of total) at 1:39 p.m. on the second day of October, which lasted thirty-two minutes.

1133. To speed Xerxes on his way out of Greece, Themistocles sent a phoney message to him from Salamis, saying that the Greeks planned to send a fleet of ships to the Hellespont to destroy his bridge. When he heard this, he hastened to get out of Europe into Asia. {*Herodotus, l. 8. c. 110. 4:113} {*Diod. Sic., l. 11. c. 19. s. 5. 4:173} {*Plutarch, Themistocles, l. 1. c. 16. s. 4. 2:47}

1134. Xerxes resolved to leave. He sent his fleet from Phalerum to the Hellespont to guard the bridge. Together with Mardonius and his army, he marched speedily toward Thessaly. {*Herodotus, l. 8. c. 107,113,115. 4:107,115,119}

1135. When Mardonius came with Xerxes into Thessaly, he chose three hundred thousand men from all of his army. These he kept with him to continue the conquest of Greece. Because the year was well advanced, he wintered in Thessaly. {*Herodotus, l. 8. c. 113,114. 4:115-117} {Justin, Trogus, l. 2. c. 13.} {*Plutarch, Aristides, l. 1. c. 10. s. 1. 2:241} However, Diodorus stated that at least four hundred thousand troops remained with him. {*Diod. Sic., l. 11. c. 19. s. 6. 4:175}

1136. In the meantime the Lacedemonians, at the command of the oracle at Delphi, sent a herald to Xerxes to require reparation from him for the death of their king, Leonidas. He answered that Mardonius should pay them their due. Then, leaving Mardonius in Thessaly, he hurried to the Hellespont. [L181] He took a large number of troops for his guard, leaving the rest to be brought after him by Hydarnes. {*Herodotus, l. 8. c. 114,115,118. 4:117-123}

1137. The army which he left behind with Mardonius was first hit by famine, then a pestilence. So many died that the highways lay strewn with their dead bodies. Both birds and beasts of prey followed the army by the smell wherever they went. {*Herodotus, l. 8. c. 115. 4:119} {Justin, Trogus, l. 2. c. 13.}

1138. In Asia, the Archaeanactidae had held the kingdom of the Cimmerian Bosphorus for forty-two years to the third year of the 85th Olympiad. {*Diod. Sic., l. 12. c. 31. s. 1. 4:439} These had their beginning from Archaeanax of Mitylene, who was said to have built Sigeum with the stones dug from the ruins of Troy. {*Strabo, l. 13. c. 1. s. 38. 6:75}

## 3525a AM, 4234 JP, 480 BC

1139. After forty-five days, Xerxes came to the Hellespont. {*Herodotus, l. 8. c. 115. 4:119} Emilius Probus said it took less time than that: {Emilius Probus, Themistocles} [E127]

> "that on the same route which had taken him six months to travel into Europe, he now took less than thirty days to make the return trip back to Asia."

1140. When Xerxes found his bridge had been smashed by the winter storms, driven by fear, he crossed in a small fishing boat. {Justin, Trogus, l. 2. c. 13.}

> "And truly it was a sight to behold and a rare example of human frailty and the fickleness of human fortunes to see him lie sulking. A short while earlier the whole sea had seemed too small to contain him. He, under the burden of whose army the very earth

itself seemed to groan, was now destitute of a page to wait on him."

1141. When the army which followed him under the command of Hydarnes found the bridge smashed, they crossed over to Abydus in boats. On the other side they found much more food than they had had along the way. They gorged themselves with food and the change in the water killed them by the score. The remainder accompanied Xerxes to Sardis. {*Herodotus, l. 8. c. 117. 4:121}

1142. While Xerxes was on the way to Sardis, he sent Megabyzus to destroy the temple of Delphi. When the latter desired to be excused, Mattacus, a eunuch, did the task and returned to Xerxes. {Ctesias}

1143. When the news that Xerxes had taken Athens came to Susa by the couriers who were sent, the Persians were so happy that they strewed myrtle boughs in all the streets and burned frankincense in them. They gave themselves totally to sacrificing and feasting. But when the news of his defeat at Salamis came, their attitude changed, so that every man rent his garments and all places everywhere were filled with their howlings and lamentations. {*Herodotus, l. 8. c. 99. 4:97} {Aeschylus, Life in Persia}

1144. When the remaining fleet and sailors had ferried the army from the Chersonesus to Abydus, they wintered at Cyme in Aeolia. {*Herodotus, l. 8. c. 130. 4:133}

1145. Artabazus, the son of Pharnabazus, accompanied Xerxes with sixty thousand soldiers to the Hellespont. When Artabazus saw that Xerxes had arrived safely in Asia, he returned and stayed near the city of Pallene, after seeing that Mardonius had wintered in Macedonia and Thessaly and had not looked after the rest of the army. While Artabazus was staying there, he found that the city of Potidaea together with Pallene had revolted from Persia, and the city of Olynthus was planning to do likewise. He besieged Potidaea and Olynthus. [L182] Having captured Olynthus and killed all its Potidaean inhabitants, he put Critobulus of Torone, a Chalcedonian, in charge of the place. {*Herodotus, l. 8. c. 126,127. 4:129}

### 3525b AM, 4235 JP, 479 BC

1146. As the Persians besieged Potidaea for three months, a large tide broke in over them in their trenches, forcing them to lift the siege. Many perished in that flood, while the Potidaeans went about in boats and knocked others on the head as they fought to swim to safety. Artabazus took those troops who escaped with him into Thessaly, to Mardonius. {*Herodotus, l. 8. c. 129. 4:131}

1147. At the beginning of spring, the rest of the Persian fleet, which had wintered at Cyme, sailed to the isle of Samos, where others of their navy, the largest part of which were Persian and Median sailors, had wintered. They were joined shortly after by certain commanders: Mardontes, the son of Bargaeus, and Artayntes, the son of Artachaees. They stayed there with three hundred ships to keep all of Ionia from revolting. This number included those Ionians who were with them under their command. {*Herodotus, l. 8. c. 130. 4:133} However, Diodorus said that there were no less than four hundred ships at Samos which awaited any Ionian revolt in this year of the 75th Olympiad. {*Diod. Sic., l. 11. c. 27. s. 1. 4:197}

1148. The Greek fleet consisted of a hundred and ten ships under two commanders: Leotychides, king of the Spartans, and Xanthippus, an Athenian. They sailed to Aegina, where messengers came to them from Ionia, begging them to come at once and relieve them in Ionia. After a while they sailed as far as to Delos. {*Herodotus, l. 8. c. 131,132. 4:135,137} However, Diodorus stated that after they stayed some days at Aegina, they sailed to Delos with two hundred and fifty ships. {*Diod. Sic., l. 11. c. 34. s. 2. 4:213}

### 3525c AM, 4235 JP, 479 BC

1149. Xerxes was said to have built both a palace and a citadel at Celaenae in Phrygia. {*Xenophon, Anabasis, l. 1. c. 2. s. 9. 3:59}

1150. Mardonius came with his army to Athens, which was not yet reinhabited ten months after it had first been taken by Xerxes. Whatever Xerxes had left standing, he destroyed and burned down. From there he marched into the country of Megara, which was as far west as the Persians went in Greece. {*Herodotus, l. 9. c. 3,13,14. 4:171,172}

### 3525d AM, 4235 JP, 479 BC

1151. While the Greek fleet was stationed at Delos, messengers came to them from Samos asking their help for themselves and all the other Greeks who lived in Asia, against the Persians. At a council of war, Leotychides, the king of Sparta, resolved to liberate all the Greek cities from the Persians. They entered into a league with the Samians, who came with their whole fleet to Samos and stayed near the temple of Juno. [E128] They prepared for a naval battle against the Persians. {*Herodotus, l. 9. c. 89,91,95. 4:263-271} {*Diod. Sic., l. 11. c. 35. s. 2-4. 4:215-271}

1152. When the commanders of the Persian navy stayed at Samos, they heard that the Greeks were coming against them. Knowing they were no match for them in a naval battle, they allowed the Phoenician ships to sail off, while the rest sailed to Mycale, which was a cape in Ionia where the army was camped. It had been left there by Xerxes to keep Ionia under submission. Sixty thousand men were under the command of Tigranes, who was the tallest and most handsome man of all the Persians. Near the temple of Ceres of Eleusis they drew up their ships and enclosed them with a rampart, which they fortified with stones and stakes and anything else they could find there. {*Herodotus, l. 9. c. 96-97. 4:271,273} They sent to Sardis and the other neighbouring places for more soldiers. With these reinforcements they had a hundred thousand troops, and prepared themselves for a battle. {*Diod. Sic., l. 11. c. 30. 4:205} [L183]

1153. In an engagement of cavalry between the Greeks and Persians near Erythrae in Boeotia, the Persian commander Masistius was killed by the Greeks. The Greeks called him Macistias. Great lamentations were made by the Persians when he died. {*Herodotus, l. 9. c. 20,22,24. 4:181-185} {*Plutarch, Aristides, l. 1. c. 14. s. 5. 2:255}

1154. At Plataea, according to Ctesias, the Greeks, under the command of Pausanias, the son of Cleombrotus, routed the Persian army which was comprised of one hundred and twenty thousand men. Emilius Probus stated there were two hundred thousand soldiers and twenty thousand cavalry. {Emilius Probus, Pausanias} Plutarch affirmed that there were no fewer than three hundred thousand men. {*Plutarch, Aristides, l. 1. c. 10. s. 1. 2:241} To this number Herodotus also added about fifty thousand Greek mercenaries hired by Mardonius. {*Herodotus, l. 9. c. 32. 4:199} Diodorus stated that besides the troops left by Xerxes, Mardonius also had over two hundred thousand soldiers from Thrace and Macedonia and other allies. In total, he had over five hundred thousand in his army. {*Diod. Sic., l. 11. c. 30. s. 2. 4:205} Herodotus and Plutarch affirmed that the Athenians had at least eight thousand men. {*Herodotus, l. 9. c. 28. 4:195} {*Plutarch, Aristides, l. 1. c. 11. s. 1. 2:245} The entire Greek army numbered a hundred thousand men, according to Diodorus Siculus, Trogus Pompeius and Orosius, or a hundred and ten thousand, according to Herodotus. {*Herodotus, l. 9. c. 29. 4:195} {*Diod. Sic., l. 11. c. 30. s. 2. 4:205} Plutarch stated the Greeks lost thirteen hundred and sixty men in the battle. {*Plutarch, Aristides, l. 1. c. 19. s. 4. 2:273} Diodorus stated they lost ten thousand men. {*Diod. Sic., l. 11. c. 33. 4:211}

1155. The Persian general of the entire army, Mardonius, the son-in-law (not of Xerxes, as Emilius Probus claimed, {Emilius Probus, Pausanias}) of Darius, who was father to Xerxes, was killed in this battle. {See note on 3510 AM. <<1088>>} He was hit by a stone flung at him by Arimnestus, a man of Sparta. {*Herodotus, l. 9. c. 63. 4:235} {*Plutarch, Aristides, l. 1. c. 19. 2:271} {Emilius Probus, Pausanias, l. 1.} Ctesias was incorrect when he said that he was only hurt and so escaped for a time. Later he was killed in a hail storm when he was destroying the temple of Apollo. However, Justin, and Orosius, who cited Justin, stated

that Mardonius was accompanied by a very small group who escaped from there as from a shipwreck. {Justin, Trogus}

1156. When the Persian army lost their general, they fled to a fortress of theirs made of wood. The Greeks overcame it and killed over a hundred thousand of them. {*Diod. Sic., l. 11. c. 32. s. 5. 4:211} Of the three hundred thousand, not three thousand men were left, in addition to the forty thousand who fled with Artabazus. {*Herodotus, l. 9. c. 66-71. 4:237-243}

1157. Leotychides, who commanded the Greek navy, came to Mycale to liberate the Ionians from the Persians. With his own army and the help of the Ionians, he gained a most memorable victory there. He killed over forty thousand Persians as well as Mardontes, the Persian naval commander, and Tigranes, the general of the army. The two other commanders of their fleet, Artayntes and Ithramitres, fled. The rest that escaped fled to the heights of Mycale. {*Herodotus, l. 9. c. 97-104. 4:273-281} {*Diod. Sic., l. 11. c. 34-46. 4:215-247}

1158. Both these battles happened near the two temples of Ceres of Eleusis on the same day of the same month. The one battle was at Plataea in Europe, early in the morning, and the other at Mycale in Asia, later in the afternoon. The news spread swiftly far and wide, so that, within a few hours, the news of the victory at Plataea came to Mycale, before the battle on that same day. {*Herodotus, l. 9. c. 100,101. 4:277} {Justin, Trogus, l. 2. c. 14.} [L184] However, Diodorus thought (which is more probable) that Leotychides heard nothing at all of what had occurred at Plataea, but cunningly spread such a rumour among his soldiers to encourage them. {*Diod. Sic., l. 11. c. 35. s. 2. 4:217,219} [E129] Aelian stated that the day of these two battles was the sixth of the month of Thargelion, the second month in the spring with the Athenians. {*Aelian, Historical Miscellany, l. 2. c. 25. 1:97} Plutarch more wisely said it was in the month of Boedromion, which was the third month in summer. It was either on the sixth day of that month, {*Plutarch, Glory of the Athenians, l. 1. c. 7. 4:519} {*Plutarch, Camillus, l. 1. c. 19. s. 4. 2:139} or on the fourth. {*Plutarch, Aristides, l. 1. c. 19. s. 7. 2:275} This battle at Mycale happened in the second year after Xerxes first entered into Greece. {*Herodotus, l. 7. c. 80. 3:389}

1159. At this time all Ionia revolted from the Persians. {*Herodotus, l. 9. c. 104. 4:281} The Aeolians and their bordering islands also revolted. {*Diod. Sic., l. 11. c. 36. s. 5. 4:221}

1160. The Greeks completely burned the Persian ships and camps. They returned to the isle of Samos and consulted together on how to move the Ionian nation from Asia. Diodorus said they planned to move the Aeolians to Greece too, since they were exposed to the danger of the Persian cruelty. Because the Athenians feared that the Ionians, who were now an independent colony, would intermix with the rest of Greece, they opposed this plan. They argued that since the Ionians were also Greeks, they could count on Greece for help against the Persians, but they desired that the Ionians remain in Asia. {*Herodotus, l. 9. c. 106. 4:283} {*Diod. Sic., l. 11. c. 37. s. 2. 4:223}

1161. The inhabitants of Greece entered into a league with those of Samos, Chios, Lesbos and the other islands who had joined in this war against the Persians. They confirmed this with a solemn oath to last forever. They sailed in a group toward the Hellespont and on their way first anchored at a cape called Lectum. When an opposing wind changed to a favourable one, they moved on to Abydus. When they found there that the bridges, which they had intended to destroy, were already broken down, Leotychides and his men of Peloponnesus returned home. The Athenians under Xanthippus, together with (as Thucydides stated) their allies from Ionia and the Hellespont who had revolted against the Persians, journeyed from Abydus to the Chersonesus and there besieged Sestus. Artayctes, a Persian, was a wicked man whom Xerxes had made governor of that province. The town was surrounded by a wall stronger than that of any other towns in the area. Ocebazus, a Persian, who had stored the cables used in the construction of the bridges at Cardia, left that place and also came to Sestus. {*Herodotus, l. 9. c. 106,114-115. 4:283,293,295}

1162. Artabazus, the son of Pharnaces, with forty thousand men who had fled from the battle at Plataea, travelled quickly to Thrace through the countries of Phocis, Thessaly, and Macedonia. They took the shortest overland route to Byzantium. Many men were left behind in his march. Some were killed by the Thracians, some died from hunger and some from the journey. When he arrived at Byzantium, he crossed over to Asia by ship. {*Herodotus, l. 9. c. 65,69,76,88. 4:237,239,249}

1163. Those who had saved themselves on the heights of Mycale retreated to Sardis, where Xerxes still was. On that journey Masistes, one of the sons of Darius Hystaspes, had charged Artayntes, one of the chief commanders of the fleet at Mycale, with cowardice. When Artayntes attacked him with his sword, Xenagoras of Halicarnassus stepped in and stopped the fight and saved Masistes from that attack. [L185] For so saving Xerxes' brother's life, he was made governor of Cilicia. {*Herodotus, l. 9. c. 107. 4:285}

1164. While Xerxes spent his time at Sardis, he there fell in love with his brother Masistes' wife. When he could not seduce her, he married her daughter, Artaynta, to

his own son, Darius, hoping to get his way with her more readily by this act. When the wedding was over, he returned to Susa and left part of his army at Sardis to continue the war against the Greeks. {*Herodotus, l. 9. c. 108. 4:287} {*Diod. Sic., l. 11. c. 36. s. 7. 4:221}

### 3526a AM, 4235 JP, 479 BC

1165. In his flight, Xerxes burned down the oracle of Apollo Didymeon in Branchidae, as he had done to all the other temples in Asia except at Ephesus. After the people of the Branchidae handed over the treasury of their god, they all went along with Xerxes, fearing that if they stayed behind, they would be punished for sacrilege and treason. {*Strabo, l. 14. c. 1. s. 5. 6:205} {Solinus, c. 40.} Herodotus stated that Xerxes left Sardis and went to Susa, but Diodorus said that he went to Ecbatana. {*Herodotus, l. 9. c. 108. 4:287} {*Diod. Sic., l. 11. c. 36. s. 7. 4:221} Ctesias wrote that he went from Babylon to Persia. {Ctesias} Arrian affirmed that after he came to Babylon, he demolished the temple of Belus and all other consecrated places, including the sepulchre of Belus. {*Arrian, Anabasis, l. 3. c. 16. s. 3. 1:275} [E130] Strabo stated that he destroyed the tomb of Belus. {*Strabo, l. 16. c. 1. s. 5. 7:199} Herodotus said that he took away the statue of Belus made of solid gold, eighteen feet high. When the priests opposed it and would not allow it to be removed, he killed them. {*Herodotus, l. 1. c. 183. 1:229}

1166. While the Athenians were besieging Sestus, autumn was approaching and they had still not taken it, so they planned to abandon the siege. However, the people within were so driven with famine that they were boiling the thongs of their beds for food. Artayctes and Oeobazus together with all of the Persians climbed over the walls by night and fled. When the inhabitants discovered this early the next morning, they surrendered to the Athenians. {*Herodotus, l. 9. c. 117,118. 4:297}

1167. A large number of prisoners were taken at Sestus and Byzantium by the Athenians and their confederates in the army. The confederates of their own accord offered to entrust the division of the spoils to Cimon, a young Athenian gentleman. He placed all the people on the one side and all the clothes and ornaments which they wore on the other. Giving the confederates first choice, he said the Athenians would take what was left. Herophytus of Samos persuaded them to take the clothes and ornaments instead of the people. Later, the friends and relatives of the prisoners came from Phrygia and Lydia and redeemed those prisoners at a high price. With the money, Cimon maintained the fleet for four whole months and brought much silver and gold into the treasury at Athens. This act gave him a reputation of wisdom with the Athenians. They received so much money from the bargain, that they laughed at their fellows who had formerly laughed at them. {*Plutarch, Cimon, l. 1. c. 9. s. 1-4. 2:431} {Polyaenus, Strategmata, l. 1.}

1168. When Oeobazus had escaped into Thrace, the Thracians, called Apsinthians, captured him and sacrificed him to their god Plistorus. His companions were killed in various ways. Artayntes and his followers were captured near the Goat's River and taken as prisoners to Sestus. By the seaside where Xerxes had built his bridge, or, as others say, on a hill near the city of Madytus, they set up gibbets and crucified them there after they had stoned Artayntes' own son to death before his eyes. [L186] Having done this, the Athenians returned to Greece. In addition to the money, they took the cables and ornaments of the bridges which had been built over the Hellespont, planning to hang them as trophies in their temples. {*Herodotus, l. 9. c. 119-121. 4:297-299} Xanthippus left a garrison in Sestus, dismissing all the strangers, while he returned to Athens with his own companies. So the war of the Medes, as they call it, came to an end after having lasted a full two years. {*Diod. Sic., l. 11. c. 37. s. 6. 4:223}

### 3526b AM, 4236 JP, 478 BC

1169. Bagapates, the eunuch, died, after he had sat by the tomb of Darius for seven years. {Ctesias}

1170. Megabyzus accused his wife, Amytis, Xerxes' daughter, of adultery. She very sharply blamed his daughter for it. {Ctesias} All the while Xerxes committed both adultery and incest. He turned his lewd affection from his brother Masistes' wife, to their daughter, Artaynta, whom he had now made his own daughter-in-law. He lay with her continually at Susa. {*Herodotus, l. 9. c. 108,109. 4:287}

### 3527 AM, 4237 JP, 477 BC

1171. Pausanias, the son of Cleombrotus, was sent as general of the Greeks from Lacedemon to free the Greek cities that were still held by the Persians. He had twenty ships from Peloponnesus and thirty more from Athens (Diodorus said fifty ships), commanded by Aristides. They sailed to Cyprus and liberated many cities held by the Persians. {*Thucydides, l. 1. c. 94. s. 1. 1:161} {*Diod. Sic., l. 11. c. 44. s. 1. 4:239}

1172. When Xerxes was celebrating his coronation day, he gave his queen Amestris any wish she wanted. She asked for the wife of Masistes, Xerxes' brother. She had her breasts, nose, ears, lips and tongue cut off and so sent her home again. Masistes conspired with his own children to steal away to the province of Bactria. He wanted to make himself governor and incite Bactria and the Sacae to rebel against the king. He was intercepted

on the way by Xerxes' soldiers and he, his children and all that were in his company were killed. {*Herodotus, l. 9. c. 109-113. 4:287-293} After the death of Masistes, the government of Bactria was given to Hystaspes, the son of Xerxes. {*Diod. Sic., l. 11. c. 69. s. 2. 4:305}

### 3528 AM, 4238 JP, 476 BC

1173. When Pausanias returned from Cyprus, he captured Byzantium. He took it upon himself to send the Persians whom he had captured (some were close friends and relatives of Xerxes) home safely to Xerxes. He maintained that they had escaped. All these matters were negotiated by Gongylus, an Eretrian, whom Pausanias also used to carry letters to Xerxes expressing his desire to marry Xerxes' daughter. [E131] In return, he promised to bring Sparta and all of Greece under his subjection. Xerxes was glad of this news, and sending his reply by Artabazus, the son of Pharnaces, he said it would be easier to communicate his counsels with Pausanias when they were closer. So he gave him the government of the province of Dascylitides and recalled Megabates, who had been governor there until that time. With these hopes, Pausanias grew more insolent than before and beginning to live like a Persian, he behaved imperiously toward those who were in league with that state. Most of them, especially the Ionians and others who had recently been liberated from their slavery under the Persians, defected to the Athenians and desired to serve under them. {*Thucydides, l. 1. c. 95. s. 1-7. 1:161,162} {*Diod. Sic., l. 11. c. 44. s. 3-5. 4:241}

### 3529 AM, 4239 JP, 475 BC

1174. When Pausanias was accused by the Spartans, he was recalled from Byzantium. He was found guilty, and was condemned for some small misdemeanours but acquitted of treason against the state. [L187] Nevertheless, he was removed from the government of the Hellespont. On his own initiative, without asking permission, he hired a ship under the pretence of aiding in the war effort on behalf of the Greeks in those parts, when in fact he wanted to advance his own interests with Xerxes. When the Athenians would not allow him to stay in Byzantium, he did not return to Sparta but stayed at Colonae in Troas. For a second time he was accused at Sparta of having consorted with the Persians and of having been up to no good while he was in those parts, and so he was once again sent for by the ephors. When he arrived there, they threw him into prison, but after a hearing, he was acquitted yet again. {*Thucydides, l. 1. c. 95. s. 3-7. 1:161,163}

### 3530 AM, 4240 JP, 474 BC

1175. In Greece, because of their hatred of Pausanias and their common dislike of the Lacedemonians, the city states favoured the Athenians. Under a pretence of avenging the wrong done to the various countries by the common enemy, the Athenians set a tax of money and ships that each city should contribute against the Persians. The cities in Greece and the Greek cities in Asia readily agreed to this for the common safety of all. The first tax amounted to four hundred and sixty (not, as Diodorus has it, five hundred and sixty) talents. It was stored on the isle of Delos, which was the common treasury of all Greece. {*Thucydides, l. 1. c. 96. s. 1,2. 1:163,165} {*Diod. Sic., l. 11. c. 46,47. 4:247,248} {Justin, Trogus, l. 16. c. 3.} {*Plutarch, Aristides, l. 1. c. 24. s. 3. 2:287} {Emilius Probus, Aristides}

1176. When Pausanias was exposed by Argilius, his homosexual lover, to whom he had committed his last letters to be sent to Artabazus, the ephors starved Pausanias to death. {*Thucydides, l. 1. c. 95. s. 2-7. 1:161,163} {*Diod. Sic., l. 11. c. 45. s. 1-7. 1:243,245} {Emilius Probus, Pausanias}

### 3531a AM, 4240 JP, 474 BC

1177. Artaxerxes was made viceroy with his father Xerxes in the twelfth year of Xerxes' reign. This time marks the first year of Artaxerxes reign. Ptolemy's Canon does not record viceroy relationships hence starts Artaxerxes reign nine years later when his father died. (Since the time when Ussher wrote his document, this new information has come to light from archaeology. We are thankful for Dr. Floyd Jones for finding the exact source of this information. Editor.) Savile wrote the following: {B. W. Savile, "Revelation and Science", Journal of Sacred Literature & Biblical Record, Series 4 (London: Williams and Norgate Pub. April 1863), p. 156.}

> "It is satisfactory to know that the idea entertained by Archbishop Ussher of dating the commencement of Artaxerxes' reign nine years earlier than the canon of Ptolemy allows, grounded upon what Thucydides says of Themistocles' flight to Persia, has been confirmed by hieroglyphic inscriptions in Egypt, showing that Artaxerxes was associated with his father in the twelfth year of Xerxes reign, so that there ought to be no longer any doubt respecting that famous prophecy of Daniel, so far as at least regards the crucifixion."

1178. Artabanus, a Hyrcanian, was captain of the guard and was in the position of enjoying more of Xerxes' trust and having more authority with him than his father Artasyras had. He conspired with Mithridates, a eunuch who was a chamberlain to the king (Ctesias called him Spamitres or Aspamitres), and who was his close friend and relative. He was let into the bedchamber with his seven young, robust sons at night, and they killed Xerxes as he lay in his bed. In the middle of the night they hastened to Artaxerxes and told him that Darius (who was the oldest of the three sons of Xerxes) had killed his father so that he would be king sooner. Aelian related this as if it were indeed the truth. {*Aelian, Historical Miscellany, l. 13. c. 3. 1:421} By this lie, he persuaded Artaxerxes to have the king's guard kill his brother Darius. {Ctesias} {*Diod. Sic., l. 11. c. 69. 4:305} {Justin, Trogus, l. 3. c. 1.}

1179. By Artabanus' plot, Artaxerxes became the next king. {Ctesias} He was a man of mild disposition and full of magnanimity to all. He was surnamed Longimanus, because his right hand was longer than his left. {*Plutarch, Artaxerxes, l. 1. c. 1. 11:129} The first seven months of his reign are attributed to Artabanus. {*Eusebius, Chronicles, l. 1. 1:192} It seems that he ruled everything in Artaxerxes' name for that period of time. Diodorus intimated that Artabanus was immediately executed for his murder of Xerxes and Darius, {*Diod. Sic., l. 11. c. 69. s. 6. 4:307} but some time elapsed before this happened, as appears from the more complete accounts of this by Ctesias and Justin.

### 3531b AM, 4241 JP, 473 BC

1180. Themistocles of Athens was suspected of the conspiracy with Pausanias for the betraying of Greece into the hands of the Persians. They searched for him and had they found him, they would have killed him. Therefore he fled from Greece and came to Pydna, a town beside the Thermaic Bay of Macedonia. There he found and boarded a merchant ship going into Ionia. A storm carried the ship into the middle of the Athenian forces which were besieging Naxos. The captain of the ship, who was being well paid by Themistocles, lay at anchor beyond the Athenian fleet for a whole night and a day. When the storm was over, he came safely to Ephesus. {*Thucydides, l. 1. c. 135-137. 1:229-233} {Emilius Probus, Themistocles} {Polyaenus, Strategmata, l. 1.} [L188] Plutarch stated that he came to Cyme and found many sea captains wanting to capture him, especially Ergoteles and Pythodorus. Xerxes had promised two hundred talents to anyone who would bring him his head. [E132] Therefore, he quietly left the area and came to a little town called Aetae in Aeolia. He hid for a few days in the house of Nicogenes, a very wealthy man in those parts who was very familiar with several of the king's most trusted attendants. {*Plutarch, Themistocles, l. 1. c. 25-26. 2:69,71} Diodorus called him Lysitheides and said further that he was a man of such great wealth that when Xerxes passed that way, he feasted both him and all his army in a very magnificent manner. By this good host's assistance, he was put into a covered wagon, such as the kings' and other great men's concubines used among the Persians. {*Diod. Sic., l. 11. c. 56. 4:269,273} He came safely into Persia, according to both Plutarch and Thucydides. However, Thucydides only said that he travelled the route from the coast into Persia in the company of a certain Persian. {*Thucydides, l. 1. c. 137. s. 3. 1:233} {*Plutach, Themistocles, l. 1. c. 27. 2:73,74} Herodotus stated that from Ephesus to Sardis is a journey of three days, and from there to Susa, three months. {*Herodotus, l. 5. c. 50,53,54. 3:55,59,61}

1181. Artabanus planned to kill Artaxerxes, just as he had killed his father and brother. He told his plan to Megabyzus, whom he knew to be unhappy out of jealousy over his wife's supposed unfaithfulness. She was Amytis, the sister to Artaxerxes. They swore secrecy to each other, but Megabyzus at once went and disclosed the matter to the king, who put Artabanus to death. Then it also became known about his hand in the death of Xerxes and his son Darius. Aspamitres, or Spamitres, the eunuch, who had been involved with him in this, was cruelly executed with certain racks and other engines in a boat. {Ctesias} (This form of torture was described by Plutarch. {*Plutarch, Artaxerxes, l. 1. c. 16. 11:163-165}) Justin wrote Becabasus for Megabyzus, as consort with Artabanus in this plot, and described the manner of Artabanus' death in this way:

"Artaxerxes, fearing the number of Artabanus' children, commanded all the army to be ready in the field the next day. He planned to review his troops, the number of them and also how every man could stand to his arms. When Artabanus was there present in his armour, Artaxerxes said that his own armour was a little short for him and that he would change with Artabanus. When Artabanus, at the command of the king, had taken off his armour, Artaxerxes ran his naked body through with his sword."

1182. From the size of his armour, we may deduce that Artaxerxes was not at this time a child, as Justin claimed, but that he was a man and old enough to be, in the seventh year of his kingdom, the father of several sons, as the scripture tells us. {Ezr 7:23}

1183. After Artabanus' death, a battle was fought between his friends and the other Persians, in which three of his sons were killed. Megabyzus, on the Persian side, was seriously wounded. This grieved Artaxerxes and his sisters, Amytis, who was the wife of Megabyzus, and Rhodogyne, as well as his mother Amestris. Megabyzus recovered, due to the great skill of Apollonius, a doctor from the isle of Cos. After this, Bactria revolted from Artaxerxes and a different Artabanus was made governor there. Between Artabanus and the Persians a battle was fought where they parted on even terms. {Ctesias} However, those words in the Greek are ambiguous, for it may mean what I have here expressed, according to how it was interpreted by Henry Stephanus, who said that either another Artabanus was made governor of Bactria instead of the former, or that at this time there was another Artabanus who was governor of that province, but

who was not the same person whom the king killed. [L189] If we take the latter sense, then this revolt of the Bactrians must refer to an earlier time, but if the first, then to the present time. For at this time Hystaspes, Xerxes' son, was governor of Bactria, according to Diodorus. He was the middle brother between Darius and Artaxerxes, according to Ctesias. It seems reasonable to assume that when Hystaspes saw his younger brother Artaxerxes preferred before him in the kingdom, he would incite not only the Bactrians, whom he governed, but also all his other friends to help him recover his right to the kingdom. {*Diod. Sic., l. 11. c. 69. s. 2. 4:305}

1184. Eusebius noted that in the fourth year of this 76th Olympiad (which we are now documenting), Themistocles fled to the Persians. {*Eusebius, Chronicles, l. 1. 1:191} This agreed with the account of Thucydides, who placed the coming of Themistocles to Artaxerxes between the siege of Naxos {*Thucydides, l. 1. c. 137. s. 2. 1:233} and that famous victory over the Persians at the mouth of the Eurymedon River by Cimon, the Athenian. {*Thucydides, l. 1. c. 98-100. 1:165,167} He took the beginning of the reign of Artaxerxes to have happened at the same time, because he said that Themistocles sent letters to Artaxerxes when he had recently been crowned king, desiring his favour and offering him his service against the Greeks. {*Thucydides, l. 1. c. 137. s. 4. 1:233} From this we may fully discern that the true beginning of Artaxerxes' reign was almost a full nine years earlier than it is commonly said to have been. (For a more exhaustive treatment of this chronological detail refer to the readily available commentary of Albert Barnes on Daniel chapter nine verse twenty-four. Barnes drew most of his material from Henstenberg's work entitled *Christology of the Old Testament*. Editor.)

1185. Plutarch, deriving his information from Phanias, reported that Themistocles was introduced into Artaxerxes' favour by Artabanus, a chiliarch. According to Eratosthenes, he obtained this favour from the chiliarch by means of his concubine, who was from Eretria. {*Plutarch, Themistocles, l. 1. c. 27,28. 2:75} [E133] He did not explain which Artabanus this was, whether he was the one killed by Artaxerxes or that Artabanus to whom Xerxes had entrusted the government of his kingdom, seven years earlier when he went to Greece. For if he meant the first, then Themistocles must have come to Artaxerxes within the first seven months of his being crowned king, according to Eusebius. If someone else, then the time he came to the king might have happened in any other month of that year. This would agree well with Thucydides, where he said: {*Thucydides, l. 1. c. 137. s. 4. 1:233}

"he was brought to Artaxerxes, when he was newly come to the throne."

*1186.* It was the right of the office of the chiliarch, as the second officer in the kingdom, to introduce those who were to be admitted into the presence of the king. {*Emilius Probus, Conon*} {*Aelian, Historical Miscellany, l. 1. c. 21. 1:43*}

*1187.* When Themistocles was thus graciously received by the king, a new danger presented itself. Mandane, a daughter of Darius Hystaspes, had lost all her children in the naval battle at Salamis. She sought revenge upon Themistocles for this, and when she could not prevail with the king or her friends and the great men in the court, she stirred up the common people. When these all rushed into the court, Artaxerxes told them fairly that he would refer the whole matter to the judgment of his lords. So, by appointing a time for a hearing, he saved Themistocles from the people's hands. {*Diod. Sic., l. 11. c. 57. 4:273*}

### 3532 AM, 4242 JP, 472 BC

*1188.* In the second battle, a strong wind in their favour helped the Persians defeat the Bactrians and again subject them to Artaxerxes. {*Ctesias*}

*1189.* Themistocles spent a whole year learning the Persian language, and the laws and customs of the country. When he came to trial, he cleared himself of all the charges and endeared himself to the king as no other Greek had done before him. *[L190]* Artaxerxes took him on hunting trips and had him attend his private delights and recreations at home. He was admitted to the presence of Amestris, the king's mother, and conversed familiarly with her. The king also bestowed on him a Persian wife of noble parentage, excellent in beauty and goodness of disposition. He had servants to wait on him and cupboards of dishes of all sorts and along with everything else he could wish for. These were for his needs and entertainment. {*Thucydides, l. 1. c. 138. 1:235*} {*Diod. Sic., l. 11. c. 57. 4:275*} {*Plutarch, Themistocles, l. 1. c. 29. s. 3,4. 2:79*}

*1190.* Demaratus, the Lacedemonian, who returned from Greece with Xerxes, displeased the king greatly when he asked if he might ride into Sardis in his chariot, wearing his turban upright on his head in a way reserved only for kings. Themistocles interceded for him and Artaxerxes' wrath was pacified, so they became friends again. {*Plutarch, Themistocles, l. 1. c. 29. s. 5. 2:81*} {*Seneca, On Benefits, l. 6. c. 31. s. 11,12. 3:431*}

*1191.* When Themistocles was made governor of the province of Magnesia, he returned into Asia. {*Thucydides, l. 1. c. 138. s. 5. 1:237*} On his return, he escaped an ambush planned by Epyxies, the Persian governor of Upper Phrygia, and the Pisidians. He was warned of it in a dream by Dindymene, the mother of the gods, while he was resting at noon. As a memorial, he built her a temple at Magnesia and caused his own daughter Muesiptolema

to become a consecrated priestess to her, {*Plutarch, Themistocles, l. 1. c. 30. s. 3. 2:83*} though some say it was his wife. {*Strabo, l. 14. c. 1. s. 40. 6:251*}

*1192.* So that Themistocles might be seen to have greater honour in Asia, the king gave him, besides the government of the province of Magnesia, the very city of Magnesia on the Meander River. This city paid the king fifty talents yearly, which paid for the food for Themistocles' table. Lampsacus in the Hellespont supplied him with wine for his meal and Myus, at the mouth of the Meander River, paid for his meat. Neanthes, Cyzicenus, Phanias and Athenaeus listed two further cities in the country of Troas, namely Percote and Palaescepsis, which supplied him with his bedding and clothing. {*Athenaeus, l. 1. (29f) 1:131*} {*Thucydides, l. 1. c. 139. 1:237*} {*Diod. Sic., l. 11. c. 57. s. 7. 4:275*} {*Plutarch, Themistocles, l. 1. c. 29. s. 6,7. 2:81*} {*Emilius Probus, Themistocles.*}

### 3533 AM, 4243 JP, 471 BC

*1193.* Cimon, the son of Miltiades, who was general in the battle at Marathon, was now made general by the Athenians against the Persians. He set out from Pyreum at Athens with two hundred warships bound for Caria. Ships from Ionia and other parts joined him to increase the size of the fleet to three hundred ships. The coastal towns, which were founded by the Greeks, revolted from the Persians to him. The rest, which were inhabited by the natives of the country and held by the Persian garrisons, he attacked and conquered. Having finished his work in Caria, he sailed into Lycia and did the same there. *[E134]* When they submitted to the Athenian government, he demanded ships of them and greatly increased his navy. {*Diod. Sic., l. 11. c. 60. s. 2-5. 4:281*}

*1194.* The Persians conscripted into the army what men they could from the king's other dominions. For naval forces they sent to the Phoenicians, Cypriots and Cilicians. The chief commander of the entire Persian fleet was Tithraustes, a son of Xerxes by a concubine. {*Diod. Sic., l. 11. c. 60. s. 6. 4:281*} Ephorus said that he was admiral of the fleet, while Pherendates was the commander on land. Callisthenes said that Ariomandes, the son of Gobryas, commanded the army. {*Plutarch, Cimon, l. 1. c. 12. s. 4. 2:441*}

### 3534 AM, 4244 JP, 470 BC

*1195.* After the Athenians had subdued Naxos, {*Thucydides, l. 1. c. 98. s. 4. 1:167*} they and their confederates, under the conduct of their general Cimon, in only one day defeated the Persians in both a naval battle, not far from the isle of Cyprus, as well as a battle on land, at the mouth of the Eurymedon River in Pamphylia. This was in the third year of the 77th Olympiad. {*Diod. Sic., l. 11. c. 60-61. 4:281,283*} *[L191]* Diodorus was of the opinion (and so was Justin {*Justin, Trogus, l. 2. c. fin.*}) that Xerxes was still alive, contrary to what Thucydides stated, who of all these writers lived closest to that time. Therefore, Eusebius was right when he said this great victory was in the fourth year of Artaxerxes. He also noted: {*Eusebius, Chronicles, l. 1. 1:193*}

> "Cimon obtained this victory by sea and land against the Persians near the Eurymedon River, and so the war with the Medes ended."

1196. From the beginning of Artaxerxes' reign (as we have noted from Thucydides' account), his fourth year was the same as the third year of the 77th Olympiad mentioned here by Diodorus. Eusebius believed the first year of his reign to coincide with the first year of the 79th Olympiad. Hence he must of necessity have placed his fourth year with the fourth year of the same Olympiad. The best way to relate this story is to record this whole matter in the same order as we find it in Diodorus and Plutarch, thus:

1197. When Cimon heard that the king's captains had taken up their position with a large army on land and a fleet at sea on the coast of Pamphylia, he stayed out at sea, so that they might not come near to the Chelidonian Islands. With two hundred ships he went from Cnidos and Triopium to the Greek city of Phaselis. When they would not allow his navy into their port and refused to defect from the Persians, he burned their country and assaulted their city. Nevertheless, at the intercession of the natives of Chios who were in the fleet, peace was made, on the condition that they should pay ten talents and follow Cimon in the war against the Persians. {*Plutarch, Cimon, l. 1. c. 12. s. 1-4. 2:439-441*}

1198. When Cimon learned that the Persian fleet was sailing around the coast of Cyprus, he immediately set sail toward them with two hundred and fifty ships against three hundred and forty of theirs. {*Diod. Sic., l. 11. c. 62. 4:287*} Ephorus said that the Persians had three hundred and fifty ships and Phanodemus stated they had six hundred. The Persians did nothing worthy of so large a navy. Those that were closest to land abandoned their ships and fled ashore to the army that was arranged in battle array there. The rest were attacked by Cimon, taken and killed. {*Plutarch, Cimon, l. 1. c. 12. s. 5,6. 2:443*} Thucydides said that they took all two hundred of the Phoenician ships and sank them. {*Thucydides, l. 1. c. 100. s. 1,2. 1:169*} Emilius Probus said that he overwhelmed and captured all the fleet of the Cypriots and Phoenicians to a total of two hundred ships. {*Emilius Probus, Cimon*} Diodorus stated that the Athenians sank many of their ships, as well as taking a hundred ships, with their crews, as prisoners. Those ships that had been abandoned by

the soldiers who had fled into Cyprus were taken without any prisoners. {*Diod. Sic., l. 11. c. 60. s. 6. 4:283*} The following verses recall this victory which the Athenians had won and offered to their god. They are found both in Diodorus and also in Plato's second oration on Aristides. {*Diod. Sic., l. 11. c. 62. s. 3. 4:287*}

> For these when soldiers all were killed at land,
> A hundred ships of the Phoenicians took,
> All full of men.

1199. Plutarch stated that Cimon brought about a hundred Phoenician ships of war from Eurymedon. {*Plutarch, Glory of the Athenians, l. 1. c. 7. 4:517*} Diodorus affirmed that he took not merely a hundred but three hundred and forty ships, that is, the whole Persian navy as well as twenty thousand men. {*Diod. Sic., l. 11. c. 62. s. 2. 4:287*} [L192]

1200. Cimon was not satisfied with this victory at sea, but attacked the land army of the Persians in Asia which he saw lined up on the shore near the mouth of the Eurymedon River. The better to achieve victory, he dressed all his soldiers in the Persian clothes which he had taken, so that the Persians would think these were their navy and welcome them. In this manner Cimon escaped detection and landed his men as soon as it was night (and it was a very dark, moonless night). They attacked the enemy's camp and killed all they met. Pherendates, one of the two chief commanders, and the king's brother's son, was killed as he lay in his pavilion. The enemy was soon put to flight. {*Diod. Sic., l. 11. c. 61. 4:283,285*} [E135] Commenting on this stratagem, Polyaenus mistakenly maintained that Cimon landed his men in Cyprus and not in Pamphylia. {*Polyaenus, Strategmata, l. 1.*} Julius Frontinus documented a similar ruse used by the Athenians. {*Frontinus, Stratagems, l. 4. c. 7. s. 23. 1:317*}

1201. Near the Hydrus River, Cimon captured eighty Phoenician ships which were not part of the battle, and before they had even heard about it. {*Plutarch, Cimon, l. 1. c. 13. s. 3. 2:445*}

## 3535 AM, 4245 JP, 469 BC

1202. Cimon sailed from Athens with four ships and captured thirteen Persian ships in the Chersonesus of Thrace. He expelled the Persians and Thracians and took possession of the place for the Athenians. The Persian army was driven out of all of Asia, from Ionia to Pamphylia. {*Plutarch, Cimon, l. 1. c. 14. s. 1. 2:447*} Pericles assumed the leadership of Athens. He himself set out with fifty ships, and Ephialtes with thirty more. They sailed beyond the Chelidonian Islands in the sea of Pamphylia and saw not one Persian ship on the entire journey, according to Plutarch, who quoted Callisthenes. {*Plutarch,

*Cimon, l. 1. c. 13. s. 5. 2:445}* Isocrates said that no Persian war ship came closer to Greece than the port of Phaselis, nor did any company of Persians cross over the Halys River by land. {*Isocrates, Panathenaicus, l. 1. (59) 2:409}* Diodorus, however, wrote that when the Persians saw the increase of the Athenian power, they started building ships faster than ever. {*Diod. Sic., l. 11. c. 62. s. 2. 4:287}*

### 3537b AM, 4247 JP, 467 BC

*1203.* Ezra the priest, a scribe or lawyer skilled in the law of Moses, obtained permission from King Artaxerxes and his seven counsellors to resettle the Jewish state and to reform the religion at Jerusalem. This grant once again made it lawful for all the willing Jews to return to Jerusalem. They could send or carry with them any gold or silver that either the king and his nobles or the Jews wanted to offer to their God. They were also given all kinds of furnishings for the Lord's house. The treasurers beyond the river were ordered to supply them from the king's treasury with everything else they would need. All who worked in the temple would be free from having to pay tribute. All the people were allowed to live according to the laws of their God. {*Ezr 7:11-26}*

### 3537c AM, 4247 JP, 467 BC

*1204.* In the seventh year of Artaxerxes, on the first day of the first month, Ezra left Babylon for Israel with a large number of Jews. {*Ezr 7:6,7,9 8:1-14,30}* Ezra gathered together at the Ahava River all those who were returning. When he found no Levites in the company, he sent and asked for some to be appointed to make this journey back to Jerusalem with them. They held a fast there for three days to seek God's protection for the journey. Ezra selected twelve of the chief priests with ten of their brethren to tabulate all the items they were taking back to the house of the Lord at Jerusalem. {*Ezr 8:15-30} [L193]*

### 3537d AM, 4247 JP, 467 BC

*1205.* On the twelfth day of the first month they set out from the Ahava River, and on the first day of the fifth month, in the seventh year of Artaxerxes' reign, they arrived at Jerusalem. They rested there for three days. {*Ezr 7:8,9 8:30,32}*

*1206.* On the fourth day of the fifth month, the gold and silver which they had brought was weighed and put into the house of the Lord along with the other furnishings. Those who had returned offered their sacrifices to God. When this was done, the king's edicts were given to the governors and rulers beyond the river, who showed much favour to the people and to the house of the Lord. {*Ezr 8:33-36}*

### 3538a AM, 4247 JP, 467 BC

*1207.* When Ezra discovered that the Israelites had intermarried with the heathen, he mourned and fasted, and

publicly made intercession to God, to avert his wrath on them. {*Ezr 9:1-15}* When many of the people sorrowed over this, Shecaniah advised Ezra to direct the people to vow to God that they would put away their heathen wives and the children whom they had fathered. This was done. {*Ezr 10:1-17}*

*1208.* Those who had returned from captivity were ordered to appear at Jerusalem within three days, and any who did not would be punished. So all the men of Judah and Benjamin gathered in the court of the temple on the twentieth day of the ninth month. They were greatly distressed over the seriousness of the matter, and because of the inclement weather. Ezra commanded every male to separate himself from his heathen wife. This they agreed to do, and asked that judges be appointed to see that the orders were followed. Two priests and two Levites were appointed to help carry this out. {*Ezr 10:7-15}*

### 3538b AM, 4248 JP, 466 BC

*1209.* This examination was held from the first day of the tenth month to the first day of the first month. In three months the matter of the heathen wives was settled. {*Ezr 10:16,17}*

### 3538d AM, 4248 JP, 466 BC

*1210.* Themistocles died a natural death at Magnesia. Others say he poisoned himself voluntarily, when he saw that he could not subdue Greece, as he had promised the king. {*Thucydides, l. 1. c. 138. s. 5. 1:237}* Cicero said, in his work on Laelius, that he killed himself twenty years after the death of Gaius Marcius Coriolanus. {*Cicero, De Amicita, l. 1. c. 12. 20:155}* According to Dionysius Halicarnassus, that would be in the third year of the 73rd Olympiad, which would place Themistocles' death in this year which is the third year of the 78th Olympiad. {*Dionysius Halicarnassus, Roman Antiquities, l. 8. c. 1. s. 1. 5:3}* {*Dionysius Halicarnassus, Roman Antiquities, l. 8. c. 62. 5:181,183} [E136]* Eusebius noted this under the current year, saying that Themistocles died from drinking bull's blood. {*Eusebius, Chronicles, l. 1. 2:192}* Valerius Maximus gave us more details when he said: {*Valerius Maximus, l. 5. c. 6. ext. 3. 1:523}*

> "Themistocles, whose own worth had made him the conqueror, had been made the general of the Persians by his own country's wrong. However, so that he might keep himself from attacking his own country, he appointed a sacrifice at which he drank a bowl full of bull's blood. Hence, he fell dead before the altar, as a noble sacrifice of piety. So memorable was his departure from this life that it effectively meant that Greece would never need another Themistocles again."

*1211.* Cicero had Pomponius Atticus tell of his death in this way: {*Cicero, Brutus, l. 1. c. 11. 5:47}*

"For just as you now tell us a tale of Coriolanus, so Clitarchus and Stratocles do the same of Themistocles. Thucydides, who was an Athenian of noble rank and an excellent man, lived not long after him. He said only that he died and that he was buried privately in some place in Attica, and that there was some suspicion that he poisoned himself. These men wrote of him that when he had sacrificed a bull, he drank its blood from a basin and died in that place."

1212. However, the Athenians themselves had heard it from Aristophanes, in his *Equitibus*, even before the writing of this history by Thucydides. *[L194]* Aristophanes wrote this in Athens during the seventh year of the Peloponnesian War, when Stratocles was ruler of Athens. He stated that Themistocles died from drinking bull's blood.

## 3540a AM, 4249 JP, 465 BC

1213. The 20th Jubilee.

## 3544 AM, 4254 JP, 460 BC

1214. Inaros, the son of King Psammetichus of Libya (not a Lydian as Ctesias has it), journeyed from Mareia, a city bordering on Pharos, and caused much of Egypt to defect from Artaxerxes. He was proclaimed king by those who defected, and he sent for the Athenians at Cyprus. The Athenians were engaged in a war with two hundred ships, some of their own and the rest were from their allies. {*Thucydides, l. 1. c. 104. 1:175}

1215. When Artaxerxes heard of the Egyptian revolt, he gathered an army and a navy from all his dominions. He spared no pains nor cost in doing this. {*Diod. Sic., l. 11. c. 71. s. 6. 4:311} This was two years earlier than the more precise account given by Thucydides.

1216. Artaxerxes planned to lead this army into Egypt, but his friends persuaded him otherwise, so he sent his brother Achemenes to head that expedition, with four hundred thousand soldiers and eighty ships. {Ctesias} Diodorus agreed with Ctesias that he sent Achemenes as general in this Egyptian war, but said that he was the son of Darius and that Artaxerxes was his uncle, and that he had only three hundred thousand troops. {*Diod. Sic., l. 11. c. 74. s. 1,2. 4:315,317} By this he meant to say that it was that Achemenes, son of Darius Hystaspes and Atossa, to whom Xerxes had given the government of Egypt after Xerxes had conquered it. {*Herodotus, l. 7. c. 7,97. 3:309,404}

## 3545 AM, 4255 JP, 459 BC

1217. When Achemenes (also called Achemenides) came into Egypt, he refreshed his army at the Nile River after the long march, and then prepared for battle. Those on the other side gathered what forces they could from Egypt and Libya and waited for the Athenians to arrive. {*Diod. Sic., l. 11. c. 74. s. 2. 4:317}

1218. The Athenians came by sea and entered the mouth of the Nile. They quickly made themselves masters of the river. {*Thucydides, l. 1. c. 104. 1:175} Inaros, together with Charamitimides, who was admiral of a fleet of forty Athenian ships, defeated the Persians. Of the fifty Persian ships, they took twenty with all their men, and sank the other thirty. {Ctesias} Diodorus Siculus stated that the entire Athenian fleet of two hundred ships at Cyprus came to Egypt, not forty ships only, as Ctesias said. {*Diod. Sic., l. 11. c. 74. s. 3. 4:317}

1219. Inaros, with his own Egyptian troops and Athenian reinforcements, fought a battle with the Persians on land, who were winning by their sheer numbers. When the Athenians came and forced the one wing of the Persian troops to retire, many Persians were killed. The rest of the Persian army fled and many were slaughtered. {*Diod. Sic., l. 11. c. 74. s. 3. 4:317} Of the four hundred thousand men whom Achemenes brought into the battle, he and one hundred thousand of his troops were killed. He died of a wound which he received from Inaros' own hand, and his body was sent to Artaxerxes. {Ctesias} Herodotus mentioned that Achemenes, a son of Darius, and other Persians, were killed by Inaros the Libyan, son of Psammetichus, at Papremes. {*Herodotus, l. 3. c. 12. 2:17} {*Herodotus, l. 7. c. 7. 3:309}

1220. The Athenians routed the Persians and took two thirds of Memphis. They attacked the third part, called the White Wall, to which the Persians and Medes had fled. {*Diod. Sic., l. 11. c. 74. s. 4. 4:317} {*Thucydides, l. 1. c. 104. 1:175} *[L195]*

## 3546 AM, 4256 JP, 458 BC

1221. When Artaxerxes heard of this great defeat, he sent Megabyzus, a Persian, to Sparta with money to pay the Peloponnesians to attack the Athenians, thinking that this would draw the Athenians away from Egypt. *[E137]* The Lacedemonians would not take his money nor agree to any of his plans. When the king realised this, he called Megabyzus home again with the money that was left. He commanded Megabyzus, the son of Zopyrus, to make provisions to go to Egypt. {*Diod. Sic., l. 11. c. 74. s. 5-7. 4:317,319} {*Thucydides, l. 1. c. 109. s. 2,3. 1:183} Megabyzus had previously been a general in Xerxes' army. {*Herodotus, l. 7. c. 82. 3:390} He married Xerxes' daughter, Amytis. {Ctesias} He was the son of Zopyrus, who recovered Babylon for Darius, the son of Hystaspes. {*Herodotus, l. 3. c. 160. 2:195}

**3547 AM, 4257 JP, 457 BC**

1222. Artabazus and Megabyzus were made commanders for the war in Egypt. They had an army of three hundred thousand troops. {*Diod. Sic., l. 11. c. 75. s. 1. 4:319} Ctesias said they only had two hundred thousand.

1223. When they came into Cilicia and Phoenicia, the commanders stayed for a time to allow the army a rest after so long a march. Meanwhile, they ordered the Cilicians, Cypriots and Phoenicians to provide the navy. The people of Thrace provided three hundred ships, fully manned and equipped for war. {*Diod. Sic., l. 11. c. 74. s. 2. 4:317} Oriscus was the admiral of the fleet. {Ctesias}

1224. They spent almost a whole year in training the troops for war. The Athenians continued to besiege the citadel of the White Wall in Memphis. The Persians manfully defended it and the Athenians saw no possibility of taking it by a direct attack. However, they besieged it for the whole of that year. {*Diod. Sic., l. 11. c. 75. s. 2-4. 4:319}

**3548 AM, 4258 JP, 456 BC**

1225. When the Persian commanders in Asia had trained their troops, they marched from there through Syria and Phoenicia. Their navy of three hundred ships sailed along the coast as they went. When they came to Memphis, their army of two hundred thousand was joined by the three hundred thousand troops left by Achemenes in Egypt. {*Diod. Sic., l. 11. c. 77. 4:323} They fought a fierce battle with the Egyptians, with many dying on each side. More Egyptians were killed than Persians. Megabyzus wounded Inaros in the thigh. Inaros fled into the stronghold called Byblus, on the isle of Prosopitis in the Nile River. He was joined by the surviving Greeks, but the Greek general Charamites was killed in this battle. All Egypt, with the exception of that citadel of Byblus, defected to Megabyzus. {Ctesias}

1226. When Megabyzus had driven both Egyptians and Greeks from the field of battle and out of Memphis, he besieged them in the little isle of Prosopitis for eighteen months. {*Thucydides, l. 1. c. 109. 1:183}

**3550a AM, 4259 JP, 455 BC**

1227. In the twentieth year of the reign of Artaxerxes, in the ninth month called Chisleu, Nehemiah was at Susa, the winter quarters of the Persian kings. {*Athenaeus, l. 12. (514f) 5:311} When he received news of how the wall of Jerusalem was still broken down and the gates burned with fire, he mourned, fasted and prayed to God. He asked that God would forgive the people's sins and give him grace in the eyes of the king. {Ne 1:1-11}

**3550c AM, 4260 JP, 454 BC**

1228. In the same twentieth year of the king, in the month of Nisan, Nehemiah's turn came to serve as cupbearer to the king. [L196] Both the king and queen (whom I suppose to be she whom Ctesias called Damaspia) noticed his sorrowful appearance. He presented his request to them and obtained permission from the king to be the governor of Judah and to rebuild Jerusalem. {Ne 2:1-6} This event marks the start of Daniel's seventy weeks. {Da 9:24,25} (For the starting date of Artaxerxes' reign, {See note on 3531b AM. <<1184>>} Editor.)

1229. Nehemiah, with a commission and supplies from the king, came to Jerusalem in spite of the opposition from two governors, Sanballat, the Horonite of Moab, and Tobiah, the Ammonite. He began the work and replied wisely to those who laughed at him for undertaking such foolish work. {Ne 2:7-20}

1230. The Persian commanders in Egypt drained the river dry which flowed around the isle of Prosopitis by diverting the water into another course. This left the Athenian ships aground and joined the isle of Prosopitis to the mainland. As soon as the Egyptians saw the Athenian ships aground, they surrendered and made peace with the Persians. When the Athenians were thus deserted by the Egyptians, they burned their ships to prevent them from falling into the hands of the enemy. [E138] The Persians crossed the dry channel and took the island, but seeing the valour of the Athenians and remembering the losses they had received at their hand previously, they allowed all six thousand of them to return home with their possessions. {*Thucydides, l. 1. c. 109,110. 1:183,185} {*Diod. Sic., l. 11. c. 77. s. 2-5. 4:323,325} {Ctesias}

1231. The fortunes of the Athenians in Egypt, where they had spent six years in war, came to naught. Egypt returned to the control of Artaxerxes, except for Amyrtaeus, who was king of those living in the low countries of Egypt. They were unable to take him because of the vastness of the low country, and because its inhabitants were most warlike. {*Thucydides, l. 1. c. 110. 1:183,185}

**3550d AM, 4260 JP, 454 BC**

1232. Eliashib, the son of Joiakim, the son of Jehu (or Jehoshua) the high priest, together with the rest of the Jews, started to build the wall of Jerusalem {Ne 3:1-32} on the fourth day of the fifth month, called Ab. {Ne 6:15}

1233. Sanballat and Tobiah, with the Samaritans and other enemies of the Jews, first laughed at this new work. When they saw the wall half up, they stopped mocking and consulted how to destroy the builders. When Nehemiah found out about this, he first prayed to God and then ordered his men to make ready for a battle, thus thwarting the plans of their enemies. {*Ne 4:1-23*}

1234. When Nehemiah heard the outcries of the people, he ordered them to be freed: the slaves from their bondage and the debtors from their debts. Those who had mortgaged their lands or goods were to be freed from their debt. He set a good example by releasing his debts and all engagements of lands or goods made to him, and freed the poor from public taxes. He gave liberally to those in need. {*Ne 5:1-19*}

1235. Nehemiah was not only in danger from Sanballat and other enemies abroad, but also from false prophets and false brethren at home. They tried to hinder the work as much as the others did. In spite of these difficulties, the wall was finished in fifty-two days, on the twenty-fifth day of the sixth month, called Elul. {*Ne 6:1-19*}

1236. The dedication of the wall was performed with much celebration and great joy. {*Ne 12:27-43*}

1237. Nehemiah took care of the various offices belonging to the house of the Lord. *[L197]* He appointed governors over the city and controlled its guards. He called the congregation together and numbered those who had returned from captivity. He selected a number of people to live in the city alongside its few remaining inhabitants, to rebuild it with the rest of its inhabitants. Everyone, according to his ability, made their various offerings to God. {*Ne 7:1-73*}

1238. When fifty Greek warships were sent to Egypt to relieve those who had been there so long, they knew nothing of what had happened to their countrymen. They anchored at the Mendesian mouth of the Nile River, where they were attacked by the Persians from the land and the Phoenicians by sea. Most of them were killed, but a few escaped to carry news to Greece. Of that large army which existed before, only a few returned to Greece again. Most were lost as they passed through the deserts of Libya to get to Cyrene. This was the sad end to which that large expedition of the Athenians came to in Egypt. {*\*Thucydides, l. 1. c. 110. s. 3-5. 1:185*}

### 3551a AM, 4260 JP, 454 BC

1239. For the Feast of Trumpets, on the first day of the seventh month, all the Jews came together at Jerusalem. The law of God was read by Ezra and expounded to them. When they heard it, they were all deeply grieved, and wept. They were encouraged by Nehemiah, Ezra and the Levites to keep that feast with joy. {*Ne 8:1-12*}

1240. On the second day of the same month, the elders of the families, the priests, and the Levites consulted with Ezra concerning questions arising from the reading of the law. They were encouraged to keep the Feast of Tabernacles outside in the fields in booths made of boughs, as stated in the law. {*Ne 8:13-15 Le 23:40*}

1241. From the fifteenth to the twenty-first day, the Feast of Tabernacles was celebrated with great care and devotion. For seven days altogether the law of God was read, and the eighth day was also kept very solemnly, according to the law. {*Le 23:36*}

> "Neither was there the like Feast of Tabernacles kept from the days of Joshua, the son of Nun, to that time, and there was great joy made." {*Ne 8:17,18*} *[E139]*

1242. The Jews wrote about this in their Greater Chronicle, in chapter thirty:

> "It may be said that Ezra compared the return of the children of Israel into the land with the days of Joshua. For as in the days of Joshua they were bound to tithes, to the year of Shemite, or Remission, and to Jubilees, and to the hallowing of their walled towns, so now, in their return in the time of Ezra, they were in like manner obliged to keep the law of tithes, of the years of Shemite, or releasings, or Jubilees, and the hallowing of their walled cities. They rejoiced greatly before the Lord."

1243. On the twenty-fourth of this month the Israelites who had returned separated themselves from all strangers, and made public profession of their repentance. {*Ne 9:1-38*} They renewed their covenant with God and bound themselves to observe the law of God, his worship, {*Ne 10:1-39*} and the law {*Le 25:4 De 15:1,2*} of the Sabbath, and the sabbatical year. {*Ne 10:31*}

1244. The chief heads of the people feasted at Jerusalem. The rest cast lots according to which every tenth man who was selected was to live in Jerusalem. {*Ne 11:1-36 1Ch 9:1-44*}

### 3551c AM, 4261 JP, 453 BC

1245. Megabyzus appointed Sartama as governor of Egypt and returned to Artaxerxes with Inaros and some other Greeks, giving them his word that they would not be harmed. Artaxerxes carefully observed this, though he was incensed against Inaros for having killed his brother Achemenes. *[L198]* When his mother, Amestris (called Amytis by Ctesias), desired vengeance on Inaros, the other Greeks and Megabyzus, the king refused her request. {*Ctesias*}

### 3554 AM, 4264 JP, 450 BC

1246. The Athenians sent Cimon, their general, with a fleet of two hundred ships, their own and their confederates, to Cyprus. Sixty went to Egypt to Amyrtaeus, who was still in Egypt. The rest besieged Citium, a city in Cyprus. {*Thucydides, l. 1. c. 112. 1:187} At this time, Artabazus and Megabyzus commanded the Persian forces. Artabazus had his fleet of three hundred ships around Cyprus. Megabyzus, with an army of three hundred thousand troops, stayed in Cilicia. {*Diod. Sic., l. 12. c. 3. s. 1. 4:379}

1247. Cimon sent messengers to the oracle at the temple of Ammon to ask about some secret matter. {*Plutarch, Cimon, l. 1. c. 18. s. 6. 2:463}

## 3555 AM, 4265 JP, 449 BC

1248. In the siege of Citium in Cyprus, {*Thucydides, l. 1. c. 112. s. 4. 1:187} Cimon died, either of a natural disease (as Emilius Probus stated) or, as others said, of a wound which he received in battle. When he was about to die, he advised those that were about him to conceal his death and to return home as fast as they could. It happened that this secret was well kept and all the Greek army returned home safely under the conduct (as Phanodemus said) of Cimon, who had been dead an entire month. Those who were sent to consult the oracle, received the answer that Cimon was already with the gods. When they returned to Egypt, they understood that Cimon had died at the very time when the oracle had answered them. {*Plutarch, Cimon, l. 1. c. 18. s. 6,7. 2:463,465} {*Plutarch, Cimon, l. 1. c. 19. s. 1. 2:465}

1249. When the Greek army returned from Egypt, those who were besieging Citium in Cyprus were short of supplies. They lifted their siege and sailed to Salamis on the same island. There, they fought with the Phoenicians, Cypriots and Cilicians, by sea and by land. In the naval battle, they sank many enemy ships, and captured a hundred others with all the soldiers and sailors still in them. They pursued the rest as far as Phoenicia. The Persians, with the remaining ships, fled into Cilicia, where Megabyzus was with his army. The Athenians sailed there as fast as possible, landed their men on the open shore and then attacked the enemy. In this battle, Anaxicrates, who commanded the fleet, behaved himself most courageously and died a most noble and heroic death. They defeated the Persians and killed many of the enemy. They returned to their ships and sailed home with those returning from Egypt. {*Diod. Sic., l. 12. c. 4. 4:381} This was in the third and fourth year of the 82nd Olympiad as Diodorus stood corrected from the records of Thucydides. Aelian wrote that the Athenians lost two hundred ships in Egypt and one hundred and fifty in Cyprus, with all their equipment. {*Aelian, Historical Miscellany, l. 5. c. 10. 1:221}

1250. When Artaxerxes heard of the loss of his men in Cyprus, he sought advice from his council concerning this war. It was resolved that for the good of the kingdom peace should be made with the Greeks. So the king wrote letters to the captains and commanders in Cyprus, telling them to make peace with the Greeks on any terms, whereupon Artabazus and Megabyzus sent messengers to Athens to seek peace. [E140] When the Athenians had consented to their conditions, they sent commissioners with full power and authority to represent them. The leader of the group was Callias, the son of Hipponicus. {*Diod. Sic., l. 12. c. 4. s. 4-6. 4:383} At this time, the men of the Argives sent their messengers to Susa to ascertain if Artaxerxes would honour the league they had made with his father Xerxes, or if he considered them enemies. [L199] Artaxerxes answered that the league would continue and that he considered no city more friendly to him than that of the Argives. {*Herodotus, l. 7. c. 152. 3:463}

1251. The peace between the Athenians and their confederates on the one side and the Persians on the other was concluded with these conditions:

> "No Persian governor would at any time come within three days' journey of the sea and no Persian warship would sail inside of Phaselis or the Cyanean Rocks, which was the entrance to the Black Sea at Byzantium."

1252. Plutarch expressed it thus: {*Plutarch, Cimon, l. 1. c. 13. s. 4. 2:445}

> "That the king would not have any warships in all the sea between the Cyanean and the Cheledonian Islands."

1253. When the king and his council of war had subscribed to these articles, the Athenians took an oath that they would not invade any of the king's provinces. {*Diod. Sic., l. 12. c. 4. s. 6. 4:383}

1254. The Athenians built an altar in memory of this peace and gave many honours to Callias, who had been its architect. {*Plutarch, Cimon, l. 1. c. 19. s. 4. 2:467}

## 3556 AM, 4266 JP, 448 BC

1255. Artaxerxes was wearied for five years with his mother's nagging and finally gave Inaros, the Egyptian king, and the Greeks that came with him, into her hand. The queen had the body of Inaros racked and stretched out and wrenched several ways. He hung on three different crosses at one time. She had the fifty Greeks (for she could catch no more) decapitated. {Ctesias} Thucydides stated that Inaros, king of Libya, was taken by treachery and crucified. {*Thucydides, l. 1. c. 110. s. 3. 1:185} Herodotus stated that his son, Thannyras, at the discretion of the Persians, held the government of Egypt which his father had held before him. {*Herodotus, l. 3. c. 15. 2:21}

*1256.* Megabyzus was exceedingly grieved by the death of Inaros and the Greeks with him. He asked permission to go to his own government in Syria, where he had secretly sent the rest of the Greeks. He followed them there, and as soon as he came to Syria, he revolted from the king and gathered an army of a hundred and fifty thousand men. {*Ctesias*}

## 3557 AM, 4267 JP, 447 BC

*1257.* Osiris was sent against Megabyzus with an army of two hundred thousand men. In the battle, Osiris wounded Megabyzus with an arrow in the thigh, two inches deep. Megabyzus, in turn, wounded Osiris, first with an arrow in the thigh and then one in the shoulder. As Osiris fell from his horse, Megabyzus caught him about his middle and saved him. Many of the Persians fell, and the two sons of Megabyzus, Zopyrus and Artipsyus, fought valiantly that day. Megabyzus won and carefully returned Osiris to Artaxerxes, who demanded his return. {*Ctesias*}

## 3558 AM, 4268 JP, 446 BC

*1258.* Another army was sent against Megabyzus. The general was Menostanes, or Menostates, son to Artarius, governor of Babylon and brother to King Artaxerxes. In the battle, Megabyzus wounded Menostanes in the shoulder and in the head. Neither of those wounds were mortal, but when it happened, he and all his army fled and Megabyzus had a most glorious victory. {*Ctesias*}

*1259.* Artarius, Artoxares the eunuch, a Paphlagonian, and Amestris, the queen mother, persuaded Megabyzus to come to terms with the king. After much effort, Artarius, his wife Amytis, and Artoxares, who was now twenty years of age and Petisas, the son of Osiris, prevailed with him to come to the king. When he came, the king sent him word that he freely pardoned him of all his past offences. A little later, while the king was hunting, a lion attacked him. When Megabyzus saw the lion raised on his hind feet, he killed him with his spear. The king was angry with him, because he had done it before the king could. He commanded that Megabyzus be decapitated. *[L200]* The intercession of Amestris, Amytis and others spared his life, and he was sent away and confined to the isle of Cirta in the Persian Gulf. Because Artoxares, the eunuch, spoke too freely with the king on Megabyzus' behalf, he was banished into Armenia. {*Ctesias*}

## 3559 AM, 4269 JP, 445 BC

*1260.* When Herodotus read his books at Athens before the council there, he was greatly honoured for his works. {*Eusebius, Chronicles, l. 1. 1:195*} Scaliger noted that Herodotus wrote his books before his going into Great Greece (Southern Italy), not in Great Greece itself, as some

thought who followed Pliny on this. We shall see more in the next year. *[E141]* But I have observed that frequent mention was made of the Peloponnesian War in these books. {*Herodotus, l. 7. c. 137. 3:439*} {*Herodotus, l. 9. c. 72,73. 4:245*} In the former reference, something is related that took place in the second year of that war. In the latter, something that happened in its nineteenth year, at Decelea. This was twenty-two years after the time assigned by Eusebius to the reading of his book at Athens. Herodotus made notes on the years 3596 AM and 3597 AM. {*See note on 3596d AM. <<1368>>*} {*See note on 3597b AM. <<1377>>*}

## 3560 AM, 4270 JP, 444 BC

*1261.* In the first year of the 84th Olympiad, when Praxiteles was the governor of Athens, and twelve years before the Peloponnesian War began, the Athenians sent a colony into Great Greece (Southern Italy) to rebuild the decayed city of Thurii. Lysias, a youth of fifteen years, was one of the men in this group, {*Plutarch, Lysias, l. 1. (835d) 10:363*} {*Dionysius Halicarnassus, Roman Antiquities, l. 1. c. 51. s. 2. 1:167*} along with Herodotus, who was forty-one years old. Although Herodotus was born at Halicarnassus in Caria, he obtained the surname of Thurius after this, because of his part in re-establishing Thurii. {*Strabo, l. 14. c. 2. s. 16. 6:283*} The 84th Olympiad coincided with the 310th year from the founding of Rome, according to Varro's account. Pliny said that it was in this year that Herodotus compiled his history, in Thurii in Italy, as mentioned under the previous year, {*Pliny, l. 12. c. 8. 4:15*} but Diodorus thought Thurii was founded two years earlier. {*Diod. Sic., l. 12. c. 9. s. 1. 4:389*}

## 3562 AM, 4272 JP, 442 BC

*1262.* In this year, all wars ceased throughout Asia, Greece, Sicily, Italy, Gaul, Spain and almost the entire world. {*Diod. Sic., l. 12. c. 26. s. 4. 4:427*}

*1263.* After Nehemiah had governed Judah for twelve years, that is from the twentieth year of the reign of Artaxerxes to the thirty-second of the same, he returned to the king. {*Ne 5:14 13:6*}

*1264.* In Nehemiah's absence, Eliashib, the priest, who was in charge of the chamber of the house of God and had made an alliance with Tobiah, prepared a room for him in the court of the temple, in the place where the gifts and tithes had formerly been kept. The son of Joiada, the son of Eliashib the high priest (who was a different man from the Eliashib whom I just mentioned), became son-in-law to Sanballat, the Horonite, after he married his daughter. When Nehemiah returned to Jerusalem with a new commission, he quickly redressed and severely punished these and other wrongdoings. {*Ne 13:1-31*}

**3563 AM, 4273 JP, 441 BC**

*1265.* After Megabyzus had lived in exile for five years, he fled from the isle where he was confined and feigning himself to be a *pisagas* (that means leper in the Persian language, and one whom no man might approach), he came home to his wife, Amytis. Through her and Amestris, the king's mother, he was at last reconciled to the king. He sat at the king's table as before and died at the age of seventy-six. The king grieved very much for him. {*Ctesias*}

**3564 AM, 4274 JP, 440 BC**

*1266.* In this year, the Samians and Milesians went to war over the ownership of the city of Priene. This was the beginning of the sixth year of the thirty years of peace, and the league between the Athenians and the Lacedemonians. {*Thucydides, l. 1. c. 115. s. 2. 1:191*} [L201] It was in the middle of the fourth year of the 84th Olympiad, according to Diodorus. {*Diod. Sic., l. 12. c. 27. 4:427*} Priene was a city in Caria, which both the Samians and the Milesians claimed. The Milesians were too weak to defeat the Samians. They drew to their side some Samians who were unhappy with things in their country. They went to Athens and complained of the behaviour of the citizens of Samos. The Athenians sent orders for them to lay down their arms and negotiate the matter at Athens. When the Samians refused to do this, Pericles prevailed to have war declared against them. He did this as a favour to his prostitute, Aspasia, that famous courtesan whom he doted on, not so much for her beauty as for her wit, and who was the daughter of Axiochus, a Milesian. The Athenians sent a fleet of forty ships under the command of Pericles and easily took the city of Samos. He changed the government from an aristocracy to a democratic government. {*Thucydides, l. 1. c. 115. s. 2,3. 1:191*} {*Diod. Sic., l. 12. c. 27. s. 1,2. 4:429*}

*1267.* After Pericles returned from Samos, a terrible sedition arose there. Some wanted a democratic government and others wanted the old aristocracy. Those who disliked the democratic form conspired with the chief men of the city and sent to Asia for Pissuthnes, the son of Hystaspes, the governor of Sardis. When they had made a league with him, he gave them a band of seven hundred soldiers. They returned in the dead of night to Samos and joined by others of like mind, they surprised and captured the town. Declaring themselves enemies of the Athenians, they took their whole garrison with the captain and officers and sent them to Pissuthnes as a gift. They immediately marched against Miletus. The inhabitants of Byzantium were also allies with them against the Athenians. [E142]

*1268.* When the Athenians heard of the revolt of Samos, they sent sixty ships. Sixteen sailed toward Caria to attack the Phoenician fleet in those parts, and into Chios and Lesbos to take on allies from there. The other forty-four vessels continued under Pericles, as the admiral, and his nine colleagues. The Samians recalled their twenty ships, which they had sent full of soldiers to assault Miletus, and these were joined by a further fifty ships. They fought with the forty-four ships of the Athenians near an island called Tragia and the Athenians were victorious. From there, the Athenians, with forty more ships from home and twenty-five more from Chios and Lesbos, went and landed with their forces on the isle of Samos. They captured the isle and made a triple ditch about the city by land, and then besieged the city with their ships. {*Thucydides, l. 1. c. 116. s. 1,2. 1:193*}

*1269.* A few days later, Pericles learned through letters from Caunus in Caria that the Phoenician fleet was coming toward him to relieve Samos. He left part of his army to maintain the siege and taking sixty ships from the navy, he went as fast as he could to meet the Phoenician navy. Stesagoras accompanied him with five ships from Samos. {*Thucydides, l. 1. c. 116. s. 3. 1:193*}

*1270.* The Samians took advantage of the absence of Pericles. Under the command of Melislus, the son of Ithagenes, an outstanding philosopher, they attacked the Athenian camp, which was neither fenced nor manned as it ought to have been. After they sank the ships which kept the island, and defeated and routed the army, they freely traded and brought in supplies for fourteen days. {*Thucydides, l. 1. c. 117. s. 1. 1:193*}

*1271.* When Pericles heard what had happened to his men at Samos, he hurried back as fast as he could with a larger fleet. [L202] Thucydides, Agnon and Phormio joined him with forty ships. Tlepolemus and Anticles brought twenty more ships from Athens. Chios and Mitylene sent him thirty ships. With these large forces, he attacked and defeated Melislus. He besieged the town by land and sea as before, and harassed them with frequent assaults on every side. Some say that those engines of battery, known as *Rams* and *Tortoises* were first invented there by Artemon of Clazomene. Ephorus, the historian, confused him with Artemon Periphresus, of whom Anacreon, the poet, made mention in his poetry. {*Athenaeus, l. 12. (533ef) 5:411*} {*Thucydides, l. 1. c. 117. s. 1. 1:193*} {*Diod. Sic., l. 12. c. 28. s. 3. 4:431*} {*Plutarch, Pericles, l. 1. c. 24-28. 3:69-83*}

**3565 AM, 4275 JP, 439 BC**

*1272.* After a nine month siege, the Samians surrendered. The town was immediately destroyed and they gave hostages to ensure their ongoing fidelity. They gave up all their ships and paid for the expense of the war by making instalment payments. The people of Byzantium submitted to the Athenian government as previously. {*Thucydides, l. 1. c. 117. s. 3. 1:195}

### 3566 AM, 4276 JP, 438 BC

1273. Spartacus succeeded the Archaeanactidae in the kingdom of Cimmerian Bosphorus. {*Diod. Sic., l. 12. c. 31. s. 1. 4:439}

### 3571 AM, 4281 JP, 433 BC

1274. Spartacus died in the fourth year of the 86th Olympiad, after reigning seventeen years. {*Diod. Sic., l. 12. c. 36. s. 1. 4:447} In the third year of the 85th Olympiad, Diodorus stated that Spartacus reigned seventeen years. The interval between these two Olympiad years assigned by Diodorus, the one interval to the beginning, the other to the end of his reign, only make up five, or at most, both intervals being included, only six years of his reign. After him came Seleucus. (Current Loeb editions of the Greek text state he reigned seven years. It appears the Greek text has been amended in the last 350 years. Editor.)

### 3572 AM, 4282 JP, 432 BC

1275. At Athens, in the year when Apseudes presided over the government, and toward the very end of the last year of the 86th Olympiad, Meton observed the summer solstice to be on the 21st day of the Egyptian month, Phamenoth (or the 27th day of June, according to the Julian calendar), in the morning. {Ptolemy, Great Syntaxis, l. 3. c. 2.} From this, he formulated the *Cyclus Lunaris*, or the cycle of the moon which we call the Golden Number of nineteen years. {*Diod. Sic., l. 12. c. 36. s. 2,3. 4:447,449} He deduced the beginning of this cycle from the next new moon following that solstice, on the fifteenth day of July, according to the Julian calendar. (This confirmed Diodorus' statement that the ancients knew the length of a year to be three hundred and sixty-five and a quarter days. Otherwise, Meton would not have known how long the cycle should have been. {*Diod. Sic., l. 1. c. 50. s. 2. 1:177} Editor.)

### 3573 AM, 4283 JP, 431 BC

1276. Arcesilaus was killed by his subjects, the Cyrenians. He was the eighth king in that state and the man who, in the third year of the 73rd Olympiad, won the thirty-first Pythian race with his chariot, for which he was made famous by Pindar, in his fourth and fifth odes. When his son should have succeeded him, he was disallowed by the Cyrenians. Thereupon, he sailed into the Hesperides, or western islands, where he died. So that kingdom of Cyrene, which had stood for two hundred years, came to an end. It had had four kings going by the name of Battus and four with the name of Arcesilaus. These interchangeably succeeded each other in the kingdom, according to the oracle at Delphi, as reported by Herodotus. {*Herodotus, l. 4. c. 163. 2:369} {Scholiast. Pindar, Ode 4. Pythion} [E143]

1277. Toward the end of the first year of the 87th Olympiad, when there were only two months remaining in the rule of Pythodorus of Athens, and at the beginning of spring, the Peloponnesian War started between the Lacedemonians and the Athenians. The countries living along the coast of Asia sided with the Athenians. All the Carians, the Dorians, the Ionians, those of the Hellespont, and all the adjoining islanders supported Athens, except for the two islands of Melos and Thera. Both sides sent their embassies to Artaxerxes, asking for help. {*Thucydides, l. 2. c. 2,9. 1:259,275}

1278. At the beginning of this war there lived three famous historians, Hellanicus, aged sixty-five, Herodotus, who was fifty-three, and Thucydides who was forty. {*Aulus Gellius, Attic Nights, l. 15. c. 23. s. 1,2. 3:113} Thucydides wrote the entire history of this war to its twenty-first year. [L203] He carefully wrote what happened by the winters and summers. He began every summer from the first day of spring and every winter from the first day of autumn.

1279. In the first summer of this war, there was a total eclipse of the sun which was so dark that the stars appeared in the sky. {*Thucydides, l. 2. c. 28. 1:309} This caused great fear among all men, and was seen as a sad and great omen in the world. When Pericles saw that the captain of the ship he was on was troubled by the eclipse, he put his cloak over his eyes. He asked him whether he was afraid at that, or whether or not he thought it portended any great event. When he said no, Pericles asked him what the difference was between this covering of the sun, and the covering of his eyes by the cloak, except that the eclipsed area was much larger than his cloak? {*Plutarch, Pericles, l. 1. c. 35. 3:101,103} He discussed with him the causes of the eclipses of the sun and moon, and the motions by which they moved, according to what he had learned from his teacher Anaxagoras. He persuaded his fellow citizens not to be troubled by a vain and needless fear. {*Valerius Maximus, l. 8. c. 11. ext. 1. 2:255,257} This eclipse happened at about five o'clock in the afternoon on August 3 at Athens. About eighty per cent (or ten digits) of the sun was covered.

### 3574 AM, 4284 JP, 430 BC

1280. A dreadful plague started first in Ethiopia and spread from there into Libya and Egypt, and especially into the regions of the Persian dominion. It raged unchecked in the city of Athens in the second year of this war. {*Thucydides, l. 2. c. 58. 1:343} Hippocrates documents the nature of this plague from a historical perspective. He was sick with it, and often in company with those who were sick. Hippocrates was a physician who lived in Athens and who was successful in the curing of various persons afflicted with the plague. He described the plague from a medical point of view. {*Hippocrates, Epidemics, l. 3. c. 3.*} Lucretius, who lived many years later, described this in his poetry.

*1281.* A sedition happened in a town of the Colophonians, called Notium. When Itamenes and his Persian soldiers were called in by one of the factions, they came and took possession of the strongest part of the town (the upper part). {*Thucydides, l. 3. c. 34. s. 1,2. 2:53*}

*1282.* Toward the end of this summer, Aristeus, the son of Adimantus, a Corinthian, and three envoys of the Lacedemonians, Aneristus, Nicolaus and Pratodamus, along with Timagoras of Tegea and Pollis of Argos, journeyed into Asia to Artaxerxes to ask for men and money for the war. They went by Thrace and came to its king, Sitalces, the son of Tereus. They planned to pass over the Hellespont and to go to Pharnaces, the son of Pharnabazus, hoping to have him convoy them safely to Artaxerxes, but they were betrayed by Sitalces and Nymphodorus of Abdera, the son of Pytheas. They were all taken to Athens where, without any formal hearing, the Athenians killed them the same day they arrived and threw their bodies into a pit. {*Thucydides, l. 2. c. 67. 1:379,381*} {*Herodotus, l. 7. c. 137. 3:439,441*}

### 3575a AM, 4284 JP, 430 BC

*1283.* The following winter, the Athenians sent six ships to Caria and Lycia under the command of Melesander. They intended to gather money from those parts and to rid the seas of pirates. These were from Peloponnesus and preyed on poor merchant ships that traded along the coast of Phaselis, Phoenicia and other ports of the continent. Melesander, with his Athenians and other confederates, did not stay at sea, but went ashore in Lycia and was defeated by the enemy. He and most of his army were killed. {*Thucydides, l. 2. c. 69. 1:385,387*}

*1284.* Seleucus, the king of Cimmerian Bosphorus, died after ruling for seven years. {*Diod. Sic., l. 12. c. 36. 4:447*} After him, Spartacus the second reigned for twenty-two years. (The Loeb edition of the text has obviously been amended to correct the defects that Ussher pointed out. It reads forty years instead of twenty-two years. However, the correction is incorrect! Editor.)

### 3576 AM, 4286 JP, 428 BC

*1285.* Pericles died in the fourth year of the 87th Olympiad, {*Diod. Sic., l. 12. c. 46. s. 1. 5:17*} thirty months after the beginning of the Peloponnesian War, of which he was the main cause. {*Thucydides, l. 2. c. 65. s. 6. 1:375*} He was the senior statesman and had continued as a prince of the

Athenian state for forty years. {*Cicero, De Oratore, l. 3. c. 16. (59) 4:47*} {*Plutarch, Pericles, l. 1. c. 39. 3:113,115*} [E144] [L204]

*1286.* In this year, Anaxagoras of Clazomene died. He was Pericles' teacher, and was born in the 70th Olympiad and died in the first year of the 88th Olympiad, according to Laertius. {*Diogenes Laertius, Apollodorus, l. 2. c. 3. (7) 1:137*} However, it was incorrectly given there as the 78th Olympiad. (Loeb edition does not have this variant reading. Editor.) He added that the men of Lampsacus bestowed on him an honourable burial with this epitaph on his tomb, as recorded also by Aelian: {*Aelian, Historical Miscellany, l. 8. c. 19. 1:279*}

> Great Anaxagoras lies here in mould,
> Who did all secrets of the heavens unfold.

### 3577a AM, 4286 JP, 428 BC

*1287.* In the winter season of the fourth year of the Peloponnesian War the Athenians sent twelve ships, commanded by Lysicles, with four commissioners, to collect their tribute from their confederate cities. Lysicles went from place to place to gather money. When he was leaving Myus through Caria, the Carians and Anaeitans ambushed and killed him and most of his army. {*Thucydides, l. 3. c. 19. 2:31*}

### 3577 AM, 4287 JP, 427 BC

*1288.* When Alcides, the commander of the Lacedemonian fleet, came to the cape of Myonnesus in the country of the Teians, he killed most of the Greeks whom he had taken prisoner from Asia. When he came to Ephesus, some messengers from the Samians, who were of the Anaeitans, rebuked him. They said he was wrong to deliver the Greeks from servitude if he planned to destroy people who had never borne arms against him nor were his enemies. Their only crime was being forced to pay tribute to the Athenians. He then spared the rest and let them go. {*Thucydides, l. 3. c. 32. 2:49,51*}

*1289.* A new broil arose between the original citizens of Notium, who lived in the lower town, and those who had recently fled there. These saw the power of the Arcadian and other barbarian mercenaries who had been sent from Pissuthnes, the governor of Lydia. They made a wall around the upper town for a fortification against the lower town. The Colophonians from the upper town, who were in sympathy with the Persians, joined them there and were admitted into citizenship. The other side sent for Paches, a captain of the Athenians, to come and help them. When he came, he defeated Hippias, the captain of the Arcadians in the citadel, and he was asked to leave the citadel for a talk. They promised him that if they could not agree, he could return safely to the citadel again. When he came, Paches took him and committed him to safe custody without manacles or fetters, while he attacked and captured the citadel. Everyone inside was killed, both Arcadians and Persians. Lastly, to keep his word with Hippias, he let him return safely to the citadel, but as soon as he had reached it, they laid hold on him again and shot him to death with arrows. So Paches restored Notium to the Colophonians, except for those who had sided with the Medes. Afterward, the Athenians established a colony there and governed the place according to their own laws. They gathered as many of the Colophonians from all parts as they could find, to live there. {*Thucydides, l. 3. c. 34. 2:53} {Polyaenus, Strategmata, l. 3.}

### 3579c AM, 4289 JP, 425 BC

1290. Artaxerxes sent Artaphernes, a Persian envoy, with a letter written in the Assyrian language, to Lacedemon. Among other things, he said that he did not know what they wanted from him, for they had sent so many envoys to him. None of them agreed with one another. Therefore, if they would have him understand what they wanted, they should send some men of their own to him. {*Thucydides, l. 4. c. 50. 2:297} [L205]

### 3579d AM, 4289 JP, 425 BC

1291. In the interim, Artaxerxes died and his son Xerxes succeeded him for only one year. {*Diod. Sic., l. 12. c. 64. 5:61,62} Xerxes' mother Damaspia died on the same day that her husband Artaxerxes did. Bagorazus, the eunuch, carried the bodies of both Xerxes' father, and mother into Persia. {Ctesias}

### 3580a AM, 4289 JP, 425 BC

1292. In the winter of the seventh year of the Peloponnesian War, Aristides, the son of Archippus, one of the captains who were sent from Athens to gather the tribute of their confederates, captured Artaphernes, the Persian envoy, as he was going to Lacedemon. This was at a place called Eion on the Strymon River. He brought him as a prisoner to Athens. The Athenians at once sent Aristides back to Ephesus accompanied by an envoy. When they arrived and heard that Artaxerxes had recently died, they returned home again. {*Thucydides, l. 4. c. 50. 2:297,299}

### 3580b AM, 4290 JP, 424 BC

1293. At the beginning of the next summer (the beginning of spring), Thucydides said there was a partial eclipse of the sun, beginning on the first day of spring in the morning (on the 21st day of March according to the Julian Calendar). This was toward the end of the fourth year of the 88th Olympiad. {*Thucydides, l. 4. c. 52. s. 1. 2:299} [E145] The sun was more than half eclipsed, according to the account of Prutenicus.

1294. The exiles from Mitylene, after their city was taken by the Athenians, joined with the exiles from Lesbos. They hired some mercenaries from Peloponnesus and went and took Rhoetium. Having received money from them, they spared the city. From there, they went to Antandros, which was betrayed into their hands. Their initial purpose was to liberate Mitylenian cities (known as the Actean cities) now controlled by Athens, and in particular, Antandros, which they fortified. They planned to build ships with timber from the hill Ida, hoping to take over the city of Lesbos and other cities in Aeolia. {*Thucydides, l. 4. c. 52. 2:299,301}

### 3580c AM, 4290 JP, 424 BC

1295. At the same time, Aristides and Demodocus (also called Symmachus,), captains of the Athenian navy, were in the Hellespont gathering tribute from the people there. Lamachus, a third captain, had gone with ten ships into Pontus. When they heard that the Mitylenians were planning to fortify Antandros, they gathered an army of their confederates and set sail for Mitylene. The enemy sallied out against the Athenians, but they defeated them in battle and captured the town. When Lamachus, who had gone into Pontus, came to the mouth of the Cales River (Diodorus called it Cachtes) in the region of Heraclea, he left his ships at anchor and plundered all the country around Heraclea. These cities favoured Persia, and had refused to pay tribute to Athens. After a heavy rain, the swollen river current drove their ships onto the rocky shore. He lost his whole fleet as well as a large part of his army. He could not return home by sea, and dared not return by land with so small a company through so many fierce and warlike countries. The Heracleans used this occasion to befriend these enemies rather than seek revenge on them. The Heracleans used the Athenian tribute to win their friendship and buy provisions for their return trip home. Lamachus, with his remaining company, went overland through the country of the Thracians, who lived on the Asian side, and came safely to Chalcedon. {*Thucydides, l. 4. c. 75. 2:341} {*Diod. Sic., l. 12. c. 72. 5:81} {Justin, Trogus, l. 16. c. 3.} [L206]

### 3580d AM, 4290 JP, 424 BC

1296. When Xerxes was roaring drunk on a festival day, he was killed in his chamber while sleeping. His brother Secundianus, born of Aloguna, a Babylonian woman, murdered him, aided by Pharnacyas, a eunuch. {Ctesias}

1297. Secundianus had for a long time borne a grudge against the eunuch Bagoras. He picked a quarrel with him for burying his father's body without his advice and ordered that he be stoned to death. His army took offence at this wicked deed, even though he gave them much money. From that time on, the army hated him for murdering his brother Xerxes. {Ctesias}

## 3581a AM, 4290 JP, 424 BC

1298. Secundianus sent for his brother Ochus, whom his father Artaxerxes had made governor of Hyrcania, but he refused to come. He sent word that he would come, but did not. This he did repeatedly. Finally he gathered a mighty army, with the intention of taking over the kingdom. Arbarius, who was general of the cavalry for Secundianus, defected to Ochus. Arxanes, the governor of Egypt, also defected. Artoxares came in person from Armenia and asked if he planned to make himself king. {Ctesias}

## 3581b AM, 4291 JP, 423 BC

1299. Ochus was made king, and subsequently after that called himself Darius. On the advice of both his wife Parysatis and his sister, he first tried to win over his brother Secundianus. Menostanes, whom he esteemed more highly than any other of the eunuchs about him, urged Secundianus not to believe his words nor have any treaty with faithless men. However, Secundianus came to make a treaty and was captured there. He died when thrown into a heap of ashes. {Ctesias} For more details on this punishment, see the following footnotes. {See note on 3485b AM. <<1025>>} {Apc 2Ma 13:5,6}

1300. When Secundianus, or Sogdianus, was dead, Ochus reigned alone and was known by the name of Darius Ochus. This happened toward the end of the first year of the 89th Olympiad. {*Thucydides, l. 8. c. 5. s. 4. 4:199} {*Diod. Sic., l. 12. c. 71. 5:79}

## 3582 AM, 4292 JP, 422 BC

1301. When the men of Delos were driven out of their country by the Athenians, Pharnaces gave them Adramyttium in Asia to live in. {*Thucydides, l. 5. c. 1. 3:3} {*Diod. Sic., l. 12. c. 73. s. 1. 5:85}

## 3583 AM, 4293 JP, 421 BC

1302. The Athenians, at the command of the oracle at Delphi, restored the people of Delos to their island again. {*Thucydides, l. 5. c. 32. 3:61}

## 3588 AM, 4298 JP, 416 BC

1303. The men of Byzantium and Chalcedon were joined by the Thracians, and crossed with a large army into Bithynia. [E146] When they had wasted the country and forced many of the smaller towns into submission, they were immeasurably cruel toward them. They gathered together a large multitude of men, women and children, and butchered every one of them. {*Diod. Sic., l. 12. c. 82. s. 2. 5:109}

## 3589a AM, 4298 JP, 416 BC

1304. The twenty-first Jubilee was the last one seen by the prophets of the Old Testament. The passage in Nehemiah is not to be understood of Darius the last, but of this Darius Nothus. {Ne 12:22} It was in his time that Johananes, also called both Johannes and Jonathan, succeeded to the high priesthood after his father Joiada (whom Josephus called Judas). {Ne 12:22,23} Jaddua's son, who succeeded his father in the priesthood, was also born then. [L207] These things Nehemiah mentioned only in passing. His book ended with the time of Artaxerxes Longimanus, the father of this Darius, whom Josephus mentions in connection with the prophetic writings: {*Josephus, Apion, l. 1. c. 8. (40) 1:179}

> "From the death of Moses to Artaxerxes, King of Persia, who succeeded Xerxes, the prophets wrote thirteen books. From Artaxerxes to our time, all things indeed have been likewise committed to writing, but not held in the same esteem as the former, because the succession of the prophets one after another has been uncertain."

1305. Eusebius made the following observation concerning the 32nd year of Artaxerxes, with whom the continued history of Nehemiah ended: {*Eusebius, Chronicles, l. 1. 1:196}

> "Hitherto, the divine scriptures of the Hebrews contain the annals of the times. Those things which were done among them after this time, we must derive from the books of the Maccabees and from the writings of Josephus and Africanus. He wrote a general history of things done among them down to the Roman times."

1306. Malachi, the last of the prophets, was a contemporary of Nehemiah. This we gather from the fact that he nowhere exhorted the people to build the temple, as Haggai and Zechariah did. Since the temple was now built, he reproved those same disorders among the Jews which Nehemiah also reproved at his second return with a new commission. These are: the marriages with foreign women, {Ne 13:23-29 Mal 2:11} withholding of tithes, {Ne 13:10-14 Mal 3:8} and abuses in the worship of God. {Ne 13:15-22 Mal 1:13 2:8} They were no longer to expect a continual succession of prophets, as before. Therefore Malachi, in the last words of his prophecy, exhorted them to hold fast to the law of Moses until Christ, that great prophet of the church, should appear with his forerunner, John the Baptist:

> "In the spirit and power of Elijah, to turn the hearts of the fathers to their children and the rebels to the wisdom of the just." {Mal 4:5 Lu 1:17 Mt 11:14 17:12}

*1307.* Jerome also stated that after Haggai, Zechariah and Malachi, he saw no other prophet till John the Baptist. *{Jerome, Commentary on Isaiah chapter 49.}* See also the Apocrypha. *{Apc 1Ma 4:46 9:27}* *{*Augustine, City of God, l. 17. c. 24. 2:360}* In the book of Pirke Abbeth we read that the men of the Great Synagogue succeeded the prophets. However, in later years the Jews count even Haggai, Zechariah and Malachi among their number, and make Ezra the head of this Great Synagogue.

## 3590 AM, 4300 JP, 414 BC

*1308.* Pissuthnes, the governor of Lydia, revolted from Darius, so Tissaphernes, Spithridates and Pharmises were sent against him. Pissuthnes went out to meet them. With him he had Lycon, an Athenian, with the Greeks under his command. The king's commanders bribed Lycon and his Greeks to abandon Pissuthnes. Then they drew in Pissuthnes with the promise of safety and the assurance that they would bring him to the king, which they did. The king ordered *Away with him to the ash heap*, and gave his government to Tissaphernes. Lycon had cities and countries given to him as a reward for his treachery. *{Ctesias}*

*1309.* Eusebius noted that Egypt rebelled from the Persians, and that Amyrtaeus Saites reigned there for six years. *{*Eusebius, Chronicles, l. 1. 1:198}* This seems to be the same Amyrtaeus whom Herodotus mentioned, when he wrote that he did the Persians much damage. *{*Herodotus, l. 2. c. 140. 1:445}* *{*Herodotus, l. 3. c. 15. 2:21}*

## 3591 AM, 4301 JP, 413 BC

*1310.* In the nineteenth summer of the Peloponnesian War, when Nicias had wanted to withdraw his army at night from before the walls of Syracuse in Sicily, an eclipse of the moon occurred about ten o'clock at night in the month of Metageition. *[L208]* This was on the 27th of August, according to the Julian calendar. He was so terrified at the sight of it, that he did not withdraw at that time, but because of that delay, he and his whole army perished. *{*Thucydides, l. 7. c. 50. s. 4. 4:101}* *{*Polybius, l. 9. c. 19. s. 1-4. 4:45}* *{*Diod. Sic., l. 13. c. 12. s. 6. 5:159}* *{*Pliny, l. 2. c. 9. (54) 1:203}* *{*Plutarch, Nicias, l. 1. c. 23. 3:289}* *{Plutarch, Superstition}*

*1311.* The next winter, Tissaphernes of Lydia and Pharnabazus of the Hellespont, two governors of Darius whose countries bordered the sea coast in lesser Asia, sought to recover the arrears of tribute from the Greek cities lying within their control, because the Athenians had recently forbidden them to pay tribute to the king. *[E147]* They made a deal with them underhandedly, to make them defect from the Athenians. They solicited the Peloponnesians in general to make a new war on Athens, and had the Lacedemonians (in particular) become allies of the Persian king. When the Athenian

power, on which Pissuthnes had founded all his hopes, was thus weakened in Asia, Tissaphernes sought by all means to capture Amorges, a bastard son of Pissuthnes, who had taken up arms in Caria. He was commanded to send him, dead or alive, to the king. When he found that the citizens of Chios and Erythrae were ready to revolt from the Athenians, he sent his messenger together with theirs to Lacedemon, to negotiate the matter by common agreement. *{*Thucydides, l. 8. c. 5. s. 4,5. 4:199}*

*1312.* At the same time, Calligeitus of Megara and Timagoras of Cyzicum, who were both banished from their country, came to Lacedemon. They were sent by Pharnabazus, who had entertained them during the time of their exile. They went in the name of the inhabitants of Cyzicum, to get ships to carry them to the Hellespont. When the messengers of Pharnabazus and Tissaphernes each made their request separately, the Lacedemonians were divided as to what to do. Some advised that Ionia and Chios should be helped first, others, the Hellespont. Alcibiades helped decide the matter. He was a condemned man from Athens who lived in Sparta, in a house with Endius, one of the ephors who was a friend of his father. At his suggestion, they made an agreement with the Chians and Erythreans and ordered forty ships to be sent to help them. Calligeitus and Timagoras, who were there on behalf of Pharnabazus and the men of Cyzicum, contributed nothing toward this fleet for Chios. They withheld the twenty-five talents which they had brought with them to hire ships for themselves, because they planned to prepare a fleet of their own. *{*Thucydides, l. 8. c. 6,8. 4:201-205}*

## 3592b AM, 4302 JP, 412 BC

*1313.* In the twentieth summer of the Peloponnesian War, Alcibiades, an Athenian, and Chalcideus, a Lacedemonian, were sent by Endius and the other ephors into Ionia with five ships. Their plan was to try to make the Greek cities defect from the Athenian side. The Clazomenians went to the mainland and built a strong citadel there, so they would have a safe place to go if their island was attacked. Similarly, the other islands which revolted from the Athenians did likewise, building citadels and preparing for war. *{*Thucydides, l. 8. c. 12,14. 4:211,213}*

*1314.* Strombichides, the commander of the Athenians, came to Samos with eight ships. *[L209]* Another ship joined him there and they sailed to Teos. They persuaded the people there not to defect from the Athenians. Chalcideus also came there with twenty-three ships and some foot soldiers from the Clazomenians and Erythreans. The men of Teos at first refused to receive the soldiers, but when they saw that the Athenians had fled, they took them in. These soldiers waited for Chalcideus to return from pursuing the Athenians, but when they did not return, they with the help of those who were under the command of Stages and Tissaphernes, pulled down the wall which the Athenians had built on the land side. When Chalcideus and Alcibiades had pursued Strombichides as far as Samos, they were joined by more ships from Chios and together they sailed to Miletus. With the help of Alcibiades, who had an important acquaintance with the noble men there, they persuaded the men of Miletus to defect from the Athenians as well. When the Athenians followed them there, they were kept out by the Milesians, and so they retreated to an island called Lade opposite Miletus. {*Thucydides, l. 8. c. 16,17. 4:217,219}

1315. Therefore, the Chians sailed with ten ships to the city of Anaea in Caria to learn the status of Miletus and to induce other cities to defect from the Athenians. They were called back by Chalcideus because Amorges, the son of Pissuthnes, was approaching with his army. They came to the small town of Dioshieron in Ionia. When they saw a fleet of sixteen Athenian ships that had been sent from there under the command of Diomedon to join with Thrasycles, they dispersed. One ship went to Ephesus, the rest to Teos. Four were captured by the Athenians, but all the men on them had escaped to shore. The rest of the ships safely reached Teos. [E148] After this, when the Athenians had gone to Samos, the Chians pursued their purpose with the remainder of their fleet and forces, and drew the cities of Lebedos and Haerae in Ionia over to their side. {*Thucydides, l. 8. c. 19. 4:221}

1316. After the foot soldiers of the Chians departed from Teos, Tissaphernes came there with his army. He pulled down what was left of the walls of Teos and went away. No sooner had he left, than Diomedon came there with ten Athenian ships, and was also received by the Teians. He went to Haerae, but when he was unable to capture it, he went on his way. {*Thucydides, l. 8. c. 20. s. 2. 4:223}

1317. When the Athenians had taken the citadel which the Clazomenians had built on the mainland, they forced them to return to their island. The leaders of the revolt escaped to Daphnus and the Clazomenians again submitted to the Athenians. {*Thucydides, l. 8. c. 23. s. 6. 4:227}

### 3592c AM, 4302 JP, 412 BC

1318. That same summer, the Athenians sailed with twenty ships from Lade, which was opposite Miletus, and landed at Panormus in the Milesian territory. They attacked Chalcideus, the Lacedemonian, and killed him and everyone with him. Two days later they returned to Panormus and erected a monument in memory of what they had done. The Milesians tore it down on the grounds that the Athenians did not have control of the the country when they set it up. {*Thucydides, l. 8. c. 24. s. 1. 4:229}

1319. At the end of the summer the Athenians, with fifteen hundred heavily armed Argive soldiers and a thousand men from Athens and many of their other confederates, sailed to Samos with forty-eight ships commanded by Phrynichus, Onomacles and Scironides. [L210] From there they sailed for Miletus and positioned their army before the city. Eight hundred heavily armed Milesian soldiers attacked them, along with Alcibiades and those whom Chalcideus had brought from Peloponnesus, and certain other soldiers who came from a foreign country and were commanded by Tissaphernes. The Argives, who led the van in their particular wing of the army, trusted too much in their valour and were routed by the Milesians, whom they held in contempt as being Ionians, and so they lost three hundred men. But eventually the Athenians won the battle and after setting up a monument in the field, they besieged the city on that peninsula. When news came that a fleet from Sicily and Peloponnesus was heading that way, they followed the advice of Phrynichus and withdrew to Samos. {*Thucydides, l. 8. c. 25. 4:231,233}

1320. When the fleet came with the ships of Chios which had formerly been beaten by Chalcideus, they were asked by Tissaphernes to attack Iasus. Amorges, the bastard son of Pissuthnes, lived there and had revolted from the king. Under the command of Astyochus, the admiral to whom Theramenes, a Lacedemonian, had brought that fleet, the Peloponnesians and the Syracusians (who were very courageous under their general, Hermocrates) suddenly attacked the Iasians and took the city. The Iasians incorrectly thought that these took them to be friends. The Peloponnesians took Amorges alive and handed him over to Tissaphernes to be sent to Darius, if he so desired. They sacked the city of Iasus, which was quite prosperous after a long peace, and took much spoil. The mercenaries hired by Amorges were spared because most of them were Peloponnesians. They enlisted them for their own service. The town with all its people was handed over to Tissaphernes. Everyone was redeemed by paying a Daric stater which was worth about twenty Attic drachmas. They returned to Miletus, and were accompanied overland by Pedaritus, who was being sent by the Lacedemonians as the governor for Chios, and by the mercenaries of Amorges. They went as far as Erythrae and left Philippus behind as the governor of Miletus. {*Thucydides, l. 8. c. 28. 4:237}

## 3592d AM, 4302 JP, 412 BC

*1321.* The next winter, after Tissaphernes had put a garrison in Iasus, he came to Miletus and there, according to a promise made at Lacedemon, paid them and their mercenaries their wages. The wage was an Athenian drachma for each man. He bargained with them for the same wages for future service. {*Thucydides, l. 8. c. 29,30. 4:239,241}*

*1322.* Astyochus, the admiral of the Lacedemonian fleet, with ten ships of Lacedemon and as many of Chios, sailed to Clazomene after the failed attack on the city of Pteleum. There he ordered all who favoured the Athenians to leave and live at Daphnus. Tamos, the governor of Ionia, gave similar orders. When they refused, he attacked the unwalled town, but was unsuccessful and left, encountering a violent storm at sea. He came safely to Phocaea and Cyme, but the rest of his ships harboured in the isles lying opposite Clazomene, Marathussa, Pele and Drymussa. They stayed there for eight days because of the storm. They plundered the goods which the Clazomenians had secretly stored there for fear of the war. The rest of the goods they put on board their ships and carried them to Astyochus at Phocaea and Cyme. {*Thucydides, l. 8. c. 31. 4:241,243}*

*1323.* That same winter, Hippocrates of Lacedemon set sail for Cnidos from Peloponnesus, with ten Thurian ships under the command of Dorieus and two others commissioned with him, one a Laconian and another from Syracuse. *[L211]* Cnidos had revolted from Tissaphernes. *[E149]* When the Milesians heard this, they sent to Hippocrates and asked him to leave half of his ships to guard Cnidos and to go with the rest and raid ships laden with cargo from Egypt. These ships lay at Triopium, which was a cape of Cnidos. When the Athenians heard of this, they went from Samos and surprised the six ships which lay at Triopium to guard those places. However, the sailors escaped and the Athenians found only empty ships. They came to Cnidos and almost took it by surprise when they attacked it. It was an unwalled town, and they decided to wait and attack again the next day. The Cnidians cast up some earth works about the town that night. Also, they were joined by the crews who were forced ashore at Triopium. When the Athenians saw it would be harder than ever to take the town, they plundered the country and returned to Samos.

{*Thucydides, l. 8. c. 35. 4:247}*

## 3593a AM, 4302 JP, 412 BC

*1324.* When the Spartans evaluated the league between Chalcideus and Tissaphernes, they considered it somewhat unfair to them. They drew up another one between the Lacedemonians and their confederates on the one side and Darius, his sons, and Tissaphernes on the other. This was in clearer terms than the previous one and was subscribed in the presence of Theramenes of Lacedemon. After Theramenes gave the command of the navy to Astyochus, Theramenes boarded a little boat and left, and was never seen again. {*Thucydides, l. 8. c. 36-38. 4:249,251}*

*1325.* Pharnabazus, the governor for the king in the Hellespont, had previously sent Calligeitus of Megara and Timagoras of Cyzicum to Sparta, asking for ships. This request was granted, and twenty-seven ships were sent under the command of Antisthenes, a Lacedemonian, in the middle of winter, from Peloponnesus into Ionia. The Lacedemonians also sent eleven commissioners of theirs (one was Lichas, the son of Arcesilaus) to advise Astyochus in the management of this war. After they came to Miletus, they were ordered to send some or all of these twenty-seven ships to Pharnabazus in the Hellespont. Clearchus was to be made commander of this fleet. If they saw cause, they could put Antisthenes in charge of the navy instead of Astyochus because Astyochus was under suspicion by Pedaritus, who had letters against him. These commissioners sailed from Malea, a port in Peloponnesus, toward the island of Melos. They gave Melos a wide birth to avoid the enemy, and landed at Caunus in Asia. {*Thucydides, l. 8. c. 39. 4:255}*

## 3593b AM, 4303 JP, 411 BC

*1326.* When Astyochus came to Cnidos, he quickly left there again to join this fleet of twenty-seven ships. On his way, he was intercepted by the Athenian fleet which had been waiting for the Peloponnesian ships coming from Caunus. The Athenians won the first battle there, but when they lost the second one, they retired and came to Halicarnassus. The victorious Peloponnesians returned to Cnidos. After this, the Athenians sailed to an island called Cyme, where they were soundly defeated. They dared not attack the Lacedemonian navy, which lay at Cnidos, but took only some tackle and baggage from Cyme. After landing at Lorymae on the mainland, they returned to Samos. {*Thucydides, l. 8. c. 42,43. 4:259,261}*

*1327.* When all the Peloponnesian navy of ninety-four ships met at Cnidos, the eleven commissioners discussed with Tissaphernes matters already transacted. They were looking for any weakness in the agreement and planning how the future war might be carried on for the best advantage to both sides. Lichas said that, in view of what had happened, neither of the two leagues which had been made with Theramenes were as they should be. *[L212]* They could not tolerate that the king should hold onto all those countries which he or his ancestors had held previously. He said that for this reason all the islands, all Thessaly, Locri and all Boeotia must not come under the king's authority again. The Lacedemonians, instead of freeing the Greek cities, would further enslave them to the might of the Persians. Therefore, they should form a new league between them, or abandon this one, and never ask nor receive any further stipend from the king of Persia as under the previous leagues. Tissaphernes grew angry and went his way in a rage. {*Thucydides, l. 8. c. 43. 4:261,263}

1328. Letters came from the Peloponnesians to Astyochus, stating that he should execute Alcibiades, because he was under suspicion and was a professed enemy of Agis, the king of Lacedemon. When Alcibiades heard about this, he fled secretly to Tissaphernes. Alcibiades persuaded him not to pay so much for the Peloponnesian navy, but rather hold matters in balance. This way, neither the Athenians nor the Lacedemonians would win the war. When each side had been exhausted by warfare, they would more easily be brought under the king's control. [E150] Pisander, with ten envoys from Athens, entreated Tissaphernes and Alcibiades for terms that would benefit both the Athenians and the Persians. However, when Alcibiades, in the name of Tissaphernes, made such intolerable demands, they thought to abandon all discussion and do nothing, even though they yielded to many of the demands. Alcibiades demanded that they should surrender all Ionia and its adjacent islands into the king's hands. When they agreed, he then demanded that the king could make as many ships as he pleased and sail them where he pleased whenever he pleased. When the Athenians discovered how intolerable these demands were, and how they were being abused by Alcibiades, they broke off the talks in a rage and returned to Samos. {*Thucydides, l. 8. c. 45,54,56. 4:265,285-289}

1329. Toward the end of this winter, Tissaphernes went to Caunus and planned to recall the Lacedemonian commissioners back to Miletus and pay them, lest the Lacedemonians become his enemies, too. When they came, he paid them all their arrears and made a third league with them. It stated:

"In the thirteenth year of the reign of Darius, when Alexipidas was ephor, the agreements were made in the field of Meander between the Lacedemonians and their confederates on the one side, and Tissaphernes and Hieramenes and the sons of Pharnaces on the other, concerning the affairs of the king and of the Lacedemonians and their confederates. These, stated that the king be permitted to retain whatever countries in Asia were his, and that he be permitted to deal with his own countries as he wished...."

1330. Concerning the payment of their yearly stipend, they agreed upon the following: {*Thucydides, l. 8. c. 58. 4:291,293}

"Tissaphernes should pay the existing fleet until the king's ships came. Once they arrived, the Lacedemonians and their confederates should maintain their navy if they wished. If they would rather have a stipend for it, then Tissaphernes should furnish the same, but on the condition that at the end of the war they should refund all the money which they had received."

1331. From this we may ascertain the full details behind what Justin stated more concisely: {Justin, Trogus, l. 5. c. 1.}

"Darius, the king of the Persians, made a league with the Lacedemonians through Tissaphernes, his governor of Lydia, and promised to bear all the cost of the war."

1332. At the very beginning of the next summer, which began the twenty-first year of the Peloponnesian War, Dercylidas, a Lacedemonian, was sent overland with a small company from Miletus into the Hellespont. He was to incite the city of Abydus, which was a colony of the Milesians, to revolt from the Athenians. First this city, then, two days later, Lampsacus, defected from Athens to Dercylidas and Pharnabazus. [L213]

1333. When Strombichides heard this news, he sailed from Chios to Lesbos with twenty-four Athenian ships. When the men of Lampsacus attacked him, he routed them and took their unwalled town on the first assault. Having settled matters there, he went to Abydus. When they repulsed his attack, he sailed to Sestus and placed a strong garrison there to defend all of the Hellespont. {*Thucydides, l. 8. c. 61,62. 4:295,297}

1334. The whole navy of the Athenians came together at Samos. They entered into a covenant with the Samians to unite in restoring the democratic state in Athens and in abolishing the newly appointed junta of four hundred. They bound themselves with a solemn oath to do this, and appointed Thrasybulus and Thrasyllus as leaders for this purpose. They consulted about calling home Alcibiades, hoping with his help to make Tissaphernes stop supporting the Lacedemonian party and to gain the king's favour for their side. {*Thucydides, l. 8. c. 63-77. 4:297-327}

1335. Among the seamen of the Peloponnesians who were at Miletus there was a general dislike for Tissaphernes and Astyochus. When the Lacedemonians were a strong naval force and the Athenians weak, Astyochus would never fight with the Athenians. Although he knew of the divisions among the Athenians, he would not assemble the Lacedemonian navy to attack. Tissaphernes was disliked because he did not send for the navy of the Phoenicians, as he had promised. Nor did he pay them their wages, except when he pleased, and then only a portion and not the full amount. Therefore they wanted the matter decided in battle. Astyochus and his confederates commanded the Milesians to march overland to the cape of Mycale, while they went by sea to the same place with the whole fleet of one hundred and twelve ships. When the Athenians, whose eighty-two ships were anchored at Glauce near Mycale, saw the fleet coming, they weighed anchor and sailed as fast as they could to Samos. On hearing of this, Strombichides hastened to come with his fleet from the Hellespont to help the Athenians. The Peloponnesians withdrew and returned to Miletus. The Athenians now had one hundred and eight ships, all strong and well-equipped. They followed the Peloponnesians home to Miletus, landed and arranged their army in the open field. When the Peloponnesians would not come to fight, they sailed back to Samos without attacking anything. *[E151]* After this, the Peloponnesians saw they were no match for the Athenian navy. Neither could they pay so many seamen, especially when Tissaphernes was so churlish in sending in their payment according to the agreement. They sent Clearchus away with forty of their ships into the Hellespont to Pharnabazus, who earnestly desired their coming and promised to pay them very liberally. {*Thucydides, l. 8. c. 78-80. 4:327-331}

### 3593c AM, 4303 JP, 411 BC

1336. When Thrasybulus left Tissaphernes, he brought Alcibiades back with him to Samos. The army made him one of their chief commanders and committed everything to his direction. Having now been made commander of the Athenian army, he sailed back to Tissaphernes in order to tell him everything. So cunningly did he handle matters to his own advantage, that he could make the Athenians afraid of Tissaphernes, and Tissaphernes of them, at his pleasure. {*Thucydides, l. 8. c. 81,82. 4:333-335}

1337. This had a disastrous effect on the morale of the Peloponnesians, who were anchored at Miletus. They hated Tissaphernes more than ever, so that they began once again to mutiny against him and Astyochus, whom they now charged with collusion with Tissaphernes, for his own personal advantage. The sailors from Syracuse and Thurii demanded, in a very rude and mutinous manner, that Astyochus pay them. *[L214]* When he replied roughly and threatened to imprison Doriecus, the commander of the Thurian squadron, for supporting his sailors, they rioted and rushed him. (The Greek commentators of Thucydides understood that Hermocrates, commander of the Syracuse squadron, was meant, not

Doriecus.) Astyochus would have been killed, had he not fled to a nearby altar. The Milesians made a surprise attack and captured the citadel which Tissaphernes had built, driving out the garrison of soldiers and taking over the citadel. This action was well received by all the rest except for Lichas, the Lacedemonian. He said that the Milesians and everyone else under the king's authority ought to obey Tissaphernes, while he governed as moderately as he did and until the war was won. {*Thucydides, l. 8. c. 83,84. 4:335,339}

1338. While they were busy in this altercation, Mindarus arrived, having been sent from Lacedemon to succeed Astyochus in the command of the navy. After he had handed over his command, Astyochus sailed home to Lacedemon. Tissaphernes sent his messenger Gaulites along with him. This man spoke both the Greek and Persian languages, although he was born in Caria. He was to charge the Milesians for the surprise attack on his citadel, and to clear Tissaphernes of the false accusations which the Milesians and Hermocrates of Syracuse had made. Tissaphernes knew that the Milesians would accuse him because he had conspired with Alcibiades against the Lacedemonians. {*Thucydides, l. 8. c. 84,85. 4:337,339}

1339. Tissaphernes saw that the Peloponnesians were against him. Among other things, they did not like the fact that he had allowed Alcibiades to return to his own people again, since he now openly favoured the Athenians. Tissaphernes went to Aspendus, where the Phoenician fleet of one hundred and forty-seven ships had come. To clear himself, he took Lichas, the Lacedemonian, along with him, leaving his agent Tamos with them, to ensure that the wages were paid to the Peloponnesian navy. Moreover, at the request of Tissaphernes, the Peloponnesians sent Philippus, a Lacedemonian, with two ships to Aspendus to see the Phoenician fleet. When Alcibiades learned that Tissaphernes was at Aspendus, he came with thirteen ships to Caunus and then to Phaselis. Everywhere, he promised his friends many supplies and much help. When he returned to Samos, he informed them that he had so arranged matters that the Phoenician fleet would not assist the Peloponnesians, and Tissaphernes had now become more friendly to the Athenians than ever. It was true that Tissaphernes met with the Phoenicians at Aspendus, but he would not let any ship go to the Peloponnesians. He put them off with the weak excuse that not as many ships had come to him as the king had commanded. However, his purpose was to hold both parties of the Greeks in suspense. By siding with neither, he hoped to make them destroy each other. {*Thucydides, l. 8. c. 87-89. 4:345-353}

*1340.* The junta of four hundred at Athens was dissolved and replaced by five thousand. The new government ratified the recalling of Alcibiades back to his home country. {*Thucydides, l. 8. c. 90-93. 4:353-365*} That same order included Thrasybulus and Theramenes in his commission, although they were absent at the time. Hence, the valour and virtue of the new government in a short time greatly reformed the Athenian state, and brought it into a better form than ever before. {*Emilius Probus, Alcibiades*} [E152]

*1341.* While the Peloponnesians waited at Miletus, none of those whom Tissaphernes had left behind when he had left for Aspendus took care to pay the navy. Neither did Tissaphernes himself pay them, nor did the fleet come, which he had promised. [L215] Both Philippus, who had been sent with Tissaphernes to Aspendus, and Hippocrates, who was at Phaselis, wrote to Mindarus, who had the charge of the navy, saying that he should not expect any ships or anything else of value from Tissaphernes. On the contrary, Pharnabazus, who served the king in those parts of the Hellespont, showed them all the favour and friendship that they could imagine. For he solicited their coming and of his own accord, incited all the Greek cities within his province to defect from the Athenians (which Tissaphernes was to have done), hoping thereby to increase his own power. Mindarus was bothered by this news and instantly made ready seventy-three ships. He gave the word that they should leave quickly, so that the Athenians at Samos would not find out. He left Miletus and sailed straight to the Hellespont. When Thrasyllus heard of this, he sailed from Samos with fifty-five ships and pursued him. {*Thucydides, l. 8. c. 99,100. 4:375,377*}

*1342.* Mindarus and the Syracuse squadron had a fierce naval battle with Thrasyllus and Thrasybulus at the cape of Cynossema, a place also known for old Hecube's monument. The Athenians won, losing only five ships, but capturing eighteen of the enemies' ships. {*Diod. Sic., l. 13. c. 38-40. 5:223-231*} {*Thucydides, l. 8. c. 104-106. 4:383-389*}

*1343.* The Athenians repaired their fleet as best they could. On the fourth day after this battle they sailed from Sestus to Cyzicum, which had revolted from them. When they saw eight ships from Byzantium at Harpagium and Priapus, they attacked them. They conquered those who defended the ships from the shore, and captured the ships for their own use. After this they sailed to the unwalled town of Cyzicum and captured it, extorting a large sum of money from its inhabitants. {*Thucydides, l. 8. c. 107. 4:389*}

## 3593d AM, 4303 JP, 411 BC

*1344.* Alcibiades sailed from Samos with twenty-one ships and exacted large sums of money from those of Halicarnassus. He sacked the island of Cos and fortified the town of Cos with a wall. Since winter was now approaching, he returned to Samos with much spoil. {*Thucydides, l. 8. c. 108. s. 1,2. 4:391*} {*Diod. Sic., l. 13. c. 42. 5:235*}

*1345.* Arsaces, a Persian and a lieutenant to Tissaphernes, harboured a secret, deadly hatred against the men of Delos, who had left their old habitation and now lived at Adramyttium. When he came that way, he sent for all the chief men among them to come and serve the king in his wars, as friends and confederates. At the time when they were all assembled together eating dinner, he surrounded them with his soldiers and had them all killed with arrows. {*Thucydides, l. 8. c. 108. s. 3,4. 4:391*}

*1346.* The people of Antandros in Aeolia feared that Arsaces might do the same to them, and they also disliked the heavy taxes which he imposed on them, so they sent for some Peloponnesian soldiers from Abydus. They secretly brought them over Mount Ida into their city and expelled the garrison of Arsaces from the citadel. {*Thucydides, l. 8. c. 108. s. 5. 4:393*}

*1347.* Tissaphernes returned from Aspendus into Ionia and was greatly disturbed, both by this last action of Antandros, and by those of Miletus and Cnidos, where the inhabitants had also expelled his garrisons. He considered himself wronged by the Peloponnesians and fearing worse things from them, he was troubled that Pharnabazus, in a shorter time and with far less cost, might appear to have done more against the Athenians than he had done. Therefore he planned to go in person to the Peloponnesians in the Hellespont, to reason with them concerning their expelling of his garrison from Antandros and to clear himself from the charges against him concerning the Phoenician fleet and other matters. As soon as he arrived at Ephesus, he sacrificed to Diana. {*Thucydides, l. 8. c. 109. 4:393*} [L216] Here ended the history of Thucydides, which Theopompus continued for another seventeen years and Xenophon for forty-eight years after that. {*Diod. Sic., l. 13. c. 42. s. 5. 5:237*} The writings of Theopompus are lost, but we do have those of Xenophon partially preserved for us. As well as the poem of his history, we lack its first two years, that is, from the end of the summer of the twenty-first year of the Peloponnesian War, where Thucydides left off, to the end of the twenty-third summer of the same war.

## 3594 AM, 4304 JP, 410 BC

*1348.* Concerning the three hundred ships sent back to Phoenicia, Tissaphernes cleared himself with the Lacedemonians by saying that he had received news that the coast of Phoenicia was in danger of attack from the Arabians and Amyrtaeus, the king of Egypt. {*Diod. Sic., l. 13. c. 46. s. 6. 5:249*} However, Thucydides stated that only a hundred and forty ships came to Aspendus from Phoenicia, and that they were all sent back again by Tissaphernes, contrary to his promise.

### 3595c AM, 4305 JP, 409 BC

*1349.* There was another naval battle between the Lacedemonians and Athenians at Cynossema. This was described by Theopompus, as a certain nameless Greek writer stated in the life of Thucydides. *[E153]*

### 3595d AM, 4305 JP, 409 BC

*1350.* Thymochares came to Athens with a small fleet of ships. The Lacedemonians and Athenians had another naval battle, which the Lacedemonians won under the command of Agesandridas. {*Xenophon, Hellenica, l. 1. c. 1. s. 1. 1:3}

*1351.* Not long after this, at the beginning of winter, Dorieus, the admiral of the Thurian fleet from Italy, sailed with fourteen ships from Rhodes to the Hellespont to meet Mindarus, who was at Abydus. He was at Abydus for a meeting of all the friends and confederates of the Peloponnesians. Dorieus had sailed as far as Sigeum, a port in Troas, when the Athenian navy at Sestus found out about his trip and destination, and sailed toward him with twenty ships. Hearing of their coming, Dorieus fled from there and beached his ships on the shores of Rhoetium. He landed his men and with the help of the men of Dardania, warded off an Athenian attack. When the Athenians saw that they could not prevail, they sailed back to Madytus to join the rest of their army. Mindarus, who at that time happened to be at old Troy sacrificing to Athena, saw this battle. He raced with eighty-four ships to the cape of Dardania to meet Dorieus and to save his ships. He also found the army of Pharnabazus ready to help the Lacedemonian navy against their enemies. The Athenian fleet of seventy-four ships came close to the shore of Abydus and there started a naval battle. Mindarus commanded ninety-seven ships, besides those of Dorieus. He placed the Syracusians in the left wing and he himself took the right wing. On the other side, Thrasybulus had the right wing and Thrasyllus the left. The battle lasted from morning to evening, neither side winning. Suddenly Alcibiades came sailing in with eighteen fresh ships from Samos, headed toward the Hellespont. When the Lacedemonians saw this, they fled toward Abydus. The Athenians chased them and captured ten of their ships, but a violent storm arose which prevented the Athenians from finishing off their enemies. The Peloponnesians all escaped safely to shore and fled to the army of Pharnabazus that was there. During the battle, Pharnabazus rode his horse into the sea up to its saddleskirts in order to fight, commanding his army to do likewise. The Peloponnesians locked their ships close together into one mass and fought against their enemies from the decks nearest the shore. *[L217]* As the night was drawing on, the Athenians returned to Samos with thirty empty ships which they had captured and their own fleet, including their damaged ships. The next morning as soon as it was light, they gathered what spoils they could from the wrecked ships of their enemies. They erected a monument to the event and then left forty ships to guard the Hellespont. The rest of the fleet was assigned to various destinations, some gathering their tribute money. One of their chief captains, Thrasyllus, sailed back to Athens to let them know what a victory they had had. He wanted a supply of men and shipping for the carrying on of the war in those parts. {*Xenophon, Hellenica, l. 1. c. 1. s. 2-8. 1:3,5} {*Diod. Sic., l. 13. c. 45-47. 5:243-249} {*Plutarch, Alcibiades, l. 1. c. 27. s. 2-4. 4:79,81}

*1352.* About the first watch of the night, Mindarus went back to the seaside and gave orders for repairing his ships which had been damaged in the battle. He urgently sent by land and sea to Lacedemon for fresh supplies. While this was happening, he made plans to join his army with Pharnabazus to capture the tributary cities of the Athenians which were in Asia. {*Diod. Sic., l. 13. c. 47. 5:249}

### 3596a AM, 4305 JP, 409 BC

*1353.* In the meantime, Tissaphernes came into the Hellespont. Alcibiades planned to magnify himself after so glorious a victory over the Lacedemonians. He came to Tissaphernes with rich presents and a princely train, but Tissaphernes was in ill repute with the Lacedemonians and so was fearful that some accusation might be made against him to Darius. He arrested Alcibiades and put him in irons at Sardis, pretending that this was the king's command and wanting to show that he counted the Athenians as enemies. Within a month, Alcibiades escaped with Mantitheus, a fellow prisoner who had been captured in Caria. He got horses and they escaped by night to Clazomene, claiming that it was with the consent of Tissaphernes. {*Xenophon, Hellenica, l. 1. c. 1. s. 9. 1:5} {*Plutarch, Alcibiades, l. 1. c. 27,28. 4:79,81}

### 3596b AM, 4306 JP, 408 BC

*1354.* Toward the end of winter, Mindarus went to Cyzicum with sixty ships and together with the army of Pharnabazus, they captured Cyzicum by force. Eighty-six ships under the command of Alcibiades, Thrasybulus and Theramenes attacked Mindarus. He was first routed at sea and then in a second battle on land, in which Mindarus fought bravely and was killed. When the troops from Syracuse saw no means of escape, they set their own ships on fire. The rest of the ships in the fleet were captured by the Athenians, who sailed them all to Proconnesus. This battle is more fully described by these authors: {*Xenophon, Hellenica, l. 1. c. 1. s. 11-18. 1:5-9} {*Diod. Sic., l. 13. c. 49-52. 5:257-267} {*Plutarch, Alcibiades, l. 1. c. 28. 4:81-85} {Polyaenus, Strategmata, l. 1.}

1355. The next day the Athenians sailed from Proconnesus to Cyzicum, and were received into the city which had been abandoned by Pharnabazus and the Peloponnesians. {*Xenophon, Hellenica, l. 1. c. 1. s. 19. 1:9} [E154] There they erected two monuments, the one for their victory at sea at the isle of Polydorus, and the other for that victory on land in which they had first put the enemies to flight. {*Diod. Sic., l. 13. c. 51. s. 7. 5:265}

1356. Alcibiades stayed at Cyzicum for twenty days. When he had extracted a vast sum of money from them, he departed without doing them any harm and returned to Proconnesus. {*Xenophon, Hellenica, l. 1. c. 1. s. 19,20. 1:9}

1357. The commanders of the Athenians who remained behind at Cyzicum came at length to Chalcedon. There they walled Chrysopolis and made it a place to gather tolls from every ship that passed by from Pontus. {*Xenophon, Hellenica, l. 1. c. 1. s. 20. 1:9} {*Polybius, l. 4. c. 44. s. 3. 2:409} {*Diod. Sic., l. 13. c. 64. s. 2. 5:301} They left a garrison and a fleet of thirty ships there under the command of Theramenes and Eumachus. This was for the purpose of keeping the town, of watching what ships came in and out at the mouth of Pontus, and of doing what mischief they could to the enemy. {*Xenophon, Hellenica, l. 1. c. 1. s. 21-22. 1:9,10}

1358. The Athenians intercepted concisely written letters from Hippocrates, the lieutenant of Mindarus, to the ephors at Lacedemon, concerning the loss they had sustained at Cyzicum. [L218] They said: {*Xenophon, Hellenica, l. 1. c. 1. s. 23. 1:10} {*Plutarch, Alcibiades, l. 1. c. 28. s. 6. 4:85}

> "All is lost. Mindarus is dead. Our men starve. We know not what to do."

1359. The Lacedemonians sued for peace, a plea which was opposed by those who made a living from the war. {Justin, Trogus, l. 5. c. 4.} For although the moderates among the Athenians were inclined to peace, those who made their living by it chose to continue the war. Cleophon, who was one of the principal leaders of this latter group, had spoken many rash things. This is how Diodorus elegantly expressed it: {*Diod. Sic., l. 13. c. 53. s. 2. 5:271}

> "He made the people proud by recounting to them the greatness of their good successes, as if fortune did not bestow her favours in the war by turns."

1360. With his fiery speeches Cleophon stirred up the people to carry on the war, though this later turned out to be to his own shame. He made lyres, and it was common knowledge that he had been a slave and been kept in irons. Later, by various devices, he had come to live in Athens. At this time, he won the people over to him by his munificence, and grew so bold as to profess openly:

> "With his own hand he would cut off the head of any man, whoever he might be, who wanted to speak any further of making peace."

1361. This is according to Eschines, in his speech *De False Legation* (that is, concerning a False Delegation).

1362. The Peloponnesians and their confederates from Syracuse, and as many as had escaped alive from the battle, went to Pharnabazus, who courteously entertained and comforted them. {*Diod. Sic., l. 13. c. 51. s. 8. 5:265} He said they should not be discouraged by the loss of a few wooden ships, since the king had more than enough wood in his kingdom to build more ships. The main thing was that the men were safe. He gave every man a new suit of clothes and two months' pay in advance. He armed the sailors and placed garrisons all along the sea coast which was under his jurisdiction as governor. He assembled all the commanders of cities and captains of every ship, and ordered them to build as many new ships at Antandros as they had lost. He paid for this and allowed them to use timber from Mount Ida. When this had been done, he sent them a fleet to relieve Chalcedon. {*Xenophon, Hellenica, l. 1. c. 1. s. 24-26. 1:11}

## 3596c AM, 4306 JP, 408 BC

1363. While this navy was being built, the men of Syracuse joined with the inhabitants of Antandros and built a wall around the town, greatly fortifying the place. In return, the Antandrians gave the Syracusians the privileges of benefactors and citizens. {*Xenophon, Hellenica, l. 1. c. 1. s. 26. 1:11}

1364. The captains of these troops from Syracuse were exiled by their countrymen at home. Their general, Hermocrates, accused Tissaphernes at Lacedemon, and they believed him, also accepting the testimony of Astyochus. Hermocrates returned to Pharnabazus and without even asking, received from him a large sum of money. When he had procured men and ships, he returned to his own country. {*Xenophon, Hellenica, l. 1. c. 1. s. 27-31. 1:11-15} {*Diod. Sic., l. 13. c. 63. 5:297}

1365. Pasippidas was condemned to be banished from Sparta because it was thought that, by his plotting with Tissaphernes, he had caused all who favoured the Lacedemonian party to be driven out. He was expelled in a riot at the isle of Thasos. Cratesippidas was sent to replace him and to take charge of the navy at Chios. {*Xenophon, Hellenica, l. 1. c. 1. s. 32. 1:15} [L219]

1366. With twenty-five ships, Cratesippidas wasted his time about the coast of Ionia and for a long time did nothing worth speaking of. Later, he was paid by the exiles from Chios to bring them home again. *[E155]* He routed out the six hundred of the opposing faction who lived at Atarneus, the most fortified place on the continent, which was opposite Chios and from where they were making daily attacks on Chios. {*Diod. Sic., l. 13. c. 65. s. 3,4. 5:305}

### 3596d AM, 4306 JP, 408 BC

1367. In the 93rd Olympiad, Eubotas, the Cyrenian, won the prize in running. Euarchippus was the ephor at Lacedemon and Euctemon was the archon at Athens. A new game was introduced in the Olympics, namely a a two-horse race called a Ξυνωρις or Συνωρις. {*Xenophon, Hellenica, l. 1. c. 2. s. 1. 1:19} {*Diod. Sic., l. 13. c. 68. s. 1. 5:311} {*Pausanias, Elis II, l. 6. c. 8. s. 3. 3:51} {Julius Africanus, Catalogue Stadionicarum} Africanus added that in the same Olympiad Pulydamas, the Seotussian, won the prize for wrestling. He was the same man whom Darius Nothus sent for by messengers with large gifts, requiring him to come to him at Susa. {*Herodotus, l. 7. c. 83. 3:391} He challenged three of the king's Immortal Guard to fight with him, three against one, and he killed all three of them. {*Herodotus, l. 7. c. 83. 3:391} {*Pausanias, Elis II, l. 6. c. 5. s. 7. 3:33} In the same book Pausanias mentioned Eubotas, surnamed Stadionicus, who, when the Oracle of Ammon had foretold that he would win the prize in running, had his own statue made beforehand. When he then won the prize, he dedicated his statue in witness of this, all in the same day. {*Pausanias, Elis II, l. 6. c. 8. s. 3. 3:51}

1368. In this year, the Medes, who had defected from King Darius of the Persians, submitted to him again. {*Xenophon, Hellenica, l. 1. c. 2. s. 19. 1:25} Herodotus stated that the Medes revolted from Darius, {*Herodotus, l. 1. c. 128. 1:167} but were defeated and brought under his control again. He made mention of the war at Decelea, {*Herodotus, l. 9. c. 73. 3:245,247} which was waged five years earlier, and of Amyrtaeus' son reigning after him. {*Herodotus, l. 3. c. 15. 2:21} From this I gather that he either wrote, or at least revised, his history at the very latter end of the Peloponnesian War.

1369. In the beginning of the summer, at Athens, Thrasyllus took command of the ships committed to his charge with five thousand sailors. These were all equipped as targeteers and he was to join with certain other targeteers at Samos. When he had stayed there three days, he sailed to the coast of Pygela in Ionia. First he wasted the country in that area, before finally coming up to the wall of Pygela with his army. Some reinforcements arrived from Miletus and attacked the lightly armed Athenians, who were busy gathering the spoil from the country. The rest of the Athenians came to relieve their troops and killed most of the Milesians. From the bodies of the dead they gathered two hundred of their bucklers and used them to erect a monument. The next day they sailed to Notium and there took on supplies. They sailed on to Colophon which yielded to them at once. The next night they entered into Lydia at the time when their grain was almost ripe, and set many villages on fire. They were scattered here and there and were concerned with nothing but their plundering. Stages, a Persian (this seems to be the same Stages mentioned previously {See note on 3592 AM. <<1314>>}), attacked them with his cavalry, taking one prisoner and killing seven of them. {*Xenophon, Hellenica, l. 1. c. 2. s. 2-5. 1:19}

1370. When Tissaphernes understood that Thrasyllus was ready to set sail for for a surprise attack on Ephesus, he gathered all the troops he could find. He sent messengers into all parts, ordering men to come in and defend Diana of the Ephesians. When Thrasyllus had spent seventeen days in Lydia, he set sail for Ephesus. He landed his heavily armed foot soldiers at Mount Coressus, but the cavalry, targeteers and all the other soldiers he put ashore near a bog on the other side of the town. *[L220]* As soon as it was light, they approached the town in two companies. The troops in the town, with the reinforcements Tissaphernes had sent them, first attacked the foot soldiers who were at Coressus. They routed them and pursued them to the seaside, killing a hundred men. After this they returned quickly and attacked those who were located near the bog. When they had routed the Athenians and killed three hundred of them, they erected one monument there and another at Coressus. They highly rewarded the companies of reinforcements from Syracuse and Selinuntia because they behaved most valiantly. They promised freedom from taxes forever to those who were expelled from their home city. {*Xenophon, Hellenica, l. 1. c. 2. s. 6-10. 1:21} Plutarch mentioned a brass monument set up to disgrace the Athenians. {*Plutarch, Alcibiades, l. 1. c. 29. s. 1. 4:85}

1371. After a truce was made, the Athenians received the bodies of their dead and buried them at Notium. They sailed away to Lesbos and the Hellespont. When they anchored at Methymna, a city of Lesbos, they spied twenty-five ships of the Syracusians with whom they had fought at Ephesus. Attacking them, they took four ships with all the men in them and routed the rest, pursuing them as far as Ephesus. Thrasyllus sent home to Athens all the prisoners which he had taken, except Alcibiades. This Alcibiades was an Athenian and the cousin and fellow exile of Alcibiades and Thrasyllus caused him be stoned to death. *[E156]* They sailed for

Sestus, where the army was, and from there the whole army went to Lampsacus for the winter, which they reckon from the beginning of autumn. When Alcibiades wanted to create one large army at Lampsacus, his soldiers refused to be mixed with those who had served under Thrasyllus. They said: {*Xenophon, Hellenica, l. 1. c. 2. s. 11-15. 1:23}

"We, who have always been conquerors, refuse to be counted with those that were beaten and routed out the other day."

### 3597a AM, 4306 JP, 408 BC

1372. While Alcibiades' and Thrasyllus' troops had wintered together at Lampsacus (Diodorus wrote, *Labdacus*, {*Diod. Sic., l. 13. c. 66. s. 1. 1:304 (footnote 4.)}) they had fortified the area. When they went to besiege Abydus, Pharnabazus came with a very large army to relieve it. He fought with the Athenians and was routed. Alcibiades chased Pharnabazus with his cavalry, and one hundred and twenty heavily armed foot soldiers followed him. He did not stop the chase until late in the night. After this victory, the whole army became friends and mixed with each other. They returned triumphantly to their camp from where they had set out. {*Xenophon, Hellenica, l. 1. c. 2. s. 16-18. 1:23,25} {*Plutarch, Alcibiades, l. 1. c. 29. s. 2. 4:85}

1373. The next day Alcibiades set up a monument and set about wasting Pharnabazus' province with fire and sword, without any opposition. He allowed all the priests whom he captured to go free without a ransom. {*Plutarch, Alcibiades, l. 1. c. 29. s. 3. 4:85}

1374. When the Lacedemonians were upset with Tissaphernes, they sent Boeotius together with other envoys to Darius. Boeotius easily obtained from Darius all that they had wanted. {*Xenophon, Hellenica, l. 1. c. 4. s. 2. 1:33}

1375. In the same winter Alcibiades' and Thrasyllus' armies attacked various countries that belonged to Darius on the continent and wreaked havock there. {*Xenophon, Hellenica, l. 1. c. 4. s. 9. 1:35}

### 3597b AM, 4307 JP, 407 BC

1376. Darius put his sixteen year old son, Cyrus the younger, in charge of all the sea coast. He was born after his father became king. {Ctesias} {*Plutarch, Artaxerxes, l. 1. c. 1. 11:129} He had the title of governor of all those countries, and headed the army that was in the plain of Castolus in Lydia. He was ordered to join with the Lacedemonians in fighting the Athenians. {*Xenophon, Hellenica, l. 1. c. 4. s. 3,4. 1:33,35} {*Xenophon, Anabasis, l. 1. c. 1. s. 1. 3:47} Justin stated: {Justin, Trogus, l. 5. c. 5.} [L221]

"Darius, king of Persia, made his younger son Cyrus governor of all Ionia and Lydia. It was he who restored the Lacedemonians to former strength."

1377. Diodorus expressly stated that Darius sent his son Cyrus for this very purpose that, in pursuing the war against the Athenians, he should relieve and help the Lacedemonians. {*Diod. Sic., l. 13. c. 70. s. 3. 5:317} He also correctly stated that Cyrus was made commander of all the governors along the sea coast, and that he was made commander-in-chief over all the provinces lying on that sea coast. It is obvious that although Tissaphernes and Pharnabazus were governors of their provinces, they were both under his command. {*Diod. Sic., l. 14. c. 12. s. 8. 6:43}

1378. We read in Eusebius that Nepherites, the king of a new dynasty, succeeded Amyrtaeus of Sais in the kingdom of Egypt. {*Eusebius, Chronicles, l. 1. 1:198} This was the twenty-ninth dynasty. {*Manetho, 1:179} However, in Diodorus we find that, before Nephereus or Nepherites, Psammetichus next reigned in Egypt. {*Diod. Sic., l. 14. c. 35. s. 4. 6:113} He was descended from the family of that former Psammetichus whom Manetho placed in the twenty-sixth dynasty, and who was also of Sais. {*Manetho, 1:169} So one may well doubt whether this was not Pausiris, the son of Amyrtaeus, who, with the help of the Persians, recovered his father's kingdom. {*Herodotus, l. 3. c. 15. 2:21} We have already discussed the number of this, and other, Egyptian kings' reigns in our Egyptian Chronology. {Ussher, Egyptian Chronology}

### 3597c AM, 4307 JP, 407 BC

1379. In the beginning of the spring when Pantacles was ephor in Sparta, and Antigenes the archon in Athens had held office for a year, the Athenians sailed into Proconnesus with all the forces they could gather. They left there and camped before Chalcedon. {*Xenophon, Hellenica, l. 1. c. 3. s. 1. 1:25} Diodorus said that they went to Theramenes, who at that time besieged Chalcedon with seventy ships and five thousand men. {*Diod. Sic., l. 13. c. 66. s. 1. 5:307}

1380. When the inhabitants of Chalcedon heard of the approach of the Athenian army, they sent away all their goods to the Thracians of Bithynia, who were their neighbours. Alcibiades heard of this and went with all his cavalry and some of his foot soldiers and demanded all those goods from them. He threatened force if they refused to deliver them. When he received the goods, he made peace with the Bithynians and returned to his camp before Chalcedon. He built a wooden wall before the city, across the neck of land from sea to sea. When Hippocrates the Lacedemonian commander saw this, he gathered all his forces and fought with Thrasyllus. [E157] The battle was undecided for a long while, until Alcibiades came in with his forces of cavalry and heavily armed foot soldiers. Hippocrates was killed and his men fled back into the city. While the battle continued,

Pharnabazus and all his army came from another direction outside the wooden stockade. He fought unsuccessfully to break through to rescue Hippocrates. He retired to Heraclium, or the Temple of Hercules, which was in the territory of Chalcedon where his own camp was well entrenched. {*Xenophon, Hellenica, l. 1. c. 3. s. 2-7. 1:27}
{*Plutarch, Alcibiades, l. 1. c. 29,30. 4:85,87}

## 3597d AM, 4307 JP, 407 BC

1381. After this, Alcibiades went into the Chersonesus and the Hellespont to gather tribute. The rest of the commanders (though Diodorus mentioned only Theramenes {*Diod. Sic., l. 13. c. 64. 5:301}) came to an agreement with Pharnabazus concerning Chalcedon. [L222] He would give them twenty talents and would convoy the Athenian envoys safely to the king. By a solemn oath, they covenanted with each other that the men of Chalcedon would pay the Athenians the same tribute as before, with all the arrears. In the meantime, the Athenians would not bother Chalcedon until the return of their envoys from the king and the return of Alcibiades. They sent two commissioners from Chalcedon, and Pharnabazus sent two more from Chysopolis. They swore to keep this covenant and pledged their support to each other. {*Xenophon, Hellenica, l. 1. c. 3. s. 8-13. 1:29}

1382. When these things had been done, Pharnabazus returned and wanted the envoys, who were to go to the king, to meet him at Cyzicum. The names of the envoys were Dorotheus, Philocydes, Theogenes, Euryptolemus, Mantitheus and both Cleostratus and Pyrolochus, who were Argives. Pasippidas and other envoys from the Lacedemonians also went. These all journeyed to the king. Hermocrates, who was banished from Syracuse, and his brother Proxenus went with the group. {*Xenophon, Hellenica, l. 1. c. 3. s. 13. 1:29,31}

1383. While Pharnabazus was escorting the envoys to the king, Clearchus, a Lacedemonian commander, came to him from across the sea. He wanted money to pay their army and to assemble into a fleet the ships that were now scattered, some at Antandros, some in the Hellespont and some in other places. He hoped to cause trouble for the confederate states of the Athenians and so draw off their forces from Byzantium. But in his absence Byzantium was betrayed and surrendered to the Athenians. {*Xenophon, Hellenica, l. 1. c. 3. s. 14-22. 1:31,33}

1384. As these Athenian envoys were on their way to the king, they met Boeotius and the rest of the Lacedemonian envoys returning from the king. Cyrus was with them on his way to become governor of all the sea coasts of those parts. When they saw him, they asked if they might safely continue their journey to the king and if not, that they be allowed to return home safely.

However, Cyrus ordered Pharnabazus either to turn over the envoys to him or to send them home again. Since Pharnabazus did not want the Athenians to know what was planned against them, he stalled for time. Sometimes he told them that he would take them to the king and sometimes that he would send them home again. So he delayed for three years (or rather, indeed for three months since the text is likely corrupted here), and in the end, by Cyrus' consent, he sent them home. {*Xenophon, Hellenica, l. 1. c. 4. s. 1-7. 1:33,35}

1385. Alcibiades took twenty ships from Samos and sailed into the Gulf of Ceramus in Caria. He gathered a hundred talents and pillaged no less than two hundred ships, which he either had searched or caused to be sunk. He returned to Athens, where he was declared general of all their armies, with full and absolute power of command, and received two hundred talents from the treasury of the city (according to Lysias, as in his speech against his son Alcibiades shows). He raised an army of fifteen hundred heavily armed foot soldiers and a hundred and fifty cavalry, with a hundred ships. {*Xenophon, Hellenica, l. 1. c. 4. s. 8-21. 1:35-41} {*Diod. Sic., l. 13. c. 68,69. 5:313-315} {Justin, Trogus, l. 5. c. 4,5.} {*Plutarch, Alcibiades, l. 1. c. 32-34. 4:93-101} {Emilius Probus, Alcibiades}

1386. Satyrus, the son of Spartacus, ruled the kingdom of Cimmerian Bosphorus for fourteen years. {*Diod. Sic., l. 14. c. 93. s. 1. 6:259} (Loeb edition has forty years, not fourteen. This number cannot be correct for it creates contradictions later in the chronology of this kingdom. Editor.)

1387. When his term expired, the Lacedemonians replaced Cratesippidas, their admiral, with Lysander, who came to Rhodes. He gathered the fleet there and sailed to the isles of Cos and Miletus. From there he went to Ephesus with seventy ships and stayed there until Cyrus came to Sardis. {*Xenophon, Hellenica, l. 1. c. 5. s. 1. 1:43} [L223] Ephesus welcomed him and the Lacedemonians, for they were grieved by the loss of trade caused by the Persians, because the Persian governors stayed most often at Miletus and attracted all the trade away from Ephesus to that city. [E158] Therefore, Lysander made Ephesus his residence and ordered all merchant ships to unload there. He made docks, and had all the ships for the navy built there. In a short time, he filled their port with ships and their city with commerce and wealth. {*Plutarch, Lysander, l. 1. c. 3. s. 2,3. 4:239}

1388. When Lysander knew that Cyrus had come to Sardis, he and the rest of the commissioners from Sparta went to him there. Lysander made grievous charges against Tissaphernes. When the king had ordered Tissaphernes to support the Lacedemonians to rid the sea of the Athenians, he on the contrary, under Alcibiades' influence, had grown remiss. He had kept back their pay from the mariners and utterly destroyed the Lacedemonian navy. Cyrus was more than willing to receive any information against Tissaphernes, who was not a good governor. Lysander befriended Cyrus. The more Lysander pressed Cyrus to do things, the bolder Cyrus was to promise that all would be done. Cyrus added that it was his father's command that it should be so, and assured him that there would be no want either of effort or money on his part. To that end, he raised the pay of the mariners and sea soldiers from three oboli per day to four oboli. {six oboli equals a drachma} He paid the whole army everything that was in arrears and advanced a whole month's pay, giving Lysander ten thousand darics for that purpose. In this way, he more than ever put heart and courage into his seamen, and left the Athenian fleet almost without sailors for the majority of their ships. Out of greed for better pay, they left the Athenians and went to Lysander. Those who stayed grew idle and careless in the service, and mutinous and troublesome to their commanders on a daily basis. {*Xenophon, Hellenica, l. 1. c. 5. s. 2-9. 1:43,45} {*Diod. Sic., l. 13. c. 70. s. 3,4. 5:317,319} {*Plutarch, Lysander, l. 1. c. 4. 4:241,243}

1389. When the Athenians heard this they were discouraged, and sent envoys to Cyrus through Tissaphernes. Cyrus refused to see them, even though Tissaphernes himself spoke for them. He told Cyrus that what he had done on the advice of Alcibiades, whose counsel had been to hold the Greeks in balance and let neither side win, allowing them to continue the war and so to consume one another to nothing. {*Xenophon, Hellenica, l. 1. c. 5. s. 9. 1:45} Although the Peloponnesians were supported by the Persian purse, nevertheless the Athenians held out against them for three whole years. {*Thucydides, l. 2. c. 65. s. 12. 1:379} Who can wonder that the Athenian state was defeated and came to nought, since the power of all the east helped in their destruction. {Justin, Trogus, l. 5. c. 1.}

1390. Lysander returned to Ephesus and rested for a while. In that time, ninety of his damaged ships were refurbished. {*Xenophon, Hellenica, l. 1. c. 5. s. 10. 1:45} He sent for the leaders from every nearby city and made an alliance with them, assuring them that if everything in this war went as he hoped, he would make every one of them a prince, with his own city. They were so enthused, that every man was ready to do more than Lysander could reasonably require of them. He had more provisions for the war effort than he could have imagined. {*Diod. Sic., l. 13. c. 70. s. 4. 5:319}

1391. When Alcibiades heard that Thrasybulus had left the Hellespont to fortify Phocaea, he sailed to him. In the meantime, he left the fleet under the charge of

Antiochus, with a strict command that he should in no way stir or fight with Lysander in his absence. [L224] However, Antiochus planned to sail to Ephesus with his own vessel and one other from Notium, as Xenophon and Plutarch stated. (Diodorus said that he selected ten of his best ships.) He skirted along under the very noses of Lysander's ships. First, Lysander set out with a small company of ships and pursued him. When more and more ships came to help Antiochus, Lysander drew out his whole fleet and the Athenians did the same from Notium and other places. They arrived there in a disorderly manner and quickly lost fifteen ships, while the rest fled to safety. Antiochus was killed in the battle. Lysander erected a monument at Notium and returned to Ephesus with the ships which he had taken. The remaining ships of the Athenians went to Samos. When Alcibiades heard what had happened, he went with his whole fleet before the port of Ephesus and there ranged it in battle array. Lysander did not stir, for he had far fewer ships than the Athenians. Alcibiades returned to Samos again. {*Xenophon, Hellenica, l. 1. c. 5. s. 10-15. 1:45,47} {*Diod. Sic., l. 13. c. 72. 5:319,321} {*Plutarch, Alcibiades, l. 1. c. 35. s. 5,6. 4:105} {*Plutarch, Lysander, l. 1. c. 5. s. 1,2. 4:243}

1392. Alcibiades sailed from Samos to Cyme. He made many false charges against them, after he had taken many of them captive. As he took them to his ships, the Cymeans rallied and attacked their enemies. Alcibiades was able to hold them off, until the rest of those in that area came to their aid. [E159] Alcibiades abandoned the prisoners and was forced to flee to his ships for safety. This distressed him so much that he sent to Mitylene for more troops. He drew his men forth in a battle array before the walls of Cyme and dared the people to come out to battle. When no man stirred, he led his men back to Mitylene, after first ravaging the surrounding country.

1393. The Cymeans sent to Athens and made their case against Alcibiades for plundering a confederate city and the surrounding area which had not offended the Athenians. When this case was made, others also complained about his conduct and misdeeds. A garrison in Samos, which did not like him, stole over to Athens and informed against him. They publicly charged him before the whole assembly of the people of being dishonest and having secret communications with the Lacedemonians. They said he had private correspondence with Pharnabazus, who had assured him that if the Lacedemonians won, he would be made ruler of Athens. {*Diod. Sic., l. 13. c. 73. s. 3-6. 5:327}

## 3598a AM, 4307 JP, 407 BC

1394. The Cymeans on the one side, and Thrasybulus on behalf of the armies on the other, accused Alcibiades of many wrong-doings in his administration. Conon, with nine assistant commissioners, was sent to replace Alcibiades as general of the army. When Alcibiades heard of this, he sailed secretly to his own lands and citadels in the Chersonesus of Thrace. {*Diod. Sic., l. 13. c. 74. 5:327,329} {*Xenophon, Hellenica, l. 1. c. 5. s. 16-20. 1:47,48} {*Plutarch, Alcibiades, l. 1. c. 36,37. 4:105-111} {*Plutarch, Lysander, l. 1. c. 5. s. 2. 4:243}

### 3598b AM, 4308 JP, 406 BC

*1395.* Lysander sent for men with leadership qualities from the nearby cities and asked them to make as many friends as they could in order to help him. He assured them, as before, that as soon as the Athenians were defeated, he would replace the democratic governments in all those cities and make each one of them a ruler in his own city. {*Plutarch, Lysander, l. 1. c. 5. s. 3. 4:243}

### 3598c AM, 4308 JP, 406 BC

*1396.* The moon was eclipsed three hours after sunset {*Xenophon, Hellenica, l. 1. c. 6. s. 1. 1:49} on the 15th of April, according to the Julian Calendar. This is verified by the astronomical calculations.

*1397.* When Pityas was ephor at Sparta and Callias was the archon at Athens, Lysander's year of command expired. Callicratidas was sent to be admiral of the navy. Although Lysander hated him, he surrendered the command of the ships, but at Sardis he gave back to Cyrus the money he had received from Cyrus for the navy. [L225] He told Callicratidas to go and ask Cyrus if he could have it and see how he could get money to pay the navy. This forced Callicratidas to go to Lydia to Cyrus and get money for the navy. Because he was not well known, he was kept waiting, day after day, in his efforts to see Cyrus, and quickly grew impatient, saying the Greeks had come to a low estate if they must now stand begging for pay from a company of barbarians. He delivered his request and left. {*Xenophon, Hellenica, l. 1. c. 6. s. 1-11. 1:49-55} {*Plutarch, Lysander, l. 1. c. 5,6. 4:245-249}

*1398.* Callicratidas sailed to Miletus and got the money from them for the navy. He sailed to Chios and took the citadel of Delphinium, which was held by five hundred Athenians, and destroyed it. After he got more money there for the sailors, he went to Teos, slipped into the town by night and sacked it. He came to Lesbos, where he took Methymna, the chief city of the island. Conon, the Athenian, hurried to their rescue but arrived too late. When he came and found the situation hopeless, he began to sail away. Callicratidas chased him with his fleet of one hundred and seventy ships, then attacked and defeated him. Conon lost thirty ships and fled to Mitylene with the forty that were left. Callicratidas followed him there and blockaded him by sea and land.

While he was besieging Mitylene, Cyrus sent him the money he had asked for. {*Xenophon, Hellenica, l. 1. c. 6. s. 12-18. 1:55,57} {*Diod. Sic., l. 13. c. 76-79. 5:335-343}

*1399.* The Athenian navy of a hundred and fifty ships sailed to Mitylene to break the blockade. Callicratidas left Eteonicus with fifty ships to continue the siege, while he sailed with a hundred and twenty ships to the Arginusa Islands which were between Malea, the bay of Lesbos, and Cape Canis in Asia. There he attacked the Athenians and was killed. The Athenians won the battle, but lost twenty-five ships and most of their crews. [E160] A few were saved by swimming to shore. The Peloponnesians lost seventy-seven ships and fled to Chios. Most of the remaining fleet retired into the countries of Curna and Phocaea. {*Xenophon, Hellenica, l. 1. c. 6. s. 24-35. 1:61-65} {*Diod. Sic., l. 13. c. 97-100. 5:397-407} This battle at the Arginusa Islands happened when Callias was archon at Athens, in the third year of the 93rd Olympiad. {*Athenaeus, l. 5. (218b) 2:487} {*Xenophon, Hellenica, l. 1. c. 6. s. 1. 1:49} {*Diod. Sic., l. 13. c. 80. s. 1. 5:347}

### 3599 AM, 4309 JP, 405 BC

*1400.* Cyrus killed his two first cousins, Autoboesaces and Mitraeus, the sons of his father Darius' sister. When they had met him, they had not pulled their hands up into their sleeves, an honour which was reserved for the king alone. Hieramenes and his wife, the parents, it seems, of those who were killed, heard about this. They told Darius that it was a shame for him to ignore so foul a deed by his son. Therefore, Darius sent for his son to come to him, pretending that he was sick. Darius was in his camp at Thamneria in the country of the Medes, where he had gone with his army against the Cadusians, a bordering country which had recently revolted from him. {*Xenophon, Hellenica, l. 2. c. 1. s. 8-13. 1:91,93}

*1401.* The Lacedemonians who were scattered in the countries of Aeolia and Ionia met together at Ephesus. They sent messengers to Lacedemon to let them know how things had gone with them in Asia, and to request that they might again have Lysander for their general, since he had proved his worth in the previous year. Cyrus also joined with them in this request. Their law stated that the same man could not be admiral of their fleet a second time. Therefore, they gave the title of admiral to Aracus, but committed the whole management of the war to Lysander as a lieutenant to Aracus. Lysander came to Ephesus and sent to Eteonicus to come to him from Chios with his ships. [L226] He was to gather all the ships that he could from Peloponnesus and other lands. Lysander repaired those which he had, and built new ones in the port at Antandros. {*Xenophon, Hellenica, l. 2. c. 1. s. 6,7,10-12. 1:91,93} {*Diod. Sic., l. 13. c. 101. s. 8. 5:409} {*Diod. Sic., l. 13. c. 104. s. 3. 5:417} {*Plutarch, Lysander, l. 1. c. 7. 4:249}

1402. Lysander journeyed to Cyrus and as before, desired money from him, which he got after much difficulty. Cyrus made it appear to him that because he had been so generous to him in the past, he was now short of funds. Lysander immediately appointed sea captains over every ship and paid every ship and sailor his due. {*Xenophon, Hellenica, l. 2. c. 1. s. 11,12. 1:93}

1403. When the Carthaginians captured Gela in Sicily, they took the large brass statue of Apollo, which was in his temple on the outskirts of the city, back to Tyre. {*Diod. Sic., l. 13. c. 107. s. 3,4. 5:429}

1404. When Cyrus received his father's message, he sent for Lysander to come to him at Sardis. He did not want him to fight the Athenians at sea until he had a far larger fleet than he had at that time. He promised that when he returned he would bring with him a very large navy from Phoenicia, Cilicia and other surrounding areas. He committed the care of all the cities of his government to Lysander. All tributes that belonged to him, he assigned to Lysander, saying that Lysander could keep for himself what was left over. {*Xenophon, Hellenica, l. 2. c. 1. s. 13,14. 1:93,95} {*Diod. Sic., l. 13. c. 104. s. 3,4. 5:417,419} {*Plutarch, Lysander, l. 1. c. 9. s. 1,2. 4:253}

1405. Cyrus journeyed to his father and took Tissaphernes along with him as a friend, as well as three hundred heavily armed Greek foot soldiers under the command of Xenias of Parrhasia. {*Xenophon, Anabasis, l. 1. c. 1. s. 2. 3:47}

1406. When Cyrus was gone, Lysander paid his army and went with his fleet to Ceramium, a bay in Caria. He attacked the town Cedreiae, which was a confederate of the Athenians, and captured it the following day. He sacked it and enslaved its inhabitants, who were a mixture of Greek and barbarian blood. {*Xenophon, Hellenica, l. 2. c. 1. s. 15,16. 1:95} However, Diodorus said that: {*Diod. Sic., l. 13. c. 104. s. 7. 5:419}

> "Lysander attacked Thasus, a city of Caria and a confederate of the Athenians, with a large number of ships. He took it by force and killed the eight hundred men of military age there. He sold the women and children as slaves and levelled the city to the ground."

1407. He wrote *Thasians* instead of *Cedrenians*. These were the inhabitants of the isle of Thasos (Loeb text shows this as a textual variation. Editor.) who lived a long way away from from there. After the defeat of the Athenians at Egos Potamos and the final ruin of Athens, the Thasians were not taken by force by Lysander, but were surprised by a ruse of his. This we may easily learn from a fragmented passage of Emilius Probus {Emilius Probus, Lysander} and the complete account of the matter by Polyaenus. {Polyaenus, Strategmata, l. 1.} [E161]

### 3599d AM, 4309 JP, 405 BC

1408. With the help of Lysander, certain men overthrew the democratic government at Miletus. On the feast of Bacchus they cut the throats of forty of those who opposed them, in their own homes. Afterward, in a crowded market, they seized a further three hundred of the richest people and cut off their heads. About a thousand of the important people, who feared for their lives, fled to Pharnabazus, the Persian governor in those parts. He entertained them very kindly and gave every one of them a gold stater (possibly a Persian daric). He gave them a citadel in Claudia, called Clauda, to live in. (I think this may be the island of Clauda mentioned in Acts, {Ac 27:16} but I am not certain.) {*Diod. Sic., l. 13. c. 104. s. 5,6. 5:419} [L227] (The Loeb edition stated it was Blaudia, which was a citadel in Lydia. Editor.)

1409. The Athenians set sail from Samos and came to Chios and Ephesus, where they laid waste to the king's countries in these areas and then prepared for a naval battle. Meanwhile, Lysander sailed with his fleet from Rhodes and leaving Ionia on the right hand, went to the Hellespont, where he planned to blockade that strait and destroy all the cities in those parts that had revolted from him. {*Xenophon, Hellenica, l. 2. c. 1. s. 16,17. 1:95}

1410. Lysander sailed with his fleet from Abydus to Lampsacus, a confederate city of the Athenians. He was met by the men from Abydus coming by land with others under the command of Thorax, a Lacedemonian captain. Together they attacked the city, captured and sacked it. It was rich, full of grain, wine and other provisions. He sent away the Athenian garrison. As he had promised, he allowed all freemen there to retain their liberty. When he had given its spoil to his soldiers, he left the place to its inhabitants. {*Plutarch, Lysander, l. 1. c. 9. s. 4. 4:255} {*Xenophon, Hellenica, l. 2. c. 1. s. 18-20. 1:95,97} {*Diod. Sic., l. 13. c. 104. s. 8. 5:419,421}

1411. The Athenian navy of a hundred and eighty ships was totally surprised and taken by Lysander at Egos Potamos, in the strait of the Hellespont, along with three thousand soldiers and their commanders. Barely ten ships escaped. {*Plutarch, Lysander, l. 1. c. 10-11. 4:255-261}

1412. Conon, their admiral, saw that the Athenian cause was now hopeless. Because he did not want to return to Athens for fear of the cruelty of his countrymen, he escaped with only nine ships to Cape Abarinders in Lampsacus. From there he took some main masts of Lysander's ships and sailed away to his good acquaintance, Evagoras, king of Cyprus, meanwhile sending a small ship to Athens to tell them what had happened to him at Egos Potamos. {*Plutarch, Lysander, l. 1. c. 11. s. 5. 4:261} {*Isocrates, Areopagiticus, l. 1. (64) 2:145} {Aristotle, Rhetoric, l. 2.} {Justin, Trogus, l. 5. c. 6.} {Aristides, Rhodiaca}

1413. Lysander had rifled the camp of the Athenians and carried away the ships, prisoners, spoils and everything else. He sailed back to Lampsacus to the sound of triumphant songs for the pipe and flute. That same day he sent Theopompus, who had been a Milesian pirate, to Lacedemon with the news of this victory. He went in the best ship, with pennants and streamers flying and every other form of magnificent attire imaginable, and in three days he reached Lacedemon. Philocles, the admiral, and three thousand Athenian prisoners all had their throats cut, except for Adimantus. {*Xenophon, Hellenica, l. 2. c. 1. s. 30-32. 1:101,103} {*Diod. Sic., l. 13. c. 106. s. 7,8. 5:425} {*Plutarch, Lysander, l. 1. c. 11. s. 6,7. 4:261}

1414. When Lysander had set all things in order at Lampsacus, he sailed to Byzantium and Chalcedon. Both cities opened their gates to him and sent away the Athenian garrisons from both places, and Lysander gave his word for their safe conduct. When those who had formerly betrayed Byzantium to Alcibiades got away, they first went into Pontus and from there to Athens, where they were all made free citizens. Lysander appointed Sthenelaus, a Lacedemonian, as governor of both Byzantium and Chalcedon, while he himself returned to Lampsacus to repair his navy. {*Xenophon, Hellenica, l. 2. c. 2. s. 1-2. 1:103}

1415. Lysander expelled from every city anyone who favoured the Athenians, and destroyed their democracies and every other form of government he came across. He left them only one *harmost*, as they were called in Lacedemon, or moderator, to govern them. Each city was divided into ten wards, and he appointed ten men to rule the city, choosing only those who were formally loyal to him or would swear allegiance to him. Thus he created a Decemvirate, or a government of ten men, in every city, composed entirely of men who were loyal to him and did his bidding. {*Plutarch, Lysander, l. 1. c. 13. s. 2-5. 4:267} {Emilius Probus, Lysander} [L228]

1416. After Lysander had spent a little time in this, he sent word to Sparta that he was ready to sail with two hundred ships. Together with Agis and Pausanias, the Spartan kings, he immediately came to besiege Athens, hoping to take it in a short time. When they defended themselves beyond his expectation, he returned into Asia. There he abolished all democracies and everywhere established his Decemviri, or government by ten men. He killed many and forced the rest to flee for their lives. At Miletus he helped his friends, who had joined an opposing party, to destroy the democracy there. [E162] He managed the matter most cunningly, so that he delivered no less than eight hundred of the democratic party to be murdered by those who stood for an aristocracy in that city. {*Plutarch, Lysander, l. 1. c. 14. s. 1. 4:269} {*Plutarch, Lysander, l. 1. c. 19. s. 2. 4:283}

### 3600c AM, 4310 JP, 404 BC

1417. The Athenians were besieged by the Lacedemonians on sea and land. They surrendered under certain conditions. However, Plutarch stated that they were told on the 16th day of Mounychion, the Attic month (the 24th of April, according to the Julian Calendar), that they had broken the articles, because they had not demolished their walls within the ten-day time limit. Hence, it is gathered that the peace treaty was made on the 6th of their month of Mounychion, that is, on April 14. {*Plutarch, Lysander, l. 1. c. 15. s. 1-3. 4:273} So the Peloponnesian War ended, after twenty-seven years of fighting. {*Thucydides, l. 5. c. 26. s. 1. 3:49} {*Diod. Sic., l. 13. c. 107. s. 5. 5:429}

1418. Shortly after this peace, Darius, the king of all Asia, died after he had reigned for nineteen years. His oldest son, Artaxerxes, reigned for forty-three years after him. {*Diod. Sic., l. 13. c. 108. s. 1. 5:429} However, Ctesias, who was the physician to Artaxerxes, said that Darius Ochus died at Babylon. He was succeeded by Arsicas or Arsaces who was born to him by Parysatis before he became king. When he became king, he changed his name to Artaxerxes. Out of respect for the greatness of that King Artaxerxes, he was surnamed Mnemon. Which, as I understand, referred to that account in Athenaeus where he said that when Ochus was dying, he was asked by his oldest son, by what wisdom and policy he had guided the state for so many years. {*Athenaeus, l. 12. (548e) 5:489} He wanted to learn from the king the correct way to rule the kingdom. The old king replied that he had done it by always doing right to both the gods and man. Darius Ochus was often urged by his wife Parysatis, who loved her younger son Cyrus more than the older, to follow the example of Darius Hystaspes. He left the kingdom to the first son that was born after he became king, not to the first son who was born before he became king. However, he would not listen to her. By his last will, he gave the kingdom to his oldest son Artaxerxes, and to his younger son Cyrus he gave all those cities and territories in Asia which were under his government at that time. {*Plutarch, Artaxerxes, l. 1. c. 2. 11:129,131} {Justin, Trogus, l. 5. c. 11.}

1419. As soon as Artaxerxes came to the throne, his wife Statira persuaded him to seize Vadiastes, who had murdered her brother Terituchmes and who was the husband of Amestris, Artaxerxes' sister. He had his tongue pulled out of his mouth and cut off, and then he was killed. He made Mitredates' or Mithridates' son (who had preserved the city Zaris for the son of Terituchmes) the governor in his place. {Ctesias}

1420. Artaxerxes went to Pasargada, where, according to the custom, he was to take off his robe and to put on the robe which old Cyrus had worn before he became king. He was inaugurated by the priests of Persia according to the ancient regal ceremonies. Tissaphernes brought him the priest who had instructed his brother Cyrus in his childhood, according to the custom of his country, and who had taught him the principles of the art of magic. The priest was trusted by Artaxerxes when he accused Cyrus of plotting against the king claiming that Cyrus planned to attack Artaxerxes as he was taking off his own robes, to murder him in the very temple itself. {*Plutarch, Artaxerxes, l. 1. c. 3. 11:131,133} [L229]

1421. Artaxerxes had his brother held captive, because he planned to have him executed. He put him in gold chains out of respect for his royal blood. When he was to be killed, his mother caught him about the middle and then threw her hair around his neck and tied him with her hair. After many tears and lamentations she secured his pardon and position back. He was sent back to his command in Lydia and the other coastal towns in Asia. {*Plutarch, Artaxerxes, l. 1. c. 3. s. 5. 11:133} {*Xenophon, Anabasis, l. 1. c. 1. s. 3. 3:47} {Justin, Trogus, l. 4. c. fin.} {Ctesias}

1422. Alcibiades feared the power of the Lacedemonians who commanded all the sea and land. He left that part of Bithynia which belonged to the Thracians and took away with him a large quantity of silver and gold, but left much more behind in the citadel where he had been. As soon as the Thracians knew about his wealth, they planned to catch him and take his money. They missed him, however, because he stole away secretly to Pharnabazus in Phrygia, who was so taken and enamoured with Alcibiades' gentle behaviour, that no one was as close to him as Alcibiades was. Hence he gave him the citadel of Grynium in Phrygia, from which place he made fifty talents a year in tribute. {*Plutarch, Alcibiades, l. 1. c. 37. s. 3,4. 4:109,111} {Emilius Probus, Alcibiades}

1423. The Lysandrian feast and games were instituted in honour of Lysander. When Antimachus and Niceratus competed in the poetry contest, Lysander gave the garland to Niceratus. Antimachus was so disappointed that he burned his own poem. A young Plato encouraged him, telling him that only the ignorant suffer from their ignorance, as the blind do from their blindness. During this period, as Apollodorus the Athenian stated, the poet Antimachus flourished. {*Plutarch, Lysander, l. 1. c. 18. s. 3-5. 4:281,283} {*Diod. Sic., l. 13. c. 108. s. 1. 5:429} [E163]

## 3600d AM, 4310 JP, 404 BC

1424. In the Olympiad following the capture of Athens by Lysander, which was the 94th Olympiad, the prize in running was won by Crocinas, a Thessalian. Xenophon stated that there was an eclipse of the sun, which the astronomical calculations show happened on the morning of September 3. {*Xenophon, Hellenica, l. 2. c. 3. s. 1-4. 1:113,115}

## 3601a AM, 4310 JP, 404 BC

1425. Cyrus, having returned safely into Lydia and remembering how his brother had shackled him, set about planning how he might avoid future problems with his brother and how he might make himself king. So he gathered as many Greek soldiers as possible and made various excuses for gathering a large army from many countries, all the while planning a surprise attack on his brother. {*Xenophon, Anabasis, l. 1. c. 1. s. 4. 3:49} {*Plutarch, Artaxerxes, l. 1. c. 3. s. 5. 11:133} He sent Lysander a gift of a ship a yard high, made entirely of gold and ivory. With this gift he congratulated him for the great sea victory that he had had. Lysander put the present in the treasury of the Brasidas and Acanthians at Delphi. {*Plutarch, Lysander, l. 1. c. 18. s. 1. 4:281} Lysander came to him at Sardis to deliver a present from all the confederate cities, and it is possible that jewel or necklace, which Aelian said was sent to Cyrus by Scopas the Younger from Thessaly, was among those things he brought for a present. {*Aelian, Historical Miscellany, l. 12. c. 1. 1:351} Cyrus welcomed him and showed him his orchard, which he had laid out and planted himself. He entertained Lysander with a discourse on husbandry, as recorded by Xenophon who used the name of Socrates instead of Cyrus in the dialogue. {*Xenophon, Oeconomicus, l. 1. c. 4. s. 20-25. 1:399,401}

1426. Among the Persians, Satibarzanes accused Orontes of keeping company with Parysatis, the king's mother, otherwise Orontes always had a good reputation for chastity. Therefore Orontes was executed. [L230] Parysatis grew unhappy with her son and had Mithridates, the son of Terituchmes' son, poisoned. {Ctesias}

1427. When Alcibiades learned that Cyrus intended to make war against his brother with the support of the Lacedemonians, he planned to hurry to Artaxerxes. He wanted to be the first to expose this treason, and hoped to get some reward for himself, as Themistocles had done before him. He also wanted the king's help to free his city of Athens from their bondage to the Lacedemonians. Meanwhile Critias, one of the thirty tyrants whom Lysander had set over the Athenians to rule them, told Lysander either to have Alcibiades killed or all that he had done at Athens would be undone.

Lysander did nothing until a scytale or an encrypted letter was brought to him from Lacedemon, ordering him to kill Alcibiades. (*Scytale*: A method of secret writing practised by the Spartans, in which the message was written on a strip of parchment wound spirally round a cylindrical or tapering staff, so that it became illegible when the parchment was unrolled, and could be read only by the use of a staff of precisely the right form and size. Hence, a secret dispatch conveyed by this method. OED.) Lysander sent to Pharnabazus to inform him that unless he immediately gave him Alcibiades, either dead or alive, the league between the king and the Lacedemonians would be broken, and war would break out again. Pharnabazus sent Magaeus, his brother, and Susamithres, his uncle (Emilius Probus called Magaeus by the name of Bagoas), to murder Alcibiades while he was in a certain place near the Deer Mountain, which is at Arginusa in Phrygia, where he was preparing for his journey to the king.

*1428.* The people of that country whom they had hired to kill him did not dare attempt it directly. In the dead of the night they surrounded the house where he was sleeping with a large pile of wood and set it on fire. When Alcibiades escaped, they shot at him with arrows and killed him, and carried his head to Pharnabazus. His sweetheart and prostitute, Timandra, wrapped the rest of his body in her own gown. (A little earlier he had dreamed that he was wrapped in it.) She cremated the body in the same fire with which the house was burned and gave him as honourable a funeral as she could afford, at the village of Melissa in Phrygia. {*Ephorus, l. 17*} {*Diod. Sic., l. 14. c. 11. 6:37,39*} {*Aristotle, History of Animals, l. 6. c. 29. s. 25. 2:337*} {*Athenaeus, l. 13. (574ef) 6:105*} {*Plutarch, Alcibiades, l. 1. c. 38,39. 4:113,115*} {*Cicero, De Divinatione, l. 2. c. 69. 20:531*} {*Valerius Maximus, l. 1. c. 7. ext. 9. 1:99*} {Justin, Trogus, l. 5. c. 8.} {Emilius Probus, Alcibiades}

## 3601b AM, 4311 JP, 403 BC

*1429.* Clearchus, a Lacedemonian, was a tyrant of Byzantium. He was overthrown by his own people under the leadership of Panthoedas and stole away by night, coming into Ionia. Learning that Cyrus planned to attack his brother, he befriended him and was made general of all his forces. Cyrus found that he was a proud, courageous and daring man. He gave him ten thousand darics, with which he raised forces and marched from the Chersonesus, attacking the Thracians that bordered on the Hellespont toward the north. Since it seemed to be to the advantage of the Greeks, the cities of the Hellespont contributed willingly to the support of the army and so these forces were maintained secretly for the service of Cyrus. {*Xenophon, Anabasis, l. 1. c. 1. s. 9. 3:51*} {*Diod. Sic., l. 14. c. 12. 6:39-43*} [E164]

## 3601c AM, 4311 JP, 403 BC

*1430.* Lysander brutally wasted the province of Phrygia and other places under the government of Pharnabazus, who complained about this at Lacedemon, where he himself was held in great esteem and was much loved, because he had great wealth and always supported their state against its enemies. Therefore the ephors were greatly displeased with Lysander, and killed Thorax, his good friend, because they found that he had a store of money in his house. They sent their scytale or encrypted letter to Lysander and recalled him from Asia, whereupon Lysander entreated Pharnabazus to write letters to justify him, which he publicly did. [L231] This was so well done, that Lysander could not have wished for better. But he also wrote one which looked similar, but which condemned Lysander's actions, and when they were sealed, he substituted this letter for the first one without Lysander's knowledge. He sent them with Lysander to Lacedemon to the ephors. In this way, Lysander was turned into his own accuser. {*Plutarch, Lysander, l. 1. c. 19,20. 4:285-291*} {Emilius Probus, Lysander} {Polyaenus, Strategmata, l. 7.}

*1431.* Not long after this, the ephors permitted him to travel to visit the temple of Jupiter Ammon. He pretended that it was to pay the vows which he had made prior to entering into certain battles he had fought in their service. However, the real purpose was to bribe the priests there for his own ends. He carried with him a large sum of money for this purpose. He had an old friend of his father there, King Libys. To mark that friendship, his father had given his younger brother the name Libys. The chief priest of that oracle could not be bribed and informed against him at Sparta, so that when he returned to Sparta, he was questioned about it, but was acquitted by the court. {*Diod. Sic., l. 14. c. 13. s. 5-7. 6:45,47*} {*Plutarch, Lysander, l. 1. c. 19. s. 4-6. 4:289*} {Emilius Probus, Lysander}

## 3602 AM, 4312 JP, 402 BC

*1432.* At this time all the cities of Ionia, with the exception of Miletus, which was under the government of Tissaphernes, defected to Cyrus. While Tissaphernes was residing at Miletus, he learned that the Milesians were also inclined toward Cyrus. He thwarted their intentions by killing some of them and expelling others, who, when they came to Cyrus, were graciously received by him. He immediately gathered an army by land and sea to restore their city to them. {*Xenophon, Anabasis, l. 1. c. 1. s. 6,7. 3:49*} Among his army was Socrates of Achaia, with five hundred heavily armed foot soldiers, and Pasion of Megara, with almost seven hundred more. {*Xenophon, Anabasis, l. 1. c. 2. s. 3. 3:55*} Cyrus' admiral, Tamos, an Egyptian, blockaded Miletus with twenty-five ships. {*Xenophon, Anabasis, l. 1. c. 4. s. 2. 3:81*}

*1433.* Cyrus sent to Artaxerxes, requesting that he entrust those cities to him rather than to Tissaphernes. His mother supported him in this. When the king learned that there was no treason behind this action, but that Cyrus had only kept an army to oppose Tissaphernes, he was content for them to forget past differences, for Cyrus duly sent to Artaxerxes the tribute from those cities which Tissaphernes had formerly held. {*Xenophon, Anabasis, l. 1. c. 1. s. 8. 3:51}

*1434.* This Cyrus was never king of either Persia or Babylon. He was not the man whom George Harvartus assumed to be that king who, after the end of the Babylonian captivity, allowed the Jews to return home with their governor Zerubbabel and with Joshua, or Jeshua, the son of Jozadak the high priest. However, it was Artaxerxes Mnemon who was then king of Persia, and while Johannes, who in Nehemiah {Ne 12:11,22,23} is called Johanan and Jonathan, was the high priest of the Jews. The governor of the Jewish country was a certain Persian governor who, Josephus said, was called Bagoses, a captain of another Artaxerxes, as Rufinus translated it. That is, another descendant of Artaxerxes Longimanus, of whom Josephus had mentioned. {*Josephus, Antiq., l. 11. c. 7. s. 1. (300) 6:459} [L232] But the connection which he made between these men was as follows:

*1435.* Jesus was brother to Johannes or John, the high priest, and Jesus was a close friend of Bagoses. Bagoses promised to bestow the next high priesthood on him, so Jesus became very bold, confident of Bagoses' support. First, he had an argument with John, and then a public brawl with his brother in the very temple itself. He provoked John so much, that his brother killed him right there. When this happened, Bagoses came and profaned the temple by entering it. He said that the high priest had already polluted it with his own brother's blood. For the next seven years he harassed the Jews for that murder and placed a heavy fine on them. {*Josephus, Antiq., l. 11. c. 7. s. 1. (300,301) 6:459} Before they offered their daily sacrifice, they were to pay fifty drachmas for every lamb (not for every year, as the common translations of Josephus, and from them Salianus, had it). This punishment continued only as long as Johannes was the high priest. [E165] We ascertain that this happened in the reign of Artaxerxes Mnemon, not Artaxerxes Ochus. We therefore reckon this from the beginning of Artaxerxes Mnemon's reign, because we find Johannes or Johanan mentioned in Ezra and Nehemiah (though not as high priest at the time). {Ezr 10:6 Ne 12:23} For between the seventh year of Artaxerxes Longimanus, to which that history of Ezra referred, and the end of the seventh year of Artaxerxes Mnemon's reign (before which we suppose and take for granted that this

Johannes did not die), there was at least a period of seventy years, according to our account. So he died after living over ninety years, and his son Jaddua succeeded him in the priesthood and held it till the reign of Alexander the Great. Jaddua died at about the age of eighty-three, if we suppose that he was born at the end of Darius Ochus' reign. This is an aside. We now return to the history of Cyrus the younger, who died before he was twenty-two years old.

### 3603a AM, 4312 JP, 402 BC

*1436.* Cyrus sent messengers to Lacedemon, asking them now to send him men, just as he from time to time had supported them with men and money against the Athenians. He bragged that if they sent him footmen, he would give them horses, if horsemen, chariots, if they had lands, he would give them towns, if towns, cities for their reward. For their wages, they would get them paid to them not by number but by weight. As a consequence, the Lacedemonians decided that what he asked for was right, and that this war would be to their advantage. They planned to send him aid, hoping to ingratiate themselves with Cyrus, and ignoring the fact that this war was against Artaxerxes. If things did not go as planned, they had a good excuse to give Artaxerxes, namely that they had decreed nothing against him in person. The ephors sent letters to their admiral, Samius, to do whatever Cyrus required. {*Xenophon, Hellenica, l. 3. c. 1. s. 1. 1:175} {*Diod. Sic., l. 14. c. 19. s. 1-5. 6:63} {Justin, Trogus, l. 5. c. fin.} {*Plutarch, Artaxerxes, l. 1. c. 6. s. 2,3. 11:139}

*1437.* Therefore, the Lacedemonian admiral sailed to Ephesus with his ships to meet with Tamos, the Egyptian who was the admiral for Cyrus, and offered Tamos his services to the best of his ability. Joining his fleet with Tamos' fleet, they sailed around the coast of Ionia to Caria, so that Syennesis, the governor of those lands, would not move to hinder Cyrus in his march overland against his brother. {*Xenophon, Hellenica, l. 3. c. 1. s. 1,2. 1:175} {*Diod. Sic., l. 14. c. 19. s. 5. 6:63} {*Xenophon, Anabasis, l. 1. c. 4. s. 2. 3:81} Diodorus said that Samius, the Lacedemonian admiral, had twenty-five ships and Tamos had fifty. Based on Xenophon's Anabasis, Tamos had only twenty-five ships and Pythagoras, the Lacedemonian, thirty-five (for he thought Pythagoras was the other admiral, and not Samius). [L233]

*1438.* Cyrus, with his army of foot soldiers, resolved to march into upper Asia under the pretence of marching against the Pisidians, who often attacked areas under his control. In consequence, he at once sent for Clearchus, the Lacedemonian, Aristippus of Thessaly, Xenias of Arcadia, the banished men of Miletus, and the army which had besieged Miletus. He sent Proxenus, a Boeotian, to go just as fast as he could to the Greeks and others, asking them to come at once to Sardis. {*Xenophon, Anabasis, l. 1. c. 1. s. 11. 3:53} {*Xenophon, Anabasis, l. 1. c. 2. s. 1. 3:53}

## 3603b AM, 4313 JP, 401 BC

1439. When Tissaphernes determined that a much larger force was being assembled than an attack on the Pisidians would require, he hurried away with five hundred cavalry as fast as he could to Artaxerxes, who, now aware of what was happening, prepared for war. {*Xenophon, Anabasis, l. 1. c. 2. s. 4. 3:55}

1440. Cyrus left some of his trusted Persian friends to manage affairs at Lydia. He trusted his good friend Tamos, the Egyptian admiral, to take care of the cities of Ionia and Aeolia in his absence, while he marched with his army toward Cilicia and Pisidia under the pretence that certain persons in those parts were unruly. {*Diod. Sic., l. 14. c. 19. s. 6. 6:63}

> "But Themistogenes of Syracuse has recorded how Cyrus gathered his army, marched against his brother, how the battle was fought and how Cyrus perished in it, and how those Greeks who went with him came back safely to the sea again, that is, into Asia Minor."

1441. This is what Xenophon wrote in the beginning of the third book of his Greek History. If we compare this part of the history with Plutarch's book, {*Plutarch, Glory of the Athenians, l. 1. c. 1. 4:495}, we find the following:

> "Xenophon wrote a history about himself, recording how he was a captain and what exploits he did. Then he said that Themistogenes of Syracuse had written it, so relinquishing the glory of having written it himself to another man, in order that the things written about himself might receive greater credibility in the world."

1442. In another place in Suidas, we find: [E166]

> "The expedition of Cyrus, which commonly went with Xenophon's history of the Greeks and some other pieces concerning his own country, were all of Xenophon's own writings."

1443. Certainly, these books about the expedition of Cyrus belonged with the rest of his Greek histories. At the end, he plainly said that its author was present at all those events. Therefore the work itself, which throughout was full of Xenophon's noble acts, was attributed to him not only by Plutarch but long before him, by Cicero, Dionysius of Halicarnassus, Hermogenes, Laertius, Athenaeus and by Arianus of Nicomedia (not to speak of our divines, Eusebius and Jerome).

Themistogenes also had the nickname of New Xenophon, as we read in Photius and Suidas, because he compiled the discourses of his teacher Epictetus into four books, as Xenophon had done for those of his teacher Socrates. Also, just as Xenophon had recorded that the above expedition of Cyrus in seven books, so Themistogenes had recorded the expedition of Alexander in seven books. [L234] Although Xenophon, in his expedition of Cyrus, as Laertius noted, has a brief preface to every book, but not to the set in general. Whereas in every book except the sixth, Themistogenes made a preface using a summary of the previous books, which Xenophon did not do in his books. Themistogenes has details in those books which do not flatter Xenophon. Therefore, I am rather inclined to think that those books were written by Themistogenes and not by Xenophon. However, I followed the authority of those ancient writers. I have all along cited him by the name of Xenophon, as they have done before me. Of those five points mentioned by Xenophon {*Xenophon, Hellenica, l. 3. c. 1. s. 1,2. 1:175} and said to have been written by Themistogenes, the first four are entirely in the first book of this expedition of Cyrus:

> a) The gathering of his army.
> b) Their marching into upper Asia and coming to the place where they fought.
> c) The details of the battle.
> d) The fall of Cyrus in that battle.

1444. Cyrus left Sardis, where Xenophon had met him after being summoned from Athens by Proxenus, the Boeotian. There Xenophon had volunteered for the action, as we find in the third book, and come to Celaenae in Phrygia, where he stayed for thirty days. During that time, Clearchus and other Greek commanders came to him from various parts and together they assembled a force of eleven thousand heavily armed foot soldiers and about two thousand targeteers. {*Xenophon, Anabasis, l. 1. c. 2. s. 9. 3:59}

## 3603c AM, 4313 JP, 401 BC

1445. From Celaenae, Cyrus came with his army to the bank of the Cayster River. He received money from Epyaxa, the wife of Syennesis, the king of Cilicia. (Cyrus was formerly thought to have had intimate relations with her.) He paid his army the three months' back wages he owed them, plus the next month in advance. Epyaxa arrived at Tartius in Cilicia five days before Cyrus. She also persuaded her husband Syennesis to come there, and to give Cyrus a vast sum of money toward the support of his army. {*Xenophon, Anabasis, l. 1. c. 2. s. 11,12. 3:61} Both Ctesias and Diodorus added that Syennesis, like a wise man, supplied both Cyrus and Artaxerxes with necessities for the war. Since he had two sons, he sent one of them to Cyrus with a competent number of men for his service. However, he had earlier secretly sent away the other to Artaxerxes, to let him know that with such an army as Cyrus had, he dared not oppose Cyrus, but publicly joined with him. Nevertheless, he declared himself loyal to Artaxerxes and would defect to him as soon as he could find an opportunity. {*Diod. Sic., l. 14. c. 20. s. 3. 6:67} {Ctesias} Cyrus stayed twenty days at Tarsus, where the Greek companies told him plainly that they would march no farther. Clearchus, using his tact, changed their minds, and so they marched to Issus. This was the remotest city of Cilicia, where Cyrus' fleet met him, bringing him seven hundred heavily armed foot soldiers, but Diodorus said eight hundred. The Lacedemonians had sent these men to Cyrus under the command of Chirosophus. {*Diod. Sic., l. 14. c. 21. 6:69} Another four hundred heavily armed foot soldiers, who had formerly served Artaxerxes under their captain Abrocomus, also came into his camp. {*Xenophon, Anabasis, l. 1. c. 4. s. 3. 3:81} However, Abrocomus left Phoenicia with three hundred thousand men and marched to Artaxerxes, arriving five days before the battle. Setting out from where he was, Cyrus crossed the passes of Syria and without halting, came to the place of the pending battle. He had travelled from Ephesus to there in ninety-three days and marched five hundred and thirty-five parasangs, or about two thousand miles, or over twenty-one miles a day. {*Xenophon, Anabasis, l. 1. c. 4. s. 5. 3:83}

1446. According to Plutarch, the battle was fought at Cynaxa, which is about sixty-three miles from Babylon. [L235] According to the second book of the expedition of Cyrus, the battle was about three hundred and eighty-three miles from Babylon. Jacobus Capellus thought it should read, from Susa. In the army of Cyrus there were about thirteen thousand Greek soldiers, although Justin said there were no more than ten thousand. Of these, there were ten thousand and four hundred heavily armed foot soldiers and twenty-five hundred targeteers. From the other nations, there were a hundred thousand men and about twenty scythe-bearing chariots. Artaxerxes had nine hundred thousand men and fifteen hundred scythe-bearing chariots. [E167] However, Ctesias of Cnidos, who was in the battle, was quoted by Plutarch; and Ephorus, who is cited by Diodorus, stated there were only four hundred thousand men. In the battle, fifteen thousand soldiers of Artaxerxes died, according to Diodorus, and three thousand on the side of Cyrus. However, Ctesias in Plutarch stated that Artaxerxes lost no more than nine thousand soldiers, and no more than twenty thousand died that day. This battle was fought in the fourth year of the 94th Olympiad, when Xenaenetus was archon in Athens, and one year before Socrates was put to death there. {*Plutarch, Artaxerxes, l. 1. c.

8. 11:143} {*Plutarch, Artaxerxes, l. 1. c. 13. 11:155} {*Diod. Sic., l. 14. c. 24. s. 5,6. 6:79} {Justin, Trogus, l. 1. c. fin.} {*Diogenes Laertius, Socrates, l. 2. c. 5. (44) 1:175}

1447. In this battle the two brothers met, and Artaxerxes was first wounded through his coat of armour. Ctesias helped him recover from this wound. Cyrus carried on with good success against his brother, fearing no danger, and was killed by an unknown hand in the battle. Artaxerxes spent his rage upon the dead body of his brother. He severed his head from his body and cut off the hand from the arm that had wounded him, carrying it about in a triumphant manner. When his sorrowful mother came to Babylon, she tearfully gathered up his remains and buried them there. The battle between the two brothers is more fully described by Plutarch, citing Ctesias and Dinon. {*Plutarch, Artaxerxes, l. 1. c. 8-13. 11:143-157}

1448. When the king came to rifle his camp, he found and took the concubine of Cyrus. She was a woman much renowned for her wit and beauty. {*Xenophon, Anabasis, l. 1. c. 10. s. 3. 3:137} She was a Phocaean who was born in Ionia, the daughter of Hermotimus. Her name had been changed by Cyrus from Milto to Aspasia, because she seemed the equal of Aspasia the Miletian, who was the mistress of Pericles. {See note on 3564 AM. <<1266>>} Artaxerxes was anxious to acquire her. When she was brought to him all tied up, he was extremely angry with those who had brought her and had them put in irons. She was the most highly esteemed of all the three hundred and sixty concubines he had, and he doted on her the most. {*Plutarch, Artaxerxes, l. 1. c. 26. s. 5. 11:191} {*Plutarch, Pericles, l. 1. c. 24. s. 7. 3:73} {*Aelian, Historical Miscellany, l. 12. c. 1. 1:353,355} {Justin, Trogus, l. 10. c. 2.}

1449. The Greeks on the opposing side did not know that Cyrus was dead, so they kept on fighting. In their quarter, they drove back Tissaphernes and all his forces with a squadron of about six thousand Greeks, according to Isocrates. He added: {*Isocrates, Panegyricus, l. 1. (146) 1:213}

> "They were not the best of the Greeks but their mere refuse, and such as could no longer live in their own homes. These were now in a strange country, and were forsaken by their companions, betrayed by their companies and bereft of their captain whom they had followed to this war."

1450. The king came with most of his army to rescue Tissaphernes. He entered their camp and rifled it. However, when the Greeks returned from pursuing Tissaphernes, they recovered their camp and drove the king away. They spent the night there with no food and also went hungry on the next day. This is the end of Xenophon's first book of Cyrus' Anabasis.

1451. The second book described how these Greeks planned to return home again under the command of Clearchus. *[L236]* Tissaphernes promised to escort them back with his own forces and to guide them, but broke this promise, rounding up Clearchus with Proxenus, Agias and Socrates, together with twenty more captains and two hundred soldiers, to be murdered. Ctesias, in his *Persian History* (which the author of this book of the Anabasis of Cyrus had undoubtedly read), had also previously told us how cunningly Tissaphernes worked. Using Menon, a Thessalian, and his own promises, he captured Clearchus and the others mentioned in the group. They were put in irons and sent to the king at Babylon. Ctesias told how he was the physician to Parysatis, the king's mother. Through her, he was able to help Clearchus while he was in prison. As a result of her request to the king, the king had promised that Clearchus would not be harmed, but at the instigation of Statira, his queen, he had Clearchus and all the rest of the commanders except Menon butchered. All the bodies were thrown out and devoured by wild beasts and birds. Only the body of Clearchus was covered and preserved by a large sand hill caused by a strong wind. {*Ctesias, Excerpts of Photius*} {*Plutarch, Artaxerxes, l. 1. c. 18. 11:167-171*}

## 3603d AM, 4313 JP, 401 BC

1452. In his third and fourth book, Xenophon described the journey back to Greece of the remainder of the Greeks whom Tissaphernes had not captured. Xenophon had the soldiers choose new captains to replace the ones they lost, and he himself was chosen to replace Proxenus. He described their journey through many enemy countries and how they endured the very cold winter and many hardships and dangers, finally returning home safely. *[E168]* This account is found in Diodorus Siculus and in Isocrates. {*Diod. Sic., l. 14. c. 27-31. 6:87-103*} {*Isocrates, Panegyricus, l. 1. (146-149) 1:213*}

1453. For his good service in this war, Artaxerxes gave Tissaphernes all the governments which his brother Cyrus had held, in addition to what Tissaphernes had held before. {*Xenophon, Hellenica, l. 3. c. 1. s. 3. 1:175*} {*Diod. Sic., l. 14. c. 25. s. 4. 6:85*} He lavished many other expensive gifts and favours on him, lastly giving him his own daughter for a wife. Tissaphernes was his most confident friend and servant. {*Diod. Sic., l. 14. c. 25. s. 4. 6:85*}

1454. For ten days, Parysatis, the king's mother, tortured the Carian who had mortally wounded Cyrus in the thigh. She had his eyes pulled out and boiling lead poured into his ear holes until he died. Mithridates, who first wounded Cyrus and bragged that he had killed him, was put between two boats. He lay there for seventeen days until he was eaten out with worms. Parysatis won

Bagabaeus, the king's eunuch, from the king at a dice game. It was he who had ordered Cyrus' head and right hand to be cut off. She had him skinned alive, and then his body was laid across three crosses and his flayed skin hung near it. After this, at the humble request of the king, Parysatis stopped mourning for her son Cyrus. {*Ctesias*} {*Plutarch, Artaxerxes, l. 1. c. 14-17. 11:157-167*}

1455. Parysatis had the queen Statira, her daughter-in-law, poisoned. Statira had a trusted maid servant called Gingis or Gigis. Dinon said she willingly helped in the death of Statira. Ctesias said she did it against her will. The one who gave the poison was called Belitaras by Ctesias and Melantas by Dinon. There is a little bird in Persia called Rhyntaces or Rhyndaces which has no excrements at all but all its innards are full of fat. Parysatis cut one of these birds in two with a knife and gave the poisoned half to Statira as they sat at dinner. This is what Ctesias thought happened. *[L237]* However, Dinon said that it was Melantas, not Parysatis, who served her the poisoned bird. When the queen subsequently died in extreme torment, the king suspected his mother for it. She was well known for her cruelty and implacable disposition of nature. He had the servants and chefs questioned and used the rack on them. Parysatis kept Gingis in her own chamber for a long time, and though the king demanded her, Parysatis would not give her up to justice. At last Gingis wanted to steal secretly to her own home by night. Artaxerxes captured her and punished her as being the poisoner. He did not harm his mother, but when she asked permission to go to Babylon, he gave it to her, telling her, however, that while she lived, he would not come there. {*Plutarch, Artaxerxes, l. 1. c. 19. 11:171,173*}

1456. Ariston, with some others, surprised the city of Cyrene. In the battle they killed five hundred of the principal men of the inhabitants, while the rest escaped and joined with three thousand of the Missenians, whom the Lacedemonians at this time had expelled from their country. They fought in an open field against those who had taken their city. In the battle, many of the Cyrenians on both sides, and almost all the Missenians, were killed. When the battle was over, the Cyrenians agreed with an oath to forget the past and live together peacefully. {*Diod. Sic., l. 14. c. 34. 6:109,111*}

## 3604a AM, 4313 JP, 401 BC

1457. Tissaphernes (Diodorus incorrectly wrote Pharnabazus) was sent by Artaxerxes to take charge of all the governments in Asia Minor. Tissaphernes also wanted all the cities of Ionia. (Loeb edition lists Pharnabazus as an alternate reading. Editor.) {*Xenophon, Hellenica, l. 3. c. 1. s. 3. 1:175*} {*Diod. Sic., l. 14. c. 35. s. 2. 6:111*}

1458. When Tissaphernes came, all the governors and cities who had followed Cyrus were afraid, and sued for peace. Tamos, the Egyptian, who was the most important of these, was governor of Ionia. {*See note on 3593 AM. <<1339>>} {*See note on 3603b AM. <<1440>>} He loaded his fleet with all his treasure and his sons, except Glos (who later became the king's general), and sailed to Egypt. He visited Psammetichus, the king, and was confident of good treatment because of how he had treated Psammetichus in the past. Psammetichus, however, disregarded the past favours done to him and butchered him and his children, to get the ships and treasure which he had brought. {*Diod. Sic., l. 14. c. 35. s. 2-5. 6:111,113} [E169]

1459. The Greeks (of whom I spoke before) left Trapezus, which was the first Greek city they had come to. It was situated on the coast of the Black Sea in the country of Colchis. After a three day march, they came to another Greek city, in the same country of Colchis, which like Trapezus, was also a coastal town, and was called Cerasus. They stayed there ten days and counted their men. Only eighty-six hundred remained of the ten thousand they had started with, the rest were lost. Either they had been killed by the enemy in the battle, or they had died in the snow, or of other sicknesses on their return journey. From there, they went through the countries of the Mossynoeci, the Chalybes and Tibareni and came to a Greek town called Cotyora, a colony of the Sinopians. [L238] This was eight months from when they started out and five months after the battle in the country of Babylon, from where they journeyed to this place in one hundred and twenty-two days, marching six hundred and twenty parasangs, or 2325 miles (about nineteen miles per day). They stayed there forty-five days. {*Xenophon, Anabasis, l. 5. c. 3-5. 3:387-425}

## 3604b AM, 4314 JP, 400 BC

1460. During their stay there, they got their provisions partly from the market of Cotyora and partly by plundering the countries around Paphlagonia. By the same token, if the Paphlagonians found any of them straggling from the camp, they attacked them. Finally Corylas, who was the governor of the Paphlagonians, made peace between them. Later, these Greeks received transport by ship from the men of Heraclea and Sinope. They came to Harmene, a port of Sinope, where they stayed five days. From there they went to Heraclea, in the country of the Mariandyni, which was a colony of the city of Megara. They came to a peninsula called Acherusia and divided themselves into three companies.

1461. The forty-five hundred or so heavily armed foot soldiers of the Arcadians and Achaeans were transported by ship by the Heracleans. They hurried aboard, hoping to take the Thracians who inhabited Bithynia by surprise, so they might get all the more spoil. They landed by night at Calpe, near the centre of their sea coast. They went to the nearby towns and villages, about six miles up the country. The Thracians, whom they attacked there, fought back and killed many of the Greeks. One of their Greek regiments, along with their captain Smicres, was entirely cut off. In another company, only eight soldiers and their captain, Hegesander, escaped. The rest fled to a hill for safety and were besieged by the Thracians.

1462. Chirosophus, with fourteen hundred heavily armed foot soldiers and seven hundred targeteers (who were Thracians and had followed Clearchus on that journey), went from Heraclea over the entire length of the country on foot. He finally came into Bithynia and although he was not feeling well, sailed to Calpe with his men.

1463. Xenophon, with his brigade of seventeen hundred heavily armed foot soldiers, three hundred targeteers and about forty cavalry, came by sea to a country which separated the Thracians of Bithynia from the country of the Heracleans. He marched through the centre of the country and arrived to rescue those who were besieged on the hill by the Thracians, so that they finally assembled again as one body at the port of Calpe. {*Xenophon, Anabasis, l. 6. c. 2. s. 16. 3:467} {*Xenophon, Anabasis, l. 6. c. 4. s. 1. 3:467}

1464. Chirosophus died there, and was replaced by Neon of Asine, who, when he saw his troops hungry and short of supplies, gathered two thousand men and went foraging all over the country of Bithynia. Pharnabazus sent his cavalry to help the Bithynians, because he hoped to keep these Greeks out of his lands. On the first attack, the cavalry killed at least five hundred Greeks and the rest fled to a hill for safety. Xenophon rescued them from the enemy and they all returned safely to the camp before sunset. When Spithridates and Rhathines came with more troops to help the Bithynians, the Greeks won a notable victory, in memory of which they erected a monument there. They returned the seven or eight miles to their camp by the sea. After this victory, their enemies provided for their own safety by carrying off their families and goods and driving their cattle to more remote parts, so that when the Greeks passed through Bithynia, they found nothing of use to them. They returned back into Bithynia again, a day and a night's journey. They found and brought with them some prisoners, sheep and other provisions for their own needs. [L239] After six days they came to Chrysopolis, a city of the Chalcedonians, and stayed there seven days, selling their plunder there. {*Xenophon, Anabasis, l. 6. 3:467-537}

1465. Pharnabazus feared that these Greeks would make war on his country. He arranged with Anaxibius, the Lacedemonian admiral, to ship them all out of Asia to Byzantium. When Anaxibius returned with Xenophon from Byzantium into Asia, he received news at Cyzicum from Aristarchus, the new governor of Byzantium. Polus had been appointed admiral in Anaxibius' place and was to sail as far as the Hellespont. *[E170]* Therefore, Anaxibius sailed from there to Patros. He sent to Pharnabazus, requesting the money which he had promised him for shipping the Greeks from Asia. When he did not get it, he planned with Xenophon to carry the Greeks back again into Asia at once. Pharnabazus prevailed upon Aristarchus, the governor of Byzantium, so that he thwarted that plan. This forced Xenophon to hire himself out to Senthes, the king of Thrace. The winter was not over and the cold was so extreme, that many Greeks lost their noses and ears from frostbite. {*Xenophon, Anabasis, l. 7. 3:539-651*} Diodorus stated that some Greeks returned into their own country, but almost five thousand followed Xenophon into Thrace. {*Diod. Sic., l. 14. c. 37. s. 1. 6:115*} Hence, it appears that the number he gave was incorrect, when he said that only eighty-three hundred men came to Chrysopolis. {*Diod. Sic., l. 14. c. 31. s. 4. 6:101*}

## 3604c AM, 4314 JP, 400 BC

1466. The Ionian and other Greek cities throughout Asia did not accept Tissaphernes' government. They wanted their freedom and feared Tissaphernes, because they had always given Cyrus preference over him. They sent messengers to the Lacedemonians, asking them for help. Since they were the protectors of all Greece, they wanted them to take over, so that their country could be free from war and they could have their liberty, like other Greeks. {*Xenophon, Hellenica, l. 3. c. 1. s. 3. 1:177*} {*Diod. Sic., l. 14. c. 35. s. 6. 6:113*}

1467. This petition was very welcome to the Lacedemonians. Like most men, the more they had, the more they wanted. They were not content to have doubled their empire by taking over Athens. Now they wanted to control all of Asia, too! {*Justin, Trogus, l. 6. c. 1.*}

1468. Therefore, the Lacedemonians promised them aid in the first message they sent back. They immediately sent to Tissaphernes, to ask him not to make war on the Asian Greek cities. Out of contempt for them, he wasted all the region around the city of Cyme and took many prisoners. Then he came with his army and besieged the city, but because the winter was coming, he could not take it at that time. So he set a large ransom on the prisoners and abandoned his siege. {*Diod. Sic., l. 14. c. 35. s. 7. 6:113*}

1469. After this, Thibron went into Asia with an army of a thousand new citizens of the Lacedemonians, four thousand of the Peloponnesians and three hundred Athenian cavalry. The cavalry had formerly served the thirty tyrants of Athens. The city desired that this group should be spent in foreign services rather than be kept at home to do greater mischief. When Thibron came into Asia, he increased his army with troops from the confederate cities there. {*Xenophon, Hellenica, l. 3. c. 1. s. 4,5. 1:177*} At Ephesus, he added two thousand more troops from these cities, to make a total army of about seven thousand men. He marched about fifteen miles into the country and on his first assault took Magnesia, a city under Tissaphernes' government. *[L240]* From there he went to Tralles, a city of Ionia, and began to besiege it, but as its location was very strongly fortified, he left it and went back to the unwalled town of Magnesia. Because he feared that, as soon as he was gone, Tissaphernes would take it again, he moved it to a hill nearby, called Thorax, which was a more easily defended position. He plundered the enemy's country and greatly enriched his army. When he heard that Tissaphernes was coming down upon him with an army of cavalry, he retired to Ephesus. {*Diod. Sic., l. 14. c. 36. 6:113,115*} He was no match for the cavalry and did not dare stay in the plain, but thought it enough if he were able to keep the countries where he was from being plundered by the enemy.

1470. When the Greeks under Xenophon had served Senthes three months in Thrace, Charminus and Polynicus were sent by Thibron to tell them that he needed their help in Asia against Tissaphernes. He offered to pay each soldier a daric a month, while each captain of a company would be paid two darics, and every colonel four. Xenophon told them that he personally planned to return home. Most of the army came to him and earnestly asked him not to leave them until he had led them to Thibron. Therefore, he boarded a ship with them and sailed to Lampsacus. There he met and conferred with Euclides, the Phliasian poet. After they had passed through the territory of Troas, they came to Pergamum, where Xenophon was entertained by Hellas, the wife of Gongylus of Eretria, and her two sons, Gorgion and Gongylus. At her counsel, he went to capture Asidates the Persian. This he failed to do, while exposing himself and his men to great danger. Finally, by chance, his soldiers captured Asidates with his wife and children and cavalry and all that they owned, and they were very rich. Thibron came and received the army from Xenophon, adding these troops to the rest of the Greeks in his army and leading them against Tissaphernes and Pharnabazus. {*Xenophon, Anabasis, l. 7. 3:539-651*} *[E171]*

1471. This point marks the end of the seven books of the Anabasis of Xenophon. Their author, whoever he was, was present for all these events. He concluded his book with this epilogue: {*Xenophon, Anabasis, l. 7. c. 8. s. 24. 3:651}

"The governors of the king's territories that we traversed were as follows: Artimas of Lydia, Articamas of Phrygia, Mithridates of Lycaonia and Cappadocia, Syennesis of Cilicia, Dernes of Phoenicia and Arabia, Belesys of Syria and Assyria, Rhoparas of Babylon, Arbacas of Media, Tiribazus of the Phasians and Hesperites; then the Carduchians, Chalybians, Chaldeans, Macronians, Colchians, Mosynoecians, Coetians, and Tibarenians, who were independent; and then Corylas governor of Paphlagonia, Pharnabazus of the Bithynians, and Seuthes of the Thracians in Europe."

"The length of the entire journey, going and coming, was two hundred and fifteen stages. The whole expedition lasted fifteen months."

1472. A stage was about five parasangs, or about fifteen miles, apart and represented a days' march or journey. They travelled 1150 parasangs or 4282 miles (4313 miles, allowing 3.75 miles per parasang).

## 3604d AM, 4314 JP, 400 BC

1473. When Thibron was strengthened with these new troops, he dared to pitch his camp in the fields under Tissaphernes' nose. Pergamum voluntarily surrendered to him. Likewise also Teuthrania and Halisarnia, which at that time were commanded by Eurysthenes and Procles, the descendants of Demaratus of Lacedemon. *[L241]* Gorgion and Gongylus, the two brothers mentioned previously, had already joined him; one held Gambrium and Palegambrium, the other Myrina and Grynium. Thibron captured the remaining weaker places by force. {*Xenophon, Hellenica, l. 3. c. 1. s. 5,6. 1:177,179}

## 3605 AM, 4315 JP, 399 BC

1474. Thibron besieged Larisa, a town in Asia called Egyptian Larisa, when it would not surrender to him. While he was besieging it with little effect, the ephors at Sparta sent him letters stating that he should leave Larisa and march to Caria and on to Ephesus. Dercylidas, who was very resourceful and was surnamed Sisyphus for his wit, was on his way to take command of the army. When Thibron returned to Sparta, he was there accused by various confederate cities for having allowed his army to plunder them. For this reason, he was banished from the city. {*Xenophon, Hellenica, l. 3. c. 1. s. 7,8. 1:179,181} {*Diod. Sic., l. 14. c. 1-3. 6:119}

1475. Mania was a woman of Dardanus of manly courage. After the death of her husband Zenis, she had managed the government of Aeolia very well under Pharnabazus, and had taken over various coastal towns, like Larisa, Hamaxitus and Colonae. She was very treacherously murdered by her son-in-law Meidias when she was about forty years old. Her seventeen-year-old son was murdered with her. Meidias seized the two strong towns, Scepsis and Gergis, where she had stored most of her treasure. The garrisons in the rest of the towns remained loyal to Pharnabazus. Meidias sent messengers to Pharnabazus with great presents, hoping to manage all the government of those parts on the same terms that Mania had done, but this was futile. Pharnabazus answered that he would never be able to rest, if he did not avenge the murder of Mania. {*Xenophon, Hellenica, l. 3. c. 1. s. 10-15. 1:181-185} (Polyaenus calls her Tania, or Phania which is a misprint for Mania. {Polyaenus, Strategmata, l. 8.})

1476. Dercylidas saw that he had to deal with both Pharnabazus and Tissaphernes, two great commanders each supported by a large army. When he saw that they were at odds with one another, he made peace with Tissaphernes. {*Xenophon, Hellenica, l. 3. c. 1. s. 8. 1:181} (Justin called him Hercylidas, instead of Dercylidas. {Justin, Trogus, l. 6. c. 1.})

1477. After Dercylidas had first conferred with Tissaphernes, he marched to Aeolia without plundering the country. Aeolia was under Pharnabazus' government. He had an old grudge against Pharnabazus, for an insult he had received from him while he had been a commander at Abydus under Lysander. Larisa, Hamaxitus and Colonae surrendered to him without a fight. (Note that Diodorus wrote Arisba instead of Larisa. {*Diod. Sic., l. 14. c. 38. s. 3. 6:119}) Neandria and Illium also surrendered to him. Cocylium did not fight with him. Cebren, a very strong and fortified city, did not wish to be assaulted and also surrendered. Leaving a large garrison there, he immediately marched to Scepsis and Gergis with the rest of his army. Meidias feared both Pharnabazus and the inhabitants of that place itself. He went out with hostages to parley, seeking to join forces against a common enemy. Dercylidas laid hold of him and told him plainly that there was no hope of any friendship between them, unless he would set free all the citizens of those places which he held, to live according to their own laws. He marched into Scepsis with him and there offered a sacrifice to Athena. {Polyaenus, Stratagmata, l. 2.} He expelled Meidias' soldiers and persuaded the inhabitants to defend their newly acquired liberty. *[E172] [L242]* He next went to Gergis with his army. When Meidias requested that he at least leave him that city, he ignored his request. Meidias ordered the gates to be opened and Dercylidas entered the city. He found the money that Mania had kept there, which was sufficient to maintain an army of eight thousand men for almost a whole year. Dercylidas took the money and sent Meidias back to live as a private citizen at Scepsis. Xenophon stated that he took nine cities in eight days. Diodorus wrote that he used both tricks and force to take over all the cities and country of Troas. {*Xenophon, Hellenica, l. 3. c. 1. s. 9-28. 1:181-193} {*Xenophon, Hellenica, l. 3. c. 2. s. 1. 1:193} {*Diod. Sic., l. 14. c. 38. s. 3. 6:119}

1478. There was a quarrel between Artaxerxes and Evagoras, the king of Salamis on the isle of Cyprus, who had expelled from there Abdemon Thyrsus, the governor of the place and a good friend of Artaxerxes. Theopompus called him Abdymon Cityces. {Theopompus, Excerpts of Photius, n. 176.} This quarrel was settled through the mediation of Conon, the Athenian, who had lived with Evagoras, and Ctesias, the Cnidian, who had lived for a long time at the court in Persia. The condition was, that Evagoras would pay a certain tribute to Artaxerxes, and that a gift would also be sent to Satibarzanes. Ctesias also sent letters to Evagoras to make amends with Anaxagoras, a king of the Cypriots. Other similar letters were written by Evagoras and Conon. {Ctesias, History of Persia}

1479. When Dercylidas had gone so far into these parts, he sent to Pharnabazus enquiring whether he wanted war or peace. Pharnabazus was afraid of what might happen to Phrygia, where he lived, since Phrygia bordered Aeolia, which was now controlled by Dercylidas. Therefore Pharnabazus wanted a truce. {*Xenophon, Hellenica, l. 3. c. 2. s. 1. 1:195}

### 3606a AM, 4315 JP, 399 BC

1480. When this truce was concluded, Dercylidas marched into that part of Bithynia which the Thracians held, and there spent the winter. Pharnabazus liked this, because the Thracians of that country often made inroads on Phrygia, and Dercylidas now plundered that part of Bithynia at will, so that he had plenty of provisions for the winter. {*Xenophon, Hellenica, l. 3. c. 2. s. 2-5. 1:195,197}

### 3606b AM, 4316 JP, 398 BC

1481. About two hundred Odrysian cavalry and three hundred targeteers were sent from Senthes, the king of Thrace, to help Dercylidas. When they first arrived, they foraged Bithynia and were almost cut off there. After this, they stayed close to the Lacedemonian army and heavily plundered the territories of the Bithynians. {*Xenophon, Hellenica, l. 3. c. 2. s. 2-5. 1:195-197}

1482. When spring arrived, Dercylidas moved from Bithynia and came to Lampsacus. Three envoys from Sparta told him that his command had been extended for another year. The ephors of Sparta told the army there that previously the soldiers had been extremely injurious to their confederates, but now they were commended for their good behaviour. Dercylidas replied that it was the same soldiers who had followed Cyrus in his wars, but that they were now under new commanders and that this was the reason for the change in behaviour. At the conclusion of this incident, Dercylidas sent the envoys from Ephesus to travel through the Greek cities and countries in those parts, telling them how glad he was that they would find them all in so peaceable and prosperous a state. {*Xenophon, Hellenica, l. 3. c. 2. s. 6-9. 1:197,199}

### 3606c AM, 4316 JP, 398 BC

1483. When the envoys left, Dercylidas sent to Pharnabazus again, wanting to know whether he would extend the truce from the previous winter, or if he wanted war. Pharnabazus wanted to continue the truce. Therefore, Dercylidas crossed over the Hellespont with his army and came into the Chersonesus of Thrace, which contained eleven or twelve towns. The isthmus, which he spanned with a strong wall, was about eight and a half miles wide. This work started in the spring and was finished before the beginning of autumn. {*Xenophon, Hellenica, l. 3. c. 2. s. 10. 1:201} {*Diod. Sic., l. 14. c. 38. s. 7. 6:121} Contrary to his custom, Diodorus combined the events of two years in one passage. [L243]

1484. Conon, the Athenian, wrote letters to Artaxerxes from Cyprus, concerning his own affairs. He desired these to be presented to the king either by Zeno of Crete, a dancer, or by Polycritus the Mendean, a physician, or, in their absence, by Ctesias, who was likewise a physician. It is said that when this letter came into Ctesias' hands, he added a letter of his own. Conon was asking the king to send Ctesias to him, as a man important to the king's service in those parts, especially in matters pertaining to the sea. Ctesias himself recorded that the king had sent and employed him in that service of his own accord. Plutarch wrote about the letters of Conon to the king and to himself, and about the speech which he had made to the king to clarify the matter. He had inserted these into his own history. He also related that at that same time, when the Lacedemonians had sent envoys to the king, the king committed them to custody and kept them there. {*Plutarch, Artaxerxes, l. 1. c. 21. s. 2,3. 11:177} [E173]

1485. After Pharnabazus had made a truce with Dercylidas, he journeyed to the king and accused Tissaphernes before him. He said that Tissaphernes had not opposed the Lacedemonian army when it came into Asia, instead he supported them there at the king's expense. He told the king that it was a shame that the king's war was not being pursued to a conclusion. He argued that his enemies should not be bribed with money, but rather driven out with armies. He persuaded the king to supply a fleet and make Conon, the Athenian, the admiral. Also employing the advice of Evagoras, the king of Cyprus, Pharnabazus persuaded the king to give him five hundred talents for this purpose. The king commanded him to commit the charge of the Phoenician fleet to Conon, making him commander-in-chief over all his naval matters. {*Diod. Sic., l. 14. c. 39. s. 1. 6:121} {*Isocrates, Evagoras, l. 1. (55-57) 3:35} {*Isocrates, Philip, l. 1. (53,64) 1:285} {*Pausanias, Attica, l. 1. c. 29. s. 15. 1:163} {Justin, Trogus, l. 6. c. 1.}

1486. When Pharnabazus returned from the court, he made Conon admiral of the seas, making many generous promises on the king's behalf. Before Conon had been fully furnished with a fleet, he took the forty ships he had ready and sailed into Cilicia, where he prepared for war. {*Diod. Sic., l. 14. c. 39. s. 1-4. 6:121,123}

### 3606d AM, 4316 JP, 398 BC

1487. Ctesias was sent to the coast by Artaxerxes. He first went into Cnidos, his own country, and from there to Sparta. He stated this toward the end of his history, which, as Diodorus said, ended with the third year of this 95th Olympiad. {*Diod. Sic., l. 14. c. 46. s. 6. 6:143}

1488. Dercylidas returned from the Chersonesus into Asia. As he reviewed the cities, he found that the exiles from Chios had taken over Atarneus. They were using this as a base to make inroads on Ionia, and were living on the spoil they found. Although Atarneus was well fortified and contained much food, he besieged it for eight months. {*Xenophon, Hellenica, l. 3. c. 2. s. 11. 1:201,203}

### 3607 AM, 4317 JP, 397 BC

1489. When Atarneus surrendered, he put Dracon of Pellene in charge of it. He supplied the city with ample provisions, so that he could use it for a good supply base when he was travelling. He then left for Ephesus. {*Xenophon, Hellenica, l. 3. c. 2. s. 11. 1:201,203}

1490. When the envoys from Ionia came to Sparta, they expressed their belief that if Caria, where Tissaphernes resided, were invaded, Tissaphernes would quickly grant them permission to live according to their own laws. The ephors wrote to Dercylidas that he should march to Caria with his army. Pharax, their admiral, was to sail the fleet into those parts, as well. {*Xenophon, Hellenica, l. 3. c. 2. s. 12. 1:203}

1491. At this time, because Tissaphernes was the chief general, Pharnabazus went to him to let him know that

he was ready to join with him in making war on the Greeks. [L244] They therefore went to Caria together, to settle matters there. When they had put garrisons there, they returned to Ionia. Dercylidas heard that they had crossed the Meander River. He conferred with Pharax and convinced him of his suspicion that Tissaphernes and Pharnabazus might both attack Ionia, which now had no garrisons. Then Dercylidas also crossed over the Meander River. {*Xenophon, Hellenica, l. 3. c. 2. s. 13,14. 1:203,205}

1492. In the Persian army there were twenty thousand foot soldiers and ten thousand cavalry. Dercylidas' army had about seven thousand men. {*Diod. Sic., l. 14. c. 39. s. 4-6. 6:123} The soldiers from the Peloponnesus were prepared to fight, whereas the ones from Priene and Achillium, the isles and the other towns of Ionia were cowards. They abandoned their weapons in the grain which grew abundantly in the fields lying around the Meander River, and fled. However, Tissaphernes remembered how well the Greeks who had been in Cyrus' army had fought against himself, and considered that not all Greeks would be cowards. Therefore, he did not attack them, as Pharnabazus wanted to do. He sent to Dercylidas and asked to meet with him to talk. After an exchange of hostages, they met to discuss a peace treaty. Dercylidas demanded that the king should allow all the Greek cities their freedom. Tissaphernes and Pharnabazus demanded that the Lacedemonian forces should withdraw from the countries of the king's dominions, and their commanders from the cities. A truce was to continue, until Dercylidas could receive an answer from Sparta. Tissaphernes and Pharnabazus were likewise waiting for an answer from the king. So both armies withdrew, the Persians returned to Tralles in Caria, and Dercylidas to Leucophrys. {*Xenophon, Hellenica, l. 3. c. 2. s. 15-19. 1:207} {*Diod. Sic., l. 14. c. 39. s. 5-6. 6:123}

### 3608 AM, 4318 JP, 396 BC

1493. A certain man called Herodas, of Syracuse in Sicily, was at that time living with a ship captain in Phoenicia. He noticed that war ships were arriving daily, while others were being outfitted and still others were being constructed. [E174] A navy of three hundred ships was being prepared. Herodas boarded the first ship bound for Greece and went to Sparta. He told them that a large fleet was being made ready at Phoenicia, and that he did not know the purpose and destination of this fleet. The Lacedemonians were very troubled by this news. Agesilaus, one of their two kings, was asked by Lysander to go with an army into Asia against the Persians. He was to take with him thirty men of Sparta whom they would choose to manage that war. The first man they picked was Lysander, who hoped to use this occasion to restore throughout all the cities in Asia the

Decemviri which he had set up before. The ephors had later abolished these, and ordered every city to live according to their own laws. So Agesilaus took two thousand of the new citizens of Sparta and six thousand from their confederate cities, with provisions for six months. They sailed from Gerastus, a port in Euboea, with all the forces that he could gather, and came to Ephesus. He did this so quickly, that he landed there before Tissaphernes and Pharnabazus heard that he had even set out. Thereby, so it happened that he found them all unprepared for his arrival. {*Xenophon, Hellenica, l. 3. c. 4. s. 1-4. 1:225,227} {*Xenophon, Agesilaus, l. 1. c. 1. s. 7,8. 7:63,65} {*Plutarch, Agesilaus, l. 1. c. 6-9. 5:13-21} {Emilius Probus, Agesilaus} {*Pausanias, Laconia, l. 3. c. 9. s. 1-5. 2:51,53} Pausanias stated that he first landed at Sardis. {*Pausanias, Laconia, l. 3. c. 9. s. 5. 2:53} [L245]

1494. Agesilaus raised a further four thousand soldiers at Ephesus, giving him an army of ten thousand foot soldiers and four hundred, or (as the Latin translation has it) four thousand, cavalry. Along with this, there was a rabble of other men, as numerous as the army, who followed the camp for pillage. {*Diod. Sic., l. 14. c. 79. s. 1-3. 6:225}

1495. Tissaphernes sent to him to find out why he had come into Asia. He replied that he had come to restore freedom to the Greek cities. Tissaphernes asked him to wait for three months, so that he might send a message to the king, at the same time assuring him of a favourable reply from the king. Agesilaus sent Herippidas, Dercylidas and Megillus to him to secure an oath from him, in which he would swear that he meant no guile, but would do what he possibly could to procure the peace which he had promised. On behalf of Agesilaus, they in turn were to swear to Tissaphernes that they would keep the truce if Tissaphernes would keep his part of the bargain. Tissaphernes disregarded his oath and sent a request to the king to increase his army. Although Agesilaus knew full well what he intended to do, he nonetheless kept the truce himself. {*Xenophon, Hellenica, l. 3. c. 4. s. 5-7. 1:229} {*Plutarch, Agesilaus, l. 1. c. 9. s. 1,2. 5:21,23} {Emilius Probus, Agesilaus}

1496. While Agesilaus was staying at Ephesus, civil disorder broke out in the cities. Neither the democratic government which the Athenians had set up, nor the Decemvirate which Lysander had set up, was being obeyed. They all made representation to Lysander, who was well known among them, asking that he would obtain for them from Agesilaus what they desired. It was from then on that Lysander always had a large court of attendants and suitors about him, so that it now seemed that Lysander was king, and Agesilaus merely a private citizen. This was a thorn in Agesilaus' side, so he began to take the administration of matters out of Lysander's hands and to reduce his authority. Then he sent him on an errand into the Hellespont. When Lysander found that Spithridates, a Persian (Plutarch called him Mithridates), was under Pharnabazus, he desired to speak with him. After a conference, Lysander persuaded him to defect from Pharnabazus, with his children and such wealth as he had, and two hundred cavalry. Spithridates left everything he had safely at Cyzicum, and came with his son to Lysander. He escorted them to Agesilaus, who was glad to see him. Spithridates told Agesilaus exactly how things were with Pharnabazus. {*Xenophon, Hellenica, l. 3. c. 4. s. 7-10. 1:229-233} {*Plutarch, Agesilaus, l. 1. c. 11. s. 2. 5:29} {*Plutarch, Lysander, l. 1. c. 24. s. 1. 4:301}

1497. When Tissaphernes received more troops from the king, he became insolent and proclaimed war against Agesilaus, unless he would leave Asia. Agesilaus was pleased about this and ordered his men to prepare for war. He sent to the Ionians, Aeolians and those of the Hellespont to send to him at Ephesus all the troops they could spare. Tissaphernes thought that he would march into Caria, but Agesilaus took his army into Phrygia. In a surprise attack on the cities there, he obtained a vast sum of money and other provisions from them and so came, safely and without stopping, near to Dascylium. His cavalry scoured the country ahead of the army and when they met with the cavalry of Pharnabazus, they were routed. In that encounter they lost twelve men and two horses. When Agesilaus came to their rescue with his foot soldiers, the Persians on the other side retired, having only lost one man. {*Xenophon, Hellenica, l. 3. c. 4. s. 11-15. 1:233-237} {*Xenophon, Agesilaus, l. 1. c. 1. s. 11-16. 7:63-67} {*Plutarch, Agesilaus, l. 1. c. 10. s. 1-3. 5:25} {Emilius Probus, Agesilaus} [L246]

1498. Agesilaus spent most of that summer plundering Phrygia and the nearby countries, and enriching his army with plunder. Toward the autumn, he returned to Ephesus and spent the winter there. {*Diod. Sic., l. 14. c. 79. s. 3. 6:225,227} {Emilius Probus, Agesilaus} [E175]

## 3609 AM, 4319 JP, 395 BC

1499. Nephereus, or Nepherites, reigned in Egypt for six years. {*Manetho, 1:179}

1500. The Lacedemonians sent to Nephereus, requesting that he join with them against the Persians. Instead, he sent them a gift of tackle, one hundred war ships and five hundred thousand bushels of grain. {*Diod. Sic., l. 14. c. 79. s. 4. 6:227} Justin called him Hercinion, as did Orosius, who related the matter in this manner: {Justin, Trogus, l. 6. c. 2.} {Orosius, l. 3. c. 1.}

> "The Lacedemonian envoys asked for naval help from Hercinion. They received a hundred war ships and six hundred thousand bushels of grain."

1501. Pharax, the admiral of the Lacedemonian fleet, set sail from Rhodes with a hundred and twenty ships and came to Sasanda, a citadel in Caria about nineteen miles from Caunus. Sailing on from there, he attacked both the town of Caunus and Conon, the Athenian, who had forty ships there. When Artaphernes and Pharnabazus came with a large army to relieve Caunus, Pharax lifted his siege and returned to Rhodes with all his fleet, while Conon assembled eighty ships and sailed toward the Chersonesus. The Rhodians, however, kept out the Peloponnesian fleet and revolted from the Lacedemonian state, instead receiving Conon with all his fleet into their port and city. It so happened that the Egyptian fleet, knowing nothing of this change of affairs, boldly anchored off the island with all their cargo of grain, which was being sent to the Lacedemonians. Conon, with the help of the Rhodians, attacked them and brought all their men and cargo into the port, storing the grain there. {*Diod. Sic., l. 14. c. 79. s. 5-8. 6:227} The soldiers rebelled against Conon because the king's officers defrauded them of their pay. They demanded their pay all the more boldly because they had been used in so great a service, and had served under so great a commander as Conon. {Justin, Trogus, l. 6. c. 2.}

1502. Agesilaus knew that he was no match for the enemy in the plains without sufficient cavalry. He raised more troops, ordering throughout all the confederate cities that any of them who were rich and did not want to fight themselves, should each send him a horse and rider to take their place. When the spring was coming, he commanded all his army to assemble at Ephesus. He carefully trained both the cavalry and foot soldiers for war. During this preparation, he gave the city of Ephesus greater importance than it had had before, by making it the centre of the war effort. {*Xenophon, Hellenica, l. 3. c. 4. s. 15-19. 1:237,239} {*Xenophon, Agesilaus, l. 1. c. 1. s. 23,24. 7:71} {*Plutarch, Agesilaus, l. 1. c. 9. s. 3-5. 5:25} {Emilius Probus, Agesilaus}

1503. A whole year had elapsed since Agesilaus had come from Sparta. The thirty commissioners assigned to him returned to Sparta and Lysander, the head of the commissioners, returned with them. Thirty others were sent to replace them, of whom Herippidas was the leader. From these, Agesilaus chose Xenocles and one other to lead the cavalry. He chose Scythes to command the heavily armed foot soldiers made up of the new citizens of Sparta. Herippidas was to lead those who had served under Cyrus. Mygdon was put in charge of those who had been sent by the cities of Asia. [L247] Agesilaus let it be known that he would march into the strongest part of the enemy country, so that his own army would be mentally prepared for a fierce battle. Tissaphernes

thought that Agesilaus had done this to amuse Tissaphernes a second time and to keep him at home. Tissaphernes marched directly into Caria, commanding his cavalry to stay behind and hold the plain of Meander. However, Agesilaus did indeed do exactly what he had said, and his whole army attacked the country of Sardis. When he had marched for three days without seeing any sign of the enemy, he gathered from that area a large supply of all types of provisions for his army. On the fourth day they spotted the enemy cavalry. They found the Greeks scattered about and busy plundering the country. They attacked and killed most of them. When Agesilaus came to their rescue, he saw that the enemies' foot soldiers had not arrived. Since he was fully prepared, he attacked the enemy near the Pactolus River and won a great victory over the Persians. He captured their camp, finding riches amounting to more than seventy talents of money, and transported all their camels into Greece. At this time, Tissaphernes stayed at Sardis, which is the reason why he was accused by the Persians of being a deserter. {*Xenophon, Hellenica, l. 3. c. 4. s. 20-25. 1:239-243}

1504. That was what Xenophon wrote. However, Diodorus stated that Tissaphernes was present in the battle with ten thousand cavalry and fifty thousand foot soldiers. {*Diod. Sic., l. 14. c. 80. s. 1-5. 6:229,231} Agesilaus came down from the hill country of Sipylus and overran all the plain around Sardis. He pillaged the land and destroyed a garden of Tissaphernes, which was enclosed and planted with all sorts of trees and other things for pleasure, infinitely sumptuous and of most exquisite workmanship and beauty. [E176] Agesilaus turned away from there and sent Xenocles with fourteen hundred men to lie in ambush, midway between Sardis and Thybarnae, to intercept some Persians who were to pass that way. In this second battle with the Persians, he defeated them and killed over six thousand men. He took a large number of prisoners and captured their camp, which was full of wealth. After all this, Tissaphernes fled to Sardis and Agesilaus returned to the coast with his army. Pausanias wrote that Agesilaus fought with Tissaphernes in the plain country of Hermus and there defeated the cavalry and foot soldiers of the Persians. {*Pausanias, Laconia, l. 3. c. 9. s. 6. 2:55} This was the largest Persian army since the time when Xerxes had gone into Greece or when Darius had gone into Scythia. It is best to trust Xenophon's account, who was not only an instructor to Agesilaus (as Cicero affirmed {*Cicero, De Oratore, l. 3. c. 34. (139) 4:111}), but was very intimate and familiar with him. {Emilius Probus, Agesilaus} {*Diogenes Laertius, Xenophon, l. 2. c. 6. (51) 1:181} Moreover, he was with him throughout all this war in Asia and returned with him to Greece the following year.

*1505.* Conon, the admiral of the Persian fleet, had repeatedly sent letters to the king asking for pay for the navy. When this failed, he went to the king in person. Pharnabazus also encouraged him to accuse Tissaphernes of treason to the king. Therefore, Conon committed the charge of the navy in his absence to Hieronymus and Nicodemus (both Athenians). He sailed into Cilicia and from there went to Thapsacus in Syria, where he travelled on a barge down the Euphrates River to Babylon. There he talked with Tithraustes, the chiliarch, which was the highest office next to the king. Conon showed him who he was, and that he desired to speak with the king, but he could not be admitted into the presence of the king or speak with him without adoration, that is, without prostrating himself before the king.

*[L248]* Therefore he did his business with him by letters and messengers, and was successful in his quest. The king declared Tissaphernes to be a traitor, and ordered Conon to take charge of the war against the Lacedemonians and to pay the navy, using whomever he was pleased to choose for that office. He was highly rewarded for his service and was sent to sea with authority to order whatever shipping he needed from the Cypriots and Phoenicians. These ships would guard the sea before the next summer, and Pharnabazus was assigned to him as an assistant, as Conon had requested. {*Diod. Sic., l. 14. c. 80,81. 6:231,233} {Justin, Trogus, l. 6. c. 2.} {Emilius Probus, Conon}

*1506.* Concerning the Cypriots, it is to be noted that at the very time while courtesies and presents passed between Artaxerxes and them, the king intended to make war against them. It lasted ten years before it ended, eight of which he spent in making preparations for it. {*Diod. Sic., l. 15. c. 9. s. 2. 6:349} Diodorus gave this deception as the reason of that war and it seems that only six years were spent in preparation. At this point, Isocrates mentioned the many vain attempts made upon Evagoras by Artaxerxes. He stated: {*Isocrates, Panegyricus, l. 1. (141) 1:205,207}

"He made war on Evagoras, who was governor of one poor city in Cyprus, and one who had formerly served him and had become his vassal and lived on an island. He suffered a great loss at sea and had no more than three thousand targeteers to defend his state with. Yet, weak as he was, the king had not been able to to get him to submit to him, though he had now spent six whole years in a war against him."

*1507.* Parysatis, the queen mother, urged the king on against Tissaphernes. She hated him because of what he had done to her son Cyrus. The king committed the war to Tithraustes and gave him letters for the cities and commanders in those parts, ordering them all to do whatever Tithraustes required of them. {*Diod. Sic., l. 14. c. 80. s. 6-8. 6:231}

*1508.* When Tithraustes left, the king gave him two letters. In the one for Tissaphernes, he requested him to continue the war against the Lacedemonians. In the other, which he sent to Ariaeus, the commander of Larisa, he requested that he help Tithraustes in the murder of Tissaphernes. Tithraustes delivered the letters to Ariaeus immediately on his arrival at Colosse in Phrygia. When Ariaeus had read them, he sent for Tissaphernes, asking him to come to Colosse, stating that he wanted to consult with him about the king's matters, especially concerning the war against the Greeks. Whereupon Tissaphernes, suspecting nothing, left his army at Sardis and came quickly to Colosse with a troop of three hundred Arcadians and Milesians and stayed at the house of Ariaeus. When he went to take a bath, he laid aside his sword. Ariaeus and his servants seized him and putting him into a closed coach, sent him away as a prisoner to Tithraustes, who took him as far as Celaenae and there cut off his head to send to Artaxerxes. *[E177]* Artaxerxes ordered it to be carried to his mother, who was overjoyed to see it, as were all the Greek women whose husbands had followed Cyrus in his war, only to be killed afterward by Tissaphernes' treachery. {*Diod. Sic., l. 14. c. 80. s. 7,8. 6:231} {Polyaenus, Strategmata, l. 7.} {*Xenophon, Hellenica, l. 3. c. 4. s. 25. 1:243} {*Xenophon, Agesilaus, l. 1. c. 1. s. 35. 7:77} {*Plutarch, Artaxerxes, l. 1. c. 23. s. 1. 11:181} {*Plutarch, Agesilaus, l. 1. c. 10. s. 4. 5:27}

*1509.* Tithraustes sent messengers to Agesilaus to let him know that Tissaphernes, who had started this war, had been punished for it. *[L249]* He stated that now the king had a good reason to withdraw his army from Asia and to leave the cities there to use their own laws and pay the king their former tribute. Agesilaus told Tithraustes that he could not do this without the consent of his country. Finally, they came to this agreement, that he would withdraw with his army into Pharnabazus' country and would receive thirty talents to support them there until he received instructions from Sparta. {*Xenophon, Hellenica, l. 3. c. 4. s. 25,26. 1:243} However, Diodorus wrote that Tithraustes and Agesilaus, following a parley, made a truce for six months. {*Diod. Sic., l. 14. c. 80. s. 8. 6:231} {*Xenophon, Agesilaus, l. 1. c. 1. s. 35. 7:77} Plutarch added that when Tithraustes offered him a large sum of money if he would withdraw out of the king's territories, Agesilaus replied: {*Plutarch, Agesilaus, l. 1. c. 10. s. 4,5. 5:27} {*Xenophon, Agesilaus, l. 1. c. 1. c. 4. s. 6. 7:105}

"Tithraustes, it is more honourable with us that a general enrich his army, rather than himself, and take spoils from his enemies, rather than rewards."

1510. While Agesilaus marched toward Phrygia, which was under Pharnabazus' command, he received a scytale or encrypted letter from the ephors of Sparta. They said that he should take charge of the navy as well as of the army, appointing as admiral of the navy whomever he saw fit. Whereupon, in a short time, he raised a navy of a hundred and twenty ships from the public contributions of the cities and the generosity of private citizens who desired to reward him personally. As admiral he appointed Pisander, his wife's brother, who was certainly a man of honour and courage and desirous of praise, but unskilled in naval matters. {*Xenophon, Hellenica, l. 3. c. 4. s. 27-29. 1:245} {*Plutarch, Agesilaus, l. 1. c. 10. s. 5,6. 5:27} {*Pausanias, Laconia, l. 3. c. 9. s. 7. 2:55}

1511. Pisander went off to the navy and Agesilaus continued on his way into Phrygia. Tithraustes knew that Agesilaus had no intention of leaving Asia, but that he rather hoped to vanquish the king's forces right there. He sent Timocrates of Rhodes (as Plutarch also called him in his life of Artaxerxes, however, even though the name of Hermocrates has crept into his *Laconical Apophthegmes*) into Greece with gold to the value of fifty talents of silver, with which he bribed the chief cities to conspire together against the Lacedemonian party, in a common war on behalf of the Athenians. {*Xenophon, Hellenica, l. 3. c. 5. s. 1. 1:245,247} {*Plutarch, Artaxerxes, l. 1. c. 20. s. 3,4. 11:175} {*Pausanias, Laconia, l. 3. c. 9. s. 8. 2:55} {*Pausanias, Messenia, l. 3. c. 17. s. 5. 2:265}

## 3610a AM, 4319 JP, 395 BC

1512. About the beginning of autumn, Agesilaus entered into Phrygia, which was under Pharnabazus' government. He pillaged all that country and took over all its cities, either by force or voluntary surrender. He was persuaded by Spithridates to march into Paphlagonia and to cause them to revolt from the Persians. Cotys, its king, had previously been sent for by Artaxerxes, but had refused to go, and now he joined with Agesilaus. Spithridates persuaded Cotys to give a thousand cavalry and two thousand foot soldiers to assist him. Agesilaus rewarded Spithridates for this, by procuring Cotys' daughter for his wife. {*Xenophon, Hellenica, l. 4. c. 1. s. 1-4. 1:265} {*Xenophon, Agesilaus, l. 1. c. 1. s. 36. 7:79} {*Plutarch, Agesilaus, l. 1. c. 11. s. 1-4. 5:29}

1513. Agesilaus was always very willing to help his friends, as it appears from this quotation attributed to him: {*Plutarch, Agesilaus, l. 1. c. 13. s. 4. 5:37} {*Plutarch, Sayings of Spartans (209ef) 3:251,253}

> "If Nicias is not guilty, let him go; but if he is guilty, let him go for my sake; but let him go anyway."

1514. He marched from Paphlagonia to Dascylium where Pharnabazus' palace was. There were many towns full of provisions around there. [L250] Here he spent the winter and maintained his army. {*Xenophon, Hellenica, l. 4. c. 1. s. 15. 1:269}

## 3610b AM, 4320 JP, 394 BC

1515. When his soldiers were foraging, they were not as wary as they should have been of their enemy, because up until now they had never been bothered by them. As it happened, Pharnabazus attacked them with two scythe-bearing chariots and four hundred cavalry as they were pillaging the area. The Greeks saw him and rallied into a troop of seven hundred men. Pharnabazus put his two chariots at the front, followed them with his cavalry and ordered them to drive into the midst of them. When the chariots had broken in and disordered them, his cavalry attacked and killed a hundred of them. The rest fled back to Agesilaus, who was not far away with his foot soldiers. {*Xenophon, Hellenica, l. 4. c. 1. s. 16-19. 1:271} [E178]

1516. Three or four days later, Spithridates found that Pharnabazus was with his army in a spacious, unwalled town called Caue, about twenty miles from there. He told Herippidas, chief of the council of war, about this. Spithridates asked Agesilaus to give him two thousand heavily armed foot soldiers, two thousand targeteers and as many of the cavalry as would voluntarily go with him. Less than half of each of the three groups of soldiers went with him. However, he set out with those he had as soon as it grew dark. He came upon Pharnabazus at the first dawning of the day and killed the Mysians who happened to be on guard at the time. The whole army was terrified and fled. Spithridates entered their camp and took much booty, including Pharnabazus' pavilion with all his luxurious furniture and wealth. Pharnabazus feared the Greeks and like the Scythian nomads, moved his camp here and there, never staying long in any one place. His main concern was that the enemy would not know where to find him. Herippidas intercepted Spithridates, stripping him and his Paphlagonians of all their plunder. After this, they spent the whole of the following night packing and went to Ariaeus at Sardis. He had formerly revolted from the king and fought against him in battle. In this Asian expedition, Agesilaus was most troubled by this loss of Spithridates with his Paphlagonian troops and the loss of Spithridates' son, Megabates, than by anything else since Agesilaus was on fire with love for the boy, Megabates. {*Xenophon, Hellenica, l. 4. c. 1. s. 20-28. 1:273-275} {*Plutarch, Agesilaus, l. 1. c. 11. s. 3-7. 5:29}

1517. After this, Agesilaus and Pharnabazus came to a parley through the mediation of Apollophanes from

Cyzicum, who was a friend to both of them. They tried to come to an agreement. Pharnabazus (as Xenophon had it in his oration concerning Agesilaus) openly stated that, unless the king would make him absolute and sole commander of the army, he would revolt from him. If he could command all the forces, then he would fight the war against Agesilaus as long as he could. Agesilaus told him that he would promptly leave his territory and not trouble him, as long as he could find business elsewhere. As soon as Pharnabazus left, his son by his wife Parapita came running to Agesilaus and entered into a league of friendship with him. They gave each other gifts as tokens of their friendship. {*Xenophon, Hellenica, l. 4. c. 1. s. 29-41. 1:275-281} {*Xenophon, Agesilaus, l. 1. c. 3. s. 2-5. 7:101} {*Plutarch, Agesilaus, l. 1. c. 12,13. 5:33-37}

1518. When spring came, Agesilaus came into the plains of Thebes and set up camp near the temple of Diana of Astyra. There he gathered an exceedingly large store of wealth. He outfitted his troops to march into the upper countries. [L251] He had no doubt that the countries which he left behind him would defect from the Persians. {*Xenophon, Hellenica, l. 4. c. 1. s. 41. 1:281} His fame was very great in Persia after spending two years in that war. {*Plutarch, Agesilaus, l. 1. c. 14. s. 1. 5:37}

## 3610c AM, 4320 JP, 394 BC

1519. The Lacedemonians learned that the Persians were bribing the principal cities in Greece to unite and revolt against them. They sent Epicidas to Agesilaus, to recall him to defend his own country. Although Agesilaus was bothered by being taken from this great war, he wrote that he would obey their command. {*Plutarch, Agesilaus, l. 1. c. 15. s. 4. 5:41} He sent to the ephors the following letter, which Plutarch inserted among his writings: {*Plutarch, Sayings of Spartans (211c) 3:261,263}

> "Agesilaus to the ephors, greetings: we have subdued a great part of Asia, routed the barbarians and provided a great store of arms in Ionia. However, because you have set a certain day to return by, I will obey your command and peradventure be back before that day. For I am king not for myself, but for you and our confederates. For a king is truly a king when he is commanded by the laws, the ephors and the other magistrates of the city."

1520. It is also said that he told his friends in jest that the king had driven him from Asia with thirty thousand archers, by which he meant that Timocrates' agent had distributed thirty thousand golden coins, stamped with archers, among the leaders of every city, to incite a common war against the Lacedemonians. {*Plutarch, Sayings of Spartans (211b) 3:261} {*Plutarch, Artaxerxes, l. 1. c. 20. s. 4. 11:175} {*Plutarch, Agesilaus, l. 1. c. 15. s. 6. 5:43}

1521. When Agesilaus returned, he left Euxenus behind as commander-in-chief, with four thousand soldiers, to assist the Ionians if needed. In order to return with a good army, he promised large rewards and honours to those cities and commanders who would send him the best cavalry and foot soldiers. Hence he caused them all to vie with one another, to see who could supply the best troops for him. {*Xenophon, Hellenica, l. 4. c. 2. s. 5-8. 1:283,285} [E179]

1522. When Xenophon was about to return with Agesilaus into Boeotia to fight against the Thebans, he deposited half the gold which he had obtained on his expedition with Cyrus at Ephesus with Megabyzus, the treasurer of the temple of Diana. He knew that he might be killed by going with Agesilaus into battle. Therefore, Xenophon ordered the treasurer that if he survived the battle he wanted the gold back, otherwise all of it was to be consecrated to the goddess Diana. The rest of his gold he sent as offerings to Apollo at Delphi. As it happened, Xenophon was killed later at Coronaea. {*Xenophon, Anabasis, l. 5. c. 3. s. 4. 3:401} {*Diogenes Laertius, Xenophon, l. 2. c. 6. (51) 1:181} Agesilaus consecrated a tenth of all that he had obtained in his two years of war in Asia to Apollo at Delphi. This amounted to about a hundred talents. {*Xenophon, Hellenica, l. 4. c. 3. s. 21. 1:305} {*Plutarch, Agesilaus, l. 1. c. 21. s. 3. 5:51}

1523. When Agesilaus had crossed the sea at the Hellespont, he received news of the Lacedemonian victory near Corinth. Thereupon, he sent back Dercylidas into Asia to inform the Ionians. [L252] This was to encourage them and strengthen their loyalty to the Lacedemonian party. {*Xenophon, Hellenica, l. 4. c. 3. s. 1-3. 1:295} {*Plutarch, Agesilaus, l. 1. c. 16. s. 1. 5:43}

## 3610d AM, 4320 JP, 394 BC

1524. About this time the famous naval battle happened at Cnidos, near Mount Dorium. {*Pausanias, Elis II, l. 6. c. 3. s. 16. 3:23} Eubulus, or Eubulidus, was governor at Athens. He took office at the very beginning of the third year of the 96th Olympiad, according to Lysias, a very good author in his work concerning the acts of Aristophanes. {Lysias, Aristophanes}

1525. The commanders of the Persian fleet lay near to Loryma, in the Chersonesus, with more than ninety ships. Pharnabazus commanded the Phoenicians, while Conon, the Athenian, commanded the Greek squadron. Pisander (for whom Diodorus incorrectly wrote Periarchus), the Lacedemonian admiral, sailed from Cnidos with eighty ships and came to a place called Physcus, in the Chersonesus. After he left there, he came upon a part of the king's fleet and won the first battle with them. When the rest of the king's fleet came to their rescue, the friends of the Lacedemonians fled ashore in a cowardly manner. Pisander with his ship attacked the thickest part of the enemy and killed many of them, but died heroically in the battle. Conon and his men fiercely pursued the Lacedemonians to land, taking no fewer than fifty of their ships. The rest fled and returned safely to Cnidos. {*Xenophon, Hellenica, l. 4. c. 3. s. 10-12. 1:297,299} {*Diod. Sic., l. 14. c. 83. s. 4-7. 6:241} {Justin, Trogus, l. 6. c. 3.} {Emilius Probus, Conon}

1526. When Agesilaus was now ready to invade Boeotia, he received news of the defeat of the Lacedemonian fleet and of the death of Pisander, his wife's brother. At that very instant, the sun was eclipsed and looked like a half moon. {*Xenophon, Hellenica, l. 4. c. 3. s. 10. 1:297} {*Plutarch, Agesilaus, l. 1. c. 17. s. 2. 5:47} This happened on August 14, 394 BC or 4320 JP, as from the astronomical accounts.

1527. After this great victory at Cnidos, Pharnabazus and Conon expelled all the Lacedemonian governors and garrisons from all the islands and coastal towns. These were told that no citadels would be put in their towns and that from now on they were to live according to their own laws. {*Xenophon, Hellenica, l. 4. c. 8. s. 1-2. 1:353} First the people of Cos, then Nisyros, then those of Teos and subsequently Chios defected from the Lacedemonians, after which the people of Mitylene, those of Ephesus and the Erythreans also defected. Almost immediately, all the rest of the cities defected from the Lacedemonians. Some expelled the Lacedemonian garrisons and set up and maintained their own government, while others put themselves into Conon's hands. From that time on, the Lacedemonians lost the sovereignty of the seas. {*Diod. Sic., l. 14. c. 84. s. 3-4. 14:243}

1528. Dercylidas, an old enemy of Pharnabazus, was at Abydus at this time. He did not yield to Pharnabazus' commands as the others did, but made a grave and pithy speech to the inhabitants, urging them to remain loyal to the Lacedemonians. When other commanders were expelled from their cities, they came to Dercylidas and were warmly received. Those that did not come of their own accord, were invited to come. When a multitude of them arrived, Dercylidas went over to Sestus on the other side of the Hellespont and there wooed all who had been expelled from their commands on the European side. He encouraged them, as he had done to the others on the Asian side. He told them that in Asia itself, which had from the beginning belonged to the king, various places, such as the small town of Temnus, Aegae in Aeolia and other places, were remaining loyal to the Lacedemonians and had not yielded to the king. {*Xenophon, Hellenica, l. 4. c. 8. s. 3-5. 1:353-357} [L253]

## 3611a AM, 4320 JP, 394 BC

1529. Pharnabazus planned to attack Ephesus and turned over forty ships to Conon, ordering him to meet him at Sestus. He himself sent threatening letters to both places, telling them that unless they expelled the Lacedemonians he would count them as his enemies. [E180] When they refused, he commanded Conon to blockade them by sea. Pharnabazus went and wasted all the country around Abydus. When they still refused to yield to him, he left and went home. He ordered Conon to deal with the cities bordering on the Hellespont. By next spring, he was to assemble the largest fleet that they could possibly make, so the winter was spent making this fleet. {*Xenophon, Hellenica, l. 4. c. 8. s. 6. 1:357}

## 3611b AM, 4321 JP, 393 BC

1530. At the beginning of spring, Pharnabazus assembled a mighty fleet and hired any ship he could. Pharnabazus took Conon with him and went through the middle of the islands of the Aegean Sea and came to Melos. From there he could easily land in Lacedemon, the country of the Spartans.

## 3611c AM, 4321 JP, 393 BC

1531. After he had wasted the country, Pharnabazus planned to return into Asia. Before he went, Conon prevailed on him to leave the navy with him. He intended to take it to Athens, to repair the long walls and fortify the port of Piraeus, saying that this would greatly trouble the Lacedemonians. Pharnabazus approved of this plan and gave him money to do that work. Conon came to Athens with eighty ships and started to repair the walls of both the city and the port. He gave fifty talents, which he had received from Pharnabazus, to his fellow citizens. {*Xenophon, Hellenica, l. 4. c. 8. s. 6-10. 1:357-361} {*Diod. Sic., l. 14. c. 84,85. 6:243,245} {*Plutarch, Agesilaus, l. 1. c. 23. s. 1. 5:63} {*Plutarch, Sayings of Spartans (213b) 3:273} {Justin, Trogus, l. 6. c. 5.} {Emilius Probus, Conon}

## 3611d AM, 4321 JP, 393 BC

1532. When the Lacedemonians heard that the Athenians were rebuilding their walls, they sent Antalcidas to Tiribazus, another chief commander of the king, who lived at Sardis. He was to try and make Tiribazus their friend and to mediate a peace between him and them. The Athenians also sent Conon and various others to him, as did the Boeotians, the Corinthians and those of Argos. When they all came before Tiribazus, Antalcidas told him that he had come to sue for a peace between the king and his countrymen, as the king desired. To that end, the Lacedemonians would not fight with him for the Greek cities in Asia, but would be content if all the islands and other countries outside Asia could be free and live according to their own laws. When all the other messengers disavowed that motion, the meeting broke up and every man returned home again. Although Tiribazus saw that it was not safe for him to make a league with the Lacedemonians without the king's consent, he nevertheless secretly furnished Antalcidas with money to build up their navy again. He did this, so that the Athenians and their confederates might be the more agreeable to a peace with the king. He imprisoned Conon at Sardis, charging him guilty of everything the Lacedemonians accused him of. They said Conon had only used the king's soldiers and money to get towns and cities for the Athenians, and to restore Ionia and Aeolia to them. After that, Tiribazus made a journey to the king to inform him of the treaty proposed by the Lacedemonians, and to tell the king what he had done to Conon, and why he had done it. He then wanted direction from the king as to what to do. {*Xenophon, Hellenica, l. 4. c. 8. s. 12-16. 1:361-365} {*Diod. Sic., l. 14. c. 85. s. 4. 6:247} {*Plutarch, Agesilaus, l. 1. c. 23. 5:63-66} {*Plutarch, Sayings of Spartans (213b) 3:273} {Emilius Probus, Conon}

1533. After Sarytus, the king of Cimmerian Bosphorus, died, his son Leucon reigned for forty years. {*Diod. Sic., l. 14. c. 93. s. 1. 6:259} [L254]

1534. Parysatis, the king's mother, had got her trusted servant to hide cuttings of palm trees in the heap of sand and dust that had buried the body of Clearchus. {See note on 3603c AM. <<1451>>} Now, after eight years, a beautiful grove of date-palm trees grew there, which shaded the entire place, as Ctesias reported in his *Persian History*. He added that when the king heard about this, he deeply regretted killing Clearchus, a man whom the gods themselves respected. {Ctesias, Excerpts of Photius} {*Plutarch, Artaxerxes, l. 1. c. 18. s. 5. 11:171}

1535. Some wrote that Conon was carried away prisoner to the king and executed. {*Isocrates, Panegyricus, l. 1. (154) 1:217,219} However, Dinon, a historian, and a man of great authority in Persian matters, said that he escaped from prison. Dinon did not know if this happened with or without Tiribazus' knowledge and consent. {Emilius Probus, Conon}

## 3612a AM, 4321 JP, 393 BC

1536. While Tiribazus was with the king, the king sent Struthas into lower Asia to take charge of naval affairs. The Lacedemonians knew that Struthas hated them, because of the many injuries which Alcibiades had inflicted on the Persians in those parts, and that Struthas favoured the Athenian party and their confederates. Therefore, they sent Thibron to attack him, so Thibron sailed to Ephesus. From there, and from other places on the Meander River, from Priene, Leucophrys and Achillium, he plundered the king's neighbouring countries. {*Xenophon, Hellenica, l. 4.

c. 8. s. 17. 1:365,365} He took over Ioada and also Coressus, a mountain five miles from Ephesus. [E181] He had eight thousand men whom he had brought with him, in addition to those whom he raised in Asia. From there, he often made incursions into and wasted all the provinces and nearby places that were under the king's control. {*Diod. Sic., l. 14. c. 99. s. 1. 6:273}

## 3612b AM, 4322 JP, 392 BC

1537. After a while, Struthas, with a large company of cavalry, five thousand foot soldiers and almost twelve thousand targeteers, camped near the Lacedemonian army. When Struthas discovered that Thibron did not keep military order in sending his men out for service, he sent some cavalry into the plain country, intending that they would attack whomever they came across. When he saw Thibron sending out forces in small numbers, and not in military order, to relieve those that were being attacked, Struthas attacked them with the main body of his cavalry, all in good battle array. Thibron and his dear friend Thersander were killed in the first attack. Thersander was an excellent minstrel and a very good soldier. As a result, the rest of the Greeks fled, with the Persians chasing them. Some were killed, others were captured and only a few Greeks escaped to Cnidos and other Greek cities. {*Xenophon, Hellenica, l. 4. c. 8. s. 18,19. 1:367} {*Diod. Sic., l. 14. c. 99. s. 2,3. 6:273}

## 3613 AM, 4323 JP, 391 BC

1538. Ecdicus was sent by the Lacedemonians with eight ships to help the exiles from Rhodes. He came to Cnidos and found that the Rhodians were very strong on land and sea, and had a fleet twice the size of his. He therefore stayed at Cnidos without attacking them. {*Xenophon, Hellenica, l. 4. c. 8. s. 20,23. 1:369} {*Diod. Sic., l. 14. c. 97. s. 3,4. 6:267,269}

1539. In the same fleet, the Lacedemonians sent Diphridas with orders to land in Asia and to man all those cities which had given allegiance to Thibron. He was to assemble the troops remaining from Thibron's defeat, and any other soldiers he could get. He started the war anew against Struthas. It was his good fortune to capture Struthas' son-in-law, Tigranes, and Tigranes' wife, as they were going to Sardis. After extracting a large sum of money from him, which he used to pay his army, he let them go. {*Xenophon, Hellenica, l. 4. c. 8. s. 21-22. 1:369} [L255]

1540. Evagoras, the king of Salamis in Cyprus, ruled almost the entire island through the exploits of his son, Pnytagoras. {*Isocrates, Evagoras, l. 1. (62) 3:39} He took over the rest of the island, partly by force and partly by persuasive words. The inhabitants of Amathus, Solos and Citium sent to ask for help from Artaxerxes. They charged Evagoras with the killing of Agyris, who, during his lifetime, had been a confederate of the Persians, and had undertaken to help the king get the whole island under his control. Artaxerxes wanted to check Evagoras, and wanted to control Cyprus for the purpose of using it as a base to defend Asia. He ordered an attack against Evagoras and sent away the envoys. He ordered all his coastal towns in Asia to start building and outfitting all the ships they could. Artaxerxes went through the cities of upper Asia and raised a large army. {*Diod. Sic., l. 14. c. 98. 6:269,271} He made Antophradates, the governor of Lydia, general of the army and Hercatomnus, the governor of Caria, admiral of the naval forces. {Theopompus, Excerpts of Photius, n. 176} Instead of making war against Evagoras, Hercatomnus secretly gave him money to hire mercenaries. {*Diod. Sic., l. 15. c. 2. 6:331}

### 3614c AM, 4324 JP, 390 BC

1541. When the Lacedemonians saw that Ecdicus did not have enough forces to help their friends, they recalled Telentias from the bay of Corinth and sent him with twelve ships to replace Ecdicus. Telentias was to support, as best he could, the Rhodians who favoured the Lacedemonian party, and to repress their enemies. When Telentias came to Samos, he added more ships to his fleet. From there he sailed to Cnidos and left Ecdicus. He set sail for Rhodes with a fleet of twenty-seven well-furnished ships. {*Xenophon, Hellenica, l. 4. c. 8. s. 23. 1:369,371} {*Diod. Sic., l. 14. c. 97. s. 4. 6:267,269}

1542. As he was on his way to Rhodes, he came upon Philocrates, who was sailing from Athens to Cyprus with ten ships, to help king Evagoras. Telentias took these and carried their spoil to Cnidos, where he sold it. So it happened that those who were themselves enemies of the king of Persia, plundered those who were going to make war against that king. {*Xenophon, Hellenica, l. 4. c. 8. s. 24. 1:371}

### 3614d AM, 4324 JP, 390 BC

1543. The Athenians saw that the Lacedemonians were recovering their naval power. They sent Thrasybulus with a fleet of forty ships against them. First he sailed into Ionia and gathered money from the Athenian confederates. He found that all the cities in Asia welcomed him, because of that arrangement which was between the king and them. Therefore, he set sail for Byzantium and farmed out to tax collectors the collection of the ten percent duty on all ships that passed through that strait. Having made a league of friendship with the Chalcedonians, he returned from the Hellespont. {*Xenophon, Hellenica, l. 4. c. 8. s. 25-27. 1:371,373} {*Diod. Sic., l. 14. c. 94. s. 2. 6:261}

1544. After this, he returned into Asia with his fleet and sent for the required tribute from the people of Aspendus, which they duly paid. He anchored his fleet at the mouth of the Eurymedon River. [E182] However, when some of his company went up into the country and plundered their goods, the men of Aspendus were furious and waited for a chance to strike back. When it came, they attacked and killed many of them, including Thrasybulus, while he was sleeping in his tent. This act terrified the Athenian captains, and they quickly boarded their ships and sailed to Rhodes. [L256] The Athenians at once sent Argyrius to replace Thrasybulus. {*Xenophon, Hellenica, l. 4. c. 8. s. 30,31. 1:375,377} {*Diod. Sic., l. 14. c. 99. s. 3,4. 6:273}

### 3615 AM, 4325 JP, 389 BC

1544a. Acoris reigned in Egypt for thirteen years. Evagoras made a league with the people of Barce. {*Manetho, 1:179} This was the beginning of the hostilities between Evagoras and the Persians. {Theopompus, Excerpts of Photius} {*Diod. Sic., l. 14. c. 98. s. 1-4. 6:269,271}

1545. Although the Lacedemonians had little reason to find fault with Dercylidas' actions, they nevertheless sent Anaxibius to replace him in the government of Abydus. Anaxibius was in favour with the ephors and promised to do wonders if he were to be furnished with men and money. They therefore gave him three ships and money to hire a thousand mercenaries. When he came to Abydus, he raised the land forces with the money which he had brought. He caused various cities of Aeolia to defect from Pharnabazus, and wasted the enemies' country. When he had acquired another three ships, he troubled the Athenians who sailed along that coast. If he happened to find any of their ships straggling away from the rest, he captured them and brought them to Abydus. {*Xenophon, Hellenica, l. 4. c. 8. s. 32,33. 1:377}

1546. When the Athenians heard of this, they sent Iphicrates, who had recently returned from Corinth, with eight ships and twelve hundred targeteers, to maintain what Thrasybulus had acquired. He sailed into those parts against Anaxibius. When he came into the Chersonesus, both he and Anaxibius established a company of pirates and land robbers, to carry on the war for them. {*Xenophon, Hellenica, l. 4. c. 8. s. 34,35. 1:377,379}

### 3616 AM, 4326 JP, 388 BC

1547. Anaxibius went to Antandros with his mercenaries, his own countrymen and two hundred heavily armed foot soldiers from Abydus. There he was very kindly welcomed and entertained. Meanwhile, Iphicrates placed ambushes for him in the mountain passages, before Anaxibius could return from there to Abydus. The vessels which had carried Iphicrates over at night, were now ordered by Iphicrates to row up the Hellespont, so that the men might think that he was on board and that he was going, as his custom was, to collect money. The men of Abydus, who were leading the troops, came into the plain which lay near a place called Cremastes (where there were gold mines), and the rest were coming down the steep hill, with Anaxibius and his Laconian troops following them, when Iphicrates, with all his men, rose from their ambush and attacked them. Anaxibius, thus entrapped, fought courageously but died, along with twelve other Lacedemonian governors of various cities. The rest fled, and Iphicrates pursued them to the very gates of Abydus. Of these, two hundred died, in addition to fifty heavily armed foot soldiers from Abydus. Iphicrates returned into the Chersonesus. {*Xenophon, Hellenica, l. 4. c. 8. s. 35-39. 1:379,381}

1548. The Lacedemonians sent Hierax to replace Teleutias as admiral of the fleet, while Teleutias, who was dearly loved and admired by his troops, returned home. {*Xenophon, Hellenica, l. 5. c. 1. s. 3,4. 2:3,5}

## 3617 AM, 4327 JP, 387 BC

1549. Shortly after this, the Lacedemonians sent Antalcidas to replace Hierax, hoping to please Tiribazus. When Antalcidas came to Ephesus, he left Nicolochus there as vice-admiral. Antalcidas and Tiribazus went together to the king to finalise the peace which was then at that time being disturbed. {*Xenophon, Hellenica, l. 5. c. 1. s. 6. 2:5} {*Diod. Sic., l. 14. c. 110. s. 2,3. 6:297}

1550. Nicolochus sailed from Ephesus to assist Abydus, and on the way he landed at Tenedos. He wasted their country and extracted a sum of money from them, before going on with his journey to Abydus. [L257] Meanwhile the Athenian generals who were at Samothracia, Thasos and other places nearby, hurried to come to the relief of Tenedos. When they found that Nicolochus had safely arrived at Abydus with twenty-five ships, they left the Chersonesus with thirty-two ships and besieged him as he was staying at Abydus. {*Xenophon, Hellenica, l. 5. c. 1. s. 7. 2:5}

1551. Chabrias, with eight hundred targeteers and ten ships, was publicly sent by the Athenians to help Evagoras. He did not leave Cyprus until he had subdued the whole island for him. On account of this, the Athenians became famous in the world. {*Xenophon, Hellenica, l. 5. c. 1. s. 10-13. 2:9,11} {Emilius Probus, Chabrias} Lysias mentioned the mission sent from the Cypriots to the Athenians, asking for aid. {Lysias, Aristophanes}

1552. Artaxerxes detested the Lacedemonians, and always said (as Dinon stated) that they were the most impudent of any men alive. However, when he saw Antalcidas had danced away among the Persians the fair fame of Leonidas and Callicratidas, he fell hopelessly in love with him. When Artaxerxes sent to Antalcidas, proposing a *guest-friendship*, he declined,

saying a public friendship was enough and that there was no need for a private one.

1553. When Antalcidas was eating supper, Artaxerxes sent him a garland, made of roses and saffron, from off his own head. It was dipped in a most costly ointment, and he was to wear it for the king's sake. Antalcidas replied: {*Plutarch, Artaxerxes, l. 1. c. 22. s. 1,2. 11:179} {*Plutarch, Pelopidas, l. 1. c. 30. s. 4. 5:417} {Plutarch, Symposium, l. 7. c. 8.} {*Athenaeus, l. 2. (48e) 1:213} {*Aelian, Historical Miscellany, l. 14. c. 39. 1:481} [E183]

> "Sir, I take and thank you for this noble gift and favour, but the perfume of its ointment mars the natural scent and fragrance of the roses."

1554. Tiribazus, together with Antalcidas, returned from the king after having made a firm league and alliance, in case the Athenians and their confederates would not take part in that peace which he had negotiated. Pharnabazus, who was in upper Asia, went to the king and married the king's daughter. {*Xenophon, Hellenica, l. 5. c. 1. s. 25,30. 2:17,19}

1555. When Antalcidas returned, he heard that Iphicrates and Diotimus had besieged Nicolochus in Abydus with all their fleet. Antalcidas went there by land and set sail at night. He made out that he had been summoned to Chalcedon, but instead besieged the port of Percote. When four captains on the Athenian side heard that Antalcidas had sailed for Chalcedon, they planned to follow him on the trade route to Proconnesus. As soon as they had sailed by, Antalcidas sailed back to Abydus. By this stratagem, he placed twelve swift ships in an ambush and intercepted the eight ships which Thrasybulus, the Athenian, brought from Thrace to join the main Attic fleet. {*Xenophon, Hellenica, l. 5. c. 1. s. 25-27. 2:17,19} {Polyaenus, Strategmata, l. 2. in Antalcidas}

1556. Antalcidas received twenty ships from Syracuse and other parts of Italy which were brought to him by Polyxenus and others, while Pharnabazus sent ships from Ionia. He also received ships from Ariobarzanes, an old friend of his. With his fleet of eighty ships he was absolute master of the sea. In this way, he could force those ships which came from the Pontus and were bound for Athens to discharge their cargo in a port friendly to the Lacedemonian party. {*Xenophon, Hellenica, l. 5. c. 1. s. 26,28,29. 2:17,19}

1557. When Tiribazus had summoned all who would subscribe to the peace treaty of Artaxerxes to come, all the Greek cities sent their envoys. He showed them the document with the king's seals attached, and had it read to them: [L258]

> "The King Artaxerxes thinks it reasonable that the cities which are in Asia, as also the islands of

Clazomene and Cyprus, should be under his government. All other Greek cities, regardless of size, should be free and live according to their own laws. This excludes Lemnos, Imbros and Sciros, which are under the control of the Athenians. Against those who shall not receive this peace, I will wage war by land and by sea, with ships and with money, together with all those who agree to this peace."

1558. The envoys returned to their respective cities with the terms of the peace. Although they were grieved to see the Greek cities in Asia under subjection, they accepted the peace. {*Xenophon, Hellenica, l. 5. c. 1. s. 31,32. 2:21,23} {*Isocrates, Panegyricus, l. 1. (135-137) 1:205} {*Diod. Sic., l. 14. c. 110. s. 2,4. 6:299} {*Plutarch, Agesilaus, l. 1. c. 23. s. 2. 5:63} {*Plutarch, Artaxerxes, l. 1. c. 21. s. 5. 11:177} {*Plutarch, Sayings of Spartans (213d) 3:275,277} {Aristides, Leuctia, l. 1,4.} This peace was proclaimed nineteen years after the sea battle at Egos Potamos and sixteen years before the battle at Leuctra in Boeotia. {*Polybius, l. 1. c. 6. s. 1. 1:15}

1559. When this peace was made, Agesilaus (according to Xenophon {*Xenophon, Hellenica, l. 5. c. 1. s. 32. 2:23}) was very earnest to see that the terms were observed. The Lacedemonians appointed themselves defenders of the peace in Greece. Artaxerxes wrote a letter to Alcibiades, which he sent by a Persian together with Callias, a Lacedemonian. He offered Alcibiades both hospitality and friendship, which offer Alcibiades declined, telling the king's messenger to tell his master that: {*Plutarch, Sayings of Spartans (213d) 3:275,277}

> "He need not trouble himself to write letters to him. For if he continued a good friend to the Lacedemonians, they would be good friends. But if he did any ill to them, he should not think that any of his letters should win him his friendship."

1560. In those articles dealing with Antalcidas' peace, previously related from the account of Xenophon, who could not have been unaware of its terms, we find that not all the islands bordering on Asia, but only two, were given to the king. However, Plutarch thought otherwise. These islands were Clazomene (which, as I showed before, was then an island {See note on 3504 AM. <<1064>>} {See note on 3509 AM. <<1084>>}) and Cyprus. {*Plutarch, Artaxerxes, l. 1. c. 21. s. 5. 11:177} {*Xenophon, Hellenica, l. 5. c. 1. s. 31. 2:21} The nature of this peace now drew Chabrias away from Cyprus, even though he had already subdued it for Evagoras. Evagoras armed almost every man on the island and mustered a large army against Artaxerxes. When Artaxerxes had made peace with the Greeks, he ordered all his forces to prepare for the conquest of Cyprus. {*Diod. Sic., l. 14. c. 110. s. 5. 6:299}

## 3618 AM, 4328 JP, 386 BC

1561. Artaxerxes mustered three hundred thousand foot soldiers and prepared three hundred ships to attack Evagoras, the king of Cyprus. Orontes, the brother-in-law of the king, was the general of the army. The admiral of his fleet was Tiribazus. These two assumed their positions at Phocaea and Cyme. [E184] They first sailed to Cilicia and from there landed in Cyprus, where they waged a fierce war against Evagoras, who procured supplies from the Egyptians, Tyrians, Arabians and others who were enemies of the Persians. He had a fleet of ninety ships, of which twenty were from Tyre and the rest were his. He had six thousand foot soldiers and a large number of auxiliaries from other parts. Since he had plenty of money, his army grew exceedingly large. {*Diod. Sic., l. 15. c. 2. s. 1-4. 6:331}

1562. Evagoras encouraged a number of pirates he had at his command to attack the enemy cargo ships. Some they captured, others they sank, and the rest did not dare sail for fear of them. When the food ran out for the Persian army, some of the mercenaries killed their commanders and the whole army was in rebellion. [L259] Hence, the officers of the army and Gaus, the chief officer at sea, were barely able to settle them down. As a consequence, the whole navy sailed for Cilicia and brought food from there for the camp. Acoris, the king of Egypt, supplied Evagoras with all the grain, money and other provisions that he could wish for. {*Diod. Sic., l. 15. c. 3. s. 1-3. 6:333}

1563. Evagoras knew that his fleet was far too weak for the enemies. Therefore, he furnished sixty more of his own ships and had fifty more sent to him from King Acoris. His fleet now totalled two hundred ships. He defeated the Persians in the first encounter on land, and routed them again at sea, where he suddenly attacked their fleet as they were sailing to Citium, sinking some of them and capturing others which had become separated from the main body of the navy. When the admiral of the Persian navy and the rest of the commanders had had time to recover, they counter-attacked and the battle was fierce. At first Evagoras had the upper hand, but when Gaus attacked with all his forces and personally fought very courageously, Evagoras' men fled, with the loss of many of his ships. After the Persians had won, they assembled their land and naval forces at Citium. When they had been outfitted, they went to besiege Salamis, the chief city, by land and sea. {*Diod. Sic., l. 15. c. 3. s. 4-6. 6:333,335}

1564. Immediately after the battle, Tiribazus went into Cilicia to carry the news of the victory to Artaxerxes. Evagoras left Salamis to be defended by his son

Pnytagoras (Protagoras perhaps, of whom I formerly made mention from Isocrates {See note on 3613 AM. <<1540>>}), to whom he committed the charge of the whole island. Evagoras escaped by night with only ten ships and sailed to Egypt. As powerfully as he could, he persuaded Acoris to make war on the Persians. {*Diod. Sic., l. 15. c. 4. 6:335,337}

## 3619 AM, 4329 JP, 385 BC

1565. Evagoras returned to Cyprus, but with far less money than he had expected. When he found Salamis strongly besieged and himself abandoned by his confederates, he sent to Tiribazus to ask for peace. Tiribazus, who was commander-in-chief, replied that he would grant peace provided that he would surrender all of Cyprus, except Salamis, into the king's hand and pay the king's tribute. He would be required to submit to the authority of the king. As hard as these conditions were, Evagoras agreed to them, but stipulated that he should be subject to the king only as one king to another, not as a slave to his master, a proposition rejected by Tiribazus. {*Diod. Sic., l. 15. c. 8. s. 1-3. 6:345,347}

1566. Orontes, the other commander-in-chief, who envied the position of Tiribazus, secretly sent letters to his father-in-law, the king. Among other matters, he accused Tiribazus of planning a rebellion. He also claimed that Tiribazus had secretly made an alliance with the Lacedemonians and had used every means to win all the main captains and commanders of the army over to himself. The king believed these lies and ordered Orontes to seize Tiribazus and have him sent to him. {*Diod. Sic., l. 15. c. 8. s. 4,5. 6:347}

1567. Orontes feared Tiribazus but devised the following plan. There was a house which had a large vault in it. Over this vault he placed a bed and removed its bottom. He covered it over with tapestry and many costly covers. [L260] Then he asked Tiribazus to come to him, pretending that he wanted a conference about some urgent matters. When Tiribazus came in, he sat down on the bed and fell through into the vault. He was caught and sent bound in chains to the king. {Polyaenus, Strategmata, l. 7.}

1568. Orontes now commanded all the forces in Cyprus. He noted that Evagoras had taken fresh courage and was enduring the siege more stoutly than before. His own soldiers were discontented by Tiribazus' misfortune, so that when Orontes received no commands, he abandoned the siege. He granted Evagoras a peace on the terms which Evagoras had proposed to Tiribazus. These were, that he would pay a yearly tribute to the king, he would continue to be king of Salamis, and as a king he would be obedient in all things to the king of Persia. Hence this war in Cyprus ended, which had

lasted ten years, of which eight years were spent in preparations and only two years in the war. The king had spent fifty thousand talents on it. [E185] When all was said and done, Evagoras was in the same state in which he had been when the war had begun. {*Isocrates, Evagoras, l. 1. (64) 3:39} {*Diod. Sic., l. 15. c. 9. s. 1,2. 6:347,349}

1569. Gaus, vice-admiral of the navy and son-in-law to Tiribazus, was fearful of meeting the same fate as Tiribazus if he were considered to be aware of Tiribazus' plans, so he thought of defecting from the king. With wealth and soldiers enough, and having the loyalty of the chief captains of the navy, he confederated with Acoris, king of Egypt, and the Lacedemonians, to make war on Artaxerxes. {*Diod. Sic., l. 15. c. 9. s. 3-5. 6:349,351}

1570. Artaxerxes followed the example of Cambyses, {*Herodotus, l. 5. c. 25. 3:27} {*Valerius Maximus, l. 6. c. 3. ext. 3. 2:43} and had certain of his judges skinned alive and their skins hung over the judgment seats. He did this so that those who judged would know what covered their judgment seats, and might be the more careful to do justice to his people. {*Diod. Sic., l. 15. c. 10. 6:351}

## 3620 AM, 4330 JP, 384 BC

1571. Artaxerxes led an army of three hundred thousand men and ten thousand cavalry against the Cadusians, a people lying between the Black and the Caspian Sea. {*Diod. Sic., l. 15. c. 10. s. 1. 6:351} {*Plutarch, Artaxerxes, l. 1. c. 24. 11:185} In this war, many important men died on each side. On the king's side, one of these was Camislates, a Carian who was a brave and valiant man. The king had made him governor of that part of Cilicia which lay next to Cappadocia and was inhabited by the Leucosytians. In his honour, the king made his son Datames governor in his place, and Datames also did great exploits for the king in this war. {Emilius Probus, Datames}

1572. In this war, Artaxerxes' army was very short of supplies. So much so, that a man could hardly buy the head of an ass for sixty drachmas. Tiribazus, who was at that time living the life of a poor, neglected and contemptible soldier in the army, helped them out in the following manner. There were two kings of the Cadusians at the time, who kept their camps separated, so Tiribazus told Artaxerxes his plan. He went to one of the kings and secretly sent his son to the other. Each deceived the king and persuaded him that the other king had secretly sent to Artaxerxes to make a peace with him for himself and to leave the other out. Thereupon, each king sent envoys, the one with Tiribazus, the other with his son, to the king, and he made peace with them both. So the war was ended. {*Plutarch, Artaxerxes, l. 1. c. 24. s. 2-4. 11:185,187} [L261]

*1573.* After this, the king referred the case of Tiribazus to three honourable persons. He so clearly demonstrated his innocence, and showed that his services to the king had been so great, that they declared him innocent. After this, the king held him in very high esteem and heaped great honours on him. Orontes was condemned as a false accuser and thrust from the king's favour. He was considered an ignominious person after that. {*Diod. Sic., l. 15. c. 11. 6:353,355}

*1574.* While Gaus was in Cyprus, the Greeks who served under him there wrote letters against him and sent them to Ionia. To find out who they were, and what they had written, he did the following. He prepared a ship with sailors and had the captain say that he was sailing for Ionia. The ship stayed for a while, to get as many letters on board as possible, and at last set out, but soon turned back into a creek not far from the place from where it had set out. Orontes went there on foot, and all the letters aboard were given to him. After Gaus had read them and found out who had sent them, he had all the men responsible executed by torture. {Polyaenus, Strategmata, l. 7.} (*Alos* or *Glos* was incorrectly written for *Gaus.*)

## 3621 AM, 4331 JP, 383 BC

*1575.* After Gaus had provoked the Egyptians and Lacedemonians to war against the Persians, he was killed, but I do not know how, nor by whom. His plans came to naught. After his death, Tachos got an army together and built the town of Leuce, on a high hill that overlooked the sea. He also built a temple for Apollo, shortly after which he died. The Clazomenians and the men of Cyme disagreed over who owned this town, but the Clazomenians were quicker and took control of it, so all rebellions in Asia ceased. After the death of Gaus and Tachos, the Lacedemonians abandoned Asia and had nothing more to do with it. {*Diod. Sic., l. 15. c. 18,19. 6:369,371}

## 3622a AM, 4331 JP, 383 BC

*1576.* When Pharnostratus was governor of Athens, in the month of Posideion in the 366th year of Nabonassar's account, on the 26th day of the Egyptian month Thoth, at 5:30 a.m. on December 23, 383 BC, there was a small eclipse of the moon observed at Babylon. {Ptolemy, Great Syntaxis, l. 4. c. fin. from Hipparchus} [E186]

## 3622c AM, 4332 JP, 382 BC

*1577.* In the same man's time, in the month of Skirophorion and in the same year of Nabonassar, on the 24th day of the month of Phamenoth, at 6:30 p.m. on June 18, 382 BC, another lunar eclipse was observed at Babylon. {Ptolemy, Great Syntaxis, l. 4. c. fin., from Hipparchus}

## 3623a AM, 4332 JP, 382 BC

*1578.* When Evander was governor of Athens, in the month of Posideion, in the 367th year of Nabonassar's account, on the 16th day of the month of Thoth, at 9:30 pm on December 12, 382 BC, there was a third lunar eclipse observed at Babylon. This was a total eclipse. {Ptolemy, Great Syntaxis, l. 4. c. fin., from Hipparchus}

## 3627 AM, 4337 JP, 377 BC

*1579.* Acoris, king of Egypt, bore an old grudge against the king of Persia. He gathered a large army of foreigners, especially from Greece, and made Chabrias, the Athenian, general of the army. Chabrias assumed this charge in Egypt without any orders or consent from Athens, and made all the preparations he could for this war against the Persians. Artaxerxes made Pharnabazus general of his army for this war. [L262] When he had made many preparations for it, he sent messengers to Athens, there to accuse Chabrias for offering his service to the Egyptians, thereby causing the Athenians to lose Artaxerxes' favour. He wanted them to send Iphicrates, their general, to him. The Athenians, who were largely desirous of endearing the king to themselves, and Pharnabazus as their good friend, recalled Chabrias from Egypt and gave Iphicrates orders to go and help Pharnabazus. {*Diod. Sic., l. 15. c. 29. s. 1-4. 7:23,25}

*1580.* Iphicrates had the charge of twenty thousand mercenaries committed to him by Artaxerxes. By continual training and exercise, he made them expert in the art of military affairs. Later, among the Romans, a skilful soldier was commonly called a Fabian soldier, after Fabius, and just so, in Greece, a good soldier was called an Iphicratian soldier, after Iphicrates. {Emilius Probus, Iphicrates} Pharnabazus spent many years in preparing for this war. One time when Iphicrates observed Pharnabazus to be a man so voluble in his speech and yet so slow in his actions, he asked him the reason why. Pharnabazus replied that it was because he was master of his words, but the king was master of his actions. {*Diod. Sic., l. 15. c. 41. s. 1,2. 7:61}

*1581.* Hecatonus Mausolus was made a governor of Caria and ruled as such for twenty-four years. {*Diod. Sic., l. 16. c. 36. s. 2. 7:337} He married Artemisia, the older of his two sisters. {*Strabo, l. 14. c. 2. s. 17. 6:286}

## 3628 AM, 4338 JP, 376 BC

*1582.* After Acoris died, Psammuthis reigned for one year in Egypt. {*Manetho, 1:179}

## 3629 AM, 4339 JP, 375 BC

*1583.* After him came Nepherites, the last of the dynasty of the Mendesians, and he reigned for four months. Then arose the first of the dynasty of Sebennytus, called Nectanabis, who reigned twelve years. {*Manetho, 1:179}

1584. Artaxerxes was now ready to make war on Egypt. To get more aid from Greece, he sent his envoys there to encourage them to make a general peace among themselves. The terms were, that every city should from that time on live according to their own laws, and that they should have no garrisons within them. All the cities of Greece accepted this, with the exception of the Thebans. {*Diod. Sic., l. 15. c. 38. s. 1,2. 7:53}

## 3630 AM, 4340 JP, 374 BC

1585. When Artaxerxes' army was assembled at Acre in Syria, he had two hundred thousand troops under Pharnabazus and twenty thousand Greeks under Iphicrates. In the navy, excluding cargo ships, he had three hundred ships with three tiers of oars and two hundred ships of thirty oars apiece. The first type were called τριρεις in Greek, the other τειαχιτιουι. At the beginning of the summer, that is, at the onset of the spring, the Persian navy sailed for Egypt and came to the frontier town near Syria called Pelusium. They found it exceedingly well fortified by Nectanabis, so they put out to sea again and when they were out of sight, they steered for Mendesium, a city on one of the mouths of the Nile River. There the shore runs a long way out from the land. They landed three thousand men, and Pharnabazus and Iphicrates set out to surprise a citadel that stood on the very mouth of the river. When they arrived there, three thousand Egyptian cavalry and foot soldiers came to defend the place. There was a fierce skirmish between them, but finally the Egyptians were overwhelmed by the number of Persians that came thronging from the ships to help their troops. They were totally surrounded and were slaughtered. Many of them were taken captive, while the rest fled to a little town nearby. Iphicrates' men pursued them and together with them entered the gate pell-mell and captured the town. [L263] They razed it to the ground and carried away its inhabitants as prisoners. {*Diod. Sic., l. 15. c. 42. s. 3-5. 7:63-67}

1586. Iphicrates advised them to go at once by sea to assault Memphis, the main city of all Egypt. It had no garrison, and he thought they should attack it before the Egyptian forces came in to defend it. Pharnabazus did not agree. He would stay until his army arrived, so they could attack them with less danger. [E187] This delay gave the Egyptians enough time to get supplies into Memphis, from where they made various attacks on the small town which the Persians had seized, as mentioned previously. They skirmished frequently with them and slaughtered many of them. When that time of the year

came, the Nile flooded all the country round about and helped fortify Memphis. Therefore, considering it foolish to fight against nature, the Persian commanders withdrew from there for the present, and so all those extensive preparations came to naught. {*Diod. Sic., l. 15. c. 43. s. 1-4. 7:67,69}

1587. As soon as they returned to Asia, Iphicrates lost favour with Pharnabazus. Iphicrates, fearing that he might be thrown into prison, as had happened to Conon, sailed secretly to Athens by night. Pharnabazus sent for him, and charged that he was the reason why Egypt had not been conquered. The Athenians replied that they would punish him, if they saw fit. Shortly after this, the Athenians made him admiral of all their fleet. {*Diod. Sic., l. 15. c. 43. s. 5,6. 7:69}

1588. Nicocles, a eunuch in Cyprus, murdered Evagoras and made himself king of Salamis, according to Diodorus in this year's account. {*Diod. Sic., l. 15. c. 47. s. 8. 7:81} Evagoras was murdered by a eunuch, but Aristotle stated that his name was Thrasydaeus. {Aristotle, Politics, l. 5. c. 10.} We learned from Theopompus that Evagoras, with this eunuch's help, got to lie with the daughter of Nicocles. {Theopompus, Excerpts of Photius, n. 176.} (Nicocles was that tyrant of Cyprus who invited Isocrates to supper, and that was the cause of Evagoras' death, according to Plutarch.) Nicocles was Evagoras' own son, according to Isocrates who received twenty talents from Nicocles for the written oration which he sent to him. {*Plutarch, Isocrates, l. 1. (838a) 10:379} We still have his oration, addressed to Nicocles, concerning the functions of a king. Another oration, entitled *Nicocles*, concerned Nicocles' duties as a prince. A third oration, called *Evagoras*, was a funeral oration made for him. Nicocles in this very year solemnified his father's funeral in a costly and magnificently pompous manner. He held all types of games of music, dancing, wrestling, ship and cavalry battles for the funeral. Therefore, Isocrates wrote this work for him, in praise and commendation of his father. He hoped that this would serve both Nicocles and his sons, and their children after them, as an example of and exhortation to well-doing. {*Isocrates, Evagoras, l. 1. (77) 3:47}

> "Supposing, that this will serve both you and your children, and the other descendants of Evagoras, for utmost encouragement to your well-doing."

1589. Hence we may correct that error in Diodorus and say assuredly that Evagoras was murdered by Thrasydaeus, a eunuch, and that Evagoras' own son Nicocles succeeded him as king in the kingdom of Salamis. [L264]

### 3633 AM, 4343 JP, 371 BC

*1590.* When Alcisthenes was governor at Athens, the Greek cities resumed their infighting. Artaxerxes sent envoys who urged them to obey the peace treaty and live peacefully with each other. All the Greek cities except Thebes swore an oath to keep the peace. When this peace had been made and agreed to by the Athenians, the Lacedemonians and Artaxerxes, then Iphicrates was recalled with his fleet. {*Diod. Sic., l. 15. c. 50. s. 4. 7:91} {*Xenophon, Hellenica, l. 6. c. 3. s. 18. 2:161} {*Dionysius Halicarnassus, Lysias, l. 1. (12) 1:43}

*1591.* Plutarch stated that this peace was concluded and made among the Greeks at Lacedemon on the 14th day of the month of Skirophorion by Athenian reckoning, and in the last month of Alcisthenes' governorship at Athens, on Thursday, July 16, 371 BC, or 4343 JP. {*Plutarch, Agesilaus, l. 1. c. 28. s. 5. 5:79}

### 3634 AM, 4344 JP, 370 BC

*1592.* The Lacedemonians were badly defeated at Leuctra by Epaminondas of Thebes. They immediately sent Agesilaus to Egypt, and Antalcidas to Artaxerxes, to get money. Artaxerxes rejected Antalcidas' request with much scorn and indignation. When he returned, he starved himself to death because he had been so spitefully used by Artaxerxes, and he feared what the ephors would do to him. {*Plutarch, Artaxerxes, l. 1. c. 22. s. 3,4. 11:179}

### 3635 AM, 4345 JP, 369 BC

*1593.* Ariobarzanes, one of Artaxerxes' governors, sent Philiscus of Abydus to Greece to resolve matters between Thebes and their confederates and the Lacedemonians. Philiscus summoned them all to Delphi. Thebes was insistent that Messenia should not be under Lacedemonian jurisdiction. Philiscus was so offended by this, that he left two thousand of his best mercenaries to assist the Lacedemonians against Thebes, and himself returned to Asia. {*Xenophon, Hellenica, l. 7. c. 1. s. 27. 2:247} {*Diod. Sic., l. 15. c. 70. s. 2. 7:147}

### 3636 AM, 4346 JP, 368 BC

*1594.* When Thebes controlled Greece, they thought it good to send their envoys to the king of Persia. They called their confederates together for this purpose, on the pretext that Euthycles of Lacedemon was already with the king. *[E188]* They sent Pelopidas from Thebes to the king, along with Antiochus the athlete from Arcadia, Archidamus of Eleus, a town in Thrace, and another man from Argos. When the Athenians heard this, they sent their envoys, Timagoras and Leon, to the king. Among them all Pelopidas was esteemed as the most gracious in the king's eyes, followed closely by Timagoras. The others were all most honourably treated by the king. {*Xenophon, Hellenica, l. 7. c. 1. s. 33,34. 2:251,253}

*1595.* Ismenias from Thebes was joint commissioner with Pelopidas in this mission. When he was brought into the presence of the king by Tithraustes, the chiliarch, he was asked to prostrate himself before the king. He dropped his ring before him and at once fell to the ground to recover his ring. The king thought he had done this to honour him, and gave him whatever he asked. {*Plutarch, Artaxerxes, l. 1. c. 22. s. 4. 11:179,181} {*Aelian, Historical Miscellany, l. 1. c. 21. 1:43,45}

*1596.* At the same time, Timagoras the Athenian sent a confidential letter at the hand of Beburis, the secretary to the king. The king was so pleased with Timagoras, that he received ten thousand darics, and had a rich supper sent to him at his lodging. Whereupon, the king's brother Ostanes said to him:

> "Remember, Timagoras, this supper, for it is not sent to you for any lowly purpose."

*1597.* This sounded as though he was upbraiding Timagoras for some treasonous intent, rather than congratulating him for the gift sent to him. {*Plutarch, Artaxerxes, l. 1. c. 22. s. 5,6.11:181} It is also said that the king gave Timagoras eight cows because he was so sickly, and the cattle would give him milk on his journey home. The king also gave him a costly bed and furniture, along with some servants to make it, because the Greeks were not skilled in such matters. *[L265]* Moreover, the king had him carried all the way to the seaside in a litter, because of his weakness. The king gave those who carried him four talents for their work. {*Plutarch, Artaxerxes, l. 1. c. 22. s. 5,6. 11:181} {*Plutarch, Pelopidas, l. 1. c. 30. s. 5,6. 5:417,419} Athenaeus stated that, after his prostration before the king, Timagoras was treated with great honour by the king. He added only: {*Athenaeus, l. 2. (48e) 1:211,213}

> "that the king sent him some food from his own table."

*1598.* As for the costly bed and furniture, and the servants to make it (as if the Greeks did not know how to make a bed) that had been sent by Artaxerxes, Athenaeus said it was sent to Timagoras of Crete, or, as Phaenias the Peripatetic called him, Entimus from Gortyn in Crete.

*1599.* By his gracious behaviour toward the king, Pelopidas got letters from him stating that the king ordered that Messenia should be exempt from the Lacedemonian jurisdiction and that the Athenians were required to withdraw their ships. If they did not obey, the king would proclaim open war against both of them.

Then, if any city refused to follow him in this war, that city would be the first among the cities to be made an example of. When Leon spoke publicly that it was time for the Athenians to look for new friends instead of the king, Artaxerxes asked that if the Athenians did not like it, they should come and state the reasons why not. {*Xenophon, Hellenica, l. 7. c. 1. s. 36,37. 2:255}

1600. When the envoys came home, the Athenians took Timagoras and decapitated him for his prostration before the king. They were insulted that the grovelling flattery of one of their citizens should subject the whole honour of the Athenian state to the domineering power of the Persians. {*Valerius Maximus, l. 6. c. 3. ext. 2. 2:43} (In the text, Darius was written by mistake for Artaxerxes.) Others say that it was because of his dishonourable acceptance of the king's gifts. Plutarch gave more details in his writings. {*Plutarch, Artaxerxes, l. 1. c. 22. s. 6. 11:181} {*Plutarch, Pelopidas, l. 1. c. 30. s. 6. 5:419} Xenophon said that he was accused by his companion Leon of not lodging with him and Leon related all his communications with Pelopidas. This no doubt was the main cause for his execution. {*Xenophon, Hellenica, l. 7. c. 1. s. 38. 2:255}

1601. Thebes summoned all the cities of Greece to hear the king's letters read. They were publicly read by the Persian who had brought them, after he had first shown them the king's seal on the letters. The letters stated that all who would be friends to the king and to Thebes were required to take an oath to observe the contents of those letters. The envoys, and later their cities, refused to take that oath. Hence that mission to Artaxerxes and the sovereignty of Greece which had been negotiated by Pelopidas and Thebes, came to naught. {*Xenophon, Hellenica, l. 7. c. 1. s. 39,41. 2:257}

### 3638a AM, 4347 JP, 367 BC

1602. The twenty-second Jubilee.

### 3638d AM, 4348 JP, 366 BC

1603. Artaxerxes sent other envoys into Greece, requiring them to stop these wars and to make a peace among themselves. In the end, he prevailed with them. {*Diod. Sic., l. 15. c. 76. s. 3. 7:163}

1604. Eudoxus, the Cnidian, surnamed Endoxos, that is the famous, was in his prime at this time. He went to Egypt with Chrysippus, a physician, carrying with him letters of commendation from Agesilaus to Nectanabis, who commended him to the priests there. After Eudoxus had spent time with Iconuphi of Heliopolis (whom Clement of Alexandria called Konuphis {*Clement, Stromateis, l. 1. c. 15. 2:315}), Apis the bull came to lick his cloak. Whereupon the priests said that he would become very famous, but that it would not be long-lived.

{Phavorinus} [L266] When Eudoxus had stayed in Egypt for sixteen months, he shaved himself all over to his very eye brows and wrote the Octocris, as some say. {Ussher, Macedonian and Asiatic Year, l. 1. c. fin.} [E189] From there he is said to have travelled to Cyzicum and Propontis, and to have spread his philosophy in those parts, finally coming to Mausolus. {*Diogenes Laertius, Eudoxus, l. 8. c. 8. (87) 2:401,403} Others say that Eudoxus went with Plato to Egypt and that they both studied for thirteen years with the priests there. {*Strabo, l. 17. c. 1. s. 46. 8:123,125}

### 3639 AM, 4349 JP, 365 BC

1605. At Heraclea in Pontus, the common people wanted all debts to be cancelled and all lands shared equally among them. The nobility sent to Timothy, prince of Athens, and also to Epaminondas of Thebes, for help against them. When these refused, they recalled Clearchus home, whom they had formerly exiled, and begged his help in repressing the common people. (This is not the same Clearchus who died about thirty years earlier.) {Justin, Trogus, l. 16. c. 4.}

### 3640 AM, 4350 JP, 364 BC

1606. Clearchus used the dissension among the people as an occasion to become ruler of the city. He dealt secretly with Mithridates, king of Pontus, who was an enemy in Greece. Clearchus agreed with Mithridates that when he was called to Heraclea, he would betray the city into Mithridates' hands and control it after this as governor under Mithridates. When Clearchus had set a time to deliver the city into Mithridates' hand, Clearchus captured Mithridates and those who accompanied him as they came to take over the city. Clearchus threw them into prison and let them go only after having extorted a large sum of money from them. So instead of maintaining the rich men's cause against the people, he made himself a patron of the common people against them. He stirred up the common people against them and behaved cruelly toward the nobility. When the people had made him ruler, Clearchus cast sixty of the chief nobility (for the rest had fled) into prison. After first taking away their goods, he had them executed. {Justin, Trogus, l. 16. c. 4.} He followed the example of Dionysius, the tyrant of Syracuse, and he ruled the city for twelve years. {*Diod. Sic., l. 15. c. 81. s. 5. 7:179} {Photius, Bibliotheca, from Memnon the Historian of Heraclea, n. 224.}

### 3641 AM, 4351 JP, 363 BC

1607. Tachos, whom Polyaenus called Thamos, {Polyaenus, Strategmata, l. 7.} Aristotle called Taos {Aristotle, Oeconomics, l. 2.} and Julius Africanus, Teos, reigned in Egypt for two years. {*Manetho, 1:183}

1608. With this year, Xenophon concluded the seven books of his Greek history. Anaximenes of Lampsacus concluded the first part of his history. He started from the birth of the gods and creation of mankind and ended with the battle of Manthinea, in which Epaminondas was killed. The history was in twelve volumes, and recorded almost everything that happened among both the Greeks and the barbarians. {*Diod. Sic., l. 15. c. 89. 7:201} In the second part, he recorded all the deeds of Philip of Macedonia and his son, Alexander the Great. {*Pausanias, Elis II, l. 6. c. 18. s. 2. 3:107}

1609. After Mithridates, the king of Pontus, died, Ariobarzanes, the governor of Phrygia under Artaxerxes, seized the kingdom of Pontus and ruled it for twenty-six years. {*Diod. Sic., l. 15. c. 90. s. 3. 7:203} {*Diod. Sic., l. 16. c. 90. s. 2. 8:87}

1610. When Clearchus, the tyrant of Heraclea, found that the chief men of Heraclea, who had fled from there, were stirring up all the neighbouring cities and states against him, he freed all their slaves. He gave them their masters' wives and daughters in marriage, and threatened death to those that would not comply. By this he made those slaves more loyal to him and more hostile to their masters. [L267] Many women reckoned these forced marriages to be worse than death itself, so that many, before their wedding, murdered their future husbands and then killed themselves. Finally, the nobles had a battle with Clearchus. He won and took the nobles as prisoners, leading them in triumph through the city in the sight of all the people. Then he put some of them in irons, others on the rack, and still others he put to death. He spared no part of the city from seeing and experiencing his cruelty. {Justin, Trogus, l. 16. c. 5.}

## 3642 AM, 4352 JP, 362 BC

1611. The Lacedemonians became the enemies of Artaxerxes when, claiming to be their friend, he nonetheless ordered them to withdraw from Messenia and to make it a distinct member in the league of Greece. {*Xenophon, Agesilaus, l. 1. c. 2. s. 29. 7:97} {*Diod. Sic., l. 15. c. 90. s. 2. 7:203} Ariobarzanes, the governor of Phrygia, joined with the Lacedemonians. He had taken over the kingdom of Pontus after the death of Mithridates. {*Diod. Sic., l. 15. c. 90. s. 3. 7:203}

1612. Autophradates, the governor of Lydia, besieged Ariobarzanes in Assos, a city of Troas. However, he lifted his siege and fled in fear when Agesilaus, who was now an old man, came into Asia only to raise money for his country. Cotys, who was besieging Sestus and was under Ariobarzanes' command, lifted his siege also. [E190] Mausolus, who was besieging Assos and Sestus with a hundred ships, was persuaded to withdraw, and returned home with his fleet. Ariobarzanes, an ally of the Lacedemonians, furnished Agesilaus with money for his country and sent him on his away. {*Xenophon, Agesilaus, l. 1. c. 2. s. 26,27. 7:97} Polyaenus mentioned the siege of Ariobarzanes by Autophradates in Adramyttium. {Polyaenus, Strategmata, l. 7.}

1613. Mausolus called his friends together and told them that unless Artaxerxes was given an excessively large sum of money, he would take away from him the country which he held by inheritance from his father. In an instant, his friends brought to him a vast sum of money. {Polyaenus, Strategmata, l. 7.} {Aristotle, Oeconomics, l. 2.} When he had the money, he decided that he was not going to give it to Artaxerxes, but allied himself with those governors and captains who were rebelling against Artaxerxes. At this time all of Ionia, Lycia, Pisidia, Pamphylia and Cilicia were in rebellion against him. In addition, the Syrians, Phoenicians and almost everyone bordering on the Asiatic sea rebelled. Also, Tachos, king of Egypt, proclaimed open war against Artaxerxes and was busy everywhere building ships and raising forces for the war. Many of these came from all over Greece, and Tachos formed an alliance with the Lacedemonians. {*Diod. Sic., l. 15. c. 90. s. 3,4. 7:203,205}

1614. When all these rebellions happened at once against Artaxerxes, he lost half of his revenues. The remainder was not enough for the war, considering that he had to support a war against the king of Egypt, all the Greek cities, and the countries in Asia. Also, he had to war against the Lacedemonians and their confederates, namely the governors who held the coastal towns and regions in all Asia under their command. {*Diod. Sic., l. 15. c. 90. s. 4. 7:205}

1615. The king of Egypt sent for Agesilaus, promising to make him general of his army. {*Xenophon, Agesilaus, l. 1. c. 2. s. 28. 7:97} He was sent there by his country, and used the money from Tachos to hire mercenaries. He loaded his ships with a thousand heavily armed foot soldiers and took with him thirty Spartan commissioners for his war council. {*Plutarch, Agesilaus, l. 1. c. 36. s. 1-3. 5:101,103} {*Diod. Sic., l. 15. c. 92. s. 2. 7:211} When the news of his landing came to the courtiers in Egypt, they vied with each other to be the first to send him presents, but when they came to him, they scorned him. [L268] They saw no attendants about him, and only a decrepit and wearisome old man, lying alone on the beach, slovenly and of small stature. They loathed his sordid and insolent behaviour all the more, when they saw that he selected only some grain and veal from all the rich foods they had sent him and gave away the dainties, sweet-meats and precious perfumes to his soldiers. {*Plutarch, Agesilaus, l. 1. c. 36. s. 4-6. 5:103} {Emilius Probus, Agesilaus} The king of Egypt did not keep his promise and did not make him general of his army, {*Xenophon, Agesilaus, l. 1. c. 2. s. 30. 7:97} but derided him for the smallness of his stature and said that whoever spoke the old proverb was correct:

"The mountain was in travail-pains and Zeus was affrighted; but it brought forth—a mouse."

1616. When Agesilaus heard this, he said in a rage: {*Athenaeus, l. 14. (616d) 6:321} {*Plutarch, Agesilaus, l. 1. c. 36. s. 6. 5:103}

"I shall one day look to you like a lion."

1617. Chabrias, the Athenian, was not sent by public authority as Alcibiades was. Tachos persuaded Chabrias to serve him as a private citizen, as admiral of the fleet. {*Diod. Sic., l. 15. c. 92. s. 2,3. 7:211} {*Plutarch, Agesilaus, l. 1. c. 37. s. 1. 5:105} When Chabrias saw the king was short of money, he advised him to take what money he could from the rich and promise them that they would be paid from his yearly taxes. By this means, Tachos gathered an enormous sum of money without injuring anyone. {Polyaenus, Strategmata, l. 3.} Aristotle thought this was only one of many schemes he had for raising money at this time. {Aristotle, Oeconomics, l. 2.}

1618. Those who rebelled in Asia made Orontes, the governor of Mysia, their commander-in-chief. When he had received enough money to pay for twenty thousand mercenaries for one year, he captured those who had contributed the money and sent them as prisoners to Artaxerxes. He then betrayed various other cities, citadels and mercenaries to the king's officers, whom the king had sent into those parts. {*Diod. Sic., l. 15. c. 91. s. 1. 7:205} Polyaenus mentioned this war by Orontes and Autophradates and other officers of the kings. {Polyaenus, Strategmata, l. 7.} Diodorus stated that in the last year of Artaxerxes Mnemon both Autophradates and Orontes and other commanders defected from Artaxerxes. Therefore, we must conclude that Autophradates stood for his son Artaxerxes Ochus, and that it was Orontes who made the war against Autophradates.

1619. Artabazus, who commanded Artaxerxes Mnemon's army, attacked Cappadocia. Datames, the governor of that province, attacked Artabazus with a strong body of cavalry and twenty thousand mercenaries on foot. [E191] Then Mithrobarzanes, his father-in-law and general of his cavalry, stole away from him at night with all his cavalry and fled to Artabazus. Mithrobarzanes and his troops were well paid for this treachery, for it happened that they were attacked and hewn in pieces by the armies of both sides. Diodorus added that when Artaxerxes was told that Datames had brought him this news, Artaxerxes, envying his success, quickly tried to rid his hands of him. Shortly after this, Artaxerxes secretly had him killed. {*Diod. Sic., l. 15. c. 91. s. 2-7. 7:207} However, it appeared from Emilius Probus that Datames lived

long after this. He acknowledged that Datames' affairs were carried out in an obscure way, which is the reason why he said that he was most careful in determining what happened. This he did in such a way that he could easily discern that everything Datames did took place in the reign of Artaxerxes Ochus. {Polyaenus, Stratagmata, l. 7.}

1620. Rheomithras was sent to Egypt by the alliance of Persian governors. He received five hundred talents and fifty ships, and returned with them to Leucae in Asia. When he sent for many of the governors and leaders to come to him there, he seized them and sent them all away as prisoners to Artaxerxes. [L269] By this act, he re-ingratiated himself with the king who was previously displeased with him. {*Diod. Sic., l. 15. c. 92. s. 1. 7:209,211}

## 3643a AM, 4352 JP, 362 BC

1621. When Tachos was fully prepared for war, he put Agesilaus in command of the ten thousand Greek mercenaries. His fleet of two hundred ships was under Chabrias, who was very skilful in naval affairs. {Polyaenus, Strategmata, l. 7.} His eighty thousand Egyptian foot soldiers were under Nectanabis, his brother's or sister's son. (The Greek word is ambiguous.) Tachos was commander over all these forces. Although Agesilaus tried to persuade him to stay in Egypt himself and to carry on the war through his officers, he refused. {*Diod. Sic., l. 15. c. 92. s. 2,3. 7:211} But even so, against his better judgment, Agesilaus went with him by sea to Phoenicia. {*Plutarch, Agesilaus, l. 1. c. 37. 5:105}

1622. While the Egyptian fleet lay off Phoenicia, Nectanabis was sent to capture some principal cities of Syria. Nectanabis had made an agreement with the man whom Tachos had left as governor of Egypt, and now Nectanabis proclaimed himself king of Egypt. He bribed the army commanders with expensive gifts and promised the soldiers many things, so they would side with him against his father. {*Diod. Sic., l. 15. c. 92. s. 3-5. 7:213}

1623. Tachos was now utterly deserted by his own subjects and also by Agesilaus, whom he had formerly offended with that mean jest he had made about him. Fearing the worst, Tachos fled from there to Sidon in Phoenicia, and from there to the king of Persia. {*Xenophon, Agesilaus, l. 1. c. 2. s. 30. 7:99} {*Plutarch, Agesilaus, l. 1. c. 38. s. 1. 5:107} Theopompus, and Lyceas of Naucratis, in his affairs of Egypt, were both cited by Athenaeus. {*Athenaeus, l. 14. (616d) 6:321} Diodorus and Aelian stated further that he was very graciously entertained by Artaxerxes. I cannot believe Diodorus, when he says that Artaxerxes presently made him general of all the forces which he had at that time raised to make war on Egypt. Nor do I think that he returned with them to Egypt, and that he was there reinstated as king by Agesilaus.

Neither can we believe Aelian, when he states that Tachos had formerly lived frugally at home, and now he died by gorging himself with food, as was the Persian custom. {*Aelian, Historical Miscellany, l. 5. c. 1. 1:215} Lynceus, or Lyceas, whom I mentioned before, stated that his Egyptian diet was far more sumptuous than that of the Persians. {*Athenaeus, l. 4. (150b) 2:185}

1624. After this, another man made himself king in Mendes, with an army of a hundred thousand men, {*Plutarch, Agesilaus, l. 1. c. 38. 5:107} and so there were now two kings in Egypt. Agesilaus followed Nectanabis, who, he thought, most favoured the Lacedemonians. {*Xenophon, Agesilaus, l. 1. c. 2. s. 31. 7:99} He was with him in a citadel during a long siege, when Nectanabis grew impatient at being confined and wanted to risk a battle. Agesilaus let him go and remained in the citadel, until the whole citadel was almost surrounded with siege works and the enemy was all around them, except for a little place where there was still a passage through. Then Agesilaus sallied out into that narrow passage and made his way through with a great slaughter of the enemy. He had their siege works at his back, so that they could not surround him. {*Plutarch, Agesilaus, l. 1. c. 38,39. 5:107-111} {Polyaenus, Strategmata, l. 2.} {*Diod. Sic., l. 15. c. 92,93. 7:211-215} Diodorus wrote Tachos, instead of the king of Mendes.

### 3643b AM, 4353 JP, 361 BC

1625. Agesilaus defeated the other king, who hated the Greeks, and took him prisoner. He restored Nectanabis to his kingdom and made him a loyal friend of the Lacedemonians. {*Xenophon, Agesilaus, l. 1. c. 2. s. 31. 7:99} [L270] However, Emilius Probus attributed this restitution of the king to Chabrias. The reason for this was because it was done jointly by the Lacedemonians and Athenians. It was twelve years from this time until Nectanabis was expelled from the kingdom, according to Diodorus. {*Diod. Sic., l. 16. c. 51. s. 1. 7:381} Hence the length of his reign was twelve years, not eighteen, as Africanus and Eusebius claim. [E192]

1626. Nectanabis entreated Agesilaus very earnestly to spend that winter with him. However, he hastened home, since Sparta was engaged in a war and he knew they needed money and were maintaining a foreign army. Therefore, Nectanabis dismissed Agesilaus very honourably, giving him, besides all the other gifts, two hundred and thirty thousand, or, as Emilius Probus has it, two hundred and twenty thousand, talents. {*Plutarch, Agesilaus, l. 1. c. 50. 5:111,113} {Emilius Probus, Agesilaus}

1627. When Agesilaus got this money, he hurried home in the dead of winter. He feared that the Lacedemonians might spend the next summer idle and do nothing against their enemies. {*Xenophon, Agesilaus, l. 1. c. 2. s. 31. 7:99}

A storm cast him onto a deserted shore called *Menelai Portus*, that is, *Port of Menelaus*, lying between Cyrene and Egypt. There he fell sick and died. Lacking wax, his friends preserved him with honey and carried him to Sparta. {*Plutarch, Agesilaus, l. 1. c. 51. 5:113} {Emilius Probus, Agesilaus} Diodorus said that his body was buried there in a most royal manner. {*Diod. Sic., l. 15. c. 93. s. 6. 7:217}

### 3643c AM, 4353 JP, 361 BC

1628. Ochus, the lawful son of Artaxerxes, had his brother Arsames, who had been born to a concubine and was dearly loved by his father, murdered by Arpates, the son of Titibazus. When Artaxerxes heard what had happened to his much-beloved son, he took it to heart and died of grief. {*Plutarch, Artaxerxes, l. 1. c. 30. 11:201,203}

1629. Ochus knew that his father was highly respected by his people while he was alive. If the news of his death were to get out, Ochus would not be respected at all. Therefore, he had all the princes and nobles, and others that were around him, keep the death of his father secret for ten months. In the meantime, he sent letters into all the provinces in the king's name and with his seal on them, requiring that every man accept Ochus for their king. {Polyaenus, Strategmata, l. 7.}

1630. Heraclea, the wife of Clearchus, the tyrant of Pontus, bore him a son whom he called Dionysus. This son lived fifty-five years. {*Athenaeus, l. 12. (538f) 5:435} {Memnon, Excerpts of Photius, c. 5.}

### 3644 AM, 4354 JP, 360 BC

1631. When everyone had acknowledged Ochus as king, he announced the death of his father and commanded a public mourning to be made for him, according to the Persian custom. {Polyaenus, Strategmata, l. 7.} He assumed the name of his father, *Artaxerxes*. {*Diod. Sic., l. 15. c. 93. s. 1. 7:213} {*Valerius Maximus, l. 9. c. 2. ext. 7. 2:318} Then he filled his court with the blood of his kindred and nobles, without regard for kin, sex or age. {Justin, Trogus, l. 10. c. 3.} He caused his own sister, whose daughter he had married, to be buried alive with her heels upward. An uncle of his, with more than a hundred children and grandchildren, was brought into a court and there shot to death with arrows. {*Valerius Maximus, l. 9. c. 2. ext. 7. 2:318} It seems this uncle was the father of Sisigambis, who was the mother of Darius, the last king of the Persians. She was the queen of whom Curtius said that she had her father and eighty brothers executed by Ochus in one day. {*Curtius, l. 10. c. 5. s. 21-23. 2:521} [L271]

### 3646 AM, 4356 JP, 358 BC

1632. The states of Chios, Rhodes, Byzantium and Cos revolted from Athens at the same time. This was called the Social War, and lasted for three years. The Athenians, in besieging Chios, received help both from their own confederates and from Mausolus, the petty king of Caria. {*Demosthenes, Peace, Liberty of Rhodes*} {*\*Diod. Sic., l. 16. c. 7. s. 3. 7:257*}

### 3648 AM, 4358 JP, 356 BC

*1633.* In the first year of the 106th Olympiad (as it is rightly read in Eusebius' *Chronicles* from Fuxius' copy, corrected by Arnaldus Pontacus), Alexander was born to King Philip at Pella in Macedonia. Alexander was called *the Great* because he conquered all of Asia. He lived thirty-two years and eight months, according to Arian's report from Aristobulus. He died at the end of the first year of the 114th Olympiad, in the month before the month of Thargelion, according to the Attic calendar, as we shall see when we come to that year. It followed that he must have been born in this year, and that in the third month, called Boedromion on the Attic calendar. Hence those who, like Aelian, have said that he was born and died on the sixth day of the month of Thargelion are incorrect. {*\*Aelian, Historical Miscellany, l. 2. c. 25. 1:97*} Plutarch said that he was born on the sixth day of the month of Hekatombaion, called Loos by the Macedonians. {*\*Plutarch, Alexander, l. 1. c. 3. s. 3. 7:229*} There was a good reason why those who lived at that time recorded that he was born on the sixth day of the month of Loos. With the Macedonians at that time, the month of Loos was the same month as Meton's Boedromion. This appeared in King Philip's epistle to the Peloponnesians, as we have already shown in our work on the Macedonian and Asiatic years. The historians and other writers of later times did not note this, and found the Syro-Macedonian month of Loos in Calippus to coincide with the month of Boedromion among the Athenians. Hence, they thought that Alexander had been born on the sixth day of the month of Boedromion. {*Ussher, Macedonian and Asiatic Year, l. 1. c. 1.*}

*1634.* This was the source of Plutarch's error, which he corrected later, but in so doing, he ended up making a more grievous mistake. He said: {*\*Plutarch, Alexander, l. 1. c. 3. s. 4,5. 7:231*} [*E193*]

> "The same day that Philip took Potidaea, there he received three reports: one from Parmenion, that he had defeated the Illyrians, the second, that he had won the race with his horses at Olympus, and the third, that his son Alexander had been born."

*1635.* For we learn from Demosthenes and Diodorus, in their reports on the third year of the 105th Olympiad, that Potidaea was not taken in that year, but two years earlier. {*Demosthenes, Against Leptines*} {*\*Diod. Sic., l. 16. c. 8. s. 5. 7:261*} If it had been true that Alexander had been born in the 105th Olympiad and on the sixth day of the month of Hekatombaion, it is incredible that Philip should not

have heard of the birth of his son a great deal sooner than he could possibly have known of winning the race of Olympus. For that race was to be run on the day of the full moon, and the decision on the race made on the sixteenth day of the same month, according to Pindar. {*Scholiast. Pindar, Ode 5. Hymn of the Olympics*} Justin, from Trogus, stated more clearly: {*Justin, Trogus, l. 12. c. 16.*}

> "The same day on which Alexander was born, news came to Philip of two victories he had, the one about the battle in Illyria and the other in a race at Olympus, where he sent his chariot with four horses to run."

*1636.* These reports appear to agree with each other. Although I grant that it may be possible that Alexander's birth was in the summer season of that year in which the Olympic games were held at Olympus in Elis. However, the testimony of Aristobulus, to whom Alexander was personally so well known, is a very strong and convincing argument to me concerning the day on which he was born. So I have no doubt that Philip, his father, was informed of the race he had won at Olympus before his son was born. [*L272*]

*1637.* On the same day that Alexander was born, the temple of Diana at Ephesus burned down. Hence the jocular remark, either from Timaeus, as Cicero has it, or from Hegesias, the Magnesian, according to Plutarch, which said that: {*\*Cicero, De Natura Deorum, l. 2. c. 27. (69) 19:191*} {*\*Cicero, De Divinatione, l. 1. c. 23. 20:277*} {*\*Plutarch, Alexander, l. 1. c. 3. s. 3,4. 7:231*}

> "The temple of Diana burned down because Diana was away from home that night, bringing Alexander into the world, and could not save her own temple."

*1638.* When the one who had started the fire was put on the rack, he confessed that he had done it on purpose, because he wanted to be world-famous for destroying so famous and excellent a work. Hence, by the common council of all Asia, it was decreed that for ever after, no man should make mention of him. {*\*Valerius Maximus, l. 8. c. 14. ext. 5. 2:277,279*} {*\*Aulus Gellius, Attic Nights, l. 2. c. 6. s. 18. 1:141*} However, Theopompus mentioned him in his history, and so we know that the man responsible was either Erostratus, as we read Strabo and Solinus, {*\*Strabo, l. 14. c. 1. s. 22. 6:225*} {*Solinus, c. 40.*} or Lygdamis, as Hesychius wrote on the word *Lygdam.* {*Hesychius, Lexicon*}

*1639.* The priests in Ephesus at that time believed that the burning of this temple was merely the harbinger of some greater evil to follow. They ran up and down as though they were mad, cutting their faces and saying that some great calamity had that day been born against all Asia. {*\*Plutarch, Alexander, l. 1. c. 3. s. 4. 7:231*}

## 3648 AM, 4358 JP, 355 BC

*1640.* Artabazus rebelled against Ochus. He joined his forces with those of Chares, the Athenian, and defeated an army of seventy thousand Persians. Chares gathered enough spoil to pay for all his army. The king took up this matter with the Athenians. When they heard a rumour that the king was about to send three hundred ships to help their enemies, against whom Chares was fighting at the time, they quickly agreed to a peace with their enemies, so that the war between them and their confederates, called the Social War, came to an end. {*Diod. Sic., l. 16. c. 22. s. 1,2. 7:299} {*Diod. Sic., l. 16. c. 7. s. 3. 7:257}

## 3650 AM, 4360 JP, 354 BC

*1641.* Leucon, the king of Cimmerian Bosphorus, died after reigning for forty years. He was succeeded by his son Spartacus, who reigned for five years. {*Diod. Sic., l. 16. c. 31. s. 6. 7:325}

## 3651 AM, 4361 JP, 353 BC

*1642.* When Artabazus was abandoned by Chares and the Athenians, he resorted to the Thebans for help. They sent him five thousand men under Pammenes, who took this army over into Asia and joined with Artabazus' forces. Together, they overthrew the king's army in two great battles. {*Diod. Sic., l. 16. c. 34. s. 1,2. 7:331}

*1643.* In the twelfth year of his reign, while he was celebrating the feast of their god Bacchus, Clearchus, the tyrant of Heraclea in Pontus, was murdered. {*Diod. Sic., l. 16. c. 36. s. 3,4. 7:337} The man behind the murder was Chion of Heraclea, the son of Matris and a scholar of Plato's, a cousin of Clearchus. Also in on the plot were Leonides and Antitheus, both scholars in philosophy, as was Euxenon. Also involved were some fifty others of Clearchus' allies and relatives. They waited for the time when the tyrant was busy and attentive to the sacrifice with the rest of the people. Then Chion ran him through with his sword. He fell, grievously tormented with pains and haunted with the apparitions and ghosts of those whom he had most barbarously murdered, and died the next day. Most of the conspirators, if not all, were shortly thereafter cut in pieces by his guards, while nevertheless stoutly defending themselves. Those that escaped were captured soon after, and died after horrible torture, which they endured with incredible constancy and patience. {Memnon, Excerpts, c. 2.} {Justin, Trogus, l. 16. c. fin.} {Suidas, Clearchus} See also the letters attributed to this Chion, as written by him to his mother Matris. [E194] [L273]

*1644.* Satyrus, brother to Clearchus, succeeded him in that government and reigned seven years. Not content with the death of the conspirators, he executed all their children as well, although they were innocent of their fathers'

deeds. He was left as guardian and protector of Timothy and Dionysius, his dead brother's children and he showed them every respect. Although he had a wife whom he loved very dearly, he would nevertheless have no children by her, lest they might in time prove dangerous to his dead brother's children. {Memnon, Excerpts, c. 3.}

*1645.* In the fourth year of the 106th Olympiad (not in the second year of the 107th Olympiad, as incorrectly reported by Pliny {*Pliny, l. 36. c. 4. (30) 10:23}), Mausolus, the petty king of Caria, died. Artemisia, his sister and wife, succeeded him and reigned for two years, since her husband had no children. {*Diod. Sic., l. 16. c. 36. s. 2. 7:337} {*Strabo, l. 14. c. 2. s. 16. 6:283} Because of the fervent love she had for his memory, she took his bones after they were burned and beat them to a powder. This was mingled with a most precious perfume and put into her drinking water, as she was zealous to be the living and breathing tomb of her deceased husband. {*Aulus Gellius, Attic Nights, l. 10. c. 18. s. 3,4. 2:263} {*Valerius Maximus, l. 4. c. 6. ext. 1. 1:407,409}

## 3652 AM, 4362 JP, 352 BC

*1646.* In the 107th Olympiad (not in the 103rd, as in Suidas {Suidas, Theodectes}) Artemisia proclaimed a contest to which all could come and show their wit and art, in praise and honour of her dead husband. Various illustrious men came to this contest: Theopompus from Chios, the best man of all the scholars of Isocrates, {*Dionysius Halicarnassus, Pompey, l. 1. (1) 2:355} Theodectes, a poet of tragedies from the city of Phaselis in Lycia and also a scholar of Isocrates, and Naucrates Erythraeus from Naucratis in Cyrene. These were all mentioned by Photius. {Photius, Bibliotheca, c. 176,260.} Plutarch and other writers said that Isocrates entered the contest too. {*Plutarch, Isocrates, l. 1. (838b) 10:379} However, this was not the Isocrates from Athens, but another by the same name. He was his scholar and successor in his office, according to Suidas, citing Callisthenes, the orator. In that contest of wits, some say Theopompus won the prize, while others say it was won by Theodectes, the tragedian, who left a tragedy entitled *Mausolus*. {*Aulus Gellius, Attic Nights, l. 10. c. 18. s. 6. 2:263} {Suidas, Theodectes} {Suidas, Isocrates} Although it seems that everything did not turn out as Theopompus may have wished, because later, when he was writing a history, he stated in it that:

> "Mausolus never refrained from using any villainy if he might get money by it."

*1647.* In all likelihood, he would never have written this, if things there had happened according to his expectation. {Suidas, Mausolus}

*1648.* About Theopompus (of whom I have spoken before), who was a historian, and Theodectes, a tragedian,

I must mention what is reported by Demetrius of Phalerum with Aristeas (and who was then quoted by Josephus and Eusebius). {**Josephus, Antiq., l. 12. c. 2. s. 14. (112-113) 7:55,57*} {*Eusebius, Gospel, l. 8. c. 5. (354d) 1:384*} {*Aristeas, Septuagint Interpreters*} Theopompus wanted to insert some things from the books of Moses into his history, but lost his mind for thirty days. During this time, before his sanity returned, he earnestly sought God to reveal to him the reason why this great judgment was upon him. He was told, in a dream, that it was because he was about to mix those divine oracles with his human studies, and publish them to the world. When he abandoned that idea, he was restored to his right mind again. *[L274]* When Theodectes planned to use some things from the Holy Writ in the tragedy he was writing, he suddenly lost his sight. When he realised the reason for this, he asked God's mercy, and was restored to his perfect sight again. (Those who publish *Reference Bibles* and intermingle their own ideas with that of the Bible, should take note. Editor.)

## 3653 AM, 4363 JP, 351 BC

*1649.* Artemisia wanted to perpetuate the memory of her husband, Mausolus, and had a stupendous tomb, which was considered one of the seven wonders of the world, built for him at Halicarnassus. However, she pined away and finally died of grief before it was completed. {*Cicero, Tusculan Disputations, l. 3. c. 31. 18:315*} {*Strabo, l. 14. c. 2. s. 16. 6:283*} {*Aulus Gellius, Attic Nights, l. 10. c. 18. s. 4,5. 2:263*} To make this tomb as grand as possible, she had the most famous and skilful workmen in the world do the construction: Scopas from the east, Bryaxis from the north, Timothy from the south and Leochares from the west. Even though she died before the work was finished, they did not stop until the work was completed, knowing that by so doing they would also immortalise their own names and glory. {*Pliny, l. 36. c. 4. (30,32) 10:23,25*} {*Vitruvius, l. 7. c. 0. s. 12. 2:73*} Therefore, for ever after, even in Rome, every sumptuous and magnificent tomb was called a *Mausolea.* {*Pausanias, Arcadia, l. 8. c. 16. s. 4. 3:427*}

*1650.* After her death, her brother Idrieus, or Hidrieus, headed the government of Caria for seven years. {*Diod. Sic., l. 16. c. 45. s. 7. 7:365*} He was the second son of Hecatomnus and married Hecatomnus' younger daughter Ada, his own sister, according to the law of Caria. {*Strabo, l. 14. c. 2. s. 17. 6:285*} {*Arrian, Anabasis, l. 1. c. 23. s. 7. 1:97*}

*1651.* When Thebes was running out of money to carry on their war against the Phocaeans, they sent envoys to Ochus and received three hundred talents from him. {*Diod. Sic., l. 16. c. 40. s. 1,2. 7:347,349*}

*1652.* The Phoenicians, and especially the inhabitants of Sidon, had been badly mistreated by Ochus and revolted from him. *[E195]* They sent to Nectanabis, king of Egypt, and formed an alliance with him in a war against the Persians. They prepared a large fleet of ships and had many foot soldiers. They cut down the king's royal park, burned the fodder that had been provided for the king's stable, and killed those Persians who had wronged them. Therefore, the governors of Syria and Cilicia made war on them. Tennes, the king of Sidon, received four thousand Greek soldiers under the command of Mentor of Rhodes from the king of Egypt. These, combined with his own forces, routed the Persians and drove them right out of Phoenicia. {*Diod. Sic., l. 16. c. 41,42. 7:351,353*}

*1653.* The petty kings of the nine cities of Cyprus, who were subject to the king of Persia, followed the example of the Phoenicians and agreed with each other to defect from the king. Each of these kings prepared for war and made himself absolute sovereign in his own city. Artaxerxes Ochus ordered these kings to be subdued by Idrieus. He had recently become king of Caria and by the long tradition of his ancestors, was loyal to the kings of Persia and helped them in their wars. He sent forty ships to Cyprus, carrying eight thousand mercenaries under the command of Phocion, the Athenian, and of Evagoras, who had formerly been the king there. These began by attacking the strongest city first, and so besieged Salamis. Many joined the battle from Syria and Cilicia, which lay opposite Cyprus, hoping to get much spoil from the battle. So the army of Phocion and Evagoras doubled in size. {*Diod. Sic., l. 16. c. 42. s. 3-9. 7:353,355*}

*1654.* Artaxerxes Ochus mustered an army of three hundred thousand foot soldiers and thirty thousand cavalry, with three hundred ships and five hundred cargo ships to carry provisions. *[L275]* He left Babylon and went toward Phoenicia and the coast. {*Diod. Sic., l. 16. c. 40. s. 6. 7:351*} Tennes, the king of Sidon, was frightened at his coming. He sent a man called Thettalion to Artaxerxes, offering to betray all the Sidonians into his hands first, and then to help him conquer Egypt. When Thettalion had delivered his message and received the king's promise, he kissed his hand to seal the agreement. He returned to Mentor and told him of the king's promise, but the Sidonians knew nothing of this. (Loeb Greek text has Mentor but the English translation uses Tennes. Ussher followed the Greek text. Otherwise the opening sentence in section 1656 makes no sense. Editor.) {*Diod. Sic., l. 16. c. 43. 7:357,359*}

*1655.* Meanwhile, Ochus sent his envoys into Greece to request their help against the Egyptians. The Athenians and Lacedemonians replied that they would keep the peace made with him, but were unable to help him at this time. Thebes, however, sent him a thousand heavily armed foot soldiers under the command of Lacrates.

Argos also sent him three thousand men, with no Greek appointed over them, because the king wanted to have Nicostratus command them. He was a high-spirited man who imitated Hercules by fighting while wearing a lion's skin and carrying a club in his hand. The Greeks who lived along the sea coast of Asia sent him six thousand men. The total Greek forces were ten thousand men. Before they arrived, the king had advanced past Syria to Phoenicia and had pitched his camp not far from Sidon. {*Diod. Sic., l. 16. c. 44. s. 1-4. 7:359}

1656. Tennes, the king of Sidon, joined with Mentor in his treason and assigned him to the guard of a certain quarter in the town, leaving him to manage the betrayal on that side. Tennes, with five hundred men, went out of the city and pretended that he would go to the common meeting of Phoenicia. In his company he had a hundred of the principal councillors of the city. He betrayed them to Artaxerxes, who had them all killed, because they were the authors of that revolt from him. Shortly after, a further five hundred of the leading Sidonians came to Artaxerxes with olive branches in their hands, to beg for mercy. Artaxerxes had them all shot with arrows, as he had done to the previous group. He had been led by Tennes, the king, to understand that the city would be unconditionally surrendered to him. The Greeks, whom Tennes had bribed, opened the gates to let the king into the city and so betrayed the city to Artaxerxes, who, once he was in, saw that Tennes was of no further service to him and had his throat cut. {*Diod. Sic., l. 16. c. 45. s. 1-3. 7:361,363}

1657. The Sidonians had burned all their ships before King Artaxerxes came, so that no one could escape by ship. When the city was taken, each man shut himself up in his own house, with his wife and children, and then set his house on fire. Over forty thousand perished in the fire. Mixed with the cinders of the place was molten silver and gold, which the king sold for many talents. The rest of the cities in the area were terrified and surrendered to the king. {*Diod. Sic., l. 16. c. 45. s. 4-6. 7:363}

1658. From there, the king went and captured Jericho. {Solinus, c. 35.} [E196] He took many from Judah along with him, to serve him in his war against Egypt. This we gather from Aristeas, {Aristeas, Septuagint Interpreters} and also from the letter of Ptolemy Philadelphus to Eleasarus. It said:

"that many of the Jews were carried away into Egypt by the Persians, while they held sway there." [L276]

1659. This saying of his was to be connected to this time of Artaxerxes Ochus. The same thing was also stated by Justin in a certain place, if there was any truth in either statement: {Justin, Trogus, l. 36. c. 3.}

"that Xerxes was the first of the Persians that subdued the Jews"

## 3654 AM, 4364 JP, 350 BC

1660. While Salamis was being besieged by Phocion and Evagoras, all the rest of the cities submitted to the Persians. Only Pnytagoras, the king of Salamis, held out against them. Evagoras wanted to be restored to his father's kingdom in Salamis. Some men treated him poorly and made accusations against him to the king. Evagoras saw that the king favoured Pnytagoras over him and gave up his request to be restored to the kingdom. He went and cleared himself of all charges before the king. He did this so well that the king gave him a far better dynasty in Asia. At last Pnytagoras voluntarily submitted to the king, after which he retained the kingdom of Salamis in peace. {*Diod. Sic., l. 16. c. 46. s. 1-3. 7:365,367} Evagoras, of whom we now speak, seems to have been the grandchild, by his son Nicocles, of another Evagoras, who had died twenty-four years earlier. We maintain this because that Evagoras the elder had a son Nicocles, who succeeded him in the kingdom of Salamis. Another, called Pnytagoras, appeared in Isocrates. This younger Evagoras, who succeeded Nicocles, seems to have been ousted from his kingdom by Pnytagoras, who was his uncle. He received a better territory than Salamis from Ochus. But because of his misdeeds there, he was forced to flee again into Cyprus, where he was captured and executed as a malefactor. {*Diod. Sic., l. 16. c. 46. s. 3. 7:367}

1661. Eusebius showed that in this third year of the 107th Olympiad, Ochus forced Nectanabis to flee into Ethiopia, and took over all Egypt, putting an end to the kingdom of Egypt. {*Eusebius, Chronicles, l. 1. 1:203} This period was the period in Manetho's commentaries covering the history of Egypt, and how Egypt was captured by Ochus. Diodorus in his record of this year gives a long account of this. {*Diod. Sic., l. 16. c. 46-51. 7:367-381}

1662. After Ochus had destroyed Sidon, the auxiliary forces came to him from the Argives, Thebes and the Greek cities in Asia. Uniting all his forces, he marched to the lake of Serbonis, but most of his army perished in the bogs of Barathra, because they had no guides. From there he marched to Pelusium, at the first mouth of the Nile River. It was held by a garrison of five thousand men under Philophron. There, the Greeks camped close to the city and the Persians camped about five miles off. Ochus divided the Greeks into three brigades, each of which was to have two commanders, one a Persian and the other a Greek. The first brigade, the Boeotians, were commanded by Lacrates of Thebes and Rhosaces, a Persian, the governor of Ionia and Lydia. The second one, the Argives, were commanded by Nicostratus, a

Greek, and Aristazanes, a Persian. The third brigade was under Mentor, who had betrayed Sidon, and Bagoas, a eunuch of Persia. To each of these Greek brigades were added various companies and troops, and sea captains with their squadrons of ships. On the opposing side, Nectanabis had twenty thousand auxiliary Greeks in his army and the same number to help him from Libya, besides the sixty thousand from his own country of Egypt who were called *Warriors*. He had an exceedingly large number of river boats, outfitted to fight in the Nile River if required. When he had supplied every place with reasonably adequate garrisons, he, with thirty thousand Egyptians, five thousand Greeks and one half of his Libyans, defended the routes which were most exposed and vulnerable to invasion. *[L277]*

1663. When things had thus been arranged on both sides, Nicostratus, who commanded the Argives, obtained some Egyptian guides, whose wives and children were kept as hostages by the Persians. With his portion of the ships, he crossed over one of the channels of the Nile River that would be least visible to the Egyptians. When the closest garrisons of the Egyptians became aware of this, they sent over seven thousand men under Clinius, who was from the isle of Cos, to cut them off. In that encounter, the Greeks on the Persian side killed almost five thousand men on the other side, along with their commander Clinius. When Nectanabis heard of this slaughter, he retired to Memphis with his army, to secure that place. Meanwhile Lacrates, who commanded the first brigade of the Greeks, hurried to attack Pelusium. He drained the water that ran around Pelusium by having a ditch dug. He raised a mound on the very channel of the original river and there planted his batteries. The Greeks within courageously defended the place, but when they heard that Nectanabis had left the field and retired to Memphis, they sued for peace. *[E197]* Binding it with an oath, Lacrates assured them that when the town was surrendered, they, with their belongings, would all be sent to Greece. When they heard this, they surrendered the town.

1664. Mentor, who commanded the third brigade, saw that all the cities were manned with two nationalities, the Greeks and Egyptians. He spread a rumour that Artaxerxes planned to deal most graciously with those who willingly submitted to him. The rest would be treated like those in Sidon. Everywhere, the Greeks and Egyptians strove to be the first to surrender their cities to the Persians. Bubastus was the first city to surrender to the Persians, followed by all the rest of the cities. They settled for the best terms they could get.

1665. Meanwhile, when Nectanabis was at Memphis, he heard how all the cities had defected to the Persians.

Despondent, he gathered all the treasure he could and fled to Ethiopia. {*Diod. Sic., l. 16. c. 51. s. 1. 7:381} Others report that he shaved his head and disguised his appearance, and so went to Pelusium, from where he sailed to Philip, king of Macedonia at Pella. (See the *Excerpta, Barbaro-Latina*, published by Scaliger, p. 58; the *Chronicle of Alexandria*, or *Fasti Siculi*, published by Raderus, p. 393; Cedrenus in the *Basil's Edition*, p. 124; and *Glycas*, p. 195 from Pseudo-Callisthenes' fabulous history of the *Deeds of Alexander*.)

1666. When Artaxerxes Ochus had taken possession of all of Egypt, he dismantled all the fortifications of the main cities and destroyed their temples. He got an immense amount of treasure. Moreover, he took away all their records from their most ancient temples. The priests bought these back again by paying a large sum of money to Bagoas, the eunuch. {*Diod. Sic., l. 16. c. 51. 7:381,383} Ochus is also said to have derided their ceremonies and their god Apis. {*Sulpicius Severus, Sacred History, l. 2. c. 14. 11:104} The Egyptians called Ochus an ass for his poor behaviour and spirit. Therefore, he violently took their god Apis, the bull, and sacrificed him to an ass. {*Aelian, Historical Miscellany, l. 4. c. 8. 1:191} Then he ordered his cooks to prepare the bull for dinner. {Suidas, Ochus}

1667. After this, Ochus rewarded his Greeks, who had helped him win this victory, with wealth and honour, each man according to his deeds. He sent them all away to their own country, and left Pherendates as his viceroy in Egypt. After so great a conquest, he was covered with glory and loaded with spoils. He returned to Babylon with his army, {*Diod. Sic., l. 16. c. 51. s. 3. 7:383} where he also took many Jews as prisoners. He settled most of them in Hyrcania, which bordered on the Caspian Sea. *[L278]* Georgius Syncellus, from Julius Africanus, stated:

> "Ochus, the son of Artaxerxes, made a journey into Egypt. He led away some Jews as captives. He settled some of them in Hyrcania, near the Caspian Sea, and the rest in Babylon. There they continue to this day, as many Greek writers stated."

1668. Hecataeus of Abdera also, in his first book *De Judais*, cited by Josephus, {*Josephus, Apion, l. 1. c. 22. (194) 1:241} mentioned many tens of thousands of Jews who were carried to Babylon. Later they were settled in Hyrcania. Paulus Orosius also wrote: {Orosius, l. 31. c. 7.}

> "Ochus, who is also called Artaxerxes, after his great and long war in Egypt was ended, carried away many of the Jews. He commanded them to settle in Hyrcania near the Caspian Sea. There, they continue to this day and prosper and increase in population. It is thought that they will one day break out from there into some other quarter of the world."

*1669.* This opinion seems to have no basis except for the passage in the Apocrypha {*Apc 2Es 13:40-46*} concerning the ten tribes who were carried away by Shalmaneser of the Jews, which speaks of certain confined Hebrews (where, I do not know) and of a river called Sabbation. Petrus Treccensis, in his scholastic history, {*Petrus Treccensis, 1 Esth. c. 5.*} and deriving his material from Vincentius Bellovacensis, {*Bellovacensis, Specul. History, l. 30. c. 89.*} mentioned those ten tribes. They were later closely confined in the Caspian Mountains. But these things do not agree with Josephus, whom he claims as his source. Rather, they agree with the writings of that false Gorion and Methodius, and even with those fictitious accounts from the Mohammedan Koran concerning Alexander.

### 3655 AM, 4365 JP, 349 BC

*1670.* Ochus rewarded Mentor of Rhodes with a hundred talents in money and very rich furnishings for his house. He made Mentor the governor over all the Asiatic shores, with full and absolute power to suppress any rebellions which happened in those parts. This great grace and favour he used well. Previously Artabazus and Memnon had made war against Ochus and been driven from Asia. {*See note on 3648 AM. <<1640>>*} {*See note on 3651 AM. <<1642>>*} They had fled to Philip, king of Macedonia, and lived with him. Mentor secured pardons for Artabazus and Memnon from the king, who sent for them both to come to him, with all their families. *[E198]* Artabazus had by the sister of Mentor and Memnon, eleven sons and ten daughters. Mentor was exceedingly delighted with so numerous a progeny, and as each of the sons grew up, Mentor gave them distinguished commands in the army. {*Diod. Sic., l. 16. c. 52. s. 1-4. 7:383,385*}

*1671.* Hermias, the archon of Atarneus, had revolted from Ochus and had many strong cities and citadels under him. Mentor invited him to a peace conference and promised him that he would get him a pardon from the king. When Hermias came, Mentor captured him and took his signet ring. He sent letters in the name of Hermias that ordered the captains and garrisons everywhere in his dominion to surrender to the bearers of these letters. This they did immediately. {*Diod. Sic., l. 16. c. 52. s. 5-8. 7:385*} {*Polyaenus, Strategmata, l. 6.*} He dealt in like manner with all the other rebels of the king, taking some by force and others by tricks, but bringing them all under the king's subjection again. He periodically sent the king Greek mercenaries. He managed the government with great wisdom, valour and loyalty for the king. {*Diod. Sic., l. 16. c. 52. s. 8. 7:385*} {*Demosthenes, Against Aristocrates*}

*1672.* When Spartacus, the king of Cimmerian Bosphorus, was dead, his brother Paerisades succeeded him to the kingdom and held it for thirty-eight years. {*Diod. Sic., l. 16. c. 52. s. 10. 7:387*} *[L279]*

### 3656 AM, 4366 JP, 348 BC

*1673.* Hermippus stated that Plato, who was the philosopher and founder of the old academy, died in the first year of the 108th Olympiad, when Theophilus was archon in Athens. {*Diogenes Laertius, Plato, l. 3. c. 1. (2) 1:279*} {*Dionysius Halicarnassus, Ammaeus, l. 1. (5) 2:317*} {*Athenaeus, l. 5. (192a) 2:369*} The saying of Numenius, the Pythagorean, as reported by Hesychius, the Milesian, was: {*Hesychius, Numenius*}

> "Whatever Plato said concerning God and the world, he stole it all from the books of Moses."

*1674.* Hence was the origin of that famous saying of his which was recorded by Hesychius and his follower Suidas. Even before them, Clement of Alexandria had said of him: {*Clement, Stromateis, l. 1. c. 22. 2:334*}

> "For what is Plato, but Moses speaking in Attic Greek?"

*1675.* Clement said that Plato translated many things from the books of Moses and put them into his own writings. Aristobulus, the Jew, said the same, so that I shall not try to defend the authority of Justin Martyr, Clement of Alexandria, Ambrose, Theodoret, Johannes Philoponus, writing on the Hexaemeron, and other Christians. {*See note on 3479b AM. <<982>>*}

*1676.* After Plato died, Aristotle, who had founded the sect of the Peripatetic philosophers, travelled to Hermias, the eunuch and ruler of Atarneus, of whom I spoke in the previous year. He lived with him for three years. {*Diogenes Laertius, Aristotle, l. 5. c. 1. (9) 1:453*} {*Dionysius Halicarnassus, Ammaeus, l. 1. (5) 2:317*} Strabo stated that he lived at Assos, which was under the dominion of Hermias, and Assos is mentioned in Acts. {*Ac 20:13*} {*Strabo, l. 13. c. 1. s. 57. 6:115,117*} Aristotle was closely related to Hermias, because he married Pythiades, the adopted daughter of Hermias. She was the natural daughter of either Hermias' sister, or brother. I do not know if Aristotle, the Peripatetic (as we find in Eusebius {*Eusebius, Gospel, l. 15. c. 2. (792d) 1:853*}), because of the affection he had for Hermias, married her after the death of Hermias. While he was staying in Asia, he met a Jew who was a man of great learning and temperance. He came from upper Asia to the coast, where he spoke in Greek with Aristotle and any others who wanted to hear him. (Clearchus of Solos, a principal scholar of Aristotle, as cited both by Josephus and in Clearchus' first book *de Somno* or *of sleep.* {*Josephus, Apion, l. 1. c. 22. (177-181) 1:235,237*}) So perhaps it is to this Jew that the Peripatetic sect of philosophers owe so many of their good sayings. They closely followed the words of Moses and the prophets, as our Clement of Alexandria affirmed from Aristobulus. {*Clement, Stromateis, l. 1. c. 22. 2:334} {*Clement, Stromateis, l. 5. c. 14. 2:467}

## 3658 AM, 4368 JP, 346 BC

*1677.* Satyrus, the ruler of Heraclea in Pontus, turned over the government to Timothy, the oldest son of his brother Clearchus. Shortly after this, Satyrus was stricken with a most grievous and incurable disease. A cancer grew in his groin which never stopped growing inward, until he died at the age of sixty-five years. He had ruled Heraclea for seven years. {Memnon, Excerpts, c. 3.} Timothy took his younger brother Dionysius into the government and appointed him to be his successor, in case he should die. {Memnon, Excerpts, c. 4.}

## 3659 AM, 4369 JP, 345 BC

*1678.* Memnon of Rhodes, a Persian commander mentioned earlier, sent for Hermias, the eunuch, and ruler of Atarneus. He came, suspecting nothing, for he was invited as a friend. Memnon seized him and sent him as a prisoner to the king, who hanged him. [L280] The philosophers, Aristotle and Xenocrates, a Chalcedonian who was born in Bithynia, were with Hermias. They got away, and fled from the Persian territories. {*Strabo, l. 13. c. 1. s. 57. 6:117} When Aristotle had lived with Hermias for three years, he went to Mitylene at the time when Eubulus was archon at Athens, in the fourth year of the 108th Olympiad. {*Diogenes Laertius, Aristotle, l. 5. c. 1. (10) 1:458} [E199] {*Dionysius Halicarnassus, Ammaeus, l. 1. (5) 2:317} Extant in Laertius there is also an epigram of Aristotle, which was on a statue of Hermias at Delphi: {*Diogenes Laertius, Aristotle, l. 5. c. 1. (6) 1:449}

> Him did the king of Persia slay
> Contrary to Jove's law or reason,
> Not by force or bloody fray,
> But by a friend's detested treason.

*1679.* Therefore, I thought it fit to insert this here, so that no man should think that Aristotle was in any way party to his death. This they might incorrectly think, based on those words of Tertullian, when he said: {Tertullian, l. 1. c. 46.}

> "Aristotle made his friend Hermias to leave his place in shame."

## 3660 AM, 4370 JP, 344 BC

*1680.* Idrieus, the prince of Caria, died. His enormous wealth is noted by Isocrates. {*Isocrates, Philip, l. 1. (103) 1:307} His wife, Ada, who was also his sister, succeeded him and ruled for four years. {*Strabo, l. 14. c. 2. s. 17. 6:285} {*Diod. Sic., l. 16. c. 69. s. 2. 8:33} It was common in Asia, after the time of Semiramis, for wives to succeed their husbands in their kingdoms. {*Arrian, Anabasis, l. 1. c. 23. s. 7. 1:97}

## 3664 AM, 4374 JP, 340 BC

*1681.* Pixodarus, the youngest son of Hecaromnus, expelled his sister Ada and ruled for five years. {*Diod. Sic., l. 16. c. 74. s. 2. 8:45} He only left her the revenues from the town of Alinda to live on. {*Strabo, l. 14. c. 2. s. 17. 6:285}

*1682.* Pixodarus sent for Orontobates, a Persian lord, to make him his consort in the government of Caria. He gave him his sister Ada in marriage. {*Arrian, Anabasis, l. 1. c. 23. s. 8. 1:99} {*Strabo, l. 14. c. 2. s. 17. 6:285}

*1683.* Philip, the king of Macedonia, and his army of thirty thousand men besieged Perinthus, a town in Thrace that was on the Propontis. They were well equipped with battering rams and other devices, and constantly tried to destroy the walls, so that the inhabitants had no time for rest or respite. The king of Persia was becoming alarmed by Philip's success, so he ordered his commanders and governors in Asia to send help to relieve Perinthus. They were to send all the help they could, which they did. {*Diod. Sic., l. 16. c. 74,75. 8:43-49} This was the main reason Alexander gave, in a letter to Darius, for invading Asia. {*Arrian, Anabasis, l. 2. c. 14. s. 1-3. 1:173,175}

## 3666c AM, 4376 JP, 338 BC

*1684.* When Artaxerxes Ochus had reigned for twenty-three years, he became sick. Bagoas was the eunuch and chief man under him as chiliarch of the kingdom, and he gave him poison to kill him, helped by Artaxerxes' physician. {*Diod. Sic., l. 15. c. 93. s. 1. 7:213}. {*Diod. Sic., l. 17. c. 5. s. 3,4. 8:131} {*Sulpicius Severus, Sacred History, l. 2. c. 16. 11:105} Bagoas was an Egyptian and thus hated Ochus for killing their god Apis, so he avenged this sacrilege (as Sulpicius termed it) done to his country by killing the king. He cut his flesh into pieces and threw it to the cats to eat. [L281] We do not know what he put into the coffin in place of his flesh. From his thigh bones he made handles for swords, thereby depicting Bagoas' propensity for blood and slaughter. {*Aelian, Historical Miscellany, l. 6. c. 8. 1:235} When Artaxerxes was dead, Bagoas was the most powerful man in the kingdom. He made Artaxerxes' youngest son, Arses, king and executed all his brothers. The young king would have no one left to help him, and would thus be forced all the more to depend on Bagoas. {*Diod. Sic., l. 16. c. 50. s. 8. 7:381} {*Diod. Sic., l. 17. c. 5. s. 3,4. 8:131}

*1685.* Timothy, the tyrant of Heraclea in Pontus, died fifteen years after his father Clearchus. {*Diod. Sic., l. 16. c. 88. s. 5. 8:85} For his great kindness, he was no longer called a tyrant, but a gracious lord and saviour. His body was honourably interred by his brother and successor, Dionysius. All sorts of athletic games and sports were held. Some were performed then, as time permitted, and some later, which were held with greater pomp and magnificence than the earlier ones. {*Memnon, Excerpts, c. 4.*}

### 3667 AM, 4377 JP, 337 BC

1686. At the general assembly of all Greece at Corinth, Philip, king of Macedonia, was made general of all the Greek forces. He had absolute power over them to make war against the king of Persia. He at once started to make many preparations for the war, assessing the number of soldiers to be levied from every city, and then he returned into Macedonia. Ariobarzanes, who reigned in Pontus for twenty-six years, died the same day. He was succeeded by Mithridates, who reigned thirty-five years. {*Diod. Sic., l. 16. c. 8. 8:85,87} {Justin, Trogus, l. 9. c. 5.}

### 3668c AM, 4378 JP, 336 BC

1687. The next spring, Philip sent three of his captains into Asia, Parmenion, Amyntas and Attalus, with part of his army. They were to plunder the king's countries and to liberate the Greek cities. {Justin, Trogus, l. 9. c. 5.} {*Diod. Sic., l. 16. c. 91. s. 2. 8:89}

1688. When Bagoas, the eunuch, knew that Arses was plotting revenge against him, he killed Arses and all his children, in the third year of his reign. When the king's family had been utterly destroyed, he set up Darius, his friend and the son of Arsames, who was a brother to Artaxerxes. Darius claimed the crown as next of kin. {*Diod. Sic., l. 17. c. 5. s. 4-6. 8:131,133} [E200] However, Justin spoke of him in this manner: {Justin, Trogus, l. 10. c. 3.}

> "Codomannus, in regard for his outstanding virtue, was made king by the people and the name of Darius was given him for majesty's sake."

1689. Alexander the Great, is quoted in Curtius as having said the following: {*Curtius, l. 6. c. 4. s. 9,11. 2:33,35}

> "For Darius did not come to the crown by succession, but by the mere procurement and favour of Bagoas, the eunuch."

1690. Again, in a letter Alexander sent to Darius, he charged him: {*Arrian, Anabasis, l. 2. c. 14. s. 5. 1:175,177}

> "As a murderer, Bagoas had Darius made king. Darius obtained that kingdom wrongfully and not according to the laws of the Persians, but by great injustice."

1691. Strabo said: {*Strabo, l. 15. c. 3. s. 24. 7:189}

> "When Bagoas had murdered Arses, he set up Darius, who was not of the king's blood, in his place."

1692. Lastly, Plutarch introduced him as speaking in this manner: {Plutarch, Fortune of Alexander, l. 1. c. 1. 4:383,385}

> "Darius, who was a slave and a courier of the kings, you (Bagoas) made king of the Persians."

1693. Also, Hesychius stated in his Lexicon: *Astandes* means *carrier* {Hesychius, Astandes}, while Suidas stated:

> "*Astandae* and *Angati*, in the Persian language, are those who carry letters from post-house to post-house until they come to the place of their destination."

1694. So Darius was one of those who in Esther {Es 8:14} are called couriers. In Aelian he is called a slave. {*Aelian, Historical Miscellany, l. 12. c. 43. 1:387} [L282]

1695. Bagoas planned to poison Darius also, but the plot was discovered and Darius sent for him. When he came, he was ordered to drink some of it. When he refused, Darius had it poured down his throat. {*Diod. Sic., l. 17. c. 5. s. 6. 8:133} He then told the people that he had killed him in self-defence. {*Curtius, l. 6. c. 4. s. 10,11. 1:35}

### 3668d AM, 4378 JP, 336 BC

1696. When Philip was still alive, Darius planned to attack him in Macedonia. {*Diod. Sic., l. 17. c. 7. s. 1. 8:135}

1697. Sanballat, a Cuthean, from whom the Samaritans had their beginning, was made governor of Samaria by Darius. He gave his daughter in marriage to Nicasus, the son of Manasses, brother to Jaddua, the high priest at Jerusalem. He hoped by this marriage to be held in better esteem by the Jews. {*Josephus, Antiq., l. 11. c. 7. s. 2. (302,303) 6:461}

1698. Philip, king of Macedonia, was celebrating the marriage of his daughter Cleopatra with Alexander, the king of Epirus, at Aegae. Philip was murdered by Pausanias, the son of Cerastes, of Orestis, a place in Macedonia. {*Diod. Sic., l. 17. c. 91-94. 8:89-101} {Justin, Trogus, l. 9. c. 6.} {*Josephus, Antiq., l. 11. c. 8. s. 1. (304) 6:461} Alexander, in his letter to Darius, stated that his father was murdered by assassins whom Darius had hired and paid with a large sum of money. {*Curtius, l. 4. c. 1. s. 12. 1:163,165} {*Arrian, Anabasis, l. 2. c. 14. s. 5. 1:175}

1699. A little before Philip was killed, Neoptolemus, a tragedian, was reported to have sung an ominous song before him. {*Diod. Sic., l. 16. c. 92. s. 3. 8:93} This very song was later sung before Caligula, the emperor, on the very day when he was murdered, according to Suetonius. {*Suetonius, Caligula, l. 4. c. 57. s. 4. 1:503} Ovid stated: {*Ovid, Metamorphoses, l. 10. (298-500) 4:85-101}

> "Mnester, the actor sang and acted that very song which previously Neoptolemus the actor had done in a play when Philip, the king of Macedonia, was killed."

*1700.* Josephus did not understand this part of the Roman history very well. {*Josephus, Antiq., l. 19. c. 1. s. 13. (94) 9:259}* Later, he had spoken of Mnester and the song which he sang, which Rufinus translated in Latin and I render it in English as:

"The actor danced the fable of Cinyras, in which both Cinyras and his daughter, Myrrha, were killed."

*1701.* Josephus deduced from this that they were both killed on the same day: {*Josephus, Antiq., l. 19. c. 1. s. 13. (95) 9:261}*

"It is known that the murder of Caligula happened on the same day that Philip, the son of Amyntas, king of Macedonia, was killed by one of his friends called Pausanias, as he was going into the theatre."

*1702.* So some men place both these murders on January 24. However, the time of Philip's death is best known by the time when Alexander succeeded him in his kingdom. *[L283]*

*1703.* After the death of Philip, Pythodemus, as Arrian called him, or Pythodorus, as he was called by Diodorus, was archon in Athens, {*Arrian, Anabasis, l. 1. c. 1. s. 1. 1:5} {*Diod. Sic., l. 16. c. 91. s. 1. 8:89}* when Alexander succeeded his father at the age of twenty. {*Plutarch, Alexander, l. 1. c. 11. s. 1. 7:251} {Justin, Trogus}* Arrian, in the beginning of his *History of Alexander*, said that he was about twenty years old when he journeyed into Peloponnesus, after his father's death. {*Arrian, Anabasis, l. 1. c. 1. s. 1. 1:5}* This may lend some doubt to his being twenty years old at the time of his father's death. Nothing is said of how long the interval was between his father's death and his journey there. *[E201]* The exact age is determined from the time of his own death, as mentioned at the end of the same history. It is said that he lived thirty-two years and eight months. Of that time, he reigned twelve years and eight months. Subtracting twelve years and eight months from the total age gives a result of exactly twenty years to the month. It appears that Philip died at the end of the Macedonian month of Daisios. I therefore gather that Alexander began his reign about the eighth month before the first of the month of Dios. Hence, Philip was murdered about the 24th of September, in which month of ours the month of Dios begins. This I have documented in my discourse on the solar year of the Macedonians and Asiatics. {*Ussher, Macedonian and Asiatic Year*} It was not the 24th of January.

### 3669a AM, 4378 JP, 336 BC

*1704.* Alexander came to Peloponnesus and following his father's example, summoned all the cities of Greece to Corinth. By the general vote of all the Greeks represented there, except the Lacedemonians, he was made general in his father's place to go to war against the Persians. {*Justin, Trogus, l. 11. c. 2.} {*Diod. Sic., l. 17. c. 4. s. 9. 8:129} {*Arrian, Anabasis, l. 1. c. 1. s. 2,3. 1:5}*

### 3669c AM, 4379 JP, 335 BC

*1705.* He returned from there into Macedonia at the very beginning of the following spring. He went through Thrace and attacked the Illyrians and the Triballi. {*Arrian, Anabasis, l. 1. c. 1. s. 4. 1:5}* In a battle on the bank of the Danube River, he defeated Syrmus, the king of the Triballi. {*Plutarch, Alexander, l. 1. c. 11. s. 3. 7:253}* Meanwhile, he received news that the Athenians, Lacedemonians and Thebans were defecting to the king of Persia. The instigator of this was Demosthenes, the orator, who had been bribed by the Persians with a vast sum of money. He made a speech assuring them that Alexander with all his forces had been defeated by the king of the Triballi. {*Justin, Trogus, l. 11. c. 2.} {Eschines, Against Ctesiphontem}* Furthermore, the Athenians sent Demosthenes' letter, by way of certain of their officials, to the Athenian captains in Alexander's army. They asked Attalus, one of the three captains sent into Asia by Philip, to revolt from Alexander. Like the other Greeks, they revoked the decision to make Alexander the general of the Greek forces. {*Demosthenes, For Ctesiphontem} {*Diod. Sic., l. 17. c. 4. s. 5. 8:129}*

### 3669d AM, 4379 JP, 335 BC

*1706.* Memnon, the commander from Rhodes, was sent into Phrygia with five thousand soldiers. After passing by Mount Ida, he suddenly attacked the city of Cyzicum. He was unable to defeat it, but wasted their territories and returned from there, loaded with a vast amount of spoil. {*Diod. Sic., l. 17. c. 7. s. 2,8. 8:135,137}*

*1707.* When Pixodarus had died, his son-in-law Orontobates succeeded him in the kingdom of Caria with the authority of the Persian king. {*Strabo, l. 14. c. 2. s. 17. 6:285} {*Arrian, Anabasis, l. 1. c. 23. s. 8. 1:99}*

*1708.* When Alexander had conquered the barbarous people to the north, he returned to Greece, where the country was all in a turmoil. On his way, he befriended the Thessalians and journeyed through the pass of Thermopylae. He won the Ambraciots over to him by his kindness. He and his army went into Boeotia and camped before Cadmia, which was being held by a garrison of Macedonians. *[L284]* The Athenians sent their officials to ask his pardon, which he gave them. However, Thebes refused his pardon when he offered it, so he besieged the city. {*Diod. Sic., l. 17. c. 4. s. 1-6. 8:125,127} {*Plutarch, Alexander, l. 1. c. 11. s. 3,4. 7:253}*

*1709.* He sent Hecataeus into Asia with an army to capture Attalus. Attalus sent the letter that he had received from Demosthenes to Alexander, with a very detailed excuse and justification for his actions. Nevertheless, Hecataeus followed his commission and captured and killed him. So the Asian Macedonian army had peace, and the rebellions ceased. {*Diod. Sic., l. 17. c. 4. s. 5. 8:129,131}

1710. Parmenion, who was always loyal to Alexander, took Grynium by force and sold all its townsmen for slaves. From there he went and besieged Pitane. When Memnon approached, he so frightened the Macedonians that they lifted their siege. {*Diod. Sic., l. 17. c. 7. s. 9,10. 8:137}

1711. Callas, with a Macedonian army and other mercenaries, fought with the Persians in the country of Troas. His small forces defeated the Persians and forced them to retire to Rhoetium. {*Diod. Sic., l. 17. c. 7. s. 10. 8:137,139}

### 3670a AM, 4379 JP, 335 BC

1712. Thebes in Boeotia was levelled to the ground by Alexander in October, which was the time when the *Mysteries* were usually observed in Athens, {*Diod. Sic., l. 17. c. 14. s. 1. 1:157} but that year they did not observe that holy solemnity, because of what happened. {*Plutarch, Alexander, l. 1. c. 13. s. 1. 7:257} {*Arrian, Anabasis, l. 1. c. 10. s. 2. 1:45} Six thousand men in Thebes were killed and thirty thousand were sold as slaves. All was destroyed, with the only exceptions being the houses of the priests, of his father Philip's friends and of Pindar, the poet. {*Aelian, Historical Miscellany, l. 13. c. 7. 1:423} [E202]

1713. At a common council of Greece, Alexander was chosen general for the second time, to go against the Persians. Alexander went to visit Diogenes, the philosopher. {*Plutarch, Alexander, l. 1. c. 14. s. 1-3. 7:259}

### 3670b AM, 4380 JP, 334 BC

1714. When he returned to Dios, a town in Macedonia, all his thoughts were on the conquest of Asia. {*Arrian, Anabasis, l. 1. c. 11. s. 1. 1:47} The likeness of the high priest of Jerusalem appeared to him in his sleep, bidding him to be courageous and bold, and telling him that he was to enter Asia quickly with his army and that he would lead his armies in the conquest of the Persian Empire. {*Josephus, Antiq., l. 11. c. 8. s. 5. (334-336) 6:477}

### 3670c AM, 4380 JP, 334 BC

1715. Therefore, at the very beginning of the spring, Alexander left his own home and after a twenty-day march, came to Sestus, from where his army crossed over into Asia. {*Arrian, Anabasis, l. 1. c. 11. s. 3-5. 1:47,49} Euaenetus was then the archon at Athens. This was eleven years before Alexander died, according to Clement of Alexandria, as he noted from the most ancient chronologies. {*Clement, Stromateis, l. 1. c. 21. 2:332} That is, this was the third month before Ctesicles was the archon in Athens. In the time while Ctesicles was archon,

Diodorus placed his trip into Asia in the third year of his reign. {*Diod. Sic., l. 17. c. 1. s. 1. 8:163} Zosimus followed Diodorus, without noting his error. {Zosimus, History, l. 1.} This entry into Asia occurred in the second year of his reign, the second year of the 111th Olympiad.

1716. He left Antipater behind in Europe with twelve thousand foot soldiers and fifteen hundred cavalry, to tend to matters there. Alexander sailed to Troas with sixty ships, {*Diod. Sic., l. 17. c. 1. s. 5. 8:165,167} but ordered Parmenion to transport most of his foot soldiers and cavalry from Sestus to Abidus. This he did with the help of one hundred and sixty ships, and a number of cargo ships. {*Arrian, Anabasis, l. 1. c. 11. s. 6. 1:49}

1717. Even those who were present do not agree on how many men Alexander took into Asia. [L285] In Polybius, Callisthenes said he had forty-five hundred cavalry and thirty thousand foot soldiers. {*Polybius, l. 12. c. 18. s. 1,2. 4:353} Plutarch stated that Aristobulus was alleged to have said that he had thirty thousand foot soldiers and four thousand cavalry. Ptolemy, the son of Lagus and later king of Egypt, said there were thirty thousand foot soldiers and five thousand cavalry. Anaximenes of Lampsacus said there were forty thousand foot soldiers and fifty-five hundred cavalry. {*Plutarch, Fortune of Alexander, l. 1. c. 3. 4:389} Livy agreed with Aristobulus and said there were four thousand cavalry. {*Livy, l. 9. c. 19. s. 5. 4:237} Diodorus, Justin and Orosius, agreed with Callisthenes that there were forty-five hundred cavalry. {*Diod. Sic., l. 17. c. 17. s. 4,5. 8:165} {Justin, Trogus, l. 11. c. 6.} {Orosius, l. 3. c. 16.} Arrian said he had more than five thousand cavalry. {*Arrian, Anabasis, l. 1. c. 11. s. 3. 1:47,49} Diodorus has a total of fifty-one hundred when you add up his numbers. As to the number of foot soldiers, he said there were thirty thousand, agreeing with Callisthenes, Aristobulus and Ptolemy. Livy said there were more than thirty thousand foot soldiers. Arrian said that there were not many more than thirty thousand soldiers. Justin and Oronus made it thirty-two thousand. The number of forty thousand foot soldiers, which Callisthenes and Anaximenes mention, is taken by Julius Frontinus to refer to his entire army, in this way: {*Frontinus, Stratagems, l. 4. c. 2. s. 4. 1:287}

> "Alexander of Macedonia, with forty thousand men, all veteran soldiers trained under his father Philip, attacked the whole world and killed an infinite number of his enemies."

1718. Aristobulus said Alexander took only seventy talents of money to pay his army. Duris said he had provisions for only thirty days. Osecritus added that he went into debt to the sum of two hundred talents to pay for his army. {*Plutarch, Alexander, l. 1. c. 15. s. 1. 7:261} {*Plutarch, Fortune of Alexander, l. 1. c. 3. 4:389}

1719. As soon as he landed on the continent, Alexander was the first among all of them to throw a spear onto the shore. This signified his taking possession of all Asia. He leaped ashore and danced about in his armour, offering sacrifices and beseeching the gods:

"that those lands might willingly receive him as their king."

1720. Then he went and sacrificed to the ghost of Achilles, from whom he was descended on his mother's side, and to Ajax and other Greek heroes, who had died in the war of Troy. {*Diod. Sic., l. 17. c. 17. s. 1,2. 8:163} {Justin, Trogus} {*Arrian, Anabasis, l. 1. c. 11. s. 5. 1:49} He commended the very good fortune of Achilles in two points: first, he had about him at his side a friend as true as Patrocles, and secondly, he had a man like Homer to sing his praises. {*Plutarch, Alexander, l. 1. c. 15. s. 4. 7:263} {*Cicero, Pro Archia Poeta, l. 1. c. 10. (24) 11:33} {*Cicero, Friends, l. 5. c. 12. s. 8. 25:375} {*Arrian, Anabasis, l. 1. c. 11. s. 1. 1:47}

1721. When he came into Illium, he sacrificed to Pallas of Troy. He hung up his own arms in her temple and in their place took some other arms from the chancel, which had been there from the time of the Trojan war. {*Diod. Sic., l. 17. c. 17. s. 6,7. 8:167} {*Arrian, Anabasis, l. 1. c. 11. s. 7,8. 1:51} Among the other relics, they displayed the lute of Paris. Alexander said he would have thanked them if they could have shown him the lute of Achilles, with which he had sung the praises of famous men. {*Plutarch, Alexander, l. 1. c. 15. s. 5. 7:263} {*Aelian, Historical Miscellany, l. 9. c. 38. 1:309}

1722. From Illium he went to Arisba to join the rest of his army, which had crossed over by sea. The next day he passed by Percote and Lampsacus, and camped at the Practius River. {*Arrian, Anabasis, l. 1. c. 12. s. 6. 1:53} [E203] He intended to utterly destroy Lampsacus and its inhabitants, because he thought they had defected, or were planning to defect to the Persians. He saw Anaximenes, the historian, a man very well known to him and to his father, coming to meet him. Guessing his errand, he swore first, vowing that:

"whatever he desired of him, that he would not do."

1723. Then Anaximenes replied:

"Sir, I beseech you to destroy Lampsacus." [L286]

1724. Alexander was caught in his own net by the wit of the man. Though much against his will, he went on his way and spared the place. {*Valerius Maximus, l. 7. c. 3. ext. 4. 2:141} {*Pausanias, Elis II, l. 6. c. 18. s. 2-4. 3:107} {Suidas, Anaximenes}

1725. After much difficulty and danger, Alexander crossed the Granicus River in Phrygia and planned a battle with the Persians in the plain of Adrastia. Justin and Orosius said that the Persians had six hundred thousand foot soldiers and twenty thousand cavalry. Arrian, somewhat improbably, added that besides the mercenaries there were less than twenty thousand foot soldiers. {*Arrian, Anabasis, l. 1. c. 14. s. 4. 1:61} Diodorus was more cautious and said that the Persian cavalry was more than ten thousand and the army was under a hundred thousand men. {*Diod. Sic., l. 17. c. 19. s. 4. 8:171} Twenty thousand Persian foot soldiers and twenty-five hundred cavalry died in the battle, according to Plutarch. {*Plutarch, Alexander, l. 1. c. 16. s. 2. 7:269} Diodorus reported that they lost ten thousand foot soldiers and no less than two thousand cavalry, and had more than twenty thousand taken prisoner. Arrian's account stated that the Persian cavalry lost a thousand men, and their foreign mercenaries were almost all killed. Two thousand were taken prisoner. Orosius' account is quite fantastic, when he said there were four hundred thousand killed. {Orosius, l. 4. c. 1.}

1726. In this battle, Alexander, who was wearing the armour which he had taken from the temple of Pallas at Illium, had his head-piece cut in pieces, to his very hair. Plutarch, from Aristobulus, stated that he lost twenty-five cavalry and nine foot soldiers. {*Plutarch, Alexander, l. 1. c. 16. 7:269} However, Justin and Orosius said that a hundred and twenty cavalry and nine foot soldiers died. According to Arrian, Alexander lost about twenty-five men in total, who were all Macedonians. Lysippus made brass statues of them. Others said that he lost sixty cavalry and thirty foot soldiers. The next day, Alexander had these men buried with all funeral rites. This great and memorable victory opened the way to the empire of all Asia. It happened in the month of Daisios with the Macedonians, and on the sixth of Thargehon with the Athenians, or Sunday May 20, 334 BC, or 4380 JP in the second year of the 111th Olympiad. This we have discussed in detail in our discourse on the Macedonian and Asiatic Solar year. {Ussher, Macedonian and Asiatic Year, c. 1. p. 4,5,11.}

1727. When Alexander had rested his army, he marched forward through Lydia and came to Sardis. This city, with all its provisions and treasures, was voluntarily surrendered to him by Mithrines or Mithrenes, its governor. {*Diod. Sic., l. 17. c. 21. s. 7. 8:179} {*Arrian, Anabasis, l. 1. c. 17. s. 3. 1:71}

## 3670d AM, 4380 JP, 334 BC

1728. He went to Ephesus and replaced the oligarchy with a democratic government, assigning all the tributes which had formerly been paid to Darius, to the goddess Diana. The Ephesians cried out for justice against those who had robbed the temple of Diana, and who had demolished the statue of Philip which was set up there.

They took Syrphax, his son Pelagon, and the sons of the brothers of Syrphax, and stoned them to death. {*Arrian, Anabasis, l. 1. c. 17. s. 10. 1:73} Moreover, they enlarged and beautified the temple itself, which had been burned down by Erostratus on the night when Alexander was born. They appointed Deinocrates, the architect, to oversee the work. Alexander later used him to build Alexandria in Egypt. {Solinus, c. 40.} Artemidorus mentioned that Alexander promised to pay for the construction of the temple if the Ephesians would allow Alexander to take the credit as the builder of the work, but they refused. {*Strabo, l. 14. c. 1. s. 22. 6:225,227}

1729. While Alexander was staying at Ephesus, envoys came to him from Magnesia and Tralles and surrendered their cities to him. [L287] He sent Parmenion to meet them, with twenty-five hundred foreign foot soldiers and twenty-five hundred of his Macedonian troops, as well as two hundred cavalry from his auxiliaries. He also sent Alcimachus, the son of Agathocles, to the cities of Aeolia and Ionia, which had previously been held by the Persians, with about the same number of troops as he had sent with Parmenion. Everywhere, he abolished the oligarchies in their cities and set up democratic governments. He gave them permission to live according to their own laws and abolished the tribute they paid to the Persians. {*Arrian, Anabasis, l. 1. c. 18. s. 1,2. 1:75}

1730. He stayed at Ephesus and sacrificed to Diana. With his whole army in battle array, he marched in a procession to her. The next day he went to Miletus with the rest of his foot soldiers, archers, Agrians, his own troops, the cavalry from Thrace and auxiliaries of his confederates. {*Arrian, Anabasis, l. 1. c. 18. s. 3. 1:75} The Persians who had escaped from the battle at the Granicus River had fled there with their general, Memnon. {*Diod. Sic., l. 17. c. 22. s. 1. 8:179,181} [E204] Three days before they arrived, Alexander had sent Nicanor, with a hundred and sixty ships, to capture the isle of Lade opposite Miletus. He held it with the Thracians and four thousand foreign mercenaries, so that when the Persian fleet of four hundred ships arrived there, they could not get to the Mount Mycale. {*Arrian, Anabasis, l. 1. c. 18. s. 3-5. 1:75,77}

1731. Alexander besieged Miletus by land and sea and battered their walls. They finally surrendered to him, and the three hundred Greek mercenaries fled from there to a small island nearby. Alexander took and enlisted them among his own troops. He gave the Milesians their freedom, but all the non-Greeks there he either killed, or sold as slaves. {*Diod. Sic., l. 17. c. 22. 8:181} {*Arrian, Anabasis, l. 1. c. 18,19. 1:77-81}

## 3671a AM, 4380 JP, 334 BC

1732. Alexander dismissed his fleet of a hundred and sixty ships. (It was a hundred and eight-two ships, according to Justin. {Justin, Trogus, l. 11. c. 6.}) He retained twenty Athenian ships with which to carry his battering rams. {Justin, Trogus, l. 11. c. 6.}

1733. Memnon of Rhodes sent his wife and children to Darius as a pledge of his loyalty, and was made general of all his army. {*Diod. Sic., l. 17. c. 23. s. 5. 8:183}

1734. Alexander marched into Caria with his army. Everywhere he went, he proclaimed liberty to all the Greek cities. He said they could live according to their own laws and be free from Persian tribute. He made it clear that this war was to liberate the Greeks from the Persian rule. {*Diod. Sic., l. 17. c. 24. s. 1. 8:183,185}

1735. While he was on his way, Ada met him. She had been expelled by her brother Pixodarus from the kingdom of Caria. She surrendered her city Alinda, which was the strongest place in all Caria. She desired to be restored to her grandfather's kingdom and also promised to help him take the rest of the citadels and cities of that country. These, she said, were in the power of her close friends. She adopted Alexander for her son, and in return, he gave her the town of Alinda and proclaimed her queen of Caria. He bade her claim Caria and did not refuse to be called her son, whereupon all the cities of Caria sent their officials to him. They gave him crowns of gold and offered him their service in whatever he would ask them to do. {*Diod. Sic., l. 17. c. 24. s. 2,3. 8:185} {*Strabo, l. 14. c. 2. s. 17. 6:285} {*Arrian, Anabasis, l. 1. c. 23. s. 8. 1:99} {*Plutarch, Alexander, l. 1. c. 22. s. 4. 7:287}

1736. Orontobates, a Persian, had held Halicarnassus, a city of Caria, ever since the days of his father-in-law Pixodarus. Memnon of Rhodes, the Persian general, had joined him with all his forces. [L288] Alexander encamped before its walls and began to assault and batter it very intensely. Ephialtes, an Athenian, behaved valiantly in the defence of the city. When he and others were killed at the breaches in the wall, Memnon and the Persian princes and captains placed a strong garrison of their best soldiers in the citadel. Then, they sailed with the rest of the people and all their belongings to the isle of Cos, near Rhodes. When they had gone, Alexander cast a trench around the citadel and built a strong wall on it. He razed the city to the ground. He left garrisons both there and in other parts of Caria, placing Ptolemy over three thousand foreign soldiers and two hundred cavalry. He left the government of that whole country of Caria to his adopted mother, Ada. {*Diod. Sic., l. 17. c. 24-27. 8:183-195} {*Arrian, Anabasis, l. 1. c. 20-23. 1:85-99}

*1737.* Alexander gave his Macedonians, who had married wives shortly before they started on this journey, leave to go home and spend the winter months with them. They could leave Caria to rejoin their wives. He appointed Ptolemy, the son of Seleucus, who was one of his captains, to be their commander. With him he sent Coenus, the son of Polemocrates, and Meleager, the son of Neoptolemus, who had recently married. He ordered them that, when they returned, they should bring all the newly married troops to him. They were to get as many cavalry and foot soldiers as possible from the country where they wintered. {*Arrian, Anabasis, l. 1. c. 24. s. 1,2. 1:99} {*Curtius, l. 3. c. 1. s. 1. 1:65}

*1738.* Alexander sent Parmenion to Sardis and made him commander over all the cavalry of his confederates. He ordered him to take all the Thessalian cavalry and auxiliaries with him, and all the wagons that he could make. They were to go ahead of him as far as Sardis, while he went to Lycia and Pamphylia. He took all the coastal towns, so that the enemy would not be able to make use of their navy. Along the way, he captured a very strong town called Hyparna on his first attack. He allowed the mercenary soldiers there to depart in safety. From there, he marched into Lycia, where the city of Telmessus conditionally surrendered to him. When he crossed the Xanthus River, the cities of Pinara, Xanthus, and Patara, and thirty smaller towns, surrendered to him.

{*Arrian, Anabasis, l. 1. c. 24. s. 3,4. 1:101} [E205]

### 3671b AM, 4381 JP, 333 BC

*1739.* In the middle of winter, Alexander went to the Milyan territory in Greater Phrygia and made a league with the envoy who came to him from Phaselis and Lower Lycia. They surrendered all their cities into his hands. A short time later, Alexander went to Phaselis and razed a strong citadel, which the Pisidians had built to harass the inhabitants of Phaselis. {*Arrian, Anabasis, l. 1. c. 24. s. 5,6. 1:101}

*1740.* While Alexander was near Phaselis, he received a rumour that Alexander Aeropus, whom he had made commander of the Thessalian cavalry, intended to kill him. He was the brother of Heromenes and Arrobaeus who had taken part in the murder of Alexander's father, Philip. Darius had received letters from Alexander Aeropus through Amyntas, who defected to him. Darius sent Sisines, a Persian, to the sea coast under the pretence of having a message for Atizyes, the governor of Phrygia. The real purpose was to assure Alexander Aeropus that if he killed Alexander, the kingdom of Macedonia would be his and Darius would give him a thousand talents of money besides. However, Sisines was intercepted by Parmenion and put to the rack. He confessed all, and was sent away heavily guarded to Alexander. Alexander looked carefully into the matter and sent Amphoterus to Parmenion with secret instructions to seize Aeropus and put him in prison. {*Arrian, Anabasis, l. 1. c. 25. s. 1-10. 1:103-107} [L289] It was about this matter that Alexander wrote in his letter to Darius, where, according to Curtius, he said: {*Curtius, l. 4. c. 1. s. 12. 1:165} {Justin, Trogus, l. 11. c. 7.}

> "When you have forces of your own, you nevertheless set out to sell your enemies' heads, since you, who were recently the king of so large an army, would hire a man to take away my life with a thousand talents."

*1741.* Alexander left Phaselis with his army and travelled along the coast to Perga. From there he came to Aspendus and besieged it. Although the city was situated on a high and rugged mountain, it surrendered to him. Next, he went into Pindia and tried unsuccessfully to take the city of Telmessus. Instead, he made a league with the Selgians who were enemies of the Telmessians. He took Salagassa by force and killed about five hundred Pisidians. He lost his captain Cleander with about twenty of his own men. From there he went to capture the other cities of Pisidia. Some of their stronger places he took by force, and others surrendered conditionally. After this, he came into Phrygia past the salt Lake Ascania. After his fifth camp, he arrived at Celaenae. {*Arrian, Anabasis, l. 1. c. 26-29. 1:107-115}

*1742.* The citadel of Celaenae was held by the Persian commander with a garrison of a thousand Carians and a hundred Greek mercenaries. After a sixty days' truce (in which time the commander expected relief from Darius), he surrendered to Alexander. {*Arrian, Anabasis, l. 1. c. 29. s. 1,2. 1:117,119} {*Curtius, l. 3. c. 1. s. 1-8. 1:65,67}

*1743.* Alexander left a garrison of fifteen hundred in Celaenae. After he had stayed there ten days, he made Antigonus, the son of Philip, governor of Phrygia. He made Balacrus, the son of Amyntas, the commander of the auxiliaries in his place. Alexander marched to Gordium, having sent a letter to Parmenion, that he should sail to meet him at Gordium. {*Arrian, Anabasis, l. 1. c. 29. s. 3. 1:117}

*1744.* Parmenion, with his army and the Macedonians who had leave to be with their new wives, came to Gordium. The army he had recently raised was under the command of Ptolemy, Coenus and Meleager. That army consisted of three thousand Macedonian foot soldiers and three hundred cavalry. Two hundred Thessalian cavalry and a hundred and fifty cavalry from Elis were led by Alcias, who was from the same country. {*Arrian, Anabasis, l. 1. c. 29. s. 3. 1:117}

1745. Darius made Memnon the admiral of his fleet and chief commander of all the sea coast. Memnon planned to carry the war from Asia into Macedonia and Greece. He outfitted a navy of three hundred ships and captured the isle of Chios and all the other cities and places on Lesbos except Mitylene. {*Diod. Sic., l. 17. c. 29. 8:199} {*Arrian, Anabasis, l. 2. c. 1. s. 1. 1:123}

1746. The elders of Jerusalem were offended that Manasseh, the brother of Jaddua, the high priest, had married a foreign wife contrary to the law. They demanded that he either divorce her or give up his priestly office. Thereupon, Jaddua was forced to forbid him to serve at the altar. Manasseh went to tell Sanaballetes, his father-in-law, that he loved his daughter very much, but did not want to lose his priesthood for her sake. This was an honour belonging to him by his birthright, and it was very highly esteemed by the Jews. Sanaballetes replied that if Manasseh would choose not to divorce his wife, he would help him stay in the priesthood, make him a high priest and prince of all his own province, and build him a temple on the hill overlooking Samaria. This temple would be at least as good as the one in Jerusalem. Sanaballetes would do all this under the authority of Darius, the king. Manasseh was encouraged by these promises, and stayed with his father-in-law. He hoped to get the priesthood as a gift, and by the authority of Darius. [L290] As a result, all the priests and other Israelites who had married foreign wives, resorted to him, and Sanaballetes furnished them with money and lands to farm. He promoted the ambition of his son-in-law as much as possible. {*Josephus, Antiq., l. 11. c. 8. s. 2. (306-312) 6:463,465} [E206]

1747. Alexander undid the Gordian knot. He either pulled out the peg, or pin, in the beam, according to Arrian, or he cut it in pieces with his sword, as others stated. {*Plutarch, Alexander, l. 1. c. 18. s. 1,2. 7:273} {*Arrian, Anabasis, l. 2. c. 3. s. 1-8. 1:129,131} {*Curtius, l. 3. c. 1. s. 11-13. 1:67,69} {Justin, Trogus, l. 11. c. 7.}

1748. Alexander departed from Gordium in Phrygia and went to Ancyra, a city in Galatia. Envoys from Paphlagonia came to him and made a league with him, surrendering their country to him. He appointed Calas, a prince of Phrygia, to be their new governor. When he had received the new troops from Macedonia, he marched into Cappadocia, where he subdued all the country on this side of the Halys River and a portion on the other side. {*Arrian, Anabasis, l. 2. c. 4. s. 1,2. 1:133} {*Curtius, l. 3. c. 1. s. 22-24. 1:71}

1749. Memnon died at the siege of Mitylene. Before he died, he appointed Autophradates and Pharnabazus, the son of Artabazus, to take over the forces until Darius would direct otherwise. They took command, subject to certain conditions. Autophradates took over the main body of the ships, while Pharnabazus sailed into Lycia with several ships, taking some mercenaries with him. {*Arrian, Anabasis, l. 2. c. 1,2. 1:121,123}

1750. After the death of Memnon, Darius conscripted soldiers from all countries and ordered them to come to him at Babylon. {*Diod. Sic., l. 17. c. 31. s. 1. 8:203} When he had set up his standard there, he pitched camp and mustered his army. He put a large circular enclosure around the camp that was capable of containing ten thousand armed men. This allowed him to number the host in increments of ten thousand. Like Xerxes had done with his troops, he went and counted all his forces. The sum came to a hundred thousand Persians, of which thirty thousand were cavalry. The Medians sent ten thousand cavalry and fifty thousand foot soldiers. From the Barcani (who were a people bordering upon Hyrcania, according to Stephanus), there were two thousand cavalry and ten thousand foot soldiers. From Armenia came forty thousand foot soldiers and seven thousand cavalry. Hyrcania sent six thousand cavalry and a thousand Tapurian cavalry. The Derbices sent him forty thousand foot soldiers and two thousand cavalry. From the Caspian Sea came eight thousand foot soldiers and two hundred cavalry. Those who were from smaller countries amounted to two thousand foot soldiers and four thousand cavalry. He also had thirty thousand Greek mercenaries. This totalled 311,200 men. {*Curtius, l. 3. c. 2. s. 1-10. 1:73,75} However, Diodorus said that there were four hundred thousand foot soldiers and at least a hundred thousand cavalry. {*Diod. Sic., l. 17. c. 31. s. 2. 8:205} This number is in the newer editions of Justin, as amended from the manuscripts. Although the older editions, together with Orosius, who followed him in every point, had only three hundred thousand foot soldiers and a hundred thousand cavalry. Both historians, Arrian and Plutarch, said that the total number of men was six hundred thousand. {*Arrian, Anabasis, l. 2. c. 8. s. 8. 1:151} {*Plutarch, Alexander, l. 1. c. 18. s. 4. 7:275}

1751. Charidemus from Athens was a man well skilled in military matters. After Alexander had expelled him from Athens, he defected to Darius. He advised Darius not to manage the army personally, but to leave it to some general who had proven himself in previous battles. He further stated that an army of a hundred thousand men, of which one-third would be Greeks, would be enough for this battle. [L291] By his sage and good counsel, he so incensed the princes with envy and angered the king, that he was executed for it. {*Diod. Sic., l. 17. c. 30. s. 2-7. 8:201,203} {*Curtius, l. 3. c. 2. s. 11-19. 1:75-79}

1752. Darius sent an energetic young man, Thymondas, the son of Mentor who was Memnon's deceased brother, to Pharnabazus, to get from him all the mercenaries whom Memnon had under his command. He was to bring them to Darius, while Pharnabazus was to replace the deceased Memnon as the head of the forces there. {*Curtius, l. 3. c. 3. s. 1. 1:79} {*Arrian, Anabasis, l. 2. c. 2. s. 1,2. 1:125}

### 3671d AM, 4381 JP, 333 BC

*1753.* Alexander committed the charge of Cappadocia to Abistenes (according to Curtius), or to Sabictas (according to Arrian), while he marched with his whole army toward the passes in Cilicia and came to a place called Cyrus' Camp. (It was either named after the older Cyrus, as Curtius stated, or after the younger Cyrus, as Arrian thought.) About seven miles from there, he found that those passes were controlled by a strong garrison of the enemy. He left Parmenion there, with troops to hold the enemies in check. In the first watch of the night, Alexander, with his company of targeteers and archers, and his band of Agrians, secretly went to attack that garrison. When the garrison heard a rumour of his coming, they threw away their weapons and fled. Arsames, the governor of Cilicia, had wasted all the country with fire and sword to prevent Alexander from getting provisions from the place. Then he left Tarsus and went to Darius. {*Curtius, l. 3. c. 4. 1:89-93} {*Arrian, Anabasis, l. 2. c. 4. s. 1-6. 1:133}

*1754.* Alexander had journeyed very quickly to Tarsus. Since he was so hot from the journey, he took off his armour and leaped into the cold water of the Cydnus River, which ran through the city. *[E207]* This so shocked his system, that he lost his voice and despairing of recovery, he waited to die, according to Justin. Curtius added that this was in the summer season, and that the heat of the day was increased by the intensity of the sun in the climate of Cilicia. Arrian reported from Aristobulus that he fell sick by over-exerting himself. Philip, a physician, gave him a potion, which he took and which cured him immediately. Parmenion had warned him that Philip had been sent to poison him. {*Arrian, Anabasis, l. 2. c. 4. s. 7-11. 1:135,137} {*Curtius, l. 3. c. 5,6. 1:93-105} {*Plutarch, Alexander, l. 1. c. 19. 7:275,279} {Justin, Trogus, l. 11. c. 8.} {*Valerius Maximus, l. 3. c. 8. ext. 6. 1:335}

*1755.* Orontobates, the Persian, held out in the citadel at Halicarnassus, with the cities of Myndus, Caunus, Thera and Callipolis all opposing Alexander. They were defeated in a battle by Ptolemy and Asander. The enemy lost about seven hundred foot soldiers and fifty cavalry, and had at least a thousand men taken prisoner. After this, the Myndians, Caunians and most of the places in that region surrendered to Alexander. {*Curtius, l. 3. c. 7. s. 4. 1:105} {*Arrian, Anabasis, l. 2. c. 5. s. 7. 1:139}

*1756.* Darius had a pontoon bridge built over the Euphrates and crossed over with his army in five days. {*Curtius, l. 3. c. 7. s. 1. 1:105}

*1757.* Alexander sent Parmenion to take the pass which divided Cilicia from Assyria or Syria. This pass was much like the pass in Cilicia mentioned previously. Alexander followed him from Tarsus and came to Anchialus on the first day. {*Arrian, Anabasis, l. 2. c. 5. s. 1-4. 1:137} From there he marched to Soli and placed his own garrison in the citadel there. He levied two hundred talents of silver from the inhabitants, since they seemed to favour Darius more than him. {*Arrian, Anabasis, l. 2. c. 5. s. 5,6. 1:139} {*Curtius, l. 3. c. 7. s. 2. 1:105} With three battalions of the Macedonians, and all his archers and Agrians, he went from there into the hill country of Cilicia. Within seven days, he won these people over to him by diplomacy and returned to Soli. He had sacrificed to Asclepius, who was the god of healing, and had his whole army march in procession. *[L292]* They had a torch relay race, and athletic and musical competitions. He allowed the city to become a democracy. {*Arrian, Anabasis, l. 2. c. 5. s. 6,7. 1:139}

*1758.* The Greek soldiers, whom Thymondas received by the arrangement with Pharnabazus, were almost Darius' only hope of victory. When they came to him, they very earnestly besought him to retire and stay in the plain country of Mesopotamia. Failing that, he should break this vast army of his into parts and not hazard everything on the chance of one battle. Darius did not like their advice, for he wanted to finish things quickly. The winter (beginning with autumn) was now drawing on, and he sent away all his money, jewels and precious belongings with a suitable guard to Damascus in Syria. The guard was under the command of Cophen, the son of Artabazus. Darius marched on with the rest of his army to Cilicia, with his wife and mother, daughter and little son, following after the camp, according to the custom of Persia. His baggage, and such people as were unfit for the war, he left at Damascus. {*Curtius, l. 3. c. 8. s. 1-12. 1:109,111} {*Arrian, Anabasis, l. 2. c. 11. s. 10. 1:165} {*Arrian, Anabasis, l. 2. c. 15. s. 1. 1:177} {*Diod. Sic., l. 17. c. 32. s. 3. 1:207}

*1759.* When Sanaballetes heard that Darius was coming into those parts, he told Manasseh that he would soon do what he had promised him concerning the high priesthood, saying he would do it when Darius returned victorious over his enemies. He said this, because all those inhabitants of Asia were absolutely certain Darius would win. {*Josephus, Antiq., l. 11. c. 8. s. 3. (313-317) 6:467}

### 3672a AM, 4381 JP, 333 BC

*1760.* Alexander wanted Philotas to bring the cavalry across the Aleian plains in Lycia to the Pyramus River.

Philotas came to Magarsus with the foot soldiers and Alexander's troops. Alexander sacrificed to Athena at a place called Athena Magarsus. {*Arrian, Anabasis, l. 2. c. 5. s. 8,9. 1:139}

1761. After building a bridge over the Pyramus River, he came to the city of Mallos in Cilicia. {*Curtius, l. 3. c. 7. s. 5,6. 1:105} He made offerings to the ghost of Amphilochus, the founder of that place, as to a demigod. When he found the inhabitants in turmoil and unrest, he befriended them, and freed them from paying tribute to Darius. {*Arrian, Anabasis, l. 2. c. 5. s. 9. 1:139,141}

1762. While he was staying at Mallos, he received news that Darius and all his army were encamped at a place called Sochi, which was a two day journey from those passes which I mentioned earlier, that divided Cilicia from Assyria or Syria. {*Arrian, Anabasis, l. 2. c. 6. s. 1. 1:141}

1763. From Mallos, Alexander came to Castabala, which was another town in Cilicia, where Parmenion met him. Alexander had sent him to find the way through a forest which he had to pass through in order to come to the town of Issus. Parmenion had seized the route in that forest and left a small company to hold it. He went forward and took the town of Issus also, which had been abandoned by the inhabitants when they heard he was coming. He went further and cleared out all those who had been set to guard the inner parts of the mountains thereabouts, and put his own garrisons everywhere in those places. When he had cleared the enemy from all that area, he returned to Alexander and told him what he had done. {*Curtius, l. 3. c. 11. s. 5-7. 1:105,107} [E208]

1764. Alexander came to Issus with his army. He held a council of war to determine whether he should march on, or stay there and expect the supplies which he knew were coming to him from Macedonia. Parmenion advised that he could not find a better place to fight than where he was. Neither side could outnumber the other while fighting because of the narrowness of the pass. {*Curtius, l. 3. c. 7. s. 8-10. 1:107} Callisthenes, as noted from Polybius, stated that when Alexander first came into Cilicia, he received five thousand foot soldiers and eight hundred cavalry from Macedonia. {*Polybius, l. 12. c. 19. s. 2. 4:355}

1765. When Darius had gone through the pass of the Amanus Mountains, he marched toward Issus. He did not know that he had left Alexander behind him. When Darius had taken the town, he cruelly tortured and put to death a poor company of Macedonians whom Alexander had left there. They had not been able, because of sickness or other infirmities, to follow the camp. [L293] The next day, Darius marched to the Pinarus River. {*Arrian, Anabasis, l. 2. c. 7. s. 1. 1:143}

1766. When Darius heard that Alexander was approaching in battle array, he immediately crossed over the Pinarus River with thirty thousand cavalry and some twenty thousand lightly armed foot soldiers, so that he might have more time to organize his army for the battle. First, he arranged those thirty thousand heavily armed Greek mercenaries. Opposite the Macedonian squadron, on both sides, he placed the sixty thousand Cardaces, who were also heavily armed foot soldiers. He could not possibly arrange them into one squadron and do battle, because the place was too narrow. As for the rest of the troops, whether heavily armed foot soldiers or those from other countries, he put them together in no particular order behind the main battle line of the Greeks and Cardaces. {*Arrian, Anabasis, l. 2. c. 8. s. 5-8. 1:151} However, Curtius stated: {*Curtius, l. 3. c. 9. s. 1-6. 1:119,121}

"Nabarzanes, who was general of Darius' army, was on the right wing with the cavalry. Next to him were almost twenty thousand slingers and archers. Thymondas was also in the same wing, commanding some thirty thousand Greek mercenaries. This was, no doubt, the very cream of the whole army and they were a match for the Macedonian phalanx. On the left wing was Aristomedes, a Thessalian, with twenty thousand foot soldiers from various countries. In the rear, he placed his reserves from the most warlike countries that he had in all his army. In that wing, the king was protected by a guard of three thousand elite cavalry and forty thousand foot soldiers. The Hyrcanian and Median cavalry followed them. Next to them were arranged the cavalry and foot soldiers of the other countries. Some were on the right hand and some on the left. Before this battalion, six thousand slingers and javelin throwers were arranged. All the ground that there was in that pass was filled up entirely with men. The wings reached from one mountain to the other, and even down to the sea. The queen and the king's mother and the rest of the women were placed in the midst of the army."

1767. Callisthenes, who was himself in this battle, said that on Alexander's side there were thirty thousand cavalry, and as many auxiliaries, all set to encounter the Macedonian phalanx. {*Polybius, l. 12. c. 18. s. 1,2. 4:353} However, Polybius said that Alexander's army consisted in total of forty-two thousand foot soldiers and five thousand cavalry. He drew attention to the many inaccuracies of Callisthenes, pointing out that, for reasons of inexperience in the marshalling of an army, Callisthenes had written many things which were not pertinent and accurate in the description of this battle. {*Polybius, l. 12. c. 19. s. 4. 4:357}

*1768.* In the morning, when Hephaestion came to Alexander to encourage him to start the battle, he forgot himself and greeted him with:

"God help you sir,"

*1769.* instead of:

"God save you sir."

*1770.* All the troops who were present were disturbed by what this meant. They thought he had meant that Alexander had not been well in his wits. Hephaestion himself was amazed by his own mistake. When Alexander realised this, he took it up and said that he thanked him for his good omen. *For this tells me, that we shall all, by God's help, come safely out of this battle today.* This is related by Eumenes of Cardia in his letter to Antipater. He was present when the words were spoken, and himself stumbled into a similar error, as it was recorded in Lucian. {*Lucian, Slip of the Tongue in Greeting (6) 6:181,183}

*1771.* Arrian said that this battle was fought when Nicostratus (or, as Diodorus Siculus wrote, when Nicocrates) was archon of Athens, in the fourth year of the 111th Olympiad. (Loeb series for Arrian does not show this name variation. Editor.) This was in the month of Maimakterion, which started on the new moon which happened on Wednesday, October 28. In this battle the Persians lost ten thousand cavalry and ninety thousand foot soldiers. A number of other writers agree with him concerning the losses of the cavalry. Concerning the foot soldiers, they all vary extremely, not only from him, but from each other. Justin said that there were sixty thousand, Orosius, eighty, Curtius, a hundred, and Diodorus, a hundred and twenty thousand. Plutarch said that they lost a hundred and ten thousand men in all. Justin and Orosius added that there were forty thousand captured. *[E209] [L294]* On Alexander's side, there were forty-five hundred wounded men. They lost three hundred and two foot soldiers and a hundred and fifty cavalry, according to Curtius. Concerning the number given for the cavalry lost, Plutarch, Justin and Orosius agreed with Curtius Diodorus said that he lost three hundred foot soldiers, while the other writers said that he lost a hundred and thirty. {*Arrian, Anabasis, l. 2. c. 11. s. 8. 1:163} {*Curtius, l. 3. c. 11. s. 27. 1:137} {*Diod. Sic., l. 17. c. 36. s. 6. 1:221} {*Plutarch, Alexander, l. 1. c. 20. s. 6. 7:281}

*1772.* Ptolemy, the son of Lagus and a captain in Alexander's army, said that in the pursuit of Darius the squadron marched over the slaughtered bodies of the enemy. {*Arrian, Anabasis, l. 2. c. 11. s. 8. 1:163} Although less than a thousand cavalry followed Alexander in this pursuit, they nonetheless killed a large number of the enemy. {*Curtius, l. 3. c. 11. s. 16,17. 1:133} When Darius was

thrown from his chariot, he climbed onto a mare. She remembered her foal at home and ran so fast, that Alexander could not catch up to him. {*Aelian, History of Animals, l. 6. c. 48. 2:67,69}

*1773.* Alexander grew weary of the pursuit of Darius and since the night was drawing on, he gave up all hope of catching him. When he had travelled twenty-five miles, he returned to Darius' camp about midnight. His men had captured it shortly before this. {*Diod. Sic., l. 17. c. 37. s. 1,2. 8:221} {*Curtius, l. 3. c. 11. s. 16,17. 1:133} They found Darius' mother, whom Diodorus called Sisygnambis, but Curtius called Sisigambis. {*Diod. Sic., l. 17. c. 37. s. 3. 8:223} His wife was there also, who Justin said was his sister as well. Darius' son Ochus, who was almost six years old, and Darius' two daughters of marriageable age were also found, as well as a few other noblemen's daughters, although most of them had sent their wives and daughters to Damascus with their baggage. Even Darius had sent most of his treasure there, as we said before. They found whatever luxurious items which were the king's custom to take with him to war. In Darius' camp, Alexander found about three thousand talents of silver. {*Arrian, Anabasis, l. 2. c. 11. s. 9,10. 1:163,165} {*Curtius, l. 3. c. 11. s. 21-26. 1:135,137}

*1774.* Early the next morning, Alexander took Hephaestion with him and went to see the two queens. When Sisigambis mistakenly fell down at Hephaestion's feet, she asked Alexander's pardon for it. He smilingly replied: {*Diod. Sic., l. 17. c. 37. s. 4,5. 8:223,235} {*Curtius, l. 3. c. 12. s. 14-17. 1:141,143} {*Arrian, Anabasis, l. 2. c. 12. s. 6-8. 1:169}

"No harm, for he too is Alexander."

*1775.* In so few words, he gave half of himself away to his friend. {*Valerius Maximus, l. 4. c. 7. ext. 2a. 1:425,427} As for the two queens and the women with them, Alexander gave them back all their wardrobe, cosmetics and ornaments, adding much more from his own belongings to this as well. He did not permit any man to mistreat the women in any way. {*Arrian, Anabasis, l. 2. c. 12. s. 3-5. 1:167} {*Plutarch, Fortune of Alexander, l. 2. c. 6. 4:451}

*1776.* In his flight, Darius came to a place called Sochi, about two days' journey from the passes of Amanus, as we noted before. Arrian stated that he collected together any Persians and others who had survived the battle, taking four thousand of them with him to Thapsacus, so that he might have the great Euphrates River between him and Alexander. {*Curtius, l. 4. c. 1. s. 1-3. 1:161} {*Arrian, Anabasis, l. 2. c. 13. s. 1. 1:169}

*1777.* Amyntas, the son of Antiochus, Thymondas, the son of Mentor, Aristomedes of Pherae and Bianor of Acarnania had previously defected to the Persians from the Greeks. They fled with eight thousand men in their company to Tripolis in Phoenicia, where they found ships which had just arrived from Lesbos. These they captured, and sailed to Cyprus and from there to Egypt. They burned the ships they did not need, so they could not be followed. {*Arrian, Anabasis, l. 2. c. 13. s. 1,2. 1:169,171} {*Diod. Sic., l. 17. c. 47. s. 2,3. 8:255} {*Curtius, l. 4. c. 1. s. 27. 1:171} [L295]

1778. Alexander had made Balacrus, the son of Nicanor and one of the leaders of his bodyguard, governor of Cilicia. Now Alexander replaced Balacrus by Menes, the son of Dionysius. He put Polyperchon, the son of Simmias, in charge of the brigade to replace Ptolemy, the son of Seleucus, who had been killed in the recent battle. He remitted the fifty talents to the men of Soli in Cilicia and returned the hostages that he had taken from them. {*Arrian, Anabasis, l. 2. c. 12. s. 2. 1:165,167} He built three altars on the banks of the Pinarus River, one to Zeus, another to Hercules and a third to Athena. Then he marched into Syria and sent Parmenion ahead of him to Damascus with the Thessalian cavalry. This was the place where Darius had all his treasure, and if they captured the city, they would be rich from the spoil, which was fitting, since the cavalry had behaved very courageously in the recent battle. {*Curtius, l. 3. c. 12. s. 27. 1:145} {*Plutarch, Alexander, l. 1. c. 24. s. 1. 7:291}

1779. As Parmenion was on his way to Damascus, he intercepted a message sent to Alexander from the governor of Damascus, offering to betray the city to Alexander. On the fourth day he came to Damascus. The governor pretended that he could not hold the city. The next morning before sunrise, he took all the king's treasure (which the Persians call his *Gaza*) and pretended that he would flee away and save it for Darius, but he gave it to Parmenion instead. As soon as he had done that, there was a heavy snow storm and the ground was frozen solid.

1780. Among the women who fled from there but were captured, there were three virgins, daughters of Ochus, the previous king before Darius. [E210] Also in the group were Ochus' queen, the daughter of Oxatris—he was the brother of Darius—and the wife of Artabanus, a chief of the courtiers, and his son; Hystanes was his name. The wife of Pharnabazus, whom Darius had made commander of all the towns and cities on the coast, was also taken, as well as three daughters of Mentor, and the wife and son of that most noble Memnon. There was hardly a family of any nobleman of the court of Persia who did not share in this calamity. {*Curtius, l. 3. c. 13. s. 12-13. 1:151} Parmenion's report to Alexander indicated that among all those he had taken were three hundred and twenty-nine of the king's women who were

skilful in music, forty-six weavers or knitters of crowns, two hundred and seventy-seven cooks and twenty-nine cooks' maids, thirteen pudding-makers, seventeen bartenders, seventy wine-clarifiers, fourteen apothecaries and confectioners. {*Athenaeus, l. 13. (608a) 6:277}

1781. Also taken were twenty-six hundred talents in coins, five hundredweight of silver bars, thirty thousand men, and seven thousand pack animals which were used as beasts of burden. {*Curtius, l. 3. c. 13. 1:145-153}

1782. The one who betrayed the city who, it seems, was Cophen, with whom Darius had sent his treasure to Damascus, had his head cut off by one of his countrymen, who then carried it to Darius. {*Curtius, l. 3. c. 13. s. 17. 1:153}

1783. Alexander made Parmenion (according to Curtius) or Memnon, the son of Cerdimmas (according to Arrian) the governor of Coelosyria, giving him his auxiliary cavalry to defend the province. Because the Syrians had not been totally subdued, they did not submit to this new governor. They were, however, quickly suppressed, whereupon they submitted to every command. {*Arrian, Anabasis, l. 2. c. 13. s. 7. 1:173} {*Curtius, l. 4. c. 1. s. 4,5. 1:161}

1784. Alexander sent Parmenion to seize the Persian fleet, while he sent others of his men who were with him to hold the cities of Asia which had surrendered to him. After the battle of Issus, Darius' own commanders, with all their gold and treasure, surrendered to Alexander. He marched into Syria and many kings of the east came and submitted to him. These he treated as each one merited. [L296] With some he made a league, while others he replaced with new kings. {Justin, Trogus, l. 11. c. 10.}

1785. At that time, Gerostratus was king of the isle of Aradus with the adjoining sea coast of the mainland, and also of some places lying farther inland. He and the kings of Cyprus and Phoenicia had consolidated their fleets under Darius' Persian commander, Autophradates. Gerostratus' son, Straton, who was viceroy of Aradus in his father's absence, met Alexander as he was on his way into Phoenicia. He placed a crown of gold on Alexander's head and surrendered the isle of Aradus, together with Marathus, a large and rich town on the mainland opposite Aradus, the city Mariamme, and whatever else belonged to his father. {*Arrian, Anabasis, l. 2. c. 13. s. 7,8. 1:173} {*Curtius, l. 4. c. 1. s. 6,7. 1:161,163}

1786. After having graciously received Straton, Alexander marched to the city of Marathus. While there, he received letters from Darius, who wanted to ransom his female captives. Alexander wrote a letter in reply which he sent Thersippus to deliver. {Justin, Trogus, l. 11. c. 12.} {*Curtius, l. 4. c. 1. s. 8-14. 1:163,165} {*Arrian, Anabasis, l. 2. c. 14. s. 1-9. 1:173-177} {*Diod. Sic., l. 17. c. 39. s. 1,2. 8:227,229} He wanted to have the

Greek envoys, who had been sent to Darius before the battle at Issus, returned to him. Alexander understood that they had been taken captive at Damascus. When Darius sent them, Alexander dismissed the two envoys of the Thebans, Thessalicus and Dionysodorus, but he kept Iphicrates of Athens, who was the son of that famous Iphicrates, in attendance, paying him special honour. Euthycles, the Lacedemonian, was first committed to custody, but later released from irons. Subsequently, when everything went well for Alexander, he was sent away too. {*Arrian, Anabasis, l. 2. c. 15. s. 2-5. 1:179}

*1787.* Alexander left Marathus and captured the city of Byblus, which conditionally surrendered to him. The Sidonians, who not long before had been so terribly abused by Ochus, sent to Alexander and desired to submit to him, as they hated the Persians and King Darius. {*Arrian, Anabasis, l. 2. c. 15. s. 6. 1:181} {*Curtius, l. 4. c. 1. s. 15. 1:165} At that time Straton was the ruler there. Because this surrender came more from the people than from Straton, Alexander replaced Straton by Abdalonymus, who lived by tending a poor garden there. Alexander gave him not only the rich furniture of Straton's house, but added various other rich gifts from what he had taken from the Persians. This new king controlled all the adjoining territories of Sidon. {*Curtius, l. 4. c. 1. s. 16-26. 1:165-169} {Justin, Trogus, l. 11. c. 10.} Plutarch called this man Abdalonymus, the king of Paphon, while Diodorus called him Ballonymus, and said that Alexander made him king of Tyre. {*Plutarch, Fortune of Alexander, l. 2. c. 8. 4:461,463} {*Diod. Sic., l. 17. c. 46. s. 6. 8:253}

*1788.* All of Syria and Phoenicia, with the exception of Tyre, were under Alexander's control. Alexander and his camp were on the mainland, and between him and Tyre there was a narrow strait. The Tyrians had sent a massive crown of gold to him for a present, congratulating him on his great success. They sent him many provisions from their city, and he received their presents as he would those from good friends. He was very gracious and friendly towards them, expressing his great desire to see their city and to sacrifice to Hercules. *[E211]* They told him that there was an altar in Palaetyros, or Old Tyre, on the continent nearby, and that it would be better to offer a sacrifice to Hercules on it, since it was the older of the two altars. When he heard this, he was so enraged that he vowed to destroy their city. It so happened that at that very time, certain select men from Carthage came to perform a yearly sacrifice to Hercules. The Tyrians were the founders of Carthage, and the Carthaginians had honoured them as the fathers of their city. These men exhorted them to hold out and to endure the siege like men. *[L297]* They assured them of speedy supplies and aid from Carthage, since the Carthaginians

at that time were a very strong naval power. {*Curtius, l. 4. c. 2. s. 2-12. 1:175-181} {Justin, Trogus, l. 11. c. 10.}

*1789.* Thus, Tyre was resolved for a war and endured a seven month siege. {*Diod. Sic., l. 17. c. 46. s. 5. 8:251} {*Josephus, Antiq., l. 11. c. 8. s. 4. (325) 6:471} {*Curtius, l. 4. c. 4. s. 19. 1:205} {*Plutarch, Alexander, l. 1. c. 2. 1:297} Their king Azelmious was absent at sea. He had left Autophradates, his son, behind him in the city. {*Arrian, Anabasis, l. 2. c. 15. s. 7. 1:181} Alexander levelled Palaetyrus, or old Tyre, to the ground. He sent for all the men in the surrounding country to come and help his men throw the stones and rubbish of the entire city into the channel that ran between the two cities. He built a causeway of half a mile long from the old city across to Tyre, according to Diodorus. Curtius agreed with him, while Pliny said it was seven hundred paces long. {*Pliny, l. 5. c. 17. (76) 2:279} {*Diod. Sic., l. 17. c. 40. s. 4,5. 8:233} {*Curtius, l. 4. c. 2. s. 16-21. 8:181,183}

*1790.* Amyntas, the son of Antiochus, had with him four thousand Greeks who had fled from the battle of Issus (as I mentioned previously). He had defected from Alexander to Darius before the battle. Sabaces, a Persian governor of Egypt, had been killed in the battle of Issus. They set sail from Cyprus to Pelusium and seized the city. Amyntas pretended that he had come to take charge of it at the order of Darius, to replace Sabaces and so deceived the garrison at Pelusium. From there, he went with his army to Memphis. At the news of his coming, the Egyptians came from the towns and the country to help him against the Persians. With their help, he routed the Persians when they attacked him and forced them into the city again. Soon after this, the Persians, followed the advice of Mazaces, their captain when he saw the Greeks scattered about and busy plundering the countryside. The Persians under Mazaces sallied forth again and in a surprise attack, they cut Amyntas and all his troops to pieces. {*Curtius, l. 3. c. 11. s. 18,19. 1:133} {*Curtius, l. 4. c. 1. s. 27-33. 1:169-173}

*1791.* Some of Darius' captains and their troops, who had escaped from the battle at Issus, along with some Cappadocians and Paphlagonians, went to retake Lydia. Antigonus, who was Alexander's commander, routed them in three battles. At the same time, the Macedonian fleet came from Greece and attacked Aristomenes, who had been sent by Darius to retake the Hellespont. They sank or captured all the Persian fleet. {*Curtius, l. 4. c. 1. s. 34-36. 1:173}

*1792.* While Alexander was besieging Tyre, he sent to Jaddua, the high priest at Jerusalem, and demanded supplies and other provisions from him, plus the tribute they had formerly paid to Darius. Jaddua replied that he was bound by a previous oath of allegiance to Darius, and that he could not be freed from that oath while Darius was alive. Alexander was very angry and swore that as soon as he had taken Tyre, he would march against Jerusalem. {*Josephus, Antiq., l. 11. c. 8. s. 3. (317-319) 6:469}

1793. At the start of the siege of Tyre, Sanaballetes, the Cushite, defected from Darius and came with eight thousand men. (Some editions of Josephus say seven thousand men. Editor.) Alexander graciously received him. Sanaballetes sought permission to build a temple on his own land and to make his son-in-law, Manasseh, who was the brother of Jaddua the high priest at Jerusalem, its high priest. When he obtained permission, and because he was now growing old, he quickly began the work. He built a temple and made Manasseh its high priest, thinking that by this he would bestow great honour on the posterity of his daughter. {*Josephus, Antiq., l. 11. c. 8. s. 4. (321-325) 6:469,471} [L298]

1794. Alexander planned to make a broader causeway from the continent for an easier approach to Tyre. After he had built new engines of war, he marched with his targeteers and a squadron of Agrians to Sidon, where he gathered as many ships as he possibly could, for he knew it would be impossible to take Tyre as long as Tyre was the master of the sea. {*Arrian, Anabasis, l. 2. c. 19. s. 6. 1:191,193}

1795. Meanwhile, when Gerostratus, the king of Aradus, and Enylus, the king of Byblus, found that all their cities had already been taken by Alexander, they abandoned Autophradates and his fleet and came with their fleets to Alexander. Some ships of the Sidonians also came with them. Alexander now had a navy of eighty ships. At the same time Rhodes sent a fleet of ten ships to Alexander, one of which was called Periplus. An additional three came from Soli and Mallus. [E212] Ten came from Lycia. Macedonia sent a ship of fifty oars under Captain Proteas, the son of Andronicus. A little later, certain kings of Cyprus sent a hundred and twenty ships to the port of Sidon. They had heard of his victory at Issus and the news that all Phoenicia had yielded to him. Alexander forgave them the previous wrongs they had done him, for they had previously sided with Darius of necessity, not of their own free choice. Azelmious, the king of Tyre, left Autophradates and returned to his own city of Tyre while it was thus besieged. He was within the city when it was later taken, according to Arrian. {*Arrian, Anabasis, l. 2. c. 20. s. 1-3. 1:193} {*Arrian, Anabasis, l. 2. c. 24. s. 4. 1:209}

1796. Alexander was cutting timber for his ships on Mount Lebanon when the wild Arabians suddenly attacked the Macedonians while they were busy at their work. They killed thirty of them and carried away almost as many prisoners. Alexander left Perdiccas and Craterus, or, as Polyaenus said, Parmenion, to continue the siege of Tyre, while he went with a lightly armed band into Arabia. {*Curtius, l. 4. c. 2. s. 24. 1:185} {*Curtius, l. 4. c. 3. s. 1. 1:185} Polyaenus confirmed that he made an excursion into Arabia. {Polyaenus, Strategmata, l. 4.} Arrian gave more details. He said that Alexander, with certain cavalry troops, lightly armed targeteers and his squadron of Agrians, went into Arabia as far as Anti-Lebanon. Plutarch stated that he marched against the Arabians who lived opposite Anti-Lebanon. {*Arrian, Anabasis, l. 2. c. 20. s. 4,5. 1:193,195} {*Plutarch, Alexander, l. 1. c. 24. s. 6. 7:293}

1797. When he came to the mountainous country of those parts, he planned to leave his cavalry and march on foot, as others did. The body of his army had gone a good distance ahead of him, the night was approaching and the enemy was close. Lysimachus, his childhood instructor, was exhausted from the journey and Alexander did not want to leave him in that condition. Alexander encouraged him and helped him along. Before he knew it, he and his group were separated from the rest of his company. He would have to pass that night in the dark, in a bitterly cold frost, and in a place devoid of all relief. Not far off, however, he saw many fires made by the enemies. Since he had a nimble and fit body, he ran to the nearest fire and killed the enemies that sat by it. He brought a firebrand back with him and kindled a fire for himself and the small group of Macedonians that were with him. This fire became so large, that the enemies were terrified and did not move against him. So he and his company lay safely all that night. This story was told about him by Plutarch, citing Chares, a Mitylenean who was one of the chroniclers of the deeds of Alexander. {*Plutarch, Alexander, l. 1. c. 24. s. 6-8. 7:295}

1798. When he had taken all that country, partly on amicable terms and partly by force, he returned to Sidon only eleven days after he had left it. He discovered that Alexander, the son of Polemocrates, had recently arrived with four thousand Greek mercenaries. {*Arrian, Anabasis, l. 2. c. 20. s. 5. 1:195}

1799. His navy was now outfitted and totalled a hundred and ninety ships, according to Curtius, or two hundred, according to Diodorus. Alexander sailed from Sidon for Tyre, in a very good formation. [L299] He was in the right wing, in a ship of five tiers of oars. The kings of Cyprus and the rest of the Phoenicians were also in that squadron, except for Pnytagoras, who, together with Craterus, commanded the left wing. {*Arrian, Anabasis, l. 2. c. 20. s. 6. 1:195} {*Curtius, l. 4. c. 3. s. 11. 1:189,191}

## 3672c AM, 4382 JP, 332 BC

*1800.* Thirty commissioners arrived from Carthage and brought Tyre word that the Carthaginians were so embroiled with war at home that they could not possibly send help to them at this time. This did not discourage the men of Tyre, but they sent away their wives and children to Carthage, considering it a safer place for them, irrespective of what might happen at Tyre. {*Curtius, l. 4. c. 3. s. 19,20. 1:193,195} {*Diod. Sic., l. 17. c. 41. s. 1.2. 8:233} {Justin, Trogus, l. 11. c. 10.}

*1801.* After Apollo had appeared to various men in dreams, signifying that he would leave the city, the superstitious men of Tyre took strong golden chains and bound his image tightly to the foot of his shrine. This image had been sent there from Syracuse, according to Curtius, or from Gela in Sicily by the Carthaginians, as we have noted from Diodorus. {See note on 3599 AM. <<1403>>} They fastened the chain to the altar of Hercules, the tutelar god of that city, as if, by his strength, he were able to keep Apollo from leaving. {*Curtius, l. 4. c. 3. s. 21,22. 1:195} {*Diod. Sic., l. 17. c. 41. s. 7,8. 8:235} {*Plutarch, Alexander, l. 1. c. 24. s. 3,4. 7:293}

*1802.* While Alexander was besieging Tyre, envoys came to him from Darius, offering him ten thousand talents (not, as Valerius Maximus wrote, a million) to ransom his mother, wife and children and all the territory lying between the Hellespont and the Halys River. Darius would give his daughter in marriage to Alexander. This offer was discussed in a council of his friends. It is reported that Parmenion said that if he were Alexander, he would not refuse those conditions, whereupon Alexander replied that neither would he, if he were Parmenion. *[E213]* Alexander wrote back to Darius that he was offering him nothing except what was already his. Therefore, he wished him to come in person to ask for his wife back, and to accept such conditions as Alexander would give him. {*Arrian, Anabasis, l. 2. c. 25. s. 1-3. 1:211,213} {Justin, Trogus, l. 11. c. 12.} {*Curtius, l. 4. c. 5. s. 1-8. 1:205-209} {*Plutarch, Sayings of Kings and Commanders (180b) 3:59} {*Plutarch, Alexander, l. 1. c. 29. s. 4. 7:311} {*Valerius Maximus, l. 6. c. 4. ext. 3. 2:51}

*1803.* Tyre was taken when Anicetes (or Nicetus, according to Dionysius of Halicarnassus, in Dinarchus) was archon in Athens, in the month of Hekatombaion. {*Arrian, Anabasis, l. 2. c. 24. s. 6. 1:211} This was in the middle of that month, at the very end of the 112th Olympiad. In Plutarch we find that it was on the 30th day of the month of Loos, according to the Macedonian calendar, and the 5th of the month of Hekatombaion, on the Athenian calendar. {*Plutarch, Alexander, l. 1. c. 25. s. 1,2. 7:295,297} This was July 24, as I have shown in my dis-

course on the solar years of the Macedonians and Asians. {Ussher, Macedonian and Asiatic Year, c. 5. fin.}

*1804.* Justin said that Tyre was taken by treason, {Justin, Trogus, l. 1. c. 10.} Polyaenus said it was by a stratagem, {Polyaenus, Strategmata, l. 1.} and Diodorus, Arrian and Curtius said it was by pure force. When the enemies had broken into the city, the townsmen still kept up the fight until seven thousand of their number had been cut to pieces. {*Diod. Sic., l. 17. c. 46. s. 3. 8:251}

*1805.* Arrian stated that eight thousand of the inhabitants were killed. Curtius said that after the battle a further two thousand were hung up all along the shore. Diodorus stated that Alexander hanged two thousand young men, all in their prime. Justin said that, mindful of the former slaughter by the inhabitants, Alexander crucified all that were captured. He put them to a death befitting a slave, because the Tyrian slaves had made a conspiracy against their own masters and had murdered both them and all the freemen of that city. *[L300]* The slaves had set up their own government and killed everyone except Straton, and an old man with his son. The slaves established the kingdom on Straton and his posterity. {*Arrian, Anabasis, l. 2. c. 24. s. 4. 1:209} {*Curtius, l. 4. c. 4. s. 17. 1:205} {*Diod. Sic., l. 17. c. 46. s. 3,4. 8:251}

*1806.* Concerning Alexander, Justin further added:

"He spared all the descendants of Straton and restored the kingdom to him and his posterity."

*1807.* (This possibly refers to Ballonymus, whom Diodorus confused with Abdalonymus, the man Alexander had made king of the Sidonians a short time earlier.)

"Alexander left the city to be repopulated by its innocent and harmless inhabitants. When he had abolished that wicked generation of slaves, he hoped to be considered the founder of a new and better people there."

*1808.* It was because of this that Justin saw Alexander as the restorer and rebuilder of Tyre. {Justin, Trogus, l. 18. c. 3,4.} All the other writers saw him not as its founder but as its destroyer. The prophecy of Isaiah concurred with this. {Isa 23:1} {Apc 1Ma 1:1} For if we believe Curtius, Alexander spared those who fled to the temples and killed everyone else, setting fire to their houses. According to Diodorus, he made slaves of anyone unable to bear arms, as well as the women and girls. This came to over thirteen thousand, even though most had been sent away to Carthage. However, according to Arrian, Alexander spared King Azemilcus (Diodorus called him Straton) and the commissioners who had come from

Carthage to sacrifice to Hercules. All the rest, which came to thirty thousand, he sold as slaves. {*Diod. Sic., l. 17. c. 46. s. 4. 8:251} {*Arrian, Anabasis, l. 2. c. 24. s. 5,6. 1:209} {*Curtius, l. 4. c. 4. s. 13,14. 1:203}

1809. Curtius said that the Sidonians, who joined up with the rest of Alexander's soldiers, did not forget their blood ties with the Tyrians. For they believed that they had all been brought there by Agenor, who was the founder of both cities. The Sidonians managed to get fifteen thousand Tyrians into their ships and saved them. Curtius stated: {*Curtius, l. 4. c. 4. s. 15,16. 1:203}

"Tyre quickly recovered and later grew to be a city again."

1810. Strabo stated: {*Strabo, l. 16. c. 2. s. 23. 7:269}

"After this enormous calamity brought on them by Alexander, they quickly overcame their misfortunes by their navigational skills and with their purple dye industry."

1811. Justin stated: {Justin, Trogus, l. 18. c. 4.}

"By their parsimony and industry, they quickly recovered their strength again."

1812. This happened so quickly that in the eighteenth year from then, they endured another siege from Antigonus, who was then lord of all Asia. This siege lasted not seven months, as in the case of Alexander, but a full fifteen months. {*Diod. Sic., l. 19. c. 61. s. 5. 9:399,401} They were no longer content with their little city which was joined to the continent by Alexander's causeways and other works. They so enlarged their boundaries, that in Pliny's time the wall of their city enclosed almost three miles. If one included Palaetyrus or Old Tyre, the whole enclosure came to no less than nineteen miles, and the actual town covered almost three miles. {*Pliny, l. 5. c. 17. (76) 2:279}

1813. Admetus, who first got onto the wall with twenty targeteers, was killed, along with his targeteers, at the very first encounter with the enemy. During the entire time of the siege, no more than four hundred Macedonians were lost. {*Arrian, Anabasis, l. 2. c. 24. s. 4. 1:209} [E214]

1814. Alexander offered sacrifices to Hercules, marching to his temple in procession, with his entire forces in full armour. He also put on a show with his ships, and staged wrestling matches, a relay torch race and other games. There was a certain Tyrian ship, consecrated to his honour, which he had captured, and this he rededicated to himself. {*Arrian, Anabasis, l. 2. c. 24. s. 6. 1:211} He took the golden chain from off the image of Apollo, and also the robes it was attired in, and gave the image a new

name, *Alexander's friend*. {*Diod. Sic., l. 17. c. 46. s. 5,6. 8:251} Timaeus stated that Alexander captured Tyre on the very same day that the Carthaginians had taken the image of Apollo from Gela in Sicily. [L301] The Greeks offered a magnificent and solemn sacrifice to Apollo, as though it had been by his power and favour that they had captured Tyre. {*Diod. Sic., l. 13. c. 108. s. 4,5. 5:429,431}

1815. As soon as Alexander had taken Tyre, he marched into Judah, {*Eusebius, Chronicles, l. 1. 1:205} {*Pliny, l. 12. c. 54. (117,118) 4:83} and subdued all that part of Syria called Syria Palestina. {*Arrian, Anabasis, l. 2. c. 25. s. 4. 1:213} He personally went to fight against those places which would not willingly submit to him. {*Curtius, l. 4. c. 5. s. 13. 1:211} When he was on his march to Jerusalem, Jaddua, the high priest, who had been terrified by his former threats and now feared his rage, resorted to God by prayers and sacrifices on behalf of the safety of everyone. God warned him in a dream that he should call a holy day in the city and open the city gates wide. He and the rest of the priests would go out in their priestly garments and all the rest of the people would be dressed entirely in white and accompany him to meet Alexander. When Alexander saw this company coming to him from a distance, he went unaccompanied to the high priest. After he had prostrated himself before that God whose name he saw engraved on the golden plate of the high priest's mitre, he greeted him. When Parmenion asked the reason for his behaviour, he replied that while he was still in Macedonia planning the conquest of Asia, there appeared to him a man clothed like this high priest, who invited him into Asia and assured him of every success in its conquest. The priests went before him as he entered into Jerusalem. He went up to the temple and sacrificed to God in the manner which the priests showed him. They showed him the book of the prophet Daniel, in which it was written that a Greek should come and destroy the Persians. {Da 8:7,20,21 11:13} He did not doubt but that he was the one in the prophecy. After this he dismissed the company. {*Josephus, Antiq., l. 11. c. 8. s. 5. (327-337) 6:473-477}

1816. The next day, he assembled the people and asked them what they wanted from him. They replied they wanted nothing but that they might live according to the laws of their own country, and that every seventh year (in the sabbatical year when there was no harvest) they might be exempt from paying any tribute. He granted all they asked. When they asked further that he would allow the Jews who lived in the countries of Babylon and Media to live according to their own rites and laws, he answered that he would grant that request as soon as he had taken those countries, too. When he told them that if any of them would follow him in his wars they could use their own rites wherever they went, many enlisted to serve him. When he had settled everything in Jerusalem, he left and went to all the other cities of that country and was joyfully received everywhere. {*Josephus, Antiq., l. 11. c. 8. s. 6. (338,339) 6:479}

1817. One of Alexander's captains, Calas, went and recaptured Paphlagonia, which had defected from Alexander after the battle at Issus. After they had defeated Darius' captain Hydarnes, Alexander's captain, Antigonus, took Lycaonia and his other captain, Balacrus, captured the city of Miletus. {*Curtius, l. 4. c. 5. s. 13. 1:211}

1818. Alexander had given the government of Cilicia to Socrates and ordered Philotas, the son of Parmenion, to govern the country around Tyre. [L302] Coelosyria was committed to Andromachus by Parmenion, who wanted to follow Alexander in the war. Alexander commanded Hephaestion to sail along the coast of Phoenicia with the fleet, while he himself went with his whole army to Gaza {*Curtius, l. 4. c. 5. s. 9,10. 1:209} and besieged the garrison of the Persians for two months. {*Diod. Sic., l. 17. c. 48. s. 7,8. 8:257} {*Josephus, Antiq., l. 11. c. 8. s. 6. (340) 6:479}

1819. According to Josephus, the name of the captain of the garrison at Gaza was Babemesis, or, according to Curtius and Arrian, Batis, a eunuch. He was very loyal to his king. He hired some Arabian mercenaries and made a good provision of food and other things. He defended the walls, which were very strong, with a small company of men. {*Josephus, Antiq., l. 11. c. 8. s. 3. (320) 6:469} {*Arrian, Anabasis, l. 2. c. 25. s. 4. 1:213} {*Curtius, l. 4. c. 6. s. 7. 1:217}

1820. Alexander received two wounds at this siege. When Batis was taken alive, Alexander had cords or thongs drawn through his ankles and tied him to a chariot. He was dragged around the city. Ten thousand Persians and Arabians died in that siege. The Macedonians also lost some men. {*Curtius, l. 4. c. 6. s. 7-31. 1:217-225} Alexander sold all the women and children there as slaves. He repopulated the place with inhabitants from the neighbouring parts and made it the location of his garrison. {*Arrian, Anabasis, l. 2. c. 27. s. 7. 1:219} [E215] The following words of Strabo are hard to understand, unless they refer to an earlier time of that city. He stated: {*Strabo, l. 16. c. 2. s. 30. 7:277}

"Gaza, which was formerly a glorious city, was destroyed by Alexander and remained desolate."

1821. We will say that this referred to a later Gaza, built in another place, which Jerome affirmed in this way: {Jerome, De Locis Hebraicis}

"The question is, how in one of the prophets it is said, *And Gaza shall be turned into an everlasting heap* and it is answered as follows. There are scarcely any signs of the old city left to be seen. The present city of Gaza was built in another place, instead of in the location of the one which was destroyed."

1822. When Alexander had done what he wanted to do to Gaza, he sent Amyntas, the son of Andremon, to Macedonia with three ships, to bring him the best of the youth for his army. {*Diod. Sic., l. 17. c. 49. s. 1. 8:259} {*Curtius, l. 4. c. 6. s. 30. 1:225}

### 3673a AM, 4382 JP, 332 BC

1823. From Gaza, Alexander marched into Egypt, as he had previously planned to do. Seven days after he left Gaza, he came to a place which he named Alexander's Camp. From there he came to the city of Pelusium. {*Arrian, Anabasis, l. 3. c. 1. s. 1. 1:223} {*Curtius, l. 4. c. 7. s. 1-3. 1:225,227} He did not go back again from Gaza to Jerusalem, as Josephus incorrectly stated. {*Josephus, Antiq., l. 11. c. 8. s. 4. (325) 6:471}

1824. A large number of the Egyptians, who were expecting Alexander's arrival, assembled at Pelusium. They had been offended by the Persians' pride, avarice, and sacrilege, and eagerly welcomed the arrival of the Macedonians. {*Curtius, l. 4. c. 7. s. 1. 1:225} {*Diod. Sic., l. 17. c. 49. s. 1. 8:259}

1825. Alexander left a garrison in Pelusium and ordered his ships to go up the river to Memphis. He marched by land to Heliopolis, having the Nile River on his right all the way. Wherever he went, all the cities opened their gates to him. He passed the desert of Egypt and came at last to Heliopolis. After crossing the river, he marched toward Memphis. {*Arrian, Anabasis, l. 3. c. 1. s. 1-3. 1:223} The Persians there did not hinder his coming when they saw the general defection of the Egyptians from them. When he was not far from Memphis, he was met by Astraces, who commanded the garrison for Darius. He gave Alexander eight hundred talents and all his master's wardrobe. {*Curtius, l. 4. c. 7. s. 4,5. 1:227} However, Curtius wrote the name Astraces instead of Mazaces, as he had written in chapter four of the same book. {*Curtius, l. 4. c. 7. s. 4. 1:226 (variant reading)} [L303] Likewise Arrian, in the beginning of his third book, stated that Mazaces, a Persian whom Darius had made governor of Egypt, received Alexander into that province and its cities in a very friendly way. {*Arrian, Anabasis, l. 3. c. 1. s. 1,2. 1:223}

1826. Alexander offered his sacrifices at Memphis and there held athletic and musical games. The most expert and skilful men of all Greece entered these games to try to win the prizes. He came down the river to the sea, where he put his targeteers, archers, Agrians and the cavalry aboard the ships of his confederates and sailed with them to Canopus. There he picked a choice site for the city of Alexandria, between the Egyptian Sea and the Lake of Mareotis, or Maria. He named the future city after himself. {*Arrian, Anabasis, l. 3. c. 1. s. 4,5. 1:223,225} In that section of the town beside the sea and the shipping docks, there was a quarter called Rhacotes where stood a temple that had previously been the location of an ancient shrine dedicated to Serapis and Isis. Rhacotes was the previous name of the location of Alexandria. {*Strabo, l. 17. c. 1. s. 6-11. 8:23-47} {*Pausanias, Elis I, l. 5. c. 21. s. 12. 2:509} {*Tacitus, Histories, l. 4. c. 84. 3:167} {*Pliny, l. 5. c. 11. (62) 2:267}

1827. Alexandria was not built in the seventh year, as Eusebius {*Eusebius, Chronicles, l. 1. 1:205} and from him, Cyril of Alexandria {Cyril, Against Julian, l. 1.} and Cedrenus stated, but in the fifth year of Alexander's reign, and in the very first year of the 112th Olympiad, according to Solinus. {Solinus, c. 32.} Diodorus incorrectly stated in the second year and Eusebius wrongly stated in the third year. For we can determine precisely the exact time when Alexandria was built, from the interval of time between the taking of Tyre and that great battle at Gaugamela, and his deeds in that interim. From this, and from the fifth year of Darius and the month of Thoth in the 417th year of Nabonassar's account, which was the 14th day of September, according to our Julian calendar, or the first year of the 112th Olympiad, Ptolemy of Alexandria deduced the years of Alexander, whom he, in the Preface of his Ποτοχειρων Κθμονων (whereof this is one), after the fashion of all Alexandrians, called *his founder*.

1828. Deinocrates was the man who designed and laid out the streets of this city. (Plutarch called him Stasicrates, and other writers called him Deinocrates, or Cheirocrates. {*Plutarch, Alexander, l. 1. c. 72. 7:425,427} {*Plutarch, Fortune of Alexander, l. 2. c. 2. 4:433}) Deinocrates was that famous architect whose skill and industry the Ephesians used in the rebuilding of their temple of Diana. For the excellency of his workmanship shown in the temple, he deserved a place of honour in the annals of the world second only to the original builders of the temple. Strabo called the architect Cheirocrates. {*Strabo, l. 14. c. 1. s. 23. 6:227} {*Valerius Maximus, l. 1. c. 4. ext. 1. 1:55} {*Vitruvius, l. 2. c. 0. s. 1. 1:73} {*Pliny, l. 5. c. 11. (62) 2:267} {*Pliny, l. 7. c. 37. (126) 2:591} {Solinus, c. 32,40.} {*Ammianus Marcellinus, l. 22. c. 16. s. 7. 2:299}

## 3673b AM, 4383 JP, 331 BC

1829. Alexander got them started and wanted them to work quickly. [E216] He journeyed to the temple of Zeus Ammon, having an ambition to go there because he had been told that Perseus and Hercules had been there. {*Plutarch, Alexander, l. 1. c. 26. s. 6. 7:301} {*Arrian, Anabasis, l. 3. c. 3. s. 1. 1:229} This was affirmed by Callisthenes in the history of Alexander which he wrote, and he was cited by Strabo. {*Strabo, l. 17. c. 1. s. 43. 8:115,117}

1830. Therefore, he followed the coastline as far as Paraetonium, finding some fresh water along the way, two hundred miles from Alexandria, according to Aristobulus. {*Arrian, Anabasis, l. 3. c. 3. s. 3. 1:229}

1831. He was met about halfway by envoys from the Cyrenians. They presented him with a crown and other costly gifts, among which were three hundred horses trained for war and five chariots, each drawn by four horses. These were the best horses that could be found. He accepted these gifts and made a league of friendship with the Cyrenians. {*Diod. Sic., l. 17. c. 49. s. 3. 8:259}

1832. He passed through the dry country from Paraetonium to Mesogabas, where the temple of Ammon was. He wandered over the plains while the hot wind blew from the south. Callisthenes claimed that he was saved from death partly by a shower of rain, which settled the sand, and partly by a flock of ravens, which led him on the way. [L304] He further added this fable to the story, that often, when the men wandered out of the way in the dark, the ravens would call them back into the right way again with their cawing. {*Strabo, l. 17. c. 1. s. 43. 8:115,117} {*Plutarch, Alexander, l. 1. c. 27. 7:303}

1833. Ptolemy, the son of Lagus, stated that there were two serpents which went before the company, making a noise, and which led them to and from the temple again. However, Aristobulus, with whom most writers agree, stated that there were two ravens which persisted in flying before the army, and that these were Alexander's guides on the way there. {*Arrian, Anabasis, l. 3. c. 3. s. 5,6. 1:231}

1834. Having come to Bitter Lake, he went on about twelve miles farther and passed by the Cities of Ammon. After a day's journey from there, they came to Zeus Ammon's grove and the temple. {*Diod. Sic., l. 17. c. 49. s. 6. 8:261}

1835. There the priests of the temple had been secretly bribed beforehand and instructed what to say. As soon as Alexander approached to enter through the temple doors, they all came and greeted him by the name of Ammon's son. {Justin, Trogus, l. 11. c. 11.} So we learn from this event that the god, although deaf and dumb, had the power, through the priests, to lie as they wished. Anyone who came to consult the oracle could be told exactly what he wanted to hear. {Orosius, l. 3. c. 16.}

*1836.* Callisthenes stated that the priests permitted no one but Alexander to come into the temple in his ordinary attire. All the rest were required to change their clothes and to hear the oracle from the outside. The oracle told Alexander various things by signs and vague language, telling him plainly, however, that he was Zeus' son. {*Strabo, l. 17. c. 1. s. 43. 8:115} Yet Alexander, in a letter to his mother Olympias, said that he had received many secret oracles there, which he would tell her alone on his return. {*Plutarch, Alexander, l. 1. c. 27. s. 5. 7:305}

*1837.* In the same letter, or in some other letter to his mother (which I am sure was what Tertullian meant {*Tertullian, De Pallio, l. 1. c. 3. 4:8}), Alexander said that he had been told by Leon, a principal priest among the Egyptians, that those who were now gods, had formerly been men. In worshipping them, the countries preserved the memory of their kings and ancestors. {*Augustine, City of God, l. 8. c. 5. 2:147,148} {*Augustine, City of God, l. 8. c. 27. 2:167} {De Consens. Evangelist, l. 1. c. 23.} {Minucius Felix, Octavius} {Cyprian, De Idolor. Vanitate.} At the beginning of the letter in which he had written this to his mother, he opened with:

> "Alexander the king, the son of Zeus Ammon, sends greetings to his mother Olympias."

*1838.* She, in her answer, very wittily replied (from Marcus Varro, in a book of his entitled *Orestes*, or *On Madness* {*Aulus Gellius, Attic Nights, l. 13. c. 4. s. 1,2. 2:423}):

> "Now, my good son, I pray thee, be content and do not accuse me, nor lay anything to my charge before Hera. For she will do me some shrewd turn, if you in your letters make me a step-queen to her."

*1839.* Alexander was well pleased at having received such an answer, as he admitted by his own confession. He returned from there to Egypt by the same way he had come, according to Aristobulus. Ptolemy said he took a shorter way to Memphis. {*Arrian, Anabasis, l. 3. c. 4. s. 5. 1:233}

*1840.* When he arrived at Memphis, he found that Antipater had sent four hundred Greek mercenaries under the command of Menoetas, the son of Hegesander and about five hundred cavalry from Thrace led by Asclepiodorus. At Memphis, Alexander sacrificed to Zeus and made oblations to him with his entire army, who were all in their complete armour. They held athletic and musical games. {*Arrian, Anabasis, l. 3. c. 5. s. 1,2. 1:233}

*1841.* Ordering the inhabitants of the neighbouring towns and cities to leave their dwellings, he moved them into Alexandria and populated that place with a large number of inhabitants. {*Curtius, l. 4. c. 8. s. 5. 1:239} {Justin, Trogus, l. 11. c. 11.} [E217] He also moved a colony of the Jews there, whose virtue and good behaviour he greatly approved

of, deeming them worthy of special trust. [L305] As a reward for their service in the war, he made them free citizens and gave them equal honours and privileges with the Greeks. The group that was there went by the name of Alexandrians as well as by the name of Macedonians. {*Josephus, Jewish War, l. 2. c. 18. s. 7. (487) 2:513} {*Josephus, Apion, l. 2. c. 4. (42) 1:309}

*1842.* He also gave lands to Sanaballetes' soldiers, whom he ordered to follow him inland into the country of Egypt as far as Thebes, entrusting them with the keeping of that territory in his absence. {*Josephus, Antiq., l. 11. c. 8. s. 6. (345) 6:481}

*1843.* Alexander had a burning desire to go and visit the inner and more remote parts of Egypt and Ethiopia, but his present war with Darius forced him to delay such expeditions. He made Aeschylus and Peucestes, the Macedonian, governors of Egypt, with an army of four thousand men, and ordered Polemon to defend the mouths of the Nile River with thirty ships. {*Curtius, l. 4. c. 8,4. s. 3,4. 1:237} Arrian stated that he made Peucestes, the son of Macatetus, and Balacrus, the son of Amyntas, commanders of the foot soldiers whom he left there. He made Polemon, the son of Theramenes, admiral of the fleet to defend the mouths of the Nile River and all the sea lying adjacent to Egypt. The civil government of the whole country he committed to Doloaspis, a native of Egypt, according to Arrian. {*Arrian, Anabasis, l. 3. c. 5. s. 2-7. 1:233-237}

*1844.* Curtius further stated that he left Apollonius to govern Africa, which bordered on Egypt, and Cleomenes to gather the tribute from both Africa and Egypt. To much the same end, Arrian stated that he left Apollonius, the son of Charinus, to govern Libya, which bordered on Egypt to the west. He appointed Cleomenes to take care of Arabia on the east from the city called Heroonpolis, which bordered on Arabia Petra. He was ordered to receive all tribute. The judicial administration he committed to the governors and justices of the country, as had been the practice before. Aristotle stated that Cleomenes of Alexandria was the governor of Egypt. {Aristotle, Oeconomics, l. 2.} He is the same person of whom Arrian said he was Cleomenes from Naucratis. {*Arrian, Anabasis, l. 3. c. 5. s. 4. 1:235} Freinshemius, who was very good at finding errors, said that in the one instance it should be *of the Nauacritians*, or *Naucratites*, and in the other, *commander of Alexandria in Egypt*. The result of this is that Cleomenes, governor of Alexandria, was a native of Naucratis, which was an ancient colony established in Egypt by the Milesians. He was in charge of the administration and of populating this city. We may in part gather this from Aristotle, who said that Alexander ordered him to populate a city near Pharos.

(Alexandria is only a mile by sea from there.) He was to redirect all the trade from Canopus to Alexandria. Justin stated that Alexander committed the building of Alexandria to Cleomenes. {*Justin, Trogus, l. 13. c. 4.} It may be added that Alexander wrote to him eight years later, ordering him to build two temples to the deceased Hephaestion, one in Alexandria and the other in Pharos. Also, all bills of lading and other contracts of merchants were to have the name of Hephaestion inscribed on them, according to Arrian, who added further that this Cleomenes was an extremely wicked man and one who did the Egyptians a thousand injustices. {*Arrian, Anabasis, l. 7. c. 23. s. 6,7. 2:285}

1845. When Alexander had gone down the Nile, Hector, a son of Parmenion, who was in the flower of his youth and a great favourite of Alexander, desired to catch up to him. He jumped into a little boat and others jumped in also, with the result that the overloaded boat sank and Hector drowned. [L306] Alexander was very grieved by the loss and when the body was recovered, he gave it a splendid funeral. {*Curtius, l. 4. c. 8. s. 7-9. 1:239}

1846. Shortly after this, Alexander received news that Andromachus had been burned alive by the inhabitants of Samaria. He immediately marched off, as quickly as he could, to exact vengeance on them. {*Curtius, l. 4. c. 8. s. 9. 1:239}

## 3673c AM, 4383 JP, 331 BC

1847. At the beginning of spring, Alexander made bridges over the Nile River and its channels around Memphis. From there, he went toward Phoenicia. {*Arrian, Anabasis, l. 3. c. 6. s. 1. 1:237} Along the way, the men who had murdered Andromachus were delivered into his hands and executed, while Memnon was sent to replace Andromachus. {*Curtius, l. 4. c. 8. s. 11. 1:241} When Alexander had captured the city of Samaria, he gave it to his Macedonians, to be inhabited by them. (Eusebius {*Eusebius, Chronicles, l. 1. 1:205} and Cedrenus derived it from him.) However, the territory belonging to it he gave to the Jews, for their loyalty to him. They did not pay him any tribute for it, according to Josephus, who based this on Hecataeus of Abdera. {*Josephus, Apion, l. 2. c. 4. (43) 1:309} The temple at Mount Gerizim was spared. [E218] If any at Jerusalem were in trouble for eating forbidden meats, breaching the Sabbath or crimes of a similar nature, they immediately defected to the Shechemites and said that they had been falsely accused. {*Josephus, Antiq., l. 11. c. 8. s. 2. (312) 6:465} Similar quarrels between the Jews and Samaritans happened not only there, but at Alexandria in Egypt as well, because of the different customs and rites used in the two temples. {*Josephus, Antiq., l. 11. c. 2. s. 1. (19) 6:323} {*Josephus, Antiq., l. 13. c. 3. s. 4. (74-76) 7:263}

1848. When Alexander reached Tyre, he met up with his fleet, which he had sent there ahead of him. He sacrificed to Hercules a second time, and held athletic and musical games, {*Arrian, Anabasis, l. 3. c. 6. s. 2. 1:237} for which the kings of Cyprus had the duty of providing suitable actors. Nicocreon, king of Salamis, sent Thessalus, a man very highly regarded by Alexander. Pasicrates, king of Soli, sent Athenodorus, who took the prize over all by a majority decision. {*Plutarch, Alexander, l. 1. c. 29. s. 1,3. 7:309} These kings of Cyprus had long before defected from Darius to Alexander and had sent him ships when he besieged Tyre. From that time on, he always treated them with the honour they deserved. {*Curtius, l. 4. c. 8. s. 14. 1:241} Concerning Nicocreon, it was also said that Anaxarchus of Abdera, the philosopher, said to Alexander while sitting at supper, that there was a certain Persian governor's head which had previously been served there. For having said this, Nicocreon later had him put to a most miserable death, after Alexander had died. {*Diogenes Laertius, Anaxarchus, l. 9. c. 10. (58,59) 2:471,473}

1849. Alexander made Coeranus, a Beroean, treasurer of Phoenicia, to gather his tribute there. In Asia, he had Philoxenus do the same in the regions of Asia on this east side of the Taurus Mountains. He put Harpalus into the position of being in charge of the money in his own treasury, and sent Menander, one of his Companion Cavalry, into Lydia to be the governor there, putting Clearchus into Menander's former job of overseeing the mercenaries. He replaced Arimmass with Asclepiodorus, the son of Eunicus, as governor of Syria. {*Arrian, Anabasis, l. 3. c. 6. s. 4-8. 1:239,241}

1850. When these tasks had been completed, Alexander made an offering at Hercules' shrine of a large vessel of gold, containing thirty dishes. Being now anxious to get after Darius, he marched on toward the Euphrates River. {*Curtius, l. 4. c. 8. s. 16. 1:243}

1851. When news reached Darius that Alexander would follow him wherever he went, he ordered all countries, no matter how far away they were, to come to him at Babylon. [L307] His army was now again grown to about half the size it had been at Issus in Cilicia, with many lacking weapons, which were normally provided for them. {*Curtius, l. 4. c. 9. s. 3. 1:243} He was said to have forty-five thousand cavalry and two hundred thousand foot soldiers. {*Curtius, l. 4. c. 12. s. 13. 1:275} At Issus, his forces in both these categories had far exceeded these in number. It is certain that the number found in Justin and in Orosius is short of what it really was, four hundred or four hundred and four thousand foot soldiers and a hundred thousand cavalry. {Justin, Trogus, l. 11. c. 12.} {Orosius, l. 3. c. 17.} Plutarch said there were ten million men, {*Plutarch, Alexander, l. 1. c. 31. s. 1. 7:315} and in another work he said a hundred million. {*Plutarch, Sayings of Kings and Commanders (180c) 3:59} (These errors in the numbers of the men do not exist in the current editions of Plutarch by Loeb. Editor.) It should be a million men. Diodorus was in general agreement with this. He said there were eight hundred thousand foot soldiers and two hundred thousand cavalry. {*Diod. Sic., l. 17. c. 53. s. 3. 8:271} Arrian attributed to the foot soldiers the same number as Plutarch did to the sum of both cavalry and foot soldiers. Arrian's figure was a million men, to which he added forty thousand cavalry. {*Arrian, Anabasis, l. 3. c. 8. s. 6. 1:249} Though some, instead of forty thousand, wrote four hundred thousand cavalry, so that the number of cavalry might be somewhat more proportional to the number of the foot soldiers, and also, so that the number of cavalry here might not seem so very much smaller than it had been at Issus. Curtius, however, said it was far in excess of it. {*Curtius, l. 4. c. 9. s. 3. 1:243} In addition, Darius had two hundred scythe-bearing chariots and fifteen elephants which the Indians had brought him. On the other side, Alexander's army did not have more than seven thousand cavalry and forty thousand foot soldiers in it. {*Arrian, Anabasis, l. 3. c. 8. s. 6. 1:249} {*Arrian, Anabasis, l. 3. c. 12. s. 5. 1:263}

1852. With this vast army, Darius moved from Babylon to Nineveh. He had the Tigris River on his left hand and the Euphrates on his right, while his army filled all that large plain of Mesopotamia. {*Diod. Sic., l. 17. c. 53. s. 3,4. 8:271,273} {*Curtius, l. 4. c. 9. s. 11-15. 1:247,249} When they had crossed the Tigris River, he heard that the enemy was not far away. He sent Satropates, leader of the Persian cavalry, with a thousand cavalry to hinder the approach of the enemy. He had ordered Mazaeus to lay waste and burn all the lands through which Alexander was to pass. Darius thought that lack of supplies might defeat Alexander, since he had nothing else but the spoil of the country for supplies. Darius marched to Arabela and leaving his baggage there, marched forward as far as the Lycus River, where he made a bridge. When he and his army had crossed over it in five days, they marched ten miles to the Bumolus River. {*Curtius, l. 4. c. 9. s. 6-10. 1:245,247} Arrian said that he pitched his camp at Gaugamela by the Bumolus River, since he called the place, Bumodus. {*Arrian, Anabasis, l. 6. c. 11. s. 6. 2:133} {*Arrian, Anabasis, l. 3. c. 8. s. 7. 1:249} It was a level field, because Darius ordered any hilly or uneven ground there to be made level, to allow his cavalry a freer range to attack, while the whole area would also be more open to his view. {*Arrian, Anabasis, l. 3. c. 8. s. 7. 1:249} {*Curtius, l. 4. c. 9. s. 10. 1:247} [E219]

### 3673d AM, 4383 JP, 331 BC

1853. Alexander advanced to Thapsacus, a large city in Syria, in the month of Hekatombaion, when Aristophanes was archon at Athens. That was in the second year of the 112th Olympiad, at the very beginning of that year. Here the Euphrates River had a ford where Alexander found two bridges already constructed. They were not completely finished, nor did they quite reach to the other bank. Mazaeus had been sent by Darius to secure that crossing, but as soon as Mazaeus heard that Alexander was coming, he fled with all his army. [L308] When he was gone, Alexander quickly completed the bridges to the other side of the river and his army crossed over and then marched toward Babylon, leaving the Euphrates River and the mountains of Armenia on their left hand. They did not take the shortest route there, as the longer route was more suitable for provisions for his army and was cooler and more comfortable for the march. On the way, he intercepted some scouts from Darius, who informed him that Darius, with all his army, was on the bank of the Tigris River to prevent him from crossing. His forces were now far more numerous than when he had fought with Alexander in Cilicia. When Alexander reached the river, he did not find Darius or anyone else. {*Arrian, Anabasis, l. 3. c. 7. s. 1-5. 1:241-245}

1854. Alexander crossed the Tigris River. Although there was no one there to hinder him, it was difficult and dangerous to cross, because the river ran quite swiftly there. He crossed safely, however, and lost nothing except a small quantity of his baggage. {*Arrian, Anabasis, l. 3. c. 7. s. 5. 1:243,254} {*Diod. Sic., l. 17. c. 55. s. 3-6. 8:277,279} {*Curtius, l. 4. c. 9. s. 14-16. 1:249} Eratosthenes calculated it to be about three hundred miles from Thapsacus, where they had crossed the Euphrates, to the place where he crossed the Tigris. {*Strabo, l. 2. c. 1. s. 24. 1:301} {*Strabo, l. 16. c. 1. s. 22. 7:231}

1855. Alexander broke camp at the bank of the Tigris River and led his army through the country of Assyria. On his left hand were the mountains of Sogdiana and on the right, the Tigris River. On the fourth day after Alexander had crossed the Tigris River, Mazaeus attacked him with a thousand cavalry. Alexander sent Aristo, who commanded the cavalry of Paeonia, to check the attack. Aristo singled out Satropates, the commander of the attacking troops, and ran a spear through his throat. Although wounded, he fled away and Aristo chased him through the middle of the enemies' troops. Knocking him off his horse, Aristo decapitated him and then brought his head and threw it down at Alexander's feet. He said:

> "Sir, in our country, such a present used to be rewarded with a cup of gold."

1856. Alexander smiled and replied: {*Plutarch, Alexander, l. 1. c. 39. s. 1. 7:339} {*Arrian, Anabasis, l. 3. c. 7. s. 1,2. 1:241,243} {*Curtius, l. 4. c. 9. s. 23,25. 1:251}

"Yes, with an empty one, but I will give you one full of wine."

1857. Alexander camped there for two days, then ordered the troops to move on the following day. That night there was an eclipse of the moon in the first watch of the night. At first the moon was dimmed, then soon after, its entire face turned a blood-like colour. The army, in considering the upcoming battle, were first troubled and later terrified at this sight. {*Curtius, l. 4. c. 10. s. 1,2. 1:253} Pliny correctly noted that: {*Pliny, l. 2. c. 72. (180) 1:313}

"The moon was eclipsed at Arbela, in the second hour of the night, and was then seen rising in Sicily."

1858. Ptolemy was incorrect when he stated that: {Ptolemy, Geography, l. 1. c. 4.}

"The moon was eclipsed in the fifth hour of the night and was seen at Carthage at the second hour of the night."

1859. Plutarch correctly stated that the eclipse happened in the month of Boedromion, about the beginning of the Great Mysteries at Athens. That was at the full moon in the very middle of that month, which was the time of the month when the Great Mysteries were set to begin and then they continued to be celebrated for a few days thereafter. The astronomical account showed that the eclipse happened on the 20th day of our September. {*Plutarch, Alexander, l. 1. c. 31. s. 3,4. 7:317}

1860. To encourage his soldiers, who were distressed at this sight, Alexander consulted the Egyptian soothsayers he had with him. Their answer was that the sun represented Greece, and the moon, Persia. Therefore, as often as the moon was eclipsed, it portended the ruin of those countries which it represented. {*Curtius, l. 4. c. 10. s. 3-7. 1:255} Alexander at once offered sacrifices to the sun, the moon and the earth, because all three must be in correct position for an eclipse of the moon. [L309] Aristander, who was Alexander's soothsayer, declared publicly that the eclipse portended nothing but good and joyous success to Alexander and the Macedonians. He said that the battle should therefore be fought in that very month, and that the sacrifices which had been offered predicted a victory for Alexander. {*Arrian, Anabasis, l. 3. c. 7. s. 6. 1:245}

1861. When Alexander knew the soldiers were now very confident of victory, he ordered them to march on the second watch of the next night. They had the Tigris River on the right hand and the Gordian Mountains on the left. The next morning, Alexander, with a small troop, attacked a thousand Persian scouts. [E220] Some they killed and the rest he took prisoner. He then sent some of his own company on to discover what was ahead. He also wanted them to put out the fires in the towns and villages which the inhabitants had set. As they had fled from the enemy, they had set fire to the barns and stacks of grain, but although the tops were burned, the fire had not consumed the piles. Hence the Macedonians saved a large quantity of food for themselves. Mazaeus, who had previously burned what he pleased, now fled before the rapidly approaching enemies, leaving much untouched. {*Curtius, l. 4. c. 10. s. 8-14. 1:255,257}

1862. Alexander knew that Darius was not more than twenty miles away. Since he had plenty of provisions for his troops, he stayed there another four days. {*Curtius, l. 4. c. 10. s. 14,15. 1:257}

## 3674a AM, 4383 JP, 331 BC

1863. During this time, Alexander intercepted certain letters sent from Darius, trying to incite the Greeks to murder or otherwise to betray Alexander. {*Curtius, l. 4. c. 10. s. 16. 1:257}

1864. Statira, the wife of Darius, was tired of this long trip and through distress and worry, aborted the child she was carrying and died. Alexander was deeply grieved by this, and prepared a very elaborate and costly funeral for her. {*Curtius, l. 4. c. 10. s. 18-24. 1:259} {Justin, Trogus, l. 11. c. 12.} {*Plutarch, Alexander, l. 1. c. 30. s. 1. 7:311} {*Plutarch, Fortune of Alexander, l. 2. c. 6. 4:451}

1865. While others were busy with the funeral, Tyrus or Tyriotes, a eunuch, stole away and carried the news of her death to Darius, who was at first deeply perplexed and troubled at it, but when he learned of the respect Alexander had always had for her and his chaste behaviour toward her, he lifted up his hands to heaven and prayed to the gods. He said that, if it were decreed and there was no option left for him, he wished that no one should sit on the throne of Cyrus other than an enemy as just and a conqueror as merciful as Alexander. {*Curtius, l. 4. c. 10. s. 25-28. 1:259,261} {*Plutarch, Alexander, l. 1. c. 30. 7:311-315}

1866. Darius was so overcome with Alexander's great clemency and chastity toward his wife that he again tried to make peace with Alexander. He sent ten of his leading men to offer Alexander new conditions. He would pay thirty thousand talents for the ransom of his mother and two daughters. He also offered Alexander his other daughter Septina, or Statipna or Sartina or Statira, for a wife. (Various editions of Curtius used all these variations.) Everything lying between the Hellespont and the Euphrates he would give as a dowry. {*Curtius, l. 4. c. 11. s. 1-6. 1:263,265} Alexander replied that he had always found the money of Darius to be soliciting, sometimes his soldiers to revolt from him, or sometimes his nearest friends to murder him. Therefore, he was resolved to pursue him to the death, no longer as a noble enemy, but as a malefactor and a poisoning murderer. Whatever Darius had already lost, or what still remained in his hands, was the reward of war. Further, war would set the bounds between their two kingdoms, and each would have what tomorrow's fortune would give. {*Curtius, l. 4. c. 11. s. 16-22. 1:269} {Justin, Trogus, l. 11. c. 12.} {*Diod. Sic., l. 17. c. 54. 8:273-277} [L310]

1867. The envoys returned and told Darius that he must fight, so he promptly sent Mazaeus ahead of him with three thousand cavalry to hold the passes through which the enemy would come. With the rest, he marched in good battle array for about two thousand yards and there made a stand, expecting the enemy to attack him there. Alexander left all his luggage within his camp and setting a reasonable guard over it, he advanced to meet the enemy. {*Curtius, l. 4. c. 12. s. 1-5. 1:271}

1868. At that very instant, a sudden panic gripped Alexander's army. The sky, since it was the summer season, seemed to sparkle and radiate like fire. They imagined that they saw flames of fire issuing from Darius' camp. With the sound of trumpets, Alexander signified to them that all was well. Ordering those that stood next to the standard in every company to lay down their weapons at their feet, he told them to pass the word along to those next to them, to do likewise. When this had been done, Alexander showed them that there was no cause for fear and that the enemy was still a long way off. They finally recovered their courage and picked up their weapons again. For extra safety, Alexander decided to make his stand there and to fortify his camp. {*Curtius, l. 4. c. 12. s. 14-17. 1:275} {Polyaenus, Strategmata, l. 4.}

1869. Alexander assembled all his forces by night and began to march about the second watch, planning to fight as soon as it was day. {*Arrian, Anabasis, l. 3. c. 9. s. 2. 1:249}

1870. Mazaeus had taken up his stand with a choice company of cavalry on the rise of a hill, to enable him to get a better view of the enemy. The next day he left the place and returned to Darius. No sooner had he gone, than the Macedonians captured it. They wanted the advantage of high ground, as well as a good vantage point from which to view the enemy forces in the plain. {*Curtius, l. 4. c. 12. s. 18-19. 1:277} [E221]

1871. Alexander commanded his mercenaries from Paeonia to march in front. He drew his phalanx of Macedonians into two wings, both flanked with cavalry. {*Curtius, l. 4. c. 12. s. 22,23. 1:277} The two camps were about eight miles apart when the army of Alexander

came to some hills from where they could view the enemy. When he consulted his captains as to whether the main battle should be fought closer to the enemy, or whether they should make a stand right there until he would be able to get a better view of the ground where they were to fight, most of them favoured the former option, but Parmenion favoured the latter, with which Alexander agreed. {*Arrian, Anabasis, l. 3. c. 9. s. 3,4. 1:251} Therefore, having resolved to camp on one of the hills there, he immediately ordered the troops to build a camp at that spot, which was quickly accomplished, while he went into his own pavilion and from there viewed the army of the enemy in the plain below. {*Curtius, l. 4. c. 12. s. 24. 1:277}

1872. Meanwhile, the horse boys, and other rag-tag boys who followed the camp, started fighting among themselves for fun, calling the captain of the one side Alexander and the captain of the other, Darius. When Alexander heard this, he stopped the others from fighting and had the two captains fight between themselves. Alexander helped captain Alexander on with his own armour, and Philotas gave captain Darius some armour. All the army watched as these two fought, believing it foreshadowed the outcome of the battle. It so happened that he who played Alexander defeated the one who played Darius. According to Eratosthenes, he was given a reward of twelve townships and the honour of wearing a Persian garment, which he was also given. {*Plutarch, Alexander, l. 1. c. 31. s. 1,2. 7:315,317}

1873. Alexander's friends now came to him and complained that the soldiers were planning in their tents to take all the spoil for themselves and to put nothing into his treasury. At this, Alexander smiled and said:

> "This is very good news, my friends, that you bring me, for I see by this they mean to fight and not to flee."

1874. Many of the common soldiers came to him to encourage him not to be afraid of the number of his enemies, since these would not be able to endure the very first noise or shout from them. [L311] Here, γρασον does not signify the smell of them, or of their arm-pits, as Xylander translated it. (The Greek text by Loeb translated this as the very smell of goat that clings to us. Editor.) {*Plutarch, Sayings of Kings and Commanders (180c) 3:59}

1875. The eleventh night after the eclipse of the moon, the two armies were stationed within sight of each other. Darius kept his men in their arms all night and reviewed them all by torch light, so that that entire plain lying between the Niphates and the Gordian Mountains shone with torches. While his army was sleeping, Alexander was up with his soothsayer Aristander before his pavilion, engaged in certain mysterious and secret rites and ceremonies, and offering a sacrifice to the god Fear. {*Plutarch, Alexander, l. 1. c. 31. s. 4. 7:317} Curtius stated:

> "Aristander, in a white robe, carrying bunches of vervain in his hand and his head covered, mumbled certain prayers which the king was to say after him, to propitiate Zeus and Minerva Victoria."

1876. Parmenion and his other friends advised him to attack Darius in the dead of night and thereby conceal from his soldiers the terror of the battle, because he was so heavily out-numbered. He replied that he had not come there to steal a victory. On the contrary, Darius feared that he might be attacked in the night. He knew his camp was not exceptionally well fortified. Therefore, he kept his men up all night in arms, so that lack of sleep was the main reason his men lost the battle on the following day. {*Plutarch, Alexander, l. 1. c. 31. s. 4-8. 7:317,319} {*Curtius, l. 4. c. 13. s. 1-16. 1:279-283} {*Arrian, Anabasis, l. 3. c. 10. s. 1-4. 1:253,255}

1877. Alexander was troubled in his mind about what might happen the next day, and did not sleep at all that night, until the early hours of the morning. Then, he fell into so deep a sleep that when it was fully day, they could not wake him. When his friends asked him what had made him sleep so soundly, he answered as follows. It was Darius, he said, who by gathering all his forces into one place, had relieved him of the trouble of having to think how to follow him into various other countries. {*Diod. Sic., l. 17. c. 56. 8:279,281} {Justin, Trogus, l. 11. c. 13.} {*Curtius, l. 4. c. 13. s. 16,17. 1:283} {*Plutarch, Alexander, l. 1. c. 32. s. 1,2. 7:319}

1878. Justin said that this battle was fought by Alexander at the very end of the fifth year and in the beginning of the sixth year of his reign, {Justin, Trogus, l. 11. c. 14.} although Jerome, in commenting on Daniel, {Da 11} disagreed, and stated that he overcame and killed Darius in the seventh year of his reign. Arrian said this battle was fought when Aristophanes was archon at Athens, in the month of Pyanopsion. The prophecy of Aristander was fulfilled in which he said that in that very month when the moon was eclipsed, Alexander should fight and defeat Darius. {*Arrian, Anabasis, l. 3. c. 15. s. 7. 1:273} Both Arrian and Diodorus stated that the battle was fought in the year when Aristophanes was archon at Athens. {*Diod. Sic., l. 17. c. 62. s. 1. 8:295} Dionysius Halicarnassus placed the battle in the following year, when Aristophon was archon at Athens. {*Dionysius Halicarnassus, First Letter to Ammaeus, l. 1. (12) 2:341} Aristander was correct when he foretold that Alexander would gain that great victory over Darius in that very month. [E222] However, Arrian mistook one month for another and said that it was in the month of Pyanopsion, while the astronomical calculations show

that the eclipse was in the month of Boedromion. On the eleventh day after the eclipse, Alexander fought that battle. {*Plutarch, Alexander, l. 1. c. 31. s. 4. 7:317} Plutarch stated that he had that victory on the fifth day of the last quarter of Boedromion, which is the twenty-fifth day of Boedromion. This month had thirty-one days and the date of the victory corresponded to October 1. (Loeb text has twenty-sixth day. Editor.) {*Plutarch, Camillus, l. 1. c. 19. s. 3. 2:139} [L312]

1879. Ptolemy Lagus and Aristobulus, who were both in the battle, stated that this battle was fought at Gaugamela, near the Bumolus River. {*Strabo, l. 16. c. 1. s. 3. 7:195,197} {*Plutarch, Alexander, l. 1. c. 31. s. 3. 7:317} {*Arrian, Anabasis, l. 6. c. 11. s. 4-6. 2:133} {*Ammianus Marcellinus, l. 23. c. 6. s. 22. 2:361} Zonaras wrote it as Gausamela. Gaugamela was only a small country village. The sound of the name is harsh on the ear. According to Strabo and Plutarch, it meant the house of a camel, or rather, the body of a camel, for this is what the word בר-גמלא meant in the Chaldee and Syriac language. This is why, according to Arrian, it came to pass that this glorious victory is said to have been won at Arbela, which was a large and famous city in those parts. Strabo, too, said the same thing: namely, that it happened this way because the other was the correct location, but Arbela was a famous city. (This city is mentioned in Hosea. {Ho 10:14}. {See note on 3276b AM. <<616>>}) For this reason, the Macedonians first wrote in their writings that the battle was fought and the victory won at Arbela, and then other historians derived it from them. These two places were not very near to each other, since there were about ten miles between the Bumolus River, where Gaugamela was, and the Lycus River, where Arbela stood. {*Curtius, l. 4. c. 9. s. 9,10. 1:245,247} Between:

a) Lycus and the country of Ardria, or Atyria (which was the old name for Assyria by which Assyria was called, as Diodorus showed in the life of Trajan),
b) the borders of the region of Babylon (in which both Nineveh and Gaugamela were located) and
c) the Capros River,

1880. at an equal distance from each of these three points, Arbela was located, as well as the hill Nicatorium (named by Alexander after this victory near it), which Strabo called Ninus. Hence it appears that, in Ptolemy's fifth table or map of Asia, Arbela should be located where Gaugamela was. Both places were located in the same place, according to him. These cities were not on the west side but on the farther side of the Lycus River. This disagreed with Eratosthenes, as reported by Strabo, as well as Curtius and Arrian. When all of these are carefully compared together, we may gather that

Gaugamela and Arbela were not sixty to seventy-five miles from each other, but a little more than just over ten miles apart. {*Strabo, l. 2. c. 1. s. 38. 1:347} {*Strabo, l. 16. c. 1. s. 3,4. 7:195,197} {*Arrian, Anabasis, l. 3. c. 8. s. 7. 1:249} {*Arrian, Anabasis, l. 6. c. 11. s. 5,6. 2:133}

1881. Aristobulus reported that when the fighting was over, a description of Darius' battle plans was found, as we read in Arrian. {*Arrian, Anabasis, l. 3. c. 11. s. 3. 1:257} Curtius detailed the battle plans for both armies. {*Curtius, l. 4. c. 11. s. 6-13. 1:273,275} {*Curtius, l. 4. c. 13. s. 26-32. 1:285-289}

1882. Darius left his chariots, threw away his weapons and mounted his mare, which had just had a new foal. He fled as fast as she could carry him, just as he had done at the battle at Issus, as I showed before from Aelian, {*Plutarch, Alexander, l. 1. c. 33. s. 5. 7:325,327} who also stated in the same place that it was for this very purpose that Darius always had mares which had recently foaled with him on the battle field. So, with very few in his company, he came to the Lycus River. When he had crossed it, some advised him to destroy the bridge after him, to hinder the pursuit of the enemy. When he considered how many there were behind him who still needed to cross, he replied that he would rather leave a way for a pursuing enemy, than take one from a fleeing friend. {*Curtius, l. 4. c. 16. s. 8,9. 1:315} {Justin, Trogus, l. 11. c. 14.} In Justin's work, we find *Cydnus* printed instead of *Lycus*. The Cydnus River ran through the centre of the city of Tarsus in Cilicia. {See note on 3671d AM. <<1754>>} From this error Orosius, who followed Justin very closely, made the mistake of saying that this last great battle between Alexander and Darius was fought at Tarsus. {Orosius, l. 3. c. 17.} [L313]

1883. When Mazaeus pressed hard against the squadron of the Macedonians, Parmenion sent to Alexander, who had chased the enemy as far as the Lycus River, because he wanted Alexander to come and help them. However, when Mazaeus heard that Darius had left the battle, he also fled. He did not go by the shortest way to Babylon, but went around over the Tigris River, which was a longer but safer route, and so he brought what was left of his army safely to Babylon. {*Curtius, l. 4. c. 15. s. 1-7. 1:313,315}

1884. About midnight, Darius came to Arbela. Many of his nobles and other soldiers resorted there too. He called them together and said that his purpose for the present was to leave all to Alexander. [E223] He would flee to the utmost borders of his kingdom and there begin the war on Alexander afresh. {*Curtius, l. 5. c. 1. s. 3-6. 1:327} He then went at once on horseback and fled over the mountains of Armenia into Media. With him were a few of his relatives and his guard. The guard was called *Melophori*, that is, *Apple Bearers*, because they each bore a spear with a golden apple carved on its butt. Later, two thousand mercenaries under the command of Paron of Phocaea, in Ionia, and Glaucus of Aetolia joined him. {*Arrian, Anabasis, l. 3. c. 16. s. 1-3. 1:275}

1885. When Alexander was returning from the Lycus River, he had his fiercest battle yet with the Parthian, Indian and some elite Persian cavalry, losing sixty men in the encounter. His captains Hephaestion, Coenus, Perdiccas and Menidas were severely wounded, but recovered. {*Arrian, Anabasis, l. 3. c. 15. s. 1,2. 1:271} {*Curtius, l. 4. c. 16. s. 32. 1:321}

1886. In the main battle, Alexander lost at most a hundred foot soldiers, although a thousand horses, of which half were his Companion Cavalry horses, died from wounds or the rigours of the chase. On the other side, three hundred thousand were killed and a much larger number taken prisoner. He captured all the elephants, and all the chariots that were not broken in the battle. {*Arrian, Anabasis, l. 3. c. 15. s. 6. 1:273} However, Diodorus stated that ninety thousand of the Persian cavalry and foot soldiers died. On the Macedonian side, five hundred were missing and a large number were wounded. {*Diod. Sic., l. 17. c. 61. s. 3. 8:293} Curtius said that forty thousand Persians and less than three hundred Macedonians died. {*Curtius, l. 4. c. 16. s. 26,27. 1:319} The total number killed in the following three battles, this battle, and those at Issus and at Granicus, over the previous forty or so months, was given as follows by Orosius: {Orosius, l. 3. c. 17.}

> "In such a multitude of calamities, it is incredible, that in the space of three years in three battles, half a million cavalry and foot soldiers should be killed. These were from a kingdom and from those countries which a few years earlier had killed nine hundred thousand men. In addition to these three battles in the three years, a number of cities in Asia had been destroyed, together with their inhabitants. All Syria was laid waste. Tyre was destroyed and all Cilicia depopulated. Cappadocia was subdued and Egypt and Rhodes sold into slavery. Many provinces bordering on the Taurus Mountains were brought into subjection. Mount Taurus was forced to receive the yoke which it had so long striven to avoid."

1887. When Alexander had rested the cavalry he had with him, he set out at midnight toward Arbela. He understood that Darius had stored all his money and royal provisions there, and Alexander planned to capture these in a surprise attack. [L314] The next day he came to Arbela, where he did not find Darius, but found all his treasure, as well as his shield and bow. {*Arrian, Anabasis, l. 3. c. 15. s. 5. 1:273} Diodorus said that he found three thousand talents there; Curtius said four thousand. {*Diod. Sic., l. 17. c. 64. s. 3. 8:301} All the wealth of the entire army had been stored in that place. {*Curtius, l. 5. c. 1. s. 10. 1:329}

1888. With this battle, the empire of Persia seemed to have come to an end. Alexander was proclaimed king of Asia and thereupon offered magnificent sacrifices to his gods and distributed houses, territories and provinces among his captains as it pleased him. {*Plutarch, Alexander, l. 1. c. 34. 7:327,329}

1889. Because he knew the air would be polluted with the stench of the dead bodies, he hurried to get away from Arbela. After four days he came to a city called Mennis, where there was a cavern from which naphtha, or liquid brimstone or bitumen, poured out. {*Diod. Sic., l. 17. c. 64. s. 3. 8:301} {*Curtius, l. 5. c. 1. s. 11-16. 1:329,331}

1890. As Alexander came toward Babylon, Mazaeus, who had fled there from the battle, humbly met him with his children, who were of age. He surrendered himself and them, along with the city of Babylon, into his hands. Alexander received him and his children very graciously. Bagophanes, who kept the citadel there containing the king's treasure, did not want to be outdone by Mazaeus. He covered the entire route along which Alexander was to pass with flowers and garlands. On each side of the path he had placed silver altars, burning frankincense and exuding all sorts of sweet odours. Alexander was guarded by armed men. He commanded all the men of Babylon who came to meet him, to follow behind him after the last of his foot soldiers. Alexander made his entrance into the city in his chariot, and went up to the king's palace, where he viewed the king's treasure on the following day. {*Curtius, l. 5. c. 1. s. 22,23. 1:333,335} {Justin, Trogus, l. 11. c. 14.} He stayed thirty-four days and refreshed and rewarded his soldiers. (This is according to the better copies, and Orosius agreed with this, as did Curtius. {*Curtius, l. 5. c. 1. s. 39. 1:341} {Orsius, l. 3. c. 17.}) His army spent the same number of days there in relaxation. Diodorus confirmed that they stayed there longer than thirty days. They liked the spaciousness of the city and the entertainment which they were given by the residents. {*Diod. Sic., l. 17. c. 64. s. 4. 8:301} [E224]

1891. Among those who entertained Alexander in this city were the Chaldeans. They talked with him concerning the movements of the heavenly bodies and the appointed changes of the seasons. {*Curtius, l. 5. c. 1. s. 22. 1:333} The Chaldeans gave Callisthenes, one of Alexander's followers, their observations of the heavenly bodies for nineteen hundred and three years of time, dating back to the founding of Babylon, about fourteen years after the birth of Peleg. Callisthenes later gave these records to Aristotle in Greece. {See note on 1771 AM. <<50>>}

1892. Alexander, consulting with the Chaldeans, followed their advice and sacrificed to Belus. He did whatever they asked of him concerning the temple repairs. Alexander commanded the Babylonians to repair the temples which Xerxes had previously demolished, and in particular the temple of Belus, that was located in the heart of the city. He ordered that all the rubbish be carried out of the temple immediately. {*Arrian, Anabasis, l. 3. c. 16. s. 4. 1:275} {*Arrian, Anabasis, l. 7. c. 17. s. 1-6. 2:261,263} This task was so great that it took ten thousand men two months to clear the place where the temple stood. {*Strabo, l. 16. c. 1. s. 5. 7:199} When Alexander commanded all his army to help with carrying away the rubbish, only the Jews refused to help in that work. Hecataeus of Abdera, who was with Alexander at the time, stated that they had gone through many other serious hardships and many other grievous inconveniences. When Alexander heard their reasons for refusing, he exempted them from the task. {*Josephus, Apion, l. 1. c. 22. (192,193) 1:241} [L315]

1893. Alexander was most amazed by that hole in the earth in Ecbatana or, as other copies have it, in Batana. (Batana was meant here, which was a city located near the Euphrates by Stephanus Byzantinus, and not Ecbatana, the city of Media.) Flames of fire continually shot forth as from a fountain, and an active spring of naphtha shot out fire not far from that hole. Plutarch described these effects in more detail. {*Plutarch, Alexander, l. 1. c. 35. 7:329-333}

1894. Alexander ordered Bagophanes, who had surrendered the citadel of Babylon, to follow him. He committed the keeping of the citadel to Agathon, who was from the town of Pydna, along with seven hundred Macedonians and three hundred mercenaries. Mazaeus, who had surrendered the city to him, was made governor of all the province of Babylon. He appointed Apollodorus from Amphipolis and Menes from Pella, in Macedonia, to be the military commanders in Babylon and all the other countries to the west, as far as Cilicia. For that purpose, he left two thousand soldiers with them, with a thousand talents of silver to hire mercenaries. He appointed Asclepiodorus, the son of Philotas, to collect his tribute in those parts, and sent Mithrines, who had surrendered the city of Sardis to him, to be governor in Armenia. {*Arrian, Anabasis, l. 3. c. 16. s. 4-5. 1:275,277} {*Curtius, l. 5. c. 1. s. 43-45. 1:341,343} {*Diod. Sic., l. 17. c. 64. s. 4,5. 8:301,303}

1895. From the money which he found in Babylon, he gave six minas to every Macedonian cavalry man, five minas to every allied cavalry-man, two minas to every Macedonian foot soldier, and two months' pay to every mercenary. {*Diod. Sic., l. 17. c. 64. s. 5. 8:303} An Attic mina contained a hundred drachmas. Curtius confused this with the Roman denarius, and said that he gave every Macedonian cavalry-man six hundred denarii and every foreign cavalry-man five hundred and every Macedonian foot soldier two hundred denarii. {*Curtius, l. 5. c. 1. s. 44,45. 1:343}

1896. Alexander was on his way from Babylon when Amyntas, the son of Andromenes, came to him with a number of men sent to him by Antipater, the governor of Macedonia. Macedonia had sent five hundred cavalry and six thousand foot soldiers. Thrace sent six hundred cavalry and thirty-five hundred foot soldiers. Peloponnesus had sent four thousand foot soldiers and three hundred and eighty cavalry. This was according to Curtius, but Diodorus has a little less than a thousand cavalry. With them had come the sons of fifty of the leading nobles of Macedonia to be Alexander's bodyguards. {*Curtius, l. 5. c. 1. s. 40-42. 1:341} {*Diod. Sic., l. 17. c. 65. s. 1. 8:303}

1897. When Alexander had received these troops, he continued on his journey. After marching six days, he came into a country called Sittacene, but Curtius called it Satrapene. As this country abounded in provisions, he stayed there many days, holding contests to test every man's prowess and dexterity in the feats of chivalry. The eight best men he put in command of a thousand troops each. He then divided his whole army into a number of brigades. Prior to this, they had been organized into companies of five hundred, and their captains had not been chosen by contests of skill. Previously, the cavalry of each country had served as a national unit of its own, but now he made no distinctions based on nationality, appointing as commanders those who were most skilled in the war, no matter what country they were from. He reformed the martial discipline of his army in many points, with the result that all the troops liked him better than ever, and were even more ready to serve him as he now continued his journey. {*Curtius, l. 5. c. 2. s. 1-7. 1:343,345} {*Diod. Sic., l. 17. c. 65. s. 2-4. 8:303,305}

1898. As Alexander approached Susa, he was met by the son of the governor of Susa and a courier with a letter from Philoxenus. Alexander had sent Philoxenus away to Susa immediately after the battle at Arbela. The letters said that the inhabitants of Susa had surrendered their city and that all the treasure had been safely kept for him. {*Arrian, Anabasis, l. 3. c. 16. s. 6. 1:277} [E225] [L316] The son of Abulites, the governor of the city, told him the same message. He either did this voluntarily or, according to some, at the orders of Darius, so that Alexander would be detained there longer, which would give Darius more time to raise a new army against him. {*Curtius, l. 5. c. 2. s. 8. 1:347} {*Diod. Sic., l. 17. c. 65. s. 5. 8:305}

1899. Alexander entertained the young man with much grace and favour. He used him as his guide to the Idaspes or Choaspes River. This river was a narrow and turbulent stream. At their meeting, Abulites had given Alexander costly gifts, including some camels known as dromedaries, which were very swift, and twelve elephants that Darius had requested to be sent to him from India. {*Curtius, l. 5. c. 2. s. 9,10. 1:347}

1900. The day after he had left Babylon, he came to Susa. After he entered the city, he received fifty thousand talents of silver, with all of the king's wardrobe and other belongings. {*Arrian, Anabasis, l. 3. c. 16. s. 7. 1:277} Curtius said that he received much more silver in bars. {*Curtius, l. 5. c. 2. s. 11,12. 1:347} Diodorus calculated that it was as much as forty thousand talents of silver and gold in bars and ingots, and nine thousand talents of gold minted into darics. {*Diod. Sic., l. 17. c. 66. s. 1,2. 8:305,307} Plutarch mentioned forty thousand talents in coins and five thousand talents' worth of purple from Hermione, which, although it had been stored there a hundred and ninety years earlier, looked as fresh as it had the first day it was put there. {*Plutarch, Alexander, l. 1. c. 36. s. 1,2. 7:333}

1901. Alexander offered sacrifices according to the Macedonian custom and held a torch relay race and athletic contests. {*Arrian, Anabasis, l. 3. c. 16. s. 7. 1:277} He sat down on the royal throne of Persia, which was too high to accommodate his size comfortably. His feet could not reach down to the step by which he had mounted the throne. One of the pages took the table which Darius used to eat his meals and put it under him for a footstool. When Philotas saw this, he persuaded Alexander to take it as a sign of good luck. {*Diod. Sic., l. 17. c. 66. s. 3-7. 8:307,309} {*Curtius, l. 5. c. 2. s. 13-15. 1:347,349}

1902. The robes and other purple clothes which were sent to Alexander from Macedonia along with those who had made them, he sent to Darius' mother Sisigambis, whom he highly respected and honoured, as a son would with his mother. With the gift he added the message that, if she liked those clothes, she would do well to let her young granddaughters learn how to make them. When he knew that she was quite distressed, he personally went to her and asked to be forgiven for his ignorance of the Persian manners and comforted her again. There is nothing that the women of Persia felt to be a greater disgrace than to work in wool. {*Curtius, l. 5. c. 2. s. 18-22. 1:349,351} So he left her, as well as Darius' two young daughters and little son Ochus, at Susa, with some tutors to instruct them in the Greek language. {*Diod. Sic., l. 17. c. 67. s. 1. 8:309}

1903. He continued on to the farthest borders of Persia, leaving Archelaus with a garrison of three thousand soldiers to keep the city. He appointed Xenophilus to hold the citadel and Callicrates to gather his tributes, while committing the civil government of the province of Susa to Abulites, who had surrendered the city to him. {*Curtius, l. 5. c. 2. s. 16,17. 1:349} He sent Menes back to the coast and made him governor of Phoenicia, Syria and Cilicia. {*Arrian, Anabasis, l. 3. c. 16. s. 10. 1:279}

1904. After a four-day march, Alexander came to the Tigris River (which the natives called the Pasitigris River), and crossed it with nine thousand foot soldiers and Agrian archers, three thousand Greek mercenaries and a thousand Thracians. He went into the country of the Uxians, which bordered on the province of Susa and extended into the main part of Persia, leaving a narrow passage between itself and Susa. Medates, the governor of this country, had married Sisigambis' niece.

1905. Alexander gave Tauron fifteen hundred mercenaries and a thousand Agrians and ordered him to set out as soon as it was dark. He was to follow his guides into the secret passes that they would show him and to advance as far as the city which Alexander planned to besiege. Alexander took the captains of his troops with him, his targeteers and some eight thousand other soldiers. [L317] They marched in the third watch of the same night and by daybreak came to those passes which opened into the Uxian country. When he had gone through them, he arrived and besieged the city. When the Uxians saw that they were besieged on all sides, they sent thirty men out from the citadel there to ask for his pardon, but he refused. At length, when he received letters from Sisigambis, he not only pardoned her kinsman, Medates, but set at liberty all whom he had taken prisoner, who had voluntarily submitted to him. He left the city untouched and all their land free from tribute. {*Curtius, l. 5. c. 3. s. 12-15. 1:355} Arrian, from Ptolemy Lagus' account, claimed that, because of Sisigambis' request, he left them their lands to till but levied a yearly tribute on them of a hundred horses, five hundred beasts of burden and thirty thousand of their flocks and herds. This whole account is related differently by Diodorus, Curtius and Arrian. {*Curtius, l. 5. c. 3. s. 1-15. 1:351-355} {*Arrian, Anabasis, l. 3. c. 17. s. 1-6. 1:281,283} {*Diod. Sic., l. 17. c. 67. 8:309,311} [E226]

1906. After he subdued the country of the Uxians, Alexander added it to the province of Susa. He divided up all his forces between himself and Parmenion, ordering that the baggage, the Thessalian cavalry, the confederates, the foreign mercenaries and the heavily armed soldiers go with Parmenion through the plain, while he took the Macedonian foot soldiers and the cavalry of his confederates, sending the light cavalry ahead, with the squadron of Agrians and the archers, to reconnoitre. They went by way of the mountains which ran along in a ridge as far as Persia. {*Curtius, l. 5. c. 3. s. 16. 1:357} {*Arrian, Anabasis, l. 3. c. 18. s. 1,2. 1:283}

1907. On the fifth day (according to Diodorus and Curtius), he came to the passes of Persia called the Susian Passes. Diodorus stated that Ariobarzanes, the Persian, held these with twenty-five thousand foot soldiers and three hundred cavalry, while Arrian stated that he had about four thousand foot soldiers and seven hundred cavalry. He repulsed Alexander's attack and made him retreat about four miles from that pass. At last Alexander captured a shepherd who had a Persian mother, but whose father had been born in Lycia, and he guided Alexander through narrow and craggy by-paths and over various snow-covered mountains. Alexander routed the enemy and took control of the pass, but Ariobarzanes broke through the army of the Macedonians with some forty cavalry and five thousand foot soldiers, resulting in a large slaughter on both sides. Ariobarzanes hurried to get into Persepolis, which was the capital city of that kingdom, but was unable to reach it, because the enemy was at his very heels. Ariobarzanes attacked them and in this second battle his forces were cut to pieces by Alexander. The following writers related this more fully in greater detail. {*Curtius, l. 5. c. 3,4. 1:355-371} {*Arrian, Anabasis, l. 3. c. 17. s. 1-6. 1:281,283} {*Diod. Sic., l. 17. c. 68. 8:311-315} {*Plutarch, Alexander, l. 1. c. 37. s. 1,2. 7:335} {Polyaenus, Strategmata, l. 4.}

1908. As Alexander was marching toward Persepolis, he received letters from Tiridates, Darius' treasurer there, telling Alexander that when the inhabitants of Persepolis heard of his coming, they were ready to take the king's treasure and share it among themselves, so he wanted Alexander to come quickly to prevent this. Alexander, leaving his foot soldiers to follow on later, travelled all night with his cavalry and although they were already tired from so long a journey, by daybreak they reached the Araxes River. After they had constructed a bridge, they crossed over it along with his army. {*Curtius, l. 5. c. 5. s. 1-4. 1:371} {*Diod. Sic., l. 17. c. 69. s. 1. 8:315}

1909. When he came within a quarter of a mile of the city, about some eight hundred (for so Diodorus, Justin and Suidas stated, in his entry under Alexander, not four thousand, as Curtius said) poor Greek slaves led by Euctemon of Cyme in Aeolia, came out as humble suppliants to meet him. These were the ones whom the former kings of Persia had taken in their wars and made slaves. They had been cruelly treated; some had their feet, hands, ears or noses cut off, and all were branded in the face with letters or other marks. These slaves pleaded with him to promise to do for them now what he had done in Greece, and to deliver them from the slavery of Persian cruelty. Later, when he offered to send an escort with them into Greece, they requested that he give them lands in that place instead. They feared that they would not prove a comfort but an abomination to their friends and relatives at home. *[L318]* Alexander approved their request and gave each of them three thousand drachmas. (Curtius wrote *denarius* instead of *drachmas*.) He gave every man and woman five changes of clothes, two yoke of oxen, fifty sheep and fifty bushels of wheat. They could now till and sow the land which Alexander had given them. Furthermore, he exempted their land from paying any tribute and left some forces to protect them and to see to it that no man would harm them. {*\*Curtius, l. 5. c. 5. s. 5-24. 1:371-379*} {*\*Diod. Sic., l. 17. c. 69. s. 2-9. 8:315-319*} {*Justin, Trogus, l. 11. c. 14.*}

*1910.* The next day, he called all the commanders and captains of his army together to tell them that this city of Persepolis, the metropolis of Persia, had always been against the Greeks, and that he was therefore resolved to give all its plunder to the soldiers, with the exception of the king's palace. After this there was a large slaughter of the prisoners whom they had taken. This he avowed in writing as his own act, since he considered it to be to his honour that he commanded that they, as enemies, be butchered in this fashion. Plutarch said that he found as much treasure there as had been at Susa. Diodorus wrote that when he came into the citadel, he found gold and silver worth a hundred and twenty thousand talents, when gold was estimated in terms of silver. (The usual ratio of gold to silver in antiquity was twelve or fifteen to one.) Curtius agreed. {*\*Plutarch, Alexander, l. 1. c. 37. s. 2. 7:335*} {*\*Curtius, l. 5. c. 6. s. 1-9. 1:379,381*} {*\*Diod. Sic., l. 17. c. 70,71. 8:319,321*}

*1911.* When Alexander first sat down on the royal throne in Persepolis, under a golden canopy, Demaratus the Corinthian, who was an old friend of his and his father's, was reported to have fallen, weeping, like an old man, exclaiming that those Greeks who had died before that day and had not lived to see Alexander sitting on Darius' throne, had missed a great event. {*\*Plutarch, Alexander, l. 1. c. 37. s. 4. 7:337*}

*1912.* Alexander committed the keeping of the citadel of Persepolis to Nicarchides with a garrison of three thousand Macedonians. *[E227]* Tiridates, who had delivered the treasure to Alexander, retained the same position which he had held under Darius. Alexander left a large part of his army and baggage there and committed the keeping of the city to Parmenion and Craterus, while he, with a thousand cavalry and lightly armed foot soldiers, went to subdue the inner parts of Persia at the time when the Seven Stars or Pleiades were setting, or the beginning of winter. Although plagued by storms and other tempestuous weather on the way, he arrived

at a place all covered with snow and frozen over with ice. Seeing that his soldiers did not want to go any farther, he leaped off his horse and went on foot over the ice and snow. When the country people, who lived in scattered huts and cabins, saw the enemy troops, they started killing their children and others who were not able to accompany them and fled to the wild woods and into the snow-covered mountains. Some of them, however, who could be persuaded to talk with Alexander, showed no fear and submitted to him. Alexander did not allow any of his troops to harm them. {*\*Curtius, l. 5. c. 6. s. 11-16. 1:383,385*}

## 3674b AM, 4384 JP, 330 BC

*1913.* After Alexander had laid waste to all the country of Persia and taken its various towns, he came into the country of the Mardi, who were a warlike people and of very different behaviour from the Persians. After he subdued the Mardi, Alexander returned to Persepolis on the thirtieth day after he had set out from there, and bestowed rewards on his captains and others, every man according to his deeds. He gave away almost everything he had acquired in Persepolis. {*\*Curtius, l. 5. c. 6. s. 17-20. 1:385*}

*1914.* This journey was undertaken, as I said before, about the time of the setting of the Seven Stars called Pleiades. Only Curtius recorded this. Plutarch stated that because the winter was now approaching, Alexander planned to give his army some rest, and so he spent four months in Persia. {*\*Plutarch, Alexander, l. 1. c. 37. s. 3. 7:335,337*} *[L319]* Pliny stated that the Greeks began their winter on the Ides of November (November 13), when the Seven Stars set in the early morning. {*\*Pliny, l. 18. c. 10. 5:221*} However, the amount of time that had elapsed since the battle at Gaugamela showed that Alexander could not have come to Persepolis before our December. Others also cast doubt upon the Mardi expedition. Curtius stated that he did not subdue them until after the death of Darius. {*\*Curtius, l. 6. c. 5. s. 11. 2:43*} This may be true, unless we distinguish the Mardi of Persia from the Mardi who bordered on Hyrcania. {*\*Herodotus, l. 1. c. 125. 1:165*} {*\*Strabo, l. 11. c. 13. s. 6. 5:309*} {*\*Arrian, Indica, l. 1. c. 40. s. 6. 2:423*} Other writers do not agree, either, with Curtius on his observation where he said:

"He gave away almost all that he got at Persepolis."

*1915.* For he spoke expressly of what he got at Persepolis not of what he got at Pasargada. (This we showed before from Jacobus Capellus. {*See note on 3674a AM. <<1910>>*}) Jacobus Capellus fully agreed with what Curtius had written earlier, that Alexander commanded horses and camels to be sent for from Babylon and Susa, to carry the hundred and twenty thousand talents which he found in this city. {*Curtius, l. 5. c. 6. s. 10. 1:318} Strabo stated: {*Strabo, l. 15. c. 3. s. 9. 7:169}

"He carried all the money of Persia from Susa, which was full of treasure and rich goods. It is known for certain that whatever he got in Babylon and in Darius' camp was never included in this total. In Persia and Susa he found forty thousand talents, some say fifty thousand talents."

1916. Diodorus Siculus stated: {*Diod. Sic., l. 17. c. 71. s. 1,2. 8:321}

"When he was forced to lay out much of the money he had found there to pay for the war, he planned to send part of it to Susa to be stored there in a bank. He had to get a multitude of draught horses, carriages and three thousand camels with pack saddles from Babylon and Mesopotamia to carry his treasure to its destined places."

1917. Plutarch stated: {*Plutarch, Alexander, l. 1. c. 37. s. 2. 7:335}

"It took ten thousand pairs of mules and five thousand camels to carry away all the money and wealth he took from there."

1918. After Darius had stayed a while at Ecbatana in Media, he gathered together all those who were left after the defeat, and replaced the weapons they had lost in the battle. He also sent letters to the governors in Bactria and other countries, requesting them to remain loyal to him. {*Diod. Sic., l. 17. c. 64. s. 1,2. 8:299,301} His purpose was that if Alexander stayed around Susa and Babylon, he would stay in Media to see whether those who were around him were prepared to unite in a new battle against Alexander. If, however, he found that Alexander planned to pursue him, he would retire to Parthia and Hyrcania, or even into Bactria. By laying waste to all the countries he passed through, he would leave Alexander no possibility of following him due to lack of forage. Therefore, he sent ahead of him all the women and the rest of excess baggage and carriages to the Caspian Gates or passes, while he himself stayed at Ecbatana with a small force, to see how things would unfold. {*Arrian, Anabasis, l. 3. c. 19. s. 1,2. 1:289}

## 3674c AM, 4384 JP, 330 BC

1919. Alexander put on a feast to celebrate his previous victories and offered magnificent sacrifices to his gods. He feasted his nobles with an extremely sumptuous banquet, at which a number of whores and courtesans were also present, each with her ruffian. Among these there was an Athenian called Thais, who was a sweetheart of Ptolemy, the son of Lagus. She thought the city should be destroyed, to which Alexander, who was as drunk as

she was, agreed. He commanded that all Persepolis, both the palace and citadel, be burned to the ground to the accompaniment of caroling and the playing of musical instruments. [E228] This was against the advice of Parmenion, if only Alexander had chosen to listen. It was true that after he had slept on it, what he had done grieved him greatly. He said: {*Arrian, Anabasis, l. 3. c. 18. s. 10-12. 1:287,289} {*Curtius, l. 5. c. 7. s. 2-12. 1:387-391} {*Diod. Sic., l. 17. c. 72. 8:325,327} {*Plutarch, Alexander, l. 1. c. 38. 7:337,339}

"The Greeks would have been more severely avenged upon the Persians, if these had been forced to see Alexander on the throne and in the palace of Xerxes." [L320]

1920. The next day, he gave thirty talents to that shepherd of Lycia who acted as his guide and showed him the way into Persia. {*Curtius, l. 5. c. 7. s. 12. 1:391}

1921. After this, Alexander took Pasargada, a city built by Cyrus. It was surrendered to him by its governor Gobares, who gave Alexander six thousand talents. {*Curtius, l. 5. c. 6. s. 10. 1:381,383} According to Strabo's account from Aristobulus, who was present at the time, Alexander visited the sepulchre of Cyrus. {*Strabo, l. 15. c. 3. s. 7. 7:165}

1922. Then he took the remaining cities of Persia, some by force, while others voluntarily surrendered. {*Diod. Sic., l. 17. c. 73. s. 1. 8:327} This seems to have been when the Seven Stars rose in the morning sky, which was the time from which the ancients reckoned the beginning of summer, not at their morning setting and the beginning of winter, when, according to Curtius, Alexander made his journey into the heart of Persia. {*Curtius, l. 5. c. 6. s. 12. 1:383}

1923. Alexander made Phrasaortes, the son of Rheomithras, governor of Persia, {*Arrian, Anabasis, l. 3. c. 18. s. 10. 1:287} and then went into Media, after getting reinforcements from Cilicia in the form of five thousand foot soldiers and a thousand cavalry under the command of Platon, an Athenian. After this he set out to find Darius. {*Curtius, l. 5. c. 7. s. 12. 1:391}

1924. Darius had planned to leave Ecbatana and flee into Bactria, but because he feared that Alexander might overtake him on the way, he changed his plans. Though Alexander was about a hundred and ninety miles away at that time, no distance seemed great enough to prevent Alexander from catching up to him. Therefore, Darius resolved that, instead of fleeing, he would try his fortune in another battle. He had thirty thousand men about him, of which four thousand were Greeks under the command of Patron, and all these men were loyal to Darius. In addition, he had four thousand archers and slingers, as well as thirty-three hundred cavalry consisting for the most part of soldiers from Bactria under the command of Bessus, the governor of Bactria. {*Curtius, l. 5. c. 8. s. 1-4. 1:391}

1925. Diodorus stated that there were thirty thousand Persians and Greek mercenaries. {*Diod. Sic., l. 17. c. 73. s. 2. 8:327} Arrian stated there were only three thousand cavalry and six thousand foot soldiers. He also said that Darius carried no more than seven thousand talents with him from Media. {*Arrian, Anabasis, l. 3. c. 19. s. 5. 1:291} However, Strabo said that, when Darius fled from Media, he took eight thousand talents. {*Strabo, l. 15. c. 3. s. 9. 7:169} The men who murdered Darius rifled and shared this money among themselves. Diodorus said that when Alexander pursued Darius, he had the same number of talents with him. {*Diod. Sic., l. 17. c. 74. s. 5. 8:333} Athenaeus, quoting Chares of Mitylene, in his fifth book of the history of Alexander, said that it was the custom of the Persian kings, wherever they went, to have a chamber with five chests in it at the head of the royal bed. In these were kept five thousand talents of gold, and they were called the royal cushion. In another chamber, at the foot of the bed, three thousand talents of silver were always kept in three chests, and this was called the king's footstool. {*Athenaeus, l. 12. (514f) 5:315}

1926. Bessus, the governor of Bactria, and Nabarzanes, the commander of a thousand cavalry who had followed Darius in his flight, commanded their soldiers to seize Darius and bind him. They resolved that if Alexander overtook them, they would purchase their freedom by delivering Darius bound into Alexander's hands. However, if they could escape from Alexander, they would renew the war against Alexander in their own names. {*Curtius, l. 5. c. 10. 1:403-407} {*Arrian, Anabasis, l. 3. c. 21. s. 3-5. 1:297} [L321] Justin stated that this happened in a town in Parthia called Thara, or rather, Dara. It was called this later by Arsaces, the first king of Parthia, in remembrance of this villainy against Darius. Justin added that this was done in accordance with a kind of fate which had determined that the Persian Empire should end in the land of those who were destined to succeed the Persians in the empire. {Justin, Trogus, l. 11. c. 15.}

1927. The king's treasure and baggage were rifled, as if it had all been enemies' goods. Bessus and Nabarzanes, with Braza (or Barzaentes), the governor of the Arachoti and Drangians, took Darius. They carried him away prisoner in a cart, but to show some respect, they placed golden chains on him. They covered the cart with a lowly, dirty covering made of skins to escape detection. They had strangers drive it, so that if any man should ask, they would not be able to tell who was in it. His captors, meanwhile, followed from a distance. The Persians were won over by Bessus' generous promises, and since there

was no one else left with whom they might unite, they joined with the Bactrians. Bessus was made general in Darius' stead by the Bactrian cavalry and the other countries who had accompanied Darius on his flight. Artabazus and his sons, with those whom he commanded, and the Greeks under Patron, did not go with Bessus. They left the roadway and went up into the mountains marching away to Parthiene. {*Curtius, l. 5. c. 12. s. 16-20. 1:415,417} {*Arrian, Anabasis, l. 3. c. 21. s. 3-5. 1:297} [E229]

1928. Alexander changed his course for Media and attacked the Paraetacenes, subduing their country, whereupon he made Oxathres, the son of Abulitus, governor over them. {*Arrian, Anabasis, l. 3. c. 19. s. 2. 1:289}

1929. Tabae was a town in the remotest border of Paraetacene. Alexander was told by some who had abandoned Darius and fled to Alexander, that Darius had hastily gone into Bactria. {*Curtius, l. 5. c. 13. s. 1-3. 1:417} When he was within three day's journey of Ecbatana, he was more accurately informed by Bisthanes, the son of Ochus who had reigned in Persia before Darius, that Darius had fled from Ecbatana four days earlier. {*Arrian, Anabasis, l. 3. c. 19. s. 4. 1:291}

1930. When Alexander reached Ecbatana, the Thessalian cavalry and others of the confederate cavalry refused to accompany him any farther. He dismissed them, giving them leave to return to their own countries. When they left, he gave them two thousand talents over and above their regular pay to be shared among them. {*Arrian, Anabasis, l. 3. c. 19. s. 5,6. 1:291} {*Plutarch, Alexander, l. 1. c. 42. s. 3. 7:349} However, Diodorus and Curtius referred to this event as happening after the death of Darius and in a general way, without any special mention of the Thessalian troops. They said that he gave everyone who served in the cavalry six talents, or six thousand denarii. {*Curtius, l. 6. c. 2. s. 17. 2:23} Curtius repeatedly called a *drachma* a *denarii*. A thousand drachmas was equal to one talent. Diodorus added that he gave every foot soldier ten minas, that is, a thousand drachmas, and abundant provisions for every man for the return journey to his home country. {*Diod. Sic., l. 17. c. 74. s. 3. 8:331} Everyone who was willing to continue in his service was given three talents in coined money. When he found that it was a large number that was staying, he appointed Epocillus to escort the rest to the coast of Asia. The Thessalians who were returning home left their horses with him. He wrote to Menes, the governor in those regions, that immediately upon their arrival they were to be furnished with shipping, and transport to the European side. {*Arrian, Anabasis, l. 3. c. 19. s. 6,7. 1:291}

1931. To pay the vast sums he gave to the soldiers that left, Alexander was forced, in spite of all his haste in the pursuit of Darius, to levy a vast quantity of money as he went along the way. Diodorus stated that he received eight thousand talents from Darius' treasurers, over and above what they had distributed among his soldiers in the form of cups and other rewards. This amounted to over thirteen thousand talents. The amount they either stole, or took by force, was calculated to be a great deal more. *[L322]* {*Diod. Sic., l. 17. c. 74. s. 5. 8:333} Curtius agreed fully when he said: {*Curtius, l. 6. c. 2. s. 10. 2:19}

"In his next plundering foray, he raised twenty-six thousand talents, from which twelve thousand talents (Justin has thirteen thousand {Justin, Trogus, l. 12. c. 1.}) were spent in one largesse which he bestowed among his soldiers. His treasurers brought him so much more."

1932. Alexander ordered Parmenion to take all the money which was brought to him from Persia and store it in Ecbatana, under the keeping of Harpalus. He was to guard it with six thousand Macedonians and some cavalry of his confederates. So this money was now brought and stored in Ecbatana. {*Arrian, Anabasis, l. 3. c. 19. s. 7,8. 1:293} Some reckon it to have amounted to a hundred and eighty thousand talents. {*Strabo, l. 15. c. 3. s. 9. 7:169} Diodorus agreed, also saying that Parmenion had charge over all that treasure. {*Diod. Sic., l. 17. c. 80. s. 3. 8:351} Justin said that the treasure amounted to a hundred and ninety thousand talents and that Parmenion was in charge of keeping it. {Justin, Trogus, l. 12. c. 1.} Diodorus and Justin were more accurate in naming Parmenion as the keeper of the treasure than Arrian, who named Harpalus as holding that office. We have previously shown that Harpalus was left behind in Babylon to gather up the tribute and perform other duties for Alexander in those parts.

1933. Alexander sent Parmenion away with certain brigades of foreigners, the Thracian cavalry and others, except for the troops of his Companion Cavalry. They were to march through the country of the Cadusians, into Hyrcania. He also wrote to Clitus, the commander of the royal squadron, ordering that as soon as Clitus was to come from Susa to Ecbatana (for he had been left behind sick at Susa), he should take all the cavalry that had been left there to guard the money and march into Parthia with them, to meet him there. {*Arrian, Anabasis, l. 3. c. 19. s. 7,8. 1:293}

1934. Alexander took with him the troops of the Companion Cavalry, vaunt cavalry and mercenaries led by Erigyius, the Macedonian squadron (except those who had been left behind at Ecbatana to guard the money), the Agrians and the archers, and went after Darius. Because he marched so fast over so great a distance, many of his foot soldiers and cavalry were not able to follow and perished, after having fainted along the way. Alexander continued on, however, and on the eleventh day he came to Rhagae. {*Arrian, Anabasis, l. 3. c. 20. s. 1,2. 1:293} In those eleven days, he covered over four hundred miles. On this long journey, the cavalry followed him very cheerfully, even though they lacked water in many places. At the end of his journey, there were only sixty with him out of that company which had set out with him from Ecbatana. {*Plutarch, Alexander, l. 1. c. 42,43. 7:349,351} [E230]

1935. This city of Rhagae, as mentioned in the Apocrypha, {Apc Tob 1:14 4:1} was a day's journey from the Caspian Gates or passes for anyone riding at Alexander's pace. Darius had already passed through them. Many of those men who had set out with Darius on his journey, slipped away and returned home, while many surrendered to Alexander along the way. {*Arrian, Anabasis, l. 3. c. 20. s. 2. 1:293,295}

1936. He gave up all hope of overtaking Darius and rested there five days. When he had refreshed his army, he made Oxydates, a Persian whom Darius had formerly committed to prison in Susa with the intention of decapitating him, governor of Media. {*Arrian, Anabasis, l. 3. c. 20. s. 3. 1:295} {*Curtius, l. 6. c. 2. s. 10,11. 2:19,21}

1937. From there Alexander went with his army into Parthia and on the first day camped near the Caspian Gates or passes. The next day he went through the passes and came to places that were well populated. *[L323]* Here he ordered provisions to be brought to him, as he had been told that he would be going through countries lacking such provisions. He sent Coenus with the cavalry and a few foot soldiers, to forage. {*Arrian, Anabasis, l. 3. c. 20. s. 4. 1:295}

1938. Meanwhile Bagistenes, a great man in Babylon, came from Darius' camp to Alexander. He told Alexander that Darius had not yet been arrested, but was in great danger of either death or bonds. {*Arrian, Anabasis, l. 3. c. 21. s. 1. 1:295} {*Curtius, l. 5. c. 13. s. 3. 1:417}

1939. Therefore, Alexander pursued him harder and did not wait for Coenus to return from foraging. He took along with him the Companion Cavalry, his vaunt cavalry {Arrian has προδρομοι. Curtius wrote dimachae which were also called αμιπποι. προδομοι and dimachae may refer to the same type of troops.} the mercenary cavalry led by Erigyius, the Macedonian battalion (except those that were to guard his treasure), as well as the Agrians and archers. Leaving Craterus to command the rest, he ordered him to come after him at a more leisurely pace. He travelled all that night and the next day until noon, when he rested for a while. Then he again travelled all night, and early next morning he came to the camp of Darius, from where Bagistenes had come to him. Continuing on, he rode all that night until noon of the next day. He came to a certain village where those who had the charge of keeping Darius had stayed the day before, according to Arrian. Curtius claimed this was the place where Bessus arrested Darius. {*Arrian, Anabasis, l. 3. c. 21. s. 2-5. 1:295,297} {*Curtius, l. 5. c. 13. s. 4-8. 1:419}

1940. When he had travelled about sixty miles from the place from where Bagistenes had first come to him and where Darius had been arrested, he found Melon, who was Darius' interpreter. He had been unable, through weakness, to follow Darius any farther. When he saw Alexander approaching so quickly, he pretended to have fled over to Alexander from Darius, fearing that he would be taken for an enemy. He told Alexander what had happened and where they had gone. However, as his men were quite weary and needed rest, Alexander took six thousand elite cavalry and added three hundred troops called *dimachae*. (Who and what they were, you may learn from Pollus and Hesychius.) These men wore heavy armour, yet rode on horse back, but if the need arose, they could get off their horses and serve as foot soldiers, according to Curtius. However, Arrian stated that when he saw that the foot soldiers could not possibly keep pace with him on horse back, Alexander made about five hundred of the cavalry get off their horses and commanded the captains and the best men of the foot soldiers to mount the horses with all their armour on. He ordered Nicanor, who commanded the targeteers, and Attalus, the captain of the squadron of Agrians, to follow, with those who were most lightly armed, on the route that Bessus had gone with his men, while commanding the rest to come later in ordinary formation. {*Arrian, Anabasis, l. 3. c. 21. s. 6-8. 1:299} {*Curtius, l. 5. c. 13. s. 4-8. 1:419}

1941. As Alexander was busy giving orders, Orsines and Mithracenes came to him. Because they abhorred Bessus for his treachery, they had fled from him to Alexander. They told him that the Persians were not more than sixty miles away and that they could lead him to them by a shorter way. He used them as guides and set out early in the evening with a select company of cavalry, ordering the Macedonian phalanx to follow him as fast as they could. When he had gone about forty miles, he was met by Brocubelus (whom Arrian called *Antibelus*), the son of Mazaeus, formerly governor of Syria under Darius. He told him that Bessus was not more than twenty-five miles ahead of him and that his army, thinking they were out of danger, was marching in no particular order. It seemed they were bound for Hyrcania. Brocubelus said that if he hur-

ried, he would be able to attack them when they were all straggling from their standards. {*Arrian, Anabasis, l. 3. c. 21. s. 7-9. 1:299} {*Curtius, l. 5. c. 13. s. 9-12. 1:421}

1942. When Bessus and his consorts found that Alexander was on their heels, they went to Darius where he was in his poor closed cart. [L324] They wanted him to get onto a horse and save himself by fleeing, but when he refused to do this, Satibarzanes and Barzaentes each shot an arrow and wounded him. They also houghed the horses that drew the cart, so that they would go no farther, and killed his two servants, who were still attending Darius. {*Arrian, Anabasis, l. 3. c. 21. s. 10. 1:299} {*Curtius, l. 5. c. 13. s. 13-17. 1:421,423} Only his dog stayed with him. {*Aelian, History of Animals, l. 6. c. 25. 2:43,45} [E231]

1943. When this was done, Satibarzanes and Barzaentes fled away as fast as possible, with six hundred cavalry. So that they could not be pursued together, Nabarzanes fled into Hyrcania and Bessus into Bactria. The rest, having lost their captains, were scattered here and there. Only five hundred cavalry stayed together, undecided as to whether to fight or flee. {*Arrian, Anabasis, l. 3. c. 21. s. 10. 1:299} {*Curtius, l. 5. c. 13. s. 18. 1:423}

1944. When Alexander saw what confusion the enemy was in, he sent Nicanor to prevent their flight, while he followed with the rest of the army. After they had killed about three thousand who refused to yield, Alexander drove the rest before him like so many cattle without harming them, and gave the word to stop the killing. He had advanced so quickly, that barely three thousand of his cavalry had followed him. The prisoners taken outnumbered those who captured them. Fear had so completely robbed them of their senses, that they never considered either their own number or how few the enemy troops were. {*Curtius, l. 5. c. 13. s. 19-22. 1:423}

### 3674d AM, 4384 JP, 330 BC

1945. Meanwhile the horses which drew Darius' cart wandered from the road, as there was no one to drive them. When they had gone about half a mile, they stopped in a certain valley, exhausted from the hot weather and sore from the injuries they had received. There was a spring of water close by. Polystratus, a Macedonian, heard about this spring from the local inhabitants and exhausted from the heat and his wounds, went there to quench his thirst. As he was taking up water in his helmet, he noticed the javelins in the bodies of the horses that drew the cart. {*Curtius, l. 5. c. 13. s. 18. 1:423} When he came nearer, he saw Darius lying in the cart, seriously wounded but not quite dead. Darius called to him for a little water. When he had drunk it, he asked him to thank Alexander for the favour he had shown to his mother, wife and children. He begged nothing for himself but a decent burial. He desired no revenge, but said that if Alexander neglected to avenge his death, it might prove both dishonourable and dangerous for him. The first concerned Alexander as being a matter of justice, the other concerned his personal safety. Darius, as a token of his sincerity, gave Polystratus his right hand and told him to pass the handshake on to Alexander, as a pledge of Darius' faith, and then, having taken hold of Polystratus' hand, he died. {*Justin, Trogus, l. 11. c. 15.} {*Plutarch, Alexander, l. 1. c. 43. s. 2. 7:351,353} {*Josephus, Antiq., l. 18. c. 9. s. 3. (328,329) 9:189}

*1946.* So Darius died at the age of fifty, in the year when Aristophontes was archon in Athens, in the month of Hekatombaion. {*Arrian, Anabasis, l. 3. c. 22. s. 2,6. 1:301,303} He had reigned for six years. Two hundred years had passed from the year of the death of Cyrus, who founded the Persian Empire, until now, which was the very beginning of the third year of the 112th Olympiad. From this time, Calippus (a man held in high regard by Aristotle who was at that time famous in his school at Athens, {Aristotle, Metaphysics, l. 12.}) began his epoch or account of seventy-six years, as we discover from various astronomical observations of Ptolemy, {Ptolemy, Great Syntaxis} [L325] although Strabo said that Darius lost his empire at the battle of Gaugamela, fought nine months earlier. {*Strabo, l. 16. c. 1. s. 3. 7:197} This was confirmed by Justin, who said that Alexander took the empire of Asia from Darius at that time. {Justin, Trogus, l. 11.} However, since it appears that Darius was murdered by his relatives, he lost his life and his kingdom at one and the same time. {Justin, Trogus, l. 10. fin.} We cannot doubt that Calippus, aware of the founding of Alexander's Empire, made this the starting point of his epoch. (We were unable to find the time from the battle of Gaugamela to the death of Darius in Strabo. Editor.)

## The Macedonian Empire

*1947.* The empire of Alexander lasted five years, according to Isidorus and Beda, from Eusebius. {*Eusebius, Chronicles, l. 1. 1:206} Africanus stated six years and the historian who wrote in the time of Alexander Severus said seven years, {Henry Cavisis, Antiq. Lectio., Tome 2., p. 600.} while Strabo allowed ten or eleven years. {*Strabo, l. 15. c. 3. s. 24. 7:189} Nicephorus Constantinopolitanus, in his *Chronicle*, stated twelve years. Clement of Alexandria was wrong when he said it was eighteen years. {*Clement, Stromateis, l. 1. c. 21. 2:329} It is most obvious that from the month of Hekatombaion, when Darius died (when Aristophontes was archon at Athens), to the month of Thargelion, when Alexander died, as we shall show presently (when Hegesias was archon in Athens), only six years and ten months elapsed. In this short period of time, Alexander did so many great feats of war in the east, that he may well be said to have flown rather than to have marched over all those regions. This is the reason why it is said that in Daniel's vision Alexander is depicted by the symbol of a goat who came from the west over the face of the whole earth. {Da 8:5} He never so much as touched the ground. In another vision, Alexander is compared to a winged leopard. {Da 7:6} Jerome noted on this passage that, of all the beasts, the leopard is the swiftest and most impetuous. He added that nothing was accomplished as swiftly as his conquest. He took everything, from the gulf of Venice and the Adriatic Sea, all the way to the Indian Ocean and the Ganges River. He did this not so much in battles as by his reputation. What he did after the death of Darius was recorded by Diodorus (second part of his book 17), Justin (book 12), Curtius (book 5), Plutarch (Alexander) and Arrian. I have inserted the accounts from the various authors in this work, according to their merits. [E232]

*1948.* Darius was no sooner dead, than Alexander rode on his horse to the place where he lay. When he saw his dead body, Alexander wept to see so unworthy a death happen to so noble a person. He took his own coat and placed it over him and immediately sent his body to his mother to be buried in a royal manner with the kings of Persia. He also took Darius' brother Oxathres into the circle of his friends and nobles, bestowing upon him every honour belonging to his high place and parentage. Alexander had planned to pursue Bessus, but since he and his army had escaped to Bactria and Alexander could not reach him at this time, he retraced his steps again. {*Plutarch, Alexander, l. 1. c. 43. s. 3. 7:353} {*Curtius, l. 6. c. 2. s. 11. 2:21}

*1949.* While he was staying at Hecatompylos, a city in Parthiene built in former times by the Greeks, he gathered a good store of provisions. All the army grew restless as they lay idle in their quarters, and they all wanted to return to Greece as soon as possible. When Alexander had allayed this desire, they all asked him to lead them wherever he wished and they would follow him. After a three days' march through the country of Parthiene, he came into the borders of Hyrcania, which Nabarzanes had captured. He left Craterus with the troops under his command, along with Amyntas' brigade of six hundred cavalry and six hundred archers. They were to keep Parthiene safe from incursions by the adjoining countries. He commanded Erigyius to take care of the carriages and to follow him through the plain with a considerable company to guard them. [L326] Alexander took his targeteers, the cream of the Macedonian squadron and some archers. When they had marched about nineteen miles, they camped in a plain near a small river. {*Arrian, Anabasis, l. 3. c. 23. s. 1,2. 1:303} {*Curtius, l. 6. c. 2,4. 2:21-33}

*1950.* After he had refreshed his army there for four days, letters came to him from Nabarzanes, who, together with Bessus, had murdered Darius, saying he would surrender to Alexander. From there Alexander moved two and a half miles through an almost impassable way, but no enemy opposed him and he got through. When he had gone almost another four miles, Phrataphernes, the governor of Hyrcania and Parthia, met him and surrendered to Alexander, along with all those who had fled to him after the death of Darius. Alexander graciously received them all. He next came to a town called Arvae, where Craterus rejoined him, having subdued all the countries which he had passed through. With him he brought Phradates, or Autophradates, the governor of the tribe of the Tapuri, whom Alexander restored to his government again and sent back home. {*Arrian, Anabasis, l. 3. c. 23. s. 4,5. 1:305} {*Curtius, l. 6. c. 4. 2:33-39}

*1951.* When Alexander came to the nearest borders of Hyrcania, Artabazus, the Persian, who was an old friend of Philip, met him. At this time he had been banished by Ochus and had always remained most loyal to Darius. He was now ninety-five years old, and came to Alexander with Cophes and eight other sons of his, all born by the same mother, who was the sister of Mentor and Memnon. Alexander received them all most graciously. Ariobarzanes and Arsames, who were governors under Darius, came and submitted to Alexander. {*Curtius, l. 6. c. 4,5. 2:39-41}

*1952.* Alexander now invaded the country of the Mardians, which bordered on Hyrcania. They held the mountain passes and met Alexander with an army of eight thousand men. Alexander attacked the army, killed many of them and took more of them prisoners. The rest fled into the craggy mountains. At length, they returned Alexander's horse Bucephalas, which they had captured, and sent fifty envoys to him to ask his pardon. When Alexander had taken hostages, he made Autophradates governor over them as well as the Tapuri. {*Arrian, Anabasis, l. 3. c. 24. s. 3. 1:305} {*Plutarch, Alexander, l. 1. c. 44. s. 3. 7:353} {*Curtius, l. 6. c. 5. 2:41-45}

*1953.* From there he returned within five days to the place from where he had set out against the Mardians. Andronicus, the son of Agerrus, and Artabazus had brought with them to Alexander fifteen hundred Greek mercenaries of Darius. Ninety envoys, who had been sent to Darius from various countries, also came to him. Alexander put four Lacedemonian envoys and Dropides, the Athenian, in prison. Democrates, the other Athenian envoy who always opposed the Macedonian party, committed suicide, because he did not expect a pardon from Alexander. The envoys from Sinope and Heraclides, who had been sent from Carthage, were freed by Alexander, along with the other envoys from Greece. To Andronicus he gave the command of the Greeks who stayed in his service. Having doubly honoured Artabazus and given him greater honours than he had held under Darius, Alexander sent him home. {*Curtius, l. 6. c. 5. 2:41} {*Arrian, Anabasis, l. 3. c. 24. s. 4. 1:309,311}

*1954.* When these matters had been taken care of, he marched against the greatest city in all Hyrcania, called Zeudracarta or Zadracarta, and remained there for fifteen days. Nabarzanes came to him there, bringing many presents with him. *[E233]* Among these was Bagoas, a young boy eunuch of rare beauty, who was later held in high regard and could do whatever he wished with Alexander. Both Darius and Alexander used Bagoas as a catamite (a boy kept for homosexual practices). {*Curtius, l. 6. c. 5. s. 23. 2:47}

*1955.* Thalestris, or Minithaea, came to Alexander at this place with three hundred ladies. She was the queen of the Amazons who lived between the two rivers of Phasis and Thermodon. She left the rest of her army at the borders of Hyrcania and came hoping to conceive a child by him. She stayed thirteen days. *[L327]* Contrary to the stream of all geographers, Curtius in this account located these Amazons on the borders of Hyrcania. {*Curtius, l. 6. c. 5. s. 24-32. 2:47,49} Justin, however, said that they bordered on Albania. {Justin, Trogus, l. 42. c. 3,25,35.} Clitarchus said that Thalestris came to Alexander from the Caspian Gates and the Thermodon River, and that it took her a twenty-five or thirty-five day journey to reach him through many countries. {Justin, Trogus, l. 12. c. 3.} The journey was at least seven hundred and fifty miles. {*Strabo, l. 11. c. 5. s. 4. 5:239} Her visit to Alexander was recorded by Polycrates, Onesicritus, Antigenes, Histor and various others. However, Aristobulus, Chares the historian, Ptolemy Lagus, Anticlides, Philo Thebanus, Philip the historian, Hecataeus Eretriensis, Philippus the historian and Duris Samius said that it was merely a fable. Alexander seemed to agree, because in his commentaries to Antigonus, in which he recorded the events exactly, he said that a certain Scythian offered him his daughter for a wife, but no mention is made of an Amazon. It is also reported that, many years later, Onesicritus was reading his fourth book to Lysimachus, who was ruling at the time. When he mentioned something about an Amazon who came to Alexander, Lysimachus smiled and said: {*Strabo, l. 11. c. 5. s. 4. 5:237,239} {*Plutarch, Alexander, l. 1. c. 46. 7:357} {*Arrian, Anabasis, l. 7. c. 13. s. 2-6. 2:247,249}

"I pray, sir, where was I all the while?"

*1956.* On returning to Parthiene, Alexander indulged himself in all kinds of Persian luxuries, also commanding his nobles to take up wearing the long Persian robe of gold and purple cloth, and if any of the common soldiers wanted to marry a Persian, he permitted it.

1957. Bessus now wore his turban upright and pointed, along with other regal attire, and assumed the titles of Artaxerxes and King of Asia. He gathered together into a body all the Persians who had fled into Bactria. As well as these, he had Bactrians, the Scythians and others who lived as far away as the bank of the Tanais River, and so he planned to make war on Alexander.

1958. Alexander made Amminapes, a Parthian, the governor of Parthia and Hyrcania in authority under himself. Amminapes, together with Mazacus, or Mazaces, had delivered Egypt into his hands. Alexander had Tlepolemus, the son of Pythophanes, one of his friends, assist Amminapes in the government. {*Arrian, Anabasis, l. 3. c. 22. s. 1. 1:301} However, Curtius said that he made Menapis (for so he called Amminapes), who had previously been banished by Ochus and had fled to Alexander's father Philip for refuge, governor of Hyrcania. {*Curtius, l. 6. c. 4. s. 25. 2:39} Justin said that when Alexander had subdued Parthia, he made a certain nobleman of Persia, called Andragoras, its governor. {Justin, Trogus, l. 12. c. 4.} It was from him that the kings of Parthia were descended, since Arsaces mentioned him as the founder of the Parthian kingdom. Justin also called him Andragoras. {Justin, Trogus, l. 41. c. 4.}

1959. After this, Alexander came to Susia, a city of the Arians. Satibarzanes, governor of the Arians, came to him, and Alexander restored his government to him. He sent Anaxippus, one of his Companion Cavalry, to run the government with him, giving him forty mounted archers to attend him, whom he could put in places which he considered most appropriate in order to keep the Arians from being plundered or injured by his army as it passed by. {*Arrian, Anabasis, l. 3. c. 25. s. 1,2. 1:311}

1960. Alexander was now ready to march against Bessus. When he saw that his army was so loaded with spoil and luxurious goods that they were in no condition to march, he first commanded his own goods to be burned, and then theirs, keeping only what was necessary for their immediate needs. {*Curtius, l. 6. c. 6. s. 14-17. 2:53}

1961. Nicanor, the son of Parmenion and captain of the Argyraspides (that is, of the silver shields, or targeteers), died suddenly, and everyone mourned his passing. [L328] Alexander was especially grieved and would have stayed to be present at his funeral, but lack of provisions made it impossible for him to do so. He therefore left Nicanor's brother Philotas there, with twenty-six hundred men, to take care of the funeral, while he went on his journey in pursuit of Bessus. {*Curtius, l. 6. c. 6. s. 18,19. 2:55}

1962. Satibarzanes, to whom Alexander had restored his government over the Arians, as mentioned earlier, murdered Anaxippus along with his forty mounted archers. He gathered all the forces he could to the chief city of the Arians called Chortacana, or Artacoana. When he heard that Alexander was coming, he planned to go and join with Bessus in a common war against the Macedonians. {*Arrian, Anabasis, l. 3. c. 25. s. 5. 1:313} {*Diod. Sic., l. 17. c. 78. s. 1. 8:343} [E234]

1963. When Alexander heard of this, he interrupted his journey into Bactria and marched seventy-five miles in two days to reach Artacoana. Satibarzanes, with two thousand cavalry (for that was all he could gather at that time), fled into Bactria to Bessus. The rest escaped to the mountains. Alexander pursued Satibarzanes for a long time, but was not able to overtake him. He attacked those who were in the mountains and took the craggy rocks to which thirteen thousand armed Arians had fled. Then Alexander returned to Artacoana, which Craterus had besieged in the meantime. Craterus was fully prepared for an assault and was waiting for Alexander to lead it, so that the honour of taking the city would fall to Alexander, not him. Joab did the same for David. {2Sa 12:27,28} When Alexander came, he found them ready to plead for his mercy, so he pardoned them and lifted his siege, restoring to every man what was his. Within thirty days, he had taken all the cities of that country and made Arsaces their governor. {*Arrian, Anabasis, l. 3. c. 25. s. 5-7. 1:315} {*Curtius, l. 6. c. 6. s. 21-34. 2:55-59}

1964. Fresh troops and supplies came to Alexander at this stage. Zoilus brought him five hundred cavalry from Greece, while Antipater sent him three thousand soldiers from Illyria. Philip, the son of Menelaus, brought him mercenary cavalry from Media, along with a hundred and thirty of the Thessalian cavalry to whom, at Ecbatana, Alexander had given leave to return home, but they had refused and stayed on with Alexander. From Lydia came twenty-six hundred foreign foot soldiers with three hundred cavalry under the command of Andromachus, according to Arrian. {*Arrian, Anabasis, l. 3. c. 25. s. 4. 1:313} {*Curtius, l. 6. c. 6. s. 35. 2:59}

1965. With these new forces, Alexander came to the capital of the Drangianes (whom Arrian calls the Zarangians), whose governor was Barzaentes. He was one of the men who, with Bessus and Nabarzanes, had turned on Darius. He feared punishment from Alexander and fled away to the Indians on the western side of the Indus River. {*Arrian, Anabasis, l. 3. c. 25. s. 8. 1:315} {*Diod. Sic., l. 17. c. 78. s. 4. 8:345}

1966. Alexander spent nine days in the capital city of the Drangian country. Some of his own people began to plot his death. Dymnus, a Macedonian, revealed to Nicomachus, his catamite and Alexander's bard, that three days from then Alexander would be murdered, and that he was in on the plot with various nobles. Although Nicomachus had been sworn to secrecy by Dymnus, he told the matter to his brother Ceballinus, asking him to tell the king about it. Since Ceballinus could not easily get to Alexander, he first told Philotas about it, but when he found that Philotas was indifferent, and possibly in on the plot, Ceballinus went to Metron, a noble young gentleman who was in charge of the artillery. He advised Metron to tell Alexander about it immediately. When Alexander heard about it, he at once ordered all those in the plot to be arrested. When Dymnus was arrested, he knew why, and killed himself with his sword. When Ceballinus was questioned, he protested that the very hour he had heard of it he had mentioned the matter to Philotas, requesting him to tell the king. *[L329]* When questioned about this, Philotas said it was true, but claimed he had meant no harm and had only done nothing through carelessness, considering it to be a baseless rumour. But when Philotas was put on the rack, he confessed all and was executed with the rest of the conspirators. Philotas was the son of Parmenion, who was next to Alexander in authority. {*Diod. Sic., l. 17. c. 79,80. 8:345-349} {*Curtius, l. 6. c. 7-11. 2:69-111}

1967. Alexander, the Lyncestian, was also called before a council of the Macedonians for his previous conspiracy, for which he was in prison for three years. {*Diod. Sic., l. 17. c. 80. s. 2. 8:349} {*Curtius, l. 7. c. 1. s. 6-9. 2:117,119} This is that same Alexander Aeropus who, before the battle at Issus four years earlier, had been put in prison for plotting Alexander's death. {*Arrian, Anabasis, l. 1. c. 25. s. 1-10. 1:103-107} {*Diod. Sic., l. 17. c. 32. s. 1,2. 8:207} {Justin, Trogus, l. 11. c. 7. s. 1.} {See note on 3671b AM. <<1740>>} Aeropus had plotted Alexander's death several times previously. Alexander spoke the following to his council of Macedonians: {*Curtius, l. 8. c. 8. s. 6,7. 2:297}

> "Alexander, the Lyncestian, was twice arraigned for two counts of treason against my life. I have twice taken him out of the hand of justice and when he was convicted a third time, I gave him a reprieve and kept him in prison these three years. (For so it should be according to the true *Palatine Manuscript* and not *two years*, as in the ordinary printed books.) Until now you desired that he be given his just punishment."

1968. When he was questioned concerning the latest attempt on Alexander's life, he could not answer without faltering. Therefore, without any more ado, he was thrust through with lances by those who stood about and heard him at the bar. {*Curtius, l. 7. c. 1. s. 8,9. 2:119}

1969. After the body of Alexander, the Lyncestian, was carried from the place, the king still remained in the judgment seat. He had Amyntas, Attalus and Simias, the sons of Andromenes and all very close to Philotas, brought to the bar. When Polemon, another son of Andromenes and the youngest of them all, heard that Philotas had been put on the rack, he fled, but was captured and brought to judgment. Finally, Alexander acquitted them all, as a result of the general intercession of all those who were present. Then he immediately sent Polydamas, whom Parmenion loved very much, with two Arabians on dromedary camels, into Media. *[E235]* They were to get there before the news of the death of Philotas reached those lands. They had letters for Cleander, Sitalces and Menidas, the commanders in the army under Parmenion, to kill him. He was the governor of Media and had the greatest reputation and authority in the army after the king himself. Parmenion was now seventy years old. After he had read Alexander's letter and was reading the second letter written to him in the name of his son Philotas, he was stabbed to death. Cleander sent his head to the king and would barely allow the rest of his body to be buried. Strabo stated that this all happened within eleven days, whereas an ordinary journey normally took thirty to forty days just in travelling time. {*Strabo, l. 15. c. 2. s. 10. 7:145} {*Curtius, l. 7. c. 1,2. 2:119-141} {*Arrian, Anabasis, l. 3. c. 26. s. 1-4. 1:315,317}

1970. Alexander feared that the glory of his actions in their entirety might be blemished by the cruelty of his most recent actions by the way he had dealt with those plotting his death, and so he did what Gaus had previously once done. {See note on 3620 AM. <<1574>>} He let it be known that he was about to send some of his friends back to Macedonia, and advised all those men who wanted to write to their friends in those parts not to miss this opportunity of sending a note back home, since they were going farther east. Every man wrote a letter, and he ordered that all the letters be brought to him. In this way he found out what everyone thought of him. He put all those whom he found to be either weary of the war or unhappy with his actions into one company, which he called the unruly company, and put Leonnidas, formerly an intimate friend of Parmenion's, in charge of it. Then he divided the Companion Cavalry into two regiments, assigning the one part to be commanded by Hephaestion and the other by Clitus. {*Curtius, l. 7. c. 2. s. 35-38. 2:141,143}

1971. When Alexander had settled matters among the Drangians, he marched toward those who formerly were called Agriaspe, or Arimaspians. In former times Cyrus, who transferred the rule from the Medes to the Persians, called them the *Benefactors*, on account of a good deed which they had done him. *[L330]* Alexander was warmly received and entertained by them. {*Diod. Sic., l. 17. c. 81. s. 1,2. 8:351,353} {*Curtius, l. 7. c. 3. s. 1. 2:143}

1972. After staying in that country five days, he received news that Satibarzanes, with two thousand cavalry from Bessus, had attacked the Arians and made them defect from Alexander, so he sent six thousand Greek foot soldiers and six hundred cavalry under the command of Erigyius and Caranus against Satibarzanes. Diodorus said that Stasanor shared the command together with Artabazus, the Persian, Andronicus and Phrataphernes, the governor of Parthia. {*Diod. Sic., l. 17. c. 81. s. 1,2. 8:351,353} {*Arrian, Anabasis, l. 3. c. 28. s. 2,3. 1:321} {*Curtius, l. 7. c. 4. s. 33-40. 2:161-163} {*Curtius, l. 7. c. 3. s. 2,3. 2:145}

1973. Alexander stayed with the Euergetae and sacrificed to Apollo. He committed Demetrius, one of the captains of his bodyguard, to prison, because he suspected him of conspiracy with Philotas, and replaced him with Ptolemy, the son of Lagus. To the Euergetae he gave a large sum of money and whatever land they desired, which was not much. When he was welcomed by the Gedrosians, who bordered on the Euergetae, he also rewarded them according to their deeds. {*Arrian, Anabasis, l. 3. c. 27. s. 5. 1:319} {*Curtius, l. 7. c. 3. s. 3. 2:145}

### 3675a AM, 4384 JP, 330 BC

1974. After he had spent sixty days with the Euergetae, he appointed Amedines, who, according to Curtius, had been Darius' secretary for some time, as their new governor. However, Arrian said he left them as a free state. Diodorus stated that he made Tiridates the governor of both the Euergetae and the Cedrosians. {*Diod. Sic., l. 17. c. 81. s. 2. 8:353} {*Arrian, Anabasis, l. 3. c. 27. s. 5. 1:319} {*Curtius, l. 7. c. 3. s. 4. 2:145}

1975. Alexander left them and marched into Bactria against Bessus, subduing the Arachosians along the way. Part of his army, which was formerly commanded by Parmenion, joined up with him. Among them were six thousand Macedonians and two hundred nobles, men of honour, and these were the very pith and marrow of all his army. He appointed Menon as governor of the Arachosians and left him four thousand soldiers and six hundred cavalry to keep order in the country. {*Curtius, l. 7. c. 3. s. 4,5. 2:145}

1976. Alexander led his army into the country of the Parapanisadae about the time of the setting of Pleiades (in the early morning), the beginning of winter. {*Strabo, l. 15. c. 1. s. 17. 7:25} All the country was covered with snow. The days were obscurely dark, rather than light, so that a man could hardly discern anything close by. In this vast wilderness, Alexander's army endured the misery

of lack of food, cold, weariness and even despair. Many died from the cold, and many men's feet rotted off their legs from frost bite. At last they came into a warmer country with more provisions. The army was relieved, and the whole country was quickly brought into subjection. {*Curtius, l. 7. c. 3. s. 6-18. 2:145-149}

1977. Alexander went to the Caucasus Mountains, which some called Parapanisus. He crossed the mountains in a sixteen or seventeen day march, and built a city near the foot of the mountains, at the place where that particular mountain pass opens into Media, naming the city after himself, Alexandria. He also built various other cities, each a day's journey from Alexandria, relocating seven thousand inhabitants of the countries in that area into these new cities. *[E236]* He put three thousand of those who followed the camp into these cities, and let as many of those who had grown unserviceable in the wars settle there, as wanted to. He made Proexes, a Persian, governor of all that region and left one of his friends, Niloxenes, as ruler over them. {*Diod. Sic., l. 17. c. 83. s. 1-3. 8:357,359} {*Curtius, l. 7. c. 3. s. 19-23. 2:149-151}

1978. When the Macedonians and Arians were fighting, Satibarzanes, who commanded the enemy, came between the two armies. Pulling off his helmet, he said who he was, and challenged to a duel any man who dared. Erigyius, the general of the Macedonian army, took up the challenge and ran his spear through his body, killing him. *[L331]* When the barbarians, who were there under compulsion rather than willingly, saw that their captain was dead, they trusted Erigyius and laid down their arms and submitted to him. {*Curtius, l. 7. c. 4. s. 33-40. 2:161,163}

### 3675b AM, 4385 JP, 329 BC

1979. Bessus and those Persians who had joined him in seizing Darius, with about seven thousand Bactrians and some of the Dahae, who lived east of the Tanais River, foraged the country bordering on the Caucasus Mountains. They hoped that by ravaging and destroying all the countries which lay between them and Alexander, they would effectively stop him from coming that way for fear of starving his army. Nevertheless, Alexander went on under extreme difficulty, in much snow, with too little food. {*Arrian, Anabasis, l. 3. c. 28. s. 8. 1:323}

1980. When winter was almost over, as he was moving north, he had India on his right and crossed over the mountains into Bactria. Not a tree was to be seen all the way, except for a few shrubs. {*Strabo, l. 15. c. 2. s. 10. 7:147} Along the route, his troops found a quantity of Indian grain, from which the common soldiers squeezed a type of juice pressed from sesame, which they used for oil to ease the pain of their cold joints. This oil was sold for two hundred and forty denarii per pitcher, while a pitcher of wine fetched three hundred denarii. There was very little wheat to make bread with. In his hunger, the common soldier sustained himself by catching river fish and eating whatever herbs he could find, but even these foods were not enough. They were told to kill their draught animals and eat them, which kept them alive until they came into Bactria. {*Curtius, l. 7. c. 4. s. 22-25. 2:157} Strabo added that they were forced to eat it raw for lack of fire to roast it with. To settle their stomachs, they had a supply of a herb called silphium, which helped their digestion.

1981. Bessus was terrified by Alexander's rapid advance. After he had first sacrificed to his gods, he feasted his friends and captains. As they ate, they discussed the war at hand. He bragged of a kingdom which he had acquired by treachery, but he was hardly in his right mind. He boasted that the cowardice of Darius had enhanced the fame and glory of the enemy. He resolved to march with his army into Sogdiana, where he would have the Oxus River as a wall between him and Alexander until help came in from other parts. When all the rest were as drunk as he was, Gobares (according to Curtius; or Bagodoras, according to Diodorus), a Median and a soothsayer by profession, advised him that when he was sober and had come to his senses, he should submit to Alexander. Bessus was so enraged that he drew his sword, and those with him could barely restrain him from killing Gobares. In the meantime, Gobares fled and came to Alexander the following night. {*Curtius, l. 7. c. 4. s. 1-19. 2:151-157} {*Diod. Sic., l. 17. c. 83. s. 7-9. 8:361}

1982. On the fifteenth day after he had set out from his new city of Alexandria and his winter quarters, he came to Adrapsa, a city of Bactria or Drapsaca, according to Arrian. {*Strabo, l. 15. c. 2. s. 10. 7:147} After he had refreshed his army, he marched to Aornus and Bactra, the two largest cities of Bactria, and took them on the first assault. He put a garrison into the citadel of Aornus under the command of his Companion Cavalry man, Archelaus. {*Arrian, Anabasis, l. 3. c. 29. s. 1. 1:325}

1983. Bessus had seven or eight thousand Bactrians in his army, who remained loyal to him and thought that Alexander would never follow them into that cold climate, but rather go into India. However, when they saw that Alexander was marching toward them, every man stole away to his own home, leaving Bessus all alone. He was left with a small retinue of his servants and tenants, who remained loyal to him. After they had crossed the Oxus River by boat, they burned the boats so that Alexander would not be able to make use of them. They went to a place called Nautaca, in the country of Sogdiana, to raise new forces from those parts. [L332] Spitamenes and Oxyartes followed him with some cav-

alry from Sogdiana and as many of the Dahae as had come to him from the bank of the Tanais River. {*Arrian, Anabasis, l. 3. c. 28. s. 8-10. 1:323,325} {*Curtius, l. 7. c. 4. s. 20,21. 2:157}

## 3675c AM, 4385 JP, 329 BC

1984. Alexander made Artabazus the governor of Bactria. He left his wagons behind there with a guard to watch them. Taking the rest of the army, he set out at night and came into the desert of Sogdiana. [E237] When he had gone about fifty miles, he found no water at all, and the next day his whole army was dying of thirst. Later, when they found water, more men died from drinking too much than he had ever lost in any battle. {*Curtius, l. 7. c. 5. s. 1-16. 2:163-167}

1985. Toward evening, Alexander came to the Oxus River, where he spent that night greatly disturbed, as he waited for the rest of his army to come.

1986. Before he crossed the river, he picked from his Macedonians those who were not fit to fight, either because of age or wounds, and selected nine hundred from the Thessalians who were following him as volunteers. He gave everyone in the cavalry two talents, and to each foot soldier he gave three thousand denarii, or drachmas. He dismissed them to go home and join their families, and thanked the rest for promising to go on with him in the war.

1987. He also sent his friend Stasanor to the Arians to seize Arsaces, their governor, because he seemed to be up to no good. He appointed Stasanor to be governor in his place. {*Arrian, Anabasis, l. 3. c. 29. s. 5. 1:327}

1988. There was no timber there for making boats. Therefore, having grown impatient at the delay, he had the hides which covered the soldiers' tents taken down, stuffed with straw and sewn or tied together. In five days, he ferried his army across the river on these leather rafts. {*Curtius, l. 7. c. 5. s. 17,18. 2:167,169}

1989. Spitamenes was Bessus' most respected and honoured friend. As soon as he heard that Alexander had crossed the Oxus River, he told Bessus that his two trusted aides, Dataphernes and Catanes, were plotting against him, but in actual fact all three were plotting against Bessus. When Bessus went to apprehend them, he was tricked and was apprehended himself. Catanes laid hold on Bessus, removed his regal diadem from his head and tore to pieces the robe which he wore, and which he had taken from the body of Darius. {*Curtius, l. 7. c. 5. s. 23-26. 2:169,171}

1990. Having crossed the Oxus River, Alexander soon marched to the place where Bessus was. On the way, he received news from Spitamenes and Dataphernes that, if he cared to send any one of his captains with a large enough guard, they would deliver Bessus into his hands, and so Alexander sent Ptolemy, the son of Lagus, with three companies of cavalry, the regiment of foot soldiers of Philotas, a thousand of the silver targeteers, the entire squadron of the Agrians and one half of the archers. In four days, Ptolemy marched with these men to the place where Spitamenes and his army had camped the day before, whereas this was normally a ten day journey. {*Arrian, Anabasis, l. 3. c. 29. s. 6,7. 1:327,329}

1991. Meanwhile, Alexander came to a little town of the Branchidae, the inhabitants of which had been relocated there from Miletus by Xerxes many years earlier, as a reward for their work on his behalf, in betraying Miletus and pulling down the temple of Apollo Didymeon. {See note on 3526a AM. <<1165>>} As this town had become the home of traitors, it was now completely plundered and then totally destroyed. All the inhabitants, men, women and children, were killed with the sword. [L333] Had this been executed on the traitors themselves, it would have been an act of justice, and not of cruelty, but now the children suffered for their forefathers' faults, even though they had never seen Miletus, much less betrayed it to Xerxes. {*Curtius, l. 7. c. 5. s. 28-35. 2:171-175} {*Strabo, l. 11. c. 11. s. 4. 5:285}

1992. As Alexander was on his march, Bessus was brought to him not only bound but stark naked, a sight delighting all the men, both Greeks and barbarians. All those bringing him were rewarded for their efforts. The prisoner was committed to the keeping of Oxathres, Darius' brother, whom Alexander had made one of the captains of his bodyguard. Oxathres planned to have him bound to a cross, after his ears and nose had been cut off and his body shot through with arrows. His dead body would be watched, so that no bird could land on it. After Bessus was scourged with whips, he was remanded to Bactria and his death deferred, because he was to be executed in the place where he had murdered Darius. {*Curtius, l. 7. c. 5. s. 36-43. 2:175,177}

1993. Alexander had reinforced his army, as he had lost many troops in crossing over the Caucasus Mountains, on the journey to the Oxus River and on his march to the Tanais River. This was not the river which divided Europe from Asia and emptied the Maeotis Lake (Sea of Azov) into the Black Sea. It is another Tanais River, also called Jaxartes, which Pliny said the Scythians called *Silis*, and according to Aristobulus, the inhabitants in the area called *Orxantes*. {*Arrian, Anabasis, l. 3. c. 30. s. 6-9. 1:331,333} {*Pliny, l. 6. c. 18. 2:375}

1994. At this place certain Macedonians went foraging and were not as careful as they should have been. They were attacked by certain natives from the mountains, who killed many of them, but captured even more. These natives numbered thirty thousand men, but Curtius said there were twenty thousand men. To fight against these natives, Alexander quickly gathered whatever companies as he had closest at hand. During this battle, he was shot in the leg with an arrow, and when the shaft was pulled out, the head stayed in. Arrian stated that the hill was taken, and that less than eight thousand of the thirty thousand enemy troops escaped. [E238] Curtius, however, stated that on the next day after he had been hurt, these barbarians voluntarily surrendered to him, sending him the prisoners which they had taken and making their peace with him. {*Arrian, Anabasis, l. 3. c. 30. s. 10,11. 1:333} {*Curtius, l. 7. c. 6. s. 1-9. 2:177,179}

1995. He moved his camp while being carried on an ordinary stretcher, which every man was happy to take turns in carrying. In four days he came to Maracanda, the principal city of all Sogdiana, whose wall was almost nine miles in circumference. He left a garrison to keep the city, while he went and wasted and burned the nearby towns. A few days later, envoys came to him from the Scythians, called Abis. These had lived as a free state ever since the death of Cyrus, but now they surrendered to him. {*Arrian, Anabasis, l. 4. c. 1. s. 1,2. 1:337} {*Curtius, l. 7. c. 6. s. 10-12. 2:179,181}

1996. The barbarians living near the river captured and killed the Macedonian soldiers that had been left there in the garrison. They started to fortify their cities, while many of the Sogdians joined with them and were encouraged by those who had taken Bessus' side. They caused some of the Bactrians to defect as well. The Susians and Bactrians had seven thousand cavalry, which helped to encourage the rest to defect. Alexander sent Spitamenes and Catanes, who had delivered Bessus into his hands, to repress them, but they turned out to be the principal ring-leaders of that rebellion. They said that Alexander had sent for all the Bactrian cavalry so that he could kill them. {*Arrian, Anabasis, l. 4. c. 1. s. 4,5. 1:337,339} {*Curtius, l. 7. c. 6. s. 14,15. 2:181}

1997. When Alexander heard about this, he attacked the city of Gaza and sent Craterus against Cyropolis. Having taken Gaza, he killed everyone in it who was of age and destroyed the city, selling the women and children into slavery. [L334] This was to be an example to others. Within two days, he had taken four other cities in those parts and treated them in the same manner, after which he marched off to Cyropolis. Eighteen thousand men had fled there, because the place was well fortified and a good refuge. Not only did he lose the bravest and best men of his army in that siege, but he himself was in extreme danger, taking such a blow to the neck with a stone, that his eyes were dazzled and he fell to the ground unconscious for a time. However, he showed invincible courage in the face of casualties that would have daunted other men. Although his wound had not yet completely healed, he assaulted the place more fiercely than ever before, his anger spurring on his natural fighting abilities. As soon as the city had been taken, eight thousand of the enemy were killed, while the rest fled into the citadel, but after Alexander had besieged it for only one day, they surrendered for lack of water. {*Arrian, Anabasis, l. 4. c. 2,3. 1:339-345} {*Curtius, l. 7. c. 6. s. 16-23. 2:183,185}

1998. Alexander ordered Cyropolis to be levelled to the ground. Of the seven cities which the natives had fortified for themselves, only one now remained to be taken, and he took it on the very first assault. Ptolemy, however, said that it surrendered to him. Aristobulus said that the men taken in it were distributed throughout the army and kept bound until Alexander left that country. This would leave no one behind who had had a part in that revolt. {*Arrian, Anabasis, l. 4. c. 3. s. 5. 1:345}

1999. Meanwhile, the Scythians of Asia came with a large army to the bank of the Tanais River, having heard that the countries on the other side were up in arms against Alexander. They planned that if the inhabitants of these countries were to revolt in large numbers, they would join with them against Alexander and attack the Macedonians. {*Arrian, Anabasis, l. 4. c. 3. s. 6. 1:345}

2000. Spitamenes stayed within the walls of Maracanda, besieging the garrison of the Macedonians who were in the citadel there. To fight against him, Alexander sent Menedemus, Andromachus and Caranus along with sixty of the Companion Cavalry, eight hundred of his mercenaries led by Caranus, and fifteen hundred mercenary foot soldiers. (Curtius said three thousand.) Alexander gave them Pharnuches as an interpreter, because he spoke the barbarians' language and could therefore best serve to negotiate with them. {*Arrian, Anabasis, l. 4. c. 3. s. 6,7. 1:345} {*Curtius, l. 7. c. 6. s. 24. 2:185}

2001. Alexander came back to the bank of the Tanais River and made a wall around his camp. He turned it into a city with walls of almost eight miles in circumference, and called the city after his own name, Alexandria. The work was done so quickly that, within seventeen days of the walls going up, it was filled with houses. {*Curtius, l. 7. c. 6. s. 25-27. 2:185,187} However, Justin said that in seventeen days he built a wall around it which was six miles in circumference. {Justin, Trogus, l. 12. c. 5.} Arrian stated that in twenty days the city was enclosed with a wall. He gave the city to his Greek mercenaries to live in, along with any of the natives in the area who wished to live there. Any of his Macedonians who had become

unserviceable for the war were allowed to live there too. He also settled some of his prisoners there, to fill this newly built city. By paying their ransom to their various masters, he made them freedmen and citizens of this city, to which he also relocated the inhabitants of three cities which Cyrus had built. {*Arrian, Anabasis, l. 4. c. 4. s. 1. 1:347}

2002. The king of the Scythians, whose kingdom lay beyond the Tanais River, knew that the city had been built purposely to restrain his ambitions. He sent his brother Carcasis to take and demolish it, and to drive away the Macedonians from beside the river. These Scythians rode up and down on the other side of the river in full view of Alexander, shooting arrows and hurling insults at him and his Macedonians. [E239] Alexander had not yet fully recovered from his wound. [L335] His voice failed him, and he could not stand unaided or sit on horseback, which meant he could not order what he wanted done. {*Arrian, Anabasis, l. 4. c. 4. s. 2,3. 1:347} {*Curtius, l. 7. c. 7. s. 1-4. 2:187}

2003. Spitamenes, besides his own men, had with him some six hundred Dahae and wild Scythian cavalry. These attacked and killed a part of the army that had been sent by Alexander to relieve those who were besieged in the citadel at Maracanda. Aristobulus said that when the Macedonians were fighting, so large a number of Scythians suddenly emerged from the neighbouring gardens that they killed almost all the Macedonians. Barely forty cavalry and three hundred foot soldiers escaped. Curtius mentioned only that two thousand foot soldiers were lost in that defeat. Alexander, however, to hide the greatness of that loss, ordered those who returned to his camp not to speak a word about it, on pain of death. {*Arrian, Anabasis, l. 4. c. 5,6. 1:353-357} {*Curtius, l. 7. c. 7. s. 30-39. 2:197,199}

### 3675d AM, 4385 JP, 329 BC

2004. Alexander put his heavily armed foot soldiers into as many boats as he could make, while the rest swam on leather bags stuffed with straw. They crossed the Tanais River with incredible courage and attacked and routed the Scythians. Even though Alexander was quite weak, he pursued them for ten miles. In this battle, sixty Macedonian cavalry and almost a hundred foot soldiers died, and about a thousand were wounded. {*Arrian, Anabasis, l. 4. c. 4. s. 4-9. 1:347-351} {*Curtius, l. 7. c. 8,9. 2:197-211}

2005. Not long after this, Scythian envoys came to him to justify what had happened. They said that this war had not been fought against him by the Scythian nation, but by only a few of their number, who lived by robbery and plundering, and that the law-abiding inhabitants would yield to him. Alexander accepted this and replied kindly. He released all the prisoners without a ransom, so that these warlike people would see that his battle with them was for honour, not revenge. {*Arrian, Anabasis, l. 4. c. 5. s. 1. 1:351} {*Curtius, l. 7. c. 9. s. 17,18. 2:211}

2006. When the Sacae saw this, they sent their envoys to him, offering him their service, and he dealt as graciously with them. He had Euxenippus, a young gentleman whom he loved very dearly and who was as close to him as Hephaestion was, to keep them company and to entertain them. {*Curtius, l. 7. c. 9. s. 17-19. 2:211,213}

2007. Alexander took half of the Companion Cavalry, all his targeteers, archers, Agrians and the best of the whole Macedonian squadron and marched to Maracanda, because he had been told that Spitamenes had returned there to besiege the Greeks in the citadel. He marched about ninety miles in three days, and came to the city early the next day. When Spitamenes heard of his approach, he lifted his siege and fled. Alexander pursued him as fast as he could. On the way he came to the place where the Scythians had killed his Macedonians, so he had their bones gathered and buried with a proper Macedonian funeral. After this, he followed the enemy until he came into the desert. {*Arrian, Anabasis, l. 4. c. 6. s. 3-5. 1:357} {*Curtius, l. 7. c. 9. s. 20,21. 2:213}

2008. By this time Craterus, marching at a slower pace, as he had been told to do, came to Alexander with the largest part of the army. To punish the Sogdians for revolting from him, Alexander divided his army into two parts and ordered them to burn every place and kill all males of age. In this manner he overran that entire region, through which the Polytimetus River ran. Beyond it, the river ran underground and all the country was a desert, totally devoid of cities and inhabitants. {*Arrian, Anabasis, l. 4. c. 6. s. 5-7. 1:359} {*Curtius, l. 7. c. 9. s. 22. 2:213} [L336]

2009. Diodorus estimated that Alexander killed a hundred and twenty thousand Sogdians. {*Diod. Sic., l. 17. c. 0. 8:111} Thirty of the most noble of them, all men of great strength, were brought to Alexander. He marvelled at their undaunted courage when in the face of death, and freed them on the condition that they would henceforth be loyal to him. They kept their word and when they returned home, they made all their people submit to Alexander. Alexander took four of them to be in his bodyguard, and no Macedonians proved more faithful to him than these men were. {*Curtius, l. 7. c. 10. s. 1-9. 2:213,215}

2010. He left Pencolaus there with a garrison of three thousand foot soldiers (since no more were needed), while he came into Bactria. Alexander called together everyone there and ordered that Bessus be brought to him. Alexander reproached him for his treachery to

Darius and had his nose and ears cut off. He sent Bessus to Ecbatana, so that he might be executed there before the Medes and Persians. Plutarch said that Alexander ordered both his arms and legs to be tied to two trees that were bent down, so that when the trees were released, they would tear him to pieces. Diodorus wrote that the brother of Darius and his other relatives railed and bitterly reproached him in many speeches, after which they cut his whole body into pieces and then put them into slings and scattered them abroad. {*Curtius, l. 7. c. 10. s. 10,11. 2:215,217} {*Arrian, Anabasis, l. 4. c. 7. s. 3. 1:361} {*Plutarch, Alexander, l. 1. c. 43. s. 3. 7:353} {*Diod. Sic., l. 17. c. 83. s. 9. 8:361} [E240]

2011. About that same time Phrataphernes, the governor of Parthia, came to him with Stasanor, who had been sent into Aria to apprehend Arsaces. Stasanor brought Arsaces, bound in chains, together with Barzaentes, whom Bessus had made governor of Persia under him, as well as other men who had been involved in the revolt of Bessus. {*Arrian, Anabasis, l. 4. c. 7. s. 1. 1:359}

2012. Epocillus and Melanidas came to Alexander from the Asian sea coast. Ptolemy, the commander of the Thracians, who had escorted the old soldiers whom Alexander had dismissed to go home as well as the money sent by Menetes, also came. Ptolemy and Melanidas brought with them four thousand foot soldiers and a thousand mercenary cavalry. Alexander or Asander came from Lycia with an equal number of foot soldiers and five hundred cavalry. Asclepidorus, the governor of Syria, sent him just as many. Antipater sent him eight thousand Greek mercenaries and six hundred cavalry under the command of Asander and Nearchus. (There are problems with the Greek text in this passage from Arrian. Editor.) {*Curtius, l. 7. c. 10. s. 11,12. 2:217} {*Arrian, Anabasis, l. 4. c. 7. s. 2. 1:359}

2013. With this larger army, he proceeded to set in order the disturbances caused by that general revolt from him. Many, especially the Sogdians, had gone into walled towns and cities and set up their own defences, and would not submit to the governor whom he had set over them. Therefore, he left Polyperchon, Attalus, Gorgias and Meleager in Bactria to keep order, so that they would not revolt again, nor draw others into rebellion. After a four day march, Alexander came to the bank of the Oxus River. Because this river had a muddy bottom and was very filthy and unhealthy to drink, the soldiers started digging wells for water, but found none. At last they saw a spring rising up in the king's pavilion, which they claimed had suddenly arisen there, because they had not seen it earlier. Plutarch reported that Proxenus, a Macedonian and master of the king's wardrobe, dug a place near the Oxus River to pitch the king's pavilion.

He found a spring of a fatty and oleaginous or oily liquor that Alexander, in his letters to Antipater, stated was one of the greatest miracles that the gods had shown him. *[L337]* Arrian went further, saying that he found two fountains, one of water and the other of oil, which had recently sprung up near the place where Alexander's tent stood. When Ptolemy brought Alexander word, he at once (as he was directed by his soothsayers) offered sacrifices to his gods. Aristander told him that the fountain of oil foreshadowed the great labour and travail that he was to endure, but in the end he would be crowned with victory. {*Arrian, Anabasis, l. 4. c. 15,16. 1:391} {*Curtius, l. 7. c. 10. s. 13,14. 2:217} {*Plutarch, Alexander, l. 1. c. 57. s. 4,5. 7:387,389}

2014. When he had crossed the Ochus and Oxus Rivers, he came to the Marginia or Magriana River, around which he built six towns, two on the south side and four on the east side. They were built close together, so each town could help the other if needed. {*Curtius, l. 7. c. 10. s. 15,16. 2:217} Strabo stated that he built eight towns in Bactria and Sogdiana. {*Strabo, l. 11. c. 11. s. 4. 5:283} Justin mentioned twelve, and noted that he put those in his army into them who were rebellious and seditious, and hence got rid of them. {Justin, Trogus, l. 12. c. 5.}

## 3676a AM, 4385 JP, 329 BC

2015. Ariamazes of Sogdiana, with a thirty-thousand-man army, climbed to the top of a high rock, called Oxus by Strabo, and made provision for a two-year siege. This rock was about nineteen thousand feet high and nineteen miles in circumference. Alexander made generous promises to three hundred gallant young lads who volunteered to climb the rock. Using cramp-irons where needed, they were able to climb the rock slowly. Thirty-two died in the attempt, because they either slipped, or the rock broke from under them. The Sogdians were astonished as if by a miracle, to see that men had managed to get up there. Since they thought there were more coming who were better armed than they were, they surrendered. Ariamazes, their leader, was quite afraid. He and the chief men of the country came down to the king in his camp. Alexander had them well whipped and later crucified at the base of the hill. He distributed the rest as slaves among the new cities which he had previously built with the money he had taken from the country. Artabazus was left to keep the Sogdians and the neighbouring countries under subjection. {*Curtius, l. 7. c. 10,11. 2:215-227} {*Arrian, Anabasis, l. 4. c. 17. 1:395-399} {Polyaenus, Strategmata, l. 4. n. 29. in Alexander} {*Strabo, l. 11. c. 11. s. 4. 5:283,285}

2016. After Alexander had taken the Oxus Rock in Sogdiana, he could see the enemies in various parts. He divided his whole army into five brigades, of which Hephaestion commanded the first, Ptolemy Lagus, the second, Perdiccas, the third, Coenus and Artabazus the fourth and Alexander the fifth. The next day Alexander marched toward Maracanda, while the rest ranged here and there as they wished. (Curtius' account differed from Arrian's account. {*Curtius, l. 8. c. 1. s. 1-4. 2:233} Editor.) If they found that any had fled to citadels or other places of strength, they attacked and captured them, but if they surrendered, they were treated mercifully. When all these five brigades had taken in most of Sogdiana, they met at Maracanda. Alexander sent Hephaestion to establish colonies in various parts. *[E241]* He sent Coenus and Artabazus to Scythia, because he had heard that Spitamenes had gone there. He took the rest of the army into Sogdiana, and easily regained any places that the rebels had fled to. Those who surrendered without fighting, he relocated in those towns which he had to subdue by force, ordering that their lands be divided among these new inhabitants. {*Arrian, Anabasis, l. 4. c. 16. s. 1-4. 1:391}

2017. While these things were happening, Spitamenes, the rebels of Bactria, and a company of Sogdians who had fled from there into Scythia, along with some six or eight hundred cavalry of the Massagetae who had come to him, went to a certain citadel which had been built and was being manned against the Bactrians. *[L338]* Making a surprise attack on the garrison, they killed everyone inside and put the commander in prison. Proud of their deeds, they went soon after to take the city of Zariaspa, which they failed to do, but they carried away much spoil from the country around it. {*Arrian, Anabasis, l. 4. c. 16. s. 4,5. 1:393}

2018. To suppress this rabble, Attinas, the governor of the country, led out some three hundred cavalry, unaware that the enemy had planned to ambush him. As well as these troops, he took some of Alexander's cavalry that had been left sick at Zariaspa and were now recovered, and who were under the command of Pithon, the son of Sosicles, and Aristonicus, a harpist. These two gathered some eighty mercenary cavalry troops from those who were left in the garrison at Zariaspa, along with some of Alexander's Companion Cavalry, since they planned to go in a company with Attinas into the country of the Massagetae. Suddenly, however, Spitamenes and his troops rose from the thickets and woods and attacked them, killing seven of Alexander's Companion Cavalry and sixty of the mercenaries. Aristonicus, who was also killed in that battle, conducted himself more like a soldier than a musician. Spitamenes killed Attinas and his entire company in this encounter, and Pithon was wounded and captured. News of this ambush quickly reached Craterus and he attacked the Massagetae with all his cavalry troops, and routed them.

He pursued them until they reached the wilderness of the country in which they were fighting. After a fierce battle, the Macedonians routed them. When the Massagetae saw that a hundred and fifty of their cavalry had been killed, they fled and easily saved themselves in that wilderness. The Dahae lost at least a thousand men. This put an end to the rebellion in those parts. {*Curtius, l. 8. c. 1. s. 3-10. 2:233,235} {*Arrian, Anabasis, l. 4. c. 16,17. 1:393,395}

2019. After Alexander had subdued all Sogdiana for the second time, he returned to Maracanda. An envoy from the king of the Scythians, who lived on the European side north of the Bosphorus, came to Alexander with a present and offered him the king's daughter in marriage. Alexander mentioned this in his letter to Antipater, as I said previously. If Alexander declined the proposal, the envoy's alternate plan was to have Alexander allow his Macedonian nobles to marry into the most important families of the Scythians. The envoy offered that, if Alexander wished, the king would come in person to receive his commands from Alexander.

2020. At the same time, Phrataphernes, or Pharoemenus, who governed the Chorasmians, a people bordering on the countries of the Massagetae and Dahae, sent his messengers to declare his readiness to receive Alexander's commands. Having graciously heard both the envoy's and the governor's errands, Alexander stayed there, awaiting the return of Hephaestion and Craterus. {*Curtius, l. 8. c. 1. s. 7-10. 2:235}

2021. As soon as Hephaestion and Craterus arrived, Alexander and his army attacked the country of Bazaria, or Basists, according to Diodorus. {*Diod. Sic., l. 17. c. 0. 8:111} Here there was virgin forest in which, as it happened, a large lion attacked Alexander. Lysimachus, who later became the king of Thrace, offered to interpose himself with his hunting spear, but the king would not allow it and asked him to stand aside. When the lion came on, Alexander held his ground and killed him with only one blow. After his army had killed some four thousand wild beasts in that forest, he and the entire army had a large feast in the woods. {*Curtius, l. 8. c. 1. s. 11-19. 2:235,237}

2022. When Alexander returned to Maracanda, Artabazus resigned as governor of Bactria because of his age. Alexander gave this command to an old soldier of his father's called Clitus, the son of Dropidas of Macedonia and the brother of Hellanica, or Lanica, Alexander's nurse. She was a woman whom Alexander had always respected and loved as his own mother. [L339] In a dream, Alexander happened to see Clitus sitting among Parmenion's sons in black robes, and all were

dead. {*Plutarch, Alexander, l. 1. c. 50. s. 3. 7:369} {*Arrian, Anabasis, l. 4. c. 17. s. 3. 1:395} {*Curtius, l. 8. c. 1. s. 11-21. 2:235,237}

2023. The third day following this dream was a holiday to Bacchus, when Alexander usually offered the yearly sacrifice to him. Someone at that time had brought him fruit from Greece, and because he marvelled at their fresh colour and good appearance, he sent for Clitus, to show him the apples and to give him some. Clitus left the sacrifice which he was about to make. As he was rushing to the king, he was followed by three sheep with flour and salt on their heads, as they had already been prepared to be offered. [E242] When the king heard of this, he asked his two principal soothsayers, Aristander and Cleomenes, the Spartan, what this meant. They told him that it was an abominable sign, whereupon Alexander remembered his dream. He ordered them to go quickly and offer a sacrifice for him. Clitus came to the feast which the king put on after he had sacrificed to Castor and Pollux. When Alexander was quite drunk, he began to brag greatly about his own acts and devalue the deeds of his father Philip. Most of those present at the feast applauded him, whereas Clitus, on the other hand, upheld the deeds of Philip and spoke honourably of his achievements, decrying the present times and sometimes saying some disgraceful things about Alexander. Alexander rose in a rage intending to kill Clitus, who (according to Aristobulus) escaped out the back door and leaving the trenches, got into the citadel to Ptolemy, the son of Lagus. Both of them returned to the feast and Clitus sat in the same seat again. Ptolemy, observing Alexander calling out for Clitus, said that Clitus was here, and what did he want to do with him? Whereupon Alexander ran Clitus through with his spear and killed him. {*Plutarch, Alexander, l. 1. c. 50,51. 7:369-373} {*Arrian, Anabasis, l. 4. c. 8. s. 1-9. 1:363-367} {*Curtius, l. 8. c. 1. s. 21-52. 2:239-247}

2024. Later, when Alexander considered the vileness of this act, he grew as angry with himself as he had formerly been with Clitus. Resolving to make amends, he secluded himself for three whole days and did not have food or drink, or pay any heed to what might become of him.

2025. When he had by now continued fasting into the fourth day, the captains of his bodyguard broke in on him. After a long time, they were able to persuade him to eat again. His soothsayers told him that this had happened because he did not sacrifice to Bacchus, so he soon went and sacrificed to him, glad to hear that this event came from the anger of the gods rather than from the malice of his heart. Aristander reminded him of his dream and of the sheep, telling Alexander that what had been done, had been done by fate and could not have been avoided. Callisthenes, the philosopher and relative of Aristotle, agreed with Aristander in this. Anaxarchus of Abdera, a subtle teacher, went much further in this shameless flattery. He quoted an old proverb that Justice and Law always sit at Zeus' elbow, from which he concluded that whatever kings did, was to be considered right and just. To lift Alexander's spirits, all the Macedonians unanimously declared that Clitus had been fairly treated and justly put to death. They would have forbidden his burial, if the king himself had not ordered it. {*Plutarch, Alexander, l. 1. c. 52. 7:375,377} {*Arrian, Anabasis, l. 4. c. 9. s. 1-9. 1:367-371} {*Curtius, l. 8. c. 2. s. 1-12. 2:247-249}

2026. When he had spent ten days in settling his mind over this, he sent Hephaestion with part of his army into Bactria, where he was to prepare Alexander's winter quarters. To fill the position which had been intended for Clitus, Alexander made Amyntas, the son of Nicolaus, governor of Bactria, and left Coenus there with his own and Meleager's brigade. He also left four hundred of the Companion Cavalry and mounted spearmen, together with the Bactrians and Sogdians who were under the command of Amyntas, ordering everyone to be subject to Coenus and to spend that winter in Sogdiana. [L340] He wanted to keep order in that country and hoped to capture Spitamenes, if should he happen to come into those parts for his winter provisions. {*Arrian, Anabasis, l. 4. c. 17. s. 3. 1:395,397} {*Curtius, l. 8. c. 2. s. 13. 2:251}

2027. Alexander journeyed to Xenippa, which bordered on Scythia, and to where the Bactrians who had revolted from him had retired to. As soon as it became known that Alexander was coming, the natives drove out the Bactrians, who therefore gathered themselves into a body of twenty-five hundred cavalry and attacked Amyntas, a commander of Alexander's. There was a long and fierce skirmish between them, until the Bactrians fled after losing seven hundred men, of whom three hundred were taken prisoner. They had killed eighty Macedonians and wounded three hundred and fifty more. However, when they yielded to Alexander again, they were pardoned. {*Curtius, l. 8. c. 2. s. 14-18. 2:251,253}

2028. After this, Alexander went with his army to a place called Nautaca, whose governor, Sisimithres, had two sons born from his own mother, since it was lawful, with those people, for children to have intercourse with their parents. Sisimithres captured the gates or passes which open through the mountains into his own country. With a strong force he had fortified the pass well, which was also naturally well defended by an extremely swift and violent river in front of it and a large rock at its back. {*Curtius, l. 8. c. 2. s. 19-22. 2:253} Arrian said that this rock was at Pareitacene and was twelve thousand feet high

and about seven and a half miles in circumference. He named the the rock, Chorienes, after the one who kept it. However, Strabo, together with Curtius and Plutarch, called it Sisimithres' Rock and located it in Bactria. These men said it was almost two miles high and ten miles in circumference. It had a large plain of good land on the top and was well able to support five hundred men. They also said that on this rock (not on that other rock in Sogdiana) Oxyartes had his daughter Roxane with him, whom Alexander later married. {*Arrian, Anabasis, l. 4. c. 21. s. 1,2. 1:407} {*Plutarch, Alexander, l. 1. c. 58. 7:389,391} {*Strabo, l. 11. c. 9. s. 4. 5:285} [E243]

2029. Although Alexander saw that this pass was naturally well fortified and strongly defended, his battering rams quickly made a breach in the fortifications. He entered the outer fortifications and approached the rock, at the base of which there was a vast bog caused by the rain which fell from the rock and was trapped there. He did not know how to fill it in quickly. Meanwhile, he had the beech trees which grew there in abundance, cut down and made into long stakes which his army drove down into the bog. All day long he stayed to encourage the work. Perdiccas, Leonnatus, and Ptolemy, the son of Lagus, the captains of his personal guard, divided the rest of the army into three parts and continued the work at night. They could not advance more than thirty feet by day and less by night, even though all the army incessantly worked at it, because the rock was so craggy and the work was very difficult. {*Arrian, Anabasis, l. 4. c. 21. s. 3-6. 1:409}

2030. At that time Oxyartes, a great man of that country, a prince and the father of Roxane, was with Alexander. When Alexander asked him about the spirit and courage of Sisimithres, he answered that he was the most cowardly man that ever lived. Alexander replied: {*Plutarch, Alexander, l. 1. c. 58. s. 2. 7:389,391}

> "Surely you have said enough to teach me that it is possible to take this rock, since you tell me that the one defending it is so weak."

2031. Alexander sent Oxyartes to Sisimithres to demand that he surrender at once with his mother, children and all that were dear to him. [L341] Sisimithres surrendered immediately. Alexander, with five hundred of his silver targeteers, went up into the rock to view its situation and strength. When he had offered sacrifices to Minerva Victoria, he left Sisimithres as the governor of that citadel and the surrounding country, as he had been before. Alexander gave him hope of a larger dominion, should he perform well and faithfully in this command. At Sisimithres' request, Alexander took along his two sons to serve Alexander in the wars. {*Arrian, Anabasis, l. 4. c. 21. s. 6-9. 1:409,411} {*Curtius, l. 8. c. 2. s. 23-33. 2:255,257}

2032. He left his Macedonian squadron behind to capture the other places which had revolted from him, while he advanced with his cavalry up a steep and rocky way. He had not gone far, but all his cavalry horses were exhausted by the journey and could not follow him any farther. Each day, his company became fewer and fewer, and even all the young gallants, who never wished to be far from him, stayed behind, except for Philip, the brother of Lysimachus. He was wearing his full body armour and other arms, an incredible thing to do. Even though he was on foot, he kept up with Alexander for over sixty miles, despite the fact that Alexander rode and often changed his horse. When they came into a wood where the enemy attacked the king, Philip stepped between them and rescued Alexander from that danger. The barbarians were routed and the woods cleared of them, but when they were gone, Philip fainted from over-exertion and collapsed between Alexander's own hands and died. No sooner had this happened, then Alexander was told that Erigyius, one of his greatest captains, had died. He had both their funerals observed with all the honour that could be given them. {*Curtius, l. 8. c. 2. s. 33-40. 2:257,259}

2033. Spitamenes came to Gabae with a rabble of three thousand wild Scythians who followed him. Gabae was a strong Sogdian town that was located near the border with the Massagetae. He easily persuaded them to join him in plundering the country of the Sogdians. When Coenus heard of his coming, he attacked him with his army and killed eight hundred of them, while he lost only twenty-five of his cavalry and twelve of his foot soldiers. The Sogdians who escaped, along with some Bactrians, deserted Spitamenes on the way and surrendered to Coenus. {*Arrian, Anabasis, l. 4. c. 17. s. 4-6. 1:397}

2034. When the Massagetean Scythians saw how badly things had gone, they plundered all the wagons of the Bactrians and Sogdians and accompanied Spitamenes into the deserts of Scythia. When they heard that Alexander was coming after them and planned to follow them into those very deserts, they decapitated Spitamenes and sent his head to Alexander, hoping by this to make him stop chasing them. {*Arrian, Anabasis, l. 4. c. 17. s. 7. 1:397,399} However, Curtius wrote that when Alexander was not far off, Spitamenes' own wife met him with her husband's head in her hand. When he saw it, he abhorred the sight and had her put out of the camp, so that the vileness of such an act would not corrupt his Greeks with these barbarian ways. {*Curtius, l. 8. c. 3. s. 1-15. 2:259-263}

2035. When the Dahae heard what had become of Spitamenes, they tied up Dataphernes, his partner in that revolt, and delivered him to Alexander, while they themselves submitted to him. Coenus and Craterus, with Phrataphernes, the governor of the Parthians, and Stasanor, the governor of the Arians, returned to Alexander at Nautaca when they had completed their missions. {*Arrian, Anabasis, l. 4. c. 18. s. 1,2. 1:399} {*Curtius, l. 8. c. 3. s. 16. 2:263} [E244]

## 3676b AM, 4386 JP, 328 BC

2036. Alexander rested his army at Nautaca because it was now the middle of winter. Arrian expressed this as *in the depth of winter*. [L342] He thought about how to avenge the subjects' wrongs, which they had suffered through the pride and avarice of their rulers. As a result of that, he ordered that Phrataphernes be governor of Hyrcania and the countries of the Mardi and Tapuri. He wanted him to bring him Phradates, who was the governor there. Alexander had often sent for him, based on complaints he received, but he would not come, so Phrataphernes was to bring him to Alexander under a sufficiently strong guard. {*Curtius, l. 8. c. 3. s. 16,17. 2:263}

2037. He removed Arsames from the government of the Drangians and put Stasanor in his place. Arsaces (according to Curtius) or Atropates (according to Arrian) was made governor over Media to replace Oxydates, because the king thought that Oxydates was not loyal to him. The province of Babylon, after the death of Mazaeus, was committed to Deditamenes, or to Stamines (according to Arrian). Sopolis, Epocillus and Menidas were sent into Macedonia to bring him a fresh supply of soldiers from there. {*Arrian, Anabasis, l. 4. c. 18. s. 2,3. 1:399} {*Curtius, l. 8. c. 3. s. 17. 2:263,265}

2038. Three months after this, he started to march into a country called Gazaca. The third day into the journey, there was a dreadful storm and it was extremely cold. His whole army was in danger of perishing in this storm. Curtius described this event in great detail, telling of the fierceness of the storm and the king's fortitude in enduring it. He showed his wisdom and humanity in keeping the army together and comforting the poor weather-beaten soldiers in that distress. However, about two thousand perished of the poorer sort of soldiers, the support personnel and hangers-on. Curtius further added what was also recorded by Valerius Maximus and Frontinus. While Alexander was warming himself at a fire, he saw an elderly common soldier of the Macedonians, half frozen with cold and benumbed in his wits no less than in his limbs. Alexander took him and sat him down in his own chair, telling him that it would be for his good, whereas in Persia, anyone who sat in the king's chair was executed. {*Valerius Maximus, l. 5. c. 1. ext. 1. 1:453,455} {*Frontinus, Stratagems, l. 4. c. 6. s. 3. 1:307} {*Curtius, l. 8. c. 4. s. 1-17. 2:265-269}

2039. The next day, he called his friends and captains together. He made a proclamation that whatever any man had lost in that storm, he would personally make good to him again. This he did to the smallest detail. For example, Sisimithres had brought along with him many beasts of burden and draught animals, two thousand camels, and whole flocks and herds, and these were now distributed among the army, compensating them for their losses and saving them from the famine. Thereupon, the king declared publicly how much he was indebted to Sisimithres for that courtesy. He ordered every soldier to take enough food for eight days, and then they went to capture the Sacae who had revolted from him. When they had gathered all the spoil of that country, Alexander gave thirty thousand head of cattle to Sisimithres from the spoil. {*Curtius, l. 8. c. 4. s. 18-20. 2:269}

2040. Alexander married Roxane, the daughter of Oxyartes. Strabo stated that this took place at the rock or citadel of Sisimithres when it was first surrendered to him. Many of his Macedonians followed Alexander's example and married foreign wives from the more illustrious families of the foreign countries. {*Diod. Sic., l. 17. c. 0. 8:111} {*Curtius, l. 8. c. 4. s. 21-30. 2:271,273} {*Strabo, l. 11. c. 11. s. 4. 5:283,285}

## 3676c AM, 4386 JP, 328 BC

2041. Now he focused completely on the war against India. So that everything would be safe and quiet behind him, he conscripted thirty thousand men from every province, whom he planned to take with him into India. They would serve both as soldiers and as pledges of the fidelity of those whom he left behind. He moved into Bactria and sent Craterus with six hundred of the Companion Cavalry, his own foot soldiers with the regiments under Polyperchon, Attalus and Alcetas, to pursue Austanes and Catanes, who were the only ones remaining of the rebels of Pareitacene. A great battle was fought between them, and Catanes was killed, while Austanes was taken prisoner and brought alive to Alexander. The Greeks lost a hundred and fifty cavalry and about fifteen hundred foot soldiers. After this, Craterus went into Bactria and Polyperchon subdued the country of Bubacene for Alexander. {*Arrian, Anabasis, l. 4. c. 22. s. 1-3. 1:413} {*Curtius, l. 8. c. 5. s. 1-3. 1:273}

2042. Alexander assumed divinity and affirmed that he was the son of Zeus. [L343] He was no longer to be addressed in the Macedonian custom, but would be adored with prostration after the fashion of the Persian kings. There were plenty of court flatterers to feed this desire of Alexander's. These are the curse of all kings, and by their tongues more kings have perished than by the sword of their enemies. [E245] The main ones around Alexander were Agis of Argos, the worst flatterer that ever was, after Choerilus, also Cleo of Sicily and

Anaxarchus, an orator. Callisthenes, an honest philosopher and a scholar of Aristotle, opposed Alexander in this and paid for it with his life. {*Plutarch, Alexander, l. 1. c. 52. s. 1,2. 7:375} {*Curtius, l. 8. c. 5. s. 5-8. 2:275}

2043. Hermolaus was a gallant youth and one of the king's company of pages, and had been instructed in the basics of philosophy by Callisthenes. He was once hunting with Alexander and killed a boar which Alexander had aimed at. Upon this, Alexander commanded him to be taken away and whipped, which the youth took badly and so started a conspiracy to kill Alexander. First, he conspired with Sostratus, the son of Amyntas, a youth like himself, of the same rank. Then he conspired with Antipater, the son of Asclepiodorus, governor of Syria and others of the same company of pages. When the conspiracy was exposed by Epimenes, one of the conspirators, they were all executed and Epimenes was rewarded. In his letters to Craterus, Alcetas and Attalus, written at that time, Alexander stated that they had confessed that the conspiracy was among themselves only, without the encouragement of anyone else. However, in another letter written later to Antipater, he accused Callisthenes also of the crime, saying:

> "The youths indeed were stoned to death by the Macedonians, but the sophist I will punish, together with those who sent him to me and those who harbour in their cities men who conspire against my life."

2044. In these words, at least, he directly revealed a hostility to Aristotle, in whose house Callisthenes, on account of his relationship, had been reared, being a son of Hero, who was a niece of Aristotle. When he had seized Callisthenes, he kept him in irons for seven months to have him judged and condemned in a court of justice when Aristotle would be present. Chares, the Mitylenian, stated that when Alexander was in the country of the Mallians and Oxydracans in India, he was recovering from a wound received in a battle. Seventeen months had passed since the conspiracy, and Callisthenes died from obesity and the disease of lice. However, Aristobulus and Ptolemy stated that the pages confessed on the rack that Callisthenes had put them up to it. Again, Ptolemy said that Callisthenes was first racked and later hanged. However, Aristobulus said that he was carried about in chains with the army, and so died. So we see that these great authors and those who were present in the army and waited on Alexander at the very time when these things happened, do not agree with each other. However, there is no doubt about the time when this happened. {*Arrian, Anabasis, l. 4. c. 13,14. 1:381-387} {*Curtius, l. 8. c. 6-8. 2:283-303} {*Plutarch, Alexander, l. 1. c. 52,53. 7:375-385}

2045. Alexander left Amyntas in Bactria with thirty-five hundred cavalry and ten thousand foot soldiers. Toward the end of spring (according to Arrian), Alexander moved with his army from there toward India to make the ocean, and the utmost border of the east, the boundary of his empire. He prepared his army in their attire for this great plan of his. He had all their shields covered with silver plate and their horse bridles made of beaten gold, and he enriched their body armour with gold or silver. *[L344]* He had a hundred and twenty thousand men with him on the Indian expedition. {*Arrian, Anabasis, l. 4. c. 22. s. 2. 1:413*} {*Curtius, l. 8. c. 5. s. 3,4. 2:273,275*}

2046. Alexander crossed the Caucasus Mountains in ten days and came to his city of Alexandria, which he had built in Parapamisadae. He replaced its governor because of his bad behaviour, and relocated more people into his new city from the neighbouring countries. Any Macedonians who were unserviceable for the war were allowed to live there. He made Nicanor the governor of the city and made Tyriespis the commander of the whole region of Parapamisadae and of all that territory as far as the Cophen River. {*Arrian, Anabasis, l. 4. c. 22. s. 4,5. 1:413,415*} {*Curtius, l. 8. c. 9. s. 3,4. 2:303,305*}

2047. From there he went to the city of Nicaea and sacrificed to Athena. He then marched to the Cophen River. He sent a herald who ordered Taxiles and the rest of the governors of the countries lying between the Cophen and the Indus Rivers to come to him. {*Arrian, Anabasis, l. 4. c. 22. s. 6. 1:415*}

## 3676d AM, 4386 JP, 328 BC

2048. Taxiles and other petty kings under his government came and met with Alexander. They received his orders and told him that he was now the third son of Zeus that had come into those parts. They had only heard of Father Liber (Dionysus or Bacchus) and Hercules, but now they were happy to see him personally present among them, which was the reason why they brought him rich presents and promised to send him twenty-five elephants. Alexander entertained them very graciously and asked them to go with him to be his guides through the passes of that country. {*Arrian, Anabasis, l. 4. c. 22. s. 6. 1:415*} {*Curtius, l. 8. c. 10. s. 1,2. 2:313*}

2049. When he saw that no one else came, he divided his army and sent Hephaestion and Perdiccas toward the Indus River, into the country called Peucelaotis. The armies led by Gorgias, Clitus and Meleager, and half the company of the Companion Cavalry, as well as all the mercenary cavalry, were told to capture any town they found, by whatever means. *[E246]* When they came to the bank of the Indus River, they were to start building boats for crossing over it into further countries. Taxiles was sent with them, as well as other commanders from those parts. {*Arrian, Anabasis, l. 4. c. 22. s. 7,8. 1:415*} {*Curtius, l. 8. c. 10. s. 2. 2:313*}

2050. Astis, the governor of the country of Peucelaotis, revolted and died in the city to which he withdrew. Hephaestion came and besieged it and one month later took and sacked it. The governor was killed and Sangaeus was made governor in his place. Previously, Sangaeus had defected from Astis and had fled to Taxiles, which fact helped Alexander trust him all the more. {*Arrian, Anabasis, l. 4. c. 22. s. 8. 1:415,417*}

2051. Alexander, with his troop of silver targeteers, the Companion Cavalry, Hephaestion and the troop of those who were called *asthetairoi*, his archers, Agrians and javelin men, all marched into the country of the Aspians, Thyraeans and Arasocans. They journeyed to the Choes River, a route which was mostly mountainous and rocky. When they had crossed that river, Alexander commanded Craterus to come after him with the foot soldiers, while he took the whole body of his cavalry and eight hundred Macedonians and targeteers on horseback and marched off quickly. He had heard that the people of that country had fled, some to the mountains and others to fortified cities, because they all planned to fight him. {*Arrian, Anabasis, l. 4. c. 23. s. 1,2. 1:417*}

2052. Alexander easily routed those who came to oppose him, driving them back into the town by the way they had come out. He easily defeated the townsmen, who all stood in battle array before their walls, and forced them to take refuge within their walls again. Craterus arrived with the foot soldiers, and so, in order to strike the greatest terror into the minds of a country of a people who did not know what kind of men the Macedonians were, he ordered the army not to spare a single life. *[L345]* They set fire to the outer works which they had made. As Alexander rode about the walls, he was wounded by an arrow in the shoulder through his armour, but it was a minor wound. Ptolemy and Leonnatus were both wounded at this same time. Then Alexander saw a place where the wall was the weakest, and pitched his camp against it. The next day, early in the morning, he easily took the outer wall, which was not very strong. The inhabitants made some resistance at the inner wall, but when the Macedonians had scaled the walls and the townsmen felt the arrows showering down on them, the soldiers within broke out of the gates and ran in all directions to the nearby mountains. Many of them escaped and saved themselves there, but were followed and overtaken by the Macedonians, who killed most of them. The townsmen who remained behind were all killed, and the city was levelled to the ground. {*Arrian, Anabasis, l. 4. c. 23. s. 1-5. 1:417,419*} {*Curtius, l. 8. c. 10. s. 4-6. 2:315*}

*2053.* After Alexander had subdued another weak country, he advanced to the city of Nysa, which was located at the foot of a hill called Meros and was said to have been built in ancient times by Bacchus. At the entreaty of Acuphis, the chief man of the city, who had been sent to him along with thirty other leaders, he spared the inhabitants of Nysa. They were only commanded to give him three hundred horses, after which he restored their freedom and allowed them to live after their own laws, having made Acuphis governor of the city and the province of Nysa. Alexander took Acuphis' son and grandchild as hostages. He sacrificed there to Bacchus under this god's other name of Dionysus. He made merry and feasted his friends and all his Macedonians, who wore garlands of ivy on their heads and sang praises to Dionysus with all his titles and names. {*Arrian, Anabasis, l. 5. c. 1,2. 2:3-7} {*Curtius, l. 8. c. 10. s. 7-18. 2:315-319}

> Calling him Bacchus, Bromius and Lyaeus,
> Born of the fire, twice born and not like others,
> But the only one that ever had two mothers.

*2054.* Ovid spoke of him in a similar fashion, although on a different occasion. {*Ovid, Metamorphoses, l. 4. (11-14) 3:179} See also Philostratus. {*Philostratus, Apollonius, l. 2. c. 2. 1:121}

*2055.* From there, he went to a country called Daedala, the inhabitants of which had all fled to the woods and mountains, so he went through Acadira, which had also been deserted by its inhabitants. {*Curtius, l. 8. c. 10. s. 19. 2:319}

*2056.* When the city of Ardaca surrendered, he left Craterus there with other commanders of the foot soldiers. They were to capture places that would not voluntarily surrender and to order matters there as they saw fit. {*Arrian, Anabasis, l. 4. c. 23. s. 5. 1:419} {*Curtius, l. 8. c. 10. s. 5. 2:315}

*2057.* Alexander took his silver targeteers, his squadron of Agrians and Coenus' and Attalus' brigades, the body of his own cavalry and at most four companies of the Companion Cavalry and one half of his mounted archers, and went to the Euaspla River, where the governor of the Aspasians was. After a lengthy journey, he and his army came the next day to a city called Arigaeum. *[E247]* As soon as the inhabitants heard that he was coming, they set their city on fire and fled to the mountains. The Macedonians chased them and killed a vast number of them, while Ptolemy killed their captain in hand-to-hand combat and brought his armour back with him. {*Arrian, Anabasis, l. 4. c. 24. s. 1-5. 1:419,421}

*2058.* Alexander came to the city of Arigaeum with his foot soldiers, who were riding on horseback. They got off their horses and attacked the natives. After a long skirmish, the natives were forced to flee for refuge to the mountains. Craterus joined Alexander with the main

body of the army when he had fully completed the task he had been sent to do. *[L346]* Alexander commanded him to rebuild Arigaeum, which the inhabitants had burnt down, and to repopulate it with people from the surrounding area who wanted to live there, and with those Macedonians who were no longer fit for military service. Alexander went to the place to where he had been told that the natives had fled. When he came to the foot of a mountain, he pitched his camp there. {*Arrian, Anabasis, l. 4. c. 24. s. 6,7. 1:421,423}

*2059.* Meanwhile Ptolemy, who had been sent to forage, went farther on with a small troop to discover what lay ahead. He sent word back to Alexander that there seemed to be more fires in the enemy's camp than there were in Alexander's camp, whereupon Alexander left part of his army in the camp and went with the remainder to view those fires for himself. When he had examined the situation well, he divided the company he had brought with him into three parts. One part he gave to Leonnatus, one of the captains of his bodyguard, with the brigade of Attalus and Balacrus. Ordering Ptolemy to take charge of the second one, he gave him a third part of his own silver targeteers, the brigade of Philip and Philotas with two thousand archers, all the Agrians and half of the whole cavalry. The third part he himself led to a spot where he noticed the largest number of the enemy to be. The enemy, having confidence in their numbers and supposing the Macedonians to be few in number, left the mountain and came down into the plain. A bloody battle ensued, which the Macedonians won. Ptolemy, who led one of the three brigades of Macedonians, reported that almost forty thousand prisoners were taken in that battle, and more than two hundred and thirty thousand oxen. Alexander selected the best of the oxen and sent them back to Macedonia, to breed them there for use in the tillage of the ground. {*Arrian, Anabasis, l. 4. c. 24,25. 1:423,425}

## 3677a AM, 4386 JP, 328 BC

*2060.* Alexander went from there into the country of the Assacenians, who were said to have mustered two thousand cavalry, thirty thousand foot soldiers and thirty elephants to fight against him. It was also said that Assacanus (which seems to have been the common name by which all their kings went) had recently died, and that his mother Cleophis commanded that entire force. {*Arrian, Anabasis, l. 4. c. 25. s. 5. 1:425,427} {*Curtius, l. 8. c. 10. s. 22,23. 2:319,321}

*2061.* When Craterus had finished rebuilding the city of Arigaeum, he brought all his heavily armed foot soldiers to Alexander with battering rams and other equipment for a siege, should that be required. Alexander advanced toward the Assacenians with the Companion Cavalry, his mounted javelin soldiers, with Coenus' and Polyperchon's companies, with the archers and a thousand Agrians. He marched through the country of the Guraeans and had great trouble crossing the Guraeus River. When the natives heard of his coming, they did not dare to fight him in one body, but divided their army and dispersed themselves. Each went into their cities, where they planned to make a stand. {*Arrian, Anabasis, l. 4. c. 25. s. 6,7. 1:425,427}

2062. First, Alexander went with his army to Massaga, the largest city of the Assacenian country. It was enclosed with a wall of about four-and-a-half miles in circumference and was defended by thirty thousand men, which included seven thousand mercenaries from the inner parts of India. These came out to fight at the foot of a hill about a mile from the Guraeus River and were forced to flee back into their city when they lost about two hundred men. Shortly after this, Alexander drew up his main battle line of the Macedonians before the gates of the city. He was wounded in the calf of his leg by an arrow shot from the wall. In pain, he cried out even though they told him he was Zeus' son, yet, when wounded, he felt pain like any other man. {*Arrian, Anabasis, l. 4. c. 26. s. 1-4. 1:427,429} {*Curtius, l. 8. c. 10. s. 23-30. 2:323} When he saw the blood running down his body, he cited a saying from Homer that this was indeed blood, but not: {Homer, Iliad, l. 5. c. 340.} {*Plutarch, Alexander, l. 1. c. 28. 7:307}

"Such blood as from the blessed gods does flow."
[L347]

2063. After nine days of the siege, the courage of the defenders began to weaken. They saw Alexander's works, the incessant labour of the besiegers, what vast valleys they filled up, what towers they built and how they made them run on wheels, so that when their captain was shot through with an arrow from a battering ram, their courage failed completely. They abandoned the idea of holding out any longer and retired into their citadel, from where they sent messengers to beg for a pardon and to surrender. [E248] Cleophis the queen, with a large number of noble ladies all pouring wine into golden basins, came out to Alexander. The queen laid her young son at his feet and not only obtained his pardon but was restored to her father's kingdom. This was due more to her good looks than to Alexander's generosity, since men commonly said that all this was merely the price of a night's lodging and that she got her kingdom back again by using her allurements to achieve what she could not achieve by force. After that, she was known among the Indians as the king's concubine. In that siege Alexander lost no more than twenty-five men. {*Arrian, Anabasis, l. 4. c. 26,27. 1:429,431} {*Curtius, l. 8. c. 10. s. 30-35. 2:323,325}

2064. The Indian mercenaries from the central regions of India, who had taken part in the siege, caused Alexander more trouble than all the rest. According to the terms of the truce, they were allowed to depart with their arms, but they camped about ten miles from there. When Alexander was told about this, he was very angry with them and attacked them. He said that he had indeed allowed them to depart with their arms, but not so that they could ever use them against the Macedonians. The Indians, unaware of the great danger they were in, locked themselves closely together to form a ring and placed their wives and children in the midst of the circle. When the enemy attacked, they withstood them very courageously. Whenever a man was killed, one of the women took up his arms and took his place in the ring. At last they were overcome by the numbers of the enemy and they all died in that spot. Alexander gave the women who were left and the rest of the rabble to his cavalry. This massacre of the Indians blemished Alexander's glory and proved a lasting blemish on all his former noble actions. {*Arrian, Anabasis, l. 4. c. 27. s. 3,4. 1:431,433} {*Diod. Sic., l. 17. c. 84. 8:361-365}

2065. Alexander sent Coenus to a strong and rich city called Bazira, supposing that the inhabitants would readily submit when they heard what had happened at Massaga, but they refused to surrender. He sent Alcetas, Attalus and Demetrius, the commander of the cavalry, to besiege the city of Ora until he arrived. The inhabitants of Ora staged an attack on Alcetas, but the Macedonians easily pushed them, repelled them, and quickly besieged them on that side. Alexander heard that Abissares was secretly intending to move more of the natives in to defend it, so he sent word to Coenus to build a strong citadel at Bazira and leave a large enough garrison in it to prevent the natives from tilling their ground, whereupon he was to return to Alexander with the rest of the army. {*Arrian, Anabasis, l. 4. c. 27. s. 5-8. 1:433}

2066. The inhabitants of Bazira saw that Coenus had gone with most of his army and had left the rest in the citadel. They ventured out into the open field, ready for battle. When five hundred had been killed and seventy more taken prisoner, the rest retreated into the city. They were more securely besieged than before and did not venture out of the gates. {*Arrian, Anabasis, l. 4. c. 27. s. 8,9. 1:433,435}

2067. Alexander took the city of Ora at the first assault and took all the elephants he could find there. When the inhabitants of Bazira heard this, they were afraid of also being taken, so they all fled out of the gates in the dead of the night, and climbed up onto a rock called Aornus. The rest of the cities in the area did likewise, every man taking his weapons there with him. Alexander put garrisons in Ora and Massaga, strengthened the walls of Bazira, and captured the towns which the inhabitants had abandoned. {*Arrian, Anabasis, l. 4. c. 27. s. 9. 1:435} {*Arrian, Anabasis, l. 4. c. 28. s. 1-5. 1:435} [E249] [L348]

## 3677b AM, 4387 JP, 327 BC

*2068.* When Taxiles died, his son Omphis, or Mophis, who had persuaded his father to submit to Alexander, sent to him inquiring as to his wishes, and wanting to know whether he would be the next king, or whether he was to live as a private citizen until Alexander should come. Although word was returned to him that he should reign, he nonetheless held off for the present. Meanwhile, when Hephaestion and Perdiccas, who had been sent to construct a bridge over the Indus River, came his way, Omphis received them with all honours and freely supplied them with provisions, but did not go out to meet them as they approached, so that he might not seem to be depending for favours on anyone other than Alexander himself. {*Curtius, l. 8. c. 12. s. 4-6. 2:333} {*Diod. Sic., l. 17. c. 86. s. 4. 8:371} {*Arrian, Anabasis, l. 4. c. 30. s. 9. 1:447}

*2069.* When Alexander came to Embolima, or Ecbolima, a city not far from the rock of Aornus, he left Craterus there with some of the army. Alexander ordered him to make provisions of grain and other necessities for a long period, in case the siege of Aornus were to last a long time and Alexander was unable to capture it on the first attack. Alexander took his Agrians and archers, Coenus' brigade, those who were the nimblest and best armed of the Macedonian squadron, two hundred of the Companion Cavalry and a hundred mounted archers, and marched to the rock. {*Arrian, Anabasis, l. 4. c. 28. s. 7,8. 1:439}

*2070.* According to legend, when Hercules was in those parts, he attempted to take that stronghold, but failed, because he was thwarted by an earthquake, and so Alexander was all the more eager to take the rock and outdo Hercules. According to Diodorus, the rock was about thirteen miles in circumference and ten thousand feet high. {*Diod. Sic., l. 17. c. 85. s. 3. 8:367} Arrian said that the rock was twenty-five miles in circumference and about seven thousand feet high at its lowest point. At the foot of it, facing south, the Indus River ran, not far from its source. {*Arrian, Anabasis, l. 4. c. 28. s. 3. 1:437} {*Strabo, l. 15. c. 1. s. 8. 7:11} The rest was covered with vast bogs and inaccessible cliffs. In one of these cliffs, in a cave containing three beds hewn out of the rock, lived a poor old man with his two sons, and Alexander promised him eighty talents if he would show him a way up the rock. The man told him there was but one way and showed him where it was. When Alexander found no other way except that one, he manned that spot so strongly that those on the rock could not possibly receive any relief

from others. Then he put his army to work, casting up a mound of earth and rubbish so high, that at least he could now come to fight with them at closer range. He launched an assault on them which lasted nine whole days and nights, without cessation. Alexander lost many of his men in the fighting and in climbing the rocks. Among those who died were Chares and a person called Alexander. Although he had no hope of taking it, he nevertheless pretended to carry on the siege, all the while leaving open one passage which led to the rock, making it possible for them to flee. Those on the rock, overcome by his persistency and resolution, took advantage of a dark night and all fled the rock. {*Arrian, Anabasis, l. 4. c. 29-30. 1:439-445} {*Curtius, l. 8. c. 11. s. 2-25. 2:325-331}

*2071.* When Alexander saw no activities on the rock the next day, he sent Balacrus to see what had happened. He brought word that the enemy had all gone, so Alexander took some of the captains of his bodyguard and seven hundred of his silver targeteers and led the way up onto the rock. The rest of the Macedonians followed, helping each other climb up as best they could. Alexander then ordered them to pursue the enemy, which they did, killing many of them in the chase, since many fell over the rocks and were dashed to pieces. When Alexander had conquered the place, he offered many sacrifices, and built altars to Minerva Victoria on the rock. He left a garrison there and made Sisicottus, or Sisicostus, the governor of that place and of the country around it. Sisicottus had previously come from India to Bessus in Bactria. When Alexander had subdued Bactria, Sisicottus with his men had joined with Alexander and served him faithfully ever since. {*Arrian, Anabasis, l. 4. c. 30. s. 3,4. 1:445} {*Curtius, l. 8. c. 11. s. 22-25. 2:331} [L349]

*2072.* Alexander left Aornus and went into the country of the Assacenians. He was told that the brother of Assacanus, the last king, with a number of elephants and a number of the local inhabitants as well as some from bordering countries, had fled to the mountains in those parts. When Alexander came to the city of Dyrta, he found no one, either there, or in the surrounding country side. {*Arrian, Anabasis, l. 4. c. 30. s. 5. 1:445}

*2073.* The next day he sent out Nearchus with a thousand silver targeteers, some lightly armed troops and the Agrians, all of whom had been assigned to him, while Antiochus was given three thousand silver targeteers. These were sent out as scouts, to see if they could find any of the natives whom they could ask, among other things, about the elephants. {*Arrian, Anabasis, l. 4. c. 30. s. 6. 1:447}

*2074.* Alexander marched on toward the bank of the Indus River, sending an army ahead of him to clear his way. Otherwise, it would have been impossible for him to have gone through. When he found that Erices controlled the narrow passes, he left Coenus to bring on the main body of the army later, at a less strenuous pace, while he advanced with his slingers and archers, cleared the forest and made a safe way for the army that would follow later. Diodorus called this Indian leader Aphrices, and said that he had twenty thousand men and fifteen elephants with him. Whether out of hatred for this Erices, or Aphrices, or to ingratiate themselves with Alexander, the Indians killed him and brought his head and arms to Alexander, who pardoned them, but did not honour them, lest others should follow their example. {*Arrian, Anabasis, l. 4. c. 30. s. 7. 1:447} {*Curtius, l. 8. c. 12. s. 1-3. 2:331,333} {*Diod. Sic., l. 17. c. 88. s. 2,3. 8:369,371}

2075. In sixteen days he reached the Indus River and captured the city of Peucelaotis, not far from there, which surrendered to him. He left Philippus there with a garrison of Macedonians to keep order. He also subdued a number of smaller towns lying along the river, while Cophaeus and Assagetes, the governors of that country, attended him as he went from place to place. From some natives whom he had taken prisoner, Alexander learned that the men of that country had all gone to Barisades (or perhaps Abisares) and that the elephants had been left grazing on the banks of the Indus River, so he ordered them to show him the way to the place where the elephants were. They caught all but two, which fell over the rocks and died. The rest were taken and trained for service, and were added to his army. He found good trees for timber there, which he ordered to be cut down for making boats. When the boats were launched, he sailed in them to the bridge of boats which Hephaestion and Perdiccas had built for him. Realising that they would have more rivers to cross, they constructed their boats in such a way that they could easily be disassembled and carried on carts. *[E250]* Besides these boats, they built two others of thirty oars apiece, and many more smaller craft. {*Arrian, Anabasis, l. 4. c. 28. s. 6. 1:437} {*Arrian, Anabasis, l. 4. c. 30. s. 7-9. 1:447} {*Diod. Sic., l. 17. c. 86. s. 3. 8:371} {*Curtius, l. 8. c. 12. s. 4. 2:333}

2076. Alexander stayed there thirty days to rest his army. In that time he offered magnificent sacrifices to his gods and entertained his cavalry and foot soldiers by the riverside. He made one of his friends, Nicanor, governor of all that region on the west side of the Indus River. After this he crossed the river with his army on the bridge that had been constructed at Peucelaotis. {*Strabo, l. 15. c. 1. s. 28. 7:47} Again he sacrificed to his gods, as was the custom of the Greeks. It was the beginning of spring when Alexander came into the region which lay between the Indus and the Hydaspes Rivers. This was recorded by Aristobulus, who was with him at that time, and by

Strabo. {*Strabo, l. 15. c. 1. s. 17. 7:25} {*Diod. Sic., l. 17. c. 86. s. 3. 8:371} {*Arrian, Anabasis, l. 5. c. 3. s. 5,6. 2:11} [L350]

### 3677c AM, 4387 JP, 327 BC

2077. When Alexander was about eight miles away, Omphis, the son of Taxiles, met him with an army and elephants spaced at equal distances among the companies. At first Alexander did not know whether he came as a friend or a foe and prepared for a battle. When Omphis saw Alexander's actions, he halted his army and rode quickly by himself to Alexander and surrendered both himself and his kingdom (which was not much larger than Egypt) into his hands. When Alexander asked him whether he had mostly labourers or soldiers in his kingdom, he replied that he was at war with two kings and hence must, of necessity, keep more soldiers than labourers in his kingdom. His enemies were Abisares and Porus, who reigned on the other side of the Hydaspes River. With Alexander's permission, Omphis assumed the title and office of a king and after the custom of his country, was known by the name of Taxiles, for that name went with whoever ruled the kingdom. {*Curtius, l. 8. c. 12. s. 4-14. 2:333,335} {*Diod. Sic., l. 17. c. 86. s. 5,6. 8:371}

2078. The city of Taxila, after which the king was named, was larger than all the other cities lying between the Indus and Hydaspes Rivers. All its inhabitants joined with Omphis in entertaining Alexander very joyfully. On the fourth day after his arrival there, Omphis told Alexander with how much grain he had furnished Hephaestion for his army. He presented both Alexander and all his friends with crowns of pure gold, in addition to giving them a large number of cattle, three thousand oxen and almost ten thousand sheep. Arrian added that he sent Alexander seven hundred Indian cavalry and two hundred talents of silver, but Curtius mentioned only eighty talents of coined silver money. {*Curtius, l. 8. c. 12. s. 11-16. 2:335,337} {*Arrian, Anabasis, l. 5. c. 3. s. 5,6. 2:11}

2079. Alexander was very impressed with this treatment, and sent him back the two hundred talents of silver, with an additional thousand talents of his own. He also sent many dinner plates of gold and silver, with a great deal of Persian attire and thirty of his own horses with their equipment. Alexander's liberality, while pleasing Omphis and obliging him to greater loyalty, deeply offended his friends. One of these, Meleager, was eating at supper when, quite drunk, he told Alexander that he was very glad to see that he had found a man here in India whom he thought worthy of a thousand talents. Alexander, remembering his regret at killing Clitus, did not seek revenge, but only said: {*Curtius, l. 8. c. 12. s. 17,18. 2:337}

"Jealous men are nothing less than their own worst tormentors."

*2080.* The next day, Abisares, king of the Indian mountaineers, sent his own brother to him with other envoys, to present him with money and elephants, submitting himself and all that he had to Alexander's disposition and pleasure. When Alexander had made a firm league with him, he sent the men back to Abisares. Other envoys with presents also came to him from Doxareus, who was a governor in those regions. {*Curtius, l. 8. c. 13. s. 1. 2:337} {*Arrian, Anabasis, l. 5. c. 8. s. 3. 2:27}

*2081.* In the country of Taxila, Alexander again offered his usual sacrifices and staged shows and contests with his cavalry and foot soldiers. He left Philip, the son of Machatas, with a garrison in the city, as the governor in those parts, while any in Alexander's army that were unfit for military service were left behind in the country of Taxila. He then went on toward the Hydaspes River. {*Arrian, Anabasis, l. 5. c. 8. s. 3. 2:27}

*2082.* Alexander thought his fame would cause Porus readily to submit to him. He sent a message to him through Cleochares, asking for tribute from him and ordering him to meet Alexander at the border of his kingdom. [L351] Porus answered that he would comply with the second of these two commands and would meet him at the border of his kingdom with his army. {*Curtius, l. 8. c. 13. s. 2. 2:337}

*2083.* There was another Porus, however, a king of a neighbouring country in India, who was the nephew of the first Porus. Because he hated his uncle, he sent envoys to Alexander, offering himself and all his kingdom at his service. {*Arrian, Anabasis, l. 5. c. 21. s. 3. 2:67} [E251]

*2084.* Alexander sent Coenus back to the Indus River with orders to dismantle the boats and bring them overland to him in carts. The smaller boats came apart in two sections, while the larger ones were in three sections, and they were all transported to the Hydaspes River. {*Arrian, Anabasis, l. 5. c. 8. s. 4,5. 2:27,29}

*2085.* When they had been reassembled and launched, he used them to return to Taxila with his army. Receiving five thousand Indians whom Taxiles and others had brought to him, he returned to the banks of the Hydaspes River. On the way, Barzaentes, who had been governor of the Drangians at various times as well as the instigator of the revolt of the Arachosians, was taken prisoner and brought to Alexander along with thirty of his elephants. This was a large prize, for the Indians trusted more in their beasts than in their men. Damaraxus, a petty king in those parts and a confederate of Barzaentes, was also taken, bound and brought to him. Both were committed to prison and the elephants enlisted into Alexander's service and sent to Taxiles, or

Omphis. Alexander advanced and came to the Hydaspes River, where he executed Barzaentes for his former treason against his master Darius. {*Curtius, l. 8. c. 13. s. 3-5. 2:337,339} {*Arrian, Anabasis, l. 5. c. 8. s. 5. 2:29} {*Arrian, Anabasis, l. 3. c. 25. s. 8. 1:315}

*2086.* Porus was camped on the other side of the Hydaspes River and planned to stop Alexander. He was a man of large stature and a brilliant mind. He was said to be seven and a half feet tall, although Plutarch said that he was six foot three inches tall. His body was so large that his coat of armour was twice as large as any other man's, and he rode on an elephant taller than all the rest, on which he sat like an ordinary man does on horseback. Curtius said that he placed eighty-five large elephants in the forefront of his battle formation. Diodorus said he had thirty, while Arrian claimed that he had almost two hundred elephants, three hundred chariots and thirty thousand foot soldiers in his army. Diodorus stated that he had more than a thousand chariots and fifty thousand foot soldiers, although Plutarch said he had twenty thousand soldiers, as well as two thousand cavalry, while Diodorus made that three thousand, and Arrian four thousand, cavalry. The Hydaspes River ran between the two armies. Porus with his elephants always appeared at the head of his army, ready to hinder the crossing of Alexander. Alexander commanded that noises be made daily in his army such that the men would become accustomed to similar noises from the barbarians and so find them less terrifying. After a while, on a dark stormy night, he crossed the river with certain of his foot soldiers and most of the choice cavalry. In the midst of a violent thunderstorm, he crossed some distance up the river onto a small island, and although he saw some of his men hit by lightning and others seriously hurt, he was determined to cross over and hide on the other side. The river was swollen with the rain and undermined its banks in many places due to the swiftness of the current. Alexander reached the bank, where he could hardly stand because of the instability of the ground and the undermining of the banks. When the Macedonians saw this, they also forced themselves onto the land, since they were up to their very arm pits in water. {*Curtius, l. 8. c. 13. s. 5-27. 2:339-345} {*Arrian, Anabasis, l. 5. c. 9-12. 2:29-37} {*Arrian, Anabasis, l. 5. c. 19. s. 1. 2:59} {*Diod. Sic., l. 17. c. 87. s. 2. 8:373} {*Plutarch, Alexander, l. 1. c. 60. 7:395,397} {*Plutarch, Alexander, l. 1. c. 62. s. 1. 7:401} [L352]

*2087.* Having crossed the river, he went ahead of his foot soldiers for two and a half miles with his cavalry and engaged a thousand enemy cavalry and sixty chariots. He captured all the chariots and killed four hundred of the cavalry. When Porus learned that Alexander had crossed the river, he attacked him with all the troops he had, except for the ones he left to take care of the Macedonian army that had not yet crossed over. Alexander feared the number of the enemy and their elephants. He attacked one wing of the enemy with some of his men and commanded the rest to attack the other wing. When the natives were hard pressed at any point, they always retired in a group to the elephants as a place of refuge. The battle grew confused on every side and Alexander could scarcely route them until about two o'clock in the afternoon. Alexander described the battle in detail in his own letters. {*Plutarch, Alexander, l. 1. c. 60. s. 5,6. 7:397}

2088. Aristobulus said that in the former of these two battles Alexander killed four hundred cavalry and captured sixty chariots, and that Porus' son was killed in the battle. However, Ptolemy, claimed Porus' son attacked with two thousand cavalry and a hundred and twenty chariots. {*Arrian, Anabasis, l. 5. c. 13. s. 3-6. 2:43,45} {*Plutarch, Alexander, l. 1. c. 60. s. 5,6. 7:397} As far as the latter engagement fought with Porus was concerned, Alexander did not go into any detail. Arrian gave more information concerning the number killed, saying that the Indians lost almost twenty thousand men and three thousand cavalry. All their chariots were scattered and two of Porus' sons were killed. Spitaces, who commanded all that region of India, and all the commanders of the elephants and the cavalry and the generals of Porus' army to a man, were killed in the battle. All the elephants not killed in the battle were captured. Of Alexander's foot soldiers, he lost eighty of the six thousand engaged in the first battle, as well as ten of the mounted archers who had led the first assault, twenty of the Companion Cavalry and two hundred other troopers. {*Arrian, Anabasis, l. 5. c. 18. s. 2,3. 2:55} [E252] Diodorus stated that about twelve thousand died, including the two sons of Porus, all the chief commanders of his army and all the bravest of his captains that he had. Nine thousand prisoners were taken and eighty elephants captured. Two hundred and eighty of the Macedonian cavalry died, along with more than seven hundred foot soldiers. {*Diod. Sic., l. 17. c. 89. s. 1-3. 8:377,379}

2089. When Porus was taken, Alexander asked him how he wanted to be treated. He replied:

"Like a king."

2090. Alexander asked him again whether he wanted anything else, and his answer was that:

"Like a king."

2091. He said that that encompassed it all. When Alexander saw his noble and royal disposition, he treated him accordingly and included him in the number of his friends. He restored him to his kingdom again, which

contained about three hundred cities and reached from the Hydaspes River to the bank of the Acesines River. {*Arrian, Anabasis, l. 5. c. 19. s. 1-3."2:59}" {*Strabo, l. 15. c. 1. s. 29. 7:49}

2092. Arrian stated that these things took place after the summer solstice, during the rainy season in India, when the Hydaspes River would swell greatly, whereas a man could wade across it in the middle of winter. {*Arrian, Anabasis, l. 5. c. 9. s. 4. 2:31} Jacobus Capellus compared another place in Arrian, {*Arrian, Anabasis, l. 7. c. 21. s. 2-5. 2:277,279} where he wrote the same thing about the Euphrates River, saying:

"It is fordable in the winter. When the spring approaches, and much more when the sun returns from its summer solstice, it grows deep and overflows its banks."

2093. The Greeks called the four seasons of the years by the name of tropics. [L353] They might just as easily have divided the year into two parts, summer and winter. Summer would start at the vernal equinox and winter from the autumnal equinox. However, Arrian was speaking after the manner of the east when he said:

"As the spring approached and after this toward the summer season, the rain began to fall there and the waters to rise."

2094. Aristobulus was an eye-witness of those Indian regions and was present with Alexander at the Hydaspes River, and he said that at the beginning of the spring, the rains began to fall and then grew stronger from day to day. Strabo said the same. {*Strabo, l. 15. c. 1. s. 18. 7:27}

2095. This battle was fought between the vernal equinox and the summer solstice, a fact plainly stated by Arrian when he said: {*Arrian, Anabasis, l. 5. c. 18. s. 3. 2:59}

"This was the end of the battle fought by Alexander against Porus and his Indians on the other side of the Hydaspes River in the year when Hegemon was archon of Athens in the month of Mounychion."

2096. In that year, that month corresponded almost entirely to our month of May, according to the Julian Calendar. The summer solstice did not happen until Alexander came to the Acesines River, as I shall show later from Nearchus.

2097. Alexander was glad of this victory, which opened the way to the farthest borders of the east, and so he had all those of his men who had died in the battle honourably buried. He sacrificed to the Sun, as the giver of this victory and held games and contests, both on foot and horseback, at the Hydaspes River near the place where he had crossed. Since there were all possible kinds of provisions available there, he stayed for thirty days to rest his wearied companies. To cheer up his soldiers for the remainder of this war, he called them together and gave them a pep talk, commending their prowess and valour. He told them that all the forces of India had been quashed by their single day's work, and everything else was a rich spoil for them to take. He gave crowns to the chief commanders of his army to wear, and each of them received a thousand pieces of gold, while he rewarded the rest according to each man's place and rank in the army. Philostratus described the monument he erected there. {*Arrian, Anabasis, l. 5. c. 20. s. 1. 2:61} {*Curtius, l. 9. c. 1. s. 1-8. 2:365,367} {*Diod. Sic., l. 17. c. 89. s. 3-6. 8:379} {*Philostratus, Apollonius, l. 2. c. 43. 1:229}

2098. Alexander planned to go and see the Indian Ocean as soon as he set foot in India, so he had his shipwrights build boats for that purpose. In the Emodian hills nearby, there was an abundance of tall fir trees with a quantity of cedar and pine trees, as well as other timber fit for ship building, but when they went to cut them down, they found very many large snakes, as long as twenty-four feet. In those wooded mountains they also found rhinoceroses, which were quite rare in other countries, as well as a large number of long-tailed apes, some quite large. When the Macedonians saw a number of the apes ranging on the side of a hill in an array somewhat like soldiers, they at first thought they had seen an enemy. Crying out *Arm, Arm*, they arranged themselves to attack them. It was not until Taxiles, who was with Alexander at the time, told them what they were, that the fray ended. {*Strabo, l. 15. c. 1. s. 29. 7:49,51} {*Diod. Sic., l. 17. c. 89,90. 8:379,381}

2099. Alexander built two cities there, one on each side of the Hydaspes River. The one, on this side of the river, was at the place where he had crossed and the other, on the other side, was the place where he had fought this battle. *[E253] [L354]* This city he named after the victory over the Indians, giving it the Greek name of Nicaea. The other one he called Bucephalon or Bucephalis, after his horse, Bucephalas. He had died there, not of any wound received in the battle (as some have it {*Aulus Gellius, Attic Nights, l. 5. c. 2. s. 5. 1:385}), but worn out from travel and old age. He was thirty years old, according to Arrian and Onesicritus, as cited by Plutarch. {*Arrian, Anabasis, l. 5. c. 19. s. 5,6. 2:61} {*Plutarch, Alexander, l. 1. c. 61. 7:399} The king gave his horse a solemn funeral and built a monument, around which he then built a city. {*Pliny, l. 8. c. 64. 3:109} Near these cities, on the Hydaspes River which ran between the two kingdoms of Porus and Taxiles, he built his navy for the ocean. Both of these men helped him greatly in building this fleet. {*Strabo, l. 15. c. 1. s. 32. 7:55} {*Curtius, l. 9. c. 3. s. 22. 2:393}

2100. Alexander left Craterus there with a part of his army to finish building these two cities and their walls, while he went further into India against those who bordered on Porus' kingdom. Aristobulus called the kingdom Glauganica, but Ptolemy called it Glausa. He took one half of the Companion Cavalry along with him, the best men from every squadron, with all his mounted archers, his squadron of Agrians and the other archers. Thirty-seven cities surrendered to him on this expedition, the smallest of which had at least five thousand inhabitants, and many had more than ten thousand. In addition, many towns and villages surrendered to him, some of which were as large as the cities. All this territory he added to Porus' kingdom and having made both Taxiles and Porus his good friends, Alexander also sent Taxiles back to his own kingdom again. {*Arrian, Anabasis, l. 5. c. 20. s. 1-4. 2:63}

2101. At the same time, envoys came to Alexander from Abisares, who promised to be at his command, provided that Alexander would not require him to give up his kingdom, for if he were enslaved to another man, he could neither reign nor live without a kingdom. Thereupon, Alexander sent back word to him that since he would not come to Alexander, Alexander and his army would take the pains to go to him, and that this would cost Abisares dearly. Envoys also came to him from those Indians who lived as free states, and from another Porus, who was also a king of the Indians. {*Arrian, Anabasis, l. 5. c. 20. s. 5,6. 2:63,65} {*Curtius, l. 9. c. 1. s. 7,8. 2:367}

2102. Phrataphernes, the governor of Parthia and Hyrcania, came to Alexander at this time with the Thracians that Alexander had left with him. Messengers came to him from Sisicottus, governor of the Assacenians, to tell him that the Indians had murdered his vice-governor and had revolted from him. Alexander sent Philippus and Tyriespis against them with an army, ordering them to suppress the rebellion of the Assacenians and to keep that province in order. About this time, Cleophis, the queen of the Assacenians, bore Alexander a son, whom she named after Alexander who later became king of that country. {Justin, Trogus, l. 12. c. 7.} {*Arrian, Anabasis, l. 5. c. 20. s. 7. 2:65} {*Curtius, l. 8. c. 3. s. 17. 2:263}

2103. The other Porus, who was the nephew of the one whom Alexander had overcome, feared his uncle Porus more than he feared Alexander. He left his kingdom and fled into the country of the Gandara, taking with him as many as would follow him and were fit to bear arms. {*Arrian, Anabasis, l. 5. c. 21. s. 3. 2:67} {*Diod. Sic., l. 17. c. 91. s. 1. 8:383}

### 3677d AM, 4387 JP, 327 BC

2104. With his army, Alexander crossed over the violent Acesines River, which was almost two miles wide. Those who crossed on bags made from skins did much better than those in the boats. Those who crossed in boats were dashed repeatedly on the rocks in the way, and some boats sank, drowning some of the army. Alexander left Coenus with his brigade on the near side, to provide for the crossing of those supplying grain and other things for the army, and to protect them from any attackers. {*Arrian, Anabasis, l. 5. c. 20,21. 2:65,67} [L355]

2105. Nearchus, who was in the army at this time and was cited by Strabo, said that Alexander first camped by the riverside, but was later forced to move his camp to higher ground to escape the flood waters. This happened at about the summer solstice. {*Strabo, l. 15. c. 1. s. 18. 7:27} Arrian said that Alexander's army escaped from the Acesines River when it flooded all the country at midsummer. {*Arrian, Indica, l. 1. c. 6. s. 4-6. 2:323}

2106. There were vast forests and shady trees of an enormous size and incredible height. Some were over a hundred feet high and so thick that five men could barely get their arms around them. They cast a shadow of three hundred feet from their limbs. For the most part, they were like large beams bowing downward to the ground, from where they then grew up again. The new plant was not nourished by the same bough, but rooted itself where the bough touched the ground. For more information about the banyan tree see Pliny. Strabo stated from Aristobulus that fifty men could sit at dinner under one of these trees. {*Pliny, l. 12. c. 11. 4:17} {*Strabo, l. 15. c. 1. s. 21. 7:33,35} {*Curtius, l. 9. c. 1. s. 9,10. 2:367} {*Arrian, Indica, l. 1. c. 11. s. 7. 2:337}

2107. There were also a large number of deadly snakes, which were small and very colourful, but their bite was so deadly that it caused sudden death to any one who was bitten. To avoid this danger, the Macedonians hung their beds from the limbs of the trees and slept above ground, which meant that they got little sleep. [E254] At length, they learned a remedy for the snake bite from the native people, who showed them a root to eat, if any man happened to be bitten. {*Curtius, l. 9. c. 1. s. 12-14. 2:369} {*Diod. Sic., l. 17. c. 90. s. 6,7. 8:383}

2108. Alexander sent Porus back to his own kingdom with orders to return with an army of the choicest and ablest Indians that he could find, along with any elephants he had. After the army had crossed the deserts, they came to the Indian river of Hyarotis or Hydraotes, which was as wide as the Acesines River, but not as violent. Everywhere he went, he left garrisons in convenient places, so that Craterus and Coenus might safely come to him with the grain which they were to gather from all the places they went. He committed part of his army to Hephaestion, giving him charge of two squadrons of foot soldiers, both his own and Demetrius' squadrons of cavalry and half his archers. He sent them into the country of that Porus who had fled away, and ordered him to transfer the kingdom to his friend King Porus. If he were to find any other Indian country, bordering on the Hydraotes River, which organized themselves as free states, he should add them all to Porus' kingdom. Alexander crossed the Hydraotes River with less trouble than he had had crossing the Acesines River. {*Arrian, Anabasis, l. 5. c. 21. s. 4-6. 2:69} {*Curtius, l. 9. c. 1. s. 13,14. 2:369}

2109. Next to this river, there was a grove of shady trees not usually seen in other parts, and wild peacocks that flew up and down in the trees. Alexander advanced and took over other countries, some of which surrendered, while others were taken by force, because in some cases he was forced to chase and overtake them, and make them yield to him. {*Curtius, l. 9. c. 1. s. 14. 2:369}

2110. Meanwhile, Alexander was told that there were other Indian states, and a people called the Cathaeans, who intended to fight him if he came into their countries. They joined with other free states of India to form an alliance with them in this action, including other countries in those regions belonging to the Oxydracans and the Mallians. A short time earlier, Abisares and Porus, with their joint armies, along with many other confederate Indians, had gone to subdue them, but had been unable to do so. [L356] These Indians awaited Alexander's arrival in Sangala, a large city of the Cathaeans, which was surrounded with a wall and a bog. These Cathaeans are called the Calthaei by Polyaenus. Diodorus called them the Cathari and stated that it was law, agreed to by all these countries, that when a husband died, his wife would be cremated with his body at the time of the husband's death. Strabo also noted this about the Cathaeans. {*Strabo, l. 15. c. 1. s. 63. 7:109} {*Arrian, Anabasis, l. 5. c. 22. s. 1,2. 2:69,71} {Polyaenus, Strategmata, l. 4.} {*Diod. Sic., l. 17. c. 91. s. 3,4. 8:385} {*Strabo, l. 15. c. 1. s. 30. 7:53}

2111. Alexander entered these parts and on the second day came to a city called Pimprama. That particular country of the Indians was named after the Adraistae or, according to Diodorus, the Andrestae. These came to him and surrendered conditionally. {*Arrian, Anabasis, l. 5. c. 22. s. 3. 2:71} {*Diod. Sic., l. 17. c. 91. s. 2. 8:383}

2112. Alexander rested his soldiers there the next day, and on the third day he marched to Sangala, where the Cathaeans and their allies awaited his arrival. They stood in battle array on the rise of a hill before the city. Instead of a trench between them and the enemy, they had positioned three rows of chariots locked closely together. Alexander quickly scattered the chariots and they all fled back into the city, where Alexander immediately besieged them. He cast up a double trench around the city, except where the bog hindered his men. He positioned Ptolemy there with three thousand of the silver targeteers, all the squadron of Agrians and one company of archers to guard that quarter. All the chariots which he had taken were placed along an escape route from the city, to prevent them from escaping. When attempting to escape in the fourth watch of the night, the inhabitants fell over those chariots and were beaten back by Ptolemy, who killed five hundred of them and forced them to retreat behind their gates again. Meanwhile, Porus came to him with the rest of his elephants and five thousand Indians. Alexander's battering rams were assembled and approached the wall. The Macedonians did not have to batter the inner wall, but only undermined the outer earthwork, made of brick. They raised their ladders against the inner wall, thus taking the city by assault. Seventeen thousand inhabitants were killed, seventy thousand taken prisoner, three hundred chariots were captured and five hundred horses were taken. Alexander lost less than a hundred men in this siege, but twelve hundred more were hurt, including Lysimachus, one of the captains of his bodyguard. {*Arrian, Anabasis, l. 5. c. 22-24. 2:71-79} {*Curtius, l. 9. c. 1. s. 15-18. 2:369}

2113. After Alexander had buried his dead according to the Macedonian customs, he sent Perdiccas with sufficient forces to ravage and plunder all the country round about. He sent Eumenes, the secretary (that is the Eumenes who was secretary to King Philip at various times, {*Plutarch, Eumenes, l. 1. c. 1. 8:79} {Emilius Probus, Eumenes}) with three hundred cavalry to two cities which had allied themselves with the men of Sangala. He was to offer them a pardon and receive them in mercy, but when the townsmen heard what had been done at Sangala, they all fled the town before he came. All those unable to escape through infirmity were killed by Eumenes, to a total of five hundred. Alexander gave up the idea of overtaking the rest and returning to Sangala, he utterly destroyed it. {*Arrian, Anabasis, l. 5. c. 24. s. 6,7. 2:79} {*Curtius, l. 9. c. 1. s. 19. 2:371} [E255]

2114. Alexander went to besiege another strong town into which a large number of people from weaker places had fled. When they asked his mercy and opened their gates to him, he pardoned them, took hostages and marched away to the next town, which was a very large and populous one. There he had the hostages presented before the walls. Since those in the town knew them as their neighbours, they desired to speak with them. By telling them what a merciful man Alexander was, and how dreadful he was to his enemies, the hostages easily persuaded them to yield to him. [L357] Prior to this, people had wrongly thought Alexander was more like a bandit,

but now that they knew that he behaved more like a conqueror, the rest of the cities surrendered without a fight. {Polyaenus, Strategmata, l. 4. n. 30. in Alexander} {*Curtius, l. 9. c. 1. s. 20-23. 2:371}

2115. From here he went into the kingdom of Sopithes, who, at more than six feet, was taller than all the men of those parts. Coming from his chief city with his two mature sons, he gave Alexander his golden rod, all set with beryl stones, and surrendered himself, his children and all his kingdom to Alexander, who gave him his kingdom back again. A few days later, he feasted Alexander and all his army in a very sumptuous manner and personally gave Alexander many large and costly gifts. He also gave him a hundred and fifty Indian dogs which were, so the saying went, a cross-breed between dogs and tigers, and very strong and courageous. To prove this, he had four of them attack a very large lion. {*Strabo, l. 15. c. 1. s. 31. 7:55} {*Aelian, History of Animals, l. 8. c. 1. 2:175,177} {*Diod. Sic., l. 17. c. 91,92. 8:383-387} {*Curtius, l. 9. c. 1. s. 24-34. 2:373-375}

2116. Meanwhile, Hephaestion returned to him with the troops he had taken with him, having subdued all the countries of the Indians far and wide, wherever he had gone. Alexander spared no honour for him, and praised him before the army. {*Curtius, l. 9. c. 1. s. 35. 2:375} {*Diod. Sic., l. 17. c. 93. s. 1. 8:387}

2117. Alexander left Sopithes in his kingdom, as he had found him. He advanced still farther to the next country, where Phegeus was king. All the inhabitants welcomed the Macedonians, and Phegeus went out personally to meet Alexander with gifts and presents, submitting himself wholly to his will. Alexander re-established him in his kingdom and was royally entertained with all his army, staying there two whole days. {*Curtius, l. 9. c. 1. s. 36. 2:375}

2118. On the third day, he departed from there and came to the Hyphasis or Hypanis River, which was almost a mile wide and thirty-six feet deep, and had a very strong current. It was very rocky under the water and quite difficult to cross. Phegeus told him what he wanted to know about the other side of the river. There was a vast desert of eleven or twelve-days' journey to cross, bounded by the Ganges River, which was the largest in all of India. Beyond the river lived various peoples, known as the Gangaridae or Gongaridae, and the Prasians, or Praendians, or Praesiaeans, or Pharrasians, or Tabraesians, for they were known by all these different names. Their king was called Aggrammes. (Diodorus called him Xandrames.) He had an army of twenty thousand cavalry, two hundred thousand foot soldiers, two thousand chariots and three or (as Diodorus said) four thousand elephants, all trained and equipped for war. {*Curtius, l. 9. c. 2. s. 1-4. 2:375,377} {*Diod. Sic., l. 17. c. 93. s. 2-1. 8:387}

2119. These things seemed incredible to Alexander, but when he questioned Porus further, Porus told him that the might and power of that king and his kingdom were very great indeed and no less than what he had been told. However, the current king was of ignoble birth and no better than a poor barber's son, and was hated and scorned by his subjects. Androcottus, who was then but a youth, had not only seen Alexander but according to Julian, had also been ordered to be executed for a certain saucy prank he had played on Alexander, and would have died had he not fled. Justin stated that he later said that Alexander had conquered almost all of India, and that the part he missed was of little note, since the king there was too wicked, base, hated and deeply scorned by his people. {Justin, Trogus, l. 15. c. 4.} {*Plutarch, Alexander, l. 1. c. 62. s. 4. 7:403} {*Curtius, l. 9. c. 2. s. 5-9. 2:377}

2120. Alexander began to reflect that his soldiers were all tired out and spent with the length of the war. [L358] Every man began to look for an end to these dangers and for the reward and fruit of all his labours. They had now been in a continual perilous war for eight full years for it had been that long since he had become king. It so happened that, for seventy consecutive days, it poured with rain, accompanied by violent thunderstorms, according to Diodorus, who said that to pacify the soldiers, Alexander gave them permission to plunder an extremely rich and bountiful country of the enemies and to take all for themselves. While they were busy doing this, he called together their wives and children and there made a law that the wives would receive their monthly allowance in grain, while their children would receive a service bonus in proportion to the military records of their fathers. {*Curtius, l. 9. c. 2. s. 8-11. 2:377,379} {*Diod. Sic., l. 17. c. 94. 8:391,393} [E256]

2121. When the soldiers returned home laden with wealth and riches, Alexander called them all together. He made a prepared speech to request them to accompany him cheerfully to the conquest of the Gangaridae. Coenus, the son of Polemocrates, replied in the name of the whole army and concluded by saying that they all desired an end to the war. The Macedonians would not listen to Alexander's request. Ptolemy reported that he went on and offered sacrifices for the crossing of the river. When the entrails portended only direful things if he proceeded, he called together his friends and those who were the oldest, and most intimate with him. He first told them and afterward declared to all the army that since all things seemed to be against his going any farther, he was now content and resolved to return home. {*Diod. Sic., l. 17. c. 94. s. 5. 8:393} {*Arrian, Anabasis, l. 5. c. 25-28. 2:81-95}

2122. Pliny wrote that, notwithstanding all this, he crossed the Hypanis River and erected altars on the other side. This is very improbable, since a similar action occurred in the same place, the mention of which in Alexander's own letters confirms as much. I think that those words refer not to his crossing over the Hypanis or Hyphasis River, but to that which had occurred previously, concerning the order and location of his camps and journeys from place to place. These were described and recorded by Diognetus and Baeton, his two principal harbingers and camp masters. For who can believe that Alexander, without his army and without any reason for going any farther, would offer to cross on his own such a dangerous river as this was? Had he done so, the enemy on the other side would have attacked him and hindered his work. Strabo noted that he went no farther eastward because he had been forbidden to cross the Hypanis or Hyphasis River. Plutarch also stated that during his time, the kings of the Praesiaeans, or Prasians, crossed the river to his side and worshipped on those altars which Alexander had set up then, offering sacrifices on them after the custom of the Greeks. {*Pliny, l. 6. c. 21. (63) 2:385} {*Strabo, l. 15. c. 1. s. 32. 7:57} {*Plutarch, Alexander, l. 1. c. 62. s. 4. 7:401}

2123. Alexander divided his army into various companies. He had twelve altars built, all of square stone, on the west side of the Hyphasis River and not on the east side. Each altar was seventy-five feet high, and together they looked like so many large towers, but were of a larger size than the towers that were usually constructed. On these altars, he offered sacrifices to his gods according to the Greek custom. After holding athletic and equestrian games for his men, he then made his camp three times larger in every respect than it had ever been done before. Making trenches fifty feet wide and ten feet deep, he had the earth cast up from the ditch and a good wall made around the trench. He commanded his foot soldiers that they should set up two bedsteads in their tents, each of them seven and a half feet long. The cavalry men were also to do this, as well as make mangers for their horses as large as they had been every other time. They were to do the same with their weapons, horse bits and other equipment which they were leaving behind. [L359] They should make them in the same proportion and hang them up. This was to give posterity a fictitious impression of his greatness. Philostratus described the inscriptions and titles of his altars. {*Philostratus, Apollonius, l. 2. c. 43. 1:229} {*Arrian, Anabasis, l. 5. c. 29. s. 1,2. 2:95} {*Diod. Sic., l. 17. c. 95. s. 1-3. 8:393,395} {*Curtius, l. 9. c. 3. s. 19. 2:393} {*Plutarch, Alexander, l. 1. c. 62. s. 3,4. 7:401,403}

2124. When these things had been done, he returned via the same route he had come to the Hydraotes River. He crossed it and came back to the Acesines River.

2125. There he found that the city which he had left Hephaestion to build, had already been built, so he relocated into this city as many of the neighbouring people as wanted to live there, and left those of his mercenary soldiers there who were unfit for military service. {*Arrian, Anabasis, l. 5. c. 29. s. 3. 2:97}

2126. Arsaces, who ruled over all the people in the province bordering on the kingdom of Abisares, came to Alexander with the brother of Abisares and his associates. They brought him presents of the most valuable items in those countries, while Abisares sent thirty elephants and a message to say that he would also have come to him but for the fact that he was sick. Alexander sent messengers to Abisares who confirmed his story, whereupon he made Abisares governor of that province under himself and made Arsaces subject to him, appointing what tribute they should pay him. Alexander again offered sacrifices at the Acesines River. {*Arrian, Anabasis, l. 5. c. 29. s. 4,5. 2:97}

2127. He crossed the Acesines River and came to the Hydaspes River. With the help of his soldiers, he repaired whatever the flooding of that unruly river had destroyed of his two cities, Nicaea and Bucephalis, which had recently been built there. From the time that he had left there until his return, it had rained continuously, with monsoon winds, according to Aristobulus as cited by Strabo. Diodorus stated that the rain lasted seventy days, with violent thunderstorms. {*Arrian, Anabasis, l. 5. c. 29. s. 4,5. 2:97} {*Diod. Sic., l. 17. c. 94. s. 2. 8:391} {*Strabo, l. 15. c. 1. s. 17. 7:25} [E257]

## 3678a AM, 4387 JP, 327 BC

2128. On the banks of the Hydaspes River, Alexander had built a large number of ships, two of which had three banks of oars, because he planned to sail down to the Indian Ocean with his cavalry and foot soldiers. For this venture, he gathered all the Phoenicians, Cypriots, Carians and Egyptians who followed his camp, and put them aboard his ships. {*Arrian, Anabasis, l. 6. c. 1. s. 6. 2:103}

2129. At the same time, Coenus, who was one of his best and closest friends, died. Alexander grieved his death and had him buried as honourably and lavishly as that time and place permitted. However, he was mindful of the speech which Coenus had made on behalf of the army requesting to return home and it gave him this biting taunt. Had Coenus known what little time he had to live, he would never have made so long a speech. {*Arrian, Anabasis, l. 6. c. 2. s. 1. 2:103}

2130. He received fresh troops from Greece, who were auxiliaries and mercenary soldiers under their various commanders, thirty thousand foot soldiers and six thousand cavalry in all. They also brought elegant suits of armour for twenty-five thousand foot soldiers and a hundred talents of medical supplies. Memnon also brought him five thousand cavalry from Thrace, beside those which came from Harpalus, and seven thousand foot soldiers. He also brought weapons inlaid with silver and gold, which Alexander distributed in the army, ordering that the old ones be burned. {*Curtius, l. 9. c. 3. s. 20,21. 2:393} {*Diod. Sic., l. 17. c. 95. s. 3-5. 8:395}

2131. Harpalus, who, according to Curtius, had sent Alexander the new supplies, was the same person whom Alexander had entrusted with the keeping of his tributes and treasure in the city and province of Babylon, and whom he had left as his overseer over that entire country. {*Plutarch, Alexander, l. 1. c. 35. s. 8. 7:333} [L360] However, he had given the government of it to Mazaeus, who had surrendered it to Alexander in the first place, and when Mazaeus died, Ditamenes succeeded him in that charge. {*Plutarch, Alexander, l. 1. c. 65. s. 3. 7:409} Although Diodorus called Harpalus the governor of that province, he further stated that Harpalus, hoping that Alexander would never return alive from India, gave himself over to all manner of intemperance and luxury, sparing no expense. First, he indulged all manner of whoredom and luxury with the women of that country, progressing to every kind of unseemly and unseasonable delights and pleasures, and squandering the king's money committed to his charge. He ordered various fish to be brought to him from as far off as the Red Sea (Persian Gulf. Editor.) and was so lavish in his feasting and everyday diet, that every man was ashamed of him. He sent for a noted strumpet, Pythonice by name, from as far away as Athens and when she died, he sent for another one, called Glycera, from the same place. Consequently, Theopompus complained to Alexander in a letter, telling him that Harpalus had spent more than two hundred talents in constructing two tombs for Pythonice when she died, one at Athens and another at Babylon. He also dedicated a grove, an altar and a temple to Pythonice, by the name of Venus Pythonica, and set up Glycera's statue in brass at Tarsus in Syria, where he let her live in the king's palace. He commanded the people to address her by the title of a queen and reverence her as such. {*Athenaeus, l. 13. (586c) 6:161} {*Diod. Sic., l. 17. c. 108. s. 4-6. 8:435,437}

2132. Cleander, Sitacles and Heracon in Media behaved similarly, hoping that Alexander would never return alive from India. They plundered private men's estates, pulled down temples and ravished the young virgins of the noblest families, as well as indulging in much other villainous conduct toward the citizens under them and their belongings. The very name of a Macedonian was odious to all the countries on account of their avarice and extravagance of every kind. Worst of all, Cleander, who had himself first ravished a noble virgin, later gave her to his slave as his concubine. {*Curtius, l. 10. c. 1. s. 1-5. 2:469} {*Arrian, Anabasis, l. 6. c. 27. s. 4,5. 2:185}

2133. Alexander prepared for his voyage to the ocean. When he saw old grudges rekindling between Porus and Taxiles, he reconciled them again, making them pledge friendship to each other, and then sent them away to their own kingdoms. He had made Porus king, as before, of all the countries lying between the Hydaspes and Acesines Rivers. In addition, he gave him all the free states which he had subdued between the Acesines and Hypanis Rivers, containing over two thousand cities. {*Arrian, Anabasis, l. 6. c. 2. s. 1. 2:103} Others said that in these fifteen countries there were more than five thousand large cities, besides towns and villages. {*Plutarch, Alexander, l. 1. c. 60. s. 8. 7:399} In fact, the region lying between the Hydaspes and Hypanis Rivers contained no more than nine countries with five thousand cities, with each city being as large as Cos in Meropis. (This was according to Apollodorus, who wrote of the affairs of Parthia, as reported by Strabo. {*Strabo, l. 15. c. 1. s. 3. 7:5}) Strabo considered his opinion to be a little excessive. {*Strabo, l. 15. c. 1. s. 32. 7:57} He said it seemed that this number was expressed somewhat hyperbolically, and therefore Pliny took it to be the number of all the cities which Alexander subdued in the whole of India. {*Pliny, l. 6. c. 21. (59) 2:383} [E258] Those who were with Alexander on his expedition reported that there were five thousand towns and cities, each as large as Cos, in that part of India which he subdued, or in these nine countries. Philippus, who was one of Alexander's company of friends, was appointed governor of a country beyond the Indus River by Alexander. {*Curtius, l. 10. c. 1. s. 21. 2:473} [L361]

2134. The cavalry from the city of Nysa was sent back home. Craterus and Hephaestion were commanded to march ahead of him into the capital city of Sopithes' kingdom and there await the arrival of Alexander's fleet. Craterus marched along one side of the Hydaspes with some of the cavalry and foot soldiers, while Hephaestion was on the other side with a larger force and two hundred elephants. The entire army at this time consisted of a hundred and twenty thousand men, including those whom he had brought from the sea coast. The men whom he had sent to levy fresh troops also returned to him, bringing with them men from various countries, with different types of weapons. {*Arrian, Anabasis, l. 6. c. 2. s. 1,2. 2:103} {*Arrian, Indica, l. 1. c. 19. s. 1-5. 2:361,363} Plutarch said that he had a hundred and twenty thousand foot soldiers and fifteen thousand cavalry at this time, and

that less than a quarter of them survived the return trip home. {*Plutarch, Alexander, l. 1. c. 66. s. 2. 7:411}

2135. Curtius said that this fleet had a thousand ships, of which, according to Diodorus, two hundred were open and the rest were barges propelled by oars. Arrian said that he had only eight hundred boats, some for transporting the horses and the rest were cargo vessels for grain and other provisions. However, according to Ptolemy Lagus, Alexander had almost two thousand boats and ships of various types. {*Arrian, Indica, l. 1. c. 19. s. 7. 2:363} {*Arrian, Anabasis, l. 6. c. 2. s. 3,4. 2:105} {*Curtius, l. 7. c. 2. s. 3,4. 2:105} {*Diod. Sic., l. 17. c. 95. s. 4,5. 8:395}

2136. The admiral of this fleet was Nearchus from Crete, while Evagoras from Corinth was in charge of all the provisions. On Alexander's ship, the captain was Onesicritus from Astypala. Arrian recorded the name of every captain for each ship. {*Arrian, Indica, l. 1. c. 18. s. 1-12. 2:357-361}

2137. When the preparations were complete, Alexander sacrificed to his native gods and to the other gods, according to the advice of the priests. These included Neptune, Amphitrite and the Nereides or Sea Nymphs. Most importantly, he sacrificed to the ocean, to the Hydaspes River, the Acesines River into which the Hydaspes flowed, and to the Indus River which received them both. He held various sorts of games, music, wrestling and the like, with prizes for those who would enter the contests. He distributed animals to every company, so that they could make their own sacrifices. {*Arrian, Anabasis, l. 6. c. 3. s. 1,2. 2:105}

2138. In the morning, the army boarded the ships. This included the silver targeteers, the archers and the Companion Cavalry, totalling eight thousand troops, and happened not many days before the setting of the Pleiades. {*Strabo, l. 15. c. 1. s. 17. 7:25} This was about the end of our October. Alexander went aboard and poured out a golden vial of wine from the prow of the ship into the river. He called on the Acesines, Hydaspes and Indus Rivers all at once. Later, when he had offered to his progenitor Hercules, to Ammon and the rest of the gods in his customary manner, the trumpet sounded at his command. This was the signal to drag down the vessels into the water and start the journey, which was duly done. An order was given as to how far every barge, horse carrier and ship of war was to stay away from every other vessel, to prevent collisions. They were to keep their rank and position and not out-row each other, as if this were a race. {*Arrian, Indica, l. 1. c. 19. s. 1-9. 2:361,363} {*Arrian, Anabasis, l. 6. c. 3. s. 1-3. 2:105}

2139. In this manner, Alexander came on the third day to the place where he had appointed Craterus and

Hephaestion to meet him. He stayed there two days, so that Philip might catch up to him with the rest of the army. Alexander had sent him to the Acesines River with orders to follow the river downstream. *[L362]* He sent away Craterus and Hephaestion again, with orders to march overland. {*Arrian, Anabasis, l. 6. c. 4. s. 1. 2:109}*

*2140.* Alexander followed the Hydaspes River, which was at least two and a half miles farther than going by land, to a spot where he landed his soldiers and from there went to Sibarus, the country of the Sibians. These were said to be the descendants of those men who had besieged the Aornus Rock with Hercules. When they were unable to take it, or to march any farther with him, they were left there by him. Their clothes were nothing but skins of wild beasts and their weapons were only clubs. Although the Greek manners and customs had long gone, nevertheless one could easily perceive some traces and marks of their Greek origin among them. When Alexander pitched his camp near the chief city of their country, their principal men came to him and were admitted into his presence. Reminding him of their Greek origin and the reverence they had for the Greeks, they offered him their service in whatever way it pleased him, bearing in mind that they were fitting for men of like blood with him and his Greeks. They testified to this with the extraordinary presents they gave to him. Alexander received them very graciously and made them a free state, entitled to live according to their own laws. {*Diod. Sic., l. 17. c. 96. s. 2,3. 8:397}* {*Curtius, l. 9. c. 4. s. 1-3. 2:395}* *[E259]*

*2141.* From there, he rode farther into the country for about thirty miles and after he laid waste to all the fields, he came to and besieged the chief city of that country. {*Curtius, l. 9. c. 4. s. 4. 2:395}*

*2142.* The Agalassians opposed him on the bank of a river with forty thousand foot soldiers and three thousand cavalry. He crossed the river and quickly routed them, after killing most of them. The rest ran into the towns, but he captured them, killed those who were of age and sold the rest as slaves. {*Diod. Sic., l. 17. c. 96. s. 3. 8:397}* {*Curtius, l. 9. c. 4. s. 4,5. 2:395}*

*2143.* Other inhabitants there also took up arms and about twenty thousand gathered together in one city. He broke into the city by brute force, but when they barricaded their streets and fought on from the battlements of their houses, he was forced to retire, leaving many of his Macedonians behind dead. In a rage he therefore set fire to the houses and burned both the city and most of the people in it. When three thousand who had fled into the citadel sued for pardon, he gave it to them. {*Curtius, l. 9. c. 4. s. 6,7. 2:397}* {*Diod. Sic., l. 17. c. 96. s. 4,5. 8:397,399}*

*2144.* He then returned to join his friends aboard ship, and proceeded at full speed into the countries of the Mallians and Oxydracans, because he had been told that they were two very populous and warlike countries. The inhabitants had carried their wives and children into fortified places and intended to meet him in battle. Therefore he hurried all the more, so that he might attack them while they were still making preparations and would not be fully ready for him. {*Arrian, Anabasis, l. 6. c. 4. s. 3. 2:109}*

## 3678b AM, 4388 JP, 326 BC

*2145.* On the fifth day of sailing down the river, he came to the confluence of the Acesines and Hydaspes Rivers, which met in a very narrow channel. This caused the river to run with an extremely violent and rapid current, creating many whirlpools. Many of their ships sprang leaks and two of the largest of them ran foul of each other, broke up and sank, drowning their passengers. Alexander's own ship was sucked into one of these whirlpools, and was in extreme danger of sinking and drowning Alexander. When they had gone a little farther, the channel became wider and the stream grew calmer. The ships approached the west bank and found a safe harbour to shelter in behind a bank which ran out into the river breaking the violence of the river and so enabling them to draw their ships to land. {*Arrian, Anabasis, l. 6. c. 4,5. 2:109-113}* {*Diod. Sic., l. 17. c. 97. 8:399,401}* {*Curtius, l. 9. c. 4. s. 6-14. 2:397,399}*

*2146.* Alexander set up altars on the river bank and sacrificed to his gods for having escaped so great a danger. He then marched about four miles farther into the country and attacked the natives who would not submit to him, thereby preventing them from helping the Mallians. He returned to his ships again, where he was met by Craterus, Hephaestion and Philip, who had brought their armies to help him. {*Curtius, l. 9. c. 4. s. 14. 2:399}* {*Arrian, Anabasis, l. 6. c. 4,5. 2:113}* *[L363]*

*2147.* The countries of the Oxydracans and Mallians lay between the confluence of the Hydaspes River with the Acesines River and the confluence of the Acesines River with the Indus River. {*Arrian, Indica, l. 1. c. 19. s. 6-8. 2:363}* These countries were usually at war with each other but had now united against their common enemy, Alexander. To make their alliance even more secure, they exchanged ten thousand virgins to intermarry. They had eighty thousand foot soldiers and ten thousand cavalry besides seven hundred chariots. Curtius said there were ninety thousand foot soldiers and nine hundred chariots. Justin and Orosius called these people the Mandri or Ambri, and the Sabracans, or Subagrans or Sugambrians and said that they had sixty thousand cavalry. The Mallians and Oxydracans (who in Diodorus were incorrectly named Sydracae) are known by all these names in various editions of the text. {*Justin, Trogus, l. 12. c. 9.} {*Orosius, l. 3. c. 19.} {*Curtius, l. 9. c. 4. s. 15,16. 2:399} {*Diod. Sic., l. 17. c. 98. s. 1,2. 8:399}

2148. The Macedonians thought that they had left all danger behind and looked forward to an end to all the fighting. When they saw themselves engaged in a new war, with fiercer and more warlike countries than they had previously faced in any part of India, they were terrified. They once again began to murmur and rebel against Alexander, who pacified them with a good speech and made them all happy again. {*Curtius, l. 9. c. 4. s. 16-24. 2:399,401}

2149. The commander-in-chief of all this native army was a man of proven valour who had been chosen from among the Oxydracans. Pitching his camp at the foot of a hill, he made many fires, in order to make his army seem all the larger. They made much loud noise and shouting, as was the custom of their country, to terrify the Macedonians. The next morning, Alexander was full of hope and confident of victory and attacked them after having encouraged his soldiers. The enemies, whether out of fear or some disagreement among themselves, all ran off, fleeing to the mountains and woods, and when the Macedonians were unable to overtake them, they started rifling their camp. {*Curtius, l. 9. c. 4. s. 24-25. 2:401,403}

2150. When Alexander had rigged his navy, he sent Nearchus down river with it into the country of the Mallians, ordering him to be there three days before the army. Alexander crossed the Hydaspes River and ordered Craterus, who was on the west bank of the river, to take charge of the elephants, of Polyperchon's brigade, of his mounted archers and of Philip's regiment. [E260] He ordered Hephaestion to march five days ahead of him, while Ptolemy was to march three days behind him. This ensured that whoever escaped from Hephaestion, would fall into the hands of either one or other of them. He ordered those going ahead of him to go to the confluence of the Acesines and Hydraotes Rivers, which was the farthest border of the Mallians, just as the confluence of the Acesines and Hydaspes Rivers was the border of the Oxydracans. They were to stay there and await his arrival, and that of the armies of Craterus and Ptolemy. {*Arrian, Anabasis, l. 6. c. 5. s. 5-7. 2:113}

2151. Alexander took his regiment of silver targeteers, his squadron of Agrians, Pithon's brigade and all his archers on horseback, as well as half of the Companion Cavalry. He went through a sandy, dry country into the region of the Mallians, to attack them before either the Oxydracans could come to help them, or they could go to the Oxydracans. {*Arrian, Anabasis, l. 6. c. 6. s. 1. 2:115}

2152. The first day, he camped near a little river about twelve miles from the Acesines River. When they had rested for a while, he ordered every man to fill all the bottles he had, with water. They marched on for the remainder of that day and the next night, covering some fifty miles. On the next morning, they attacked a large number of the Mallians who, never thinking that he would come through that dry wilderness, were walking abroad idly outside the city. [L364] He killed most of them, and the rest fled into the city and locked the gates. Instead of using a trench, Alexander had his cavalry surround the walls until his foot soldiers arrived. {*Arrian, Anabasis, l. 6. c. 6. s. 2,3. 2:115}

2153. As soon as the foot soldiers came, he sent Perdiccas away with his own troops, Clitus' cavalry and the Agrians, to besiege another town of the Mallians, where he understood many of the Indians to have gathered together. He did not want them to make any assault until he came, but to keep them entrapped, and so prevent them from spreading the news that he had come into the country. He began to make his approaches, and to assault the city which he had besieged. {*Arrian, Anabasis, l. 6. c. 6. s. 4. 2:115,117}

2154. He killed many of them in the assault, and the rest left the walls and fled to the citadel. When he took that, he killed two thousand people. {*Arrian, Anabasis, l. 6. c. 6. s. 5. 2:117}

2155. When Perdiccas came to the city which he had been commanded to besiege, he found that all the inhabitants had fled. When he found that they had only recently escaped, he followed them as fast as he could, killing all the ones he overtook, while the rest escaped into the bogs and marshes. {*Arrian, Anabasis, l. 6. c. 6. s. 6. 2:117}

2156. When Alexander had rested and refreshed himself and his army, he set out at the first watch of the night. At daybreak they came to the Hydraotes River, where he found that many of the Mallians had already crossed, but he attacked and killed the rest who were crossing the river. Then he crossed the river with his army and overtook those that had crossed earlier, killing many of them and taking others prisoner. Most of them, however, escaped into a well fortified city. {*Arrian, Anabasis, l. 6. c. 7. s. 1,2. 2:117,119}

2157. When his foot soldiers came up, Alexander sent Pithon against the enemy with his own and two other regiments of cavalry. On the first attack, he chased them into the town and took it. All those who were not killed, were taken as slaves, and Pithon then returned to the camp. {*Arrian, Anabasis, l. 6. c. 7. s. 3. 2:119}

2158. Alexander led his army against a city of the Brachmanes, where he understood more of the Mallians to have fled. As soon as he arrived, he besieged it very securely on all sides with his squadrons. The soldiers immediately left the walls and fled to the citadels. When this city was captured, some of the inhabitants set their own houses on fire and threw themselves into the flames, while others died fighting. About five thousand perished and few were captured alive. {*Arrian, Anabasis, l. 6. c. 7. s. 4-6. 2:119,121}

2159. Alexander stayed there one day, to give his soldiers a rest. The next day he marched against the other towns of the Mallians, but found that all the cities had been abandoned and the inhabitants had all fled to the desert. He stayed there one day. {*Arrian, Anabasis, l. 6. c. 8. s. 1. 2:121}

2160. The next day he sent Pithon and Demetrius, the captain of a regiment of cavalry, back to the riverside, also sending other troops and companies with them, because he wanted them to deal with any that had escaped to the woods. If they did not surrender, they were to be killed, and so a great many were killed by them. {*Arrian, Anabasis, l. 6. c. 8. s. 2-4. 2:121} [E261]

2161. Alexander marched against the capital city of the Mallians, having learned that many others had fled there. When this large city heard of his coming, the inhabitants fled and crossed over the Hydraotes River, forming themselves into battle array on its high cliffs, as if to stop him from crossing there. [L365] Alexander immediately followed them with his cavalry, ordering his foot soldiers to come later. When he was in the middle of the river, the Indians, although they were in good battle array, abandoned the place and fled. There were at least fifty thousand of them, and Alexander saw that they were in a strong compact body. Since his foot soldiers had not come to him, he kept circling around and making charges without coming into close quarters with the Indians. He did not think it wise to fight with them at that time. {*Arrian, Anabasis, l. 6. c. 8. s. 2-6. 2:121,123}

2162. As soon as the Agrians, the other well-ordered squadrons and the archers came, the main battle using the foot soldiers began. The Indians all fled and ran away to the next fortified city, with Alexander in pursuit. When they arrived there, Alexander at once surrounded the city with his cavalry before the foot soldiers came, and killed many of those who had fled. {*Arrian, Anabasis, l. 6. c. 8. s. 7,8. 2:123}

2163. Demophon, a soothsayer, spoke with Alexander and told him that he had observed, by certain signs and prodigies, that Alexander was in great danger. He wanted Alexander to stop, or at least to defer this siege. Alexander reproached him sharply for disheartening the

soldiers while they were in action. He divided his army into two parts, with himself leading one part and Perdiccas commanding the other. Together they went to scale the wall. The Indians could not endure the attack and all fled into the citadel, abandoning their stations on the wall. Alexander himself, with those about him, broke open the first gate and entered into the city. He began to set ladders against the citadel wall, and when he saw that his Macedonians were not following as quickly as he would have wished, he took a ladder himself and setting it against the wall, climbed onto its top. Peucestes was carrying Alexander's shield, which Alexander had taken from the temple of Athena in Troy. In all previous encounters, he had always been ahead of Alexander, but this time he was behind him. After him on the same ladder came Leonnatus, one of the captains of his bodyguard. Abreas, one of the soldiers who was receiving double pay, was on another ladder. When the silver targeteers heard of the danger Alexander was in, they fought to set up the ladders so thickly, that the ladders broke and everyone came tumbling to the ground. In this way, they were of no use and hindered others, who could have helped, from getting up. {*Curtius, l. 9. c. 4. s. 26-33. 2:403,405} {*Arrian, Anabasis, l. 6. c. 9. s. 1-4. 2:125,127} {*Appian, Civil Wars, l. 2. c. 21. (152) 3:509}

2164. Alexander was shot at from every direction from the adjoining towers, though no man dared come and fight hand to hand with him on the wall. Alexander leaped off the wall down into the citadel yard and putting his back to a wall there, killed with his own hand those who came to attack him. After he had killed the captain of the Indians who came boldly to attack him, no one dared come near him, but all shot at him from a distance. {*Arrian, Anabasis, l. 6. c. 9. s. 5,6. 2:127}

2165. Meanwhile, Peucestes, Leonnatus and Abreas leaped down from the wall into the yard after him and came to his rescue. Abreas was shot in the head through his face and died there. Alexander, as Ptolemy reported, received so great a wound in his chest, that his very breath came out at the wound with his blood. Peucestes, who interposed with Athena's buckler in his hand, and Leonnatus, who took in his own body the blows which were meant for Alexander, were likewise seriously wounded. All agreed that Peucestes had defended him with his Palladian buckler, which is the reason why Pliny called him the saviour of Alexander the Great. {*Pliny, l. 34. c. 19. (67) 9:177} Not everyone agrees concerning the actions of Leonnatus and Abreas. Ptolemy, the son of Lagus, was present to rescue him, which was affirmed by Clitarchus, Timagenes and Pausanias. [L366] Ptolemy, however, denied this claiming that he had been fighting with the enemy elsewhere all the while. Curtius said that the carelessness of those old historians was so great, it was hard to know what to believe. {*Pausanias, Attica, l. 1. c. 6. s. 2. 1:29} {*Arrian, Anabasis, l. 6. c. 10. s. 1-4. 2:127-131} {*Arrian, Anabasis, l. 6. c. 11. s. 8. 2:135} {*Curtius, l. 9. c. 5. s. 1-21. 2:405-411} {*Pausanias, Attica, l. 1. c. 6. s. 2. 1:29}

2166. At last, the Macedonians broke into the citadel and killed everyone there with the sword. They spared neither man nor woman, old nor young. They brought Alexander out upon their shields, not knowing whether he was dead or alive. The treatment of his wounds was more excruciating than the wounds themselves, but he endured the pain and started to recover. It was almost impossible to convince the army of this, as it was widely rumoured that he had died from his wounds. So, as soon as he possibly could, he had himself carried to the riverside, from where he sailed down in a barge to the place where his army was camped at the confluence of the Hydraotes and the Acesines Rivers. Hephaestion was in charge of the army there, and Nearchus of the navy. As soon as he stepped ashore, he permitted his soldiers to kiss his hand and refusing his stretcher, mounted his horse so all could see him. [E262] Then he alighted and went on foot to his pavilion. {*Curtius, l. 9. c. 5. s. 19-30. 2:411-415} {*Arrian, Anabasis, l. 6. c. 10,11. 2:129,131}

2167. When Alexander's wounds had been healing for seven days, he heard that the Indians were convinced he was dead. He had two barges joined together and had his royal pavilion spread across them, open on every side, so all could see he was still alive. This would put an end to the rumour of his death among the enemies. From there, he travelled down the river and ordered that no boats should come near the barge he was in, for fear of jolting his weak body with the beating of the oars. In this manner, they came on the fourth day to a country that had been deserted by its inhabitants. It had abundant provisions of grain and cattle, and since the place pleased him well, he stayed there to refresh both himself and his army. {*Curtius, l. 9. c. 6. s. 1-5. 2:415}

2168. Nearchus, the admiral, reported that Alexander's friends accused him for acting like a soldier, rather than a king or captain in the army. When Alexander grew angry at this remark, his disapproval was obvious in his expression on his face. A certain old Boeotian put him in good humour again by reciting an old limerick: {*Arrian, Anabasis, l. 6. c. 13. s. 4,5. 2:139}

"It stands to reason that he who would do a great thing, must suffer something too."

2169. Curtius mentioned a speech made to him by Craterus in the name of his friends for the same purpose.

Alexander replied that a man must never be without an occasion by which to win glory: {*Curtius, l. 9. c. 6. 2:415-423}

"Having conquered both continents in the ninth year of my reign and twenty-eighth year of my life, does it seem to you that I can pause in the task of completing my glory, to which alone I have devoted myself?" {*Curtius, l. 9. c. 6. s. 21. 2:421}

2170. Curtius quoted him as having said this. However, the chronologically correct time was the tenth year of his reign (which agrees well enough with this saying), in his thirtieth year.

2171. Alexander stayed there many days, until he was fully recovered from his wounds, and built more ships. There were about three thousand Greek soldiers whom he had located in certain cities he had built in the countries of Bactria and Sogdiana. They grew tired of living among those barbarous people and encouraged by the supposed news of Alexander's death, they defected from the Macedonian government and killed some of the leaders among their own countrymen. They took up arms and seized the citadel of the city of Bactra, which was not as carefully guarded as it should have been. They drew the inhabitants into this revolt with them. [L367] The leader of this conspiracy was Athenodorus, who assumed the title of a king, not so much out of a desire for a kingdom, but to bolster his plan to have the men follow him back to Greece. Biton, or Bicon, was a Greek. Because of a grudge, and out of envy against Athenodorus, he invited him to a banquet and had Boxus kill him. The next day, Biton called a company together and there persuaded some that Athenodorus would have killed him. Others, who thought it was nothing but mere roguery on Biton's part, quickly persuaded still others, and they all took up arms to kill him. The leaders among them persuaded the rest against this, and everything settled down again. {*Diod. Sic., l. 17. c. 99. s. 5,6. 8:405} {*Curtius, l. 9. c. 7. s. 1-6. 2:423,425}

2172. Biton, having escaped this action, began to plot the deaths of those who had saved his life. When they discovered this, they seized him and Boxus, killing Boxus immediately. They planned to put Biton on the rack, but suddenly, and for no apparent reason, the Greeks, like madmen, all rose up in arms, so they did not rack Biton for fear of a rescue by the multitude. Although he was naked, he fled to the Greeks. When they saw his distress and that he was ready to be racked, they changed their minds and rescued him from the danger he was in. Biton returned to his native land with the rest of the Greeks who defected from Alexander. {*Curtius, l. 9. c. 7. s. 7-11. 2:425,427}

*2173.* Meanwhile the Mallians, who were left, sent their messengers to Alexander to surrender their country to his mercy, and the Oxydracans likewise surrendered, sending the captains and chief men of every city, and with them a hundred and fifty of the principal men of the whole country, to Alexander. He wanted them to send him a thousand of their principal men, or as Curtius said, twenty-five hundred cavalry, whom he would keep as hostages, or as soldiers to serve him until he had ended his war with the Indians. {*Arrian, Anabasis, l. 6. c. 14. s. 1-3. 2:141} {*Curtius, l. 9. c. 7. s. 12-14. 2:427}

*2174.* Alexander invited all the principal men and petty kings of these countries to a feast where he ordered a hundred golden beds to be set up at a reasonable distance from each other. Each one of those beds was enclosed with curtains made of purple and gold. The purpose of the feast was to display whatever the old luxury of the Persians together with the new extravagances of the Macedonians, could afford. {*Curtius, l. 9. c. 7. s. 15. 2:427}

*2175.* Dioxippus, the Athenian, was at this feast. Dioxippus was a famous athlete and one of whom Alexander made much of, for his great strength of body and courage. *[E263]* Choragus was a Macedonian of mighty strength, who had shown his courage in many a battle. When Choragus was drunk, he challenged Dioxippus to a fight. The next day Dioxippus came, stark naked and anointed all over with oil, with nothing but a truncheon and a cloak for his armour. He approached the Macedonian, who came in armed with sword, buckler, pike and a javelin, and Dioxippus laid him to the ground at his feet. Aelian said Dioxippus killed the man. {*Curtius, l. 9. c. 7. s. 16-22. 2:427-431} {*Diod. Sic., l. 17. c. 100. 8:407,409} {*Athenaeus, l. 6. (251a) 3:131} {*Aelian, Historical Miscellany, l. 10. c. 22. 1:329} {*Aelian, Historical Miscellany, l. 12. c. 58. 1:401} {*Plutarch, On Being a Busybody, l. 1. c. 12. 6:505} {?Pliny, l. 35. c. 11. Dioxippus not mentioned in this book. Editor.}

*2176.* The Macedonians and Alexander took this defeat as a disgrace on the Macedonian nation before these barbarians, and were embarrassed by it. A short time later, at another feast, a golden cup disappeared and was planted in Dioxippus' room. Dioxippus, who was suspected of taking it, was so upset by this, that he wrote a letter to Alexander and then killed himself. {*Curtius, l. 9. c. 7. s. 23-26. 2:431} {*Diod. Sic., l. 17. c. 101. 8:409,411}

*2177.* Alexander shipped his cavalry, seventeen hundred of the Companion Cavalry and about ten thousand of his foot soldiers downstream. *[L368]* He travelled only a short distance on the Hydraotes River, until he came to the confluence of this river and the Acesines River. He sailed down the Acesines River, finally coming to the confluence of the Acesines and Indus Rivers, where he stayed with his navy until Perdiccas reached him with the main body of the army. Along the way he subdued the Abastanes, who were a free state among these Indians. {*Arrian, Anabasis, l. 6. c. 14. s. 4,5. 2:143} {*Arrian, Anabasis, l. 6. c. 15. s. 1. 2:143}

*2178.* While he stayed there, other ships of thirty oars apiece came to join him, and certain cargo ships recently built in the country of the Xathrians, which was another free state in those regions. Envoys came and submitted to him from the Ossadians, also a free state. {*Arrian, Anabasis, l. 6. c. 15. s. 2. 2:143}

*2179.* Likewise, the messengers of the Oxydracans and Mallians returned to him with presents, among which were a small quantity of linen cloth, a thousand Indian shields and a hundred talents of white iron. They also brought large lions and tigers which had been tamed, the skins of large lizards, and tortoise shells. There were three hundred cavalry and one thousand and thirty chariots as well, each drawn by four horses. {*Curtius, l. 9. c. 8. s. 1-3. 2:433} Arrian also mentioned that they sent him a thousand men for hostages, who were the bravest and best men they could find from among them. They also sent five hundred manned chariots equipped with soldiers to fight, which was more than what Alexander had asked of them. Arrian added that Alexander accepted their chariots and returned their hostages again. {*Arrian, Anabasis, l. 6. c. 14. s. 3. 2:141}

*2180.* Alexander commanded them to pay him such tribute as they had formerly paid to the Arachosians, and appointed Philip to be their governor. His government was to extend to the confluence of the two rivers, the Indus and Acesines, and no farther. We can hardly believe Plutarch, where he said that the extent of Philip's government was three times the size of Porus' kingdom, especially if it was as large as Plutarch stated it to have been. To guard that province, Alexander left him all the Thracian cavalry and such companies of foot soldiers as he thought fit and necessary for the purpose. Moreover, he had a city built at the confluence of those two rivers. Thinking it would quickly grow quite large and famous, he constructed a large number of docks for ship building. {*Arrian, Anabasis, l. 6. c. 15. s. 2. 2:143,2:145}

*2181.* At that time Oxyartes, the father of Roxane whom Alexander had married, came to him. Alexander cleared him of all suspicion of having had any part in the revolt of the Greeks who were in Bactria. {*Arrian, Anabasis, l. 6. c. 15. s. 3. 2:143-145} {*Curtius, l. 9. c. 8. s. 10. 2:435}

## 3678c AM, 4388 JP, 326 BC

*2182.* After this, Polyperchon was sent to Babylon with an army. {*Justin, Trogus, l. 12. c. 10.*} Craterus was ordered to take the elephants with most of the remaining army and to march down on the east bank of the Indus River. This route was easier for the heavily armed foot soldiers and since not all the bordering countries were friendly. Alexander took some choice companies and sailed down the Indus River to the ocean. {*Arrian, Anabasis, l. 6. c. 15. s. 4. 2:145*} It is said that he went at least seventy-five miles a day on the river, and yet the journey lasted a full five months. {*Pliny, l. 6. c. 21. (60) 2:383*}

*2183.* In the voyage down the river, the first country Alexander came to was that of the Sabracans or Sambestans. This was a country as large as any in India, both in total population and in the number of warriors. It was governed by a democratic government throughout all their cities. When they heard of the coming of the Macedonians, they armed sixty thousand foot soldiers and six thousand, or (as Curtius said) eight thousand, cavalry with five hundred chariots. (Loeb copy of Curtius had six thousand. Editor.) These were under the command of their three most skilled captains. When the navy arrived there, they were frightened by the strangeness of the sight. [L369] They recalled the invincible glory of the Macedonians and took the advice of the old men among them, who said they should avoid so imminent a danger by submitting to the Macedonians. [E264] Thereupon, they sent messengers and surrendered themselves wholly into Alexander's hands, and he graciously received them. They gave him many gifts and the honour befitting a demigod. {*Curtius, l. 9. c. 8. s. 4-8. 2:433*} {*Diod. Sic., l. 17. c. 102. s. 1-3. 8:411,413*} {*Pliny, l. 19. c. 5. 5:435*}

*2184.* Four days later, he came to a country which lay on both sides of the river, belonging to the Sodrians (or Sogdians, as in Arrian) and Massanians. Alexander received them as graciously as he had received the previous group of people. Here, on the bank of the Indus River, he built another Alexandria and selected ten thousand men to populate it. He made places for merchants and docks for shipping, and repaired any of his ships which were damaged. He made Oxyartes, his father-in-law, and Pithon, governors of all the country from the confluence of the Acesines and Indus Rivers to the sea, and also included all the sea coast. He sailed down the river and quickly came into the country of King Musicanus, and he was arriving before Musicanus the king had even heard of his coming. Not knowing what else to do, Musicanus immediately went out to meet him and presented him with the choicest gifts that India had to offer, and in particular, with all his elephants. He surrendered himself and all his kingdom into his hands

and asked a pardon for not having done it sooner. Alexander pardoned him and asked about the country, and the city there. (For more details see Strabo's account, which he based on Aristobulus and Onesicritus.) Alexander restored him to his kingdom, as he was in his previous role. {*Strabo, l. 15. c. 1. s. 21. 7:33*} {*Strabo, l. 15. c. 1. s. 33,34. 7:57-61*} {*Curtius, l. 9. c. 8. s. 8-10. 2:435*} {*Arrian, Anabasis, l. 6. c. 15. s. 2-7. 2:143-147*} {*Diod. Sic., l. 17. c. 102. s. 4,5. 8:413*}

*2185.* It was there that he heard in person the complaints, brought by his accusers, Tyriespis or Terioltes, whom he had made governor over the Parapanisadae. Finding him guilty of many acts of cruelty and avarice, he executed him there and gave that government to his father-in-law, Oxyartes. {*Curtius, l. 9. c. 8. s. 9,10. 2:435*} {*Arrian, Anabasis, l. 6. c. 15. s. 3. 2:145*}

*2186.* He ordered Craterus to build a citadel at the city of Musicanus. This was completed before Alexander left the region. He saw that that location was excellent to keep the neighbouring tribes in check and to maintain order. {*Arrian, Anabasis, l. 6. c. 15. s. 7. 2:147*}

*2187.* From there, he sailed on with his archers, the Agrians and all the cavalry he had on board, until he came to another country of the Indians, called Praestans. He marched against their king, Porticanus or Oxycanus, because the king did not come to meet him, nor did he send envoys to him. Alexander captured two of the largest cities in the kingdom. Porticanus was in one of these, which Alexander took on the third day of his siege. Porticanus fled into the citadel and sent envoys to treat for conditions, but before they reached Alexander, two large pieces of the wall fell down to the ground. The Macedonians rushed into the citadel through these breaches, and Porticanus, with the few who were with him, stood his ground on their guard. They were all killed and the citadel was pulled down, while all those in the town were sold as slaves. The spoil was given to the soldiers, and Alexander kept only the elephants for himself. {*Arrian, Anabasis, l. 6. c. 16. s. 1,2. 2:149*} {*Curtius, l. 9. c. 8. s. 11-14. 2:435,437*}

*2188.* Diodorus said that Alexander first gave those two cities over to his soldiers to be plundered, and then he burned them. After that, he went and captured all the rest of the cities and towns and destroyed them. By this action, he struck terror into all the neighbouring countries, so the rest of the countries merely had to hear of his coming to send envoys and surrender to Alexander without any resistance, as Arrian noted. {*Diod. Sic., l. 17. c. 102. s. 5. 8:413*} [L370]

*2189.* After this, Alexander entered the country of the Brachmanes, where Sambus or Sabus or Samus, according to Curtius, or Sabbas, according to Plutarch, or Ambigerus, according to Justin, or Ambiras, according to Orosius, was king. When he heard that Alexander was coming, he fled. When Alexander came near his main city, called Sindomana or Sindonalia, he found the gates wide open for him. Sambus' servants came to meet him, with presents of money and elephants. They told him that Sambus had fled, not out of hostility toward Alexander, but because Sambus feared Musicanus, as they were enemies, and Alexander had pardoned him and let him go.

*2190.* Alexander captured this and many other places. He went and took another city by force which had revolted from him, putting to death many of the Brachmanes who had caused the revolt, since it had been at their instigation that Sambus, who had recently submitted to him, and the cities of his kingdom, had revolted from him. Curtius said that Alexander took the city by undermining the wall, and that the natives stood amazed to see men rise from the ground in the middle of the city.

*2191.* Clitarchus, according to Curtius, said that there were eight thousand, or rather (as Diodorus and others stated) eighty thousand men killed in that country. A large number were sold as slaves. The Brachmanes had brought these disasters on themselves, but the rest, who simply submitted to him and asked for his pardon, were not harmed. *[E265]* King Sambus saved himself and got away as far as he could with thirty elephants. {*Arrian, Anabasis, l. 6. c. 16. s. 3-5. 2:149*} {*Curtius, l. 9. c. 8. s. 14-16. 2:437*} {*Diod. Sic., l. 17. c. 102. s. 6,7. 8:413,415*}

*2192.* Alexander captured ten men of the gymnosophists, who had persuaded Sambus to flee, and had caused much trouble for Alexander and his Macedonians. He asked them some hard and obscure questions, and threatened to hang every man if they did not answer these questions, which were recorded by Plutarch. When Alexander heard their replies, he gave them many honours for their trouble and dismissed them. {*Plutarch, Alexander, l. 1. c. 64. 7:405-409*}

*2193.* In the meantime, Musicanus revolted and Alexander sent Pithon against him with an army. He destroyed some of the cities in his kingdom and put garrisons in others, building citadels to keep the inhabitants in line. He captured Musicanus and brought him to Alexander, who immediately had him crucified in his own kingdom, along with as many of the Brachmanes as had encouraged him to revolt. {*Curtius, l. 9. c. 8. s. 16. 2:437*} {*Arrian, Anabasis, l. 6. c. 17. s. 1,2. 2:151*}

*2194.* Alexander returned to the Indus River, where he had ordered his navy to wait for him. They sailed down

the river again and came to a city called Harmatelia or Harmata, which belonged to Sambus and the Brachmanes. The inhabitants trusted in their strength and the fortifications of their city, and so shut their gates to him. Alexander ordered five hundred of his Agrians to go beneath the walls with their arms. If the townsmen sallied out against them, they were to retreat. Three thousand attacked the five hundred, who fled as they had been ordered to. The enemies pursued them and unsuspectingly came across the other companies, which were waiting in ambush for them. Alexander was personally waiting for them. In the ensuing battle, six hundred were killed, a thousand captured and the rest fled back into the city and stayed there. On Alexander's side, many were grievously wounded, almost to the point of death. The Indians had poisoned the heads of their weapons with a deadly poison. Ptolemy, the son of Lagus, was among the wounded, and almost died. It is said that in his sleep Alexander saw a herb which was a remedy for that type of poison. The herb was squeezed into a drink and taken to neutralise the poison, and many of the wounded made use of that medicinal herb and recovered. It is most likely that someone who knew the medical value of that herb told Alexander about it, and that this fable was made up to flatter and honour him. *[L371]* So said Strabo, who stated that this story happened among the Oritae, of whom we shall speak later. {*Curtius, l. 9. c. 8. s. 17-28. 2:437-441*} {*Diod. Sic., l. 17. c. 103. 8:415-419*} {*Strabo, l. 15. c. 2. s. 7. 7:139*}

*2195.* When Alexander started to besiege Harmatelia, which was a strong and well fortified city, all the inhabitants came out to him and humbly begged his pardon. They surrendered themselves and their city to his will, and so he pardoned them. {*Curtius, l. 9. c. 8. s. 28. 2:441*}

### 3678d AM, 4388 JP, 326 BC

*2196.* Moeris, the king of Patala, which was the neighbouring country, came to Alexander and put himself and his kingdom wholly into his hands. When Alexander had freely restored him to his kingdom again, he ordered Moeris to provide for his army. {*Arrian, Anabasis, l. 6. c. 17. s. 2. 2:151*}

*2197.* Alexander commanded Craterus to take with him the regiments of Attalus, and Meleager and Antigenes with some of his archers, and those of the Companion Cavalry and Macedonians who were unfit for the war. He was ordered to take them to Macedonia by way of Carmania, through the countries of the Arachotians and Zarangians, or Drangians. Some of the rest of the army were led by Hephaestion along one side of the Indus River, while the mounted javelin men and the Agrians were led by Pithon along the other side. He was ordered to get inhabitants for the cities which Alexander had built, and if any new revolts happened in those parts, he was to put them down. When that was done, he was to come and join the rest of the army at Patala. {*Arrian, Anabasis, l. 6. c. 17. s. 3,4. 2:151,153}

2198. When Alexander had now sailed down the river for three days, he received news that Moeris, with a large number from Patala, had left the city and fled to the mountains and woods, so he hurried as fast as he could to get there. {*Arrian, Anabasis, l. 6. c. 17. s. 3. 2:153}

2199. Strabo stated from Aristobulus that Alexander came into Patala at about the setting of the Dog Star (Sirius), having spent ten full months on his trip down the river. He had set out shortly before the setting of the Seven Stars (Pleiades). Alexander arrived in Patala at about the end of our July, having set sail at the beginning of the tenth month prior to this. Hence, it appears that he spent nine full months sailing down the Hydaspes, Acesines and Indus Rivers, which we determine from the rising and setting of these stars. We find Plutarch's account in this matter inaccurate. He stated: {*Strabo, l. 15. c. 1. s. 17. 7:25} {*Plutarch, Alexander, l. 1. c. 66. s. 1. 7:411}

"that his sailing down the rivers to the sea took him up to seven months." [E266]

2200. Alexander came to Patala and found no inhabitants in the city or the countryside, but he found large numbers of flocks and herds of cattle there, and grain in great abundance. He quickly sent his fastest soldiers to overtake those who had fled. As they overtook them, they were to send them off to catch up with the rest, and to persuade them to return. They were promised peace, and their home and belongings, in both the city and country. {*Arrian, Anabasis, l. 6. c. 17. s. 4. 2:153}

2201. Alexander ordered Hephaestion to build a citadel at Patala, and sent others into a region of theirs which was totally destitute of water, to dig wells to make it more habitable. Some of the natives attacked and killed them, but since the natives had lost many of their own in the battle, the rest fled away to the woods and mountains. When Alexander heard what had happened to his men, he sent more men to help them complete the work. {*Arrian, Anabasis, l. 6. c. 18. s. 1. 2:153}

2202. Alexander asked Nearchus, his admiral, to select some suitable season of the year to set out from the mouth of the Indus River, and to sail along until he came to the Persian Gulf and to the mouth of the Euphrates and Tigris Rivers. {*Arrian, Indica, l. 1. c. 21. s. 1. 2:367} [L372] Plutarch said Alexander made Nearchus the admiral of the fleet and Onesicritus its chief pilot. {*Plutarch, Alexander, l. 1. c. 66. s. 2. 7:411} Onesicritus, in his

account, said that Nearchus was the admiral. {*Arrian, Anabasis, l. 6. c. 21. s. 3. 2:163} Pliny called Onesicritus a commander of the fleet. {*Pliny, l. 6. c. 24. (81) 2:399} Strabo more correctly called him the chief pilot, and Nearchus the admiral. {*Strabo, l. 15. c. 1. s. 28. 7:49} {*Strabo, l. 15. c. 2. s. 4. 7:133,135} {*Arrian, Anabasis, l. 7. c. 5. s. 6. 2:217} {*Arrian, Indica, l. 1. c. 18. s. 9. 2:359,361}

2203. At Patala, the Indus River divided into two large branches, both of which retained the name of the Indus River until they emptied into the sea. These two branches created a triangular shaped island between them, after which the city of Patala was named. This island was larger than the Nile delta in Egypt. Onesicritus stated that each side of this island was two hundred and fifty miles long, while Aristobulus said that the side facing the ocean was about a hundred and twenty-five miles long. The land was marshy where the rivers emptied into the sea. Nearchus, and later Arrian, said that this side was two hundred and twenty-five miles wide, while Pliny said that it was two hundred and twenty miles wide. {*Strabo, l. 15. c. 1. s. 33. 7:59} {*Pliny, l. 6. c. 23. (80) 2:399} {*Arrian, Anabasis, l. 6. c. 20. s. 2. 2:159}

2204. Alexander planned to sail down to the sea by the western branch. He selected his fastest ships, all of two decks, all his galleys of thirty oars apiece, and some fast barques. He captured some guides who knew the river, and set out, telling Leonnatus to keep up with him, with a thousand cavalry and eight thousand foot soldiers, along the river bank. {*Arrian, Anabasis, l. 6. c. 18. s. 3,4. 2:155}

2205. The morning after he set out, a violent wind arose. The wind and tide crossed each other to create large waves on the river, so that his ships collided with each other. Most of them were leaking, and many of the ships of thirty oars apiece broke apart before they could reach an island in the middle of the channel. {*Arrian, Anabasis, l. 6. c. 18. s. 5. 2:155}

2206. Alexander was forced to stay there a long time to build new vessels to replace those that had been lost. His river guides had fled, and as he was unable to replace them, they were forced to go on without them. When they had gone fifty miles, the pilots were all agreed and told Alexander that they could smell the sea, which meant the ocean could not be far away. So he sent some men ashore to get some of the natives who, he thought, might be able to confirm this. They searched for a long time for people in their huts. Finally they found some people, whom they asked how far away the sea was. They replied that they did not know what the sea was, nor had they ever heard of any such thing, but if they went on for three days, they would come to salt water which mixed with the fresh. {*Curtius, l. 9. c. 9. s. 1-6. 2:441,443}

*2207.* Arrian stated that when certain Macedonians went ashore, they found some Indians whom Alexander used for guides on the river for the rest of the journey. They came to the place where the river widened to twenty-five miles, which was its greatest width. The wind blew very strongly from off the sea, and they were again forced to take refuge in a creek into which his guides directed him. Curtius said that he came to salt water on the third day, as he had been foretold. There he found another island in the river, and they observed that the boats did not move as fast there as they had been travelling because of the incoming tide. {*Arrian, Anabasis, l. 6. c. 18. s. 4,5. 2:155} [L373]

*2208.* While they lay there at anchor, some of the men went foraging, unaware that a new danger now confronted them. A very large tide (which to this day was usual in Cambay, where the Indus River emptied into the sea) came in upon them and flooded all the countryside. Only the tops of some hills were above water, like so many little islands, and those who had gone ashore resorted to these hills. *[E267]* When the sea had gone out again and had left the land dry, as before, their ships were left high and dry. Either they were stuck nose first into the bank, or they had fallen over on their side. When the next tide came in, those ships which had stood upright on their keels in the mud, floated again with the rising of the water and were not damaged, but those that had settled on hard ground when the sea had gone out, had fallen on their sides. When the tide returned, these ships were driven against one another, or smashed and broken on the shore. {*Arrian, Anabasis, l. 6. c. 19. s. 1-3. 2:157} {*Curtius, l. 9. c. 9. s. 2-27. 2:443-449}

*2209.* Everything was repaired as well as time and place would permit. Alexander sent two barques down the river to view the island at which the guides had told him that he must land, if he wanted to sail out into the ocean. The natives called this island Cilluta, Alexander called it Scillustis and others, Psiltucis. They brought word back to him that the island was large and afforded excellent ports and lots of fresh water. Alexander ordered the whole navy to sail to this island, while he took some of the better vessels and went ahead, to ascertain whether there was a barrier at the mouth of the river, or a safe passage out into the open ocean. When he had gone fifty miles, he saw yet another island lying farther out in the open ocean. {*Plutarch, Alexander, l. 1. c. 66. s. 1,2. 7:411} {*Arrian, Anabasis, l. 6. c. 19. s. 3,4. 2:157}

*2210.* Alexander returned to the former island lying at the mouth of the river, and came ashore at one of its capes. He offered sacrifices to certain gods, to whom he claimed Jupiter Ammon had commanded him to sacrifice. The next day he sailed to another island lying out in the same

ocean, and offered more sacrifices to other gods in the same manner as he had done previously, saying that what he had done was at the command of Jupiter Ammon. He sailed far out of the mouth of the Indus River into the open ocean. There he sacrificed to Neptune certain oxen he had on the ship, and threw them overboard into the sea, after having also made a drink offering and having first poured that into the sea. Then, he threw a golden vial into the ocean, followed by various golden bowls, for a thank offering. Since he planned to send Nearchus to the Persian Gulf, he prayed that he might arrive there safely. {*Arrian, Anabasis, l. 6. c. 19. s. 4,5. 2:157,159}

*2211.* Justin stated that when Alexander returned to the mouth of the Indus River, he built a new city called Barce there as a memorial, and erected some altars. {*Justin, Trogus, l. 12. c. 10.*} Curtius said that he set out at midnight with a small company of ships when the tide began to go out, and went about fifty miles into the open sea, far out from the mouth of the Indus River. When he had gone this far, he sacrificed to the gods of those seas and the neighbouring lands, and then returned to the rest of his navy. {*Curtius, l. 9. c. 9. s. 27. 2:443-449} Diodorus stated that he went out into the main ocean with some of his closest friends, landed at two little inlets and there offered a magnificent sacrifice to the gods. He threw into the sea a number of very expensive golden cups and made drink offerings to the sea. When he was finished, he built some altars in honour of Tethys and Oceanus. Now that he had finished his intended voyage into the east, he returned with his navy up the river. On that journey he came back to a prosperous and famous city called Patala, which had a government that was very similar to that of Sparta. {*Diod. Sic., l. 17. c. 104. s. 1,2. 8:419}

*2212.* Like Sparta, they had two kings, who were descended from two houses and inherited their office from their fathers. The kings were in charge of military matters, while civil affairs were managed by a council of elders. {*Diod. Sic., l. 17. c. 104. s. 2. 8:419}

*2213.* When Alexander returned up river to Patala, he found the citadel completed according to his directions, and Pithon had returned with his army, having completed his assigned task. *[L374]* Alexander planned to leave a part of his navy at Patala, which is the name by which the city is known to the Indians of Cambais to this very day. Hephaestion was put in charge of constructing the ports and docks for the navy, at this spot where the Indus River divided into two branches. {*Arrian, Anabasis, l. 6. c. 20. s. 1,2. 2:159}

*2214.* Meanwhile, Alexander made another journey to the ocean along the the eastern channel of the same river, to determine which of the two channels afforded the better and easier journey to the ocean and back again. When he was almost at the mouth of the second channel, he came across a lake in the channel, which had been formed either by the river's meandering or by water flowing in there from other parts and making the river wider there than elsewhere. The lake looked like an arm of the sea. He left Leonnatus there with most of his army and with all his smaller ships, while he went on with his ships of thirty oars apiece and those with two tiers of oars. Again he sailed out into the vast ocean, and found that this was the more spacious channel of the two to navigate for taking commerce to Patala. *[E268]* He went ashore with some of the cavalry and made a three day journey along the sea coast, exploring the coast where he had sailed. He had wells dug in various places to provide fresh water for his navy, should they need it. {*Arrian, Anabasis, l. 6. c. 20. s. 2-4. 2:159,161}

2215. Curtius said that the next day, following his return from the ocean, he sailed up the river to a certain salt water lake. Some of the men went into it, not knowing anything about it, and developed an infectious scab that spread to others. However, they quickly found an oil which cured it. If this was the same lake which I previously mentioned from Arrian, then in all this history concerning Alexander's last return from the ocean, it was not mentioned by any author except for Arrian. {*Curtius, l. 9. c. 10. s. 1,2. 2:451} {*Arrian, Anabasis, l. 6. c. 20. s. 3. 2:161}

2216. When Alexander returned to Patala the second time, he sent a part of his army to dig those wells mentioned before, by the seaside, ordering them to return to Patala as soon as they were done. He sailed into the lake again and there constructed new ports and more docks for his ships. He left a garrison there and stored a four month supply of grain and other supplies for the coastal voyage. {*Arrian, Anabasis, l. 6. c. 20. s. 5. 2:161} Now it seems that he built the city called Potana at this lake, in order to provide him with a good port for his navy in that part of the ocean. (Diodorus {*Diod. Sic., l. 3. c. 47. s. 9. 2:233} compared with Agatharchides, *Excerpts of Photius*, Cod. 250. c. 51 and with this place in Arrian.)

2217. Curtius wrote that Alexander stayed on the island of Patala with his army, awaiting the arrival of spring, and during that time he built many cities there. As winter was drawing to an end, he burned his ships, which were now unserviceable, and marched away by land. {*Curtius, l. 9. c. 10. s. 4. 2:451} Strabo stated that he left India toward the summer season (which, in his reckoning, always began with the spring). {*Strabo, l. 15. c. 2. s. 5. 7:135} I think he would not have said this, had he better considered what he said later about Alexander concerning this voyage, and which was affirmed by Nearchus, who was his admiral. He said: {*Strabo, l. 15. c. 2. s. 5. 7:135}

"When the king was now completing his journey, Nearchus himself began his voyage in the autumn when the Pleiades or Seven Stars began to appear in the evening."

2218. It is therefore obvious that Alexander had sent Leonnatus ahead of him in September, to dig wells in suitable places for the army in their overland march through a dry and desert country. He burned his ships, which were leaky, and marching from Patala, he came with all his army to the bank of the Arbies or Arabis River. *[L375]* This river separated India and the Arbites, or the Arabites (whom Dionysius Periegetes called the Aribes, and others call Abrite), from the Oritans. For the Arbites inhabited that part of the coastline of India which lay between the Indus and Arbis Rivers, a distance of a hundred and twenty-five miles, according to Nearchus. {*Strabo, l. 15. c. 2. s. 1. 7:129} {*Arrian, Indica, l. 1. c. 25. s. 3. 2:381} These were the Indian people living farthest to the west. {*Arrian, Indica, l. 1. c. 25. s. 3. 2:381} {*Pliny, l. 7. c. 2. 2:527} They were neighbours to the Oritans and spoke their own language, which was different from that of the Indians. {*Pliny, l. 6. c. 25. (95) 2:411} {*Arrian, Indica, l. 1. c. 22. s. 10. 2:373}

2219. These Arbites or Arabites were a free state living under their own laws. Since they were not strong enough to withstand Alexander, nor willing to submit to him, they fled away to the woods and wildernesses as soon as they heard of his coming. {*Arrian, Anabasis, l. 6. c. 21. s. 4. 2:163,165}

2220. Alexander turned the rest of his army over to Hephaestion, while Alexander took half of his silver targeteers, some of his archers, some regiments called *Asthetairoi* and a troop of the Companion Cavalry. Taking one troop from every regiment of cavalry, and all his mounted archers, he kept the ocean on his left and journeyed westward. He ordered a number of wells to be dug along the coast, to supply his navy with fresh water when they passed by on their way to the Persian Gulf. {*Arrian, Anabasis, l. 6. c. 21. s. 3,4. 2:163}

2221. As soon as Alexander had left, the inhabitants of Patala were inspired with fresh courage and the desire for liberty. They attacked Nearchus and the army that was left with him, forcing him to flee to his ships. He had no wind to sail with, {*Strabo, l. 15. c. 2. s. 5. 7:135} because it was a poor time for sailing before the beginning of winter, which in those parts began with the setting of the Pleiades in the month of our November. {*Arrian, Anabasis, l. 6. c. 21. s. 1,2. 2:163}

## 3679a AM, 4388 JP, 326 BC

2222. Therefore, Nearchus prepared to make the voyage as soon as the Etesian or trade winds had ended. All summer long, these winds blew from the sea to land

and made all navigation along that coast impossible. When Nearchus had sacrificed to Zeus, the deliverer, and held certain gymnastic games, he set sail from there in the 11th year of Alexander's reign. This was the time when Cephisodorus was the archon of Athens. He left on the 20th day of the month of Boedromion, or October 1 according to the Julian Calendar. (This I have already shown in my discourse of the solar year among the Macedonians. {*Ussher, Macedonian and Asiatic Year, l. 1. c. 2.} [E269] {*Arrian, Indica, l. 1. c. 21. s. 1. 2:367}) We find the name of Cephisodorus four years earlier, in the third year of the 113th Olympiad, and also three years later, in the second year of the 114th Olympiad. This was the year following Alexander's death, according to the tables of the archons of Athens. If this name was correctly recorded by Arrian at this point, then this Cephisodorus may be the same person, because of the closeness of the times. The following discrepancies occurred between Diodorus Siculus, Dionysius of Halicarnassus and Arrian for in the recording of the names of the archons of Athens in the fourth year of the 113th Olympiad: [L376]

### OLYMPIAD 113

| Year | Diodorus | Dionysius | Arrian |
|------|----------|-----------|--------|
| 1 | Euthycritus | Hegemon | Hegemon |
| 2 | Chremes | Hegemon | Chremes |
| 3 | Anticles | Chremes | Cephisodorus |
| 4 | Sosicles | Anticles | Anticles |

2223. Pliny stated that Alexander built a city at the place where Nearchus and Onesicritus started on their intended voyage. It is the same city we find called Xylinepolis. {*Pliny, l. 6. c. 26. (96) 2:411} It is amazing that at the same time Pliny said that no one could tell where or on what river it had been built, for where should it be, but on the island of Patala, where they were left by Alexander to wait for a suitable season to begin their voyage? Where else but on the Indus River, where along which the navy sailed and on which the fleet made its way down to the ocean. {*Arrian, Indica, l. 1. c. 21. s. 2. 2:369}

2224. The first day after they sailed from the port of Xylinepolis to go down the Indus River, they came to a good, deep channel called Stura, about thirteen miles from the port, and there they anchored for two days.

2225. The third day they sailed and came to another channel about four miles downstream, where they found the water to be a little brackish, because the tide had come up that far and mixed with the fresh water, leaving a taste of salt in the place even at low tide. The name of the place was Caumana.

2226. They went on from there and came to a place about three miles farther down on the river, called Coreetis.

2227. Setting sail again, they had not gone far when they spied a rocky reef just inside the mouth of the Indus River and stretching to the shore, which was also very rocky. They put in with the tide where the ground was softer and provided a better landing-place for the ships. Then they made a ditch about a thousand yards long through the reef to the sea, and sailed the ships through this channel.

2228. Sailing on for another nineteen miles, they came to a sandy island called Crocala and stayed there another day. On the mainland near the island lived the Indian tribe called the Arabies, from the Arabius River. This river divided them, as mentioned before, from the Oritans. {*Arrian, Indica, l. 1. c. 21. s. 3-8. 2:369}

2229. Their journey was described in detail by Arrian from Nearchus' accounts, {*Arrian, Anabasis, l. 6. c. 21. s. 3. 2:163} and later by Jo. Baptisa Ramusius. {Ramusius, Navigations. l. 1. fol. 169.} The high points of the voyage were described by Pliny, as recorded from Onesicritus by King Juba. The following words of his indicate this: {*Pliny, l. 6. c. 26. (96) 2:411}

> "It is fit I should here set down what Onesicritus recorded of this voyage, wherein he sailed from India into the very centre of Persia at the command of Alexander. From him the story is related again by King Juba."

2230. This also helps us to understand these next words of Pliny:

> "The voyage of Nearchus and Onesicritus had neither names of places where they landed, nor distances from one place to another."

2231. That is, as it was described by Juba or Onesicritus himself. For both accounts were derived from Nearchus, as from Arrian noting from his account and had recorded his history using these accounts.

2232. The night after Alexander had crossed the Arbis or Arabius River, he marched through a large part of the sandy country and came, on the following morning, into places that were well inhabited and civilised. Leaving the foot soldiers to follow in good array, he went on horseback with several troops and squadrons in very good order. They were widely spread out, to enable them to take in and clear all the country before them, but when they were attacked by the Oritans, many of them were killed or taken prisoner. Then they came to the bank of a small river and camped there. {*Arrian, Anabasis, l. 6. c. 21. s. 4,5. 2:165} [E270]

2233. Alexander divided his company into three brigades. He gave one to Ptolemy to lead along the coast, and a second to Leonnatus to take through the middle of the country and across its plain, while he took the third brigade and marched into the hilly and mountainous country of that region. [L377] He wasted everything he came across, thereby enabling the soldiers to enrich themselves, and killed many tens of thousands of the inhabitants. {*Diod. Sic., l. 17. c. 104. s. 5-7. 8:421,423}

2234. When Alexander was joined by Hephaestion, who had the larger part of the whole army under his command, he marched forward to Rhambacia, which was the principal division of all that country. When he found a spot by the seaside that was safe from every wind and weather, he at once ordered Hephaestion to build a city there, which on completion was called Alexandria, and into which he relocated the Arachosians. {*Diod. Sic., l. 17. c. 104. s. 8. 8:423} {*Arrian, Anabasis, l. 6. c. 21. s. 5. 2:165}

2235. Alexander took half of his silver targeteers, the Agrians, and a squadron of cavalry and mounted archers, and marched away to the borders of the Oritans and Gedrosians, where he had been told there was a narrow pass separating the two countries. Both countries were camped there with their armies to keep the pass. No sooner had they heard of his coming, than most of them abandoned the place and fled, whereupon the leaders of the Oritans went to him and submitted themselves and their whole country to him. The only command which Alexander gave them, was to recall their countrymen to their homes. They were to assure them that in so doing, they would receive no harm and all would be well with them. {*Arrian, Anabasis, l. 6. c. 22. s. 1,2. 2:165,167}

2236. Alexander made Apollophanes joint governor of the Oritans with Leonnatus, a captain of his bodyguard, with whom he left all his Agrians and some of his archers. He ordered Leonnatus to await the coming of the fleet into those parts. In the meantime, they were to go and help with the building of a new city and to arrange everything there for the well-being of the people. {*Arrian, Anabasis, l. 6. c. 22. s. 3. 2:167}

2237. He then marched with most of his army, for now Hephaestion had joined up with him again, into the country of the Gedrosians, which had largely been abandoned by its inhabitants. Aristobulus said that the Phoenicians who followed the army as traders, bought up what was being offered for sale there in this desert. They loaded their camels with myrrh and spikenard which grew in abundance there. The whole army used them for bed coverings. The spikenard, over which they walked, gave off a delightful smell, that spread far and wide. {*Arrian, Anabasis, l. 6. c. 22. s. 3-8. 2:167,169} {*Strabo, l. 15. c. 2. s. 3. 7:133}

2238. He sent Craterus ahead of him into the midland countries with a part of the army. He was to subdue

Ariana or Aria (this is what all the regions to the west of India, even as far as Carmania, were called) and to go into those places through which Alexander planned to go. Craterus marched through the countries of the Arachotians and the Drangians, and subdued by force the country of the Chaarene, who refused to submit. {*Strabo, l. 15. c. 2. s. 5. 7:135} {*Strabo, l. 15. c. 2. s. 11. 7:147,149} When Ozines, whom Arrian called Ordanes, and Tariaspes, two Persian nobles, revolted in Persia, Craterus subdued them by force and placed them in irons. {*Curtius, l. 9. c. 10. s. 20. 2:457} {*Arrian, Anabasis, l. 6. c. 27. s. 3. 2:183}

2239. Alexander, with another part of the army, went through the country of Gedrosia, which was about sixty miles from the sea. He marched up to seventy-five miles at night through a barren, craggy, dry and desolate country. Alexander wanted to go all along the sea coast to discover suitable places where he could build ports and make provision for his fleet which was to come that way by his orders. He had wells dug and ports made for his navy. {*Arrian, Anabasis, l. 6. c. 23. s. 1. 2:169} {*Strabo, l. 15. c. 2. s. 5,6. 7:135,137}

2240. To this end, he sent Thoas ahead of him with a competent company of cavalry, to scout the sea coast. He was to see whether there were any good landing places or fresh water near the shore, or other suitable provisions for them. [L378] When he returned to Alexander, he told him that he had found some poor fishermen there, who lived in little cottages built from shells and covered over with the bones of fish and their backbones served as rafters. What little water these men used, they had to dig for in the sand, and the water was not always fresh. {*Arrian, Anabasis, l. 6. c. 23. s. 2,3. 2:171}

2241. Alexander finally came into a country of the Gedrosians where there was a supply of grain. Seizing it all and sealing the sacks with his own signet, he placed it on wagons and sent it all away to the coast. While he went on to the next ports, the soldiers broke the seals, opened the sacks and ate all the grain to satisfy their extreme hunger. [E271] Those who were the leaders in this matter, were the ones who had been entrusted with guarding the grain. When Alexander realised that it had been done out of hunger, he overlooked it. He sent all over the country to get more grain and had Cretheus carry it away to the coast to supply the fleet and the army. At that very time, the fleet landed in those parts. Alexander ordered the natives to go farther up into the country to bring from there as much flour, dates and sheep as they possibly could, and to carry this to the seaside, where it was to be sold to the army. He sent Telephus, one of his friends, to get additional provisions of flour, and when he found a quantity of it, although not much, he carried it to another port, according to his orders. {*Arrian, Anabasis, l. 6. c. 23. s. 4-6. 2:171,173}

2242. Meanwhile, some of the Oritans who lived in the mountains attacked Leonnatus' brigade, killing a large number of them, and then withdrew to safety again, according to Diodorus. Then the whole country of the Oritans joined with other neighbouring countries to make an army of about eight thousand foot soldiers and four hundred cavalry, and led a general revolt. Leonnatus attacked and killed six thousand of their foot soldiers and all their leaders. He himself lost fifteen cavalry, a few foot soldiers and Apollophanes. He was the governor of that country and had been appointed by Alexander, as we noted before. {*Diod. Sic., l. 17. c. 105. s. 8. 8:427} {*Curtius, l. 9. c. 10. s. 19. 2:457} {*Arrian, Anabasis, l. 7. c. 5. s. 5. 2:217} {*Arrian, Indica, l. 1. c. 23. s. 5. 2:375,377}

2243. Nearchus landed at this place with his fleet and loaded provisions of grain provided by Alexander, which would serve the army on board for ten days. He repaired his ships that were leaking, and left any unfit sailors to serve on land with Leonnatus, taking others from his companies in their place. {*Arrian, Indica, l. 1. c. 23. s. 6-8. 2:377}

2244. Philip, whom Alexander had made governor over the Oxydracans and Mallians, was attacked and murdered by his own mercenary troops. The murderers were attacked by the Macedonians, who were his guard, and were soon seized and cut to pieces for their deeds. {*Arrian, Anabasis, l. 6. c. 27. s. 2. 2:183}

2245. It is said that Alexander endured more hardships and suffered more losses in the country of the Gedrosians than he had in all of Asia. Of that army with which he went into India, he scarcely brought a quarter back with him out of Gedrosia. They endured grievous diseases, poor diet, burning heat, deep sands, famine and shortages of water. Nearchus said that Alexander had known of the difficulties of going that way. Purely from self-willed ambition, which reigned, or rather raged, in him, he was determined to force his way through. Someone had told him that Semiramis and Cyrus had gone that way into India. Therefore he was determined to return by that same way out of India, although he had been told that she was forced to save herself by fleeing from there with only twenty men in her company, and Cyrus with only seven. Alexander thought he would enhance his reputation if he were able to get out with his army safe and sound, when they had suffered there so much. [L379] Therefore, Nearchus claimed that the desire to return home by this route was partly due to this ambition and partly in order to favour and relieve his navy, which had been appointed to meet him in those parts. His guides lost their way through those vast sands, because the wind had covered all the tracks which led through the desert. Alexander had a hunch that the way must lie to his left, and so, taking a small company of cavalry with him, he went to see whether he could find the seashore. All their horses except for five were exhausted by the length and heat of the journey, so he left them behind and went with those five and came to the sea coast. He dug for a while and found fresh water to drink. He then immediately sent back for his whole army to come there to him, and when they arrived, he marched forward for seven days along the sea coast, finding plenty of fresh water all the way. Once his guides recognised the way again, they led him up into the midland countries, as he had wanted. {*Strabo, l. 15. c. 1. s. 5. 7:7} {*Strabo, l. 15. c. 2. s. 5,6. 7:135,137} {*Arrian, Anabasis, l. 6. c. 24-26. 2:173-183}

2246. After two months he left the country of the Oritans and came to the chief city of the Gedrosians, called Pura. He rested his army there and refreshed them with feasting, which was very fitting and a good time for him to do so. {*Strabo, l. 15. c. 2. s. 7. 7:139} {*Arrian, Anabasis, l. 6. c. 27. s. 1. 2:183} {*Plutarch, Alexander, l. 1. c. 66. s. 3. 7:411}

2247. From Pura he sent away the swiftest couriers that he could possibly find to Phrataphernes, whom he had left as governor of Parthia, and to the two governors of the provinces of Drangiane and Aria, which lay at the foot of the Taurus Mountains. They were ordered to assemble as many camels, dromedaries and others, with all kinds of beasts of burden, as they possibly could, and these were all to be loaded with all manner of supplies and sent at once to meet him as soon as he entered into the country of Carmania. [E272] These letters were speedily carried to them and obeyed, so that when he came into Carmania, he found abundant provisions at the appointed place, ready for him and his army. {*Diod. Sic., l. 17. c. 105. s. 7. 8:425} {*Curtius, l. 9. c. 10. s. 22. 2:457}

2248. Menon, the governor of the Arachosians, had recently died. Alexander appointed Sibyrtius as governor of both Arachosia and Gedrosia. {*Curtius, l. 9. c. 10. s. 20. 2:457}

## 3679b AM, 4389 JP, 325 BC

2249. As Alexander was marching toward Carmania, he received news of the death of Philip, the governor of the Oxydracans and Mallians, so he wrote to Eudamus and Taxilas and in his letters gave them the charge of those two provinces, until he would send a governor to replace Philip. {*Arrian, Anabasis, l. 6. c. 27. s. 2. 2:183}

2250. As soon as he entered Carmania, Astaspes, the governor of that province, met him. It was suspected that he planned to revolt from Alexander while the latter was in India. Alexander concealed his anger toward him and received him very graciously and while treating him according to his rank and station, all the while tried to determine if the charges were true. {*Arrian, Anabasis, l. 6. c. 27. s. 2. 2:183} {*Curtius, l. 9. c. 10. s. 21. 2:457}

2251. Craterus came to Alexander with the rest of the army and the elephants, bringing with him Ordanes, or Ozines, and Zariaspes, whom he had taken into custody for trying to revolt in Persia. Stasanor, the governor of the provinces of Parthia and Hyrcania, came to him with the captains and commanders of all those forces which he had previously left with Parmenion in the province of Media, namely Cleander, Sitalces, Heracon and Agathon, who brought him five thousand foot soldiers and a thousand cavalry. {*Arrian, Anabasis, l. 6. c. 27. s. 3. 2:183,185} {*Curtius, l. 10. c. 1. s. 1. 2:469}

2252. Various governors in different parts of India sent him a large number of horses and other beasts of burden. Some were for pack animals and others for military use, and they came from every country of his dominions in India. [L380] Stasanor and Phrataphernes brought him a large number of draft horses and camels, which Alexander distributed among those who wanted to use these animals to carry their goods. He gave some to select captains and the rest he distributed among the soldiers, by troops and companies, as he saw the need. He also armed his soldiers with new weapons because they were now drawing near to Persia, which was a peaceful and very wealthy country. {*Arrian, Anabasis, l. 6. c. 27. s. 6. 2:187}

2253. Alexander (as Arrian reported from Aristobulus) offered a sacrifice of thanksgiving to his gods for his victory over the Indians and for the safe journey of his army from Gedrosia. He entertained his armies with sports of music, wrestlings and the like. He also added Peucestes to his bodyguard, the one who had covered him with his shield in the country of the Mallians. At that time, only seven men had this honour: Leonnatus, Hephaestion, Lysimachus, Aristonous (all born in Pella), Perdiccas, a Macedonian, Ptolemy, the son of Lagus, and Pithon. The eighth man was Peucestes, for his bravery in saving the king from the Mallians. Other writers, including Diodorus, Curtius and Plutarch, stated that Alexander imitated Bacchus by spending seven days crossing through Carmania with his army in a drunken manner. {*Diod. Sic., l. 17. c. 106. s. 1-3. 8:427} {*Plutarch, Alexander, l. 1. c. 67. 7:413} {*Plutarch, Fortune of Alexander, l. 1. c. 11. 4:415} {*Curtius, l. 9. c. 10. s. 23-30. 2:457-461} {*Curtius, l. 3. c. 12. s. 18. 1:143} {*Curtius, l. 8. c. 10. s. 13-18. 2:317,319} Arrian thought this was unlikely, since neither Ptolemy, Aristobulus or any other credible writer mentioned it. {*Arrian, Anabasis, l. 6. c. 28. s. 1-4. 2:187,189}

2254. Astaspes, the governor of Carmania, was put to death and was replaced by Tlepolemus. {*Curtius, l. 9. c. 10. s. 29,30. 2:461} {*Arrian, Anabasis, l. 6. c. 27. s. 1. 2:183} {*Arrian, Indica, l. 1. c. 36. s. 8. 2:413}

2255. Cleander and Sitalces, who had killed Parmenion at Alexander's orders, were accused before Alexander for many villainies (which I mentioned before), which they had done, along with their subordinates and the army. Their act of killing Parmenion could not atone for the large number of villainies and the gross misbehaviour with which they were charged. Therefore Alexander put them in chains, to be executed when he thought fit, but he executed the six hundred private soldiers whom they had used to perform their villainies. At the same time, Alexander had Ozines and Zariaspes, whom Craterus had brought as prisoners, executed for attempting to rebel in Persia, as we noted before. {*Arrian, Anabasis, l. 6. c. 27. s. 3-5. 2:185} {*Curtius, l. 10. c. 1. s. 2-9. 2:469}

2256. Meanwhile, Nearchus had sailed along the coast of the Arabians, the Oritans, the Gedrosians and the Icthyophagians (so called because they lived only on fish), and arrived in the Persian Gulf. He came to Harmozia or Armusia (which is now called Orus or Ormusa) and there brought his ships to land. He went overland with a small retinue to Alexander, since a Greek from Alexander's army told Nearchus that Alexander was not more than a five days' journey from there. [E273] He found Alexander in a coastal town called Salmus, sitting in the open theatre, occupied with putting on a stage play there. {*Arrian, Anabasis, l. 6. c. 28. s. 5,6. 2:189,191} {*Arrian, Indica, l. 1. c. 33-36. 2:403-413} {*Diod. Sic., l. 17. c. 106. s. 4. 8:429}

2257. Alexander there sacrificed to Zeus, the Saviour, to Hercules and Apollo, the deliverers from evil, and to Poseidon, for bringing his army safely across the ocean. He conducted sports events, games of music and other gymnastic exercises, and held a pageant that was led by Nearchus. All the army sought to get flowers and garlands to bestow on him. {*Arrian, Indica, l. 1. c. 36. s. 1-3. 2:411,413}

2258. When Alexander had heard the entire story of the voyage, he sent Nearchus back to the fleet with only a small army to escort him, as the whole country through which he was to pass was considered to be friendly. Alexander wanted him to sail up as far as the mouth of the Euphrates and be ready to row up to Babylon when ordered to do so. {*Curtius, l. 10. c. 1. s. 10-16. 2:471,473} [L381]

2259. Tlepolemus had barely been made governor of Carmania, when the natives rebelled and took over the strategic and strongest places in the country. On his return journey, they also attacked Nearchus in various places, so that he was forced to flee, as often as two or three times in a day, but after much trouble, he safely reached the coast. He sacrificed to Zeus, the Saviour, and held athletic games. Then he set sail from Organa and following the coast of the Persian Gulf, finally came to the mouth of the Euphrates River. {*Arrian, Indica, l. 1. c. 36,37. 2:413,415}

2260. When Alexander received letters from Porus and Taxiles saying that Abisares was dead, he gave his kingdom to Abisares' son. He sent Eudemon or Eudamus, who was commander of the Thracians, to take over the government of the Oxydracans and Mallians and to replace Philip, who had been killed. {*Curtius, l. 10. c. 1. s. 20. 2:473} {*Arrian, Anabasis, l. 6. c. 27. s. 2. 2:183}

2261. Alexander sent Hephaestion, with the larger part of the army and with the wagons and elephants, to go from Carmania to Persia by sea. The Persian Gulf was always calm in the winter and there were abundant supplies in those parts. {*Arrian, Anabasis, l. 6. c. 28. s. 7. 2:191}

2262. Stasanor was sent back to his government. Alexander, with the choicest of his foot soldiers, the Companion Cavalry and some of his archers, marched to Pasargada in Persia. He gave money to the women as was the custom of the Persian kings, who, whenever they came into Persia, gave every woman there a piece of gold. {*Arrian, Anabasis, l. 6. c. 29. s. 1. 2:191} {*Plutarch, Alexander, l. 1. c. 69. s. 1. 7:417}

2263. As soon as he entered Persia, he was met by Orsines, or Orxines, who had been appointed governor there after the death of Phrasaortes, and had held that position since the time of Alexander's absence while in India. Under Orsines' authority, the Persians had been kept in subjection and in allegiance to Alexander until he would appoint another governor to replace the dead one. Orsines was descended from one of the seven princes of Persia and traced his lineage from Cyrus. He came and met Alexander, and presented him and all his friends with rich gifts, but failed to give anything to Bagoas, the eunuch, and Alexander's other homosexual lovers, saying it was not the Persian custom to show any respect to men who allowed themselves to be sexually used as women. This proved, later, to be the reason for his death. {*Curtius, l. 10. c. 1. s. 22-26. 2:475} {*Curtius, l. 4. c. 12. s. 8. 1:273} {*Arrian, Anabasis, l. 6. c. 29. s. 1,2. 2:191}

2264. While he was at Pasargada, Atropates, the governor of Media, arrived, bringing with him the prisoner Baryaxes, a Median who had worn his turban upright and had called himself king of the Medes and Persians. For this reason he brought him as a prisoner to the king, along with all those who had been part of the conspiracy, and Alexander had them all executed immediately. {*Arrian, Anabasis, l. 6. c. 29. s. 3. 2:191,193}

2265. Alexander was offended most of all at the vandalism of Cyrus' monument, which he found to be completely broken down and spoiled. All the precious things which he had previously seen there, except for a lector and a golden coffin in which his body had been placed, had been stolen. The coffin had been broken and the lid of the coffin taken off by those sacrilegious thieves, and the body itself tumbled from it. They had also tried to hew in pieces and smash the coffin, so that they could carry it away more easily in pieces, but as this had proved impossible for them, they had left it behind. Alexander ordered Aristobulus to rebuild the sepulchre. The parts of Cyrus' body which remained were to be placed into the coffin again, and a new cover made for it. He was to restore everything as it had been before, and then he was to seal the door which led into the mausoleum where the body lay, with lime and stone and place the impression of Alexander's seal upon it. {*Strabo, l. 15. c. 3. s. 7,8. 7:165-169} {*Arrian, Anabasis, l. 6. c. 29. s. 4-11. 2:193-197} {*Curtius, l. 10. c. 1. s. 30-35. 2:477} [E274] [L382]

2266. After this, Alexander commanded that the magi who guarded the sepulchre be racked, to make them confess who had committed this sacrilege. When they told him nothing, they were let go. Plutarch, however, said that Polymachus, a noble from Pella, was put to death by Alexander for pillaging the sepulchre. {*Plutarch, Alexander, l. 1. c. 69. s. 1,2. 7:417}

2267. From Pasargada, Alexander marched to Persepolis, the royal seat of the kings of Persia. On his previous visit he had set it on fire and burned it to the very ground. However, on his return there, he regretted having done this. Orsines, their governor, was falsely accused of many misdeeds. He was said to have spoiled and robbed the king's houses and the sepulchres of the dead, and executed many of the Persian nobility. In particular, Bagoas, the eunuch, put it into the king's head that perhaps it had also been Orsines who had robbed the sepulchre of Cyrus, for he said that he had heard Darius say there were three thousand talents stored there. Bagoas persisted so far with Alexander that he immediately caused the noblest person of all the Persian nation, and Alexander's most affectionate servant, to be crucified without delay. Hence, Bagoas had revenge against Orsines because he disapproved of Bagoas' homosexual lifestyle. Not content, Bagoas laid his hand on Orsines as he was being led away to be executed. Orsines, with a glance at him, said: {*Arrian, Anabasis, l. 6. c. 30. s. 1,2. 2:197} {*Curtius, l. 10. c. 1. s. 30-38. 2:477,479}

"I have heard that women once reigned in Asia; this, however, is something new, for a eunuch to reign!"

2268. At the same time, Phradates, who had formerly been governor of the Hyrcanians, Mardians and Tapurians, was suspected of making himself a king and was executed. {*Curtius, l. 10. c. 1. s. 39. 2:479} {*Curtius, l. 8. c. 3. s. 17. 2:263}

2269. Alexander made Peucestes the governor of Persia. He had proven his worth many times over, especially in that danger which had befallen Alexander among the Mallians. Of all the Macedonians, only Peucestes adopted the Median clothes and started to learn the Persian language and set out to manage everything dressed in Persian attire. Alexander commended him highly for this, and the Persians were pleased to see him use the Persian rather than the Macedonian manner of dress. {*Arrian, Anabasis, l. 6. c. 30. s. 2,3. 2:197,199}

2270. A new fancy now struck Alexander. He wanted to go down the Euphrates and Tigris Rivers to see the Persian Gulf and see how those rivers entered into the ocean. This he had done before at the mouth of the Indus River. He also planned to sail around the coast, first of Arabia and then of all Africa, intending to return into the Mediterranean Sea and to Macedonia by the way of Pillars of Hercules. {*Arrian, Anabasis, l. 7. c. 1. s. 1-3. 2:203} Since he was in this frame of mind, he ordered the governors of Mesopotamia to cut timber in Mount Libanus (Lebanon) and to carry it to Thapsacus, a city in Syria. They were to make keels on which to construct large ships. These were not all of seven banks of oars high, as Curtius said, but some were of one size and some of another, as we shall see shortly from Aristobulus. Seven hundred ships were to be constructed, and all were to be brought overland to Babylon, while the kings of Cyprus were ordered to provide brass, equipment and sails for this fleet. {*Curtius, l. 10. c. 1. s. 17-19. 2:473}

2271. Nearchus and Onesicritus arrived with the fleet at the mouth of the Euphrates River and anchored at Diridotis, the main market town of the whole province of Babylon, where the merchants of Arabia sold their frankincense and spices. When they heard that Alexander wanted to go to Susa, they went back and over to the mouth of the Pasitigris River. They rowed up that river and came to a country that was well inhabited and with plentiful provisions. When they had rowed about nineteen miles, they came to a harbour, where they stayed and waited for the return of those men whom Nearchus had sent to find out where Alexander was. While he was waiting, Nearchus sacrificed there to the gods, who had delivered him, and held games. All the sailors were involved in this pastime and merriment. {*Arrian, Indica, l. 1. c. 41,42. 2:425-429}

2272. Calanus was an Indian and belonged to the gymnosophists, or the sect of philosophers who went naked. In all his seventy-three years, he had never felt an ache in his bones or other sickness in his body. It so happened that he now became ill with his first sickness, at Pasargada. He began to feel sick and grew weaker every day. [L383] When he came to the borders of Susa (for it was there that this happened, according to Diodorus, and not in a suburb of the city of Babylon, as Aelian claimed), he asked Alexander if he would make a large pile of wood. When he had climbed on top of it, he wanted some of his servants to set it on fire. At first, Alexander endeavoured to dissuade him from his plan, but he could not. Calanus told him he would simply die some other way. Alexander ordered a pile of wood to be arranged as Calanus desired and had Ptolemy, the son of Lagus, take care of this. {*Aelian, Historical Miscellany, l. 5. c. 6. 1:217,219} {*Diod. Sic., l. 17. c. 107. 8:431,433} {*Strabo, l. 15. c. 1. s. 4. 7:7} {*Strabo, l. 15. c. 1. s. 64. 7:109-113} {*Strabo, l. 15. c. 1. s. 68. 7:119-121} {*Arrian, Anabasis, l. 7. c. 3. s. 1-6. 2:207-211} As Calanus was going to the pile of wood, he greeted all the rest of his friends and kissed their hands and bade them farewell, but he would not kiss Alexander's hand, for he said that he would meet with him at Babylon and greet him there, by which he meant that Alexander would die at Babylon, and so he predicted his death there. {*Plutarch, Alexander, l. 1. c. 69. s. 3,4. 7:419,421} {*Arrian, Anabasis, l. 7. c. 18. s. 6. 2:267} {*Cicero, De Divinatione, l. 1. c. 23. 20:275,277} {*Valerius Maximus, l. 1. c. 8. ext. 10. 1:121} [E275]

2273. Nearchus stated that as soon as the fire was started, Alexander had the trumpets sound. All the army who were there gave a shout, as if ready to join in a battle, while the elephants, at the same time, made a noise like they were in the habit of doing when they entered into a battle. It was as if all had planned to honour the funeral of Calanus. {*Arrian, Anabasis, l. 7. c. 3. s. 6. 2:211}

2274. Chares of Mitylene added that Alexander, to honour Calanus' funeral, proclaimed a prize for the musicians and wrestlers. To please the Indian nation, he held a drinking match, which was a custom of theirs, awarding a crown worth one talent to the one who could drink the most, thirty minas for the second prize and ten minas for the third prize. Alexander held a feast for his friends and captains, at which Promachus drank the most. He drank about three gallons and was awarded first prize, but he died three days later. Thirty-five of the rest were chilled by the event and died immediately, while six others died shortly thereafter in their tents. {*Plutarch, Alexander, l. 1. c. 70. s. 1. 7:419} {*Aelian, Historical Miscellany, l. 2. c. 41. 1:113} {*Athenaeus, l. 10. (437ab) 4:479}

## 3679c AM, 4389 JP, 325 BC

2275. Nearchus and Onesicritus continued their course up the Pasitigris River with their naval forces and came to a recently built bridge over which Alexander was to pass with his army. They sailed into the land of Susia and laid anchor. {*Arrian, Indica, l. 1. c. 42. 2:427,429} Pliny said they found him at Susa, observing a holiday. This was seven months after Alexander had left them at Patala, and in the third month after they had set sail from there. But it was really in the sixth month, since we have already shown that they left Patala in the next month after he had left them behind at the city of Patala. {*Pliny, l. 6. c. 26. (100) 2:415}

2276. When the naval and land forces came together, Alexander again offered sacrifices for both his navy's and army's preservation, holding athletic games as a part of the proceedings. Wherever Nearchus went throughout the camp, every man scattered flowers and placed garlands on him. {*Arrian, Indica, l. 1. c. 42. 2:429}

2277. After Alexander had sent Atropates away to his province, he marched to Susa. Abulites, who had made no preparation at all for his entertainment, only presented him with three thousand talents of silver, which Alexander ordered him to lay before his horses. When they would not do it, Alexander asked for what purpose this money was, then. Plutarch said that Alexander laid Abulites in irons and ran his son Oxathres, or Oxyartes, through with a javelin. Arrian said that he put both the father and the son to death for their bad conduct in the government at Susa. {*Arrian, Anabasis, l. 7. c. 4. s. 1. 2:211} {*Plutarch, Alexander, l. 1. c. 68. s. 4. 7:415,417}

2278. Many of the people of the countries which he had conquered came in and complained about their governors. [L384] These governors had never even dreamed that Alexander would ever return alive from India, and so they had committed many and monstrous outrages on the temples of their gods, the sepulchres of the dead and on the persons and property of their subjects. Alexander ordered all of those governors to be executed in full view of those who had come to complain against them, without any regard for nobility, favour or service they had done. He executed Cleander and Sitalces, whom he had condemned while he was still in Carmania, because they were as guilty as the rest. Heracon, who up to this time had escaped scot-free, but was now being accused by the men of Susa of robbing and ransacking their temple, was convicted and executed. Alexander was ready to listen to even the slightest accusation about trivial matters, and to punish it with death and torment. He did this even for small offences, because he thought that those who acted improperly in small matters, intended greater evils in their mind. {Lu 16:10} {*Arrian, Anabasis, l. 7. c. 4. s. 1-3. 2:211,213}

2279. When the fame of Alexander's severity against his officials spread, many feared what would become

of them, knowing how they had behaved. Some got all the money they could and fled to parts unknown, while others, who commanded mercenary troops, openly revolted from Alexander. This prompted Alexander to send letters to all the governors of the countries throughout all Asia, ordering them to disband and send away all the mercenary troops. {*Diod. Sic., l. 17. c. 108. s. 6-8. 8:437}

2280. No sooner had the mercenary troops been discharged, than they wandered all over Asia, without any work. They lived from the spoil of the country, until at length they all came together in one body at Taenarum in Laconia. Likewise, all the remaining commanders and governors of the Persians gathered together what men and money they could and came to Taenarum, where they all combined their forces. {*Diod. Sic., l. 17. c. 108. s. 6-8. 8:437,439} {*Diod. Sic., l. 18. c. 21. s. 1. 9:73}

2281. Alexander married Statira, the eldest daughter of Darius, and according to Aristobulus, he married Parysaris, the youngest daughter of Ochus, as well. He gave Drypates, the youngest daughter of Darius and his own wife's sister, in marriage to Hephaestion. [E276] To Craterus he gave Amestrine, the daughter of Oxyatres, the brother of Darius. Perdiccas married the daughter of Atropates, the governor of Media. Nearchus married the daughter of Spitamenes, the Bactrian. To Ptolemy, the son of Lagus and the captain of his bodyguard, and to Eumenes, he gave the two daughters of Artabazus and sisters of Barsine, by whom, though not in lawful wedlock, Alexander had a son called Hercules. Ptolemy's wife was called Artacama, or Apama, while Eumenes married Artonis. In Arrian the name *Barsine* was written for *Statira*. However, Plutarch called Eumenes' wife *Barsine* instead of *Artonis*. {*Plutarch, Eumenes, l. 1. c. 1. s. 1. 8:81} {*Arrian, Anabasis, l. 7. c. 4. s. 4-8. 2:213,215}

2282. Alexander gave wives from the most illustrious families among the Medes and Persians to all the rest of his friends. The number, according to Arrian, was eighty or ninety according to Aelian, or ninety-two, according to Chares, or a hundred, according to Plutarch. {*Plutarch, Fortune of Alexander, l. 1. c. 7. 4:401} These marriages of Alexander and his friends were all made and solemnised at the same time, and Alexander bestowed a dowry on each one of them. For five days they celebrated these marriages with pomp, magnificent feasts and parties, according to Aelian. He gave a golden vial to each of the nine thousand guests, with which to make the sacrifice of a drink offering. [L385] He gave wedding gifts to each one of the rest of the ten thousand Macedonians who had previously married wives from Asia. {*Arrian, Anabasis, l. 7. c. 4. s. 4-8. 2:213,215} {*Aelian, Historical Miscellany, l. 8.

c. 7. 1:267} {*Athenaeus, l. 12. (538c) 5:433} {*Plutarch, Alexander, l. 1. c. 70. s. 2. 7:419}

2283. Moreover, he considered it appropriate at this time to pay every one of his soldiers' debts from his own funds. He ordered that each one should submit a bill for what he owed, and they would be given the money to pay their debt. At first very few handed in their bills, because they feared that this was merely a scheme of Alexander's to find out who among them could not live on their pay, because of their riotous living. Among those who submitted a bill was Antigenes, who had only one eye since he had lost the other under Philip at the siege of Perinthus by an arrow shot from the wall. He pretended to be more in debt than he actually was, and brought a man to the pay master who affirmed that he had lent Antigenes so much money, whereupon Antigenes received the money he had asked for. Alexander, who was later informed of this abuse, was very angry and removed him from his office, forbidding him ever to come within his court again. Antigenes took this ignominy to heart and contemplated committing suicide. When Alexander heard of this, he forgave him and allowed him to enjoy his money.

2284. When Alexander discovered that many who were truly in debt would not turn in their names to be given money to pay their debts, he publicly denounced them for being so distrustful of him. He said that a king should only be honest with his subjects just as the subjects should believe the king was totally honest and fair to them. Then he had tables with money on them set out in various places of the camp, and whoever brought in his bill of what he owed received his money immediately, without so much as being asked what his name was. Then they began to believe that Alexander was a man of his word.

2285. The money he distributed among his soldiers, according to Justin and Arrian, amounted to about twenty thousand talents. It is likely that Diodorus was more accurate when he said it was less than ten thousand talents. Curtius and Plutarch said that of the ten thousand talents brought, there were only a hundred and thirty left after all the debts had been paid. {*Plutarch, Alexander, l. 1. c. 70. s. 2-4. 7:421} {*Arrian, Anabasis, l. 7. c. 5. s. 1-4. 2:215,217} {*Diod. Sic., l. 17. c. 109. s. 1. 8:439} Curtius said: {*Curtius, l. 10. c. 2. s. 9-11. 2:485,487}

> "So that army, the conqueror of so many of the richest countries, carried off from Asia more victory than booty."

2286. Alexander at this time gave other gifts to various men in the army, either according to the honour that rank conferred or to conspicuous courage displayed in dangers. To those who had excelled in bravery he gave, in addition, crowns of gold to wear. The first one was given to Peucestes, who had protected him with his shield against the Mallians. The next he gave to Leonnatus, who on that same occasion had also fought most courageously in his defence, and had at numerous times behaved most bravely in the country of the Oritans. The third he gave to Nearchus, who had brought his navy and army safely from India over the ocean on ships. The fourth crown was given to Onesicritus, the pilot of the king's ships, and Hephaestion and the other captains of his bodyguard also received crowns. {*Arrian, Anabasis, l. 7. c. 5. s. 4-6. 2:217}

2287. Meanwhile, the governors of various cities he had built and of various provinces he had subdued brought thirty thousand troops to him at Susa from Persia and other countries. {See note on 3676c AM. <<2040>>} These were all good, strong young men, who were selected by the king's command and trained in the Macedonian military manner. [E277] They were all gloriously armed and camped before the walls of Susa. When they had proven their readiness and skill in military discipline before Alexander, he richly rewarded them and called them the Epigoni (Successors), that is members of a later troop, replacing those who had gone before them in feats of chivalry and conquering the world. {*Arrian, Anabasis, l. 7. c. 6. s. 1. 2:217} [L386]

## 3679d AM, 4389 JP, 325 BC

2288. Alexander had turned over most of his army to Hephaestion, to be led to the coast of the Persian Gulf. He had ordered his navy to come to the country of Susa, and he himself sailed there with his silver targeteers, his phalanx, or main squadron, and part of his Companion Cavalry. They sailed down the Eulaeus River into the Persian Gulf. Before he arrived there, he abandoned many of his ships, which were leaking or damaged. With some of the remainder, he sailed from the mouth of that river by sea to the Tigris River. The rest he sent up the channel connecting the Tigris with the Eulaeus River, and so they all reached the Tigris River. {*Arrian, Anabasis, l. 7. c. 7. s. 1,2. 2:221,223}

2289. Alexander sailed along the shore of the Persian Gulf which lay between the mouth of the Eulaeus and Tigris Rivers, and came to his camp. Hephaestion was waiting with the army for his arrival. Alexander returned again to the city of Opis on the bank of the Tigris River, and as he went along, he had all the dams, locks and sluices removed which the Persians had constructed on that river to hinder enemy access by sea to Babylon, saying they were devices of little worth. {*Arrian, Anabasis, l. 7. c. 7. s. 3-7. 2:223,225} {*Strabo, l. 16. c. 1. s. 9. 7:205}

*2290.* As soon as he came to Opis, he called all his army together and disclosed his plans to them. He wanted to discharge all those who through age or for any other reason, found themselves unfit for military service. These would be free to return home, while he promised to make conditions for those who stayed extremely good and to bestow such gifts upon them as would make the eyes of those who were idle at home, ache. This would encourage the rest of the Macedonians to come and share with them in their fortunes.

*2291.* His intention in all this was to honour the Macedonians, but they took it to mean that he was ashamed of them and counted them no better for his wars than a company of useless men. They seemed anxious to recall every other grievance and occasion for discontent which he had caused them. He was wearing a Median robe, and all those marriages he had made had all been solemnised after the Persian manner. Peucestes, his governor of Persia, had turned completely Persian, both in clothing and language, and Alexander delighted too much in these new customs and foreign fashions. The Bactrians, Sogdians, Arachosians, Zarangians, Arians, Parthians and Persian cavalry, who were called Euaca, were mixed with and counted among the Companion Cavalry. A fifth brigade of cavalry had been set up, which was not made up entirely of foreigners, but an increasing number of his cavalry were from foreign countries, nevertheless. Cophes, the son of Artabazus, Hydarves and Artiboles, the two sons of Mazaeus, Itanes, the son of Oxyartes and brother to Roxane, Alexander's wife, Aegobares and his brother Mithrobaeus were in this new regiment, while Hydaspes, a Bactrian, was the commander over that regiment. Instead of the Macedonian spear, they used a javelin, after the custom of the foreign countries. He had created a new company of young foreigners whom he called *Epigoni* and had armed them after the Macedonian manner. Finally, he despised and scorned the Macedonian discipline and customs in all things, and even the Macedonians themselves. Therefore the army all cried out, desiring to be discharged and no longer wishing to serve in the wars. They told him that he and his father Ammon could go and fight from now on if they wanted to, since he had grown weary of his own soldiers and no longer cared for those who had previously fought for him.

*2292.* In this revolt, Alexander, enraged as he was, leaped down from the place where he had stood speaking to them. With whatever captains he had around him, he flew in among them and took thirteen of the chief rebels who had stirred up this sedition among the rest. *[L387]* He handed them over to the sergeants, to be bound hand and foot and thrown into the Tigris River. So great was either the dread of Alexander upon them, or Alexander's own resolution in executing them according to the marshal discipline, that they took their death with resignation. Then Alexander went to his lodging, accompanied only by his friends and the captains of his bodyguard. He neither ate nor slept, nor allowed any man to come into his presence, throughout that day and the next one.

*2293.* On the third day, he ordered the Macedonians to stay in their tents and called his foreign soldiers together. *[E278]* When they came, he spoke to them through an interpreter and ordered their perpetual loyalty to himself and to their former kings. Recalling all the many favours and honours which he had conferred upon them, he reminded them that he had never treated them as conquered persons, but as fellow soldiers and partners in all his conquests and he had mixed the conquered with the conquerors through intermarriage. He said:

> "Therefore, count not yourselves as made, but born my soldiers. The kingdoms of Asia and Europe have all become one. What was novelty before, is now grown natural by long use and custom, and you are no less my countrymen than you are my soldiers."

*2294.* After this he chose a thousand tall young men from among them and appointed them as his personal bodyguards. He gave the chief commands of the army to the Persians, also calling these his relatives and friends, and called the various troops and companies by Macedonian names. He allowed only them the privilege to be admitted to kiss his hand. {*Polyaenus, Strategmata, l. 4. n. 7. Alexander*}

*2295.* The Macedonians saw the king emerge guarded only by Persians, and noted that all the sergeants and other attendants were Persians. Only Persians were promoted to all the places of dignity and honour, while the Macedonians were set aside with scorn and infamy, and so their courage failed and they conferred some time among themselves. Then, running all together to the king's lodging, they threw off all their clothes right down to their waistcoats. Throwing down their arms at the court gates, they stood outside, begging to be admitted. They offered to turn over every instigator of that rebellion and asked the king to be satisfied with their deaths rather than their disgrace. Although Alexander was no longer angry, he would not admit them. They continued their crying and howling all the more and would not go away, but remained there two whole days and nights. They called on him by the name of lord and master, and vowed not to leave his gate until he would show them mercy. On the third day, he came out to them and saw their humiliation and dejection before him, together with their genuine sorrow. He heard their pitiful complaint and the lamentation they were making, and moved with compassion for them, he wept a long time over them. He stood for some time as if he would speak to them, but could not, and they continued before him all the while on their knees.

2296. Callines, a man venerable on account of his age and held in great esteem in the regiment of the Companion Cavalry, spoke to him:

> "This, oh king, is what grieves your Macedonians, that now you have made some of the Persians your cousins and have received these to kiss your hand and have deprived your Macedonians of this honour."

2297. He would have proceeded, but Alexander interrupted him, saying:

> "I now make you all my cousins, and from henceforth will call you by that name."

2298. When he had said this, Callines stepped forward and went up to kiss his hand, and as many others as wanted to, did likewise. Every man took up his arms again and they all returned with joy and triumph into the camp.

2299. Then Alexander sacrificed to the gods as he was accustomed to do. He made a general feast for all the army, at which he sat down first, then his Macedonians were seated, and then the Persians. After them, the rest were seated according to their various ranks and stations in the army. Then Alexander took from the bowl and drank, and so it went round among the Macedonians. [L388] The Greek prophets and Persian priests poured forth their prayers, and among all the favours they asked for him from their gods, was that they grant a concord and unity of empire between the Macedonian and Persian kingdoms. It is said that there were nine thousand guests who sat at this feast, and that they all pledged this concord and sang the same Paeana, or song of joy and gladness to Apollo, which they used to sing when they returned to their camp from a victory. {*Arrian, Anabasis, l. 7. c. 8-11. 2:225-241} {*Plutarch, Alexander, l. 1. c. 71. 7:421,423} {*Curtius, l. 10. c. 2,3. 2:487-501}

2300. Alexander crossed over the Tigris River and camped in a country called Cares. Crossing the region called Sittacene in a four day march, he came to Sambana, where he camped seven days and then arrived at Celones after a further three day journey. Xerxes had earlier formed a colony there with the people whom he had brought from Boeotia. Then, turning aside from the route to Babylon, he went to see the country of Bagisthane, which abounded with fruit and every other commodity that was good for one's health and pleasure. {*Diod. Sic., l. 17. c. 110. s. 4,5. 8:441,445}

2301. Meanwhile, Harpalus, a Macedonian who was the chief baron and treasurer of all the king's money in Babylon, and of the revenues of that whole province, was well aware of his wastefulness and bad conduct in that office. He also knew what Alexander had done to many other governors when complaints had been made about them by their subjects. Taking five thousand talents of silver and six thousand mercenaries, he fled from Asia and came with them to Taenarum in Laconia, where he left them. Others, who had not been able to stay in Asia, had already exiled themselves there. {See note on 3679b AM. <<2280>>} [E279] He went to Athens in a humble manner, but when Antipater and Olympias wished to be rid of him, he handled people of Athens by bribing Demosthenes and other orators there, and so was able to escape and return safely to his company at Taenarum. {*Diod. Sic., l. 17. c. 108. s. 6-8. 8:437,439} {*Diod. Sic., l. 18. c. 21. s. 1. 9:73} {*Pausanias, Attica, l. 1. c. 35. s. 5. 1:199,201} {*Plutarch, Demosthenes, l. 1. c. 25. 7:61,63} {*Plutarch, Phocion, l. 1. c. 21,22. 8:191-195} In Arrian there is a blank left where Harpalus' flight from Babylon should have been recorded, together with the subsequent journey of Alexander, as appeared in Photius. {Photius, Bibliotheca, c. 91.} {*Arrian, Anabasis, l. 7. c. 12. s. 7. 2:245} There was an action brought against Harpalus for bribes he had received, according to Dionysius Halicarnassus, as recorded at the end of his letter to Ammaeus concerning Demosthenes, when Anticles was archon at Athens. This was, as I said before, in this fourth year of the 113th Olympiad, according to his account. {*Dionysius Halicarnassus, Ammaeus, l. 1. (12) 2:345}

2302. Hephaestion and Eumenes had an argument about a certain gift and exchanged many harsh words. Alexander settled their differences and made them friends again, even though Hephaestion was unwilling at first and Alexander had to threaten him. Eumenes, however, was content with the settlement. {*Arrian, Anabasis, l. 7. c. 13. s. 1. 2:245} {*Plutarch, Eumenes, l. 1. c. 2. s. 4,5. 8:83}

## 3680a AM, 4389 JP, 325 BC

2303. From there, Alexander went into a country where large herds of horses belonging to the Persian kings grazed. In this place, called the Nesean country, a hundred and fifty or sixty thousand of the king's horses had been kept in the past. When Alexander came there, he found about fifty thousand horses, {*Arrian, Anabasis, l. 7. c. 13. s. 1. 2:245} {*Strabo, l. 11. c. 13. s. 7. 5:311} while Diodorus stated there were about sixty thousand horses. Most of the horses had been stolen. {*Diod. Sic., l. 17. c. 110. s. 6. 8:443}

*2304.* When Alexander had camped there thirty days, he marched on again and seven days later came to Ecbatana, the chief city of all Media, which had a circumference of over thirty-one miles. After he transacted the business that was urgent, he was once more occupied with theatres and festivals, since three thousand artists had come to him from Greece. {*Diod. Sic., l. 17. c. 110. s. 6. 8:443} {*Arrian, Anabasis, l. 7. c. 13. s. 2,3. 2:249} {*Plutarch, Alexander, l. 1. c. 72. s. 1. 7:425}*

*2305.* Apollodorus of Amphipolis, one of Alexander's Companion Cavalry officers, was commander of the force Alexander left behind with Mazaeus the governor of Babylon. *[L389]* When Apollodorus heard what had happened to other governors Alexander had placed over his kingdom, he was afraid, just as his friend Harpalus had been before him. Apollodorus had a brother called Pythagoras, who was a soothsayer. When he consulted him by letters to find out what was likely to happen to him, Pythagoras wrote back wanting to know whom it was he feared, since he wanted his fortune told. He replied that it was for fear of Alexander and Hephaestion, whereupon Pythagoras looked into the entrails of a beast for Hephaestion. When he found that its liver had no lobes, he wrote a reply and sent it from Babylon to his brother in Ecbatana, telling him not to fear Hephaestion for he would die soon. Aristobulus stated that this letter was written the very day before Hephaestion died. {*Arrian, Anabasis, l. 7. c. 18. s. 1-3. 2:263,265} {*Appian, Civil Wars, l. 2. c. 21. (152) 3:511}*

*2306.* Hephaestion loved wine too much and became sick because of this. He was a young soldier who would not keep any diet he was told to follow. While his physician Glaucias was away for a time, he ate dinner just as he did every other time. He had a roasted guinea fowl and took a large draught of chilled wine after it, causing him to become sick and to die seven days later.

*2307.* On the same day, gymnastic games were being performed before Alexander by the pages of the court. When he was told of Hephaestion's illness, he suddenly arose from the games and went to see Hephaestion. When he got there, he found him dead. As a result, he did not eat for three days nor take care of himself, but lay all the while either sullenly silent, or impatiently lamenting the loss of his friend Hephaestion. Later, he changed his attire and shaved himself, ordering that all the soldiers and even the horses and mules be totally shorn. He had the pinnacles taken from the walls in Ecbatana and all other cities and towns around there, because he wanted them to look poorly so they would appear to lament and bewail his death. He crucified Hephaestion's poor physician, because he had been unable to help him, as well as ordering that no sound of pipe or flute be heard in all the camp and a general mourning be observed for Hephaestion in all the provinces. {*Arrian, Anabasis, l. 7. c. 14. s. 1-7. 2:249-253} {*Diod. Sic., l. 17. c. 110. s. 7,8. 8:445} {*Plutarch, Alexander, l. 1. c. 72. s. 1.3. 7:425} {*Plutarch, Pelopidas, l. 1. c. 34. s. 2,3. 5:429} {Epictetus, l. 2. c. 22.} {*Aelian, Historical Miscellany, l. 7. c. 8. 1:251}*

*2308.* Alexander gave Hephaestion's body to Perdiccas to be carried to Babylon. *[E280]* He intended to give him a most magnificent funeral and often spoke with the principal architects around him about making a most splendid monument for him. He spoke most with Stasicrates, who knew of innovations used in designing and erecting vast buildings. {*Plutarch, Alexander, l. 1. c. 72. s. 3. 7:425}*

*2309.* Eumenes was afraid that Alexander might think that he was glad about Hephaestion's death, so he encouraged Alexander all the more in this project and suggested to him new ways of honouring Hephaestion. He dedicated himself and his arms to Hephaestion. Various others of Alexander's friends followed Eumenes' example and did likewise. {*Plutarch, Eumenes, l. 1. c. 2. s. 4,5. 8:83} {*Arrian, Anabasis, l. 7. c. 14. s. 9. 2:253}*

*2310.* Moreover, since Hephaestion had been the colonel of the regiment of Alexander's Companion Cavalry, Alexander did not replace him, lest the name of Hephaestion should be forgotten among them. He called that regiment Hephaestion's regiment, just as he named the standard after him which he presented to them to go before them whenever they went into battle. {*Arrian, Anabasis, l. 7. c. 14. s. 10. 2:253}*

## 3680b AM, 4390 JP, 324 BC

*2311.* Finally, to lift his spirits, Alexander started a needless war. He split his army with Ptolemy and went off to hunt men, determining to clear the country as he would clear a forest of wild beasts. He attacked the Cossaeans, a people who bordered on the Uxians and lived in the mountainous parts of Media. *[L390]* The Persian kings had never managed to bring them under their subjection. Nor, in all these wars, had these people ever become discouraged or thought that the Macedonians were such great warriors that they needed to be afraid of them. First, he took the passes leading through the mountains into their country and wasted their borders. Then, he went farther on and routed them in various conflicts. He destroyed them mercilessly wherever he went and called that Hephaestion's funeral feast. According to Arrian, Nearchus also stated that Alexander attacked these Cossaeans in the depths of winter, when they little dreamed of any enemy coming upon them. {*Arrian, Anabasis, l. 7. c. 15. s. 1-3. 2:255} {*Arrian, Indica, l. 1. c. 40. s. 1-11. 2:423,425} {*Strabo, l. 11. c. 13. s. 6. 5:307,309} {Polyaenus, Strategmata, l. 4. n. 31. in Alexander}*

2312. The Cossaeans saw that they were being badly defeated, and were grieved to see what large numbers of them were being taken prisoner. They were forced to redeem the lives of their fellows with their own slavery, and surrendered entirely to Alexander's will and pleasure. He granted them peace on the condition that they would always obey the king, and do whatever he commanded. So Alexander returned with his army after he had subdued all that country in the space of forty days. He built various cities in the most difficult passes of the country. {*Diod. Sic., l. 17. c. 111. s. 4-6. 8:447,449} {*Arrian, Anabasis, l. 7. c. 15. s. 1-3. 2:255}

2313. Alexander sent Heraclides into Hyrcania with certain shipwrights, to cut timber there for building ships. These were all to be *men of war*, some with decks, some without, after the Greek design. He had a great desire to see the Caspian Sea and to establish to whom it belonged. {*Arrian, Anabasis, l. 7. c. 16. s. 1-4. 2:257,259}

## 3680c AM, 4390 JP, 324 BC

2314. When he had crossed with his army over the Tigris River, he marched straight toward Babylon, making many camps along the way and resting his army in various places. Whenever he was on the move, he made easy marches. When he was about forty miles from Babylon, he was met by the Chaldean priests and prophets, who had been sent to him by one of their own company, called Bellephantes. They advised him that under no circumstances should he go to Babylon, for if he did, he would die there. {*Diod. Sic., l. 17. c. 112. s. 1-3. 8:449}

2315. When Alexander was told by Nearchus (for Bellephantes was not bold enough to speak directly with Alexander) what the Chaldean's message was, he sent many of his friends to Babylon, but he turned aside from Babylon and would not enter it. He camped about twenty-five miles from it at a place called Bursia. This is possibly the same place which Ptolemy called Bersita, a city long since destroyed. {*Diod. Sic., l. 17. c. 112. s. 4. 8:451}

2316. At that place, Anaxarchus and other Greeks persuaded him not to regard these predictions of the priests and magicians, but rather to reject and despise them as vain and false, whereupon he quoted that iambic verse of Euripides:

"Who best can guess, he the best prophet is."

2317. Then the Chaldeans requested that if he must enter the city, he should at least not enter it with his face toward the west, but should rather take the trouble to go around it and enter it looking toward the east. Aristobulus stated that he heeded this request. On the first day he marched as far as the Euphrates River. On the next day, he had the river on his right hand and marched south along its bank. He wanted to march along that side of the city which faced the west so that he might come in facing the east. [E281] When he found that way to be marshy and hard for his army to pass over, he neglected that express point of their counsel also, and entered Babylon with his face toward the west. {*Seneca the Elder, Suasoriae, l. 4. 2:545-551} {*Appian, Civil Wars, l. 2. c. 21. (152) 3:511} {*Arrian, Anabasis, l. 7. c. 16-19. 2:259-269} [L391]

2318. When Alexander arrived at the walls of the city, he looked and he noticed a flock of crows, fighting and killing each other. As some fell down dead close to him, Apollodorus told him that he had a brother in the city called Pythagoras. He was skilled in the art of soothsaying by looking into the entrails of beasts offered for sacrifice, and had already consulted the gods that way concerning Alexander. Whereupon Alexander immediately sent for him and asked him what he had found out concerning him. He told Alexander that he had found the liver of the beast to be without any lobes, and when Alexander asked what that meant, Pythagoras replied that some great evil was hanging over his head. (Appian wrote that he said to Alexander that he would die shortly.) Alexander was not offended by him. In fact, from that time on, Alexander consulted him all the more because of his candour in dealing with him. This much Aristobulus related as having learned directly from Pythagoras. {*Arrian, Anabasis, l. 7. c. 18. s. 3-6. 2:265,267} {*Plutarch, Alexander, l. 1. c. 73. s. 1,2. 7:427}

2319. The Babylonians entertained his army in a very courteous manner, as they had done the last time he had been there. They all indulged in ease and luxury, and there was no lack of anything that their hearts desired. {*Diod. Sic., l. 17. c. 112. s. 6. 8:451}

2320. While Alexander resided at Babylon, envoys came to him from all the different regions and countries of the world. For beside those who came out of Asia representing cities, princes and countries there, many others came from countries in Europe and Africa. From Africa came the Ethiopians who lived near the temple of Ammon, as well as envoys from the Carthaginians and other Punic countries bordering all along the Mediterannean coast of Africa from as far west as the Pillars of Hercules and the western sea. Envoys also came from Europe, from various cities of Greece and Macedonia, and from the Thracians, Illyrians and Scythians. The Bruttians, Lucanians and Etruscans came from Italy along with representatives from the islands of Sicily and Sardinia. They also came from Spain and Gaul, names and countries which the Macedonians had never even heard of before. {*Arrian, Anabasis, l. 7. c. 15. s. 4-6. 2:255,257} {*Diod. Sic., l. 17. c. 113. s. 1,2. 8:453}

*2321.* Alexander had them all placed on a list and determined whom he would see first in order, in the process of hearing them all. He decided he would see those first who had come about religious matters, followed by those who had brought him presents. Next, he would see those who had come about wars they were having with neighbouring countries, after which he would hear those who had come about private and particular interests. Lastly, he intended to see those who had come to show why they had not restored to their homes and estates again any Greeks who had been banished by them from their cities and countries. Athenaeus cited Ephippius Olynthius, who stated that in order to hear them, he had a throne of gold set up there in the garden, and seats of silver for his friends, with whom he then took his place to hear these envoys. His main purpose was to hear them out, and then to answer them in such a way that they would be content and he could send each man away satisfied and well-pleased. {*Diod. Sic., l. 17. c. 113. s. 3,4. 8:453,455} {*Athenaeus, l. 12. (537d) 5:429}

*2322.* The first ones to see him were those who had come from the city of Elis. After that, he saw those who had come from the temple and city of Ammon, from Delphi, from Corinth, Epidaurus and other places, and heard each of them in order of the dignity and fame of their various temples, rather than of the cities from which they came. {*Diod. Sic., l. 17. c. 113. s. 4. 8:455}

*2323.* When he had heard the envoys from Epidaurus and granted their request, he sent a present and oblation with them to their god Aesculapius, adding these words:

> "Esculapius had dealt unfavourably with him, in recently taking away from him a friend whom he loved as dearly as his own life."

*2324.* He took all the statues of illustrious persons, images of the gods or any other consecrated thing that Xerxes had previously taken from Greece and which he had set up or otherwise placed in Babylon, Susa, Pasargada and elsewhere in all Asia. Alexander ordered the envoys of Greece to take these statues back home again with them. Among all those sent back, he had the brass statues of Harmodius and Aristogiton returned to Athens, with the image of Celcaen Artemis. {*Arrian, Anabasis, l. 7. c. 19. s. 1,2. 2:267,269}

*2325.* Concerning the restitution of the exiles from Greece, he sent this short letter by Nicanor, a native of the city of Stagyra, to be read and proclaimed at the next Olympic games: {*Diod. Sic., l. 18. c. 8. s. 2-5. 9:35} {*Diod. Sic., l. 17. c. 113. s. 1. 8:453} [L392]

> "King Alexander, to the exiles of Greece sends greeting: We were not the reason that you were banished,

but we will take care to see that you are all restored to your former estates except such as are banished for outrageous crimes. [E282] Concerning these things, we have written to Antipater and ordered him to proceed, by way of force, against all such as shall oppose your restitution."

*2326.* When he had taken care of all the envoys, he started to prepare for Hephaestion's funeral, ordering all the cities in the region to contribute whatever they possibly could to the funeral. Moreover, he expressly ordered all the cities and countries of Asia to put out the fire which the Persians called the *Holy Fire*, until after the funeral, a custom associated with the funerals of the kings of Persia. This action was taken as an ill omen about the king himself, and as portending his death. {*Diod. Sic., l. 17. c. 114. s. 4,5. 8:457}

*2327.* Thereupon, all his chief commanders and friends made medallions of Hephaestion carved from ivory or cast in gold or some other costly metal. Alexander called together the best workmen available, and a large number of them broke down the wall of Babylon for about two thousand yards. Removing its brick, they first levelled the spot and then built a square funeral pyre sixty-five yards high and two hundred yards long on which the body was to be burned. Diodorus described the work in detail, giving the total cost of this splendid funeral. The mourners, the soldiers, the envoys and natives of the country tried to outdo each other in giving to this project, and more than twelve thousand talents were collected. {Justin, Trogus, l. 12. c. 12.} Plutarch and Arrian said that it was about ten thousand talents. {*Diod. Sic., l. 17. c. 115. 8:457-461} {*Plutarch, Alexander, l. 1. c. 72. s. 3,4. 7:425,427} {*Arrian, Anabasis, l. 7. c. 14. s. 8-10. 2:253,255}

*2328.* Alexander first threw Hephaestion's weapons into the fire and then threw in the gold and silver, along with a robe of great value and esteem among the Persians. {*Aelian, Historical Miscellany, l. 7. c. 8. 1:251} Beside this, Alexander held athletic and musical games far beyond all that he had ever done before. The number of the winners and value of the prizes was larger than anything done previously. It is said that there were no less than three thousand who entered the games for all types of prizes. {*Arrian, Anabasis, l. 7. c. 14. s. 10. 2:253,255}

*2329.* It so happened that Philip, one of the king's friends, returned to him from the temple of Ammon where he had been sent. He brought word from the oracle there that Hephaestion could be sacrificed to as a demigod. This greatly pleased Alexander, who first of all offered to him according to that custom, then sacrificed to him ten thousand beasts of all kinds and put on a magnificent feast for all the people. {*Diod. Sic., l. 17. c. 115. s. 6. 8:461}

He ordered Cleomenes, the governor of Egypt and a lewd man, to erect temples in Hephaestion's name. {*See note on 3673b AM. <<1844>>} He also ordered that no written contract would be good or valid, if Hephaestion's name was not subscribed to it, adding the following in the letter which he wrote to Cleomenes about this matter: {*Arrian, Anabasis, l. 7. c. 14. s. 7. 2:253} {*Arrian, Anabasis, l. 7. c. 23. s. 6-8. 2:285,287} [L393]

> "For if I shall find that you have duly erected temples to Hephaestion in Egypt as to a demigod, I will not only pardon you of all your past offences, which you have committed in your government, but whatever you shall do after this shall never be laid to your charge by me."

2330. As a result, many cities started building temples and shrines to Hephaestion, erecting altars, offering sacrifices and observing holidays in his name. The most religious oath that a man could take was if he swore by Hephaestion that *it is true or false*. Death was the reward for any man who faltered or failed in his devotion to him. Many dreams were said to have been of him, and his ghost was said to have appeared to many. Many words were recorded which his ghost had spoken and the answers which it gave. Sacrifices were offered to him as to a tutelar god and a revenger of all evil. Initially, Alexander was wonderfully pleased with such fancies in other men, but after a while he began to believe them himself. He bragged that not only was he himself Zeus' son, but he could also make gods of other men. At this time it happened also that Agathocles, a Samian and one of Alexander's best captains, was in extreme danger of losing his life. He was accused of having been seen to weep as he passed by Hephaestion's tomb. He would undoubtedly have died for it, had not Perdiccas helped him out by making up a lie and swearing to it by Hephaestion. He said that Hephaestion had appeared to him as he was hunting and told him that Agathocles had indeed wept for him, but not as for one who was dead and now vainly being called upon and worshipped as a god. He wept only out of an appropriate remembrance of the former intimacy and familiarity that had existed between the two of them. But for this tale, Agathocles, a great soldier and loyal to Alexander, would have died for being so kind to his deceased friend. {*Lucian, Slander, l. 1. (17) 1:379}

### 3680d AM, 4390 JP, 324 BC

2331. The 114th Olympiad was celebrated at Elis, and all agree that Alexander died in that year, {*Josephus, Apion, l. 1. c. 22. (185) 1:239} which was the time when Agesias or Hegesias was the archon at Athens. {*Diod. Sic., l. 17. c. 113. s. 1. 8:453} [E283] It was confirmed by Arrian that

Alexander died toward the end of the year of his archonship, in that same Olympiad year, which shall be confirmed by the month when he died. {*Arrian, Anabasis, l. 7. c. 28. s. 1. 2:297}

2332. At the general assembly of all Greece at the Olympic games, Alexander's letter ordering that all exiled persons be restored to their homes and estates again was read publicly by the one who announced the winners in the games. Nevertheless, the Athenians and Aetolians protested against it. {*Diod. Sic., l. 18. c. 8. s. 6,7. 9:35,37} {Justin, Trogus, l. 13. c. 5.}

2333. According to Aristobulus, Alexander received his fleet while he was at Babylon. Part of it sailed down the Euphrates into the Persian Sea under the command of Nearchus. Some of the ships had been built in Phoenicia and Cyprus. Two of the Phoenician ships had five tiers of oars, while three ships were four tiers high and twelve were three tiers high. Thirty ships had thirty oars each. All these ships had been taken apart and carried overland in pieces to the city of Thapsacus, where they had been reassembled and sailed down the Euphrates River to Babylon. Alexander also had some other ships built at Babylon from the cypress trees which he found in the gardens there, because there was no other timber in those parts fit for ship building. Moreover, all other provisions for shipping were brought to him at Babylon from Phoenicia and other cities lying along the sea coasts in Asia, whilst shipwrights and mariners of all types came to him. {*Arrian, Anabasis, l. 7. c. 19. s. 3,4. 2:269} {*Strabo, l. 16. c. 1. s. 11. 7:209}

2334. Alexander had a port made at Babylon that was large enough to hold a thousand warships. [L394] He had built dockyards there and sent Miccalus, a Clazomenian, into Phoenicia and Syria with five hundred talents, to persuade or hire as many seamen as he possibly could to come and serve him. Alexander planned to make several colonies on the Persian Gulf and assured them that these places would be as lavish to dwell in as any places in Phoenicia. {*Arrian, Anabasis, l. 7. c. 19. s. 4-6. 2:269,271}

2335. All these naval preparations were made to attack the Arabians, with the pretext that, among all other countries, they alone had not sent envoys to him or shown him any respect. The real reason was that he had an inordinate desire to be sovereign over all. He had heard that they worshipped only two gods, Juno and Bacchus, and he considered himself worthy to be worshipped as a third god among them, if he could overcome them and restore their pristine liberty to them, as he had done to the Indians. {*Arrian, Anabasis, l. 7. c. 19. s. 6. 2:271} {*Strabo, l. 16. c. 1. s. 11. 7:211}

*2336.* Alexander was told that Arabia, which bordered on the sea coast, was as large as all India and had many islands lying along its coast. He ordered Archias, Androsthenes (this was that Androsthenes of Thasos mentioned by Strabo and Theophrastus {*Strabo, l. 16. c. 3. s. 2. 7:301,303} {Theophrastus, Plants, l. 2. c. 7.}) and Hieron of Solos to set sail from Babylon with three ships of thirty oars apiece, and sail around the peninsula of Arabia. They were to find out what they could about all the ports in that region. Concerning these ports, Arcmas brought him word that there were two islands which lay out in the sea at the mouth of the Euphrates River. The smaller one, which was fifteen miles offshore, he consecrated to Artemis, and Alexander named this island Learus, according to Aristobulus. The larger island was a day's and a night's sailing from the shore in the same latitude, and was called Tylos. Hieron, however, who went farther than any of the rest, brought him word that the peninsula was of a vast size and had a cape which ran far out into the ocean. Those who had come by sea from India with Nearchus maintained that they had not sailed a great distance from that peninsula before arriving at the mouth of the Euphrates River. {*Arrian, Anabasis, l. 7. c. 20. s. 1-10. 2:271-277} {*Arrian, Indica, l. 1. c. 43. 2:429-433}

*2337.* While his ships of war were being built and a harbour was being dug at Babylon, Alexander sailed from there down the Euphrates River for a distance of a hundred miles, to the mouth of the Pollacopas River. They rowed up and down and according to Aristobulus, Alexander sometimes steered his own boat. He saw some ditches which he had scoured by those that were with him. They dammed up the mouths of some and opened others. They saw one dike among the rest on the Arabian side, toward its marshy places, the outlet of which was difficult to dam because of the weakness of the soil. So Alexander opened a new mouth about four miles from the other, in firmer and harder ground, forcing the water course in that direction. He saw many monuments there of the old Assyrian kings and princes who lay buried in that marshy country and in the middle of those lakes. {*Arrian, Anabasis, l. 7. c. 21,22. 2:277-281} {*Strabo, l. 16. c. 1. s. 11. 7:209}

*2338.* They sailed through those lakes into the body of Arabia, where Alexander built a walled city and planted a colony of mercenary Greeks, volunteers and anyone who because of age or for other reasons had grown unfit for the war. {*Arrian, Anabasis, l. 7. c. 21. s. 7. 2:279} [E284]

*2339.* He began to laugh and scoff at the Chaldeans and their predictions, because he had entered Babylon and left it safely with his fleet. Therefore, he sailed all the more boldly through those lakes in the direction of Arabia, having Babylon on his left hand. {*Arrian,

*Anabasis, l. 7. c. 21. s. 7. 2:279} {*Appian, Civil Wars, l. 2. c. 21. (152) 3:511} [L395]

*2340.* When some of his army wandered up and down in those parts and were lost for lack of a pilot, Alexander sent them one who brought them into the right channel again. Then, there arose a strong wind which separated Alexander's ship from the rest of the fleet and hurled the king's hood off from his head and into the water. His turban or diadem which was fastened to it, was rent from it and driven by the wind onto a large reed growing close to the sepulchre of one of the kings who was buried there, as mentioned before. One of the mariners saw it and swam to it. He picked it up and put it on his own head on his return, for fear of getting it wet. Aristobulus said that the mariner who did this was a Phoenician, and that he was well scourged for presuming to put the king's turban on his head. After this accident Alexander consulted a soothsayer and was advised to offer a magnificent sacrifice to the gods and to be very diligent and devout in it. {*Diod. Sic., l. 17. c. 116. s. 5-7. 8:465} {*Arrian, Anabasis, l. 7. c. 22. s. 2-5. 2:281} {*Appian, Syrian Wars, l. 11. c. 9. (56) 2:211}

*2341.* When Alexander was told that the Athenians and Aetolians would not obey his edict concerning the restoring of their exiles, he ordered a thousand warships to be built. He planned to make a war in the west and to begin it with the destruction of Athens, but died before he could do this. {Justin, Trogus, l. 13. c. 5.} {*Curtius, l. 10. c. 2. s. 1-7. 2:485}

## 3681a AM, 4390 JP, 324 BC

*2342.* When Alexander returned to Babylon, he indulged in its luxuries. He was so addicted to gluttony and drunkenness that in the diaries that were kept by Eumenes Cardianus and Diodorus Erythraeus, it is often found that on such and such a day or night Alexander was carried to bed drunk. {*Athenaeus, l. 10. (434b) 4:467} {Plutarch, Symposium, l. 1. c. 6.} One example of this was cited by Aelian, based on Eumenes' account. {*Aelian, Historical Miscellany, l. 3. c. 23. 1:157} I thought it good to insert it here, so that it may show that there is an application for my treatise on the Macedonian year, compared with the days of our Julian Calendar. I first corrected that place in Aelian where it is recorded without making any sense, and where it is given as the month called Dios. (Current Loeb text amended and omitted the last sentence and changed the 24th to the 27th. Editor.) {Ussher, Macedonian and Asiatic Year}

> "On the fifth of the month of Dios (our September 28), he drank until he was drunk at Eumaus' house. He did nothing at all that day except to rise and order his captains where they should march tomorrow.

He told them that he would be going very early. On the seventh day (our September 30), he dined with Perdiccas and started drinking again. On the eighth (our October 1), he slept all day and on the 15th of the same month (our October 8), he was drinking again. The next day (our October 9), he slept it off all day, according to his custom. Upon the 24th (our October 17), he ate at Bagoas' lodging, which was two hundred yards from the king's palace. Then on the third (or rather the 5th), he slept it off again."

## 3681b AM, 4391 JP, 323 BC

*2343.* When Alexander saw Babylon excel both in greatness and in every other aspect, he planned to embellish it as much as he could and to make it the place of his residence for the rest of his life. {*Strabo, l. 15. c. 3. s. 10. 7:169*} He resolved to rebuild the temple of Belus and raise it from its ruins. Some say he planned to make it more magnificent than it had ever been before, but because the Babylonians in his absence went on more slowly with that work than he would have liked, it was his intention to have all his army work on it. As the work would require much labour and lots of time, he was not able to go through with it as he wanted to, because he died soon after this. {*Strabo, l. 16. c. 1. s. 5. 7:199*} {*Arrian, Anabasis, l. 7. c. 17. s. 1-6. 2:261,263*}

*2344.* Alexander dreamed that Cassander had killed him. He had never seen the man in all his life, but when he happened to see him shortly after this, he recalled his dream. *[L396]* At first this alarmed him, but when he understood that he was a son of Antipater, he dispelled any fear of harm from him, especially from poison, which was even at that time being prepared for him. He cheerily uttered a certain Greek verse purporting: {*Valerius Maximus, l. 1. c. 7. ext. 2. 1:91,93*}

So many dreams,
So many lies.

*2345.* When Cassander saw the foreign people prostrating themselves as they came to him, he started to snicker, since he had never seen this done before. Alexander was furious and wrapping both his hands in Cassander's long hair, he beat his head against the wall. {*Plutarch, Alexander, l. 1. c. 74. 7:429,431*}

## 3681c AM, 4391 JP, 323 BC

*2346.* A rumour was circulated that Antipater had sent a poison by Cassander to deliver to Antipater's brother, Iollas, the cupbearer to the king. Iollas was supposed to have poisoned Alexander's last drink. It was also said that Antipater had at the same time sent Craterus back with a company of old soldiers to kill Alexander. {*Curtius, l. 10. c. 10. s. 14,15. 2:557*} *[E285]* Concerning the poison of

which Alexander is said to have died, see Andreas Schottus' collections on the subject from various authors, compiled as part of his comparison of the lives of Aristotle and Demosthenes (to the first year of the 114th Olympiad. See also Mathaus Raderus, on Curtius. {*Curtius, l. 10. c. 3. 2:501*}) As far as Craterus and his old soldiers, who had been sent away with him into Macedonia, are concerned, Justin, Arrian and Plutarch reported that this event happened before the death of Hephaestion. It nevertheless must have happened at this time and not before, as is shown by many other arguments, in particular, that Craterus, with his old maimed soldiers, had not come into Macedonia but was still in Cilicia at the time of Alexander's death. {*Arrian, Anabasis, l. 7. c. 12. s. 3,4. 2:243*} {*Plutarch, Alexander, l. 1. c. 71. s. 5. 7:423*}

*2347.* Those among the Macedonians who found themselves unable through age or other weaknesses of body to follow the war any longer, and who were willing, were dismissed by Alexander to return into their own country. Their number, at this time, came to ten thousand. {*Diod. Sic., l. 18. c. 4. s. 2. 9:19*} {*Diod. Sic., l. 17. c. 109. s. 1,2. 8:439*} Justin stated that it was eleven thousand. {*Justin, Trogus, l. 12. c. 12.*} To each he gave not only his full pay for the time of service, but also money for the journey home. Any who had children from Asian wives, were asked by Alexander to leave them with him, since he feared the possibility that the half breeds might in time stir up some rebellion in Macedonia by contending with the wives and children who already lived there. He promised that when the children were grown up, they would be trained in marshal discipline after the Macedonian custom, and then they would be sent home to them. Justin said that those who returned had received their full pay for the duration of their journey. Plutarch stated that the children of the deceased continued to receive their fathers' pay. He further added that Alexander wrote to Antipater ordering that those who returned should have the best places given to them in the theatres, and should sit there with garlands on their heads. When they parted, they all wept, including Alexander. {*Arrian, Anabasis, l. 7. c. 12. s. 1,2. 2:241*} {*Plutarch, Alexander, l. 1. c. 71. s. 5. 7:423*} {*Curtius, l. 10. c. 3. 2:501*}

*2348.* Together with these, various friends were sent home, including Clitus, Gorgias, Polydamas, Adamas and Antigenes. They were all under the command of Craterus, but if Craterus should happen to die on the way, as he was at that time quite weak and sickly, Polyperchon was to assume command. He ordered Craterus to take over the government of Macedonia, Thrace, Thessaly and of free Greece from Antipater, who in turn was to come to Alexander and bring with him an army of lusty young Macedonians to replace the old men whom he had sent home to him. {*Arrian, Anabasis, l. 7. c. 12. s. 3,4. 2:242} [L397]

2349. When Craterus was sent to lead some old, worn-out soldiers into Cilicia, he also received written orders from Alexander. Diodorus, using Alexander's own commentaries, stated the main points to have been these: He was to have a thousand war ships of three tiers of oars built, that would be a little larger than ships of that type were normally. These were to be constructed in Phoenicia, Syria, Cilicia and Cyprus for his wars against the Carthaginians and others bordering on the sea coasts of Africa, Spain and the islands as far as Sicily. He was to give orders that Alexander's route along the sea coast of Africa, as far as the Pillars of Hercules, was to be prepared for him. He was to set aside fifteen hundred talents to build six magnificent temples, and in various places he was to make ports suitable to receive such a large fleet. He was to take men from Europe into Asia, and likewise from Asia into Europe, to live in any new cities that he would build on either continent. Alexander hoped that by intermarriage he might establish a peace between the two main continents of the world. {*Diod. Sic., l. 18. c. 4. s. 1-6. 9:19-23} These were his plans, of which Lucan spoke in this manner: {*Lucan, l. 10. (36-44) 1:593}

His purpose was the Atlantic Sea to sail;
Nor fire, nor water, nor the Libyan sand,
Nor Ammon's Syrtes could bound his vast desires.
He would into the western clime wave have gone,
Where the sun stoops to fall into Tethys' lap;
And to have marched quite round about the poles,
And drunk the Nile's water, where it first doth rise,
Had not death met him and his journey stayed.
Nothing but nature could a period bring,
To the vast projects of this mad-cap king.

2350. A little before his death, envoys came to him from Greece to acknowledge him as a god. They wore crowns of gold and placed them on his head. {*Arrian, Anabasis, l. 7. c. 24. s. 3. 2:287}

2351. Peucestes returned from Persia with about twenty thousand Persians, and along with them also brought a large company of Cossaeans and Tapurians to Babylon for his service. [E286] These countries bordered on Persia and were considered to be more warlike than any other countries. Philoxenus came with an army from Caria and Menander from Lydia with another army, while Menidas brought an army of cavalry. Alexander commended the devotion of the Persian nation, and especially Peucestes for his just and discreet government among them. He ranked both them and those who came from the coast with Philoxenus and Menander on a par

with his Macedonian squadrons. He had frequent naval exercises in which there were often naval battles on the Euphrates River between the ships of three and those of four tiers of oars, while the mariners and the commanders in these exercises worked hard to outdo their opponents, because Alexander always bestowed crowns upon and honoured those that did the best. {*Diod. Sic., l. 17. c. 110. s. 2. 8:441} {*Arrian, Anabasis, l. 7. c. 24. s. 1. 2:287}

2352. Once, when he was ordering those companies who had come with Philoxenus and Menander among his Macedonian squadrons, he happened to be thirsty. He left his throne, and some of his friends seated on the thrones next to his also left, to attend him. It so happened that a certain lowly man (some say that he was committed to custody, but had no irons on him) came through the middle of all the bodyguards and other officers who stood closely around the throne, and sat down on Alexander's throne. The bodyguards dared not pull him off the throne because there was a Persian law to the contrary, but they tore their clothes, beat their faces and pounded their breasts, taking this as an exceedingly ominous omen against the king. [L398] When Alexander heard this, he caused the man to be racked, to ascertain whether or not he had done it as part of a plot with others, and for what purpose. When he answered that what he had done had only been out of a light humour and fantasy which came into his head, the soothsayers told him that it was all the worse a sign for that reason. Diodorus said that at their advice the poor fellow was killed for this act, in the hope that if there were any bad luck in this, it might happen to him and not to Alexander. Plutarch stated the same, adding that when he was on the rack and asked to give his name, he replied that he was Dionysius of Messenia. {*Diod. Sic., l. 17. c. 116. s. 2-4. 8:463} {*Arrian, Anabasis, l. 7. c. 24. s. 2,3. 2:287,289} {*Plutarch, Alexander, l. 1. c. 73. s. 3,4. 7:429}

2353. A few days later Alexander sacrificed to his gods in thanksgiving for his good successes, this time adding more to the sacrifices than normal, at the advice of the priests. After that, he started feasting with his nobles and sat up doing this until late into the night. He also distributed beasts for sacrifices among the soldiers and gave them wine to drink. When he was leaving the feast, he was told that Medius, a Thessalian, had prepared a banquet to which he was inviting him and all his company. At the banquet sat twenty guests, and Alexander drank to their health as they did likewise to his, according to Athenaeus as recorded from certain memorials, commonly attributed to Nicobule. {*Athenaeus, l. 10. (434c) 4:467,469} {*Athenaeus, l. 12. (537d) 5:429}

2354. Alexander had called for a cup containing six quarts, according to Ephippius, from a book which he wrote about the death and burial of Alexander and Hephaestion, as recorded by Athenaeus. {*Athenaeus, l. 10. (434a) 4:465,467} He ordered Proteas, a Macedonian, to drink to him. Proteas called out for the cup to be brought to him and spoke many words greatly honouring Alexander. He took the cup and drank from it with such grace that all the table commended him highly for it. After a while, Proteas called for the same cup again and drank it to Alexander, who took it and pledged him a large draught, but could not drink it and let the cup fall from his hand. He slumped on the cushion and presently fell sick and later died. This was that Herculean cup that proved fatal to Alexander. {*Diod. Sic., l. 17. c. 117. s. 1. 8:465,467} {*Plutarch, Alexander, l. 1. c. 75. s. 3. 7:433} {*Seneca, Epistles, l. 1. c. 83. s. 22,23. 5:273} {*Athenaeus, l. 11. (469d) 5:71} {Macrobius, Saturnalia, l. 5. c. 21.}

2355. Aristobulus said that when he grew light-headed with his fever and very thirsty, he called for a draught of wine, which cast him into a frenzy. So, on the 30th day of the month of Daisios, that is, on the 24th of our May, Alexander died. Others say that he died on the 6th day of the Athenian month of Thargelion, {*Aelian, Historical Miscellany, l. 2. c. 25. 1:97} which would be on May 18. In the diaries that were kept of the king's actions, it is said that he died on the 28th day of the month of Daisios, or the 22nd of our May. Therefore, it is certain that he died in the month of Daisios according to the Macedonian account, and in our month of May, although the writers disagree on the day of the month.

2356. From the diaries, Arrian and Plutarch described in detail the events that happened during his last sickness. No one can tell us who wrote those diaries about Alexander's deeds. Whether Eumenes Cardianus or Diodorus Erythraeus or Strattis Olynthius did this, we do not know. [E287] The author kept a diary of his deeds in four books, and one additional book relating to Alexander's death, according to Suidas. Whoever it was that owned the diaries, they contain the clearest account of what happened, which is the reason why I thought it best to include what I found in Plutarch from these diaries. I compared them with the days of the Macedonian month of Daisios and our month of May using my own discourse of the Macedonian year. (The footnote in the Loeb series of Curtius agreed with the date Ussher gave for Alexander's death. The footnote in Plutarch stated it was June 13, 323 BC. Editor.) {*Plutarch, Alexander, l. 1. c. 76. 7:435 (footnote)} {*Curtius, l. 10. c. 5. s. 6. 2:516 (footnote)} {*Arrian, Anabasis, l. 7. c. 25,26. 2:289-295} Plutarch wrote: {*Plutarch, Alexander, l. 1. c. 76. 7:433,435} [L399]

"The 18th of the month of Daisios (May 12), he slept in a bath for his fever. The next day (May 13), after he had washed, he went to his chamber and spent that day there playing dice with Medius, and then washed again. Toward the evening, after his customary sacrifice, he ate a little of his supper and the next night had a grievous bout of fever. On the 20th day (May 14), when he had walked, he again very solemnly offered sacrifices. While reclining in a bath, he listened to Nearchus as he told him of the things that had happened to him on his voyage, and what wonders he had seen in the ocean. On the 21st (May 15), while doing the same things as on the previous day, his fever increased. The next day (May 16), his fever grew very high and he was carried to lie in a chamber near the large bath. There he talked with his commanders about putting approved men in, to fill vacancies in the army. On the 24th (May 18), his sickness grew much worse, and he offered sacrifices, to which he was carried. He ordered the principal commanders who were then in the court to stay with him, but the commanders of the divisions and companies were to remain outside and watch. On the 25th (May 19), he was carried to the palace on the other side of the river which gave him a little relief, but his fever did not leave him. When the commanders came to him, he did not speak to them at all, and the same happened on the 26th (May 20). Thereupon the Macedonians, thinking that he had died, came flocking to the chamber door with a loud noise and threatened his friends who were there, should they refuse to let them in. The doors were opened and every common soldier passed by his bedside. That same day, Pithon and Seleucus were sent to Serapis' temple to find out whether Alexander should be moved there, or not. They brought back the answer from the oracle that he should stay where he was. He died on the 28th day (May 22), in the evening."

2357. Now, whereas I said that all the Macedonians passed by Alexander's bedside, it is to be understood that they came in at one door and went out by another. {Lucian, Pseudomenos} Although he had grown weak and faint with the severity of his sickness, he nevertheless raised himself upon his elbow and gave every one of them his hand to kiss as he passed by. {*Valerius Maximus, l. 5. c. 1. ext. 1b. 1:455} This may seem more incredible in itself, considering the position into which he put himself. He stayed in that position while every man in the army, from the first to the last, had passed by and kissed his hand. {*Curtius, l. 10. c. 5. s. 3. 2:515}

2358. When the soldiers had gone, he then turned to his friends and asked them, After I am gone, will you find a king worthy of such men? When no man answered that question, then again he spoke, saying that he could not answer it either. Therefore, he foresaw how much Macedonian blood would be shed before this matter would be settled, and with what large slaughters and shedding of blood they would solemnise his funeral and sacrifice to his ghost when he was gone. He ordered his body to be carried to the temple of Ammon and to be buried there. {*Justin, Trogus, l. 12. c. 15.} When his friends asked him to whom he would leave his kingdom, his answer was *To the strongest.* Then he took off his signet and gave it to Perdiccas. They all took this to mean that he was commending the government of his kingdom to Perdiccas' care and trust until his children should come of age. {*Emilius Probus, Eumenes} Again, when Perdiccas asked Alexander when he wished divine honours to be paid to him, he replied that he wished it at the time when they themselves were happy. {*Curtius, l. 10. c. 5. s. 2-6. 2:515,517}

*2359.* Eratosthenes, in his *Canons* (mentioned by Clement {*Clement, Stromateis, l. 1. c. 21. 2:332}), said that twelve years had passed between the death of Philip and the change, that is, the death of Alexander. This is the same number given him in these sources {Apc 1 Ma 1:7} {*Chronicles of the Jews} {*Tertullian, Answer to the Jews, l. 1. c. 8. 3:159} {L400} {Porphyry, Scaliger's Greek Eusebius, p. 124} {*Josephus, Antiq., l. 12. c. 2. s. 1. (11) 7:7} {Orosius, l. 3. c. 23.} {Jerome, Daniel 11} {Theodoret, Daniel 11} although Gellius allowed him only eleven years. {*Aulus Gellius, Attic Nights, l. 17. c. 21. s. 34,35. 3:283} Julius Africanus, and from him Eusebius, said that it was twelve years and six months, while Diodorus said that it was twelve years and seven months, but Livy, and after him Emilius Probus, said it was thirteen years. {*Diod. Sic., l. 17. c. 117. s. 5. 8:467} {Emilius Probus, Eumenes} {*Livy, l. 9. c. 18. s. 10,11. 4:235}

*2360.* There are just as many differences among writers concerning the years of his life, as there are of his reign. Cicero stated: {*Cicero, Philippics, l. 5. c. 17. 15:305} [E288]

> "What shall I say of Alexander the Macedonian, when he set himself the goal of great achievements from his very youth and was not deterred from them except by death in the thirty-third year of his life."

*2361.* Justin said that he died at the age of thirty-three years and one month. {Justin, Trogus, l. 12. c. fin.} However, Philostratus, Eusebius, Jerome and other writers who followed Eusebius, said that he only lived thirty-two years. {*Philostratus, Sophists Herodes, l. 2. c. 1. (557) 3:165} {*Eusebius, Chronicles, l. 1. 1:206} {*Eusebius, Constantine, l. 1. c. 7. 1:483} {Jerome, Daniel 8,11} All of whom can nevertheless be reduced to that period given by Arrian, who said that he lived thirty-two years and took up eight months of the thirty-third year, as Aristobulus said. However, he

reigned twelve years and eight months. {*Arrian, Anabasis, l. 7. c. 28. s. 1. 2:297}

*2362.* Immediately after Alexander's death, a great dispute arose between the cavalry and foot soldiers of the army concerning the settling of the present state of things. They were ready to fight and to take up arms about it, but on the advice of the nobles and commanders, the matter was settled. It was agreed that the supreme authority, or rather a bare name and shadow of such, should be committed to Aridaeus, the brother of Alexander and son to his father Philip. He was the son of Philinna of Larisa, a common dancer, as mentioned by Ptolemy, son of Agesarchus, in his history of Philopator. {*Athenaeus, l. 13. (578a) 6:121} She had been Philip's mistress. {Justin, Trogus, l. 13. c. 2.} {*Plutarch, Alexander, l. 1. c. 77. s. 5. 7:437} When he was proclaimed king by common consent, they called him by the name of Philip. Joint ruler with him was the son that Roxane would bear. She was eight months pregnant with Alexander's son, according to Justin, while Curtius said she was six months pregnant. {*Curtius, l. 10. c. 6. s. 9. 2:529} No consideration was given to his son Hercules, who was then living at Pergamum, because he was born of Barsine who was never married to Alexander. Aridaeus was deficient in intellect owing to a bodily disease. This, however, did not come upon him in the course of nature or of its own accord, indeed, it is said that as a boy he displayed an exceeding gifted and noble disposition: but afterwards Olympias gave him drugs which injured his body and ruined his mind. For this reason, Perdiccas, to whom Alexander had handed his signet in the hour of his death, was made regent and in effect, absolute king. The charge of the army and of all its affairs was committed to Meleager, the son of Neoptolemus, together with or under Perdiccas. The command of the cavalry, which was the most honourable position in all the army and which, after Hephaestion's death, had been given to Perdiccas, was now assigned to Seleucus, the son of Antiochus, but like the other, together with or under Perdiccas. Added to this, the oversight of the kingdom and its treasure was commended to Craterus' trust. See also Dioxippus and Arrian, in their books written about what happened after the death of Alexander. {*Diod. Sic., l. 18. c. 1-3. 9:13-19} {Justin, Trogus, l. 13. c. 1-4.} {*Curtius, l. 10. c. 6,7. 2:525-539} {*Plutarch, Eumenes, l. 1. c. 3. 8:85} {*Plutarch, Alexander, l. 1. c. 77. s. 5. 7:437} {Photius, Bibliotheca, cod. 82,92} {*Appian, Syrian Wars, l. 11. c. 9. (52) 2:203} {*Appian, Syrian Wars, l. 11. c. 9. (57) 2:213} [L401]

*2363.* Censorinus noted that the years of Philip were reckoned from the death of Alexander, and always started from the first day of that month which the Egyptians call Thoth. {Censorinus, De Die Natali} The Egyptian astronomers applied this calculation of times to their own epochs, to simplify calculations. They set this period as beginning with the first day of Thoth, at the start of the 425th year of Nabonassar, that is, on the 12th of November in 324 BC. This was in the seventh month prior to the true time of Alexander's death. It was from the beginning of that month of Thoth that Ptolemy, in his manual *Canons of Astronomy* (not yet published), deduced the epoch or rising of all the stars of which he in his Preface *Ad Syrus* said:

> "Here were fixed the epochs, or start of all accounts, according to the meridian of Alexandria which was in Egypt, from the first day of the Egyptian month of Thoth in the first year of Philip who succeeded Alexander, the founder of this city."

2364. This was not Philip, the father of Alexander (as some have imagined), but was referring to Philip, Alexander's brother and nearest successor to Alexander. The Alexandrians, for honour's sake, called Alexander their founder, as indeed he was. It was added:

> "For from the first day of his (meaning Philip Aridaeus') reign, the times of the Manual Canons of Ptolemy (who in them followed the common account or calendar of the Egyptians) were taken."

2365. This is according to the rectifying of the Egyptian year (reduced to the Alexandrian account, which Theon also used in his canon) are calculated. This we also find in the Greek collections published by Scaliger in his Eusebian Fragments. {*Eusebius, Scaliger's Greek Eusebius, p. 48*} Hence it was that in the letter to Apollophanes, falsely attributed to Dionysius, the Areopagite, as found in Hilduinus {*Hilduinus, Areopagatica*}) these astronomical tables are called *The Canon of Philip Aridaeus*.

2366. The dead body of Alexander had lain on his throne for seven days, according to Justin. (Aelian said thirty days. {*Aelian, Historical Miscellany, l. 12. c. 64. 1:405*}) All the while, men's thoughts were taken up with the settling of the present state, and so they did not give Alexander a proper burial. Yet, in all that time, no putrefaction, or the least discolouring of the flesh of his body, could be seen. The very vigour of his countenance, which is the reflection of the spirit that is in a man, still remained the same. *[E289]* The Chaldeans and Egyptians were commanded to take care of the body, but when they came to do it, they did not at first dare approach to touch him, because he looked alive. After saying their prayers, so that it might be no sin for them, as mere mortals, to lay their hands on so divine a body, they started to work and dissected him. The golden throne, where he lay, was all stuffed with spices and hung about with pennants and banners and other emblems of his high estate and fortune. {*Curtius, l. 10. c. 10. s. 9-13. 2:555,557*}

2367. (Recently the theory has been put forward that Alexander died from typhoid fever. This disease is caused by drinking impure water and can be fatal in twenty to thirty per cent of the cases. Historical accounts stated that before he died, Alexander had chills, sweat, exhaustion, extremely high fever and severe pain. He eventually fell into a coma and died. This fits the description of typhoid fever. The severe pain may have been caused by typhoid fever perforating the bowel. History notes that his body did not begin to decay until several days after he died. There is a rare complication caused by typhoid fever, called ascending paralysis. The paralysis gradually seizes the whole body and depresses the breathing. Alexander may have appeared to have been dead before he actually died. {*Discover, Alexander the Infected, October 1998, 1:22*} Editor.)

2368. Aridaeus was in charge of his funeral and of providing a chariot to carry the body into the temple of Ammon. We do not know whether this Aridaeus was Alexander's brother, as Justin stated, {*Justin, Trogus, l. 13. c. 4.*} and Dexippus also, as from Scaliger {*Eusebius, Scaliger's Greek Eusebius (Ad Fragmenta), p. 84.*}, or whether he was another Aridaeus, of whom we shall see more later from Diodorus. {*Diod. Sic., l. 18. c. 3. s. 5. 9:19*} Aridaeus spent two whole years in preparation. {*Diod. Sic., l. 18. c. 28. s. 2. 9:93*} *[L402]* When Alexander's mother Olympias learned that he was unburied for so long, she cried out in great grief of heart and uttered these words: {*Aelian, Historical Miscellany, l. 13. c. 30. 1:437,439*}

> "Oh my son, you who would needs be counted among the gods and was in earnest about it, could you not now have that which every poor man has, a little earth and a burial?"

2369. Meanwhile, when Sisigambis, the mother of Darius, heard of his death, she was very sorrowful and dressed herself in mourning attire. When her niece and nephew, Drypates and Oxathres, came and fell at her knees, she looked away from them and refused either to eat or to go outside any more, and as a consequence she died of hunger five days later. {*Diod. Sic., l. 17. c. 118. s. 3,4. 8:469,471*} {*Justin, Trogus, l. 13. c. 1*} {*Curtius, l. 10. c. 5. s. 21-25. 2:521,523*}

2370. Roxane, who was quite pregnant, was favoured by the Macedonian army. She grew envious of Statira, the eldest daughter of Darius, who was also one of Alexander's wives, so she sent letters inviting her to come to see her, but as soon as she came, Roxane had both her and her sister Drypetis, Hephaestion's widow, murdered. She threw both their bodies into a well and covered them with earth. All this she did with Perdiccas' knowledge and assistance. {*Plutarch, Alexander, l. 1. c. 77. s. 4,5. 7:437}

*2371.* Later, Roxane gave birth to a son whom they named Alexander and whom the common soldiers proclaimed as king. {Photius, Bibliotheca, c. 92., from Arrian} {*Pausanias, Attica, l. 1. c. 6. s. 3. 1:29} {Eusebius, Scaliger's Greek Eusebius (Ad Dexippus), p. 48.}

*2372.* Perdiccas ordered a purification of cleansing by a solemn sacrifice for the whole army, because there had been many disputes among them since the death of Alexander. The Macedonian manner of cleansing the army was as follows. They cut a dog in two and laid the one half on the one side and the other on the other side of the field to which the army was to come, after which the army was to pass between the parts in solemn procession. As the army passed, Perdiccas had some three hundred soldiers thrown among the elephants to be trampled to death, and Curtius stated that thirty of them died. These men had followed Meleager when, at the first assembly of the Macedonians after the death of Alexander, he had got up and left them in a rebellious manner. All this had taken place in full view of the army and in the presence of Aridaeus. Meleager had Aridaeus wrapped in purple clothes like a child and put on the royal throne. {*Plutarch, Fortune of Alexander, l. 2. c. 5. 4:445} Meleager did not move for the present because no violence threatened him, but when he saw they were after his life, he fled to a temple, where he was seized and killed. {Justin, Trogus, l. 13. c. 4.} {*Curtius, l. 10. c. 9. s. 16-21. 2:551,553} {Photius, Bibliotheca, from Arrian}

*2373.* Diodorus stated that Alexander had made his last will and testament and had left it at Rhodes for safekeeping. {*Diod. Sic., l. 20. c. 80. s. 3. 10:355} Ammianus thought that in his will he wanted to leave everything in the hands and power of one man. {*Ammianus Marcellinus, l. 23. c. 6. s. 8. 2:353} Curtius stated: {*Curtius, l. 10. c. 9. s. 5. 2:553}

> "Some have the opinion that a distribution of the provinces was made by Alexander in his last will and testament. However, we have found that this was false, although stated by various writers."

*2374.* Nevertheless, the writer of the first book of Maccabees seemed to be of the first opinion, as reported and believed by so many writers. They say that Alexander, in his own lifetime, divided his kingdom among his most illustrious and noble officers. {Apc 1Ma 1:6,7} The chronologer of Alexandria (from whom those barbarous and broken Latin fragments published by Scaliger are taken {Eusebius, Scaliger's Greek Eusebius, p. 58,59}) affirmed the division of the provinces, which Justin and other writers report to have been carried out by Perdiccas in the following manner, based on Alexander's will.

[L403] {Justin, Trogus, l. 13. c. 4.} {*Curtius, l. 10. c. 10. s. 1-4. 2:553} {Photius, Bibliotheca, cod. 92., from Arrian} {Photius, Bibliotheca, col. 82., from Dexippus}

*2375.* In Europe, all of Thrace with the Chersonesus and other countries bordering upon Thrace as far as Salmydessus, a city on the edge of the Black Sea, were committed to Lysimachus, the son of Agathocles, a Pellean. [E290] The region which lay beyond Thrace belonging to the Illyrians, Triballi, and Agros, together with Macedonia and Epirus, stretching as far as the Ceraunian Mountains, as well as all of Greece, was assigned to Antipater and Craterus. This was the division of Europe. {*Curtius, l. 10. c. 9. s. 1-4. 2:553} {*Diod. Sic., l. 18. c. 3. 9:15-19}

*2376.* In Africa, all of Egypt and everything else Alexander had captured in Cyrene or Libya, with all of that part of Arabia which borders on Egypt, was allotted to Ptolemy, the son of Lagus, of whom Pausanias said that he was honoured with the surname of *Deliverer* by the people of Rhodes. {*Pausanias, Attica, l. 1. c. 8. s. 6. 1:41} The truth is, that the Macedonians always believed that Ptolemy was a bastard son of Philip, Alexander's father, because when his mother Arsinoe was pregnant by Philip, she was cast off by him and married a poor fellow of Macedonia called Lagus. This is the reason why it happened that some while later (as Plutarch stated), when Ptolemy wanted to mock a pedant by asking him: {*Plutarch, On Anger, l. 1. c. 9. 6:123}

> "Who was Peleus' father?"

*2377.* The pedant replied:

> "I shall tell you, if you will first tell me who Lagus' father was."

*2378.* By this, he intimated the baseness of Ptolemy's birth on his father's side. {*Curtius, l. 9. c. 8. s. 22-24. 2:439} {*Pausanias, Attica, l. 1. c. 6. s. 1. 1:29} {Suidas, Lagus}

*2379.* Cleomenes, who had been left by Alexander to gather up the tributes and other incomes of those parts, was ordered to turn over that province to Ptolemy and to hold his office as under him. Ptolemy entered that province shortly after the death of Alexander and died about forty years later. Hence, many writers stated that he reigned in Egypt for forty years. {*Lucian, Octogenarians, l. 1. (12) 1:231} {*Eusebius, Chronicles, l. 1. 1:207} {Porphyry, Scaliger's Greek Eusebius, p. 225.} {*Clement, Stromateis, l. 1. c. 21. 2:329} {Epiphanius, De Mensuris et Ponderibus} After him, his posterity down to Cleopatra held that kingdom under the title and name of Ptolemy.

*2380.* In Asia Minor, Eumenes Cardianus was assigned all of Cappadocia, Paphlagonia and all the regions lying on the Black Sea as far as Trapezus, a colony of the

Sinopians. Alexander had not subdued these people because he had been involved in a major war against Darius. Now Eumenes was ordered to make war on Ariarathes, who had been the only one of these peoples to have resisted Alexander. Antigonus was made governor of Pamphylia, Lycia, Lycaonia, and Greater Phrygia. Lesser Phrygia, which lies on the Hellespont, was committed to Leonnatus. The government of Lydia, both the inland country and the parts on the sea coast taking in Aeolia and Ionia, was given to Menander, who had previously received it by grant from Alexander. {*Arrian, Anabasis, l. 3. c. 6. s. 7,8. 1:241} Diodorus incorrectly wrote the name of Meleager here. Caria was given to Cassander, the son of Antipater, while Cilicia and Isaura were given to Philotas.

2381. In upper and greater Asia, all of Syria and Phoenicia was committed to Laomedon of Mitylene. The petty kings of the isle of Cyprus ruled as it had been granted them by Alexander. Neoptolemus was set over Armenia, and Arcesilaus was over Mesopotamia, as well as becoming governor over the province of Babylon. [L404] Atropates, the father-in-law of Perdiccas, had been left as governor of Media by Alexander himself. Justin and Orosius said that, in this division, Atropates was made the governor of Greater Media and Perdiccas' father-in-law of the Lesser, {Justin, Trogus, l. 13. c. 4.} {Orosius, l. 3. c. 23.} {*Diod. Sic., l. 18. c. 3. s. 3. 9:19} whereby Orosius forgot that Atropates and Perdiccas' father-in-law were one and the same person. Later, when Antipater had better considered the matter, Antipater made a second distribution in Triparadisus, acknowledging that Media had been assigned to Pithon. {Orosius, l. 15. p. 660.} {*Diod. Sic., l. 18. c. 39. s. 6. 9:121,123} {*Diod. Sic., l. 19. c. 11. s. 12. 9:259,261} Nor is it likely that the son-in-law would in any way diminish the authority of his father. The rule and government of nearer Bactria and Sogdiana was put into the hands of Philip, and Oropius jointly held the government of Sogdiana with him. Dexippus said that after Oropius had received that kingdom through Alexander's generosity, he was removed from it again for treason. The government of Persia was given to Peucestes. Hyrcania and Parthia (for they went together {*Strabo, l. 11. c. 9. s. 1. 5:271}) were given to Phrataphernes. In Carmania, Tlepolemus held the government, while in the Parapamisus, the government was given to Oxyartes, or Oxathres, the father of Roxane, Alexander's wife. In Aria and Drangiane, bordering on the Taurus Mountains, the government was given to Stasanor of Solos. The provinces of Susa, consisting of Scynus, Arachosia, Gedrosia and Sibyrtius, continued with the governors that Alexander had assigned. All the coast of India from Parapanisus and the junction of the Acesines and Indus Rivers right down to the ocean, was given to Pithon, the son of Agenor. The Oxydracans and Mallians were given to Eudemus, or Eudemon, the commander of the Thracian companies. The rest of India was given to King Porus, to Taxiles and to the son of Abisares, who each ruled the same territories that Alexander had assigned to them. [E291]

2382. When this division had been made, every man had his share as if it had been allotted to him from heaven. They used the opportunity to increase their power and their pleasure, for not long after, they behaved more like kings than governors. They added to their kingdom, and left it to their posterity. {Justin, Trogus, l. 13. c. 4.} Immediately upon the death of Alexander, that vast empire bearing the name of the Macedonians was divided into several kingdoms. {*Livy, l. 45. c. 9. s. 7. 13:273} However, no man assumed the title of a king as long as any of Alexander's children were alive, because of the great respect they had for him. Although they had the power of a king, they willingly refrained from using the title while ever Alexander had a lawful biological heir alive to succeed him. {Justin, Trogus, l. 15. c. 2.} All of this was foretold long before by the Holy Spirit. {Da 11:4}.

## 3681d AM, 4391 JP, 323 BC

2383. The instructions given by Alexander to Craterus were referred by Perdiccas to the general assembly of the Macedonians for consideration. Although they did not disapprove of them in principle, they nevertheless ordered by general consent that none of them be followed up, because they were so exceedingly grand and difficult to carry out. {*Diod. Sic., l. 18. c. 4. s. 1-3. 9:19,21}

2384. The old Greek soldiers, whom Alexander had left in garrisons and colonies in upper Asia and various provinces, became homesick and desired to see their native country. Because they saw themselves as having been ejected, as it were, and cast out into a distant and remote corner of the world, they joined together and revolted from the Macedonian state, choosing Philon, an Aenian, to head up this conspiracy. They assembled twenty thousand foot soldiers and three thousand cavalry, all of whom were old, proven and expert soldiers. Against these, Perdiccas sent Pithon, who had been one of the captains of Alexander's bodyguard. He was a man full of spirit and able to command. He had three thousand Macedonian foot soldiers and eight hundred cavalry, chosen by lot. He went to the governors in all those parts, with letters and instructions to furnish him with an additional ten thousand foot soldiers and eight thousand cavalry. [L405] Pithon planned to win over those old Greeks to himself by all possible means. He hoped that with their help and his forces, he might be able to establish himself all the better and subdue all those upper provinces. When Perdiccas perceived this, he tried to thwart his plan by ordering that when he had overcome the rebels, Pithon was to kill them all and divide their spoil among his soldiers. Pithon, corrupted Letodorus, who commanded a rebel brigade of three thousand men and defeated the rebels when Letodorus' troops suddenly withdrew from the battle. After Pithon had defeated the rebels and did not kill them, but gave them permission to return to their own places. However, the rest of the Macedonians, remembering the order Perdiccas had given them, killed every one of the rebels and shared their spoil. So Pithon failed in his scheme and returned to Perdiccas with his Macedonians. {*Diod. Sic., l. 18. c. 7. 9:29-33} {Justin, Trogus, l. 13. Prologue}

2385. When Ptolemy had quietly taken possession of Egypt, he acted fairly in all things toward the people of the land. He used eight thousand talents to hire a mercenary army and to pay those who came to him as a result of observing how justly he administered Egypt. When he was told that Perdiccas planned to take over Egypt, he joined himself firmly in league with Antipater, {*Diod. Sic., l. 13. c. 14. s. 1,2. 9:51} and won the loyalty of the neighbouring kings and princes by favours and good deeds. {Justin, Trogus, l. 13. c. 16.} Having discovered that Cleomenes, whom Perdiccas had given to him for a lieutenant, was a spy, he cut his throat and placed strong garrisons of his own all over Egypt. {*Pausanias, Attica, l. 1. c. 6. s. 3. 1:29}

## 3682a AM, 4391 JP, 323 BC

2386. Leonnatus and Antigonus were commanded to use force to make Eumenes the governor of Cappadocia and Paphlagonia. Antigonus, however, because he was proud and wanted the position for himself, refused to obey Perdiccas' command, as opposed to Leonnatus who came down with his army from the upper provinces to Phrygia and promised Eumenes help. Here, however, Hecataeus, the tyrant of Cardia, joined with Leonnatus and advised him to go rather to the assistance of Antipater and the Macedonians who were besieged in Lamia. Leonnatus therefore determined to cross over to Greece, invited Eumenes to go with him, and tried to reconcile him with Hecataeus. For they had a hereditary distrust of one another arising from political differences; and frequently Eumenes had been known to denounce Hecataeus when he was a tyrant and to exhort Alexander to restore its freedom to Cardia. Therefore at this time Eumenes declined to go on that expedition against the Greeks, saying he was afraid that Antipater, who had long hated him, would kill him to please Hecataeus. Then Leonnatus took him into his confidence and revealed to him all his purposes. He really planned to go and take over Macedonia. When he

was unable to win over Eumenes, he planned to secretly murder him. [E292] Eumenes, either because he was afraid of Antipater, or because he despaired of Leonnatus as a capricious man full of uncertain and rash impulses, or he found out about the plot against him, escaped by night with his carriages. He had only three hundred cavalry with him and two hundred of his bodyguard, as well as gold worth five thousand talents in money. When he came to Perdiccas, he told him all Leonnatus' plans, causing Perdiccas to receive him as a loyal friend and make him a member of his council. Perdiccas appointed him as governor over Cappadocia. {*Plutarch, Eumenes, l. 1. c. 3. s. 2-7. 8:85-89} {Emilius Probus, Eumenes}

2387. When Leonnatus arrived to help Antipater, he was killed in a battle by the Greeks. {*Diod. Sic., l. 18. c. 15. s. 1-4. 9:53,55} {Justin, Trogus, l. 13. c. 5.} {*Plutarch, Phocion, l. 1. c. 25. s. 3. 8:201} {Photius, Bibliotheca, from Arrian}

2388. When Thibron captured Harpalus in a battle in Crete, he killed him. Harpalus had fled there from Asia and had taken all the king's money with him. Thibron got all the treasure, his army and the fleet. He left Cydonia, a city in Crete, and sailed with six or (as Diodorus stated) seven thousand men to the country of Cyrene, having been invited there by the exiles of the Cyrenians and the Barcenses. {*Diod. Sic., l. 17. c. 108. s. 4-8. 8:435-439} {*Diod. Sic., l. 18. c. 19. s. 2-5. 9:69} {*Strabo, l. 17. c. 3. s. 17. 8:203} {Photius, Bibliotheca, from Arrian} [L406]

2389. In a battle against the Cyrenians, Thibron slaughtered them and took many prisoners. He then seized their port and prepared to take the city itself, but agreed to a peace if they would pay him five hundred talents of coined money and give him half their chariots equipped for service. He sent envoys to the other neighbouring cities to join with him, pretending that he would make war on Libya and subdue it. As well as this, he seized all the merchants' goods that were in the port and gave them to the soldiers as plunder, thereby making them more eager to follow him. {*Diod. Sic., l. 18. c. 19. s. 3-5. 9:69}

2390. Mnasicles, a man of Crete and one of Thibron's captains, had a fiery disposition. He defected from Thibron to the Cyrenians, and by pointing out Thibron's cruelty and unfaithfulness, he persuaded them to break their covenant with him and to fight for their former freedom. Consequently, when they had paid only sixty of the five hundred talents, they refused to pay any more. Thibron planned to destroy them and seized eighty of their men whom he found in the port. With his own men, and the men from Barca and Hesperis, he came up to the walls of the city, where they did all they could to take it, but when they failed, they retired to the port. {*Diod. Sic., l. 18. c. 20. s. 1,2. 9:71}

*2391.* The Cyrenians left sufficient troops to keep the town and with the remainder went foraging into the neighbouring parts. When the people sent to Thibron for help, he immediately went with all the troops that he could muster to relieve them against the Cyrenians. When Mnasicles saw that there were very few soldiers left in the port, he wanted those who were left in the city to sally out and attack the port. The people of the city were easily persuaded to do this and followed him and attacked the port, which they easily took, because Thibron and most of his men were absent. Any goods they found there belonging to the merchants were faithfully restored to the owners. Mnasicles started to fortify the port against Thibron, in case he should return. Things went badly for Thibron, for he had not only lost the port, but with it all the provisions stored there. However, when he captured another town, called Taruchira, his hopes were raised again. {*Diod. Sic., l. 18. c. 20. s. 3-6. 9:71,73}

*2392.* Thibron's sailors and sea-going soldiers were expelled from the port. They had no food and were forced to plunder the country for it on a daily basis. After a time, the men of the country discovered their camps and lay in wait for them. They slaughtered many, and took prisoner as many again as they had killed. Those who survived escaped to their ships and sailed for other confederate places. On their way, a violent storm arose which sank many of the ships. Of those which escaped, some were driven ashore in Egypt and some on the isle of Cyprus. Those who had encouraged the Cyrenians now fought against Thibron and killed many of his men. {*Diod. Sic., l. 18. c. 20,21. 9:73,75}

*2393.* Craterus left Cilicia with six thousand of those old soldiers who had first accompanied Alexander into Asia. Along the way, he gathered four thousand troops, besides a thousand Persian archers and slingers and fifteen hundred cavalry, as he hurried to help Antipater. Arriving in Thessaly, he yielded authority to Antipater and they both camped on the bank of the Penius River. In the month of Mounychion (our April), they fought a battle with the Greeks and defeated them. {*Diod. Sic., l. 18. c. 16. s. 4,5. 9:59} {*Plutarch, Phocion, l. 1. c. 26. s. 1. 8:201} {*Plutarch, Demosthenes, l. 1. c. 28. s. 2. 7:71} {Photius, Bibliotheca, from Arrian} [L407]

*2394.* After Jaddua, his son Onias succeeded him in the priesthood at Jerusalem and held the position there for twenty-one years. {*Josephus, Antiq., l. 11. c. 8. s. 7. (347) 6:483} {*Eusebius, Chronicles, l. 1. 1:207} [E293]

*2395.* Thibron had hired new soldiers from Taenarum in Laconia, soldiers who wandered around Laconia and were out of pay. He started a new war with the Cyrenians, who asked for help from the Africans and

Carthaginians. Together, they assembled an army of thirty thousand men. After a long and bloody battle, they lost many men and Thibron won. The Cyrenians lost all their own commanders and made Mnasicles their general. Thibron grew proud of this victory and attacked and captured the port of Cyrene. Every day he assaulted the city. As the siege continued, causing shortages of provisions, the Cyrenians began to fight among themselves. The common people carried the day and expelled the rich from the city. Some of those who were expelled defected to Thibron and others went into Egypt. {*Diod. Sic., l. 18. c. 21. s. 1-7. 9:73,75}

*2396.* Those who fled into Egypt asked Ptolemy to restore them to their country. With his help, they returned with an army and naval forces under the command of Ophellas, a Macedonian. When those who had defected to Thibron heard this, they prepared to defect to Ophellas, but Thibron, hearing of their intentions, executed them. When the leaders of the common people of Cyrene were frightened by the return of their exiles, they made peace with Thibron and joined with him. In a major battle they were all utterly vanquished by Ophellas. {*Diod. Sic., l. 18. c. 21. s. 8-7. 9:73,75}

*2397.* In his escape, Thibron was attacked by some Africans who seized him and carried him off to Epicides, who held the town of Teuchira in those regions, under Ophellas. The men of that place, with Ophellas' permission, first scourged him with whips and then sent him to be crucified at the port of Cyrene. Since many of the Cyrenians were still fighting among themselves, Ptolemy made a journey there by sea. When he had settled everything there, he returned by the same seaward route. {Photius, Bibliotheca, from Arrian}

*2398.* When Perdiccas had Philip and the royal army at his command, he went against Ariarathes, the petty king of Cappadocia, who had not accepted Eumenes as governor there, as he had been ordered. At that time, Ariarathes gathered a large army of thirty thousand foot soldiers and fifteen thousand cavalry. In two battles, Perdiccas killed four thousand men and took five thousand prisoners, including Ariarathes himself. He first tortured him and all who were allied with him, and then crucified them, but pardoned the rest. When he had settled all matters in Cappadocia, he committed its government to Eumenes, as had originally been determined. {Photius, Bibliotheca, from Arrian} {*Diod. Sic., l. 18. c. 16. s. 1-3. 9:57,59} {*Plutarch, Eumenes, l. 1. c. 3. s. 6. 8:87} {*Appian, Mithridatic Wars, l. 12. c. 2. (8) 2:253}

*2399.* Eumenes committed the various cities of his government to his most trusted friends and gave them garrisons. Without imposing on Perdiccas, he appointed judges and tax collectors as he saw fit, but having done this, Eumenes returned with Perdiccas out of respect for him and so that he would not be a stranger at court. {*Plutarch, Eumenes, l. 1. c. 3. s. 7. 8:89}

2400. Perdiccas and King Philip left Cappadocia and went into Pisidia. They planned to destroy two cities, one belonging to the Larandians, the other to the Isaurians. [L408] In Alexander's lifetime, these cities had killed Balacrus, the son of Nicanor, whom he had placed over them. They took Laranda on the first assault, killing all who were of age and selling the rest for slaves, and laid the city level with the ground. When the people of Isaura saw that they were besieged, they set the city on fire, planning to kill themselves and destroy the city. The soldiers, however, to whom Perdiccas had given the spoil of the city, quenched the fire and found a large accumulation of silver and gold there. {*Diod. Sic., l. 18. c. 22. 9:77-81} Justin said that this was done by the Cappadocians, when they saw that Ariarathes had been taken. {Justin, Trogus, l. 13. c. 6.} Orosius agreed. {Orosius, l. 3. c. fin.}

2401. Antipater's son Jollas accompanied by Archias, came to Perdiccas from Macedonia. Jollas brought them Nicaea, Antipater's daughter, to be Perdiccas' wife. Long before this, when his affairs had been more uncertain Perdiccas had betrothed her, thereby hoping to secure Antipater's loyalty. Now that he had quietly managed to get the royal army and the administration of the kingdom into his hands, he planned to marry Cleopatra, the daughter of Philip, the father of Alexander and thus Alexander's sister. Eumenes urged him to marry Nicaea, so that he would more easily have access to a ready supply of the Macedonian youth and that he would not have Antipater for an opponent in his undertakings. Therefore, he married Nicaea when she came, doing this mainly on the advice of his brother Alcetas. {*Diod. Sic., l. 18. c. 23. s. 1-3. 9:81} {Justin, Trogus, l. 13. c. 6.} {Photius, Bibliotheca, from Arrian} [E294]

2402. Cynna was another daughter of Philip's and a sister of Alexander, but not by the same mother, and Cynna brought her daughter Adea who was later called Eurydice, and was to be married to Philip Aridaeus. However, Perdiccas and his brother Alcetas had Cynna killed, whereupon the Macedonians became enraged, and in order to pacify them, Perdiccas was forced to give her daughter to Aridaeus in marriage. {Photius, Bibliotheca, from Arrian} There she was named, not Cynna, but Cynane, yet that same Arrian, in another place, called her Cyna. {*Arrian, Anabasis, l. 1. c. 5. s. 4. 1:21} Diodorus and Athenaeus called her Cynna. {*Diod. Sic., l. 19. c. 52. s. 5. 9:373} {*Athenaeus, l. 13. (557c) 6:13}

2403. Perdiccas sent Eumenes away from Cilicia, under the pretence of having him take care of his own government in Cappadocia, but his real reason was that Perdiccas might have control of the government of Armenia. Neoptolemus had thrown the country into confusion, but using flattery, Eumenes prevailed with him to such an extent that although he was of a high and intemperate spirit, Eumenes was able to keep him under control. {*Plutarch, Eumenes, l. 1. c. 4. s. 1,2. 8:89}

2404. When Eumenes found that the Macedonian squadron had grown insolent and hostile, he raised an army of cavalry from the provinces in those regions, by remitting to them all payment of tribute and granting them other immunities. He furnished cavalry to those whom he most trusted and put them under his command. Encouraging their loyalty to him with his generosity and the bounteous favours he bestowed on them, he kept them in shape by continual labours and journeys which he had them undertake, and so, in a short time, he had about six thousand cavalry troops. {*Plutarch, Eumenes, l. 1. c. 4. s. 2,3. 8:89,91}

### 3683a AM, 4392 JP, 322 BC

2405. In Greece, Antipater and Craterus made war on the Aetolians. When continual battles forced Craterus' old soldiers to spend the winter in regions covered with snow, they almost perished due to lack of supplies. {*Diod. Sic., l. 18. c. 24,25. 9:83,85}

2406. Eumenes carried Perdiccas' gifts to Cleopatra at Sardis. Perdiccas was now resolved to rid himself of Nicaea, Antipater's daughter, and to take Cleopatra to be his wife, a fact which Menander, the governor of Lydia, mentioned to Antigonus, who was an intimate friend of Antipater. {Photius, Bibliotheca, from Arrian} Perdiccas repeatedly made false charges against Antigonus and tried to have him unjustly executed. [L409] Antigonus indicated that he was coming to the hearing, but secretly sailed off with his son Demetrius and some other friends in an Athenian ship. They fled to Europe to join Antipater there. {*Diod. Sic., l. 18. c. 23. s. 3,4. 9:81,83}

### 3683 AM, 4393 JP, 321 BC

2407. Aristander, a soothsayer of Telmessus, proclaimed that it had been revealed to him by the gods that the land in which Alexander's body would rest would be the happiest of all countries and forever free from all foreign invasions. Consequently, there was much strife among the leaders of Macedonia about who should get the body. The main disagreement was between Perdiccas and Ptolemy, the son of Lagus. {*Aelian, Historical Miscellany, l. 12. c. 64. 1:405,407} Perdiccas arranged with his friends to have the body carried to Aegae. {*Pausanias, Attica, l. 1. c. 6. s. 3. 1:29}

2408. However, Aridaeus, who had custody of the body, thwarted Perdiccas and carried it to Ptolemy as he was journeying from Babylon via Damascus to Egypt. Although he met with many impediments from Polemon, a good friend of Perdiccas, he nevertheless carried it into Egypt, as he had planned to do. {*Photius, Bibliotheca, from Arrian*}

2409. Aridaeus spent two full years in preparations for this funeral, and its magnificence was recorded in detail by Diodorus. Finally, he moved the body from Babylon with a very large number of workmen to clear the way and level it where needed. Many others attended the funeral and followed him. Ptolemy, with his whole army, went as far as Syria to meet him. {*Diod. Sic., l. 18. c. 28. s. 2-6. 9:93,95*} He took the corpse and first buried it at Memphis with all rites and ceremonies after the Macedonian custom. According to Pausanias, it was moved to Alexandria a few years later, not by this Ptolemy Lagus, but by his son, Ptolemy Philadelphus. {*Curtius, l. 10. c. 10. s. 20. 2:559*} {*Pausanias, Attica, l. 1. c. 6. s. 3. 1:29*} {*Pausanias, Attica, l. 1. c. 6. s. 8. 1:35*} {*Strabo, l. 17. c. 1. s. 8. 8:35,37*}

2410. Perdiccas called a council of captains and friends in Cappadocia and asked them whether he should first march with his army into Macedonia against Antipater, or into Egypt against Ptolemy. Some were of the opinion to go into Macedonia first, but it was resolved that it was best to begin with Ptolemy in Egypt, otherwise Ptolemy might come and take over Asia while Perdiccas was engaged in Europe. Therefore Perdiccas gave Eumenes, in addition to what he had already, the provinces of Caria, Lycia and Phrygia, with the government of all that part of Asia lying between the Taurus Mountains and the Hellespont. Eumenes was ordered to take charge of all the garrisons in Cappadocia and Armenia, and to use them to check the actions of Antipater and Craterus, to fortify every place on the Hellespont, and to prevent their landing in case they were to come into those parts by sea. *[E295]* Perdiccas further ordered his brother Alcetas, and Neoptolemus, to obey Eumenes in all matters. He wanted Eumenes for the present to use his discretion to do things as he thought best. Cilicia was taken from Philotas and committed to Philoxenus. Perdiccas left Damascus to conceal his actions better. He took Aridaeus and Alexander, the son of Alexander the Great by Roxane, along with him, and marched toward Egypt to fight with Ptolemy. {*Diod. Sic., l. 18. c. 25. s. 6. 9:87*} {*Diod. Sic., l. 18. c. 29. s. 1-6. 9:95,97*} {*Justin, Trogus, l. 13. c. 6.*} {*Plutarch, Eumenes, l. 1. c. 5. s. 1,2. 8:91*} {*Emilius Probus, Eumenes*} {*Photius, Bibliotheca, from Arrian*} {*Pausanias, Attica, l. 1. c. 6. s. 3. 1:29,31*}

2411. Antipater and Craterus were told by Antigonus that Perdiccas had married Cleopatra and planned to invade Macedonia, with the intention of setting himself up as absolute king and removing them from their governments. *[L410]* So they made peace with the Aeolians and left Polyperchon to manage affairs in Greece and Macedonia, while they hurried into the Hellespont on the Asian side, and kept those who had been appointed to keep that passage busy by sending daily embassies to them. They also sent envoys to Ptolemy, who was just as much a deadly enemy to Perdiccas as they were, desiring him to join with them. They sent to Eumenes and Neoptolemus as well, who at that time were both in good standing with Perdiccas. Neoptolemus defected from Perdiccas and joined them, but they could not win over Eumenes. {*Diod. Sic., l. 18. c. 29. s. 4,5. 9:97*} {*Justin, Trogus, l. 13. c. 6.*} {*Photius, Bibliotheca, from Arrian*}

2412. Alcetas, Perdiccas' brother, flatly refused to bear arms against Antipater and Craterus. Neoptolemus envied the power of Eumenes and while secretly joining Antipater and Craterus, he also plotted to kill Eumenes and betray all his army into their hands. When Eumenes discovered this, he was forced to fight it out with the traitor in a battle. He made a large slaughter of Neoptolemus' men, took all his baggage and won the remainder of his troops over to his side. Eumenes became stronger with the addition of so many good Macedonian soldiers to his former army. Neoptolemus escaped with only three hundred cavalry and fled to Antipater and Craterus, who again sent envoys to Eumenes to win him over, promising that he should not only hold what he had but also have more provinces given to him. When he replied that he would rather lose his life than break his word to Perdiccas, they responded by dividing their army in two. Antipater marched with one into Cilicia and from there to Egypt, to join forces with Ptolemy against Perdiccas, while the other stayed behind with Craterus to fight with Eumenes.

2413. When Eumenes saw the enemy coming on, he feared lest his soldiers, knowing against whom he was to fight, would not go with him but disband and desert him. Therefore he led them about by an unfamiliar way, where they might not easily hear how the matters went. There were already rumours buzzing in their midst that Neoptolemus was approaching, together with Pigris, with an army of Cappadocian and Paphlagonian cavalry. By carefully choosing his ground everywhere he went, Eumenes arranged it so that he could force the enemy to fight with the cavalry rather than the foot soldiers, because Eumenes had a much stronger cavalry, but was weaker than the enemy in foot soldiers. He had twenty thousand foot soldiers from various countries and some five thousand cavalry, and he trusted the latter to carry the day. Craterus had a little more than two thousand cavalry and as many foot soldiers as Eumenes. However, his soldiers were all old veteran Macedonians who had proved their valour, and he trusted that they would secure the victory for him.

*2414.* These armies met in Cappadocia. Craterus had the right wing and Neoptolemus the left. Eumenes put none of his Macedonians to fight against Craterus, but only two regiments of foreign cavalry led by Pharnabazus, the son of Arabazus, and Phoenix of Tenedos. He wanted them to attack the enemy quickly, without any shouting or words. Eumenes, with a company of three hundred cavalry, attacked Neoptolemus like lightning. Craterus acted very bravely and valiantly, but his horse stumbled and a certain Thracian, or rather, according to Arrian, a Paphlagonian, put a lance through his side and knocked him to the ground. As he fell, one of Eumenes' captains recognised him and did what he could to save him, but he died of his wound. Meanwhile, Eumenes and Neoptolemus met and fought with each other. Both got off their horses to the ground, so that they might easily see with what deadly hatred they encountered each other. *[L411]* Their spirits were more hostile than their bodies could be. Eumenes wounded Neoptolemus in one of his hamstring muscles, and even though his hamstrings were cut and he fell, his courage held him up and he raised himself up on his knees. He continued fighting and gave Eumenes three wounds, one in his arm and the other two in his thigh, none of which was mortal. After the second blow, Eumenes made a full blow at him and struck off his head. *[E296]* This was about ten days after the earlier victory that he had had over him. {*Plutarch, Eumenes, l. 1. c. 6-8. 8:93-101} {*Diod. Sic., l. 18. c. 29-31. 9:97-103} {Photius, Bibliotheca, from Arrian} {Justin, Trogus, l. 13. c. 6.}

*2415.* When Eumenes saw Craterus brought half dead from the battle, he did all he possibly could to save his life. When he died, he wept bitterly over him and with outstretched arms lamented his fate. He had held a high position and the two liked each other very much. He gave him an honourable burial and sent his bones home to Macedonia to his wife and children. {*Plutarch, Eumenes, l. 1. c. 7. 8:101} {Emilius Probus, Eumenes}

*2416.* Both the leaders were killed and many others, especially of the better troops, were taken prisoner. The rest of the cavalry fled back to the main squadron of the foot soldiers to a more secure defence. Eumenes was content with what he had done, sounded a retreat and setting up a monument in the place, buried his dead. The enemy foot soldiers were trapped and could not escape without Eumenes' permission, so they surrendered. They swore oaths of loyalty to him and received permission to buy food in the surrounding area, but as soon as they had acquired food and recovered their strength, they broke their oath and returned to Antipater. {*Diod. Sic., l. 18. c. 32. s. 2-4. 9:103,105} {Photius, Bibliotheca, from Arrian} {Emilius Probus, Eumenes}

*2417.* Perdiccas, with the two kings, Aridaeus and the young child Alexander, came into Egypt with his army and camped near Pelusium. While he was busy in clearing an old ditch, an extraordinary flood of the Nile destroyed all his works. Although Ptolemy had cleared himself publicly of all those crimes with which Perdiccas had charged him and the army was not enthused with this campaign, Perdiccas was still determined to make war on him. {*Diod. Sic., l. 18. c. 33. s. 1-4. 9:105} {Photius, Bibliotheca, from Arrian}

*2418.* When Perdiccas finally realised that many of his friends had abandoned him and had fled over to Ptolemy, he assembled all his commanders and captains. He tried to win them over with gifts, generous promises, fair words and his good behaviour toward them. Then he noiselessly moved his camp in the night and camped on the bank of the Nile River, not far from a certain citadel called the Citadel of Camels. At day break, he crossed the river with his army and elephants and attacked the citadel, but was valiantly repulsed by Ptolemy and gladly retreated into his camp again. The next night, he moved as quietly as possible and came to a place opposite Memphis. There the river parted and made an island suitable to camp on. In crossing the river to the island, he lost more than two thousand men. At least a thousand, who were being tossed up and down in the water for a long time, were devoured by the crocodiles and other large animals in the river. Ptolemy took these bodies as they were cast ashore on his side of the river and gave them a proper funeral, then he sent their bones to their friends and kinsmen in the army. As a result, the minds of the soldiers became much more fiercely enraged against Perdiccas and were more inclined to Ptolemy than ever before. {*Diod. Sic., l. 18. c. 33-36. 9:105-113}

*2419.* Then a rebellion arose in the camp in which about a hundred of the chief commanders, including Pithon, defected from Perdiccas. *[L412]* Pithon was a very brave man, noted for his virtue and valour, and was held in highest esteem among all of Alexander's Companion Cavalry. Some of the cavalry conspired secretly together and went to Perdiccas' pavilion and killed him. He had now held that government three full years, or at least, for the third year running. {*Diod. Sic., l. 18. c. 36. s. 2-5. 9:113,115} {Photius, Bibliotheca, from Arrian} {Justin, Trogus, l. 13. c. 8.} {*Pausanias, Attica, l. 1. c. 6. s. 3. 1:29,31} {Emilius Probus, Eumenes}

*2420.* The next day, when the whole army had been called together, Ptolemy crossed the river and came to the two kings. He presented both them, and others of the nobles, with expensive gifts and behaved himself fairly and in a humble manner toward them all. When he had apologised for what he had done, he realised that the army was destitute of provisions, so he supplied them with plenty of grain and all other necessities, making it publicly evident that he was heartily sorry and bemoaned the present state and condition of Perdiccas' friends. If he saw any Macedonian in any distress or danger, he did what he could to relieve and help him. By such gracious behaviour, he could easily have become the guardian of the two kings, as Perdiccas had been, but he persuaded them to make Pithon and Aridaeus, who transported the body of Alexander, the guardians of the two kings, Aridaeus and the young child, Alexander, to which they all agreed. Pithon was the man who had previously quieted the disturbances of the Greeks in upper Asia, while Aridaeus had formerly had the duty of conveying the body of Alexander from Babylon. They had supreme power over all the armies, as Perdiccas had, when this had first been established. {*Diod. Sic., l. 18. c. 36. s. 6,7. 9:115} {Photius, Bibliotheca, from Arrian} [E297]

2421. Two days after the death of Perdiccas, news arrived of Eumenes' victory in Cappadocia and of the death of Neoptolemus and Craterus. Had this come two days earlier, it would no doubt have saved Perdiccas' life. For who, after that success, would have dared to stir against him? The Macedonians were enraged at the death of Craterus and declared Eumenes a public enemy, along with fifty of his friends. Included on this list were Pithon Illyrius (for so I find in Justin, as also in Arrian {*Arrian, Indica, l. 1. c. 18. s. 6. 2:359}), Pithon, the son of Craterus, who was from Alcomene, a city in Illyria, {Stephanus, de Urbibus} and Alcetas, the brother of Perdiccas. The generals who were against them were Antigonus and Antipater. For this reason Antigonus was sent for from Cyprus and ordered, along with Antipater, to come quickly to the two kings. {Photius, Bibliotheca, from Arrian} {Justin, Trogus, l. 13. c. 8.} {*Plutarch, Eumenes, l. 1. c. 8. s. 1,2. 8:101} {*Diod. Sic., l. 18. c. 37. s. 1,2. 9:117}

2422. In Egypt, all who had any association with Perdiccas were executed, including his sister Atalanta, whom Attalus, the admiral of Perdiccas' fleet at Pelusium, had married. When he heard of the deaths of his wife and of Perdiccas, he weighed anchor and sailed to Tyre. Archelaus, a Macedonian and the governor there, entertained him with every respect and affection. He surrendered the city and gave him the eight hundred talents which Perdiccas had deposited there.

2423. Attalus stayed at Tyre, receiving and helping all of Perdiccas' friends who had escaped from the camp at Memphis. {*Diod. Sic., l. 18. c. 37. s. 3,4. 9:117}

2424. Eurydice, the wife of King Aridaeus, did not want the two guardians to make any important decisions without her. At first, they refused to comply with her request. Later they told her plainly that she had nothing to do with matters of state, and that they would be responsible for her only until Antigonus and Antipater were to come. {Photius, Bibliotheca, from Arrian} [L413]

2425. Pithon and Aridaeus, who were the two guardians, left the Nile River with the two kings and the army and came to Triparadisus in upper Syria. Eurydice was meddling in matters of state and would cross the guardians on many occasions. Pithon was offended by this, and all the more so, when he saw that the Macedonians were inclined to obey her commands. He called the Macedonians together and resigned his guardianship before them all, whereupon they chose Antipater to be the guardian in his stead, with all the sovereign power associated with it. {*Diod. Sic., l. 18. c. 39. s. 1-4. 9:119,121}

2426. The army now demanded of Antipater all the rewards for their long labour in all those wars in which Alexander had made them serve. When Antipater had nothing to give them at the time, he told them that their demands were just and reasonable, and that he would shortly look into the king's treasury and find out whatever he had laid aside. This speech gave the army little satisfaction, so that when Eurydice also helped foment discontent with him, the minds of the common soldiers were stirred up to rebel against him. At the same time, Eurydice made a public declamation against him, which was read to the people by Asclepiodorus, her secretary. When Attalus agreed and made a speech of his own, Antipater barely escaped out of their hands with his life, while Antigonus and Seleucus stood up in his defence, thereby risking their own lives also.

2427. Therefore, when Antipater had escaped to his own army, the chief commanders of the cavalry came together. After much ado, they pacified the multitude, and so Antipater was sent for again and asked to resume the sovereign power and use it as he had formerly done. {Photius, Bibliotheca, from Arrian} {*Diod. Sic., l. 18. c. 39. s. 3,4. 9:121}

2428. After this, at Triparadisus, Antipater made a new distribution of the governments of the provinces. He partly ratified what had formerly been done in that region and made some alterations as required. He left Ptolemy what he had, for it was hard to remove him to any other government, since he was firmly entrenched in Egypt. Mesopotamia and the country of Arbela were assigned to Amphimachus, the king's brother. Babylon went to Seleucus, Parthia to Philip, Aria and Drangiane to Atasander of Cyprus. Bactria and Sogdiana went to Stasanor of Solos in Cyprus. Media, as far as to the Caspian Gates, was taken from Atropates, the son-in-law of the deceased Perdiccas, and given to Pithon, the son of Crateas, or Craterus. Thereupon, Atropates named the Lesser Media Atropatene after himself, and revolted from the Macedonian government, declaring himself its absolute king, and his posterity held it until the time of Strabo. {*Strabo, l. 11. c. 13. s. 1. 5:303} Antigenes (whose name was incorrectly recorded as Antigonus by Diodorus), captain of the silver targeteers, was given the province of Susa, because he had been the first to go against Perdiccas. [E298] To him were given three thousand of the most active Macedonians in the recent sedition. The rest of the provinces of upper Asia were left in the hands of those who formerly had them, with the exception of Patala, which was the largest city of all India and was assigned to King Porus by this settlement, according to Arrian. This we find hard to believe.

2429. In Asia Minor, Cappadocia and Paphlagonia were taken from Eumenes and given to Nicanor. Lydia (not Lycia, as Diodorus wrote) was given to Clitus. Lesser Phrygia, extending all the way to the Hellespont, went to Aridaeus. Caria, with Greater Phrygia, Lycaonia, Pamphylia, and Lycia, went to Cassander to govern, as he had previously done. Diodorus wrote Cilicia, instead of Lycia, even though a little earlier he had said Cilicia was given to Philoxenus. More correctly, as Arrian has it, the province was confirmed to him, since I showed, a little before, from Justin, {Justin, Trogus, l. 13. c. 6.} that Perdiccas had taken that province from Philotas and given it to Philoxenus. {*Diod. Sic., l. 18. c. 39. s. 5-7. 9:121-125} {Photius, Bibliotheca, from Arrian} [L414]

2430. Antigonus was nicknamed the *Cyclops*, because he had only one eye. {*Aelian, Historical Miscellany, l. 12. c. 43. 1:387} Antipater made him general of the king's army and in particular commander of those forces which Perdiccas had formerly. He also committed to him the care of the two kings and sent him to make war on Eumenes, which he was anxious to do. Based on this, Appian said that Antipater made him overseer of all Asia. {*Appian, Syrian Wars, l. 11. c. 9. (53) 2:203,205} Diodorus called him absolute commander, or general, of all Asia but Antipater attached his own son, Cassander, the governor of Caria, with Antigonius as his general of the cavalry. He did this so that if Antigonus should go about establishing himself, he might have someone to keep an eye on him. {*Diod. Sic., l. 18. c. 39. s. 7. 9:123} {*Diod. Sic., l. 18. c. 40. s. 1. 9:125} {Photius, Bibliotheca, from Arrian}

2431. At the same time, Antipater made Autolychus, the son of Agathocles, Amyntas, the son of Alexander and brother to Pencesta, as well as Ptolemy, the son of Ptolemy, and Alexander, the son of Polyperchon, captains of the bodyguard to the two kings. He received great approval among all the men for his good management and proper administration of affairs in his guardianship. Then he journeyed with the two kings to Macedonia. {Photius, Bibliotheca, from Arrian} {*Diod. Sic., l. 18. c. 39. s. 7. 9:123,125}

2432. When Eumenes heard that he had been declared an enemy by the Macedonians and that Antigonus had been sent against him, he voluntarily announced the matter to the army. He feared that if the news were to reach them from another source, it might possibly make matters worse than they were, or that their courage would be dampened if they were taken by surprise. At least in this way he would find out how his army took the news and what their attitude was toward him. He told them plainly that if anyone was afraid because of this news, he was free to leave and go wherever he wished. With these words he so won over the men and secured their loyalty to him, that they all bade him be of good cheer, declaring that they would cut that decree of the Macedonians into pieces with their swords. {Justin, Trogus, l. 14. c. 1.}

2433. Moreover, when news of that decree came to Alcetas, the brother of Perdiccas, he fled and ingratiated himself with the Pisidians. For while he was among them, whenever he got plunder from the enemy, he gave them half. He was always friendly and courteous to them in his speeches and often invited their principal men to feasts, honouring them with gifts and presents, and in this way won their hearts to him. {*Diod. Sic., l. 18. c. 46. s. 1,2. 9:139}

2434. Attalus, who was the chief admiral of the navy and who had been among the first to defect from Antipater, fled and banded himself with the rest of the exiles. He got together an army of ten thousand foot soldiers and eight hundred cavalry, and with these troops he set out to capture Cnidos, Caunus and Rhodes, but Demaratus, the admiral of Rhodes, valiantly held him off. {Photius, Bibliotheca, from Arrian}

## 3684a AM, 4393 JP, 321 BC

2435. Eumenes took as many horses as he wanted from the king's herd, which was on Mount Ida. When he sent an account of their number in writing to the king's revenue officers, Antipater laughed at it. He said that he was surprised to see Eumenes so cautious that he should either think himself to be accountable to them for the king's goods, or expect that others would account for them. {*Plutarch, Eumenes, l. 1. c. 8. s. 3. 8:103}

2436. From there he marched with his army, not into Aetolia, as written in the printed copies of Justin, but as a manuscript copy has it, into Etulia or Etulane. This is a part of Lesser Armenia in Cappadocia (according to Isaacus Vossius, a most learned young man and my very good friend, who noted this from Ptolemy). Here he levied money from the cities in those regions, and if any refused to pay their contribution, he plundered them as though they were enemies. [L415] Moving on again from there, he went to Sardis, to Cleopatra, the sister of Alexander the Great. He hoped that her presence, as royalty by his side, would strengthen the loyalty of the officers of his army toward him. {*Justin, Trogus, l. 14. c. 1.*} When it happened that Antipater also passed through Sardis on his way to Macedonia, Eumenes decided to fight in the plains of Lydia. *[E299]* He was the stronger in cavalry and was keen to let Cleopatra see of what mettle he was made. Cleopatra, however, fearing that Antipater and the Macedonians might charge her with being the instigator of this war against them, persuaded Eumenes to leave Sardis. But when Antipater came, he nevertheless rebuked her for having any association with Eumenes and Perdiccas. She stood her ground, however, and defended her actions, blaming Antipater for this state of things. Finally, they parted on good terms with each other. {*\*Plutarch, Eumenes, l. 1. c. 8. s. 4,5. 8:103*} {*Photius, Bibliotheca, from Arrian*}

*2437.* Therefore Eumenes left the country of Lydia and marched away into upper Phrygia. He made his winter quarters in Celaenae and sent a message to Alcetas and his associates, {*\*Plutarch, Eumenes, l. 1. c. 8. s. 5. 8:103*} advising them to assemble their forces into one body and to make a united attack on a common enemy. When they could not agree among themselves, nothing was done. {*Photius, Bibliotheca, from Arrian*} Alcetas, Polemon and Docimus could not agree about who should be the leader, whereupon Eumenes cited the old proverb: {*\*Plutarch, Eumenes, l. 1. c. 8. s. 5. 8:103*}

"Of perdition no account is made."

*2438.* Eumenes promised to pay his army within three days and sold all the towns and cities of that country, which were filled with men and cattle. Thereupon, the captains and commanders took them off his hands and having received battering rams from him, went and entered the towns by force, sold everything and fully paid each man. {*\*Plutarch, Eumenes, l. 1. c. 8. s. 5,6. 8:103*}

*2439.* Antipater did not yet dare fight with Eumenes, but sent Cassander to fight with Alcetas and Attalus. They fought and departed on equal terms, but Cassander fared the worse in the battle. {*Photius, Bibliotheca, from Arrian*}

*2440.* Cassander broke off his friendship with Antigonus, but his father Antipater persuaded him to befriend him again. When Cassander met with his father in Phrygia, he advised his father not to go too far away from the kings, nor to rely too much upon Antigonus. But by his temperate and discreet behaviour on all occasions, Antigonus did what he could to make Antipater trust him. Whereupon Antipater set aside his displeasure toward him and turned the forces which he had brought with him from Asia over to Antigonus. These were eighty-five hundred Macedonians and just as many cavalry from

his confederates, as well as some seventy of his elephants. Antigonus, who was to use these forces to make war against Eumenes, accepted the task, while Antipater journeyed to Macedonia together with the kings. {*Photius, Bibliotheca, from Arrian*}

*2441.* The whole army cried out for their wages, and Antipater promised to pay them when he came to Abydus. He told them that perhaps he would give them the whole amount which Alexander had promised, and if not, at least most of it. Encouraging them with this hope, he quietly marched to Abydus. When he came there, he stole away by night with the two kings in his company, and crossed over the Hellespont to Lysimachus. On the next day, the army followed him without any further demands for their pay. *[L416]* So said Arrian, and here Arrian ends his ten books which he wrote about the deeds of Alexander. {*Photius, Bibliotheca, c. 92. from Arrian*}

### 3684b AM, 4394 JP, 320 BC

*2442.* Antigonus assembled all his forces from their winter quarters to march against and subdue Eumenes, who at that time was in Cappadocia. Everywhere in Eumenes' camp there were notices promising a hundred talents, good conditions and positions of authority as well to the one who would bring Eumenes' head to Antigonus. {*Justin, Trogus, l. 14. c. 1.*} {*\*Plutarch, Eumenes, l. 1. c. 8. s. 6,7. 8:103,105*} When Eumenes discovered this, he immediately called all the soldiers together and first thanked them all that there was no one in so large a number who would break his oath with Eumenes for the sake of a reward. Eumenes cleverly intimated to them that these notices were his own, and that he had used them to determine their loyalty to him. Consequently, if the enemy should do the same again later, the army would imagine it to be just another ploy by Eumenes to determine their loyalty. Thereupon, they all called out and vowed their service to protect his life. {*Justin, Trogus, l. 14. c. 1.*} They decreed among themselves that a thousand men should be chosen from the main part of the army for his daily guard and that they would take turns every night to watch over him. Those who were chosen were glad of the service and willingly received from Eumenes the kind of gifts that the the Macedonian kings normally bestowed on their friends. For Eumenes gave them purple hats and robes which, among the Macedonians, was always deemed a great favour from their kings. {*\*Plutarch, Eumenes, l. 1. c. 8. s. 6,7. 8:103,105*} *[E300]* However, one of his chief commanders, Perdiccas, defected from him, along with three thousand foot soldiers and five hundred cavalry. When Perdiccas had journeyed three days, Eumenes sent Tenedos, a Phoenician, with four thousand select foot soldiers and a thousand cavalry to overtake them. This he did, attacking them by surprise at night, while they were all asleep. He took Perdiccas prisoner and brought all the soldiers back to Eumenes, who picked out the chief instigators of this revolt and executed them, while the rest were distributed in small numbers among his other companies. He spoke kindly to them and treated them courteously, thereby again winning over their affections. {*Diod. Sic., l. 18. c. 40. s. 2-4. 9:125}

2443. After this, Antigonus communicated through a secret messenger with Apollonides, one of the commanders of the cavalry under Eumenes. By making generous promises, he had him betray Eumenes and forsake and turn against him in the middle of the battle. At this time, Eumenes was camped in the country of Orcynia in Cappadocia, which was a place suitable to fight in with the cavalry. Antigonus went there with his army and took over all the upper ground near the foot of the mountains. His army had consisted of ten thousand foot soldiers who were mainly Macedonians and men of admirable strength and courage, as well as two thousand cavalry and thirty elephants. In Eumenes' army there were at least twenty thousand foot soldiers and five thousand cavalry. The battle began very fiercely and Eumenes' side was winning, but when Apollonides defected to the enemy with his regiment of cavalry, Antigonus won. Eumenes lost eight thousand men and all his supply train in that battle. {*Diod. Sic., l. 18. c. 40. s. 5-8. 9:125,127} {*Plutarch, Eumenes, l. 1. c. 9. s. 2. 8:105}

2444. Eumenes did not allow the traitor to escape, but seized him and hanged him while he was in the very act of his villainy. Eumenes fled in the opposite direction from the way that his pursuers took. He turned back shortly after, passed by the enemy and returned to the place where the battle had been fought. There he camped and gathered together the dead bodies, but since the place lacked firewood, he took the doors and gates of the towns and villages in the area, had them broken up, and made piles on which to burn his dead. The captains were burned separately from the common soldiers. When Antigonus later returned to the place, he was amazed at this bold act of his and the undauntedness of his great courage. {*Plutarch, Eumenes, l. 1. c. 9. s. 2. 8:105,107} [L417]

2445. By chance, Eumenes came across Antigonus' wagons. Although he could have taken many prisoners, and a substantial number of slaves with many goods, he did not. He feared lest his men, when they had acquired so much wealth, would grow less keen to fight and to move quickly, because of all the goods they had picked up. Eumenes ordered that each man should feed his horse well and refresh himself, after which they were to be ready to attack the enemy. Meanwhile, he secretly sent to Menander, who had been positioned to guard the

enemy's luggage, to move immediately from the plain to the foot of the mountain, because he feared that Menander might suddenly be surrounded by hostile cavalry. When Menander saw the potential danger, he moved quickly. The enemy said that they were very much indebted to Eumenes for sparing their children from slavery and their wives from rapine. Antigonus, however, told them that Eumenes had not done it for their sakes, but so as not to burden his troops with useless goods in their flight. {*Plutarch, Eumenes, l. 1. c. 9. s. 3-6. 8:107,109}

2446. Eumenes went from there and secretly persuaded a great many of his men to leave him for the present. This was either from an honest concern for them, or because they had now become too few to oppose the enemy and yet were too many to conceal with him in his flight. He came to Nora, which was a strong citadel and which Strabo said was called Neroassus in his time. It was located near Cappadocia and Lycaonia. {*Strabo, l. 12. c. 2. s. 6. 5:357} He had five hundred cavalry and two hundred foot soldiers with him. (Although Diodorus said that there were not more than six hundred in total.) As many of his friends as asked his permission to leave, were each embraced in a fair and courteous manner and dismissed. They wanted to leave either because of the desolation of the place or the scarcity of fresh provisions. He freely gave them the food that they found there. The place was not more than about four hundred yards in circumference and contained abundant provisions of grain, salt and water, but there was no supply of fresh food to be had. {*Diod. Sic., l. 18. c. 41. s. 1-3. 9:127,129} {Justin, Trogus, l. 14. c. 2.}

2447. Antigonus arrived at this spot and before he besieged it, he sent to Eumenes to come to a talk. When Eumenes required hostages, Antigonus refused, but asked him to come out to his superior. Eumenes again sent him word:

> "As long as he wore a sword by his side, he would acknowledge no superior."

2448. Thereupon, when Antigonus sent him his own brother's son, called Ptolemy, as had been requested, Eumenes came out and they embraced each other very warmly and genuinely. As they discussed various matters, Antigonus noticed that Eumenes never mentioned anything concerning his own security or pardon, but still continued to demand that his former governments be confirmed and he be compensated for his losses. The bystanders stood amazed at this and wondered at the constancy of his courage and the magnanimity that he demonstrated. [E301] Antigonus told him that he would talk with Antipater concerning these matters. So, with much ado, he returned to his citadel again, safe from the violence of the crowd. Antigonus built a double wall with trenches around the citadel and left enough men to maintain the siege, after which he then moved his camp. {*Diod. Sic., l. 18. c. 41. s. 4-7. 9:129,131} {*Plutarch, Eumenes, l. 1. c. 10. 8:109,111} {Justin, Trogus, l. 14. c. 2.}

2449. After a while, Eumenes sent messengers to Antipater to make peace. One of these was Hieronymus, the historian, who was born in Cardia, as Eumenes was. In the meantime, he provided food for his company and though he was short on provisions, he nonetheless cheerfully accepted what he had. He invited them all in their turn to his table, where he entertained them with pleasant discourses and good speeches, instead of better food. As often as he chose to, he would sally forth and either burn or destroy Antigonus' works. {*Diod. Sic., l. 18. c. 42. 9:131,133} {*Plutarch, Eumenes, l. 1. c. 11. 8:111} {Emilius Probus, Eumenes} {Justin, Trogus, l. 14. c. 2.} [L418]

2450. He feared that he might lose all his horses from lack of exercise, since they were always confined to one place. He ordered every day that his horses be propped up with their front feet above ground and be made to stand on their hind feet, so that with striving and much struggling, they might get exercise, and sweat. He gave them boiled barley to eat, so that they could digest it more easily. When at last he came out of the citadel, everyone was amazed to see his horses so fat and sleek, as if they had been kept in the best pasture of the country all the while. {*Frontinus, Stratagems, l. 4. c. 7. s. 34. 1:323} {*Diod. Sic., l. 18. c. 42. s. 3-5. 9:131,133} {*Plutarch, Eumenes, l. 1. c. 11. s. 3,5. 8:113} {Emilius Probus, Eumenes}

2451. Ptolemy, the son of Lagus, knew that Phoenicia and Coelosyria would be very advantageous to him for the defence of Egypt and also for the capture of Cyprus. He thought much about how he could take them over. Therefore he tried to persuade Laomedon, who had been made governor of those two provinces, first through Perdiccas and later through Antipater, to turn them over to him, offering him a vast sum of money in return. When this did not work, he raised a large army and having made his trusted friend, Nicanor, its general, he sent him to take this area by force. Nicanor marched into Syria and took Laomedon prisoner, but he bribed his keepers and escaped to Alcetas in Caria. In a short time, Nicanor had subdued all Phoenicia and Syria, stationing garrisons there before returning to Egypt. {*Diod. Sic., l. 18. c. 43. 9:133} {*Appian, Syrian Wars, l. 11. c. 9. (52) 2:203} {*Pausanias, Attica, l. 1. c. 6. s. 4. 1:31}

2452. Ptolemy attacked the various regions of Phoenicia and Syria. When he had captured Jerusalem by deceit, he deported a hundred thousand men into Egypt. Of these he selected thirty thousand of the ablest, whom he armed and took into his army at greater than normal

pay. He committed his garrison towns and citadels in Egypt into their trust, and sold the rest for slaves among his soldiers. This was not necessarily Ptolemy's doing, but came from the desire of the soldiers, who wanted the Jews, rather than any other people, to help to do the menial tasks related to war. {Aristeas, Septuagint Interpreters} {Aristeas, Letter to Ptolemy Philadelphus} {*Josephus, Antiq., l. 12. c. 1. s. 1. (1-10) 7:3-7} {*Eusebius, Chronicles, l. 1. 1:207}

2453. Concerning the capture of Jerusalem, Agatharchides of Cnidos described it in his book about the successors of Alexander the Great: {*Josephus, Antiq., l. 12. c. 1. s. 1. (1-10) 7:3-7} {*Josephus, Apion, l. 1. c. 22. (209-212) 1:247,249}

"They, who are called Jews, live in a most fortified city which the natives call Jerusalem. They keep every seventh day as a holiday. They do not involve themselves in war, husbandry or any other type of work on this day. They only hold up their hands in hallowed places and stay there praying until the evening with outstretched hands. When Ptolemy, the son of Lagus, entered their city with his army, all men observed the folly of them that were observing the Sabbath. So the country became enslaved under a bitter master and their law was found to be nothing else but a foolish custom."

2454. Appian added that Ptolemy demolished the walls of the city. When he had left garrisons in Syria, he returned to Egypt by sea. {*Appian, Syrian Wars, l. 11. c. 8. (50) 2:199} {*Appian, Syrian Wars, l. 11. c. 9. (53) 2:203}

2455. Concerning this Jewish deportation into Egypt, Josephus wrote: {*Josephus, Antiq., l. 12. c. 1. s. 1. (7-10) 7:5,7}

"Ptolemy carried away many captives from the hill country of Judea, the places bordering on Jerusalem, from Samaria and from Mount Gerizim into Egypt. He made them to dwell there. [L419] He found that the men of Jerusalem kept their oaths from the reply which they made to Alexander's messengers after the last defeat of Darius. Therefore, he decided to put many of them in his garrisons and citadels. When he had settled many of them in Alexandria, he gave them the same privileges which the Macedonians had. He bound them all with an oath to be loyal to his posterity because he had bestowed such generous favours on them."

2456. Again, Josephus said: {*Josephus, Apion, l. 2. c. 4. (44) 1:309,311}

"Ptolemy Lagus committed all his citadels and places of strength to his Alexandrian Jews. He thought they would be kept most safely in their hands because of their fidelity and integrity. [E302] So that he might reign most securely in Cyrene and other parts of Libya, he sent many of those Jews to live in that country."

2457. Jason of Cyrene, from whose writings the second book of the Maccabees was collected, {*Apc 2Ma 2:23*} was descended from these Jews, as well as Simon of Cyrene, who bore the cross of Christ, {*Mt 27:32*} and of whom mention is made in Acts. {*Ac 2:10 6:9*}

## 3685a AM, 4394 JP, 320 BC

2458. While Eumenes was trapped in Nora, Antigonus besieged it, putting a double wall around him. He marched with his army against Alcetas and Attalus, first going into Pisidia, where Alcetas and his forces were. In seven days he marched about three hundred miles to the city of Cretopolis. Because he came upon them so suddenly and unexpectedly, he was able to take over some suitable hills and places of advantage there. In his army, besides his elephants, were forty thousand foot soldiers and seven thousand cavalry. However, Alcetas dared to meet him in the open field with only sixteen thousand foot soldiers in his army and nine hundred cavalry from his friends. Because Antigonus had the advantage of the ground and had a much stronger force, he routed him and took both Attalus and Docinius, Polemon and many other chief captains as prisoners. He showed them his mercy and exercised great clemency and humanity toward them. He distributed the rest of the prisoners among his own companies, thereby greatly increasing his own army. {*Diod. Sic., l. 18. c. 44,45. 9:135,137*}

2459. Alcetas fled to Telmessus, a city of Pisidia, with his bodyguard, his sons and other Pisidians who served him. The Pisidians numbered about six thousand and were all very strong and valiant men, who promised never to forsake him. Therefore, when Antigonus with all his army came before the walls of Telmessus, he demanded that Alcetas be delivered to him. The older men wanted to turn him over but the younger men met together at night and swore an oath not to forsake him, in spite of any danger that might ensue. Nevertheless, the elders of the city secretly sent a messenger to Antigonus to let him know that they would deliver Alcetas into his hands, dead or alive. The plan was that he would send the soldiers to a skirmish and pretend to flee and retreat to a reasonable distance from the walls of their city. This was done, drawing the young men out of the city. In the meantime, the elders with their men attacked Alcetas, who killed himself rather than fall into the hands of the enemy. His body was placed on a funeral bier and wrapped in a coarse cloth. While the young men were fighting, his body was sent to Antigonus. For three days, Antigonus exposed it to all the contumelies and indignities that

could be imagined, and finally had it cast out unburied. When the young men returned from the battle and heard what had happened in their absence, they were enraged at the elders. They seized part of the city and resolved at first to set it all on fire, but changed their minds and started plundering and wasting the enemies' country in the area. When they learned that Antigonus had left the corpse of Alcetas behind, they took it up and gave it an honourable burial. {*Diod. Sic., l. 18. c. 45-47. 9:137-143*}

## 3685b AM, 4395 JP, 319 BC

2460. Antipater became sick, and before his death made Polyperchon guardian of the kings and sovereign commander in his place. *[L420]* Polyperchon was almost the oldest man of all who had served under Alexander, and was held in very great esteem among the Macedonians. However, Cassander, Antipater's son, was not content with his office of general of the cavalry. He was enraged to see that Polyperchon was preferred over him as the guardian and sovereign of the realm. He began to plot with his friends to get the kingdom into his own hands and secretly sent his agents to Ptolemy to renew his former friendship with him. He wanted him to enter into an alliance with him and sail with his fleet from Phoenicia into the Hellespont. He did the same with the other commanders and cities, and urged them to join forces with him. {*Diod. Sic., l. 18. c. 47-49. 9:143-147*} {*Plutarch, Phocion, l. 1. c. 31. 8:217*}

2461. When Antigonus returned with his army from Pisidia into Phrygia to the city of the Cretenses, he was there informed about all these matters by Aristodemus of Miletus. This pleased him greatly, for he also aspired to supreme sovereignty. {*Plutarch, Eumenes, l. 1. c. 12. s. 1. 8:115*} He had been left as sole and absolute commander of all Asia by Antipater and had a larger army there than anyone else. He planned to seize all the king's treasure there while there was no one to oppose him. He had in his army, at the time, sixty thousand foot soldiers, ten thousand cavalry and thirty elephants, and realised that he had the means, if needed, to increase his army at his pleasure. He could get troops from foreign countries, and Asia was well able to feed and pay them all abundantly. So he called a council of his friends, declaring to them that his purpose was for the good of them all, and then assigned them to various offices and commands. With generous promises he secured them to be loyal to him and help him do what he planned. He resolved to go throughout all Asia, putting out the governors and replacing them with ones of his own choosing. {*Diod. Sic., l. 18. c. 50. 9:149-151*} *[E303]*

2462. When Aridaeus, who had the government of Phrygia on the Hellespont, knew what Antigonus was up to, he went and attacked the large city of Cyzicum, which would be most suitable for his needs. He had an army of more than ten thousand mercenary foot soldiers, a thousand Macedonians, five hundred Persian archers and slingers and eight hundred cavalry, as well as every kind of battering ram. The men of Cyzicum, under the pretence of a treaty for peace, obtained a truce for a time. They dragged out the discussions for the surrender, while they secretly sent to Byzantium for help and supplies of men and equipment of all types for their defence. As they sailed along their own coasts with their warships, they gathered men from the country and put them in the city, along with any supplies they brought with them. Aridaeus, as he later found out, had been fooled by the men of Cyzicum, and had to return to his own government again. {*Diod. Sic., l. 18. c. 51. 9:151-155}

2463. When Antigonus was at Celaenae, he hurried away with twenty thousand select foot soldiers and three thousand cavalry to relieve Cyzicum, hoping to ingratiate the city to him, but he came too late. He sent messengers to Aridaeus to rebuke him for his actions. He required Aridaeus to give up his government and to live henceforth as a private citizen with only the revenue from one city to live on. When Aridaeus refused to comply, he placed guards about the gates and on the walls and various other places of the city where he was. Then he sent away a part of his army, under a commander, to side with Eumenes. They were to raise the siege from the citadel of Nora and help Eumenes out of that danger. This was to help Aridaeus make a league with Eumenes against Antigonus. {*Diod. Sic., l. 18. c. 52. s. 1-4. 9:155,157} [L421]

2464. Probus stated that Eumenes, toward the beginning of the spring, under the pretence of submitting himself to Antigonus, daily entreated for conditions. At last Eumenes tricked him, and he and all his people escaped from the citadel. {Emilius Probus, Eumenes} However, Justin said that Antigonus raised the siege when he found that Antipater had sent relief to Eumenes. {Justin, Trogus, l. 14. c. 2.} Diodorus and Plutarch stated that Eumenes, through the mediation of Hieronymus Cardianus, his countryman and true friend, was allowed to come out on his word, and so it was. {*Plutarch, Eumenes, l. 1. c. 12. s. 2,3. 8:115,117} {*Diod. Sic., l. 18. c. 50. s. 4,5. 9:151}

2465. Antigonus, wondering how to get everything under his control, sent for Hieronymus, the historian, to come to him, and used him to send a message to Eumenes to cut a deal. He wished to forget what had happened between them in the battle at Cappadocia, and would now be pleased to join with him in a firm league of love and friendship, and an association of arms. He offered to give him far more wealth than he

had lost and a better province than he had ever had before. He would make him the best among all his friends and partaker of all his plans and fortunes. {*Diod. Sic., l. 18. c. 50. s. 4,5. 9:151} When Antigonus had drawn this up in the form of an oath, to bind each other to strict observance of the conditions, he sent it to Eumenes. Eumenes took it and amended it in some points, then he asked those Macedonian captains who were in the siege against him, to judge which of the two was the better and less ambitious. Among everything else, Antigonus made mention of the kings in a formal manner, but in the performance of all services and conditions, he referred only to himself, and they were made in his own name. Whereas Eumenes, in his draft, mentioned Olympias first, with the two kings. Secondly, he arranged the oath on such terms as purported that he would reckon all those to be friends and foes, who were friends and foes not only to Antigonus, but to Olympias and the two kings as well. When this seemed to them to be the more reasonable of the two, Eumenes took his oath. Because he had taken the oath, they promptly raised their siege and sent to Antigonus, asking him to bind himself to the same oath as Eumenes had. Meanwhile, Eumenes sent back home again whatever Cappadocian hostages he had. Antigonus wrote back a sharp and taunting letter to those Macedonians for presuming to amend anything in the wording of the oath which he had prescribed for Eumenes to take. He wanted them to besiege Eumenes again, but this order came too late. {*Plutarch, Eumenes, l. 1. c. 12. s. 2,3. 8:115,117}

2466. When Eumenes, against all his expectations, had escaped after a year's close siege, he stayed for a time in Cappadocia, gathering together his old friends and soldiers who were now scattered about the country. {*Diod. Sic., l. 18. c. 50. s. 4,5. 9:151} He started all over again from nothing. The friends of those hostages whom he had released lent him horses, wagons and tents, and in a short time about a thousand cavalry, from the old regiments which were foraging up and down the country, came to him. {*Plutarch, Eumenes, l. 1. c. 12. s. 3. 8:115} [E304] Eumenes was a most active and industrious man, and there were others there who were just as devoted to the state as he was, and so it happened that large numbers of soldiers came flocking to him. Within a few days, in addition to the five hundred friends who were with him in the citadel, he had acquired two thousand men who were all ready to serve him. {*Diod. Sic., l. 18. c. 53. s. 4,5. 9:157-161}

2467. Antigonus sent some of his forces to besiege Aridaeus, the governor of Lesser Phrygia. He personally marched with most of the army into Lydia to expel Clitus from his government. Clitus, however, had been forewarned and immediately packed every one of his towns and places of defence with strong garrisons. He went into Macedonia to acquaint the kings and Polyperchon, their guardian, of Antigonus' doings and his planned revolt from the Macedonian government. He asked for help against him. {*Diod. Sic., l. 18. c. 52. s. 5,6. 9:157}

2468. Antigonus captured Ephesus at his first coming, because some within the city betrayed it into his hands. [L422] Later, Aeschylus of Rhodes arrived there, bringing four ships from Cilicia with six hundred talents that were to be sent to the kings in Macedonia. Antigonus seized it all for his own use, saying that he had need of it to raise and pay foreign soldiers with. By this act, he plainly showed his intention to be independent and to rebel against the kings. After this, he proceeded to take the rest of the cities, some by force and others by fair words. {*Diod. Sic., l. 18. c. 52. s. 6,7. 9:157} It is from the time of this revolt that Dexippus, Porphyry and Eusebius calculated the eighteen years of his rule. {Porphyry, Scaliger's Greek Eusebius, p. 48,164,226.}

2469. When Cassander had crossed the Hellespont, he went to Antigonus in Asia, to seek his help and assure him of Ptolemy's support. Antigonus was glad of his coming and at once offered to help him by land and sea. This he did under a pretence, as if he intended to him for his father Antipater's sake. Whereas his main purpose was to embroil Cassander in as many wars and troubles as he possibly could in Europe thereby enabling Antigonus to move about more freely, take over Asia and make himself king there. {*Diod. Sic., l. 18. c. 54. 9:161,163}

2470. Polyperchon, the guardian of the kings and curate of the Macedonian empire, sent letters to Eumenes in the two kings' names, requiring him to be loyal to the kings and fight against Antigonus, as he had done before. He gave Eumenes the choice of coming into Macedonia and there being a guardian of the two kings, jointly with him, or of staying in Asia. If he stayed, he would receive supplies of men, money and equipment to oppose Antigonus, who had now openly declared himself a rebel against the kings. If he needed larger forces, Polyperchon would be ready, with the kings and all the power that the kingdom of Macedonia could muster, to cross the seas and to come into Asia to join forces with him. Similar letters were sent to the treasurers in Cilicia, requiring them, from the money which was at Quinda or Cyinda (where the kings' treasure for Asia was kept, according to Strabo), immediately to pay him five hundred talents toward his recent losses. From the rest of the kings' money, they were to give him as much as he should ask for, to hire and pay for foreign soldiers. He also wrote letters to Antigenes and Tentamus, who between them commanded three thousand silver targeteers under Antigonus. They were to

defect to Eumenes and help him all they could. Polyperchon did this as the man who had been made absolute commander and governor of all Asia under the kings. Olympias, the mother of Alexander the Great, did her part and wrote similar letters, requiring all men to come and aid both herself and the kings. {*Diod. Sic., l. 18. c. 57,58. 9:167-173} {Emilius Probus, Eumenes} {*Plutarch, Eumenes, l. 1. c. 13. 8:117} {*Strabo, l. 14. c. 5. s. 10. 6:341,343}

2471. Eumenes left Cappadocia with only five hundred cavalry and two thousand foot soldiers. He could not wait for the arrival of those who had promised to enlist themselves under him. They had not yet come because Menander was coming with a large army and would not permit Eumenes to stay in Cappadocia, as he had been declared a public enemy of Antigonus. This army arrived three days later and went after Eumenes, but when they saw that they could not possibly overtake him, they returned into Cappadocia. {*Diod. Sic., l. 18. c. 59. s. 1,2. 9:173}

2472. Eumenes made long marches and having passed the Taurus Mountains, came into Cilicia, where he was met by Antigenes and Tentamus, captains of the silver targeteers, with their friends. They obeyed the command of the kings. Congratulating him on his fortunate escape from so many great dangers, they offered him their service and promised to stand by him in his worst dangers. [L423] Then the regiment of about three thousand Macedonian silver targeteers arrived and pledged their loyalty to him. {*Diod. Sic., l. 18. c. 59. s. 3-6. 9:173,175} [E305]

### 3686 AM, 4396 JP, 318 BC

2473. Eumenes feared the envy of the Macedonians if he were to assume the role of absolute governor of the place, since he was a foreigner born in Cardia in the Chersonesus of Thrace. First, he declined to accept the five hundred talents which had been given to him for his losses, saying that he did not need so large a sum, since he was not assuming any government there. {*Diod. Sic., l. 18. c. 60. s. 1-3. 9:175,177} {*Plutarch, Eumenes, l. 1. c. 13. s. 2,3. 8:117} Then he pitched his tent in the name of Alexander and called it Alexander's pavilion, pretending that he had been warned to do so by a vision in a dream. He had a golden throne placed there, with a sceptre and a diadem. They met there every day to consult about matters, and he hoped to minimise any envy toward himself by seeming to administer all things under the majesty and title of Alexander. {*Diod. Sic., l. 18. c. 60,61. 9:177,179} {*Plutarch, Eumenes, l. 1. c. 13. s. 3,4. 8:117,119} {Emilius Probus, Eumenes} {Polyaenus, Strategmata, l. 4.} By behaving as an ordinary man in all the meetings and speaking to every man with good, courteous language, he removed all thoughts of envy toward him. He behaved like this toward the silver targeteers, who were all Macedonians, and was highly esteemed by them, so much so that every man said that he, of all men, was most worthy to have the guardianship of the kings. {*Diod. Sic., l. 18. c. 61. s. 2,3. 9:179,181} He was so honourable in his speech that he did not hesitate to call them his fellow soldiers or his masters, and his companions in those eastern wars. He told them that they were the only men who had conquered the east, the only men to have outdone Bacchus and Hercules with their victories. They were the men who had made Alexander great, and it was through them that he had attained divine honours and immortal glory in the world. Eumenes desired that they should not look on him as their commander, but as their fellow soldier and a man of their own company. {Justin, Trogus, l. 14. c. 2.}

2474. Eumenes selected certain choice men from his friends and giving them much money, he sent them to hire soldiers, promising generous pay. Thereupon, some went into Pisidia, Lycia and the places bordering these countries. Others went into Cilicia, Coelosyria, Phoenicia and the isle of Cyprus, doing their best to hire as many soldiers as they could. Many Greeks, who saw what generous pay was being offered, also came, so that in a short time they had gathered ten thousand foot soldiers and two thousand cavalry, besides the silver targeteers and the men whom Eumenes had brought with him from Cappadocia. {*Diod. Sic., l. 18. c. 61. s. 4,5. 9:181}

2475. Ptolemy came with his navy to a port called Zaphyrium in Cilicia. He sent some of his agents to solicit the silver targeteers to defect from Eumenes, since he had been proclaimed as an enemy, with the death sentence awaiting him. He also sent to the chief officers at Quinda and advised them not to issue any money to Eumenes. No one listened to Ptolemy, because the kings, their governor Polyperchon and Olympias, Alexander's mother, had written to them, requiring them in all things to obey Eumenes as the commander-in-chief of the kingdom. {*Diod. Sic., l. 18. c. 62. s. 1,2. 9:181,183}

2476. After this, Antigonus sent one of his good friends, Philotas, with thirty Macedonians in his company, to the silver targeteers, to sound them out. They first asked their captains and chief soldiers if they could be bribed to kill Eumenes, now that he was in their hands. They found no man agreeable to their desires except for Teutamus, who was one of the captains of the silver targeteers. He agreed and tried to win over Antigenes, his colleague, to help in this foul deed. Antigenes was not at all interested, and prevailed with Teutamus to abandon his plan. He showed him that there were better things and better reasons for trusting Eumenes, a man of moderate fortune and limited power, than trusting Antigonus, who had already grown too powerful.

[L424] Antigonus would cast them aside once he had managed to get everything into his hands, and would replace them with his own friends. Philotas then sent to the chief captains a letter from Antigonus that was directed to the soldiers in general, requiring them to kill Eumenes on sight. It threatened that if they did not do it, Antigonus would come shortly and attack them with his army to make examples of them for their disobedience. This terrified the soldiers, but Eumenes came to them and persuaded them to follow the orders of their kings and not listen to the words of a man who had now openly proclaimed himself a rebel. After speaking many things, Eumenes saved himself from imminent danger and made the troops more loyal to him than ever. {*Diod. Sic., l. 18. c. 63,64. 9:185-189}

2477. Eumenes ordered them to march into Phoenicia, where he assembled all the ships he could from all the coastal towns, to make a strong navy. He planned that Polyperchon, with a fleet at his command, should, at any time, sail with his forces from Macedonia to Asia to fight against Antigonus. For this reason Eumenes stayed even longer in Phoenicia. {*Diod. Sic., l. 18. c. 64. s. 6. 9:189} [E306]

2478. Meanwhile Polyperchon made Clitus, the governor of Lydia, admiral of the fleet and sent him into the Hellespont with the order to stay there and ensure that no ships passed that way from Asia into Europe. He wanted him to help Aridaeus, the governor of Lesser Phrygia, who had fled with whatever men he had into the city of the Cyonians for fear of Antigonus. {*Diod. Sic., l. 18. c. 72. s. 2,3. 9:207}

2479. Clitus came into the Hellespont to protect the cities of Propontis, having joined Aridaeus' army together with his own. Then Nicanor, the captain of the garrison of Munychia, welcomed Cassander, who had put all his navy to sea. He took Antigonus' fleet with him, so that he had more than a hundred ships in his fleet. In a naval battle not far from the city of Byzantium, Clitus won, sinking seventeen of the enemy's ships and capturing at least forty more, with all the men in them. {*Diod. Sic., l. 18. c. 72. s. 2-4. 9:207,209} Clitus was overjoyed. Previously, he had merely taken three or four ships of the Greeks near the isle of Amorgus, one of the Cyclades. He allowed himself to be called Poseidon and carried a trident. {*Plutarch, Fortune of Alexander, l. 2. c. 5. 4:447}

2480. When Antigonus heard of the loss of his navy at sea, he sent for some ships from Byzantium and put as many archers, slingers, targeteers and other such lightly armed men in them as he thought would fit. They landed on the European side and attacked Clitus' men, who had gone ashore and were busy making their camp. They frightened them and forced them to retreat to their ships again, in the process of which their baggage was lost and many men were taken prisoner. In the meantime, Antigonus procured other ships of war, into which he put many of his best soldiers. He sent them to the same place with a strict charge to attack their enemies valiantly, and then they would no doubt overcome them. These came by night under the command of Nicanor, their captain, and attacked at the break of day. *[L425]* He routed them on the very first assault and sank some of their ships with the prows of their own ships. They captured other ships complete with the men in them, who surrendered. Finally they took all the rest of the ships and men, except for Clitus, who abandoned his ship and fled to land, hoping to get into Macedonia, but on the way he was attacked by Lysimachus' soldiers, who killed him. {*Diod. Sic., l. 18. c. 72. s. 5-9. 9:209,211}

2481. After Antigonus had given this great defeat to the enemy, he became master of the sea, and hurried to make himself absolute monarch of all Asia. To this end, he selected twenty thousand of the best foot soldiers and four thousand cavalry from his army and marched toward Cilicia, with the intention of scattering those companies of Eumenes that were there, before his whole army came together. {*Diod. Sic., l. 18. c. 73. s. 1,2. 9:211}

## 3687a AM, 4396 JP, 318 BC

2482. Twenty-third Jubilee.

2483. When Eumenes heard about Antigonus' plans, he tried to persuade Phoenicia, where he then was, and which was at that time unjustly occupied by Ptolemy, to obey the kings. When he was unsuccessful in this, he left and went through Coelosyria, hoping to get into those regions which are called the upper provinces. {*Diod. Sic., l. 18. c. 73. s. 2,3. 9:211} He had the silver targeteers with him, including their captain, Antigenes. These had wintered in the villages of Babylonia known as the villages of the Carians. {*Diod. Sic., l. 19. c. 12. s. 1. 9:259}

## 3687b AM, 4397 JP, 317 BC

2484. Eumenes sent from there to Seleucus, the governor of Babylonia, and to Pithon, the governor of Media, to come with him to help the kings against Antigonus, who had rebelled against them. Seleucus sent him word that he would do what he could for the kings, but he would not help Eumenes, who had for a long time been a person condemned by the council of Macedonians. He secretly sent to Antigenes and the silver targeteers, to kill Eumenes, but they refused. {*Diod. Sic., l. 19. c. 12. s. 2,3. 9:259,261}

2485. Eumenes had the loyalty of his soldiers. He marched to the bank of the Tigris River and camped there, about forty miles from Babylon, where he lost some of his men

in an uprising of the natives against him. From there, he planned to go forward to Susa to gather his soldiers from the upper provinces and to take the kings' money, which was stored there, for his own needs. Seleucus caught up with him near the Euphrates River. Eumenes almost lost his whole army in a sudden flood caused by Seleucus when he opened the head of an old dam and let in the water, flooding his camp and almost drowning everyone. Consequently, Eumenes and his men were forced to flee from there to higher ground. They spent that day figuring out how to recover things. The next day they got about three hundred flat-bottomed boats and transported the main part of the army, without being hindered by the enemy, because Seleucus had nothing but cavalry with him and they were out-numbered by Eumenes. *[E307]* When night came, Eumenes returned with his Macedonians to take care of the wagons which had been left behind. They crossed the river and there, with the help of the natives, found a place to let out the water by another way, to make all that country dry and passable again. When Seleucus heard about this, he wished to rid his country of such guests. As soon as he possibly could, he sent messengers to offer them a truce, and thus he allowed them to march away without bothering them. So once again, beyond all his expectations, Eumenes escaped from Seleucus and came with his army into Persia, to the country of Susa. *[L426]* He had sixteen thousand foot soldiers and thirteen hundred cavalry. When he had refreshed his army after their hard and miserable march, he sent to the commanders of the upper provinces, requesting them to send men and money to him for the service of the kings. {*Diod. Sic., l. 19. c. 12,13. 9:261-265}

2486. Attalus, Polemon, Antipater and Philotas, all of them captains who had been captured in the defeat of Alcetas, had been committed to prison in an exceedingly strong citadel. When they heard that Antigonus had marched up into the upper provinces (Diodorus said that at that time he was in Mesopotamia), they found a sword for each man. Although there were only eight in their group, at midnight they attacked four hundred men who were in the garrison. First they seized Xenopithes, the captain of the garrison, and threw him off the rock of the citadel, which was about two hundred yards high. When they had killed some and overpowered the rest, they set fire to the houses within the citadel, at which point those who were outside waiting to see how the matter would go, made a move, and about fifty were received into the citadel. When they came in, they could not agree among themselves as to whether they should hold the place and await supplies from Eumenes, or abandon it and every man go his own way, since the soldiers of the other garrisons were not far off. About five hundred foot soldiers and four hundred cavalry, as well as about three thousand natives, appointed a new captain and came to besiege the citadel. Docimus, who had advised that they leave the place, saw an unguarded way down the hill and sent a messenger to Statomice, the wife of Antigonus, who was close by. He and another man got out and went to her. However, she did not keep her word with him and held him captive again. The man who had gone with him guided the enemy up to the citadel. They outnumbered the defenders and took over a strong place inside, but Attalus, with the rest who had been of the opinion to defend the citadel, nevertheless kept on fighting bravely from day to day for sixteen months. {*Diod. Sic., l. 19. c. 15. s. 6. 9:271} {*Diod. Sic., l. 19. c. 16. 9:273,275}

2487. When Pithon, the governor of Media, had killed Philotas, who was governor of the upper provinces, he replaced him with his own brother, Eudamus. Thereupon the other governors united their forces, fearing they would be treated in the same way, because they knew that Pithon was a man of a violent disposition. They attacked and defeated him and having killed many of his men, they drove him from all of Parthia. He went into Media, hoping to get relief there, but finding none, he went to Babylon and there sought help from Seleucus. {*Diod. Sic., l. 19. c. 14. s. 1,2. 9:265}

2488. Eumenes stayed in the country of Susa. Lacking supplies, he divided his whole army into three brigades. Even so, as he marched through the country, he found a great scarcity of grain everywhere. He was forced to give them rice instead, and a variety of Indian wheat and the fruit of the palm tree, which was in great abundance there. He had previously sent the kings' letters to the governors of the upper provinces, requesting help. Again, he sent more letters of his own to them, requesting them to come to him into the country of Susa with all their forces. His messengers, however, found them all in one place, fighting Pithon. {*Diod. Sic., l. 19. c. 13. s. 6,7. 9:265}

2489. The leader of them all, and the man most watched, was Peucestes, whom Alexander had previously made the chief captain of his bodyguard and the governor of Persia. He had with him ten thousand Persian archers and slingers. From the other countries he had taken three thousand Macedonians, with six hundred cavalry from the Greeks and Thracians, along with four hundred Persian cavalry. Tlepolemus (or Polemon, Loeb variant reading. Editor.), a Macedonian and governor of Carmania, had fifteen hundred foot soldiers and seven hundred cavalry. [L427] Sibyrtius, the governor of Arachosia, had a thousand foot soldiers and six hundred and ten cavalry. Androbazus had twelve hundred foot soldiers and four hundred cavalry that had been sent by Oxyartes, the governor of Parapanisada. Stasanor, the governor of Aria and Drangiane, had fifteen hundred Bactrian foot soldiers and a thousand cavalry. Eudamus (whom Arrian called Eudemus and Curtius calls Eudemon), the governor of the Oxydracans and Mallians, brought three hundred foot soldiers and five hundred cavalry from India, plus a hundred and twenty elephants. He had acquired these animals when he had treacherously killed Porus, the king of the Indians. In total, they had eighteen thousand and seven hundred foot soldiers (although the numbers add up to twenty-one thousand) and forty-six hundred cavalry. {*Diod. Sic., l. 19. c. 14. s. 5-8. 9:267,269} [E308]

2490. When they had all come to Eumenes in the country of Susa, they called a public council. There was a hot dispute, especially between Peucestes and Antigenes, the captain of the silver targeteers, about the choice of a general. Eumenes removed the reasons for that dispute by erecting a pavilion for Alexander and putting his throne in it. All meetings about public affairs were conducted there, and all the governors and generals jointly decided what to do. {*Diod. Sic., l. 19. c. 15. s. 1-3. 9:269}

2491. When they were all together at Susa, Eumenes took from the kings' treasury as much as the kings' service required. (The kings' letters to the keepers of their treasure had ordered that they give money only to Eumenes, and only as much as he needed.) He gave the Macedonians six months' advance pay, and gave two hundred talents to Eudamus, who had brought the elephants from India. This was under the pretence of defraying the cost of the beasts, but it was intended to secure his loyalty, because Eumenes knew that if any controversy occurred, the side with the elephants would most likely win. The rest of the governors paid for their own soldiers, whom they had brought with them. When this was done, Eumenes stayed in Susiana for a while to refresh his army after their hard journey. {*Diod. Sic., l. 19. c. 14. s. 4-6. 9:271}

2492. Olympias, the mother of Alexander the Great, murdered Philip Aridaeus, one of the two kings, and his wife Eurydice. He had reigned for six years after the death of Alexander, {Justin, Trogus, l. 14. c. 5.} or six years and four months, according to Diodorus. {*Diod. Sic., l. 19. c. 11. s. 4,5. 9:257} Porphyry said that this happened about the 22nd day of our September. {Porphyry, Scaliger's Greek Eusebius, p. 228.}

## 3688 AM, 4398 JP, 316 BC

2493. Cassander, the son of Antipater, besieged Olympias, with her grandchild Hercules, the son of Alexander the Great and his mother Barsine, in the Macedonian town of Pydna. At the beginning of the next spring, they ran out of provisions and Olympias was forced to dismiss her soldiers. She surrendered to Cassander on the condition that she would be allowed to live. {*Diod. Sic., l. 19. c. 36. s. 1-5. 9:329} {*Diod. Sic., l. 19. c. 49,50. 9:363-369} {Justin, Trogus, l. 14. c. 6.}

2494. Antigonus left Mesopotamia and came into the country of Babylonia, where he allied himself with Seleucus and Pithon. After receiving some supplies from them, he made a bridge of boats over the Tigris River and crossed it there. He quickly marched off to fight against Eumenes. However, Eumenes was notified ahead of this and ordered Xenophilus, the keeper of the citadel in Susa, to pay Antigonus none of the kings' money, nor was he even to talk to him. Eumenes went with his armies and manned the bank of the Tigris River along its entire length, from its source to the sea, with citadels, which were built on its bank. Since that was a considerable undertaking, Eumenes and Antigenes had Peucestes send them ten thousand more archers from Persia. {*Diod. Sic., l. 19. c. 17. s. 2-4. 9:275,277} [L428]

2495. Antigonus went with his army to the king's palace in Susa and made Seleucus the governor of that country. He left a sufficiently large army with him and wanted him to besiege the citadel. Xenophilus, the treasurer, refused to obey his commands. About the rising of the dog star (Sirius), Antigonus and his army marched at night to the Coprates River where it joins the Tigris River. He lost a large number of his men, because the season was so hot. Finding that river to be about four hundred feet wide, he got together a small quantity of flat-bottomed boats and used them to get some of his foot soldiers across, telling them to wait for the rest to cross. Eumenes was notified of this by his scouts as he was about ten miles from the place. He crossed the Tigris River on a bridge and came with four thousand foot soldiers and thirteen hundred cavalry. He found that three thousand foot soldiers and four hundred cavalry of Antigonus' army had already crossed over, but there were at least six thousand who were foraging about the country. He suddenly attacked them and routed them, forcing the Macedonians who fought, into the river. They ran headlong into their boats, which sank from overloading, and few escaped. About four thousand, who did not venture into the river, were taken prisoner, according to Diodorus. Plutarch, however, said that when Antigonus crossed the Pasitigris River, the rest of the commanders did not know what had happened. Eumenes himself met him with his own company and killing many of his men, filled the river with dead bodies and took four thousand prisoners. {*Diod. Sic., l. 19. c. 17. s. 2-4. 9:279-283} {*Plutarch, Eumenes, l. 1. c. 14. s. 1-3. 8:121}

2496. When Antigonus saw that he could not cross that river, he retired with his army toward a city of Badace

that was located on the Eulaeus River. He stayed there for a few days to refresh his army, which was exhausted from the extreme heat, after which he planned to go to Ecbatana. He did not follow the highway because of the extreme heat, and because the journey would take at least forty days. He went instead by way of the Cossaeans, which was shorter and not so hot. In spite of this, he lost a large number of men and risked the lives of the rest. [E309] After nine days, when they had yet to come to any habitable place in Media, the whole army began to grumble, for they had received three major setbacks within forty days. Antigonus ordered Pithon to go throughout all Media, which he did, bringing him two thousand cavalry, a thousand equipped cavalry horses, and enough equipment to outfit his army again. He also brought five hundred talents from the king's treasury. Antigonus distributed the cavalry among his other troops and gave the horses to those who had lost their own. He gave the beasts of burden freely to those who wanted them. By this, he quickly regained the love and favour of his army again. {*Diod. Sic., l. 19. c. 18-20. 9:279-287}

2497. Eumenes and his men left Pasitigris for Persia and after a twenty-four day march, came to the royal seat of the kingdom called Persepolis. There his whole army was entertained and most magnificently feasted by Peucestes, the governor of that province. Sacrifices were offered to the gods, including Alexander and Philip. Plutarch added that each man was given a sheep for his own particular sacrifice. Eumenes alone knew that it was Peucestes' intention to ingratiate himself with the army and to gain command of it, and sovereign power for himself. In the name of Orontes, the governor of Armenia and a good friend of Peucestes, he forged a letter addressed to himself, and written in the Syriac script. It stated that Olympias, with Alexander's youngest son, had defeated Cassander and had recovered the kingdom of Macedonia again. It said also that Polyperchon, with the main force of the king's army and his elephants, had crossed into Asia against Antigonus. {*Diod. Sic., l. 19. c. 21-23. 9:287,293} {*Plutarch, Eumenes, l. 1. c. 14. s. 3. 8:121} {Polyaenus, Strategmata, l. 4.} [L429] These letters passed as authentic, and so everyone thought that Eumenes would be the most important man and in a position to advance whom he pleased and to punish whom he thought fit. Therefore they resolved to depend on him, and any that opposed him were called into question by him before the courts. He started with Sibyrtius, the governor of Arachosia, and so made them all afraid. In the meantime, he courted Peucestes' loyalty and told him of the great honour and wealth he would give to him when the time came, and with this tactic he prevented him from doing anything else against him. {*Diod. Sic., l. 19. c. 23. s. 2-4. 9:293}

2498. Because he wished to ingratiate the rest of the commanders and governors of the provinces to himself, he made out as though he needed more money and consequently exhorted them to contribute what they could spare for the king's service. Having thus collected four hundred talents, he now made those who had previously seemed most fickle toward him, most loyal to him, for fear of losing the money which they had lent him. {*Diod. Sic., l. 19. c. 24. s. 1-3. 9:295} {*Plutarch, Eumenes, l. 1. c. 13. s. 6. 8:119}

## 3689a AM, 4398 JP, 316 BC

2499. In Asia Minor, Attalus and the rest of the commanders with him were at last forced to surrender. They had endured a siege of sixteen months and suffered much hardship. {*Diod. Sic., l. 19. c. 16. s. 5. 9:275}

2500. In Greater Asia, Antigonus moved with his army from Media into Persia. Eumenes prepared to march against him, and offered sacrifices and started feasting with his captains. He enjoyed their pleasure and became quite drunk and sick, which delayed his march for a few days. As a result, his soldiers said that while other generals could feast, Eumenes could do nothing but command and fight. After a little while, he recovered and went on his march. Peucestes and Antigenes led the troops, and Eumenes was on a litter, following on behind with the elephants. The two armies were within a day's journey of each other, when the scouts came in and brought news of their approach. They reported the number of the enemy and the way by which they were coming, whereupon both armies prepared for the battle. When Eumenes, who was lying on his litter, did not come into the camp, the chief soldiers in every company resolved not to go any farther unless Eumenes came into the camp to move among them. Consequently he was carried on his litter and went in this manner from one quarter to another throughout the army, giving orders everywhere for the arranging of the troops. Meanwhile Antigonus looked on and laughed at him for his efforts. So each side prepared for the battle which never happened, because the ground between the two armies was so poor to fight on. {*Diod. Sic., l. 19. c. 25. 9:297,299} {*Plutarch, Eumenes, l. 1. c. 14. 8:121,123}

2501. They approached within six hundred yards of each other and spent four days in small skirmishes and foraging in the surrounding country, as each side was very hungry and needed supplies. On the fifth day, Antigonus again tried to make Eumenes' army betray him, by offering large rewards, but his agents were sent away by the enraged Macedonians, who threatened them with harm if they were to come again on that errand. After this, Eumenes received news that Antigonus planned to move his camp by night and take a three-day journey to a place called Gabene, which had an abundant supply of provisions. So Eumenes sent some trusted men, who pretended to be deserters, to inform Antigonus that Eumenes would attack his camp that night. [E310] While Antigonus was preparing for the attack, Eumenes stole away with his army to go to Gabene before Antigonus, so he could find a good location for his camp. When Antigonus learned that Eumenes had tricked him, he followed him, even though Eumenes had a six-hour head start. He wanted Pithon to follow safely later with the main body of the army. Antigonus, with a company of the swiftest cavalry that he could choose, got ahead of Eumenes and showed himself upon a hill where Eumenes could see him. Eumenes assumed that Antigonus was there with all of his army and made his stand before he had reached the exact spot where he had intended to pitch his camp and there arranged his army in battle array. [L430] In the meantime, Antigonus' army came upon him, and so these two great generals used their wits and tricked each other. {*Diod. Sic., l. 19. c. 25,26. 9:297-303}

2502. In the country of Paraetacene, these two generals arranged their army in excellent formation and with great judgment, as Diodorus described in detail. Eumenes had with him thirty-five thousand foot soldiers, sixty-one hundred cavalry and a hundred and fourteen elephants. Antigonus had twenty-eight thousand foot soldiers, more than eighty-five hundred cavalry and sixty-five elephants. The battle was bravely fought on each side until almost midnight, as the moon was almost full. When each side was exhausted from fighting, they stopped and went back to their camps. Antigonus lost thirty-seven hundred foot soldiers and fifty-four cavalry, and had about four thousand wounded men. Eumenes lost five hundred and forty foot soldiers and a very small number of his cavalry, while more than nine hundred were wounded. {*Diod. Sic., l. 19. c. 27-31. 9:303-317}

2503. Eumenes wanted to bury the dead as a sign of a total victory, but the army would not allow it, because they wanted to go to the place where their belongings were. Since that was some distance away, Eumenes was forced to allow them to do it.

2504. Antigonus forced his men to camp near the place where the battle had been fought and where his men lay dead. They buried them and Antigonus said he had the victory, claiming:

> "He who had power to bury his dead, was ever to be counted conqueror of the field."

*2505.* The bodies were buried by the break of day. He detained the herald who came to him from Eumenes to beg the bodies of the dead. He sent him back again at night and gave them permission to come and bury the bodies the next day.

*2506.* When he had sent away the herald, he marched away with all his army and by a series of long marches came to Gamarga in Media, which was far away from Eumenes. Pithon was governor of this country, which had abundant provisions and was able to maintain a very large army. When Antigonus had been defeated by Eumenes in the country of Paraetacene, he went away to take up his winter quarters in Media, in a place called *Gadamala* or *Gadarla* according to Diodorus, or *Gadamarla* according to Polyaenus. {*Diod. Sic., l. 19. c. 31,32. 9:315-319} {*Diod. Sic., l. 19. c. 37. s. 1. 9:331} {Emilius Probus, Eumenes} {Polyaenus, Stratagemata}

*2507.* Eumenes heard through his scouts that Antigonus had not followed him. His army was not up to it, and he wanted to bury his dead. Among these dead was Ceteus, who had commanded those who had come to join him from India. His burial caused a fierce argument between his two wives, as each wanted to have the honour of being burned alive with him. The younger of the two won the argument and went into the fire, because the older wife was pregnant. She was given the choice to live, but she pined away from grief and also died. Diodorus described this in detail. {*Diod. Sic., l. 19. c. 33,34. 9:319-323}

*2508.* When Eumenes had finished burying his dead, he went to Gabene. This was some distance from where Antigonus was with his army. It was about a twenty-five day journey if one went through the inhabited country, but if one went through the desert, they were only a nine days' journey apart. They wintered far from each other and gave their armies a chance to rest and recover their spirits again before the next spring. {*Diod. Sic., l. 19. c. 34. s. 7,8. 9:323,325}

*2509.* Meanwhile, Cassander, the son of Antipater, was keen to make himself absolute king of Macedonia. He had Olympias, the mother of Alexander the Great, murdered, and married Thessalonice, the daughter of Philip (not of Aridaeus, as Justin thought) and Alexander's half-sister. Having done this, he sent Alexander, the son of Alexander the Great, with his mother, Roxane, who was very great with child, to be kept in the citadel at Amphipolis. {*Diod. Sic., l. 19. c. 52. s. 1-4. 9:371,373} {Justin, Trogus, l. 14. fin.} [L431]

*2510.* While Eumenes' soldiers were resting, they grew heady and insolent. In spite of their commanders, they camped where they wanted to, all over the country of Gabene. Some of their tents were more than a hundred and twenty-five miles from their headquarters, {*Plutarch, Eumenes, l. 1. c. 15. s. 3. 8:125} as they had chosen their own quarters, not according to any discipline or order of war, but to satisfy their own wishes and preferences. {Emilius Probus, Eumenes} [E311]

*2511.* When Antigonus was told of the disorder in Eumenes' camp, he decided to attack. He let it be known that he would march with his army from Media into Armenia. However, in the depth of winter, at about the winter solstice, he departed from the customary route and marched through the desert. He made fires in the daytime and put them out at night to escape detection, but after they had spent five days on this tedious journey, the soldiers started making fires at night as well as by day, because of the extreme cold. Some of those who lived in the desert saw this and using dromedaries, which commonly run two hundred miles in a day, they notified Eumenes and Peucestes of this. {*Diod. Sic., l. 19. c. 37. 9:331,333} {*Plutarch, Eumenes, l. 1. c. 15. s. 3,4. 8:125} {Emilius Probus, Eumenes}

## 3689b AM, 4399 JP, 315 BC

*2512.* Peucestes was terrified when he heard this and thought of running away, but Eumenes calmed things down and said he would take charge. The enemy would not be coming into those parts for at least three or four days, or as Emilius has it, more than five days. Therefore, he sent messengers into every part to require his troops to come to their headquarters. Then, he went about with certain speedy officers and had fires made everywhere on the hilly countryside so Antigonus would see them. When Antigonus was within nine miles from Eumenes, he saw those fires and began to think that he had been betrayed and his purposes revealed by some of his own people. He thought Eumenes was coming to attack him with his whole army. Not wanting to risk his tired army against Eumenes' fresh and lusty soldiers, he turned aside from the plain into a more winding way, where he stayed one whole day to rest his men and to refresh his beasts, so that they would be in better shape to fight, if they had to. {*Diod. Sic., l. 19. c. 38. 9:333-337} {*Plutarch, Eumenes, l. 1. c. 15. s. 3-7. 8:125,127} {Polyaenus, Stratagemata, l. 4.}

*2513.* Meanwhile, most of Eumenes' army came to their headquarters. When his soldiers saw his surpassing skill and wisdom in organizing things, they wanted him to organize everything himself. As a result, Antigenes, who had always been loyal to him, and Teutamus, the two commanders of the silver targeteers, were envious, and plotted with the other captains of the army to kill him. When Eudamus, who commanded the regiment of the elephants, and Phaedimus (being two of those who had lent Eumenes money and so feared losing it if he died) found out about this, they immediately told Eumenes. Eumenes said that he had to deal with a large herd of wild beasts. He set about making his will and then burned his cabinet of papers, lest after his death they should tell tales and prove dangerous to the people that had written them. {*Plutarch, Eumenes, l. 1. c. 16. s. 1-3. 8:127,129}

2514. Diodorus described in detail the day of the battle between Antigonus and Eumenes. Antigonus had with him twenty-two thousand foot soldiers and nine thousand cavalry, with sixty-five elephants. Eumenes' army consisted of thirty-six thousand and seven hundred foot soldiers, six thousand and fifty cavalry and a hundred and fourteen elephants. The field where they fought was very spacious, and a sandy desert. Such a dust was stirred up when the cavalry first charged, that any man standing only a short way off would not be able to see what was going on. [L432] When Antigonus saw this, he promptly sent some Median cavalry and some Tarentines from Italy to attack the baggage of the enemy, which was about a thousand yards from the battle. Peucestes, the governor of Persia, was frightened by Antigonus and got out of the dust cloud with his horse, taking with him some fifteen hundred more troops. However, the silver targeteers on Eumenes' side made a strong attack on Antigonus' main battle line, killing more than five thousand and routing the rest, and this happened without losing a single man. So Eumenes won, and did not lose more than three hundred men in the battle. {*Diod. Sic., l. 19. c. 39-43. 9:337-347} {*Plutarch, l. 1. c. 16. s. 3-6. 8:129,131} {Polyaenus, Strategmata, l. 4.}

2515. After the battle, the Macedonians saw that their wagons had all been taken, with their wives, children and everything else that was dear to them, so there was great sorrow in the camp. Eumenes sought to pacify them by reminding them that they had killed five thousand of the enemy and if they would only be patient, the enemy would be forced to ask for peace and then all would be well again. They had lost about two thousand women, a few children and servants, and these would more readily be regained by pressing the victory, than by letting it go, now that victory was so close at hand. [E312] However, the Macedonians started railing at him and told him plainly that they would neither flee, now that they had lost their wives and children, nor bear arms against them. Then Teutamus, of his own accord, sent a messenger to Antigonus to request him to send back to them again the goods he had taken. So the bargain was driven between them that if they surrendered Eumenes into his hands, they would get back their belongings, whereupon the Macedonians, ten thousand Persians who had come with Peucestes, the various governors of other regions

and most of the soldiers, left Eumenes and went to Antigonus' camp. {*Diod. Sic., l. 19. c. 43. s. 7-9. 9:349} {*Plutarch, Eumenes, l. 1. c. 17. 8:131} {Justin, Trogus, l. 14. c. 3.}

2516. Before they went, the silver targeteers broke in on Eumenes, took his sword from his hand and bound his hands behind him with a garter. On the fourth day after the battle, they delivered him bound to Nicanor, who had been sent by Antigonus to receive him. Eumenes requested nothing of Nicanor except that he would lead him through the midst of the Macedonians and give him permission to speak his last words to them. When this had been done, he walked ahead of his keepers into Antigonus' camp, followed by the army which had betrayed their own commander and who were now themselves no better than so many captive slaves. They went proudly into their conqueror's camp, and to make it a complete triumph, the elephants and the auxiliaries from India brought up the rear. Antigonus, out of real shame and reverence for the old friendship that had been between them, did not allow Eumenes to be brought into his sight, but assigned him into the custody of certain soldiers. {*Plutarch, Eumenes, l. 1. c. 17,18. 8:131-135} {Justin, Trogus, l. 14. c. 4.}

2517. Among those who were wounded, they brought Hieronymus of Cardia, the historian. He had always been held in great esteem by Eumenes, and after Eumenes' death, Antigonus held him in great favour also. {*Diod. Sic., l. 19. c. 44. s. 3. 9:351} Hieronymus wrote a book concerning the successors of Alexander the Great and the general history of his own time. {*Diod. Sic., l. 18. c. 42. s. 1. 9:131} {*Dionysius Halicarnassus, Roman Antiquities, l. 1. c. 5. s. 1. 1:19} {*Diod. Sic., l. 18. c. 42. s. 1. 9:131} {*Josephus, Apion, l. 1. c. 23. (213) 1:249}

2518. Antigonus, who now had Eumenes and all his army in his hands, first laid hold on Antigenes, the commander of the silver targeteers. He put him alive into a coffin and burned him to ashes. [L433] Then he executed Eudamus, who had brought Eumenes elephants from India, along with Celbanus and some others who had opposed him. {*Diod. Sic., l. 19. c. 44. s. 1-3. 9:349,351}

2519. When Onomarchus, the captain of the watch, asked Antigonus how he wanted Eumenes to be kept, he replied that he was to be kept as one would keep a raging lion or an unruly elephant. Later he relented and ordered that his heavy chains be removed and a boy of his own be allowed to attend him and to help to bathe him. He also allowed Eumenes' friends to visit him and to supply him with necessities. Although his own son Demetrius and Nearchus the Cretian wanted to spare him and tried to save his life, almost all the others that were around Antigonus urged him to kill Eumenes. In spite of all this, Antigonus took seven days to think about it, but when he feared that his army might rebel, he ordered that no man would be allowed to go near Eumenes. He ordered him to be given no food, because he said that he would not kill the man who had formerly been his friend. When Eumenes had neither eaten nor drunk anything in eight days, and the camp was suddenly to be moved, a man was sent who cut Eumenes' throat. Antigonus knew nothing of this and out of respect for his former friendship, ordered his corpse to be turned over to his closest friends to be buried as they thought fit. They burned it in an honourable and military way, with all the army following the bier and witnessing the burning. They gathered his bones into a silver urn and took care to deliver them to his wife and children in Cappadocia. {*Diod. Sic., l. 19. c. 44. s. 1-3. 9:349,351} {*Plutarch, Eumenes, l. 1. c. 18,19. 8:135,137} {Emilius Probus, Eumenes}

2520. Antigonus returned into Media with his whole army and spent the rest of the winter in a town not far from Ecbatana. He distributed his army here and there all over that province, and especially in the country of Rages. It was called that from רעש, because more than two thousand cities and towns in those regions had been destroyed by earthquakes, according to Strabo, based on Posidonius' account. {*Strabo, l. 11. c. 9. s. 1. 5:273} Antigonus discovered that Pithon, the governor of Media, was trying to ingratiate himself with many of Antigonus' soldiers with generous gifts and promises, and trying to encourage them to revolt from him. Antigonus handled the matter very astutely. He let it be known that he planned to make Pithon the governor of the upper provinces and give him a sufficiently large army for that purpose. [E313] He also wrote letters to Pithon and earnestly asked him to come quickly to him, to enable them to consult together on some important matters, so that he could march at once into Asia Minor. Persuaded by these and other letters sent to him from his supposed friends, Pithon, who was then in the remotest parts of all Media in his winter quarters, came to Antigonus. As soon as Antigonus had him, he called him before a council of war, who quickly found him guilty and chopped off his head. {*Diod. Sic., l. 19. c. 44. s. 4,5. 9:351} {*Diod. Sic., l. 19. c. 46. s. 1-4. 9:355,357}

### 3689c AM, 4399 JP, 315 BC

2521. Antigonus gathered all his army together and committed the government of Media to Orontobates, a Median. He made Hippostratus the general of his army, with thirty-five hundred foreign foot soldiers under him, but Antigonus took the main body of his army to Ecbatana, where he acquired five thousand talents of solid silver. Then he marched into Persia and after a twenty day march, arrived at Persepolis, its capital city. {*Diod. Sic., l. 19. c. 46. s. 5,6. 9:357}

2522. While Antigonus was on his way there, the friends of Pithon (those who had been in on Pithon's conspiracy, of which Meleager and Menoetas were the most notable) and followers both of Pithon and of Eumenes who were scattered abroad, met together. [L434] They had about eight hundred cavalry, with which they first attacked the lands and possessions of the Medes who refused to join with them in this rebellion. Then they attacked the camp of Hippostratus and Orontobates by night. They almost overcame the outer works, but had to retire because they were outnumbered, since they had only been able to persuade a few Medes to follow them. Some of the nimblest of the cavalry made many incursions on the country people and raised many disturbances among them. Eventually they were trapped in a place surrounded by rocks and cliffs, where some were killed and the rest captured. Meleager, Ocranes and the most valiant men among those who would not surrender, died fighting. {*Diod. Sic., l. 19. c. 47. 9:357,359}

2523. As soon as Antigonus came to Persia, the people honoured him like a king and proclaimed him master of all Asia. Calling a council of his friends, he propounded to them the matter of the government of the various provinces to be considered. They decided to give Carmania to Tlepolemus, Bactria to Stasanor and Parapanisada to Oxyartes, the father of Roxane, since they could not easily remove them from their positions. Evitus was sent to Aria, but died soon after he arrived there, so Evagoras, who was a man of outstanding valour and sober judgment, replaced him. {*Diod. Sic., l. 19. c. 48. s. 1,2. 9:359}

2524. Antigonus sent for Sibyrtius from Arachosia, who was his friend. He confirmed him in his government of that province and gave him a thousand of the most rebellious silver targeteers, who had betrayed Eumenes. He appointed them to him under the pretence of their helping Sibyrtius in the war, but his real reason was to kill them, for he ordered Sibyrtius to use them in the riskiest work, until he had killed them all. Antigonus did not want any of them ever to return to Macedonia or see Greece again. {*Diod. Sic., l. 19. c. 48. s. 3,4. 9:359,361} {*Plutarch, Eumenes, l. 1. c. 19. s. 2. 8:137} {Polyaenus, Strategmata, l. 4.}

2525. When Antigonus found that Peucestes was highly respected in Persia, he planned to remove him from his government. When all the Persians complained about this, Thespius, one of their leaders, spoke up publicly against it, saying that the Persians would only be governed by Peucestes. Antigonus had Thespius killed and made Asclepiodorus the governor of Persia. He strung Peucestes along with vain hopes of better things, until he had drawn him from Persia. {*Diod. Sic., l. 19. c. 48. s. 5,6. 9:361}

2526. While Antigonus was on his way to Susa, Xenophilus, who had the keeping of the king's treasure at Susa, was sent by Seleucus to meet Antigonus at Pasitigris, offering him his service in whatever he required. Antigonus received him very graciously and pretended that he honoured him more than all his friends, because he feared that Seleucus might happen to change his mind and keep him out when he came to Susa. After he entered the citadel of Susa, he took it over for himself. He also took the golden vine and a number of objects of art totalling fifteen thousand talents, and made all of it into coins. In addition to the crowns of gold and other presents, and spoil taken from the enemy, which amounted to a further five thousand talents, he took twenty-five thousand talents out of Media. {*Diod. Sic., l. 19. c. 48. s. 6-8. 9:361,363}

### 3689d AM, 4399 JP, 315 BC

2527. Antigonus appointed Aspisas, a native of the country, as the new governor of the province of Susa. He planned to carry away all this money to the sea coast in Asia. He had wagons made for this purpose and journeyed toward Babylon. {*Diod. Sic., l. 19. c. 55. s. 1. 9:381}

2528. After twenty-two days, he arrived at Babylon, and Seleucus, the governor of that province, received him with every kind of royal present imaginable and feasted his whole army. [E314] Antigonus wanted him to give an account of all the money in the public treasury which he had received while there, since he had been appointed to his position. [L435] Seleucus replied that he was not bound to give an account for what had been given to him by the Macedonians for the service which he had done for Alexander in his lifetime. When hostilities grew daily between them, Seleucus knew he was too weak to tackle Antigonus and feared that he might be killed like Pithon. So he stole away with only fifty cavalry in his company and fled to Ptolemy in Egypt. All the world spoke of how good Ptolemy was to all those that fled to him for refuge. {*Diod. Sic., l. 19. c. 55. s. 2-5. 9:381,383} {*Appian, Syrian Wars, l. 11. c. 9. (53) 2:205}

2529. Antigonus was quite happy that he had been able to take over Babylon without having to kill his old friend, but the Chaldeans told him that if he let Seleucus go, all Asia would be his and he would one day lose his life in a battle against him. He regretted that he had let him go and sent men after him to capture and bring him back again. After they had pursued him for a time, they gave up and returned to Antigonus, {*Diod. Sic., l. 19. c. 55. s. 6-9. 9:383,385} who thereupon removed Blitor, the governor of Mesopotamia, for allowing Seleucus to pass that way. {*Appian, Syrian Wars, l. 11. c. 9. (53) 2:205}

2530. When Seleucus arrived safely in Egypt, Ptolemy entertained him very graciously. When he told Ptolemy all the things Antigonus had done against him, he persuaded Ptolemy to fight against Antigonus. {*Diod. Sic., l. 19. c. 55. s. 6-9. 9:383,385} {*Pausanias, Attica, l. 1. c. 6. s. 4,5. 1:31}

### 3690a AM, 4399 JP, 315 BC

2531. From there, Seleucus went to Europe with some of his closest friends to persuade Cassander, who at that time commanded everything in Macedonia, and Lysimachus, who was over Thrace, to wage war on Antigonus. Antigonus suspected his intentions and sent his agents to Ptolemy, Cassander and Lysimachus, to request their loyalty and friendship to him as in former times. {*Diod. Sic., l. 19. c. 56. s. 1-4. 9:385,387} However, Seleucus carried the day, so that they all joined together with him in a firm league against Antigonus. {*Appian, Syrian Wars, l. 11. c. 9. (53) 2:205}

2532. Antigonus had made Pithon, who came from India and was the son of Agenor, governor of Babylon. Then he marched toward Cilicia and came to Mallos, a city in Cilicia. There he distributed his army into their winter quarters, since it was the time when Orion set in the early morning, in our month of November. He received ten thousand talents in the city of Quinda, in the same province, while he received a further eleven thousand talents from the yearly revenue of the province. {*Diod. Sic., l. 19. c. 56. s. 4,5. 9:387}

2533. When Antigonus had gone into upper Syria, envoys came to him from Ptolemy, Cassander and Lysimachus. They came to him as he sat in council and made their demands according to the instructions given them. Antigonus was to surrender all Cappadocia and Lycia to Cassander. Phrygia, bordering on the Hellespont, was to be turned over to Lysimachus, while all Syria was to be given to Ptolemy and the province of Babylon to Seleucus. All the public money which he had taken since the death of Eumenes was to be shared equally among them. Antigonus replied roughly that he was now making war on Ptolemy, and that it was his purpose not to have any partners, in either the peril or the profit. {*Diod. Sic., l. 19. c. 57. s. 1,2. 9:387,389} {*Appian, Syrian Wars, l. 11. c. 9. (53) 2:205} {Justin, Trogus, l. 15. c. 1.}

### 3690b AM, 4400 JP, 314 BC

2534. When the envoys returned with this answer, Ptolemy, Cassander and Lysimachus immediately prepared to fight against Antigonus by sea and land. [L436] When Antigonus realised what a gathering storm was about to break over his head, he sought the alliances of other cities, countries and princes to help him in this war. To this end, he sent Agesilaus to the king of Cyprus and Idomeneus and Moschion to Rhodes. He sent his nephew Ptolemy to Cappadocia with an army. Aristodemus was sent into Peloponnesus with a thousand talents to hire soldiers there. He placed couriers and watchmen throughout all Asia, which he controlled, to quickly send him news of anything that happened. {*Diod. Sic., l. 19. c. 57. s. 2,5. 9:389,391}

2535. When this was done, he marched into Phoenicia and camped near Tyre. He ordered them to provide him with a fleet and sent for the petty kings and governors of those parts to come to him. When they came, he asked them to join with him in providing a fleet and in building more ships, since all the ships that belonged to Phoenicia were at that time with Ptolemy in Egypt. He ordered them to bring him four and a half million measures of wheat, which was the annual cost of keeping his army. He then had men fell timber and build ships, using eight thousand men and a thousand beasts of burden to move the materials for the ships from Mount Libanus (Lebanon) to the seaside. {*Diod. Sic., l. 19. c. 58. s. 1-4. 9:391,393} {*Appian, Syrian Wars, l. 11. c. 9. (53) 2:205} {Justin, Trogus, l. 15. c. 1.} [E315]

2536. While Antigonus was busy building a fleet and had his camp by the seaside, Seleucus sailed past with a hundred well-outfitted ships, sailing along in a scornful manner under their very noses. Antigonus' new associates were greatly troubled by this, but Antigonus encouraged them by saying that by the end of the summer, they would see him put to sea with a fleet of five hundred ships as good as those. Meanwhile, Agesilaus returned with his embassy from Cyprus, bringing word that Nicocreon and the most powerful kings of that island had already confederated with Ptolemy, but that Cition, Lapithus, Marion and Cerynia would join with Antigonus. So Antigonus left three thousand men under the command of Andronicus to maintain the siege against Tyre, while he marched with the rest of the army against Gaza and Joppa, which held out against him, and took them by force. Any of Ptolemy's men that he found there, he distributed among his own companies to serve him in his wars. He placed garrisons in both places to keep them in submission, then returned to his standing camp before Tyre and made all necessary preparations for a siege against it. {*Diod. Sic., l. 19. c. 58,59. 9:393,395} {*Appian, Syrian Wars, l. 11. c. 9. (54) 2:207} {Justin, Trogus, l. 15. c. 1.}

2537. At the same time Ariston, who had been entrusted to carry Craterus' bones, delivered them to Phila, the daughter of Antipater, who had first been married to Craterus and now to Demetrius. Antigonus had persuaded her father to have his son Demetrius marry her. Demetrius was not happy with the match, because she was so much older than he. Antigomus would always toast Demetrius in the feast with that saying from Euripides:

"Where there is gain, against nature's dictates must one wed."

2538. He substituted off-hand must one wed for the similar inflection must one serve. He meant that a man must do anything to serve his own ambitions. Phila was a woman who was reputed to excel both in wit and wisdom, by which she often repressed the tumultuous spirits of the most turbulent soldiers in the army. At her own cost, she arranged for marriages for the sisters and daughters of the poorer people among them. {*Diod. Sic., l. 19. c. 59. s. 3-6. 9:395} {*Plutarch, Demetrius, l. 1. c. 14. 9:33,35}

2539. Aristodemus was sent with other captains into Laconia, where he got permission from the Spartans to raise soldiers, and so acquired eight thousand troops from Peloponnesus. [L437] Aristodemus, in a conference with Polyperchon and his son Alexander made a firm alliance with Antigonus. Aristodemus made Polyperchon commander over the forces which he had raised in Peloponnesus and had Alexander sail over into Asia to Antigonus. {*Diod. Sic., l. 19. c. 60. s. 1,2. 9:395,397}

2540. Ptolemy, another of Antigonus' captains, went with an army into Cappadocia. He found the city of Amisus besieged by Asclepiodorus, a captain of Cassander. He raised the siege and secured the place, and Asclepiodorus left under a truce. Subject to certain conditions, he recovered that whole province for Antigonus. He marched through Bithynia and came up behind Zibytes, king of Bithynia, while he was busy in the siege of two cities at once. One city belonged to the Astacenians, and the other to the Chalcedonians. Ptolemy forced him to raise his siege from both cities, whereupon they both surrendered to Ptolemy and gave him hostages as a pledge of their loyalty. Then Ptolemy moved toward Ionia and Lydia, because Antigonus had written to him to secure that coast as quickly as possible. He had been informed that Seleucus was sailing into those parts with his fleet, but Seleucus had indeed already come, and had besieged the city of Erythrae which was on the peninsula opposite Chios. When he heard that Ptolemy, the nephew of Antigonus, was coming, he left it and went away as he had come. {*Diod. Sic., l. 19. c. 60. s. 2-4. 9:397}

2541. Meanwhile, Alexander, Polyperchon's son, came to Antigonus. Before the whole army, including the Macedonians who were not in the army, Antigonus publicly announced to them what Cassander had done, saying that he would avenge the murder of Olympias by Cassander and deliver Roxane and her son, Alexander, from the prison in Amphipolis. He would break off the yoke which Cassander had laid upon all the cities of Greece by putting his garrisons into them. Antigonus sent back Alexander, Polyperchon's son, into

Peloponnesus with a further five hundred talents. {*Diod. Sic., l. 19. c. 61. s. 1-5. 9:397,399} {Justin, Trogus, l. 15. c. 1.}

2542. When Antigonus had received a fleet from Rhodes to go with his other recently built ships, he sailed for Tyre. Since he was master of the sea, he blockaded the people of Tyre by sea and starved them, thereby throwing that city into great distress. {*Diod. Sic., l. 19. c. 61. s. 5. 9:399,401}

2543. When Ptolemy of Egypt heard the declarations Antigonus had made before the Macedonians, about delivering all the Greeks from the rule of Cassander, Ptolemy did the same. He wanted all the world to know that he was no less zealous for the liberty of all the Greeks than Antigonus was. [E316] Asander, the governor of Caria, who was a man of great power and had many large cities under his command, joined with Ptolemy. Although Ptolemy had previously sent three thousand soldiers to the kings of Cyprus, he now sent them ten thousand more under the command of Myrmidon, an Athenian, along with a hundred ships commanded by Polyclitus, making his brother Menelaus general over the whole force. {*Diod. Sic., l. 19. c. 62. s. 1-4. 9:401}

2544. When these came to Cyprus, Seleucus and his fleet met them. In a council of war, they determined their plan of action. They decided that Polyclitus would sail to Peloponnesus with fifty ships and there make war on Aristodemus, Polyperchon and Polyperchon's son, Alexander. Myrmidon with an army of mercenaries would go into Caria to help Asander, the governor of that province, against Ptolemy, a captain of Antigonus who was warring with Asander. Seleucus and Menelaus would stay in Cyprus to support Nicocreon, the king, and the rest of their confederates, against their enemies who were making war against them. When they had divided their forces, Seleucus went and took Cerynia and Lapithus. When he persuaded Stasioecus, king of the Marenses, to join his side, he then forced the prince of the Amathusians to give him hostages to ensure his future safety. The city of Cition would not come to an agreement with him, so he besieged it with his whole army. {*Diod. Sic., l. 19. c. 62. s. 5,6. 9:401,403} [L438]

2545. About the same time, forty ships sailed to Antigonus from the Hellespont and Rhodes, under the command of one Themison their admiral. Then Dioscorides came with eighty more ships. Antigonus already had a navy of a hundred and twenty ships of his own, which had recently been built in Phoenicia, so now, counting the ones besieging Tyre, he had a navy of two hundred and forty ships. Of these, ninety were of four tiers of oars, ten of five, three of nine, ten of ten and thirty were open galleys. He divided this navy and sent fifty of them into

Peloponnesus, and the rest he committed to help his friends as required. He wanted the isles which were still holding out against him to join his side. {*Diod. Sic., l. 19. c. 62. s. 6-9. 9:403,405}

2546. Polyclitus, Seleucus' lieutenant, sailed from Cyprus and came to Cenchrea, which was the port of Corinth. When he found that Alexander, Polyperchon's son, had defected from Antigonus to Cassander and was no longer an enemy, he sailed for Pamphylia. From there, he sailed to Aphrodisia in Cilicia, where he learned that Theodotus, the admiral of Antigonus' navy, had sailed from Patara, a port of Lycia, with the Rhodian fleet which was manned by sailors from Caria. He also learned that Perilaus, with a land army, was following along the shore for the defence of the fleet, if required. In this case he used his wits to defeat him. He landed his men and placed them near a suitable place where the land army would have to pass. He and his fleet went and anchored behind a cape nearby and awaited the coming of the enemy. It so happened that when Perilaus' army came, he fell into the ambush that had been laid for him. He was taken prisoner, while some of his men were killed and the rest were captured alive. When the fleet at sea saw the land army engaged, they hurried to their relief. In this confusion, Polyclitus attacked them with his ships in good formation and easily routed them. So Polyclitus captured all their ships and most of the men in them. Theodotus, their admiral, died shortly after this from his wounds. {*Diod. Sic., l. 19. c. 64. s. 4-7. 9:407,409}

2547. When Polyclitus had had such good success, he first sailed back to Cyprus and later to Pelusium in Egypt, where Ptolemy richly rewarded him for so great a service. He promoted him to a far higher elevation in rank and position of honour than he had before, because he was responsible for such a great victory. He released Perilaus and some other prisoners whom Antigonus had asked for through a messenger he had sent to him. Ptolemy went to Ecregma to confer with Antigonus, but when Antigonus refused to grant him what he demanded, he left and returned to Egypt. {*Diod. Sic., l. 19. c. 64. s. 8. 9:409,411}

## 3691a AM, 4400 JP, 314 BC

2548. Cassander sent an army from Macedonia into Caria, wanting to help the cities which had allied themselves with Ptolemy and Seleucus. He also wanted to prevent Antigonus from coming into Europe. The commanders of this army, Asander, the governor of Caria, and Prepelaus, heard that Ptolemy, Antigonus' general in those regions, had the winter quarters for his army there, and was also busy at the time in burying his father who had recently died. They sent Eupolemus with eight thousand foot soldiers and two hundred cavalry to a place near Caprima in Caria, to lie in ambush for him. Ptolemy found out about it through some men who defected to him and after getting together eighty-three hundred foot soldiers and six hundred cavalry, he attacked them in their trenches and found them off guard and asleep. *[E317]* He took Eupolemus prisoner and forced all the rest to surrender unconditionally. {*Diod. Sic., l. 19. c. 68. s. 2-8. 10:17,19}

## 3691b AM, 4401 JP, 313 BC

*2549.* When Antigonus saw that Cassander wanted to be master of Asia, he left his son Demetrius in Syria with instructions to intercept Ptolemy's men, because he suspected that they were coming farther up into Syria with an army. *[L439]* He left his son with ten thousand mercenaries, two thousand Macedonians, five hundred from Lycia and Pamphylia, four hundred Persian archers and slingers, five thousand cavalry and forty-three elephants. He left four men as counsellors, Nearchus, Pithon who had recently come from Babylon and was the son of Agenor, Andronicus and Philip. These were all men of mature age and judgment, who had served Alexander the Great in his exploits, while Demetrius was a young man, not more than twenty-two years old. {*Diod. Sic., l. 19. c. 69. s. 1,2. 10:19,21}

*2550.* Antigonus took the rest of the army and went to cross the Taurus Mountains. He encountered very deep snow and lost many of his men, prompting him to return to Cilicia. He was told of an easier, less dangerous way to cross the mountains. He came to Celaenae in Phrygia and set up the winter quarters for his army. {*Diod. Sic., l. 19. c. 69. s. 3. 10:21}

*2551.* After Tyre had withstood a fifteen-month siege, it conditionally surrendered to Antigonus. The men of Ptolemy, the king of Egypt, were allowed to leave with their belongings. Andronicus was stationed there to hold the place with a garrison. {*Diod. Sic., l. 19. c. 61. s. 5. 9:399,401} {*Diod. Sic., l. 19. c. 86. s. 1. 10:69}

*2552.* Antigonus sent for Medius to come to him with his fleet, which he had in Phoenicia. On his way, he met with the fleet from the city of Pydna, which he captured and brought to Antigonus with all the men in it. {*Diod. Sic., l. 19. c. 69. s. 3. 10:21}

*2553.* Asander, the governor of Caria, was overwhelmed by the enemy and came to the following agreement with Antigonus. He would give all his army to Antigonus, all the Greek cities there could live according to their own laws, and Asander would continue to hold the government, which he had there, as a grant from Antigonus and would be a loyal friend to Antigonus. As security,

he gave his own brother Agathon as a pledge, but a short time later he changed his mind. He freed his brother from them and sent his agents to Ptolemy and Seleucus, asking them to come speedily and help him. Antigonus took this rather badly, and sent his naval and land forces to attack the free Greek cities. To this end, he made Medius the general of his army, and Docimus the admiral of his navy. When they came to the Milesians, they encouraged the inhabitants to fight for their freedom. The Milesians captured the citadel, placed a garrison there and restored the city to her original freedom again. {*Diod. Sic., l. 19. c. 75. s. 1-4. 10:39,41}

*2554.* Meanwhile, Antigonus besieged and took Tralles and attacked the city of Caunus. He sent for his fleet and took the city, except for the citadel. He made a trench around it and made continual assaults on it in places where it seemed he might be able to break through. He had sent his nephew Ptolemy to the city of Iasus, to compel that city to support Antigonus, so that at that time all these cities came under his control. {*Diod. Sic., l. 19. c. 75. s. 5,6. 10:41}

## 3692 AM, 4402 JP, 312 BC

*2555.* The Cyrenians defected from Ptolemy Lagus and fiercely besieged the citadel there. They had almost taken it, when messengers from Alexandria came and tried to persuade them to stop, so they decapitated them and worked harder than ever to take the citadel. Ptolemy was rather upset by this and sent his captain Agis there with an army, as well as sending a navy, under the command of Epaenetus, to help Agis. Agis vigorously pursued the war against the rebels and took the city of Cyrene. *[L440]* He imprisoned the instigators of this sedition and then sent them bound to Alexandria, while disarming the rest. When he had set things in order there, he returned to Egypt. {*Diod. Sic., l. 19. c. 79. s. 1-3. 10:51}

*2556.* After this success in Cyrene, Ptolemy sailed with his fleet to Cyprus, to fight against those who were rebelling there against their kings. He captured and executed Pygmalion, who was negotiating with Antigonus. He imprisoned Praxippus, king of Lapithia and the ruler of Cerynia, who was suspected of a revolt. He also imprisoned Stasioecus, a petty king of Marion, and destroyed their city, relocating the inhabitants from there to Paphos. After this, he made Nicocreon the commander over all Cyprus, giving him the cities, together with the revenues of all the kings whom he had expelled from their dominions. Then he went with his army into upper Syria and sacked the cities of Poseidium and Potamos in Caria, after which he sailed quickly and took Malus in Cilicia. He sold all the inhabitants into slavery and wasted all the region around there. When he had made his army rich from plunder, he sailed back again to Cyprus. {*Diod. Sic., l. 19. c. 79. s. 4-7. 10:51,53} [E318]

2557. Meanwhile, Demetrius, the son of Antigonus, stayed in Coelosyria, awaiting the coming of the Egyptians. When he heard what damage Ptolemy had done to so many cities in Syria, he left Pithon, the son of Agenor, in command of that region, leaving his heavily armed soldiers and elephants with him, while he, with his cavalry and companies of lightly armed soldiers, rushed toward Cilicia to help save them from Ptolemy. He arrived too late and found that the enemy had already gone. He speedily returned to his camp again, but lost many of his horses on the way because he pressed them too hard to make the journey so quickly. In six days, he marched from Malus, which is normally a twenty-four day journey by ordinary marches. So that through rapid travel, none of the servants of the cavalry were able to keep up to them. {*Diod. Sic., l. 19. c. 79. s. 4-7. 10:51,53}

2558. When Ptolemy saw that everything was going according to his plans, he returned to Egypt. Not long after, Seleucus urged him to attack Antigonus, because Seleucus hated Antigonus. Therefore Ptolemy planned to march into Coelosyria and attack Demetrius. After he had gathered all his army together, he marched from Alexandria to Pelusium. He had eighteen thousand foot soldiers and four thousand cavalry, of which some were Macedonians and some were mercenaries. Some Egyptians helped carry their arrows and weapons, and other baggage of the army, and some went as soldiers. When they crossed the desert from Pelusium, Ptolemy camped near the old city of Gaza and awaited the enemy's arrival. {*Diod. Sic., l. 19. c. 80. s. 4,5. 10:55}

2559. In the 117th Olympiad, Ptolemy defeated Demetrius, the son of Antigonus, in a major battle near Gaza. After this, Ptolemy was also called Poliorcetes, that is, the city taker, according to Castor, the historian, as cited by Josephus. {*Josephus, Apion, l. 1. c. 22. (185) 1:237,239} Diodorus gave the details of the battle in his history of that Olympiad. He said that eight thousand were taken prisoner and about five hundred were killed, but this should be amended from Plutarch, who said that five thousand were killed. Among the nobles who were killed was Pithon, the son of Agenor, who was at that time joint commander with Demetrius, and Boeotus. He had had spent a long time with Antigonus, Demetrius' father, and was most knowledgeable about his plans and affairs. {*Diod. Sic., l. 19. c. 81-85. 10:55-67} {*Plutarch, Demetrius, l. 1. c. 5. s. 2. 9:13}

2560. Ptolemy and Seleucus took Gaza, but Demetrius, escaped aided by a good pair of spurs, reached Azotus at around the following midnight, after riding about

thirty-four miles. [L441] From there, he sent messengers to request the bodies of his dead for burial. Ptolemy and Seleucus readily granted this, and also sent back his own pavilion with all its furniture, gratis and without seeking ransom. They added a generous message that they were not fighting for pay but for honour, and to determine who should wear the garland. {*Diod. Sic., l. 19. c. 85. s. 3. 10:67,69} {*Plutarch, Demetrius, l. 1. c. 5. s. 3,4. 9:15} {Justin, Trogus, l. 15. c. 1.}

2561. Demetrius was no longer able to hold out in the position he was in. He sent a messenger with letters to his father, who was in Phrygia, asking for help and wanting him to come quickly. Demetrius said he was coming to Tripolis in Phoenicia. He sent for the soldiers who were in Cilicia and elsewhere in garrisons remote from the enemy's quarters, to come to him. {*Diod. Sic., l. 19. c. 85. s. 5. 10:69}

2562. When Antigonus heard the news, he said that Ptolemy had this time gained a victory over beardless boys, but that next time he would be fighting against men. In order not to discourage his son, and because his son wanted another battle with Ptolemy, Antigonus said he could fight with him alone if he wanted to. {*Plutarch, Demetrius, l. 1. c. 6. s. 1. 9:15}

2563. Ptolemy sent the prisoners whom he had taken, to Egypt, where they were distributed among the various regiments of his fleet. When he had honourably interred his dead troops, he marched on and attacked the cities and fortified locations of Phoenicia, some of which he besieged, while others were persuaded to yield to him. When he had captured Sidon, he went and camped before Tyre. He sent to Andronicus, the captain of the garrison, to surrender the city to him, while making him generous promises of wealth and honour. He, however, replied that he would never betray the trust which Antigonus and his son Demetrius had put in him, and said many harsh things against Ptolemy. But a little later, his soldiers rebelled and he was taken by Ptolemy, who overlooked the harsh words he had spoken against him and greatly rewarded him. He took Andronicus into the number of his friends and regarded him highly. {*Diod. Sic., l. 19. c. 86. 10:69,71}

2564. Seleucus took with him a thousand foot soldiers from Ptolemy and three hundred cavalry, according to Appian. Diodorus said they were only eight hundred foot soldiers and two hundred cavalry. With so small a force, he went to recover his government of the province of Babylon. When he came with them into Mesopotamia, he dealt with the Macedonians he found living there in Carrhae. [E319] He persuaded some to follow him, while others had to be forced to go along with him on his journey. No sooner had he set foot within the territory of Babylon, than the inhabitants came flocking to him, offering him their service in the recovery of his government. Polyarchus also, who held some office among them, came to him to receive his commands, and brought a thousand armed troops to him. When those who sided with Antigonus realised his popularity with the people, they all fled to the citadel which was commanded by Diphilus, but Seleucus besieged it and took it by force. He released from there the children and friends of his that Antigonus had imprisoned when Seleucus had fled to Egypt for fear. When this had been accomplished, he began raising soldiers in the country. He bought horses and distributed them among those who were able to ride them. He behaved fairly and in a friendly manner toward all of them, securing their loyalty so that they were all prepared to risk any hazard with him. So, once again, for the third time, he recovered all his government of Babylon. {*Diod. Sic., l. 19. c. 90,91. 10:77-81} {*Appian, Syrian Wars, l. 11. c. 9. (54) 2:207}

2565. Nicanor, whom Antigonus had made governor of the province of Media, marched against Seleucus with ten thousand foot soldiers and seven thousand cavalry. Seleucus immediately went to meet him with a little over three thousand foot soldiers and four hundred cavalry. [L442] When he had crossed the Tigris River, he heard that the enemy was not far off, so he hid his men in the marshes around there and planned to ambush Nicanor. When Nicanor came to the bank of the Tigris River, he could not find the enemy and camped near a royal station. Little did he think that the enemy was so near. The following night he was not even thinking about the enemy, and so did not post a proper military watch. Seleucus attacked him and raised a great tumult in his army. When the Persians joined the battle, Euager, their general, was killed, as were some of their other commanders. After this battle, most of Nicanor's army abandoned him and defected to Seleucus. They did not like the strait they were in, nor did they care for Antigonus. Whereupon Nicanor, fearing what would happen next if his soldiers were to turn him over to Seleucus, stole away with a few of his friends and fled home again through the desert into Media. {*Diod. Sic., l. 19. c. 92. 10:81,83}

2566. Even though Seleucus had acquired this powerful army, he still behaved well toward everyone and easily subdued the provinces of Media, Susa and the other bordering countries. He quickly sent Ptolemy word about how he had regained his full regal power and majesty. {*Diod. Sic., l. 19. c. 92. s. 5. 10:83} Based on this, Eusebius counted this as the first year of Seleucus' reign. All the historians noted that the Edesseni began their epoch here. The story of the Maccabees' account of the

Greek reign also began here. Without a doubt this is from the autumn of this very year, that is, from September or October of the year 312 BC or 4402 JP. The writer of the second book of Maccabees calculated his Greek years by starting at that time, and the Jews reckon their *Eram Contractium*, that is, their *Account of Contracts* from this time, and those of Edessa, and other Syrians, their *Epoch of the Seleucian Kingdom*, and the Arabians, *the years of Alexander Dehiplarnain*, as they called them. The writer of the first book of Maccabees, however, began his account of the Greek year from the previous spring to this autumn, and Ptolemy of Alexandria began his Chaldean account from the next spring. {Ptolemy, Great Syntaxis}

## 3693a AM, 4402 JP, 312 BC

2567. While Ptolemy of Egypt stayed behind in Coelosyria, he sent one of his friends, a Macedonian called Cilles, against Demetrius with a large army. Demetrius was camped in upper Syria, and Ptolemy wanted Cilles to fight with him and either drive him from Syria, or confine him there and destroy him. Demetrius was told by his spies that Cilles and his army were carelessly camped at Myus, without keeping a proper watch. So Demetrius left his baggage behind him and marched away with a company of lightly armed troops. They travelled all night, and a little before daybreak they attacked Cilles' camp, turning it into chaos, and captured Cilles together with seven thousand soldiers, as well as much booty. Since he thought Ptolemy was coming later with all his army, Demetrius pitched his camp in a place where he had a swamp on one side and large marshes on the other to protect him. {*Diod. Sic., l. 19. c. 93. s. 1-3. 10:81,83} {*Plutarch, Demetrius, l. 1. c. 6. 9:15,17}

2568. Demetrius sent news of this good success to his father Antigonus at Celaenae in Phrygia. He asked him quickly to send an army, or to come in person into Syria. When Antigonus read the letter, he was overjoyed by the news of the victory and his son's conduct in managing the battle. He had shown himself a man worthy of wearing the crown after Antigonus. {*Diod. Sic., l. 19. c. 93. s. 3,4. 10:83} Demetrius, with his father's permission, sent Cilles and all his friends back to Ptolemy again, and so was no longer indebted to Ptolemy for his former kindness to him. {*Plutarch, Demetrius, l. 1. c. 6. s. 3. 9:17} [E320] [L443]

2569. Antigonus moved from Phrygia with his army and in a few days crossed the Taurus Mountains and came to his son Demetrius. Ptolemy followed the advice of his council and decided to leave Syria. Before he left, he laid waste and destroyed the main cities which he had captured. These included Ace (later called Ptolemais) in Phoenician Syria, Joppa, Samaria and Gaza in Syria.

He took whatever he could carry from there, and returned to Egypt loaded with wealth. {*Diod. Sic., l. 19. c. 93. s. 3-7. 10:85,87}

2570. A large number of men who lived there noticed his good temperament and mild nature, and so wanted to return with him to Egypt. Among these was Ezechias, a high priest of the Jews. (Perhaps a secondary one, for the chief high priest at that time was Onias I.) Ezechias was about sixty-six years old and highly respected among his people, very eloquent and with much experience in the affairs of the world. This and much more concerning this Ezechias was recorded by Hecataeus, the historian (who conversed with him in Ptolemy's army), in a peculiar treatise which he wrote about the Jews. {*Josephus, Apion, l. 1. c. 22. (186-190) 1:239} He told a long story about another Jew with whom he became acquainted, named Mosollamus. His story was this:

> "When I went toward the Red Sea, there was one among the rest of a troop of cavalry of the Jews, who escorted us, a man called Mosollamus. He was a very intelligent man and the best archer of the entire company. He noticed a certain seer in the company stand still and request that all the company do the same, while he observed a certain bird flying, so that he could divine by it. Mosollamus asked him why he was standing still. The seer showed him the bird he was watching and said that it would be best for the company to stay there, if the bird were to stay where it was. If it arose and flew ahead of them, then they should go forward too. If it flew back, then all the company ought to return also. Mosollamus said nothing, but drew his bow and shot and killed the bird. The seer and others present there were angry about this and reproved him for his actions. He replied by asking why they were angry with him, and why they had picked up this unlucky bird. How could this bird, which had not known what was about to happen to it, predict what would happen to them on their journey? If it had had any knowledge of things to come, it would never have come there to be shot to death by Mosollamus, a Jew."

2571. Many things besides this are told by Josephus {*Josephus, Apion, l. 1. c. 22. (200-204) 1:245,247} in the same book concerning the Jews. He said that at that time there were fifteen hundred priests who received tithes, and governed all things belonging to the commonwealth. Demetrius of Phalerum, in his letter to Ptolemy Philadelphus (found in Aristeas and Josephus), gave the reason why no heathen poet or historian mentioned either of those sacred books, or anything about those men who lived according to the rules set down in them. These books contained a sacred and venerable rule which was not to be uttered by unhallowed mouths. {Aristeas, Septuagint Interpreters} {*Josephus, Antiq., l. 12. c. 2. s. 14. (111) 7:55}

### 3693b AM, 4403 JP, 311 BC

2572. Antigonus had recovered all Syria and Phoenicia without fighting a battle. He journeyed to the country of the Arabians, called the Nabateans, and because he thought they had never really favoured his actions, he appointed one of his friends, Athenaeus, with four thousand foot soldiers and six hundred light cavalry, to attack them and get as much spoil as he could. About that time of the year, all the neighbouring countries came together to a common market, to sell their wares. [L444] It was the custom of the Nabateans to go to this market. They left their wealth and the old men, with their wives and children, on the top of a rock. Athenaeus waited for this opportunity and quickly marched to this rock. He left the province of Edom and marched about two hundred and seventy-five miles in the space of three days and three nights. At about midnight, he surprised the Arabians and captured the rock, killing some of the soldiers there and taking some prisoners, but leaving their wounded behind. He took a large quantity of their myrrh and frankincense, with five hundred talents of silver, but he did not stay there more than three hours, lest the neighbouring countries attack him, instead returning immediately. When they had gone about twenty-five miles and could go no farther because they were so tired, they rested and did not set a watch, because they thought the people could not reach them for two or three days. {*Diod. Sic., l. 19. c. 94. s. 1. 10:87} {*Diod. Sic., l. 19. c. 95. s. 1-3. 10:91,93}

2573. When the Arabs heard what had happened from those who had seen the enemy army, they left the market and returned to the rock. The wounded told them which way the army had gone, and the Arabs followed them. [E321] Athenaeus' men were keeping no watch, because they were weary and fast asleep after their long journey, so some of their prisoners stole away from them and told the Arabs where the enemy camp was. They hurried to the place and arrived about the third watch in the morning. They attacked their trenches and killed eight thousand of them as they lay sleeping in their tents. Any who resisted were killed. They utterly destroyed all their foot soldiers and only fifty of their cavalry escaped, and most of them were wounded, too. {*Diod. Sic., l. 19. c. 95. s. 4-7. 10:93,95} So the Nabateans recovered their goods and returned to the rock. They sent a letter to Antigonus written in Syriac, in which they complained about Athenaeus and his wrong-doing, and apologised for their actions. Antigonus wrote back again, cunningly telling them that Athenaeus had been treated well enough by them. He blamed Athenaeus for his actions, assuring them that he had issued no such order. When he had appeased and deceived these poor Nabateans, Antigonus a little later selected four thousand foot soldiers from all his army. They were lightly armed and the swiftest on their feet that he could find. He added four thousand cavalry to the troops and wanted them to take a supply of food that would not need to be cooked, in their knapsacks for the journey. He had his son Demetrius command them, and sent them away early in the night with orders to avenge his loss. {*Diod. Sic., l. 19. c. 96. 10:95,97} Demetrius travelled three days' journey through the desert and hurried to attack them by surprise. However, the scouts saw them coming and made fires to signal their coming into that country, whereupon the Arabs at once climbed to the top of their rock. There was only one way to get up, and that was by climbing by hand. They left their belongings there with a sufficiently large guard to keep them. The rest went and drove away their cattle, some to one place, some to another, in the desert. When Demetrius came to the rock and saw that all the cattle had been driven away, he started to besiege the rock. They manfully defended it and due to the advantage of the position, had the upper hand that day. Finally Demetrius was forced to withdraw. Since he saw that he could not defeat them, he made peace with them. They gave him hostages and the gifts that had been agreed upon between them. He moved about forty miles with his army and camped near the Dead Sea. {*Diod. Sic., l. 19. c. 97. 10:95,97} Plutarch said that he went there with a large booty and seven hundred camels. {*Plutarch, Demetrius, l. 1. c. 7. s. 1. 9:17} [L445]

2574. When Demetrius returned to Antigonus, he told his father what had happened. Antigonus blamed him for making peace with the Nabateans, and said that those barbarous people would become more insolent because they had escaped. However, he commended him for discovering the Dead Sea, as he might raise some yearly revenue for himself from there. He made Hieronymus Cardianus, the historian, his treasurer for that revenue. Josephus noted that he was made governor of Syria by Antigonus. Josephus deservedly condemned Hieronymus for making no mention of the Jews in his writings, since he lived near them and almost among them. {*Josephus, Apion, l. 1. c. 23. (214) 1:249,251} Hieronymus was commanded to build ships and to gather together in one place all the bitumen or liquid brimstone that could be extracted from that lake. Six thousand Arabians attacked them as they were in their ships gathering this brimstone, and killed almost all of them with arrows, and so Antigonus lost all hope of making any regular revenue that way. {*Diod. Sic., l. 19. c. 100. s. 1,2. 10:103,105}

2575. Antigonus learned from letters sent by Nicanor, the governor of Media, and others, how Seleucus was

prospering in those parts. He sent his son Demetrius with five thousand Macedonian foot soldiers, ten thousand mercenaries and four thousand cavalry, with orders to march to the very walls of Babylon. After he had recovered that province, he was to march down to the sea. Demetrius left Damascus in Syria and went to execute his father's commands. As soon as Patrocles, whom Seleucus had left as governor of Babylon, heard that Demetrius was coming into Mesopotamia, he did not dare to impede his coming, because he had only a small force with him. He ordered the rest of the people to leave the city, and to flee when they had crossed the Euphrates River. Some should go into the desert, while others should go over the Tigris River into the province of Susa and to the Persian Sea. He, with the forces he had, would trust in the sandbars of the rivers and dikes of the country as defences, instead of so many fortresses and bulwarks. He stayed within the bounds of his own government and planned how to entrap his enemy. He kept Seleucus in Media informed of how things were going with him and requested that help be speedily sent to him. {*Diod. Sic., l. 19. c. 100. s. 3-6. 10:105,107}

2576. When Demetrius came to Babylon and found the city itself devoid of inhabitants, he started to besiege the citadels that were there. When he had taken one, he gave its spoil to the soldiers. [E322] He turned out Seleucus' men and put his garrison of seven thousand soldiers in their place, but was not able to take any other citadels, and after a long siege he departed and left Archelaus, one of his loyal friends, to maintain the siege with five thousand foot soldiers and a thousand cavalry. When Demetrius had run out of the time that his father had allowed for this expedition, he ordered his soldiers to steal for themselves whatever they could from that province, after which he journeyed back to Asia. By this action, he left Seleucus more firmly established and better settled in his government than before. Men questioned why Demetrius would waste and spoil the country, if he planned to take it over. For this reason, the Chaldeans reckon the beginning of the Seleucian reign in Babylon from this time, rather than an earlier time. {*Diod. Sic., l. 19. c. 100. s. 3-6. 10:107,109} {*Plutarch, Demetrius, l. 1. c. 7. s. 2,3. 9:17,19}

2577. Demetrius returned to Asia and quickly raised the siege which Ptolemy had laid to Halicarnassus. {*Plutarch, Demetrius, l. 1. c. 7. s. 3. 9:19}

2578. Cassander, Ptolemy and Lysimachus made peace with Antigonus on the following conditions. Cassander would command everything in Europe until Alexander, the son of Roxane, came of age. Lysimachus would hold Thrace, and Ptolemy Egypt, along with the bordering countries of Libya and Arabia. [L446] Antigonus would have the command of all Asia to himself. This agreement did not last long, for they all used any excuse to encroach on one another's territory. {*Diod. Sic., l. 19. c. 105. s. 1. 10:117,119}

2579. Cassander saw that Alexander, the son of Roxane, was growing up, and heard a rumour among the Macedonians that they thought it was about time that the young king should now be freed from his prison and rule the kingdom. Alarmed by this, he ordered Glaucias, the keeper, to murder Roxane and her son, the king, and to bury their bodies in some secret place, concealing their deaths by every possible means, all of which he did. {*Diod. Sic., l. 19. c. 105. s. 2-4. 10:119}

2580. Parysades, the king of Cimmerian Bosphorus, died after ruling for thirty-eight years. He left his kingdom to his oldest son, Satyrus, who held the kingdom for only nine months. {*Diod. Sic., l. 20. c. 22. s. 1. 10:197,199} {*Diod. Sic., l. 20. c. 23. s. 7. 10:203}

## 3694 AM, 4404 JP, 310 BC

2581. In Peloponnesus, Ptolemy, one of Antigonus' captains, defected from him to Cassander's side. He sent soldiers to a very loyal friend of his called Phoenix, to whom he had also committed the management of the government of the Hellespont, advising him to man his citadels and cities and to be on the alert and no longer serve Antigonus. {*Diod. Sic., l. 20. c. 19. s. 2. 10:193}

2582. On the other side, Ptolemy of Egypt complained about Antigonus, who, contrary to the agreement, had put his garrisons into various Greek cities on the asian side. Consequently, he sent Leonides, his captain, to Cilicia Trachea, to take over some cities and places that belonged to Antigonus, while also sending his agent to some cities held by Cassander and Lysimachus, to say that they should follow his advice and not allow Antigonus to become too powerful. {*Diod. Sic., l. 20. c. 19. s. 3,4. 10:193}

2583. Antigonus sent his younger son Philip to fight against Phoenix and others who had revolted from him in the Hellespont. His son Demetrius was sent into Cilicia against Ptolemy of Egypt, and both routed the captains of Ptolemy and recovered the cities which he had taken. {*Diod. Sic., l. 20. c. 19. s. 5. 10:193}

2584. Polyperchon, in Peloponnesus, complained about Cassander and his government of Macedonia. He sent for Hercules, a son of Alexander the Great by Barsine, who was now seventeen years old, as well as sending to those who were enemies of Cassander, to seek their help in establishing this young man in his father's kingdom. {*Diod. Sic., l. 20. c. 20. s. 1. 10:195}

2585. When Ptolemy of Egypt had all Cyprus under his command, he learned that Nicocles, the king of Paphos, had negotiated secretly with Antigonus. Ptolemy sent two confidants of his, Argaeus and Callicrates, with orders to kill Nicocles. They crossed over into Cyprus, taking with them a certain number of soldiers from Menelaus, who commanded the army there. They surrounded the house of Nicocles and then told him what Ptolemy wanted Nicocles to do, and advised him to find another kingdom. First, he tried to clear himself of the charges. When he realised that no one was listening to him, he drew his sword and killed himself. When his wife, Axiothea, heard of her husband's death, she took her daughters, who were all young virgins, and killed them, and tried to make the wives of Nicocles' brothers die with her. Ptolemy had not requested this, but had ordered that they be spared. The brothers of Nicocles died when they shut themselves in the palace and set fire to it. So the entire family of the kings of Paphos came to a tragic and lamentable end. {*Diod. Sic., l. 20. c. 21. 10:195,197} {Polyaenus, Strategmata, l. 8.} [E323]

2586. Around this time, Agathocles, king of Sicily, was sailing toward Africa to make war upon the Carthaginians. [L447] A total eclipse of the sun occurred and it was so dark, that the stars appeared in the sky and the day was turned into night. This happened on August 15, 310 BC or 4404 JP, according to the astronomical tables. {*Diod. Sic., l. 20. c. 5. s. 5. 10:155,157} {Justin, Trogus, l. 22. c. 6. s. 2.}

2587. When Epicurus was thirty-two years old, he taught publicly for five years, in both Mitylene and Lampsacus. {*Diogenes Laertius, Epicurus, l. 10. c. 10. (15) 2:543}

2588. In Cimmerian Bosphorus, Eumelus, the younger brother of Satyrus, allied himself with some of the neighbouring natives and laid claim to the kingdom of his elder brother. When Satyrus discovered this, he went against him with a large army and crossed the Thapsis River. Satyrus approached Eumelus' quarters and surrounded Eumelus' camp with his carts and wagons, in which he had brought a large quantity of provisions. He arranged his army in the field for battle and as was the custom of the Scythian kings, led the centre of his army's battle line. He had less than two thousand Greeks and as many Thracians, while all the rest were Scythians who had come to help him. They numbered twenty thousand foot soldiers and at least ten thousand cavalry. Eumelus was being helped by Aripharnes, king of Siraces, with twenty thousand cavalry and twenty-two thousand foot soldiers. Satyrus routed Aripharnes and then defeated his brother Eumelus, with his foot soldiers. He forced them all to retreat to Aripharnes' palace, which was surrounded by a river with steep rocks and thick woods. {*Diod. Sic., l. 20. c. 22. 10:197-201}

2589. At first, Satyrus went and wasted the enemy's country and set fire to their villages, from which he gathered much spoil. Then, making his way through their marshy country, he came to their wooden citadels and took them. He crossed the river and cut down a large forest through which he had to pass to get to the king's palace. He had his whole army work at this for three days, until they came to the walls of the citadel. Meniscus, who was leading the mercenary companies, got through a passage in the wall, and although he fought very courageously, he was outnumbered and was forced to retreat. Satyrus, who had come to his aid, was wounded in the arm with a spear and was forced to retire to his camp, where he died the following night of his wound. Meniscus broke off the siege and withdrew the army to a city called Gargaza, from where he carried the king's body down the river to a city called Panticapaeum, to Satyrus' brother Prytanis. He gave it a magnificent burial and laid the body in the king's sepulchre, after which he went to Gargaza and took over the army and the kingdom. {*Diod. Sic., l. 20. c. 23. 10:201,205}

2590. Agents from Eumelus came to Prytanis to propose that the kingdom be divided between them. Prytanis would have none of it and left a strong garrison at Gargaza. He returned to Panticapaeum to settle the affairs of his kingdom. After a while, Eumelus, with the help of some barbarians, captured Gargaza and various other towns and citadels. Later, he defeated Prytanis in a battle and trapped him in an isthmus near Lake Maeotis (Sea of Azov). He forced Prytanis to surrender, imposing the condition that he give up all his army and leave the kingdom. Nevertheless, when Prytanis returned to Panticapaeum, where the kings of Bosphorus kept their standing court, he again endeavoured to recover his kingdom. He was foiled in this, and fled to a place near there called the *Gardens*, where he was killed. His brother Eumelus reigned in his place for five years and five months. {*Diod. Sic., l. 20. c. 24. s. 1,2. 10:205} {*Diod. Sic., l. 20. c. 25. s. 3. 10:209}

### 3695 AM, 4405 JP, 309 BC

2591. To establish his kingdom, Eumelus killed all the friends, wives and children of both his brothers, Satyrus and Prytanis. *[L448]* Only Parysades, Satyrus' son, who was only a youth, escaped. Using a swift horse, he fled to Agarus, king of the Scythians. When Eumelus saw that the people grieved over the loss of their friends whom he had murdered, he called them all together. He apologised for his actions and gave them back their ancient form of government as well as restoring to the citizens of Panticapaeum their former exemptions, promising to free them from all tribute. He was not sparing in his use of persuasive words to win over the hearts of the people

to him once again, and so he regained their good will. He ruled with justice and moderation and was held in esteem by them. {*Diod. Sic., l. 20. c. 24. s. 3-5. 10:205,207}

2592. When Ptolemy Lagus of Egypt heard that he had again lost everything in Cilicia, he sailed over with his fleet to Phaselis and took that city by force. From there, he passed into Lycia and in an assault took Xanthus and the garrison of Antigonus that was there. Then he attacked Caunus, which surrendered to him, after which he also attacked the citadels that were within it and took them by assault. He utterly destroyed Heracleum, whereas Persicum was surrendered to him by the soldiers who held it. {*Diod. Sic., l. 20. c. 27. s. 1,2. 10:211,213} [E324]

2593. Then, Ptolemy Lagus sailed to Cos and sent for Ptolemy, Antigonus' nephew, who had an army committed to him by Antigonus, to come to him. He defected from his uncle and completely sided with Ptolemy Lagus. He left Chalcis, and arrived at Cos. At first, Ptolemy Lagus received him in a very courteous manner, but after a while he observed his indolence and how he tried to win over his officers by gifts and secret meetings with them. Fearing the worst, he put him in prison, where he poisoned him with a drink of hemlock. Ptolemy Lagus secured Ptolemy's soldiers with generous promises and distributed them in small numbers among the rest of his army. {*Diod. Sic., l. 20. c. 27. s. 3. 10:213}

2594. Cassander feared that the Macedonians might defect to Hercules, the son of Alexander the Great, who was then fourteen years old (according to Justin, or else seventeen, according to Diodorus). Cassander befriended Polyperchon and used him to have Hercules and his mother Barsine secretly murdered and their bodies hidden deeply enough in the ground to prevent the truth from accidently coming to light during their solemn funerals. Now that Alexander's two sons were both dead and there was no biological heir left to succeed him, every governor made himself king of the province which he held, just as if he had captured it in battle. {*Diod. Sic., l. 20. c. 28. 10:213,215} {Justin, Trogus, l. 15. c. 2.}

### 3696 AM, 4406 JP, 308 BC

2595. Ptolemy sailed from Myndus along the islands which were along his way, and came to Andros, where he expelled the garrison that was there and restored the city to her former liberty. {*Diod. Sic., l. 20. c. 37. s. 1. 10:241}

2596. Cleopatra, the daughter of Philip and sister of Alexander the Great, was incensed against Antigonus. Of her own accord, she planned to go to Ptolemy and tried to leave Sardis, but the governor there, whom Antigonus had charged not to hurt her, prevented her from leaving. Later, at Antigonus' command and with the help of some of the women about her, Cleopatra was murdered. To allay suspicion, Antigonus had some of these women who had murdered her executed, while he buried Cleopatra with all the magnificence possible to him. {*Diod. Sic., l. 20. c. 37. 10:241,243}

2597. Ophellas, who had expelled Thibron and subdued the Cyrenians for Ptolemy, now claimed Cyrene with the cities and adjoining regions as his own. [L449] Still not content, he began to look for greater things. While he was thinking about this, Orthon of Syracuse came to him with a message from Agathocles, asking him to join in arms with him against the Carthaginians, and telling him that if he subdued them, Agathocles would make him sovereign of all Africa. This fuelled his ego and he listened to him. He sent his agent to Athens, the former home of his wife Eurydice, the daughter of Miltiades, to ask for their help and alliance in this war. {*Diod. Sic., l. 20. c. 40. 10:249,251}

### 3697 AM, 4407 JP, 307 BC

2598. Many Athenians and other Greeks willingly listened to this motion. They hoped through this to gain a share of the richest pieces of all Africa, with all the wealth of Carthage for themselves. Ophellas was outfitted for this expedition, and was given an army of ten thousand foot soldiers, six hundred cavalry and a hundred chariots, with more than three hundred charioteers and men to fight beside them. Not counting the followers of the camp, he had more than ten thousand with him, who brought along their wives and children, with their baggage. This looked more like a colony going to be established than an army marching against an enemy. When they had marched for eighteen days and gone about thirty-seven miles, they came to a city called Automula on the western border of Cyrene, where they camped and rested themselves. Then, they moved on again and travelled through a dry desert country that was full of poisonous snakes. At last, after two months of miserable travel, they came to Agathocles' camp and pitched their own camp close to his. {*Diod. Sic., l. 20. c. 41,42. 10:251-255}

2599. When Agathocles heard of Ophellas' coming, he went to meet him, and advised him to rest and relax after so tedious and difficult a journey. When they had dined together many times, Ophellas adopted Agathocles as his son. Later, when most of Ophellas' army was foraging in the country, Agathocles suddenly called an assembly of his own army and in their presence accused Ophellas, who was to have helped him in this war, of betraying him. When he had incensed the multitude, he drew out his whole army in formation against Ophellas and his Cyrenians. Ophellas was shocked at this unexpected turn of affairs and had his

men defend themselves, but the enemy was too quick for him and he too weak for them, and so he was killed. [E325] After his death, Agathocles persuaded those who were left to lay down their arms and then told them what great things he would do for them. He persuaded them to take their pay from him and so took over Ophellas' army. Those whom he found to be unfit for the war, he sent to Syracuse. Some arrived there, but most perished in a fierce storm on the way. {*Diod. Sic., l. 20. c. 42. s. 3-5. 10:255,257} {Justin, Trogus, l. 22. c. 2.}

2600. After Ophellas' death, Cyrene and all Libya returned to Ptolemy's government again. {Suidas, in Δημητρ}

### 3698 AM, 4408 JP, 306 BC

2601. Demetrius Poliorcetes, or as Pliny rendered it, *Expugnator Urbum*, that is, the *City Taker*, was furnished with two strong armies, one on land and another at sea. Equipped with all the weapons and every other provision for the war, they left Ephesus with five thousand talents of silver, to liberate the Greek cities. {*Diod. Sic., l. 20. c. 45. s. 1. 10:265} They came to Piraeus, the port of Athens, with two hundred and fifty ships on the 26th day of the month of Thargelion, about May 31. They were received into Athens and took the city of Megara. Since Cassander had put a garrison under the command of Dionysus into Munychia, which was the citadel of Athens, Demetrius razed it to the ground. {*Plutarch, Demetrius, l. 1. c. 8,9. 9:21-25} [L450]

2602. This happened in the year when Anaxicrates was archon at Athens. Philochorus, who lived at this very time, recorded this, among others. {Philochorus, Attic, l. 8.} This was cited by Dionysius Halicarnassus. {*Dionysius Halicarnassus, Dinarchus, l. 1. (3) 2:259} It was toward the end of Anaxicrates' archonship, in the second year of the 118th Olympiad.

2603. Eurydice returned to Athens. She was the widow of Opheltas, or Ophellas, who was governor of Cyrene and who had been killed the previous year. Demetrius, the son of Antigonus, married her, which the Athenians considered a great honour for them. They were the first to address Demetrius and Antigonus by the title of king. Otherwise, they had denied that title to anyone else, because they saw it as the only mark of royalty which belonged exclusively to Philip, Alexander and his posterity. {*Plutarch, Demetrius, l. 1. c. 14. s. 1,2. 9:33} {*Plutarch, Demetrius, l. 1. c. 10. s. 2,3. 9:25}

2604. Demetrius was recalled from Greece by his father Antigonus to make war upon the captains of Ptolemy in Cyprus. He sailed first to Caria and then to Cilicia, from where he got supplies of ships and men, and then sailed to Cyprus with fifteen thousand foot soldiers, four hundred cavalry and a fleet of a hundred and ten very fast ships, of three tiers of oars apiece, and fifty-three that were slower. The rest were cargo ships to transport the men, horses and equipment.

*2605.* He landed and first camped near the shore not far from Carpasia. He drew up his ships to land and there fenced them with a deep trench and ramparts. Then he went and took Urania and Carpasia by force. Leaving a sufficiently large guard to defend his trenches around the fleet, he marched at once to Salamis. {*Diod. Sic., l. 20. c. 47. s. 1,2. 10:271*}

*2606.* At that time Menelaus, the brother of Ptolemy and chief commander of the island, was at Salamis. When he saw the enemy within five miles of the city, he drew out twelve thousand foot soldiers and eight hundred cavalry from the adjoining garrisons, and went to attack him, but was overcome by the enemy and fled. Demetrius hotly pursued him to the very gates of the city and there captured three thousand men and killed a thousand. He distributed the prisoners among his own companies to serve him. When he found they were constantly ready to defect to Menelaus again, because their wealth was in Ptolemy's hands in Egypt, he shipped them all away to Antigonus, his father. {*Diod. Sic., l. 20. c. 47. s. 3,4. 10:271,273*}

*2607.* Antigonus at that time was building a city in upper Syria by the Orontes River. He called it Antigonia, after himself, and spent large amounts of money on its construction. The walls were about nine miles long, and the place was very well located to control Babylon and the upper provinces, and also the lower ones as far down as Egypt. {*Diod. Sic., l. 20. c. 47. s. 5,6. 10:273*}

*2608.* Menelaus fled back to Salamis and determined to endure a siege. He sent a messenger to Ptolemy for more help and told him what danger he was in. Demetrius set to work preparing his battering rams to take the city by force. He had one special machine which he called the *Helepolis*, that is, the *City-Taker*. It was about a hundred and thirty-five feet high and had a base half that length. Each of its four wheels was twelve feet high. He also had various other large rams, and galleries for them. At night, those within the city threw wood down on them and shot fire brands which consumed many of the machines, with most of the men that guarded them. Yet Demetrius would not stop, but pressed the siege both by sea and land, believing that in time he would capture the city. {*Diod. Sic., l. 20. c. 48. 10:275,277*} *[E326]*

*2609.* When Ptolemy heard of the loss of his men, he sailed with a well-furnished army for sea and land and arrived at Paphos in Cyprus. *[L451]* He took boats from the neighbouring cities and went to Citium, about

twenty-five miles from Salamis. His whole fleet consisted of a hundred and forty or, as Plutarch has it, a hundred and fifty ships. The largest was of five tiers of oars and the smallest had four tiers of oars. These were accompanied by two hundred cargo ships containing at least ten thousand soldiers. He sent orders to Menelaus that, at the moment when he saw them in the heat of the battle, he was to attack from the port of Salamis with sixty ships, assaulting the rear of the enemy and disorganizing them in any way he could. Demetrius foresaw what would happen. He left part of his army to maintain the siege by land and ordered Antisthenes, his admiral, to lie at the mouth of the harbour of Salamis with ten ships of five tiers of oars apiece to hem the fleet in, so they could not get out. When he had arranged his land army on the shore of the forelands overlooking the sea, he arranged his fleet of a hundred and eight or, as Plutarch has it, of a hundred and eighty ships in battle formation. Some were of seven tiers of oars, but most four tiers of oars. {*Diod. Sic., l. 20. c. 49,50. 10:277,279*} {*Plutarch, Demetrius, l. 1. c. 15. s. 1,2. 9:37*}

*2610.* Ptolemy was in the wing, where he utterly routed the enemy and sank some of their ships, while he captured others with their men in them. When he returned, he intended to do the same with the rest of the enemy forces, but he found that his left wing had been completely routed by Demetrius, and that he was in hot pursuit of them. Therefore, he sailed back to Citium. Demetrius committed his warships to Neon and Burichus, to pursue the enemy and rescue those who were swimming in the sea, while he returned to his own port, from where he had set out. {*Diod. Sic., l. 20. c. 52. s. 2,3. 10:287*}

*2611.* Meanwhile, Menelaus sent out his sixty ships, as he had been commanded, under the command of Menoetius, who fought with those ten ships that had been sent to keep him in. He broke through them and caused them to flee for safety to the army that was on land. When Menoetius' men saw that they had come too late to act according to their instructions, they returned again to Salamis. {*Diod. Sic., l. 20. c. 52. s. 4,5. 10:287*}

*2612.* Ptolemy saw he could do no good in Cyprus and returned to Egypt with only eight ships, whereupon Menelaus surrendered the city as well as all his land and sea forces to Demetrius. He had twelve hundred cavalry and twelve thousand heavily armed foot soldiers. In a short time, Demetrius captured all the island's remaining cities and citadels and distributed the garrison soldiers among his own companies, which amounted to sixteen thousand foot soldiers and six hundred cavalry. {*Diod. Sic., l. 20. c. 53. s. 1-4. 10:289*} {*Plutarch, Demetrius, l. 1. c. 16. s. 1,2. 9:37*} {*Justin, Trogus, l. 15. c. 2.*}

2613. He had taken a hundred cargo ships containing almost eight thousand soldiers, and forty warships with their crews. About eighty ships had been damaged in the battle and leaked, and they drew these to land below their camp near the city. Demetrius had twenty of his own ships badly damaged in this battle, but these were repaired and were as good as new again, according to Diodorus. However, Plutarch said seventy of Ptolemy's ships were captured with their crews and soldiers, while the rest, who were in the cargo ships, were mainly slaves, friends and women. They had weapons and money to pay the soldiers and engines of war. Nothing escaped, and Demetrius took it all and carried it to his camp. Among the rest, there was a lady named Lamia, who was initially famous for her excellent skill in playing upon the recorder, and later became a notorious harlot. *[L452]* Although she was well past her prime, Demetrius, who was much younger than she was, fell in love with her. She caught and enamoured him to such an extent with the pretence of her talk and behaviour, that he became as much in love with her as other women were with him. {*Diod. Sic., l. 20. c. 52. s. 6. 10:289} {*Plutarch, Demetrius, l. 1. c. 16. s. 3,4. 9:37,39}

2614. Demetrius buried the bodies of the enemy who had been killed with a very honourable burial. He dismissed those he had taken prisoner and gave the Athenians arms enough to furnish twelve hundred men. {*Plutarch, Demetrius, l. 1. c. 17. s. 1. 9:39} He sent home Leontiscus, Ptolemy's son, Menelaus' brother and his other friends, with suitable provisions for their journey along the way. He did not forget what Ptolemy had formerly done to him in a similar situation. He engaged in these reciprocal displays of affection and kindness in the very heat of war, that it might be evident that their dispute was for the sake of honour, and not from hatred. It was the fashion in those days to wage war more religiously than men are now inclined to observe the laws of friendship in time of peace. {Justin, Trogus, l. 15. c. 2.}

2615. Demetrius sent Aristodemus, the Milesian, to his father, with news of this victory. This Aristodemus was considered to be the foremost flatterer in the entire court. When he came to Antigonus, he stood still for a while and held him in suspense as to what the news might be. Finally, he burst out with these tidings:

> "God save the King Antigonus, we have overthrown King Ptolemy at sea. Cyprus is ours. We have taken prisoner twelve thousand and eight hundred of his men."

2616. Antigonus replied to him: {*Plutarch, Demetrius, l. 1. c. 17. s. 2-5. 9:39,41}

> "God save you, too. Nevertheless, because you held me in suspense so long before you told me your good news, you shall be punished in the same way, too. For you shall stay a while, before you receive your reward for your good news." *[E327]*

2617. Antigonus was puffed up with pride by this victory and subsequently assumed to himself a crown and the title of king. Thereupon, Ptolemy did the same, lest he should in any way seem to have been defeated by this or be held in less regard by his subjects. In all his letters from that time on, he swore himself to be king. Other governors of the provinces followed their example. Seleucus, who had recently subdued the upper provinces to himself, did likewise, as did Lysimachus and Cassander, when they saw that now there was neither mother nor brother nor son of Alexander the Great left alive. {*Appian, Syrian Wars, l. 11. c. 9. (54) 2:207} {Justin, Trogus, l. 15. c. 2.} {*Diod. Sic., l. 20. c. 53. 10:289} {*Plutarch, Demetrius, l. 1. c. 18. s. 1,2. 9:41}

### 3699 AM, 4409 JP, 305 BC

2618. Seleucus proclaimed himself king of Babylon and Media, since he had personally killed Nicator, or Nicanor, whom Antigonus had placed there as governor. He assumed the surname of Nicator or Nicanor (for this is what we find stamped on his coins, also), not from that Nicator or Nicanor whom he killed, but from the many great victories which he had gained. After he had subdued the Bactrians, he proceeded and took in all the rest of the countries which Alexander had formerly subdued, as far as the Indus River, and added them to his own dominion. {Justin, Trogus, l. 15. c. 4.} {*Ammianus Marcellinus, l. 23. c. 6. s. 3. 2:351} {*Appian, Syrian Wars, l. 11. c. 9. (55) 2:207}

2619. King Antigonus' (for so we must call him from now on) youngest son died and Antigonus buried him in royal style. He called Demetrius home from Cyprus and commanded his whole army to meet at his new city of Antigonia, as he planned to march from there into Egypt. Leading the foot soldiers himself, he went through Coelosyria. He had an army of eighty thousand foot soldiers and about ten thousand cavalry, and he made Demetrius the admiral of his fleet, ordering him to keep close to the shore, within sight of the army. He had a hundred and fifty warships and a hundred cargo ships that carried an enormous supply of all types of weapons. The pilots told him that now was the time that the seven stars (Pleiades) were ready to set, and that they would set on the eighth day from then, at the beginning of November. Hence, it was not a good time to sail. Antigonus replied that they were too timid to make good sailors. {*Diod. Sic., l. 20. c. 73. 10:337,339} *[L453]*

2620. Antigonus came to Gaza with his army and planned to attack Ptolemy before Ptolemy was ready for him. He commanded his soldiers to take ten days' supply of food with them. With the camels from Arabia, he loaded a hundred and thirty thousand bushels of grain and an enormous supply of fodder for the beasts of burden. He carried his weapons in wagons and went through the desert, which caused some trouble for the army. They crossed various marshy places on the way, especially around the place called Barathra. {*Diod. Sic., l. 20. c. 73. s. 3. 10:339}

2621. Demetrius sailed with his ships from Gaza at about midnight and had calm weather for several days. The taller ships were forced to tow the cargo ships with ropes. After this, and as soon as the seven stars had set, a northerly wind rose upon them. Many of the ships of four tiers of oars were driven ashore near the city of Raphia, where there was no good harbour for them. Of those carrying the weapons, some sank and the rest retired to Gaza again. Some of the best of them bore up and came to below the cape of Casius. That cape is not far from the Nile River and is not suitable for shipping, especially if there are any storms. There was no way to get near it, so every ship dropped anchor a quarter of a mile from land and was forced to ride out the storm in a heavy sea. In the midst of all this danger, they were driven to extremity, for had the storm lasted only one day longer, they would have used all their fresh water and would have died of thirst. The storm ceased and Antigonus arrived at the place with his army and camped there. The weather-beaten men came ashore and refreshed themselves in the camp. Nevertheless, this storm claimed three ships of five tiers of oars, from which some men escaped alive to reach land. {*Diod. Sic., l. 20. c. 74. 10:339,341}

2622. Antigonus moved from there and placed his army a quarter of a mile from the Nile River. But Ptolemy, who had manned all the banks of the river with strong garrisons, sent some men in river boats to go as close to the farther bank as they safely could and proclaim that if any of Antigonus' army would come to him, he would give a common soldier two minas and a captain a whole talent for his trouble. No sooner had this proclamation been made than a large number of Antigonus' mercenaries wanted to leave. Some of his captains also wanted to go. But when Antigonus realised that a large number of his men were deserting him, he positioned archers, slingers and various engines of war, to keep them from crossing over the water in boats. If they found any that went, he put them to death with horrible torments. {*Diod. Sic., l. 20. c. 75. s. 1-3. 10:341,343} [E328]

2623. Antigonus gathered together his ships, which had come to him, although they were late. He went to a place called Pseudostomon, where he planned to land some of his men. However, he found a strong garrison of the enemy there and was beaten off with bows and slings

and other engines of war. Therefore, as the night drew on, he went his way and ordered the captains of every ship to follow the lantern of the admiral. So they came to the mouth of the Nile River, which is called Phatniticum. The next morning, he found that many of his ships had lost their way and he did not know where they had gone. He was forced to anchor there and send the swiftest ships he had all over the sea to look for them and bring them back. Meanwhile, as time wore on, Ptolemy had been alerted to the approach of the enemy. He immediately went to the aid of his men and arranged his army all along the shore, in sight of the enemy. Demetrius could find no landing place there, either. He was told that if he were to land in the surrounding area, the country was naturally fortified with marshes and moorish grounds. [L454] He set sail and returned home. {*Diod. Sic., l. 20. c. 75,76. 10:343}

2624. As he was going, a violent wind came up from the north and drove three of his ships of four tiers of oars and some other transports onto the shore, where they all fell into Ptolemy's hand. After much trouble, the rest got to Antigonus' camp. Ptolemy had placed strong garrisons at each of the mouths of the Nile River and had an enormous number of river boats everywhere. These were supplied with arrows and slings and men who knew how to use them well. These troubled Antigonus very greatly, for the mouth of the river at Pelusium was strongly guarded by Ptolemy. Antigonus could make no use of his ships at all, and his land forces were also in trouble. The Nile River started swelling at the coming of the sun into Cancer. When the sun entered Leo, the Nile River overflowed all its banks, and was now so high that they could do little. What was worse, he was running out of food for the men and fodder for the animals, because they had stayed there so long. {*Diod. Sic., l. 20. c. 76. s. 2-4. 10:343,345}

2625. When Antigonus saw that his army was demoralised, he called them all together. Before them all, he asked the captains whether it was better to stay and fight, or to return to Syria for the time being. They would then return next year, better prepared and when the waters would be lower. When every man wanted to go, he ordered his soldiers to gather up their belongings. His navy followed them along the shore, and he returned to Syria. {*Diod. Sic., l. 20. c. 76. s. 5,6. 10:345} The pointlessness of this expedition had been foreseen in a dream by Medius, one of Antigonus' friends. For it appeared to him that he saw Antigonus with all his army compete in a race at Olympus, called *Diaulus*, that is, *a double course*. When they first set out, they seemed to run very well. After a while they grew weaker. When they came to the race-post around which they had to turn to return to the barriers from where they had set out (for that was the nature of this double course), they were so out of breath that they could go no farther. {*Plutarch, Demetrius, l. 1. c. 19. s. 1,2. 9:43}

2626. Ptolemy was glad to see that the enemy was gone. He offered sacrifices to his gods for this great benefit they had bestowed on him. He made a magnificent feast for his friends and wrote letters to Seleucus, Lysimachus and Cassander, telling of his good success. He did not forget to tell them how large an army had defected over to him from Antigonus. Now that he had rescued Egypt a second time and acquired it by his sword, he thought he might lawfully consider it his own, and returned in triumph to Alexandria. {*Diod. Sic., l. 20. c. 76. s. 6,7. 10:345,347} Hence it was, that Ptolemy started the beginning of his reign over Egypt from this time. He calculated that the time from the death of Alexander the Great to this time was nineteen full years. For the nineteenth year from the death of Alexander the Great ended, according to his account, with the date of November 6, 305 BC or 4409 JP. {Ptolemy, Canon of Kings}

2627. While these things were happening in Egypt, Dionysius, the tyrant of Heraclea in Pontus, died. He reigned thirty-three years, according to Athenaeus, although Memnon said that he reigned only thirty years, and Diodorus said thirty-two years. He was incredibly fat. Besides being mentioned by Memnon and Nymphis of Heraclea, this fact was noted by Athenaeus in his twelfth book of the city of Heraclea, in the place mentioned, as well as by Aelian. He had two sons by Amastris or Amestris, the daughter of Oxyartes, brother of Darius, the last king of Persia. She had first been given in marriage to Craterus by Alexander. The older of the sons was called Clearchus, the younger Oxathres, according to Diodorus, Zathras and Dionysius. [L455] Therefore, in his last will, he joined some others with her in the administration, so that the government of his kingdom and the charge of his two children, who were still very young, would not go entirely to his wife. {*Aelian, Historical Miscellany, l. 9. c. 13. 1:291,293} {*Athenaeus, l. 12. (549d) 5:493} {Memnon, Excerpts of Photius, l. 1. c. 5.} {*Diod. Sic., l. 20. c. 77. s. 1. 10:347}

### 3700 AM, 4410 JP, 304 BC
2628. Menedemus sailed to Patara in Lycia with the command of three ships, each of which was between two and three tiers of oars apiece. [E329] He captured a ship of four tiers of oars coming from Cilicia, that had on board royal robes and the rest of an outfit that Phila had taken great pains to make ready and send off to her husband Demetrius Poliorcetes. All of this was sent by Menedemus to Ptolemy in Egypt, an affront that enraged Demetrius against the Rhodians, causing him to besiege their city. When this had been going on for a

year, the Athenians mediated an agreement that the Rhodians would help Antigonus and Demetrius in their wars against any country except for Ptolemy's, and so the siege was lifted. {*Diod. Sic., l. 20. c. 93-100. 10:389-407} {*Plutarch, Demetrius, l. 1. c. 21,22. 9:49-53}

2629. As soon as this war was over, the Rhodians sent some of their priests to consult the oracle of Ammon, wanting to know whether or not they should worship Ptolemy as a god. When they were told they should, they consecrated a square grove in their city to him. They built a gallery about two hundred yards long on each side and called it Ptoleum or Ptolemy's Gallery. They were also the first to surname Ptolemy Soter, or Saviour, because he had saved them from the violence of Antigonus and Demetrius, and that not with his soldiers. {*Pausanius, Attica, l. 1. c. 8. s. 6. 1:41} Also, Ptolemy had saved Alexander the Great in the city of the Oxydracans, as some have thought. {See note on 3678b AM. <<2165>>} {*Arrian, Anabasis, l. 6. c. 10. s. 1-4. 2:127-131} {Stephanus, On the word Ὀξυδραχ} {*Diod. Sic., l. 20. c. 100. 10:407,409}

2630. After reigning six years, Eumelus, the king of Cimmerian Bosphorus, died in an accident. He was hurrying home from Scythia to a certain solemn sacrifice that was to be offered at the time. He was in a four-wheeled coach, drawn by four horses and covered with a canopy. As he approached his palace, the horses took a fright and ran away with him. When the driver could not hold them, Eumelus feared that they might run down some precipice and leaped from the coach. His sword caught in the wheel and he was dragged along with the coach and killed. His son Spartacus succeeded him and reigned twenty years. {*Diod. Sic., l. 20. c. 100. s. 7. 10:409} {*Diod. Sic., l. 20. c. 25. s. 4. 10:209}

### 3701 AM, 4411 JP, 303 BC
2631. Seleucus crossed the Indus River and made war on Sandrocottus, or Androcottus. After Seleucus had restored his government in the east, Sandrocottus had murdered all the governors whom Alexander had appointed, and taken over all of India. {Justin, Trogus, l. 15. c. 4.} {*Appian, Syrian Wars, l. 11. c. 9. (55) 2:209}

2632. As Seleucus was going to make this war, a wild elephant of enormous size met him along the way and approached him as if it were tame. He went up to it and the animal allowed him to get on and ride it. This beast proved to be a prime and singularly good elephant for the war. {Justin, Trogus, l. 15. c. 4.} Sandrocottus crossed over all India with an army of six hundred thousand men and subdued it. {*Plutarch, Alexander, l. 1. c. 62. 7:401} He made himself king over them and freed them from a yoke of strangers, only to bring them under his yoke. {Justin, Trogus, l. 15. c. 4.}

*2633.* Megasthenes lived with Sibytrius, governor of the Arachosians, and often speaks of his visiting Sandracottus, the king of the Indians. *[L456]* {*\*Arrian, Anabasis, l. 5. c. 6. s. 2. 2:19*} Megasthenes said that Sandrocottus had an army of forty thousand men. {*\*Strabo, l. 15. c. 1. s. 53. 7:87*} (The original copy of Ussher had *four hundred* not *forty* as the modern Loeb editions of Strabo have. Editor.)

## 3702 AM, 4412 JP, 302 BC

*2634.* Cassander, king of Macedonia, sent his envoys to Antigonus, wishing to make a peace with him. Antigonus refused, unless Cassander would surrender unconditionally to him. After a conference between Cassander and Lysimachus, king of Thrace, they both agreed to send their envoys to Ptolemy, king of Egypt, and to Seleucus, king of the upper provinces of Asia. Decrying the pride and arrogance of Antigonus expressed in his answers, they showed these two kings how this war involved them, too. {*\*Diod. Sic., l. 20. c. 106. s. 2,3. 10:423,425*} Consequently, they realised that Antigonus planned to take them on, one at a time, because they were not united against him. So they appointed a place where they all agreed to meet, having resolved to contribute their various forces to carry on this war. Cassander could not be there, because the enemy was so close to him, so he sent Lysimachus with all the forces he was able to spare, together with abundant provisions for them. {*Justin, Trogus, l. 15. c. 2.*}

*2635.* Seleucus made a marriage alliance with Sandrocottus, the king of India, and gave him all those regions bordering the Indus River which Alexander had taken from the Arians. Seleucus received from Sandrocottus a gift of five hundred elephants in return. (Seleucus had previously made these regions his colonies and had set governors over them.) {*\*Strabo, l. 15. c. 2. s. 8. 7:143*} {*\*Plutarch, Alexander, l. 1. c. 62. s. 2. 7:401*} {*\*Appian, Syrian Wars, l. 11. c. 9. (55) 2:209*} When Seleucus had thus made peace in the east, he prepared for the war in the west against Antigonus with his allies, according to their agreement. {*Justin, Trogus, l. 15. c. 4.*}

*2636.* Lysimachus crossed over into Asia with his own army and came up against Lampsacus and Parium. Because they readily submitted to him, he restored their ancient liberty to them. When he had taken Sigeum by force, he put a strong garrison in it. *[E330]* He then committed six thousand foot soldiers and a thousand cavalry to Prepelaus and sent him to take the cities of Ionia and Aeolia. Lysimachus besieged Abydus with all types of battering rams and other weapons of war, but when Demetrius sent an army to defend the place, he lifted the siege. After having captured the Hellespont and

Phrygia, he went on and besieged the city of Synnada, where Antigonus stored his treasure. Lysimachus persuaded Docimus, a commander of Antigonus, to defect to his side. Docimus helped take Synnada and other citadels belonging to Antigonus and captured Antigonus' treasure. {*\*Diod. Sic., l. 20. c. 107. s. 1-3. 10:425,427*}

*2637.* Meanwhile, Prepelaus, who had been sent to make war upon Ionia and Aeolia, took Adramyttium on the way, and besieged Ephesus, where he so terrified the inhabitants that they submitted to him. He found Rhodian hostages there, whom he sent home again to their friends, nor did he harm any of the Ephesians. He only burned all the ships which he found in their harbour, because the enemy still controlled the sea, and the whole outcome of the war was uncertain. After this, the people of Teos and Colophon joined the common cause against Antigonus. But the Erythreans and Clazomenians were helped by forces sent by sea, and he was not able to overcome them, so he wasted their territories and went to Sardis. There he was able to persuade Antigonus' captains and Phoenix to defect, enabling him to take all the city except for the citadel, which was held by Philip, a friend of Antigonus, and so would not defect to him. {*\*Diod. Sic., l. 20. c. 107. s. 1-3. 10:425,227*} *[L457]*

## 3703 AM, 4413 JP, 301 BC

*2638.* Antigonus was at that time fully occupied holding games and feasts at his new city of Antigonia. He had proclaimed expensive prizes for those who would enter the contests, and offered large wages to all the skilled artisans that he could hire. When he heard how Lysimachus had come into Asia and what large numbers of his soldiers had defected to him, he stopped the games, but distributed over two hundred talents among the athletes and the artisans who had come. Then he went as quickly as he could, making long marches with his army to meet the enemy. As soon as he arrived at Tarsus in Cilicia, he advanced his army three months' pay from the money which he had taken with him from the city of Quinda. Besides this, he had brought three thousand talents along with him from Antigonia, so he would not run out of money. He crossed over the Taurus Mountains and hurried into Cappadocia. He subdued those who had revolted from him in upper Phrygia and Lycaonia, and made them help him in the wars, as they had previously done. {*\*Diod. Sic., l. 20. c. 108. s. 1-3. 10:429,431*}

*2639.* When Lysimachus heard of the enemy's approach, he consulted with his council concerning this imminent danger and what to do. Their advice was not to risk a battle until Seleucus came from the upper provinces, but to get into the strongest, most fortified place. He should entrench himself in the strongest manner that he possibly could, with ramparts and palisades, and await the coming of the enemy. Lysimachus followed this advice. As soon as Antigonus came within sight of Lysimachus' camp, he drew out in battle formation and tried unsuccessfully to provoke Lysimachus to a battle. Antigonus captured all the passes that could be used to supply food for the camp, causing Lysimachus to fear that he might be taken alive by Antigonus when his food ran out. So he moved his camp by night and marched about fifty miles to Dorylaeum and camped there, as there was an abundant supply of grain and other provisions in those parts, and he had a river at his back. Therefore, they raised a work there and enclosed it with an exceedingly deep trench with three rows of stakes on the top of it. He made the camp as secure as he could. When Antigonus found that the enemy had gone, he pursued as fast as he could and approached the place where Lysimachus was entrenched. When he realised that Lysimachus did not want to fight, he started to make another trench around his camp to besiege him there. To that end, he had all types of instruments brought there for a siege, such as missiles, arrows and catapults. Although many skirmishes were fought around the trenches, because Lysimachus' men fought from their works to hinder the enemy, Antigonus' side prevailed. {*Diod. Sic., l. 20. c. 108. s. 1-3. 10:431} {*Diod. Sic., l. 20. c. 109. s. 1. 10:431,433}

2640. In time, Antigonus' works were almost finished around him and Lysimachus' provisions began to run out. Therefore, Lysimachus took the advantage of a stormy night and got away with his army. They travelled through mountainous country and came to his winter quarters. The next morning, when Antigonus saw that the enemy was gone, he marched after him through the plain of the country, but because there had been so much rain and the way was poor and very muddy, he lost many of his pack animals and some of his men on that journey. [E331] The whole army was greatly distressed, and so, to spare his army and because the winter was approaching, he abandoned the pursuit for that time. He looked around for the best places in which to winter, and distributed his army there. {*Diod. Sic., l. 20. c. 109. s. 2-5. 10:433}

2641. Similarly, Lysimachus sent his army to winter in the country of Salonia. He had made generous provisions for them from Heraclea, because he had made an alliance with that city by marrying Amastris, who was the widow of Craterus and the guardian of his two young children, as well as the governess of that city. {*Diod. Sic., l. 20. c. 109. s. 6,7. 10:433} {Photius, Bibliotheca, c. 5. from Memnon} [L458]

2642. At this time, Demetrius made a truce with Cassander and was sent for by his father from Greece. He steered a straight course through the isles of the Aegean Sea and came to Ephesus, where he landed his army and camped before the city, making it submit to him as before. He allowed the garrison which Prepelaus had put there to depart safely, while he put a strong garrison of his own into the citadel, and then marched away with the rest of his army as far as the Hellespont. He subdued Lampsacus and Parium, and from there went to the entrance of Pontus and camped near a place called the *Temple of the Chalcedonians*. He fortified it and left three thousand foot soldiers, with thirty warships, to keep it, while he sent the rest of his army to winter in various places around there. {*Diod. Sic., l. 20. c. 111. s. 2,3. 10:439,441}

2643. About this time, Mithridates, who was subject to Antigonus, was suspected of favouring Cassander's party and was killed at the city of Cius in the country of Mysia. He had reigned for thirty-five years over Cius and Myrlea, {*Diod. Sic., l. 20. c. 111. s. 4. 10:441} and various authors mention him. This Mithridates was the son of Ariobarzanes, a man of the royal blood of Persia. He was descended from one of those seven men who had destroyed the Magi there, as noted by Polybius, Florus and Sextus. {*Polybius, l. 5. c. 43. s. 2. 3:105} {*Florus, l. 1. c. 40. s. 1,2. 1:179} {Sextus Aurelius, l. 1. c. 76.} He was surnamed the *Founder*, and left the succession of the kingdom of Pontus after him to a line of men culminating in Eupator, or that Mithridates who maintained so long a war against the Romans. {*Strabo, l. 12. c. 3. s. 42. 5:453} This fact was also mentioned by Tertullian, who wrote: {*Tertullian, De Anima, l. 1. c. 46. 3:224}

"I learn from Strabo that Mithridates got the kingdom of Pontus by a dream."

2644. Antigonus had dreamed that he had a field full of a golden harvest, but that Mithridates came and cut it and carried it away into Pontus. As a result, Antigonus planned to capture and kill him. When Mithridates was told this by Demetrius, he fled away with only six cavalry in his company and fortified a certain town in Cappadocia. There, many men joined his cause and so he obtained Cappadocia and also many other countries of Pontus. He left them to the eighth generation after him, before the Romans took over his kingdom. {*Plutarch, Demetrius, l. 1. c. 4. 9:11,13} {*Appian, Mithridatic Wars, l. 12. c. 2. (9) 2:253} Lucian, from Hieronymus Cardianus and other writers, stated that he lived for eighty-four years and that his son, also called Mithridates, succeeded him in his kingdom. He added Cappadocia and Paphlagonia to his dominions, and held them for thirty-six years.

{*Lucian, Octogenarians, l. 1. (13) 1:233} {*Diod. Sic., l. 20. c. 111. s. 4. 10:441}

2645. Cassander sent Plistarchus into Asia to help Lysimachus with an army of twelve thousand foot soldiers and five hundred cavalry. When he came to the entrance of Pontus, he found that the strait was held by the enemy. Giving up his attempt to get through that way, he went to Odessus, which was between Apollonia and Callantia, opposite Heraclea. Some of Lysimachus' men were there. He did not have enough ships there to transport his army, so he divided his army into three parts. The first part that set out, landed safely at Heraclea. The second part was defeated by the enemy, who held the strait of Pontus. The third part, which included Plistarchus, almost completely perished in a violent storm. Most of the ships with their men were lost, and his ship also sank. It was a large warship of six tiers of oars, and only thirty-three of the five hundred men in it escaped. Plistarchus held on to part of the wreckage from the ship when it sank and was cast ashore, half dead. He recovered a little and was carried to Heraclea, where he regained his strength and went to Lysimachus' winter quarters. He had lost most of his army on the way. {*Diod. Sic., l. 20. c. 112. 10:441,443} [L459]

2646. About the same time, Ptolemy came from Egypt with an extremely well-outfitted army and subdued all the cities of Coelosyria. While besieging Sidon, he heard a false rumour that a battle had been fought in which Seleucus and Lysimachus had been beaten, that they had fled to Heraclea and that Antigonus was moving quickly into Syria with his victorious army. Ptolemy believed the rumour and made a truce with the Sidonians for five months. After putting garrisons into the other cities in those parts which he had taken, he returned into Egypt. {*Diod. Sic., l. 20. c. 113. s. 1,2. 10:443}

2647. While these things had been going on, twenty-eight hundred of the soldiers had defected to Antigonus, who entertained them very courteously and furnished them the pay that they claimed Lysimachus owed them. [E332] In addition, he gave them a large amount of money as a reward for their actions. {*Diod. Sic., l. 20. c. 113. s. 3,4. 10:443,445}

2648. At the same time, Seleucus came down from the upper provinces into Cappadocia with a large army, and wintered his army in tents which he had brought already made for them. His army consisted of twenty thousand foot soldiers, twelve thousand cavalry including his mounted archers, four hundred and eighty elephants and a hundred scythed chariots. These kings' forces assembled to fight it out in the following summer, to see who would be the master. {*Diod. Sic., l. 20. c. 113. s. 4,5. 10:445}

2649. Pythagoras had been the former soothsayer of Alexander the Great and of Perdiccas, and was now employed by Antigonus. He started his divinations of the bowels of beasts that were being offered in sacrifices. When he found the strings or filets in the liver missing, he told Antigonus that this indicated his death. {*Arrian, Anabasis, l. 7. c. 18. s. 5. 2:267}

2650. Alexander the Great also appeared to Demetrius in his sleep. He was gloriously armed and asked Demetrius what rallying cry he and his father planned to give to his army prior to battle. Demetrius replied:

"Zeus and Victory."

2651. Then Alexander replied: {*Plutarch, Demetrius, l. 1. c. 29. s. 1,2. 9:69,71}

"Therefore, will I go over to your enemies, for they will take me for theirs."

2652. When Antigonus heard that there were so many kings assembled against him, he boastfully said that he would scatter them all like so many birds out of a bush, but when the enemies approached, he was observed to be more quiet than usual. He showed his son to his army and told them that this was the man that must be his successor, at which they marvelled even more, especially Demetrius. Antigonus talked with him alone in his tent many times, whereas prior to this, he would never share any secret at all with his son. When his army was fully ready in battle array, and Antigonus was leaving his pavilion to go to them, he stumbled and fell flat on his face, a fact which greatly troubled him. He got up again and begged the gods to send him either a victory that day, or a death devoid of pain. {*Plutarch, Demetrius, l. 1. c. 28. s. 2. 9:67,69} {*Plutarch, Demetrius, l. 1. c. 29. s. 2. 9:71}

2653. The battle between these many kings was fought at the beginning of the year at Ipsus, a town in Phrygia. {*Arrian, Anabasis, l. 7. c. 18. s. 5,6. 2:267} {*Plutarch, Pyrrhus, l. 1. c. 4. s. 2,3. 9:355} {*Appian, Syrian Wars, l. 11. c. 9. (55) 2:209} {*Diod. Sic., l. 21. c. 1. s. 1. 11:3} {Porphyry, Chronology, Olympiad 119. Year 4.} In this battle Antigonus and Demetrius had more than seventy thousand foot soldiers, ten thousand cavalry, seventy-five elephants and a hundred and twenty chariots between them. {*Plutarch, Demetrius, l. 1. c. 28. s. 3. 9:69} Demetrius, with most of his cavalry, charged Antiochus, who was the son of Seleucus and later, his successor in the kingdom. [L460] Demetrius most valiantly routed him, but rashly pursued him too far. This was the reason for his father's defeat that day. {*Plutarch, Demetrius, l. 1. c. 29. s. 3. 9:71} In that pursuit Pyrrhus conspicuously displayed his valour and his worth. He was only seventeen years old and had been expelled from his kingdom by the

Molossians. He had allied himself with Demetrius, who had married his sister Deidamia, who had been intended for Alexander, the son of Alexander the Great, by Roxane. {*Plutarch, Pyrrhus, l. 1. c. 4. s. 1-3. 9:353,355}

2654. When Seleucus saw that Antigonus' battalion was destitute of all help from their cavalry, he acted as if he was going to attack them, but instead he wisely invited them to defect to him. A large number of them did so and the rest fled, while Seleucus turned on Antigonus. One of them cried out, saying:

"These come upon you, oh king."

2655. He answered:

"But Demetrius will come and help us."

2656. While he stood waiting for Demetrius to come back and rescue him, the enemy came on and showered their javelins as thick as hail on him. In that storm he fell and died, whereupon all forsook him and fended for themselves. Only Thorax of Larisa stayed by Antigonus' body, {*Plutarch, Demetrius, l. 1. c. 29. s. 3-5. 9:71,73} which was later taken up and buried in a royal manner. {*Diod. Sic., l. 21. c. 1. s. 4b. 11:5,7} Plutarch stated that when Antigonus was on his recent expedition into Egypt, he was then a little less than eighty years old. Appian stated that he was over eighty years old on that expedition. He lived eighty-six years, according to Porphyry. {Porphyry, Scaliger's Greek Eusebius, p. 226. last line} However, the historian Hieronymus Cardianus, who lived with him, stated that he only lived eighty-one years. {*Lucian, Octogenarians, l. 1. (11) 1:231}

2657. When Demetrius saw that all was lost, he fled away to Ephesus as fast as he could, with five thousand foot soldiers and four thousand cavalry. Everyone there began to fear that, because of a lack of money, he might plunder the temple of Diana. When he thought he would not be able to restrain his soldiers from doing this, he left there as quickly as he could. {*Plutarch, Demetrius, l. 1. c. 30. s. 1,2. 9:73} Taking his mother Stratonice and all his treasure with him, he sailed to Salamis on the isle of Cyprus, which at that time was under his command. {*Diod. Sic., l. 21. c. 1. s. 4b. 11:7}

2658. After the kings had achieved this great victory, they started dividing up the large kingdom of Antigonus and Demetrius among themselves, and adding these new lands to their existing kingdoms. {*Plutarch, Demetrius, l. 1. c. 30. s. 1. 9:73} {*Appian, Syrian Wars, l. 11. c. 9. (55) 2:209} {*Polybius, l. 5. c. 67. s. 7-13. 3:165,167} [E333]

2659. When they could not agree on how to divide the spoil, they split into two sides. Seleucus allied himself with Demetrius, and Ptolemy joined with Lysimachus. {Justin, Trogus, l. 15. c. 4.} Seleucus and Ptolemy were the two strongest of the whole group. Consequently, the dispute between them was continued by their posterities under the names of the Seleucians, or kings of the north, and the kings of Ptolemy, or the kings of the south. This was foretold in Daniel. {Da 11:5-20}

2660. Simon, the son of Onias, succeeded him in the priesthood at Jerusalem. He was surnamed *The Just*, because of his great zeal and fervency in the worship of God and the great love which he had for his countrymen, the Jews. {*Josephus, Antiq., l. 12. c. 2. s. 5. (44) 7:25} In the Apocrypha we find this testimony given about him:

"Simon was the high priest, the son of Onias, who in his lifetime repaired the house again and in his days fortified the temple. He had built the foundation for the high double walls and the high fortress of the wall about the temple. In his days, the cistern to hold water, which was round like the sea, was covered with plates of brass. He took care of the temple, that it should not fall, and fortified the city against besieging. [L461] How he was honoured in the midst of the people at his coming from the sanctuary!" {Apc Sir 50:1-5}

2661. See Salianus and Scaliger. {Salianus, Annals - 3675 AM, Tom. 5.} {Eusebius, Scaliger's Greek Eusebius (Animadversions), num. 1785.} This man was said to have been high priest for nine years. {Eusebius, Scaliger's Greek Eusebius, p. 50.}

## 3704 AM, 4414 JP, 300 BC

2662. On April 23, Seleucus offered sacrifices to Zeus on Mount Casius and consulted him concerning a place to build a city. An eagle came and caught away a piece of flesh from the altar. She was said to have let it fall in a place near the sea below Palaeopolis (this was a little city built in previous times by Syrus, the son of Agenor, on a hill there), in a coastal town of Pieria. Immediately after that, Seleucus started to lay the foundation of a large city which he built there and named Seleucia, after himself. {Johannes Malela, Chronology} However, others say that it was not the action of the eagle that he followed, but the flash of lightning that appeared to him which was the reason why lightning, from then on, was always celebrated with set hymns and praises in that place, as if it were itself a god. {*Appian, Syrian Wars, l. 11. c. 9. (58) 2:215,217}

2663. Seleucus came to Iopolis, a city built in the hill country of Silphium. There, on the third day after his arrival, which was the first of the month of Artemisios, or our May, he offered sacrifices to Zeus the Thunderer in a certain shrine said to have been built there in ancient times by Perseus, the son of Danae. Later, when he arrived at Antigonia, he offered sacrifices to Zeus on the altars recently built there by Antigonus. Seleucus, with

Amphion the priest, prayed that Zeus would show him by some sign whether he should live in Antigonia and rename the place, or whether he should go and build a new city in another place. It is said that at that moment, once again, an eagle came and caught away a piece of the flesh from the altar and let it fall near the hill of Silphium. So it was that he laid the foundation of his wall opposite the hill on which Iopolis was built, near the Orontes River, where there was a town called Botzia. This was at sunrise on the 22nd day of the month of Artemisios. He named this city after his son, Antiochus and later built a temple there to Jupiter Botzius. This and other things are related by Johannes Malela of Antioch, concerning the origin of that city. {*Johannes Malela, Chronology*} Eusebius also stated that this city was built by Seleucus in the twelfth year of his reign. {*Eusebius, Chronicles, l. 1. 1:209*} This Syrian city was later made into a tetrapolis, that is, a fourfold city. It was divided into quarters, creating four cities, each of which had a proper wall built around it, while one common wall enclosed them all. The first city was built by this Seleucus Nicator, the second was the work of the inhabitants themselves, while the third was finished by Seleucus Callinicus and the fourth by Antiochus Epiphanes. {*Strabo, l. 16. c. 2. s. 4. 7:241,243*}

*2664.* Seleucus named this city after his son Antiochus. This is confirmed by Malela, Cedrenus and Julian the Apostate. {*Julian, Misopogone*} However, Strabo, Appian and Trogus Pompeius stated that he called it Antioch after his father, Antiochus. Justin said that he consecrated the memorial of a twofold beginning there, {*Justin, Trogus, l. 15. c. 4.*} saying that he called the city by the name of his father Antiochus, and consecrated its fields to Apollo. This he did because his mother Laodice wanted him to believe that he was born of her by Apollo, and so Daphne was consecrated to Apollo. Daphne is a suburb of Antioch, a place famous for the grove of laurel trees that grew there over an area of no less than ten miles around. Therefore it is to this day called Daphne near Antioch, {*Apc 2Ma 4:33*} while the city of Antioch itself is referred to as Antioch near Daphne by other writers. *[E334]*

*2665.* Seleucus utterly demolished Antigonia and carried the materials down the Orontes River to Antioch. He relocated fifty-three hundred Macedonians and Athenians whom Antigonus had moved there to his new city. {*Johannes Malela, Chronology*} *[L462]* Diodorus said that Seleucus did destroy Antigonia and added that he relocated its inhabitants to his new city of Seleucia. {*Diod. Sic., l. 20. c. 47. s. 5,6. 10:273*} However, while Strabo also mentioned the inhabitants of Antigonia being relocated to Antioch, he added that some of the families and offspring of Triptolemus and those Argives who had long

ago been sent with him to seek out Io, were settled there by Seleucus. {*Strabo, l. 16. c. 2. s. 5. 7:243*} These were those Greeks from Peloponnesus of whom Stephanus Byzantius said that they were settled in Antioch near Daphne. Johannes Malela also stated that: (cf. Scaliger's notes on the 1713. number of the Eusebius' Chronicles)

> "Seleucus personally sought out some of the Greeks from Ionia and relocated those Greeks who lived in Iopolis, to Antioch. He made them citizens there as men who were more sacred and generous than the rest."

*2666.* Lysimachus, the king of Thrace, married Arsinoe, the daughter of Ptolemy. This was not Ptolemy Philadelphus, as Memnon stated {*Memnon, c. 5.*} but Ptolemy I, the son of Lagus, surnamed *The Deliverer*. {*Plutarch, Demetrius, l. 1. c. 31. s. 1. 9:77*} {*Justin, Trogus, l. 17. c. 2.*} {*Justin, Trogus, l. 24. c. 2.*} {*Memnon, Excerpts, c. 9.*} Ptolemy had married Eurydice. {*Pausanias, Attica, l. 1. c. 6. s. 6. 1:33*} His former wife, Amastris, the widow of Dionysius, the tyrant or usurper of Heraclea, grew so offended, that she left him and returned to Heraclea. There she built a city near the Black Sea which she called Amastris, after herself, and sent for people from Selsamus, Cytorum, Cromna, Teos and other places to live there. {*Memnon, Excerpts, c. 5.*} {*Strabo, l. 12. c. 3. s. 10. 5:385*}

## 3705 AM, 4415 JP, 299 BC

*2667.* Seleucus followed the example of Lysimachus and sent his envoys to express his desire to marry Stratonice, the daughter of Demetrius and Phila, whereupon Demetrius took his daughter along with him and sailed for Syria with his whole fleet, which was attending him at Athens. On the way they landed in Cilicia, which was held by Plistarchus, the brother of Cassander, to whom it had been allotted by general consent of the kings, after the battle in which Demetrius' father Antigonus was killed. Plistarchus, offended that Demetrius had landed in his territory, complained to him about Seleucus. For Seleucus, without the consent of the other kings, Ptolemy and Lysimachus, had entered into a league with Demetrius, a common enemy to them all. Demetrius was quite upset by this and went from there to Quinda, where he found what remained of the old treasury of Alexander's twelve hundred talents. Taking it all away with him, he weighed anchor and sailed away as fast as he could. {*Plutarch, Demetrius, l. 1. c. 31,32. 9:77*}

*2668.* Seleucus came to meet Demetrius and his wife Phila at a place called Orossus, and invited them to dine with him at his pavilion in his camp. Demetrius subsequently invited him aboard his ship of thirteen tiers of oars high. They spent whole days together in friendly conversation, without arms or guards around them. At length, Seleucus married Stratonice and with great pomp returned with her to Antioch. {*Plutarch, Demetrius, l. 1. c. 31. 9:77}

2669. When Demetrius had taken over Cilicia, he sent his wife Phila to her brother Cassander to make apologies for such matters as Plistarchus may have charged him with. While she was away, his other wife, Deidamia, came to him from Athens and she died shortly thereafter. {*Plutarch, Demetrius, l. 1. c. 32. 9:77,79}

## 3706 AM, 4416 JP, 298 BC

2670. Seleucus wanted Demetrius to sell him Cilicia for a certain sum of money, but he refused. Seleucus, in anger, demanded that Sidon and Tyre be given to him by Demetrius. This seemed an injurious act on his part, that, having made himself lord and possessing everything from India to the Syrian Sea, he was nevertheless of so poor a spirit as to trouble his father-in-law, who was under a cloud of adverse fortune, for two cities as poor as Tyre and Sidon. [L463] Consequently, Demetrius stoutly answered that even if he were defeated a thousand times over, he still would never buy a son-in-law at so dear a price. So he started to fortify those two cities, which were such thorns in Seleucus' side. {*Plutarch, Demetrius, l. 1. c. 32. 9:77}

## 3707a AM, 4416 JP, 298 BC

2671. Cassander died after ruling Macedonia for nineteen years. He left three sons, Philip, Antipater and Alexander, who were born by Thessalonice, the sister of Alexander the Great. All these reigned after their father for only forty-two months. This is according to Dexippus and Porphyry, as recorded in Eusebius. {Eusebius, Scaliger's Greek Eusebius, p. 48,228.} {*Eusebius, Chronicles, l. 1. 1:208} [E335]

2672. Philip, the oldest of the three, died of consumption shortly after his father's death. His two younger brothers, Antipater and Alexander, died fighting about the kingdom. {Justin, Trogus, l. 16. c. 1.} {*Pausanias, Boeotia, l. 9. c. 7. s. 1-4. 4:203,205} {*Plutarch, Pyrrhus, l. 1. c. 6. s. 2,3. 9:361} {*Plutarch, Demetrius, l. 1. c. 36. s. 1. 9:87}

2673. Dexippus and Eusebius called this Antipater by the name of Antigonus. {*Eusebius, Chronicles, l. 1. 1:209} Hermippus meant the same person when he said that Demetrius of Phalerum, after the death of Cassander and out of the fear he had of Antigonus, fled to Ptolemy, surnamed The Deliverer. {*Diogenes Laertius, Demetrius, l. 5. c. 5. (78) 1:531}

2674. At the same time, Pyrrhus remained in exile, with Ptolemy in Egypt. He married Antigone, the daughter of Berenice, the queen, by Philip, her former husband. {*Plutarch, Pyrrhus, l. 1. c. 4. s. 4. 9:355,357} {*Pausanias, Attica, l. 1. c. 6. s. 8. 1:33}

## 3707b AM, 4417 JP, 297 BC

2675. With the help of Antigone, his wife, Pyrrhus obtained a fleet of ships and money from Ptolemy and set sail for his old kingdom of Epirus. He came to an agreement with Neoptolemus, who had usurped his kingdom, to hold it jointly with him. {*Plutarch, Pyrrhus, l. 1. c. 5. s. 1,2. 9:357} {*Pausanias, Attica, l. 1. c. 6. s. 8. 1:33}

2676. Eupolemus, the historian, wrote a chronology from Adam and the coming of the children of Israel from Egypt down to the fifth year of Demetrius. He calculated that the death of Demetrius' father Antigonus occurred in the twelfth year of Ptolemy as reckoned from the death of Alexander the Great's children. {See note on 3695 AM. <<2165>>} He did this in his book of the kings of Judah, according to Clement. {*Clement, Stromateis, l. 1. c. 21. 2:332}

## 3708 AM, 4418 JP, 296 BC

2677. Demetrius Poliorcetes, that is City Besieger, or City Taker, wasted the city of Samaria, which Perdiccas had formerly rebuilt. {*Eusebius, Chronicles, l. 1. 1:209,210}

## 3709 AM, 4419 JP, 295 BC

2678. Velleius Paterculus stated that Pyrrhus began his reign when Quintus Fabius was in his fifth consulship and Decius Mus was consul for the fourth time. {*Velleius Paterculus, l. 1. c. 14. s. 6. 1:37} That was the time when Neoptolemus was killed and Pyrrhus took sole possession of Epirus. He remembered how much he had been indebted to Berenice and Ptolemy, through whose favour he had recovered his kingdom, and named the son, whom Antigone gave him, after Ptolemy. When he had built a new city on a neck of land in Epirus, he named it after his wife's mother, Berenice. {*Plutarch, Pyrrhus, l. 1. c. 5,6. 9:357-361}

## 3710a AM, 4419 JP, 295 BC

2679. In the thirty-sixth year of the first Calippic period, the 25th day of the month of Posideion, in the 454th year of Nabonassar, the 16th day of Paophus, three hours after midnight on the 21st day of our December, Timocharis at Alexandria in Egypt observed the following: the moon rose to her farthest height north and touched the most northerly star in the head of Scorpio. {Ptolemy, Great Syntaxis, l. 7. c. 3.}

## 3710b AM, 4420 JP, 294 BC

2680. In the same year, on the 15th day of the month of Elaphebolion, the fifth of the month of Tybus, four hours before midnight on the ninth of our May, Timocharis observed the conjunction of the moon with Spica in Virgo. {Ptolemy, Great Syntaxis, l. 7. c. 3.}

2681. Thessalonice, the queen and widow of Cassander, the daughter of Philip who was the father of Alexander the Great, born to the daughter of Nicasipolis, was murdered by Antipater, her own son. She pleaded for her life because she was his mother, but to no avail. The reason was that when the kingdom had been divided between him and his brother, she had seemed to favour her youngest son, Alexander. *[L464]* Alexander sought to avenge the murder of his mother and asked for help from his friends, Pyrrhus, king of Epirus, and Demetrius Poliorcetes in Peloponnesus. {*Justin, Trogus, l. 16. c. 1.*} {*\*Plutarch, Pyrrhus, l. 1. c. 6. s. 2. 9:361*} {*\*Pausanias, Boeotia, l. 9. c. 7. s. 3. 4:203,205*}

2682. Lysimachus, the king of Thrace, feared Demetrius' arrival. He persuaded his son-in-law, Antipater to fight an old common enemy and set past differences aside. {*Justin, Trogus, l. 16. c. 1.*} Knowing full well that Pyrrhus would do anything for Ptolemy's sake, he sent some forged letters to Pyrrhus from Ptolemy. These advised him to accept a gratuity of three hundred talents from Antipater and to stop his expedition into Macedonia in support of Alexander against his brother. Pyrrhus recognised this trick of his. When he opened the letter, he did not find the usual greeting from Ptolemy to him, which was, *The father, to the son, health and happiness.* Instead of this, it said, *King Ptolemy to King Pyrrhus, health and happiness.* When Demetrius suddenly attacked Macedonia, he foiled all these schemes of Lysimachus. {*\*Plutarch, Pyrrhus, l. 1. c. 6. s. 3,4. 9:361,363*}

2683. Ptolemy of Egypt captured the whole isle of Cyprus from Demetrius, except for the city of Salamis, where he besieged Demetrius' mother and children, who were there. When he finally captured the city, he sent them home to Demetrius with an honourable escort and with rich presents for their journey. {*\*Plutarch, Demetrius, l. 1. c. 34. s. 3,4. 9:87*}

2684. When Demetrius captured Alexander, he killed him and took over the kingdom of Macedonia. *[E336]* {*Justin, Trogus, l. 16. c. 1.*} {*\*Pausanias, Boeotia, l. 9. c. 7. s. 3. 4:205*} {*\*Plutarch, Pyrrhus, l. 1. c. 7. s. 1. 9:363*} {*\*Plutarch, Demetrius, l. 1. c. 36. 9:87-91*} {*Plutarch, Shamefacedness*} He held it for seven years, as Plutarch affirmed. {*\*Plutarch, Demetrius, l. 1. c. 44. s. 7. 9:113*}

## 3711 AM, 4421 JP, 293 BC

2685. At that time, Lysimachus was fighting a war started against him by Dromichaetes, the king of the Getes. So he would not be forced to fight against the king of the Getes and Demetrius at the same time, he gave up that part of Macedonia which belonged to his son-in-law Antipater and so made peace with Dromichaetes. {*Justin, Trogus, l. 16. c. 1.*} {*\*Strabo, l. 7. c. 3. s. 8. 3:203*}

2686. Dromichaetes captured Lysimachus, but treated him very kindly. {*\*Strabo, l. 7. c. 3. s. 8. 3:203*} {*\*Diod. Sic., l. 21. c.*

*12. 11:17-32*} Lysimachus gave him his daughter in marriage, and that part of Thrace which lay beyond the Ister River, for a dowry. {*\*Pausanias, Attica, l. 1. c. 9. s. 6. 1:45,47*}

2687. Clearchus, the king of Heraclea in Pontus, had gone to help Lysimachus in his war against the Getes and was taken prisoner together with Lysimachus. When Lysimachus had achieved liberty for himself, he wisely secured Clearchus' liberty also. {*Mennon, Excerpts, c. 6.*}

## 3712 AM, 4422 JP, 292 BC

2688. When Simon, surnamed the Just, who was the high priest at Jerusalem, died, he left behind him only one son, Onias. Simon's brother, Eleazar, became the high priest of the Jews. {*\*Josephus, Antiq., l. 12. c. 2. s. 5. (43,44) 7:25*} He was said to have held that office for thirty-two years. {*Eusebius, Scaliger's Greek Eusebius, p. 50,162.*} {*\*Eusebius, Chronicles, l. 1. 1:210*}

2689. After Lysimachus returned from the war with the Getes, Agathocles, his oldest son, who, as some report, had been taken prisoner in the first battle in which he took part, was married. He took Lysandra for a wife, who was the daughter of Ptolemy of Egypt, surnamed *The Deliverer*, and Ptolemy's wife, Eurydice. {*\*Pausanias, Attica, l. 1. c. 9. s. 6,7. 1:47*}

2690. After this, Lysimachus sailed into Asia with his navy and captured those who were in subjection to Antigonus and Demetrius. {*\*Pausanias, Attica, l. 1. c. 9. s. 6,7. 1:47*} {*\*Plutarch, Demetrius, l. 1. c. 44. s. 1,2. 9:109*} While he besieged Ephesus, the Ephesians were helped by Mardro, an old pirate who often brought them rich prizes which he had captured. Lysimachus bribed him and had him betray the city to him. He gave Mardro some valiant Macedonians, whose hands were then bound behind them by Mardro, before he brought them like prisoners into Ephesus. *[L465]* These men waited for an opportune time to get weapons from the citadel in which they were kept, and so took the city for Lysimachus. {*\*Frontinus, Stratagems, l. 3. c. 3. s. 7. 1:217*} The city of Ephesus was located on low ground, and some time later was completely flooded by the sea. In Stephanus Byzantinus we may read an epigram made by Duris, concerning this flood. Lysimachus moved the city to another place and rebuilt it, calling it after his new wife Arsinoe, but after his death the city quickly assumed its old name of Ephesus. {*\*Strabo, l. 14. c. 1. s. 21. 6:221*} {*Stephanus, de Urbibus, on Ephesus*} To populate his new city, he destroyed the two cities of Lebedos and Colophon and relocated their inhabitants to the new city. Phoenix, in his poetry, grievously deplored this action involving the destruction of these two famous cities. {*Phoenix, Iambics*} {*\*Pausanias, Attica, l. 1. c. 9. s. 7. 1:47*}

**3713 AM, 4423 JP, 291 BC**

*2691.* Seleucus wanted to populate the cities he had built in Asia and lower Syria, especially Antioch, which was the metropolis of all the rest. He relocated the Jews from their own dwellings into these cities and gave them the same privileges, prerogatives and immunities that the Macedonians had both in towns and cities. {*Eusebius, Chronicles, l. 1. 1:210} {*Josephus, Antiq., l. 12. c. 3. s. 1. (119) 7:61} {*Josephus, Apion, l. 2. c. 4. (38,39) 1:307} Seleucus named sixteen of the cities Antioch, after his father Antiochus. Five of them he named Laodicea, after his mother Laodice. He named nine of them Seleucia, after himself, while three of them were named Apamea, after his wife. He named one after his former wife, Stratonice, and to the rest he gave Greek and Macedonian names as he thought best, that is: Berrhoea, Edessa, Pella and so forth. {*Appian, Syrian Wars, l. 11. c. 9. (57) 2:213,215}

**3715 AM, 4425 JP, 289 BC**

*2692.* When Agathocles, the tyrant of Sicily, was about to die, he shipped his wife Thoxena off to Egypt with his two children, whom he had had by her and who were very young, and sent along with them all his treasure, his family and costly furniture. Because he was one of the richest kings, and his wife had originally come from Egypt, he feared that as soon as he was dead, they would suffer and his kingdom would be plundered. His wife begged to stay with him to the end, for she said she had married him for better or worse. At last she and her children left him, but not without much sorrowing. Even his young children could scarcely be pulled away from him. As soon as they were gone, he died. {Justin, Trogus, l. 23. c. 2.} [E337]

*2693.* Clearchus and Oxathres, the two kings of Heraclea in Pontus, murdered their mother. When Amastris was on board a ship to leave them, she was thrown overboard in a most barbarous manner and drowned in the sea. {Memnon, Excerpts, c. 6.}

**3716 AM, 4426 JP, 288 BC**

*2694.* Lysimachus desired to revenge the death of Amastris, to whom he had been married for a long time. He came into Heraclea and showed every fatherly affection toward Clearchus and those who were closest to him, but then first killed him and after that his brother Oxathres. {Memnon, Excerpts, c. 7.} This was seventeen years after the death of the father of Clearchus, as recorded in Diodorus. {*Diod. Sic., l. 20. c. 77. s. 1. 10:347} When he had conquered that city and its territory, he took all the treasure belonging to those kings and whatever they had of value and leaving the city in full liberty, he returned to his own kingdom. {Memnon, Excerpts, c. 7.}

*2695.* Strato of Lampsacus, the son of Arcesilaus, and surnamed Physicus, succeeded Theophrastus in his school. Strato was the teacher and tutor to Ptolemy Philadelphus, who gave Strato eighty talents for educating him. {*Diogenes Laertius, Strato, l. 5. c. 3. (58) 1:511}

*2696.* Demetrius Poliorcetes was trying to recover all the dominions of his father Antigonus. [L466] He was now ready to land in Asia with an army so large that no man since the days of Alexander the Great up to that time, had had a larger army. He had more than ninety-eight thousand foot soldiers and a little less than twelve thousand cavalry. His fleet consisted of five hundred ships, some of which were extremely large, as they had fifteen or sixteen tiers of oars. Before he left on this expedition, he made a firm league with Pyrrhus, because he feared that Pyrrhus might possibly create trouble in his absence and interfere with his plans. {*Plutarch, Demetrius, l. 1. c. 43. s. 2-5. 9:107,109} {*Plutarch, Pyrrhus, l. 1. c. 7. s. 1,2. 9:363}

**3717 AM, 4427 JP, 287 BC**

*2697.* Seleucus, Ptolemy and Lysimachus also feared what Demetrius' intentions might be. Combining their forces into one body, they made war on Demetrius in Europe. All three sent envoys to Pyrrhus in Epirus and requested that he invade Macedonia. They urged him to disregard the league he had made with Demetrius, since Demetrius had no intention of peace, but planned to be free to wage war where he pleased. Pyrrhus readily agreed to this. He defeated Demetrius' army, routed him and took over the kingdom of Macedonia. This was the first time that Pyrrhus acquired any elephants. {*Plutarch, Demetrius, l. 1. c. 44. 9:109-113} {*Plutarch, Pyrrhus, l. 1. c. 7. s. 3-5. 9:365} {Justin, Trogus, l. 16. c. 2.} {*Pausanias, Attica, l. 1. c. 10. s. 2. 1:49}

*2698.* Lysimachus came and pretended that he, as well as Pyrrhus, had a hand in the defeat of Demetrius and wanted half the kingdom of Macedonia. Pyrrhus doubted the loyalty of the Macedonians toward himself and agreed, and so Macedonia was divided between the two by cities and regions. {*Plutarch, Demetrius, l. 1. c. 44. s. 7. 9:113}

*2699.* Lysimachus found that his son-in-law Antipater complained publicly that his father-in-law had, by these machinations, cheated him of the kingdom of Macedonia. So Lysimachus killed him, and when his daughter Eurydice, Antipater's widow, was grieved by the death of her husband, he committed her to prison. Thus the whole house of Cassander paid for the destruction of Alexander the Great's family, either by their own deaths or in the destruction of Cassander's own family by various murders, torments or parricides until his own family line was utterly destroyed. {Justin, Trogus, l. 16. c. 2.}

2700. When Demetrius was stripped of his kingdom, he fled to Cassandria. His wife Phila was consumed with grief and unable to endure seeing her husband become a private citizen in a foreign country, she gave up all hope for the future and poisoned herself. {*Plutarch, Demetrius, l. 1. c. 45. s. 1. 9:113}

2701. When Demetrius besieged Athens, which had revolted from him to Pyrrhus, Crates, the philosopher, was sent to him in an embassy, and persuaded Demetrius to lift his siege. So he assembled all his ships and boarded them with his eleven thousand foot soldiers in addition to his cavalry, sailed away into Asia and captured all Caria and Lydia from Lysimachus. There, not far from Miletus, Eurydice, the sister of his wife Phila, met him and brought with her Ptolemais, her daughter by Ptolemy of Egypt. Demetrius' son-in-law Seleucus had previously spoken to Ptolemy, asking that he give her to him. Therefore Demetrius now married her through the good will of Eurydice, and fathered a son by her, also called Demetrius, who later reigned in Cyrene. {*Plutarch, Demetrius, l. 1. c. 46. s. 2,3. 9:117} {*Plutarch, Demetrius, l. 1. c. 53. s. 4. 9:135}

2702. In this expedition, Demetrius captured many towns and cities. Some he persuaded to defect to him, while others he took by force. Some defected to him from Lysimachus, and these gave him a good supply of men and war materials. When Agathocles, the son of Lysimachus, came toward him with an army, he marched up into Phrygia. He planned to invade Armenia and thereby provoke a rebellion in Media. [E338] He wanted to see how loyal the upper provinces of Asia were to him, because he hoped to find a good refuge there, if required. He had often beaten Agathocles, who was following him, in small battles, but had never engaged him in a major battle. {*Plutarch, Demetrius, l. 1. c. 46. s. 4,5. 9:117}

2703. Nevertheless, he often lacked food for himself and fodder for his horses. He found himself under severe pressure, especially through an error he made in crossing the Lycus River, whereby he lost many of his soldiers, who were swept away by the violence of the river. [L467] After a famine, a pestilence killed eight thousand of his troops, forcing him to return with the remainder to Tarsus in Cilicia. He planned to refrain from any oppression of the people of Seleucus, whom he did not want to offend in any way, but this was not to be. When he considered the extreme necessity that his army was in and the fact that Agathocles controlled all the passes of the Taurus Mountains, he wrote letters to Seleucus. He complained of his own poor fortune and humbly besought Seleucus to be compassionate to him, since he was a poor relative of his, and one who had suffered

enough to be pitied even by an enemy. {*Plutarch, Demetrius, l. 1. c. 46,47. 9:119}

## 3718a AM, 4427 JP, 287 BC

2704. Seleucus had compassion on the distressing state of his father-in-law. He wrote to his commanders and officers in those parts to supply Demetrius with all supplies in a kingly manner, and not to allow his army to be short of anything. But Patrocles, an intimate friend of Seleucus, planted suspicions against Demetrius in Seleucus' head, so that Seleucus led an army against him into Cilicia. Demetrius wondered at this sudden change in Seleucus and withdrew into the craggy Taurus Mountains, from where he sent his agents to Seleucus to request that he be given permission to attack some free state of the barbarians. He would then spend the remainder of his life there, without ranging over the world any longer. If Seleucus would not permit this, then he asked permission to winter quietly where he was, and not to be exposed to the force and fury of his enraged enemy in the extremity in which he now was. Seleucus was suspicious of these requests, and so granted him only that after he had surrendered his best friends to him for hostages, he could then spend two months of his winter quarters in Cataonia, a country bordering upon Cappadocia. Meanwhile Seleucus blocked all the passes which led from there into Syria. {*Plutarch, Demetrius, l. 1. c. 47,48. 9:119,121}

2705. Demetrius was now trapped like a wild beast in a den. He had Agathocles, the son of Lysimachus, on the one hand and Seleucus on the other, to watch him. He then used force and wasted some of the provinces which belonged to Seleucus, in every encounter getting the better of Seleucus. When Seleucus let his scythe-bearing chariots attack him, Demetrius on several occasions routed them also and put his enemies to flight. He took the mountain passes and drove out the garrisons which Seleucus had placed there to hold them. Growing confident of his own strength, he now resolved to settle the matter in a pitched battle with Seleucus. Suddenly he became very sick, which laid him low and dashed his hopes of better things in this world. In that sickness, all his soldiers abandoned him, with some defecting to his enemies and others disbanding and going where they pleased. {Justin, Trogus, l. 16. c. 3.} {*Plutarch, Pyrrhus, l. 1. c. 12. s. 6. 9:381} {*Plutarch, Demetrius, l. 1. c. 48. s. 2-4. 9:121,123} {*Pausanias, Attica, l. 1. c. 10. s. 3. 1:51}

## 3718b AM, 4428 JP, 286 BC

2706. While Demetrius was trapped by Seleucus in Syria, Lysimachus attacked Pyrrhus in Macedonia, and won all of it from Pyrrhus within five years and six months. {Justin, Trogus, l. 16. c. 3.} {*Pausanias, Attica, l. 1. c. 10. s. 3. 1:51} {Dexippus} {Porphyry}

2707. After a period of forty days, Demetrius recovered from his sickness. He took the remaining soldiers and moved his camp, letting on that he would march into Cilicia. The next night, without the sound of a trumpet, he turned around another way. When he had crossed the range of Amanus, he ravaged and plundered all that country as far as Cyrrhestica, a region in Syria. When Seleucus came there with his army and camped not far from him, Demetrius and his men attacked him at night, while he slept. Seleucus, however, had received notice of his coming through some who had defected to him. He got out of his bed and commanded an alarm to be sounded. While he was putting on his shoes, he cried out to his friends that they had to deal with a fierce, wild beast. [L468] When Demetrius realised, by the noise which he heard in the enemy camp, that his attack was no longer a surprise, he retired and went his way. {*Plutarch, Demetrius, l. 1. c. 49. s. 1,2. 9:123,125}

2708. As soon as it was day, Seleucus followed and overtook him. Demetrius ordered one wing of his army to be led by a captain of his, and led the other himself. He routed the wing of the enemy on his side. Then Seleucus leaped off his horse and took off his helmet. With a shield in his hand, he showed himself bare-faced to the mercenaries of Demetrius' army and exhorted them to leave Demetrius and defect to him. He urged them to know that it was more as a favour to them than to Demetrius that he had for so long refrained from attacking them. [E339] Whereupon they welcomed him and hailed him as their king, and abandoned Demetrius to serve Seleucus. {*Plutarch, Demetrius, l. 1. c. 49. s. 2,3. 9:125}

2709. Demetrius thought this would be the last reversal of his fortunes and the worst thing that could befall him. He retired to the passes of the Amanus Mountain and spent that night in a dense forest with the few friends whom he had left. He planned to go from there to the city of Caunus in the hope of finding his fleet and fleeing to some other country. Just when he realised that he did not have so much as one day's provision for those who were with him, it so happened that an old friend of his, Sosigenes, came and brought him four hundred pieces of gold. Hoping that this money would pay for his needs on his journey to the coast, he set out by night to cross the top of the mountain, but when he saw the enemy campfires everywhere and realised that the enemy was blocking his way, he was forced, in great despair, to return to the place from where he had set out. When one of the company told him that he would do well to surrender to Seleucus, Demetrius drew his sword and would have killed himself on the spot. But his friends persuaded him not to, and he sent to Seleucus and surrendered himself to

him, together with all that he had. {*Plutarch, Demetrius, l. 1. c. 49. s. 3-5. 9:125,127}

2710. When Seleucus heard the message, he ordered his servants to outfit a royal pavilion in a most regal manner to welcome Demetrius. He sent Apollonides, who had formerly been an intimate friend of Demetrius, to comfort him and to tell him that there was no cause for fear, since he was coming to an old friend and son-in-law of his. When Seleucus' servants heard this, first one by one and then later they all flocked in large numbers to Demetrius. Their action provoked envy instead of compassion toward Demetrius, which caused his foes to thwart Seleucus' good intentions to him. They told Seleucus that no sooner would Demetrius be seen in their camp than Seleucus would be faced with a great revolution in the camp. {*Plutarch, Demetrius, l. 1. c. 50. s. 1-3. 9:127}

2711. Consequently, Pausanias was sent with a company of about a thousand men, made up of cavalry and foot soldiers. They separated him from everyone else and instead of bringing him to Seleucus, carried him away to a certain cape in Syria, where he was kept under a strong guard for the rest of his days. He was given an adequate allowance and lacked neither money, nor the freedom to enjoy walks, gardens, places of hunting, or any other recreations that his heart could desire. His friends, who had followed him, were free at any time to see him and talk with him. Not a day passed, while he was there, that someone did not come to see him with friendly messages from Seleucus, to encourage him to be of good comfort and to hope for further liberty on reasonable terms. Seleucus said that he would free Demetrius as soon as Antiochus (who was Seleucus' son) came with his wife Stratonice. {*Plutarch, Demetrius, l. 1. c. 50. s. 4-6. 9:129} However, Diodorus stated that he was kept prisoner at Pella all this time. {*Diod. Sic., l. 21. c. 20. 11:39}

2712. Finding himself in this position, Demetrius wrote to his son, and to other captains and friends of his at Athens, Corinth and other places, saying that they should give no credence to any letters that might happen to come to them as being sent in his name or sealed with his seal. They should act as if he were dead and respect his son Antigonus in the kingdom. {*Plutarch, Demetrius, l. 1. c. 51. s. 1. 9:129} Thus Porphyry started Antigonus' reign over Greece from this time, that is, from the tenth year before Antigonus added the kingdom of Macedonia to his other dominions. [L469] Porphyry further stated that Antigonus was surnamed Gonatas after a place called Goni in Thessaly, where he grew up. {Eusebius, Scaliger's Greek Eusebius, p. 226.} {*Eusebius, Chronicles, l. 1. 1:211} When Antigonus heard the news of his father's captivity, he took it very hard. He clothed himself in mourning clothes and wrote letters to various kings, as well as to Seleucus. He did this in a humble manner, offering himself, and whatever he could call his, as a pledge to Seleucus for his father. Similar letters and messages came to Seleucus from various cities and kings on Demetrius' behalf. {*Plutarch, Demetrius, l. 1. c. 51. s. 2. 9:131}

2713. Only Lysimachus in his letters advised Seleucus to be careful how he let the man go. He said Demetrius was ambitious and a turbulent spirit, too ambitious of sovereignty and too inclined to encroach upon the rights of all the other kings. He offered Seleucus two thousand talents if he would kill him, but Seleucus, who had never had a good opinion of Lysimachus, utterly detested him after reading his letter and thought he was a barbarous and loathsome person. He told Lysimachus' envoys in no uncertain terms what he thought of their attempts to persuade him to break the promise he had given and to murder someone who was so closely related to him. Nevertheless, Seleucus immediately wrote letters to his son Antiochus, who was in Media at the time, advising him how to deal with Demetrius now that he had him. Seleucus planned to free him and restore him to his former glory as a king, and so he thought it fitting to share this honour with Antiochus, since he had married Demetrius' daughter Stratonice and had children by her. {*Plutarch, Demetrius, l. 1. c. 51. s. 2,3. 9:131} {*Diod. Sic., l. 21. c. 20. 11:39} [E340]

## 3719 AM, 4429 JP, 285 BC

2714. Demetrius was confined to that cape in Syria. At first he exercised himself in hunting and other sports, but gradually he grew idle and reckless and spent most of his time eating and playing dice. {*Plutarch, Demetrius, l. 1. c. 52. s. 1. 9:131}

2715. Ptolemy of Egypt, surnamed *Soter* (or *Saviour*), had children first by Eurydice, the daughter of Antipater, and then by Berenice, whom Antipater had only sent into Egypt as a companion with his daughter. He was now near death and appointed Ptolemy, surnamed Philadelphus, one of his sons, whom he had by Berenice, to succeed him in the kingdom. {*Pausanias, Attica, l. 1. c. 6. s. 8. 1:33} Justin stated that he turned his kingdom over to his son while he was still in very good health, and that he told the people his reasons for doing this. {Justin, Trogus, l. 16. c. 2.} However, Lucian and Porphyry stated that when he had reigned thirty-eight years by himself, he then made his son viceroy in the kingdom and so held the kingdom jointly with him for two years. {*Lucian, Octogenarians, l. 1. (12) 1:231} {Eusebius, Scaliger's Greek Eusebius, p. 225.} However, I calculated that it was in the thirty-ninth year after the death of Alexander that he took his son, Philadelphus, into the consortship of the kingdom with him. To mark this, Dionysius, the astronomer, began a new era starting from the summer of this year, 3719 AM, as Ptolemy

showed in his work from Dionysius' celestial observations. {Ptolemy, Great Syntaxis} This Dionysius was none other than that same man Dionysius whom Ptolemy Philadelphus sent into India. {*Pliny, l. 6. c. 21. (59) 2:383}

2716. Hermippus said that Demetrius of Phalerum advised Ptolemy to appoint one of his sons born by Eurydice as viceroy, and not a son by Berenice Heraclides. In his epitome of the successions of Sotion, he stated that when Ptolemy wanted the kingdom to be given to his son, Philadelphus, Demetrius said to him: {*Diogenes Laertius, Demetrius, l. 5. c. 5. (79) 1:531}

> "Sir, take heed what you do; if you give it away once, you will never have it again."

2717. In spite of this, the father publicly gave his son the kingdom and served him as one of his ordinary guard. He said that it was much better to be the father of a king than to have a kingdom. {Justin, Trogus, l. 16. c. 2.} [L470]

2718. Ptolemy was surnamed *Ceraunus*, that is *Lightning*. This was either for his speed and promptness in handling business or for his fierceness of nature, and he was the other son of Ptolemy but by Eurydice. Memnon stated that when he saw his younger brother made king ahead of him, he fled to Seleucus out of fear. Seleucus pitied him in his situation, seeing him as the son of a friend, and entertained him with a generous and honourable allowance. He promised that as soon as his father died, he would set him on his throne in Egypt. {Memnon, Excerpts, c. 9,13.} {*Appian, Syrian Wars, l. 11. c. 10. (62) 2:225}

## 3720 AM, 4430 JP, 284 BC

2719. Cyril stated that in the 124th Olympiad the image of Serapis was brought to Alexandria from Sinope on the Black Sea, in the reign, as some thought, of Ptolemy Philadelphus. {Cyril, Against Julian, l. 1.} But this should be under Ptolemy I, his father, since, as was noted before, they reigned jointly in the beginning of this Olympiad. Envoys were sent from Ptolemy I to Scydrothemis, who was the king of Sinope in Pontus at that time, dealing with this very matter. Cornelius Tacitus described this in detail. {*Tacitus, Histories, l. 4. c. 81-84. 3:159-167}

2720. In the same Olympiad, Sostratus of Cnidos built the lighthouse on Pharos at Alexandria. {*Eusebius, Chronicles, l. 1. 1:211} Pliny stated: {*Pliny, l. 36. c. 18. 10:65}

> "The lighthouse built by a king on the isle of Pharos, at the port of Alexandria, is very famous. This cost eight hundred talents to build. Ptolemy, the king, was very generous in that he allowed Sostratus, the architect of that great work, to name it. The use of the tower was to hold a beacon of light in it to help those who travelled by sea at night. By day, it showed

them the entrance into the port and warned of the shoals near it."

2721. When Strabo called Sostratus the *friend of kings*, he was referring to the two Ptolemys, father and son, who, as I have shown before, held that kingdom in consortship together at this time. He cited the inscription which Sostratus himself had made there: {*Strabo, l. 17. c. 1. s. 6. 8:25}

"Sostratus of Cnidos, the son of Dexiphanes, a friend of the kings, for the safety of the seamen."

2722. Lucian stated the same, except that he said that Sostratus somewhere cunningly inserted *and of himself*, and not, as Pliny claimed, *by the permission and good liking of the two kings.* For when he built the lighthouse, he engraved this inscription somewhere on the inside of it. Then, he plastered it over and on that plaster wrote the name of that Ptolemy who was reigning at the time. He thought that in a short time it would come to pass (as indeed it did) that the upper inscription would fall off together with the plaster and then his own name, which was engraved underneath in good stone, would appear. {*Lucian, How to Write History (62) 6:71,73} [E341]

2723. To ensure a safe means of getting supplies to Pharos, which lay about a mile from the mainland, a large causeway was constructed to join the island to the continent. Hence it was no longer a distinct island but was joined to the continent at Rhacotes, a suburb of the city of Alexandria. Julius Caesar stated: {*Caesar, Civil Wars, l. 3. (112) 2:357}

"On the island there is a tower called Pharos, of great height, a work of wondrous construction, which took its name from the island. This island, lying opposite Alexandria, makes a harbour, but it is connected with the town by a narrow roadway like a bridge, piers nine hundred feet in length having been thrown out seawards by former kings."

2724. The Latin for the last phrase, "by former kings" is *superioribus regibus.* For that is what it should say, as Broadaeus, Scaliger and Salianus have noted, and not a *superioribus regionibus,* as the common printed copies have it.

2725. For we can in no way give credence to that fable of Ammianus Marcellinus {*Ammianus Marcellinus, l. 22. c. 16. s. 9. 2:299} [L471] or Johannes Malela, {Johannes Malela, l. 9. c. 2.} or the author of the Fasti Siculi or George Cedrenus and Johannes Tzetza, who imagined that both the lighthouse itself and its causeway were the work of Cleopatra, the last queen of Egypt.

2726. Spartacus, the king of Cimmerian Bosphorus, died after he had reigned twenty years. It seems he was succeeded by his son, Parysades. {See note on 3694 AM. <<2588>>} {*Diod. Sic., l. 20. c. 100. s. 7. 10:409}

2727. Demetrius Poliorcetes, who had been confined in a cape of Syria for three whole years, became sick and died. This was caused partly by laziness and partly by overeating, {*Plutarch, Demetrius, l. 1. c. 52. s. 4. 9:133} and occurred seventeen years after his father Antigonus died. Dexippus, Porphyry and Eusebius said that Seleucus was ill-spoken of throughout the world because of his death. Indeed, he regretted it often and blamed himself for having been so jealous and suspicious of him. When Demetrius' son Antigonus heard that the body of his father was on its way to him, he put to sea with all the ships that he could find and met them around the isles. There he received the ashes of his body and placed them in a golden urn, which he then covered with a purple veil and put a diadem or golden crown on it. He gave him a royal funeral after having first carried the urn along with him to Corinth. Then he went to Demetrias, a city named after his father and populated by him with men taken from the smaller towns and villages of Iolcus in Thessaly. {*Plutarch, Demetrius, l. 1. c. 52. s. 4. 9:133}

2728. Seleucus had now acquired all that Demetrius had possessed in Syria and Asia, and he made both these kingdoms into one unified empire. {*Eusebius, Chronicles, l. 1. 1:210,211} At that time, while the Jews paid him three hundred talents yearly for their tribute, they did not, however, have a foreign ruler over them, but were governed by their high priests and according to the customs of their country. {*Sulpicius Servius, Sacred History, l. 2. c. 17. 11:106}

## 3721a AM, 4430 JP, 284 BC

2729. In this year, Ptolemy, the son of Lagus, surnamed Soter, died. He had made his son viceroy with him in the kingdom for almost fifteen months, according to the calendar of Dionysius. This was about thirty-nine years and four months after the death of Alexander the Great. (Others said it was a full forty years, but Claudius Ptolemy said that it was thirty-nine years. {Ptolemy, Canon of Kings}) He had lived a full eighty-four years. {*Lucian, Octogenarians, l. 1. (12) 1:231} The countries and kingdoms which he had held in his possession were all listed by Theocritus, the poet. {Theocritus, Idyll. 17.} These were— Egypt, Phoenicia, Arabia, Syria, Libya, Ethiopia, Pamphylia, Cilicia, Lycia, Caria and the isles of the Cyclades. The truth is that he was said to have allied himself with Seleucus against Demetrius on the express condition that the dominion of all Asia should go to Seleucus but that Phoenicia and Coelosyria would be his. However, the Seleucians denied this and said that Ptolemy entered into an alliance against Antigonus not to gain anything by it for himself but to help Seleucus in the claim which he laid to Coelosyria. After the death of Antigonus, Cassander and Lysimachus gave Coelosyria to Seleucus. {*Polybius, l. 5. c. 67. s. 6-8. 3:165} There is no doubt, as Theocritus also stated, that at certain times Phoenicia and Syria belonged to Ptolemy. After the death of Antigonus, Ptolemy again subdued Syria for himself. {*Pausanias, Attica, l. 1. c. 6. s. 8. 1:33} Yet we have already shown that Tyre and Sidon were in the possession of Demetrius Poliorcetes. After his death, if not before, both those places and all the rest of Syria were controlled by Seleucus.

2730. Josephus said that Ptolemy Philadelphus reigned for thirty-nine years. {*Josephus, Antiq., l. 12. c. 2. s. 1. (11) 7:7,9} [L472] It seems he counted from the time that he first reigned jointly with his father, for Clement of Alexandria said he reigned only thirty-seven years after his father's death. Claudius Ptolemy said it was thirty-eight years {Ptolemy, Canon of Kings} and so did Porphyry, Eusebius and others. Whereas, according to my account, he reigned thirty-seven years and almost eight months after his father's death, but one month short of thirty-nine years in all. Although the length of his reign is uncertain, it is known for sure that he put to death his younger brother Argaeus because the latter had been guilty of plotting his death. He executed another brother of his, born of Eurydice, because he was found to be instigating a revolt in the isle of Cyprus. {*Pausanias, Attica, l. 1. c. 7. s. 1. 1:35} [E342] Going by those actions, he little deserved that generous name of *Philadelphus*, that is, *a Lover of His Brethren*. Theocritus said that he had 33,339 cities in his dominions and was said to have been so great a power that he exceeded his father, Ptolemy I. {Theocritus, Idyll. 17.} Jerome confirmed this from his histories in commenting on Daniel, {Da 11} and so did Appian from the records of the kings of Egypt, in his preface to his history of the Romans. {*Appian, l. 1. c. 0. s. 10. 1:15,17} To support this further we could add what Athenaeus said about his fleets and the incredible size of his ships. {*Athenaeus, l. 5. (203-206) 2:421-433}

## 3721b AM, 4431 JP, 283 BC

2731. In the forty-seventh year of the first period of Calippus, in the eighth day of the month of Anthesterion, in the 465th year of Nabonassar's account, the 29th day of the month of Athyr, three hours before midnight, at the end of the 29th day of our January according to the Julian calendar, Timocharis observed at Alexandria that the fourth part of the moon covered a third part of a star in Virgo (or Pleiades), or nearly a half. {Ptolemy, Great Syntaxis, l. 7. c. 3.}

2732. Lysimachus, who was now king of Thrace and Macedonia, was persuaded by his wife Arsinoe (by whom he also had children) to murder his oldest son Agathocles, even though he had intended him to be his successor in his kingdom, and Lysimachus had achieved so many glorious victories through him. It is uncertain whether he was killed by poison or at the hands of Ptolemy Ceraunus, the brother of his wife Arsinoe. {*Strabo, l. 13. c. 4. s. 1. 6:165} {Justin, Trogus, l. 17. c. 1.} {*Pausanias, Attica, l. 1. c. 10. s. 3. 1:51} {Memnon, Excerpts, c. 9.}

2733. After his son was killed, he did not hesitate to kill those nobles of his who lamented his son's death, whereupon those who escaped, as well as the captains of his armies in all regions, defected to Seleucus. {Justin, Trogus, l. 17. c. 1.} The murders of his nobles made all the people abhor him, with the result that whole cities defected from him to Seleucus. {Memnon, Excerpts, c. 9.}

2734. Lysandra, the daughter of Ptolemy Soter and sister to Arsinoe, defected to Seleucus along with her brothers and her children born to her through Agathocles. Alexander, another son of Lysimachus' other wife Odryssias, also fled to Seleucus. They all came to Babylon and petitioned Seleucus to make war on Lysimachus. {*Appian, Syrian Wars, l. 11. c. 10. (64) 2:229} {*Pausanias, Attica, l. 1. c. 10. s. 4. 1:51}

2735. At the same time, Philetaerus of Paphlagonia, a eunuch who had a good education in his youth, was the keeper of all Lysimachus' treasure that was stored at Pergamum. Grieved by the murder of Agathocles and by Arsinoe, who daily accused him to Lysimachus, he seized the city of Pergamum, which stood on the Caicus River. He then sent to Seleucus, offering Seleucus both himself and all the treasure belonging to Lysimachus which he had there under his charge. He made a practice of siding with the strongest and keeping them in line with good promises and offices as opportunities arose, and so he held the citadel there and the government of the place for twenty years. {*Pausanias, Attica, l. 1. c. 10. s. 4,5. 1:51,53} {*Strabo, l. 13. c. 4. s. 1. 6:163,165} Appian called him *The Prince of Pergamum*, {*Appian, Syrian Wars, l. 11. c. 10. (63) 2:227} but some old annals of Huber Goltsis Thesauro, called him *Regem*, that is, *King*, for this indeed was the man who was the founder of that new government in Pergamum. He was sixty years old, according to Lucian. {*Lucian, Octogenarians, l. 1. (12) 1:231,233} [L473]

## 3722a AM, 4431 JP, 283 BC

2736. In the 48th year of the first Calippic period, on the 25th day of the month of Pyanopsion, the 466th year of Nabonassar, the 7th day of the month of Thoth, three and a half hours before midnight, on the 9th day of our November, Timocharis at Alexandria observed the conjunction of the moon with Spica in Virgo, in its northern parts. {*Ptolemy, Great Syntaxis, l. 7. c. 3.}

## 3722b AM, 4432 JP, 282 BC

2737. Antiochus, also surnamed Soter, son of Seleucus Nicator, fell in love with Stratonice, one of his father's wives by whom his father had a son. Aware of the strength of his own desire, he neither attempted anything on her nor revealed anything of what was troubling him, but lay in bed and would have died in that melancholy, had not the cause of his problem been discovered by Leptines, a mathematician, or as others say, Erasistratus. (He was a physician, Aristotle's grandchild by his daughter and a disciple of Chrysippus, according to Pliny. {*Pliny, l. 29. c. 3. (5) 8:185} That was the Chrysippus who was a Cnidian and a physician, {*Diogenes Laertius, Chrysippus, l. 7. c. 7. (186) 2:295} although some others say he was a scholar under Theophrastus, as Laertius stated elsewhere. {*Diogenes Laertius, Theophrastus, l. 5. c. 2. (57) 1:509} [E343] His followers went by the name of Erasistrataeans. Later Galen wrote a book on Phlebotomie. {Galen, Bloodletting}) Erasistratus, who was sitting with Antiochus, noticed that when Stratonice came in, his colour always rose and his pulse beat high. When she went away, he grew pale and waned again and was short of breath and panted. He discovered what his problem was and told Seleucus about it, whereupon Seleucus was content to part with her to his son, although he loved her most dearly. Calling his army together, Seleucus married her to his son before them all. At that time, Seleucus had seventy-two provinces under him, the larger part of which he gave to his son, namely the upper provinces, which were all east of the Euphrates River. He reserved for himself only those countries which lay to the west, between the Euphrates River and the Mediterranean Sea. {*Appian, Syrian Wars, l. 11. c. 10. (59-62) 2:217-225} {*Valerius Maximus, l. 5. c. 7. ext. 1. 1:529,531} {*Plutarch, Demetrius, l. 1. c. 38. 9:93-97} {Lucian, De Syria Dea} {Galen, On Foreknowing} {Julian, Misopogone}

## 3723 AM, 4433 JP, 281 BC

2738. Lysimachus crossed over into Asia to make war on Seleucus. This was the last battle fought between the survivors of Alexander the Great, of whom thirty four were already dead and these were the last two alive. This battle was fought in Phrygia, which bordered on the Hellespont, Ποι Κορουπεδιον, according to Porphyry. {Eusebius, Scaliger's Greek Eusebius, p. 228.} Lysimachus personally fought very bravely. After he had lost many of his men, he was wounded with a large spear by Malacon, a Heraclean. Lysimachus had lived to see the death of fifteen of his children and was one of the last surviving members of his family. {*Pausanias, Attica, l. 1. c. 10. s. 5. 1:53} {*Appian, Syrian Wars, l. 11. c. 10. (62) 2:225} {*Appian, Syrian Wars,

l. 11. c. 10. (64) 2:229} {Memnon, Excerpts, c. 9.} {Justin, Trogus, l. 17. c. 1,2.} {Orosius, l. 3. c. fin.} Appian said he lived seventy years, Justin and Orosius said seventy-four, but Hieronymus Cardianus, the historian who lived at that time and was held in great esteem, said that he died at eighty. {*Lucian, Octogenarians, l. 1. (11) 1:231}

2739. When Lysimachus had fallen, his dog stayed by the body and drove all the birds and animals away from it. Finally, Thorax, from the country of Pharsalia, found the almost putrefied body after a long search and recognised it by his dog lying beside it. Alexander, his son by Odrysias, got the body from Lysandra after much ado and many requests. He carried it into the Chersonesus of Thrace and buried it there, but the bones were later moved to the temple in Lysimachia by its citizens, where they were placed in an urn, and from henceforth the name of the temple was Lysimachium. {*Appian, Syrian Wars, l. 11. c. 10. (64) 2:229} {*Pausanias, Attica, l. 1. c. 10. s. 5. 1:53}

2740. After Lysimachus' death, his kingdom became part of Seleucus' kingdom. {Memnon, Excerpts, c. 9.} Seleucus was very pleased with himself after so great a victory, because he now saw himself as the last one alive of all that company which had been known as Alexander's companions in arms. He said that to be a Conqueror of Conquerors was a gift from the gods, not man. {Justin, Trogus, l. 17. c. 1,2.} [L474]

2741. The men of Heraclea in Pontus heard that Lysimachus was dead and that he had been killed by a countryman of theirs. In the eighty-fourth year after Clearchus I had subdued them, they wanted to recover their native liberty, which Lysimachus had again taken from them after the deaths of their local tyrants. They behaved valiantly to recover it. After the death of the two brothers, Clearchus II and Oxathres, Lysimachus had restored their liberty for a while, but afterward, at the requests of his wife Arsinoe, he had made a new war on them. {Justin, Trogus, l. 17. c. 3.} When he had taken their city, he appointed Heraclitus Cimaeus, a man loyal to Arsinoe, governor over them. After Lysimachus' death, the men of Heraclea offered Heraclitus a safe passage and a large sum of money to leave, on the condition that they would again have their liberty. He was very angry at this and ordered some of them to be executed. When the citizens discovered this, they secretly made a deal with the chief officers of the garrison under Heraclitus to free them and to pay them all their back wages. The officers took Heraclitus and put him in prison, where they kept him for a while until, realising they were free from all danger, they demolished the citadel which Lysimachus had built to control them. Then they sent an embassy to Seleucus to tell him what they had done, and they made Phocritus the governor of their state. {*Memnon, Excerpts, c. 8-10.*}

*2742.* Zipoetes, a petty king of Bithynia, was angry with the men of Heraclea, first on account of Lysimachus and now Seleucus, because both of these were his enemies, so he attacked them and did as much damage as he could. Although his men were not caught, they often received as much harm as they inflicted. {*Memnon, Excerpts, c. 11.*} *[E344]*

*2743.* Meanwhile, Seleucus sent Aphrodisias to the cities of Phrygia and nearby places to take care of his tribute and affairs. After he had settled the business he was sent on, he returned to Seleucus, praising many cities but accusing the Heracleans of many things, especially of not being loyal to Seleucus. At this, the king was enraged and scorned the embassy sent to him by the Heracleans. He spoke harshly to them, but there was one of them, called Camaeleon, who was not intimidated. He spoke thus to Seleucus:

"Sir, Hercules, Carron."

*2744.* (The word *Carron*, in the Dorian dialect or language, means *he that is the strongest*.) Seleucus, not knowing what the word meant, continued his tirade against them and ordered them to leave. Consequently, these messengers who had been sent knew that it was of no use for them either to stay there or to return home again. When Heraclea heard the news, they fortified their city as best they could and sought foreign aid by sending their envoys for help to Mithridates, king of Pontus, and to the states of Byzantium and Chalcedon. {*Memnon, Excerpts, c. 12.*}

*2745.* Those who had been banished and were living in exile from the state of Heraclea met together and came to an agreement among themselves. The deal was this. At this meeting Nymphidius persuaded them to work toward a restitution to their country, by telling them it would not be hard to do this if they would seek restitution in a fair and non-violent way. They were all easily persuaded by him, whereupon everything happened as they had desired. It was hard to tell who was happier, the returning exiles or the citizens who received them. Those who were returning treated the citizens who had expelled them very kindly, while the citizens allowed none of them to be short of anything they required for daily living. In this way they grew more united into one body again and returned to their original state of government. {*Memnon, Excerpts, c. 12.*} *[L475]*

### 3724 AM, 4434 JP, 280 BC

*2746.* Seleucus planned to end his days in his old and his former native country of Macedonia and so, he crossed

over the Hellespont and went to Lysimachia. There by chance he noticed a certain altar standing in a conspicuous place and asking what the name of this altar was, he was told it was called *Argos*. Now it is said that he had been forewarned by an oracle to beware of Argos. When he further asked why it was called Argos, he was told that it had been built either by the Argonauts on their way to Colchis, or by the Achaeans who had besieged Troy, for which reason the people in the neighbourhood still called it *Argos*, either as a corruption of the name of the ship *Argo*, or stemming from the native place of the sons of Atreus. As he was still listening to this story, Ptolemy Ceraunus, who was standing behind him, ran him through with his sword and killed him. Ptolemy was the son of Ptolemy I by his wife Eurydice, and brother to Arsinoe, the widow of Lysimachus, and now he had killed his great benefactor, who had kept him and had always wanted him with him. So, within seventeen months after the death of Lysimachus, Seleucus lost both the kingdom of Macedonia, which he had taken from Lysimachus, and his own life. {*Memnon, Excerpts, c. 13.*} {*Justin, Trogus, l. 17. c. 2.*} {**Appian, Syrian Wars, l. 11. c. 10. (63) 2:225,227*}

*2747.* Arrian stated that Seleucus was the greatest man who had lived after Alexander the Great, and that he had the most noble spirit of them all, as well as having the largest dominions of any of them. {**Arrian, Anabasis, l. 7. c. 22. s. 5. 2:281*} He died in the forty-third year after the death of Alexander, in the thirty-second year of the Greek, or Seleucian, Calendar. Appian said he lived seventy-three years, but Justin said it was seventy-eight years. His body was burned by Philetaerus, the king of Pergamum, who redeemed it from Ceraunus with a large sum of money. He sent his ashes to his son Antiochus who buried it at Seleucia-by-the-Sea, where he erected a temple to his father, and made a precinct around it. The precinct was called *Nicatorium*, after his surname. {**Appian, Syrian Wars, l. 11. c. 10. (63) 2:227*} Justin stated that both he and his sons and grandchildren after him were all born with the sign of an anchor on one of their thighs, which was a natural birthmark of that family. {*Justin, Trogus, l. 15. c. 4.*} In his book *Catalogue of Famous Cities* Ausonius, in speaking of Antioch, said: {*Ausonius, Ordo Urbium Nobilium, l. 2*}

She for her founder did Seleucus praise,
Who wore a native anchor on his thigh;
A true impress of his nativity,
And birthmark on all his progeny.

*2748.* Polybius noted that Ptolemy I, Lysimachus, Seleucus and Ptolemy Ceraunus all died in the 124th Olympiad. {**Polybius, l. 2. c. 41. s. 1-3. 1:343*} *[E345]* Ptolemy I died in the first year of that Olympiad and Lysimachus and Seleucus in the last year. However, since Ceraunus did not die until the latter end of the first year of the next Olympiad, Polybius seems to have omitted him when mentioning the concurrence of their deaths later in the same book. {*Polybius, l. 2. c. 71. s. 1-6. 1:413,415}

2749. After Ceraunus had murdered Seleucus, he escaped on a swift horse to Lysimachia, where he proclaimed himself king and surrounded himself with bodyguards. He went to the army, who of pure necessity received him and hailed him as king, even though they had sworn allegiance to Seleucus only a short time before. {Memnon, Excerpts, c. 13.}

2750. When Antigonus, surnamed Gonatas, the son of Demetrius Poliorcetes, heard how Seleucus had been murdered, he made an expedition into Macedonia, planning to get there with his army and naval forces before Ceraunus could. However, Ceraunus had all Lysimachus' fleet in readiness, and set out and met him at sea in a good battle formation. [L476] As a part of his navy, ships had been sent from Heraclea in Pontus, some of six, some of five tiers of oars. These types of ships were called *Aphracta*, but the largest ship of all had eight tiers of oars and was called the *Leontifera*. She was admired by all for her large size and exquisite construction. In her were a hundred oars per tier, so that on each side there were eight hundred rowers, which made sixteen hundred in all. On the upper deck or hatches there were twelve hundred fighting men who were under two special commanders. When the battle began, Ceraunus won and Antigonus was forced to flee with all his navy. In this battle, the ships from Heraclea performed the best and among them the Leontifera proved to be the best of all. After being routed, Antigonus fled into Boeotia, while Ptolemy Ceraunus went into Macedonia, where he stayed quietly for two years. {Memnon, Excerpts, c. 14,15.} That was for seventeen months, according to Dexippus and Porphyry, who related this matter more precisely. (Ptolemy Philopator [c. 244-205 BC] built an even larger warship. It was four hundred and twenty feet long, fifty-seven feet wide and seventy-two feet high to the top of her gunwale. From the top of her stern-post to the water line was seventy-nine and a half feet. It had four steering oars forty-five feet long, and had forty banks of oars, with the oars on the uppermost tier being fifty-seven feet long. The oars were counterbalanced with lead to make them easier to handle. It had a double bow and a double stern and carried seven rams, of which one was the leader and the others were of gradually reducing size. It had twelve under-girders nine hundred feet long. She was manned by four hundred sailors to handle the rigging and the sails, four thousand rowers and two thousand eight hundred and fifty men-in-arms to make up a total of seven thousand and fifty men. This ship was too large to be of much practical use. {*Athenaeus, l. 5. (203f-204b) 2:421,423} {*Plutarch, Demetrius, l. 1. c. 43. s. 4. 9:109} Editor.)

2751. Ceraunus grew in favour in the eyes of the people because of his father Ptolemy I of Egypt and for the revenge which he had taken for Lysimachus' death. He first tried to win over Lysimachus' sons and desired to marry Arsinoe, their mother, and his own sister. He told them that he would adopt them as his children, hoping they would not attempt anything against him out of respect for their mother or to him as their new father. He sent letters to his brother Ptolemy Philadelphus, king of Egypt, soliciting his friendship. He claimed that he had utterly forgotten the loss of his father's kingdom and that he would never seek to get from his brother that to which he had already more honestly attained by getting it from an enemy. {Justin, Trogus, l. 17. c. 2.} He also made peace with Antiochus, whose father, Seleucus, he had murdered. {Justin, Trogus, l. 24. c. 1.}

2752. Neither did he forget to solicit the friendship of Pyrrhus, the king of Epirus, thinking that Pyrrhus' support would sway many to his side. Pyrrhus made generous use of everyone else's property and used it as if it were his own. In this spirit, he began to help the Tarentines in Italy against the Romans. He sent to borrow ships from Antigonus Gonatas to transport his army into Italy, while sending to Antiochus, the son of the deceased Seleucus, to borrow money, because he seemed to have much more wealth than he had men. He asked Ptolemy Ceraunus to furnish him with some companies of soldiers from Macedonia, so Ceraunus lent Pyrrhus five thousand foot soldiers, four thousand cavalry and fifty elephants for two years of service only. For this favour, Pyrrhus married his daughter and left him as protector of his kingdom of Epirus during his absence, because he feared that while he was away with the best of his army in Italy, someone might take advantage of his absence and plunder his kingdom. {Justin, Trogus, l. 17. c. 2.}

2753. Therefore Pyrrhus nonetheless made Ptolemy, his fifteen-year-old son by Antigone the daughter of Berenice, governor of his kingdom, and placed him under the authority of Ptolemy Ceraunus, the king of Macedonia. Pyrrhus sailed with his army and landed in the port of Tarentum, now called Otranto, in Italy. He took his two younger sons with him, Alexander and Helenus. They were very young and he took them for comfort in this distant war. {Justin, Trogus, l. 18. c. 1.} He did not wait for spring but sailed there in the middle of the winter, according to Zonaras' account from Dionysius

Halicarnassus. This was in the fourth year of the 124th Olympiad. {*Polybius, l. 2. c. 41. s. 11,12. 1:345}

2754. Following the death of his father Seleucus, Antiochus Soter held the kingdom of Syria for nineteen years. {*Eusebius, Chronicles, l. 1. 1:212} {Porphyry} {*Sulpicius Severus, Sacred History, l. 2. c. 19. 11:106} After many battles, he barely recovered all his father's dominions. In the end he sent an army, under the command of Patrocles, to cross the Taurus Mountains, choosing Hermones, born at Aspendus, to serve as his captain. [L477] Patrocles was to attack Heraclea in the country of Pontus, but when he received satisfaction from an embassy sent to him by the Heracleans, he halted the expedition and made a firm league with them. [E346] He altered his course and passing through the country of Phrygia, came into Bithynia, where he was ambushed by the Bithynians and perished with all his army. In this battle, Patrocles behaved most valiantly and personally did many exploits against the enemy. {Memnon, Excerpts, c. 16.} When Zipoetes, the king of Bithynia, had thus destroyed Antiochus' army, he built the city of Liparus at the foot of the hill and named it after himself. {Memnon, Excerpts, c. 21.}

2755. At the end of the 50th year of the first Calippic period, which was the 44th year from the death of Alexander the Great, Aristarchus of Samos observed the summer solstice. This was after Meton had first observed the lunar cycle a hundred and fifty-two years or eight complete lunar cycles earlier (from Hipparchus' book *De Anni Magnitudine*, as quoted by Ptolemy). {Ptolemy, Great Syntaxis, l. 3. c. 2.} {See note on 3572 AM. <<1275>>}

2756. Arsinoe, the widow of Lysimachus, married her own brother, Ptolemy Ceraunus and received him into her city of Cassandria. He seized the citadel and took and killed her two sons, whom she had by Lysimachus. The one, who was sixteen years old, was called Lysimachus, and the other, who was only three years old, was called Philip. He killed them both in the arms of their mother, who then tore her clothes and pulled out her hair. She was hauled out of the gates of the city with only two servants and banished to the isle of Samothracia. {Justin, Trogus, l. 24. c. 2,3.} {Memnon, Excerpts, c. 15.}

## 3725 AM, 4435 JP, 279 BC

2757. In the beginning of the second year after Pyrrhus' arrival in Italy, the Gauls invaded Greece. {*Polybius, l. 1. c. 6. s. 5,6. 1:17} They divided their whole army into three parts and assigned each part a task. One part, led by Cerethrius, attacked Thrace and Triballi. The second group attacked Paenonia and were led by Brennus and Acichorius. The third group, led by Belgius, attacked Macedonia and Illyria. {Justin, Trogus, l. 24. c. 5.} {Justin, Trogus,

l. 25. c. 2.} Pausanias incorrectly called him Bolgius. {*Pausanias, Phocis, l. 10. c. 19. s. 7. 4:475}

2758. Ptolemy Ceraunus (meaning *Thunderbolt*, because he was so rash) was driven on by the madness of his wicked mind. He and a small, poorly organized company went to war with Belgius. Ptolemy thought wars were as easily waged as murders were committed. When the king of the Dardanians offered to help him against these newly arrived Gauls with twenty-thousand men, Ptolemy refused the offer. When the Gauls sent messengers to him offering him peace for money, he replied that he would not give them peace unless they surrendered their arms and the leaders of their army for hostages, as signs of their loyalty to him. Not able to agree, the two sides fought a battle in which the Macedonians were defeated and fled. Ptolemy was grievously wounded, and when the elephant on which he rode was also wounded, it became unruly and threw him off its back. He was captured by the Gauls and torn to pieces. His head was cut off, put on the point of a spear and carried about to terrify the enemy. Few of the Macedonians escaped, while the majority were either killed or taken prisoner. {Justin, Trogus, l. 24. c. 4,5.} {Justin, Trogus, l. 25. c. 2.} {Memnon, Excerpts, c. 15.} {*Diod. Sic., l. 22. c. 3,4. 11:49,51} {*Pausanias, Phocis, l. 10. c. 19. s. 7. 4:475}

2759. Ptolemy's brother Meleager succeeded him in the kingdom of Macedonia, but after two months the Macedonians kicked him out as not being worthy of the position. They replaced him with Antipater, the son of Philip, who was brother to Cassander. {Justin, Trogus, l. 12. c. 14.} He was nicknamed *the Etesian* because he held the office for only forty-five days, which is about how long the Etesian winds used to blow on that coast each year. {Porphyry, Scaliger's Greek Eusebius, p. 228.}

2760. When Brennus (who, some say, was by birth a Prausian, {*Strabo, l. 4. c. 1. s. 13. 2:205}) heard of this great victory by Belgius, he did not want to let this golden opportunity of getting all the riches of the east slip from his hands. [L478] He gathered together a hundred and fifty thousand foot soldiers and fifteen thousand cavalry of his Gauls and marched quickly into Macedonia. {Justin, Trogus, l. 24. c. 6.} When he came into the country of the Dardanians, a people in Illyria, he was forced to stay there because of a rebellion which arose in his army. About twenty thousand of his men (Suidas also has this number under the entry *Galatae*), with Leonorius and Lutarius as their captains, defected from him and went into Thrace. By fighting, and selling peace to those who would buy it from them, they finally came to Byzantium. After they had wasted the country of Propontis for a while and made it a tributary to them, they took over all the cities in those parts. {*Livy, l. 38. c. 16. s. 1-4. 11:51}

## 3726a AM, 4435 JP, 279 BC

*2761.* Sosthenes, a leader in Macedonia, assembled the youth and brave men of the country and attacked the Gauls that were in the land, quelling them after many encounters and defending the country against their further plundering. [E347] For this great service, he was chosen to be king at a time when many of the nobles were striving for the kingdom. He was selected, even though he was a man of humble birth and parentage and not of royal blood. When they wanted to make him king, he refused, insisting that they take their oath that they swear allegiance to him as their captain only, {*Justin, Trogus, l. 24. c. 5.*} a capacity in which he then governed the country for two years. {*Porphyry*} {*Eusebius, Chronicles, l. 1. 1:211,213*}

*2762.* When Brennus came into Macedonia, he started plundering the country. Sosthenes met him with his army, but was hopelessly outnumbered, so that the Macedonians were quickly defeated and fled to their cities. While they stayed confined to their cities, Brennus and his army overran and plundered all the country. {*Justin, Trogus, l. 24. c. 6.*}

*2763.* Leonorius and Lutarius used trickery to capture Lysimachia and so took over the whole region, and when they came down from there into the Hellespont and saw how short a distance it was across to Asia, they planned to go there. They sent their agents to Antipater, the governor of the Hellespont, to help them make the journey. {*Livy, l. 38. c. 16. s. 4,5. 2:53*}

*2764.* When Zipoetes had reigned in Bithynia for a full forty-eight years and had lived seventy-six years, he died, leaving four sons. The oldest was Nicomedes, and he succeeded his father in the kingdom. He proved to his brothers that he was not a brother, but a butcher. {*Memnon, Excerpts, c. 21.*} The youngest, who was called Zipoetes and whom Livy called Ziboetas, held the sea coast of Bithynia, {*Livy, l. 38. c. 16. s. 9. 11:53*} which was known as Thracian Thyniaca or Asiatica. {*Memnon, Excerpts, c. 18.*}

*2765.* After the death of Zipoetes, Antiochus Soter prepared to make war upon Bithynia. Nicomedes sent and asked for help from the city of Heraclea, promising to help them should the need arise, whereupon they sent him help. This provided the opportunity for them later to recover Cierus, Teos and the land of Thinis at great cost. When they went to recover the city and territory of Amastris (which had also been taken from them) they did not consider either war or money too great a cost to pay for its recovery. Eumenes, however, who only held it as governor, chose, out of sheer spite, to turn it over gratis to Ariobarzanes, the son of Mithridates, king of Pontus. He did this, rather than surrender it to the state of Heraclea on any terms. {*Memnon, Excerpts, c. 18.*}

## 3726b AM, 4436 JP, 278 BC

*2766.* Brennus and Acichorius left Macedonia with the Illyrians (as Appian stated,) whom they called Autarians, and the Celts, whom they called Cimbrians. They went into Greece with an army of a hundred and fifty-two thousand foot soldiers and twenty thousand and four hundred cavalry. Every cavalryman had two footmen attending him, so that if the cavalryman was killed, one of them could take his place. [L479] When they went to plunder the temple at Delphi, they were driven off by thunder and lightning. They experienced earthquakes and the ground sank from under them on Mount Olympus. Because it was winter, there were bitter frosts and snow, and they were miserably distressed in many ways. The Phocians killed almost six thousand of them, and panic and fear struck the whole army. That night, a frost killed more than ten thousand men and as many again perished there from hunger. Brennus, their leader, was wounded. Because of this shameful defeat, he drank himself drunk, fell on his own sword and died. When Acichorius saw how the leaders of this war had been punished, he hastily left Greece with a company of ten thousand poor, maimed soldiers. But the continual storms of rain and snow, with bitter frosts and famine and what was worst of all, the perpetual walking, utterly wasted the bodies of this unlikely army. All the countries through which they passed on their return journey attacked them as they went, scattering them and making a prey of them. {*Pausanias, Phocis, l. 10. c. 19-23. 4:473-507*} {*Pausanias, Attica, l. 1. c. 4. s. 1-6. 1:19-23*} {*Justin, Trogus, l. 24. c. 6-8.*} {*Diod. Sic., l. 22. c. 9. 11:61-65*} {*Appian, Illyrian Wars, l. 10. c. 1. (5) 2:61*} {*Polybius, l. 2. c. 20. s. 6,7. 1:291*} This disaster happened in the second year of the 125th Olympiad, when Anaxicrates was archon of Athens. {*Pausanias, Phocis, l. 10. c. 23. s. 14. 4:507*}

## 3726c AM, 4436 JP, 278 BC

*2767.* When those of Illyria, called Autarians, who survived this misfortune, arrived home in their own country, they found themselves plagued with a large number of frogs. They killed so many that they polluted the very rivers with the rotting bodies. The foul air rising from their dead bodies caused a pestilence to spread throughout all the country. They were forced to flee from their native land but carried the plague along with them, so that no country would receive them and they were forced to go on a twenty-three day journey, until they came into the country of the Bastarnians. There, they built cities in which to live. But the land of the Celts was plagued with earthquakes and whole cities were swallowed up. [E348] These disasters continued to happen to the Celts, until at last they, too, were forced to leave their habitation and went wandering until they came to the country of the Illyrians, who had been partners with them in their action at Delphi. They easily defeated them, since the Illyrians were consumed with the plagues. However, they also caught the infection by touching their goods. Once again they were forced to leave, and so they wandered until they came to the Pyrenees Mountains. {*Appian, Illyrian Wars, l. 10. c. 1. (4) 2:59} All these horrid, strange and supernatural plagues and punishments happened to these Gauls and others for the sacrilegious acts they had committed against their idols. We can indeed affirm that truth spoken by the wise man about those who swore falsely by their idols:

> "For it was not the power of those by whom they swore: (nor of the gods whom these men have robbed) but it is the just vengeance upon sinners from the true God, that punishes the offence of the ungodly." {Apc Wis 14:31}

2768. The Cordistae had been a part of those Gauls who had attempted the plundering of Delphi. It is said that Bathanattus, their captain, settled them near the bank of the Ister River, and it is after him that the way by which they returned was later called Bathanattus' way. {*Athenaeus, l. 6. (234b) 3:53,55} These are the same Gauls whom Strabo called the Scordisci. They settled on the bank of the Ister River, expelling the Autarians or Autoriates from their lands. {*Strabo, l. 7. c. 5. s. 2. 3:253,255} {*Strabo, l. 7. c. 5. s. 11. 3:271,273}

2769. Those Gauls, as I said before, went from Thrace down to the strait of the Hellespont. After a rebellion among them, Leonorius, with most of his men, returned to Byzantium, from where he had come. Lutarius took five ships from the Macedonians who had been sent to him by Antipater as envoys, but they were really spies. He used these ships to transport his men into Asia, a few at a time. {*Livy, l. 38. c. 16. s. 3-8. 11:51,53}

2770. Zipoetes (the son of the deceased King Zipoetes) and the Bithynians defeated the state of Heraclea. When help came to them from other parts, Zipoetes was forced to flee. The Heracleans gathered the bodies of their dead, burned them and carried their bones into the city. They laid them up in their sepulchres together with the bones of other men who had excellently served their country. {Memnon, Excerpts, c. 18.}

### 3726d AM, 4436 JP, 278 BC

2771. About the same time, Antiochus Soter and Antigonus Gonatas made elaborate preparations to go to war against each other. [L480] Because Nicomedes, the king of Bithynia, sided with Antigonus, but other kings with Antiochus, Antiochus for the present set aside the war with Antigonus and first marched against Nicomedes. He in turn was forced to get what help he could from other parts, sending to his friends, the Heracleans, from whom he got thirteen ships of three tiers of oars apiece, with which he went to engage Antiochus at sea. They met at sea, but after looking at each other for a while, each side withdrew and nothing happened. {Memnon, Excerpts, c. 19.}

2772. The men of Byzantium were worn out with the continual attacks and plundering of the Gauls. They sent envoys to their friends, the Heracleans, and received a thousand pieces of gold from them. (Some say that it was four thousand pieces.) Not long after this, Nicomedes came to an agreement with these Gauls, the terms of which were: {Memnon, Excerpts, c. 20,21.}

> "Thus they should forever continue firm and fast friends to Nicomedes and his heirs. That they should not, without his knowledge and consent, lend a helping hand to any who by embassies should seek assistance from them in their wars. They should be friends to his friends and foes to his foes. Furthermore, that they should help those of Byzantium, if the occasion arose. Likewise, that they should maintain league and friendship with the Tianians, Heracleans, Chalcedonians, Cierians and some other states which had other countries under their jurisdiction."

2773. Leonorius, with the help of Nicomedes, king of Bithynia, crossed from Byzantium into Asia. {*Livy, l. 38. c. 16. s. 7. 11:53} {*Strabo, l. 12. c. 5. s. 1. 5:469} This crossing of the Gauls into Asia happened in the third year of the 125th Olympiad. {*Pausanias, Phocis, l. 10. c. 23. s. 14. 4:507}

2774. However, the people of Byzantium were not rid of those plundering Gauls yet, for some of those who had been at Delphi with Brennus and had escaped that danger, came into the Hellespont under their captain, Comontorius. They planned to go no farther, since they liked the country around Byzantium, and so they settled there. After they had conquered the Thracians, they made Tylis the capital city of their kingdom, and caused Byzantium to fear them just as the other Gauls before them had done. {*Polybius, l. 4. c. 46. s. 1-3. 2:413,415}

### 3727 AM, 4437 JP, 277 BC

2775. Ptolemy Philadelphus was a great patron of learning and all liberal arts and sciences. He built a very famous library at Alexandria, in that quarter of the city known as Brachium. He committed the task of getting books of every kind and from every country to Demetrius of Phalerum, upon whose advice he also sent to have the holy writings of the Jews translated from Hebrew into Greek, a task undertaken by seventy-two translators in the seventh year of his reign. *[E349]* This translation was called the Septuagint, {*Epiphanius, De Mensuris et Ponderibus*} and Tertullian wrote concerning it: {*\*Tertullian, Apology, l. 1. c. 18. 3:32*}

> "The most learned king of all the Ptolemys was surnamed Philadelphus and was most interested in all forms of literature. I think he endeavoured to outdo Pisistratus in the matter of libraries. These are but monuments, which either antiquity or curiosity could provide for perpetuating man's fame to posterity. He was guided in this by Demetrius of Phalerum, a most excellent scholar and humanitarian in those days, whom he had set over that work. He asked the Jews if he could have their books also."

2776. Ptolemy was very zealous in the study of human learning. This was confirmed by Phylarchus the historian, as related by Athenaeus, {*\*Athenaeus, l. 12. (536e) 5:425*} and is given in more detail by Vitruvius, {*\*Vitruvius, l. 7. c. 0. s. 4,5. 2:65,67*} who showed that Ptolemy, when he had finished this large library at Alexandria, instituted certain games in honour of Apollo and the Muses. He invited all the writers in the common arts and sciences (not as others were wont to do, wrestlers and the like) to compete for the prizes, and awarded generous prizes to the winners. *[L481]* Vitruvius also related how Ptolemy entertained Zoilus, surnamed *Homeromastix*, that is, the *Scourge of Homer*, when he came to him. {*\*Vitruvius, l. 7. c. 0. s. 8. 2:69*}

2777. Ptolemy acquired Aristotle's books. When Aristotle died, he left his library to Theophrastus, and Theophrastus, in his last will and testament, left it to Nileus, {*\*Diogenes Laertius, Theophrastus, l. 5. c. 2. (53) 1:505*} who took it to the city of Scepsis. {*\*Strabo, l. 13. c. 1. s. 54. 6:111*} {*\*Plutarch, Sulla, l. 1. c. 26. 4:407*} Ptolemy bought these books from him, as well as buying others at Athens and Rhodes, and brought them all to Alexandria. {*\*Athenaeus, l. 1. (3b) 1:11*} But Strabo and Plutarch, and elsewhere in his writings Athenaeus also, stated that Theophrastus' books, and with them Aristotle's entire library, came into the hands of Nileus and his heirs, and that much later, in the days of Sulla, his descendants sold them for a large sum of money to Apellicon of Teos. {*\*Strabo, l. 13. c. 1. s. 54. 6:111*} {*\*Plutarch, Sulla, l. 1. c. 26. 4:407*} {*\*Athenaeus, l. 5. (214e) 2:471*}

2778. Demetrius of Phalerum was a great grammarian, commended by Tertullian, and an outstanding philosopher, as well as having previously been a great statesman and an excellent governor in Athens. He was succeeded by Zenodotus of Ephesus, who, according to Suidas, was the first editor of Homer's books. After him came Aristophanes, who read, with great diligence and industry, all the books of that large library in the order in which

they had been placed, a fact which was affirmed by Vitruvius. {*\*Vitruvius, l. 7. c. 0. s. 6,7. 2:67*} This was at a much later time. {*Aristeas, Septuagint Interpreters*} {*\*Josephus, Antiq., l. 12. c. 2. s. 1. (12) 7:9*} {*\*Eusebius, Gospel, l. 9. c. 42. (458b) 1:486*}

2779. When Demetrius of Phalerum was asked by King Ptolemy how many myriads, or tens of thousands, of books he had collected, he answered about two hundred thousand, but that he hoped before long to have half a million books. So he had accumulated about two hundred thousand books, a fact we learn from Aristeas and from those copies of Aristeas' writings which Josephus and Eusebius used. The smaller sum of fifty-four thousand and eight hundred, which was found in Epiphanius, who wrote long after these other writers, was incorrect.

2780. Demetrius of Phalerum advised the king, as I said before, to acquire the sacred writings of the Jews. Aristeas, who was an attendant in the king's presence at that time, advised him to buy them by giving all the Jews who were then slaves in Egypt their freedom and sending them home. It is said that their number came to a hundred thousand. In our copy of Aristeas it is said that each one of them cost the king twenty drachmas, but in Josephus it is a hundred and twenty. {*\*Josephus, Antiq., l. 12. c. 2. s. 3. (28) 7:17*} One hundred and twenty drachmas make thirty shekels in silver. This was the full price of a slave in Exodus, {*Ex 21:32*} and was also the amount for which our Saviour was sold by Judas the traitor. The twenty drachmas, which we find in our Aristeas, when multiplied by a hundred thousand, amounts to two million drachmas. When divided by six thousand, it makes an Attic talent. The total amount was about three hundred and thirty-three Attic talents. The price which Ptolemy paid to redeem the Jews from their masters came to more than four hundred talents, as was affirmed by Josephus and by Aristeas. There were more than ten thousand slaves freed. *[L482]* In this redemption of the Jewish slaves from their masters, a similar price was paid for every nursing child among them together with the mothers who nursed them. Hence it was that Josephus said that Ptolemy paid about four hundred and sixty talents, instead of six hundred and sixty talents, which our common editions of Aristeas state. {*Aristeas, Septuagint Interpreters*} {*\*Josephus, Antiq., l. 12. c. 2. s. 3. (33) 7:19*}

2781. From among these Jews, Ptolemy selected the youngest and ablest for his army, and employed the rest in his private affairs. This was confirmed in his letters to Eleazer, the high priest. For in addition to the one true letter of the king's, Epiphanius recorded two forged ones. *[E350]* They are different both in style and meaning from the one we find recorded in Aristeas and Josephus. This latter one begins thus:

"For a treasure that is hidden and a fountain sealed up, what profit is there?"

2782. Whereas in the Greek letter attributed to the king, he did not know a Hebrew proverb that was taken from the Apocrypha. {*Apc Sir 20:30 41:14*}

"wisdom if be hidden, and a treasure unseen, what profit is there of either of them?"

"...for wisdom that is hid, and a treasure that is not seen, what profit is in them both?"

2783. With his letter, he also sent expensive gifts for the use of the temple at Jerusalem. His two servants, Andreas and Aristeas, delivered these to Eleazer, the high priest. One of the gifts was a golden table two cubits long (two and a half cubits, according to Josephus) and not less than half a cubit thick, of solid gold and not gold plate. He also sent twenty goblets of solid gold and thirty of solid silver. To make these, he used more than fifty talents of gold, seventy talents of silver and five thousand precious stones. The value of these stones was about two hundred and fifty talents of gold. Besides all this, he sent a hundred talents toward sacrifices and other uses in the temple. {*\*Josephus, Antiq., l. 12. c. 2. s. 5. (40-42) 7:23*}

2784. Eleazer, the priest, received these presents. After the captivity, some people were still left from the ten northern tribes of the twelve tribes of Israel. {*See note on 3468c AM. <<952>>*} From each of the twelve tribes he chose six men who surpassed all others in eminence. These men, who were mature in age, of noble birth and well educated, were to translate God's Law from Hebrew into Greek. The names of these seventy-two elders are recorded by Aristeas. The last one was called Ezekiel. I think he was the same man of whom Eusebius {*\*Eusebius, Gospel, l. 9. c. 38. (436d) 1:467*} said that he had written a tragedy about the deliverance of the children of Israel from Egypt. The name of Ezekiel shows that he was Jewish and not a Greek, as Clement of Alexandria and Eusebius thought.

2785. Eleazer also wrote a letter back to the king. Aristeas gave us the salutation, *God save you.* Eusebius more correctly had: *If you and the Queen Arsinoe your sister are well, then all is well and as we desire it should be.* Philadelphus was married to Arsinoe, the daughter of Lysimachus, king of Thrace and Macedonia, by whom he had Ptolemy Euergetes and Berenice. After she died, he married a second Arsinoe, his own sister. [L483] After the death of Lysimachus, her first husband, she was married to Ptolemy Ceraunus, her own brother. But she died before she bore any child to Philadelphus. He loved her so much that he named a district in Egypt *Arsinoites*, after her. {*\*Pausanias, Attica, l. 1. c. 7. s. 1.-3. 1:35,37*} He made a

statue of her out of topaz, six feet high, and consecrated it in a temple known as the golden temple. {*\*Pliny, l. 37. c. 32. 10:253*} At his orders, Timochares, the architect, made an arched roof entirely of lodestone, so that beneath it an image of her made of iron would cling to it and seem to hang there in mid air. {*\*Pliny, l. 34. c. 42. 9:235*} Concerning Timochares, Ausonius said: {*Ausonius, Idyllion, 9.*}

Who for a monument of incestuous love,
By Ptolemy's command did make to hang
Arsinoe in the air of an Egyptian temple.

2786. These seventy-two translators came to Alexandria and gave the king the things Eleazer had sent to him. These included various parchments on which the law was intricately written with golden letters in the language of the Jews. The parchments were so joined together that the seams could not be discerned by the eye of man. It so happened that they arrived there at the time when Ptolemy received news of a great victory gained by him at sea against Antigonus. The writers who wrote of this naval battle said that it happened about this time. I cannot agree with those who relate it to that time when Antigonus Gonatas made war on the Athenians and besieged their cities by sea and land. What we find recorded in Justin and Pausanias did not happen until after the death of Pyrrhus, and before the death of Aretas, or Areus, the first king of Lacedemon. {*Justin, Trogus, l. 26.*} {*\*Pausanias, Laconia, l. 3. c. 6. s. 4. 2:35*} This was between the years 272 and 264 BC (4442 - 4450 JP). For although this Areus came at that time with his army and Patrocles with Ptolemy's fleet to help the Athenians, Areus returned home without any battle having been fought. Pausanias stated that Patrocles did not do anything either to relieve them. {*\*Pausanias, Attica, l. 1. c. 1. s. 1. 1:3*} {*\*Pausanias, Laconia, l. 3. c. 6. s. 4,5. 2:35,37*}

2787. Ptolemy entertained and feasted the seventy-two translators for seven days (Josephus stated twelve days), in a most sumptuous and magnificent manner. After that, he appointed Dorotheus to take care of them and to supply them with everything they needed, ensuring that they did not lack anything. [E351] Now and then, the king himself would question them concerning affairs of state and of morality. They extemporaneously answered him with very prudent and well-thought-out answers, according to Aristeas, who derived everything he wrote from the king's diaries. The king gave them each three talents and a boy servant. {*\*Josephus, Antiq., l. 12. c. 2. s. 12. (94-100) 7:51*}

2788. Three days later, Demetrius walked with the translators along the causeway called the Heptastadium, which was fourteen hundred yards long. He led them over the bridge onto the isle of Pharos, where he settled them in a good house on the north shore of the island, far from any noise or tumult. They started to work on the translation as exactly as possible from the original manuscripts. Demetrius had each day's work copied precisely. Every day they worked until three o'clock in the afternoon and then they went and relaxed. They had everything abundantly provided for them. Their meals were of the same lavish kind that was provided for the king's own table, since Dorotheus had them fed by orders of the king. Moreover, very early every morning, they came to court and bade the king good morning, before returning to their place, where they washed their hands, as was their custom, and said their prayers. Then they applied themselves to read and to interpret, point by point. *[L484]* Epiphanius differed in his account from Aristeas and Josephus. He said that they were put into thirty-six rooms, two to a room, where they worked from the break of day until the evening, when they were put into thirty-six boats, two to a boat, and brought back to the king's palace to eat supper. I do not know whom he followed in the earlier part of this narration, but the latter, it seems, was a product of their fables, since they imagined that the causeway had not been made, or at least not been finished, until Cleopatra's time. {*Josephus, Antiq., l. 12. c. 2. s. 13. (101-109) 7:51-55}*

2789. It happened that the work of the seventy-two translators was finished in seventy-two days, as if it had been deliberately so planned. When it was completed, Demetrius called all the Jews together in the location where the translation had taken place and read it all in the presence of the translators. Having completed such a good work, they were highly commended and magnified by all the Jews who were there. Demetrius was also highly praised by the Jews. They asked him to deliver a copy of the translated Law to their rulers. When it had been read to them right through, the priests and elders among the translators and the officers of the Jews stood up and said:

> "Forasmuch as this translation was carefully and accurately done, it is befitting that it should remain as it is, and that no changes be made to it."

2790. When all had approved of this with great acclamation, Demetrius declared a great curse (as was customary) on any man who should alter it, either by adding anything to it, or by taking anything from it.

2791. When the king had read it through completely, he greatly admired the wisdom of God, and commanded that all possible care be taken of these books and they be carefully stored and kept. He also expressed his desire that the translators, after they had returned home, should often come and visit him. He gave each of them

three good changes of clothes, two talents of gold, a cup of one whole talent and the complete furnishings for a room.

2792. In addition he gave them for Eleazar, the high priest, ten beds with silver feet and expensive furnishings to go with them. He also sent a cup of thirty talents, ten garments, a purple robe, an expensive crown, a hundred pieces of linen as fine as silk, shallow bowls, cups, libation bowls and two golden goblets to sacrifice with. In his letters he requested Eleazar to permit any of these men to come and visit him, should they desire to do so at any time. Ptolemy really wanted to talk with such men, and would rather spend his money on them than in any other way. {Aristeas, Septuagint Interpreters} {*Josephus, Antiq., l. 12. c. 2. s. 13-15. (107-118) 7:53-59}

2793. The Gauls who had been left by Brennus to keep Macedonia when he went into Greece, did not want to be idle while their companions were working. So they outfitted fifteen thousand foot soldiers and three thousand cavalry and attacked the Getes and the Triballi and routed them. {Justin, Trogus, l. 25. c. 1.}

### 3728 AM, 4438 JP, 276 BC

2794. When Antigonus Gonatas had lost a battle at sea, as was said before, to Ptolemy Philadelphus, he made a peace with Antiochus Soter. {Justin, Trogus, l. 25. c. 1.} He went into Macedonia, where his father Demetrius Poliorcetes had reigned at times. Antigonus went there in the tenth year after he first became king of Greece, and reigned for thirty-four years. {Porphyry, Scaliger's Greek Eusebius, p. 229.} His heirs reigned there until Perseus was defeated by the Romans, and so the kingdom of Macedonia ended. {*Plutarch, Demetrius, l. 1. c. 53. s. 4. 9:135} [L485]

2795. When the Gauls had defeated the Getes and Triballi, they sent their envoys to Antigonus, king of Macedonia, to offer him peace in return for his money. *[E352]* At the same time they wanted to spy on his army and see his camp. Antigonus entertained and feasted them in a sumptuous manner, but the Gauls, seeing an enormous amount of silver and gold brought out for the feast, were greedy and wanted it. Therefore, they went back more his enemies than when they had come, and they all resolved to attack him. Antigonus suspected this, and ordered that every man should take with him what he could and hide in a nearby wood. When the Gauls came, they took what they found there and went on to the coast. While the Gauls were busy preparing the ships, the sailors and a part of Antigonus' army who had fled there with their wives and children to save themselves, attacked them suddenly. They killed them and wrought such havoc among them that Antigonus subsequently had quite a reputation among the Gauls and in all the surrounding countries. {*Justin, Trogus, l. 25. c. 1,2.}*

*2796.* These Gauls were under seventeen commanders, of whom Leonorius and Lutarius were the main leaders. Several times they passed over into Asia, before they all came together again into one body and offered their assistance to Nicomedes against Ziboetas, the younger, who held that part of Bithynia lying along the coast. These forces, and others who came from Heraclea in Pontus, crushed poor Ziboetas to pieces, and so all Bithynia came into the hands of Nicomedes. When the Gauls had wasted all that country, they shared its spoil among themselves, dividing the kingdom between themselves and Nicomedes and calling their portion *Gallogracia*, which later became known as Galatia. {*Livy, l. 38. c. 16. s. 9. 11:53} {*Livy, l. 38. c. 17. s. 10. 11:59} {Justin, Trogus, l. 25. c. 2.} {Memnon, Excerpts, c. 20.}*

*2797.* Of the twenty thousand men the Gauls had, only ten thousand were armed, but even these few troops struck terror into all the countries on this side of the Taurus Mountains. Not only the places they went into, but also the ones into which they did not go, submitted to them, whether they were far away or close to them. They consisted of three countries of their own, the Tohstobogians or the Tolostobogians (coming, as was thought, from the Gauls, who were called the Boii), the Trocmians and the Tectosagians. They divided all Asia between them and settled there. The Trocmians settled in the Hellespont and all that region, Aeolia and Ionia was allotted to the Tolostobogians, and the Tectosagians occupied the inland or middle part of Asia, making their headquarters on the bank of the Halys River. {*Livy, l. 38. c. 16. s. 10-13. 11:53,55} {Suidas, Galatia}*

*2798.* Demetrius Byzantius wrote thirteen books concerning this crossing of the Gauls from Europe into Asia. {*Diogenes Laertius, Demetrius, l. 5. c. 5. (83) 1:537}* Phaennis, who lived forty or so years before this happened, was said to have foretold this event by way of an oracle in these words: {*Pausianus, Phocis, l. 1. c. 15. s. 3. 4:451}*

> The Gauls shall pass the straits of the Hellespont,
> And ravage all the land of Asia.
> Yet worse things have the gods in store for them
> Who on the sea coast of that land do dwell.

## 3729 AM, 4439 JP, 275 BC

*2799.* In the 126th Olympiad, Eratosthenes of Cyrene, the son of Aglai or, according to others, of Ambrosius, was born. *[L486]* He was a scholar of Aristo Chius, the philosopher, and of the grammarian Lysanias of Cyrene, and of Callismachus of Cyrene, a poet. {*Suidas, Eratosthenes}*

## 3730a AM, 4439 JP, 275 BC

*2800.* In this year, Curius Dentatus fought with Pyrrhus in Italy. He killed twenty-three thousand of his men and captured his camp, forcing Pyrrhus to retreat to Tarentum. {*Eutropius, l. 2.}*

*2801.* The envoys, whom Pyrrhus had sent to the kings of Asia and to Antigonus Gonatas for help with men and money, returned without either. Pyrrhus called the princes of the Epirotes and Tarentines together and concealing the contents of the letters, told them that supplies would come very speedily. When news of this came to the Roman camp that there were many supplies coming to him from both Macedonia and Asia, the Romans did not attempt any more actions against him. {*Pausanias, Attica, l. 1. c. 13. s. 1. 1:63}* Pyrrhus acted as if he would move with his army from Tarentum, but never said why. Meanwhile, he wanted his confederates to continue the war, and committed the keeping of the citadel at Tarentum to his son Helenus and to Milo, one of his friends. {*Justin, Trogus, l. 25. c. 3.}* After having spent six whole years on the war in Italy and Sicily, he had lost many of his men, and so, with no hope left of doing any good, he returned to Epirus with the eight thousand foot soldiers and five hundred cavalry remaining to him. {*Plutarch, Pyrrhus, l. 1. c. 26. s. 2. 9:431} [E353]*

## 3730b AM, 4440 JP, 274 BC

*2802.* When Curius was consul, he held a triumph for the defeat of Pyrrhus. He was the first to bring elephants (four in total) to Rome. {*Eutropius, l. 2.}* The people were eager during that triumph to get a look at these beasts that had turrets on their backs, and of which they were very afraid. The beasts themselves seemed to have sensed their captivity by holding down their heads as they followed the victorious horses in the triumph. {*Florus, l. 1. c. 17. s. 28. 1:67}* This triumph happened in the month of January or February, as gathered from the marble fragments of the record of their triumphs.

*2803.* With the help of some of the Gauls, Pyrrhus made some inroads upon Macedonia, where Antigonus Gonatas reigned. He captured many cities, and two thousand of Antigonus' soldiers revolted from him. This raised Pyrrhus' hopes still more, so that he marched directly against Antigonus himself to force a battle with all his forces, both Macedonians and Gauls. The Gauls, who brought up the rear, fought very bravely that day. Many were cut to pieces and died there. The captains of the elephants were vexed by the enemy and surrendered to Pyrrhus with their elephants. The Macedonian foot soldiers were shocked at this defeat and heard Pyrrhus both calling them all in general, and calling on their captains and chief officers by name, to surrender to him.

They left Antigonus and defected to Pyrrhus. Antigonus saved himself by fleeing, but Pyrrhus pursued him to the coast. {*Plutarch, Pyrrhus, l. 1. c. 26. s. 2-5. 9:431,433} {*Pausanias, Attica, l. 1. c. 13. s. 2. 1:63,65}

2804. After this victory, Pyrrhus took the richest and best spoils from the Gauls and hung them in the temple of Athena in Itonia, which was between Phera and Larisa. He subdued all upper Macedonia and Thessaly, {*Plutarch, Pyrrhus, l. 1. c. 26. s. 5-8. 9:433,435} {*Pausanias, Attica, l. 1. c. 13. s. 3,4. 1:65} figuring this made up for the loss of Italy and Sicily. He sent for his son Helenus from the citadel of Tarentum, where he had left him. {Justin, Trogus, l. 25. c. 3.}

2805. Pyrrhus had plundered the city of Aegae, which was the royal seat and the burial ground of the former kings of Macedonia. To keep it, he left the Gauls there who had followed him in this war. [L487] They were told that much treasure was stored in the tombs of the kings, according to the custom of the times. So they broke into the tombs and took away any treasure that was there. They threw the kings' bones about the streets and trampled them under their feet. When Pyrrhus found that their actions caused the Macedonians to murmur against him, he did not rebuke them publicly, because he knew he needed them for future wars. {*Plutarch, Pyrrhus, l. 1. c. 26. s. 6,7. 9:433} {*Diod. Sic., l. 22. c. 12. 11:73}

2806. Antigonus, with a small number of cavalry that followed him, came to Thessalonica, where he waited to see how events would unfold, and what would become of Macedonia, now that he had lost it. He planned to capture it back again with the help of any mercenary Gauls he was able to hire, but Ptolemy, the young son of Pyrrhus, utterly defeated him, so that he escaped with only seven in his company. He skulked up and down and did not try to recover his kingdom any longer, but only sought to save his own skin. {Justin, Trogus, l. 25. c. 3.} Pyrrhus reproached him and called him an impudent fellow, for in spite of the condition he was in, Antigonus would not wear a common cloak as other Greeks did, but persisted in wearing his purple robe. {*Plutarch, Pyrrhus, l. 1. c. 26. s. 7. 9:435}

### 3731 AM, 4441 JP, 273 BC

2807. In the year when Gaius Fabius Licinius and Gaius Claudius Caninas were consuls of Rome, Ptolemy Philadelphus heard of the great defeat of Pyrrhus by the Romans, and how the Roman power was beginning to grow in the world, so he sent his envoys with presents from Alexandria to Rome and made a league with them. {Eutropius, l. 2.} {*Livy, Fragments, l. 14. 4:551} {*Dionysius Halicarnassus, Roman Antiquities, l. 20. c. 14. 7:425} {Zonaras, l. 2.} The Romans were glad to see that so great a king as he, had sought their friendship. So they, likewise, sent him

their envoys, Quintus Fabius Maximus, Numerius Fabius Pictor and Quintus Ogulnius, who received expensive presents from the king. (Valerius Maximus wrote Gurges for Maximus. Editor.) As soon as they came home and before they went to the Senate to relate what had happened, they went and put everything they had received from him into the treasury. They rightly knew that they should reap no benefits except praise and honour from a public service for the commonwealth. Everything was restored to them again by a decree of the Senate and by the general vote of the people, and the quaestors were commanded to go and return to each of them what the king had given them. So that in these things the bounty and magnificence of Ptolemy, the sincerity of the envoys, the equity of the Senate and the entire population of Rome, they had the praise and honour due to them. {*Dionysius Halicarnassus, Roman Antiquities, l. 20. c. 14. 7:425} {*Valerius Maximus, l. 4. c. 3. s. 9. 1:175,177}

### 3732 AM, 4442 JP, 272 BC

2808. In the 13th year of Dionysius' calendar, on the 25th day of Aegon or Capricorn, in the 52nd year from the death of Alexander the Great, the 476th from the beginning of Nabonassar's account, on the 20th day of Athyr (17th of our January), in the morning, Dionysius observed the planet of Mars to be under the northerly part of the forehead of Scorpio. {Ptolemy, Great Syntaxis, l. 10. c. 9.} [E354]

2809. When Pyrrhus had subdued the kingdom of Macedonia, he now began to look for the sovereignty of all Greece and Asia. {Justin, Trogus, l. 25. c. 4.} Before he had entirely subdued all Macedonia, he was sent for by Cleonymus of Sparta to come and help him in his wars at Laconia. {*Pausanias, Attica, l. 1. c. 13. s. 4. 1:65} Areus, their king, was away in Crete helping the men of Gorryna, who were at that time oppressed with a war. Therefore, Pyrrhus went to help him with twenty-five thousand foot soldiers, two thousand cavalry and twenty-four elephants. With so large an army, Pyrrhus thought that instead of recovering Sparta for Cleonymus, he could take over all of Peloponnesus. {*Plutarch, Pyrrhus, l. 1. c. 26,27. 9:435,437}

### 3733a AM, 4442 JP, 272 BC

2810. In the 13th year of Ptolemy Philadelphus (in some copies it is incorrectly written, and a half) in the 476th year of Nabonassar, on the 17th day of the month of Mesore, the 11th of our October, twelve hours after the setting of the sun, Timocharis observed the planet of Venus to be completely eclipsed in the morning. {Ptolemy, Great Syntaxis, l. 10. c. 4.} [L488]

2811. While Pyrrhus besieged Sparta, a company of women led by Archidamia defended it against him until the return of Areus from Crete. Acrotatus, the son of

Areus, valiantly drove back Ptolemy, the son of Pyrrhus, when he made an assault and would have broken through into Sparta with two thousand Gauls and some select companies from Chaonia. Whereupon Pyrrhus despaired of accomplishing anything and withdrew, taking the spoil of the country and planning to winter there. {*Plutarch, Pyrrhus, l. 1. c. 27-30. 9:437-447}

2812. While the war was going on in Laconia, Antigonus recovered the cities of Macedonia and marched down with his army into Peloponnesus. He wanted to fight with Pyrrhus again because he knew if Pyrrhus succeeded there, he would return to continue the war in Macedonia. {*Pausanias, Attica, l. 1. c. 13. s. 7. 1:69} When Pyrrhus was on his way to Argos, he was attacked from the rear by Areus, the king, who then cut off some of the Gauls and Molossians who were bringing up the rear. Oryssus of Crete killed Ptolemy, the son of Pyrrhus, who fought valiantly for his father. {*Plutarch, Pyrrhus, l. 1. c. 30. 9:447,449} When Pyrrhus saw his son's dead body, he said that this death happened to him not as soon as he had feared it would, nor as soon as it had been deserved, because of his son's great rashness in actions. {Justin, Trogus, l. 25. c. 4.}

2813. It is said that on the very night that Pyrrhus entered into Argos, a screech owl came and sat on the top of his spear. {*Aelian, History of Animals, l. 10. c. 37. 2:333} The next day, Pyrrhus was killed by a tile which a poor old woman threw down on his head. His head was cut off by Zopyrus, a soldier of Antigonus, and carried to Aleyoneus, the son of Antigonus, who took it and dashed it on the ground at Antigonus' feet, as he sat with his friends about him. Antigonus rebuked him very sharply for so greatly insulting so great a person, because he did not consider the frailty of human life. He took the head and put his hood over it, and then wore it for a garment in the manner of the Macedonians. He buried Pyrrhus' body very honourably. When Helenus, the son of Pyrrhus, was brought to him as a prisoner, Antigonus wanted him to adopt both the manner and the spirit of a king. He gave him the bones of his father in a golden urn, which he wanted him to carry into Epirus to his brother Alexander. Antigonus treated Pyrrhus' friends, who had been captured, with every respect. {*Plutarch, Pyrrhus, l. 1. c. 34. 9:457-461} {Justin, Trogus, l. 25. c. 5.} {*Valerius Maximus, l. 5. c. 1. ext. 4. 1:459}

### 3733b AM, 4443 JP, 271 BC

2814. When the people of Tarentum heard of the death of Pyrrhus, they sent to Carthage to ask for help against the Romans and against Milo, who was holding the city with a strong garrison of Epirotes. When Milo was besieged on all sides, by the Romans on land and the Carthaginians at sea, he surrendered the citadel to Papirius Cursor, the Roman consul. They agreed to let Milo and his soldiers leave safely for their own country with their money and other baggage. The city was also surrendered to Papirius by its townsmen, who gave up their arms, their ships and themselves to him. This was the end of the war of Tarentum against the Romans. {*Dio, l. 10. (42) 1:373 (Zonaras, l. 8. c. 7.)} {Orosius, l. 4. c. 3.} {*Frontinus, Stratagems, l. 3. c. 3. s. 1. 1:213}

### 3734 AM, 4444 JP, 270 BC

2815. After the death of Strato, who was the master of the school of the Peripatetics for eighteen years, Lyco of Troas, the son of Astyanax, succeeded him. He was an eloquent man and very capable to instruct and bring up the youth. {*Diogenes Laertius, Strato, l. 5. c. 3. (58) 1:511} {*Diogenes Laertius, Lyco, l. 5. c. 4. (65) 1:519}

### 3735 AM, 4445 JP, 269 BC

2816. Attalus the younger, the brother of Philetaerus, had a son born whom he also called Attalus. This son later reigned in Pergamum, and lived for seventy-two years. {*Polybius, l. 18. c. 41. s. 8,9. 5:177} {Suidas, Attalus} {*Livy, l. 33. c. 21. s. 1. 9:335}

### 3736a AM, 4445 JP, 269 BC

2817. The Twenty-fourth Jubilee. [E355]

### 3738 AM, 4448 JP, 266 BC

2818. Mithridates died after reigning in Pontus for thirty-six years, and his son Ariobarzanes succeeded him. {*Diod. Sic., l. 20. c. 111. 10:441} {Memnon, Excerpts, c. 17,25.} [L489]

### 3740a AM, 4449 JP, 265 BC

2819. In the 21st year of Dionysius' calendar, on the 22nd and 26th day of the sign of Scorpio, in the 484th year of Nabonassar, on the 18th and 22nd day of the month of Thoth and on the 14th and 18th of November according to the Julian calendar, Dionysius observed the planet Mercury in the morning. {Ptolemy, Great Syntaxis, l. 9. c. 10,11.}

### 3741 AM, 4451 JP, 263 BC

2820. Philetaerus, the Teian who was born at Teium in Pontus, ruled Pergamum for twenty years and died when he was eighty years old. He was succeeded by Eumenes I, the son of his older brother. He ruled for twenty-two years. {*Strabo, l. 12. c. 3. s. 8. 5:381} {*Strabo, l. 13. c. 4. s. 2. 6:165,167} {*Lucian, Octogenarians, l. 1. (12) 1:231}

2821. The first Punic or Sicilian war started this year between the Romans and the Carthaginians. This was the first time the Romans had left Italy and fought their first naval battle. The Carthaginians had invaded Sicily. This war lasted twenty-four years without stopping. {*Polybius, l. 1. c. 12. s. 5-9. 1:31}

2822. In this same year, Diognetus was the archon at Athens. The chronologer of Paris noted this in his canon, or order of times. Mr. Selden recently published this in his *Marmora Arundelliana*.

## 3742 AM, 4452 JP, 262 BC

2823. Dionysius, the astronomer, observed Mercury three times. The first time was in the 23rd year of Dionysius' calendar, on the 29th (it should be the 19th or 20th, according to the position assigned to the sun) of the sign Hydra or Aquarius, in the 486th year of Nabonassar on the 17th of the month Choiak (on the 11th of our February), in the morning. The second time was on the fourth of the sign Taurus, or the first of Phamenoth the Egyptian month (for in Claudius Ptolemy we must here write *A* for Λ). This was on the 26th of our April, in the first hour of the evening. The third time was in the same year of Nabonassar, but the 24th day of the Dionysian account, on the 24th day of Leonion, or 30th day of Paynus, or the 23rd of our August, in the evening. Dionysius' observations were recorded by Claudius Ptolemy from the writings of Hipparchus. {*Ptolemy, Great Syntaxis, l. 9. c. 7.*}

2824. Nicomedes, king of Bithynia, enlarged the city of Astacus and renamed it Nicomedia after himself. {*Eusebius, Chronicles, l. 1. 1:213*} {*Pausanias, Elis I, l. 5. c. 12. s. 7. 2:449*} {*Trebellius, Pallio, in Gallienis.*} {*Ammianus Marcellinus, l. 22. c. 9. s. 3. 2:245*} Memnon said that he built Nicomedia opposite the city of Astacus, as did both Strabo and Pliny. {*Memnon, Excerpts, c. 21.*} They thought they were really two distinct cities.

2825. When Eumenes I had taken many cities and places around Pergamum, he defeated Antiochus, the son of Seleucus, near Sardis. {*Strabo, l. 13. c. 4. s. 2. 6:165*}

## 3743 AM, 4453 JP, 261 BC

2826. Antiochus of Syria died after he had killed one of his sons and declared the other his successor. {*Justin, Trogus, l. 26. c. 0.*} For his great victory over the Gauls who came across to Asia from Europe, Antiochus was surnamed *Soter*, that is *Their Deliverer*. {*Appian, Syrian Wars, l. 11. c. 11. (65) 2:229*} Lucian described this victory over the Gauls in more detail. {*Lucian, Slip of the Tongue in Greeting (9) 6:183*} {*Lucian, Zeuxis or Antiochus (8-12) 6:163-169*} He was succeeded by his son Antiochus, whom he had by Stratonice, the Milesian. The Milesians were the first who surnamed him *Theos* because he ridded them of their tyrant, Timarchus. {*Appian, Syrian Wars, l. 11. c. 11. (65) 2:229*} Tatian, the Assyrian, inferred in his writings that Berosus, who was a priest of Bel in Babylon, dedicated his three books of the Chaldean history to this Antiochus. {*Tatian, Address to the Greeks, l. 1. c. 36. 2:80*} Berosus published the observations of the stellar motions among the Babylonians for a period of four hundred and ninety years. {*Pliny, l. 7. c. 56. 2:637*} (Loeb edition incorrectly translated the number as four hundred and ninety thousand. The Loeb Latin text has four hundred and ninety. Editor.) This is the number of years from the beginning of the epoch of Nabonassar's account, as other learned men understand this. We also find this to have ended six years before the start of the reign of this Antiochus. *[L490]* Porphyry, Eusebius, Sulpicius Severus, Johannes Malela of Antioch and all others agree that Antiochus reigned fifteen years.

2827. Antiochus gave the Jews living in Ionia equal rights and privileges with the Gentiles, and allowed them to live according to their own religion and the customs of their country. {*Josephus, Antiq., l. 12. c. 3. s. 3. (132-134) 7:67*} At various times, he made war on Ptolemy Philadelphus and fought against him with all the forces he could raise from Babylon and all the east. Ptolemy wanted to end this bloody war and gave him his daughter Berenice for a wife, while Antiochus' former wife Laodice was still living. Laodice had borne him two sons, Seleucus Callinicus and Antiochus Hierax, that is, *Hawk*. Ptolemy accompanied his daughter as far as Pelusium and there, with her, gave Antiochus an enormous quantity of gold and silver for a dowry. Hence Ptolemy was called the dowry giver. {*Jerome, Da 11*} At great expense, he supplied her with water from the Nile River, which was to be carried to her, so that wherever she was, she would only drink that water. {*Athenaeus, l. 2. (45c) 1:197*} Appian was incorrect in saying that Berenice and Laodice were both daughters of this Ptolemy. {*Appian, Syrian Wars, l. 11. c. 11. (65) 2:231*} *[E356]*

## 3745 AM, 4455 JP, 259 BC

2828. Josephus wrote that Eleazar, the son of Onias, was succeeded in the priesthood at Jerusalem by his uncle Manasseh, the son of Jaddua. {*Josephus, Antiq., l. 12. c. 4. s. 1. (157) 7:83*} He was the high priest for twenty-six years. {*Eusebius, Scaliger's Greek Eusebius, p. 50.*} {*Eusebius, Chronicles, l. 1. 1:213*}

## 3746 AM, 4456 JP, 258 BC

2829. Laodice bore to Antiochus Theos a son called Antiochus who, as mentioned before, was called *Hierax*. {*See note on 3760 AM. <<2845>>*}

## 3747 AM, 4457 JP, 257 BC

2830. In the 28th year of Dionysius' calendar, the 7th day of the month of Didymon, in the 491st year of Nabonassar, on the 5th day of the month Pharmuthi, and the 28th of our July, Dionysius observed the planet Mercury in the evening near the sign of Gemini, toward its southern head. {*Ptolemy, Great Syntaxis, l. 9. c. 7.*}

**3750 AM, 4460 JP, 254 BC**

*2831.* The second period of Calippus began in this year.

**3753 AM, 4463 JP, 251 BC**

*2832.* Aratus of Sicyon, at the age of twenty, delivered his native city from the tyranny and oppression of Nicocles and joined with the Achaean League. {*Polybius, l. 2. c. 43. s. 3. 1:347} He sent to Ptolemy Philadelphus in Egypt and from him got a hundred and fifty talents, which he bestowed among his poor countrymen. This was partly used in redeeming those who had been taken prisoner. Those who had been expelled from their country were now restored, but they would give no rest to those who now possessed their lands and estates. Therefore, Aratus made another journey to Ptolemy and asked him for money to settle all the differences among his countrymen and all legal actions between them. On the journey, he sailed through a violent storm and contrary winds. He finally came to Egypt where he obtained a boon of a further one hundred and fifty talents for his country's good. He took forty talents along with him and returned into Peloponnesus. {*Plutarch, Aratus, l. 1. c. 13. s. 4. 11:31}

**3754 AM, 4464 JP, 250 BC**

*2833.* This year, Manlius Vulso and Attilius Regulus were consuls in Rome. {*Polybius, l. 1. c. 39. s. 15. 1:111} This was the fourteenth year of this first Carthaginian war. The Parthians, under their captain Arsaces, broke off the Macedonian rule and revolted from them. {Justin, Trogus, l. 41.} This man, Arsaces, is called *Aski* or *Askam* by the later Persian writers, and Mircondus calls him *Chapur*. He began his reign there in the seventy-second year after the death of Alexander the Great, which was one year before the consulship of Manlius and Attilius in Rome and three years before the 133rd Olympiad. Eusebius noted that this Arsaces and his Parthians defected at that time and rebelled against Antiochus Theos. {*Eusebius, Chronicles, l. 1. 1:214} However, the Parthians observed a holiday when Arsaces defeated Seleucus Callinicus, the son and successor of Antiochus, and took Callinicus himself prisoner. This holiday was celebrated with a great festival and was observed on the anniversary of their liberty. {*Athenaeus, l. 4. c. 14. (153a) 2:197} {Justin, Trogus, l. 41. c. 4.} [L491] Therefore both Justin and Appian thought that the Parthians began their revolt under Seleucus and not under Antiochus, his father. {*Appian, Syrian Wars, l. 11. c. 11. (65) 2:231} Moreover, the Parthians honoured Arsaces by calling their dynasty of kings after him, by the name of Arsaces. {Justin, Trogus, l. 41. c. 5.} {*Strabo, l. 16. c. 1. s. 28. 7:237}

*2834.* The Parthians, together with the Persians, which the later Persian writers confound, and make one people with the Parthians (for more about this see {Schikard, Tarich, p. 101,102} and our third note on the *Acts of Ignatius*), revolted from the Persian Empire. Arrian noted this in his annals as preserved by Photius. {Arrian, Parthicus} {Photius, Bibliotheca, cod. 58.} Arrian mentioned the reason for this revolt from the Persian Empire. It was because this Arsaces and Tiridates, the sons of Phripites or Priapatius who was the son of Arsaces, had first killed Pherecles (or Agathocles, as we find him called by Georgius Syncellus). He was the governor of that country and had been appointed by Antiochus Theos. The governor and five others had wanted to have homosexual intercourse with Tiridates. Arsaces and Tiridates expelled the Macedonians and took over the kingdom. Their successors later fought with the Romans and contended with them for the empire of the world. {*Strabo, l. 11. c. 6. s. 4. 5:247}

*2835.* At the same time, Theodotus, who had a thousand cities of the Bactrians under his control, revolted from the Macedonians. The whole east followed their example and revolted. {Justin, Trogus, l. 41. c. 4.} Others say that the two kings of Syria and Media defected. Euthydemus persuaded the Greeks who inhabited Bactria to revolt from the Macedonians. Thereupon when Arsaces saw Diotus, or Theodotus, grow so powerful among the Bactrians, he persuaded the Parthians also to revolt from the Macedonians. Apollodorus, in his books of the Parthian affairs, stated that the Greeks who lived in Bactria became very strong and invaded India. They went so far that, after they had crossed the Hypanis River, they went as far as the Isamus River, farther than Alexander had gone in his conquest of India. {*Strabo, l. 11. c. 9. s. 2. 5:273,275} {*Strabo, l. 15. c. 1. s. 3. 7:5} [E357]

**3758 AM, 4468 JP, 246 BC**

*2836.* Seleucus, king of Syria, was overcome with love for his former wife Laodice and her children and began to court her again. A short time later she began to fear his fickleness and thought that his affections might again turn to Berenice, his second wife, so she poisoned him. {Jerome, Da 11} {*Appian, Syrian Wars, l. 11. c. 11. (65) 2:231} To conceal this wicked deed of hers, she had Artemo, who looked very much like him, lie in his bed and pretend to be sick. By his face and the imitation of Seleucus' speech, he deceived all that came to see and visit him in his sickness. In this way, she concealed the death of the true king until she had arranged a suitable successor. {*Valerius Maximus, l. 9. c. 14. ext. 1. 2:389} {*Pliny, l. 7. c. 12. (53) 2:541} {Solinus, c. 1.} Through her, Seleucus, the oldest son of Seleucus by Laodice, succeeded him in the kingdom. He was surnamed *Callinicus* because of the many victories which he won. (There were none that I know of.) Due to his large beard, he was called *Pogon*, meaning a *beard*. {*Polybius, l. 2. c. 71. s. 3,4. 1:413} He ruled for twenty years. {*Eusebius, Chronicles, l. 1. 1:214}

*2837.* In Egypt, Ptolemy Philadelphus died. He had lived luxuriously and had not hesitated to say that he would live for ever, and that he alone had found the way to immortality. He died forty years after the death of Ptolemy Lagus, his father. {*Athenaeus, l. 12. (536e) 5:425} [L492] Ptolemy, surnamed Euergetes, his son, succeeded him. He was born of Arsinoe, the daughter of Lysimachus, and reigned twenty-five years. {Ptolemy, Canon of Kings} {*Clement, Stromateis, l. 1. c. 21. 2:329} {Jerome, Da 9} It is said that in his time a phoenix appeared, which came to Heliopolis, followed by a large flock of other birds. Everyone marvelled at the beauty of the phoenix. {*Tacitus, Annals, l. 6. c. 28. 4:201}

*2838.* Laodice turned Berenice and her young son, whom she had by Ptolemy, over to Icadion and Genneus (or Coeneus) to have them murdered. These were two important men in Antioch. {Jerome, Da 11} {*Appian, Syrian Wars, l. 11. c. 11. (65) 2:231} When Berenice heard that they were coming to murder her, she shut herself up in Daphne, a citadel or suburb of Antioch which I mentioned earlier. When the cities of Asia heard that she and her young son were besieged, they remembered her and respected her high calling and that of her son. Out of compassion, they sent her help from every direction. Her brother Ptolemy also, who was surnamed Euergetes, was fearful of the danger his sister was in. Leaving his kingdom, he went as quickly as he could, with as many forces as he could gather, to help her. {Justin, Trogus, l. 27. c. 1.} Before any help arrived, the young son was taken through the schemes of Laodice and carried off. When Berenice, his mother, heard of this, she armed herself and got into a chariot. She pursued Coeneus, the perpetrator of that act of butchery. When she overtook him, she was helpless against him with her spear, so she took a stone and knocked him down. She forced her chariot over the actual body of the knave and breaking through the middle of the companies, she went directly to the house where she had heard that they had laid the body of her murdered son. {*Valerius Maximus, l. 9. c. 10. ext. 1. 2:357,359}

*2839.* The murderers of the child took another child very much like him and brought him out to show him to the people, with a royal guard around him, as though it were the same child. However, they had a strong guard of mercenary Gauls attack Berenice. These turned the strongest part of the place, or the citadel of Antioch, over to her. They swore their loyalty to her and entered into a covenant with her. She heeded the advice of Aristarchus, her physician, who persuaded her to make a covenant of friendship with them. But they simply used their oath as a stratagem, to get near her, and tried to cut her throat. The women about her defended her as

well as they could, and many of them died in the battle. However three of them who survived—Panariste, Maria and Gethosyne—took her body and laid it in her bed as if she had only been wounded and was not quite dead. They let it be known that she might recover, and held the people in suspense until the coming of Ptolemy. {Polyaenus, Strategmata, l. 1.}

*2840.* All the cities of Asia which had revolted from Seleucus sent their ships and joined with Ptolemy. They were either going to defend Berenice if she were still alive or to avenge her murder, if she were dead. {Justin, Trogus, l. 27. c. 1.} When Ptolemy came, he killed Laodice and entered Syria, marching as far as Babylon. {*Appian, Syrian Wars, l. 11. c. 11. (65) 2:231} He took over Coelosyria from Seleucia. {*Polybius, l. 5. c. 58. s. 11. 3:145} Syria, Cilicia, the upper provinces beyond the Euphrates and almost the whole of Asia became his. {Jerome, Da 11} Even from the Taurus Mountains to India, he took everything without fighting a battle. That is, if we can believe Polyaenus' account, given in the record cited above, with which we may also compare what we find on the monument of Euergetes, called *Monumentum Adulitanum*, published at Rome in the year 1631 by Leo Allatrus. It said:

> "After his father died, Ptolemy became king of Egypt, Libya, Syrian Phoenicia, Cyprus, Lycia, Caria, and the Cycladian Isles. He gathered an army of foot soldiers and cavalry with a fleet of ships and elephants from Troglodyte and Ethiopia. [E358] He had some elephants from his father and he brought the rest from there into Egypt. He trained these forces in the art of war and they were well equipped. [L493] With these forces he sailed into Asia and conquered all the land on this side of the Euphrates River, Cilicia, Pamphylia, Ionia, the Hellespont and Thrace, together with all their forces and other elephants from India and all the kings of these countries. He crossed over the Euphrates River and conquered Mesopotamia, Babylonia, Susia, Persia, Media and all the countries as far as Bactria."

*2841.* When Euergetes had conquered all Syria, he came down to Jerusalem and offered many sacrifices of thanksgiving to God. He dedicated to him gifts worthy of such a great victory. {*Josephus, Apion, l. 2. c. 5. (48) 1:311,313}

## 3759 AM, 4469 JP, 245 BC

*2842.* Euergetes was called back by a rebellion of his own people in Egypt. {Justin, Trogus, l. 27. c. 1.} While he himself held Syria, he entrusted Cilicia to his friend Antiochus and put Xanthippus in control of the provinces beyond the Euphrates. He wasted all the kingdoms of Seleucus and carried off forty thousand talents of silver and all the rich vessels that were there, as well as taking twenty-five hundred images of their gods. Among these images were the images which Cambyses had previously taken from Egypt to Persia. On account of this action, the Egyptians surnamed him *Euergetes*, when they saw their gods come home. {*Jerome, Da 11*} In that monument mentioned earlier, called *Monumentum Adulitanum*, we find written concerning him:

> "Ptolemy had returned those gods which the Persians had previously taken and carried from Egypt, along with other treasures stored there. He sent his army to let in the water in ditches recently dug for that purpose."

*2843.* After the departure of Ptolemy from Syria, Seleucus outfitted a large fleet to attack the cities that had revolted from him. A sudden storm sank the whole fleet, causing all the cities and countries which had defected to Ptolemy because they hated Seleucus, to return to him out of sympathy for this great disaster at sea. {*Justin, Trogus, l. 27. c. 2.*}

### 3760a AM, 4469 JP, 245 BC

*2844.* In the 67th year according to the Chaldean calendar, on the fifth day of the month of Apellaios, and in the 504th year of Nabonassar, 27th of the month of Thoth, the 18th day of our November, the planet Mercury was observed in the morning to have been toward the north of the uppermost star in the head of Scorpio. {*Ptolemy, Great Syntaxis, l. 9. c. 7.*}

### 3760 AM, 4470 JP, 244 BC

*2845.* Seleucus Callinicus began to make war on Ptolemy Euergetes, but after being utterly routed he fled to Antioch. From there, he wrote to his brother Antiochus and begged his help, offering him all of Asia on this side of the Taurus Mountains for his trouble. At this time, Antiochus was not more than fourteen years old and was very greedy for a kingdom. He seized on the occasion, but not out of brotherly love. He acted like a robber (*laron*, Ussher cited in Oxford English Dictionary as using this term) and sought to strip his brother of all that he had in his time of need. Although he was a child, he nonetheless behaved more like a man with this impious resolve. On account of this, he was surnamed *Hierax*, that is, *Greedy Hawk*. He was more like a rapacious and filthy eagle, because he was always ready to fall upon every man's estate. {*Justin, Trogus, l. 27. c. 2.*} {*Strabo, l. 16. c. 2. s. 14. 7:259*}

### 3761 AM, 4471 JP, 243 BC

*2846.* At this time, the people of Smyrna and Magnesia, in the month of Lenaeon, entered into a league between themselves to maintain the honour and greatness of Seleucus. We find this league preserved to this very day, transcribed from the *Marmora Arundelliana*, those marble stones which the Earl of Arundel brought from those parts, and published by Mr. J. Selden, as noted before.

*2847.* When Ptolemy saw that this young Antiochus sided with Seleucus, he made a ten-year truce with Seleucus, lest he should be forced to fight both of them. {*Justin, Trogus, l. 27. c. 2.*} In this long time of peace, he sent for Eratosthenes of Cyrene from Athens and made him the keeper of his library at Alexandria. {*Suidas, Eratosthenes*} {*Suidas, Apollonius*} Ptolemy Euergetes followed after his father Philadelphus in promoting the magnificence of this library and with it, all types of learning. *[L494]* He was a scholar of Aristarchus, the philosopher, and wrote certain historical commentaries himself. {*\*Athenaeus, l. 2. (71b) 1:311*} About his diligence in getting works into his library from the ancient writers, Galen in commenting on the third book of Hippocrates (of *Epidemic Diseases*) said:

> "He ordered all their books which came into Egypt to be brought to him. He had copies made of them and gave the copies back to the owners who brought the originals. The originals were placed in his own library with this inscription, *from out of ships* so that it might appear that they came from such ships as had arrived there."

*2848.* He left fifteen talents in Athens as a security deposit, so he could borrow the works of Sophocles, Euripides and Eschylus, to transcribe them. He was to get his money back when he returned them. He had them written out most exquisitely on excellent parchment, and then kept the originals. *[E359]* He sent these copies back to them again and asked them to keep his deposit of fifteen talents and allow the originals to remain with him.

### 3762a AM, 4471 JP, 243 BC

*2849.* Antigonus Gonatas died after he had reigned in Macedonia for thirty-four years and in Greece for forty-four years. He lived eighty years, according to Medius and other writers. Porphyry said he lived eighty-three years. {*\*Lucian, Octogenarians, l. 1. (11) 1:231*} {*Porphyry, Scaliger's Greek Eusebius, p. 229.*}

*2850.* Antigonus Gonatas was succeeded by his son Demetrius, who reigned ten years. {*Porphyry, Scaliger's Greek Eusebius, p. 229.*} {*\*Polybius, l. 2. c. 44. s. 1,2. 1:349*} During this time he subdued all of Cyrene and Libya. After the death of her husband and brother Alexander, Olympias, the daughter of Pyrrhus, who was the king of Epirus, gave her daughter Pthias to Demetrius. He was already married to the sister of Antiochus, king of Syria. When Demetrius turned her out, she went to her brother

Antiochus and stirred him up to make war on her husband, because of the wrong he had done to her. {*Justin, Trogus, l. 28. c. 1.*} During all this time there was no other king named Antiochus, apart from Antiochus Hierax. He wanted to take the whole kingdom from Seleucus, his older brother. Justin called both these brothers kings. {*Justin, Trogus, l. 44. c. 1.*} Justin and Polyaenus stated that Antiochus went into Mesopotamia, where Seleucus had built a city called Callinocopolis, according to the Fasti Seculi, in the first year of the 134th Olympiad. At that time, neither Antiochus nor Seleucus controlled Syria, {*Justin, Trogus, l. 27. (Prologue)*} {*Polyaenus, Strategmata, l. 4. Antiochus Hierax*} for Ptolemy Euergetes, the king of Egypt, governed it.

### 3762b AM, 4472 JP, 242 BC

*2851.* At this time, Antiochus tried to take over all Asia proper from his brother Seleucus. Antiochus raised a mercenary army of the Gauls to fight against Seleucus. They fought near the city of Ancyra and Seleucus was defeated by the extraordinary prowess of the Gauls. The Gauls then supposed that Seleucus had been killed in the battle and turned on Antiochus who had hired them. When he knew what was happening, he bought their loyalty and was forced to make a league with these mercenaries. However, Eumenes, with a fresh army of his own, attacked and routed Antiochus and his Gauls, who were all tired out, with many having been wounded from the recent battle with Seleucus. In this way, Eumenes got most of Asia under his control. {*Justin, Trogus, l. 27. c. 2,3.*} {*Justin, Trogus, l. 27. c. 0.*}

### 3763 AM, 4473 JP, 241 BC

*2852.* Eumenes, who was the nephew (the son of Philetaerus' older brother Eumenes) and adopted son of Philetaerus, king of Pergamum, drank until he was drunk and died as recorded by Ctesicles in his third book of *Chronicles*. {*Athenaeus, l. 10. (445d) 4:517,519*} Attalus, the cousin and adopted son of Eumenes, succeeded him. Attalus was son of Attalus, the the younger brother of Philetaerus, and born of Antiochis, the daughter of Achaeus. [L495] Attalus used his great wealth cautiously and magnificently. He thought that he should be called a king and then convinced other men, also, that he deserved to be a king. So, after he had defeated the Gauls, he assumed the title of a king. He ruled wisely and his house continued to the third generation. {*Polybius, l. 18. c. 41. 5:175,179*} {*Livy, l. 33. c. 21. s. 1,2. 9:335*} {*Strabo, l. 13. c. 4. s. 2. 6:165,167*} Suidas reported an oracle which was given to him by the prophetess at Delphi, which said:

> Go on Taurocerus, thou a crown shalt wear,
> And thy sons' sons, and there an end shall be.

*2853.* Now it is thought that this Eumenes was surnamed Taurocerus, because there were a pair of bull's horns

added to a statue of him. Also in the oracle by Phaennes, he foretold the slaughter which Attalus would one day make of the Gauls. Attalus is called *Tauri Filius*, that is, the *Son of a Bull*. {*Pausanias, Phocis, l. 10. c. 15. s. 3. 4:451*} It said this:

> For Jove shall quickly send them a saviour.
> Son of a Bull and by Jove nurtured,
> Which on the Gauls shall bring a dismal day.

*2854.* Concerning this battle fought between Attalus and the Gauls, Livy said: {*Livy, l. 38. c. 16. s. 14,15. 11:55*}

> "Attalus was the first in Asia who refused to pay tribute to the Gauls. Fortune there, beyond all expectation of men, favoured this bold attempt of his and in a battle he fought and defeated them."

*2855.* However, Polyaenus told of a scheme which Sudines, a Chaldean soothsayer, used to motivate his soldiers for this battle when they were quite dispirited. {*Polyaenus, Strategmata, l. 4. Attalus*} Sudines was the Babylonian mathematician whom we find mentioned by Strabo. {*Strabo, l. 16. c. 1. s. 6. 7:203*} [E360] Vettius Valens of Antioch said he used Sudines' astronomical tables to determine the motions of the moon.

*2856.* In the 45th year according to Dionysius' calendar, on the 10th day of the month of Parthenion or the sign of Virgo, eighty-three years after the death of Alexander, on the 17th day of the month of Epeiph (September 3), the planet Jupiter eclipsed the southern star of the constellation of Asellus, that is, *Little Asses*. {*Ptolemy, Great Syntaxis, l. 11. c. 3.*} (The Aselli are two stars in the constellation of Cancer the Crab. {*Pliny, l. 18. c. 80. 5:411*})

### 3764 AM, 4474 JP, 240 BC

*2857.* Lacydes of Cyrene, the rector of the new academy in Aeolia, succeeded Arcesilaus of Potana in the 4th year of the 134th Olympiad. Lacydes kept his academy in a certain garden which Attalus, the king, had provided there for that purpose. {*Diogenes Laertius, Lacydes, l. 4. c. 8. (59,61) 1:435,437*}

### 3768 AM, 4478 JP, 236 BC

*2858.* In the 75th year according to the Chaldean calendar, on the 14th day of the month of Dios in the 512th year of Nabonassar, the ninth of the month of Thoth (July 29), in the morning, the planet of Mercury was seen near the beam star in the sign of Libra. {*Ptolemy, Great Syntaxis, l. 9. c. 7.*}

### 3771 AM, 4481 JP, 233 BC

*2859.* Onias II became high priest. He was the son of Simon the Just. After Simon, Eleasarus had carried out the office of the high priest at Jerusalem, because Onias was still quite young. After Eleasarus, Manasses became high priest until Onias came of age. Josephus said Onias was a dim-witted man and in his old age finally came to be prince and high priest among the Jews. In this office, he behaved in a most unworthy and base manner, and was only concerned about money. {*Josephus, Antiq., l. 12. c. 4. s. 1. (157,158) 7:83} {Eusebius, Scaliger's Greek Eusebius, p. 50.} {*Eusebius, Chronicles, l. 1. 1:215} It is said that he was the high priest for fourteen years. [L496]

2860. In his days, the Samaritans grievously vexed the Jews. They plundered the country and carried the people away as captives. Onias refused to pay the twenty talents of silver imposed upon the land by the kings, because he was very covetous of money. This sum had been paid by his predecessors from their own wealth, to relieve the people. In a rage, Ptolemy Euergetes sent a messenger to Jerusalem and threatened Onias that if he did not quickly send in his arrears of tribute, he would immediately distribute the land among his soldiers and settle new colonies of his own there. At that time, there was a man named Joseph, the son of Tobias, who, although only a young man, was held in high regard among all men for his prudence, justice and other virtues. He lived in the country at a place called Phicola, where he had been born. He was told of the arrival of these envoys at Jerusalem by his mother, who was the daughter of Simon the Just and sister to this Onias the priest. So he came to Jerusalem and undertook to be part of an embassy to Euergetes concerning this matter. He so ingratiated himself to King Ptolemy and his queen, Cleopatra, that he appeased the king's wrath. He also obtained a company of two thousand soldiers to collect the tributes and other profits for the king from Coelosyria, Phoenicia, Samaria and Judea. He held that office for twenty-two years and in that time doubled the king's revenues, increasing them from eight thousand to sixteen thousand talents a year. He brought this into the king's treasury along with all the goods of the thieves and confiscated goods which the tax collectors had previously kept and divided among themselves. {*Josephus, Antiq., l. 12. c. 4. s. 2-10. (160-227) 7:83-115}

## 3772 AM, 4482 JP, 232 BC

2861. In Macedonia, Demetrius died, leaving his very young son, Philip, as king. Antigonus was made his guardian. He was known for the great and extraordinary promises which he made to all sorts of men. He was nicknamed *Doson*, that is, one who was ever full of promises and no action. He married the mother of Philip and took over the kingdom. {Justin, Trogus, l. 28. c. 3.} He ruled for twelve years. {Dexippus} {Porphyry, Scaliger's Greek Eusebius} {*Eusebius, Chronicles, l. 1. 1:215}

## 3773 AM, 4483 JP, 231 BC

2861a. Spurius Carvilius divorced his wife for barrenness. This was the first divorce that occurred in Rome since the city was founded over five hundred years earlier. {*Valerius Maximus, l. 2. c. 1. s. 4. 1:131} {*Aulus Gellius, Attic Nights, l. 4. c. 3. s. 2. 1:323}

## 3774 AM, 4484 JP, 230 BC

2862. Lyco of Troas died. He was head of the school of the Peripatetics for forty-four years. Strato of Lapsacus was the previous head of the school until his death. Lyco lived for seventy-four years. {*Diogenes Laertius, Lyco, l. 5. c. 4. (68) 1:521}

## 3775 AM, 4485 JP, 229 BC

2863. In the 82nd year according to the Chaldean calendar, the 5th day of the month of Xanthikos, in the 519th year of Nabonassar, the 14th day of the month of Tybi (March 1), in the evening, Saturn was observed to be two fingers width below the southern shoulder of Virgo. {Ptolemy, Great Syntaxis, l. 11. c. 7.}

## 3778a AM, 4487 JP, 227 BC

2864. When Antiochus Hierax was in trouble, he fled to Ptolemy Euergetes in Egypt, who threw him into prison. He escaped with the help of a certain harlot who used to come to him. On his escape, he fell into the hands of some thieves, who killed him. {Justin, Trogus, l. 17. c. 3.}

## 3778 AM, 4488 JP, 226 BC

2865. At about the same time, Seleucus Callinicus, the older brother of Antiochus, fell off his horse, broke his neck and died, {Justin, Trogus, l. 17. c. 3.} leaving two sons. The older one was Seleucus Ceraunus, who was physically weak and poor, and could not keep order in his army. The younger was called Antiochus and was later surnamed the Great. After the death of his father, he went into upper Asia. {*Polybius, l. 4. c. 48. s. 5,6. 2:417} {*Polybius, l. 5. c. 40. s. 4-7. 3:99} {*Appian, Syrian Wars, l. 11. c. 11. (66) 2:231} [E361] Seleucus Ceraunus reigned only three years. {Porphyry, Scaliger's Greek Eusebius} {*Eusebius, Chronicles, l. 1. 1:215} {*Sulpicius Severus, Sacred History, l. 2. c. 19. 11:107}

## 3781a AM, 4490 JP, 224 BC

2866. Seleucus Ceraunus marched against Attalus, who had controlled all of Asia on the western side of the Taurus Mountains. He left his kingdom in the care of Hermias, a Carian, and crossed over the Taurus Mountains with a large army. {*Polybius, l. 4. c. 48. s. 7. 2:417} {*Polybius, l. 5. c. 40. s. 5-7. 3:99}

## 3781b AM, 4491 JP, 223 BC

2867. In Phrygia, Seleucus was poisoned by his two friends, Apatarias and Nicanor. {*Polybius, l. 5. c. 40. s. 5-7. 3:99} {*Appian, Syrian Wars, l. 11. c. 11. (66) 2:231} {Jerome, Da 11}

{*Justin, Trogus, l. 29. c. 1.} [L497] In his army was Achaeus, the son of Andronicus, who was the brother of Laodice, Seleucus' wife. She was at that time in exile with Ptolemy in Egypt. Achaeus, as a kinsman to Seleucus, avenged his death and killed the two men who had murdered Seleucus. He managed all matters in the army with extraordinary skill, wisdom and magnanimity. Even though he could now crown himself king and all men wanted him to do so, he would not, choosing instead to reserve the role for Antiochus, the young son of Seleucus Callinicus. Achaeus marched with the army from place to place throughout Asia and recovered all that his father had lost on the western side of the Taurus Mountains. {*Polybius, l. 4. c. 48. s. 8-20. 2:419}

2868. The army that was in Syria sent to Antiochus, who was in Babylon, wanting him to come and assume the kingdom. {Jerome, Da 11} This he did when he was less than fourteen years old. {Justin, Trogus, l. 29. c. 1.} {*Polybius, l. 4. c. 2. s. 5-8. 2:301} Porphyry and Eusebius said that he reigned thirty-six years.

2869. Antiochus committed to Achaeus the whole rule and government of all Asia on the western side of the Taurus Mountains. He made Molon the governor of Media, and Alexander, Molon's brother, governor of Persia. In court, Hermias the Carian controlled all. A man of a fierce and cruel nature, he punished even small offences very severely and made them seem all the greater by the aggravating words he said. He made false charges against various people and proved to be merciless and an inexorable judge. {*Polybius, l. 5. c. 40,41. 3:99}

2870. Cleomenes, the king of Lacedemon, was defeated by Antigonus Doson, king of Macedonia near Sellasia. He was expelled from his kingdom and sailed from Gythiom in a ship he had prepared beforehand in case it should be needed. Taking some of his friends along with him, he sailed into Egypt to Ptolemy Euergetes. (He had previously sent his children and his mother Cratesiclea to Ptolemy as pledges, when Ptolemy had initially promised him help.) When he arrived, Ptolemy honourably entertained him. {*Polybius, l. 2. c. 69. s. 10,11. 1:411} {Justin, Trogus, l. 28. c. 4.} {*Pausanias, Corinth, l. 2. c. 20. s. 8-9. 1:353,355} {*Plutarch, Cleomenes, l. 1. c. 27-32. 10:113-125}

### 3782 AM, 4492 JP, 222 BC

2871. The two brothers—Molon, the governor of Media, and Alexander, the governor of Persia—despised the youth of Antiochus, their king. They thought that Achaeus could easily be persuaded to join with them, since all of them feared the power of Hermias in the court and his malice and cruelty. The two brothers together conspired with their provinces to revolt from Antiochus. {*Polybius, l. 5. c. 41. s. 1. 3:99}

2872. In the regions of Caria and the isle of Rhodes, there was a very strong earthquake which destroyed their houses along with the large colossus or image of Zeus at Rhodes. {*Eusebius, Chronicles, l. 1. 1:216} {Orosius, l. 4. c. 13.}

2873. Ptolemy Euergetes gave Cleomenes some hopes that he would send him back into Greece with a well-furnished navy and restore him to his kingdom again. Because of his loving nature, Ptolemy gradually developed a closer, warmer relationship with him day by day. Meanwhile, he gave him twenty-four talents yearly for his entertainment. With this he lived frugally and maintained himself and those with him. {*Plutarch, Cleomenes, l. 1. c. 32. s. 2. 10:123,125}

### 3783 AM, 4493 JP, 221 BC

2874. Ptolemy died before he could help Cleomenes regain his kingdom. {*Plutarch, Cleomenes, l. 1. c. 33. s. 1. 10:125} He either died of a natural sickness, {*Polybius, l. 2. c. 71. s. 2,3. 1:413} [L498] or through the wicked action of his own son, called Philopator, which name means *lover of his father* and is said to have been given to him in a sarcastic manner. Justin stated: {Justin, Trogus, l. 29. c. 1.}

> "When Ptolemy had murdered his father and his mother (whom Strabo called Agathoclia {*Strabo, l. 17. c. 1. s. 11. 8:43}), he took Egypt into his hands. Because of his vile deed of murdering his parents, he was surnamed *Philopator* by the country."

2875. Pliny stated that this Ptolemy was called by another nickname, *Tryphon*, from his effeminate and luxurious lifestyle. {*Pliny, l. 7. c. 56. (208) 2:647} The Fasti Siculi stated:

> "Ptolemy Philopator, who was also called Gallus, son of Ptolemy Euergetes, was also surnamed Tryphon...."

2876. Justin incorrectly attributed the surname of *Tryphon* to his father Euergetes. {Justin, Trogus, l. 27. c. 0.} {Justin, Trogus, l. 30. c. 0.} [E362] The collector of the Great Etymology concurred with him that the other name of *Gallus* was given to Philopator. He noted that Philopator was called Gallus because he was inclined to go about with an ivy bush around his head and other parts of his body, as was the custom of the Gauls, who were priests of Cybele. He did this when he observed the holy days of Bacchus. He was so effeminate and debauched with drinking, that when he was in his best state and uncommonly sober, he would even then run about the streets with the dancers, and bells jangling about him. {*Plutarch, Cleomenes, l. 1. c. 33. s. 1,2. 10:125} Polybius noted that he spent the whole of his reign in revellings. He gave himself over to every imaginable sensual and filthy lust of the flesh, and to daily drinking and carousing. {*Polybius, l. 5. c. 34.

3:83,85} {*Polybius, l. 5. c. 37. s. 10,11. 3:93} Strabo added that he, and all the Ptolemys who came after him, grew rich, and never managed that state well. {*Strabo, l. 17. c. 1. s. 11. 8:43} Ptolemy Philopator reigned for seventeen years. {Ptolemy, Canon of Kings} {*Clement, Stromateis, l. 1. c. 21. 2:329} {Porphyry} {*Eusebius, Chronicles, l. 1. 1:216}

2877. Philopator feared his brother Magas who, with the help of his mother Berenice, had ingratiated himself with the army. So he consulted with Sosibius, his right-hand man, and with others, how to get rid of both of them, which worried these men greatly. They feared lest the great courage of Berenice should prevail and all this matter would come to nothing. Therefore, they were forced to flatter all the court and to give them their agreement in important matters, in case their plot progressed and went on and succeeded as they had planned. However, Sosibius went further. He talked to Cleomenes, the king of Sparta, who at that time greatly needed the king's help, and who was a very wise and politically astute man with much experience in matters of the world. When he told Cleomenes of the plot, Cleomenes dissuaded him from it. He said that the king had need of more sons and brothers for the security and preservation of his kingdom, rather than to destroy those whom he already had. Sosibius had told him that the king could never be sure of the mercenary soldiers as long as Magas was alive. Cleomenes told him not to worry about that, for among his mercenaries Cleomenes had three thousand Greeks from Peloponnesus and a thousand from Crete, who would follow him if he gave the word. This encouraged Sosibius, so that he murdered Berenice and her son Magas and all their relatives. {*Polybius, l. 5. c. 36. 3:89,91} {*Polybius, l. 14. c. 12. 4:461} {*Plutarch, Cleomenes, l. 1. c. 33. 10:125,127}

2878. Philopator had first murdered his father, then his mother, and now had killed his brother, too. As though all had been well with him, he gave himself over more than ever to wanton living. All the court followed him in this lifestyle, including his friends at court and his main commanders in the army. The whole body of the army, from the highest to the lowest, eschewed martial discipline and indulged themselves in taverns and brothels. {Justin, Trogus, l. 30. c. 1.} [L499]

2879. Antiochus was advised by his counsel how to put down that rebellion of the two brothers, Molon and Alexander, in Media and Persia. Epigenes was the man who secured for Antiochus the loyalty of the army that had been gathered together for Seleucus. A man of great credit and reputation in the army, Epigenes advised that Antiochus should personally march against them with his army. Hermias, however, advised the king to go into Coelosyria himself and recover it, and instead send Xenon and Theodotus, surnamed Hemiolius, to subdue the two brothers. {*Polybius, l. 5. c. 41,42. 3:101-105}

2880. During this rebellion, and while Antiochus was besieging Zeugma in Seleucia, Diognetus, his admiral, came to him from Cappadocia escorting Laodice, the daughter of Mithridates, the king of Pontus. As soon as she arrived, Antiochus married her. When he came to Antioch from the upper regions, he had her proclaimed queen, and then he prepared for the war. {*Polybius, l. 5. c. 43. s. 1-4. 3:105}

2881. At the same time Molon, who had his brother Alexander to help him in all his affairs, marched with a large army against Xenon and Theodotus, the king's commanders. Molon and Alexander were sent into those parts and scared Xenon and Theodotus so much that they did not dare stay in the fields, but secured themselves in walled cities. At this time, Molon controlled the country of Apollonia and had plenty of provisions. {*Polybius, l. 5. c. 43. s. 5-8. 3:105,107}

### 3784a AM, 4493 JP, 221 BC

2882. Meanwhile Philip, the son of Demetrius, became king in Macedonia after the death of Antigonus, his guardian and father-in-law. He was fourteen years old and reigned forty-two years. {Justin, Trogus, l. 28. c. fin.} {Justin, Trogus, l. 29. c. 1.} Dexippus, Porphyry, Eusebius and Polybius noted that these three, Philip of Macedonia, Ptolemy Philopator of Egypt and Antiochus the Great of Syria, all came to their kingdoms within the time of the 139th Olympiad. {*Polybius, l. 2. c. 71. s. 5,6. 1:415} Antiochus became king in the first year of this Olympiad, Ptolemy Philopator succeeded his father in the third year, and Philip of Macedonia became king in the fourth year. Polybius noted that around that time almost all the kingdoms of the world had new kings. {*Polybius, l. 4. c. 2. s. 5-11. 2:301} [E363] Justin and Polybius also noted that Ariarathes became king of Cappadocia at around the same time. {Justin, Trogus, l. 29. c. 1.}

2883. After the death of Antigonus, the Aetolians united with the Lacedemonians and together fought the Achaeans and Macedonians. Cleomenes asked Philopator of Egypt if he would furnish him with means and some soldiers and allow him to return to his own country. When he realised that Philopator was not going to do this, he began asking the king more often to allow him and his small company to leave. The king cared little for the business of the state or what the result of his actions would be, and paid no attention to Cleomenes. However, Sosibius, who was the chief man of all those around the king as far as the matters of the kingdom were concerned, advised him, as well as the rest of the council, to keep Cleomenes. {*Polybius, l. 5. c. 35. 3:85-89}

2884. Molon tried to cross the Tigris River to besiege Seleucia, but was prevented in this by Zeuxis, who had taken all the boats on the river. So Molon changed his plans, went to Ctesiphon and made his winter quarters there. {*Polybius, l. 5. c. 45. s. 3,4. 3:109}

2885. Antiochus was told that Molon was coming and that his men had yielded ground to him. So he resolved to abandon going against Ptolemy in Coelosyria and instead to march in person against Molon. However, Hermias did not change his original plans and sent Xenoetas, an Achaean, against Molon with a well-outfitted army. Xenoetas had absolute power to use the army to accomplish his ends. [L500] Hermias brought the young king back again to Apamea and there assembled an army for him. {*Polybius, l. 5. c. 45. s. 5-7. 3:109,111}

2886. Xenoetas came to Seleucia with his army and sent for Diogenes, the king's governor of the province of Susa, and for Pythiades, the governor of the coasts of the Persian Gulf. Together with their forces, he marched with the Tigris River at his back. He camped with his army in the very face of the enemy. The next day, he seized Molon's camp, which Molon had left that night. The invading army started drinking and rioting in the camp. When Molon saw his opportunity, he came back the following night and attacked and recovered his camp in the dead of night, also capturing the enemy camp. Xenoetas was killed by an unknown soldier while fighting in the darkness. Molon came with his army up to Seleucia and took it with the first assault, because Zeuxis had fled the city along with Diomedon, the governor of the place. He then subdued the whole province of Babylonia, as well as the one bordering the Persian Gulf, and took the city of Susa. Leaving some troops there to besiege the citadel into which Diogenes, their commander, had fled, he returned to Seleucia on the Tigris River and refreshed his army. He took over the country that bordered the river as far as Europus, a city in those regions. In Mesopotamia, he controlled everything as far as Dura. {*Polybius, l. 5. c. 46-48. 3:113-119}

2887. After that meeting held by Sosibius, Cleomenes was committed into custody. He waited for the time when Philopator had gone to Canopus with his court, and led his keepers to believe that the king would let him go free soon. While they grew careless about him and lay fast asleep as a result of their heavy drinking, he and his friends broke out of prison at noonday. He wanted to instigate a rebellion among the people but finding himself unable to do so, and having no hope of escape left, both he and his followers killed themselves. {*Polybius, l. 5. c. 38,39. 3:95,99} This was three years after his defeat in Laconia. {*Polybius, l. 4. c. 35. s. 7,8. 2:387} When Philopator

heard of this, he commanded Cleomenes' body to be hung on a cross and executed Cleomenes' mother Cratesiclea and her sons, with all the women who attended her. {*Plutarch, Cleomenes, l. 1. c. 38. s. 2,3. 10:137}

2888. Antiochus set out from Laodicea with his whole army and having crossed the desert, he came to the defile of Marsyas, which was between Lebanon and Anti-Lebanon. He spent many days in marching his army through this defile and captured those places that were on his way, or close to it. He finally came to Gerra and Brochi, two citadels built on the narrow pass which led into this defile. These were held by Theodotus, who was an Aetolian and governor of Coelosyria for Philopator. When Antiochus saw these citadels, he planned to attack them, but when he found out that they were very strong fortifications and that Theodotus was very courageous, he abandoned the place and left. {*Polybius, l. 5. c. 59,60. 3:145-151} Theodotus was not rewarded by Philopator for this. On the contrary, when he was summoned to Alexandria, he barely escaped with his life. {*Polybius, l. 5. c. 40. s. 1-3. 3:97,99} [E364]

2889. Antiochus heard of the utter destruction and slaughter of his men with their general Xenoetas, and of Molon's victory. Through this action, all the upper provinces were now lost, and controlled by Molon. He abandoned his intended journey and thought about how to regain this lost territory. {*Polybius, l. 5. c. 48. s. 17. 3:117} Hermias could not oppose the general vote of all the rest in the council, who persuaded the king to go, but he had his way in one thing. He forged certain letters as written from Molon to Epigenes, and put them in a packet with other letters to him. By that means, he had Epigenes put to death as an informer for Molon. The king marched against Molon and coming to the Euphrates River, he added to his army the rest of his forces that were there, before arriving at Antioch, which is in Mygdonia. This was about the beginning of winter and he stayed there almost until the next spring. {*Polybius, l. 5. c. 49-51. 3:121-125} [L501]

## 3784 AM, 4494 JP, 220 BC

2890. After spending forty days there, he went on to Libba and held a council. Following the advice of Zeuxis rather than that of Hermias, he crossed over the Tigris River with all his army and marched toward Dura. At the news of his approach, the captains of Molon raised the siege of Dura. Advancing hence and marching continuously for eight days, Antiochus' troops crossed the Oreicum Mountain and came to Apollonia. {*Polybius, l. 5. c. 51,52. 3:125,127}

2891. Although Molon seriously feared that his army might abandon him, he still attacked the king. Making two wings, he put his brother Neolaus in charge of the left wing and led the other himself. When the battle started, his right wing remained loyal to him and fought very stoutly against their countrymen, but the left wing defected to the king. When Molon realised this, and saw that he was about to be wholly surrounded by the enemy, he fell upon his own sword. The rest of his friends who had been part of this conspiracy against the king, escaped to their homes and killed themselves. When the wing which Neolaus was leading surrendered to the king, Neolaus escaped to Persia to Alexander, Molon's brother. Having first killed Molon's mother and his children, Neolaus advised Alexander to kill himself and then he, too, committed suicide. The king commanded Molon's body to be hung on a cross in the most conspicuous place in Media, while he castigated his rebel army with bitter words for their foul and disloyal actions toward him. Finally, he gave them his right hand and received them back into his favour and service again. He appointed some to escort them back into Media from where they had come, and to settle them in that province again. Meanwhile, he went down from those upper parts to Seleucia, where Hermias was treating the inhabitants very harshly. Hermias planned to extract a fine of a thousand talents from them. The king reduced the fine to a hundred and fifty talents and left Diogenes to govern Media. He made Apollodorus governor of the province of Susiana and sent Tychon, the chief secretary of the army, to govern the regions bordering the Persian Gulf. {*Polybius, l. 5. c. 52-54. 3:127-135}

2892. At the time when Antiochus made this war on Molon, Theodotus, the Aetolian, who was governor under Philopator of Coelosyria, returned from Alexandria. He thought that Philopator was a worthless fellow and that he would get nothing of value from his princes. With the troops he had with him, he seized Ptolemais and Tyre through Panaetolus. Theodotus resolved to come to some agreement with Antiochus to place all Coelosyria under his control, and this he did a little later. {*Polybius, l. 5. c. 61,62. 3:151-155} {*Polybius, l. 5. c. 40. s. 1-3. 3:97,99}

2893. Attalus, king of Pergamum, had a son born of Apollinis of Cyzicum called Attalus Philadelphus, who lived eighty-two years. {*Lucian, Octogenarians, l. 1. (12) 1:233} About the same time, Antiochus had a son born to him, called Seleucus who was surnamed Philopator.

## 3785a AM, 4494 JP, 220 BC
2894. Jubilee 25

2895. After his son was born, Antiochus planned to attack Artabarzanes, who had obtained the kingdom of Atropatene and the other countries in that area.

Artabarzanes feared the coming of the king. Since he was now old and decrepit, he made peace with the king on the best terms he could get. {*Polybius, l. 5. c. 55. 3:135,137}

2896. While the war went on between Antiochus and Artabarzanes, Achaeus besieged Attalus in his capital city of Pergamum and took all the places around there. He made a league with Ptolemy Philopator of Egypt and planned to capture Syria before Antiochus could return to defend it. With the help of the Cyrrhestians, who had revolted from Antiochus, he planned to take over that kingdom. [E365] To that end, he left Lydia with his whole army and marched in the direction of Syria. [L502] When he came to Laodicea in Phrygia, he placed a crown on his head and there began to assume the title of a king. He did this whenever he received envoys from other princes and whenever he had the opportunity of writing to them. He entertained Siveris, who had been banished from his own country and who was the main one urging him on to be a king. Continuing his journey toward Syria, he approached Lycaonia, where his army began to rebel, complaining that they were fighting against Antiochus, who was their natural king. So Achaeus, seeing that his plans incited such a response, abandoned his schemes and went no farther. Moreover, he told the army that he had never planned to lead them into Syria against Antiochus, but only to waste the country of Pisidia where he was leading them. This they did, and when they had enriched themselves with its spoil, they returned home again as loyal as ever to him. {*Polybius, l. 4. c. 2. s. 5,6. 2:301} {*Polybius, l. 4. c. 48. s. 1-5. 2:417} {*Polybius, l. 5. c. 57. 3:141,143}

2897. After the war between Antiochus and Artabarzanes was over, Apollophanes, a physician of Seleucia, greatly feared Hermias. So he figured out a way to bring him into disfavour with the king. Thereupon, the king feigned to be sick and had Hermias taken from his house and murdered by some men to whom he had assigned the task. At the same time, the women of Apamea stoned Hermias' wife to death, while the boys did the same to his sons. {*Polybius, l. 5. c. 56. 3:137-141}

2898. When Antiochus had returned home and had sent his soldiers to their winter quarters, he sent many threatening letters to Achaeus. {*Polybius, l. 5. c. 57. 3:141,143}

## 3785 AM, 4495 JP, 219 BC
2899. The Jewish high priest, Onias II, died and was succeeded by his son, Simon II. {*Josephus, Antiq., l. 12. c. 4. s. 10. (225) 7:115} He was high priest for twenty years. {Eusebius, Scaliger's Greek Eusebius}

2900. At the beginning of spring, Antiochus called all his army to Apamea. Apollophanes, his physician, persuaded him to go to Seleucia, which was called Pieria.

So he sent Diognetus, his admiral, there with his fleet, and sent Theodotus Hermiolius with a suitable force to take over the passes into Coelosyria. He had received information from some informers among the Seleucians in the town, whom he had won over to him by large amounts of money and generous promises. He captured one of the suburbs and then the inhabitants opened the gates of the city to him. When he was inside, he treated the inhabitants very kindly, but put garrisons into their citadel and port. {*Polybius, l. 5. c. 58-61. 3:143-151}

2901. While the king was busy in settling matters there, he received letters from Theodotus, the Aetolian, to ask him to go into Coelosyria. He was now ready to turn it over to the king. Consequently, the king marched there, but Nicolaus, a captain of Philopator's, discovered this plot and besieged Theodotus in Ptolemais. When Nicolaus heard of Antiochus' arrival, he raised the siege and sent Lagoras, a Cretian, and Dorymenes of Aetolia, with troops to hold the pass that led into Coelosyria near Berytus. Antiochus easily defeated these troops. When Theodotus and Panaetolus saw the siege raised from before Ptolemais, where they and their friends had been confined, they went and met Antiochus on the way. They turned over Tyre and Ptolemais and all that was in them to Antiochus. In these two ports, they found forty ships which were turned over to Diognetus, the admiral. {*Polybius, l. 5. c. 61,62. 3:151-155} {*Polybius, l. 4. c. 37. s. 4,5. 2:393}

2902. Antiochus was told that Philopator had gone to Memphis, that all Ptolemy's forces were gathered at Pelusium and the sluices of the Nile had all been opened to let the sea in to spoil all the fresh water there. So he changed his plans of marching to Pelusium and went into Coelosyria, where he went from one place to another and sought to subdue them all. Some he took by force and others surrendered, based on the reasonable conditions he offered them. The weaker places generally yielded to him when he first asked. The rest remained loyal to Philopator, their king, and Antiochus spent much time in besieging them. {*Polybius, l. 5. c. 62. s. 4-6. 3:155} [L503]

2903. Meanwhile, Philopator did not concern himself with anything. But Agathocles and Sosibius, who managed everything under him, prepared for war. They kept everything as secret as they could, so Antiochus would not know what was happening. They secretly solicited help from the states of Cyzicum, Byzantium, Rhodes, Aetolia and others to mediate for a peace between the two kings. In the interim, they made every provision possible for the war that they could. To the best of their ability, they trained and exercised their men in all types of feats of chivalry and martial discipline. {*Polybius, l. 4. c. 38. s. 5,6. 2:393} {*Polybius, l. 5. c. 62,63. 3:155,157} [E366]

2904. At this time, there was a new war between the Byzantines and the Rhodians. The cause of the war was the fact that the Byzantines were being forced to pay a heavy tribute to the Gauls, and hence were charging a toll on every ship that passed by them into the Pontus Sea. {*Polybius, l. 1. c. 6. s. 6. 1:17} {*Polybius, l. 4. c. 37,38. 2:393,395} {*Polybius, l. 4. c. 46,47. 2:413,415}

2905. Thereupon, the Rhodians sent to Prusias, king of Bithynia. (That was the Prusias whom Memnon surnamed *The Lame*.) {Memnon, Excerpts, c. 29.} They made an alliance with him, even though, previously, he had normally been their enemy. But because the Byzantines were trying to form an alliance with Attalus and Achaeus, who were hostile to Prusias, he now came to this agreement with the Rhodians. They would take charge of the war at sea and he would conduct the war on land. He immediately seized Hieron, which had been a port of theirs on the Asian side. This place had previously been owned by the merchants who traded in the Pontus, but the Byzantines had recently bought them out. They themselves used it, as well as all that portion of Mysia in Asia which they had controlled many years earlier. {*Polybius, l. 4. c. 47-50. 2:415-421}

2906. When the Byzantines saw the Rhodians had an alliance with Prusias, they tried to get help from Attalus and Achaeus. Attalus wanted to help, but because Achaeus was pressing so heavily on him, he could offer very little help. Achaeus, whose dominions stretched far and near on the west side of the Taurus Mountains and who had recently assumed the title of king, promised them all the help that he could give. {*Polybius, l. 4. c. 48. s. 1-3. 2:417} They also sent for Tiboetes from Macedonia to be their general in this war against Prusias. They thought that the whole kingdom of Bithynia belonged as much to Tiboetes as to Prusias, the nephew of Tiboetes. {*Polybius, l. 4. c. 50. s. 9,10. 2:423}

2907. Prusias feared the coming of his uncle Tiboetes and pulled down all citadels and places of any strength that existed in the kingdom. {*Polybius, l. 4. c. 52. s. 8,9. 2:427}

2908. The Rhodians tried to draw away Achaeus from helping the Byzantines. They sent to Ptolemy, because they wanted him to give them Andromachus, who at that time was a prisoner in Alexandria. They wanted to present him to his son Achaeus as a gift from them. When this had been done, along with some other deeds of honour extended to him by the Rhodians, the Byzantines lost their main supporter in the war. When Tiboetes was being escorted from Macedonia, he died on the way, which greatly thwarted their purposes. Cavarus was a petty king of the Gauls who lived in Thrace. {*Polybius, l. 8. c. 22. 3:505} {*Athenaeus, l. 6. (252d) 3:137}

He came to Byzantium at that time and mediated a peace between Byzantium and Prusias and the Rhodians. *[L504]* The Byzantines agreed to stop charging any more tolls on their ships and Prusias was to restore what he had taken from Byzantium. {*Polybius, l. 4. c. 52. s. 3-10. 2:425,427*}

*2909.* At the same time, Mithridates, king of Pontus, made war on the people of Sinope. These had borrowed a hundred and forty thousand drachmas from the Rhodians, money which they used to fortify their city and the whole of the peninsula on which their city was located. {*Polybius, l. 4. c. 56. 2:433,435*}

## 3786a AM, 4495 JP, 219 BC

*2910.* Antiochus besieged Dura in Phoenicia, a city which Claudius Ptolemy called Adora. But because the place was naturally well fortified, he could not take it. Nicolaus, a captain of Philopator's, sent them relief. Because winter was coming, Antiochus was content to make a truce with them for four months, which some envoys sent by Philopator had persuaded him to do. He would not grant a longer truce, nor spend more time there than necessary, away from his own dominions. It was obvious that Achaeus intended to invade his kingdom and there was no doubt that Philopator was helping Achaeus. Therefore, he sent away the envoys and put garrisons in suitable places. He left everything there to the care of Theodotus, while he returned to Seleucia. He sent his army to their winter quarters but made no effort to keep them in military condition. He thought that the rest of the cities would submit to him without a great deal of fighting, because he had already acquired a part of Coelosyria and Phoenicia. So he thought he could win the war with words, rather than by fighting. {*Polybius, l. 5. c. 66. 3:159-163*}

## 3786 AM, 4496 JP, 218 BC

*2911.* In the spring, however, events did not unfold as he had planned. He took his army from their winter quarters and intended to attack his enemies by sea and land, and to subdue by force the remainder of Coelosyria that was withstanding him. {*Polybius, l. 5. c. 68. s. 1,2. 3:167*}

*2912.* Philopator committed the charge of all his wars to Nicolaus, the Aetolian, and made Gaza the storehouse for the war effort, placing all his provisions for the war there. *[E367]* He sent his armies by land and sea, appointing Perigenes as the admiral of his naval forces. Even though he only had thirty war ships, he had four hundred cargo ships. {*Polybius, l. 5. c. 68. s. 2-6. 3:167,169*}

*2913.* Antiochus had marched as far as Marathus when envoys came to him from the isle of Aradus, desiring his friendship. He agreed to this, and also settled the differences between them and their neighbours who lived on the continent, making them good friends after that. Antiochus entered into Phoenicia by way of Theuprosopon and came to Berytus. On his way, he attacked Botrys and took it. He burned Trieres and Calamus to the ground. {*Polybius, l. 5. c. 68. s. 6-8. 3:169*}

*2914.* Before the main battle, he divided his army into three parts. He gave one part to Theodotus, the other to Menedemus and the third he reserved for the naval battle under the command of Diocles. He had made Diocles the governor of Parapotamia, which bordered on the Euphrates River. Antiochus, with bodyguards around him for protection, went to see how the battle was going and to help if needed. Diognetus prepared the naval forces for Antiochus and Perigenes did the same for Philopator. Each kept as close to the land as he possibly could. At last, when a general signal was given, the battle was joined on land and sea. At sea, neither side won and they parted on even terms. On land, Theodotus routed Nicolaus after a strong fight. In the chase, two thousand of Nicolaus' men were killed and at least that many taken prisoner, while the rest fled into Sidon. *[L505]* When Perigenes saw that the land battle had been lost, he retreated by sea to Sidon. Without delay, Antiochus came there with his whole army and besieged it. He did not attack it, because there were many men inside it and they had many provisions to keep them alive. {*Polybius, l. 5. c. 69,70. 3:171,173*}

*2915.* When Publius Cornelius Scipio and Tiberius Sempronius Longus were consuls at Rome, Hannibal made a difficult crossing of the Alps and came down into Italy in the summer of that year. {*Livy, l. 21. c. 18. s. 1. 5:49*} {*Livy, l. 21. c. 38. 5:111,113*} This was in the latter end of the second year of the 140th Olympiad, and it is from that time that we indicate the start of the second Carthaginian War, or the War of Hannibal. This is described in detail by Polybius and Livy. Silius Italicus described it in poetry, and Appian in his history. {*Appian, Hannibalic War, l. 7. c. 1-9. (1-61) 1:305-399*} This war enhanced the fame of the Carthaginians and Romans all over the world. The effect was first felt in Greece, then in Asia, properly so called, and its islands. All men began to look to them and no longer to Philip, Antiochus or Ptolemy. {*Polybius, l. 5. c. 105. s. 7,8. 3:253*}

*2916.* In the same summer that Hannibal came into Italy, Antiochus attacked Palestine. He ordered Diognetus, his admiral, to take his foot soldiers to Tyre. Antiochus himself marched with his army to Philoteria, a city seated on the Lake of Tiberias, into which the Jordan River flowed. From there, the river ran through the country adjoining the city of Scythopolis, which Josephus called Bethshan in the tribe of Manasseh. When he had captured both of these cities and left garrisons to hold them, he crossed the mountains and came to Atabyrium. This was the city called Tabor, which was located on a hill whose top was almost two miles in circumference. Antiochus drew them out in small skirmishes. He had his vanguard go close to the walls and then feign to flee, all of which they did. When the townsmen came out and pursued them, they were attacked by those who lay in ambush, so that many were killed. With the remainder of the army, Antiochus then attacked and captured the city. {*Polybius, l. 5. c. 70. s. 1-10. 3:173,175}

2917. At the same time, Ceraeas, a commander of Ptolemy Philopator, defected from him to Antiochus. Antiochus received him so graciously that Hippolochus of Thessaly defected with his entire cavalry of four hundred. Antiochus left a strong garrison in Atabysium and went and subdued Pella, Camus and Gephrus, which surrendered to him. After this great success, the Arabians, who bordered on those parts, unanimously joined their forces with those of Antiochus. Antiochus was encouraged by these events and trusted in the resources of Arabia. He marched into the country of Galatis, subdued the area and took the city of Abila. All the men who were under the command of Nicias came to help them. Only Gadara remained to be taken, and it was reputed to be by far the strongest city in all that region. So Antiochus came and showed himself before it. He began to cast up his works against them, and the very sight of this so terrified the inhabitants that they surrendered to him. {*Polybius, l. 5. c. 70,71. 3:175}

2918. In the same summer in Pamphylia, the people of Pednelissus were besieged by the Selgians and were in danger of being taken. They sent and asked for help from Achaeus, who immediately sent six thousand foot soldiers and five hundred cavalry under the command of Garsieres. [E368] He planned to enter the town by way of the pass of Milyas, but found that the Selgians controlled the passes, so he made out as if he were leaving. When the Selgians saw him go, they went on their way too. Some went to the camp and others to their harvest, which was ready to be gathered. [L506] Once Gasieres was sure of this, he turned back quickly and without any opposition, crossed the pass of Milyas near Climax. There he left a strong guard and then committed the whole war and defence of Pednelissus to Phaylus. He was going to Perga, and stirred up all the people of Pamphylia and Pisidia to come and help the distressed citizens of Pednelissus. Thereupon, the people of Aspendus sent them four thousand foot soldiers and those of Aetenna sent eight thousand men. Because of their rash actions, the Selgians were badly defeated and

lost ten thousand men. They fled home to Selge with Phaylus in close pursuit. They were so afraid that they immediately sent Logbasis to sue for peace, but instead he betrayed them. When a truce was declared, the enemy soldiers came freely into Selge. The townspeople secretly sent to Achaeus and put themselves at his mercy, to deal with them as he thought best. Meanwhile, Logbasis plotted to betray the town to their enemies. When his plan was ready to be carried out, his plot was discovered and they executed him, his fellow conspirators and all the enemies in the area. Then Achaeus began seriously to negotiate a peace between them, to which the men of Selge were agreeable. It was agreed that they were to pay four hundred talents initially and a further three hundred later. The Pednelissians were to restore all their prisoners to them without ransom. When Achaeus had acquired control of Milyas and the greater part of Pamphylia, he immediately marched to Sardis. After having constantly harassed Attalus in war, he now began to threaten Prusias. {*Polybius, l. 5. c. 72-77. 3:179-191}

2919. While Achaeus was busy in making war against the men of Selge, Attalus was not idle. He enlisted the Gauls of Europe, called the Tectosagians. He had sent for them from Europe to fight against Achaeus, because of their reputation for valour. He marched through the cities of Aeolia and other nearby cities, which had all submitted to Achaeus out of fear. All Cyme, Smyrna and Phocaea voluntarily yielded to Attalus. Those of Aegae and Temnus yielded to him out of fear at his first approach. Envoys came to him from the Teians and Colophonians, and when they had given hostages, he controlled them subject to the conditions they had been under before. Continuing on, he crossed the Lycus River and came into the country inhabited by the Mysians. Passing through that, he came to the borders of the Carseae. He so frightened these people, and the men who kept Didymatiche and Themistocles, whom Achaeus had left to be held for him, that they surrendered them to Attalus. He moved on from there and ravaged all the plain of Apia, passed Mount Pellicas and camped on the bank of the Megistus River. While he was there, the moon was totally eclipsed. The Gauls were weary of so long an expedition with their wives and children in their company, and so pretended that this eclipse was a bad omen and refused to go any farther. On September 1, near the beginning of the night, the moon was eclipsed for more than an hour. {*Polybius, l. 5. c. 77,78. 3:191,193}

2920. Attalus feared that his Gauls might defect to Achaeus and so attack his countries. He did not kill them because they came from Europe to Asia on the promise he would not harm them. So he escorted them all back safely to the Hellespont where they had first landed, gave them lands to live on and promised that, if at any later time they should need his help, he would be ready to aid them. He summoned the men of Lampsacus, Alexandria, Troas and Illium and commended them for remaining loyal to him, after which he returned with his army to Pergamum. {*Polybius, l. 5. c. 78. 3:193,195}

### 3787a AM, 4496 JP, 218 BC

2921. Antiochus was told that a large enemy army was assembled in the Arabian city of Rabbatamana, or Rabbath-Ben-Ammon. [L507] After Antiochus had plundered all the country around there, he marched toward the city. He approached the little hills where the city stood, and went and viewed the enemy. He learned that there were only two ways to get into the city, so he located his batteries against those two places to break down the wall. Nicarchus was in charge of the one site and Theodotus the other. When they breached the wall, much to their surprise, the inhabitants quickly repaired the breaches. Though Antiochus' men laboured day and night without stopping, and with all their might, to get into the city, they were unable to do so, because the damage was repaired as fast as they could inflict it. Finally, one of the prisoners in the camp showed them an underground way that the inhabitants used to get their water. [E369] He quickly sealed it up and the city was forced to surrender for lack of water. When the king had captured the place, he left Nicarchus, with an adequate garrison, to hold it. He sent Hippolochus and Ceraeas, who had defected from Ptolemy, with five thousand foot soldiers to the country adjoining Samaria, to govern that province and to protect his friends in those regions. He himself went with his army to Ptolemais to winter there. {*Polybius, l. 5. c. 71. s. 3-12. 3:175-179}

### 3787b AM, 4497 JP, 217 BC

2922. Gnaeus Servilius started his consulship at Rome on the Ides of March (March 15). Among the omens that were told to the Senate was the fact that in Sardinia the sun was dimmer than it normally was. In Apri, the sun and the moon seemed to fight with each other. {*Livy, l. 22. c. 1. s. 5-13. 5:199-203} Gaius Flamminius, the other consul, who was with the army in the spring of this year, was disastrously defeated by Hannibal at Lake Trasimene in Etruria. He and fifteen thousand of his men were killed. {*Livy, l. 22. c. 4-7. 5:213-223} On February 11 there was an eclipse of the sun in Sardinia.

### 3787c AM, 4497 JP, 217 BC

2923. Polybius stated that as well as that great battle at Trasimene, another battle was fought in the east between Antiochus and Philopator, over Coelosyria.

{*Polybius, l. 5. c. 105. s. 3. 3:253} This was fought toward the latter end of the third year of the 140th Olympiad, at a place called Raphia. He described it thus: {*Polybius, l. 5. c. 80. s. 3-6. 3:197}

"In the beginning of this spring, Antiochus and Ptolemy had made final preparations for war. The fate of Coelosyria was to be decided in the next battle. Therefore, Ptolemy left Alexandria with seventy thousand foot soldiers, five thousand cavalry and seventy-three elephants. {*Polybius, l. 5. c. 79. s. 1-3. 3:197} First, he camped at Pelusium, where he stayed until the rest of his army came to him. When he had given every man his allowance of grain, he marched on through a desert country near the Casius Mountains and Barathra and came to Gaza. After a five-day march, he came to his planned destination and camped within six miles of Raphia. This is the first city of Coelosyria, except for Rhinocolura, which a man would meet when he leaves Egypt for Coelosyria."

2924. At the same time, Antiochus arrived there with his army of sixty-two thousand foot soldiers, six thousand cavalry and a hundred and two elephants. Passing the walls of Raphia, he camped on the first night about two thousand yards from Ptolemy's camp, while the next day he came within a thousand yards of it. {*Polybius, l. 5. c. 80. s. 4-7. 3:197,199}

2925. At that time, Theodotus, the Aetolian, who had previously been well-known in Ptolemy's court and knew his daily routine well, tried to kill Ptolemy. [L508] About the break of day, he and two others came inside his trenches. The next night they got into the king's pavilion, hoping to kill him while he was alone. However, Dositheus, who was a Jew by birth but no longer observed the Jewish religion, had moved the king to another tent. He had common men occupy the king's bed that night. When Theodotus broke into the king's tent that night, he wounded two of the guards and killed Andreas, the king's chief physician. So the king returned untouched to his own tent again. {*Polybius, l. 5. c. 81. 3:199} {RApc 3 Ma 1:2,3}

2926. After the armies had camped there for five days, the battle started. {*Polybius, l. 5. c. 82. s. 1,2. 3:199,201} When Antiochus appeared to be winning, Arsinoe, Ptolemy's sister, went among the soldiers with her hair hanging about her ears and cried to them that they should fight bravely and defend their own wives and children. She promised them that if they won, they would each be given two minas in gold. This revitalised the army and they killed many of the enemy and took many prisoners. {*Polybius, l. 5. c. 83. 3:203,205} {RApc 3 Ma 1:4,5}

2927. In that battle, Antiochus lost almost ten thousand foot soldiers and more than three hundred cavalry, while more than four thousand were taken prisoner. Three elephants were killed in the battle and two died later from their wounds. Ptolemy lost fifteen hundred foot soldiers and seven hundred cavalry. Sixteen of his elephants were killed and the rest were captured. {*Polybius, l. 5. c. 86. s. 4-6. 3:211}

2928. When Antiochus had buried his dead, he returned home with the rest of his army. Ptolemy went back again to Raphia and the rest of the places that had been taken from him. They voluntarily surrendered to him and vied with each other to be the first to recognise his kingship. This was particularly true of the Coelosyrians, because they had always been inclined to serve the Ptolemys. On this occasion, they exceeded all others in honouring him with crowns, sacrifices, altars and other expressions of their affection. {*Polybius, l. 5. c. 86. s. 7-11. 3:211,213} Ptolemy visited the nearby cities and bestowed gifts on their temples, thereby encouraging the people to remain loyal to him. {RApc 3Ma 1:6,7} [E370]

2929. The Jews sent some of their Sanhedrin and elders to offer him their service and to present him with gifts. They congratulated him after so great a victory, but he happened to be more anxious to visit their city and honour it with his presence. When he came, he greatly admired the beauty of their temple and would have gone into the Holy of Holies. Only the high priest could enter there, and then only once a year. When the Jews refused that request, the king wanted all the more to enter it. He went into the temple, and all the temple was filled with crying and howling, and the city was in a tumult. Then Simon, the high priest, knelt down in the temple, that is between the temple and the altar, and prayed to God for help in this time of trouble. Thereupon, the king fell into such a horror of mind and body that he was unable to speak, and was carried half dead from the temple. {RApc 3Ma 1:8-2:33}

2930. As soon as Antiochus had returned to Antioch, he sent Antipater, his brother's son, and Theodotus Hemiolius as his envoys to Ptolemy to sue for peace between them. [L509] Ptolemy was content with this surprise victory and with the recovery of Coelosyria. After a few sharp words with the envoys and complaining about the unjust dealings of Antiochus, he granted a truce for a year. He sent Sosibius to ratify it with Antiochus. {*Polybius, l. 5. c. 87. s. 1-6. 3:213} {Justin, Trogus, l. 30. c. 1.}

### 3787d AM, 4497 JP, 217 BC

2931. When Ptolemy had spent three months in Syria and Phoenicia settling matters there, he left Andromachus from Aspendus in Asia to govern all that country, while he returned to Alexandria with his friends and his sister Arsinoe. His subjects, knowing his lifestyle, marvelled at his success in this war against Antiochus. Antiochus ratified the truce in the presence of Sosibius and began a war on Achaeus, as he had previously planned to do. {*Polybius, l. 5. c. 87. s. 6-8. 3:213,215}

### 3788 AM, 4498 JP, 216 BC

2932. Antiochus spent the winter in making his provisions with every possible care. The next spring he crossed the Taurus Mountains and having made a league with Attalus, he started his war on Achaeus, {*Polybius, l. 5. c. 107. s. 4. 3:257} by besieging him in Sardis. Daily there were skirmishes between the two sides, as each side tried to get the upper hand by any means they could. {*Polybius, l. 7. c. 15. s. 1. 3:437}

2933. When the Gauls whom Attalus had settled in the Hellespont besieged the city of Illium, the inhabitants of Alexandria Troas sent their captain Themistes with four thousand men. He expelled them from all the territories of Troas. He took all their provisions and attacked them on every side. When the Gauls could no longer stay there, they went and took over the city of Arisba and the territories of Abydus, using them as a base to take over the rest of the surrounding country. Thereupon, Prusias, king of Bithynia, went out and attacked them. After he had defeated them, he attacked their camp and slaughtered their wives and children and any of them that remained, giving their spoil to his soldiers as their reward. {*Polybius, l. 5. c. 111. s. 1-7. 3:265}

2934. When Ptolemy returned to Egypt, he resumed his old lifestyle and wallowed in all manner of gluttony and luxury. {*Polybius, l. 14. c. 12. s. 3. 4:461} He grew increasingly mad because of this way of living, in which he indulged himself with uncleanness and lechery. He also vexed the Jews of Alexandria with infamous and false reports spread against them. He tried by every means to turn them away from the true worship of the living God, and commanded that those who refused be killed. He expelled them from all offices of dignity, and with hot irons branded them in the face with the sign of an ivy leaf, which was the sign of Bacchus. He allowed those that abandoned their religion, to enjoy equal rights and privileges with the native Macedonians in Alexandria. {RApc 3Ma 2:25-30}

2935. Many abandoned their religion and others bought their peace with money. They saved their lives and escaped having their faces branded. Those who continued in the religion of their forefathers, while remaining loyal to the king, excommunicated and had no dealings with those who had apostatised from their religion. By this action, the Jew's enemies assumed that they really opposed the king and were trying to make his subjects defect. *[E371]* *[L510]* Philopator became very angry with the Jews in Alexandria and throughout all Egypt. He ordered that they be gathered into one place so he could destroy them all. The king's officers were allowed forty days to do this, from the 25th day of the month of Pachon to the 4th day of the month of Epeiph, according to the fixed year of Alexandria. Some later historians assumed, without any basis, that this calendar was never used until after the naval battle at Actium between Augustus and Antony. This period was from May 20 to June 29. Three days were allotted for the massacre, that is, from the 5th to the 7th of Epeiph, inclusively. {*RApc 3Ma 2:31-4:21 6:38,39*}

2936. At the appointed time, the Jews of Alexandria were all brought into the hippodrome. They were first reviled and humiliated by all that passed by. Then the king called for Hermon, the master of the elephants. He ordered him to cause his five hundred elephants to drink wine mingled with myrrh or frankincense before the following day. This would make them become more fierce and completely mad. He would then let them go and drive them on the Jews, to tear and trample them all to pieces. The next day, the king fell into a dead sleep and did not awake until dinner-time. By that time all the people that had come there to see the event had gone home again. On the third day, when the elephants were all prepared and ready to attack the Jews, two angels appeared, who were very terrible to look at. They came down from heaven and so amazed all the people who were there, that they stood still and did not move. The king fell into a trance and relented of his fury toward those poor prisoners. Most interestingly, the elephants did not attack the Jews, but turned around and attacked and trampled the soldiers behind them. {*RApc 3Ma 5:1-6:21*}

2937. Then the king commended the Jews for their loyalty and released them from their fetters. He acknowledged that their God had delivered them. For a period of seven days, from the 7th to the 14th of Epeiph (July 2-9), he feasted them. After this, the Jews obtained permission from the king to execute those Jews who had apostatised from their religion. They maintained that those who, for their belly's sake, had forsaken the laws and commandments of their God, would never prove loyal to their king. They killed three hundred on the way as they moved around from place to place, before finally coming to Ptolemais on the Nile River in Arsinoise's Nome. (A Nome is an administrative division of ancient Egypt. Editor.) It is called *Rhodophorus* from the abundance of roses which grew there. Their fleet attended them there for seven days, while they all made a feast of thanksgiving together. The king himself gave every man a generous allowance for his homeward expenses, and so they returned home joyfully. Some went by land, others by sea, and some by the river. {*RApc 3Ma 6:22-7:23*}. Phlostorgius, in the beginning of his *Ecclesiastical History*, called his book the *Librum Portentosum*, that is a *Book of Miracles*.

2938. The Egyptians grew insolent and proud because of their success against Antiochus at the battle of Raphia. They never liked Philopator after that, so they sought a captain of their own, with enough power to quell the likes of him. This they did shortly thereafter. {*Polybius, l. 5. c. 107. s. 1-3. 3:257*}

### 3789 AM, 4499 JP, 215 BC

2939. Philopator was now forced to make war on his rebellious subjects. {*Polybius, l. 5. c. 107. s. 1. 3:257*} His recent actions ensured the loyalty of the Jews. Eusebius and Jornandes stated that about this time there were approximately sixty thousand Jews killed in a battle. {*Eusebius, Chronicles, l. 1. 1:216*} {*Jornandes, De Regnorum ac Temporum Succession*} *[L511]* Such a large slaughter may have been what prompted Demetrius, who wrote a book of the Kings of the Jews, to think it reasonable to record the years from the captivity of Babylon, or the carrying-away of the Jews into Assyria, down to the reign of this Philopator. This was noted by Clement of Alexandria. {*Clement, Stromateis, l. 1. c. 21. 2:332*} From there we gather that Demetrius, the historian, wrote after the days of Philopator but before that vast desolation brought upon the Jews by Antiochus Epiphanes. Had he known of the latter, he would have described it in the same terms in which he described the earlier calamities of the Jews.

2940. With the exception of the citadel, the city of Sardis was taken by Antiochus through the work of Lagoras, the Cretian, in the second year after Antiochus besieged it. {*Polybius, l. 7. c. 15-18. 3:437-445*}

2941. Sosibius managed all the affairs in Egypt, under Philopator. He conferred with Bolis, a Cretian, how to deliver Achaeus, who was besieged in the citadel at Sardis, from this danger. *[E372]* Bolis made an arrangement with Cambylus, the captain of the Cretians who served under Antiochus, and got Achaeus out of the citadel, but Sosibius delivered him alive into Antiochus' hands. Antiochus first had his hands and his feet cut off. Then he had his head chopped off and sewn into an ass's belly, while his body was hung on a cross. In the citadel, some sided with Ariobazus, the governor of Sardis, others with Laodice, the widow of Achaeus and daughter of Mithridates, king of Pontus, since these two were at odds with each other, but they quickly resolved to surrender themselves and the citadel to Antiochus. {*Polybius, l. 8. c. 15-34. 3:481-501*}

## 3790 AM, 4500 JP, 214 BC

*2942.* Lacydes of Cyrene was the head of the new academy for twenty-six years. He was the only man who resigned the position while he was alive. He turned it over to Telecles and Evander, both from Phocaea. {*Diogenes Laertius, Lacydes, l. 4. c. 8. (60,61) 1:437*}

## 3792 AM, 4502 JP, 212 BC

*2943.* Antiochus attacked Media and Parthia, and other provinces which had revolted from his ancestors. {*Appian, Syrian Wars, l. 11. c. 11. (65) 2:231*} He made an expedition against Arsaces, who was the main founder of the Parthian Empire. {*Polybius, l. 10. c. 27-31. 4:165-179*}

## 3793 AM, 4503 JP, 211 BC

*2944.* When Publius Sulpicius and Gnaeus Fulvius were consuls of Rome, the praetor Laevinus made a league with the Aetolians in Greece and Attalus, king of Pergamum, in Asia. {*Livy, l. 26. c. 26. 7:91-95*} {*Justin, Trogus, l. 29. c. 4.*} {*Eutropius, l. 3.*} Attalus kept the agreement with the Romans until he died. {*Polybius, l. 18. c. 41. s. 9,10. 5:177*}

## 3794 AM, 4504 JP, 210 BC

*2945.* Marcus Atilius and Manius Acilius were sent as envoys from Rome to Ptolemy and Cleopatra at Alexandria in Egypt, to remind them of the league and to renew it. They gave him a purple toga and tunic, and a throne made entirely of ivory, while she received an embroidered palla and a purple cloak. {*Livy, l. 27. c. 4. s. 10. 7:215*} {*Justin, Trogus, l. 30. c. 1,4.*} {*OED—palla: A loose outer garment or wrap worn out of doors by women (sometimes by men); an outer robe, mantle.*}

## 3795 AM, 4505 JP, 209 BC

*2946.* Ptolemy Epiphanes was born to Ptolemy Philopator by his wife Eurydice, who was also his sister. When Ptolemy Epiphanes was five years old, he succeeded his father in the kingdom of Egypt. {*Justin, Trogus, l. 30. c. 1,2.*} First, his birthday was solemnly celebrated by all the great men and other citizens of Syria and the countries in his dominion. [L512] Every man made the journey to Alexandria to congratulate him on the birth of his son. Among these was Joseph, the Jew, the son of Tobias and of the daughter of Simon the Just, the high priest. Joseph was the collector of Ptolemy's tributes throughout Syria, Phoenicia and Palestine. He sent his youngest son Hyrcanus, who was born of the daughter of Solimius, his older brother, to kiss the king's hand. He sent letters to his agent Arion, who managed all his money at Alexandria, where he had over three thousand talents. Arion was to supply him with money to buy the most expensive present for the king that that money could buy. The most expensive present the king had received to that point was not worth more than ten talents. Hyrcanus brought with him a hundred beautiful boys and as many

maidens, and gave them a thousand talents to offer to the king. The boys were a gift for the king and the girls a gift for Cleopatra, the queen. The king greatly admired so magnificent and unexpected a present as this, and royally entertained the young man with every honour and royal gifts. He wrote royal letters of commendation to Joseph's father and brethren, and to all his commanders and chief officers in those parts, and then dismissed Joseph in a most honourable fashion. But Joseph's brethren (who were seven in number but begotten by another wife) were jealous of the great honour the king had extended to him, so they met him on the way, intending to murder him. Though his father was aware of this, he did not care, because he was angry with him for the extravagant cost of the gift he had given to the king. When his brothers attacked him, he killed two of them, along with various others in their company. When he reached Jerusalem, no man there would look upon him, so, fearing the worst, he exiled himself to the regions beyond Jordan. {*Josephus, Antiq., l. 12. c. 4. s. 7-9. (196-222) 7:101-113*}

## 3796a AM, 4505 JP, 209 BC

*2947.* Philip, king of Macedonia, fought two battles against the Aetolians. Although they received help from Rome, and from Attalus the king, as well as receiving ships from Prusias, king of Bithynia, they were defeated both times. Attalus and Publius Sulpicius, the proconsul in those regions, wintered that year in the isle of Aegina. {*Livy, l. 27. c. 33. 7:343*} {*Polybius, l. 10. c. 41. 4:203-207*}

## 3796 AM, 4506 JP, 208 BC

*2948.* At the beginning of spring, Sulpicius and Attalus joined together and sailed to Lemnos. From there, they came into Euboea and captured the cities of Oreum and Opus. When Attalus heard that Prusias, the king of Bithynia, had invaded his kingdom, he left the Romans and the war in Aetolia and sailed into Asia. Philip came to Aetolia, where he had arranged for some envoys from Ptolemy and from the Rhodians to meet him. [E373] While they tried to end the war in Aetolia, news arrived that Machanidas, the tyrant of Lacedemon, was ready to attack the Eleans while these were busy about their solemn games at Olympus. {*Livy, l. 28. c. 5-7. 8:17-29*} This summer began the 143rd Olympiad.

## 3797 AM, 4507 JP, 207 BC

*2949.* Polybius stated that Arsinoe, the queen and sister of Ptolemy, was murdered by Philammon, as arranged for by Sosibius. {*Polybius, l. 15. c. 25. s. 1-13. 4:519-523*} Justin stated that Philopator killed Eurydice, who was his wife and sister. {*Justin, Trogus, l. 30. c. 1.*} It seems that Polybius' Arsinoe, Justin's Eurydice and Livy's and Josephus' Cleopatra were all the same person.' {*See note on 3794 AM. <<2945>>*} {*See note on 3795 AM. <<2946>>*}

*2950.* When she was dead, whatever her name was, Philopator fell in love with Agathoclia, a female musician, and with her brother Agathocles in a homosexual way. To everyone's amazement, he put Agathocles in charge of his kingdom. But he was not familiar with the ways of the court or state affairs, so Agathoclia and Agathocles had the assistance of their mother Oenanthe. She endeared herself to the king, winning his affection through her children. Agathocles always stayed near the king and ruled the whole state, while the two women gave all the offices and military positions of the state to whomever they pleased. The king himself, who was now in their hands, had the least power and authority of anyone in his own kingdom. {*Polybius, l. 15. c. 25. s. 1-24. 4:519-527} {Justin, Trogus, l. 30. c. 1,2.} {Plutarch, Eroticus (Dialogue on Love?)} {*Plutarch, Cleomenes, l. 1. c. 33. s. 4. 10:125} {*Athenaeus, l. 6. (251e) 3:135} {*Athenaeus, l. 13. (576f) 6:113} {Jerome, Da 11} [L513]*

*2951.* The people were looking for someone who could execute their anger on Agathocles and Agathoclia. They were forced to bide their time for the present, and placed their hopes on Tlepolemus. {*Polybius, l. 15. c. 25. s. 25. 4:527}* This young man conducted himself well and had done military exploits. At that time, he was managing the king's treasure. But because he used the funds not as an officer, but rather like a young heir, he was soon disliked, then hated, by the royal court. Ptolemy, the son of Sosibius (of whom I spoke earlier), returned with the other envoys from Philip in Macedonia, where it seems they had been sent the previous year. When he began to speak his mind rather freely about Tlepolemus, he found that every man at court agreed with him. {*Polybius, l. 16. c. 21,22. 5:43-47}*

## 3798 AM, 4508 JP, 206 BC

*2952.* This discontent was fanned when the courtiers complained about Tlepolemus in a public assembly. In his defence, Tlepolemus planned to accuse them all to the king. Sosibius heard this. He had both the keeping of the king's seal and custody of the king. He gave the seal to Tlepolemus, who thereafter ran everything in the state just as he pleased. {*Polybius, l. 16. c. 22. s. 7-11. 1-5:47,49}*

## 3799 AM, 4509 JP, 205 BC

*2953.* During the consulship of Publius Cornelius Scipio and Publius Licinius Crassus, the college of the Decemviri found the following written in Sibylline books which they kept:

> "Whenever a foreign enemy were to make war on Italy, he might be driven out again and overcome if the image of the mother of the gods at Ida, which had fallen from heaven, were sent for and brought to Rome."

*2954.* Consequently, five envoys were sent to King Attalus to desire the image from him and to bring her to them by sea. These five each had a ship of five tiers of oars for the journey. To obtain a favourable reply, they were to ingratiate themselves as soon as they arrived and to promote a good opinion of the Roman name and the majesty of their state. Attalus received and entertained these envoys very benevolently at Pergamum. He led them to Pessinus in Phrygia and turned the sacred stone over to them which the people who lived there said was the mother of the gods. He asked them to take it to Rome as they had requested. {*Livy, l. 29. c. 10,11. 8:245-249}*

*2955.* Justin stated that Antiochus' expedition subdued all the upper provinces of Asia as far as Bactria. There he spent a long time trying unsuccessfully to expel Euthydemus from that province. He was finally forced to come to an agreement and make a league with him. To ratify this, Euthydemus sent his own son Demetrius to Antiochus. Antiochus saw his behaviour and judged him a man worthy to be a king. First, he promised to give him one of his daughters to marry, then he gave his father permission to assume the title of king. Lastly, they subscribed to the other articles of the league between them, and Antiochus took his oath for their true observance. Then Antiochus distributed provisions generously among his soldiers and moved his camp. Euthydemus had given him all the elephants which he had with him. {Justin, Trogus, l. 30. c. 0.} {*Polybius, l. 11. c. 39. s. 1-11. 4:303} [E374]*

*2956.* Antiochus crossed the Caucasus Mountains and re-entered India. He renewed the league and friendship he had made previously with King Sophagasenus, who then gave Antiochus more elephants. Hence, Antiochus had a hundred and fifty elephants in all. He distributed more grain among his army and so returned. He left Androsthenes of Cyzicum to bring him the treasure later, which Sophagasenus had promised him. {*Polybius, l. 11. c. 39. s. 12,13. 4:303}*

## 3800a AM, 4509 JP, 205 BC

*2957.* He then came to Arachosia. When he had crossed the Erymanthus River, he went through the country of Drangiane and came into Carmania. [L514] Since winter was coming, he placed his troops around the country. {*Polybius, l. 11. c. 39. s. 13-16. 4:303,305}*

## 3800 AM, 4510 JP, 204 BC

*2958.* The Romans made a peace with Philip, king of Macedonia. The parties to the league were Philip, Prusias, king of Bithynia, the Romans, the state of Illium and Attalus, king of Pergamum. {*Polybius, l. 11. c. 6. s. 9,10. 4:243}*

*2959.* Philopator died at Alexandria. Ptolemy, surnamed *Epiphanes*, that is *The noble* succeeded him. Appian surnamed him Philopator also, after his father's surname. {*Appian, Syrian Wars, l. 11. c. 1. (1) 2:105} He assumed the throne when he was four years old, according to Jerome. {Jerome, Da 11}. Justin said he was five years old at the time. He reigned twenty-four years. {Ptolemy, Canon of Kings} {*Clement, Stromateis, l. 1. c. 21. 2:329} {Porphyry} {Jerome} {*Eusebius, Chronicles, l. 1. 1:217}

*2960.* Philopator's death was concealed for a long time, while Agathoclia and Oenanthe, her mother, rifled the king's treasury. They got all his money and put the affairs of state under the control of their lewd companions. {Justin, Trogus, l. 30. c. 2.} Finally, Agathocles assembled the leaders of the Macedonians. He came with his sister Agathoclia and the young king, and told them that when the king was dying he had committed the care of the child to his sister. He produced the testimony of Critolaus, who said that Tlepolemus was about to invade the kingdom and become the next king of Egypt. He said the same things wherever he went, but the people scorned him. To make his disagreement with Tlepolemus more obvious to everyone, he took Danae, Tlepolemus' mother-in-law, from the temple of Demeter (or Ceres). He dragged her through the open streets and put her in prison. He seized Moeragenes, one of the guard, because he gave information about all these things to Tlepolemus and favoured him. (He could do no less, out of regard for the friendship which existed between him and Adaeus, the governor of Bubastus.) Agathocles turned him over to his secretary, Nicostratus, to be tortured, but he mysteriously escaped the rack and got away stark naked. He fled to the Macedonians and stirred them up against Agathocles. {*Polybius, l. 15. c. 26-28. 4:531-537}

*2961.* When all the people came flocking to the court in a tumultuous manner, Agathocles took the king with him and went and hid himself in a place called *Syringes*. This was a gallery or walkway which, on every side, had three walls and gates to go through before one could enter it. The Macedonians forced him to hand the king over to them. Once they had him, they brought him out to the people and sat him on a royal throne, which brought great joy and comfort to all who saw him. Shortly after this, they brought out Agathocles, who was well-fettered. The first person who met him cut his throat. Then Nicostratus was brought, and then Agathoclia with her sisters and their entire generation. Finally, Oenanthe was hauled from the temple of Thesmophoria. They were all stark naked and were placed on horses and brought into the stadium. Here they were all turned over to the people, to do with as they liked. Some started tearing them with their teeth, some lanced them with their knives and oth-

ers pulled out their eyes. Those who had been killed, were pulled to pieces until there was nothing left. At that same time, also, the maidens who had attended Arsinoe while she was alive, heard that Philammon had come from Cyrene to Alexandria. Since he was chiefly responsible for her murder, they broke into his house and killed him with staves and stones. They found and strangled his little child, then dragged his wife stark naked into the street and cut her throat. {*Polybius, l. 15. c. 29-33. 4:537-551} When the fury of the people had been exhausted, the management of the affairs of the kingdom was committed to Aristomenes, who was born in Acarnania. {*Polybius, l. 15. c. 31. s. 6,7. 4:545} {*Polybius, l. 18. c. 53-55. 5:201-209} [L515] He was made governor over the king and the kingdom, and administered its affairs with a great deal of moderation and wisdom. {*Diod. Sic., l. 28. c. 14. 11:241}

*2962.* When Antiochus, the king of Syria, and Philip, the king of Macedonia, heard of the death of Philopator, they plotted how to get his kingdom and divide it between them. They encouraged one another and planned to murder the young king. {*Polybius, l. 15. c. 20. s. 1-2. 4:509} {*Livy, l. 31. c. 14. s. 5. 9:43} {Justin, Trogus, l. 30. c. 3.} Polybius stated: {*Polybius, l. 3. c. 2. s. 8. 2:7} [E375]

> "When King Ptolemy had died, Antiochus and Philip agreed together to divide the estate of the young king between them. Philip started this wicked deed by capturing Egypt and Caria and Antiochus took over Coelosyria and Phoenicia."

*2963.* Jerome, on Daniel, {Da 11} said:

> "Philip, king of Macedonia, and Antiochus the Great conspired together and made war on Agathocles (he should have said, Aristomenes) and the young king, Ptolemy Epiphanes. The condition was that each would take those of his dominions which bordered his own kingdom."

*2964.* Josephus gave more detail when he said: {*Josephus, Antiq., l. 12. c. 3. s. 3. (129-137) 7:65-71}

> "When Antiochus the Great reigned in Asia, both Judea and Coelosyria lived in a continual state of trouble. There was a constant war going on. First, Antiochus fought with Philopator and later with Epiphanes, his son. Whether he won or lost, these countries were blighted by him and were tossed and tumbled between his prosperous and adverse fortunes like a ship in the sea between contrary waves. Finally, Antiochus had the upper hand and added Judea to his dominions. When Philopator was dead, Epiphanes sent a large army into Coelosyria under his general, Scopas. He recovered both Coelosyria and our country for him again...."

*2965.* He basically said that Antiochus, after a long war with Philopator and Epiphanes over of the land of Judea, finally took it from Epiphanes. Epiphanes, through his general, Scopas, recovered it from him again. However, he lost it a second time to Antiochus. Eusebius missed this and said that in the tenth year of Philopator:

"Antiochus had overcome Philopator and added Judea to the rest of his dominions."

*2966.* Eusebius wrote that in the first year of Epiphanes: {*Eusebius, Chronicles, l. 1. 1:217}

"Ptolemy Epiphanes, by his General Scopas, took Judea."

*2967.* However, after Antiochus' defeat at Raphia, we do not find anywhere that he made war on Philopator again. The league which was made after that battle, was first broken by Antiochus in the very first year of Epiphanes. Scopas was not in charge of that war, as appeared later. This is shown by Jerome, where he said: {*Jerome, Da 11}*

"When Ptolemy Philopator was dead, Antiochus broke the league he made with him. He led an army against Ptolemy's son, who was then only four years old and was surnamed Epiphanes."

### 3801 AM, 4511 JP, 203 BC

*2968.* When Gnaeus Servilius Caepio and Gaius Servilius Geminus were consuls in Rome, it was observed at Frusino that the sun seemed to be surrounded with a little circle and then that circle again was surrounded by a larger body of the sun. {*Livy, l. 30. c. 2. s. 12. 8:373} This seems to have been the total eclipse of the sun that happened on May 6, according to the Julian Calendar. *[L516]*

*2969.* The Carthaginians were worn down by the continual victories of Publius Scipio and gave up hope of defeating him. So they recalled Hannibal from Italy to help them. After Hannibal had been in Italy for sixteen years, he now left and returned to Africa. {*Livy, l. 30. c. 9. s. 5-9. 8:393,395} {*Livy, l. 30. c. 38. s. 1,2. 8:465}

*2970.* Philip, king of Macedonia, sent Heraclides, a Tarentine and an extremely vicious fellow, to Rhodes to destroy their fleet. He then sent envoys to Crete to stir them up to a war against the Rhodians. {*Polybius, l. 13. c. 4. 4:415,417} [E376]

*2971.* There was a naval battle near the isle of Lade between Philip, king of Macedonia, and the Rhodians. He captured two of their ships of five tiers of oars apiece. The rest of their fleet fled into the open sea, where they were beset by a bad storm and driven ashore, first at Myndus and the next day at Cos. The Macedonians fol-

lowed behind the sterns of the ships they had taken and went into Lade, which was opposite Miletus. There they refreshed themselves in the Rhodian camp which had been abandoned by them. When the Milesians heard about this, they gave Philip and Heraclides crowns as they entered Miletus. {*Polybius, l. 16. c. 15. 5:31}

### 3802 AM, 4512 JP, 202 BC

*2972.* Philip needed grain and continued to waste all Attalus' country, even to the very walls of Pergamum. He was unable to take any of his cities, because they were so well fortified. Neither could he get grain or other spoil from the country, because Attalus had anticipated his actions. So he attacked the temple and altars and destroyed them. He even broke their stones in pieces, so that they could never be put together again. He utterly destroyed the Nicephorian Grove, which was growing near the city of Pergamum, and levelled many temples and shrines in the area to the ground. Upon leaving there, Philip first went toward Thyatira, but then turned back again. He went to a field called Thebes, where he hoped to get some booty, but being unsuccessful, he went on to a place called Hiera Come. He sent messengers to Zeuxis, the governor of Lydia under Antiochus, and asked him for provisions for his army under the peace treaty between Antiochus and Philip. At first Zeuxis acted as if he would honour the treaty, but then resolved to do nothing to help Philip. {*Polybius, l. 16. c. 1. 5:3,5} {*Diod. Sic., l. 28. c. 6. 11:233}

*2973.* Philip conducted another naval battle against Attalus and the Rhodians near the isle of Chios, in which sixty Rhodians and seventy of Attalus' men were killed. Philip lost three thousand of his Macedonians and six thousand sailors, while two thousand Macedonians and seven hundred Egyptians were taken prisoner. Even though Philip had been defeated, he maintained his honour in two ways. First, he forced Attalus to flee to Erythrae and had driven the admiral's ship ashore and captured his ships. Secondly, when he landed on the shore at Argennus, a cape in Ionia, he made his stand to recover what he could of his navy. {*Polybius, l. 16. c. 2-7. 5:5-19}

*2974.* When Philip besieged Prinassus, a city of Caria, he was unable to take it by force, but captured it at length by a stratagem. {*Polybius, l. 16. c. 11. 5:23,25} He put garrisons into Iasus, Bargylia and the city of Euromus. {*Polybius, l. 16. c. 12. 5:26,27} {*Polybius, l. 17. c. 2. s. 3,4. 5:89}

### 3803a AM, 4512 JP, 202 BC

*2975.* Publius Cornelius Scipio utterly defeated Hannibal in Africa in the last battle of the second Carthaginian war. We read in Zonaras that the Carthaginians were amazed by a total eclipse of the sun which happened at this time. {*Dio, l. 17. (78) 2:267 (Zonaras, l. 9. c. 14.)} However, there was no total eclipse. *[L517]* Livy said that the body of the sun at Zama did indeed seem to be somewhat darkened. {*Livy, l. 30. c. 29. 8:469-473} {*Livy, l. 30. 8:551 (Appendix)} From the astronomical tables we know that there was a very small eclipse of the sun in this year, on the 19th of our October. Some say that Hannibal fled from the battle and reached the sea coast, where he found a ship ready for him. He sailed directly into Asia, to King Antiochus. When Scipio demanded that the Carthaginians hand over Hannibal, they replied that he was no longer in Africa. {*Livy, l. 30. c. 37. s. 13. 8:509} Others more correctly stated that Scipio in fact never did demand him from them. {*Plutarch, Flamininus, l. 1. c. 9. s. 6. 10:347}

### 3803b AM, 4513 JP, 201 BC

*2976.* When Philip came toward Abydus, they shut their gates against him. They would not even let the messengers in whom he sent to them. So he besieged the place for a long time. For them to be able to be delivered from him, they wanted Attalus and the Rhodians to hurry to their aid. But Attalus sent them only three hundred men, and the Rhodians, who were anchored at Tenedos with their whole fleet, sent them only one ship of four tiers of oars to help. The walls of the city were surrounded with engines of war. At first, the men in Abydus held Philip's men off very courageously making it impossible for them to get in by land or by sea. Later, a breach was made in the main wall, but they had cast up another within it. The Macedonians went to undermine that wall also. Consequently, the people of Abydus were forced to send to Philip, seeking a conditional surrender. They wanted safe conduct for the Rhodian ship together with the soldiers and mariners on board, and for Attalus' men who were in the town. Lastly, they asked that they themselves might leave with only their clothes on their backs. But they could get no answer from him, unless they were prepared to unconditionally surrender to him. Therefore, becoming very angry in their indignation and despair, they made fifty of their leaders swear publicly that if they saw the inner wall taken by the enemy, they would go and kill every man's wife and children and throw his silver, gold and jewels into the sea. When this had been agreed upon, the soldiers determined that they would either vanquish their enemies or die fighting for their country. {*Livy, l. 31. c. 14. s. 4. 9:43} {*Polybius, l. 16. c. 30,31. 5:67-71}

*2977.* About that same time, Attalus and the Rhodians sent envoys to Rome, to complain of the wrongs done to them by Philip and his Macedonians. They were told that the Senate would take care of the affairs of Asia. {*Livy, l. 31. c. 2. s. 1-3. 9:7} {Justin, Trogus, l. 30. c. 3.}

*2978.* Three envoys were sent from Rome to Ptolemy and Antiochus, to put an end to all differences between them.

The envoys were Gaius Claudius Nero, Marcus Aemilius Lepidus and Publius Sempronius Tuditanus. They came to Rhodes and hearing of the siege of Abydus, they wanted to talk with Philip. {*Livy, l. 31. c. 2. s. 3,4. 9:7} However, they followed their orders for the present, and continued on their journey to Ptolemy and Antiochus. They sent Aemilius, the youngest of the three, to Philip. When he met with him at Abydus, Aemilius told him that the Senate of Rome wanted him to stop making war on any Greek city. He was not to lay hands on anything that belonged to Ptolemy, the king of Egypt. *[E377]* If he complied, he would live in peace, but if he did not, he should know that the Romans were resolved and ready to make war on him. Philip returned this reply: {*Livy, l. 31. c. 18. s. 4,5. 9:55} {*Polybius, l. 16. c. 34. 5:73-77} {*Polybius, l. 16. c. 27. s. 4,5. 5:61}

> "Your age, good appearance and above all, the name of a Roman, make you speak so boldly. However, I would tell you to remember the league and to keep peace with me. *[L518]* If not, I am also resolved to do my best and to make you know and feel that the power and name of a Macedonian is in no way inferior to, or less noble than, that of a Roman."

*2979.* Justin stated that Marcus Aemilius Lepidus was also sent into Egypt by the Romans to govern the kingdom of Egypt on behalf of this young Ptolemy Epiphanes. {Justin, Trogus, l. 30. c. 3.} This may have happened for one of two possible reasons. They may have received an embassy sent to them from Alexandria to take over the guardianship of the young king and to defend the kingdom of Egypt. Antiochus and Philip were said already to have divided the kingdom between them. {Justin, Trogus, l. 30. c. 2.} Another possibility is that the father committed this charge to them on his deathbed. {Justin, Trogus, l. 31. c. 1.} Concerning this, Valerius Maximus said: {*Valerius Maximus, l. 6. c. 6. s. 1. 2:67}

> "The King Ptolemy had left the people of Rome as the guardian of his son while he was under age. Therefore, the Senate sent Marcus Aemilius Lepidus, the High Pontiff and then twice elected as consul, to Alexandria. He was to take care of the child's estate. He was a very honest and most upright man. He was well versed in their own affairs and exercised his duty for the benefit of Egypt, not for himself."

*2980.* He said this because he thought that this man had executed the office of a guardian in Egypt while he was High Pontiff, and when he had already been consul in Rome twice. But Epiphanes had died before that happened. The reason for the error was this: he had seen some coins depicting both the title of Lepidus' position and his office as a guardian in Egypt. For to this day there are still some silver coins to be found, bearing the following inscription. Each of these coins said on one side *Alexandrea*, while on the other it had *S.C.M. Lepidus Pont. Max. Tutor Reg.* On the image side is a picture of a man putting a crown on the head of a young man who is standing on his right with a sceptre in his hand.

*2981.* When the Athenians saw their territory wasted by Philip, they sent and asked for aid from every country, from the Romans, the Rhodians, Attalus and Ptolemy. {*Livy, l. 31. c. 5. s. 7. 9:17} {*Livy, l. 31. c. 9. s. 1-3. 9:17}

*2982.* Therefore, the envoys of the Romans and Rhodians met with Attalus in Athens, where they agreed, by common consent, to help them. For this, the Athenians at once decreed excessive honours, both to Attalus and to the Rhodians, going so far as to name one of their own tribes after Attalus and to add it to the ten that they they already had. {*Livy, l. 31. c. 15. 9:47} {*Polybius, l. 16. c. 25,26. 5:55-59}

*2983.* While the Romans were busy preparing for war against Philip, envoys from Ptolemy, or rather from his guardians, arrived in Rome, to inform them that the Athenians had sought help from the king against Philip. Although the Egyptians were confederates both of the kings and of the Romans, Ptolemy would not send any military support without the consent and authority of the people of Rome. The envoys said that if the Romans would help the Athenians, Egypt would keep out of it. But if the Romans did not want to get involved, Egypt could easily supply the Athenians with enough forces to overcome Philip. The Senate decreed that the king should be thanked for his kindness and be told that the Romans planned to defend and maintain their own friends and confederates themselves. Should they need anything for the war, they would tell him. They knew very well that the king's military forces were very large and were required for the defence of his own state. The Senate ordered presents to be sent to the king's envoys, with each one receiving five thousand *asses* of money. {*Livy, l. 30. c. 9. s. 1-5. 9:27}

*2984.* In the fifty-fourth year, for so it was written in the Greek manuscript at Lambeth (not the fifty-second, as in the common edition), of the second period of Calippus, in the 547th year of Nabonassar, on the 16th day of the month of Mesore, the 22nd of our September, seven hours after noon, the moon was eclipsed at Alexandria. {*Ptolemy, Great Syntaxis, l. 4. c. 11.} [L519]

### 3804a AM, 4513 JP, 201 BC

*2985.* Toward the latter end of autumn, Consul Publius Sulpicius Galba crossed over into Macedonia against Philip with an army. He was met by envoys from Athens who desired that he would raise the siege on Athens.

Thereupon, he sent Gaius Claudius Cento with twenty warships and a thousand soldiers to relieve Athens. Philip himself was not involved in this siege, as he was engaged with the siege of Abydus. {*Livy, l. 31. c. 14. s. 1-4. 9:43}

*2986.* The men of Abydus recalled their oath and fought so hard that when the night should have ended the battle between them, Philip was amazed at their courage, or rather at their rage, in fighting. [E378] He was forced to withdraw and to sound a retreat. Glaucides and Theognetus conferred with some of the elders of the town, who had the hardest part to play in this tragedy. They saw that there were but few of their men left after the battle, and that these were wearied from wounds and loss of blood. As soon as it was day, they sent their priests, in their robes, to surrender the town to Philip. When the inhabitants heard this, they were so desperate with rage that each man immediately ran to kill his wife and children, and then they killed each other. The king was amazed at their fury and ordered his soldiers to stay away, saying that he would give the Abydenians three days to die. In that time, they carried out more barbarous acts of cruelty on each other than they would have expected from an enraged enemy. No one who was not in prison and who was free to kill himself, was taken alive by the enemy. The king seized all their wealth, which they had gathered into one place for the purpose of destroying it, and departed, after leaving a garrison in the place. {*Livy, l. 31. c. 17. 9:51,53} {*Polybius, l. 16. c. 33. 5:73}

*2987.* When he came to Bargylia, he was very troubled to see the Romans, the Rhodians and Attalus allied to make war against him. When his army was almost famished, Zeuxis, the governor of Lydia, and the cities of Mylasa, Alabanda and Magnesia sent him some small provisions to relieve them. Against his nature, he flattered any who brought him supplies, and when they stopped, he plotted against them. Philocles formed a plan to take Mylasa but when it failed through his own folly, Philip went and wasted the territory of Alabanda. Although these were his good benefactors, he treated them like public enemies. The only reason he gave was that his soldiers needed food. {*Polybius, l. 16. c. 24. 5:53,55}

### 3804b AM, 4514 JP, 200 BC

*2988.* In the 55th year of the second period of Calippus, in the 548th year of Nabonassar, on the 9th of the month of Mecheir, at about midnight of the beginning of March 20, there was a total eclipse of the moon at Alexandria. {*Ptolemy, Great Syntaxis, l. 4. c. 11.}

*2989.* The next summer, the Romans, with the help of Attalus and the Rhodians, made war on Philip and his associates in Macedonia. {*Livy, l. 31. c. 28. 9:81,83}

2990. Scopas, a prominent man in Aetolia, was sent from Alexandria by Ptolemy with a large amount of money with which he hired six thousand foot soldiers, in addition to cavalry, and shipped them away to Egypt. He would have left no one in Aetolia who could serve in the military, if he would have had his way, but Damocritus reminded them of the war in which they were ready to engage, and of the vulnerability of the country should they all leave. For this reason, a large number of the men who were going changed their minds and stayed at home. It is uncertain whether he did this out of a true zeal for his country, or if Scopas did not bribe him to the same extent as he had the others. {*Livy, l. 31. c. 43. 9:125,127}

2991. About this time Joseph, the son of Tobias, died, and the people of Jerusalem were thrown into an uproar by the quarrelling of his sons. The older brothers tried to make war on their youngest brother Hyrcanus, of whom I have spoken before. [L520] Many of the Jews favoured the older brothers, and the rest favoured Simon, the high priest, because of his family ties. {*Josephus, Antiq., l. 12. c. 4. s. 10. (223-227) 7:113,115}

2992. In the 55th year of the second period of Calippus, in the 548th year of Nabonassar, on the 5th of the month of Mesore, at three o'clock after midnight, on September the 12th, there was a total eclipse of the moon at Alexandria. {Ptolemy, Great Syntaxis, l. 4. c. 11.}

2993. Before the autumnal equinox, Oreus surrendered to Attalus. Attalus was present at the feast of Ceres in Athens. When he had sent home Agesimbrotus and the Rhodians, he returned into Asia. {*Livy, l. 31. c. 47. s. 1-4. 9:137,139}

## 3805 AM, 4515 JP, 199 BC

2994. After Simon II died, his son Onias III succeeded him in the high priesthood of the Jews. {*Josephus, Antiq., l. 12. c. 5. s. 1. (237) 7:121} He was a good man, who was gracious, well respected, meek and very cautious in his speech. From his youth he behaved in a very virtuous manner. {Apc 2Ma 15:12} In the Fasti Siculi (for here Scaliger's Greek Eusebian Fragments fail us), he was said to have been high priest for twenty-four years.

## 3806a AM, 4515 JP, 199 BC

2995. Ptolemy Epiphanes sent a large army into Coelosyria under the command of Scopas. With the use of force, he recovered many cities for Ptolemy, including Jerusalem. {*Josephus, Antiq., l. 12. c. 3. s. 3. (131-137) 7:67-71} Polybius added: {*Polybius, l. 16. c. 39. 5:81,83}

"Scopas, the general of Ptolemy's army, marched into the upper regions and subdued the country of the Jews in the winter season."

2996. Jerome said this: {Jerome, Da 11}

"When Antiochus held Judea, Scopas, the Aetolian, was sent as general of Ptolemy's forces. He fought valiantly against Antiochus and captured Judea and returned into Egypt." [E379]

2997. Meanwhile, Antiochus invaded Attalus' kingdom, which was undefended at that time, because its forces were being employed for the Romans in the Macedonian war. {*Livy, l. 32. c. 8. s. 9-11. 9:175}

## 3806b AM, 4516 JP, 198 BC

2998. When the Senate of Rome had considered complaints made by Attalus, they sent their envoys to Antiochus. They told him that at that time the Romans were making use of Attalus' military forces against the Macedonians, a common enemy to them both, and so they would be pleased if he did not meddle with the kingdom of Attalus. It was befitting that these kings, who were in league and friendship with the people of Rome, should also live in peace among themselves. Antiochus, when he heard this, withdrew and ceased from any further war against Attalus. Attalus sent his envoys to the Senate of Rome to thank them for this great favour they had done for him. He gave them a crown of gold for the Capitol, weighing two hundred and forty-six pounds. {*Livy, l. 32. c. 8. 9:175,177} {*Livy, l. 32. c. 27. 9:237}

## 3806c AM, 4516 JP, 198 BC

2999. At this time, two fleets from Asia joined the Roman fleet, the one under Attalus, the king, consisting of twenty-four ships of five tiers of oars apiece, and the other from Rhodes, of twenty decked ships, commanded by Agesimbrotus. These pursued Philip as fast as they could. {*Livy, l. 32. c. 16. s. 6-8. 9:197}

## 3806d AM, 4516 JP, 198 BC

3000. That summer, Antiochus took in all the cities of Coelosyria which Ptolemy controlled. {*Livy, l. 33. c. 19. s. 8,9. 9:331} When Antiochus defeated Scopas in a battle, he recovered all the cities of Syria and grew friendly and well disposed toward the Jews. {*Eusebius, Chronicles, l. 1. 1:218}

3001. Antiochus met Scopas at the head of the Jordan River, where the city of Panium was later built, and there defeated him. When he had recovered the cities which Scopas had taken from him, along with Samaria, the Jews voluntarily submitted to him. [L521] They received his whole army, with his elephants, into their city, and supported and helped them in the siege of the citadel where Scopas had put a garrison. Josephus confirmed this from a letter which Antiochus had written to Ptolemy, the captain of the garrison. He stated, from Polybius, that Antiochus took in Batanea, Samaria,

Abila and Gadara after the defeat of Scopas. The Jews who lived at Jerusalem, where the famous temple was, surrendered to him. Antiochus took and destroyed Gaza, which had withstood him and had sided with Ptolemy. All this was also written in the same book by Polybius. {*Josephus, Antiq., l. 12. c. 3. s. 3. (132-136) 7:67,69} {*Polybius, l. 16. c. 39. 5:81,83}

3002. Zeno of Rhodes, in his *Local History* mentioned by Laertius, had described in detail this battle between Antiochus and Scopas at Panium, near the source of the Jordan River. {*Diogenes Laertius, l. 7. c. 35. 2:145,147} This, along with other excerpts of his from Polybius, was given to us by the most learned Henric Valesius. Antiochus routed Scopas and pursued him to Sidon, where he besieged him with ten thousand troops. Ptolemy sent three famous captains, Europus, Menocles and Damozenus, to rescue him, but they were unable to raise the siege. Finally Scopas surrendered due to hunger, and he and his troops were allowed to leave the place, stark naked. {*Polybius, l. 16. c. 18-20. 5:37-43} {Jerome, Da 11}

### 3807a AM, 4516 JP, 198 BC

3003. With that victory at Panium, Antiochus recovered all Phoenicia, Coelosyria and the other cities in the country of Syria. Although these territories rightfully belonged to the kings of Egypt, {Justin, Trogus, l. 31. c. 1.} Antiochus left these lands to be held by the kings of Syria from then on. {*Polybius, l. 28. c. 1. 6:3} Antiochus himself returned to winter in Antioch. {*Livy, l. 33. c. 19. s. 8. 9:331}

3004. In the 551st year of Nabonassar and the three proceeding years, on the 17th day of the month of Athyr, which day is unmoveable, the Egyptians celebrated the feast of Isis. {*Plutarch, Isis and Osiris, l. 1. c. 13. (356D) 5:37} {*Plutarch, Isis and Osiris, l. 1. c. 39. (366E) 5:95,97} This was on December 28. {Ussher, Macedonian and Asiatic Year, c. 7.} Eudoxus placed the winter solstice at this time. Dositheus noted this in his *Octaeris* (which, Censorinus stated, was attributed to Eudoxus) or in his *Parapegma* appended to it, which he published at Coloniae near Athens (or rather, at Coloni in Aeolia). This is how it came to pass, as mentioned by Geminus, that the Greeks were of the opinion that the feast of Isis was always kept on the winter solstice, {Geminus, l. 6.} which was the shortest day of the year. He also stated there that this error had previously been noted by Eratosthenes, in his commentary *De Octaeteride*.

3005. In this winter season, Philip came to talk with the Roman consul Titus Quinctius Flamininus. He wanted to know the conditions for peace. Among the conditions that Flamininus mentioned was that Philip should restore to Ptolemy, king of Egypt, all the cities which he had taken since the death of Ptolemy Philopator, his

father. {*Polybius, l. 18. s. 12-14. 5:87} {*Livy, l. 32. c. 35. s. 9-12. 9:261,263} [E380]

### 3807b AM, 4517 JP, 197 BC

3006. In the same year there was an earthquake in the middle of the stretch of sea between the two islands of Theramenes (or Thera) and Therasia. This created a new island with hot springs. [L522] That same day, an earthquake in Asia shook Rhodes and many other cities, and destroyed many houses there. Some cities were completely swallowed up. Thereupon, their priests and soothsayers predicted that the rising Roman Empire would swallow up and devour both the kingdoms of Macedonia and Asia. {Justin, Trogus, l. 30. c. 4.}

### 3807c AM, 4517 JP, 197 BC

3007. At the beginning of spring, Flamininus sent for Attalus to join him in Elatia. Together they went to Thebes to try to persuade the Boeotians to join the league with the Romans. Attalus addressed them in a speech and spoke with more force than his voice could endure. He had grown old by now, and he suddenly lost the ability to speak and collapsed. He was sick there in Thebes, and one side of his body was paralysed. Flamininus saw that he was in no danger of dying, but needed time to recover from the weakness of his body. So he left him there and returned to Elatia, from where he had come. {*Livy, l. 33. c. 1,2. 9:279-283} {*Plutarch, Flamininus, l. 1. c. 6. s. 3. 10:339}

3008. At the same time, Antiochus sent his two sons, Ardyes and Mithridates, ahead of him by land with instructions to wait for him at Sardis. He set sail with a hundred decked ships and other smaller vessels, planning to try to do what he could to win over the cities of Caria and Cilicia, which were controlled by Ptolemy. He hoped to assist Philip by sea and land. First he took over Zephyrium, Soli and Aphrodisia, and then rounded the cape of Anemurium, a foreland of Cilicia. Selinus, and the other towns, cities and citadels all along that coast, surrendered without resistance, either from fear, or to gain his favour. At length he came to Coracesium, which shut its gates to him, much to his surprise. {*Livy, l. 33. c. 19,20. 9:331,333}

3009. While Antiochus besieged Coracesium, Rhodes sent envoys to him. They told him that they would oppose him if he did not stay on the other side of Nephelis, a cape of Cilicia. This was not because they had any grudge against him, but to keep him from joining with Philip, and so that he might not interfere with the Romans, who had now undertaken to procure and maintain the liberty of Greece. When he heard this, he controlled his anger, telling them only that he would send his envoys to Rhodes to deal with this matter. They had instructions to renew the leagues that had formerly been made between them and him and his forefathers. They were to tell the Rhodians not to fear his coming to them, for he would do neither them nor any of their friends any harm, and he would not infringe on his friendship with the Romans. His reply satisfied them. {*Livy, l. 33. c. 20. s. 7-10. 9:333}

3010. The Rhodians laid claim to Peraea, on the continent of Asia, opposite Rhodes. It had always been in the possession of their ancestors, but had now been invaded and was being occupied by Philip. At this time Pausistratus, the Rhodian general, had routed Deinocrates and the Macedonians. Had he followed up on his victory and marched straight to Stratonicia, it would have been his for the asking. But they returned to their camp, which gave Deinocrates and the remainder of his army time to get into the city. So the Rhodians were unable to take it. This story is described in more detail by Livy. {*Livy, l. 33. c. 18. 9:323-329}

3011. Attalus was carried sick from Thebes by sea to his city of Pergamum, where he died. {*Livy, l. 33. c. 21. s. 1,2. 9:335} {*Polybius, l. 18. c. 41. 5:175,177} {*Plutarch, Flamininus, l. 1. c. 6. s. 3. 10:339} He lived seventy-two years and was king for forty-four years, according to Livy, Polybius, and Suidas. {Suidas, Attalus} Strabo said that he only reigned for forty-three years. [L523] He was survived by his wife, Apollonis, of the city of Cyzicum, and four children, Eumenes, Attalus, Philetaerus and Athenaeus. {*Strabo, l. 13. c. 4. s. 2. 6:167} {*Livy, l. 33. c. 21. s. 4,5. 9:335} Eumenes, who was the oldest, succeeded him in the kingdom. {*Strabo, l. 13. c. 4. s. 2. 6:167} Plutarch stated that the two younger brothers, both of a brave and lusty spirit, nonetheless exhibited a deep respect for Eumenes. {*Plutarch, On Brotherly Love, l. 1. c. 5. 6:259} They were like guards about him to protect his crown and dignity. {*Polybius, l. 18. c. 41. s. 9.10. 5:177} {Suidas, Attalus} This is the reason why their mother would often say that she was a happy woman, not because of her wealth, or because she was a queen, but because she saw her two younger sons being excellent guards of the oldest son. [E381] The two sons always had their swords with them, yet Eumenes lived in their midst without the least dread or fear of them. {*Plutarch, On Brotherly Love, l. 1. c. 5. 6:259} The filial duty and respect which they all bore to Apollonis or Apollonias, their mother, was recorded in more detail in Polybius and Suidas. {*Polybius, l. 22. c. 20. 5:387,389} {Suidas, Apollonius}

## 3807d AM, 4517 JP, 197 BC

3012. Philip's army of foot soldiers and cavalry were defeated in the battle fought at Cynoscephalae, in the country of Thessaly. {Apc 1Ma 8:5,6} Flamininus offered him a truce because he understood that Antiochus was marching from Syria with an army, to come into Europe. So he made a truce with him for four months, to give Flamininus time to send to Rome and submit everything to the will and pleasure of the Senate. {*Polybius, l. 18. c. 39. s. 4-7. 5:173,175} {*Livy, l. 33. c. 13. s. 14,15. 9:311,313}

3013. When the Rhodians heard of the defeat of Philip, they still defended the cities that were allied with Ptolemy and were in danger of being invaded by Antiochus. To some they sent help and to others a letter telling them they would defend them against the aggression of Antiochus. Letters were sent to Caunus, Myndus, Halicarnassus and Samos. {*Livy, l. 33. c. 33. s. 10-13. 9:333,335} However, this was not sufficient. Antiochus, in spite of this, surprised Coracesium, Corycus, Andriace, Limyra, Patara and Xanthus, all of which belonged to Ptolemy. Lastly, he took the city of Ephesus. {Jerome, Da 11}

## 3808a AM, 4517 JP, 197 BC

3014. Antiochus spent his winter at Ephesus and tried to subdue all of Asia into the empire his forefathers once had. He saw that the rest of the cities would easily be taken but found that Smyrna in Aeolia and Lampsacus in the Hellespont were planning to fight, hence, he advised them to surrender, like the rest. He threatened them in case they would not, fearing that the rest might follow their example in opposing his plans. When this did not work, he sent some companies from Ephesus to besiege Smyrna, and others from Abydus to besiege Lampsacus. {*Livy, l. 33. c. 38. 9:379,381} Consequently, both these cities, as well as others that joined with them, sent their commissioners to Flamininus to ask for help against Antiochus. {*Appian, Syrian Wars, l. 11. c. 1. (2) 2:107}

3015. When Marcus Claudius Marcellus assumed his office of consul, envoys arrived at Rome to ask for a league to be made with Philip. As a result of this, the Senate passed the following decree:

"Everywhere the Greeks in both Europe and Asia should be free and live after their own laws. Those who were under Philip's dominion, or had any garrisons of his in them, should, before the celebration of the next Isthmian games, turn them over into the hands of the Romans. From those who were in Asia, such as Euromum, Pedasa, Bargylia, Iassus, Abydus, Thasos, Myrina and Perinthus, Philip should withdraw his garrisons and leave them free. He should not renew his war with Eumenes, the new king (for Valerius Antias observed that special notice was taken of him) who was the son of Attalus. [L524] Concerning the liberation of the Ciani, Titus Quinctius Flamininus should write letters to Prusias that the will and pleasure of the Senate was...."

*3016.* To ensure the execution of this decree, the Senate sent ten commissioners into Greece. {*Polybius, l. 18. c. 44. 5:183} {*Livy, l. 33. c. 30. 9:359,361}

## 3808b AM, 4518 JP, 196 BC

*3017.* After the Isthmian games were over, the general liberty of Greece was proclaimed by the public crier. Flamininus and the ten commissioners who had come from Rome, listened to Hegesianax and Lysias, who were envoys from Antiochus to Flamininus. These were told to tell Antiochus that he must not meddle with any free city in Asia, much less make war upon them. He must get out of any places he now controlled which had formerly belonged to either Ptolemy or Philip. He was ordered not to enter Europe himself and not to send any of his forces there. They added that they would soon journey to Antiochus themselves. {*Polybius, l. 18. c. 47. s. 1-6. 5:191,193} {*Livy, l. 33. c. 33,34. 9:367,369}

*3018.* When the assembly was dismissed, the ten commissioners divided among themselves the work they had to do. Every man went to see the region assigned to him, to be liberated according to the decree. Publius Lentulus went by sea to Bargylia in Asia, and freed that city to live according to their own laws. Lucius Stertinius did the same at Hephaestia, in Thasos and the cities of Thrace, and wherever he went. Publius Villius and Lucius Terentius journeyed to Antiochus, and Gnaeus Cornelius went to King Philip. {*Polybius, l. 18. c. 48. s. 1-3. 5:195} {*Livy, l. 33. c. 35. 9:371} {*Plutarch, Flamininus, l. 1. c. 12. s. 1. 10:355}

## 3808c AM, 4518 JP, 196 BC

*3019.* At the beginning of spring, Antiochus went by sea from Ephesus to the Hellespont. With his land army, he crossed from Abydus and added them to his naval forces. He landed in the Chersonesus and took over any cities that surrendered to him out of fear. From there he went to Lysimachia, which had been utterly destroyed a short time earlier by the Thracians. *[E382]* He began to rebuild it and to make it the capital for his son Seleucus' kingdom in those regions. {*Livy, l. 33. c. 33. s. 8-14. 9:381} {*Appian, Syrian Wars, l. 11. c. 1. (3) 2:109}

*3020.* Everything was going as well as Antiochus could have imagined. However Lucius Cornelius, who had been sent by the Senate of Rome to make peace between Antiochus and Ptolemy, came to Selymbria. Publius Lentulus from Bargylia, Lucius Terentius and Publius Villius from Thasos were three of the commissioners who had gone to Lysimachia. Lucius Cornelius came from Selymbria and met them there at Lysimachia. A few days later, Antiochus came there from Thrace and met them. Hegesianax and Lysias, who had previously been sent as envoys from Antiochus to Flamininus, happened to be there at the same time. In the conference,

Lucius Cornelius said that he thought it reasonable that Antiochus should restore to Ptolemy all the cities and places of Ptolemy's kingdom that he had recently taken from him. Further, he should withdraw his garrisons from all the places which belonged to Philip, because the Romans had now defeated him. They warned him not to meddle with any free state. Antiochus replied that he first of all wondered what right the Romans had to quarrel with him about the cities in Asia, since he did not question them on what they did in Italy. He was content that the cities in Asia should enjoy their liberty, but they should thank him for it, and not the Romans. As far as Ptolemy was concerned, they were already good friends and he was about to make a marriage alliance with him. {*Polybius, l. 18. c. 49-51. 5:197-201} {*Livy, l. 3. c. 49,50. 9:383-387} {*Appian, Syrian Wars, l. 11. c. 1. (3) 2:109}

*3021.* Lucius Cornelius continued, and told him that it was reasonable that the envoys of Lampsacus and Smyrna should be called and allowed to speak for themselves, and so they were summoned. Parmenion and Pythodorus represented the city of Lampsacus, and Coeranus spoke for Smyrna. *[L525]* They spoke boldly and freely for their own cause. Antiochus was enraged to see that he was being called before the Romans for what he had done in Asia, as if they were his judges. He ordered Parmenion to hold his peace and said that he moved that the controversy be decided before the Rhodian judges, and not the Romans, whereupon that conference broke up and nothing was done. {*Polybius, l. 18. c. 52. 5:201}

*3022.* Polycrates, who was governor of Cyprus, was in charge of collecting the the king's revenue. He handed the government over to his successor, Ptolemy of Megalopolis, and returned to Alexandria. He turned over a large sum of money to King Epiphanes, who was glad to receive it, and Polycrates was thought highly of by all. {*Polybius, l. 18. c. 54. 5:203}

*3023.* Shortly after this, the Aetolians revolted under their captain Scopas, who had a large company of soldiers under him. Since the king was but a child, Scopas could do what he liked. While he dawdled his time away, his plans were cut short. When Aristomenes found out that Scopas' friends went to him in his own house and used to sit in council together with him, he sent a company of the guards and summoned him before the king's council. Scopas was surprised and grew so wild and devoid of reason that he did not carry out his plans, nor did he obey the summons of the king, as he should have done. Aristomenes knew what state Scopas was in, and sent a company of soldiers who surrounded the house. Ptolemy, the son of Eumenes, brought him before the king. {*Polybius, l. 18. c. 53. s. 4-11. 5:203}

3024. He was brought before the council. First the king charged him and then Polycrates and Aristomenes did. He was quickly found guilty and condemned by the king's council and by all the envoys of the foreign countries who were there. For Aristomenes, having intended to accuse him, had purposely brought together various illustrious personages of the Greeks and the Aetolian envoys, who had been sent there at that time to work out a peace between the king and themselves. Dorimachus, the son of Nicostratus, was one of these envoys. After these had all spoken, Scopas and all his cohorts were cast into prison. The next night, Aristomenes had him and all his family poisoned. He had Dicaearchus, who was a most impious wretch, racked to death. Dicaearchus had been the admiral of Philip's navy and had harassed the Cyclades Islands. He had erected two altars in a certain port there, the one to *Impiety* and the other to *Lawlessness*, and he had sacrificed to them both as to two gods. To the rest of the Aetolians who wanted to return, the king gave them permission to do so, and to take with them what belonged to them. {*Polybius, l. 18. c. 54. 5:203-207}

3025. When this business of the Aetolians had been settled and all was quiet, the whole court started the solemn revels which they used to have when anyone was made king. This event was called the *Proclamation* or *Anacleteria*. The king was then not old enough to run the government, but the court thought that if it were known abroad that the king had now attained to ruling in his own person, things would go better and it would be more peaceful in the kingdom. [E383] So they made every provision they could to perform this solemnity for the honour of the kingdom. {*Polybius, l. 18. c. 55. 5:207,209}

3026. While the conference at Lysimachia was going on between Antiochus and the commissioners from Rome, an unconfirmed source reported what had happened to Scopas at Alexandria, and that Ptolemy was dead. [L526] Hence that conference came to naught, since neither party would act until they knew exactly what had happened. Lucius Cornelius, whose proper errand was to make peace with both the kings, desired some time to talk directly with Ptolemy. He wanted to get there as soon as possible, before anything could be resolved there after the king's supposed death, to help establish the state. Antiochus made no doubt of his intentions. If the king were indeed dead, Egypt would be his. So he sent away the commissioners and left his son Seleucus with his army to continue rebuilding Lysimachia. He himself sailed to Ephesus with his whole fleet and from there sent envoys to Flamininus, to ask him to continue the league and friendship between them. He set sail again

and stayed close to the coast of Asia until he came to Lycia. At Patara, he was told for certain that Ptolemy was alive, and so he abandoned his journey to Egypt. {*Livy, l. 33. c. 41. s. 1-6. 9:387} {*Appian, Syrian Wars, l. 11. c. 1. (4) 2:111}

### 3809a AM, 4518 JP, 196 BC

3027. Antiochus hurried toward Cyprus, which he certainly hoped to get. When he had rounded the cape of the Chelidonian foreland, his sailors mutinied and he was forced to stay in Pamphylia for a while, at the mouth of the Eurymedon River. From there, he sailed to a place called the *Head of the Saris River*. A severe storm almost drowned him and all his fleet. Many of his ships were driven ashore, and many sank with all hands. A number of sailors and common soldiers, as well as his nobles and leaders, died in that storm. He salvaged what he could from the wreck, and since he was in no position to go on to Cyprus, he sailed to Seleucia in Syria and there started to rebuild his navy. He married his two children, Antiochus and Laodice, to each other, then sailed again for Antioch because winter was approaching. {*Livy, l. 33. c. 41. s. 6-9. 9:387,389} {*Appian, Syrian Wars, l. 11. c. 1. (4) 2:111}

### 3809b AM, 4519 JP, 195 BC

3028. The Decemviri, or ten commissioners, returned to Rome and told the Senate about Antiochus and his return into Syria. {*Livy, l. 33. c. 43. s. 5,6. 9:395} Hannibal's enemies at Carthage informed the Senate of Rome that he and Antiochus were sending letters to each other on a daily basis. Although this was false, those who feared these men believed the false report. So they sent envoys to the council at Carthage, complaining to them that Hannibal was working with Antiochus, and telling them to get rid of Hannibal by any means. {Justin, Trogus, l. 31. c. 1,2.} {*Livy, l. 33. c. 45. s. 6-8. 9:397,399} {*Livy, l. 33. c. 47. s. 6-10. 9:3403}

3029. Flamininus' reply to Antiochus' envoys, when they asked for a league, was that he could do nothing now that the ten commissioners were gone. The envoys would do well to go after them and make their application to the Senate at Rome. {*Livy, l. 34. c. 57. 9:561,563}

3030. Hannibal stole away from Carthage and came safely to Tyre. There he was received by the founders of Carthage as though he were in his home country. After he had rested there for a few days, he sailed to Antioch. When he found that Antiochus had left, he spoke with his son there, who was celebrating a solemn festival in Daphne. Having been courteously entertained by him, he set sail again and followed Antiochus, overtaking him at Ephesus. Antiochus, who was trying to decide whether or not he should make war on the Romans, was completely taken by surprise when Hannibal came to him.

From now on he thought not so much of the war itself, as of what great things he would get by conquering the Romans. {*Livy, l. 33. c. 48,49. 9:403-407} {Justin, Trogus, l. 31. c. 1,2.} {Emilius Probus, Hannibal}

3031. Phormio, a philosopher of the Peripatetic text, had in his school disputed at great length on the subject of the duty and office of a commander of an army, and of the military art and the ordering of a battle. [L527] Finally, Hannibal could contain himself no longer, and cried out that he had heard many a doting fool in his days, but a bigger fool than this Phormio was, he had never heard. {*Cicero, De Oratore, l. 2. c. 18. (75) 3:255}

## 3809c AM, 4519 JP, 195 BC

3032. Titus Quinctius Flamininus joined with Eumenes and the Rhodians and fought very successfully against Nabis, the tyrant of Lacedemon. {*Livy, l. 34. c. 29-37. 9:491-515}

3033. When Marcus Porcius Cato was consul, the city of Smyrna began to build a temple to the city of Rome. {*Tacitus, Annals, l. 4. c. 56. 4:101} At their example, the Alabandians not only built another temple to her, but instituted some anniversary plays and games in honour of her as a proper goddess. {*Livy, l. 43. c. 6. s. 5,6. 13:23} [E384]

## 3810 AM, 4520 JP, 194 BC

3034. Eratosthenes of Cyrene, the son of Aglaus, died. He was not only a grammarian, though that was his main profession, but also a poet, a philosopher and a geometrician, for he excelled in all these areas. {*Lucian, Octogenarians, l. 1. (27) 1:243} Apollonius Alexandrinus succeeded him in managing the library at Alexandria. He was a scholar of Callimachus, who wrote the *Argonautica*. Because he lived at Rhodes for many years, he was surnamed *Rhodius*. {Suidas, Apollonius}

3035. Antiochus was aware of the loyalty of the Jews for him. He conferred more great favours on them and he highly commended them in his letters. {*Eusebius, Chronicles, l. 1. 1:218} Josephus preserved these letters in his works. {*Josephus, Antiq., l. 12. c. 3. s. 3. (129-153) 7:65-79} In an address to Ptolemy's government, he mentioned many gifts of his and immunities granted, both to the city of Jerusalem and also to the temple there. In another letter to Zeuxis, he ordered that two thousand Jewish families living in the provinces of Babylonia and Mesopotamia be settled in Phrygia and Lydia. He hoped their presence would keep order there.

## 3811 AM, 4521 JP, 193 BC

3036. Antiochus prepared to make war in Greece and to begin his war against the Romans there. When he told

Hannibal what he planned to do, Hannibal told him that the Romans could only be conquered in Italy. Hannibal asked for a hundred of his warships with ten thousand foot soldiers and a thousand cavalry. With this fleet he would first sail into Africa, where he knew he could instigate a fresh rebellion among the Carthaginians. If that failed, he would land in some part of Italy and there begin the war against them anew. When he had persuaded the king to let him do this, he did not personally go to Africa (as Emilius Probus thought {Emilius Probus, Hannibal}), but sent Aristo, a Tyrian born at Ephesus, under the guise of a merchant, to trade at Carthage. He was to prepare their minds for a revolt against the Romans. However, Hannibal's enemies laid hold of Aristo at Carthage. They spent many days in consultation, trying to determine what to do with him and whether they should send him to Rome to demonstrate their innocence in this matter. Aristo escaped, however, and sailed back to Hannibal again, whereupon they sent envoys to the consuls and the Senate at Rome to tell them what had happened. {Justin, Trogus, l. 31. c. 3,4.} {*Livy, l. 34. c. 60,61. 9:569-575} {*Appian, Syrian Wars, l. 11. c. 2. (7,8) 2:115-119}

3037. Meanwhile, Antiochus sent Lysias, Hegesianax and Menippus as his envoys to Rome to determine the feelings of the Senate. [L528] They went under the pretence of trying to arrange a league and friendship between him and them. They told the Senate that the king wondered why they should order him to get out of the cities of Aetolia and Ionia, to forego the tributes due to him from other places, and not to meddle with matters in Asia and countries of his ancient inheritance in Thrace. These were not commands that ought to be given to friends of theirs, such as he was, but to conquered enemies. They were told that they should go and ask Flamininus and the ten commissioners who had formerly been sent into Greece. When they came to the commissioners, the commissioners insisted that Antiochus should either stay out of Europe, or allow the Romans to take care of what they already had in Asia and acquire more there if they could. The envoys told them plainly that they could not negotiate a deal by which the king's rights and dominions might be impaired in any way. So this matter was left unresolved and the envoys were sent away. {*Livy, l. 34. c. 57-59. 9:561-569} {*Appian, Syrian Wars, l. 11. c. 2. (6) 2:113,115}

3038. Scarcely had the envoys left, when news came from Carthage that Antiochus was busy preparing for war against the Romans, and that Hannibal was his general. They were afraid that a fresh war might start from Carthage. {*Livy, l. 34. c. 60. s. 1-3. 9:569}

## 3812a AM, 4521 JP, 193 BC

*3039.* Antiochus gave his daughter to Ptolemy in marriage at Raphia in Phoenicia, or rather in Palestine, and returned to Antioch. {*Livy, l. 35. c. 13. s. 4,5. 10:39} He was now fully resolved to make war against the Romans and thought it best to league himself by marriages and alliances with as many kings and princes in the area as he could. Therefore he sent his daughter Cleopatra, surnamed Syra, to Egypt, to marry Ptolemy. He gave Ptolemy a dowry for her, consisting of all Coelosyria, which he had previously taken from Ptolemy. This he did to pacify Ptolemy and to keep him from joining with the Romans in this war. {*Appian, Syrian Wars, l. 11. c. 1. (5) 2:111,113} Jerome cited Eucles of Rhodes as saying that when Antiochus planned to get Egypt for his dominion, he espoused his daughter Cleopatra in the seventh year of the young Ptolemy's reign. {Jerome, Da 11} However, Jerome followed Eusebius, who said it was the thirteenth year of Ptolemy's reign. {*Eusebius, Chronicles, l. 1. 1:218} [E385] According to our calculations, it was in the twelfth year that he sent her to him. Ptolemy received a dowry of all Coelosyria and Judea. Antiochus did not get Egypt, however. Ptolemy and his council perceived his plans and were more cautious in their affairs, while Cleopatra took her husband's side, rather than her father's. Josephus wrote that Antiochus gave his daughter Cleopatra as a wife for Ptolemy, along with her dowry of Coelosyria, all of Phoenicia, Judea and Samaria. The tribute from these places was equally divided between the two kings. The prominent men in each of these countries gathered the tribute for them and paid it to them. {*Josephus, Antiq., l. 12. c. 4. s. 1. (154.155) 7:81}

*3040.* He offered another daughter, Antiochis, in marriage to Ariarathes, the king of Cappadocia. His third daughter he sent to Eumenes, the king of Pergamum. When Eumenes saw that he planned to make war against the Romans and that this was the reason for the marriage, he refused the offer. When his two brothers, Attalus and Philetaerus, wondered why he should refuse such an offer made to him by a neighbouring king as important as Antiochus, Eumenes told them a great war was coming. He said that if the Romans won, as he truly thought they would, he would be able to hold his own with them. If Antiochus won, then Eumenes' fortune would either be to be turned out of his kingdom by a powerful neighbouring prince, or to be forced to live under him. Concerning this, see Eumenes' speech in Polybius. {*Polybius, l. 21. c. 18-21. 5:269-279} {*Appian, Syrian Wars, l. 11. c. 1. (5) 2:113} {*Livy, l. 35. c. 14. 10:39,41}

## 3812b AM, 4522 JP, 192 BC

*3041.* Antiochus crossed the Taurus Mountains and marched through Cilicia, reaching Ephesus at the very end of winter. {*Livy, l. 35. c. 13. s. 4. 10:39}

*3042.* From there, at the beginning of spring, he sent his son, Antiochus, back into Syria to take care of matters both there and in the remote parts of his eastern dominions, while he himself was busy in the west. Antiochus and his whole army went to invade the Pisidians who lived around Sida. {*Livy, l. 35. c. 13. s. 5. 10:39} [L529]

*3043.* At that time, envoys from Rome arrived at Elaea to see Antiochus. They came under the pretence of an embassy, but were there to see first-hand what preparations he had made. They spent much time in speaking with Hannibal to try to cool his anger toward them. In case that failed, they hoped to make Antiochus jealous of Hannibal because he frequently spoke with the Romans. The envoys who, along with others, met with Antiochus at Lysimachia were Publius Sulpicius and Publius Villius. {*Livy, l. 34. c. 59. s. 8. 9:569} {*Livy, l. 35. c. 13. s. 6,7. 10:39} {Justin, Trogus, l. 31. c. 4.} {*Frontinus, Stratagems, l. 1. c. 8. s. 7. 1:61} {*Appian, Syrian Wars, l. 11. c. 2. (9) 2:119}

*3044.* The envoys went up from Elaea to Pergamum, where Eumenes' palace was. Their instructions were to confer with Eumenes first, before they went to Antiochus. Eumenes did the best he could to have them make war on Antiochus. Sulpicius stayed behind sick at Pergamum, but when Publius Villius heard that Antiochus was warring against Pisidia, he went to Ephesus. During the few days that he stayed there, he made it a point to speak to Hannibal as often as he could. He wanted to know his intentions and to mitigate his anger toward the Romans by assuring him that they intended him no further harm. {*Livy, l. 35. c. 13,14. 10:39,41}

*3045.* Claudius Quadrigarius, who followed the account of the Greek history of Acilius, stated that Publius Scipio Africanus was in this embassy, and that he was the one who spoke with Hannibal at Ephesus. He mentioned one talk of theirs in particular. Africanus asked Hannibal whom he believed to be the greatest general in the world? Hannibal replied that Alexander the Great was the greatest. When asked whom he thought was second, he answered Pyrrhus. When asked who, then, was third, he replied, he himself. At that, Scipio burst out laughing and asked him what he would have done, had he defeated Scipio. To which Hannibal replied that he would have counted himself ahead of both Pyrrhus and Alexander, and all the others that had ever existed. His perplexing and intricate answer was but a trick of Punic wit, and Scipio was taken in by it as with a pretty form of flattery. He was not considered to be better than all the generals, yet he had vanquished a better man than Alexander. {*Livy, l. 35. c. 14. s. 5-12. 10:41-45} {*Plutarch, Flamininus, l. 1. c. 21. s. 3. 10:383} {*Appian, Syrian Wars, l. 11. c. 2. (10) 2:119,121}

## 3812c AM, 4522 JP, 192 BC

*3046.* Villius went from Ephesus to Apamea and there Antiochus heard about the Roman envoys coming to meet them. They discussed almost the same points which had been discussed between Flamininus and the other commissioners on one side, and his envoys on the other, at Rome. When news came of the death of his son Antiochus, who had recently been sent into Syria, the conference was suspended. Villius did not want to be there at this sad time and went to Pergamum while the king and court were all in mourning. The king stopped all preparations for the war and went to Ephesus. {*Livy, l. 35. c. 15. 10:45,47} [E386]

*3047.* The Roman envoys were told to come to Ephesus. They met in conference with Minnio, a principal counsellor and favourite of the king. In his discourse, Minnio accused the Romans of intending to make war against Antiochus under the pretence of setting Greece at liberty. The Romans were holding so many famous countries, which had formerly lived in freedom and according to their own laws, in subjection to them and were making them pay tribute to Rome. Sulpicius replied for the Romans, for he had now recovered from his sickness. He called the envoys of the other states present there as witnesses for the Romans, as they had been instructed to do by Eumenes. Then the conference degenerated into a brawl. {*Livy, l. 35. c. 16-17. 10:47-51}

*3048.* When Antiochus had heard the embassy of the Rhodians, he told them that if he and the Romans came to an agreement and a league, they would all be free, along with the people of Byzantium and Cyzicum, as well as other Greeks living in Asia. The Aetolians and Ionians would still be under the control of the kings of Asia. [L530] Therefore, when they could get nowhere with the king, the Roman envoys returned to Rome, since this had indeed been the least part of their errand, as they had primarily come to spy on him. {*Appian, Syrian Wars, l. 11. c. 3. (12) 2:123}

## 3813a AM, 4522 JP, 192 BC

*3049.* After this, the Aetolian envoys came to the king. They offered to make him commander of all the forces they had raised and persuaded him by every means to go over to Greece. They said that Greece was ready to receive him, and that he should not stay until his armies came down to him from the remote and inner parts of Asia. This made Antiochus all the more eager to go into Greece as soon as possible. {*Appian, Syrian Wars, l. 11. c. 3. (12) 2:123,125} {*Polybius, l. 3. c. 3. s. 3. 2:9} {Justin, Trogus, l. 30. c. 4.} {Justin, Trogus, l. 32. c. 1.}

*3050.* Before he sailed, he went up to Illium and sacrificed to Athena. He returned to his fleet and sailed with forty decked ships, sixty open vessels and two hundred cargo ships. These were loaded with all types of provisions and sailed at the rear of the fleet. His whole army consisted of ten thousand foot soldiers and five hundred cavalry, with six elephants. This was barely enough to take over Greece, if no one was there to defend it. How inadequate were these forces to stand up against the Roman military might. {*Livy, l. 35. c. 43. s. 3-6. 10:127}

*3051.* Eumenes sent his brother Attalus to Rome to let them know that Antiochus had crossed over the Hellespont with his army. So the Aetolians were ready to rise up in arms as soon as he landed. The Senate thanked Attalus and his absent brother Eumenes, while Attalus was housed at public expense, and given presents. {*Livy, l. 35. c. 23. s. 10,11. 10:67}

## 3813b AM, 4523 JP, 191 BC

*3052.* About the middle of winter, Antiochus consulted with Demetrius on how to carry on the war. Hannibal gave sound advice, if only it had been followed. It was not, except that Polyxenidas was sent to bring the rest of the fleet and army from Asia. {*Livy, l. 36. c. 5-8. 10:169-181} {Justin, Trogus, l. 31. c. 5,6.} {*Appian, Syrian Wars, l. 11. c. 3. (13,14) 2:125-129}

*3053.* Antiochus fell in love with a young maiden of Chalcis, the daughter of Cleoptolemus, his host. Even though Antiochus was almost fifty, he set aside the matters of the war and thought only of marrying her. He called her by the name of Euboea and spent all the next winter in banqueting and revels. Likewise, his army spent all that season in luxury and pleasure. {*Polybius, l. 20. c. 8. 5:223} {*Athenaeus, l. 10. (439ef) 4:491,493} {*Diod. Sic., l. 29. c. 2. 11:247} {*Livy, l. 36. c. 11. s. 1-3. 1:189,191} {*Appian, Syrian Wars, l. 11. c. 3. (16) 2:133}

*3054.* Manius Acilius Glabrio, the consul, left Rome dressed in military uniform, to go against Antiochus. This was on the 5th day of the Nones of May (May 3). We deduced this date from an eclipse that happened the following January. {*Livy, l. 36. c. 3. s. 14. 10:165}

*3055.* About the same time, envoys came to Rome from two kings, Philip of Macedonia and Ptolemy of Egypt. Both offered their help against Antiochus with money and grain. Ptolemy brought a thousand pounds in gold and twenty thousand pounds in silver. Nothing was accepted, and the Senate thanked them for their good will. When both of them offered to come into Aetolia in person with their armies, the Senate answered that they would not trouble Ptolemy. However, the Senate and people of Rome would be happy if Philip would assist Manius Acilius, their consul, with whatever he needed. {*Livy, l. 36. c. 4. s. 1-5. 10:165,176}

## 3813c AM, 4523 JP, 191 BC

*3056.* Antiochus was defeated at Thermopylae in a battle against the consul Marcus Acilius, and Cato, a general in that army. {*Livy, l. 36. c. 15-19. 10:201-219} {*Plutarch, Cato Major, l. 1. c. 13,15. 2:337-343} {*Appian, Syrian Wars, l. 11. c. 4. (17-20) 2:133-141} {*Frontinus, Stratagems, l. 2. c. 4. s. 4. 1:127} [E387] [L531] He was forced to flee back to Asia and came to Ephesus with his new wife. {*Livy, l. 36. c. 21. s. 1. 10:221} {Justin, Trogus} {*Appian, Syrian Wars, l. 11. c. 4. (20) 2:139} {*Polybius, l. 20. c. 8. 5:223} {*Athenaeus, l. 10. (439ef) 4:491,493} Cicero wrote that Cato, in speaking of himself, said that he fought at Thermopylae under Manius Acilius Glabrio in the fourth year that he (Cato) had been military tribune. {*Cicero, De Senectute, l. 1. c. 10. (32) 20:41} Plutarch and Livy stated that he was sent to Rome by the consul Acilius with the news of that victory. {*Plutarch, Cato Major, l. 1. c. 14. s. 3,4. 2:343} {*Livy, l. 36. c. 21. s. 4,5. 10:223} Antisthenes, the historian, noted the actions by Buplagus the Syrian and Publius a Roman captain after this battle at Thermopylae as recorded by Phlegon. {Phlegon, De Mirabilibus, c. 3.}

*3057.* When Antiochus was at Ephesus, he became careless and unafraid of the Romans, believing that they would never cross over into Asia. When Hannibal had roused him from these idle thoughts, he sent for his forces from the inland countries to come down quickly to the coast. He prepared his navy and made Polyxenidas, an exile of Rhodes, his admiral. He again crossed over into the Chersonesus and fortified it, putting garrisons into Sestus and Abydus, where he thought the Romans would try to cross over into Asia. {*Livy, l. 36. c. 26. 10:235,237} {*Appian, Syrian Wars, l. 11. c. 4. (21) 2:141}

## 3814a AM, 4523 JP, 191 BC

*3058.* Gaius Livius Salinator was sent to succeed Attalus in the navy. On his way to Asia, Eumenes routed Polyxenidas, Antiochus' admiral. He sank ten of his ships and captured thirteen more, losing only one ship himself, and that one was from Carthage! They pursued Polyxenidas as far as Ephesus. They then sent back the Rhodian fleet of twenty-five ships, which had arrived after the battle. Eumenes and his ships came to Canas, a town of Lycia. Because the winter was coming, they drew their ships to land and fortified the place where they were staying with works for their defence. {*Livy, l. 36. c. 43-45. 10:277-285} {*Appian, Syrian Wars, l. 11. c. 5. (22) 2:143,145}

*3059.* While this naval battle was being fought at Coricus, Antiochus had gone to Magnesia near the mountain of Sipylus to gather his land forces together. When he heard of his naval defeat, he began to prepare a new navy, so that he might not appear to have been vanquished from the sea. He sent Hannibal into Syria to get ships from the Phoenicians, and ordered Polyxenidas to make up his fleet again by repairing those ships that had been damaged in the battle and building new ones. Meanwhile, he made his winter quarters in Phrygia. He sent for help from all his regions, even from Galatia. {*Livy, l. 36. c. 41. s. 6,7. 10:275} {*Livy, l. 37. c. 8. s. 1-4. 10:313} {*Appian, Syrian Wars, l. 11. c. 5. (22) 2:145} Using both fear and his money, he also convinced them to join in arms with him, because he thought their height and courage would terrify the Romans. {*Appian, Syrian Wars, l. 11. c. 2. (6) 2:115}

*3060.* The envoys from Ptolemy and Cleopatra arrived at Rome to congratulate them on having driven Antiochus out of Europe. The envoys persuaded them to cross into Asia, all the way to Syria. They declared that they were ready to do whatever the Romans would request. The Senate sent thanks to the king and queen for their good will and gave each of the envoys four thousand *asses* of money. {*Livy, l. 37. c. 3. s. 9-11. 10:299,301}

*3061.* Antiochus left his son Seleucus in Aeolia with the army, to hold the sea coast there in order. They were being bothered from every direction, by the Romans on one side and Eumenes on the other. Seleucus spent all that winter at times helping his friends and at other times plundering those whom he could not win over to his side. {*Livy, l. 37. c. 8. s. 5,6. 10:313,315}

## 3814b AM, 4524 JP, 190 BC

*3062.* About the middle of winter, Eumenes, with a company of two thousand foot soldiers and a hundred cavalry, came to Canas where the Roman fleet was wintering. [L532] There he told them that, if they wanted to, they could get much spoil from the country around Thyatira. He did not leave until he had persuaded Livius, the admiral, to let him have five thousand men. He set out with these and brought them back again within a short time, loaded with an enormous amount of plunder. {*Livy, l. 37. c. 8. s. 6,7. 10:315}

*3063.* In the interim, a rebellion took place in Phocaea, where some were trying to draw the common people to Antiochus. The wintering of the Roman navy there had taxed them very heavily. They had been required to furnish them with five hundred outer garments and five hundred undergarments. Grain had become scarce, so that the ships and garrison were forced to move from there and quarter elsewhere. After this, the faction siding with Antiochus was no longer afraid, even though the elders and chief men of the city stood firmly for the Romans. However, the leaders of the faction for Antiochus prevailed with the common people. {*Livy, l. 37. c. 9. s. 2-5. 10:315} [E388]

*3064.* Consequently, the magistrates of Phocaea feared the opinion of the common people. They wisely sent their agents to Seleucus, to ask him not to come near their city because they were resolved to do nothing until they saw the outcome of the war. When Seleucus was told that the common people were wholly for his father and that they were short of grain, he did not reply, but immediately marched toward them with his army. {*Polybius, l. 21. c. 6. s. 4-6. 5:245}

3065. At Rome, both the new consuls, Lucius Scipio and Gaius Laelius Nepos, were keen to go into Greece. Publius Scipio Africanus, speaking on behalf of his brother Lucius, said that if they wished to send his brother there, he would go with him as his lieutenant. His words carried the day. They said who was more appropriate to fight against Hannibal, as the brother of Scipio Africanus who had already vanquished him once? {*Cicero, Philippics, l. 11. c. 7. 15:475} {*Livy, l. 37. c. 1. s. 7-10. 10:293} {*Valerius Maximus, l. 5. c. 5. s. 1. 1:509} {Justin, Trogus, l. 31. c. 7.}

3066. In those days, when Lucius Scipio was on his way against Antiochus and while the anniversary games were being celebrated in honour of Apollo, an eclipse occurred on the 5th of the Ides of July (July 11). On a very clear day, it suddenly grew dark through an eclipse of the sun. {*Livy, l. 37. c. 4. s. 4,5. 10:301} This eclipse of the sun at Rome was confirmed by the astronomical account and happened on March 14 of the Julian calendar. Hence, the calendar was out by a hundred and twenty-five days. January 1 really occurred on August 29! So great was the confusion of the Roman calendar in those days. This is treated in more detail in Livy. {*Livy, Appendix, l. 33. 13:87,89}

## 3814c AM, 4524 JP, 190 BC

3067. At about the beginning of spring, Pausistratus with thirty-six Rhodian ships, Livius with thirty Roman ships and Eumenes with seven of his, sailed into the Hellespont. Livius first sailed into the port which was known as the harbour of the Achaeans. From there Livius went up to Illium and sacrificed to Athena. Livius made a speech to, and a good impression on, the envoys of some of the neighbouring cities, Eleus, Dardanus and Rhoetium. These all came and voluntarily surrendered themselves to Livius. He left ten ships to blockade Abydus and went with the rest of the ships to the other side, to besiege Sestus. After these had surrendered, he prepared to return to the Asian side to besiege Abydus. {*Livy, l. 37. c. 9. s. 6-11. 10:315,317} {*Appian, Syrian Wars, l. 11. c. 5. (23) 2:147}

3068. While these things were happening in the Hellespont, Polyxenidas, the admiral of King Antiochus, told Pausistratus, the admiral of Rhodes, that he would betray the whole of Antiochus' fleet, or most of it, into his hands. Pausistratus believed Polyxenidas and went to Samos. Because he did not keep a proper watch, as he should have done, he was killed and the twenty-nine

ships which he had under his command were lost. [L533] Of all his fleet, only five ships from Rhodes escaped, and two from the Isle of Cos. {*Livy, l. 37. c. 9-11. 10:315-325} {*Appian, Syrian Wars, l. 11. c. 5. (24) 2:147,149}

3069. At the same time, Seleucus recovered Phocaea after a gate of the city was opened to him, and he and his army gained entry that way. While these things were happening in Aeolia, Abydus had endured the siege for a number of days and continued to hold out through the valour of the king's garrison. Finally, everyone grew weary of the business and the chief magistrates of the city, with the ready consent of the captain of the garrison, sent to Livius to ask for conditions of surrender. It was at that very time that Livius heard of the destruction of the Rhodian navy, and so would no longer stay to take in Abydus and to keep the Hellespont. He and all his fleet set sail for Phocaea. When he found that it was held by a strong garrison of the king and that Seleucus was not far off with his army, he started wasting the sea coast. Taking what spoil he could find in the area, he stayed only until Eumenes could reach him with his fleet. Then he planned to go to Samos, where he finally arrived, badly weather-beaten. Here he united his fleet with that of the Rhodians, which now consisted of twenty ships under the command of Eudamus. {*Livy, l. 37. c. 11,12. 10:325,327}

3070. After Livius had added the Rhodian ships to his fleet, he immediately sailed to Ephesus. There he arranged his ships in battle array before the very mouth of the port. When no one came out against him, he divided his fleet into two parts. One part anchored in the very haven of the enemy, while the other landed their men. These had ranged far and wide in that vicinity and gathered a vast amount of spoil and were just returning with it to their ship when Andronicus, a Macedonian (Appian called him Nicander) and captain of the garrison in Ephesus, sallied out against them and forced them to retire to their ships. They abandoned most of their booty and at once returned to Samos, where they were to be met by Lucius Aemilius Regillus, the praetor, who was to succeed Livius in the charge of the navy. As Regillus was coming there from the Isle of Chios, Livius sent out two good ships of Rhodes, of four tiers of oars each, along with Eumenes himself, in person, with two more ships of five tiers of oars each, to meet him. {*Livy, l. 37. c. 13. 10:325-331} {*Appian, Syrian Wars, l. 11. c. 5. (25) 2:149,151} [E389]

3071. After sitting at Samos in council about naval matters, Aemilius sailed with all his fleet to the very mouth of the port of Ephesus to terrify the enemy. Livius went to Patara in Lycia. Aemilius was driven from Ephesus by a storm and so returned to Samos. The cities of Miletus, Myndus, Halicarnassus, Cnidos and Cos, which Livius sailed passed, readily accepted him. Lycia did not welcome him, for he encountered not only a storm at sea but also the enemy at land. Therefore, he returned to Greece again. After this, he spoke with the two Scipios, who were in Thessaly at the time, so that he might then return to Italy. {*Livy, l. 37. c. 14-16. 10:331-339}

3072. At Samos, Aemilius, the praetor, and Eumenes received letters from the Scipios, saying there was a truce with the Aetolians and they were to march toward the Hellespont. The Aetolians had informed Antiochus and his son Seleucus about this, also. {*Polybius, l. 21. c. 8. 5:249}

3073. Eumenes sent his agents into Achaia to make an alliance with them which the people had ratified in a general assembly, and also sent him a company of tall young men to assist him. {*Polybius, l. 21. c. 3. 5:239}

3074. Aemilius with all his fleet sailed past Miletus and the other cities of that coast and landing in the Bay of Bargylia, they went to Iasus. The city was held by a garrison of Antiochus' men, so they sent to the magistrates and other chief men of the city to persuade them to surrender. When they were told that they would do nothing, Aemilius drew up to the walls in order to besiege it. But the exiles of Iasus, who were among the Rhodians, prevailed with them and through Eumenes' mediation, they pulled back and abandoned the siege. {*Livy, l. 37. c. 17. s. 1-8. 10:339,341} [L534]

3075. The people of Heraclea in Pontus sent envoys to Aemilius. He sent them a very kind and favourable answer in writing, purporting that the Senate of Rome would be their good friends. Further, neither their counsel nor their concerns would be ignored whenever the Heracleans should have an occasion to use them. {Memnon, Excerpts, c. 28.}

3076. While Eumenes was away helping the Romans and Rhodians attack the sea towns of Lycia, Seleucus and his army invaded his country. They first came in a hostile manner to Elaea. When they were unable to take the city, they wasted all the country around it. From there, Seleucus marched with all his forces to Pergamum itself, the capital city of this kingdom. Attalus, Eumenes' brother, drew out and pitched his camp before the city walls, where he had engaged in many skirmishes with the enemy. He was too weak to fight them, so he withdrew behind the walls and remained there and the city was besieged. {Memnon, Excerpts, c. 28.}

3077. About the same time, Antiochus went from Apamea and first camped at Sardis, not far from his son Seleucus, near the head of the Caicus River. He had with him a large army made up of men from various countries. The strongest, most frightening squadron in it was from the Galatians, and consisted of four thousand soldiers. With these and a few others, he went to ravage and waste all the country about Pergamum from one end to the other. {Memnon, Excerpts, c. 28.}

3078. At Samos, Eumenes heard this and so was called away to take care of his own affairs at home. He sailed with all his men and came to Elaea, from where he went to Pergamum before the enemy heard of his arrival. He frequently sailed out from there and engaged in some small skirmishes with the enemy. A few days later, both the Roman and the Rhodian fleet came from Samos to Elaea to help him. {Memnon, Excerpts, c. 28.}

3079. Antiochus heard that there were so many fleets coming together into the same port. A consul was already in Macedonia with his army and making provisions at the Hellespont for his crossing into Asia. Antiochus thought it a good time to try for a peace with Eumenes, the Romans and the Rhodians all at once. So he moved his camp and came to Elaea. After taking a little hill opposite the city, he left all his foot soldiers and with his cavalry (about six thousand men) went down into a plain close to the walls of the city. He sent some commissioners into the city to ask for peace. Whereupon Lucius Aemilius sent for Eumenes to come there to him from Pergamum. Eumenes advised what he considered to be the best course of action. Eudamus and Pamphilidas, the commanders of the Rhodian fleet, were also there, giving advice, and said the Rhodians were not against a peace. Eumenes said that it was not in the interests of their honour to make a peace treaty. However, they were unable to settle the matter at that time, so Aemilius sent Antiochus word that no peace could be made before the coming of the consul. [E390] When he heard this reply, Antiochus started wasting the country all around Elaea. He left Seleucus to continue the siege before Pergamum and marched away in a rage with the rest of his army. He did not stop until he came into that rich country which was called Thebes' Campus, that is, the plain of Thebes. He created all manner of havock there and greatly enriched all his army for the time being. {*Polybius, l. 21. c. 10. 5:251,253} {*Livy, l. 37. c. 18,19. 10:341-347}

3080. At the same time, the Achaeans sent Diophanes of Megalopolis, with a thousand foot soldiers and a hundred cavalry, to Elaea for Eumenes. {*Polybius, l. 21. c. 3b. 5:239,241} These were old veterans and their captain had been trained under Philopoemen, the most famous commander of all the Greeks in his time. {*Livy, l. 37. c. 20. s. 1-3. 10:347} {*Polybius, l. 21. c. 9. 5:249} [L535]

*3081.* As soon as they had landed, Attalus sent some men to show them the way and so brought them to Pergamum. As soon as these Achaeans arrived, they made continual sallies against Seleucus to make him withdraw and leave that country. Nevertheless, Seleucus stayed in the area and annoyed his foes and helped his friends in those regions. {*Appian, Syrian Wars, l. 11. c. 5. (26) 2:151,153*} {*Livy, l. 37. c. 20,21. 10:347-351*}

*3082.* While Antiochus marched in a hostile manner to Adramyttium, Aemilius and Eumenes came by sea to rescue it. Consequently, Antiochus did not attack the town, but started plundering the country around it. He captured Peraea, a colony of the Mitylenians. Likewise, he took Cottos, Corylenus, the Aphrodisians and Prinne on the first assault. He then returned to Sardis by way of Thyatira. {*Livy, l. 37. c. 21. s. 4-7. 10:351,353*}

*3083.* The Roman fleet, together with the Rhodians and Eumenes, first went to Mitylene and from there returned to Elaea. They sailed to Phocaea and anchored at Bacchium, an island very close to the city of Phocaea. They plundered their temples and monuments, which they had previously spared. When they came to the city, they found that a company of three thousand of Antiochus' foot soldiers had managed to get in there before they came. Hence, they did not besiege the place, but returned to the island where they had been before. After first ravaging the country around there, the Roman fleet returned to Elaea, and Eumenes and the Rhodians to Samos. {*Livy, l. 37. c. 21,22. 10:353*}

## 3814d AM, 4524 JP, 190 BC

*3084.* About midsummer, the Rhodian fleet fought with Antiochus' navy. The Rhodian fleet had thirty-two ships of four tiers of oars and four others of three tiers of oars. Hannibal brought a fleet of thirty-seven ships from Syria, some of which were of an extraordinary size. The battle took place at Sida, a cape of Pamphylia. The Rhodians routed Hannibal, but could not pursue him, because their sailors were weak and sickly. However, to prevent him from joining with the old fleet, they sent Chariclitus and twenty ships to Patara and the harbour of Megiste. Shortly after this, they sent Pamphilidas with four more ships, {*Livy, l. 37. c. 23,24. 10:357-361*} and so Hannibal was blockaded in Pamphylia. {*Appian, Syrian Wars, l. 11. c. 6. (28) 2:157*} {*Emilius Probus, Hannibal*}

*3085.* When Antiochus came to Sardis, he sent envoys with letters to Prusias, the king of Bithynia, who was surnamed *Cynegus*, that is, *The Hunter*. He wanted Prusias to join with him against the Romans. This initially worried Prusias. However, other letters came to him from the two brothers, Lucius and Publius Scipio, telling him not to fear the Romans. This was confirmed to him when, shortly after this, an embassy was sent to him from Rome. Its leader was Gaius Livius, who had recently commanded their fleet. When Prusias spoke with them, he resolved to side with the Romans and to break off entirely with Antiochus. {*Polybius, l. 21. c. 11. 5:253-257*} {*Livy, l. 37. c. 25. s. 5-14. 10:363,365*} {*Appian, Syrian Wars, l. 11. c. 5. (23) 2:147*} {*Appian, Mithridatic Wars, l. 12. c. 1. (2) 2:241,243*}

*3086.* When Antiochus saw no further hope of getting Prusias on his side, he moved from Sardis to Ephesus. There, he inspected his fleet, which had been in preparation for a long time. He saw no other way of preventing the Romans from moving their land army into Asia than to make himself absolute master of the sea. He resolved to do what he could and to risk a naval battle. {*Polybius, l. 21. c. 11. s. 13. 5:257*} {*Livy, l. 37. c. 26. s. 1-3. 10:365*} [L536]

*3087.* Therefore, he immediately went to see whether he could take Notium, which was a town of the Colophonians not far from where he was at Ephesus. He hoped that when the Romans came by land to relieve their confederate town, Admiral Polyxenidas would then have an opportunity for a major naval victory. Polyxenidas at that time had eighty-nine or ninety good ships under his command. Aemilius and the Rhodians fought with him at Myonnesus. Livy said that Aemilius had fifty-eight ships and the Rhodians, twenty-two. Appian said the Rhodians had twenty-five. Polyxenidas was defeated and with a good wind at his back, fled quickly back to Ephesus. He lost forty-two ships (not twenty-nine only, as Appian stated) of which thirteen quickly came into the hands of the enemy with all their men on board. The Roman fleet had only two leaking ships and a few others damaged. *[E391]* Polyxenidas captured a Rhodian ship and took it with him to Ephesus. This battle took place in December (as the year went at that time in Rome). {*Livy, l. 37. c. 30. 10:377-381*} {*Appian, Syrian Wars, l. 11. c. 5. (27) 2:153,155*} This was the time stated by Macrobius: {*Macrobius, Saturnalia, l. 1.*}

> "...the 11th of the Calends of January (December 20) was a feast dedicated to their Lares (that is, their household gods). At this time, Lucius Aemilius Regillus, praetor, in the war against Antiochus, vowed to build a temple in the Campus of Mars."

*3088.* Livy stated that his vow was performed eleven years later. {*Livy, l. 40. c. 52. s. 4,5. 12:161*} There is also a copy (but most inaccurately written) of:

> "a table, containing the manner of this victory, hung up by him on the doors not only of his new temple but also in Jupiter's temple in the Capitol."

*3089.* Antiochus, who was disturbed by the news of this defeat, was poorly advised to withdraw his garrison from

Lysimachia, lest the garrison should fall into Roman hands. Raising his siege from Colophon, he retired to Sardis. He sent letters to Ariarathes, his son-in-law in Cappadocia, to bring him troops, both from there and everywhere else that he could find men. {*Livy, l. 37. c. 31. s. 1-4. 10:381} Meanwhile, he lay idly at Sardis wasting his time, which might have been better spent in ordering his affairs elsewhere. {*Polybius, l. 21. c. 13. 5:257}

## 3815a AM, 4524 JP, 190 BC

3090. After this naval victory, Aemilius sailed straight to Ephesus and arranged his ships in battle formation before the very mouth of the port. This publicly showed that Antiochus had lost the mastery of the sea. Aemilius sailed to Chios and repaired his ships which had been damaged in the battle. He sailed to Phocaea, which had recently revolted from the Romans. First he tried to take it directly, but it later surrendered to him. He could not prevent his soldiers from plundering it, but he returned their city, their lands and their laws to them. With the approach of winter, he stayed there because the place had two ports. {*Livy, l. 37. c. 31,32. 10:381-387}

3091. About the same time, Lysimachia, which was well supplied with all types of provisions, welcomed the Roman generals and the two Scipios when they arrived. The Romans continued through the Chersonesus to the Hellespont and found everything already prepared by Eumenes for their crossing. They crossed over as if into a friend's country, and no one hindered their journey. {*Livy, l. 37. c. 33. 10:387,389}

3092. Antiochus was at his wits' end and did not know what to do, so he sent Heraclides of Byzantium to sue for peace with the Romans. He had instructions both to the council of war there in general, and to Publius Scipio Africanus in particular. The council answered him that he must pay the cost of this war and surrender all Asia on the west side of the Taurus Mountains to the Romans. Antiochus could not imagine anything worse than if he were to be utterly defeated, so he abandoned any attempts for peace and prepared for war. {*Polybius, l. 21. c. 13-15. 5:257-265} {*Diod. Sic., l. 29. c. 6. s. 7-9. 11:253,255} {*Livy, l. 37. c. 34-37. 10:389-399} {*Appian, Syrian Wars, l. 11. c. 5. (29) 2:157-161} [L537]

3093. Lucius Scipio, the consul, journeyed to the Hellespont or Dardanus and Rhetaeus. All the people of both places came joyfully from their cities to greet him and his men. From there he went to Illium and pitched his camp in the plain opposite the city walls. He went up into the city and the citadel, and sacrificed to Athena as the goddess and protector of that place. There was much joy and mutual congratulations between the men of Illium and the Romans. They recounted how

Aeneas and his captains, who had set out from Troy to eventually found Rome, were their countrymen. The Romans were just as proud that they were descended from them. They were like parents and children who had been separated by a long absence and were now joyfully reunited. {*Livy, l. 37. c. 37. s. 1-3. 10:395,397} {Justin, Trogus, l. 31. c. 8.} Demetrius of Scepsis said of himself that when he had come to Illium as a boy, he had seen their houses lying in such a poor state that they did not so much as have roof tiles with which to cover them. {*Strabo, l. 13. c. 1. s. 27. 6:53}

3094. Scipio left there and on the sixth day of marching, came to the head of the Caicus River, where Eumenes met him with his forces. They made provision for food to carry with them for many days, as they planned to attack Antiochus and settle the business before winter came. {*Livy, l. 37. c. 37. s. 4,5. 10:397}

3095. Publius Scipio Africanus became sick and was carried to Elaea. He left his substitute, Gnaeus Domitius, to take over his responsibilities. Antiochus intercepted Scipio's son in a plain near Thyatira, not far from the enemy. He sent the young Publius Scipio home to his father without a ransom. This was to ease his mind and to help him get well again. {*Polybius, l. 21. c. 15. 5:262,263} {*Livy, l. 37. c. 37. s. 6-11. 10:397,399} {Justin, Trogus, l. 31. c. 7.} {*Appian, Syrian Wars, l. 11. c. 6. (30) 2:161} {Aurelius Victor, De Viris Illustribus, c. 64.} {*Dio, l. 19. (62) 2:317} [E392]

3096. The Senate and people of Heraclea in Pontus sent an embassy to the Scipios, and desired that they would ask them to ratify and confirm the league which Aemilius had previously made with them. This was done. They also requested that Antiochus might be received into the favour and friendship of the people of Rome. Having drawn up a general decree of the people at Heraclea, they sent it to Antiochus and advised him to abandon the war against the Romans. {Memnon, Excerpts, c. 28.}

3097. Florus stated that Antiochus had equipped his army with very large elephants all decked out and glittering with gold, silver, purple and ivory from elephants. {*Florus, l. 1. c. 24. s. 16,17. 1:123} In the Apocrypha we read that he had a hundred and twenty elephants. {Apc 1Ma 8:6} This is likely correct, for he had a hundred and two when he fought with Ptolemy and a hundred and fifty later. {See note on 3787c AM. <<2923>>} {See note on 3800a AM. <<2956>>} Livy said he had only fifty-four elephants, sixty thousand foot soldiers and almost twelve thousand cavalry. {*Livy, l. 37. c. 37. s. 9. 10:399} {*Livy, l. 37. c. 39. s. 13. 10:405} Appian stated that he only had seventy thousand troops in all. {*Appian, Syrian Wars, l. 11. c. 6. (32) 2:165} However, Florus greatly exaggerating when he said: {*Florus, l. 1. c. 24. s. 16. 1:123}

"He had three hundred thousand foot soldiers and an equal number of cavalry and scythed chariots in the field that day."

*3098.* Appian stated that the Romans had only thirty thousand foot soldiers. {*Appian, Syrian Wars, l. 11. c. 6. (31) 2:163} Livy said that of these, about two thousand Macedonians and Thracians were left to defend the camp. {*Livy, l. 37. c. 39. s. 12,13. 10:405}

*3099.* This battle was fought near Magnesia at the foot of the Sipylus Hill. Hannibal was not there, since he was still bottled up in Pamphylia with the fleet which he had brought from Syria. Publius Scipio Africanus was not there either, because he was sick and in the city of Elaea. The day of the battle was misty. Antiochus, with so large an army, could not see both wings of his army at once. The dampness ruined the strings of the bows and thongs with which they shot their arrows. Nevertheless, they forced the right wing of the Roman army to run and flee to their camp. *[L538]* When Aemilius, who was on the left wing, saw them coming, he sent out his men to meet them. They threatened to kill them with their swords unless they returned into the battle. Thereupon, they found themselves hemmed in with their friends ahead of them and the enemies behind. Aemilius also offered to go with them himself with two thousand of his men. So they turned around and ran desperately into the throng of the enemy and made a vast slaughter of them. This was the turning point in the battle. Antiochus lost fifty thousand foot soldiers and three thousand cavalry. {*Livy, l. 37. c. 41-43. 10:409-419} {Eutropius} Livy said fourteen hundred were taken prisoner, while Justin said there were eleven thousand captured. A few of the elephants were killed and fifteen were taken with their masters. A few of the Romans were wounded. They lost not more than three hundred foot soldiers and twenty-four cavalry. {*Livy, l. 37. c. 44. s. 1,2. 10:419} Eumenes lost twenty-five men.

*3100.* Antiochus escaped with a few in his company. More joined him along the way and he arrived at Sardis with a moderately sized army about midnight. He heard that his son Seleucus and various of his friends had fled to Celaenae, near which the new city of Apamea had been built. Before day, he went on horseback with his wife and daughter and joined him there, having left Xeno to hold Sardis. He made Timo the governor of the province of Lydia and left some of his captains there to salvage what they could from this disaster. The next day he went to Syria. {*Livy, l. 37. c. 44. s. 5-7. 10:419} {*Appian, Syrian Wars, l. 11. c. 6. (36) 2:173} {*Dio, l. 19. (2) 2:321 (Zonaras, l. 9. c. 20.)}

*3101.* When Polyxenidas, Antiochus' admiral, heard of this defeat, he left Ephesus and sailed as far as Patara in Lycia. For fear of the Rhodian fleet, which lay not far

from Megiste, he went ashore with a few of his company and reached Syria by land. {*Livy, l. 37. c. 45. s. 1-3. 10:421}

*3102.* After this victory, envoys from all parts flocked to Scipio. They first came from Thyatira and Magnesia. {*Livy, l. 37. c. 44. s. 5. 10:419} Then they came from Sardis, Tralles, Ephesus and that Magnesia which was on the Meander River. They all surrendered themselves to him, after which all the cities of Asia did likewise. They submitted themselves wholly to his mercy and the sovereignty of the people of Rome. {*Livy, l. 37. c. 45. s. 1-3. 10:421}

*3103.* The consul then went to Sardis, and his brother Publius Scipio came from Elaea to meet him as soon as he was able to travel. About the same time Musaeus was sent as a herald from Antiochus. Through the mediation of Publius Scipio, he obtained permission for Antiochus to send envoys to the consul to sue for peace. Shortly after this, Antiochus sent envoys from Zeuxis, the governor of Lydia, and Antipater's brother's son came to Publius Scipio. They first talked with Eumenes, who was not friendly toward them because of the former quarrels between Antiochus and Eumenes himself. So the envoys worked through Publius Scipio, to address the consul directly. *[E393]* The consul called a full council and having listened to them, offered the king the same conditions that he had sent him from the Hellespont, before the battle at Magnesia. Publius Scipio publicly proclaimed that the Roman custom was not to be humiliated by defeat nor to become haughty in victory. Therefore, Antiochus was to leave Europe and part with all of Asia on the west side of the Taurus Mountains. He would have to pay the cost of this war. He was to pay fifteen thousand Euboean talents, five hundred immediately, twenty-five hundred when the Senate and people of Rome had ratified the peace, and a thousand talents a year in twelve instalments over twelve years. He was to pay four hundred talents to Eumenes for his damages and the balance of grain which was owing to Eumenes' father. He had to surrender to the consul, Hannibal, the Carthaginian, and to Thoas, the Aetolian, and some others who had been the first instigators of this war. Lastly, Antiochus would have to deliver twenty hostages, to ensure compliance with these conditions. *[L539]* When Antipater and Zeuxis had accepted these conditions, it was unanimously agreed to send envoys to Rome for their ratification, whereupon the meeting adjourned. {*Polybius, l. 21. c. 16,17. 5:265-269} {*Diod. Sic., l. 29. c. 8. s. 10. 11:255,257} {*Livy, l. 37. c. 45. 10:421-427} {Justin, Trogus, l. 31. c. 8.} {*Appian, Syrian Wars, l. 11. c. 7. (38,39) 2:177-181}

*3104.* After this, the consul divided his army and sent them away to their winter quarters. Some went to Magnesia, and some to Tralles and Ephesus. {*Livy, l. 37. c. 45. s. 19,20. 10:425} {*Polybius, l. 21. c. 17. s. 11,12. 5:269}

*3105.* The consul went to Ephesus and Antiochus sent him five hundred talents as agreed for a down payment, as well as the hostages whom he was to hand over. {*Livy, l. 37. c. 45. s. 20. 10:425}* Among them was Antiochus, the king's youngest son. {*Appian, Syrian Wars, l. 11. c. 7. (39) 2:181}* However, Zonaras stated that it was Gnaeus Manlius Vulso, who succeeded Scipio, who first demanded the king's youngest son for a hostage. {*Dio, l. 19. (2) 2:321 (Zonaras, l. 9. c. 20.)}*

## 3815b AM, 4525 JP, 189 BC

*3106.* Marcus Aurelius Cotta was sent to Rome by the consul, with Antiochus' envoys. Eumenes and his envoys also went, as well as envoys from Rhodes, Smyrna, and almost all of the cities and states on the west side of the Taurus Mountains. {*Livy, l. 37. c. 52. s. 1,2. 10:441,443}*

*3107.* Manius Acilius Glabrio entered Rome in a triumph over Antiochus and the Aetolians. {*Livy, l. 37. c. 46. s. 2,3. 10:427}*

## 3815c AM, 4525 JP, 189 BC

*3108.* Gnaeus Manlius Vulso, the consul, went into Asia to take over the army which was under Lucius Scipio. He brought with him from Rome four thousand foot soldiers and two hundred cavalry, while the Latins sent eight thousand foot soldiers and four hundred cavalry. {*Livy, l. 37. c. 50. s. 1,2. 10:437}* At almost the same time as Manlius, the consul, landed in Asia, Quintus Fabius Labeo came as the praetor to take charge of the fleet. {*Livy, l. 37. c. 60. s. 1. 10:477}* When the new consul arrived at Ephesus at the beginning of the spring, Lucius Scipio turned the army over to him. After he had reviewed the troops, he made a speech to incite them to prepare for a war against the Gauls, or Galatians. {*Livy, l. 37. c. 60. s. 1,2. 10:477}* {*Livy, l. 38. c. 12. s. 2. 11:37,39}* Fabius set sail with the fleet for Crete, to liberate any Romans and other Italians who were slaves there, after which he returned to Ephesus and sent three ships to Thrace. He ordered Antiochus' garrisons to withdraw from Aenos and Maronea, and then these places were restored to their original liberty. {*Livy, l. 37. c. 60. s. 3-7. 10:477,479}*

*3109.* About the beginning of summer, Eumenes and the envoys came to Rome. Cotta first told the Senate and later the common people what had happened in Asia. Then Eumenes was asked by the Senate to speak. He told them what he had done in their service and what his request to them was, while being very moderate in his presentation. The Rhodians, however, opposed him because of their own interests and because they sought the liberty of the Greek cities and states in Asia. After both parties had been heard, the Senate decreed that all the regions on the west side of the Taurus Mountains which belonged to Antiochus would be given to Eumenes. But Lycia and Caria, as far as the Meander River, were given to the Rhodians. The rest of the cities in Asia, which had been tributaries to Attalus, would pay tribute to Eumenes, whereas those that were tributaries of Antiochus would be free and pay no tribute at all. {*Polybius, l. 21. c. 18-24. 5:269-287}* {*Livy, l. 37. c. 52-56. 10:441-467}* {*Livy, l. 38. c. 38. 11:123-131}* {*Appian, Syrian Wars, l. 11. c. 7. (44) 2:191}* {*Diod. Sic., l. 29. c. 11. 11:257}*

*3110.* Antipater and Zeuxis, the envoys of Antiochus, had a session in the Senate and obtained a confirmation of peace for Antiochus on the same conditions that Scipio had given him in Asia. A while later, the people also ratified this. Then they made a solemn league with Antipater, chief of the embassy for Antiochus, with sacrifices in the Capitol to confirm the agreement. {*Polybius, l. 21. c. 24. 5:285,287}* {*Livy, l. 37. c. 55. s. 1-3. 10:461}* [L540] This league was etched in brass and solemnly hung up in the Capitol, as other leagues were. A copy of it was sent to Manlius Vulso, the consul, who had succeeded Scipio in Asia. {*Appian, Syrian Wars, l. 11. c. 7. (39) 2:181}* [E394]

*3111.* Under this treaty, Antiochus himself and his successors would pay a large tribute to the Romans. {*Apc 1Ma 8:7}* He would give hostages for security, as well as a part of his kingdom. According to this agreement, Antiochus was to pay twelve thousand talents over twelve years. These were Euboic talents, not Attic talents, as Livy seems to have misunderstood from Polybius. They were of the purest Attic silver and weighed eighty Roman pounds each. In addition, he had to give five hundred and forty thousand bushels of grain and twenty hostages. The hostages would be changed every three years. Even though he lost part of the kingdom, he still controlled Commagene, Syria and Judea. {*Memnon, Excerpts, c. 28.}* In addition, he had all the upper provinces beyond the Euphrates River, like Babylonia, Assyria, Susiana, and the rest. In lower Asia he had Cilicia, although he was forbidden to come into the ports of Cilicia with his ships; he also had the territory west of the Calycadnus River and the cape of Sarpedon, with the condition that he could not wage war there. {*Polybius, l. 21. c. 42. 5:333-339}* {*Livy, l. 38. c. 38. 11:123-131}* {*Appian, Syrian Wars, l. 11. c. 7. (38,39) 2:177-181}*

*3112.* When the Senate heard from the envoys of Smyrna and the other states of Asia, they sent ten commissioners, as was their ancient custom, to manage all matters in Asia and to settle any differences between the states. {*Polybius, l. 21. c. 41. s. 6-10. 5:333}* {*Diod. Sic., l. 29. c. 11. 11:257}* {*Livy, l. 37. c. 55. s. 7. 10:463}*

## 3815d AM, 4525 JP, 189 BC

*3113.* At the time that there was peace between the Romans and Antiochus, there was a riot in Rome. In Asia,

Gnaeus Manlius did what he could to stir up trouble there. He tried to get his hands on Antiochus if at all possible, but failed, because Antiochus knew the consul's real intentions. Although he was often asked to come to a conference with the consul, he kept himself aloof and would not come to him. The consul was keen to get him and came with his army to the divide almost at the top of the Taurus Mountains, but he was unable to pick any quarrel against him or his allies. Therefore, the consul attacked the Galatians, under the pretence that they had previously helped Antiochus in his war. There was no point driving Antiochus beyond the Taurus Mountains unless these fierce and warlike people were also subdued. Since Eumenes was at that time out of the country at Rome, the consul, who had moved from Ephesus to Magnesia, sent for Eumenes' brother, Attalus, to come to him from Pergamum. When Attalus received this summons, he came to him with a thousand foot soldiers and about five hundred cavalry. Together they went to the Harpasus River. Athenaeus, another brother of Eumenes and Attalus, came to him with Leusus of Crete and Corragus, a Macedonian. Between them, they brought an additional thousand foot soldiers from various countries and three hundred cavalry. {*Livy, l. 38. c. 12,13. 11:37-41}

3114. Envoys from the state of Alabanda came to the consul and requested help in subduing a citadel that had recently revolted from them. The consul helped them recover the citadel, after which he continued on to the city of Antioch on the Meander River. Seleucus, the son of Antiochus, also came there, as he was legally entitled to do by the articles with Scipio. He came to supply grain for the Roman army. The inhabitants of Taba, a city of Cilicia bordering upon Pisidia, attacked the army of the Romans and for their pains paid twenty-five talents and ten thousand bushels of wheat. The inhabitants asked for mercy. On the third day after the Romans came back to the Casus River, they went to attack the city of Eriza, which they took on the first assault. {*Livy, l. 38. c. 13,14. 11:41-45} [L541]

3115. Moagetes, the tyrant, who had three cities under him, Cibyra, Syleium and Ad Limnen, was a cruel and crafty man. He could barely be persuaded to purchase his peace at the price of a hundred talents and ten thousand bushels of grain. {*Livy, l. 38. c. 13,14. 11:41-45} {*Polybius, l. 21. c. 33,34. 5:315-319}

3116. When the consul had crossed the Colobatus River, envoys came to him from Isiodenses, asking for help. The men of Termessa, a city in Pisidia, had joined with the inhabitants of Philomelus and plundered their country and city. They had besieged their citadel, into which all their citizens had fled for safety with their wives and children. The consul took control of the situation and marched toward Pamphylia. He raised the siege of Isiodenses and pardoned the men of Termessa, after they had paid fifty talents of silver. The people of Aspendus and of Pamphylia were treated likewise. {*Livy, l. 38. c. 15. 11:45,49} {*Polybius, l. 21. c. 33,34. 5:319,321}

## 3816a AM, 4525 JP, 189 BC

3117. The consul returned from Pamphylia to start his war against Galatia. He captured the city of Cormasa, where he found a great deal of booty. He left there and as he proceeded on his way through the marshes of that country, envoys came to him from the city of Lysinoe and submitted to him. After having granted them his mercy, he came to the plain of Sagalassus in Pisidia. Since no embassy came out to meet him, he sent out parties to plunder the fields. [E395] Envoys came to him and presented him with a crown of gold of fifty talents in weight and with twenty thousand bushels each of barley and wheat, so he made peace with them. {*Livy, l. 38. c. 15. s. 7-12. 11:49} {*Polybius, l. 21. c. 35,36. 5:319,321}

3118. From there he went to the Rhotrine Springs, the source of the Obryma River, and camped at a place called the Acordos Come. The next day Seleucus came to him from Apamea. The consul sent away to Apamea those of his soldiers who were sick, or otherwise unserviceable. He was supplied with guides, but found the cities everywhere abandoned by their inhabitants, in fear of his coming. His army had so much spoil, that they were barely able to march five miles a day. Marching at this rate, they came to the Old Beudos and on the third day after that, into the country of Galatia. {*Livy, l. 38. c. 15. s. 12-15. 11:49}

3119. There the consul camped for a few days, during which time he sent his envoys to Eposognatus, who alone of all the kings of that country had remained loyal to Eumenes and had never helped Antiochus against the Romans. Eposognatus subsequently went to the rest of the kings of that country and asked them to submit to the Romans on fair and reasonable terms. {*Livy, l. 38. c. 18. s. 1-3. 11:61} {*Polybius, l. 21. c. 37. 5:321} At that time three kings were ruling these Gauls, who were still known by their old names of the Tolostobogians, Tectosagians and Trocmians. The three kings were Ortiagon, Combolomarus and Gaulotus. {*Livy, l. 38. c. 19. s. 1-3. 11:65,67} Of the three, Ortiagon was a man of great reputation for his bounty, prudence and martial valour, and was believed at that time to be harbouring the ambition of controlling the whole country. {*Polybius, l. 22. c. 21. 5:389} {Suidas, Ortiagon}

3120. Meanwhile, envoys came from Oroanda to the consul as he camped in a village called Tyscon. They wanted his friendship, which he finally gave to them for two hundred talents. {*Livy, l. 38. c. 18. s. 1-3. 11:61}

3121. While the Romans besieged Cuballum, which was a citadel of the Galatians, the enemy's cavalry arrived. They attacked and killed some of the Roman army and caused quite a disruption. The consul repelled the attack and killed some of them as they were fleeing. Without stopping anywhere on the way, he came with his army to the Sangarius or Sagaris River, which is a river in Galatia running through Phrygia into the Pontic Sea. {*Livy, l. 38. c. 18. s. 5-8. 11:63}

3122. Since the river was too deep to ford, he made a bridge, by means of which he crossed the river. Two Galli, or eunuchs of Cybele, the mother of the gods, were sent from Pessinus by her priests, Attis and Battacus, and met him there with ornaments and other trinkets on them. They prophesied in a fantastic way and told him that the mother of the gods had sent them to offer the Romans the victory and sovereignty over that country. [L542] The consul replied that he accepted the offer and pitched his camp in that very spot. {*Livy, l. 38. c. 18. s. 9-11. 11:63,65} {*Polybius, l. 21. c. 37. s. 4-7. 5:321,323}

3123. The next day he came to Gordium, which had been abandoned by the inhabitants, but was full of all kinds of provisions. While he was there, Eposognatus came to him and said that he had spoken with the kings of the Gauls, but could not bring them to listen to reason. They, with their wives and children and most of their wealth, were all retiring to Mount Olympus, where they planned to defend themselves, trusting in their arms and the location of the place. {*Livy, l. 38. c. 18. s. 12-15. 11:65} {*Polybius, l. 21. c. 37. s. 8,9. 5:323} Some men of the tribe of Oroanda came soon after with more detailed news. The Tolostobogians had already taken Mount Olympus and the Tectosagians had taken another hill, called Magaba. The Trocmians had left their wives and children with the Tectosagians and had joined forces with the Tolostobogians. {*Livy, l. 38. c. 19. 11:65,67}

3124. The camp of these Gauls, on Mount Olympus, was attacked and taken by the consul and Attalus. Claudius Quadrigarius said that they fought twice on Mount Olympus. Forty thousand men were killed. However, Valerius Antias said only ten thousand were killed. There is no doubt that forty thousand were killed, since they had all sorts of people, young and old, of either sex on the mount, making it more like a colony than an army for fighting against an enemy. The consul burned all their arms in one large fire and had all their spoil brought to him. He either sold all that could be sold or

equally divided it among his soldiers. {*Livy, l. 38. c. 20-23. 11:67-81}

3125. However, the war with the Tectosagians still waited to be fought. So the consul marched toward them and came to a place called Ancyra, which was a large city thereabouts. They camped less than ten miles from the enemy. There, Chiomara, Ortiagon's (or Orgaigo's) wife, was taken prisoner. [E396] A certain centurion had ravished her and when she got her chance, she cut off his head and took it to her husband who had gone home from Mount Olympus. She threw the head at his feet, at which he was astonished and said, "Ah my wife, it is good to keep faith." "Yes," she replied, "but it is better still that only one man who has lain with me should remain alive." {*Livy, l. 38. c. 24. 11:83.85} {*Florus, l. 1. c. 27. s. 6. 1:129} {*Polybius, l. 21. c. 38. 5:323,325} {Aurelius Victor, De Viris Illustribus, l. 1. c. 55.} {*Valerius Maximus, l. 6. c. 1. ext. 2. 2;13} This story was more fully related by Polybius, who said that he spoke with Chiomara herself at Sardis. He added that he was amazed at the wisdom of the woman. {*Plutarch, Bravery of Women Chiomara, l. 1. c. 22. (258e) 3:557,559}

3126. While the consul camped at Ancyra, some envoys from the Tectosagians came to him, asking him not to move his army from there, but to come out for a parley. They wanted this done before their kings agreed to a treaty with him about a peace. Under the pretence of a parley, they ambushed a party of the Romans, and since they outnumbered the Romans, they killed many of them. They would have done more damage, had not others of their number, who were abroad foraging, heard their cry and come to their rescue. {*Polybius, l. 21. c. 39. 5:325,327} {*Livy, l. 38. c. 25. 11:85-89}

3127. The Romans were enraged at this. The next day the whole army marched and came to where they were. They spent two days in viewing and considering the situation of the hill where they were. On the third day, the consul drew out his army and divided them into three brigades. The main force of the enemy was in the Tectosagians and Trocmians, who numbered fifty thousand foot soldiers plus the cavalry. Since they could make no use of their cavalry on that craggy ground, they added ten thousand of them to their foot soldiers. The Cappadocians who were sent by Ariarathes and others in the left wing who were sent by Morzius, added a further four thousand troops. [L543] When the battle began, the Gauls were defeated and the Romans slaughtered a great many of them. The rest fled and every man fended for himself. In the chase, the Romans killed another eight thousand and the rest escaped over the Halys River.

3128. The next day, the consul viewed the spoil, as well as the prisoners. The men were gnawing the chains they were tied to, using their teeth, and were offering themselves to be choked by each other. The spoil was very great, as this was a most greedy and rapacious country, which for so many years had taken spoil from all Asia on their side of the Taurus Mountains. The Gauls who had escaped came together later, naked and wounded, having lost all they had. So they agreed among themselves to send to the Romans and sue for peace. The consul wanted them to follow him to Ephesus. It was past mid-autumn and he was anxious to get out of that cold air near the snowy Taurus Mountains and go to the sea coast to winter his army. {*Livy, l. 38. c. 26,27. 11:89-93} {*Appian, Syrian Wars, l. 11. c. 7. (42) 2:187,189} {*Florus, l. 1. c. 27. s. 1-5. 1:127}

3129. At Rome, on the Calends or 1st of February (according to their year, but September 27 by ours), Lucius Aemilius Regillus held a triumph over Antiochus for the victory which he had won at sea. {*Livy, l. 37. c. 58. s. 3-5. 10:473}

3130. About this time, the ten commissioners left Rome for Asia, accompanied by, among others, those envoys who had come from Asia. They came to Brundisium. Lucius and Publius Scipio came from Asia to land in Italy, and a few days later they entered Rome with a triumph. {*Polybius, l. 21. c. 24. s. 16,17. 5:287} Lucius Scipio held a triumph over Antiochus on the last day before March of the intercalary month, or the 16th of our November. This was almost a year after his consulship had expired. So that he might not appear inferior to his brother Africanus in any point, everyone surnamed him *Asiaticus.* {*Livy, l. 37. c. 58,59. 10:473-477}

3131. Gnaeus Manlius Vulso remained in Asia as a proconsul for another year after his term as consul had expired. {*Livy, l. 38. c. 37. s. 1. 11:121}

## 3816b AM, 4526 JP, 188 BC

3132. In the fourth year of the 147th Olympiad, envoys came to Manlius the proconsul while he was wintering at Ephesus. They came from all the cities, states and countries in Asia on the west side of the Taurus Mountains, to congratulate him on his victory over the Gauls. They presented him with crowns of gold, while he entertained them all with so much respect and favour, that he sent them away more glad and joyful than when they had come. Envoys from the Gauls came to him as he had arranged, to find out on what conditions they could have their peace. He said that he would speak with them about that matter when Eumenes came, and not before. Envoys also came from Ariarathes, king of Cappadocia, to ask the consul's pardon and to make good his offence with money in that he had assisted Antiochus, his father-in-law, in his war. He was fined six hundred talents of silver, although Appian said it was only two

hundred. Musaeus also came to him from Antiochus. Manlius answered that he would meet with him at the borders of Pamphylia, and would take the twenty-five hundred talents and the grain which he was to pay, according to the agreement made with him by Lucius Scipio. {*Polybius, l. 21. c. 40. 5:329,331} {*Livy, l. 38. c. 37. 11:121,123} {*Appian, Syrian Wars, l. 11. c. 7. (42) 2:187,189} [E397]

## 3816c AM, 4526 JP, 188 BC

3133. At the beginning of the spring, the consul reviewed his army. He and Attalus left Ephesus and on the eighth day came to Apamea. When they had spent three days there, they left and in a further three days came with their army into Pamphylia to the place which the consul had appointed for his meeting with Antiochus. He stayed there for three days and distributed among his army the wheat which Antiochus had sent, while the money he had sent was consigned to one of the officers to be conveyed to Apamea. [L544] He next went to Perga, the only place in all that country which was defended by a garrison. As he approached it, the captain of the garrison came out to meet him and asked for a truce for forty days, to enable him to ask Antiochus what he should do about the surrender of the place to the consul and to receive his answer. This was granted and on the set day, the garrison left. {*Livy, l. 38. c. 37. s. 9-11. 11:123}

3134. About the same time, near the beginning of summer, the ten commissioners arrived at Ephesus with Eumenes. They stayed for only two days to settle their stomachs after the voyage, then they left and came to Apamea. When the proconsul heard of their coming, he sent his brother Lucius Manlius with four thousand soldiers to Oroanda to demand of them the money that was in arrears. The proconsul requested that the envoys of Antiochus follow him, and returned to Apamea with his army. Finding Eumenes there with the ten commissioners, he held a meeting with them to determine what should be done. First, all agreed to ratify the peace previously made with Antiochus, that it be observed just as it had been drawn up by the Senate. (The details of the agreement were accurately given by Polybius and Livy.) Manlius, the proconsul, took a solemn oath in the presence of the king's envoys to observe the agreement. After that, he sent Quintus Minucius Thermus, a colonel, and his own brother Lucius Manlius, who had just returned from Oroanda with the money which he had been sent for, to Antiochus. They were to take the same oath from Antiochus and to ratify all its conditions. {*Polybius, l. 21. c. 41-43. 5:331-339} {*Livy, l. 38. c. 38,39. 11:123-131} {*Appian, Syrian Wars, l. 11. c. 7. (39) 2:181}

3135. The proconsul wrote letters to Quintus Fabius Labeo, who commanded the navy, to go at once to

Patara. He was to burn or destroy all the king's ships that were there. {*Polybius, l. 21. c. 43. 5:339} {*Livy, l. 38. c. 39. s. 1-3. 11:131}

3136. Labeo left Ephesus and came to Patara, where he burned or destroyed fifty of the king's ships. On the same journey, he recovered Telmessus, surprising the men there by the sudden coming of the Roman fleet. He sailed from Lycia, sending word to Ephesus for ordering those who were left there to follow him. Passing through the middle of the islands on his way into Greece, he stayed a few days at Athens until his ships from Ephesus arrived, and then the whole fleet sailed for Italy. {*Livy, l. 38. c. 39. s. 3,4. 11:131}

3137. In accordance with the peace treaty, the proconsul received from Antiochus the elephants which were at Apamea, according to Polybius. He then gave them all to Eumenes, after which he mediated in the disagreements between the cities and states resulting from the war and the new peace. Ariarathes, the king of Cappadocia, had half his fine removed for Eumenes' sake, to whom he had then recently betrothed his daughter. {*Livy, l. 38. c. 39. s. 5-7. 11:131}

3138. At Apamea, the proconsul and the ten commissioners heard all the representatives that came to them. With the consent of all parties, they selected neutral places in which to hear about the differences between city and city with respect to boundaries, revenue and the like. The proconsul and the commissioners relieved the Colophonians, who lived in Notium, as well as the inhabitants of Cyme and Mylasa, from ever having to pay tribute. The Clazomenians were freed from tribute and the isle of Drymussa, lying opposite their city, was assigned to them. The Milesians were given back the place called *Sacer Ager*, that is, the *Sacred Land*, which they had abandoned for fear of their enemies. For their zeal and readiness to help in the war, the peoples of Chios, Smyrna and Erythrae were given all the lands they wanted to have, and were given a singular recommendation for their actions. The inhabitants of Phocaea had their laws and liberties fully restored to them, along with all the territory which they had possessed before the war began. {*Livy, l. 38. c. 39. s. 8-15. 11:133} {*Polybius, l. 21. c. 45. 5:339,341}

3139. To Illium, they gave the cities and lands of Rhoetium and the Gergithes, not so much for any great service which they had done, but because the people of Illium were related to the Romans from the distant past. {*Livy, l. 38. c. 39. s. 10. 11:133}

3140. Previously, there had been a few places belonging to Eumenes at Pergamum and under its jurisdiction. [L545] These extended only to the seaside near the Elaitic and Adramyttium Gulfs, according to Strabo. {*Strabo, l. 13. c. 1. s. 51. 6:103} [E398] To Eumenes they gave Lysimachia and the Chersonesus of Thrace on the European side, while in Asia he received all Lycaonia, Myllus, Greater and Lesser Phrygia and all the countries of Lydia and Ionia. The towns which were free when the battle was fought with Antiochus were exempted. They also gave him Tralles, Ephesus and Telmessus in Lycia. Since he had previously controlled Mysia, before King Prusias had captured it, this land was restored to him. They deferred the allocation of Pamphylia to the Senate, as Eumenes' envoys said it was on the west side of the Taurus Mountains and the envoys of Antiochus said it lay beyond it. {*Livy, l. 38. c. 39. s. 14-17. 11:133,135} {*Livy, l. 37. c. 56. s. 1-4. 10:463,465} {*Polybius, l. 21. c. 45. s. 9-12. 5:341,343}

3141. The two Rhodian envoys, Theaedetus and Philophron, wished to have Lycia and Caria, according to a former decree of the Senate. Hipparchus and Satyrus, the envoys from Illium, most earnestly asked the commissioners to consider the blood ties between them and the Lycians, and to pardon the Lycians. The commissioners tried to satisfy both parties as best they could. They did not fine the Lycians as a favour to those from Illium. However, they assigned the whole country of the Lycians to the Rhodians to satisfy their wishes, as well. The city of Telmessus and its citadels, and the country belonging to Ptolemy of Telmessus, were not given to Rhodes. Caria and everything beyond the Meander River was given to the Rhodians, with the exception of those places which had been free on the day before the battle against Antiochus at Magnesia. {*Livy, l. 38. c. 39. s. 13. 11:133} {*Livy, l. 37. c. 56. s. 5,6. 10:465} {*Polybius, l. 22. c. 5. 5:351,353}

3142. The Lycians protested publicly that they would risk anything rather than be subject to Rhodes. They claimed that they were assigned by the commissioners as friends and associates to them, not as subjects. {*Polybius, l. 22. c. 5. s. 10. 5:353}

3143. The commissioners, according to the articles of the peace, demanded Hannibal from Antiochus. When Antiochus told Hannibal this, he fled from there and went to Gortyna in Crete. {Justin, Trogus, l. 32. c. 4.} {Emilius Probus, Hannibal} Yet the story is that, when Antiochus was defeated by the Romans, Hannibal first fled to Artaxas (or Artaxias), the Armenian, whom he gave much good counsel. He told Artaxas to build the capital city, which was named after him and called Artaxata or Artaxiasata, in Armenia. {*Plutarch, Lucullus, l. 1. c. 31. s. 3,4. 2:573} {*Strabo, l. 11. c. 14. s. 6. 5:325,327} Artaxas and Thariadis or Zariadris were two captains in Antiochus' army. By his consent they had previously ruled over all Armenia. The one had ruled over Greater Armenia and the other over Lesser Armenia. After Antiochus' defeat, they had joined with the Romans and had each obtained from them the title of a king in his own dominions. {*Strabo, l. 11. c. 14. s. 5. 5:323,325} It is most likely that, at the time when they made friends with the Romans, Hannibal escaped from there also and fled into Crete.

3144. When Antiochus had lost all of Asia, he said that he was very grateful to the Romans for taking that troublesome area from him and confining him to a more manageable estate. {*Cicero, Pro Dejotaro, l. 1. c. 13. 14:535} {*Valerius Maximus, l. 4. c. 1. ext. 9. 1;359,361}

## 3817a AM, 4526 JP, 188 BC

3145. When Gnaeus Manlius and the ten commissioners had now settled all issues, they went toward the Hellespont with the entire army and planned to settle matters in Galatia on the way. {*Livy, l. 38. c. 40. s. 1-3. 11:135} {*Polybius, l. 21. c. 45. s. 12. 5:343}

3146. They summoned these petty kings to them and gave them such conditions of peace as they thought fit, the substance of which was this: they were to keep peace with Eumenes and were warned to stop their warring customs and stay within their own lands. {*Livy, l. 38. c. 40. s. 1-3. 11:135} [L546] These lands were that part of Phrygia, Paphlagonia, and Mysia, which bordered on Mount Olympus and Cappadocia. This had previously been occupied by them, and was now called Galatia. {*Dio, l. 19. (63) 2:323 (Zonaras, l. 9. c. 20.)} The Romans imposed a tribute on them. {Apc 1Ma 8:2} to chastise the Galatians for their insolence toward them, after which the Romans assumed the entire sovereignty of Asia on the west side of the Taurus Mountains. They made the mountains the eastern boundary of the empire for that time, in this way sparing the inhabitants there from having to live in terror of those fierce and barbarous Gauls, as they had formerly done. {*Polybius, l. 3. c. 3. s. 4,5. 2:9} {*Cicero, Pro Lege Manilia, l. 1. c. 6. (14) 9:27} {*Livy, l. 38. c. 40. s. 1-3. 11:135}

3147. Manlius gathered all the ships which he could get along that entire coast. Eumenes came to him with his ships, and he used them to cross into Europe with his army. {*Livy, l. 38. c. 40. s. 3,4. 11:135}

3148. Antiochus marched with his army into his upper provinces (or, as Jerome on Daniel stated, *going to the remotest cities of his dominions.*) {Jerome, Da 11} He proclaimed his son, Seleucus Philopator, as his successor. {Apc 2Ma 9:23} [E399]

## 3817 AM, 4527 JP, 187 BC

3149. Antiochus committed a sacrilege on his gods, either because he felt over-burdened by the heavy tribute imposed by the Romans or simply because he was greedy and used the Roman tribute as an excuse. He had heard that the temple of Zeus Belus in Elymais

had large quantities of silver, gold and other precious jewels stored there, so he planned to seize everything. He came into Elymais and pretended that the inhabitants there had revolted from him. His army raided the temple at night and took an enormous amount of wealth from there. When the people heard about this, the peasants of the country came in and attacked his army and killed him with his entire army. {*Diod. Sic., l. 28. c. 3. 11:231} {*Diod. Sic., l. 29. c. 15. 11:259,261} {*Strabo, l. 16. c. 1. s. 18. 7:223} {Justin, Trogus, l. 32. c. 2.} Jerome said that he was killed in a battle against the inhabitants of Elymais. {Jerome, Da 11} Aurelius Victor, however, stated that he was killed by his drinking companions, some of whom he had beaten in a drunken fit and misused at a feast. {Aurelius Victor, De Viris Illustribus, c. 54.} Zonaras noted that this happened in the year when Gaius Flamininus and Aemilius Lepidus were consuls of Rome. {*Dio, l. 19. (64) 2:327 (Zonaras, l. 9. c. 21.)}

3150. After his death, Seleucus, surnamed Philopator, or, according to Josephus, Soter (which was indeed the surname of his son, Demetrius), succeeded him in the kingdom. {*Josephus, Antiq., l. 12. c. 4. s. 11. (234) 7:119} He reigned twelve years and was a lazy man, who also had little power because of his father's great defeat by the Romans. {*Appian, Syrian Wars, l. 11. c. 8. (45) 2:191} {Porphyry} {*Eusebius, Chronicles, l. 1. 1:219} {*Sulpicius Severus, Sacred History, l. 2. c. 19. 11:107} When he assumed the kingdom, he had a son called Demetrius, whose surname was Soter. According to Polybius, he was twenty-three years old when his uncle Antiochus Epiphanes died. {*Polybius, l. 31. c. 2. s. 5,6. 6:167} It is this Seleucus who is referred to in the Apocrypha: {Apc 2Ma 3:1-3}.

> "When the Holy City lived in complete peace, its laws were excellently well executed because of the piety of Onias, the high priest. He was utterly opposed to all ungodliness. It came about that even kings themselves honoured this place and adorned the temple with many rich offerings. Seleucus, king of Asia, himself furnished all the cost for the public ministry of the sacrifices out of his own coffers."

3151. When Philopoemen was the chief magistrate of the Achaeans, Demetrius of Athens came as an envoy of Ptolemy from Alexandria to renew his league with the Achaeans. They were very glad about this and sent him their envoys, Lycortas, the father of Polybius the historian, Theodoridas and Rositeles of Sicyon. [L547] They were to take their oath to the king and also to receive his oath to them. {*Polybius, l. 22. c. 3. s. 5,6. 5:345,347}

## 3818a AM, 4527 JP, 187 BC

3152. Gnaeus Manlius Vulso, contrary to the votes of the ten commissioners, held a triumph in Rome over the Gauls in Asia, on the fifth day of March. {*Livy, l. 39. c. 6. s. 3-5. 11:235} {*Livy, l. 38. c. 58. s. 11,12. 11:205} Hannibal, having nothing else to do, wrote a book in Greek about the consul's deeds in Asia. He learned Greek at Illium from Sosilus, a Lacedemonian, who recorded the deeds of Hannibal in seven volumes. {*Diod. Sic., l. 26. c. 4. 11:183}

### 3818b AM, 4528 JP, 186 BC

3153. When Aristaenus was the chief magistrate in Achaia, the envoys who had been sent from there to king Ptolemy returned home. The general assembly of that country met at Megalopolis, and before this assembly Lycortas declared that they had taken their oath to the king according to their commission and had received his oath to them. He added that they had brought a present from the king to the people of Achaia. They had received two hundred talents of coined bronze and enough brass arms to furnish six thousand targeteers. {*Polybius, l. 22. c. 9. s. 1-3. 5:361}

3154. Eumenes also sent his envoys to that meeting, to renew the league with them which had formerly existed between them and his father. He promised to give them a hundred and twenty talents which they could lend at interest, so that its income would help defray the cost of those who periodically came to their assemblies. They were all tempted by his generosity, but declined it. {*Polybius, l. 22. c. 7. s. 2,3. 5:357} {*Diod. Sic., l. 29. c. 17. 11:261,263} [E400]

### 3819 AM, 4529 JP, 185 BC

3155. Eumenes' envoys came to Rome to request the ownership of the cities of Thrace, Aenus and Maronea, which they claimed belonged to Eumenes, having been given to him by the Romans. They complained that Philip, the king of Macedonia, had seized them by force and put garrisons in them. He had also taken some inhabitants from there and settled them in Macedonia. To settle the matter, the Senate sent Quintus Caecilius Metellus, Marcus Baebius and Tiberius Sempronius as a commission to Thessaly to hear both sides of the dispute. {*Polybius, l. 22. c. 11. s. 2-4. 5:369} {*Polybius, l. 23. c. 1. 5:393,395} {*Livy, l. 39. c. 24. s. 12-14. 11:291}

### 3820 AM, 4530 JP, 184 BC

3156. When they returned to Rome, the envoys on either side told the Senate that there was nothing but what they had already said before the commissioners at Thessaly. The Senate decreed a second commission, under Appius Claudius, with instructions to expel all the garrisons from Aenus and Maronea and to remove all the sea coast of Thrace from the jurisdiction of Philip and his Macedonians. {*Polybius, l. 22. c. 11,12. 5:367-373} {*Polybius, l. 23. c. 4. s. 7,8. 11:401} {*Livy, l. 39. c. 33. s. 3,4. 11:323}

3157. At the same time, the two head men of Sparta, Arcus and Alcibiades, came to Rome. They complained bitterly in the Senate about the Achaeans, whereupon the Senate thought fit to refer that cause to those same commissioners. {*Polybius, l. 23. c. 4. s. 1-7. 5:401} {*Pausanias, Achaia, l. 7. c. 9. s. 1-7. 3:217-221}

3158. Lycortas of Megalopolis, Polybius' father and the praetor of Achaia, called an assembly of the country. At that assembly, Arcus and Alcibiades, who had gone to complain about them at Rome, were condemned to die for this act. {*Livy, l. 39. c. 35. s. 7,8. 11:329} {*Pausanias, Achaia, l. 7. c. 9. s. 1-7. 3:217-221} [L548]

3159. Some time later, the Roman envoys came into Achaia and the common council of Achaia met before them at Clitor in Arcadia. {*Livy, l. 39. c. 35. s. 8. 11:329} {*Polybius, l. 22. c. 12. s. 10. 5:373} Their coming did not please the Achaeans, especially when they saw Arcus and Alcibiades (whom they in a recent assembly had condemned to death) come with the envoys. Lycortas, like a magistrate, very boldly pleaded and upheld the cause of the Achaeans. The commissioners, however, did not pay much attention to what he said and declared publicly and with joint consent that Arcus and Alcibiades were honest men. They had done the Achaeans no wrong at all and prevailed even to the point of having the sentence against them reversed. {*Livy, l. 39. c. 36,37. 11:329-341} {*Pausanias, Achaia, l. 7. c. 9. s. 7. 3:221}

3160. When Hannibal had lived very quietly at Gortyna in Crete for a long time, many envied him because of his great wealth. In desperation, he filled some large chests with lead and deposited them in the temple of Diana. As a result, when the people had been given such a pledge as that, they were less envious of him. In the meantime, he stole away to Prusias, surnamed the *The Hunter*, king of Bithynia. Hannibal had melted his gold into hollow statues of brass which he carried away with him. {Justin, Trogus, l. 32. c. 4.} {Emilius Probus, Hannibal}

3161. A little later, Prusias broke his league with Eumenes, the king of Pergamum, now that he had Hannibal to manage his war for him. {Justin, Trogus, l. 32. c. 4.} There was a fierce war between them, both on land and sea, but with the help of the Romans, Eumenes overpowered him. Because Prusias was poor and weak, Hannibal procured for him the help of some other kings and states, and those peoples from very warlike countries. {Emilius Probus, Hannibal} Among others, he got the help of Philip, the king of Macedonia, who sent him Philocles, his general, with a large army, to help him. {*Polybius, l. 23. c. 3. s. 1,2. 5:399}

### 3821a AM, 4530 JP, 184 BC

*3162.* In the 149th Olympiad, when Marcus Claudius Marcellus and Quintus Fabius Labeo first entered into their consulship, an embassy came to Rome from Eumenes, carried by his youngest brother, Athenaeus. Bringing with him a crown of gold of fifteen thousand gold staters, he complained that Philip had not withdrawn his garrisons from Thrace and that he had sent help to Prusias, the king of Bithynia, who had wilfully broken his league and made war on Eumenes. {*Polybius, l. 23. c. 1. s. 4-7. 5:395} {*Livy, l. 39. c. 46. s. 9. 11:367} With the other envoys from Lacedemon, Arcus and Alcibiades came to the Senate. {*Polybius, l. 23. c. 4. s. 1-3. 5:401}

### 3821b AM, 4531 JP, 183 BC

*3163.* After Prusias had been defeated by Eumenes on land, he tried to defeat him at sea, but he was too weak for Eumenes. Hannibal advised him to try to accomplish by craft what he could not do through sheer force. So he put a number of all kinds of snakes into earthen vessels, which were to be hurled aboard the enemy's ships in the thick of the battle. He ordered his soldiers and sailors to attack only the ship that Eumenes was in and defend themselves against the rest as well as they could, using these snakes. So that they would know for certain which ship Eumenes was in, Prusias sent a letter to him beforehand by a herald, which was full of contempt and abuses against Eumenes. So when the battle started, Prusias' men fought only against the ship in which Eumenes was in, forcing him to flee. He would have died, had he not landed on a shore where he had beforehand placed a company of troops for such emergencies. When Eumenes' other ships pressed close to the enemy, these threw their earthen pitchers full of snakes at them. They landed on the decks and broke, releasing the snakes. At first this seemed ridiculous to them, but when they could not move anywhere in the ship for the snakes and found themselves as bothered by their bites as by the arrows of their enemy, they abandoned the battle and fled to their sea camp on the shore. {Justin, Trogus, l. 32. c. 4.} {Emilius Probus, Hannibal} [E401] [L549]

*3164.* Hannibal's tricks defeated Eumenes in that battle. In various other engagements, Hannibal used different tricks to overcome Eumenes. Once, when he advised Prusias to fight, he refused, because he said the entrails of the beasts forbade him to. Hannibal replied: {*Cicero, De Divinatione, l. 2. c. 24. 20:431} {Plutarch, On Exile} {*Valerius Maximus, l. 3. c. 7. ext. 6. 1:315}

> "Really? Would you rather trust a lump of calf flesh, than a veteran general?"

*3165.* When news of these events reached Rome, envoys were immediately sent by the Senate to make a peace between the two kings and to demand that Prusias hand over Hannibal. {Justin, Trogus, l. 32. c. 4.} Polybius stated that at that time Titus Quinctius Flamininus was sent as an envoy both to Prusias and also to Seleucus, the king of Syria. {*Polybius, l. 23. c. 5. s. 1. 5:403} Livy said that Lucius Scipio Asiaticus and Publius Scipio Nasica were sent with Flaminius to Prusias as a commission. {*Livy, l. 39. c. 56. s. 6. 11:399}

*3166.* Agesipolis, who was a minor and too young to be the king of Sparta, was sent to Rome with others from among those who had been banished from Lacedemon. On the way he was killed by pirates. {*Polybius, l. 23. c. 6. 5:407,409} Agesipolis was the son of Cleomenes, the king of Sparta, who had been killed in Alexandria. {See note on 3784 AM. <<2887>>} He had legally been appointed for their king by the ephors, but had been turned out again by those usurping tyrants who had taken over the state, namely Lycurgus, Machanidas and Nabis. {*Polybius, l. 4. c. 35. s. 10-13. 2:389} Since the lawful king was now dead, Arcus (whom I mentioned before from Polybius, Livy and Pausanias) was a most earnest and strong defender of his country's liberty against the Achaeans, whose power was now controlled by the Romans. He seems to have acquired the title of a king among them, since both Josephus and Eusebius stated that Arcus, the king of Lacedemon, sent an embassy with his letters to Onias III, the son of Onias the high priest at Jerusalem. {*Josephus, Antiq., l. 12. c. 4. s. 10. (225) 7:115} {*Eusebius, Chronicles, l. 1. 1:217} These letters were preserved in Josephus and in the Apocrypha. {*Josephus, Antiq., l. 12. c. 4. s. 10. (225-227) 7:115} {Apc 1Ma 12:1-23} This book was translated from the Hebrew (for it was originally written in Hebrew, as Jerome stated) and retained throughout the brevity and Hebrewisms characteristic of it. In these letters, mention was made of the blood relationship between the Jews and Lacedemonians. This seems to have been taken from the mythological writings of the Greeks such as was that of Claudius Iolaus in Stephanus Byzantinus in the word *Judea*. The name of the Jews came from Judeus Spartones, a fellow soldier of Bacchus in his wars, although Pausanias stated that Spartones' names were completely unknown to the Spartans or Lacedemonians of his time. {Pausanias, Corinth, l. 2. p. 58.}

*3167.* Eumenes started to make war with Prusias, king of Bithynia, and Ortiagon, one of the kings of the Gauls. {Justin, Trogus, l. 32. Prologue} {*Polybius, l. 3. c. 3. s. 6,7. 2:9}

### 3822a AM, 4531 JP, 183 BC

*3168.* I think the death of Hannibal occurred in the consulship of Lucius Aemilius Paulus and Gnaeus Baebius Tamphilus, for Polybius and Valerius Antias both stated this. It was not in the year before, as stated by Atticus and by Livy, who copied him. Nor was it in the following year, as Sulpicius and Probus wrote. {*Emilius Probus, Hannibal*} Livy described in detail how he died. {*Livy, l. 39. c. 51. 11:379-383*} {*Justin, Trogus, l. 32. c. 4.*} {*Plutarch, Flamininus, l. 1. c. 20. 10:379,381*} {*Dio, l. 19. (65) 2:331 (Zonaras, l. 9. c. 21.)*} {*Emilius Probus, Hannibal*} {*Appian, Syrian Wars, l. 11. c. 2. (11) 2:121*}

3169. Hannibal stayed in a little citadel Prusias had given him. In it he made seven doors which did not look like doors from the outside. *[L550]* If anyone should come to attack the place, they would not place any guards there, because these did not appear to be doors. Consequently, when he heard that the king's soldiers were in the porch to break in on him, he went to get out at one of these blind back doors. When he found that, contrary to his expectation, men were there to take him and the place was totally surrounded, he poisoned himself with the poison he always carried with him. He died at the age of seventy years. Concerning his death, it is said that this oracle was uttered long before:

"The Libyssan earth, Hannibal's remains shall cover."

3170. He had always understood the word *Libya*, or *Libyssa*, as referring to *Libya* in Africa. However, there was a little village in Bithynia near the seaside by the same name. Pliny said: {*Pliny, l. 5. c. 53. 2:333*}

"There was in those parts a little town called Libyssa, where now there is nothing worth seeing, except for Hannibal's tomb." *[E402]*

3171. Pharnaces, the king of Pontus, suddenly attacked the city of Sinope and captured it. It remained his possession, and that of his successors, from that time on. {*Strabo, l. 12. c. 3. s. 11. 5:387,389*}

## 3822 AM, 4532 JP, 182 BC

3172. In the second year of the 149th Olympiad, envoys came to Rome from the two kings, Eumenes and Pharnaces, who were at war with each other. Envoys came from Rhodes and complained of the injustice done to them by Pharnaces at Sinope. Thereupon, Quintus Marcius and others in commission with him were sent as envoys to examine the case of Sinope and to settle all differences between the two kings. {*Livy, l. 40. c. 2. s. 6-8. 12:7*} {*Polybius, l. 23. c. 9. 5:411-415*}.

3173. During the reign of Seleucus, Hyrcanus (the son of Joseph and the nephew of Tobias) went and subdued the Arabs on the east side of the Jordan River. He built a good and extremely well fortified citadel, entirely of white marble, which he called Tyre. It was located in the regions of Arabia and Judea on the other side of the Jordan River, not far from the land of Heshbon. He was governor of all that region during the last seven years of Seleucus' reign. During that entire time, there

was a constant war with the Arabians and he on numerous occasions slaughtered large numbers of them, besides taking many prisoners and slaves. {*Josephus, Antiq., l. 12. c. 4. s. 11. (229-233) 7:117,119*}

3174. Marcius and his commissioners returned to the Senate after they had investigated the situation between Eumenes and Pharnaces, and reported what they had found. They said that Eumenes was fair and temperate in all his ways, but that Pharnaces was very greedy and hot-tempered. They said he was the most violent and dangerous king they had ever come across. {*Polybius, l. 24. c. 1. s. 2,3. 5:437*} {*Diod. Sic., l. 29. c. 22. 11:273*}

## 3823a AM, 4532 JP, 182 BC

3175. Ariarathes, the king of Cappadocia, joined with Eumenes, of Pergamum, to make war on Pharnaces, king of Pontus. All three sent their envoys to Rome at the same time. When the Senate had heard them all, they said that they would send commissioners into those countries once more, with power to hear and determine all matters between them. {*Polybius, l. 40. c. 1. 5:437,439*} {*Livy, l. 40. c. 20. s. 1,2. 12:63,65*}

## 3823b AM, 4533 JP, 181 BC

3176. Pharnaces scorned the Romans and in the middle of winter sent Leocritus with an army of ten thousand men to harass and ravage all the country of Galatia. {*Polybius, l. 24. c. 14. s. 1,2. 5:461,463*}

3177. The next spring, Pharnaces personally mustered all his forces as if to attack Cappadocia. {*Polybius, l. 24. c. 14. s. 2. 5:463*}

3178. Eumenes was grieved to see him transgress all bounds of law and honesty in this manner. He and his brother Attalus, who had recently returned from Rome, marched into Galatia against Leocritus, but they did not find him there. *[L551]* Cassignatus (or rather Eposognatus, as Fulvius Ursinus thought it should be) and Gaezatarix sent their envoys, asking them not to harm them, as they were ready to do whatever they were told to do. Eumenes rejected them, as men who had previously lied and broken their faith and word to him, and he and his brother continued on against Pharnaces. {*Polybius, l. 24. c. 14. s. 3-7. 5:463*}

3179. In four days, Eumenes and his brother marched from Calpitus or Calpia, a city of Bithynia, to the Halys River. On the sixth day, they came to Parnassus, a city in Cappadocia. There Ariarathes, the king of that country, joined his army with theirs. They all came into the plain of Mocissus and there pitched camp. They were barely settled, when news came that the commissioners had come from Rome to make a peace between them. So Eumenes sent away his brother Attalus to welcome them into those regions, while he in the meantime doubled his army and put them all into the best shape he could. {*Polybius, l. 24. c. 14. s. 8-11. 5:463}

3180. The commissioners arrived and asked both parties to be at peace. Eumenes and Ariarathes replied that they wanted peace with all their hearts and would do anything else that the commissioners might be pleased to ask. When the commissioners asked that during the treaty they withdraw their forces from the enemy's country, Eumenes readily assented and the following morning ordered his forces back into Galatia. {*Polybius, l. 24. c. 15. s. 1-6. 5:465}

3181. The commissioners then talked with Pharnaces and could not get him to come to any conference if Eumenes was to be there. After much ado, they persuaded him to send his envoys to some place on the coast with full power to make an agreement there, and to give his word that he would abide by the agreement. When his envoys came to the appointed place, the conference began. Eumenes was ready to yield to any conditions, but the envoys of Pharnaces behaved in such a way that the commissioners easily realised that Pharnaces had no intention of coming to any agreement. {*Polybius, l. 24. c. 15. s. 7-11. 5:465,467}

3182. Therefore, the conference broke off and no peace was made between them. When the commissioners left Pergamum and Pharnaces' envoys departed, the war went on between them as before. [E403] Eumenes on his part started to prepare everything necessary for it, but at the earnest insistence of the Rhodians, who sought his help against the Lycians, he left Pharnaces alone for that time and went to help them. {*Polybius, l. 24. c. 15. s. 12,13. 5:467}

3183. Leocritus, the general of Pharnaces' forces, besieged Tius (or rather, Teos), a town in Pontus. He forced the garrison, which consisted entirely of mercenary soldiers, to surrender the town to him on the condition that they would be granted safe conduct. Later, Leocritus received an order from Pharnaces to kill them all, because they had previously offended him. He pursued them on their way and killed them all. {*Diod. Sic., l. 29. c. 23. 11:273}

3184. When Seleucus had assembled a reasonably sized army, he went to help Pharnaces. He was ready to cross the Taurus Mountains when he remembered that he was breaking the peace agreement with the Romans. So he followed good advice, stopped the expedition and returned home again. {*Diod. Sic., l. 29. c. 24. 11:273}

## 3824 AM, 4534 JP, 180 BC

3185. After this, Pharnaces entered into an agreement with Attalus and those associated with him. They entered into a solemn league between themselves. Eumenes

was sick at Pergamum at the time, but had now recovered. He ratified what Attalus had done and then sent Attalus and the rest of his brothers to Rome. Everyone who knew what service they had done for the Romans in the wars in Asia welcomed them heartily. The Senate provided lodgings and a generous allowance for them at the public expense. [L552] Attalus complained to the Senate of the wrongs that Pharnaces had done to them, desiring the Senate to chastise him commensurate with the severity of his offence. They answered him graciously and promised to send then commissioners who would make a final accord between them. {*Polybius, l. 24. c. 5. 5:441} {*Diod. Sic., l. 29. c. 22. 11:271,273}

3186. Ptolemy Epiphanes desired a closer alliance with the Achaeans, so he sent his envoys to them and promised them ten ships, each of fifty oars apiece and fully outfitted. The Achaeans, considering this an offer too good to be refused, as it amounted to the value of almost ten talents, willingly accepted it. They sent him their envoys, Lycortas with his son, Polybius (that is, the historian), even though he was legally too young to be an envoy. With them, they sent Aratus, the son of Aratus the Sicyonian, with instructions to thank the king for both the arms and the money he had previously sent them through Lycortas. They were to receive from him the ten promised ships and to bring them into Peloponnesus. However, the embassy never went farther than Achaia because they received news that Ptolemy had died. {*Polybius, l. 24. c. 6. 5:443,445}

3187. At the time when Ptolemy laid a trap to deceive Seleucus, he sent an army on foot to go against him. When one of Ptolemy's captains asked him where he would get the money to go through with what he planned to do, Ptolemy replied: {*Diod. Sic., l. 29. c. 29. 11:271}

"My friends are my money bags."

3188. This saying spread quickly and his friends and captains in the army heard it. Thinking it meant that he planned to enrich himself by impoverishing them, they poisoned him. {Jerome, Da 11} Ptolemy Epiphanes, in Priscian, the grammarian, is said by Cato to have been a most excellent and bountiful king. The truth is that, for a long time, he behaved himself very nobly and well. Later he was influenced by some followers of the court. He forced Aristomenes, whom he had formerly honoured like a father, to drink hemlock, which killed him. He did other acts of violence and cruelty and ruled his people more like a tyrant than a king. Because of these actions, he was so hated and despised by his subjects that they were ready to depose him. {*Diod. Sic., l. 28. c. 14. 11:241} {*Diod. Sic., l. 29. c. 29. 11:271}

*3189.* When he died, he left two sons who were not of legal age. The older was called Philometor; the younger, Physcon. {*Josephus, Antiq., l. 12. c. 4. s. 11. (235,236) 7:119} Ptolemy Philometor (whom Epiphanius incorrectly called *Philopator*) reigned after his father for thirty-five years. {Ptolemy, Canon of Kings}. {*Clement, Stromateis, l. 1. c. 21. 2:329} {*Eusebius, Chronicles, l. 1. 1:220} Others tell us the same length of time, minus only three months.

### 3825 AM, 4535 JP, 179 BC

*3190.* Pharnaces laid waste to Galatia and planned to invade Cappadocia. (There is a missing fragment in this part of Polybius' account, so we do not have all the details. Editor.) Eumenes counterattacked and Pharnaces found himself outpowered by this unexpected and violent attack of the enemy. He sent his envoys to Eumenes and Ariarathes and sued for peace. So this war between Eumenes and Ariarathes on the one side and Pharnaces and Mithridates, the king of Armenia, on the other concluded on the following conditions. Pharnaces would not enter Galatia, and would break off all former agreements and leagues made with the Galatians. He would likewise leave Paphlagonia, but would now send back home, with their arms, those inhabitants whom he had deported from there. He would restore to Ariarathes all the places he had taken from him, along with any hostages he had received from him. He would restore all the prisoners whom he had taken without a ransom, and would turn over those who had left their king and defected to him. [E404] He would restore to Morzius and Ariarathes the nine hundred talents which he had taken from them, and give a further three hundred to Eumenes for his war expenses. Mithridates, the king of Armenia, would pay three hundred talents for having made war on Ariarathes and thereby breaking the league which he had made with Eumenes. This league included all the important men of Asia as well as Artaxias, a petty king of Greater Armenia, and Acusilochus. [L553] On the European side, Gatalus, a Sarmatian, was part of this league, as were the free states of Heraclea, Mesembria, Chersonesus and Cyzicum. As soon as the hostages arrived from Pharnaces, the armies disbanded and every man went home. {*Polybius, l. 24. c. 14. 5:461,467} {*Polybius, l. 25. c. 2. 5:469,471}

### 3826a AM, 4535 JP, 179 BC

*3191.* Teos was a town in Pontus which Prusias had been required to restore to Eumenes, according to the league. Eumenes freely gave it back to him again, for which Prusias was grateful. {*Polybius, l. 25. c. 2. s. 7. 5:469}

*3192.* After the death of Philip, the king of Macedonia, his son Perses, or Perseus, succeeded him in the year when Quintus Fulvius and Lucius Manlius were consuls at Rome. He reigned eleven years, {*Livy, l. 45. c. 9. s. 3,4. 13:271} or rather, ten years and eleven months, as Porphyry more exactly said. {Eusebius, Scaliger's Greek Eusebius, p. 229.} {*Eusebius, Chronicles, l. 1. 1:220}

### 3826b AM, 4536 JP, 178 BC

*3193.* The third period of Calippus began.

*3194.* The Lycians sent their envoys to Rome to complain of the cruelty of the Rhodians, to whom they had been made subject by Lucius Cornelius Scipio. The envoys said that the bondage which they had endured under Antiochus was, in comparison to this, an excellent form of liberty and freedom. They claimed there was now no difference between them and the very slaves whom they bought in the market. The Senate was moved by this piteous complaint and gave them their letters to carry to the Rhodians. They reminded the Rhodians that the Romans had put the Lycians under their rule and protection, but that they were still to be free states under the sovereignty of the people of Rome. {*Livy, l. 41. c. 6. s. 8-12. 12:203,205}

### 3827 AM, 4537 JP, 177 BC

*3195.* Prusias married the sister of Perseus, and Perseus married Laodicea, the daughter of Seleucus. The Rhodians used their fleet to to pick her up and convey her into Macedonia to her husband. {*Livy, l. 42. c. 12. s. 3-4. 12:325} {*Polybius, l. 25. c. 4. s. 9,10. 5:475,477} {*Appian, Syrian Wars, l. 11. c. 9. (57) 2:213}

*3196.* The Rhodians persisted in their ways and now made open war on the poor Lycians. The men of Xanthus sent their embassy to the Achaeans and to the people of Rome for help. Nicostratus headed up the embassy. {*Polybius, l. 25. c. 4. s. 1-4. 5:475}

*3197.* The Lycians had already been subdued by the Rhodians before their envoys could get a hearing with the Senate of Rome. It was not until Tiberius Sempronius Gracchus and Gaius Claudius Pulcher, the consuls of that year, had gone out against the Histrians and Ligurians, that they saw the Senate. When they were admitted, they plainly showed them the cruelty and oppression of the Rhodians against the poor Lycians. They prevailed with the Senate to send envoys to Rhodes. They were to let them know that when the Senate had perused the acts and records which the ten commissioners had drawn up in Asia, they had found the following. The Lycians had been consigned by the Romans to the Rhodians, not as a gift to do with as they liked, but to use them as friends and associates. This message met with the approval of the common people in Rome, who had been offended with the Rhodians for their officiousness in bringing Perseus' wife home to him. They would have been pleased to have seen the Rhodians and the Lycians fight it out, so that the Rhodians might have some opportunity to spend their treasure and provisions, of which they had so much. {*Livy, l. 41. c. 6. s. 8-12. 12:201} {*Polybius, l. 25. c. 4. s. 4-8. 5:475}

## 3828a AM, 4537 JP, 177 BC

*3198.* When the Roman commissioners came to Rhodes, the inhabitants were in an uproar. They said that since everything was now well settled in Lycia, why did they want to create an opportunity for more trouble there? When the Lycians heard the content of the declaration the Senate had made on their behalf, they began to revolt and protest publicly that they would endure anything to recover their just rights and liberty again. The Rhodians thought that the Senate had been misinformed and misused by some false accusations from the Lycians, so they sent Lycophron, their envoy, to Rome. When the Senate had heard his errand, they gave him an immediate answer. {*Polybius, l. 25. c. 5. 5:477}

## 3828b AM, 4538 JP, 176 BC

*3199.* Simon was a man of the tribe of Benjamin and the head keeper of the temple. He had a disagreement with Onias III, who was the high priest. *[L554]* When he could not get his way, he went to Apollonius, the governor of Coelosyria and Phoenicia, and told him that there was an enormous amount of money in the treasury of the temple, of which the priests made no use. Therefore, it would be better in the king's coffers. When Apollonius told Seleucus this, he sent his treasurer Heliodorus to Jerusalem to get the money from there. When he arrived, Onias, the high priest, told him that it was true that there was some money in the temple, but that it was the money of widows and orphans, who had deposited it there for safe-keeping. *[E405]* Some of the money belonged to Hyrcanus, the nephew of Tobias, who was a most honourable person. {See note on 3822 AM. <<3173>>} He said that what was there amounted to less than four hundred talents of silver and two hundred of gold. Such was the holiness of the place and of the matter itself that no man should take the money. When Heliodorus disregarded the words of Onias, resulting in a tumult of the people who lamented the profaning of their temple, he was struck down by the angel of God in that very spot. He was carried half-dead to his lodging by his own servants who were close by. After he was restored to health through the intercession and prayers to God made by Onias, the high priest, he returned to Seleucus. He magnified the holiness of the temple and the power of the God who lived there. This story is recorded in the Apocrypha {Apc 2 Ma 3} and by Josephus in his book, πσθι αυτοχρατορος λογιομου. Josephus wrote Apollonius for Heliodorus. (So also did the Fasti Siculi.) This showed that this event happened a little before the death of Seleucus; otherwise Heliodorus would have returned after the death of Seleucus. By the articles between Antiochus and the Romans, Antiochus was to change his hostages and send new ones in place of the old at the end of every three years. To replace Antiochus Epiphanes, who was then a hostage at Rome and who was the younger son of the former Antiochus, Seleucus sent his son Demetrius. {Apc 1 Ma 1:10} {*Appian, Syrian Wars, l. 11. c. 8. (47) 2:195}

*3200.* Simon, the Benjamite, that traitor of his country and the one who told of the money deposited in the temple, brought an accusation against Onias, the high priest. Onias was a man who was well respected both in the city and the country of the Jews. Simon said Onias had incited Heliodorus against the Jews and plotted all the evil against himself and the king. When matters went so far that many murders were committed by Simon and his faction in the city, Apollonius grew very angry and backed Simon up in what he did. Onias went to Seleucus. {Apc 2 Ma 4:1-6} The writer of Jason of Cyrene seems to indicate that Seleucus was dead before Onias arrived, although Eusebius said that he found the king alive and had Simon banished by him. {*Eusebius, Chronicles, l. 1. 1:219,221}

*3201.* So I have brought this chronicle of Asia and Egypt to the beginning of the time of Antiochus Epiphanes and the history of the Maccabees. I shall continue it until the time of the utter destruction of Jerusalem under the Emperor Vespasian. This, together with the Annals of the New Testament and a brief history of the church during that time until the beginning of the fourth century after Christ, I plan to write following this, if God grant me life and health.

**Glory be to God on High.**

**FINIS**

# VOLUME II

The Latter Part
of
THE ANNALS
of
JAMES USSHER,
Archbishop of *Armagh:*
Containing besides that of the
M A C C A B E E S
AND
N E W T E S T A M E N T
the History of all the remarkable
Occurrences transacted during the
R O M A N  E M P I R E, which began
under *Gaius Julius* and *Octavius Caesar,*
With the most considerable Events
in all *Asia* and *Egypt:*
CONTINUED
From the beginning of the Reign of
*Antiochus Epiphanes,*
to the beginning of the Empire
of *Vespasian,* and the utter
Destruction and Abolition
of the Temple and Commonwealth
of the Jews.

*L O N D O N,*
Printed by *E. Tyler,* for *F. Crook,*
and *G. Bedell,* 1658

*(From the original Title Page)*

# The Epistle to the Reader

3202. You have here the other volume of my annals, which you will find records more fully the history of Rhodes and the isles between Asia and Europe. Whereas previously, to make the work more manageable, I decided to associate these with Greece, I later also considered it appropriate to place them with Asia, since, in the division of the Eastern Empire, the province of the isles is counted as part of Asia. The facts which I put forward as a part of this history, are presented to you on the authority of the authors who related them. I have left the judgment of such things to those learned men who make it their business to deal with them. In the citing of Cornelius Tacitus, I have followed the edition of Bereggerus and Freinshemius, since that edition is divided into chapters. But since its dealing with the history of the apostolic times does not appear to be adequate, I shall (if God Almighty affords me life and strength to finish that work) give you an account in my Sacred Chronology. *[E409]* *[K1]*

A CHRONICLE
OF
The Asiatic and Egyptian Affairs,
carried on from the
beginning of the times of the MACCABEES,
until the Destruction of the
Jewish Commonwealth
under Vespasian.

## 3829 AM, 4539 JP, 175 BC

3203. Antiochus, son of Antiochus the Great, returned from Rome (where he had been held hostage) and came to Athens. His brother Seleucus had been murdered through the treachery of Heliodorus. But Eumenes and Attalus expelled Heliodorus, who had intended to take over the kingdom of Syria. They gave Antiochus that kingdom, hoping by this good turn to obligate him to be their friend. They began to grow jealous of the Romans because of some small injustice they received. {*Appian, Syrian Wars, l. 11. c. 8. (45) 2:191,193}

3204. Demetrius, son of Seleucus, to whom the kingdom rightly belonged, was ten years old and was being held hostage at Rome at this time. Apollonius had been raised with him and was a good friend of Seleucus. After the death of Seleucus, Apollonius left the court to go to Miletus. {*Polybius, l. 31. c. 13. s. 2-4. 6:187} The Syrians called their new king Antiochus *Epiphanes*, or *Illustrious*, because when strangers tried to take over the kingdom,

he appeared very brave to his people, vindicating his ancestor's title. {*Appian, Syrian Wars, l. 11. c. 8. (45) 2:193} Polybius thought he should more correctly be called *Epimanes*, or *the Madman*, because of his wild behaviour. {*Athenaeus, l. 2. (45c) 1:197} {*Athenaeus, l. 5. (193d) 2:377} {*Athenaeus, l. 10. (439a) 4:489}

3205. When he became king of Syria, he behaved most unusually for a king. First, he secretly left his royal palace, and without the knowledge of his servants. He unadvisedly wandered about the city in the company of only one or two companions. Moreover, he was pleased to talk and drink with the common people and with foreigners and strangers of the lowest estate. If he heard of any young men that were having a merry party, he came to the revels with his wine and music. This so startled those present with the strangeness of the action that they either fled when he came, or from fear sat still in silence. Lastly, he put aside his royal garment and donned a coat like the ones worn by the officials of Rome. He greeted every ordinary man that he came across and sometimes asked to be given the position of an aedile, or that of a tribune of the people. *[K2]* At last, by the will of the people, he obtained the place of a magistrate. According to the Roman custom, he sat in his ivory chair and gave judgment. *[E410]* He settled the law suits and disputes of the citizens with such industry and diligence, that everyone who was wise had grave doubts about his actions. Some thought he was indiscrete, some imprudent and others mad. {*Diod. Sic., l. 29. c. 32. 11:277,279} Athenaeus made similar observations. {*Athenaeus, l. 5. (193d) 2:377} {*Athenaeus, l. 10. (439a) 4:489} {*Polybius, l. 26. c. 1. 5:481-485} Livy recorded this also, as one may see in the fragment which Charles Sigonius falsely attributed to Perseus. {*Livy, l. 41. c. 20. 12:246-251}

3206. Antiochus began his reign in the 137th year, and died in the 149th year of the kingdom of the Greeks, or the Macedonians, from the time of Seleucus. {Apc 1Ma 1:10 6:16} Johannes Malela of Antioch, in his Chronicle, said he ruled twelve years, but Porphyry, Eusebius, Jerome, Sulpicius Severus and others say only eleven. To reconcile this, we must say that Antiochus began to rule at the end of the 137th year and ended his reign at the beginning of the 149th year from the spring of the season, as this author tends to reckon, that is, eleven years plus a few months.

3207. At first, Antiochus was not acknowledged as king by those who favoured Ptolemy Philometor, but some time later he obtained the title under the pretence of clemency. {Jerome, Da 11} He made an alliance with Eumenes and powerfully ruled over Syria and the neighbouring countries. The government of Babylon was committed to Timarchus, but the custody of the treasury to Heraclides' brother. Heraclides and his brother had previously been his favourites in immorality. {*Appian, Syrian Wars, l. 11. c. 8. (45) 2:193}

3208. Hyrcanus, the son of Joseph and grandchild of Tobias, saw Antiochus becoming very strong. Since he was afraid of coming under his rule and possibly being punished for what he had done against the Arabians, he killed himself, and Antiochus seized his entire estate. {*Josephus, Antiq., l. 12. c. 4. s. 11. (234-236) 7:119,121}

3209. Jason, son of Simon II, the high priest, coveted the high priesthood of Onias III, his brother. In order to obtain the priesthood for himself, he promised Antiochus three hundred and sixty talents of silver and eighty talents from other sources. Moreover, he added a further one hundred and fifty talents if he in return was given authority to set up a gymnasium to train the youth at Jerusalem and subdue the people of Jerusalem under the same conditions as applied to the citizens of Antioch. The covetous king readily agreed to these proposals. Jason removed his brother Onias and became the high priest. When he had taken over the government, he began to treat his own countrymen like Greeks and eliminated the royal privileges which had been granted by special favour to the Jews and which had been obtained through John the father of Eupolemus, who later went to Rome as an envoy. He dismantled the governments which were the lawful governments and brought in new customs contrary to the law. {Apc 2Ma 4:7-11} Josephus affirmed that Onias III, who died about this time, was removed and replaced by his brother Jesus, who changed his name to Jason. After three years, Jason was removed from the high priesthood by the actions of Menelaus, the new high priest, and Tobias' sons (or grandchildren of Hyrcanus' brother). (This passage is quite confused in Josephus' account according to the footnote in Loeb edition of Josephus. Editor.) At this time, the Greek customs were introduced. {*Josephus, Antiq., l. 12. c. 5. s. 1. (237-241) 7:121,123} However, the same writer, in his small treatise of the Maccabees, stated matters differently and close enough to the Maccabean account (except for the error in the annual tribute): [K3]

> "Antiochus removed Onias from the high priesthood and substituted Jason, his brother. Jason promised to pay him the sum of three thousand six hundred and sixty talents yearly. When he became priest and leader of the people, he subdued the country and abandoned their ancient customs and institutions and led them into every conceivable iniquity. He established a gymnasium in the fortress of our country and abolished the care of the temple."

## 3830 AM, 4540 JP, 174 BC

3210. In the seventh year of Philometor, the 574th year of Nabonassar and on the 27th day of the month of Phamenoth, according to the Egyptians (May 1), the moon was eclipsed two hours after midnight at Alexandria. {Ptolemy, Great Syntaxis, l. 6. c. 5.}

3211. The Greeks made a six month truce in their hostilities, but later a more serious war started. However, when Quintus Minucius, the commissioner, arrived with ten ships from the Romans to settle their disputes, they again hoped for peace. {*Livy, l. 41. c. 25. s. 7,8. 12:273}

3212. About the same time, Eumenes incited the Lycians to revolt from the Rhodians. Eumenes' garrisons attacked certain citadels and lands located in the farthest reaches of the continent opposite the Rhodians. {*Polybius, l. 25. c. 5. s. 5. 5:477} {*Polybius, l. 27. c. 7. s. 6-8. 5:501} {*Livy, l. 41. c. 25. s. 7,8. 12:273} {*Livy, l. 42. c. 42. s. 6-8. 12:419}

3213. King Antiochus granted those apostate Jews who agreed with Jason, the false high priest, the right to live according to the ordinances of the Gentiles. They erected a gymnasium beneath the very tower of Zion. [E411] They forced the leading young men to obey the laws of the school by wearing a hat and by concealing their circumcision, so that when they were fighting naked, they would still look like Greeks. The Greek fashions and the heathen customs became so popular, that the priests no longer had the courage to serve at the altar. They despised the temple and neglected the sacrifices, and eagerly became involved in the games. {Apc 1Ma 1:11-15 2Ma 4:12-15} {*Josephus, Antiq., l. 12. c. 5. s. 1. (241) 7:123}

3214. When Antiochus attended the games that were held every fifth year at Tyre, the impious Jason sent there from Jerusalem special messengers who were inhabitants of the city of Antioch. They carried three hundred (or, as it is much more correctly recorded in the manuscript book of the Earl of Arundel's library, three thousand and three hundred) drachmas of silver for the sacrifice to Hercules. However, the bearers of the money used it to build ships. {Apc 2Ma 4:18-20}

## 3831 AM, 4541 JP, 173 BC

3215. King Antiochus' envoys came to Rome, with Apollonius as the head of the delegation. The Roman envoys who returned from Syria said that he was highly regarded by the king and most friendly toward the Roman people. When they came before the Senate, they brought the tribute due from the king and excused its late payment. They also brought a gift in the form of vessels of gold weighing five hundred pounds. Apollonius added:

"The king requested that the association and friendship which they had with his father, should be renewed with himself. The Roman people should lay such injunctions on him as were right to impose on a faithful and confederate king. He would not be found wanting in any area of service to them. The king noted that the attitudes of the Senate had been so great toward him while he was at Rome and such had been the civility of the youth that he was treated by all as a king and not as a hostage." *[K4]*

3216. The envoys received a kind answer and Aulus Attilius, praetor of the city, was asked to renew the league with Antiochus which had existed with his father. The praetors of the city received the money, the censers and the golden vessels. It became their duty to distribute these among the temples at their discretion. The envoy Apollonius was sent a reward of a hundred thousand *ass* — pieces of coin. His lodging was given to him gratis and his expenses were paid while he stayed in Italy. {*Livy, l. 42. c. 6. s. 6-12. 12:309,311}

3217. Antiochus had a son, Antiochus Eupator. The father died when his son was nine years old. {*Appian, Syrian Wars, l. 11. c. 8. (46) 2:193} {*Appian, Syrian Wars, l. 11. c. 11. (66) 2:233}

3218. Cleopatra, the beloved mother of Ptolemy Philometor, the daughter of Antiochus the Great and the sister of Antiochus Epiphanes, died. As a dowry, she had received all of Coelosyria from her father (or at least a large part of it). Lomus and Eulaeus, the eunuch and foster-father of Philometor, governed Egypt. Eulaeus persuaded Ptolemy to demand Coelosyria from Antiochus Epiphanes, claiming it had been fraudulently seized. This constituted the basis of the war between the uncle and the youth, as Porphyry related from the *Alexandrian Histories* of Callinicus Sutorius. {Jerome, Da 11} The justification for Philometor in demanding Coelosyria back was that Antiochus the Great, father of Epiphanes, had unjustly taken Coelosyria away from Ptolemy Epiphanes, father of Philometor, when he had been under age. Later, Antiochus had restored it to him with his daughter Cleopatra, as her dowry. Antiochus Epiphanes, on the contrary, asserted that from the time when his father had overcome the father of Philometor at Parium, Coelosyria had always been subject to the kings of Syria, and he firmly denied that it had been given by his father to Cleopatra, the mother of Philometor, for her dowry. {*Polybius, l. 28. c. 20. 6:41,43} {*Polybius, l. 28. c. 20. s. 8,9. 6:41,43}

3219. It was at that time that Philometor began to reign and the coronation ceremonies were performed. {Apc 2 Ma 4:21} Ptolemy, son of Dorymenes, surnamed Macron,

displayed his wisdom. At the time that he had received the government of the isle of Cyprus, when the king was a child, he had given none of the king's money to the stewards, and now, when the king had come of age, he sent an enormous amount of money to Alexandria. The king and all the courtiers very highly commended his earlier parsimony. {*Polybius, l. 27. c. 13. 5:513}

3220. Antiochus sent Apollonius, son of Menestheus, to Egypt to the coronation of Philometor, the king. When Antiochus realised that he was in disfavour with Philometor, he fortified himself against him. After he came to Joppa, he journeyed to Jerusalem, where he was honourably received by Jason and the city. He entered the city by torchlight accompanied by great shouting. From there, Antiochus went into Phoenicia with his army. {Apc 2 Ma 4:21,22}

## 3832 AM, 4542 JP, 172 BC

3221. Three years after Jason had been made high priest by Antiochus, he sent Menelaus, the brother of Simon the Benjamite, a traitor, to bring the promised money to the king and to advise him of essential matters. Menelaus used the opportunity provided by this his embassy for his own advantage. *[E412]* In the same way that Jason had usurped his brother Onias, Menelaus usurped Jason. He promised the king three hundred talents of silver over and above what Jason had promised, so that he would be the high priest instead of Jason. {Apc 2 Ma 4:23-25} {*Sulpicius Severus, Sacred History, l. 2. c. 18. 11:106} *[K5]* Josephus stated that Menelaus was first called Onias and was brother to Onias III and to Jason himself, and the youngest son of Simon II, the high priest. {*Josephus, Antiq., l. 12. c. 5. s. 1. (239) 7:121} {*Josephus, Antiq., l. 15. c. 3. s. 1. (41) 8:21}

3222. When Menelaus secured the government of Judah, he expelled Jason to the country of the Ammonites. He did not pay any of the money he had promised to the king. {Apc 2 Ma 4:25-27}

3223. When Gaius Popilius Laenas and Publius Aelius Ligur were consuls, Valerius Antias stated that Attalus, the brother of Eumenes, came to Rome. He accused Perseus, the king of the Macedonians, of crimes and wanted to know who was backing his war effort. (The annals of most of the historians and those to whom you would give the greater credit, affirmed that Eumenes came to Rome in person. Livy.) Eumenes was entertained with the highest honour and brought into the Senate. He said that the reason he had come to Rome, apart from the desire to see the gods and men by whose benevolence he was in such a good position, was that he might publicly advise the Senate to oppose the actions of Perseus. {*Livy, l. 42. c. 11. 12:321-325} {*Appian,

*Macedonian Affairs, l. 9. c. 11. (1,2) 2:29,31}* This matter was kept so secret, that prior to the war being finished and the capture of Perseus, it was not known what Eumenes had said or what the Senate had replied. {*Livy, l. 42. c. 14. s. 1. 12:331} {*Valerius Maximus, l. 2. c. 2. s. 1b. 1:137}

3224. Some days later, Satyrus, a leader of the envoys of the Rhodians, accused Eumenes before the Senate. He said Eumenes had stirred up the country of the Lycians against the Rhodians and caused more trouble in Asia than Antiochus. Although Satyrus made a good speech, Eumenes continued to be held in high regard by the Romans. He was shown every honour and given very generous gifts, with a chariot of state and an ivory staff. {*Livy, l. 42. c. 14. s. 6-10. 12:333,335} {*Appian, Macedonian Affairs, l. 9. c. 11. (3) 2:31,33} {*Diod. Sic., l. 29. c. 34. 11:279}

3225. Eumenes returned to his kingdom from Rome. He left Cirra for the temple of Delphi in order to sacrifice to Apollo. On the way he was ambushed by men hired by Perseus. They rolled two large stones down on him, one bruising the king's head and the other injuring his shoulder. They heaped many stones on him after he fell from a steep place. The next day, when he revived, his friends brought him to the ship, and they sailed from there to Corinth. From Corinth, their ships were carried across the neck of the isthmus to Aegina. His recovery was kept so secret, that the news of his death was reported in Asia and Rome. {*Livy, l. 42. c. 15,16. 12:335-339} {*Appian, Macedonian Affairs, l. 9. c. 11. (4) 2:33}

3226. Attalus gave more credit to these reports than he should have done. He did not confer with the governor of the citadel of Pergamum as to who should be the next king, but assumed the kingdom himself and married Stratonice, his brother's wife, the daughter of Ariarathes, king of the Cappadocians. He rushed too quickly into her embraces, for not long afterward he heard that his brother was alive and was coming to Pergamum. He set aside his diadem and carrying a halberd according to custom, he and the guard went to meet Eumenes. Eumenes greeted him in a friendly and honourable manner and cheerfully greeted the queen. However, he nonetheless whispered into his brother's ear:

> Until thou seest that I am dead,
> Approach not rashly to my bed. [K6]

3227. Eumenes treated Attalus with the same friendship as before for the rest of his life, in spite of these events. {*Livy, l. 42. c. 15,16. 12:335-339} {*Diod. Sic., l. 29. c. 34. s. 2. 11:281} {*Plutarch, Sayings of Kings and Commanders (184b) 3:83} {*Plutarch, On Brotherly Love, l. 1. c. 18. 6:311}

3228. Because of the recent wickedness of Perseus against him, as well as the ancient hatred between their countries,

Eumenes prepared for war with all his strength. Envoys came to him from Rome and congratulated him on his escape from so great a danger. {*Livy, l. 42. c. 18. s. 4,5. 12:343}

3229. After that, Ariarathes, the king of the Cappadocians, had two daughters and one son by his wife Antiochis, daughter of Antiochus the Great. The son was first named Mithridates and later called Ariarathes. [E413] As his wife had thought she would be barren, she had procured two other sons for him. Hence the king sent Ariarathes, the older of the two procured sons, to Rome with a good estate. The younger was called Holophernes, or Horophernes, and was sent into Ionia. Ariarathes did not want them to contend with his genuine son for the kingdom. {*Diod. Sic., l. 31. c. 19. s. 6-8. 11:369,371} Therefore, in this year he sent Ariarathes, his genuine son, to be educated at Rome, so that from childhood he might be accustomed to the manners and men of Rome. He requested that they would permit him not to be under the custody of hosts, as was the custom with private individuals. He wanted him under the charge of public care and tuition. The embassy of the king was well received by the Senate and they decreed that Gnaeus Sicinius, the praetor, should appoint a furnished house, where the king's son and his retinue might live. {*Livy, l. 42. c. 19. s. 3-8. 12:345,347}

3230. The Romans sent envoys to their confederate kings, Eumenes, Antiochus, Ariarathes, Masanissa and to Ptolemy, king of Egypt. Others were sent into Greece, Thessaly, Epirus, Acarnania and the islands. They were to unite in a war against Perseus. {*Appian, Macedonian Affairs, l. 9. c. 11. (4) 2:33} Tiberius Claudius Nero and Marcus Decimius were sent to confirm the loyalty of Asia and the islands, and were also commanded to go to Crete and Rhodes to renew the friendships with them. They were to find out whether their confederates had been swayed by King Perseus. {*Livy, l. 42. c. 19. s. 7,8. 12:347}

## 3833a AM, 4542 JP, 172 BC

3231. When the envoys that had been sent to the confederate kings returned from Asia, they reported that they had conferred with Eumenes in Asia, Antiochus in Syria and Ptolemy in Alexandria. Each of these men had been solicited by the embassies of Perseus, but had remained loyal to the Romans and promised to do what the Romans thought best. Likewise, they reported that the confederate cities remained loyal, with the possible exception of Rhodes, which was inclined toward Perseus. The Rhodian envoys came to clear themselves of these charges, which they knew to be circulating as rumours. It was thought fitting that when the new consuls entered their office, a Senate should be convened for them. {*Livy, l. 42. c. 26. s. 7-9. 12:365,367}

## 3833b AM, 4543 JP, 171 BC

*3232.* The consuls, Publius Licinius Crassus and Gaius Cassius Longinus, along with all the kings and cities in Asia and Europe, now turned their attention to the pending war between Macedonia and Rome. Eumenes was eager for the war because of long-standing animosities between the two peoples and because Perseus had almost killed him at Delphi. Prusias, the king of Bithynia, resolved to stay out of the conflict. He did not think it right to fight with the Romans against his wife's brother. If Perseus should win, he could easily obtain pardon through his wife, who was the sister of Perseus. Ariarathes, the king of the Cappadocians, promised to help the Romans. He had an alliance with Eumenes and joined all councils of war and peace. *[K7]* Antiochus eyed the kingdom of Egypt, for he despised the youth of the king and the sloth of his tutors. He thought the dispute over Coelosyria would be a good reason for the war against Egypt. He could fight this war, while the Romans were busy in the Macedonian war. However, he generously promised help to all the kings, the Senate and their envoys through his own envoys. The young Ptolemy was still controlled by his tutors. These prepared for war against Antiochus, with the intention of retaking Coelosyria. They also made generous promises for the Macedonian war. {*Livy, l. 42. c. 29. s. 1-7. 12:373,375}* Ptolemy, king of Egypt, Ariarathes of Cappadocia, Eumenes of Asia and Masanissa of Numidia all helped the Romans. {Orosius, l. 4. c. 20.}

*3233.* Three envoys, Aulus Postumius Albinus, Gaius Decimius and Aulus Licinius Nerva, were sent from the Romans to Crete, which had sent archers for the war. {*Livy, l. 42. c. 35. s. 7. 12:397}*

*3234.* Three other envoys, Tiberius Claudius, Spurius Postumius and Marcus Junius, were sent into the islands and the cities of Asia. They were to urge their confederates to help fight against Perseus. They concentrated their efforts on the larger cities first, for they knew that the smaller cities would follow the lead of the larger ones. The Rhodians were judged to be the wealthiest and to have the most business interests in that region. They supplied forty ships by the authority of Hegesilochus, who was at that time the *Prytanis*, or head of the government. As soon as he knew the Romans planned to wage war with Perseus, he exhorted his citizens to ally themselves with the Romans. They should send the same help to the Romans that they had given in the war with Antiochus and before that, with Philip. The Rhodians should enlist the help of their naval allies to assemble this fleet. They should eagerly do this, to effectively kill the rumours spread against them by Eumenes. Consequently, when the envoys from Rome came, the Rhodians showed them a fleet of forty ships prepared and equipped for war. *[E414]* Their action had a great influence on the rest of the cities of Asia. {*Livy, l. 42. c. 45. 12:427,429} {*Polybius, l. 27. c. 3. 5:493}*

*3235.* After Perseus had a conference with the Romans, he wrote down all the reasons supporting his position, and what the other side had alleged. This was contrived in such a way as to put him in a favourable light, and was copied and sent by couriers to the other cities. However, he ordered Antenor and Philip to go as envoys to Rhodes. When they arrived there, they gave the letters to the magistrates. After a few days, the envoys from Perseus were to request the Rhodians that for the present they would not take sides in this war. If the Romans were to undertake a war with Perseus and the Macedonians, contrary to the laws of the league, the Rhodians should endeavour to bring them back to the terms of the agreement, which would be in everyone's interest. The Romans ought to be more intent than others on preserving law and liberty, since they were the guardians of the liberty of Greece and Rhodes. Therefore, they ought to enforce the compliance of those who were not so inclined. *[K8]* When the envoys had spoken these things, their speech seemed reasonable to everyone, but the opposing side prevailed, nonetheless. On the other points, they yielded courteously to the envoys. In reply, the Rhodians requested that Perseus not demand anything that would be against the will of the Romans. Antenor did not accept this, and used the courtesy of the Rhodians to return to Macedonia. {*Polybius, l. 27. c. 4. 5:495,497} {*Livy, l. 42. c. 46. s. 1-7. 12:429,431}*

*3236.* While the navy was stationed around Cephallenia, Gaius Lucretius, the Roman praetor, sent a letter with the Romans requesting the ships to be sent to him. This letter, which he gave to Socrates, a gymnastic trainer, to deliver, came to Rhodes at the time when Stratocles was the head of the council, or Prytanis, in the latter half of that year. When the matter was debated, it seemed fitting to Agathagetus, Rhodophon, Astymedes and many others that the Rhodians should, without any further delay, send the ships and ally themselves with the Romans. However, Dinon and Polyaratus, who did not approve of those things which had previously been decreed in favour of the Romans, argued that the letter had not been sent from the Romans but from Eumenes, the enemy of the Rhodians. They claimed Eumenes was determined to draw them into the war and engage the people in unnecessary expenses and troubles. They said that the letter had been brought to Rhodes by an obscure person, a gymnastic trainer. However, the Romans used great care to pick out men most suitable for such a task. Stratocles, the chief officer or Prytanis opposed these men by speaking at length against Perseus and generously commending the Romans. He prevailed with the Rhodians that a decree should be made to send the ships. Therefore, of the six ships that were ready, they sent five to Chalcis under the command of Timagoras, and one to Tenedos, under the command of Nicagoras. Nicagoras was unable to capture Diophanes at Tenedos, where he had been sent by Perseus, but he captured Diophanes' ship with all its crew. {*Polybius, l. 27. c. 7. 5:499-503}

3237. From the embassy that came from Asia, the Romans heard about the state of the Rhodians and the rest of the cities. They convened a Senate for the envoys of Perseus. {*Polybius, l. 27. c. 6. 5:497,499} {*Livy, l. 42. c. 46. s. 7. 12:431} So it was at that time that these envoys, Solon and Hippias endeavoured to relate all the circumstances and to lessen the tension. However, they defended the crime and treachery against Eumenes with special zeal, because the matter was well known. When they had finished their speech, the Senate, who had previously decreed the war, denounced them and whoever else had happened to come to Rome from Macedonia. They were to depart immediately from within the walls of Rome and be out of Italy within thirty days. {*Polybius, l. 27. c. 6. 5:497,499} {*Livy, l. 42. c. 46. s. 1-7. 12:429,431} {*Diod. Sic., l. 30. c. 7. s. 1. 11:283}

3238. Notice was sent to Eumenes that he should, with all his strength, help in the war against Perseus. {Justin, Trogus, l. 33. c. 1.} He came by sea to Chalcis in Boeotia with his brothers, Attalus and Athenaeus. His brother Philetaerus stayed at Pergamum to safeguard the kingdom. Together with Attalus and four thousand foot soldiers and a thousand cavalry, Eumenes went from Chalcis into Thessaly, to Gaius Licinius Crassus, the consul. [E415] [K9] Meanwhile, Athenaeus was left behind at Chalcis with two thousand foot soldiers, and when Marius Lucretius came there with an army of ten thousand soldiers, he took these troops with him to the siege of Haliartus. {*Livy, l. 42. c. 45,46. 12:463,465}

3239. About the same time, warships arrived at Chalcis from their other confederates: two Phoenician ships of five tiers of oars, two from Heraclea in Pontus of three tiers of oars, four each from Chalcedon and Samos. Furthermore, Rhodes sent five ships of four tiers of oars. {*Livy, l. 42. c. 46. s. 6,7. 12:465} Gaius Lucretius, the praetor, and brother of Marcus, returned the ships to the confederates when he saw that there would be no naval war. {*Livy, l. 42. c. 46. s. 7. 12:465} {*Polybius, l. 27. c. 7. s. 16. 5:503} However, together with his brother, the praetor attacked Haliartus and after it had surrendered to him, levelled it to the ground and then took Thebes without any opposition. {*Livy, l. 42. c. 63. s. 3-12. 12:489}

3240. While these affairs were going on in Boeotia, Licinius, the consul, Eumenes and Attalus engaged Perseus in Thessaly. In the first conflict, no one won a clear victory. About thirty men were killed on Eumenes' side, including Cassignatus, the captain of the Gauls. In the second battle, Perseus was victorious. {*Livy, l. 42. c. 58-62. 12:469-487} But even though he won and asked for peace from Licinius, he did not get it. {*Livy, l. 42. c. 62. s. 15. 12:487} {*Polybius, l. 27. c. 8. 5:503-507} {*Appian, Macedonian Affairs, l. 9. c. 12. (1) 2:41}

3241. Perseus sent Antenor to Rhodes to redeem the captives that had sailed with Diophanes. There was a long discussion over this issue by those who governed the country, about what ought to be done. It seemed best to Piplophron and Theaedetus that the Rhodians should not entangle themselves in the affairs of Perseus. However, Dinon and Polyaratus wanted to get involved. At last they came to an agreement with Perseus concerning the captives. {*Polybius, l. 27. c. 14. 5:515}

3242. When Antiochus clearly saw Egypt preparing to wage war over Coelosyria, he sent Meleager to Rome as an envoy. Through him he declared to the Senate that he was being wrongly invaded and that since Ptolemy was an ally of Rome, just as he was, allies should not be fighting with each other. {*Polybius, l. 27. c. 19. 5:521} {*Polybius, l. 28. c. 1. 6:3,5}

3243. When the war began between Antiochus and Ptolemy over Coelosyria, the envoys of both kings came to Rome. Antiochus sent Meleager, Sosiphanes and Heraclides. Ptolemy sent Timothy and Damon. Meleager came in order to tell the Senate that Ptolemy had first wrongly provoked Antiochus and wanted to put him out of a country that was rightfully his. Timothy was sent to renew the friendship with the Romans and to observe Meleager's dealings with them. When he had renewed the friendship and received favourable answers to his requests, he returned to Alexandria. The Senate told Meleager that they would have Quintus Marcius write to Ptolemy as he thought best on his own authority. {*Polybius, l. 28. c. 1. 6:3,5} {*Diod. Sic., l. 30. c. 2. 11:283,285}

3244. Antiochus defeated Ptolemy's commanders between Pelusium and Mount Casius. He spared the king because of his youth and pretended to be his friend. He went up to Memphis and took over the kingdom, claiming that he would be careful about the affairs of the land. Therefore with a small company of people, he subdued all of Egypt. {Porphyry, Callinicus Sutorius} {Jerome, Da 11} Ptolemy Macron, the son of Dorymenes, to whom Philometor had committed the government of Cyprus, seems to have defected to Antiochus at this time and surrendered the island to him, {Apc 2 Ma 10:13} [K10] whereupon the care of Cyprus was committed to Crates. {Apc 2 Ma 4:29} Antiochus made Ptolemy the governor of Coelosyria and Phoenicia, {Apc 2 Ma 8:8} and admitted him into his inner circle of friends. {Apc 1 Ma 3:38}

### 3834a AM, 4543 JP, 171 BC

3245. Jubilee 26.

3246. Perseus was defeated by Licinius the consul, Eumenes, Attalus and Misagenes, the prince of the Numidians. When Perseus reached Pella, he sent his army into their winter quarters. The consul returned to Latissa and sent Eumenes and Attalus home. He placed Misagenes with his Numidians and the rest of his own army in their winter quarters throughout Thessaly. {*Livy, l. 42. c. 65-67. 12:495-505}

3247. Sostratus, the governor of the citadel of Jerusalem, was in charge of collecting the king's revenues there. When he requested the money promised to Antiochus by Menelaus, both of them were summoned to Antioch by the king. Menelaus left his brother Lysimachus in charge of the high priesthood, while Sostratus left Crates, who was governor of Cyprus, in his place. {Apc 2 Ma 4:27-29} [E416]

3248. In Cilicia, the men of Tarsus and Mallos revolted because Antiochus had given the cities to Antiochis, his concubine, as a gift. The king hurriedly came to appease them, leaving Andronicus in charge at Antioch. {Apc 2 Ma 4:30,31}

3249. Menelaus took advantage of the king's absence. With the help of Lysimachus, the king's deputy, he stole some gold vessels from the temple at Jerusalem. Some he gave to Andronicus and some he sold in Tyre and the surrounding cities. When Onias III, the legal high priest, knew of this, he impeached Menelaus for this sacrilege. Onias hid himself in a sanctuary at Daphne, which was near Antioch. {Apc 2 Ma 4:32,33} This sanctuary was in the middle of a grove and was dedicated to Apollo and Artemis. {*Strabo, l. 16. c. 2. s. 6. 7:245} It was a spacious facility and had been built by Antiochus. {*Ammianus Marcellinus, l. 22. c. 13. s. 1. 2:269}

3250. At the request of Menelaus, Andronicus had Onias leave the sanctuary and promised him his safety, but then had him murdered. {Apc 2 Ma 4:34,35}

3251. When Antiochus returned to Antioch from Cilicia, the Jews of that city and those in many other countries complained to him of the unjust murder of that most holy old man. Antiochus was deeply moved, to the point of tears, and commanded that Andronicus be stripped of his royal attire and led around the city. He was killed in the same place where he had murdered Onias. {Apc 2 Ma 4:35-38}

### 3834b AM, 4544 JP, 170 BC

3252. After many sacrileges had been committed at Jerusalem by Lysimachus, with the consent of Menelaus, the people assembled against Lysimachus, since many gold vessels had already been taken away. To protect himself, he gathered three thousand troops under Auranus, who was an old and foolish man. In the riot, some picked up stones, some large clubs, some picked up dirt and threw this at Lysimachus and his soldiers. In the uproar, many were wounded, some were killed and the rest fled. [K11] Lysimachus was killed near the treasury. {Apc 2 Ma 4:39-42}

3253. When Antiochus came to Tyre, three men were sent from the elders at Jerusalem to testify against Menelaus, as having been a partner in the sacrileges and wickedness of Lysimachus. However, even though Menelaus was convicted, the king freed him when he was promised large sums of money by Ptolemy, the son of Dorymenes. Menelaus had bribed Ptolemy to help him. Through Ptolemy, Menelaus was acquitted and allowed to continue as the high priest. The three innocent persons who pleaded for the city, the people and the holy vessels, were condemned to die. The men of Tyre gave them a magnificent funeral. {Apc 2 Ma 4:44-50}

3254. About that time, Antiochus prepared his second expedition into Egypt. It happened that for forty days strange visions were seen at Jerusalem of armed horsemen and of foot soldiers in battle in the air, portending their future problems. {Apc 2 Ma 5:1-4}

3255. Antiochus planned to add the kingdom of Egypt to his own. He entered Egypt with a vast company, with chariots, elephants, horsemen and a large navy. He made war against Ptolemy, king of Egypt, who turned and fled away, and many were killed. Afterward, the victors seized the fortified cities in the land and Antiochus took the spoils of Egypt. {Apc 1 Ma 1:16-19}

3256. A false rumour of Antiochus' death was circulated. Jason took with him no less than a thousand men and made a surprise attack on the city of Jerusalem. Menelaus fled into the citadel, but Jason slaughtered his own citizens unashamedly. However, he was unable to take over the government and was forced to flee in shame. He returned back to the country of the Ammonites, but having been accused before Aretas, the king of the Arabians, he did not dare show his face there. He was forced to flee from one city to another and was hated by all men because he had forsaken their laws. He was proclaimed a public enemy of his own country. {Apc 2 Ma 5:5-10}

*3257.* Antiochus, in Egypt, heard that the rumour of his death had made the people of Jerusalem very glad. Because he suspected from the rebellion of Jason that Judea would revolt, he was very angry. {*Apc 2Ma 5:11*} {*Josephus, Maccabean War*} After having subdued Egypt in the 143rd year of the Greeks, or Seleucus, he went up against Israel and Jerusalem with a large army. {*Apc 1Ma 1:20,21*}

*3258.* Josephus wrote that, in the 143rd year of the Seleucians, he took the city without a battle. {*Josephus, Antiq., l. 12. c. 5. s. 3. (246,247) 7:125*} [*E417*] The men of his own faction opened the gates to him. However, in the Apocrypha, the city was said to have been taken by force of arms. {*Apc 2Ma 5:11*} Elsewhere, Josephus contradicts himself and stated that Antiochus took the city by force, and added that Antiochus was enraged at the memory of the things which he had endured in the siege. {*Josephus, Jewish War, l. 1. c. 0. s. 7. (19) 2:11,13*} Moreover, the men of Jerusalem made an attack against Antiochus while he besieged the city, and were killed in the conflict. {*Josephus, Jewish War, l. 6. c. 10. s. 1. (436) 4:303*} [*K12*]

*3259.* When the city had been captured, the soldiers were ordered to kill anyone they met. Cruelly, they killed everyone, regardless of age or sex. In three days, eighty thousand men were missing, forty thousand of whom had been killed and the rest sold into slavery. {*Apc 2Ma 5:11-14*}

*3260.* Antiochus was not content with this and went into the temple, with Menelaus, who had betrayed their laws and country, as his guide. He wickedly seized the holy vessels and anything else that had been dedicated by other kings to the glory and honour of the place. {*Apc 2Ma 5:15,16*} He took the golden altar, the lampstand with all its vessels, the table of the showbread, the pouring vessels, the vials, the censers of gold and the veil. He removed the crowns and the golden ornaments that were fastened to the temple doors. He pulled off the gold from everything that was covered with gold, and stole all the silver, the lovely vessels and all the hidden treasures that he found. {*Apc 1Ma 1:23,24*}

*3261.* Polybius of Megalopolis, Strabo of Cappadocia, Nicolaus Damascene, Timagenes, Castor the historian and Apollodorus wrote that Antiochus was short of money and broke his league. He assaulted the Jews, his confederates and friends, and plundered the temple that was full of gold and silver, sparing nothing of value. {*Josephus, Apion, l. 2. c. 7. (84,85) 1:327*} His large tribute to the Romans forced him to gather money by pillaging and not to miss any opportunity of plundering. {*Sulpicius Severus, Sacred History, l. 2. c. 19. 11:107*} Those who were the enemies of the Jews affirmed that many other things were done by him because he hated the Jews and had contempt for their religion. Diodorus stated: {*Diod. Sic., l. 34. c. 1. s. 3,4. 12:55*}

"When Antiochus Epiphanes had overcome the Jews, he entered into the Holy of Holies of God, where only the priests could lawfully go. There he found a marble statue of a man with a long beard, holding a book in his hand and sitting on an ass. He thought him to be Moses, who had built Jerusalem, founded the nation and established those laws that are hated in all nations. He desired to remove this reproach to the nations and endeavoured to abrogate the laws. Therefore, he sacrificed a large sow to the statue of the founder, Moses. He poured blood on the altar of God that stood in the open air, as well as on the statue. He boiled the flesh of the sow and commanded that the holy books containing their laws be marred and obliterated with the broth. He commanded that the eternal flame, which always burned in the temple, be extinguished. He compelled Menelaus, the high priest, and other Jews to eat swine's flesh."

*3262.* However, we disagree with the testimony of all who would reproach the Jews as being a wicked people, for even Strabo commended the Jews as being just and religious persons. {*Strabo, l. 16. c. 2. s. 37. 7:285*}

*3263.* When Antiochus had captured the city, he sacrificed swine on the altar and with the broth of its flesh he sprinkled the temple. {*Josephus, Antiq., l. 13. c. 8. s. 2. (243) 7:349*}

*3264.* Antiochus carried eighteen hundred talents from the temple and quickly returned to Antioch. He appointed governors to vex the country. He appointed Philip, who was a Phrygian and more of a barbarian than Antiochus, to be over Jerusalem. He also appointed Andronicus at Gerizim in Samaria. In addition to these, he left Menelaus, who was worse than all the rest and who had a most malicious attitude toward the Jews, to rule the citizens with a heavy hand. {*Apc 2Ma 5:21-23*} [*K13*]

*3265.* The envoys of Asia were heard in the Senate at Rome. The Milesians, mindful of the fact that they had so far done nothing, promised their readiness to do whatever the Senate should command, to help the war against Perseus. The Alabandians stated that they had erected a temple to the city of Rome and instituted anniversary games to the goddess. They brought a golden crown weighing fifty pounds, which they might place in the Capitol as a gift to Jupiter. They also brought three hundred shields for the cavalry, which they were willing to give to whomever the Senate should appoint. The people of Lampsacus brought an eighty pound crown and made the following reasoned appeal:

"How that they had defected from Perseus when the Roman army had come into Macedonia. They had been under the jurisdiction of Perseus and before that, of Philip. With regard for this, and in return for having handed everything over to the Roman commanders, they requested only that they might be received into the friendship of the Roman people. [E418] Should a peace be made with Perseus, they did not wish to be under Perseus' authority any longer."

3266. A civil answer was returned to the rest of the envoys. Quintus Maenius, the praetor, was commanded to enrol Lampsacus as allies. Rewards were given to them all, amounting to more than two thousand *asses* of money for each of them. The Alabandians were commanded to carry the shields back with them to Aulus Hostilius Mancinus, the consul in Macedonia. {*Livy, l. 43. c. 6. s. 1-10. 13:21-25}

## 3835a AM, 4544 JP, 170 BC

3267. It was decided by the common agreement of the Achaeans that all the honours of Eumenes which were considered by them as unseemly and repugnant to the laws, should be removed. Sosigenes and Diopithes from Rhodes were judges in the matter at that time, and because they were offended by Eumenes, they destroyed all his honours in the cities of Peloponnesus. {*Polybius, l. 28. c. 7. s. 1-11. 6:15-17}

## 3835b AM, 4545 JP, 169 BC

3268. While Aulus Hostilius, the consul, wintered in Thessaly with his forces, Attalus, who at that time was wintering at Elatia, was informed that his brother Eumenes had been most distressed because they had taken away his grandest honours by a public decree. After Archon, the leader of the Achaeans, had been told by Attalus about this matter, he agreed to help Attalus. Attalus sent envoys to the common council of the country, to negotiate with them concerning restoring the honours to the king. Thereupon, through the persuasion of Polybius, the historian, a decree was made that the magistrates be commanded to restore everything connected with the honour of Eumenes. Those honours that were not in the common interest of the Achaeans, or were contrary to the laws, were not to be restored. In this way, Attalus rectified at that time the miscarriages that had been rashly committed in Peloponnesus concerning his brother Eumenes' honour. {*Polybius, l. 28. c. 7. 6:15-19} {*Polybius, l. 16. c. 25,26. 5:55-59}

3269. At the beginning of the spring, Quintus Marcius Philippus, the consul, was sent against Perseus. {*Livy, l. 44. c. 1. s. 1. 13:91}

3270. The Achaeans published a decree concerning the sending of auxiliaries to Marcius, the consul, which was brought to him by Polybius. Telocritus was to be their envoy to Attalus, to bring him that decree whereby the honours of Eumenes had been restored to him. At the same time, the Achaeans heard that the *Anacleteria* had been celebrated in honour of Ptolemy, the king, as was the custom for the kings of Egypt when they reached legal age. As a token of their joy in this, they sent envoys for the renewing of the friendship that existed between the Achaeans and the kings of Egypt. Alcithus and Parsiadas were chosen to do this. {*Polybius, l. 28. c. 12. 6:25,27}

3271. About that time a wicked act, and most abhorrent to the institutions of the Greeks, was committed on the island of Crete. [K14] Between the people of Cydonia and Apollonia there was a common bond of friendship and a league of peace. When the tables of that league were ratified on each side by oath, they were fastened to the image of Idaean Zeus for all to see. In spite of this, the people of Cydonia broke the league at a time of peace, when they were being treated by Apollonia as friends. They surprised their city, killed all the men with the sword and plundered their goods. They divided their wives, their children and all their land among themselves. {*Polybius, l. 28. c. 14. 6:31} {*Diod. Sic., l. 30. c. 13. 11:297}

3272. The people of Cydonia were afraid of the Gortynians. Previously, their city had almost been taken by a surprise attack by Nothocrates, so they sent envoys to Eumenes asking for help based on their league with him. The king chose Leon as captain, sending him there speedily with a band of three hundred soldiers. When these forces arrived, the people of Cydonia gave the keys of the gates to Leon and put the whole city under his control. {*Polybius, l. 28. c. 15. 6:31,33}

3273. At the urging of Eulaeus, the eunuch, Ptolemy started a new war to recover Coelosyria. So Antiochus made his third expedition into Egypt and subdued it. {*Polybius, l. 28. c. 18-20. 6:39-43} When the Egyptians fled, Antiochus could have killed them all with his cavalry, but he restrained his troops and ordered that they should be taken alive. For this kindness, he gained both Pelusium and a little later, all of Egypt. {*Diod. Sic., l. 30. c. 14. 11:297}

3274. The opposing factions at Rhodes grew daily after they had heard about the Roman Senate's decrees that from now on, those matters were to be done according to the dictates of the Senate, and not of their own magistrates. Philophron and Theaedetus persuaded them to send envoys to Rome. [E419] At the beginning of the summer, Hegesilochus, the son of Hegesias, Nicagoras and Nicander were sent as envoys to Rome. Hagepolis, Ariston and Pasicrates were sent to Quintus Marcius

Philippus, the consul, and to Gaius Marcius Figulus, the admiral of the fleet. They had all been commanded to renew the friendship with the Roman people and to answer the accusations of some against Rhodes. Hegesilochus had also been ordered to request permission to send grain. Hagepolis overtook Quintus Marcius, who was camped at Heraclea in Macedonia. When he had carried out his orders, the consul said that he paid no heed to those who slandered the Rhodians and asked the envoys not to put up with anyone who did such things. He treated them very kindly and wrote to the Roman people about this. Hagepolis was overwhelmed by the courtesy of the consul. Marcius took him into a private meeting, where he said he wondered why the Rhodians did not try to reconcile the kings who were fighting over Coelosyria, since they were in a position to do so. [K15] Hagepolis subsequently went to Gaius, the admiral of the fleet, and was even more favourably entertained by him than he had been by Marcius. He returned to Rhodes a short time later and related both what had happened and how well he had been treated by both the Roman commanders. The expectations of all the Rhodians were raised to a high pitch, but not in the same way. Most of the older ones were very pleased about the friendship of the Romans, while the younger ones were troubled by these actions. They thought that this excessive kindness of the Romans was a sign that they were terrified by the imminent danger and that matters were not unfolding as they should. Later, Hagepolis sided against them and secretly took orders from Marcius to propose, in the council of the Rhodians, the making of a peace treaty agreement between the kings. Dinon had no doubts at all but that the affairs of the Romans must be in a dreadful mess. So envoys were sent to Alexandria to put an end to the war between Antiochus and Ptolemy. {*Polybius, l. 28. c. 16,17. 6:33-37}

3275. Toward the end of the summer, Hagesilochus and other envoys from Rhodes came to Rome and were very graciously entertained. It was common knowledge that the Rhodians were divided by civil disputes. Agathagetus, Philophron, Rhodophon and Theaedetus placed all their hopes in the Romans. Dinon and Polyaratus, on the other hand, trusted in Perseus and the Macedonians. It happened frequently that, when matters had been debated equally well on either side and with different conclusions, the Senate ignored the internal differences at Rhodes, although they were well aware of them. The Senate granted a licence to them to export a hundred thousand bushels of wheat from Sicily. {*Polybius, l. 28. c. 16. 6:33,35}

3276. After Egypt had been subdued by Antiochus, Comanus and Cineas discussed with king Ptolemy what was to be done. It was decided that a council be created, composed of the chief captains who would be in charge of settling matters. The council decided that any Greeks whom they might be able to find there should go as envoys to Antiochus, to negotiate with him about a peace. {*Polybius, l. 28. c. 19. s. 1,2. 6:39}

3277. At that time two envoys arrived from the country of the Achaeans. Alcithus, the son of Xenophon of Aegina, was to renew their friendship with the king. Pasiadas had been sent about the matter of the war between Ptolemy and Antiochus. The Athenians sent envoys, headed by Demaratus, concerning a certain donation, and these men brought up two religious matters, as well. The first, concerning the feast of Athena, called *Panathenaea*, was mentioned by Callias, the pancratiast, or conqueror at the games. The other, concerning the mysteries, was handled by Cleostratus, who, in the course of the discussion, made a speech to the king. Miletus was represented by four envoys, Eudemus, Icesius from Clazomene, Apollonides and Apollonius. {*Polybius, l. 28. c. 19. s. 3-6. 6:39}

3278. Together with these, Ptolemy, the king, sent his own envoys, Tlepolemus and Ptolemy, the teacher of rhetoric. They sailed and came to Antiochus, who received them courteously and on the first day invited them to a sumptuous feast. The next day he gave them the liberty of a personal conference and asked them to declare their purpose. The envoys of the Achaeans were the first to speak with him. [E420] Then Demaratus spoke, who had been sent by the Athenians. [K16] He was followed by Eudemus, from Miletus. All affirmed that the war had been started at the instigation of Eulaeus, the eunuch. After they had emphasised how young Ptolemy was, they all deplored the war between the kings. Antiochus agreed with their speeches and more fully explained himself, defending his rights. With great earnestness he sought to prove that Coelosyria belonged to the kings of Syria. He denied what the envoys from Alexandria alleged, namely that Coelosyria had been given as a dowry with Cleopatra, the mother of Philometor, who now reigned. After much discussion, he proved his point to everyone present. At that time, he sailed to Naucratis. There he spoke in a kindly manner, and treated the citizens well. To each Greek resident he gave a gold stater, which was valued at 16 shillings eight pence. (Value at 1650 AD. Editor.) He journeyed to Alexandria and promised to reply to the envoys after Aristides and Theris had returned because he wanted the Greeks to know and witness his actions. {*Polybius, l. 28. c. 19. s. 7-13. 6:39-43}

3279. Philometor was being taught by Eulaeus, the eunuch, in pleasure and effeminate ways. He became so slothful that, since he was so far removed from all danger and separated from the enemy by a great distance, he surrendered his large and wealthy kingdom without fighting for it. {*Diod. Sic., l. 30. c. 17. 11:301,303}

3280. Antiochus took the crown from Philometor after he had reigned eleven years. The Alexandrians committed the management of affairs to Euergetes, his younger brother. {Porphyry, Scaliger's Greek Eusebius, p. 54,225.} They later nicknamed him *Cacergetes*, or the *Malefactor*, as opposed to *Euergetes*, which means *Benefactor*. {*Athenaeus, l. 4. (184c) 2:313} {*Athenaeus, l. 12. (549d) 5:493} However, from the large size of his body and the largeness of his paunch, he was nicknamed Physcon, or Gore-belly. This was added after his name and is read on his coins. ΠΤΟΛΕΜΑΙΟΥ ΦΥΣΚΩΝΟΣ ΕΥΕΡΓΕΤΟΥ

3281. Epiphanius called this Ptolemy *Ptolemy Philologus*, because of his love of knowledge. {Epiphanius, De Mensuris et Ponderibus} He was one of Aristarchus' scholars and he wrote historical observations which were frequently cited by Athenaeus. {*Athenaeus, l. 2. (71b) 1:311} This second Euergetes wrote the things we took from Athenaeus and Galen about the first Ptolemy Euergetes. {See note on 3761 AM. <<2847>>} At this time Eumenes, the son of Attalus, reigned in Asia, of whom Strabo stated that he furnished Pergamum with libraries. {*Strabo, l. 13. c. 4. s. 2. 6:167} It is likely that the following things which Vitruvius mentioned refer to this same Ptolemy: {*Vitruvius, l. 7. c. 0. s. 4. 2:65}

> "The Attalian kings were inclined to the wonderful delights of learning when they had erected a famous library at Pergamum for the common enjoyment of all. Ptolemy was zealous to do the same at Alexandria."

3282. Pliny stated: {*Pliny, l. 13. c. 21. (70) 4:141}

> "Subsequently, parchment was invented at Pergamum when, according to Varro, owing to the rivalry between King Ptolemy and King Eumenes about their libraries, Ptolemy suppressed the export of paper."

3283. Ptolemy Philometor was driven from his kingdom and fled to his younger brother Ptolemy Euergetes at Alexandria. {Justin, Trogus, l. 34. c. 2.} Since Alexandria was not under the power of Antiochus, they made him co-ruler with his brother in the kingdom. [K17] This was in the twelfth year of Philometor's reign and the fourth year of Euergetes' reign. {Porphyry, Scaliger's Greek Eusebius, p. 54,225.} After a while, however, they expelled Philometor and banished him. {*Polybius, l. 28. c. 21,22. 6:43,45} {*Polybius, l. 29. c. 23. s. 3-5. 6:81,83}

3284. Antiochus seized on that occasion and took over the government of the banished prince. He used the specious pretence of bringing him home again to justify his Egyptian war. This is what he told the envoys whom he sent into all the cities of Asia and Greece. {*Livy, l. 44. c. 19. s. 6-14. 13:151,153} {*Livy, l. 45. c. 11. s. 8. 13:279}

## 3836a AM, 4545 JP, 169 BC

3285. Antiochus, through the pretence of bringing the older Ptolemy back to his kingdom, fought a war with his younger brother Euergetes, who at that time possessed Alexandria. He defeated him in the naval battle at Pelusium. He crossed the Nile with his army on a bridge which he hastily built, and besieged Alexandria. Thereupon, the younger Ptolemy and Cleopatra, his sister, sent envoys to Rome. They asked the Senate to send assistance to the kingdom and to those princes who were friends to the empire, and reminded them that the people of Rome had this obligation to Antiochus. So great was their authority with all the kings and nations that if they were but to send envoys declaring that it did not please the Senate that a war was being fought between their allies, Antiochus would immediately depart from Alexandria and withdraw his army into Syria. {*Livy, l. 44. c. 19. s. 6-11. 13:151} [E421]

3286. When Antiochus was unable to break down the wall of Alexandria, he left. {*Livy, l. 45. c. 11. s. 1. 13:277} In spite of his withdrawal, Meleager, Sosiphanes and Heraclides were sent to Rome as envoys. They were given a hundred and fifty talents, of which fifty talents were to be spent on a crown to be given to the Romans, and the remainder was to be divided among certain Greek cities. {*Polybius, l. 28. c. 22. 6:45}

3287. About that time, the envoys of the Rhodians, headed by Praxon, arrived at Alexandria to negotiate a peace. Shortly after this, they went to the camp of Antiochus, where they were permitted to see the king. They had a long discourse about the mutual alliances between both the kings and the advantages that would accrue to each if peace were made. But the king interrupted the envoy in his speech and said that there was no need of any further discussion, as the kingdom belonged to the older Ptolemy, and he had long since made a peace with him and was his friend. If the Alexandrians now wished to recall him from banishment, Antiochus would not prevent it. {*Polybius, l. 28. c. 23. 6:45}

3288. Leaving the older Ptolemy at Memphis, Antiochus pretended to fight for Ptolemy's kingdom and gave him the rest of Egypt. After that, he left a strong garrison at Pelusium and withdrew his army into Syria, considering it prudent to allow the civil war in Egypt to continue. He could always use it as a pretence to re-enter Egypt with his army to help the older brother. {*Livy, l. 45. c. 11. s. 2. 13:277}

3289. King Eumenes came from Elaea with twenty decked ships to the shores of Cassandria, where he met with Gaius Marcius Figulus, who was a praetor and the admiral of the Roman fleet. Prusias sent five ships there. {*Livy, l. 44. c. 10. s. 12. 13:123} At the same time Marcius, with the help of Demetrius, tried in vain to take the city of Cassandria. {*Livy, l. 44. c. 11,12. 13:123-129} It was rumoured that Cydas, the Cretian, and Antimachus, the commander in Demetrias, were negotiating a peace between Eumenes and Perseus. Cydas, who was one of Eumenes' intimate friends, had previously been seen talking with a certain countryman of his, Chimarus, at Amphipolis. [K18] Later, at Demetrias, he was seen talking with a certain captain of Perseus by the name of Menecrates, and then again with Antimachus, under the very walls of the city. Eumenes left Demetrias and sailed to Quintus Marcius, the consul, to congratulate him on his arrival into Macedonia, after which he left for his own kingdom of Pergamum. Gaius Marcius Figulus, the praetor, sent part of the fleet to winter at Sciathum and went with the rest of the ships to Oreus in Boeotia. {*Livy, l. 44. c. 24. s. 9-11. 13:169} {*Livy, l. 44. c. 13. s. 9-11. 13:131,133}

3290. Reports varied concerning Eumenes. Valerius Antias wrote that although the praetor summoned the king with frequent dispatches, he had not even received the naval assistance from him. Neither did Eumenes, on his way to Asia, part on good terms with the consul, being indignant because he was not permitted to encamp in the Roman area. He could not even be persuaded to leave behind any of the Galatian cavalry he had brought with him. Attalus, his brother, remained with the consul and was loyal to him throughout the war. {*Livy, l. 44. c. 13. s. 12-14. 13:133} Velleius Paterculus wrote that King Eumenes was indifferent to that war and lent his brother no assistance. {*Velleius Paterculus, l. 1. c. 9. s. 2. 1:21}

3291. At Rome, the envoys of Pamphylia brought a golden crown into the Senate, made of twenty thousand philips. At their request, they were allowed to put the crown in the temple of Jupiter and to sacrifice in the Capitol. Their desire of renewing friendship was graciously granted and each received a gift of two thousand asses of money. {*Livy, l. 44. c. 14. s. 1-4. 13:133,135}

3292. At that time, envoys came from King Prusias to help make a peace with King Perseus. They received an audience with the Senate. Prusias said that he supported the Romans then, and that he would stand by them during the war. However, when the envoys had come to him from Perseus with the desire to end the war, he had promised them to intervene on their behalf with the Senate. He hoped that if they could be persuaded to end their displeasure with himself, he could be of assistance to them in making a peace with both parties. {*Livy, l. 44. c. 14. s. 5-8. 13:135}

3293. The embassy from Rhodes was more arrogant over the same issue. They recounted the deeds which they had done for the Roman people and how they had been largely responsible for the victory over Antiochus. They added that, at the same time there had been peace between the Macedonians and the Romans, they had an alliance between themselves and King Perseus. [E422] This they had broken against their will, not through any provocation against them on his part, but because it had pleased the Romans to draw them into the war. Now, in the third year of the war, they were feeling the brunt of it. Because of the interruption of commerce, their island was being reduced to poverty, as they had lost their revenues that came by sea and their food supply had been cut off. When they had no longer been able to endure this, they had sent envoys into Macedonia to Perseus, telling him that the Rhodians would be happy if he would make peace with the Romans. The Rhodians indicated to Perseus that they would send to the Romans to declare this, and would consider what should be done against those who failed to end the war. Claudius Quadrigarius said that no answer was given to these persons. A decree of the Senate was recited in which the Roman people announced that the Carians and Lycians were now free, and that letters should immediately be sent to both countries to inform them of this. When they heard this, the head of the Rhodian delegation, whose magniloquence the Senate house had scarcely been able to contain just a moment earlier, fell down astonished. Others said that the Senate replied that from the beginning of the war, the Roman people had been told by reputable persons that the Rhodians had secret talks against Rome with King Perseus. [K19] If this had been doubtful before, the envoys' words had made it plain. This fraud, which had been secret in the beginning, had now largely been exposed. What the Rhodians were about to consider, the Romans knew themselves. Most certainly the people of Rome would appropriately reward each city for its part in the war when Perseus was defeated, which they hoped would be soon. However, each of the envoys was offered a gift of two thousand asses of money, which they refused. {*Livy, l. 44. c. 14,15. 13:135-139}

3294. Dio gave the following account of the matter. King Perseus had requested peace from the Romans and might have obtained it except for the presence in his embassy of the Rhodians. The Rhodians feared lest the Romans should lack an adversary and had joined their envoys with the envoys of Perseus. The envoys from

Rhodes were anything but moderate and behaved most unsuitably for people purporting to be looking for peace. They had more than just requested a peace for Perseus, they had virtually given it to him. They proudly spoke of other things and finally threatened that they would attack those who failed to make peace. So it happened that although the Romans suspected them of siding with Perseus, the Rhodians' behaviour caused the Romans to consider them more odious, and blocked Perseus' chances of getting peace. {*Dio, l. 20. (66) 2:339,341 (Zonaras, l. 9. c. 22.)}

## 3836b AM, 4546 JP, 168 BC

3295. About the beginning of the consulship of Lucius Aemilius Paulus and Gaius Licinius, the Alexandrian envoys from Ptolemy and Princess Cleopatra were called into the Senate. They were dressed in dirt-stained white clothing and had long straggling beards and hair. They entered the Senate with olive branches and then prostrated themselves, requesting that the Senate help their kingdom and princess, who were Roman allies. {*Livy, l. 44. c. 19. s. 6-14. 13:151,153}

3296. They told the Senate that Antiochus had seized the rest of Egypt and still remained there, hoping to conquer Alexandria as well. The Senate was concerned at the power of this king, so they decreed to send an embassy to help make peace and to determine firsthand what was happening there. {*Polybius, l. 29. c. 2. 6:47}

3297. They therefore immediately sent Gaius Popilius Laenas, Gaius Decimius and Gaius Hostilius as envoys to conclude the war between the kings. They were ordered to go to Antiochus first, then to Ptolemy. They were to say that if they did not stop this war, they would no longer be considered allies of Rome. {*Livy, l. 44. c. 19. s. 13,14. 13:153}

3298. These men accompanied the envoys from Alexandria and left on their journey within three days. Envoys from Macedonia arrived on the last day of the Quinquatria, or the feast of Athena's birthday. They said that Eumenes and his fleet came and went like an unpredictable storm, as the king was not constant in his loyalties. Although they said many things against Eumenes, they attested to the extraordinary loyalty of Attalus. {*Livy, l. 44. c. 20. 13:153,155}

3299. At the time when the envoys who had been sent to Egypt left Rome, the following was recorded in an ancient diary of this year (which Pighius had inserted into the second book of his annals in the 585th year of the city):

"The third day of the Nones of April (April 3), Gaius Popilius Laenas, Gaius Decimius and Gaius Hostilius were sent as envoys to the kings of Syria and Egypt to discuss the war between them. [E423] These envoys, with a number of their adherents and kindred, sacrificed early in the morning in the temple of Castor to the household gods of P. R. (People of Rome. Editor.) They offered a bull and so completed their sacrifice."

3300. However, the 3rd day of the Nones of April (April 3), as the year at Rome then stood, was January 23. [K20] This is according to the Julian account, as we deduce from the eclipse of the moon which happened five months later, on June 21.

3301. After Antiochus and his army had returned into Syria, Ptolemy Philometor wisely considered the danger he was in. He sent envoys first to Alexandria to his sister Cleopatra and then to his brother Euergetes and his friends, confirming a peace with them. His sister helped him greatly through her advice and intercession on his behalf. After a peace had been made by the public and common consent, he returned from Memphis and was received into Alexandria. He reigned together with his brother and the common people accepted this. In this war, they had no supplies from Egypt, either during the siege, or after it was lifted. Their condition was brought very low. {*Livy, l. 45. c. 11. s. 1-7. 13:277,279} {*Polybius, l. 29. c. 23. s. 4,5. 6:81,83}

3302. This should have been reason for Antiochus to be glad, had he actually brought his army into Egypt to restore Ptolemy to the throne. However, he was so offended that he prepared for war against them both more eagerly and maliciously than he had done against them individually. Then he sent his fleet to Cyprus and defeated the Egyptian ships and the captains of Ptolemy. {*Livy, l. 45. c. 11. s. 8-11. 13:279,281} {*Polybius, l. 29. c. 26. 6:89}

3303. Both brothers shared the throne and were militarily quite weak. They sent envoys to Eumenes, to Dionysodorus and to the Achaeans, to request a thousand foot soldiers and two hundred cavalry. They wanted Lycortas to be captain of all the auxiliary forces and his son Polybius to be captain of the cavalry. They also wrote to Theodoridas of Sicyon, to hire a thousand mercenary soldiers. {*Polybius, l. 29. c. 23. s. 5-7. 6:83}

3304. Perseus, king of the Macedonians, and Gentius, king of the Illyrians, united in league together by giving pledges to each other. They decreed that envoys should be sent to Rhodes, in the hope that the city which at that time was the major naval power might, by the authority of two kings, go to war against the Romans. The envoys were sent to Thessaly and ordered to be ready to sail. There they met with Metrodorus who had recently come from Rhodes, and who affirmed that on the authority of Dinon and Polyaratus, principal men of the city, the Rhodians were prepared for war. The brothers Hippocritus and Diomedon from among the men of Cos, and Dinon and Polyaratus in Rhodes, spoke boldly for the Macedonians and accused the Romans, while publicly advising an alliance with Perseus. Metrodorus was made the leader of this confederate embassy with the Illyrians. {*Livy, l. 44. c. 23. s. 7-10. 13:165} {*Polybius, l. 30. c. 7. s. 9,10. 6:113} {*Diod. Sic., l. 30. c. 9. 11:291,293}

3305. Perseus had sent Telemnastus, the Cretian, as envoy to Antiochus, and advised him not to miss the opportunity, nor to think that the proud and insolent injunctions of the Romans pertained only to Perseus. Rather, he should know that the Romans would shortly treat him in the same way, unless he helped Perseus settle matters between the Romans and the Macedonians. Should this not prove possible, then at least he could help Perseus against the Romans. {*Polybius, l. 29. c. 4. s. 8-10. 6:53} {*Livy, l. 44. c. 24. s. 1-6. 13:167}

3306. At the same time, Perseus again sent Herophon as an envoy to Eumenes, who had already been on two embassies to Eumenes. {*Livy, l. 44. c. 24. s. 11. 13:169} [K21] He hoped that by offering money, he could solicit Eumenes either to side with Perseus, or to reconcile Perseus to the people of Rome, or failing that, simply to remain neutral. He hoped that he would be able to succeed in one of these points or at the very least achieve by that solicitation what he did in fact achieve, namely that Eumenes would become more suspect to the Romans. However, Eumenes despised the friendship of Perseus. For making peace, he demanded fifteen hundred talents and for remaining neutral to both sides, a thousand talents. Perseus promised to give the sum required for his help in getting a peace, but not before it had been accomplished. He would, however, deposit it in the temple at Samothracia until the peace had been concluded. {*Appian, Macedonian Affairs, l. 9. c. 18. (1) 2:45} As that island was under Perseus' own jurisdiction, Eumenes saw that it signified nothing more than if the money had been at Pella, and insisted that he should bring part of the money for the present. This did not happen either. {*Livy, l. 44. c. 25. 13:169-173} Herophon returned home and the negotiations were kept secret. To avoid suspicion, both sides said that the negotiations had concerned the redemption of captives. [E424] Eumenes told the same to the consul. {*Livy, l. 44. c. 27. s. 13. 13:179}

3307. The Rhodians disagreed among themselves, but the party which favoured Perseus prevailed. It seemed good that envoys should be sent to settle the war between Perseus and the Romans. So the main leaders of their councils immediately sent Hagepolis, Diocles and Clinombrotus as envoys to Rome, while sending Damon, Nicostratus, Hagesilochus and Telephus to the consul and Perseus. They also sent envoys to Crete to renew the friendship with all the Cretians. They were to advise them to be mindful of the times and the imminent danger. They should be friends with the people of Rhodes and they should have the same friends and enemies as the Rhodians had. They were sent to each city, as well, to entreat with them about these same matters. {*Polybius, l. 29. c. 10. 6:63,65}

3308. The envoys of the Ptolemys, the kings, came into Peloponnesus while it was still winter. Then, in an assembly of the Achaeans celebrated at Corinth, they renewed their ancient friendship after much discussion. Presenting their view of the afflicted condition of the kings, they requested aid. The multitude were ready to give their assistance, not with a part of their forces only but if need be, with all their strength. However, Callicrates, Diophanes and Hyperbatus opposed this decision. So, in debating against them, Lycortas and Polybius pointed out the imminence of the peril that threatened Egypt. They exhorted the Achaeans not to neglect this opportunity, but mindful of their agreement, of the benefits they had received and especially of their sworn word, to confirm the proposed treaty. When the multitude had again jointly agreed that assistance should be given, Callicrates frustrated that debate by intimidating the magistrates with the assertion that the laws gave no authority to such assemblies to commit auxiliary troops. {*Polybius, l. 29. c. 23,24. 6:81-85}

3309. A little later, a council was called in the city of the Sicyonians, in which the magistrates and everyone over the age of thirty were present. Andronidas and Callicrates spoke for a time about making peace. After much discussion, a courier arrived at the theatre. He brought letters from Quintus Marcius, the proconsul, in which he was supposed to exhort the Achaeans. They were to comply with the desire of the Romans and endeavour to reconcile the kings. [K22] Polybius, out of respect for Marcius, retired from the discussion. Thereupon the Achaeans sent as envoys: Archon of Aegira, with Arcesilaus and Ariston of Megalopolis, to make a peace between the Ptolemys and Antiochus. The envoys from Alexandria lost all hope of help and returned home. {*Polybius, l. 29. c. 25. 6:87,89}

3310. Perseus had his winter quarters at Phila. He drew his forces into Ionia, where he could intercept the wheat that was being conveyed from there to the Romans. {*Appian, Macedonian Affairs, l. 9. c. 18. (1) 2:49} Antenor and Callippus were the admirals of the navy, and Perseus sent them with forty small boats and five larger cutters called *Pristes* (because they resembled a large fish), to Tenedos. From there they dispersed around the Cyclades

Islands, in order to capture the ships that came into Macedonia with wheat. These ships sailed from Cassandria, after which they first came to the havens which lay opposite Mount Athos, and from there they sailed in a calm sea to Tenedos. Perseus' men sent away the Rhodians' open vessels under Eudamus, their captain, without any harm and treated them very civilly. These were later told that fifty of their cargo ships had been blockaded by the warships of Eumenes under the command of Damius at the very mouth of the haven at Mount Athos. Perseus' fleet dispersed their enemies and opened the blockade, escorting them into Macedonia with ten small scout ships. {*Livy, l. 44. c. 28. s. 1-5. 13:179,181}

3311. Nine days later, those small vessels returned to the fleet lying at Sigeum. From there, they sailed to Subota, which is an island lying between Elaea and Chios. However, the following day, thirty-five ships arrived which they called horse-transports. They came from Elaea with the cavalry of the Gauls and horses sent from Eumenes to Attalus. These were bound for Phanae, a cape of Chios, from where they were to sail over into Macedonia. Antenor set sail from Subota, between the cape of Erythrae and that of Chios, where the sea is very narrow, and suddenly attacked these ships. When there was no hope of resisting, some who were near the shore of the continent, swam to Erythrae. Some hoisted sail and beached their ships on Chios. They left their horses behind and fled to the city. The small vessels of Perseus' fleet had delivered their armed men nearer the city, at a spot more convenient for landing. The Macedonians defeated the Gauls and killed some as they fled, while others were intercepted in front of the gate and killed. About eight hundred Gauls were killed (seven hundred, as Gruter's edition had it), and two hundred were taken alive. Some of the horses drowned in the sea when the ships sank and some were hamstrung by the Macedonians on the shore. [E425] Antenor commanded those same ten vessels that he had sent before, to convey twenty of the best horses to Thessaly with the captives and to return to the fleet as soon as possible. He would meet them at Phanae. The navy stayed almost three days at the city. From there they went to Phanae and sailed across the Aegean Sea to Delos, transported in the ten vessels which had returned earlier than expected. {*Livy, l. 44. c. 28. s. 6-16. 13:181-185}

3312. While these things were happening, the Roman envoys, Gaius Popilius, Gaius Decimius and Gaius Hostilius, came to Delos after they had sailed from Chalcis with three ships of five tiers of oars. There they found forty ships of the Macedonians and five ships from King Eumenes which had five tiers of oars. The sanctity of the temple and the island gave security to all

people. Therefore, the Romans, the Macedonians and the naval allies of Eumenes all intermingled and talked together in safety, because respect for the temple made this place a safe haven. {*Livy, l. 44. c. 29. s. 1-3. 13:185}

3313. Antenor, Perseus' admiral, received word from the watch-towers that cargo ships were seen at sea. He pursued them with some of his ships, while he sent the rest around the Cyclades Islands. He either sank or plundered all the ships, except those bound for Macedonia. [K23] Popilius and the navy of Eumenes helped as many as they could. They escorted them by night in groups of two or three vessels and so deceived the Macedonians. {*Livy, l. 44. c. 29. s. 3,5. 13:185}

3314. About that time, Parmenion and Morcus, the envoys of Gentius, king of the Illyrians, came to Rhodes along with Metrodorus, the envoy of Perseus. Perseus' authority had increased at the sight of the warships which passed up and down along the Cyclades Islands and the Aegean Sea, and because of the large number of the horsemen who had been killed. His prestige was further enhanced by the alliance between Gentius and himself and the rumour that large numbers of the Gauls' cavalry and foot soldiers were coming to help him. These things encouraged Dinon and Polyaratus, who favoured Perseus, but depressed Theaedetus, who did not support him. Therefore, the Rhodians decreed to give a friendly answer to both the kings and to indicate to them that they had resolved to use their authority to put an end to the war. They encouraged them to agree to a peace. Moreover, the envoys of Gentius were entreated with great courtesy in their public place of assembly. {*Livy, l. 44. c. 29. s. 6-8. 13:185-189} {*Polybius, l. 29. c. 11. 6:65}

## 3836c AM, 4546 JP, 168 BC

3315. In the beginning of the spring, Antiochus set out for Egypt with his army and came into Coelosyria near Rhinocolura. He met the envoys of Ptolemy Philometor, who thanked Antiochus for restoring him to his kingdom. They asked that Antiochus should not undo his act of kindness, but say what he wanted done, rather than turn from an ally into an enemy by taking military action. Antiochus replied that he would recall his fleet and reduce his army under no other terms than that Ptolemy would surrender all of Cyprus to him, as well as Pelusium and the land that was adjacent to that mouth of the Nile River. He named a day by which he had to receive an answer. {*Livy, l. 45. c. 11. s. 9-11. 13:279,281}

3316. Antiochus sent Apollonius, the overseer for the collection of his tribute (called μεριδαρχη {*Josephus, Antiq., l. 12. c. 5. s. 5. (261) 7:135} or μυσαρχη in the Apocrypha {Apc 1Ma 1:29 2Ma 5:24}), with an army of twenty-two thousand men into the cities of Judea. This was two full years after he had plundered the temple at Jerusalem. They had been ordered to kill all the mature young men and sell the women and children. {*Apc 1Ma 1:30 2Ma 5:24*}

*3317.* Apollonius subsequently arrived at Jerusalem without any sign of hostility. He restrained himself until the Sabbath day, when he killed all who came to perform religious duties. He marched about the city with his forces and killed a large number of people. After he had plundered the city, he set it on fire and pulled down the houses and the walls. He led away the women and children as captives and seized the cattle. {*Apc 1Ma 1:31-34 2Ma 5:25,26*} Josephus attributed to Antiochus himself the things that were done by his officers. He mentioned the following: {*\*Josephus, Antiq., l. 12. c. 5. s. 4. (248-256) 7:127-133*}

> "...after the sacking of the whole city, either to have killed the inhabitants or to have led them away captive together with their children and wives to the number of ten thousand...."

*3318.* Judas Maccabeus left with nine others and spent his life in the mountains, where they foraged like wild beasts. They fed on herbs, so that they would not be involved with the pollution, or the prohibited meats, or the idolatry, or the contamination and desolation of the sanctuary, which had now happened. {*Apc 2Ma 5:27 1Ma 1:39-41*} It was three and a half years later before the restitution and purification of the temple was made by this same Judas Maccabeus. {*Apc 1Ma 4:43-54*} *[E426] [K24]* Josephus implied that during this time the city of Jerusalem was oppressed by Antiochus, and stated that the service of the daily sacrifice ceased and the sanctuary was desolate. {*\*Josephus, Jewish War, l. 1. c. 0. s. 7. (19) 2:13*} {*\*Josephus, Antiq., l. 12. c. 7. s. 6. (321) 7:167*} He mentioned the length of the time of this desolation of the sanctuary, as Hippolytus affirmed. {*Caten. Grac., Da 8:11-14*}

*3319.* Later, they built a large wall in the city of David, or Zion, secured with strong towers, which was to form a citadel for them. A garrison of wicked men held the place, and there they deposited the spoils of Jerusalem. Those Jews who visited the temple often risked their lives in so doing. Much innocent blood was shed and the sanctuary was defiled. The inhabitants of Jerusalem fled and the city became a habitation of strangers, and foreign to her own citizens. {*Apc 1Ma 1:33-40*}.

*3320.* The envoys of the Rhodians came to the camp of the Romans with the same instructions concerning peace which had so highly incensed the senators at Rome. They were heard with much more discontent by the council of war. However, though some would have had them violently expelled from the camp, the council declared that they would give them an answer after fifteen days.

In the meantime, so that it would be evident how little they regarded the authority of the Rhodians to broker for peace, they began to plan how to carry out the war. {*\*Livy, l. 44. c. 35. s. 4-7. 13:205*}

*3321.* The day before Perseus was defeated, Gaius Sulpicius Gallus, the tribune of the soldiers of the second legion, assembled the soldiers with the permission of Lucius Aemilius Paulus, the consul. He told them that on the following night they should not be alarmed by an eclipse of the moon. This eclipse would occur from the second to the fourth hour of the night and was a natural event that could be predicted, not a sign or evil omen. {*\*Livy, l. 44. c. 37. s. 5-7. 13:215*} Concerning eclipses, Pliny wrote that Gallus was the first of the Romans to discover the reason for solar and lunar eclipses. {*\*Pliny, l. 2. c. 9. (54) 1:203*} Cicero quoted Cato, when talking to Scipio, as saying about Gallus: {*\*Cicero, De Senectute, l. 1. c. 14. (49,50) 20:61*}

> "We beheld Gaius Gallus, the intimate acquaintance of your father (Aemilius Paulus), even to greatly exhaust himself in his endeavours of measuring, almost bit by bit, the heavens and the earth. How often did the morning surprise him, when he began to observe anything at night? How oft did the night come on him, when he began to observe in the morning? How was he delighted when he foretold to us the eclipses of the sun and moon a great while before they happened?"

*3322.* The eve of the day before the Nones of September (September 4), the moon was eclipsed at the appointed hour. To the Roman soldiers, this seemed to be almost a divine thing. The Macedonians took it as a sad omen, portending the fall of their kingdom and a disaster for their country. {*\*Livy, l. 44. c. 37. s. 8,9. 13:217*} {*Justin, Trogus, l. 33. c. 1.*} {*\*Valerius Maximus, l. 8. c. 11. s. 1. 2:255*} {*\*Frontinus, Stratagems, l. 1. c. 12. s. 8. 1:83*} The astronomical account showed that the eclipse of the moon was on the 21st day of June, according to the Julian account, in the eighth hour after noon. At this hour in Macedonia, the soldiers were about to retire for the evening. {*\*Plutarch, Aemilius Paulus, l. 1. c. 17. s. 7. 6:399*} When Paulus entered into his second consulship, the Ides of March (March 15) happened on January 4, according to the Julian reckoning.

*3323.* The next day, Perseus was defeated and the kingdom of the Macedonians came to an end. {*Apc 1Ma 8:5*} *[K25]* From the time of Caranus, it had stood for six hundred and twenty-six years. However, while the Roman empire was rising, the remains of the Macedonian empire survived in the Seleucids of Syria and the Ptolemys of Egypt. {*\*Livy, l. 45. c. 9. 13:271,273*} {*Justin, Trogus, l. 33. c. 2.*} {*Eusebius, Chronicles, Col. 242.*} {*\*Eusebius, Chronicles, l. 1. 1:222*}

*3324.* The third day after the battle, Perseus and about five hundred Cretians fled to Amphipolis in Thrace, but were not allowed to enter the city. Their money, in the form of gold and silver, was brought to the ships which were anchored at Strymon. Perseus arrived at the river. To those Cretians who were following him only for his money he gave fifty talents from his own treasure. He sent cups and goblets, with other gold and silver vessels, and left them on the bank to be scrambled for by these Cretians, while Perseus and his followers boarded the ships in a disorderly manner. One ship was overloaded and sank right there in the mouth of the river. On that day, he came to Galipsus, or Alepsus. The next day, he reached the island of Samothracia with two thousand talents, and humbly sought refuge in the temple of Castor and Pollux. {*Livy, l. 45. c. 2. s. 5,6. 13:253} {*Plutarch, Aemilius Paulus, l. 1. c. 23. 6:415-419} [E427]

*3325.* When news of the Roman victory had reached Asia, Antenor, who was waiting at Phanae with a fleet of ships, sailed from there to Cassandria. {*Livy, l. 45. c. 10. s. 1. 13:273}

## 3836d AM, 4546 JP, 168 BC

*3326.* Gaius Popilius was anchored at Delos to safeguard ships bound for Macedonia. After he had heard of the Roman victory in Macedonia and the departure of the enemy's ships from that area, he dismissed the ships of Attalus. He set sail for Egypt to finish the job he had started. He wanted to meet with Antiochus before he captured Alexandria. After the envoys had sailed past Asia, they came into Loryma, which was a haven about twenty miles from Rhodes and directly opposite the city. The leaders of the Rhodians met them and asked them to put in at Rhodes. The rumour of the Roman victory had reached even Rhodes. They said that it affected the honour and safety of the city and that the Romans should understand that everything that had previously occurred at Rhodes, was currently causing unrest at Rhodes. They could report at Rome what they had learned first-hand, not what they heard through rumour. Although the envoys at first refused, the Rhodians, after a time, persuaded them to make a short interruption in their voyage for the safety of a confederate city. When they arrived at Rhodes, the same persons, by their urging, convinced them to come into their public assembly. {*Livy, l. 45. c. 9. s. 1.-8. 13:273,275}

*3327.* The arrival of the envoys increased, rather than diminished, the fear of the citizens. Popilius recounted everything that anyone had spoken or done in a hostile manner during the time of the war. Since he was a man of a harsh disposition, his stern countenance and incriminating voice aggravated the grievousness of the things that had been spoken. So, because there was no

basis for his personal displeasure with the city, they concluded from the bitterness of one single Roman senator how the whole Senate felt toward them. The speech of Gaius Decimius was more mild, as in most of the things alleged by Popilius he said that the fault lay not with the people, but with a few rebellious men who had stirred them up. These men, whose tongues were for sale, had produced decrees full of flattery of the king, and the envoys they had sent had been such, that the Rhodians were no less ashamed of this than they were repentant. The people heartily approved of this speech, because it laid the blame on a few guilty parties and not on the people in general. [K26] Therefore, when the leader replied to the Romans, the speech of those who endeavoured to mitigate the charges brought by Popilius was in no way as popular as the view of those who agreed with Popilius in singling out for punishment the persons responsible for the crimes. Thereupon, those Rhodians who had previously been arrogant, acting as if they had conquered Philip and Antiochus, and were stronger than the Romans, were now terrified in the presence of the envoys. A decree was quickly passed that whoever proved to be guilty of having favoured Perseus and having said anything against the Romans, should be condemned to death. When the Romans came, some left the city and others committed suicide. The envoys did not stay at Rhodes for more than five days and then went on to Alexandria. After they had left, the Rhodians were no less zealous in carrying out this decree. The cause of the action was mainly due to the clemency of Gaius Decimius. {*Livy, l. 45. c. 9. s. 8-15. 13:275,277} {*Dio, l. 20. (68) 2:355}

*3328.* After the news of Perseus' flight had been brought to Rome, the Senate thought it appropriate that the Rhodian envoys who had come to negotiate a peace with Perseus should be called before their assembly. The envoys, of whom Hagepolis was the leader, entered the Senate. They said that they had been sent to bring to an end a war that would have been grievous and incommodious to the whole of Greece and costly and harmful to the Romans themselves. Now, since it had been concluded in a way the Rhodians had always desired, they congratulated the Romans on it. When Agesipolis had briefly spoken these words, he left the assembly. The Senate made use of that occasion, because they planned to disgrace the Rhodians publicly and make an example of them. They replied that the Rhodians had dispatched that embassy neither for the benefit of Greece, nor out of concern for the Roman people, but on behalf of Perseus. If their care had been as it was claimed, envoys would then have been sent denouncing the war, when Perseus' army entered into Thessaly and for two years, either besieged or terrified the cities of Greece. At that time, no mention of peace had been made by the

Rhodians. But after they had heard that the forest had been crossed and that the Romans had passed into Macedonia and Perseus was hemmed in, the Rhodians had sent their embassy. Their purpose had been to deliver Perseus from his imminent danger. *[E428]* It was therefore the senators' judgment that they ought not to bestow the accustomed rewards or any benefit upon, nor give a courteous answer to, the envoys. {*Polybius, l. 29. c. 19. 6:73} {*Livy, l. 45. c. 20. s. 4-10. 13:311,313}

3329. Thoas had been sent as a courier from Rhodes by Dinon to Perseus, and had often sailed into Macedonia. With the turn of affairs in Rhodes, he fled in fear to Cnidos, where the Cnidians granted him safe custody. After the Rhodians granted him safety, he was returned to Rhodes. When examined, he confessed everything. He fully admitted to all the notes of the letters which had been intercepted and to the letters sent each way from Dinon and Perseus. Consequently, Dinon was convicted, and executed, as an example to others. {*Polybius, l. 30. c. 8. s. 5-8. 6:115}

3330. Gnaeus Octavius had managed the Macedonian war with Paulus Aemilius. When Octavius' fleet arrived at Samothracia, he honoured the sanctity of the temple of Castor and Pollux and left Perseus alone. But he kept him from the sea and so prevented him from escaping. {*Plutarch, Aemilius Paulus, l. 1. c. 26. s. 1. 6:423} All the while he endeavoured to make him surrender, sometimes by threats and sometimes by raising his hopes. Whether accidental or contrived, this business was assisted by Lucius Attilius, an illustrious young man. *[K27]* When he saw the people of Samothracia assembled together, he addressed them with the permission of the magistrate. He complained that the supposed sanctity of the island was being violated by the presence of Evander, the Cretian. It was he who had almost murdered Eumenes at Delphi and now, together with Perseus, was seeking refuge in the temple. Theondus, who was the chief magistrate among them (and whom they called king), saw that the whole island was in the power of the Romans. He demanded of Perseus that Evander surrender himself for trial. Perseus did not want to do this, because he saw that the crime would also involve him. He had Evander murdered and bribed Theondus to tell the people that Evander had committed suicide. However, by killing his only remaining friend, who had been involved with him in so many enterprises, he alienated the affections of all who were with him. When everyone else defected to the Romans for their own safety, he was forced to think about how to escape. {*Livy, l. 45. c. 5,6. 13:259-263}

3331. Therefore, Perseus secretly arranged an escape with Oroandes, the Cretian, to whom the coast of Thrace was well known, because he once used to trade in that country. Perseus was to board a ship that was anchored at the cape of Demetrias, so that Oroandes might convey him to Cotys, the king of the Thracians. At sundown, as much money was brought to the ship as could secretly be transported. When it was on board, Oroandes sailed for Crete as soon as it was dark. Later, around midnight, the wretched Perseus went himself out with his children and his wife by a back door into a garden next to his bedroom. After scrambling with difficulty over a wall, they reached the sea. Unable to find the ship in the harbour, he walked a while on the shore. Finally, fearing the approach of dawn, he hid in a dark corner in the side of the temple. {*Livy, l. 45. c. 6. s. 2-6. 13:263,265} {*Plutarch, Aemilius Paulus, l. 1. c. 26. s. 2-6. 6:423,425}

3332. After that, at the command of Octavius, the praetor, it was proclaimed by the crier that if the royal children of the princes who had been chosen to wait on the king and other Macedonians, and who were from Samothracia, would come over to the Romans, they would be safe. They would have their freedom, and all that they had with them or had left behind in Macedonia would be theirs. They all came over and gave their names to Gaius Postumius, the tribune of the soldiers. Ion, the Thessalian, surrendered to Octavius the young children of the king, who had been committed to his trust. No children were left with the king except Philip, the oldest. Thereupon, Perseus surrendered himself and his son to Octavius. He blamed fortune and the gods in whose temple he was, because they had not helped him. He was ordered to be put aboard the flagship and whatever money was left was brought there. The fleet at once sailed back to Amphipolis. {*Livy, l. 45. c. 6. s. 7-12. 13:265,267}

3333. Antiochus came to take over Pelusium. When he had crossed over the Leusines River, which was four miles from Alexandria, he met the Roman envoys. As they approached, he greeted them and put out his right hand to Popilius. He gave Antiochus the documents which he held in his hands, containing that decree of the Senate which said he was to end the war against Ptolemy at once. Popilius urged him to read it before he did anything else. When he had read the documents, he said that he would consult with his friends as to what he ought to do. With a vine twig that he had in his hand, Popilius drew a circle around the king and demanded his answer before he left the circle. The king was astonished at this unusual and imperious action. After he had thought a while, he said: *[E429] [K28]*

"I will do what the Romans command."

3334. Thereupon, Popilius put out his right hand to the king as to a confederate and friend. Antiochus felt secretly that he had been humiliated but withdrew his forces from Egypt into Syria on the appointed day. (For instead of αγριαν in Polybius, we assume that συριαν ought to be substituted from Livy.) He thought it expedient to yield for the present. {*Polybius, l. 29. c. 27. 6:89-93} {*Livy, l. 45. c. 12. s. 1-8. 13:281,283} {*Cicero, Philippics, l. 8. c. 8. 15:385} {*Velleius Paterculus, l. 1. c. 10. s. 1,2. 1:25} {*Valerius Maximus, l. 6. c. 4. s. 3. 2:47} {Justin, Trogus, l. 34. c. 3.} {*Appian, Syrian Wars, l. 11. c. 11. (66) 2:231,233} {*Plutarch, Sayings of Romans (202f) 3:203,205}

3335. When the Samaritans saw the Jews being most miserably oppressed by Antiochus, they claimed to be descendants of the Sidonians. In this way, they obtained letters from Antiochus to Apollonius, the king's governor, and Nicanor, the king's steward, stating that they should not be subject to the same oppression as the Jews were. Since the temple at Gerizim had not yet been honoured with the name of any god, it was from this time on to be called by the name Διος Ελληνιος, or *Zeus Hellenios*. This was discussed in Josephus where both the letter and the reply from Antiochus were given. This was dated in the 46th year (but I do not know from what epoch the account is determined), on the 18th day of the month Hekatombaion. {*Josephus, Antiq., l. 12. c. 5. s. 5. (257-264) 7:133-137}

3336. After Antiochus had left Egypt, the Roman envoys, by the authority invested in them, confirmed the union between the two brothers, who were barely friends with each other. {*Livy, l. 45. c. 12. s. 5. 13:283} Gaius Popilius requested as a favour from the kings that they free Menalcidas, the Lacedemonian who had energetically availed himself of the distressed condition of the kingdom to obtain his own restoration. {*Polybius, l. 30. c. 16. 6:129} Popilius commanded them to send Polyaratus, who had been the chief supporter of Perseus at Rhodes, to Rome. Menalcidas was dismissed by Ptolemy, but he hesitated to send Polyaratus to Rome, as he had great respect for Polyaratus and Rhodes. Therefore, he sent him to Rhodes and delivered him into the custody of one of his friends, Demetrius. He sent him to Rhodes with letters for the Rhodians explaining his journey. However, Polyaratus arrived at Phaselis. He took herbs with him, for strewing on the altar, and priestly ornaments, and fled to the sanctuary of the town. {*Polybius, l. 29. c. 27. s. 9. 6:91} {*Polybius, l. 30. c. 9. s. 1-5. 6:115,117} {*Polybius, l. 30. c. 16. s. 1,2. 6:129}

3337. When Popilius had settled affairs at Alexandria, he sailed to Cyprus and sent back to Syria the fleet and army of Antiochus, who were there because they had recently captured Cyprus from the Egyptians. {*Polybius, l. 29. c. 27. s. 9,10. 6:91,93} {*Livy, l. 45. c. 12. s. 7.8. 13:283}

3338. The kings of Egypt had now been delivered from the war against Antiochus. One of the first things they did was to send Numenius, one of their friends, as an envoy to Rome, to thank them for the favours which they had received from them. {*Polybius, l. 30. c. 16. 6:129}

3339. When the Phaselites sent to Rhodes, asking them to take Polyaratus from them, the Rhodians did indeed send a ship. However, they forbade Epichares, the captain of the ship, to allow him aboard the vessel, because the Alexandrians had been ordered to set the man ashore at Rhodes. Therefore, the ship came to the Phaselites. Epichares refused to allow Polyaratus onto his vessel, while on the other hand Demetrius, into whose custody he had been entrusted by the king, ordered the man to get on. The Phaselites urged him to go, fearing that they might become offensive to the Romans. Polyaratus was grieved and went aboard the ship again with Demetrius. [K29] However, at the first opportunity when they landed, he quickly fled directly to Caunus. He complained of his situation and begged their assistance, but they refused, because they were tributaries to the Rhodians. He secretly sent to the people of Cibyra, requesting admission into their city. He asked for someone to come and safely escort him there. He was known in that city because the children of Pancrates, the tyrant, had been educated with him. The people of Cibyra consented and Polyaratus was brought to Cibyra. {*Polybius, l. 30. c. 9. s. 5-15. 6:117,119}

3340. Popilius and the embassy returned to Rome from Antiochus. They reported about the differences they had settled between the kings and that Antiochus' army had left Egypt for Syria. Later, the envoys of the kings themselves came. The envoys of Antiochus declared that the peace which had been approved by the Senate seemed more appropriate to the king than any victory. They also reported that he had obeyed the commands of the Roman envoys as if they had been direct commands from the gods. [E430] After this, they congratulated the Senate on the conquest of Perseus. Had they asked the king for anything, he would have gladly given it. The envoys of Ptolemy, in the name of the king and Cleopatra, thanked them also, saying that they were more indebted to the Senate and the Roman people than to their parents or to the immortal gods. They had been delivered from a most miserable siege and had received their paternal kingdom back, which they had almost lost. The Senate replied that Antiochus had acted correctly in obeying the envoys and that it was acceptable to the Senate, the Roman people and to the princes of Egypt. If any benefit and advantage came to Ptolemy and Cleopatra because of Rome, the Senate was glad of it. The Senate told them that if they wished to preserve their kingdom, the best way was to maintain the friendship with the Roman people. Gaius Papirius, the praetor, was commanded to take care of the gifts that were sent to the envoys according to the custom. {*Livy, l. 45. c. 13. s. 1-11. 13:287}

*3341.* A joint embassy came to Rome from the brothers Eumenes, Attalus and Athenaeus, to congratulate them on the overthrow of Perseus. {*Livy, l. 45. c. 13. s. 12. 13:287}

## 3837 AM, 4547 JP, 167 BC

*3342.* By a public edict, Antiochus ordered all the countries that were subject to him to observe the same way of divine worship and set aside their peculiar customs. They were all to adopt the same religion as the Greeks under the punishment of death to those who refused. Over every country he appointed overseers who were to compel them to do this. {Apc 1Ma 1:43-52,63}

*3343.* Antiochus sent an old man of Athens into Judea and Samaria, that he might force the Jews to stop observing the divine law and defile the temple at Jerusalem. He called their temple *Zeus Olympus* and the temple at Gerizim *Zeus Hospitable*, or the *friend of strangers*. He thought this was a more appropriate name for the Samaritans, since they were strangers in the Jewish land. {Apc 2Ma 6:1-6}

*3344.* Through envoys, the king sent proclamations to Jerusalem and the cities of Judah, that they were to follow the rites of the Gentiles and remove the sacrifices from the temple. They were forbidden to keep the Sabbaths and feast days. They were to pollute the sanctuary and its priests and to erect altars, groves and temples to idols. They were to sacrifice swine and other unclean beasts, and they had to allow their children to remain uncircumcised. *[K30]* They were, in other words, to defile themselves with every impure thing, so that they would forget the law and change all the ordinances of their God. {Apc 1Ma 1:44-51} From now on, it would be a crime to observe the Jewish religion. {Apc 2Ma 6:6}

*3345.* A decree also came to the neighbouring cities of the Greeks at the suggestion of Ptolemy, the son of Donymenes. {Apc 2Ma 4:45} They should proceed against the Jews in like manner and compel them to partake in their sacrifices. Those who did not adopt Greek customs were to be executed. {Apc 2Ma 6:8,9}

*3346.* The other countries obeyed the instructions of the king. Many Israelites agreed to his religion, sacrificed to idols and profaned the Sabbath. {Apc 1Ma 1:44 2:18} For many of the people who forsook the law joined them and drove the Israelites into hiding in dens and every place of refuge they had. {Apc 1Ma 1:51-53} Others were forced by bitter compulsion to eat of the sacrifices on the monthly celebration of the king's birthday. When the feast of Bacchus was held, they were compelled to be in a procession to Bacchus, carrying ivy. {Apc 2Ma 6:7}

*3347.* The temple was filled with riot and revelling by the Gentiles who riotously spent their lives with harlots and defiled themselves with women in the holy precinct of the temple. They brought in things that were not lawful and the altar, too, was filled with profane things which the law forbade. {Apc 2Ma 6:4,5}

*3348.* On the 15th day of the month of Chisleu (which is part of our November and part of December) in the 145th year of the kingdom of the Greeks, they erected the abomination of desolation, the detestable idol of Zeus Olympus, on the altar. They built altars for idols throughout the cities of Judah and burned incense at the doors of their houses and in the streets. {Apc 1Ma 1:54-56} [E431]

*3349.* When they had cut to pieces any books of the law which they found, they burned them in the fire. By the king's command, they executed anyone they found with a book of the testament or who approved of the law. {Apc 1Ma 1:56,57} In referring to books of the law, we do not mean just the Mosaic Pentateuch. With the later Hebrews, who from hence derive the origin of that *Petaroth* or *ordinary lecture* after which the people were dismissed (according to Elias Levita, in his Tischbi, on the word פטר), the whole scripture of the Old Testament is meant. {Joh 10:34 15:25 1Co 14:21} Josephus said of the same events: {*Josephus, Antiq., l. 12. c. 5. s. 4. (256) 7:133}

> "Wherever any holy book was found, both the copy of the law and those in whose possession it was found, perished miserably."

*3350.* Sulpicius Severus wrote: {*Sulpicius Severus, Sacred History, l. 2. c. 19. 11:107}

> "The holy volumes of the law and the prophets were consumed in our fires."

*3351.* On the 25th day of the month of Chisleu, sacrifices were offered on the idol altar which had been erected on the altar of God. {Apc 1Ma 1:54,59} This was the 145th year of the reign of the Seleucids in the 153rd Olympiad. {*Josephus, Antiq., l. 12. c. 5. s. 4. (248) 7:127} {*Josephus, Antiq., l. 12. c. 7. s. 6. (321) 7:167}

*3352.* At the same time, two women who had circumcised their children, were accused. Their children were clinging to them, their arms about their mothers' necks. After they had been publicly led through the city, they were thrown down headlong from a wall. *[K31]* Their families and those who had circumcised the infants were killed. {Apc 1Ma 1:61 2Ma 6:10}

*3353.* The Galatians under Advertas, their leader, attacked the kingdom of Eumenes and caused quite a disruption, until a truce was made for the time of winter. The Gauls went home again and the king withdrew to

Pergamum to his winter quarters, where he became sick with a serious disease. {*Polybius, l. 30. c. 1. s. 1-3. 6:95} {*Livy, l. 45. c. 19. s. 3. 113:303}

## 3837b AM, 4547 JP, 167 BC

3354. When Antiochus saw that his edicts were despised by the people, he forced everyone, by using torture, to eat unclean meats and to renounce Judaism. {Josephus, Maccabean War} However, many of the Israelites were fully resolved not to eat any unclean thing and chose to die, so that they would not be defiled with those meats, or profane the holy covenant. {Apc 1Ma 1:62,63}

3355. Therefore, Antiochus sat in a prominent place, as a king with his assessors and his army complete with their weapons around them. He ordered every Hebrew to be seized and be forced to eat swine's flesh and things that had been offered to idols. If any should refuse the profane meat, they were to be executed, after being racked on wheels. {Josephus, Maccabean War}

3356. Among the many that were taken, a leader, Eleazar, was captured. He was a ninety-year-old priest who was a famous scribe and most expert in the knowledge of the laws. He was well-known to many of the followers of Antiochus and was brought before them. He refused to eat swine's flesh, nor did he pretend to have eaten it. He chose to undergo the most cruel torments rather than to violate the law. {Josephus, Maccabean War} {Apc 2Ma 6:18-31}.

3357. After him, seven young brothers were brought before Antiochus, along with their most courageous mother. Because they refused to taste swine's flesh, they were tortured to death with newly invented torments and treated with extreme cruelty. The most noble martyrdom of these persons is found described in the Apocrypha {Apc 2Ma 7} and in the small treatise of Josephus, dealing with the subject of the Maccabees, entitled Of the Empress Reason. In the Latin paraphrase of this, written by Rufinus, these persons were reported to have been brought from their citadel, named Sasandrum, to the king at Antioch. Their names were Maccabeus, Aber, Machir, Judas, Achas, Areth and Jacob. The mother's name was said to be Solomona. However, the later Hebrew historians called her Hannah.

3358. In Judah at about this time, an elder of Jerusalem, named Razis, gave a notable example to others. He risked his body and soul for the defence of the Jewish religion. For this love to his country he was called The Father of the Jews. {Apc 2Ma 14:37,38}

3359. The king's officers, who were forcing men in Judea to this apostasy, came to the city called Modin, with the intention of compelling the Israelites to sacrifice to idols. {Apc 1Ma 2:15} Modin was a city near Diospolis, as Eusebius related in his book. Mattathias, the son of Jonathan, who was the son of Simeon, lived there at that time. He was a priest of Jerusalem of the family of Jehoiarib, who was the first among the twenty-four courses of priests. {1Ch 24:7} He had five sons, John called Caddis or Gaddis, Simon called Thassi, Judas called Maccabeus, Eleazar called Abaron or Avaran, and Jonathan called Apphus. {Apc 1Ma 2:1-5} Those seven martyrs who died at Antioch, were called Maccabean Brethren after their older brother Maccabeus. [E432] [K32] So the custom prevailed that all of Mattathias' five sons, from Judas Maccabeus, to the rest were called by this surname, as Josephus thought. {*Josephus, Jewish War, l. 1. c. 2. s. 3. (37) 2:21} Because of the record of the prowess and glory they achieved, {Apc 1Ma 2:66 3:4,9 4:25} they all became known by the common name of Maccabees. But their father Mattathias, or Matthias, was called the son of Asamonaeus by Josephus, Eusebius and the lesser Seder Olam of the Hebrews. {*Josephus, Jewish War, l. 1. c. 1. s. 3. (36) 2:21} {*Eusebius, Chronicles, l. 1. 1:223} {Seder Olam} Josephus also called him the son of John, the son of Simeon, the son of Asamonaeas. {*Josephus, Antiq., l. 12. c. 6. s. 1. (265) 7:137} The ordinary Hebrews thought Mattathias was called Asamonaeus and that from him that surname had descended to his posterity. R. David Kimchi thought this was based on the Psalms {Ps 68:5-32} where he renders the word חשמנים as princes.

3360. Antiochus' officers earnestly exhorted Mattathias, when he was brought to them, to set an example by yielding obedience to the king because he was a prince and an illustrious person, and a great man in the city of Modin. He was strengthened by the presence of his sons and brethren. Mattathias refused to do as he was asked and killed a certain Jew whom he saw sacrificing on the heathen altar, at the same time also killing Apelles, the king's commissioner, who was forcing men to sacrifice there. He threw down the altar and after that exhorted all who were zealous of the law to follow him. He fled with his sons into the mountains, leaving all their goods behind in the city. {Apc 1Ma 2:16-28} {*Josephus, Antiq., l. 12. c. 6. s. 2. (268-272) 7:139,141}

3361. Then many who desired justice went down into secret places and together with their children and wives and cattle, lived in caves. When this was made known to Philip (the Phrygian whom Antiochus had left as governor at Jerusalem {Apc 2Ma 5:22}), the king's commanders pursued them with the garrison of the citadel of Jerusalem. When they could not persuade them to obey the king's commandment, they threw fire into the cave on the Sabbath day. They killed about a thousand people, including their wives and children with their cattle. Those who were trapped there, offered no resistance and honoured the Sabbath day. {*Apc 1 Ma 2:29-38 2 Ma 6:11} {*Josephus, Antiq., l. 12. c. 6. s. 2. (272-276) 7:141,143}

3362. When Mattathias and his friends were told of this, they grieved for them. They decided that from then on they would attack the enemy and drive them out. {Apc 1 Ma 2:39-41} {*Josephus, Antiq., l. 12. c. 6. s. 2. (276-278) 7:143}

3363. The company of the Assideans joined them. These were religious men who voluntarily offered themselves to defend the law with arms, along with all those who had been compelled to flee from the wicked. After setting up an army, they killed some of the impious men and forced others to flee to other countries. Meanwhile, Mattathias and his friends marched up and down the country and threw down altars. They circumcised all the uncircumcised children they found in the land of Israel. They chased the enemy and had good success. {Apc 1 Ma 2:42-48}

3364. Fearing the Romans, the people of Cibyra did not want Polyaratus, the Rhodian, among them. [K33] They were unable to take him to Rome, because they were not skilled sailors. They sent an embassy to Rhodes as well as into Macedonia to Lucius Aemilius Paulus, the proconsul, asking them to take the man. The proconsul wrote to the people of Cibyra that they should keep Polyaratus in custody and deliver him to Rhodes. He ordered the Rhodians that he should secretly be brought to Rome by sea. So this was done and Polyaratus was at last brought to Rome. {*Polybius, l. 30. c. 9. s. 16-19. 6:119}

3365. King Eumenes sent his brother Attalus to Rome for help to settle the invasion of the Galatians. He was also to congratulate the Senate on the victory over Perseus. Attalus happily led this embassy, because he had assisted the Romans in that war and had exposed himself to all kinds of danger as a willing and devoted confederate. Perhaps he might find out, through some evidence of favour and benevolence, just how acceptable that service had been to the senators. In case he should also be tempted to procure the kingdom for himself, Eumenes sent Stratius the physician to Rome after his brother. He was a person who was highly trusted by Eumenes and had great authority with him. He was to be a faithful spy of the things done by his brother and a trusty monitor, if he should see him depart from his fidelity to Eumenes. {*Polybius, l. 30. c. 1,2. 6:95,97} {*Livy, l. 45. c. 19. s. 1-9. 13:303,305}

3366. All men at Rome received Attalus with kindness, for they knew him and what he had done for them in the war, and considered him a friend. [E433] When a

larger number than he expected came to honour him, he became proud, not knowing the true reason for which he was being so kindly entertained. Most of the Romans did not like Eumenes. They believed that he had acted deceitfully in this war, had previously had conferences with Perseus and had been waiting to take advantage of any difficulty the Romans may have had. Some high officials were eager to draw Attalus into a private discussion and encourage him to lay aside the mission he had undertaken for his brother and to entreat on his own behalf. They said that the Senate was alienated from his brother and keen to give Attalus his brother's kingdom. As a result of this, it happened that Attalus' mind became so puffed up, that he even asked some of these officials to bring the matter to the Senate for debate. However, Stratius the physician, a person of outstanding prudence and powerful eloquence, persuaded him otherwise. He told him that in actual fact he was even now reigning with his brother and would, in the future, be left the undoubted successor to the kingdom. This may not have been too far off, since Eumenes was quite sick and was expected to die at any time. He reminded him that the new disruption in the kingdom, from the insurrection of the Gauls, could scarcely be handled by both of them acting together, much less if there was a civil war in the kingdom. So, when Attalus came into the Senate, he first expressed joy at the overthrow of Perseus and then talked of his own active part in that war. Lastly, he requested the Senate to send envoys to the Galatians. By their authority they should make them stop this war and return to their own lands. He also spoke of the cities of the Enions and the Maronites, requesting that they be given to him. [K34] Concerning the accusation against his brother and the division of the kingdom, he said nothing. {*Polybius, l. 30. s. 2,3. 6:97-101} {*Livy, l. 45. c. 19,20. 13:305-311}

3367. The Senate thought that Attalus would come to them again and discuss the matter of the kingdom, so they promised him to send envoys. They were very generous in the gifts they gave him, which were given according to custom. Moreover, they promised to give him the cities he had asked for. After all this had been done for him, Attalus left the city, and the things the Senate hoped for did not happen. The senators were frustrated and while Attalus was still in Italy, they declared Aenus and Maronea to be free and reneged on the promise they had made to Attalus. However, the embassy headed by Publius Licinius Crassus was sent to the Galatians. {*Polybius, l. 30. c. 3. s. 5-8. 6:101}

3368. Among the many embassies that had come from Asia and Greece, after Attalus, the envoys of the Rhodians drew the most attention. They had a two-fold mission at this time. First came Philocrates and then later Philophron and Astymedes. When the Rhodians had received the reply that had been given to Hagepolis shortly after the battle with Perseus, they knew the senators were angry with them. When they heard their threats, they immediately sent these embassies. {*Polybius, l. 30. c. 4. s. 1,2. 6:101} {*Livy, l. 45. c. 20. s. 4,5. 13:311}

3369. The envoys first appeared in white clothing, as a sign of rejoicing over the Roman victory. Had they come in dirty clothes, they might have looked like mourners for the misfortune of Perseus. The senators had consulted with Marcus Junius, the consul, while the envoys stood in the public assembly. They wanted to determine whether they would give them accommodation, a hearing and rewards. They decided that no rite of hospitality should be given to them. The consul left the Senate and the Rhodians told them they had come to congratulate them on their victory and clear the accusations against their city. When they requested permission to appear before the Senate, they were told that the Romans usually gave their confederates and friends hospitality, lodging, entertainment and also a Senate hearing. However, the Rhodians had not been considered confederate friends in that war. On hearing this, they all prostrated themselves on the ground and begged the consul and everyone present. They requested that they should not consider new and false incriminations that were injurious to them any more than they considered their previous service, to which the Romans were witnesses. They immediately put on mourning clothes and went up and down with prayers and tears to the houses of the chief persons. They pleaded with them that they might first be told the reason before they were condemned. {*Livy, l. 45. c. 20. s. 4-10. 13:311,315} [E434]

3370. Marcus Juventius Thalua, the praetor whose job it was to oversee the affairs between the citizens and foreigners, stirred up the people against the Rhodians. He set a dangerous precedent of not going through the Senate or the consuls. He made a motion that Rome should declare war on Rhodes and one of the magistrates of that year should be sent with a fleet to manage the war, in the hope that he would be the one to lead the force. Marcus Antonius and Marcus Pomponius, the tribunes of the people, opposed this motion. The praetor and tribunes disputed this matter. The tribunes succeeded in persuading the assembly to defer the matter until the arrival of Aemilius, the general. {*Livy, l. 45. c. 21. 13:313,315} Antonius violently removed the praetor from the desk and brought the envoys of the Rhodians to the Senate, where they made their speeches. Philophron spoke first, and then Astymedes. {*Polybius, l. 30. c. 4. s. 5,6. 6:103} {*Diod. Sic., l. 31. c. 5. 11:319-323} [K35] The latter part of Astymedes'

speech is found in Livy, but the first part is missing. Polybius stated that Astymedes put his speech among his letters and gave them to the public. However, the same author observed about this speech that it was not liked by the more prudent persons because (perhaps in the first part of it, which is missing in Livy) he undertook the defence of his own country in such a way as to accuse the rest of the Greeks.

3371. After the speech was over, all the envoys fell down on their faces and in a humble manner cast down the olive branches. At length, they got up again and left the assembly. When the vote was held, those who held the office of consuls or praetors or envoys in Macedonia, or who had been involved in the war, were most enraged against the Rhodians. But the Rhodian cause was advanced by Marcus Porcius Cato, who, in spite of his naturally stern disposition, at that time proved himself to be a gentle and meek senator. He added the speech which he spoke in the Senate on their behalf, to the fifth book of his *Beginnings*. Finally, the senators severely upbraided the Rhodians with many things. The reply given to the Rhodians was so phrased that while they were not turned into enemies, they did not continue to be allies. {*Polybius, l. 30. c. 5. s. 1-2. 6:105,107} {*Diod. Sic., l. 31. c. 5. s. 3. 11:321} {*Livy, l. 45. c. 25. s. 1-4. 13:329,331}

3372. When the answer was given, Philocrates immediately went to Rhodes while Astymedes remained at Rome, so that he might know what was going on and notify his countrymen accordingly. The Rhodians were relieved that the fear of war had passed and while they took the rest of the news sadly, they accepted the situation. {*Polybius, l. 30. c. 5. s. 1-2. 6:105,107} {*Livy, l. 45. c. 25. s. 5,6. 13:331}

3373. Publius Licinius and the rest of the envoys who had been sent with Attalus to end the war between the Gauls and King Eumenes, arrived at Synnada. At this time Eumenes, who in the beginning of the spring had now recovered, was up and around and had gathered his army together at Sardis from various places. At Synnada, the Roman envoys conferred with Solovettius, the captain of the Gauls, and Attalus went along with them. He would not enter into the camp of the Gauls, lest his presence should inflame the situation. Publius Licinius talked with the captain of the Gauls, and found that he was even fiercer after his talk. So much so, that it seemed strange that the words of the Roman envoys should prevail to such an extent among those rich kings, Antiochus and Ptolemy, that they had been prepared to make peace, when they carried no weight whatsoever with the Gauls. {*Livy, l. 45. c. 34. s. 10-14. 13:367}

3374. Toward summer, the Rhodians sent Theaedetus (the copies of Livy have Theodotus), the admiral of the fleet, with a crown to the value of ten thousand or, as we read it in Livy, twenty thousand gold pieces, to enable them by all means to procure the friendship with the Romans. They hoped that this could be asked of the Romans in such a way that the Rhodian people would not need to vote on it, in the event that it should be committed to writing. They feared that should they also fail to obtain it, over and above the failure of their embassy, this refusal would disgrace them further. In actual fact, however, the Rhodians had assisted the Romans for over forty years. *[K36]* They had continued in their friendship, but had never bound themselves to them by a league of amity. *[E435]* They had not at any time wanted to cut off from the kings the hope that the Rhodians might come to their assistance, should the need arise. Nor did they want to deprive themselves of the chance of profiting from the goodwill and good fortune of these kings. Now, however, they most earnestly endeavoured to procure this honour, though not because they were enamoured with new confederates or stood in fear of anyone other than the Romans themselves, but because they hoped thereby to reduce the Roman suspicion of them. {*Polybius, l. 30. c. 5. s. 3-10. 6:107,109} {*Livy, l. 45. c. 25. s. 5-10. 13:331,333} {*Dio, l. 20. (68) 2:355,357}

*3375.* Theaedetus had barely arrived at Rome from Rhodes when the Caunians revolted from Rhodes. The people of Mylasa occupied the towns of the Euromenses. The Rhodians quickly sent Lycus with an army and with the help of Cibyra, forced the Caunians to submit to their government. In a battle near Orthosia, they defeated both the Mylasians and the Alabandians, who had taken away the province of the Euromenses. {*Polybius, l. 30. s. 11-16. 6:109} {*Livy, l. 45. c. 25. s. 11-13. 13:333}

*3376.* At the same time, the Senate published a decree granting liberty to the Carians and Lycians, which, after this war, made the Rhodians fearful, as they thought they had wasted their money in giving the crown and had entertained vain hopes of friendship with the Romans. So the Rhodians lost Lycia and Caria, after they had been forced to endure their wars to gain them. {*Polybius, l. 30. c. 5. s. 11,12. 6:109} {*Livy, l. 45. c. 25. s. 5,6. 13:331} {*Appian, Syrian Wars, l. 11. c. 7. (44) 2:191}

*3377.* When Theaedetus was granted a hearing in the Senate, he entreated them concerning the issue of entering into a league with the Rhodians. While the senators made delays, he died at the age of eighty years. Later, the Caunians and Stratonicians, who were in exile, came to Rome. When they had been heard by the Senate, the Senate decreed that the Rhodians had to withdraw their garrisons from Caunus and Stratonicia. As soon as this answer became known, Philophron and Astymedes quickly returned to their country, fearing that if the

Rhodians were not to recall their garrisons, new calamities would befall their city. {*Polybius, l. 30. c. 20. 6:137}

*3378.* About the same time, the Cnossians and Gortynians waged war with Rhaucus. They made a league among themselves, confirmed by an oath, that they would not end the war before they had taken Rhaucus by force. {*Polybius, l. 30. c. 23. s. 1,2. 6:141}

*3379.* When the Rhodians were notified about the Caunians, they realised the Romans were still angry with them, and so they obeyed the decree of the Senate. {*Polybius, l. 30. c. 23. s. 2,3. 6:141} Thus, they lost Caunus, which they had bought from the commanders of Ptolemy for two hundred talents, and they also lost Stratonicia, which they had received as a generous gift from Antiochus and Seleucus. Both cities had been paying a hundred and twenty talents yearly to the Rhodians. {*Polybius, l. 30. c. 31. s. 6,7. 6:157}

*3380.* The Rhodians sent an embassy to Rome, headed by Aristoteles. They were earnestly to ask for friendship with the Romans. About midsummer, the envoys arrived and were heard before the Senate, where they said that the Rhodians had obeyed everything they had been asked to do, and so with many reasons they urged the senators to grant them amity. *[K37]* However, the Senate's reply contained no mention of amity for the Rhodians. {*Polybius, l. 30. c. 23. s. 3,4. 6:141}

## 3838a AM, 4547 JP, 167 BC

*3381.* At the beginning of autumn, Lucius Aemilius Paulus appointed Gaius Sulpicius Gallus to oversee the army, while he went with a small retinue to view Greece. His son Scipio and Athenaeus, a brother of Eumenes the king, were his bodyguards. He granted liberty to Macedonia and enacted laws befitting for confederates. After settling the matters of state, he instituted games at Amphipolis, for which he had long been preparing. He had sent messengers into the cities of Asia and notified their kings but in Greece he personally visited the cities and notified their governors. For this great gathering of Europe and Asia, a multitude came from every quarter. While some came to congratulate the Romans, others came to see the sight of such a large army and naval force. Provisions were abundant and cheap, so that most received gifts of food for their needs and enough to take back home. {*Livy, l. 45. c. 27-33. 13:339-361}

*3382.* Labeo was sent by the Romans to destroy Antissa on the island of Lesbos and to resettle the inhabitants in Methymna. When Antenor, Perseus' admiral, had sailed near Lesbos, the inhabitants received him and furnished him with supplies. {*Livy, l. 45. c. 31. s. 12-15. 13:357} *[E436]*

3383. Prusias (Venator), the king of Bithynia, came to Rome with his son, Nicomedes. The Senate sent Lucius Cornelius Scipio, the quaestor, to meet him at Capua and decreed that a most excellent house should be rented for him at Rome. Provisions were to be charged to the public account for himself and all his retinue. He was entertained and treated like a good friend by the whole city of Rome. {*Livy, l. 45. c. 44. s. 4-7. 13:405} {*Valerius Maximus, l. 5. c. 1. s. 1e. 1:441}

3384. After he entered the city with a long train, he went from the gate and the judgment seat of Quintus Cassius, the praetor, to the forum. A large crowd was on every side. He said that he had come to worship the gods who lived at Rome, as well as to greet the Senate and the Roman people. He congratulated them on their victory over Perseus and Gentius, the kings, who had increased their empire by subduing the Macedonians and Illyrians. When the praetor had told him that, if he pleased, he would hold a Senate for him that day, he requested a delay of two days, so that he might visit the temples of the gods, the city and his friends. Lucius Cornelius Scipio, the quaestor, was appointed to him as a guide. On the third day, Prusias came to the Senate and congratulated them on their victory. He mentioned his part in that war and requested that he might be allowed to perform his vow by offering ten large sacrifices in the Capitol at Rome and one at Praeneste to the god, Fortune. These were his vows for the conquest won by the people of Rome and that his friendship with the Romans would be renewed. He wanted the land that had been taken from King Antiochus and was now occupied by the Gauls, although the Romans had given it to no one. Last of all, he entrusted his son Nicomedes to the Senate. Because he was supported by all those who had been commanders in Macedonia, his remaining requests were granted. Concerning the land, they said they would send envoys to inquire whether it belonged to the Roman people and had been assigned to anyone. They willingly accepted Nicomedes. Ptolemy, king of Egypt, whose kingdom had been preserved by the Romans when Antiochus had invaded it, testified to the care the Roman people took of the children of their confederate kings. It was commanded, moreover, that beasts and other things that were needed for sacrifices, whether to be offered by the king at Rome or at Praeneste, should be given to him at the public expense, just as to the Roman magistrates. [K38] Twenty warships from the fleet which lay at Brundisium should be given to him, which he could use until he reached the fleet that had been assigned to him. Also, Lucius Cornelius Scipio should accompany him and should pay all his expenses until they were to sail. It is reported that the king was overjoyed at the kindness of the Roman people.

He refused the gifts that were given to him, but commanded his son to accept the gift of the Roman people. These things about Prusias were related by the Roman writers. {*Livy, l. 45. c. 44. s. 4-21. 13:405-411}

3385. Polybius and other Greek authors wrote that when he came into the Senate, he bowed low and kissed the threshold of the Senate, and called the senators his tutelary gods. It was not so much that he spoke honourably to the hearers, as that he spoke in a manner demeaning to himself. For this extraordinary action, he received a more courteous answer from the Senate. {*Livy, l. 45. c. 44. s. 20,21. 13:409,411} {*Polybius, l. 30. c. 18. 6:131} {*Diod. Sic., l. 31. c. 15. 11:345,349} {*Dio, l. 20. (69) 2:357} However, after he had stayed in the city about thirty days, he left for his kingdom. {*Livy, l. 45. c. 44. s. 21. 13:411}

3386. About this time news arrived that Eumenes was on his way to Rome. If he were to be excluded from Rome, he might be thought to be an enemy because he had remained neutral in the Macedonian war. If he were to be admitted, people would think he had been exonerated. Consequently, a general law was passed that no king should be permitted to come to Rome. {*Polybius, l. 30. c. 19. s. 1-9. 6:131,133} {*Livy, l. 46. 14:11} After it became known that Eumenes had arrived at Brundisium in Italy, they sent the quaestor to him to bring him this decree. He was to ask whether Eumenes had to address the Senate about anything, and if he had no request to make to the senators, then he should tell the quaestor and quickly leave Italy. After the king had met with the quaestor and understood the wishes of the Senate, he said nothing to him about business and assured him that he needed nothing. In this way, the Romans prevented Eumenes' arrival at Rome and procured something else that was of great concern to them. The kingdom of Pergamum was in great danger from the Galatians. There was no doubt that by this disgraceful rejection of Eumenes, the courage of all his friends would be lessened, while the Galatians would be twice as courageous in waging war. This happened at the beginning of winter. {*Polybius, l. 30. c. 19. s. 7-14. 6:133,135} [E437]

## 3838b AM, 4548 JP, 166 BC

3387. Mattathias exhorted his sons to the study of piety and to defend the law of God. He commended Simon to them as a counsellor and father, but Judas Maccabeus as the commander of their wars, because from his youth he had been very brave. After this, he blessed them and died, in the 146th year of the kingdom of the Greeks. For one year he had governed their miserable and banished troops. His sons buried him in the sepulchres of their fathers at Modin and all the Israelites bewailed him with great lamentation. {Apc 1Ma 2:49-70} {*Josephus, Antiq., l. 12. c. 6. s. 3,4. (279-284) 7:143-147}

3388. Judas Maccabeus' brothers, and all who had followed his father, helped him as he took his father's place. {Apc 1Ma 3:1,2} He went secretly into the villages and exhorted his countrymen and gathered them together with those who had remained loyal to the Jewish religion. [K39] They assembled six thousand men and called on the Lord to take pity on his profaned temple and the ruined city, and to hear the blood that cried to him and remember the unjust death of the innocent infants and the blasphemies that were being committed against his name. They asked that he would demonstrate his hatred against the wicked. {Apc 2Ma 8:1-4}

3389. In the meantime, when Antiochus heard of the games held by Aemilius Paulus in Macedonia, he planned to hold more magnificent games than Paulus had held. He sent envoys and observers into the cities to declare that games would be held by him at Daphne, near Antioch. It was his intention that from all Greece, {*Polybius, l. 30. c. 25. s. 1,2. 6:143} or from all parts of the world, {*Diod. Sic., l. 31. c. 16. 11:351,353} famous men would eagerly come to that show. Polybius described the games in detail.

3390. First there were five thousand men in their prime dressed like Roman soldiers, with hooked breastplates. These were followed by just as many Mysians. Next came three thousand lightly armed Cilicians, wearing golden crowns, followed by three thousand Thracians and five thousand Gauls. Next came twenty thousand Macedonians, of whom ten thousand bore golden shields. Then came two hundred and fifty pairs of gladiators, who were followed by a thousand horsemen from Nisa and three thousand horsemen from Antioch. Most had crowns and trappings of gold, and the rest, trappings of silver. These were followed by about a thousand cavalry of their confederates and friends, who were all furnished with golden trappings. Next came a thousand more cavalry of their associate friends, adorned in the same way. Besides these, a thousand choice men marched, who were excellent horsemen. They were followed by about a thousand called *Agema* by the Greeks, who were the crack cavalry troops. Lastly came fifteen hundred horsemen in complete armour from head to toe, called the *Cataphracti* by the Greeks, because both men and horses were covered with arms of mail. All these persons wore purple coats, some of which were interwoven with gold and bore the image of beasts. After these paraded a hundred chariots with six horses abreast and forty chariots with four horses abreast. There was a chariot drawn by a pair of elephants and another with two horses. These were followed by thirty-six elephants in single file with their trapping.

3391. Next came about eight hundred youths with golden crowns and almost a thousand fat oxen with three hundred cows for sacred purposes, plus men carrying eight hundred elephants' tusks. Then, men carried whatever they said or believed were gods or demigods. Many carried images of their heroes, some of which were gilded over while others were clothed in golden robes, and each one was gallantly adorned with his eulogy and motto, according to the legend written about him. To these were added the images of the *Night*, of the *Day*, of the *Earth*, of the *Heaven*, of the *Morning* and of the *Noon*. The slaves belonging to Dionysius, the king's secretary, walked in this pompous train carrying silver vessels, none of which weighed less than a thousand drachmas. These were followed by six hundred more of the king's slaves, carrying vessels of gold. Then came about two hundred women, whose job it was to sprinkle the spectators with sweet ointments from their golden urns. In the rear came eighty women gloriously clothed and adorned with costly garments, who were carried in litters with golden legs. Five hundred came in litters with silver legs. These were the most remarkable things in the pageantry. [K40]

3392. After this, a large number of sporting contests, and fencing and hunting events were held for thirty days. Throughout this time, a variety of ointments was provided by the king for all who played for any prize. To this end, fifteen golden jars were supplied, full of ointments of saffron. An equal number contained cinnamon and spikenard. These ointments were given out freely for the first five days. For the rest of the games, ointments of fenugreek, marjoram and orris were given out freely. At times a thousand, and at other times fifteen hundred tables were most richly spread for the guests. All these things were magnificently executed. He paid for these from what he had cheated King Philometor out of, in Egypt, while he was still a minor. [E438] Other funds came from the spoils of the many temples he had plundered. {*Athenaeus, l. 5. (210d-211a) 2:451,453} {*Athenaeus, l. 10. (289f-290a) 4:301,303} {*Polybius, l. 30. c. 25,26. 6:143-149}

3393. However, the glory of this preparation was eclipsed and debased by the unworthy conduct of the king. For he went riding up and down on a little riding pony ordering some to stand, others to pass, just as it suited him. He did this in such a way that, had it not been for his diadem, no one would have thought him a king, since he barely qualified as a servant. During the whole time of the feast, he stood at the doors of the rooms where the feast was being held. He escorted some in, others he seated at the tables, as well as ushering in the servants who brought in the dishes. Sometimes he walked around, sometimes he sat down and at times he lay on the floor. Often he would run around to remove a dish or a cup from the table. In drinking with his guests, he now and then drank to those who drank to him. He sported and jested with those who were so inclined. Moreover, many had left because the feast went on for such a long time. He came in a disguise brought in by the actors and lay on the ground along with them as if he had been one of their company. Finally, roused by the sound of music, he got up and started dancing and acting his part with ridiculous gestures. All were so ashamed of the king's behaviour, that they left the feast. {*Polybius, l. 30. c. 26. s. 5-8. 6:149} {*Diod. Sic., l. 31. c. 16. s. 2,3. 11:353,355}

3394. The show finally finished. Tiberius Gracchus was sent by the Senate as an envoy to Antiochus. He was to determine what the king was up to and spy on his affairs. The king entertained him with such cheerfulness and alacrity, that he did not suspect a plot, or discover the least hint of alienation in him for what had happened at Alexandria. Tiberius opposed those who wanted to impeach him. Antiochus gave his royal palace to the envoys of Rome, which was as good as giving them his very diadem. Notwithstanding all this ceremony, his will and affection were most irreconcilably alienated against the Romans. {*Polybius, l. 30. c. 27. 6:149,151} {*Diod. Sic., l. 31. c. 17. 11:255}

3395. While Antiochus was at leisure in the games at Daphne, Judas Maccabeus was busy in Judea. Greatly helped by his brothers, he drove out the enemy, killed his apostate countrymen and purged the land of its uncleanness. {*Josephus, Antiq., l. 12. c. 6. s. 4. (286) 7:147} He made surprise attacks on cities and villages and burned them. He controlled the most strategic places and routed large numbers of his enemies. [K41] He usually attacked by night to avail himself of the element of surprise. The fame of his valour spread everywhere. {Apc 1Ma 3:8,9 2Ma 8:6,7}

3396. Envoys were sent from the Galatians in Asia to Rome. The Senate granted them freedom to rule themselves, as long as they stayed within their land and did not attack other lands. {*Polybius, l. 30. c. 28. 6:151}

3397. Python was sent to Rome on a mission from Prusias, the king of Bithynia. He complained to the Senate about Eumenes, who had pillaged Prusias' territories and seized some places for himself. He further accused Eumenes of refusing to stop his encroachment on Galatia and of not submitting to the decrees of the Senate, but instead only advancing his own interests. Whereas Prusias, on the other hand, was obeying the desires of the Roman people and wanted his country to be governed by the precepts of the Senate. Others, likewise, came from the Asiatic cities with fresh accusations, hinting at an alliance between Eumenes and Antiochus against the Romans. When the Senate had heard these

things, they neither refuted the accusations nor said what they would do. They kept everything secret and carefully monitored the actions of Eumenes and Antiochus with increasing suspicion. Meanwhile, they satisfied the Galatians in some matters and helped them affirm their freedom. {*Polybius, l. 30. c. 30. 6:153,155} {*Livy, l. 46. 14:11}

3398. Astymedes, the Rhodian envoy, pleaded his country's cause at Rome before the Senate. He was more moderate now and not as heated in his speech as during his previous embassy. He omitted all recriminations and made it his only business at the time to show that his countrymen had suffered sufficiently and well beyond the degree of the offence. His main complaint was that the Rhodians had lost the revenue from their harbour. In regard to that, the Romans had discharged Delos from paying tribute and had also taken from the people the liberty which they had formerly enjoyed of determining tariffs and other matters of public concern. The custom duties, which had in former times netted a million drachmas, now barely amounted to a hundred and fifty thousand. [E439] He said that the Senate knew that only a few were engaged in criminal behaviour and these had been punished by the people. So he requested that they would not show their displeasure against those who had not been involved in any way, but to receive them into their grace and favour as they had done before. Their country stood more in need of friends in peacetime than an ally for war. His speech seemed so appropriate for the present condition of the Rhodians. Tiberius Gracchus (who had recently returned from Asia, where he had been an envoy) said that the Rhodians had submitted themselves to the decrees of the Senate, and that all those had been executed who previously had anything to do with bringing the Rhodians into disfavour with the Romans. He silenced his adversaries and prevailed with the Romans that they should take the Rhodians into their alliance. {*Polybius, l. 30. c. 31. 6:155-159}

3399. Tiberius could not tell the Senate anything more about the plans of Eumenes and Antiochus than what they had known before Tiberius had left Rome. The kings had entertained him most graciously. {*Polybius, l. 30. c. 30. s. 6-8. 6:155}

3400. Apollonius, the governor of Samaria, raised a large army from among the Gentiles and Samaritans and attacked the Jews. However, Judas Maccabeus killed him and many others, while the rest fled. [K42] Judas took the spoil, including Apollonius' own sword, which from then on he always used in the war. {Apc 1Ma 3:10-12} {*Josephus, Antiq., l. 12. c. 7. s. 1. (287) 7:147}

3401. Seron, who governed Coelosyria, heard that Judas was well-equipped with an army and that large numbers were coming to him from all parts. Seron mustered all the forces under his command, including the renegade Jews, and camped near the route to Bethhoron. Judas routed his whole army and eight hundred of them were killed. The rest fled into the land of the Philistines near the sea coast. {*Apc 1Ma 3:13-24*} {*Josephus, Antiq., l. 12. c. 7. s. 1. (288-292) 7:149,151*}

### 3839a AM, 4548 JP, 166 BC

*3402.* As soon as the news of this defeat reached Antiochus, he was so furious that he immediately levied all the troops of his kingdom. He gave them a year's pay and ordered them to be ready for service. After this salary had been paid, he saw that his treasury was empty. The Jewish revolt was depriving him of three hundred talents of silver each year. Also, intense persecution raged in the Greek cities and in many regions, thus reducing his revenues, as he did not spare the Gentiles either, while he tried to make them forsake their ancient superstitions and conform to his worship. He persecuted them to such an extent, that he feared he would not find enough to defray his expenses and gratuities. In this regard, he was very generous and surpassed all the kings that had gone before him. So he determined to go into Persia to get money there. {*Apc 1Ma 3:27-31*} {*Josephus, Antiq., l. 12. c. 7. s. 2. (293,294) 7:151,153*} {*Sulpicius Severus, Sacred History, l. 2. c. 21. 11:107*}

*3403.* Before he left, he appointed Lysias, of Syrian royalty, as governor over all the regions from the Euphrates River to the borders of Egypt and entrusted him with the care of his son Antiochus Eupator. He committed half of all his forces and his elephants to him, ordering him utterly to root out the name of the Jews and to give their country to strangers. Antiochus left with the rest of his sons from Antioch near Daphne in the 147th year of the kingdom of the Greeks. He crossed over the Euphrates River and marched into the high countries. {*Apc 1Ma 3:32-37*}

*3404.* Philip, whom Antiochus had appointed over Jerusalem, saw how Judas Maccabeus grew stronger and stronger every day. He wrote to Ptolemy (son of Dorymenes), the governor of Coelosyria, for help. Ptolemy immediately sent Nicanor, the son of Patrocles, a most trusted friend, with more than twenty thousand soldiers from all countries. He was to exterminate the Jews. Ptolemy also sent Gorgias, a captain who was quite experienced in military affairs, as a joint commander. {*Apc 2Ma 5:22 8:8,9*}

*3405.* Lysias also sent them Ptolemy as a reserve. Under these three commanders, Ptolemy, Nicanor and Gorgias, were forty thousand foot soldiers and seven thousand cavalry. They marched with their entire army and camped near Emmaus in the plain country. {*Apc 1Ma 3:38-40*}

*3406.* Since Antiochus was two thousand talents in arrears to the Romans, Nicanor intended to settle the account from the sale of the captive Jews. For that purpose, he invited a thousand merchants from the cities near the sea coast, and promised them ninety slaves for one talent. {*Apc 2Ma 8:10,11,14,34,36*} [K43] No sooner did this become known, than the merchants of the country came to the camp with their attendants, to purchase the Jews for slaves. [E440] Large numbers also came from Syria and from the Philistines to barter for slaves. {*Apc 1Ma 3:41*}

*3407.* Jerusalem had now been abandoned by its inhabitants and the temple profaned. In these distressing times, Judas Maccabeus moved with his army to Maspha, or Mizpah, where the Jews used to worship before the temple was built. {*Jud 11:11 20:1 21:5,8 1Sa 7:5,6 10:17*} He proclaimed a fast and with most fervent prayers asked the Lord's protection for his small army. He had only six thousand men (seven thousand, in the Latin edition) against this large force. After this, in accordance with the law, he sent away any who had betrothed wives or planted vineyards or were afraid. {*De 20:6-8*} He divided his army into four squadrons of fifteen hundred men and gave command of each squadron to one of his brothers. The army moved and camped on the south side of Emmaus, opposite the enemy. Judas earnestly exhorted them to behave valiantly, even to the point of dying for their country and the laws of their God. He ordered them to be ready for the battle the next day. {*Apc 1Ma 3:42-60 2Ma 8:12-22*}

*3408.* That night, Gorgias planned a surprise attack. He took five hundred foot soldiers and a thousand choice cavalry and came toward the Jewish camp. He had the garrison soldiers of the citadel of Zion for his escort. When Judas found this out, he wisely used this opportunity to attack the enemy while they were divided. He marched immediately to Emmaus against Nicanor, while Gorgias, their normal commander, was absent. When Gorgias came to the Jewish camp by night, no one was there. He thought they had fled and searched for them in the mountains. At the break of day, Judas showed himself in the plains of Emmaus with three thousand men who had neither armour nor swords. {*Apc 1Ma 4:1-6*}

*3409.* Judas encouraged his soldiers for the battle and gave the word to fight. By the help of God, he led the troops against Nicanor and killed more than nine thousand and wounded and maimed most of Nicanor's army. They were all routed. The Jews pursued some of them from Emmaus as far as Gazara (as the Greek copy of the Maccabees, in the end in Arundel's library, had it) or Gadara (according to Josephus). Others fled to the plains of Idumea, still others as far as Palestine, Azotus and Jamnia. In all, about three thousand stragglers were killed. {*Apc 1Ma 4:8-15 2Ma 8:23,24*}

3410. Among those that fled were the merchants, who had been certain of victory and of getting a good bargain in slaves, but who now became targets themselves. The Jews seized their money with which they had intended to buy them. When they had pursued them for a great distance, they sounded a retreat for the evening on which the Sabbath began. After they had gathered up the arms of the vanquished army and taken the spoils from them, they prepared for the observance of the Sabbath. *[K44]* They praised the mercy of God for this marvellous deliverance. {*Apc 2Ma 8:25-27*}

3411. Judas restrained his Jews, who were eager for plunder, because he feared an encounter with Gorgias, who had now returned from his fruitless expedition and whose forces were in the mountains. From the smoke of the burning tents, the enemy knew what had happened and that the other division of their army had been routed. When they saw Judas on the plain, standing in battle array ready to engage them, they all scattered into the neighbouring countries. The land was thus cleared of the enemy. Judas returned to the spoil, where he found plenty of gold, blue silk, purple of the sea, which the Phoenician merchants had left behind them, and much wealth. {*Apc 1Ma 4:16-23*} All this the soldiers shared among themselves, having first set aside a portion for the maimed, widows and orphans. Then, together, they earnestly entreated the Lord that he would continue to be gracious and reconciled to his servants. {*Apc 2Ma 8:28,29*}

3412. After this, the Jews fought with Timothy and Bacchides, Antiochus' captains, and in that battle killed more than twenty thousand of the enemy. They took over the citadels and divided much spoil among themselves. They set aside some for the maimed, orphans, widows and aged persons, dividing it into portions equal with their own. Then they had gathered up the arms and disposed of them in the most convenient places. They carried the remainder of the spoil to Jerusalem. They also killed Philarches, one of Timothy's men, who was a most wretched fellow and a notorious persecutor of the Jews. In the midst of the solemn festival which they had instituted for their recent victory, they burned Callisthenes alive, after he had taken sanctuary in a little house. He had burned the holy gates. *[E441]* Nicanor stripped himself of all his glorious clothes, to be less conspicuous. After fleeing like a solitary fugitive through the midland country to Antioch, he confessed that the Jews were utterly unconquerable, because they had God for their protector. {*Apc 2Ma 8:30-36*}

3413. Lysias was told of what had happened by one who had escaped. He was perplexed and discouraged because the things which he had wanted to happen in Is-

rael did not occur, and the king's orders had been thwarted. {*Apc 1Ma 4:26,27*}

### 3839b AM, 4549 JP, 165 BC

3414. Therefore, the next year, which was the 148th of the kingdom of the Greeks, Lysias hurried into Judea through Idumea with sixty thousand foot soldiers and five thousand cavalry. Judas Maccabeus marched toward him as he was camped at Bethsura, on the borders of Judea. First, he publicly implored the help of God and then started the battle. Lysias saw how the Jews broke through their enemy's ranks, like so many madmen, without fear of death. His men fled and five thousand were killed there. He returned to Antioch and planned a new expedition after he had gathered a larger army. {*Apc 1Ma 4:28-35*}

3415. Antiochus Epiphanes undertook an expedition against Artaxias, the king of the Armenians, who was marching from the eastern parts. Antiochus killed most of his army and took Artaxias prisoner. {*\*Appian, Syrian Wars, l. 11. c. 8. (45) 2:193*} {*Porphyry*} {*Jerome, Da 11*}

3416. Prusias, the king of Bithynia, strongly condemned Eumenes, the king of Pergamum, who was already under suspicion by the Romans. Letters had been intercepted that intimated an alliance with Perseus against the Romans. Prusias had also prevailed with the Galatians, the Selgenses and many other people of Asia, to complain about Eumenes. *[K45]* Attalus and Athenaeus were sent to Rome by their brother Eumenes, where, in an audience with the Senate, they cleared him of all the crimes of which he had been accused. Then they returned to their country with many honours conferred on them. However, for all this, the Senate still suspected an alliance between Eumenes and Antiochus. They sent Gaius Sulpicius Gallus and Marius Sergius as envoys with instructions to examine closely the affairs of Antiochus and Eumenes. They were to see if there were any preparations being made for war and if there was any alliance between them against the Romans. {*\*Polybius, l. 31. c. 1. 6:165,167*} {*\*Diod. Sic., l. 31. c. 17. 11:357,359*}

3417. When Gaius Sulpicius Gallus entered Asia, he unwisely made a proclamation throughout the chief cities there. He asked anyone who had any accusations against King Eumenes to come to Sardis at a set time. When he arrived, he sat on the bench made for that purpose and spent ten days hearing all sorts of things against Eumenes. He was looking for something to impeach him with, because he was a vain person and hoped to be honoured by finding fault with Eumenes. {*\*Polybius, l. 31. c. 6. 6:173*}

3418. When they had some relief from their enemies, Judas Maccabeus and his brothers came up to Jerusalem with all their forces. They retook the temple and the city, except for the citadel of Zion. They demolished the altars and shrines that the Gentiles had built in the public streets. Judas commanded some men to attack those who were in the citadel of Zion. He spent most of his time in cleansing the temple. His spirit was stirred up by the ravages and devastation he saw. {*Apc 1 Ma 4:36-41 2 Ma 10:1,2*}

## 3840a AM, 4549 JP, 165 BC

*3419.* Judas assigned the priests, who knew the law, to cleanse the sanctuary and move the defiled stones into an unclean place. They pulled down the altar of burnt offerings, which had been profaned by the Gentiles. Its stones were stored in the mount of the temple until the time when a prophet should come who might tell them what ought to be done with them. They built another of whole stones on which no iron tool had been used, according to the law. {*De 27:5,6*} They repaired the Holy Place and the Holy of Holies. They hallowed the courts and made new holy vessels. They brought the lampstand, the altar of incense and the table into the temple. They burned incense on the altar and lit the lamps on the lampstand. They placed the showbread on the table, hung the curtains and saw through to its conclusion everything they had started. {*Apc 1 Ma 4:42-51 2 Ma 10:3*}

*3420.* On the 25th day of the 9th month, called Cisleu, or Chisleu, in the 148th year of the kingdom of the Greeks, they rose early in the morning and started a fire by striking stones one against the other. On their new altar of burnt offering, they offered sacrifices according to the law. {*Apc 1 Ma 4:52,53 2 Ma 10:3*} [E442] This was two years after Judas had succeeded his father Mattathias in the government, but three whole years since the Gentiles had first sacrificed in that place. For on the very same day of the same month on which they had profaned the old altar, Judas consecrated the new one. {*Apc 1 Ma 4:54 2 Ma 10:3-5*} {*\*Josephus, Antiq., l. 12. c. 7. s. 6. (316-322) 7:163-167*}

*3421.* This dedication was joyfully celebrated with songs, hymns, citherns, harps, and cymbals. All the people fell prostrate on the ground and worshipped and blessed the God of heaven who had given them good success. They entreated him that he would not allow them to fall into such calamities ever again. [K46] They prayed that if at any time they should provoke him, he himself would chasten them in mercy and that they might not be delivered up to the blasphemous and barbarous Gentiles. They kept the dedication of deliverances, or peace offerings, and of praise. They decked the forefront of the temple with golden crowns and shields. They repaired the gates and chambers on the sides of the temple and made doors for them. {*Apc 1 Ma 4:54-58 2 Ma 10:4-6*}

*3422.* Then, Judas and his brethren and all the congregation of Israel ordained a feast to be observed throughout the whole country of the Jews. The days of the dedication of the altar were to be observed annually with mirth and gladness for eight days, starting with the 25th day of the month of Chisleu. {*Apc 1 Ma 4:59 2 Ma 10:8*} After they had kept the eight days, they kept the feast of tabernacles. They recalled how not long ago they had kept that feast while living around the mountains and caves like wild beasts. Now, they carried green boughs, fair branches and palms. They sang praises to him who had brought the purification of his holy place to such a good conclusion. {*Apc 2 Ma 10:6,7*} Hence it was that in the letters which the council at Jerusalem wrote to the Jews in Egypt, these days were called the days of tabernacles of the month of Chisleu. {*Apc 2 Ma 1:9,18*} In the gospel they are called the feast of dedication of the Jews, or the feast of lamps. {*Joh 10:22*} This festival commemorated either unexpected removal of their religion and liberties, as Josephus intimated, or the relighting of the lamps in the temple for both events occurred on the same day of the year. {*\*Josephus, Antiq., l. 13. c. 2. s. 3. (46-57) 7:249-255*} {*Apc 1 Ma 4:49,50 2 Ma 10:3*} Also, to this very day, the Jews in their synagogue still continue their custom of celebrating this feast with the lighting of lamps.

*3423.* When they had repaired the temple, they fortified Mount Zion with high walls and strong towers to contain the enemy. They feared that the men garrisoned in that citadel would sally out against those worshipping at the temple. They fortified Bethsura, which was about half a mile away, {*Apc 2 Ma 11:5*} so that the people might have a garrison as a defence against Idumea. {*Apc 1 Ma 4:60,61 6:7-26*}

## 3840b AM, 4550 JP, 164 BC

*3424.* When the surrounding countries heard of the building of the altar and the dedication of the sanctuary, they were very displeased. So they plotted how they could destroy all the Jews, and began to massacre all the Jews who lived in any of their quarters. {*Apc 1 Ma 5:1,2*}

*3425.* Antiochus Epiphanes crossed the high country beyond the Euphrates River. He heard that the city of Elymais in Persia (called Persepolis {*Apc 2 Ma 9:2*}) was a very wealthy city. Its temple was richly appointed and had gold coverings, breast plates and arms left there by Alexander the Great, Philip's son. Appian stated that the temple was dedicated to Venus of Elymais, but Polybius and Diodorus said that it was to Artemis (or Diana) in Elymais. {*\*Appian, Syrian Wars, l. 11. c. 11. (66) 2:233*} {*\*Diod. Sic., l. 31. c. 18a. 11:361*} {*\*Polybius, l. 31. c. 9. 6:117*} {*\*Josephus, Antiq., l. 12. c. 9. s. 1. (354) 7:185*} {*Jerome, Da 11*} When Antiochus greedily tried to plunder the city, the citizens rose up in arms against him. He was defeated and forced to retreat with much dishonour. {Apc 1Ma 6:1-4 2Ma 9:1,2} [K47]

3426. When he arrived at Ecbatana, he was told of the defeat of Nicanor and Timothy in Judea. He left there for Babylon. Near the borders of Persia, he also heard of the great defeat inflicted on Lysias' army, how the image of Jupiter Olympius had been cast out of the temple at Jerusalem, and that the sanctuary and Bethsura had been fortified. Therefore, full of fury, he set out to avenge himself on the Jews for the disgrace he had recently suffered at their hands. He ordered his chariots to go at full speed, to hasten the journey home. He proudly bragged that as soon as he arrived at Jerusalem, he would make that city a common burying place for the Jews. {Apc 1Ma 4:4-7 2Ma 9:3,4} Tacitus stated: {*Tacitus, Histories, l. 5. c. 8. 3:189}

> "King Antiochus endeavoured to reform their religion and to bring in the cities of the Greeks. [E443] He was hindered by the Parthian war in his plan of destroying that most base nation."

3427. Scarcely had these proud words left Antiochus' mouth, when he was struck with an incurable disease in the bowels and extreme pains. Although his body was quite sick, his mind was still sharp. Still breathing out his threats against the Jews, he ordered his chariot driver to increase his pace. It happened that he fell out of his chariot on this fast journey. He was badly hurt, his whole body was bruised and his limbs put out of joint. After he was taken up from the ground, he was carried about on a horse litter. Worms bred so fast in his body, that whole streaks of flesh sometimes dropped from him. While he was still alive in such a pitiful state and because of his stench, none could endure to carry him and he became offensive to his whole army. {Apc 2Ma 9:5-10} He was forced to stop his journey to Babylon and to stay at Tabis, a town of Persia. {*Polybius, l. 31. c. 9. 6:177} {Jerome, Da 11} He continued bedridden for many days, and pined away. {Apc 1Ma 6:8,9} {*Appian, Syrian Wars, l. 11. c. 11. (66) 2:233}

### 3840c AM, 4550 JP, 164 BC

3428. In the 149th year of the kingdom of the Greeks, which began from the beginning of the spring, Antiochus Epiphanes gave up any hope of recovering. He called his friends to him and publicly acknowledged that all these miseries had happened to him because of the harm he had done to the Jews. Now, to his great grief, he had to die in a strange land. {Apc 1Ma 6:10-13,16} When he could no longer endure his own smell, he said:

> "It is appropriate to be subject to God and a man who is mortal should not proudly think of himself as if he were God."

3429. In this prayer to God, he vowed that he would allow the people of Jerusalem and all other Jews everywhere the free use of their own constitutions, and that in future they should enjoy the freedom of being able to live by their own laws and customs. He promised he would beautify the temple with the rarest of gifts and restore all the holy vessels. The costs of the sacrifices would be defrayed from his own treasury and he himself would also become a Jew. He promised to go through all the inhabited world and declare the power of God. When he saw no lessening of his pains, he wrote very courteous letters to the Jews and earnestly entreated them to remain loyal to him and to his son. While Antiochus was still alive, he had already, as was the normal custom, appointed his son to be the next king. {Apc 2Ma 9:11-27}

3430. He called Philip to him, who was his close friend and had been raised with him. {Apc 2Ma 9:29} He appointed him over the whole kingdom and committed his crown, his robe and his signet to him. It was his intention that after he had brought back his son Antiochus from Antioch, where he had left him with Lysias, Philip should raise him to be the next ruler of the kingdom, since he was only nine years old. {*Appian, Syrian Wars, l. 11. c. 11. (66) 2:233} [K48] So in the 149th year of the kingdom of the Greeks, Antiochus died a miserable death in a strange land on the mountains of Parata near Babylon. {Apc 1Ma 6:14-16 2Ma 9:28} Curtius cited Grotius as saying that the town of Tabae was located there. {*Curtius, l. 5. c. 13. s. 2. 1:417} Polybius said that he died at Tabae in Persia. {*Polybius, l. 31. c. 9. 6:177} Jerome told, from Polybius and Diodorus, how Antiochus was frightened by certain phantoms and visions, went mad and at last had a disease which killed him. {Jerome, Da 11} He attributed Antiochus' calamity to his sacrilegious designs on Diana's temple, but Antiochus himself professed in the presence of all his friends that the basis of all his misery was the fact that:

> "He had robbed the temple at Jerusalem and sent forces to destroy the Jews without any cause." {Apc 1Ma 6:12,13}

3431. His corpse was carried out by Philip, who, because he feared Antiochus' son, then withdrew himself into Egypt to Ptolemy Philometor. {Apc 2Ma 9:29} He planned to raise forces against Lysias. When Lysias had heard of Antiochus Epiphanes' death, he had set up the king's son Antiochus, who had been under his guardianship during his minority years, on the throne in his father's place, and called him Eupator. {Apc 1Ma 6:17} Appian stated that the Syrians gave him that surname in honour of his father and confirmed that Lysias was his guardian and responsible for his upbringing. {*Appian, Syrian Wars, l. 11. c. 8. (46) 2:193}

3432. Antiochus Eupator was now in actual possession of the crown and preferred to let Lysias manage the realm. In particular, he gave him control of Coelosyria and Phoenicia. Ptolemy Macron, Dorymenes' son, who had formerly had that honour under Antiochus Epiphanes, {Apc 2Ma 8:8 1Ma 3:38} poisoned himself when he was accused to Eupator of favouring the Jews. He saw the great injustices that had been done to them and tried to see to it that they would be shown justice and that their affairs might be managed in a peaceable manner. [E444] He had been called a traitor for turning over Cyprus, which had been committed to his trust by Philometor, to Antiochus Epiphanes. {Apc 2Ma 10:11-13} Polybius gave him this commendation: {*Polybius, l. 27. c. 13. 5:513}

> "Ptolemy Macron, the governor of Cyprus, behaved himself not like a typical Egyptian, but was prudent and valiant among the best."

3433. Gorgias, who had the command of all the regions around Judea, hired soldiers and continually pressed the war against the Jews. The Idumeans were allied with him and got control of the best places. They accepted the Jerusalem renegades and attacked the Jews, doing all they could to keep the war going. {Apc 2Ma 10:14,15}

3434. Consequently Judas Maccabeus attacked the sons of Esau who had besieged the Jews, at Arabattine, a region of Idumea. He stormed their garrisons and took control of them. Over twenty thousand were killed and he seized all their spoils. {Apc 1Ma 5:3 2Ma 10:16,17}

3435. He recalled the injury done to the Jews by the children of Baean, who had hidden themselves in secret ambushes along the way where the Jewish army was to pass. After their last defeat, the Baeanites had escaped with nine thousand men to two very strong citadels which were well supplied with everything necessary to endure a siege. [K49] So Judas Maccabeus left his brother Simon, with Joseph and Zacchaeus, to besiege them. He marched away to relieve some other places that stood in more need of his help. The men who were with Simon were greedy for money, so they made a deal with the besieged for seventy thousand drachmas and allowed some to escape. As soon as Maccabeus learned this, he convened the governors of the people and in their presence executed all those who were involved in this treachery. He took both the garrisons with little trouble and burned them to the ground, utterly destroying more than twenty thousand of their number. {Apc 1Ma 5:4,5 2Ma 10:16-23}

3436. From there, he passed over to the Ammonites, where he found a very large force under Timothy's command. He had often fought them and defeated them. He took Jazer and its towns and returned to Judea. {Apc 1Ma 5:6-8}

3437. After his last defeat, Timothy recruited multitudes of foreign forces and cavalry from Asia. He returned confident of being able to conquer Judea. Maccabeus and those who were with him, after a serious humiliation and supplication to God, marched from Jerusalem and fought the enemy a great distance from the city. They were encouraged by visions of some horsemen in the heavens fighting for them. They killed twenty and a half thousand of the enemy's foot soldiers and six hundred cavalry. Timothy escaped to a very strong garrison called Gazara, where his brother Chereas was governor, but the garrison was finally taken. Timothy and his brother were found hiding together with Apollonius in a pit and all three were killed with the sword. {Apc 2Ma 10:24-38}

3438. The Trocmians, a people of Galatia, tried to get a foothold in Cappadocia. When this failed, they sent letters to the Romans hoping to turn them against King Ariarathes. The Romans soon sent an embassy there, headed by Marcus Junius. {*Polybius, l. 31. c. 8. 6:175}

## 3841a AM, 4550 JP, 164 BC

3439. The autumn began the 149th year of the *account of the contracts* or *Dhilkarnain*, as noted by the writer of Second Maccabees. In the Chaldee account used in the king's edicts, {Apc 2Ma 11:21} and in Ptolemy's account, the number 148 was used. {Ptolemy, Great Syntaxis, l. 9. c. 7.} {Ptolemy, Great Syntaxis, l. 11. c. 8.} This was also a sabbatical year.

3440. The Gentiles around the region of Gilead assembled against the Jews who were near their borders and planned to exterminate them. They killed a thousand Jews who lived in the land of Tob. {Jud 11:3} They led away their wives and children as captives and took their goods and household belongings. Timothy hurried with an army to besiege the Jews of Gilead who had taken refuge in the garrison in Dathema. This was not the same Timothy who was killed with his brother Chereas, but another man with the same name. At the same time, others from Ptolemais, Tyre, Sidon and all of Galilee of the Gentiles held a meeting to wipe out the Galilean Jews. {Apc 1Ma 5:9-15}

3441. The Gileadites and Galileans sent letters to Judas and his brothers, earnestly asking them to hurry to their aid to help them. Thereupon Judas, having first consulted with those at Jerusalem, divided his whole army into five brigades. He sent his brother Simon with three thousand men to help the Galileans, while he and his brother Jonathan took along eight thousand to help the Gileadites. [E445] [K50] He left the rest of the army with Joseph, the son of Zacharias, and with Azarias, for the defense of Judea. He strictly charged them not to fight with the Gentiles under any circumstances until he and the other men returned. {Apc 1Ma 5:16-20}

3442. As soon as Simon entered Galilee, he attacked the Gentiles and chased them to the very gates of Ptolemais. There they killed three thousand men and took their spoil. After he had rescued the Galileans and the men of Arbattis in the plain with their wives, children and all they had, he brought them into Judea with great joy. {Apc 1Ma 5:21-23}

3443. Before Judas could get to the Gileadites, many of them were besieged in Bosora, Bosor, Alema, Casphor, Maked, Carnaim and other cities in Gilead. {Apc 1Ma 5:26,27}

3444. By that time, Judas and his brother had crossed the Jordan River and had gone on a three day march through the Arabian Desert. The Nabateans met him and told of what had happened to the Gileadites. They added that on the next day, the enemy planned to attack the garrisons and to kill everyone in them, all in one day, just as fast as they could capture them. At this news, Judas turned aside with his army to Bosora, by way of the wilderness. After they had captured the city, they killed all the males, pillaged the city and then burned it to the ground. He left at night and marched toward the citadel, where he found the enemy around daybreak, engaged in placing the battering rams against the citadel. Those within the city prayed to God for help. Judas' men marched in three divisions to the rear of the enemy. They blew trumpets and lifted up their voice in prayer. Timothy's camp knew that it was Maccabeus who was so near and fled from him as fast as they could. In the pursuit, Judas killed eight thousand of the enemy. After this, he went to Maspha and took it by storm. He killed all the males and after they had plundered the place, they set it on fire. From there he went and took Casphor, Maked, Bosor and the other cities of the country of Gilead. {Apc 1Ma 5:24-36}

3445. While Judas and Jonathan were in Gilead and Simon was in Galilee opposite Ptolemais, Joseph, the son of Zacharias, and Azarias, who had been left behind to hold Judea, heard of their gallant achievements. They were ambitious to get themselves a name as great as the others, so, contrary to orders, they took their army as far as Jamnia, planning to fight the Gentiles. However, Gorgias assembled all his forces from the city against them and drove them back to the very borders of Judea. Two thousand Jews were killed that day. {Apc 1Ma 5:55-62}

### 3841b AM, 4551 JP, 163 BC

3446. Lysias was the protector and kinsman of the young king, Eupator, and he effectively ran the kingdom. He was greatly upset at what had happened and mustered almost eighty thousand men with all his own cavalry and eighty elephants. He marched against the Jews with the intention of making Jerusalem a Greek city, with the temple a tributary, and selling the office of the high priest every year. When he entered Judea, he besieged Bethsura, a strong citadel about half a mile from Jerusalem. However, Maccabeus' army was guided by an angel and killed eleven thousand of the enemy's foot soldiers and sixteen hundred cavalry. All the rest fled, including Lysias. Many were badly wounded and others threw away their arms and fended for themselves. {Apc 2Ma 11:1-12} [K51]

3447. Lysias thought about his defeat and about God, who fought the battles for the Jews. He sent envoys to them to sue for peace and said that he would agree to all reasonable terms. He said he would use his influence to gain favour with the king. Judas Maccabeus agreed and wrote what he thought would be in the best interest of the Jews. This letter was sent at the hands of John and Absalom and contained what Lysias should ask the king for, on behalf of the Jews. The king granted every request. {Apc 2Ma 11:13-15} Both the letter from King Antiochus to Lysias and from him to the Jews are contained in the Apocrypha. {Apc 2Ma 11:22-26} These are dated in the year (of the Chaldee account) 148, on the 24th day of the month of Dioscorinthius, as it is in the Greek copies. In the Latin copy, {Apc 2Ma 11:16-21} this month in the Chaldee year seems to be intercalated between Dystos and Xanthikos (in which are written the following letters of the King and of the Romans to the Jews, concerning this peace). Therefore, in the Greek edition of the book of Esther (now seen in the noble Earl of Arundel's library), this is called the month of Adar-Nisan and Dystos-Xanthikos, and by the modern Jews, Veadar, or the other, Adar. However, our Syriac interpreter of the second book of the Maccabees has substituted in its place the Syrian name of *Latter Tishri*.

3448. In this same 148th year (of the Chaldee account), on the 15th day of the month of Xanthikos, according to the Chaldean reckoning, letters were sent to the Jews from King Antiochus {Apc 2Ma 11:27-33} [E446] and from Quintus Memmius and Titus Manlius (otherwise called Manius or Manilius), the envoys from Rome. At that time, they came to the king at Antioch. {Apc 2Ma 11:34-38} Then Lysias came to the king, after the covenants from the king to the Jews had been drawn up. {Apc 2Ma 12:1}

### 3841c AM, 4551 JP, 163 BC

3449. At about the beginning of the spring, the 150th year of the kingdom of the Greeks began, which was the mode of reckoning used by the writer of the first book of the Maccabees.

3450. Demetrius, the son of Seleucus Philopator, had been held hostage at Rome for many years and was now twenty-three years old. He requested of the Senate that, with the help of the people of Rome, he be restored to his own kingdom, which had been unjustly usurped by the son of Antiochus Epiphanes, his uncle. He said that he would always look on Rome as his native country, consider the senator's sons as brothers and the senators as fathers. Notwithstanding all this flattery, the Senate esteemed it more expedient for them to have Syria governed by a child rather than a man. They voted that Demetrius should be detained at Rome and the kingdom be confirmed to the child which Antiochus had left behind. However, before long they sent Gnaeus Octavius, Spurius Lucretius and Lucius Aurelius as envoys to run that kingdom according to the wishes of the Senate. They thought no one would oppose them, since the king was still only a child and the princes of the court would be inclined to the Senate, because the Romans had not turned the kingdom over to Demetrius, which the princes had greatly feared might happen. The Senate was told that Antiochus had acquired elephants in Syria and many more ships than the Senate had allowed him to have. They ordered their envoys to burn the ships and hamstring the elephants. In other words, they were to do what they could to bankrupt the king's treasury. {*Polybius, l. 31. c. 2. 6:167,169} {*Appian, Syrian Wars, l. 11. c. 8. (46) 2:193} {*Dio, l. 20. 2:361 (Zonaras, l. 9. c. 25.)} {Justin, Trogus, l. 34. c. 3.}

3451. The envoys also received instructions to visit the Macedonians, who were not accustomed to a democratic government and had made no use of a common council. There were factions and seditions among them. In addition, the envoys had orders to make a diligent enquiry into the affairs of the Galatians and the kingdom of Ariarathes. {*Polybius, l. 31. c. 2. s. 12-14. 6:169} [K52] However, by his great civility in a conference with Junius and the former envoys, Ariarathes sent them away with a good opinion of himself. {*Polybius, l. 31. c. 3. 6:169,171}

3452. The peace between Eupator and the Jews had no sooner been made than it was broken by those who had command in the adjacent lands. Timothy, Apollonius, the son of Genneus, Hieronymus, Demophon and Nicanor, the governor of Cyprus, would not allow the Jews to live in peace. The citizens of Joppa tricked more than two hundred Jews, who lived among them, onto their ships. They sailed from shore and threw them all overboard. {Apc 2Ma 12:2-4}

3453. When Judas Maccabeus heard of this piece of treachery, he came to Joppa by night and burned their port and their ships. He killed all those who had fled there. When he learned that the Jamnites had plotted against the Jews who lived among them, he did the same by night to their port and fleet. The flames of the fire

were visible as far away as Jerusalem, which was thirty miles away. {Apc 2Ma 12:5-9}

3454. When Judas' army had gone about a mile from there on their march against Timothy, the nomads of Arabia attacked them with at least five thousand foot soldiers and five hundred cavalry. After a fierce battle, the Arabians were defeated. They agreed to supply them with cattle and other needs and hence made peace with Judas. {Apc 2Ma 12:10-12}

3455. Judas' soldiers stormed the city of Caspis and took it. The city was fortified with a bridge and surrounded with walls and inhabited by people from various countries. So great was the slaughter of the citizens that an adjacent lake, a quarter mile wide, was red with blood. {Apc 2Ma 12:13-16}

3456. Leaving there, they travelled about a hundred miles to Characa, to the Jews who were called Tubieni, because they lived in the land of Tob. Timothy had left the place, although he had not finished his business there, but he had left behind a very strong garrison. Dositheus and Sosipater, two of Judas' captains, attacked the garrison and killed about ten thousand of the men that Timothy had left to hold it. {Apc 2Ma 12:17-19}

3457. After this defeat, Timothy raised a new army of a hundred and twenty thousand foot soldiers and twenty-five hundred cavalry from all the surrounding countries, with mercenaries from the Arabians. He sent away the women and children and other supplies to Carnion, or Carnaim, a place that was hard to besiege and difficult to approach because of the narrowness of the entrance. Timothy camped opposite Rhaphon, on the other side of the brook. Judas, placing himself in the vanguard, crossed the brook with all his forces and advanced toward the enemy. He totally routed that Gentile army. [E447] Some fled this way and others that way, in such a great disorder that they were often harmed by their own men and wounded by the points of their own swords. Judas eagerly pursued them and killed nearly thirty thousand men. {Apc 1Ma 5:37-43 2Ma 12:20-23}

3458. Timothy was captured by Dositheus and Sosipater. He craftily persuaded them to let him escape with his life because he had many of the Jews' parents and brothers in his power. If he were put to death, these would likewise be killed. When he agreed to their safe return, they let him go for the sake of their brethren. {Apc 2Ma 12:24,25} [K53]

3459. Judas marched on to the city of Carnaim and to the temple of Atargatis which was located there and to which many of the enemy had fled for refuge. Judas burned the temple along with everyone in it and demolished the city, killing twenty-five thousand. {Apc 1Ma 5:43,44 2Ma 12:26,27}

3460. Judas brought back all the Israelites who were in Gilead with their wives, children and all their belongings. He planned to bring them into Judea. They came as far as Ephron, a very large and well-fortified city that stood in their way. It was inhabited by people from many countries. The walls were well-manned and the city had in it a good supply of engines and ammunition. When Judas and his army had to pass through it, the citizens closed their gates against them and barricaded them up with stones. However, after a day and a night's battery they forced their way through and demolished the city to the ground. They took all the spoil, killed all the males, numbering almost twenty-five thousand, and marched over the dead bodies to get through it. {Apc 1Ma 5:45-51 2Ma 12:27,28}

3461. After this, they passed over Jordan into a large plain before Bethshan, {Apc 1Ma 5:52} which the Greeks called Scythopolis, {*Josephus, Antiq., l. 12. c. 8. s. 5. (348) 7:181} about seventy-five miles from Jerusalem. As soon as they entered the town, the Jews who lived among them, met them and told them how friendly the Scythopolitans had always been with them. They related how kindly they had treated them in their adversities. Thereupon, they thanked them sincerely and requested that their friendship toward their country might continue in times to come. {Apc 2Ma 12:29-31}

3462. Judas brought up the rear of his army and encouraged them all the way until he came back to Judea. {Apc 1Ma 5:53} They arrived at Jerusalem about the feast of Pentecost {Apc 2Ma 12:31} and went up to Mount Zion with joy and gladness. They offered burnt offerings because they had not lost a man and all returned to their homes in peace. {Apc 1Ma 5:54}

3463. After Pentecost, Judas and his brothers, with three thousand foot soldiers and four hundred cavalry, marched against Gorgias who commanded Idumea, intending to fight with him. {Apc 2Ma 12:32,33 1Ma 5:65}

3464. In that battle, some of the Jews were killed. Dositheus, one of Bacenor's troops and a strong man, had taken Gorgias prisoner. Having grabbed him by his coat of mail, he was leading him away when a Thracian soldier came to him and cut off his shoulder, so rescuing Gorgias, who escaped into Marisa. The men who followed Judas were wearied with the long battle. When Judas had called on the Lord and sung psalms and hymns in his mother tongue, he made a sudden attack on Gorgias' forces, putting them to flight. {Apc 2Ma 12:33-37}

3465. After this victory, he called together his army and withdrew to the city of Adullam. When the Sabbath came, they purified themselves and kept that day. The next day, Judas' soldiers gathered up the bodies of those

who had died in the battle, intending to bury them. Under each man's coat, they found things consecrated to the idols of the Jamnites, which was a thing prohibited by Jewish law. {De 7:25,26} It was now clear to all why they had died, so they prayed and beseeched God that the sin might be utterly rooted out. [K54] Arundel's book and the Aldin edition stated that they beseeched God that they might not be utterly destroyed for that sin. Moreover, they made a contribution of two thousand or three thousand drachmas of silver (as the Greek copy of Arundel's and my own Syriac book have it, or twelve thousand, as the Latin copies have it) and sent it to Jerusalem to make a sin offering. {Apc 2Ma 12:38-43}

## 3841d AM, 4551 JP, 163 BC

3466. Then Judas and his brethren went against the Edomites and attacked them in the south of Judea, smiting Hebron and its villages. They dismantled the fortifications and burned the towns around the area. From there, they went through Samaria, planning to go into the land of the Philistines. At that time, some priests who had been keen to show their valour in a skirmish and had acted unwisely, were killed. [E448] Judas went down into the land of the Philistines, toward Azotus. After he had overturned their altars, burned their graven images and taken away the spoils of the cities, he returned into Judea. {Apc 1Ma 5:65-68}

3467. Antiochus' soldiers, who were garrisoned in the tower at Jerusalem, confined the Jews in the temple area and always tried to find ways to annoy them and strengthen the Gentiles. Judas and all the people besieged them in the 150th year of the Greeks. He placed his battering rams and engines against them. However, some of the besieged escaped, and some wicked Jews also allied themselves to these men. They persuaded Antiochus Eupator, the king, swiftly to subdue the rising power of the Jews. {Apc 1Ma 6:18-27}

3468. As a result, the king summoned together all his friends and the commanders of his army and his cavalry and also acquired forces from other kingdoms. His whole force consisted of a hundred thousand foot soldiers and twenty thousand cavalry, as well as thirty-two elephants trained for war. {Apc 1Ma 6:28-30} In the second book of the Maccabees we read that in the 149th year of the account, that is, of the contracts, Judas Maccabeus received news that Antiochus Eupator had gone against Judea. His Greek forces numbered a hundred and ten thousand foot soldiers and fifty-three hundred cavalry, twenty-two elephants and three hundred scythed chariots. {Apc 2Ma 13:1,2}

3469. Menelaus, the usurping high priest, sided with this power in the hope that he would obtain from

Eupator that honour which he had previously in name only. {Apc 2Ma 13:3}

3470. King Eupator was highly enraged and came resolved to bring far greater harm on the Jews than his father had ever done. When Judas heard about this, he commanded the people to call on God night and day for protection. After he had called a council of war, he resolved to march against the king and camped near Modin. {Apc 2Ma 13:9-14}

3471. When the king's army had marched through Idumea, they attacked Bethsura with their engines of war, but the men of Bethsura sallied forth valiantly and burned the engines. Judas camped in Bethzachariah opposite the king's camp. {Apc 1Ma 6:31,32} He told his men that victories were from God. Then he took with him the most valiant men and attacked the enemy's camp by night, advancing as far as the king's own pavilion. [K55] In this battle, he killed almost four thousand men and their best elephants, along with all who attacked him. When the morning dawned, he withdrew victoriously. The entire enemy camp was filled with dread and horror at his exploits. {Apc 2Ma 13:15-17}

3472. Early in the morning, the king marched with his army and camped near Bethzachariah. He drew up his men into battle array and ordered that the juice of grapes and mulberries be placed before the elephants, as he thought that this would make them more fierce in the battle. These beasts were distributed throughout the army and to each beast were assigned a thousand well-armed foot soldiers and five hundred cavalry. Each elephant's back carried a wooden room that held thirty-two soldiers plus the Indian to steer the elephant. Their armour made such a glorious show, that the neighbouring hills glittered from the reflection of the sun on their shields of gold and brass. {Apc 1Ma 6:33-41}

3473. Judas and his army engaged the enemy and killed six hundred men of the king's party. At this point, Eleazar, surnamed Savaran (or Avaran, Judas' brother {Apc 1Ma 2:5}), saw an elephant in royal harness and taller than any of the others. Thinking the king was riding on its back, he went for it and slaughtered his enemies on both sides. He crept under its belly and killed the beast, but was himself killed as the beast fell on him. When the Jews saw the vast forces of the king and their strength, they retired from battle. {Apc 1Ma 6:42-47}

3474. When the king returned to besiege Bethsura, he was engaged by Judas in skirmishes in which the king was sometimes driven off and sometimes Judas had to retreat with losses. However, Judas tried to relieve the besieged and sent them the things they needed.

Rhodocus, a person in the Jewish army, told the enemy of this, and so, after the Jews had inquired into the matter, Rhodocus was seized, put on the rack and kept in prison. Then the king talked a second time with the men of Bethsura and persuaded them to surrender to him. {Apc 2Ma 13:19-22} After the peace had been concluded between them, the Jews all marched out of the city. They had been forced to surrender for lack of provisions to sustain the siege, because that year was the sabbatical year, in which it was not lawful to sow their land. After the king had taken Bethsura, he placed a garrison there to keep it. {Apc 1Ma 6:49,50} [E449]

(Since this was a sabbatical year, it verifies Ussher's calculations that a Jubilee was every forty-nine, not every fifty years. Otherwise, this would not have been a sabbatical year. This also confirms the date for the first sabbatical year. {See note on 2560a AM. <<334>>} {See note on 2609a AM. <<344>>} Editor.)

3475. From there, the king's army went up to Jerusalem and camped against Mount Zion and the sanctuary for many days. They used their artillery with engines, and had instruments to cast fire, machines to shoot arrows and catapults to lob stones. The besieged also made engines to thwart the enemies' weapons. They held them off for a long time, but supplies began to grow scarce for both parties because this was the Sabbatical year. Those in Judea who had been delivered from the Gentiles had eaten up the supply of their store. Very little was left in the sanctuary because the famine was so severe among them, and so they were forced to disperse into various places. {Apc 1Ma 6:51-54} {*Josephus, Antiq., l. 12. c. 9. s. 5. (375-378) 7:195,197}

3476. Meanwhile Philip, whom Antiochus Epiphanes, by his last will and testament, had named as guardian of his son Eupator and who had been appointed ruler under him over the whole kingdom, had already returned from Egypt. He came from Media and Persia with the forces which Epiphanes had left there and planned by force to recover his rights, which Lysias had usurped. {Apc 1Ma 3:37 6:55,56 2Ma 13:23}

3477. When Lysias heard of this, he persuaded the king and the commanders of the army to make peace with the whole country of the Jews and to permit them to enjoy their own laws as in former times. [K56] He said that their own army was growing weaker every day, the provisions for the camp running out, the place they were besieging was well-fortified and the affairs of their own kingdom were more urgent and important. {Apc 1Ma 6:57-59}

3478. The king and his nobles agreed with Lysias and sent to the besieged about terms of peace. The conditions were accepted and the covenants confirmed with an oath. Upon that, the besieged marched from the garrison and the king entered Mount Zion, offered sacrifice, honoured the temple and behaved benevolently towards the place. A little later, when he had contemplated the strength of the place, he broke his oath and ordered the walls to be pulled down. {Apc 1Ma 6:60-62 2Ma 13:23}

3479. The king appointed Maccabeus, or Higemonides (according to the Greek context and my Syriac version), to be the governor from Ptolemais to the Gerrhenians, or as far as Egypt. The boundary of his jurisdiction was Mount Gerar, according to Ptolemy's account. {Apc 2Ma 13:24}

3480. While the king was visiting Ptolemais, the citizens there, who had always hated the Jews, were quite upset by the peace made with Judas. {Apc 1Ma 12:48} In a rage, they wanted to nullify the covenant, but Lysias went up to the judgment seat and defended the matter. He calmed the tumult and pacified the citizens. {Apc 2Ma 13:25,26} Josephus stated that the rule of the Asmoneans lasted a hundred and twenty-six years, to the taking of Jerusalem by Herod and the killing of Antigonus. {*Josephus, Antiq., l. 14. c. 16. s. 4. (490) 7:703} In another place, Josephus stated that the time was a hundred and twenty-five years. {*Josephus, Antiq., l. 17. c. 6. s. 3. (162,163) 8:447} However, this happened in the 126th year from this time, so that the start of this rule was from the time of the peace agreed on between Antiochus and Maccabeus.

## 3842a AM, 4551 JP, 163 BC

3481. From this autumn began the year of accounts of the contracts, the 150th year, which the writer of the second book of the Maccabees used.

3482. Antiochus Eupator hurried to Antioch with Lysias, his guardian, and brought Menelaus, the high priest, along with him as a prisoner. {Apc 1Ma 6:63 2Ma 13:26} {*Josephus, Antiq., l. 12. c. 9. s. 7. (385) 7:201} Lysias had accused him of being the sole cause of the whole Jewish war and the primary instigator of all their evils. Thereupon, by orders of the king, Menelaus was sent to Berea in Syria, where he was let down into a tower filled with ashes and so died the kind of death his life deserved. {Apc 2Ma 13:4-8}

3483. This wretched Menelaus was killed in the tenth year after he first usurped the priesthood at Berea. This was correctly written in Josephus, in the first instance, but not the second instance when he erroneously wrote Berytus. (This variant was removed in the modern Greek text of Josephus. Editor.) The king substituted another in his place, one who was just as wicked, called Alcimus, or Jacimus. He was descended from Aaron, but not of the high priest's bloodline. Lysias persuaded the king to

transfer that honour to another family. {*Josephus, Antiq., l. 12. c. 9. s. 7. (385) 7:201} {*Josephus, Antiq., l. 20. c. 10. s. 3. (235) 10:125}

3484. When Onias, son of Onias III the high priest, saw that the high priesthood had been given to Alcimus, he went into Egypt. After he had ingratiated himself with Ptolemy Philometor and his wife Cleopatra, he obtained permission to build a temple of God in the city of Heliopolis similar to the one at Jerusalem. They would also appoint him the high priest there. Josephus wrote this in his Jewish Antiquities, contradicting what he had formerly written in his work on the Jewish Wars. [E450] [K57] There he had said that Onias' flight and his building of the temple in Egypt happened while Antiochus Epiphanes was still living. {*Josephus, Antiq., l. 12. c. 9. s. 7. (387,388) 7:201} {*Josephus, Jewish War, l. 1. c. 1. s. 1. (31-33) 2:19} {*Josephus, Jewish War, l. 7. c. 10. s. 2. (422-424) 4:425}

3485. About this time, Ptolemy Philometor and his younger brother Ptolemy Euergetes II had a falling-out. The Senate of Rome wrote letters to their envoys, Gnaeus Octavius, Spurius Lucretius and Lucius Aurelius, to do what they could to make peace. {*Polybius, l. 31. c. 2. s. 13,14. 6:169} After they had ruled together peacefully for six years as joint rulers, the younger brother expelled Philometor and ruled alone. {Porphyry, Scaliger's Greek Eusebius, p. 54,225.}

3486. When the older Ptolemy was expelled from his kingdom, he went to Rome for help. He had very few in his retinue and travelled in poor clothes. {*Valerius Maximus, l. 5. c. 1. s 1f. 1:443} As he was on his way to the city on foot, he was noticed by Demetrius, Seleucus' son, who was very troubled at this sight and promptly provided a royal robe and a diadem for him, and a horse adorned with golden fittings. He went with his own servants and met Ptolemy twenty-six miles from the city. After a civil greeting, he advised him to put on these trappings and to enter Rome more like a king, lest he appear contemptible. Ptolemy thanked him very much for his goodwill toward him, but he did not accept these things for himself. Ptolemy wanted rather to be allowed to rest a while with Archias in one of the towns along the way. {*Diod. Sic., l. 31. c. 18. 11:359}

3487. Finally, he came to Rome and lodged at an Alexandrian painter's house. As soon as the Senate heard of it, they sent for him and made a most thorough apology because they had not, according to the usual custom, sent the quaestor to wait upon him, nor had they entertained him at the public expense. They assured him that those omissions were not to be imputed to any disrespect of theirs toward him but merely to his own coming to them so suddenly and so privately. Upon that, they conducted him from the court to the house of public entertainment and persuaded him to take off his sordid clothes. They settled on a day for a meeting. They also took care that presents were sent to him daily by the treasurers. By their kind treatment of him, they restored Ptolemy from the low condition he was in to his former kingly eminence. This caused him to hope more for Rome's assistance than to fear his low estate. {*Valerius Maximus, l. 5. c. 1. s. 1f. 1:443}

3488. As soon as Gnaeus Octavius and Spurius Lucretius, the Roman envoys, came to Ariarathes, the king of the Cappadocians, they enquired into the battles between him and the Galatians. He told them the whole matter in a few words, adding that he was willing to agree to use them as arbitrators. Most of his speech concerned Syria, for he knew that Octavius was going there. He showed them also what a weak condition that state was in and how great the similarity was between his own weak state and Syria. As well as this, he expressed his preference to escort them with his forces and to be ready on all occasions to help them, until they had returned safely from Syria. The king's goodwill and desire to accommodate them was much appreciated by the envoys. They told him that at present they had no need of his company, but in case of some future emergency, should the need arise, they would not hesitate to inform him. They said that after this they would always include him as a most sincere friend to the Romans. {*Polybius, l. 31. c. 8. s. 4-8. 6:175,177} [K58]

3489. King Eupator, with the help of his guardian Lysias, had quickly pacified the disturbances in Syria. When he returned to Antioch, he found Philip in command there, so he fought him and took the city. {Apc 1Ma 6:63} After he had captured Philip, he had him killed. {*Josephus, Antiq., l. 12. c. 9. s. 7. (386) 7:201}

## 3842b AM, 4552 JP, 162 BC

3490. Octavius, Lucretius and Aurelius, the three Roman envoys, followed their instructions from the Senate when they came into Syria. They saw to it that the elephants were killed and the ships of the navy burned, and then attended to everything else with the interests of Rome in mind. This grieved Leptines, who therefore stabbed Gnaeus Octavius, the head of the embassy, at Laodicea, as he was preparing himself in the gymnasium. Leptines testified that the deed had been carried out lawfully and at the instigation of the gods. Octavius was the first one, of that family from which Caesar Augustus later descended, to have the consulship. Lysias, Eupator's guardian, who was reputed to be the chief instigator of the people against the Romans, took care of the funeral for Octavius. [E451] In the king's name, he at once sent envoys to Rome to apologise for the deed and testify to

the king's innocence, as not having been an accessory to this in any way. {*Polybius, l. 31. c. 2. s. 11-14. 6:169} {*Polybius, l. 31. c. 12. s. 4. 6:183} {*Cicero, Philippics, l. 9. c. 2. 15:405} {*Appian, Syrian Wars, l. 11. c. 8. (46) 2:193,195} {*Dio, l. 20. 2:361,363 (Zonaras, l. 9. c. 25.)} Julius Obsequens confirmed that the killing of Octavius happened when Gaius Marcius and Publius Scipio Nasica were consuls. {*Julius Obsequens, Prodigies, l. 1. c. 15. 14:249}

3491. At that time there lived in Syria a grammarian named Isocrates, who belonged to a company of men who made public recitations. He was a prating braggart who was hated by the Greeks. Alcaeus, in his public speeches, used to make fun of him. As soon as Isocrates had come to Syria, he had begun to reproach the Syrians as being stupid. He did not stay within the bounds of his profession and began to talk of state matters and pass his judgment on them. He defended the justice of the murder of Octavius and wanted the other Roman envoys killed as well, so no one would be left to take the news back to Rome. Through this, the Romans might be made more humble and might cease interfering in the business of others. {*Polybius, l. 32. c. 2. s. 4-8. 6:235}

3492. Through their envoys, Canuleius and Quintus, the Romans restored Ptolemy Philometor to his kingdom and reconciled him to his younger brother, Euergetes, having decreed that the kingdom should be divided between them. Philometor was to take Egypt and Cyprus as his share, Euergetes was to get Cyrene. This agreement was confirmed by all manner of religious ceremonies and by the mutual pledging of their faith to each other. Euergetes, however, hurried away to Rome to try to have the covenant voided. After which Philometor sent Menyllus of Alabanda there also, as his envoy. He was to be his advocate and representative in his quarrel with Euergetes. {*Polybius, l. 31. c. 19,20. 6:201,203} {*Livy, l. 46. 14:11} {*Dio, l. 20. 2:359,361 (Zonaras, l. 9. c. 25.)}

3493. Ariarathes, the king of Cappadocia, died and his son Ariarathes, surnamed Philopator, succeeded him by right of inheritance. As soon as he had performed his father's funeral with the utmost magnificence, he sent his envoys to Rome to renew the league and alliance with the people of Rome. He had first been called Mithridates, but after he came of age, he was known by his father's name of Ariarathes. When he was crowned, he treated his friends, nobles and subjects with due respect, so that he soon won the affections of all. [K59] He was experienced in Greek and studied philosophy, with the result that Cappadocia, never before known to the Greeks, soon became a home for learned men. {*Livy, l. 46. 14:11} {*Dio, l. 20. 2:359 (Zonaras, l. 9. c. 24.)} {*Diod. Sic., l. 31. c. 19. s. 6-8. 11:369}

## 3842c AM, 4552 JP, 162 BC

*3494.* This spring began the 151st year of the kingdom of the Greeks, which is used in the first book of the Maccabees.

*3495.* When the envoys of Ariarathes, the new king of Cappadocia, arrived at Rome, they asked the Senate to embrace their king fully, with love and affection, as he had always wished the Romans well. The Senate renewed the league and amity, as the envoys requested, and highly commended the king's affections to them. They entertained the envoys very civilly. After this, Tiberius Gracchus returned from his embassy in Asia and related many notable expressions of the affections of this king and of his father, and indeed, of the whole kingdom, toward the people of Rome. {*See note on 3833b AM. <<3232>>} {*Polybius, l. 31. c. 3. 6:170,171}

*3496.* The Rhodians requested through Cleagoras and Lygdamis, their envoys at Rome, that they might be permitted to retain Lycia and Caria on the same terms as before. {*Polybius, l. 31. c. 4. 6:171}

*3497.* At that time, Calynda in Caria revolted from Caunus, whereupon the Caunii attempted to besiege them. The Calyndians first requested help from the Cnidians and they were able to hold the enemy off for a while. Since the outcome of the war was uncertain, they sent an embassy to the Rhodians and surrendered themselves and their city into their hands. The Rhodians accepted this and accordingly sent supplies by both sea and land. They raised the siege and took the city into their own jurisdiction. Soon after this, the Senate confirmed the right to and possession of the city to them. {*Polybius, l. 31. c. 5. 6:171,173}

*3498.* Ariarathes, the king of Cappadocia, had heard from his envoys, who had returned from Rome, that he was in good favour with the Romans. He considered himself secure in his kingdom and offered sacrifices to the gods and feasted his nobles. Moreover, he sent envoys to Lysias at Antioch to get the bones of his sister and his mother Antiochis, the daughter of Antiochus the Great. He gave the envoys instructions before they left and prayed for their success. He told them it would be best not to mention the death of Octavius, even though he was quite displeased by it, as he thought this might provoke Lysias and he would not grant his request. [E452] Lysias allowed him to have the bones and as soon as they were brought to him, he carried them out very solemnly and placed them very carefully in his father's tomb. {*Polybius, l. 31. c. 7. 6:173,175}

*3499.* After the two Ptolemys (brothers) had divided the kingdom between them, the younger Ptolemy went to Rome to invalidate the partition agreed upon with his brother. He said that he had not voluntarily done as he was commanded but had yielded from necessity, having been forced to by the difficult circumstances. Therefore he requested the Senate to give him Cyprus, otherwise his portion would be much less than his brother's. For the other side, Menyllus, Philometor's envoy, stated what was also confirmed by the Roman envoys' testimony, how the younger Ptolemy had retained not only Cyrene but also his very life because of the help of his brother. [K60] Since he was generally hated, he saw it as a great favour that the kingdom of Greece had sided with him, which was more than he could have hoped for, or any man would have dreamed of. After Ptolemy's reply the Senate was urged to consider that the sharing of the kingdom was not quite finalised, partly out of their own interest in seeing that kingdom divided. For, should the occasion arise, they would have less trouble subduing it if it were divided than if it were united. So they granted the younger brother's demands and immediately sent their envoys, Titus Torquatus and Gnaeus Merula, with instructions to reconcile the two brothers and to give Cyprus to the younger brother. {*Polybius, l. 31. c. 10. 6:177-181}

*3500.* News reached Rome of the killing of Gnaeus Octavius. When the envoys of Antiochus Eupator, whom Lysias had sent, arrived at Rome, they showed that their king was in no way involved in the murder. The Senate sent the envoys back again and decided nothing on the issue, because they were determined not to reveal their thinking on the matter. {*Polybius, l. 31. c. 11. s. 1,2. 6:181} However, they ordered that a statue in memory of Octavius be erected in the place of common pleas. {*Cicero, Philippics, l. 9. c. 2. 15:405}

*3501.* Demetrius was greatly disturbed by the news of that accident. He sent for Polybius the historian and asked him whether or not it was wise to ask the Senate again about his own affairs. Polybius warned him to be careful of dashing himself twice against the same stone. He told him that he had better attempt some noble exploit worthy of a kingdom, hinting by this that Demetrius should steal away from Rome as soon as he could. However, Demetrius followed the counsel of Apollonius, his close friend, who was a good man, but very young. Demetrius came into the Senate and requested that he might at least have his liberty and no longer be detained as a hostage at Rome, seeing that they had confirmed the kingdom to Antiochus Eupator. The Senate, for all this, stood by their decree. As a result, Demetrius consulted first with Diodorus, who was a crafty fellow who had recently arrived from Syria and had previously educated him. Then he talked with Polybius about how he might make his escape. Menyllus,

Ptolemy Philometor's agent, who by Polybius' means (since Polybius was intimately acquainted with him) had been admitted into the discussion under the pretence of providing for Demetrius' return home. Menyllus publicly hired a Carthaginian ship which was about to sail to Tyre to bring the firstfruits of the Carthaginians to their ancestral gods, according to their custom. When everything was ready, Demetrius sent his tutor, Diodorus, ahead into Syria to hear what was being said and to feel the pulse of the people. Demetrius only took a few with him as companions on his journey. He dined at a friend's house with them and sent the rest away to Anagnia, where he said he would come hunting the next day. {*Polybius, l. 31. c. 11-13. 6:181-187}

3502. At the time, Polybius was sick in bed. He was afraid that Demetrius might spend too much time drinking and miss the opportunity to escape. Since the night was passing, he sent him a sheet sealed up with these lines written on it: {*Polybius, l. 31. c. 13. s. 7-14. 6:187,189}

> He that delays, incurs the fates
> Of a deadly night—boldness success creates.
> Adventure, come what can, let all,
> Rather than thou, thyself, shouldest fall.

3503. [E453] [K61] Polybius added this saying of Epicharmus: {*Polybius, l. 31. c. 13. s. 13,14. 6:189} {*Cicero, Atticus, l. 1. c. 19. 22:89}

> Be sober and remember to distrust;
> These are the very sinews of the mind.

3504. As soon as Demetrius read the note, he understood immediately what these instructions meant and from whom they came. So, pretending to be sick, he and his friends left the company. He told his plan to Nicanor and the rest of his friends. He came by night to Ostia, at the mouth of the Tiber River. Menyllus had preceded them and communicated with the officers of the ship, saying that he had a message from the king (Ptolemy) to the effect that he must himself remain in Rome for the present, but must send on to him in advance the most trustworthy of his young soldiers, who would give him all the news about his brother. About the end of the third watch of the night, Demetrius arrived with eight friends, five servants and two lackeys. Menyllus commended these to the captain of the ship, who knew nothing of the plot, and they set sail around daybreak. No one at Rome missed him until four days later, when they looked for him, but could not find him. On the fifth day, the Senate met over the matter, but Demetrius was now six days from the city by sea and had gone as far as the Straits of Messenia. The Senate thought it would be of no use to pursue him, since he had such a

head start on them. A few days later, they sent Tiberius Gracchus, Lucius Lentulus and Servilius Glaucia as envoys whose business it was to see how things were going in Greece. After that, they were to find out what Demetrius was up to, see how the kings felt toward Rome and settle their differences with the Galatians. {*Polybius, l. 31. c. 14. 6:189-193}

3505. In the meantime, Demetrius had arrived in Lycia, from where he wrote the Senate that he was not marching against Antiochus, his uncle's son, but against Lysias, with a resolution to avenge Octavius' death. He won Tripolis in Syria over to his side by saying he had been sent by the Senate to take possession of the kingdom, for no one dreamed of his escape. He captured Apamea and having mustered all his forces together, marched toward Antioch. He killed the young king, Antiochus Eupator, and Lysias, when they came out to give him a friendly greeting. They had not wanted to take up arms for fear of displeasing the Romans. He won the approval of all in Syria and took over the kingdom. {*Dio, l. 20. 2:363,365 (Zonaras, l. 9. c. 25.)} {Justin, Trogus, l. 34. c. 3.} {*Appian, Syrian Wars, l. 11. c. 8. (47) 2:195}

3506. We read in the Apocrypha that in the 151st year of the kingdom of the Greeks, Demetrius, the son of Seleucus, escaped from Rome and came with a few men to a city on the sea coast that is Tripolis of Phoenicia and began to reign there. He entered into the palace of his ancestors at Antioch near Daphne, the metropolis of Syria. His soldiers seized Antiochus and Lysias and killed them at his orders. {Apc 1Ma 7:1-4} In the Apocrypha {Apc 2Ma 14:1,2} we read that after three years, or in the third year, from the beginning of Antiochus Eupator, or the purging of the temple by Judas Maccabeus as mentioned in the Apocrypha, {Apc 2Ma 10:1-10} Judas was told of the arrival of Demetrius at Tripolis, and that he had taken the country with a large army and navy and had killed Antiochus and Lysias, his tutor. However, both Josephus and Eusebius stated that Antiochus Eupator only reigned two years. {*Josephus, Antiq., l. 12. c. 10. s. 1. (390) 7:203} {*Eusebius, Chronicles, l. 1. 1:223} [K62] On the other hand, Porphyry and Sulpicius Severus stated that he reigned only eighteen months. {Porphyry, Scaliger's Greek Eusebius, p. 228.} {*Sulpicius Severus, Sacred History, l. 2. c. 23. 11:108}

3507. Demetrius removed Heraclides from the charge of the treasury in Babylon. Antiochus Epiphanes had appointed him to that position. Demetrius also killed Heraclides' brother, Timarchus, who had been appointed governor of Babylon by Antiochus Epiphanes. Timarchus had rebelled against Demetrius and was running the place poorly. The Babylonians were the first to surname Demetrius *Soter*, or *Protector*. {*Appian, Syrian Wars, l. 11. c. 8. (47) 2:195}

**3842d AM, 4552 JP, 162 BC**

*3508.* Alcimus had obtained the high priesthood from Antiochus Eupator, but was not accepted by the people. In the period of the confusion under Antiochus Epiphanes, he had wilfully defiled himself. {*Apc 2 Ma 14:3*} In an attempt to get the priesthood confirmed to him by Demetrius Soter, he addressed the king. He was accompanied by other wicked and apostate Israelites who maligned their countrymen, especially the Asmoneans. They said the Asmoneans were guilty of killing the king's friends and banishing them out of the country. Demetrius resented the substance of their complaints. Thereupon, he sent a large force into Judea under Bacchides, the governor of Mesopotamia and an intimate and faithful friend of his, along with Alcimus, to whom he had given the priesthood. When they had entered the land, they thought they had won over Judas Maccabeus and his brethren with their talk about peace. However, the Jews did not believe them when they saw their large forces. {*Apc 1 Ma 7:5-11*} [E454]

*3509.* A company of scribes headed by the Assideans came to Alcimus and Bacchides and desired peace from them. They said:

> "One who is a priest of the seed of Aaron has the charge of this army, and he will not do us any wrong."

*3510.* After they had committed themselves to his safety, that wicked priest broke the agreement and his oath and executed sixty of their scribes in one day. The historian applied the saying of the psalmist to this event: {*Ps. 79:2, 3*}

> "The dead bodies of thy servants have they given to be meat unto the fowls of the heaven, the flesh of thy saints unto the beasts of the earth. Their blood have they shed like water round about Jerusalem; and there was none to bury them."

*3511.* Many were terrified by this act of wickedness and fled from the city. {*Apc 1 Ma 7:12-19*}

*3512.* Bacchides left Jerusalem and camped in Bezeth, or Bethzetha, from where he sent out men to capture many of those who had forsaken him. He killed some of the Jews and cast them into a deep pit. After that, he committed the country to Alcimus' care and left him a sufficiently large force to help him, while he himself returned to the king. All the rebellious among the people joined Alcimus, who had done everything to ensure the priesthood for himself. When they had subdued Judea, they created great havoc in Israel. Thereupon, Judas Maccabeus went throughout the whole land of Judea and took vengeance on all who had revolted from him. He was so successful, that the enemies were confined to their garrisons and did not make any more incursions into the country. {*Apc 1 Ma 7:19-24*}

*3513.* The younger Ptolemy left Italy and came into Greece, where he hired an army of very strong men. He also hired Damasippus, a Macedonian who, after having killed the members of the council at Phacus, a town of Macedonia, had escaped from there as fast as he could with his wife and children. Ptolemy left and came to Peraea, a land opposite Rhodes. After he had been courteously treated by the people, he planned to set sail for Cyprus. However, when Torquatus and the rest of the Roman envoys saw the large number of mercenary soldiers he had, they remembered their instructions from the Senate, in which they had been expressly charged to control him without fighting. [K63] Eventually, they prevailed upon him to disband his mercenaries as soon as he came to Sida and not to make his intended voyage to Cyprus. He was to do his best to meet with them over the matter of Cyprus. In the meantime, they would be going to Alexandria to persuade the king to agree to his requests. They would meet him at the appointed place and bring the king himself along with them. These propositions had such influence on the younger Ptolemy, that he gave up the idea of conquering Cyprus and dismissed his mercenary soldiers. He went directly to Crete, taking Damasippus along with him and Gnaeus Merula, one of the envoys. As soon as he had hired a thousand soldiers, he departed to Libya and kept them at the port of Apis. {*\*Polybius, l. 31. c. 17. 6:195,197*}

*3514.* In the interim, Torquatus and Titus came to Alexandria and did what they could to persuade the older Ptolemy to come to an agreement with his brother and give him Cyprus. Ptolemy gave in on some things, while he listened to others merely to buy time. His younger brother, who was camped before Apis in Libya as agreed, was very displeased that nothing had as yet been concluded concerning the surrender of Cyprus. He sent Gnaeus Merula to Alexandria, hoping to accomplish his plans through him and Torquatus. {*\*Polybius, l. 31. c. 18. s. 1-5. 6:197*}

**3843a AM, 4552 JP, 162 BC**

*3515.* Hipparchus of Bithynia attempted to transmit to posterity the exact number of the stars and to catalogue the constellations using particular instruments he had invented. He showed their positions and their magnitudes. Pliny maintained that his work never received sufficient recognition. {*\*Pliny, l. 2. c. 24. 1:239*} In his book, Hipparchus wrote that in the 27th year of the third Calippic period, on the 30th day of the Egyptian month of Mesore (September 27), around sunset, he observed the autumnal equinox. {*Ptolemy, Great Syntaxis, l. 3. c. 2.*}

*3516.* This autumn began the 151st year of the account of the contracts as used in the second book of the Maccabees. In this year (for so the Greek copies compute, and my Syriac Interpreter, whereas the Latin edition reads 150), Alcimus came to King Demetrius and gave him a golden crown, a palm and boughs which were used in the temple. {*Apc 2Ma 14:3,4*} He saw how Judas Maccabeus and the Assideans who were with him had greatly increased in power. They would not allow him to come near the holy altar. Using this opportunity, he eagerly accused them to the king as the instigators of all the rebellions and as disturbers of the common peace in Judea. He complained most bitterly about this, claiming he had been divested of the high priesthood, which had been the glory of his ancestors. *[E455]* He was confident that as long as Judas was alive, Demetrius would never enjoy the kingdom in peace. This was confirmed by his friends and other implacable enemies of Judas. Demetrius was so angry that he sent Nicanor, his general, into Judea with orders to destroy Judas and disperse his associates, the Assideans. He was to place Alcimus in the high priesthood. The Gentiles who had fled from Judea for fear of Judas, flocked to Nicanor. They were pleased about the calamities which were likely to befall the Jews. {*Apc 2Ma 14:3-14 1Ma 7:25,26*}

*3517.* When the Jews heard of Nicanor's coming and of the alliance of the Gentiles with him, they cast dust on their heads and prayed to God. *[K64]* There was a short skirmish between Simon, Judas' brother, and Nicanor near the village of Dessaro. Nicanor had heard of the prowess and valour of Judas and his company in defending their country and was afraid of fighting with him. So he sent Poseidonius, Theodotus and Matthias to make a peace with him. When they had discussed the matter among themselves, Judas presented it to the people, who unanimously approved the articles. A day was appointed in which Judas and Nicanor were to meet but Judas did not trust the enemy, and placed some armed men in several convenient places for security in case of any violence. However, the conference was very peaceful and concluded in a league without the king's knowledge. Nicanor then stayed a while in Jerusalem and dismissed the companies which he had earlier collected. He lived on such friendly and familiar terms with Judas, that Judas persuaded him to marry a wife from among their people. {*Apc 2Ma 14:15-25*}

*3518.* As soon as Alcimus saw what had happened, he spoke to Demetrius a third time, to complain about Nicanor and accuse him of plotting against the king. Demetrius was so disturbed by all this, that he immediately wrote to Nicanor to let him know how very upset he was by his dealings with Judas Maccabeus. He ordered

Nicanor to send Judas bound to Antioch. This Nicanor was very reluctant to do, since it would break their articles of peace and since Judas had done nothing wrong. However, he knew enough not to cross the king and so watched for a convenient time to execute the king's command through craft. {*Apc 2Ma 14:26-29*}

*3519.* Ptolemy Philometor detained the Roman envoys at Alexandria for forty days with his entertainment. This was against their will, since no business was transacted. The Cyrenians and some other cities revolted from Euergetes, the younger brother. Ptolemy Sympetesis, whom Euergetes had appointed over the whole realm when he himself had sailed away to Rome, had taken the side of the insurgents, and news of this reached Euergetes. He was also told that the Cyrenians already had an army prepared for war. He feared that while he was trying to add Cyprus to his kingdom, he would lose Cyrene. He set aside all other matters and left Apis, where his navy was anchored in the harbour. He marched to the Great Slope, as they called it, and planned to go to Cyrene from there. He found that the pass was being held by the Libyans and the Cyrenians, so he shipped half his men with orders to sail around the pass and to make a surprise attack on the enemy. He led the vanguard and with the rest of the army tried to capture the hill. As soon as the Libyans realised they were surrounded, they abandoned their stations. Hence, the king took the top of the hill and captured the citadel and the place beneath it called Four Towers, which contained plenty of water. {*Polybius, l. 31. c. 18. s. 1-12. 6:197,199*}

*3520.* From there, he marched through the wilderness in six days, while the soldiers under Mochyrinus followed him by sea. When the Cyrenians heard of his coming, they drew out their army of eight thousand foot soldiers and five hundred cavalry against him. They could guess Philometor's disposition by what he had done at Alexandria. They saw no traces of a king in Euergetes, only a tyrant, and could not be persuaded to voluntarily submit to him. *[K65]* Therefore, they fought and defeated him. {*Polybius, l. 31. c. 18. s. 12-16. 6:199,201*}

## 3843b AM, 4553 JP, 161 BC

*3521.* Judas Maccabeus noticed that Nicanor had grown more reserved than before and that his dealings had become more harsh than they usually were. Believing he was up to no good, Judas gathered many of his associates and withdrew himself from Nicanor's sight. {*Apc 2Ma 14:30*}

*3522.* Nicanor came to Jerusalem with large forces and with his persuasive speeches drew Judas to a meeting. However, the enemy planned to seize Judas and carry him away, while they were greeting one another. *[E456]* When Judas became aware of this, he was very afraid of him and did not want to see him any more. Nicanor, realising that his plan had been discovered, marched against Judas to fight him beside Capharsalama. Nicanor's side lost five thousand men and the rest fled to the city of David. {*Apc 1Ma 7:27-32*}

*3523.* After this, Nicanor went to Mount Zion, where he was met by some of the priests and elders of the people. They came from the sanctuary to greet him peaceably and to show him the burnt sacrifice that had been offered for the king. He scoffed at and slighted them, commanding them to turn over Judas. They swore with an oath that they did not know where he was. Nicanor stretched out his right hand toward the temple and swore that unless Judas and his forces were delivered into his hands, he would, when he returned in peace, burn the house of God, destroy the altar and erect in its place another glorious temple to Bacchus. Thereupon, the priests entered the temple and stood before the altar, with great lamentations beseeching God to frustrate Nicanor's threats and avenge his blasphemies. {*Apc 1Ma 7:33-38 2Ma 14:31-36*}

*3524.* Razis, one of the elders of Jerusalem, who was called *The Father of the Jews* on account of his love and affection for the citizens, came to Nicanor. Therefore, because of who this man was, Nicanor thought that if the man was killed, he would be able to do what he pleased with the Jews. He sent about five hundred soldiers to seize him. When they had forced the outer gates of the tower where he was and were ordered to burn the other doors, Razis stabbed himself with his own sword. When he realised that, because of his haste, his wound was not mortal, he threw himself headlong from the wall. Afterward, running to a steep rock when he was almost dead, he ripped out his bowels and with both his hands threw them among the throng, and so he died. {*Apc 2Ma 14:37-46*} Concerning this event, see Augustine. {*Augustine, Epistle to Dulcitius, n. 61.*} {*Augustine, Against Gaudentius, l. 2. c. 23.*}

*3525.* When Nicanor saw that Judas was not in Jerusalem, but in the regions of Samaria, he marched from Jerusalem and camped in Bethhoron, while more troops came from Syria to join him. Judas camped in Adasa, about four miles from the enemy, with three thousand men. Nicanor tried to start the battle on the Sabbath day, but was before long admonished by some Jews who were compelled to march with him, to reverence that day and the God who instituted it. He railed on them with a most horrid blasphemy, but was unable to carry out his plan of fighting on the Sabbath. Maccabeus encouraged his troops from the law and the prophets. Moreover, he had them remember their former encounters and told them about his dream. *[K66]* He had seen Onias III praying for the people and the prophet

Jeremiah reaching out to him with a golden sword. In this way, he encouraged the troops. After that, being well-armed with prayers and a sure confidence in God, they attacked the enemy on the 13th day of the 12th month of Adar. Nicanor was the first to die in the battle, whereupon the rest threw away their arms and fled. The Jews chased them for a whole day from Adasa to Gazara and sounded an alarm after them with their trumpets. At this, all the Jews from the various surrounding towns hurried to the slaughter of their fleeing enemies. At least thirty-five thousand were killed and not one of the enemy army survived. Then, they fell on the spoil and took the prey. They cut off Nicanor's head and arms with the shoulder and brought them to Jerusalem. They hung his head on a high tower by his right hand, which he had so proudly stretched forth against the house of God. Judas ordered the tongue of this wicked fellow to be cut out, chopped in pieces and fed to the birds. In commemoration of this victory, it was enacted by a general decree that a great holiday should be kept annually on the 13th day of the 12th month, called Adar in the Syriac, the day before the feast of Mordecai. {*Apc 1Ma 7:39-49 2Ma 15:1-37*} {*\*Josephus, Antiq., l. 12. c. 10. s. 5. (406-412) 7:211-215*}

*3526.* This ends the history contained in the second book of the Maccabees and is a summary of the five books of Jason, a Jew of Cyrene. After Nicanor's death, Judea had rest from wars for a while. {*Apc 1Ma 7:50*} During that time, Judas Maccabeus heard of the great power of the Romans and their humanity toward any who were in distress. He also knew how greatly Demetrius feared the Romans. Therefore, he sent Eupolemus the son of John, and Jason the son of Eleazar, as agents to the Senate at Rome, in his own name, as well as that of his brother and the commonwealth of the Jews. They were to negotiate an association and alliance with the people of Rome by which they hoped to free themselves of the heavy yoke of King Demetrius and the empire of the Greeks. {*Apc 1Ma 8:1,17,18,31,32*}

*3527.* Gnaeus Merula finally returned from Alexandria to Euergetes and told him that his brother Philometor would not agree to any of his demands. *[E457]* He impressed upon him that the brothers had to abide by the covenants which had initially been ratified. When Euergetes heard this, he ordered Comanus and his brother Ptolemy to go to Rome as his envoys, along with Merula. They were to entreat the Senate concerning the wrongs done to him by his brother and to tell them of Philometor's contempt for the Romans. On their way they met Titus Torquatus, who was Gnaeus Merula's colleague in the embassy. He had also left Alexandria, without having completed the business for which he had gone there. At the same time,

Philometor sent Menyllus of Alabanda as an envoy to the Senate. {*Polybius, l. 31. c. 19,20. 6:201}

3528. After Demetrius heard that Nicanor and his whole army had been destroyed in the battle, he sent Bacchides and Alcimus into Judea for the second time and gave them the right wing, or the better part of his army. They marched on the route to Gilgal, and camped at Masaloth, or Massadoth, which is in Arbela. When they captured it, they killed many people. {Apc 1Ma 9:1,2}

### 3843c AM, 4553 JP, 161 BC

3529. In the first month of the 152nd year of the kingdom of the Greeks, they marched toward Jerusalem to find Judas Maccabeus and from there they marched to Berea (or Beerzath, as it is in Arundel's copy), with twenty thousand foot soldiers and two thousand cavalry. [K67] Judas was camped in Eleasa with three thousand choice men. When they saw the large number of the enemy, they were very afraid and many deserted him, so that he had only eight hundred left in the camp. With these few he attacked Bacchides' vast army and fought from morning till night. At last he routed the enemy's right wing, where Bacchides was, and pursued them to Mount Azotus. However, those in the left wing chased Judas and the men with him. Judas died fighting valiantly and the rest promptly fled. Then Jonathan and Simon took up the body of their brother Judas and buried it in the sepulchre of their fathers at Modin, and Israel mourned over him for many days. {Apc 1Ma 9:3-21} Judas was killed in the sixth year after the death of his father Mattathias.

3530. After the death of Judas, wicked men, who previously had stayed out of sight for fear of Judas, appeared all over Israel. There was a severe famine in those days, which caused the whole country to side with them and submit to Bacchides, in order to have access to more provisions. Bacchides promoted these wicked men to the position of rulers in the land. When they found any of Judas' friends, they brought them to Bacchides to be tormented and reviled, so that there was great affliction in Israel. There had been nothing like this since the time of the last prophets of the Old Testament. {Apc 1Ma 9:23-27}

3531. In the meantime, the envoys who had been sent to Rome by Judas Maccabeus concluded a peace and an association with the people of Rome. The articles were written in tables of brass and said that the Jews should assist the Romans, and the Romans the Jews, against the common enemy. The Senate also wrote letters to King Demetrius, advising him to stop oppressing the Jews, or else they would wage war with him both by sea and on land to support this people, who were now their friends and confederates. {Apc 1Ma 8:19-32} Justin stated: {Justin, Trogus, l. 36. c. 3.}

> "When they had revolted from Demetrius (having procured an alliance with the Romans), they were the first among all the eastern people to obtain their liberty. At that time, the Romans were very free in giving away what was not their own."

3532. Josephus noted that this was the first league ever known to exist between the Romans and the Jews. {*Josephus, Antiq., l. 12. c. 10. s. 6. (419) 7:219} It was written differently, with the following forged subscription appended.

> "This decree of the Senate was written by Eupolemus, son of John, and Jason, son of Eleazar (the Jewish agents): *when Judas was high priest and his brother Simon was the general.*"

3533. Jonathan was the most likely one to have been the general while Judas was alive. It was not until Jonathan died that Simon became the general. A little earlier, Josephus incorrectly wrote that when Alcimus died, the people voted Judas to be the next high priest. {Apc 1Ma 9:54-56} That was incorrect, because this passage shows that Alcimus died after Judas, and Josephus later admitted his error, saying that Jacimus or Alcimus had no successor at all and Jerusalem had no high priest for seven whole years. {*Josephus, Antiq., l. 20. c. 10. s. 3. (235) 10:125}

3534. There was a long and acrimonious debate in the Senate between the envoys of both the Ptolemys. Titus and Gnaeus, who had been sent as envoys by the Romans, testified on Euergetes' behalf and promoted his cause. [K68] The Senate ordered that Menyllus, Philometor's envoy, should leave Rome within five days and the league between them and Philometor was void. The Senate sent Publius Apustius and Gaius Lentulus as envoys to Euergetes. [E458] They went to Cyrene at once and with great care informed him of what had been done. This inflated his hopes so that he soon levied an army and plotted how to take over Cyprus. {*Polybius, l. 31. c. 20. 6:201,203}

### 3843d AM, 4553 JP, 161 BC

3535. All Judas Maccabeus' friends met and chose Jonathan as the general in his place. He was the brother of Judas and was surnamed Apphus. As soon as Bacchides heard this, he planned to kill him. Jonathan, his brother Simon, and the men who were with him found out about this. To thwart him, they fled into the desert of Tekoa and camped by the pool of Asphar. Jonathan sent his brother John, surnamed Gaddis, with a band of soldiers, to ask the Nabatean Arabs to leave their wagons with them, for they had many wagons.

However, the children of Jambri from Medeba met them on the way and attacked and killed John and his company. They seized the spoil and went on their way, but their victory was short lived. Jonathan and his brother Simon heard that these sons of Jambri were having a large wedding and were bringing the bride from Nadabatha with great pomp and a long train of nobles, as she was the daughter of a prince in Canaan. They attacked them from an ambush and killed four hundred, while the rest fled to the mountains. They seized all their spoil and marched back to the marshes of Jordan, having now fully avenged the blood of their brother. {*Apc 1Ma 9:28-42} {*Josephus, Antiq., l. 13. c. 1. s. 1-4. (1-21) 7:229-237}

3536. Bacchides followed Jonathan closely and on the Sabbath day came to the banks of the Jordan River with a large army. The two armies met in battle and Jonathan tried to kill Bacchides, but he deflected the blow. However, a thousand of Bacchides' men were killed, although Josephus said two thousand. Jonathan knew he could not cope with such a large force, so he and his men leaped into the Jordan River and crossed over to the other side, and the enemy did not attempt to follow him. Bacchides returned to Jerusalem and built fortified cities in Judea and citadels in Jericho, Emmaus, Bethhoron, Bethel, Thamnatha, Pharathoni and Taphon. He strengthened them with high walls, gates and bars and put garrisons in all of them, then used these places as bases from which to attack and annoy the Jews. He fortified Bethsura, Gazara and the tower at Jerusalem, and supplied them with men and provisions. He seized the sons of the country's chief men as hostages and imprisoned them in the tower at Jerusalem. {Apc 1Ma 9:43-53} {*Josephus, Antiq., l. 13. c. 1. s. 5. (22-25) 7:235,237}

3537. Mithrobuzanes, one of the sons of Zadriades, king of Lesser Armenia, had escaped to Ariarathes, king of Cappadocia. Artaxias, the king of Greater Armenia, who had been conquered by Antiochus Epiphanes, wanted his old kingdom back, so he sent an embassy to Ariarathes and asked him to side with him. They would murder one of the two brothers whom he had under his power at that time and Artaxias would divide Sophene between himself and Ariarathes. Ariarathes detested this treachery and sharply rebuked the envoys. [K69] He sent letters to Artaxias, admonishing him not to do such a wicked act. As well as that, he restored Mithrobuzanes to his father's kingdom. {*Diod. Sic., l. 31. c. 21,22. 11:369,371}

### 3844a AM, 4553 JP, 161 BC

3538. Ariarathes very royally received the Roman envoys, Tiberius Gracchus, Lucius Lentulus and Servilius Glaucius, in Cappadocia. Demetrius Soter sent Menocharis there, so that he could seriously debate with the Roman envoys about the settling of his kingdom. {*Polybius, l. 31. c. 32,33. 6:229} He also offered King Ariarathes a marriage with his sister, who was related to Perseus, king of the Macedonians, but he declined, for fear of offending the Romans. {*Diod. Sic., l. 31. c. 28. 11:389,391} {Justin, Trogus, l. 35. c. 1.}

### 3844b AM, 4554 JP, 160 BC

3539. Menocharis returned to Demetrius at Antioch and gave an account of his conferences with the Roman envoys. The king, deeming it very necessary in his present situation to gain the favour of the Roman envoys, set aside all other matters and sent an embassy to them, first into Pamphylia, then again to Rhodes. He said he would do whatever he could for the Romans if they would only confirm his title as king. Tiberius favoured him and helped him considerably to obtain the legal right to his kingdom. {*Polybius, l. 31. c. 33. 6:229,231}

3540. Leptines, who had stabbed Gnaeus Octavius, the Roman envoy, at Laodicea, went to King Demetrius and told him not to be troubled by the death of Gnaeus, nor to act harshly toward the Laodiceans because of this. He planned to go to Rome and state before the Senate that he had done this act and that the gods approved of it. He went cheerfully, of his own accord, and was conveyed from there to Rome without any guard or bonds. As for Isocrates, the grammarian, who had got himself into trouble with his vicious tongue, he went completely mad when he realised the trouble he was in. [E459] When he saw the irons being put about his neck and the shackles on his hands, he totally neglected his personal duties, including his appearance and clothes. {*Polybius, l. 32. c. 3. 6:235,237}

### 3844c AM, 4554 JP, 160 BC

3541. In the 153rd year of the kingdom of the Greeks, in the second month, Alcimus commanded the wall of the inner court to be pulled down. This wall divided the court of the people from that of the Gentiles and had been built by Zerubbabel and the prophets. However, God shut the mouth of this profane high priest by striking him with a sudden palsy. He could not speak another word or give any orders concerning his own house. He died in great torment in the third year after having usurped the high priesthood. {Apc 1Ma 9:54-56} Josephus said in one place that he was high priest for four years, but later said it was only three years. {*Josephus, Antiq., l. 12. c. 10. s. 6. (413) 7:215} {*Josephus, Antiq., l. 20. c. 10. s. 3. (237) 10:127} He added that after Alcimus' death, Jerusalem went seven whole years without a high priest. Seven years and five months elapsed between the second month of the 153rd year, in which Alcimus died, and the seventh month of the 160th year, when Jonathan became the high priest. {Apc 1Ma 10:21}

*3542.* When Alcimus died, Bacchides returned to King Demetrius and Judea had two years of peace. {*Apc 1 Ma 9:57*}

## 3845a AM, 4554 JP, 160 BC

*3543.* About the 155th Olympiad, envoys came to Rome from Ariarathes, the king of Cappadocia, with a crown valued at ten thousand pieces of gold. *[K70]* They told the Senate how their king had graciously received Tiberius Gracchus and that on their account he had refused any alliance with Demetrius and the offer of marriage with his sister. They added that he was most willing to serve the Romans in whatever they wanted him to do. When Tiberius Gracchus and the rest of the envoys confirmed this as to be true, the Senate accepted the crown and received it as a great favour. The Senate gave them a staff and an ivory seat which the Romans highly esteemed. These envoys had been sent to the Senate by Ariarathes immediately before the beginning of winter. {*\*Polybius, l. 30. c. 32. 6:229*} {*\*Polybius, l. 31. c. 1. s. 1,2. 6:233*} {*\*Diod. Sic., l. 31. c. 28. 11:391*}

## 3845b AM, 4555 JP, 159 BC

*3544.* When the new consuls, Gnaeus Cornelius Dolabella and Marcus Fulvius Nobilior, assumed office, a joint embassy arrived from Prusias, the king of Bithynia, and the Galatians and complained to the Senate against Eumenes, the king of Pergamum. Attalus, who had been sent there by his brother, Eumenes, to plead his cause, was also heard. He was completely cleared of all the accusations and a great deal of honour bestowed on him. He was received and dismissed with great courtesy, for although the hearts of the senators were opposed to King Eumenes, whom they hated, they really liked Attalus. They hoped he would take over the kingdom from his brother and so they treated him royally. {*\*Polybius, l. 30. c. 32. 6:332*} {*\*Polybius, l. 31. c. 1. 6:233*}

## 3845c AM, 4555 JP, 159 BC

*3545.* Menocharis and other envoys came to Rome from Demetrius Soter, the king of Syria. They brought a crown worth ten thousand pieces of gold as a present, sent by the king as a token of his gratitude for the kind treatment he had received while he was a hostage at Rome. They turned over Leptines, who had killed Gnaeus Octavius, the envoy, and Isocrates, the grammarian, who had publicly defended the murder. Isocrates presented a strange spectacle to everyone. His face looked frightful, and as fierce as the face of any man must of necessity look who, in the space of a whole year, had neither washed, nor trimmed his nails or cut his hair. The movement of his eyes showed that he was mad. Any who had met him by chance, would have preferred the attack of a wild beast instead. Leptines, on the other hand, was totally unaffected and ready to come into the Senate at any time. He freely confessed the murder to anyone who talked with him. He was confident the Romans would not harm him, and he was right. The senators had debated about this for a long time. At length, the Senate heard the envoys and received the crown from them. The senators made no mention of these two men, as if this was a fault chargeable to all the Syrians. It was the policy of the Senate to keep this matter to themselves, so that they might avenge this crime as often as they pleased. They replied to Demetrius that the Senate was ready to be friendly to him, provided he became their tributary again, as before. {*\*Polybius, l. 31. c. 2,3. 6:235-239*} {*\*Diod. Sic., l. 31. c. 29,30. 11:391*} {*\*Appian, Syrian Wars, l. 11. c. 8. (47) 2:195*}

*3546.* Orophernes, or Holophernes, spoke to Demetrius Soter, the king of Syria, and complained that Ariarathes, his younger brother, had driven him out of the kingdom of Cappadocia. *[E460]* Although Ariarathes was not the lawful heir, he had either been put in by Queen Antiochis or adopted by her, as Zonaras related from Dio, as we said before and which we quoted previously from Diodorus. {*See note on 3832 AM. <<3229>>*} Demetrius still bore a grudge against Ariarathes for having slighted the offer of his sister in marriage, so he agreed to the request and gave Oropherenes a thousand talents to help dethrone Ariarathes. *[K71]* This was over and above the help he had received from Eumenes, the king of Pergamum. {*\*Polybius, l. 3. c. 5. s. 1,2. 2:13*} {*\*Livy, l. 47. 14:13*} {*Justin, Trogus, l. 35. c. 1.*} {*\*Appian, Syrian Wars, l. 11. c. 8. (47) 2:195*} {*\*Dio, l. 20. 2:359 (Zonaras, l. 9. c. 24.)*}

*3547.* When Eumenes, the king of Pergamum, was on his deathbed, he bequeathed his wife Stratonice, the sister of Ariarathes, who had recently lost his kingdom, to his brother Attalus. {*\*Plutarch, Sayings of Kings and Commanders (184b) 3:83*} Eumenes reigned for thirty-eight years. If we subtract the years, as computed by Strabo, of the reigns of his brother and son, who succeeded him from the interval inserted in the Roman history between his becoming king and the time when Pergamum ceased to be a kingdom, more than thirty-eight years elapsed. Therefore, Eumenes died in the very beginning of the thirty-ninth year. However, Strabo incorrectly stated that he reigned forty-nine years. He left Attalus Philometor, whom his wife Stratonice had borne to him, to inherit the kingdom after him. However, since his son was so young, he appointed his brother Attalus Philadelphus as guardian over him and the kingdom, and he managed its affairs for twenty-one years. {*\*Strabo, l. 13. c. 4. s. 2. 6:167*}

## 3846a AM, 4555 JP, 159 BC

*3548.* In the morning at about sunrise on the first day of the Egyptian Additionals, or September 27, in the 20th year of the Calippic Period, Hipparchus made a second observation of the autumnal equinox. {*Ptolemy, Great Syntaxis, l. 3. c. 2.*}

3549. After Orophernes had expelled his brother Ariarathes, it was necessary for him to manage things with great prudence and ingratiate himself into the people's hearts by acts of forbearance and graciousness. This he did not do, but tried to get as much money together as he could, at the same time most wickedly killing many people. He gave fifty talents to Timothy, whom he later sent to Rome as an envoy. He gave Demetrius seventy and promised to pay another six hundred talents soon, along with another four hundred later. When he realised that he was hated by the Cappadocians, he started to plunder all the people and take the wealth of the nobility into his treasury. {*Diod. Sic., l. 31. c. 32. 11:393*}

3550. Orophernes had been educated in Ionia. {*See note on 3832 AM. <<3229>>*} He had little regard for the traditional customs of his country and introduced: {*Polybius, l. 32. c. 11. s. 10. 6:253*} {*Athenaeus, l. 10. (440b) 4:493*}

"The refined debauchery of Ionia."

3551. After amassing a vast sum of money, he deposited four hundred talents with the Prienians, in case events should turn against him. They later faithfully returned the money to him. {*Polybius, l. 33. c. 6. 6:269*} {*Diod. Sic., l. 31. c. 32. 11:393,395*}

## 3846c AM, 4556 JP, 158 BC

3552. After Jonathan and his company had lived in peace for two years, some lying Jews suggested to Bacchides that there was a good chance of taking them all by surprise in one night. Therefore, Bacchides approached them with a large force and secretly sent letters to all his friends in Judea, asking for help with his plan of capturing Jonathan and his company. However, their plot was discovered by Jonathan and his men, who seized and executed the fifty men in the country who were involved in this plot. {*Apc 1Ma 9:57-61*}

3553. Then Jonathan and Simon and the men with him moved to Bethbasi (or Bethlagan, as Josephus wrote), situated in the wilderness. They repaired its walls, which were in ruins, and fortified it. As soon as Bacchides heard about this, he mustered up all his forces and summoned his adherents in Judea to come join him. [K72] Then, he went and laid siege to Bethbasi, fighting against it for many days with his engines of war. Meanwhile Jonathan left his brother Simon in the city and crossed the country with a small troop. He killed Odoarkes, or Odomera, and his brethren, and the sons of Phasiron, in their tents. When he began to kill all he met and break into the enemy forces, Simon and his company sallied forth from

the city and burned the engines. Defeated in this fight and enraged to see his plans thwarted, Bacchides directed his anger against the wicked wretches who were the cause of this expedition and killed many of them. When Jonathan learned that he planned to return into his own land, he sent envoys to him to negotiate with him about making a peace and to ask him to return the prisoners he had taken from Judea. Bacchides very readily agreed to the proposal and said he would do nothing against Jonathan all the days of his life. Therefore he returned to his own land and never again entered Judea with an army and so the wars ended in Israel. [E461] Jonathan lived in Michmash, in the tribe of Benjamin, and began to judge his people and uproot the wicked from the land. {*Apc 1Ma 9:62-73*}

## 3847a AM, 4556 JP, 158 BC

3554. Hipparchus made a third observation of the autumnal equinox in the 21st year of the Calippic Period, about noon on the first day of the Egyptian Additionals, on September 27. {*Ptolemy, Great Syntaxis, l. 3. c. 2.*}

## 3847b AM, 4557 JP, 157 BC

3555. When Ariarathes was deprived of his kingdom, he came to Rome as a humble suppliant and sought the help of the consul, Sextus Julius Caesar. His clothes showed the great distress he was in. Demetrius sent an embassy under Miltiades, who came to oppose Ariarathes' accusations against Demetrius and to bring charges against Ariarathes. Orophernes also sent his envoys, Timothy and Diogenes, to present a crown at Rome and to renew their alliance and association. Their main purpose was to justify and defend Orophernes' actions and to accuse Ariarathes. Diogenes and Miltiades had the upper hand in the private conferences. They were bold and told whatever lies suited them, so they prevailed over Ariarathes. When the matter was discussed publicly, they dared to contradict him and said whatever they liked, whether it was true or not, because there was no one there to refute what they said. {*Polybius, l. 32. c. 10. 6:249,251*} Finally, the Senate decreed that since Ariarathes was a friend and associate of the people of Rome, he and Orophernes should reign together as brothers and partners in the kingdom. {*Appian, Syrian Wars, l. 11. c. 8. (47) 2:195*} {*Dio, l. 20. 2:359 (Zonaras, l. 9. c. 24.)*}

3556. Ptolemy Euergetes tried to capture Cyprus and was defeated there in a battle with his brother Philometor. Philometor besieged him in the city of Lapithus until the city was in dire straits. When Philometor captured him, he spared him because he was his brother and was of a mild disposition. He also feared the Romans. He forgave him, entered into a covenant with him and gave him back the rule of the Cyrenians. Instead of Cyprus, he gave him some cities with an annual allowance of grain. He also promised to give him his own daughter. *[K73]* Thus, after many hard feelings, this war between the two brothers was quickly settled in a peaceful manner. {*Polybius, l. 33. c. 11. s. 6. 6:277,279} {*Polybius, l. 39. c. 7. s. 5-7. 6:451} {*Dio, l. 20. 2:361 (Zonaras, l. 9. c. 25.)} {*Diod. Sic., l. 31. c. 33. 11:397} {*Livy, l. 47. 14:13}

*3557.* When Orophernes realised that the Romans had taken away what he had formerly enjoyed, he resolved to pay his mercenary soldiers as soon as possible, because he feared that they might rebel for want of pay. Since he was short of money, he pillaged the temple of Zeus located at the foot of Mount Ariadne, which, up until that time, had never been touched. From the plunder, he was able to pay his soldiers what he owed them. {*Diod. Sic., l. 31. c. 34. 11:397,399}

*3558.* Attalus, Eumenes' brother and successor in the kingdom of Pergamum, drove Orophernes and Demetrius Soter from Cappadocia and restored Ariarathes to the throne. {*Polybius, l. 32. c. 12. 6:253} {*Dio, l. 20. 2:359 (Zonaras, l. 9. c. 24.)}

*3559.* Demetrius Soter offered Archias five hundred talents in return for betraying Cyprus to him, also promising him other rewards and honours, provided he would help him. As Archias was going about this task, he was apprehended by Ptolemy Philometor. When he was questioned about what he was doing, he hung himself with the rope of the curtain which was drawn before the hall. {*Polybius, l. 33. c. 5. 6:267,269} {Suidas, Ρρστεινειν, Ρρσσαγγελια}

*3560.* After Ariarathes had been restored to the kingdom of Cappadocia, he demanded that the Prienians pay the four hundred talents which Orophernes had deposited with them. They replied honestly that as long as Orophernes was alive, they would not give the money to anybody but the one who had entrusted it to them. Consequently, Ariarathes sent troops to pillage the country and Attalus helped him. Indeed, Attalus instigated this, since there was a private grudge between him and the Prienians. There was a large slaughter of men and beasts and some were killed at the very gates of the city. However, the Prienians could not defeat them, so they sent their envoys to the Rhodians and finally asked the Romans for protection, but Ariarathes did not regard all this news seriously. The Prienians had faithfully restored to Orophernes the money that he had deposited with them, for which act Ariarathes imposed a large fine on them and without just cause afflicted them with extremely oppressive miseries. {*Polybius, l. 33. c. 6. 6:269,271} *[E462]*

## 3848 AM, 4558 JP, 156 BC

*3561.* When Prusias Venator, the king of Bithynia, had some differences with Attalus, Attalus sent Andronicus, Prusias Nicomedes and Antiphilus as envoys to Rome. As a result, the Senate sent Publius Lentulus to find out what was happening. When Andronicus had arrived before from Attalus, he began to charge Prusias with having been the first to invade but the Romans were not impressed with what he said. Prusias' envoys had protested that no such thing had happened, which made the Senate give less credit to what was being alleged against Prusias. After a more detailed enquiry into the business, the Senate was uncertain about how well they could trust these envoys. They sent two more envoys of their own, Lucius Apuleius and Gaius Petronius, to see how matters stood between these two kings. {*Polybius, l. 32. c. 16. 6:259,261}

## 3849a AM, 4558 JP, 156 BC

*3562.* When Prusias had defeated Attalus, he entered Pergamum and having made expensive sacrifices, he went into the temple of Asclepias. *[K74]* As soon as he had concluded his offerings, he returned to the camp. The next day, unable to capture Attalus, he brought his forces to Nicephorium, which was near the walls of Pergamum. He began to pillage all the temples and rifled and ransacked the images and statues of the gods. In the end, even the image of Asclepias, to whom he had offered so many vows and sacrifices on the previous day, was not spared. It was an excellent piece made by Philomachus, or Phyromachus, and Prusias had his soldiers carry it away. From there, he marched with his army to Elaea and tried to besiege the city. He saw that this was not going to be successful because Sosander, the foster brother of Attalus, was in the city with a strong garrison and drove him off. He went away by ship to Thyatira and on the way sacked the temple of Artemis, or Diana, at Hiera Come. The temple of Apollo Cynnius at Temnus was also sacked and burned to the ground. When he had done this, he returned home, having lost most of his foot soldiers to famine and dysentery. He had no better luck with his fleet. A violent storm at Propontis wrecked most of his ships and most of the soldiers and mariners drowned, while the rest were cast ashore. {*Polybius, l. 32. c. 16. 6:257,259} {*Diod. Sic., l. 31. c. 35. 11:399} {Suidas, Προυιας}

*3563.* After Attalus had been beaten by Prusias, he sent his brother Athenaeus along with Publius Lentulus, to tell the Senate what had happened to him. {*Polybius, l. 33. c. 1. 6:263}

## 3849b AM, 4559 JP, 155 BC

*3564.* When these two had told the Senate what Prusias had been up to, the senators immediately ordered that

Gaius Claudius Cento, Lucius Hortensius and Gaius Aurunculius should go as envoys with Lentulus. They were to order Prusias to stop his hostilities against Attalus. {*Polybius, l. 33. c. 1. 6:263}

3565. When Publius Scipio and Marcus Marcellus were consuls, the Athenians sent three of the most famous philosophers of that age as envoys to the Senate and people of Rome. Carneades, an academic from Cyrene, Diogenes, the Stoic from Babylon, and Critolaus, the Peripatetic, were sent to obtain a release from the fine of five hundred talents. This had been the judgment against the Sicyonians and had been ordered by the Senate for their devastation of Oropus. When the envoys were brought into the Senate, they used Caecilius, or Gaius Acilius, a senator, as their interpreter, even though each of them had previously shown their abilities and discoursed in a large assembly of people. At the time, Rutilius and Polybius stated that it was admirable to hear the eloquence of these three philosophers as they spoke. Carneades was hot and fiery, Critolaus was witty and smooth and Diogenes grave and sober in his style. Clitomachus, in his history written in Greek, related how Carneades, for whom Clitomachus was the speaker, and Diogenes, the Stoic, had stood before the Senate in the Capitol. Antony Albinus, who was then the praetor, had said in jest to Carneades:

> "In your view, oh Carneades, I am not a real praetor [because I am not a wise man], nor is this a real city, nor its state a real state."

3566. He replied to the praetor:

> "In the view of our Stoic friend here you are not."

3567. (The humour in this requires an understanding of Stoic philosophy. Editor.) As soon as Carneades had finished speaking, Cato the Censor thought it best to send these envoys away at once, because while he argued, the truth could not easily be discerned. The fame of these philosophers spread all over the city and the Roman youth set aside all other pleasures and delights and followed after philosophy as if they were mad. [K75] Cato feared that the youth would pursue all their studies in this area and prize the glory of eloquence more than that of action and martial discipline. He moved that all philosophers should be sent out of the city in a civil manner. When he came into the Senate, he rebuked the senators for having allowed these envoys, who were able to persuade them of whatever they pleased, to stay so long among them without being given an answer. [E463] Therefore, he also advised that they should, without further delay, end the matter and decree something concerning the embassy, so that they could send them

home to argue among their young Greeks, rather than spoil the youth of Rome. These were to be ordered strictly to obey the laws and magistrates, as in former times. {*Cicero, Academica, l. 2. c. 45. 19:645} {*Cicero, Tusculan Disputations, l. 4. c. 3. 18:333,335} {*Cicero, De Oratore, l. 2. c. 37. (155,156) 3:311} {*Pliny, l. 7. c. 30. 2:579,581} {*Plutarch, Cato Major, l. 1. c. 22. 2:369,371} {*Aulus Gellius, Attic Nights, l. 7. c. 14. s. 1-9. 2:127-131} {Macrobius, Saturnalia, l. 1. c. 5.}

# 3850 AM, 4560 JP, 154 BC

3568. At the same time that the Senate sent Quintus Opimius, the consul, to wage war with the Oxybians of Liguria, the younger Ptolemy Euergetes came to Rome. {*Polybius, l. 33. c. 9. s. 8. 6:273} No sooner had he entered the Senate than he accused his brother Philometor of having set an ambush for him, showing them the scars from the wounds he had received. He tried to use inflammatory language to stir up the people and so create sympathy for himself. The elder Ptolemy had sent Neolaides and Andromachus as envoys to answer the charges made by his brother. The Senate, however, because they seemed to believe the claims of the other brother, would not allow them to speak, but ordered them to leave Rome at once. Five envoys were selected, headed by Gnaeus Merula and Lucius Thermus, and each was assigned a ship of five tiers of oars. Their commission was to escort the younger Ptolemy and give him Cyprus. The Senate also wrote to their allies in Greece and Asia requesting them to help Ptolemy recover Cyprus. {*Polybius, l. 33. c. 11. 6:277,279}

3569. When the envoys from Rome met with Prusias, they forbade him in the Senate's name to take any further hostile action against Attalus, an ally and confederate of the Romans. They charged him strictly either to submit to the Senate's decree or to come to the borders with a thousand cavalry and there to argue the case with Attalus, who was coming there with the same number. Prusias saw Attalus' small retinue and hoped to surprise him. He sent his envoys a little ahead, as if intending to follow after with his thousand men. However, he drew up his whole army as if he had come to fight, and not to talk. Attalus and the Roman envoys were warned and hurried away. Prusias, however, seized the Roman wagons, took Nicephorium and demolished it. He burned the temples within the city and forced Attalus and the Roman envoys to flee to Pergamum for refuge, which he then besieged. {*Appian, Mithridatic Wars, l. 12. c. 1. (3) 2:243,245}

3570. When Hortensius and Aurunculius returned to Rome from Pergamum, they declared with what great contempt Prusias had received the injunctions of the Senate. In violation of the league between them, he had used every violence against them and Attalus, after he had besieged them in Pergamum. The senators were so highly incensed and moved by this affront, that they decreed that ten envoys should be sent at once, among whom were Lucius Anicius, Gaius Fannius and Quintus Fabius Maximus. These were ordered to end the war and to compel Prusias to make reparation to Attalus for the damages he had sustained in this war. {*Polybius, l. 33. c. 7. 6:271} [K76]

3571. While it was still winter, Attalus gathered a large army. Ariarathes and Mithridates, his confederates, had sent both foot soldiers and cavalry under the command of Demetrius, Ariarathes' son. While Attalus was preparing for war, the Roman envoys met him at Cadi. After they had talked with him, they went directly to Prusias. As soon as they arrived there, they told him he had displeased the Senate greatly. Prusias promised he would do some of the things the Senate required of him, but rejected most of them. Whereupon the Roman envoys, whom he had offended greatly by his obstinacy, renounced the friendship and alliance which had formerly existed between them. They all left him and journeyed to Attalus. Prusias meanwhile regretted what he had done and went after the envoys, begging and beseeching them for a long time. When he saw that it was all to no avail, he let them go and returned home. He did not know what to do. In the meantime, the Romans advised Attalus to keep his army within the boundaries of his kingdom and not commit any acts of hostility against anyone. He should secure his own cities and villages against invasion. Then the envoys went their separate ways. While some went to Rome to tell the Senate of King Prusias' impertinence, others went into the country of Ionia and still others to the Hellespont and into adjacent lands to Byzantium. All of them went with the intention of making the rulers break their alliance with Prusias and join Attalus, to help him in whatever way they could. {*Polybius, l. 33. c. 12. 6:279,281}

3572. Soon after this, Attalus' brother Athenaeus came with a large fleet of eighty decked ships. Five of them, which had been used in the war in Crete, came from the Rhodians. [E464] Twenty came from the Cyzicenians, twenty-seven from Attalus, while the rest were from his confederates. He sailed directly to the Hellespont. When he sailed past any cities that were under Prusias' command, he went ashore and wasted their surrounding countryside. {*Polybius, l. 33. c. 13. s. 1-3. 6:281}

3573. As soon as the Senate had heard the envoys who had returned from Prusias, they sent three others, Appius Claudius, Lucius Oppius and Aulus Postumius. When these arrived in Asia, they concluded the war and prevailed with both the kings to agree on these conditions:

"Prusias would immediately give Attalus twenty decked ships. He would pay him five hundred talents over twenty years. Each was to keep what had belonged to him before the start of the war. Moreover, Prusias was to make good the damage he had done to the countries of Methymna, Aegae, Cyme and Heraclea and to pay them a hundred talents."

3574. After both parties had signed the covenants, Attalus returned home with all the forces he had brought by sea or land. {*Polybius, l. 33. c. 13. s. 4-10. 6:281,283} When Prusias saw how his subjects hated him for his tyranny and how his son Nicomedes was loved by them, he grew jealous of his son and sent him away to Rome to live. {*Appian, Mithridatic Wars, l. 12. c. 1. (4) 2:245}

3575. When Antioch revolted from Demetrius Soter, Orophernes entered into a league with them and plotted to dethrone him. Demetrius had recently been restored to his kingdom and had not fully established himself. When Demetrius learned about his plans, he spared his life because he did not want Ariarathes to be saved from the fear of war at the hands of his brother. [K77] However, he seized him and commanded him to be kept as a prisoner at Seleucia. The people of Antioch were not put off by the discovery of the plot, but applied themselves all the more to their plan. They allied themselves with Ptolemy, king of Egypt, Attalus, king of Asia and Ariarathes of Cappadocia, who was attacked by Demetrius. The men of Antioch bribed a certain obscure youth, a foreigner, who was to lay claim to the kingdom of Syria as being his father's kingdom, and to try to recover it by force. So that the affront would be complete, they called him Alexander and said that he was a son of King Antiochus. Such was the universal hatred of Demetrius, that the strength and power befitting a king, as well as the royal extraction, was conferred on his rival with everyone's consent. {Justin, Trogus, l. 35. c. 1.}

3576. Livy said about this Alexander: {*Livy, l. 52. 14:43}

"He was an obscure person, whose descent was not very well known."

3577. Athenaeus stated: {*Athenaeus, l. 5. (211a) 2:453,455}

"He was the supposed son of Antiochus Epiphanes."

3578. Appian said: {*Appian, Syrian Wars, l. 11. c. 11. (67) 2:233}

"He was a person who added himself into the family of those who were descended from Seleucus."

3579. Sulpicius Severus stated: {*Sulpicius Severus, Sacred History, l. 2. c. 24. 11:109}

"He was a youth raised at Rhodes, who falsely bragged about himself as being the son of Antiochus."

*3580.* Strabo surnamed him Balas, and Josephus, Balles. {*Strabo, l. 16. c. 2. s. 8. 7:247*} {*Josephus, Antiq., l. 13. c. 4. s. 8. (119) 7:285*} (The Loeb edition does not have the spelling variation of Balles. Editor.)

*3581.* In the middle of the summer, Heraclides, whom Antiochus Epiphanes had formerly appointed over the treasury at Babylon, brought Alexander Balas, the pretended son of Antiochus Epiphanes, with him to Rome along with Laodice, the daughter of Antiochus Epiphanes. While Heraclides stayed at Rome, he wore the clothes of some great person and conducted himself very craftily, purposely stretching out the time, in the hope of influencing the Senate to favour his plans. {*Polybius, l. 33. c. 15. 6:283*}

### 3851a AM, 4560 JP, 154 BC

*3582.* While Attalus, the son of King Eumenes (in whose name his uncle Attalus was governing the kingdom of Pergamum), was still a child, he came to Rome to ingratiate himself with the Senate and renew the friendship and right of hospitality that had formerly existed between his father and the people of Rome. He was treated with most extraordinary civility by the Senate. His father's friends received an answer according to their wishes. After being shown suitable honours for a child of his age, he left Rome within a few days for the return journey. All the cities of Greece through which he passed gave him a cordial and generous reception. {*Polybius, l. 33. c. 18. s. 1-4. 6:287*}

*3583.* Demetrius, later called Nicator, son of the then reigning Demetrius Soter in Syria, was in Rome at the same time. His reception was ordinary, since he was a child, and he did not stay long. {*Polybius, l. 33. c. 18. s. 5. 6:2897,289*}

### 3851b AM, 4561 JP, 153 BC

*3584.* Heraclides stayed a long time in Rome and came into the Senate with Laodice and Alexander Balas. First, the youngster made a short speech in which he asked the Romans kindly to remember that friendship and alliance which had formerly been in place between them and his father Antiochus, and that they would consequently help him recover his kingdom. Failing that, he sought permission to return to Syria and asked that they would not oppose any of those who were ready to help him regain his father's kingdom. *[E465]* Heraclides spoke next. After he had extolled the merits of Antiochus for a long time, he condemned Demetrius (Soter). He concluded that it was right and just to grant the youth (Alexander) and Laodice, who were the lawful seed of King Antiochus, permission to return to their country. Very little, if anything, of what he said was liked by the sober-minded senators, who thought that everything he had said was fiction.

*[K78]* They utterly detested Heraclides. The least of the senators, whom Heraclides had made his friends by means of his deceptions, all agreed that a decree of the Senate should be made to this end:

> "The Senate had given to Alexander and Laodice, children of a king who had been a friend and an associate of the people of Rome, permission to return to their father's kingdom by right of former inheritance and to assist them, according to their decrees."

*3585.* After this, Heraclides soon hired soldiers and drew a very large number of persons to his side. He came to Ephesus, where he began to prepare in earnest for the war which he had planned so long for. {*Polybius, l. 33. c. 18. s. 6-14. 6:289*}

### 3851c AM, 4561 JP, 153 BC

*3586.* In the 160th year of the kingdom of the Greeks, Alexander Balas, who was pretending to be the son of Antiochus Epiphanes, captured Ptolemais, a city of Phoenicia, which was betrayed to him by the soldiers who were garrisoned there. {*Apc 1Ma 10:1*} {*Josephus, Antiq., l. 13. c. 2. s. 1. (35) 7:243*} They detested Demetrius' behaviour, because he was of a harsh disposition and very insolent. He secluded himself in the royal palace with four towers which he had built not far from Antioch, and allowed no one to see him. He did not care about public matters, but trifled his time away in idleness. {*Josephus, Antiq., l. 13. c. 2. s. 1. (35,36) 7:243,245*}

*3587.* When Demetrius Soter heard that Alexander had been received into Ptolemais and had begun to reign there, he mustered together a very large force and planned to march against him and fight with him. {*Apc 1Ma 10:1,2*} After considering the hazards of the war, Demetrius sent two of his sons, Demetrius Nicator and Antiochus Sideres, who were later kings of Syria, to his army at Cnidos with a large amount of gold. This was to protect them, should the war turn out badly, in which case, they would be alive to avenge their father's quarrel. {*Livy, l. 52. 14:43*} {*Justin, Trogus, l. 35. c. 2.*}

*3588.* Demetrius wrote letters to Jonathan, renewing peace with him and giving him authority to levy forces and to provide arms to help him in the war against Alexander. He ordered that the hostages who were being kept in the citadel, be released. When Jonathan read the letters publicly at Jerusalem, those who held the citadel became fearful and turned the hostages over to him, and he then gave them to their parents. {*Apc 1Ma 10:3-9*}

### 3851d AM, 4561 JP, 153 BC

*3589.* Jonathan wisely made good use of this opportunity and began to repair Jerusalem. He took care to build up the walls and Mount Zion all around and surround Mount Zion with square stones to fortify it. The foreigners who were in the citadels that Bacchides had built left their strongholds and hurried away to their own land. Only some of the apostates and deserters of the law were left who used Bethsura as their place of refuge. {Apc 1Ma 10:10-14}

3590. When Alexander had, in the meantime, heard of the good promises which Demetrius had made to Jonathan through his letters, he also sent letters courting his friendship and association. He ordained him as the high priest of that country and honoured him with the title of being called the king's friend, sending him a purple robe and a crown of gold. {Apc 1Ma 10:15-20}

### 3852a AM, 4561 JP, 153 BC

3591. Jonathan assumed the high priesthood in the seventh month of the 160th year of the kingdom of the Greeks at the Feast of Tabernacles. {Apc 1Ma 10:21} This was the ninth, not the fourth, year (as Josephus stated) after the death of his brother Judas. {*Josephus, Antiq., l. 13. c. 2. s. 3. (46) 7:249} [K79] For by Josephus' account, Judas did not die before the 164th year of the Greeks. This contradicted the history of the Maccabees. {Apc 1Ma 9:3,18,54} This error generated another, in that Judas supposedly succeeded Alcimus in the high priesthood. We have shown previously that this was wrong, and it was later acknowledged by Josephus also. He clearly stated later that no one succeeded Jacimus, or Alcimus, but that the city was without a high priest for seven whole years. {*Josephus, Antiq., l. 20. c. 10. s. 3. (237) 10:127} After seven years and five months had expired, Jonathan now assumed the office of the high priesthood. He was the first of the Asmoneans who descended from Jehoiarib, who was of the priestly line, to hold the office of the high priest. He was not descended from Jaddua, the high priest, whose heir, Onias, was living in Egypt with Ptolemy Philometor at this time.

3592. Demetrius Soter was grieved that the Jews were inclined to side with Alexander. He hoped to win them over by forgiving the arrears of tribute and all the tribute by which the Macedonians had previously so miserably oppressed that country. He made generous promises of other honourable concessions, but Jonathan and the Jewish people were not greatly influenced by this. [E466] They knew that this offer came from a man who, by his former actions, had clearly shown his hatred of them. They realised Demetrius would not keep his word if he were to escape the troubles he was in, so they abandoned him and sided with Alexander. He had been the first to make an offer of peace with them and from that time on, they were his confederates in the war. {Apc 1Ma 10:22-47}

### 3852b AM, 4562 JP, 152 BC

3593. Andriscus of Adramyttium, a contemptible person, claimed that he was the son of Perseus, the last king of the Macedonians, and changed his name to Philip. He tried to create a rebellion in Macedonia. When no one paid any attention to him, he went into Syria and spoke to Demetrius Soter, whose sister was Perseus' wife, thinking he might get some help from him. To accomplish this more readily, he devised the following tale. He said he was descended from King Perseus by a concubine and had been given to a woman of Crete to receive his education. This had been done so that some of the royal family might be preserved, in case Perseus lost his war against the Romans, in which he had been engaged at the time. After Perseus' death, he had been kept in ignorance of his lineage and had believed until he was twelve that the man with whom he had been brought up at Adramyttium was his father. Later, the man became sick and was about to die, and before he died, he told him the truth. He gave him a little book which his reputed mother had signed with King Perseus' signet, and which he was to have given him when he came of age. Until then, everything was to have been kept secret. When he had come of age, the book, in which two treasures were left to him by his father, was to be given to him. Then, the woman who knew that he was not her own son, but a secret son, had told him of his true descent. She had begged him earnestly to withdraw from those regions before Eumenes, who was Perseus' sworn enemy, found out about it, since she feared that they might be put to death. For this lie, he was arrested by King Demetrius and sent to Rome. When it became obvious that he was neither the son of Perseus nor had possessed anything else of note, he was slighted and condemned. He later left Rome and took over Macedonia. {*Livy, l. 48. 14:27,29} {*Dio, l. 21. 2:383 (Zonaras, l. 9. c. 28.)}

### 3854 AM, 4564 JP, 150 BC

3594. Alexander Balas assembled a large army made up of the soldiers who had revolted from King Demetrius in Syria and the auxiliaries of Attalus, Ariarathes, Jonathan and especially of Ptolemy Philometor. He fought against Demetrius and was routed by the left wing of Demetrius' army which pursued him so hard that they also had the plunder from his camp. [K80] Whereas the right wing, in which Demetrius himself fought, was forced to give ground. Even though many of his troops fled, Demetrius conducted himself very valiantly by killing some of his enemies and chasing others, who were not able to withstand the violence of his charge. He was caught in a deep and impassable slough from which he could not escape, because his horse kept falling as he went. Though the enemy surrounded him and shot him with arrows, he nevertheless fought very gallantly on foot, until he fell down dead from his many wounds. {*Apc 1Ma 10:48-50} {*Josephus, Antiq., l. 13. c. 2. s. 4. (58-61) 7:255,257} {Justin, Trogus, l. 35. c. 1.} {*Appian, Syrian Wars, l. 11. c. 11. (67) 2:233} Demetrius died after having reigned in Syria for twelve years. When the rest of the kings conspired against him, he lost his life and his kingdom together at the same time. {*Polybius, l. 3. c. 5. s. 2,3. 2:13} Porphyry, who knew Demetrius well, and Eusebius and Sulpicius Severus all agree that he ruled twelve years. However, Josephus said he ruled for only eleven. {Porphyry, Scaliger's Greek Eusebius, p. 228.}

3595. After the death of Demetrius, who was survived by his two sons, Demetrius and Antiochus, and just prior to the Macedonian War, a comet the size of the sun appeared. At first its orb was fiery and ruddy, casting a clear light that brightened up the night. After that, it began to lessen in size and its brightness waned, until it finally disappeared. {*Seneca, Natural Questions, l. 7. c. 15. s. 1. 10:259}

3596. After Alexander, with (as Appian stated) the special help of Ptolemy Philometor, had killed Demetrius and taken his kingdom, he sent envoys to Ptolemy to arrange a marriage between him and his daughter. Ptolemy readily agreed and with his daughter Cleopatra immediately left Egypt for Ptolemais. She was a woman born to ruin the kingdom of Syria. This marriage happened toward the end of the 162nd year of the kingdom of the Greeks. {Apc 1Ma 10:51-58}

3597. Jonathan was invited to this wedding by Alexander. He presented the two kings and also their friends with gold, silver and many other gifts, hoping to ingratiate himself to them. [E467] At the same time, some wicked men came from the land of Israel to accuse Jonathan, but Alexander refused to listen to them and commanded that Jonathan be clothed in purple and be seated next to him. He also ordered the peers of his realm to accompany him into the centre of Ptolemais. A proclamation was made, forbidding anyone to speak against him or to molest him in any way, whereupon his accusers vanished from his sight. The king also showed him a great deal of honour by promoting him among those who were said to be his most intimate friends. He made him general over his forces in Judea and shared the dominion with him in his own court. So Jonathan returned to Jerusalem in peace and great joy. {Apc 1Ma 10:59-61}

3598. Onias, the son of the high priest Onias III, lived as a renegade with Ptolemy Philometor at Alexandria. He saw that there was no hope of recovering the high priesthood of Jerusalem, since it had been passed to the family of the Asmoneans. He aspired to make a name for himself for all of posterity. He petitioned King Ptolemy and Queen Cleopatra, who was not only the king's wife but also his sister, at a time when Ptolemy was waging war in various countries. [K81] He noted that the Jews had their temples in Coelosyria, Phoenicia and Leontopolis, in the nome of Heliopolis in Egypt, and in various other places. This was the cause of all the strife that they so frequently experienced. Onias therefore requested that he might have permission to purify an old ruined temple, not yet consecrated to any god, which he had found standing near the citadel of Bubastus in the plain. He also wanted to build another temple in the same spot to the Almighty God, patterned exactly like the one at Jerusalem in size and shape. Then the Jews who lived in Egypt would be able to keep their assemblies there. This would be a good means of preserving unity among themselves and preparing them to serve the king when required to do so. He justified his actions by saying that the prophet Isaiah had foretold that in the latter days an altar to the Lord God would be erected in Egypt. Isaiah had also prophesied many other things concerning that land. {*Josephus, Antiq., l. 13. c. 3. s. 1-3. (62-73) 7:257-263}

3599. Onias had not planned to build a new temple when he had first come into Egypt to Philometor and Cleopatra. Only later did he decide to do this, after he had served them well in the Egyptian and Syrian wars. Josephus stated that Philometor and Cleopatra committed the management of their whole kingdom to the Jews and appointed Onias and Dositheus (both Jews) over the whole army. {*Josephus, Apion, l. 2. c. 5. (49) 1:313} Again, that prophecy of Isaiah which Onias wrested to support his sacrilegious ambition, really concerned the spiritual kingdom of our Lord Christ. It is found in Isaiah: {Isa 19:18,19}

> "In that day shall there be five cities in the land of Egypt speaking the language of Canaan, and sworn to the Lord of Hosts; one shall be called a city of destruction (of Heres, or, of the sun). In that day shall there be an altar to the Lord in the middle of the land of Egypt and a pillar to the Lord at its border."

3600. Here for עיר ההרם, city of destruction, is the similar עיר ההרם, which was rendered the city of the sun, where the only difference between sun and destruction is that the ע is pointed differently. This is how Symmachus interpreted it and Jerome rendered it:

> "One of them shall be called the city of the sun."

3601. The Chaldee Paraphrase joined them together:

> "The city of the sun which shall be destroyed."

*3602.* This may be the reason, as Scaliger guessed, why Onias chose the nome of Heliopolis to build the temple. (Heliopolis means *city of the sun.* Editor.)

*3603.* When Onias was given a plot of land in the nome of Heliopolis, about twenty-three miles from Memphis, he built a temple there. This was not as large or as costly as the one at Jerusalem. The towers were similar, made of large stones and rising to a height of ninety feet. The altar was a copy of the one at Jerusalem and was furnished with the same utensils, except for the lampstand. Instead of the lampstand, he made a golden lamp which sparkled, as it were, with a beam of light, and hung it on a chain of gold. He surrounded the temple with a wall of brick containing gates of stone. The king gave a grant of a large portion of land and revenue, so that the priests might be supplied with necessities for the worship of God. Onias also found some Jews living in the same area as he, who were priests and Levites, so he employed them in his temple. {*Josephus, Antiq., l. 13. c. 3. s. 3. (72,73) 7:261,263} {*Josephus, Jewish War, l. 7. c. 10. s. 2,3. (420-432) 4:425-429} {*Josephus, Jewish War, l. 1. c. 9. s. 4. (190) 2:89}* The priests who ministered in Onias' temple were considered little better than the priests of the high places, who were not permitted (as appears from Second Kings {2Ki 23:9}) to offer burnt offerings on the altar of the Lord at Jerusalem, but only to eat unleavened bread like the unclean priests among their brethren. {*Meshna, Minhoth, c. 13. s. 10.*} [E468] [K82]

*3604.* At Alexandria, a dispute arose between the Jews and the Samaritans concerning their holy rites. One contended that the temple at Jerusalem was the only lawful temple, and ordained by Moses, while the other party contended for Gerizim. Both sides appealed to Ptolemy Philometor and his friends for a hearing and decision on the matter. They wanted the losers to be executed. Sabbaeus and Theodosius pleaded for the Samaritans and Andronicus, the son of Messalamus, for the Jews. They took their oaths by God and the king that they would use no arguments other than those which they found in the law. They asked the king that he would put to death whoever lost. The king, with many of his friends at the council, heard the whole debate. Finally, they were persuaded by Andronicus' arguments and determined that the temple in Jerusalem was the one which had been built according to Moses' directions. Sabbaeus and Theodosius were sentenced to death, as it had been agreed. {*Josephus, Antiq., l. 13. c. 3. s. 4. (74-79) 7:263,265}*

*3605.* At the same time Aristobulus, a Jew who was a Peripatetic philosopher, became famous at Philometor's court in Egypt. He wrote a commentary on Moses which he dedicated to the king. In its preface there is a famous passage that was quoted by Clement of Alexandria and by Eusebius. {*Eusebius, Gospel, l. 13. c. 7. (653d) 1:710} {*Clem-*

*ent, Stromateis, l. 1. c. 22. 2:334}* In his book, Aristobulus copied large sections from the books of Aristotle. {*Eusebius, Gospel, l. 8. c. 9. (375d) 1:406}*

## 3855 AM, 4565 JP, 149 BC

*3606.* The third Carthaginian war started this year. Mithridates Euergetes, who was the first of the kings of Pontus and a confederate of the people of Rome, brought a number of ships against the Carthaginians. {*Appian, Mithridatic Wars, l. 12. c. 2. (10) 2:255}* Both the consuls were sent to manage this war. Marcus Manilius managed the army and Lucius Marcius Censorinus was admiral of the fleet. They were secretly instructed not to stop the war until Carthage was demolished. {*Livy, l. 49. 14:29,31} {*Appian, Punic Wars, l. 8. c. 11. (75) 1:527}*

*3607.* Andriscus, or the false Philip, secretly escaped from Rome. He levied an army and captured all Macedonia and the royal ensigns. Where he could not achieve this with the consent of the inhabitants, he used force of arms, and this took place in the third year of the 157th Olympiad. He also thought of invading Thessaly and adding it to his domains, but at the instigation of the Roman envoys, it was defended with the help of the Achaeans. {*Livy, l. 49,50. 14:31-37} {*Velleius Paterculus, l. 1. c. 11. s. 1-3. 1:27} {Porphyry, Scaliger's Greek Eusebius, p. 229.}*

*3608.* When Prusias Venator, the king of Bithynia, learned that his son Nicomedes was in good favour at Rome, he ordered him to go to the Senate, as he wanted the arrears of the money which he owed to Attalus to be cancelled. He also sent an envoy, Menas, as his assistant, who was secretly ordered to murder Nicomedes if the king failed to get his request. {*Appian, Mithridatic Wars, l. 12. c. 1. (4) 2:243}* This would give the kingdom to his younger sons, who were his by a second wife. {Justin, Trogus, l. 34. c. 4.} One, who was named after his father, had no teeth in his upper jaw, which instead was one bone that grew out so evenly, that it did not disfigure him or cause him any problems when chewing. {*Livy, l. 50. 14:31} {*Valerius Maximus, l. 1. c. 8. ext. 12. 1:123} {*Pliny, l. 7. c. 16. (69) 2:551}*

*3609.* Prusias sent out his envoy Menas with some small ships and two thousand soldiers, while Attalus sent Andronicus as an envoy to oppose the request. [K83] He demonstrated quite clearly that the fine which had been imposed on Prusias, was far less than the booty he had obtained by pillaging the country. Menas saw that there was little hope of obtaining his request of getting Prusias' fine removed, and he also realised in what high esteem Nicomedes was held in Rome. He did not know what to do, as he dared not kill Nicomedes or return to Bithynia. In this state of indecision, he remained at Rome. Nicomedes called him to a meeting which he did not find too disagreeable. They conspired against Prusias and drew Andronicus into their confederacy, in order that he might persuade Attalus to help establish Nicomedes in Bithynia. They all met together at Bernice, a little town in Epirus, and went aboard a ship by night. They wanted to determine what was the best way to accomplish this business. After the discussion, they went their way that same night. In the morning, Nicomedes came ashore in his purple robe and with his crown on his head, like a king. Andronicus, attended by five hundred soldiers, met him a little later and greeted him as a king. Menas pretended not to know that Nicomedes was in the company until then. Menas ran around the two thousand soldiers he had brought with him and encouraged them to side with the one who seemed most deserving. *[E469]* He intimated that Prusias was now an old man and Nicomedes was in his youth. The Bithynians were weary of Prusias and wished for his son. The leading Romans liked this youth extremely well. Andronicus, who was now captain of his guard, had assistance promised from Attalus, a neighbouring king of a large kingdom, who was also a bitter enemy to Prusias. Menas reminded them of Prusias' cruelty and antics, for which he was hated by everybody. As soon as Menas saw the dislike of Prusias' villainies in these soldiers, he took them all to Nicomedes. He was the second after Andronicus to greet him as king, and he brought two thousand soldiers with him as a guard. {*Appian, Mithridatic Wars, l. 12. c. 1. (4,5) 2:245-249}

3610. Attalus was very eager to accept the youth and sent orders to Prusias to turn over to his son some cities to dwell in and fields for provisions. Prusias answered that he would soon give Attalus' whole kingdom to him, for whose sake it was that he had formerly invaded Asia. After saying this, he sent some envoys away to Rome to accuse Nicomedes and Attalus and summon them both to a trial. {*Appian, Mithridatic Wars, l. 12. c. 1. (6) 2:249}

3611. Nicomedes was encouraged by Phaellon, or rather Phaennis, Epirus' seer, who predicted success, as well as by the instigation of Attalus, and so he waged war with his father Prusias. {Zosimus, History, l. 2.} As soon as he and Attalus arrived in Bithynia with their forces, the Bithynians began to revolt. Because of this, Prusias did not dare to entrust himself to any of his own subjects. Hoping that the Romans would relieve him, he waited for this and secured himself in a citadel at Nicaea. From his father-in-law Diegylis, a Thracian, he had received five hundred Thracians, whom he appointed to be his bodyguard. {*Appian, Mithridatic Wars, l. 12. c. 1. (6) 2:249}

### 3856a AM, 4565 JP, 149 BC

3612. The praetor of Rome did not conduct the envoys from Prusias to the Senate as soon as they arrived, since he hoped to show Attalus a courtesy. After he had ushered them into the Senate, the Senate chose some envoys who might settle the war. One had been wounded in the head with a large stone and was badly disfigured from the scars. A second one was lame in his feet and the third was a fool. Cato Censorinus, who died soon after this at the age of ninety-four, said in jest that the Romans sent an embassy that had neither head, feet nor heart. {*Livy, l. 50. 14:33} {*Plutarch, Cato Major, l. 1. c. 9. s. 1,2. 2:327} {*Plutarch, Cato Major, l. 1. c. 1. s. 6. 2:305} {*Plutarch, Cato Major, l. 1. c. 27. s. 4. 2:385}

3613. When the envoys came into Bithynia, they ordered both sides to lay down their arms. *[K84]* Nicomedes and Attalus indicated they would submit to the authority of the Senate. However, the Bithynians, who had been instructed and previously told by Nicomedes and Attalus what they should do, said obstinately that they could no longer endure Prusias' tyranny, especially as they had shown him by this present engagement how much they disliked his government. Since the Bithynians had not as yet made these grievances known to the Senate, the envoys returned home again, having accomplished nothing. Prusias gave up expecting help from the Romans, nor had he sought help elsewhere, because he had believed that the Romans would help him. He crossed over to Nicomedia, planning to fortify it and from there to prevent the enemy from getting in. However, the townsmen deserted their king and opened the gates to the enemy. Thereupon, Prusias fled to the temple of Zeus and trusted he would be protected by the religion and respect associated with such a place. In spite of this, Nicomedes sent some of his party, who killed Prusias there. {*Appian, Mithridatic Wars, l. 12. c. 1. (7) 2:249,251} Diodorus Siculus stated that Prusias had fled, for his own security, to the altar of Zeus, where he was killed by the hand of his son, Nicomedes. {*Diod. Sic., l. 32. c. 21. 11:433} Strabo stated he was killed by Attalus. {*Strabo, l. 13. c. 4. s. 2. 6:167,169} Livy said he was killed by his son, with the help of Attalus. {*Livy, l. 50. 14:35} Zonaras from Dio said he was killed by his own subjects. {*Dio, l. 21. 2:383 (Zonaras, l. 9. c. 28.)} Polybius stated that he was so hated by the Bithynians, that they all rose up against him in such numbers and with such violence as if it were their plan not only to revolt from him but mostly to avenge themselves upon him for the notable injustices of his government. {*Polybius, l. 36. c. 15. 6:379} {Suidas, Προυσιας}

3614. In Macedonia, Andriscus, or the false Philip, fought with Juventius, the Roman praetor, who had been sent against him with a legion. He won the battle and killed Juventius and most of the Roman army. From there, he invaded Thessaly and wasted most of the country, then took the Thracians into an alliance. {*Livy, l. 50. 14:31}

{*Florus, l. 1. c. 30. 1:133} {Eutropius, l. 4.} {*Dio, l. 21. 2:383,385 (Zonaras, l. 9. c. 28.)} {Orosius, l. 4. c. 20.} With these successes, he began to commit acts of cruelty and tyrannical deeds. There was not a wealthy person whom he did not put to death on false accusations. [E470] He did not spare even his most intimate friends, killing many of them. Naturally of a fierce and bloody disposition, he was proud and haughty in his everyday behaviour, and in the end he was deeply engaged in covetousness and all manner of vice. {*Diod. Sic., l. 32. c. 17. s. 1. 11:429}

## 3856b AM, 4566 JP, 148 BC

3615. In Syria, Alexander Balas gave himself over entirely to riotous living and luxury, while his friend Ammonius managed the affairs of the kingdom. He killed all the king's friends, as well as Laodice, the queen, who was the daughter of Antiochus Epiphanes and Antigonus, who was the son of Demetrius. {*Livy, l. 50. 14:33} {*Josephus, Antiq., l. 13. c. 4. s. 6. (106-108) 7:279} {*Athenaeus, l. 5. (211a-e) 2:453-457}

3616. In the 165th year of the Greeks, Demetrius, the oldest son of Demetrius Soter, was now in his prime. He heard of the degenerate lifestyle and luxury of Alexander, to whom were coming those vast incomes of the kingdom, of which he could scarcely dream. All the while he stayed like a prisoner in his own palace, among a company of courtesans. He raised a large force of mercenary soldiers from Lasthenes, a Cretian, who sailed with this army from Crete to Cilicia. Alexander was so terrified at this news, that he hurried away from Phoenicia to Antioch to settle things before Demetrius arrived. The government of Antioch had been committed to Hierax and Diodotus, also called Tryphon. {Apc 1Ma 11:39 10:67,68} {*Josephus, Antiq., l. 13. c. 4. s. 3. (86-90) 7:269,271} {Justin, Trogus, l. 35. c. 2.} {*Diod. Sic., l. 32. c. 27. s. 9c. 11:445}

3617. Apollonius, the governor of Coelosyria who was surnamed Daus by Josephus, joined Demetrius and made him general over the forces which he was sending against those Jews who had remained loyal to Alexander. When Apollonius had raised a large army, many defected from Alexander to Demetrius out of fear. [K85] He camped at Jamnia and sent to Jonathan, the Jewish general and high priest, boastfully challenging him to meet him in the plain and fight, if he dared. This inflamed Jonathan so much, that he immediately marched from Jerusalem with ten thousand men. His brother Simon met him to help him. They camped before Joppa, but Apollonius' soldiers, who were garrisoned there, shut them out. So they laid siege to the place and began to use their batteries against it, which so dismayed the citizens that they immediately opened the gates and surrendered the city. {Apc 1Ma 10:69-76}

3618. As soon as Apollonius heard of the loss of Joppa, he marched to Azotus with three thousand cavalry and his eight thousand foot soldiers, according to Josephus. He placed in ambush a thousand cavalry who were to attack Jonathan's rearguard, as soon as he had passed the place where the ambush lay. Then Apollonius would charge the enemy's vanguard, so that the Jews were to be attacked at both ends. As soon as Jonathan passed the place, he saw the ambush coming to surround his camp. He commanded his men to stand still and deflect the enemies' arrows with their shields. The cavalry had worn themselves out and exhausted their arrows, because they had been attacking from the morning until night. Then, Simon led his forces up against the enemy's foot soldiers and defeated and routed them. The enemy cavalry fled to Azotus and entered Bethdagon, their idol temple, seeking safety. Jonathan, however, burned Azotus and the surrounding cities and took much spoil. He burned Dagon's temple to the ground and all who had fled there died in the flames. Nearly eight thousand men were killed by the sword and in the fire. Jonathan left there and camped before Askelon, where the men of the city treated him very nobly. After this victory, Jonathan returned to Jerusalem as a conqueror, with his army loaded with much booty and spoil. When King Alexander heard the news of Jonathan's successes, he continued to show his respects to him and sent him a golden buckler, which was usually given only to those of royal blood. He also gave him Accaron with its territories (a city of the Philistines), to belong to him and his heirs for ever. {Apc 1Ma 10:77-89}

3619. After the Carthaginians had defeated Calpurnius Piso, the consul, at Hippagreta, they sent their envoys to Macedonia to Andriscus, the alleged son of Perseus. They urged him to persist courageously in his war against the Romans and promised that he would never lack money or shipping from Carthage. {*Appian, Punic Wars, l. 8. c. 16. (110,111) 1:595,597}

3620. Quintus Caecilius Metellus, the Roman praetor (not the consul, as both Florus and also the Latin interpreter of Pausanias' Achaia had it), was sent against Andriscus with a large army and came into Macedonia. There he persuaded the commissioners, whom the Senate had sent to gather information on the affairs in Asia, that before they went to Asia, they would go first of all to the commanders of the Achaeans and order them to stop the war they were fighting with the Lacedemonians. [E471] They sent the message they had received from Metellus to Damocritus and the Achaeans, who were just about to attack the Lacedemonians. When the commissioners saw that they had no effect on the Achaeans, they went on to Asia. {*Florus, l. 1. c. 30. s. 5. 1:135} {*Pausanias, Achaia, l. 7. c. 13. s. 1-3. 3:239,241}

3621. When Metellus entered Macedonia, Attalus brought his fleet to help him and so kept Andriscus away from the sea coast. Andriscus brought up his army a little beyond Pydna. [K86] Although his cavalry had defeated the enemy, he nevertheless pulled back for fear of the Roman foot soldiers. He divided his army into two brigades and sent one of them into Thessaly to waste that country, while keeping the other with him. Metellus put little stock in the enemy forces and marched toward them. When he had beaten Andriscus' troops, Andriscus fled into Thrace. After he had levied a new army, he fought with Metellus, but was defeated. He fled to Byzes, a petty king of Thrace, who betrayed him into the hands of Metellus. One Alexander, who also was pretending to be the son of Perseus, gathered an army and seized part of the country beside the Nestus River. Metellus pursued him as far as Dardania. {*Strabo, l. 13. c. 4. s. 2. 6:169} {*Velleius Paterculus, l. 1. c. 11. s. 1,2. 1:27} {*Florus, l. 1. c. 30. 1:133,135} {*Dio, l. 21. 2:385 (Zonaras, l. 9. c. 28.)} The false Philip was utterly defeated, with the loss of twenty-five thousand of his soldiers. He was taken prisoner and Macedonia was recovered by the Romans. {Eutropius, l. 43.} This happened when Spurius Postumius and Lucius Piso were consuls, in the 4th year of the 157th Olympiad, at the close of the year. {*Julius Obsequens, Prodigies, l. 1. c. 19. 14:253} {Porphyry, Scaliger's Greek Eusebius, p. 229.}

## 3857 AM, 4567 JP, 147 BC

3622. Publius Cornelius Scipio, the consul, fought a naval battle at Carthage. In addition to his own ships, his fleet had five ships from the Sidetes which Mithridates, the king of Pontus, had sent to him. {*Appian, Punic Wars, l. 8. c. 18. (123) 1:621} {*Appian, Mithridatic Wars, l. 12. c. 2. (10) 2:255}

3623. The inhabitants of Aradus planned to destroy the city of Marathus in Phoenicia. They communicated secretly with Ammonius, who at that time was viceroy in Syria under Alexander Balas, and offered him three hundred talents to betray Marathus to them. After that, Ammonius sent Isidorus to Marathus, with instructions to pretend he was there on business, when the true reason was to seize Marathus and give it to the Aradians. The Marathians were aware that the king favoured the Aradians more than themselves and denied the king's soldiers entrance into their city. From among their oldest citizens, they selected ten of the most distinguished and sent them as suppliants to the isle of Aradus. These men took along some of the oldest images of their gods that they had in their city, in the hope of thereby appeasing the fury of the Aradians. The Aradians were extremely displeased and ignored their humble speeches.

Disregarding all reverence for the gods, they broke the images and most shamefully trampled them under their feet. When they tried to stone the envoys to death, some of the older men who intervened, had trouble getting them to prison safely. The envoys protested and pleaded the privileges of suppliants and of the sacred gods. Even though the rights of envoys were not to be violated, these men were massacred by a company of impudent young fellows. Immediately afterwards, the authors of this villainy came into the assembly. Having taken the signet rings from the Marathians whom they had killed, they now forged letters to the Marathian people in the envoys' names, in which they said that the Aradians would quickly send them some supplies. They hoped to deceive the Marathians and have the Aradian forces admitted into their city, in the belief that they had come to help them. For this reason, the Aradians seized all the ships belonging to private men, in the fear that someone might possibly reveal their plot to the Marathians. In spite of all this, a certain sailor who was a friend of the Marathians, pitied their sad situation. He usually sailed in the neighbouring sea. But since his ship had also been taken, he boldly swam across the mile wide strait by night and told the Marathians that the Aradians planned to attack them. When the Aradians realised that their plot had been revealed, they abandoned their plan of sending them letters. {*Diod. Sic., l. 33. c. 5. 12:13-17} Instead, they openly attacked Marathus and captured the city, demolishing it and sharing its territory among themselves. {*Strabo, l. 16. c. 2. s. 13,14. 7:257,259} [K87]

## 3858a AM, 4567 JP, 147 BC

3624. A fourth observation of the autumnal equinox was made by Hipparchus at midnight, in the 32nd year of the 3rd Calippic period, on the 3rd day of the Egyptian Additionals (at the beginning of September 27), in the 178th year from the death of Alexander. The 177th year was ending and the 178th was about to start in two days. {Ptolemy, Great Syntaxis, l. 3. c. 2.}

## 3858b AM, 4568 JP, 146 BC

3625. In the same year of the same Calippic Period, the 178th year from the death of Alexander, on the 27th day of the Egyptian month of Mecheir (March 24), in the morning, Hipparchus wrote that he observed the vernal equinox. {Ptolemy, Great Syntaxis, l. 3. c. 2.} [E472]

3626. When Gnaeus Cornelius Lentulus and Lucius Mummius were consuls, Carthage was demolished. {*Velleius Paterculus, l. 1. c. 12. s. 5. 1:31} On this occasion, Scipio, considering the changeableness of human affairs, was fearful lest the same fate should happen sometime to Rome. He said this:

The day shall come when sacred Troy shall fall,
And Priam with his stock sink therewithal.

3627. He told this to his teacher Polybius, who was present at the time and had inserted this passage in his history. {*Appian, Punic Wars, l. 8. c. 19. (132). 1:637}

3628. Lucius Mummius, the consul, who had been sent by the Senate to end the Achaean war, came to the Roman army at early dawn with a small company. He ordered Metellus who was in charge of the Achaean war to go and settle the Macedonian War. When Metellus had finished that war, he was to march with all his forces within Macedonia to the isthmus. Mummius stayed in the isthmus until he had drawn up his whole army, which consisted of thirty-five hundred cavalry and twenty-three thousand foot soldiers. There were some archers from Crete in this army, while Philopoemen came from Pergamum on the Caicus to bring him a brigade from Attalus. At the isthmus, the consul defeated Diaeus, who was the last Achaean leader and the prime instigator of these Achaean disorders. On the third day after the battle, the consul entered Corinth with his trumpets sounding. After he had taken the spoils of the city, he levelled it to the ground, nine hundred and fifty-two years after it had been founded by Aletes, the son of Hippos, in 1097 BC. {*Livy, l. 52. 14:41} {*Velleius Paterculus, l. 1. c. 13. s. 1,2. 1:33} {Justin, Trogus, l. 34. c. 2.} {*Florus, l. 1. c. 32. 1:141,143} {*Pausanias, Achaia, l. 7. c. 16. s. 1-10. 3:255-261} {Orosius, l. 5. c. 3.} This occurred in the 3rd year of the 158th Olympiad (for so it is in Pliny, and not the 156th), and according to Varro's calculations, in the 608th year since Rome had been built. {*Pliny, l. 34. c. 3. (6,7) 9:131}

3629. When Polybius came from Africa to help his country, he noticed some pictures by the most talented artists lying on the ground at Corinth and the soldiers were playing dice on them. In his history he mentioned two pictures. One was of Hercules being tortured in the robe of Dianira. The other was a picture of Dionysus, drawn by Aristides of Thebes. Some think it was Aristides who coined the proverb, *Nothing in comparison with Dionysus*, and this was Aristides' picture of Dionysus. {*Strabo, l. 8. c. 6. s. 23. 4:201} When Lucius Mummius found out that King Attalus had bought this picture of Dionysus from among the spoils that were about to be shipped away, for six thousand sesterces or a hundred talents, he marvelled at the high price that had been paid. {*Pliny, l. 7. c. 38. (126) 2:591} {*Pliny, l. 35. c. 8. 9:277,279} Suspecting that there might be some rare virtue which he did not know about, he revoked the sale, in spite of Attalus' protests, and placed the picture in Ceres' temple at Rome. {*Pliny, l. 35. c. 8. 9:277,279} He knew so little of the value of such things that when he had culled out some exquisite pieces and statues of the best artists to be carried into Italy, he told

those who had responsibility for them, that if they lost any of them on the way, they would have to replace them with new ones. {*Velleius Paterculus, l. 1. c. 13. 1:33,35} [K88] Any hangings and other ornaments that seemed admirable were sent to Rome. Others of less value were given to Philopoemen and shipped to Pergamum. {*Pausanias, Achaia, l. 7. c. 16. s. 8. 3:259}

3630. Ptolemy Philometor assembled large naval and land forces and left Egypt for Syria under the pretence of helping Alexander Balas, his son-in-law. His real reason was to annex the kingdom of Syria, of which Alexander had been deprived, to his own dominions. When all the cities had received him peaceably in accordance with Alexander's orders, Ptolemy placed a garrison of soldiers in every one of them, pretending this to be in Alexander's interests. {Apc 1Ma 11:1-3}

3631. As soon as Ptolemy came to Azotus, the people showed him the temple of Dagon, which had recently been burnt, and the ruins of Azotus and its surrounding lands. He was shown the piles of the dead bodies of those who had been killed in the war and burnt at Jonathan's command, for they had laid them in heaps along the way that he was to come. Although they had given a biased account of everything Jonathan had done with the deliberate intention of maligning him, the king said nothing. Jonathan met the king at Joppa with great pomp and was very courteously received by him. From there they went together as far as the Eleutherus River, where Jonathan took his leave of the king and returned to Jerusalem. {Apc 1Ma 11:4-7}

3632. Ptolemy had taken all the cities along the sea coasts as far as Seleucia, which is located on the coast at the mouth of the Orontes River. He thought Alexander had plotted an ambush against him because [E473] Ammonius had set an ambush at Ptolemais to trap him. When Ptolemy demanded justice for this act by Ammonius, Alexander would not surrender Ammonius. Consequently, Ptolemy took his daughter Cleopatra away from Alexander and gave her in marriage to Demetrius Soter, also promising to restore him to his father's kingdom. {Apc 1Ma 11:8-12} {*Josephus, Antiq., l. 13. c. 4. s. 6,7. (106-110) 7:277,281} {*Livy, l. 52. 14:43}

3633. The men of Antioch deserted Alexander because of Ammonius, from whom they had received much abuse. Ammonius planned to make an escape dressed as a woman, but was attacked and killed. Ptolemy went into Antioch and was greeted by the people. He crowned himself with two diadems, the one of Asia (or Syria), the other of Egypt. He told them that he, for his part, was satisfied with his own dominion of Egypt, and persuaded the men of Antioch to receive Demetrius. He said that their present situation affected him far more than the recent provocations and disputes which had happened between them and his father Seleucus. {*Josephus, Antiq., l. 13. c. 4. s. 7. (111-115) 7:281} {Apc 1Ma 11:13} Hence, the men of Antioch gave their loyalty to the son, to atone for the actions they had taken against his father. The old soldiers of his father loved Demetrius and followed him. {Justin, Trogus, l. 35. c. 2.}

3634. Alexander was in Cilicia at this time, where he consulted the oracle of Apollo and claimed to have received the following answer. {Apc 1Ma 11:14} The oracle said that he should beware of that place which had a rare sight, an object having two shapes. This was generally thought to refer to Abas, a city in Arabia where Alexander was killed not long after. In this city there was a certain woman called Herais, who was the daughter of Diophantus, a Macedonian, and who had an Arabian woman for her mother. She married Samiades but subsequently changed her sex and became a man, assuming her father's name of Diophantus. She was a hermaphrodite, that is, she developed male sexual parts as she matured. {*Diod. Sic., l. 32. c. 10. 11:447-453}

## 3859a AM, 4568 JP, 146 BC

3635. Hipparchus observed the fifth autumnal equinox in the 33rd year of the third Calippic period, on the fourth day of the Egyptian Additionals (September 27), in the morning. {Ptolemy, Great Syntaxis, l. 3. c. 2.} [K89]

3636. Alexander had gathered together a powerful army. He invaded Syria and wasted all the territories of Antioch, pillaging and burning wherever he went. Ptolemy and his son-in-law Demetrius marched toward him and defeated his forces in a battle near the Oenopara River. Alexander escaped from the battle with five hundred of his soldiers and quickly headed toward Abas, a city of Arabia. He wanted to see Zabdiel, an important person of Arabia. {Apc 1Ma 11:17} Josephus called him Zabel and Diodorus Siculus, Diocles. Two commanders of Alexander's band, Heliades and Casius, treacherously killed Alexander. They had previously arranged this with Demetrius, to whom they had sent an embassy to look after their own interests. In the final battle it happened that Ptolemy's horse was scared by the trumpetting of an elephant and threw him to the ground. When he was down, the enemy attacked him and seriously wounded him in the head. They would have killed him, had not his bodyguard saved him. Even so, he lay so senseless for four whole days, that he could neither speak nor understand what others spoke to him. Zabdiel, the Arabian, cut off Alexander's head and presented it to Ptolemy. About the fifth day, he had some relief from the pain of his wounds and returned to his senses. He

was encouraged by the pleasing story of the death of Alexander and the sight of Alexander's head. On the third day after that, Ptolemy died while his wounds were being dressed and the physicians were endeavouring to set his bones. {Apc 1Ma 11:14-18} {*Polybius, l. 39. c. 7. s. 1-3. 6:451} {*Diod. Sic., l. 32. c. 10. 11:445,447} {*Livy, l. 52. 14:43} {*Strabo, l. 16. c. 2. s. 8. 7:247} {*Josephus, Antiq., l. 13. c. 4. s. 8. (116-119) 7:281-285}

3637. Josephus said Alexander ruled for five years after the death of Demetrius Soter, from which we suppose that about five months are to be deducted. {*Josephus, Antiq., l. 13. c. 4. s. 8. (119) 7:283,285} Based on the authority of the Maccabean writer, the death of this man appears to have happened at the same time as Philometor's. After Alexander's death, Demetrius, son of Demetrius Soter, controlled the government of Syria in the 167th year of the kingdom of the Greeks. {Apc 1Ma 11:19} Since he had defeated one who was not descended from their family, he received the same surname, Nicator, or the conqueror, as the first Seleucus of that kingly line. {*Appian, Syrian Wars, l. 11. c. 11. (67) 2:233}

3638. As soon as Ptolemy Philometor was dead, the soldiers whom he had placed in the citadels and cities for the security of Syria, were all killed by the other soldiers in the same garrisons at the instigation of Demetrius. {Apc 1Ma 11:18} Demetrius treated the rest of Ptolemy's soldiers very unkindly, forgetting the help that Ptolemy had given him and his alliance by marriage with Cleopatra. [E474] These soldiers hated his ingratitude and they all retreated to Alexandria and left only the elephants under his control. {*Josephus, Antiq., l. 13. c. 4. s. 9. (120,121) 7:285}

## 3859b AM, 4569 JP, 145 BC

3639. In Egypt, Cleopatra, the wife and sister of Philometor who had just died, negotiated with the nobles of the realm and tried hard to get the kingdom given to her son. {*Josephus, Apion, l. 2. c. 5. (49) 1:313} {Justin, Trogus, l. 38. c. 8.} However, they sent for Ptolemy, the younger brother of Philometor who was surnamed Euergetes II along with Physcon who reigned in Cyrene, to come from there to oppose her in her plans. Onias, who had recently built the temple in the nome of Heliopolis, took up the war for Cleopatra and marched with a small army of Jews to the city of Alexandria. [K90] This happened when Lucius Thermus was an envoy there for the Romans. {*Josephus, Apion, l. 2. c. 5. (50) 1:313}

3640. Physcon ended the quarrel and forced Cleopatra, who was his older sister and wife to their own brother, to marry himself. {*Valerius Maximus, l. 9. c. 1. ext. 5. 2:305} As soon as he entered Alexandria, he commanded all those who favoured the young child to be killed. He also killed the young child, while he was in his mother's arms on

the wedding day, in the midst of their feasting and religious solemnities. So he went up to his sister's bed covered with the blood of her own son. Nor was his behaviour
any milder toward his countrymen, who had invited him
to the kingdom and helped him secure the throne. He gave
the foreign soldiers permission to kill as they pleased, and
many were killed everywhere. {*Justin, Trogus, l. 38. c. 8.} He
executed many of them with the cruellest tortures based
on false charges of treason. He banished others and confiscated their estates, based on false charges he had made
up and forged. {*Diod. Sic., l. 33. c. 6. 12:19}

3641. When Jonathan had assembled those who were in
Judea, he prepared many engines of war and besieged
the tower at Jerusalem. Demetrius Nicator was told
about this by some ungodly persons who hated their
own country. At this, the king was incensed and wrote
to Jonathan to break off the siege and quickly meet him
at Ptolemais, so they could have a conference about the
matter. Jonathan did not break off his siege, but did go
to the king. He was accompanied by the elders and the
priests, and they took along some presents with which
they soon pacified the king's wrath. Jonathan made so
good an apology for himself, that the king dismissed
the informers, conferred the high priesthood on him and
counted him as one of his best friends. Moreover,
Jonathan promised to give the king three hundred talents, while procuring from him a release for all Judea
and the three countries annexed to it, namely Apherma,
Lydda and Ramoth. They no longer had to pay tithes
and tributes, which had formerly been paid to the kings.
The king sent letters about this to Lasthenes, who, with
the auxiliaries from Crete, had restored Demetrius to
the kingdom and whom he considered his cousin and
father. {Apc 1Ma 10:30 11:20-37} {*Josephus, Antiq., l. 13. c. 4. s. 9.
(120-128) 7:285,289}

3642. When Demetrius saw that there was now peace
throughout the kingdom and no opposition against him,
he disbanded his old native soldiers. He kept in arms
only those bands of foreigners whom he had levied in
Crete and the other islands. This turned the hearts of
his father's soldiers against him, because they continued to receive their salaries from previous kings in times
of peace, so that they might be all the more willing and
more cheerful to serve them in all dangers and emer-
gencies. {Apc 1Ma 11:38} {*Josephus, Antiq., l. 13. c. 4. s. 9. (129,130)
7:289,291}

3643. Diodotus, one of Alexander Balas' commanders,
who later was made king and assumed the name of
Tryphon, noticed the alienation of the soldiers from
Demetrius. He was born at the citadel of Casiana in the
country of Apamea and was raised at Apamea. {Apc 1Ma
11:39} {*Strabo, l. 16. c. 2. s. 10. 7:251,253} {*Livy, l. 52. 14:45} {*Livy,

l. 55. 14:55} {*Josephus, Antiq., l. 13. c. 5. s. 1. (131,132) 7:291} {*Appian,
Syrian Wars, l. 11. c. 11. (68) 2:233} Tryphon went to Simalcue,
the Arabian, who had been entrusted with the education of Antiochus, the son of Alexander Balas, and told
him all that Demetrius Nicator had done and the disagreements between him and the soldiers. He urged him
very strongly to give him the young child and he would
undertake to establish him in his father's kingdom. The
Arabians were opposed to this, and he stayed there many
days. {Apc 1Ma 11:39,40} [E475] [K91]

3644. In the meantime Demetrius Nicator, supposing
himself secure and out of danger, executed anyone who
appeared to oppose him, using unusual ways of death.
Lasthenes, who was a wicked and rash fellow and who
had been appointed over the whole kingdom, corrupted
Demetrius with his flattery and put him up to all types
of villainy. {*Diod. Sic., l. 33. c. 4. s. 1. 12:7,9 (footnote 1)}

## 3860a AM, 4569 JP, 145 BC

3645. Jonathan sent envoys to Demetrius, asking him to
remove his garrison of soldiers from the tower of Jerusalem and all other citadels, because they continued to
attack the Israelites. Demetrius replied that he would
grant Jonathan his request and would also make him
and his country glorious when the time was more suitable for him. For the present, he wanted Jonathan to
send him some soldiers to help him against his own soldiers, who had revolted from him. Jonathan quickly satisfied his request and sent three thousand strong men
to him in Antioch, for which the king was grateful. {Apc
1Ma 11:41-44}

3646. Demetrius was well-supplied with foreign mercenaries, in whom he placed greater confidence than in
his own troops. He commanded them to disarm the citizens of Antioch, but the people of Antioch refused to
surrender their arms and assembling in the middle of
the city, began to attack him in the palace. The Jews
hastened to relieve him and dispersed themselves within
the city. On that day, they killed nearly a hundred thousand men, burned the city and took much booty. After
that, the citizens laid down their arms and made peace
with the king. For this service, the Jews received much
honour from the king and the kingdom, and returned
to Jerusalem richly laden with spoils. {Apc 1Ma 11:45-52}
{*Diod. Sic., l. 33. c. 4. s. 2,3. 12:9}

3647. After the destruction of most of Antioch by fire, the
execution of many for sedition and the confiscation of
estates into the king's treasury, many of the citizens were
forced to escape. Out of fear and hatred of Demetrius,
they wandered about Syria and used every opportunity
to avenge themselves on Demetrius. Meanwhile
Demetrius, whose actions had made him detestable to all

men, persisted in his massacres, banishments and confiscations, far surpassing his father in cruelty. {*Diod. Sic., l. 33. c. 4. s. 3. 12:9} Moreover, he lied to Jonathan. In spite of his flattery, he turned away his friendship from him and afflicted him very grievously. {Apc 1Ma 11:53} He furthermore threatened to wage war with him, unless he would pay all the tributes which the country of the Jews had paid his predecessors. {*Josephus, Antiq., l. 13. c. 5. s. 3. (142,143) 7:295}

## 3860b AM, 4570 JP, 144 BC

3648. Finally, Diodotus, also called Tryphon, returned to Syria from Arabia with the young Antiochus, who was the son of Alexander Balas and Cleopatra, the daughter of Ptolemy Philometor. He set the crown on his head and proclaimed him to be the rightful heir of the kingdom, surnaming him *Theos*, or *Divine*. He returned with a large force, many of whom had been discharged by Demetrius. He attacked and defeated Demetrius in a plain and forced him to flee to Seleucia. Diodotus seized his elephants and took Antioch. {Apc 1Ma 11:54-56} {*Livy, l. 52. 14:43,45} {*Josephus, Antiq., l. 13. c. 5. s. 3. (143,144) 7:295,297} {*Appian, Syrian Wars, l. 11. c. 11. (68) 2:233}

3649. Then Antiochus, or rather Diodotus, in Antiochus' name, sent letters at the hand of envoys to Jonathan, confirming the high priesthood to him and granting him the four territories. [K92] (Perhaps Ptolemais was added to the three territories.) {See note on 3859b AM. <<3643>>} {Apc 1Ma 10:30,39} He honoured Jonathan as one of the king's friends. He also sent him chargers of gold from which to be served and gave him permission to drink from vessels of gold, to be clothed in purple and to wear the golden buckle. Moreover, he appointed his brother Simon as general of all the king's forces from the land of Tyre to the borders of Egypt. {Apc 1Ma 11:57-59} Jonathan was very grateful for the favours and honours Antiochus had so bountifully bestowed on him and sent his envoys to Antiochus and his guardian Tryphon. He promised that he would be their friend and associate and join in arms against their common enemy, Demetrius. He complained about Demetrius' ingratitude, in that he had repaid his civilities and courtesies with many shrewd actions and injustices. {*Josephus, Antiq., l. 13. c. 5. s. 4. (145-147) 7:297,299}

3650. After all of Syria had revolted from their king, Diodotus used Coracesium, a citadel in Cilicia, as his headquarters. He had the Cilicians join him in piracy at sea. {*Strabo, l. 14. c. 5. s. 2. 6:327} [E476]

3651. Demetrius stayed at Laodicea and spent his time idly in revelling and luxury. He did not change his wicked ways and had learnt nothing from his recent calamities. {*Diod. Sic., l. 33. c. 9. 12:25}

3652. At this time, Ptolemy Euergetes II, or Physcon, was made king at the palace at Memphis according to the solemn rites of the Egyptians. Queen Cleopatra, who was both his sister and wife and also the sister of Philometor, bore him a son. He was so overjoyed at this that he named him Memphites, because he was born while his father was observing the holy solemnities at Memphis. However, even during the celebration of his son's birth, he did not refrain from his cruel practices, but gave orders to execute some of the Cyrenians, who were the ones who had first brought him into Egypt. They had been too free and sharp in reproving him for his courtesan Irene, the prostitute. {*Diod. Sic., l. 33. c. 13. 12:27}

3653. When Jonathan had received permission from Antiochus to wage war against Demetrius' captains, he assembled his soldiers from Syria, Phoenicia and elsewhere. He quickly passed through all the cities located beyond the Jordan River. With all his Syrian auxiliaries, he marched to Askelon, where the citizens very conscientiously came out to meet him. He left there for Gaza, where he was denied entrance, the citizens shutting their gates against him. Thereupon, Jonathan besieged the city and plundered and burned its outskirts, forcing them by these actions to sue for peace. This was granted when they handed over hostages, whom Jonathan sent to Jerusalem. Jonathan then marched through the country as far as Damascus. {Apc 1Ma 11:60-62} {*Josephus, Antiq., l. 13. c. 5. s. 5. (148-153) 7:299,301}

3654. The princes of Demetrius came to Kadesh, a city of Galilee, and planned to draw Jonathan away from attacking Syria by making him come to the aid of the Galileans. Jonathan marched against them and left his brother Simon behind in Judea. Simon vigorously assaulted Bethsura for many days and after a long siege, forced them to surrender. He expelled Demetrius' soldiers and put in a garrison there instead. {Apc 1Ma 11:63-66 14:7,33} {*Josephus, Antiq., l. 13. c. 5. s. 6. (154-157) 7:301,303}

3655. Jonathan and his army camped by the Lake of Gennesaret. Early in the morning they came to the plain of Asor, where Demetrius' forces attacked him from an ambush they had placed in the mountains. [K93] As soon as the ambush showed itself, the Jews feared they might be trapped and could all be killed. So they all fled, leaving Jonathan in great danger. Only Mattathias, the son of Absalom, and Judas, the son of Calphi, who were the two chief commanders of the army, remained with him with a band of fifty very brave men. First, Jonathan begged for God's help, and then he and the men charged the enemy and defeated them. When those who had deserted Jonathan saw that the enemy was fleeing, they returned into the field and pursued the enemy to their own camp, as far as Kadesh. About three thousand of the enemy were killed that day, after which Jonathan returned to Jerusalem. {*Apc 1Ma 11:67-74*} {*\*Josephus, Antiq., l. 13. c. 5. s. 7. (158-162) 7:303,305*}

*3656.* Jonathan saw that things were now going well and sent Numenius, son of Antiochus, and Antipater, son of Jason, as envoys to Rome to confirm and renew the alliance and association which had formerly been started with Judas Maccabeus. {*Apc 1Ma 12:1,16*} He gave them orders that on their return home from Rome, they should visit the Lacedemonians, to remind them of the alliance and ancient league previously made with the high priest, Onias III. He sent a letter for the same purpose, wherein the people of Judea said, among other things, that they continually remembered them as their own brethren when they made their holy sacrifices and observed their devotions. {*Apc 1Ma 12:2,5-18*} {*\*Josephus, Antiq., l. 13. c. 5. s. 8. (163-170) 7:307-311*}

*3657.* Jonathan got word that Demetrius' commanders had returned to fight against him with an army far larger than they previously had. He left Jerusalem and marched against them in the country of Amathus, which is located in the farthest borders of Canaan. When he camped within six miles of the enemy, he sent out his scouts to spy on the enemy's position and fortifications. Jonathan learned through some prisoners whom the scouts had brought back, that the enemy planned a surprise attack on them. He ordered his soldiers to stand all night with their armour in a position of readiness to receive the enemy attack. He placed his guards throughout the camp. When the enemy heard that Jonathan was drawn up in battle array and was prepared for their attack, they began to be afraid. So they stole away secretly by night, leaving campfires throughout the camp to deceive the Jews. In the morning, Jonathan pursued them, but was unable to overtake them because they had already crossed the Eleutherus River. *[E477]* Therefore, Jonathan went into Arabia against the Zabadeans or Nabateans, according to Josephus, killing them and taking their spoil. From there, he went to Damascus and travelled through the whole country hunting and chasing the followers of Demetrius. His brother Simon was not idle, either. He made an expedition as far as Askelon and the adjacent garrison. From there, he went to Joppa and captured it. He put his garrison of soldiers in it to hold it. There was a rumour that the citizens planned to turn the garrison over to Demetrius' party. {*Apc 1Ma 12:24-34*} {*\*Josephus, Antiq., l. 13. c. 5. s. 10. (174-180) 7:313-317*}

*3658.* The envoys of the Jews were brought into the Senate, where they renewed their amity and league with the Romans, who gave them letters for the governors of their various allies, asking them to conduct them safely to Judea. {*Apc 1Ma 12:3,4*} On their return home, the envoys called on the Lacedemonians, who treated them very civilly and gave them a public decree concerning the renewing of their amity and the preserving of the friendship between their two countries. A copy of this is found on another occasion in the Apocrypha. {*Apc 1Ma 14:22,23*}

> "Numenius, the son of Antiochus, and Antipater, the son of Jason, the Jews' envoys, came to us to renew the friendship that was between us. *[K94]* It pleased the people to receive the men honourably and to enter a copy of their embassy among the public records, so that the people of the Lacedemonians might have a memorial of this."

*3659.* As soon as Jonathan returned to Jerusalem, he assembled the elders of the people and consulted with them about the building of citadels in some suitable locations around Judea. He also wanted the wall around Jerusalem strengthened and a high and strong wall erected between the citadel of Zion and the city, to prevent anyone from carrying provisions from the city to the citadel. They began their repairs and brought their new work to join up with the remains of the old wall, toward the east by the brook Kidron. They repaired the place known as Chaphenatha. Simon, meanwhile, went into other places of Judea, and built Adida in Sephelah, or the plain, and reinforced it with gates and bars. {*Apc 1Ma 12:35-38*}

## 3861a AM, 4570 JP, 144 BC

*3660.* In the 169th year of the account of the contracts, in the reign of Demetrius, the Jews in Jerusalem and Palestine wrote to the Jews in Egypt about the keeping of the feast of tabernacles in the month of Chisleu. {*Apc 2Ma 1:7-9*} This was the feast of the Maccabean dedication, which was observed according to the ordinance of the Mosaic feast of tabernacles in the month of Tishri. {*See note on 3840a AM. <<3422>>*}

*3661.* Tryphon planned to kill Antiochus and feared that Jonathan would come to the defence of the young king. So he marched with his forces to Bethshan, which the Gentiles called Scythopolis, hoping to surprise him. When Jonathan heard of his coming, he marched toward him with forty thousand good men. This so disheartened Tryphon that he did not lay hands on him, but treated him very nobly and recommended him to all his friends. He gave Jonathan many presents and ordered his soldiers to guard Jonathan as they guarded him. After the meeting, he persuaded Jonathan to dismiss his army and with a few selected men accompany him to Ptolemais, which he promised to turn over to him along with the other garrisons and forces he had in the area. Jonathan believed him and sent two thousand of his soldiers to Galilee and the rest to Judea, keeping only a thousand for himself. As soon as he entered Ptolemais, Tryphon commanded the gates to be shut. Jonathan was captured and all who had come with him were killed. Not satisfied, however, with the massacre of those thousand, Tryphon sent his army and some cavalry into Galilee to attack the two thousand men that Jonathan had sent there. As soon as they heard what had happened at Ptolemais, they prepared for battle. Tryphon's soldiers knew they were dealing with desperate men and retreated back again. So Jonathan's soldiers safely reached Judea and all Israel mourned the loss of their countrymen with great lamentation. {*Apc 1 Ma 12:39-52*}

3662. After this, Tryphon raised a large army to attack Judea and destroy it. When Simon saw how discouraged the people were at this, he went up to Jerusalem, assembled the people and offered to help them. So they chose him as general in place of Judas and Jonathan, his brothers. He gathered all the men of war and quickly completed the walls of Jerusalem, fortifying it on every side. He spent large sums of money from his own purse to arm, and pay, all the men of war from his own country. {*Apc 1 Ma 12:52,53 13:1-10 14:31,32*} [*E478*] [*K95*]

3663. In addition, Simon sent Jonathan, the son of Absalom, with a reasonably large army to Joppa. He drove out the inhabitants and occupied and fortified the place, to use it as his sea port. {*Apc 1 Ma 13:11 14:5,34*} From this, Strabo, too, has noted that the Jews used this harbour. {*\*Strabo, l. 16. c. 2. s. 28. 7:275*}

3664. Tryphon left Ptolemais with his army to march against Judea, taking Jonathan along with him as his prisoner. Simon was camped in Adida, opposite the plain. When Tryphon saw that the Jews were prepared for battle, he pretended that he was keeping Jonathan prisoner for a ransom of a hundred talents of silver. He promised to release Jonathan when this was paid, provided that he sent two of his sons as hostages, to guard against Jonathan's attempt to revenge his imprisonment after he was freed. However, as soon as Simon had sent both the money and his brother's sons to him, Tryphon broke his word. {*Apc 1 Ma 13:12-19*}

3665. When Tryphon marched against Judea, he went in the direction of the road to Adora, or Dora, a city of Idumea, according to Josephus. However, Simon's army followed him wherever he went. The men in the citadel of Zion at Jerusalem sent some agents to Tryphon, very earnestly asking him to hurry through the desert as fast as he could and to supply them with food. Tryphon was quite ready for the expedition with his cavalry. That night, however, there happened to be such a large snowfall that he could not possibly get to them, so he altered his journey and marched into the country of Gilead.

As soon as he came close to Bascama, or Bascha, he killed Jonathan. After he had buried him, Tryphon retreated back into Syria. {*Apc 1 Ma 13:20-24*} {*\*Josephus, Antiq., l. 13. c. 6. s. 6. (208-212) 7:331,333*} Jonathan lived seventeen years and seven months after the death of his brother Judas Maccabeus. He was the high priest for nine years and a month or two.

## 3861b AM, 4571 JP, 143 BC

3666. Simon sent men to bring back the bones of his brother Jonathan, which he then buried at Modin, the city of their ancestors. All Israel lamented for him for many days. Simon built a monument over the sepulchre of his father and his brothers. It was very high, and made of polished white stone. He built seven pyramids, all in a row, in memory of his father, his mother, and his four brothers. To these he added a porch of large stone pillars, on which he had a picture of arms and ships engraved. These were conspicuous to all who sailed by that way. {*Apc 1 Ma 13:25-30*} {*\*Josephus, Antiq., l. 13. c. 6. s. 6. (208-212) 7:331,333*} Josephus said that this rare sepulchre at Modin lasted to his time, as did Eusebius of Caesarea, in his book πζει πω ποπικω ονοματων. (Greek almost unreadable in the original. Editor.)

3667. The Romans and the Lacedemonians were very deeply grieved by the death of Jonathan. As soon as they learned through Simon's envoys that he had been made the high priest in his brother's place, they wrote to him in tables of brass concerning the renewing of the amity and league which they had formerly made with his brothers, Judas and Jonathan. {*Apc 1 Ma 14:16-19*} The Romans considered the Jews their allies, friends and brethren, and most honourably entertained Simon's envoys. {*Apc 1 Ma 14:40*} The inscription of the letters which the Lacedemonians returned through the envoys, and to which they also attached a copy of the reply they had previously sent to Jonathan, was this: [*K96*]

> "The magistrates and cities of the Lacedemonians to Simon the high priest and the elders and to the rest of the people of the Jews our brethren, greetings." {*Apc 1 Ma 14:20-24*}

3668. The letters from the Romans and the Lacedemonians were read before the congregation at Jerusalem. {*Apc 1 Ma 14:19*}

3669. Antiochus Theos, or the Divine, the son of Alexander Balas, was murdered by his guardian, Diodotus, or Tryphon. He bribed the surgeons to kill Antiochus and say that he had died of a fit while they were operating on him. Tryphon began with his own country and seized Apamea, Larisa, Casiana, Megara, Apollonia and the other neighbouring cities first. From there he went on to invade the rest of Syria. He placed the royal crown on his own head and created great desolation in the country. {*Apc 1Ma 13:31,32*} {*Livy, l. 55. 14:55*} {*Strabo, l. 16. c. 2. s. 10. 7:253*} {*Justin, Trogus, l. 36. c. 1.*}

3670. When Tryphon had made himself king, he hurried to have his kingdom confirmed by decree of the Roman Senate. To accomplish this, he sent his envoys to the Romans with a golden statue of Victory that weighed ten thousand gold staters. He did not doubt the success of his mission, because he had sent such a rich gift and because it carried the name of Victory. His hopes were dashed by the subtlety of the Senate. When they received the present, they ordered that instead of Tryphon's name, the title of the princely youth who had been killed by Tryphon's treachery should be engraved on it. {*Diod. Sic., l. 33. c. 28a. 12:47*} [E479] Not dismayed by this, he caused money to be minted of which some pieces still exist. It had this inscription: ΒΑ ΙΛΕΩ ΤΡΥΦΩΝΟ and ΤΡΥΦΩΝΟ ΑΥΤΟΚΡΑΤΟΡΟ ΒΑ ΙΛΕΩ: *King Tryphon* and *Tryphon, the Autocratic King.* After he had taken over the kingdom, he was bold enough to assume the title of king. He changed his old name from Diodotus to Tryphon. {*Appian, Syrian Wars, l. 11. c. 11. (68) 2:233*}

3671. Sarpedon, general of Demetrius' forces, was defeated by Tryphon's army, to whom the inhabitants of Ptolemais were allied. He retired with his soldiers into the Mediterranean country. As the victorious forces of Tryphon were marching along the sea coast between Ptolemais and Tyre, they were suddenly hit by a giant tidal wave from the sea, which rose to an incredible height and rushed onto the land with great force. Many were drowned. Some were pulled out to sea by the retreating wave and others were left dead in hollow places. The retreating wave left a large number of fish mingled with the dead bodies. When Sarpedon's soldiers heard of this disaster, they quickly returned to the scene, very pleased to see the destruction of the enemy. They gathered up a great number of the fish and sacrificed them to Poseidon, the deliverer, before the gates of Ptolemais, where the battle had been fought. {*Strabo, l. 16. c. 2. s. 26. 7:273*} {*Athenaeus, l. 8. (333cd) 4:4:13,15*}

3672. Simon, the Jewish general and high priest, repaired the garrisons in Judea. He fortified them all around with high towers, large walls, gates and bars, and supplied them all with provisions. His greatest concern was to see that Bethsura, which was located within the borders of Judea and had formerly been the enemy's armoury, would be well-fortified. He put a garrison of Jews there to secure it. {*Apc 1Ma 13:33 14:7,33*}

3673. Simon saw that all Tryphon did was plunder everything. He sent a crown of gold to King Demetrius Nicator, requesting him to release Judea from having to pay tribute. {*Apc 1Ma 13:34,37 14:10,33*} [K97]

3674. Demetrius heard that Simon's envoys had been very nobly entertained by the Romans and that the Jews and the priests had passed the right to the government and the high priesthood to Simon and his heirs. So Demetrius also confirmed the high priesthood to Simon and made him one of his friends. {*Apc 1Ma 14:38-41*} He wrote a letter to him:

"King Demetrius to Simon, the high priest, and friend of the king, and to the elders and country of the Jews, greetings:"

3675. In this way, he made a peace with them. He promised an amnesty for all past actions, a ratification of all former covenants that had been made with Jonathan and a grant to them of all the citadels which they had built. {*Apc 1Ma 11:32-37*} He granted to all in general a release from tribute, as well as granting release from the custom taxes arising from the sale of commodities to those at Jerusalem. Hence the yoke of the Gentiles was removed from Israel in the 170th year of the kingdom of the Greeks. The people began to date their instruments and contracts as: {*Apc 1Ma 13:35-42*} {*Josephus, Antiq., l. 13. c. 6. s. 7. (213,214) 7:333,335*}

"In the first year that Simon was the great high priest, general, and leader of the Jews:"

3676. In those days, Simon besieged Gazara, which had rebelled following Jonathan's death. After he had forced the tower with his battering engines, he compelled the city to surrender. When the city humbly asked for his mercy, he did not kill the citizens but drove them out of the city. After he had cleared the houses of all their idols and other impurities, he entered the city and praised God with hymns. He repopulated the city with those who worshipped the true God. He fortified it and built a house in it for himself. {*Apc 1Ma 13:43-48*}

## 3862a AM, 4571 JP, 143 BC

3677. Hipparchus observed the sixth autumnal equinox in the 36th year of the Calippic period, on the fourth day of the Egyptian Additionals (September 26), in the evening around sunset. {*Ptolemy, Great Syntaxis, l. 3. c. 2.*}

3678. Alexandra, who later became the queen of the Jews, was born at this time, if she lived seventy-three years, as Josephus claimed. {*Josephus, Antiq., l. 13. c. 16. s. 6. (430) 7:445*} This is also found in the thirty-third chapter of the Jewish History which is printed at the end of the Paris Bibles in many languages, under the title of the second book of the Maccabees. From Eusebius' Chronicle, we find that she was called Salina in Arabic, as we also do from

Epiphanius in the 29th heresy of the Nazarenes, and from Jerome {Jerome, Da 9:1-17 11:1-12} and Sulpicius Severus. {*Sulpicius Severus, Sacred History, l. 2. c. 26. 11:109} Eusebius seems to have taken it, as was his practice, from Julius Africanus, and he from Justus Tiberiensis, or some other ancient writer of the affairs of the Jews.

## 3862b AM, 4572 JP, 142 BC

3679. The garrison of soldiers in the citadel at Jerusalem surrendered after being deprived of all provision for two years. Simon expelled them all and cleared the citadel of all the pollutions of their idols. [E480] He entered it on the 23rd day of the second month, called Iyyar, in the 171st year of the kingdom of the Greeks, with palm branches, harps, cymbals, viols, hymns and songs. He ordained this day as a holy day, to commemorate the day they were freed from a wicked enemy who troubled them greatly whenever they went to the temple. Moreover, he made the citadel stronger than it had been and fortified the temple mount which the citadel overlooked. This was for the greater security of the country and the city. He lived there with his troops. {Apc 1Ma 13:49-53 14:7,36,37} [K98]

3680. Simon knew that his son John, later surnamed Hyrcanus, was a very valiant man and appointed him captain of all his forces, while Simon lived in Gazara in the borders of Azotus, where the enemies had formerly lived. {Apc 1Ma 13:53} Simon had dislodged them and repopulated the place with Jews. {Apc 1Ma 14:7,34} This was the Gadara which Strabo said the Jews later made their own. {*Strabo, l. 16. c. 2. s. 29. 7:277}

3681. Ptolemy Philometor's daughter, Cleopatra, and Demetrius Nicator had a son, Antiochus, later surnamed Grypus, because of his hook nose. This event happened at this time if he lived for forty-five years, as Josephus stated. {*Josephus, Antiq., l. 13. c. 13. s. 4. (365) 7:409}

## 3863 AM, 4573 JP, 141 BC

3682. Two hours before midnight, Hipparchus observed an eclipse of the moon in Rhodes, in the 37th year of the third Calippic period, in the 607th year of Nabonassar, on the 20th day of the Egyptian month of Tybi (January 27). {Ptolemy, Great Syntaxis, l. 6. c. 5.}

3683. When Demetrius learned that most of his cities had revolted from him, he thought to remove this reproach by fighting against the Parthians. At that time, the Parthians were ruled by Mithridates, son of King Pampatius, called Arsaces or Arsacides. This was a name common to all the Parthian kings. Mithridates was not inferior to Arsaces, his great-grandfather and the founder of the Parthian monarchy, from whom that surname was passed to all his successors. By his prowess, Mithridates extended the Parthian empire as far as the Indus River to the east and the Euphrates River to the west. {Justin, Trogus, l. 36. c. 1.} {Justin, Trogus, l. 41. c. 5,6.} {Orosius, l. 5. c. 4.} Before we discuss Demetrius' Parthian expedition, we shall show how Mithridates obtained his vast dominion.

3684. At the time when Mithridates began to reign over the Parthians, Eucratides became ruler of the Bactrians. They were both gallant men, but good fortune was on the side of the Parthians. During the rule of Mithridates, he led them to the highest pinnacle of sovereignty. The poor Bactrians were involved in wars which eventually led to the loss of their dominions and liberty. After the Sogdians, the Arachats, the Drangians and the Indians had thoroughly weakened them by their continual wars with them, the feeble Parthians attacked them while they were in this weakened state and overcame them. {Justin, Trogus, l. 41. c. 6.} Arsaces, or Mithridates, followed up on his victory as far as India and had no difficulty in subduing the country where Porus of old had reigned, and the other countries lying between the Hydaspes and Indus Rivers. {*Diod. Sic., l. 33. c. 18. 12:35,37} {Orosius, l. 5. c. 4.} These Bactrians were the survivors of the Greeks who had taken Bactria from the kings of Syria, the successors of Seleucus Nicator. They also seized Ariana and India. They controlled Pattalena and all the sea coasts along with the kingdoms of Tessariostus and Sigartis. Apollodorus (against the common opinion, in actual fact) affirmed in his book of the Parthian Affairs that they were masters of a greater portion of India than Alexander and his Macedonians had been. He added, moreover, that Eucratides had a thousand cities in India under his own jurisdiction. {*Strabo, l. 11. c. 9. s. 2. 5:275} {*Strabo, l. 15. c. 1. s. 3. 7:5} Eucratides was always at war, for he was engaged in many wars and behaved himself with much prowess. When he was worn out from constant warfare, he was closely besieged by Demetrius, king of the Indians. Although Eucratides had no more than three thousand soldiers with him, he wasted an enemy army of sixty thousand by his daily sallies against them. [K99] When he gained his freedom in the fifth month, he subdued all India under his command. On his journey homeward, he was killed by his own son, whom he had made viceroy in the kingdom. His son did not try to hide his actions, but drove his chariot through the blood and commanded that the dead body be cast aside into some place or other and left unburied, as if he had killed an enemy and not murdered his father. While these things were happening among the Bactrians, a war started between the Parthians and the Medes. The initial conflicts were indecisive, but finally the Parthians got the upper hand. Mithridates was strengthened by this victory and appointed Bacasis over Media while he marched into Hyrcania. As soon as he returned from there, he fought and defeated the king of the Elymeans and annexed that country to his other dominions. *[E481]* By his various conquests, he enlarged the dominion of the Parthians from the mountain of Gaucasus as far as the Euphrates River. {*Justin, Trogus, l. 41. c. 6.*} After he had defeated Demetrius Nicator's general, he invaded the city of Babylon and all its regions. {*Orosius, l. 5. c. 4.*}

*3685.* The Greeks and Macedonians of the upper provinces did not like the insolence of those strangers, the Parthians. They repeatedly sent embassies to Demetrius Nicator, promising that if he would come to them, they would yield to him and join with him in fighting Arsaces, the king of Persia and Media. Encouraged by this, Demetrius hurried to them. In the 172nd year of the kingdom of the Greeks, he assembled all his forces and marched into Mesopotamia. He thought that he would soon have Babylon and Media, and that with the help of the upper provinces he could easily expel Tryphon from Syria. When he arrived in those regions, he was quickly joined by the auxiliaries of the Persians, Elymeans and Bactrians, and defeated the Parthians many times. He was at last outsmarted by one of Arsaces' nobles, who was sent to capture Demetrius on the pretence of concluding a peace. Demetrius was surprised by an ambush and was captured alive, after losing his whole army. They led him through the streets of the city and showed him to the people, who mocked him. Finally, he was imprisoned under tight security. {*Apc 1Ma 14:1-3*} {*\*Josephus, Antiq., l. 13. c. 5. s. 11. (181-186) 7:317,319*} {*Justin, Trogus, l. 36. c. 1.*} {*Justin, Trogus, l. 38. c. 9.*} Georgius Syncellus added that he was kept in Troas, and was surnamed *Siderites* from that occasion.

*3686.* Although Arsaces was in control of such a vast dominion, he did not succumb to luxury and pride, which was the usual practice of most princes. He acted with valour against his enemies and a great deal of clemency toward his subjects. When he had brought various countries under his command, he selected the best institutions and laws from each of them, and introduced them to his Parthians. {*\*Diod. Sic., l. 33. c. 18. 12:35,37*} Demetrius, who was sent away into Hyrcania, was treated with respect too. Arsaces gave him his daughter for a wife and promised to restore the kingdom of Syria to him, which had been taken from him by Tryphon. {*Justin, Trogus, l. 36. c. 1.*} {*Justin, Trogus, l. 38. c. 9.*} However, Appian wrote that Demetrius lived at the court of Phraates, the brother and successor of Mithridates, and married his sister, Rhodoguna. {*\*Appian, Syrian Wars, l. 11. c. 11. (67) 2:233*}

*3687.* In the 172nd year of the kingdom of the Greeks, on the 18th day of the sixth month, called Elul, about the end of the third year of Simon's high priesthood after the death of his brother Jonathan, a large assembly of the priests and the people, and the rulers and the elders of the country, was held. A notice was published that said how well Simon had served the Jewish people, and the right of sovereignty was granted to him and his posterity. *[K100]* He should be their governor and have control over those who managed the temple, over the governors in the country, over the commanders in the army and the captains of the garrisons. He should also have the charge of the holy things and should be obeyed by all men. All contracts in the country should be signed in his name. He should be clothed in purple and wear gold. It should not be lawful for any of the priests or the people to repeal any of these decrees, or contradict anything he spoke, or to hold any assembly in the country, without his permission. No one should wear purple or use the golden buckle. Simon accepted this and was quite content to carry out the high priest's office and to be general and commander over the Jews, the priests and the rest of the people. Then they commanded that this writing be put in tables of brass and be hung on the pillars in the porches of the temple, in a public place. A copy of this should be kept in the treasury of the temple, so that these edicts might be available to Simon and his sons. {*Apc 1Ma 14:26-49*}

## 3864 AM, 4574 JP, 140 BC

*3688.* The soldiers grew weary of Tryphon's conduct and revolted from him to Cleopatra, the wife of Demetrius Nicator. At that time, she was confined in Seleucia with her children. She sent to Antiochus, the brother of her imprisoned husband Demetrius, and offered to marry him and give him the kingdom. She did this partly on the advice of her friends and partly because she feared that some of the Seleucians might surrender the city to Tryphon. {*\*Josephus, Antiq., l. 13. c. 7. s. 1. (222) 7:339*}

*3689.* Josephus called this Antiochus, the son of Demetrius Soter, *The Pious* because of his religion. {*\*Josephus, Antiq., l. 7. c. 5. s. 3. (393) 5:569,571*} {*\*Josephus, Antiq., l. 13. c. 8. s. 2. (244) 7:351*} Elsewhere, Josephus called him by his father's surname, *Soter*. {*\*Josephus, Antiq., l. 13. c. 7. s. 1. (222) 7:339*} Justin called him *Pompey*. {*Justin, Trogus, l. 39. Prologue*} Eusebius called him *Sidetes*, or *Sedetes*. {*\*Eusebius, Chronicles, l. 1. 1:227*} *[E482]* This was either from his great love of hunting, as Plutarch thought, which in Syriac is צירה, or from the city of Sidon, from where (as Georgius Syncellus wrote) he came to besiege Tryphon. Justin related that he was at first brought up in Asia by his father, Demetrius Soter, and then, with his older brother Demetrius Nicator, entrusted to an army at Cnidos. {*Justin, Trogus, l. 35. c. 2.*} {*Justin, Trogus, l. 36, c. 1.*} Appian wrote that when he was being educated at Rhodes, he was told the news of his brother's confinement and what happened subsequently. {*\*Appian, Syrian Wars, l. 11. c. 11. (68)*}

*2:233,235}* After he had assumed the title of king, he wrote letters to Simon, the high priest and ruler, and to the whole country of the Jews. {*Apc 1Ma 15:1,2}*

*3690.* In these letters, he complained much about the harsh treatment he had received from his enemies and showed that he was now ready to avenge himself, lest he seem to be a king in name only. He wanted to make Simon his friend and so he confirmed to him all the immunities and privileges which other kings had granted. To these he added the right to coin money with his own stamp. Moreover, he decreed that Jerusalem should be exempted from being under the king's jurisdiction and also promised that he would confer more and greater favours, as soon as he was in possession of his kingdom. {*Apc 1Ma 15:3-9}*

## 3865 AM, 4575 JP, 139 BC

*3691.* Numenius, the son of Antiochus, and some other envoys came to Rome from Simon, the high priest, and the people of the Jews, about renewing their league and friendship with the Romans. They brought a large gold shield with them, weighing a thousand pounds. The present was well received and Lucius, the consul, gave them letters to the kings and to the provinces, prohibiting these from attempting anything which might prejudice the Jews or help any of their enemies. *[K101]* If at any time any renegade Jews should flee from Judea and come into their land, they should turn them over to Simon, the high priest, to be prosecuted according to the laws of their country. {*Apc 1Ma 14:1-49 15:15-21}*

*3692.* This Lucius was the same Lucius Calpurnius Piso, the colleague of Lucius Popilius Laenas, who was sent into Spain against the Numantians. Concerning his consulship, Valerius Maximus stated: {*\*Valerius Maximus, l. 1. c. 3. s. 3. 1:47}*

> "Publius Cornelius Hispalus, the praetor for visitors when Popilius Laenas and Lucius Calpurnius were consuls, by his edict commanded that within ten days all those Chaldeans were to depart from the city and from Italy, whose profession it was, with their lies to cast mists on vain and foolish minds, by their false interpretation of the influence of the stars."

*3693.* Even though Stephanus Pighius (from Cassodorus' *Fasti Consulares*) had written the name of Gnaeus for Lucius of the name Lucius, which is against the authority of the received manuscripts.

*3694.* Five kings received these letters: Ptolemy Euergetes II or Physcon of Egypt, Demetrius Nicator of Syria (even though he was a prisoner of the Parthians at this time), Attalus Philadelphus of Pergamum in Asia, Ariarathes of Cappadocia, and Arsaces or Mithridates of Parthia. Nineteen cities, countries and islands also received these letters: Sampsames (or, as in the Latin, Lampsacus), Sparta, Delos, Myndus, Sicyon, Caria, Samos, Pamphylia, Lycia, Halicarnassus, Rhodes, Phaselis, Cos, Sida, Aradus, Gortyna, Cnidos, Cyprus and Cyrene. {*Apc 1Ma 15:16,22,23}*

*3695.* In the 174th year of the kingdom of the Greeks, Antiochus Sidetes returned to the land of his fathers, where he married Cleopatra, his brother's wife. {*Apc 1Ma 15:10}* {*Justin, Trogus, l. 36. c. 1.}* She was upset at Demetrius for marrying Rhodoguna. {*\*Appian, Syrian Wars, l. 11. c. 11. (68) 2:235}* From this time, Antiochus reigned for nine years. {*Porphyry, Scaliger's Greek Eusebius}*

*3696.* Tryphon had a very small following, because almost all his forces had defected to Antiochus. After his soldiers deserted him, he hurried to get into Adora, which was a maritime city of Phoenicia. Antiochus pursued him there and very tightly besieged the place, so that no one could get in or out. Antiochus had an army of a hundred and twenty thousand foot soldiers, with eight thousand cavalry and a fleet. {*Apc 1Ma 15:10-14}*

*3697.* Meanwhile, Numenius and his company came from Rome and brought with them letters to the kings and provinces and a copy of these same letters to Simon, the high priest. {*Apc 1Ma 15:15,24}*

*3698.* Simon sent two thousand choice men with silver and gold and many engines of war to Antiochus at the siege of Adora. He refused them all and breaking whatever covenants he had previously made with Simon, made him his enemy. He sent Athenobius to him to demand that he surrender Gazara, Joppa and the citadel in Jerusalem. Antiochus also wanted the tributes of those places beyond the borders of Judea which were occupied by Simon. In lieu of this, he demanded five hundred talents of silver and in consideration of the harm Simon had done and the tributes of the cities, a further five hundred talents. He threatened war unless everything was done according to his commands. {*Apc 1Ma 15:25-31}*

*3699.* Athenobius, a friend of the king's, came to Jerusalem. *[E483]* As soon as he saw Simon's splendour, his tables set with gold and silver plates, and other furnishings of the house, he was astonished and told Simon the king's message. *[K102]* Simon denied that they had seized any towns that belonged to others, and claimed they had only recovered from the enemy by law of arms some of their own towns which had been withheld from them. As for Joppa and Gazara, in spite of the fact that the people had sustained much damage at the hands of the enemy, he offered a hundred talents. In a rage,

Athenobius returned to Antiochus and told him both what he had heard and seen. Nor was the king any less passionate, when he saw that his commands had not been submitted to, nor his great threat of war heeded. {Apc 1Ma 15:32-36}

3700. Meanwhile, Tryphon set sail and escaped to Orthosia, which was another maritime city of Phoenicia. {Apc 1Ma 15:37}

3701. Antiochus made Cendebeus the governor of the sea coast and gave him foot soldiers and cavalry. He was to build Kidron (or, as the Latin edition has it, Gedor, as in the Bible {Jos 15:58}) and to wage war on the Jews, while the king pursued Tryphon. {Apc 1Ma 15:38,39}

3702. Cendebeus went as far as Jamnia and began to invade Judea. He took some prisoners and killed others. When he had built Kidron (or Gedor), he stationed some cavalry there and some companies of foot soldiers, who were to raid the highways of Judea as the king had ordered him to do. {Apc 1Ma 15:40,41}

### 3866a AM, 4575 JP, 139 BC

3703. John Hyrcanus came from Gazara and told his father, Simon, what wicked acts Cendebeus had done. Simon was now old and so he committed the war to his two oldest sons, Judas and John. They duly selected twenty thousand men of war from throughout the country and together with some cavalry, marched against Cendebeus. That night they camped at Modin, their birth place, from where, on the following morning, they engaged the enemy's powerful army. However, as there was a brook between them, John waded across first and the rest of the people quickly followed. He then divided his forces so that the cavalry was in the midst of the foot soldiers and they mutually protected each other from the enemy attacks. Then they sounded their holy trumpets and Cendebeus was routed, while many of his army were killed. Some fled to his citadel of Kidron, which he had recently built, and others escaped to other places. John's brother Judas was wounded and could not give chase, but John pursued them as far as the towers which were in the fields of Azotus, killing about two thousand men in the chase. When he had burned the towers to the ground, he led his army safely back into Judea. {Apc 1Ma 16:1-10}

### 3866b AM, 4576 JP, 138 BC

3704. At length, Tryphon retired to his own countrymen at Apamea. Frontinus recorded the following about this event: {*Frontinus, Stratagems, l. 2. c. 13. s. 3. 1:197}

"All the way that he went, he scattered money on purpose to slow down Antiochus' soldiers in their pursuit of him and so he escaped from their hands."

3705. Josephus stated that Apamea was taken by assault and Tryphon killed in the third year after Demetrius was taken prisoner by the Parthians. {*Josephus, Antiq., l. 13. c. 7. s. 3. (224) 7:341} Appian wrote that he was at length taken by Antiochus and killed, but not without much trouble. {*Appian, Syrian Wars, l. 11. c. 11. (68) 2:233,235} Strabo stated that he was besieged in a certain citadel and driven to such extremities that he killed himself. {*Strabo, l. 14. c. 5. s. 2. 6:327} Georgius Syncellus wrote that when he was driven from Orthosia, he leaped into the fire and died.

3706. Hierax was the general for the war in Egypt because he was an excellent soldier and very popular with the people. He was ambitious and controlled the kingdom of Ptolemy Physcon. [K103] When he realised that Ptolemy had little money and that the soldiers were ready to revolt to Galaestes for lack of pay, he put down the rebellion by personally paying the soldiers. The Egyptians publicly despised the king when they saw how childish he was in his talk, how impudent and prone to the vilest jests, and how effeminate he was. {*Diod. Sic., l. 33. c. 22,23. 12:41,43}

3707. In that part of Asia where Pergamum was, Attalus Philadelphus, the brother of Eumenes, grew so restless through long idleness and peace that Philopoemen, one of his friends, was able to influence him in any direction he pleased. Likewise, the Romans, to mock him, would often ask of those who sailed from Asia whether the king had any interest in Philopoemen, because he would not leave his kingdom to any of his own sons. {*Plutarch, Old Men in Public Affairs, l. 1. c. 16. 10:125} However, in his lifetime, he gave the kingdom to his brother Eumenes' son, whose guardian he was until his nephew came of age. {*Plutarch, Sayings of Kings and Commanders (184b) 3:83} {*Plutarch, On Brotherly Love, l. 1. c. 18. 6:311}

3708. After the death of his uncle Attalus, Attalus who was surnamed Philometor, ruled the kingdom of Pergamum for five years. He was the son of Eumenes by Stratonice, who was the daughter of Ariarathes, the king of the Cappadocians. {*Strabo, l. 13. c. 4. s. 2. 6:169} [E484]

3709. He had no sooner become king, than he marred the kingdom by killing his friends and turning against his relatives. At one time he pretended that his mother, who was an old woman, and at another time, that Berenice, his wife, had died through their enchantments. {Justin, Trogus, l. 36. c. 4.} He was jealous of the best and most eminent of his father's friends. Lest they should engage in some treasonable act against him, he planned to kill them all. To that end, he selected the most bloody and covetous from among his barbarous mercenary soldiers and placed them in various private rooms in the palace. When he called together to court those of his friends whom he held in greatest suspicion, he turned them over to these barbarians, who killed them. Immediately after this, he ordered them to do the same to the men's wives and children. His other friends either had command of the army or were appointed over cities. Some of them he killed by treachery and when he located others, he beheaded them with their whole families. By this cruelty, he became detestable to his own subjects and to his neighbouring countries, so much so that all under his dominion were anxious for a new king. {*Diod. Sic., l. 34/35. c. 3. 12:91}

### 3867a AM, 4576 JP, 138 BC

*3710.* After this mad and furious fit was over, he put on a dirty garment and let his hair and his beard grow, as criminals used to do. He did not appear in public and would not show himself to the people. He did not entertain at home and gave the appearance of being mad, seeming to be haunted by the ghosts of those he had recently murdered. {Justin, Trogus, l. 36. c. 4.}

### 3867b AM, 4577 JP, 137 BC

*3711.* When Attalus had resigned the government of the kingdom to his nephew, he took up gardening and growing herbs. He mixed good plants with poisonous ones, from which he made poisonous juices and sent them as rare presents to his friends. {Justin, Trogus, l. 36. c. 4.} He planted hendoryenium, which was used to make poisoned arrows. He also studied the plants to know the nature of their juices, seeds and fruits and to harvest them in their proper season. {*Plutarch, Demetrius, l. 1. c. 20. s. 2. 9:47} [K104] Varro, Columella and Pliny stated that he wrote some books about husbandry. {Varro, Human Antiquities, l. 1. c. 2.} {Columella, De Re Rustica, l. 1. c. 1.} {*Pliny, l. 18. c. 5. 5:203}

*3712.* Antiochus Sidetes attacked those cities which had revolted in the beginning of his brother's reign. When he had conquered them, he added them to his own kingdom. {Justin, Trogus, l. 36. c. 1.}

### 3868 AM, 4578 JP, 136 BC

*3713.* Ptolemy Euergetes II, or Physcon, killed many of those Alexandrians who had first called him to the kingdom. He banished a large number who had now come of age who, in their youth, had been raised with his brother Philometor, with whom he previously had differences. He let his foreign soldiers kill as they pleased and blood was daily shed everywhere. {Justin, Trogus, l. 38. c. 8.} {*Athenaeus, l. 4. (184c) 2:313} Moreover, he divorced Cleopatra herself, who was both his sister and wife. He first ravished her daughter, a virgin, and then married her. These wicked deeds so appalled the people that, in fear of death, they left their country and went into exile. So many left, that Ptolemy and his company were left alone in that vast city. When he saw that he was a

king of empty houses rather than of men, he by his edicts invited strangers to live there. {Justin, Trogus, l. 38. c. 8.} In this way, he repopulated the cities and islands with grammarians, philosophers, geometricians, musicians, school teachers, artists, physicians and many other artisans. By teaching their arts to make their living, they produced many excellent men. It came to pass that the liberal arts and sciences were revived in these lands. This knowledge had been interrupted and advancement hindered by the continual wars that had occurred during the times of Alexander's successors. {*Athenaeus, l. 4. (184c) 2:313}

*3714.* Publius Scipio Aemilianus, who after the destruction of Carthage was called Africanus, Spurius Mummius and Lucius Metellus were made envoys by the Roman Senate to ascertain the condition of the kingdoms and cities of their allies and to settle their differences. They made a thorough survey of Egypt, Syria, Asia and Greece. {*Strabo, l. 14. c. 5. s. 2. 6:329} {Justin, Trogus, l. 38. c. 8.} {*Plutarch, Sayings of Romans (200f) 3:191} {*Athenaeus, l. 6. (273a) 3:227} {*Athenaeus, l. 12. (549e) 5:493} Cicero wrote that Scipio was in this famous embassy before he was made a censor, but in Somnio Scipionis this same Cicero said that it was after he was censor and a little before his second consulship. {*Cicero, Academica, l. 2. c. 2. 19:471} Valerius Maximus stated that this embassy took place after his two consulships and his two chief triumphs, the Carthaginian and Numantian. {*Valerius Maximus, l. 4. c. 3. s. 13. 1:379} Polybius, in a work describing the Numantian war (as mentioned in Cicero {*Cicero, Friends, l. 5. c. 12. 25:367}), referred to this embassy. [E485] This we gather from Athenaeus {*Athenaeus, l. 6. (273a) 3:227} and from Suidas under the word Βαπος, when compared with Diodorus. {*Diod. Sic., l. 33. c. 28b. 12:49,51} Polybius said that after Scipio had been part of that embassy, he was sent to settle the Numantian war. Given these three conflicting opinions, we thought it best to choose the middle one.

*3715.* On this embassy, Scipio took a friend along with him. This was not Gaius Lelius, as was stated in the corrupt copies of Aurelius Victor, but Panaetius, the philosopher. {Aurelius Victor, De Viris Illustribus, l. 1. c. 58.} {*Cicero, Academica, l. 2. c. 2. 19:471} {*Plutarch, Sayings of Romans (201a) 3:193} {*Plutarch, Philosophers and Men in Power (777ab) 10:33,35} Athenaeus incorrectly thought it was Posidonius, the Stoic but he lived long after Scipio. {*Athenaeus, l. 12. (549de) 5:493} [K105] In his retinue Scipio had only five servants, according to Posidonius and Polybius (so that from these sources both Valerius Maximus, who assigned seven to him, and Aurelius Victor, who allowed only two, should be amended). Of those, one died on the journey. Scipio did not buy another servant, but wrote home for another one to be sent from Rome to replace him. {*Athenaeus, l. 6. (273ab) 3:227} {*Plutarch, Sayings of Romans (201a)

*3:193}* As he passed through the countries of both allies and strangers, they were not so much impressed by his slaves as by his various victories. Nor were they as interested in the amount of the gold and silver that he brought with him, as in the greatness of his reputation. {*Valerius Maximus, l. 4. c. 3. s. 13. 1:379}*

### 3869a AM, 4578 JP, 136 BC

*3716.* On receiving Ptolemy Euergetes' proclamation, foreigners came to Alexandria. The envoys from Rome also arrived there. {*Justin, Trogus, l. 38. c. 8.}* When Scipio left the ship to come ashore, he walked with his head covered with his cloak, but the Alexandrians flocked about him and asked him to show himself, because they wanted to see this great man. As soon as he uncovered himself, they shouted with great acclamation. {*Plutarch, Sayings of Romans (200f) 3:191}*

*3717.* When the king came to meet the envoys, he appeared somewhat ridiculous to the Romans. He looked horrible, short in stature, swag belly and more like a beast than a man. This ugliness was made worse by the thin, transparent garment he wore, as if to expose what modest men conceal. Justin described the man whom Athenaeus, from the seventh book of Poseidonius the Stoic, and Natalis Comes, described thus: {*Justin, Trogus, l. 38. c. 8.}* {*Athenaeus, l. 12. (549e) 5:493}*

> "His body, by reason of his luxurious living, had become gross and offensive and his belly so big that a man could hardly encircle him with his arms. This forced him to wear a long garment with sleeves reaching down to his ankles. He rarely walked on foot except for this time, out of respect for Scipio."

*3718.* Scipio saw that the king, because of lack of exercise, could barely keep pace with him without greatly straining himself. He whispered in Panethius' ear: {*Plutarch, Sayings of Romans (200f) 3:191,193}*

> "Now the Alexandrians have reaped some fruits from our travels here, since they, by their king's civility to us, have seen their king walking."

*3719.* From this we see how well Dalechamp, who translated Athenaeus, had rendered those words:

> "He never walked on foot without leaning on his staff."

*3720.* The king entertained the envoys very well and showed them his palace and his treasury. Because they were virtuous, they were content with plain, wholesome food and scorned the rich provisions as prejudicial both to the mind and body. Those things which the king esteemed as rarities and admirable, they only glanced at with their eyes and counted them as things of no value.

They looked at things of real worth very carefully. They noted the location of the city and its industry, and particularly looked at Pharos and what belonged to it. From there, they sailed to Memphis and noticed the goodness of the country, the convenience of the Nile River, the number of the cities, the very large population and the fortifications of Egypt. They noted the wealth and richness of the country, and how well it was provided for in security and size. In brief, having sufficiently admired both the populousness of Egypt and the good locations of its cities, they thought that the kingdom of Egypt could easily grow into a vast empire if it were fortunate enough to have good leadership. *[K106]* After they had viewed Egypt well, they went to Cyprus and from there to Syria. {*Diod. Sic., l. 33. c. 28b. 12:49}*

*3721.* To Mithridates Euergetes, king of Pontus, was born that famous Mithridates who was surnamed Dionysus, or Bacchus, or Eupator. Consequently, he called the city which he subsequently built Eupatoria. {*Appian, Mithridatic Wars, l. 12. c. 2. (10) 2:255}* {*Appian, Mithridatic Wars, l. 12. c. 11. (78) 2:387}* This Mithridates was both born and raised in the city of Sinope and therefore always held it in high esteem, also making it the capital of his whole kingdom. {*Strabo, l. 12. c. 3. s. 11. 5:389}* *[E486]*

*3722.* In the same year that Mithridates was born, there appeared a large comet. {*Justin, Trogus, l. 37. c. 2.}* This is the very same comet which Seneca mentioned: {*Seneca, Natural Questions, l. 7. c. 15. 10:259}*

> "In the time of Attalus' reign, there appeared a comet which at first was small. Later it elevated and spread itself and came as far as the equator. Its vast extent equalled the size of the Milky Way."

*3723.* Eutropius and Orosius, who usually followed Livy, stated that Mithridates lived seventy-two years. {*Eutropius, l. 6.}* {*Orosius, l. 6. c. 5.}* If Appian is correct when he stated that he lived only sixty-eight or nine years, then this comet appeared after Attalus was dead and not in his reign. {*Appian, Mithridatic Wars, l. 12. c. 16. (112) 2:457}*

### 3869b AM, 4579 JP, 135 BC

*3724.* Simon, the high priest and the ruler of the Jews, visited the cities of Judea and provided for their orderly government. He came down to Jericho with his sons, Mattathias and Judas, in the 177th year of the kingdom of the Greeks, in the eleventh month, which is called Shebat. There Ptolemy, the son of Abubus and the son-in-law to Simon, the high priest, entertained them in the citadel of Doc, which he had fortified. Ptolemy had been appointed by his father-in-law over the province of Jericho and was a very wealthy man who had wanted to take over the government of the country for himself. Thereupon, while he was treating Simon and his sons to a banquet at which they drank somewhat freely, he and his army of ruffians, whom he had placed in some secret spot, entered the house and treacherously killed Simon, his sons and some of his servants. {*Apc 1Ma 16:11-17*} Josephus stated that Simon was killed at a banquet through the treachery of his own son-in-law, after Simon had ruled the Jews for just eight years. {*Josephus, Antiq., l. 13. c. 7. s. 4. (228,229) 7:343*} However, we learn from the story of the Maccabees that Simon was the high priest for eight years and three months after his brother Jonathan died.

3725. Ptolemy immediately told King Antiochus Sidetes of this villainy and requested him to send an army to help him. He would soon deliver the country and cities of the Jews into his hands. {*Apc 1Ma 16:18*} Since all of this and the promise of getting the country for himself was known to the king so quickly, it was suspected that the king was in on this plot all along, and that the place of honour which the traitor wanted so much was prearranged by the king as a reward for this deed. Jacobus Salianus observed this in the epitome of his Annals, from which is derived that passage in Justin: {*Justin, Trogus, l. 36. Prologue*}

"After Hyrcanus was killed, Antiochus subdued the Jews."

3726. Hyrcanus, the son of Simon, was incorrectly written for Simon. On the contrary, Eusebius confused the father Simon with the son Hyrcanus when he wrote concerning the history of the conquest of Judea by Antiochus: {*Eusebius, Chronicles, l. 1. 1:227*}

"He forced Simon the high priest to submit to conditions." [K107]

3727. This wicked Ptolemy sent his vile men to Gazara to surprise John Hyrcanus and to kill him. He tried to influence the captains of the Jewish army and wrote letters to them, making them generous promises if they would revolt. He sent others to seize Jerusalem and the temple mount. However, someone ran ahead to Gazara and told John that his father and his brothers had been killed and that others were coming to kill him. Although John was greatly shocked by the sad news, he killed the murderers by attacking them first. He was made high priest in the place of his father. {*Apc 1Ma 16:19-24*}

3728. Here ends the first book of the Maccabees, containing the history of forty years, which Josephus continued. He begins with an improbable account, for he said that John Hyrcanus escaped to the city in the very nick of time and was received into it by the people. He then shut out Ptolemy, who was attempting to enter in by another gate. After John had performed the holy services, he led his army from the city against Ptolemy and besieged him in the citadel of Dagon, above Jericho. While John was endeavouring to take the citadel, Ptolemy ordered that John's mother and his two brothers, who were with him in the citadel, be brought out. They were to scourge them soundly with whips and threaten to throw them down over the wall, unless he broke off the attack. John was touched by their plight and started to lose his resolve. His mother very resolutely exhorted her son not to stop out of his love for her, but to do what he could to take vengeance on the traitor. However, he stopped his batteries as often as he saw his mother being whipped. Since the sabbatical year was approaching, in which the Jews rested from their works just as on the Sabbath, John lifted his siege and Ptolemy escaped. After he had killed Hyrcanus, his mother and his brothers, Ptolemy fled to Zeno, surnamed Cotylas, who was the governor of Philadelphia. {*Josephus, Jewish War, l. 1. c. 2. s. 4. (57-60) 2:31*} {*Josephus, Antiq., l. 13. c. 8. s. 1. (230-235) 7:343*} [E487]

3729. Salianus, in the book of his Annals, has a similar account with a great deal of variation concerning the people, times and places. {*Salianus, Annals - 3919 AM, Tom. 6. c. 5-7.*} {*Salianus, Annals - 3920 AM, Tom. 6. c. 5,6.*} He noted that waging war or besieging cities or building fortifications in a sabbatical year was not prohibited by the law of God. We add that this year was indeed the sabbatical year, but that it began not after Simon's death, but four months before it. That is, in the beginning of the 177th year of the account of the contracts, as is evident from the list of the sabbatical years kept by the Jews to these very times.

3730. Hipparchus observed the vernal equinox in the 43rd year of the third Calippic period, after midnight, on the 29th day of the Egyptian month of Mecheir (the beginning of March 24). At the end of the same year of the same period, he observed the summer solstice. {*Ptolemy, Great Syntaxis, l. 3. c. 2.*}

3731. At the end of the fourth year of Antiochus Sidetes' reign and at the beginning of the first year of Hyrcanus, Antiochus Sidetes' army invaded Judea and wasted the country. He forced Hyrcanus to retire to Jerusalem and then besieged it in seven places. [K108] He divided his whole army into seven brigades, so that he could block all routes into the city. {*Josephus, Antiq., l. 13. c. 8. s. 2. (236,237) 7:347*}

3732. Scipio and the other Roman envoys travelled through very many parts of the world and were generally received with much affection and love. Wherever they went, they did their utmost to settle differences by reconciling some and persuading others to yield to what was just and fair. Those who were obstinate were forced to yield, and any causes they met with that were too difficult to be decided by them, they referred to the Senate.

After they had visited various kings and countries and renewed their ancient friendship and alliance with all of them, they returned home. Those whom they had visited sent envoys to Rome and praised the Senate for sending such men to them. {*Diod. Sic., l. 33. c. 28b. s. 3,4. 12:51}

3733. The siege of Jerusalem lasted a long time because of the strength of the walls and the courage of the defendants. At last, on the other side of the wall, where the ground was more level, Antiochus built a hundred towers, three stories high. In them he placed bands of soldiers who daily attempted to cross the walls. He also made a long, wide double trench, so that the besieged Jews could not get out. However, the Jews made frequent sallies out. If at any time they found the enemy's camp unguarded, they attacked them; but if there was good resistance, they retreated back to the city. {*Josephus, Antiq., l. 13. c. 8. s. 2. (237-239) 7:347}

3734. Hyrcanus knew that the large number of people in the city would hinder his cause by consuming the provisions. He expelled the weaker ones from the city and only kept those who were able to fight. Antiochus would not allow them to pass, so they were forced to wander about the walls and many died from hunger. {*Josephus, Antiq., l. 13. c. 8. s. 2. (240,241) 7:349}

## 3870a AM, 4579 JP, 135 BC

3735. When the feast of tabernacles came, the Jews took pity on the ones around the walls and allowed them back into the city again. They also requested Antiochus to respect their feast and stop the hostility for seven days. This he did and with very great pomp, he brought bulls with gilded horns to the very gates of the city, and gold and silver cups filled with all manner of spices. When he had given these sacrifices to the priests of the Jews and made a feast for his army, he returned to his camp. {*Josephus, Antiq., l. 13. c. 8. s. 2. (241-244) 7:349,351} {*Plutarch, Sayings of Kings and Commanders (184f) 3:87}

3736. At the time of the setting of Pleiades, plentiful showers supplied the besieged with water. Prior to this, they had been badly distressed from lack of water. Also, the sabbatical year was over and if the Jews were to be hindered from sowing their grounds, a famine would undoubtedly follow. Hyrcanus considered Antiochus' justice and piety and sent envoys to him, requesting him that he would give them permission to live according to the laws of their forefathers. Many of the king's friends urged him to demolish the city and kill all the Jews, because they were unsociable and distinct from all other countries in their laws. Failing that, they urged him at least to abrogate their laws and force them to change their manner of life. The king, however, who was of a noble spirit and gentle in his conduct, rejected their

counsel and approved of the Jews' piety. He commanded that the besieged should deliver up their arms to him, dismantle the city walls, pay all the tribute due from Joppa and the other cities outside of Judea and have a garrison stationed among them. [E488] [K109] On these conditions he would make a peace with them. They agreed to all the king's propositions, except the one of having a garrison among them, since they avoided all business with strangers. In lieu of that, they chose to give hostages, among whom would be Hyrcanus' own brother, as well as five hundred talents. Of this, three hundred were paid immediately and the rest later. So the enemy removed the battering rams from the wall, raised the siege and freed the Jews from further threats of hostilities. {*Josephus, Antiq., l. 13. c. 8. s. 3. (245-248) 7:351} {*Diod. Sic., l. 34/35. c. 1. 12:53,55}

3737. When Hyrcanus opened the sepulchre of David, who had been the richest of all the kings, he removed three thousand talents from it. Using this treasure, he began to employ foreign auxiliaries, which the Jews had never done before. {*Josephus, Jewish War, l. 1. c. 2. s. 5. (61) 2:31} {*Josephus, Antiq., l. 7. c. 15. s. 3. (393,394) 5:571} {*Josephus, Antiq., l. 13. c. 8. s. 4. (249) 7:353} {*Josephus, Antiq., l. 16. c. 7. s. 1. (179) 8:281} Concerning this, see Salian's remarks. {Salianus, Annals - 3921 AM, Tom. 6. c. 8,9.}

3738. In the first year of Hyrcanus, Matthias surnamed Ephaeus, the son of Simon Psellus of the course of the priests of Joiarib, had by the daughter of Jonathan the high priest, Matthius, surnamed Curtus, who was the great-grandfather of Josephus. {*Josephus, Life, l. 1. c. 1. (1-6) 1:3,5}

## 3870b AM, 4580 JP, 134 BC

3739. When Publius Africanus and Gaius Fulvius were consuls, the slave war started in Sicily. {*Livy, l. 56. 14:59} {*Julius Obsequens, Prodigies, l. 1. c. 27b. 14:261} It was started by Eunus, a Syrian slave, born in the city of Apamea. Fascinated by magical incantations and juggling, he pretended to have received the knowledge of future events by the inspiration of the gods. This first appeared to him in his sleep, but later when he was awake. Although he failed in many of his predictions, because by chance he got some right, nobody noticed his errors. His correct predictions were diligently noted and applauded, so that his name became famous. At last, he pretended to be mad while he observed the ceremonies of the goddess of Syria. He said that she had appeared to him in his sleep and promised to promote him to regal honour. He stirred up the slaves to appeal for their liberty and to take up arms at the command of the gods. To prove that this was no design of his, but had first come from the gods, he concealed a nutshell in his mouth, crammed with sulphur and fire. His breath caused him to send out a flash of fire as often as he spoke. This very miracle at first raised two thousand men for him from the common people. He quickly had acquired an army of sixty thousand and broke open the prisons by force. Thereupon, Eunus was made king by his slaves. After he was crowned and his wife, who was also a Syrian, was proclaimed queen, he selected the wisest from the whole company to be his council. He called himself Antiochus and his rebels, Syrians. These men succeeded so well that Cleon, another slave, was encouraged by this also to raise an army. He was born in Cilicia, not far from the Taurus Mountains and had been a highway robber from his youth. However, he submitted himself to Eunus, who made him his general. He had an army of fifty thousand of his own soldiers (or, as it says in Livy, seventy thousand). This took place about thirty days after the first outbreak of the rebellion. Since the praetors were not able to quell it, the matter was turned over to Gaius Fulvius, the consul. {*Diod. Sic., l. 34/35. c. 2. 12:57-71} {*Livy, l. 56. 14:59} {*Florus, l. 2. c. 7. 1:237} [K110] Eunus caused similar rebellions in other places, and particularly at Delos. {*Diod. Sic., l. 34. c. 2. s. 19. 12:67} This island was a shopping place for slaves. Myriads were traded there each day, so much so, that it became a proverb: {*Strabo, l. 14. c. 5. s. 2. 6:329}

> "Merchant, put in here, display your slaves, you shall sell them all off immediately."

3740. Scipio Africanus, the other consul, marched into Spain to put an end to the Numantian war. King Attalus sent very expensive presents to him from Asia. {*Cicero, Pro Dejotaro, l. 1. c. 7. 14:517,519} Scipio accepted these gifts in the sight of all his army. Antiochus Sidetes did the same thing as Attalus, as appears from Livy: {*Livy, l. 57. 14:61}

> "Though it was the fashion of other generals to conceal kings' gratuities, yet Scipio said he would receive in public court the rich gifts which Antiochus Sidetes sent him. He commanded the treasurer, moreover, to register them all in the public tables, so that he might have this money to reward the gallantry of his soldiers."

### 3871 AM, 4581 JP, 133 BC

3741. Attalus Philometor was the last king of Pergamum in Asia. He dedicated himself to working in the art of brass, and decided to make a sepulchre for his mother. He was too intent on the work, and he became sick from exposure to the violent heat of the furnace. He died seven days later. {Justin, Trogus, l. 36. c. 4.} [E489]

3742. Eudemus of Pergamum brought Attalus' will to Rome and gave it to Tiberius Gracchus, the tribune of the people. He also gave him the crown and purple robes of the king of Pergamum. {*Plutarch, Tiberius Gracchus, l. 1. c. 14. 10:177} The will said:

> "Let the people of Rome be the heir of my goods."

3743. Hence, the people of Rome thought that the kingdom was part of the king's goods and held that province, not by force of arms, but by virtue of that will. {*Florus, l. 1. c. 35. 1:159} By this will Attalus bequeathed Asia to the people of Rome, if it really was bequeathed, in order that it might be free. {*Livy, l. 59. 14:65} Indeed, the Romans were charged with the counterfeiting of this will in Mithridates' letter to Arsaces. {*Sallust, Letter of Mithridates, l. 1. (8) 1:435} Horace hints that they were not the lawful heirs to Attalus. Acron noted this in his notes on the 18th ode of the second book of verses. {*Horace, Odes, l. 2. c. 18. (5,6) 1:157}

> Neither have I, as an obscure heir,
> invaded Attalus' court.

3744. Tiberius Sempronius Gracchus wanted to buy the favour of the people. He put through an agrarian law which was named after him as the Sempronian law. The land in Asia was to be farmed out by the Roman censors, and to this end he published a law to the people. It said that as soon as the money bequeathed by King Attalus had arrived, it should be divided among the citizens, who, in line with the Sempronian law, were to rent the lands for farming and to buy farming implements. He denied that the Senate had anything to do with the cities of the kingdom of Attalus. He intended to refer them to an assembly of the people. {*Cicero, Against Verres II, l. 1. c. 58. 7:285} {*Livy, l. 58. 14:61,63} {*Plutarch, Tiberius Gracchus, l. 1. c. 14. 10:177} {Orosius, l. 5. c. 8.} In an assembly of the tribunes held that summer, it was moved that he might continue as tribune of the people for the next year. He was stabbed while in the Capitol at the arrangement of Publius Cornelius Nasica, the Pontifex Maximus. {*Appian, Civil Wars, l. 1. c. 2. (16) 3:33,35} Scaevola and Pison were consuls in the same summer when Attalus died. {Asconius Pedianus, Against Verres II, l. 2.} [K111]

### 3872a AM, 4581 JP, 133 BC

3745. Aristonicus pretended to be descended from royal blood, according to Velleius Paterculus. He was, indeed, the son of King Eumenes and the brother of the dead Attalus, although not by lawful wedlock, but by an Ephesian courtesan, the daughter of a harpist. He invaded Asia to obtain the right of his father's kingdom. Most of the cities that had previously lived under the king's government were easily persuaded to side with him. Those few that feared the Romans and so opposed him, he took by force. {*Livy, l. 59. 14:65} {*Velleius Paterculus, l. 2. c. 4. 1:55} {*Strabo, l. 14. c. 1. s. 38. 6:247} {*Florus, l. 1. c. 35. 1:159}

{*Justin, Trogus, l. 36. c. 4.*} {*Plutarch, Flamininus, l. 1. c. 21. s. 6. 10:385*} {*Appian, Civil Wars, l. 1. c. 3. (18) 3:35,37*} {*Appian, Mithridatic Wars, l. 12. c. 2. (12) 2:259*} {*Eutropius, l. 4.*}

*3746.* The first place which he persuaded to revolt was a little town called Leucae. However, he was soon driven out, after losing a naval battle with the Ephesians near Cyme. {*Strabo, l. 14. c. 1. s. 38. 6:247*}

## 3872b AM, 4582 JP, 132 BC

*3747.* From there, Aristonicus marched into the midland, where he assembled a large company of poor persons and slaves, whom he incited to stand up for their liberty. He called them the Heliopolitans. {*Strabo, l. 14. c. 1. s. 38. 6:247*} Wherever slaves lived under a hard master, they stopped serving him and ran away to Aristonicus, who defeated many cities. Aristonicus first attacked Thyatira, then Apollonia and later the other garrisons. {*Strabo, l. 14. c. 1. s. 38. 6:247*} He took Myndus, Samos and Colophon by force. {*Florus, l. 1. c. 35. 1:161*}

*3748.* To stop him, all the cities around there sent their forces. Nicomedes, king of Bithynia, Ariarathes of Cappadocia, Phylaemenes of Paphlagonia and Mithridates of Pontus brought their forces to join the Romans in opposing him. As well as that, five envoys came from Rome. {*Strabo, l. 14. c. 1. s. 38. 6:247,249*} {*Justin, Trogus, l. 37. c. 1.*} {*Eutropius, l. 4.*}

*3749.* This was the 38th year under Ptolemy Euergetes II or Physcon, the start of his reign being counted from the time he began to reign with his brother Philometor. {*See note on 3835b AM. <<3280>>*} Jesus, the son of Sirach, who was born at Jerusalem, came into Egypt and lived there. He translated the book of his grandfather, Jesus, whom the Greeks called *Panaretos* and *Ecclesiasticus*, from Hebrew into Greek, as he stated in the preface to his translation. Jerome, in his 115th Epistle, said he had seen this very book in the Hebrew, with this inscription:

"The parables of Jesus, son of Sirach."

*3750.* Publius Rupilius was promoted from the position of a Sicilian tax collector to the honour of consulship. [E490] He then put down the insurrection of the slaves in Sicily. {*Livy, l. 59. 14:65*} {*Asconius Pedianus, Against Verres II, l. 4.*} {*Valerius Maximus, l. 2. c. 7. s. 3. 1:181*} {*Valerius Maximus, l. 6. c. 9. s. 8. 2:87,89*} When he besieged Tauromenium, he took Comanus, Cleon's brother, prisoner as he was stealing out of the city. A little later, at Sarapion, a Syrian betrayed the citadel to him and he was able to seize all the fugitives in the city. After he had racked them, he killed them all. From there he marched to Enna, where he fought with Cleon, the general, who had marched out of the city to fight him. Cleon conducted himself very gallantly and received many wounds before he fell. As soon as the general was killed, that city was also betrayed to the consul. Eunus, the king of the rebels, took a thousand of his bodyguards along with him and escaped as fast as he could to the craggy mountains for his safety. For fear of the pursuers they hid in caves, from where he and four more of his company were dragged out and cast into prison at Morgantina. He lay there so long, that his body putrefied and was infested with lice. This was a lamentable death, but his rash actions deserved no better. {*Diod. Sic., l. 34/35. c. 2. s. 20-23. 12:67-71*} [K112]

## 3873 AM, 4583 JP, 131 BC

*3751.* In the eighth year of Antiochus Sidetes, about ten o'clock in the morning on the 21st day of the month of Peritios, or February, there was an earthquake at Antioch in Syria. This is recorded in the Chronicles of Johannes Malela of Antioch.

*3752.* When Lucius Valerius Flaccus and Publius Licinius Crassus were consuls, the question was put to the people as to whom they wanted to have in charge of managing the war against Aristonicus. Crassus, who was both consul and Pontifex Maximus, threatened to impose a fine upon Flaccus, his colleague in the consulship and a priest of Mars, if he left the holy services. The people removed the fine, but enjoined the priests to obey the Pontifex. For all that, the people would not consent that the managing of the war should be given to a private person. Although Scipio Africanus, who the year before had triumphed over the Numantians, was the man they wanted, they voted that the war should be entrusted to Crassus, the consul, rather than to Africanus, who was merely a private citizen. {*Cicero, Philippics, l. 11. c. 8. 15:477*} So, for the first time ever, the Pontifex Maximus left Italy. {*Livy, l. 59. 14:65*}

*3753.* Antiochus Sidetes marched with his army against Phraates, who had succeeded his brother, Arsacides or Mithridates, in the kingdom of Parthia. He intended to get back his brother Demetrius Nicator. Twice Phraates had captured him as he was fleeing away and sent him back into Hyrcania to his wife Rhodoguna and his children. This was not out of kindness toward them, or respect for his own alliance with them, but because Phraates aspired to the kingdom of Syria. Therefore, he wanted to use Demetrius against Antiochus, his brother, as the opportunity might present itself and as the events of the war might require. Consequently, Antiochus thought it best to strike first; so he led his army, which he had already hardened in the wars he had fought with his neighbours, into Media against the Parthians. {*Justin, Trogus, l. 38. c. 9,10.*} {*Justin, Trogus, l. 42. c. 1.*} {*Livy, l. 59. 14:67*} {*Athenaeus, l. 10. (439e) 4:491*} {*Athenaeus, l. 12. (540b) 5:443*} {*Appian, Syrian Wars, l. 11. c. 11. (68) 2:235*}

3754. As he lived, so he waged war. He had three hundred thousand (Orosius said two hundred thousand) menial servants who followed his army of eighty thousand (Orosius said a hundred thousand) men. {*Orosius, l. 5. c. 10.*} Most of these servants were cooks, bakers and actors. {*Justin, Trogus, l. 38. c. 10.*} Antiochus regularly each day entertained such a large number of guests that, besides what was eaten at table and taken off by heaps, every one of the guests carried away whole joints of meat untouched. They had meat from four-footed beasts, birds and sea fish already dressed. Moreover, many desserts of candied honey were provided, and many coronets of frankincense and myrrh, with knots and ribbons of gold which were let down at length and were as long as a man. {*Athenaeus, l. 12. (540c) 5:443*} {*Athenaeus, l. 5. (210d) 2:451*} The soldiers imitated his blind and mad excesses. They drove silver nails into the soles of their shoes, prepared silver vessels for kitchen service and adorned their tents with tapestries. All this would seem more like a booty to encourage the enemy, than a means to slacken the hands of a courageous man or to discourage him from pursuing a victory. {*Valerius Maximus, l. 9. c. 1. ext. 4. 2:305*} {*Justin, Trogus, l. 38. c. 10.*}

3755. As soon as Antiochus came into those regions, many of the eastern kings surrendered themselves and their kingdoms to him and cursed the insolence of the Parthians. He soon engaged the enemy and having won three battles, he was about to seize Babylonia. He became so famous that the Parthians had nothing left but their own country and the people generally defected to Antiochus. {*Justin, Trogus, l. 38. c. 10.*} [K113]

3756. In this expedition, John Hyrcanus, the Jewish high priest and ruler, followed Antiochus with his supplies. Nicolaus Damascene, in his general history, stated this concerning him:

"Antiochus had erected a monument near the Lycus River where he had defeated Indates, the Parthian general. [E491] There he waited for two days, at the request of Hyrcanus, the Jew. It happened to be the time of one of the Jews' solemn festivals, during which it was not lawful for the Jews to travel."

3757. It was the feast of Pentecost, which occurred after the Sabbath. During this time, the Jews were prohibited from taking any journey. {*Josephus, Antiq., l. 13. c. 8. s. 4. (253) 7:355*} When it was over, John defeated the Hyrcani and because of this was surnamed Hyrcanus, as Eusebius and Sulpicius Severus assumed. {*Eusebius, Chronicles, l. 1. 1:228*} {*Sulpicius Severus, Sacred History, l. 2. c. 26. 11:109*} He returned home again with a great deal of honour.

3758. Publius Crassus, the consul, came into Asia to put down King Aristonicus. Through his studiousness, he became so expert in the Greek language, that he knew it exactly, even down to the five dialects into which it was divided. This earned him a great deal of respect and love among the allies, when they noticed him answer their requests in the very same dialect that they themselves had used. {*Valerius Maximus, l. 8. c. 7. s. 6. 2:227*} {*Quintilian, l. 11. c. 2.*}

3759. When Crassus was preparing to besiege Leucae, he wanted a strong and large beam to make a battering ram for the walls of the town. He wrote to the chief carpenter of the Mylatta (or Mylasa? Loeb text corrupted at this point. Editor.), who were confederates and allies of the Romans. He wanted the larger of the two masts which he had seen there sent to him. The carpenter understood what he wanted, but sent the smaller of the two masts, thinking it more suitable for the purpose and easier to ship. Crassus ordered him to be sent for. When he demanded why he had not sent the mast he asked for, Crassus was not put off by his excuses and reasons and commanded him to be stripped and whipped. Crassus thought that all respect due to superiors would soon disappear, if a man were allowed to respond to a command, not with the exact obedience which is expected, but with a meddlesome interpretation of his own. {*Aulus Gellius, Attic Nights, l. 1. c. 13. s. 11-13. 1:69*}

## 3874a AM, 4583 JP, 131 BC

3760. Antiochus Sidetes divided his army up among the cities for their winter quarters because it was so large. When he expected these cities to provide free board for his soldiers and the soldiers behaved themselves poorly, the cities defected from him. {*Justin, Trogus, l. 38. c. 10.*} Athenaeus, one of Antiochus' captains, was the most intolerably insolent of all, no matter where he went to spend the winter. {*Diod. Sic., l. 34/35. c. 17. s. 2. 12:105*}

3761. Publius Crassus, the proconsul of Asia, had a very strong force and had troops sent to him from the kings of Bithynia, Pontus, Cappadocia and Paphlagonia. Nevertheless, when he fought with the enemy at the end of the year, he was defeated. After a large slaughter of his army, the army was forced to flee. He himself was captured by an ambush of Thracians near Leneas, between Elea and Smyrna, where Aristonicus had a number of troops garrisoned. The consul, mindful of the fact that he was descended from an honourable family and that he was a Roman citizen, thrust the stick he was using to guide his horse into the eye of the Thracian who had charge of him. The man was so enraged because of the pain, that he ran his sword into Crassus' side, who thus died in a way that avoided disgrace and servitude. His head was presented to Aristonicus and

his body interred at Smyrna. *[K114]* {*Livy, l. 59. 14:65}
{*Velleius Paterculus, l. 2. c. 4. s. 1. 1:55} {*Strabo, l. 14. c. 1. s. 38. 6:249}
{*Valerius Maximus, l. 3. c. 2. s. 12. 1:247} {*Florus, l. 1. c. 35. s. 4-6.
1:159,161} {Justin, Trogus, l. 36. c. 4.} {*Julius Obsequens, Prodigies, l.
1. c. 28. 14:263} {Eutropius, l. 4.} {Orosius, l. 5. c. 10.}

### 3874b AM, 4584 JP, 130 BC

*3762.* When Marcus Perperna, the consul who succeeded
Crassus, heard of his death and the defeat of the Roman army, he hurried into Asia. He surprised
Aristonicus, who was taking a holiday as it were, because of his recent conquest, and routed him because
he was without his forces. He escaped to Stratonicia, to
where the consul followed him and then besieged the
city so tightly, that he forced it to surrender for lack of
provisions. He took Aristonicus prisoner and kept him
in bonds. {*Livy, l. 59. 14:65} {*Velleius Paterculus, l. 2. c. 4. s. 1.
1:55} {*Strabo, l. 14. c. 1. s. 38. 6:249} {*Valerius Maximus, l. 3. c. 4. s. 5.
1:285} {*Florus, l. 1. c. 35. s. 6,7. 1:161} {Justin, Trogus, l. 36. c. 4.}
{Eutropius, l. 4.} {Orosius, l. 5. c. 10.}

*3763.* Belossius Cyme thought so highly of Tiberius
Gracchus that he said if Gracchus had commanded him
to set fire to the Capitol, he would have done it with no
regrets. After the death of Tiberius Gracchus, he left
Rome for Asia and went to Aristonicus. When he witnessed the reversal of Aristonicus' fortunes, he killed
himself. {*Plutarch, Tiberius Gracchus, l. 1. c. 20. s. 4. 10:193,195}

*3764.* Just before the capture of Aristonicus, news came
to Rome that the image of Apollo at Cyme had wept
for four days. The soothsayers were so appalled at this
sign that they would have thrown the image into the
sea, had not the old men of Cyme interceded. *[E492]*
The most expert soothsayers said that this sign showed
the downfall of Greece, from where the image had been
brought. At this, the Romans sacrificed and brought
offerings into the temple. {*Julius Obsequens, Prodigies, l. 1. c.
28. 14:263} {*Augustine, City of God, l. 3. c. 11. 2:47}

*3765.* Phrygia was recovered by the Romans. {*Julius
Obsequens, Prodigies, l. 1. c. 28. 14:263}

*3766.* Phraates sent Demetrius Nicator into Syria with a
company of Parthians to seize that kingdom. He hoped
thereby to draw Antiochus from Parthia and so to save
his own country. In the meantime, since he could not overcome Antiochus in battle, he endeavoured by every means
to surprise him with stratagems. {Justin, Trogus, l. 38. c. 10.}

*3767.* The cities in which Antiochus' army had taken up
their winter quarters, found it a burden to supply quarters to the insolent troops, and so revolted to the Parthians.
On a set day, all of them attacked the army as it was dispersed in the various quarters. They placed ambushes so
that they could not come to help one another. As soon

as Antiochus heard of this, he marched to relieve those
who were nearest to him, taking that company which
was with him. {Justin, Trogus, l. 38. c. 10.}

*3768.* The swallows built nests in Antiochus' pavilion, but
he ignored the portent and fought with the enemy. {*Julius
Obsequens, Prodigies, l. 1. c. 28. 14:263} He behaved more gallantly than both his army and Phraates, whom he met
in the way. At the end, his army deserted him. {Justin,
Trogus, l. 38. c. 10.}

*3769.* The first man who deserted Antiochus was
Athenaeus, who fled to some of those villages which he
had provoked by his insolence when he was quartered
among them. They shut their gates against him and he
was denied food by everyone. He was forced to wander
up and down the country until he died from hunger.
{*Diod. Sic., l. 34/35. c. 17. s. 2. 12:105,107}

*3770.* Julius Obsequens, Justin, Josephus, Eusebius and
Orosius stated that Antiochus was killed by the
Parthians in that battle. {*Julius Obsequens, Prodigies, l. 1. c. 28.
14:263} {Justin, Trogus, l. 38. c. 10.} {Justin, Trogus, l. 39. c. 1.}
{*Josephus, Antiq., l. 13. c. 8. s. 4. (253) 7:355} {*Eusebius, Chronicles, l.
1. 1:228} {Orosius, l. 5. c. 10.} *[K115]* Appian stated he killed
himself after losing the battle. {*Appian, Syrian Wars, l. 11. c.
11. (68) 2:235} Aelian said that after he lost the battle, he
threw himself down headlong from a steep place. {*Aelian,
History of Animals, l. 10. c. 34. 2:331} Some modern writers think
he was stoned to death by the priests of the temple of
Nannea in Persia, where he went with the remainder of
his army to plunder the temple. They agreed with Rupert
Tuitiensis, who thought that this was the same Antiochus
who was mentioned in the letter written by the Jews at
Jerusalem to their brethren in Egypt. {Tuitiensis, De Victoria
Verbi Dei, l. 10. c. 6,16,24.} {Apc 2Ma 1:10-17}

*3771.* Arsaces, as Phraates was known by the common name
of the kings of Parthia, buried the body of Antiochus.
Athenaeus quoted Posidonius of Apamea as stating, in
the sixteenth book of his histories, that Phraates reproved
Antiochus' debauchery: {*Athenaeus, l. 10. (439e) 4:491}

> "Your wine and your rashness, oh Antiochus, your
> two great confidences, have deceived you. For you
> hoped, in your large cups, to have swallowed down
> the kingdom of Arsaces."

*3772.* After Phraates conducted Antiochus' funeral in a
royal manner, he was enamoured with Demetrius'
daughter, whom Antiochus had brought along with him
and married her. He began to regret having sent
Demetrius away, so he quickly sent some cavalry to bring
him back. The attempt was a waste of time, as they
found Demetrius already established in his kingdom,
so they returned back to the king.

*3773.* Antiochus and his army were defeated in Parthia and his brother Demetrius was freed from his captivity under the Parthians and restored to his kingdom. At the time, all Syria bemoaned the loss of the army. However, Demetrius seemed to consider it a stroke of good luck, as he could not have managed it better himself. One of them was taken prisoner and then freed, while the other was killed. {*Justin, Trogus, l. 39. c. 1.*}

*3774.* After the death of Antiochus, the Jews never permitted a Macedonian king to rule over them, but created magistrates from among their own number. They annoyed Syria with continual wars and subdued many parts of Syria and Phoenicia. {*Justin, Trogus, l. 36. c. 1.*} {*Strabo, l. 16. c. 2. s. 37. 7:285*} After the death of Antiochus, Hyrcanus revolted from the Macedonians and never again sent them any supplies, either as a subject or a friend. At the first rumour of Antiochus' death, Hyrcanus led his whole army against the cities of Syria, on the assumption that they would have few troops to defend them, and this was indeed true. He stormed Medeba, which is mentioned in the Apocrypha, {*Apc 1 Ma 9:36*} and captured it with some difficulty after a six-month siege. He next conquered Samega and its adjacent towns. {*Josephus, Antiq., l. 13. c. 9. s. 1. (254,255) 7:355*} [E493]

*3775.* In the meantime, Phraates resolved to start a war in Syria in vindication of Antiochus' attempt to take over the kingdom of Parthia. He was thwarted and was called home to put down a rebellion of the Scythians. The Scythians had been hired by the Parthians to help them against Antiochus. However, since they did not arrive with their supplies until the war was over, the Parthians reduced their pay and justified it by saying they had come too late. The Scythians were upset after they had marched so long for nothing. They asked that they might be given their pay because of their tedious march, or else be given some other work to do. When the Parthians gave them a rough answer which offended them, they started plundering the country. {*Justin, Trogus, l. 42. c. 1.*}

*3776.* While Phraates was away fighting the Scythians, he left Himerus behind as viceroy. A Hyrcanian by birth, Himerus had been highly favoured by Phraates as a young man, but he now forgot his former lowly position and the fact that he was acting on behalf of another. He instigated a great deal of tyranny and vexed the Babylonians and many other cities, for no reason at all. {*Justin, Trogus, l. 42. c. 1.*} [K116] He made many of the Babylonians his slaves and with their whole families, dispersed them into Media. He set the market place on fire, and some temples of Babylon, as well as pulling down all the most beautiful places in the city. {*Diod. Sic. l. 34/35. c. 21. 12:109*} Posidonius of Apamea, in the sixteenth book of his histories, also mentioned the extravagant government of Himerus. {*Athenaeus, l. 11. (466b) 5:33*} He stated that Lysimachus, a Babylonian, invited him and three hundred others to supper. When the food had been taken away, he presented to each one of those three hundred the silver cup from which they had been drinking, which weighed four pounds.

*3777.* In Egypt, Ptolemy Euergetes II, or Physcon, had reigned for fifteen years after his brother Philometor. {*Diod. Sic., l. 33. c. 6. 12:19*} His cruelty made him so odious to those same foreigners whom he had invited to Alexandria, that they set his royal palace on fire. They stole away secretly to Cyprus with his son Memphites, whom his sister Cleopatra had borne him, and with his wife, the daughter of the same Cleopatra. The people then conferred the kingdom on Cleopatra, his sister and divorced wife, so Ptolemy hired an army and waged war against his own sister and his native country. {*Livy, l. 59. 14:67*} {*Justin, Trogus, l. 38. c. 8.*} {*Orosius, l. 5. c. 10.*}

## 3875a AM, 4584 JP, 130 BC

*3778.* John Hyrcanus took Sichem and Gerizim and demolished the temple of the Cuthites, two hundred years after it had been built by Sanballat. {*Josephus, Antiq., l. 13. c. 9. s. 1. (255) 7:355*}

*3779.* Marcus Perperna was careful to have Aristonicus and the treasure which Attalus had given in his legacy to the people of Rome, shipped away from there. Manius Aquilius, the consul who was his successor, did not take kindly to this action. He immediately hurried to Perperna, intending to get Aristonicus from him, because he thought Aristonicus belonged in his triumph, rather than to Perperna's. However, Perperna's death settled the matter, as he took sick at Pergamum on his return and died. {*Strabo, l. 14. c. 1. s. 38. 6:249*} {*Valerius Maximus, l. 3. c. 4. s. 5. 1:285*} {*Justin, Trogus, l. 36. c. 4.*} {*Eutropius, l. 4.*} {*Orosius, l. 5. c. 10.*}

## 3875b AM, 4585 JP, 129 BC

*3780.* Aquilius, the consul, finished the remainder of the Asian war. He forced some cities to surrender by poisoning their water supply. Although this made for a quick victory, it spoiled his reputation and made him dishonourable. {*Florus, l. 1. c. 35. s. 7. 1:161*}

*3781.* Most of the Asians, who for four whole years had helped Aristonicus against the Romans, turned their loyalty back to Rome from fear. {*Appian, Mithridatic Wars, l. 12. c. 2. (12) 2:259*} {*Appian, Mithridatic Wars, l. 12. c. 9. (62) 2:353,355*} Lydia, the ancient seat of the kings, Caria, the Hellespont and Greater and Lessor Phrygia by joint surrender, all put themselves under the power of the Romans. {*Sextus Rufus, Breviary*}

*3782.* The people of Massilia (which is Marseilles) sent their envoys away to Rome to mediate on behalf of their founders, the Phoenicians, whose city and name the Senate had ordered to be totally destroyed, because they had fought against the people of Rome, both in the war with Aristonicus and previously with Antiochus the Great. The Senate granted them their pardon. {*Justin, Trogus, l. 37. c. 1.*}

*3783.* The Romans gave Greater Phrygia to Mithridates Euergetes, king of Pontus, as a gift for helping them against Aristonicus. {*Justin, Trogus, l. 37. c. 1.*} {*Justin, Trogus, l. 38. c. 5.*} It is generally believed, however, that Manius Aquilius was generously bribed for his pains, and therefore gave it to him. *[K117]* Consequently, after the death of Mithridates, the Senate took Phrygia away from his son, who was not of legal age, and made it a free and independent state. His complaints about this were noted by Justin. {*Appian, Mithridatic Wars, l. 12. c. 2. (12) 2:259*} {*Appian, Mithridatic Wars, l. 12. c. 8. (57) 2:343*} {*Appian, Civil Wars, l. 1. c. 3. (22) 3:43*} {*Justin, Trogus, l. 38. c. 5.*} *[E494]*

*3784.* Aquilius with ten commissioners reorganized Attalus' dominion into the form of a province and made it a tributary. They called it Asia, after the name of the continent. {*Strabo, l. 13. c. 4. s. 2. 6:169*} {*Strabo, l. 14. c. 1. s. 38. 6:249*}

*3785.* Ariarathes, the king of Cappadocia, was killed in the war against Aristonicus and left behind six sons by his wife Laodice. The people of Rome gave them Lycaonia and Cilicia for their father's good service. Laodice was jealous of her sons and because she feared that when they came of age she would be deprived of the kingdom, she poisoned five of them. But one young son escaped his mother's cruelty through the help of his family. He became ruler after the people had killed Laodice for her cruelty. {*Justin, Trogus, l. 37. c. 1.*}

*3786.* John Hyrcanus took Adora and Marisa, which were cities of Idumea. When he had subdued all the Idumeans, he had them circumcised under penalty of losing their country. They loved their native country and so were circumcised and kept all the other Jewish laws, after which they were counted as Jews. {*Josephus, Antiq., l. 13. c. 9. s. 2. (257,258) 7:357*} {*Josephus, Antiq., l. 15. c. 7. s. 9. (254) 8:119,121*} {*Josephus, Jewish War, l. 4. c. 4. s. 4. (281,282) 3:241*} Strabo stated that these Idumeans were originally Nabateans, but had been driven from there after some sedition. They had joined themselves to the Jews and submitted to their laws. {*Strabo, l. 16. c. 2. s. 34. 7:281*} He added that Herod, the king of the Jews, came from there, *virum indigenam, A stranger born.* {*Strabo, l. 16. c. 2. s. 46. 7:299*} Antigonus said he was an Idumean, that is, a half Jew. {*Josephus, Antiq., l. 14. c. 15. s. 2. (403) 7:661*} For although Stephanus Byzantinus wrote (in voc. Ιδουμαιος) that the Idumeans were originally Hebrews, yet Ammonius, the grammarian, in his book *De Differentius Verborum*, from Ptolemy's first book, *De Rege Herode* (perhaps that Ptolemy who was Herod's lieutenant {*Josephus, Antiq., l. 16. c. 7. s. 2. (191) 8:285*}), noted this difference between the Idumeans and the Jews:

> "The Jews are such as were so naturally from the beginning. The Idumeans were not Jews from the beginning, but Phoenicians and Syrians who were conquered by the Jews. They were compelled to be circumcised, to unite their country to the Jews' country and to be subject to their laws. Therefore, they were called Jews."

*3787.* They were called Jews, not because of their descent, but in regard to their religion and manner of life. For there were other men who were called Jews, though they were born strangers, because they lived according to the Jewish rites and constitutions. {*Dio, l. 37. (17) 3:127*} Hence it was that the kingdom of Herod and his posterity were called מלכות הגרים, *The Kingdom of the Proselytes,* by the Hebrews. (It was not *Hagarens,* as it was rendered by Munster in *Seder Olam Minore,* and by Scaliger in *Judaici Computi Spicilegio* book seven of *de Emendatione Temporum.*) For among the Jews, the term *proselytes of righteousness,* as they called them, came to be used of the Idumeans at this time. These proselytes were always counted as and given the same honour as other Jews.

*3788.* Ptolemy Physcon recalled his oldest son from Cyrene and killed him, because he feared the Alexandrians would set him up as king against him. *[K118]* Thereupon, the people pulled down his statue and his images. {*Justin, Trogus, l. 38. c. 8.*} Ptolemy thought that this had been done at the instigation of his sister Cleopatra and not knowing how to be avenged in any other way, he ordered his son Memphites, who was a promising young child he had by Cleopatra, to be killed before his eyes. He had his head, hands and feet cut off and put into a chest covered with a soldier's coat. He gave them to one of his servants to carry to Alexandria and to present them to Cleopatra on her birthday, when she was at the height of her happiness over a birthday gift. This was a grievous and sad spectacle for the queen and the entire city. The whole merry mood of the celebration was changed and the court mourned this act. The nobles turned their festival into a funeral and showed the mangled limbs to the people, to let them see what they themselves might expect from their king, who had murdered his own son. {*Justin, Trogus, l. 38. c. 8.*} {*Diod. Sic., l. 34/35. c. 14. 12:101,103*} {*Livy, l. 59. 14:67*} {*Valerius Maximus, l. 9. c. 2. ext. 5. 2:317*}

3789. Ptolemy saw how detestable he had become in his country and feared the worst, so he tried to secure his throne with more cruelty. He thought that if the common people were killed, his throne would be more secure. At a time when the public place of exercise was full of young men, he surrounded it and burned it. Those that escaped the fire were killed by the sword. {*Valerius Maximus, l. 9. c. 2. ext. 5. 2:317}

3790. In his war against the Scythians, Phraates led the army of those Greeks whom he had captured in the war against Antiochus. He behaved himself very arrogantly toward them and did not consider their hostility toward him because of their captivity. [E495] He had exasperated them with new indignities, so that as soon as they saw the Parthian army give ground, they wheeled around to the enemy and carried out the long-desired revenge for their captivity. Phraates was killed and the Parthian army put to the sword. {Justin, Trogus, l. 42. c. 1.}

3791. Artabanus, his uncle, succeeded Phraates in the kingdom of the Parthians. The Scythians were contented with their victory and after they had pillaged the country of the Parthians, they returned home again. Artabanus had started a war with the Thogarii or Tochari, who were a people descended from the Scythians. He was wounded in his arm and died shortly after, leaving his son, Mithridates the Great, as his successor. Shortly after this, Mithridates waged war with Ortoadistes, the king of Armenia. {Justin, Trogus, l. 42. c. 2.}

3792. At Rhodes, Hipparchus, at six o'clock in the morning, observed the sun in Leo, at eight degrees thirty-five minutes, and the moon in Taurus, at twelve degrees two minutes. This was in the 50th year of the third Calippic period, on the 16th day of the Egyptian month of Epeiph (August 5). {Ptolemy, Great Syntaxis, l. 5. c. 3.}

## 3876 AM, 4586 JP, 128 BC

3793. Hipparchus observed the vernal equinox in that same 50th year, on the first day of the Egyptian month of Phamenoth (March 23). {Ptolemy, Great Syntaxis, l. 3. c. 2.}

3794. Hipparchus, also in the same year, observed the star in the heart of Leo, twenty-nine degrees fifty minutes from the point of the summer solstice. {Ptolemy, Great Syntaxis, l. 7. c. 2.}

3795. Hegelochus, Ptolemy Physcon's general, was sent against Marsyas, the Alexandrians' general, and captured him alive, but killed his troops. When Marsyas was brought into the king's presence, everyone believed the king would give him a cruel death. However, Ptolemy spared him against all expectations, for he was now beginning to regret his previous bloody actions and was very keen by such acts of grace to reconcile himself to the people, who were extremely alienated from him. {*Diod. Sic., l. 34/35. c. 20. 12:109} [K119]

3796. After the days of mourning for her son were over, Queen Cleopatra was aware that her brother Physcon was marching against her and sent her envoys to ask for help from Demetrius Nicator, the king of Syria. He was her son-in-law, for Cleopatra, the wife of Demetrius, was the daughter of this Cleopatra and Philometor. She promised him that he should have the kingdom of Egypt for his trouble. In hope of this reward, he marched into Egypt and made his first attack on Pelusium. {Justin, Trogus, l. 38. c. 9.} {Justin, Trogus, l. 39. c. 1.} {Porphyry, Scaliger's Greek Eusebius, p. 227.}

## 3877a AM, 4586 JP, 128 BC

3797. In this year, Alexander Jannaeus, who later became the king of the Jews, was born to John Hyrcanus. He lived for forty-nine years. {*Josephus, Antiq., l. 13. c. 15. s. 5. (404) 7:431} As soon as he was born, he fell out of favour with his father. For it is said that Hyrcanus enquired of God, who appeared to him in his sleep, about his successor. He was very anxious to gain favour for Aristobulus and Antigonus, whom he loved far more than their brothers. When God told him that Jannaeus would succeed him, he was very perplexed and sent Alexander into Galilee to receive his education. He never allowed him into his presence again as long as he lived. {*Josephus, Antiq., l. 13. c. 12. s. 1. (320-323) 7:389,391}

3798. About this time, Simon the son of Dositheus, Apollonius the son of Alexander and Diodorus the son of Jason were sent as envoys from Hyrcanus and the people of the Jews to renew their friendship and amity with the Romans. Fannius, the son of Marcus, was praetor and arranged a meeting of the Senate for them on the 8th of the Ides of February (February 6). This was really in November (Julian Calendar) because of the mess the Roman calendar was in. It was ordered by a decree of the Senate that Joppa and its regions, as well as Gazara, Pegae and the other cities which Antiochus Sidetes had taken from them, should be restored, contrary to the former decree of the Senate. It was further ordered that the king's soldiers were not to travel through their country, or through any country under their command. Whatever Antiochus had gained in that war was to be set aside. The envoys, who were being sent by the Senate, were to take care to ensure that whatever Antiochus had taken away was restored and to give an estimate of the damage the country had sustained in that war. Letters of commendation were to be given to the envoys for the kings and free people, so that these might be able to return to their home country in greater safety. Fannius, the praetor, was also ordered to supply the envoys with money from the public treasury, to provide for their needs on their return journey. {*Josephus, Antiq., l. 13. c. 9. s. 2. (259-266) 7:357-361}

## 3877b AM, 4587 JP, 127 BC

3799. On the island of Rhodes, Hipparchus observed the sun at seven degrees forty-five minutes in Taurus and the moon at twenty-one degrees forty minutes in Pisces. This was in the 197th year after Alexander's death and the 621st year of Nabonassar, on the 11th day of the Egyptian month of Pharmuthi (May 2), in the morning at 5:20 a.m. {Ptolemy, Great Syntaxis, l. 5. c. 5.} [E496]

3800. In the same year, on the 17th day of the Egyptian month of Pauni (July 7), in the afternoon at 3:20 p.m., in the same place, Hipparchus observed the sun at ten degrees fifty-four minutes in Cancer and the moon at twenty-one degrees forty minutes in Pisces. {Ptolemy, Great Syntaxis, l. 5. c. 5.}

3801. In the ninth year of Hyrcanus' high priesthood and reign, Alexander, the son of Jason, Numenius, son of Antiochus, and Alexander, son of Dorotheus, who were the envoys for the Jews, presented the Senate with a chalice and buckler of gold, valued at fifty thousand staters, as a testimony of their ancient amity with the people of Rome. When the envoys had received letters for the free cities and kings, asking them to grant the men safe passage through their countries and ports, they returned home. [K120] A copy of this decree of the Senate was recorded in Josephus but linked to a different occasion. {*Josephus, Antiq., l. 14. c. 8. s. 5. (143-155) 7:523-531} For Josephus had said earlier that Julius Caesar's letters contained a decree giving permission to Hyrcanus II to repair the walls of Jerusalem which Pompey had demolished. I do not know through what oversight he connected this decree instead of the other, which in no way concerned the repair of the walls of Jerusalem. Moreover, Josephus said that this was done in the ninth year of Hyrcanus' high priesthood and reign, in the month of Panemos. This occurred when, as the acts themselves confirm, this decree had been published on the Ides of December (December 13), which was in the Julian September and the Macedonian month of Hyperberetaios. If Caesar had made that decree in favour of Hyrcanus II, then it should have been recorded as the twenty-seventh year of Hyrcanus, rather than the ninth. As for his reign, nothing at all should have been noted, because Josephus himself stated that Pompey had removed him as king and left him only in the high priest's office. Therefore, that decree should be taken as referring to the ninth year of Hyrcanus I, when the Jewish country was still a free state and confederate with the people of Rome, and not to the ninth year of Hyrcanus II. This is because it was conquered in the time of Hyrcanus II and made a tributary of the Romans. {*Josephus, Antiq., l. 14. c. 4. s. 4. (73) 7:485}

3802. In King Demetrius Nicator's absence, the Antiochians first revolted because of his pride which had grown intolerable through his experiences with the cruel Parthians. Later, the people of Apamea and the other cities of Syria were encouraged by the Antiochians' example and also revolted from him. {Justin, Trogus, l. 39. c. 1.} Demetrius was told of this while he was in Egypt, and so he had to march back to Syria.

3803. When Cleopatra, the Egyptian queen, had lost her best defender, Demetrius Nicator, she packed up all her goods and hurried to Syria to her daughter, Cleopatra the Syrian and Demetrius, her son-in-law. {Justin, Trogus, l. 39. c. 1.}

3804. Demetrius was detested both by the Syrians and by his soldiers. They sent to Ptolemy Physcon, asking him to appoint someone who was descended from Seleucus and whom they might appoint as king over them. {*Josephus, Antiq., l. 13. c. 9. s. 3. (267) 7:361} He sent them an Egyptian youth, the son of Protarchus, a merchant, who was to seize the kingdom of Syria through force of arms. He made up a very elegant story about how he had been adopted by King Antiochus into the royal bloodline. The Syrians were very willing to submit to any king whatever, rather than live under Demetrius any longer, because of his insolence. {Justin, Trogus, l. 39. c. 1. s. 4.} Porphyry stated that this youth was sent as the son of Alexander Balas, who alleged himself to be the son of Antiochus Epiphanes. The youth also called himself Alexander, but the Syrians surnamed him Zebinas, because he was generally thought to be one of Ptolemy's slaves, whom he had purchased. {Porphyry, Scaliger's Greek Eusebius, p. 227.} Among the Syrians, the Hebrew word זבינא, to speak the truth, meant both bought and redeemed. This king was not ashamed of having been bought, always putting this inscription on his coins: ΑΛΕΞΑΝΔΡΟΥ ΖΕΒΕΝΝΟΥΣ ΒΑΣΙΛΕΩΣ.

## 3878a AM, 4587 JP, 127 BC

3805. It is reported that after this new king had arrived from Egypt with his numerous forces, the remains of Antiochus Sidetes, who had been killed by the king of the Parthians, were sent to Syria in a silver coffin to be interred there. These were received with a great deal of reverence both by the cities and by King Alexander. This ingratiated him very much with the countrymen, who truly believed that the tears he shed at the funeral were not fake, but real. {Justin, Trogus, l. 39. c. 1.} [K121]

## 3878b AM, 4588 JP, 126 BC

3806. The two armies fought near Damascus and Demetrius Nicator was defeated. When he realised that he was almost surrounded, he withdrew from the battle and hurried to his wife Cleopatra at Ptolemais. She, however, shut the gates against him. After he had been deserted by his wife and his sons, he fled to Tyre with a very small retinue, hoping for sanctuary in the temple. {*Justin, Trogus, l. 39. c. 1.*} {*Porphyry, Scaliger's Greek Eusebius, p. 227.*} {*Josephus, Antiq., l. 13. c. 9. s. 3. (268) 7:361,363*} [E497]

3807. Porphyry stated that when Demetrius was denied entrance there, he was killed as he was sailing to some other place. This was after he had reigned for four years since his return from Parthia. Justin stated that he was killed at the command of the governor, as he was first landing. Josephus stated that he was taken prisoner by the enemy. They treated him badly and he died in custody. Livy and Appian stated that his wife Cleopatra killed him. {*Livy, l. 60. 14:71*} {*Appian, Syrian Wars, l. 11. c. 11. (68) 2:235*} In fact, it is very probable that he was killed at Tyre and that she was an accessory. For by doing this, the citizens of Tyre obtained their freedom and the liberty to live according to their own laws, either from her or from Alexander Zebinas. From this very year they began a new epoch in the reckoning of their history. Eusebius stated that the 402nd year of Tyre was the same as the second year of the Emperor Probus, which was 277 AD. {*Eusebius, Chronicles, l. 1. 1:228*} The judgment of Tyre inserted into the ninth action of the council of Chalcedon was in the year after the consulship of Flavius Zeno and Postumius, and which was in 449 AD, is reckoned as the 574th year of the epoch of Tyre. Moreover, in the inscriptions recorded by Grotius we find the city of Tyre honoured with the commendation of being the religious and the independent metropolis of Phoenicia. {*Gruter, Inscriptions, p. 1105.*}

3808. When Alexander Zebinas was in control of that kingdom, he entered into a league with John Hyrcanus, the high priest, and things went very well for Hyrcanus during the reign of Alexander. {*Josephus, Antiq., l. 13. c. 9. s. 3. (269) 7:363*} {*Josephus, Antiq., l. 13. c. 10. s. 1. (273) 7:365*}

3809. Manius Aquilius, the proconsul, returned in triumph from Asia on the 3rd of the Ides of November (November 13), which was August in the Julian year. This may be deduced from the fragments of the triumphal tables of marble. In reference to this, Mithridates, in a letter to Arsaces, stated: {*Sallust, Letter of Mithridates, l. 1. (8,9) 1:435*}

> "The Romans unjustly pretended a will, that is King Attalus' will, and led in triumph Aristonicus, Eumenes' son, who had attempted to recover his father's kingdom by force of arms."

3810. Velleius Paterculus intimated that Aristonicus was led in triumph by Manius Aquilius and later beheaded. {*Velleius Paterculus, l. 2. c. 4. 1:55*} He was strangled in the prison at Rome by an order from the Senate. {*Strabo, l. 14. c. 1. s. 38. 6:249*} {*Eutropius, l. 4.*} {*Orosius, l. 5. c. 10.*}

3811. Manius Aquilius was accused of bribery and, knowing that he was guilty, bribed his judges and so was acquitted. {*Appian, Civil Wars, l. 1. c. 3. (22) 3:43,45*}

## 3879 AM, 4589 JP, 125 BC

3812. When Marcus Plautius Hypsaeus and Marcus Fulvius Flaccus were consuls, a large army of locusts in Africa was blown into the sea and washed ashore at Cyrene. This caused such an intolerable stench, that many cattle died because of the noxious air. It is also reported that eight hundred thousand men died from the same infection. {*Julius Obsequens, Prodigies, l. 1. c. 30. 14:265*} {*Orosius, l. 5. c. 11. s. 2.*}

3813. Mithridates Euergetes, king of Pontus, sent Dorylaus of Pontus and a man expert in military affairs to Crete to hire foreign mercenaries. While he was there, a war was started in those regions, by the Cnossians against the Gortynians. The Cnossians appointed Dorylaus as their general, who quickly ended the war, but this was more through luck than skill. He was highly honoured by the Cnossians for his good service and subsequently lived among them with his whole family. A little later he received news that Mithridates had died. Dorylaus was the great-grandfather of the mother of Strabo, the geographer. {*Strabo, l. 10. c. 4. s. 10. 5:133-137*} {*Strabo, l. 12. c. 3. s. 33. 5:433*} [K122]

## 3880a AM, 4589 JP, 125 BC

3814. In the 188th year of the account of the contracts, the Jews of Palestine with Judas and the elders of Jerusalem were about to celebrate the feast of the dedication of the cleansing of the temple on the 25th day of the month of Chisleu. They wrote to Aristobulus Ptolemy, Physcon's master, who was descended from the family of the priests according to Aaron, and to the Jews in Egypt, that they should likewise keep the feast. {*Apc 2 Ma 1:10,18*} Rupert Tuitiensis thought that this Judas was that same Judas the Essean, whom Josephus noted had foretold nineteen years later the sudden death of Antigonus, the son of John Hyrcanus. {*Rupert Tuitiensis, De Victoria Verbi, l. 10. c. 15.*} He seldom failed in his prophecies. {*Josephus, Antiq., l. 13. c. 11. s. 2. (310,311) 7:383*} Clement of Alexandria and Eusebius of Caesarea thought that Aristobulus was that certain Jewish philosopher, the Peripatetic, of whom we made mention before. {*Clement, Stromateis, l. 5. c. 14. 2:467*} {*Eusebius, Gospel, l. 8. c. 9. (375d) 1:406*} {*Eusebius, Scaliger's Greek Eusebius*} {*See note on 3854 AM. <<3605>>*}

## 3880b AM, 4590 JP, 124 BC

3815. Seleucus, Demetrius Nicator's son, seized the crown without his mother Cleopatra's permission and reigned one year in Syria. {*Livy, l. 60. 14:71*} {*Porphyry, Scaliger's Greek Eusebius, p. 227.*}

*3816.* After much trouble, Alexander Zebinas defeated Antipater, Clonius and Aeropus, three of his most eminent commanders, who had revolted against him and had seized the city of Laodicea from him. *[E498]* Nevertheless, he showed a great deal of gallantry toward them, taking them prisoner and eventually pardoning all their apostasy. He was naturally of a mild disposition and pleasing temper, and displayed a wonderful disposition in all his meetings. Hence, he was extremely well-liked by all men. {*Diod. Sic., l. 34/35. c. 22. 12:109,111}*

## 3881a AM, 4590 JP, 124 BC

*3817.* Mithridates Euergetes, king of Pontus and Lesser Armenia, was killed through the treachery of some of his closest friends. He left his wife and sons to succeed him in the kingdom. Mithridates, surnamed Eupator, the older brother of the two, laid claim to the whole kingdom for himself. {*Strabo, l. 10. c. 4. s. 10. 5:135} {Justin, Trogus, l. 37. c. 1.}* For shortly after, he imprisoned his mother, whom his father had intended to be viceroy with him in the kingdom. He kept her there in bonds and because of the harsh treatment and long imprisonment, she died there. *{Memnon, Excerpts, c. 32.}* Sallust stated in his history that Mithridates was a child when he became king, after having poisoned his mother. *{Servius, Virgil's Aeneid, l. 6.}*

*3818.* Strabo stated that Mithridates was eleven years of age when he succeeded his father in the kingdom. Memnon said he was thirteen. We selected twelve, based on Eutropius' account, who said that Mithridates reigned sixty years and lived seventy-two years. Although Pliny said he reigned fifty-six years, while Appian said fifty-seven. {*Pliny, l. 25. c. 3. 7:141} {*Appian, Mithridatic Wars, l. 12. c. 16. (112) 2:455} {See note on 3869a AM. <<3722,3273>>}*

*3819.* Just as there appeared a comet in the year when Mithridates was born, so one also appeared in the first year of his reign. For seventy nights and days the whole heaven seemed to be all on fire, because its tail covered a quarter part of the heaven, or forty-five degrees of the upper hemisphere, and outshone the sun in brightness. Its rising and setting took four hours. {*Justin, Trogus, l. 37. c. 2.} [K123]*

## 3881b AM, 4591 JP, 123 BC

*3820.* In Syria, Cleopatra killed her son Seleucus with an arrow. She did this either because he had seized the crown without her consent, or because she feared that he might in time avenge the death of his father Demetrius, or simply because she had managed all things with the same fury and violence as her son did. When Seleucus was dead, she made her other son Antiochus Grypus king, whom she had by Demetrius and whom she had sent to Athens to receive his education. She gave him the title of king, but ran the kingdom herself. {*Livy,*

*l. 60. 14:71} {Justin, Trogus, l. 39. c. 1.} {*Appian, Syrian Wars, l. 11. c. 11. (69) 2:235}* Porphyry stated that when Seleucus was killed through his mother's treachery, Antiochus, the younger brother, succeeded him in the kingdom, in the second year of the 164th Olympiad. *{Porphyry, Scaliger's Greek Eusebius, p. 227.}* He added that he was called both Grypus and Philometor. Josephus referred to him by the first surname. {*Josephus, Antiq., l. 13. c. 9. s. 3. (269) 7:363}*

## 3882 AM, 4592 JP, 122 BC

*3821.* Alexander Zebinas was puffed up with good fortune and in his insolence now began to despise Ptolemy himself, through whom he had come to the kingdom. As a result, Ptolemy reconciled himself to his sister Cleopatra. He tried to ruin Alexander's kingdom, which the latter would never have been able to obtain had not Ptolemy sent him supplies, out of his hatred for Demetrius. To that end, he sent a very considerable force to Grypus and offered his daughter Tryphena to him in marriage. He hoped that the people would side with his new son-in-law, which would be out of respect for the former confederacy and association between them and also by virtue of his new relation and alliance. It worked. When it was evident that Grypus was backed by as much strength as Egypt could muster, they began by degrees to defect from Alexander. {*Justin, Trogus, l. 39. c. 2.}*

*3822.* Alexander did not have much confidence in his army. They were not well-trained militarily, so he did not risk a battle. After having first collected the king's treasuries and pillaged the temples, he planned to steal away into Greece by night. While he attempted to plunder Zeus' temple with the help of some of his barbarians, he was seized and both he and his whole army would likely have been destroyed, had he not soon escaped from their hands and headed toward Seleucia. The Seleucians, however, had heard a rumour of his sacrilege and shut their gates against him. Unable to do anything there, he went to Posideium and remained on the sea coast. {*Diod. Sic., l. 34/35. c. 28. 12:117}*

*3823.* Finally, Antiochus Grypus and Alexander Zebinas met in battle. Alexander was defeated and forced to flee to Antioch. As soon as he arrived there, he needed money to pay his soldiers, so he ordered that the statue of Victory, which was made of beaten gold, be taken from Zeus' temple. He justified his sacrilege with a jest:

"Zeus has lent me Victory."

*3824.* A few days later, he had his soldiers begin to pull down the image of Zeus. This was to be done as quietly as possible. *[E499]* However, he was surprised by the common people, who caught him in the very act, so that he was forced to flee. At sea, he was caught in a violent storm and became separated from his company. He was captured by pirates and turned over to Grypus, who had him executed. {*Justin, Trogus, l. 39. c. 2.*} Josephus stated that he was killed in a battle with Grypus. {*Josephus, Antiq., l. 13. c. 9. s. 3. (269) 7:363*} Porphyry stated that he poisoned himself when he was depressed at the loss of his army, in the fourth year of the 164th Olympiad. {*Porphyry, Scaliger's Greek Eusebius, p. 227.*}

*3825.* Cleopatra knew that her authority would be diminished by the victory which her son Antiochus Grypus had won over Alexander Zebinas. *[K124]* As he came from exercising or from the army (original uncertain), she presented him with a cup of poison. Grypus had been warned of this treachery and pretended that it was out of respect for his mother that he insisted that she drink first. When she refused, he persistently urged her to drink. Finally he charged her with plotting to poison him and showed her the one who had informed him of the plot. He told her that the only way she could prove her innocence was to drink the cup which she had prepared for her son. The queen was forced to yield and so she died from the poison which she had prepared for another. After her death, Grypus quickly assumed the throne and enjoyed eight peaceful years. {*Justin, Trogus, l. 39. c. 2.*} {*Appian, Syrian Wars, l. 11. c. 11. (69) 2:235*}

## 3883 AM, 4593 JP, 121 BC
*3826.* The 27th Jubilee.

*3827.* Lucius Opimius was the consul in the year when the tribune Gaius Gracchus, brother of Tiberius Gracchus, was killed as he was encouraging the common people to revolt. The air was so warm and sunny that Pliny, about two hundred years later, reported how wines made then lasted to his time and had the consistency of honey. {*Pliny, l. 14. c. 6. 4:223*} {*Pliny, l. 14. c. 16. 4:249*} In the same year a bow appeared around the sun. {*Pliny, l. 2. c. 29. 1:241,243*}

## 3888a AM, 4597 JP, 117 BC
*3828.* Ptolemy Euergetes II, or Physcon, died twenty-nine years after the death of his brother Philometor. {*Ptolemy, Canon of Kings*} {*Clement, Stromateis, l. 1. c. 21. 2:329*} {*Eusebius, Chronicles, l. 1. 1:229*} {*Epiphanius, De Mensuris et Ponderibus*} {*Jerome, Da 9*} He was survived by three sons, of whom one, Ptolemy Apion, the son of a harlot, was bequeathed the kingdom of the Cyrenians. {*Justin, Trogus, l. 39. c. 5.*} {*Appian, Mithridatic Wars, l. 12. c. 17. (121) 2:477*} Cleopatra bore him the other two sons. She was the daughter of the former Cleopatra, who had been both his sister and wife. The younger was called Alexander and the older, Ptolemy. {*Ptolemy, Canon of Kings*} {*Porphyry, Scaliger's Greek Eusebius*} {*Jerome, Da 9*} {*Epiphanius, De Mensuris et Ponderibus*} He was called *Soter* by Strabo. {*Strabo, l. 17. c. 1. s. 11. 8:43*} He

was called *Lathurus* or *Lathyrus* by Justin, Pliny, Clement and Josephus. {*Justin, Trogus, l. 39,40. Prologue*} {*Pliny, l. 2. c. 67. 1:305*} {*Pliny, l. 6. c. 35. 2:479*} {*Josephus, Antiq., l. 13. c. 13. s. 4. (370) 7:411*} {*Clement, Stromateis, l. 1. c. 21. 2:329*} He was called *Philometor* by Athenaeus and Pausanias. {*Athenaeus, l. 6. (252f) 3:139*} {*Pausanias, Attica, l. 1. c. 9. s. 1. 1:41*} He was called Philopator, which is a variation on Philometor, by Natalis Comes, who translated Athenaeus. This last name was given to him because he was so despised. Pausanias noted that no king was ever more hated by his mother than he. {*Pausanias, Attica, l. 1. c. 9. s. 1. 1:41*}

*3829.* On his deathbed, Physcon left the kingdom of Egypt to his wife Cleopatra and to the son of her choice. He hoped by this to make Egypt more quiet and free from rebellions than the kingdom of Syria. However, in choosing either son, the mother was sure to make the other her enemy. {*Justin, Trogus, l. 39. c. 3.*} She thought that Alexander, the younger son, would prove more pliable to her requests and asked the Egyptians to ratify this choice. She was unable to prevail with the common people and was forced to select her older son Lathurus, who had been banished to Cyprus by his father upon her request. The two reigned together in Egypt for ten years. {*Justin, Trogus, l. 39. c. 3.*} {*Pausanias, Attica, l. 1. c. 9. s. 1,2. 1:41*} {*Porphyry, Scaliger's Greek Eusebius, p. 225.*}

## 3888b AM, 4598 JP, 116 BC
*3830.* Before Cleopatra would give the kingdom to Lathurus, she took his wife away from him, by forcing him to divorce his most beloved sister, Cleopatra, and at the same time ordering him to marry the younger sister, Selene. In this action she showed more partiality toward her daughters than was appropriate for a mother, in that she took away the husband from one and gave him to the other. {*Justin, Trogus, l. 39. c. 3.*} These girls had another sister, Tryphena, who was married to Grypus.

## 3890 AM, 4600 JP, 114 BC
*3831.* After Antiochus Grypus, the son of Seleucus, had enjoyed the kingdom of Syria for eight peaceful years, his half-brother Antiochus of Cyzicenus rose up as his rival in the kingdom. They both had the same mother, but Cyzicenus' father was his paternal uncle Antiochus Sidetes. *[K125]* (The royal Syrian genealogy was quite complicated due to excessive intermarriage. Editor.) Grypus planned to poison his rival. Faster than Grypus thought he would be able to, his brother raised an army to fight for the kingdom. Antiochus of Cyzicenus had been sent away to Cyzicum by his mother Cleopatra for fear of Demetrius Nicator, her former husband, whom she had abandoned. Antiochus had been raised there by Craterus, the eunuch, and from there had received the surname of Cyzicenus. {*Justin, Trogus, l. 39. c. 2.*} {*Appian,

*Syrian Wars, l. 11. c. 11. (69) 2:235} {Porphyry, Scaliger's Greek Eusebius, p. 227.} {\*Josephus, Antiq., l. 13. c. 13. s. 4. (365-369) 7:411} [E500]*
When Grypus heard that his brother was raising forces against him in Cyzicum, he abandoned his intended expedition against the Jews and prepared to meet him. {*\*Josephus, Antiq., l. 13. c. 13. s. 4. (369) 7:411*}

## 3891 AM, 4601 JP, 113 BC

*3832.* That Cleopatra who was the former wife of Ptolemy Lathurus and was later divorced from her husband by Cleopatra, queen of Egypt, was married to Antiochus Cyzicenus in Syria. As her dowry, she brought him the army stationed at Cyprus. He thought that with these forces he was a match for his brother, but when they fought, he was defeated and fled to Antioch. Grypus pursued him to Antioch and besieged it. Cleopatra, the wife of Cyzicenus, was in the town. As soon as it was taken, Tryphena, the wife of Grypus ordered that her sister, Cleopatra, should be found. She did not intend to release her, but wanted to see her suffer, because she had invaded this kingdom mainly out of envy of her and had, by her marriage with the sworn enemy of her sister, made herself her enemy also. Moreover, she accused her of being responsible for bringing in the foreign forces and for the differences between the two brothers. Since she had been divorced from her brother, she had married out of the kingdom and one who was not an Egyptian against her mother's will. Grypus endeavoured to prevent his wife from acting cruelly toward her. He told her that it was against the law of arms after a victory to act violently against women, especially those that are blood relatives, as Cleopatra was. She was Tryphena's own sister and his first cousin, as well as aunt to Tryphena's children. In addition to being a blood relative, she had sought sanctuary in the temple, which had to be respected. He concluded by saying that killing her would not reduce Cyzicenus' power, nor would returning her to him unharmed gain Cyzicenus any advantage. Tryphena, on the other hand, thought his words were the result of love and not from pity. She sent some soldiers into the temple who killed Cleopatra. They first cut off her hands as she embraced the image of the goddess, so that there would not appear to be any less hostility between the two sisters than there was between the brothers. {*Justin, Trogus, l. 39. c. 3.*}

*3833.* In the fourth year of her reign, Cleopatra, the queen of Egypt and the mother of these two sisters, made Alexander, her younger son, king of Cyprus and sent him there. She hoped that through this she would appear more formidable to her older son Lathurus, who was her partner in the kingdom. {*\*Pausanias, Attica, l. 1. c. 9. s. 2. 1:43} {Porphyry, Scaliger's Greek Eusebius, p. 225.*}

## 3892a AM, 4601 JP, 113 BC

*3834.* At the age of sixteen, Alexander Jannaeus had a son Hyrcanus by his wife Alexandra. Years later, when Herod heard of Caesar's victory at Actium, he killed this Hyrcanus when he was over eighty years old. {*\*Josephus, Antiq., l. 15. c. 6. s. 2. (173) 8:83*} From this we gather that this Alexandra, who is also called Salina by the ecclesiastical writers, {*See note on 3862 AM. <<3678>>*} was not the same as that Salome, the wife of Aristobulus, whom the Greeks called Alexandra. After the death of her husband, Alexandra made Alexander Jannaeus, who was twenty-two years old, king in his place. Josephus stated that he reigned twenty-seven years and lived for forty-nine years. {*\*Josephus, Antiq., l. 13. c. 15. s. 5. (404) 7:431} [K126]*}

## 3892b AM, 4602 JP, 112 BC

*3835.* Antiochus Cyzicenus fought with Grypus and won. He captured Tryphena, Grypus' wife, who a little earlier had killed her sister, his wife. He did the same to her and sacrificed her to the ghost of his wife. {*Justin, Trogus, l. 39. c. 3.*} He also chased his brother from his kingdom and reigned over the Syrians in his place. {*\*Appian, Syrian Wars, l. 11. c. 11. (69) 2:235,237*} After this defeat, Grypus withdrew to Aspendus and from there assumed the surname of Aspendius. Cyzicenus started to reign in the first year of the 167th Olympiad. {*Porphyry, Scaliger's Greek Eusebius, p. 227.*}

## 3893 AM, 4603 JP, 111 BC

*3836.* In the second year of the same Olympiad, Antiochus Grypus returned from Aspendus and regained Syria, but Cyzicenus held Coelosyria, and so the kingdom was shared between them. {*Porphyry, Scaliger's Greek Eusebius, p. 227.*}

*3837.* As soon as Antiochus Cyzicenus had taken over the kingdom, he gave himself up to revellings and luxury and conduct altogether unseemly for kings. He was very fond of acting and stage players and all sorts of jugglers. He learned their arts very well, also applying himself to playing with puppets. His main delight was in making the images of living creatures to a size of seven to eight feet, which he then covered over with gold and silver, enabling them to move by themselves with various machines. Moreover, he was very fond of hunting. He would often steal away secretly by night with a servant or two to hunt boars, lions and leopards. Many times he risked his life by his rash encounters with wild beasts. {*\*Diod. Sic., l. 34/35. c. 34. 12:133,135} [E501]* Antiochus Grypus also engaged in luxurious living, as described by Athenaeus. {*\*Athenaeus, l. 12. (540b) 5:443} {\*Athenaeus, l. 5. (210ef) 2:453*} Athenaeus derived his material from the twenty-eighth book of the histories of Poseidonius of Apamea.

**3894 AM, 4604 JP, 110 BC**

*3838.* The war between those two brothers weakened both of them and proved a great advantage to John Hyrcanus. In this way, he acquired the incomes and revenues of Judea and stored up this money for future use. He saw what contemptible havoc Cyzicenus was creating in his brother's country, and how Grypus received no supplies from Egypt to help him. Grypus and his brother were draining their resources fighting one another, so that, in time, John stopped worrying about either of them. {*Josephus, Antiq., l. 13. c. 10. s. 1. (273,274) 7:365}

*3839.* Thereupon, he marched with his army against the Samaritans, who were under the dominion of the kings of Syria. The Samaritans had attacked the Marisieni, who were Idumeans, and had subdued them. These had previously been under the Jews as farmers to them, and had been in league with them. Hyrcanus besieged Samaria, which was a well-fortified city with a trench and a double wall ten miles long. He left his sons, Antigonus and Aristobulus, to manage the siege, which they maintained so well, that famine raged within Samaria. The people were driven to such extremity that they were forced to eat food not fit for human consumption. Finally, they begged for help from Antiochus Cyzicenus. {*Josephus, Antiq., l. 13. c. 10. s. 2. (275-277) 7:365-367}

**3895a AM, 4604 JP, 110 BC**

*3840.* Cyzicenus came as fast as he could to relieve the Samaritans. He was routed by Aristobulus' soldiers and the two brothers pursued him closely as far as Scythopolis, so that he barely escaped. It is reported that on that very day Hyrcanus, the high priest, as he was alone in the temple offering incense, heard a voice that told him of the recent victory which his sons had won over Antiochus. After they had beaten Antiochus, they returned back to Samaria and forced the Samaritans to retreat within their walls. So they were constrained once more to beg for help from Antiochus. {*Josephus, Antiq., l. 13. c. 10. s. 2. (277) 7:367}

**3895b AM, 4605 JP, 109 BC**

*3841.* Antiochus Cyzicenus had about six thousand soldiers that Ptolemy Lathurus had sent him in spite of his mother, Cleopatra. *[K127]* She had not yet deposed him. These soldiers wandered up and down Hyrcanus' dominions and Antiochus plundered with his Egyptians wherever he went. He did not dare fight with John, who was far too strong for him. He hoped that, by his pillaging of the country, he would draw Hyrcanus away from the siege of Samaria. After he had lost many of his men through an ambush laid by the enemy, he marched away to Tripolis. He committed the war with the Jews to two of his commanders, Callimandrus and Epicrates.

Callimandrus fought the enemy with greater resolution than discretion, with the result that his troops were routed and he was killed. Epicrates betrayed Scythopolis and some other towns to the Jews, after having been paid well for the task. All of this did not help the Samaritans. After Hyrcanus had spent a full year besieging Samaria, he was not content with the bare surrender of the city, but levelled it to the very ground. {*Josephus, Antiq., l. 13. c. 10. s. 2. (278-280) 7:367,369}

*3842.* The Seleucians who lived near Antioch in Syria had obtained the liberty of living according to their own laws. They started their epoch from that time. {Fasti Siculi, Olympiad 167., Year 4.}

**3896 AM, 4606 JP, 108 BC**

*3843.* Hyrcanus belonged to the sect of the Pharisees and as a disciple, he favoured them. He invited some of the most eminent among them to a feast. He took exception to Eleazar, who falsely charged that when Hyrcanus' mother had been taken prisoner in the time of Antiochus Epiphanes, she had been forced to become a harlot. Since the scandal was not as deeply resented by the rest of the company as he felt it should have been, he became enraged against the whole sect of the Pharisees. At the instigation of Jonathan, a Sadducee, he deserted the Pharisees and became a Sadducee. The Pharisees commended to the people many commandments which they had received from their ancestors through tradition and which were not to be found written among Moses' laws. The Sadducees said that therefore these customs were not binding and that only what was found in Moses' law was legally valid. As a result of this, a great dispute arose between the two parties. The rich sided with the Sadducees, while the Pharisees appealed to the common people. Therefore, Hyrcanus wanted to punish some of the Pharisees, who were zealous for their laws even though Hyrcanus had abrogated them, and so a rebellion arose among them. Although he soon settled it at the time, he and his sons were nevertheless hated by the common people for this action. {*Josephus, Antiq., l. 13. c. 10. s. 6. (293-298) 7:375} [E502]

**3897 AM, 4607 JP, 107 BC**

*3844.* John Hyrcanus died after serving as high priest for twenty-nine years, according to Eusebius, quoting from Josephus. {?Eusebius, Gospel, l. 8. c. 2.} Jerome repeated that age in his commentaries when translating Eusebius into Latin. {Jerome, Da 9} Even though in our books, and in the old translation of Rufinus, Josephus in his *Jewish War* stated this was thirty-one years (Loeb edition has thirty-one years but the Hendrickson edition has thirty-three. Editor.), {*Josephus, Jewish War, l. 1. c. 2. s. 8. (68,69) 2:35} but in his *Antiquities* he says it was thirty-one years. {*Josephus, Antiq., l. 13. c. 10. s. 7. (299) 7:377} {*Josephus, Antiq., l. 20. c. 10. s. 3. (240,241) 10:129} His father Simon died in the 177th year of the kingdom of the Greeks, in the 11th month called Shebat, {Apc 1 Ma 16:14} about February 135 BC, or 4579 JP. His wife Alexandra died about November 70 BC, or 4644 JP. There is a difference of almost sixty-five years and nine months, so that, subtracting the thirty-seven years which Josephus assigns to the reign of his sons and his wife, there remain only twenty-eight years and nine months for Hyrcanus. Some of the modern men are of the opinion, but with no good reason, that John was the writer of the first book of the Maccabees. They say that these words in the end of the book were added by someone else.

> "As for the other things of John, both his wars, and his noble acts, in which he behaved himself manfully, and his building of the walls [K128] (viz. of Jerusalem, which were demolished by command of Antiochus Sidetes), and his other deeds, behold, they are written in the chronicles of his priesthood from the time he was made high priest after his father."

3845. These chronicles are probably what is recorded in the fourth book of the Maccabees, which Sextus Senensis, in the end of the first book of his *Bibliotheca Sanctae*, said he saw in a manuscript at Lyons, in Sontes Pagninus' library among the Predicants, translated from the Hebrew into Greek. It began like this:

> "And after Simon was killed, John his son was made high priest in his place."

3846. It is supposed that Josephus took his information from that book. He told of three offices which Hyrcanus held at the same time—the kingship over the Jews, the high priesthood and the prophetic office. For Josephus stated that because Hyrcanus often spoke with God, he obtained such a good insight into the future that, much earlier, he had foretold the short time which his two oldest sons would have in the kingdom that their father left them. {*Josephus, Jewish War, l. 1. c. 2. s. 8. (68,69) 2:35} {*Josephus, Antiq., l. 13. c. 10. s. 7. (299,300) 7:377,379}

3847. Concerning the tower built by John, which Herod later called the Tower of Antonia and where he placed the robe and the rest of the high priest's ornaments, Josephus stated: {*Josephus, Antiq., l. 18. c. 4. s. 3. (91) 9:65}

> "Hyrcanus was the first high priest by that name. He built a tower near the temple and lived in it most of his time. Since he kept the high priest's robe, used by nobody else but himself, in his own custody, he took it off in that place when he put on his ordinary

clothes. This custom was also observed by his sons and their posterity."

3848. After Hyrcanus died, the stones which were set in the high priest's breastplate and the onyx stone upon his right shoulder grew dim and lost their lustre. The light from these stones showed God's approval of the conduct of the Jews. Josephus stated that this showed God's displeasure with the Jews for transgressing his laws. {*Josephus, Antiq., l. 3. c. 8. s. 9. (218) 4:421} This was two hundred years before Josephus began to write his books concerning the Jewish history. At the end of those books, he stated that he completed them in the 13th year of Domitian's reign, in 94 AD, or 4807 JP.

3849. Judas, the oldest son of Hyrcanus, was otherwise called Aristobulus and surnamed Philellen from his familiarity and commerce with the Greeks. He succeeded his father in the government and the high priesthood, but he held them for only a year. He was the first of anyone, after the return from the Babylonian captivity, to place the crown on his head and change the state to a monarchy. {*Josephus, Jewish War, l. 1. c. 3. s. 1. (70) 2:35} {*Josephus, Antiq., l. 13. c. 11. s. 1. (301) 7:379} {*Josephus, Antiq., l. 20. c. 10. s. 4. (243) 10:131} However, Strabo wrote that Judas' brother and successor, Alexander, was the first to make himself king. {*Strabo, l. 16. c. 2. s. 40. 7:289} It is likely that he disregarded Aristobulus, because he only held office for such a short time.

3850. Aristobulus promoted his second brother, Antigonus, whom he liked far more than the rest, to be a partner in the kingdom. He committed the other three to be bound in prison. He also cast his mother into prison, as she quarrelled with him for the government, because Hyrcanus had left her over the entire government. He sank to new depths of cruelty when he starved her to death in the prison. {*Josephus, Jewish War, l. 1. c. 3. s. 1. (71) 2:35} {*Josephus, Antiq., l. 13. c. 11. s. 1. (302) 7:379}

3851. Cleopatra in Egypt was greatly troubled that her son Ptolemy Lathurus shared the government of the kingdom with her, so she stirred up the people against him. {Justin, Trogus, l. 39. c. 4.} She selected those whom she trusted from among her eunuchs and brought them into the public assembly, pitifully cut and slashed. [K129] She accused Ptolemy of having secretly hired men to ambush her and disfigure her eunuchs. [E503] The Alexandrians were so enraged at the sight, that they would have killed him. However he had secretly sailed away out of danger and they greeted Alexander as king, who had returned from Cyprus shortly after this event happened. {*Pausanias, Attica, l. 1. c. 9. s. 1,2. 1:43}

3852. Before Ptolemy Lathurus was banished from the kingdom, his mother Cleopatra had taken his wife

Selene from him. The indignity was the greater, because he had two sons by her. {*Justin, Trogus, l. 39. c. 4.*} As for Alexander, who was called in by his mother and made king of Egypt in his brother's place, he was at that time in the eighth year of his reign in Cyprus, while his mother was in the eleventh year of her reign in Egypt. {*Porphyry, Scaliger's Greek Eusebius, p. 225.*} Athenaeus noted that Alexander grew as fat and swag-bellied as his father Physcon. He mentioned this passage concerning him, from Poseidonius of Apamea, in the forty-seventh book of his histories: {*\*Athenaeus, l. 12. (550b) 5:495*}

> "The king of Egypt was not popular with the common people. He was blinded by the insinuations and flatteries of his friends and lived in continual luxury. He could not walk a step unless he was supported by two men. In the dancing which was the custom at the feasts, he would leap bare-foot from the higher beds and move his body in dancing, as nimbly and actively as the best."

## 3898 AM, 4608 JP, 106 BC

*3853.* Aristobulus marched with an army into Iturea and added it to Judea. Under penalty of banishment, he forced the inhabitants to be circumcised and to keep the other Jewish ceremonies. Strabo affirmed this in the following words from Timagenes, the historian: {*\*Josephus, Antiq., l. 13. c. 11. s. 3. (318,319) 7:387*}

> "He (Aristobulus) was an upright man and one who furthered the Jews' interests very much. He enlarged their territories and annexed part of Iturea to them and secured it by the covenant of circumcision."

## 3899a AM, 4608 JP, 106 BC

*3854.* Antigonus returned in triumph from the wars at the time the Jews held their solemn feast of tabernacles. It so happened that king Aristobulus fell sick and stayed in his bed in the tower, which was later called the Tower of Antonia. His brother Antigonus, however, intending to be present at the holy solemnities, went up to the temple very gloriously attired. The main purpose of his going there was to pray for the sick king's recovery. Aristobulus was told, by some wicked persons who meant no good to Antigonus, that he should beware of his brother who had a plot against him. He placed some of his guard in a dark underground vault near the tower and gave orders that if his brother came unarmed, no one should touch him. Otherwise, they should attack and kill him. However, he secretly sent to him a man who was to tell him he should not come armed. However, Salome, the queen, and the rest of wicked men who were plotting with her against Antigonus, persuaded the messenger to tell him just the opposite, namely that the king wanted to see him dressed in his military attire.

Judas, one of the sect of the Essenes, was famous as a person who could tell the future. He had foretold that Antigonus would die that very day in Straton's Tower. He did not know that there was any other Straton's Tower besides the one which was later called the Straton's Tower in Caesarea, about seventy-five miles from Jerusalem. Therefore, when he saw Antigonus going up to the temple that day, he wished himself dead on the spot, because he was afraid that he might be proved a false prophet and ruin his reputation. Shortly after this, Judas Aristobulus heard that Antigonus had been killed in that underground place, which was known by the same name of Straton's Tower as was that other tower in Caesarea on the sea coast. {*\*Josephus, Antiq., l. 13. c. 11. s. 2. (303-313) 7:381-385*} {*\*Josephus, Jewish War, l. 1. c. 3. s. 1-5. (70-80) 2:35-41*} [K130]

*3855.* Aristobulus' sickness grew worse and worse, out of remorse over his horrid murder of his brother. At last his pains were so violent that he vomited blood. As one of his servants was carrying out the blood to empty it, it so happened that his foot slipped and he spilt Aristobulus' blood on the very same spot which was stained with Antigonus' blood. Aristobulus was told of the accident and acknowledged the just judgment of God by it. He immediately gave up the ghost in extreme anguish of body and soul. {*\*Josephus, Antiq., l. 13. c. 11. s. 3. (314-318) 7:385,385*} {*\*Josephus, Jewish War, l. 1. c. 3. s. 6. (81-84) 2:41,43*}

*3856.* After Aristobulus died, his wife Salome, or Salina, whom the Greeks called Alexandra, released his brothers, whom he had kept prisoners for a long while. She made Alexander Jannaeus king because he was the oldest and most moderate of them. As soon as he had the kingdom, he killed one of his brothers when he discovered that he was plotting against him. However, he acted quite civilly toward the other brother, who was content to live a retired life and at ease. {*\*Josephus, Antiq., l. 13. c. 12. s. 1. (320-323) 7:389,391*} He was called Absalom and forty-two years later was taken prisoner at Jerusalem by Pompey. {*\*Josephus, Antiq., l. 14. c. 4. s. 4. (71) 7:483*}

## 3899b AM, 4609 JP, 105 BC

*3857.* Alexander Jannaeus ordered the affairs of the kingdom in the way that seemed to him most appropriate. He marched with an army against Ptolemais and defeated the enemy in a battle. He forced the enemy to retreat within the walls and then besieged them while he made his battering rams. *[E504]* At the same time, the two brothers, Philometor, or Grypus, and Cyzicenus in Syria, were so weakened by their battles with each other, that they took no notice of the problems of Ptolemais. Zoilus, a tyrant, saw the dissensions between the two brothers and used the opportunity to seize Straton's

Tower and Adora. He helped the besieged, but not very much. Ptolemy Lathurus, who had been thrown out of the kingdom of Egypt by his mother Cleopatra, had taken over Cyprus. The men of Ptolemais sent envoys to him, asking him to come and rescue them from the danger they were in from Alexander. They promised that as soon as he entered into Syria, he would have the men of Gaza and of Sidon, as well as Ptolemais' and Zoilus' men, and many others, on his side to help. Encouraged by their good promises, he prepared for the voyage. {*Josephus, Antiq., l. 13. c. 12. s. 2. (324-329) 7:391,393}

3858. Meanwhile Demenaetus, a popular and eminent authority, persuaded the men of Ptolemais to alter their resolutions. He told them that they would be better to take the fortunes of war with the Jews, where they might win, than to submit to certain bondage by calling in a king over them. Moreover, in doing the latter they would not only suffer the brunt of the present war, but would have to expect another war from Egypt. Cleopatra would not stand by and allow Ptolemy to gather forces from the adjacent regions, but would quickly march with a strong force to hinder his efforts. For the queen was endeavouring to drive him out of Cyprus, as well. {*Josephus, Antiq., l. 13. c. 12. s. 3. (330,331) 7:393} His conjecture proved true. Cleopatra was not content with having banished her son, but persecuted him up and down with war and not only chased him out of Cyprus, but killed the general of her own army when he let him escape, after having taken him prisoner. Justin said, if we can believe him, that Ptolemy did not leave the island, not because he thought himself equal to her in power, but because he was ashamed to fight against his mother. {Justin, Trogus, l. 39. c. 4.}

3859. Although Ptolemy had heard on the way that the people of Ptolemais had changed their minds, he still sailed on to Sycamina, where he landed his forces, which consisted of thirty thousand cavalry and foot soldiers. He marched to Ptolemais with all his forces and camped there. When he saw that the citizens of Ptolemais would not allow his envoys into the town, nor would they so much as hear them speak, he was all the more perplexed. After that, Zoilus and the Gazeans came to him and sought his assistance against the Jews. After he had raised the siege of Ptolemais for fear of Ptolemy, Alexander pillaged their country. {*Josephus, Antiq., l. 13. c. 12. s. 3. (332,333) 7:395} [K131]

## 3900a AM, 4609 JP, 105 BC

3860. After Alexander Jannaeus had led his army home, he began to play tricks. He made a secret alliance with Cleopatra against Ptolemy, but in public proclaimed him to be his friend and ally. He promised him four hundred talents of silver if, for his sake, he would remove Zoilus, the tyrant, and give his country to the Jews. Ptolemy

very willingly struck up the bargain with him, but when he later realised how Alexander had negotiated secretly with his mother Cleopatra, he broke the league he had made with him. {*Josephus, Antiq., l. 13. c. 12. s. 4. (334,335) 7:395}

3861. The Senate had given permission to Marius, who was on an expedition against the Cimbrians, to request supplies from the countries beyond the seas. He wrote to Nicomedes, the king of Bithynia, for help. Nicomedes replied that most of the Bithynians had been carried away and kept as slaves by the tax gatherers in various places. Whereupon the Senate issued a decree, prohibiting any free man of the allies of the people of Rome to serve as slaves in any province. In addition, they sent orders to the governors of the provinces, to free those who were so enslaved. {*Diod. Sic., l. 36. c. 3. s. 1,2. 12:151}

## 3900b AM, 4610 JP, 104 BC

3862. This decree of the Senate was duly and strictly observed as soon as it was issued. When it was later neglected by Licinius Nerva, the praetor of Sicily, this caused the second slave war in Sicily. The rebels made Salvius, a soothsayer and a minstrel, their king, whom they later called Tryphon. {*Diod. Sic., l. 36. c. 3. s. 2,3. 12:151,153} {*Dio, l. 27. (93) 2:449}

3863. When Gaius Marius and Gaius Flaccus, or rather Flavius, were consuls, there was an eclipse of the sun at about three minutes before the seventh hour. {*Julius Obsequens, Prodigies, l. 1. c. 43. 14:277} There was an almost total eclipse of the sun and the astronomical calculation shows that this happened on July 19, 104 BC, or 4610 JP.

3864. When Askelon became a free state, they computed time from that point, as was noted in the Cicilian Chronicles where they deal with the 169th Olympiad. Eusebius' Chronicle agreed, and said that the 380th year of their epoch was the second year of Probus, the emperor. This happened in 277 AD, or 4990 JP. [E505]

3865. Ptolemy Lathurus left his commanders with a brigade of his army to besiege Ptolemais, which had shut its gates against him. They finally took the city. Meanwhile he marched away with the remainder of his forces against Judea, to pillage and subdue it. Alexander Jannaeus received news of his coming and his actions. He gathered about fifty thousand (some writers rather think eighty thousand) men and marched to meet him. Ptolemy made a surprise attack on Asochis, a city of Galilee, on the Sabbath and took it. He carried away with him about ten thousand prisoners, besides much plunder. Next, he attacked Zephoris, which was close to Asochis. When he had lost many men in front of the place, he withdrew to fight with Alexander Jannaeus, whom he met at the Jordan River opposite Asophon.

Alexander had eight thousand men who fought in the vanguard, carrying shields covered with bronze, whom he called *Hundred-Fighters*. These faced Ptolemy's vanguard, who also used shields of brass. Ptolemy's men were pushed back by the first charge of the enemy, but in the end they were persuaded by Philostephanus, who was a skilled military man, to cross over the river to the place where the Jews were camped. *[K132]* The battle was waged and no side was the victor. Finally, Ptolemy's soldiers routed the Jews and killed so many in the pursuit, that their arms were wearied and the edges of their swords became dull. It is said that thirty thousand Jews died in that battle. (Timagenes stated fifty thousand in his writings.) The rest were either taken prisoner or escaped. After the victory, Ptolemy roved about the country all that day. At evening he retired into some of the villages belonging to the Jews. When he saw they were crowded with women and children, he commanded his soldiers to attack and kill indiscriminately. They chopped them in pieces to put them into scalding cauldrons. They did this, so that those who had escaped would believe that the enemy ate human flesh, which would make them appear more dreadful and formidable to the onlookers. This act of cruelty was recorded by Strabo and Nicolaus Damascene in their histories. {*Josephus, Antiq., l. 13. c. 12. s. 4-6. (334-347) 7:395-401}

### 3901 AM, 4611 JP, 103 BC

3866. Cleopatra, the queen of Egypt, saw her son Lathurus daily increasing in power. He subdued the city of the Gazeans and plundered the Jews at will. She did not consider it wise to let him go on like this, especially when he was doing these things so close to Egypt and longed to have the kingdom. Therefore, to check him, she promptly raised land and naval forces which she entrusted to Chelcias and Ananias. These were both Jews and sons of the Onias who had built the temple in the region of Alexandria. {*Josephus, Antiq., l. 13. c. 10. s. 4. (287) 7:371} {*Josephus, Antiq., l. 13. c. 13. s. 1. (348,349) 7:401} The queen did everything on the advice of these two favourites. Josephus confirmed this from the history of Strabo the Cappadocian:

> "Most of those who first entered Cyprus with us, and of those also who were sent there later by Cleopatra, defected to Ptolemy Lathurus. Only those Jews who were on Onias' side remained loyal. In that regard, their countrymen Chelcias and Ananias were held in high esteem by the queen."

3867. Cleopatra deposited a considerable portion of her wealth on the isle of Cos, where she also left her grandchildren and her last will and testament. {*Appian, Mithridatic Wars, l. 12. c. 4. (23) 2:281} She ordered her son

Alexander to sail toward Phoenicia with a large fleet. After the country had revolted and flocked to her, she came to Ptolemais, where she was denied entrance and so she resolved to take it by storm. It so happened, in the meantime, that Chelkias, one of her chief commanders, died as he was pursuing Lathurus in Coelosyria. Lathurus had left Syria and was hurrying to get into Egypt because he thought that the garrisons would all have been emptied by Cleopatra. Hence, he dreamed he could take them by surprise, but he was mistaken. {*Josephus, Antiq., l. 13. c. 13. s. 1. (349-351) 7:401}

3868. In the territory of Segesta and Lilybaeum, the fugitives in Sicily appointed Athenio, a Cilician shepherd, as their king. He pretended that the gods had told him by the stars that he would be king of all Sicily. Therefore, it was incumbent upon him to favour the country and to spare its cattle and fruits as if they were his own. However, as soon as Tryphon sent for him, he submitted himself to Tryphon as king and was content with being general over the army under Tryphon. {*Diod. Sic., l. 36. c. 5-7. 12:161-167} {*Cicero, Against Verres II, l. 2. c. 54. 7:437} {*Florus, l. 2. c. 19. s. 10. 1:239,241} {*Dio, l. 27. (93,94) 2:451,453}

### 3902 AM, 4612 JP, 102 BC

3869. Cleopatra heard that her son Lathurus had attempted to take over Egypt, but had failed. She sent a brigade of her army there and drove him out of the country. After he had again been driven from Egypt, he spent the following winter at Gaza. {*Josephus, Antiq., l. 13. c. 13. s. 2. (352) 7:403}

3870. In the meantime, Cleopatra captured Ptolemais with its garrisons. Alexander Jannaeus came to her bearing gifts. *[E506] [K133]* She entertained him in a manner appropriate for someone who had been oppressed by Lathurus and had no other refuge to turn to. Some of the queen's favourites tried to persuade her to seize that country, also, and not to allow such a large number of good Jews to be at the command of one single person. Ananias advised her to the contrary, and told her that it would be most unjust for her to strip of his fortunes a man who was her fellow warrior and Ananias' kinsman. If she did so, she would, in a very short time, lose the affections of the whole country of the Jews. Cleopatra followed his counsel and did him no harm at that point, while shortly after this she renewed their former league at Scythopolis, a city of Coelosyria. {*Josephus, Antiq., l. 13. c. 13. s. 2. (353-355) 7:403,405}

3871. As Alexander Jannaeus was now free of any danger from Ptolemy Lathurus, he undertook an expedition into Coelosyria and besieged Gadara. {*Josephus, Antiq., l. 13. c. 13. s. 3. (356) 7:405}

*3872.* Lucius Licinius Lucullus was sent by the Senate against the slaves that had revolted. He came into Sicily with an army of seventeen thousand men consisting of Italians, Bithynians, Thessalians, Acarnanians and Lucanians. Athenio, the Silician, marched out to meet him with forty thousand men. He lost twenty thousand of his men, and although he himself was badly wounded, he escaped by feigning to be dead. {*Diod. Sic., l. 36. c. 8. s. 1-4. 12:169,171}

*3873.* The Jews and the Arabians raided Syria by land and the Cilicians started a war at sea with their piracy. The Romans waged war against them in Cilicia through Marcus Antonius, the praetor. {Justin, Trogus, l. 39. Prologue} He was the orator and grandfather of Mark Antony, who held the triumph. Marcus was sent to that war instead of the consul and stayed at Athens many days because of poor sailing weather. He heard Mnesarchus, Charmadas and Menedemus, who were three very learned men, disputing there, as he later also heard Metrodorus of Scepsis in Asia. When, with the help of the Byzantines, he arrived in the province, he fought the pirates with good success. But in the battle he lost Marcus Gratidius, his admiral. {*Cicero, De Oratore, l. 1. c. 18,19. 3:59,61} {*Cicero, De Oratore, l. 2. c. 88. 3:471} {*Cicero, Orator, l. 1. c. 16. 5:343} {*Cicero, Brutus, l. 1. c. 45. 5:145} {*Livy, l. 68. 14:81} {*Tacitus, Annals, l. 12. c. 62. 4:407} This happened in the consulship of Gaius Marius and Quintus Lutatius. {*Julius Obsequens, Prodigies, l. 1. c. 44. 14:277} The pirates in Sicily (sic. Cilicia) were defeated by the Romans. In another passage, Livy stated that Antonius, the praetor, chased the pirates at sea in Sicily. (It must be read Cilicia, as in the former citation. Loeb edition does not have this reading. Editor.) {*Livy, l. 68. 14:81} For this action he held a triumph, according to Pighius, about the end of the 661st year of Rome. {Pighius, Annals of Rome, Tom. 3.}

*3874.* The fourth Calippic period begins.

*3875.* Alexander Jannaeus took Gadara, after he had spent ten months besieging it. {*Josephus, Antiq., l. 13. c. 13. s. 3. (356) 7:405}

*3876.* When Marius and Catulus were consuls, Archias, the poet of Antioch, came to Rome. He later described the Mithridatic war in Greek verse and many of his epigrams are still extant in the Greek anthology. He was chiefly responsible for teaching Cicero. {*Cicero, Pro Archia Poeta, l. 1. c. 3. (4) 11:11}

*3877.* Although Gaius Marius was ready to fight the Cimbrians in Gaul, he delayed the battle. He pretended that, on the advice of certain oracles, he was only delaying for a convenient time and place for a victory. He carried Martha, a Syrian woman, around with him on a litter. She was reported to have skills in prophesying. *[K134]* He held her in great reverence and never sacrificed without her approval. She had formerly been with the Senate to entreat about such matters and foretell what would happen. However the Senate ignored her and would no longer give her a hearing. {*Plutarch, Marius, l. 1. c. 17. s. 1,2. 9:507}

*3878.* About the same time, Bataces or Batabaces, a priest of the Great Mother, Cybele, came to Rome from Pessinus in Phrygia. (Pessinus was the main sanctuary of Cybele.) He came into the Senate and told them that he had been ordered there by his goddess with tidings of a great victory which was to happen to the people of Rome and of the fame they would get in a war. He added that the religious rites of the goddess had been profaned and therefore public expiation ought to be made for the rites at Rome. He also brought along with him a garment and other body ornaments that were new and had never before been seen by any Roman. He also brought a golden crown of an unusual size and a long robe interwoven with flowers and gilded. It was all very glorious and regal in appearance. After he had made a speech to the people from the orator's speaking-desk and persuaded them to receive his superstitious worship, he was entertained at the public places of receipt for strangers. He was prohibited by Aulus Pompeius, the tribune of the people, from bringing his crown with him. The other tribune brought him to the court and questioned him about the expiation of the temple. He responded with a very superstitious answer. After Pompeius had called him an impostor and driven him from the court, he disbanded the assembly and went home. *[E507]* He suddenly became sick with a violent fever, so that soon after this he became speechless and was most severely tormented with a swollen throat. He died on the third day (or, as others stated, the seventh day). Some interpreted all this to have happened to him by a divine providence because of the indignant manner in which he had treated the priest and the goddess. For the Romans were naturally inclined to superstitions, which is the reason why Bataces in his holy dress was treated so magnificently by the men and women. When he left Rome, he was accompanied out of town with great pomp. {*Plutarch, Marius, l. 1. c. 17. s. 4-6. 9:509} {*Diod. Sic., l. 36. c. 13. 12:175-179}

*3879.* A servant belonging to Quintus Servilius Caepio made himself a eunuch for the worship of the Great Mother. He was sent overseas and never again returned to Rome. {*Julius Obsequens, Prodigies, l. 1. c. 44a. 14:279}

### 3903a AM, 4612 JP, 102 BC

*3880.* Alexander Jannaeus captured Amathus, which was the strongest fortified citadel of any near the Jordan

River. There Theodorus, the son of Zenon, had stored whatever he had of value. When Theodorus attacked Alexander without warning, he recovered what he had lost and pillaged Alexander's wagons, killing ten thousand Jews. As soon as Alexander had recovered from this loss, he attacked the countries along that sea coast and captured Raphia and Anthedon, which Herod later renamed Agrippias. {*Josephus, Jewish War, l. 1. c. 4. s. 2. (86,87) 2:43} {*Josephus, Antiq., l. 13. c. 13. s. 3. (356,358) 7:405}

## 3903b AM, 4613 JP, 101 BC

3881. Manius Aquilius, who was in his fifth consulship and was the colleague of Gaius Marius, was sent as general against Athenio, the Cilician, who had been made king of the renegades in Sicily after Tryphon's death. Manius behaved himself gallantly in the service and won a very famous victory over the rebels. He fought personally with King Athenio and finally overcame him. When the soldiers strove among themselves over whose prisoner he should be, Athenio was torn in pieces by them in the strife. {*Diod. Sic., l. 36. c. 10. 12:173} {*Florus, l. 2. c. 19. s. 11,12. 1:241}

3882. Ptolemy Lathurus left Gaza and returned to Cyprus, while his mother Cleopatra returned to Egypt. {*Josephus, Antiq., l. 13. c. 13. s. 3. (357,358) 7:405} [K135] Her harsh treatment of Lathurus frightened her younger son Alexander so much, that it caused him to leave Cyprus. He preferred a secure and safe life to the hazards of a kingdom. Because of this, Cleopatra feared that her older son Lathurus might get Antiochus Cyzicenus' help in recovering Egypt. So she sent supplies to Antiochus Grypus and also sent him Selene, Lathurus' wife, to be married to the enemy of her former husband. She also had her envoys recall her son, Alexander, to the kingdom. {Justin, Trogus, l. 39. c. 4. s. 4.} This was the cause of their civil wars, mentioned by Livy, which arose between the kings of Syria. {*Livy, l. 68. 14:83}

## 3904a AM, 4613 JP, 101 BC

3883. Julius Obsequens noted that the fugitives in Sicily were all killed in various battles, at the time when Gaius Marius and Lucius Valerius were consuls. {*Julius Obsequens, Prodigies, l. 1. c. 44a. 14:279} Aquilius, the proconsul, pursued the remaining ten thousand fugitives until he had subdued them all. Thus the second war of the slaves ended, after it had lasted almost four years. {*Diod. Sic., l. 36. c. 10. 12:173,175} Athenaeus stated that a million slaves were killed in these wars. {*Athenaeus, l. 6. (272f) 3:225}

## 3904b AM, 4614 JP, 100 BC

3884. Gaius Marius became consul for the sixth time, mainly through the help of Lucius Apuleius Saturninus, the tribune of the people. He banished Quintus Metellus Numidicus, who went to Rhodes, where he devoted himself to the study of philosophy and had time to read authors and hear the discourses of the most eminent scholars. {*Cicero, In Pison, l. 1. c. 9. 14:165} {*Cicero, Pro Sestio, l. 1. c. 47. 12:173} {*Livy, l. 69. 14:83,85} {*Plutarch, Marius, l. 1. c. 28. 9:539-543} {*Appian, Civil Wars, l. 1. c. 4. (29-31) 3:57-63}

3885. Envoys came to Rome from Mithridates with a good sum of money, hoping to bribe the Senate. Saturninus, tribune of the people and a sworn enemy of the whole order of senators, noticed their arrival. He thought he had a reason to attack the Senate and berated the embassy with reproaches. The envoys, at the instigation of the senators, called him into question for this and so muzzled him. The Senate welcomed the embassy and promised them their help. Saturninus was in great danger of capital punishment for violating the rights of the envoys, whose privileges the Romans at all times held in a most religious esteem. But the people rescued him from this danger and again made him tribune of the people. {*Diod. Sic., l. 36. c. 15. 12:181} This action caused a new rebellion, however, in which he was killed. This was the very year when Gaius Marius (for the sixth time) and Valerius Flaccus were consuls. {*Cicero, Philippics, l. 8. c. 5. 15:377} {*Cicero, In Pison, l. 1. c. 2. 14:147} {*Appian, Civil Wars, l. 1. c. 4. (32) 3:63,65} {Orosius, l. 5. c. 17.} [E508]

## 3906 AM, 4616 JP, 98 BC

3886. In every assembly, for two whole years, the matter of ending the banishment of Quintus Metellus was debated. Quintus Metellus' son crossed the forum, with his beard and hair overgrown and dressed in a dirty garment. With tears in his eyes, he prostrated himself before the citizens and begged them to recall his father home again. The people refused to raise the hopes of Quintus Metellus by doing anything on his behalf that was contrary to law. However, out of compassion for the young man and his earnest pleas, they recalled Quintus Metellus from his banishment and gave his son the surname of Pius, on account of the outstanding affection and care he had shown for his father. {*Diod. Sic., l. 36. c. 16. 12:181} Aurelius Victor, however, wrote that the father, Quintus Metellus, was banished to Smyrna and was later recalled home by the Calidian law. The letters of recall were brought to him as he sat in the theatre, and although he glanced at the letters, he would not even read them until the show was over. {Aurelius Victor, De Viris Illustribus, l. 1. c. 62.} [K136]

3887. After Metellus returned home, Gaius Marius could not face him and so sailed to Cappadocia and Galatia. He pretended he wanted to worship the Great Mother, but his real plan was to start a new war. To accomplish this, he thought it good to egg Mithridates on. He was received with every civility and respect, while

Mithridates at the time was obviously busy preparing for war. Gaius Marius said this to the king:

"Either endeavour, oh king, to put yourself into such a state that you may be too hard for the Romans, or else quietly submit to their commands."

*3888.* This saying amazed the king. He had heard of Gaius' name, but never before had he experienced the the free-spokenness of the Roman tongue. {*\*Plutarch, Marius, l. 1. c. 31. 9:549,551*}

*3889.* Alexander Jannaeus was enraged against the citizens of Gaza, because they had called Ptolemy Lathurus in to help them against him. So he attacked their city and wasted the country. In the meantime Apollodotus, the commander of the men of Gaza, with two thousand mercenaries and ten thousand of the townsmen he had armed, sallied forth by night into the Jewish camp. In this night battle, the men of Gaza had the upper hand since the Jews believed that Ptolemy had come to the enemy's relief. As soon as it was daybreak and the truth of the matter became evident, the Jews rallied forth in a body and attacked the townsmen with all their might, killing about a thousand of them. In spite of all this, and though their supplies grew scarce, the Gazeans would not surrender to the Jews. They were ready to undergo any hardship rather than submit to the enemy. Aretas, the king of the Arabians, raised their spirits for a while by saying he would help them, which he did not end up doing. {*\*Josephus, Antiq., l. 13. c. 13. s. 3. (359,360) 7:407*}

### 3907 AM, 4617 JP, 97 BC

*3890.* Lysimachus envied the great regard in which his brother Apollodotus was held by the citizens of Gaza, and killed him. He then gathered a band of soldiers and delivered the city over to Alexander Jannaeus. At first, he marched in very calmly, but shortly after he turned the soldiers loose to attack the townsmen and to kill without restraint. The Gazeans were slaughtered in every street. However, they did not die unrevenged, but struggled with their assailants and killed an equal number of Jews. Others retired to their houses and set them on fire to prevent the enemy from plundering them. Still others killed their wives and their children with their own hands, so that they might not be led away captive. The five hundred councilmen retired to Apollo's temple, for it so happened that at the very time that the enemy was let into the city, a council was being held there. But Alexander cut all their throats. When he had destroyed the city, he returned to Jerusalem, about a year after he had started his siege of Gaza. {*\*Josephus, Antiq., l. 13. c. 13. s. 3. (361-364) 7:407,409*}

*3891.* At the same time, Antiochus Grypus was killed through the treachery of Heracleon. He had lived for forty-five years and reigned for twenty-nine, {*\*Josephus, Antiq., l. 13. c. 13. s. 4. (365) 7:409*} or, twenty-six according to Porphyry. Eleven of those twenty-six years he had reigned alone, the other fifteen years in joint partnership with Cyzicenus. He died in the fourth year of the 180th Olympiad. {*Eusebius, Scaliger's Greek Eusebius, p. 227.*} Grypus was survived by five sons, the first named Seleucus, who, Josephus said, succeeded his father. Antiochus and Philip were the second and third and were twins by Tryphena, the daughter of Ptolemy Physcon, king of Egypt. Demetrius Eucarus was the fourth and Dionysius the fifth.

### 3908a AM, 4617 JP, 97 BC

*3892.* Mithridates Eupator, the king of Pontus, had a son born to him, named Pharnaces, who lived fifty years. {*\*Appian, Mithridatic Wars, l. 12. c. 17. (120) 2:475*}

### 3908b AM, 4618 JP, 96 BC

*3893.* When Gnaeus Domitius and Gaius Cassius were consuls, Ptolemy, who was the king of the Cyrenians and Physcon's son by a courtesan, died. He left the people of Rome as his heir. {*\*Livy, l. 70. 14:87*} {*\*Julius Obsequens, Prodigies, l. 1. c. 49. 14:285*} {*Cassidorus, Chronicle*} [K137] The cities of that kingdom were enfranchised by a decree of the Senate, according to Livy. Although Plutarch stated that the Cyrenians were miserably harassed soon after with continual rebellions and wars. {*\*Plutarch, Lucullus, l. 1. c. 2. s. 3,4. 2:475,477*} [E509]

### 3909 AM, 4619 JP, 95 BC

*3894.* Anna, the prophetess, daughter of Phanuel, of the tribe of Asher, was married and lived with her husband for seven years after her marriage. {*Lu 2:36,37*}

*3895.* Tigranes, son of Tigranes, who had been turned over to the Parthians as a hostage, was restored by them to his father's kingdom of Armenia. The Parthians received seventy valleys of land in his country as a gratuity. {*\*Strabo, l. 11. c. 14. s. 15. 5:339*} {*Justin, Trogus, l. 38. c. 3.*} {*\*Appian, Syrian Wars, l. 11. c. 8. (48) 2:197*} This is deduced from the 25th year of his reign and mention will be made later. {*See note on 3439b AM. <<4214>>*}

### 3910a AM, 4619 JP, 95 BC

*3896.* Quintus Mucius Scaevola was sent as the proconsul into Asia and selected his most intimate friend, Publius Rutilius Rufus, as his associate. Pomponius erroneously stated that Rufus was the proconsul of Asia. {*Pomponius, Civil Law*} Scaevola relied on his advice and counsel in managing the affairs of the province and making laws. Scaevola played a significant role in restraining the injustices and exactions of the tax collectors, who mercilessly oppressed that province. As often as anyone who had been wronged by these tax collectors brought their cause to him, he condemned them, no matter who they were, through upright judges. The condemned were then turned over to the persons they had injured, to be confined to prison by them. As well as this, he paid his own expenses and the expenses of his retinue from his own wealth. He soon won the hearts of all in the province toward the people of Rome. {*Cicero, De Oratore, l. 1. c. 53. 3:165} {*Diod. Sic., l. 37. c. 5. 12:203,205}

## 3910b AM, 4620 JP, 94 BC

*3897.* Seleucus, son of Antiochus Grypus, assembled a considerable force and marched against his uncle, Antiochus Cyzicenus. Cyzicenus came from Antioch with his army and fought with him, but was defeated. His horse ran away with him into the enemy's camp, and when he saw no possibility of escape, he killed himself. He had reigned eighteen years. When Seleucus had won the kingdom, he retired to Antioch. {Porphyry, Scaliger's Greek Eusebius, p. 227.} Josephus related that Cyzicenus was taken prisoner in the battle by Seleucus, and was later killed. {*Josephus, Antiq., l. 13. c. 13. s. 4. (365,366) 7:409} However, Trogus stated that he died in the battle which was fought between him and Grypus' sons. {Justin, Trogus, l. 40. Prologue}

*3898.* When Gnaeus Lucius Domitius and Gaius Caelius were consuls, the Senate decreed that it was forbidden for anyone to lend money to the Cretians. {Asconius Pedianus, Pro Cornelio} {*Dio, l. 30-35. (111) 2:499} {See note on 3935b AM. <<4259>>}

*3899.* Quintus Mucius Scaevola resigned the government of Asia after nine months, fearing lest he should become a financial burden to the treasury. {*Cicero, Atticus, l. 5. c. 17. 22:381} {Asconius Pedianus, In Pison} While he held his office in Asia, he managed it so uprightly and justly, that the Senate by decree held up Scaevola's administration as a model and form after that time to be imitated by all those who should succeed him in that province. {*Valerius Maximus, l. 8. c. 15. s. 6. 2:283} The Greeks also inserted a festival day in their calendar in honour of him, which the Asians called Mucia. {Asconius Pedianus, Against Verres II, l. 3.} {Asconius Pedianus, Against Divinations} Concerning this, Cicero wrote: {*Cicero, Against Verres II, l. 2. c. 22. 7:351}

> "Although Mithridates was master of all that province in Asia, he did not suppress the Scaevola Festival. Although he was an enemy and very violent and cruel in other matters, he would not violate the great honour of the man who was hallowed with the ceremonies of the gods." [K138]

*3900.* However, his associate, Publius Rutilius Rufus, a person of high integrity who had helped in ridding Asia of unjust exactions and wrongs by the tax collectors, was called into question about receiving bribes. This was orchestrated by a factious party of the rich land-owners whom he, together with the proconsul, had punished for exorbitantly extracting rents. He had such complete trust and innocence that he did not let his beard grow, nor put on unfashionable clothes, nor set aside his senatorial robes from the day that his accusers had appointed to accuse him about this. He was not intimidated by his adversaries, nor did he try to influence his judges. When the praetor granted him permission to make his defense, he made a speech worthy of his position. His attitude was such as would be appropriate for any good man, whose lot it was to be burdened with troubles and who was more concerned about the sad state of the republic than his own situation. He did not speak one word which could be seen as detracting from the splendour of his previous years. {*Livy, l. 70. 14:87} {*Velleius Paterculus, l. 2. c. 13. s. 2. 1:77} {Orosius, l. 5. c. 17. s. 12,13.} {Asconius Pedianus, Against Verres II} {*Valerius Maximus, l. 6. c. 4. s. 4. 2:47,49} {*Dio, l. 28. (97) 2:455,457} Cicero stated: {*Cicero, De Oratore, l. 1. c. 53. 3:165}

> "Since the man was the very pattern of innocence and not one person in the whole city of greater integrity or sanctimony: he did not petition the judges' favour and would not so much as allow his advocates to plead his cause with greater flourishes and embellishments than the bare account of the truth itself would permit. In some few particulars of his defence, he used Cotta, an eloquent man and his sister's son. Quintus Mucius also pleaded some things on his behalf after his accustomed manner, without any flourish, his diction simple and crystal clear."

*3901.* Cicero elsewhere stated: {*Cicero, Brutus, l. 1. c. 30. 5:103,105}

> "At which time that most innocent person was called to trial, by whose conviction we know the state to have been shaken. Although those two eloquent men, Lucius Crassus and Marcus Antonius, were then in the city, he would not have either of them for his advocate. He pleaded his own cause for himself and Gaius Cotta said a few things, since he was the son of his sister. [E510] Although he was a youth, he nevertheless showed himself an orator. Quintus Mucius also spoke in court, clearly indeed and smoothly, as he always did, yet not with such zeal and volubility as that process and the graveness of the cause required."

*3902.* Thus the rich land-owners of Rome, by means of the Gracchian laws, had gained control of the judicial system. To the great grief of the city, they condemned Rutilius as being guilty of bribery. There was never a man alive who was more innocent than he was. {*Velleius Paterculus, l. 2. c. 13. 1:77} No sooner was sentence passed on him and an estimate made in monetary terms of what he stood charged of in court, than he immediately parted with all that he had. By this he demonstrated that he was altogether innocent of the crime he was charged with. For everything that he could gather together did not approach the amount his accusers said he had extorted in Asia. He showed that every part of his estate had been conveyed to him on just and lawful titles. Gaius Marius was envious of this man and hated his integrity. Rutilius did not like how matters had gone at Rome and could not stand Marius. Therefore, he voluntarily left his country and went into Asia to live in exile at Mitylene. {*Dio, l. 28. (97) 2:455-459} One of his friends tried to comfort and cheer him up in his banishment by telling him that the civil wars would soon happen, and then all the banished would be able to return home. He replied: {*Seneca, On Benefits, l. 6. c. 37. 3:443}

> "What wrong did I ever do to you, that you should wish me a more unhappy return home than I had going into banishment? I had rather that my country should blush at my banishment, than weep at my return home."

3903. His banishment in no way marred his former glory and wealth. All the cities of Asia sent their envoys to wait on him. [K139] Quintus Mucius and all those cities and kings that had formerly been under an obligation to him for any courtesy shown them, sent him very many presents. He now had more wealth than before his banishment. {*Valerius Maximus, l. 2. c. 10. s. 5. 1:225} {*Dio, l. 28. (97) 2:459}

### 3911 AM, 4621 JP, 93 BC

3904. Antiochus Eusebes, or *Pius*, the son of Antiochus Cyzicenus, escaped a plot by Seleucus, his first cousin. A courtesan, who fell in love with Antiochus on account of his good looks, helped foil the plot. But the Syrians ascribed his escape to his piety, for which he had the surname of *Pius*. He went to Aradus and set a crown on his head, and then started a war against Seleucus. In one battle he gave him so great a defeat, that Seleucus was never able to fight with him again and was chased from Syria. {*Josephus, Antiq., l. 13. c. 13. s. 4. (365-367) 7:409,411} {*Appian, Syrian Wars, l. 11. c. 11. (69) 2:237}

3905. Seleucus fled to Cilicia and was received by the Mopsuestians. After a while, he began to exact tribute from them. They were so offended by his taxes, that they set fire to his palace and burned both him and his friends alive. {*Josephus, Antiq., l. 13. c. 13. s. 4. (368) 7:411} Appian stated that he was burned alive in the public place of exercise, because he behaved so violently and tyrannically. {*Appian, Syrian Wars, l. 11. c. 11. (69) 2:237} Eusebius stated that he was burned alive by Antiochus Cyzicenus' son. {*Eusebius, Chronicles, l. 1. 1:231} Porphyry, however, wrote that after

he had fled to the city and discovered that the Mopsuestians planned to burn him alive, he committed suicide. {*Eusebius, Scaliger's Greek Eusebius, p. 227.}

3906. The twin brothers of Seleucus, Antiochus and Philip, drew up their forces against Mopsuestia and took it, levelling it to the ground in revenge for their brother's death. This had no sooner been done than Antiochus Pius, the son of Cyzicenus, attacked and defeated them. When Antiochus fled from the battle on horseback, he drowned in trying to cross the Orontes River. His brother Philip (to whom Scaliger attributes a coin to belong, which had this inscription: ΙΛΙΠΠΟΥ ΕΥΕΡΓΕΤΟΥ ΦΙΛΛΑΔΕΛΦΥ ΒΑΣΙΑΕΩΣ) and Antiochus Pius began their reigns together from the 3rd year of the 171st Olympiad. Both of them had considerable forces and fought to see who would be the sole ruler of Syria. {Porphyry, Scaliger's Greek Eusebius, p. 227.}

### 3912 AM, 4622 JP, 92 BC

3907. Ptolemy Lathurus sent to Cnidos for Demetrius Eukairos (the Ill-Timed), the fourth son of Antiochus Grypus, and made him king of Damascus. Antiochus Pius fought the forces with those of Demetrius and Philip and opposed them very valiantly for a while. {*Josephus, Antiq., l. 13. c. 13. s. 4. (370,371) 7:411,413} At length, Antiochus was defeated and was forced to flee to the Parthians for refuge. {Porphyry, Scaliger's Greek Eusebius, p. 227.} [E511]

### 3913a AM, 4622 JP, 92 BC

3908. When Mithridates, the king of Pontus, had seized Cappadocia, he killed the two sons of Ariarathes, the king of Cappadocia. Ariarathes had died in the war against Aristonicus and had two sons by Mithridates' sister, Laodice, who was not Ariarathes' sister of the same name. Mithridates turned the kingdom of Cappadocia over to his own eight-year-old son, Ariarathes, and appointed Gordius as his guardian. Nicomedes Philopator, the king of Bithynia, was worried lest after Mithridates had captured Cappadocia, he should attempt to invade Bithynia, which bordered on it. He bribed a very handsome youth to say that he was the third son of Ariarathes, and that he had more than two sons. He was to petition the Senate about restoring him to his father's kingdom. He also sent to Rome Ariarathes' wife Laodice, who was Mithridates' sister, and who, after the death of her former husband, Ariarathes, was now married to Nicomedes. She was to testify that Ariarathes had three sons. As soon as Mithridates heard about this, he, with equal impudence, sent Gordius to Rome, as well. [K140] He was to tell the Senate that the youth whom he had placed in the kingdom of Cappadocia was descended from that Ariarathes who had died in the war with Aristonicus. This

Ariarathes had brought supplies to the Romans and had died while doing this. {*Justin, Trogus, l. 38. c. 1,2.}*

## 3913b AM, 4623 JP, 91 BC

*3909.* The queen of the Samenians waged war with the Parthians. Josephus wrote that Antiochus Pius, Cyzicenus' son, was called on to help her and fought gallantly, but was killed in a battle. After his death, the kingdom of Syria remained in the power of Grypus' sons: the two brothers, Philip, and Demetrius Eukairos. {*Josephus, Antiq., l. 13. c. 13. s. 4. (371) 7:411,413}* But Eusebius ended the reign of Seleucus' family in the two years which he attributed to Philip, Grypus' son. {*Eusebius, Chronicles, l. 1. 1:231}* Appian, however, stated that after this time Antiochus Pius was driven out of his kingdom by Tigranes. {*Appian, Syrian Wars, l. 11. c. 11. (69) 2:237}* Josephus stated that Philip, with his brother, Demetrius Eukairos, waged war on Antiochus and took over the kingdom of Syria. {*Josephus, Antiq., l. 13. c. 13. s. 4. (371) 7:411,413}* It seems more probable that when Antiochus Pius returned from the Parthians, as Porphyry and Eusebius confirmed, he did not go against his enemies but to a sanctuary and refuge for himself. He recovered that part of Syria which Philip had usurped for two years. Philip, to recover that loss, fought with his two brothers, Demetrius and Antiochus, and hoped to add the kingdom of Damascus to his government. These battles between the kings of Syria seem to be those which Livy has described. {*Livy, l. 70. 14:87}* Philip claimed for himself all the remaining parts of Syria which were not in the hand of Cyzicenus' son. The Syrians finally grew quite weary of the various skirmishes that Philip had with Antiochus Pius and with his brothers over eight years. They deserted the Seleucians and voluntarily put themselves under the command of Tigranes, king of Armenia. {*Justin, Trogus, l. 40. init.}* Appian stated that the surname of Pius, which was given to Antiochus, was given to him in derision by the Syrians because he had married Selene, who had formerly been the wife both of his father Cyzicenus and his uncle Grypus. Appian plainly stated that it was for this reason he was thrown out of the kingdom by Tigranes and that it was the just judgment of God. {*Appian, Syrian Wars, l. 11. c. 11. (69) 2:237}*

*3910.* The Senate of Rome was well aware of the plans of the two Asiatic kings to steal away another man's kingdom by producing bogus heirs. They took Cappadocia away from Mithridates and to even the score, they took Paphlagonia from Nicomedes. So that neither king could claim a victory, they made both these places a free state. The Cappadocians refused this liberty and sent envoys to Rome to tell them that it was utterly impossible for them to live without a king. The Romans were puzzled at this and gave them permission to elect a king, whereupon

Ariobarzanes was made king. {*Justin, Trogus, l. 38. c. 2.}* {*Strabo, l. 12. c. 3. s. 1. 5:371,373}* The Romans denounced Gordius, whom Mithridates had commended to them. {*Justin, Trogus, l. 38. c. 5.}*

## 3914a AM, 4623 JP, 91 BC

*3911.* Lucius Cornelius Sulla's office as a praetor expired. Velleius Paterculus stated that he was praetor the year before Lucius Caesar and Publius Rutilius were consuls. {*Velleius Paterculus, l. 2. c. 15. 1:79,81}* He was appointed over Cilicia and was sent as an envoy to Cappadocia. His trip was ostensibly to establish Ariobarzanes in his kingdom as the newly elected king. His real intention was to crush the designs of Mithridates, whose head was full of plots. Sulla brought no large force with him but with the help of the allies, who readily offered their services, he killed a large company of Cappadocians and a far larger number of Armenians, who came to assist Gordius. He threw out Gordius and the young king Ariarathes, to whom Gordius had been assigned as guardian by Mithridates. [E512] [K141] Sulla proclaimed Ariobarzanes the king, according to the decree of the Senate. Mithridates did not say anything against it at the time. {*Livy, l. 70. 14:87}* {*Plutarch, Sulla, l. 1. c. 5. s. 3. 4:335}* {*Appian, Mithridatic Wars, l. 12. c. 8. (57) 2:343,345}* {*Appian, Civil Wars, l. 1. c. 9. (77) 3:141}*

## 3914b AM, 4624 JP, 90 BC

*3912.* The Parthian envoys came to Sulla from their King Arsaces, to ask for friendship with the people of Rome. {*Livy, l. 70. 14:87}* {*Sextus Rufus, Breviary}* There had never been any communication between these two peoples before that. Orobazus, the Parthian, headed the embassy which met with Sulla, who was near the Euphrates River. Sulla is said to have had three seats set up, one for Ariobarzanes, another for Orobazus and the third for himself. So he sat in between them and listened to what the envoys said. Soon after this, the Parthian king killed Orobazus. Some say that he killed Orobazus because he had exposed the barbarians to public derision, while still others stated the reason for killing him was that Orobazus was an arrogant, ambitious man. It is also recorded that a certain Chaldean in Orobazus' retinue looked carefully at Sulla's countenance, observing the the mood, inclination and movement of his mind and body and noting his character, by artfully observing him. He declared publicly that it was impossible for Sulla not to become a great man soon. He was surprised that he could tolerate his present office and that he was not already head of everything. {*Plutarch, Sulla, l. 1. c. 5. s. 4-6. 4:335,337}* {*Velleius Paterculus, l. 2. c. 24. s. 3. 1:101}*

*3913.* As soon as Sulla returned home to Rome, Censorinus impeached him for bribery, alleging that Sulla had illegally taken a large sum of money from a kingdom, in return for getting friendship and amity for them with the Romans. However, he did not pursue the allegation, but but let it drop. {*Plutarch, Sulla, l. 1. c. 5. s. 6. 4:337}

3914. Mithridates used Gordius to persuade Tigranes, the king of Armenia, to side with him in the war which he had long been planning against the Romans. Tigranes never dreamed that the Romans would take any exception to their war with Cappadocia and with Ariobarzanes, whom the Romans had set up as king over the Cappadocians. Gordius flattered him as if he were only a stupid fellow and one who had no spirit or life in him at all. In order to appear to be playing fair, Mithridates offered his daughter Cleopatra to Tigranes in marriage. {Justin, Trogus, l. 38. c. 3.}

## 3915a AM, 4624 JP, 90 BC

3915. The commanders of Mithridates, Bagoas and Tigranes drove out Ariobarzanes. As soon as they came, he packed and fled to Rome. Mithridates set up Ariarathes in the kingdom. So, with Tigranes' help, Cappadocia was once again under Mithridates' jurisdiction. {Justin, Trogus, l. 38. c. 3.} {*Appian, Mithridatic Wars, l. 12. c. 2. (10) 2:255}

3916. At the same time, when Nicomedes Philopator died, the Senate of Rome made his son Nicomedes the king of Bithynia. He was his son by Nisa, who was a common dancer of Mithridates, as Justin called her. {Justin, Trogus, l. 38. c. 5.} Mithridates sent an army to Bithynia under Nicomedes' older brother Socrates, who was also called Nicomedes, and surnamed Chrestus, or *The Thrifty*. After Socrates had beaten his brother Nicomedes, he took over the kingdom. {Justin, Trogus, l. 38. c. 5.} {*Appian, Mithridatic Wars, l. 12. c. 2. (10) 2:255} {Memnon, Excerpts, c. 32.}

3917. When Nicomedes was stripped of his kingdom, he made his humble address to Rome. Whereupon it was decreed in the Senate that both he and Ariobarzanes should be restored to their kingdoms. To do this, Manius Aquilius, who had quelled the slave war in Sicily, and Malthius (or, as it reads in the MS., Marcus Altinius), {Justin, Trogus, l. 38. c. 5.} {*Appian, Mithridatic Wars, l. 12. c. 2. (11) 2:255} [K142] and Lucius Cassius, who controlled the country around Pergamum in Asia with a small army, were sent as envoys. Mithridates was ordered to help them. But Mithridates did nothing, because the ownership of Cappadocia was in dispute at the time and the Romans had taken Phrygia away from him. {*Appian, Mithridatic Wars, l. 12. c. 2. (11) 2:255,257} He put them off with a long story of his grievances and showed the envoys what vast expenses he had incurred in both public and private accounts. {*Dio, l. 30-35. (99) 2:467} Trogus recorded

this speech, in which Mithridates affirmed that his son had been turned out of Cappadocia, which, by the law of nations, belonged to him as the victor, and also that he had killed Chrestus, the king of Bithynia, as a favour to the Romans. {Justin, Trogus, l. 38. c. 5.}

## 3915b AM, 4625 JP, 89 BC

3918. Mithridates soon planned to fight with the Romans and drew Tigranes into his plans through the alliance he had with him. Mithridates was to get the cities and the fields as his share and Tigranes the people and the plunder. Mithridates realised what a great task he had undertaken and sent his envoys abroad for help. Some he sent to the Cimmerians, others to the Galatians, to the Samatians and the Bastarnians. He had secured each of these countries beforehand with gifts and favours, at the time when he had first conceived the idea of fighting the Romans. [E513] He also commanded that an army be sent to him from Scythia. {Justin, Trogus, l. 38. c. 3.} All those who inhabited Tanais, the regions of the Ister River and Lake Maeotis (Sea of Azov) were ready to help him. He also sent into Egypt and Syria, to make an alliance with their kings. He already had three hundred ships with decks and was building more every day, while he sent for captains and pilots from Phoenicia and Egypt. He also had his father's kingdom, which was twenty-five hundred miles wide. He got many of the neighbouring countries on his side, including the warlike country of the Colchians. {*Appian, Mithridatic Wars, l. 12. c. 3. (15,16) 2:263-267} He seized the country which is bounded by the Halys River as far as Amastris, and some parts of Paphlagonia. He also annexed to his kingdom the sea coast toward the west as far as Heraclea. On the other side, he added to Pontus, all the land between Pontus, the Colchians and Lesser Armenia. {*Strabo, l. 12. c. 3. s. 1. 5:371,373} Aulus Gellius wrote about the fact that he had twenty-five countries which paid homage to him as subjects. {*Aulus Gellius, Attic Nights, l. 17. c. 17. s. 2. 3:263} Valerius Maximus, Quintilian and Pliny state that he had twenty-two countries under his control. {*Valerius Maximus, l. 8. c. 7. ext. 16. 2:241} {Quintilian, l. 11. c. 2.} {*Pliny, l. 7. c. 24. 2:563} {*Pliny, l. 25. c. 3. 7:139} Mithridates was so well-skilled in every one of their various languages, that he never used an interpreter on any occasion that he had to speak with the people. Sextus Aurelius Victor stated that Mithridates could speak twenty-two different languages. However, in the cited reference the manuscripts stated fifty, instead of twenty-two. {Aurelius Victor, De Viris Illustribus, l. 1. c. 76.}

3919. The Roman envoys, together with Cassius' soldiers and some other forces levied from Galatia and Phrygia, had re-established the kingdoms for Nicomedes in Bithynia and Ariobarzanes in Cappadocia. They advised both of them to attack Mithridates' country, which bordered on theirs, and by so doing start a war. They assured them of their help if Mithridates retaliated. Neither of them really wanted or dared to provoke so powerful a neighbour by outright acts of hostility but the envoys prevailed on Nicomedes to attack Mithridates. Nicomedes owed large sums of money to the general treasury and to the envoys themselves, in return for his restitution to the kingdom. He also owed other money, which he had borrowed on interest from the Romans in Asia, who now called in the loan. By this pinch and much against his own will, he was thus forced to make inroads into Mithridates' kingdom. He destroyed and pillaged the country as far as the city of Amastris without any resistance. *[K143]* For although Mithridates was well-prepared for a battle, he restrained himself and allowed the enemy to range at will. This way, all the world would see that he had not started the war against the Romans, but had just cause to retaliate. {*\*Appian, Mithridatic Wars, l. 12. c. 2. (11) 2:257*} {*\*Livy, l. 74. 14:93*} {*\*Dio, l. 30-35. (99) 2:467*} Regarding the arrogance of the Romans, Mithridates wrote to Arsaces stating: {*\*Sallust, Letter of Mithridates, l. 1. (10) 1:435,437*}

> "Although I was separated from their empire on every side by kingdoms and tetrarchies, yet because it was reported that I was rich and would not be a slave, they provoked me to war through Nicomedes. I was not unaware of their design, but had previously given warning of what occurred subsequently...."

*3920.* As soon as Nicomedes had returned home with his rich plunder, Mithridates sent Pelopidas, the orator, to the Roman generals and envoys. He knew well enough that Nicomedes had done what he did at their instigation. He reasoned with them over the injuries and injustices done to him by Nicomedes. Nicomedes' envoys laid all the blame on Mithridates for starting this war. The Romans replied that they were not happy that Nicomedes should molest Mithridates in any way, but neither would they allow Mithridates to recover his losses by waging war with Nicomedes. Mithridates did not receive any better satisfaction. Since he realised that the Romans planned to thwart his actions, he sent his son Ariarathes, with a large army, to capture Cappadocia. His son soon drove out Ariobarzanes and reigned in his place. {*\*Appian, Mithridatic Wars, l. 12. c. 3. (15) 2:263*} {*\*Livy, l. 76,77. 14:95,97*} {*Eutropius, l. 5.*} {*Orosius, l. 6. c. 2.*} Maltius or Marcus Altinius, the Roman envoy, was defeated there at the same time. {*Justin, Trogus, l. 38. c. 4.*}

*3921.* Mithridates sent his envoys to Rome to ask that, if the Romans counted Nicomedes their friend, they would either persuade or compel him to do what was right and fair. If they considered him an enemy, they should give Mithridates permission to avenge himself upon him. The Romans did not satisfy him on any of his demands, but threatened him instead, if he did not give back Cappadocia to Ariobarzanes and make peace with Nicomedes. They ordered his envoys out of Rome that very day and strictly prohibited him from sending envoys to Rome again, unless he submitted to their injunctions. {*\*Dio, l. 31. (99) 2:467,469*} *[E514]*

*3922.* In the meantime, Mithridates sent Pelopidas to the Roman generals to tell them that he had sent some envoys to the Senate to complain about them and was therefore warning them to be present to explain their actions. They were not to dare to do anything until they had received a decree from the Senate and people of Rome. Since Pelopidas sounded somewhat harsh and insolent, the Romans warned Mithridates not to meddle with Nicomedes and to leave Cappadocia, because they would take care of restoring Ariobarzanes. They ordered Pelopidas from the camp and warned him not to return until the king had done what he was told to do. He was sent away with an escort, in case he should try to bribe anyone along the way. {*\*Appian, Mithridatic Wars, l. 12. c. 3. (15,16) 2:263-267*}

*3923.* The Roman generals did not wait for the decree from the Senate and the people about this war. They drew their forces from Bithynia, Cappadocia, Paphlagonia and Galatia, and after adding to them the army that Lucius Cassius had for securing Asia, they arranged their forces into several divisions. Cassius camped around Bithynia and Galatia, while Manius Aquilius used his brigade to secure the passage which Mithridates would have to use to enter Bithynia. Quintus Oppius, meanwhile, camped in the borders of Cappadocia. Each of them had forty thousand foot soldiers and cavalry, and they had a fleet as well. It sailed near Byzantium under the command of Minucius Rufus and Gaius Popilius, who were to secure the entrance to the Pontus. *[K144]* Nicomedes also sent fifty thousand foot soldiers and six thousand cavalry to help them. {*\*Appian, Mithridatic Wars, l. 12. c. 3. (17) 2:267,269*}

*3924.* Mithridates had a quarter of a million foot soldiers and forty thousand cavalry in his army, three hundred ships with decks and a hundred galleys with two tiers of oars. He had made other preparations essential for so large an army. Two brothers, Neoptolemus and Archelaus, had the command of these forces. The king personally took charge of many things. Among the auxiliaries, Mithridates' son Arcathias had brought ten thousand cavalry from Lesser Armenia. Dorylaus commanded the phalanx and Craterus had the command of a hundred and thirty chariots with scythes. {*\*Appian, Mithridatic Wars, l. 12. c. 3. (17) 2:269*}

3925. As soon as the generals of Nicomedes and Mithridates located each other in the plain near the Amnias River, they drew into battle array. Nicomedes used every man he had, but Neoptolemus and Archelaus only used their lightly armed foot soldiers and Arcathias' cavalry, along with some chariots. They made a phalanx of eight thousand men who had not yet arrived, but were on the march. The victory was uncertain. Sometimes one side had the upper hand, then the other side. At last Mithridates' commanders, with their smaller number of soldiers, unleashed their chariots armed with scythes and mowed the enemy down. It was hard to believe how many were killed. Nicomedes was forced to flee into Paphlagonia with his troops. The deserted enemy camp was plundered and the victors took the money. {*Appian, Mithridatic Wars, l. 12. c. 3. (18) 2:269,271} {Memnon, c. 33.} {*Strabo, l. 12. c. 3. s. 40. 5:449}

3926. When Nicomedes was chased from the field of battle, he camped near the place where Manius Aquilius was with his brigade. Mithridates took Mount Scoroba, which divided Bithynia and Pontus. He sent as his scouts a hundred cavalry of Sarmatians, who attacked eight hundred of Nicomedes' cavalry and took some of them prisoner. Neoptolemus and Nemanes, an Armenian, overtook Manius Aquilius as he was drawing off his forces after Nicomedes had gone to Cassius. This occurred at the stronghold of Protopachium, around the seventh hour. They forced him to fight when he only had four thousand cavalry and forty thousand foot soldiers with him. Of these, ten thousand were killed and three thousand taken prisoner. After this disaster, Aquilius fled as fast as he could toward the Sangarius River, which he crossed by night, and so escaped to Pergamum. {*Appian, Mithridatic Wars, l. 12. c. 3. (19) 2:273} {*Livy, l. 77. 14:97}

3927. Cassius, Nicomedes and all the Roman envoys moved their camps and marched to Lion's Head, which was the most well-fortified citadel in all Phrygia. They exercised a company of new soldiers whom they had gathered together from among the tradesmen, the husbandmen and the dregs of the people, as well as having made a levy of the Phrygians. When they saw that these would make poor soldiers, they dismissed them all and retreated from there. Cassius marched off with his forces to Apamea, Nicomedes to Pergamum and Aquilius toward Rhodes. As soon as news of this reached those who had been sent to guard the entrance into Pontus, they scattered and handed over the inlets of Pontus and Nicomedes' ships as a prize to Mithridates. {*Appian, Mithridatic Wars, l. 12. c. 3. (19) 2:273,275} [E515]

3928. Mithridates sent home all the prisoners that he had taken in this war, with provisions for the journey. With this act of clemency, he hoped to gain a good reputation among his enemies. {*Appian, Mithridatic Wars, l. 12. c. 3. (18) 2:271} This kind gesture was so admired by everyone, that all the cities came flocking to his side. Envoys from all the cities came to him and by their public decrees invited him to come to them, calling him their god and deliverer. Whenever Mithridates approached a city, the people from the surrounding cities came flocking in white garments to greet him and received him with great joy and acclamation. {*Diod. Sic., l. 37. c. 26. 12:231} The titles of honour which they conferred on him, too notable and lofty for a mere mortal, were more befitting a god. Calling him their god, they asked for his help. {*Athenaeus, l. 5. (212d) 2:461} [K145] They called him their Lord, Father, Saviour of Asia, Euhius, Dionysus or Bacchus, Nysius, Bromius and Liber. {*Cicero, Pro Flacco, l. 1. (60,61) 10:509} Plutarch, in the first book of his Symposium, gave the reason why the title of Bacchus was given more than all the rest. {Plutarch, Symposium, l. 1.}

3929. After Nicomedes had withdrawn to Italy, Mithridates seized all of Bithynia, so that he had nothing else to do there but to ride in circuit from city to city, to settle things and put them in order. {Memnon, c. 33.} {*Livy, l. 76,77. 14:95,97} {*Strabo, l. 12. c. 3. s. 40. 5:449,451} {*Appian, Mithridatic Wars, l. 12. c. 3. (20) 2:275} From there he marched with a considerable army into Phrygia, a province belonging to the people of Rome. {*Livy, l. 77. 14:97} He stayed in the same quarters which Alexander the Great had used before him, considering it a very good omen that it so happened that he should lodge at night where Alexander himself had slept. So he overran all Phrygia, Mysia and Asia, including the provinces which had recently been taken over by the Romans, extending as far as to Caria and Lycia. {*Appian, Mithridatic Wars, l. 12. c. 3. (20) 2:275}

## 3916a AM, 4625 JP, 89 BC

3930. Mithridates sent his commanders around to subdue Lycia, Pamphylia and other places, as far as Ionia. {*Appian, Mithridatic Wars, l. 12. c. 3. (20) 2:275} He also invaded Paphlagonia and drove out King Pyloemen, who was a confederate of the people of Rome. {Eutropius, l. 5.} {Orosius, l. 6. c. 2.} {*Appian, Mithridatic Wars, l. 12. c. 8. (58) 2:345}

3931. The Athenians sent an envoy to Mithridates. He was Athenion, the son of Athenion the Peripatetic by an Egyptian slave girl. After his master died, he was left as the heir, whereupon he enrolled as a free citizen of Athens. He assumed the name of Aristion and taught young boys rhetoric and the Peripatetic philosophy. No sooner had he wormed his way into the list of the king's favourites, than he immediately solicited them, through his letters, to new ways of running the state. {*Athenaeus, l. 5. (211d-215b)

2:455-473} He was a most impudent and cruel person, who imitated the vilest of Mithridates' vices. {*Plutarch, Sulla, l. 1. c. 13. s. 1,2. 4:367} {Dio, Excerpts of Valesius, p. 649}

3932. Mithridates promised security and protection to the Laodiceans who lived near the Lycus River, on the condition that they turn over the proconsul Quintus Oppius. The proconsul of Pamphylia had retreated with his cavalry and mercenary soldiers. So they disbanded the mercenaries and brought Oppius to Mithridates, who ordered the lictors to walk ahead of Oppius in derision. Mithridates took him wherever he went and was extremely proud that he had taken a Roman general prisoner. {*Livy, l. 78. 14:99} {*Athenaeus, l. 5. (213a) 2:463} {*Appian, Mithridatic Wars, l. 12. c. 3. (20) 2:275}

3933. Mithridates' side swept all before them in Asia as they went about unopposed. All the cities quickly revolted from the Romans. The Lesbians resolved to surrender to the king and turn Aquilius over to him, as he had fled to Mitylene to recover from a disease. So they sent a company of strong youths to Aquilius' lodging, who burst into the room where Aquilius was and seized and bound him. The Lesbians thought that he would be a most unusual and very gratifying present for Mithridates. {*Diod. Sic., l. 37. c. 27. 12:231} Along with Aquilius, the Mitylenians also turned other prisoners over to Mithridates. {*Vellerius Paterculus, l. 2. c. 18. s. 3. 1:85}

3934. The king took Aquilius, tied onto an ass, wherever he went, because he had been the head of the embassy and the chief instigator of this war. He forced him to proclaim to the onlookers with his own mouth that he was Manius Aquilius. He was tied to a Bastarnian who was about seven and a half feet tall. Sometimes he had to walk while being led on a chain by a man on horseback. [K146] Finally, after Aquilius had been scourged and put on the rack at Pergamum, Mithridates ordered molten gold to be poured down his throat in atonement for Roman corruption and bribery. {*Athenaeus, l. 5. (213b) 2:465} {*Appian, Mithridatic Wars, l. 12. c. 3. (21) 2:275,277} {*Livy, l. 78. 14:99} {*Pliny, l. 33. c. 14. (49) 9:41} {*Cicero, Pro Lege Manilia, l. 1. c. 5. (11) 9:23} {*Cicero, Tusculan Disputations, l. 5. c. 5. 18:439} [E516]

3935. After the king had appointed governors of the various places he had subdued, he went to Magnesia, Ephesus and Mitylene, where he was royally welcomed. When he came to Ephesus, the Ephesians took down all the statues of the Romans which they had set up in their midst. {*Appian, Mithridatic Wars, l. 12. c. 3. (21) 2:275,277}

3936. Mithridates' generals were received favourably by the cities. In these, they found a good supply of gold and silver which the former kings had hoarded up, as well as a good provision for war. Because he used this,

Mithridates did not need any tribute, so he forgave the cities their arrears in both public and private accounts and granted a release from tribute for five years. {Justin, Trogus, l. 38. c. 3.} He said this about himself in his letter to Arsaces: {*Sallust, Letter of Mithridates, l. 1. (11,12) 1:437}

"I, in revenge of the injuries done to me, drove Nicomedes from Bithynia, recovered Asia and King Antiochus' spoil, and eased Greece of that heavy burden under which it groaned."

3937. When Mithridates returned from Ionia, he captured Stratonicia, imposed a fine on it and left a garrison within it. Here he saw a very beautiful virgin called Monima, Philopoemen's daughter, whom he took along with him, putting her among his women. He continued his war with the Magnesians, the Paphlagonians and the Lycians, because they made some resistance and would not allow him to place his garrisons among them. {*Appian, Mithridatic Wars, l. 12. c. 3. (21) 2:277} In this dispute near Mount Sipylus, the Magnesians wounded Archelaus, Mithridates' general, who was pillaging their borders, and killed many of his men. {*Pausanias, Attica, l. 1. c. 20. s. 5. 1:101}

3938. Cleopatra, the Egyptian queen, thought she had thwarted a plot by her son Alexander and planned his overthrow. But she was seized by him and put to death. Nor was she, who had done such wicked deeds, to be pitied in any way. She had driven her own mother from her marriage bed and had made her two daughters widows by forcing them to barter their husbands. She had engaged in a war against one of her sons and had not stopped until she had banished him. She had deprived the other of his kingdom and his father had plotted his murder. {Justin, Trogus, l. 39. c. 4.} {*Pausanias, Attica, l. 1. c. 9. s. 3. 1:43} {*Athenaeus, l. 12. (550a) 5:495} {*Eusebius, Chronicles, l. 1. 1:231} However, Alexander reigned together with his mother for eighteen years. {Porphyry, Scaliger's Greek Eusebius, p. 225.}

3939. As soon as it became known that Cleopatra had been killed by her son Alexander, the people were in an uproar, which forced Alexander to flee the place. After he left, the Alexandrians sent envoys to Cyprus to Ptolemy Lathurus, the older brother, and turned the kingdom of Egypt over to him. He ruled for eight years, or, as Porphyry has stated more exactly, seven years and six months. {Justin, Trogus, l. 39. c. 5} {*Pausanias, Attica, l. 1. c. 9. s. 3. 1:43} {*Eusebius, Chronicles, l. 1. 1:232} {Porphyry, Scaliger's Greek Eusebius, p. 225.}

## 3916b AM, 4626 JP, 88 BC

3940. After the death of her husband, Anna the prophetess, the daughter of Phanuel, did not leave the temple, but served God with fastings and prayers night and day for eighty-four years, until the time she saw Christ in the temple. {*Lu 2:37*}

*3941.* The Italians, who had revolted from the Romans, sent to Mithridates, asking him to march with his forces into Italy, against the Romans. They thought that, with his help, their united forces could easily defeat the Romans. Mithridates replied that it was his intention to march into Italy after he had completed his conquest of Asia, which was fully occupying him at the moment. After Mithridates' refusal to help, the Italians began to despair and lost courage. Because of this, the war with the confederates, or the Marian War, came to an end. {*\*Diod. Sic., l. 37. c. 2. s. 11. 12:193*} Livy mentioned that two galleys with four tiers of oars, sent from Heraclea in Pontus, were among the supplies sent to the Romans from foreign lands during this war. {*\*Livy, l. 72. 14:89*} *[K147]* Memnon mentioned this in his history also. {*Memnon, c. 31.*} On the Italian side, Agamemnon, the Cilician pirate, was among those who helped them. {*\*Diod. Sic., l. 37. c. 16. 12:223*} {*Orosius, l. 5. c. 18.*}

*3942.* Mithridates found that the citizens of Rome who were scattered throughout the cities of Asia were a hindrance to his plans. He sent private letters from Ephesus to the governors and magistrates of the cities, ordering that in thirty days, all on the same day, they were to kill all the Roman and Italian citizens with their wives and children, as well as all other free-born citizens of Italy. Their bodies were to be left unburied, while one part of their goods was to go to the king and the other to the assassins. He also had a public crier threaten to fine anyone who dared to bury any of the dead, or who hid any who had escaped the massacre. *[E517]* He promised a reward to those who found anyone doing this, while promising slaves their liberty if they would murder their Roman masters and debtors one half of their debt to kill their creditors. These instructions were secretly sent to all of them. When the appointed day came, it was impossible to count the large numbers of Roman citizens who were massacred at that time, or to assess what a sad state most of the provinces were in. How pitiful was the state of those that were killed and those who killed them. Everyone was forced to choose between betraying his innocent guests and friends, or being fined. {*\*Appian, Mithridatic Wars, l. 12. c. 4. (22,23) 2:279,281*} {*\*Appian, Mithridatic Wars, l. 12. c. 7. (48) 2:327*} {*\*Appian, Mithridatic Wars, l. 12. c. 8. (54) 2:339*} {*\*Appian, Mithridatic Wars, l. 12. c. 9. (62) 2:355*} {*\*Cicero, Pro Lege Manilia, l. 1. c. 3. (7) 9:21*} {*\*Cicero, Pro Flacco, l. 1. (57,61) 10:507,509*} {*Memnon, Excerpts, c. 33.*} {*\*Livy, l. 78. 14:99*} {*\*Velleius Paterculus, l. 2. c. 18. 1:85*} {*\*Florus, l. 1. c. 40. 1:181*} {*Eutropius, l. 5.*} {*Orosius, l. 6. c. 2.*}

*3943.* In Ephesus, the Ephesians dragged those who had taken sanctuary in Diana's temple away as they were in the very act of embracing their shrines and killed them. The people of Pergamum were killed with arrows as they clung to the statues in the temple of Aesculapius, to which they had fled for help and which they had steadfastly refused to leave. The people of Adramyttium killed the Italians among them as well as their children, in the water as they attempted to swim across the sea. The Caunians, after their victory over Antiochus, had been placed under the Rhodians and a little before that, had been restored to their privileges by the Senate and counted as Italians. They had escaped to the sacred court of that city from the very altars. After their infants had been killed before their mothers' eyes, the mothers themselves were killed and then their husbands. The Trallians, to avoid the scandal of killing those who lived with them, did not kill anyone themselves, but hired a bloody fellow, Theophilus of Paphlagonia, to do the job. He acted so savagely, that he shut them up in the temple of Concord and then attacked them with his sword, cutting off their hands as they embraced the statues. {*\*Appian, Mithridatic Wars, l. 12. c. 4. (22,23) 2:279,281*} {*\*Dio, l. 31. (101) 2:469,471*}

*3944.* Publius Rutilius Rufus, who had been the consul, lived in banishment among the Mitylenians. He escaped the king's fury against all Roman men by dressing like a philosopher. {*\*Cicero, Pro Rabirio Postumo, l. 1. c. 10. 14:391*} The fable of Theophanes, the Mitylenian, who recorded the affairs of Pompey the Great, cannot be credited at all. He wrote that in the citadel of Caenum, captured by Pompey, a speech of Rutilius was found among other precious secrets of Mithridates, in which Rutilius blamed the king for this cruel massacre of the Romans. {*\*Plutarch, Pompey, l. 1. c. 37. 5:213*} Like Rutilius, other Romans also changed their clothes to aid them in escaping the danger which was so imminent at the time. {*\*Athenaeus, l. 5. (213b) 2:465*} *[K148]* The floating Reed Islands in Lydia saved many of the citizens. {*\*Pliny, l. 2. c. 96. 1:341*} However, in spite of all this, eighty thousand were killed on that one day. {*Memnon, c. 33.*} {*\*Valerius Maximus, l. 9. c. 2. ext. 3. 2:315*} It was not a hundred and fifty thousand, as stated by Plutarch and by Dio. {*\*Plutarch, Sulla, l. 1. c. 24. s. 4. 4:405*} {*Dio, Legat., 36. or 37.*}

*3945.* Mithridates sailed over to Cos, where he found a party willing to receive him. The people of Cos gave him Alexander, the son of that Alexander who had previously reigned in Egypt. This was the Alexander whom his grandmother, Cleopatra, had left in Cos with a large supply of money. He adopted him and raised him as his own son. From Cleopatra's treasures, Mithridates was well-supplied with wealth, exquisite pieces made by craftsmen, jewels, everything associated with women's dresses and a large hoard of money. All this he sent away to Pontus. {*\*Appian, Mithridatic Wars, l. 12. c. 4. (23) 2:281*}

{*Appian, Mithridatic Wars, l. 12. c. 17. (115) 2:465} {*Appian, Civil Wars, l. 1. c. 11. (102) 3:189} Josephus, from the books of Strabo's histories, stated that, in addition to the treasures which belonged to Cleopatra, Mithridates carried away eight hundred talents of the Jews' money. He thought that it had been deposited by the Jews on that island in Asia out of fear of the Mithridatic War, and that the money was intended for the temple of Jerusalem. {*Josephus, Antiq., l. 14. c. 7. s. 2. (112,113) 7:505}

3946. In the 19th year of his reign in Egypt and his 26th in Cyprus, Alexander, the father of this young Alexander, was defeated in a naval battle by the Egyptians under their admiral, Tyrrus, who was of royal blood. Alexander was forced to flee to Myra, a city in Lycia, with his wife and daughter. As he was sailing from there toward Cyprus, he was found by Chaereas, a sea captain, and was killed. {Porphyry, Scaliger's Greek Eusebius, p. 225.}

3947. Athenion or Ariston, the Athenian envoy, was returning home to the Athenians from Asia after having seen Mithridates. He was driven by a storm to Carystus in Euboea. [E518] To bring him home, the Athenians sent some warships and a chair supported by silver feet. Most of the city ran out to greet him. No sooner had he gained control of the city, than he began to act like a tyrant. He either killed those who favoured the Romans, or else turned them over to Mithridates. To avoid this, many escaped to Amisus, a colony of the Athenians in Asia, where they were allowed into the city. {*Athenaeus, l. 5. (212bc) 2:459,461} {*Plutarch, Lucullus, l. 1. c. 19. s. 6. 2:531} {*Pausanias, Attica, l. 1. c. 20. s. 5. 1:99,101}

3948. The Italians who escaped from Asia found a sanctuary at Rhodes. Lucius Cassius, the proconsul of Asia, was one of these. The Rhodians fortified their walls and ports and positioned their engines of war, helped by men from Telmessus and Lycia. They destroyed the suburbs when Mithridates and his fleet approached, so that they might not be a shelter to the enemy or useful to them. They put their ships into battle formation, some in the front and others on the flanks. {*Appian, Mithridatic Wars, l. 12. c. 4. (24) 2:281,283} The Rhodian ships were outnumbered, but in everything else, the Rhodians were superior. They had experienced pilots and knew better how to arrange their ships and work the oars. They had more valiant soldiers and their commanders were more skilled and courageous. By comparison, the Cappadocians were but freshwater soldiers who had little experience in naval battles. They did everything in a disorderly way, which proved their undoing. {*Diod. Sic., l. 37. c. 28. 12:233}

3949. The Cappadocians were now ready to engage the enemy at sea in the presence of their king, desiring to prove their loyalty and affection to him. Since their only advantage was in the number of their ships, they swarmed about the enemy ships and sought to encircle and cut them off. {*Diod. Sic., l. 37. c. 28. 12:233} [K149] Finally, after sunset, Damagoras, the admiral of the Rhodian fleet, attacked twenty-five of the king's ships with his six. He sank two and forced another two to flee to Lycia. After spending the night at sea, he returned to engage the enemy again. In this encounter, one of the Chian ships, an ally of Mithridates, accidently bumped Mithridates' ship as he was going about encouraging his soldiers. As the king almost fell into the enemy's hands, he later punished the captain and pilot and was displeased with all the Chians. Then, as Mithridates' land forces were sailing to him from Asia in ships and galleys, a sudden storm drove them onto Rhodes. While they were disordered and dispersed by the storm, the Rhodians attacked them. They boarded some ships, sank some and burned others. They also captured four hundred prisoners. At last, Mithridates brought his engines and scaling-ladders to take the city. He was driven off and forced to retreat from Rhodes in disgrace. {*Appian, Mithridatic Wars, l. 12. c. 4. (25,26) 2:283-287} {Memnon, c. 33.} {*Livy, l. 78. 14:99}

3950. From there he went to Patara and besieged it. Because he did not have materials for engines, he began to cut down Latona's grove. He had a dream ordering him to stop and not to cut down those consecrated trees. He left Pelopidas to carry on the war in Lycia and sent Archelaus into Greece, in order to draw into his alliance, by any means at all, as many cities as he could. While he entrusted his commanders with many great tasks, he busied himself in levying soldiers, making arms and sporting about with his wife from Stratonicia. He was also busy in the investigation of all persons who had been charged with treason, for attempting either to kill him or to overthrow the state, or for being in any way so inclined. {*Appian, Mithridatic Wars, l. 12. c. 4. (27) 2:287,289}

3951. Archelaus, the king's general, was sent ahead into Achaia with a hundred and twenty thousand foot soldiers and cavalry. The city of Athens was surrendered to him by Aristion, the Athenian. {*Livy, l. 78. 14:99} {Eutropius, l. 5.} {Orosius, l. 6. c. 2.} From there he went with his fleet and provisions to Delos, which had revolted from the Athenians and he destroyed other citadels as well. He also took money, dedicated to Apollo, and sent it away with Aristion to the Athenians, with an escort of two thousand soldiers for safety. {*Appian, Mithridatic Wars, l. 12. c. 5. (28) 2:289} Apellicon of Teos, an Athenian citizen, was a most intimate friend of Athenion or Aristion, as they were both Peripatetics. He quickly came to Delos with some companies of foot soldiers. He stayed there a while and believing he was safe enough, did not position his guards with the care he should have taken and did not secure the rear of the island with a garrison or trench. Orobius, or Orbius, the general of the Roman army, had been entrusted with Delos. He saw the man's negligence and imprudence and arrived with his forces on a dark night. He attacked them when they had been drinking and were in a deep sleep. He cut the throats of six hundred of the Athenians and their auxiliaries, as if they had been so many sheep. He took about four hundred alive. Apellicon himself, however, who had so unworthily commanded that force, escaped. *[E519]* Many of them fled to the nearby villages for safety, but Orobius pursued them and set fire to the houses. He burned both them and their siege engines, together with other engines that belonged to the league. When he was all done, he erected a monument and altar with this inscription: {*Athenaeus, l. 5. (214d-215b) 2:271,273} [K150]

> Here lies with the sea, a foreign nation near
> The shores of Delos; which died fighting here.
> When those of Athens spoiled the holy isle,
> The Cappadocian king received a foil.

## 3917a AM, 4626 JP, 88 BC

3952. Mithridates sent Metrophanes with another band of soldiers and so slaughtered many in Euboea, the territories of Demetrias and Magnesia, who were opposed to the king. Bruttius, a lieutenant of Sentius the praetor, attacked Metrophanes at sea with some small forces he had brought from Macedonia. He sank one large ship and one ship called the Hemiolia. He killed all the men that were on board, while Metrophanes was forced to stand by looking on. The sight seemed so dreadful to him that he hoisted sail and got away as fast as he could. Bruttius gave chase, but the wind favoured Metrophanes. Bruttius was happy to give up the chase and instead attack Sciathos, an island which was well-known as a den for barbarian thieves and robbers. As soon as he had conquered the place, he crucified some of the slaves he discovered there and cut off the hands of the freemen. {*Appian, Mithridatic Wars, l. 12. c. 5. (29) 2:291} {*Plutarch, Sulla, l. 1. c. 11. s. 4. 4:361}

3953. One of the sons of Mithridates held the ancient kingdom of Pontus and Bosphorus as far as the deserts above Lake Maeotis (Sea of Azov), and no one opposed him. The other Ariarathes continued with the conquest of Thracia and Macedonia. The various generals, whom Mithridates sent out with armies, stayed in other quarters. Archelaus was in charge of them and with his fleet controlled almost all of the sea. He brought the islands of Cyclades under his jurisdiction and all the other islands that lay to the east of Cape Malea. {*Plutarch, Sulla, l. 1. c. 11. s. 2,3. 4:359} Eretria, Chalcis and all Euboea came and sided with Mithridates. {Memnon, c. 34.}

## 3917b AM, 4627 JP, 87 BC

3954. Lucius Sulla, the proconsul, with Lucius Cornelius Cinna, the consul, marched into Greece with five legions and several other companies to manage the Mithridatic war. {*Plutarch, Sulla, l. 1. c. 11. s. 5. 4:361} {*Dio, l. 31. (102) 2:471} {*Appian, Mithridatic Wars, l. 12. c. 5. (30) 2:293} {*Appian, Civil Wars, l. 1. c. 7. (55) 3:103} Mithridates remained at Pergamum during that time, where he was very busy distributing his wealth, his principalities and places of command among his friends. The following incident was among the many signs which happened to Mithridates while he was staying at Pergamum. It was said that at the same instant that Sulla put to sea with his fleet from Italy, the men of Pergamum were in the theatre, using an engine to lower a statue of Victory bearing a crown to place upon Mithridates' head. It happened that when the crown was just in line with his head, it fell to the ground and was shattered. This accident was seen as a bad omen and the people were struck with horror. Although everything was going well for him at the time, Mithridates was also greatly dejected. {*Plutarch, Sulla, l. 1. c. 11. s. 1,2. 4:359}

3955. Among the other strange visions that appeared to Mithridates when he first planned his war against the allies of the people of Rome, were these. Julius Obsequens said this happened at the time of the consulship of Lucius Sulla and Quintus Pompey. At Stratopedon, where the Senate usually sat, the crows killed a vulture with their beaks. The form of Isis seemed to strike *the harp*, which was a siege engine Mithridates used at Rhodes, with a thunderbolt. A large meteor fell from heaven on the same spot. At the time that Mithridates was busy in burning the grove dedicated to the Furies, a great laughing was heard, but no one could be found who had laughed. *[K151]* When, at the advice of the soothsayers, he was about to sacrifice a virgin to the Furies, a sudden fit of laughing burst forth from the throat of the maiden, disturbing the sacrifice. {*Julius Obsequens, Prodigies, l. 1. c. 56. 14:293,295}

3956. At Rome, Marcus Cicero studied under Molo of Rhodes, who was the best instructor and the most famous one for the pleading of causes. {*Cicero, Brutus, l. 1. c. 90. 5:271} *[E520]* Molo was the orator from Alabanda, in Caria, who had moved to Rhodes. {*Strabo, l. 14. c. 2. s. 26. 6:299} {See note on 3927b AM. <<4088>>}

3957. When Sulla entered Attica, he sent some of his forces to oppose Aristion in the city, while he personally marched at once to Piraeus, where Archelaus, Mithridates' general, had retreated within the walls. {*Appian, Mithridatic Wars, l. 12. c. 5. (30) 2:293}

## 3918a AM, 4627 JP, 87 BC

*3958.* The winter season was drawing on and Sulla camped near Eleusis, where he constructed a deep trench from the mountains to the sea. He wanted supplies brought to him in ships that he sent to Rhodes. {*Appian, Mithridatic Wars, l. 12. c. 5. (33) 2:299}

*3959.* Finally, in March, Sulla took Athens, which was very short of provisions. In his commentaries he related that he took Athens: {*Plutarch, Sulla, l. 1. c. 14. s. 6. 4:371,373}

"On the Calends of March (March 1), a day which corresponds very nearly with the first of the month of Anthesterion; in this month, as it happened, the Athenians performed many rites corresponding to the destruction and devastation caused by the Flood, believing that the ancient deluge occurred at this time."

*3960.* Comparing that day with the beginning of the month of Anthesterion, it was the time when the memory of the Ogygian Flood was celebrated by the Athenians. In Plutarch's time, the Athenian lunar month of Anthesterion corresponded to March. However, in the incorrect calendar of the Romans, the month of March coincided with the Athenian month of Posideion, which was December on the Julian calendar.

## 3918b AM, 4628 JP, 86 BC

*3961.* The Rhodians found it impossible to bring supplies to Sulla by sea because of Mithridates' fleets, which patrolled the seas. They advised Lucius Lucullus, a man of great repute among the Romans and one of Sulla's envoys, to sail secretly to Syria, Egypt and Libya. He was to gather whatever ships he could from the king's cities and bring them to add to the Rhodian fleet. He set out in the midst of winter, undeterred by the unfavourable sailing weather. Setting out with three Greek and three Rhodian galleys, he risked his life both on the sea and with the many enemy ships that patrolled the area. In spite of this, he arrived at Crete and got that island to help him. {*Appian, Mithridatic Wars, l. 12. c. 5. (33) 2:299} {*Plutarch, Lucullus, l. 1. c. 2. s. 1-3. 2:475}

*3962.* When Athens was taken, Aristion, the tyrant, and others retreated into the citadel of Athens. After they had been besieged by Curio for a long time, they were forced to surrender for lack of water. On the same day, and at the very time, that Curio was bringing the tyrant from the citadel, the sky suddenly became overcast and there was a violent rainstorm that supplied the citadel with fresh water. Sulla executed Aristion and his company and any who held an office among them, or had in any way violated the constitutions which the Romans had established among them after their conquest of Greece. To all the others, he granted his free pardon.

{*Appian, Mithridatic Wars, l. 12. c. 6. (39) 2:309} {*Plutarch, Sulla, l. 1. c. 14. s. 7. 4:373} {*Strabo, l. 9. c. 1. s. 20. 4:269,271} Pausanias reported that when Aristion fled to the temple of Athena for sanctuary, Sulla commanded him to be dragged from there and put to death. {*Pausanias, Attica, l. 1. c. 20. s. 7. 1:103} Others say that he was poisoned by Sulla. {Plutarch, Sulla}

*3963.* Magnesia was the only city in all Asia that remained loyal to the Romans and valiantly fought against Mithridates. {*Livy, l. 81. 14:103} [K152]

*3964.* Lucullus observed that the Cyrenians had always been ruled by tyrants and were continually embroiled in war. He settled the affairs of their state and enacted laws to secure the peace of the state for the future. {*Plutarch, Lucullus, l. 1. c. 2. s. 3,4. 2:475,477} After they had been taken over by the Romans ten years earlier, they had been grievously oppressed by Nicocrates and his brother Leander. They had recently been relieved from this oppression through Aretaphila, Nicocrates' wife. {*Plutarch, Bravery of Women - Aretaphila, l. 1. c. 19. (255e-258c) 3:541-551} Ten years later, Cyrene was made a province by the Romans, as noted by Appian. {See note on 3929a AM. <<4099>>} Josephus stated, from the books of Strabo's histories, that at this time Cyrene was being disturbed by a rebellion of the Jews and that Lucullus was quickly sent there by Sulla to pacify it. {*Josephus, Antiq., l. 14. c. 7. s. 2. (114) 7:507}

*3965.* As Lucullus was sailing from Cyrene to Egypt, he nearly lost all his ships through a sudden attack by pirates. He personally escaped safely to Alexandria, where he was received with a great deal of honour. The whole fleet was gloriously decorated and went out to meet him, as was their custom any time their king returned from the sea. Ptolemy Lathurus, whom Plutarch incorrectly called a youth, treated him very courteously. He gave him his lodging and his table at court, which had never before been known to occur for any foreign commander. [E521] He allowed him four times the usual amount, to pay his expenses. Lucullus only took what was necessary and refused all presents, although some were worth eighty talents. It is said that he did not go to Memphis nor went to see any of the famous wonders of Egypt. He considered those things to be sights for tourists, but not for one who had left his general in the open field, marching against the garrisons of the enemy. {*Plutarch, Lucullus, l. 1. c. 2. s. 5,6. 2:477}

*3966.* Aurelius Victor wrote that Lucullus won Ptolemy, the king of Alexandria, over to his side along with Sulla, the consul. {Aurelius Victor, De Viris Illustribus, l. 1. c. 74.} However, Sulla was not a consul at the time, but a proconsul. Also, Ptolemy would not ally himself with Sulla for fear of being attacked, but he allowed Lucullus' ships to take him to Cyprus. As Lucullus was leaving, Ptolemy greeted him and gave him an emerald set in gold. Lucullus at first refused this, but when the king showed him the king's own picture engraved on it, Lucullus dared not refuse, in case the king thought that he had been unhappy with him when he left and would therefore attack him at sea. {*Plutarch, Lucullus, l. 1. c. 3. s. 1. 2:477,479}

3967. Lucullus gathered a multitude of ships from among the port towns as he sailed by, except from those who had been engaged in piracy. He sailed over into Cyprus, having been told that the enemy was lurking around the promontories to catch him. He sailed his fleet into the harbour and wrote to the cities round about to provide him with winter quarters and provisions, pretending that he would stay there with his fleet until spring. But as soon as the wind was favourable, he put to sea again, sailing with low sails by day, while spreading all the canvas he had by night. With this trick, he brought his fleet safely to Rhodes. {*Plutarch, Lucullus, l. 1. c. 3. s. 2,3. 2:479}

3968. Cinna, the consul, sent his colleague Lucius Valerius Flaccus into Asia with two legions, to govern the province and to manage the war against Mithridates. Because he was a novice soldier, Gaius Fimbria, one of the senators, went along with him. He was a man of reputation among the soldiers. [K153] Livy, Aurelius, Victor and Orosius called him Flaccus' envoy, but Dio, as well as his lieutenant, Strabo, and his quaestor, Velleius Paterculus, called him commander of the cavalry. When they undertook this task, the Senate ordered them to help Sulla as long as he was loyal to the Senate, otherwise they should fight with him. Soon after they had put to sea from Brundisium, many of their ships were ravaged by a storm, and those that were damaged were burned by ships belonging to Mithridates. {Memnon, c. 36.} {*Livy, l. 82. 14:103} {*Strabo, l. 13. c. 1. s. 27. 6:55} {*Velleius Paterculus, l. 2. c. 24. 1:99} {*Dio, l. 31. (104) 2:477} {*Appian, Civil Wars, l. 1. c. 8. (74) 3:139} {*Appian, Mithridatic Wars, l. 12. c. 8. (51) 2:333} {Orosius, l. 6. c. 2.}

3969. Mithridates' general, Taxiles, marched from Thrace and Macedonia with a hundred thousand foot soldiers, ten thousand cavalry and ninety chariots with scythes. He asked Archelaus to help him, so they combined their forces. They had a hundred and twenty thousand men (Memnon stated more than sixty thousand) consisting of Thracians, Pontics, Scythians, Cappadocians, Bithynians, Galatians, Phrygians and others who had come from Mithridates' new provinces. Sulla brought Lucius Hortensius along with him, who had six thousand men from Italy. They fought with Taxiles near Chaeronia, even though Sulla only had about fifteen hundred cavalry and fifteen thousand foot soldiers, according to Plutarch. However, Appian stated that his entire force was so small that it was less than a third the size of the enemy. Sulla won, killing a hundred and ten

thousand of the enemy (or a hundred thousand, as in Livy's Epitome) and pillaging their camp. Archelaus escaped to Chalcis with not many more than ten thousand men. Sulla stated that he lost about fourteen men, others say fifteen. Two of those presumed dead returned to the camp at evening. {Memnon, c. 34.} {*Livy, l. 82. 14:103} {*Plutarch, Sulla, l. 1. c. 15-19. 4:373-391} {*Appian, Mithridatic Wars, l. 12. c. 6. (41-45) 2:311-319} {Eutropius, l. 5.} {Orosius, l. 6. c. 2.}

3970. Sulla received news that Flaccus, the consul, who was in an opposing political party, was sailing across the Ionian Sea with some legions on the pretext of coming against Mithridates, but that he was in actual fact coming to fight Sulla. Sulla marched into Thessaly to meet him. {*Plutarch, Sulla, l. 1. c. 20. s. 1. 4:391} Flaccus was an unsuitable person to lead the army. He was poorly qualified, covetous, rigorous and cruel when punishing his soldiers. His soldiers detested him so much, that some of those whom he sent into Thessaly defected to Sulla. The rest would also have revolted, had it not been for Fimbria, who was reputed to be the better soldier and of a softer temper. {*Appian, Mithridatic Wars, l. 12. c. 8. (51) 2:333}

3971. Since the Romans had no navy, Archelaus roved about the islands, quite secure, causing havock anywhere he pleased, all along the coast. He ventured ashore and laid siege to Zacynthus, where he was attacked in the night by some Romans who were strangers in those parts. [E522] He hurried to his ships again and sailed back to Chalcis, more like a pirate than a warrior. {*Appian, Mithridatic Wars, l. 12. c. 6. (45) 2:319}

3972. Mithridates was deeply dismayed by the news of his defeat, but not totally discouraged. He imposed new levies on all the countries under his dominion. Because he feared that his defeat might encourage some to revolt from him, he thought it best to arrest all those he suspected, before the war broke out afresh. {*Appian, Mithridatic Wars, l. 12. c. 7. (46) 2:321}

3973. He began with the tetrarchs of the Galatians, both those whom he had about him as his friends, as well as those who had not as yet been subdued by him. He killed them all, with their wives and children, except for three who escaped. [K154] Some he surprised by treachery and the rest he massacred in one night at a party. He jealously believed that none of them would remain loyal to him if Sulla should chance to come into those regions. When he had confiscated their goods, he placed garrisons into their cities and made Eumachus governor over the whole country. Shortly after the tetrarchs escaped, they gathered a force together and drove him and his garrisons from Galatia. Hence, Mithridates had gained nothing from that country but money. {*Appian, Mithridatic Wars, l. 12. c. 7. (46) 2:321}

3974. He had been angry with the Chians ever since in the naval battle with the Rhodians, a ship of theirs accidently happened to run against the king's ship. First he made plans to sell the goods of all the citizens who had defected to Sulla, after which he sent some persons to spy on the Roman faction among the Chians. At last, Zenobius, or, as Memnon wrote, Dorylaus, arrived with an army on the pretext of going into Greece. He surprised the Chians by night and captured their strongest citadels. Then he placed guards at the gates of the city and assembled the citizens. He compelled them to turn over their arms, while the most important men's sons were taken as hostages and sent to Erythrae. After this, Mithridates sent letters to the Chians, asking for two thousand talents in compensation. To pay this, they were forced to take down the ornaments from their temples and make their women give up their jewellery. In spite of this, Zenobius picked a quarrel with them, pretending that their money was not enough. He ordered the men to separate themselves from the women and children, to be carried by ship to the Black Sea to Mithridates, while he divided their lands among the Pontics. {*Appian, Mithridatic Wars, l. 12. c. 7. (46,47) 2:321-325} {Memnon, c. 35.}

3975. The Heracleans, who were good friends of the Chians, attacked the Pontic ships carrying the captives on their way and brought them into their city. These did not offer any resistance at all, as they were out-numbered. At that time, the Heracleans relieved the Chians by giving them what they needed, and eventually they restored them to their own country, after being very generous to them. {Memnon, c. 35.}

3976. The Ephesians ordered Zenobius, as he approached the city with his soldiers, to lay down his arms at the gate of the city and to enter with a very small company. He was happy enough to do so and went to Philopoemen, the father of Monima, one of Mithridates' favourite concubines. From there, he had a town crier summon the Ephesians to assemble themselves together. Since they expected nothing good from him, they deferred the assembly until the next day, while they met together that night and urged each other to attack Zenobius. So they cast him into prison and killed him there. They placed guards on the walls and armed the common people, arranging them into companies which then brought home the grain from the fields. They also made sure that the youth of the city were prevented from causing any riots. The people of Tralles, Hypaepa, Mesopolis and some others, among whom Orosius mentioned the people of Smyrna, Sardis and Colophon, were all terrified by the terrible disaster that had recently happened to the Chians. Therefore when they heard of the Ephesians' exploits, they followed their example. {*Appian, Mithridatic Wars, l. 12. c. 7. (48) 2:325} {Orosius, l. 6. c. 2.}

### 3919a AM, 4628 JP, 86 BC

3977. Fimbria outdistanced Flaccus and got a long way ahead of him in his march. He thought that now was a good time for some civil disorder, so, to gain the affection of his soldiers, he permitted them to make incursions into the countries of their allies. They could do what they pleased and take captive anyone they met. The soldiers really liked this idea, so that within a few days they had gathered an abundance of wealth from their plundering. [E523] [K155] Those who had been robbed of their goods went to meet the consul Flaccus and complained bitterly to him about the wrongs they had received. Very upset by this, he ordered them to follow him, as he would personally see that restitution was made to everyone who had been robbed. He threatened Fimbria and ordered that he immediately return to the owners whatever had been taken away from them. Fimbria placed full blame on the soldiers, claiming they had done this without any orders from him. Secretly, however, he told them to ignore the consul's commands and not allow anything which they had acquired by law of arms to be taken from them. Thereupon, when Flaccus demanded that restitution be made for their plundering, even adding threats to his commands, the soldiers refused to obey and there was a great rebellion in the camp. {*Diod. Sic., l. 38/39. c. 8. s. 1. 12:251}

3978. When Sulla, on his march to meet Flaccus, had come as far as the town of Meliteia, he received news from various places that the country which he had just left was again overrun, to the same extent as before, by another army of Mithridates. Dorylaus had arrived at Chalcis, with a large fleet carrying eighty thousand armed men who were the most disciplined and best-trained of all Mithridates' soldiers. He attacked Boeotia and after he had captured all that region, he marched to fight with Sulla. {*Plutarch, Sulla, l. 1. c. 20. s. 1,2. 4:391,393}

3979. Dorylaus was the son of Philetaerus, who was the brother of Dorylaus, the general. {See note on 3879 AM. <<3813>>} He had been raised by Mithridates, who was very fond of him. When he was a man, the king promoted him to the highest honours, the highest of which, in turn, was his appointment to the priesthood of Comana, in Pontus. The king invited his relatives, the sons of Dorylaus, the general, and Steropa, a Macetan woman, to come with him to Cnossus. Dorylaus, the general, had two sons by her, Lagetas and Stratachas, and a daughter. The daughter was later the mother of Strabo, the geographer. After the death of Mithridates, the family lived at Cnossus. {*Strabo, l. 10. c. 4. s. 10. 5:133,135} {*Strabo, l. 12. c. 3. s. 33. 5:433}

*3980.* Dorylaus, with his eighty thousand (Plutarch and Appian) or with seventy thousand (Eutropius and Orosius) choice soldiers, joined his forces to those of Archelaus, who had only ten thousand of his former army left and tried in vain to convince Dorylaus not to attack Sulla. They attacked Sulla near Orchomenus and lost fifteen thousand men (Appian and Orosius) or twenty thousand. (Eutropius) Archelaus' son, Diogenes, was killed and when, soon after this, they had a second battle, the rest of Mithridates' forces were destroyed. Twenty thousand were driven into a nearby moor, where they were butchered. They cried for mercy, but the Romans did not understand their language and so they killed them. Many more were forced into a river and drowned. The rest of the miserable wretches were killed on every side. Plutarch stated that the marshes overflowed with the blood of the dead and that a pool was filled up with dead bodies. So much so, that, two hundred years later, in his time, many of the barbarians' bows, helmets, pieces of steel breast-plates and swords were found buried in the mud. {*Plutarch, Sulla, l. 1. c. 20,21. 4:391-397} {*Appian, Mithridatic Wars, l. 12. c. 7. (49) 2:327,329} {*Livy, l. 82. 14:103} {Eutropius, l. 5.} {Orosius, l. 6. c. 2.}

*3981.* Archelaus spent two days (Plutarch) or three days (Eutropius), stripped naked, hiding in the marshes of the Orchomenians. At last, he found a little boat and sailed into Chalcis. Wherever he came across any of Mithridates' forces, he hastily assembled them into a body of troops. {*Plutarch, Sulla, l. 1. c. 22. s. 4. 4:399} {Eutropius, l. 5.} {*Appian, Mithridatic Wars, l. 12. c. 7. (50) 2:329,331} [K156] Sulla pillaged and created what havock he could in Boeotia which was inclined to revolt to one side or the other at every new crisis. From there, he moved on into Thessaly, where he constructed his winter quarters. He was expecting Lucullus to arrive with ships, but when he heard no news of his coming, he built other ships. {*Appian, Mithridatic Wars, l. 12. c. 8. (51) 2:331} Livy stated that Archelaus surrendered himself and the king's fleet to Sulla. {*Livy, l. 82. 14:103} Aurelius Victor wrote that through Archelaus' treachery, Sulla was able to intercept the fleet. {Aurelius Victor, De Viris Illustribus, l. 1. c. 76.} It is evident that there were secret communications between Sulla and Archelaus for other reasons, as well. For Sulla had given Archelaus two thousand acres in Euboea, where Chalcis was. Sulla, however, tried to remove all those suspicions in his commentaries. {*Plutarch, Sulla, l. 1. c. 23. s. 2. 4:401} {Dio, Legat., 33. or 34.} Although, in a letter of Mithridates to Arsaces, some expressions implied that those suspicions were so firmly rooted in men's minds that they were not easily removed. {*Sallust, Letter of Mithridates, l. 1. (12) 1:437}

"Archelaus, the most unworthy of those that were under me, thwarted my plans by his betrayal of my army."

*3982.* Strabo stated that Archelaus, who waged war against Sulla, was greatly admired by the Romans, Sulla and the Senate. {*Strabo, l. 12. c. 3. s. 34. 5:437} {*Strabo, l. 17. c. 1. s. 11. 8:45} [E524]

*3983.* In the interim, Flaccus reached Byzantium, where Fimbria had caused the soldiers to revolt against him. Flaccus ordered his soldiers to stay outside the walls while he entered the city. Consequently, Fimbria began to accuse Flaccus of having received money from the citizens of Byzantium and of having gone to pamper himself in the city while his soldiers endured the harshness of the winter in the open fields in their tents. These speeches so greatly enraged the soldiers, that they broke into the city and killed a few people whom they chanced to meet on the way. They dispersed themselves into various houses. {*Dio, l. 31. (104) 2:479}

*3984.* Lucius Valerius Flaccus passed through the region of Byzantium into Bithynia and camped at Nicaea. {Memnon, c. 36.} Cicero, in his speech for that Flaccus who was this man's son, stated: {*Cicero, Pro Flacco, l. 1. (61) 10:509}

"It was the same time when all Asia shut her gates to Lucius Flaccus, the consul, or now rather proconsul, but not only received that Cappadocian (Mithridates) into their cities, but deliberately sent to invite him to them."

## 3919b AM, 4629 JP, 85 BC

*3985.* When some differences arose between Fimbria and Flaccus' quaestor, Flaccus was chosen as an arbitrator. He had so little regard for Fimbria's honour, that Fimbria threatened to return home to Rome (Appian) or Flaccus threatened to send him to Rome, whether he wanted to go or not. (Dio) Thereupon, Fimbria so vilely reproached Flaccus, that Flaccus took away his command and assigned someone else to replace him. {*Appian, Mithridatic Wars, l. 12. c. 8. (52) 2:333} {*Dio, l. 31. (104) 2:479}

*3986.* After this dispute, Fimbria was discharged and went to the soldiers at Byzantium. {Aurelius Victor, De Viris Illustribus, l. 1. c. 70.} He greeted them as if he were going to Rome and wanted letters from them, to take to their friends there. He also complained about the great injustice done to him and reminding them of the good turns he had done for them, he cautioned them to take heed and look out for themselves. By this, he secretly hinted that Flaccus had some plot against them. His words were well received and they wished him well, but they were jealous of Flaccus. Then, Fimbria ascended the platform and in plain words incited them against Flaccus, among other things charging Flaccus with having bribed him to betray them. {*Dio, l. 31. (104) 2:479}

*3987.* When Fimbria had again crossed the Hellespont, he stirred up his soldiers to acts of plunder and every form of villainy. *[K157]* He exacted money from the cities and divided it among the soldiers, whom he let do as they wished, without restraint. Attracted by hopes of a large income, they loved Fimbria all the more. {*Diod. Sic., l. 38/39. c. 8. s. 2. 12:251,253}

*3988.* When Flaccus had gone toward Chalcedon with his fleet, Fimbria took advantage of his absence. He first began with Thermus, the propraetor who had been left in charge. He took the fasces, the ensigns of his authority, away from him, as if he had taken that office upon himself from the army. Then Fimbria chased after Flaccus, but Flaccus fled and hid in a private citizen's house. In the night, he scaled the wall and stole away, first to Chalcedon and from there to Nicomedia, where he had the gates shut. Fimbria followed him closely and forced the Roman consul (or rather, one who had been consul, as Velleius stated) and the commander-in-chief of this war, to hide himself in a well. Fimbria dragged him from there and killed him. When he had cut off Flaccus' head, he threw it into the sea, but left the body lying unburied on the ground. {*Appian, Mithridatic Wars, l. 12. c. 8. (52) 2:333,335} {Memnon, c. 36,42.} {*Livy, l. 82. 14:103} {*Velleius Paterculus, l. 2. c. 24. 1:99} {*Strabo, l. 13. c. 1. s. 27. 6:55} {Aurelius Victor, De Viris Illustribus, l. 1. c. 70.} {Orosius, l. 6. c. 2.} Fimbria then allowed his soldiers to plunder Nicomedia. {*Diod. Sic., l. 38/39. c. 8. s. 2. 12:253}

*3989.* Mithridates sent an army against those who had revolted from him. After he had defeated them, he behaved very harshly toward them. {*Appian, Mithridatic Wars, l. 12. c. 7. (48) 2:325} He took by force all the cities in Asia and miserably pillaged the province. {*Livy, l. 82. 14:103} Fearing lest others should prove disloyal, he made the cities of Greece free. Through a public crier, he promised to cancel every debt of every debtor, all prisoners would be allowed to live freely in their own cities and all slaves would be set free. Through these acts of grace, he hoped that he could buy the loyalty of all debtors, prisoners and slaves, so that they would help keep him in power. They indeed helped him not long after this. {*Appian, Mithridatic Wars, l. 12. c. 7. (48) 2:325,327}

*3990.* Meanwhile the king's intimate friends, Mynnio and Philotimus, who were from Smyrna, and Clisthenes and Asclepiodotus, who were from Lesbos, conspired against Mithridates. Asclepiodotus had at times been the commander of his mercenary soldiers. Asclepiodotus himself was the first to talk. To obtain credence for what he was saying, he had the king lie under a couch and listen to what Mynnio would say. The treason was thus exposed and all the conspirators died on the rack. *[E525]* Many others were shrewdly suspected to have had a hand in it. Eighty citizens of Pergamum, as well as others in other cities, were seized because they were thought to be in on this conspiracy. Then the king sent his inquisitors into all the regions, where they executed about sixteen hundred men for this conspiracy. Each of the inquisitors charged their personal enemies with treasonable conduct. Not long after this, the accusers were either punished by Sulla, or took their own lives, or accompanied Mithridates in his flight to Pontus. {*Appian, Mithridatic Wars, l. 12. c. 7. (48) 2:327} {Orosius, l. 6. c. 2.}

*3991.* Diodorus, Mithridates' general, who claimed to be an academic philosopher, a lawyer and a rhetorician, killed among others all the elders of Adramyttium to please the king. When the king was deposed, he accompanied him into Pontus. He starved himself to death to prevent the disgrace which was likely to happen to him, because of some great crimes with which he was charged. {*Strabo, l. 13. c. 1. s. 66. 6:129}

*3992.* Lucius Lucullus, with the help of some Rhodian ships and the fleet he had gathered together from Cyprus, Phoenicia and Pamphylia, laid waste to all the enemy's coasts. Now and then, along the way, he fought with Mithridates' fleet. {*Appian, Mithridatic Wars, l. 12. c. 8. (56) 2:343} He persuaded the citizens of Cos and Cnidos to expel the king's garrisons and to take up arms with him against the Samians. *[K158]* He drove the king's party from Chios, and brought relief to the Colophonians by setting them at liberty and seizing Epigonius, their king. {*Plutarch, Lucullus, l. 1. c. 3. s. 3. 2:479} Through Marena's help, he brought Mithridates' fleet to Sulla. {Aurelius Victor, De Viris Illustribus, l. 1. c. 74.}

*3993.* After Gaius Fimbria had killed Flaccus in Bithynia and taken his army, the men made him their general. {*Velleius Paterculus, l. 2. c. 24. 1:99} He gained control of a number of cities. Some voluntarily submitted to him, while others were forced to submit. {Memnon, c. 36.} He killed many people, not for any just reason, but merely out of cruelty and to gratify his passion. At one time he ordered some posts to be put into the ground, to which he then used to have men bound and scourged to death. When he saw that there were more posts than condemned persons, he ordered his soldiers to seize some of the crowd standing by and bind them to the posts, so that it would not seem that the posts had been set up in vain. {*Dio, l. 31. (104) 2:481}

*3994.* When Fimbria entered Cyzicum, he claimed to be their friend. As soon as he was inside, he began to charge all their wealthiest persons with some crime or other. After he had condemned two principal men of the city, he had them whipped with rods to terrify the rest, and then he had them decapitated and sold their goods. This forced others, out of fear, to give him all that they had. {*Diod. Sic., l. 38/39. c. 8. s. 3. 12:253}

3995. Mithridates, the son of Mithridates, joined with Taxiles, Diophantus and Menander, three most highly skilled commanders. With a good army they marched against Fimbria. Because of the large number of enemy soldiers, Fimbria lost some men in this battle. They came to a river which separated the two armies. In a great rainstorm that occurred before morning, Fimbria crossed the river and so completely surprised the enemy as they lay asleep in their tents, that they never knew he was there. He made such a wholesale slaughter of them, that very few escaped, and those only from among the commanders and cavalry. {Memnon, c. 36.}

3996. Among those who escaped was Mithridates, the king's son. He was chased from Asia to Mileropolis, from where he safely came to his father at Pergamum with a company of cavalry. Fimbria attacked the king's ships as they lay in the harbour and drove him from Pergamum. After he had taken the city, he pursued him as he fled into Pitane. He besieged him and endeavoured to make a trench around the place. {Memnon, c. 36.} {*Livy, l. 83. 14:105} {*Appian, Mithridatic Wars, l. 12. c. 8. (52) 2:335} {*Plutarch, Lucullus, l. 1. c. 3. s. 4. 2:479} {Aurelius Victor, De Viris Illustribus, l. 1. c. 70.} {Orosius, l. 6. c. 2.}

3997. Mithridates had now been driven from the land by Fimbria and was trapped in a corner facing the sea. He summoned together all his fleet from their various places. He did not want to fight with Fimbria, because the latter was clever and a conqueror. When Fimbria saw what was happening, he quickly sent to Lucullus to ask him to bring his fleet and unite with him in taking this king, who was the most bitter and cruel enemy of the people of Rome. If Lucullus had placed the public good ahead of his private animosities, they would have captured Mithridates. As it was, he did not, and Mithridates escaped. {*Plutarch, Lucullus, l. 1. c. 3. s. 4-7. 2:479,481} {Orosius, l. 6. c. 2.} [E526]

3998. After Mithridates escaped with his fleet to Mitylene, Fimbria went up and down the province and levied fines on those who had supported Mithridates, and destroyed the grounds of any who would not let him into their city. {*Appian, Mithridatic Wars, l. 12. c. 8. (53) 2:335} [K159] He recovered most of Asia for the Romans, due to the various defections of the cities from Mithridates. {Memnon, c. 36.} {*Livy, l. 83. 14:105}

3999. When Fimbria tried to take Illium, which was built on the site of Troy, the citizens sent to Sulla for help. After Sulla agreed to help, he warned Fimbria not to meddle any further with those who had submitted to him. He commended Illium for returning to the alli-

ance they had formerly had with the people of Rome. He also said it did not really matter to whom they submitted, since both Sulla and Fimbria were Roman citizens and they were all descended from the Trojans. In spite of all this, Fimbria stormed the city and entered it on the eleventh day. He bragged that he had taken the city in only eleven days, when Agamemnon, with a fleet of a thousand ships and the whole power of Greece, previously had a great deal of trouble taking it in ten years. A certain man said that the reason for this was:

"There was not among us a Hector who would stand bravely to defend the city."

4000. Fimbria indiscriminately killed everyone he came across and burned almost the whole city. He tormented to death those who were a part of the embassy to Sulla. He spared neither the holy artifacts nor the people who had fled to the temple of Athena for sanctuary, but burned both them and the temple together. Moreover, he pulled down the walls and on the following day, surrounded the city and looked for anything that had escaped his fury. He did not allow any fair court or consecrated house or statue to remain in the city. {*Livy, l. 83. 14:105} {*Strabo, l. 13. c. 1. s. 27. 6:55} {*Appian, Mithridatic Wars, l. 12. c. 8. (53) 2:335,337} {*Dio, l. 31. (104) 2:481} {Orosius, l. 6. c. 2.}

4001. Fimbria ordered Illium to be burned because they had been somewhat slow in opening the gates to him. Aurelius Victor wrote that Athena's temple stood untouched. {Aurelius Victor, De Viris Illustribus, l. 1. c. 70.} He said:

"It was without all doubt preserved by the goddess herself."

4002. However, Julius Obsequens and Appian affirmed that the temple was burned, but that the ancient image of Athena, called the Palladium, which was supposed to have been taken by Diomedes and Ulysses at the time of the Trojan war, was found safe and unharmed among its ruins. Fimbria discovered this, as Servius noted, and it was later carried to Rome. {*Virgil, Aeneid, l. 2. (162-168) 1:305} However, Strabo stated that several similar images of Athena were displayed at Lavinium, Luceria and Siris, as having been brought from Troy. Appian wrote that this destruction of Troy occurred in the 173rd Olympiad, one thousand and fifty years after its destruction by Agamemnon. However, according to Eratosthenes, Apollodorus and Diodorus Siculus, there were one thousand and ninety-nine years between the first destruction of Troy and the fourth year of the 173rd Olympiad, when Troy, or Illium, was again destroyed. {*Julius Obsequens, Prodigies, l. 1. c. 56b. 14:297} {*Appian, Mithridatic Wars, l. 12. c. 8. (53) 2:335,337} {*Strabo, l. 6. c. 1. s. 14. 3:49,51} {*Diod. Sic., l. 1. c. 4. s. 5. 1:21,32}

4003. Lucullus first routed the king's fleet near Lectum, in Troas. At Tenedos, he saw Neoptolemus sailing toward him with a larger fleet than before. Lucullus was sailing some distance ahead of his fleet, in a Rhodian ship with five tiers of oars. Damagoras, who was the captain of the ship and was very skilled in naval battles, favoured the Romans. Neoptolemus sailed toward him at high speed, ordering the pilot to direct his forecastle against the enemy ship. Damagoras feared the size of the king's ship and the force of its brazen prow. Not daring to close the gap between them, he ordered the pilot to stop the course of the ship by hastily turning her about. By breaking the blow in this way, he caused the enemy to sail quickly on. His ship was not harmed because he had only made contact with some sections of the ship which were underwater. [K160] As soon as the rest of the fleet reached him, Lucullus commanded the pilot to steer about. After displaying his valour, he compelled the enemy to hoist sail, while he sailed as fast as he could in pursuit of Neoptolemus. {*Plutarch, Lucullus, l. 1. c. 3. s. 8-10. 2:481,483}

4004. The citizens of Damascus invited Aretas, king of Coelosyria, to take over the government, because they disliked Ptolemy Mennaeus. Aretas entered Judea with an army. After he had defeated Alexander Jannaeus at Adida and had secured terms of peace with him, he marched home. {*Josephus, Antiq., l. 13. c. 15. s. 2. (392) 7:423,425}

4005. When Cinna and Carbo started a civil disorder in Rome, they violently attacked the most eminent persons of the city, without any restraint. Most of the nobility stole away, first into Achaia and later to Sulla in Asia. Within a short time, there were many senators in his camp. {*Velleius Paterculus, l. 2. c. 23. s. 1-3. 1:97} {*Plutarch, Sulla, l. 1. c. 22. s. 1. 4:397} {*Dio, l. 31. (102) 2:471-477} They all urged him to come to the relief of his own country, which was in extreme danger and almost lost. {Eutropius, l. 5.} {Orosius, l. 15. c. 20.} [E527] His wife Metella stole away with great difficulty to him barely escaping with her own life and her children. She told Sulla that his house and its villa had been burned by the enemy and begged him, therefore, to come and help the city. {*Plutarch, Sulla, l. 1. c. 22. s. 2. 4:397}

4006. Mithridates, having considered how many men he had lost in the very short time since first he had advanced into Greece, wrote to Archelaus, instructing him to make peace with Sulla on the most honourable conditions he could get. {*Appian, Mithridatic Wars, l. 12. c. 8. (54) 2:337} Sulla was now faced with a deep dilemma. He did not want to abandon his country when it was in such a sad state, nor did he want to leave Asia with an unfinished war with Mithridates. Then a merchant from Delos, by the name of Archelaus, offered to negotiate the treaty and had carried some hopes and secret instructions from Archelaus, the king's general. Sulla was very pleased at this and hurried to go and confer with Archelaus the general himself. They met at the seacoast near Delos at the site of Apollo's temple. Archelaus began by urging Sulla to abandon his Asian and Pontic expedition, and to go home to put down the civil war there. He said that his master, the king, would supply him with whatever silver, ships, or men, he needed. Sulla replied by telling Archelaus to abandon Mithridates and reign in his stead. He said that he would consider Archelaus an ally and friend of Rome, if he would turn over the king's fleet to him. But when Archelaus detested so treacherous an act, Sulla finally proposed some conditions of peace to be made with the king. {*Plutarch, Sulla, l. 1. c. 22. s. 2-5. 4:397,399} Among these conditions was one demanding that the king withdraw all his garrisons, except from those places in which he previously had soldiers before the war broke out. When Archelaus heard this, he immediately removed the garrisons. Archelaus wrote to the king concerning the other articles to find out what the king wanted to do. {*Appian, Mithridatic Wars, l. 12. c. 8. (55) 2:341}

4007. When the articles had been agreed on, Sulla withdrew to the Hellespont, and crossed through Thessaly and Macedonia. Archelaus accompanied him and Sulla treated him very civilly. When Archelaus became quite sick near Larisa, Sulla stopped his march and took just as much care of him as if he had been one of his own commanders or praetors. All this increased the suspicion that Mithridates had about Archelaus, namely, that he had not fought as well as he could have, in the battle at Chaeronia. {*Plutarch, Sulla, l. 1. c. 23. s. 1,2. 4:399,401} {Dio, Legat., 33. or 34.}

4008. The envoys from Mithridates came to Sulla. They said the terms about the surrender of Paphlagonia and of the ships were unacceptable, adding that they could get easier conditions from the other general, Fimbria. In a rage, Sulla replied that Fimbria would smart for this, and that as soon as he was to come into Asia, he himself would see what Mithridates wanted more, peace or war. [K161] Archelaus interceded with Sulla, taking him by the hand and calming his fury with his tears. At last he begged earnestly to be sent to Mithridates. He promised that Mithridates would either conclude a peace on Sulla's terms or else, if he refused to sign those articles, he would kill Mithridates, or possibly (for the Greek copies vary) kill himself. {*Plutarch, Sulla, l. 1. c. 23. s. 3-5. 4:401,403} {Dio, Legat., 34. or 35.} {*Appian, Mithridatic Wars, l. 12. c. 8. (56) 2:341}

### 3920a AM, 4629 JP, 85 BC

4009. Six years before he died, Alexander Jannaeus, after he had concluded a peace with Aretas, led an army against the neighbouring people and took the city of Dium by storm. {*Josephus, Antiq., l. 13. c. 15. s. 3. (393) 7:425}

*4010.* Archelaus returned from Mithridates and met with Sulla at Philippi in Macedonia. He told him that everything had gone as he had wished and that Mithridates wanted to meet with him. Consequently, Sulla marched through Thrace to Cypsella and sent Lucullus, who had joined him with his fleet, ahead of him to Abydus. Lucullus provided Sulla with a safe passage from the Chersonesus and helped him in transporting the army. {*Plutarch, Sulla, l. 1. c. 23. s. 6. 4:403} {*Plutarch, Lucullus, l. 1. c. 3. s. 9,10. 2:483} {*Appian, Mithridatic Wars, l. 12. c. 8. (56) 2:341,343}

*4011.* Sulla met with Mithridates at Dardanus, a town of Troas. Mithridates had two hundred ships with oars, twenty thousand foot soldiers and six thousand cavalry there with him, and a number of chariots armed with scythes. Sulla had four regiments of foot soldiers and two hundred cavalry. Both of them went aside to talk in the field, each with a small retinue, while their armies looked on. Mithridates came to him and extended his right hand. Sulla asked him whether he would accept a peace on the conditions negotiated with Archelaus. The king demurred for a while and each of them hurled complaints and accusations at each other. Finally, Mithridates was frightened by Sulla's passionate speeches and consented to the articles of peace that had been offered to Archelaus. After this, Sulla greeted him, embracing and kissing him. {Memnon, c. 37.} {*Plutarch, Sulla, l. 1. c. 24. 4:403,405} {Dio, Legat., 35. or 36.} {*Appian, Mithridatic Wars, l. 1. c. 8. (56-58) 2:343-347}

*4012.* The articles of peace were as follows. Mithridates would be content with what had been his father's kingdom in Pontus and would not have anything to do with Asia or Paphlagonia. *[E528]* He would release all commanders, envoys, prisoners, renegades, fugitives, the Chians and any he had carried away as captives with him into Pontus from the various cities. He would give the Romans seventy or (as Memnon has it) eighty ships with brass beaks and with all their equipment. Lastly, the cities which were currently under Roman jurisdiction, would not be questioned for having defected to the Romans. However, shortly after, the Romans brought many of them under slavery and bondage, contrary to the tenor of the articles for peace. {Memnon, c. 37.} {*Plutarch, Sulla, l. 1. c. 24. 4:405} {Dio, Legat., 33. or 34.} {*Appian, Mithridatic Wars, l. 12. c. 8. (58) 2:347} {*Livy, l. 83. 14:105} {*Velleius Paterculus, l. 2. c. 23. s. 6. 1:99} *[K162]* So the first Mithridatic war, which had begun four years earlier, was ended by Sulla. In less than three years, Sulla killed a hundred and sixty thousand of the enemy, recovered Greece, Macedonia, Ionia, Asia and various other countries which Mithridates had captured. He took the king's fleet and confined the king himself to his father's kingdom. {*Appian, Civil Wars, l. 1. c. 8. (76) 3:139} {*Appian, Mithridatic Wars, l. 12. c. 8. (54-58) 2:337,347} The most remarkable thing about Sulla was his discipline. Although factions of Canna and Marius had been in Italy for three years, Sulla nonetheless did not conceal his intention of coming against them to fight with them. Nor did he lay aside the business he currently had in hand. He considered that it was best first to crush the enemy and then to avenge a citizen; first to secure from fear abroad by defeating a foreigner and only after that to repress a rebellion at home. {*Velleius Paterculus, l. 2. c. 24. s. 4. 1:101} {*Plutarch, Lysander and Sulla, l. 1. c. 5. s. 1-4. 4:455,457}

*4013.* Mithridates surrendered his ships to Sulla with five hundred archers, as well as the other things required in the covenant. Then he sailed with the remainder of his ships to Pontus into his father's kingdom. {Memnon, c. 37.} {*Strabo, l. 13. c. 1. s. 27. 6:55} {*Plutarch, Sulla, l. 1. c. 24. s. 3. 4:405} {Dio, Legat., 36. or 37.} {*Appian, Mithridatic Wars, l. 12. c. 8. (58) 2:347} Sulla saw that this peace did not sit well with his soldiers. They were grieved to see the king, who was their most bitter enemy, and who in one day had killed so many thousands of Roman citizens living in Asia, sail away freely out of Asia. He was leaving Asia, with his treasure and the spoils he had acquired in the war, after having almost exhausted it for some years through plunder and force. Sulla justified himself by telling them that he was glad to be rid of Mithridates at any cost, as he had feared he might join up with Fimbria. Had he done that, Sulla would have been too weak to fight both of them. {*Plutarch, Sulla, l. 1. c. 24. s. 4. 4:405} {Dio, Legat., 36. or 37.}

*4014.* From there, Sulla moved to within four hundred yards of Fimbria's camp at Thyatira. Sulla demanded that he turn over the armies to him, since he had illegally assumed that command. Fimbria replied resolutely that he did not take orders from Sulla, whereupon Sulla laid siege and began to make his trench. Fimbria's soldiers came running from their garrison to greet Sulla's men and were very helpful to them in making the trench. {*Plutarch, Sulla, l. 1. c. 25. s. 1. 4:405} {*Appian, Mithridatic Wars, l. 12. c. 9. (59) 2:349} {Orosius, l. 6. c. 2.}

*4015.* Fimbria was taken aback by this sudden turnaround of events and assembled the rest of the soldiers to ask them to be loyal to him. When they absolutely refused to fight against their fellow citizens, he tore his garment and shook every one of them by the hand. He begged them not to desert him. When that was to no avail and he saw that very many were stealing away to the enemy, he went to the tribunes' tents, where he bribed some of them and then summoned the soldiers again to force an oath of allegiance. When those who had been bribed cried out that every soldier ought to be called to the oath by name, he ordered the crier at first to name only those who were under an obligation to him for past favours. Nonius, who had been his accomplice in every kind of villainous exploit, was called and refused to swear. Fimbria drew his sword at him and threatened to kill him, but because the soldiers with a united shout expressed their disapproval of that action, he was happy to stop. {*Appian, Mithridatic Wars, l. 12. c. 9. (59) 2:349}

4016. After this, Fimbria bribed a slave with money and the promise of obtaining his freedom. He was to go to Sulla's camp and pretend to be a renegade and so use the opportunity while there to stab Sulla. But the man's heart began to fail him in the process and Sulla suspected by his trembling that he had not come with good intentions. So he arrested him and the slave confessed the whole business. This filled Sulla's army with anger and scorn. The men standing about Fimbria's trench called him Athenio by way of reproach, because this had been the name of the one who had, for a few days, been king over the slaves in Sicily. {*Appian, Mithridatic Wars, l. 12. c. 9. (59) 2:349,351} [E529]

4017. When Fimbria saw that this plot had failed, he gave up all hope and fled to a strong citadel, from where he invited Sulla to a talk. Sulla would not go himself, but sent Rutilius in his place. It cut Fimbria to the heart that Sulla would not come to him, as this was never denied even to common enemies. He had earnestly sought pardon on account of of his immaturity. [K163] Rutilius replied that Sulla was willing to pardon him and allow him safe passage to the seacoast, on the condition that he sail away and leave Asia to Sulla, since Sulla was the proconsul there. Fimbria told him he knew of a better way than that. He returned to Pergamum and went into Aesculapius' temple, where he stabbed himself with his sword. When he found that the wound was not fatal, he asked his servant to kill him. The servant did as he was asked and thereafter killed himself. Sulla gave Fimbria's body to his chief servants, to be buried by them. {*Appian, Mithridatic Wars, l. 12. c. 9. (60) 2:351} {*Livy, l. 83. 14:105} {*Velleius Paterculus, l. 2. c. 24. s. 1. 1:99} {*Plutarch, Sulla, l. 1. c. 25. s. 1. 4:405} {Aurelius Victor, De Viris Illustribus, l. 1. c. 70.} {Orosius, l. 6. c. 2.}

4018. Fimbria's army came and offered their services to Sulla, who entertained them and added them to his own troops. Soon after, he sent Cunio with a command to establish Nicomedes and Ariobarzanes in their kingdoms. He also sent a full account of all the events to the Senate and took no notice at all of the fact that they had declared him an enemy of the state. {*Appian, Mithridatic Wars, l. 12. c. 9. (60) 2:351}

## 3920b AM, 4630 JP, 84 BC

4019. Sulla rebuilt Illium, formerly called Troy, which had been destroyed by Fimbria. {Orosius, l. 6. c. 2.} {*Strabo, l. 13. c.

l. s. 27. 6:55} He also settled the affairs of the province of Asia and bestowed freedom on the inhabitants of Illium, Chios, Rhodes, Lycia, Magnesia and various other people. He enrolled them among the allies of the people of Rome either as payment for their help in the wars or to cheer them up after the great calamities they had undergone because of their loyalty to the Romans. He sent his soldiers to all the other towns to proclaim that all slaves who had received their freedom from Mithridates had to return to their masters immediately. Many ignored the edict, while many cities revolted because of it. Many slaves and free-born were killed in the ensuing massacres. The walls of many towns in Asia were demolished and some of the inhabitants were sold. Any men or cities found favouring the Cappadocians were severely fined. The Ephesians, who in scorn had taken the Roman offerings down from their temples, were especially punished. {*Appian, Mithridatic Wars, l. 12. c. 9. (61) 2:351}

4020. When everything was peaceful again, criers were sent throughout the province to summon the leaders of all the cities in Asia to come to Sulla at Ephesus on a set day. As they were gathered together, Sulla made a speech to them from the judgment seat. He told them how much the Romans had helped the Asians and how poorly the Asians had responded. At the end of his speech, he pronounced this sentence on them:

> "I fine you a whole five years of tribute, which I charge you to pay at once, down to the last penny. Moreover, you shall pay out the money spent on this war and whatever further amount the present state and condition of the province shall require. I shall lay the tax on the cities proportionally and appoint a time for the payment. Any who default on this, I shall consider as enemies."

4021. Having said this, he distributed the fine by portions to the lieutenants and also assigned persons to collect it. {*Appian, Mithridatic Wars, l. 12. c. 9. (61-63) 2:351-357} To this end, he divided Asia into forty-four regions. {Cassidorus, Chronicle} This took place when Lucius Cinna was consul for the fourth time and Gnaeus Papirius was consul for the second time. Cicero stated that this tribute was imposed on all regions alike, {*Cicero, Quintus, l. 1. c. 11. 28:423} but in another place he said that Sulla imposed it proportionally upon all the cities of Asia. {*Cicero, Pro Flacco, l. 1. (32) 10:477}

4022. Plutarch wrote that Sulla, besides this fine of twenty thousand talents which he levied from the whole, annoyed various individuals among them by quartering his insolent and unruly soldiers in their private houses. [K164] He ordered every landlord to pay sixteen drachmas a day to a soldier quartered in his house. He was to provide his supper for him, as well as for any friends he brought along to supper. A captain was to have fifty drachmas a day and two suits of clothes, one for wearing at home and another for outside. {*Plutarch, Sulla, l. 1. c. 25. s. 2. 4:407} Lucullus was in charge of collecting the general tax of twenty thousand talents and of coining the money. To the cities of Asia, this seemed a relief from Sulla's hard usage. Lucullus always behaved himself in an inoffensive and upright manner and dealt mercifully and mildly with them. This was befitting the sad state of affairs in Asia. {*Plutarch, Lucullus, l. 1. c. 4. s. 1. 2:483}

4023. The cities, oppressed by poverty, borrowed money to pay Sulla at high rates of interest from Roman loan sharks and mortgaged their theatres, their gymnasiums, their walls, their harbours, and every other scrap of public property. [E530] The soldiers were very harsh with them and pressed them for their money. After payment had been made, they carried the money to Sulla, while Asia bemoaned its sad state. {*Appian, Mithridatic Wars, l. 12. c. 9. (63) 2:357}

4024. At this same time, pirates were busy in all parts of Asia. They moved about as openly as if they had been nothing more than so many legal fleets. They had first been put to sea by Mithridates, who, since he was likely to lose all he had gained in those regions, had resolved to do what mischief he could. Now they had increased to so large a number that they were dangerous to ships and threatened the ports, citadels and towns. It is certain that Iasus, Samos, Clazomene and Samothracia were taken while Sulla was staying in these regions. It is generally reported that they took many ornaments, estimated to have been worth a thousand talents, out of the temple at Samothracia. Sulla did nothing, either because he thought these places were unworthy of his protection because they had behaved basely toward him, or because he hurried to Rome to settle the civil disorders there. In either case, Sulla sailed to Greece. {*Appian, Mithridatic Wars, l. 12. c. 9. (63) 2:357}

4025. Sulla offered to take Publius Rutilius Rufus, who had lived as an exile at Mitylene, back home to Rome. He refused, however, choosing rather to stay in exile in case he might do something that was not lawful. Rufus moved to Smyrna, {*Valerius Maximus, l. 6. c. 4. s. 4. 2:49} {*Seneca, Epistles, l. 1. c. 24. s. 4. 4:167} {Quintilian, l. 11. c. 1.} {*Dio, l. 28. (95) 2:459} where he was made a free citizen of that city. {*Cicero, Pro Bablo, l. 1. c. 10. 13:659} He spent his years there in study, {Orosius, l. 5. c. 17.} and could never be persuaded to return home to his country. {*Dio, l. 28. (95) 2:459} Seneca said of him: {*Seneca, On Providence, l. 1. c. 3. s. 7. 1:19}

"Is Rutilius to be looked on as unfortunate, because those who condemned him will plead his cause

through all ages? Because he preferred to allow himself to be expelled from his country rather than to give up his banishment? Because he alone, of all the rest, dared to deny Sulla, the dictator, something when he was called home, not only would not come back but went farther away?"

4026. Ovid stated of Rutilius: {*Ovid, Pontus, l. 1. c. 3. s. 60,61. 6:285}

Rutilius his fortitude admire,
Who, being called home, had rather still retire
In banishment at Smyrna, than return;
For Sulla's proffer he alone did scorn.

4027. Alexander, son of Ptolemy Alexander the previous king of Egypt, fled from Mithridates. The Chians turned him over to Sulla, who entertained him and treated him as a close friend. Alexander accompanied Sulla from Asia into Greece, and from there to Rome. {*Appian, Civil Wars, l. 1. c. 11. (102) 3:189,191} {Porphyry, Scaliger's Greek Eusebius, p. 225. fin.}

4028. Alexander Jannaeus led his army against Essa, or Gerasa, where Theodorus, son of Zenon, had stored everything that was of greatest value to him. After he had surrounded the place with a triple wall, he finally captured it. {*Josephus, Antiq., l. 13. c. 15. s. 3. (393) 7:425} {*Josephus, Antiq., l. 13. c. 13. s. 3. (356) 7:405} {*Josephus, Jewish War, l. 1. c. 4. s. 2. (86) 2:43} {*Josephus, Jewish War, l. 1. c. 4. s. 8. (103,104) 2:51}

4029. Lucius Murena was left behind by Sulla with the two Fimbrian (or Valesian) legions, to arrange matters in Asia. {*Appian, Mithridatic Wars, l. 12. c. 9. (64) 2:357,359} [K165] Julius Exuperantius said this concerning Sulla: {Exuperantius, Opusculum}

"He left Murena, his lieutenant, in charge of the province and appointed him over the Valesian soldiers whose loyalty he could not be sure of in the civil wars. With the other part of the army he marched away to suppress the Marian faction which had revolted."

4030. Julius wrote that passage as having taken place before Sulla started the war with Mithridates. But at that time there were no Valesian or Fimbrian legions, as these did not exist until after the war had ended.

4031. Lucius Lucullus was left as governor in Asia with Lucius Murena, the praetor. Lucullus conducted himself with such discretion while he had the command of the province, that he received much credit for it. {*Cicero, Academica, l. 2. c. 1. 19:465} {*Plutarch, Lucullus, l. 1. c. 4. s. 1. 2:483} Lucullus was kept busy in Asia and was not involved with the fighting of Sulla and Marius in Italy. {*Plutarch, Precepts of Statecraft, l. 1. c. 12. (806de) 10:201}

4032. Sulla sailed from Ephesus with his fleet and arrived at Piraeus on the third day. After he had performed his religious duties, he went to the library of Apellicon, the Teian, who had many rare books of Aristotle and Theophrastus. {*Plutarch, Sulla, l. 1. c. 26. s. 1,2. 4:407} [E531] Apellicon was rich and had purchased Aristotle's library, as well as many other good libraries. He had also managed to acquire, by stealth, from Metroon the originals of the decrees that had been published in the temple of the Mother of the Gods by their ancestors. From other cities he gathered anything that was either ancient or secret and valued as a rarity. {*Athenaeus, l. 5. (214de) 2:471} For all this, he was a person who was more taken with the sight of the books than the study of them. For a large sum of money, he had purchased the books of Aristotle and Theophrastus from the heirs of Nileus of Scepsis. Many were spoiled by water and were worm-eaten. He repaired the places which were eaten out and transcribed the books again, supplying the missing passages as best he could, with the result that the books he had were full of errors. When he died, Sulla took his library and with it enriched his own library at Rome. {*Strabo, l. 13. c. 1. s. 54. 6:111,113} {?Lucian, Adversus Indoctum, l. 1. (Ussher p. 531.)}

4033. Mithridates returned to Pontus and quickly subdued many of the countries that had revolted from him when he had been in his low estate. {Memnon, c. 37.} He began with Colchis. When they saw him marching toward them, they asked that his son Mithridates might be appointed king over them. As soon as this was done, they returned to their obedience. The king was jealous that his son's ambition was the reason for this action and recalled him. He kept him bound for a while with chains of gold and killed him not long after. This was in spite of the outstanding service his son had done for him in Asia against Fimbria. {*Appian, Mithridatic Wars, l. 12. c. 9. (64) 2:357}

4034. While Sulla was at Athens, he became sick and experienced numbness in his feet. So he sailed to Aedepsus and used the hot baths there, passing his time by watching stage plays. {*Plutarch, Sulla, l. 1. c. 26. s. 3,4. 4:409}

## 3921a AM, 4630 JP, 84 BC

4035. Sulla arrived at Brundisium with his army in the 174th Olympiad, {*Appian, Civil Wars, l. 1. c. 9. (79) 3:145} when Lucius Scipio Cinna and Gaius Papirius Carbo were consuls. {*Livy, l. 83. 14:105} {*Julius Obsequens, Prodigies, l. 1. c. 57. 14:297} {Eutropius, l. 5.} He returned into Italy in the fourth year after leaving and not, as Julius Obsequens stated, *after the fifth year.*

4036. When the Thebans revolted from Ptolemy Lathurus, he waged war against them. {*Pausanias, Attica, l. 1. c. 9. s. 3. 1:43}

4037. Lucius Lucullus was very keen to have the Mitylenians, who had publicly revolted from Sulla, acknowledge their wrongdoing and submit to some easy punishment for having followed Manius. [K166] When he realised that this suggestion only made them more furious, he attacked and defeated them with his fleet, so that they were forced to retire within their walls. In the course of attacking the town in daylight, he sailed off in plain view toward Elea. However, in the night he came back secretly and after he had cast anchor, he placed an ambush near the city. The Mitylenians came rushing furiously from the town in great disorder intending to seize the enemy camp because they thought the enemy had deserted it. Lucullus attacked them before they knew what was happening and captured a large number of prisoners. He killed any who resisted and led away six thousand as slaves, while taking much plunder with him. {*Plutarch, Lucullus, l. 1. c. 4. s. 2,3. 2:483,485}

4038. Mithridates provided a fleet and a large army to go against the Bosphorus, which had revolted from him. The preparation he made was so considerable, that most thought (as Cicero intimated {*Cicero, Pro Lege Manilia, l. 1. c. 4. (9) 9:21}) that it was never his intention to make use of it against the Bosphorus, but against the Romans. For he had not surrendered the whole of Cappadocia to Ariobarzanes, but had kept some parts of it for himself. He also suspected that when Archelaus was in Greece, he had conceded more to Sulla than was appropriate, in the articles of peace. Archelaus hurried away in fear to Lucius Murena and at his instigation prevailed with Lucius to wage war on Mithridates before he did. {*Appian, Mithridatic Wars, l. 12. c. 9. (64) 2:359} So Archelaus defected to Sulla, whose deputy in Asia was Murena. {*Dio, l. 39. (57) 3:393} Orosius stated that he defected to Sulla, together with his wife and children. {Orosius, l. 6. c. 2.} Hence, as far as this matter is concerned, little credit should be given to Memnon, who stated that Archelaus stayed with Mithridates and stood with him in the last Mithridatic war. {See note on 3919a AM. <<3981>>}

4039. Lucius Murena had a burning desire for a triumph, so he renewed the war with Mithridates. {*Livy, l. 86. 14:109} He passed through Cappadocia and invaded Comana, the largest city under Mithridates' command, which was famous for its religion and costly temple. He killed some of the king's cavalry. {*Appian, Mithridatic Wars, l. 12. c. 9. (64) 2:357,359} [E532]

4040. Mithridates sent envoys to Murena, who were Greek philosophers and they condemned the king rather than commending him in their pleading the articles of peace that had been concluded with Sulla. Murena denied ever having seen any such covenants. Sulla had never written down any treaty, but had been content with the carrying out of what had been agreed on between them, and left the country. After this, Murena started plundering and not sparing the money that had been consecrated for holy uses. Making his winter quarters in Cappadocia, he established the kingdom more securely for Ariobarzanes than it had ever been previously, and built the city of Ecinina on the frontiers of Mithridates' kingdom. {*Memnon, c. 38.*} {*Appian, Mithridatic Wars, l. 12. c. 9. (64) 2:359*}

### 3921b AM, 4631 JP, 83 BC

*4041.* By the mutual enmity of the Seleucians, the kingdom of Syria had been quite exhausted by a futile war between the two Seleucian kings, and so the people looked to foreign kings for help. Some thought to ask for help from Mithridates, the king of Pontus, others wanted to invite Ptolemy from Egypt, but thought better of it. Mithridates was already engaged in a war with the Romans and Ptolemy had always been a professed enemy of Syria. Hence, they decided on Tigranes, king of Armenia. In addition to his own strength at home, he was allied with the Parthians and with Mithridates. He was called into the kingdom of Syria and held it for eighteen years, until the time that Pompey took it from him and added it to the Roman Empire. {*Justin, Trogus, l. 40. c. 1,2.*} [K167]

*4042.* For fourteen of those eighteen years, Magadates was over Syria with an army as Tigranes' viceroy, until the time he was forced to march off with that army to help his king. After the defeat of Tigranes, Lucullus gave the kingdom of Syria to Antiochus Asiaticus. {*Appian, Syrian Wars, l. 11. c. 8. (48,49) 2:197*} {*Appian, Syrian Wars, l. 11. c. 11. (69,70) 2:237*} In the interim, Antiochus Pius, the father of Asiaticus, had by Tigranes been dispossessed of Syria as far as from the Euphrates River to the sea coast, as well as part of Cilicia. He stayed quietly for a while in another part of Cilicia, in which neither Tigranes nor the Romans showed any interest. {*Appian, Mithridatic Wars, l. 12. c. 15. (105) 2:439,441*} {*Justin, Trogus, l. 40. c. 2.*} His wife Selene and her two sons reigned in Phoenicia and some other parts of lower Syria. {*Josephus, Antiq., l. 13. c. 16. s. 4. (419,420) 7:439*} {*Cicero, Against Verres II, l. 4. c. 27. (61) 8:355*}

*4043.* Mithridates sent envoys both to the Senate and to Sulla, to complain about Murena. {*Appian, Mithridatic Wars, l. 12. c. 9. (65) 2:361*} He and Murena sent envoys to oppose each other, and asked the Heracleans for supplies. These saw the dreadful power of the Romans on the one side, while they feared the closeness of Mithridates on the other side. So they told the envoys that in such a storm of war as this, it was all they could do to protect their homes, much less help others. {*Memnon, c. 38.*}

*4044.* Alexander Jannaeus captured Gaulana and Seleucia. {*Josephus, Antiq., l. 13. c. 15. s. 3. (393,394) 7:425*}

### 3922a AM, 4631 JP, 83 BC

*4045.* Lucius Murena crossed over the large Halys River while it was swollen by heavy rains and overran four hundred of Mithridates' villages. The king did not oppose him, since he was expecting the return of his envoys from Rome. When Murena thought he had obtained enough booty, he went back into Phrygia and Galatia again. Calidius, who had been sent to Murena from Rome after Mithridates' complaints, brought Murena no decree of the Senate, but instead publicly denounced him, saying that he should not molest the king, who was a confederate of the Romans. After this, he took him aside and was seen talking with him privately. In spite of this, Murena continued to invade the frontiers of Mithridates. {*Appian, Mithridatic Wars, l. 12. c. 9. (65) 2:361*}

### 3922b AM, 4632 JP, 82 BC

*4046.* Some advised Murena to invade Sinope and attempt to capture the king's palace because, once that was taken, the other places would be subdued without any difficulty. However, Mithridates had fortified that place well with garrisons and now began to take action. {*Memnon, c. 38.*} He ordered Gordius to attack the neighbouring villages, while he got together many beasts of burden, wagons and countrymen as well as soldiers and camped on the other side of the bank, opposite Murena's camp. Neither side fought until Mithridates had come with a larger army, and then there was a bloody battle between them. The king crossed over the river in spite of Murena's fighting. He defeated Murena and forced him to retreat to a naturally fortified hill and then to move quickly through the mountains to get to Phrygia. He lost many of his men in the flight, as well as the battle. {*Appian, Mithridatic Wars, l. 12. c. 9. (65) 2:361*} [E533]

*4047.* News spread quickly of this famous and swift victory and on hearing it, many sided with Mithridates. He drove all of Murena's garrisons of soldiers out of Cappadocia and made a large bonfire on the top of a high hill, according to his country's custom. [K168] The fire was so large, that it could be seen at a distance of one hundred and twenty-five miles from the sea and nobody came near it for several days on account of the heat. He offered sacrifices to Zeus Stratius, that is, the *God of Armies*. {*Appian, Mithridatic Wars, l. 12. c. 9. (66) 2:361,363*}

### 3923a AM, 4632 JP, 82 BC

*4048.* Lucius Cornelius Sulla was appointed dictator of Rome so that he might restore the state to its ancient customs. He allowed Marcus Tullius and Cornelius Dolabella to be elected as consuls, although he was in charge of everything and so also had authority over them. {*Appian, Civil Wars, l. 1. c. 11. (99,100) 3:183,185*} In the beginning of their consulship, he triumphed gloriously over King Mithridates {*Eutropius, l. 5.} on the 3rd of the Calends of February (January 28), as was recorded on the pieces of the marble on which the triumph was engraved. This day occurred in the Julian month of November. Although that triumph was very great in regard to its stateliness and the rarity of the spoils they had taken from the king, it was nevertheless made more excellent by the exiles. For the most eminent and chief men of the city wore crowns on their heads and attended Sulla's chariot. They called him their deliverer and their father, because it was through him that they had been brought back to their native country and their wives and children had been restored to them. {*Plutarch, Sulla, l. 1. c. 34. 4:433}

4049. There is one thing for which Sulla deserved commendation. When he resigned the command in Asia, he rode in triumph and did not have around him anyone from the towns belonging to the Romans, as he had done in many cities in Greece and Asia. {*Valerius Maximus, l. 2. c. 8. s. 7. 1:207,209} Sulla transferred to the treasury fourteen thousand pounds of gold and six thousand of silver which his son, Gaius Marius, had brought to Palestrina after the burning of the Capitol and other dedicated places. On the previous day, he had also transferred all the other spoils of the victory, that is fifteen thousand pounds of gold and a hundred and fifteen thousand pounds of silver. {*Pliny, l. 33. c. 5. 9:15} From this it is evident that the triumph lasted for two days.

4050. After Alexander Jannaeus had subdued the valley known as Antiochus' Valley and the citadel of Gamala, he removed Demetrius from the position of governor of these places, because he had received many accusations against him. Just at the end of the third year of his expedition, he led his army home again. The Jews gave him a hearty welcome home for his good success. At this time, the Jews held on to many of the cities of Syria, Idumea and Phoenicia. On the sea coast in the Mediterranean region they captured the towns of Straton's Tower, Apollonia, Joppa, Jamnia, Azotus, Gaza, Anthedon, Raphia and Rhinocolura. In the interior of the country, toward Idumea, they captured Adora, Marisa and the whole of Idumea and Samaria, as well as Mount Carmel, Mount Tabor, Scythopolis and Gadara. In Gaulanitis, they took Seleucia and Gamala. In Moab, they captured Essebon, Medeba, Lemba, Oronaim, Agalain (Ajalon?), Thona, Zoara, the valley of the Cilicians and Pella. They demolished this last city, because the inhabitants refused to submit to the Jewish ceremonies. They occupied some other major cities of Syria which had only recently been annexed to their kingdom. {*Josephus, Antiq., l. 13. c. 15. s. 3,4. (394-397) 7:425,427}

4051. Lucius Cornelius Sulla thought it was unjust that Mithridates, a confederate of Rome, should be both-

ered by war. He sent Aulus Gabinius earnestly to charge Murena to stop fighting with Mithridates and to try to reconcile Mithridates and Ariobarzanes to each other. At that meeting, Mithridates betrothed his four-year-old daughter to Ariobarzanes. This was only a pretence, as he still retained a part of Cappadocia which he had garrisoned. He organized a general entertainment for the company, during which he offered a certain weight of gold to those who could win at drinking or eating, jesting, singing and other solemn sports. Everyone participated except Gabinius. {*Appian, Mithridatic Wars, l. 12. c. 9. (66) 2:363} [K169]

4052. Thus the second Mithridatic war ended in its third year. {*Appian, Mithridatic Wars, l. 12. c. 9. (66) 2:363} In this war, Murena had caused much harm to Mithridates. He withdrew, leaving Mithridates weaker, but not crushed. In his speech for Murena's son, Cicero said that he had been a help to his father in his difficulties, a comfort in his labours and a rejoicer in his victories. Cicero also stated that, on Murena's orders, the people of Milesia built ten ships from the revenues of the people of Rome, as well as from taxes gathered from various Asian cities. This fleet was to serve the Romans in all wars at sea. Asconius Pedianus noted this also. {*Cicero, Against Verres II, l. 1. c. 35. 7:217} {Asconius Pedianus, Against Verres}

4053. Lucius Lucullus spent the time of his quaestorship under the peaceful conditions existing in Asia, while Murena was waging war in Pontus. {*Cicero, Academica, l. 2. c. 1. 19:465,467}

4054. Sulla recalled Murena from Asia, {*Cicero, Pro Lege Manilia, l. 1. c. 3. (8) 9:21} and Marcus Thermus succeeded him in the praetorship of Asia. {*Suetonius, Julius, l. 1. c. 2. 1:39} [E534] It is likely that Lucullus was recalled from his quaestorship at the same time, together with Murena. We think this because he sat on the bench at Rome with Aquilius Gallus, who was the judge in Quintus' case. Gellius and Jerome said this case was pleaded by Cicero in his 26th year, when Marcus Tullius and Gnaeus Dolabella were consuls. {*Aulus Gellius, Attic Nights, l. 15. c. 28. s. 3. 3:121} {*Eusebius, Chronicles, l. 1. 1:233}

## 3923b AM, 4633 JP, 81 BC

4055. As soon as Alexander Jannaeus had a little relief from wars, he became sick for three years with a fever, or Quartan Ague, caused in part by his intemperance. In spite of this he kept up his military activities. {*Josephus, Jewish War, l. 1. c. 4. s. 8. (105,106) 2:51,53} {*Josephus, Antiq., l. 13. c. 15. s. 5. (398) 7:427,429}

4056. When Lucius Murena came to Rome, he was given an honourable triumph. His son graced his triumph with some military presents. He had served under him while he was general and had made his father's victory and triumph the only purpose in his fighting. {*Cicero, Pro Lege Manilia, l. 1. c. 3. (8) 9:21}

4057. Mithridates was now at peace and subdued the Bosphorus, appointing Machares, one of his sons, to be king over that country. {*Appian, Mithridatic Wars, l. 12. c. 10. (67) 2:365}

4058. Molo, the rhetorician, came with envoys to the Senate concerning the reward for the Rhodians. He was the first of any foreign nationality to speak in the the Senate without an interpreter. He deserved that honour for he had aided Roman eloquence at its highest power. At that time, Cicero studied under him as he had done also some six years earlier. {See note on 3917b AM. <<3956>>} {*Cicero, Brutus, l. 1. c. 90. 5:271} {*Valerius Maximus, l. 2. c. 2. s. 3. 1:139,141}

4059. Julius Caesar was sent by Marcus Thermus to be the praetor of Asia. He sent to Bithynia to get the fleet, and stayed a while with Nicomedes. It was rumoured that he had prostituted his chastity for the king's lust. The rumour was strengthened when he returned to Bithynia in a very short time, on the pretext of getting some money which was due to a certain freedman who was one of his clients. {*Suetonius, Julius, l. 1. c. 2. 1:39} Suetonius cited the elder Curio as testifying to Caesar's immoral behaviour. {See note on 3957c AM. <<5014>>} Curio said in one of his speeches that Caesar was: {*Suetonius, Julius, l. 1. c. 52. s. 3. 1:103}

"every woman's man and every man's woman."

4060. Whenever Lucius Cornelius Sulla found a strong young man among the slaves, he made him a free man. He freed more than ten thousand men who formerly belonged to the proscribed men and called them Cornelians, after his name. It was his plan to have the loyalty of at least ten thousand men in the city among the common people, to side with him in all emergencies. {*Appian, Civil Wars, l. 1. c. 11. (100) 3:187} {*Appian, Civil Wars, l. 1. c. 12. (104) 3:195} [K170] Servius thought that Polyhistor was one of those who were made free citizens by Sulla. Alexander Polyhistor lived in Sulla's time and was made free and surnamed Cornelius. {Servius, Virgil's 10th Aeneid} Suidas in Ἀλεξάνδρω τω Μιλησιω confirmed that he was named after his patron, Cornelius Lentulus, to whom he was sold and whose schoolmaster he was. For Suidas called him Melesium and said he was that grammarian Craterus' scholar. However, Stephanus Byzantinus claimed that he was the son of Aselepiades of Cotyaeum, a city in Lesser Phrygia and that he had written forty-two books on many subjects. Eusebius cited him where he also cited many passages from the book which Polyhistor wrote about the Jews. {*Eusebius, Gospel, l. 9. c. 17. (418c) 1:450}

4061. After Ptolemy Lathurus had subdued the Thebans in the third year of their revolt, he fined them so heavily that, while they had previously been one of the richest cities in Greece, they now were among the poorest. Pausanias related this as if it pertained to the Boeotian Thebes, and not to the Egyptians. {*Pausanias, Attica, l. 1. c. 9. s. 3. 1:43} Whereas we have noted from Appian that, almost at the very same time in which the Thebans revolted from Ptolemy, the greater Thebes of Boeotia defected from Archelaus, Mithridates' general, to the Roman general, Sulla. {*Appian, Mithridatic Wars, l. 12. c. 5. (30) 2:293}

4062. Ptolemy Lathurus died not long after this, six years and six months after the death of his brother Philometor. {*Pausanias, Attica, l. 1. c. 9. s. 3. 1:43} His daughter Cleopatra succeeded him and had previously been viceroy with him. She was the wife of Ptolemy Alexander, who was the younger brother of Lathurus and who had killed his mother. She only reigned for six months. {Porphyry, Scaliger's Greek Eusebius, p. 225.} Pausanias stated that of all Lathurus' descendants, only Berenice was legitimate and she died before her father. {*Pausanias, Attica, l. 1. c. 9. s. 3. 1:43} His bastard son Ptolemy seized the kingdom of Cyprus and Cleopatra's kingdom. After this, he seized the kingdom of Egypt and was called the New Dionysus, or Ptolemy Auletes. That is, unless it is possible that the one whom Porphyry called Cleopatra was the same one whom Pausanias called Berenice.

4063. Sulla sent Alexander back to Alexandria in Egypt, to be their king. He was the son of that Ptolemy Alexander who had killed his mother. He was a good friend of Sulla and had accompanied him from Asia. There were no longer any male heirs and the women wanted a man of the same lineage. In this way, Sulla hoped to get a good stash of gold from that wealthy kingdom. {*Appian, Civil Wars, l. 1. c. 11. (102) 3:189} [E535]

4064. When Gaius Julius Caesar captured Mitylene, he was rewarded by Marcus Thermus with the Civic Crown. {*Suetonius, Julius, l. 1. c. 2. 1:39} Mitylene was demolished to the ground, when it had been the only city still in arms after Mithridates was defeated. {*Livy, l. 89. 14:113} So, by the law of war and right of conquest, this noble city was brought under the jurisdiction of the people of Rome. {*Cicero, Agrarian Law II, l. 1. c. 15. 6:413}

## 3924 AM, 4634 JP, 80 BC

4065. After Alexander had lived with his new wife Cleopatra, queen of Egypt, for nineteen days, he killed her. {Porphyry, Scaliger's Greek Eusebius, p. 225.} Appian wrote that this king was very domineering and insolent, because he had the backing of Sulla. She was dragged out of his palace by the Alexandrians and killed in the place of exercise. It appears, from Suetonius and Cicero, that he reigned fifteen years after the death of his wife. {*Suetonius, Julius, l. 1. c. 11. s. 1. 1:47} [K171] This refutes the common error of historians who begin the reign of Ptolemy Auletes here and so confound his years with the years of Alexander.

4066. Mithridates made raids on the Achaeans beyond Colchis (who were supposed to be descended from those who had lost their way when returning from the Trojan War). He lost two divisions of their army, some in battle, some in an ambush and the rest to the harshness of the weather. {*Appian, Mithridatic Wars, l. 12. c. 10. (67) 2:365}

4067. When Mithridates returned home, he sent some envoys to Rome to ratify the articles of the league between him and Sulla. Ariobarzanes also sent other envoys, either voluntarily or at the instigation of others, to report that Cappadocia was not entirely under his control, since Mithridates had kept back the larger part for himself. Sulla ordered Mithridates to leave Cappadocia, before the articles could be ratified. {*Appian, Mithridatic Wars, l. 12. c. 10. (67) 2:365}

4068. After the province of Cilicia was established, Gnaeus Dolabella was sent there as proconsul. Cicero stated that in addition to the three territories of Pamphylia, Isaura and Cilicia, three other territories in Asia were added. {*Cicero, Friends, l. 13. c. 67. s. 1. 27:155} These were the Cibyratic, Synnadensian and Apameensean, located in the regions of Phrygia, Pisidia, and Lycaonia. Dolabella brought Gaius Malleolus along with him as his quaestor and Gaius Verres as his lieutenant. When they had come as far as Delos, Verres ordered that some ancient images be stolen at night and secretly taken from the temple of Apollo and put aboard one of the cargo ships. A violent storm suddenly struck and Dolabella could not possibly sail. He had a great deal of trouble even remaining at anchor in the harbour, because the large waves beat against the ships. The ship carrying the images was wrecked by the violence of the waves and the images of Apollo were found floating toward the shore. Dolabella ordered that they should be returned to the temple. After that, the storm let up and Dolabella sailed from Delos. {*Cicero, Against Verres II, l. 1. c. 17,18. 7:167-171}

4069. Verres carried away some very beautiful images from Chios, Erythrae and Halicarnassus, as well as taking the statue of Tenes, which was also a beautiful work, from the city of Tenedos, to the great grief of that city. It is said that Tenes built the city and that the city was named after him. {*Cicero, Against Verres II, l. 1. c. 19. 7:173}

4070. Verres asked Dolabella to send him to the kings Nicomedes of Bithynia and Sadala of Thrace, who were allies of the people of Rome. He came to Lampsacus in

the Hellespont, and there Rubrius, one of his pages, attempted to bring Verres the daughter of one Philodamus, a most eminent citizen. The Lampsacens, stirred up by Themistagoras and Thessalus, came in a crowd at night to protect the virgin's chastity. In the resulting uproar, Verres' lictor, Cornelius, was killed and some of his servants, including Rubrius, received some injuries. They had a great deal of trouble to prevent Verres' house from being burned. At Verres' request, Dolabella turned the war, which was at that time being managed by Dolabella in Cilicia, over to him. Verres marched from that province into Asia and had Gaius Nero, who had succeeded Marcus Thermus in the praetorship of Asia, convict and behead Philodamus and his son. {*Cicero, Against Verres II, l. 1. c. 24-30. 7:185-203} {Asconius Pedianus, Against Verres}

### 3925a AM, 4634 JP, 80 BC

4071. Charidemus, a ship captain at Chios, was ordered by Dolabella to accompany Verres' march from Asia. He came with him as far as Samos, where Verres attacked the most ancient temple of Juno of Samos and carried off the pictures and the images from there. [K172] The Samians went to Chios and charged Charidemus with this sacrilege. However, he clearly showed it was not his doing, but Verres' action, whereupon envoys from Samos came to Gaius Nero in Asia to complain about him. They were told that complaints such as these, which concerned the Roman envoy, should not be handled by the praetor but by the Roman Senate. {*Cicero, Against Verres II, l. 1. c. 19,20. 7:173-177} [E536]

4072. The Milesians had a fleet that the Romans, by a treaty made with them, could make use of at any time. When Verres demanded one of these ships to escort him to Myndus, they immediately sent him the best ship they had. As soon as Verres arrived at Myndus, he ordered the soldiers and the sailors to return to Miletus by foot overland while he sold the ship to Lucius Magius and Lucius Fannius. These men had left Marius' army and came to live at Myndus, but had later sided with Sertorius and Mithridates with the result that the Senate had declared them public enemies. When the captain of the ship reported what Verres had done, the Milesians caused a declaration to be entered into the public registry. However, at Verres' request, Gnaeus Dolabella did his best to punish the captain and those who had made the declaration. In addition, he ordered that the declaration be removed from the records. {*Cicero, Against Verres II, l. 1. c. 34. 7:213-217} {Asconius Pedianus, Against Verres}

4073. Gaius Malleolus, Gnaeus Dolabella's quaestor, was killed in the war. Verres immediately assumed the office of quaestor for Dolabella. Once he had that office, he began to steal Asia's wealth. {*Cicero, Against Verres II, l. 1. c. 36,37. 7:219,223}

## 3925b AM, 4635 JP, 79 BC

*4074.* When the provinces were assigned to the consuls, Cilicia was given to Servilius and Macedonia to Appius. Claudius Servilius went to Tarentum to visit his colleague, who was sick. He journeyed to the city of Corycus and was ordered to set out to subdue the pirates. {*Sallust, History, l. 1.} {Priscian, l. 15.} Under the leadership of Isidorus, they sailed about in the adjacent sea between Crete, Cyrene and Achaia, and the sea off Cape Malea. Because of the plunder the pirates accumulated there, that sea was called the Golden Sea. {*Florus, l. 1. c. 41. s. 3,4. 1:191} Julius Caesar served under Servilius for a very short time, {*Suetonius, Julius, l. 1. c. 3. 1:39} and Lucius Flaccus was the tribune of the soldiers. {*Cicero, Pro Flacco, l. 1. 10:447 (Bobbio Fragment)}

*4075.* Gnaeus Dolabella was recalled home from his province of Cilicia and accused of extortion at Rome by the young man Marcus Aemilius Scaurus. He was condemned and sent away into banishment. The amount was estimated at three million sesterces, based on the following. His quaestor, Gaius Verres, had exacted more than was required from the cities of Lycia, Pamphylia, Pisidia and Phrygia in grain, hides, clothes of fur, sacks and similar wares. He did not receive the goods, but demanded to be given the money they were worth. Verres was the main witness against him. Verres was unwilling to give account of his lieutenantship and his quaestorship until such time as Dolabella, who was the only one who was aware of his crimes, had been condemned and banished. {*Cicero, Against Verres II, l. 1. c. 38. 7:223-227} {Pighius, Annals of Rome, Tom. 3. p. 280,281,286,287.}

## 3926a AM, 4635 JP, 79 BC

*4076.* Alexander Jannaeus died in the garrisons of a fever and exhaustion from his battles. *[K173]* He had reigned twenty-seven years. At the time, he was besieging the citadel of Ragaba, which was located beyond the Jordan River. On his death bed, he advised his wife Alexandra to hide his death from the soldiers for a time and after she had returned victorious to Jerusalem, to give the Pharisees a little more freedom than before. The Pharisees were able greatly to influence the Jews, if they chose to do so, either as friend or as foe. The common people placed a great deal of confidence in them, even though they were inclined to impeach anyone out of envy. Alexander was disliked by the Jews because he had offended the Pharisees, so he persuaded her to yield and allow them to have his funeral, and that she not do anything in matters of government without their knowledge and approval. In this way, he would receive an

honourable burial and she and her son would reign without problems. {*Josephus, Jewish War, l. 1. c. 4. s. 8. (106) 2:53} {*Josephus, Antiq., l. 13. c. 15. s. 5. (398-404) 7:427-431} {*Josephus, Antiq., l. 20. c. 10. s. 4. (242) 10:129}

## 3926b AM, 4636 JP, 78 BC

*4077.* Queen Alexandra, also called Selene by the ecclesiastical writers, captured the citadel of Ragaba. She did everything her husband had requested. She let the Pharisees make the funeral arrangements and control the kingdom, whereby she made them her friends, when before they had been her worst enemies. The Pharisees assembled the common people and made a speech to them, praising the famous exploits of Alexander and bemoaning what a good king they had lost. They so moved the people, that they all grieved in their hearts and cried. No king before him had ever had such a stately funeral. {*Josephus, Antiq., l. 13. c. 16. s. 1. (405,406) 7:431}

*4078.* When Alexander was dying, he made his will. He left the administration of the kingdom to his wife Alexandra and also left the election of the high priest to her discretion. She declared Hyrcanus, her oldest son, as high priest. *[E537]* She did not do this because he was the oldest, but because he was quite pliable and would not threaten her power in any way, while her younger son, Aristobulus, was quite content to live as a private citizen and had a more fiery disposition than his brother. She governed the kingdom for nine years, while her son Hyrcanus held the high priesthood. She was very gracious with the people because of the favour she held with the Pharisees, and she seemed to be greatly troubled by her husband's excesses. She was a queen in name only, for the Pharisees managed all the state affairs and the people had been expressly charged to obey them. In effect, she restored all the laws that had been made by the Pharisees according to the traditions of their elders and which her father-in-law, Hyrcanus, had set aside. The Pharisees ordered the recall of all the exiles and called for the release of prisoners. She managed some things herself and directly maintained a large number of mercenary soldiers. She increased her strength to such an extent that she was a formidable force to the neighbouring princes and took hostages from them. {*Josephus, Antiq., l. 13. c. 16. s. 1,2. (407-409) 7:433} {*Josephus, Antiq., l. 13. c. 16. s. 6. (430) 7:445} {*Josephus, Jewish War, l. 1. c. 5. s. 1. (107-109) 2:53}

*4079.* Mithridates restored all Cappadocia to Ariobarzanes, in accordance with Sulla's orders. After this, he sent embassies to Rome to have the articles of the peace ratified. {*Appian, Mithridatic Wars, l. 12. c. 10. (67) 2:365}

*4080.* When Marcus Lepidus and Quintus Catulus were consuls, Sulla died. {*Livy, l. 90. 14:113,115} {*Appian, Civil Wars, *l. 1. c. 12. (104) 3:195}* He finished the twenty-second book of his commentaries just two days before his death. *[K174]* He said that the Chaldeans had foretold for him that after he had lived very splendidly for a while, he would die at the height of his greatness. *{*Plutarch, Sulla, l. 1. c. 37. 4:441}* He bequeathed his commentaries to Lucullus in his will. On his death bed, he appointed him as the guardian of his son and did not appoint Pompey, which was thought to be the cause of the animosity between Pompey and Lucullus in their quest for greatness. *{*Plutarch, Lucullus, l. 1. c. 4. s. 4. 2:485}*

*4081.* Marcus Cicero had spent six months at Athens with Antiochus of Askelon, who was a most famous and wise philosopher of the ancient academies and along with Demetrius Syrus, a highly experienced and extraordinary orator. When Cicero heard of Sulla's death, he sailed into Asia and travelled across that country. He exercised his gift of oratory with the best orators in those lands. The best of these were Menippus of Stratonicia (surnamed Catocas of Caria), Dionysius Magnes, Aeschylus, a Cnidian, and Xenocles of Adramyttium. *{*Cicero, Brutus, l. 1. c. 91. 5:273}* *{*Plutarch, Cicero, l. 1. c. 4. s. 1,2. 7:89,91}* *{*Strabo, l. 14. c. 2. s. 25. 6:299}* *{*Strabo, l. 13. c. 1. s. 66. 6:131}* *{*Diogenes Laertius, Menippus, l. 6. c. 8. (101) 2:105}*

*4082.* At this time, a certain woman of Miletus was sentenced to death, because she had induced an abortion with some medicines. She had been paid to do this by those who were the second heirs to her estate. She got what she deserved, for with that action she destroyed her hope of being a parent. Her name would not be carried on and she would not have the support of a son or daughter, the heir of a family and in all likelihood, a citizen of the state. *{*Cicero, Pro Aulus Cluentio, l. 1. c. 11. 9:255}*

*4083.* Publius Servilius, the proconsul, subdued Cilicia. He overwhelmed the pirates' lightly armed ships with his larger warships and gained a bloody victory over them. *{*Livy, l. 90. 14:115}* *{*Florus, l. 1. c. 41. s. 4. 1:191}* *{Eutropius, l. 6.}* He attacked Cilicia and Pamphylia with such force that he almost utterly destroyed them, when in fact he only wanted to subdue them. *{Orosius, l. 5. c. 23.}*

*4084.* When Julius Caesar heard of the news of Sulla's death, he left Cilicia and quickly returned to Rome. *{*Suetonius, Julius, l. 1. c. 3. 1:39}*

*4085.* After Sulla's death, Mithridates heard nothing from the magistrates at Rome concerning the embassy he had sent to the Senate. The king bribed Tigranes, his son-in-law, to invade Cappadocia. The plot was not carried out all that secretly, since the Romans had an idea of what was going on. *{*Appian, Mithridatic Wars, l. 12. c. 10. (67) 2:365}* Sallust mentioned this in a speech Lucius Philippus gave at the time before the Senate, against Lepidus. He said this: *{*Sallust, Philippus, l. 1. (8) 1:401}*

"Mithridates lies at the borders of our revenues, which, while we yet enjoy, he is watching for an opportunity to make war on us."

## 3927a AM, 4636 JP, 78 BC

*4086.* Tigranes surrounded Cappadocia so that no one could escape from him. From there, he carried away captive with him about three hundred thousand people whom he resettled in Armenia. One such place was the city where he had been crowned king of Armenia, called Tigranocerta, that is, the *City of Tigranes.* *{*Appian, Mithridatic Wars, l. 12. c. 10. (67) 2:365}* *[E538]* He had built that city between Iberia and Zeugma, which lay near the Euphrates River. It was populated with the men whom he had deported from the twelve cities of Greece which he had conquered. *{*Strabo, l. 11. c. 14. s. 15. 5:339}* In that city there were a number of Greeks who had been driven out of Cilicia and many barbarians who shared the same fate as the Greeks. He resettled the Adiabenians, Assyrians, Gordians and Cappadocians there after he had wasted their various countries. *{*Plutarch, Lucullus, l. 1. c. 26. 2:553}* Simultaneously as he was wasting Cappadocia with his raids, he drove the Mazacenians from their land. He deported them to Mesopotamia and populated the larger part of Tigranocerta with these inhabitants. *{*Strabo, l. 12. c. 2. s. 9. 5:367}* *[K175]*

*4087.* Geminus, an excellent mathematician, wrote his book of astronomy from which which Proclus *Sphere* was derived. Geminus' book was written one hundred and twenty years after the Egyptians celebrated the festival of Isia. This happened, according to Eudoxus, on the winter solstice, or the 28th of December. *{Geminus, l. 6.}* *{See note on 3807a AM. <<3004>>}*

## 3927b AM, 4637 JP, 77 BC

*4088.* When Marcus Cicero came to Rhodes, he studied under Molo, whom he had previously heard at Rome. Molo was an excellent lawyer for honest causes, and a good writer. He was also a wise instructor, very discreet in correcting and noting faults. In teaching Cicero, he did the best he could to keep Cicero on the right track and to repress his youthful licentiousness and excesses. *{*Cicero, Brutus, l. 1. c. 91. 5:275}*

*4089.* Apollonius, a great teacher of oratory, became famous at the same time. Strabo surnamed him Μαλαχος, or *the soft,* and others called him, Molo. This is the reason that some, including Quintilian, confused him with the other man, Molon. *{Quintilian, l. 12. c. 6.}* They were both Alabandians from Caria and students of Menecles, the Alabandian. They both came from his school and practised their art at Rhodes. Molon arrived there later than the other, which was the reason why Apollonius, like Homer, named him Οψε μολων. {*Strabo, l. 14. c. 2. s. 3. 6:267} {*Strabo, l. 14. c. 2. s. 13. 6:281} {*Strabo, l. 14. c. 2. s. 25. 6:299} Cicero always called one of them Molo and the other Apollonius, the Alabandian. Mark Antony is introduced speaking of him as follows: {*Cicero, De Oratore, l. 1. c. 28. 3:89}

> "For this one thing, I have always liked that famous teacher, Apollonius, the Alabandian. Although he taught for money, he yet did not allow any whom he thought incapable of being made an orator, to waste their time with him, but sent them home again. His custom was to exhort and persuade everyone whom he judged most suited and inclined to it, to apply himself to that art."

4090. It was said that Apollonius was not well-versed in Latin and desired Cicero to speak in Greek. Cicero was satisfied with the request and thought that Apollonius would be better able to correct his mistakes. While many stood in amazement and admired Cicero, and others strived to outdo one another in praising him, it was observed that Apollonius did not look cheerful at any time while Cicero was speaking. When he had finished speaking, Apollonius thought for a good while and looked as if he were musing and pensive. At last, when he was aware that Cicero had noted his behaviour, he said: {*Plutarch, Cicero, l. 1. c. 4. s. 4. 7:91,93}

> "Truly, Cicero, I commend and admire you. Yet I cannot but pity Greece's sad fortune when I see that the only glories which were left to us, learning and eloquence, are through you to belong also to the Romans."

4091. Plutarch stated that Cicero heard Posidonius, the philosopher at Rhodes, and considered himself a pupil of Posidonius. {*Plutarch, Cicero, l. 1. c. 4. s. 4. 7:91} {*Cicero, De Natura Deorum, l. 1. c. 3. (7) 19:9} {*Cicero, De Fato, l. 1. c. 3. 4:197,199} Posidonius was a philosopher of the Stoic sect and had been born at Apamea in Syria. In time, he was made a citizen of Rhodes and was called a Rhodian. {*Strabo, l. 14. c. 2. s. 13. 6:279} {*Athenaeus, l. 6. (246c) 3:109} However, Josephus wrote that Posidonius and Apollonius of Malon, or *Molon* (as it is written elsewhere), gave Apion, the grammarian, the material for the stories about the Jews and their temple. {*Josephus, Apion, l. 2. c. 7. (79) 1:325} With the first name, he was referring to this Posidonius of Apamea, Cicero's teacher in the Stoic philosophy, from the books of whose histories we have previously quoted so many passages. [K176] With the latter name, he meant that Apollonius of whom we last spoke, or rather Molo, his equal. Cicero stated that Molo was most accomplished and

was by some deemed to be one and the same person as that Apollonius. {*Cicero, Brutus, l. 1. c. 91. 5:275}

4092. Publius Servilius, the proconsul in Cilicia, subdued several cities of the pirates. {*Livy, l. 93. 14:117} He demolished the city of Isaura and destroyed many citadels which the pirates had held along the sea coast. Strabo said that Servilius was an acquaintance of his. {*Strabo, l. 12. c. 6. s. 2. 5:475} {*Strabo, l. 14. c. 3. s. 3. 6:315} [E539] He also took Lycia and its cities of note, besieging them and forcing them to surrender. In addition, he roved all over Mount Olympus and levelled three large cities to the ground, Olympus, Phaselis and Corycus. He was the first Roman to lead an army through the Taurus Mountains. He ended his march there and controlled the side of the mountains which faced Cilicia. He brought the Isaurians, who were quite worn out from the wars, under the power of the Romans. {Orosius, l. 5. c. 23.} {*Florus, l. 1. c. 41. s. 4,5. 1:191} {Sallust, History, l. 1.} {Priscian, l. 15.} {Asconius Pedianus, Against Verres II, l. 3.} {Eutropius, l. 6.} Cicero confirmed that the countries of Attalia, Phaselis, Olympus and the land of Agera, Oroanda and Gedusa were added to the people of Rome by Servilius' victory. {*Cicero, Agrarian Law I, l. 1. c. 2. 6:347} {*Cicero, Agrarian Law II, l. 1. c. 18. 6:423} Cicero particularly added the following information concerning Phaselis. {*Cicero, Against Verres II, l. 4. c. 10. 8:305,307} Phaselis, which Publius Servilius took, had not always been a city of Cilicians and thieves. The Lycians, who were Greeks, had previously lived there. Because it had a good location and was so elevated and strongly fortified, the pirates who came from Sicily resorted there. The pirates were first associated with this town by commerce and later through an alliance.

### 3928 AM, 4638 JP, 76 BC

4093. Lucius Magius and Lucius Fannius were renegades from Fimbria's army and allied themselves with Mithridates. They persuaded him to ally himself with Sertorius, who was then fighting to subdue a Spanish rebellion against the Romans. Mithridates sent these two men to Sertorius as his envoys, with letters promising him a supply of money and ships for the war and in return wanting to confirm all of Asia to him. Mithridates had surrendered Asia to the Romans in accordance with the articles of peace between him and Sulla.

4094. The envoys came to Italy in the small ship which the Mindians had bought from Verres. From there they hurried to get to Sertorius. The Senate declared them enemies of the state and ordered them to be apprehended. In spite of all that, they safely reached Sertorius, who assembled his friends and called the meeting of his senate. He would not allow the last condition, although all the rest were favourable. He maintained that he would never give away Asia, which Mithridates had unjustly taken from the Romans and Fimbria had recaptured in war. He referred them back to the articles with Sulla, which said Asia should never be under Mithridates' power again. Sertorius would allow Mithridates to keep Bithynia and Cappadocia, which had always been under his command and did not belong to the people of Rome. An alliance based on the following terms was concluded between them and confirmed by mutual oaths. Mithridates would supply Sertorius with three thousand talents and forty ships; Sertorius, in return, would make him a grant of Cappadocia and Bithynia. (In addition, Appian added Paphlagonia and Galatia and even all Asia.) Sertorius would send him a general and soldiers. Sertorius sent Marcus Marius, who was one of the banished senators, to Asia as a general for Mithridates. *[K177]* (Appian called him Varius.) He sent Lucius Magius and Lucius Fannius with him, to be his advisers. They sailed from Dianium, a coastal town of Spain, and arrived at Sinope in Pontus, where Mithridates was. When they told the king that Sertorius had denied him Asia, the king said to his friends:

> "What will Sertorius sitting in the Palatine demand after this? Although he is as far away from us as the Atlantic Ocean, he thinks he can set the boundaries of our kingdom and denounce us if we should attempt to recapture Asia?"

4095. In spite of all this, Marcus Marius made a league with him that was in agreement with Sulla's peace treaty. The king kept Marius with himself and in a very short time made him his general in place of Archelaus, who had deserted him and defected to Sulla. {*Cicero, Pro Lege Manilia, l. 1. c. 4. (9-11) 9:21,23} {*Cicero, Pro Murena, l. 1. (33) 10:229} {*Cicero, Against Verres II, l. 5. c. 59. 8:637} {Asconius Pedianus, Against Verres} {*Livy, l. 93. 14:117} {*Plutarch, Sertorius, l. 1. c. 23,24. 8:63,65} {*Appian, Mithridatic Wars, l. 12. c. 10. (68) 2:365,367} {Orosius, l. 6. c. 2.}

4096. The Capitol, which, along with the Sibylline books, had been destroyed seven years earlier by a fire, was rebuilt. Gaius Curio, the consul, asked the Senate to send some envoys to Erythrae to get another copy of the Sibylline books and bring them to Rome. Publius Gabinius, Marcus, Otacilius and Lucius Valerius were sent on that errand. They had those verses transcribed by private hands and then brought them to Rome. Curio and Octavius, the consuls, stored them in the Capitol, which had been repaired again by Quintus Catulus. This was recorded by Fenestella and cited by Lactantius Firmianus. {*Lactantius, Divine Institutions, l. 1. c. 6. 7:16} {*Lactantius, De Ira Dei, l. 1. c. 22. 7:278} Based on this account, Varro said that Erythrae was believed to have written these Sibylline books which the Romans had copied. *[E540]* He thought this because these verses were found

on the island of Erythrae, after Apollo's temple, where the books were normally kept, was burned, if we can believe Servius. {*Servius, Virgil's Aeneid, l. 6.} For the temple which was burned was not Apollo's, but Jupiter Capitoline's temple. After the temple was repaired, envoys were sent by order of the Senate to Erythrae in Asia to get those verses transcribed. However, those books which were still extant after the fire, were brought to Rome. These did not come only from Erythrae, but were also procured from other Italian and Greek cities. In addition, they were found in private men's libraries under whatever name the Sibylline books went by. These books contained many things that were found to be suppositions. The differences in the books were detected using acrostics, as determined from Varro's own books of divine things, as related by Dionysius Halicarnassus and by Lactantius Firmianus. {*Dionysius Halicarnassus, Roman Antiquities, l. 4. c. 62. s. 5,6. 2:469,471} {*Lactantius, Divine Institutions, l. 1. c. 6. 7:16} Tacitus stated that: {*Tacitus, Annals, l. 6. c. 12. 4:175,177}

> "Where the Sibylline verses differed, the correct rendering was contended for in Samos, Troy, Erythrae, through all Africa, Sicily and the Italian colonies. The priests were responsible to take all the care that mortal men could take, to discover the true from the false."

4097. Pliny stated that during the time when Gnaeus Octavius and Gnaeus Scribonius Curio were consuls, Licinius Syllanus, the proconsul, and his company, saw a spark fall from a star. It increased in size as it came nearer the earth, until it became as large as the moon and gave off as much light as if it had been a cloudy day. It went up toward the heaven again and changed into the shape of a torch. Since Syllanus was not found to be a Roman surname for that family, Pighius thought that, instead of Licinius Syllanus, as it was stated in Pliny, it should be Lucius Junius Syllanus. Junius, who, about this time, was sent into Asia with the authority of a proconsul, to replace Gnaeus Nero with his company, may have been an eye witness of this sign. {*Pliny, l. 2. c. 35. 1:239,241} [K178]

## 3929a AM, 4638 JP, 76 BC

4098. Nicomedes, King of Bithynia, died without any descendants and in his will gave his kingdom to the people of Rome, whereupon his kingdom was reorganized into a province. {*Livy, l. 93. 14:117} {*Velleius Paterculus, l. 2. c. 4. s. 1. 1:55} {*Velleius Paterculus, l. 2. c. 39. s. 2. 1:135} {*Appian, Civil Wars, l. 1. c. 13. (111) 3:207} {*Appian, Mithridatic Wars, l. 12. c. 1. (7) 2:251} {*Appian, Mithridatic Wars, l. 12. c. 10. (71) 2:371} Relating to this issue, Mithridates' complaint about the Romans in a letter to Arsaces went as follows: {*Sallust, Letter of Mithridates, l. 1. (9) 1:435}

"After Nicomedes was dead, they seized all Bithynia, although Nysa, whom he called queen, unquestionably had a son."

*4099.* In the same year, which ended the 176th Olympiad, the Romans added Cyrene to their empire. Ptolemy Apion, its king, who was of the house of Lagidae, had bequeathed it to the Romans. {*Appian, Civil Wars, l. 1. c. 13. (111) 3:207} This king was an illegitimate son of the house of the Lagidae. {*Appian, Mithridatic Wars, l. 12. c. 17. (121) 2:477} Appian showed that he was the same person as the one that Justin said was the son of a courtesan and who turned over Cyrene to the Romans. {Justin, Trogus, l. 39. c. 5.} However, Justin added that part of Libya was made a province, whereas Livy had previously stated that after Ptolemy Apion's death, the Senate of Rome enfranchised all the cities of the kingdom of Cyrene. {See note on 3908 AM. <<3893>>} It seems that they may have received their grant of freedom at that earlier time, but only now been established as a province. At that time:

"Ptolemy, the king of Cyrene, on his death bed made the Romans his heirs in his will, in the first year of the 171st Olympiad."

*4100.* After this:

"Libya was left to the Romans as a legacy by King Apion."

*4101.* This was in the fourth year of the 178th Olympiad, as Jerome noted, {*Eusebius, Chronicles, l. 1. 1:235} which was almost eleven years later than Apion's account stated. Eutropius had related this very thing nine years later, at the time of Caecilius Metellus' Cretian triumph. At that time he stated: {Eutropius, l. 6.}

"Libya was also annexed to the Roman empire by the last will of Apion, who was its king. Berenice, Ptolemais and Cyrene were its largest cities."

*4102.* Jornandes wrote:

"Libya, that is to say, all Pentapolis, was granted to the Romans by that first Ptolemy. It later rebelled and in Apion's last will it was given to the people of Rome."

*4103.* Before him, Sextus Rufus stated: {Sextus Rufus, Breviary}

"We were beholden to Ptolemy the elder's bounty for Cyrene and the other cities of Libya's Pentapolis. Libya came to be ours by King Apion's last will and testament."

*4104.* Ammianus Marcellinus agreed with him and said: {*Ammianus Marcellinus, l. 22. c. 16. s. 4. 2:297,299}

"We obtained the dryer parts of Libya by King Apion's last will. Ptolemy gave us Cyrene and the other cities of Libya's Pentapolis."

*4105.* The learned Valerius noted this event in his history. He denied that there were two Ptolemy Apions. In addition, Cicero mentioned: {*Cicero, Agrarian Law II, l. 1. c. 19. 6:425}

"the Cyrenian lands which were Apion's."

*4106.* Cornelius Tacitus stated: {*Tacitus, Annals, l. 14. c. 18. 5:135}

"The land which was once King Apion's was bequeathed by him to the people of Rome, together with his kingdom." [E541]

*4107.* The rest of the summer and the following winter were spent by Mithridates in preparation for war against the Romans. He cut timber, built ships and made arms. {*Appian, Mithridatic Wars, l. 12. c. 10. (69) 2:367} He reduced his forces to the minimum and sent away the rabble from among the multitudes. [K179] The barbarians stole all the weapons that were gilded and set with precious stones, so Mithridates replaced these with swords similar to the Roman ones and made good, substantial shields. He assembled a well-managed and experienced cavalry, rather than one made up of those who were neat and handsome. In addition, he built ships that were not adorned with gilded cabins or fitted with baths for courtesans or delicate rooms in which to keep his women, but were equipped with arms, arrows and munitions for war. {*Plutarch, Lucullus, l. 1. c. 7. s. 3-5. 2:491,493} He distributed two million medimni (a medimn equals about 12 gallons) of grain along the coast. In addition to his old forces, he had other forces readily available to him: Chalybes, Armenians, Scythians, Taurians, Achaeans, Heniochi, Lencosyrians and those who lived near the Thermodon River, which was commonly called the land of the Amazons. His old forces came to him from Asia. He also had supplies from beyond the sea from Europe, from the Sarmatians, Basilians, Iazyges, Corallians, Thracians and all the countries around the Danube River and the mountains of Rhodope and Haemus. The Basternians, who were the most gallant men and the bravest of them all, also helped him. {*Appian, Mithridatic Wars, l. 12. c. 10. (69) 2:367,369}

### 3929b AM, 4639 JP, 75 BC

*4108.* When Julius Caesar was twenty-five years old, he planned to sail to Rhodes to study under Apollonius Molon, who was the most eminent teacher of oratory at that time. While he was on his way in the winter time, the pirates captured him near the island of Pharmacussa, which was near the Asian shore, north of Miletus. These pirates were so well-equipped with ships, that they controlled the seas. When the pirates demanded twenty talents from him for his ransom, Caesar laughed at them, because they did not know how important a man he was. He promised that he would give them fifty talents. He immediately sent his companions and servants to the cities of Asia to get the money for his release. He only kept a physician and two others with him, to attend to his personal needs. He was alone with these three for thirty-eight days in a company of Cilicians who were the most savage people in the world. He behaved himself so well that he filled them with both terror and reverence. He did not remove his shoes or unclothe himself, in case this should happen to cause some extraordinary change of appearance and they would suspect him of something. He had no guard other than their watchful eyes. Whenever he went to rest, he sent someone to them to tell them to be quiet. He would play and exercise with them as if they had been in his retinue and not he a prisoner of theirs. He wrote verses and orations which he recited to them. If any of them did not admire and applaud them, he would publicly call them dull fellows, barbarians, and often in jest, would threaten to crucify them. His humour pleased them greatly and they attributed his free-spokenness to his simplicity and youth. {*Velleius Paterculus, l. 2. c. 41. 1:141} {*Suetonius, Julius, l. 1. c. 4. 1:39,41} {*Plutarch, Caesar, l. 1. c. 3. 7:447} It was reported that, while he was in custody, he cried out: {*Plutarch, Crassus, l. 1. c. 7. s. 5. 3:333}

> "Oh Crassus, how great a pleasure will you taste, when you hear of my captivity."

4109. The money from all the cities was brought to Caesar from Miletus. Caesar would not pay the fifty talents until he had forced the pirates to release the hostages to the cities. After this, he was put ashore. The next night, he got as large a fleet as he could quickly assemble and sailing out from the port of the Milesians, he went toward the same island where the pirates were still anchored. He forced part of their fleet to flee while he sank most of the other ships. He captured the remaining ships with their crews. He was overjoyed with the victory of the night's expedition and handed over to his company the pirates' money he had seized as his own booty. He imprisoned the pirates at Pergamum. When he had finished that, he went to Junius, the proconsul of Asia, who was in Bithynia. Junius had command of Asia and Bithynia, which had recently been established as a province. [K180] Demanding that justice be done to the captives, he had them crucified. This he had foretold the pirates while he was a prisoner, but they had thought he was just joking. {*Velleius Paterculus, l. 2. c. 41. 1:141} {*Suetonius, Julius, l. 1. c. 4. 1:39,41} {*Plutarch, Crassus, l. 1. c. 7. s. 5. 3:333} Before he captured them, he had sworn that he

would crucify them. He ordered that their throats be cut first and they then be fastened to the crosses. {*Suetonius, Julius, l. 1. c. 74. s. 1. 1:125}

4110. As spring was arriving, the third Mithridatic war started. It lasted for eleven and a half years and ended with the death of Mithridates. Mithridates assembled all his fleets together and sacrificed, as was his custom, to Zeus Stratius, that is, the *God of Armies*. He drowned his chariot with white horses in the sea, as a sacrifice to Poseidon. After this, he hurried to Paphlagonia with Taxiles and Hermocrates, the generals of his army. {*Appian, Mithridatic Wars, l. 12. c. 10. (70) 2:369} [E542] He had in his army a hundred and twenty thousand (or, as Appian has it, a hundred and forty thousand) foot soldiers, who were trained according to the Roman discipline. He had sixteen thousand cavalry and a hundred chariots with scythes. A further large company followed the camp to guard the ways and carry the burdens. {*Plutarch, Lucullus, l. 1. c. 7. s. 4,5. 2:493}

4111. As soon as Mithridates had arrived at Paphlagonia, he made a haughty speech to the soldiers. When he saw that he had aroused their hatred of the Romans, he invaded Bithynia, which had recently been bequeathed to the Romans in Nicomedes' will. {*Appian, Mithridatic Wars, l. 12. c. 10. (70,71) 2:369,371} Livy said that Mithridates got it all into his hands. {*Livy, l. 93. 14:117} Plutarch said that he was very willingly greeted by all the cities of Bithynia. {*Plutarch, Lucullus, l. 1. c. 7. s. 5,6. 2:493}

4112. All Asia was being most intolerably oppressed by the Roman money-lenders and tax collectors and defected to Mithridates. {*Plutarch, Lucullus, l. 1. c. 7. s. 5,6. 2:493} With Marcus Marius, or Varius, whom Sertorius had sent to him from Spain to be his general, Mithridates captured some of its cities. When they entered the cities, the king put Marius ahead of him with the rods and fasces, as if he were the supreme magistrate, while the king followed behind, as if he were one of his officers. He enfranchised some of the cities on his own terms, while he granted immunity to others, but said these grants were not from him, but from Sertorius. So Asia, which previously had been plagued by the tax collectors and oppressed by the covetousness and abuses of the garrisoned soldiers, began to be encouraged by this change of government. {*Plutarch, Sertorius, l. 1. c. 24. s. 3,4. 8:67}

4113. Julius Caesar saw what havock Mithridates was making in the adjacent countries and was ashamed to sit idly by when the allies were in such trouble. He left Rhodes, where he had gone, and crossed over to Asia. Assembling what forces he could, he drove the king's lieutenant clear out of the province. By so doing, he kept those cities which, before that, had been wavering and ready to revolt, loyal to Rome. {*Suetonius, Julius, l. 1. c. 4. s. 2. 1:41} Junius, whom the people of Rome had appointed as their chief magistrate in Asia, offered very little resistance to Mithridates because he was a coward. {*Velleius Paterculus, l. 2. c. 42. s. 3. 1:143}

4114. Based on Livy, Eutropius and Orosius stated that Publius Servilius ended the war in Cilicia and Pamphylia within three years and because of this was called *Isauricus*. Cicero stated that Servilius had commanded the army for five years. {*Cicero, Against Verres II, l. 3. c. 90. 8:259} Consequently, we have connected his first going into the province to the year before this fifth year, in which he was also consul. Cicero affirmed that this man took more of the robbers' commanders alive than all those had done who had gone before him. {*Cicero, Against Verres II, l. 5. c. 26. 8:541} [K181] Among others, he recaptured Nico, a famous pirate, who had broken his chains and escaped with the same gallantry that he had exhibited when he was first taken prisoner. {*Cicero, Against Verres II, l. 5. c. 30. 8:555} Ammianus Marcellinus wrote: {*Ammianus Marcellinus, l. 14. c. 8. s. 4. 1:67}

> "Cilicia and Isaura were mutually engaged in a war of piracy and had some troops of land robbers. Servilius, the proconsul, made them submit to him and after that he made them a tributary."

4115. Jornandes wrote that Servilius overcame Pamphylia, Lycia (or rather Cilicia and Pisidia), and reduced them all to provinces. {Jornandes, De Regnorum ac Temporum Succession} Octavius, who was this year's consul, was sent into the province of Cilicia. {*Plutarch, Lucullus, l. 1. c. 6. s. 1. 2:487}

4116. Wherever Servilius marched, it was a splendid sight to see the various prisoners and captives whom he took along with him. People came flocking to him from everywhere. They came from the towns through which they marched and also from all the adjacent places for the express purpose of seeing this spectacle. This pleased the people of Rome all the more, and they were more delighted with this victory than with any that had ever been before. {*Cicero, Against Verres II, l. 5. c. 26. 8:541,543} In this triumph he displayed the various images and ornaments which he had taken away from the city of Olympus after he had captured it. They were carried in state on chargers that rode ahead of him in the triumph. All of this he later caused to be entered into the public records and brought into the treasury. The number of those images, and the size, shape and condition of each image were specified. {*Cicero, Against Verres II, l. 1. c. 21. 7:179,181} {Asconius Pedianus, Against Verres} Valerius Maximus mentioned this triumph of Servilius. {*Valerius Maximus, l. 8. c. 5. s. 6. 2:219} Eutropius and Sextus Rufus also referred to the triumph. Claudian, the poet, said this of him: {Eutropius, l. 1.} [E543]

> "Servilius charioted the untamed Isaures."

## 3930 AM, 4640 JP, 74 BC

4117. Marcus Antonius, the father of Mark Antony who was in the triumvirate, obtained an unlimited commission to guard all the Roman sea coasts. He obtained this through the favour of Cotta, the consul, and Cethegus' faction in the Senate. Marcus Antonius Senior was an extremely vile person and his wicked companions pillaged Sicily and all the provinces. {*Cicero, Against Verres II, l. 3. c. 91. 8:261,263} {*Lactantius, Divine Institutions, l. 1. c. 11. 7:22} {Asconius Pedianus, Divination} {Asconius Pedianus, Against Verres}

4118. The province of Cisalpine Gaul had been allotted to Lucius Lucullus, the consul. When Octavius, who held Cilicia, died, Lucullus befriended Cethegus by means of Praecia, a common strumpet. Cethegus had a great deal of influence in Rome and caused the province of Cilicia to be assigned to Lucullus. Since Cappadocia was close to Cilicia, they voted that Lucullus should undertake the Mithridatic War. However, Marcus Cotta, his colleague in the consulship, prevailed with the Senate after much pleading, that he might be sent with a fleet to guard the Propontis and defend Bithynia. {*Plutarch, Lucullus, l. 1. c. 6. 2:487-491} So both the consuls were sent to this war, the one to secure Bithynia and the other to pursue Mithridates in Asia. {*Cicero, Pro Murena, l. 1. (33) 10:229} {Memnon, c. 39.} {Eutropius, l. 6.} Lucullus, the consul, not only had Cilicia allotted to him, but Asia, also (properly so called), and he had the command of it for seven years. {*Velleius Paterculus, l. 2. c. 33. 1:121}

4119. Lucullus obtained a legion in Italy and with it crossed over into Asia. He added Fimbria's legions and two other legions to his force. However, these new additions had long ago been spoiled with luxury and covetousness, while the Fimbrians had for a long time gone without leadership and were more intractable and impudent. [K182] However, they were very warlike, and were very skilled and experienced in military undertakings. Lucullus reformed the one legion and settled the fierceness of the other. {*Plutarch, Lucullus, l. 1. c. 7. s. 1,2. 2:491} {*Appian, Mithridatic Wars, l. 12. c. 11. (72) 2:373} He did the best he could to punish the money-lenders and Roman tax collectors and make them more moderate in their dealings, as their extortions had been the main reason for Asia's revolt. He put down all the various rebellions of the people when almost every country was in revolt. {*Plutarch, Lucullus, l. 1. c. 7. s. 5,6. 2:493}

4120. Mithridates had another large army on the march, with four hundred ships of thirty oars plus a large number of smaller ships, commonly called Pentecouteri and Cercura. He sent away Diophantus Mathaerus into Cappadocia with a large force, to put garrisons into the cities and to intercept and stop Lucullus, should he attempt to enter Pontus. Mithridates kept for his own force a hundred and fifty foot soldiers, twelve thousand cavalry and a hundred and twenty chariots with scythes, which followed the cavalry. He had a good supply of all types of war engines. With all of these, he marched quickly through Timonitis, Cappadocia and Galatia and reached Bithynia within nine days. Lucullus, in the meantime, commanded Cotta and all his fleet to stay at a port of the Chalcedonians. {*Memnon, c. 39.*}

4121. Mithridates' fleet stayed near Heraclea in Pontus, but were denied use of the harbour. However, the citizens gave them access to their market. After some disputes between them, as are usual in such places, two of the most prominent men of Heraclea, Silanus and Satyrus, were taken away as prisoners by them. They would be freed only on the condition that they help Mithridates in this war against the Romans with five frigates. Through this, the Heracleans lost favour with the Romans. The Romans had appointed the public sale of the citizens' goods in other cities, and they now also subjected Heraclea to sale. The tax collectors who were to carry out this business arrived and started exacting money, contrary to the customs of the state. The citizens grew very perplexed, viewing this action as a prelude to slavery. Then, finding themselves in this situation, they knew they would have to send an embassy to the Roman Senate to ask for their favour in stopping the sale of their goods. Persuaded by a bold, desperate fellow in the city, they murdered the tax collectors so secretly, that no one knew of their death. {*Memnon, c. 40.*}

4122. Marcus Cotta heard the news of Lucullus' coming, and that he was already camped in Phrygia and was very confident of victory over Mithridates. Cotta hurried to fight with Mithridates before Lucullus could, so that Lucullus would not share in the victory with him. {*Plutarch, Lucullus, l. 1. c. 8. s. 1,2. 2:493,495*} In a short time, Mithridates' generals, Marius (or Varius) and Eumachus, had assembled a large army. They fought with Publius Rutilius, Marcus Cotta's lieutenant, at Chalcedon. [E544] Rutilius, along with the best part of his army, was killed in the battle. {*Orosius, l. 6. c. 2.*} The Basternians routed the Italian foot soldiers and killed many of them. {*Memnon, c. 41.*}

4123. Mithridates marched up to Chalcedon, where the Romans from everywhere were coming to Cotta. Since Cotta was a novice soldier, he did not fight with him. However, Nudus, the admiral of his fleet, with a brigade of the army, took to the field where it was most fortified. They were beaten off from there and fled back to the gate of Chalcedon. [K183] When they reached the gate, there was such a crowd of them trying to get in,

that those who chased them could not shoot an arrow without missing the enemy troops. Every arrow found its target. As soon as they had let down the bolts to secure the gates for fear of the enemy, they drew Nudus and some other commanders up to them with ropes. All the rest were killed in the midst of their friends and enemies. In vain they held up their arms to them, begging also to be drawn up. {*Appian, Mithridatic Wars, l. 12. c. 10. (71) 2:371,373*}

4124. Mithridates thought it would be best to follow up on this victory at once and move his fleet toward the harbour. When they had broken the brazen chain that was at the entrance of the harbour, they burned four of the enemy's ships. They towed away another sixty by tying them to the sterns of their own vessels. Neither Nudus nor Cotta offered any resistance, but stayed securely within the walls. In this battle, the Romans lost about three thousand men, among whom was Lucius Manlius, a senator. Mithridates lost twenty of the Basternians, who had been the first to assault the harbour. {*Appian, Mithridatic Wars, l. 12. c. 10. (71) 2:373*} Plutarch stated that Cotta lost four thousand foot soldiers on land, besides those sixty ships with their men. {*Plutarch, Lucullus, l. 1. c. 8. s. 2. 2:495*} Memnon said that in one day the land and sea were most disgracefully filled with the bodies of the Romans. Eight thousand were killed in the naval battle and forty-five hundred were taken prisoner. Fifty-three hundred of the army of Italian foot soldiers were killed. Mithridates' side lost only about thirty Basternians and seven hundred others from his whole company.

4125. This was the battle near Chalcedon where Marcus Aurelius Cotta, the consul, was defeated {*Livy, l. 93. 14:117*} and in a letter to Arsaces Mithridates said: {*Sallust, Letter of Mithridates, l. 1. (13) 1:437*}

> "I totally routed Marcus Cotta, the Roman general, near Chalcedon on land and have deprived him of a most gallant fleet at sea."

4126. The sad condition of Cotta, on both sea and land, greatly increased Mithridates' wealth and prestige, {*Cicero, Pro Murena, l. 1. (33) 10:229*} while his success depressed the enemy. Lucullus, who was camped along the Sangarius River, heard of this great defeat and seeing his soldiers' morale failing, encouraged them with a speech. {*Memnon, c. 41.*}

4127. Archelaus, who had formerly been one of Mithridates' commanders, had now sided with the Romans. He tried to convince Lucullus that he could easily take the whole kingdom of Pontus, now that Mithridates was in Bithynia with his army. Lucullus replied that he would not be deemed a greater coward than the common huntsmen, who did not dare to fight with wild beasts, but were brave enough to go into their empty dens. After saying this, Lucullus marched against Mithridates with his company of thirty thousand foot soldiers and twenty-five hundred cavalry. When he first came in sight of the enemy, he was astonished to see such a vast number and therefore chose not to fight but play for time. When he remembered that Marius, whom Sertorius had sent from Spain to be Mithridates' general, was marching up against him, he decided to fight and drew his troops into battle array. Just as the army was set to fight, the sky suddenly split apart and between both armies there seemed to fall a large flaming meteor, resembling a hogshead in shape and silver-fiery hot. This strange sight so frightened both armies, that they decided not to fight. They say this sign happened in Phrygia, near Otryae. {*Plutarch, Lucullus, l. 1. c. 8. s. 3-7. 2:495,497}

4128. With his cavalry, Lucullus, the consul, fought some skirmishes with Mithridates' cavalry and won. He also made some other raids in which he was fortunate. This so encouraged his soldiers and made them so eager to fight, that he had a lot of trouble in keeping them under control. {*Livy, l. 94. 14:117}

4129. Mithridates saw that the city of Cyzicum was his door of entry into all of Asia. If he were able to take it, the whole province would be open to his attacks, so he resolved to make it the centre of his war effort. {*Cicero, Pro Murena, l. 1. (33) 10:229} It was the most famous city of all Asia and was a faithful friend to the people of Rome. {*Cicero, Pro Lege Manilia, l. 1. c. 8. (20) 9:33} In the recent defeat at Chalcedon, it had lost three thousand citizens and ten ships. [K184] When he thus made up his mind, the king decided to give Lucullus the slip. As soon as he had dined, he took the opportunity of a dense fog at night and moved his camp, so that by daybreak he had reached the top of the Adrastia Mountain Range. This is also called Dindymus, and is located opposite the city. {*Plutarch, Lucullus, l. 1. c. 9. s. 1. 2:497} [E545] Strabo wrote that Mithridates invaded the Cyzicenians with a hundred and fifty thousand foot soldiers and a large body of cavalry, taking the Adrastia Mountain Range and the suburbs. {*Strabo, l. 12. c. 8. s. 11. 5:501} Appian stated that Lucullus, with thirty thousand foot soldiers and sixteen hundred cavalry, camped opposite Mithridates' force of about three hundred thousand men. {*Appian, Mithridatic Wars, l. 12. c. 11. (72) 2:373} Orosius stated: {Orosius, l. 6. c. 2.}

> "Indeed, it was reported that in the siege of Cyzicum he lost more than three hundred thousand men through famine and sickness."

4130. Plutarch stated that Lucullus killed at least three hundred thousand of Mithridates' men and support staff. {*Plutarch, Lucullus, l. 1. c. 11. s. 6. 2:505} Eutropius recorded that, in the following winter and summer, Lucullus killed almost a hundred thousand men of the king's forces. {Eutropius, l. 6.}

4131. Mithridates surrounded the Cyzicenians with ten brigades and also attacked them by sea with a fleet of four hundred ships. {*Strabo, l. 12. c. 8. s. 11. 5:502} {*Plutarch, Lucullus, l. 1. c. 9. s. 3. 2:499} Since the Cyzicenians did not know what had become of Lucullus, Mithridates' forces told them that Lucullus' tents, which were pitched before them, were the forces of the Armenians and Medes, which Tigranes had sent to join Mithridates. Demonax was sent to the city from Archelaus and was the first to tell them that Lucullus was nearby. They did not believe him, thinking this was a ruse to cheer them up. However, a boy who had been taken prisoner by the enemy escaped and with his finger pointed out to them the place where the Romans were camped, after which they believed the report. {*Plutarch, Lucullus, l. 1. c. 9. s. 5,6. 2:501} Lucullus sent one of his soldiers to those who understood their language, telling them to be encouraged. This soldier had come on a raft made of two water skins. {*Florus, l. 1. c. 40. s. 16. 1:185} {Orosius, l. 6. c. 2.}

### 3931a AM, 4640 JP, 74 BC

4132. Lucullus attacked Mithridates from the rear and defeated the Pontics, gaining a glorious victory. He killed more than ten thousand soldiers and took thirteen thousand prisoners. {Memnon, c. 42.}

4133. Lucullus saw a very convenient mountain on which to make his camp. If he could capture it, he would have ample provisions for his army and would be able to starve the enemy. There was one very narrow pass to it at which Mithridates had placed a guard to secure it, on the advice of Taxiles and some of his other commanders. Lucius Manius, or Magius, the arbitrator of the league between Mithridates and Sertorius, secretly sent a messenger to Lucullus. He then persuaded Mithridates to allow the Romans to pass by and to camp wherever they chose. He lied to Mithridates by saying that Fimbria's legions, which had formerly served Sertorius in the wars, would defect to him within a day or two, so that he would be spared the effort of a battle and get a victory without fighting. Mithridates did not suspect anything and allowed the Romans quietly to enter the pass and to fortify the mountain against him. In this way, the Romans had plentiful provisions from all the lands lying behind them, while Mithridates was blocked by a lake, mountain and river, and able to get few supplies by land for his camp. [K185] He could neither get out, nor force Lucullus out, and the winter season was approaching and would likely hinder all supplies from coming to him by sea. {*Appian, Mithridatic Wars, l. 12. c. 11. (72) 2:373,375}

4134. Plutarch wrote that Lucullus camped in Thrace at a place called *Comes*, which was the place most suitable for obstructing all the supply lines to Mithridates. Mithridates sent some men to Fimbria's legions to bring them over to him. Memnon said they pretended to defect to Mithridates and then killed all of Mithridates' envoys.

## 3931b AM, 4641 JP, 73 BC

4135. Nicomedes, a Thessalian, had built notable engines to batter Cyzicum. {*Plutarch, Lucullus, l. 1. c. 10. s. 2. 2:501,503} One of these was called the *Helepolis*, that is, *The City-Taker*. It was a hundred and fifty feet high and was the most remarkable one. On this, another tower was erected on which were placed other sorts of weapons and engines to sling stones. Before they positioned the engines, Mithridates ordered that three thousand of the Cyzicenians, whom he had taken, be sent to the city to urge them to surrender. However, this did not work, because Lysistratus, their general, ordered a crier to exhort them from the walls, saying that since it was their bad luck to have fallen under the power of a foreigner, they should bear up under this as well as they could. Mithridates used all the strength he could, both by sea and land, to subdue the city. The townsmen were very busy on the inside, defending it. *[E546]* The attacking forces were not able to breach the walls and could not enter through the part that fell near the evening, because the heat of the fire was so scorching. The Cyzicenians, meanwhile, repaired the breach at night. {*Appian, Mithridatic Wars, l. 12. c. 11. (73) 2:377}

4136. At last Lucullus found a way of sending some auxiliaries to the city by night. {*Strabo, l. 12. c. 8. s. 11. 5:503} On the Dascylitis Lake there were very large boats. He took one of the largest and carried it in a wagon to the seaside and put as many soldiers in it as it could hold. Under cover of darkness, they secretly got into the city and the enemy knew nothing about it. {*Plutarch, Lucullus, l. 1. c. 9. s. 6. 2:501}

4137. This was the time of Proserpina's festival, when the Cyzicenians offered a black heifer. Although they did not have one, they made one of dough and brought it to the altar. The heifer which had been intended for the festival was feeding with the rest of the Cyzicenians' herds on the other side of the sea. On the day of the festival, she left the other herds and swam over alone to Cyzicum. She passed all the way through the enemy's fleet and by diving underwater got through the bars which were at the mouth of the harbour. She passed through and came into the midst of the city, to the temple of Proserpina, where she presented herself before the altar. The Cyzicenians sacrificed her and were greatly encouraged. {*Julius Obsequens, Prodigies, l. 1. c. 60a. 14:301} {*Plutarch, Lucullus, l. 1. c. 10. s. 1. 2:501} {*Appian, Mithridatic Wars, l. 12. c. 11. (75) 2:379}

4138. It was reported that Proserpina appeared in a vision by night to Aristagoras, who, according to Julius Obsequens, was the chief magistrate. Plutarch gave him the title of the town clerk. She told him that she had provided a piper against the pipers. Plutarch related it in such a way as to indicate that she immediately sent a Libyan piper against the Pontic trumpeter. The Cyzicenians wondered what this meant. About daybreak, there was foul weather at sea, as from a stormy wind. The king's engines had now been drawn up to the walls and by their creaking and crashing it was evident that there was a storm brewing. Soon after this, an extremely violent south wind arose which, within an hour, destroyed the rest of the king's engines. It so shook the wooden tower erected on the engine, that it was overturned and thrown to the ground. {*Julius Obsequens, Prodigies, l. 1. c. 60a. 14:301} {*Plutarch, Lucullus, l. 1. c. 10. s. 2,3. 2:501,503} {*Appian, Mithridatic Wars, l. 12. c. 11. (75) 2:379} [K186]

4139. It was also reported that Athena appeared to many at Illium in their sleep, dripping with sweat and showing that part of her shawl was cut off. She told them that she had come from providing relief for the Cyzicenians. The people of Illium used to show the pillars on which the decrees and letters telling of this matter had been engraved. {*Plutarch, Lucullus, l. 1. c. 10. s. 3. 2:503}

4140. Mithridates was advised by his friends to take his fleet and sail away from the city. He, however, was not dismayed in the least by what had happened. He went up to Mount Dindymus and cast up a bank from there all along to the walls of the city, on which he built towers and from there tried to undermine the walls. {*Appian, Mithridatic Wars, l. 12. c. 11. (75) 2:379} In spite of all this, the Cyzicenians held out so stoutly, that they very nearly captured Mithridates alive in his own tunnel. The Cyzicenians also dug a tunnel to him, but when he became aware of the danger he was in, he managed to get away safely. {*Strabo, l. 12. c. 8. s. 11. 5:503}

4141. When winter set in, Mithridates was cut off from supplies by sea. The army was so short of supplies, that many of them died from famine. While some were content to eat human flesh, others fed on herbs as their only food and became sick. All the while, the dead bodies were lying about unburied, which caused a plague to break out. {Memnon, c. 42.} {*Strabo, l. 12. c. 8. s. 11. 5:503} {*Florus,

*l. 1. c. 40. s. 16,17. 1:185}* {*Plutarch, Lucullus, l. 1. c. 11. s. 1. 2:503}*
{*Appian, Mithridatic Wars, l. 12. c. 11. (76) 2:381}* {*Orosius, l. 6. c. 2.}*

4142. While Lucullus had gone to capture some citadel or other, Mithridates tried to make use of the opportunity. So he ordered some of his forces to march home with their arms, but without being seen by the enemy. Most of his cavalry he sent into Bithynia, as well as those horses which were beasts of burden, his foot soldiers and all who were unfit. The horses were now weak from lack of food and lame because, lacking shoes, their hooves were worn away. When Lucullus heard about this, he hurried to the camp by night as fast as he could. At daybreak, he went after them with ten companies of foot soldiers and all his cavalry. At that instant, a violent storm struck, so that many of the soldiers, because of the snow and other hardships, were forced to lie down from the very cold, unable to follow. With the rest of his troops, he overtook the enemy at the passage of the Rhyndacus River and slaughtered so many of them, that the women of Apollonia came out and plundered the wagons and stripped the dead. In this battle, six thousand horses, an enormous number of beasts of burden and fifteen thousand men were captured. Lucullus carried everything away with him, besides the pillage of the enemy's camp. If we can believe him, Orosius reported that: [E547]

"In this battle, Lucullus killed more than fifteen thousand men."

4143. Sallust thought that this was the first time the Romans had ever seen any camels. However, those who had been under Scipio, the general who defeated Antiochus, and those who had fought with Archelaus at Orchomenus and Chaeronia, would most certainly have seen camels. {*Plutarch, Lucullus, l. 1. c. 11. s. 2-4. 2:503,505}* {*Appian, Mithridatic Wars, l. 12. c. 11. (75) 2:379,381}* {*Orosius, l. 6. c. 2.}*

4144. Fannius, who had joined in with Mithridates, and Metrophanes, the king's general, were defeated by Mamercus. They escaped into Moesia with two thousand cavalry and went from there to Moeonia, reaching the dry, parched hills and plains of Inarime. After they had been there a long time, they finally got out and arrived at the king's camp without being noticed by the enemy. {*Orosius, l. 6. c. 2.}*

4145. Eumachus, the general, and the rest of Mithridates' generals fought in Phrygia, killing many Romans with their wives and children. They subdued the Pisidians, the Isaurians and also Cilicia. [K187] As they were roving about, one of the tetrarchs of Galatia, Dejotarus, attacked them and killed them along with many of their soldiers, thus bringing their actions to an end. {*Livy, l. 94. 14:117}* {*Appian, Mithridatic Wars, l. 12. c. 11. (75) 2:381}* {*Orosius, l. 6. c. 2.}*

## 3932a AM, 4641 JP, 73 BC

4146. The 28th Jubilee.

4147. The Cyzicenians undermined the mounds which the king had cast up all along from the Dindymus Mountain to the city and burned his engines. They knew that the enemy was severely weakened by famine and made many sallies against them, so that Mithridates resolved to withdraw and leave. {*Appian, Mithridatic Wars, l. 12. c. 11. (76) 2:381}* He wrote about this in a letter to Arsaces: {*Sallust, Letter of Mithridates, l. 1. (14) 1:437}*

"In besieging Cyzicum with a large army, I lacked provisions, since there were none available in the area. I could get nothing from all the regions around there and winter had blocked the sea, so that none could be expected from that direction. I was forced (not by any compulsion of the enemy) to march back into my own kingdom."

4148. Plutarch stated from Sallust that for two whole winters Lucullus camped first at Cyzicum and later at Amisus. See Cicero concerning the raising of the siege of Cyzicum. {*Cicero, Pro Lege Manilia, l. 1. c. 8. (21) 9:33}* {*Cicero, Pro Murena, l. 1. (33) 10:229}* {*Cicero, Pro Archia Poeta, l. 1. c. 9. (21) 11:29,31}*

4149. Mithridates suddenly resolved to leave. To keep Lucullus from following after him too swiftly, he sent Aristonicus, the Greek admiral of his fleet, to put out to sea. However, by some foul play, Lucullus took him prisoner just as he was setting out from shore and seized the ten thousand pieces of gold he was carrying with him for the purpose of bribing some of the Roman army. {*Plutarch, Lucullus, l. 1. c. 11. s. 5,6. 2:505}*

4150. The king left his land forces with the generals to march to Lampsacus. Hermaeus and Marius, the generals who had been sent by Sertorius, led thirty thousand men to Lampsacus. However, Lucullus followed close behind them and at last overtook them, surprising them as they were crossing the Aesepus River, the level of which was higher than normal at the time. He took many of them as prisoners and killed twenty thousand of them. More than eleven thousand of these were reported to have been Marius' soldiers. The Granicus and Aesepus Rivers ran red with blood. One of Mithridates' nobles, who knew how very covetous the Romans were, ordered the soldiers to scatter their knapsacks and money about deliberately, to slow down the pursuers. {*Memnon, c. 42.}* {*Polyaenus, Stratagmata, l. 7.}* {*Florus, l. 1. c. 40. s. 18. 1:185}* {*Plutarch, Lucullus, l. 1. c. 11. s. 6. 2:505}* {*Appian, Mithridatic Wars, l. 12. c. 11. (76) 2:381,383}* {*Orosius, l. 6. c. 2.}*

4151. Mithridates planned to return by sea and sail by night to Parium. {*Appian, Mithridatic Wars, l. 12. c. 11. (76) 2:381}*

His soldiers were determined to leave with him and crowded into the ships on every side. Some were already full and others filled soon after. It happened that so many tried to get on the ships, that some ships sank and others capsized. The Cyzicenians saw this and attacked the enemy's camp. They cut the throats of the sick who were left behind and carried away whatever they could find. {Memnon, c. 42.}

4152. Lucullus entered Cyzicum and was received with great joy and magnificence. {*Plutarch, Lucullus, l. 1. c. 12. s. 1. 2:505,507} In his honour, they later instituted some games, which they called the Lucullian Games. {*Appian, Mithridatic Wars, l. 12. c. 11. (76) 2:381,383} The Romans conferred a great deal of honour on the city and granted them their freedom. {*Strabo, l. 12. c. 8. s. 11. 5:503} {*Tacitus, Annals, l. 4. c. 36. 4:65}

4153. After Mithridates' men had been driven to Lampsacus by Lucullus and besieged there, Mithridates sent his fleet to transport them and the Lamsacenians from there. He left fifty ships with ten thousand men on board for Marius or Varius, the general from Sertorius, Alexander, a Paphlagonian, and Dionysius, the eunuch. [K188] With the larger part, Mithridates made for Nicomedia, but many of these, as also of those left behind, were drowned in a storm. {*Appian, Mithridatic Wars, l. 12. c. 11. (76) 2:383} [E548]

4154. As best he could, Mithridates assembled some forces in Pontus and besieged Perinthus. He made some attempts against it, but when he was unable to take it, he sent his forces away to Bithynia. {Memnon, c. 42.}

4155. Antiochus Asiaticus and his brother, who were the young sons of king Antiochus Pius and who controlled part of the kingdom of Syria which had not been seized by Tigranes, came to Rome. They requested the kingdom of Egypt, which they believed rightly belonged to them and their mother Selene. They stayed there almost two whole years and retained their royal retinue. {*Cicero, Against Verres II, l. 4. c. 27. 8:355}

## 3932b AM, 4642 JP, 72 BC

4156. Antipas or Antipater, the Idumean, was the foremost citizen of their country with regard to birth and wealth. He was the son of the other Antipas or Antipater, who they say was the son of Alexander, the king of the Jews, and his wife Alexandra. Antipater was made governor of all Idumea and was married to Cyprus, who was born at a famous place among the Arabians. He had a son called Herod, who later became the king of Judea. Herod was twenty-five years old when his father placed him over Galilee. {See note on 3957c AM. <<5026>>} {See note on 3875b AM. <<3786>>} Nicolaus Damascene recorded Herod's life while Herod

was still living. To gain favour with Herod, he derived Antipater's pedigree from the princes of the Jews who had come from Babylon into Judea. {*Josephus, Antiq., l. 14. c. 1. s. 3. (8,9) 7:453} This is also in the 35th chapter of the Arabic History of the Jews, which is written at the end of the Parisian Bible. There we read that Antipater was a Jew who was descended from those who came from Babylon with Ezra, the priest. He was appointed by Alexander Jannaeus as governor of the country of the Idumeans and married a wife from there. However, Julius Africanus, in a letter of his to Aristides (found in Eusebius {*Eusebius, Ecclesiastical History, l. 1. c. 6,7. 1:49-65}) and Ambrose, who followed him, {Ambrose, Commentary on Luke 3, l. 3} stated a tradition of those who were called the kinsmen of our Saviour according to the flesh, that Antipater was the son of Herod from Askelon, who had charge of Apollo's temple there. He was carried away from Askelon by some Idumean robbers, and so Antipater was instructed in the manners and customs of the Idumeans. This was the most common opinion of all the Christian fathers. {*Julius Africanus, Aristides, l. 1. c. 4. 6:126}

4157. Barba came with a strong band of Italians and with Triarius, one of Lucullus' commanders, besieged Apamea. The citizens held out for a long time, but finally surrendered, according to Memnon. However, Appian wrote that when Triarius arrived there, he took the city by storm and killed many of the people of Apamea in their temples, where they had fled for sanctuary. Soon after this, the Roman army, under Barba, took Prusias, a very well-fortified city at the base of Mount Olympus, and pillaged it. From there, Triarius went with his army to the city of Prusias which bordered on the sea. Prusias, the king of Bithynia, had taken it from the Heracleans and named it after himself, but it had previously been called Cierus, or Chius, after the river on which it bordered. As soon as he drew near the city, the Prusians expelled the Pontics and welcomed them in. From there Triarius and his army came to Nicaea, in which there was a garrison of Mithridates. The Pontics knew full well that the citizens favoured the Romans, so they stole away by night to Mithridates at Nicomedia. Hence, the Romans got that city under their command without any trouble. (Memnon and Appian have conflicting details for the events in this paragraph. We left it as close to the original as possible. Editor.) {Memnon, c. 43,49} {*Appian, Mithridatic Wars, l. 12. c. 11. (77) 2:383} {Orosius, l. 6. c. 2.} [K189]

4158. Lucullus came to the Hellespont and prepared his fleet. He arrived at Troas and went into the temple of Venus. That same night in his sleep he dreamed that he saw the goddess standing by him and saying:

Sleep'st thou now, lion stout?
Whole herds of fawns rove here about.

*4159.* While he was telling this dream to his friends, some men came to him from Illium before daybreak, to tell him that thirteen of the king's ships, each with five tiers of oars, had appeared at a port of the Achaeans and were bound for Lemnos. Lucullus sailed from Troas, captured all the thirteen ships and killed Isidorus, their admiral. {*Plutarch, Lucullus, l. 1. c. 12. s. 1-4. 2:507} {*Appian, Mithridatic Wars, l. 12. c. 11. (77) 2:383,385} [E549]

*4160.* Lucullus followed up on his victory by going after the generals Alexander and Dionysius, and Marius or Varius, whom Sertorius had sent to be general. He overtook them near Lemnos, which was on the deserted island where Philoctetes' altar with the brazen serpent was located. As he approached them, he ordered his soldiers, prior to the battle, not to kill anyone who had only one eye. He was referring to Marius, who had lost an eye and whom Lucullus planned to deride before killing him. When Lucullus noticed that the enemy did not move and had drawn all their ships to the shore, he stopped and sent two ships, to try to draw them into a battle. They would not budge, but defended themselves from their decks, which really galled the Romans. The place was such that they could not turn around, nor was it possible for the ships, tossed about by the waves as they were, to do much harm to the enemy. The enemy fleet was beached and they had good, sure footing. So Lucullus sent a squadron of ships to the island by another way. He landed all his best foot soldiers there, who then attacked the enemy from the rear. Some were killed and others retreated to their ships. They were so fearful of Lucullus, that they dared not launch into the deep, but sailed along the coast. Consequently, they were now attacked from both land and sea and many were killed as they tried to get away. {*Plutarch, Lucullus, l. 1. c. 12. s. 2-5. 2:507,509} {*Appian, Mithridatic Wars, l. 12. c. 11. (77) 2:383,385} Lucullus either sank or captured thirty-two of the king's ships, besides a number of cargo ships. Among those killed were very many who had been proscribed by Sulla. {Orosius, l. 6. c. 2.}

*4161.* The next day, the three generals were found hidden in a cave. Lucullus had Marius, or Varius, killed. {Orosius, l. 6. c. 2.} {*Appian, Mithridatic Wars, l. 12. c. 11. (77) 2:385} Alexander was reserved to be killed later and Dionysius died soon after, from poison that he carried with him. {*Appian, Mithridatic Wars, l. 12. c. 11. (77) 2:385}

*4162.* These were the two naval victories which Lucullus had, one at Tenedos, the other in the Aegean Sea. Memnon mentioned them as two distinct battles. {Memnon, c. 44.} Cicero stated that there was just one battle: {*Cicero, Pro Lege Manilia, l. 1. c. 8. (21) 9:33}

"The large and well-equipped fleet, which Sertorius' commanders were in all zeal sailing to Italy, was defeated by Lucullus and the proconsul, Lucius Murena. Do you think that the naval battle at Tenedos (when the enemy fleet in good hopes and spirits made a direct course for Italy under the most experienced generals) was defeated after a small battle or a light skirmish?"

*4163.* In another speech, Cicero stated: {*Cicero, Pro Archia Poeta, l. 1. c. 9. (22) 11:31} [K190]

"Lucullus defeated the enemy's fleet at that incredible naval battle at Tenedos."

*4164.* Lucullus sent letters to the Senate recounting his achievements, as was the custom of conquerors. {*Appian, Mithridatic Wars, l. 12. c. 11. (77) 2:385} When the Senate decreed to send him three thousand talents to procure a fleet, he wrote back that he had no need of the money. He boasted that he was able to drive Mithridates from the sea with the ships of the Roman allies. {*Plutarch, Lucullus, l. 1. c. 13. s. 4. 2:509,511}

*4165.* After this, he hurried to catch Mithridates, thinking he might find him around Bithynia. He secured the place with the help of Voconius, whom he had sent to Nicomedia with a squadron of ships to pursue Mithridates. However, Voconius was busy in the religious ceremonies and holy festival days at Samothracia and arrived too late. Mithridates set sail, hurrying to get to Pontus before Lucullus could catch him. A storm struck and wrecked part of his fleet. Some ships were damaged and others were sunk, so that for many days all the coasts around there were littered with the wreckage that washed ashore. They said that this storm was caused by Artemis of Priapus, in revenge against the Pontics for having plundered her temple and taken down her image from its place.

*4166.* Dio wrote that Mithridates was wrecked twice as he was sailing to Pontus. Through these accidents, he lost about ten thousand men and sixty ships. The rest were scattered by the winds. Mithridates wrote to Arsaces and said: {*Sallust, Letter of Mithridates, l. 1. (14) 1:437,439}

"I lost my best soldiers and my fleet by two wrecks at Parium and Heraclea."

*4167.* Orosius said:

"After Mithridates had manned his fleet and sailed against Byzantium (where Eutropius said he was chased by Lucullus), he was caught by a storm and lost eighty ships with brass prows."

4168. To conclude, Florus stated: {*Florus, l. 1. c. 40. s. 18,19. 1:185}

> "A storm struck this fleet of more than a hundred ships and a very large military force in the Pontic sea. The storm so battered it, that it looked like it had been done by a real naval battle."

4169. The pilot of the large ship which carried Mithridates considered it impossible to beach the ship in so violent a storm, since the ship was already leaking and almost full of water. [E550] Mithridates, against the advice of his friends, leaped into the ship of Selemus, a pirate who helped him get on board. Mithridates entrusted himself to the pirates, who brought him safely to Heraclea in Pontus, after first going to Sinope and then to Amisus. {*Plutarch, Lucullus, l. 1. c. 13. 2:509,511} {Orosius, l. 6. c. 2.} {*Appian, Mithridatic Wars, l. 12. c. 11. (78) 2:385}

4170. Cotta, wanting to atone for his former losses, moved his forces from Chalcedon, where he was camped at the time, to Nicomedia. He camped eighteen miles from the city and was cautious how he engaged the enemy. Triarius, of his own accord, quickly brought his army to Cotta using running marches. Then both the Roman armies prepared to attack the city. The king, aware that Lucullus had already obtained two notable victories over the Pontics at sea, knew that he was no match for the Roman forces. He moved his fleet back into the river, where he lost some ships with three tiers of oars in a storm. However, he escaped with most of his ships to the Hypius River. {Memnon, c. 44.}

4171. Mithridates remained there because of the storm. On hearing that Lamachus of Heraclea, an old and trusted friend of his, ruled that state, he flattered him with many fair promises, influencing him to let him enter the city and to do the best he could for him. [K191] Mithridates also sent him some money for this purpose. Lamachus prepared a large feast for the citizens outside the city. During this feast, he promised Mithridates that the gates would not be shut. He made the people drunk, so that Mithridates might come as planned on that very day. Mithridates came and took them by surprise as they were sleeping, and so the city became his own while no one even dreamed of his coming. On the next day, the king summoned the city together and spoke to them in a very friendly manner. After he had exhorted them to remain loyal to him, he committed the city to Connacoriges and placed a garrison there of four thousand men. His pretence was, merely to defend and protect the citizens in case the Romans should attack the place. From there, he sailed directly toward Sinope. Before he left, he distributed some money among the citizens and especially among the magistrates. {Memnon, c. 44.}

4172. After Lucullus had recovered Paphlagonia and Bithynia, he passed through Bithynia and Galatia to invade Mithridates' kingdom. At Nicomedia, he joined his forces with the troops of Cotta and Triarius, so that together they could attack Pontus. {Eutropius, l. 6.} {*Plutarch, Lucullus, l. 1. c. 14. s. 1. 2:511} {Memnon, c. 45.} They received news of the taking of Heraclea when as yet they knew nothing of the plot. They thought it had been surrendered when the citizens voluntarily abandoned the whole city. Lucullus thought it best that he, with the might of his entire army, should march through the midlands and Cappadocia against the king and his whole kingdom. Cotta thought they should try to recapture Heraclea, while Triarius thought they should take the fleet and intercept Mithridates' ships, which had been sent into Crete and Spain, on their return through the Hellespont and Propontis. {Memnon, c. 45.}

4173. When Mithridates heard of their plans, he prepared for war. He quickly sent for forces from his son-in-law, Tigranes, the Armenian, and his son Machares, who was reigning in Bosphorus, as well as from the Parthians. He also ordered Diocles to go to the neighbouring Scythians, to solicit them with many gifts and a large weight of gold. However, he ran away to Lucullus with the gifts and the gold. The others also refused to meddle, while Tigranes delayed for a long time. (Mithridates wrote that this war was begun and that from the start Tigranes refused to help. {*Sallust, Letter of Mithridates, l. 1. (15) 1:439}) However, he promised to send supplies, because Mithridates' daughter wore him down until he yielded. {Memnon, c. 45.} {*Appian, Mithridatic Wars, l. 12. c. 11. (78) 2:385}

4174. The envoy whom Mithridates sent to Tigranes was Metrodorus Scepsis, who had left his philosophy and become a politician. Mithridates had him as such a close friend, that he was called the king's father. He had been made a judge and it was not lawful for any man to appeal his sentence to the king. Tigranes asked the king's envoy what he thought of this business of sending forces against the Romans. The envoy replied:

> "As I am an envoy I advise you to send, as I am a counsellor I am against it."

4175. Tigranes sent Metrodorus back to Mithridates with his answer, but Metrodorus died on the way. Either the king had him killed or he died of some disease, for there was talk of both. Tigranes had informed the king of what Metrodorus had said, believing that Mithridates would never think any the worse of Metrodorus. To express his sorrow for what he had done, Tigranes interred his body very nobly, sparing no expense for the funeral of one whom Tigranes had betrayed when he was alive. {*Strabo, l. 13. c. 1. s. 55. 6:113} {*Plutarch, Lucullus, l. 1. c. 14. 2:511-515}

## 3933a AM, 4642 JP, 72 BC

*4176.* Mithridates sent several generals against Lucullus. *[K192]* They fought some battles, but the Romans won most of them. {*Memnon, c. 45.*} *[E551]* At first, Lucullus was very short of food. There were thirty thousand Galatians following the camp who were each to bring a measure of grain on their shoulders. After he had marched a little farther, he subdued and plundered all the way. A little later, he came to a country that had not been ravaged by war for many years, so that a slave was sold for four drachmas and an ox for one drachma. Goats, sheep, clothes and other things were equally cheap. They were not able to carry away all the booty, because there was so much of it. Therefore they left some of it behind and destroyed the rest. {*Plutarch, Lucullus, l. 1. c. 14. s. 1. 2:511*} {*Appian, Mithridatic Wars, l. 12. c. 11. (78) 2:385,387*}

*4177.* After this, Lucullus attempted to subdue Amisus and Eupatoria, which Mithridates had built near Amisus. He had named it after his own surname and made it his royal palace. A brigade of Lucullus' army was sent to take Themiscyra, on the Thermodon River. They used towers against Themiscyra and cast up works, digging such large mines that the two sides often fought underground. The townsmen opened their mines from the top and through these holes, let down bears, other wild beasts and swarms of bees among the invaders. The Romans met stiff resistance at Amisus, as the Amisians fought bravely in their own defence. They sometimes sallied out in force and at other times just a few went out. {*Appian, Mithridatic Wars, l. 12. c. 11. (78) 2:387*}

*4178.* Lucullus spent much time before Amisus in a long siege. His army began to complain at the delay and grumbled considerably that they were not allowed to plunder any of the cities they captured. It did not matter whether the city surrendered freely or was taken by storm. Lucullus replied that he had good reasons for drawing out the siege. In this way, he hoped to wear down Mithridates' forces little by little. He did not want Mithridates to think he had overpowered him, lest he go to Tigranes for help and thus make another enemy with whom they would have to fight. Plutarch quoted Lucullus as having said this: {*Plutarch, Lucullus, l. 1. c. 14. s. 4,5. 2:513*}

> "It is but a few days' march from Cabira into Armenia, where Tigranes lives, who is that lazy king of kings. He is so powerful that he wrests Asia from the Parthians, carries the Greek cities into Media, holds Syria and Palestine, dethrones the kings, Seleucus' successors, and steals their daughters and wives from their palaces, taking them with him as prisoners. This Tigranes is a neighbour to Mithridates, and is his son-in-law."

*4179.* Cotta moved his camp and first marched with his Romans to Prusia, which was formerly called Cierus. From there he went down to the Pontic Sea, and moved along the sea coast. He camped before the walls of Heraclea, which stood on the top of a hill. The Heracleans did not put too much trust in the strength of their location, but joined with the soldiers whom Mithridates had garrisoned among them and fought against Cotta, who made valiant attempts against them. More fell on the Roman side than on the other, but the Heracleans received many wounds from the Roman arrows. Therefore, Cotta gave up the attack and sounded a retreat to his soldiers. He camped farther off and started to besiege the city. When the Heracleans were short of food, they sent their envoys to the colonies around them to buy food. The envoys were well received. {*Memnon, c. 49.*}

*4180.* A little before this, Triarius, who was equipped with the Roman fleet from Nicomedia, attacked the Pontic ships which Mithridates had sent toward Crete and Spain. When he heard that the rest of the ships had returned to Pontus, he chased them. *[K193]* Many of them had been lost in storms and naval battles in various places. He overtook them at Tenedos and attacked them. Lucullus had seventy ships and the Pontics less than sixty. After they had violently rammed one another with their prows, the king's side endured the enemy attack very well for a while, but later they were forced to retire and the Romans obtained a complete and famous victory. This was the end of the large fleet that Mithridates had brought with him into Asia. {*Memnon, c. 50.*}

## 3933b AM, 4643 JP, 71 BC

*4181.* Mithridates sent abundant provisions, arms and soldiers to the besieged Amisians from Cabira. He made Cabira his winter quarters and levied another army of forty thousand foot soldiers and four thousand cavalry. {*Plutarch, Lucullus, l. 1. c. 15. s. 1. 2:515*} {*Appian, Mithridatic Wars, l. 12. c. 11. (78) 2:387*} Memnon said there were eight thousand cavalry.

*4182.* Olthacus, whom Appian called Olcaba, was a Scythian and prince of the Dandarians, who lived around Lake Maeotis (Sea of Azov). He was highly commended for warlike exploits, counsel and civil conduct. He was in some of Mithridates' garrisons and contested with some of the princes and his countrymen for superiority. He promised to do a great exploit for Mithridates by killing Lucullus. The king highly commended him, but pretended to be angry with him over it and very formally reproached him. *[E552]* Thereupon, he rode off to Lucullus, where he was treated very cordially. {*Plutarch, Lucullus, l. 1. c. 16. s. 1,2. 2:519*}

4183. The first year of the 177th Olympiad was now approaching. In the spring, Lucullus left Murena with two legions to continue the siege at Amisus, while he, with three other legions, marched through the mountains against Mithridates. {*Phlegon, Chronicles} {Photius, Bibliotheca, cod. 97., l. 5.} {*Plutarch, Lucullus, l. 1. c. 15. s. 1. 2:515} {*Appian, Mithridatic Wars, l. 12. c. 12. (79) 2:387,389} Murena was a lieutenant to Lucullus, who was the general. He was the son of that Murena whom Sulla had left as praetor in Asia. Cicero, in a speech on his behalf, said: {*Cicero, Pro Murena, l. 1. (11) 10:199}

> "During the time when he was lieutenant, he led an army, fought battles, defeated the enemy forces, took many cities, some by storm, others by siege. He behaved himself so well in Asia, which at that time was well provided with every luxury, that he left not the least hint of his covetousness or luxury. He demeaned himself so gallantly in that great war, that he did many noble acts without the general's assistance and the general did nothing without him."

4184. Mithridates had ordered his guards to keep Lucullus out and give notice by fires in case any unusual thing should happen. Phoenix, who was a member of the royal blood, was in charge of the guards. According to agreement, he warned of Lucullus' approach, but then he and all his forces defected to Lucullus. Due to this action, the mountains could be crossed safely and Lucullus marched down to Cabira. {*Appian, Mithridatic Wars, l. 12. c. 12. (79) 2:387,389}

4185. After Mithridates crossed the Lycus River, he came into a wide plain, where he tried to provoke the Romans to battle. {*Plutarch, Lucullus, l. 1. c. 15. s. 1,2. 2:515} He sent Diophantus and Taxiles against them. At first, their armies only tested each other's strength in daily skirmishes. {Memnon, c. 45.} Later, their cavalries fought and the Romans fled. Lucullus was forced to retreat to the mountains. In this battle, Pompeius, or Pomponius, who was the general of the cavalry, was taken prisoner and brought to Mithridates in a seriously wounded state. When Mithridates asked him whether, if he allowed him to live, he would be his friend in the future, he replied:

> "Truly I shall, if you will conclude a peace with the people of Rome, but if not, I shall remain your enemy."

4186. After this reply, the barbarians would have killed him, but the king would not allow them to do so. [K194] He said that he would not allow any cruelty to a valiant man, merely because of misfortune. {*Appian, Mithridatic Wars, l. 12. c. 12. (79) 2:389} {*Plutarch, Lucullus, l. 1. c. 15. s. 1,2. 2:515}

4187. After this, Mithridates drew his forces into battle array and stood in that posture for many days. Since Lucullus would not come down to fight, he looked for a way to march up to him. {*Appian, Mithridatic Wars, l. 12. c. 12. (79) 2:389}

4188. In the meantime, Olcaba, or Olthacus, the Scythian, who had saved many Romans in the last battle of the cavalry, had been admitted into Lucullus' inner circle at meal time and knew their counsels and secrets. With his usual short dagger by his side, he came to Lucullus as he was sleeping at noon in his tent. He said he had some matter of great importance to tell Lucullus, but Menedemus, Lucullus' chamberlain, refused to let him in. Olcaba, fearing that he might be questioned, stole away from the camp and rode on horseback to Mithridates. {*Appian, Mithridatic Wars, l. 12. c. 12. (79) 2:389,391} {*Plutarch, Lucullus, l. 1. c. 16. 2:519,521} He revealed to the king that another Scythian, named Sobadacus, intended to run away to Lucullus, and so he was immediately seized. {*Appian, Mithridatic Wars, l. 12. c. 12. (79) 2:391}

4189. Lucullus was afraid to come down to the plain, because the enemy cavalry was too strong. However, he was at a loss as to how to pass through the mountainous region, which was a long trek, covered in woods and quite dangerous. By chance, he came upon some Greeks who had hidden themselves in a certain cave around there. The oldest of them was Artemidorus who, as Appian said, was a hunter and knew the mountains well. He guided Lucullus and his army to a place where he could safely camp and which also had a citadel overlooking Cabira. Lucullus used this guide, kindled fires in the camp and marched away. He went through the woods by an unused path without any difficulty and finally arrived at that citadel. At daybreak, he was seen pitching his tents above the enemy. He chose his place in such a way that, if he wanted to fight, he could, and if not, he could not be forced into a battle. He still avoided the plains for fear of the enemy's cavalry and camped where there was plenty of water. {*Appian, Mithridatic Wars, l. 12. c. 12. (80) 2:391} {*Plutarch, Lucullus, l. 1. c. 15. s. 3,4. 2:515,517}

4190. Neither army thought of fighting at present. It was reported that as the king's party was chasing a deer, the Romans came that way and stopped their chase. A skirmish began and more came flocking in from both sides. Finally, the Romans fled. Lucullus came down alone to the plain and ran up to the forest from where the Romans came running. He ordered them to stop and march back again with him against the enemies. The soldiers submitted to their general and the others stopped fleeing also. The Romans rallied together and easily made the enemy flee, pursuing them to their very camp. When

Lucullus returned from pursuing the enemy, he publicly disgraced those who had run away. *[E553]* He took away their weapons and ordered them to dig a twelve foot trench, while all the other soldiers stood by and looked on. {*Plutarch, Lucullus, l. 1. c. 15. s. 5-7. 2:517,519}

4191. When Lucullus ran short of food, he sent a party into Cappadocia to forage. He often skirmished with the enemy, until at one time the king's troops began to flee. Mithridates ran from the camp and deriding them for fleeing, forced them back again. That put such a dread into the Romans, that they ran back to the mountains without stopping. Although the king's troops abandoned the chase, the Romans were so terrified, that they still kept running, thinking the enemy was at their heels. Mithridates sent messengers to every place to tell of his victory. {*Appian, Mithridatic Wars, l. 12. c. 12. (80) 2:391}

4192. Sornatius, with ten cohorts of foot soldiers, was sent by Lucullus to get provisions. He saw Menander, one of Mithridates' commanders, and followed after him. *[K195]* He stopped until Mithridates' men came to him. Then he fought with them and killed many, putting the rest to flight. {*Plutarch, Lucullus, l. 1. c. 17. s. 1. 2:521}

4193. After this, Lucullus again sent Adrian with some forces into Cappadocia to supply the army with food. Taxiles and Diophantus, Mithridates' generals, sent Menemachus and Myron against him with four thousand foot soldiers and two thousand cavalry. They hoped to ambush the Roman wagons as they returned to Lucullus. {Memnon, c. 45.} {Phlegon, Chronicles, Year 1. Olympiad 177.} {*Plutarch, Lucullus, l. 1. c. 17. s. 1. 2:521} Since Cappadocia was the only place where Lucullus could expect to get supplies, Mithridates hoped to subject him to the same kind of distress that he had been subjected to at the siege of Cyzicum. {*Appian, Mithridatic Wars, l. 12. c. 12. (81) 2:393}

4194. The king's party chanced to attack a party of the foragers in some narrow passes. Because they did not wait until they came to a more open place, the cavalry could not help them, whereupon the Romans drew themselves up into battle array as fast as they could. The roughness of the places helped them. They attacked the king's troops, killing some of them and forcing others down the rocky precipices, while the rest fled away. {*Appian, Mithridatic Wars, l. 12. c. 12. (81) 2:393} After having received some troops from Lucullus, the Romans pursued the king's troops to the very camp of Diophantus and Taxiles. In a fierce battle, the Pontics stood their ground for a while, but as soon as their commanders began to give ground, the whole army retreated. The commanders were the first to tell Mithridates of this defeat. {Memnon, c. 45.} Plutarch said that all the cavalry and foot soldiers who had come with Menemachus and

Myron were killed, with the exception of only two. {*Plutarch, Lucullus, l. 1. c. 17. s. 2. 2:521} Eutropius wrote that thirty thousand of the king's best soldiers were routed by five thousand of the Romans. {Eutropius, l. 6.} Livy stated that Lucullus fought against Mithridates in Pontus with very good success and killed more than sixty thousand of the enemy. {*Livy, l. 97. 14:121} In this figure he was including those who were killed a little later, when Mithridates was forced to flee.

4195. Mithridates heard this news before Lucullus did. {*Appian, Mithridatic Wars, l. 12. c. 12. (81) 2:393} Adrian had marched by Mithridates' camp in great pomp and brought a large number of wagons along with him, laden with provisions and spoil. This sight depressed Mithridates, and his soldiers began to fear and tremble. {*Plutarch, Lucullus, l. 1. c. 17. s. 2,3. 2:521} However, the king was sure Lucullus would suddenly attack him, now that he had lost his cavalry. He started to fear and thought of fleeing. In his pavilion, he told his friends of the trouble they were in. They did not wait until the trumpet sounded before gathering up their baggage, and so they had moved all their goods from the camp before daybreak. They made up such a large company, that the beasts of burden began to crowd one another. No sooner was this noticed by the army, who knew the drivers of the beasts of burden, than they feared the worst. They had not been notified and quite upset, they violently stampeded, destroying their own fortifications. {*Appian, Mithridatic Wars, l. 12. c. 12. (81) 2:393} They mobbed the gates and rifled the packs. They attacked those who were carrying them away and killed them all. Dorylaus, the general, was killed. He only had a purple garment on his back and was killed for that very garment. Hermaeus, the priest, was trampled to death in the gates. {*Plutarch, Lucullus, l. 1. c. 17. s. 3. 2:521,523}

4196. The soldiers ran away over the fields in disorder and everyone cared only about himself, not waiting for orders from their generals and commanders. As soon as the king realised the disorder and speed with which they were fleeing, he ran out of his pavilion, hoping to say something to them. *[K196]* Nobody would listen, but the mob pressed so hard on him that he fell down in the crowd. {*Appian, Mithridatic Wars, l. 12. c. 12. (81) 2:393,395} Memnon wrote that he stayed at Cabira for some time and later made his escape. {Memnon, c. 46.} *[E554]* Appian stated that he soon left on horseback and fled away to the mountains, accompanied by only a small retinue. Plutarch stated that Mithridates had not lost a soldier and abandoned the camp with the rest of the throng. Nor had anyone in the king's party prepared a horse for him. Finally, though late in the proceedings, Ptolemy, the eunuch, who had a horse, saw Mithridates tossed to and fro in the disorder. He leaped off his horse and offered it to the king. {*Plutarch, Lucullus, l. 1. c. 17. s. 4. 2:523}

4197. When Lucullus heard of the victory of his foragers and saw the flight of their enemy, he sent a good brigade of cavalry to pursue them in their flight. With his legions, he surrounded those who had remained in the camp and had put themselves in a defensive position. He told his troops not to pillage the enemy camp until such time as they had killed as many of them as possible. However, when the soldiers saw the gold and silver vessels and the rich garments, they ignored the general's prohibition. {*Appian, Mithridatic Wars, l. 12. c. 12. (82) 2:395} The king had been overtaken by a company of Galatians, who had caught up with him in the chase. They would not have recognised him, had it not been for one of his mules which carried the king's treasure. It had been placed between the king and his pursuers, either of its own accord or by the king's plan, to slow them down. For while they were busy in gathering up the gold and quarrelling among themselves about the spoil, the king escaped. {Memnon, c. 46.} {*Appian, Mithridatic Wars, l. 12. c. 12. (82) 2:395} {*Plutarch, Lucullus, l. 1. c. 17. s. 5,6. 2:523} When they had taken Callistratus, the king's secretary, Lucullus ordered that he be brought to the camp. Those who escorted him, found he had five hundred pieces of gold in the belt he wore, so they killed him along the way and took the money. {*Plutarch, Lucullus, l. 1. c. 17. s. 7.'2:523,525} Cicero wrote this of the escape of Mithridates from Pontus:

> "Mithridates fled away and left a very large store of gold and silver and other precious things behind in Pontus. Some of this he had received from his ancestors and some he had taken in his first war in Asia and added it to his other treasures. While our men were too busy in gathering up all they found, the king escaped."

4198. Lucullus came as far as Talaura in pursuing Mithridates. This was now the fourth day, and as Mithridates had a head start, he escaped into Armenia to Tigranes. {*Plutarch, Lucullus, l. 1. c. 19. s. 1. 2:527} (He did not go to Iberia, as Josephus incorrectly stated. {*Josephus, Antiq., l. 13. c. 16. s. 4. (421) 7:439}) Lucullus marched back again and gave the soldiers the plunder of the king's camp. {*Plutarch, Lucullus, l. 1. c. 17. s. 7. 2:525} He sent Marcus Pompey as commander-in-chief against Mithridates while he, with all his forces, moved to Cabira. {Memnon, c. 47.} Mithridates, in a letter to Arsaces, reported the matter in this way: {*Sallust, Letter of Mithridates, l. 1. (15) 1:439}

> "After I recruited my army at Cabira and had many battles between myself and Lucullus, both of us were short of food. He was supplied from Ariobarzanes'

kingdom of Cappadocia, which had not been touched by the war. Since all regions around me were wasted and destroyed, I withdrew into Armenia."

4199. Mithridates went safely to Comana and from there hurried away to Tigranes with two thousand cavalry. {*Appian, Mithridatic Wars, l. 12. c. 12. (82) 2:395} He could not, by any means, get his son-in-law to help him, for Tigranes had disowned him, because he had lost so great a kingdom. Tigranes would not help him in his fight, nor acknowledge him as his kinsman. However, Mithridates procured from him a grant for the protection of his person and was assigned a princely table in some of his citadels, nor did he lack any such obligations of hospitality. {Memnon, c. 48.} {*Appian, Mithridatic Wars, l. 12. c. 12. (82) 2:395} [K197] However, Plutarch wrote that Tigranes dismissed him with a great deal of contempt and scorn. Mithridates was cooped up in some remote corner of the kingdom in the swampy and unhealthy regions. {*Plutarch, Lucullus, l. 1. c. 22. s. 1. 2:539}

4200. When Mithridates was fleeing, he sent Bacchus, or Bacchides, one of his eunuchs, to kill his sisters, wives and concubines, who were kept at Pharnacia, in any way he could. {Memnon, c. 46.} {*Appian, Mithridatic Wars, l. 12. c. 12. (82) 2:395} {*Plutarch, Lucullus, l. 1. c. 18. s. 2. 2:525}

4201. Among these were two of the king's sisters, Roxane and Statira, who had lived as virgins for almost forty years. There were also two of his Ionian wives: Berenice, a Chian, and Monima, a Milesian. Bacchides came to them and told them that they must die, but that they should have the freedom to choose what type of death they thought would be the easiest and most painless. Monima took the diadem from off her head, made it fit her neck and hung herself by it. But when it broke, she said:

> "Oh you cursed band, will you not serve for this use?"

4202. Then she kicked it about and spat on it, and exposed her throat to Bacchides. [E555] Berenice took a cup of poison and gave part of it to her mother, who was also present and asked for it. So they both drank it together. The poison worked on the weaker body, but it did not kill Berenice, since she had not taken her full dose. Therefore, when Bacchides saw her in pain taking a long time to die, he strangled her. It is also reported of these two virgin sisters that Roxane drank her poison after many a curse and reproach against her brother. However, Statira spoke nothing bitter or unworthy of him, instead praising him highly, in that, when his own life was in danger, he should think of them and make provision for them to die as free women and not be raped. {*Plutarch, Lucullus, l. 1. c. 18. s. 2-6. 2:525,527}

*4203.* When Lucullus besieged Cabira, the barbarians surrendered conditionally. He made peace with them and took over their strongholds. {*Memnon, c. 47.*} After the surrender of Cabira and many other cities, he found rich treasures and prisons in which many Greeks, as well as many of the king's friends, were locked up. They had long considered themselves to be dead men and were now released to new life by Lucullus' favour. Among all these, they found Nyssa, Mithridates' sister, and freed her. {*Plutarch, Lucullus, l. 1. c. 18. s. 1,2. 2:525*}

*4204.* Most of the governors of Mithridates' garrisons defected to Lucullus. {*Appian, Mithridatic Wars, l. 12. c. 12. (82) 2:395*} Among these was Moaphernes, Strabo's mother's uncle on her father's side, who had been the governor of Colchis under Mithridates. {*Strabo, l. 11. c. 2. s. 18. 5:213*} He defected, because Mithridates had recently killed his first cousin Tibius and his son Theophilus. By this action, Moaphernes was instrumental in the defection of fifteen other garrisons from Mithridates to Lucullus. {*Strabo, l. 12. c. 3. s. 33. 5:435*} So Pontus was wide open to the Roman legions, when previously it had been blocked on all sides, preventing the Romans from entering it. {*Cicero, Pro Lege Manilia, l. 1. c. 8. (21) 9:33*} {*Cicero, Pro Archia Poeta, l. 1. c. 9. (21) 11:29*}

*4205.* When the Romans had finished their work with Mithridates, they attacked the Cretians, simply because they were ambitious to subdue that noble island. As a reason for the attack, they gave the fact that the Cretians had favoured Mithridates and had let him have mercenaries for his army against the Romans. Mithridates had entered into an alliance with the pirates, whom Marcus Antonius was chasing at the time. The Cretians had offended Antonius when he had been an envoy and had given him two arrogant replies. *[K198]* As a result of that, Antonius soon confidently invaded the island, so sure of victory that he carried more chains than arms in his ships. But the Cretians intercepted many of his ships and bound any prisoners they took with sails and ropes, then hung them up and in this manner, hoisted sail and returned back triumphantly to their harbours. Antonius became sick and died, thus ending the war which he had begun with little success. In spite of this, he obtained the surname of *Creticus.* {*Livy, l. 97. 14:121*} {*Florus, l. 1. c. 42. 1:195*} {*Asconius Pedianus, Against Verres*} {*Appian, Sicily and the Other Islands, l. 5. c. 6. (1) 1:135*}

*4206.* Antiochus Asiaticus, the son of Antiochus Pius, had stayed at Rome with his brother for almost two whole years without as yet having received a promise from the Senate of the things he had demanded concerning the kingdom of Egypt. On his return home, he journeyed through Sicily and came to Syracuse, where he stayed in the house of Quintus Minucius Rufus. He had brought along with him to Rome a very elaborate lampstand covered with bright gems, with the intention of bestowing it in the Capitol. Since the temple there was not yet completed, he was carrying it back with him again into Syria. He intended to send it back to the Capitol by his envoys, together with some other presents, at the time of the dedication of Jupiter's image, which was carried out in the following year by Quintus Catulus. Verres, the governor of Sicily, cheated him of this lampstand, of many other cups of gold inlaid with gems and of another cup for wine which was cut from one large gem. When he demanded them back, Verres ordered him to leave the province before nightfall and told him that he had received news that the pirates were coming from his kingdom into Sicily. {*Cicero, Against Verres II, l. 4. c. 27-29. 8:357-361*} {*Cicero, Against Verres II, l. 4. c. 31. 8:367*}

*4207.* After frequent massacres in Judea by the Pharisees, the old friends of Alexander Jannaeus went to Queen Alexandra and told her what was happening. Their leader was Alexandra's younger son, Aristobulus. *[E556]* They made their addresses to the court and asked the queen if either they might all be killed there, or that they might be dispersed into various citadels, where they could spend the rest of their lives, safe from their enemies' treacheries. As a result of this, and for want of better counsel at the time, she entrusted the command of all the citadels to them, with the exception of Hyrcania, Alexandrion and Machaerus, where she had stored her best treasures. {*Josephus, Antiq., l. 13. c. 16. s. 2,3. (408-417) 7:433-437*}

*4208.* Cotta was still besieging Heraclea and had not yet made an assault against it with his whole army. He had only brought a few of his Romans up against the town and had placed the Bithynians in the front lines. When he saw how many of them were wounded or dead, he resorted to his engines. None terrified the besieged as much as the one which they called their *turtle* (Latin word was *testudo*). This was an engine enclosed with boards and raw hides, under the shelter of which they could safely scale the walls. Thereupon, Cotta brought up all his troops from the camp and led them up against a tower in which they were very hopeful of making a breach. This tower had so far endured one or two batteries, without sustaining any damage at all. Contrary to all their expectations, the ram broke off from the engine. While the Heracleans were encouraged, Cotta began to despair of ever taking the town. When, on the next day, they used their engine again, but with little result, Cotta burned the engine and cut off the head of the carpenter who had made it. Leaving an adequate guard at the walls of the city, he camped with the rest of his army in the plain of Lycia, which had plenty of provisions. He thereby reduced the city to dire need, since all the country around Heraclea was utterly destroyed. *[K199]* So they at once sent an embassy to the Sevthians, who were the inhabitants of the Chersonesus, to the Theodosians and to the princes around the Bosphorus. Heraclea wanted to make a league, to which they agreed. {*Memnon, c. 51.*}

4209. While the enemies attacked the city from without, the Heracleans were almost as badly plagued by disputes among themselves within the town. Mithridates' garrison was not content to eat what the townsmen lived on. They scourged the citizens and made them provide things which at the time were quite scarce. Conacorix, the governor, was worse than his soldiers, because he did not restrain their insolence, but freely permitted them to do what they wanted. {*Memnon, c. 51.*}

### 3934a AM, 4643 JP, 71 BC

4210. Lucullus subdued the Chaldeans and the Tibareni. {*Plutarch, Lucullus, l. 1. c. 19. s. 1. 2:527*} He captured Lesser Armenia, which Mithridates had previously controlled. {*Plutarch, Lucullus, l. 1. c. 19. s. 1. 2:527*} {*Eutropius, l. 6.*} After he had gone over all Pontus and subdued the province, he approached its coastal cities with his fleet. {*Appian, Mithridatic Wars, l. 12. c. 12. (82) 2:395*}

4211. Amisus was still under siege. Callimachus, the governor, had worn out the Romans with his engine devices and his plots. {*Plutarch, Lucullus, l. 1. c. 19. s. 1,2. 2:527,529*} Lucullus came to besiege them and exhorted them to surrender. When he realised that they would not, he moved the siege to Eupatoria and acted as if he had been very careless in the attack. Those who kept the garrison of Eupatoria also became careless and persisted in their false sense of security, whereupon Lucullus commanded his soldiers quickly to scale the walls. Therefore, Eupatoria was taken and immediately pulled down to the ground. {*Memnon, c. 47.*}

### 3934b AM, 4644 JP, 70 BC

4212. Not long after this, Amisus, which (as Plutarch confirmed from Sallust) had held out for another winter's siege, was taken. For at the very hour of the day in which Callimachus usually withdrew his soldiers to allow them to refresh themselves, Lucullus scaled the walls with his ladders. {*Memnon, c. 47.*} {*Plutarch, Lucullus, l. 1. c. 19. s. 2,3. 2:529*} When a small section of the wall had been taken by the enemy, Callimachus burned the city, either out of envy that the Romans should have so large a booty, or else contriving to escape by this means. For nobody prevented any who wanted to from sailing away. As soon as the flames caught hold on the walls, the soldiers immediately started plundering. Out of pity for the burning city, Lucullus tried to stop the fire from outside the walls and ordered his soldiers to help quench

it. They disregarded him, only shouting and rattling their armour. So Lucullus was forced to give the plunder to the soldiers, in an effort to save the city from being burned to the ground. However, the soldiers did the exact opposite, for when the fire was almost everywhere, they themselves set fire to some houses. While the city was being taken, the fire was put out by a storm that occurred miraculously. Lucullus repaired many places before he left. {*Plutarch, Lucullus, l. 1. c. 19. s. 3-6. 2:529,531*} He prevented his soldiers from any further slaughter of the citizens and gave both the city and the surrounding country to those who survived. {*Memnon, c. 47.*}

4213. Tyrannio, the grammarian, was also taken prisoner at this time. Lucullus did not want to make him a slave, so he gave him to Murena, who freed him. *[E557]* Tyrannio was a citizen of Amisus by birth and Strabo was one of his students. {*Strabo, l. 12. c. 3. s. 16. 5:399*} {*Plutarch, Lucullus, l. 1. c. 19. s. 7. 2:531*} *[K200]*

4214. Selene, the queen, asked the Syrians to help drive out Tigranes. She was also known as Cleopatra, and after the death of her husband Antiochus Pius, reigned jointly with her sons in that part of Syria which had not been captured by Tigranes, the king of Armenia. She had some cities of Phoenicia defect from him, as a result of which, Tigranes entered Syria with a vast army to quell the rebellion. {*Josephus, Antiq., l. 13. c. 16. s. 4. (419-421) 7:439*} {*Plutarch, Lucullus, l. 1. c. 21. s. 1,2. 2:535*} It is likely that it was in this expedition that Tigranes recovered those seventy valleys of Armenia which were naturally fortified with hills and mountains. When Tigranes had been a Parthian hostage, he had given this to the Parthians as a gift. He now wasted the countries of the Parthians around Ninus and Arbela. {*Strabo, l. 11. c. 14. s. 15. 5:339*} This was undoubtedly that recent war of Tigranes against the Parthians which is mentioned by Mithridates in his letter to Arsaces in the next year. {*Sallust, Letter of Mithridates, l. 1. (3) 1:433*} Dio stated that a certain disputed country was taken from the Parthians. {*Dio, l. 36. (1) 3:5 (Xiphilinus)*}

4215. In the ninth year of Alexandria, queen of the Jews, Joseph was born to Matthias Curtus, the priest's son. Joseph was the grandfather of Josephus, the historian. {*Josephus, Life, l. 1. c. 1. (4,5) 1:5*}

4216. Alexandra sent her son Aristobulus to Damascus with an army, against Ptolemy Mennaeus, who had been a very troublesome neighbour to that city. Alexander marched back again without any results. {*Josephus, Antiq., l. 13. c. 16. s. 3. (116) 7:437,439*}

4217. About this same time, it was rumoured that Tigranes had entered Syria with an army of half a million men and that he would suddenly come into Judea. (Some copies of Josephus read three hundred thousand. Editor.) This news so terrified the queen and the Jews, that they dispatched envoys to him with rich presents as he was besieging Ptolemais, which he captured soon after. When the envoys found him there, they told him the queen and the Jews would deal honestly and fairly with him. He commended them for coming on so long a journey to to pay him homage, and wished them all well. {*Josephus, Antiq., l. 13. c. 16. s. 4. (419,420) 7:439} Appian wrote that Tigranes overran all the countries of the Syrians west of the Euphrates River, as far as Egypt. {*Appian, Syrian Wars, l. 11. c. 8. (48) 2:197} Plutarch stated that he captured Palestine. {*Plutarch, Lucullus, l. 1. c. 21. s. 1,2. 2:535} However, Eutropius stated that he did not march toward Egypt beyond Phoenicia and that Tigranes was master of only part of Phoenicia. {Eutropius, l. 6.}

4218. Lucullus sent his wife's brother, Appius Claudius, as an envoy to Tigranes, to demand that he hand over Mithridates. {Memnon, c. 48.} {*Plutarch, Lucullus, l. 1. c. 21. s. 1. 2:535} The king's captain brought Claudius through the upper countries by a circuitous and roundabout way. Finally one of his own freemen, a Syrian, showed him the right way. Using him as their guide, they reached the Euphrates River in five days and came to Antioch, which was called Epidaphne. He had been ordered to wait there for Tigranes, who had gone to subdue some other cities of Phoenicia that were not yet under his power. He caused many of the princes in those parts, who did not heartily obey the Armenians, to side with the Romans. Zarbienus, king of the Gordians, was one of them. {*Plutarch, Lucullus, l. 1. c. 21. s. 1,2. 2:535}

4219. Appius promised Lucullus' help to many other cities under Tigranes' control, that had secretly sent envoys to him, ordering them not to rebel at the present time. The Armenians were treating the Greeks very badly. [K201] The king was worse than the rest and grew more arrogant and conceited with his success. He thought that whatever mortal men admire and long to have for themselves, was there for him and specifically created for him. Many kings waited upon him as his servants. He had four in his retinue as his attendants and guards who, on their errands, ran on foot at his horse's side. When he sat on his throne and answered any questions the countries had asked of him, these men stood with their arms crossed. This posture, more than any other, was a sign of their submission to him. {*Plutarch, Lucullus, l. 1. c. 21. s. 3-5. 2:535,537}

4220. Lucius Metellus was appointed to succeed Verres as the governor of Sicily. {Asconius Pedianus, In Divination} Metellus set out against the pirates in Sicily (not Cilicia, as is incorrectly written in Livy's Epitome) and was victorious.

{*Livy, l. 98. 14:121} {Orosius, l. 6. c. 3.} When the Sicilians impeached Verres for extortion, Cicero was appointed to represent them. Cicero had to argue against Hortensius, who was the consul elect. {*Cicero, Brutus, l. 1. c. 92. 5:277} In this, Quintus Cecilius Niger tried his best to prosecute the impeachment of Verres in Cicero's stead. Quintus Cecilius Niger was Verres' quaestor on that island. [E558] He was a Sicilian by descent (as Pedianus noted {Asconius Pedianus, Against Cecilius}), and a freeman and a Jew by religion. Plutarch, writing in the life of Cicero, related the jest which Cicero made about Cecilius, who was suspected of Jewish practices. It was based on a play on the word Verres, which means castrated pig in Latin. {*Plutarch, Cicero, l. 1. c. 7. s. 4,5. 7:99}

"What has a Jew got to do with a pig?"

4221. This passage of Cicero stated the condition of things at that time: {*Cicero, Against Verres II, l. 2. c. 31. 7:377}

"Notwithstanding all this, let him come if he please, let him engage with the Cretians in a battle, let him free the Byzantines, let him call Ptolemy king, let him speak and think whatever Hortensius would have him do."

4222. This agreed with another passage in a letter which Mithridates wrote the next year to Arsaces: {*Sallust, Letter of Mithridates, l. 1. (12,13) 1:437}

"The Cretians were at that time the only people who retained their freedom and their king Ptolemy. A little later, Ptolemy avoided hostilities from day to day by the payment of money, while the Cretians have already been attacked once, and will find no respite from war until they are defeated."

4223. By comparing the two passages, we may gather that the Romans used to their own advantage the right that Antiochus Asiaticus claimed to the kingdom of Egypt. They deemed it convenient that Ptolemy Alexander should be called king, as long as he would purchase the quiet possession of that kingdom by paying a constant tribute. Also, the Romans were fully resolved to start anew the first war with Crete, which had ended in the death of Marcus Antonius. This all happened in the following year, as we shall see.

4224. Lucullus marched into Asia, which was still in arrears of the fine imposed by Sulla, and imposed a twenty-five per cent tax on the crops. There was already a tax on slaves and house property. {*Appian, Mithridatic Wars, l. 12. c. 12. (83) 2:399} The tax collectors and money-lenders had made havock of the cities of Asia and had treated them very slavishly. They had been compelled to sell their sons and their daughters into slavery and sell their ornaments, pictures and images. In the end, they themselves became slaves to their creditors.

4225. Lucullus took such action with these pestilent fellows that, within four years, all obligations were satisfied and the possessions were restored free to their owners, to inherit. The public debt, which Sulla had imposed upon Asia, was twenty thousand talents. The creditors were allowed only double this sum, which, together with the interest they charged, had amounted to a hundred and twenty thousand talents. [K202] The creditors, considering this to be too hard a measure, slandered Lucullus at Rome and set the most influential Romans against him. However, Lucullus was very well-liked by those countries to which he had rendered these good services. He had inspired great affection for himself in all the other provinces, as they considered those people to be very fortunate, whose lot it was to have such a good governor over them. {*Plutarch, Lucullus, l. 1. c. 20. 2:533,535}

4226. After Lucullus had fully settled Asia with many excellent laws and a universal peace, he relaxed and enjoyed himself. He lived at Ephesus and delighted the cities with processions, triumphal festivals, athletic contests and gladiators. The cities held the holiday of the Lucullian Games to honour him. He was not as touched by this as by the affection they bore him. {*Plutarch, Lucullus, l. 1. c. 23. s. 1. 2:543}

4227. Tigranes killed Selene, surnamed Cleopatra, after having kept her securely as a prisoner in the citadel at Seleucia. {*Strabo, l. 16. c. 2. s. 3. 7:241} Antiochus Asiaticus, who had held some hopes of recovering the kingdom of Egypt by right of his mother, was dispossessed of the part of Syria which she had held.

4228. As soon as Tigranes returned to Antioch, Appius, the envoy, declared publicly that he had come to take Mithridates, as belonging to Lucullus' triumph. If Tigranes refused to surrender him, Appius was to proclaim war against Tigranes. Tigranes was somewhat troubled by the envoy's outspoken behaviour, but held his peace to see what else he would say. In almost twenty-five years, he had not heard anyone speak freely to him, until now. It was for so many years he had reigned and shown his wanton tyranny. {*Plutarch, Lucullus, l. 1. c. 21. s. 6. 2:537,539} He answered Appius that he knew very well that Mithridates was a very wicked man, but that he had to respect the alliance between them. All the world might well cry out against him, if he should surrender his wife's father into the hands of his enemies. He was therefore resolved not to desert Mithridates and if the Romans started a war, he could put up a good fight. He was very offended at Lucullus, because in his letter he had only greeted him as King and not as King of Kings.

To get even, therefore, he did not, when writing back, address Lucullus by the title of Imperator. Appius returned quickly to the general. Of the many presents the king had offered him, he had accepted only one bowl made of gold, fearful of offending the king if he were to refuse all the presents. {*Plutarch, Lucullus, l. 1. c. 21. s. 7. 2:539} {Memnon, c. 48.} [E559]

4229. When Tigranes learned that Zarbienus, the king of the Gordians, had secretly allied himself with Lucullus, he killed him along with his wife and children. {*Plutarch, Lucullus, l. 1. c. 29. s. 6. 2:569}

4230. As soon as Appius had returned and the war with Tigranes had been planned, Lucullus paid his holy vows to his gods at Ephesus, as if the victory had already been won. He marched back into Pontus again and camped before Sinope, or rather, besieged the king's party of Cilicians who were garrisoned there. {*Plutarch, Lucullus, l. 1. c. 23. s. 2. 2:543} {*Appian, Mithridatic Wars, l. 12. c. 12. (84) 2:399} Just as the city was being assaulted from outside the walls by the Romans, it was being assaulted within the walls by the commander whom Mithridates had appointed to keep the town. This commander was called Cleochares, according to Orosius, or Bacchides, according to Strabo. He feared treachery among the citizens and so committed various massacres among the people. Hence, the citizens neither had heart courageously to resist the enemy, nor were they in a position to surrender conditionally. {*Strabo, l. 12. c. 3. s. 11. 5:391}

4231. Memnon described what happened as follows. The king had entrusted the defence of the city to Leonippus and Cleochares. Leonippus saw that things were hopeless and sent to Lucullus about surrendering the city. [K203] However, the plot was discovered by Cleochares and Seleucus, the chief pirate, who was Mithridates' envoy and had equal authority with the others. They called a council and accused Leonippus. The citizens paid no attention to the accusation, since they had a very high opinion of the man's integrity. As a result of this, Cleochares' faction was afraid of Leonippus' following among the common people and treacherously killed him at night. Although the common people were deeply disturbed by this, Cleochares and his party prevailed nonetheless and did what they pleased. They thought that by acting so high-handedly, they could avoid being called to account for the murder of Leonippus. {Memnon, c. 55.}

4232. Meanwhile, Censorinus, the admiral of the Roman fleet, set sail with fifteen galleys of three tiers of oars, loaded with provisions. They sailed from Bosphorus for the Roman camp and arrived near Sinope. Cleochares' and Seleucus' Sinopian ships, under the command of

Seleucus, put to sea and fought with Censorinus. The Italians were defeated and their ships with their provisions were taken away as a prize. Cleochares and his colleague were elated with this success and behaved more tyrannically than before. They summoned the townsmen to execution without any legal processes and cruelly abused them in other ways. It happened that Cleochares and Seleucus fell out with each other. Cleochares deemed it best to continue the war, but Seleucus wanted to kill all the Sinopians and surrender the city to the Romans for a good gratuity. Since they could not agree on this matter, they put everything they had into ships and sent them away to Machares, Mithridates' son, who was at that time living at Colchis. {*Memnon, c. 55.}

4233. About that time, Lucullus drew closer to the city and made a most intense attack on it. Machares, Mithridates' son, sent an embassy to Lucullus, requesting a league of friendship between them. The petition was courteously received and he was told that there should be a firm league between them, provided that they send no more supplies to the Sinopians. Machares kept to this agreement, ordering that whatever was intended for the relief of Mithridates' party, be sent to Lucullus. {*Memnon, c. 56.} Machares, the king of Bosphorus, gave Lucullus a crown valued at a thousand pieces of gold and was admitted as an ally and confederate of the Romans. {*Livy, l. 98. 14:121} {*Plutarch, Lucullus, l. 1. c. 24. s. 1. 2:545} {*Appian, Mithridatic Wars, l. 12. c. 12. (83) 2:397,399}

4234. Cleochares and Seleucus saw how things were going and realised they were in a desperate situation. So they massacred many of the citizens and carried an abundance of wealth to their ships. They let their soldiers plunder the town, before burning it. After this, they burned their larger ships and with the smaller ones sailed away by night to the inner parts of Pontus, where they settled near the Sanegians and the Lazians. When Lucullus saw the fire, he guessed what had happened and ordered his soldiers to scale the walls. As soon as he entered the town, he killed eight thousand of the king's party who had been left behind. He had great pity on the rest and hurried to put out the fires, after which he restored the citizens' goods. Thus, by the hands of friends and foes, this unfortunate city was ruined by those who had come to defend it, and preserved by those who had come to ruin it. {*Memnon, c. 56.} {*Orosius, l. 6. c. 3.} {*Plutarch, Lucullus, l. 1. c. 23. s. 2,3. 2:543} {*Appian, Mithridatic Wars, l. 12. c. 12. (83) 2:395,397}

4235. The reason why Lucullus took such care in preserving Sinope and later enfranchising it, was this. It was rumoured to be because of some admonition that he received in a dream. [E560] For in his sleep, someone appeared at his bedside and spoke these words: [K204]

"Go a little forward, Lucullus, for Autolychus is coming to meet you."

4236. When he awoke, he could not possibly imagine what this meant. On the same day that he took the city, and as he was pursuing the Cilicians, who fled away by ship, he came across a statue lying by the sea shore. The Cilicians had intended to make it their companion in their escape and for that reason had wrapped it up in clothes and bound it up with cords, but had not had enough time to get it onto the ship. When the Romans unwrapped it, Lucullus saw that it looked like the one who had appeared to him in a dream the previous night. Later, he learned that it was the statue of Autolychus, who was the founder of the city of Sinope. When he heard this, he remembered the warning of Sulla, who wrote in his commentaries that nothing is to be esteemed as so sure and certain as what is shown in dreams. {*Plutarch, Lucullus, l. 1. c. 23. s. 2-6. 2:543,545} {*Appian, Mithridatic Wars, l. 12. c. 12. (83) 2:397} This statue of Autolychus had been made by Sthenis. Lucullus took both it and Billarus' sphere with him, but left all other ornaments of the city behind. {*Strabo, l. 12. c. 3. s. 11. 5:391}

4237. After he was finished at Sinope, he restored Amisus to its inhabitants who had fled away in ships. He gave them their freedom and granted the city the right to use their own laws. {*Appian, Mithridatic Wars, l. 12. c. 12. (83) 2:397} He repopulated cities for other Greeks, even for as many as asked that favour of him, and to each city he added fifteen miles of land. Moreover, he was kind to the Athenians who had escaped there to live in the time of Sulla, because of Aristion's tyranny. To those still living, he gave clothes and two hundred drachmas each and sent them back to their country. {*Plutarch, Lucullus, l. 1. c. 19. s. 4-7. 2:529,531}

4238. Amasea, the country of Strabo the geographer, was still holding out against the Romans, but yielded soon after. {Memnon, c. 56.}

4239. After Cotta had destroyed everything around Heraclea, he again attacked the walls. Since the soldiers lacked enthusiasm for this, he gave up on it. He sent for Triarius and ordered him quickly to blockade the way and intercept any supplies for the townsmen, that might come by sea. {Memnon, c. 51.}

4240. Triarius arrived with his twenty-three ships and twenty Rhodian ships, and with this fleet sailed to Pontus. When he notified Cotta of his arrival, Cotta drew up his army to the walls of the city while Triarius showed himself at sea. Consequently, the Heracleans, somewhat troubled at Triarius' sudden arrival with his fleet, put to sea with thirty ships. These were not as well-manned as they should have been, since all the other men were occupied in defending the city against the enemy's assaults. The Rhodians first attacked the Heraclean ships, as a result of which three Rhodian ships and five of the Heracleans' ships were sunk. After this, the Romans entered the battle and although soundly defeated in the battle, did more harm than they received from the enemy. At the end, they routed the Heracleans and forced them to retreat back to the city, with the loss of fourteen of their ships. The conquering fleet rode into the large port and Cotta withdrew his foot soldiers from storming the town. {Memnon, c. 52.}

4241. Each day, Triarius' men made their sallies from the port, to prevent supplies from reaching the besieged. There was such a shortage of food in the city that a bottle of grain was sold for eighty attics. To make matters worse, a pestilence broke out among them that may have been caused by the unhealthy air, or a poor diet. They did not all die in the same way, but appeared to be suffering from different diseases. [K205] Lamachus' pangs of death were more violent and wearying than any of the others. This disease raged most among the soldiers of the garrison, so that a third of the three thousand soldiers died. {Memnon, c. 52.}

## 3935a AM, 4644 JP, 70 BC

4242. Conacorix was now ready, because of the siege, to betray the city to the Romans. He bought his own safety at the expense of the Heracleans. Damopheles, a Heraclean, helped to execute the plot. He had been a great rival of Lamachus in everything and after Lamachus' death, he was appointed over the garrison. Conacorix did not trust Cotta, who was a devious man, but confided the matter to Triarius. Damopheles was also anxious to conclude the matter and arrived at a fair bargain for the surrender. When they thought they were safe, the conspirators went about their work. However, it happened that the conspirators' business became public knowledge, whereupon the citizens came together and called for the governor of the city, and then for Brithagoras, who was an eminent person of authority among his countrymen. [E561] They earnestly asked Conacorix to secure their safety from Triarius, as well. He was very much opposed to this, but very craftily led the Heracleans on for a while with his flattering words. {Memnon, c. 53.}

4243. Then, in the dead of the night, Conacorix put all his men aboard ships and left the town, which was the agreement he had made with Triarius, that they would march away quietly with all their baggage. Damopheles opened the gates and let in the Roman army with Triarius. Some of them came rushing in at the gate and others clambered up the walls. When the Heracleans saw that they had been betrayed, some of them surrendered,

but the rest were killed. They plundered their household goods and whatever things they had laid aside in hopes of saving them. Indeed, the enemy acted very cruelly against the citizens, for the Romans remembered the large losses they had received in the recent naval battle and what great trouble they had encountered in assaulting the town. In revenge, they did not spare those who had escaped to the consecrated places for sanctuary. They killed them near the altars and the temples, even though they begged for mercy. Their situation seemed so desperate, that many escaped over the walls and dispersed themselves about the country, while others were forced to flee to Cotta. {Memnon, c. 53.}

4244. Cotta was told by those who had fled to him that the city had been taken, many men had been killed and the town plundered. Upset by this news and with extreme indignation, he marched to the city as fast as he could. His army was also very deeply discontented because they had missed out on the glory of their valiant achievements and been cheated of all their plunder. So they attacked Triarius' men most fiercely and outdid one another in killing each other. When Triarius heard of the rebellion, he put an end to the battle by pacifying Cotta with good words and faithfully promising them an equal share of all the plunder they had taken in the town. {Memnon, c. 53.}

4245. Cotta was told that Conacorix had seized Teium and Amastus and at once sent Triarius to take their cities out of his hands again. Cotta stayed at Heraclea and took the prisoners, and any that surrendered themselves, into his custody. He went on to other matters, and all his administration was accomplished with great cruelty. He searched up and down in every corner for the wealth of the city and did not spare the consecrated things. He took down the statues and images, even the very good ones, and amassed a good number of them. [K206] He carried Hercules from the market place, ripping off his ornaments from the pyramid, as well as various other things from the temple and city that were every bit as rare and beautiful as these, and put them on his ships. For his farewell, he ordered his soldiers to bring fire and they burned the city in many places. So Heraclea was taken and subdued, after withstanding a two-year siege. {Memnon, c. 54.}

4246. Triarius arrived at the cities assigned to him by Cotta and recovered them when they surrendered conditionally. He allowed Conacorix, who had meant to conceal his betrayal of Heraclea by seizing these two cities, to sail away. {Memnon, c. 54.}

4247. After Cotta had finished matters, he turned over all his foot soldiers and cavalry to Lucullus, dismissed the auxiliaries he had with him from the various allies of the Romans and then sailed away with his fleet. It so happened that part of the fleet, which carried the spoils of Heraclea, was overloaded and sank not far from shore, while the other part was dashed against the sands by a contrary north wind and lost much of its cargo. {*Memnon, c. 54.}

4248. Lucullus left Sornatius behind with six thousand soldiers to control the province, while he took twelve thousand foot soldiers along with him and less than three thousand cavalry. (Appian stated it was two legions and five hundred cavalry.) He entered Cappadocia, where Ariobarzanes was his friend, and made forced marches to the Euphrates River, where Cappadocia bordered Armenia. {*Sallust, Letter of Mithridates, l. 1. (15) 1:439} {Nonius Marcellus, see word Naves Codicaria} {Memnon, c. 58.} {*Plutarch, Lucullus, l. 1. c. 24. s. 1-4. 2:545,547} {*Appian, Mithridatic Wars, l. 12. c. 12. (84) 2:399}

4249. At that time during the winter, the Euphrates River was swollen and rough. Around evening, the water began to recede and by daybreak the river was running within its own banks. At this, the inhabitants fell down in adoration of Lucullus. The waters did not go down before, but only at the very time he came, to allow him an easy crossing. As soon as he had crossed over with his army, another favourable prodigy occurred. One of the oxen came to Lucullus. These animals were consecrated to the Persian god Artemis, whom the barbarians beyond the Euphrates River worshipped with great reverence. [E562] Usually, these beasts could not be captured without considerable trouble. However, this one came to him of its own accord and he sacrificed the bull to the Euphrates River, for his easy crossing. He camped there all that day. {*Plutarch, Lucullus, l. 1. c. 24. s. 4-7. 2:547,549}

4250. During the time he was marching through Sophene, he did not offend the inhabitants in any way, and they surrendered to him and cheerfully entertained his army. {*Plutarch, Lucullus, l. 1. c. 24. s. 8. 2:549} He only requested some money from them. The inhabitants of these countries did not like fighting, so they would not interfere when Tigranes and Lucullus were fighting. {*Appian, Mithridatic Wars, l. 12. c. 12. (84) 2:399}

4251. There was a citadel in those parts, where a great deal of treasure was thought to be stored. The soldiers wanted to attack the place, but Lucullus pointed at Taurus, which could be seen in the distance, and said:

> "Let us rather attack that stronghold. What is stored here is only reserved to reward conquerors."

4252. So they marched on, and he crossed the Tigris River and entered Armenia. {*Plutarch, Lucullus, l. 1. c. 24. s. 8. 2:549}

4253. At the same time as Lucullus was invading Armenia, Alexandra, the queen of the Jews, became very sick.

Consequently, Aristobulus, her young son, desired the kingdom and stole out in the night, taking only one servant along with him. He went to the citadels that were controlled by his father's friends. Only his wife, whom he had left at home with his children, knew of his plans. The first place he came to was Agaba, where Palaestes was in command, and he received Aristobulus very enthusiastically. {*Josephus, Antiq., l. 13. c. 16. s. 5. (422-424) 7:441} {*Josephus, Jewish War, l. 1. c. 5. s. 4. (117) 2:57} [K207]

4254. The next day, the queen noticed Aristobulus' absence, but did not imagine that he was plotting to take over the kingdom. When messenger after messenger came and brought the news of this citadel and then of that citadel being seized by her son, both the queen and the whole country were in confusion. They feared that if he were to take over the kingdom, he would call them to account for their harsh treatment of his close friends. It was therefore thought best to lock up Aristobulus' wife and children in the citadel which was near the temple. In the meantime, there was a large crowd of men who defected to Aristobulus in the hope of getting something out of this revolution. Aristobulus behaved like a king, gathering an army from Lebanon, Trachonitis and the local princes. {*Josephus, Antiq., l. 13. c. 16. s. 5. (424-428) 7:441,443}

4255. Thereupon, Hyrcanus, the high priests, and the elders of the Jews addressed the queen, wanting her advice about this emergency. She told them to do whatever they thought best in the public interest and to use the present strength and treasure of the kingdom to carry it out. She was in such a weak state of mind and body, that she could not help in the public administration, and died not long after this. {*Josephus, Antiq., l. 13. c. 16. s. 5. (428-430) 7:443,445}

4256. Hyrcanus, her oldest son, succeeded her in the third year of the 177th Olympiad, when Quintus Hortensius and Quintus Metellus (later surnamed Creticus) were consuls. {*Josephus, Antiq., l. 14. c. 1. s. 2. (4) 7:451} During her lifetime, his mother had turned the kingdom over to him. Aristobulus, however, exceeded him in strength and authority. {*Josephus, Jewish War, l. 1. c. 6. s. 1. (120) 2:57}

4257. When the consuls cast lots for their provinces, the managing of the war against the Cretians fell to Hortensius. However, he was more interested in the city and the forum, in which he had the next place after Cicero, and willingly gave this expedition to Metellus. {*Dio, l. 36. (1a) 3:3}

### 3935b AM, 4645 JP, 69 BC

4258. When the Senate declared war on Crete, the wisest of the Cretians thought it best to send envoys to Rome. The envoys were to clear them of all the allegations, to pacify the Senate with acceptable words and secure their reconciliation. When this was agreed to, they sent thirty of their most eminent men in this embassy to Rome. They hoped through them to obtain a new ratification of their former contract and be thanked for the favour they had shown the Roman quaestor and the soldiers whom they had taken prisoner in the recent battle with Marcus Antonius. By privately visiting the senators at their houses, the envoys won them over to their side. When they were brought into the Senate, they answered the charges against them and reminded them about the good services they had rendered them and their alliance in war under the Roman general. *[E563]* It was resolved that the Cretians' impeachments should be removed and that after this they would be allies of the Romans. However, Lentulus, who was surnamed Spinther, had this decree reversed, whereupon this particular business was debated several times by the Senate. It was concluded that, since the Cretians had sided with the pirate ships and had shared in the booty, they should send to Rome all their pirate ships, even including boats of four tiers of oars, and should also return the ships they had taken from the Romans. They were to return all prisoners, renegades and the three hundred hostages taken from among the prominent citizens. Lasthenes and Panares, who had both fought against Antonius, were to be surrendered. In addition to this, the Romans also demanded four thousand talents of silver. {*Diod. Sic., l. 40. c. 1. 12:275} {*Appian, Sicily and the Other Islands, l. 5. c. 6. (1) 1:135} {*Dio, l. 34. (111) 2:499} [K208]

4259. The Romans did not wait for a reply from the Cretians back home. They soon sent one of the consuls to collect what was being demanded and to wage war with them should they refuse. It was certain they would not comply. For was it not imaginable that these people—who at the beginning, before any such things were exacted from them or before they had obtained a victory, refused to admit to any wrong they had committed—would now, after having won a victory, meekly submit to such haughty demands? The Romans knew full well what the outcome would be and suspected that the envoys would try to bribe some people to obstruct the wars. Hence, they made a decree in the Senate, prohibiting any person from lending the envoys anything. {*Dio, l. 34. (111) 2:499}

4260. When the commands of the Senate were being debated by the Cretians, the most politically astute were of the opinion that every detail should be observed. Those belonging to Lasthenes' faction were somewhat disagreeable, fearing that they would be sent to Rome and there be punished for what they had done. So they stirred up the people and exhorted them earnestly to fight for their liberty. {*Diod. Sic., l. 40. c. 1. 12:275}

4261. When Cotta had returned to Rome, he was highly honoured by the Senate and given the surname of *Ponticus*, because he had taken Heraclea. {*Memnon, c. 61.}

4262. Mithridates had lived in various places in Armenia for twenty months, but had not yet been admitted to see Tigranes, his son-in-law. At last, overcome by his desire to present himself, Mithridates met Tigranes with a gallant train who received his father-in-law with princely splendour. Nevertheless, three days passed without any conference between them. Later, he gave adequate indication of his affection toward him by the sumptuousness of the entertainments. {*Memnon, c. 57.} Then, in the conference that was held very privately at court, they allayed the suspicions of Metrodorus of Scepsis and other friends on both sides. {*Plutarch, Lucullus, l. 1. c. 22. s. 1,2. 2:539} So Mithridates was sent back again into Pontus with ten thousand cavalry. {*Memnon, c. 57.}

4263. Lucullus drew up a company of troops against the city in which he had been told that Tigranes had secured his courtesans and most of his precious things. {*Memnon, c. 58.}

4264. Tigranes hung a man as a trouble maker who brought the first news of Lucullus' coming with his army. (Plutarch said he cut off his head.) After that, no one brought him any news. At last, when he found that it was true, he sent Mithrobarzanes against Lucullus with two thousand (as Appian) or three thousand (as Plutarch has it) cavalry and a vast number of foot soldiers. He was ordered to take Lucullus alive and bring him to Tigranes, to deter others from doing the same. {*Plutarch, Lucullus, l. 1. c. 25. s. 1,2. 2:549,551} {*Appian, Mithridatic Wars, l. 12. c. 12. (84) 2:399}

4265. Part of Lucullus' forces were camped and the remainder were on their march when the scouts brought news of the enemy's approach. This made Lucullus fear that the enemy could attack his men at a time when they were not ready for battle. He halted the march and started to fortify his camp. He sent Sextilius, the envoy, with sixteen hundred cavalry and almost as many foot soldiers with orders to stop when he reached the enemy. He was not to move until he received word that the camp was thoroughly fortified. However, Mithrobarzanes came upon him so quickly, that he was forced to fight. Mithrobarzanes was killed in this battle and most of the rest fled and were killed in the pursuit. {*Plutarch, Lucullus, l. 1. c. 25. s. 3,4. 2:551} [E564] [K209]

4266. Tigranes left Tigranocerta and committed the custody of the city to Mancaeus. He went about the country to levy an army and retreated to Taurus, making that place his headquarters. {*Plutarch, Lucullus, l. 1. c. 25. s. 5. 2:551,553} {*Appian, Mithridatic Wars, l. 12. c. 12. (84) 2:399}

Lucullus followed him so closely, that he could not assemble an army, as Lucullus sent Murena to attack and take all the troops he found marching to Tigranes. Sextilius was sent another way to attack a large band of Arabians to prevent them from coming to the king. {*Plutarch, Lucullus, l. 1. c. 25. s. 5,6. 2:553}

4267. Sextilius attacked the Arabians as they were camped before they knew what had happened, and captured most of them. Murena marched after Tigranes, who had a very large force, and overtook him in a rough and narrow defile. Murena gained some advantage from the terrain and fought with Tigranes who abandoned all his wagons and fled as fast as he could. Many Armenians died in the battle but far more were taken prisoner. {*Plutarch, Lucullus, l. 1. c. 25. s. 5,6. 2:553}

4268. Sextilius forced Mancaeus to retreat into Tigranocerta and started plundering the king's palace located outside the walls. He made a trench around the city and the citadel to position the batteries and undermine the walls. {*Appian, Mithridatic Wars, l. 12. c. 12. (84) 2:401} Finally, Lucullus came to join them and closely besieged the city. He thought that Tigranes would not allow him to besiege the city, but would come down in a rage to fight him. {*Plutarch, Lucullus, l. 1. c. 26. s. 1,2. 2:553} The barbarians hindered his actions greatly. They shot many arrows and shot their naphtha or fire-pitch from their engines. This naphtha was a pitchy kind of substance and was so scalding that it burned anything it stuck to. Water would barely quench it. {*Dio, l. 36. (1b) 3:3}

4269. Mithridates sent envoys with letters (as Plutarch stated, and not in person), and then met with Tigranes (as Appian has it) and warned him not to fight the Romans. He advised him to rove around the country with his cavalry. He was to lay it waste if possible and by so doing, deprive the enemy of food. This was what Lucullus had done to Mithridates a short time earlier at Cyzicum, causing him to lose an army without fighting a stroke. {*Plutarch, Lucullus, l. 1. c. 26. s. 3. 2:553,555} {*Appian, Mithridatic Wars, l. 12. c. 12. (85) 2:401}

4270. The Armenians and the Gordians joined with Tigranes. Every man of the Medes and Adiabenians was brought by their kings. The Arabians also came in numbers from the Babylonian Sea. Many Albanians came from the Caspian Sea, along with the Iberians, their neighbours, who were a free people living near the Araxes River. Some came out of love for their king and others came because they were induced by gifts. {*Plutarch, Lucullus, l. 1. c. 26. s. 3,4. 2:553,555} Others came out of fear. For the barbarians thought the Roman army was coming solely to ransack their countries and their wealthy temples. For this reason many countries, including the larger ones, went to fight against Lucullus. {*Cicero, Pro Lege Manilia, l. 1. c. 9. (23) 9:35,37}

4271. All these forces came together. At Tigranes' banquets and council rooms, they talked only of victory and of how roughly they would handle the enemy when they had captured them. Taxiles, who was Mithridates' envoy and his assistant, was in danger of losing his head because in a council of war he alone opposed fighting with the Romans maintaining that the Romans were unconquerable. Mithridates was thought to envy the glory of the victory Tigranes would have, should he not wait until Mithridates came and so neglect to share the glory of the day with him. {*Plutarch, Lucullus, l. 1. c. 26. s. 3,4. 2:553,555} However, Tigranes sent for Mithridates to come quickly to help him. {Memnon, c. 58.} [K210]

4272. Tigranes ordered about six thousand soldiers to go and defend the city where his concubines were kept. These charged through the Roman brigades and got into the town but when they found their return trip intercepted by a valley of archers, they sent the king's concubines and his treasures safely away by night to Tigranes. At daybreak the Romans and the Thracians fought with these Armenians. They killed many of them and took at least as many prisoners. {Memnon, c. 58.} {*Appian, Mithridatic Wars, l. 12. c. 12. (85) 2:401,403} Appian's account was corrected from Memnon's account.

4273. Tigranes marched against Lucullus with the rest of his army. He was very troubled that he would now fight with only one of the Roman generals, Lucullus, and not with the whole army. In his army, Tigranes had twenty thousand archers and slingers, fifty-five thousand cavalry, and a hundred and fifty thousand heavily armed foot soldiers, who were divided, some into regiments and some into squadrons. There were thirty-five thousand who were set aside for the task of barricading passes. {*Plutarch, Lucullus, l. 1. c. 26. s. 5,6. 2:555,557}

4274. As soon as Tigranes appeared at Taurus with all his host, he could overlook from the top of a hill the Roman army that was besieging Tigranocerta. [E565] The barbarians in the city welcomed the king's arrival with howlings and acclamation, jeering at the Romans from the top of the walls and pointing to the Armenians on the hill. {*Plutarch, Lucullus, l. 1. c. 27. s. 1. 2:557}

4275. Lucullus left Murena to continue the siege of Tigranocerta with six thousand foot soldiers, while he marched against Tigranes. In his army, Lucullus had twenty-four cohorts of foot soldiers consisting of about ten thousand heavily armed foot soldiers, along with all his cavalry, as well as slingers and archers, who numbered about a thousand. He camped in a large spacious field near a river. {*Plutarch, Lucullus, l. 1. c. 27. s. 1,2. 2:557} No sooner had Tigranes seen the Roman camp, than he promptly mocked their small numbers and reproached them, saying: {Memnon, c. 59.} {*Plutarch, Lucullus, l. 1. c. 27. s. 3,4. 2:557,559} {*Appian, Mithridatic Wars, l. 12. c. 12. (85) 2:401} {*Dio, l. 36. (1b) 3:5 (Xiphilinus)}

"If these men came as envoys, there are a large number of them indeed, but if as enemies, there are but forty companies of them."

4276. As Lucullus was wading across the river with his army, some of his commanders advised him to be careful what he did on that day, because it was a black or unlucky day on their calendar. For on that very day, the Cimbrians had defeated the army under Caepio. Lucullus replied:

"We ought therefore to fight all the more bravely now, in the hope of perhaps turning this black and dismal day into a day of rejoicing for the Romans."

4277. That day was the day before the Nones of October (October 6), {*Plutarch, Lucullus, l. 1. c. 27. s. 7. 2:561} {*Plutarch, Camillus, l. 1. c. 19. s. 7. 2:141} {*Plutarch, Sayings of Romans (Lucullus) (203) 13:205} according to the Roman calendar at that time. However, according to the Julian calendar, it was July 5 and the beginning of the fourth year of the 177th Olympiad. This was the time of this battle according Phlegon.

4278. Lucullus knew that his soldiers were afraid of the heavily armed foot soldiers, so he encouraged them by saying that they would have more trouble in stripping them than in defeating them. He first charged them on the hill and when he saw the barbarians give ground, he cried out: {*Plutarch, Sayings of Romans (Lucullus) (203) 13:205}

"We have overcome them, fellow soldiers."

4279. No sooner was Tigranes' right wing forced to flee, than the left also began to retreat. In the end, they all turned their backs and so the Armenians fled in confusion and haste and the army was slaughtered. {Memnon, c. 59.} The Romans continued the killing for fifteen miles, trampling the whole way on bracelets and chains until night came forcing them to give up the chase. So they started stripping the dead bodies which Lucullus had ordered them not to do until the enemy had been soundly defeated. {*Appian, Mithridatic Wars, l. 12. c. 12. (85) 2:401,403} [K211]

4280. Phlegon said Tigranes' forces lost five thousand men and that a greater number than this were taken prisoner. Orosius said that thirty thousand men were reported killed in that battle. {Orosius, l. 6. c. 3.} Plutarch said that more than a hundred thousand foot soldiers were

killed and very few of the cavalry escaped. The Roman army had five dead and a hundred wounded. Antiochus, the philosopher, mentioned this battle in his treatise *Concerning Gods*, saying that there had never been a day like it. Strabo related in the first book of his *Historical Commentaries* that the Romans themselves were ashamed of what they had done and jeered themselves for fighting against such cowardly slaves. Livy said that never in all their history had the Romans been as heavily outnumbered as twenty to one. {*Plutarch, Lucullus, l. 1. c. 28. s. 6-8. 2:565}

4281. If we say, with Eutropius, Sextus Rufus and Jornandes, that Lucullus had eighteen thousand men in his army, then that number, multiplied by twenty, would make three hundred and sixty thousand in Tigranes' army, not a hundred and fifty thousand, as Plutarch stated, but two hundred and fifty thousand foot soldiers, according to Appian. He would not have had fifty thousand cavalry as Appian stated but fifty-five thousand as noted by Plutarch. To this host Plutarch added twenty thousand archers and thirty-five thousand support personnel. The total would have been three hundred and sixty thousand. If this is correct, then neither Phlegon's nor Memnon's account are accurate, but are far too low. The one writer assigned forty thousand foot soldiers and thirty thousand cavalry to Tigranes' army, while the other allowed him a total of eighty thousand foot soldiers and cavalry altogether. As much as their accounts were underrated so much was that of Eutropius' overrated. The Clibanarii were cavalry in impenetrable armour as they are described by Sallust in the fourth book of his history as cited by Nonius. {Nonius Marcellus, see word Cataphracti} Plutarch intimated that Lucullus himself had written to the Senate that Tigranes had only seventeen thousand of these Clibanarii in his army. So there is no doubt that Eutropius was very much mistaken in stating that the total was six hundred thousand. Sextus Rufus, in his Breviary, said that there were not more than seventy-five hundred of these Clibanarii, but one hundred and twenty or thirty thousand archers.

4282. At the beginning of the battle, Tigranes fled from the field and ran as fast as he could to one of his citadels with barely a hundred and fifty cavalry with him. He found his son as depressed as he was and taking off the diadem and turban from his head, he turned his men over to his son. He tearfully urged him to fend for himself and to try any possible strategy that had not yet been tried. [E566] Since the young prince dared not carry the royal ensigns with him, he committed them to a highly trusted friend to keep for him. However soon after this, it was his friend's misfortune to be taken prisoner and brought to Lucullus. The soldiers took the turban and the diadem and gave them to Lucullus. {*Memnon, c. 59.*} {*Plutarch, Lucullus, l. 1. c. 28. s. 5,6. 2:563,565*} {*Orosius, l. 6. c. 3.*} {*Dio, l. 36. (1b) 3:5 (Xiphilinus)*} Lucullus marched back to Tigranocerta and continued the siege with more zeal than before. {*Memnon, c. 59.*}

4283. Mithridates did not hurry to the battle, because he thought that Lucullus would manage this war with the same caution and delay as he had shown before. Acting on this belief, he was not very fast in coming when sent for by Tigranes. Soon after this, he chanced upon some Armenians along the way who were terrified and ready to collapse from fear. Mithridates suspected that all was not well with Tigranes' side. Soon after this, he met with other companies of stripped and wounded men who told him of the great defeat. Mithridates hurried as fast as he could to find Tigranes. [K212] When he found him desolate and depressed, he did not gloat over his misfortune. He dismounted his horse and after mutually bemoaning each other's sad misfortune, Mithridates turned his own princely retinue over to him, who attended him, and encouraged him for the future. {*Plutarch, Lucullus, l. 1. c. 29. s. 1,2. 2:565,567*} After he had cheered him up a little, he gave him royal robes as rich as anything he had ever worn and also made some proposals about levying new forces. Since Mithridates already had a considerable army, he said there would be another battle to reverse this misfortune. Tigranes ascribed more prowess and discretion to Mithridates than himself and thought that he would be the better one to deal with the Romans. Therefore he put Mithridates in charge of the war effort. {*Memnon, c. 59.*}

4284. From the walls of Tigranocerta, Mancaeus saw the dismal scene of his defeated friends. He started to disarm all the Greek mercenaries, because he suspected they would not remain loyal. The Greeks, fearing that they could be arrested, took precautions and drew themselves up into a body and so remained together in this way day and night. When they saw Mancaeus marching against them with his armed barbarians, they wrapped their clothes about their arms as bucklers and bravely charged them. After this they had enough weapons so they seized some citadels on the walls and called in the Romans who were besieging them and received them into the town. {*Plutarch, Lucullus, l. 1. c. 29. s. 2. 2:567*} {*Appian, Mithridatic Wars, l. 12. c. 12. (86) 2:403*} Dio related that most of the inhabitants were Cilicians. When these had a disagreement with the Armenians, they opened the town by night to the Romans who plundered everything except what the Cilicians owned. {*Dio, l. 36. (2) 3:7*} However, Memnon stated that when Mithridates' or rather Tigranes' commanders saw how desperate things were for their side, they conditionally surrendered the town to Lucullus. {*Memnon, c. 59.*}

4285. After Lucullus had captured Tigranocerta and taken the king's treasures that were there, he let his soldiers plunder the city. In addition to everything else they found, they discovered eight thousand talents of coined money. As well, Lucullus gave eight hundred drachmas from the spoil to every soldier. He found many players there, whom Tigranes had brought together from all over since he was about to dedicate the theatre he had built. Lucullus used them for his contests and spectacles. {*Plutarch, Lucullus, l. 1. c. 29. s. 3,4. 2:567*} He preserved from harm many wives of the chief officers who were taken and in this way won their husbands over to his side. {*Dio, l. 36. (2) 3:7*} He fitted out the Greeks for their journey back to their country and also permitted the Cappadocians, Cilicians and other barbarians, who had been forced to live there, to return home. So it happened that, through the ruin of one city (for the city was only half finished and Lucullus had demolished it and left only a small village), many cities received back their former citizens and hence many cities were restored. These cities later esteemed Lucullus as their founder. {*Plutarch, Lucullus, l. 1. c. 29. s. 4. 2:567*} {*Strabo, l. 11. c. 14. s. 15. 5:339*} {*Strabo, l. 12. c. 2. s. 9. 5:367*}

4286. Envoys arrived there from almost the entire east, begging his friendship. {*Orosius, l. 6. c. 3.*} The countries of the Sophenians allied themselves to him. Antiochus, the king of Commagene (part of Syria near the Euphrates and Taurus Rivers), also came. Alchaudonius, a petty prince of Arabia, and some others sued for peace through their envoys and Lucullus received them. He added a large part of Armenia to Rome. {*Plutarch, Lucullus, l. 1. c. 29. s. 4. 2:567*} {*Dio, l. 36. (2) 3:7*}

4287. Gaius Metellus went to the Cretian war with three legions and defeated Lasthenes near the city of Cydonia. [K213] He was called *Imperator* and destroyed the whole island with fire and the sword. He forced the Cretians into their citadels and cities and refused to make peace with them. {*Florus, l. 1. c. 42. 1:197*} {*Appian, Sicily and the Other Islands, l. 5. c. 6. (2) 1:135,137*} {*Phlegon, Chronicles, Year 4. Olympiad. 174.*} {*Dio, l. 36. (19) 3:29*} {*Photius*} [E567]

4288. Cleopatra, the daughter of Ptolemy, was born at Auletta. She was the last queen of Egypt of the Macedonian family and lived thirty-nine years. {*Plutarch, Antony, l. 1. c. 86. s. 4,5. 9:331*} Tigranes and Mithridates went around various countries and raised another army which was placed under the command of Mithridates. {*Plutarch, Lucullus, l. 1. c. 29. s. 2. 2:567*} {*Appian, Mithridatic Wars, l. 12. c. 13. (87) 2:405*}

4289. Magadates, who managed the army in Syria for Tigranes for fourteen years, set out from there with an army to help his king. Because of this move, Antiochus

Asiaticus, the son of Antiochus Pius and Selene, obtained the kingdom of Syria with the help of the Syrians. He was surnamed Asiaticus because he had been educated there. Lucullus, who had recently defeated Tigranes, did not interfere with Antiochus' actions in Syria. {*Appian, Syrian Wars, l. 11. c. 8. (49) 2:197} {*Appian, Syrian Wars, l. 11. c. 11. (70) 2:237} However, Strabo wrote that Lucullus drove Tigranes out of Syria and Phoenicia and later defeated Tigranes. {*Strabo, l. 11. c. 14. s. 15. 5:339} Antiochus, the son of Cyzicenus (or rather, his grandchild by his son), was called king of Syria, until Pompey took away from him what Lucullus had given to him. Justin stated that four years elapsed between the time that he received the kingdom of Syria and the time it was taken away by Pompey. {Justin, Trogus, l. 40. c. 2.}

4290. Tigranes and Mithridates sent envoys begging aid from their neighbours and from Arsaces, the Parthian king. They condemned the Romans suggesting that the Romans had conquered them at a time when they were destitute and forsaken by others, and that the Parthians would be next to be attacked. {*Dio, l. 36. (3) 3:7}

4291. Arsaces was called by this name because it was the common name of the kings of Parthia. His proper name was Pacorus, according to Xiphilinus, but he was called Phradates by Memnon. Photius cited Phlegon of Tralles as saying that in the year before, which was in the third year of the 177th Olympiad, Phraates had succeeded Sinatrucus, the deceased king of the Parthians. {Photius, Bibliotheca, cod. 97.} However, Dio stated that Phraates succeeded Arsaces. {*Dio, l. 36. (45) 3:75} Appian said he succeeded Sintricus, which was correct, as we shall see. {*Appian, Mithridatic Wars, l. 12. c. 15. (104) 2:439} Arsaces had ruled the empire for six years before the third war of Mithridates started. These words are mentioned in a letter he wrote to Arsaces (of which we shall say more later) to prove this: {*Sallust, Letter of Mithridates, l. 1. (13) 1:437}

"You are far removed and all others had submitted, so I again renewed the war."

4292. From this, we conclude that his proper name was either Sintricus, or Sinatrux.

4293. Arsaces was offended with Tigranes for starting a new war about a certain country over which they were in dispute. Tigranes gave this country back to him again. As well as that, the Parthian king also wanted to have the large valleys of Mesopotamia and Adiabene given to him as the reward for his alliance. When Lucullus heard of the embassy that Tigranes and Mithridates had sent to Arsaces, he also sent some envoys. These threatened Arsaces, if he assisted Tigranes, and made him promises if he would side with the Romans. [K214]

Lucullus' envoys urged him either to help the Romans, or remain neutral. Arsaces secretly promised friendship to both sides but ended up giving it to neither. {Memnon, c. 60.} {*Dio, l. 36. (3) 3:7} {*Plutarch, Lucullus, l. 1. c. 29. s. 2. 2:567} {*Appian, Mithridatic Wars, l. 12. c. 13. (87) 2:405}

4294. Among the remains of the fourth book of Sallust's History, there is an entire letter of Mithridates that was sent to Arsaces about this very affair. In it, he seems to turn the indignation Arsaces had against Tigranes for waging the recent war, to his own advantage. He said:

"For being guilty, you shall receive what alliance you please."

4295. He excused the great victory the Romans had won against him, by saying: {*Sallust, Letter of Mithridates, l. 1. (15) 1:439}

"They forced the multitude into such narrow places, that they attributed their victory to their own strength, when in fact it was but his imprudence."

4296. Later, Mithridates stirred up Arsaces against the Romans, by saying: {*Sallust, Letter of Mithridates, l. 1. (20-32) 1:441}

"You, for whom Seleucia is the greatest city, and to whom the kingdom of Persia and very great riches belong, what can you look for, but deception for the present and war in the future. The Romans have waged war everywhere but it is most violent where the victory over their adversaries affords the richest spoil. They invade and they beguile. One war gives rise to another. By these means, they either thwart the schemes of, or destroy, those that fight with them. This is not difficult, if you in Mesopotamia and we in Armenia surround their armies while they are without food and allies and who have been saved so far only by their good fortune and our own errors. You would then have the reputation of bravely having assisted great kings and suppressed great robbers. This I desire and exhort you to do, unless you had rather by our ruin enlarge the Roman empire than by our friendship become a conqueror yourself."

4297. As soon as the unwelcome news of what Marcus Cotta had done at Heraclea arrived at Rome, he was in public disgrace and his great riches increased their envy. To avoid this, he brought most of the spoils back to the treasury. However the Romans remained just as suspicious, assuming he had handed over only a small portion of the great abundance he had taken. They also learned that the prisoners at Heraclea were suddenly to be freed by a public decree. {Memnon, c. 61.} [E568]

4298. Furthermore, Thrasymedes from Heraclea publicly accused Cotta before an assembly, praising the benevolence of his city to the Romans. He demonstrated that if they had transgressed in any way, it had not been with the consent of the city, but through the fraud of their magistrates and the power of their adversaries. He cried as he told them about the burning of the city and tearfully told them how Cotta had plundered everything for his private gain. A large number of men and women captives also came with their children. They came dressed in mourning clothes and kneeled down, holding up their hands with much weeping. The Roman nobles were inclined to sympathise with their case when Cotta came. After he had pleaded a little in his own language, he left again. Carbo arose and said:

"We, oh Cotta, gave you commission to take, not to destroy the city."

4299. Others arose after him and made similar statements, expressing their indignation against him, so that many thought he should be banished. In the end, they only took away his dignity. To the Heracleans, they restored their lands, sea and harbours, on the condition that none of them should be made slaves. {Memnon, c. 61.}

4300. After this was over, Thrasymedes sent the people back to their country but he stayed for some years with Brithagoras and his son Propylus at Rome. Together they did the things required to represent their country. {Memnon, c. 62.} [K215]

4301. Lucullus was condemned, both by strangers and by his own citizens, for not having pursued Tigranes, but having allowed him time to escape when he might easily have subdued him. They believed that he had wanted to prolong his own command. Therefore, the government of Asia (properly so called) which had previously been committed to him, was assigned to the praetors. {*Dio, l. 36. (2) 3:7}

4302. Lucullus went to the land of the Gordyenes and attended the funeral of their King Zarbienus, whom Tigranes had killed. Zarbienus had secretly entered into a league with Lucullus. Lucullus lit the fire to the pile of wood that was decorated with royal robes, gold and the spoils which had been taken from Tigranes. At the funeral in the presence of his friends and kindred, Lucullus declared him his friend and a confederate of the Romans, commanding that a beautiful monument be paid for from the king's treasury and dedicated to him. As a result of this, the Gordyenes were so devoted to Lucullus that they would have left their homes and followed him with their wives and children. {*Plutarch, Lucullus, l. 1. c. 29. s. 7,8. 2:569}

4303. They found much silver and gold in the palace of Zarbienus and three million bushels of grain were stored in his granaries. This was used to supply the soldiers and it was a matter of great honour for Lucullus that he had taken nothing from the treasury but had financed the war solely from the spoils of the war. {*Plutarch, Lucullus, l. 1. c. 29. s. 8. 2:569,571}

4304. Lucullus welcomed the envoys from Arsaces, king of the Parthians, and they who sought his friendship and alliance. He sent Sicilius, or Sextilius, to Arsaces. However Arsaces, from his expertise in military matters, suspected that he had been sent to spy out the military strength of the land rather than to confirm the treaty. So he did not give the Romans any help but remained neutral in the war. {*Plutarch, Lucullus, l. 1. c. 30. s. 1. 2:571} {*Dio, l. 36. (3) 3:7,8}

### 3936a AM, 4645 JP, 69 BC

4305. When Lucullus had learned that Arsaces was wavering in his loyalty and that he had secretly requested Mesopotamia from Tigranes as a reward for his friendship, Lucullus decided to consider Tigranes and Mithridates as defeated enemies. He hurried to march against the Parthians to test their valour and strength. Therefore, he sent a message to Sornatius, his envoy in Pontus, and to several others there. They were to bring him the forces they had there since he intended to advance eastward from Gordyene against the Parthians. However, their soldiers were obstinate and could not be persuaded, saying that if they were left there without help, they would go away leaving Pontus undefended. Lucullus' soldiers were dejected when they heard this news. Riches and luxury had made them long for ease and they hated the hardships of war. As soon as they perceived the fury of the Pontics, they said these men were fit to be imitated and esteemed, maintaining they had already deserved their rest and discharge because of their many achievements. Hence Lucullus was forced to forgo his expedition into Parthia. {*Plutarch, Lucullus, l. 1. c. 30. 2:571,573}

### 3936b AM, 4646 JP, 68 BC

4306. The island of Delos, located in the Aegean Sea, was a main centre for merchants. This island was full of riches but although small and without a wall it was secure and the inhabitants feared nothing. {*Cicero, Pro Lege Manilia, l. 1. c. 18. (55) 9:67} Then the pirate Athenodorus captured it, took the inhabitants captive and destroyed the images of their gods. Gaius Triarius repaired the ruins and built a wall around it, in the fourth year of the 177th Olympiad. {Phlegon, Chronicles, l. 5.} {Photius, Bibliotheca, cod. 97.} [E569] [K216]

4307. Mithridates levied troops from every town and when he called a muster, he established that this force consisted almost entirely of Armenians. From these troops, he selected seventy thousand foot soldiers and half as many cavalry and sent the rest home. He had the men arranged into companies and troops according to the Italian discipline and he had the Pontics train them. {*Appian, Mithridatic Wars, l. 12. c. 13. (87) 2:405}

4308. In that year, when Quintus Marcius was the sole consul, Lucullus was not able to attack Tigranes until the middle of summer because it was too cold before then. After he had passed the Taurus Mountains and had seen the green fields, he was astonished that the season was so late there because of the cold. However, he nonetheless came down into the plains and after being attacked by the Armenians in two or three battles, he routed and dispersed them. {*Plutarch, Lucullus, l. 1. c. 31. s. 1,2. 2:573} {*Dio, l. 36. (4) 3:9} While Mithridates remained on a hill with the foot soldiers and some of the cavalry, Tigranes attacked the Roman foragers with the remainder and was defeated. After this the Romans got their provisions in greater security. They moved their camp nearer to Mithridates and intercepted the supplies for Tigranes. {*Appian, Mithridatic Wars, l. 12. c. 13. (87) 2:405} They caused great hardship for the enemy due to a lack of provisions. {*Plutarch, Lucullus, l. 1. c. 31. s. 1,2. 2:573}

4309. Lucullus destroyed one section of the country, thinking that the barbarians would be goaded into fighting for it. When he found that they would not he marched out against them. While his cavalry was distressed by the enemy cavalry, there was no conflict with the foot soldiers. Lucullus came in with his shields to their relief and scattered the enemy who were not greatly harmed by the encounter but shot their arrows back toward their pursuers. Of these, many were killed and wounded. Their wounds were very serious and difficult to heal because the arrows had a double point and were poisoned. They were so constructed that the second iron point remained in the wound when the arrow was pulled out. {*Dio, l. 36. (5) 3:9,11}

4310. In Crete, Lasthenes, the governor of Cydonia, was besieged by Gaius Metellus, the proconsul, and fled from Cydonia to Cnossus. Panares, another governor of the city, made peace and surrendered the city to Metellus. When Metellus later besieged Cnossus, Lasthenes put all his wealth into a house, set fire to it and fled from Cnossus. {*Appian, Sicily and the Other Islands, l. 5. c. 6. (2) 1:135,137} Cnossus, Cydonia and Eleutherna were taken by Metellus along with many other cities. {*Livy, l. 99. 14:123} {*Florus, l. 1. c. 42. 1:197} {*Appian, Sicily and the Other Islands, l. 5. c. 6. (2) 1:135,137} The Cretians were besieged by Metellus for a long time, and were brought to great extremity. They were forced to quench their thirst with their own urine and with their cattle's urine. {*Valerius Maximus, l. 7. c. 6. ext. 1. 2:169}

4311. Lucullus brought his army against Artaxata, Tigranes' royal residence, where his wife and children were. Unable to stand for this, Tigranes broke camp and after a four-day march came and camped by the Romans. Between them was the Arsania River which the Romans had to cross to attack Artaxata. {*Plutarch, Lucullus, l. 1. c. 31. s. 4. 2:575}

4312. After Lucullus had performed his sacrifice to his gods, he drew out his army as if he were certain of victory. He placed twelve cohorts in the vanguard and kept the rest in reserve in case they should be surrounded by the enemy. [K217] The enemy had a large number of cavalry while ahead of the cavalry were the Mardian and Iberian lancers, who used arrows, also on horseback. Tigranes had the greatest confidence in these, as being the most valiant among his mercenaries. However, they did nothing remarkable and only skirmished for a while with the Romans. They were not able to endure the force of the legions and ran away with the cavalry in pursuit. {*Plutarch, Lucullus, l. 1. c. 31. s. 5,6. 2:575}

4313. As soon as they were dispersed and Lucullus saw Tigranes' cavalry advance, he restrained his soldiers from chasing the fleeing troops, suspecting that Tigranes had a large number of well-trained cavalry. In the meantime, with those accompanied by nobles and officers he had around him, Lucullus marched up against the forces advancing toward him. The enemy was terrified and fled even before the Romans started to charge. Of the three kings in the field at the time, Mithridates, the king of Pontus, ran away most shamefully and could not even tolerate the the shout of the Romans. The Romans pursued them all night and grew weary of killing and taking prisoners and became tired from taking and carrying away their money and spoil. Livy reported that in the former battle more of the enemy were taken or killed but in this one it was the best soldiers and a large number of them. {*Plutarch, Lucullus, l. 1. c. 31. s. 6-8. 2:575,577}

4314. The pirates were so powerful at this time, that they controlled the entire sea. They intercepted provisions intended for the fleet and made a habit of coming ashore destroying provinces and islands. The Romans, who had conquered the whole world, could not control the seas. {*Plutarch, Pompey, l. 1. c. 14. s. 1-5. 5:173,175} {*Appian, Mithridatic Wars, l. 12. c. 14. (91) 2:413} {*Dio, l. 36. (20) 3:31} {Eutropius, l. 6.} {Orosius, l. 6. c. 4.} The next year, Cicero, in his speech for the Manilian Law, reminded them of this: {*Cicero, Pro Lege Manilia, l. 1. c. 12. (32,33) 9:45} [E570]

"What province have you defended? Who was protected by your ships? How many islands do you think are deserted? How many cities are either forsaken for fear or have been taken from your friends by pirates?

It was the ancient custom of the Romans to wage war far from home and rather use their forces in the defence of their friends' fortunes than of their own. Shall I say that for these many years your sons have been a help to your friends and though our army was at Brundisium, they dare not cross over but in the midst of winter? Why should I complain about the fact that those who came to us from abroad were taken, when the very envoys of the people of Rome are being redeemed? Shall I say the sea is not safe for our merchants when twelve of our guard (there were two praetors, Sextilius and Bellinus captured {*Plutarch, Pompey, l. 1. c. 24. s. 6. 5:177}) have fallen into the hands of the pirates? Why should I remind you of Colophon and Samos, those two noble cities, or of many more that have been taken, when you know your own harbours and those very parts you yourselves inhabit have been taken by these enemies. Where was this government, when the Roman envoys, praetors and quaestors were intercepted, when public and private commerce from old provinces was forbidden us, when the merchandise was so confined, that we were unable to trade either in private or in public?"

*4315.* In this, as in all other things, he expressed himself most eloquently.

*4316.* The common base of these pirates, and the main base for their activities, was Cilicia, which was called Trachea, meaning *Craggy.* They had citadels, towers and deserted islands everywhere, with secret creeks for their ships. Many of them came from this part of Cilicia, which was called Trachea. It had no harbours and had very high mountain peaks rising from the shore. For this reason, these men were known to everyone by the common name of Cilicians. *[K218]* This evil, which began in Cilicia, attracted the Syrians, Cypriots, Pamphylians, Pontics and all the eastern countries together. Because of Mithridates' war, they were more inclined to do mischief than to endure it. They exchanged the land for the sea, so that in a short time there were many tens of thousands of them. {*Appian, Mithridatic Wars, l. 12. c. 14. (92) 2:415}

*4317.* The pirates had more than a thousand ships and captured more than four hundred cities. They pillaged the temples at Claros, Didyma and Samothracia, which had previously been sacred and untouched. They plundered what was dedicated to Chthionian Earth at Hermione, to Asclepias at Epidaurus, to Poseidon at the isthmus, at Taenarum and Calauria, Apollo at Actium and Leucae, Hera at Samos, Argos and Lacinium. At Mount Olympus (a pirate stronghold in southern Asia Minor), they offered strange sacrifices of their own and some secret mysteries of those who worshipped Mithras

or the Sun. They went out of their way to insult any Romans. If any one of their prisoners called himself a Roman, they at once feigned fear and knocking their knees together and falling down at his feet, humbly implored his pardon. While he believed them to be real and sincere, some of them furnished him with shoes, others with garments, so that he should no longer remain unknown. When they had mocked and deluded the man for a long time, they put down a ladder into the sea and bade him go down in safety. If he refused, they threw him down headlong and drowned him. {*Plutarch, Pompey, l. 1. c. 24. s. 5-8. 5:175,177}

## 3937a AM, 4646 JP, 68 BC

*4318.* About the autumnal equinox, severe storms unexpectedly struck Lucullus' army. It snowed for most of the time and when it was clear, there was hoar frost and ice. The ice was troublesome because the frozen rivers gave them little water for the horses. If they broke through the ice, the pieces cut their legs and made it difficult to cross. Because the country was forested, they were daily covered with the snow that fell from the trees and were forced to rest uncomfortably while still wet. Therefore they petitioned Lucullus through their tribunes and later there was a riot in the night. Lucullus begged them earnestly, but to no avail, and pleading with them not to give up until they had destroyed what was the greatest work of their enemy, the Armenians, since Carthage had been taken. For it was reported that Artaxata was built on the advice of Hannibal, the Carthaginian. {See note on 3816c AM. <<3143>>} Lucullus failed in his efforts and was forced to retreat. {*Plutarch, Lucullus, l. 1. c. 32. s. 1-3. 2:577,579} Concerning this retreat of the Roman army, Cicero, in his speech for the Manilian Law, tried to excuse this retreat of the Roman army as follows: {*Cicero, Pro Lege Manilia, l. 1. c. 9. (24) 9:37}

"Although our army had taken a city in Tigranes' kingdom called Tigranocerta and had fought several successful battles, yet were they nonetheless discouraged by the tediousness of their march. I will not say any more here. The result was, that our soldiers were more anxious for an early return from these regions, than for a further advance."

*4319.* Lucullus returned through Armenia to Mesopotamia and crossed the Taurus Mountains at another spot. He descended into the country of Mygdonia which was a very warm and fruitful country. It contained a large and populous city, called Nisibis by the barbarians, and Antioch in Mygdonia by the Greeks. {*Plutarch, Lucullus, l. 1. c. 32. s. 3,4. 2:579} {Orosius, l. 6. c. 3.} [K219]

*4320.* The city had been built by the Macedonians, but Tigranes had taken it and all Mesopotamia from the

Parthians. {*Josephus, Antiq., l. 20. c. 2. s. 3. (68) 10:37} There he had placed his treasure and many other valuable things. It was surrounded by a very thick double-brick wall and a ditch so deep and broad that the wall could neither be shaken nor undermined. {*Dio, l. 36. (6) 3:11} [E571] Tigranes' brother, Gouras, was commander and under him was Callimachus, a brilliant engineer. He had performed noble exploits at Amisus and was respected as a person of great knowledge in fortifications and of much experience in war. Callimachus caused Lucullus many problems at both places, here, as well as at Amisus. {*Plutarch, Lucullus, l. 1. c. 32. s. 4,5. 2:579}

4321. Lucullus besieged the city with all manner of engines. {*Plutarch, Lucullus, l. 1. c. 32. s. 4. 2:579} At the beginning of the winter, the barbarians were so sure of victory, that they started to become careless. The Romans had already departed; however, Lucullus returned one night when the moon was not out and a fierce thunder storm was in progress, so that the barbarians could neither see nor hear what was happening. For this reason they had left only a few men there and had almost deserted the outer wall and the ditch between the walls. Lucullus, by his siege works, easily scaled over the wall and without much trouble killed the few sentinels he found. He filled up part of the ditch by throwing in earth, for the enemy had previously destroyed their bridges. When the enemy was unable to harm them with their arrows or with fire because of the rain, he occupied the ditch and promptly captured the city. Their inner walls had not been made as strong because they were placing most of their confidence in the outer wall. {*Dio, l. 36. (7) 3:11,13}

4322. Those who fled into the citadel, he received on terms. {*Dio, l. 36. (7) 3:13} Gouras, the brother of Tigranes, surrendered and was treated civilly. Lucullus put Callimarchus in chains to be punished even though he promised to show him where large sums of money were hidden. Callimarchus had burned Amisus and robbed Lucullus of the opportunity of showing kindness to the Greeks. {*Plutarch, Lucullus, l. 1. c. 32. s. 5. 2:579} Much money was later found and Lucullus wintered at Nisibis. {*Dio, l. 36. (7) 3:13}

4323. In the meantime, the men who were the popular leaders at Rome envied Lucullus and accused him of having prolonged the war out of greed and a desire for power. One of them said that Cilicia, Asia, Bithynia, Paphlagonia, Galatia, Pontus, Armenia and all the provinces as far as Phasis, had already been conquered. Now he said Lucullus was only foraging in Tigranes' countries as though he had been sent to plunder princes rather than to vanquish them. It was reported that Lucius Quintus, one of the praetors, had said this and had per-

suaded the people of Rome to order another commander to replace him and to disband many of the soldiers who had faithfully served under Lucullus. {*Plutarch, Lucullus, l. 1. c. 33. s. 4,5. 2:581}

4324. In Lucullus' camp, Publius Clodius was a man of great insolence and dissoluteness, who severely disturbed the camp. He was the brother of Lucullus' wife, with whom he was said to be intimate for she was a lewd woman. Lucullus removed him from his command because he had degenerated so much in his behaviour. Clodius stirred up the Fimbrians (or Valerians) against him. By this we mean those whom he had brought from Fimbria who had killed Lucius Valerius Flaccus, the consul. Clodius wanted to command them. After they had been seduced by Clodius, these men would not follow Lucullus against Tigranes or Mithridates. [K220] Since it was winter, they extended the time at Gordyene expecting another commander to come and replace Lucullus. {*Plutarch, Lucullus, l. 1. c. 34. 2:581,583}

4325. When Lucullus was besieging Nisibis, Tigranes did not go to its relief because he thought the city was invincible. He sent Mithridates into his own country while he marched into Armenia. For a while, he besieged Lucius Fannius until Lucullus heard about it and marched to his rescue. {*Dio, l. 36. (8) 3:13,15}

4326. Mithridates marched into Pontus which was the only kingdom he had remaining to him. He had four thousand of his own men and four thousand from Tigranes. {*Appian, Mithridatic Wars, l. 12. c. 13. (88) 2:407} He invaded the other Armenian and neighbouring regions. He killed many straggling Romans in a surprise attack. He fought fairly and quickly defeated and recovered many places. The men were inclined toward him because he had been born in that country and his father had previously ruled there, whereas they did not like the Romans, because they were strangers and some of their governors were tyrants. Hence, they freely came to Mithridates. {*Dio, l. 36. (9) 3:15} Cicero, in a speech, said about this: {*Cicero, Pro Lege Manilia, l. 1. c. 9. (24) 9:37}

> "Mithridates had now acquired his own soldiers and those from his kingdom who had joined with him, along with large numbers supplied by foreign countries and kings. He was reinforced in this by what we have heard does in fact frequently happen, that a prince's calamities do easily generate compassion in most men. This is especially true if they are either kings themselves, or live under the government of such a king, because the name of a king is very reverend and sacred. In this way, he has done more by being defeated, than if he had been victorious in all that he did."

4327. Mithridates defeated Marcus Fabius whom Lucullus had left as governor of these regions. In this, he was helped by the Thracians who were angry with Fabius, although they had previously been paid by him. *[E572]* The slaves in the Roman camp also helped in the defeat of the Romans. {*Dio, l. 36. (9) 3:15} {*Appian, Mithridatic Wars, l. 12. c. 13. (88) 2:407}

4328. Fabius had sent out some of the Thracian scouts, who had returned with imprecise information so that Fabius advanced without due care and was suddenly attacked by Mithridates. At that moment, the Thracians revolted and attacked the Romans, routing them and killing five hundred of their number. After that, when Mithridates promised liberty to the slaves, Fabius was afraid of all the slaves in his camp. These also defected to Mithridates' side and would doubtless have killed all the troops of Fabius, had not Mithridates been hurt with a stone in the knee. Because of that, he was hit under his eye with an arrow and was suddenly carried off the field. While the barbarians were taking care of their king, Fabius used the opportunity to retreat safely with the rest of his men. The Agari were a people of Scythia who were well-skilled in medicines made from the poison of serpents, for which reason they always accompanied the king, and they now had the care of the king. {*Dio, l. 36. (9) 3:15,17} {*Appian, Mithridatic Wars, l. 12. c. 13. (88) 2:407}

4329. After this, Fabius was besieged in Cabiris and was relieved by Gaius Triarius, as he was marching that way from Asia to join Lucullus. He had heard of Mithridates' success and assembled as many troops as he could. This terrified Mithridates to such an extent that he moved his camp because he imagined that he had the entire Roman army against him. *[K221]* Encouraged by this, Triarius pursued them into the country of the Commagenians (or rather Comana in Cappadocia, of which Dio said more later), where he fought and defeated them. Mithridates had camped on one side of a river and the Romans came down on the other. Hoping to find them weary after their march, Mithridates advanced immediately, and ordered the rest to attack over another bridge while the first group were fighting. They fought a long time but the battle was indecisive. Because so many men had crossed over the bridge, it collapsed, preventing Mithridates' troops from helping him, and so Mithridates was defeated. Since it was now winter, both sides established their winter quarters after this battle. {*Dio, l. 36. (10) 3:17}

4330. Aulus Gabinius, a tribune, persuaded the people that a commander should be chosen from those who had been consuls. This man's command would last for three years and he would have full and absolute power against the pirates. He would be supplied with very large

forces and many deputies. It is not certain whether Pompey put him up to this (even though he did not ask for Pompey), or if it was his own idea, to ingratiate himself to Pompey. Gabinius was a very wicked man and nothing that he did was for the benefit of the republic. {*Dio, l. 36. (23) 3:35,37} Cicero, in his speech about him after his return to the Senate, said:

> "Had he not been protected by his being a tribune, he could neither have avoided the power of the praetor, the number of his creditors, nor the proscription of his goods. At that time, had he not got that order concerning the war with the pirates, necessity and wickedness would have constrained him to become a pirate himself. This would have been less dangerous and detrimental to the commonwealth, since their adversary would have been from without, not within."

4331. The Senate confirmed this order of the people although unwillingly. {*Dio, l. 36. (37) 3:61} Velleius Paterculus related that this was like a war and not like attacking common thieves, for the pirates had terrified the whole world with their ships and they had achieved this not through any sudden or secret expedition on their part. As well as that, they had destroyed some cities in Italy. Gnaeus Pompey was sent to suppress them and was given an equal authority with the proconsuls within fifty miles of the sea. By this decree of the Senate, the government of the whole world was placed on one man. However the same thing had been decreed two years earlier in the praetorship of Marcus Antonius, as Velleius stated. (Current Loeb edition reads *seven years* and shows *two years* as a variant reading. Editor.) {*Velleius Paterculus, l. 2. c. 31. 1:117} However, it seems to me that it should be six years earlier, rather than two, since it appears that Marcus Antonius had died three years before in the Cretian war. Marcus Antonius died in the Cretian war, two years before the commission of *the great care of all the sea coasts within the Roman empire* was committed to Pompey, in the consulship of Lucullus and Cotta. Asconius Pedianus stated this, in his speech about Verres' praetorship in Sicily. {See note on 3930 AM. <<4117>>} {See note on 3934b AM. <<4220>>}

4332. Under the Gabinian Law, Pompey had the command of the navy for three years and as Plutarch said, command over all men in the provinces within fifty miles of the sea throughout the Mediterranean. {*Plutarch, Pompey, l. 1. c. 25. s. 2,3. 5:179} He had the power to command all the kings, governors and cities around this sea to help him. {*Appian, Mithridatic Wars, l. 12. c. 13. (88) 2:407} Appian, Velleius and Plutarch said it was about fifty miles. *[K222]* Xiphilinus said it was fifty miles. {*Dio, l. 36. (36a) 3:61 (Xiphilinus)} Dio said it was three days' journey from the sea, {*Dio, l. 36. (17a) 3:27 (Xiphilinus)} and they considered a day's journey to be about sixteen miles. [E573]

4333. Under the same law, Pompey had the power to choose fifteen deputies from the Senate, to whom he would assign the charge of various provinces. He was also able to take as much money as he needed from the treasury, as well as take two hundred ships and levy what forces he pleased. However, he called an assembly of the people, where he prevailed with them for much more and then doubled his preparation. He outfitted five hundred ships, although Appian said he had only two hundred and seventy, including the smaller vessels. He raised a hundred and twenty thousand foot soldiers and five thousand cavalry (four thousand, according to Appian). From the Senate, he chose twenty-four captains for the troops (twenty-five, according to Appian) and made them officers under him. He had two quaestors given to him and six thousand Attic talents because the task of pursuing so many navies in so large a sea seemed so considerable. There were many hiding places to which they could escape if attacked and then later suddenly launch an attack from there. {*Appian, Mithridatic Wars, l. 12. c. 14. (93) 2:419} {*Plutarch, Pompey, l. 1. c. 26. s. 1,2. 5:181}

### 3937b AM, 4647 JP, 67 BC

4334. Pompey was very well supplied with his own ships and those of his confederates from Rhodes. He and his commanders controlled both sides of the sea and together they boxed up the pirates in every port, bay, creek, recess, promontory or island. {*Florus, l. 1. c. 41. s. 11. 1:193} When he had managed the matters at sea, he gave ships, cavalry and foot soldiers, along with the praetorian standards, to the officers he had chosen from the Senate. Each one of them had absolute authority in the place to which he was assigned. Those pirates who were taken by one group were turned over to others, to prevent any from having too long a pursuit or possibly prolonging the war by sailing too far away. {*Appian, Mithridatic Wars, l. 12. c. 14. (95) 2:421}

4335. To Tiberius Nero and Manilius Torquatus, Pompey assigned Spain and the Pillars of Hercules. Marcus Pompey, his son, was assigned the Gallic and Ligurian waters. Africa, Sardinia, Corsica and the adjacent islands were assigned to Publius Attilius and Lentulus Marcellinus. The coasts of Italy were assigned to Lucius Gellius and Gnaeus Lentulus. Sicily and the Adriatic, as far as Acarnania, was assigned to Plotius Varus and Terentius Varro. According to Pliny, the latter was the most learned of the Togatians and was presented with a naval crown by Pompey for his efforts in this war. {*Pliny, l. 3. c. 11. (101) 2:75} {*Pliny, l. 7. c. 30. (115) 2:581} {*Pliny, l. 16. c. 3. (7) 4:391} Lucius Sisenna had the oversight of

Peloponnesus, Attica, Euboea, Thessaly, Macedonia and Boeotia. Lucius Lollius was given all the Aegean Sea and the Hellespont. However, Florus assigned the Asiatic Sea to Caepio. Metellus Nepos was assigned Lycia, Pamphylia, Cyprus and Phoenicia. Publius Piso was assigned Bithynia, Thrace and Propontis. Cato besieged the straits so tightly with his ships, that he blocked up the Propontis as if it had been a gate. {*Florus, l. 1. c. 41. s. 8-12. 1:193} {*Appian, Mithridatic Wars, l. 12. c. 14. (95) 2:421} Pompey, like a king of kings, oversaw everything and demanded that everybody stay in their areas lest, while he found that the pirates had been defeated in one place, he should be attacked from another area. He ordered that, while all were to be ready to relieve one another, they should not, by sailing around, make it possible for the enemy to escape. {*Appian, Mithridatic Wars, l. 12. c. 14. (95) 2:421} [K223]

4336. When his forces had been dispersed over the whole sea in this manner, Pompey began from the lower part and surrounding the enemies' navy, dragged them as with a net into their harbours. Those who escaped, fled into Cilicia to hide themselves like bees in a hive. {*Plutarch, Pompey, l. 1. c. 26. s. 3. 5:183} In forty days, he and his officers had cleared the Tyrrhenian Sea, the Libyan Sea, and the sea around Sardinia, Corsica and Sicily. He returned to Rome and did what he wished. {*Livy, l. 99. 14:123} {*Appian, Mithridatic Wars, l. 12. c. 14. (95) 2:421} {*Plutarch, Pompey, l. 1. c. 26. s. 3. 5:183}

4337. Pompey sailed from Brundisium with sixty very good ships to start the war in Cilicia. The enemy prepared to fight him, not because they thought they could beat him, but because they were very oppressed and had little to lose. They only attacked once and then found themselves surrounded. They threw away their arms and oars and with a general shout as a sign of their submission begged for their lives. {*Florus, l. 1. c. 41. s. 12,13. 1:193} {*Appian, Mithridatic Wars, l. 12. c. 14. (96) 2:421,423} {*Plutarch, Pompey, l. 1. c. 26. s. 3,4. 5:183} Cicero stated that he had brought all Cilicia into subjection to the Romans within forty-nine days from when he had set sail from Brundisium. This story of the recovering of all of Cilicia in so short a time should be seen as a rhetorical device to praise Pompey. {*Cicero, Pro Lege Manilia, l. 1. c. 12. (35) 9:47} {See note on 3941b AM. <<4557>>}

4338. After news arrived that Mithridates had defeated Fabius and was marching against Sornatius and Triarius, the Fimbrian (or Valerian) soldiers were ashamed and followed Lucullus when he went to their relief. {*Plutarch, Lucullus, l. 1. c. 35. s. 1. 2:585} Mithridates, in the meantime, when Manius Acilius Glabrio and Gaius Piso were consuls, camped opposite Triarius near Gaziura. [E574] He trained and exercised his men in full view of the Romans. He tried to provoke him to fight, in order to engage him before Lucullus came in the hope of defeating the Romans and thereby recovering the remainder of the kingdom. Mithridates was not able to draw him out. Therefore he sent some of his men to Dadasa to besiege a citadel where the Romans had stored their baggage. He hoped that the Romans would come to its relief so that he could attack them. Triarius was not fooled for he feared the number of troops Mithridates had. Since he expected that Lucullus for whom he had sent, would soon come, he stayed in his camp. When his soldiers heard that Dadasa was under siege, they were afraid of losing the goods they had there. So they threatened, in a rebellious manner, that unless he would lead them out, they would go to defend Dadasa without his permission. Due to this, he marched out against his will. {*Dio, l. 36. (12) 3:19}

4339. When Triarius had come out against Mithridates, there was a violent storm that was worse than anyone could remember. It blew the tents over in both camps, drove the cattle from the way and knocked some of the soldiers down from the hills. This storm forced both sides to retire. When Triarius was told that Lucullus was near, he attacked Mithridates' camp before day, as if he wanted to snatch the victory from Lucullus. After they had fought for a long time with equal fortune and courage, the king trusted his own wing of troops and at length prevailed and pressed upon the enemy. He forced their foot soldiers into a dirty ditch where they were cut down because they had poor footing while Mithridates lost only a few men. After his victory, he courageously pursued their cavalry through the fields, until a Roman centurion in the guise of a servant ran by his side as fast as his horse and gave him a deep wound in his thigh. *[K224]* The centurion could not kill him because of his breastplate but was himself quickly killed by Mithridates' troops. Mithridates was carried to the rear of the army. {*Appian, Mithridatic Wars, l. 12. c. 13. (88,89) 2:407,409} {*Plutarch, Lucullus, l. 1. c. 35. s. 1,2. 2:585} {*Dio, l. 36. (12,13) 3:19,21}

4340. After this, the king's friends sounded a retreat and called the soldiers back from this notable victory. This was unexpected and made the men fearful that something bad might have happened somewhere else. They gathered tumultuously around the body of their king. Finally, Timothy the physician stopped the bleeding and held him up on high in their sight. Had it not been for this accident, the Romans would have been utterly destroyed but they escaped as a result of this delay. When Mithridates came to his senses, he reproved those who had sounded the retreat. That same day Mithridates broke camp and marched against the Romans. The Romans were very afraid and felt utterly deserted. More than seven thousand soldiers were killed in this battle including a hundred and fifty centuries and twenty-four tribunes. In no other battle before this had so many officers been lost. {*Appian, Mithridatic Wars, l. 12. c. 13. (89) 2:409,411} {*Plutarch, Lucullus, l. 1. c. 35. s. 1. 2:585} {*Dio, l. 36. (13) 3:21} Appian said this encounter happened near Mount Scotius: {*Appian, Mithridatic Wars, l. 12. c. 17. (120) 2:473}

"It was a famous place in those parts by reason of Mithridates' victory, Triarius' defeat and the loss of the Roman army."

4341. Hirtius stated that this was about three miles from Zela, a town in Pontus. {*Caesar, Alexandrian War, l. 1. (73) 3:127}

4342. This was the defeat to which Cicero referred in his speech for the Manilian Law, a year and a half later: {*Cicero, Pro Lege Manilia, l. 1. c. 9. (25) 9:37}

"Your army was resolute and victorious but Mithridates attacked them. Allow me in this place, like those who write of the Roman affairs, to skip over our misfortunes, which were so great, that the news did not come to Lucullus by a messenger from the battle but by rumour."

4343. Later, he said: {*Cicero, Pro Lege Manilia, l. 1. c. 15. (45) 9:57}

"After we were defeated in Pontus, about which I reminded you a little earlier against my will, our friends and confederates were afraid and the wealth and courage of the enemies increased. The province had no garrison or troops in which to trust and Asia would have been lost, oh Romans, had not fortune, in the nick of time, brought Pompey from heaven, as it were, to the relief of those countries. His arrival stopped Mithridates though swelled with his success, and held back Tigranes, who was threatening Asia with great strength."

4344. When Mithridates was healed of his wounds, he suspected there might be more of the enemy among his men. He had a troop review on another pretext and unexpectedly ordered everyone to their tents. The Romans were found alone and killed. {*Dio, l. 36. (13) 3:21}

4345. From there, he went into Lesser Armenia. He took with him all the provisions he could carry and spoiled the rest in case it might be useful to Lucullus. About that time, Attidius, a Roman senator, was found guilty of conspiracy by Mithridates. He had fled to Mithridates long ago out of fear of justice and had been received into his favour. Out of respect for his former office, Mithridates would not torture him but was satisfied merely with his death. He grievously tormented his fellow conspirators but sent Attidius' servants away untouched even though Attidius had been made privy to his plans. {*Appian, Mithridatic Wars, l. 12. c. 13. (90) 2:411} *[K225]*

4346. Lucullus came and hid Triarius from the search of his angry soldiers. {*Plutarch, Lucullus, l. 1. c. 35. s. 2. 2:585} [E575] They had left unburied those who had died in the battle which was thought to have been the reason that first alienated the affections of his own soldiers. {*Plutarch, Pompey, l. 1. c. 31. s. 5. 5:195,197}

4347. Mithridates waited with his army on a hill near Talaura for Tigranes who was coming to him with large forces. He refused to fight until he came, but Mithridates the Mede, one of Tigranes' sons-in-law, suddenly attacked the Romans as they were scattered abroad and soundly defeated them. {*Plutarch, Lucullus, l. 1. c. 35. s. 2. 2:585} {*Appian, Mithridatic Wars, l. 12. c. 13. (90) 2:411} {*Dio, l. 36. (14) 3:21}

4348. Quintus Marcius, who had been the sole consul in the previous year, was sent as proconsul into Cilicia, Lucullus' main province. Marcius marched through Lycaonia with three legions and Lucullus asked him for his help but Marcius said his soldiers would not follow him. {Sallust, History, l. 5.} {Priscian, l. 18.} {*Dio, l. 36. (17) 3:25}

4349. When Marcius entered into Cilicia, he graciously received Menemachus who had revolted from Tigranes, and also made Publius Clodius commander of the navy. Marcius had married Clodius' sister and Lucullus had married another sister of Clodius. Clodius had fled from Lucullus in fear because of the offences he had committed at Nisibis. {*Dio, l. 36. (17) 3:25,27}

4350. Clodius suffered a surprise attack by the Cilician pirates in which he was taken prisoner. When they demanded a ransom for him, he sent to Ptolemy, the king of Cyprus, to see if he would pay it. Ptolemy only sent two talents which the pirates despised. However they feared Pompey and thought it best to free him for nothing. {*Strabo, l. 14. c. 6. s. 6. 6:385} {*Appian, Civil Wars, l. 2. c. 3. (23) 3:269} {*Dio, l. 36. (17) 3:25,27} {*Dio, l. 38. (30) 3:261,263}

4351. Under the Gabinian Law, Manius Acilius Glabrio, who was the sole consul that year, was made successor to Lucullus in the command of Bithynia and Pontus. The Valerian or Fimbrian legion, which had previously been discharged and re-employed, was again disbanded. These troops began to rebel and despised Lucullus, as they luxuriated with the fruits of victory, living at ease and with plenty when Lucullus was not around. {Sallust, History, l. 5.} {Priscian, l. 18.} {*Dio, l. 36. (14,15) 3:23}

4352. Dio stated that Publius Clodius was the main instigator of this rebellion. Cicero affirmed this in his speech. {*Cicero, De Haruspicum Responsis, l. 1. c. 20. 11:371} He said that when Clodius was freed by the pirates, he treacherously corrupted Lucullus' army and he fled from there to Rome. Dio said that he went to Antioch in Syria to help them against the Arabians with whom they were at war. Again he stirred up a rebellion and was very nearly killed. {*Dio, l. 36. (17) 3:27}

4353. Lucullus was in trouble daring neither to move from his place nor to stay there. Finally, he resolved to march against Tigranes, hoping to attack him unexpectedly or when he was tired after his march. He hoped that this would settle the rebellions in his camp but it did not. His soldiers followed him for a while but when they realised they were heading for Cappadocia, they all unanimously turned their backs without speaking one word. When the Valerians or Fimbrians heard they had been discharged at Rome and that Lucullus' command had been given to others, they all deserted from their colours. [K226] In the meantime, Lucullus tried to reconcile them and in great dejection with tears in his eyes, he went to their tents and begged everyone to come back. He took some of them by the hand but they refused his embraces. Throwing down their empty purses, they declared that as he through them had enriched himself alone, he should also fight alone with his enemies. {*Dio, l. 36. (15) 3:23} {*Plutarch, Lucullus, l. 1. c. 34. 2:583,575}

4354. This rebellion of the soldiers who refused to follow Lucullus, kept him from pursuing Mithridates and Tigranes and completing his victory over them. The Valerian Legions cried out that they had been disbanded and forsook him. {*Livy, l. 98. 14:123} Finally, they were won over by the entreaty of their fellow soldiers. They agreed to keep to their colours that summer on the condition that if no one came to fight them during that time they might depart. Lucullus was forced to agree with these men or leave that province with no garrison to defend it against the barbarians. He did not command them or lead them out into battle but thought it sufficient if they only stayed. He allowed Tigranes to forage in Cappadocia and Mithridates to range over the whole province. {*Plutarch, Lucullus, l. 1. c. 35. s. 4,5. 2:587}

4355. Lucullus had written to the Senate that he had finished the war with Mithridates. Officers came to Lucullus to settle the affairs in Pontus assuming everything would be peaceful there. {*Plutarch, Lucullus, l. 1. c. 35. s. 5. 2:587} {*Dio, l. 36. (43) 3:71} However, they found that he was not even in control of his troops but was being mocked and derided by his soldiers. By the time the summer was over, they had become so insolent and contemptuous of their commander that they took up their arms and drew their swords. They called for their enemies which they could not find anywhere. Shouting and throwing up their arms they retired from the camp. They declared that the time to stay, which they had promised Lucullus, had expired. {*Plutarch, Lucullus, l. 1. c. 35. s. 5,6. 2:587,289} [E576]

4356. When Acilius Glabrio, the consul, arrived at the province that was assigned to him, he sent criers about announcing that the Senate had discharged Lucullus' army and confiscated his goods because he had prolonged the war and refused to obey their commands. When the soldiers heard this most of them forsook him. Only a few who were very poor and did not fear their punishment stayed with him. {*Appian, Mithridatic Wars, l. 12. c. 13. (90) 2:411} As a result of this, Mithridates recovered most of his kingdom and did much damage to Cappadocia. Lucullus did not fight with Mithridates, nor did Acilius defend the country. For although he had hurried, as if wanting to rob Lucullus of his victory, when he understood their condition, namely, that Lucullus came with no army, he then prolonged his stay in Bithynia. {*Dio, l. 36. (17) 3:25}

4357. In his Manilian speech to the Romans, in which, as a favour to Lucullus, he excused what had happened, Cicero said: {*Cicero, Pro Lege Manilia, l. 1. c. 9. (26) 9:39}

"Lucius Lucullus—a man who might perhaps have been able in some measure to repair these losses—was by your orders compelled to disband a part of his troops, who had served their time, and to hand over a part to Manius Glabrio."

4358. We conclude this section about Lucullus and will return to the war with the pirates, or the maritime war (as Sallust and Cicero called it) that Pompey completed this summer. [K227]

4359. Most of the pirates had sent their children, their wealth and a large number of less useful people into their citadels and strongholds near the Taurus Mountains. They fought with Pompey at Coracesium in Cilicia where they were soon defeated and besieged. Finally, they sent out commissioners and surrendered themselves, their islands and their towns, which, because of their strength, would have been very difficult to capture. {*Plutarch, Pompey, l. 1. c. 28. s. 1. 5:185}

4360. Pompey advanced into Cilicia with a very large number of engines, intending to attack the pirates who were located on the rocks. This he did not need to do, for his fame and the news of his preparation terrified the pirates who thought that he would be more merciful if they did not fight him. Those who commanded the large citadels of Cragus and Anticragus were the first to come in and submit themselves, later followed by all the Cilicians on the mountains. They turned over many arms that were either finished or still being made, including many ships, half completed in the docks, and others ready for sail. As well, they turned over brass and iron prepared for these ships and sails, ropes and

other material. They surrendered a large number of captives who had been forced to ransom themselves or work in their prisons. Pompey burned the materials, carried away the ships and sent the prisoners home. Many of them saw their own tombstones, made for them by their relatives when they had assumed them to be long dead. {*Appian, Mithridatic Wars, l. 12. c. 14. (96) 2:423} Thus the pirates were vanquished and all the might of the pirates was subdued in every part of the sea in no more than three months, {*Plutarch, Pompey, l. 1. c. 28. s. 2. 5:187} or two months, if we are prepared to follow Lucan. {*Lucan, l. 2. (576) 1:101}

Before twice Cynthia did wax and wane,
The frightened rover left the all horrid main
To seek a dwelling in some private plain.

4361. Pompey burned more than thirteen hundred boats and destroyed their settlements. {*Strabo, l. 14. c. 3. s. 3. 6:315} Seventy-two ships were taken by force and three hundred and six surrendered. {*Appian, Mithridatic Wars, l. 12. c. 14. (96) 2:423} Plutarch stated that eight hundred surrendered and of these, ninety had prows of brass. {*Plutarch, Pompey, l. 1. c. 28. s. 2. 5:187} Pliny affirmed that eight hundred and forty-six ships were taken or sunk. {*Pliny, l. 7. c. 25,26. 2:567,569} A hundred and twenty towns, citadels and storehouses were taken and ten thousand pirates were killed in the battle. {*Appian, Mithridatic Wars, l. 12. c. 14. (96) 2:423}

4362. Twenty thousand of the pirates were left alive because Pompey determined to let them live. However, he did not think it was wise to permit them to leave or to allow many soldiers and desperate persons to stay together. {*Plutarch, Pompey, l. 1. c. 28. s. 2,3. 5:187} In case poverty might constrain them to future piracy, he relocated them into a certain place remote from the sea and gave them the abandoned fields for farming. He put some in cities that were in need of inhabitants and gave them a capacity to live without resorting to thievery. {*Livy, l. 99. 14:123} {*Velleius Paterculus, l. 2. c. 32. s. 4-6. 1:119,121} {*Florus, l. 1. c. 41. s. 14,15. 1:195} {*Dio, l. 36. (37) 3:63} He ordered them to settle in Mallus, Adana, Epiphanea and other remote towns in Cilicia Trachea. {*Appian, Mithridatic Wars, l. 12. c. 14. (96) 2:423} He also settled them in a coastal town of Cilicia which had formerly been called Soli, but which he called Pompeiopolis and which he repaired, as it had been destroyed by Tigranes, the Armenian king. He also transferred many to Dyme in Achaia, which lacked inhabitants. {*Strabo, l. 14. c. 3. s. 3. 6:315} {*Plutarch, Pompey, l. 1. c. 28. s. 4. 5:187} {*Dio, l. 36. (37) 3:63} [E577] [K228]

4363. Thus, the war that had lasted so long and been so large in its extent that it had affected all countries was concluded. Pompey prepared for it in the middle of winter, began it in the spring and finished it in the middle of summer. Cicero stated: {*Cicero, Pro Lege Manilia, l. 1. c. 11. (31) 9:43,45}

"Who ever supposed that a war of such dimensions, so inglorious and so long-standing, so widespread and so extensive could be brought to an end either by any number of generals in a single year or by a single general in any number of years?"

4364. Florus also said that, besides the swiftness of execution and the satisfaction in the success, not one ship was lost. From this point on, there would be no more pirates. This was achieved by the singular conduct of the captain in removing those who had been so used to the sea from the sight of it and resettling them in the midland countries. Should he not be listened to, when he speaks of the speediness of the conquest, because what had happened only of his success in the lower seas (which indeed in itself was truly amazing), he attributes to the general's prowess? He said this was all finished in forty days. {*Florus, l. 1. c. 41. s. 15. 1:195} Cicero denied this and so did Dio, saying that the greater part of the seas was made safe by Pompey in that very year. {*Dio, l. 36. (37) 3:61} {*Cicero, Pro Lege Manilia, l. 1. c. 11. (31,32) 9:45}

4365. In Crete (which Plutarch stated was the next haven of the pirates, after Cilicia), the prisoners were so harshly dealt with, that most of them poisoned themselves. Others sent to Pompey, although he was absent, and said that they would surrender to him. {*Florus, l. 1. c. 41. s. 12,13. 1:193,195} At the time, Pompey was in Pamphylia, so their envoys came there and promised that all the cities in Crete would surrender themselves to him. He did not disappoint them but he demanded hostages. {*Cicero, Pro Lege Manilia, l. 1. c. 12. (35) 9:49} In the meantime, he forbade Metellus from interfering in this war and wrote to the cities that they should not obey him. {*Plutarch, Pompey, l. 1. c. 29. s. 2,3. 5:189} He also ordered Metellus to leave the island since Pompey would take that charge upon himself as part of the charge committed to him. {*Appian, Sicily and the Other Islands, l. 5. c. 6. (2) 1:137} He sent one of his officers, Lucius Octavius, without an army there since he was not to go to wage war but to receive the cities into the favour of the people of Rome. However, he shut himself up within the walls together with those that were besieged by Metellus. He fought alongside them and made Pompey's name odious and contemptible. {*Plutarch, Pompey, l. 1. c. 29. s. 3,4. 5:189} {*Dio, l. 36. (18,19) 3:27,29}

4366. Metellus despised the command of Pompey, who was in another province, and continued to pursue his intended war. He was all the more severe in the war because he was exercising the right of a conqueror on his enemies and hurrying to subdue them before Pompey

could come. {*Plutarch, Pompey, l. 1. c. 29. s. 4,5. 5:189,191} {*Dio, l. 36. (17a) 3:27} {*Florus, l. 1. c. 42. s. 4-6. 1:197} He sent letters to Rome, complaining that Pompey had deprived him of the glory of his actions who had sent his envoy into Crete to accept the surrender of the cities. Pompey justified his actions. {*Livy, l. 99. 14:123}

4367. Cornelius Sisenna, who was governor of Greece at this time, came into Crete with his army and admonished Metellus to spare the people. However, Cornelius could not persuade him and did nothing that compelled him to be more tolerant. {*Dio, l. 36. (18) 3:29}

4368. Aristion marched from Cydonia after he had defeated Lucius Balsas, who had come out to attack him. [K229] He took Hierapydna and defended that city against the Romans. {*Dio, l. 36. (19) 3:29}

4369. Metellus bribed many within the city of Eleuthera and took it by treachery. The conspirators softened a large tower of brick with vinegar for several nights. Otherwise, the tower would have been extremely hard to take. Later, he extorted money from Eleuthera and took Lappa by force. He was not deterred by the fact that Octavius was in command there and did him no harm. He only killed the Cilicians he found about him. {*Dio, l. 36. (18,19) 3:29} Metellus dismissed Octavius, after he had been mocked and abused with many degrading actions in the camp. {*Plutarch, Pompey, l. 1. c. 29. s. 5. 5:189,191}

4370. Octavius did not like this treatment and did not waste time as before. He took command of Sisenna's army, as the latter had recently died of a disease. He relieved those who were being oppressed by Metellus and then went to Aristion where he managed their war by mutual consent and continued in that position for some time. When they heard that Metellus was advancing against them, they forsook their citadels and sailed away. However they were hit by a storm and were forced to put ashore and lost many of their men. {*Dio, l. 36. (19) 3:29}

4371. Marcus Cotta had dismissed his quaestor, Publius Oppius, on suspicion of defrauding the treasury and conspiring against him. However, Cotta himself had gathered a large amount of money in Bithynia, for which he was accused by Gaius Carbo, who was made consul, although previously he had only been a tribune. {*Dio, l. 36. (40) 3:67} {See note on 3935b AM. <<4298>>} [E578]

## 3938a AM, 4647 JP, 67 BC

4372. After Sinatruces (whom Appian called Sintricus, and Dio referred to by the common name of the kings of Parthia, Arsaces) died, his son Phraates succeeded him. He was the second king of Parthia by that name, and was, by a most impious title, called *the god*. {*Appian, Mithridatic Wars, l. 12. c. 15. (104) 2:439} {*Dio, l. 36.

*(45) 3:75}* {*Phlegon, Photius' Bibliotheca, cod. 97.*} {*See note on 3935b AM. <<4291>>*}

4373. Hyrcanus was driven from his kingdom by Aristobulus, his younger brother, three months after the death of his mother Alexandra. {*Josephus, Antiq., l. 15. c. 6. s. 4. (180) 8:87}* However, it appears that there were six years from the time Hyrcanus began to reign, which occurred when Quintus Hortensius and Gaius Metellus were consuls, to the latter end of the reign of Aristobulus. It was in that year that Jerusalem was taken by Pompey, when Gaius Antonius and Marcus Tullius Cicero were consuls. Josephus allowed three years and three months to Aristobulus. Therefore, Hyrcanus must have ruled for about three years, not three months. From these three years we think we must deduct two months to make the time exact. {*Josephus, Antiq., l. 14. c. 1. s. 2. (4-7) 7:451,453}*

4374. About this time, they fought at Jericho and many of Hyrcanus' men defected to his brother Aristobulus. Hyrcanus fled into the citadel where the wife and children of Aristobulus had been placed by Alexandra, his mother. The rest fled to the temple in fear of Aristobulus and surrendered a short time later. Finally, the brothers came to a peace treaty. Aristobulus would rule and his brother would be allowed to lead a private life and enjoy the wealth he had acquired by his wits. *[K230]* They made this covenant in the temple and after all oaths had been made, they embraced each other in the sight of the people. Aristobulus took over the court and Hyrcanus retired as a private person to Aristobulus' house. {*Josephus, Antiq., l. 14. c. 1. s. 2. (4-7) 7:451,453}* Thus Aristobulus held the kingdom and the chief priest's office for three years and three months. {*Josephus, Antiq., l. 20. c. 10. s. 4. (243,244) 10:131}*

4375. Lucius Tullius and Aemilius Lepidus were consuls at the beginning of their consulship in January, which was really October on the Julian calendar. At this time, the Senate annulled a law that the night before had been passed by the people and sponsored by Gaius Manilius, a tribune of the people. He had bribed some of the populace to vote for this law which stated that any freed slaves should be allowed the same voting privileges as their masters. For this reason, Manilius feared for his safety because the common people were very angry. To ingratiate himself with Pompey, he proclaimed another law, which stated that the charge of the war with Tigranes and Mithridates should be given to Pompey. He was to be assigned the legions and provinces which were under Lucullus, as well as Cilicia, which was under the command of Marcius, the sole consul, and Bithynia, under Acilius Glabrio. Also, there would be no change in Pompey's maritime command. {*Dio, l. 36. (42) 3:69,71}* {*Livy, l. 100. 14:125}* {*Velleius Paterculus, l. 2. c. 33. 1:121}* {*Asconius Pedianus, Pro Cornelio}* {*Plutarch, Pompey, l. 1. c. 30. s. 1. 5:191}*

4376. Livy noted that this law was passed with great indignation from the nobility. {*Livy, l. 100. 14:125}* To the Senate, it seemed no less than an obvious insult to Lucullus. Pompey was not so much being sent to succeed him in the war as in the victory and to take possession of the spoils he had taken rather than the administration of the war. {*Plutarch, Lucullus, l. 1. c. 35. s. 7. 2:589}* Nor did it please those who were forced to recall Marcius and Acilius from their commands before the time they had given them had expired. {*Dio, l. 36. (43) 3:71}* They were chiefly jealous of Pompey's power to whom the whole Roman Empire was subjected by this means. For those provinces which he did not control under the former Gabinian law, like Phrygia, Lycaonia, Galatia, Cappadocia, Cilicia, the upper Colchis and Armenia, were now under his power, through this law. {*Plutarch, Pompey, l. 1. c. 30. s. 2. 5:191}* Furthermore, he received the power to make war and settle a peace and by his own will, and at his pleasure, judge anyone his enemy or make any his friend and associate, as he thought best. He also had the command of all the armies from Italy. No Roman before him had ever had so much power. {*Appian, Mithridatic Wars, l. 12. c. 15. (97) 2:425}*

4377. At this time, Cicero, who was then a praetor, made his speech for the Manilian Law, in the 23rd year after that cruel slaughter of the citizens of Rome which had been perpetrated in Asia in a single day, on Mithridates' order: {*Cicero, Pro Lege Manilia, l. 1. c. 3. (7) 9:21}*

> "He now reigns, the 23rd year from that time, and reigns not so as to hide himself in Pontus or Cappadocia but to break out and invade the tributaries and breathe your Asian air."

4378. Pompey was still following up on his victory over the pirates in Cilicia. Plutarch, however, stated that the war was over and since Pompey had nothing to do, he was visiting the cities around there. {*Plutarch, Pompey, l. 1. c. 30. s. 1. 5:191}* When he received letters from Rome, he learned what had happened there and his friends congratulated him on the news. However, he was reported to have frowned and struck his thigh, as though he were already weary and discontented with his command. *[K231]* But they all knew he really wanted that opportunity. {*Plutarch, Pompey, l. 1. c. 30. s. 5,6. 5:193}* {*Dio, l. 36. (45) 3:75}* *[E579]* Although he had earlier made a plan of sailing into Crete to Metellus, he now abandoned that and all his maritime business, as if nothing had been left undone. Instead, he applied himself fully to the war with the barbarians, {*Dio, l. 36. (45) 3:75}* recalling the soldiers to him and requesting the assistance of all the kings and potentates he had received as friends. {*Plutarch, Pompey, l. 1. c. 31. s. 1. 5:193}*

4379. Tigranes, the younger, grandchild of Mithridates by his daughter, revolted from his father Tigranes and was defeated but not captured. He joined up with the chief men, who were discontented with his father, and defected to Phraates, the king of the Parthians. {*Livy, l. 100. 14:125} {*Appian, Mithridatic Wars, l. 12. c. 15. (104) 2:439} {*Dio, l. 36. (45) 3:75}

4380. Pompey continued in his war with Mithridates and renewed his league with Phraates, the king of Parthia {*Livy, l. 100. 14:125} on the same conditions which had previously been offered by Sulla and Lucullus. Pompey said that: {*Lucan, l. 8. (218,220) 1:463}

"If our ancient treaty holds good—the treaty which I swore to observe in the name of the Roman Thunderer...."

4381. According to the agreement, Phraates and Tigranes, the younger, together invaded Armenia which was subject to Tigranes. They advanced as far as Artaxata overcoming all opposition on the way and besieged it. Tigranes, the elder, withdrew into the mountains in fear. {*Dio, l. 36. (45) 3:75,77}

## 3938b AM, 4648 JP, 66 BC

4382. Pompey wanted to find out Mithridates' intentions and sent Metrophanes to him with very friendly proposals. Mithridates had hoped that Phraates, who was the new king of Parthia, would have joined with him and rejected the proposals. But when he found out that Phraates had a league with Pompey and had been engaged to invade Armenia, he had second thoughts and promptly sent envoys with propositions of peace. Pompey demanded that he lay down his arms and surrender those who had defected from the Romans. {*Dio, l. 36. (45) 3:75}

4383. As soon as Mithridates' army heard this, the many Roman deserters suspected they would be turned over to Pompey. The barbarians rebelled too who thought they would have to continue the war without their help. This would have been disastrous for Mithridates had he not pretended that he had sent his envoys to spy out the strength of the enemy rather than to seek peace. {*Dio, l. 36. (45) 3:77} He swore, moreover, that he would not enter into friendship with the Romans because they were so covetous nor would he surrender any of them or do anything that was not for the common good. {*Appian, Mithridatic Wars, l. 12. c. 15. (98) 2:425}

4384. When Pompey arrived in Galatia, Lucullus came to meet him at the citadel of Danala. {*Dio, l. 36. (46) 3:77} {*Strabo, l. 12. c. 5. s. 2. 5:469,471} Lucullus, with regard to his age and the dignity of his consulships, was the better man. However, Pompey's dignity, with respect to the

number of his commands and the two triumphs that he had enjoyed, was greater than that of Lucullus. Both of them had garlands of laurel carried before them in honour of their victories, but Pompey's laurels were dead and withered, because he had come on a long journey through dry and squalid countries. When Lucullus' lictors saw this, they courteously presented him with some of theirs which were fresh and green. [K232] Pompey's friends looked on this sign of friendship as a good omen signifying that he should carry the rewards of Lucullus' victories. {*Plutarch, Lucullus, l. 1. c. 36. s. 1-3. 2:589,591} {*Plutarch, Pompey, l. 1. c. 31. s. 1-4. 5:195}

4385. Lucullus told him that everything had already been subdued and that there was no reason for this expedition at all. Also, he said that the persons sent by the Senate had come to settle affairs. But when he failed to persuade Pompey to go back, he started to complain and to slander him so much so that a great argument arose between them. {*Dio, l. 36. (46) 3:77} Pompey objected to Lucullus' covetousness and Lucullus complained about Pompey's insatiable desire for command. Neither of them could be accused of saying anything untrue. {*Velleius Paterculus, l. 2. c. 33. s. 3,4. 1:121,123} {*Plutarch, Pompey, l. 1. c. 31. s. 3,4. 5:195}

4386. For this reason, Lucullus disposed of the lands he had taken from the enemy as he pleased besides giving away many good gifts. Pompey sharply reproved him for this, in that he was settling and conferring honours and rewards while the enemy was not yet defeated, something not normally done until the war was over. Offended, Pompey moved his camp a little farther from him and ordered that no one should obey or come near Lucullus. He made a public edict forbidding the confirmation of Lucullus' acts or any counsel his officers might put forward. [E580] Since Pompey had the larger army, he was the more formidable. Pompey left Lucullus only sixteen hundred men for his triumph and took away all his soldiers but due to their rebellious behaviour they were as useless to him as they had been to Lucullus. {*Plutarch, Lucullus, l. 1. c. 36. s. 4-6. 2:591} {*Plutarch, Pompey, l. 1. c. 31. s. 5-7. 5:195,197} Only the Valerian or Fimbrian legions served Pompey faithfully, although they had been rebellious under Lucullus. {*Dio, l. 36. (46) 3:77} {*Dio, l. 36. (16) 3:25}

4387. Lucullus returned from there to Rome bringing along with him a good number of books which, according to Isidorus, were part of his spoil from Pontus. {Origen, l. 6. c. 3.} He placed them in his library, which was always open to everyone, especially the Greeks. {*Plutarch, Lucullus, l. 1. c. 42. s. 1. 2:605} He was also the first one to bring cherries into Italy. {*Pliny, l. 15. c. 30. 4:359} In spite of his poor treatment by Pompey, he was received very honourably by the Senate. {*Plutarch, Lucullus, l. 1. c. 38. s. 2. 2:595,597}

*4388.* When Metellus had defeated the island of Crete, he took away their laws from an island which, before that time, had been free. {*Livy, l. 100. 14:125}* He deprived them of the liberty they had for so long enjoyed, by imposing his taxes on them. {*Velleius Paterculus, l. 2. c. 38. 1:133}* Orosius stated that Metellus subdued that island in two years wearing it out with continual skirmishes. {Orosius, l. 6. c. 4.} Eutropius said that he overcame the whole country in three years in several large battles. {Eutropius, l. 6.} Velleius Paterculus agreed with him and said this: {*Velleius Paterculus, l. 2. c. 34. 1:123}*

> "About that time, the island of Crete was subdued by the Romans. They had resisted with an army of twenty-four thousand young men who were pernicious in their agility, patient in respect to labour and skilful in respect to the management of their arms. Under the command of Panares and Lasthenes, together they had worn out the Roman armies for three years."

*4389.* Lucius Flaccus, along with the commander-in-chief, bore the brunt of that war. {*Cicero, Pro Flacco, l. 1. (6) 10:447}* Gaius Nasennius, a freedman from Suessa, was the first centurion of the eighth cohort. {*Cicero, Letters to Brutus, l. 1. c. 15. s. 2. 28:671}* Gnaeus Plancius was a person highly regarded by the envoys, Gaius Sacerdos and Lucius Flaccus. He was a soldier under Quintus Metellus. {*Cicero, Pro Plancio, l. 1. c. 11. 11:441}*

*4390.* Hence, the men of Crete, who had previously been free and had never known any foreign command, were brought under the yoke and Metellus received the name of *Creticus* in recognition of this from the Senate. {*Dio, l. 36. (17a) 3:27} [K233]*

*4391.* Antipas, also called Antipater, was the governor of Idumea and father of Herod, the king of Judea. Antipater was a rich and energetic man and a troublemaker. He feared Aristobulus' power because of some grudges between them and so sided with Hyrcanus' party. When the secret slander of Aristobulus proved effective, Antipater stirred up the chief of the Jews to enter into a conspiracy against him. He suggested it would be very unwise to let Aristobulus occupy a position he had usurped by force, having displaced his older brother and robbed him of the prerogative of his birth. Antipater continually worked away on Hyrcanus. He added that his very life was in danger unless he fled, for Aristobulus' friends were continually scheming how they would be able to confer his authority on someone else once they had removed him out of the way. Hyrcanus, however, was a good man and not easily moved by rumours and so gave little credence to his information. His quiet disposition and gentleness of mind had given him the reputation of being slothful. Antipater continued to complain about Aristobulus as if he had plans to kill Hyrcanus. {*Josephus, Antiq., l. 14. c. 1. s. 3. (8-13) 7:453}*

*4392.* Phraates decided it was likely that the siege of Artaxata would last a long time, so he left some of his troops with Tigranes' son and returned home. {*Dio, l. 36. (51) 3:87}*

*4393.* Farther Spain was allocated to Gaius Julius Caesar when he was a quaestor. He was ordered by the praetor to travel around the various countries and decide matters of law. When he came to Gades, he saw Alexander the Great's statue in Hercules' temple. He was grieved that he had done nothing of note by the time he was thirty-four, the age at which Alexander had conquered the world. He became greatly depressed and begged that he might be sent back to Rome so that he could attempt some noble thing at the first opportunity. He left before his time expired and went to some Italian colonies that were in rebellion. He would have stirred them to do something had not the consuls kept them under control with their legions which had been raised to go into Cilicia. {*Suetonius, Julius, l. 1. c. 7,8. 1:43,45}*

*4394.* With his navy, Pompey controlled all the seas between Phoenicia and the Bosphorus. He advanced against Mithridates with a select army of thirty thousand foot soldiers, arranged in a phalanx, for the safekeeping of his country. Plutarch said that he also had two thousand cavalry, Appian said three thousand. {*Plutarch, Pompey, l. 1. c. 32. s. 1,2. 5:197} {*Appian, Mithridatic Wars, l. 12. c. 15. (97) 2:425}* Since Lucullus had recently pillaged that country, Mithridates' troops was very short of provisions. Many fled to Pompey although Mithridates used all the severity he could to prevent this. He crucified some, put out their eyes, or burned them alive. *[E581]* This prevented many from defecting but they were very short of provisions. {*Appian, Mithridatic Wars, l. 12. c. 15. (97) 2:425}*

*4395.* Pompey placed some troops in an ambush and sent others out to face the king's camp and provoke him to battle. They had orders to turn and flee after the enemy came out, thereby drawing Mithridates into his trap. *[K234]* The king suspected it and drew out his foot soldiers otherwise they might possibly have pursued them as far as their camp. This was the first skirmish between the cavalries. {*Appian, Mithridatic Wars, l. 12. c. 15. (98) 2:427}*

*4396.* Because Mithridates was outnumbered, he avoided fighting Pompey and instead destroyed the countries through which he came. By marching up and down, he tried to wear out his enemy or cause them to run short of provisions. Pompey went into Lesser Armenia which was subject to Mithridates, partly to get food and partly to take it over, since it was without enemy troops. Finally,

Mithridates also went there to prevent the province from falling into the hands of his enemies in his absence. {*Dio, l. 36. (47) 3:77,79}

4397. Mithridates camped opposite his enemy in a strong and secure position on a hill. He stayed there quietly with his whole army, hoping by intercepting their provisions to cause the Romans distress and thereby to defeat them. Mithridates was in his own country and was being kept well supplied from every region. Below this hill there was a plain into which he sent some cavalry to confront and cut off everyone they met. This is how it came about that many from the enemy defected to him. {*Dio, l. 36. (47) 3:79}

4398. Pompey did not dare attack the enemy in that place and moved his camp to another spacious area surrounded by woods. In this way he protected himself from their troops and arrows. He laid an ambush in a convenient place then made a few advances and faced their camp. After raising a tumult, he drew the enemy from their works to the place he had planned and soundly defeated them. The Romans were encouraged by this victory and Pompey sent his men to the other regions of the country to bring in provisions. {*Dio, l. 36. (47) 3:79}

4399. Mithridates left the hill where he was camped, because he thought it was a dry barren place. Pompey then came and occupied it and when he observed that the plants grew so well and that there was a hollowness and convex shape of the place, he thought there must be water there. He ordered his troops to dig wells up and down the hill. They soon had so much water in their camp that he wondered why Mithridates had not found it long ago. {*Plutarch, Pompey, l. 1. c. 32. s. 1,2. 5:197,199}

4400. Mithridates camped on a mountain near Dastira in Acilisene which had abundant water and was not far from the Euphrates River which divides Acilisene and Lesser Armenia. {*Strabo, l. 12. c. 3. s. 28. 5:425} Orosius wrote that Pompey blockaded the king's camp near the Dastracus Mountain in Lesser Armenia and made a line around the king of about eighteen miles. {Orosius, l. 6. c. 4.} He built several citadels there, so that he could intercept their foragers. The king did not hinder the work either out of fear or folly which were often the forerunners of disaster. {*Appian, Mithridatic Wars, l. 12. c. 15. (99) 2:427} Plutarch said that Mithridates was besieged for forty-five days but Appian said it was for fifty days. They could barely keep themselves alive, having killed all the cattle they had only sparing the horses. {*Appian, Mithridatic Wars, l. 12. c. 15. (99) 2:427} {*Plutarch, Pompey, l. 1. c. 32. s. 3. 5:199}

4401. Finally, Mithridates discovered that the enemy had been supplied with provisions and had captured a

country in Armenia called Anaitis. Many of his men defected to Pompey and Marius' army. The legions which Suetonius had said were raised for Cilicia, where Pompey was governor, were coming to Pompey. Mithridates was afraid and decided to leave that country. {*Dio, l. 36. (48) 3:79} He killed those who were sick and of no use to him. With the entire army he went out very quietly in the night and escaped. {*Appian, Mithridatic Wars, l. 12. c. 15. (99) 2:427} {*Plutarch, Pompey, l. 1. c. 32. s. 3. 5:199} {Orosius, l. 6. c. 4.} [K235] By marching through the night, he planned to go into Greater Armenia, which was subject to Tigranes, and there to drive off Pompey should he pursue him. {*Dio, l. 36. (48) 3:79} {Orosius, l. 6. c. 4.}

4402. The following day after much trouble Pompey caught up to him and attacked him from the rear. The king would not fight in spite of his friends' advice and was satisfied merely to beat back the enemy with some cavalry. In the evening he retired into the woods. {*Appian, Mithridatic Wars, l. 12. c. 15. (99) 2:427,429}

4403. The next day Mithridates occupied a strong position that was surrounded on all sides by rocks and had only one way in which he guarded with four cohorts of foot soldiers. The Romans also guarded the entrance to prevent the escape of the king. {*Appian, Mithridatic Wars, l. 12. c. 15. (99) 2:429} [E582]

4404. When they arrived at the border Pompey feared that Mithridates would get ahead of him, cross the Euphrates River and make his escape, so he resolved to force a battle with him at night. {*Plutarch, Pompey, l. 1. c. 32. s. 3,4. 5:199} {*Dio, l. 36. (48) 3:81} By moving his camp, he deceived the barbarians who were taking their noonday rest. He marched ahead by the same way that they were to come. Occupying a convenient place among the hills, he drew up his men into the highest area and waited for the enemy. The barbarians did not suspect this and since the Romans had not fought with them, they did not even send scouts ahead to spy out their way. {*Dio, l. 36. (48) 3:81}

4405. It is said that Mithridates had a vision in his sleep at the time which forewarned him of what was to happen. He seemed to be sailing with a fair wind on the Pontic Sea and came within sight of the Bosphorus. He was joyfully overcome with a certain and unquestionable sense of safety and pleasantly began to make conversation with those who carried him. Suddenly he found himself deserted and tossed about on a small part of the wreckage. While he was thinking about this vision, his friends who were close to him awoke him and told him that Pompey was nearby. Therefore, forced to fight for his camp, he brought out his army and both sides drew into battle array. {*Plutarch, Pompey, l. 1. c. 32. s. 4,5. 5:199}

*4406.* When Pompey saw that they were prepared for a battle, he thought it best not to fight during the night but to surround them so they could not escape. He could attack them the next morning with his army which was much stronger. However the more senior and leading men among his officers provoked him with their urging to attack in the night. {*Plutarch, Pompey, l. 1. c. 32. s. 5. 5:199,201}

*4407.* Therefore, it was agreed that all the trumpets would together sound a charge. After this, the soldiers and the whole multitude would give a shout and then some would strike their spears against their brass vessels. The mountains echoed and made the noise more horrible. When the barbarians suddenly heard this at night in a deserted place, they were extremely dismayed and supposed that some misery inflicted by the gods had befallen them. In the meantime the Romans were throwing stones, arrows and javelins down from above on every side. Since there were so many barbarians almost every object hit someone. After they had shot all their arrows, they ran down violently at the barbarians. These were kicking and pressing each other forward and so were killed because they were neither able to defend themselves nor to attack the enemy. Most of them were cavalry men and archers who could do little in the dark and in a confined space. {*Dio, l. 36. (49) 3:81,83} [K236]

*4408.* As soon as the moon was up, the barbarians were encouraged, thinking they could possibly repel the enemy by its light. This might have helped them except for the fact that the moon was on the Romans' backs so that as the moon began to rise, their shadows appeared a long way ahead of their bodies and close to the enemy. They judged their distance by these long shadows and so did not shoot their arrows far enough to hit the Romans who later attacked them and easily defeated them. {*Dio, l. 36. (49) 3:83,85} {*Plutarch, Pompey, l. 1. c. 32. s. 6,7. 5:201} {*Florus, l. 1. c. 40. s. 23,24. 1:187} {Eutropius, l. 6.}

*4409.* This battle took place at night. {*Livy, l. 100. 14:125} {*Dio, l. 36. (49) 3:83,85} {*Plutarch, Pompey, l. 1. c. 32. s. 6,7. 5:201} {*Florus, l. 1. c. 40. s. 23,24. 1:187} {Eutropius, l. 6.} {Orosius, l. 6. c. 4.} Only Appian said it was in the day and happened as follows. Both armies were drawn up early in the morning when some soldiers from both sides advanced and skirmished among the rocks. Some of the king's cavalry men came running on foot without orders to relieve their fellow soldiers. They were charged by a large number of the Roman cavalry and ran back to their camp in one company to get their horses to enable them better to confront their enemy. From a high place, the Pontics who were on guard witnessed the noise and haste as they ran and thinking their camp had been breached in some other part, took this to be the reason for their flight. They threw away their arms and fled but there was nowhere

to escape. They ran afoul of one another until they threw themselves down the rocks in their haste. It was easy for Pompey to carry out the rest, killing and taking prisoner all those that were unarmed and so entangled among the rocks. Ten thousand were killed and their camp was taken, along with all their ammunition and baggage. {*Appian, Mithridatic Wars, l. 12. c. 15. (100) 2:429,431}

*4410.* Plutarch stated that many more than ten thousand were killed. {*Plutarch, Pompey, l. 1. c. 32. s. 7. 5:201} Dio said that there were very many killed and just as many taken prisoner. {*Dio, l. 36. (49) 3:85} Eutropius stated the total was forty thousand. {Eutropius, l. 6.} Orosius stated that this many were either killed or captured. {Orosius, l. 6. c. 4.} Eutropius said Pompey lost only twenty or thirty of his men and two of his captains, while Orosius claimed the Romans had a thousand wounded and about forty killed.

*4411.* Mithridates broke through the Roman lines with a troop of eight hundred cavalry. At length, when all the rest had abandoned him, he was left with only three in his company. [E583] One of these was Hypsicratia, whom the king called Hypsicrates because of her masculine spirit. Plutarch called her his concubine but Valerius Maximus and Eutropius said she was his wife. Although she wore a Persian man's clothes and rode on horseback, she was not tired either by the tediousness of her own flight or by care and concern for the king. {*Plutarch, Pompey, l. 1. c. 32. s. 8-7. 5:201} {*Valerius Maximus, l. 4. c. 6. ext. 2. 1:409} {Eutropius, l. 6.} His daughter Dripetine accompanied him in this distressing time. She had been born to him by Laodice, the queen, but was very deformed by a double row of teeth. {*Valerius Maximus, l. 1. c. 8. ext. 13. 1:123}

*4412.* Hence Mithridates, aided by a clear night, escaped through the confusion of the battle. He walked his horse when he came into remote places and trembled at every noise he heard. {Orosius, l. 6. c. 4.} Finally he came across some mercenary cavalry and three thousand foot soldiers who escorted him into the citadel of Sinorex where he had stored a great deal of money. {*Appian, Mithridatic Wars, l. 12. c. 15. (101) 2:431} This citadel, which Plutarch called Sinora, but Strabo called Sinoria, or Synoria, was located on the border of Greater and Lesser Armenia. {*Plutarch, Pompey, l. 1. c. 32. s. 8. 5:201} {*Strabo, l. 12. c. 3. s. 28. 5:425} [K237]

*4413.* Mithridates gave gifts and a year's pay to those who had escorted him in his flight while he himself took six thousand talents along with him. {*Appian, Mithridatic Wars, l. 12. c. 15. (101) 2:431} He also gave expensive garments to those who came to him from the rout, as well as giving deadly poison to his friends to carry about with them, in case any of them should fall into the enemy's hands. From there he marched into Armenia to Tigranes. {*Plutarch, Pompey, l. 1. c. 32. s. 8,9. 5:201}

4414. Tigranes was pestered by the envoys from Mithridates but would not receive Mithridates, instead throwing his envoys into prison. He pretended that Mithridates was responsible for his son's rebellion. Since his hopes were thus frustrated, Mithridates crossed over the Euphrates River and fled into Colchis which had formerly been subject to him. {*Appian, Mithridatic Wars, l. 12. c. 15. (101) 2:431} {*Dio, l. 36. (50) 3:85} {*Plutarch, Pompey, l. 1. c. 32. s. 9. 5:203} {*Strabo, l. 12. c. 3. s. 28. 5:425} {*Plutarch, Pompey, l. 1. c. 32. s. 9. 5:203}

4415. Mithridates did not stop and on the fourth day he crossed the Euphrates River. They armed themselves for three days and assigned the troops he had with him or who came to him. He came to Chotene, the chief town in Armenia. The Choteneans and Iberians had tried to impede his march with slings and arrows but he was able to beat off their attack. Then he advanced to the Absarus River. {*Appian, Mithridatic Wars, l. 12. c. 15. (101) 2:431}

4416. Pompey sent out troops to pursue Mithridates but he had crossed the Phasis River and escaped. So Pompey built a city at the same site where he had won his victory between the two rivers which had their source in the same mountain. These were the Euphrates and Araxes Rivers, located in Lesser Armenia, and he called the city, Nicopolis which means *Victory*. With his soldiers' consent, he gave this city to those who were old or lame, sick or wounded, or who had been disbanded. Also many of the neighbouring people moved there and the Nicopolitans lived according to the customs of the Cappadocians. {*Dio, l. 36. (50) 3:85,87} {*Strabo, l. 12. c. 3. s. 28. 5:425} {*Appian, Mithridatic Wars, l. 12. c. 15. (105) 2:441} {*Appian, Mithridatic Wars, l. 12. c. 17. (115) 2:463} {Orosius, l. 6. c. 4.}

4417. Tigranes, the father, advanced against Tigranes, his son, who had been left alone to besiege Artaxata and defeated him. First, he fled toward Mithridates, his grandfather. But when he heard that he too had been defeated and was more likely to be in need of help than in a position to help him, Tigranes defected to the Romans. {*Dio, l. 36. (51) 3:87} He was willing to help them, even though he was Mithridates' grandson by his daughter. {*Appian, Mithridatic Wars, l. 12. c. 15. (104) 2:439} He met Pompey at the Araxes River and guided Pompey and his army into Armenia against his father who was considered a confederate of Mithridates. {*Plutarch, Pompey, l. 1. c. 33. s. 1. 5:203} {*Dio, l. 36. (51) 3:87} They went to Artaxata to the court of Tigranes. {*Appian, Mithridatic Wars, l. 12. c. 15. (104) 2:437}

4418. When Tigranes, the father, found out about this, he was filled with great alarm. When he heard that Pompey was of a gentle and pleasant nature, he sent a herald to him through whose agency he turned over Mithridates' envoys whom he had imprisoned. His son

prevented him from obtaining any tolerable conditions and Pompey still crossed the Araxes River and approached Artaxata. At length, Tigranes surrendered the city and the entire garrison that was in it. With his friends and kindred, he went out to meet Pompey without so much as sending a herald ahead of them. He surrendered all his rights to him and appealed for justice against his son. {*Plutarch, Pompey, l. 1. c. 33. s. 2-4. 5:203} {*Dio, l. 36. (52) 3:87,89} {*Appian, Mithridatic Wars, l. 12. c. 15. (104) 2:437,439} [K238]

4419. So that he might appear deserving of respect and compassion in Pompey's eyes, he said he would retain a mediocre position, somewhere between his former dignity and his present misery. He had taken off his gown that was half white and his royal robe of purple but still wore his diadem and the ornaments for his head. {*Dio, l. 36. (52) 3:89} When Pompey sent the captains and officers of his cavalry to meet and honour him, Tigranes' friends, who were with him, fled for they worried about their safety because they had sent no heralds ahead of them. {*Appian, Mithridatic Wars, l. 12. c. 15. (104) 2:439} [E584]

4420. When Tigranes came to Pompey's camp, which was sixteen miles away from Artaxata, two lictors from Pompey came to him and ordered him to get off his horse. For no man alive had ever been observed entering a Roman camp on horseback and he had entered the works themselves, according to the customs of his country. Tigranes obeyed unbuckling his sword and handed it over to them. {Eutropius, l. 6.} {*Plutarch, Pompey, l. 1. c. 33. s. 3. 5:203} {*Dio, l. 36. (52) 3:89} Pompey saw him enter on foot after he had thrown away his crown and prostrate himself on the ground according to the custom of the barbarians. Touched with compassion, Pompey ran over to him, caught him by the hand, lifted him up and replaced the crown that he had thrown aside. Pompey ordered him to sit down on one side of him and his son on the other side, but Tigranes' son did not rise up to greet his father, nor show him any respect. {*Cicero, Pro Sestio, l. 1. c. 27. 12:113,115} {Eutropius, l. 6.} {*Plutarch, Pompey, l. 1. c. 33. s. 3-6. 5:203,205} {*Dio, l. 36. (52,53) 3:89,91} {*Appian, Mithridatic Wars, l. 12. c. 15. (104) 2:439} {*Plutarch, Lucullus and Cimon, l. 1. c. 3. s. 3,4. 2:619}

4421. Tigranes surrendered himself and his kingdom to Pompey for he had previously stated that there was no man in Rome, or any other country, to whom he would have surrendered, other than to Pompey. He said that he would be content with whatever happened to him, whether it be good or bad. He also said that it was no disparagement to be conquered by him, whom it was a sin to conquer, nor was it dishonourable to submit to him, whom fortune had exalted above everyone. {*Velleius Paterculus, l. 2. c. 37. s. 3-5. 1:129,131} He and his son were later invited to supper by Pompey but the son excused himself and thereby gave Pompey a reason to be offended at him. {*Dio, l. 36. (52,53) 3:89}

4422. The next day, after their disputes had been heard, Pompey restored the kingdom of Armenia (the ancient possession of his forefathers) to Tigranes, the elder. Strabo said that he added the greatest and best part of Mesopotamia but took away the countries Tigranes had gained in the war. {*Strabo, l. 16. c. 1. s. 24. 7:231,233} He imposed a fine on him of six thousand talents of silver to be paid to the people of Rome because he had waged war with them without a cause. He gave his son the command of Gordyene and Sophene, with the freedom of joining the rest of Armenia to it when his father died. He gave the treasure in Sophene (a country in the borders of Armenia) to the father, otherwise he would not be able to pay his fine. {*Cicero, Pro Sestio, l. 1. c. 27. 12:113,115} {Eutropius, l. 6.} {*Plutarch, Pompey, l. 1. c. 33. s. 5,6. 5:205} {*Dio, l. 36. (53) 3:89,91} {*Appian, Mithridatic Wars, l. 12. c. 15. (104,105) 2:439,441} {*Velleius Paterculus, l. 2. c. 37. s. 3-5. 1:129,131} {*Plutarch, Lucullus and Cimon, l. 1. c. 3. s. 3,4. 2:619}

4423. Tigranes, the father, was very pleased about these conditions and the fact that he had been called a king by the Romans. He left and went through Cappadocia, some regions of Cilicia and all of Syria and Phoenicia, from the Euphrates River to the sea. He had controlled these provinces, together with part of Cilicia, after he had driven out Antiochus Pius. {Eutropius, l. 6.} {*Livy, l. 101. 14:125} {*Plutarch, Pompey, l. 1. c. 33. s. 4-6. 5:203,205} {*Dio, l. 36. (53) 3:89,91} {*Appian, Mithridatic Wars, l. 12. c. 15. (104,105) 2:439,441} {*Velleius Paterculus, l. 2. c. 37. s. 3-5. 1:129,131} [K239]

4424. The younger Tigranes was badly disappointed and plotted to escape. Pompey was aware of this and restrained him but with liberty to move around. He sent messengers to those who kept the money to demand it for Tigranes, the elder. They refused and stated they only took orders from the younger Tigranes, to whom they thought this country belonged. The younger Tigranes was sent to the citadel but was shut out. Against his will, he ordered them to open to him but the keepers refused and said he was only giving the order because Pompey was forcing him to do so. Displeased, Pompey put the younger Tigranes in chains and finally obtained the treasure for his father. {*Dio, l. 36. (53) 3:91}

4425. The Armenians, who had deserted the king on his journey to the Roman camp, asked his son, who was staying with Pompey, to dispose of his father but the son was taken and put in irons. However, while he was bound, he used his messengers to persuade the Parthians to fight the Romans and pretended he had been imprisoned for the triumph. {*Appian, Mithridatic Wars, l. 12. c. 15. (105) 2:441}

4426. After the father received his money, he handed over a greater portion of money than had been agreed on by Pompey. He freely gave every soldier fifty drachmas or, as Strabo said, a hundred and fifty or, according to Plutarch, half a mina of silver. Each centurion received a thousand drachmas or, as Plutarch said, ten minas of silver. Each tribune received ten thousand drachmas or, as Strabo and Plutarch have it, a talent, which is six thousand drachmas. Because of this, he was counted among the friends and confederates of the people of Rome. {*Strabo, l. 11. c. 14. s. 10. 5:331} {*Plutarch, Pompey, l. 1. c. 33. s. 5-6. 5:205} {*Dio, l. 36. (53) 3:91} {*Appian, Mithridatic Wars, l. 12. c. 15. (104) 2:439} According to his custom, Pompey delivered to the quaestor for the public use, the money that was owing to the people of Rome. {*Velleius Paterculus, l. 2. c. 37. s. 5. 1:131}

4427. Pompey gave Ariobarzanes the whole kingdom of Cappadocia, Sophene and Gordyene, which he had first assigned to the younger Tigranes. This area was later known as the province of Cappadocia. [E585] Pompey also gave him Castabala or Gabala, a city of Cilicia, along with some others, which Ariobarzanes later left to his sons. {*Appian, Mithridatic Wars, l. 12. c. 15. (105) 2:441}

## 3939a AM, 4648 JP, 66 BC

4428. A few days before Gaius Julius Caesar assumed the office of aedile, he was suspected of involvement in a conspiracy with Marcus Crassus, the consul. Publius Sulla and Lucius Antronius were also suspected, when their term as consuls expired. They were condemned for having tried to overthrow the republic at the beginning of the year. (January 1 corresponded to October on the Julian calendar, when Cotta and Torquatus entered the consulship.) They had planned to invade the Senate and kill whomever they pleased, while Crassus was to become the dictator and Caesar would be called the master of his cavalry. The whole state would be run as they saw fit and the consulship would be restored to Sulla and Antronius. It was with reference to this that Cicero, in a letter to Axius, stated that when Caesar was consul, he settled the kingdom as he had planned to do when he was an aedile. {*Suetonius, Julius, l. 1. c. 9. s. 1,2. 1:45}

4429. Pompey left Armenia under the command of Afranius and pursued Mithridates through the countries around the Caucasus. Of these, the largest countries belonged to the Albanians and Iberians, who allowed him to pass through when he first came. {*Plutarch, Pompey, l. 1. c. 34. s. 1,2. 5:205} Livy, however, said that Pompey fought and overcame them because they refused to allow him access. {*Livy, l. 101. 14:125} [K240] This battle is mentioned briefly by Plutarch and Appian, whereas Dio gives more details. Pompey divided his army into three parts and took his winter quarters near the Cyrnus River in the country around Tanais. In spite of this, he did not have peace. Oroeses, or Oroezes, the king of the Albanians, inhabited the country above the Cyrnus or Cyrus River. Florus, Eutropius and Orosius called him Orodes. {*Florus, l. 1. c. 40. s. 27,28. 1:187,189} {*Eutropius, l. 6.} {Orosius, l. 6. c. 4.} Oroeses advanced against the Romans, partly to gratify his friend, the younger Tigranes, but mostly because he feared the Romans would invade Albania. He hoped that if he made a surprise attack in the winter, they would not have pitched their camp all in one place. Because he wanted to do some brave exploit, he and his army advanced against the Romans in the midst of their Saturnalia. He himself marched against Metellus Celer who had Tigranes with him. Others went against Pompey, while still others went against the commander of the third army, under Lucius Flaccus, because the king wanted to attack all three at once, so they could not help one another. {*Dio, l. 36. (54) 3:93} Appian stated that Oroeses, the king of the Albanians, and Otoces (or rather Artoces), the king of the Iberians, set an ambush for Pompey near the Cyrnus River with seventy thousand men. {*Appian, Mithridatic Wars, l. 12. c. 15. (103) 2:435,437} Plutarch stated that at least forty thousand barbarians crossed the river against Pompey in the Roman Saturnalia festivals, which were celebrated in the month of December. {*Plutarch, Pompey, l. 1. c. 34. s. 2-5. 5:205,207} (In that year they occurred in September, or the Julian October, that is, at the beginning of autumn, or winter, according to those that divide the year into two parts only, summer and winter. This we saw in Thucydides' history of the Peloponnesian War.)

4430. Metellus defeated Oroeses. Flaccus made an inner ditch around his camp because the first ditch around his camp was too large to be defended. The enemy, thinking he did this out of fear, advanced into the outer ditch. Flaccus made an unexpected sally and killed many of them, both in the conflict and in the chase. Pompey, aware of the barbarian attacks on the two camps, attacked those who were marching against him and defeated them. He went directly against Oroeses himself, but could not find him because after Oroeses had been beaten by Metellus Celer and had heard that the others had also been defeated, he had fled. {*Dio, l. 36. (54) 3:93}

4431. Pompey camped where they had crossed the Cyrnus River. He finally agreed to their supplications and granted them peace but planned to revenge their attacks by invading their country. Since it was winter, this would be difficult to do. {*Dio, l. 36. (54) 3:95} Plutarch wrote that Pompey routed a large number of them and killed nine thousand, while taking ten thousand prisoners. Later,

their king sent envoys and Pompey made peace with him. {*Plutarch, Pompey, l. 1. c. 34. s. 2-5. 5:205,207}

4432. Mithridates wintered in Dioscurias, where the isthmus between the Black and the Caspian Seas begins. {*Appian, Mithridatic Wars, l. 12. c. 15. (101) 2:431} {*Strabo, l. 11. c. 2. s. 16. 5:209}

4433. Antipater urged Hyrcanus to flee to Aretas, the king of the Arabians, and promised to help him. He was barely able to convince him but Hyrcanus did finally go. [K241] Arabia bordered on Judea and Antipater was sent ahead to the king to get his promise that he would not turn Hyrcanus over to his enemies. As soon as the king had given his word, Antipater quickly returned to Hyrcanus at Jerusalem. He took Hyrcanus and stealing with him from the city by night, they came, after a long journey, to a city called Petra where Aretas' palace was. {*Josephus, Antiq., l. 14. c. 1. s. 4. (15-17) 7:457}

4434. Antipater was very close to Aretas and requested that he would restore Judea to Hyrcanus. [E586] His constant urgings and his presents finally convinced him to help Hyrcanus. If the king would help him get his kingdom back, Hyrcanus promised he would give him back a country with twelve cities which his father Alexander Jannaeus had taken away from the Arabians. These cities were: Medeba, Libba, Dabaloth, Arabatha, Agalla, Athone, Zoara, Oronain, Gabalis, Arydda, Alusa and Orybda. (The Loeb edition of Josephus lists many spelling variations for the names of these cities. Oronain could be Oronaim. Editor.) {*Josephus, Antiq., l. 14. c. 1. s. 4. (16-18) 7:457,459}

### 3939b AM, 4649 JP, 65 BC

4435. Ptolemy Alexander II, king of Egypt and son of Ptolemy Alexander I, was expelled by the Alexandrians. {*Suetonius, Julius, l. 1. c. 11. s. 1. 1:47} Ptolemy, a natural son, replaced him and he was the son of Ptolemy Lathurus. {Justin, Trogus, l. 39.} He was called the New Dionysus or Bacchus, and Auletes because he followed the ways of Dionysus in a most effeminate way. He put on women's clothes and danced to the cymbals in the celebrations of Bacchus. {*Lucian, Slander, l. 1. (16) 1:379} He also practised their piping so much that he boasted about it. He was not ashamed to celebrate contests in his court in which he contested with others. {*Strabo, l. 17. c. 1. s. 11. 8:43,45}

4436. Aretas, the king of the Arabians, defeated Aristobulus with an army of fifty thousand men. After this battle, many of Aristobulus' men ran away to Hyrcanus so that Aristobulus found himself abandoned and fled to Jerusalem. Aretas brought his army with him and besieged him in the temple. The people helped Hyrcanus while only the priests were loyal to

Aristobulus. Aretas continued the siege very vigorously with both the Jewish and Arabian armies. {*Josephus, Antiq., l. 14. c. 2. s. 1. (19,20) 7:459}

4437. These things took place before the time of the feast of unleavened bread. The leaders of the Jews abandoned their country and fled into Egypt. Onias in Judea was an honest and just man who, in a great drought, had prevailed for rain through the piety of his prayers. When he foresaw the civil war that was to follow, he hid himself in a cave but the Jews caught him and brought him into their camp. They wanted him to curse Aristobulus and his side, just as he had prayed for rain. For a long time he refused. Finally, the multitude compelled him and he stood in their midst and prayed:

"Oh God, you who are the king of the whole universe, for as much as these that are with me are your people and those who are besieged are your priests, I beseech you that you would neither hear these against them nor them praying against these."

4438. After this, some wicked men of the Jews surrounded him and stoned him to death. God immediately revenged this wickedness and punished the slaughter of Onias in this way. {*Josephus, Antiq., l. 14. c. 2. s. 1. (21-24) 7:459,461}

4439. While Aristobulus was besieged with his priests, the feast of the passover arrived, during which it was the custom for them to make many sacrifices to their God. [K242] Because of the siege, they asked the Jews who were besieging them, if they would give them sacrifices at whatever price they wanted to set. When they demanded a thousand drachmas for every ox, Aristobulus and his priests willingly agreed to this and let down their money from the wall. But when the Jews below had the money, they gave them no animals for the sacrifice in return. This was the height of impiety in that they had broken their faith with men and robbed God of his due honour. But the priests who had been defrauded prayed to God that he would take vengeance on them and this soon happened. A violent storm caused extensive damage to their grain so that a bushel of wheat was sold for fifteen drachmas. {*Josephus, Antiq., l. 14. c. 2. s. 1. (21-24) 7:459,461}

4440. Pompey waged war with the Iberians. They very much wanted to gain the favour of Mithridates and to drive out Pompey. Up to that point, they had never been subject either to the Medes or to the Persians, to Alexander or the Macedonians. {*Plutarch, Pompey, l. 1. c. 34. s. 4. 5:207} When Lucius Cotta and Lucius Torquatus were consuls, Artoces, the king of the Iberians, feared that Pompey might attack him. So he sent envoys to Pompey on the pretence of treating for peace but in the mean-

time prepared to make a surprise attack on them. Pompey was aware of this and attacked their country before Artoces had sufficiently prepared himself and secured the passes. {*Strabo, l. 11. c. 3. s. 5.5:221} Before Artoces knew anything of his coming, Pompey had advanced as far as the city of Acropolis, located in the passes of the Caucasus Mountains. It was fortified for the defence of that particular pass. Artoces, having lost the opportunity of strengthening himself, became greatly alarmed. He crossed the Cyrnus River and burned the bridge. When the city saw him flee and realised that they were beaten, they surrendered the town. By this means, Pompey gained control of the passes and put a garrison over them. He marched from there and subdued the whole country on that side of the river. {*Dio, l. 37. (1) 3:99}

4441. Pompey was about to cross the Cyrnus River, when Artoces begged a truce through his envoys. He offered to make him a bridge, as well as furnishing him with all the supplies he needed. This he did to obtain peace. [E587] As soon as Pompey had crossed that river, Artoces promptly fled to the Pelorus River. He ran from Pompey whom he had helped to cross the river when he might have prevented his crossing. Aware of this, Pompey pursued him and when he caught up to him, he fought and easily defeated him. Before the bowmen came to fight, he had routed them. When Artoces had crossed the Pelorus River and burned that bridge also, he fled while the remainder were cut off. Some died in the battle and some attempted to cross the river on foot. Many fled to the woods and held out for some days by shooting arrows from the large trees. But Pompey had the trees cut down and they also died. {*Dio, l. 37. (2) 3:99,101} Plutarch reported that nine thousand were killed in the battle and more than ten thousand were taken prisoner. {*Plutarch, Pompey, l. 1. c. 34. s. 5. 5:207}

4442. Artoces sent envoys to Pompey to sue for peace. They brought gifts of a bed, a table and a chair, all of gold, which he begged Pompey to accept. Pompey took the presents and turned them over to the quaestors to be recorded in the public records. [K243] He refused to give them peace unless Artoces was prepared to hand over his sons as hostages. Artoces hesitated until in the summertime, the Romans had found a ford in the river, which they crossed with much trouble, even though no one hindered their crossing. Then Artoces sent his sons for hostages and made peace with Pompey. {*Dio, l. 37. (2) 3:101} {*Plutarch, Pompey, l. 1. c. 34. s. 3,4. 5:207} {*Florus, l. 1. c. 40. s. 28,29. 1:187,189} Eutropius stated that Pompey defeated Arthaces, the king of Iberia in battle and received him into favour while setting some conditions. Sextus Rufus and Jonandes stated that both Iberia and their king

Arthaces, surrendered to Pompey. However, Orosius stated that he defeated Artoces, the king of the Iberians, and subdued all of Iberia. {*Orosius, l. 6. c. 4.*}

4443. Mithridates travelled through the country of the Scythians, who were offended by his presence. Some he persuaded to help him, while others had to be forced. He went to the Heniochi but the Archaeans tried to resist him and were defeated. Later, he entered into the countries around Lake Maeotis (Sea of Azov) and defeated many of their commanders. Because of the fame of his achievements, he was warmly welcomed. He gave and received many gifts and formed marriage alliances with the most powerful men there. {*Livy, l. 101. 14:125*} {*Appian, Mithridatic Wars, l. 12. c. 15. (102) 2:433*} {*Dio, l. 36. (50) 3:85*} Strabo also referred to this place. {*Strabo, l. 11. c. 2. s. 1. 5:191*} The Heniochi had four kings at the time when Mithridates fled through their country into Bosphorus from Pontus. He gave up any hopes of passing through the territory of the Zygians because the way was difficult and the people were fierce. Therefore, he was frequently forced to follow the sea and march along the shore with much trouble until he finally arrived among the Achaeans who received him. (Appian said they resisted him.) There he ended his journey of almost five hundred miles, which had begun at Phasis. Strabo listed the countries he passed through, based on those writers who wrote about the affairs of Mithridates. The countries, mentioned in this order were: the Achaeans, the Zygians, the Heniochi, the Cercetans, the Moschians and the Colchians. {*Strabo, l. 11. c. 2. s. 1. 5:191*} Hypsicratea, his queen, went through all these uncivilised countries with an indefatigable mind and body, following her distressed husband. To enable her to share in his labour and pains more easily, she shaved her hair. She was accustomed to ride on horseback and bear arms. Faithful in all his distresses, she was Mithridates' greatest and most pleasant asset. He seems to have wandered with his entire fortune and family while his wife accompanied him in his banishment. {*Valerius Maximus, l. 4. c. 6. ext. 2 1:409*}

4444. Machares, the son of Mithridates, reigned in Cimmerian Bosphorus and favoured the Romans. He heard that in a very short time his father had overcome so many fierce and warlike countries and crossed the borders of Scythia itself, which had never been crossed before. He sent envoys to his father to let him know that it was of necessity that he had been forced to agree to a friendship with the Romans. Knowing his father's animosity, he fled into the Pontic Chersonesus and burned his ships to prevent his father from following him. When Mithridates procured other ships and sent them after his son, his son killed himself. Mithridates killed all the friends that he had sent with his son as companions when Machares had first gone off into his kingdom. Mithridates sent his son's other friends away unharmed. {*Appian, Mithridatic Wars, l. 12. c. 15. (102) 2:435*} However, Dio stated that the father corrupted his son's friends with promises of safety and with bribes, persuading them to kill his son. {*Dio, l. 36. (50) 3:85*} [K244] Orosius said that Machares was killed by his father. {*Orosius, l. 6. c. 5.*}

4445. Pompey made his journey into the northern parts of Scythia, navigating by the stars as if he had been at sea and attacked Colchis. He camped at the foot of the Caucasus Mountains and ordered their king, Orodes, to come down into the plains. {*Florus, l. 1. c. 40. s. 28. 1:189*} [E588] Florus said that Orodes was king of the Alcans, as did Eutropius and Orosius. For *Orodes* refers to the name *Olthaces*, who, according to Appian, was the king of Colchis and who was led in triumph by Pompey. {*Appian, Mithridatic Wars, l. 12. c. 17. (117) 2:467*} Appian and Eutropius stated that *Aristarchus* was made king of Colchis in the place of Orodes. {*Appian, Mithridatic Wars, l. 12. c. 17. (114) 2:463*} {*Eutropius, l. 6.*}

4446. Plutarch said that Servilius met Pompey at the Phasis River with the fleet which had been left for the defence of Pontus. {*Plutarch, Pompey, l. 1. c. 34. s. 5. 5:207*} The pursuit of Mithridates, who had hidden himself in the countries around Bosphorus and Lake Maeotis (Sea of Azov), had caused him a great deal of trouble. Pompey went to Colchis in order to see the places of the journeys of the Argonauts, Dioscuri and Hercules. He especially wanted to see the place where Prometheus was said to be bound to the Caucasus Mountains. These sights drew him from the neighbouring countries. {*Appian, Mithridatic Wars, l. 12. c. 15. (103) 2:435*} He also won Colchis and the hostile countries to his side, partly by fair words and partly through fear. He realised that his journey would be difficult by land, through many warlike and unknown countries, but that it would be worse if he were to go by sea, because the inhabitants were hostile and the country lacked ports. So Pompey commanded his ships to stay there and watch Mithridates to prevent him from escaping and to block all provisions going to him. Pompey headed off against the Albanians, but took a roundabout way, so that they would think they were safe and he could come upon them suddenly and thereby easily defeat them. However, Plutarch stated that the Albanians finally revolted and that Pompey was incensed with anger and a desire for revenge. He marched against them immediately but he then returned to Armenia and crossed the Cyrnus River which was fordable at that time of the year. {*Dio, l. 37. (3) 3:103*} {*Plutarch, Pompey, l. 1. c. 35. s. 1. 5:207*}

4447. He crossed this river with great difficulty. The barbarians had fortified it with long stretches of palisades.

{*Plutarch, Pompey, l. 1. c. 35. s. 1,2. 5:207,209} At a spot where the river was calm, Pompey first crossed over with his cavalry, followed by his train and then his foot soldiers. He used the horses to break the force of the river with their bodies and if the current should happen to carry any part of the train away, it would land against those who were escorting the train and so be carried no farther. {*Dio, l. 37. (3) 3:103} Since he had come by a long, dry and rocky route, he filled ten thousand water bottles before continuing on his journey. {*Plutarch, Pompey, l. 1. c. 35. s. 2. 5:209}

4448. Finally, with no resistance from the enemy, he arrived at the Cambyses River. His whole army was badly affected by the heat and by thirst, although they had marched mainly in the night. He had selected guides from among the prisoners but they had not shown him the easiest way. Moreover, the river proved harmful too. The water was extremely cold and they drank too much, which made them quite sick. They did not rest until they came to the Abas River. For all of that time, they carried only water with them, as the inhabitants generously supplied their needs. For this reason, they marched through and did them no harm. {*Dio, l. 37. (3) 3:103,105}

4449. When they had crossed the river, they heard that Oroeses was coming toward them. {*Dio, l. 37. (4) 3:105} He had sixty thousand foot soldiers in his army and twelve thousand, or twenty-two thousand, cavalry (according to Strabo). Most of these were poorly armed and clothed only with the skins of wild beasts. They were under the command of Cosis, the king's brother. {*Plutarch, Pompey, l. 1. c. 35. s. 2. 5:209} {*Strabo, l. 11. c. 4. s. 5. 5:227} Pompey wanted to draw them into a battle before they realised the numbers of the Romans. First, he drew up his cavalry and told them what to do. Behind them he placed his foot soldiers. He had them lie down and cover themselves with their shields, telling them to lie still without making any noise. In this way, Oroeses was totally unaware of them until he was engaged in battle. He despised the cavalry believing them to be all alone and attacked them. In an instant they fled, as they had been ordered to do by Pompey, and Oroeses chased them furiously. The foot soldiers rose up suddenly and made a space to allow the cavalry to retreat through their midst. Charging the enemy, they surrounded a large number of them and killed them. The rest were killed by the cavalry, who came around on the right hand and the left and attacked their rear. So the cavalry also killed a large number. The enemy fled to the woods but were killed when these were set on fire. The Romans shouted to them to remember what had happened at the Saturnalia. At around that time, as was mentioned previously, the Albanians had laid an ambush and made a surprise attack on the Romans. {*Dio, l. 37. (4) 3:105,107} [K245]

4450. In the battle, Cosis, the king's brother, charged Pompey himself and with his javelin struck him through the joint of his breastplate. Pompey ran him through with his spear and killed him. It was reported that in this battle certain Amazons, who lived in the mountains beside the Thermodon River, came to help the barbarians. While the Romans were taking the plunder in the field, they found some Amazon shields and buskins, but found no women. {*Plutarch, Pompey, l. 1. c. 35. s. 2-4. 5:209} [E589] Appian also claimed that this battle and the previous one with the Albanians were one and the same battle. {*Appian, Mithridatic Wars, l. 12. c. 15. (103) 2:435,437} However, Orosius, like Eutropius and Sextus Rufus, stated that Pompey defeated Oroeses, the king of the Albanians, and his commanders. {Orosius, l. 6. c. 4.} (This paragraph in both the English and Latin copy is almost unreadable in the original. Editor.)

4451. Pompey destroyed the country all around there. Finally, he was persuaded to accept a peace from Orodes, or Oroeses, who sent Pompey a golden bed and other gifts to make peace. {*Florus, l. 1. c. 40. s. 28. 1:189} {*Dio, l. 37. (5) 3:107} {Eutropius, l. 6.} {Orosius, l. 6. c. 4.} They commemorated their Italian origins because they had followed Hercules from Mount Albanus and so they now greeted Pompey as one of the fathers of their country. {Justin, Trogus, l. 42. c. 3.} Pompey made peace with the Albanians and all the inhabitants along the Caucasus Mountains near the Caspian Sea, even as far as the mountain that was in Pontus. These people had requested peace through their envoys. {*Dio, l. 37. (5) 3:107} Strabo wrote that, from all regions including the Caspiane, which was named after the Caspian Sea, Pompey warred against the Iberians and Albanians. {*Strabo, l. 11. c. 1. s. 6. 5:187} Pompey wanted to see the Hyrcanian or the Caspian Sea. [K246] That plan was thwarted by the number of deadly snakes in the area when Pompey was only three days into his journey from there, so he went instead into Lesser Armenia. {*Plutarch, Pompey, l. 1. c. 33. s. 3. 5:215} (This paragraph in both the original English and Latin copies is almost unreadable. Editor.)

4452. After Pompey had crossed the Taurus Mountains, he advanced to Antiochus Commagene and finally received him into favour. He had surrendered to Pompey at Seleucia, a citadel in Mesopotamia with everything that he had captured in his excursion there. {*Appian, Mithridatic Wars, l. 12. c. 16. (106) 2:441} {*Appian, Mithridatic Wars, l. 12. c. 17. (117) 2:469} {*Appian, Mithridatic Wars, l. 12. c. 17. (121) 2:475} {*Strabo, l. 16. c. 2. s. 3. 7:241} Pompey defeated Darius and the Medes, either because he had recently helped Antiochus or because he had previously helped Tigranes. Appian stated that Darius and the Medes were counted among the princes and peoples that

Pompey defeated. {*Appian, Mithridatic Wars, l. 12. c. 16. (106) 2:441} {*Appian, Mithridatic Wars, l. 12. c. 17. (117) 2:469} Velleius Paterculus numbered Media among the countries Pompey had successfully invaded. {*Velleius Paterculus, l. 2. c. 40. s. 1. 1:135} However, Plutarch stated that Pompey only sent a polite reply to the kings of the Medes and Elymeans who had sent envoys to him. {*Plutarch, Pompey, l. 1. c. 36. s. 2. 5:209}

4453. Phraates, the king of the Parthians, saw Pompey warring so successfully that Armenia and the part of Pontus adjoining his country ended up being taken by Pompey's commanders. Gabinius had crossed the Euphrates River and was advancing toward the Tigris River. Phraates was frightened and sent envoys to Pompey to renew the peace with the Romans that they had previously. But the embassy was unsuccessful, because Pompey, elated with his present successes, had hopes of future conquests and for this reason had little respect for Phraates. Among his arrogant demands was an order that the territory of Corduene, or Gordyene, be given to him. This was a country disputed between Phraates and Tigranes and because the envoys did not have the authority to act on this, they did not reply. So Pompey wrote to Phraates. {*Dio, l. 37. (5) 3:107}

4454. In his letters, Pompey neglected to give Phraates the title of King of Kings. Everyone else gave him this title, including the Romans, and Pompey later gave this title to the captive Tigranes when celebrating his triumph over him at Rome. He addressed him only as a King. Phraates scorned the letter also because his kingdom had been plundered. Pompey did not wait for a reply, but immediately sent Afranius with an army into Gordyene. They defeated the Parthians who had invaded it and pursued them as far as Arbela, thus restoring the country to Tigranes. {*Dio, l. 37. (6) 3:109} {*Plutarch, Pompey, l. 1. c. 36. s. 2. 5:209,211}

4455. Josephus stated that Gabinius was sent by Pompey from Armenia into Syria. {*Josephus, Jewish War, l. 1. c. 6. s. 2. (127) 2:61} {*Josephus, Antiq., l. 14. c. 2. s. 3. (29,30) 7:463} We believe this was Lesser Armenia, where, according to Plutarch, Pompey retired when he had finished the war with the Albanians. Josephus was misled by the similarity of the names and mistakenly thought it was Greater Armenia, which is why he wrote that Gabinius was sent into Syria at the same time that Pompey was fighting with Tigranes. This would not have been possible unless, with Appian, he made Tigranes' defeat come after Pompey's expedition against the Albanians. But from Livy, Velleius, Florus, Plutarch, Eutropius and Orosius we have shown this defeat to have been before, not after, that expedition.

4456. As soon as Scaurus came to Damascus, he found that it had recently been captured by Metellus and Lollius. So he left there and when he had been informed that something was happening in Judea, he went there because it was convenient for him. As soon as he had entered the country, he met envoys from Hyrcanus who had besieged the temple of Jerusalem, as well as from his brother Aristobulus, who was besieged there. Both asked for his help. When Aristobulus offered four hundred talents, Hyrcanus offered him an equal amount. [K247] But Scaurus preferred Aristobulus and when he received his money, he sent envoys to Hyrcanus and Aretas, the Arabian king. They were being helped by many of the Nabateans although these were not very fitted for the war. In the name of the Romans and of Pompey, Scaurus commanded them to lift the siege. [E590] Frightened, Aretas withdrew from Judea into Philadelphia and Scaurus returned to Damascus. Aristobulus gathered together all the forces he had, planning to punish Aretas and Hyrcanus. He fought with them at Papyron and defeated them. About six thousand of the enemy were killed, including Phallion, the brother of Antipater. {*Josephus, Antiq., l. 14. c. 2. s. 3. (29-33) 7:463,465} {*Josephus, Jewish War, l. 1. c. 6. s. 3. (128-130) 2:61}

4457. Pompey returned from Armenia and met with certain kings and rulers. Plutarch stated that they were twelve barbarian kings. {*Plutarch, Pompey, l. 1. c. 38. s. 2. 5:215} He heard their complaints and pronounced his judgments. He confirmed some in their kingdoms, increasing some kingdoms while removing others from their kingdoms. {*Dio, l. 37. (7a) 3:113} Valerius Maximus referred to this famous time in history in recording the following.

4458. Ariobarzanes turned over his kingdom of Cappadocia to his son in the presence of Gnaeus Pompey. Ariobarzanes had taken the throne at Pompey's invitation. But when he sat on the throne, he saw his son placed with his secretary in a place inferior to his dignity and fortune. Because he could not stand to see his son beneath himself, he arose from his seat and put the crown upon his head, urging him to go up to the throne. The young man at once began to weep and as his body trembled, the crown fell to the ground. He could not bring himself to ascend to the throne and even when his father urged him to receive the kingdom, he refused. This matter was not settled until Pompey concurred with his father. Pompey called his son King and ordered him to take the crown and sit in the ivory chair. {*Valerius Maximus, l. 5. c. 7. ext. 2. 1:531}

4459. From there, Pompey went into Coelosyria and Phoenicia, which had recently been liberated from their kings and had been invaded by the Arabians and Tigranes. He stayed there, although Antiochus tried in vain to recapture them. Pompey subdued them and made them into one province. They received their laws from him and were administered according to the custom of the people of Rome. {*Dio, l. 37. (7a) 3:113}

4460. Justin, Appian and Porphyry stated that this was Antiochus Pius, the son of Antiochus Cyzicenus. {Justin, Trogus, l. 40. c. 2.} {*Appian, Mithridatic Wars, l. 12. c. 16. (107) 2:443} {Porphyry, Scaliger's Greek Eusebius, p. 227.} However, Appian had earlier stated more correctly that he was Antiochus Asiaticus, the son of Antiochus Pius and Selene. {*Appian, Syrian Wars, l. 11. c. 8. (49) 2:197} {*Appian, Syrian Wars, l. 11. (69,70) 2:235,237} Four years earlier, either by favour or consent of Lucullus, he had been given permission to acquire the kingdom of Syria which Tigranes had abandoned. While Pompey was busy with other matters, Antiochus kept it for one whole year. {*Appian, Syrian Wars, l. 11. c. 11. (69,70) 2:235,237} This was after Tigranes had very rightly surrendered what he had in Syria to the people of Rome. Although he asked for his father's kingdom in Pompey's presence, Pompey did not give it to him, even though he had done nothing against the people of Rome. It was, of course, easy for such a large army to oppress an unarmed prince. [K248] However, another reason was given, namely that it seemed unfair that, after the ancient kings had been defeated by Tigranes' armies and been driven from Syria, the kingdom should go to the defeated Seleucians rather than to the Romans who had defeated them. Pompey did not think it was right to give Antiochus what he had been unable to defend when invaded by the Jews and Arabians. {Justin, Trogus, l. 40. c. 2.} {*Appian, Syrian Wars, l. 11. c. 8. (49) 2:197} {*Appian, Syrian Wars, l. 11. c. 11. (69,70) 2:237} {*Valerius Maximus, l. 5. c. 7. ext. 2. 1:531}

4461. When Julius Caesar was an aedile, he won the favour of the people and tried, through some of the tribunes, to acquire the government of Egypt by an order from the people. There was a reason for this command, in that the Alexandrians had driven out their prince, who was an associate and friend of the Romans. But the Senate disallowed this commission by the people because a large number of the aristocratic party opposed it. {*Suetonius, Julius, l. 1. c. 11. 1:47,49}

4462. Pompey was called into Egypt by Alexander II, who had been expelled, to quell some rebellions there. He was presented with many gifts of money, as well as clothes for his whole army. But Pompey did not go there, either out of consideration for the envy of his enemies, or because the Sibylline oracle forbade it, or for some other reasons. {See note on 3948a A.M. <<4658>>} {*Appian, Mithridatic Wars, l. 12. c. 17. (114) 2:461}

4463. Pompey came to Damascus and moved around in Coelosyria. At that time, envoys came to him from every

place in Syria, Egypt and Judea. It appears that it was at this same time that the twelve kings mentioned by Plutarch came to him. Josephus mentioned this from Strabo's history: {*Josephus, Antiq., l. 14. c. 3. s. 1. (34-36) 7:465,467}

"An embassy came from Egypt with a crown worth four thousand pieces of gold. Judea sent a vine, or a garden, which was a piece of workmanship entitled *The Delight*. We saw this gift at Rome, where it was dedicated in the temple of Jupiter Capitoline with this inscription: *From Alexander, the king of the Jews*. It was valued at five hundred talents." [E591]

4464. This present, which had been placed in the temple at Jerusalem by Alexander Jannaeus and which was sent to Pompey by his son Aristobulus, was described by Pliny, in connection with the record of his *Acts of Pompey's Triumphs*, as follows: {*Pliny, l. 37. c. 6. (14) 10:175}

"It was a square mountain of gold, with deer, lions and every variety of fruit on it and a golden vine entwined around it; and a grotto of pearls, on top of which there was a sundial."

## 3940a AM, 4649 JP, 65 BC

4465. Envoys again came to Pompey from Judea: Antipater for Hyrcanus and Nicomedes for Aristobulus. Aristobulus' envoy complained about Gabinius, who had received three hundred talents of money and later about Scaurus, who had received four hundred talents. In so doing, Aristobulus made these men his enemies. Pompey commanded both parties, Hyrcanus and Aristobulus, to appear before him. {*Josephus, Antiq., l. 14. c. 3. s. 2. (37) 7:467}

4466. After the treaty between Pompey and Phraates came into effect, Afranius came to Syria. He lost his way as he went on the journey and endured much hardship because it was winter and supplies were scarce. He would have died, had he not been rescued by the Macedonian colony of Carrhae who helped him on his journey. {*Dio, l. 37. (5) 3:107,109}

4467. Pompey made his winter quarters at Aspis in Pontus and received into favour all the places in the country which had previously been hostile, a fact we gather from the fragments of Dio. {*Dio, l. 37. (7) 3:113} The reader may easily compare them and deduce that this happened in the consulship of Lucius Caesar and Gaius Figulus. {*Dio, l. 37. (6) 3:109} [K249] Pompey did not touch any of Mithridates' concubines who were brought to him but sent them back to their parents and kindred. They were mainly the wives and daughters of rulers and commanders. {*Plutarch, Pompey, l. 1. c. 36. s. 2. 5:211}

4468. Dio stated that Stratonice was found in the citadel of Symphorian, or Sinoria, and brought to Pompey. She was the daughter of a musician and one of the king's wives or concubines. She was furious at having been abandoned by Mithridates while he was wandering about Pontus. She sent most of the garrison out for provisions and let the Romans in, on this single condition. If Pompey captured her son Xiphares, he was to keep him safe for his mother. She knew of a large treasury, that was hidden underground in numerous iron-bound brass vessels and told Pompey where it was. He only selected the items which he thought would add most splendour to the temple and to his triumph, then gave the rest to Stratonice. {*Plutarch, Pompey, l. 1. c. 36. s. 3-7. 5:211,213} {*Appian, Mithridatic Wars, l. 12. c. 16. (107) 2:443,445} {*Dio, l. 37. (7) 3:113}

4469. When Mithridates found out about this, he had her son Xiphares killed while his mother watched from the other side of the river. He then threw away his body without burial and refrained from all dutiful reverence in order to make her repent of what she had done. {*Appian, Mithridatic Wars, l. 12. c. 16. (107) 2:445}

4470. Pompey also took that almost impregnable citadel, called *Kainon Chorion*, or the *New Place*, where Mithridates had stored his most valuable things which Pompey later dedicated to the Capitol. {*Strabo, l. 12. c. 3. s. 31. 5:429,431} Pompey took many of Mithridates' most secret records from there and freely examined them to determine the numbers of Mithridates' troops and the extent of his wealth. {*Plutarch, Pompey, l. 1. c. 37. 5:213} Among the records there were also some physical inventions of Mithridates which Pompey ordered Lenaeus, a learned grammarian, to translate into Latin. {*Pliny, l. 25. c. 3. 7:139}

4471. Phraates sent envoys to Pompey, through whom he complained of the wrongs he had received. Pompey had kept the younger Tigranes prisoner and Phraates asked that his son-in-law be returned. He saw the Euphrates River as being the boundary of his empire and warned Pompey against crossing it. Pompey replied that Tigranes ought to be turned over to his father, rather than his father-in-law, and that he would respect his boundaries. {*Plutarch, Pompey, l. 1. c. 38. s. 2. 5:215} {*Dio, l. 37. (7) 3:111}

4472. In the spring, when Lucius Caesar and Gaius Figulus were consuls, Phraates made an expedition against Tigranes. Even though he was defeated in one battle, he later defeated his enemy. {*Dio, l. 37. (6) 3:109}

4473. At the beginning of spring, Pompey drew out his forces from their winter quarters and marched into Damascus. On the way, he demolished a citadel in Apamea which Antiochus Cyzicenus had fortified. Pompey also attacked the country of Ptolemy Mennaeus, who was no less dangerous than Dionysius

of Tripolis, who had been allied to him and had been beheaded. Ptolemy redeemed himself by payment of a thousand talents, which Pompey distributed among his soldiers. Then Pompey also destroyed the citadel of Lysias, whose governor was a Jew named Silas. After that, he marched past Heliopolis and Chalcis and crossed the middle of the mountain. He came into Coelosyria from the rest of Syria and arrived at Damascus. {*Josephus, Antiq., l. 14. c. 3. s. 2. (38-40) 7:467,469}

4474. Pompey listened to the Jews and to Hyrcanus and Aristobulus, their princes. [E592] [K250] They were at odds with each other, as their country was with both of them. In their ancient laws, the Jews had a precept that they should give obedience to the priests of God and refuse to be governed by kings. These two men were of the priestly line but planned to change the government and bring the people into servitude. Hyrcanus complained that his younger brother had taken most of the country by force and invaded and usurped it. On land, he had made hostile invasions on Hyrcanus' borders and at sea he had harbours for his pirates. Antipater had persuaded more than a thousand of the leaders of the Jews to confirm that what Hyrcanus said was true. On the other side, Aristobulus pleaded that Hyrcanus had been removed because of his laziness and that he was held in general contempt among the people of his own country. He himself had been compelled to take over the government to prevent it from being transferred to some other family. To attest to this, he called some insolent young men who offended everybody by the fineness of their clothes, the exactness of their hair and their other accoutrements. Their dress would have been much more appropriate for a festive procession, than for a court. {*Josephus, Antiq., l. 14. c. 3. s. 2. (41-45) 7:469-471}

4475. Pompey heard their cases and rebuked the violence of Aristobulus. He dismissed them peaceably with the promise that he would come into their country himself, as soon as he had settled the affairs of the Nabateans. In the meantime, he urged them to be peaceful and treated Aristobulus with great civility, fearing he might oppose Pompey's journey, if provoked. However he gained no favour from Aristobulus, who had arrayed himself with as much splendour as possible. Aristobulus did not like the way he was being treated, because he thought it intolerable to endure anything beneath the majesty of a king, so he left Diospolis and went to the town of Dium. From there, he went to Judea to order his own affairs. {*Josephus, Antiq., l. 14. c. 3. s. 2. (41-45) 7:469-471} {*Josephus, Jewish War, l. 1. c. 6. s. 4. (131,132) 2:61,63}

4476. When Ptolemy Alexander II was driven from Egypt, he went to Tyre and died there. In his will, he left his kingdom of Egypt to the people of Rome. In his first speech, made on the first day of his consulship, Cicero said this: {*Cicero, Agrarian Law I, l. 1. c. 1. 6:343}

"The Decemviri said what was often spoken by many, that Alexander, the king, had left his kingdom to the Romans in his last will. Will you therefore privately give Alexandria to those whom you opposed publicly and fought with in battle?"

4477. In his second speech, he said more fully: {*Cicero, Agrarian Law II, l. 1. c. 16. 6:415,417}

"What about Alexandria and all Egypt, how secretly does it lie? How privately is it kept? How obscurely reported to the Decemviri? Who of you are ignorant of the fact that it is said that this kingdom was conferred on the Romans by Alexander's last will? In this case I, though a Roman consul, am so far from determining anything, that I withhold my opinion. For it seems to me no small matter, not only to judge but to speak of this thing. I see him who will assert the making of the will. I suppose there are still records in the Senate concerning their possession of their heritage. After the time when Alexander died, we sent envoys to Tyre for the restitution of the money that was disposed of by us. This, I remember, I have often heard Lucius Philippus affirm in the Senate. It is granted, almost by all sides, that he who rules at this time (Ptolemy Auletes) is neither of the royal family nor of the honour of a king. On the other side, it is said there is no will and that the people of Rome ought not to appear covetous of every kingdom. It was the richness of the place and the abundance of everything that would have attracted our citizens there. Concerning so great an affair, Publius Rufus, with the rest of his colleagues on the Decemviri, will judge." [K251]

4478. It was also reported that when Marcus Crassus, the censor, who tried to make Egypt a tributary to the people of Rome, strongly opposed Lutatius Catulus, his colleague in his office as censor, the dissension became so sharp that they voluntarily laid down their offices and power. {*Plutarch, Crassus, l. 1. c. 13. s. 1. 3:353}

4479. Pompey wanted to recover Syria and to pass through Arabia to the Persian Gulf. In his pursuit of the Albanians, he had extended the Roman Empire almost to the Hyrcanian or Caspian Sea, just as it was bounded by the Atlantic in the west. Likewise, in his conquest in the east, he now wanted to extend it to the Persian Gulf. He foresaw great difficulty in taking Mithridates, as he was more troublesome in his flight than when he stood and fought him. He hoped to starve him out by having his ships intercept merchants who traded into the Bosphorus with Mithridates. He threatened them with death if he should catch them helping Mithridates. Then, Pompey took most of his army and began his journey. {*Plutarch, Pompey, l. 1. c. 38,39. 5:215}

4480. He invaded Coelosyria and Phoenicia. First, he overran Idumea and Iturea. {*Appian, Mithridatic Wars, l. 12. c. 16. (106) 2:443} {Eutropius, l. 6.} {Orosius, l. 6. c. 6.} These people lived in the hilly country around Libanus (Lebanon), and invaded and plundered their neighbours, and their retreats were very strongly fortified. On the hills were Sinna, Borrama and other strongholds. In the valleys were Botrys and Gigartus, besides caves by the seaside. [E593] There was a citadel on a mountain called Θεου προσωπω, or *The Face of God*. Pompey destroyed these places and overran Byblus, or Palaeybyblus, which was the royal residence of Cinyras. He gave the place its liberty by cutting off the governor's head. {*Strabo, l. 16. c. 2. s. 18. 7:263}

4481. After Afranius had subdued the Arabians near Amanus, Pompey came down to Syria, which had no king. He subdued it and made it a Roman province. {*Appian, Mithridatic Wars, l. 12. c. 16. (106) 2:443} He received a sum of money from Antioch and enfranchised their city but left them to use their own laws. {Porphyry, Scaliger's Greek Eusebius, p. 227.} He indulged the citizens of Antioch by restoring the place of their public confession which was in decay. He had great respect for them because they traced their lineage from the Athenians. {Johannes Malela, Chronicle}

4482. Pompey gave the very strong city of Seleucia (Pieria), which was adjacent to Antioch, its liberty, because it had refused to admit Tigranes. {*Strabo, l. 16. c. 2. s. 8. 7:249} {Eutropius, l. 6.} He released the hostages from Antioch, and gave to Daphne a certain parcel of open land for the enlargement of their grove. This place was delightfully pleasant and had plenty of water. {Eutropius, l. 6.} Strabo noted that the grove was ten miles in circumference and well-watered with springs. {*Strabo, l. 16. c. 2. s. 6. 7:245} Sextus Rufus recorded that Pompey consecrated this grove of Daphne and enlarged it. {Sextus Rufus, Breviary} Jerome added that it was planted by the hands of his soldiers, at Pompey's orders. In his chronicle, Jerome said it was consecrated to Apollo, which may be true, if it was in reference to the new trees that were added. {Jerome, Eze 16} Concerning the old grove, see our notes. {See note on 3704 AM. <<2664>>} {See note on 3834a AM <<3249>>}

4483. Cato Minor was in Syria and was later called Uticensis. [K252] He was a philosopher belonging to the sect of the Stoics. Although only a young man, he was held in great esteem. Because of the great friendship between his father and him, he was invited to Syria by Dejotarus, king or tetrarch of the Galatians. He travelled through Asia and observed the manners, customs and strength of every province he passed through. He always walked on foot, while his friends, who accompanied him, rode. He came to see Antioch in Pompey's absence and saw a large throng of people in white before the gate. The men were on one side of the road and the children on the other. Thinking this ceremony was for him, he ordered his friends to get off their horses and walk with him. As they approached, an old man, who was ordering and commanding the whole multitude, approached, carrying a rod and a crown in his hand. He spoke first, addressing Cato, and without so much as greeting him, he and his followers inquired how Demetrius was and when he would come there. Demetrius had been Pompey's servant, but had been freed, and because he had considerable influence with Pompey, he was revered by everybody. Cato's friends burst out laughing but Cato cried out *Oh miserable city*, and passed on without giving any other reply. Whenever he remembered it, he started laughing at himself. {*Plutarch, Pompey, l. 1. c. 40. s. 1-3. 5:219} {*Plutarch, Cato Minor, l. 1. c. 12,13. 5:261-265}

4484. When Tigranes, the Armenian, was defeated by Phraates, the Parthian, he requested help from Pompey, who was then in Syria. Phraates promptly sent envoys to Pompey and these so earnestly accused both the Romans and Tigranes, that they made Pompey afraid, as well as ashamed. So he did not help Tigranes, nor did he later wage war against Phraates although many urged him to do so. He said he had no commands from the people of Rome for that expedition and that Mithridates was still at large. For the present, he was satisfied that Tigranes would finally meet with misfortune. He extenuated Phraates' accusations and did not refute them, saying he hoped to arbitrate the differences between Phraates and Tigranes about their boundaries. This worked and he promised to send three commissioners who would judge the matter. Pompey sent them and they were received as arbitrators by the kings and settled all differences between them. Tigranes was angry that he did not get help from the Romans. However, Phraates wanted Tigranes to survive, since he would need his help some day, as an ally against the Romans. It was obvious to both of them that whoever overcame the other, was certain to have a battle with the Romans and fall more easily into their power. When they considered this, they made peace. {*Dio, l. 37. (7) 3:111} {*Plutarch, Pompey, l. 1. c. 39. s. 3,4. 5:217} {*Appian, Mithridatic Wars, l. 12. c. 16. (106) 2:443}

4485. While Pompey was thus occupied, Mithridates went around Pontus and took over Panticapaeum, which was a market town in Europe, at the outlet of the Black Sea. (A footnote in the Loeb edition suggests an error in Appian and states the city was located at the outlet of the Sea of Azov. Editor.) {*Appian, Mithridatic Wars, l. 12. c. 16.

(107) 2:443} He also sent envoys to Pompey, who was in Syria and did not know if Mithridates was still alive. They promised that if Pompey would restore him to his father's kingdom again, he would become a tributary to the people of Rome. When Pompey urged that the king should come to him, as Tigranes had done, he refused, saying this was not appropriate for Mithridates, but said he would send his sons and some of his friends. {*Appian, Mithridatic Wars, l. 12. c. 16. (107) 2:445} [E594] [K253]

4486. After these events, Mithridates summoned all the people indiscriminately, servants, as well as free. He also made a large supply of arms, arrows and other engines. He spared nothing, not even their oxen for the ploughing. These he killed for their sinews to make strings for the bows. He also imposed a tax on all the people, which was raised but did great harm to many although Mithridates was unaware of this. Because he was troubled at the time with a certain ulcerous disease on his face, no one was allowed to see him, except the eunuch who was his doctor. He was finally cured and at that same time his army was ready. It consisted of sixty cohorts, each of them containing six hundred men, and a numerous multitude of ships, as well as strongholds which his commanders had captured while he was sick. He led part of his army to Phanagoria, another town also located at the mouth of the sea, so that he might secure the pass on all sides. All this time, Pompey was in Syria. {*Appian, Mithridatic Wars, l. 12. c. 16. (107,108) 2:445,447}

4487. In Bosphorus, while Mithridates was celebrating in honour of Ceres, there was suddenly a violent earthquake which was the greatest in the memory of man and which destroyed many cities and caused great damage to the fields. {*Dio, l. 37. (11) 3:119} {Orosius, l. 6. c. 5.} This was not the same earthquake that Justin mentioned, which killed a hundred and seventy thousand men and destroyed many cities in Syria. The prognosticators said this sign predicted a great change in affairs. {Justin, Trogus, l. 40. c. 2.}

4488. At the same time, Castor, who was commander-in-chief for Mithridates in Phanagoria, killed Trypho as he was entering the town. Trypho was the king's eunuch who had previously maltreated Castor. Then, stirring up the people to fight for their liberty, Castor led them against the citadel that was being held by Artaphernes and the rest of Mithridates' children. They gathered wood and other combustible things together from everywhere and set the citadel on fire, forcing Artaphernes, Darius, Xerxes, Oxathres and Eupatra, who were the children of Mithridates, to surrender. Among these, Artaphernes was the only older person, at forty years of age. The rest were attractive youths. Cleopatra, another daughter, resisted against them. Her courage so delighted her father that Mithridates sent a squadron of galleys and rescued her. After Castor had gained control of the citadel, he sent the children to the Romans. {*Appian, Mithridatic Wars, l. 12. c. 16. (108) 2:447,449} {Orosius, l. 6. c. 5.}

4489. Those citadels which were nearby and had recently been taken by Mithridates, followed the bad example of Phanagoria and also revolted. These were at the Chersonesus and at Theodosia, Nymphaeum and other places around Pontus that were good military positions. {*Appian, Mithridatic Wars, l. 12. c. 16. (108) 2:447}

4490. Mithridates was very angry and killed some of the renegades that he had taken, as well as many of his friends, including Exipodras, one of his children. {*Dio, l. 37. (12) 3:119} {Orosius, l. 6. c. 5.} Mithridates saw their great problems and suspected the entire army because they were being forced and were under extraordinary taxes. He thought the adversity of his fortune would always be in the minds of a changeable and coerced people. Therefore, he sent his eunuchs to the princes of Scythia to ask about marrying their daughters. He wanted them to come quickly to his relief with their forces. The eunuchs, who were escorted by five hundred soldiers, had not gone far from Mithridates, when the soldiers killed them. They did this, because the eunuchs had great authority with the king and had always been troublesome to them. After this, they carried the ladies to Pompey. {*Appian, Mithridatic Wars, l. 12. c. 16. (108) 2:447,449}

4491. Pompey left Syria and crossed into Asia, where he furthered his ambition. He did the very thing for which he had so much reprehended Lucullus. [K254] While Mithridates still controlled the Bosphorus and had gathered a very considerable army, Pompey disposed of several provinces and conferred gifts. {*Plutarch, Pompey, l. 1. c. 38. s. 1. 5:213}

4492. Livy stated that Pompey organized Pontus into the form of a province in Mithridates' lifetime. {*Livy, l. 102. 14:125} It was added to Galatia, was divided into eleven regions and was called Bithynia. {*Strabo, l. 12. c. 3. s. 1. 5:373}

4493. Pompey captured Mithridatium from Pontus and gave it to Bogodiatarus. {*Strabo, l. 12. c. 5. s. 2. 5:469} He made Archelaus, son of the Archelaus who was honoured by Sulla and the Senate, {See note on 3919a AM. <<3982>>} the chief priest of Luna, who was a goddess of Comana in Pontus. Pompey restored the princely dynasty and added to the sacred revenue of that office the amount of two schoeni (about seven and a half miles) of land. He ordered the inhabitants of Comana to obey Archelaus and so he was their governor and the head of all the priests of that temple. More than six thousand temple servants lived in the city. However, he

did not have the power to sell them. {*Strabo, l. 12. c. 3. s. 34. 5:435} {*Strabo, l. 17. c. 1. s. 11. 8:45} {*Appian, Mithridatic Wars, l. 12. c. 17. (114) 2:463} [E595]

4494. Appian stated that Attalus had the kingdom of Paphlagonia given to him by Pompey. {*Appian, Mithridatic Wars, l. 12. c. 17. (114) 2:463} Eutropius said it was given to Attalus and Polaemenes, and Sextus Rufus and Jornandes stated that Polaemenes, on his deathbed, left the kingdom of Paphlagonia to the people of Rome. Pompey gave Lesser Armenia to Dejotarus, the king of Galatia (or rather the tetrarch), because he was an ally in the Mithridatic war. {Eutropius, l. 6.} Pompey thought that Dejotarus was the best friend the Romans had. {*Cicero, Philippics, l. 11. c. 13. 15:495} Therefore, Pompey gave him Gazelonitis, which was part of Pontus, Pharnacia and Trapezus as far as Colchis and Lesser Armenia, and declared him king of that region. Prior to this, he held the tetrarchy of the Tolostobogians of Galatia which he had received by inheritance from his father. {*Strabo, l. 12. c. 3. s. 13. 5:393} Pompey left Galatia to the tetrarchs of his family. {*Strabo, l. 12. c. 3. s. 1. 5:373} {*Appian, Mithridatic Wars, l. 12. c. 17. (114) 2:463} A little later, it came into the hands of only three, then of two, and last of all into the sole power of Dejotarus. {*Strabo, l. 12. c. 5. s. 1. 5:469}

4495. Even though Mithridates had lost most of his children, many citadels and his whole kingdom, he was not discouraged. He did not dwell on his debased condition, considering that he had lost his dignity as well and had no hope of getting any help from Scythia. He planned to journey to the European Gauls, whom he had befriended before, and get their help. He planned to go through Scythia and along the Ister River, so that with the Gauls he might cross the Alps into Italy. He hoped that many Italians who also hated the Romans would join him. {*Florus, l. 1. c. 40. s. 24. 1:187} {*Appian, Mithridatic Wars, l. 12. c. 16. (109) 2:449} {*Dio, l. 37. (11) 3:117,119}

4496. The soldiers disliked these grand plans and were afraid of the boldness of the enterprise and the length of the march. They were to fight against men whom they were not able to handle even in their own country. They believed Mithridates to be in such a desperate situation that he was intending to end his life valiantly rather than as a defeated man. They stayed with him for a while and quietly let him go on planning because he was no lowly or contemptible prince, even under the greatest of misfortunes. {*Appian, Mithridatic Wars, l. 12. c. 16. (109) 2:449,451} [K255]

4497. Aretas, the king of Arabia Petra (extending to the Red Sea), had often invaded Syria previously. The Romans came to help the Syrians and defeated him. However he still continued the war, so Pompey made an expedition against him and his neighbours. Phraates was now behaving himself, and Syria and Phoenicia were now tranquil. {*Dio, l. 37. (15) 3:123,125} The soldiers were not very happy about this expedition for they thought that they should be going after Mithridates, their old enemy, who even then was recruiting his forces. He was preparing to march through Scythia and Paenonia to invade Italy with an army. Pompey, however, was satisfied that it was nobler to defeat a warring foe than to take the body of a conquered and fleeing enemy. {*Plutarch, Pompey, l. 1. c. 41. s. 1,2. 5:221}

4498. Before Pompey began his journey, he gave a very noble and handsome burial to the dead who had fallen under Triarius in that unlucky battle they had fought with Mithridates in Pontus and whom Lucullus had left unburied. Aretas, who had earlier condemned the Roman arms, was now terrified and wrote to Pompey that he would do whatever he should command. However, Pompey, in order to ascertain his true feelings, attacked Petra. {*Plutarch, Pompey, l. 1. c. 39. s. 1. 5:215,217} {*Plutarch, Pompey, l. 1. c. 41. s. 1. 5:221} He easily defeated the king and his allies and took them into custody, after having captured their city of Petra. {*Dio, l. 37. (15) 3:125} {Orosius, l. 6. c. 6.} However, Josephus wrote that he did not fight them and went to fight Aristobulus. {*Josephus, Antiq., l. 14. c. 3. s. 3. (46-48) 7:471,473} Plutarch stated that when Pompey had gone a little distance from Petra, he heard the news of Mithridates' death and returned from Arabia, arriving at Amisus. {*Plutarch, Pompey, l. 1. c. 41,42. 5:221,223}

4499. When Publius Servilius Rullus, the tribune of the people at Rome, assumed his office, he passed the Agrarian law which created a commission of Decemviri. They were to sell or distribute among the colonies all the public revenues in Italy and Syria and the land gained by Pompey. This law was passed in January which, as the year then went at Rome, took place in the beginning of the Julian October. This occurred when Cicero became consul. He spoke against Rullus and freed everyone from the widespread fear they had of this law. {*Cicero, Agrarian Law I, l. 1. c. 1-9. 6:343-367} {*Cicero, Atticus, l. 2. c. 1. 22:103} {*Plutarch, Cicero, l. 1. c. 12. s. 1-3. 7:109}

4500. The Decemviri had the power to sell: {*Cicero, Agrarian Law I, l. 1. c. 2. 6:349}

"All those lands which Mithridates had possessed in Paphlagonia, Pontus and Cappadocia."

4501. In his second Agrarian speech before the people, Cicero reprehended the injustice of that popular decree in this way: {*Cicero, Agrarian Law II, l. 1. c. 19. 6:425,427} [E596]

"Is it not so? Without terms having been arranged, without the general's report having been heard, before

the war is finished, while King Mithridates, without an army, driven from his kingdom, nevertheless contemplating some new enterprise against us at the end of the world, and is defended from the invincible troops of Pompey by the Maeotis (Sea of Azov) and those marshes, by the narrow defiles and lofty mountains; while our commander is still engaged in war and even now the name of a war is heard in those districts—shall the Decemviri sell those lands, over which, according to the custom, Gnaeus Pompey still ought to possess all civil and military authority?"

4502. Lucius Valerius Flaccus, who was the praetor at Rome, was sent as praetor into Asia. His office in Asia was for one year. Quintus Cicero succeeded Flaccus and was the fifth one to hold that position, as Marcus Cicero, his brother, stated in the speech in which he accused Flaccus of bribery. {*Cicero, Pro Flacco, l. 1. (33) 10:479} [K256]

## 3941a AM, 4650 JP, 64 BC

4503. Pharnaces plotted against Mithridates. He was his most dearly loved son, whom he had often confirmed as his heir to his kingdom. Pharnaces did this either because he thought the Italian expedition would permanently alienate the Romans, or for some other reason, or out of covetousness. Those who were guilty of involvement in the plot were put to the rack but Menophanes persuaded Mithridates to pardon his son. {*Appian, Mithridatic Wars, l. 12. c. 16. (110) 2:451} Dio, as Salianus noted, said nothing of the pardon and stated that men who were sent to take Pharnaces were persuaded by him to join his side. After they had taken Panticapaeum, they captured his father. He also noted that although Mithridates was generally a very wise king, he never stopped to consider that all the arms and the vast numbers of his subjects were of little value, without their goodwill and love. On the contrary, if they were unfaithful, there was the least safety in the largest numbers. Appian made the same observation. {*Dio, l. 37. (12) 3:119,121}

4504. Pharnaces knew that the soldiers were very much against the expedition into Italy. At night, he went to the Romans who had defected to Mithridates and told them of the great danger involved in their crossing into Italy, which they well knew. He promised them great things if they would refuse to go and persuaded them to defect from his father. Then that same night, he sent messengers to nearby camps and persuaded them to join him. In the morning, first the Italian fugitives and then all the other adjoining camps talked about this and so did the naval forces. With a loud shout, they proclaimed their defection. They had not been told of this beforehand, nor were they bribed. Either, they were induced by the example of so many whom they realised they could not withstand, or they were overcome by the extremity of the old king's misfortunes.

*4505.* When Mithridates heard the shout of the army, he sent some men to find out what they wanted. The men were told they wanted Mithridates' son to be king, because they wanted a young man, instead of an old one who was fond of eunuchs and who caused the deaths of many sons, generals and friends. When Mithridates heard this, he went out to speak to them himself. Many of his guard defected to the fugitives, but were not accepted unless they were prepared to do something to show their unfaithfulness to the king. They pointed to Mithridates' horse which was killed as he was fleeing. They now greeted Pharnaces as king, as if they had obtained their heart's desire. Some of them took a very large skin of parchment, which they had brought from the temple, and put it around his head instead of a diadem.

*4506.* The old man saw this from the upper porch and sent one person after another to Pharnaces, to request a safe passage for himself, but none returned. He was afraid that he might be turned over to the Romans. After praising those men and his friends who still stood by him, he sent them to the new king. Some were killed by the army on the way, contrary to all expectations. {*\*Appian, Mithridatic Wars, l. 12. c. 16. (110,111) 2:451,453*} When he had begged his son in vain from the walls and realised that he would not give in, Mithridates is said to have uttered these words when he was about to die:

> "Oh country gods, if you so grant, that, at one time or another, he may receive the same words from his children."

*4507.* He went to his wives and concubines and gave them poison. {*Orosius, l. 6. c. 5.*} [K257]

*4508.* Two virgin daughters had been brought up with him, Mithridatis and Nyssa, who were betrothed to the kings of Egypt and Cyprus. They earnestly entreated their father to let them drink their poisoned potion before him. They wanted him to wait until they had done this. {*\*Appian, Mithridatic Wars, l. 12. c. 16. (111) 2:455*} But as for Mithridates, neither the poison he always carried about in his sword, nor the wound he had given himself with the sword, were sufficient to kill him. Even though he walked about most strenuously, so that the poison would spread itself through his veins and would act more quickly, nothing happened. He had vaccinated his body against poison with daily antidotes of medicines, which to this day are called *Mithridatic Drugs.* His sword wound had been poorly executed, because of his age, his present distresses and the partial effect of the poison, so that he had not killed himself but still lingered.

[E597] The wall had now been broken down and Bitocus, or Bituitus, a Galatian soldier, wandered about. He was terrified by the majesty of Mithridates' countenance. Mithridates called him back and caused the soldier's trembling hand to put an end to his life. {*\*Dio, l. 37. (13) 3:121*} {*\*Livy, l. 102. 14:125,127*} {*\*Florus, l. 1. c. 40. s. 25,26. 1:187*} {*\*Valerius Maximus, l. 9. c. 2. ext. 3. 2:315*} {*\*Pliny, l. 25. c. 3. 7:139,141*} {*Justin, Trogus, l. 37. c. 2.*} {*\*Aulus Gellius, Attic Nights, l. 17. c. 16. s. 1-6. 3:261,263*} {*\*Appian, Mithridatic Wars, l. 12. c. 16. (111) 2:455*} {*Aurelius Victor, De Viris Illustribus, l. 1. c. 76.*} {*Orosius, l. 6. c. 5.*}

*4509.* In this way Mithridates ended his life at Panticapaeum in Cimmerian Bosphorus: {*\*Velleius Paterculus, l. 2. c. 18. s. 1. 1:85*}

> "A man neither to be passed over in silence, nor to be spoken of without respect. He was most eager for war, of exceptional bravery, great in spirit and sometimes in achievement, in strategy—a general, in bodily prowess—a soldier, in hatred of the Romans—as Hannibal."

*4510.* Cicero called him: {*\*Cicero, Academica, l. 2. c. 1. 19:467*}

> "The greatest king since the time of Alexander the Great."

*4511.* Because of these eulogies, I have been as careful about recording his life as I was about recording that of Alexander the Great.

*4512.* Orosius wrote the following about the time of the Mithridatic war: {*Orosius, l. 6. c. 1. fin.*}

> "The Mithridatic war, or rather, to the end of the Mithridatic war, which involved many provinces, was carried on for forty years. It began in the 662nd year after the foundation of Rome, as I said before, {*Orosius, l. 5. c. 19.*} in the same year as the first civil war began. This was in the consulship of Cicero and Antonius. (I use the words of that excellent poet, Lucan.) The war was *scarcely ended by the infamy of the poison by Mithridates.* {*\*Lucan, l. 1. (337) 1:29*} The war lasted thirty years. It is difficult to know why most write forty."

*4513.* Justin stated that Mithridates warred with the Romans for forty-six years. {*Justin, Trogus, l. 37. c. 1.*} Appian, in the beginning of his Mithridatic Wars, said that the Mithridatic War lasted nearly forty-two years. {*\*Appian, Syrian Wars, l. 11. c. 8. (48) 2:197*} {*\*Appian, Mithridatic Wars, l. 12. c. 3. (17) 2:269*} {*\*Appian, Mithridatic Wars, l. 12. c. 17. (118) 2:469*} Florus agreed with Appian. {*\*Florus, l. 1. c. 40. s. 1,2. 1:179*} (Loeb edition reads *forty,* not *forty-two,* in Florus. Editor.) However, Eutropius only allowed forty years. {*Eutropius, l. 6.*} In Pliny, the record placed by Pompey in the temple of Athena, showed that this war lasted only thirty years. {*Pliny, l. 7. c. 26. 2:569} From the beginning of the first Mithridatic war to the death of Mithridates is only twenty-six years. This time period included the years of peace between the two wars. To make it a round number the war may be said to have lasted thirty years. Another example to illustrate this tendency: Cicero, in his consulship, stated that when Gaius Rabirus was standing his trial for treason, he upheld and defended against detraction the authority of the Senate which had been interposed forty years before Cicero's consulship. (Gaius Rabirius was on trial for the murder of Saturninus thirty-six years earlier.) {*Cicero, In Pison, l. 1. c. 2. 14:147} [K258] However, Dio more accurately said that this had happened thirty-six years earlier. {*Dio, l. 37. (26) 3:141,143} For more information, consult Asconius Pedianus. {Asconius Pedianus, In Pison}

4514. At the time when Pompey was in Judea, he was angry with Aristobulus and marched against him, having been urged to do so by Hyrcanus. Taking the Roman legions and the auxiliaries he had raised in Damascus and other parts of Syria, he went through Pella and Scythopolis and came to Coreae, near the border of Judea toward the Mediterranean. When he learned that Aristobulus had fled into Alexandrion, a good citadel which was located on the top of a hill, he summoned Aristobulus to come to him. He, in turn, came to Pompey, having been persuaded by many of his friends not to start a war against the Romans. After he had argued with his brother Hyrcanus about the kingdom, Pompey gave him permission to retire to his citadel again. He did this two or three times always flattering Pompey and in the hope of getting the kingdom, feigning that he would obey Pompey in everything. In the meanwhile, he returned to the citadel and fearing that the kingdom might be given to his brother Hyrcanus, fortified it and prepared for war. {*Josephus, Jewish War, l. 1. c. 6. s. 5. (133-137) 2:63,65} {*Josephus, Antiq., l. 14. c. 3. s. 4. (48-51) 7:473}

4515. Pompey commanded Aristobulus to surrender the citadels and wrote to the governors about this. These would not have obeyed him, had the letters not been written with Aristobulus' own hand. Aristobulus unwillingly submitted but then went to Jerusalem, fully intending to prepare for war. Pompey immediately followed him with his army, as he thought it best not to give him any time for preparation. {*Josephus, Jewish War, l. 1. c. 6. s. 5. (137) 2:65} {*Josephus, Antiq., l. 14. c. 3. s. 4. (52,53) 7:475}

4516. As Pompey was marching near Jericho, a messenger came and told him that Mithridates had been killed by his son, Pharnaces. {*Josephus, Jewish War, l. 1. c. 6. s. 6. (138) 2:65} {*Josephus, Antiq., l. 14. c. 3. s. 4. (53) 7:475} The men who brought the news had wreathed their javelins' heads with laurels. There was no high place from where Pompey could speak to the soldiers. Since as the camp was made with turfs that had been cut and laid, one on top of the other, they made a mound which Pompey ascended to tell his soldiers that Mithridates had killed himself and that Pharnaces had acted on behalf of himself and the Romans. {*Plutarch, Pompey, l. 1. c. 41. s. 3-5. 5:221,223} [E598]

4517. At this, the army greatly rejoiced and spent their time in sacrificing and feasting, as though, with Mithridates' death, large numbers of their enemies had died. Pompey was very glad that putting an end to all Mithridates' acts and expeditions had proved much easier for him than he had thought it would be. {*Plutarch, Pompey, l. 1. c. 42. s. 1. 5:223} Mithridates had worried Pompey so much that, although he had conquered all his kingdom, he did not consider the war to be over, as long as Mithridates was alive. {*Cicero, Pro Murena, l. 1. (34) 10:231} Lucan mentioned Pompey bragging about this: {*Lucan, l. 2. (580) 1:101}

> Skulking about Pontus,
> and while he watched to bring
> Ruin to the Romans,
> that untamed king,
> With better luck than Sulla,
> I have made to die.

4518. Pompey first camped at Jericho, where the very best dates were to be had, and balsam, which was the most precious of all ointments. The following morning, he marched toward Jerusalem. [K259] Aristobulus was sorry for what he had done and came to meet him. He promised him money and that he would surrender himself and the city to him. He only asked that there be no war and for things to be settled peaceably. Pompey pardoned him and sent Gabinius with the soldiers to receive the money but they returned without either because Aristobulus' soldiers would not honour his promise. Pompey became very angry, committed Aristobulus to custody and marched in person against the city. It was strongly fortified except on the northern side, which could most easily be battered. {*Josephus, Antiq., l. 14. c. 4. s. 1. (54-57) 7:475,477}

4519. The citizens within the city were divided. Those who sided with Hyrcanus said that the city should be surrendered to Pompey. Many, who feared the determination of the Romans, agreed. However, Aristobulus' side ordered the gates to be shut and the people to prepare for war because Pompey was holding the king prisoner. Aristobulus' men first seized the temple and cut down the bridge by which they had come into the city then stood, prepared to fight. Hyrcanus' party welcomed the army into the city and turned the city and the king's palace over to Pompey. Pompey committed these to Piso, his lieutenant, who fortified the houses and other buildings that were near the temple. First, he offered the besieged people conditions of peace. When they refused, Pompey prepared for a general assault and was given every assistance by Hyrcanus. {*Josephus, Jewish War, l. 1. c. 7. s. 2. (142-144) 2:67} {*Josephus, Antiq., l. 14. c. 4. s. 2. (58-60) 7:475,477}

4520. Pompey camped on the north side of the city, which was the easiest side to attack. There were also high towers and a handmade ditch, in addition to a deep valley around the temple. All places around the city sloped down quite steeply, especially where the bridge had been removed and on the side where Pompey was camped. However, the Romans daily raised mounts for their engines of war and cut down trees around there, filling up the trench with materials that the soldiers brought. The work was very difficult because the trench was so deep and because the Jews were fighting from above. {*Josephus, Jewish War, l. 1. c. 7. s. 3. (145-147) 2:67,69} {*Josephus, Antiq., l. 14. c. 4. s. 2. (61-63) 7:479}

4521. Josephus stated that if the Jews had not observed the Sabbath, the Romans could not have finished the earthworks, because of the Jewish resistance. The law permitted the Jews to defend themselves against an attacking enemy on the Sabbath but not to hinder any work that the enemy was doing. This was not a written law but one that had been received by tradition from their doctors. When the Romans became aware of how the Jews behaved on the Sabbath, they did not shoot any arrows against the Jews nor fight with them in any way. They only erected their mounds and towers and planted their engines to be able to use them against the Jews on the next day. {*Josephus, Antiq., l. 14. c. 4. s. 3. (64) 7:479,481} King Agrippa said that Pompey had especially chosen those days to carry on the war to prevent the Jews from attacking the Romans on their Sabbath. {*Josephus, Jewish War, l. 2. c. 16. s. 4. (392) 2:477}

4522. Pompey's letters about the death of Mithridates and the end of that war were read in the Senate. Cicero, the consul, proposed a procession lasting twelve days to be decreed in honour of Pompey. {*Cicero, De Provinciis Consularibus, l. 1. c. 11. 13:571} The Romans kept these festival days, to celebrate being freed from a great enemy. {*Appian, Mithridatic Wars, l. 12. c. 16. (113) 2:459} [E599] [K260]

4523. Titus Ampius and Titus Labienus, who were the tribunes of the people, proposed a law that Pompey should wear a golden crown and the full dress of a triumphator at the circus. At the theatre, he could wear a purple-bordered toga and the golden crown. He only availed himself of this honour once. {*Velleius Paterculus, l. 2. c. 40. s. 4. 1:137} {*Dio, l. 37. (21) 3:135}

4524. At Jerusalem, the trench was being filled and the tower fitted onto the mounts. The engines from Tyre were positioned and the Romans shot large stones to batter the temple stones. But the towers, which were exceedingly strong and beautiful withstood the assaults of the besiegers. The Romans were very tired and Pompey wondered at the faithful perseverance of the Jews. Among other things, he especially marvelled at their constantly observing the whole service of God amid all their enemies' attacks as if they were at peace. Throughout the duration of the attacks, they performed the daily sacrifices. Twice a day, in the morning and at the ninth hour, the priests offered sacrifices on the altar. They did not stop their sacrifices no matter what happened. {*Josephus, Jewish War, l. 1. c. 7. s. 4. (148) 2:69} {*Josephus, Antiq., l. 14. c. 4. s. 2. (61,62) 7:479}

4525. The Latin Feriae was held at Rome. (This feast was not on a set day, but was appointed by the magistrates.) At this feast, a comet appeared and the moon was eclipsed on November 7, two hours after midnight. Cicero referred to this in the second book of his consulship, mentioning it in these verses:

> When Alban's snowy heaps thou viewed, and when
> With glad milk the Latina celebrated, then
> Comets of fire did tremble in thy sight,
> And thou a conflict fancied in the night.
> Which time scarce escaped inauspicious; when
> The moon withdrew her light and sight from men,
> And on a sudden, left a starry night.

4526. In the third month of the siege of Jerusalem, the largest tower fell, after having been shaken by repeated battering with the ram. A large part of the wall fell with it and through this breach, large numbers of the enemy broke into the temple. The first man to climb the wall was Faustus Cornelius, the son of Sulla, with his band of soldiers. Immediately after him came the centurion, Furius, with his regiment who followed him on either side, and between them, the centurion Fabius with a valiant band of his soldiers. These surrounded the temple while some of the Jews tried to hide themselves. Others offered some resistance and were killed. Although many priests saw the enemies rushing in with their drawn swords, they were not at all dismayed and continued their sacrifices. They were killed even as they made offerings and burned incense in the temple because they preferred to observe their religious duty rather than save their own lives. {*Josephus, Jewish War, l. 1. c. 7. s. 4. (148,149) 2:69} {*Josephus, Antiq., l. 14. c. 4. s. 4. (69,70) 7:483}

4527. All the places were full of the dead. Some of the Jews were killed by the Romans and others by their own countrymen of the opposing faction. Many threw themselves headlong down the rocks. Others set their houses on fire and burned themselves alive. They could not bear to watch the things being done by the enemy. About twelve thousand Jews died, whereas very few of the Romans were killed, but many were wounded. Among the captives was Absalom, the uncle and father-in-law of Aristobulus and the son of John Hyrcanus, of whom Josephus wrote that he was honoured by Alexander Jannaeus because he was content to live a private life. {*Josephus, Antiq., l. 13. c. 12. s. 1. (320-323) 7:389,391} {*Josephus, Jewish War, l. 1. c. 7. s. 4. (148,149) 2:69} {*Josephus, l. 14. c. 4. s. 4. (69-71) 7:483} [K261]

4528. The temple was taken on the day of the fast, when Gaius Antonius and Marcus Tullius Cicero were consuls, in the 179th Olympiad. {*Josephus, Antiq., l. 14. c. 4. s. 3. (66) 7:481} Eusebius stated that it was at the start of the year, in the holy fast of the third month, that the city was later taken by Sossius. {?Eusebius, Gospel, l. 8. c. 2.} {*Josephus, Antiq., l. 14. c. 16. s. 4. (487) 7:701} This is to be understood as the third month of the civil year, which started in the autumn, according to the Hebrews and other eastern accounts. {*Josephus, Antiq., l. 1. c. 3. s. 3. (80,81) 4:37} {Jerome, Eze init.} That is, it was the third month of the Syrians, which was called the *former Canun* by them and called *Chisleu* by the Hebrews. It was on the 28th day of this month that the Jews kept, and still keep even to this very day, a fast to commemorate the burning of the sacred roll by the wicked Jehoiakim. {Jer 36:9,22,23} {See note on 3398 AM. <<773-776>>} [E600] This fast was appointed to remember the day Nebuchadnezzar captured Jerusalem when the Jews first began to serve the Babylonians. A cycle (or *peritrope*, OED noted the word is rare and cited this sentence in Ussher as an example. Editor.) was noticed when, on the same day of the same month, after five hundred and forty-three years, the temple was taken by Pompey at the time when the Jews began to serve the Romans. Again, twenty-six years later, it was taken by Sossius when the Jews began to serve Herod, the Idumean, and his posterity. The 28th day of the month of Chisleu corresponded to the 28th day of the Julian December that year and (which is also worth noting) it was on a Saturday, or the Jewish Sabbath, that the temple was taken by assault. Dio noted that this was calculated to have been the 79th year from the 170th of the Greek empire, of which year it was written that the yoke of the heathen was removed from Israel. {Apc 1 Ma 13:41} From this it can be seen for how short a time they enjoyed their liberty.

4529. Pompey and many others entered the temple and saw those things which was not lawful for anyone but the high priest to see. In the temple there was the table, the lampstand with the lamps, all the vessels for sacrifice, the censers, entirely made of gold, and a large pile of spices. In the treasuries of sacred money, they found about two thousand talents. Pompey did not touch any of this but on the next day ordered those who had the charge of the temple to purify and cleanse it and to offer their solemn sacrifices to God. {*Josephus, Jewish War, l. 1. c. 7. s. 6. (152,153) 2:71} {*Josephus, Antiq., l. 14. c. 4. s. 4. (71-73) 7:483,485}

4530. Pompey restored the high priesthood back to Hyrcanus, because he had willingly helped him in the siege and had hindered the Jews who were spread over the whole country from joining with Aristobulus. {*Josephus, Jewish War, l. 1. c. 7. s. 6. (153) 2:71} {*Josephus, l. 14. c. 4. s. 4. (73) 7:485} Pompey also gave him the kingdom but forbade him to wear a crown. From this time, plus the previous nine years, in which he had been high priest during the reign of his mother Alexandra, he held the high priest for an additional twenty-four years which we take to be twenty-three and a half years. {*Josephus, Jewish War, l. 1. c. 7. s. 6. (153) 2:71} {*Josephus, Antiq., l. 20. c. 10. s. 4. (244,245) 10:131}

4531. Pompey put to death those who were the main instigators of the war and gave great honours and rewards to Faustus and the others who had been the first to ascend the wall. {*Josephus, Jewish War, l. 1. c. 7. s. 6. (154) 2:73} {*Josephus, Antiq., l. 14. c. 4. s. 4. (73,74) 7:485}

## 3941b AM, 4651 JP, 63 BC

4532. Pompey made the Jews tributary to the Romans. {*Josephus, Antiq., l. 14. c. 4. s. 4. (74) 7:485,487} {*Eusebius, Chronicles, l. 1. 1:236} {*Sulpicius Severus, Sacred History, l. 2. c. 26. 11:110} [K262] He took away the cities in Coelosyria which they had previously conquered and ordered them to obey their own governors and reduced the boundaries of the country to their ancient limits. As a favour to Demetrius of Gadara, a freedman of his (of whose insolence Plutarch made mention {*Plutarch, Pompey, l. 1. c. 40. 5:217-221}), he rebuilt Gadara, which the Jews had previously destroyed. He restored the inhabitants to their inland cities of Hippos, Scythopolis, Pella, Dium, Samaria, Marisa, Azotus, Jamnia and Arethusa, as well as restoring the inhabitants to any city that had been destroyed. He did the same with the coastal towns of Gaza, Joppa, Adora and Straton's tower. This tower was later magnificently rebuilt by Herod and called Caesarea. Pompey gave these cities their liberty and annexed all of them to the province of Syria. {*Josephus, Jewish War, l. 1. c. 7. s. 7. (155,156) 2:73} {*Josephus, Antiq., l. 14. c. 4. s. 4. (75,76) 7:487}

4533. Josephus stated: {*Josephus, Antiq., l. 14. c. 4. s. 5. (77,78) 7:487}

"Hyrcanus and Aristobulus, through their quarrelling and dissensions, were the cause of this calamity to the inhabitants of Jerusalem. For it was at that time, that we first began to lose our liberty and were made subject to the government of the Romans. In addition, we were forced to surrender to the Syrians the country we had recently taken from them in war. The Romans have also exacted from us more than ten thousand talents in a short time."

4534. After this, Josephus stated that Crassus alone took this much from the temple. He can be understood to be speaking here of the tributes and taxes imposed on the people. {*Josephus, Antiq., l. 14. c. 7. s. 1. (105-109) 7:503,505}

4535. It is interesting to compare what Josephus wrote about Pompey's action against the Jews, with the writings of other non-Jewish historians. Cicero, during whose consulship these things happened, was the main writer and we found this testimony of Pompey's restraint. {*Cicero, Pro Flacco, l. 1. (68) 10:517}

"When Gnaeus Pompey had taken Jerusalem, he removed nothing from the temple. From the beginning as in all things, he acted most wisely. In so large and rebellious a city, he gave no occasion for the speeches of slanderous detractors. I think that the religion of the Jews was no restraint to him but this excellent commander acted out of respect for public opinion."

4536. As much as could be expected from a heathen, he made a comparison between the Roman and the Jewish religion in this manner: {*Cicero, Pro Flacco, l. 1. (69) 10:517,519}

"Every city has its particular religion and we have ours. While Jerusalem stood and the Jews were in league with us, their religion abhorred the splendour of the sacred rites of our empire, the majesty of our name and the institutions of our ancestors. Now, which is worse, that nation has shown their opinion of us by their arms. It is sufficiently obvious how dear they are to the immortal gods in that they are conquered, farmed out to tax collectors and enslaved." [E601]

4537. Livy stated: {*Livy, l. 102. 14:127}

"Gnaeus Pompey subdued the Jews and took their temple, which until that time had been kept sacred."

4538. Unless we believe that (as they have done in other parts of their histories) Eutropius and Orosius borrowed the following comment from Livy. It was Eutropius who said: {Eutropius, l. 6.}

"...passing over against the Jews, he took Jerusalem, the capital of the country, in the third month. Twelve

thousand Jews were killed and the rest were taken into league."

4539. Orosius wrote that Pompey went from Petra in Arabia against the Jews: {Orosius, l. 6. c. 6.}

"over whom Aristobulus reigned after he expelled his brother, Hyrcanus (who was the first king born of a priest)."

4540. This showed that he did not take this part of his history from Josephus, but rather from someone less knowledgeable in Jewish affairs. In spite of this, he accurately related what Pompey did: [K263]

"He sent Gabinius with an army to Jerusalem, their city. He himself arrived later and was received into the city by the chief elders. He was driven from the walls of the temple by the common people which made him determined to take it. The place was well fortified by its natural location and was surrounded by a very large wall. Even so, one legion after another attacked the walls, night and day, without stopping. It took three months until he finally captured it after much trouble. Thirteen thousand (Josephus and Eutropius say twelve thousand) Jews were killed and the rest made a truce. Pompey ordered the walls of the city to be levelled to the ground. After he had beheaded some princes of the Jews, he restored Hyrcanus to the high priesthood and brought Aristobulus to Rome as a prisoner."

4541. Strabo wrote:

"When Judea was now openly being oppressed with tyranny, Alexander was the first who made himself king, instead of just a priest. His sons, Hyrcanus and Aristobulus, fought for the government. Pompey came in and deposed and demolished their bulwarks, after first taking Jerusalem by force. That wall was entirely of stone and well guarded. Inside, they were well supplied with water but outside it was very dry. Outside the wall a ditch had been cut in the rock, sixty feet deep and two hundred and sixty feet wide. The walls of the temple were made of the stones that had been removed from the ditch. Pompey took it, so the report goes, by taking the opportunity of a day of fasting, in which they abstained from every type of work. When he had filled in the ditch, he crossed the wall using his scaling ladders. He commanded all the walls to be demolished, and as much as he was able, destroyed all the dens of robbers and all the places where the tyrant's treasures were stored. Two of them were located at the entrance to Jericho, that is Threx and Taurus. The rest were Alexandrion, Hyrcanium, Macharus, Lysias, and some places near Philadelphia, Scythopolis and adjacent to Galilee. {*Strabo, l. 16. c. 2. s. 40. 7:289,291} Later, Pompey took away some places that the Jews had captured by force and made Hyrcanus the high priest. (Josephus incorrectly said it was Herod, not Hyrcanus, who was made the high priest. Editor.) {*Strabo, l. 16. c. 2. s. 46. 7:297,299}

4542. In Lucan, listed among the other countries that Pompey conquered, Judah was described as follows: {*Lucan, l. 2. (590-600) 1:101}

To the Arabs and the war-like Heniochi tamed
And the fleece-deprived Colchi I am known: my famed
Ensigns the Cappadocians, and the Jews, who adore
An unknown God, and soft Sophene fear full sore:
Taurus, Armenia and Cilicia I have subdued.

4543. Plutarch stated: {*Plutarch, Pompey, l. 1. c. 39. s. 2. 5:217}

"He subdued Judea and took their King, Aristobulus."

4544. Appian said: {*Appian, Mithridatic Wars, l. 12. c. 16. (106) 2:441,443}

"He made war upon Aretas, the king of the Nabatean Arabians, and also on the Jews, who had revolted from their king, Aristobulus. He took Jerusalem, a city which, in their conceit, they thought most holy."

4545. Appian also stated elsewhere: {*Appian, Syrian Wars, l. 11. c. 8. (50) 2:199}

"Only the country of the Jews remained unconquered, whose King, Aristobulus, the conquering Pompey sent to Rome. He overthrew the walls of Jerusalem, the greatest and most holy city in all that country."

4546. Tacitus stated: {*Tacitus, Histories, l. 5. c. 9. 3:191}

"Gnaeus Pompey was the first Roman that conquered the Jews and entered the temple by right of conquest. At that time it was first known that their temple was without any images on the inside and had an empty seat. The walls of Jerusalem were thrown down but the temple still stood."

4547. Florus said, concerning the same event: {*Florus, l. 1. c. 40. s. 29,30. 1:189}

"Pompey marched through Libanus (Lebanon) in Syria and through Damascus, placing the Roman ensigns there. He passed through those sweet-smelling groves of frankincense and balms. The Arabians were at his service. The Jews were afraid to defend Jerusalem. He also entered the temple and saw openly the grand mystery of that wicked nation as under a sky of beaten gold. (Concerning this, see Lipsius. {Lipsius, Elector., l. 2. c. 5.}) [E602] [K264] The brothers were at odds about the kingdom and Pompey was made the judge. He gave the kingdom to Hyrcanus and put irons on Aristobulus, for refusing to abide by the agreement."

4548. Dio said that, in the consulship of Marcus Tullius Cicero and Gaius Antonius, {*Dio, l. 37. (15,16) 3:125,127}

"Pompey marched into Syria Palestina because their inhabitants had invaded Phoenicia. This country was governed by two brothers, Hyrcanus and Aristobulus, who were at odds with each other at the time about the priesthood of God, which is the same as ruling the kingdom, with them. One of them filled the city with seditions. Therefore, Pompey conquered Hyrcanus without fighting because there were no forces able to resist him. Aristobulus was besieged in a certain citadel and was forced to accept conditions of peace. Since he would neither give him money, nor surrender the citadel, Pompey cast him into prison and then easily conquered the rest. The taking of Jerusalem caused Pompey much trouble. He easily took the city and was let in by those who favoured Hyrcanus. However, he did not easily take the temple which had been seized by the opposing faction. It was located on a hill and fortified with a wall of stone. Had they defended it every single day, it would never have been conquered but they did not defend it on Saturdays. Because they rested from all work on those days, they gave the Romans the opportunity of overthrowing the wall. Once the Romans observed this custom of the enemies, they did nothing against the wall on the other days. But when the week was past and Saturday arrived, they started working heartily and took the temple by force. Finally, the Jews were overcome and did not defend themselves. Their treasures were taken away and the kingdom was given to Hyrcanus, while Aristobulus was carried away prisoner. These things happened in Palestine at this time."

4549. While Pompey made war around Judea, Ptolemy (Auletes) maintained eight thousand cavalry at his own expense and feasted a thousand guests with as many gold drinking cups. He always changed the cups as they changed the dishes, as Varro related. {*Pliny, l. 33. c. 47. 9:103} In a speech which is now lost, Cicero said that Ptolemy was paid twelve thousand five hundred talents in tribute annually from Egypt. {*Strabo, l. 17. c. 1. s. 13. 8:53} However, Diodorus Siculus stated that the revenue of Egypt was only six thousand talents at this time.

*4550.* Seleucis, in Palestine, was built by Pompey. {*Appian, Mithridatic Wars, l. 12. c. 17. (117) 2:469*}

*4551.* Pompey left the government of Coelosyria, from the Euphrates River as far as the borders of Egypt, to Scaurus, along with two legions. Pompey left for Cilicia and took Aristobulus along with him as a prisoner together with his two sons and two daughters. {*Josephus, Antiq., l. 14. c. 4. s. 5. (79) 7:489*} One son, called Alexander, escaped on the journey but the younger son, called Antigonus, and his sisters were taken to Rome. {*Josephus, Jewish War, l. 1. c. 7. s. 7. (158) 2:73,75*}

*4552.* Appian wrote that when Pompey left Syria, he put his quaestor, Scaurus, in charge. {*Appian, Syrian Wars, l. 11. c. 8. (51) 2:199*} {*Appian, Civil Wars, l. 5. c. 1. (10) 4:393*} {*Josephus, Jewish War, l. 1. c. 6. s. 2. (127) 2:61*} Josephus added that he gave the government of Syria, as well as Judea, to Scaurus. {*Josephus, Jewish War, l. 1. c. 7. s. 7. (157) 2:73*} Ammianus Marcellinus affirmed this: {*Ammianus Marcellinus, l. 14. c. 8. s. 12. 1:71*}

> "After Pompey had conquered the Jews and taken Jerusalem, he organized Palestine into a province and committed its jurisdiction to a governor."

*4553.* Hyrcanus retained the name of king, but without a crown. He was so dull-witted, that the governors of Syria took the power to themselves. *[K265]* They managed the tributes and all other matters in Palestine according to their own pleasure. We shall see this later, in the government of Gabinius.

*4554.* When Cicero and Antonius were consuls, on the 9th day before the month of October, a son, Octavius, was born to Octavius and his wife Atia, who was the sister of Gaius Julius Caesar. {*Suetonius, Augustus, l. 2. c. 4,5. 1:155,157*} Octavius was later called Caesar Augustus and it was in his reign that our Lord Jesus Christ, the Saviour of the world, was born. {*Lu 2:1,6,7*} Julius Marathus reported that a few months before Augustus was born, a prodigy or oracle happened at Rome and became publicly known. It stated that nature was about to bring forth a king over the people of Rome. The Senate was afraid and made a law that no male child born that year should be raised. Those whose wives were pregnant objected, for everyone thought this sign might apply to his or her future son. They said this act should not be brought into the treasury and then enrolled as law. Suetonius confirmed that Octavius' birthday was on the 9th day before the month of October. {*Suetonius, Augustus, l. 2. c. 5. 1:155*} Augustus agreed with Suetonius in a letter to his nephew, Gaius. {*Aulus Gellius, Attic Nights, l. 15. c. 7. s. 3. 3:79*} The new calendar, {*Gruter, Inscriptions, p. 133.*} the Narbon stone, {*Gruter, Inscriptions, p. 229.*} as well as Dio,

state that he was born on the 23rd of September. {*Dio, l. 56. (30) 7:69*} In the Julian September of thirty days, the 9th of the Calends of the month of October is the 23rd of September, although in the Pompilian September, which only has twenty-nine days, it is the 22nd of the same month. However, September, as the year was at Rome (before the corrections of Julius Caesar), happened in June 63 BC, or 4651 JP.

*4555.* The Catiline conspiracy broke out at Rome. Quintus Marcius Rex and Quintus Metellus Creticus were both generals in the city. *[E603]* They were both prevented from celebrating a triumph by the false accusation of a certain few, whose custom it was to assail everything, whether true or false. {*Sallust, Catiline, l. 1. c. 30. s. 3,4. 1:51*}

*4556.* The Philadelphians calculated their years from the second year of the 179th Olympiad. {*Fasti Siculi*} This Philadelphia was not far from Judea, as noted by Josephus, and the area was the den of many thieves. However it was captured that year and the thieves were taken away by Pompey. This may explain the reason for the institution of this epoch. {*Josephus, Jewish War, l. 1. c. 6. s. 3. (129,130) 2:61*} {*Strabo, l. 16. c. 2. s. 34. 7:281*} {*Strabo, l. 16. c. 3. s. 40. 7:291*}

*4557.* Pompey marched around the rest of Cilicia, which did not acknowledge the Roman power. He subdued it all to Roman authority without a fight, except the part which was occupied by the Eleuthero-Cilicians. {*Appian, Mithridatic Wars, l. 12. c. 17. (118) 2:469*} Their town was located in Mount Amanus and they were later conquered by Cicero, the proconsul of Syria.

*4558.* Pharnaces sent Pompey the embalmed body of his father Mithridates and surrendered himself and his kingdom to him. {*Dio, l. 37. (14) 3:123*} Appian wrote that he sent it to Pompey, at Sinope, in a galley, along with those who had captured Manius Aquilius and many Greek and barbarian hostages. Pharnaces desired to retain either his father's kingdom or the Bosphorus, which only his brother Machares had received from Mithridates. {*Appian, Mithridatic Wars, l. 12. c. 16. (113) 2:459*} Plutarch said that when Pompey came to Amisus, he found many gifts sent by Pharnaces and many members of the royal family. *[K266]* The corpse of Mithridates was not very easily recognisable by his face but could be identified from the scars by those who wanted to see that sight. Pompey did not see the corpse but sent it to Sinope. {*Plutarch, Pompey, l. 1. c. 42. 5:223*}

*4559.* Pompey believed that all hostility had died with Mithridates and so did no harm to the corpse but ordered that it be buried in the sepulchre of his fathers. {*Dio, l. 37. (14) 3:123*} He turned the corpse over to those who were to take care of it and paid for the funeral, with orders that it should be royally interred at Sinope. He commended Mithridates for the excellence of his exploits and declared him to have been the most famous king of his time. {*Appian, Mithridatic Wars, l. 12. c. 16. (113) 2:459}

4560. Pompey admired the wonderfully rich apparel and the arms that Mithridates wore. However, Publius stole the scabbard of his sword, which was worth four hundred talents, and sold it to Ariarathes. Gaius, the foster-brother of Mithridates, privately gave Mithridates' tiara, the product of wonderful workmanship, to Faustus, the son of Sulla, who asked him for it. Pompey did not know about this but when Pharnaces later found out, he punished the thieves. {*Plutarch, Pompey, l. 1. c. 42. s. 3. 5:223,225}

4561. Pompey registered Pharnaces and Castor of Phanagoria among the friends and allies of the people of Rome. {*Appian, Mithridatic Wars, l. 12. c. 16. (113) 2:461,463} {*Dio, l. 37. (14) 3:123} He also gave the kingdom of Bosphorus to Pharnaces, because he had freed Italy from many difficulties, but he was not given Phanagoria. Pompey granted that country its liberty, because they had been the first to trouble Mithridates by revolting from him when he was gathering up his forces again and when he had an army and a fleet. By their example to others, they had been the cause of his downfall. {*Appian, Mithridatic Wars, l. 12. c. 16. (113) 2:461} After Pompey left, Pharnaces attacked Phanagoria and their neighbours until they were forced through famine to come out and fight with him and were defeated. He did not harm them, but received them into friendship with him and only took hostages from them. {*Appian, Mithridatic Wars, l. 12. c. 17. (120) 2:473}

4562. Pompey recovered the citadels in Pontus. They were surrendered to Pompey personally by the garrisons which controlled them, because they thought that if they turned them over to anyone else, the treasure would be looted and they would be held accountable. {*Dio, l. 37. (14) 3:123} The city of Talauri was the place where Mithridates had stored his belongings. There they found two thousand cups of onyx stone which were welded together with gold. They also found many cups, wine-coolers and drinking horns, as well as couches and chairs, which were all exceptionally splendid. They found bridles for horses, as well as trappings for their breasts and shoulders, that were all covered with gold and precious stones. The treasurer spent thirty days recording what was found. Part of the treasure came from Darius, the son of Hystaspes, and had been handed down to his successors. Cleopatra had deposited part of the Ptolemy family treasure at Cos, from where Mithridates had carried it when the citizens handed it over to him. Some of the treasure belonged to Mithridates, who was extremely keen to have rich household furniture. {*Appian, Mithridatic Wars, l. 12. c. 17. (115) 2:463,465}

4563. At Rome, at the time when the consuls were elected, Cicero, the consul, made a speech for Murena, who was chosen consul for the following year. He was accused of unlawful bribery to get the office. In the speech, Cicero said that the army of Lucius Lucullus, which had come to Lucullus' triumph, came to help Murena by demanding the consulship. Concerning this triumph, Cicero stated: {*Cicero, Academica, l. 2. c. 1. 19:469}

"When he returned as the conqueror from the Mithridatic war, he triumphed three years later than he ought to have done, due to the false accusations of his enemies. [K267] We who are consuls were most honoured to bring the chariot of this famous man into the city."

4564. Gaius Memmius had set the people of Rome against Lucullus, as maintaining that he had embezzled much of the spoils and had protracted the war. Hence, he persuaded the people that they should deny Lucullus his triumph. [E604] But the noblemen and those that had the most authority mingled with the tribes. They entreated them so much by solicitation and persuasion, that they finally persuaded them to allow Lucullus' triumph. {*Plutarch, Lucullus, l. 1. c. 37. s. 1. 2:593}

4565. He did not make his triumphant entry burdensome by a lengthy show, or with the number of things he brought there with him, as many captains had done before him. Instead, he decorated the circus of Flamininus with a large number of the enemy's weapons and with the king's battering engines. This sight was a pleasant one to see. In this triumph, there was a certain company of mail-clad cavalry men, ten chariots with scythes and sixty friends and generals of the two kings, as well as a hundred and ten bronze-beaked ships. Also displayed was a six foot high solid gold statue of Mithridates, a shield set with precious stones, the crown of Tigranes, and twenty litters of silver vessels and thirty-two litters of golden beakers, armour and coins, which were carried upon men's shoulders. Eight mules carried golden couches, fifty-six carried silver bullion and a hundred and seven carried silver coins worth a little less than two million, seven hundred thousand pieces of silver. Moreover, books of accounts were carried, recording what he had given to his own soldiers, which was nine hundred and fifty drachmas apiece. Then Lucullus feasted all the cities and villages around there. {*Plutarch, Lucullus, l. 1. c. 37. s. 2-4. 2:593,595}

4566. After the triumph, an account was given of the Mithridatic war. Lucullus engaged in a lifestyle that was far more magnificent than had been the ancient practice of temperance and the manner of life of the Romans of old. He was the first Roman to bring in all manner of luxuries, after having received the riches of the two kings, Tigranes and Mithrides. {*Nicolaus Damascene, History, l. 27.} {*Athenaeus, l. 6. (274e) 3:235} {*Athenaeus, l. 12. (543a) 5:459} Velleius Paterculus also confirmed that he was the first to introduce the excessive luxury in buildings and household goods. {*Velleius Paterculus, l. 2. c. 33. s. 4. 1:123}

### 3942a AM, 4651 JP, 63 BC

*4567.* Pompey rebuilt Eupatoria, which Mithridates Eupator had built and named after himself, and then destroyed it again, because it entertained the Romans. Pompey gave it lands and inhabitants and called it Magnopolis. {*Strabo, l. 12. c. 3. s. 30. 5:429} {*Appian, Mithridatic Wars, l. 12. c. 17. (115) 2:463} He built Cabira into a city and called it Diospolis. {*Strabo, l. 12. c. 3. s. 31. 5:431} He appointed laws and statutes for the Bithynians and the people of Pontus. Pliny, the praetor of Bithynia, mentioned these in his letter to Trojan. {*Pliny, Letters, l. 10. c. 69. 2:265}

*4568.* Pompey marched from Pontus into Asia (properly so called) and wintered at Ephesus. {*Dio, l. 37. (20) 3:131} {*Plutarch, Cato Minor, l. 1. c. 14. s. 1. 8:265} When he had finished his task on sea and land, he ordered the cities of Asia to furnish him with a fleet equivalent to the price Lucius Sulla had imposed. {*Cicero, Pro Flacco, l. 1. (32) 10:477}

*4569.* Lucius Valerius Flaccus, who had been praetor at Rome in the previous year, was praetor of Asia that year. {*Cicero, Pro Flacco, l. 1. (100,101) 10:551}

### 3942b AM, 4652 JP, 62 BC

*4570.* Around the end of winter, Pompey distributed the rewards to his conquering army. Each man received fifteen hundred Attic drachmas. Plutarch confirmed that each man received at least this much, while the tribunes and centurions received amounts commensurate with their position. The total sum of money was calculated to have been sixteen thousand talents. {*Appian, Mithridatic Wars, l. 12. c. 17. (116) 2:465} {*Plutarch, Pompey, l. 1. c. 45. s. 3. 5:231} [K268] He gave a hundred million sesterces to the commanders and quaestors defending the sea coast and six thousand sesterces to each of the soldiers, according to Pliny. {*Pliny, l. 37. c. 6. 10:177}

*4571.* When Decimus Julius Silanus and Lucius Murena were consuls, Metellus had a triumph in the month of June for having conquered Crete. {Eutropius, l. 6.} (This is as much as we can gather from the *Marble Fragments of the Triumphal Records*.) This triumph was in the Julian March and one of the attractions in the triumph was to have been the captured generals, whom Pompey had taken from Metellus. {*Velleius Paterculus, l. 2. c. 40. s. 5. 1:139}

With the help of one of the tribunes, whom he had persuaded to assist him, Pompey had taken Lasthenes and Panares, because he claimed these two generals had submitted to him in the settlement, and not to Metellus. {*Dio, l. 36. (19) 3:29,31} However, the triumph of Lucullus and Metellus much enjoyed the favour of every good man because of the merits of the two generals and especially on account of the general unpopularity of Pompey. {*Velleius Paterculus, l. 2. c. 34. s. 2. 1:123,125} Appian also mentioned the triumph of Metellus Creticus. {*Appian, Sicily and the Other Islands, l. 5. c. 6. (2) 1:137}

*4572.* Cato came to Ephesus, to greet Pompey as someone older and greater in dignity than he. When Pompey saw him come, he would not allow him to come to him while he sat in his seat but went to meet Cato, as one of the most important noblemen. Taking Cato by the hand, he embraced and greeted him. He commended Cato in the presence of all men, both when he was present and in his absence. But Pompey was nevertheless glad when he was gone, almost as though he could not command as freely when Cato was there. He also commended the care of his wife and children to Cato, a thing Pompey never did to any others who sailed to Rome, although, indeed, Cato was related to him. {*Plutarch, Cato Minor, l. 1. c. 14. s. 1-3. 8:265,267} [E605]

*4573.* Pompey had overcome many princes and kings, partly by war and partly by allying them to himself with firm conditions of peace. He had taken no less than nine hundred cities, rebuilt thirty-nine cities that had either been ruined or destroyed in war (as was Mazaca, the capital city of Cappadocia), and had enlarged eight cities and repopulated countries with colonies. Most of the countries throughout Asia belonging to the Romans he instructed in his own laws and ordained a commonwealth for them. Finally, he sailed from Ephesus, passing through the islands and Greece, and travelled toward Italy in very great pomp. {*Dio, l. 37. (20) 3:131} {*Appian, Mithridatic Wars, l. 12. c. 17. (117) 2:467,469} {*Plutarch, Pompey, l. 1. c. 45. 5:231,233}

*4574.* When Pompey reached Lesbos, he released the city of Mitylene of all taxes. {*Plutarch, Pompey, l. 1. c. 42. s. 4. 5:225} The Mitylenians had surrendered Marius Aquilius and other prisoners, and were granted liberty by Pompey as a favour to Theophanes. {*Velleius Paterculus, l. 2. c. 18. s. 3. 1:85} This was Balbus Cornelius Theophanes, a Mitylenian and a writer of Pompey's deeds. Pompey esteemed him as one of his most intimate friends and in the presence of the whole army, made him a citizen of Rome. When he died, the Greeks bestowed divine honours on Theophanes. {*Cicero, Pro Archia Poeta, l. 1. c. 10. (24) 11:33} {*Strabo, l. 13. c. 2. s. 3. 6:143} {*Valerius Maximus, l. 8. c. 14. s. 3. 2:273} {*Tacitus, Annals, l. 6. c. 18. 4:185} {Julius Capitoline, Maximus and Balbus}

4575. At Mitylene, Pompey watched the poets perform plays in which Pompey's deeds and acts were the theme of all the performances. Pompey was delighted with the theatre and recorded the plans for it so that he could build a similar one at Rome, only larger and more magnificent. {*Plutarch, Pompey, l. 1. c. 42. s. 4. 5:225} [K269]

4576. When he came to Rhodes, he heard the sophists dispute and gave each of them a talent. Posidonius had written the discourse he made before Pompey against Hermagoras, the rhetorician, on *Investigation in General*. {*Plutarch, Pompey, l. 1. c. 42. s. 4. 5:225} As Pompey was about to go into Posidonius' house, he forbade his lictor to knock on the door in the customary manner and he himself, to whom both the East and the West had submitted, dipped his standard to the portals of learning. {*Pliny, l. 7. c. 30. 2:579} Based on Pompey's own account, Cicero related the following about that meeting: {*Cicero, Tusculan Disputations, l. 2. c. 25. 18:215}

"I have often seen Posidonius myself but I will tell you what Pompey has often said to me. When he came from Syria and arrived at Rhodes, he intended to hear Posidonius. When he heard that he was very sick and in great pain with the gout, he still wanted to see this famous philosopher. When Pompey had met him and greeted him, he paid him great compliments. Pompey told him how very sorry he was that he could not hear him. Posidonius replied that he might still hear him, since he would not allow the pain of his body to frustrate the visit to him of so great a man. So Pompey told me that the philosopher disputed very gravely and fully on this subject: *That there is nothing good, but what is honest.* He was all on fire, as it were, with pain, as if so many torches had been put to him. He often said of his pain, *All that you do is nothing, although you are troublesome, yet I will never admit you are an evil.*"

4577. Some also say that Pompey came to Rhodes on his way to the Mithridatic war, and that the time when he was about to march against Mithridates was the time when he spoke to Posidonius. As Pompey was leaving, he asked him if he would give him some advice. Posidonius repeated that verse in Homer:

"Act nobly and remember to excel over others."

4578. This was recorded from Strabo. {*Strabo, l. 11. c. 1. s. 6. 5:189}

4579. When Valerius Flaccus was praetor, he commanded the cities of Asia to furnish him with money and sailors for a fleet. This fleet was half the size of the one Pompey used. Flaccus divided it into two squadrons, one of which was to sail north of Ephesus and the other south.

With this fleet, Marcus Crassus sailed from Aenus, in Thrace, to Asia and Flaccus sailed from Asia into Macedonia. Each year, in the name of the Jews, gold was exported to Jerusalem from Italy and all the Roman provinces. For this reason, Flaccus ordered that no gold should be exported from Asia. When almost a hundred pounds of gold was intercepted at Apamea, it was weighed before the praetor himself in the court of Sextus Caesius, a Roman equestrian. At Laodicea, more than twenty pounds of gold were seized by Lucius Peducaeus. At Adramyttium, a hundred pounds of gold were seized by Gnaeus Domitius, one of Flaccus' subordinate officers. At Pergamum, not much gold was taken. All this gold was duly accounted for and stored in the treasury. There was no evidence of any theft of the gold. {*Cicero, Pro Flacco, l. 1. (32) 10:477} {*Cicero, Pro Flacco, l. 1. (68,69) 10:517}

4580. Scaurus, who had been left governor of Syria by Pompey, marched into Arabia. Because the way was difficult, he did not go as far as Petra, but nevertheless wasted the country around there. [E606] He endured much suffering, as his army was affected by famine, even though Hyrcanus, through Antipater, supplied him from Judea with grain and other things he had need of. Antipater was also sent as an envoy from Scaurus to Aretas, because he was his very close friend. He tried to persuade him that he could redeem his country from destruction by paying a sum of money, so Aretas paid him three hundred talents on condition that the war was ended. So the war ended, to the satisfaction of neither Scaurus nor Aretas. {*Josephus, Jewish War, l. 1. c. 8. s. 1. (159) 2:75} {*Josephus, Antiq., l. 14. c. 5. s. 1. (80,81) 7:489} [K270] Scaurus had a silver coin stamped during his aedileship. One side showed a king in barbarous clothes kneeling before Scaurus. This king was wearing a loose coat and hose. He was being presented with a crown by Scaurus who was riding on a camel's back. These letters were written around the image: *M. SCAVRVS AED. CVR. EX. S. C.* This meant *Marcus Scaurus aedile by the decree of the Senate.* Below it was written *REX ARETAS*, or King Aretas. {Pighius, Annals of Rome, Tom. 3. p. 341,362.}

4581. When Pompey had sent his lieutenant Piso to seek the consulship, the Romans deferred the request until Piso arrived. They chose Piso as consul by general consent. This commendation of Piso by Pompey was confirmed by both his friends and his enemies because they were all afraid of Pompey before he had dismissed his army. {*Dio, l. 37. (44) 3:169}

## 3943a AM, 4652 JP, 62 BC

4582. Around the time of Publius Piso's consulship (in the Julian November), Pompey came into Italy. {*Cicero,

*Atticus, l. 1. c. 12. 22:29-33}* {*Cicero, Atticus, l. 1. c. 14. 22:39}* It was feared that he would come with his army and would order public affairs after his own pleasure, making himself lord of all Italy and over all the might of the Romans. But as soon as he came to Brundisium, he voluntarily discharged all his forces before any decree reached him, either from the Senate or the people. {*Velleius Paterculus, l. 2. c. 40. s. 3. 1:137}* {*Plutarch, Pompey, l. 1. c. 43. s. 1,2. 5:227}* {*Appian, Mithridatic Wars, l. 12. c. 17. (116) 2:465}* {*Dio, l. 37. (20) 3:133}* Plutarch said that when Pompey had discharged his soldiers in a kindly manner, he ordered them to meet him again at his triumph. {*Plutarch, Pompey, l. 1. c. 43. s. 2. 5:227}* However, Dio affirmed that he did not intend to use them in his triumph. {*Dio, l. 37. (20) 3:133}*

*4583.* In a speech at Rome, Pompey declared that he had made war, in the East, with twenty-two kings. {*Orosius, l. 6. c. 6.}* At the time that he had received command for Asia, it had been the outermost province, but now, when he had restored it to his country again, it was the most central one. {*Pliny, l. 7. c. 26. 2:571}* {*Florus, l. 1. c. 40. s. 31. 1:189}*

*4584.* Quintus Tullius Cicero, the younger brother of Marcus, was chosen by lot to be praetor over Asia and succeeded Lucius Valerius Flaccus. {*Cicero, Pro Flacco, l. 1. (33) 10:479}* {*Cicero, Atticus, l. 1. c. 15. 22:47}*

*4585.* When he was to go into his province, he wanted Titus Pomponius Atticus, his wife's brother, to go with him as his lieutenant. Atticus did not consider it fitting for him, if he could not be a praetor, to be a servant of the praetor. {*Cornelius Nepos, Life of Atticus, l. 1. c. 5,6. 1:295,297}* Cicero was offended by this. {*Cicero, Atticus, l. 1. c. 17. 22:67}*

*4586.* Publius Clodius was accused of the revolt of Nisibis, of having entered a temple (which it was unlawful for a man to enter) dressed as a woman, of having defiled the wife of Metellus, the high priest, and of Gaius Caesar, and of unseemly behaviour with his own sister. He was acquitted by the judges who had been bribed with money. {*Cicero, Atticus, l. 1. c. 13. 22:35}* {*Livy, l. 103. 14:127}* {*Plutarch, Cicero, l. 1. c. 28. 7:151,153}* {*Dio, l. 37. (44,45) 3:169,171}*

*4587.* Cicero wrote to Atticus that he had taken Syria which had been assigned to Piso, the consul, away from Piso. {*Cicero, Atticus, l. 1. c. 16. 22:57}* Therefore, Marcius Philippus, who had been praetor, was sent out as the successor to Scaurus, whom Pompey had left in Syria. For two years Philippus had skirmished with the Arabians, who lived near there and who had invaded Syria. {*Appian, Syrian Wars, l. 11. c. 8. (51) 2:199}* [K271]

*4588.* In the ninth year of the priesthood and government of Hyrcanus (that is, from the death of his mother Alexandra, before Gabinius took the government from him), in the month of Panemos, or June, the decree of

the Athenians in honour of Hyrcanus seems to have been published, as recorded by Josephus. {*Josephus, Antiq., l. 14. c. 8. s. 5. (148-155) 7:527-531}* However, Josephus connected that time to a former decree of the Roman Senate. It was set out both in the time of the previous Hyrcanus, the son of Simeon, and as well as on the Ides of December (December 13). {See note on 3877a AM. <<3798>>} However, this particular decree, made in honour of Hyrcanus, the second son of Alexander, was written on the 11th day of the Athenian month of Mounychion (about the 28th day of the Julian April), by Eucles, the son of Xenander, the Almusian. He was the secretary and on the πεμπη απιοντος of the Macedonian month of Panemos, or the 27th day (corresponding to the 20th day of the Julian June), he delivered it to the governors and to Agathocles, who was the praetor at Athens. {Ussher, Macedonian and Asiatic Year, l. 1. c. 1.}

### 3943b AM, 4653 JP, 61 BC

*4589.* First, Quintus Cicero relieved the cities of Asia of the financial burden of having to provide sailors and a fleet. {*Cicero, Pro Flacco, l. 1. (33) 10:479}* [E607] He restored many cities that were almost deserted. Two of these were Samos, a most illustrious city of Ionia, and Halicarnassus, a city of Caria. {*Cicero, Quintus, l. 1. c. 8. 28:413}*

*4590.* Pompey deferred his triumph until his birthday, which he celebrated the day before the month of October. (His birthday happened either in July or June, of the Julian account.) Marcus Messala and Marcus Piso were consuls when this took place as may be gathered from the *Marble Fragments of the Triumphal Records*. It can be more fully deduced from the official records of Pompey's triumphs. {*Pliny, l. 7. c. 26. 2:569}* {*Pliny, l. 37. c. 6. 10:173}* He had a most magnificent triumph of so many kings for two whole days. {*Velleius Paterculus, l. 2. c. 40. s. 3. 1:137}* {*Appian, Mithridatic Wars, l. 12. c. 17. (116) 2:465}* Even though this triumph lasted for two days, Plutarch said its greatness was not fully displayed because a large part of the preparation, sufficient to have furnished another triumph, was not presented. {*Plutarch, Pompey, l. 1. c. 45. s. 1. 5:231}*

*4591.* Those who tried to compare Pompey with Alexander the Great in all things, would have us believe he was not yet thirty-four years old, when he was in fact nearly forty, if we accept Plutarch's account. {*Plutarch, Pompey, l. 1. c. 46. s. 1. 5:233}* Due to the talk of his flatterers, Pompey believed, even from his youth, that he was like Alexander and so he imitated both his actions and advice. {*Sallust, Speech of Macer, l. 1. (23) 1:429}* {Nonius Marcellus, under word, Aemulus} However, Velleius very elegantly observed that some men were altogether too taken up with the age of that great man. {*Velleius Paterculus, l. 2. c. 53. s. 4. 1:169}*

"...who were deceived by five years. Whereas setting these things right could easily be done by calculating from the consulships of Gaius Atilius and Quintus Servilius."

4592. While he corrected others, Plutarch made the same mistake. He said that Pompey was nearly forty years old, when in actual fact he was about forty-five.

4593. Pompey had made his first triumph over Africa, the second over Europe and the third over Asia. He had established the three parts of the world as monuments of his victory. {*Velleius Paterculus, l. 2. c. 40. s. 4. 1:137} {*Plutarch, Pompey, l. 1. c. 45. s. 5. 5:233} Consequently, this great triumph was called *The Triumph of the Whole World*. {*Dio, l. 37. (21) 3:135} Due to this, the whole assembly greeted him by the surname of *Great*. {*Livy, l. 103. 14:129} He was pleased with this surname, even though he could have been given many new names because of his famous deeds. {*Dio, l. 37. (21) 3:135} [K272]

4594. The preface of the triumph (as it was described by Pliny from Pompey's own records) was this: {*Pliny, l. 7. c. 26. 2:569,571}

"When he had freed the seacoast from pirates and had restored control of the sea to the people of Rome, he triumphed over Asia, Pontus, Armenia, Paphlagonia, Cappadocia, Cilicia, Syria, the Scythians, Jews and Albanians, over Iberia, the Isle of Crete, the Bastarnians and above all these, over the kings, Mithridates and Tigranes."

4595. Plutarch added: {*Plutarch, Pompey, l. 1. c. 45. s. 2. 5:231}

"Media, Colchis, Mesopotamia and Arabia."

4596. Appian added: {*Appian, Mithridatic Wars, l. 12. c. 17. (116) 2:465}

"the Heniochi and Achaeans."

4597. Pompey brought seven hundred ships that were intact. There was a vast number of wagons that carried the armour and also the ramming prows of the ships. After these came a multitude of captives and pirates, who were not bound, but clothed in their countries' clothes. After them came noblemen, captains or sons of the kings, some of them captives and others hostages, for a total of three hundred and twenty-four. These walked ahead of Pompey, who sat on a lofty chariot. {*Appian, Mithridatic Wars, l. 12. c. 17. (116,117) 2:465,467}

4598. Among these was Tigranes, the son of Tigranes, the king of Armenia, with his wife and daughters and Zosime, the wife of Tigranes himself. Moreover, the sister and five sons of Mithridates (Artaphernes, Cyrus, Oxathres, Darius and Xerxes) and two daughters of his (Orsabaris and Eupatra) were also in the procession. As well as this, there was Olthaces, the king of the Colchians, Aristobulus, the king of the Jews, and the tyrants of the Cilicians. There were women of the royal family of the Scythians, three chiefs of the Iberians, two of the Albanians, along with Menander of Laodice, who was the general of Mithridates' cavalry. There were also the hostages of the Albanians and Iberians and of the king of the Commagenians. He had many other trophies in the procession, consistent with the number of battles that either he or his lieutenants had won in various places. {*Appian, Mithridatic Wars, l. 12. c. 17. (117) 2:467} {*Plutarch, Pompey, l. 1. c. 45. 5:231,233}

4599. Although Tigranes and Mithridates were not present, pictures of them were carried, showing how they had fought, given ground and fled. The attacks of Mithridates were depicted and how he had secretly fled away by night. Last of all came pictures showing his death and that of his daughters, who were his companions in death. Tables were carried with the images of his sons and daughters who had died before him and the figures of the barbarian gods in their own country's attire. {*Appian, Mithridatic Wars, l. 12. c. 17. (117) 2:467,469}

4600. Pompey, who was being carried in a chariot set with precious stones, was clothed, so it was reported, in the armour of Alexander the Great. Following his chariot came the officers who had accompanied him in this expedition, some on horseback, while others walked. {*Appian, Mithridatic Wars, l. 12. c. 17. (117) 2:469} [E608] The day before the month of October, which was the day of his birthday, Pompey brought a gaming-board with a complete set of pieces made of two precious minerals and measured three feet wide and four feet long. On it was a thirty pound golden Moon. Also displayed were three gold dining couches, enough gold vessels inlaid with gems to fill nine display stands. There were three golden images of Minerva, Mars and Apollo, as well as thirty-three pearl crowns. There was a square mount of gold, covered with stags, lions and all types of fruit. These were surrounded by a golden vine. {See note on 3939b AM. <<4464>>} There was a grotto of pearls, on the top of which was a sundial. Pompey's own image made of pearls was there. {*Pliny, l. 37. c. 6. 10:173,175} Pompey also recorded that he carried trees in the triumph, namely the ebony tree and the balsam tree, which only grew in Judea. {*Pliny, l. 12. c. 9. 4:15} {*Pliny, l. 12. c. 54. 4:81} [K273]

4601. There were also carts and other vessels laden with gold and various other ornaments. Among them was the bed of Darius, the son of Hystaspes, the throne and sceptre of Mithridates Eupator, and a solid gold statue of him twelve feet high. {*Appian, Mithridatic Wars, l. 12. c. 17. (116) 2:467} There was a silver statue of Pharnaces, who was the first ruler in Pontus, and gold and silver chariots. {*Pliny, l. 33. c. 54. 9:113} There were also seventy-five million, one hundred thousand drachmas in silver coins. {*Appian, Mithridatic Wars, l. 12. c. 17. (116) 2:467} Moreover, it was shown in the records that, prior to this, all the tribute of the people of Rome had totalled only fifty million drachmas, but together with these, which Pompey had gained for the people of Rome, it now amounted to eighty-five million. {*Plutarch, Pompey, l. 1. c. 45. s. 3. 5:231}

4602. A tablet was also carried, containing a summary of the things Pompey had achieved in the east. It was inscribed with this superscription. {*Appian, Mithridatic Wars, l. 12. c. 17. (117) 2:469}

"Eight hundred ships with prows were taken; eight cities built in Cappadocia, twenty in Cilicia and Coelosyria, and in Palestine the city which is now called Seleucis. Kings conquered: Tigranes the Armenian, Artoces the Iberian, Oroeses the Albanian."

4603. Pliny mentioned a similar one that was placed in the temple of Minerva and dedicated from the spoils: {*Pliny, l. 7. c. 26. 2:569}

"Gnaeus Pompey the Great, Commander-in-Chief, finished a war of thirty years. He overthrew, routed, killed and had yielded to him twelve million one hundred and eighty-three thousand men, sank and took eight hundred and forty-six ships, had fifteen hundred and thirty-eight towns and citadels surrendered to him. He conquered from the Lake Maeotis (Sea of Azov) to the Red Sea and deservedly offers this vow to Minerva."

4604. He brought twenty thousand talents into the public treasury in plate and in gold and silver coins. {*Plutarch, Pompey, l. 1. c. 45. s. 3. 5:231} Among the other gifts that were dedicated by him in the Capitol was the cabinet of King Mithridates, as Varro and other authors of the time confirmed. This first gave the Romans an appetite for pearls and jewels. {*Pliny, l. 37. c. 5. 10:171,173} They dedicated all the most precious things of Mithridates that had been found in Kainon Chorion. {*Strabo, l. 12. c. 3. s. 31. 5:429} Also dedicated was that golden vine which had been brought from Judea. {*Josephus, Antiq., l. 14. c. 3. s. 1. (34,35) 7:465} At this time, six cups of the mineral murrhine (maybe fluorspar or agate) were first brought to Rome. These were soon commonly used and became popular material for plates and dishes. {*Pliny, l. 37. c. 7. 10:177}

4605. When Pompey entered the Capitol in his triumph, he put none of the captives to death, as those who had triumphed before him used to do. Instead, he paid their expenses from the public money and sent everyone home to his own country, except those who were of royal extraction. {*Appian, Mithridatic Wars, l. 12. c. 15. (105) 2:441} {*Appian, Mithridatic Wars, l. 12. c. 17. (117) 2:469} It appears incorrect that Appian added that Aristobulus was put to death, and later Tigranes, because Aristobulus subsequently returned to his country. Josephus and Dio confirmed both this and the fact that Tigranes was kept in chains with Flavius, a senator, on Pompey's orders. He was released from his custody by Clodius, the tribune of the people, a fact which Asconius Pedianus confirmed in his writings. {*Josephus, Antiq., l. 14. c. 4. s. 5. (79) 7:489} {*Dio, l. 38. (30) 3:261} {Asconius Pedianus, Pro Milone}

## 3944a AM, 4653 JP, 61 BC

4606. After the city of Gaza was freed from the rule of the Jews, the citizens began the epoch of their times from this event. {Fasti Siculi, Olympiad 179. Year 4.} The city of Gaza began its year about the 27th day of the Julian October, as we gathered from Marcus, a deacon of Gaza, in the biography of Porphyry, the bishop of Gaza.

4607. Cicero's brother, Marcus, was the reason that no one would excel Quintus Cicero in the praetorship of Asia. [K274] Cicero showed this, in a letter to him. Among other things that he had done well in the province, he listed that the thieveries of the Mysians had been stopped and murders suppressed in many places. Peace had settled throughout the whole province. Robbing and stealing from travellers in the countryside, the towns and cities had also been suppressed. {*Cicero, Quintus, l. 1. c. 8. 28:413,415}

4608. Marcus Cicero had sent his memoirs about his consulship, written in Greek, to Posidonius in Rhodes. (He was from Apamea and was a philosopher and historian. Cicero wanted him to rewrite these in better style.) When he read what Cicero had written, he wrote back to him that he did not have the courage to write, but that he was clearly afraid. {*Cicero, Atticus, l. 2. c. 1. 22:101}

4609. Ptolemy Auletes had a son born to him in his old age, who succeeded him in his kingdom. Hence, he was no older than thirteen years when Pompey fled to him after the battle of Pharsalia. {*Dio, l. 42. (3) 4:119} [E609]

## 3944b AM, 4654 JP, 60 BC

4610. Pompey requested that the Senate ratify all the things he had granted to kings, governors and cities. {*Appian, Civil Wars, l. 2. c. 2. (9) 3:245}

4611. Lucullus had spent his time in luxurious living. When the Senate asked him to use his authority to involve himself in matters of state, he soon attacked Pompey's legislation. {*Plutarch, Pompey, l. 1. c. 46. s. 3. 5:235} Lucullus and Metellus Creticus had not forgotten the wrongs Pompey had done them and so they and some of the nobility resisted Pompey. They did not want to see what had been promised to cities distributed in accordance with Pompey's own wishes, nor see rewards bestowed on any who should have received retribution at his hands. {*Velleius Paterculus, l. 2. c. 40. s. 5. 1:139} Lucullus requested that Pompey should have to detail his proposals to the Senate and not demand that they all be approved in one measure. Otherwise, it would be unfair to approve all his acts before knowing what they were, as though they had been the actions of some god. Since Pompey had disannulled some of Lucullus' acts, Lucullus demanded that Pompey's acts should be individually proposed in the Senate, so that the Senate could ratify those worthy of approbation. Cato, Metellus Celer, who was the consul, and others who were of the same opinion, vigorously supported Lucullus. {*Dio, l. 37. (49,50) 3:177,179} Lucullus also bragged that the victory over Mithridates belonged to him, and won Crassus to his side. {*Appian, Civil Wars, l. 2. c. 2. (9) 3:245} As a result, Lucullus obtained ratification of those decrees which Pompey had disannulled. {*Plutarch, Pompey, l. 1. c. 46. s. 3. 5:235} He overturned all the constitutions that Pompey had made after having defeated the kings. Lucullus and Cato thwarted Pompey's request that the lands be divided among his soldiers. {*Plutarch, Lucullus, l. 1. c. 42. s. 6. 2:607}

4612. Thwarted in the Senate, Pompey was compelled to appeal to the tribunes of the people. {*Plutarch, Pompey, l. 1. c. 46. s. 4. 5:235} He realised that Lucius Flavius, the tribune, demanded that the lands be divided among Pompey's soldiers and that all the citizens should be allowed to have their say. He saw that, in this way, the measure might be granted more readily. Flavius also wanted all Pompey's acts confirmed. Metellus, the consul, so vigorously opposed him, that he was confined to prison by the tribune. The consul, notwithstanding, resolutely persisted in his opinion, as did others also, with the result that Pompey was finally forced to yield to his demands. Pompey regretted that he had discharged his soldiers and thereby exposed himself to be wronged by his enemies. {*Dio, l. 37. (50) 3:179}

4613. Meanwhile, Gaius Julius Caesar came to Rome to demand the consulship. [K275] Pompey allied himself with him and promised that he would do his best to help Caesar become a consul. By so doing, Pompey hoped that the acts he had done in the provinces beyond the seas, which were opposed by so many, would finally be confirmed by Caesar when he was consul. Pompey and Crassus had been at great odds ever since they had held the consulship together. Caesar reconciled them and entered into an alliance with both of them. According to this contract, nothing would be done in the state which displeased any of the three. This conspiracy proved destructive to the city, to all the world

and to themselves, also. {*Livy, l. 103. 14:127} {*Velleius Paterculus, l. 2. c. 44. 1:145,147} {*Suetonius, Julius, l. 1. c. 19. s. 2. 1:57} {*Plutarch, Lucullus, l. 1. c. 42. s. 6. 2:607} {*Plutarch, Crassus, l. 1. c. 14. s. 1,2. 3:355} {*Plutarch, Pompey, l. 1. c. 47. s. 1,2. 5:237} {*Plutarch, Caesar, l. 1. c. 13. s. 2,3. 7:471,473} {*Appian, Civil Wars, l. 2. c. 2. (9) 3:245,247} {*Dio, l. 37. (54,55) 3:187,189}

4614. Varro, who was the best writer of this period of history, wrote about this conspiracy of the three principal men of the city and called it τρικαρανον, or the *three-headed monster.* {*Appian, Civil Wars, l. 2. c. 2. (9) 3:247} Asinius Pollio also began to write his history of the civil war from the same book of Varro's, which was written during the consulship of Metellus Celer. {*Horace, Odes, l. 2. c. 1. (Title) 1:107} His interpreters, Acron and Porphyry, confirmed this, for neither believed (as many at the time thought) that it was the dissension between Caesar and Pompey which sparked the civil wars. The cause was their initial agreement to conspire together to root out the aristocracy, and then subsequently, they disagreed with each other. {*Plutarch, Caesar, l. 1. c. 13. s. 2,3. 7:471,473}

4615. In this very year, the 180th Olympiad was solemnised and Herodes was archon in Athens (a person other than that Herod of Athens, of whom Pausanias and Gellius say that he was the most famous man of his time). {*Pausanias, Attica, l. 1. c. 19. s. 6. 1:97} {*Aulus Gellius, Attic Nights, l. 1. c. 2. s. 1. 1:5} Diodorus Siculus began the history of Caesar's affairs, and wrote that he travelled over Egypt in the reign of that Ptolemy who was called *New Bacchus.* {Photius, Bibliotheca, l. 1. part. 1,2.}

## 3945a AM, 4654 JP, 60 BC

4616. A third year was added to the praetorship of Quintus Cicero in Asia. Suetonius stated that he governed the proconsulate of Asia with little distinction. {*Suetonius, Augustus, l. 2. c. 3. s. 2. 1:155} In this year, an excellent letter was written by Marcus Cicero relating to the good government of a province. This was placed first among the letters that he wrote to his brother Quintus. {*Cicero, Quintus, l. 1. c. 8,9. 28:413,415}

4617. The Senate sent Lentulus Marcellinus, who had been praetor, to succeed Marcius Philippus in the government of Syria. [E610] He had spent two years fighting off the Arabians, who adjoined Syria and repeatedly invaded the country. {*Appian, Syrian Wars, l. 11. c. 8. (51) 2:199}

## 3945b AM, 4655 JP, 59 BC

4618. Julius Caesar, the consul, confirmed all Pompey's acts, just as he had promised him, without slandering Lucullus or anyone else. {*Appian, Civil Wars, l. 2. c. 2. (13) 3:251} {*Dio, l. 38. (7) 3:211}

4619. Pompey obtained the promise from the Senate that they would not confirm the honours that Lucullus had promised to some in Pontus. He said it was unjust that the distribution of rewards and honours should be given to one who had not finished the war. {*Strabo, l. 12. c. 3. s. 33. 5:435} After filling the city with arms and soldiers, he expelled Cato and Lucullus from the forum and confirmed his acts by violence and force. {*Plutarch, Pompey, l. 1. c. 48. s. 1,2. 5:239} {*Plutarch, Lucullus, l. 1. c. 42. s. 6. 2:607,609}

4620. Suetonius wrote that Caesar, in his first consulship, made alliances and thrones a matter of barter. [K276] He took six thousand talents from Ptolemy alone in his own and Pompey's name. {*Suetonius, Julius, l. 1. c. 54. 1:103,105} Dio related that Ptolemy (Auletes) spent vast sums of money (both his own and borrowed) on certain Romans, in the hope that the kingdom of Egypt might be confirmed to him through them and that he might be called their friend and ally. {*Dio, l. 39. (55) 3:387} Plutarch related that Auletes owed Caesar seventeen million, five hundred thousand drachmas. Ten million of this Caesar extracted when he came into Egypt, after Pompey had been killed. He released Auletes' children from the rest of the debt. {*Plutarch, Caesar, l. 1. c. 48. s. 4. 7:557}

4621. In this year, when Caesar was first consul, Auletes was taken into the alliance of the people of Rome by a law and a decree of the Senate. {*Caesar, Civil Wars, l. 3. (107) 2:349} Caesar obtained this honour from the Senate before the proscription of Ptolemy's brother, Ptolemy of Cyprus (which happened in the next year.) {*Cicero, Pro Sestio, l. 1. c. 26. 12:111,113} {*Cicero, Atticus, l. 2. c. 16. 22:155}

4622. Gaius Antonius was condemned and Cicero (his colleague in the consulship) defended him in vain. {*Dio, l. 38. (10) 3:215} He lived as a banished man in Cephallenia and had all the island under his command, as his own possession. He began to build a city, but did not finish it before being recalled from exile. {*Strabo, l. 10. c. 2. s. 13. 5:47}

4623. It was decreed that Publius Clodius should go as an envoy to Tigranes, the king of Armenia. When he objected, he, who was a patrician, was made a plebian by adoption, so that in this way he could be chosen as a tribune of the people. {*Cicero, Atticus, l. 2. c. 7. 22:129} {*Cicero, De Domo Sua, l. 1. c. 13. 11:177} {*Dio, l. 37. (51) 3:181}

4624. Brithagoras was a man of great authority among the Heracleans in Pontus. He and his son Propylus went to Julius Caesar and became his friends. They followed him as he passed up and down through all the lands for twelve years, so that Caesar might do good to his fellow citizens. {Mennon, c. 62.}

## 3946a AM, 4655 JP, 59 BC
4625. Publius Clodius was made tribune of the people. To draw the new consuls to his side, he decreed large provinces for them. To Gabinius he gave Syria, with

Babylon and Persia. To Piso he gave Achaia, Thessaly, Greece, Macedonia and all Boeotia. {*Cicero, Pro Sestio, l. 1. c. 43. 12:161-165} {*Cicero, De Domo Sua, l. 1. c. 21. 11:201} {*Cicero, De Provinciis Consularibus, l. 1. c. 1,2. 13:541} {*Plutarch, Cicero, l. 1. c. 30. 7:157}

## 3946b AM, 4656 JP, 58 BC
4626. When Quintus Cicero had governed Asia for three years, he left the province. {*Cicero, Friends, l. 2. c. 15. s. 4. 25:141} {*Cicero, Atticus, l. 6. c. 6. 22:473} Marcus Cicero was in exile in Thessaly at the time and wrote to Atticus concerning his brother's journey. {*Cicero, Atticus, l. 3. c. 9. 22:209}

> "My brother Quintus had departed from Asia before the Calends of May (at the end of April, which was really about the end of the Julian February), and came to Athens on the Ides of May (May 15). He was forced to hurry lest another calamity happen in his absence, if perchance anyone should not be content with the ills we already suffered. Therefore, I would rather that he hurry to Rome than come to me."

4627. The Sibylline priest in Pessinus, a city of Phrygia, was expelled from his priesthood by a tribunal law of Publius Clodius. Brogitarus was a Galatian and was considered to be that Bogodiatarus to whom, according to Strabo, Pompey gave Mithridatium, after having taken the region away from Pontus. {*Strabo, l. 12. c. 5. s. 1. 5:469} He was a wicked man, who wanted the priesthood not out of reverence for the temple, but for the power it offered. Through his envoys to Clodius, he bought the office of the priesthood with a large sum of money. [K277] In ancient times, the priests of Pessinus had been petty kings. {*Strabo, l. 12. c. 5. s. 3. 5:471} By the same tribunal law, Dejotarus was often thought worthy of that title by the Senate, just as much as his son-in-law Brogitarus, who had never asked the Senate for it. When Brogitarus simply agreed with Clodius that so much money be paid to Clodius by bond, he had then been ordained by Clodius to be called king. Dejotarus, however, accepted that part of the law which agreed with the Senate that he should be a king, without giving any money to Clodius. Dejortus preserved Pessinus in their ancient religion and would rather have his son-in-law enjoy the title by way of a gift from Clodius, than the temple should lose her ancient religion. {*Cicero, De Haruspicum Responsis, l. 1. c. 13. 11:351-355} {*Cicero, Pro Sestio, l. 1. c. 26. 12:111} [E611]

4628. Clodius wanted to get his revenge on Ptolemy, the king of Cyprus, who was the brother of Auletes, the king of Alexandria. (If we believe Velleius Paterculus, he was very much like his brother in every aspect of his depraved lifestyle.) Previously, when Clodius had been captured by pirates, Ptolemy had neglected him. Now, even though Clodius lived at peace and enjoyed his ease, he favoured a law for reducing Ptolemy's kingdom into the form of a province, without giving any reason, or mentioning any specific wrong Ptolemy had done. All Ptolemy's goods and money would be confiscated under this law, which would send out Marcus Cato from the commonwealth, under an honourable title, to carry out the law. Although Cato was also in favour of this law, he went unwillingly to Cyprus with a quaestor, to exercise command there with praetorian power. {*Cicero, Pro Sestio, l. 1. c. 27. 12:115} {*Cicero, De Domo Sua, l. 1. c. 8. 11:157} {*Livy, l. 104. 14:131} {*Florus, l. 1. c. 44. 1:199} {*Plutarch, Cato Minor, l. 1. c. 34. s. 2-4. 8:319} {*Strabo, l. 14. c. 6. s. 6. 6:385} {*Velleius Paterculus, l. 2. c. 45. s. 4,5. 1:149} {*Appian, Civil Wars, l. 2. c. 3. (23) 3:269} {*Dio, l. 38. (30) 3:261} Cicero, in his speech for Publius Sestius, said this of Ptolemy: {*Cicero, Pro Sestio, l. 1. c. 27. 12:115}

> "That miserable Cypriot, who was always an ally, was always a friend, against whom there was never so much as the least suspicion expressed against him, either to the Senate or to our generals, lives (as they say) to see himself, in a situation where even his food and clothes have been confiscated. Behold, why should other kings think that their fortune is secure, when, by this wicked example of that regrettable year, they may see themselves stripped of all their fortunes and all their kingdom by one tribune and six hundred artificers."

4629. Consequently, Ammianus Marcellinus was not ashamed to say that the people of Rome invaded that island out of covetousness or because of a shortage of money in their treasury, rather than in pursuit of justice. {*Ammianus Marcellinus, l. 14. c. 8. s. 15. 1:73} Sextus Rufus said that the poverty of the people of Rome and the shortage of money in the treasury provoked them to seize this island which was so famous for its riches. Their gaining command of it was motivated more by covetousness than justice. {Sextus Rufus, Breviary}

4630. Tigranes, the son of Tigranes, a king and an enemy, was still being kept prisoner at the house of Lucius Flavius, who was the praetor, on Pompey's command. Clodius, the tribune of the people, was bribed to ask Flavius to give Tigranes permission to dine with them, so that he might see him. When Tigranes came, he feasted him and took him from prison and let him go free. Clodius would not hand him over when Pompey demanded him. Tigranes had escaped by ship but was driven back by a storm. Clodius, the tribune, sent Sextius Clodius to bring Tigranes to him. As soon as Flavius heard of it, he went to apprehend Tigranes. Within four miles of the city, there was a skirmish and while many were killed on both sides, Flavius' party fared the worse. Papirius, who was a Roman equestrian, a tax collector and a very close friend of Pompey, was killed. Flavius

only just escaped to Rome alone. [K278] Clodius, the tribune, contemptuously treated Pompey and Gabinius, who did not approve of this action. Clodius beat and wounded their companion, then broke the fasces of Gabinius, the consul, and confiscated his goods. {*Cicero, De Domo Sua, l. 1. c. 25. 11:213,215} {Asconius Pedianus, Pro Milone} {*Plutarch, Pompey, l. 1. c. 48. s. 6. 5:241} {*Dio, l. 38. (30) 3:261}

4631. Piso and Gabinius, who were the consuls, expelled Syrapis, Isis, Harpocrates and Cynocephalus and forbade them to come to the Capitol. The consuls overthrew their altars and curtailed the vices of their filthy and idle superstitions. {*Tertullian, Apology, l. 1. c. 6. 3:23}

4632. Ptolemy Auletes was told by the Egyptians to request the island of Cyprus from the Romans or to renounce the alliance he had with them, but he did not agree to do this. So he incurred their hatred for this reason, as well as for the high taxes he imposed on the Egyptians to pay the debt he had incurred by purchasing the Roman alliance. Therefore, when he could neither persuade them, nor compel them by force, to be quiet (as he had no mercenaries), he fled from Egypt and sailed to Rome. {*Livy, l. 104. 14:131} {*Dio, l. 39. (12) 3:325} He wanted Caesar and Pompey to use their army to restore him to power. {*Plutarch, Cato Minor, l. 1. c. 35. s. 2. 8:321} However, Timagenes, who, under Augustus' reign, wrote some histories of which Seneca made mention, affirmed that Ptolemy left the kingdom without any good reason, or that he was not compelled to leave of necessity. {*Seneca, On Anger, l. 3. c. 23. s. 4. 1:313} Theophanes convinced him to leave Egypt by saying he would give Pompey an opportunity to get money and to start new wars. {*Plutarch, Pompey, l. 1. c. 49. s. 6,7. 5:245,247}

4633. When Cato sailed to Cyprus, Clodius, the tribune, would not give him any ships, soldiers or servants to go with him. He only had two secretaries, one was a notorious thief and the other a lackey of Clodius. As if the business in Cyprus were but a minor matter, Clodius ordered him to restore the exiles of Byzantium as well to keep Cato away from Rome as long as he possibly could. {*Plutarch, Cato Minor, l. 1. c. 34. s. 3. 8:319}

4634. Cato, through his friend Canidius, whom he sent to Cyprus ahead of him, talked with Ptolemy and tried to persuade him to yield without fighting. [E612] He gave Ptolemy the promise that he would neither live poorly nor in contempt and that the people would give him the priesthood of the goddess Paphos. In the meantime, Cato stayed at Rhodes to make preparations and to wait for an answer. {*Plutarch, Cato Minor, l. 1. c. 35. s. 1,2. 8:321} When Ptolemy knew what had been decreed against him, he did not dare fight the Romans. Nor did he think he could go on living, if he were to be expelled from his kingdom, so he put all his treasure into ships and set sail. He hoped to sink his ships and to die as he chose with his treasure so that his enemies would not get their hands on it. However, because he could not endure to sink his gold and silver, he returned home again and killed himself by drinking poison. Although he held the title of a king, he was a slave to his money. {*Plutarch, Cato Minor, l. 1. c. 36. s. 1. 8:323} {*Florus, l. 1. c. 44. 1:199} {*Strabo, l. 14. c. 6. s. 6. 6:385} {*Velleius Paterculus, l. 2. c. 45. 1:149} {*Valerius Maximus, l. 9. c. 4. ext 1. 2:333} {*Appian, Civil Wars, l. 2. c. 3. (23) 3:269} {*Dio, l. 39. (22) 3:337} {*Ammianus Marcellinus, l. 14. c. 8. s. 15. 1:73} {Sextus Rufus, Breviary}

4635. Ptolemy Auletes sailed for Rome. When he arrived at Rhodes, he wanted to meet Cato and sent for him hoping that Cato would come to him. However Cato replied that if Ptolemy wanted to see him, Ptolemy would have to come to him, since he was not well. [K279] As Ptolemy came, Cato neither went to meet him nor rose from his seat, but greeted him as he would greet one of the common people and asked him to sit down. At first, it amazed Ptolemy and he marvelled at such haughtiness and severity in someone who had so simple and lowly a retinue. When they began to talk of his business, Cato accused him of being foolish for leaving his own rich country and being willing to subject himself to such dishonour and such great pains, simply to satisfy the covetousness of the chief men of Rome. This he would never be able to do, even if all the kingdom of Egypt were coined into money. Therefore, Cato counselled him to return with his navy and to reconcile himself to his subjects, even offering to go along with him and to help him be reconciled. The king was brought to his senses by this speech and perceiving the truth of Cato's wisdom, intended to follow his advice. However, his friends turned him from this good advice. As soon as Ptolemy arrived in Rome and was approaching the door of a magistrate, he began to lament his rash enterprise and the fact that he had scorned the divine oracles of such a great man. {*Plutarch, Cato Minor, l. 1. c. 35. s. 2-5. 8:321,333} However his coming later caused the Romans so much trouble that Crassus used that speech of the tragedian: {*Cicero, Pro Caelio, l. 1. c. 8. 13:427}

"Would that in the forest of Pelion (the ship) had not...."

4636. The Alexandrians did not know of Ptolemy's journey to Italy and thought that he was dead. So they set his legitimate daughter Berenice over the kingdom, along with her older sister Tryphena, who was also older than Cleopatra. {*Strabo, l. 17. c. 1. s. 11. 8:47} {*Dio, l. 39. (13) 3:327} {Porphyry, Scaliger's Greek Eusebius, p. 226.} They sent Menelaus, Lampon and Callimachus to Antiochus Pius (or rather, Asiaticus, his son, whom Pompey had dis-

possessed of his kingdom) to ask him to reign together with the women but he became sick and died. {Porphyry, Scaliger's Greek Eusebius, p. 227.}

4637. Both the consuls went into the provinces as soldiers, Piso into Macedonia and Gabinius into Syria. The people followed them as they left Rome with their curses. {*Cicero, Pro Sestio, l. 1. c. 33. 12:131} {*Cicero, In Pison, l. 1. c. 14. 14:181} When Gabinius was about to set sail for Syria, he invited Antony, who was later in the triumvirate, to accompany him to the wars. Antony refused to do this as a private soldier but when he was put in command of the cavalry, he then went with him to the wars. {*Plutarch, Antony, l. 1. c. 3. s. 1. 9:143}

4638. Titus Ampius obtained the province of Cilicia with the help of the tribune Publius Clodius, which was contrary to custom. {*Cicero, De Domo Sua, l. 1. c. 9. 11:161} {*Cicero, Friends, l. 1. c. 3. 25:15}

4639. Cicero mentioned the following about Gabinius' journey to Syria and his first arrival: {*Cicero, De Provinciis Consularibus, l. 1. c. 4. 13:551}

"His journey into the province was like this. King Ariobarzanes hired your consul to commit murders as if he had been a Thracian. When he first came into Syria, he lost many of his cavalry and later the best of his foot soldiers."

4640. Cicero, in his speech for Sestius, also mentioned the loss of Gabinius' cavalry and foot soldiers. {*Cicero, Pro Sestio, l. 1. c. 33. 12:131}

## 3947a AM, 4656 JP, 58 BC

4641. Although it was said that the king of Cyprus had left a vast sum of money behind him, Cato still determined to go to Byzantium first. Marcus Brutus, his sister's son (and later, the murderer of Julius Caesar), was in Pamphylia, where he was living at the time to recover his health. [K280] Cato wrote to him that he should come to him at once from there to Cyprus because he suspected that Canidius was meddling with the money and would appropriate some for himself. Brutus undertook this journey very much against his will, because he thought Cato had slandered Canidius and that this job was too menial and unsuited for him. Though a young and studious man, Brutus conducted himself so well that Cato commended him. {*Plutarch, Cato Minor, l. 1. c. 36. s. 1,2. 8:323} {*Plutarch, Brutus, l. 1. c. 3. 6:131,133} [E613]

## 3947b AM, 4657 JP, 57 BC

4642. Alexander, the son of Aristobulus, who had escaped from Pompey while on the way to Rome, bothered Judea with his raids. At the time, Hyrcanus was not able to resist him, because he was determined to rebuild the walls of Jerusalem that Pompey had thrown down. The Romans, who were there, hindered the work. Alexander travelled through the country, arming many Jews. In a short time, he had ten thousand heavily armed foot soldiers and fifteen hundred cavalry. He strongly fortified Alexandrion, a citadel located near Corea, as well as Hyrcania and Michaeron, not far from the mountains of Arabia. {*Josephus, Jewish War, l. 1. c. 8. s. 2. (160,161) 2:75} {*Josephus, Antiq., l. 14. c. 5. s. 2. (82,83) 7:491}

4643. Aulus Gabinius, the governor of Syria, undertook an expedition against Alexander. He sent Mark Antony ahead with some commanders, and they joined up with some Jews who were under their command, whose captains were Pitholaus and Matichus. They also took some auxiliaries from Antipater and then fought with Alexander, while Gabinius followed with the rest of the army. Alexander drew near to Jerusalem, where the battle was then fought. The Romans killed three thousand of the enemy and took as many prisoners. When Gabinius came to the citadel of Alexandrion, he offered the besieged men conditions of peace and promised them a pardon for everything that was in the past. Many of the enemy had camped outside the citadel. When they refused all the peace overtures, the Romans attacked them. Mark Antony behaved very valiantly and killed many of the enemy. {*Josephus, Jewish War, l. 1. c. 8. s. 3,4. (162-165) 2:75,77} {*Josephus, Antiq., l. 14. c. 5. s. 2,3. (84-86) 7:491,493} Antony was courteously entertained by Antipater and sixteen years later, when Antony was in the triumvirate and came into Syria, he showed that he remembered this courtesy by acting kindly toward Antipater's sons, Phasael and Herod. {*Josephus, Jewish War, l. 1. c. 12. s. 5. (244) 2:113} {*Josephus, Antiq., l. 14. c. 13. s. 1. (325,326) 7:621}

4644. Gabinius left part of the army at the siege of Alexandrion and went to visit the rest of Judea. He ordered that any cities he came across that had been destroyed, should be rebuilt. By this means, Samaria, Azotus, Scythopolis, Anthedon, Apollonia, Jamnia, Gamala, Raphia, Adora, Marisa, Gaza and many others were rebuilt. These were later peacefully inhabited, after having been deserted for so long.

4645. Having so ordered these things in the country, Gabinius returned to Alexandrion. When the Romans intended to attack the citadel, Alexander requested pardon through his envoys. He offered Gabinius the citadels of Hyrcania and Machaerus and finally, Alexandrion. Gabinius, on the advice of the mother of Alexander, levelled these to the ground, lest they should be a reason for new wars. The woman was solicitous for her husband and children, who had been carried captive to Rome, and favoured the Romans. She used all her charms toward Gabinius and obtained from him

whatever she desired. {*Josephus, Jewish War, l. 1. c. 8. s. 4,5. (165-168) 2:77,79} {*Josephus, Antiq., l. 14. c. 5. s. 3,4. (89-90) 7:493,495}

4646. After Gabinius had settled his affairs, he took Hyrcanus to Jerusalem and committed the care of the temple and the priesthood to him. He made others of the nobility rulers of the Jewish state. [K281] He appointed five seats for courts and divided the whole province into so many equal parts. Some went to court at Jerusalem, some at Gadara (otherwise Adora), some at Amathus, some at Jericho and some at Sepphoris. Thus the Jews were freed from the command of one single man and were willingly governed by an aristocracy. {*Josephus, Jewish War, l. 1. c. 8. s. 4,5. (169,170) 2:79} {*Josephus, Antiq., l. 14. c. 5. s. 4. (91) 7:495}

4647. Philip Euergetes, the son of Grypus, and Tryphena, the daughter of Ptolemy, the eighth king of the Egyptians (who thirty-five years before had been king of Syria), were sent for by the Alexandrians, to take over the kingdom of Egypt. However he was hindered from doing this by Gabinius, the governor of Syria. {Porphyry, Scaliger's Greek Eusebius, p. 227.}

4648. At Rome, Pompey took up Ptolemy Auletes' cause, commended it to the Senate and asked for his restoration. {*Strabo, l. 17. c. 1. s. 11. 8:45} However, Ptolemy requested that he might be restored by Cornelius Lentulus Spinther, the consul, who had been given charge of the province of Cilicia. {*Dio, l. 39. (12) 3:325,327} Spinther was also in favour of restoring Ptolemy to his kingdom as the sole ruler. A decree of the Senate was made to that end. {*Cicero, Friends, l. 1. c. 1. s. 1,2. 25:3,5} {*Cicero, In Pison, l. 1. c. 21. 14:201} {*Cicero, Pro Rabirio Postumo, l. 1. c. 8. 14:385,387}

4649. It was said that the following advice was given by the same consul, that greater authority be given to Pompey to provide grain through all the Roman Empire by sea and land. He hoped that Pompey would be occupied in this greater charge and that he himself would be sent to help Ptolemy. {*Plutarch, Pompey, l. 1. c. 49. 5:245}

4650. The Alexandrians sent a hundred men to Rome, to defend their cause against the accusations of Ptolemy as well as accuse him of the wrongs he had done to them. The leader of the embassy was Dio, an academic. {*Strabo, l. 17. c. 1. s. 11. 8:48} {*Dio, l. 39. (13) 3:327}

4651. Ptolemy sent out certain men in various directions and laid ambushes for the envoys. Most were killed on their journey, but some of them he killed in the city of Rome itself. The rest, he bullied or bribed into submission. [E614] He arranged matters in such a way, that they did not so much as dare to bring their cause before the magistrates to whom they had been sent, or even once make any mention of those who had been killed. {*Dio, l.

*39. (13,14) 3:327}* Cicero mentioned the murdering of the Alexandrian envoys, against all law and honesty. {*Cicero, De Haruspicum Responsis, l. 1. c. 16. 11:361}* He also mentioned the beating of the Alexandrians at Puteoli. {*Cicero, Pro Caelio, l. 1. c. 10. 13:433}*

*4652.* This business was so commonly known, that the Senate was very angry, especially Marcus Favonius, who stirred them up. Many envoys of their allies who were sent to Rome, were violently killed. Cicero mentioned one in particular, Theodosius, who was sent as an envoy from a free city. He was stabbed at the hands of Publius Clodius and Hermarchus, a Chian. {*Cicero, De Haruspicum Responsis, l. 1. c. 16. 11:361}* Many Romans were, at that time, corrupted by bribes, so the Senate called Dio, the leader of the embassy, to them, so that he could testify before them to the truth of the matter. However Ptolemy's money had prevailed to such an extent, that neither did Dio come into the Senate, nor was any mention made, all the while that Dio was at Rome, of those who had been killed. {*Dio, l. 39. (14) 3:327,329}*

*4653.* Finally, Dio himself was murdered. A very learned man, he had lodged with Lucceius. *[K282]* (He, too, was a most learned man, whom Cicero engaged to write the history of his consulship. {*Cicero, Friends, l. 5. c. 12. 25:365}*) Dio had known Lucceius from Alexandria. Publius Asicius was not found guilty of this murder, nor was Ptolemy punished. Asicius was acquitted in his trial. Pompey entertained Ptolemy at his house and helped him all he could. Although many had taken bribes and were later accused before the judges, very few were condemned, since there were so many who were guilty of the same fault. Everyone helped the others, out of fear for himself. Hence, men committed wicked deeds for the love of money. {*Cicero, Pro Caelio, l. 1. c. 10. 13:435} {*Dio, l. 39. (14) 3:329}*

*4654.* After Marcus Cato had reconciled the banished men with the rest of the citizens and established a firm agreement in Byzantium, he sailed into Cyprus. The Cypriots willingly received him in the hope that they would now become friends and allies of the people of Rome, instead of servants, as they had been. Cato found a large and royal preparation there, in plates, tables, jewels, and purple. All of this was to be sold for money and so he gathered a little less than seven thousand talents of silver. {*Plutarch, Cato Minor, l. 1. c. 36-38. 8:323-329} {*Plutarch, Brutus, l. 1. c. 3. 6:131} {*Strabo, l. 14. c. 6. s. 6. 6:385} {*Dio, l. 39. (22) 3:337,339}*

*4655.* Cato was very careful to check out and to set the highest price and account for every last penny. He did not trust the ways of the forum but suspected all apparitors, criers, appraisers and friends. He also talked with those who set the price privately and he forced many to buy. He sold many things by these means. But in this

way, he offended many of his friends by distrusting them, especially his most intimate friend, Munatius, whom he provoked almost to an implacable offence. This gave Julius Caesar the occasion for accusing Cato as recorded in the book that Munatius wrote, called Anticaron. This Munatius (who was called Rufus {*Valerius Maximus, l. 4. c. 3. s. 2. 1:367,369}*) wrote a commentary about Cato and his journey to Cyprus. Thrasea mainly followed Munatius' account. In the book, Munatius did not record that this difference between them arose from any distrust on Cato's part. However, when Munatius later came to Cyprus, Cato did not entertain him and preferred Canidius over him, who was already there and who had proved his fidelity to Cato. {*Plutarch, Cato Minor, l. 1. c. 36,37. 8:323,325}*

*4656.* In the last month of his consulship (then happening in the Julian September), when the new tribunes of the people entered their office, Publius Cornelius Spinther prepared to take a journey to his province of Cilicia. Ptolemy Auletes departed from Rome, according to the passage from Fenestella, as cited by Nonius Marcellus: {*Nonius Marcellus, Fenestella, l. 22.}*

> "As soon as the tribunes entered their office, Gaius Cato, who was a troublesome and bold young man and one who could speak reasonably well, began to stir up the people with his speeches against Ptolemy, who had now left the city and against Publius Lentulus Spinther, who was now preparing for his journey."

*4657.* However, Ptolemy's cause was defended by Cicero, as he himself seemed to show, in his speech for Caelio, and as Fortunatianus more clearly confirmed, by quoting by name that very speech of his on behalf of King Ptolemy. *[K283]*

## 3948a AM, 4657 JP, 57 BC

*4658.* In the beginning of the consulship of Lucius Marcius Philippus and Gnaeus Lentulus Marcellinus, the statue of Jupiter Capitoline was struck by lightning. This halted the restoration of Ptolemy, for when the Sibylline books were consulted, it was reported that they had foretold that a king of Egypt with crafty councils (as it says in Cicero {*Cicero, Pro Rabinius Postumus, l. 1. c. 2. 14:371}*) would come to Rome. Dio recorded the Sibylline sentence relating to this suspicion of Ptolemy as follows: {*Dio, l. 39. (15,16) 3:329.331} [E615]*

> "If a king of Egypt needs your help and shall come here, you shall not deny him friendship, but you shall not help him with any large forces. If you shall do otherwise, you will have labours and dangers."

*4659.* The oracle was leaked to the people by Gaius Cato, the tribune of the people. It was not lawful to disclose any Sibylline prophecies to the people, unless the Senate had so decreed it. It seemed even less lawful, considering how badly the people took it. Because of this, Cato feared that the sentence of the oracle would be suppressed, so he compelled the priests to translate it into Latin and to declare it to the people before the Senate had decreed anything relating to it. {*Dio, l. 39. (15) 3:329,331} Notwithstanding, it was the opinion of the people of Rome that this name of a pretended omen had been introduced by those who were against Lentulus Spinther, the proconsul of Cilicia. This was not so much to hinder him, as to prevent anyone from going to Alexandria out of a selfish desire for military command and among all the rest, Pompey was the most keen in this regard. {*Cicero, Friends, l. 1. c. 4. 25:17}

4660. Ammonius, Ptolemy's envoy, publicly opposed the restoring of the king by Spinther and used money to help convince others. Those few who were for the king wanted the matter committed to Pompey. The Senate approved the forgery of the religious oracle, not for religious reasons, but out of ill-will and hatred of the king's large bribes. {*Cicero, Friends, l. 1. c. 2. 25:13} {*Cicero, Quintus, l. 2. c. 2. 28:485} {*Appian, Syrian Wars, l. 11. c. 8. (51) 2:201} {Appian, Parthian Wars, p. 134.}

4661. Pompey understood from the oracle that Ptolemy requested that Pompey might come to his aid, instead of Spinther. There were little notes found, thrown about in the forum and the Senate house, that indicated the same. Thereupon, the king's letter relating to this business was read publicly by Aulus Plautius, the tribune of the people. His colleague Caninius (Plutarch incorrectly called him Canidius) proposed a law that Pompey, without an army and only accompanied by two lictors, should bring the king back into favour with the Alexandrians. Although the law did not seem to displease Pompey, it was nevertheless decreed by the senators partly under the guise of the grain law that had already been committed to him, as well as the pretence of a false concern for the safety of Pompey's person (as they pretended to be afraid for him). {*Plutarch, Pompey, l. 1. c. 49. s. 6. 5:245} {*Dio, l. 39. (16) 3:331}

4662. The Senate had various opinions about this business. Bibulus thought that Ptolemy should be established in his kingdom, not with an army, but by three envoys who were only private citizens. Crassus thought that the three envoys should either be private citizens or men holding office. When Lupus proposed this law, Volcatius, the tribune of the people, thought Pompey should go. Afranius, Libo, Hypsaeus and all the close friends of Pompey agreed. Hortensius, Cicero and Lucullus thought that it ought to be done by Lentulus Spinther. However Servilius denied that the king ought to be established at all. {*Cicero, Friends, l. 1. c. 1,2. 25:3-13} [K284]

4663. In the month of February (or the Julian November), Gaius Cato published a law to deprive Lentulus of his office. This gave his son a reason to change his garment for poorer ones, as mentioned by Cicero. {*Cicero, Quintus, l. 2. c. 3. 28:485} This meant the law of re-establishing Ptolemy in his kingdom, according to the decree of the Senate, was granted to him in his consulship. It is obvious from the letters of Cicero written to him, from the first book and the seventh and subsequent letters, that, after the passing of this law, Lentulus retained the proconsulship of Cilicia with the addition of Cyprus, as Cato had already left Cyprus. Cyprus was now made a tributary by the Romans and organized into a province. {*Cicero, Friends, l. 1. c. 7. s. 4. 25:31} {*Ammianus Marcellinus, l. 14. c. 8. s. 15. 1:73} {*Strabo, l. 14. c. 1. s. 11. 8:47}

4664. When Ptolemy saw that he would not be established in his kingdom again, either by Pompey (as was his preference) or by Lentulus, he now despaired of ever returning at all. He went to Ephesus where he stayed in the temple of Diana. {*Dio, l. 39. (16) 3:331}

4665. Aristobulus and his son Antigonus escaped from Rome and returned to Jerusalem. A large number of Jews sided with him again, as they wanted a change and he still commanded their affections. He planned to rebuild the citadel of Alexandrion which had been torn down. {*Josephus, Jewish War, l. 1. c. 8. s. 6. (171) 2:79} {*Josephus, Antiq., l. 14. c. 6. s. 1. (92) 7:495}

4666. Gabinius, the governor of Syria, sent soldiers under their captains, Sisenna (his son), Antony and Servilius, to prevent Aristobulus from seizing Alexandrion and to capture him, if they could. For many other Jews had resorted to him, because of the reputation that he had. Pitholaus also, the second in command at Jerusalem, had left the Roman party and came to him with a thousand well-armed men. Since many of those who came to him were not well-armed, Aristobulus dismissed them as unsuitable for war. [E616] He took only eight thousand armed men (among whom were those that Pitholaus had brought), and marched to Machaerus. The Romans pursued them and fought with them. Aristobulus' side valiantly held out for a good while, but after they had lost five thousand men, they were forced to flee. Nearly two thousand fled to a certain hill. From there, they got away and provided for their own safety as well as they could. Another thousand, with Aristobulus, broke through the ranks of the Romans and fled to Mathaerus, where they began to fortify the citadel. They were not able to hold out in the siege for more than two days. After many had been wounded, Aristobulus was taken prisoner, along with his son Antigonus, and brought to Gabinius. {*Josephus,

*Jewish War, l. 1. c. 8. s. 6. (171-174) 2:79,81}* {*Josephus, Antiq., l. 14. c. 6. s. 1. (93-97) 7:497-499}*

4667. Plutarch gave more details of this event and ascribed the whole victory to the honour of Antony. {*Plutarch, Antony, l. 1. c. 3. s. 1. 9:143}*

"When Antony was sent against Aristobulus, who caused the Jews to rebel, he was the first man that climbed the wall of an extremely strong citadel of Aristobulus. Antony drove him from all his strongholds. Then, with a few men of his, he fought and overthrew a large army, putting them all to the sword except for a handful. Aristobulus and his son were taken prisoner."

4668. Dio incorrectly wrote that Gabinius went into Palestine and captured Aristobulus (who had fled from Rome and incited a rebellion). Gabinius sent him to Pompey and imposed a tax on the Jews. From there, he went into Egypt to re-establish Ptolemy in his kingdom. {*Dio, l. 39. (56) 3:391}*

4669. Tyrannio, who was teaching in Cicero's house, organized Cicero's library with the help of Dionysius and Menophilus, who were two bookbinders sent to him by Atticus. {*Cicero, Quintus, l. 2. c. 4. 28:497}* {*Cicero, Atticus, l. 4. c. 4a. 22:281,283}* {*Cicero, Atticus, l. 4. c. 8. 22:293}* [K285] This was Tyrannio Amisenus, who (fourteen years earlier) had been taken by Lucullus and who had now become rich and famous in Rome and had accumulated about thirty thousand books. {Suidas, In Voc., Tyrannio} Tyrannio had the books of Aristotle copied from the library of Sulla. It was reported that Andronicus of Rhodes received the copies and that he published the copies we now have. {*Strabo, l. 13. c. 1. s. 54. 6:111,113}* {*Plutarch, Sulla, l. 1. c. 26. 4:407}*

4670. Valerius produced witnesses testifying to the help that Marcus Cato had been in administering the business of Cyprus. {*Valerius Maximus, l. 4. c. 3. s. 2. 1:367,369}*

"...Epirus, Achaia, the Cyclades Islands, the sea coasts of Asia, the province of Cyprus. When he undertook the charge of bringing away the money, he took no bribes and handled the matter fairly. For although he had the king's riches in his own power and the required places of lodging on his trip were most delightful cities, he behaved most discretely. Munatius Rufus, his faithful companion in that journey, indicated as much in his writings."

4671. Cato feared a tedious journey and prepared various coffers, each of which held two talents and five hundred drachmas. He tied each of these to a long rope and fastened it at the end with a large piece of cork. If the ship was sunk, the cork would indicate the place.

Thus, all the money, except for a very little, was transported very safely. Cato made two books in which he recorded the accounts of everything he had obtained. Philargyrus, a freedman of Cato's, was carrying one of these books when he sailed from Cenchrea and was drowned with all his belongings. Cato took the other book himself. He came to Corcyra, where he stayed in the market-place in his tent. The sailors made many fires because of the cold and accidently set the tents on fire. So Cato lost that book, also. Although the royal stewards could easily have silenced his enemies and detractors, it bothered Cato. He had not kept these accounts to vindicate his fidelity but to give an example of diligence to others. {*Plutarch, Cato Minor, l. 1. c. 38. 8:327,329}*

### 3948b AM, 4658 JP, 56 BC

4672. Cato, with great diligence, travelled up the Tiber River in light boats that carried the riches of Cyprus as if they had been spoils taken from an enemy and carried in a fleet. {*Florus, l. 1. c. 44. s. 5. 1:199}* {*Valerius Maximus, l. 4. c. 1. s. 14. 1:351}* {*Ammianus Marcellinus, l. 14. c. 8. s. 15. 1:73}* This brought more money to the treasury of the people of Rome than any triumph. {*Florus, l. 1. c. 44. s. 5. 1:199}*

4673. When the news of Cato's arrival became known, all the magistrates and priests, along with the consuls (one of whom was Lucius Marcius Philippus, the father of Marcia, Cato's wife), the whole Senate, and many of the people went to the riverside to meet him. His arrival differed very little from the show and splendour of a triumph. Notwithstanding, his arrogance was observed in his arrival. He did not come ashore to the consuls and praetors who had come to meet him, nor altered his course, but sailed past the shore in one of the king's galleys with six tiers of oars. [K286] He did not come ashore until he and his fleet reached the place where the money was to be landed. {*Velleius Paterculus, l. 2. c. 45. s. 5. 1:151}* Plutarch stated that when he landed, the consuls and the rest of the magistrates were ready to receive him with great favour. They were happier to see Cato safely home again, than they were to see the vast sum of gold and silver the fleet had brought. {*Plutarch, Cato Minor, l. 1. c. 39. 8:329}* {*Valerius Maximus, l. 8. c. 15. s. 10. 2:287}* [E617]

4674. As the money was being carried through the market place, the people marvelled at the treasure, which was far greater than they had hoped for. {*Plutarch, Cato Minor, l. 1. c. 39. s. 3. 8:329}* Cato could not be accused by anyone, because although he had gathered together many slaves and much money out of the king's riches, he had honestly declared everything. Cato received no less honour than if he had returned as a conqueror from the wars. Indeed, many men had allowed themselves to be corrupted with bribes, but because of him it was accounted a rarer virtue to despise money than to conquer an enemy. {*Dio, l. 39. (22) 3:339}

4675. Pliny stated that Cato brought a philosopher with him when he came back from this Cypriot expedition. {*Pliny, l. 7. c. 30. 2:581} Cato had the Senate grant Nicias, the king's steward, his freedom, and Cato himself testified to his fidelity and diligence. {*Plutarch, Cato Minor, l. 1. c. 39. s. 3. 8:331} Clodius intended that the slaves who had been brought from Cyprus, should be called *Clodians*, because he had been the one who had sent Cato there. However Clodius was thwarted, when Cato opposed this. So they were called *Cyprians*, for Cato would not allow them to be called *Porcians*, after his own surname, although some were of the opinion that this should be the case. {*Dio, l. 39. (23) 3:339}

4676. Clodius was angry with Cato, because he had opposed him, so he slandered the service that Cato had done and demanded an account of his deeds. Even though he did not think he could accuse Cato of any unjust act, he thought he could get something against him, since almost all the records had been lost in the shipwreck. Caesar helped Clodius in this business, although he was absent and (as some reported), sent accusations against Cato to Clodius by letters. {*Dio, l. 39. (23) 3:339,341} However, Cato told them that he had brought so much money from Cyprus but had not received so much as one horse or soldier, compared to Pompey, who had brought horses and soldiers from so many wars and triumphs, when all the world had been in turmoil. {*Plutarch, Cato Minor, l. 1. c. 39. s. 3. 8:329}

4677. Cato opposed Cicero, who insisted that none of the things that Clodius had done in his tribuneship should be confirmed in the Senate. He did not do this as a favour to Clodius, but because Cato's commission for Cyprus was among the acts that were to be revoked because the tribune who had sent him had been chosen unlawfully. {*Plutarch, Cato Minor, l. 1. c. 40. 8:331} {*Plutarch, Cicero, l. 1. c. 34. 7:169,171}

4678. Phraates II was wickedly put to death by his sons. Orodes succeeded him in the kingdom of the Parthians and expelled his brother, Mithridates, from Media, where he governed. {*Dio, l. 39. (56) 3:391} The sons contended for the kingdom and it seems that Orodes was banished first and then Mithridates as well. However Surenas, who was a rich man and among the Parthians, second only to the king in blood and authority, brought Orodes back again from banishment. It was his prerogative by birth that he should always crown the new king of the Parthians. He subdued Seleucia on the Tigris River, bringing it under the king's dominion. Surenas was the first man to scale the walls and with his own hands he defeated those who defended it. [K287] Although he was not yet thirty years old, he was held in esteem for his advice in council and for his wisdom. {*Plutarch, Crassus, l. 1. c. 21. s. 6,7. 3:379} {Appian, Parthian Wars, p. 140,141.} However, at another time Appian stated that Mithridates was driven from his kingdom by his brother Orodes. {Appian, Parthian Wars, p. 134.} {*Appian, Syrian Wars, l. 11. c. 8. (51) 2:201} Justin, on the other hand, noted that Mithridates was deposed from his kingdom by the Parthian nobility because of his cruelty, and that his brother Orodes seized the kingdom when the throne was vacant. {Justin, Trogus, l. 42. c. 4.} However Justin incorrectly thought this Mithridates was the same as Mithridates, the king of the Parthians, whose famous acts gave him the surname of *Great*. Between this Mithridates the Great and the one who was the brother of Orodes, there was a succession of many kings among the Parthians. This appeared in the prologue of Justin's history. {Justin, Trogus, l. 42. Prologue}

4679. Mithridates was driven from his kingdom, either by the Parthian nobility or by his brother Orodes, and came to Gabinius, the proconsul of Syria, when he was preparing for an expedition against the Arabians. He reasoned with Gabinius that he should leave the Arabians alone and go against the Parthians instead to help restore him to his kingdom. {Appian, Parthian Wars, p. 134.} {*Appian, Syrian Wars, l. 11. c. 8. (51) 2:201} {*Dio, l. 39. (56) 3:391}

4680. On the Ides of May (May 15, which happened in the Julian February), the letters of Gabinius were read in full to the Senate. These letters concerned the war that he was having with the greatest countries and tyrants of Syria (among whose names) the princes of Judea, Commagene, Chalcis, Emesa, Thrachonitis, Batanea, and Abilene, are usually mentioned. However, the report was not believed and so the Senate denied him the triumph he wanted at Rome. {*Cicero, Quintus, l. 2. c. 8. 28:509} {*Cicero, De Provinciis Consularibus, l. 1. c. 6. 13:555,557} {*Cicero, In Pison, l. 1. c. 17. 14:189}

4681. When Gabinius had sent King Aristobulus and his sons to Rome, the Senate kept the king prisoner but immediately sent his sons back into Judea, because they understood from Gabinius' letters that he had promised the king's mother this in return for the surrender of the citadels. {*Josephus, Jewish War, l. 1. c. 8. s. 7. (173,175) 2:81} {*Josephus, Antiq., l. 14. c. 6. s. 1. (97) 7:499} [E618] Josephus further added that Aristobulus held the kingdom and the priesthood for forty-two months. The Arabian collector of the Jewish History (as set forth by this same man in chapter forty at the end of the Parisian Bibles of many languages) understood it to refer to the time of the former government, until he was taken prisoner for the first time. However, it seems rather that it should be taken as meaning the former and the latter time were both taken together, so that he reigned thirty-nine months before the former captivity and three months before his second captivity. {*Josephus, Antiq., l. 20. c. 10. s. 4. (245) 10:131}

4682. Marcus Cicero, in a speech before the Senate, advised that Lucius Piso and Aulus Gabinius (in whose consulship Cicero was banished) should be recalled and their provinces of Macedonia and Syria assigned to the future consuls. Among other things, he voiced the following objections against Gabinius: {*Cicero, De Provinciis Consularibus, l. 1. c. 4,5. 13:551,553}

"When he was governor in Syria, nothing was done but some work for money with the tyrants, confiscations, plundering, thieveries and murders. When his army was in battle array, he, as general of the people of Rome, did not exhort his soldiers to gain honour, but stretched out his right hand and cried that all things had already been bought or were about to be bought by him for money. Now he has delivered the wretched tax collectors to slavery and turned them over to Jews and Syrians, countries that were themselves born to slavery. [K288] He has continued in this, in that he will not do justice to a tax collector, but has revoked all agreements made between them in which there was no unfairness. He took away guards and released many, who were paying tribute, from the obligation to pay. In whatever town he was, or wherever he went, he forbade any tax collector or tax collector's servant to be there."

4683. Gabinius had afflicted Syria with many wrongs and had done more wrong to the province than the thieves, who were very strong at that time. However, as he considered all his achievements to be trifles, he planned an expedition against the Parthians and made preparations for that journey. {*Dio, l. 39. (56) 3:391}

4684. Pompey made Archelaus, the friend of Gabinius, the high priest of Comana in Pontus. {See note on 3940a AM. <<4493>>} Archelaus was living there with Gabinius and the latter hoped that he would be Pompey's companion in the Parthian wars for which he was preparing, but the Senate would not allow it. {*Strabo, l. 12. c. 3. s. 34. 5:435} {*Strabo, l. 17. c. 1. s. 11. 8:45}

4685. Gabinius led his army against the Parthians and in so doing, crossed the Euphrates River. Ptolemy came with letters from Pompey, promising that he would give a large sum of money to Gabinius and his army, a down payment now and the rest when he had been restored to his kingdom. It was ten thousand talents that Ptolemy promised Gabinius, as confirmed by Plutarch and

Cicero. Cicero reckoned the sum to be two million one hundred and sixty thousand sesterces. {*Cicero, Pro Rabirio Postumo, l. 1. c. 8. 14:387} (Loeb text stated two hundred and forty million. Editor.) Most of the commanders were against it and Gabinius was also hesitant about doing it, although he would have liked to have lightened Ptolemy of those ten thousand talents. However, Antony, who longed to do great exploits and was keen to gratify Ptolemy's request, was quite prepared to go, and persuaded Gabinius to undertake this war. The law forbade any provincial governor to go beyond the bounds of his own government, or to undertake any war on his own initiative. Based on the oracle of the Sibylline verses, the people of Rome had totally forbidden the restoration of Ptolemy at all. However the more he knew it to be wrong, the more he viewed the potential gains in wealth. Hence, he abandoned the Parthian expedition and undertook the expedition against the Alexandrians. {*Josephus, Jewish War, l. 1. c. 8. s. 7. (175,176) 2:83} {*Josephus, Antiq., l. 14. c. 6. s. 2. (98,99) 7:499} {*Plutarch, Antony, l. 1. c. 3. 9:143} {*Appian, Syrian Wars, l. 11. c. 8. (51) 2:201} {Appian, Parthian Wars, p. 134.} {*Dio, l. 39. (56) 3:391}

4686. At that time, Bernice, the daughter of Auletes, held the kingdom of Egypt. She had sent for Seleucus from Syria, who, as he said himself, was of the stock of the Syrian kings. She married him and made him a partner in the rule of the kingdom and of the war. He was a most repulsive man and in contempt was surnamed Ptolemy Cocces, and Cybiosactes, meaning *dealer in salt fish.* {*Suetonius, Vespasian, l. 8. c. 19. 2:295,297} He broke open the golden coffin in which the body of Alexander the Great was buried, but did not profit by the thievery. When the queen saw that he was such a base man, she strangled him within a few days, because she could no longer endure his sordidness and niggardliness. She looked for another husband of royal extraction. Some friends brought Archelaus, the high priest of Comana, who was in Syria at the time. He pretended to be the son of Mithridates (under whom his father Archelaus had waged war against Sulla and the Romans). [K289] She married him and deemed him fit to rule the kingdom under the same conditions that Seleucus had enjoyed. He ruled the kingdom together with her for six months. {*Strabo, l. 17. c. 1. s. 11. 8:45,47} {*Strabo, l. 12. c. 3. s. 34. 5:437} {*Dio, l. 39. (57) 3:393} [E619]

4687. Gaius Clodius, a praetor and the brother of Publius Clodius, obtained the province of Asia through Publius Clodius. (Dio said Gaius held office that year. {*Dio, l. 39. (21) 3:337}) {?Cicero, Atticus, l. 4. c. 14.} Gaius Scribonius Curio was his quaestor in that province. Cicero sent many letters to him which are still extant. {*Cicero, Friends, l. 2. c. 1-7. 25:93-115}

## 3949a AM, 4658 JP, 56 BC

*4688.* Through a law made by Gaius Trebonius, the tribune of the people, the provinces were assigned to the new consuls. Gnaeus Pompey was given Spain and Africa and Marcus Licinius Crassus was assigned Syria with its adjacent countries. Power was given to both of them to take as many soldiers as they wanted from Italy and from their allies and to make peace or war with whomever they wished. {*Livy, l. 105. 14:131} {*Plutarch, Crassus, l. 1. c. 15. s. 5. 3:361} {*Plutarch, Pompey, l. 1. c. 52. s. 3. 5:251} {*Plutarch, Cato Minor, l. 1. c. 43. s. 1. 8:339} {*Appian, Civil Wars, l. 2. c. 3. (18) 3:261} {*Dio, l. 39. (33) 3:355}

*4689.* As soon as Crassus had, by lot, obtained his province, he could not conceal his joy and supposed that nothing better could ever have happened to him. He would talk so vainly and childishly among his close friends, that it was not becoming his age and wisdom. He planned the conquest of Syria and Parthia and even had vain hopes of conquering the Bactrians, the Indians and the Eastern ocean. However, in the decree made by the people about his government, no mention was made of the Parthians, yet everyone knew that Crassus longed for that conquest. When Caesar wrote to him from Gaul, he commended his resolution and advised him to pursue it. {*Plutarch, Crassus, l. 1. c. 16. s. 1-3. 3:361}

*4690.* Aulus Gabinius left his son Sisenna, who was very young, with very few soldiers, so exposing the province he governed to the actions of pirates. Gabinius went through Palestine to Egypt {*Dio, l. 39. (56) 3:391} against Archelaus, whom the Egyptians had chosen to be their king. {*Livy, l. 105. 14:131} In this expedition he used his friends, Hyrcanus and Antipater, to supply him with all the things that were necessary for the war. Antipater helped him with money, arms, men and grain. {*Josephus, Jewish War, l. 1. c. 8. s. 7. (175,176) 2:83} {*Josephus, Antiq., l. 14. c. 6. s. 2. (99) 7:499}

*4691.* They came to a place where they had to cross through deep, dry, sandy areas around the Serbonian fens and marshes, which the Egyptians call the *blasts of Tryphon*. (Tryphon was the evil Egyptian deity buried under the Serbonian marshes.) Mark Antony was sent ahead with the cavalry. Gabinius had made Antony the commander of the cavalry, even though he was very young. {*Appian, Civil Wars, l. 5. c. 1. (8) 4:389} Antony took the pass, as well as the very large city of Pelusium. {*Plutarch, Antony, l. 1. c. 3. s. 2,3. 9:143} The Jews who inhabited Pelusium and were the guards of the pass into Egypt, were drawn to his side. {*Josephus, Jewish War, l. 1. c. 8. s. 7. (175,176) 2:83} {*Josephus, Antiq., l. 14. c. 6. s. 2. (99) 7:499}

*4692.* After the garrison of Pelusium had been conquered, Antony secured the way for the army and settled the victory for the general with fairness. As soon as Ptolemy had entered Pelusium, he was so inflamed with anger and hatred, that he would have put all the Egyptians to the sword, but Antony interceded and would not allow him to do so. {*Plutarch, Antony, l. 1. c. 3. s. 4,5. 9:143,145}

*4693.* When Gabinius had marshalled his army into two battalions, he marched from Pelusium and on that same day, routed the Egyptians who opposed him. {*Dio, l. 39. (58) 3:393} [K290]

*4694.* In a speech he made at Rome, Cicero extorted the little town of Zeugma, located on the Euphrates River, from the ignoble King Aniochus of the Commagenians. He also said many things against him and made everyone laugh when he ridiculed the purple toga which the king had received during the consulship of Caesar. {*Cicero, Quintus, l. 2. c. 12. 28:521}

*4695.* On the Ides of February (February 13, which happened in the Julian November), the Tyrians were admitted into the Senate, but opposing them were many of the Syrian tax collectors. (There is a textual variation of Syrians for Tyrians in the Loeb edition. Editor.) Gabinius was fiercely abused. However, the tax collectors were denounced by Domitius because they had honoured Gabinius with an escort of cavalry. {*Cicero, Quintus, l. 2. c. 13. 28:525}

## 3949b AM, 4659 JP, 55 BC

*4696.* About the 4th of the Calends of May (April 27, which happened in the Julian February), the rumour was widely circulated at Puteoli that Ptolemy was in his kingdom. {*Cicero, Atticus, l. 4. c. 10. 22:297} He was indeed in Egypt and Gabinius had taken Archelaus, who had come out against him sooner than had been anticipated, so that there was no more business to be done. But now Gabinius feared that, because he had done nothing, he should receive less money from Ptolemy than had been agreed upon. He also hoped that he would receive more money because Archelaus was a brave man and of good reputation. He had received a large sum of money from Archelaus, so that he let him go, as if he had escaped from him. {*Dio, l. 39. (57,58) 3:393,395}

*4697.* Mark Antony had performed many noble deeds in the fights and battles. By this, he showed himself to be a valiant and wise commander. He was honoured with many excellent gifts, especially for his tactic of surrounding the enemy from the rear and by that means giving the victory to those who were attacking from the front. {*Plutarch, Antony, l. 1. c. 3. s. 5. 9:145}

*4698.* The people of Egypt marched against Gabinius from the walls of Alexandria, under the command of

Archelaus. Archelaus had ordered that the camp should be fortified with a rampart and a ditch. *[E620]* They all cried out that the work should be done with public money and not by themselves. Therefore, their minds were so engrossed with pleasure that they could not withstand the attack of the Roman army. {*Valerius Maximus, l. 9. c. 1. ext. 6. 2:305} So Gabinius once again obtained a victory by sea and land. The Alexandrians were brave and daring, and were by nature heady and inclined rashly to speak anything that came into their minds. However they were most unfit for war, although in seditions (a frequent occurrence among them and very serious) they soon started to murder each other, because they thought it good to die in this way. {*Dio, l. 59. (58) 3:393,395}

4699. When Gabinius had conquered them and killed many in the battle, including Archelaus, he was master of all Egypt, which he then turned over to Ptolemy. {*Dio, l. 59. (58) 3:395} {*Livy, l. 105. 14:131} {*Strabo, l. 12. c. 3. s. 34. 5:437} {*Strabo, l. 17. c. 1. s. 11. 8:47} Cicero, in a speech, related all of this to the madness of Gabinius: {*Cicero, In Pison, l. 1. c. 21. 14:199,201}

> "That vast wealth, which he had squeezed from the fortunes of the tax collectors, from the countries and cities of the allies, was now squandered. Part of it was devoured by his insatiable lust, part by his new and unheard-of luxury, part by the purchases that he had made in those places that he had totally plundered, part by bartering, and all this just for building up that mountain of a villa at Tusculum. When the intolerable building was stopped for a time, he sold everything out to the Egyptian king: his person, his fasces, *[K291]* the army of the people of Rome, the power and the interdiction of the immortal gods, the responses of the priests, the authority of the Senate, the mandate of the Roman people and the fame and dignity of this empire. Whereas the bounds of his province were as large as he wanted, as great as he could desire, as great as he could buy with the price of my banishment, yet he could not contain himself within them. He brought his army from Syria. How dared he lead it out of the province? He made himself a mercenary soldier to the king of Alexandria and what was more vile than this? He came into Egypt and fought with the Alexandrians. When had either the Senate or the people undertaken this war? He took Alexandria. What more could we expect from his madness but that he would send letters to the Senate, telling of all the famous acts that he had done?"

4700. Dio observed that he did not send the letters, lest he himself should end up testifying to his own villainies. {*Dio, l. 39. (59) 3:395}

4701. Mark Antony contended for the dead body of Archelaus (who was his close friend) and gave it a royal burial. He was famous among the Alexandrians for this deed. {*Plutarch, Antony, l. 1. c. 3. s. 5,6. 9:145} In Pontus, the son of Archelaus received the priesthood of Comana after his father. {*Strabo, l. 12. c. 3. s. 35. 5:437}

4702. Gabinius left some of his soldiers with Ptolemy at Alexandria as a guard. These later lived according to the Alexandrian manner of life, with its licentiousness. They forgot the name and discipline of the people of Rome and married wives, by whom they had many children. {*Caesar, Civil Wars, l. 3. (110) 2:353} Lucan added: {*Lucan, l. 10. (400) 1:621}

> …The greater part were Latins born,
> But they, corrupted into foreign manners,
> Did so forget themselves, they did not scorn
> To obey a sergeant, follow a servant's banners,
> Whom the Pharian tyrant's rule was much below.

4703. When Ptolemy was restored to his kingdom, he put his daughter, the queen Bernice, to death. {*Strabo, l. 17. c. 1. s. 11. 8:47} {*Dio, l. 39. (58) 3:395} {Porphyry, Scaliger's Greek Eusebius, p. 226.} He also killed many of the rich noblemen because he needed much money. {*Dio, l. 39. (58) 3:395}

4704. Gaius Rabirius Postumus was a Roman equestrian who had rashly trusted Ptolemy, both when he was in his kingdom and when he came to Rome. Ptolemy left with his money and the money of his friends. In order to recover the money, he was forced to change his Roman attire for the Greek attire at Alexandria. There he had to undertake the proctorship and stewardship for the king, having been made the king's overseer by the king. Notwithstanding, he was later put in prison and saw many of his close friends put in bonds. Death was always before his eyes and finally he was forced to flee from the kingdom, naked and poor. {*Cicero, Pro Rabirio Postumo, l. 1. c. 9. 14:389,391}

4705. While Gabinius stayed in Egypt, Alexander, the son of Aristobulus, again seized the government by force and caused many of the Jews to revolt. *[E621]* He gathered a large army and foraged the country, killing all the Romans he found and besieging all those who fled to Mount Gerizim. When Gabinius returned, he sent Antipater, who was known for his great wisdom, to the rebellious Jews. He was able to make many submit to him in obedience. However, Alexander, who had thirty thousand Jews with him, fought with Gabinius near Mount Tabor, where the Jews then lost ten thousand men. *[K292]* After Gabinius had settled the affairs of Jerusalem by following Antipater's advice, he marched against the Nabateans, whom he overcame in one battle. {*Josephus, Antiq., l. 14. c. 6. s. 2,3. (100,101) 7:501*}

4706. King Mithridates, the son of Phraates II, was abandoned by Gabinius and did not recover the Parthian kingdom with the help of the Arabians. (This was commonly believed, from an incorrect interpretation of the words of Appian. {*Appian, Syrian Wars, l. 11. c. 8. (51) 2:201*}) In fact, Justin stated that he retired to Babylon. When his brother Orodes had besieged Mithridates for a long time, the latter was forced to surrender the city because of the famine. Mithridates trusted in the fact that Orodes was his brother and surrendered to him. However, Orodes treated him as an enemy rather than a brother and commanded him to be killed before his eyes. {*Justin, Trogus, l. 42. c. 4.*}

4707. Gabinius secretly sent back Mithridates III and Orsanes, who were men of renown among the Parthians and who had fled to him. He spread rumours among his soldiers that they had fled. {*Josephus, Jewish War, l. 1. c. 8. s. 7. (178) 2:83*} {*Josephus, Antiq., l. 14. c. 6. s. 4. (103) 7:501*}

4708. The Syrians did much complaining about Gabinius. They complained, among other things, that they were grievously bothered with thieves because of his absence. The tax collectors also complained that, because of the thieves, they could not gather the tribute and so were deeply in debt. Angry at this, the Romans determined to have the matter judged and were prepared to condemn him. Cicero also vehemently accused Gabinius and was of the opinion that the Sibylline verses should be read again. He convinced himself that there was some punishment determined for the one who had violated the oracles. However, both Pompey and Crassus, who were still consuls, favoured Gabinius. Pompey favoured him for his own interests, while Crassus did it to gratify his colleague, and as well as in return for the money that Gabinius had sent him. Since both of them publicly defended him, they allowed nothing to be decreed against him and had Cicero banished. {*Dio, l. 39. (59,60) 3:395,297*}

4709. In his second consulship, Pompey dedicated his theatre by exhibiting most magnificent plays and shows. {*Cicero, De Officiis, l. 2. c. 16. 21:229*} {*Cicero, Friends, l. 7. c. 1. 26:5*} {*Asconius Pedianus, In Pison*} However, it was reported that this theatre had not been built by Pompey himself, but by his freedman Demetrius, who was a Gadarene, with the money that he had obtained when he was a soldier under him. He gave the honour of this work to Pompey, lest he should be ill-spoken-of, in that a freedman of his should get so much money and that he was able to spend so much. {*Dio, l. 39. (38) 3:363*}

4710. Gabinius did not allow the lieutenant, who had been sent ahead by Crassus, to succeed him in the province of Syria. He retained the province as if he had received a perpetual government. {*Dio, l. 39. (60) 3:397*}

4711. The tribunes of the people hindered Crassus, the consul, from raising any soldiers and endeavoured to annul the expedition that had been decreed to him. However when Crassus took up arms, the tribunes of the people saw that their liberty was threatened and that they were helpless to withstand his actions for lack of arms. So they stopped their actions, but cursed him to the pit of hell. As Crassus went into the Capitol to make his accustomed prayers for a prosperous journey, they told him what unlucky signs and prodigies had happened. {*Dio, l. 39. (39) 3:363-367*} *[K293]*

4712. Ateius, the tribune of the people, was prepared to hinder Crassus' departure, as were many others, who were offended that he should plan to make war against men who were at peace with them and who were confederates. Crassus feared this and wanted Pompey to go with him from the city, for Pompey was held in high esteem with the common people. Although many were prepared to hinder Crassus, when they saw Pompey go ahead of him with a pleasant and smiling countenance, they nevertheless held their peace and made a path for them. {*Plutarch, Crassus, l. 1. c. 16. s. 3,4. 3:363*}

4713. When Ateius, the tribune, met Crassus, he forbade him to go any farther. Then he ordered his attendant to arrest him and carry him to prison. However, the rest of the tribunes would not allow it and Crassus managed to get outside the walls. {*Plutarch, Crassus, l. 1. c. 16. s. 4,5. 3:363*} {*Dio, l. 39. (39) 3:365,367*} However, Ateius ran to the gate and there started a fire. As Crassus passed by, he cast in incense and libations upon it, pronouncing horrible curses and calling on the terrible and strange names of the gods. *[E622]* The Romans considered these secret and ancient exhortations to be of such force that anyone so cursed could not escape their power, nor that he who cursed anyone would ever prosper. Therefore this procedure was not employed at random nor by many. {*Plutarch, Crassus, l. 1. c. 16. s. 5,6. 3:363*}

4714. Florus wrote that Metellus, the tribune of the people, pronounced hostile curses on Crassus when he started his journey. {*Florus, l. 1. c. 46. s. 3. 1:211*} Velleius Paterculus stated that all the tribunes of the people cursed Crassus. {*Velleius Paterculus, l. 2. c. 46. s. 2. 1:151*} Appian and Dio also noted this event. {*Appian, Civil Wars, l. 2. c. 3. (18) 3:261*} {*Dio, l. 39. (39) 3:367*} Lucan stated: {*Lucan, l. 3. (126) 1:123*}

…The tribunes so ill befriended
Crassus, with curses he his march attended.

*4715.* Cicero said that it was mainly Gaius Ateius who pronounced those curses and set a sign before him, warning him of what would happen unless he took heed. {*Cicero, De Divinatione, l. 1. c. 16. 20:257,259*} Crassus left for the province from the house where he had attended a dinner party given by Cicero, for Cicero had dined with him in the gardens of his son-in-law Crassipes. {*Cicero, Friends, l. 1. c. 9. s. 20. 25:79*} From there, Cicero went to his Tusculan villa around the 17th of the Calends of December (or November 14, which fell in the Julian August), and Crassus went on his journey, clad in his armour. {*Cicero, Atticus, l. 4. c. 12,13. 22:301,303*} Crassus shipped his army from Brundisium. {*Cicero, De Divinatione, l. 2. c. 40. 20:465*}

*4716.* Crassus sailed from Brundisium before the storms on the seas were over and so lost many of his ships. He landed his army, made up of those who survived, and marched by land through Galatia. When he found King Dejotarus, a very old man, building a new city, he mocked him by saying:

"Do you begin to build in the twelfth hour?"

*4717.* The king smilingly answered:

"Truly I think, oh Imperator, you do not go against the Parthians early in the day!"

*4718.* Crassus was sixty years old and his face made him seem older than he was. {*Plutarch, Crassus, l. 1. c. 17. s. 1,2. 3:365*}

## 3950a AM, 4659 JP, 55 BC

*4719.* In his absence, Cicero very earnestly defended the cause of Crassus against the new consuls and many who had been consuls. {*Cicero, Friends, l. 5. c. 8. 25:349*}

## 3950b AM, 4660 JP, 54 BC

*4720.* Crassus did not have much to do in Syria, for the Syrians were quiet and those who had troubled Syria were afraid of the power of Crassus and did not stir, so Crassus undertook an expedition against the Parthians. There was no reason for making war upon them, only that he had heard that they were rich. *[K294]* He hoped that Orodes, who now reigned, would easily be overcome. {*Dio, l. 40. (12) 3:421*}

*4721.* When he heard of the riches of the temple of Jerusalem, which Pompey had left untouched, he turned aside into Palestine, came to Jerusalem and took away the riches. {*Orosius, l. 6. c. 13.*}

*4722.* In the temple was a wedge of solid gold weighing three hundred minas, or seven hundred and fifty common pounds. It was enclosed in a hollow beam of wood on which they hung the hangings of the temple, which were admired for their beauty and the esteem in which they were held. Only Eleazar, a priest, who was the keeper of the sacred treasure, knew about this. When he saw Crassus so greedy in gathering up the gold, he was afraid that he would take away all the ornaments of the temple. He turned the golden beam over to him, as a ransom for all the rest, having first bound him by an oath, that he would not take anything else. In spite of this, Crassus took the oath and immediately broke it, taking from the temple two thousand talents, which Pompey had not touched, as well as all the rest of the gold, which added up to eight thousand Attic talents. Josephus tried to prove the existence of these vast riches, for he was convinced that it would scarcely be believed among people of other countries. He cited the historical writings of Strabo of Cappadocia, which are now lost, and others, that in olden times gold had been found there, sent from the Jews who lived in Europe, Asia and Cyrene. {*Josephus, Antiq., l. 14. c. 7. s. 1. (105-109) 7:503*}

*4723.* Crassus built a bridge over the Euphrates River and easily and safely crossed the river with his army. He controlled many towns which voluntarily yielded to him. {*Plutarch, Crassus, l. 1. c. 17. s. 2. 3:365*} They had not expected Crassus' arrival, so that there were scarcely any established garrisons in all of Mesopotamia. {*Dio, l. 40. (12) 3:423*}

*4724.* Talymenus Ilaces (or Sillaces), the governor of that country, fought against Crassus with a few cavalry and was defeated. He was wounded and retired to the king, to inform him of the expedition of Crassus. {*Dio, l. 40. (12) 3:423*}

*4725.* In the meantime, Crassus recovered many cities, especially those that belonged to the Greeks, including Nicephorium. For many of the inhabitants who were Macedonians, and Greeks who had served under the Macedonians in the wars, feared the tyranny of the Parthians. *[E623]* They hoped for a better deal from the Romans, and Crassus knew the Greeks favoured Rome, so they very willingly revolted from the Parthians. {*Dio, l. 40. (13) 3:423*}

*4726.* Only the citizens of Zenodotia, where Apollonius was the ruler, killed a hundred Roman soldiers, after having allowed them within their walls as though they meant to surrender to them. Thereupon, Crassus brought his whole army there and captured the city. He sacked it because of this outrage and sold the inhabitants. Although this was Crassus' first encounter with an enemy, he allowed himself to be called *Imperator*, or captain general. This turned out to his disgrace, and resulted in his being thought of as a lowly man who did not hope for any great things, since he was puffed up by so small a success. {*Dio, l. 40. (13) 3:423*} {*Plutarch, Crassus, l. 1. c. 17. s. 3. 3:365*}

4727. Gabinius returned into Italy when Lucius Domitius and Appius Claudius were consuls. {Asconius Pedianus, In Pison, Init.} These same consuls were there again who had given judgment against Gabinius in his absence. [K295] Although Pompey very earnestly stood up for him, the opinion of many of the judges was against him, since Domitius was an enemy of Pompey because of the dispute over the demanding of the consulship and because he had taken that office against Domitius' will. Although Appius was a relative of Pompey, he planned that by flattering the people that if he made any move, he would be bribed by Gabinius. To that end he directed all his actions. For this reason, it was decreed that the Sibylline verses should be read over again, although Pompey was very much against it. In the meantime, the money that had been sent by Gabinius arrived in Rome. This money achieved so much, that Gabinius was certain not to suffer any great loss, whether he was absent or present. For there was such confusion in Rome at the time, that when Gabinius had given but part of that money to bribe the magistrates and some of the judges, they did not want to bring the matter to justice. Others had learned that they could be wicked with impunity and that money easily bought *justice* and removed the threat of punishment. {*Dio, l. 39. (60,62) 3:397-401}

4728. On the 12th of the Calends of October (September 19, which was around the Julian July), Gabinius came into the city. On the 4th of the Calends of October (September 27), he entered the city again by night, {*Cicero, Quintus, l. 3. c. 1. s. 5,6. 28:563,571} for his conscience so tormented him over his ugly actions, that it was late when he came into Italy. He entered the city by night and did not dare leave his own house for many days. {*Dio, l. 39. (62) 3:401}

4729. Various factions accused Gabinius. Lucius Lentulus, the son of the *flamen*, or priest, accused him of treason. Tiberius Nero joined in this accusation with various good men, among whom were Gaius Memmius, the tribune of the people, and Lucius Capito. After he was accused of treason, he appeared by the edict of Gaius Alfius, the praetor. He was almost trampled by the large crowd and was hated by all the people. {*Cicero, Quintus, l. 3. c. 1. s. 5,6. 28:563,571}

4730. On the tenth day after coming into the city, Gabinius had to give an account of the numbers killed, of both enemies and his own soldiers. He entered the Senate when it was poorly attended and was quite surprised by what happened. Appius, the consul, accused him of treason. When his name was called, he answered not a word. When he wanted to leave, he was detained by the consuls while the tax collectors were brought in. He was accused on all sides. When he was wounded more

than anything by the words of Cicero, he could not endure it any longer. With a trembling voice he called Cicero an exile. All the Senate rose to support Cicero and to turn against Gabinius. With a shout, they came to where he stood to attack him. The tax collectors did likewise, with a similar shout and with violence. On the 6th of the Ides of October (October 10), Memmius angrily put Gabinius before the people, so that Calidius could not speak for him. The next day, there was a divination before Cato at the praetor's house to appoint an accuser against Gabinius. They selected from among Memmius, Tiberius Nero, and Gaius and Lucius Antonius, the sons of Marcus. {*Cicero, Quintus, l. 3. c. 2. 28:573,575}

4731. There were many accusations against Gabinius and not a few accusers. The first thing that was debated involved the crime of restoring Ptolemy to his kingdom. Almost all the people flocked to the tribunal and they often had a mind to pull him to pieces, especially because Pompey was not there. Cicero had accused him most severely. {*Dio, l. 39. (62) 3:401} Cicero denied that he had accused him. {*Cicero, Quintus, l. 3. c. 2. 28:575} {*Cicero, Quintus, l. 3. c. 4. 28:583} He did this either from fear of having any quarrels with Pompey, or because he did not doubt that justice would be done, whether he was there or not, or he feared that he would be forever disgraced if such an infamous and guilty person were to escape justice if he pleaded against him. {*Cicero, Quintus, l. 3. c. 4. 28:585} [K296]

> "I was much delighted with this moderation, and this also pleased me that, when I had sharply spoken according to both condolence and religion, the defendant said that if he might be in the city he would give me satisfaction. Neither did he ask me anything."

4732. Cicero stated elsewhere: {*Cicero, Quintus, l. 3. c. 9. 28:605}

> "All that I did, I did with much dignity and the same tenderness that everyone feels. I neither attacked him, nor helped him. [E624] I was a forcible witness, but beyond that, I did and said nothing."

4733. In this trial for treason, Gabinius was very slow in answering and was hated by all men. Alfius was a strong and sterling character as he presided over the trial. Pompey was very earnest in seeking to solicit the judges to favour him. {*Cicero, Quintus, l. 3. c. 3. 28:581} Gabinius said that he had restored Ptolemy for the good of the state, because he was afraid of the fleet of Archelaus, and because he thought the sea would be filled with pirates. He also said that he was permitted to do it by law. {*Cicero, Pro Rabinius Postumus, l. 1. c. 8. 14:385,387} The friends of Caesar and Pompey were very eager to help him and said that the Sibylline verses referred to another king and another time. They pleaded this the most because no specific punishment was mentioned in the oracle. {*Dio, l. 39. (62) 3:401} Lucius Lentulus was incredibly young to be a prosecutor. Everyone said he had deliberately been brought in, so that Gabinius might win. In spite of this, there had been great disputes and entreaties by Pompey and a rumour of a dictatorship, which caused much fear. Gabinius had not replied to Lucius Lentulus. When the judges gave their sentence, there were thirty-two who condemned him and thirty-eight who absolved him. {*Cicero, Atticus, l. 4. c. 18. 22:327} {*Cicero, Quintus, l. 3. c. 4. 28:583}

4734. Dio stated that when Gabinius stood on trial for very serious crimes, he spent large sums of money on bribes. {*Dio, l. 39. (62) 3:401} When he was absolved, he spent little for bribes on the minor crimes, since he thought he would get off on these, also. However, the people almost killed the jurors, but they escaped. Gabinius was brought to trial before the people by Memmius and freed because of the intercession of Laelius, the tribune of the people. Valerius Maximus stated what happened. Aulus Gabinius, in the midst of his infamy, was subjected to trial by the people by Gaius Memmius, his accuser. It seemed as if all his hopes were dashed because the accusation was fully proved and his defence was very weak. Those who judged him, were very anxious to punish him because of an over-hasty anger on their part. The lictor and prison were ever before him. All this was thwarted by the intervention of an auspicious happening. Sisenna, the son of Gabinius, simply through the mental impulse of amazement, fell humbly prostrate before Memmius. From there, he hoped for some assuaging of the storm at its source. Memmius, the insolent conqueror, rejected him with a stern countenance and taking his ring from his finger, let it lie on the ground a long while. This spectacle was the reason that Laelius, the tribune of the people, ordered that Gabinius be dismissed. We can learn from this example, neither insolently to abuse the success of prosperity, nor that anyone need be too cast down by adversity. {*Valerius Maximus, l. 8. c. 1. absol. 3. 2:191,193}

4735. In spite of this acquittal, Gabinius was on trial again for other reasons, as well as that he had wrongfully extorted a hundred thousand (either drachmas or denarii) from the province. He was condemned for extortion. [K297] Pompey, who was away from the city to provide grain (for much grain had been ruined by the flooding of the Tiber River), was still in Italy. He hurried to be present at the trial but when he saw that he had come too late, he did not leave the suburbs until the trial was finished. Pompey called the people together outside the walls of the city (because it was not lawful for a proconsul to come into the city) and spoke to them on behalf of Gabinius. He read them the letters that he had received from Caesar concerning the safety of Gabinius and used many entreaties with the judges. He prevented Cicero from prosecuting Gabinius and even persuaded Cicero to defend him! However, all these things did not help Gabinius. The judges condemned him, partly from fear of the people and partly, because they had not received any large bribes from Gabinius (who, standing accused of small wrongs, did not bestow much money on them, confidently believing that he would be freed). They condemned him to banishment and Caesar later restored him and brought him back. {*Dio, l. 39. (63) 3:401,403}

4736. Cicero acknowledged that he had very earnestly defended Gabinius, after which these two men, who had formerly been great enemies, became friends. {*Cicero, Pro Rabirio Postumo, l. 1. c. 8. 14:385} Although this favour was commended by Valerius Maximus, Dio stated that Cicero was branded with the name and crime of a turncoat. {*Valerius Maximus, l. 4. c. 2. s. 4. 1:363} {*Dio, l. 39. (62) 3:401} Truly, Marcus Cicero quite forgot what he had previously written to his brother Quintus: {*Cicero, Quintus, l. 3. c. 5. s. 5. 28:595}

"I would be ruined, had I defended Gabinius, as Pansa thought I ought to have done."

4737. Although Cicero gave this account of his actions: {*Cicero, Pro Rabirio Postumo, l. 1. c. 8. 14:385}

"The renewing of our friendship was the reason that I defended Gabinius. Neither does it ever grieve me to have a mortal hatred and immortal friendship."

4738. Timagenes, the Alexandrian (or the Egyptian, according to some), was the son of the king's treasurer. He was captured in the war and brought to Rome by Gabinius. He was redeemed by Faustus, the son of Sulla, after which he taught rhetoric at Rome under Pompey, Julius Caesar and the triumvirs, and wrote many books. {Suidas, in Τιμαγενης}

4739. When Publius Cornelius Lentulus Spinther, the proconsul of Cilicia, had done well in the war, his army greeted him as Imperator, or captain general. {*Cicero, Friends, l. 1. c. 8. s. 7. 25:45} {*Cicero, Friends, l. 1. c. 9. s. 2. 25:49} [E625]

## 3951a AM, 4660 JP, 54 BC

4740. The Senate decreed that Appius Claudius Pulcher, at about the end of his term as consul, was to replace Publius Cornelius Lentulus. This law was not ratified by the people (lex curiata) and so he went into Cilicia at his own expense. {*Cicero, Friends, l. 1. c. 9. s. 25. 25:87} {*Cicero, Quintus, l. 3. c. 2. s. 1. 28:577} {*Cicero, Atticus, l. 4. c. 18. s. 12. 22:331} Lentulus went to meet him when he came into the province. {*Cicero,

*Friends, l. 3. c. 7. s. 5. 25:193}* When Appius took over the command, he afflicted the province most miserably and almost destroyed it. {*Cicero, Atticus, l. 5. c. 16. 22:377,379} {*Cicero, Atticus, l. 6. c. 1. 22:415,417}*

4741. When he first took the places in Mesopotamia, Crassus should have followed up on these initial successes with the full force of his army and so made good use of the fear the barbarians had of him. He should have attacked Babylon and Seleucia, two cities that were always enemies of the Parthians. Instead, he was weary of being in Mesopotamia and longed for the ease and idleness in Syria. *[K298]* He gave the Parthians time to prepare for war and opportunities to attack the Roman soldiers that were left in Mesopotamia. {*Plutarch, Crassus, l. 1. c. 17. s. 4,5. 3:365,367} {*Dio, l. 40. (13) 3:423,425}*

4742. In the cities that had surrendered to him, he had placed garrisons amounting to seven thousand foot soldiers and a thousand cavalry, after which he returned to Syria, to winter there. His son Publius Crassus came to him from Julius Caesar in Gaul, who had bestowed upon him the kind of gifts that generals usually give. He brought with him a thousand choice cavalry. {*Plutarch, Crassus, l. 1. c. 17. s. 4. 3:365,367}*

4743. Crassus spent his time in Syria more like a tax collector than a general. He did not spend his time in getting arms or training his soldiers, but instead, tallied up the revenues of the cities and spent many days weighing and measuring the treasures of the goddess of Hierapolis. He also demanded soldiers from various people and then discharged them for a sum of money. These actions brought him into contempt. As they were leaving the temple of the goddess Venus, or Juno, at Hierapolis, the young Crassus fell on the threshold and his father fell on top of him. This was taken as an ill omen. {*Plutarch, Crassus, l. 1. c. 17. s. 5,6. 3:367}* Hierapolis was the city that some call Bambyce, others Edessa and the Syrians, Mabog. The Syrian goddess, Atargatis, called Derceto by the Greeks, was worshipped there. {*Strabo, l. 16. c. 1. s. 27. 7:235} {*Pliny, l. 5. c. 19. 2:283}*

4744. Rabirius Postumus was accused of treason before the judges, because he had followed Ptolemy to Alexandria to get the money that he owed him. {*Suetonius, Claudius, l. 5. c. 16. s. 2. 2:33}* After Gabinius had been condemned of extortion and had gone into banishment, Gaius Memmius accused Rabirius, because the king had made him his *dioecetes*, or treasurer. He had worn the clothes of Alexandria and had gathered money from the tribute which had been imposed by Gabinius and Memmius himself. Cicero defended him at a time when it was very cold. This may be deduced from his speech, which is still extant. {*Cicero, Pro Rabirio Postumo, l. 1. c. 10. 14:393}*

## 3951b AM, 4661 JP, 53 BC

4745. Marcus Crassus and his son Publius were killed and the army was routed beyond the Euphrates River, where it perished in shame and disgrace. {*Cicero, De Divinatione, l. 2. c. 9. 20:395}* Dio mentioned this defeat, but Plutarch treated it more fully. {*Dio, l. 40. (27) 3:447} {*Plutarch, Crassus, l. 1. c. 31. s. 6,7. 3:417}* Appian in his writings copied Plutarch word for word. {*Appian, Parthian Wars}* Therefore, it will be worth the effort to record the main points of this very famous history, taken from these accounts as Salianus has done.

4746. Orodes, the king of the Parthians, sent envoys to Crassus in Syria. They were to find out why Mesopotamia was invaded and demand the reasons why he had started this war. Orodes also sent Surana with an army, to recover those places that had been taken or had revolted. He personally made an expedition into Armenia to frighten Artabazes, the son of Tigranes, lest he send any help to the Romans. {*Dio, l. 40. (16) 3:429}*

4747. The envoys of Orodes came to Crassus in Syria as he was drawing his forces from their winter quarters. (However, Florus stated that this took place in Mesopotamia, when Crassus was camped at Nicephorium.) They reminded him of the league they had made with Pompey and Sulla, thereby declaring to him that if this army had been sent against the Parthians by the people of Rome, then they would have no peace with the Romans. However if Crassus had initiated this war against the Parthians for his own private gain and had seized his cities, then their king would deal with him more favourably, considering Crassus' old age, and would send his soldiers back to the people of Rome. *[K299]* Crassus was blinded by the king's treasures and did not reply, nor did he pretend to excuse the war. Crassus said that he would answer them at Seleucia. Then Vageses, the chief of the envoys, smiled and striking the palm of his right hand with the fingers of his left, said that hairs would sooner grow there, than that Crassus would see Seleucia. So the envoys returned and told King Orodes that he must prepare for war. {*Florus, l. 1. c. 46. 1:211} {*Plutarch, Crassus, l. 1. c. 18. s. 1,2. 3:367,369} {*Dio, l. 40. (16) 3:429}*

4748. In the meantime, certain soldiers who had been left in garrisons in Mesopotamia, had barely escaped in dangerous circumstances to bring Crassus news. *[E626]* They told of the approach of a formidable multitude of the Parthians, recounting what weapons they used and how they fought. They spoke from experience! This so discouraged the Romans, that some of the captains were of the opinion that Crassus should stay and hold a council about the whole business. Cassius, the treasurer of

Crassus, was one of those who urged this. The soothsayers also tried to deter him, but Crassus would not listen to any of them. {*Plutarch, Crassus, l. 1. c. 18. s. 2-5. 3:369,371}

4749. Crassus was greatly encouraged by Artabazes, the king of the Armenians, when he came into his camp with six thousand cavalry who were said to be the king's own guard. He promised him another ten thousand mail-clad cavalry and thirty thousand foot soldiers, whom he would pay. He also persuaded Crassus that he should invade Parthia through Armenia and that he would abundantly supply his army. The march that way would be safer, because of the unevenness of the terrain, and so not as much in danger of the large numbers of Parthian cavalry. Crassus neglected this very wise counsel and thanked the Armenian. He sent him back and told him that he would march through Mesopotamia, where he had left many good Roman soldiers. {*Plutarch, Crassus, l. 1. c. 19. s. 1-3. 3:371,373}

4750. When he came to Zeugma, on the bank of the Euphrates River, he ignored many bad prodigies, which Plutarch and Dio mentioned. {*Plutarch, Crassus, l. 1. c. 19,20. 3:373,375} {*Dio, l. 40. (18,19) 3:431-435} Julius Obsequens noted the main one: {*Julius Obsequens, Prodigies, l. 1. c. 64. 14:305}

> "A sudden wind snatched the standard from the standard bearer, and it sank in the water. A sudden black storm of fog, that poured in on them, hindered their crossing."

4751. In spite of this, Crassus was determined to go on. Florus stated this: {*Florus, l. 1. c. 46. s. 3. 1:211}

> "When the army had passed Zeugma, a sudden whirlwind threw the standard into the Euphrates River, where it sank."

4752. Crassus also ignored the counsel of Cassius. He advised him that he should refresh his army in some of the cities where he had a garrison, until he heard some definite news of the Parthians. Otherwise, he should march to Seleucia along the river, so that the ships could supply him with food and follow the camp, while the river would keep the enemy from surrounding him. {*Plutarch, Crassus, l. 1. c. 20. 3:375}

4753. As Crassus was considering these things, Auganus, or Abgarus, of Osroene dissuaded him from this good advice. He was correctly named by Dio. {*Dio, l. 40. (20) 3:435} Florus called him Mazaras, the Syrian. {*Florus, l. 1. c. 46. s. 6. 1:211} The copies of the Breviary of Sextus Rufus vary. He was called Mazarus, Marachus, Macorus and also Abgarus. In Plutarch, he was called Ariamnes, a captain of the Arabians. Although in some copies of

Plutarch, and in those which Appian used, he was called Acbarus. {Appian, Parthian Wars} This man had formerly been in league with the Romans in Pompey's time, but now followed the Parthians. Although he was on the Parthians' side, he pretended that he was a good friend to Crassus and generously gave him much money. He found out all Crassus' plans and passed them to the Parthians. [K300] When Crassus was determined to march to Seleucia and from there to go to the city of Ctesiphon, Auganus persuaded Crassus not to follow that plan, because it would take too long. Instead, he should lead his army directly against Sillaces and Surenas, two of Orodes' captains. In doing this, he would turn his back on the Euphrates River, which was his only supply line and fortification. {*Dio, l. 40. (20) 3:435} {*Plutarch, Crassus, l. 1. c. 21. 3:377}

4754. He then led his army through a vast, sandy desert plain that lacked water and any vegetation. Crassus began to suspect treason, especially when Artabazes sent envoys to him and told him that he could send him no forces, because he was fighting a major war, for Orodes had now wasted the country of the Armenians. He very earnestly advised Crassus to come into Armenia and to join forces with him, so that together they might fight with Orodes. If he was not willing to do this, then he should be sure to avoid any terrain that was most suitable for cavalry. Crassus angrily rejected this advice and did not write to the king. He told them that he had no time to think about Armenia, but that on his return he would punish Armenia for its treachery. Abgarus left immediately, before his treachery was discovered. He had persuaded Crassus to surround the enemies and rout them. {*Dio, l. 40. (21) 3:435,437} {*Plutarch, Crassus, l. 1. c. 22. 3:379-383}

4755. They had not gone far, when a few scouts returned (for the rest were killed by the enemy) and told them that large forces were courageously marching on toward them. At this, Crassus was astonished and all the army was paralysed with fear. At first, Crassus followed Cassius' advice and set his battle formation wide. Presently he changed his mind and contracting his forces, made it square and deep. He gave the leading of one wing to Cassius and the other to his son, Gaius Publius. He led the battle in the middle. As soon as they came to the Balissus River, most of the commanders tried to persuade him to camp and to lodge there for the night. In the meantime, they should send scouts to see what forces the enemy had and how they were armed. Crassus ignored this good advice because his son and some of his cavalry were eager for a battle. [E627] So he commanded them to eat and drink while standing in their ranks. Before everyone was able to finish this, he marched on quickly with a sustained pace until the enemy came into view. {*Plutarch, Crassus, l. 1. c. 22. 3:379-383}

4756. Surenas had camouflaged his main forces behind his advance guard, concealing the gleam of their armour by having ordered them to cover themselves with robes of skins. He positioned his troops in a suitable place to terrify the Romans. When they tried with their lances to make the Romans break rank, they could not. As soon as they saw the depth of the Roman forces and that the soldiers kept their ranks, they withdrew. Then, while appearing to be in disarray, they surrounded the Romans before the Romans were aware of it. Crassus commanded his light cavalry to attack but they had not marched very far before being showered with arrows, forcing them to retire to the main body of troops. This was the beginning of fear and disorder among the Romans, especially when they saw the force of the weapons that broke through everything and caused many nasty wounds. {*Plutarch, Crassus, l. 1. c. 23,24. 3:387,389}

4757. The Parthians left them and began to shoot with their arrows at the whole body of the army on every side. No arrow fell in vain. They impacted so forcefully that it either made a horrible wound or, most commonly, resulted in death. The Parthians continued shooting, even while they were withdrawing from the Romans. [K301] The Romans took heart from the knowledge that once the enemy had shot all their arrows, the battle would be fought by hand-to-hand combat. However, they soon realised that there were many camels loaded with arrows, from which they went to replenish their supply once they had shot all their initial stock. Crassus began to despair, aware that there would be no end to their shooting until they had all been killed with their arrows. As a result, he ordered his son to endeavour by every means to join battle with the enemy, before they were surrounded. {*Plutarch, Crassus, l. 1. c. 25. s. 1. 3:389,391}

4758. The young Publius Crassus took with him thirteen hundred cavalry (a thousand of which he had received from Caesar), five hundred archers and eight cohorts of the men-of-arms who were closest to him. He charged at the Parthians, who deliberately fled, to draw him a good way off from his father. Then they turned around and shot them through with their arrows on every side. Publius (whom Orosius commended as a very famous and excellent young man {Orosius, l. 6. c. 13.} {Eutropius, l. 6.}) commanded a gentleman to thrust him through the side, because he could not use his hand, which had been shot through. Censorinus, a senator and orator, was said to have died in a similar way. Magabacchus, who was a valiant man both in body and mind, thrust himself through, as did the rest of the nobility. The remainder fled to a hill and were killed in the battle by the spears of the Parthians. Five hundred were said to have been taken prisoner. {*Plutarch, Crassus, l. 1. c. 25. 3:391-397}

4759. They cut off Publius' head and marched toward Crassus, who was expecting the return of his son during the time the enemy did not press them so hard. However, messenger came upon messenger, saying that Publius was totally defeated unless he was to receive help immediately from a very strong force. Crassus was planning to march with the whole army when the enemy came upon him. Because they had become more fierce as a result of their victory, they were making a terrible noise as they brought the head of his son on a spear. That spectacle broke the hearts of the Romans, in spite of Crassus' endeavours to encourage his men to wipe the joy of their victory from the enemy and to revenge their cruelty. The battle was renewed, but the Romans were again wounded on every side with their arrows. Many died miserably, because those, who in desperation believed they could escape the arrows, were charged with large lances by the enemy, who had forced the Romans into a small area. With one thrust, they struck through two bodies. This continued as night approached and the Parthians retired. They bragged that they would allow Crassus one night to bemoan his son. {*Plutarch, Crassus, l. 1. c. 26,27.'3:397-401}

4760. That same night, Octavius and Crassus called together the centurions and soldiers. Crassus was overwhelmed with sorrow at the army's defeat and the death of his son. He lay on the ground by himself in the dark with his head covered. They feared what was yet to come and forced the rest of the army to consider fleeing. The army everywhere began to break camp without any sound of trumpet. When those who were weak knew they were being abandoned, there was great tumult and confusion and all the camp was filled with howling and lamentations. Then fear and terror seized those who were marching because they thought the enemy would be aroused by this noise and would come and attack them. The enemy did, indeed, know that they were leaving but did not pursue them. Three hundred light cavalry under their captain Egnatius reached Carrhae late at night. He called to the watch and ordered them to tell Coponius, the governor, that Crassus had just had a major battle with the Parthians. That was all he said, before quickly riding off to Zeugma. Coponius assumed by the vagueness of the message that this was not good news. He promptly armed his men and met Crassus, who was marching slowly because of his wounded men. He received him and his army into the city. {*Plutarch, Crassus, l. 1. c. 27. 3:401-405} [E628] [K302]

4761. As soon as it was day, the Parthians went to the Roman camp, killing four thousand men who were still there. Many men of their cavalry were also captured as they were wandering in the plain. Among these, there were four cohorts led by Vargontinius, a lieutenant, who had lost their way in the night. These retired to a hill, which the Parthians quickly surrounded. They killed them all in a battle except for twenty soldiers. These broke through the midst of the enemy and safely reached Carrhae. {*Plutarch, Crassus, l. 1. c. 28. s. 1,2. 3:405,407} Orosius also mentioned this slaughter of Vargontinius. {Orosius, l. 6. c. 13.}

4762. Surenas was uncertain whether Crassus and Cassius were at Carrhae, or had fled to some other place. So he sent some men to Carrhae that he might discover the truth, on the pretext of making a league with the Romans if they would surrender Mesopotamia. The Romans approved of this because they were in a desperate situation. The Parthians demanded a time and a place to be determined for Crassus and Surenas to meet. When Surenas knew that the enemy was shut up in Carrhae, he came up to the city the next day with his whole army and besieged the place. He commanded the Romans that, if they wanted any truce, they should deliver up Crassus and Cassius as prisoners. At this, the Romans were deeply grieved that they had been cheated so. They gave up all hope of any help from the Armenians and considered how they might escape by fleeing. {*Plutarch, Crassus, l. 1. c. 28,29. 3:405,407}

4763. This meeting was to be kept secret from any of the residents of Carrhae, but Crassus told it to Andromachus, who was the most treacherous of men. Crassus used him as their guide on his march, consequently the Parthians knew all their plans because of the treachery of Andromachus. Since it was not their custom, nor was it safe for the Parthians, to fight at night, Crassus went out by night. In case the enemy would not be able to catch up, Andromachus led them back and forth circuitously. Finally, he led them into deep bogs and places that were full of ditches. There were some who suspected Andromachus' frequent turnings and would not follow him, as Cassius had retired to Carrhae and had made his way from there into Syria with five hundred men. Others, who found trustworthy guides, took the way of the hill country, called Sinnaca, and before day, retired into a safe place. These were almost five thousand men under Octavius, who was their commander and a valiant man. {*Plutarch, Crassus, l. 1. c. 29. 3:407,409}

4764. Daylight overtook Crassus, who was entangled in those difficult places and bogs because of the treachery of Andromachus. With much difficulty, he got through these areas, together with four cohorts of legionary soldiers, a few cavalry and five lictors. When the enemy approached, he fled to another hill within a mile and a half of Octavius. It was not as well-fortified, nor was it too steep for horses. It was below the country of Sinnaca and joined to it by a long ridge of land that stretched

through the middle of the whole plain. Hence, Octavius could easily see the danger that Crassus was in, so that first he himself, then some others, came to his aid. The rest chided one another and followed him, and drove the enemy from the hill. He received Crassus into their midst and surrounded him with their shields and encouraged him. No Parthian weapon could touch the body of their commander until the Parthians had killed every last man who defended him. {*Plutarch, Crassus, l. 1. c. 29. 3:409,411}

4765. Surenas saw that the Parthians were not as courageous as they should be and that it was a dangerous thing to fight with desperate men, especially when they fought from higher ground. If night should overtake them, they would not be able to take the Romans, who would then keep to the hills and go to the Armenians, with whose help they might then renew the war. {*Dio, l. 40. (25,26) 3:445} Consequently, Surenas plotted another treacherous deed. [K303] He released some prisoners who had deliberately been allowed to overhear some of the barbarians say that their king was not altogether against making peace with the Romans and that he would treat Crassus with all the civility that might be possible if he could make peace. In the meantime, the barbarians stopped fighting and Surenas, with some noblemen, approached the hill with his bow unbent. He held out his right hand and invited Crassus to make a league with him. He told him that while Crassus had, to this point, experienced the force of the Parthians, he could now, if he so chose, experience his humanity. Crassus did not go to him because he feared him and saw no reason for this sudden change of heart. {*Plutarch, Crassus, l. 1. c. 30. s. 1-3. 3:411,413}

4766. However, the soldiers demanded peace, even using harsh words to Crassus. He tried to persuade them and reason with them, saying that if they could hold out for the rest of the day, they could march through the mountainous terrain that night. They should not abandon the hope of safety that was so close at hand. They started to rebel and beat their harnesses and began to threaten him. Afraid, he went toward the enemy, but turned around to his own men and said: {*Plutarch, Crassus, l. 1. c. 30. s. 3-5. 3:413} [E629]

> "Indeed, even though you, Octavius and Petronius and all you Roman commanders that are here with me, see what violence is being done to me, yet, if ever any of you should get away safely, say that Crassus was deceived by his enemies and not that he was delivered up by his own citizens."

4767. It appears as though he was trying, in saying this, to assuage their obstinate minds by this friendly speech, while providing for their honour. However, Octavius and the rest did not remain on the hill, but went down with him. Crassus forbade the lictors, who wanted to follow him for his honour's sake, to go. {*Plutarch, Crassus, l. 1. c. 31. s. 1. 3:413}

4768. The first of the barbarians who came to meet him were two half-breed Greeks. Dismounting from their horses, they greeted him in Greek and asked him to send some men ahead to see if Surenas and the others who were coming to the parley, had arrived safely. Crassus sent the two brothers Roscii, whom Surenas then detained. Surenas came on horseback, but Crassus was walking. Surenas ordered that he should be brought a horse to take him to the riverside to write the articles of the peace. Because the Romans were not very observant of their covenants, Surenas gave him his right hand. When Crassus sent for a horse, Surenas told him there was no great need, as the king had given him one. Soon a horse with a golden bridle was brought to him. The grooms mounted Crassus and followed along behind him, lashing the horse. First, Octavius took hold of the bridle and then Petronius, one of the tribunes. Then the rest of the Romans surrounded him to steady the horse and to take him away from those who were pressing around Crassus on every side. {*Plutarch, Crassus, l. 1. c. 31. s. 1-4. 3:413,415}

4769. At first they were jostling and thrusting one another until finally they started fighting. Octavius drew his sword and killed a groom, one of the barbarians. Another struck Octavius from behind and killed him. Petronius had no weapon and was being hit on his coat of mail. He got off his horse and was not harmed. A Parthian, by the name of Pomaxathres, or Maxarthes, killed Crassus. Others said that another man killed Crassus, cutting off his head and right hand as he lay dead. {*Plutarch, Crassus, l. 1. c. 31. s. 5-7. 3:415,417} Dio left it in doubt whether he was killed by his own men, for fear of falling alive into the enemies' hands, or whether he was killed by the enemies. Some reported that the Parthians poured molten gold into Crassus' mouth in mockery. {*Dio, l. 40. (27) 3:447} Livy stated: {*Livy, l. 106. 14:133}

"He was taken and resisted, lest he be captured alive, and then he was killed. He was lured to a parley by a sign given by the enemy. He would have quickly fallen into their hands, had not the resistance of the tribunes stirred the barbarians to prevent the flight of the general."

4770. Florus said what was then also copied by Sextus Rufus in his Breviary to Valentinian, the emperor: {*Florus, l. 1. c. 46. s. 9. 1:211} {Sextus Rufus, Breviary} [K304]

"Crassus himself was lured to a parley and might have been taken alive, except for the resistance of the tribunes; he escaped and while he fled, he was killed."

4771. Surenas, the general of the Parthians, took Crassus by treachery and killed him at Sinnaca, a city of Mesopotamia, {*Strabo, l. 16. c. 1. s. 23. 7:231} although he would rather have taken him alive. {Orosius, l. 6. c. 13.} Velleius Paterculus stated that he was killed with most of the Roman army. {*Velleius Paterculus, l. 2. c. 46. s. 4. 1:153} Pliny stated that all the Lucanian soldiers, of which there were many in the army, were killed with him. {*Pliny, l. 2. c. 56. 1:285} Jornandes wrote that they lost almost eleven legions and their general. {Jornandes, De Regnorum ac Temporum Succession} It was said that the number of those killed was twenty thousand. Only ten thousand were taken alive by the enemy, according to Plutarch and Appian. {*Plutarch, Crassus, l. 1. c. 31. s. 7. 3:417} Of the one hundred thousand in the army, barely ten thousand escaped into Syria. {*Appian, Civil Wars, l. 2. c. 3. (18) 3:261} This happened in the month of June. {*Ovid, Fasti, l. 6. (465) 5:355} Dio said it was in the middle of summer. He also added that the Parthians, at this time, again recovered all their country that was in the vicinity of the Euphrates River. {*Dio, l. 40. (28) 3:447}

4772. The survivors of the Roman army shifted for themselves. Their flight had scattered them into Armenia, Cilicia and Syria, and there was scarcely a man alive to bring the news of the overthrow. {*Florus, l. 1. c. 46. s. 10. 1:213} As soon as this major defeat became known, many provinces of the east would have revolted from their alliance with, and the protection of, the people of Rome, had Cassius not gathered together a few soldiers from those who had fled. He went to Syria, which was beginning to grow proud, and managed the province with great virtue and moderation. {Orosius, l. 6. c. 13.} This was the same Cassius who had refused to accept the command that the soldiers had offered him at Carrhae, out of the hatred they had for Crassus. Crassus had been willing to yield to him when he knew the greatness of his loss but Cassius had refused. Now he was compelled, by necessity, to assume the government of Syria. {*Dio, l. 40. (27) 3:445,447} He was also the treasurer of Crassus, who kept Syria under Roman control, as well as being the same Gaius Cassius who, together with Brutus, later killed Julius Caesar. {*Velleius Paterculus, l. 2. c. 46. s. 4. 1:153} {*Velleius Paterculus, l. 2. c. 56. s. 3. 1:173} {*Velleius Paterculus, l. 2. c. 58. s. 1,2. 1:175}

4773. Surenas sent the head and the right hand of Crassus to Orodes in Armenia. Through his messengers, he spread a rumour at Seleucia that he had taken Crassus alive. He dressed up Gaius Paccianus, a captive who looked very much like him, and so made a ridiculous show which they mockingly called a triumph. {*Plutarch, Crassus, l. 1. c. 32. s. 1-3. 3:417,419}

4774. In the meantime, Orodes was reconciled to Artabazes, or Artavasdes, the Armenian, and betrothed his sister to his son Pacorus. [E630] They made feasts and revels during which many Greek verses were sung, for Orodes understood Greek and was a scholar. Artavasdes had written tragedies, speeches and histories. Jason, the tragedian of Tralles, was there, singing some verses from the Bacchus of Euripides, where Agave is about to appear. Sillaces came into the dining room and threw the head of Crassus down before them. Pomaxathres, or Maxarthes, rose from supper and took it for himself, since he thought the honour belonged to him more than to anyone else. {*Plutarch, Crassus, l. 1. c. 33. s. 1-4. 3:421,423}

4775. Some reported that, among other indignities, the Parthians poured molten gold down the mouth of Crassus and verbally insulted him. *[K305]* Florus recorded this about what happened: {*Florus, l. 1. c. 46. s. 10. 1:213}

> "The head and right hand of Crassus was brought to the king and they made sport of him. They poured molten gold down his open mouth, so that the dead and bloodless carcass of him whose mind had been on fire with the desire for gold while he was alive, might be burned with gold."

4776. Sextus Rufus Jornandes said similar things about this. {Sextus Rufus, Breviary} {Jornandes, De Regnorum ac Temporum Succession}

4777. Not long after, Surenas was punished for his treachery to Crassus. He was killed by Orodes, who envied his honour. {*Plutarch, Crassus, l. 1. c. 33. s. 5. 3:423}

4778. At Rome, Marcus Cicero was made augur in place of young Crassus, who had been killed in the Parthian war. {*Plutarch, Cicero, l. 1. c. 36. s. 1. 7:173}

4779. With the death of Crassus, one head of Varro's triumvirate was cut off and the foundation was laid for the civil wars between Pompey and Caesar. After Crassus was killed, who had been above them both, it remained for Caesar to eliminate Pompey, who was above him, so that he would be the greatest. {*Plutarch, Caesar, l. 1. c. 28. s. 1. 7:511} {*Plutarch, Pompey, l. 1. c. 53. s. 6,7. 5:255} Lucan wrote: {*Lucan, l. 1. (125) 1:13}

> Caesar would no superior fear,
> Nor Pompey any equal bear.

### 3952a AM, 4661 JP, 53 BC

4780. During the interim, the Senate decreed that neither any consul nor any praetor should have any foreign province by lot, until after the fifth year of his magistracy. A little later, Pompey confirmed this. {*Dio, l. 40. (46) 3:477} Interrex, Servius Sulpicius, on the 5th of the Calends of March (February 25), in an intercalary month (about the beginning of the Julian December), appointed Pompey as consul. {Asconius Pedianus, Pro Milone}

### 3952b AM, 4662 JP, 52 BC

4781. The Parthians invaded Syria with only a small army because they thought the Romans lacked soldiers and a general. Consequently, Cassius easily repulsed them. {*Dio, l. 40. (28) 3:447}

4782. Cassius came to Tyre and also arrived in Judea. When he came the first time, he captured Tarichea and led away about thirty thousand Jewish prisoners. He executed Pitholaus because he had sided with Aristobulus' faction at the persuasion of Antipater, who could do whatever he wished with Pitholaus. For Antipater realised that Pitholaus was in great standing with the Idumeans and was sought after, through courtesies and friendship, by others who were in power. He particularly made an alliance with the king of the Arabians, into whose custody he had committed his children during the war that he had fought with Aristobulus. Cassius had forced Aristobulus, the son of Alexander, to make peace, before he moved his camp to the Euphrates River to keep the Parthians from crossing over. {*Josephus, Jewish War, l. 1. c. 8. s. 9. (180-182) 2:85} {*Josephus, Antiq., l. 14. c. 7. s. 3. (119-122) 7:511,513}

### 3953 AM, 4663 JP, 51 BC

4783. When Marcus Marcellus and Gaius Sulpicius were consuls, the league with the Rhodians was renewed. It provided that one people should not make war on the other, but that they should send each other mutual help. The Rhodians also swore to have the same enemies that the Senate and the people of Rome had. {*Cicero, Friends, l. 12. c. 15. s. 2. 26:569} {*Appian, Civil Wars, l. 4. c. 8. (61) 4:245} {*Appian, Civil Wars, l. 4. c. 9. (66) 4:251} Because of this, Posidonius of Apamea, who had a school at Rhodes, seems to have come to Rome when Marcus Marcellus was consul. {Suidas, in voc. ποσιδωνις} *[K306]* He was a very noble philosopher, mathematician and historian. Cicero mentioned a globe he made: {*Cicero, De Natura Deorum, l. 2. c. 34. (87) 19:207}

> "If anyone should carry into Scythia or Britain this globe which was recently made by a close friend of mine, whose every turning performs the same actions as the sun and moon and the other five planets do in the heavens each day, who, in that barbarous land, would doubt but that this was a most exact representation, created by a rational being?"

4784. By the decree of the Senate and by the law of Pompey which had been made the year before, none could obtain either a consular or praetorian province, unless he had been consul or praetor five years or more prior to the appointment. Marcus Calpurnius Bibulus, who had been consul seven years earlier, and Marcus Tullius Cicero, who had been consul eleven years ago, and yet neither had ever been sent into any province, were assigned provinces by lot. *[E631]* Bibulus was given Syria {*Dio, l. 40. (30) 3:451} {*Dio, l. 40. (46) 3:477} and Cicero had Cilicia. {*Cicero, Friends, l. 3. c. 2. s. 1,2. 25:169} Cicero wrote that he had now been appointed proconsul to Appius Pulcher, the Imperator (captain general), whom he was to succeed. (For the army had given him the title, because he had done well in the wars in Cilicia.) Cicero also indicated that this had happened against his will and that he had never desired to be forced by the decree of the Senate to go and govern in his province. As his lieutenants, Cicero had his brother, Quintus Tullius, Gaius Pomponius, Lucius Tullius and Marcus Anneius. His quaestors were Lucius Messinius and Gnaeus Volusius.

4785. Plutarch said that Cicero had twelve thousand foot soldiers in his army and twelve hundred cavalry. {*Plutarch, Cicero, l. 1. c. 36. s. 1. 7:173} Cicero himself said that he had the command of only two legions and these were so undermanned, {*Cicero, Atticus, l. 5. c. 15. 22:375} that they were barely able to hold one pass, as Marius Caelius stated. {*Cicero, Friends, l. 8. c. 5. s. 1. 26:117}

4786. On the 11th of the Calends of June (May 22, as the year was then accounted at Rome, which fell on the 6th day of the Julian March), Cicero left for his province and arrived at Brundisium. There he met with Quintus Fabius Vergilianus, the envoy of Appius Claudius Pulcher, whom he was to succeed. When he told him that he needed a larger force to govern that province, almost all were of the opinion that the legions of Cicero and Bibulus should be supplied from Italy. The consul Servius Sulpicius vehemently denied this request. Such was the general agreement in the Senate that Cicero and Bibulus should be sent quickly, that at length they were forced to yield and make do with what troops they had. {*Cicero, Friends, l. 3. c. 3. s. 1. 25:171}

4787. Before the civil war of Caesar and Pompey on the Julian March 7, a little after noon, there was an almost total eclipse of the sun of ten and a half digits (88%). Dio said the whole sun was eclipsed. {*Dio, l. 41. (14) 4:27} Lucan wrote: {*Lucan, l. 1. (540) 1:43}

> …Titan hides
> (When mounted in the midst of heaven he rides)
> In clouds his burning chariot, to enfold
> The world in darkness quite: day to behold
> No nation hopes.…

4788. Cicero sailed from Brundisium and came to Actium on the 17th of the Calends of July (June 14, or the 29th day of the Julian March). He journeyed overland and reached Athens on the 6th of the Calends of July (June 26, or Julian April 9). {*Cicero, Atticus, l. 5. c. 9. 22:355} {*Cicero, Atticus, l. 5. c. 10. 22:355} The day before he arrived there, Memmius had set out for Mitylene. He had been condemned for unlawful bribery and banished. {*Cicero, Atticus, l. 5. c. 11. 22:365} [K307]

4789. In the month of the Julian April, Ptolemy Auletes died. Marcus Caelius mentioned this in a letter to Marcus Cicero, written from Rome on the Calends of August (August 1, or the 15th day of the Julian May). {*Cicero, Friends, l. 8. c. 4. s. 5. 26:117} Gaius Marcellus was chosen consul for the next year. News was brought to Rome confirming definitely that the king of Alexandria was dead. Of his two sons and two daughters, he left the oldest son and daughter as heirs. To ensure that this would be so, Ptolemy, in the same will, humbly and earnestly entreated the people of Rome, by all the gods and by the league that he had made with them at Rome, to make sure the will was carried out. One copy of his will was sent to Rome with his envoys, to be placed in the treasury, and the other was left sealed up and kept at Alexandria. {*Caesar, Civil Wars, l. 3. (108) 2:351}

4790. His will directed that his oldest son, Ptolemy, after the ancient custom of the Egyptians, should be married to Cleopatra, his oldest daughter, and that both of them should rule the kingdom. However, they were to be under the guardianship of the people of Rome. {*Dio, l. 42. (35) 4:171} Cleopatra spoke to Caesar concerning this: {*Lucan, l. 10. (90) 1:597} [E632]

> I am not the first woman to have swayed
> The Pharian sceptre: Egypt has obeyed
> A queen; not sex excepted: I desire
> Thee read the will of my deceased sire
> Who left me there a partner to enjoy
> My brother's crown and marriage bed.…

4791. The copy of this will was brought to Rome. Because of public practices, it could not be put in the treasury and was deposited with Pompey. {*Caesar, Civil Wars, l. 3. (108) 2:351} Eutropius stated that because the new king was so young, Pompey was appointed his tutor. {Eutropius, l. 6.}

4792. Marcus Cicero stayed a few days at Athens. On the day before the Nones of July (July 6, or Julian April 19), he sailed from the harbour of Piraeus. {*Cicero, Friends, l. 2. c. 8. s. 3. 25:119} He was carried to Zoster by a contrary wind, which detained him there until the 7th. On the 8th of July (April 25), he came to the village of Ceos and from there went to Gyaros, Syros and Delos. {*Cicero, Atticus, l. 5. c. 12. 22:367} On the 11th of the Calends of August (July 22, or Julian May 5), he reached Ephesus. He sailed more slowly because the Rhodian ships were frail. He was met by a very large crowd and the Greeks very readily offered themselves to him as if he had been the praetor of Ephesus. {*Cicero, Atticus, l. 5. c. 13. 22:369} Quintus Minucius Thermus was at Ephesus. He was the propraetor of the Asian governments which were separated from the province of Cilicia. He met with Cicero about a matter involving Cicero's lieutenant, Marcus Anneius, who had a dispute with the Sardinians. Cicero later wrote many letters to Thermus. {*Cicero, Friends, l. 13. c. 53-57. 27:129-139} {*Cicero, Atticus, l. 5. c. 20. 22:397,399} Publius Silius was propraetor of Bithynia at the time. {*Cicero, Friends, l. 13. c. 61. 27:143}

4793. Publius Nigidius was expecting Cicero at Ephesus and returned to Rome from his embassy. He was a very learned man. Cratippus also came there from Mitylene to see and greet Cicero. At that time, Cratippus was the most highly respected of all the Peripatetics, as Cicero stated in the preface to Plato's Timaeus, which he himself translated into Latin. [K308]

4794. Cicero left Ephesus and travelled to Tralles by a very dry and dusty route. {*Cicero, Atticus, l. 5. c. 14. 22:371} On the 6th of the Calends of August (July 27, or Julian May 10), he arrived at Tralles, where Lucius Lucilius met him with letters from Appius Pulcher. {*Cicero, Friends, l. 3. c. 5. 25:177} From these he learned that Appius had averted a rebellion of the soldiers and that the soldiers had all been paid to the Ides of July (July 15). {*Cicero, Atticus, l. 3. c. 14. 22:371}

4795. The day before the Calends of August (July 31, or Julian May 14), when Sulpicius and Marcellus were consuls, Cicero came to Laodicea, into a province which had been almost destroyed by Appius. That day marked the first day of the term of office that had been assigned to him by the Senate. {*Cicero, Atticus, l. 5. c. 15. 22:373} {*Cicero, Atticus, l. 5. c. 16. 22:377} {*Cicero, Atticus, l. 5. c. 20. 22:389} {*Cicero, Atticus, l. 5. c. 21. 22:405} {*Cicero, Friends, l. 3. c. 6. s. 6. 25:189} {*Cicero, Friends, l. 15. c. 2. s. 1. 27:235} {*Cicero, Friends, l. 15. c. 4. s. 2. 27:247} Cicero was told by the Cypriot envoys who came to meet him at Ephesus, that Scaptius, Appius' governor in Cyprus, was besieging the senate in their senate-house in Salamis, with some cavalry troops, hoping to starve the senators out. The same day that Cicero first entered the province, he sent letters ordering that the cavalry should immediately leave the island. {*Cicero, Atticus, l. 5. c. 21. 22:407} {*Cicero, Atticus, l. 6. c. 1. 22:421}

4796. He saw, by the time of year, that he must soon go to the army. After he had stayed three days at Laodicea (while the money was received which was owed him from the public treasury), on the 3rd of the Nones of August (August 3, or Julian May 17), he journeyed to Apamea. He stayed there four or five days, then three at Synnada and five at Philomelus. At that town, there was a large gathering of people. He freed many cities from the most

heavy tributes, exorbitant interest payments and large debts. {*Cicero, Friends, l. 3. c. 5. 25:181} {*Cicero, Friends, l. 15. c. 4. s. 2. 27:247} {*Cicero, Atticus, l. 5. c. 15. 22:375} {*Cicero, Atticus, l. 5. c. 16. 22:377} {*Cicero, Atticus, l. 5. c. 20. 22:389}

4797. Appius Claudius was allowed to stay in the province thirty days after his successor arrived. This was according to the law of Cornelius Sulla, the dictator. During those days he sat judging at Tarsus, while Cicero judged at Apamea, Synnada and Philomelus. {*Cicero, Friends, l. 3. c. 6. s. 3,4. 25:185} {*Cicero, Friends, l. 3. c. 8. s. 5. 25:203} {*Cicero, Atticus, l. 5. c. 16. 22:379} {*Cicero, Atticus, l. 5. c. 17. 22:381}

4798. Marcus Bibulus, the proconsul, sailed from Ephesus around the Ides of August (August 13, or Julian May 25) and came to his province, Syria, with the aid of a very favourable wind. {*Cicero, Friends, l. 15. c. 3. s. 2. 27:245} When the Senate had permitted him to raise soldiers in Asia, he had not done so. {*Cicero, Friends, l. 15. c. 1. s. 5. 27:233} [E633] The auxiliaries of the allies due to the harshness and injustice of the Roman government, had either been so weakened that they could be of little help, or so alienated from them, that little could be expected of them. So it did not seem wise to trust the allies for troops. {*Cicero, Friends, l. 15. c. 1. s. 5,6. 27:233,235}

4799. Before Cicero arrived in the province, the army was scattered due to a rebellion. Five cohorts were without lieutenant, or colonel or centurions. Cicero stayed at Philomelus, while the rest of the army was in Lycaonia.

4800. Cicero commanded his lieutenant, Marcus Anneius, to escort these five cohorts to the rest of the army and rally the whole army into one place and camp at Iconium, in Lycaonia. When Anneius had carried this out precisely, Cicero came into the camp on the 7th of the Calends of September (August 24, or Julian June 7). A few days before, in accordance with the decree of the Senate, he had received a good band of newly recruited soldiers, a number of cavalry, as well as voluntary auxiliaries of the free people, from the kings who were their allies. {*Cicero, Friends, l. 15. c. 4. s. 3. 27:247,249} [K309]

4801. Dejotarus, the son, who was declared king by the Senate, took Cicero's sons with him into his kingdom, while Cicero made war during the summertime. {*Cicero, Atticus, l. 5. c. 17. 22:379,381} {*Cicero, Atticus, l. 5. c. 18. 22:385} Plutarch stated that Dejotarus, the father, had killed all his other sons in order to establish the kingdom for this one son. {Plutarch, De Stoicorum Repugnantiis} Both the father and son reigned together and Cicero greatly commended both of them. {*Cicero, Philippics, l. 11. c. 13. 15:495}

4802. Pacorus, the son of Orodes, king of the Parthians, who was married to the sister of the king of the Armenians, came with large forces of the Parthians and a large band from other countries. They crossed the Euphrates River and attacked the province of Syria. {*Cicero, Friends, l. 15. c. 1. s. 2. 27:231} {*Cicero, Friends, l. 15. c. 2. s. 1. 27:235,237} {*Cicero, Friends, l. 15. c. 3. s. 1. 27:245} {*Cicero, Friends, l. 15. c. 4. s. 7. 27:251,253} {*Cicero, Atticus, l. 5. c. 18. 22:381,383} Orsaces was the general and Pacorus only held the title of general, for he was barely fifteen years old. {*Dio, l. 40. (28) 3:449}

4803. The Parthians went into Syria and when they had subdued all the territories, they came as far as Antioch. They hoped to win it, too, for the Romans held that province with only a small army. The citizens barely tolerated the domineering Romans and were inclined toward the Parthians, since they were their neighbours and close friends. {*Dio, l. 40. (28,29) 3:349} The proconsul Bibulus had not yet arrived in the province. For although the province had been appointed to him for one year only, as in Cicero's case, it was reported that the reason he arrived so late in the province was so that he could leave later. {*Cicero, Atticus, l. 5. c. 16. 22:379} {*Cicero, Atticus, l. 5. c. 18. 22:383}

4804. Cicero, on the 3rd of the Calends of September (August 28, or Julian June 11), reviewed his army at Iconium. {*Cicero, Atticus, l. 5. c. 20. 22:389} On the Calends or the 3rd of the Nones of September (September 1 or 3), the envoys that had been sent by Antiochus, the king of the Commagenians, arrived at the camp at Iconium. They were the first to bring Cicero the news that large forces of the Parthians had begun to cross the Euphrates River. It was said that the Armenian king would make an invasion on Cappadocia. When the news was brought to him, Cicero was troubled. Although there were some who thought that not much credit should be given to the king's planned invasion, Cicero did not think so. He was worried about Syria, his own province, and indeed for all Asia. Therefore, he thought it best that the army should march through Lycaonia, the country of Isaura, and that part of Cappadocia which bordered Cilicia. {*Cicero, Friends, l. 15. c. 1. s. 2. 27:231} {*Cicero, Friends, l. 15. c. 2. s. 1,2. 27:237} {*Cicero, Friends, l. 15. c. 3. s. 1. 27:245} {*Cicero, Friends, l. 15. c. 4. s. 3,4. 27:249}

4805. After he had stayed ten days at Iconium, he moved his army and camped at the town of Cybistra, in the remotest part of Cappadocia, not far from the Taurus Mountains. He did this to demonstrate to Artavasdes, the Armenian king, that no matter what he intended to do, there was a Roman army not far from his border. In this way, he and the Parthians would think themselves shut out of Cappadocia and so Cicero could defend Cilicia, which bordered their country, and hold Cappadocia. This would hinder any new plans of the neighbouring kings who, although they were friends with the people of Rome, did not dare to be overt enemies to the Parthians. {*Cicero, Atticus, l. 5. c. 20. 22:389,391}

{*Cicero, Friends, l. 15. c. 2. s. 2. 27:237} {*Cicero, Friends, l. 15. c. 4. s. 4. 27:249} [K310]

4806. Cicero sent his cavalry from Cybistra into Cilicia, so that the news of his coming would be conveyed to the cities in that part and the citizens would be more loyal to him. This would allow him quickly to stop what was being done in Syria. {*Cicero, Friends, l. 15. c. 2. s. 3. 27:237}

4807. He was careful of the charge given to him by the Senate, that he was to defend Ariobarzanes, the king of the Cappadocians, and ensure that he and his kingdom were safe. With his brother, Ariarathes, and some of his father's old friends, the king came to the proconsul in the camp and stayed there three or four days. {*Cicero, Atticus, l. 6. c. 2. 22:449} [E634] They complained of treasons that had been plotted against his life and requested that some cavalry and Roman foot soldiers come and guard him. Cicero exhorted his friends to protect the life of their king taking every care and diligence, and learn from the sad example of his father. Cicero exhorted the king that he should learn to reign by protecting his own life from whomever he was certain was plotting treason against him. With these, he could do as he wished, punishing those who needed punishing and freeing the rest from fear. He should use the protection of the Roman army more to incite terror in those who were at fault, than for fighting. Then it would come about that they would understand, when they heard the decree of the Senate, that Cicero would be a protector to the king whenever needed. Concerning the king, Cicero wrote to the consuls and Senate that he was more careful to inform them because in King Ariobarzanes, there were such signs of virtue, wit, fidelity and goodwill toward them, that they were wise to give Cicero such a charge to protect him. {*Cicero, Friends, l. 15. c. 2. s. 6,7. 27:239-243}

4808. Cicero established Methras and Athenaeus, men whom King Ariobarzanes had banished because of the hostility of Athenais, into supreme favour and authority. A great war would have ensued in Cappadocia if the priest of Comana would have defended himself with armies. Hirtius stated that the priest was considered second only to the king in majesty, command and power, by common consent in that country. {*Caesar, Alexandrian War l. 1. (66) 3:117,119} The priest was a young man and some thought he might start a war, since he had cavalry, foot soldiers and money, as well as allies who wanted to see a revolution. However, Cicero brought it about that he left the kingdom, so that the king obtained the kingdom with honour and without any revolt or war, while the authority of his court was confirmed to him even more. {*Cicero, Friends, l. 15. c. 4. s. 6. 27:251} Even though in another letter Cicero thought that there was nothing more pillaged than that kingdom and no one poorer than that king. {*Cicero, Atticus, l. 6. c. 1. 22:419}

4809. In this way, the kingdom of Ariobarzanes was preserved for the king. {*Cicero, Friends, l. 15. c. 5. s. 1. 27:265,269} Cappadocia was reconciled to obedience to him, without fighting and with a great deal of goodwill. {*Plutarch, Cicero, l. 1. c. 36. s. 1,2. 7:173} As far as Ariobarzanes was concerned, Cicero bragged about himself to Atticus: {*Cicero, Atticus, l. 5. c. 20. 22:395}

"Ariobarzanes lives and reigns by my means, by my advice and authority. This happened because I kept myself away from those who lay in wait for him and free from bribes. Hence, I preserved both the king and the kingdom."

4810. In the meantime, Cicero heard, through many letters and messages, that Cassius (Bibulus had not yet arrived in Syria) was at Antioch with an army. Large forces from the Parthians and Arabians had come to Antioch. There was a large body of cavalry who had passed into Cilicia and had all been killed by those cavalry troops Cicero had sent there, assisted by a praetorian cohort stationed in a garrison at Epiphanea. [K311] The Parthians were in Cyrrhestica, a part of Syria that bordered on Cilicia. Therefore, when he realised that the forces of the Parthians had turned from Cappadocia and were not far from the borders of Cilicia, he left Cybistra in Cappadocia, after having camped for five days, and led the army into Cilicia. At the borders of Lycaonia and Cappadocia on the 13th of the Calends of October (September 18, or Julian June 30), he received letters from Tarcondimotus and from Jamblichus, a leading tribesman from the Arabians, who were considered friends of the Roman commonwealth. They said that Pacorus had crossed the Euphrates River with a large body of Parthian cavalry and was camped at Tyba. Cicero, shortly after, wrote to the consuls and Senate about this. {*Cicero, Friends, l. 15. c. 1. s. 2. 27:231} {*Cicero, Friends, l. 15. c. 2. s. 3. 27:237} {*Cicero, Friends, l. 15. c. 4. s. 7. 27:251,253} {*Cicero, Atticus, l. 5. c. 18. 22:383} {*Cicero, Atticus, l. 5. c. 20. 22:391}

4811. A rumour of the arrival of Cicero encouraged Cassius, who was besieged in Antioch, and filled the Parthians with fear, so that they left Antioch before the arrival of Bibulus and were driven back by Cassius. He pursued them in their retreat from the town and killed many of them. {*Cicero, Atticus, l. 5. c. 20. 22:389,391} {*Cicero, Atticus, l. 5. c. 21. 22:399} {*Cicero, Friends, l. 2. c. 10. s. 2,3. 25:123,125} Dio gives a fuller account of this.

4812. When the Parthians were hoping to capture Antioch, Cassius drove them off, for they were very awkward at storming cities. They marched toward Antigonia. The suburbs of that city were planted with trees and so they dared not come near it, nor were they able to. They intended to cut down the trees and to clear the place of forest, so that they could attack the city more boldly on that side. This did not happen, because it was a lot of work, time was quickly passing and Cassius attacked any stragglers. So they retreated from Antigonia and planned to attack another place. In the meantime, Cassius had placed ambushes in the way along which they were to pass. First he showed himself to them with a few troops to draw them into pursuing him, then he turned on them. {*Dio, l. 40. (29) 3:449,451} Orsaces, the great commander of the Parthians, was wounded and died a few days later. {*Cicero, Atticus, l. 5. c. 20. 22:391} [E635]

4813. In Justin, this story is not recorded as accurately: {Justin, Trogus, l. 42. c. 4.}

"Pacorus was sent to pursue the remainder of the Roman army after he had achieved many things in Syria. He was recalled home because of the mistrust of his father. In his absence, the Parthian forces that had been left in Syria, along with all their captains, were wiped out by Cassius, the quaestor of Crassus."

4814. Livy stated that Gaius Cassius, the quaestor of Marcus Crassus, killed the Parthians who had marched into Syria. {*Livy, l. 108. 14:135} Velleius said that he very successfully routed the Parthians that had come into Syria. {*Velleius Paterculus, l. 2. c. 46. s. 4. 1:153} Sextus Rufus said that he valiantly fought against the Persians (which is what he called the Parthians) who had made an invasion into Syria, and utterly destroyed them, driving them beyond the Euphrates River. {Sextus Rufus, Breviary} Eutropius said that, with singular valour and great courage, he restored the state when it was as good as lost, in that he overcame the Persians in various battles. {Eutropius, l. 6.} Orosius added, concerning Cassius: {Orosius, l. 6. c. 13.}

"He overcame Antiochus in battle, killing him and his large forces, and through war he drove out the Parthians who had been sent into Syria by Orodes. They had advanced as far as Antioch. He killed their general, Orsaces."

4815. Cicero stated: {*Cicero, Philippics, l. 11. c. 14. 15:495}

"He did many gallant things before the arrival of Bibulus, the chief commander. He utterly routed the greatest commanders and the large forces of the Parthians thereby freeing Syria from a horrible invasion of the Parthians." [K312]

4816. The 41st chapter of the Jewish History, written in Arabic and entitled the second book of the Maccabees, adds something about Cassius that should not be accepted:

> "He crossed over the Euphrates River and conquered the Persians and brought them under the obedience of the Romans. He also secured the obedience of the twenty-two kings that Pompey had subdued and brought the countries of the east under their obedience."

*4817.* Orosius mentioned how Pompey bragged that he had made war with twenty-two kings. {*Orosius, l. 6. c. 6.*}

*4818.* The day before the Calends of October (September 29, or Julian July 11), the Senate was convened in the temple of Apollo. (Loeb edition translated it as September 30. The translator forgot that in the Republican calendar, September only had twenty-nine days, not thirty. Editor.) They decreed that henceforth propraetors who had formerly been praetors at Rome and had never had any command in any province should be sent into Cilicia and into eight other provinces. {*Cicero, Friends, l. 8. c. 8. s. 6. 26:137*}

*4819.* Cicero marched with his army through the pass of the Taurus Mountains into Cilicia, on the 3rd of the Nones of October (October 5, or Julian July 16). On the Nones of October (October 7, or Julian July 18), the Senate read the letters of Cassius, telling of his victory. He wrote that he had single-handedly ended the Parthian war. The letters of Cicero telling of the Parthian uprising, were also read. Thereupon, little credit was given to Cassius' letters. {*Cicero, Atticus, l. 5. c. 21. 22:399*} The same day, Cicero went from the Taurus Mountains toward the Amanus Mountain. {*Cicero, Friends, l. 3. c. 8. s. 10. 25:209,211*} This mountain belonged both to him and to Bibulus and divided Syria from Cilicia. It formed a divide for the watershed and was full of perpetual enemies to both provinces. {*Cicero, Friends, l. 2. c. 10. s. 2. 25:123,125*} {*Cicero, Atticus, l. 5. c. 20. 22:391*}

*4820.* The next day (October 8, or Julian July 19), he camped in the plain of Mopsuestia. He wrote his eighth letter to Appius Pulcher, whom he had succeeded in the proconsulship, and stated: {*Cicero, Friends, l. 3. c. 8. s. 10. 25:209,211*}

> "If you ask concerning the Parthians, I think there were none. The Arabians who were there and lived like Parthians, are all said to have pulled out. They deny that there was any enemy in Syria."

*4821.* When Cicero came to Amanus, he heard that the enemy had retreated from Antioch and that Bibulus was at Antioch. At Amanus, he learned that Dejotarus was fast approaching him with a large army of cavalry, foot soldiers and his entire forces. Cicero saw no reason why Dejotarus should leave his kingdom, so he immediately sent letters and messengers to him to stay there in case anything unusual should occur in his kingdom. {*Cicero, Friends, l. 15. c. 4. s. 7. 27:253*}

*4822.* Cicero considered that it was a matter of great concern for both provinces to secure Mount Amanus and eliminate the perennial enemy from that mountain. So he pretended to enter some other parts of Cilicia but when he had gone about a day's journey from Mount Amanus, he camped at Epiphanea. On the 4th of the Ides of October (October 12, or Julian July 23), toward evening, he marched so quickly with his army, that on the next day, at daybreak, he was able to go up the Amanus Mountain. {*Cicero, Friends, l. 15. c. 4. s. 8. 27:253*}

*4823.* He marshalled his cohorts and auxiliaries. He and his brother Quintus, his lieutenant, commanded some of these, while others were under his lieutenant, Gaius Pomptinus, and the rest under Marcus Anneius and Lucius Tullius. They came on the enemy suddenly, before they were aware of them, and many were killed or captured and the rest were scattered. *[K313]* Fugerana (or rather, Erana) which was more like a city than a village, because it was the main place in Amanus, along with Sepyra and Ceminoris (or Commoris), very stoutly resisted for a long time. Pomptinus attacked that part of Amanus from the break of day till ten o'clock. It was taken and a large number of the enemy were killed. Six well-fortified citadels were captured through their sudden arrival and more were burned. When they had done this, Cicero camped at the foot of the Amanus Mountain, at the altars of Alexander by the Issus River, where Darius had been defeated by Alexander. *[E636]* He stayed four days, destroying the remainder of Amanus that belonged to his province and in wasting the country. For this well-deserved victory, he was called *Imperator*, or *Captain General*, by the army. After he had spoiled and wasted Amanus, he left it on the sixth day. {*Cicero, Friends, l. 2. c. 10. s. 3. 25:125*} {*Cicero, Friends, l. 15. c. 4. s. 8,9. 27:253,255*} {*Cicero, Atticus, l. 5. c. 20. 22:391*} {*Plutarch, Cicero, l. 1. c. 36. s. 4,5. 7:175*}

*4824.* In the meantime, when Bibulus came to Amanus, he began to look for a needle in a haystack in seeking after the vain name of Imperator. However, he suffered a great defeat. He wholly lost his first cohort and a centurion of the vanguard who was a noble man and his relative, Asinius Dento. He also lost Sextus Lucilius, a colonel, who was the son of Titus Gravius Caepio, a rich and renowned man. {*Cicero, Atticus, l. 5. c. 20. 22:391,393*}

*4825.* Cicero brought his army to the most dangerous part of Cilicia, which was inhabited by the

Eleutherociles. They were a cruel and fierce people, who were well-armed. They had never obeyed their kings and at this time were hosting fugitives. They were daily expecting the arrival of the Parthians. Cicero attacked their town of Pindenissus, which was located in a steep and well-fortified site on the 12th of the Calends of November (October 20 or Julian August 1). They surrendered on the 57th day, on the day of the Saturnalia (the 14th of the Calends of January, or December 17, or the Julian September 27). He surrounded it with a rampart and a trench and contained them with six citadels and very large brigades. He attacked it with a mount, engines and an extremely high tower, employing many archers and a large number of battering rams. On the 25th day of the siege (November 14 or Julian August 25), Cicero wrote about this in a letter to Marcus Caelius Rufus, who had been chosen as aedile. {*Cicero, Friends, l. 2. c. 10. 25:123} This is also mentioned in his letters, written after the capture of the city, to Marcus Cato {*Cicero, Friends, l. 15. c. 4. s. 10. 27:255,257} and to Pomponius Atticus. {*Cicero, Atticus, l. 5. c. 20. 22:393}

### 3954a AM, 4663 JP, 51 BC

4826. Cicero accomplished what he had set out to do after much work and preparation, but at no cost to the allies. Many of his men were wounded, but the army was safe. On the very day of the Saturnalia (the 14th of the Calends of January, or December 17, or Julian September 26), his forces had the city of Pindenissus at their mercy. The entire city was either torn down or burned. He granted his soldiers all of the spoil from it except for the horses. The slaves were sold on the third day of the Saturnalia. He took hostages from the Tibareni, who were the next door neighbours to the city of Pindenissus and just as wicked and audacious. After this, he sent his army to their winter quarters under his brother, Quintus. The army was to be quartered in those places that had been taken from the enemy or that had not been fully subdued. {*Cicero, Atticus, l. 5. c. 20. 22:393} When he settled his affairs for the summer, he appointed his brother Quintus to command in the winter quarters and to be over Cilicia. {*Cicero, Atticus, l. 5. c. 21. 22:403} He had planned to use the summer months to carry out this war and the winter months to sit in judging cases. {*Cicero, Atticus, l. 5. c. 14. 22:373}

4827. Publius Lentulus Spinther held a triumph at Rome for Cilicia, as we gather from Cicero. {*Cicero, Atticus, l. 5. c. 21. 22:401} {*Cicero, Friends, l. 1. c. 9. s. 2. 25:49} [K314]

4828. The son of Orodes, king of the Parthians, came into Cyrrhestica, a country of Cilicia where the Parthians also wintered. {*Cicero, Atticus, l. 5. c. 21. 22:399} {*Cicero, Atticus, l. 6. c. 1. 22:431}

4829. Cicero sent Quintus Volusius, who was a trusted man and not liable to corruption by bribes, to Cyprus to stay there a few days. Hence, the few Roman citizens who had business to do there, would not be able to say they had not been handled fairly. The inhabitants could not be summoned to courts outside of their own island. {*Cicero, Atticus, l. 5. c. 21. 22:403}

4830. After being well received by the cities of Cilicia, Cicero went from the Taurus Mountains into Asia on the Nones of January (January 5, or Julian October 13), crossing over the Taurus Mountains in the sixth month of his command. Wherever he went, without using any violence or reproach, but only his authority and advice, he managed to achieve that the Greek and Roman citizens who had withheld their grain, promised to supply the people. For this was necessary because a great famine raged in much of that part of Asia since there had been no harvest. {*Cicero, Atticus, l. 5. c. 21. 22:403,405}

4831. Dejotarus (whose daughter was betrothed to the son of Artavasdes, the king of Armenia) helped Cicero greatly. He came to Laodicea to live with Cicero's children, and brought him news that Orodes intended to come into those regions at the beginning of summer with all the Parthian forces. {*Cicero, Atticus, l. 5. c. 20. 22:397} {*Cicero, Atticus, l. 5. c. 21. 22:399} {*Cicero, Atticus, l. 6. c. 1. 22:431}

4832. At Laodicea, from the Ides of February (February 13, or Julian November 29) to the Calends of May (May 1 or Julian February 26), Cicero held court for the part of Asia that belonged to him. From the Ides of February (February 13), he held it for Cibyra and Apamea, and from the Ides of March (March 15), for Synnada and Pamphylia. [E637] Many cities were freed from their debts and many had their financial burdens considerably eased. All of them used their own laws and judgments after being given permission to do so. They were all greatly restored to their former condition. {*Cicero, Atticus, l. 5. c. 21. 22:405} {*Cicero, Atticus, l. 6. c. 2. 22:447}

### 3954b AM, 4664 JP, 50 BC

4833. When Lucius Aemilius Paulus and Gaius Claudius Marcellus were consuls, the Senate at Rome decreed a triumph for Cicero because he had been victorious in Cilicia. {*Cicero, Friends, l. 2. c. 15. s. 1. 25:139} {*Cicero, Friends, l. 8. c. 11. s. 1. 26:155} {*Cicero, Friends, l. 15. c. 5. s. 2. 27:267} {*Cicero, Friends, l. 15. c. 6. s. 2. 27:271} {*Cicero, Friends, l. 15. c. 13. s. 3. 27:285} {*Cicero, Atticus, l. 7. c. 1. 23:7}

4834. When Gaius Cassius, who had been Marcus Crassus' quaestor, was about to leave Syria after the Parthian war, he commended Marcus Fadius to Cicero who was then at Laodicea. {*Cicero, Friends, l. 9. c. 25. s. 2. 26:279} {*Cicero, Friends, l. 15. c. 14. s. 1. 27:287} Cicero wrote back and congratulated him on the greatness of his deeds and the timing of his departure, for he was leaving the province while he carried great approval and was held in high esteem. Cicero advised him to hurry to Rome for his arrival would be very well-received because of his recent victory.

*4835.* Cicero commended his lieutenant Marcus Anneius, whose wisdom, virtue and fidelity had been proven in the war in Cilicia, to Quintus Thermus, the praetor of Asia. Thermus was to go and settle a dispute he had with the Sardinians and wanted Anneius to come with him. Cicero wanted him returned by the Calends of May (May 1), when he intended to go into Cilicia. {*Cicero, Friends, l. 13. c. 55. s. 1. 27:131,133} {*Cicero, Friends, l. 13. c. 57. s. 1. 27:137,139}

*4836.* Publius Cornelius Dolabella, who, a little later, was married to Tullia, the daughter of Cicero, accused Appius Claudius Pulcher of treason and bribery in his office, when he demanded a triumph at Rome for the good work he had done in Cilicia. *[K315]* As soon as Dolabella appeared before the tribunal, Appius entered the city and withdrew his demand for a triumph. Finally, when Quintus Hortensius and Marcus Brutus defended Appius, he was acquitted of both crimes. {*Cicero, Friends, l. 8. c. 6. s. 1. 26:121} {*Cicero, Friends, l. 8. c. 13. s. 1. 26:165} {*Cicero, Friends, l. 3. c. 10. s. 1. 25:217} {*Cicero, Friends, l. 3. c. 11. s. 1. 25:233} {*Cicero, Friends, l. 3. c. 12. s. 1. 25:239} {*Cicero, Atticus, l. 6. c. 6. 22:471} {*Cicero, Brutus, l. 1. c. 94. 5:281}

*4837.* The cavalrymen, whom Gabinius had left in Egypt, killed two sons of Marcus Bibulus, the proconsul. {*Caesar, Civil Wars, l. 3. (103) 2:345} {*Valerius Maximus, l. 4. c. 1. s. 15. 1:351,353} Cleopatra, the queen, sent the murderers to Bibulus in bonds for him to punish them as he wished. He soon sent them back to Cleopatra without harming them, saying that the authority to punish them belonged to the Senate and not to him. {*Valerius Maximus, l. 4. c. 1. s. 15. 1:351,353} {*Seneca, Ad Marciam, l. 1. c. 14. s. 2. 2:45}

*4838.* Cicero thought of going into Cilicia on the Nones of May (May 7). (Loeb English edition incorrectly wrote May 15. Editor.) {*Cicero, Friends, l. 2. c. 13. s. 4. 25:137} {*Cicero, Atticus, l. 6. c. 2. 22:447} However, he did not arrive at the Taurus Mountains before the Nones of June (June 5, or Julian April 2). Many things troubled him. A great war was on in Syria and there were many robbers in Cilicia. {*Cicero, Atticus, l. 6. c. 4. 22:463}

*4839.* He left there and while he was camped by the Pyramus River, Quintus Servilius sent him letters from Taurus that had been written by Appius Claudius Pulcher. They were dated at Rome on the Nones of April (April 5, or Julian February 1), and he wrote that he had been cleared of the charge of treason. {*Cicero, Friends, l. 3. c. 11. s. 1. 25:231,233}

*4840.* Syria was in turmoil with the Parthian war and there was great fear at Antioch. In spite of his sorrow over the murder of his sons, Bibulus managed the war. Although there were great hopes of having Cicero and his army to help them, Bibulus was reported to have said that he would rather endure anything than get help from Cicero. Hence, while he wrote to Thermus, the praetor of Asia, about the Parthian war, he never wrote to Cicero for help even though he knew that the greatest part of the war threatened Syria the most. Notwithstanding, his lieutenants sent letters to Cicero, asking him to come and help them. {*Cicero, Friends, l. 2. c. 17. 25:151-157} {*Cicero, Atticus, l. 6. c. 5. 22:469}

*4841.* Although Cicero's own army was weak, he had good auxiliaries from the Galatians, Pisidians and Lycians. He considered it his duty to have his army as near as possible to the enemy while he was in command in that province by the decree of the Senate. Since the term of his office only lasted a year and had almost expired, he agreed with Dejotarus that the king should be in his camp with all his forces. {*Cicero, Atticus, l. 6. c. 1. 22:431} {*Cicero, Atticus, l. 6. c. 5. 22:469} Cicero said about Dejotarus: {*Cicero, Philippics, l. 11. c. 13. 15:495}

> "I and Bibulus were both in command of the nearby and neighbouring provinces. Both of us were often helped by that king with cavalry and foot soldiers."

### 3954c AM, 4664 JP, 50 BC

*4842.* The Parthians kept Bibulus besieged. {*Caesar, Civil Wars, l. 3. (31) 2:241} As long as the Parthians were in the province, he stayed within the extremely well-fortified town with his men. {*Cicero, Friends, l. 12. c. 19. s. 2,3. 26:589} *[E638]* He never set foot outside the town as long as the Parthians were on the west side of the Euphrates River. {*Cicero, Atticus, l. 6. c. 8. 22:479} {*Cicero, Atticus, l. 7. c. 2. 23:17}

*4843.* The Parthians left Bibulus half dead with fright. {*Cicero, Atticus, l. 7. c. 2. 23:19} By an incredible stroke of good luck, Bibulus had set the Parthians at odds with one another. {*Cicero, Atticus, l. 6. c. 6. 22:473} {*Cicero, Atticus, l. 7. c. 1. 23:5} {*Cicero, Friends, l. 2. c. 17. 25:151} He befriended Ornodapates, who was a nobleman, and an enemy of Orodes. *[K316]* Through messengers who went back and forth between them, he persuaded him that he should make Pacorus king and with Bibulus' help, make war on Orodes. {*Dio, l. 40. (30) 3:451}

*4844.* Bibulus, in the letter he wrote to the Senate concerning the things that he had done, claimed to have done by himself alone those things which, in actual fact, he and Cicero had done together. He also said that those things, which Cicero had done alone, had been done by both of them together. Cicero complained of this in a letter he wrote to Sallust, Bibulus' quaestor. He also noted the mark of a poor, malicious and vain spirit, which he attributed not to Ariobarzanes, the king, but to his son (whom the Senate called king and whom it had commended to Cicero). {*Cicero, Friends, l. 2. c. 17. s. 7. 25:157} When Bibulus, who had done no great deeds, tried to obtain a triumph, Cicero thought it would be a disgrace to him not to obtain the same also. Bibulus' army set their hopes on Cicero's army. On the advice of his friends, Cicero also began to think of a triumph. {*Cicero, Atticus, l. 6. c. 6. 22:475} {*Cicero, Atticus, l. 6. c. 8. 22:479} {*Cicero, Atticus, l. 7. c. 2. 23:17}

4845. After the danger of the Parthians had passed, Cicero withdrew all the garrisons that he had provided for Apamea and other places which were good and strong. {*Cicero, Friends, l. 2. c. 17. s. 3. 25:153}

4846. About the 3rd of the Calends of August (July 30, or Julian May 26), Cicero's term of office was almost over, since it had only been for a year. According to the decree of the Senate, someone had to replace him when he left. So Cicero placed Gaius Caelius Caldus over the government of the province which had now been freed from the fear of the Parthian war. He had recently been sent to him from Rome to be his quaestor in place of Gnaeus Volusius, and was a noble young gentleman indeed, but one who lacked gravity and self-control. {*Cicero, Friends, l. 2. c. 15. s. 4. 25:141} {*Cicero, Friends, l. 2. c. 19. s. 1. 25:161} {*Cicero, Atticus, l. 6. c. 4. 22:465} {*Cicero, Atticus, l. 6. c. 6. 22:471}

4847. The 3rd of the Nones of August (August 3, or Julian May 29), when his annual command had expired, Cicero sailed to Sida, a city of Pamphylia. {*Cicero, Friends, l. 3. c. 12. s. 4. 25:243} From there, he went to Laodicea, the farthest boundary of the province. There he ordered his quaestor, Messinius, to wait for him while he went to leave his accounts in the province, according to the Julian law, in the two cities of Laodicea and Apamea. {*Cicero, Atticus, l. 6. c. 7. 22:475} {*Cicero, Friends, l. 2. c. 7. 25:115} {*Cicero, Friends, l. 5. c. 20. s. 2. 25:409} Cicero had not taken a penny of the plunder from Mount Amanus but had left it all, just as he had also left the yearly salary which was given to him. It amounted to a million sesterces and was put into the treasury. His cohort grumbled at this, thinking it ought to be distributed among them. He also safeguarded all the public money at Laodicea that it might be safely returned to him and to the people without any danger of loss. {*Cicero, Atticus, l. 7. c. 1. 23:9} {*Cicero, Friends, l. 2. c. 17. s. 4. 25:153}

4848. When the Senate had received Bibulus' letters, Cato persuaded the Senate to decree that a very large parade be held, lasting twenty days, for Marcus Bibulus. {*Cicero, Atticus, l. 7. c. 2. 23:17,19} {*Cicero, Atticus, l. 7. c. 3. 23:21} Those

legions were detained, which the Senate had decreed should be sent into Syria by Marius, who was to succeed Sallust in the office of quaestor. The province had now been freed from the fear of the Parthian war. {*Cicero, Friends, l. 2. c. 17. s. 1. 25:151} The Senate decreed that one legion from Gnaeus Pompey and another from Julius Caesar should be sent to Bibulus for the Parthian war. Pompey would not release any of the legions that he had with him. However, he commanded the commissioners of this matter to demand from Caesar the legion which Pompey had lent to Caesar. [K317] Caesar, although he did not doubt that his adversaries intended him to be left without any legions, sent Pompey back his legion and also gave another from his own number to satisfy the decree of the Senate. Hence these two legions were outfitted as though they were to be sent against the Parthians. However, since there was no need of them for that war, the consul Marcellus, fearing that they would be sent back to Caesar, kept them in Italy and gave them to Pompey. Although Caesar knew full well why these things had happened, he determined to endure everything, because he did not wish to be charged with disobedience and because it gave him an excuse to levy more soldiers. {*Caesar, Civil Wars, l. 1. (3) 2:5,7} {*Caesar, Gallic War, l. 8. (54,55) 1:589,591} {*Plutarch, Pompey, l. 1. c. 52. s. 3,4. 5:251} {*Dio, l. 40. (65,66) 3:505-509}

## 3954d AM, 4664 JP, 50 BC

4849. Cicero persuaded Quintus Thermus, the praetor, who was to depart from Asia, to leave his quaestor, a noble young gentleman, as governor of that province. [E639] His name was Gaius Antonius, as Pighius wrote in his annals. {Pighius, Annals of Rome, Tom. 3. p. 431.} {*Cicero, Friends, l. 2. c. 18. s. 2. 25:159}

4850. Cicero gave the tax collectors at Ephesus all the money which had lawfully come to him there, which was twenty-two hundred sesterces. {*Cicero, Friends, l. 5. c. 20. s. 9. 25:419} He was seriously hindered by the Etesian winds and sailed from Ephesus on the Calends of October (October 1, or Julian July 25). He landed at Rhodes for the sake of his children. {*Cicero, Atticus, l. 6. c. 8. 22:477} {*Plutarch, Cicero, l. 1. c. 37. s. 5. 7:175} {*Cicero, Atticus, l. 6. c. 7. 22:475} {*Cicero, Friends, l. 2. c. 17. s. 1. 25:151} There he heard of Hortensius' death. {*Cicero, Brutus, l. 1. c. 1. 5:19}

4851. With the winds against him, Cicero arrived at Athens on the day before the Ides of October (October 14, or Julian August 7). {*Cicero, Friends, l. 14. c. 5. s. 1. 27:201} {*Cicero, Atticus, l. 6. c. 9. 22:479}

4852. As the civil war between Caesar and Pompey approached (Julian August 21), a little after sunrise, the sun was eclipsed almost two digits (about 17%). Pertronius seems to make reference to this in the signs of this war:

For blondy Sol appeared with visage like to death,
Thou d'st think the civil wars just then began to
    breathe.

4853. Bibulus left Asia on the 5th of the Ides of December (December 9, or Julian October 1). {*Cicero, Atticus, l. 7. c. 3. 23:25}

## 3955a AM, 4664 JP, 50 BC

4854. On the Calends of January (January 1, or Julian October 22), when Gaius Claudius Marcellus and Lucius Cornelius Lentulus assumed the office of consuls, the Senate decreed that Caesar should dismiss his army before a certain day and that, were he to refuse, this action would be assumed to be against the state. In vain had Mark Antony and Quintus Cassius, the tribunes of the people, interceded against this decree, which marked the beginning of the civil war between Caesar and Pompey. {*Caesar, Civil Wars, l. 1. (2) 2:5} {*Cicero, Philippics, l. 2. c. 21. 15:115} {*Velleius Paterculus, l. 2. c. 49. s. 1. 1:159} {*Dio, l. 41. (1) 4:3,5}

4855. On the day before the Nones of January (January 4, or Julian October 25), Cicero came to the city. He was given such a welcome, that nothing could have conferred greater honour. This took place just before the civil war. {*Cicero, Friends, l. 16. c. 11. s. 2. 27:341} [K318] He did not enter the city. Amid these troubles, a packed Senate earnestly demanded a triumph for him. Lentulus, the consul, deferred this request, in order to intensify his own honour. {*Cicero, Friends, l. 16. c. 11. s. 3. 27:341,343} {*Cicero, Atticus, l. 7. c. 1. 23:9} Since the Senate had decreed a triumph for him, Cicero said that he would rather see peace made and follow Caesar's chariot in a triumph than hold his own triumph. {*Plutarch, Cicero, l. 1. c. 37. s. 1. 7:175} However, the discord increased and neither Bibulus nor Cicero ever received a triumph. {*Cicero, Atticus, l. 9. c. 2. 23:181-185} {*Cicero, Atticus, l. 9. c. 6. 23:199} {*Cicero, Atticus, l. 11. c. 6. 23:367}

4856. On the 7th of the Ides of January (January 7, or Julian October 28), the Senate decreed that the consuls, praetors, tribunes of the people, and all the proconsuls who were in the city (of whom Cicero was one) should do their utmost to prevent the state from being harmed. The tribunes of the people, who had opposed that decree of the Senate, immediately fled from the city and went to Caesar. {*Caesar, Civil Wars, l. 1. (5) 2:9} {*Cicero, Friends, l. 16. c. 11. s. 2. 27:341} {*Dio, l. 41. (2) 4:7,9}

4857. The next day, when the Senate convened outside the city and Pompey was also present, the provinces were assigned to private men; two of them were for the consuls, the rest were assigned to the praetors. Syria was given to Scipio. {*Caesar, Civil Wars, l. 1. (6) 2:11,13} This was Metellus Scipio who had married his daughter Cornelia, the widow of Publius Crassus who had been killed by

the Parthians, to Pompey. {*Velleius Paterculus, l. 2. c. 54. s. 2. 1:169} Scipio, who three years before had been Pompey's colleague in the consulship, this year shared Syria with him (that is, this year being two years before Pompey was killed). {*Plutarch, Pompey, l. 1. c. 55. s. 1. 5:261} {*Dio, l. 40. (51) 3:485} Sextius, or Sestius, succeeded Cicero in the province of Cilicia. {*Cicero, Friends, l. 5. c. 20. s. 6. 25:415} {*Cicero, Atticus, l. 11. c. 7. 23:369} He was sent to Cyprus, which from this time on was distinct from Cilicia, as the first quaestor with praetorian authority. {*Cicero, Friends, l. 13. c. 48. 27:121} The three governments of Asia—Cibyra, Synnada and Apamea—were taken from the province of Cilicia and given to the new proconsul of Asia, Publius Servilius Sigonius. {*Cicero, Friends, l. 13. c. 67. 27:155} {*Cicero, De Provinciis Consularibus, l. 1. c. 12. 13:577}

4858. On the same day, on the 8th of the Calends of March (February 22, or Julian December 11), the Feralia was celebrated. {Gruter, Inscriptions, p. 133.} [E640] Caesar came from Corsinium to Brundisium in the afternoon of that day and Pompey came from Canusium in the morning. Autumn was already past. {*Cicero, Atticus, l. 8. c. 14. 23:163} {*Cicero, Atticus, l. 9. c. 1. 23:177} {*Dio, l. 41. (14) 4:27}

4859. Pompey sent his father-in-law Scipio and his son Gnaeus from Brundisium to Syria to raise a fleet. {*Plutarch, Pompey, l. 1. c. 62. s. 2. 5:279} In a letter that Cicero wrote on the day before the Nones of March (March 6, or Julian December 23), he stated that Scipio went into Syria either because the lot fell to him, or for the honour of his son-in-law, or because he was fleeing from an angry Caesar. {*Cicero, Atticus, l. 9. c. 1. 23:179}

4860. On the 7th of the Ides of March (March 9, or Julian December 26), Caesar came to Brundisium and camped before its walls, as he wrote in a letter to Oppius and Cornelius Balbus. {*Cicero, Atticus, l. 9. c. 13a. 23:251}

## 3955b AM, 4665 JP, 49 BC

4861. On the 16th of the Calends of April (March 17, or Julian January 3), according to Cicero (not three days before March, as is recorded in Lipsius, in the 31st epistle of the century to the Germans and Frenchmen), the Liberalia was celebrated. {*Cicero, Atticus, l. 9. c. 9. 23:225} This is recorded in the marble records. {Gruter, Inscriptions, p. 133.} [K319] Pompey, with all the forces at his disposal sailed from Brundisium to Epirus on the very day of the Liberalia, or Dionysia. Pompey's sons were defeated at the battle of Munda in Spain, exactly four years after the time when their father was said to have gone to war. {*Plutarch, Caesar, l. 1. c. 56. s. 1-3. 7:571,573} This was the same day when their father Pompey left Italy and made Greece the centre of the civil war. It was not that he fled from the city to make war, as Orosius mistakenly wrote. {Orosius, l. 6. c. 16.}

*4862.* The next day Caesar entered Brundisium, made a speech and marched toward Rome. He wanted to be at the city before the first of the next month. {*Cicero, Atticus, l. 9. c. 15. 23:261}

*4863.* From there, Caesar sent Aristobulus to his own country of Palestine to do something against Pompey. {*Dio, l. 41. (18) 4:35} Josephus stated that Caesar sent Aristobulus into Syria after freeing him from prison. He gave him two legions to enable him to keep the province in order more easily. Both their plans were thwarted. Aristobulus was poisoned by Pompey's supporters and buried by Caesar's faction. {*Josephus, Jewish War, l. 1. c. 9. s. 1. (183,184) 2:85,87} {*Josephus, Antiq., l. 14. c. 7. s. 4. (123,124) 7:513}

*4864.* Alexander, the son of Aristobulus, was beheaded at Antioch by Scipio, according to Pompey's letters. First, he was publicly accused of what he had done against the Romans. But Ptolemy, the son of Mennaeus, governor of Chalcis, which was located at the foot of Mount Lebanon in the Lebanon valley, had sent his son Philippion to Askelon to the wife of Aristobulus. He sent for her son Antigonus and her two daughters. The younger daughter was called Alexandra and Philippion fell in love with her and married her. {*Josephus, Jewish War, l. 1. c. 9. s. 2. (185,186) 2:87} {*Josephus, Antiq., l. 14. c. 7. s. 4. (126) 7:515} Pompey had a year in which to raise forces. Since he was free from war and as his enemy was not active, he assembled a large fleet from Asia, the Cyclades Islands, Corcyra, Athens, Pontus, Bithynia, Syria, Cilicia, Phoenicia and Egypt. He saw to it that a large navy was built in every place and he also exacted large sums of money from Asia, Syria, and all the kings, governors, tetrarchs and the free people of Achaia. He forced the provinces that had been allocated to him to pay him large sums of money. {*Caesar, Civil Wars, l. 3. (3) 2:199} It was reported that sixty ships were sent to him from Egypt by Cleopatra and Ptolemy, who were but a child king and queen of Egypt at the time. He also had auxiliaries from Ionia, archers from Crete, javelin throwers from Pontus and cavalry from Galatia. The Commagenians were sent from Antiochus. Cilicians and Cappadocians and Lesser Armenia supplied some troops. The Pamphylians and Pisidians also came to him. {*Appian, Civil Wars, l. 2. c. 8. (49) 3:319} {*Appian, Civil Wars, l. 2. c. 10. (71) 3:359}

*4865.* Marcus Cato was sent into Asia by Pompey to help those who were gathering the fleet and soldiers. He took his sister Servilia along with him and a son that Lucullus had by her. After he had persuaded the Rhodians to side with Pompey, he left Servilia and her son with them and returned to Pompey. Pompey was well furnished with very strong land and naval forces. {*Plutarch, Cato Minor, l. 1. c. 54. s. 1,2. 8:363,365} It was Pompey's intention to make

war across the whole world on land and sea and to stir up barbarous kings and bring armed and cruel nations into Italy. {*Cicero, Atticus, l. 8. c. 11. 23:131}

*4866.* Pompey also tried to draw Orodes, the king of the Parthians, onto his side. Although Pompey was considered an enemy after the death of Crassus, Orodes promised him his help if he were given Syria. [K320] Because Pompey did not grant him Syria, he brought no forces, although otherwise the Parthians were on Pompey's side. {*Dio, l. 41. (55) 4:95} They favoured Pompey because of the friendship they had made in the Mithridatic War and also because they had heard, after the death of Crassus, that Crassus' son was on Caesar's side and they knew that his son would revenge his father's death, if Caesar won the war. {Justin, Trogus, l. 42. c. 4.} [E641]

*4867.* Pompey used a large fleet which he had together from Alexandria, Colchis, Tyre, Sidon, Andros (or rather, Aradus), Cyprus, Pamphylia, Lycia, Rhodes, Byzantium, Lesbos, Smyrna, Miletus and Cos. They were to intercept the provisions from Italy and to seize the provinces from where the grain was coming. {*Cicero, Atticus, l. 9. c. 9. 23:219}

*4868.* Pompey's son was the admiral of the Egyptian fleet. Decius Laelius and Gaius Triarius were in charge of the Asiatic fleet, while Gaius Cassius was over the Syrian fleet and Gaius Marcellus over the Rhodian fleet. Gaius Coponius commanded the light ships and the Achaean fleet was under Scribonius Libo and Marcus Octavius. Marcus Bibulus was the chief admiral over all the naval forces. {*Caesar, Civil Wars, l. 3. (5) 2:203}

## 3956a AM, 4665 JP, 49 BC

*4869.* Julius Caesar was made dictator. After eleven days, he and Publius Servilius Isauricus were declared consuls and so Caesar resigned his dictatorship. {*Caesar, Civil Wars, l. 3. (1,2) 2:197,199} {*Plutarch, Caesar, l. 1. c. 37. s. 1. 7:531,533} {*Appian, Civil Wars, l. 2. c. 7. (48) 3:317}

*4870.* It was from this first dictatorship of Caesar that the Macedonians of Syria began their reckoning of the time of the Caesars. (This fact was mentioned on an old marble monument. {Gruter, Inscriptions, p. 287.}) The date was the 24th of the Julian September. {Ussher, Macedonian and Asiatic Year} From that day, not only the Macedonian, but also the Roman, emperors began their indictions, or their cycle of fifteen years. The people of Antioch reckoned the same way, which was divided by fifteen and always showed the indictions of the emperors although the form of the year was later changed and the Macedonian months brought into conformity with the Italian ones. The Antiochians identified the beginning of their period, and the rest of the Eastern people the beginning of their indictions, with the beginning of their new year, and moved it from the 24th of September to the first of September. No matter what may have been said concerning the origin of the indictions (which they commonly attributed to the times of Constantine), it ought to be beyond controversy, that the start of the Antiochian period is to be determined from September 49 BC, or 4665 JP.

4871. At the end of the year when Marcellus and Lentulus were consuls, Pompey was made general of the Romans, and the Senate, which was with him in Ephesus, bestowed honours on kings and other people who had earned them. Lucan mentioned: {*Lucan, l. 5. (50-60) 1:243}

> Phoebus sea-powerful Rhodes rewarded was,
> And Spartans rough, praised were the Athenian
> Phocis made free where Massilians:
> Faithful Dejotarus, young Sadala,
> The valiant Cotys and Rhascyporlis [K321]
> Of Macedonia were praised: Juba to thee
> The Senate gives all Libya by decree.

4872. (Salala was the son of Cotys, king of Thrace, Rhascypolis, was a commander from Macedonia. {*Caesar, Civil Wars, l. 3. (4) 2:201}) Lucan affirmed that it was by the same method that the kingdom of Egypt was confirmed to Ptolemy at this time though he was little more than a child. Lucan mentioned the words attributed to Pothinus, the governor of Ptolemy, referring to Pompey: {*Lucan, l. 8. (518) 1:475}

> …The Senate gave to me
> The sceptre, when persuaded to it by thee.

4873. About the winter solstice, Caesar sent messengers to the army telling them to meet him at Brundisium. He departed from Rome in the month of December, not expecting to assume his office as consul on the first day of the next year. This is why Appian thought that the account of the Roman year was the same at that time as it was later in his own time. {*Appian, Civil Wars, l. 2. c. 9. (48) 3:337} However, the first of January, when Caesar was to begin his second consulship, corresponded to the Julian October 11. [E642] Florus made a similar mistake and asserted that Caesar had sailed to go to the war, even though it was the middle of winter. {*Florus, l. 2. c. 13. s. 36,37. 1:279} Plutarch also wrote that Caesar arrived at Brundisium shortly after the winter solstice and left there in the beginning of the month of January, which he said corresponded to the Athenian month of Posideion. {*Plutarch, Pompey, l. 1. c. 65. s. 2,3. 5:285} Indeed, Caesar confirmed that he set sail with seven legions on the day before the Nones of January (January 4) and the next day he landed at the Ceraunia Rocks. {*Caesar, Civil Wars, l. 3. (6) 2:203} However, this was not the Julian

January, on which the Athenian month of Posideion fell in the time of Plutarch, but it corresponded to the month of the Roman year used then. The 5th of January, when Caesar landed at the Ceraunia Rocks, corresponded to the Julian October 15, with winter approaching. Thereupon, Pompey marched to his winter quarters from Ephesus to Apollonia and Dyrrachium, as Caesar showed later. By no means was it the height of winter.

4874. Pompey provided for a large quantity of grain from Thessaly, Asia, Egypt, Crete, Cyrene and other countries. He planned to winter in Dyrrachium, in Apollonia and in all the coastal towns in order to prevent Caesar from crossing the sea, although this did not prevent Caesar from coming. {*Caesar, Civil Wars, l. 3. (5) 2:203}

4875. Scipio, the governor of Syria and the father-in-law of Pompey, received some casualties near Mount Amanus and declared himself Imperator. After this, he imposed large sums of money on the cities and the tyrants, as well as extracting two years of taxes from the tax collectors of the province. From them, he borrowed the money for the following year, while ordering the whole province to provide him with cavalry. When all the forces had come together, he turned his back on the Parthians, who were enemies on his border, and marched from Syria with his legions and cavalry. When the soldiers complained that they would go against an enemy but not against the consul and their fellow-citizens, he brought the legions into the richest cities, like Pergamum, for their winter quarters. He gave large bribes and to bind the soldiers more firmly to him, he allowed them to plunder these cities. {*Caesar, Civil Wars, l. 3. (31) 2:239,241}

4876. In the meantime, the taxes that had been imposed on the cities, was collected in a very cruel manner. Generally speaking, many things were done out of covetousness. The tribute was imposed on both bond and free. [K322] A tax was imposed on pillars and doors, for soldiers and mariners, for arms and engines and wagons. The fact that anything had a name, was sufficient reason for taxing it. Governors were appointed, who were given commands, not only over cities and citadels, but even villages. The one who did any given thing most outrageously and cruelly, was considered the best man and the best citizen. The province was full of lictors and commanders and was over-burdened with petty governors and tax collectors, who collected the money they were supposed to and also lined their own pockets. They said that they had been expelled from their own houses and country and so needed all the things necessary. This excuse was to whitewash their business with some honest pretence. In addition to these exactions, large interest-bearing loans were incurred, which mainly happen in wartime. In the matter of loans, they said that postponing the day of payment was termed a free gift. As a result, the debt of the whole province was multiplied greatly in these two years. No less money was exacted for this cause from the Roman citizens of the province than was exacted upon all the guilds, and a fixed amount of money was demanded from every city. They told them that they were borrowing this money by the decree of the Senate. {*Caesar, Civil Wars, l. 3. (32) 2:241,243}

4877. Moreover, at Ephesus, Scipio ordered that the money, which had been deposited in the temple of Diana, should be taken from there. As he entered the temple, accompanied by all the senators whom he had called together for this purpose, he received letters from Pompey saying that Caesar had crossed the sea with his legions and that he should set everything else aside and quickly come to Pompey with his army. As soon as he had received these letters, he dismissed the men whom he had called to him and began to prepare for his march into Macedonia. A few days later, he left, thereby sparing the money at Ephesus. {*Caesar, Civil Wars, l. 3. (33) 2:243}

4878. In the meantime, besides the Roman and Italian legions, Pompey had two legions in his army which Lentulus the consul had raised. He also had archers from Crete, Lacedemon, Pontus, Syria and other countries, making a total of three thousand and two cohorts of six hundred slingers each. He had seven thousand cavalry, of which Dejotarus had brought five hundred Galatians and Ariobarzanes had brought five hundred from Cappadocia. From Egypt came five hundred Gauls and Germans, whom Gabinius had left at Alexandria to guard King Ptolemy and the son that Pompey had brought with the fleet. Tarcondarius Castor and Domnilaus sent three hundred troops from Galatia. One of them came along himself, the other sent his son. [E643] Antiochus, the Commagenian, on whom Pompey had bestowed large rewards, sent two hundred, among whom were many archers on horseback. It was anticipated that Scipio would bring two legions from Syria. {*Caesar, Civil Wars, l. 3. (4) 2:201}

### 3956b AM, 4666 JP, 48 BC

4879. After Caesar arrived at Ephesus, many months passed and winter came on. Neither the ships nor legions that had left Brundisium ever reached Caesar. However, Mark Antony and Fusius Calenus sailed with a fair south wind and brought three legions of veterans with them to Caesar and one recently raised legion, along with eight hundred cavalry. When Quintus Coponius, who was commanding the Rhodian fleet at Dyrrachium, tried to hinder the ships, a storm arose and so troubled the fleet. Sixteen ships were driven

against one another and perished through shipwreck. Most of the mariners and soldiers were dashed against the rocks and killed. Some, who were dispersed by Caesar's forces, were saved alive by Caesar and sent home again. {*Caesar, Civil Wars, l. 3. (26,27) 2:233,235} [K323]

4880. In Egypt, the young Ptolemy, with help from his relatives and friends, expelled Cleopatra, who was his wife and sister, from the kingdom. {*Caesar, Civil Wars, l. 3. (103) 2:343,354} {*Livy, l. 111. 14:139} Lucan recorded the complaint of Cleopatra: {*Lucan, l. 10. (95) 1:597}

> But all his power, will and affections be
> Under Pothinus' belt....

4881. Strabo stated how she was expelled by the lad's friends who instigated a rebellion. {*Plutarch, Caesar, l. 1. c. 48. s. 3. 7:557} This affair was attributed to Pothinus (as his name reads in Caesar), who was the governor at the time that Ptolemy ruled the kingdom and whom the Greek writers call Potheinus, which is more likely to be correct. After Cleopatra was expelled, she left for Syria with her sister to raise an army. {*Strabo, l. 17. c. 1. s. 11. 8:47} {*Appian, Civil Wars, l. 2. c. 13. (90) 3:393}

4882. When Pharnaces, the son of Mithridates, king of Pontus, and himself king of Cimmerian Bosphorus, heard that there was civil war among the Romans, he hoped it would continue for a long time. Since Caesar was not nearby, he revolted from the Romans in the hope of regaining all his father's former possessions. He committed the government and defence of Bosphorus to Asander. Without meeting much resistance, he subdued Colchis and all Armenia, along with the kingdom of Moschis, where he plundered the temple of Leucothea, as Strabo noted. {*Strabo, l. 11. c. 2. s. 17. 5:213} Since Dejotarus was absent, he added to these conquests some cities of Cappadocia and Pontus that belonged to the jurisdiction of Bithynia. {*Dio, l. 41. (63) 4:109} He also captured Sinope and marched toward Amisus but was at that time not able to capture it. {*Appian, Mithridatic Wars, l. 12. c. 17. (120) 2:473}

4883. Pompey secretly sent his wife Cornelia to the isle of Lesbos, so that she could live quietly at Mitylene, free from all the troubles of the wars. {*Lucan, l. 5. (785) 1:299} She was accompanied by her son-in-law Sextius and the younger son of Pompey. {*Plutarch, Pompey, l. 1. c. 66. s. 3. 5:287} {*Dio, l. 42. (2) 4:117} Lucan, however, said that the younger son stayed in the camp with his father. {*Lucan, l. 6. (825) 1:365}

4884. Lucius Hirtius (otherwise called Hirrius) was sent as an envoy to the Parthians (as we understand from Caesar {*Caesar, Civil Wars, l. 3. (82) 2:313}), but did not get any help from Orodes. Instead he was thrown into prison by him contravening the universally accepted law concerning the treatment of envoys. {*Dio, l. 42. (47) 4:189} Orodes did this, because he was not given Syria. {*Dio, l. 41. (55) 4:95}

## 3956c AM, 4666 JP, 48 BC

4885. Caesar besieged Pompey in Dyrrachium for four months with large siege works. The fighting at Dyrrachium was intense; in one day, six battles were fought, three at the outer works and three at Dyrrachium. Over two thousand of Pompey's troops were killed, while Caesar lost about twenty men. However, almost everyone of Caesar's troops was wounded. To prove how intense the battle was, Caesar's troops counted over thirty thousand arrows which they collected after the battles. They showed Caesar the shield of Scaeva, a centurion, which had a hundred and twenty holes in it! Caesar promoted Scaeva and gave him two hundred thousand sesterces. {*Caesar, Civil Wars, l. 3. (53) 2:271,273} Finally, Pompey was utterly defeated in the battle of Pharsalia. {*Suetonius, Julius, l. 1. c. 35. s. 1. 1:79}

4886. Caesar came into Thessaly (when the battle at Palaeo-Pharsalia had been fought), and a few days later Pompey also came, when the grain started to ripen. {*Caesar, Civil Wars, l. 3. (49) 2:267} Appian also confirmed that Caesar was very short of food at the time that the battle was fought, implying that the harvest was not yet ready. On the other hand, Pompey had secured the roads and controlled the sea. Provisions came to him in abundance from every quarter. {*Appian, Civil Wars, l. 2. c. 10. (66) 3:349} Lucan stated that it was approaching the time of the grain harvest. {*Lucan, l. 7. (98) 1:377} It was in the middle of summer and very hot weather, if we believe Plutarch. {*Plutarch, Brutus, l. 1. c. 4. s. 6,7. 6:135}

4887. On the same day that the battle was being fought at Pharsalia, people at Antioch twice heard such a shouting of an army, such sounding of alarms and rattling of arms that the whole city ran up to the wall with their weapons. [K324] The same thing happened at Ptolemais. At Pergamum, from the vestry of the temple of Bacchus, which it was only lawful for the priests to enter, a loud noise of drums and cymbals started and went through the whole city. A growing palm tree sprang up to full grown size in Tralles in the Temple of Victory between the joints of the stones below the statue of Caesar. [E644] The Syrians also had two young men appear to them who declared the result of the battle and then were never seen again. {*Caesar, Civil Wars, l. 3. (105) 2:347} {*Julius Obsequens, Prodigies, l. 1. c. 65a. 14:307} {*Plutarch, Caesar, l. 1. c. 43. s. 2,3. 7:547} {*Dio, l. 41. (61) 4:105}

4888. Almost all the countries which lived around the sea toward the east were represented in the army of Pompey. There were troops from the Thracians, Hellespontians, Bithynians, Phrygians, Ionians, Lydians, Pamphylians, Pisidians, Paphlagonians, Cilicians, Syrians, Phoenicians, Hebrews and their neighbours the Arabians, Cypriots, Rhodians, Cretian slingers and other islanders. There were kings and governors: Dejotarus, the tetrarch of Galatia and Ariarathes, the king of the Cappadocians, Taxiles, who led the Armenians on this side of the Euphrates and Megabates, the lieutenant of King Artapates, who led those beyond the Euphrates. Other minor princes helped also, according to their power. {*Appian, Civil Wars, l. 2. c. 10. (71) 3:359} Since most of his army consisted of Asians, who were not used to the wars, Pompey was defeated. {*Dio, l. 41. (61) 4:105} Petronius also stated:

> He who made Pontus and Hydaspes quake,
> Did quell the pirates, by his triumph shake
> Three times great Jove, to whom Pontus submits wave
> And likewise Posphors their submission gave
> To his shame! has fled and left the name Imperator.

4889. Though Caesar had taken Pompey's files, he did not read the private letters showing their goodwill toward Pompey, or their displeasure with Caesar, nor did he make copies of them. In a gesture of goodwill, he soon burned them all lest he should be compelled by the content of the letters to act too severely against any man. {*Pliny, l. 7. c. 25. 2:567} {*Dio, l. 41. (63) 4:109,111} He later pardoned the kings and the people who had helped Pompey and did not impose any punishment on them, except for two monetary fines. For Caesar considered that he had previously either very few, or no dealings with any of them. However Pompey had deserved very much at their hands and Caesar commended those far more highly who had received favours from Pompey and yet had forsaken him in his greatest dangers. {*Dio, l. 41. (63) 4:109,111}

4890. Pompey left the camp and fled to Larisa, with very few accompanying him. He did not enter the city, although invited to do so by the citizens, lest the city should be punished for receiving him. At a later time, he would even ask them to seek the victor's friendship. When he had received the necessary supplies from them, he set off toward the sea. {*Dio, l. 42. (2) 4:117}

4891. Gaius Cassius came into Cilicia with a fleet of Syrians, Phoenicians, and Cilicians. After having burned Caesar's ships, he learned of the battle that had been fought in Thessaly and departed with his fleet. {*Caesar, Civil Wars, l. 3. (101) 2:339,341}

4892. After the battle of Pharsalia, the Rhodian fleet under Gaius Coponius deserted Pompey's side and returned home. {*Cicero, De Divinatione, l. 1. c. 32. 20:299} [K325]

4893. Lucius Lentulus (Crus), who the previous year had been consul to Publius Lentulus (Spinther), and others who had followed Pompey from the flight, arrived at Rhodes. They were not received into either the town or the port. After they had sent messengers to them, they were ordered, against their will, to get out of Rhodes. {*Caesar, Civil Wars, l. 3. (102) 2:343}

4894. Caecilius Bassus, an equestrian on Pompey's side, withdrew to Tyre. He hid himself in the market where merchants used to trade, according to Livy. {*Dio, l. 47. (26) 5:169} {*Appian, Civil Wars, l. 3. c. 11. (77) 4:99}

4895. Marcus Claudius Marcellus was afraid of Caesar and went to Mitylene. He lived there quite happily in the study of good arts. (Seneca related this from Brutus, in his conciliation to Albina.) Cicero tried in vain to persuade him to return from there to Rome and ask pardon of Caesar. {*Cicero, Friends, l. 4. c. 7.8. 25:281-291}

4896. Labienus left the battle at Pharsalia and brought news of the defeat of Pompey's army to Dyrrachium, where Marcus Cato was, with fifteen cohorts and three hundred galleys. Thereupon, both he and Cicero, and others who were with them, sailed away in fear. As they looked back toward the town, they saw all their cargo ships on fire because the remaining soldiers had burned them since they would not follow them. [E645] Cato crossed to Corcyra (an island located south of Epirus, in the Ionian and Adriatic sea), where the fleet was containing those who had fled in fear. He took the remainder that had fled from the battle of Pharsalia, or had simply followed Pompey. Lucius Scipio, the father-in-law of Pompey, Labienus, Africanus and many other famous men, escaped from the battle. A little later Octavius, who was guarding the Ionian sea, had taken Gaius Antony with him and joined himself with Cato's fleet. Also, Gnaeus Pompey (oldest son of Pompey the Great), who was sailing in the Egyptian fleet, had made incursions into Epirus. But when his father was defeated, the Egyptians went home and he went to Corcyra. Cassius, who had attacked Sicily, fled along with others to Cato whom they had observed to surpass all others in virtue. {*Cicero, De Divinatione, l. 1. c. 32. 20:301} {*Plutarch, Cato Minor, l. 1. c. 55. s. 3. 8:371} {*Appian, Civil Wars, l. 2. c. 12. (87) 3:387} {*Dio, l. 42. (10) 4:131}

4897. There, Cato resigned his command to Cicero, since Cato was only a praetor and the others had been consuls, which was a higher rank. When Cicero refused, as he was not suited for military life and wanted to leave the wars, he was almost killed. {*Livy, l. 111. 14:139} The young Pompey and his friends called him a traitor and drew their swords to kill him. Cato withstood them and

kept Cicero from being killed by withdrawing him from the camp. {*Plutarch, Cato Minor, l. 1. c. 55. s. 3. 8:371} {*Plutarch, Cicero, l. 1. c. 39. s. 1,2. 7:181}

4898. After this, the fleet was divided among Pompey's main friends. Cassius sailed into Pontus to Pharnaces, with the intent of stirring him up against Caesar. Scipio sailed into Africa, with Varus and his forces accompanying him, as well as the auxiliaries of Juba and Moor. {*Appian, Civil Wars, l. 2. c. 12. (87) 3:387}

4899. Cato, surmising that Pompey had fled either into Africa or Egypt, hurried after him. Before he sailed, he gave all those who were not willing to follow him, permission either to leave him or go with him. {*Plutarch, Cato Minor, l. 1. c. 56. s. 1,2. 8:371} Lucan described the voyage like this: {*Lucan, l. 9. (32-41) 1:507} [K326]

> He sails to Corcyra's shore,
> And in a thousand ships carries away
> The conquered remnant of Pharsalia.
> Who would have thought so large a fleet had held
> All fleeing men? That conquered ships had filled
> The straitened seas? From there they sailed away
> To Ghost field Taenarum, and long Malea,
> There to Cythera: Boreas blowing fair,
> Crete flies and getting a good sea they clear
> The Cretan coast; Phycus, that dared deny
> Their men to land, they sack deservedly.

4900. Phycus was a promontory of the country of Cyrene and a town, as the poet noted, whose plunder Cato gave to his soldiers. Leaving Cato, we will now continue the narrative of Pompey the Great's flight and Julius Caesar's pursuit of him.

### 3956d AM, 4666 JP, 48 BC

4901. Caesar stayed two days at Pharsalia to offer sacrifices for the victory he had won and to refresh his soldiers, who were tired after the battle. {*Appian, Civil Wars, l. 2. c. 13. (88) 3:389} On the third day, he pursued Pompey, for he thought it best to set aside everything else and to pursue Pompey wherever he went, lest he should be forced to raise new forces and so renew the war against Pompey. Each day, therefore, he went with his cavalry as far as he possibly could, while commanding one legion to follow him in shorter marches. {*Caesar, Civil Wars, l. 3. (102) 2:341}

4902. Pompey came to the sea and rested all night in a fisherman's cottage. [E646] About daybreak, he boarded a ferry and taking all the freemen with him, ordered all the slaves to go to Caesar without any fear; then he left the land. {*Plutarch, Pompey, l. 1. c. 73. s. 3. 5:307} Concerning this, Lucan wrote: {*Lucan, l. 8. (33-36) 1:439}

Now to the shore he came where Peneus ran
Red with Pharsalia's slaughter to the main;
There a small barque unfit for seas and winds,
Scarce safe in shallowest rivers Pompey finds
And goes aboard....

4903. As he sailed along the shore in this boat, he saw a large ship under sail, whose captain was Peticius, a Roman citizen. He knew Pompey and took him from the boat into the ship, together with the two Lentuli (who had been consuls who, as we have shown from Caesar's writings, were prevented from landing in Rhodes), Favonius (who had been praetor {*Velleius Paterculus, l. 2. c. 53. s. 1. 1:167}), and all the others who had wanted to come. Shortly after this, King Dejotarus, who trusted the omens deduced from the flight of birds, came to Pompey when he thought the birds portended good success for Pompey. {*Cicero, De Divinatione, l. 1. c. 15. 20:253,255} When the men saw him riding toward them from the land, they took him in as well. {*Plutarch, Pompey, l. 1. c. 73. s. 5-7. 5:307,309}

4904. At anchor one night, Pompey called on his friends at Amphipolis. After he had received money from them for his necessary expenses and realising that Caesar was coming after him, he left that place. {*Caesar, Civil Wars, l. 3. (102) 2:341,343}

4905. When he sailed past Amphipolis, he reached shore at the isle of Lesbos within a few days. {*Caesar, Civil Wars, l. 3. (102) 2:343} {*Plutarch, Pompey, l. 1. c. 74. s. 1. 5:309} {*Dio, l. 42. (2) 4:117}

4906. He sent for his wife to come from Mitylene to the shore where together they bewailed their bad fortune. Then she ordered her baggage to be brought from the town and called her maidservants to come to her. [K327] Pompey, however, refused to come into the town of the Mitylenians, even though they came to greet him and invited him in. He advised them to obey the conqueror and not to be afraid because Caesar was merciful and generous. Then he turned to Cratippus, the philosopher, for he had come from the town to visit him, and bewailed his misfortune and disputed some things concerning providence with him. The philosopher affirmed that:

"Because of the poor government of the commonwealth, there was need of a monarchy."

4907. He asked Pompey: {*Plutarch, Pompey, l. 1. c. 75. 5:311,313}

"How and by what token can we believe that you would have used your good fortune better than Caesar, if you had overcome Caesar?"

4908. He was detained there for two days by a storm. Taking other light ships, he put all his belongings into four galleys, which came from Rhodes and Tyre, and sailed along the coast to Cilicia with his wife and friends, stopping at harbours along the way to take on fresh water and supplies. {*Caesar, Civil Wars, l. 3. (102) 2:343} {*Plutarch, Pompey, l. 1. c. 76. s. 1. 5:313} {*Appian, Civil Wars, l. 2. c. 12. (83) 3:381} {*Dio, l. 42. (2) 4:117}

4909. Lucan added: {*Lucan, l. 8. (203-210) 1:453}

So hid the stars, and land discovered
When those that from Pharsalia's battle fled
To Pompey came, and first from Lesbos' shores
He met his son; then kings and senators:
For Pompey yet (although at that sad time
Vanquished and fled) had kings to wait on him;
Proud sceptred kings that in the east did reign
Attended there in banished Pompey's train.
Then Pompey King Dejotarus commands,
To go for help to farthest eastern lands. [E647]

4910. Pompey issued Dejotarus with instructions to go and request help from the Parthians (which he never did). Lucan, the poet, continued to describe Pompey's journey: {*Lucan, l. 8. (243-254) 1:455}

...The king took leave at shore
And by the Icarian rocks great Pompey gone
Leaves Ephesus and sea calm Colophon,
Shaving small Samos' foamy rocks he goes,
A gentle gale blows from the shore of Cos:
Cnidos and sun-honoured Rhodes he leaves
And sailing straight in the mid-ocean saves
Telmessus' long and winding circuits. First
Pamphylia greets their eyes: but Pompey durst
Commit his person to no town but thee,
Little Phaselis: thy small company
And few inhabitants could not cause fear:
More in thy ships than in thy walls there were. [E648]

4911. The first town that Pompey entered was Attalia, in Pisidia. Some ships reached him there from Cilicia, bringing some soldiers, also, and about sixty senators. When he heard news that his navy was safe and that Cato had crossed into Africa with a strong force of soldiers that he had collected from the flight, he began to regret that he had fought with Caesar so far away from the help of his fleet. But it was too late now to change what had been done. {*Plutarch, Pompey, l. 1. c. 76. s. 1-3. 5:313,315} Lucan stated that, at Selinus in Cilicia, Pompey began to discuss with Lentulus, who had been the previous year's consul, and with the rest of the senators, about a safe place to retreat. {*Lucan, l. 8. (262-265) 1:455,457} [K328]

4912. Pompey sailed to Cyprus from Cilicia. {*Caesar, Civil Wars, l. 3. (102) 2:343} Those who came to offer him their service at Paphos, assured him that Cicero had very honourably referred to him. {*Cicero, Philippics, l. 2. c. 15.

15:103} He also knew that, with the general agreement of all the Antiochians and Roman citizens who traded there, the citadel of Antioch had already been taken, simply to keep him out. It was also reported that these people had sent messengers to all the neighbouring cities to tell any who had retired there from the flight not to come to Antioch. If they did, it would be at the risk of their lives, because a report was circulating around the cities about Caesar's coming there. When Pompey heard this, he set aside his intentions of going into Syria. Taking away the money that belonged to the guilds, as well as taking from private persons, he shipped this large sum of money to defray the charges of the army. He took two thousand well-armed soldiers some of whom he took from the families of the guilds or forced from the merchants, together with anyone else he thought fit for this purpose and sailed to Pelusium. {*Caesar, Civil Wars, l. 3. (103) 2:343}

4913. Theophanes from Lesbos and Pompey's other friends persuaded him to forget about every other place and go into Egypt. It was within a three days' journey and was a rich and powerful country. He could expect help from the king, who was his charge, especially since Pompey, with the help of Gabinius, had restored his father to his kingdom, and the son was not ungrateful but had sent ships to Pompey to use against Caesar. {*Velleius Paterculus, l. 2. c. 53. s. 1,2. 1:167} {*Plutarch, Pompey, l. 1. c. 76. s. 5,6. 5:315,317} {*Appian, Civil Wars, l. 2. c. 12. (84) 3:381} {*Dio, l. 42. (2) 4:117,119} As soon as that opinion prevailed, Pompey and his wife boarded a ship of Seleucis and set sail from Cyprus. Some accompanied him in warships and others in merchant ships. {*Plutarch, Pompey, l. 1. c. 77. s. 1. 5:317} Lucan described this voyage thus: {*Lucan, l. 8. (460-466) 1:471}

> Pompey departing thence, his course he bend,
> Round all the Cypriot Rocks that southward tend,
> And got into the interposed main;
> Nor by the night's weak light could he attain
> Mount Casius, but with struggling sails and strength,
> A lower port of Egypt reached at length,
> Where parted Nile's greatest channel flows,
> And to the ocean at Pelusium goes.

4914. Lacking galleys, Caesar crossed the Hellespont in small ships. As he was crossing in a ferry boat, Cassius was coming to Pharnaces with ten warships and met Caesar in the middle of the crossing. Caesar did not avoid him but heading straight toward him, advised his adversary to surrender. Cassius was astonished at the incredible boldness of Caesar and thought that Caesar had deliberately sailed against him. He held Caesar's hand to help him from the galley and humbly asked his pardon. He immediately turned over the fleet of seventy ships to him—if we can believe Appian. {*Suetonius, Julius, l. 1. c. 63. 1:115} {*Appian, Civil Wars, l. 2. c. 13. (88) 3:389,391} {*Dio, l. 42. (6) 4:125,127}

4915. As soon as Caesar arrived in Asia, he granted liberty to the Cnidians as a favour to Theopompus, who had collected fables. {*Plutarch, Caesar, l. 1. c. 48. s. 1. 7:555} He received the Ionians and Aeolians into favour and pardoned those other countries, living in the lesser Asia, who asked Caesar's pardon through their envoys. {*Appian, Civil Wars, l. 2. c. 13. (89) 3:391} [K329] Caesar only asked money from them and rewarded them with a further benefit. He freed Asia from the tax collectors who had caused it distress and converted a portion of the customs into a convenient payment of tribute. {*Dio, l. 42. (6) 4:127} A third of the tribute he remitted to all the inhabitants of Asia. {*Plutarch, Caesar, l. 1. c. 48. s. 1. 7:555}

4916. Titus Ampius intended to remove the money from the temple at Ephesus and called the senators of that province to witness how much money he took. But when he heard that Caesar was coming, he was forced to flee. Thus, Caesar twice saved the money at Ephesus. {*Caesar, Civil Wars, l. 3. (105) 2:347}

4917. Since no one knew for certain where Pompey planned to flee, Caesar took part of his journey alone with Marcus Brutus, who had defected to him from Pompey's side and whom Caesar esteemed among his best friends. Caesar asked his opinion and because they could make no certain conjecture about Pompey's flight, they intended to take the most probable journey and, setting aside all other places, headed straight for Egypt. {*Plutarch, Brutus, l. 1. c. 6. s. 3-6. 6:137} They feared that if Pompey should get control of that kingdom, he could again rally his forces. {*Dio, l. 42. (7) 4:127} Therefore, Caesar crossed to Rhodes and without waiting until all his army had arrived, he continued on with the ships of Cassius and the Rhodian galleys, with only the forces he had with him. He told no one where he planned to go and set sail about evening, ordering all the ships' captains to follow the light of the admiral's galley by night, and his own flag by day. Once they were far from land, he ordered his ship's captain to direct his course for Alexandria and they arrived there on the third day. {*Appian, Civil Wars, l. 2. c. 13. (89) 3:391}

4918. Lucan described this voyage of Caesar more like a poet than a historian. He mentioned that Caesar stayed at Illium and the places around there, then sailed from there and came into Egypt on the seventh night. {*Lucan, l. 9. (1003-1007) 1:579,581} [E649]

> …This said, to shore
> He hastens, takes shipping, and to Coreus lends
> His full-spread sails, with haste to make amends

For these delays and with a prosperous wind,
Leaves wealthy Asia and fair Rhodes behind:
The west wind blowing still, the seventh night
Discovers Egypt's shore by Pharian light;
But ere they reach the harbour, day appears,
And dims the night by fires....

*4919.* Caesar more clearly explained what happened: {*Caesar, Civil Wars, l. 3. (106) 2:347,349}

"After Caesar had spent a few days in Asia, he heard that Pompey had been seen at Cyprus. Caesar conjectured that Pompey had sailed to Egypt, since he had ties with that kingdom and other opportunities in that place. Caesar came to Alexandria with two legions, one which he had ordered to follow him from Thessaly, and another, under his lieutenant, Fusius, which he had ordered to come to him from Achaia, with eight hundred cavalry in the ten Rhodian ships and a few from Asia. In these legions were thirty-two hundred men. The rest were so weakened by their wounds from battle and by the hardship and length of the journey, that they could not catch up to Caesar. *[K330]* Caesar trusted in the fame of what he had done and did not hesitate to advance with weak supports, thinking that every place would be equally safe for him."

*4920.* Lucan described in detail when Pompey came into Egypt, ahead of Caesar: {*Lucan, l. 8. (467-469) 1:471}

That time was come wherein just Libra weighs
The hours and makes the nights equal with days;
Then pays the winter nights' hours which the spring
Had taken away....

*4921.* Lucan knew that it was the end of September, as the year was then accounted, that Pompey came into Egypt. He also knew that, in the Julian year which was being used in his time, the sun was entering Libra at the end of the same month. Consequently, not considering the different account of the times, he wrote that Pompey came into Egypt at about the autumnal equinox. This was the time when the sun began to enter into Leo, around the beginning of the Dog Days, and the Nile River began to flood. It was in Libra when the river usually receded within its banks.

*4922.* Not far from Pelusium, one of the mouths of the Nile, around Mount Casius, which is located between the borders of Egypt and Arabia, King Ptolemy, with large forces, was waging war with his sister Cleopatra, whom he had expelled from the kingdom a few months earlier. His camp was not far from Cleopatra's camp. {*Caesar, Civil Wars, l. 3. (103) 2:343,345} {*Plutarch, Pompey, l. 1. c. 77. s. 1,2. 5:317} {*Appian, Civil Wars, l. 2. c. 12. (84) 3:381} {*Dio, l.

42. (3) 4:119} Caesar stated that Ptolemy was only a boy in age. Hirtius said he was a boy in his middle years. {*Caesar, Alexandrian War, l. 1. (24) 3:47} Strabo said he was a very young boy. {*Strabo, l. 17. c. 1. s. 11. 8:47} Dio stated he was only a boy. {*Dio, l. 42. (3) 4:119} Orosius stated he was a young man. {Orosius, l. 6. c. 15.} Plutarch stated he was a very young man. {*Plutarch, Pompey, l. 1. c. 77. s. 2. 5:317} Velleius said he was nearer a boy than a man. {*Velleius Paterculus, l. 2. c. 53. s. 1. 1:167} Appian wrote that he was, at most, only thirteen years old. {*Appian, Civil Wars, l. 2. c. 12. (84) 3:383}

*4923.* When Pompey saw such a large army on the shore, he dared not land unless it were safe for him to do so. {*Lucan, l. 8. (470,471) 1:471}

Finding the king to keep within the Casian Mount,
He turned aside.

*4924.* He sent some of his followers to the king to tell him humbly of his arrival. They were to entreat him, for the sake of the friendship he had held with his father and the benefits confirmed on the king, that to receive Pompey into Alexandria and protect him with his forces from this calamity. {*Caesar, Civil Wars, l. 3. (103) 2:345} {*Plutarch, Pompey, l. 1. c. 78. s. 1,2. 5:319} {*Appian, Civil Wars, l. 2. c. 12. (84) 3:381,383} {*Dio, l. 42. (3) 4:119} *[E650]* After the men who had been sent from Pompey had delivered their message, they began to talk more freely with the king's soldiers encouraging them to perform their duty to Pompey and not despise his ill-fortune. Among their number were many of the soldiers whom Gabinius had received from Pompey's army in Syria and had taken to Alexandria to establish Ptolemy. At the conclusion of that war, he had left them with Ptolemy, the father of the lad. {*Caesar, Civil Wars, l. 3. (103) 2:345}

*4925.* The king did not reply, but his friends, who had the administration of the kingdom, did: Achillas an Egyptian, who was the general, and Pothinus, a eunuch, who was the treasurer of the kingdom. They began to discuss Pompey's situation and held a council in which they talked with other officers, including Theodotus. *[K331]* He was from either Cos, or Samos, and was a mercenary teacher of rhetoric. He exercised great authority with the king since he was the king's schoolteacher. {*Livy, l. 112. 14:141} {*Plutarch, Pompey, l. 1. c. 77. s. 2,3. 5:317} {*Appian, Civil Wars, l. 2. c. 12. (84) 3:383}

*4926.* In this council, some were of the opinion that Pompey was to be received, while others thought that he should be kept from entering Egypt. However, Theodotus, who boasted of his eloquence and skill in arguments, stated that both sides were mistaken. There was only one expedient thing to do: they should receive him and put him to death. At the close of his speech, he added: {*Plutarch, Pompey, l. 1. c. 77. s. 4. 5:319} {*Plutarch, Brutus, l. 1. c. 6. s. 5,6. 6:137}

"A dead man does not bite."

4927. The rest, in fear, followed his opinion, later claiming to have done so to prevent Pompey from tampering with the king's army and thereby seizing Alexandria and Egypt. If they were to condemn his misfortune, as is commonly done in times of trouble, many of his friends would become enemies. Hence, publicly, they gave a kind answer to those who had been sent to them from Pompey and invited him to come to the king. However, secretly, they sent the following men to kill Pompey: Achillas, the king's general and a man of singular audacity, and Lucius Septimius, who had been a centurion under Pompey in the wars against the pirates. {*Caesar, Civil Wars, l. 3. (104) 2:345}

4928. These men, together with Salvius, another centurion, and three or four such officers, went aboard a little ship and came to Pompey. Meanwhile, the whole army lined the shore in battle formation, as if in honour of his arrival. The king was at their head and clothed in his robes. There were many of the king's ships around, full of men, to make sure Pompey could not escape, should he change his mind. As the little ship approached, Septimius arose first and greeted Pompey in Latin by the name of *Imperator*. Achillas greeted him in Greek and asked him to come aboard their little ship, as it would be impossible to land in Pompey's large ship, because the sea was full of sand bars. He said the king wished to see him as soon as he could, along with all the chief men in Pompey's entourage. All those who had sailed with him, came and advised him to sail out to sea again while they were out of danger from the Egyptian's weapons. When Pompey saw the army in battle array, noted the small ship that was sent to him, and that the king had not come to meet him, nor any of the chief noblemen, he also began to suspect foul play. However, he embraced Cornelia, who had already bewailed his death. He ordered two centurions, and his freeman Philip and a servant called Scynes, to board the little ship ahead of him. Then Achillas helped him with his hand while Pompey also entered the ship. Just before turning to his wife and son, Pompey spoke those lines of Sophocles:

> Who deal with tyrants, they shall surely be
> Enslaved, though before they be never so free.

4929. As they sailed, there was a dead silence and his suspicion increased. He held a book in his hand, in which he had written the speech he intended to give to Ptolemy, and he began to read it as they approached the shore. [K332] The men had determined to kill Pompey before they reached land because they feared that, when he

met with Ptolemy, he would be rescued either by the king, or by the Romans he had with him, or by the Egyptians, who bore him much goodwill. Cornelia stood with his friends from the ship and in great suspense watched the whole thing. Pompey began to be encouraged because, at his landing point, he saw many of the king's friends come running to greet him with honour. [E651] However, as Philip lent him his hand to help him up, Septimius first came at him from behind and ran him through, after which Salvius and Achillas thrust him through with their swords. Pompey had no way of defending himself, or escaping. With both his hands, he hid his face with his gown. He neither spoke, nor did anything unworthy of himself, but only gave a groan as he patiently received all their thrusts. {*Caesar, Civil Wars, l. 3. (104) 2:345} {*Plutarch, Pompey, l. 1. c. 78,79. 5:319,323} {*Appian, Civil Wars, l. 2. c. 12. (85) 3:383} {*Dio, l. 42. (4) 4:121,123}

4930. When his wife and his friends on the ships saw this, they gave a great shriek which was heard even on the shore. They held up their hands to heaven and implored the gods, who were the revengers of covenant breaking. Then they quickly weighed anchor and fled. {*Plutarch, Pompey, l. 1. c. 80. s. 1. 5:323} {*Appian, Civil Wars, l. 2. c. 12. (85) 3:385} Some of them were taken by the Egyptians, who pursued them, while some escaped and sailed as far as Tyre, where they were shown hospitality by the Tyrians in their flight. {*Dio, l. 42. (5) 4:125} {*Dio, l. 42. (49) 4:193} Of those who escaped, his wife Cornelia and his son Sextus Pompeius fled to Cyprus. {*Livy, l. 112. 14:141} The rest of Pompey's fleet was captured and everyone in it was very cruelly murdered. Then Quintus Pompey, the Bithynian, was killed. Cicero mentioned that he lived at that time. {*Cicero, Brutus, l. 1. c. 68. 5:207} Lentulus, who had been consul, was killed at Pelusium. {Orosius, l. 6. c. 15.} He was the same Lucius Lentulus who had been the consul in the previous year and of whom Caesar wrote that he was captured by the king and killed in prison. {*Caesar, Civil Wars, l. 3. (104) 2:345} Plutarch noted that he went to Cyprus together with Pompey, but did not leave Cyprus for Egypt until a long time after the burial of Pompey. A little after leaving Cyprus, he was captured at sea and killed. {*Plutarch, Pompey, l. 1. c. 80. s. 4. 5:325}

4931. Gaius Caesar and Publius Servilius were consuls when Pompey was killed in his fifty-eighth year, the day before his birthday. {*Velleius Paterculus, l. 2. c. 53. s. 2,3. 1:167} On that very day, in earlier times, he had triumphed over Mithridates and the pirates. {*Dio, l. 42. (5) 4:125} That triumph had lasted for two days and had started on the 3rd of the Calends of October (September 28). {*Pliny, l. 7. c. 26. 2:569} {*Pliny, l. 37. c. 6. 10:173} Plutarch was incorrect when he said Pompey lived fifty-nine years and died the day after his birthday. {*Plutarch, Pompey, l. 1. c. 79. s. 4. 5:323}

The last day of September, which was the last day of the life of Pompey, was the Julian July 25. The Roman calendar was in such a mess at that time.

4932. Septimius cut off the head of Pompey and kept it until Caesar arrived, as he hoped for a large reward. {*Lucan, l. 8. (606,607) 1:483} The body was thrown naked from the ship, to be seen by all who wanted to see it. Philip, his freedman, stayed by it until all had satisfied their eyes. Then he washed it with sea water and wrapped it in a coat of his own. Because he had nothing at hand, he looked around the shore and found the broken planks of an old fishing boat. [K333] This was enough to burn the naked body, but not completely. As he was gathering the planks together and laying them in order, a grave old citizen of Rome, who had served under Pompey in his younger days, came and helped him to perform the funeral rites. {*Plutarch, Pompey, l. 1. c. 80. s. 1-3. 5:323,325} Appian wrote that a certain man buried Pompey on the shore and made a little monument for him, and another man added this inscription: {*Appian, Civil Wars, l. 2. c. 12. (86) 3:385}

...Scarce would the temples hold
That which is covered over with a little mould.

4933. The trunk of Pompey's body was cast into the Nile and later burned. {Aurelius Victor, De Viris Illustribus, l. 1. c. 77.} It was buried by Servius Codrus, who wrote this on his tomb: *HERE LIES POMPEY THE GREAT.* Lucan wrote: {*Lucan, l. 8. (715-720) 1:491}

...To the shore did fearful Codrus come
Out of his lurking hole that was before
Great Pompey's quaestor, and from Cyprus' shore
Had followed him; he by the shades of night
Durst go true love had vanquished terror quite
To find his slaughtered lord, along the sand,
And through the waves to bring the trunk to land.

4934. [E652] For the poet was more correct when he said that his body was in the sea, than was Aurelius Victor, who said it was in the Nile River. It was shown by other writers that Pompey was killed and buried not far from Mount Casius. {*Strabo, l. 16. c. 2. s. 33. 7:279} {*Pliny, l. 5. c. 12. 2:269} This was the end of the great Pompey's life, who was considered to be the most powerful of the Romans. He was surnamed *Agamemnon*, because he also had the command of a thousand ships, but then died near Egypt in a little ship, like one of the smallest Egyptian boats. He had been given an oracle a long time earlier, that had made him suspect all the clan of the Cassian family. In the end, he was killed and buried near Mount Casius. {*Dio, l. 42. (5) 4:125} This mountain is located not far from the border of Judea, which he first subjected to the Roman yoke.

4935. Those who were together with Cato arrived in Cyrene and heard of the death of Pompey. {*Dio, l. 42. (13) 4:135} Cornelia and her son-in-law, Sextus Pompeius, sailed to Cato from Cyprus. Lucan stated: {*Lucan, l. 9. (117-119) 1:513}

They first arrived on Cyprus' foamy shore,
From there a mild east wind commanding bore
Their ships to Cato's Libyan Camp.

4936. Lucan added, furthermore, that the son of Pompey (Gnaeus, the elder), who was with Cato, there learned from his younger brother Sextus, who was with Cornelia, about the death of his father. Cornelia burned the remains of Pompey. At her example, the rest of the army made funeral piles and performed funeral rites to the ghosts of those who had died at Pharsalia. Cato made a funeral speech in memory of Pompey.

4937. After this, they had different ideas about what to do. Those who had no hope of obtaining pardon from Caesar, stayed with Cato. Others left and went where chance took them. [K334] Still others went directly to Caesar and obtained pardon. {*Dio, l. 42. (10,11) 4:131} Cornelia was given a pardon and returned safely to Rome. {*Dio, l. 42. (5) 4:125} In Mount Albanus, she buried the remains of her husband that were brought to her. {*Lucan, l. 8. (769,770) 1:495} {*Plutarch, Pompey, l. 1. c. 80. s. 6. 5:325}

4938. Cato's soldiers, who were chiefly mariners of Cilicia under their King Tarcondimotus, had been ready to leave him, but stirred by the words Cato spoke to them, they returned to their duty. {*Lucan, l. 9. (219-229) 1:521}

4939. Cato was permitted by the citizens to enter Cyrene, when, only a few days earlier, they had shut their gates against Labienus. {*Plutarch, Cato Minor, l. 1. c. 56. s. 2,3. 8:371,373} Lucan stated: {*Lucan, l. 9. (296-301) 1:527}

Their second labour is
To scale Cyrene's lofty walls, on whom
Cato no vengeance took when overcome
Though they against him shut their gates to him
Revenge sufficient did their conquest seem.
He hence to Libyan Juba's kingdom goes.

4940. Cato was told that Scipio, the father-in-law of Pompey, had been welcomed by King Juba and that Attius Varus, to whom the province of Libya was given by Pompey, had joined them with his army. {*Plutarch, Cato Minor, l. 1. c. 76. s. 3. 8:373}

4941. Three days into his pursuit of Pompey, Caesar reached Alexandria. King Ptolemy was still around Mount Casius. {*Appian, Civil Wars, l. 2. c. 13. (89) 3:391} Lucan said it was seven days, not three. {*Lucan, l. 9. (1004) 1:581} He found that the Alexandrians were in rebellion over the death of Pompey, so that he dared not go ashore immediately, but left the shore and stayed off-shore for some time. {*Dio, l. 42. (7) 4:127} Lucan stated: {*Lucan, l. 9. (1007-1010) 1:581} [E653]

> …where, when he saw the shore
> With giddy tumult all confused over,
> Doubting if safe to trust them, did forbear
> To bring his ships to land.…

4942. When he found out that Pompey was dead, Caesar first left his ship and heard the shouting of the soldiers whom Ptolemy had left as a garrison in the town. He saw them come running out to him, because his fasces was being carried before him. The crowd claimed that, by this act, the royal authority had been infringed. {*Caesar, Civil Wars, l. 3. (106) 2:349} {*Dio, l. 42. (7) 4:127} Concerning this event, Lucan wrote: {*Lucan, l. 10. (11-13) 1:591}

> But perceiving that the throng
> Of people murmured that in Egypt he
> Bare the ensigns up of Rome's authority
> He finds their wavering faiths.…

4943. In spite of this, Caesar entered Alexandria while it was in a turmoil, without any danger to himself. {*Livy, l. 112. 14:141} He withdrew by fleeing into the palace but the weapons were taken from some of his soldiers. The crowd retreated, as all the ships came to shore. {*Dio, l. 42. (7) 4:127}

4944. Caesar was very angry when Theodotus offered him the head and signet of Pompey. He took the ring and started to weep. {*Livy, l. 112. 14:141} {*Plutarch, Caesar, l. 1. c. 48. s. 1,2. 7:555} [K335] We read that the head of Pompey was presented to Caesar with the ring by Achillas, the captain of Ptolemy's guard, and was wrapped in an Egyptian covering. {Aurelius Victor, De Viris Illustribus, l. 1. c. 77.} Caesar had it burned with many and very precious fragrances, while he did not stop weeping. Lucan made mention of the head that was given to him by the captain of the guard: {*Lucan, l. 9. (1011,1012) 1:581}

> Bringing his king's dire guise, great Pompey's head,
> With an Egyptian mantle covered.

4945. Both Dio and Lucan thought Caesar was being a hypocrite and the tears were not genuine. {*Dio, l. 42. (8) 4:129} {*Lucan, l. 9. (1035-1041) 1:583}

> Caesar at his first gift would not refuse
> Nor turn his eyes away, but fixedly views
> Till he perceived it was true, and plainly saw,
> It was safe to be a pious father-in-law:
> Then shed forced tears and from a joyful breast
> Drew sighs and groans, as thinking tears would best
> Conceal his inward joy.

4946. Concerning the burial of the head, Lucan introduced Caesar, commanding: {*Lucan, l. 9. (1089-1093) 1:587} [E654]

> …But do you inter
> This worthy's head, not that the earth may bear
> And hide your guilt; bring fumes and odours' store,
> To appease his head, and gather from the shore
> His scattered limbs; compose them in one tomb.

4947. However, Caesar ordered the head to be buried in the suburbs and there dedicated a temple of Nemesis, or Revenge. {*Appian, Civil Wars, l. 2. c. 13. (90) 3:393}

4948. To demonstrate more of his goodwill toward Pompey, he kindly entertained Pompey's friends and associates, who had been captured by the king as they wandered in that country. He won them to himself by favours he did for them and wrote to his friends at Rome that the greatest and most pleasant fruit he derived from his victory, was that he was daily able to save some citizens who had opposed him. {*Plutarch, Caesar, l. 1. c. 58. s. 2. 7:577}

4949. Before his army reached him and because he lacked the companionship of his own friends, Caesar gave himself to idle pursuits. He courteously entertained everyone he met and walked about to see the city. He admired its beauty and stood to hear many of the philosophers. His leisure gained him favour and good reputation with the people of Alexandria. {*Appian, Civil Wars, l. 2. c. 13. (89) 3:393} Lucan said that he visited the temples and the tomb where the body of Alexander the Great lay: {*Lucan, l. 10. (14-22) 1:591}

> Then with a look still hiding fear goes he,
> The stately temple of the old god to see;
> Which speaks the ancient Macedonian greatness.
> But there delighted with no objects' sweetness,
> Nor with their gold nor gods' majestic dress,
> Nor lofty city walls, with greediness,
> Into the burying-vault goes Caesar down.
> There Macedonian Philip's mad-brained son,
> The prosperous thief, lies buried: whom just fate
> Killed in the world's revenge.… [K336]

4950. Caesar transferred the government of Asia and the neighbouring provinces to Gnaeus Domitius Calvinus, {*Caesar, Alexandrian War, l. 1. (34) 3:65} and ordered him to take the armies that were in Asia with him and make war on King Pharnaces. {*Dio, l. 42. (46) 4:187} When Caesar saw that there were many riots daily at Alexandria, because of the great gathering of the multitude, and that many soldiers were being killed in various areas of the city, he ordered that the legions he had gathered from Pompey's soldiers be brought to him from Asia. He was detained in Alexandria by the Etesian winds, which blow contrary to those who sail from there. {*Caesar, Civil Wars, l. 3. (107) 2:349} These are the northern winds, which stop blowing about the end of the Julian August, as we may learn from the Ephemerides of Geminus and Ptolemy, as well as in Pliny and Columella. {*Pliny, l. 2. c. 47. 1:265} {Columella, De Re Rustica, l. 2.} From this source we also discover the error of Lucan, who stated {*Lucan, l. 8. (167-169) 1:449} that Pompey came to Egypt at the time of the autumnal equinox. Lucan also told of Cato's weary march with the legions through the African desert (concerning this, see Livy {*Livy, l. 112. 14:141}), after he heard of the death of Pompey. {*Lucan, l. 9. (250-949) 1:523-575} He said it was undertaken by him in the winter that followed this equinox.

4951. When Cato left Cyrene, he tried to cross the Gulf of Surtis with his fleet, but a storm cast him into the marshes of Tritonis. [E655] So Sextus Pompeius was left with some of the forces in the more fruitful places of Africa while Cato intended to march overland because the sea was now impassable because of storms. He wanted to find the king of Mauritania, as Lucan described: {*Lucan, l. 9. (368-374) 1:533}

> Part of the fleet got off from hence again,
> And from the Syrtes driven, did remain
> Under great Pompey's oldest son's command,
> On this side Garamantians in rich land:
> But Cato's virtue brooking no delay,
> Through unknown regions led his troops away,
> To encompass round the Syrtes by land, for now
> The stormy seas unnavigable grow
> In winter time....

4952. Plutarch affirmed that this overland march took place in the winter. {*Plutarch, Cato Minor, l. 1. c. 76. s. 3. 8:373}

4953. His army suffered miserably in the country of the Nasamones, which was near the Syrtes. The winds blew the sand about, water was scarce and they encountered a large number of different varieties of snakes. Cato arrived at the temple of Jupiter Ammon, where he was advised by Labeinus to consult the oracle about his future fortune. He refused and finally, after wandering two months through the sandy deserts of Africa, he reached Leptis and spent the winter there. {*Lucan, l. 9. (379-949) 1:533-575} After winter, he assembled his ten thousand soldiers again. {*Plutarch, Cato Minor, l. 1. c. 76. s. 4. 8:373}

4954. Caesar was detained at Alexandria by the Etesian winds and spent his time in Egypt in raising money and deciding the controversy between Ptolemy and Cleopatra. {*Dio, l. 42. (9) 4:129} Some of the vast sum of money that was owed to him by Ptolemy Auletes, the father of the young king, he collected, to pay the costs of his army. {*Plutarch, Caesar, l. 1. c. 48. s. 4. 7:557} The Egyptians did not take kindly to Caesar's collection procedures. They, of all people, were extremely superstitious worshippers of a multitude of gods and did not approve of Caesar taking the things that were dedicated to their gods. {*Dio, l. 42. (34) 4:167} [K337] Although in this he was deceived by the king's guardians, who claimed that the king's treasury was empty, in order to stir up the people to hate Caesar. {Orosius, l. 6. c. 15.} To encourage this unrest, Pothinus, the eunuch, a man who held greatest authority, spoke and did many things in public. For he gave the soldiers old and musty grain and told them that they should be satisfied because they were being fed at the expense of another. He ordered that his own supper should be served up in wooden and earthen dishes and said that Caesar had taken away all the gold and silver plate for the payment of the debt. {*Plutarch, Caesar, l. 1. c. 48. s. 3,4. 7:557}

4955. Caesar thought that the controversies of the king and queen belonged to the people of Rome and to him, because he was a consul. They were associated with his office because, in his former consulship, an alliance had been formed with the elder Ptolemy, both by legislative enactment and by decree of the Senate. Therefore, he told them that it was his wish that both King Ptolemy and his sister Cleopatra dismiss their armies. They should settle their controversies before him, through the law, rather than between themselves, by fighting. {*Caesar, Civil Wars, l. 3. (107) 2:349}

4956. The death of Pompey was not believed at Rome until later, when his signet ring was sent there. It had three trophies engraved on it or, as Plutarch thought, a lion holding a sword. {*Plutarch, Pompey, l. 1. c. 80. s. 5,6. 5:325} Then the Romans strove to see who would give Caesar the greatest number of honours. He was given power to deal with Pompey's side as he wished. He was given authority to make war and peace with whomever he wanted, without consulting the Roman people. He was made consul for five years. He was made dictator for a whole year, not the normal six month period. He was to have the authority of a tribune as long as he lived and to sit with the tribunes and together with them determine any action that was to be taken. This had never been done before. {*Dio, l. 42. (20) 4:145} [E656]

4957. When Caesar had accepted these honours, he immediately entered into the office of dictator, although he was out of Italy. {*Dio, l. 42. (21) 4:149} Josephus correctly began his rule from this time, assigning it a period of three and a half years. {*Josephus, Antiq., l. 14. c. 11. s. 1. (270) 7:593} In Syria, while the Antiochians seem to reckon the times of the Caesars from his first dictatorship, the Lacedemonians appear to do so from his second dictatorship. Eusebius, in his Chronicle (at the second year of the empire of Probus), showed that the Laodicean epoch was later than the Antiochian epoch, but only by one year.

## 3957a AM, 4666 JP, 48 BC

*4958.* Velleius Paterculus stated that the king and those who exercised authority over him, attempted treason against Caesar. {*Velleius Paterculus, l. 2. c. 54. s. 1. 1:169*} Suetonius affirmed this of King Ptolemy himself. {*Suetonius, Julius, l. 1. c. 35. s. 2. 1:81*} Eutropius and Plutarch stated that the eunuch Pothinus was the instigator of the treasons plotted against him. Caesar began to feast whole nights in his own defence. Pothinus would tell him that it was now time to stop and attend to his important business and return to his feasting later. Caesar replied that he did not need any advice from any of the Egyptians. He secretly sent for Cleopatra from the country. {*Eutropius, l. 6.*} {*Plutarch, Caesar, l. 1. c. 48. s. 5. 7:559*}

*4959.* Previously, Cleopatra had pleaded her case before Caesar through other men. As soon as she knew that women were his weakness, she requested that she personally might plead her case before him. {*Dio, l. 42. (34) 4:167*} [*K338*] This was granted and she took only one of her friends with her, Apollodorus Siculus. They sailed to the palace in a light ship as soon as it was dark. Since she could not easily hide herself, she laid herself inside a bed-sack that was then folded up and tied up with a cord by Apollodorus and carried up through the gate to Caesar. {*Plutarch, Caesar, l. 1. c. 49. s. 1,2. 7:559*} Lucan described her arrival to Caesar like this: {*Lucan, l. 10. (53-60) 1:595*}

> Now the young king, came from Pelusium,
> Had pacified the people's wrath: in whom
> As hostage of his peace in Egypt's court
> Caesar was safe; when, lo, from Pharos' port,
> Bribing the keeper to unchain the same,
> In a small galley Cleopatra came,
> Unknown to Caesar entering the house
> The stain of Egypt, Rome's pernicious
> Fury, unchaste to Italy's disgrace.

*4960.* Cleopatra fell at Caesar's feet and asked for her part of the kingdom. She was an exceedingly beautiful woman and this act enhanced her beauty a great deal. She did seem to suffer an injury as great as the hatred of the king himself who had murdered Pompey. The king had not done this on account of Caesar and would just as easily have killed Caesar had he been able to. {*Florus, l. 2. c. 13. s. 56. 1:285*} When Caesar saw Cleopatra and heard her speak, he at once became her slave. As soon as it was day, he sent for Ptolemy and mediated a peace between them. He became Cleopatra's advocate when previously he was her judge. Both this and the

fact that Ptolemy saw his sister with Caesar before he had known about it, so inflamed the lad with anger that he ran out to the people. He shouted that he had been betrayed and took his crown and threw it to the ground. {*Dio, l. 42. (35) 4:169*}

*4961.* After this, a large uproar resulted. Caesar's soldiers took Ptolemy and carried him inside, but the Egyptians were all in an uproar. Had Caesar, who was afraid, not gone to talk to them from a safe position and promised them that he would do what they wanted, they could easily have captured the palace on the first assault, as they had infiltrated it by sea and land. The Romans, who had thought they were among their friends, had no way of resisting. {*Dio, l. 42. (35) 4:169,171*}

*4962.* After these events, Caesar went out to the people, together with Ptolemy and Cleopatra, and read the will of their father. It stated that, according to the ancient custom of the Egyptians, the two should be married to one another and should hold the kingdom in common while being under the protection of the people of Rome. [*E657*] Caesar added that it was his role, since he was now dictator and had all the power of the people of Rome, both to take care of the children and to see that their father's will was followed. Therefore, he gave the kingdom of Egypt to Ptolemy and Cleopatra. He gave Cyprus to Arsinoe and Ptolemy, the younger, for he was so afraid at the time, that he would willingly have given anything of his own, rather than have taken away anything that belonged to the Egyptians. In this way, the riot was appeased. {*Dio, l. 42. (35) 4:171*} {*Caesar, Civil Wars, l. 3. (108) 2:351*} {*Caesar, Alexandrian War, l. 1. (33) 3:63,65*} {*Livy, l. 112. 14:141*} {*Plutarch, Caesar, l. 1. c. 49. s. 1,2. 7:559*} [*K339*]

*4963.* King Dejotarus came to Gnaeus Domitius Calvinus, Caesar's lieutenant in Asia, and requesting him not to allow Lesser Armenia, his own kingdom, nor Cappadocia, the kingdom of Ariobarzanes, to be occupied and plundered by Pharnaces. Unless Pharnaces' activities were checked, they would not be able to do as they had been commanded, nor pay the money that they had promised to Caesar. Domitius immediately sent messengers to Pharnaces, ordering that he should get out of Armenia and Cappadocia. Thinking this order would carry greater weight if he came closer to these countries with his army, he selected a legion from the three legions he had with him. He took the thirty-sixth and sent the other two into Egypt to Caesar, who had written to him, asking for them. In addition to the thirty-sixth legion, he added two more that he had received from Dejotarus. They were disciplined and armed after the Roman manner. Dejotarus gave him a hundred cavalry as well, and Domitius took an equal number of troops from Ariobarzanes. He sent Publius Sestius to

Gaius Plaetorius, his quaestor, to bring him a legion which he had hastily raised and also sent to Quintus Patiscius in Cilicia, to bring more troops. All these forces were ordered by Domitius to meet at Comana as quickly as possible. {*Caesar, Alexandrian War, l. 1. (34) 3:65,67}

4964. In the meantime, the envoys brought back an answer from Pharnaces, saying that he had left Cappadocia and that he had recovered Lesser Armenia, which he ought to keep, since it had belonged to his father. Furthermore, all the business to do with Pharnaces should be referred to Caesar himself, for he was prepared to do whatever Caesar should decide. He had left Cappadocia because he could more easily defend Armenia since it was nearer to his own kingdom than Cappadocia. When Domitius heard his reply, he still thought that he should get out of Armenia, since he had no more right to Armenia than to Cappadocia. His request, that the whole business should be tabled until Caesar came, was unjust, for nothing would change in the meantime. After Domitius had replied, he marched with his forces into Armenia. In the meantime, Pharnaces sent many embassies to Domitius, entreating for peace and offering him expensive presents. Domitius constantly refused them all and answered the envoys that he did not consider that nothing was dearer to him than to recover the dignity of the people of Rome and the kingdom for their allies. {*Caesar, Alexandrian War, l. 1. (35,36) 3:67,69}

4965. While Caesar carried on the war at Alexandria, Dejotarus did what he could for Caesar and supplied Gnaeus Domitius' army with lodgings. He added his own forces to those of Domitius, as Cicero confirmed in a speech he made on his behalf. {*Cicero, Pro Dejotaro, l. 1. c. 5. 14:513}

4966. In Egypt, the eunuch Pothinus, who had the oversight of all the king's treasure and of the whole kingdom, was afraid that he might be punished for the earlier sedition of the Egyptians, of which he had been the chief ringleader. He was the instigator of a new and difficult war. He first complained among his own friends that the king had been called to plead his cause before Caesar. In others, whom he planned to have on his side, he sowed a suspicion that Caesar, to appease the riot, had indeed given the kingdom to both parties but that in the process of time, he would give it to Cleopatra alone. By letters and messengers he solicited Achillas, who was commander-in-chief of all the king's forces. He first appealed to him with his own promises and flattered him with promises from the king, that he alone should lead the king's entire army of foot soldiers and cavalry from Pelusium to Alexandria. {*Caesar, Civil Wars, l. 3. (108) 2:351} {*Dio, l. 42. (36) 4:171,173} [K340]

4967. Caesar did not have enough troops to overcome the enemy, if he were forced to fight outside the town. The only thing that he could do, was to stay within Alexandria and wait and see what Achillas planned to do. He wanted the king to send some of his most confident friends, who also held the greatest authority, as envoys to Achillas. Dioscorides and Serapion, who had been envoys at Rome and had exercised great authority under his father, were sent to Achillas by the king to declare Caesar's intentions. As soon as they came to him, and before Achillas knew why they came, he ordered them to be taken and killed. Dioscorides was wounded and taken away by his own men for dead and Serapion was killed. After this, Caesar arranged matters so that he got the king under his own power. [E658] He thought that the king's title would hold great authority among his own countrymen and that this war might then appear to have been undertaken through the outrage of a few private men and thieves, rather than on the advice of the king. {*Caesar, Civil Wars, l. 3. (109) 2:351,353} {*Caesar, Alexandrian War, l. 1. (26) 3:53}

4968. Achillas had substantial forces with him. They were twenty thousand trained and armed troops. These included the soldiers of Gabinius, who were now accustomed to the life and licentiousness of the Alexandrians and had forgotten the name and discipline of the people of Rome. They were joined by a company of thieves and robbers from Syria, Cilicia and the neighbouring provinces. Moreover, there were many condemned persons and banished men present. All Roman fugitives were safe and well taken care of at Alexandria, on the condition that, when required, they enlisted with the soldiers. If anyone was apprehended by his master, he was rescued again by a concourse of soldiers. They defended the violence of their companions, because they were just as guilty and feared their own punishment. According to the old custom of the Alexandrian army, these men used to demand that the king's friends be put to death, and to plunder rich men's goods to increase their pay. They were in the habit of besieging the king's palace, of banishing some and recalling others from banishment. There were also two thousand cavalry, many of whom had served a long time in the wars of Alexandria. {*Caesar, Civil Wars, l. 3. (110) 2:353,355}

4969. Achillas trusted in these forces and despised the small number of Caesar's soldiers. He captured Alexandria and attempted to break into Caesar's house. However, Caesar had stationed his cohorts in the passes and they withstood the assault, while simultaneously fighting at the harbour, where the fiercest fighting of all took place. At the same time, the enemy brought their forces to fight in many passes and also endeavoured, with many troops, to seize the warships. Fifty of these ships had been sent to help Pompey and when the battle in Thessaly was over, they had returned. They were all galleys of three or five tiers of oars, well-rigged and all fitted out with tackling for sailing. In addition to these, twenty-two ships were always stationed there at Alexandria to guard the city. They were all decked and fitted out with ramming prows. If the enemy had seized these and robbed Caesar of his fleet, they would have had the harbour and the whole sea at their command and would have kept all provisions and any help from coming to Caesar, which is why this was the hottest part of the battle. *[K341]* Caesar recognised the importance of the fleet and the harbour for their safety, so he overcame the problem by burning these ships and the rest that were in the arsenal because he could not defend them with the few troops that he had. {*\*Caesar, Civil Wars, l. 3. (111) 2:355,357*} Lucan stated: {*\*Lucan, l. 10. (497-503) 1:627,629*}

> Nor over the ships alone do flames prevail;
> But all the houses near the shore assail,
> The south winds feed the flame, and drive it on
> Along the houses with such motion,
> As through the heavens fiery meteors run,
> That, wanting fuel, fed on air alone.

*4970.* When this fire had spread to part of the city, it burned four hundred thousand books that were stored in the adjoining houses. This was a singular monument to the care and industry of their ancestors, who had gathered together so many great works of famous writers. {*Orosius, l. 6. c. 15.*} Seneca quoted Livy as saying that this was a famous tribute to the glory of and the care taken by the earlier Egyptian kings. Seneca stated that only forty thousand books were destroyed. {*\*Seneca, De Tranquillitate Animi, l. 1. c. 9. s. 4,5. 2:247*} Aulus Gellius and Ammianus Marcellinus stated that seven hundred thousand were burned. {*\*Aulus Gellius, Attic Nights, l. 7. c. 17. s. 3. 2:139*} {*\*Ammianus Marcellinus, l. 22. c. 16. s. 13. 2:303*} Indeed, at the end of the Alexandrian war, the city was plundered by the soldiers. However, Plutarch stated that the fire was increased by the arsenal and the library was burned at the beginning of this war. {*\*Plutarch, Caesar, l. 1. c. 49. s. 3,4. 7:561*} Dio confirmed that the storehouses, granaries and library were burned, together with the arsenal. {*\*Dio, l. 42. (38) 4:175*} *[E659]*

*4971.* After the fleet was burned and the enemy was still engaged in fighting, Caesar landed his soldiers from the other ships at the island of Pharos (which was joined to the city by a narrow neck of land, nine hundred feet long, and formed the harbour) and placed a garrison there. As soon as he had done this, he was able to bring grain and troops to him by ship. {*\*Caesar, Civil Wars, l. 3. (112,113) 2:357*} Lucan wrote of the taking of Pharos by Caesar: {*\*Lucan, l. 10. (512-514) 1:629*}

> Two helps on Caesar both that citadel bestow:
> Commands the seas, the foe's incursions stayed,
> And made a passage safe for Caesar's aid.

*4972.* In other parts of the town, they fought so that neither of them had the upper hand. Neither side gave ground because of the narrowness of the places and only a few were killed on either side. After Caesar had taken the most important places, he fortified them by night. On that side of the town, there was a small section of the palace where they had first brought him to live. A theatre, which was joined to the house, was like a citadel and had a road to the harbour and the arsenal. He daily strengthened these fortifications so that they would be like a strong wall for him and so that he might not be forced to fight except when he wanted to. {*\*Caesar, Civil Wars, l. 3. (112) 2:359*}

*4973.* The Egyptians feared that Caesar, who had won the battle at sea, would now seize the harbour of the city. So they built a rampart to bar his entrance and only left a little space. But Caesar blocked that space by sinking cargo ships filled with stones. *[K342]* This blocked all the enemy's ships in the harbour so they could not leave. In this way, he could get what he needed with less trouble. He was now also able to get water because Achillas had taken all water from him by cutting the conduits. {*\*Dio, l. 42. (38) 4:175*}

*4974.* Caesar sent into all the neighbouring countries and called for help from there. {*\*Caesar, Civil Wars, l. 3. (112) 2:357*} He sent for the whole fleet from Rhodes, Syria and Cilicia. He ordered them to bring archers from Crete and cavalry from Malchus, the king of the Nabateans. He ordered battering-rams, grain and other supplies to be brought to him. {*\*Caesar, Alexandrian War, l. 1. (1) 3:11*} He told Domitius Calvinus of his danger and requested that he send him supplies by every means, as soon as he possibly could. He wanted him to come to Alexandria through Syria. {*\*Caesar, Alexandrian War, l. 1. (9) 3:23*} Mithridates of Pergamum was a man of great nobility in his country, with knowledge and valour in the wars, who was held in great esteem and who enjoyed personal honour and friendship with Caesar. He was sent into Syria and Cilicia to expedite the supplies. {*\*Caesar, Alexandrian War, l. 1. (26) 3:51*} {*\*Josephus, Antiq., l. 14. c. 8. s. 1. (127,128) 7:515*} {*\*Dio, l. 42. (41) 4:181*}

*4975.* In the meantime, a eunuch named Ganymedes stole away Arsinoe, who was only carelessly guarded, and carried her to the Egyptians. They made her queen and fought the war with more enthusiasm than before, because they had acquired one of the family of the Ptolemys as a commander. {*\*Dio, l. 42. (39) 4:175*} Lucan wrote thus: {*\*Lucan, l. 10. (519-522) 1:629*}

Arsinoe, from court escaped, goes
By Ganymedes' help to Caesar's foes,
The crown (as Lagus' daughter) to obtain.

4976. Caesar wrote this: {*Caesar, Civil Wars, l. 3. (112) 2:359}

"The young daughter of King Ptolemy hoped to take over the kingdom and escaped from the palace to join Achillas and commanded in the war together with him. Immediately, there was a dispute as to who would be the chief commander. The matter was aggravated by many bribes among the soldiers. Each strove to get the goodwill of the soldiers to their own detriment."

4977. While these things were being done among the enemies, Pothinus, the king's governor and administrator of the kingdom for Ptolemy, sent messengers to Achillas telling him to pursue the issue and not desist in the war. But when the messengers were approached and apprehended, Pothinus was put to death by Caesar. {*Caesar, Civil Wars, l. 3. (112) 2:359} [E660] After this, Caesar kept the young king in strict custody, thus further exasperating the minds of the Egyptians. {*Dio, l. 42. (39) 4:177}

4978. While these things were happening in Egypt, Domitius Calvinus marched against Pharnaces with long and continual marches. He camped not far from Nicopolis, a city of Lesser Armenia built by Pompey, which Pharnaces had already seized to live in. About seven miles from there, Pharnaces had made ambushes for him which failed. The next day, Domitius moved closer and brought his camp to the very edge of town. Pharnaces set his men in battle array after his own custom and fashion. The following night, Pharnaces intercepted the messengers who were bringing the letters to Domitius concerning the Alexandrian affairs. From this, he learned of the danger Caesar was in and the recalling of Domitius. He considered it as good as a victory if he stalled for time. Domitius, now more concerned with the danger of Caesar than his own, brought his soldiers from the camp and prepared to fight. He placed the thirty-sixth legion in the right wing, the Pontic troops on the left and the legions of Dejotarus in the middle of the battle formation. [K343] When both armies were in battle array, the battle started. The Pontic legion was almost entirely lost and most of Dejotarus' soldiers were killed. The thirty-sixth legion retreated into the mountains and only lost about two hundred and fifty men. In spite of this, Domitius rallied the remains of his scattered army and returned to Asia by safe journeys through Cappadocia since winter was now approaching. {*Caesar, Alexandrian War, l. 1. (36-40) 3:69-77} {*Appian, Civil Wars, l. 2. c. 13. (91) 3:395} {*Dio, l. 42. (46) 4:187}

4979. Caesar and the Alexandrians fought hard against one another with fortifications and works. Most of all, Caesar tried to isolate that section of the city which a marsh had made the narrowest, from the the rest of the city. Using works and ramparts, he hoped that the city would first be divided into two sectors. Then his army would be united under him again although in two adjacent sectors of the city. Also, should they find themselves in any danger, help could be brought to him from the other sector of the city. Most importantly, he wanted the abundant freshwater supply from the marsh. The Alexandrians sent messengers into every part of Egypt to enlist men. They brought all sorts of engines and weapons into the town which were described in detail by Hirtius. {*Caesar, Alexandrian War, l. 1. (1-3) 3:11-15}

4980. When Caesar saw the numbers of the enemy increasing, he began to entertain the idea of an agreement between them. He ordered that Ptolemy be placed where he might be heard by the Egyptians. He was to tell them that he was not harmed in any way and that there was no need for this war. They should make peace and he would take care that the conditions were kept. The Egyptians, however, suspected that he had been deliberately coerced into this by Caesar and still carried on their war. {*Dio, l. 42. (39) 4:177} They said that Caesar had to be driven out quickly. Because of the storms and the season of the year, Caesar was unable to receive help by sea. {*Caesar, Alexandrian War, l. 1. (3) 3:15}

4981. In the interim, the dissension increased between Achillas, the general of the old army, and Arsinoe, the younger daughter of Ptolemy Auletes. Both were plotting and scheming against each other. While Achillas aimed at taking over the kingdom, Arsinoe thwarted him with the help of Ganymedes, the eunuch, and her foster-father. She took over the kingdom and put to death Achillas, pretending that he would have betrayed the fleet. After he was killed, she alone enjoyed the whole kingdom and Ganymedes was made the general of the army. Once he had assumed that charge, he increased the soldiers' pay and acted with similar care and discretion in all things. {*Caesar, Alexandrian War, l. 1. (4) 3:15,17} {*Dio, l. 42. (40) 4:177,179}

4982. Alexandria was riddled with underground channels that connected to the Nile River, by means of which, water was brought into private houses. The water settled with time and became drinkable. Ganymedes blocked those channels in all the places of the city where Caesar's forces were besieged. He pumped salt water into these channels so Caesar's forces did not have fresh water to drink. They began to think of fleeing, but this advice was not well received and Caesar ordered that wells should be dug in the night. A large quantity of fresh water was found and all the laborious work of the Alexandrians came to nought. {*Caesar, Alexandrian War, l. 1. (5-9) 3:17-23} [K344]

4983. The next day, the thirty-seventh legion arrived. It was made up of those soldiers of Pompey's army who had surrendered themselves and been shipped by Domitius Calvinus. They came to the shores of Africa a little above Alexandria, with supplies of grain, arms, weapons and engines. The other legion, which he had sent by overland through Syria, had not yet reached Caesar. With the Etesian winds continually blowing, these ships rode at anchor and could not get into the harbour. When Caesar realised this, he sailed and ordered his fleet to follow him. He did not take any soldiers with him, in case he might leave the citadels short of men to defend them. [E661] When he came to a steep place called the Chersonesus, he sent some sailors ashore for fresh water. Some of them were intercepted, and told the enemy that Caesar was indeed in the fleet and had no soldiers in the ships. Therefore, they rigged their whole navy and met up with Caesar as he returned with the legion of Domitius. Although Caesar did not want to fight that day, a Rhodian ship, which was positioned in the right wing and at some distance from the rest, was attacked by four decked warships of the enemy and some open ones. Caesar was forced to help them and got the victory. If night had not fallen and stopped the battle, Caesar would have defeated the whole fleet of the enemy. {*Caesar, Alexandrian War, l. 1. (9-11) 3:23-27}

4984. Although the Egyptians had been defeated, they were nevertheless encouraged again by Ganymedes. Even though they had lost a hundred and ten warships in the harbour and arsenal, they earnestly started to repair their fleet. To that end, they gathered together all the ships from all the mouths of the Nile River and from the private arsenals belonging to the king. In a few days, beyond all expectations, they made a fleet of twenty-two ships. They had galleys with four tiers of oars and five with five tiers, plus many smaller and undecked ones. They furnished them with soldiers and outfitted them for battle. {*Caesar, Alexandrian War, l. 1. (12,13) 3:27,29} They opened the entrance of the harbour and placed their ships in the path of the Romans, causing them much trouble. {*Dio, l. 42. (40) 4:177}

4985. Caesar had nine Rhodian ships (for of the ten that had been sent, one was lost on the voyage along the Egyptian shore), eight ships from Pontus, five Lycian ships and twelve from Asia. Of these, ten were with five tiers and four tiers of oars respectively. The rest were cargo ships and many were not decked. With these, Caesar sailed about Pharos and took up a position opposite the enemy's ships. There were sandbars between the two fleets with a very narrow passage. They stayed in that position for a long time, while they waited to see who would be the first to cross the passage. The one who crossed first would easily be overcome by the whole enemy fleet before the rest could pass and come to the battle. The Rhodian ships asked that they might be the first to cross. By their singular skill, they withstood the whole fleet of the enemy and never turned their sides to them, thus making a safe passage for the rest to follow and so come to the battle. {*Caesar, Alexandrian War, l. 1. (13-15) 3:29-33}

4986. Caesar won the victory and did not lose a single ship. On the Alexandrian side, one galley with five tiers of oars was captured and one with two tiers of oars. All the soldiers and sailors on these were captured, too. Three ships were sunk and the rest fled to the nearby town of Pharos where the citizens defended them from the citadels and buildings which were above them and so kept Caesar from getting close. They were routed out of there immediately by the hard work of the Romans and lost both the town and the island and many of their men. The island was joined to the continent by a double bridge, one of which was abandoned by the enemy and so the Romans easily captured it. On the other bridge, through the rashness of some, the Romans were attacked and routed, so that they fled to their ships. Some of them got to the ships, which sank due to the number and weight of the men. Some fought and not knowing what to do, were killed by the Alexandrians. [K345] Some Romans escaped to safety on the ships that were at anchor. A few swam to the next ships. Caesar retired onto his own ship. When a large number who were following him tried to get onto his ship, he guessed what would happen. He jumped from the ship and swam to those ships which were farther off. From there, he sent boats to help those who were in danger and saved some of them. His own ship sank when it was overloaded with the large number of soldiers and a number of troops drowned. {*Caesar, Alexandrian War, l. 1. (16-21) 3:33-45}

4987. Although Hirtius never mentioned it, the following interesting detail of the battle was noted by Suetonius and by Orosius, who copied Suetonius. When Caesar escaped by swimming to the next ship, he held up his left hand so that his war commentaries should not get wet. This is also mentioned by Plutarch and Dio, while Appian related the story thus: Caesar, alone on the bridge, was surrounded by the enemy that was pressing on him. He cast off his purple coat and leaped into the sea. The king's soldiers pursued him and he swam a long time underwater, only lifting his head to get air. He swam to a lone ship nearby and by holding up his hands to them, was recognised and saved. But Suetonius wrote that he held his soldier's coat in his mouth and dragged it behind him so that the enemy could not get it. However, Florus and Plutarch stated that he left it in the waves, either by chance or on purpose, so that the enemies, who were pursuing him, would shoot at it with their arrows and stones. When the Egyptians got the coat, they fastened it to a monument, which they had erected for their routing of the enemy, as if they had taken the general himself. So said Appian and Dio. {*Suetonius, Julius, l. 1. c. 64. 1:115} {Orosius, l. 6. c. 15.} {*Dio, l. 42. (40) 4:179} {*Plutarch, Caesar, l. 1. c. 49. s. 4. 7:561} {*Appian, Civil Wars, l. 2. c. 13. (90) 3:393} {*Appian, Civil Wars, l. 2. c. 21. (150) 3:505,507} {*Florus, l. 2. c. 13. s. 59,60. 1:285,287}

4988. In this battle, about four hundred soldiers from the legions were killed. [E662] A few more of the soldiers, who belonged to the fleet, as well as some sailors, were also killed. The Alexandrians built a citadel there and strengthened it with many engines of war. They took the stones from the sea and made use of the place more freely, as the base for sending out their ships. {*Caesar, Alexandrian War, l. 1. (21) 3:43,45}

4989. Meanwhile, Mithridates of Pergamum quickly gathered large forces from Syria and Cilicia through the extreme goodwill of the cities and his own diligence. {*Caesar, Alexandrian War, l. 1. (26) 3:51} When he came to Askelon by himself, he sent for Antipater, the governor of Judea, to come to him. He brought three thousand soldiers with him and through his influence managed to achieve in getting Hyrcanus, the high priest, and other governors to join their forces together. Strabo related this from Hypsicrates, who was a historian of the Phoenicians. For Antipater had agreed with the princes of the Arabians that they should also come to Caesar's aid. Through Antipater's efforts and exceptional determination Iamblicus, the governor, Ptolemy's son and Tholomy, the son of Soemus, who lived at Mount Libanus (Lebanon), and almost all the cities of Syria, sent help for Caesar. They did not want to be outdone by Antipater in their zeal for Caesar. {*Josephus, Antiq., l. 14. c. 8. s. 1. (127-132) 7:515-519}

4990. When the Alexandrians saw that the Romans became more zealous through the losses they had recently sustained and that they were encouraged by losses as well as by success, they sent envoys to Caesar. They wanted him to let their king go free and come to them, for a large number were weary of the war and would do whatever the king wished them to do. [K346] Caesar thought that, through the king, they might become Caesar's friends and stop fighting. Although Caesar knew that the fidelity of both the king and the Alexandrians was suspect, he let him go. He knew that the enemy's strength would not be increased by the king's

going to them and the war against a king would be all the more glorious. Caesar advised him to take care of his kingdom and to honour the fidelity that he owed to Caesar and the people of Rome. The king tearfully faked his joy and asked not to be released. But when Caesar sent him away, he eagerly pursued the war against Caesar. {*Caesar, Alexandrian War, l. 1. (23,24) 3:45-49} {*Dio, l. 42. (42) 4:181}

4991. The Alexandrians found that their new general made them no stronger and the Romans were no weaker. Worse, the soldiers daily mocked the king's youth and weakness. They were very distressed and did not know how to help themselves. There were reports that large forces were coming to Caesar by land from Syria and Cilicia about which Caesar had heard nothing. They determined to intercept the provisions which were being brought to the Romans by sea. So they rigged their ships, stationed them in convenient places in the channel around Canopus and watched for ships bringing the provisions. {*Caesar, Alexandrian War, l. 1. (25) 3:49} Since the soldiers from Syria, whom Caesar had sent for, were now approaching, they guarded all the shores and did much harm to these forces. Those who were on the Libyan side, brought some help to Caesar. At the mouths of the Nile River, the Egyptians made many fires, as though they were Romans. By this deceit, they took many, so that the rest did not dare to come there. {*Dio, l. 42. (40) 4:179}

4992. Thereupon, Caesar commanded that his fleet, over which Tiberius Nero was the commander, be rigged. In this fleet, the Rhodian ships included their flagship, the Euphranor, which had been in every battle and had always been victorious, but was unlucky in this battle. When they came to Canopus, both fleets were positioned facing one another. The Euphranor, according to Nero's custom, started the battle and sank one of the enemy's ships. She followed the chase of the next ship too far and Nero's own side was too slow in following him. He was all alone surrounded by the Alexandrians. He fought valiantly in the battle and died alone with his conquering ship. However, the enemies were defeated in this battle which Tiberius Claudius Nero had started so that his own side could safely sail to land. {*Caesar, Alexandrian War, l. 1. (25) 3:49,51} {*Dio, l. 42. (40) 4:179}

4993. About the same time, Mithridates from Pergamum came overland from Syria across its border with Egypt bringing large forces to Pelusium. {*Caesar, Alexandrian War, l. 1. (26) 3:51} He tried to go upstream by the mouth of the Nile River which is at Pelusium. The Egyptians had blocked the entrance by night with their ships, which they had carried into the channel. He transported his ships there, for the channel did not reach all the way to the sea, and went into the Nile River with his ships. He suddenly attacked those who were guarding the mouths of the Nile River from the sea and from the river simultaneously. He took control of the mouths and attacked Pelusium with his fleet and his land forces. {*Dio, l. 42. (41) 4:181} This town had been controlled by Achillas with a strong garrison because of its strategic position. All Egypt was thought to be sufficiently fortified by Pharos against any access by sea, and by Pelusium, against any access by land. But he suddenly surrounded Pelusium with large forces. The defenders stoutly defended it with a strong garrison of men but were overcome. Mithridates constantly maintained the large number of the attackers. He replaced any men who were wounded and weary and in this way maintained a constant attack. *[E663] [K347]* He overcame the city in the same day that he attacked it and stationed a garrison of his own there. {*Caesar, Alexandrian War, l. 1. (26) 3:51,53} Antipater acted valiantly, by breaking down a piece of the wall. He was the first to break in, thus allowing the rest to follow. {*Josephus, Antiq., l. 14. c. 8. s. 1. (130,131) 7:517} After these great exploits, Mithridates marched to join Caesar in Alexandria. {*Caesar, Alexandrian War, l. 1. (26) 3:53} As he advanced toward Alexandria, he learned that Dioscorides was coming to fight them. Mithridates ambushed and killed him. {*Dio, l. 42. (41) 4:181} By the authority which normally belonged to the victor, he peacefully subdued all the districts along his line of march and won them over to friendship with Caesar. {*Caesar, Alexandrian War, l. 1. (26) 3:53}

*4994.* The Egyptian Jews, who lived in that part of the country called Onias, would not allow Mithridates and Antipater to march to Caesar. Antipater tried to win them over to his side, since they were fellow countrymen. He showed them the letters from Hyrcanus, the high priest, in which they were invited to be friends to Caesar and to provide him with food and supplies for his army. {*Josephus, Antiq., l. 14. c. 8. s. 1. (131,132) 7:517,519} However, Asinius Pollio (that is, Trallianus, a writer of the civil war) wrote that Hyrcanus, the high priest, himself invaded Egypt with Mithridates, as Josephus related from Strabo. {*Josephus, Antiq., l. 14. c. 8. s. 3. (130) 7:521} Also, the words of Caesar about Hyrcanus, which were inscribed by him on a brazen table in memory of Hyrcanus' deeds, seem to confirm this: {*Josephus, l. 14. c. 10. s. 2. (192,193) 7:551}

> "In the last Alexandrian war, he came to our aid with fifteen hundred soldiers and was sent by me to Mithridates. He surpassed all those in his company in valour."

*4995.* The Jews, the inhabitants of the country of Onias, willingly submitted, because of the authority of Antipater and Hyrcanus. When those who lived around Memphis heard this, they sent for Mithridates to come

to them also, and when he came, they, too, joined his side. {*Josephus, Antiq., l. 14. c. 8. s. 1. (131,132) 7:517,519}

*4996.* King Ptolemy knew that Mithridates was rapidly approaching the place which is called Delta because of its similarity to the Greek letter Δ, and which was not far from Alexandria. Ptolemy knew that he would have to cross the Nile River. Therefore, he sent large forces against him so that he could either defeat him or prevent him from joining Caesar. The forces that first crossed over the river at the delta, met with Mithridates and began the battle. They hurried, to prevent those who followed from sharing in the victory. Mithridates withstood their attack with great prudence. He entrenched his camp after the Roman custom. When he saw the attackers carelessly and proudly coming right up to his fortifications, he made a general sally and killed a large number of them. The rout was so complete, that they would all have been killed had the rest not hidden themselves in secret places or retired to the boats they had used to cross the river. After they had recovered somewhat from their defeat, they joined with those who were following and began a fresh attack on Mithridates. {*Caesar, Alexandrian War, l. 1. (27) 3:53,55}

*4997.* This battle was fought near the place which is called the *Camp of the Jews.* Mithridates commanded the right wing and Antipater the left wing. Mithridates' wing began to waver and would very likely have been routed, had not Antipater quickly marched along the riverside with his forces. They had already defeated the forces opposing them and now came to Mithridates' rescue. They forced the Egyptians, who were defeating Mithridates, to flee. *[K348]* They so hotly pursued those who fled, that Antipater took over the enemies' camp. He shared the plunder with Mithridates, then pursued the enemy, leaving Mithridates far behind him. Mithridates lost eight hundred of his men and Antipater only fifty (or eighty {*Josephus, Jewish War, l. 1. c. 9. s. 4. (190-192) 2:89}). When Mithridates told Caesar of these things, he stated plainly that Antipater was the cause of the victory and of their preservation. {*Josephus, Antiq., l. 14. c. 8. s. 2. (133-136) 7:519}

### 3957b AM, 4667 JP, 47 BC

*4998.* King Ptolemy marched out to surprise Mithridates, almost at the same time that Caesar came to rescue him. The king took the quickest route by the Nile River where he had a large fleet already rigged. Caesar did not take the same route so that he would not be forced to fight a naval battle on the river. {*Caesar, Alexandrian War, l. 1. (28) 3:55} Therefore, he sailed by night as though he were hurrying to one of the mouths of the Nile. He carried many lights on all his ships, so that the Egyptians would think he was sailing in that direction. At first, he went out with his fleet but later he put out his lights and sailed back again. He sailed around the city and arrived at a peninsula on the Libyan side where he landed his soldiers. They marched around the marsh and met with the king's forces before these could attack Mithridates. {*Dio, l. 42. (43) 4:183} He defeated them and was received safely with his army. {*Caesar, Alexandrian War, l. 1. (28) 3:55}

4999. The king and his army took up the higher ground in a place that was naturally well-fortified. Caesar was about seven miles from him and there was a river between them. If he crossed the river, he would have to fight with the Alexandrians. He crossed it and killed a large number of the Alexandrians who tried to hinder his crossing. Caesar camped a short distance from the king's camp, which he had joined to his camp by the outer works. His soldiers pursued the Alexandrians, who fled from there, right up to their camp and came up to their fortifications. [E664] They began to fight bravely at a distance but were wounded with arrows coming from various places. The men, who were behind them, fought from the river where there were many ships that were well-manned with slingers and archers. {*Caesar, Alexandrian War, l. 1. (29,30) 3:57,59}

5000. Caesar knew that his men were fighting as well as they could, yet they could not prevail, because of the difficulty of the terrain. He saw that the highest place of the camp was deserted by the Alexandrians because it was naturally well-fortified. They had come down to where the battle was, partly to see and partly to fight. So he commanded his cohorts to go around the camp and capture the highest ground. He put Carfulenus in command of this, for he was an excellent man both in valour and knowledge of military affairs. As soon as they arrived at the camp, they found that only a few were left in it. Caesar's soldiers fought bravely and the Alexandrians, frightened by the shouting and fighting of their adversaries, began a general rout. The Romans were so encouraged by their disorder, that they captured almost the whole camp on all sides. First they took the highest place of the camp and then the Romans ran down and killed a large number in the camp. To escape this danger, the Alexandrians fled and cast themselves in large numbers over the rampart on the side facing the river. The other side was being overwhelmed with the great violence of the battle, so that the rest on the side facing the river had the easier escape. {*Caesar, Alexandrian War, l. 1. (31) 3:59,61} [K349]

5001. It is certain that the king fled from the camp, that he was received into a ship and that he died there when the overloaded ship sank, because of the large number who swam to the ships that were nearest. {*Caesar,

Alexandrian War, l. 1. (31) 3:61} {*Livy, l. 112. 14:141} {*Dio, l. 42. (43) 4:185} {Orosius, l. 6. c. 16.} His body wallowed in the mud and rolled to the bank of the Nile. It was identified by the golden breastplate which he wore (such as the Ptolemys used to wear, as Julius Capitoline confirmed, in his work on Maximinius the Younger). {*Florus, l. 2. c. 13. s. 60. 1:287} {Eutropius, l. 6.} {Orosius, l. 6. c. 16.} After the death of his father, Auletes, he lived three years and eight months, which is why Porphyry attributed four years to his reign. {Porphyry, Scaliger's Greek Eusebius, p. 226.}

5002. In this battle, twenty thousand men were killed and twelve thousand surrendered. Seventy warships were captured. Caesar lost five hundred men. {Orosius, l. 6. c. 16.} Antipater, whom Caesar had used for valiant service in the most dangerous tasks he faced, was also wounded in this battle. {*Josephus, Antiq., l. 14. c. 8. s. 2. (136) 7:519}

5003. Because of this great victory, Caesar confidently marched to Alexandria by land the next day with his cavalry. As conqueror, he entered that part of the town which was being held by a garrison of the enemies. However, all the townsmen tossed away their arms and left the citadel. They put on the clothes they usually wore when they wanted to supplicate their governors. Bringing out all the sacred things of their religion, with which they were accustomed to appease the offended and enraged minds of their kings, they came and met Caesar and submitted to him. Caesar placed them under his protection and comforted them. Passing through the enemy's fortifications, he reached his own part of the town, with great shouting from his own soldiers. They not only rejoiced that the battle had been successful, but also, that his arrival was so joyful. {*Caesar, Alexandrian War, l. 1. (32) 3:61,63}

5004. In the marble calendar records, {Gruter, Inscriptions, p. 133.} on the date of the 6th of the Calends of April (March 27), it is thus noted: *HOC DIE CAESAR ALEXAND. RECEPIT. This day Caesar recovered Alexandria.* However, that day was the 14th of the Julian January. Hence, the Alexandrian war was over. Caesar had fought this war in an unfavourable place and at a poor time for fighting since it was in the winter. {*Suetonius, Julius, l. 1. c. 35. s. 1. 1:81}

5005. After Caesar had conquered Egypt, he did not subject it to the dominion of the Romans, but gave it to Cleopatra, for whose sake he had carried on the war. He was fearful that the Egyptians might not like being under a queen and that by this he would stir up the Romans against him, both on account of his actions and for being too familiar with Cleopatra. Therefore, he ordered that she should marry her other brother, who was still alive, and that they should hold the kingdom in common between them. This he did only for appearance's sake. For, in actual fact, the whole kingdom had been entrusted to Cleopatra, for her husband was only a child of age eleven. Hence, Strabo said he was exceedingly young. {*Strabo, l. 17. c. 1. s. 11. 8:47} However, she could do anything with Caesar. Therefore, under the pretence of marriage with her brother and of sharing the kingdom equally with her husband, she alone ruled over all. She was also too familiar with Caesar. These things Dio had related more honestly. {*Dio, l. 42. (44) 4:185} Hirtius stated them more mildly, in favour of Caesar, thus: {*Caesar, Alexandrian War, l. 1. (33) 3:63}

"After Caesar had conquered Egypt, he made those kings, whom Ptolemy had appointed in his will and earnestly asked the people of Rome that they would not alter it. Since the king, the older of the two sons, was dead, he turned over the kingdom to the younger son and to Cleopatra, the older of the two daughters. [E665] [K350] She remained under his protection and quarters."

5006. Suetonius stated: {*Suetonius, Julius, l. 1. c. 35. s. 1,2. 11:81}

"After Caesar had gained the victory, he granted the kingdom of Egypt to Cleopatra and her younger brother. He was afraid to make it a province lest, at some time or another, they had a rebellious leader, who might start a new rebellion."

5007. Cleopatra and Caesar often feasted together and sat up until daybreak. He sailed with her on the Nile River with four hundred ships. He was in the same galley with her, which was called Thalamegos. He crossed Egypt as far as Ethiopia, but his army refused to follow him any farther. {*Suetonius, Julius, l. 1. c. 52. s. 1,2. 1:101} {*Appian, Civil Wars, l. 2. c. 13. (90) 3:393}

5008. At Alexandria, Caesar erected a brazen pillar which recorded the liberties that he had granted to the Jews. {*Josephus, Antiq., l. 14. c. 10. s. 1. (188,189) 7:549} {*Josephus, Apion, l. 2. c. 4. (37) 1:307}

5009. Pharnaces had become famous because of his successes. He hoped all things would happen to Caesar as he wanted it to. Pharnaces seized Pontus with all his forces and conquered it. He was a most cruel king. Because he thought he should have better luck than his father had, he conquered many towns and plundered the goods of the citizens of Rome and of Pontus. He decreed punishments worse than death itself for those who deserved praise for either beauty or age. He captured Pontus when there was no one to defend it and bragged that he had recovered his father's kingdom. {*Caesar, Alexandrian War, l. 1. (41) 3:77}

5010. He displayed his cruelty particularly on Amisus, a city of Pontus. After it had resisted for a long time, he won it by storm, then put all the adult men to death and made all the boys, eunuchs. {*Appian, Civil Wars, l. 2. c. 13. (91) 3:395} {*Dio, l. 42. (46) 4:187}

### 3957c AM, 4667 JP, 47 BC

5011. Asander, to whom Pharnaces had committed the government of Bosphorus, tried to curry favour with the Romans, in the hope of getting the kingdom of Bosphorus for himself. He organized an insurrection against his master. {*Dio, l. 42. (46) 4:187,189}

5012. Caesar sent letters from Egypt to Marcus Cicero telling him to stay where he was and to retain the name of Imperator for the victory he had won in Cilicia. Gaius Pansa carried these letters to him. Cicero postponed the grant of the laurelled fasces and the ceremony for such a time as he considered more appropriate. {*Cicero, Pro Ligario, l. 1. c. 3. 14:465} For after he had left the province of Cilicia, he had not as yet entered Rome, but was accompanied everywhere by his lictors, hoping in vain for a triumph. {*Cicero, Atticus, l. 11. c. 6. 23:367} Caesar's letters were delivered to Cicero on the 3rd of the Ides of August (August 11, or Julian May 31). {*Cicero, Friends, l. 14. c. 24. 27:223}

5013. After Pharnaces had captured Bithynia and Cappadocia, he planned to take Lesser Armenia. So he incited all the kings and tetrarchs of that country to rebel. {*Plutarch, Caesar, l. 1. c. 50. s. 1. 7:561} He also marched into Asia hoping for the same success that his father Mithridates had enjoyed there. {*Dio, l. 42. (46) 4:187}

5014. Appian stated that Caesar spent nine months in Egypt, {*Appian, Civil Wars, l. 2. c. 13. (90) 3:393} and that Cleopatra would have kept him there longer or accompanied him on his voyage to Rome. Pharnaces forced him to leave Egypt against his will and held up his rapid march into Italy. {*Dio, l. 42. (47) 4:189} A short time later, Cleopatra gave birth to a son by him whom the Alexandrians called Caesarion. {*Plutarch, Caesar, l. 1. c. 49. s. 5. 7:561} This name was given to the son by the mother, with the permission of Caesar himself. {*Suetonius, Julius, l. 1. c. 52. s. 1,2. 1:101} [K351] Plutarch seemed to intimate that, after Caesar's death, she had too much familiarity with his enemy, Gnaeus Pompey, the oldest son of Pompey the Great. {*Plutarch, Antony, l. 1. c. 25. s. 3. 9:193} Suetonius cited the elder Curio as witnessing to Caesar's immoral behaviour. Curio said in one of his speeches, that Caesar was: {*Suetonius, Julius, l. 1. c. 52. s. 3. 1:103} {See note on 3923b AM. <<4059>>}

"every woman's man and every man's woman."

5015. Caesar removed Arsinoe, the younger sister of Cleopatra, from the kingdom in whose name

Ganymedes had, for a long time, reigned most tyrannically. He wished to prevent a future rebellion that might arise through seditious men, so he wanted to keep her away until time had confirmed the authority of the king. He took his sixth veteran legion and left three other legions there, so that the king's authority might be confirmed. But the king could not retain the affections of his own subjects, because both he and his queen were staunch friends of Caesar. Nor could they claim any basis for their authority, since they were new to the throne. {*Caesar, Alexandrian War, l. 1. (33) 3:63,65} {*Suetonius, Julius, l. 1. c. 76. s. 3. 1:129,131}

5016. After Caesar had settled everything, he marched overland into Syria. {*Caesar, Alexandrian War, l. 1. (33) 3:65} {*Suetonius, Julius, l. 1. c. 35. s. 2. 1:81} {*Plutarch, Caesar, l. 1. c. 49. s. 5. 7:561} {*Appian, Civil Wars, l. 2. c. 13. (91) 3:395} {Orosius, l. 6. c. 16.} Josephus wrote that he sailed to Syria. {*Josephus, Antiq., l. 14. c. 8. s. 3. (137) 7:521} Hirtius later confirmed this.

5017. The news of Caesar's departure from Alexandria reached Italy on the 3rd of the Nones of July (July 5, or Julian April 23). {*Cicero, Atticus, l. 11. c. 20. 23:411} Gaius Trebonius left Caesar at Antioch and set out from Seleucia Pieria. After a twenty-eight day journey, on the 16th of the Calends of September (August 15, or Julian June 3), Trebonius arrived in Italy. {*Cicero, Atticus, l. 11. c. 23. 23:419} From this it is deduced that Caesar was at Antioch on the 15th of the Calends of August (July 18, or Julian May 6). (Loeb edition of text has 17th of Calends of September. Editor.)

5018. Johannes Malela of Antioch noted that on the 12th day of the month of Artemisios, or May, an edict was publicly proposed in the city of Antioch, concerning the empire of Julius Caesar. {Johannes Malela, Chronicle (Unpublished), l. 9.} On the 20th of the same month, another edict was sent out from Julius Caesar concerning the liberty of the same city. It said: *Julius Caesar to the metropolis of Antioch, the holy and privileged asylum and refuge against the vigour of the law.* Finally, on the 23rd day, Caesar, the dictator, entered Antioch. [E666] However, that edict clearly shows that he was in Antioch on the 20th day. It should be said that he left the city on the 23rd day, having arrived before that.

5019. Antigonus, the son of Aristobulus, came to Caesar to complain to him about his father's misfortune. For siding with Caesar, he was poisoned by Pompey's side. His brother had been beheaded by Scipio. Antigonus wanted Caesar to have pity on him because he had been expelled from his father's kingdom. As well, he accused Hyrcanus and Antipater of having used force to take over the government. They did not hold back from wronging him. He also accused them of having sent help

into Egypt to Caesar, not so much out of goodwill, but in fear of the ancient animosity and so that they would not be punished for their loyalty to Pompey. However, Antipater pleaded his own cause, justifying himself and accusing Antigonus. He recalled what work he had undertaken for Caesar in the most recent wars. He showed all the wounds he had sustained and let them testify to the truth of his words. When Caesar heard this, he made Hyrcanus the high priest and having offered Antipater any government he asked for, made him governor of Judea. {*Josephus, Jewish War, l. 1. c. 10. s. 1-3. 2:91,93} {*Josephus, Antiq., l. 14. c. 8. s. 4,5. (140-144) 7:521-525} [K352]

5020. Caesar also decreed that Hyrcanus and his children should retain the government and high priesthood of the Jews in perpetuity according to the custom of the country. Hyrcanus was included in the number of Caesar's friends and allies. If any controversy was to arise involving the discipline of the Jews, Hyrcanus should decide it. Moreover, he would not be forced to quarter soldiers in winter, nor would he pay taxes. A brazen table containing these things was to be erected in the Capitol and in the temples at Tyre, Sidon and Askelon. It was engraved in Latin and Greek. These decrees were to be sent into every place. {*Josephus, Antiq., l. 14. c. 10. s. 3. (196-198) 7:553}

5021. After Caesar had stayed in almost all the cities of Syria that were of any note, he distributed rewards both publicly and privately to those who deserved them. He was made aware of and settled old controversies. He also took kings and tyrants, governors of the provinces and borders (who all came to him) under his protection, on conditions which he imposed on them for the keeping and defending of the provinces. He dismissed his friends and the friends of the people of Rome. {*Caesar, Alexandrian War, l. 1. (65) 3:115,117}

5022. At Tyre, Caesar took away all the things that were dedicated to Hercules because they had received Pompey and his wife during their flight. He did not do this out of malice but because he needed the money. {*Dio, l. 42. (49) 4:193}

5023. After some days had been spent in the province of Syria, he handed the command of the legions and Syria over to Sextus Caesar, his friend and relative. {*Caesar, Alexandrian War, l. 1. (66) 3:117,119} Dio wrote that he committed all matters to the charge of Sextus, his praetor and cousin. {*Dio, l. 47. (26) 5:171} Appian stated that a legion was left in Syria by him, even when he was thinking about the Parthian war. The honour of governor was granted to his relative, Sextus Julius, who was a young man. {*Appian, Civil Wars, l. 3. c. 11. (77) 4:97,99} {*Appian, Civil Wars, l. 4. c. 8. (58) 4:239}

*5024.* After Caesar had ordered the affairs in Syria, he went to Cilicia in the same fleet with which he had come. {*\*Caesar, Alexandrian War, l. 1. (66) 3:117*} {*\*Josephus, Antiq., l. 14. c. 9. s. 1. (156) 7:531*} He called all the cities of this province to him at Tarsus. There, he set in order all matters to do with the province and the neighbouring cities but did not stay there long, because he wanted to settle the war in Pontus. {*\*Caesar, Alexandrian War, l. 1. (66) 3:117*}

*5025.* There he pardoned King Tarcondimotus (mentioned previously {*\*Cicero, Friends, l. 15. c. 1. s. 2. 27:231*}), who had a region of Cilicia under him and had greatly helped Pompey by sea. {*\*Dio, l. 41. (63) 4:109*}

*5026.* After Antipater had followed Caesar from Syria, he returned into Judea. As he was making his rounds through the province, he repressed, by using both threats and reasoning, all those who were rebellious. He told them that if they were content with their prince Hyrcanus, they would live happily in their own land. But if they thought they could do better by rebelling, they would have himself as master instead of governor, Hyrcanus as a tyrant instead of a king, and Caesar and the Romans would be their very bitter enemies, instead of princes. *[E667]* Because of this, Antipater would definitely not allow anything to be changed from what they agreed on. When Antipater realised that Hyrcanus was dull and idle, he settled the state of the province as he pleased. He made his older son, Phasael, the governor of Jerusalem and the neighbouring countries and gave the care of Galilee to Herod, who was his second oldest son and a very young man. {*\*Josephus, Jewish War, l. 1. c. 10. s. 4. (201-203) 2:93,95*} {*\*Josephus, Antiq., l. 14. c. 9. s. 1,2. (156-158) 7:531,533*}

*5027.* Josephus stated that Herod was only fifteen years old at that time. {*\*Josephus, Antiq., l. 14. c. 9. s. 2. (158) 7:533*} *[K353]* The following references retain the same number. {*Rufinus, in his translation of Josephus*} {*Photius, Bibliotheca, cod. 258.*} {*Pseudogoronides the Hebrew, l. 5. c. 3.*} {*Nicephorus Callistus, Ecclesiastical History, l. 1. c. 6.*} However, Ptolemy and Nicolaus Damascene, the first historians who wrote of Herod, and from whom Josephus took his information, wrote twenty-five instead of fifteen. It was an easy mistake for the transcribers to confuse: κε for ιε. It was forty-three and a half years from this time to the death of Herod. If we add twenty-five years to this, we get his age at death as being sixty-eight and a half years. Had he lived six months longer, he would have been in his seventieth year. Josephus himself acknowledged that, when Herod was dying, he was almost in his seventieth year. {*\*Josephus, Antiq., l. 17. c. 6. s. 1. (147) 8:439*}

*5028.* Phasael had a son born to him who was also called Phasael by the mother, Salampsio, the daughter of Herod and Mariamme. {*\*Josephus, Antiq., l. 18. c. 5. s. 4. (130)*}

9:89} He was only seven years old when his father died. {*\*Josephus, Antiq., l. 14. c. 14. s. 1. (371,372) 7:645*}

*5029.* Pharnaces planned an expedition against Asander, who had revolted from him in the Bosphorus. When he heard that Caesar was rapidly approaching Armenia, he was terrified and more afraid of Caesar, who was leading the invasion, than of his army. He sent many envoys to negotiate for peace before Caesar came too close. Hoping to avoid this immediate danger by any means, he made the fact that he had never helped Pompey his main pretence. He also hoped to be able to induce Caesar to some peace terms because he was hurrying into Italy and Africa. Then, after his departure, he would be free to renew his planned war. Caesar suspected as much and courteously entertained his first and second envoys, to enable him to take him by surprise while he was still hoping for peace. {*\*Dio, l. 42. (47) 4:189,191*}

*5030.* Caesar made long marches through Cappadocia and stayed two days at Mazaca. Then he came to Comana, the most ancient temple of Enyo, or Bellona (goddess of war), in Cappadocia. She was worshipped with such great devotion that her priest was considered by the whole country to be second only to the king in majesty, command and power. {*\*Strabo, l. 12. c. 2. s. 3. 5:351,353*} Caesar decreed this priesthood on Lycomedes of Bithynia, who was a most noble man and of the family of the Cappadocian kings. He thus recovered the right that was undoubtedly his, although it had long been interrupted. {*\*Caesar, Alexandrian War, l. 1. (66) 3:117,119*} Although Caesar confirmed to others, who had sided with Pompey against him, the positions of authority which they had received from Pompey, he transferred the priesthood of Comana from Archelaus to Lycomedes. {*\*Appian, Mithridatic Wars, l. 12. c. 17. (121) 2:475*} Pompey had given it to Lycomedes' father Archelaus, the husband of Cleopatra's elder sister, whom Gabinus had killed in Egypt. {*\*Strabo, l. 12. c. 3. s. 34. 5:437*}

*5031.* When Caesar neared Pontus and the borders of Galatia, Dejotarus, the tetrarch of Galatia, came to him. He was claiming the state of Lesser Armenia which the Senate had granted to him, but which was being disputed by the rest of the tetrarchs, who said it had never belonged to him, either by law or custom. Dejotarus set aside his royal robes and dressed like a common man who was guilty. He fell prostrate at Caesar's feet and begged his pardon for having served in Gnaeus Pompey's army. He made the excuse that he had not known what was happening in Italy and that he had been forced to do this because he had been surrounded by Pompey's armies. *[K354]* Caesar rejected his excuse but said he would grant him his request because of his old acquaintance and friendship, on account of the dignity and age of the man and at the entreaty of many of Dejotarus' friends and acquaintances, who came to intercede on his behalf. Caesar restored his royal robes to him, saying that he would later decide the controversies of the tetrarchs. However, he ordered that Dejotarus' legion be brought to him, which Dejotarus had formed from his own men, who were trained in the Roman discipline. Caesar also wanted all his cavalry to be brought to him to serve him in the Pontic war. {*Caesar, Alexandrian War, l. 1. (67) 3:119} Caesar fined his old acquaintance, Dejotarus, a sum of money and gave Lesser Armenia, which had been given to Dejotarus by the Senate and was currently occupied by Pharnaces, to Ariobarzanes, the king of Cappadocia. {*Cicero, Philippics, l. 2. c. 37. 15:157,159} {*Cicero, De Divinatione, l. 1. c. 15. 20:255} {*Cicero, De Divinatione, l. 2. c. 37. 20:461} {*Dio, l. 42. (46) 4:187}

5032. Cicero made a speech on behalf of this king Dejotarus, saying that Domitius had paid his fine two or three times over, by selling his own private goods at a public sale. Caesar could then use the money in the war. [E668] Also, to gain Caesar's favour, he spoke to Caesar thus about the matter: {*Cicero, Pro Dejotaro, l. 1. c. 13. 14:535}

"He remembers what you have helped him to retain, not what you have helped him to lose. Nor does he think that he was punished by you, but since he thought that many things were to be given by you to many men, he did not oppose your taking some from him who was on the opposing side. Oh Caesar, you have given all things to Dejotarus, since you have granted the name of king even to his son. As long as he retains and keeps this title, he thinks that kindness of the people of Rome and the opinion held of him by the Senate has been no whit diminished."

5033. When Caesar arrived in Pontus, he made a rendezvous of all his forces in one place. They varied in number and in martial discipline, except for the sixth legion, which was a veteran legion that he had brought with him from Alexandria. However, due to the labours and hazards they had undergone, difficulties both by sea and land and numerous skirmishes, they were so undermanned that they were less than a thousand men. The remainder were three legions, one from Dejotarus and two that had been in the battle which Gnaeus Domitius had fought with Pharnaces. {*Caesar, Alexandrian War, l. 1. (69) 3:121}

5034. Pharnaces was frightened by the approach of Caesar and sent envoys to negotiate for peace. They brought him a golden crown when he was twenty-five miles away and very foolishly offered him their king's daughter in marriage. {*Appian, Civil Wars, l. 2. c. 13. (91) 3:395} First of all, they begged that he would not come as an enemy, for Pharnaces would do anything whatever he ordered him

to do. They especially reminded him that Pharnaces had sent no forces to Pompey against Caesar, whereas Dejotarus had sent some troops, but had still been received into Caesar's favour. Caesar replied that he would be very favourably inclined toward Pharnaces, if he would do everything as he had promised. But he advised the envoys in mild terms, as was his custom, that they should not object to him about Dejotarus, nor brag too much about the favour that they had not sent help to Pompey. {*Caesar, Alexandrian War, l. 1. (69,70) 3:123,125} He also accused Pharnaces of having been wicked and ungrateful toward his benefactor. {*Dio, l. 41. (63) 4:109} {*Dio, l. 42. (47) 4:189,191} In summing up, he ordered him to get out of Pontus and to send back the household slaves of the tax collectors. He was to restore to him the allies and citizens of Rome who were in his possession. If he would do this, Caesar said that he would then accept those presents which generals were accustomed to receive from their friends after a war was happily ended. {*Caesar, Alexandrian War, l. 1. (70) 3:125}

5035. Pharnaces freely promised all things, hoping that Caesar would want to hurry to Rome and so believe his promises more willingly. [K355] He began to go more slowly about his business, to ask for more time for his departure, to interpose new conditions and in short, to disappoint Caesar. Caesar recognised his craftiness and rushed through his business all the more, so that he would be able to come and fight with him sooner than anyone would expect. {*Caesar, Alexandrian War, l. 1. (71) 3:125}

5036. As soon as Caesar arrived at Pharnaces' camp, he said: *Shall not now this parricide (murderer of a parent) be punished?* Mounting his horse, he routed the enemy at the first shout that was given, and carried out a large slaughter. Caesar was helped by a thousand cavalry who followed him when he first rushed into the battle. {*Appian, Civil Wars, l. 2. c. 13. (91) 3:395} {*Dio, l. 42. (47) 4:189} The same day that he reached the enemy after his march, Caesar went to fight with the enemy. He was troubled at times by the enemy's cavalry and their chariots armed with scythes, but he finally obtained the victory. Julius Frontinus noted that Caesar marshalled his army on a hill, which made for an easier victory. {*Frontinus, Stratagems, l. 2. c. 2. s. 4. 1:99} The arrows, which were shot from above onto the barbarians below, quickly made them flee. Dejotarus was in the battle with Caesar against Pharnaces, risking his life. {*Cicero, Pro Dejotaro, l. 1. c. 5. 14:513}

5037. This battle was fought around Mount Scotius, which was not more than three miles from the city of Zela. It was near there that Mithridates, the father of Pharnaces, had defeated Triarius and the Roman army with a large slaughter. {*Caesar, Alexandrian War, l. 1. (72) 3:125,127} {*Plutarch, Caesar, l. 1. c. 50. 7:561} {*Appian, Mithridatic

*Wars, l. 12. c. 17. (120) 2:473*} {*\*Dio, l. 42. (47) 4:191*} On this mountain, Pharnaces (that we may report the story of this battle more accurately from Hirtius) had repaired the old works of his father's camp, five miles from the enemy, so that he could control the valleys adjoining the king's camp. The next night, in the fourth watch, Caesar left his camp with all his legions, but without any baggage, and captured the very place where Mithridates had fought against Triarius.

5038. As soon as it was day and Pharnaces became aware of this, he drew out all his forces in front of his camp. They were either encouraged by the good fortune Mithridates had enjoyed in that place, or persuaded by tokens and ceremonies (which, as Caesar later heard, he scrupulously observed), or filled with contempt for the number of the Roman forces. Many of these had already been defeated under Domitius. Pharnaces, taking the initiative, attacked the Romans in an uneven place as they were fortifying their camp and terrified them. *[E669]* As they were suddenly called from their work, they were not set in battle array. The king's chariots, which were armed with scythes, created chaos among the soldiers. But these chariots were quickly overcome by a large number of arrows. The main body of the enemy followed the chariots and fought hand to hand. They were overcome first in the right wing, where the sixth legion composed of old veterans had been placed, then the left wing and then the main body, where the entire forces of the king were routed. Many of the soldiers were either killed or trampled by their own men. Those who hoped to escape through their swiftness, threw away their arms and crossed the valley. But they were met by the Romans coming from the higher ground and perished. The Romans, encouraged by this victory, did not hesitate to climb up that steep place and attack their works, thereby quickly capturing the enemy's camp from the cohorts that Pharnaces had left for its defence. {*\*Caesar, Alexandrian War, l. 1. (73-76) 3:127-133*} *[K356]*

5039. In this way, Caesar ground Pharnaces into the dust in a single battle or rather, part of a battle, like lightning which came, hit and departed, all in one instant. Nor was it a vain boast of Caesar's that he had overcome the enemy before having set eyes on him. {*\*Florus, l. 2. c. 13. 1:287*} Caesar bragged that he had come to the enemy, he had seen him, and he had conquered him, all on the same day and in the same hour. {*\*Dio, l. 42. (48) 4:191*} In his letters sent to Rome, he wrote these three words to his friend Amanitius: *VENI, VIDI, VICI, I came, I saw, I conquered.* {*\*Plutarch, Caesar, l. 1. c. 50. s. 2. 7:563*} {*\*Appian, Civil Wars, l. 2. c. 13. (91) 3:395*} Within five days of his arrival and within four hours of having come in sight of him, he had vanquished Pharnaces in only one battle.

{*\*Suetonius, Julius, l. 1. c. 35. s. 2. 1:81*} He often remarked on the good luck of Pompey, who happened to get his greatest honour in the Mithridatic War over so cowardly an enemy. {*\*Suetonius, Julius, l. 1. c. 35. s. 2. 1:81*} {*\*Appian, Civil Wars, l. 2. c. 13. (91) 3:395*}

5040. Pharnaces fled with a few cavalry after his whole army had been either killed or captured. When the Romans invaded his camp, it gave him an opportunity to escape. Otherwise, he would have been brought alive into Caesar's hands. {*\*Caesar, Alexandrian War, l. 1. (76) 3:133*} He fled to Sinope with a thousand cavalry. {*\*Appian, Mithridatic Wars, l. 12. c. 17. (120) 2:473*}

5041. Caesar was overjoyed that he had ended so major a war in so short a time. In recalling the sudden danger, he was all the more joyous, because the victory had come so easily, after so many difficulties. {*\*Caesar, Alexandrian War, l. 1. (77) 3:133*} Caesar gave the soldiers all the king's baggage and the spoils, even though they were considerable. {*\*Caesar, Alexandrian War, l. 1. (77) 3:135*} {*\*Dio, l. 42. (48) 4:191*} On this site, Mithridates had set up a monument for the victory he had won over Triarius. Since it had been consecrated to the gods, it was not lawful for Caesar to pull it down. So he set up one in front of it for his victory over Pharnaces, whereby he obscured it and in a way, threw down the monument which Mithridates had erected. After this, he recovered everything Pharnaces had taken from the Romans or their allies. He restored to everyone what each had lost, except for a part of Armenia, which he gave to Ariobarzanes, as well as requiting the city of Amisus for the calamity it had endured, by giving it its liberty. {*\*Dio, l. 42. (48) 4:191*} He ordered the sixth legion to go to Italy to receive the rewards and honours due to them and sent home the supplies that Dejotarus had brought. The two other legions he left in Pontus with Caelius Vinicianus. He passed through Galatia and Bithynia into Asia. He paid attention to and settled all the controversies of all these provinces and gave laws to tetrarchs, kings and cities. {*\*Caesar, Alexandrian War, l. 1. (78) 3:135*}

5042. As he passed through Asia, he collected money, which raised great anger against the tax collectors who exacted it secretly from all the people. {*\*Appian, Civil Wars, l. 2. c. 13. (92) 3:397*} (Publius Servilius Isauricus, the colleague of Caesar and Cicero in the Augurship, was proconsul there. {*\*Cicero, Friends, l. 13. c. 68. 27:157*})

5043. Brithagoras was a man of great authority among the Heracleans in Pontus and had followed Caesar wherever he went. He had even returned to this place again about a matter that concerned his countrymen. When Caesar was preparing to return to Rome, Brithagoras died. He was worn out with old age and continual labours, and his death was greatly mourned by his countrymen. {*Memnon, Excerpts of Photius, c. 62.*}

5044. Caesar made Mithridates of Pergamum the king of Bosphorus (who had carried on the war in Egypt to a good conclusion and very speedily). *[K357]* He was of the family of the kings and had a royal education. Mithridates, the king of all Asia, had taken him away from Pergamum when he was only a child and carried him into his camp and kept him for many years. By this action, namely by putting a king over them who was very friendly toward them, Caesar greatly strengthened the provinces of the people of Rome against the barbarians and enemy kings. {*Caesar, Alexandrian War, l. 1. (78) 3:135*} {*Strabo, l. 13. c. 4. s. 3. 6:169*} {*Appian, Mithridatic Wars, l. 12. c. 17. (121) 2:475*}

5045. He ordered Mithridates to make war upon Asander and become the master of Bosphorus, in order to revenge Asander's treachery against his friend. {*Dio, l. 42. (48) 4:191,193*} *[E670]* Caesar also granted him the tetrarchy of the Trocmians in Galatia, which bordered on Pontus and Cappadocia. This belonged to him by his mother's right, but had previously been seized by Dejotarus and been in his possession for some years. {*Cicero, Philippics, l. 2. c. 37. 15:159*} {*Cicero, De Divinatione, l. 2. c. 37. 20:461*} {*Caesar, Alexandrian War, l. 1. (78) 3:135*} {*Strabo, l. 12. c. 5. s. 2. 5:469*} {*Strabo, l. 13. c. 4. s. 3. 6:169,171*} {*Dio, l. 42. (48) 4:191*}

5046. After this, Caesar sailed into Greece and Italy, raising large sums of money under any pretence whatever, as he had done before. He exacted some money that had previously been promised to Pompey, as well as feigning other excuses to raise money. He also received many golden crowns from the princes and kings, in honour of his victories. He declared that there were two things by which empires were gained, retained and increased: soldiers and money. Each helped the other and if one of them failed, the other must also fail. {*Dio, l. 42. (49) 4:193*}

5047. It does not appear that he was at Athens on the Calends of September (September 1, or Julian June 17), for many things were reported to have detained him in Asia, especially Pharnaces. {*Cicero, Atticus, l. 11. c. 21. 23:413,415*} However, Pharnaces was conquered so suddenly, according to Livy, and everything settled so quickly, that he came to Italy sooner than anyone had imagined. {*Livy, l. 113. 14:143*} {*Caesar, Alexandrian War, l. 1. (78) 3:135*}

5048. Caesar came to Rome just at the end of the year in which he had been made dictator. (This office had never been an annual office.) He was declared consul for the next year. {*Plutarch, Caesar, l. 1. c. 51. s. 1. 7:563*}

5049. Pharnaces turned over Sinope to Domitius Calvinus, who had been left by Caesar to continue the war against him. Domitius Calvinus accepted the peace terms and dismissed him with his thousand cavalry. Pharnaces then killed the horses of the cavalry, which grieved his men. From there, Pharnaces sailed and fled into Pontus. {*Appian, Mithridatic Wars, l. 12. c. 17. (121) 2:475*} Appian stated that Pharnaces fled back into the kingdom of Bosphorus that had been given to him by Pompey. {*Appian, Civil Wars, l. 2. c. 13. (92) 3:395*}

5050. Herod, the prefect of Galilee, captured Hezekiah, a Jew, and his many accomplices in thievery who were accustomed to invade Syria with his bands. Herod put him to death and this gained him much favour with the Syrians. Then he governed the province of Syria. {*Josephus, Jewish War, l. 1. c. 10. s. 5. (204,205) 2:95*} {*Josephus, Antiq., l. 14. c. 9. s. 2. (158-161) 7:533,535*} *[K358]*

5051. Phasael was jealous of his brother's glory and won the favour of the inhabitants of Jerusalem by doing all public business personally and not abusing his power to harm anyone. In this way, it came to pass that Antipater, his father, was reverenced by the whole country as if he had been the king. However, the fidelity and goodwill that was shown him by the people, and which he owed to Hyrcanus, was maintained. {*Josephus, Jewish War, l. 1. c. 10. s. 5. (206,207) 2:95,97*} {*Josephus, Antiq., l. 14. c. 9. s. 2. (161,162) 7:535*}

# 3958a AM, 4667 JP, 47 BC

5052. Caesar undertook an expedition against Publius Scipio, the father-in-law of Pompey the Great, Marcus Cato, and Juba, the king of Numidia. On the 14th of the Calends of January (December 17th, or Julian September 30), he came to Lilybaeum. He sailed from there on the 6th of the Calends of January (December 25), and after four days came within sight of Africa. {*Caesar, African War, l. 1. (1,2) 3:147,149*} (Loeb English translation has three days, whereas the Latin has four days. Editor.) This was the year before the institution of the new calendar, counting backward from the following long year of four hundred and forty-five days which made the Calends of January (January 1) the first day of the new Julian year. This will be shown later. Plutarch and Dio did not note this fact. Plutarch stated that Caesar crossed into Sicily around the winter solstice. {*Plutarch, Caesar, l. 1. c. 52. s. 1. 7:565,565*} Dio said that he went into Africa in the middle of winter. {*Dio, l. 43. (4) 4:217*} However, Cicero clearly affirmed that he went into Africa before winter: {*Cicero, De Divinatione, l. 2. c. 24. 20:431*}

> "When Caesar was advised that he should not go into Africa before winter, did he not go? No, if he had not gone, all the forces of his adversaries would have made their rendezvous in one place."

*5053.* On the Calends of January (January 1, or Julian October 13), Caesar camped at a town called Ruspina. On the day before the Nones of January (January 4, or Julian October 16), the third day after he landed in Africa, there was an extremely fierce battle, which lasted from five o'clock in the morning until sunset, in which Caesar defeated Labienus and Petreius. On the 6th of the Calends of February (January 25, or Julian November 6), he again defeated the enemy's army under the command of Labienus and Scipio. {*Caesar, African War, l. 1. (6-40) 3:155-209}

*5054.* Dio noted that Pharnaces tried to enter into the Bosphorus by force, whereupon he was cast into prison and put to death by Asander. {*Dio, l. 42. (47) 4:191} Appian gave more details. [E671] Pharnaces had gathered together a band of Scythians and Sarmatians and had captured Theodosia and Panticapaeum. When he made war on Asander, his cavalry men, who had no horses and were not used to fighting on foot, were defeated. Pharnaces fought valiantly, even though he was now fifty years old. He was wounded and killed. He had reigned fifteen years in Bosphorus, as Appian stated, or rather, seventeen years. That was the elapsed time from the murder of his father Mithridates. {*Appian, Mithridatic Wars, l. 12. c. 17. (120) 2:475}

*5055.* Caecilius Bassus was an equestrian who had fled from the battle of Pharsalia after Pompey was defeated. He lived as a private citizen at Tyre, where some of his own side joined him. He won the favour of these men and of the soldiers of Sextus, the governor of Syria, who came at various times to guard the city. Since a great deal of news was brought of Caesar's ill-fortune in Africa, Bassus became discontented and tried to instigate a revolt. Sextus arrested him for this, before he was completely ready. Bassus excused himself by saying that he had only raised forces to help Mithridates of Pergamum capture Bosphorus. So Sextus believed him and let him go. {*Dio, l. 47. (26) 5:169,171} [K359]

*5056.* The noblemen of the Jews began to detest Antipater and his sons, because they were so highly honoured by the Jewish nation and became rich through the money from Hyrcanus and the revenues from Judea. Antipater befriended the Roman generals and persuaded Hyrcanus to send them money. He got the credit for this gift, as if he had sent it from his own treasury rather than having received it from Hyrcanus. When Hyrcanus heard about this, he was not angry, but accepted it. However, the violence and bold nature of Herod, who wanted the government for himself, terrified the princes of the Jews the most. For this reason, they went to Hyrcanus and publicly accused Antipater. Most of all, they complained about Herod because he had put Hezekiah to death,

along with many others, without having received any order from Hyrcanus. This was in contempt of the laws, by which no man was punished, no matter how wicked, unless he had first been condemned by the judges. Every day, the mothers of those who had been killed did not stop complaining and crying in the temple, thereby persuading both the king and the people that Herod should give an account of his actions before the Sanhedrin. Because of this, Hyrcanus yielded to their requests and ordered that Herod be summoned before the council to plead his own case. {*Josephus, Antiq., l. 14. c. 9. s. 3. (163-167) 7:535-539}

*5057.* When Herod had arranged the affairs of Galilee as he thought best for himself, he was warned by his father that he should not go into the council alone. He should take with him a moderate but adequate guard, in case he should terrify Hyrcanus if he brought too many. Neither should he leave himself exposed to any danger from the trial. When Herod presented himself before the Sanhedrin in his royal robes with his guard in arms, they were all astonished. Nor did anyone, who had accused him when he was absent, dare to speak a word against him now that he was present. Everyone was silent not knowing what to do. Then Samaias spoke, who was one of the council. He was a just man and for this reason not afraid and that old proverb of the Hebrews shows that he was not a hot-spirited man.

"Be thou humble as Hillel, and not
קפדן angry as Sameas"

*5058.* He accused Herod of presumption and violence, but laid the blame on the judges and the king himself, who had granted him such great liberty. He later said that, by the just judgment of God, they would be punished by Herod himself. This actually happened, for the judges of that council and Hyrcanus were put to death by Herod when he was king. When Hyrcanus saw that the judges were inclined to condemn Herod, he deferred the business until the next day. He privately advised Herod to take care of himself. So Herod left for Damascus, as though he were fleeing from the king, and presented himself before Sextus Caesar. Having secured his own affairs, Herod professed publicly that he would not appear, if he were to be cited again before the judges. The judges took this with great disdain and tried to convince Hyrcanus that all these things would be his downfall. {*Josephus, Antiq., l. 14. c. 9. s. 4,5. (168-184) 7:539-547}

## 3958b AM, 4668 JP, 46 BC

*5059.* When Caesar was in Africa, on the 12th of the Calends of April (March 21, or Julian January 21), he ceremonially purified his army. The next day he brought out all his forces and set them in battle array. After he had waited long enough for his enemies to come to battle, he realised they were not willing to fight, so he returned his forces to their camp. {*Caesar, African War, l. 1. (75) 3:261} [K360]

5060. Caecilius Bassus, from letters he forged, claimed to have received news from Scipio that Caesar had been defeated in Africa and was dead, and that the government of Syria had been committed to his charge. Therefore, with the soldiers he had secured for that purpose, he seized Tyre and from there marched toward Sextus' forces. He was wounded and defeated and after that, did not try to take Sextus by force. {*Dio, l. 47. (26) 5:171} [E672]

5061. On the day before the Nones of April (April 4, or Julian February 4), in the third watch of the night, Caesar left the town of Aggar and marched sixteen miles that night. He began to fortify Thapsus that day, then had a famous battle there, in which he defeated Juba and Scipio. After this battle, Cato committed suicide in Utica. {*Caesar, African War, l. 1. (79-93) 3:269-295}

5062. After Sextus Caesar had been bribed by Herod, he made Herod the governor of Coelosyria. Herod was quite upset that he had been called before the council and planned to lead an army against Hyrcanus. However, the entreaties of his father Antipater and brother Phasael prevented him from invading Jerusalem. They tried to appease him and wanted him to be content with giving them a good fright, but doing them no harm. He was to do no more, and obey his father, who had given him his power and government. Herod obeyed this advice, believing that he had done sufficient for his future plans and had shown the country that he was a force to be reckoned with. {*Josephus, Antiq., l. 14. c. 9. s. 5. (180-184) 7:543-547}

5063. In Africa, Caesar was reported to have seen a large army in his sleep, calling to him and weeping. He was so moved by this dream, that he immediately recorded it in his books of memoirs. He sent some colonists from Rome to rebuild Carthage and Corinth. {*Appian, Punic Wars, l. 8. c. 20. (136) 1:645}

5064. Hyrcanus, through his envoys, requested Julius Caesar to confirm the alliance and friendship which was existing between them. {*Josephus, Antiq., l. 14. c. 10. s. 1. (185) 7:547}

5065. Caecilius Bassus sent some of his party to Sextus Caesar's soldiers. They were to raise their hopes and cause them to ally themselves to Bassus. After they had killed Sextus, they won over his own legion to Bassus' side. {*Josephus, Antiq., l. 14. c. 11. s. 1. (268) 7:593} {*Livy, l. 114. 14:143} {*Appian, Civil Wars, l. 3. c. 11. (77) 4:99} {*Dio, l. 47. (26,27) 5:171} However, this story was reported by others like this: Sextus was a young man who liked pleasure. He

poorly mistreated the legion that Julius Caesar had left for him in Syria. Bassus, to whom the care of the legion had been committed, reprehended him for this. Sometimes Sextus reproachfully rejected this advice. Later, on one occasion when Sextus had ordered Bassus to come, he obeyed slowly and Sextus ordered him to be dragged before him. In this tumult, the two started fighting. When the army could not endure this insolence any longer, they killed Sextus with their arrows. They soon regretted what they had done and because they were afraid of Caesar, they made a conspiracy to fight it out to the last man if they did not receive a pardon and adequate assurance of it. They also forced Bassus to join the conspiracy. After this, they raised a new company and trained them in the same discipline that they kept. {*Appian, Civil Wars, l. 3. c. 11. (77) 4:97,99} {*Appian, Civil Wars, l. 4. c. 8. (58) 4:239,241}

5066. Bassus took over all the army, except for a few who, having wintered at Apamea, had left for Cilicia before his arrival. In vain he followed them there. When he returned to Syria, he was nominated praetor and fortified Apamea so that he could make it the seat of the war. He enlisted all who were of full age for the war, both freemen and servants, and gathered money and made arms. {*Dio, l. 47. (27) 5:171,173} [K361]

5067. When Caesar had finished the African war on the Ides of June (June 13, or Julian April 14), he sailed from Utica. After the third day, he came to Caralis in Sardinia. On the 3rd of the Calends of July (June 27, or Julian April 29), he sailed by ship close to the shore. Twenty-eight days later (Julian May 26), because he had been hindered by storms, he arrived at the city of Rome. {*Caesar, African War, l. 1. (98) 3:299}

5068. Caesar triumphed at Rome four times in the same month, with a few days between each triumph. Each one displayed different equipment and provisions. {*Suetonius, Julius, l. 1. c. 37. s. 1. 1:83} The chariot for the Gallic triumph was made of citrus wood, for the Pontic one, of acanthus, for Alexandria, of tortoise shell, and for Africa, of ivory. {*Velleius Paterculus, l. 2. c. 56. s. 1,2. 1:173} In the Pontic triumph, among the pageants and shows, he carried before him a banner with these words, *VENI, VIDI, VICI, I came, I saw, I conquered.* This did not signify the acts achieved by him, as with other conquerors, but the quick execution of this war. {*Suetonius, Julius, l. 1. c. 37. s. 2. 1:83} In this particular triumph, the flight of Pharnaces made the people laugh. The Alexandrian triumph for Egypt was held between the Gallic and the Pontic ones. The people applauded the deaths of Achillas and Pothinus. {*Appian, Civil Wars, l. 2. c. 15. (101) 3:415} Arsinoe, the Egyptian woman who at that time was considered a queen, was led along as one of the number of the captives. This had never happened at Rome before and raised much pity for her with the people. After the triumph, she was released, as a favour to her relatives. {*Dio, l. 43. (19) 4:245,247}

5069. Her family, that is, her older sister Cleopatra and younger brother Ptolemy, the husband of Cleopatra, came to Rome this year, at Caesar's invitation. Caesar appointed Cleopatra her lodging in his own house, and sent her away with great honours and rewards, not at all perturbed about the gossip he created by this. {*Dio, l. 43. (27) 4:261} {*Suetonius, Julius, l. 1. c. 52. s. 1,2. 1:101} [E673] Also, in the temple of Venus Genetrix, which he built because of a vow he had made during the battle of Pharsalia (Dio confirmed it was dedicated by him in this year), Caesar set up an image of Cleopatra beside Venus. {*Appian, Civil Wars, l. 2. c. 15. (102) 3:417}

5070. In Syria, Gaius Antistius (Vetus) and others of Caesar's captains, came against Caecilius Bassus with cavalry and foot soldiers. He besieged Bassus in Apamea. The neighbouring countries that favoured Caesar's party sent forces to help. Antipater sent forces with his sons, as well, both for the sake of Sextus Caesar, who had been killed, and Julius Caesar, who was alive, because he was a friend to both of them. They fought for a long time, to no one's advantage. A truce was made with no articles or covenants and they suspended the war to bring in more auxiliaries. {*Josephus, Jewish War, l. 1. c. 10. s. 10. (216,217) 2:101} {*Josephus, Antiq., l. 14. c. 11. s. 1. (268) 7:593} {*Dio, l. 47. (27) 5:173}

5071. Mithridates of Pergamum again plundered the temple of Leucothea (in the country of the Moschi, near the Phrixus River), which had previously been plundered by Pharnaces. {*Strabo, l. 11. c. 2. s. 17. 5:213} Like Pharnaces before him, he tried to seize Bosphorus. Asander (referred to by Strabo as Calander and Lysander) defeated him and after he had eliminated both of them, Asander quietly enjoyed the kingdom of Bosphorus. {*Strabo, l. 11. c. 2. s. 17. 5:213} {*Strabo, l. 13. c. 4. s. 3. 6:169} [K362]

5072. When Julius Caesar was high priest in his third year and in the consulship of Marcus Aemilius Lepidus, he ordered the amendment of the Roman year. He had the help of Sosigenes in astronomical matters and of the scribe, Flavius, in arranging the calendar. There were twenty-three days intercalated in the month of February. Between November and December, he interposed two other intercalary months of sixty-seven days, so that this year had fifteen months, or four hundred and forty-five days. {Censorinus, De Die Natali, l. 1. c. 8.} {*Suetonius, Julius, l. 1. c. 40. 1:87} {*Pliny, l. 18. c. 57. (211) 5:323} {*Dio, l. 43. (26) 4:259} {Macrobius, Saturnalia, l. 1. c. 14.}

## 3959a AM, 4668 JP, 46 BC

5073. On the 5th of the Calends of the first intercalary month (Julian September 26), Cicero made a speech before Caesar for Quintus Ligarius. {*Cicero, Friends, l. 6. c. 14. s. 2. 25:499}

## 3959b AM, 4669 JP, 45 BC

5074. From the month of January, when Caesar started his fourth consulship, the year was reckoned to start on the first day of the new Julian year. He decreed that this time would mark the beginning of the year in the future. {Censorinus, De Die Natali, l. 1. c. 8.}

5075. Caesar made war in Spain with Pompey's sons on the 11th of the Calends of March (February 19), and captured the town of Ategna. He was called Imperator when the Liberalia (or Lupercalia, as it was called by Plutarch {*Plutarch, Caesar, l. 1. c. 61. s. 1. 7:585}) was celebrated on the 16th of the Calends of April (March 17, as is shown from the old calendar). He achieved a memorable victory at the city of Munda when thirty thousand men on Pompey's side, along with the two generals, Labienus and Attius Varus, and almost three thousand equestrians, were killed in the battle. Caesar lost about a thousand men and had about five hundred wounded. After young Gnaeus Pompey, who had assumed the office of the consul and the government, was killed, his head was presented to Caesar as he was marching to Hispalis. This was on the day before the Ides of April (April 12), and the head was publicly displayed to the people. {*Caesar, Spanish War, l. 1. (1-42) 3:311-389} In the battle against Pompey's son, his army was afraid to join battle. Caesar dashed ahead into the space between the armies and received two hundred arrows on his shield, until his army, moved with shame and fear for his safety, rushed forward and rescued him. {*Appian, Civil Wars, l. 2. c. 21. (152) 3:509,511}

5076. The day before the Parilia, on the 12th of the Calends of May (April 20), around evening, the news of this victory reached Rome. {*Dio, l. 43. (42) 4:287} The day before the Calends of May (April 30), at Hispalis, Caesar wrote a consolatory letter to Marcus Cicero on the death of his daughter Tullia. {*Cicero, Atticus, l. 13. c. 20. 24:143} After the divorce of her mother, Terentia, Tullia died in childbirth at Publius Lentulus' house while her husband, Publius Cornelius Dolabella, was in Spain with Caesar. {Asconius Pedianus, In Pison} {*Plutarch, Cicero, l. 1. c. 41. s. 4,5. 7:189} {*Cicero, Atticus, l. 13. c. 20. 24:143} {*Cicero, Philippics, l. 2. c. 30. 15:143}

5077. Gaius Octavius, the grandchild of his sister Julia, accompanied Caesar in this war. He was eighteen years old and always stayed in the same house with Caesar and rode in the same coach with him. Caesar honoured this lad with the high priesthood. {*Velleius Paterculus, l. 2. c. 59. s. 3. 1:177,179}

5078. When King Dejotarus was in some trouble, he sent Blesamius, his envoy, to Spain to Caesar. Caesar sent him letters, which he sent to him from Tarraco, bidding him to be of good hope and good courage. {*Cicero, Pro Dejotaro, l. 1. c. 14. 14:537}

5079. While the war with Caecilius Bassus was going on in Syria, Lucius Statius Murcus, who was a former praetor, was sent by Julius Caesar as the successor to Sextus. (In Velleius and Appian, he was called Staius, and in Appian, Sextius. Josephus called him Marcus. Loeb editions do not have some of these variations. Editor.) He left Italy with three legions, but was valiantly defeated by Bassus. {*Velleius Paterculus, l. 2. c. 69. s. 2. 1:199} {*Josephus, Jewish War, l. 1. c. 10. s. 10. (216,217) 2:101,103} {*Josephus, Antiq., l. 14. c. 11. s. 1. (268,269) 7:593} {*Appian, Civil Wars, l. 3. c. 11. (77) 4:99} {*Appian, Civil Wars, l. 4. c. 8. (58) 4:241} The country had well supplied the army of Bassus. [K363] Many Arabian princes were also allied with him in this war and they controlled many fortified places nearby. [E674] Among these places was Lysias, which was located beyond the lake near Apamea, and Arethusa, the country of Sampsiceramus and his son Jamblichus, whom Cicero mentioned. {*Cicero, Friends, l. 15. c. 1. s. 2. 27:231} These princes governed the countries of the Emiseni, of Heliopolis and Chalcis. They were close to the countries who were under the command of Ptolemy, the son of Mennaeus. He also governed Massyas and the mountainous places of the Itureans. {*Strabo, l. 16. c. 2. s. 10. 7:253}

5080. Alchaudonius, the Arabian (called Alchaedamnus by Strabo), was the king of the Rhambaean nomads, who lived near the Euphrates River. They had earlier made a league with Lucullus, but later, had sent forces to the Parthians against Crassus. Now, both Bassus and his enemies appealed to them for help, so Alchaudonius went into Mesopotamia. When he reached a place that was between Apamea and the camp of Caesar's supporters, before he would answer either side, he proposed that he would help those who gave him the most. In the battle, his troops greatly overpowered the enemy with their archery. {*Strabo, l. 16. c. 2. s. 10. 7:253,255} {*Dio, l. 47. (27) 5:173}

5081. On the Ides of September (September 13), Caesar made his last will and testament in his own house at Laticum and committed it to the keeping of the head vestal virgin. In it, he appointed as his heirs three grandchildren of his sister. Gaius Octavius received three-quarters (not half, as Livy wrote) and Lucius Pinarius and Quintus Pedius received a quarter of the estate. He also adopted Gaius Octavius into his family, as well as naming many of those, who would later prove to be his murderers, as tutors to his sons should he happen to have any. He appointed Brutus to be one of his secondary heirs together with Mark Antony, in case the primary heirs were deceased. {*Livy, l. 116. 14:147} {*Suetonius, Julius, l. 1. c. 83. s. 1,2. 1:141} {*Dio, l. 44. (35) 4:367} {*Florus, l. 2. c. 15. s. 1. 1:301,303} {*Appian, Civil Wars, l. 2. c. 20. (143) 3:491}

## 3960a AM, 4669 JP, 45 BC

5082. In the month of October Caesar, who had now conquered all, entered Rome and pardoned all who had fought against him. {*Velleius Paterculus, l. 2. c. 56. s. 1. 1:173} After he had performed the triumph for Spain, at the beginning of this month, he retired from the consulship. He instituted a new order by substituting honorary consuls. He made Quintus Fabius Maximus and Gaius Trebonius the consuls for three months. {*Dio, l. 43. (46) 4:293} {Gruter, Inscriptions, p. 298.} The former of these had been consul and had triumphed for Spain on the 3rd of the Ides of October (October 13). {Gruter, Inscriptions, p. 297.} Thereupon, when Chrysippus had seen the ivory towns carried before Caesar in his triumph, and then, a few days later, the wooden ones of Fabius Maximus, he said the latter were nothing more than the cases for Caesar's towns. {Quintilian, l. 6. c. 4.}

5083. Very many and great honours were decreed to Caesar by the Senate. He was declared to be the perpetual dictator and was called Imperator, or Emperor. {*Livy, l. 116. 14:145} {*Suetonius, Julius, l. 1. c. 76. s. 1. 1:129} This was not in the sense in which, both before and after, the title was given to generals for any victory they had obtained in the wars. This signified the highest power and authority in the state, for it was granted to him that he alone should have soldiers and the command of the militia; {*Dio, l. 43. (44) 4:289} he alone was to take charge of the public money, and it would not be lawful for any other person to make use of either of these. All the magistrates were to be subject to him, including the magistrates of the common people. They were to swear that they would never infringe on any of his decrees. {*Dio, l. 43. (45) 4:291} {*Appian, Civil Wars, l. 2. c. 16. (106) 3:423} Velleius declared the time from this point to his last return to the city to have been: {*Velleius Paterculus, l. 2. c. 56. s. 3. 1:173} [K364]

"His five months of his supreme power."

5084. Caesar thought of repressing the Getae, or Daci, who had made a large invasion into Pontus and Thrace. {*Suetonius, Julius, l. 1. c. 44. s. 3. 1:93} {*Appian, Civil Wars, l. 2. c. 16. (110) 3:429} To prepare for this expedition, he sent Octavius, the son of Atia by his sister Julia's daughter, ahead to Apollonia. He was to study there and learn martial discipline, as it was Caesar's intention later to make him his fellow soldier in the Getic and Pontic war. {*Velleius Paterculus, l. 2. c. 59. s. 4,5. 1:179} {*Suetonius, Augustus, l. 2.

*c. 8. s. 2,3. 1:161}* {*\*Plutarch, Brutus, l. 1. c. 22. s. 1. 6:175}* {*\*Appian, Civil Wars, l. 3. c. 2. (9) 3:533}* {*\*Dio, l. 45. (2) 4:407}* Octavius led some very old squadrons of Pergamum from the city to Apollonia. {*\*Suetonius, Augustus, l. 2. c. 8,9. 1:159,161}* {*\*Suetonius, Augustus, l. 2. c. 89. s. 1. 1:281}* {*\*Strabo, l. 13. c. 4. s. 3. 6:171}* Some squadrons of cavalry from Macedonia came to Apollonia and Octavius trained them. By entertaining them courteously, he developed a very affable manner with the army. {*\*Appian, Civil Wars, l. 3. c. 2. (9) 3:533}*

*5085.* Castor, a young man, was incited by his father, Saocondarius (as Strabo called him), and his mother, the daughter of King Dejotarus, so that he went to Rome to accuse his grandfather. He corrupted Philip, Dejotarus' servant and a physician with hopes and promises to get him to accuse his master falsely of treason by saying that the king would have killed Caesar when he entertained him in his tetrarchy. *[E675]* The king's envoys, Hieras, Blescenius, Antigonus and Dorylaus, opposed this plan and offered their own lives to Caesar for the safety and security of the two kings. (The father and son then reigned together.) Cicero made a speech in Caesar's house in his defence in memory of their old friendship and familiarity. He prefaced his remarks with the statement that it was so unusual for a king to be guilty of treason, that it had never been heard of before. However, because of this false accusation, Dejotarus killed Castor (that noble chronographer) and his own daughter in his palace at Gorbeus. {*\*Strabo, l. 12. c. 5. s. 3.5:473}* {*Suidas, in voc. Καστορ}* For more about all this business, see our dear friend, Vossius. {*Vossius, Greek Historians, l. 1.}*

*5086.* On the Ides of December (December 13), Quintus Pedius triumphed for Spain (the third time within three months), in which (as Fabius had done before him) he used wooden pageants instead of ivory ones, which caused much laughter. {*Gruter, Inscriptions, p. 297.}* {*\*Dio, l. 43. (42) 4:285}*

*5087.* The Parthians came to help Caecilius Bassus, but did not stay long, because it was winter, and did not do anything outstanding for him. Dio stated that their arrival effectively freed Bassus from that close siege by Antistius Vetus, as Vetus himself confirmed in his letters to Balbus. {*\*Dio, l. 47. (27) 5:173}* Concerning this, Cicero wrote: {*\*Cicero, Atticus, l. 14. c. 9. 24:233}*

> "Balbus was here with me, to whom letters from Vetus were delivered on the day before the month of January. Vetus stated that Caecilius was besieged by him and had almost been taken, Pacorus the Parthian came with numerous forces, and so he escaped from him with the loss of many of his men. He blamed Volcacius for this. So it seems to me that war is near, but let Nelcias and Dolabella take care of it."

*5088.* When Cicero wrote this letter, Nelcias and Dolabella had been entrusted with the care of the province of Syria and of the Parthian war, after the death of Caesar.

*5089.* At Rome, the day before the Calends of January (December 31), after Quintus Fabius Maximus, the consul, was dead, Gaius Caninius Rebilus demanded the consulship for the few remaining hours. {*\*Cicero, Atticus, l. 14. c. 9. 24:233}* {*\*Pliny, l. 7. c. 53. 2:627}* {*\*Suetonius, Julius, l. 1. c. 76. s. 2. 1:129}* {*\*Suetonius, Nero, l. 6. c. 15. s. 2. 2:105}* {*Trebellius, Pallio and Tyrants, c. 30.}* *[K365]* Concerning whom Cicero sarcastically wrote the following about him to Curtius: {*\*Cicero, Friends, l. 7. c. 30. s. 1. 26:85,87}* (See Macrobius also. {*Macrobius, Saturnalia, l. 2. c. 3.}* {*Macrobius, Saturnalia, l. 7. c. 3.}*)

> "Know that all the time that Caninius was consul, no one dined. However, no harm was done the whole time that he was consul, for he was very vigilant, for he never slept during his consulship."

## 3960b AM, 4670 JP, 44 BC

*5090.* The next day, Caesar assumed his fifth and last consulship. He made an edict that thanks should be expressed to Hyrcanus, the high priest and prince of the Jews, as well as to the country of the Jews, for their affection toward him and the people of Rome. Caesar also decreed that Hyrcanus should have the city of Jerusalem and should rebuild its walls and govern it after his own will. He also granted to the Jews that every second year there should be a reduction in their rents and that they should be free from impositions and tributes. {*\*Josephus, Antiq., l. 14. c. 10. s. 7. (217,212) 7:561}* Josephus seems to have been mistaken when, in the previous chapter, he said that Caesar was in Syria and sent letters to Rome to the consuls. The letters said that authority should be given to Hyrcanus to rebuild the walls of Jerusalem which Pompey had thrown down. Josephus said that shortly after this, Caesar left Syria and Antipater started to rebuild the walls. That decree of the Senate, which Josephus recorded, did not apply to Hyrcanus nor to the rebuilding of the walls of Jerusalem. {*See note on 3877a AM. <<3798>>}* {*Salianus, Annals - 4007 AM, c. 36,37.}*

*5091.* In the same fifth consulship, in the second Julian year, the month of Quintilis was renamed July, in honour of Julius Caesar. Mark Antony, his colleague in the consulship, proposed this law, because Julius was born on the 4th of the Ides of Quintilis (July 12). {*\*Appian, Civil Wars, l. 2. c. 16. (106) 3:423}* {*\*Dio, l. 44. (5) 4:317}* {*Censorinus, De Die Natali, l. 1. c. 9.}* {*Macrobius, Saturnalia, l. 1. c. 12.}* Thereupon, in the following month of Sextilis, Marcus Brutus, who was the city's praetor and was to hold the games in honour of Apollo after Caesar had been murdered by him, wrote *Nonis Jul.*, the *Nones of July*. Cicero wrote to his friend Atticus: {*\*Cicero, Atticus, l. 16. c. 1. 24:369}*

"I could go on cursing all day. Could they have insulted Brutus worse than with their *July*?"

5092. After Brutus was admonished for this by Cicero, he said that he would write that the hunting which was to take place on the day after the games to honour Apollo, should be on the 3rd of the Ides of Quintilis (July 13). Thus, he wrote Quintilis instead of July. {*Cicero, Atticus, l. 16. c. 4. 24:381}

5093. Caesar rebuilt Carthage and Corinth, both of which had previously been demolished, by bringing Roman colonies there. {See note on 3858b AM. <<3626,3628>>} {*Dio, l. 43. (50) 4:301,303} {*Strabo, l. 8. c. 6. s. 23. 4:203} {*Strabo, l. 17. c. 3. s. 15. 8:189} [E676] Pausanias, Solinus and Appian stated that a hundred and two years had elapsed between the overthrow and the rebuilding of Carthage. This would bring us to this year, when Mark Antony and Publius Dolabella, whom Solinus named, were consuls. Appian wrote that these cities were again rebuilt by Augustus Caesar. {*Pausanias, Corinth, l. 2. c. 1. s. 2. 1:249} {Solinus, Carthage, c. 30.} {*Appian, Punic Wars, l. 8. c. 20. (136) 1:645,647}

5094. At this time, the people of Rome were in a mood to revenge the death of Crassus and the army he had lost. They hoped utterly to conquer the Parthians. As a result, it was decreed, by general consent, that this war was to be headed by Caesar, and so they very earnestly made preparations for it. [K366] The following action was taken for the execution of that war, so that Caesar should have sufficient officers with him and that, in his absence, the city would not be left without magistrates. So that the city would not choose them while he was away and cause problems for Caesar, Caesar intended to appoint magistrates beforehand for the whole three years, which was how long they thought the war would last. Caesar chose half of these, as the law allowed him to do, but in truth, he chose all the rest as well. {*Suetonius, Julius, l. 1. c. 41. 1:87} {*Dio, l. 43. (51) 4:303}

5095. Caesar planned to attack the Getes, or Dacians, first. He sent sixteen legions and ten thousand cavalry ahead of him across the Adriatic Sea. Then he planned to make war on the Parthians by going through Lesser Armenia. He did not want to come to a pitched battle until he had tried his troops. {*Suetonius, Julius, l. 1. c. 44. s. 3. 1:93} {*Appian, Civil Wars, l. 2. c. 16. (110) 3:429}

5096. Caesar sent Cornificius to make war in Syria against Caecilius Bassus, and gave him the province of Syria. {*Cicero, Friends, l. 12. c. 18,19. 26:585,587} While the legions were being brought to Cornificius, Caesar was murdered. After that, the province was assigned to Publius Cornelius Dolabella, the consul, and old Africa was given to Cornificius. {*Cicero, Friends, l. 12. c. 19. 26:587} {*Cicero, Friends, l. 12. c. 21. 26:591} {*Appian, Civil Wars, l. 4. c. 8. (57) 4:239}

5097. Caesar committed the charge and command of three legions that he had left in Alexandria to Rufinus, the son of a freedman of his and a former catamite (boy kept for homosexual purposes) of his. {*Suetonius, Julius, l. 1. c. 76. s. 3. 1:129,131}

5098. On the 7th of the Calends of February (January 26), Caesar entered the city in an ovation from Mount Albanus for it had been decreed that during the performance of the Latin Feriae, he should be brought into the city in this way. {Gruter, Inscriptions, p. 297.} {*Dio, l. 44. (4) 4:315}

5099. Some had greeted him as king, as he was returning from the sacrifice of the Latin Feriae and entering the city from Mount Albanus. He was offended that the people took it poorly and told them that he was Caesar, and not a king. When they all held their peace, he passed by them, very sad and melancholy. One of the company put a laurel crown, tied with a white ribbon (something they used to do to their kings), on his statue. Epidius Marullus and Caesetius Flavus ordered that the crown be untied and the man put into prison. Caesar was grieved that the mention of a kingdom was not well received, or that the glory of denying it was taken from him. He severely reprimanded the tribunes and removed them from their office. {*Suetonius, Julius, l. 1. c. 79. s. 1,2. 1:133} {*Plutarch, Caesar, l. 1. c. 60. s. 2. 7:583} {*Dio, l. 44. (4) 4:315} {*Livy, l. 116. 14:145,147} {*Appian, Civil Wars, l. 2. c. 16. (108) 3:425}

5100. On the Lupercalia (which, according to the old calendar, was celebrated on the 15th day of February), Mark Antony, his colleague in the consulship, came running stark naked into the midst of those who were celebrating the feast. He fell down before Caesar, who sat in the rostrum on his golden chair, clothed in purple and crowned. He presented him with a diadem in the name of the people of Rome. This was twice put on his head by Antony, but Caesar took it off again and laid it on his golden chair. He said that Jupiter alone was the king of the Romans and sent the diadem into the Capitol to Jupiter. He ordered that it should be written in the records:

"That at the Lupercalia, Mark Antony, the consul, offered a kingdom to Caesar, the dictator, but he would not take it."

5101. As a result of that, it was suspected that this had only been a trick between them and that Caesar did in fact desire the name of king, but that he would pretend to have been forced to take it. {*Appian, Civil Wars, l. 2. c. 16. (109) 3:429} {*Cicero, Philippics, l. 2. c. 34. 15:149} {*Cicero, Philippics, l. 3. c. 5. 15:201} {*Cicero, Philippics, l. 13. c. 8. 15:563} {*Velleius Paterculus, l. 2. c. 56. s. 4. 1:173,175} {*Plutarch, Antony, l. 1. c. 12. 9:165,167} {Cassidorus, Chronicle} [K367]

*5102.* After this, a rumour circulated which was neither true nor false (which was how fables usually came about to be made), that the priests, called Quindecimviri, had found in the Sibylline book that the Parthians would be overcome by the Romans, if a king were general. Otherwise they were unconquerable. Consequently, Lucius Cotta, one of the Quindecimviri, would propose a law in the next Senate that Caesar should be called king. Some thought that he ought to be called either dictator, or emperor of the Romans, or any other name that sounded more agreeable than the name of a king. Since all other nations were under the command of the Romans, he should certainly be called king. {*Suetonius, Julius, l. 1. c. 79. s. 3. 1:133} {*Plutarch, Caesar, l. 1. c. 60. s. 1. 7:581,583} {*Dio, l. 44. (15) 4:331} {*Appian, Civil Wars, l. 2. c. 16. (110) 3:429} Cicero also referred to this: {*Cicero, De Divinatione, l. 2. c. 54. 20:495}

> "We note this in the Sibylline verses, which she was reported to have spoken in a fury and which were interpreted by Lucius Cotta. *[E677]* These interpretations were recently thought to be a man's fabrications, as if it were maintaining that the one we now already have for a king, must be called a king, if we will want to be secure."

*5103.* Caesar prepared to leave the city as soon as he could without having given any thought to where he would go. However, four days before he had intended to leave, he was stabbed in the Senate. {*Appian, Civil Wars, l. 2. c. 16. (111) 3:431} Sixty senators and equestrians were involved in this conspiracy. {*Suetonius, Julius, l. 1. c. 80. s. 4. 1:135,137} {Eutropius, l. 6. fin.} {Orosius, l. 6. c. 17.} Marcus Brutus, Gaius Trebonius and Gaius Cassius, as well as Decimus Brutus, one of Caesar's party, were the leaders in the conspiracy. {*Livy, l. 116. 14:147} Caesar had come into the Senate on the Ides of March (March 15), with the intention of advocating the Parthian war, but as he sat in the ivory chair, the senators stabbed him and he received twenty-three wounds. {*Livy, l. 116. 14:147} {*Florus, l. 2. c. 13. s. 94,95. 1:299} He was fifty-six years old. {*Suetonius, Julius, l. 1. c. 81. s. 4. 1:139} {*Suetonius, Julius, l. 1. c. 88,89. 1:147,149} {*Plutarch, Caesar, l. 1. c. 69. s. 1. 7:605} {*Appian, Civil Wars, l. 2. c. 21. (149) 3:503} {*Appian, Civil Wars, l. 2. c. 16. (117) 3:445}

*5104.* Thus he, who had fought in fifty battles, was killed in that Senate by a number of the senators he himself had chosen. {*Pliny, l. 7. c. 25. 2:565} He was killed in Pompey's hall, in front of the statue of Pompey, and many of his own centurions witnessed this. So he fell at the hands of the noblest citizens, many of whom also had been promoted by him. None of his friends and none of his servants dared approach his body. {*Cicero, De Divinatione, l. 2. c. 9. 20:395}

*5105.* Publius Cornelius Dolabella was twenty-five years old and had been appointed by Caesar to be consul for the remainder of Caesar's term, when Caesar left the city. He snatched up the fasces and the consular ensigns. Before them all, he vilely reproached the author of his honour. Some say that he proposed a law, that that day should be considered the birthday of the city. {*Appian, Civil Wars, l. 2. c. 17. (122) 3:453} {*Velleius Paterculus, l. 2. c. 58. s. 3. 1:177}

*5106.* The third day after the murder of Caesar, {*Cicero, Philippics, l. 2. c. 35. 15:153} when the Liberalia was being celebrated, that being the 16th of the Calends of April (March 17), the Senate convened in the temple of Tellus. {*Cicero, Atticus, l. 14. c. 10. 24:235} {*Cicero, Atticus, l. 14. c. 14. 24:255} The consul Antony, Plancus and Cicero spoke in favour of an act of amnesty and peace. *[K368]* It was decreed that the memory of all wrongs should be blotted out, a firm peace should be established among the citizens and Caesar's acts should be ratified. {*Cicero, Philippics, l. 1. c. 7. 15:35} {*Velleius Paterculus, l. 2. c. 58. 1:175,177} {*Plutarch, Cicero, l. 1. c. 42. s. 2,3. 7:191} {*Plutarch, Brutus, l. 1. c. 21. s. 1,2. 6:173} {*Plutarch, Antony, l. 1. c. 14. s. 1,2. 9:169} {*Appian, Civil Wars, l. 2. c. 18. (135) 3:477} {*Dio, l. 44. (34) 4:363,365}

*5107.* On that very day, Mark Antony first of all set aside all hostility and accepted that Dolabella should be his colleague in the consulship. {*Cicero, Philippics, l. 1. c. 11. 15:47} Although Caesar had previously shown that he had planned, before he left the city, that Dolabella should be consul and Antony had strongly opposed it. {*Cicero, Philippics, l. 2. c. 32. 15:145} {*Plutarch, Antony, l. 1. c. 11. s. 2,3. 9:163} At first, Antony had determined not to allow him to be consul, since he was still too young, but fearing that he might cause a riot, he allowed it to happen. {*Dio, l. 44. (53) 4:403}

*5108.* The next day, the Senate met again and assigned provinces to Caesar's murderers. Crete went to Marcus Brutus, Africa to Cassius, Asia to Trebonius, Bithynia to Cimber and Cisalpine Gaul to Decimus Brutus. {*Plutarch, Brutus, l. 1. c. 19. s. 4,5. 6:169}

*5109.* Of these, the last two still held the office of praetors of the city. They did not think it wise to enter the provinces before their term of office as praetors in Rome had expired. When they also saw that it was not safe for them to exercise any authority in the city, they planned to spend the rest of the year in Italy as private citizens. When the Senate realised this, they appointed them to be overseers of the grain shipments to Rome. {*Appian, Civil Wars, l. 3. c. 1. (2) 3:521} Brutus was in charge of the grain shipments from Asia and Cassius from Sicily, but Cassius scorned this office. {*Cicero, Atticus, l. 15. c. 9. 24:319} {*Cicero, Atticus, l. 15. c. 11. 24:323} {*Cicero, Atticus, l. 15. c. 12. 24:327}

*5110.* Some had a plan that a private fund should be established by the Roman equestrians for those who had killed Caesar. They thought that this could easily be done if the leaders of their number would bring in their money. So Atticus was called upon by Flavius, a close friend of Brutus, to take the lead in this business. Atticus was always mindful of doing his friend a favour, without causing any friction. He replied that if Brutus wished to make use of his estate, he could do so to the extent that his estate would permit. However, he himself refused even to speak with anyone about this matter, let alone join them in it. So their whole plot was spoiled by one man's dissent. {*Cornelius Nepos, Life of Atticus, l. 1. c. 8. s. 1-4. 1:299,301} [E678]

*5111.* In the temple of Castor, some letters in the inscriptions of the names of the consuls, Antony and Dolabella, were struck down by lightning. Julius stated that this portended their alienation from their country. {*Julius Obsequens, Prodigies, l. 1. c. 68. 14:311}

*5112.* The consul Antony persuaded his colleague, Dolabella, since he was an ambitious young man, to request to be sent into Syria, and to the army that had been raised against the Parthians. He managed to achieve that the province of Syria was allocated to Dolabella by the votes of the people, along with the Parthian war and the legions that had been assigned by Caesar for that purpose. Those who had been sent ahead into Macedonia were also given to him. Antony then obtained Macedonia, which was not being defended by an army, from the Senate. {*Appian, Civil Wars, l. 3. c. 1. (8) 3:531} {*Appian, Civil Wars, l. 3. c. 3. (24) 3:563}

## 3960c AM, 4670 JP, 44 BC

*5113.* Cicero feared Antony's power and at first determined to go with Dolabella into Syria as his lieutenant. {*Plutarch, Cicero, l. 1. c. 43. s. 1,2. 7:191} On the 4th of the Nones of April (April 4), Cicero was given the lieutenancy, so that he could enter the position whenever he wanted to. {*Cicero, Atticus, l. 15. c. 11. 24:325} He was persuaded otherwise by Hirtius and Pausa, who were appointed consuls for the next year, and so changed his mind. [K369] He left Dolabella and planned to spend the summer at Athens. {*Plutarch, Cicero, l. 1. c. 43. s. 2,3. 7:193} He intended to journey into Greece before the time that the Olympian games were celebrated. {*Cicero, Atticus, l. 15. c. 26. 24:359} {*Cicero, Atticus, l. 16. c. 7. 24:399} The 184th Olympiad was celebrated in this year.

*5114.* In the sixth month after Octavius had come to Apollonia, he received news of his uncle's death. He left Epirus for Italy and at Brundisium, was received by the army, that had gone to meet him as Caesar's son. Without any further delay, he immediately assumed the name

of Caesar and took to himself the role of being his heir. All the more so, because he had brought a large amount of money with him, as well as the numerous forces that had been sent to him by Caesar. At Brundisium, he was adopted into the Julian family, from which point on he called himself Gaius Julius Caesar Octavius, instead of Gaius Octavius. {*Livy, l. 117. 14:147} {*Julius Obsequens, Prodigies, l. 1. c. 68. 14:309} {*Appian, Civil Wars, l. 3. c. 2. (9-11) 3:533-537} {*Dio, l. 45. (3,4) 4:413,415}

*5115.* On account of this very name, just as if he had been a true son, a large number of friends, both freedmen and slaves, flocked to him. They also brought soldiers to Brundisium, who either carried provisions and money into Macedonia, or brought the tributes and other money that they had exacted from the provinces. He was encouraged and emboldened by the large number of people who came to him. Because of the authority of the name of Caesar, he was held in high esteem by the common people. He journeyed toward Rome with a considerable following, which increased daily like a flood. {*Appian, Civil Wars, l. 3. c. 2. (12,13) 3:537,539}

*5116.* On the 14th of the Calends of May (April 18), Octavius came to Naples and the following day, he visited Cicero at Cyme. {*Cicero, Atticus, l. 14. c. 10. 24:235,237} Cicero wrote a letter to Atticus on the 10th of the Calends of May (April 22): {*Cicero, Atticus, l. 14. c. 12. 24:241}

"Octavius was with us and was very noble and friendly. His own followers greeted him by the name of Caesar, but Philippus would not."

*5117.* Octavius' mother, Atia, and his step-father, Philippus, did not approve that he should take the name associated with the envied fortune of Caesar. {*Velleius Paterculus, l. 2. c. 60. s. 1. 1:179} {*Suetonius, Augustus, l. 2. c. 8. s. 2,3. 1:161} {*Appian, Civil Wars, l. 3. c. 2. (13) 3:539}

*5118.* A vast company of friends met Octavius as he was coming to Rome. As he entered the city, the globe of the sun seemed to be on his head, and bent round just like a bow, putting a crown, as it were, upon the head of the man who was later to be so famous. {*Velleius Paterculus, l. 2. c. 59. s. 5,6. 1:179} {*Julius Obsequens, Prodigies, l. 1. c. 68. 14:309}

"When he entered the city with a large number around him, the sun was included in the circle of a pure and unclouded sky and surrounded him with the inmost part of the circle."

*5119.* Rainbows are usually bent in the clouds. That is, a circle of various colours, as is usual in the rainbow, surrounded the sun. {*Seneca, Natural Questions, l. 1. c. 2. s. 1. 7:23} {*Pliny, l. 2. c. 28. 1:241} {*Suetonius, Augustus, l. 2. c. 95. s. 1. 1:295} {*Dio, l. 45. (4) 4:415} {Orosius, l. 6. c. 20.}

*5120.* Octavius called his friends together and that night ordered them all to be ready the next morning, with a good number of followers, to meet him in the forum. Octavius went to Gaius, the brother of Antony, the city praetor. Gaius told him he accepted his adoption. It was the Roman custom to interpose the authority of the praetor in an adoption, and his acceptance was registered by the scribes. Then Octavius immediately left the forum and went to Antony, the consul. {*Appian, Civil Wars, l. 3. c. 2. (14) 3:541} [K370]* The consul entertained him haughtily (but this was not out of contempt, but fear), scarcely admitting him into Pompey's gardens and gave him little time to speak with him. {*Velleius Paterculus, l. 2. c. 60. s. 3. 1:181}*

*5121.* The annual Circus games, which had been decreed to be solemnised in honour of Caesar in the Parilia on the 11th of the Calends of May (April 21), were neglected. The day before that holiday was the day the news of Caesar's victory in Spain reached Rome. {*Dio, l. 43. (42) 4:287} {*Dio, l. 45. (6) 4:419} [E679]* Quintus and Lamia wore crowns in Rome in honour of Caesar. {*Cicero, Atticus, l. 14. c. 14. 24:253} {*Cicero, Atticus, l. 14. c. 20. 24:285}*

*5122.* When the murderers of Caesar were sent into the provinces which had been allocated to them by lot, {*Dio, l. 44. (51) 4:401}* Gaius Trebonius went into his province {*Cicero, Atticus, l. 14. c. 10. 24:233}* to succeed Quintus Philippus as the proconsul of Asia. {*Cicero, Friends, l. 13. c. 73,74. 27:167,169}* cf. {*Cicero, Friends, l. 13. c. 43,45. 27:115-119}* Patiscus went with him as an ordinary proquaestor. However, Publius Lentulus, the son of Publius Lentulus Spinther, was sent by the Senate into Asia as an extraordinary quaestor, to gather in the tribute and to raise money. {*Cicero, Friends, l. 12. c. 14. s. 1. 26:557} {*Cicero, Friends, l. 12. c. 15. s. 2. 26:569}*

*5123.* On the 11th of the Calends of June (May 22), Trebonius came to Athens and there found young Cicero earnestly at his study under Cratippus. He invited them both into his province of Asia. Cicero mentioned this in his letters to his father, dated on the 8th of the Calends of June (May 25). {*Cicero, Friends, l. 12. c. 16. s. 2. 26:579}* His father replied by letter. {*Cicero, Friends, l. 12. c. 30. 26:617}*

*5124.* On the 4th of the Nones of June (June 2), a law was passed, granting the consuls the right to decide on Caesar's statutes, decrees and proceedings. {*Cicero, Atticus, l. 16. c. 18.'24:435}*

*5125.* After Antony was appointed executor to oversee the things which Caesar had ordered to be done, he altered the instructions and changed them as it suited him. He did everything the way he wanted it, as if assigned to do so by Caesar. In this way, he gratified cities and governors and amassed a large fortune. He sold fields and tributes, as well as freedoms, even those of the city of Rome and other immunities. These he sold to individuals as well as to whole provinces and anyone who wanted it. A record of these things was inscribed on tables and hung up in the Capitol. {*Cicero, Philippics, l. 2. c. 38. 15:159,161} {*Cicero, Friends, l. 12. c. 1. s. 1. 26:519} {*Velleius Paterculus, l. 2. c. 60. s. 4,5. 1:181} {*Plutarch, Antony, l. 1. c. 15. 9:171} {*Appian, Civil Wars, l. 3. c. 1. (5) 3:525,527} {*Dio, l. 44. (53) 4:403,405}* In one of those tabled records, the richest cities of the Cretians were freed from tributes and it was decreed that, after the proconsulate of Brutus, Crete would no longer be a province. {*Cicero, Philippics, l. 2. c. 38. 15:159,161} {*Cicero, Friends, l. 12. c. 1. s. 1. 26:519}* Antony also received a large sum of money to amend a register to make it appear as if Caesar had made the law that the Sicilians would be made citizens of Rome. {*Cicero, Atticus, l. 14. c. 12. 24:241}*

*5126.* As soon as King Dejotarus heard of Caesar's death, he recovered everything by his own initiative that had been taken from him. However his envoys were fearful and unskilful. Without the consent of the rest of the king's friends, they gave Fulvia ten million sesterces as a bond and had a decree hung in the Capitol. It ridiculously pretended that everything had been restored to him by Caesar himself. {*Cicero, Atticus, l. 14. c. 12. 24:241} {*Cicero, Philippics, l. 2. c. 37. 15:157,159}*

### 3960d AM, 4670 JP, 44 BC

*5127.* Games were to be performed to commemorate Caesar's victory on the 13th of the Calends of August (July 20). {Gruter, Inscriptions, p. 133.} [K371]* Those who had been appointed to celebrate these games, did not dare do it, so Octavius held them himself. {*Suetonius, Augustus, l. 2. c. 10. 1:163}* He committed the responsibility for preparing for them to Gaius Matius, a very learned man, who gave the following reason to Cicero for accepting this task: {*Cicero, Friends, l. 11. c. 28. s. 6. 26:509} {*Cicero, Atticus, l. 15. c. 2. 24:299,301}*

> "I have taken responsibility for the games that the young Caesar made for the victory of Caesar. However, it was part of my private service to him and not to the state of the commonwealth. Yet this service I ought to perform to the memory and honour of my best friend, although now dead. Neither could I refuse the request of that hopeful young man and most worthy Caesar."

*5128.* Dio added this: {*Dio, l. 45. (7) 4:419}*

> "They sacrificed with certain processions on a particular day consecrated to Caesar for his victories."

*5129.* Dio confirmed that it had previously been decreed that the days on which Caesar had obtained his victories should be celebrated with solemn sacrifices. {*Appian,

*Civil Wars, l. 2. c. 16. (106) 3:423*} {*\*Dio, l. 43. (42) 4:287*} It seems that all the victories he had obtained were remembered and commemorated on this one day and consecrated as his victory sacrifices. Lucan stated that the day of the victory of Pharsalia, the most famous of them all, was not included among the feast days. {*\*Lucan, l. 7. (410,411) 1:399*}

> Rome hath oft celebrated times less dire,
> But this would in oblivion have retire. *[E680]*

5130. Marcus Brutus and Gaius Cassius sent private letters to advise Trebonius in Asia and Tullius Cimber in Bithynia that they should secretly gather money and raise an army. {*\*Appian, Civil Wars, l. 3. c. 1. (6) 3:527*} Cimber obeyed and provided a navy as well. {*\*Cicero, Friends, l. 12. c. 13. s. 3. 26:555*} This was the drunken Cimber who, according to Seneca, made this joke about himself: {*\*Seneca, Epistles, l. 1. c. 83. 5:267*}

> "Am I able to deal with anyone who cannot bear wine?"

5131. At age nineteen, Caesar Octavius gathered an army, of his own accord and at his own expense. This occurred on the 12th of the Calends of October (September 20). He himself wrote about this in the breviary of his affairs and it was inscribed in the Ancyran Marble. {*\*Augustus, l. 1. c. 1. 1:345*} {*Gruter, Inscriptions, p. 230.*} Before the departure of Antony from the city (which took place in the following October), Octavius was commended to the Senate through Cicero and others who hated Antony. Octavius tried to gain the favour of the people and to gather an army. {*\*Plutarch, Antony, l. 1. c. 16. s. 3. 9:173*} He prepared forces against Antony, both for his own safety and that of the state. He stirred up the old soldiers who had been sent into the colonies. {*\*Livy, l. 117. 14:149*} Florus stated: {*\*Florus, l. 2. c. 15. s. 4,5. 1:303*}

> "Octavius Caesar was pitied for his youth and the wrongs he endured. He was gracious for the sake of the majesty of the name that he had assumed. He called the old soldiers to arms and then, as a private citizen (who would believe it?), took on the consul."

5132. Florus was incorrect in stating that he was: {*\*Florus, l. 2. c. 15. s. 2. 1:303*}

> "but eighteen years old"

5133. Nor was Dio correct, who wrote that he was eighteen years old when he assumed the name of Caesar. {*\*Dio, l. 45. (4) 4:515*} Nor is it accurately set forth by Seneca: {*\*Seneca, On Mercy, l. 1. c. 9. s. 1. 1:381*}

> "he was just past his eighteenth year"

5134. Neither is Velleius Paterculus correct: {*\*Velleius Paterculus, l. 2. c. 61. s. 1. 1:181*}

> "he had entered his nineteenth year"

5135. Paterculus stated: {*\*Velleius Paterculus, l. 2. c. 61. s. 1. 1:181,183*}

> "Octavius Caesar had turned nineteen. He dared bold exploits and attained the highest position by his own initiative. He had a greater mind for the safety of the state than the Senate had." *[K372]*

5136. When he began to prepare an army, he was almost twenty, and it was fifty-seven years from that time to his death. Maximus the monk, in his calculations, also assigned the same length of time to his government.

5137. Antony was afraid and held a meeting with him in the Capitol, at which the two were reconciled. That same night, in his sleep, Antony dreamed that his right hand was struck by lightning. A few days later, it was secretly whispered to him that Caesar was seeking to betray him. Because he did not believe Caesar when he tried to clear himself, their old enmity broke out again. {*\*Plutarch, Antony, l. 1. c. 16. s. 3,4. 9:173*}

5138. Antony thought that he needed a larger force. He knew that the six legions in Macedonia were the best soldiers and that they outnumbered his legions. There was a large band of archers, lightly armoured men and cavalry. All were excellently equipped. These had been allocated to Dolabella because the Parthian war had been assigned to him when Caesar had made preparation against the Parthians. Antony intended to draw these to his side because they were so close and by crossing the Adriatic Sea, could soon be in Italy. A false rumour was spread that the Getae had heard of the death of Caesar and had wasted Macedonia in an invasion. Antony demanded an army from the Senate for the purpose of taking vengeance on the enemy. He said that the Macedonian army had been raised by Caesar against the Getae before he had planned to attack the Parthians and that all things were now quiet on the Parthian border. They eventually agreed to send one legion over to Dolabella and Antony was chosen as the general of the Macedonian army. {*\*Appian, Civil Wars, l. 3. c. 3. (24,25) 3:563,565*} He forced the passing of a law which changed the way the provinces were allocated. Gaius Antony, his brother, would take Macedonia, which had been assigned to Marcus Brutus. The consul Mark Antony would take Cisalpine Gaul, that had been assigned to Decimus Brutus. Antony would also command the Macedonian army, which had been sent ahead by Caesar to Apollonia. {*\*Dio, l. 45. (9) 4:434*} {*\*Livy, l. 117. 14:149*} {*\*Appian, Civil Wars, l. 3. c. 4. (27) 4:3,5*} {*\*Appian, Civil Wars, l. 3. c. 4. (30) 4:9,11*}

*5139.* It was reported that the legions of Alexandria were in arms, Bassus had been sent for from Syria and Cassius was expected. {*Cicero, Atticus, l. 15. c. 13. 24:331*}

*5140.* When the time had arrived for the games which the aedile, Critonius, was to hold, Caesar prepared to display his father's golden throne and a crown. It had been ordered by decree of the Senate that this custom be carried on for ever, in all plays. Critonius would not allow Caesar to be honoured in those plays, even when Octavius held them at his own private expense. Octavius brought him before Antony, the consul. The consul told him that he would refer the matter to the Senate. Octavius was vexed and said:

> "Refer it and I will place the throne there as long as the decree is in force."

*5141.* Antony was exasperated and forbade this in all future plays. Julius Caesar had solemnised these plays and they had been instituted in honour of his mother, Venus Genetrix, when he had dedicated both a temple in the forum, as well as the forum itself, to her. Antony publicly hated this. {*Appian, Civil Wars, l. 3. c. 4. (28) 4:5*} [E681] [K373]

*5142.* On the 6th of the Calends of October (September 26), in the marble inscriptions of the old calendar, {*Gruter, Inscriptions, p. 135. fin.*} compared with another whole one, {*Gruter, Inscriptions, p. 133.*} it was engraved, *VENERI. GENETRICIIN. FORO. CAESAR.* Therefore, Octavius held those games on that day to gain the people's favour. These games had been instituted for the completion of the temple of Venus, and he paid for them personally, since he came from the same family, some of whom had promised, during Caesar's lifetime, to solemnise the temple, but had not done it. {*Dio, l. 45. (6) 4:417,419*} Seneca stated that while Octavius was doing this, a comet suddenly appeared. {*Seneca, Natural Questions, l. 7. c. 17. s. 2,3. 10:263*} {*Suetonius, Julius, l. 1. c. 88. 1:147*} Pliny quoted Octavius as saying: {*Pliny, l. 2. c. 23. 1:237*}

> "In the very days of my plays there was a comet seen for seven days altogether in the northern part of the heaven. It arose about the eleventh hour of the day. It was clear and conspicuous in all lands. The people generally thought that by this star, it was signified that Caesar's soul had been received into the number of the gods. It was because of this notion that that word was added to the image of his head which we recently consecrated in the forum."

*5143.* This was also seen on some coins that were minted after his death with the inscription *DIVI JULII*, or *The Divine Julius*, and noted by Virgil: {*Virgil, Aeneid, l. 8. (680) 2:107*}

> "Thy father's star appeared in the north."

## 3961a AM, 4670 JP, 44 BC

*5144.* On the 7th of the Ides of October (October 9), Antony came to Brundisium to meet four or five of the Macedonian legions that he hoped to win over to his side with money. {*Cicero, Friends, l. 12. c. 23. s. 2,3. 26:597*} {*Appian, Civil Wars, l. 3. c. 6. (40) 4:31*} {*Dio, l. 45. (12) 4:429,431*} These legions had been granted to him by the Senate and the people of Rome, to be used against the Getae, but he transported them to Italy. {*Velleius Paterculus, l. 2. c. 61. 1:183*} {*Appian, Civil Wars, l. 3. c. 4. (27) 4:3*} {*Appian, Civil Wars, l. 3. c. 4. (30) 4:9,11*} {*Appian, Civil Wars, l. 3. c. 7. (46) 4:41*}

*5145.* Octavius, also, sent his friends with money to hire those same soldiers for himself. {*Dio, l. 45. (13) 4:429,431*} He sent into Campania to enlist for his cause those soldiers that his father had sent into the colonies to war. First, he drew the old soldiers of Galatia to his side, then the men of Casilinum, which was situated on either side of Capua. He gave them five hundred denarii each (which Appian and Dio, after the custom of the Greeks, translate as drachmas). He gathered together about ten thousand men, but they were not well-armed or marshalled into companies. He marched with them under one ensign as a guard. {*Cicero, Atticus, l. 16. c. 8. 24:401*} {*Cicero, Philippics, l. 3. c. 2. 15:193*} {*Velleius Paterculus, l. 2. c. 61. 1:183*} {*Appian, Civil Wars, l. 3. c. 6. (40) 4:31*} These troops were the first to be called the *Evocati*, because after they had received permission to retire from the army, they were again called into service. {*Cicero, Friends, l. 10. c. 30. s. 1,2. 26:393,395*} {*Dio, l. 45. (12) 4:429*} {*Dio, l. 55. (24) 6:457*}

*5146.* In the meantime, the four legions from Macedonia accused Antony for his delay in avenging Caesar's death on the murderers. Without any acclamations, they conducted him to the tribunal, as if demanding to hear an explanation of this business above all else. Antony did not handle their silence well. Unable to contain himself, he upbraided them for their ingratitude because they did not acknowledge how much better it had been to go into Italy than into Parthia, nor had they shown any vestige of thankfulness. He also complained that they had not brought certain disturbers of the peace to him that had been sent by that wicked young man, for that was what he called Caesar, but he vowed that he would find them. [K374] He said he would march with the army to the province that had been decreed to him by the Senate, even that fortunate Gaul. He said he would give everyone present a hundred denarii or drachmas. The niggardliness of his promises was greeted with laughter. When he reacted badly to this, he was deserted, and the general disorder increased. {*Appian, Civil Wars, l. 3. c. 7. (43) 4:35*} {*Dio, l. 45. (13) 4:431*} {*Cicero, Atticus, l. 16. c. 8. 24:401*}

*5147.* When, according to the discipline of war, Antony had demanded the rebels from the tribunes, he drew out every tenth man by lot. He did not punish them all, but only some of them, with the intention of terrifying them little by little. {*Appian, Civil Wars, l. 3. c. 7. (43) 4:37} Also, in the house of his host on the bay of Brundisium and in the presence of his extremely greedy and cruel wife, Fulvia, he put to death some centurions who had been taken from the Martian legion. {*Cicero, Philippics, l. 3. c. 2. 15:193} {*Cicero, Philippics, l. 5. c. 8. 15:277,279} {*Cicero, Philippics, l. 13. c. 8. 15:565} {*Dio, l. 45. (13) 4:431}

5148. When those of Caesar's party, who had been sent to bribe the legions, saw that they were more incensed by this deed, they spread handbills among the army. They asked them to recall Caesar when considering this business, and the cruelty of Antony, and invited them to benefit from the liberality of the young man. Antony promised to reward any who would tell him about them and to punish those who did not expose the offenders. He reacted rather poorly when none were discovered which suggested that the army was defending them. {*Appian, Civil Wars, l. 3. c. 7. (44) 4:37} [E682]

5149. When Octavius Caesar came to hold office, he endeavoured to win the people to himself. Both Marcus Brutus and Gaius Cassius gave up all hope of controlling the opinion of the people and afraid of Caesar, they sailed from Italy and landed at Athens, where they were magnificently entertained. {*Dio, l. 47. (20) 5:157,159} Cornelius Nepos wrote that when Antony began to get the upper hand, they abandoned the government of the provinces that had been assigned to them by the consuls and went into exile. Nepos stated: {*Cornelius Nepos, Life of Atticus, l. 1. c. 8. s. 5,6. 1:301}

"Fearing both the arms of Antony and that they might again increase the envy they had against Antony, they pretended they were afraid and protested by their edicts that they would willingly live in perpetual exile, as long as the commonwealth was in peace. Nor would they provide any cause for a civil war."

5150. Velleius Paterculus stated that they departed from Italy. {*Velleius Paterculus, l. 2. c. 62. s. 3. 1:185}

5151. When some joined Octavius' side and some went to Antony's, the armies sided with whoever gave them the most. Brutus, intending to leave Italy, went through Lucania and travelling overland, reached the sea at Elea. From there he sailed to Athens, where he became a student of Theomnestas, the Academic, and of Cratippus, the Peripatetic (the Mitylenian). He studied together with them and appeared to forget all business and live in idleness. However, he was preparing for the war, and within a few days, the navy of Cassius caught up with Brutus. {*Plutarch, Brutus, l. 1. c. 23,24. 6:177} {*Cicero, Philippics, l. 10. c. 4. 15:431}

5152. Brutus and Cassius made up their minds to invade Macedonia and Syria by force, even though these provinces had previously been assigned to Dolabella and Antony. As soon as this became known, Dolabella hurried into Syria, visiting Asia along the way to gather money from there. {*Appian, Civil Wars, l. 3. c. 3. (24) 3:563} For Appian thought, as Florus did, that, before he was killed by them, Julius Caesar had decreed Macedonia to Brutus and Syria to Cassius. {*Florus, l. 2. c. 17. s. 1-4. 1:307,309} There were other letters granting other provinces to them in place of the ones that were later taken from them by the consuls. That is, Cyrene and the isle of Crete. [K375] Some attribute both of these to Cassius, while they attribute Bithynia to Brutus, but claim that while they had been assigned these, they had gathered an army and money with the intention of invading Syria and Macedonia. {*Appian, Civil Wars, l. 3. c. 1. (2) 3:521} {*Appian, Civil Wars, l. 3. c. 1. (6,7) 3:527,529} {*Appian, Civil Wars, l. 3. c. 1. (8) 3:531} {*Appian, Civil Wars, l. 3. c. 2. (12) 3:537,539} {*Appian, Civil Wars, l. 3. c. 2. (16) 3:545} {*Appian, Civil Wars, l. 3. c. 5. (36) 4:23} {*Appian, Civil Wars, l. 4. c. 8. (58) 4:239}

5153. However, Syria had been appointed to Cornificius by Julius Caesar, as we gather from Cicero. The fourth day after Caesar's murder, the Senate decreed Crete to Brutus and Africa to Cassius, as we have previously learned from Plutarch. Cicero stated of Brutus: {*Cicero, Philippics, l. 11. c. 12. 15:489,491}

"Nor did he go into his own province of Crete, but hurried into Macedonia, which was another's. Cassius obeyed the law of greed when he went into Syria. This was in fact another's province, if men would abide by written laws. But these were violated, so he lived by the law of greed."

5154. Velleius Paterculus confirmed that both of them seized provinces without any public authority or decree from the Senate. {*Velleius Paterculus, l. 2. c. 62. 1:185} He also said that both of them lived at Athens. Dio wrote that they heard that Caesar had increased in strength. Crete and Bithynia, where they had been sent, were neglected, because they thought that these provinces would not be of much help. Instead, they planned to take Syria and Macedonia, which did not belong to them. At that time, both of them had men and money. {*Dio, l. 47. (21) 5:159}

5155. Dolabella travelled through Achaia, Macedonia and Thrace, but arrived too late in Asia. However, he had foot soldiers and cavalry in Achaia. He met Veterus Antistius, who had returned from Syria and had dismissed his army, which he had mainly used against Caecilius Bassus. He was prepared to suffer any danger, rather than appear to give any money to Dolabella,

either willingly or by compulsion. {*Dio, l. 47. (29) 5:175}
{*Cicero, Letters to Brutus, l. 1. c. 16. s. 2. 28:673}

5156. On the Calends of November (November 1), Octavius sent letters to Cicero, seeking his advice. He asked whether it would be best for him to come to Rome with those three thousand old soldiers, or if he should keep them at Capua and keep Antony from there, or whether he should go to the three legions of Macedonia, which had arrived by way of the Adriatic Sea. Because they would not accept the bribes that Antony offered them, he thought he might be able to win them to himself. {*Cicero, Atticus, l. 16. c. 8. 24:401} Octavius numbered the centuries at Capua, {*Cicero, Atticus, l. 16. c. 9. 24:403} and journeyed to Samnium and arriving at Cales, stayed at Teanum. There was a marvellous crowd to meet him there and cheer for him. {*Cicero, Atticus, l. 16. c. 11. 24:411}

5157. Octavius went to the common people, who had already been prepared for this purpose by Cannutius, the tribune of the people. In a long speech to them, Octavius renewed the memory of his father and the brave acts he had done. He modestly said many things about himself, too, while accusing Antony. He commended the soldiers who had followed him for being ready to help the city and for having chosen him for that purpose. By this act they should signify this to so large a crowd. [E683] Caesar was commended for the good equipment his soldiers had and for the large number of soldiers that were following him. He then went into Etruria to get more soldiers. {*Dio, l. 45. (12) 4:429,431}

5158. At this time, Marcus Cicero dedicated his three famous books, De Officiis, to his son Marcus, who had been a scholar of Cratippus for a whole year. {*Cicero, De Officiis, l. 1-3. 21:1-403} (This was not the first time he had been sent there, as Dio thought. {*Dio, l. 45. (15) 4:435} {*Cicero, Atticus, l. 16. c. 11. 24:409}) [K376] Some of the son's letters to Tiro, in which he mentioned those who boarded with him, still exist: {*Cicero, Friends, l. 16. c. 21. s. 5,6. 27:367}

> "I have hired a place for Brutus close to me and as much as I can from my poverty, I sustain his needs. Moreover, I intended to make my speech in Greek before Cassius, but I will do my practising in Latin with Brutus. My close friends and boarders are those whom Cratippus brought with him from Mitylene, learned men and well approved by him."

5159. When Brutus was in financial need, he made friends with Cicero's son and other young men who were studying at Athens. He sent Herostratus into Macedonia to win the favour of those who were the captains of the armies. When he received news that some Roman ships laden with money were sailing from Asia toward Athens and that the admiral was an honest man and his close friend, he went to meet him at Carystus. He persuaded him to turn the ships over to him. {*Plutarch, Brutus, l. 1. c. 24. s. 2-5. 6:179}

5160. On his birthday, Brutus held a large feast for the admiral. When they began the toasts, they drank to the health of Brutus and the freedom of the people of Rome. Brutus took a large cup and spoke this verse aloud without any apparent reason: {Homer, Iliad, l. 16. (849)}

> Letona's son (Apollo) and cruel fate
> To my success have put a date.

5161. This was taken as an ill omen of his defeat. When he went to fight his last battle at Philippi, he gave his soldiers the watchword, Apollo. {*Plutarch, Brutus, l. 1. c. 24. s. 5-7. 6:179} {*Appian, Civil Wars, l. 4. c. 17. (134) 4:367}

5162. After this, Antistius gave Brutus five hundred thousand drachmas of the money he was carrying into Italy. {*Plutarch, Brutus, l. 1. c. 25. s. 1. 6:181} The Latin interpreter rendered it twenty thousand sesterces while Brutus himself acknowledged the sum that Vetus Antistius had of his own accord promised him and gave him from his money. Brutus commended him to Cicero in a letter, since Antistius was going to Rome to request the praetorship. {*Cicero, Letters to Brutus, l. 1. c. 16. s. 1. 28:671} We read in Cornelius Nepos that Pompey Atticus also sent a present of a hundred thousand sesterces when Brutus was expelled and left Italy and in his absence he commanded that three hundred thousand sesterces should be given to him in Epirus. {*Cornelius Nepos, Life of Atticus, l. 1. c. 8. s. 6. 1:301}

5163. Cassius and Brutus parted company in Piraeus. Cassius went into Syria to keep out Dolabella and Brutus went into Macedonia to enable him to control Macedonia and Greece. {*Cicero, Philippics, l. 11. c. 12. 15:489} {*Plutarch, Brutus, l. 1. c. 25. s. 3. 6:181} {*Dio, l. 47. (21) 5:159} Without any public authorization, they seized the provinces and armies and pretended that they were the legitimate government in each place respectively. From those who were prepared to give it to them, they collected money which the quaestors were sending to Rome from the lands beyond the seas. {*Velleius Paterculus, l. 2. c. 62. 1:185}

5164. Cassius got ahead of Dolabella and sailed into Asia to Trebonius, the proconsul. After the proconsul had been bribed, he sided with Cassius and gave him many of those cavalry who had been sent ahead into Syria by Dolabella. Publius Lentulus bragged in his letters to Cicero that he was the first to turn these over to Cassius. {*Cicero, Friends, l. 12. c. 14. s. 6. 26:563} A large number from Asia and Cilicia also joined him. Cassius persuaded Tarcondimotus and the inhabitants of Tarsus to join an alliance with him, but the city of Tarsus did so unwillingly. *[K377]* The citizens so favoured the first Caesar and for his sake, Octavius, that instead of Tarsus, they called their city Juliopolis. {*Dio, l. 47. (26) 5:169}

5165. Brutus received from Apuleius all the forces he had at the time. He also received sixteen thousand talents in coined money, which had been collected from the payments and tributes of Asia that Apuleius had received from Trebonius. Brutus went into Boeotia. {*Appian, Civil Wars, l. 3. c. 8. (63) 4:73,75} {*Appian, Civil Wars, l. 4. c. 10. (75) 4:267} {*Dio, l. 47. (27) 5:159} There he gathered soldiers from among those he found wandering about Thessaly since the battle of Pharsalia. Some of those who had come with Dolabella from Italy had either been left there because of sickness, or had deserted their regiments. He took five hundred cavalry from Cinna, which the latter was taking to Dolabella to Asia. {*Plutarch, Brutus, l. 1. c. 25. s. 1,2. 6:181} {*Dio, l. 47. (21) 5:159} *[E684]* This was the occasion of which Cicero wrote, when speaking about Brutus: {*Cicero, Philippics, l. 11. c. 12. 15:489}

"He raised new legions and welcomed the old ones. He took Dolabella's cavalry for himself, before Dolabella murdered Trebonius. Brutus counted him an enemy by his own standards. For if it were not so, how could he take the cavalry away from the consul?"

5166. Brutus was thus appointed under the pretence of serving the state and of undertaking a war against Antony. He seized Greece where there were no forces worth mentioning to oppose him. {*Dio, l. 47. (21) 5:159} {*Livy, l. 118. 14:149}

5167. From there he went to Demetrias, where he found a large supply of arms that had been stockpiled for the Parthian war on Julius Caesar's orders and should have been turned over to Antony. {*Plutarch, Brutus, l. 1. c. 25. s. 2. 6:181} {*Appian, Civil Wars, l. 3. c. 8. (63) 4:75}

5168. Brutus went into Macedonia at the time when Gaius Antony, the consul's brother, had recently arrived there and Quintus Hortensius, the proconsul of Macedonia, was preparing to leave. This did not bother Brutus, as Hortensius would soon join with him and Antony was forbidden to meddle with anything that belonged to the chief magistrate (Caesar now controlled everything at Rome), and because Antony had no forces. {*Dio, l. 47. (21) 5:159,161} {*Cicero, Philippics, l. 10. c. 5. 15:433,435}

5169. A muster was held in Macedonia through the great care and efforts of Quintus Hortensius. The legion led by Lucius Piso, the lieutenant of Antony, was turned over to Cicero's son, whom Brutus brought with him from Athens. The cavalry were led into Syria in two brigades. One brigade left its commander, the quaestor, in Thessaly and went to Brutus, while Gnaeus Domitius took away the other one in Macedonia from the lieutenant of Syria. {*Cicero, Philippics, l. 10. c. 6. 15:437}

5170. Brutus heard that Antony would march at once to join the forces Gabinius had at Dyrrachium and Apollonia. Brutus wanted to prevent this, so he quickly journeyed through rough ways and much snow, outdistancing those who were bringing his provisions. As he approached Dyrrachium, he was stricken with a bulimia because of the strain and the cold. This is a disease that affects those who are worn out from going through the snow and the cold. When this became known, the soldiers left the guard and came running with food for him. As he was being taken to the town, Brutus behaved kindly to all for this courtesy. {*Plutarch, Brutus, l. 1. c. 25. s. 3-6. 6:181,183} Publius Vatinius, who was commanding in nearby Illyria, came from there to Dyrrachium, which he had previously captured. *[K378]* He had been an adversary to Brutus throughout the entire civil war. Because of Brutus' sickness, Vatinius' soldiers despised him and defected to Brutus, so Vatinius opened the gates to him and turned his army over to him. {*Dio, l. 47. (21) 5:161} {*Cicero, Philippics, l. 10. c. 6. 15:437} {*Livy, l. 118. 14:149}

5171. When a safe route became available for Dolabella to go into Syria, he invaded Asia, which was another man's province and was also unprepared for war. He sent Marcus Octavius, a poor senator, with a legion to waste the countries and attack their cities. {*Cicero, Philippics, l. 11. c. 2. 15:459,461}

5172. Trebonius would not allow Dolabella into Pergamum or Smyrna, but out of respect for his office as a consul, allowed him to buy provisions outside the walls. When, in a passion, Dolabella had attacked Smyrna in vain, he went away, but by night he returned secretly and captured Smyrna and Trebonius. Trebonius, the proconsul of Asia, who had fortified the cities as a refuge for Brutus and Cassius, promised that he would let him into Ephesus. He told the soldiers he would follow them at once to Dolabella. {*Appian, Civil Wars, l. 3. c. 3. (26) 3:565,567}

5173. After this, there were friendly conferences with Trebonius. However, these were but false tokens of great kindness in feigned affection. {*Cicero, Philippics, l. 11. c. 2. 15:461} In this way, Trebonius was deceived into promising Dolabella every courtesy. He made provision for his soldiers and lived together with them without any fear. {*Dio, l. 47. (29) 5:175,177}

5174. In Egypt, the young Ptolemy, who was fifteen years old, was poisoned in the fourth year of his reign by his wife and sister, Cleopatra. This was the eighth year of his sister's reign from the death of their father, Auletes. {*Josephus, Antiq., l. 15. c. 4. s. 1. (88,89) 8:43} {Porphyry, Scaliger's Greek Eusebius, p. 226.}

*5175.* After Mark Antony, the consul, had returned from Brundisium to Rome, he ordered the Senate to meet on the day before the 8th of the Calends of December (November 24). When they failed to meet on that day, he deferred it until the 4th of the Calends of December (November 28), and then ordered them to meet in the Capitol. {*Cicero, Philippics, l. 3. c. 8. 15:209,211}

*5176.* In the meantime, Antony's Macedonian legions rebelled on their way into Cisalpine Gaul, despising the lieutenant who commanded them. Many of them defected to Caesar. {*Dio, l. 45. (12,13) 4:429-433} The entire Martian legion removed their colours and came to Caesar and stayed in Asia. The fourth legion rebelled against their commander, Lucius Egnatuleius, the quaestor, and also defected to Caesar. {*Dio, l. 45. (13) 4:429,433} {*Cicero, Philippics, l. 3. c. 3. 15:197} {*Cicero, Philippics, l. 4. c. 2. 15:241} {*Cicero, Philippics, l. 5. c. 19. 15:311} {*Cicero, Philippics, l. 11. c. 8. 15:479,481} {*Cicero, Philippics, l. 13. c. 16. 15:587} {*Cicero, Friends, l. 11. c. 7. s. 2. 26:447} {*Livy, l. 117. 14:149} {*Velleius Paterculus, l. 2. c. 61. 1:183} {*Appian, Civil Wars, l. 3. c. 7. (45) 4:39,41} [E685] Caesar received them and gave them money, as he had previously done, thereby drawing many to his side. By chance, he also got all of Antony's elephants as they were being driven along. {*Dio, l. 45. (13) 4:429,431}

*5177.* When Antony was going into the Senate in the Capitol on the appointed day, to complain of Caesar's actions, he received news at the very entrance of the court of the revolt of the legions. He was terrified and did not dare to speak a word in the Senate concerning Caesar. He had planned to make a motion in the Senate, as one who had been a consul, that Caesar be considered an enemy. {*Cicero, Philippics, l. 3. c. 8. 15:211} {*Cicero, Philippics, l. 5. c. 8,9. 15:279} {*Cicero, Philippics, l. 13. c. 9. 15:567} {*Appian, Civil Wars, l. 3. c. 7. (45) 4:39} [K379] At evening on the very same day, the lots were cast among the friends of Antony for the provinces for the next year, so that everyone would have the province that best suited Antony. {*Cicero, Philippics, l. 3. c. 10. 15:217}

*5178.* Antony went to Alba to see if he could get the soldiers of the Martian legion, who were quartered there, to obey him again. When they shot at him from the walls, he sent five hundred drachmas for each man in all the remaining legions. With what forces he had around him, he marched in warlike array to the Tiber River and then on to Ariminum, on the border of Cisalpine Gaul. He had three Macedonian legions with him, since the rest had now arrived. He also had one legion of the old veterans with the auxiliaries who wanted to follow them, in addition to the praetorians and young soldiers. {*Appian, Civil Wars, l. 3. c. 7. (45,46) 4:41}

*5179.* Antony besieged Decimus Brutus in Mutina, because he would not leave Cisalpine Gaul, since it was his province. {*Appian, Civil Wars, l. 3. c. 7. (45) 4:41} {*Appian, Civil Wars, l. 3. c. 8. (49) 4:47} Caesar Octavius sent help to him, even though he was one of Caesar's murderers. But then, politics makes strange bedfellows. {*Dio, l. 45. (14) 4:433} Octavius had the two valiant legions that had come to him from Macedonia, and one legion of new soldiers and two other legions of veterans. The latter were not at full strength, so he added the young soldiers to their ranks. When the army wanted to make him propraetor, he refused the honour they offered him. However, he hired the mercenaries with a gift and gave each man in the two Macedonian legions (that fought a mock battle before him) five hundred denarii. He promised five thousand more to the conquerors, should there be any need for a battle. {*Appian, Civil Wars, l. 3. c. 7. (47,48) 4:43,45} Cicero referred to this: {*Cicero, Philippics, l. 10. c. 10. 15:445}

> "The veterans who followed the authority of Caesar first repressed the attacks of Antony. Later the Martian legion abated his fury and the fourth legion routed him."

*5180.* At Rome the Senate was convened on the 13th of the Calends of January (December 20), when neither of the consuls was present. Antony had sent Dolabella ahead into Macedonia, while he besieged Mutina. On this day, Cicero persuaded the Senate that the things Octavius had done against Antony should be confirmed. Praises and rewards should be given to the rebels, the Martian legion, the fourth legion and to the veterans that had defected to Octavius. {*Cicero, Philippics, l. 3. c. 3,4. 15:195,197} Also, Cicero proposed (without taking any notice of the allocation of provinces which Antony had made by lots) that Decimus Brutus and all the rest should retain their provinces and turn them over to no one without a decree from the Senate. The Senate passed this decree. Cicero called the people together and told them what had been done in the Senate. {*Cicero, Philippics, l. 3. c. 15. 15:227-231} {*Cicero, Philippics, l. 5. c. 13. 15:293} {*Cicero, Philippics, l. 6. c. 3. 15:319,321} {*Cicero, Friends, l. 11. c. 6. 26:443,445} {*Cicero, Friends, l. 12. c. 22. 26:593} {*Dio, l. 45. (15) 4:435}

## 3961b AM, 4671 JP, 43 BC

*5181.* On the Calends of January (January 1), when Hirtius and Pausa began their consulship, Cicero made a speech in the Senate, persuading them to make war on Antony, and declared that honours should be decreed to those who defended the state against him. {*Cicero, Philippics, l. 5. c. 16. 15:301} The next day, the Senate gave Caesar Octavius an extraordinary command (as Cicero called it {*Cicero, Philippics, l. 11. c. 8. 15:479,481}), with consular authority and lictors and the ensigns of a praetor. He and the consuls were to go to the assistance of Decimus Brutus against Antony. Further, he should tell the quaestors and the former consuls that he was to have authority to hold the consulship ten years before the legal age of a consul. The Senate also honoured him with a gold statue of himself on horseback. *[K380]* It was placed in the rostrum and had his age on the inscription. By the same decree, all the money that he had given to the soldiers was refunded to him from the public treasury. (Although he had done it as a private citizen, it had nevertheless been for the service of the state.) The gift he had promised to give to the two Macedonian legions after the victory, was to be given to them in the name of the state. Also, the legions and the other soldiers that had been hired by Caesar, were to be exempt from military service as soon as the war was over and to have lands divided among them. {*Cicero, Philippics, l. 5. c. 17. 15:303} {*Cicero, Letters to Brutus, l. 1. c. 24. s. 6,7. 28:709,711} {*Livy, l. 118. 14:149} {*Velleius Paterculus, l. 2. c. 61. 1:183} {*Suetonius, Augustus, l. 2. c. 10. s. 2-4. 1:163} {*Plutarch, Antony, l. 1. c. 17. s. 1. 9:175} {*Appian, Civil Wars, l. 3. c. 8. (50,51) 4:49,51} {*Dio, l. 46. (29) 5:57} [E686]*

5182. The office of propraetor, which had formerly been offered to him by the army and which he had refused to accept, was granted to Caesar Octavius by the Senate. (A propraetor would have no authority when consuls were serving with him.) The Senate gave him the same power as the consuls had, in managing the war. However, a secret order was given to the consuls to take the two Macedonian legions which were most militarily fit, away from him. For this was the intent of their plan: When Antony was defeated, Caesar weakened and all Caesar's side despised, then Pompey's side should again be restored to the government of the state. When Pansa, the consul, was on his deathbed, he told Octavius this. {*Appian, Civil Wars, l. 3. c. 9. (64,65) 4:77} {*Appian, Civil Wars, l. 3. c. 11. (80) 4:103}

5183. When Octavius heard what had been decreed, he accepted the honours with great joy. He was even more overjoyed because, on the same day that he had assumed the office of praetor, he had made a sacrifice in which the livers of six of the sacrifices appeared double, or folded inwards from the lowest fillets. This meant that within the year his command would be doubled. But he was displeased that envoys were sent to Antony and that the consuls did not seriously prosecute the war on the pretext that it was winter, which meant he was compelled to spend all the winter at Forum Cornelii. {*Dio, l. 46. (35) 5:69} {*Julius Obsequens, Prodigies, l. 1. c. 69. 14:313} {*Pliny, l. 11. c. 73. 3:551}

5184. Gaius Trebonius was the first of all Caesar's murderers to be punished. He had governed Asia by consular power and was killed at Smyrna through the treachery of Dolabella. Trebonius was most ungrateful for the honours Caesar had given him and was one who had

helped murder him. It was Caesar himself who had promoted Trebonius to the height of consular dignity. {*Cicero, Philippics, l. 11. c. 2. 15:461,463} {*Cicero, Philippics, l. 12. c. 10. 15:533} {*Strabo, l. 14. c. 1. s. 37. 6:247} {*Velleius Paterculus, l. 2. c. 69. s. 1,2. 1:197,199} {*Appian, Civil Wars, l. 3. c. 3. (26) 3:565,567} {*Appian, Civil Wars, l. 4. c. 8. (60) 4:243} {*Dio, l. 47. (29) 5:175} {Orosius, l. 6. c. 8.} Dolabella entered Smyrna at night and took the proconsul. After he had censured him, he turned the proconsul over to the banished man, Samiarius. After he had questioned him about the public money, he tortured him with imprisonment and scourgings and with the strappado. (A form of punishment or torture to extort confession, in which the victim's hands were tied across his back and secured to a pulley. He was then hoisted from the ground and let down halfway with a jerk.) After two days of this, Samiarius commanded that he be beheaded and his head carried on a spear. The rest of his body was to be dragged and torn, then cast into the sea. Cicero's account is more accurate than that of Appian, who stated that this murder was committed at the command of Dolabella when he entered into Asia having just become consul. {*Cicero, Philippics, l. 11. c. 2. 15:461,463}

5185. Dio wrote that Dolabella cast his head before the statue of Caesar. {*Dio, l. 47. (29) 5:177} *[K381]* Appian stated that the order was given to place it in the praetorian chair from where Trebonius had dispensed justice. But the soldiers and the drudges were angry with him for having been a partner in the conspiracy because he had detained Antony in a conversation before the doors of the court while Caesar was being killed. The soldiers abused the other part of his body in various ways, while making a football of his head in a spot that was paved with stones. They so marred the head, that no sign of the face remained. Strabo affirmed that there were many parts of the city of Smyrna that were destroyed by Dolabella. {*Strabo, l. 14. c. 1. s. 37. 6:247} (In Loeb edition footnote, it stated the word *destroyed* was translated by some as *freed*. Editor.)

5186. After Asia was seized by Dolabella, Publius Lentulus, the extraordinary quaestor, quickly sent a large amount of money to Cassius, to help him seize Syria. Lentulus went into the adjoining province of Macedonia to Brutus and tried, with his help, to recover the province of Asia and its tributes. He stated this in two letters, one of which was sent publicly to the Senate and the other privately to Cicero. He told Cicero that he did not see his son, because he had gone into winter quarters with the cavalry. {*Cicero, Friends, l. 12. c. 14. s. 5. 26:563} {*Cicero, Friends, l. 12. c. 15. s. 1. 26:567,569}

5187. Dolabella carried on most cruelly in the province of Asia. {*Cicero, Letters to Brutus, l. 1. c. 2. s. 5. 28:629} {*Cicero,

*Letters to Brutus, l. 1. c. 4. s. 3. 28:635}* He took away the Roman tributes and taxed and vexed the Roman citizens. {*\*Cicero, Friends, l. 12. c. 15. s. 1. 26:567,569}* He burdened the cities with new exactions of tributes and with the help of Lucius Figulus, hired a navy of the Rhodians, Lycians, Pamphylians and Cilicians. {*\*Appian, Civil Wars, l. 4. c. 8. (60) 4:243}*

*5188.* The Rhodians were concerned about the lands that they controlled on the continent. They sent two embassies to Dolabella to protest his actions, because these were against their laws and the magistrates had forbidden it. {*\*Cicero, Friends, l. 12. c. 15. s. 4. 26:571}* Brutus wrote that Publius Lentulus was excluded from Rhodes by the Rhodians. {*\*Cicero, Letters to Brutus, l. 1. c. 4. s. 3. 28:635}*

*5189.* Aulus Allienus, Dolabella's lieutenant, joined him after the death of Trebonius. {*\*Cicero, Philippics, l. 11. c. 12. 15:491}* Dolabella sent Aulus to Egypt to Queen Cleopatra, who favoured him because of the acquaintance he had previously with the former Caesar. She sent him four legions with Allienus. These were the remainder of the troops after the defeat of Pompey and Crassus, and were the number of those that had remained with Cleopatra after Caesar had left. *[E687]* She also had a navy ready to help him, but which could not set sail as yet, because of the contrary winds. {*\*Appian, Civil Wars, l. 3. c. 11. (78) 4:99}* {*\*Appian, Civil Wars, l. 4. c. 8. (59) 4:241}* {*\*Appian, Civil Wars, l. 4. c. 8. (61) 4:243,245}* {*\*Appian, Civil Wars, l. 5. c. 1. (8) 4:389}*

*5190.* Cicero made a speech about Bassus: {*\*Cicero, Philippics, l. 11. c. 13. 15:493}*

> "The valiant and victorious army of Quintus Caecilius Bassus, a private citizen, had prevailed for some time in Syria."

*5191.* Quintus Marcius Crispus, the proconsul in Bithynia (as Cicero called him {*\*Cicero, Philippics, l. 11. c. 12. 15:491}*), sent troops to Statius Murcus. (Appian wrote Minucius for Marcius. This variation is not in the Loeb edition. Editor.) {*\*Appian, Civil Wars, l. 3. c. 11. (77) 4:99}* {*\*Appian, Civil Wars, l. 4. c. 8. (58) 4:241}* {*\*Dio, l. 47. (27) 5:173}* Murcus governed Syria by the decree of Julius Caesar and the approval of the Senate. Although this year, Cimber also tried to govern this province by the right of Antony's lottery. Marcius arrived with three legions of his own to aid the three legions of Murcus. He besieged the two legions of Bassus (called ταυγματα by Strabo, τιλη by Appian, for it was obvious, from Cassius' letters to Cicero, that they made only one legion. {*\*Cicero, Friends, l. 12. c. 11. s. 1. 26:545}* {*\*Cicero, Friends, l. 12. c. 12. s. 3. 26:549}*) *[K382]* Bassus so bravely withstood the siege of the two Roman armies, that he was not subdued until he had obtained the conditions he wanted. Then he surrendered.

{*\*Strabo, l. 16. c. 2. s. 10. 7:253}* Gaius Cassius had come with his forces after having been called there with the consent of Murcus, Marcius and the army, as Brutus related in his letters to Cicero. {*\*Cicero, Letters to Brutus, l. 1. c. 2. s. 3. 28:627}* Bassus would not turn his army over to Murcus. If the soldiers had not sent messengers to Cassius, Bassus would have held Apamea, without Cassius' consent, until it would have been taken by assault, as Cassius himself wrote to Cicero. {*\*Cicero, Friends, l. 12. c. 12. s. 3. 26:549}*

*5192.* Cassius raised the siege before Apamea, and Bassus and Murcus were reconciled. Cassius won the two troops that had been besieged and the six others that had besieged them, over to his side. Cassius assumed the ensigns of a general and commanded them by proconsular power. {*\*Velleius Paterculus, l. 2. c. 69. s. 2,3. (271,272) 1:199}* {*\*Josephus, Jewish War, l. 1. c. 11. s. 1. (218,219) 2:103}* {*\*Josephus, Antiq., l. 14. c. 11. s. 2. (271,272) 7:595}* {*\*Appian, Civil Wars, l. 3. c. 11. (78) 4:99}* {*\*Dio, l. 47. (29) 5:177}*

*5193.* From this time he assumed the title of proconsul, as appeared on the inscriptions of his letters to Cicero. {*\*Cicero, Friends, l. 12. c. 11. 26:545 (Latin Title)}* {*\*Cicero, Friends, l. 12. c. 12. 26:547 (Latin Title)}* Cicero, in his letters to him, did not give him that title, because the Senate had not yet given him that title. {*\*Cicero, Friends, l. 12. c. 7. 26:535 (Latin Title)}* {*\*Cicero, Friends, l. 12. c. 8. 26:539 (Latin Title)}* {*\*Cicero, Friends, l. 12. c. 9. 26:539 (Latin Title)}* {*\*Cicero, Friends, l. 12. c. 10. 26:541 (Latin Title)}* However, Appian stated otherwise. {*\*Appian, Civil Wars, l. 3. c. 11. (78) 4:99}* {*\*Appian, Civil Wars, l. 4. c. 8. (59) 4:241}*

*5194.* While Cassius was encamped with all those forces, torrential rain suddenly fell and wild swine rushed through every part of the camp and greatly disorganized everything. Some thought this was an omen about his sudden rise to power and of his sudden overthrow, a little later. {*\*Dio, l. 47. (28) 5:175}*

*5195.* When Cassius was strengthened with these forces, he immediately subdued all the cities of Syria. Some of those cities he was able to subdue by his prestige and position as the quaestor. {*\*Dio, l. 47. (21) 5:159,161}* {*\*Dio, l. 47. (28) 5:173,175}* Taking arms and soldiers, he went to the cities and exacted very heavy taxes from them. {*\*Josephus, Antiq., l. 14. c. 11. s. 2. (272) 7:595}* Livy wrote that he took control of Syria with three legions which were in that province. {*\*Livy, l. 121. 14:153}* Velleius Paterculus stated that he brought them under his control with the legions in that country. {*\*Velleius Paterculus, l. 2. c. 69. s. 2. 1:199}*

*5196.* Marcus Brutus undertook an expedition against Gaius Antony, who was keeping Apollonia with seven cohorts. Brutus sent public letters to Rome about the things that he had done in Greece and Macedonia, which were read in the Senate by the consul, Pansa. In a speech made by Cicero, {*Cicero, Philippics, l. 10. c. 1. 15:423} the Senate passed a decree that Brutus should retain Macedonia, Illyria, and all of Greece, as proconsul. {*Cicero, Philippics, l. 10. c. 6. 15:437} {*Appian, Civil Wars, l. 3. c. 8. (63) 4:73} {*Appian, Civil Wars, l. 4. c. 8. (57,58) 4:239} {*Appian, Civil Wars, l. 4. c. 10. (75) 4:265,267}

5197. The body of Trebonius was brought to Rome. When the Senate saw how disgracefully it had been treated, they declared Dolabella an enemy of the state. {*Cicero, Philippics, l. 11. c. 12. 15:491} {*Livy, l. 119. 14:151} {*Appian, Civil Wars, l. 3. c. 8. (61) 4:71} {Orosius, l. 6. c. 8.} A day was appointed for those on his side to leave him, otherwise they, too, would be deemed enemies. {*Dio, l. 47. (29) 5:177} [K383]

5198. The next day, the Senate debated about the choice of a general to carry out the war against Dolabella. Lucius Caesar thought that, contrary to the normal procedure, this war should be committed to Publius Servilius. Others thought that the consuls should cast lots for Asia and Syria, to determine who would fight against Dolabella. Cicero, in a speech, railed fiercely against Dolabella. {*Cicero, Philippics, l. 11. c. 12. 15:491,493} Dolabella had previously been Cicero's son-in-law, but shortly after he had left Italy, they had had a great falling-out. Cicero persuaded the senators that this war should be committed to Publius Cassius. Scaliger, in his notes on Eusebius (under the number MDCCCCLXXIII), was not correct in his report about the decree of the Senate concerning the command for Cassius. He thought that Cicero's opinion had not prevailed and that Pansa, the consul, had resolutely opposed it. [E688] However, Cicero himself testified in his letters to Cassius about this, and added the following about himself: {*Cicero, Friends, l. 12. c. 7. 26:537}

> "I promised and also acted on it, that you had not expected, nor should you expect anything other from our decrees, except that you yourself should defend the commonwealth. Although, as of yet, we had heard nothing, either of where you were or what forces you had, yet it was nevertheless my opinion that all the auxiliaries and forces which were in those regions should be under your command. I was confident that you would recover the province of Asia for the commonwealth."

5199. When it was not yet known at Rome that Cassius had control of Syria, the war against Dolabella was committed to the consuls to be fought at a time when the present war against Antony should come to an end. The governors of the neighbouring countries were told not to help Dolabella. {*Dio, l. 47. (29) 5:177} With the consuls' consent, the government of Asia was confirmed to Publius Lentulus Spinther, who currently governed it under the title of proquaestor and propraetor. This may be seen in Spinther's letters to Cicero, written after the death of Pansa and Hirtius. (He did not know of their deaths at that time.)

5200. This decree against Dolabella was passed and letters were sent from Antony to Hirtius, the consul, and Octavius Caesar, the propraetor. These are given and refuted by Cicero. Antony's letter which Cicero refuted reads as follows:

Antony, to Hirtius and Caesar:

> "When I heard of the death of Gaius Trebonius, my joy was not greater than my grief. That a criminal has paid the penalty to the ashes and bones of a most illustrious man, and that the power of the gods has been revealed before the end of the year (From this we deduce that Trebonius was killed shortly before the Ides of March less than a year after the murder of Caesar.) the punishment for murder being either already inflicted or impending, is matter for rejoicing. That Dolabella has at this crisis been adjudged an enemy for killing an assassin, and that the son of a buffoon seems dearer to the Roman people than Gaius Caesar, the father of his country, is a matter for lament. But the bitterest thing is that you, Aulus Hirtius, though you have been distinguished by Caesar's benefits, and left by him in a position which you wonder at yourself—and you, oh boy—you who owe everything to a name—that you should strive to show that Dolabella was rightly condemned! And that this she-poisoner should be liberated from a siege. That you should strive that Cassius and Brutus may be as powerful as possible. Truly you regard these things as you did the former (what things, pray?): you used to call the camp of Pompey the Senate. {*Cicero, Philippics, l. 13. c. 10,11. 15:569-575} You have had the vanquished Cicero for your general. You are fortifying Macedonia with garrisons. Africa you have entrusted to Varus, a man twice a captive. [K384] You have sent Cassius into Syria. You have allowed Casca to hold the tribuneship. You have taken from the Luperci the Julian revenues. You have taken away the veterans' colonies, though planted by law and by decree of the Senate. You are promising to restore to the Massilians what has been taken from them by the laws of war. You repeat that no surviving adherent of Pompey is bound by the Hirtian law. You supplied Brutus with the money of Apuleius. You approved of the execution of Petraeus and Menedemus, men who had been given the citizenship, and guest-friends of Caesar. You did not care that Theopompus was stripped and driven

out by Trebonius, and took refuge in Alexandria. You look on Servius Galba in the camp girt with the identical dagger. You have enlisted soldiers, either mine or veterans, on the plea that it was for the destruction of Caesar's murderers; and then these same soldiers you have set on unexpectedly to endanger him who had been their quaestor, or their general, or those who had been their own fellow soldiers. In short, what is there you have not approved or done, which, should he come to life again, would be done by—Gnaeus Pompey himself—or his son, should he be able to live at home. Lastly, you say peace is impossible unless I either let out Brutus or supply him with grain. What! is this the opinion of those veterans of yours to whom all courses are still open? Although you have set out to pervert them with flatteries and poisoned gifts. But you say you are bringing aid to the besieged soldiers. I do not mind their being safe, and going where they wish, provided only they suffer him to perish who has deserved it. You write that mention has been made of peace in the Senate, and that the envoys are five consulars. It is difficult to believe that those who drove me headlong though I was offering most equitable terms—and even so thinking of yielding as to some of them—to imagine they will do anything moderate or humane. It is hardly likely too that those who adjudged Dolabella an enemy on account of a most just deed can at the same time spare me who am of the same sentiments. Wherefore do you rather consider which is in better taste and more beneficial to your party, to avenge the death of Trebonius or that of Caesar; and whether it is more fitting that we would join battle so that the cause, so often slaughtered, of the Pompeians should more easily come to life, or should agree together, that we may not be a derision to our enemies. For whichever of us falls those enemies will profit. Such a spectacle Fortune herself so far has avoided, that she might not see two armies of one body fighting with Cicero as trainer, who is so far fortunate that he has deceived you with the same flowers of speech with which he boasted Caesar was deceived. Whichever fall, will be our profit. *[E689]* I am resolved to endure no insults to myself or to my friends, and not to desert the party Pompey hated, nor to permit the veterans to be removed from their abodes, nor to be dragged one by one to torture, nor to betray the pledged faith I have given to Dolabella, Nor to be false to my alliance with Lepidus, the most loyal of men, Nor to betray Plancus, the partner of my counsels. If, as I tread the path of an upright purpose, the immortal gods shall, as I hope, assist me, I will

gladly live. But if another fate await me, I anticipate joyfully the punishments you will suffer. For if, when conquered, Pompeians are so insolent, what they will be as conquerors it is you rather who will discover. Finally, the sum of my decision tends to this: I can bear injuries inflicted by my friends, if either they themselves are willing to forget the commission of them, or are ready with me to avenge Caesar's death." {*Cicero, Philippics, l. 13. c. 15-22. 15:581-599}

5201. (The preceding was taken directly from the translation of Cicero's speech as translated in the Loeb history books. In the original speech, Cicero reads this letter to the Senate and comments on it as he reads it, refuting Antony point by point. We have only included the text of the original letter. Ussher's Latin edition of the Annals contains this speech. The English translation was poorly done so we decided to use the copy from Loeb rather than retranslate it ourselves. Editor.)

5202. The envoys, who were sent by the Senate to Antony to make peace, were unable to reach an agreement with him. The whole city of Rome (even those who did not go to the war) put on their soldiers' uniforms and made a general muster through all Italy. The armies of Aulus Hirtius and Gaius Caesar, the propraetor, were sent against Antony. {*Cicero, Philippics, l. 6. c. 1. 15:317} {*Cicero, Philippics, l. 10. c. 10. 15:445} {*Cicero, Philippics, l. 13. c. 17,18. 15:589,591} {*Livy, l. 118. 14:149} {*Appian, Civil Wars, l. 3. c. 8. (62) 4:71} {*Dio, l. 46. (29) 5:59} [K385] From the start of this campaign against Mark Antony, Eusebius and Cassodorus derive the beginning of the government of Caesar Octavius, assigning fifty-six years and six months to it.

5203. Gaius Antony was defeated at a battle which was fought at the Byllis River by Cicero's son, a captain of Brutus. A little later, Antony's soldiers surrendered both him and themselves to Brutus. For a long time, Brutus very honourably entertained Antony, even to the extent that he did not take the ensigns of his office from him. {*Plutarch, Brutus, l. 1. c. 26. s. 1-6. 6:183}

5204. From Illyria, Marcus Brutus received three legions from Vatinius, whom he had succeeded in the province of Illyria by a decree of the Senate. Brutus also received one legion that he had taken from Antony in Macedonia and four others, which he had gathered. In all, he had eight legions, and in them were many of Gaius Caesar's old veterans. Beyond that, he had a large number of cavalry, lightly armed men and archers. He praised the Macedonians and trained them after the Italian manner. {*Appian, Civil Wars, l. 4. c. 10. (75) 4:267}

5205. As Brutus was gathering soldiers and money, he met with some good fortune in Thrace. Polemocratia, the wife of a certain king who had been killed by Brutus' enemies, was afraid lest some harm might come to her son. So she went to Brutus and commended her son to him, giving him her husband's treasure. He committed the lad to the inhabitants of Cyzicum to be raised, until he had time to restore him to his father's kingdom. Among these treasures, he found a large quantity of gold and silver, which he coined. {*Appian, Civil Wars, l. 4. c. 10. (75) 4:267}

5206. After Gaius Cassius had seized Syria, he travelled toward Judea, because he heard that the soldiers who had been left in Egypt by Caesar were coming there. He easily won these troops and the Jews to his side. {*Dio, l. 47. (28) 5:175} In Palestine, he surrounded Allienus, the lieutenant of Dolabella, as he was returning from Egypt with four legions, before he was even aware of him. He forced Allienus to take his side, since Allienus did not dare oppose his eight legions with the four he had. Hence, Cassius controlled twelve legions in all, which was more than he had hoped for. As well, he had some Parthian cavalry who were archers. He was held in high esteem by the Parthians, ever since the time that he had been the quaestor for Crassus because they thought he was wiser than Crassus. {*Appian, Civil Wars, l. 3. c. 11. (78) 4:99} {*Appian, Civil Wars, l. 4. c. 8. (59) 4:241}

5207. As soon as he had received the forces that Aulus Allienus had brought from Egypt, Cassius wrote some letters to Cicero concerning these forces. {*Cicero, Friends, l. 12. c. 11,12. 26:545-551} This letter was dated on the Nones of March (March 7), from the camp at Tarichea in Galilee: {*Cicero, Friends, l. 12. c. 11. 26:545,547}

Gaius Cassius, Proconsul, sends hearty commendations to Marcus Tullius Cicero:

"If you are well, all is right; I too am well. You must know that I have started for Syria to join Lucius Murcus and Quintus Crispus, commanders-in-chief. When those gallant officers and admirable citizens heard what was going on in Rome, they handed their armies over to me, and are themselves administering the affairs of the State side by side with me, and with the utmost resolution. I beg to inform you also that the legion which Quintus Caecilius Bassus had, has come over to me, and I beg to inform you that the four legions Aulus Allienus brought out of Egypt have been handed over by him to me. [E690] For the present I do not suppose there is any need of my exhorting you to defend us while we are away, and the Republic too, as far as in you lies. [K386] I should like you to be assured that neither all of you, nor the Senate are without strong safeguards, so that you may defend the Republic in the best of hopes and with the highest spirit. What business remains will be transacted with you by Lucius Carteius, an intimate friend of mine. Farewell. Dated the Nones of March (March 7), from camp at Tarichea."

5208. After these things, Cassius dismissed Bassus, Crispus and any others who would not serve under him. He did not harm them in any way. He left Statius Murcus in the office that he had originally had and committed the charge of his navy to him. So stated Dio. {*Dio, l. 47. (28) 5:175} But it appears from Cassius' own letters to Cicero that Crispus was firmly loyal to him. {*Cicero, Friends, l. 12. c. 11. s. 1. 26:545} {*Cicero, Friends, l. 12. c. 12. s. 3. 26:549}

5209. Cassius exacted seven hundred talents of silver from Judea (not of gold, as may be read in the forty-fifth chapter of the Jewish Histories, as recorded in Arabic by the Parisians, in the Bible of many languages). When Antipater saw that his state was in trouble, he feared Cassius' threats. Antipater appointed two of his sons to gather part of the money, and Malichus, a Jew who was his enemy, to gather another part, with some others to gather the rest. First of all, Herod brought a hundred talents from Galilee, which he governed. He was greatly favoured by Cassius. Even at that time, it was considered a good policy to win the favour of the Romans at the expense of other men. The officers of the other cities, every last man of them, were sold as slaves and at that time, Cassius sold into servitude the cities of Gophna, Emmaus, Lydda and Thamna. Cassius was also greatly enraged, so that he was about to put Malichus to death, but Hyrcanus sent a hundred talents through Antipater and appeased his fury. {*Josephus, Jewish War, l. 1. c. 11. s. 2. (220-222) 2:103,105} {*Josephus, Antiq., l. 14. c. 11. s. 2. (271-276) 7:595,597}

5210. Caesar Octavius finished the war against Antony that had been committed to him, in three months. {*Suetonius, Augustus, l. 2. c. 10. s. 2,3. 1:163} The war around Mutina was so well managed by him, when he was only twenty years old, that Decimus Brutus was freed from the siege and Antony was forced to leave Italy in dishonourable flight and without his baggage. {*Velleius Paterculus, l. 2. c. 61. s. 3,4. 1:183} Cicero described the battle in his writings. {*Cicero, Philippics, l. 14. c. 9,10. 15:631-635} Servius Galba, who was in the battle, stated in the beginning of his letters to Cicero that the battle was fought on the 17th of the Calends of May (April 15). {*Cicero, Friends, l. 10. c. 30. s. 1. 26:393} So then they seem to have started the time of Caesar Octavius from the third day after the victory of Mutina. They calculated it to be fifty-six years, four months and one day. This may be seen in Theophilus of Antioch, {*Theophilus, Ad Autolycum, l. 3. c. 28. 2:120} as well as Clement of Alexandria, if the errors of his printer, who wrote forty-six for fifty-six, are corrected. {*Clement, Stromateis, l. 1. c. 21. 2:333}

*5211.* Aulus Hirtius, the consul (the author of the Alexandrian and African war, that had been fought by Julius Caesar), died in the battle. The other consul, Pansa, died from his wounds a little later. {*Cicero, Friends, l. 12. c. 25. s. 6. 26:607} {*Dio, l. 46. (39) 5:79} {*Cicero, Friends, l. 11. c. 9. s. 1. 26:451} {*Livy, l. 119. 14:151} {*Velleius Paterculus, l. 2. c. 61. s. 4. 1:183} Tibullus assigned this date to the birthday of Ovid. {Tibullus, l. 3. c. 5.} Ovid wrote that his birthday occurred: {*Ovid, Tristia, l. 4. c. 10. (5-7) 6:197}

"When both the consuls fell with the same fate." *[K387]*

*5212.* Both the armies of the dead consuls obeyed Caesar. {Eutropius, l. 7.} {Orosius, l. 6. c. 18.}

*5213.* The Senate was very ungrateful to Caesar, who was the only one of the three generals to survive. In a triumph that was decreed to Decimus Brutus, for having been freed from the siege at Mutina by Caesar, the Senate made no special mention of Caesar and his army. {*Livy, l. 119. 14:151} {*Velleius Paterculus, l. 2. c. 62. s. 4,5. 1:185} The envoys were sent to the army with orders to speak to the soldiers when Octavius was out of the way. But the army was not as ungrateful as the Senate was. When Caesar quietly bore this wrong, the soldiers said they would not obey any commands unless their general was present. Without a doubt, the Senate would have taken the legions he had from Octavius, except that they were afraid to decree this publicly. They were well aware of the loyalty and love the soldiers had toward Caesar. {*Velleius Paterculus, l. 2. c. 62. s. 5,6. 1:185,187} {*Dio, l. 46. (39) 5:79}

*5214.* On their own initiative, the city of Tarsus invited Dolabella into Syria and the city of Laodicea called Dolabella into Cilicia. {*Cicero, Friends, l. 12. c. 13. s. 4. 26:555} *[E691]*

*5215.* When Dolabella was about to leave Asia, he sent five cohorts into the Chersonesus. Brutus easily captured these, because he had five legions, very good cavalry and numerous auxiliaries. {*Cicero, Letters to Brutus, l. 1. c. 14. s. 1. 28:669} This letter was dated the 12th or the 14th of the Calends of May (April 20 or 18). Dolabella left Asia for Syria by land with two legions and Lucius Figulus followed him with the navy. {*Appian, Civil Wars, l. 4. c. 8. (60) 4:243}

*5216.* On the 5th of the Calends of May (April 27), the Senate debated the issue of making war on those who were considered enemies of the state. Servilius, a tribune of the people, thought that Cassius should make war on Dolabella. Caesar agreed, and decreed that Marcus Brutus, too, should pursue Dolabella, if he thought it profitable and for the good of the state. Brutus was to do what he thought was best for the state. Nothing was decreed about Cassius, nor had any letters from him come to Rome, as yet. {*Cicero, Letters to Brutus, l. 1. c. 9.

*s. 1. 28:651,653*} Cassius explained the reasons for this delay in his letters to Cicero. {*Cicero, Friends, l. 12. c. 12. s. 2,3. 26:549}

*5217.* Dolabella went into Cilicia and Tarsus freely yielded to him. He defeated some guards of Cassius who were in Aegae. {*Dio, l. 47. (30) 5:177}

*5218.* Cassius was in Palestine at the time. {*Dio, l. 47. (30) 5:177} From there, he wrote his second letter to Cicero from the camp, dated on the Nones of May (May 7). He described the state of his affairs like this: {*Cicero, Friends, l. 12. c. 12. s. 2. 26:549}

> "I have all the armies that were in Syria. I made some delay, while I paid the soldiers all what I promised them, but now there is nothing to hinder me."

*5219.* He then exhorted Cicero to defend the dignity of his soldiers and of the generals, Murcus and Crispus. He added: {*Cicero, Friends, l. 12. c. 12. s. 3-5. 26:549,551}

> "I have heard, through letters that were written, that Dolabella has come into Cilicia with all his forces. I will go into Cilicia. Whatever I shall do, I will do my best to give you prompt notification of it. I very earnestly hope that we shall be worthy of the well-being of the state, for then we shall be contented."

*5220.* As soon as Cassius had left Judea, Malichus plotted Antipater's death. He thought that, with his death, Hyrcanus' government would be more secure. When Antipater found out about the plot, he went beyond Jordan and gathered an army from the inhabitants there and from the Arabians. *[K388]* Malichus was an astute politician and denied that he had intended any treason, swearing before Antipater and his sons that no such thing had ever entered his mind. This was especially necessary since Phasael had a garrison in Jerusalem and Herod had the army at his command. So he was reconciled to Antipater. Murcus, the governor of Syria, wanted to execute him, but Antipater spared his life. Murcus had found out that Malichus was going around in Judea, seeking to create a rebellion against Rome. {*Josephus, Antiq., l. 14. c. 11. s. 3. (277-279) 7:597}

*5221.* When Cassius and Murcus had gathered an army, they made Herod governor of all Coelosyria. They gave him large forces of foot soldiers, cavalry and naval ships. They promised him the kingdom of Judea after the end of the war they were having against Antony and the young Caesar. {*Josephus, Antiq., l. 14. c. 11. s. 4. (280) 7:599} {*Josephus, Jewish War, l. 1. c. 11. s. 4. (225) 2:105}

*5222.* Cassius appointed many tyrants in Syria, as well as leaving Marion, the tyrant of the Tyrians in his position, who then also ruled in Syria. Marion ejected the garrisons that were there and captured three citadels in

Galilee, which were next to Syria. {*Josephus, Jewish War, l. 1. c. 12. s. 2. (238) 2:111} {*Josephus, Antiq., l. 14. c. 12. s. 1. (297.298) 7:607}

5223. A certain Cicereius wrote to Satrius, the lieutenant of Gaius Trebonius, that Dolabella had been killed by Tullius and Dejotarus and his army had been routed. This Greek letter relating to these events was sent by Brutus to Cicero on the 17th of the Calends of June (May 16), {*Cicero, Letters to Brutus, l. 1. c. 12. s. 3. 28:665} but its information turned out to be false.

5224. Dolabella left Asia and went through Cilicia into Syria. He was refused entry into Antioch by the garrison defending the city. {*Dio, l. 47. (30) 5:177,179} He tried many times to enter by force, but was repulsed each time, with the loss of men. After he had lost about a hundred men, he left many behind sick, while he fled by night from Antioch toward Laodicea. That night, almost all the soldiers he had enrolled in Asia left him. Some returned to Antioch and surrendered to the men whom Cassius had left there to control the city. Some went down the hill of Amanus into Cilicia. Of these, thirty came into Pamphylia, where they were told that Cassius, with all his forces, was only a four-day journey away, just at the time when Dolabella was arriving there. {*Cicero, Friends, l. 12. c. 15. s. 7. 26:575,577}

5225. Dolabella had intelligence about Cassius' forces and came to Laodicea, a city that was friendly to him. It was located on a peninsula and faced toward the continent. It was well-fortified and had a good harbour facing the sea. It was very suitable for bringing in provisions and also very convenient for sailing out when and where they pleased. {*Appian, Civil Wars, l. 4. c. 8. (60) 4:243} [E692] He did not take this city by assault because the citizens truly surrendered themselves to him on account of the love they had for the former Caesar. {*Dio, l. 47. (30) 5:177,179}

5226. At Jerusalem, when Antipater was feasting at Hyrcanus' house, Malichus bribed the king's butler and poisoned Antipater. He gathered a band of soldiers and seized the government of the city. Phasael and Herod were very angry and Malichus firmly denied everything. Herod planned soon to revenge his father's death and to raise an army for that purpose. However, Phasael thought it better to defeat Malichus with guile in case that Herod should start a civil war. [K389] Phasael therefore accepted Malichus' defence, pretending to believe him when Malichus said that he was not involved in his father's death. Malichus built a splendid monument for Antipater. {*Josephus, Antiq., l. 14. c. 11. s. 4. (281-284) 7:599}

5227. Meanwhile, Herod went to Samaria and found it in a desperate situation. He restored order and subdued the dissensions that existed among the inhabitants. Not long after this, when the feast of Pentecost was approaching, he came into the city of Jerusalem with soldiers. Malichus was afraid and persuaded Hyrcanus not to let him enter. Hyrcanus did this on the pretext that, among the holy people, it was not lawful to bring in a mixed multitude of profane men. Herod discounted this excuse and entered the city by night, which greatly terrified Malichus. Consequently, consistent with his hypocrisy, he publicly and with tears bewailed the death of Antipater as his great friend. Therefore, it was thought good by Herod's friends to take no notice of this hypocrisy, but again courteously to entertain Malichus. Herod sent letters to Cassius, notifying him of Antipater's death. Cassius knew the character of Malichus all too well, and wrote back to Herod suggesting that he revenge his father's death. He secretly ordered the tribunes that were at Tyre to help Herod in doing this. {*Josephus, Antiq., l. 14. c. 11. s. 5,6. (285-288) 7:601,603}

5228. In Gaul, on the 4th of the Calends of June (May 29), Marcus Lepidus allied himself with Marcus Antony. {*Cicero, Friends, l. 10. c. 23. s. 2. 26:367,369}

5229. When Publius Lentulus, the proquaestor of Asia and propraetor extraordinary, saw that Brutus was slow in getting into Asia and that Dolabella had left Asia, he thought it best to return to his office from Macedonia as soon as he could. This would enable him to collect the tribute that was owing and gather up the money he had left there and send it to Rome. In the meanwhile, as he was sailing about the islands, he learned that the navy of Dolabella was in Cilicia (or Lycia), and that the Rhodians had furnished him with many ships which were already being used by him. Therefore, he returned to Rhodes with the ships that he had, or which Patiscus, the proquaestor of Asia, had provided. He relied on the decree of the Senate, by which Dolabella had been declared an enemy, and on the league that had been renewed with the Rhodians. But the Rhodians would not strengthen the proquaestor's navy with their ships. His soldiers were forbidden to come into the city or the port, or anywhere in Rhodes. They were prevented from getting any provisions, or even fresh water. Even Lentulus himself had a difficult time getting into the city with his ship. When he was brought into their city and to the elders, he could obtain nothing from them. He complained of this in public letters he sent to the Senate and in the private ones he sent to Cicero. {*Cicero, Friends, l. 12. c. 14. s. 2,3. 26:559} {*Cicero, Friends, l. 12. c. 15. s. 2. 26:569}

5230. While Lentulus and Patiscus were detained at Rhodes, Sextus Marius and Gaius Titius, the lieutenants of Dolabella, found out about their coming and soon hurriedly fled from Cilicia (or Lycia) in a galley from the navy. They left their cargo ships, which they had spent much time gathering. There were more than a hundred cargo ships and the smallest could carry two thousand tons. Dolabella had provided them for this purpose: If his hopes in Syria and Egypt were frustrated, then he could use these ships to transport all his soldiers and all his money and go directly into Italy. *[K390]* He would ally himself with the two Antonys, who were his relatives. For this reason, Lentulus and Patiscus came there from Rhodes with the ships they had, captured all these cargo ships and restored them to their rightful owners. Then, from there, they pursued the navy that had fled as far as Sida, the remotest country of the province of Asia. They knew that some of Dolabella's fleet had fled there and that the rest, which were scattered, had sailed into Syria and Cyprus (or Egypt). When Lentulus heard that Cassius had a very large fleet prepared in Syria, he returned to his office. {*Cicero, Friends, l. 12. c. 14. s. 1. 26:557,559} {*Cicero, Friends, l. 12. c. 15. s. 2. 26:569}

5231. However, Patiscus and Cassius of Parma assembled a fleet from the seacoast of the province of Asia and from all the islands that would give them ships. They soon had sailors, although the cities were very uncooperative. They pursued the fleet of Dolabella, which Lucilius was commanding. They encouraged them, in the hope that Lucilius would surrender, and sailed as fast as they could. Finally, Lucilius came to Corycus in Pamphylia and burned the harbour and stayed there. *[E693]* So they left Corycus and thought it best to go to Cassius' camp. Another fleet, which Tullius Cimber had assembled in Bithynia the previous year, under the command of Turullius the quaestor, was following them and so they came to Cyprus. {*Cicero, Friends, l. 12. c. 13. s. 3. 26:555}

5232. Cicero received letters about what Dolabella was doing and his arrival in the city of Laodicea. Two letters, written to Cicero, are extant. One is the fourteenth letter from Publius Lentulus, sent from Pamphylia on the 4th of the Nones of June (June 4), not the 4th of the Calends of June (May 29). {*Cicero, Friends, l. 12. c. 14. s. 1. 26:557} This is shown from the following letter to the Senate, which was dated from Perga and to which the letter from Lentulus referred. {*Cicero, Friends, l. 12. c. 15. s. 1. 26:567} The thirteenth letter was later sent from Cassius on the Ides of June (June 13), from Cyprus. {*Cicero, Friends, l. 12. c. 13. s. 1. 26:551} In the first letter, Cassius told of the trouble that Dolabella encountered after he entered Laodicea. {*Cicero, Friends, l. 12. c. 14. s. 4. 26:561}

> "I hope I shall quickly bring him to punishment, for he neither has any place to flee to, nor can he resist so large an army as Cassius has."

5233. The second letter was from Cassius (if I am not mistaken) of Parma, who was also one of the murderers of Julius Caesar. He wrote that taunting letter to Octavius which is mentioned by Suetonius, and we know the letter was not from Cassius Longinus, who at the time held the office of proconsul of Syria and whom he also mentioned at the end of this letter. {*Suetonius, Augustus, l. 2. c. 4. s. 2. 1:155} From him we have a more accurate description of Dolabella's camp: {*Cicero, Friends, l. 12. c. 13. s. 4. 26:555,557}

> "The people of Tarsus are the very worst allies and the citizens of Laodicea are even crazier. Of their own authority they sent for Dolabella, who had acquired a number of Greek soldiers from both cities and made an army. He has placed his camp before the city of Laodicea, has broken down part of the wall and has joined his camp to the town. Our Cassius, with ten legions, twenty companies of auxiliaries and four thousand cavalry, has his camp at Paltus, within twenty miles of him. He thinks he may defeat him without once striking a blow because wheat is now selling for three tetradrachmas in Dolabella's camp. Unless he has received some supplies from the ships of Laodicea, he must shortly perish from famine. He cannot supply himself, because of the large navy which Cassius has, under the command of Quintilius Rufus. Those ships that I myself, Turullius, and Patiscus have brought, will easily assist Rufus."

5234. Dolabella had been at Laodicea some time in a good situation. His navy had followed him quickly from Asia. However, when he went to the Aradians to receive money and shipping from them, he was surprised by a few soldiers and was in extreme danger. *[K391]* As he fled, he met the army of Cassius and was defeated, so he retired to Laodicea. {*Dio, l. 47. (30) 5:179}

5235. Cassius, fearing that Dolabella might escape from there, raised a rampart a quarter mile long across the isthmus. It was made with stones and materials brought from the villages beyond the city and from the sepulchres. The messengers he sent to request ships from Phoenicia, Lycia and Rhodes, were slighted by all except the Sidonians. Cassius engaged in a naval battle with Dolabella in which, after the loss of many ships on both sides, five were taken by Dolabella, together with all the sailors. {*Appian, Civil Wars, l. 4. c. 8. (60,61) 4:243}

5236. Again, Cassius sent messengers to those who had slighted his first commands and to both Cleopatra, the queen of Egypt, and Serapion, who commanded her forces in Cyprus. The people of Tyre, Aradus and Serapion sent as many ships as they had, without the queen's consent, while the queen excused herself and said that the Egyptians were troubled with famine and pestilence, so that she sent no ships at all. The Rhodians, too, refused in any way to assist toward the civil wars. They said that even the ships they had given to Dolabella had only been to transport him and that they did not know whether or not he used them for war. {*Appian, Civil Wars, l. 4. c. 8. (61) 4:243,245} {*Appian, Civil Wars, l. 5. c. 1. (8) 4:389}

5237. The people of Tarsus tried to keep Tullius Cimber (who was also one of Caesar's murderers) from crossing the Taurus Mountains as he was hurrying to help Cassius. Fearing that Cimber had large forces with him, they left the passes and made an agreement with him but later, when they knew the small size of his force, they refused him entrance into their city and did not supply him with provisions. So Cimber thought it better to take his forces to Cassius, than to assault Tarsus. He built a citadel against them and returned into Syria. When the people of Tarsus took soldiers there, they seized the citadel and attacked the city of Adana. (It was nearby and they had a standing controversy with the city because they said Adana favoured Cassius' side.) When Cassius heard of this, he sent Lucius Rufus against Tarsus. {*Dio, l. 47. (31) 5:181}

5238. After Cassius had repaired his fleet as best he could, and after Statius Murcus arrived with the navy he had assembled, Cassius had two more naval battles with Dolabella. In the first, there were equal losses on both sides, but in the second battle, he was more successful. On land, he had finished his rampart and now brought the battering rams to the walls, so that Dolabella was prevented from getting supplies by land or sea. [E694] Lacking supplies, he soon made an attack, but was driven back into the town. {*Dio, l. 47. (30) 5:179} {*Appian, Civil Wars, l. 4. c. 8. (62) 4:245}

5239. Unable to bribe the night-watch, whom Marsus commanded, Cassius bribed the day-watch, whom Quintus commanded, so that, while Marsus slept by day, Cassius got in through some of the smaller gates and the city was taken. Dolabella asked one of his guards to cut his throat and then to escape. The guard cut Dolabella's throat, then cut his own. {*Appian, Civil Wars, l. 4. c. 8. (62) 4:245} {*Appian, Civil Wars, l. 5. c. 1. (4) 4:381,383} Seneca the Elder stated that Dellius (or Quintus Dellius, the historian): {*Seneca the Elder, Suasoriae, l. 1. c. 7. 2:495,497}

> "was about to defect from Dolabella to Cassius on the promise of immunity if he would kill Dolabella."
> [K392]

5240. Thus Cassius forced Dolabella to commit suicide at Laodicea. {*Livy, l. 121. 14:153} {*Strabo, l. 16. c. 2. s. 9. 7:249} {*Velleius Paterculus, l. 2. c. 69. s. 1,2. 1:197,199} {*Dio, l. 47. (30) 5:179}

{Orosius, l. 6. c. 18.} Marsus also committed suicide. {*Appian, Civil Wars, l. 4. c. 8. (62) 4:245} Marcus Octavius, Dolabella's lieutenant, did likewise. Cassius afforded them a proper burial, even though they had cast out Trebonius, unburied. He gave those who had followed the camp, although they had been declared enemies at Rome, both lodgings and immunity. He did not punish Laodicea any more than to impose a sum of money on them. {*Dio, l. 47. (30) 5:179,181} However, Appian said that he plundered both the temples and the treasury and exacted very large tribute from the rest of the population. Also, that he executed every nobleman and so reduced that city to a most miserable state. {*Appian, Civil Wars, l. 4. c. 8. (62) 4:245}

5241. Cassius commanded the army of Dolabella to take the military oath of loyalty to him. {*Appian, Civil Wars, l. 4. c. 8. (62) 4:245} Then he went to Tarsus. When he saw that the city of Tarsus had already surrendered to Lucius Rufus, he fined them all the private and public money, but laid no other punishment on them. {*Dio, l. 47. (31) 5:181} He imposed an extremely heavy tax of fifteen hundred talents on them, with the result that when the soldiers violently tried to collect it, the people were forced to sell all their public and sacred ornaments for lack of money, and broke down the sacred and the dedicated things. When this was not enough to pay the sum, the magistrates sold those who had been born free, first virgins and boys. Later, they sold women and old men, which fetched very little. Finally, they sold the young men, many of whom killed themselves. {*Appian, Civil Wars, l. 4. c. 8. (64) 4:247,249}

5242. After the capture of Laodicea, the governors came from every place and brought crowns and presents to Cassius. Herod expected that Malichus would be punished there, for the murder of his father Antipater. However, Malichus suspected this and planned to make the Phoenicians around Tyre revolt. Since his son was being kept in that city as a hostage, he meant to steal him away privately into Judea. While Cassius was preparing for war against Antony, he would stir the Jews to revolt from the Romans and to depose Hyrcanus, so that he could get the kingdom for himself. Herod was a shrewd politician and when he learned of this treachery, he invited both Malichus and Hyrcanus to supper with their companions. At that time he sent out one of his servants on the pretext of providing for the banquet. But instead, he sent him to the tribunes, that these might kill Malichus. The tribunes remembered the orders of Cassius, so they went out and found him on the shore near the city, where they ran him through and killed him. Hyrcanus was so astonished, that he fainted. He had barely come to, when he asked who had killed Malichus. One of the tribunes said that it had been done on the orders of Cassius. Then Hyrcanus replied:

> "Truly, Cassius has preserved me and my country, by killing the one who was a traitor to both."

5243. It is uncertain whether he spoke from fear, or approved of the action. {*Josephus, Jewish War, l. 1. c. 11. s. 7,8. (231-235) 2:109,111} {*Josephus, Antiq., l. 14. c. 11. s. 6. (288-293) 7:603,605}

5244. On the day before the Calends of July (June 30), Marcus Lepidus was decreed an enemy of the state because he had entertained Antony. The others who had revolted from the state were also declared to be enemies, but if they chose to obey the Senate before the Calends of September (September 1), they would be forgiven. {*Cicero, Friends, l. 12. c. 10. s. 1. 26:541} Thus Cicero wrote to Gaius Cassius, the relative of Lepidus: {*Cicero, Friends, l. 12. c. 10. s. 8. 26:543} [K393]

> "We would gallantly have overcome all, had not Lepidus entertained Antony after he was pillaged, disarmed and fleeing. For this reason, Antony was never hated by the city as much as Lepidus. He raised war from a state that was in trouble but Lepidus when it was in peace and quiet."

5245. In the same letter, Cicero showed that he had received letters from Cassius, from the camp, dated on the Nones of May (May 7). {*Cicero, Friends, l. 12. c. 10. s. 2. 26:543} Cassius stated that he held Syria and that he was preparing for his expedition into Cilicia, against Dolabella. The news of the success of that expedition and of the defeat of Dolabella had not yet reached Rome. He had written to Caesar of his returning to favour, as Brutus had written to the Senate in the same way, concerning the state of affairs. {*Dio, l. 47. (29) 5:175,177} Brutus, in his letters sent to Caesar, persuaded him to oppose Antony and to side with him. {*Dio, l. 47. (22) 5:161,163} [E695] However, in his letters to Cicero, Brutus said something quite different, for when Cicero wrote to Caesar:

> "that there was one thing desired and expected from him, namely that he would allow those citizens to live in peace, of whom good men and the people of Rome thought well."

5246. Brutus wrote back to Cicero in a rage: {*Cicero, Letters to Brutus, l. 1. c. 25. s. 1. 28:719}

> "What if he will not, shall we not be? It is better not to live, than to live with his help. I, by my loyalty, do not think all the gods to be so opposed to the safety of the people of Rome, that Octavius must be entreated for the safety of one private citizen. I will not say for the deliverers of the whole world."

5247. When the Senate was informed of the affairs of Cassius, it confirmed him in the government of Syria (which he held at the time) and committed the war against Dolabella to him (which they knew had already been ended). {*Dio, l. 47. (29) 5:175} So all the governments beyond the sea were committed to the care of Brutus and Cassius, in that a decree was issued that all the provinces and armies who obeyed the Romans, from the Ionian Sea to the east, should be obedient to these two. The Senate approved of all the things that these men had done and praised the armies that had surrendered to them. {*Velleius Paterculus, l. 2. c. 62. s. 1,2. 1:183,185} {*Appian, Civil Wars, l. 3. c. 8. (63) 4:73,75}

5248. Octavius saw that the actions of the Senate were obviously to the advantage of Pompey's side and to the detriment of Caesar's. He thought it a disgrace that Decimus Brutus had been chosen, instead of himself, as general in the war against Antony. Concealing his discontent, he requested a triumph for the victory at Mutina. He was slighted by the Senate, as though he were demanding greater things than were appropriate for his age. He feared that if Antony were to be utterly vanquished, he would be slighted even more, so he began to have some thoughts of siding with Antony, in line with the advice which Pansa had given him on his deathbed. {*Appian, Civil Wars, l. 3. c. 9. (64,65) 4:75-79} {*Appian, Civil Wars, l. 3. c. 12. (86) 4:113} An agreement with Antony was made by Marcus Lepidus. {*Livy, l. 119. 14:151} {Orosius, l. 6. c. 18.}

5249. Therefore, an alliance for controlling the government was started between these three. They began by sending letters among themselves and relating how they had been treated. Antony warned Caesar, what formidable enemies Pompey's side had been to him and to what heights they had risen. Brutus and Cassius were extolled by Cicero. Antony told Caesar that he would join his forces with those of Brutus and Cassius, who were commanders of seventeen legions, if Caesar refused his alliance. [K394] He added, that it was even more important that Caesar avenge the death of his father, than that he avenge the death of his friend. At the advice and entreaty of the armies, an alliance was made between Antony and Caesar, as a part of which, the step-daughter of Antony was betrothed to Caesar. {*Velleius Paterculus, l. 2. c. 65. s. 1. 1:189,191} She was Claudia, the daughter of Fulvia by a former husband, Publius Clodius, and was scarcely of marriageable age. {*Suetonius, Augustus, l. 2. c. 62. s. 1. 1:241,243}

5250. When Octavius made an agreement with Mark Antony and Marcus Lepidus, then Octavius sent four hundred soldiers to Rome to demand the consulship for him in the name of the army. When the Senate began to vacillate, Cornelius, a centurion, the leader of the men that had brought the message, thrust his soldier's coat behind him and showed the hilt of his sword. He boldly said before the Senate:

"This shall do it, if you will not do it."

5251. The Senate was forced by Octavius' soldiers to submit, after which Octavius went toward Rome with them. {*Suetonius, Augustus, l. 2. c. 26. s. 1,2. 1:187} {*Appian, Civil Wars, l. 3. c. 12. (88) 4:117} {*Dio, l. 46. (43) 5:87}

5252. While he was on his journey, the praetors placed guards in various locations of the city and seized Janiculum, with a guard of soldiers they already had in the city and with two legions that had come from Africa. When Octavius entered the city, the praetors came down from Janiculum and surrendered themselves and their soldiers to him, while the legions voluntarily gave their ensigns to him. {*Appian, Civil Wars, l. 3. c. 13. (91) 4:123} {*Dio, l. 46. (45) 5:91,93} In the month of August, the legions which had been brought from Janiculum followed Octavius, just as it was in the decree of the Senate. {Macrobius, Saturnalia, l. 1. c. 12.}

5253. On the first day of the choosing of consuls, as Octavius was making an augury in the field of Mars, six vultures appeared to him. When he had been selected as consul and was speaking to the soldiers from the rostrum, six vultures again appeared (some say twelve). This was what happened to Romulus in his auguries, when he was about to build Rome. Based on this, Octavius hoped that he would found the city anew. {*Julius Obsequens, Prodigies, l. 1. c. 69. 14:315} {*Suetonius, Augustus, l. 2. c. 95. s. 1. 1:295} {*Appian, Civil Wars, l. 3. c. 13. (94) 4:129} {*Dio, l. 46. (46) 5:93} After he was chosen as consul, those with him hurried to Quintus Pedius, his colleague, whereupon he gave Octavius his rightful portion from the inheritance of Julius Caesar. {*Velleius Paterculus, l. 2. c. 95. s. 2,3. 1:191} {*Appian, Civil Wars, l. 3. c. 13. (93) 4:129} {*Dio, l. 46. (46) 5:93}

5254. Livy said that Octavius was made consul when he was only nineteen years old. {*Livy, l. 119. 14:151} However, Suetonius more correctly wrote that he became the consul in his twentieth year. {*Suetonius, Augustus, l. 2. c. 26. s. 1. 1:187} [E696] Eutropius agreed with this and Plutarch also confirmed this about Octavius, in stating: {Eutropius, l. 7.} {*Plutarch, Brutus, l. 1. c. 27. s. 1,2. 6:185}

"when his army was placed around the city, he received the consulship, having scarcely come to a man's estate, since he was only twenty years old, as he relates in his own commentaries."

5255. Velleius wrote: {*Velleius Paterculus, l. 2. c. 65. s. 2. 1:191}

"he was made consul the day before he was twenty years old, on the 11th of the Calends of October (September 22)."

5256. However, Velleius was mistaken about the day he became consul. For there was a whole month and five days to go before Octavius turned twenty. He was not born in the month of September, but he first obtained the consulship in August which was why the month of Sextilis was first called August, as was stated by Suetonius. {*Suetonius, Augustus, l. 2. c. 31. s. 1,2. 1:197} {*Dio, l. 55. (6) 6:395} The decree of the Senate, as recorded by Macrobius, also confirmed this. {Macrobius, Saturnalia, l. 1. c. 12.}

5257. Dio noted that he was made consul for the first time on the 14th of the Calends of September (August 19), and that he later died on the same day, fifty-six years later. {*Dio, l. 56. (30) 7:69} [K395] Tacitus noted: {*Tacitus, Annals, l. 1. c. 9. 3:259}

"The same day marked the beginning of his acceptance of the empire and the end of his life (many years later). He died at Nola in the same house and room as his father Octavius had."

5258. His empire is not incorrectly calculated starting from this first consulship, which he extorted from the Senate against their will, as Tacitus wrote, and laid down at his own pleasure and relinquished when he pleased. {*Tacitus, Annals, l. 1. c. 10. 3:263} Octavius hypocritically thanked the Senate, pretending to consider it a favour bestowed on him, as though the things he had extorted by force had been freely offered to him. The senators bragged that they had conferred these things on him of their own volition. Moreover, they conferred on him whom they did not think worthy of the consulship, the right to have precedence over the consuls after his consulship was over, whenever he commanded the army. The consuls commanded the other armies to obey him whom they had earlier threatened to punish for having gathered forces on his own private authority. The Senate assigned the legions of Brutus to Octavius to disgrace Brutus, as they had committed the war against Antony to Octavius to repress Brutus. In short, the custody of the city was given to him and it was granted that, even without any direction from the law, he should have power to do whatever he wanted. {*Dio, l. 46. (47) 5:97,99} He retained this power as long as he lived, for the next fifty-six years. There was good reason why Brutus warned Cicero about this: {*Cicero, Letters to Brutus, l. 1. c. 9. s. 4. 28:661}

"I am afraid, that your Caesar will think himself to have risen so high by your decrees that he will not be likely to come down again once he is made a consul."

5259. Octavius was not content with his earlier adoption, made by the last will of Julius Caesar, and so he had it confirmed by a decree of the people in a full assembly of their wards (which Antony had prevented the previous year). By public authority, he then assumed the name of Gaius Julius Caesar Octavius. {*Appian, Civil Wars, l. 3. c. 13. (94) 4:129} {*Dio, l. 46. (47) 5:97}

5260. Octavius soon passed another law absolving Dolabella (whose death was not yet known in Rome), who had been declared an enemy by the Senate and sentenced to die for the death of Caesar. {*Appian, Civil Wars, l. 3. c. 13. (95) 4:129} Octavius did this, so that it would be thought that he did nothing by force, but only by law. Quintus Pedius, his colleague in the consulship, made the law called the Pedian Law, which decreed that all those who were involved in the murder of Caesar would be banished and their goods confiscated. {*Livy, l. 120. 14:151} {*Velleius Paterculus, l. 2. c. 69. s. 5,6. 1:199} {*Suetonius, Nero, l. 6. c. 3. s. 1. 2:87} {*Dio, l. 46. (48) 5:97,99} He appointed Lucius Cornificius to accuse Marcus Brutus, and Marcus Agrippa to accuse Gaius Cassius. Since they were absent, they were condemned without any hearing of their case. {*Plutarch, Brutus, l. 1. c. 27. s. 4,5. 6:185} Capito, the uncle of Velleius Paterculus and one of the senatorial order, supported Marcus Agrippa against Gaius Cassius. {*Velleius Paterculus, l. 2. c. 69. s. 5. 1:199}

5261. Decimus Brutus, one of the murderers of Caesar, was absent and was also condemned. On the orders of Mark Antony and in the house of a certain guest of his, a nobleman called Camelius, Decimus was killed by Capenus, a Burgundian, a year and a half after the death of Caesar. {*Livy, l. 120. 14:151,153} {*Velleius Paterculus, l. 2. c. 64. s. 1. 1:189} {*Appian, Civil Wars, l. 3. c. 14. (98) 4:135,137} {Orosius, l. 6. c. 18.} Cicero said Decimus excelled in this particular virtue: {*Cicero, Friends, l. 11. c. 21. s. 4. 26:485}

"He was never afraid, nor ever disturbed."

5262. However, Seneca stated that he showed a cowardly fear when facing death. {*Seneca, Epistles, l. 1. c. 82. s. 12. 5:249} To encourage him, Helvius Blasio, a man who had always loved him, because they had always been fellow soldiers, killed himself. [K396] Decimus witnessed this and so was strengthened to endure his own death. {*Dio, l. 46. (53) 5:109} Camelius sent the head of the dead Brutus to Antony. When he saw it, he gave it to his friends to bury. {*Appian, Civil Wars, l. 3. c. 14. (98) 4:135}

5263. Trebonius was the next to die for the murder of Caesar. He had been the closest friend of the murderers and he had thought it best to keep the things he had received from Caesar, even though he had thought Caesar, who had given him those things, had to die. [E697] While Caesar was alive, Trebonius was the master of the cavalry and commanded Farther Gaul. He was also elected consul by Caesar in the year following the consulship of Hirtius and Pansa, as well as being made

governor of Nearer Gaul. {*Velleius Paterculus, l. 2. c. 69. s. 1. 1:197} {*Appian, Civil Wars, l. 3. c. 14. (98) 4:135}

5264. At the same time also, Minucius Basillus, one of the murderers of Caesar, was killed by his own servants, because he had castrated some of them in his anger. {*Appian, Civil Wars, l. 3. c. 14. (98) 4:137} {Orosius, l. 6. c. 18.}

## 3962a AM, 4671 JP, 43 BC

5265. When Marcus Brutus had appeased the army that was likely to rebel at the instigation of Gaius Antony, Brutus turned him over to Gaius Clodius at Apollonia to be guarded. Brutus went into the higher Macedonia with the largest and strongest part of his army and from there crossed into Asia. He wanted to take them as far away from Italy as possible, so that he could better control the troops. In Asia, he received many auxiliaries, including those from Dejotarus, a man who was now very old and who had previously denied help to Gaius Cassius. {*Dio, l. 47. (24) 5:165}

5266. Mark Antony and Marcus Lepidus left their lieutenants in Gaul and went to Caesar in Italy with the largest and best part of the army. {*Dio, l. 46. (54) 5:109} When those three armies met at Bononia, an eagle sat on Caesar's tent and drove off two ravens, which he struck to the ground. All the army noted this and thought it portended that a time was coming when a difference would arise among the colleagues and that Caesar would get the victory over the other two. {*Dio, l. 47. (1) 5:119} {*Suetonius, Augustus, l. 2. c. 96. s. 1. 1:295}

5267. These three had a three-day private conference at the confluences around Bononia and Mutina, on a certain little island formed by the Lavinius River. They made peace among themselves and agreed that they should jointly govern the state's affairs for five years. {*Livy, l. 120. 14:153} {*Florus, l. 2. c. 16. 1:305} {*Plutarch, Cicero, l. 1. c. 46. s. 2. 7:201} {*Plutarch, Antony, l. 1. c. 19. s. 1. 9:179} {*Appian, Civil Wars, l. 4. c. 1. (2) 4:143} {*Dio, l. 46. (55,56) 5:111-115}

5268. By a common decree, they decided the following things: Caesar would turn over the consulship to Ventidius for the rest of the year. A new office of the triumviri would be established to avoid all civil disorder. Lepidus, along with Antony and Caesar, would hold that office for five years, with consular power. The triumviri would immediately be the annual magistrates for the city for a five year period. The provinces were to be divided in such a way that Antony should have all of Gaul, as well as Togata on this side of the Alps and Comata on the other side, excluding the province of Narbon. Lepidus should have the command of Narbon, together with Spain. Africa, along with Sardinia and Sicily, should be Caesar's share. In this way the Roman

Empire was divided among the triumviri. They deferred the division of those provinces over which Brutus and Cassius had the command. *[K397]* Moreover, it was agreed among them that they should put their enemies to death and that Lepidus should be chosen consul for the following year, in place of Decimus Brutus. He would have the responsibility of guarding Rome and all Italy, while Antony and Caesar would carry on the war against Brutus and Cassius. {*Appian, Civil Wars, l. 4. c. 1. (2) 4:143*} {*Dio, l. 46. (55,56) 5:111,113*}

5269. On the third day, the triumviri entered Rome, each separately with his praetorian cohort and one legion. When Publius Titius, the tribune of the people, called an assembly of the wards, he passed a law for the establishing of the new office. The triumviri were given consular power for five years, to restore order to the state. {*Appian, Civil Wars, l. 4. c. 2. (7) 4:151*} {*Dio, l. 47. (2) 5:119*}

5270. When the triumviri arrived, Cicero left the city and was assured, which also came to pass, that he could no more escape Antony, than Brutus and Cassius could escape Caesar. {*Livy, l. 120. 14:153*} {*Seneca the Elder, Suasoriae, l. 7. 2:595-611*}

5271. The triumvirate of Marcus Aemilius Lepidus, Mark Antony and Caesar Octavius commenced its rule on the 5th of the Calends of December (November 27). This was to continue to the days before the month of January of the sixth year. This was evident from the Colatian Marble. {*Gruter, Inscriptions, p. 298.*} At that time, Marcus Terentius Varro had a vision in which he saw Rome rise up with three heads. It is from that time that Suetonius and Eutropius derive the beginning of the government of Caesar Octavius. This was almost twelve years (less three months) before the victory at Actium, from which they began his monarchy. {*Suetonius, Augustus, l. 2. c. 8. s. 3. 1:161*} {*Eutropius, l. 7.*}

5272. On the 7th of the Ides of December (December 7), when Caesar Octavius substituted himself and Quintus Pedius as the consuls in place of Pansa and Hirtius, Marcus Cicero was killed by some men who were sent from Mark Antony. One of his ungrateful murderers was Popillus, a tribune whom Cicero had successfully defended against the charge of parricide. {*Plutarch, Cicero, l. 1. c. 49. 7:207*} The writer of the dialogue of the *Causes of Corrupted Eloquence*, which was ascribed to Gaius Tacitus, confirmed this from the writings of Tiro, a freedman of Cicero's. {*Tacitus, Oratory, l. 1. c. 17. 1:273,275*} *[E698]* This was the end of the life of one who was the first to deserve in peace the triumph and laurel of the tongue, and who was the father of eloquence and Latin learning. Julius Caesar had previously written about him that he had obtained a laurel far beyond all triumphs, and how much greater an achievement it was, to have extended the bounds of Roman learning than those of the empire. {*Pliny, l. 7. c. 30. 2:583*} These things were recorded about Cicero by the following writers. {*Velleius Paterculus, l. 2. c. 66. 1:191,193*} {*Seneca the Elder, Suasoriae, l. 7. 2:595-611*} {*Plutarch, Cicero, l. 1. c. 48,49. 7:205-209*}

5273. Cleopatra brought no forces to Cassius, although he demanded auxiliaries from her with threats. {*Appian, Civil Wars, l. 5. c. 1. (8) 4:389*}

5274. While Brutus was in Asia, Gellius Publicola conspired against him. Mark Antony also sent some men to rescue his brother, Gaius Antony. Therefore, Gaius Clodius, who had been left as Antony's guard, killed Gaius when he could no longer keep him safe. He did this either on his own authority or on the orders of Brutus. It was reported that Brutus had a great concern for the safety of Gaius Antony. After he learned of Decimus Brutus' death, he took no more care of Antony. However, Brutus did not punish Gellius, although he was guilty of treason against him. Gellius knew that Brutus had always considered him among his closest friends and that Marcus Messala, his brother, was on very good terms with Cassius. Therefore, Brutus left Gellius alone. {*Dio, l. 49. (24) 5:165,167*}

5275. As soon as Brutus heard of the acts of Mark Antony and the death of Gaius Antony, he feared that some new rebellion might arise in Macedonia, so he hurried back into Europe. {*Dio, l. 47. (25) 5:167*} *[K398]*

5276. The triumviri at Rome decreed the construction of a temple to Isis and Serapis. {*Dio, l. 47. (16) 5:147*}

5277. When Octavius had resigned the consulship and his colleague Quintus Pedius was dead, the triumviri appointed as consuls, Publius Ventidius (Bassus), the praetor, along with Gaius Carrinatus. This may be shown from the inscription in the Colatian Marble. {*Gruter, Inscriptions, p. 298.*} They gave the praetorship to one who was aedile. Later they removed all the praetors from their office, five days before the office was to expire and sent them into the provinces and appointed others in their places as praetors. {*Dio, l. 47. (15) 5:147*} This was what Paterculus referred to: {*Velleius Paterculus, l. 2. c. 65. s. 3. 1:191*}

> "This year saw Ventidius as both consul and praetor in that city through which he had been led in a triumph among the captives from Picencum."

5278. As a boy, he had been led in a triumph by Pompey. This is described in more detail by Valerius Maximus, Gellius and Pliny. {*Valerius Maximus, l. 6. c. 9. s. 9. 2:89*} {*Aulus Gellius, Attic Nights, l. 15. c. 4. s. 1-4. 3:69-73*} {*Pliny, l. 7. c. 43. 2:597*} Maximus added that, as a young man, Ventidius had made his living very humbly, by providing mules and coaches for the magistrates who were to go into the provinces. As a result, these verses were commonly written through all the streets:

> You *augurs* and *haruspices* draw near,
> We have an uncouth wonder happened here;
> He that rubbed mules is made consul here.

*5279.* At the end of the year, those who had recently been elected consuls held a triumph. Lucius Munatius Plancus triumphed for Gaul on the 4th of the Calends of January (December 29), and Marcus Aemilius Lepidus held a triumph for Spain on the 2nd of the Calends of January (December 31). This is evident from the Marble Records of Triumphs. {*Gruter, Inscriptions, p. 297.*} {*\*Velleius Paterculus, l. 2. c. 67. s. 3,4. 1:195*} {*\*Appian, Civil Wars, l. 4. c. 5. (31) 4:193*}

## 3962b AM, 4672 JP, 42 BC

*5280.* In the fourth Julian year, a day was incorrectly added to February. Only three years had elapsed from the first February of the first Julian year until that time. This error continued until the 37th Julian year. They should have added a day at the end of every four years, before the fifth year began. But the priests added a day at the beginning of the fourth year rather than at its end. So the year, which had been correctly ordered by Julius Caesar, was disordered by their negligence. {*\*Suetonius, Augustus, l. 2. c. 31. s. 2. 1:197*} {*Macrobius, Saturnalia, l. 1. c. 14. fin.*}

*5281.* After Marcus Brutus had settled everything in Macedonia, he went back into Asia again. {*\*Dio, l. 47. (25) 5:167*} He took a large army with him and arranged a fleet in Bithynia and at Cyzicum. He went by land and settled all the cities and heard the complaints of the governors. {*\*Plutarch, Brutus, l. 1. c. 28. s. 3. 6:187*} He appointed Apuleius, who had fled to him from the proscription by the triumviri, governor over Bithynia. {*\*Appian, Civil Wars, l. 4. c. 6. (40) 4:207*} [E699]

*5282.* The letters which Brutus wrote in a laconic style to those who were in Asia, are still extant. Aldus preserved them in Greek and Rainutius Florentius translated and recorded them in Latin. Plutarch recorded three in his writings. {*\*Plutarch, Brutus, l. 1. c. 2. s. 5-8. 6:131*} The first one, to the Pergamenian, can be found in the beginning of the collection that has already been published. Another one, which we shall recite, was to the Rhodians. [K399] The third and shortest of all was inscribed in the published Greek copies, to the Bithynians and in the Latin copy of Rainutius, to the Galatians and in Plutarch, to the Samians. It said this:

> "Your councils are paltry, your subsidies slow; what do you think will be the end of this?"

*5283.* Cassius intended to go into Egypt when he heard that Cleopatra, with her large navy, was about to side with Caesar and Antony. He thought that he could punish her and prevent her from doing this. She was troubled with a famine and had almost no foreign help because of the sudden departure of Allienus with four Roman legions. {*\*Appian, Civil Wars, l. 4. c. 8. (63) 4:245,247*} {*\*Appian, Civil Wars, l. 5. c. 1. (8) 4:389*}

*5284.* Crassus hoped that he would have a suitable occasion for this venture, until Brutus recalled him to Syria through one messenger after another, who reported that Octavius and Antony were crossing the Adriatic Sea. {*\*Appian, Civil Wars, l. 4. c. 8. (63) 4:247*} {*\*Plutarch, Brutus, l. 1. c. 28. s. 3,4. 6:187,189*} He gave up on his Egyptian plans and again sent his lightly armed cavalry with bribes to the king of the Parthians, sending his envoys with them to request more help. {*\*Appian, Civil Wars, l. 4. c. 8. (63) 4:247*}

*5285.* Cassius left his brother's son in Syria with one legion and sent his cavalry ahead of him to Cappadocia. They made a surprise attack on Ariobarzanes and took away a large amount of money and other provisions. Cassius on his return from Syria took pity on Tarsus, which was most miserably oppressed and he freed the city from paying any tribute in the future. {*\*Appian, Civil Wars, l. 4. c. 8. (63,64) 4:247,249*} Once his affairs were settled in Syria and Cilicia, he went to Asia to Brutus. {*\*Dio, l. 47. (32) 5:183*}

*5286.* After Cassius had left Syria, there was a sedition at Jerusalem. Helix, who had been left there with soldiers by Hyrcanus, revenged Malichus' death and attacked Phasael, causing the people to take up arms. Herod was there with Fabius, the governor of Damascus, and planned to help his brother, but was prevented by illness from doing so. Phasael withstood Helix's attack and first forced him into the town, then, after agreeing on conditions, allowed him to leave. Phasael was very angry with Hyrcanus, who had received so many benefits from him and had still favoured Helix and allowed the brother of Malichus to seize some citadels for he had held many citadels, of which Masada was the strongest. {*\*Josephus, Jewish War, l. 1. c. 12. s. 1. (236,237) 2:111*} {*\*Josephus, Antiq., l. 14. c. 11. s. 7. (294-296) 7:605,607*}

*5287.* Brutus and Cassius were very joyful and confident when they met at Smyrna and considered the forces which they had. When they had left Italy, they were poor and without arms and like abject exiles. They did not have so much as one ship rigged, one soldier or one friendly town. In a short time, they had met together with a fleet and were outfitted with cavalry and foot soldiers, as well as money to pay them. They were ready to fight for the Roman Empire. Cassius wanted to give

Brutus the same honour that he had. Brutus frequently prevented Cassius from doing this and often came to him, because Brutus was the older and his body could not endure the same amount of hardship. {*Plutarch, Brutus, l. 1. c. 28,28. 6:189}

5288. Together they planned the war against the triumviri. {*Livy, l. 122. 14:153} Brutus wanted to go into Macedonia with their combined forces and settle everything in one large battle. The enemy had forty legions, of which eight had been transported across the sea to Iconium. [K400] Cassius, on the other hand, thought the forces of the enemy were contemptible and that he and Brutus would not have adequate provisions for so large a force. He believed that the best way forward was to quell those who favoured the enemy, such as the Rhodians and Lycians, who were strongest at sea. Otherwise, they themselves would be attacked from behind, while they were attacking the enemy. Cassius' opinion prevailed. {*Appian, Civil Wars, l. 4. c. 9. (65) 4:249} When they heard that the triumviri were busy settling the affairs at Rome, Cassius and Brutus assumed that they would be kept busy enough with Sextus Pompey who was lying in wait against them near by. {*Dio, l. 47. (32,33) 5:183,185}

5289. Moreover, at Smyrna, Brutus desired that he might have some of the money, of which Cassius had a large amount. Brutus said that he had spent all he had in preparing a fleet with which they might control the whole inland sea. Cassius' friends, however, were against Cassius giving Brutus any money, saying it was unjust that what they had saved by frugality and acquired through hard work should be spent in bribing soldiers. In spite of this, Cassius gave him a third of everything. So both of them set about their own work. {*Plutarch, Brutus, l. 1. c. 30. s. 1-3. 6:193} [E700]

5290. They either went themselves or sent their envoys to draw those who had opposed them to their side. They gathered more men and money to fight the war. All those who lived in those parts and had formerly been not so much as spoken to, presently came to side with them. Although Ariobarzanes, the Rhodians and Lycians did not oppose them, they nonetheless refused Cassius' and Brutus' alliance. Brutus and Cassius suspected them of favouring the opposing side because they had received so many favours from the former Caesar. They feared that, in their absence, these might create some disturbances and thereby incite all the others not to keep their promise. They determined to attack them first of all, in the hope that with their superior forces they would easily convince them to side with them, either willingly or through force. {*Dio, l. 47. (33) 1:183,185}

5291. As soon as Herod had recovered, he went against the brother of Malichus and recaptured all the citadels he had seized. Herod also recovered three citadels in Galilee which had been seized by Marion, the tyrant of Tyre. He allowed all the garrison soldiers of the tyrants to leave, on conditions. He sent some of them home well-rewarded, thereby winning the affection of Tyre and fostering hatred for the tyrant. {*Josephus, Antiq., l. 14. c. 11. s. 7,8. (296-298) 7:607} {*Josephus, Jewish War, l. 1. c. 12. s. 2. (238) 2:111}

5292. The citizens of Tyre who had resisted Cassius, were commended by the triumviri, and given the hope that they would receive something for the losses they had sustained. In the same manner, because Cleopatra had sent help to Dolabella, she was granted that her son Ptolemy, whom she said she had by Caesar and who was therefore called Caesarion, should be called king of Egypt. {*Dio, l. 47. (31) 5:181,183}

5293. Brutus demanded men and money from the Lycians, because Naucrates, the popular leader, had persuaded the cities to revolt. They had positioned themselves on some hills to keep Brutus from passing through. First, he sent his cavalry against them while they were eating breakfast and the cavalry killed six hundred of them. Later, he took some citadels and smaller towns and then let them all go free without ransom, so that he might win the favour of the country. [K401] But they were obstinate and discontented on account of the losses they had sustained and so despised his clemency and good will. {*Plutarch, Brutus, l. 1. c. 30. s. 3-6. 6:193,195}

5294. In a battle, Brutus defeated the common army of the entire country of the Lycians. He also took over their camp, entering it as they fled. Many cities surrendered to him. {*Dio, l. 47. (34) 5:185}

5295. Then he besieged the most warlike of them and forced them to retire within the walls of Xanthus. {*Plutarch, Brutus, l. 1. c. 30. s. 6,7. 6:195} These people had destroyed their suburbs, intending that Brutus should have neither lodging nor materials. They fortified their city well and drove the enemy from the fortifications. They made a ditch fifty feet deep and equally as broad, so that when they stood on the bank they could use their javelins and arrows as if separated from the enemy by an unfordable river. Brutus besieged the city, pushing forward mantelets (a movable shelter used to cover the approach of men-at-arms when besieging a fortified place) for his men and dividing his army into two, to continue the assault by day and night. He brought his materials from a long distance and still urged them on to hasten the work. They did whatever had to be done with great earnestness and labour. Therefore, even though he had thought at first that he would not be able to overcome the strong resistance of the enemy for many months, he finished the task within a few days. With his cohorts, he assaulted and besieged the walls with engines, close to the gate. He continually replaced those of his men who were wearied or wounded, with fresh men. The enemy, likewise, held out manfully as long as the fortifications held, but they lost heart when these were destroyed. The town was battered with the engines. When Brutus saw what would happen, he ordered those who were besieging the gate to retreat. The men of Xanthus, thinking this had occurred through negligence on the part of the guard, sallied out by night with torches and burned the engines. However, the Roman cohorts hurried back there, as had been pre-arranged, and the enemy quickly fled back to the gate. Those who kept the gate had shut it, in case the enemy should break in together with those who were fleeing, and so there was a great slaughter of the men who were shut out of the town. {*Appian, Civil Wars, l. 4. c. 10. (76,77) 4:269,271}

5296. A river ran past the city. As some tried to escape by swimming underwater, they were captured again by the nets which had been let down into the river across the channel. These nets had bells hanging at their top, which signalled when anyone was entangled. {*Plutarch, Brutus, l. 1. c. 30. s. 6,7. 6:195}

5297. The men of Xanthus sallied out again around noon, drove back the guards and burned all the engines. Since the gate was open for them to return, two thousand Romans rushed in together with the townsmen, and others entered in a chaotic fashion. The portcullis (a heavy iron grate) fell upon them, due either to the action of the men of Xanthus or to the breaking of the ropes by which it was let down. [E701] Therefore, all the Romans who had broken in, were either beaten down or shut in, since they could not draw it up again without ropes. They were attacked from above by the men of Xanthus and barely managed to get into the forum, even though it was nearby, because the area around there was full of archers. Since the Romans had neither bows nor arrows, they fled into the temple of Sarpedon to avoid being surrounded. In the meantime, the Romans outside the city were very anxious for those who were trapped within. Brutus was running up and down, trying at every conceivable place to rescue them. But they could not break open the portcullis and they had lost their ladders and wooden towers through the fire. [K402] However, before long, some men made ladders and others brought tree trunks to the walls and used them for ladders. Some fastened hooks to ropes and tossed them up onto the walls and whenever any held, they climbed up on them. {*Appian, Civil Wars, l. 4. c. 10. (78) 4:271,273}

5298. The Oenandeses, their neighbours and enemies, were at that time the allies of Brutus. They climbed up the steep rocks with the Romans following them at once with determination. Many fell down as they lost their footing, but some got over the wall and opened a little gate. In front of the gate was a very dense palisade. With the help of these men, the most daring got up. As more men joined them, they went to break the portcullis, which was not protected with iron on the inside. Others also tried to do the same on the other side, since the Xanthians were busy attacking those who had fled into the temple of Sarpedon. The men broke it open from both sides of the gate. At sunset, accompanied by a frenzied noise, they all rushed in as one company. They gave a loud shout, as a sign to those trapped in the temple. {*Appian, Civil Wars, l. 4. c. 10. (79) 4:273}

5299. The Romans rushed into the city and set some houses on fire. First, the fire terrified those who witnessed this being done. Those who were farther off, thought that the city had been taken and so the neighbours, voluntarily set their own houses on fire, but most killed one another. {*Dio, l. 47. (34) 5:187} They withdrew inside their own houses, killing everyone who was dear to them as these willingly offered their throats to be cut. Such a lamentable cry went up at that time that Brutus thought the soldiers were sacking the city, a practice he had forbidden through public criers. When he was better informed, he so pitied the generous character of these men who had been born to liberty, that he sent messengers inviting them to peace. But they drove them back with their arrows and having first killed all that belonged to them and laid them on funeral piles and set them on fire, they cut their own throats. This was Appian's account of the story. {*Appian, Civil Wars, l. 4. c. 10. (80) 4:273} However, Plutarch related it as follows.

5300. Brutus was afraid that the city would be destroyed and ordered the soldiers to put out the fire and help the city. But a massive and incredible desperation suddenly took hold of the Lycians, which could well be compared to a desire for death. For, from the wall, both freemen and slaves, old and young, with women and children, assailed the enemy who came to quench the fire. The Xanthians themselves brought reeds and anything combustible to set the city on fire. Having done this, they used every means available to fan the flames. When all the city was ablaze, Brutus was grieved about this and went through the city seeking to help it. He stretched out his hands to the Xanthians and entreated them to spare the city, but no one obeyed him. In fact, they killed themselves in all manner of ways, including men and women and even little children. With loud cries and howlings, they threw themselves into the fire and some headlong from the wall. Some offered their naked throats to their fathers' swords, wanting to be killed by them. After the city had been consumed in this manner, one woman was seen hanging by a rope, her dead child hanging at her neck. She had a fiery torch with which she had set her house on fire. The sight appeared so tragic, that Brutus could not bear to look at it. *[K403]* When he was told of it, he started weeping and offered a reward to any of the soldiers who had saved a Lycian. They counted only a hundred and fifty who had surrendered. {*Plutarch, Brutus, l. 1. c. 31. 6:195,197}

5301. Appian wrote that Brutus saved some slaves. Of the freeborn, scarcely a hundred and fifty men were saved, and any women who did not have husbands to kill them. He added that Brutus saved all the temples he possibly could. {*Appian, Civil Wars, l. 4. c. 10. (80) 4:273,275}

5302. From there, Brutus went to Patara, a city which seemed to have been the port for the Xanthians where their ships were anchored. He ordered them to surrender to him, or expect a similar fate to that of the Xanthians. But the citizens would not surrender. The slaves had recently obtained their liberty and the freemen, who were poor, had recently had all their debts cancelled, so they resisted surrendering to Brutus. *[E702]* Therefore, Brutus sent them the Xanthians whom he had taken captive, because they were related to each other, thinking that when they saw their miserable condition, the Patarenses would have a change of heart. But they were just as steadfast as before, although he had granted everyone his relatives as a gift. Brutus allowed them the rest of the day for consultation and withdrew. However, the next morning, he again brought his forces there. {*Appian, Civil Wars, l. 4. c. 10. (81) 4:275} {*Dio, l. 47. (34) 5:187} He set up an auction block in a safe place under the wall and began selling the leaders of the Xanthians. He brought them out one by one to see whether this would move the people of Patara. When, after he had sold a few of them, they would not yield in spite of all this, he let the rest go free. {*Dio, l. 47. (34) 5:187}

5303. Since Brutus had taken some of the women of Patara captive, he let them go free, also, without any ransom. They told their husbands and fathers, who were the leaders of the city, that Brutus was a very modest and just man and persuaded them to surrender to him. {*Plutarch, Brutus, l. 1. c. 32. s. 1-3. 6:197,199} When he entered the town, he did not kill or banish anyone. He ordered all the public gold and silver to be brought to him and took everyone's own personal treasure, as well, promising to punish those who would not co-operate and to reward those who did. {*Appian, Civil Wars, l. 4. c. 10. (81) 4:275,277}

5304. A slave betrayed his master, who had hidden some gold, by telling a centurion who had been sent to collect the money. When they were all brought out, the master was silent. However, to save her son, his mother followed and cried that she had hidden the money. Without having been asked, the slave replied that she was lying and that the master had hidden the money. After Brutus had commended the young man's patience and the mother's piety, he dismissed both of them with the gold. But he crucified the servant who against every system of justice had betrayed his master. {*Appian, Civil wars, l. 4. c. 10. (81) 4:277}

5305. At the same time, Lentulus was sent to Andriace, which was the port of Myra, where he broke the chain barring the mouth of the harbour and captured the general of Myra. When Brutus had released the general, the people of Myra surrendered and paid the money imposed on them. {*Appian, Civil Wars, l. 4. c. 10. (82) 4:277} {*Dio, l. 47. (34) 5:189} All the countries of the Lycians were subdued in the same manner, and sent envoys to Brutus. They promised to send both men and money, according to their ability. They found Brutus to be bountiful and indulgent beyond all their expectations, for he sent home all the freeborn of the Xanthians and only imposed a fine of a hundred and fifty talents upon the Lycians, while doing violence to no one. {*Plutarch, Brutus, l. 1. c. 32. s. 3,4. 6:199} {*Appian, Civil Wars, l. 4. c. 10. (82) 4:277} {*Dio, l. 47. (34) 5:189} *[K404]*

5306. After Brutus had conquered the Lycians, {*Velleius Paterculus, l. 2. c. 69. s. 6. 1:199} he wrote some letters, among which this one was said to have been sent to the Rhodians:

> "We have severely punished the Xanthians when they revolted from us. We punished everyone, including their children, and we destroyed the city with fire and sword. As for the people of Patara, who were faithful to us, we have released their tributes and granted them the freedom to live after their own laws. We have given them fifty talents toward the rebuilding of the things that were demolished. You have the freedom to see for yourselves whether you will be accounted enemies, like the Xanthians, or friends, like the people of Patara."

5307. Plutarch recorded this letter more concisely:

> "The Xanthians despised our bounty and have made their country the sepulchre of their desperation. The citizens of Patara, who have submitted to me, have their liberty in governing their state. Therefore, it is in your power either to choose the opinion of the citizens of Patara, or the fortune of the Xanthians."

*5308.* The Rhodian noblemen were afraid to contend with the Romans, but the common people held a high opinion of their own abilities, mindful of the ancient victories which they had won over other such men. {*Appian, Civil Wars, l. 4. c. 9. (66) 4:249,251}* They trusted so much to their skill in navigation, that they first went to Cassius on the continent and showed him the fetters they had brought, as if intending to take many of their enemies alive. {*Dio, l. 47. (33) 5:185}*

*5309.* Cassius had to fight these people, who were skilful at sea. For this reason, he exercised his fleet at Myndus, having rigged and furnished it with soldiers. The Rhodians sent envoys to him who were to entreat him not to attack Rhodes, which had always revenged the wrongs done to her, nor to break the league that existed between the Romans and the Rhodians, which stated clearly that neither people should make war on the other. They also sent him Archelaus as an envoy, who had formerly been his teacher at Rhodes for the Greek language. He more humbly asked the same things of him. Cassius replied that the league had first been broken by the Rhodians and that he would punish them for it, if they did not immediately surrender. {*Appian, Civil Wars, l. 4. c. 9. (66-68) 4:251-259}*

*5310.* This answer terrified the wiser citizens, but the people were more influenced by the speeches of Alexander and Mnaseas and recalled with how much larger a fleet Mithridates and before him, Demetrius, had invaded Rhodes. Both had been very powerful kings. Consequently, they appointed Alexander as Prytanis, which is a magistrate among them of very great power, and made Mnaseas the admiral. {*Appian, Civil Wars, l. 4. c. 9. (66) 4:251,253}* {*Appian, Civil Wars, l. 4. c. 9. (67) 4:253}* [E703]

*5311.* Alexander and Mnaseas, the commanders of the Rhodians, sailed to Myndus with thirty-three good ships. They hoped to make Cassius afraid through this boldness. Since they had defeated Mithridates near this town, they hoped to defeat Cassius also. To show their skill in sailing, they went to Cnidos the first day. The next day, Cassius' soldiers left the shore and sailed out against them. {*Appian, Civil Wars, l. 4. c. 9. (66) 4:251}* {*Appian, Civil Wars, l. 4. c. 9. (71) 4:259}*

*5312.* A fierce battle took place between them. With their small, nimble ships, the Rhodians sailed here and there, sometimes through the enemies' ranks and sometimes around them. On the other side, the Romans trusted their heavier ships. As often as they laid hold with their iron hook on any ship that sailed too close, they prevailed as in a land battle. [K405] Cassius had the larger number of ships and the Rhodians could not for long use their swiftness and usual tactics, to play with their

enemies, as Cassius' more numerous ships surrounded the Rhodian fleet. Since the Rhodians could now only attack them from the front and then retreat, it did them little good. Their enemies still kept themselves close together. Also, the attacks of their armoured prows were ineffectual against the heavy ships of the Romans. On the other hand, the Roman ships attacked these light ships with a direct attack, until three Rhodian ships were taken with all the soldiers in them. Two were damaged and sank, while the rest fled to Rhodes, badly damaged. {*Appian, Civil Wars, l. 4. c. 9. (71) 4:261}*

*5313.* The Roman fleet successfully fought with the Rhodians at Myndus. {*Appian, Civil Wars, l. 4. c. 9. (71) 4:261}* {*Dio, l. 47. (33) 5:185}* Cassius watched the sea-battle from a mountain. After the battle, he repaired his fleet at once and went to Loryma, a citadel of the Rhodians on the other side of the continent. From there, he conveyed his land forces over in cargo ships under the command of Fannius and Lentulus. Then, with eighty warships, Cassius set out to strike terror into the Rhodians. He trusted that his sea and land forces would reduce the hostility of the enemy. {*Appian, Civil Wars, l. 4. c. 9. (72) 4:261}*

*5314.* When they again met him boldly, Cassius defeated them with the help of Statius Murcus, by overcoming their skill with the size and number of his ships. Once they had lost two ships, the Rhodians were then surrounded on every side. {*Appian, Civil Wars, l. 4. c. 9. (72) 4:261}* {*Dio, l. 47. (33) 5:185}*

*5315.* At once, all the walls were filled with soldiers to repulse Fannius' attack from the land. Cassius was prepared for an assault on the walls from the sea, with his navy. Having thought that such a thing would happen, he had brought towers with him that were in sections, and now set them up there. Thus Rhodes, twice beaten at sea, was now under attack both by sea and land. They were unprepared for a sustained double attack and it appeared that in a short time the enemy would overpower them, or they would be starved out by famine. When the wiser among the Rhodians realised this, they held a secret conference with Fannius and Lentulus. Since Cassius had suddenly come right into the middle of the city with his best soldiers, it was believed that some of the smaller gates had been opened to him by citizens who secretly favoured him, so that the city would not be miserably destroyed. {*Appian, Civil Wars, l. 4. c. 9. (72,73) 4:263}*

*5316.* Cassius replied to the Rhodians, who called him king and lord, that he was neither lord nor king, but the killer and avenger of a lord and king. {*Plutarch, Brutus, l. 1. c. 30. s. 3. 6:193}* He sat under a spear for his tribunal, because he wanted to be seen as having taken the city by force of arms. He ordered his army to be peaceful and through his public criers, threatened death to plunderers. He summoned fifty Rhodian citizens to appear before him, whom whom he ordered to be executed. He ordered another twenty-five, who did not appear, to be banished. {*Appian, Civil Wars, l. 4. c. 9. (73) 4:263}

5317. He plundered the Rhodians of their ships and money. He took all the gold that belonged to either the temples or the treasury. He even took away all the things which were dedicated to the gods, except for the Chariot of the Sun. {*Appian, Civil Wars, l. 4. c. 9. (73) 4:263,265} {*Dio, l. 47. (33) 5:185} However, not content with all that, he took whatever gold or silver anyone owned. Through a crier, he proclaimed a punishment to anyone who hid any and offered a reward to those who told of it. They would get a tenth part of it and the slaves would get their liberty. [K406] At first, some concealed their money, in the hope that his threats would go no further than words. When they saw that rewards were being given to informers, they asked that the time he had granted be extended. Some dug up what they had hidden in the earth and others retrieved their money from wells. This collection brought in more than the previous one had! {*Appian, Civil Wars, l. 4. c. 9. (73) 4:263,267} He had extorted eight hundred talents from private individuals and publicly fined the city five hundred talents more, {*Plutarch, Brutus, l. 1. c. 32. s. 4. 6:199} thus leaving the Rhodians with nothing but their lives. {Orosius, l. 6. c. 18.}

5318. Therefore, Cassius, in a fierce and most prosperous war, defeated Rhodes, an undertaking of great difficulty. {*Velleius Paterculus, l. 2. c. 69. s. 6. 1:199} [E704] Rejoicing at his quick victory and the large amount of money he had obtained, he left Lucius Varus at Rhodes with a garrison. {*Appian, Civil Wars, l. 4. c. 9. (74) 4:265} After this, he put Ariobarzanes, whom he had captured, to death {*Dio, l. 47. (33) 5:185} and ordered ten years of tribute from all the provinces of Asia, which he collected in full. {*Appian, Civil Wars, l. 4. c. 9. (74) 4:265}

5319. Cassius was told that Cleopatra was about to sail to join Caesar and Antony with a large navy and many forces. She had always followed that side before, on account of the love she previously had to the former Caesar. Now she did so far more eagerly, because of her fear of Cassius. To prepare for her invasion, Cassius sent Murcus into Peloponnesus with one legion and some archers in sixty decked ships, to guard the sea lanes around Cape Taenarum. Avoiding Cassius and Murcus, Cleopatra set sail toward the Ionian Sea, but her fleet was wrecked by a large storm off the coast of Libya. The waves carried evidence of her shipwreck even into the country of Laconia. Cleopatra became sick and therefore returned home. {*Appian, Civil Wars, l. 4. c. 9. (74) 4:265} {*Appian, Civil Wars, l. 4. c. 10. (82) 4:277} {*Appian, Civil Wars, l. 5. c. 1. (8) 4:389}

5320. Among Brutus' letters, there was one that had been sent to the Coans, concerning his and Cassius' victories:

> "Rhodes now truly obeys Cassius, a city more bold than strong through her own strength. All of Lycia is now at our command, partly conquered in war and partly through fear of extreme hardships. This choice was truly to their advantage. They willingly chose what, a little time later, they would have been forced to do. You choose, therefore, whether you would prefer to be forced to serve, or rather be called our friends by receiving us."

5321. Brutus returned from Lycia into Ionia and did many memorable deeds in honouring those who deserved to be honoured and in punishing others according to their actions. Among others, he tortured and killed Theodorus, the rhetorician, who was wandering in Asia. He had been instrumental (as he himself bragged) in the death of Pompey the Great. {*Plutarch, Brutus, l. 1. c. 33. 6:199,201} {*Plutarch, Pompey, l. 1. c. 77. s. 3,4. 5:317,319}

5322. Brutus sent for Cassius to come to Sardis. As he was approaching, Brutus went to meet him with his friends. All the soldiers were fully armed and greeted them both as Imperators. As often happens between two who have many troops and friends, mutual suspicion and accusations arose between them. First, they went alone into a private room, shut the doors after them and asked everyone to leave. They began to talk, then to argue and accuse each other. Their friends were afraid of what the outcome would be, because Cassius and Brutus were all the more free and vehement in chiding one another, as they became very sharp in their arguments with each other. {*Plutarch, Brutus, l. 1. c. 34. s. 1-3. 6:201} [K407] All these suspicions between them arose through false accusations, but they finally settled everything wisely. {*Dio, l. 47. (35) 5:189}

5323. Marcus Favonius, whom Cicero mentioned to have been a close friend of Brutus, was present there. {*Cicero, Atticus, l. 15. c. 11. 24:323} He followed in the footsteps of Marcus Cato, who was a philosopher. However he was not as reasonable and was governed by some passionate and mad purpose. He considered it a lowly office to be a consul of Rome. With his cynical and harsh language, he frequently alleviated the tedium his importunity brought upon many. At this meeting between Brutus and Cassius, he violently shoved aside the porters who forbade him entrance and entered the room where Brutus and Cassius were having their private conference. With an impersonating voice, he pronounced the verses that Homer said Nestor had used:

> "But both obey me, for I your senior am"

*5324.* He also quoted the verses that follow on from there. This made Cassius laugh, but Brutus kicked him out and called him an:

"unlearned and adulterous dog"

*5325.* After this difference had been resolved, Cassius arranged a supper, to which Brutus invited his friends. As they were about to sit down, Favonius came in, fresh from his bath. Brutus protested that he came uninvited and asked him to use the farthest couch, but he pushed himself in and placed himself on the central couch at the table between them. There was both hilarity and good conversation at the feast. {*Plutarch, Brutus, l. 1. c. 34. s. 4-8. 6:201,203.}

*5326.* The next day, in public judgment and with a note of dishonour, Brutus condemned Lucius Pellius, who had been praetor. Brutus had previously employed him and now he was being accused of bribery by the Sardinians. Cassius was not innocent in this matter, either. Only a few days earlier, Cassius had privately chastised two who had been found guilty of the same fault and having absolved them publicly, was still making use of them. Thereupon, Cassius accused Brutus of being too strict and righteous, when, at such a time, he ought to behave more civilly and with benevolence. Brutus again admonished him to remember the Ides of March (March 15), when they had killed Caesar, who had not so much himself plundered all men, but had been a patron of those who did. {*Plutarch, Brutus, l. 1. c. 35. 6:203,205} [E705]

*5327.* Labienus the younger, the son of Titus Labienus (Caesar's lieutenant in Gaul), was sent by Cassius and Brutus to request aid from Orodes, the king of the Parthians. He stayed there with them for a long time without any notice being taken of him, for the king had no intention of helping them, but dared not deny them. {*Dio, l. 48. (24) 5:269,271} {*Florus, l. 2. c. 19. s. 3,4. 1:317} {*Velleius Paterculus, l. 2. c. 78. s. 1. 1:215}

*5328.* Brutus ordered the whole fleet of the Lycians to sail for Abydus, while he marched there with his land forces. They were to wait for Cassius' arrival from Ionia, so that they could both go to Sestus together. {*Appian, Civil Wars, l. 4. c. 10. (82) 4:277}

*5329.* When Cassius and Brutus were about to leave Asia for Europe and to transport their army to the opposite continent, Brutus had a horrible dream. [K408] In the dead of the night, when the moon was not shining very brightly and all the army was in silence, a black image of a large and horrid body stood silently beside Brutus. It was said to offer itself to Brutus, since his lamp was burning low. Brutus boldly asked if he was a man or a god. The spirit replied, *Oh Brutus, I am thy evil genius,*

*you shall see me again at Philippi.* So as not to appear afraid, Brutus said, *Then I shall see you.* {*Florus, l. 2. c. 17. s. 8,9. 1:309} {*Appian, Civil Wars, l. 4. c. 17. (134) 4:367} Plutarch gave a more complete account in his work on Brutus. He added that the next morning Brutus told Cassius what he had seen and that Cassius, from the doctrine of the Epicureans, expounded to him what was to be thought about such dreams. {*Plutarch, Brutus, l. 1. c. 36,37. 6:207,209} {*Plutarch, Caesar, l. 1. c. 69. s. 6-8. 7:607,609}

## 3963a AM, 4672 JP, 42 BC

*5330.* Antigonus, the son of Aristobulus (the brother of Hyrcanus), invaded Judea with the help of Ptolemy, the son of Mennaeus, Fabius the governor of Damascus, whose friendship he had bought, and Marion, the tyrant of Tyre, who followed him because he hated Herod. Herod met Antigonus when he had barely crossed the borders of the country and drove him from there, after having defeated him in battle. Therefore, Hyrcanus honoured Herod with crowns as soon as he returned to Jerusalem. He had already promised that Herod was to be considered a member of Hyrcanus' family for marrying Mariamme (in Syriac called סרים or Mary). She was the daughter of Alexander, the son of Aristobulus (the brother of Hyrcanus) and Alexandra, the daughter of Hyrcanus. {*Josephus, Jewish War, l. 1. c. 12. s. 2,3. (239-241) 2:111,113} {*Josephus, Antiq., l. 14. c. 12. s. 1. (298-300) 7:607} {*Josephus, Antiq., l. 15. c. 2. s. 5. (23,24) 8:13}

*5331.* At the Gulf of Melos, Cassius and Brutus numbered their army and found they had eighty thousand foot soldiers. Brutus had four thousand Gallic and Lusitanian cavalry, two thousand cavalry from Thrace, Illyria, Parthia and Thessaly. Cassius had two thousand cavalry from the Spaniards and the Gauls and four thousand mounted cavalry archers from Arabia, Media and Parthia. (Justin confirmed that the Parthians had sent help there. {Justin, Trogus, l. 42. c. 4.}) Tetrarchs from Galatia and the kings who were allies, brought five thousand cavalry, in addition to foot soldiers. {*Appian, Civil Wars, l. 4. c. 11. (88) 4:289}

*5332.* These forces met the army of the triumviri under Marcus Antony and Octavius Caesar at Philippi in Macedonia. (The city was just as famous for Paul's letter to it, as for this battle.) {*Velleius Paterculus, l. 2. c. 70. s. 1. 1:201} Each side had the same number of legions. Brutus and Cassius had twenty thousand cavalry and Antony and Caesar had thirteen thousand. Cassius' side did not fight the enemy for many days, hoping to starve them through lack of provisions. They themselves had abundant supplies from Asia, which were being brought to them by sea, whereas the enemy troops were in need of supplies, since they were in the country of an enemy.

The merchants could get nothing from Egypt, as there was a great famine there. Nor would Sextus Pompeius allow anything to be brought from Spain or Africa. Statius Murcus and Domitius Ahenobarbus guarded the sea lanes to Italy, aware that Macedonia and Thessaly could not long sustain the enemy. So Antony tried to hinder supplies from coming to the enemy from Thasos, in their rear. Within ten days, he made a secret passage in a narrow marsh and erected many citadels with trenches on the far side. Later, Cassius ran a trench from his camp to the sea through all the marshes and made Antony's works useless. {*Appian, Civil Wars, l. 4. c. 14. (109) 4:323,325} [K409]

5333. When the battle began (from which Caesar and Antony were said to have withdrawn themselves), the wing which Brutus commanded beat back the enemy and captured Caesar's camp. However, Cassius and his wing was routed and his camp was taken by Antony's troops. {*Florus, l. 2. c. 17. s. 10,11. 1:311} {*Velleius Paterculus, l. 2. c. 70. s. 1. 1:201} {*Plutarch, Antony, l. 1. c. 22. s. 1-3. 9:183} Cassius lost eight thousand men, including the servants who followed the camp, whom Brutus called *Briges*. Messala Corvinus, who was present in Brutus' camp at the time, but surrendered to Caesar a little later, said he thought twice as many if not more were killed. {*Plutarch, Brutus, l. 1. c. 45. s. 1. 6:227} {*Appian, Civil Wars, l. 4. c. 14. (112) 4:329}

5334. After Cassius had lost his camp, he could not return to it, but went up to a hill near Philippi to get a better view of what was going on and what he should do. {*Appian, Civil Wars, l. 4. c. 15. (113) 4:329,331} [E706] Believing that the whole army had been routed, he killed himself. {*Livy, l. 124. 14:155} He used the same dagger with which he had killed Caesar. {*Plutarch, Caesar, l. 1. c. 69. s. 3. 7:605} Although in another place, Plutarch, along with other historians, stated that his head was cut off by his freedman, Pindarus, whom Cassius had appointed for that task after the defeat of Crassus in Parthia. {*Plutarch, Brutus, l. 1. c. 43. s. 7,8. 6:225} {*Plutarch, Antony, l. 1. c. 22. s. 3,4. 9:185} {*Velleius Paterculus, l. 2. c. 70. s. 1-3. 1:201} {*Appian, Civil Wars, l. 4. c. 15. (113) 4:331} {*Dio, l. 47. (46) 5:211,213} Valerius Maximus stated: {*Valerius Maximus, l. 6. c. 8. s. 4. 2:77}

"Pindarus had recently been freed by Cassius. When Cassius was defeated in the battle at Philippi, Pindarus spared him the insults of his enemies by cutting off his head at the request of Cassius. He hid his body so it could not be found. The gods, the revengers of so great a wickedness, had bound Cassius' right hand, which was used in the murder of the father of his country, with such a weakness that he came trembling to Pindarus' knees, lest he should pay that punishment which he had deserved at the hand of the pious conqueror. Truly, deified Julius, you have exacted the revenge your heavenly wounds deserve by compelling the head that was wickedly set against you to beg for help from a common man. Cassius was forced, by the rage of his mind, not to retain his life, but neither did he dare take it with his own hand."

5335. Brutus gave the body of Cassius to his friends and had it privately buried at Thasos, so that the army would not be provoked to mourning and become dejected at the sight of his funeral. {*Plutarch, Brutus, l. 1. c. 44. s. 1,2. 6:225,227} {*Appian, Civil Wars, l. 4. c. 15. (114) 4:331,333} {*Dio, l. 47. (47) 5:213} Cassius died on the same day as he had been born. {*Appian, Civil Wars, l. 4. c. 15. (113) 4:331} In the evening, Cassius' servant came to Antony, bringing the soldier's coat and the sword he had recently taken from Cassius' body. When Antony saw these, he was greatly encouraged and set the army in battle array as soon as it was day. {*Plutarch, Brutus, l. 1. c. 45. s. 1,2. 6:227}

5336. On the same day that the army of Caesar was defeated in the battle at Philippi, the Martian legion and other large forces that were coming to Caesar with Domitius Calvinus from Italy, were defeated by Murcus and Domitius Ahenobarbus in the Ionian sea. {*Plutarch, Brutus, l. 1. c. 47. s. 1-3. 6:233} {*Appian, Civil Wars, l. 4. c. 15. (115) 4:333,335} Brutus did not know of this victory for twenty days. During that time, the soldiers of Caesar and Antony were mired in the marshes of Philippi. They were bothered by autumn showers that happened after the battle and turned to ice. {*Plutarch, Brutus, l. 1. c. 47. s. 4-6. 6:233} During that time, many Germans fled to Brutus. But at the same time, Amyntas, the general of Dejotarus, and Rhascyporis, the Thracian, left Brutus' side. When Brutus heard about this, he feared a larger revolt and decided to gamble everything on one battle. {*Dio, l. 47. (48) 5:215} [K410]

5337. It was reported that the ghost came to Brutus again on the night before the battle, in the same way as before. It spoke nothing and silently vanished away. However, Publius Volumnius made no mention of this, even though he was a man who studied wisdom and was in Brutus' camp and wrote about other prodigies that happened. {*Plutarch, Caesar, l. 1. c. 69. s. 7,8.'7:607,609} {*Plutarch, Brutus, l. 1. c. 48. s. 1. 6:235} {*Appian, Civil Wars, l. 4. c. 17. (134) 4:367}

5338. Antony was involved in the second battle, as well as Caesar Octavius, even though he was weak and sickly. Ovid wrote about the things that were done in this war of Philippi. {*Ovid, Fasti, l. 3. (709,710) 5:173}

Caesar's first work, or worthy action rather,
Was, by just arms he did revenge his father.

*5339.* Ovid also wrote: {*\*Ovid, Fasti, l. 5. (569-573) 5:303*}

> This the youth vowed, when first to arms he ran,
> Being the leader of them, he then began.
> His stretched out hand to the soldiers while he
>     shook,
>   He, them confederated, thus bespoke....

*5340.* Brutus was defeated in the battle and fled to a hill by night. The next day he wanted Strabo of Aegaeae, an Epirote, with whom he was friendly because they studied rhetoric together, to help him kill himself. *[E707]* He put his left arm over his head and held the point of the sword in his right hand. He directed it to his left breast, where the heart beats, and forced it through himself. So he died, after being run through with only one thrust. {*\*Livy, l. 124. 14:155*} {*\*Velleius Paterculus, l. 2. c. 70. s. 4,5. 1:201,203*} {*\*Plutarch, Brutus, l. 1. c. 52. 6:243,245*} {*\*Appian, Civil Wars, l. 4. c. 16. (130,131) 4:359,361*}

*5341.* Thus this war ended the careers of Brutus and Cassius, the murderers of Julius Caesar, their Imperator, by whom they had been spared in the Pharsalia battle, only to commit suicide later. {*\*Appian, Civil Wars, l. 4. c. 17. (131,132) 4:361*} They killed themselves using the same swords they had used to kill Julius Caesar. {*\*Dio, l. 48. (1) 5:219*} With the murder of Caesar, they lost the very liberty they had so much wanted to see restored. {*\*Florus, l. 2. c. 17. s. 1. 1:307*} In under two years, they had gathered more than twenty legions, about twenty thousand cavalry and more than two hundred warships. They had made great preparations and had extorted large sums of money from men, regardless of whether these had wanted to give it or not. They had often been victorious in the wars that they had waged with many cities and with opposing countries. They had exercised the command over everything from Macedonia to the Euphrates River. Whomever they had made war with, they had drawn to their side. They had made use of the help of all who were faithful to them, like kings and governors, and even of the Parthians, despite the fact that they were enemies. {*\*Appian, Civil Wars, l. 4. c. 17. (133) 4:363,365*}

*5342.* Antony stood by the body of Brutus and modestly upbraided him for the death of his brother Gaius, whom Brutus had killed in Macedonia. However, Antony had often said that he imputed the death of his brother to Hortensius, who was the proconsul of Macedonia, rather than to Brutus, which was why he ordered Hortensius to be killed on Antony's brother's grave. {*\*Plutarch, Brutus, l. 1. c. 53. s. 4. 6:247*} {*\*Plutarch, Antony, l. 1. c. 22. s. 4. 9:185*} *[K411]* Placing his purple soldier's coat of great value over Brutus' body, Antony committed the care of his funeral to one of his freedmen, but later he killed that man, when he learned that he had not burned that coat with him. Antony sent Brutus' ashes to his mother, Servilia. {*\*Plutarch, Brutus, l. 1. c. 53. s. 4. 6:247*} {*\*Plutarch, Antony, l. 1. c. 22. s. 4. 9:185*} {*\*Appian, Civil Wars, l. 4. c. 17. (135) 4:369*} Octavius sent Brutus' head to Rome, so that it could be placed under Caesar's statue. {*\*Suetonius, Augustus, l. 2. c. 13. s. 1. 1:167*} However, on the voyage from Dyrrachium, a storm arose and the head was cast into the sea. {*\*Dio, l. 47. (49) 5:217*}

*5343.* The nobility who escaped to Thasos now sailed away from there. Others surrendered themselves to the power and mercy of Messala, Corvinus and Lucius Bibulus. Still others agreed to side with Antony for their security. Antony himself came into Thasos and they turned whatever money, arms, provisions or other preparations were left, over to him. {*\*Appian, Civil Wars, l. 4. c. 17. (136) 4:371*}

*5344.* Lucius Julius Mocilla, who had been praetor, along with his son and Aulus Torquatus and others who had suffered this defeat, went to Samothracia. Pomponius Atticus ordered that all they needed should be sent for them from Epirus. {*\*Cornelius Nepos, Life of Atticus, l. 1. c. 11. s. 2,3. 1:307*}

*5345.* After Brutus and Cassius had gone to the war, Cassius of Parma was left in Asia with a fleet and an army, to raise money. After the death of Cassius, he hoped for better things from Brutus. He chose thirty of the Rhodian ships, planning to fill them with the sailors of the allies, and burned the rest in case the city should rebel. After this, he set sail with his own and the Rhodian ships. However, as soon as Brutus saw the Rhodians were about to rebel, he sent Clodius. Once Brutus was dead, Clodius withdrew the garrison of three thousand men and left with Cassius of Parma. Turullius joined them with many other ships and the money he had exacted from the Rhodians before their revolt. {*\*Appian, Civil wars, l. 5. c. 1. (2) 4:379*}

*5346.* Anyone who had some naval forces scattered throughout Asia, joined this fleet. They put as many legions of soldiers on board as they possibly could. From the islanders of the ports to which they came, they enlisted rowers of bondmen and slaves. Cicero, the younger, and as many of the nobility as had fled from Thasos, also joined them. In a short time, there was a large fleet with a large army under competent commanders. {*\*Appian, Civil Wars, l. 5. c. 1. (2) 4:379*}

*5347.* They sailed on the Ionian Sea to Statius Murcus and Gnaeus Domitius Ahenobarbus, who commanded large forces. They took Lepidus with them, with another band of soldiers who had kept Crete with one of Brutus' garrisons. When they parted company, some stayed with Ahenobarbus, making a faction of their own, which controlled the Ionian Sea and did much harm to their enemies. The rest went with Murcus and joined forces with Sextus Pompeius. When Murcus added his large fleet and the remains of Brutus' army to him, he doubled Sextus' forces. {*Appian, Civil Wars, l. 5. c. 1. (2) 4:379} {*Velleius Paterculus, l. 2. c. 72. s. 3-5. 1:205} {*Velleius Paterculus, l. 2. c. 77. s. 3. 1:215} {*Dio, l. 48. (19) 5:259} {*Dio, l. 48. (16) 5:251} [E708]

5348. Caesar and Antony dismissed the soldiers who had served out their time, except for eight thousand, whom they entreated to serve under them for a further period. [K412] They divided these between them and took one in every hundred of their number for their bodyguard. Of eleven legions and fourteen thousand cavalry of Brutus' army who were left, Antony took six legions and ten thousand cavalry, while Caesar took four legions and four thousand cavalry. {*Appian, Civil Wars, l. 5. c. 1. (3) 4:381} Moreover, it was agreed that Caesar should give two legions of his own to go along with Antony and that he in turn should receive two others, which consisted of his soldiers under the command of Calenus and which were left back in Italy at the time. {*Appian, Civil Wars, l. 5. c. 1. (3) 4:381} {*Dio, l. 48. (2) 5:223}

5349. Octavius took the matter of getting the legions from Italy upon himself so that he would be able to repress Lepidus, the triumvir, if he caused any problems. He also wanted to carry on the war against Sextus Pompeius and apportion the lands promised to the old soldiers who had been retired. Octavius returned to Italy, but became sick on the way, so that those who were at Rome thought that he was dead. Antony stayed to move about the provinces beyond the sea, both to subdue the enemies' pride and to get money for the soldiers, which they had been promised. {*Livy, l. 125. 14:155} {*Velleius Paterculus, l. 2. c. 74. s. 1. 1:207} {*Plutarch, Antony, l. 1. c. 23. s. 1,2. 9:185} {*Appian, Civil Wars, l. 5. c. 1. (3) 4:381} {*Dio, l. 48. (3) 5:223} Since they had promised every soldier twenty thousand sesterces, they had to ensure that they got paid. {*Plutarch, Antony, l. 1. c. 23. s. 1,2. 9:185} {*Dio, l. 47. (42) 5:205}

5350. For this reason, Antony went into Greece with a large army and at first behaved kindly toward the Greeks. He was happy to be considered a friend of the Greeks, especially of the Athenians, on whose city he bestowed many gifts. {*Plutarch, Antony, l. 1. c. 23. s. 2,3. 9:185,187}

## 3963b AM, 4673 JP, 41 BC

5351. Lucius Censorinus was in Greece and went into Asia. {*Plutarch, Antony, l. 1. c. 24. s. 1. 9:187} There he travelled about sending others to exact money from the cities and to sell their territories. {*Dio, l. 48. (34) 5:291} Also, kings keenly courted his favour and the kings' wives, vying with each other in their gifts and their beauty, would yield up their honour for his pleasure. Anaxenor, a harper, Xuthus, a musician, Metrodorus, a dancer, and

all the Asian comics and actors attended Censorinus' court, where everything was very luxurious. Antony was here too. Eventually, Antony was ready to go to the Parthian war and sent Dellius into Egypt to Cleopatra. Dellius was the historian, as Plutarch later referred to him, and was also the one who, according to Seneca, left Cassius and went to Antony. Dellius ordered Cleopatra to appear before Antony in Cilicia to explain herself, because she was said to have given much help to Cassius. {*Plutarch, Antony, l. 1. c. 24,25. 9:187-193} {*Seneca the Elder, Suasoriae, l. 1. c. 7. 2:497}

5352. Apuleius, who had been proscribed by the triumviri, was restored to his country when he turned Bithynia over to Antony. He had been made governor of Bithynia by Brutus. {*Appian, Civil Wars, l. 4. c. 6. (46) 4:217,219}

5353. In Bithynia, Antony met embassies from many different countries. The rulers of the Jews were there to accuse Phasael and Herod, as maintaining that Hyrcanus reigned only as a puppet and that, in actual fact, the two brothers had all the power. However, Antony greatly honoured Herod, who had come there to clear himself of these accusations, and so it came about that his adversaries were not so much as even admitted to speak to Antony. Herod had arranged this by bribing Antony. {*Josephus, Antiq., l. 14. c. 12. s. 2. (301-303) 7:609,611}

5354. When Antony came to Ephesus, women walked ahead of him, dressed in the clothes of the Bacchanals, and men in the clothes of Satyrs and Pans. All the city was full of ivy garlands and instruments of music, flutes and pipes. They called him: {*Plutarch, Antony, l. 1. c. 24. s. 3. 9:187,189} [K413]

"Dionysus, Giver of Joy and Beneficent"

5355. He made a magnificent sacrifice to the goddess Diana, the protector of that place, and absolved the followers of Cassius, who had fled into sanctuary there, when they petitioned him. But he did not forgive Petronius, who was guilty of the conspiracy against Caesar, and Quintus, who had betrayed Dolabella to Cassius at Laodicea. {*Appian, Civil Wars, l. 5. c. 1. (4) 4:381,383}

5356. The envoys of Hyrcanus, the high priest, and of the Jews also came to him at Ephesus. These were Lysimachus, the son of Pausanias, Joseph, the son of Mennaeus, and Alexander, the son of Theodorus. They gave him a crown of gold and requested the same thing from him as the embassy at Rome had done. They wanted to have the Jews freed whom Cassius had taken prisoner, contrary to the laws of war. They wanted him to send letters to the provinces to effect this. They also wanted their country, which had been taken from them by Cassius, to be restored. Antony considered their requests to be fair and granted them, writing letters to this effect to Hyrcanus, as well as to Tyre, Sidon, Antioch and Aradus. Josephus recorded these letters. {*Josephus, Antiq., l. 14. c. 12. s. 2-6. (303,323) 7:611-619}

5357. The Greeks and other nationalities living in Asia at Pergamum, were called to Ephesus. Antony told them what generous promises he had made to his twenty-eight victorious legions, some of whom they had supplied. He had a hundred and seventy thousand men. Considering that they had given to Cassius and Brutus, his enemies, ten years' tribute in two years, he demanded that they should give him as much in one year. [E709] They complained that they had been impoverished by their former enemies and with difficulty eventually obtained the concession that they could pay nine years' tribute in two years. {*Appian, Civil Wars, l. 5. c. 1. (5,6) 4:385,387}

5358. Antony took the estates of many noblemen and gave them to knaves and flatterers. Many begged to be given the fortunes of some who were alive and they were given to them, while some wanted and received the estates of those who had died. It was reported that he gave the goods of a citizen of Magnesia to a cook who had excellently prepared only one supper for him. Finally, when Antony had burdened the cities with another tribute, Hybreas, who caused discontent in Asia, was so bold as to say:

"If you can exact a tribute from us twice in one year, you must also be able to make two summers and then to yield fruits for us twice."

5359. When Asia brought in two hundred thousand talents, Hybreas said:

"If you have not received them, demand it from those who took it; but if you received it and do not have it, we are undone."

5360. With this saying, he was sharply rebuking Antony, who naively believed his own servants and was ignorant of many things that were being done. {*Plutarch, Antony, l. 1. c. 24. s. 4-6. 9:189}

5361. On the orders of Antony, other tributes were imposed in like manner on kings, governors and free cities, each according to their abilities. {*Appian, Civil Wars, l. 5. c. 1. (7) 4:387}

5362. As Antony was going about the provinces, Lucius, the brother of Cassius, and all who had heard of his clemency at Ephesus, were afraid. They humbly came and presented themselves to him and Antony forgave them all, except those who were guilty of Caesar's murder. These he would not forgive. {*Appian, Civil Wars, l. 5. c. 1. (7) 4:387}

5363. He released the Lycians and Xanthians from tribute and urged them to rebuild their city. To Rhodes, he gave the places of Andros, Tenos, Naxos and Myndus, but not long after this, he took them from them, because he said Rhodes was ruling them too harshly. He also gave liberty and freedom from tributes to the citizens of Laodicea and Tarsus. [K414] To the Athenians who came to him, Antony first gave Tenos and then Aegina, Icos, Ceos, Sciathos and Patepathos. {*Appian, Civil Wars, l. 5. c. 1. (7) 4:387}

5364. He journeyed though Phrygia, Mysia, Galatia, Cappadocia, Cilicia, Coelosyria, Syria Palestina, Iturea and the other provinces of the Syrians, imposing very heavy tributes on them all. He settled all differences of kings and cities just as it suited him. In particular, in Cappadocia he settled the matter of Sisina and Ariarthes in favour of Sisina, who received the kingdom as a favour to his beautiful mother. However, in Syria, he removed tyrants from various towns. {*Appian, Civil Wars, l. 5. c. 1. (7) 4:387} He committed the government of Cyprus to Demetrius, the freedman of Julius Caesar. {*Dio, l. 48. (40) 5:305}

5365. Antony promised the city of Tyre an office of gymnasiarch, but appointed Boethus, instead of a gymnasiarch, to be over the city. He was a poor poet and a bad citizen, but Antony liked the poem which he wrote about his victory at Philippi. The citizens preferred him, because he was able to speak without notice and unceasingly on any subject. When the recording of the expenses to be paid in the university was committed to his care, he was found to have stolen the oil, among other things. When he was being accused before Antony, he answered:

"As Homer sang the praises of Agamemnon and Achilles and also Odysseus, so have I sung yours, therefore it is not fit that I should be accused of these crimes before you."

5366. The accusers replied:

"Homer stole no oil from Agamemnon and Achilles, which you have done, and because of which you shall be punished."

5367. Nevertheless, Boethus appeased Antony's anger with some services and retained the government of the city, continuing to plunder it until Antony's death. {*Strabo, l. 14. c. 5. s. 14. 6:349}

5368. Dellius brought Cleopatra to Antony in Cilicia. She put her confidence in her beauty and deportment. {*Plutarch, Antony, l. 1. c. 26. 9:193,195} {*Josephus, Antiq., l. 14. c. 13. s. 1. (324) 7:621} {*Appian, Civil Wars, l. 5. c. 1. (8) 4:389} {*Dio, l. 48.

*(23) 5:269}* Her fabulous arrival is described by Plutarch more in the manner of a poet than that of a historian. She came up the Cydnus River, which runs by the city of Tarsus, in a ship that was covered in gold. It had purple sails fully spread, and silver oars. They arrived to the accompaniment of the music of flutes, pipes and harps. She rested under a canopy of cloth of gold, in a beautiful dress, like Venus is painted. Boys stood here and there like cupids, fanning her. Her maidens, in the clothes of Nereides and Graces, stood at the helms and others plied the oars. All along the river banks, the air was filled with most fragrant smells, because of the abundance of perfumes. Men on both sides of the shore accompanied her along the river's edge. The people in the city came to see the sight, so that Antony was left alone, sitting in the forum on his tribunal. There was a general rumour that Venus was coming to feast with Bacchus for the preservation of Asia. Antony sent certain men to invite her to supper. However, she thought it was his place to come to her, instead. To show his gentleness and courtesy on her arrival, he obeyed her and came.

5369. Antony accused Cleopatra of not having sided with Caesar in the last war. She objected that she had sent four legions to Dolabella, but that her fleet had been wrecked by storms. *[E710] [K415]* She told him how often Cassius had threatened her and how she had been forced to send aid to him. Antony was overcome and began to fall in love with her like a young man, although he was then forty years old. A long time ago, he had wantonly cast his eyes on her when she had been but a girl and he a young man who had followed Gabinius to Alexandria. At that time he had been in charge of the cavalry. Antony's ancient diligence and ambition promptly failed him and no one did anything other than carry out the commands of Cleopatra, without regard for either human or divine law. *{*Appian, Civil Wars, l. 5. c. 1. (2) 4:379}* *{*Appian, Civil Wars, l. 5. c. 1. (8,9) 4:389}*

5370. At Cleopatra's request, Antony sent murderers to Miletus to kill her sister Arsinoe, who was a suppliant in the temple of Artemis at Leucophrys. *{*Appian, Civil Wars, l. 5. c. 1. (9) 4:389}* (The footnote in Josephus on this event stated it was at Ephesus, not Miletus. Editor.) However, Josephus said that she was at her prayers in the temple of Artemis. (Loeb edition does not give that translation. Editor.) *{*Josephus, Antiq., l. 15. c. 4. s. 1. (89,90) 8:43,45}*

5371. Antony commanded the inhabitants of Tyre to turn Serapion, the governor of Cyprus, who had sent aid to Cassius and now came to beg Antony's pardon, over to Cleopatra. Antony ordered the Aradians to turn over another suppliant, whom they were holding at the time, who had said that he was Ptolemy, when Ptolemy, the brother of Cleopatra, had disappeared at the battle with Julius Caesar on the Nile River. He also commanded Megabyzus, the priest of Artemis of the Ephesians, to be brought before him, because he had entertained Arsinoe as a queen. At the entreaty of the Ephesians to Cleopatra, Antony let him go. *{*Appian, Civil Wars, l. 5. c. 1. (9) 4:391,393}*

5372. In the meantime, Fulvia, the wife of Antony in Italy, who was a woman in body only and more like a man, raised a large rebellion against Caesar Octavius. *{*Velleius Paterculus, l. 2. c. 74. s. 2. 1:207}* This action dissolved the alliance between Octavius and Antony and the state was involved in a full-scale war between them. Caesar could not endure the insolence of his mother-in-law (for he had seemed to disagree rather more with her than with Antony). He divorced her daughter Claudia, who, he swore, was still a virgin. *{*Dio, l. 48. (5) 5:229}* *{*Suetonius, Augustus, l. 2. c. 62. s. 1. 1:241,243}*

5373. Thereupon, Caesar sent Cocceius and Caecina as envoys to Phoenicia to Antony. When Caecina's task was finished, he returned to Caesar, but Cocceius stayed with Antony. *{*Appian, Civil Wars, l. 5. c. 6. (60) 4:477,479}*

5374. One hundred of the most honourable men among the Jews came to Daphne, near Antioch in Syria, to Antony, who was now doting on the love of Cleopatra. They came to accuse Phasael and Herod, having selected for this purpose the most eloquent of their whole number. Messala undertook to defend the young men's cause. Hyrcanus, who had betrothed his daughter to Herod, assisted him. After Antony had heard both sides, he asked Hyrcanus which side he considered to be better at governing a state. When he answered in favour of Phasael and Herod, Antony, who loved them because he had been kindly entertained by their father, made them both tetrarchs. He left them the government of all Judea and also wrote letters to this end, as well as putting fifteen of their adversaries in prison. He would have put them to death, had Herod not interceded for them. *{*Josephus, Jewish War, l. 1. c. 12. s. 5,6. (243-245) 2:113,115}* *{*Josephus, Antiq., l. 14. c. 13. s. 1. (324-326) 7:621,623}*

5375. A thousand men came from Jerusalem to Tyre to meet with Antony, who had already been well-bribed by Herod and Phasael, and Antony ordered the magistrates of Tyre to punish the envoys. He said the men were instigators of seditions and that the magistrates should help the tetrarchs. However, Herod and Hyrcanus came to them at the time, outside the city on the seashore, and earnestly advised them to withdraw. *[K416]* They warned them of the danger that would ensue if they followed this plan, but they ignored this advice. Thereupon, certain Jews and the inhabitants of that city rose up against them and the Romans killed and wounded some of them. However, Hyrcanus helped the wounded to recover and had the dead buried, while the rest fled home. When the people did nothing but rail against Herod, Antony, in his displeasure, killed those he was holding in prison. {*Josephus, Jewish War, l. 1. c. 12. s. 6,7. (245-247) 2:115} {*Josephus, Antiq., l. 14. c. 13. s. 2. (327-329) 7:623}

5376. Cleopatra returned to Egypt. Antony sent cavalry to plunder Palmyra, a city located not far from the Euphrates River. This crime against them was committed because they had sided neither with the Romans nor with the Parthians. Antony hoped to enrich his cavalry. The people of Palmyra, who lived on the frontier between the Romans and the Parthians, were merchants who carried Indian and Arabian wares to the Romans from Persia. When the inhabitants of Palmyra, who excelled in archery, had an inkling of what was afoot, they carried their goods to the other side of the river and positioned archers to keep the Romans off. So the cavalry found the city empty and returned without any plunder or bloodshed. As a result, the Parthian war started, shortly after this. Many tyrants from Syria, whom Antony had expelled, fled to the Parthians and asked them to seize Syria. {*Appian, Civil Wars, l. 5. c. 1. (9,10) 4:391,393} [E711]

## 3964a AM, 4673 JP, 41 BC

5377. When Antony had imposed heavy tributes on the people and thereby offended the city of Palmyra, he did not stay to settle the troubles of the province. He divided his army into its winter quarters, while he went into Egypt to Cleopatra. {*Appian, Civil Wars, l. 5. c. 1. (10) 4:393} Antony left Plancas in Asia and Saxa in Syria. {*Dio, l. 48. (24) 5:269} Decidius Saxa was the man Cicero mentioned as having been one of Mark Antony's guards. {*Cicero, Philippics, l. 13. c. 13. 15:577} Livy stated he was Antony's deputy in Syria. {*Livy, l. 127. 14:157}

5378. These actions caused seditions. The inhabitants of the island of Aradus did not obey those sent to them to collect tributes and the islanders even killed some of them. The Parthians, who even before had been rebellious, now initiated many more insurrections against the Romans. The Parthian forces were under the command of Labienus and Pacorus, the son of Orodes. {*Dio, l. 48. (24) 5:269}

5379. Eusebius wrote this about the Aradians: {*Eusebius, Chronicles, l. 1. 1:240}

"Curtius Salassus was burned alive with four cohorts in the island of Aradus, because he exacted their tributes too zealously."

5380. Livy noted that Labienus belonged to Pompey's party. {*Livy, l. 127. 14:157} Plutarch wrote: {*Plutarch, Antony, l. 1. c. 28. s. 1. 9:197}

"When the forces of the Parthians were prepared to attack, Labienus was made their general for the expedition of the Parthians. When the king's general was about to attack Syria, Antony was drawn away to Alexandria by Cleopatra."

5381. From this, the compiler of the Parthian account should be corrected. {Appian, Parthian Wars, p. 155,156.} He foolishly insinuated that Labienus was brought to Alexandria by the king's captains. However, Dio explained both the origin and progress of this expedition as follows.

5382. After the defeat of Philippi, Labienus thought that the conquerors would not pardon any of their opponents. He thought it better to live with the barbarians than to die in his own country and therefore he stayed with the Parthians. As soon as he understood the carelessness and indolence of Antony, his love for Cleopatra and his journey into Egypt, he advised the Parthians to make war against the Romans. [K417] The Roman armies were partly cut off and partly under strength, while the remainder disagreed among themselves, so that it looked like civil war would break out at any time. Therefore, he persuaded the king to subdue Syria and the countries around it, while Caesar was detained in Italy because of Sextus Pompeius and Antony was giving himself over to his love in Egypt. He also promised him that he would go as the general of this war, in order to provoke many countries to revolt from the Romans. This was because they were offended with the Romans for the continual damages and tributes with which they were afflicting them. {*Dio, l. 48. (24) 5:269,271}

5383. When he had persuaded the king to make war, he received many forces from him, along with his son Pacorus. Labienus invaded Phoenicia, where he attacked Apamea and was repulsed from its wall. He took the garrisons that were stationed in that country by their voluntary surrender to him. These consisted of the soldiers of Cassius and Brutus, whom Antony had chosen for his army and had left there to keep Syria, since they knew the country well. Therefore, Labienus easily persuaded them to join his side, because they already knew him. Everyone did, except Saxa, who commanded them. He was the brother of Decidius Saxa, the deputy of Antony and his quaestor. {*Dio, l. 48. (25) 5:271,273}

5384. Labienus defeated Saxa in a battle due to the size and valour of his cavalry, and pursued him as he fled from his camp by night. He had earlier shot notices into his camp to draw his soldiers to his side. Saxa feared this greatly and fled. Labienus overtook him and killed most of the men with him. When Saxa had fled to Antioch, Labienus took Apamea, which no longer resisted him, because it was generally reported that Saxa was dead. He also took Antioch after Saxa deserted it. {*Dio, l. 48. (25) 5:273}

5385. Mark Antony was splendidly entertained by Cleopatra and wintered in Egypt without his imperial ensigns. He did this either because he was in another person's government and royal city, or because he wanted to solemnise the festival days in his winter quarters. He set aside all business for his country and wore the Greek four-cornered robe and the white Attic shoes called *Phaecasium*, which the Athenian and Alexandrian priests used. When he went out, he went only to the temples or places of exercise, or to the meetings of philosophers. He always kept company with the Greeks and courted Cleopatra, who was the main reason for his coming, as he himself said. {*Appian, Civil Wars, l. 5. c. 1. (11) 4:393,395}

5386. Antony gave himself over to luxurious living with Cleopatra and the Egyptians. He whiled his time away, even to the point of his utter destruction. {*Dio, l. 48. (27) 5:275,277} Plutarch described at length how he indulged himself and his son. Plutarch's account is based on what Philotas, the Amphissian physician, who was at Alexandria at the time, pursuing his studies, told Plutarch's grandfather, Lamprias.

5387. Cleopatra was with him day and night. *[E712]* She played dice with him, drank with him, hunted with him and watched him exercising himself in the skilful use of his weapons. She accompanied him by night through the streets, as he was eavesdropping at the gates and windows of the citizens and talked to those who were inside. She walked with him as he was clad in the clothes of a serving maid, for he often wore such clothes himself. Consequently, he often returned home well-jeered or thoroughly beaten. {*Plutarch, Antony, l. 1. c. 29. s. 1,2. 9:201,203} *[K418]*

5388. Antony detained the envoys that were sent to him from the Italian colonies, either because it was winter or because he wanted to conceal his intentions. {*Appian, Civil Wars, l. 5. c. 6. (52) 4:463} In the meantime, Caesar Octavius besieged the consul Lucius Antony, Antony's brother, at Perusia in Etruria. {*Appian, Civil Wars, l. 5. c. 4. (32) 4:427}

## 3964b AM, 4674 JP, 40 BC

5389. When Gnaeus Domitius Calvinus and Asinius Pollio were consuls, Perusia was taken by Octavius. {*Dio, l. 48. (15) 5:249}

5390. Labienus followed Saxa as he fled into Cilicia and killed him there. {*Dio, l. 48. (25,26) 5:273} Paterculus stated: {*Velleius Paterculus, l. 2. c. 78. s. 1. 1:215}

"Labienus went from Brutus' camp to the Parthians and led an army of them into Syria. He killed the deputy of Antony, who had very badly oppressed the transmarine provinces."

5391. Florus stated: {*Florus, l. 2. c. 19. s. 4. 1:317,319} (Loeb text has been amended with no footnote to remove incorrect name. Editor.)

"Saxa (for thus it is to be read there, not Casca), the deputy, committed suicide, so that he might not fall into his enemies' hands."

5392. After Saxa was dead, Pacorus subdued all Syria, with the exception of Tyre. {*Velleius Paterculus, l. 2. c. 78. s. 1. 1:215} {*Florus, l. 2. c. 20. s. 5. 1:319} {*Livy, l. 127. 14:157} {*Dio, l. 48. (25,26) 5:273} The Romans who had been left, along with the friendly Syrians, had occupied it before. They could not be persuaded or forced to yield because the Parthians had no fleet with them. {*Dio, l. 48. (26) 5:273}

5393. In the second year from the time of the coming of Antony into Syria, when Pacorus, the king's son, and Barzapharnes, a ruler of the Parthians, had seized Lysia, Ptolemy, the son of Mennaeus, died. His successor in the kingdom of Lysia was his son, Lysanias. (Dio said he was made king of the Itureans by Antony. {*Dio, l. 49. (32) 5:407}) He became friends with Antigonus, the son of Aristobulus, a nobleman. Lysanias found him useful and was able to influence him significantly. (Greek text unclear. See Loeb footnote. Editor.) {*Josephus, Antiq., l. 14. c. 13. s. 3. (330) 7:623}

5394. At the beginning of the spring, Antony set out against the Parthians. He came as far as Phoenicia and reached Tyre. {*Plutarch, Antony, l. 1. c. 30. s. 2. 9:205} {*Appian, Civil Wars, l. 5. c. 6. (52) 4:463} He sailed there as if he was intending to bring help to the city. When he saw that all the surrounding country had been seized by the enemy, he left on the pretext of engaging in the war against Sextus Pompeius. On the contrary, he used the excuse of the Parthian war as the reason why he had not gone against Pompeius sooner. Therefore, he pretended that it was on account of Sextus, that he gave his allies no assistance. Likewise, he gave none to Italy on account of his allies. {*Dio, l. 48. (27) 5:277}

5395. As he was passing the continent and sailed by Cyprus and Rhodes to Asia, he heard of the news of the siege of Perusia. He accused his brother Lucius and his wife Fulvia, but more especially Manius, who had been his representative in Italy in his absence. He then sailed into Greece, where he met his mother Julia and his wife Fulvia, who had fled from Italy. As he sailed into Italy from there, he took Sipontum. {*Dio, l. 48. (28) 5:277} {*Appian, Civil Wars, l. 5. c. 3. (19) 4:407,409} {*Appian, Civil Wars, l. 5. c. 6. (52) 4:463,465}

*5396.* After Fulvia died at Sicyon, her husband Antony was persuaded by his mother Julia and Lucius Cocceius to make peace with Caesar. Antony recalled Sextus Pompeius (with whom he had already entered into a league) into Sicily, to arrange, as it were, for those things that they had agreed upon. He sent Domitius Ahenobarbus into Bithynia to govern there. {*Appian, Civil Wars, l. 5. c. 7. (60) 4:479} {*Appian, Civil Wars, l. 5. c. 7. (63) 4:485} He knew that Marcellus, the husband of Octavia, the most dearly beloved sister of Caesar, although by another mother, had recently died. [K419] To more firmly ratify a peace, Octavia was betrothed to Antony. He did not hide his involvement with Cleopatra but he denied that she was his wife. {*Appian, Civil Wars, l. 5. c. 7. (64) 4:487} {*Livy, l. 127. 14:159} {*Plutarch, Antony, l. 1. c. 31. s. 1,2. 9:205,207}

*5397.* They divided the Roman Empire between them. They established Scodra, a town of Illyria located midway up the Adriatic Gulf, as the boundary of each of their dominions. All the eastern countries, as well as the islands and provinces of both Europe and Asia, as far as the Euphrates River, were allocated to Antony. The western areas of Sardinia, Dalmatia, Spain and Gaul were allocated to Caesar. Caesar had given the provinces of Africa to Lepidus, the triumvir, and Sextus Pompeius had seized Sicily. {*Plutarch, Antony, l. 1. c. 30. s. 3,4. 9:205} {*Appian, Civil Wars, l. 5. c. 7. (65) 4:487} {*Dio, l. 48. (28) 5:279,281}

*5398.* The war against Pompeius was assigned to Caesar, unless something else should happen, while Antony took on the Parthian war to revenge the wrong done to Crassus. Domitius Ahenobarbus, although he was one of the murderers of Julius Caesar, was taken into a league by Caesar, on the same condition as he had formerly been taken into a league by Antony. It was added to the league that it could be lawful for both the generals to muster the same number of legions from Italy. It was on these articles that this last league was made between Caesar and Antony. {*Appian, Civil Wars, l. 5. c. 7. (65) 4:487} [E713]

*5399.* Caesar and Antony entered Rome and made a speech about the good news of the peace established between them. {Gruter, Inscriptions, p. 297.} The citizens entertained them as in a triumph and clothed them in triumphal robes. They had them watch the plays and seated them in ivory chairs. {*Dio, l. 48. (31) 5:285} The marriage was solemnised between Antony and Octavia, who was quite obviously pregnant. The law forbade any woman to marry until ten months after the death of her husband but the time was reduced by a decree of the Senate. {*Velleius Paterculus, l. 2. c. 78. s. 1. 1:215} {*Plutarch, Antony, l. 1. c. 31. s. 2,3. 9:207} {*Appian, Civil Wars, l. 5. c. 7. (64) 4:487} {*Dio, l. 48. (31) 5:285} Antony put Manius to death because he had exasperated Fulvia by his frequent complaining

about Cleopatra and because he had been the cause of so many evils. {*Appian, Civil Wars, l. 5. c. 7. (66) 4:489}

*5400.* Asinius Pollio had a son born during his consulship, whom he called Salonius. He was named after the city of Salo of Spalato in Dalmatia. Virgil wrote singing verses about the birth of Salonius Pollio, from the Cymean or Sibylline poems. He classified the ages of the world by metals and foretold that, in the tenth and last age of the world, in which Solar Apollo was to rule, all things would be restored, while also stating that in this year the golden age would return again (and with it the Virgin Erigone, or Aftraea, who had left the earth in the Iron Age). {*Virgil, Eclogue 4. 1:29-33} In his description, the poet seems to have inserted the things he had heard spoken about by the Jews, since Cicero said that there were many Jews who lived at Rome, around the Aurelian stairs. [K420] Or else, Virgil would have read this in the books of the Jewish prophets, which were available in the Greek language. {*Cicero, Pro Flacco, l. 1. (66) 10:515}

*5401.* Pacorus, son of the king of Parthia, captured Syria and went into Palestine, where he deposed Hyrcanus, who had been appointed by the Romans to govern that country, and put Hyrcanus' brother Aristobulus in his place. This is how Dio confused Aristobulus, the father, with Antigonus, his son, when he later invariably called this Antigonus the king, rather than Aristobulus. {*Dio, l. 48. (26) 5:273} {*Dio, l. 48. (41) 5:307} {*Dio, l. 49. (22) 5:387,389} Josephus described the matter in detail.

*5402.* Antigonus, the son of Aristobulus, said that he would give the Parthians a thousand talents and five hundred women, if they would give Hyrcanus' kingdom to him and kill Herod and all his relatives. Antigonus did not in fact give them these, but nevertheless the Parthians marched with their army toward Judea to claim the kingdom for Antigonus. Pacorus, the king's son, went by sea and Barzapharnes by land. The Tyrians shut their gates against him but the Sidonians and the people of Ptolemais opened their gates to him. He sent a squadron of cavalry ahead of him into Judea under the cupbearer of King Pacorus, to see what had to be done, and ordered that they should help Antigonus. {*Josephus, Antiq., l. 14. c. 13. s. 3. (331-333) 7:625} {*Josephus, Jewish War, l. 1. c. 13. s. 1. (248,249) 2:117}

*5403.* The Jews who lived at Mount Carmel allied themselves with Antigonus and were prepared to invade the enemies' country with him. He began to get some hope that with their help he could subdue the country of Drymus, which was also called *The Grove* and may have been the Plain of Sharon. He encountered his enemies and chased them right up to Jerusalem. {*Josephus, Antiq., l. 14. c. 13. s. 3. (334) 7:625,627} {*Josephus, Jewish War, l. 1. c. 13. s. 2. (250) 2:117}

5404. Antigonus' side had greatly increased in numbers and besieged the king's house. However, Phasael and Herod came to the assistance of the besieged, and in the battle which was fought in the market place the young men defeated the enemy. After pursuing them into the temple, Herod and Phasael sent sixty men to guard them, after they had placed them in the adjoining houses. However, the people bore a grudge against these men and burned them with fire. Herod was very angry and killed many of the people. Daily skirmishes killed many. {*Josephus, Antiq., l. 14. c. 13. s. 3. (335-336) 7:627} {*Josephus, Jewish War, l. 1. c. 13. s. 2. (251,252) 2:117,119}

5405. When the day of Pentecost arrived, many thousands of men, armed as well as unarmed, gathered around the temple from all parts of the country. They seized the temple and the city, except the king's house. Herod guarded the king's house with a few soldiers, while his brother Phasael held out on the walls. Aided by his brother, Herod attacked his enemies in the suburbs and forced many thousands to flee, either into the city or the temple, or the outer rampart, which was near the city. {*Josephus, Antiq., l. 14. c. 13. s. 4. (337-339) 7:627,629} {*Josephus, Jewish War, l. 1. c. 13. s. 3. (253) 2:119}

5406. In the meantime, Antigonus asked that Pacorus, the general of the Parthians, might be admitted, to arrange a peace between them. Pacorus was entertained by Phasael and urged him to go as an envoy to Barzapharnes. He had laid an ambush for Phasael, who did not go, because he suspected as much. Herod did not approve of this planned meeting because of the perfidiousness of the barbarians. He suggested, instead, that he should kill Pacorus and those who had come with him. In spite of this, Hyrcanus and Phasael went on with their embassy. To allay suspicions, Pacorus left Herod with two hundred horsemen and ten whom they call *Freemen*, and took the envoys with him. {*Josephus, Antiq., l. 14. c. 13. s. 4. (340-342) 7:629} {*Josephus, Jewish War, l. 1. c. 13. s. 3. (254,255) 2:119} [E714] [K421]

5407. As soon as they had come into Galilee, the governors of those towns came out against them in arms. Barzapharnes welcomed them with a cheerful countenance and gave them gifts, but later made ambushes against them. Phasael and his entourage were brought to a place near the seaside, called Ecdippa. Ophellius learned from Saramalla, the richest of all the Syrians, that ambushes had been set for Phasael and offered him boats to escape. Phasael was unwilling to leave Hyrcanus and his brother Herod in jeopardy and expostulated with Barzapharnes concerning the wrongs done to the envoys. Barzapharnes swore that these things were not true and soon left to go to Pacorus. {*Josephus, Antiq., l. 14. c. 13. s. 4. (343-347) 7:631,633} {*Josephus, Jewish War, l. 1. c. 13. s. 4,5. (256-259) 2:119,121}

5408. He had no sooner gone than Hyrcanus and Phasael were thrown into prison, after protesting the perjury of the Parthians. A eunuch was sent to Herod also, with orders to surprise him, if he could get him out of the city. When Herod learned from others what had happened to his brother, he took with him what forces he had and put the women on horses, that is, his mother Cybele, his sister Salome, his wife Mariamme, and her mother, Alexandra, the daughter of Hyrcanus. Together with these and his youngest brother Pheroras, their servants and the rest of the company, Herod fled by night into Idumea, unknown to his enemies. {*Josephus, Antiq., l. 14. c. 13. s. 4-7. (347-354) 7:633-637} {*Josephus, Jewish War, l. 1. c. 13. s. 5,6. (260-263) 2:123}

5409. On the journey, his mother was almost killed when her coach overturned. Herod was so terrified in case the enemy should overtake them while they were staying there that he intended to kill himself with his own sword. He was restrained by those around him and went toward Masada, a very strongly fortified place located in the country of Arabia and Palestine. He took the shortest way possible. First, the Parthians pursued him and then the Jews. When he was only about eight miles from Jerusalem, he defeated both of them in a battle. {*Josephus, Antiq., l. 14. c. 13. s. 8,9. (355-359) 7:637,639} {*Josephus, Jewish War, l. 1. c. 13. s. 7,8. (264,265) 2:123,125}

5410. After he reached Rhesa, a village of Idumea, his brother Joseph came to him. He saw that together they were bringing so large a multitude with them, as well as mercenary soldiers, that the citadel at Masada, to which they were planning to flee, would not be able to hold them. So Herod dismissed most of them. He told nine thousand to take care of themselves in Idumea and gave them food. He selected the best men and his closest friends and went into the citadel. There he left the women with the rest of their companions, because there was plenty of grain, water and other provisions, while he went to Petra, a city of Arabia. {*Josephus, Antiq., l. 14. c. 13. s. 9. (360-362) 7:639,641} {*Josephus, Jewish War, l. 1. c. 13. s. 8. (266,267) 2:125}

5411. The day after he had fled from Jerusalem, the Parthians plundered all the goods of the citizens of Jerusalem, including the king's house. Only the treasure of Hyrcanus, which was three hundred talents, was untouched, and a large part of Herod's wealth, that he had providentially carried into Idumea. Not content with the plunder of the city, the Parthians went out of the city and plundered the country also. They destroyed the rich city of Marisa. {*Josephus, Antiq., l. 14. c. 13. s. 9. (363,364) 7:641} {*Josephus, Jewish War, l. 1. c. 13. s. 9. (268) 2:125,127}

5412. Antigonus was brought back into his country by the king of the Parthians and received Hyrcanus and

Phasael, who were prisoners at the time. He was deeply grieved that the women, whom he had intended to turn over to the Parthians, had escaped. The money, too, which he had promised to give the Parthians, was gone. Fearing that Hyrcanus, whom the Parthians were holding prisoner, might be restored into his kingdom again by the favour of the people, he cut off his ears to render him unfit for the priesthood. *[K422]* The law forbade any disfigured person from being in the priesthood. {*Le 21:17-21*} {*Josephus, Antiq., l. 14. c. 13. s. 10. (365,366) 7:641,643*} {*Josephus, Jewish War, l. 1. c. 13. s. 9. (269,270) 2:127*}

*5413.* Phasael knew that he was to be executed. Since he could not easily commit suicide because his hands were chained, he beat out his own brains against a stone. Before he was dead, he heard from a woman that his brother Herod had escaped. He rejoiced greatly that someone was left to revenge his death. Although the Parthians had missed the women whom they had wanted the most, they settled everything at Jerusalem with Antigonus and took Hyrcanus along with them as a prisoner into Parthia when they left. {*Josephus, Antiq., l. 14. c. 13. s. 10. (367-369) 7:643*} {*Josephus, Jewish War, l. 1. c. 13. s. 10,11. (271,272) 2:127,129*}

*5414.* At the same time, Labienus took Cilicia and all the cities which were located in the continent of Asia, except Stratonicia. In fear of him, Plancus, Antony's lieutenant in Asia, had fled to the islands. Most of the cities Labienus took without a fight, but Mylasa and Alabanda he took by force. When those cities had entertained a garrison from Labienus, they revolted on a certain festival day and killed the garrison. After capturing Alabanda, Labienus executed the citizens. He destroyed Mylasa after it had been abandoned by its inhabitants. Although he besieged Stratonicia for a long time, he was unable to take the city. *[E715]* At length, when he had taken their money and robbed their temples, he called himself *Imperator* and *Parthicus*. With regard to the latter, he acted directly contrary to the Roman custom, in that he took his title from those whom he was leading against the Romans, as though it were the Parthians and not his fellow citizens that he had defeated. {*Dio, l. 48. (26) 5:275*}

*5415.* Thus, the Parthians made conquests for themselves, under the pretence of being auxiliaries for Labienus, their captain. They invaded from the Euphrates River into Syria as far as Lydia and Ionia and behaved more like thieves than enemies. {*Florus, l. 2. c. 19. s. 3,4. 1:317*} {*Plutarch, Antony, l. 1. c. 30. s. 1,2. 9:205*} {*Appian, Syrian Wars, l. 11. c. 8. (51) 2:201*} {*Appian, Parthian Wars, p. 134,156*} {*Appian, Civil Wars, l. 5. c. 7. (65) 4:489*} {*Appian, Civil Wars, l. 5. c. 14. (133) 4:597*} To stop this, Antony sent his lieutenant, Marcus Ventidius Bassus, into Asia.

{*Plutarch, Antony, l. 1. c. 33. s. 1. 9:209*} {*Appian, Parthian Wars, p. 156.*} {*Appian, Civil Wars, l. 5. c. 7. (65) 4:489*}

*5416.* Ventidius quickly reached Labienus, before the latter knew anything about it. Labienus, who was without his forces, was terrified by his sudden arrival. He had no forces with him except some soldiers gathered from Asia, and because he did not have any Parthians, he did not dare meet him, but fled. Ventidius followed him with his lightly armed soldiers as he fled. When he caught up with him at the Taurus Mountains, he would not let him go any farther. {*Dio, l. 48. (39) 5:303*}

*5417.* They stayed quietly in that spot for many days in their camps opposite each other. Labienus was waiting for the Parthians and Ventidius expected his legions. In those days both wanted to hide. Ventidius feared the Parthian cavalry and stayed up on high ground where he had made his camp. The Parthians trusted in their numbers and despised those whom they had defeated in the past. Before joining with Labienus, they approached the hill early in the morning. The Romans boldly came out to meet them and the Parthians intended to go to the very top of the hill. As they came up, the Romans ran toward them and without much effort, forced them into a disorderly retreat. The Romans killed some of the Parthians, but the majority were killed in their retreat by their own side, because they saw that some were fleeing, while others had only just arrived at the hill. {*Dio, l. 48. (39,40) 5:303,305*} *[K423]*

*5418.* Ventidius followed the Parthians, who fled into Cilicia to their camp, rather than going toward Labienus. Ventidius noticed that Labienus was still standing there. When Labienus had set his men in array, he saw that his men were astonished at the flight of the barbarians and so he dared not fight. He intended instead to escape somewhere by night. When Ventidius found out about this from some fugitives from Labienus, he killed many of Labienus' men as they left by setting ambushes. All the rest deserted Labienus and he fled. {*Dio, l. 48. (40) 5:305*}

*5419.* Labienus disguised himself and after he had hidden in Cilicia for some time, he was sought out and taken by Demetrius, who was governing Cyprus for Antony at the time. {*Dio, l. 48. (40) 5:305*}

*5420.* After this, Ventidius recovered and settled Cilicia. He sent Pompedius Silo ahead of him with cavalry to Mount Amanus, which was located on the border between Cilicia and Syria. Silo went to take control of the passes, but was unable to capture a citadel there. He was also in extreme danger from Phranapates, the lieutenant of Pacorus, who held that pass. Silo had been utterly routed, but Ventidius arrived by chance, as they were fighting. He brought him help by suddenly attacking the outnumbered Parthians. Phranapates was killed, along with many others. Ventidius recovered Syria without fighting, after the Parthians had abandoned it and only the Arabs remained. The Arabians, fearing the punishment for their bold attacks against Antony, did not surrender to Ventidius, even though he attacked them for some time. {*Dio, l. 48. (41) 5:305,307}

5421. Unaware of his brother Phasael's death, Herod went to Malchus, the king of the Arabians (Nabateans), who was obliged to him for many favours Herod had done for him. Herod was willing to spend three hundred talents to redeem his brother from the enemy as soon as he could. For this reason, he took Phasael, his brother's son, with him, a child of seven years old, to leave as a pledge with the Arabians. However, he was met by some men who had been sent to him from Malchus. They told him he should leave Malchus' kingdom because this had been ordered by the Parthians. However, this was only a pretence upon which he and his nobles had agreed, so they could defraud Herod of the treasure that his father, Antipater, had committed to their custody. Herod was very discouraged and returned to a certain temple where he had left many of his followers. The next day, when he came to Rhinocolura, he heard of his brother's death. {*Josephus, Antiq., l. 14. c. 14. s. 1. (370-373) 7:643,645} {*Josephus, Jewish War, l. 1. c. 14. s. 1,2. (274-278) 2:129,131}

5422. Malchus was sorry for his ingratitude and quickly sent after Herod. He could not overtake him, for he had already covered a great distance on his way to Pelusium. Some sailors, who were about to sail to Alexandria, denied him passage. Herod was honourably entertained by the magistrates of Pelusium and was brought to Cleopatra, the queen at Alexandria. [E716] She was unable to detain him because he was in a hurry to go to Rome, although the sea was very stormy and the political affairs in Italy at that time were in a sorry state. It was not yet winter time. {Salianus, Against Forniellus, 4014 AM, num. 26,27.} Ignoring the storms, Herod sailed from Alexandria toward Pamphylia, but ran into a violent storm and was nearly shipwrecked, so that he had to throw most of his goods overboard and barely got to Rhodes. {*Josephus, Antiq., l. 14. c. 14. s. 2,3. (373-377) 7:647} {*Josephus, Jewish War, l. 1. c. 14. s. 2,3. (278-280) 2:131,133}

5423. He was met at Rhodes by two of his best friends, Sappinas and Ptolemy. They found that the city had suffered a great deal in the war against Cassius. [K424] He could not be restrained, even in his present poverty, but wanted to do something for Rhodes even beyond his capacity. He had an immense trireme built, after which he embarked with his friends, arriving at Brundisium in Italy. From there, he went to Rome and told Antony everything that had happened to him and his family. He mentioned the violent storms and recounted all the dangers, saying that he had withdrawn to Antony, his only refuge, in whom all his hopes lay. {*Josephus, Antiq., l. 14. c. 14. s. 3. (378-380) 7:647,649} {*Josephus, Jewish War, l. 1. c. 14. s. 3. (280,281) 2:133}

5424. Antony was stirred by the story and also recalled the friendship of Antipater, Herod's father. He was especially moved both by the promise of money if he made Herod king, and by his hatred of Antigonus, who was a man of a turbulent spirit and an enemy to the Romans. This made him more inclined toward Herod. Octavius was also sympathetic because Antipater had been a fellow soldier with his father in Egypt and because of other courtesies which Antipater had shown his father. To satisfy Antony, who he knew, was well disposed toward Herod, Octavius was willing to promote his endeavours. Therefore the Senate was convened. Messala and Atratinus brought out Herod. After they had praised him, they recalled the services and goodwill that both his father and he had done for the Romans. They accused Antigonus for previous crimes and for his recent sedition against the Romans, in which he had received the kingdom from the Parthians. Antony declared to the Senate how helpful it would be to the Parthian war that was still raging, if Herod were to be made king. Antigonus was declared an enemy and the title of King was given to Herod by their general consent. {*Josephus, Antiq., l. 14. c. 14. s. 4. (381-385) 7:649,651} {*Josephus, Jewish War, l. 1. c. 14. s. 4. (282-285) 2:133,135}

5425. After the Senate was dismissed, Antony and Caesar emerged, leading Herod between them. Accompanied by the consuls and other magistrates, they went up to the Capitol to sacrifice and to place the decree of the Senate there. Antony feasted the new king on the first day of his reign. Hence, Herod obtained the kingdom in the 185th Olympiad, not the 184th, as Josephus wrote. Gnaeus Domitius Calvinus and Asinius Pollio were consuls. Within seven days, Antony dismissed Herod from Italy, who was honoured with this unexpected friendship. {*Josephus, Antiq., l. 14. c. 14. s. 5. (386-389) 7:653}

5426. During this time of Herod's absence, Antigonus attacked Herod's family in Masada, who, while they had plenty of provisions, lacked water. For this reason, Herod's brother Joseph planned to escape to the Nabateans with two hundred of his friends because he had heard that Malchus now regretted the ingratitude he had shown toward Herod. However, that night it rained and he changed his mind when the cisterns were filled with water. They made a gallant sally out and killed many of Antigonus' men, both in the open field and in surprise attacks. {*Josephus, Antiq., l. 14. c. 14. s. 6. (390,391) 7:655} {*Josephus, Jewish War, l. 1. c. 15. s. 1. (286,287) 2:135}

## 3965a AM, 4674 JP, 40 BC

*5427.* After frightening King Antigonus out of the country, Ventidius occupied Palestine with little trouble. Besides accomplishing all this, he exacted large sums of money from all men but especially from Antigonus, Antiochus (Commagene) and Malchus, the Nabatean, because they had given help to Pacorus. {*Dio, l. 48. (41) 5:307} He had also come into Palestine with the pretext of helping Joseph, but his real purpose had been to extort money from Antigonus. Therefore, he camped near Jerusalem and extorted as much money from him as he wanted. [K425] In order to conceal his fraudulent dealing, he left Silo there with some of his forces. Antigonus was to obey Silo, so that he would not create some new troubles. Antigonus, meanwhile, hoped the Parthians would come to his aid. {*Josephus, Antiq., l. 14. c. 14. s. 6. (391-393) 7:655} {*Josephus, Jewish War, l. 1. c. 15. s. 2. (288-290) 2:135,137}

*5428.* There was, in the company of Antony, an Egyptian astrologer who told him that although his fortune was indeed splendid and great, it was being obscured by the fortune of Caesar. Therefore, he persuaded him to get as far away from that young man as he could, because he claimed that Antony's guardian genius was afraid of Caesar's genius. While Antony's genius was tall and erect when he was alone, it became more languid whenever Caesar drew near. {*Plutarch, Antony, l. 1. c. 33. s. 1-3. 9:209,211}

*5429.* After these events, Antony went to the Parthian war. He had all his acts, both past and future, confirmed by the Senate. Once again, he dismissed many of his commanders and settled all matters as he wished. He appointed some kings on his own authority, who were merely to pay a certain tribute. [E717] He made Herod king of both Idumea and Samaria, Darius (the son of Pharnaces and grandson of Mithridates) king of Pontus, Amyntas of Pisidia, Polemon of part of Cilicia and appointed other kings in other countries. {*Appian, Civil Wars, l. 5. c. 8. (75) 4:505,507} When he had committed the care of his family to Caesar, he left Italy and took Octavia with him into Greece. He had one son by her. {*Plutarch, Antony, l. 1. c. 33. s. 3,4. 9:211} He stayed in Greece for many days. {*Dio, l. 48. (39) 5:301,303}

*5430.* Normally, Antony would winter his army around him. However, to get them accustomed to plunder and exercise, he sent some of them against the Partheni, a tribe in Illyria who, in previous times, had been greatly attached to Brutus. He sent others against the Dardanians, who also lived in Illyria and were in the habit of invading Macedonia. He ordered still others to stay with him in Epirus, so that he would have them all around him, since he planned to make Athens his winter quarters. He also sent Furnius into Africa to get the four legions from Sextius to use against the Parthians, since he had not as yet heard that Lepidus had taken them from Sextius. When all this had been done, he wintered at Athens with Octavia, just as he had done before at Alexandria with Cleopatra. {*Appian, Civil Wars, l. 5. c. 8. (75,76) 4:507}

*5431.* While wintering at Athens, he heard early reports about Ventidius' military success. He learned that the Parthians had been defeated and Ventidius had killed Labienus and Phranapates, or Phraates, the chief general of king Hyrodes, or Orodes. To celebrate these victories, Antony put on a feast for the Greeks and held games for the people of Athens. As he was the main person in the games, he left his imperial ensigns at home and was seen in public with the wands that a gymnasiarch used, clothed with coats and shoes called *Phaecasium.* He joined the young gamesters and when they had contended as long as he thought good, he ended the games. {*Plutarch, Antony, l. 1. c. 33. s. 3,4. 9:211}

*5432.* Antony was praised at Rome and triumphs were decreed in his name. Ventidius received no reward, as decreed by the Senate, because he was not a general, but was carrying on the war under the authority of another. {*Dio, l. 48. (41) 5:307}

*5433.* Castor received the countries of Attalus and Dejotarus after their deaths. {*Dio, l. 48. (33) 5:289}

*5434.* When Herod returned from Italy to Ptolemais, he gathered a number of mercenaries and the men of his own country and hurried through Galilee against Antigonus. He was helped by Silo and Ventidius, to whom Antony had sent Dellius (for so his name is to be read, {*Josephus, Antiq., l. 15. c. 2. s. 6. (25) 8:13} [K426] not Gellius. Loeb edition corrected the Greek text. Editor.) with orders that they should help Herod get his kingdom. As it happened, Ventidius was detained by the need to settle the uprisings that the Parthians had caused in various cities. Silo was in Judea, but had been bribed with money from Antigonus. Nonetheless, Herod's forces increased daily and all of Galilee, with few exceptions, stood by Herod. {*Josephus, Antiq., l. 14. c. 15. s. 1. (394,395) 7:657} {*Josephus, Jewish War, l. 1. c. 15. s. 3. (290,291) 2:137}

*5435.* As Herod was marching to Masada to help his family, Joppa refused to let him pass. He first had to take the city out of the hands of the enemy because he would not leave any fortification behind him on his march to Jerusalem. Silo used this fact that Herod was fighting at Joppa to leave Jerusalem. When the Jews pursued him, Herod met them with a small band of men and saved Silo, who fought very poorly. {*Josephus, Antiq., l. 14. c. 15. s. 1. (395-397) 7:657,659} {*Josephus, Jewish War, l. 1. c. 15. s. 3. (292) 2:137}

*5436.* After Joppa was taken, Herod hurried to Masada to deliver his family from the siege. His army had greatly increased in size and many of the country people joined with him. When he freed his friends from Masada, he approached Jerusalem in spite of Antigonus, who had made ambushes for him in every suitable location. The soldiers of Silo followed him, as well, and many of the Jews were terrified by his power. When he had camped on the west side of the city, those who held the walls on that side shot at him with arrows and javelins, while various men came out in troops and attacked their quarters. Herod commanded a herald to proclaim around the walls that he had come for the public good and the preservation of the city and that he would pardon all former wrongs. On the opposing side, Antigonus talked to Silo and the Romans. He told them that it was unjust to give the kingdom to Herod, who was not of the royal family, and only an Idumean, that is, a half-Jew. By custom, it ought to be given to the priests. Antigonus allowed his men to fight the enemy from the wall, but the enemy shot their arrows so valiantly and fought with so much spirit, that Antigonus' men were driven from the towers. Antigonus secretly bribed some of Silo's soldiers, whom he knew, to demand more provisions and money to buy them with, as well as request to be withdrawn into more commodious winter quarters. As a result, the army was troubled and was preparing to leave, but Herod entreated the captains and soldiers of Silo's army not to leave him now, as he had been sent both by Caesar and Antony and all the rest of the Senate. Soon he sent his soldiers into the country and removed any pretext for Silo to leave. They returned with an abundant supply of provisions, greater than anyone could hope for. *[E718]* He ordered those of his friends who lived around Samaria to bring grain, wine, oil, cattle and other necessities to Jericho, so that there would be enough for the soldiers for the future. {*Josephus, Antiq., l. 14. c. 15. s. 1-3. (398-408) 7:659-663} {*Josephus, Jewish War, l. 1. c. 15. s. 4-6. (293-299) 2:139,141}*

*5437.* When Antigonus became aware of this, he sent troops into the country to intercept those bringing supplies. However, Herod captured them with his ten cohorts, five of which were made up of Romans and five of Jews. Herod intermixed some foreign soldiers and a few cavalry with them and went to Jericho, but found the city empty of its inhabitants. Five hundred had fled with their families to the tops of the hills. Herod captured these and let them go again. The Romans entered the city and plundered it, finding the houses full of all manner of precious things. *[K427]* Herod left a garrison and returned to Jerusalem and dismissed the Roman army to winter in the countries that had recently surrendered to him, which were Idumea, Galilee and Samaria. By bribing Silo, Antigonus was granted that some of the Roman army should be lodged in Lydda to please Antony. Thus the Romans lived in plenty and were freed from having to bear arms. {*Josephus, Antiq., l. 14. c. 15. s. 3. (409-412) 7:663,665} {*Josephus, Jewish War, l. 1. c. 15. s. 6. (300-302) 2:141,143}*

### 3965b AM, 4675 JP, 39 BC

*5438.* Herod was not idle. He sent his brother Joseph into Idumea with two thousand foot soldiers and four hundred cavalry. He himself went into Samaria and there settled his mother and the rest of his family, whom he had taken from Masada. He then marched into Galilee and surprised some places that were being held by Antigonus' garrisons. When he came to Sepphoris in snowy weather, Antigonus' men deserted it and Herod took large amounts of provisions. From Sepphoris, he sent a cavalry troop and three companies of foot soldiers against some thieves, living in caves near the village of Arbela, whom he wanted to keep in check. On the fortieth day, Herod arrived there with the whole army and was boldly met by the enemy. They caused his left wing to waver, until he arrived with the main body of troops and helped them. He forced his enemy, who was winning, to flee, and his own men, who were fleeing, to stand. But not content with this, he followed the chase as far as the Jordan River. Through this, he subdued all Galilee, except for those inhabiting the caves. He gave every soldier a hundred and fifty drachmas and considerably more to the captains. Then he dismissed them into their winter quarters. {*Josephus, Antiq., l. 14. c. 15. s. 4. (413-417) 7:667} {*Josephus, Jewish War, l. 1. c. 16. s. 1-3. (303-308) 2:143,145}*

*5439.* In the meantime, Silo, who had wintered with Antigonus, came to Herod with his captains, because Antigonus would not provide supplies for them for longer than one month. Antigonus had sent to the inhabitants around the country and ordered them to destroy all the supplies in the country and to flee to the mountains. He had done this so that the Romans would perish through famine. Herod, however, committed the care of the provisions to his youngest brother, Pheroras, and ordered him to rebuild Alexandrion. In a short time, Pheroras had furnished the soldiers with abundance of all necessities and rebuilt Alexandrion, which had previously been destroyed. During this time, Antony stayed at Athens. {*Josephus, Antiq., l. 14. c. 15. s. 4,5. (418-420) 7:667,669}*

*5440.* When Publius Ventidius heard that Pacorus was gathering an army and coming into Syria, he was afraid, because the cities were not guarded and the armies were still dispersed in their winter quarters. Therefore, to stop Pacorus and buy time to get his own forces together, he went to Channaeus, a certain governor with whom he was well acquainted and whom he knew to be friendly to the Parthians. Nevertheless, he treated him with great honour, as though he were his faithful friend, and asked his advice in some affairs. He pretended that he was in on his most secret plans. So he pretended to be afraid that the Parthians would not follow their usual crossing over the Euphrates River at Zeugma, but would use some lower part of the river, since that area was a plain and better for the Parthian cavalry, while the other place was hilly and favoured him. By this means, he persuaded Channaeus and through him deceived Pacorus, so that the Parthians took the longer march through the plain, through which Ventidius pretended he did not want them to do. This gave Ventidius time to collect his forces, which was how Dio related the story. {*Dio, l. 49. (19) 5:381} [K428] Frontinus stated that it happened as follows. {*Frontinus, Stratagems, l. 1. c. 1. s. 6. 1:11,13} In the Parthian war against King Pacorus, Ventidius knew that Pharnaeus, who was from the province of Cyrrhestica and pretended to be one of his allies, told the Parthians whatever went on in Ventidius' camp. Ventidius used the perfidiousness of the barbarian to his own advantage, by pretending that he was afraid that those things which he in actual fact most wanted, would happen. Those he was most afraid of, he pretended to want. He was really in fact afraid that the Parthians would cross the Euphrates River before the legions, which he had in Cappadocia, on the other side of the Taurus Mountains, could come to him. He very carefully deceived the traitor, by utilising his normal spying, into thinking that he wanted him to persuade the Parthians that they should cross over with their army at Zeugma, where the journey was shorter and the channel not so deep. If they came that way, he affirmed that he could make good use of the hills to evade the archers, but that he was very afraid if they were to come by the plain. [E719]

5441. Antony spent the winter at Athens in great luxury and enjoying the pleasure of Octavia, as though he were a different man. He returned to the old Roman virtues. Now, the lictors were around the gates and the captains and his guards were with him. He arranged everything in such a way as to put men in fear of him. Envoys who had waited a long time, now received an audience. Justice was administered, the ships were launched and everything was carried out promptly. {*Appian, Civil Wars, l. 5. c. 8. (76) 4:507,509} Finally, he took a crown from the sacred olive tree and was ready to go to war. To satisfy a certain oracle, he carried a vessel with him, filled from the sacred spring called Clepsydra, near the Athenian Acropolis. {*Plutarch, Antony, l. 1. c. 34. s. 1. 9:213}

5442. In Syria, Ventidius sent for Silo to go to war against the Parthians. He ordered him to help Herod first and then to bring Herod along with the rest of the auxiliaries of those provinces. However Herod sent Silo to Ventidius while he himself marched with his soldiers against the thieves that lived in the caves. Josephus gave more details about this. {*Josephus, Jewish War, l. 1. c. 16. s. 4. (309-313) 2:145,147} {*Josephus, Antiq., l. 14. c. 15. s. 5. (420-430) 7:669-673}

5443. Herod made Ptolemy governor of the country, but his government was disturbed when the country was invaded by those who had previously bothered it. Ptolemy was killed, after which the invaders retired to the marshes and inaccessible places and robbed and invaded all that country. When Herod returned, he made them pay dearly for their thievery. Some of the rebellious persons were killed and others fled into fortified places. Herod conquered them and punished them by razing their strongholds, getting rid of the leaders of these revolts and fining the cities a hundred talents. {*Josephus, Jewish War, l. 1. c. 16. s. 4. (314-316) 2:149} {*Josephus, Antiq., l. 14. c. 15. s. 6. (431-433) 7:673}

5444. Pacorus arrived in Syria with numerous Parthian forces that had taken the shorter route at Zeugma while he had brought his army around by the plain. Even though the barbarians made a bridge between the wider banks, it was rather unwieldy. It took forty days for their army to arrive with its engines. Ventidius used this time to gather his forces, which he received only three days before the Parthians arrived. Ventidius had allowed them to cross the river without attacking them in their crossing, thereby making them think that the Romans were effeminate and cowards. [K429] Ventidius pretended fear and did not attack them, but endured the insults of the Parthians for a long time. At last, he sent some of the legions against them when they were feeling secure and were not watchful. On the first attack, the Parthians were defeated and routed. When Pacorus saw his men fleeing, he thought that all the legions had attacked them. Therefore, he attacked Ventidius' camp with the main body of his army thinking that the camp had been left without anyone to defend it. It was located on a hill and when the Parthian cavalry attacked it, they were easily pushed down the precipice by a sudden sally the Romans made. However, Ventidius did not lead the rest of the legions out from the camp again, until the enemy had come within half a mile of him. Then, when they were near him, he made so sudden an assault, that their arrows were no use against him, because he was still too far away. With this plan, he quickly attacked the barbarians, who were over-confident. His slingers helped him very greatly and severely afflicted the barbarians from a distance with their violent strokes. However, the Parthians, many of whom were heavily armed, fought stoutly. Pacorus himself fought valiantly and was killed.

A few courageously strove in vain for his body. Ventidius killed all the Parthian cavalry along the entire distance between the Orontes and Euphrates Rivers. He killed over twenty thousand, which was the most the Parthians had lost in any war. Any who tried to get home over the bridge were prevented by their enemies from doing so and were killed. Others fled into Commagene to King Antiochus. Thus, Ventidius again pursued the Parthians within Media and Mesopotamia, but would not drive them any farther for fear of the envy of Antony. {*Livy, l. 128. 14:159} {*Florus, l. 2. c. 19. s. 5-7. 1:319} {*Strabo, l. 16. c. 2. s. 8. 7:247,249} {*Velleius Paterculus, l. 2. c. 78. s. 1. 1:215} {*Josephus, Antiq., l. 14. c. 15. s. 7. (434) 7:673} {*Aulus Gellius, Attic Nights, l. 15. c. 4. s. 4. 3:73} {Justin, Trogus, l. 42. c. 4.} {*Plutarch, Antony, l. 1. c. 33. s. 4. 9:211} {*Frontinus, Stratagems, l. 1. c. 1. s. 6. 1:11} {*Frontinus, Stratagems, l. 2. c. 2. s. 5. 1:101} {*Dio, l. 49. (20) 5:381,383} {Eutropius, l. 7.} {Sextus Rufus, Breviary} {Orosius, l. 6. c. 18.}

5445. This very famous victory occurred in Syria Cyrrhestica. {*Plutarch, Antony, l. 1. c. 34. s. 1. 9:213} {*Dio, l. 49. (19) 5:381} {*Strabo, l. 16. c. 2. s. 8. 7:247,249} Pacorus was killed on the same day of the year on which, fourteen years earlier, his father Orodes had killed Crassus through his captain, Surenas. {*Dio, l. 49. (21) 5:385} {Eutropius, l. 7.} {Sextus Rufus, Breviary} {Orosius, l. 6. c. 18.} This happened in the month of June. {*Ovid, Fasti, l. 6. (465-468) 5:355}

5446. Ventidius made an expedition against those who had revolted and subdued them. {*Plutarch, Antony, l. 1. c. 34. s. 2. 9:213} The Syrians had loved Pacorus very much for his justice and clemency and had never had a king like him. {*Dio, l. 49. (21) 5:383} So when Syria was uncertain about the outcome of the war, Ventidius carried about Pacorus' head to all the cities that had revolted, thereby easily restoring order without any fighting. {*Dio, l. 49. (21) 5:383} {*Florus, l. 2. c. 19. s. 7. 1:319} [E720]

5447. Orodes, having previously heard that Syria had been wasted and Asia had been seized by the Parthians, gloried in the fact that Pacorus had conquered the Romans. When he suddenly heard of his son's death and the destruction of his army, he went mad out of sheer grief. For many days, he spoke to no one, nor ate anything. He was speechless, so that he seemed to have been stricken dumb. After many days, when grief had restored his voice, he did nothing but call out to Pacorus to speak and stand beside him. Then again, with many tears, he would bewail his loss. {Justin, Trogus, l. 42. c. 4.} [K430]

5448. At Rome, the Senate decreed processions and a triumph for this victory against the Parthians. As of yet, Ventidius had never triumphed, because, according to the laws, he was not the general in charge of the province. These things were decreed for Antony, because,

with the death of Pacorus, he seemed to have amply atoned for the defeat of Crassus. {*Dio, l. 49. (21) 5:385}

5449. Ventidius led his army against Antiochus, the Commagenian, on the pretext that he had not given him the refugees, but what he really wanted was all of Antiochus' treasure. {*Dio, l. 49. (20) 5:383}

5450. Ventidius attacked Antiochus and besieged him in Samosata. Antiochus promised to give Ventidius a thousand talents and obey Antony. Ventidius ordered him to send envoys to Antony to ask him for peace, because Antony had now advanced into the neighbourhood and would not allow Ventidius to make peace with Antiochus. {*Plutarch, Antony, l. 1. c. 34. s. 2,3. 9:213}

5451. Antony ordered Ventidius to send Machaeras to help Herod with two legions and a thousand cavalry. {*Josephus, Antiq., l. 14. c. 15. s. 7. (434) 7:673} Antony was happy about, but envious of, both the victories Ventidius had gained over Labienus and Pacorus. Ventidius had previously had great success all by himself. Although processions and a triumph were decreed to Antony for both the victories that Ventidius had won, Antony nevertheless removed him from his charge and from the government of Syria, and never used his help again. Thus wrote Dio. {*Dio, l. 49. (21) 5:385} However, Plutarch wrote that Ventidius was honoured by Antony and that he was sent to the triumph by Antony. {*Plutarch, Antony, l. 1. c. 34. s. 4. 9:215}

5452. Antigonus wrote to Machaeras, seeking his support and offering him a large bribe. Machaeras was not prepared to show such contempt for his superior's orders and declined. Also, Herod had offered him a larger bribe. However, against Herod's wishes, he feigned friendship and went to Antigonus to spy into his actions. Antigonus suspected him and did not allow him in, but drove him from the walls. Machaeras realised that Herod had given him good advice and that he had been wrong for not following it. So he was forced to retire to Emmaus and rejoin Herod. On his march, he killed all the Jews he encountered, whether friend or foe, for he was angry at the things that had happened. Herod was grieved by his actions and went to Samaria, planning to go to Antony to say that he needed different men from those who were doing him more harm than his enemies. Herod determined to subdue Antigonus by himself. Machaeras caught up to him and begged him to stay or, if he was determined to go on, at least to give him his brother Joseph, so that together they could make war against Antigonus. After much entreaty, Herod was reconciled to Machaeras. He left Joseph, his brother, with the army and ordered him, in his absence, to fight with Antigonus, but take no unnecessary risks. Herod hurried to Antony, whom he found assaulting Samosata, a city near the Euphrates River. Herod brought auxiliaries of foot soldiers and cavalry with him. {*Josephus, Antiq., l. 14. c. 15. s. 7,8. (435-438) 7:675,677} {*Josephus, Jewish War, l. 1. c. 16. s. 6,7. (318-320) 2:149,151} (The details in these two footnotes conflict with each other. Editor.)

5453. When Herod arrived at Antioch, he found many there who wanted to help Antony, but did not dare to go, because the barbarians were lying in wait along the way. Herod offered to escort them and so he came to Samosata to Antony, who had defeated the barbarians once or twice. Antony entertained Herod very honourably and he was much praised for his valour. {*Josephus, Antiq., l. 14. c. 15. s. 8,9. (439-446) 7:677,679} {*Josephus, Jewish War, l. 1. c. 16. s. 7. (321) 2:151}

5454. The siege of Samosata lasted for a long time and the besieged acted valiantly, because they had given up hope of peace. {*Plutarch, Antony, l. 1. c. 34. s. 3,4. 9:213} [K431] Antony suspected that his soldiers were alienated from him, because he had treated Ventidius very poorly, as Dio wrote. Privately, he mentioned some hope of peace to enable him to depart with honour. When he could only receive two hostages who were not noblemen and refused to give him any money, he granted peace to Antiochus and was satisfied with three hundred talents. Antiochus yielded to him so that he could put Alexander to death, who had earlier fled from him to the Romans. {*Dio, l. 49. (22) 5:385,387} {*Plutarch, Antony, l. 1. c. 34. s. 4. 9:213,215} {Orosius, l. 6. c. 18.} [E721]

## 3966a AM, 4675 JP, 39 BC

5455. Therefore this war was concluded. Antony made Gaius Sossius the governor of Syria and Cilicia, leaving him an army. {*Dio, l. 49. (22) 5:387} {*Josephus, Antiq., l. 14. c. 15. s. 9. (447) 7:681} He had repeatedly been most successful while engaged in fighting in Syria. {*Plutarch, Antony, l. 1. c. 34. s. 6. 9:215}

5456. Plutarch wrote that after the affairs in Syria had been settled somewhat, Antony returned to Athens. Josephus said that he went into Egypt, while Dio said he intended to go to Italy. It seems that he may first have returned to Athens and from there crossed over to Italy, after having been called there by Caesar, and then have returned to Athens to sail to Egypt, to spend the winter with Cleopatra. He was sent for by Caesar from Athens, to enable them to consult together about the war against Sextus Pompeius. He came as far as Brundisium with a few men, but did not find Caesar there on the appointed day. He was frightened by a certain prodigy: a wolf had entered his headquarters and killed some soldiers. Therefore, he sailed back to Greece under the pretence of the urgency of the Parthian war.

Caesar was not pleased that he had not waited for him. {*Appian, Civil Wars, l. 5. c. 9. (78,79) 4:511,513} {*Dio, l. 48. (46) 5:319}

5457. Joseph forgot his brother Herod's orders and while he was away, went toward Jericho with his own men and five Roman cohorts given to him by Machaeras. He wanted to harvest the enemies' grain, which was now ripe, and so he camped in the mountains. The Roman cohorts were mostly raw soldiers, unskilled in the art of military matters, because most of them had been taken from Syria. He was surrounded by the enemies there and lost six cohorts. He fought valiantly, but was killed. When Antigonus found the dead bodies, he was so enraged that he whipped the dead body of Joseph, even though Pheroras, his brother, offered fifty talents to redeem it. After this, the Galileans revolted from their governors and drowned any who belonged to Herod's side in the lake. Idumea, where Machaeras was fortifying Gitta at the time, also had many seditions. {*Josephus, Jewish War, l. 1. c. 17. s. 1. (323-326) 2:151,153} {*Josephus, Antiq., l. 14. c. 15. s. 10. (448-450) 7:681,683}

5458. Antony ordered Gaius Sossius to help Herod against Antigonus and sent two cohorts with him to Judea. {*Josephus, Jewish War, l. 1. c. 17. s. 2. (326) 2:151} {*Josephus, Antiq., l. 14. c. 15. s. 9. (447) 7:681} He subdued the Aradians, who had endured a siege, but were now worn out with famine and sickness. {*Dio, l. 49. (22) 5:387} Herod was at Daphne, in the suburbs of Antioch, when he found out about his brother's death and the military defeat. Herod had expected this, because of some dreams that he had previously, so he hurried and came to Mount Libanus (Lebanon). From there, he took eight hundred men with him, as well as leading one cohort of the Romans, and arrived at Ptolemais. He left Ptolemais by night with the army and crossed Galilee. {*Josephus, Jewish War, l. 1. c. 17. s. 3. (328,329) 2:155} {*Josephus, Antiq., l. 14. c. 15. s. 11. (451,452) 7:683}

5459. He met his enemies and defeated them, forcing them into the citadel from which they had come the day before. [K432] When Herod attacked at daybreak, he was forced to stop, because of a severe storm, and led his men into the adjoining villages. When another cohort arrived from Antony, those who held the citadel were dismayed and abandoned it at night. Herod hurried to Jericho intent on avenging his brother's death. When he arrived, he arranged a feast for the noblemen. After the feast was over and the guests had been dismissed, he retired to his lodging. The room where they had eaten, which was now empty, collapsed and no one was hurt. By this event, everyone considered Herod to be beloved by God since he had so providentially preserved him. {*Josephus, Jewish War, l. 1. c. 17. s. 3. (329-331) 2:155,157} {*Josephus, Antiq., l. 14. c. 15. s. 11. (453-455) 7:683,685}

5460. The next day, six thousand of the enemies came down from the tops of the mountains to fight with Herod. They terrified the Romans with their arrows and stones and chased Herod's soldiers, so that the king himself received a wound in his side. {*Josephus, Jewish War, l. 1. c. 17. s. 4. (332) 2:157} {*Josephus, Antiq., l. 14. c. 15. s. 12. (456) 7:685}

5461. Antigonus sent a captain by the name of Pappus into Samaria who was eager to show off the size of his forces and fought against Machaeras. Herod had taken five towns and killed two thousand of the garrison soldiers. Then he set the towns on fire and marched against Pappus, who was camped at a village called Isana, or Cana. {*Josephus, Jewish War, l. 1. c. 17. s. 5. (332,333) 2:157} {*Josephus, Antiq., l. 14. c. 15. s. 12. (457,458) 7:685}

5462. Many joined Herod from Jericho and Judea. When he saw that the enemy was so bold as to come to battle with him, he fought and defeated them. He was so inflamed with a desire to revenge his brother's death, that he killed those who fled, following them right into the village. The houses were filled with soldiers and some fled to the tops of the houses for safety. They, too, were overcome and the houses thrown down. He found every conceivable place filled with soldiers who had been miserably crushed to death. The rest fled in companies and were very afraid. Herod at once went to Jerusalem and would have ended the war, had not a severe winter storm hindered him. Now Antigonus began to think of fleeing and abandoning the city. {*Josephus, Jewish War, l. 1. c. 17. s. 6. (335-339) 2:157,159} {*Josephus, Antiq., l. 14. c. 15. s. 12. (458-461) 7:687}

5463. In the evening, when Herod had dismissed his friends to refresh themselves, he was still sweating in his armour and went into a chamber to wash himself, accompanied only by one servant. [E722] Some of his enemies, who were armed, were inside hiding in fear. While he was naked and washing himself, one of these men, with his sword drawn, hurried to escape through the doors, followed by a second and then a third—all of them were armed. They were so astonished, that they were glad to save themselves and did Herod no harm. The next day, Herod cut off Pappus' head and sent it to his brother, Pheroras, in revenge for Herod's brother's death, whom Pappus had killed; for it was Pappus who had killed Joseph with his own hand. {*Josephus, Jewish War, l. 1. c. 17. s. 7,8. (340-342) 2:159,161} {*Josephus, Antiq., l. 14. c. 15. s. 13. (462-464) 7:689}

5464. At Rome, on the 5th of the Calends of December (November 27), Publius Ventidius Bassus had a triumph for his victory at the Taurus Mountains and then over the Parthians, as recorded in the Marble Records of the Triumphs. {Gruter, Inscriptions, p. 297.} Ventidius Bassus was a man of lowly parentage who, through the favour of Antony, rose to such heights of honour, that he was made governor of the eastern provinces. He triumphed for his conquests over Labienus and Pacorus and the Parthians, when he himself had twice (if we may believe Massurius in Pliny) been led in triumph with other captives. {*Velleius Paterculus, l. 2. c. 65. s. 3. 1:191} {*Valerius Maximus, l. 6. c. 9. s. 9. 2:89} {*Pliny, l. 7. c. 43. 2:597} {*Aulus Gellius, Attic Nights, l. 15. c. 4. s. 4. 3:73} {*Plutarch, Antony, l. 1. c. 34. s. 4,5. 9:215} {*Dio, l. 49. (21) 5:385} {Eutropius, l. 7.} [K433] {See note on 3962a AM. <<5277>>}

## 3966b AM, 4676 JP, 38 BC

5465. Spain was now controlled by Caesar Octavius, after having been subdued by Domitius Calvinus, the proconsul. The Spaniards began their computation of time from the first of January of this year, as may be understood from others and as well as from Eulogius, the archbishop of Toledo, in his Memorial of the Saints.

5465a. In the beginning of spring, Antony arrived at Tarentum with three hundred ships, from Syria, according to Dio, or from Athens, according to Appian. He came to help Caesar against Sextus Pompeius and when Caesar refused his help, Antony took it badly. However, he stayed there nonetheless, since he had unwillingly spent so much on this navy and because he needed the Italian legions for the Parthian war, he intended to exchange his fleet for them. Even though, by the agreement, both of them had power to raise soldiers in Italy, this would, in fact, be very difficult for him, since Italy had been allocated by lot to Caesar. Therefore, he sent Octavia (who had accompanied him from Greece, who was also with child at the time and by whom Antony previously had a second daughter) to her brother, Caesar, in the hope that she would make peace between them. She helped arrange matters so that Antony would deliver a hundred and twenty ships to Caesar at Tarentum. (Plutarch wrote a hundred warships.) For these, Caesar promised that he would send Antony from Italy δυο ταγματα (as it is in Plutarch), or twenty thousand soldiers (as Appian wrote). Moreover, besides the covenants, Octavia obtained twenty small ships for her brother from Antony, as Plutarch stated, or ten combination warship and merchant vessels, which were galleys of three tiers of oars, as Appian stated. In return, Caesar gave Octavia a thousand men for Antony's guard and let Antony choose them. {*Plutarch, Antony, l. 1. c. 35. 9:215,217} {*Appian, Civil Wars, l. 5. c. 10. (93-95) 4:539} {*Dio, l. 48. (54) 5:335,337} To strengthen the alliance, Caesar betrothed his daughter Julia to Antyllus, the son of Antony, and Antony betrothed his daughter by Octavia to Domitius Ahenobarbus, although he was guilty of the murder of Julius Caesar and had been proscribed. These things were only done for show and they had no intention of following through on them, but simply did them for expediency's sake. {*Dio, l. 48. (54) 5:337}

5466. After the five year term of the triumvirate had expired, they extended their power for another five years without asking for the people's consent. {*Dio, l. 48. (54) 5:337} {*Appian, Civil Wars, l. 5. c. 10. (95) 4:539} Antony sent Octavia back to Italy, out of fear of exposing her to danger in the Parthian war. He commended the children that he had, both by her and Fulvia, to Caesar, and went into Syria. {*Plutarch, Antony, l. 1. c. 35. s. 5. 9:217} {*Appian, Civil Wars, l. 5. c. 10. (95) 4:539} {*Dio, l. 48. (54) 5:337}

5467. Cleopatra built a new library in the same spot where the old one at Alexandria had been burned in Julius Caesar's time. The library was called the daughter of the former one, as Epiphanius affirmed. {Epiphanius, De Mensuris et Ponderibus} From the seventh year of Ptolemy Philadelphus, in which we have shown, in the year 277 BC, or 4437 JP, that the previous library was built, Epiphanius incorrectly calculated two hundred and forty-nine years to this time, which would bring us to the year 29 BC, or 4686 JP, which was one year after Cleopatra's death. The main cause of his error was this: Epiphanius attributed thirty-two years to the reign of Cleopatra, instead of twenty-two. [K434] If we deduct ten years from both, we make the time between the founding of the two libraries, two hundred and thirty-nine years. Plutarch wrote that, at this time, Calvisius objected to Antony: {*Plutarch, Antony, l. 1. c. 59. s. 5,6. 9:271}

"that Antony had given to Cleopatra the libraries that were at Pergamum, which contained two hundred thousand entire books or single volumes."

5468. Strabo spoke of κατοικιαν του Περγαμου, the settlement of Pergamum, not of libraries that were extant in his time. {*Strabo, l. 13. c. 4. s. 2. 6:167} Lipsius incorrectly thought this. {Lipsius, Syntagma of Libraries, l. 4.}

5469. In the beginning of the third year after Herod had been declared king at Rome, he came with an army to Jerusalem and camped near the city. [E723] He soon moved closer to the place where he first planned to assault the walls. Placing his tents before the temple, he intended to assail the walls where Pompey had done in the past. To that end, he surrounded the place with three bulwarks and erected his batteries with the help of many workmen. He brought materials from every nearby place. He placed suitable men to oversee the works, while he went to Samaria to solemnise his marriage with Mariamme, the daughter of Alexander, son of Aristobulus. She had earlier been betrothed to him. {*Josephus, Antiq., l. 14. c. 15. s. 14. (465-467) 7:689} {*Josephus, Jewish War, l. 1. c. 17. s. 8. (343,344) 2:161}

5470. After the marriage, Sossius came through Phoenicia, after he had sent his army overland. He arrived there himself with many cavalry and foot soldiers. Herod also came, from Samaria, with a considerable army of thirty thousand men. He had eleven legions of foot soldiers and six thousand cavalry in addition to the Syrian auxiliaries, who were not included in the total. He made their camp at the north wall of the city. Two generals were over the army, Herod and Sossius, as Sossius had been sent by Antony to help Herod. Herod started this war to oust Antigonus, who was an enemy of the people of Rome, and to enable him to be king in his place as the Senate had decreed. {*Josephus, Antiq., l. 14. c. 16. s. 1. (468,469) 7:691} {*Josephus, Jewish War, l. 1. c. 17. s. 9. (345,346) 2:161,163}

5471. The Jews from the whole country had gathered together at Jerusalem and were being besieged within the walls. They offered valiant resistance, boasted much about the temple of the Lord and wished the people well, saying that God would not forsake his people in their danger. They destroyed all the provisions, for both men and animals, which were outside the city, secretly stole supplies and made provisions very scarce for the besiegers. However, Herod provided well for this. He placed ambushes in suitable places and prevented their thievery, while sending his soldiers to fetch provisions from afar, so that in a short time the army was well-furnished with all their supplies. {*Josephus, Antiq., l. 14. c. 16. s. 2. (470-472) 7:691,693} {*Josephus, Jewish War, l. 1. c. 18. s. 1,2. (347-349) 2:163,165}

5472. The large number of workmen easily finished the three bulwarks. It was now summer and the work went on and he was unhindered by bad weather. He often battered the walls with his engines and attacked every part of it. The besieged fought valiantly and used all their cunning to evade their enemies' endeavours. They often sallied out and set fire to their works, some of which had been completed, while some were still under construction. They fought valiantly hand-to-hand with the Romans and were just as brave, but not as well-trained, as the Romans were. {*Josephus, Antiq., l. 14. c. 16. s. 2. (473-475) 7:693,695} {*Josephus, Jewish War, l. 1. c. 18. s. 1. (349-351) 2:163,165}

## 3967a AM, 4676 JP, 38 BC

5473. The sabbatical year was now approaching and brought a famine to the Jews who were besieged. In spite of this, they built a new wall to replace the sections which had been battered down by the engines. [K435] They countermined the enemies' mines, so that sometimes they fought hand-to-hand underground and using despair rather than courage, they held out to the last. {*Josephus,

*Antiq., l. 14. c. 16. s. 2. (475) 7:695}* Pollion, the Pharisee, and his disciple, Samaias, advised them to let Herod into the city, saying that, because of their sins, it was inevitable that Herod would be their king. {*Josephus, Antiq., l. 14. c. 9. s. 4. (175,176) 7:543} {*Josephus, Antiq., l. 15. c. 1. s. 1. (3,4) 8:3,5}*

*5474.* For five months they held out in the siege in spite of the large army besieging them. {*Josephus, Jewish War, l. 1. c. 18. s. 1. (351) 2:165}* Finally, twenty of Herod's best soldiers got on the wall and were followed by the centurions of Sossius. {*Josephus, Antiq., l. 14. c. 16. s. 2. (476) 7:695}*

*5475.* The first wall was taken on the fortieth day and the second one on the fiftieth. Some galleries around the temple were burned, for which Herod blamed Antigonus, so that the people would hate him. The outer part of the temple was taken and then the lower city. The Jews fled into the inner part of the temple and the upper city. Fearing that they would be hindered from offering the daily sacrifices to God, they sent envoys to ask permission that those beasts only might be brought in. Herod granted this, in the hope that they would then be less obstinate and submit themselves. {*Josephus, Antiq., l. 14. c. 16. s. 2. (476,477) 7:697}*

## 3967b AM, 4677 JP, 37 BC

*5476.* When Herod saw that this was not going to happen and that the besieged were obstinately fighting to protect the government of Antigonus, Herod made a general assault and took the city. {*Josephus, Antiq., l. 14. c. 16. s. 4. (487) 7:701}* This was on the Calends of January (January 1), 37 BC, or 4677 JP, on the 2nd day of the month of Chisleu. According to the eastern people's records of the civil year, this was in the 3rd month, on the 28th day, when the Jews kept a solemn fast in memory of the holy scroll that was burned by Jehoiakim. {*See note on 3941a AM. <<4528>>}*

*5477.* The Calends of January (January 1), because of the incorrect intercalating done at Rome at that time, was really the last day of December. This concluded the first five years of the triumviri and also the consulship of Claudius and Norbanus, to whom this calamity of the Jews was mentioned by Dio. {*Dio, l. 49. (22,23) 5:387,389}* The next day, Marcus Vipsanius Agrippa and Lucius Caninius Gallus entered their consulships at Rome. Josephus stated: {*Josephus, Antiq., l. 14. c. 16. s. 4. (487) 7:701} [E724]*

> "This calamity of Jerusalem happened in the consulship of Marcus Agrippa and Caninius Gallus in the 185th Olympiad (that is, in the third year), in the third month, on a solemn fast day. It was as if the calamity that had happened to the Jews twenty-seven years earlier was about to repeat itself again

at the same time for the city was taken by Herod on the same day."

*5478.* However, this interval of time exceeded the true account by one year, unless you interpret μεταετη κζ as being in the year after the twenty-seventh, as in Mark. {*Mr 8:31}* It was said that Christ would rise again, μετα πτιριετη Χηονοκ, *after three days,* which is more clearly explained in Matthew as τηπειτη ιμιρα, *on the third day* {*Mt 16:21}.* In the Apocrypha {*Apc 2Ma 14:1}* μοθριετη χηιρτη, *after the time of three years,* is explained by the interpreters as being the third year. In the Catalogue of the Station of Julius Africanus, 211th Olympiad, the games of Olympus are said to have been celebrated by Nero, not at a lawful time, but μιτα ξτη δυο, that is, in the second year of that Olympiad. {*Eusebius, Scaliger's Greek Eusebius, p. 221}* Even Josephus himself, in his Jewish War, stated μτι ετη δυο and in his Antiquities said δευ τιρω ουτει. {*Josephus, Jewish War - Greek Copy, l. 1. c. 11.} {Josephus, Antiq. Greek Copy, l. 14. c. 23} [K436]* (References are to original 1654 publication of Josephus. Greek in this passage is almost unreadable in the original document. Editor.)

*5479.* After the city was captured, it was filled with the bodies of the murdered. The Romans were incensed that they had been forced to continue the siege for so long and the Herodian Jews tried to eliminate the opposing faction, so there were continual slaughters through the porches and houses. The reverence of the temple did not save the suppliants. They spared no one, regardless of age or gender, not even children. Although Herod begged and entreated them to stop, no one obeyed him, but they all continued as if mad and showed their cruelty without respect of age. {*Josephus, Antiq., l. 14. c. 16. s. 2. (479,480) 7:697} {*Josephus, Jewish War, l. 1. c. 18. s. 2. (351,352) 2:165}*

*5480.* Antigonus came down from the town and fell at Sossius' feet. Sossius did not show him any pity because of the change in his fortune, but insulted him by calling him Madam Antigone. He put him in prison and set keepers over him. {*Josephus, Antiq., l. 14. c. 16. s. 2. (481) 7:697,699} {*Josephus, Jewish War, l. 1. c. 18. s. 2. (353) 2:165,167}*

*5481.* When a number of mercenaries rushed into the temple and even into its inner sanctuary, Herod restrained them by entreaty, some by threats and some by force of arms. He thought his victory would be worse for him than if he had been defeated, if any of those things which it was not lawful to see, were to be seen by the common people. He forbade any plundering in the city, as much as he was able. He entreated Sossius, as well, and asked if the Romans wanted to make him king of a wilderness, since the city was so depopulated by pillaging and murders. Sossius replied that the soldiers wanted the plunder of the city because of the long siege they had endured. Herod answered that he would reward every man from his own treasury and so he freed the city from any further trouble. He kept his promise and generously gave gifts to the soldiers and proportionally to the commanders and royally to Sossius. Hence, Sossius offered a crown of gold to God and left Jerusalem, taking Antigonus with him as a prisoner to Antony. {*Josephus, Antiq., l. 14. c. 16. s. 3,4. (482-488) 7:699,701} {*Josephus, Jewish War, l. 1. c. 18. s. 3. (354-357) 2:167}

5482. Herod made a distinction between the people of the city. He promoted those on his side and daily killed some of those on the opposing side. {*Josephus, Jewish War, l. 1. c. 18. s. 4. (358) 2:167,169} {*Josephus, Antiq., l. 15. c. 1. s. 1. (1,2) 8:3} Among those whom he killed were all those judges of the great Sanhedrin who had accused him of some capital crime before he was king. He spared Pollion, the Pharisee, and his disciple, Samaias, and highly honoured them. {*Josephus, Antiq., l. 14. c. 9. s. 4. (175,176) 7:543} {*Josephus, Antiq., l. 15. c. 1. s. 1. (3,4) 8:3,5}

5483. He gathered together all the royal ornaments. By collections and by taking away from rich men, he acquired a large amount of gold and silver, which he gave to Antony and his soldiers. He put to death forty-five of Antigonus' chief noblemen and set a watch at the doors so that none of the noblemen would be carried out under the pretence of being dead. All the gold or silver that was found was brought to Herod, so that there was no end to these miseries. The covetousness of the needy conqueror consumed all their goods. Since it was a sabbatical year, the fields were not being tilled, for it was unlawful to sow them. {*Josephus, Jewish War, l. 1. c. 18. s. 4. (359) 2:169} {*Josephus, Antiq., l. 15. c. 1. s. 2. (5-7) 8:5}

5484. These miserable times were witnessed by the priest Zacharias and his wife Elizabeth. Of the remains of David's family, Heli and Joseph saw these things. It was also witnessed by Anna, the prophetess, of the tribe of Asher, and by Simeon the Just, who received an answer from the Holy Spirit that he should not see death until he had seen the Lord's Christ. {Lu 2:26} [K437]

5485. Antony received Antigonus, intending to keep him prisoner with him until his triumph. He realised that Herod was afraid in case Antigonus, when he was brought to Rome by Antony, would contend with Herod before the Senate for his right to the kingdom. Antony heard that the country was ready to revolt out of hatred for Herod and that they favoured Antigonus. Antony received large sums of money from Herod and cut off Antigonus' head at Antioch, after having given him the vain hope of life right up to the end. Once this had been done, Herod was totally free from fear. The government of the Asmoneans had now ended. {*Josephus, Jewish War, l.

l. c. 18. s. 3. (357) 2:167} {*Josephus, Antiq., l. 14. c. 16. s. 4. (489-491) 7:701,703} {*Josephus, Antiq., l. 20. c. 10. s. 4. (245,246) 10:131} [E725]

5486. Two years and seven months elapsed from the beginning of the priesthood and government of Antigonus to the taking of Jerusalem. Also reckoning from this starting point, Antigonus was killed by Antony in the third year of the reign of both Antigonus and Herod. This was written in the fifty-second chapter of the Jewish History, which was written in Arabic and set forth in the Paris Bible of many languages. However, Josephus attributed three years and three months to Antigonus. {*Josephus, Antiq., l. 20. c. 10. s. 4. (245) 10:131} If this included the time up until his death, it would extend to August of this year. According to our account, from the beginning of the rise of Judas Maccabeus until now, a hundred and twenty-six years and two or three months elapsed. Josephus agreed, writing that the time from the founding of the government of the Asmoneans, until it ended and Antigonus was killed, was one hundred and twenty-six years. {*Josephus, Antiq., l. 14. c. 16. s. 4. (490) 7:703} However, Josephus contradicted himself, stating elsewhere that from the beginning of Judas Maccabeus to the beginning of the third year of the reign of Herod, when the siege of Jerusalem began, was a hundred and twenty-five years. {*Josephus, Antiq., l. 17. c. 6. s. 3. (162) 8:447}

5487. Other foreign writers have written concerning the taking of Jerusalem and the death of Antigonus. Livy referred to this event in his epitome: {*Livy, l. 128. 14:159}

"The Jews were also subdued by Antony's deputies."

5488. So said the old books, where it was written:

"The envoys of the Jews were killed by Antony."

5489. We have the following record of the death of Antigonus preserved by Josephus from the books of Strabo, the Cappadocian: {*Josephus, Antiq., l. 15. c. 1. s. 2. (8-10) 8:5,7}

"Antony brought Antigonus, the Jew, to Antioch and had him beheaded. He was presumed to be the first of the Romans to have put a king to death in this manner, because he thought that the Jews could not tolerate Herod as their king while Antigonus was alive. No matter how Herod oppressed them, they would not recognise him as king because they held Antigonus in such high esteem. Therefore, it was thought fit to blot out his memory by some ignominious death and lessen the public hatred against Herod."

5490. Plutarch wrote: {*Plutarch, Antony, l. 1. c. 36. s. 2. 9:219}

"He bestowed tetrarchies of great countries on many private men and took away kingdoms from many, such as from Antigonus, the Jew, whom he brought forth and beheaded. No king was ever killed in this way before."

5491. Dio, when writing about Sossius, also mentioned this: {*Dio, l. 49. (22) 5:387}

"He conquered Antigonus, who had killed a garrison of the Romans which he had with him. Sossius was defeated in battle at Jerusalem and forced to flee. The Jews (a country of implacable anger, once it is stirred) did many wrongs to the Romans, but suffered much more themselves. First of those who were taken were fighting for the temple of their God and then rested on a Saturday. So excessive were they in their devotion to religion that the first set of prisoners, those who had been captured along with the temple, obtained leave from Sossius, when the Sabbath day came around again, and went up into the temple and there performed all the customary rites, together with the rest of the people. [K438] Antony made Herod king over these people. Antony killed Antigonus, after he had scourged him and tied him to a post. This had never before been done to any king by the Romans."

5492. That is, he was beheaded at a post. Concerning this, see the following work. {Excercitation of Causabon on Baronius, l. 1. c. 7.} This event happened when:

"Claudius and Norbanus were consuls"

5493. Dio implied this. {*Dio, l. 49. (23) 5:389} It is true of Antigonus' defeat and of the taking of Jerusalem, but not as far as the death of Antigonus is concerned. He died when Marcus Agrippa and Caninius or Canidius Gallus were consuls, in the next year.

5494. Nothing of note was done by the Romans this year in Syria, for Antony spent the whole year in going into and returning from Italy. Sossius, fearing the envy and anger of Antony, whiled away that time and did no gallant actions, so as not to offend Antony. He hoped to curry favour with Antony by doing nothing. {*Dio, l. 49. (23) 5:389} When Antony returned from Italy, he replaced him with Plancus as the governor of Syria and appointed Gaius Furnius as his lieutenant in Asia. {*Appian, Civil Wars, l. 5. c. 14. (137) 4:603} {*Appian, Civil Wars, l. 5. c. 14. (144) 4:615} {*Dio, l. 48. (26) 5:275} {*Dio, l. 49. (17) 5:377}

### 3968a AM, 4677 JP, 37 BC

5495. After Orodes, the king of the Parthians, had long mourned for his son, he had more problems. He had to select a successor from his thirty sons to replace Pacorus. Many of his concubines, who had borne him many sons, pestered the old man to make their son the new king.

Finally, he selected the oldest, who was the worst of them all, and made him king. {Justin, Trogus, l. 42. c. 4.} {*Dio, l. 49. (23) 5:389} This was Phraates III, called Phraortes by Plutarch. {*Plutarch, Antony, l. 1. c. 52. s. 1. 9:255} He is called Phraates by the compiler of Appian's Parthian History, which he transcribed word for word from Plutarch, and by Plutarch himself at the end of his book. {*Plutarch, Crassus, l. 1. c. 33. s. 5. 3:423} Horace, too, referred to this time: {*Horace, Odes, l. 2. c. 2. (17) 1:111} [E726]

"Phraates was restored to Cyrus' throne."

5496. He received the kingdom by treachery and killed his brothers, who had been born to the daughter of Antiochus. He did this, because they surpassed him in every virtue and related to him on his mother's side. He also killed his father Orodes. {*Dio, l. 49. (23) 5:389} He poisoned him as he lay sick with the dropsy. Orodes was beginning to recover, so Phraates stopped the slow poisoning and took a shorter route by strangling him. {*Plutarch, Crassus, l. 1. c. 33. s. 5. 3:423}

5497. After Phraates had killed his father, he killed all his brothers. When he saw that the nobility hated him for his wicked acts, he ordered that his son, who was now fully grown, also be killed, so that there would be no one else to make king. {Justin, Trogus, l. 42. c. 5.}

5498. After this, Phraates set about killing the nobility and doing many wicked things. Many of the chief men fled from him, going where they could, and some, like Monaeses, who was a powerful nobleman, fled to Antony. {*Plutarch, Antony, l. 1. c. 37. s. 1. 9:219} {*Dio, l. 49. (23) 5:389} This happened when Agrippa and Gallus were consuls. {*Dio, l. 49. (24) 5:389}

### 3968b AM, 4678 JP, 36 BC

5499. The rest of the winter, when Gellius and Nerva were consuls, Publius Canidius Crassus was left as deputy by Antony. [K439] Around the region of Armenia, he led his army against the Iberians. He defeated their king, Pharnabazus, in battle and compelled him to join forces with him. He went into Albania with him and likewise allied that country to himself, along with Zober, their king. {*Dio, l. 49. (24) 5:391} He went as far as the Caucasus Mountains with the conquered Armenians and the kings of the Iberians and Albanians, making Antony's name famous among the barbarous countries. {*Plutarch, Antony, l. 1. c. 34. s. 6. 9:215} {*Strabo, l. 11. c. 3. s. 5.5:221} (In Loeb, the footnote for Strabo incorrectly attributed this to Crassus the triumvir. Editor.)

5500. Antony was puffed up with these successes and relied very heavily on Monaeses, committing the Parthian war to him. Antony promised him the kingdom of the Parthians and granted him the revenues of those cities of theirs which were subject to the Romans. He was to receive this as long as the war lasted. {*Dio, l. 49. (24) 5:391} Antony compared the fortune of Monaeses with that of Themistocles and equally, his own riches and magnificence to that of the kings of Persia. He gave Monaeses three cities: Larisa, Arethusa and Hierapolis, formerly called Bambyce. {*Plutarch, Antony, l. 1. c. 37. s. 1. 9:221}

5501. Phraates, the king of the Parthians, courteously entertained the captive king, Hyrcanus, because of his noble descent. He took him from prison and allowed him to live in Babylon, where many Jews lived. These Jews honoured him as their king and high priest. All those millions of Jews, who in olden times had been deported beyond the Euphrates River by the Assyrians (or Babylonians) also honoured Hyrcanus. Once he realised that Herod had been made king, he began to hope for a favour from Herod, as Hyrcanus had saved Herod when he had been on trial for his life. Therefore, he began to consult with the Jews, who, out of duty, came to visit him, about his journey. In spite of all their wise admonitions, he could not be persuaded against his desire to return to his own country. The tetrarchy of Herod had been added to his former country. Herod wanted to get his hands on Hyrcanus and wrote him that he would request his release from Phraates and the Jews of that land. Herod said that the Jews ought not to envy the joint power that he would enjoy with his son-in-law. Herod said that the time had now come, when he would be able to repay the one who had preserved him in the past. Herod also sent Saramalla, his envoy, to Phraates himself, with large presents to win his favour, so that Phraates would not prevent Herod from showing kindness to Hyrcanus. Herod then received Hyrcanus, who had been sent by the Parthians. He had been honourably provided for by the Jews for the expenses of his journey. Herod entertained him with every honour and gave him the upper seat in all the assemblies and the most honourable place at all the feasts. He called him father and so in this way lulled him into a false sense of security. {*Josephus, Antiq., l. 15. c. 2. s. 1-4. (11-22) 8:7-13}

5502. Herod saw to it that none of the nobility would be appointed high priest. He sent to Babylon for a priest of lowly parentage, with whom he was well-acquainted. He was of the family of the priests, but descended from those Jews who had been transported beyond the Euphrates River. This man's name was Ananel (or Hananeel) and Herod gave him the high priesthood. {*Josephus, Antiq., l. 15. c. 2. s. 4. (22) 8:13} [E727]

5503. Mark Antony rejected all honest and salutary counsel and sent Fonteius Capito to bring Cleopatra into Syria. {*Plutarch, Antony, l. 1. c. 36. s. 1. 9:217} She had no sooner arrived in Syria, than she thought about how she might get it into her possession. {*Josephus, Antiq., l. 15. c. 4. s. 1. (88) 8:43} [K440] She accused the Syrian noblemen to Antony and persuaded him to put them to death, so that she would more easily be able to take over their estates. {*Josephus, Jewish War, l. 1. c. 18. s. 4. (360) 2:169}

5504. She accused Lysanias, the son of Ptolemy (Mennaeus), the king of Chalcis and Iturea, of favouring the Parthians and had Antony execute him. {*Josephus, Antiq., l. 15. c. 4. s. 1. (92,93) 8:45} {*Dio, l. 49. (32) 5:407} (In Dio, Parthians should be read for Pacorus.) This was fifteen years after the death of his father Auletes, a fact which is derived from Porphyry, where the name of Lysanias is incorrectly written for Lysimachus. {Porphyry, Scaliger's Greek Eusebius, p. 226.}

5505. Antony made Amyntas, the secretary of Dejotarus, the prince of Galatia, to which he added part of Lycaonia and Pamphylia. {*Dio, l. 49. (32) 5:407} {*Strabo, l. 12. c. 5. s. 1. 5:469}

5506. Antony also made Archelaus, who was not descended from royalty, the king of Cappadocia. This Archelaus deposed Ariarathes (who was descended from those Archelauses who had waged war against the Romans), and his mother was the harlot called Glaphyra. {*Dio, l. 49. (32) 5:407} {*Strabo, l. 12. c. 2. s. 11. 5:371} From that lascivious epigram of Octavius Caesar, it appears that Antony was involved with Glaphyra. {Martial, l. 11. c. 21.}

5507. Alexandra, the daughter of Hyrcanus and wife of Alexander the son of Aristobulus and mother-in-law of Herod, took it badly that her son Aristobulus, the brother of Mariamme, was being condemned because during his lifetime someone from another place had usurped the high priesthood. She wrote to Cleopatra through a certain musician, asking her to request the priesthood from Antony for her son, but Cleopatra failed to do this. Quintus Dellius, a friend of Antony, who travelled into Judea from time to time, persuaded Alexandra to send the pictures of her son Aristobulus and her daughter Mariamme to Antony, maintaining that once Antony saw them, he would not deny them anything. These were sent. Dellius also added that they seemed to be of divine origin rather than of the human race, for he was busy on his own account, trying to entice Antony into sexual pleasures. {*Josephus, Antiq., l. 15. c. 2. s. 5,6. (23-27) 8:13,15} Dellius was the historian whom Plutarch mentioned and whose wanton letters to Cleopatra were common, as attested by Seneca. {*Seneca the Elder, Suasoriae, l. 1. c. 7. 2:497} Dio also implied as much and stated that Antony used him for immoral purposes. {*Dio, l. 49. (39) 5:421}

5508. Since Antony did not want to make Cleopatra jealous, he did not think it proper to send for a lady who was married to Herod. He wrote to Alexandra that she should send her son to him on some honest pretext, but added she should not do it if this would be burdensome to her. When Herod found out about this, he did not think it safe that Aristobulus, a young man of sixteen years, in the flower of his youth, should be sent to Antony, who was the most powerful of all the Romans and also very much given to lust. He therefore wrote back that if the youth left the kingdom, the whole country would be up in arms because the Jews wanted to revolt and have a new king. Antony was satisfied with Herod's reply. {*Josephus, Antiq., l. 15. c. 2. s. 6. (28-30) 8:15,17}

5509. In the Sicilian war, Caesar Octavius and Marcus Lepidus defeated Sextus Pompeius. Marcus Lepidus became proud about the ability of his twenty legions and attributed the whole victory to himself. [K441] He was bold enough to oppose Caesar and to claim Sicily for himself, but his army abandoned him and he was put out of the triumvirate. He was glad to beg Caesar for his life and goods and Caesar banished him to Circei. {*Livy, l. 129. 14:159,161} {*Velleius Paterculus, l. 2. c. 79,80. 1:217-221} {*Suetonius, Augustus, l. 2. c. 16. 1:169,171} {*Suetonius, Augustus, l. 2. c. 54. 1:235} {*Appian, Civil Wars, l. 5. c. 11-13. (97-127) 4:541-587} {*Dio, l. 49. (1-18) 5:339-380} {Orosius, l. 6. c. 18.}

5510. Sextus Pompeius, who had previously had a fleet of three hundred and fifty ships, now fled into Asia with only six or seven. {*Florus, l. 2. c. 18. s. 9. 1:317} Appian and Orosius wrote that he had seventeen ships. {*Appian, Civil Wars, l. 5. c. 12. (121) 4:579} {Orosius, l. 6. c. 18.} He intended to flee to Antony because the latter had saved his mother from a similar danger. {*Appian, Civil Wars, l. 5. c. 12. (122) 4:579}

5511. He put his daughter, his friends, his money and all his best things into the fastest ships he had left. Pompeius sailed by night and no one pursued him because he left secretly and Caesar was continually preoccupied with troubles from Lepidus. {*Dio, l. 49. (11) 5:363} In spite of this, after he had left Messana, Pompeius feared being followed and suspected the treachery of his companions. After he told them that he would set sail for the main sea, he put out the light which admirals' ships usually carry, and sailed along the coast of Italy. {*Dio, l. 49. (17) 5:375} When he arrived at the cape of Lacinium, he robbed the temple of Juno of all its offerings. {*Appian, Civil Wars, l. 5. c. 14. (133) 4:597}

5512. From there he sailed to Corcyra and into Cephallenia. He received others of his men who had been washed in there by a storm. [E728] After he had called them together, he took off his general's attire and told them that if they all stayed together, it would come about that they would not be able to be of sufficient help to each other nor would they be able to remain

hidden. If they dispersed, however, they could flee more easily, and so he advised everyone to fend for himself. Most of them followed his advice and went their various ways. He, together with some who stayed with him, went to Lesbos. {*Dio, l. 49. (17) 5:375,379} He stayed at Mitylene, where his father had left him before the battle of Pharsalia and from where he had picked him up again after the defeat. {*Appian, Civil Wars, l. 5. c. 14. (133) 4:597}

5513. The Parthians were troubled by the defection of Monaeses to Antony and Phraates was quite worried. He sent messengers to Monaeses to ask for peace and with generous promises persuaded him to come back again. When this became known, Antony was angry but he did not kill Monaeses, whom he still had in his power. He thought that if he did, none of the barbarians would ever trust him, so he used politics against the enemy. He dismissed Monaeses as if wanting to make peace with the Parthians through him. He sent envoys with him to Phraates. They were to make peace, if the king would restore the ensigns and those captives who were still alive, whom the Parthians had taken in the defeat of Crassus. He thought he would catch the king unprepared for war by giving him reasons to hope for peace. {*Plutarch, Antony, l. 1. c. 37. s. 2. 9:221} {*Dio, l. 49. (24) 5:391,393}

5514. In the meantime, Antony prepared for war. He came to the Euphrates River, which he presumed would be unguarded. When he found a strong garrison there, he changed his plan, intending soon to go into Armenia to make war with Artavasdes, the king of the Medes. The king of Greater Armenia had suggested it, since Artavasdes was the enemy of the king of Armenia. Both kings had the same name. {*Dio, l. 49. (25) 5:393}

5515. Artavasdes, the king of the Medes, was called Artabazes, the son of Tigranes, by Josephus. {*Josephus, Jewish War, l. 1. c. 18. s. 5. (363) 2:171} {*Josephus, Antiq., l. 15. c. 4. s. 3. (104) 8:51} [K442] Orosius called him Artabanus. {Orosius, l. 16. c. 19.} Antony had used him as his counsellor, guide and chief for the management of the war, but then he betrayed Antony and later created problems for the Romans. {*Strabo, l. 11. c. 13. s. 4. 5:307} {*Strabo, l. 16. c. 1. s. 28. 7:237}

5516. Antony sent Cleopatra back into Egypt, while he went through Arabia into Armenia. He had ordered that his own forces and the auxiliaries of the kings meet him there. Among these were many friends and allies, including Artavasdes or Artabazes, the king of Armenia, with six thousand cavalry and seven thousand foot soldiers. When the soldiers were mustered, the Romans and the allies of Italy had six thousand foot soldiers, with ten thousand of the ordinary cavalry of the Iberians and Celts. The auxiliaries from other countries numbered thirty thousand cavalry and lightly armed soldiers. This was according to Plutarch. However, Velleius Paterculus said Antony had thirteen legions. Florus stated he had sixteen, Justin and Livy said eighteen legions and sixteen thousand cavalry. {*Plutarch, Antony, l. 1. c. 37. s. 3. 9:221} {*Velleius Paterculus, l. 2. c. 82. s. 1. 1:223} {*Florus, l. 2. c. 20. s. 10. 1:323} {Justin, Trogus, l. 42. c. 5.} {*Livy, l. 130. 14:161}

5517. The guide of Antony's army led them from Zeugma to the Euphrates River almost as far as Atropatene, which was separated from Armenia by the Araxes River. This was a journey of a thousand miles and almost twice as far as the shorter way. The guide led them over mountains and byways. {*Strabo, l. 11. c. 13. s. 4. 5:307} Antony should have refreshed his army, who were weary from this thousand mile trek, in the winter quarters of Armenia. Since spring was coming, he should have invaded Media before the Parthians left their winter quarters. He could not tolerate any delay because he wanted to be back with Cleopatra, and so he thought more about returning quickly than about gaining a victory. {*Plutarch, Antony, l. 1. c. 37,38. 9:221,223}

5518. Therefore, when he found out that the king of Media had gone far from his country to bring help to the Parthians, he quickly set out with the best part of his cavalry and foot soldiers, leaving part of his army and baggage with Oppius Statianus. He ordered them to follow him, hoping that he would conquer Media on the first attack. {*Dio, l. 49. (25) 5:393}

5519. Among the things that were left behind were the battering engines, which were carried in three hundred wagons. One ram was eighty feet long. If any of the machines were damaged, they could not be repaired due to the scarcity of materials in those countries because the trees were too short and not strong enough. {*Plutarch, Antony, l. 1. c. 38. s. 2. 9:223}

5520. After Antony had crossed the Araxes River, he faced problems and hardships on all sides. {Orosius, l. 6. c. 19.} As soon as he came into Artopatene, he harassed that country and then besieged the large city of Phraata. The wife of the king of the Medes lived there with her children. When Antony realised his error in leaving his engines behind, he was forced to raise a mount near the city. This took a long time and was a lot of work. {*Plutarch, Antony, l. 1. c. 38. s. 2. 9:223} This was the royal city of the Medes and was called *Praaspa* by Dio, and *Vera* by Strabo, who cited Dellius, the historian. Dellius accompanied Antony on this expedition and wrote about it and commanded part of the army. [E729] Dellius said this city was three hundred miles from the Araxes River. {*Dio, l. 49. (25) 5:393} {*Strabo, l. 11. c. 13. s. 3. 5:305}

5521. The Parthians and Medes knew that Antony was wasting his time in attacking that city because it was so well-fortified with walls and men. They attacked Statianus suddenly when he was tired from his journey, and killed both him and all who were with him. Plutarch reckoned they killed ten thousand men. [K443] Velleius Paterculus said two legions were killed and all the baggage and engines of war were taken. Polemon, the king of Pontus, and an ally of the war, was captured and released when he paid a ransom. This was an easy victory for the barbarians because the king of Armenia, who might have helped the Romans, was not at the battle. He did not come but left Antony in order to return to his own kingdom. {*Dio, l. 49. (25) 5:393} {*Velleius Paterculus, l. 2. c. 82. s. 2. 1:223} {*Plutarch, Antony, l. 1. c. 38. s. 2,3. 9:223,225}

5522. Although Antony hurried to help Statianus when he heard the first news, he arrived too late, for he found nothing but dead men. He was terrified with this defeat but none of the barbarians opposed him, so he thought that they had left in fear of him and was encouraged. Soon after this, they fought and Antony routed them. His slingers, of whom he had a large number, put them to flight. The slingers' arrows went farther than the enemies' arrows, so the heavily armed cavalry were not safe from them. Not many barbarians were killed, however, because of the swiftness of their cavalry troops. {*Dio, l. 49. (26) 5:395}

5523. Antony resumed the assault on Praaspa. He did little damage to the enemy and the garrison inside the city strongly repelled their attacks, while the enemy that was outside the city hindered them with hand-to-hand combat. {*Dio, l. 49. (25) 5:395} The Parthians, who came to help the besieged, threatened the Romans most contemptuously. Antony did not want his soldiers to lose any of their animosity. He took ten legions, three praetorian cohorts and all his cavalry with him and went foraging, in the hope that the enemy would then attack him and he would be able to fight them. {*Plutarch, Antony, l. 1. c. 39. s. 2. 9:225}

5524. When he had gone a day's journey, he noticed the Parthians wheeling about behind him to hinder his return. He ordered the signal for battle to be sounded, but packed up his tents, as though he were preparing for his march, not to fight. Then he marched past the barbarians, who were drawn up in a half-moon. He gave orders to his cavalry that the legions, as soon as they had come together, should attack the enemy and that the cavalry should begin the charge. The Parthians were perplexed at the well-ordered army of the Romans. They saw the soldiers passing by, keeping their ranks and brandishing their javelins at them, but not speaking a word. After the signal and a loud shout were given, the cavalry began the attack. The Parthians resisted a little, although the Romans were so close to them from the start, that they were unable to use their arrows. Soon, the legions joined the battle with great shouting and the clattering of armour. The Parthian cavalry were frightened and the Parthians fled before they reached hand-to-hand combat. Antony hoped that now he would overcome them, or at least finish the greatest part of the war. He followed the chase very hard. After his foot soldiers had pursued them about six miles and his cavalry three times that distance, he counted the number of the dead and the prisoners. They found they had taken thirty and killed only eighty. This greatly discouraged them, for they thought it was very hard if they could kill so few when they were conquerors, and yet, when conquered, they could lose as many as they had lost when the baggage was taken. The next day, as they were returning to their camp, they met a few of their enemies at first, then more came and finally all of them, as if they had not been routed earlier, but were all fresh men. They reviled them and broke in upon them on every side, so that the Romans were barely able to return to their camp. {*Plutarch, Antony, l. 1. c. 39. s. 3-6. 9:225,227} [K444]

5525. In Antony's absence, the Medes at Praaspa attacked the mount and terrified those defending it. Antony was so enraged, that he decimated those who had forsaken the place and gave the rest of them barley instead of wheat. He killed one in ten of his own troops who had fled. {*Plutarch, Antony, l. 1. c. 39. s. 7. 9:227}

5526. In the beginning, the foragers sent out by Antony brought enough provisions for the Romans. Later, when the Romans had consumed all the supplies nearby, the soldiers themselves were forced to go foraging. It so happened that if only a few were sent out, they brought back nothing and often the foragers were killed, but if many left, then Praaspa was short of besiegers and the sallies of the barbarians killed many of the Romans and many engines were destroyed. Consequently it came about that Antony's men, who were besieging the city, ran as short of supplies as those inside the city. The townsmen, as well as the enemy on the outside, looked for opportune times for sallies. With their sudden incursions and quick retreats, they seriously troubled those who remained in the camp each time the Roman forces were divided. The foragers who went to the villages were never molested, but the Parthians attacked them unexpectedly when they were scattered on their return to the camp. {*Dio, l. 49. (28) 5:395,397} [E730]

**3969a AM, 4678 JP, 36 BC**

5527. Sextus Pompeius heard that Antony was in Media and was making war with the Medes and Parthians.

Pompeius intended to commit himself to Antony's protection when the latter returned. In the meantime, he wintered in Lesbos and the people of Lesbos entertained him very willingly on account of the good memory they had of his father. {*Dio, l. 49. (17) 5:377} {*Appian, Civil Wars, l. 5. c. 14. (133) 4:597}

5528. As Antony prolonged the siege of Praaspa, the war became very troublesome to both sides. Antony could not get any supplies without having his men killed or wounded. Phraates knew that the Parthians would endure anything except a winter in the camp in a strange country. Therefore, he was afraid that if the Romans continued the war, his men would leave him, since the weather would grow very cold after the autumnal equinox. {*Plutarch, Antony, l. 1. c. 40. s. 1,2. 9:229} (English translation by Loeb stated it was the summer equinox, which makes no sense. Summer has a solstice, not an equinox. Editor.) He was also afraid that if the siege were continued, either by Antony himself or else with outside help, Antony would seriously weaken the city. So he secretly sent some agents to promote the idea of a peace between them, in the hope that it would readily be granted. {*Dio, l. 49. (27) 5:397}

5529. Therefore, the Parthian king commanded his men to treat the foragers more courteously when they met with them, and to talk to them about peace. This persuaded Antony to send a friend to request the restitution of his ensigns and prisoners, so that he would not appear to be satisfied only merely to depart in safety. They replied that he should forget about those things. If he wanted peace and security, he should leave promptly. {*Plutarch, Antony, l. 1. c. 40. s. 3,4. 9:229,231} Phraates was sitting on his golden throne and twanging a bow string. After he had railed considerably against the Romans, he promised Antony's envoys peace on the condition that he immediately withdraw his army. {*Dio, l. 49. (27) 5:397}

5530. Antony received this reply. Although very eloquent in both civil and military speeches, he nevertheless, out of shame and sorrow, did not speak to his soldiers at that time, but got Domitius Ahenobarbus to speak to the soldiers for him and encourage them. Within a few days they had packed the baggage and he departed. {*Plutarch, Antony, l. 1. c. 40. s. 5. 9:231} [K445] The works that he had raised for the assault of Praaspa he left intact, as if he had been in a friend's country. The Medes burned everything and cast down the mount. {*Dio, l. 49. (27,28) 5:397,399}

5531. They were to return through the same plain country, where there were no forests. A certain Mardian, who knew the customs of the Parthians and had fought well for the Romans at the battle where the engines were taken, persuaded Antony that he should march with his army via the mountains on their right hand. He should not hazard the plain and the open fields because the Romans were heavily armed and thus good targets for the number of Parthian cavalry, who were all archers. The Parthians used this occasion to draw him from the siege by good words, so that the Mardian would show Antony a shorter way with more plentiful supplies for his soldiers. Antony told his council these things and confessed that he trusted little in the peace with the Parthians. However, he commended the shorter way, especially since the journey would be through a plentiful country. He asked for some assurance from the Mardian, who surrendered himself to be bound until he had brought the army into Armenia. Once he was bound, he led them without problems for two days. {*Plutarch, Antony, l. 1. c. 41. s. 1-3. 9:231,233}

5532. On the third day, Antony gave little thought to the Parthians and marched confident of the peace. The Mardian noticed that a dam of the river had recently broken and that all the way they were to go, was flooded. He knew that this had been done by the Parthians to force the Roman army to halt, so he warned Antony about it and told him to prepare for the arrival of the enemy. Antony ordered his battle and set distances between the ranks. In this way, those that used arrows and slings could make an attack on the enemies, when the Parthians opened their ranks to surround and disorder the army. When the light-horsemen attacked them, they were beaten back, after having given and received many wounds. They came on again until the cavalry from the Celts, who had been held in reserve, gave them a fierce charge and routed them, so that they attempted nothing more that day. {*Plutarch, Antony, l. 1. c. 41. s. 4,5. 9:233}

5533. Antony learned from this what had to be done. He made his army march in a square body and had a strong guard of archers and slingers in the rear and in the flanks. He ordered his cavalry to drive the enemy back, if they attacked them. However, if they fled, they were not to follow the chase too far. For four days, the Parthians received as many casualties as they caused. They began to ease off and thought about going back, since it was winter. {*Plutarch, Antony, l. 1. c. 42. s. 1. 9:235}

5534. On the fifth day, Flavius Gallus, one of the captains and a valiant and industrious man, asked Antony for permission to take some lightly armed men from the rear and some cavalry from the front because he planned to do some gallant act. [E731] With this rash attempt, he broke in on the enemy by taking a great risk. The Romans sent him help in small companies, which were too weak and so were cut off by the enemy, until Antony came with the whole strength of the army and rescued the rest from obvious danger. {*Plutarch, Antony, l. 1. c. 42. s. 2-4. 9:235}

5535. Florus stated that two legions fell victim to the Parthian arrows. {*Florus, l. 2. c. 20. s. 3. 1:321} Plutarch said that at least three thousand were killed and five thousand wounded men were brought back into the tents. Gallus was shot in four places and later died from his wounds. Antony was very troubled to see this and went and comforted the wounded. They cheerfully took him by his right hand and asked him to take care of himself and no longer trouble himself about them. [K446] They called him their Imperator and told him that if he was well, then they were all safe and in good health. {*Plutarch, Antony, l. 1. c. 43. 9:237,239}

5536. This victory made the Parthians, who earlier had been weary and in despair, so proud, that they lodged near the Roman camp all night, in the hope that they would soon be able to plunder all their money and ransack their tents. {*Plutarch, Antony, l. 1. c. 44. s. 1. 9:239} On that night, a certain Roman, whose life had been spared in Crassus' defeat, came in Parthian clothes to the Roman trenches and greeted them in Latin. Once they trusted him, he informed them of the danger at hand and that the king was coming with all his forces. He advised them not to march by the way they had intended, but to go back again and take the way through the woods and the mountains. He told them that they might also meet with the enemy that way. {*Florus, l. 2. c. 20. s. 4,5. 1:321} {*Velleius Paterculus, l. 2. c. 82. s. 2,3. 1:225}

5537. As soon as it was day, many of the enemy came together, with at least forty thousand cavalry. Because they were so confident of victory, the king also sent along his bodyguard, even though he had never been at any previous battle. Then Antony lifted up his hands to heaven and offered his prayers to the gods. He prayed that if any god had been offended at his former good fortune, the god would lay all the adversity on Antony's head but give health and victory to the rest of the army. {*Plutarch, Antony, l. 1. c. 44. s. 2,3. 9:239}

5538. The next day, the army marched on in a more secure guard. The Parthians attacked them and were greatly deceived in their expectations. They thought that they had only come to pillage and plunder and not to fight. They lost heart when they were greeted by Roman arrows. {*Plutarch, Antony, l. 1. c. 45. s. 1,2. 9:241}

5539. As they were going down a certain hill, the Parthians, who were lying in ambush for them, overwhelmed them with their arrows as thick as hail. Then the soldiers who carried large shields took in the lightly harnessed men under their shields. Kneeling down on their left knee, they held their shields over their heads and made a roof over them. This formation is called a *testudo*. In this manner, they defended themselves and their friends from the enemies' arrows, which fell on the convex shields and slid off the slippery surfaces. {*Plutarch, Antony, l. 1. c. 45. s. 2,3. 9:241} {*Florus, l. 2. c. 20. s. 6-8. 1:321,323} {*Frontinus, Stratagems, l. 2. c. 3. s. 15. 1:115} {*Dio, l. 49. (29,30) 5:401,403}

5540. The Parthians had never seen such a thing before and thought that they had all fallen down because of their wounds, or that they would soon all fall. They cast away their bows and leaping off their horses, they took their spears and came to kill them with their naked swords. Then the Romans rose up again and at the signal, widened their army and gave a shout. They attacked their enemies in the front, killing the nearest of them with their arrows and making them all flee. This thing struck such amazement into the barbarians, that one of their number said: {*Florus, l. 2. c. 20. s. 6-8. 1:321,323} {*Dio, l. 49. (29,30) 5:401,403} {*Plutarch, Antony, l. 1. c. 45. s. 3. 9:241}

> "Go, Romans, and farewell. Fame has with good reason called you, who can withstand the Parthian weapons, the conquerors of nations."

5541. There were continual skirmishes between them, which slowed the Roman march down greatly. {*Plutarch, Antony, l. 1. c. 45. s. 3. 9:241} When they marched at break of day, they were constantly bothered by the Parthian arrows. Therefore, Antony deferred his march until the fifth hour, thereby making his own soldiers more confident. The Persians withdrew and they marched without any trouble for that day. {*Frontinus, Stratagems, l. 2. c. 13. s. 7. 1:199} [K447]

5542. The army then began to be troubled by food shortages, because their frequent skirmishes hindered them from foraging. They also lacked grinding mills, which had largely been left behind. The beasts of burden were either dead or were being used to carry the sick and wounded men. It was reported that little more than a quart of wheat was sold for fifty drachmas and barley loaves for their weight in silver. Then they were forced to eat roots and herbs. By chance, they encountered one that, when eaten, made them mad. Those who ate it, only dug up stones and removed them, and thought they were doing some serious business. [E732] At last, they vomited up a great deal of bile and died, because they lacked wine which was the only remedy. {*Plutarch, Antony, l. 1. c. 45. s. 4-6. 9:241,245}

5543. The famine raged in the camp and they began to flee to the enemy but the Parthians killed these runaways before the eyes of the rest. They had all planned to defect but the cruelty of the Parthians stopped the revolt. {*Dio, l. 49. (29) 5:399,401}

5544. Antony saw large numbers of his own soldiers dying and the Parthians continually attacking them. It was reported that he often cried out: *Oh the Ten Thousand!*, and expressed admiration for the army of Xenophon, who had marched a far longer march from Babylon and had often fought with their enemies but had still come home safely. {*Plutarch, Antony, l. 1. c. 45. s. 6. 9:243}

5545. The Parthians could break neither the spirit of the Romans, nor their ranks, but were themselves often defeated and repulsed. They again began to talk peaceably with those who went to forage and fetch water. They showed them their unbent bows and told them that they were departing and that they would follow them no more. If, however, they should have some Medes follow them for a day or two, they would not do them any great harm, but would only secure some of the remoter villages. They won them over with this talk and gently took their leave of them. The Romans were very joyful. Antony wanted to march through the plain rather than the mountains because it was said that that route lacked water along the way. {*Plutarch, Antony, l. 1. c. 46. s. 1,2. 9:243,245}

5546. While he was thinking this way, Mithridates came to him from the enemy camp. He was a cousin of Monaeses, to whom Antony had given the three cities. Antony asked that some men be sent to him who understood the Syriac or Parthian language. When Alexander came, who was from Antioch and a good friend of Antigonus, he was told by Mithridates that the Parthians were lying in ambush with all their forces in those hills which he could see beside the plains. They were waiting to attack them as they passed across the plains. He advised them to travel through the mountains, which had no other inconvenience than lack of water for one day. Antony took his advice and the Mardian guided them through the mountains by night. He ordered his soldiers to carry water with them, which many did, in their helmets and leather bags. {*Plutarch, Antony, l. 1. c. 46,47. 9:245,247}

5547. The Parthians found out about this and contrary to their custom, pursued them by night. At sunrise, they overtook the rearguard of the Romans, who were tired from the hard march and from watching. They had gone thirty miles that night and did not think the enemy would attack them so soon. This made them more dejected and their thirst also increased with their fighting because they were forced to march while fighting. {*Plutarch, Antony, l. 1. c. 47. s. 2,3. 9:247}

5548. In the interim, the vanguard found a cool, clear river, but it was salty. [K448] The water from it just increased the thirst of those who drank it. Although the Mardian had forewarned them of this, they nonetheless pushed aside those who would have kept them from drinking of it and drank freely. Antony, too, was very urgent with them and begged them to stop, telling them that there was a river only a short way off from which they could drink and that the rest of the way was so rough and uneven, that the enemy could not possibly follow them. He also sounded a retreat, so that the soldiers could at least refresh themselves in the shade. {*Plutarch, Antony, l. 1. c. 47. s. 3,4. 9:247} {*Florus, l. 2. c. 20. s. 8,9. 1:323}

5549. As soon as the tents were pitched, the Parthians departed, according to their custom and Mithridates returned. Alexander came to him and he told Alexander that after they had refreshed themselves for a while, they should all arise and hurry over the river. The Parthians would not pursue them beyond that point. For this, Antony gave him a large number of gold plates and drinking cups. He took as much as he could hide in his clothes and departed. {*Plutarch, Antony, l. 1. c. 48. s. 1,2. 9:249}

5550. They were not bothered on the following day's journey, but that night they became their own worst enemies. Those who had any gold or silver, were killed and robbed. The pack animals (sumpters), which carried the treasure, were plundered. Finally, all Antony's household belongings, such as his plates and precious tables, were broken and divided among themselves. As a result of this tumult and uproar in the army, they thought that the enemy had attacked the sumpters to rob them. Antony called a freedman and ordered him to kill him and to cut off his head, so that he would not be taken alive by the enemy, or identified when he was dead. {*Plutarch, Antony, l. 1. c. 48. s. 2,3. 9:249} {*Florus, l. 2. c. 20. s. 9,10. 1:323} {Sextus Rufus, Breviary}

5551. As his friends were weeping around him, the Mardian encouraged Antony, for he knew there was a river nearby. Others told Antony that this tumult had arisen from their own covetousness and doing wrong to one another. [E733] Consequently, Antony gave the signal to make camp, in order to quell these tumults and disturbances in the army. It began to grow light and the army fell into good order again. When the rearguard was hit by enemy arrows, the light cavalry were signalled to fight. The men who carried the large shields, came together as they had done before and defended them from the Parthian arrows. The Parthians did not dare come too close. As they marched on a little distance, the vanguard spotted the river. Antony interposed his cavalry between the enemy and the army and arranged for all the sick men to cross over first. The men that fought were now braver and strengthened. As soon as the Parthians saw the river, they unbent their bows and bade them cross over with good courage and highly commended their valour. So they took their time crossing the river and were glad they had not trusted in the promises of the Parthians. {*Plutarch, Antony, l. 1. c. 48,49. 9:249,251}

5552. After Caesar Octavius had settled his affairs in Sicily, he entered Rome from Sicily on the Ides of November (November 13), and made a speech. This was noted in the marble triumphal records. {Gruter, Inscriptions, p. 297.} {*Suetonius, Augustus, l. 2. c. 22. 1:181} {*Dio, l. 49. (15) 5:371} {Orosius, l. 6. c. 18.} He had a gold statue erected for him in the rostrum which showed his image, with this inscription: {*Appian, Civil Wars, l. 5. c. 13. (130) 4:593}

"Peace, long disturbed, he re-established on land and sea."

5553. He was twenty-eight years old, according to Appian: {*Appian, Civil Wars, l. 5. c. 13. (132) 4:595}

"This seemed to be the end of the civil dissensions. Octavius was now twenty-eight years of age." [K449]

5554. He also received the tribunal power for life by a decree of the Senate, who with this honour invited him to lay down the triumvirate. He wrote privately to Antony about this through Bibulus. {*Appian, Civil Wars, l. 5. c. 13. (132) 4:595,597} {Orosius, l. 6. c. 18.}

5555. Antony's men came to the Araxes River, that divided Media from Armenia, on the sixth day after the battle. The crossing was very difficult because of the depth and swiftness of the river. There was a rumour that the enemy was lying in ambush to attack them during their crossing. After they had crossed over safely and entered Armenia, it was as if they had recently landed from the sea. They kissed the earth and embraced one another with tears of joy. When they marched through a fruitful country after such a long famine, they so gorged themselves with food, that many began to fall sick with dropsies and dysenteries. {*Plutarch, Antony, l. 1. c. 49. s. 3,4. 9:253}

5556. Antony numbered his army and found that he had lost twenty thousand foot soldiers and four thousand cavalry. Half of these had died of diseases and not from fighting against the enemy. {*Plutarch, Antony, l. 1. c. 50. s. 1. 9:253} Of the whole army, at least a quarter of the men were dead or missing. The grooms and slaves had lost about a third of their staff and hardly anything remained of the baggage. However, Antony called this flight his victory because he was still alive. {*Velleius Paterculus, l. 2. c. 82. s. 3. 1:225}

5557. In twenty-one days, he had fled three hundred miles. {*Livy, l. 130. 14:161} The march from Phraata, or Praaspa, continued for twenty-seven days altogether. During that time, the Parthians had been repelled eighteen times in battle. The cavalry of sixteen thousand, who were armed after the Parthian custom and were used to fighting with the Parthians, had been of no help to the Romans.

Artavasdes had brought them from Armenia. The Parthians would not have been able to rally as often after their battles, considering that they had so often been beaten by the Romans if the Romans had the Armenian cavalry to pursue the Parthians. Therefore, all the men encouraged Antony to punish the Armenians. He did not do this, nor did he upbraid Artavasdes for his treachery but showed him the same honour and courtesy that he had always done. He did this because he knew the army was weak and lacked provisions. {*Plutarch, Antony, l. 1. c. 50. s. 2,3. 9:253,255}

5558. Now that Antony was no longer troubled by enemies, and unwilling to winter in Armenia, he hurried to Cleopatra. He took a quick journey in cold winter weather and continual snows. He hurried his soldiers on and lost eight thousand men to the extremities of the weather. {*Livy, l. 130. 14:161} {*Plutarch, Antony, l. 1. c. 51. s. 1. 9:255} As they crossed over the mountains of Armenia, which were covered with snow, their many wounds greatly bothered them and many died or became unfit for service. Antony could not bear to hear of these things and forbade anyone to speak to him about it. Although Antony was angry with the king of Armenia and wished for revenge because the king had deserted him, he tried to win the king's favour in order to get provisions from him. Finally, the soldiers could not endure this journey in winter any longer. Antony persuaded the king with flatteries and promises that if he would let his army winter in his country, he planned to have the army attack the Parthians again the next spring. {*Dio, l. 49. (31) 5:403,405} [K450]

### 3969b AM, 4679 JP, 35 BC

5559. Finally, Antony reached Syria with barely a third of the original sixteen legions. He returned to Antioch, {Orosius, l. 6. c. 19.} where he foolishly began to brag as if he had gained the victory because he had escaped. {*Florus, l. 2. c. 20. s. 10. 1:323} [E734]

5560. He came down to the seaside with a few of his company and stayed in a citadel between Berytus and Sidon, called White Village. He awaited Cleopatra's arrival, pining away because of her absence. To pass the time, he started feasting and drinking excessively. During this time, he would arise and run to see if she were coming, until at last she finally arrived. {*Plutarch, Antony, l. 1. c. 51. 9:255}

5561. Cleopatra brought a large amount of money and apparel for the soldiers. Some reported that Antony took the apparel she had brought, but gave his own private money to the soldiers, as if it had been a gift from her. {*Plutarch, Antony, l. 1. c. 51. s. 2. 9:255} Concerning this matter, Dio wrote that the money which Cleopatra brought him, he gave to the soldiers. He divided four hundred sesterces

to every soldier of the legions, and to others proportionally. When that money ran out, he made up the rest from his own funds and gave credit for what he had received from Cleopatra. He also received much money from his friends and exacted much from his allies. When he had done this, he went into Egypt. {*Dio, l. 49. (31,32) 5:405}

5562. Herod was continually pestered with the nagging of his wife Mariamme. She wanted him to restore the high priesthood to her brother Aristobulus, according to his due. So he called a council of his friends and bitterly complained against his mother-in-law Alexandra, as if she had secretly committed treason against his kingdom and had endeavoured, through Cleopatra, to make her son the new king. However, so that he would not appear to be disrespectful to her and the rest of the family, he said that he would now restore the priesthood to her son. Before this, Ananel had been preferred, because Aristobulus was so young. Alexandra was almost beside herself for joy and grieved that she was being suspected of treason. She wept and cleared herself of these accusations, thanking Herod many times for her son's honour and promising that after this she would be most obedient to the king. Thus Herod gave the priesthood to Aristobulus in the lifetime of Ananel. He was only seventeen years old. {*Josephus, Antiq., l. 15. c. 2,3. (31-41) 8:17-21}

5563. Sextus Pompeius learned of Antony's ill fortune in Media. Because Gaius Furnius, who was governor of Asia at that time, was not friendly toward him, Sextus did not stay in Lesbos. He began to hope that he should either succeed Antony to all his power (if he were to die), or at least receive some part of it. He was especially encouraged by the fact that many came to him from Sicily and from other places. Some came because of his father's reputation, while others came because they did not know where else to live. Hence, he took the trappings of a general and prepared to capture Asia, always keeping in mind the recent example of Labienus, who had quickly overrun it. {*Appian, Civil Wars, l. 5. c. 14. (133) 4:597} {*Dio, l. 49. (17) 5:377}

5564. When Antony came into the country of his friends, he heard what Pompeius had done, but promised to pardon him and make him his friend, if he would lay down his arms. Pompeius promised he would and wrote him back accordingly. However, since he despised Antony for the disastrous defeat he had received and the fact that he had gone into Egypt so soon, Pompeius carried on his plans anyway. {*Dio, l. 49. (18) 5:377} [K451] Not wishing to burn his bridges, he sent messengers to Antony and offered to be his friend and ally but the real purpose was to spy on Antony. In the meantime, he sent envoys to the governors of Thrace and Pontus, thinking that if he failed to take Asia, he could flee through

Pontus into Armenia. He also sent envoys to the Parthians in the hope that they would willingly use him for their captain in the war against Antony, which had not yet ended. Pompeius was a Roman and also the son of Pompey the Great. He provided for ships and exercised the mariners, pretending that he was afraid of Caesar and that this preparation was for the service of Antony. {*Appian, Civil Wars, l. 5. c. 14. (133) 4:597}

5565. As soon as Antony heard what Pompeius was up to, he continued on his journey but sent Marcus Titius, who had formerly revolted from Sextus Pompeius to him, as the general against him. He had received a fleet and army from Syria for this purpose and was to use all his power to resist Pompeius if he started any war. If Pompeius would submit himself, he was to receive him with all honour. {*Appian, Civil Wars, l. 5. c. 14. (134) 4:599} {*Dio, l. 49. (18) 5:377}

5566. Pompeius' envoys, who had been sent to the Parthians, were captured by Antony's captains and brought to Alexandria. When Antony had learned all these things from these envoys, he called the other envoys, who had been sent to him, and brought them face to face. They excused Pompeius as being a young man in a desperate situation who had feared he would not be accepted by Antony and had been forced to try the goodwill even of countries that were the greatest enemies of the Romans. Had he known Antony's mind, there would have been no need of all the solicitations and craft. Antony believed this, since he was not a malicious man, but well-meaning and generous. {*Appian, Civil Wars, l. 5. c. 14. (136) 4:603} [E735]

5567. When Octavia was at Rome, she intended to sail to Antony and Caesar agreed. The reason was not, as most have written, out of any regard for Antony but to give Caesar a legitimate excuse to make war against him if he slighted or harmed her. {*Plutarch, Antony, l. 1. c. 53. s. 1. 9:257} She went to Athens and wintered there. {*Appian, Civil Wars, l. 5. c. 14. (138) 4:607}

5568. At this time, the king of the Medes (Artarasdes) went to war against Phraates, the king of the Parthians, and Artabazes or Artavasdes, king of the Armenians. Artarasdes was angry with the Armenians, because the Romans had invaded him with their help. He was upset with the Parthians because he had received neither any substantial amounts of the Roman spoil, nor any honour whatsoever. Artavasdes was also afraid that the Parthians would take his kingdom away from him, so he sent Polemon, the king of Pontus, as an envoy to Antony, asking for his friendship and alliance. He wanted Antony to come to him and promised him the help of all his forces. Antony was pleased, for the only thing that seemed to prevent the overthrowing of the Parthians was his lack of cavalry and archers. He thought that he would now benefit more from receiving them than the king would in giving them to him. Consequently, Antony had great expectations and once again set out to go through Armenia. He called the king of the Medes to the Araxes River and then started the war with Parthia. {*Plutarch, Antony, l. 1. c. 52. 9:255,257} {*Dio, l. 49. (33) 5:409}

5569. Antony wrote to Octavia, who was now at Athens, telling her to stay there and informing her of an expedition that he was about to take. She took this badly and thought it was just an excuse. However, she wrote to him, wanting to know what he wanted her to do with the things she had brought for him. [K452] She had brought a great deal of apparel for the soldiers, many cavalry, a large sum of money and presents for his captains and friends. In addition, she had two thousand men, all of them armed like the praetorian cohorts. Niger, a friend of Antony, was sent by Octavia to tell Antony this. He added the deserved commendations for Octavia. Antony accepted both her own and others' gifts and also the soldiers that she had begged from her brother for this purpose. {*Plutarch, Antony, l. 1. c. 53. s. 1,2. 9:257} {*Dio, l. 49. (33) 5:409}

5570. Cleopatra was afraid that Octavia might draw Antony from her and seemed to languish out of love for him. She made her body so weak by her feminine tricks that it appeared as though she could not live if she were deprived of him. Antony, overcome by this, abandoned his journey to the king of the Medes even though he had received news that the Parthians were embroiled in civil wars, and returned to Alexandria. {*Plutarch, Antony, l. 1. c. 53. s. 3-6. 9:257,259} From that time on, he gave himself over to the love and wishes of Cleopatra. {*Dio, l. 49. (34) 5:409}

5571. Antony summoned Artavasdes, king of Armenia, into Egypt as a friend. He hoped to get him into his power, in order to be able to kill him more easily, but when the king did not come, he suspected some deceit. He then found other means to deceive him. Antony did not publicly show his anger against him, so that he would not provoke him to war. {*Dio, l. 49. (33) 5:409}

5572. Gaius Furnius, the governor of Asia (of whom we read in Plutarch's Antony, and Jerome's Chronicle, that he was a man of great authority and the most eloquent among the Romans), entertained Pompeius, who came to him at this time. Furnius was not strong enough to drive him out, nor did he know what Antony wanted to do. When he saw Pompeius' soldiers exercising, he also mustered the forces who were in his province and sent for Ahenobarbus, who commanded the army in the vicinity. He also called for Amyntas to help him. When they came at once, Pompeius complained that he was being considered an enemy when he was merely expecting an answer from Antony through the envoys he had sent to him. However, Pompeius was planning to take Ahenobarbus through the treachery of Curius, a close friend of his. He hoped to hold the general hostage to exchange for himself in case of need. The treason was discovered and Curius was put to death after being condemned in the council chambers of the Romans. Pompeius also killed Theodorus, a freedman of his, who alone knew about this business, on the assumption that he had been the one who had told his secret. {*Appian, Civil Wars, l. 5. c. 14. (137) 4:603,605} {*Plutarch, Antony, l. 1. c. 58. s. 6. 9:271} {*Eusebius, Chronicles, l. 1. 1:241}

5573. Pompeius gave up hope that Furnius would receive him and using treachery, seized Lampsacus, where many Italians lived, who had been brought there as a colony by Gaius Caesar. Pompeius paid the Italians large wages to entice them to serve under him, so that he now had two hundred cavalry and three legions. He attacked Cyzicum by sea and land, but was repulsed on both fronts, because there was a very large band of soldiers to guard the walls, who had been brought there for Antony. Pompeius returned to the harbour of the Achaeans and planned to provide grain for his troops. {*Appian, Civil Wars, l. 5. c. 14. (137) 4:605}

5574. Furnius would not fight, but always stayed near his camp with many cavalry. He would not allow Pompeius to get any grain or seize any cities. Pompeius concealed attacked his camp in front and sent some around to attack from the rear, so that when Furnius went out against him, he had his camp at his back. [E736] Pompeius killed many as they fled through the fields of Scamander. The fields were very wet because a great deal of rain had fallen. Those who escaped, retreated into a safe place, but were unable to prepare for a new war. Pompeius received men from Mysia, Propontis and other places. [K453] These were poor men, who had been exhausted with taxes, and served under Pompeius for money. He was now famous for the victory he had won at the harbour of the Achaeans. {*Appian, Civil Wars, l. 5. c. 14. (138) 4:605,607}

5575. Pompeius, who lacked cavalry and therefore could not go very far to forage, heard that a squadron of Italian cavalry had been sent to Antony from Octavia, who was wintering in Athens, so he sent at once to bribe them with gold. Antony's governor of Macedonia apprehended them and divided the money among the soldiers. {*Appian, Civil Wars, l. 5. c. 14. (138) 4:607}

5576. Pompeius captured Nicaea and Nicomedia, where he gathered money in abundance because of his great and unexpected successes. {*Appian, Civil Wars, l. 5. c. 14. (139) 4:607}

5577. Furnius was camped near him. As soon as it was spring, a fleet of seventy ships reached him from Sicily. This was the remainder of the fleet that Antony had lent to Caesar against Pompeius, and when the Sicilian war had ended, Caesar had dismissed them. Titius, too, came from Syria, with a hundred and twenty ships and a large army. They all arrived at Proconnesus. {*Appian, Civil Wars, l. 5. c. 14. (139) 4:607}

5578. Pompeius, because he was not fully prepared, was very afraid and selected the places which were most convenient for his flight. When he was apprehended in Nicomedia, he asked for peace through his envoys, hoping that the favours he had previously done for Titius would make him well disposed towards him. Titius absolutely refused to grant any peace unless he agreed to surrender all his ships and forces to him. {*Dio, l. 49. (18) 5:377,379}

5579. Consequently, giving up any hope of safety by sea, Pompeius put all his heavy provisions into his ships and set them on fire. He armed his sailors, who would be of more use to him on land with the others. {*Dio, l. 49. (18) 5:379} {*Appian, Civil Wars, l. 5. c. 14. (139) 4:607}

5580. Herod feared that his mother-in-law Alexandra would seek opportunities to create new problems. He ordered that she be kept within the palace and not be permitted to do anything on her own authority. She was guarded so strictly, that nothing she did was concealed from him, not even what she did in her daily life. She took this captivity very badly and sent letters to Cleopatra, in which she complained of her harsh treatment and sought her help. Therefore, Cleopatra said that she should flee with her son to her in Egypt. Alexandra had two coffins made to accommodate her and her son similar to those which are used when men die. She ordered the servants who were aware of the plot to carry them out by night and take them to a ship which had been prepared to carry them into Egypt. Aesop, a servant, told Sabbion, a friend of Alexander's, about this, because he thought that he was already aware of all this before. Because Sabbion had been considered an enemy of Herod's, ever since he had been suspected of having been in on the plot to poison Antipater, he took this opportunity to be restored to the king's favour by revealing this matter. Herod played along in the scheme until it was being executed, then surprised her during her flight and brought her back. He pardoned her, however, not daring to punish her for fear that Cleopatra would not be easily satisfied but would seek any reason for hatred against him. Therefore, under the pretence of a magnanimous spirit, he made a show of pardoning her solely out of clemency. {*Josephus, Antiq., l. 15. c. 3. s. 2. (42-49) 8:21-25}

5581. Cassius of Parma, Nasidius, Saturninus, Thermus, Antistius and other honourable friends of Sextus Pompeius, as well as his dear friend, Fannius, and his father-in-law, Libo, could not persuade Pompeius to abandon the war against someone more powerful than himself, especially when Titius arrived, whom Antony had sent. [K454] They began to despair and defected to Antony. {*Appian, Civil Wars, l. 5. c. 14. (139) 4:607,609}

5582. After Pompeius had been forsaken by his friends, he departed into the midland country of Bithynia, intending (as was reported) to go into Armenia. He stole away secretly from the camp by night. Furnius, Titius and Amyntas pursued him and by marching excessively fast, overtook him around evening. Both parties camped around a hill, but with neither a ditch nor a trench, because it was late at night and they were weary. While they were in this condition, Pompeius sent three hundred light troops by night, who attacked them as they were in their beds or running out from their lodgings. In most cowardly fashion, they all fled naked. If Pompeius had attacked them with all his forces, or pursued them as they were fleeing, he might have had an absolute victory, but since he did not do this, he gained nothing whatsoever by all this. He continued on his way to the midland country. {*Appian, Civil Wars, l. 5. c. 14. (140) 4:609} [E737]

5583. His enemies joined together and kept him from foraging, so that he was very short of food. He was forced to demand a parlay with Furnius, who had in earlier times been a friend of Pompey the Great and who was a man of exceptional honour and gravity. Therefore, standing on the bank of a river that ran between them, Pompeius told him that he would place himself under his protection on the condition that he be brought to Antony. Furnius answered that this was not a matter for him but for Titius to decide. Pompeius suspected Titius' trustworthiness and again offered to surrender, pleading that he be accepted. When he did not get what he wanted, he asked to be received by Amyntas. Furnius told him that Amyntas would do nothing to offend the person Antony had entrusted with his business. So the parlay broke off. {*Appian, Civil Wars, l. 5. c. 14. (140-142) 4:609,613}

5584. Furnius' soldiers thought that, because of a very serious shortage of food, Pompeius would surrender to Titius the next day. As was the custom in camps, Pompeius made many fires in the night and used trumpeters to distinguish the watches of the night, but he secretly withdrew with his army, without taking any baggage or so much as telling them where they were going. It was his intention to return to the sea and burn Titius' fleet. He might have been able to do this, if Scaurus had not run away from him and told of his departure and of the way he was going, although he did not know what Pompeius intended to do. Then Amyntas pursued him with fifteen hundred cavalry, while Sextus had none. As soon as he overtook him, Pompeius' soldiers went over to him, some secretly and some openly. Pompeius, now almost forsaken and afraid of his own soldiers, surrendered himself without any conditions, when he had earlier refused the conditions of Titius. {*Appian, Civil Wars, l. 5. c. 14. (143) 4:613}

5585. Dio wrote that Pompeius was taken by surprise, surrounded and captured by Titius and Furnius at Midaeum, which was a town of Phrygia. {*Dio, l. 49. (18) 5:379} Appian said that his army was forced by Titius to take a solemn oath to Antony. {*Appian, Civil Wars, l. 5. c. 14. (144) 4:615}

5586. When Antony heard what had happened, he at once sent letters ordering that Pompeius be executed. A little later, he changed his mind and ordered that he be spared but the carrier of the last letters arrived before the one that was bringing the first. Titius only later received the letters dealing with his death, so that he either supposed they had actually been written last, or else he was aware of the truth, but would not believe it. He followed the orders of the letters as they were delivered and not as Antony had intended. {*Dio, l. 49. (18) 5:379} [K455]

5587. There were some who reported that it was not Antony who ordered the death of Pompeius, but Plancus. He was the governor of Syria and was accustomed to signing for Antony in letters of importance, as well as using Antony's seal with his knowledge. (Yet Antony himself would not write, either because of the reputation of Pompeius, or because Cleopatra supported him because of the memory of his father, Pompey the Great.) In the event that Antony did not know, then Plancus may have done it himself, either because he was afraid that Pompeius could be an instigator of dissension between Caesar and Antony, or in case Cleopatra should favour Pompeius over himself. {*Appian, Civil Wars, l. 5. c. 14. (144) 4:615}

5588. Sextus Pompeius was executed at Miletus. {*Appian, Civil Wars, l. 5. c. 14. (144) 4:615} {*Strabo, l. 3. c. 3. s. 2. 2:23} This happened when Lucius Cornificius and another Sextus Pompeius were consuls. {*Dio, l. 49. (18) 5:379} Livy wrote this note about him: {*Livy, l. 131. 14:161}

> "When Sextus Pompeius had surrendered to Antony while still making war against him in Asia, he was conquered by Antony's lieutenants."

5589. We read in Orosius: {*Orosius, l. 6. c. 19.*}

"Pompeius fled, after being defeated numerous times on sea and land. He was captured and a little later put to death."

5590. Velleius Paterculus wrote with reference to Antony: {*Velleius Paterculus, l. 2. c. 87. s. 2,3. 1:233,235*}

"When Antony promised that he would preserve the dignity of Sextus Pompeius, he then killed him."

5591. He wrote in more detail: {*Velleius Paterculus, l. 2. c. 79. s. 5,6. 1:219*}

"Pompeius fled into Asia and was killed on the order of Antony, whose help he implored. Pompeius had been undecided whether to be a general or a petitioner and now, endeavouring to retain his dignity, he begged for his life. Antony had Pompeius' throat cut by Titius. Due to this act, Titius was unpopular for a long time. When he was celebrating the games in Pompey's theatre, he was driven out of it by the curses of the people taking part in the games he was holding."

5592. Caesar Octavius held games in the Circus because of the death of Sextus Pompeius. He set up a chariot before the rostrum in Antony's honour and set up statues in the temple of Concord. He gave Antony permission to banquet there with his wife and children, as had previously been decreed to Octavius. For as yet he pretended to be his friend and comforted Antony over the Parthian expedition. In this way, Octavius tried to cure Antony's jealousy over Octavius' victory in Sicily and the honours decreed to him for it. {*Dio, l. 49. (18) 5:387,389*}

## 3970a AM, 4679 JP, 35 BC

5593. At the feast of tabernacles, the new high priest, Aristobulus, who had just turned seventeen, offered the sacrifice according to the law. Clothed in the priestly attire, he approached the altar and performed the ceremony with propriety. He was quite handsome and taller than usual for someone his age. His features displayed the honour of his lineage and he won the affection of all the multitude. Everyone recalled the worthy and memorable actions of his grandfather Aristobulus. [E738] They were overcome with affection for him and were so overjoyed, that they could not contain themselves. They prayed publicly for him and wished him much joy. They publicly proclaimed the memory of that family and the thanks they owed it for all their benefits, doing this more freely than was fitting while under a king like Herod. {*Josephus, Antiq., l. 15. c. 3. s. 3. (50-52) 8:25,27*}

5594. As soon as the feast was over, he was entertained at a banquet by his mother Alexandra. King Herod

courteously enticed the young man into a convenient place and pretended to jest with him in the style of young men. Because that place was too hot and they were quickly weary, they left their games and went to the swimming pools that were near the court, to take in the fresh air at noon. At first, they watched some of their friends and servants as they were swimming. At length, the young man, at Herod's insistence, also went in to join them. Toward evening, those who had been given this charge, dunked him as he was swimming, as if in sport and jest. They held him underwater and did not stop until he drowned. [K456] This was the end of Aristobulus, in the eighteenth year of his life and the first year of his high priesthood. The high priesthood immediately reverted back to Ananel. {*Josephus, Antiq., l. 15. c. 3. s. 3. (53-56) 8:29*}

5595. When this accident was reported to the women, they were all in an uproar and did nothing but weep and wail over the dead body of the young man. Sorrow seized the whole city as soon as the rumour had spread abroad. Every house bewailed the calamity, as if it had been their own. Herod attempted by every means to make people believe that this accident had happened without his knowledge. He pretended to be sorrowful and tearful. In order to give the women more comfort, he buried the body with a most magnificent funeral. He was extremely generous in adorning his monument and in providing perfumes and other precious things. {*Josephus, Antiq., l. 15. c. 3. s. 4. (57-61) 8:29,31*}

5596. Aristobulus' mother Alexandra, although often ready to commit suicide because she was aware of all that had happened, nonetheless repressed her passion. She behaved as though she were not suspicious, as though she thought that her son had not been deliberately killed, until some opportunity for revenge might offer itself. {*Josephus, Antiq., l. 15. c. 3. s. 5. (62) 8:31*}

## 3970b AM, 4680 JP, 34 BC

5597. Antony sought some way in which he could more easily be revenged on Artavasdes, the king of Armenia. He sent Quintus Dellius to him to ask for a marriage between his daughter and Antony's son Alexander, whom he had by Cleopatra, also adding many promises. Finally, at the beginning of spring, he suddenly came to Nicopolis, a city in Lesser Armenia that had been built by Pompey. From there he sent for Artavasdes to come, as if wanting to make use of both his advice and help in the Parthian war but Artavasdes suspected treachery and did not come. {*Dio, l. 49. (39) 5:421*}

5598. Alexandra was enraged with grief and a desire for revenge. She told Cleopatra in letters about the treachery of Herod and of the lamentable death of her son.

Cleopatra, who had for a long time wished to help her and now pitied the woman's misfortune, took particular care of this matter herself. She never stopped nagging Antony to revenge the young man's death. She told him it was an unpardonable act that Herod, who, thanks to Antony's help, enjoyed a kingdom that rightfully belonged to another and had behaved with such insolent rage against the lawful family of the kings. Antony was persuaded by these words and after he had come into Laodicea in Syria, he sent for Herod to appear before him to answer to the crime against him over the death of Aristobulus. {*Josephus, Antiq., l. 15. c. 3. s. 5. (63,64) 8:33}

5599. Herod committed the care of the kingdom to his uncle Joseph, and secretly ordered him to execute his wife Mariamme if Antony should do him any harm. He told Joseph that he loved her so much, that he would consider it a wrong done to himself, if anyone else were to enjoy her beauty, even after his death. {*Josephus, Antiq., l. 15. c. 3. s. 5. (65-67) 8:33,35}

5600. Herod went to Antony and appeased him with the presents he had brought from Jerusalem for this purpose. He appeased Antony's anger through many conferences he had with him, after which Cleopatra's charges carried less weight with him. Antony maintained that it was not appropriate for a king to give an account of his actions, otherwise he would cease to be a king. Once he had been given the honour of being a king, he should have the free power to do as he wished. He also said that Cleopatra should not meddle too much with other men's governments. {*Josephus, Antiq., l. 15. c. 3. s. 8. (74-76) 8:37} [K457]

5601. While Joseph was governing the kingdom that had been committed to him, he talked at various times with Mariamme. Sometimes it was about business and partly to honour her. He often mentioned how much Herod loved her, which made the other ladies laugh, especially Alexandra. He was trying so hard to vindicate the king's love to them, that he told them about the secret command the king had given him. [E739] He thought that this was the best argument in support of Herod's love, because he could neither endure to live without her nor be parted from her in death. The ladies did not interpret it as an indubitable sign of Herod's love, but abhorred the tyrannical mind of one who, even though he were dead, would still seek to take their life. {*Josephus, Antiq., l. 15. c. 3. s. 6. (68-70) 8:35}

5602. In the interim, a rumour spread in the city that the king had been put to death by Antony. This disturbed all the court, especially the ladies. Alexandra also persuaded Joseph to take them with him and to flee to the ensigns of the Roman legions who were around the city.

Joseph should seek the protection of the tribune Julius, so that they would be safe and the Romans would be well disposed towards them, if initially, there might be any troubles around the court. Moreover, it was hoped that Mariamme would be able to obtain anything she wanted, if only she could get to see Antony and might even recover the kingdom and whatever belonged to the royal family. {*Josephus, Antiq., l. 15. c. 3. s. 7. (71-73) 8:35,37}

5603. As they were holding this meeting, Herod's letters arrived, which quashed the rumour. He wrote about the honours Antony had shown him, in public assemblies and by inviting him to feasts. He said that Antony was doing this in spite of the accusations of Cleopatra, who was keen to have that country and fought with every means she had to destroy him, so that she could usurp his kingdom. However, since Antony had shown that he was just, no great danger was to be expected. He would return shortly, once he had his kingdom and alliance confirmed by Antony. Now the covetousness of Cleopatra no longer had any hope, since Antony had granted her Coelosyria, instead of what she had demanded. It had been given on the condition that she would never again demand Judah or mention this matter to him. {*Josephus, Antiq., l. 15. c. 3. s. 8. (77-79) 8:39}

5604. The moment these letters were received, the reason for fleeing to the Romans vanished but the resolution to do so was not kept concealed. As soon as Herod had brought Antony a part of the way as a precaution against the Parthians (for so he pretended), he returned into Judea. At once his sister Salome and his mother Cypros told him what Alexandra and her friends had intended to do. Not content with this, Salome accused her husband Joseph of having been too familiar with Mariamme. She was motivated to do this by an old grudge because the queen was a woman of a proud spirit and among other women's chatter, had upbraided Salome's family for their lowly birth. {*Josephus, Antiq., l. 15. c. 3. s. 9. (80,81) 8:39,41} {*Josephus, Antiq., l. 14. c. 7. s. 3. (121) 7:511}

5605. Mariamme had sworn to Herod on an oath, attesting to her chastity, and Herod had told her again how much he loved her. She denied that it was wrong for a lover to order that if he should die, his wife should also be put to death. Herod thought this secret could never have been known unless she had committed adultery with Joseph. He wanted to kill her for this but he was overcome with love and barely restrained himself from doing it. He ordered Joseph to be put to death, however, without so much as allowing him to come into his presence, and also put Alexandra into prison, since she was the cause of all these evils. {*Josephus, Antiq., l. 15. c. 3. s. 9. (82-87) 8:41,43} [K458]

5606. In the meanwhile, the affairs of Syria were unsettled. Cleopatra never failed to prejudice Antony against everyone and persuaded him to take the government of every other ruler from him and to give it to her. She wanted Judea and Arabia to be taken from the two kings, Herod and Malchus, and given to her, and so she plotted their destruction. Antony, however, thought it was unjust to put two such great kings to death as a favour to an importunate woman. In spite of this, he no longer considered them his friends and took part of their country from them which he gave to Cleopatra. Besides this, he gave her all the cities which were between the Eleutherus River and Egypt, except for Tyre and Sidon. He knew that these two cities had always been free, although she tried to get them also, with her earnest entreaties. {*Josephus, Jewish War, l. 1. c. 18. s. 4,5. (359-362) 2:169} {*Josephus, Jewish War, l. 7. c. 8. s. 4. (300-302) 4:391,393} {*Josephus, Antiq., l. 15. c. 4. s. 1. (88-95) 8:43-47}

5607. In this way Cleopatra, through the generosity of Antony, enjoyed a large part of Cilicia, the country of Judea where the balsam grows, Arabia, Nabatea, which was Malchus' country (that is, all the part bordering the sea), Iturea, Phoenicia, Coelosyria, Cyprus and a part of Crete. With his generous gifts, Antony greatly offended the people of Rome, who were upset by the immorality of Cleopatra, from whom he had earlier had twins, Alexandra and Cleopatra. He named one the *Sun*, and the other the *Moon*. She also had a son Ptolemy, whom she named Philadelphus. {*Plutarch, Antony, l. 1. c. 36. s. 2,3. 9:217,219} {*Plutarch, Antony, l. 1. c. 36. c. 54. s. 3-6. 9:261,263} {*Dio, l. 49. (41) 5:425} {*Livy, l. 132. 14:163} Cleopatra was said to have understood many languages, so that she did not need an interpreter, but could speak any of the following: Ethiopian, Troglodyte, Hebrew, Arabian, Syrian, Median and Parthian. Her predecessors, the kings of Egypt, had scarcely understood the Egyptian languages, and some of them had also forgotten the Macedonian language. {*Plutarch, Antony, l. 1. c. 27. s. 3,4. 9:197} [E740]

5608. Cleopatra accompanied Antony, who was going with his army into Armenia, as far as the Euphrates River, before she returned. On the way back she visited Apamea and Damascus, and then came into Judea. {*Josephus, Antiq., l. 15. c. 4. s. 2. (96) 8:47}

5609. In the third summer after Lepidus had been removed from office in Sicily by Caesar Octavius, Antony had undertaken his expedition into Armenia. {*Velleius Paterculus, l. 2. c. 82. s. 3. 1:223} After the death of Sextus Pompeius, he again sent Quintus Dellius to the king of Armenia to confer with him, while he quickly went to Artaxata. {*Appian, Civil Wars, l. 5. c. 14. (145) 4:617} {*Dio, l. 49. (39) 5:421}

5610. In Judea, Cleopatra was entertained by Herod, who assured her of that part of Arabia that had been granted to her by Antony, while the revenues of Jericho were also hers. This country grew balsam, which was the most precious of all ointments and only grew there. There was also a large supply of dates. {*Josephus, Antiq., l. 15. c. 4. s. 2. (96) 8:47} The balsam was only grown in the land of Judea and only in two gardens, both of which belonged to the king. One was twenty *iugera* (about thirteen acres) in size and the other was smaller. {*Pliny, l. 12. c. 54. 4:79}

5611. Through this, Herod became good friends with Cleopatra. She tried to entice him with her wiles, either due to the intemperance of her lust, or else because she was seeking an opportunity for her treachery through this, too. She only pretended love and Herod refused her. He had a meeting with his friends about killing her but they restrained him from this attempt. [K459] He appeased Cleopatra with generous presents and paid her every kind of polite attention and then accompanied her as far as Pelusium. {*Josephus, Jewish War, l. 1. c. 18. s. 5. (362,363) 2:171} {*Josephus, Antiq., l. 15. c. 4. s. 2. (97-103) 8:47-51} Because he was afraid of her and also of the Jewish people, he turned the citadel of Masada into a refuge for himself and stored sufficient arms there for ten thousand men. {*Josephus, Jewish War, l. 7. c. 8. s. 4. (300-302) 4:391,393}

5612. In Armenia, Antony prevailed upon King Artavasdes to come to him, through his friends' persuasion. Antony also frightened him with the size of his forces. The king was deceived by his many promises, since Antony, in his letters and deeds, always behaved like his friend. He came into Antony's camp on his assurance and was apprehended. {*Dio, l. 49. (39) 5:421} {*Livy, l. 131. 14:161} {*Strabo, l. 11. c. 14. s. 15. 5:339,341} {*Velleius Paterculus, l. 2. c. 82. s. 3,4. 1:225} {*Plutarch, Antony, l. 1. c. 50. s. 4. 9:255} {Orosius, l. 6. c. 19.}

5613. As soon as Antony had captured him, he took him around to the citadels where his treasure was stored. He did not put him in fetters because he hoped to get the treasure without any fighting. He pretended that he had only taken him captive to get his money from the Armenians, in return for their freedom and his kingdom. This was all in vain because the men who kept the treasure would not obey the king. {*Dio, l. 49. (39) 5:421,423}

5614. Those Armenians who bore arms, made his oldest son Artaxes, or Artaxias, king instead of Artavasdes, or Artabazes, who had been taken prisoner. {*Dio, l. 49. (39) 5:421} {*Josephus, Antiq., l. 15. c. 4. s. 3. (104,105) 8:51} Antony bound Artavasdes with silver chains, as if it were a lowly thing for a king to be restrained with iron fetters. {*Dio, l. 49. (40) 5:423} By these chains, he compelled him to confess where the royal treasure was. When he had captured the town where the king told him the treasure was stored, he took a large amount of gold and silver from there. {*Orosius, l. 6. c. 19.*}

5615. After all this, Antony subdued all of Armenia, either by force or through voluntary surrender. {*Dio, l. 49. (40) 5:423*} {*Josephus, Antiq., l. 15. c. 4. s. 3. (104) 8:51*} When Artaxes engaged him in a battle, Artaxes was defeated and fled to the Parthians. {*Dio, l. 49. (40) 5:423*} Antony led Artavasdes bound into Egypt, together with his sons, who were princes, as a present for Cleopatra, along with whatever had been valuable in their kingdom. {*Josephus, Jewish War, l. 1. c. 18. s. 5. (363) 2:171*} {*Josephus, Antiq., l. 15. c. 4. s. 3. (104) 8:51*}

5616. At Rome, on the Ides of September (September 13), Gaius Sossius, the proconsul, triumphed for Judea. (Latin copy by Ussher stated the 3rd of the Nones, or September 3. Editor.) This appeared in the marble triumphal records. {*Gruter, Inscriptions, p. 297.*}

## 3971a AM, 4680 JP, 34 BC

5617. Antony, to create a firmer tie of friendship, obtained the daughter of Artarasdes, the king of Media, for a marriage with his son. He left his army in Armenia and returned into Egypt with his enormous plunder. When he entered Alexandria in a chariot, among other captives, he led Artavasdes or Artabazes, the king of Armenia, before him, with his wife and children. {*Dio, l. 49. (40) 5:423*} The Romans were unhappy about this because it seemed that the best possessions of their country had to be shared with the Egyptians, as a favour to Cleopatra. {*Plutarch, Antony, l. 1. c. 54. s. 2,3. 9:261*}

5618. Antony presented Artavasdes and his family in chains of gold before Cleopatra, at an assembly of the people. She was on a silver-plated platform and sat in a chair of gold. The barbarians did not show her any respect or fall to their knees (although they were often ordered to do so, with threats and promises). [K460] They only called her by her own name, for which they were considered to be high-spirited and so suffered all the more. {*Dio, l. 49. (40) 5:423,425*}

5619. Antony feasted the Alexandrians and assembled the people in the arena where the young men exercised themselves. On the high silver platform he placed two golden chairs, one for himself and another for Cleopatra, and smaller chairs for his children. [E741] He then made a speech to the people and decreed that Cleopatra should be called Queen of Kings, and her son and partner in the kingdom, namely Ptolemy Caesarion, King of Kings. He gave them Egypt and Cyprus, in a different division from the one he had previously made. He also told them that Cleopatra was the wife of Caesar, the dictator, and that Caesarion was his lawful son. He pretended that he spoke this in love for Caesar, so that he might cause Octavius to be hated because Octavius was not Caesar's son, but only an adopted son. Antony allocated lands to the children he had by Cleopatra. He gave Cyrene in Libya to their daughter, Cleopatra. He gave Armenia to her brother, Alexander, and also promised him Media and Parthia and all the countries that lie beyond the Euphrates River as far as India, after he had conquered them. Also, to Ptolemy (surnamed Philadelphus) he gave Phoenicia, Syria, Cilicia, and all the countries on this side of the Euphrates River, to the Hellespont. {*Plutarch, Antony, l. 1. c. 54. s. 3-6. 9:261,263*} {*Dio, l. 49. (41) 5:425*}

5620. Antony also brought out his sons: Alexander wearing Median clothing which included a tiara and an upright head-dress. Ptolemy came in boots, short cloak, and a broad-brimmed hat surmounted by a diadem. These were the clothes of Alexander the Great's successors and of the Medes and Armenians respectively. As soon as the lads had greeted their parents, the Macedonians were to guard the one and the Armenians the other. Whenever Cleopatra appeared in public, she wore the clothes of the goddess Isis and so spoke to all her subjects in the name of the New Isis. {*Plutarch, Antony, l. 1. c. 54. s. 3-6. 9:263*} She also ordered that she should be called Isis, or Selene, and Antony, the New Osiris and Father Bacchus (Liber), or Dionysus, since he was crowned with ivy and wore buskins. He was carried about at Alexandria in a chariot, like Father Liber. {*Velleius Paterculus, l. 2. c. 82. s. 4. 1:225*} {*Dio, l. 50. (5) 5:445*}

## 3971b AM, 4681 JP, 33 BC

5621. Antony went as far as the Araxes River, as though intending to make war on the Parthians. He thought he had accomplished enough by making an alliance with Artarasdes, the king of the Medes. Antony and the Mede promised each other mutual assistance, the one against the Parthians and the other against Caesar. To seal the pact, they exchanged some soldiers. Antony also gave the Mede the part of Armenia that he had recently seized. In return, Antony received the king's daughter, Iotape, who was very young, to be the future wife for his son Alexander (born of Cleopatra), to whom he had given the kingdom of Armenia. The Mede also gave him the ensigns that had been taken from Statianus. {*Dio, l. 49. (44) 5:431,433*} {*Plutarch, Antony, l. 1. c. 52. 9:255,257*} {*Livy, l. 131. 14:161*}

5622. After peace had been made with the Medes, Antony gave Lesser Armenia to Polemon. He also gave the consulship to Lucius Flavius (or Cluvius), who was with him, and took him along with him. {*Dio, l. 49. (44) 5:431,433*}

5623. Caesar Octavius frequently accused Antony in the Senate and before the people and incensed the people against him. Antony also sent recriminations against Octavius. {*Plutarch, Antony, l. 1. c. 55. s. 1. 9:263} [K461] Among other things, Caesar complained that Antony held Egypt which had not been assigned to him. He had killed Sextus Pompeius, whom he (as he said) had willingly spared. He had treacherously captured and imprisoned Artavasdes and had brought great infamy upon the people of Rome by this deed. Caesar also demanded some of the spoils. Above all, Caesar upbraided him for his conduct with Cleopatra for having had children with her and for having given her all those countries. He was especially upset because Antony had brought Caesarion, the son of Cleopatra, into the family of Caesar. {*Dio, l. 50. (1) 5:437} Antony affirmed to the Senate that Caesarion had been acknowledged by Julius Caesar as his son, and that Gaius Matius, Gaius Oppius, and the other friends of Julius Caesar were aware of this. Gaius Oppius, as though the matter needed defending, wrote a book to say that Caesarion was not, as Cleopatra maintained, Caesar's son. {*Suetonius, Julius, l. 1. c. 52. s. 2. 1:101}

5624. When Antony was in Armenia, he ordered Canidius to go to the coast with sixteen legions, while he took Cleopatra with him and went to Ephesus, where all his fleets were to meet. There were eight hundred ships, of which Cleopatra had promised two hundred ships, twenty thousand talents and provisions for all the army during the war. {*Plutarch, Antony, l. 1. c. 56. s. 1,2. 9:265}

5625. Antony, on the advice of Domitius and some others, ordered Cleopatra to return to Egypt and there to await the result of the war. But fearing that Antony and Octavia might be reconciled, she persuaded Canidius with large bribes to speak to Antony for her. He was to say that it was not fair that she should be sent back when she had brought so much for the war effort. It would not be good for the Egyptians, who made up a large part of the naval forces, to be discouraged. Antony was convinced and they assembled their forces and sailed to Samos where they gave themselves over to pleasure. Just as the order was given that all kings, governors, tetrarchs, countries and cities located between Syria, Lake Maeotis (Sea of Azov), Armenia and Illyria were to help in the war, so it was ordered that all the dramatic artists meet at Samos. [E742] Whereas almost all the world was filled with weeping and wailing, this one island alone resounded with piping and singing for many days. The entire theatre was full of these common players. Every city sent contributions over for sacrifices and the kings vied among themselves as to who would put on the greatest feast and give the greatest presents, so that it was commonly said: {*Plutarch, Antony, l. 1. c. 56. s. 2-5. 9:265,267}

"What will they do when they are conquerors in a triumph, when the very preparation for the war is made with such sumptuousness?"

5626. Antony sailed from there to Athens and gave himself wholly over to seeing plays and shows. {*Plutarch, Antony, l. 1. c. 57. s. 1. 9:267} He carried a golden sceptre, had a Persian scimitar by his side and wore a purple robe studded with precious gems. Only a crown was lacking to make him a king dallying with a queen. {*Florus, l. 2. c. 21. s. 3,4. 1:325}

5627. The king of Media used the help of the Roman forces that Antony had left with him to defeat the Parthians and Artaxes (or Artaxias, the Armenian), who came against him. {*Dio, l. 49. (44) 5:433}

### 3972a AM, 4681 JP, 33 BC

5628. Herod duly paid the tributes of the countries of Judea and Arabia, which Cleopatra had received from Antony, because he did not think it safe to give her any reason for ill-will against him. Herod had undertaken to collect the tribute from Arabia and for some time, had paid two hundred talents annually. [K462] Later he was slow and remiss, scarcely paying her half, and that very negligently. {*Josephus, Antiq., l. 15. c. 4. s. 4. (106,107) 8:51}

5629. Caesar and Antony accused each other while each defended himself. This was sometimes done by private letters sent between them. (Among these, the ones that Antony sent to Caesar were the more petulant. Suetonius said that he began to live with Queen Cleopatra, whom he affirmed to have been his wife for nine years. {*Suetonius, Augustus, l. 2. c. 69. 1:253,255}) Other letters were sent openly. Caesar pleaded his case publicly and Antony through his letters. On these occasions, they often sent envoys to one another to demonstrate more fully that their cause was just and to spy on the affairs of the adversary. In the meantime, they got money together, as if for some other purpose, and prepared for war as though it were to be against other enemies. {*Dio, l. 50. (1,2) 5:437,439}

### 3972b AM, 4682 JP, 32 BC

5630. The new consul at Rome, Gaius Sossius (who had triumphed for Judea), made a long speech in the Senate on the Calends of January (January 1), praising Antony and criticising Caesar. Gnaeus Domitius, his colleague, because he had previously endured many calamities, did not get involved. Sossius was ready to make an edict against Caesar, who would have resolutely left the city, had not Nonius Balbus, the tribune of the people, opposed it. {*Dio, l. 50. (3) 5:439}

5631. Antony wrote to Rome to confirm the allocation of countries that he had made at Alexandria between

Cleopatra and her children. In spite of this, these letters were not read publicly. The consuls, Domitius and Sossius, who favoured Antony, forbade it. Caesar wanted everything to be made public, but since their opinion prevailed, Caesar had the Senate agree that none of the letters would be read that had been written about Artavasdes, with whom Caesar had privately consulted against Antony. Caesar also begrudged Antony a triumph. {*Dio, l. 49. (41) 5:425,427}

5632. The Senate convened and Caesar sat between the consuls in the curule chair, surrounded by his friends and soldiers carrying concealed weapons. When at length he defended himself, accusing Sossius and Antony, and saw that no one else, not even the consuls themselves, dared say a word, he ordered them to meet again on a certain day, when he would show them the wrongs of Antony in writing. The consuls did not dare to oppose him but neither were they able to hold their peace. They left the city privately before that day arrived and went to Antony and many of the senators followed them. When Caesar heard of this, he said that anyone on his side was also free to go in safety to Antony, so that he would not appear to have been deserted by them, because of some wrong he had done them. {*Dio, l. 50. (3) 5:439,441} {*Suetonius, Augustus, l. 2. c. 17. s. 2. 1:173}

5633. After the consuls left, Caesar convened the Senate and did and said what he pleased. When Antony heard this, he called a council of his friends and after many arguments on both sides, he declared war. {*Dio, l. 50. (3) 5:441} He divorced his wife Octavia, the sister of Caesar. {*Dio, l. 50. (3) 5:441} {*Livy, l. 132. 14:163} {Eutropius, l. 7.} {Orosius, l. 6. c. 19.} [K463]

5634. Later, Antony sent some men to Rome, to put Octavia out of his house. She left, taking with her all the children Antony had previously by Fulvia, except the oldest, who lived with his father. She wept and was most distressed because it seemed that she was one of the causes of the civil war. [E743] The people of Rome pitied Antony even more than her, and those all the more who had seen Cleopatra, because she was not superior to Octavia in beauty or youth. {*Plutarch, Antony, l. 1. c. 57. s. 2-3. 9:267,269}

5635. When Caesar heard of Antony's rapid and extensive preparations, he was very astonished and feared he would be forced to fight that summer. Caesar was very short of funds and vexed the people of Italy with his extractions of money. Antony's most serious mistake was that he delayed the battle, as this gave Caesar time to prepare and to settle the uproar over his extractions. {*Plutarch, Antony, l. 1. c. 58. s. 1. 9:269}

5636. After King Herod had settled the troubles of Judea and had taken Hyrcanium (a town which the sister of

Antigonus had retained), the war started at Actium in the 187th Olympiad, which was this summer. Herod made great preparations to help Antony but Antony relieved him of this obligation by saying he did not require help. When Antony heard from Cleopatra and others of the wrongdoings of the Arabians, who refused to pay the tribute Antony had imposed, he ordered Herod to make war on them. Cleopatra also persuaded Antony that it would be to her advantage. She hoped that if Herod were to defeat the Arabians, she would be the mistress of Arabia, and conversely, if the Arabians defeated Herod, she would be the mistress of Judea. As a result, Herod returned home on Antony's orders and kept his army there. He soon invaded Arabia, with a good army of foot soldiers and cavalry. He went to Diospolis, where the Arabians met him, and after a fierce battle, the Jews won. {*Josephus, Jewish War, l. 1. c. 19. s. 1,2. (364-366) 2:171} {*Josephus, Antiq., l. 15. c. 5. s. 1. (108-111) 8:53,55}

5637. Titius and Plancus, who had previously been consuls, were Antony's best friends. They knew all of Antony's plans and Cleopatra secretly hated them because they were strongly against her presence in this war. They fled to Caesar, who readily entertained them and got to know all Antony's actions and counsels from them, as well as the contents of his will and its location, as they had been witnesses to it and knew its contents. {*Plutarch, Antony, l. 1. c. 58. s. 2,3. 9:269} {*Dio, l. 50. (3) 5:441} Velleius described the actions of Plancus (who had formerly been secretary to Antony and later Antony had made him proconsul of Asia and then of Syria), as well as his and Titius' flight. {*Velleius Paterculus, l. 2. c. 83. s. 1-4. 1:225}

5638. Antony's will had been deposited with the vestal virgins, who refused to turn it over to Caesar, but said they would not stop him if he were to come and take it; so he did just that. {*Plutarch, Antony, l. 1. c. 58. s. 3. 9:269} At first he read it privately and noted some places which were objectionable. Later, he read it publicly in the Senate and then to the people. Many were offended that a man should give an account of things to be done after his death, while he was still alive. Even though it was considered very unjust to do this, the things contained in the will were of such a nature as to remove all envy from Caesar for his actions. Antony's will stated that Caesarion was indeed the true son of Caesar, the dictator. [K464] He numbered the children he had by Cleopatra among his heirs and bestowed large gifts on them. Concerning his funeral, it said that even if he should die at Rome, he was to be carried through the forum and sent to Alexandria to Cleopatra. {*Plutarch, Antony, l. 1. c. 58. s. 3,4. 9:269,271} {*Suetonius, Augustus, l. 2. c. 17. s. 1,2. 1:173} {*Dio, l. 50. (3) 5:441,443}

5639. These things so enraged everyone against Antony, that they believed everything that was said about him to be true. They believed that Antony would give Rome itself to Cleopatra and move the empire to Egypt, if he were to get the power into his hands. Besides, everyone was so angry with him, that not only his enemies, but also his friends, severely blamed him. They were astonished at the reading of the will and came to the same conclusion about Antony as Caesar did. {*Dio, l. 50. (4) 5:443}

5640. The recent runaway, Plancus, said many horrible things against Antony in the Senate. {*Velleius Paterculus, l. 2. c. 83. s. 3. 1:227} Calvius, or Clavisius, a friend of Caesar's, upbraided Antony's actions, done as favours to Cleopatra, but most of his charges were believed to be false. Antony's friends, however, acted as intercessors to the people for him. They sent Geminius into Greece to Antony, to implore him not to allow himself to be voted out of office and declared an enemy of the state. During supper, Geminius, when provoked by Cleopatra, told her that everything would go well if she returned to Egypt but then he feared the queen's anger and was forced to flee to Rome as fast as he could. {*Plutarch, Antony, l. 1. c. 59. s. 1-3. 9:271,273}

5641. As soon as Caesar was sufficiently prepared, he proclaimed open war against Cleopatra, but not against Antony. [E744] The consulship (for Antony had been appointed consul for the next year) was also taken from him, as well as all his other power, which he had handed over to the pleasure of a woman. It is also said that Cleopatra had so besotted Antony with her charms, that he was not his own man. {*Plutarch, Antony, l. 1. c. 60. s. 1. 9:273,275} {*Dio, l. 50. (4) 5:443,445} She had so enthralled him that she made him the overseer of the exercises of the Alexandrians, while he called her queen and lady. She had Roman soldiers in her guard and all of them had Cleopatra's name written on their shields. She also went into the forum with Antony and helped him put on plays. She sat with him in judgment and she rode on horseback with him. In the cities, she rode around in a chariot, while Antony followed her on foot with the eunuchs. In short, she was so bold as to entertain hope of gaining the government over the Romans. She always swore by a great oath, as she hoped to make laws in the Capitol. {*Dio, l. 50. (5) 5:445,447} Her womanish desire, as well, caused her to want to reign in Rome. {Eutropius, l. 7.} Horace wrote about this: {*Horace, Odes, l. 1. c. 37. (6-12) 1:99}

> This Queen did to
>    The Capitol provide,
> And Empire, ruin,
>    Joining to her side
> The dregs of the World,
>       being above hope now,
>    Ravished with madam fortune's
>       pleasing brow.

5642. Ovid stated: {*Ovid, Metamorphoses, l. 15. (826-829) 4:423} [K465]

> ...The Egyptian spouse shall fall,
> Ill trusting to her Roman General,
> To make our stately Capitol obey
> Of proud Canopus shall in vain assay.

5643. If Antony had been declared an enemy, those who were with him would also have been considered enemies, with the exception of those who had defected from him. To avoid this happening (for the power of his friends was to be feared), he was not verbally declared an enemy, though he was in fact an enemy. Impunity and commendations were propounded to those who were prepared to forsake Antony, but war was publicly proclaimed against Cleopatra, who, they knew, would never forsake him. The charge against him was that he had freely chosen to undertake a war against his own country, which had never offended him. He had done this for the sake of an Egyptian woman. As if there had now been an actual war, the Romans took their soldiers' coats and went to the temple of Bellona. There Caesar, as though he were a herald at their request, carried out all the things according to the tradition of the Romans before a war was begun. {*Dio, l. 50. (5,6) 5:443-447} Caesar added, moreover, that those in charge of the war against the Romans were Mardon, the eunuch, and Pothinus, and Iras, who trimmed Cleopatra's hair, and Charmion, who managed the highest affairs of the government. (Galen stated that Nairas and Carmio were Cleopatra's maids. {Galen, De Theriaca ad Posonem}) {*Plutarch, Antony, l. 1. c. 60. 9:273,275}

5644. After this, the youth were earnestly called to arms by both sides. Money was coined and everything necessary for the war was provided. The preparation for this war was far greater than for any of the previous wars because so many countries sent help to each side. Caesar had help from all of Italy, Gaul, Spain, Illyria, both the Africas, Sardinia, Sicily and other islands located near the previously mentioned mainlands. {*Dio, l. 50. (6) 5:447,449} He had two hundred and fifty warships, eighty thousand foot soldiers and twelve thousand cavalry. Antony had more than five hundred warships, of which some had eight or ten tiers of oars. They were sumptuously equipped and fit for a triumph. He had a hundred thousand foot soldiers and twelve thousand cavalry. [E745] Antony got help from the kings who were his subjects: Bocchus, king of Libya (who had been ousted from his kingdom by the Romans), Tarcondemus (or Tarcondimotus) of Upper Cilicia, Archelaus of Cappadocia, Philadelphus of Paphlagonia, Mithridates of Commagene and Sadalas, king of Thrace, who were all personally present in the war. Polemon sent help from Pontus, Malchus from Arabia, and Herod from Judea, as well as Amyntas, the king of Lycaonia and Galatia. Antony also commanded all the region from the Euphrates River and Armenia right to the Ionian Sea and Illyria, as well as from Cyrene to Ethiopia. {*Plutarch, Antony, l. 1. c. 61. s. 1-3. 9:275,277} Consequently, all the countries of the continent of Asia obeyed the Romans, namely, Thrace, Greece, Macedonia, Egypt, Cyrene, with the borders and all the neighbouring islands. Almost all kings and princes, and all who only bordered on these lands of the Roman Empire, obeyed Antony. Some came in person, others sent their generals (as it was said) to help Antony. {*Dio, l. 50. (6) 5:449}

5645. The king of the Medes sent an auxiliary force to Antony. {*Plutarch, Antony, l. 1. c. 61. s. 2. 9:277} When Antony saw this, he sent them back and recalled his own soldiers, whom he had lent to the Medes. That king had defeated Phraates, the king of the Parthians, and Artaxes (or Artaxias), the king of the Armenians. [K466] Without Antony's troops, however, he was soon defeated. In this way, the Romans lost control of Armenia which Antony had recently conquered, together with Media. {*Dio, l. 49. (44) 5:433}

5646. Antony feared even the over-attentiveness of Cleopatra herself when he was preparing for the war at Actium. He would not eat anything that had not been previously tasted, so she was said to have used the following means to cure him of this fear. She dipped the uppermost flowers of her garland in poison and put the garland on his own head. Immediately, at the height of their mirth, she invited Antony to drink their garlands. When Antony took it from his head, put it into the cup and began to drink, she stopped him with her hand and said:

> "Look, I am the woman, Mark Antony, against whom, with your new craze for tasters, you are carefully on your guard. Such my lack of opportunity or means to act if I can live without you!"

5647. Then she called for a prisoner and ordered him to drink it. He died on the spot. {*Pliny, l. 21. c. 9. 6:169,171}

5648. Herod had routed the greater part of the Arabian army at Cana in Coelosyria. Athenion, the general of Queen Cleopatra in that country, hated Herod, so he assembled a number of the natives and joined with the Arabians. They carried out a large slaughter of the Jews in the rough and difficult places, with which the enemy was better acquainted. When the king saw that his men were put to the worse, he sent men on horseback to bring new troops. He, however, hurried as fast as possible to the Jewish camp, only to find the enemy had taken it. {*Josephus, Antiq., l. 15. c. 5. s. 1. (112-119) 8:55-59}

## 3973a AM, 4682 JP, 32 BC

5649. From that time on, Herod began to make incursions on the Arabians and to prey on them. He always camped on the mountains and always avoided coming to a set battle. He was successful with this tactic, in that he accustomed his men to labour and continual exercise. He was preparing himself to blot out the infamy of his former defeat. {*Josephus, Antiq., l. 15. c. 5. s. 1. (120) 8:59} {*Josephus, Jewish War, l. 1. c. 19. s. 3. (369) 2:173}

5650. Antony intended to go into Italy before his enemies were aware of it, and carry on the war there. When he came to Corcyra, he heard that some light ships, that had been sent out to spy, were anchored near the Ceraunian Mountains. Suspecting that Caesar had come with his whole fleet, he went back into Peloponnesus and wintered at Patrae, since it was now the end of autumn. He sent his soldiers into all the various locations, to enable them to guard them better and to ensure a better supply of food for them. {*Dio, l. 50. (9) 5:453,455}

## 3973b AM, 4683 JP, 31 BC

5651. Caesar sailed from Brundisium and went as far as Corcyra. It was his intention to attack the enemy by surprise as they made their way to Actium. However, he was thwarted by a storm and forced to return, so that he missed his chance. {*Dio, l. 50. (11) 5:457}

5652. While Herod made inroads on the land of Arabia in the seventh year of his reign (this was calculated, both here and later on, from the death of Antigonus in the month of August, 38 BC or 4676 JP), the war at Actium had now begun. In the beginning of the spring, Judea was shaken by an earthquake such as it had never experienced before. Thirty thousand people were killed in the ruins of their houses. The soldiers were unharmed, because they were in the open fields. This calamity was made much worse, when the Arabians, who were their enemies, found out about it. They became quite proud, as if all the cities of the Jews had been overthrown and all the men were dead, so that there were no enemies left. For this reason, they apprehended the envoys of the Jews who, due to this affliction, had come to ask for peace. They killed them and then prepared for war with renewed determination. {*Josephus, Jewish War, l. 1. c. 19. s. 3. (370-371) 2:173,175} {*Josephus, Antiq., l. 15. c. 5. s. 2. (121-124) 8:59,61} [E746] [K467]

5653. Herod encouraged his men and offered sacrifices according to the custom. He quickly crossed over the Jordan River with his army and camped at Philadelphia. The battle started over the citadel which was located between him and the Arabians. The Jews won, forcing the dismayed enemy to another battle. After continual skirmishes, the Arabians were put to flight and in their rout, trampled their own men when the Jews pursued them. They lost five thousand men, while the rest were besieged in their camp and were very short of water. They sent envoys to Herod, who treated them with disdain. They merely became more earnest, offering fifty talents for their freedom, because they were so short of water. Finally, they came out in companies and surrendered to the Jews, so that four thousand captives were taken in five days. On the fifth day, those remaining in the camp came out to fight but they were defeated and seven thousand men died. With this defeat, the courage of the Arabians was diminished and they declared Herod governor of their country. He returned home with great glory. {*Josephus, Jewish War, l. 1. c. 19. s. 5,6. (380-385) 2:179,181} {*Josephus, Antiq., l. 15. c. 5. s. 4,5. (147-160) 8:71-77}

5654. Hillel, a Babylonian of the family of David, lived at Jerusalem a hundred years before the Jewish account of the destruction of the temple. {Gemara Babylonic. tractat. שבת c. 1.} He had a large number of disciples, one of whom was Jonathan, the son of Uzziel and the famous author of the Chaldee Paraphrase of the prophets. The Pharisees were divided into two sects, springing from a difference that arose between Hillel and Shammai, or Sameas, whom Josephus mentioned previously. Jerome stated: {Jerome, l. 3. on Isa 8:14}

> "The Nazarites (such are those who received Christ and yet observed the old law) interpret the two houses of Shammai and Hillel as two families from whom sprang the scribes and Pharisees."

5655. He added, moreover:

> "Shammai and Hillel (or their two houses, of which mention is so often made in the Talmud) sprang up not long before the Lord was born."

5656. Phraates, the king of the Parthians, became more insolent as a result of the victory he had over Antony. He behaved more cruelly than before and was driven into exile by his own subjects, whereupon Tiridates was made the new king. {Justin, Trogus, l. 42. c. 5.} {*Dio, l. 51. (18) 6:51}

5657. Medeius persuaded the Mysians of Asia to revolt from Antony, and with their help he made war against Antony. {*Dio, l. 51. (2) 6:7}

5658. Antony went to Actium, the place where he had appointed to meet his fleet. He was not unperturbed when he found that almost a third of his sailors had starved to death, and simply said: {Orosius, l. 6. c. 19.}

> "Well, the oars are safe, for I will not lack rowers as long as Greece has any men."

5659. Consequently, the captains conscripted travellers, mule drivers, harvesters and young men, but even so the ships were not fully manned and many were empty. {*Plutarch, Antony, l. 1. c. 62. s. 1. 9:277}

5660. Asinius Pollio had stayed in Italy the whole time after the peace had been concluded at Brundisium and had never seen Cleopatra, nor taken an active part on Antony's side, after Antony had been so taken with her love. When Caesar asked if he would go with him to the war at Actium, he replied: {*Velleius Paterculus, l. 2. c. 86. s. 3. 1:233} [K468]

> "My services to Antony are too great, his favours to me are better known, therefore I will have nothing to do with your difference with him, but will be the prize of the conqueror."

5661. Marcus Agrippa had been sent ahead by Caesar and captured many cargo ships loaded with grain and arms, as they were coming from Egypt, Syria and Asia to help Antony. He crossed over the bay of Peloponnesus and conquered Methone, which had been fortified by Antony with a strong garrison. {Orosius, l. 6. c. 19.} He killed Bogud there. He also determined the best places for the cargo ships to arrive. From there, he went into various places in Greece, troubling Antony greatly. {*Dio, l. 50. (11) 5:459}

5662. Caesar was encouraged by these results and set out from Brundisium with all his forces and two hundred and thirty ships with armed prows. He sailed into Epirus after having crossed the Ionian Sea. {*Dio, l. 50. (12) 5:459} {*Livy, l. 132. 14:163} {*Plutarch, Antony, l. 1. c. 62. s. 2,3. 9:279} {Orosius, l. 6. c. 19.} He met his foot soldiers, whom he had conscripted from around the Ceraunian Mountains and drawn together to Actium. Using his ships, he seized Corcyra, which had been left without a garrison. He anchored at Fresh Harbour, because the harbour was not salty. From there he went with his fleet to Actium, where most of Antony's fleet was also anchored. Then he camped at the spot where he later built Nicopolis. {*Dio, l. 50. (12) 5:461,463}

5663. At daybreak, when Antony saw his enemies sailing toward him, he feared that they would take his ships. Lacking men to defend them, he placed his sailors in arms on the forecastle and ordered them to hold up their oars on both sides of the ships as if they were soldiers. [E747] So he kept them in the mouth of the harbour at Actium with the prows toward the enemy, as if they were well equipped with rowers and ready for a fight. Caesar was fooled by this stratagem and turned back. {*Plutarch, Antony, l. 1. c. 63. s. 1. 9:279}

5664. Marcus Agrippa sailed to Leucas and took the island and the ships that were there from under the very nose of Antony's fleet. He also seized Patrae, after defeating Quintus Nasidius in a naval battle, and later took Corinth. {*Velleius Paterculus, l. 2. c. 84. s. 2. 1:229} {*Dio, l. 50. (13) 5:465}

5665. Marcus Titius and Statilius Taurus suddenly attacked Antony's cavalry and routed them. They also joined in a league with Philadelphus, King of Paphlagonia. {*Dio, l. 50. (13) 5:465}

5666. Gnaeus Domitius was a very gallant man, the only one of all of Antony's party who refused to greet Cleopatra by anything other than her own name, for which he was intensely hated by the queen. In defecting to Caesar, he incurred great and imminent dangers. {*Dio, l. 50. (13) 5:465} {*Velleius Paterculus, l. 2. c. 84. s. 2. 1:229} While he was sick with a fever, he took a little boat and crossed over to Caesar. Although Antony took it badly, he opposed Cleopatra's wishes and sent him all his baggage, together with his friends and servants. Domitius, as though regretting his public treasons, died soon after. {*Plutarch, Antony, l. 1. c. 63. s. 2,3. 9:281} He seemed to have fled from Antony because he had lost hope in Antony's chances of success, and many followed his example. {*Dio, l. 50. (13) 5:465}

5667. Beginning to despair, Antony suspected all his friends, some of whom he put to death by torture, including among others Jamblichus, a king of part of Arabia. He ordered that some be torn in pieces, including Quintus Postumius, a senator. [K469] Antony feared that Quintus Dellius and Amyntas, King of Galatia, who had been sent into Macedonia and Thrace to hire soldiers, would defect to Caesar. He went after them as if wanting to help them, in case the enemy should attack them. {*Dio, l. 50. (31) 5:465,467}

5668. In the meantime, on Antony's side, Sossius hoped that he would be victorious if he were to attack Lucius Taurius, who was keeping guard against Antony's fleet with a few ships. He wanted to do this before the arrival of Agrippa, Caesar's admiral, to enable him to do some great exploit. Therefore he attacked him suddenly, early in the morning, taking advantage of a fog, in case Taurius should flee when he saw how many ships he had. He defeated Taurius in the first conflict and chased him but when he happened to be met by Agrippa, he did not overtake Taurius or receive any reward for his victory. Instead, Sossius was killed along with Tarcondimotus and many others. (Dio was inconsistent, for later he stated that Octavius pardoned Sossius. Editor.) {*Dio, l. 50. (14) 5:467}

5669. This defeat, as well as the defeat of his cavalry by Caesar's guard, changed Antony's mind about having his camp opposite the enemies' camp. Therefore, he left it by night and went to the other side of the narrows where his larger forces were camped. Since he was being blockaded from getting provisions, he held a council to decide whether they should go to battle now, or leave that location and fight the war later. {*Dio, l. 50. (14) 5:467}

5670. Canidius, who commanded the legions and who had encouraged Antony to bring Cleopatra with him, now changed his mind and persuaded him to send her back again. Antony should then go into Thrace or Macedonia and decide the matter in a land battle because he was stronger on land and could then also make use of the fresh troops sent by Dicomes, the king of the Getae. {*Plutarch, Antony, l. 1. c. 63. s. 3. 9:281}

5671. Cleopatra and Antony, however, had been frightened by some prodigies. Because of these and the low morale, Cleopatra succeeded in persuading Antony that the war should be decided in a naval battle. However she prepared for her flight and packed her baggage, as if all was lost and she did not think they would win. She planned how she could escape more easily. They determined not to steal away secretly, as though they were fleeing, in case they should strike fear into the army, which was already prepared for battle. However, if anyone were to oppose them, they intended to use brute force to make their way into Egypt. {*Plutarch, Antony, l. 1. c. 63. s. 5,6. 9:281,283} {*Dio, l. 50. (15) 5:469}

5672. Velleius Paterculus stated that King Amyntas defected to Caesar, while Plutarch stated that both Amyntas and Dejotarus defected. Quintus Dellius, the historian, also defected to Caesar, and Horace wrote an ode about him. Either Dellius was afraid of the treacheries of Cleopatra, of which he said Glaucus, her physician, had told him, or else he was following his old pattern. He had defected from Dolabella to Cassius and from Cassius to Antony, and finally gone over from Antony to Caesar. Messala Corinus called him the pole vaulter of the civil wars. {*Seneca the Elder, Suasoriae, l. 1. c. 7. 2:495,497} {*Velleius Paterculus, l. 2. c. 84. s. 2. 1:229} {*Plutarch, Antony, l. 1. c. 63. s. 3. 9:281} {*Dio, l. 50. (23) 5:485} {*Horace, Odes, l. 2. c. 3. (1-4) 1:113}

5673. Antony's fleet was defeated twice, prior to the last great battle. {*Velleius Paterculus, l. 2. c. 84. s. 2. 1:229} There was a captain of the foot soldiers, a valiant man, who had numerous scars on his body from having fought many battles under Antony's command. [E748] Just as they were going to the last battle, he cried out in Antony's presence: [K470]

"Oh noble Imperator, why do you distrust these wounds and our swords, and put your trust in these wooden ships? Let the Egyptians and Phoenicians fight by sea but give us permission to fight by land, where we would either die standing, or defeat our enemies."

5674. Antony did not reply but with a gesture and a look as it were, bade the man be of good courage, while he passed by without any great courage himself. {*Plutarch, Antony, l. 1. c. 64. s. 2. 9:283}

5675. Of the Egyptian ships, Antony and Cleopatra only kept sixty and burned the rest. They did not have enough soldiers to guard them because of the number of runaways and defeats. By night, they carried aboard all their most valuable possessions. The captains of the galleys would only have taken their oars into the battle and left their sails but Antony compelled them to take the sails with them and put them on their ships. He said it had to be done, in case any of his enemies should escape. However, in doing this, Antony was really providing a means for his own escape. {*Plutarch, Antony, l. 1. c. 64. s. 1. 9:283} {*Dio, l. 50. (15) 5:469}

5676. Caesar had two hundred beaked warships and thirty without beaks. His galleys were as swift as light ships. Eight legions were in his fleet, as well as five praetorian cohorts. Antony's fleet consisted of a hundred and seventy ships and although they were fewer in number, they were much larger in size and some had ten tiers of oars. {Orosius, l. 6. c. 19.} Florus stated: {*Florus, l. 2. c. 21. s. 5,6. 1:325}

> "We had four hundred ships and the enemy had not less than two hundred, but what they lacked in number was made up for in size. All the ships they had were from six to nine tiers of oars. Moreover, they were so raised with turrets and decks, that they resembled citadels and cities and made the sea groan under them and the wind out of breath to move them. Their very size was their weakness."

5677. Caesar, in his commentaries, noted by Plutarch, denied these statements concerning the number of Antony's ships. He said that he took three hundred of them. Vegetius stated that the size can be calculated from the number of tiers of oars: {Vegetius, De Re Militaris, l. 4. c. 17.}

> "At Actium, there were ships of six and more tiers of oars."

5678. Florus stated that: {*Florus, l. 2. c. 21. s. 6. 1:325}

> "Caesar's ships had from two to six tiers of oars and none larger."

5679. Strabo, along with Plutarch and Dio, positively said that Antony had some ships that had ten tiers. Scaliger also noted this. {Eusebius, Scaliger's Greek Eusebius, num. 1230.} {*Plutarch, Antony, l. 1. c. 64. s. 1. 9:283} {*Dio, l. 50. (23) 5:485}

5680. It was reported that Sextus Pompeius had been defeated in Sicily by the larger size of Caesar's ships. Antony had built his ships much larger than his enemies'. He had some of three tiers of oars, but all the rest were from four to ten tiers. He also built high towers on them and put large numbers of men inside, who could then fight as if from a wall. He put all the noblemen he had with him on board ship, in case they should defect from him if they were left on their own, as Dellius and some others had done, who had fled to Caesar. He also put some archers, slingers, and armed soldiers on board. {*Dio, l. 50. (23) 5:485} He filled his best and largest ships, from three to ten tiers of oars, with twenty thousand foot soldiers and two thousand archers. {*Plutarch, Antony, l. 1. c. 64. s. 1,2. 9:283}

5681. When Caesar saw the preparations of the enemy and learned of his intentions from others, but especially from Dellius, he also prepared for the battle. {*Dio, l. 50. (23) 5:485} For the first four days, the sea was so rough that the battle was delayed. On the fifth day, when the sky cleared and the storm ceased, they came to battle. [K471] Antony and Publicola were in the right wing, Coelius in the left, while the middle was commanded by Marcus Octavius and Marcus Insteius. Caesar placed Agrippa in the left wing and managed the right wing himself. {*Plutarch, Antony, l. 1. c. 65. s. 1,2. 9:283} However, Velleius Paterculus stated: {*Velleius Paterculus, l. 2. c. 85. s. 1-3. 1:229}

> "The right wing of Caesar's ships was committed to Marcus Larius (or Lurius) and the left to Arruntius. Agrippa directed the whole battle at sea. Caesar was present anywhere he felt his presence was needed to help the battle. The command of Antony's fleet was committed to Publicola and Sossius."

5682. All historians agreed on the commanders of the land forces: Taurus commanded Caesar's forces and Canidius commanded Antony's.

5683. Antony sailed about in a row-boat, exhorting his soldiers, encouraging them to fight valiantly, as if they were on firm land, because the ships were so heavy and large. Antony ordered the captains of the galleys to receive their enemies' charge as if their ships were at anchor, and to stay in the mouth of the gulf. {*Plutarch, Antony, l. 1. c. 65. s. 1,2. 9:285}

5684. It was reported that Caesar left his tent while it was still dark, to visit his fleet. On his way he met an ass, named Nicon (meaning Victor), and his driver, Eutychus (meaning Prosper). After the victory, he erected their images in brass in a temple which he built in the very spot where he had camped. {*Suetonius, Augustus, l. 2. c. 96. s. 2. 1:297} {*Plutarch, Antony, l. 1. c. 65. s. 3. 9:285} It so happened, too, that, as he was sacrificing before the battle, a beast was sacrificed that had its liver tissue folded back inward. {*Pliny, l. 11. c. 73. 3:551} [E749]

5685. Caesar went in a small boat to the right wing of Antony's fleet, wondering why the enemy lay so still in the gulf, and decided that they must be at anchor and so he restrained his galleys. About noon the wind was rising from the sea and Antony's soldiers began to get angry that they were being held back from fighting. Trusting in the large size of their ships, as though they were invincible, they advanced their left wing and as soon as they left the gulf, Caesar's men started the battle. {*Plutarch, Antony, l. 1. c. 65. s. 4,5. 9:285,287}

5686. Caesar's ships were more agile and easier to manoeuvre in battle, either in attack or retreat. The enemy ships were heavy and unwieldy and each one of them was attacked by many of Caesar's ships, which used arrows and rams and shot fire-brands to overcome them. {*Florus, l. 2. c. 21. s. 6. 1:325} On the other side, Antony's soldiers shot arrows and stones from the wooden towers with their crossbows. They also cast grappling-irons on the enemy's ships, if they came too near. If the irons grabbed, they overcame the enemy, otherwise they made a hole in their own ships and sank them! This is how the naval battle went, both sides using various methods to stir up the skill and courage of their soldiers. They also heard the cries of the soldiers on land, who gave them heart by shouting *Courage!* {*Dio, l. 50. (32) 5:505,507} {*Plutarch, Antony, l. 1. c. 66. s. 1,2. 9:287}

5687. Agrippa extended one of his wings to surround the enemy. On the other side, Publicola was also forced to widen his wing and so was divided from his main body. Antony was attacked and fought with Arruntius, but on equal terms. Cleopatra, who for a long time had wondered what to do and now feared that they might lose the battle, signalled her ships. She, in a galley whose poop deck was of gold and her sails of purple, along with sixty of the swiftest Egyptian ships, hoisted their main sails. They had a good wind and set sail for Peloponnesus. As soon as Antony saw the ships of Cleopatra under sail, he forgot everything else and embarked in a galley with five tiers of oars. [K472] He removed the admiral's ensign from the galley and accompanied only by Alexas, the Syrian, and Scellius, followed his fleeing wife. {*Florus, l. 2. c. 21. s. 8,9. 1:327} {*Plutarch, Antony, l. 1. c. 66. s. 3-5. 9:287,289} {*Dio, l. 50. (33) 5:507,509} {Orosius, l. 6. c. 19.} Thus the general, who ought to punish runaways, deserted his own army. No doubt he would have arranged the victory according to the wishes of Cleopatra since she was able to cause his flight at her command. {*Velleius Paterculus, l. 2. c. 85. s. 3. 1:229,231}

5688. When Cleopatra saw that Antony was coming, she raised a signal from her ship and Antony was taken on board. He did not see her, nor was seen by her, but went and sat down alone in the prow of the ship. He never said a word and clapped both his hands over his head. {*Plutarch, Antony, l. 1. c. 67. s. 1. 9:289}

5689. Antony's soldiers were astonished at the flight of their general and also began to think of fleeing. Some hoisted sail and others cast the towers and tacklings of their ships into the sea, so that the lightened ships could flee faster. Caesar's soldiers, who had no sails on their ships and were only prepared for a naval battle, did not follow those who fled. They attacked those preparing to flee, for now they were equal to their enemies in number. They surrounded each of their enemies' ships with many of their own and fought with those close by and those who were afar off. {*Dio, l. 50. (33) 5:509} Antony's soldiers were very brave for a long time after their general had gone and when they lost hope of victory, they fought in order to die. Caesar tried to pacify with words, those men whom he could have killed with his sword. He shouted to them, telling them that Antony had fled and demanding to know from them, for whom and with whom they were fighting. {*Velleius Paterculus, l. 2. c. 85. s. 3,4. 1:231} Finally, he was forced to order that fire be brought from the camp, for now there was no other way of getting the full victory. He had refrained from setting fire to the ships in hope of getting the enemies' treasure. Caesar's men could no longer control themselves when the enemy's ships were on fire, much less do any more harm to their enemies. They sailed over to them, greedy for their money, and endeavoured to quench the fire. Many perished by being burned with their ships and in fighting with their enemies. {*Dio, l. 50. (34,35) 5:511-515}

5690. When the fleet of Antony had long resisted Caesar and was seriously damaged by the waves that were beating against the prows of their ships, they were defeated at about the tenth hour. {*Plutarch, Antony, l. 1. c. 68. s. 1. 9:293} Thus the soldiers, who had long fought for their absent general, at last very unwillingly laid down their arms and surrendered. Caesar soon granted them life and pardon, before they could even be persuaded to ask for it. It was generally conceded that the soldiers had performed the duties of an excellent general, and the general those of a cowardly soldier. {*Velleius Paterculus, l. 2. c. 85. s. 5. 1:231}

5691. From the fifth hour (as Orosius said) to the seventh, the battle on both sides went without any clear outcome. [E750] However, the rest of the day and the subsequent night, Caesar got the upper hand. {Orosius, l. 6. c. 19.} The battle continued until late at night, so that the conqueror was forced to stay on board all night. {*Suetonius, Augustus, l. 2. c. 17. s. 2. 1:173}

5692. The battle at Actium was fought when Caesar and Messala Corvinus were consuls. {*Velleius Paterculus, l. 2. c. 84. s. 1. 1:227} The battle was on September 2, and it was from this time that Dio began the reign of Caesar. {*Dio, l. 51. (1) 6:3,5} [K473] In another place, Dio said his reign lasted forty-four years minus thirteen days, the time between his death, on the 19th of August, and the 2nd of September, when he had started to rule. {*Dio, l. 56. (30) 7:68} Both of those days were excluded after the custom of Suetonius, Aurelius Victor and Eutropius. {*Suetonius, Augustus, l. 2. c. 8. s. 3. 1:161} They said that Caesar governed the state on his own for forty-four years.

5693. As soon as it was day, Caesar completed his victory. Twelve thousand of the conquered had been killed and six or seven thousand wounded, of whom a thousand died of their wounds. {Orosius, l. 6. c. 19.} Plutarch stated that not more than five thousand died and three hundred ships were captured. The remains of this large armada was carried up and down over the whole sea in its wreckage, for the seas were cleared by the wind and daily washed up gold and purple on the shores, from the spoils of the Arabians, the Sabeans and a thousand other peoples of Asia. {*Plutarch, Antony, l. 1. c. 68. s. 1. 9:293} {*Florus, l. 2. c. 21. s. 7. 1:327}

5694. This famous naval battle was much spoken of by the poets of that time. {*Virgil, Aeneid, l. 8. (675-705) 2:107,109} {*Ovid, Metamorphoses, l. 15. (826-831) 4:423} {*Horace, Epodes, l. 1. c. 9. (1-38) 1:389,391} {Propertius, Elegies, l. 4. c. 6.} Propertius had this memorable saying:

The cause it is the soldier animates,
Which if not good, his courage shame abates.

5695. The rejoinder is that which Messala Corvinus was reported to have said, when commended by Caesar, with whom he was colleague this year in the consulship. Messala was once praised by Caesar because, though at Philippi he had been most hostile to him and Antony for the sake of Brutus, at Actium he had been a most zealous adherent of his. Messala replied: {*Plutarch, Brutus, l. 1. c. 53. s. 3. 6:247}

"Oh Caesar, you shall always find me on the better and more just side."

5696. From the spoils of the enemy, Caesar dedicated ten ships from Actium to Apollo, ranging from a ship of one tier of oars up to a ship with ten tiers. {*Strabo, l. 7. c. 7. s. 6. 3:305} {*Dio, l. 51. (1) 6:5}

5697. Caesar sent part of his fleet in pursuit of Antony and Cleopatra, but when they could not overtake them, they returned. {*Dio, l. 51. (1) 6:5} Some lighter ships overtook Antony, which he was able to repulse. Only Eurycles, a Lacedemonian, the son of Lachares, who had been beheaded by Antony for thievery, shook a lance at him from the deck of the ship, as if he intended to throw it at him. He did not attack Antony's ship, but with his prow struck another galley of the admiral (for there were two of them). He turned her around and captured both her and another ship, which was loaded with very rich items and baggage. {*Plutarch, Antony, l. 1. c. 67. s. 2,3. 9:289,291}

5698. When he was gone, Antony returned to his former silence and resumed his previous posture. After he had spent three days in the prow of the ship, he was smitten with either anger or shame. He arrived at Taenarum, where Cleopatra's women first succeeded in getting them to speak to each other. Later they ate and slept together. {*Plutarch, Antony, l. 1. c. 67. s. 4. 9:291}

5699. Many merchant ships arrived there, as well as some of Antony's friends, who had escaped through flight. They brought news that the fleet was indeed scattered, but that they believed the land forces were intact. Antony sent messengers to Canidius, ordering him to retire with the army through Macedonia into Asia, as quickly as possible. {*Plutarch, Antony, l. 1. c. 67. s. 5. 9:291} [K474]

5700. Many of the army on land did not know of Antony's flight. When they heard of it, it seemed incredible to them that he should flee and leave nineteen whole legions of foot soldiers and twelve thousand cavalry behind. His soldiers hoped that he would show up again somewhere else. They showed so much loyalty to him, that when his flight was known for a certainty, they stayed for seven days and rejected the messengers sent to them by Caesar. {*Plutarch, Antony, l. 1. c. 68. s. 2,3. 9:293}

5701. Caesar overtook them as they were marching into Macedonia and without fighting, joined them to his army. {*Dio, l. 51. (1) 6:5} When it was night, the general, Canidius, left the camp and fled to Antony in great haste. Destitute of all things and betrayed by their leaders, they surrendered themselves to the conqueror. {*Velleius Paterculus, l. 2. c. 85. s. 6. 1:231} {*Plutarch, Antony, l. 1. c. 68. s. 3. 9:293} Caesar added them to his own army. {*Dio, l. 51. (1) 6:5,7} [E751]

5702. Even then, many of the Roman nobility fled to Antony, but the auxiliaries fled into their own countries and never again waged war against Caesar. Along with all the people who had previously been subject to the Romans, in the course of time they accepted conditions of peace from Caesar. {*Dio, l. 51. (1) 6:5,6}

5703. Caesar demanded money from the cities and took away their power over the citizens, which they had usurped in the councils of the people. From the kings and governors, with the exception of Amyntas and

Archelaus, he took all the towns they had received from Antony. He deposed from their thrones: Philopator, the son of Tarcondimotus (the prince of Cilicia), Lycomedes, who had obtained the kingdom of Pontus in a part of Cappadocia, and Alexander, the brother of Jamblichus, who had received a kingdom in Arabia. Alexander had received his kingdom for accusing Caesar. He gave the country of Lycomedes to Medeius, who had instigated the revolt of the Mysians of Asia from Antony. He granted freedom to the people of Cydonia and Lampe (in Crete), because they had helped him, and rebuilt the city of the Lampeans, which had been destroyed. The senators and equestrians and other noblemen who had in any way helped Antony, were either fined, put to death, or pardoned. {*Dio, l. 51. (2) 6:6}

5704. Among those to whom he granted life, was Sossius, who had often made war against Caesar, but had fled and hidden, only to be found later. Caesar let him go free. Caesar spared Marcus Scaurus, the half-brother of Sextus Pompeius, who had also been condemned to death, for the sake of his mother, Mucia. Among those who were put to death was Curio, the son of that Curio whose help Julius Caesar had often used. Caesar had only ordered that one of the Aquilii Flori was to die, namely the one who drew the lot; but before the lots were cast, the son offered to die and was executed. Out of grief, the father killed himself over his dead son's body. {*Dio, l. 51. (2) 6:7,9}

5705. Cassius of Parma fled to Athens and was executed. {*Valerius Maximus, l. 1. c. 7. s. 7. 1:89} {*Velleius Paterculus, l. 2. c. 87. s. 3. 1:235} Horace asked of Albius Tibullus the poet: {*Horace, Epistles, l. 1. c. 4. (2,3) 2:277}

> "Writing something to outshine the pieces of Cassius of Parma?"

5706. Orpheus, a poem recorded by Achilles Statius at the end of the commentaries on the book of Suetonius, a famous rhetorician, was thought to be one of Cassius' poems. [K475] A poem called Brutus is also cited by Varro. {*Varro, De Lingua Latina, l. 6. (7) 1:179} It stated that, at Athens, Cassius was terrified by a ghost similar to the one said to have appeared to Brutus before the battle at Philippi. In an earlier place, Valerius described it in these words. In the dead of the night, as he lay in bed, while his mind was wrought with grief and cares, he thought he saw a very large man coming towards him. He was of a black hue with an ugly beard and long hair. When Cassius asked who he was, he answered, your bad angel. Terrified at so horrible a vision and a more horrid name, Cassius called his servants and asked them if they had seen anyone coming or going. They replied that no one had come and he went back to bed, but the

same vision was constantly in his mind; so he gave up trying to sleep, ordered that a light be brought in and forbade his servants to leave him. Valerius added that not long after this night, he was executed by Caesar. He was among the last to be put to death for the murder of Julius Caesar, as Trebonius was the first to die. {*Velleius Paterculus, l. 2. c. 87. s. 3. 1:235} {Orosius, l. 6. c. 19.} We know this from the earlier account of Valerius Maximus, that he was executed at Athens a little after the victory at Actium. {*Valerius Maximus, l. 1. c. 7. s. 7. 1:89}

5707. At that time, Caesar sailed to Athens and was reconciled with the Greeks. He distributed the grain that was left from the war to the cities which were suffering from famine and had been stripped of money, servants and horses. {*Plutarch, Antony, l. 1. c. 68. s. 4. 9:295}

5708. Antony wanted to leave Taenarum for Libya and selected one good cargo ship to hold his enormous treasure. He gave the remaining valuable articles made of gold and silver to his friends and ordered them to divide them among themselves and go their own way. When they tearfully refused, he comforted them very politely and at length dismissed those who agreed to provide for themselves. He wrote letters to Theophilus, his steward in Corinth, asking him to keep them safe and give them some hiding place until they could make their peace with Caesar. Theophilus was the father of Hipparchus, whom Antony greatly respected. [E752] He was the first of his freedmen to defect to Caesar and later went and lived in Corinth. {*Plutarch, Antony, l. 1. c. 67. s. 5-7. 9:291,293}

5709. So that Cleopatra could safely sail to Egypt, she put garlands on the prows of her ships and ordered those songs to be sung to a pipe that are usually sung when a victory has been won. {*Dio, l. 51. (5) 6:17}

## 3974a AM, 4683 JP, 31 BC

5710. When they arrived safely in Egypt, she put to death many noblemen who had always been her enemies and who, at that time, were elated over her defeat. She took what they had, including the sacrifices to their gods, even removing them from temples. When she had gotten an enormous amount of money this way, she prepared an army and looked for foreign mercenaries. In the hope of making an alliance with the king of Media, she sent him the head of the king of Armenia, Artavasdes, or Artabazes. {*Dio, l. 51. (5) 6:17}

5711. She also embarked on a bold and great enterprise. She planned to have her fleet cross over the isthmus which divided the Red Sea from the Mediterranean Sea off Egypt and is considered to be the boundary between Asia and Libya. This isthmus is about thirty-eight miles wide at its narrowest point. She sent her forces to the Arabian Gulf (Red Sea) with a large amount of money, to enable her to find some remote country with her ships, where she could be free from slavery and war. {*Plutarch, Antony, l. 1. c. 69. s. 2,3. 9:295,297} [K476] The first ships which were carried over, however, and others that were built for sailing into the Red Sea, were burned by the inhabitants of Arabia Petra at the instigation of Quintus Didius, the governor of Syria. {*Plutarch, Antony, l. 1. c. 69. s. 3. 9:297} {*Dio, l. 51. (7) 6:21}

5712. Antony landed in Libya and went into the desert. He wandered up and down, alone except for his two friends, Aristocrates, a Greek rhetorician, and Lucilius, a Roman. {*Plutarch, Antony, l. 1. c. 69. s. 1. 9:295} Later, he sailed to Pinarius Scarpus in Libya to the army he had previously raised for the defence of Egypt. Scarpus told those who were sent to him that he would not entertain Antony, then killed them and also put to death some soldiers who disagreed with his actions. {*Dio, l. 51. (5) 6:17}

5713. When Antony learned of this revolt, he decided to kill himself, but was prevented by his friends from doing so. He went to Alexandria, still believing that the legions at Actium were intact. Canidius later brought him news that this was not so. Therefore, Cleopatra abandoned her plans of sailing into the Red Sea and instead, fortified the mouths of the Nile River with garrisons. {*Plutarch, Antony, l. 1. c. 69. s. 3. 9:297}

5714. Antony left the city and the company of his friends and built a house on the sea beside the isle of Pharos. He created a mound in the sea to build on and lived there as an exile from all men, saying he would lead the life of Timon, the man-hater, because his situation was so like his. He, too, had been abused by his friends and had experienced their ingratitude. Therefore, he would trust no man and angry with all men, called his house Timonium. {*Plutarch, Antony, l. 1. c. 69-71. 9:297-301} {*Strabo, l. 17. c. 1. s. 9. 8:39}

5715. Herod sent to Antony, advising him to put Cleopatra to death. He suggested that if it were done at an opportune time, Antony could enjoy her estate and obtain more favourable conditions of peace from Caesar. {*Josephus, Antiq., l. 15. c. 6. s. 6. (191) 8:91}

5716. Caesar dismissed his veteran soldiers and Antony's army into Italy, without giving them anything, and sent the rest into various places. He was afraid that those who had been companions of his victory and were dismissed without any reward, could raise some seditions, so he sent Agrippa after them into Italy, seemingly on some other business. Caesar settled the affairs of Greece, as though there were no danger to be expected from the

soldiers who had been discharged. He went into Asia to settle things there and awaited what Antony would do. {*Dio, l. 51. (3) 6:9,11}

5717. All the people and kings refused to send Antony and Cleopatra any help, although many of them had received generous favours from them both. The gladiators were a people in a most wretched state. They had been training in Cyzicum where Antony planned to hold triumphal games when he defeated Caesar. {*Appian, Civil Wars, l. 5. c. 14. (137) 4:605} They had valiantly fought for Antony and Cleopatra. As soon as they heard what had happened, they decided to go to Egypt to help them. Their journey upset Amyntas in Galatia and the sons of Tarcondimotus in Cilicia, who had formerly been good friends to Antony and Cleopatra, but had revolted from them. Quintus Didius, the governor of Syria, also forbade them to go through his land, so that they were boxed in and able neither to go into Egypt, nor to cause a revolt in Syria. Although Didius gave them many good promises, they sent for Antony to come to them. [K477] They thought that they could wage war in Syria more easily, if Antony were with them. Antony did not go, nor did he send any messengers to them, so they reluctantly yielded to Didius, on the condition that they would never fight as gladiators again. Didius gave them Daphne, a suburb of Antioch, to live in, until he knew what Caesar wanted to do. {*Dio, l. 51. (7) 6:21,23} [E753]

5718. Didius wrote to Caesar that troops had been sent to him by Herod, to suppress these gladiators. Caesar also mentioned this fact in a letter he sent to Herod. {*Josephus, Jewish War, l. 1. c. 20. s. 2. (392) 2:185} Caesar also wrote that Capidius had written to tell him how much Herod had helped him in the war against the monarchs of Syria. {*Josephus, Antiq., l. 15. c. 6. s. 7. (195) 8:93} In the first instance, I have written gladiators for monarchs; so it is clear that, in both places, the name of Quintus Didius should have been written for Ventidius and Capidius. As a result of this action, news reached Antony at his house at Timonium that Herod the Jew had defected to Caesar with some legions and cohorts. {*Plutarch, Antony, l. 1. c. 71. s. 1,2. 9:301}

5719. Many things were decreed at Rome to honour Caesar for his victory at sea. A triumph was given to him for Cleopatra and a triumphal arch was erected at Brundisium, with another one in the Roman forum. The base of the Julian Temple was to be decorated with the prows of captured ships. Every four years, a festival was to be held in his honour. There were always to be processions on his birthday and on the day the news of his victory had first been brought. The vestal virgins and the Senate, with their wives and children, were to go and meet him as he entered the city. All the honours associated with Antony were to be pulled down and demolished and his birthday considered an unlucky day. An edict was passed that no one in any family was to have the surname of Marcus. {*Dio, l. 51. (19) 6:51,53}

5720. Caesar retired to Samos to winter there. {*Suetonius, Augustus, l. 2. c. 17. s. 3. 1:173} Antony had taken away the three colossal statues made by Myron that had stood on one base. Caesar put two of them back on the the same base, namely Athena and Hercules, while he carried the third, Jupiter or Zeus, into the Capitoline and erected a temple just for it. {*Strabo, l. 14. c. 1. s. 14. 6:213,215}

5721. When Caesar was viewing the prisoners there, an old man, Metellus, was brought out. He had long hair and was otherwise deformed, due to his hard life. When the crier called his name as he stood among the prisoners, his son, who was one of Caesar's captains, leaped from his seat and with tears went and embraced this man, whom he barely recognised. Then he stopped weeping and said:

> "My father, oh Caesar, was an enemy to you, I, a companion. He has deserved punishment, I, a reward. I request that you either grant my father his life, for my sake, or put me to death together with him."

5722. Caesar felt pity toward them and granted Metellus his life, even though he was his mortal enemy and had spurned many previous offers to defect from Antony. {*Appian, Civil Wars, l. 4. c. 6. (42) 4:211,213}

5723. Antony left his cottage by the sea, which he called Timonium, and went to the palace. He was entertained by Cleopatra and turned all the city to revelling and banqueting and liberally bestowed gifts. {*Plutarch, Antony, l. 1. c. 71. s. 2. 9:301} [K478] He enrolled Caesarion, the son of Caesar and Cleopatra, among the young men. He gave Antyllus, his own son by Fulvia, the *toga virilis*, without the purple hem. He did this, so that the Egyptians would be happier in that they had a man to reign over them. The others, who would have them for commanders, would also be more satisfied, in case anything should happen to Antony and Cleopatra. {*Plutarch, l. 1. c. 71. s. 2. 9:301} {*Dio, l. 51. (6) 6:17,19}

5724. After this, there was great feasting and banqueting at Alexandria for many days. However, they turned this gathering into another, which was not inferior to the other in delights, luxury and splendour, and which they called the society of:

> "Partners in Death"

5725. This was for the friends of all those who would die together. They registered their names and when it came round to each one's turn, passed the time in pleasures and in feasting. {*Plutarch, Antony, l. 1. c. 71. s. 3. 9:301}

5726. Cleopatra, furthermore, gathered various sorts of deadly poisons, testing them on condemned persons and animals and watching how they died. She did this daily and of everything that she tried, she found that the bite of the asp was the best way to die. It only brought a sleepiness and heaviness over one, without any spasms or pain. It caused only a gentle sweating of the face and a languishing dullness of the senses. {*Plutarch, Antony, l. 1. c. 71. s. 4,5. 9:301,303}

5727. Although Antony and Cleopatra made preparations as if they were about to make war both by sea and land, they made provision for an alternative plan, as well. If for any reason it should become urgently necessary, they planned to set sail for Spain, in the hope of being able to cause a revolt, using their money; otherwise, they would go to the Red Sea. {*Dio, l. 51. (6) 6:19} Florus indicated this with these words: {*Florus, l. 2. c. 21. s. 9. 1:327} [E754]

> "of whose preparation to flee into the ocean"

## 3974b AM, 4684 JP, 30 BC

5728. Caesar entered into his fourth consulship in Asia. {*Suetonius, Augustus, l. 2. c. 26. s. 3. 1:187} For the sixth time, he was called Imperator and for the fourth time now, was consul with Marcus Licinius Crassus. Caesar arrived at Brundisium after having been recalled to Italy through letters written by Agrippa from Rome. He was to repress a sedition of the soldiers, who were demanding rewards for their services. {Orosius, l. 6. c. 19.} {*Plutarch, Antony, l. 1. c. 73. s. 3. 9:305} They had been discharged after the victory at Actium, out of the whole number Caesar had earlier sent to Brundisium. {*Suetonius, Augustus, l. 2. c. 17. s. 3. 1:173}

5729. In crossing the seas, Caesar was twice bothered by storms, first between the cape of Peloponnesus and Aetolia, then once again, near the Ceraunian Mountains. In both places, some of his smaller ships were lost, while the tackling on his ship was ripped and the helm was broken. {*Suetonius, Augustus, l. 2. c. 17. s. 3. 1:173}

5730. Caesar came to Brundisium in the middle of winter, but went no farther. He was met by the whole Senate. (The tribunes of the people had appointed two praetors for the government of the city, by a decree of the Senate.) He also met with the equestrians and a great many of the people, along with many envoys. The very soldiers in question came there also, with some coming out of fear of such a large crowd and fear of Caesar himself. Germanicus said about the soldiers: {*Tacitus, Annals, l. 1. c. 42. 3:317}

> "That he daunted the Actium legion with his look."

5731. Some came, hoping for pay, while others were sent for. Caesar gave some of them money and to some, who had been with him in all his wars, he gave lands. {*Dio, l. 51. (4) 6:13}

5732. Suetonius wrote that he did not stay at Brundisium more than twenty-seven days, only until he had settled his business with the soldiers. *[K479]* Dio said that he went into Greece again on the thirtieth day after having come into Italy. Because it was winter, the ships were brought over the isthmus of Peloponnesus. He came into Asia so quickly, that Cleopatra and Antony heard of his departure and return at the same time. {*Dio, l. 51. (5) 6:15} {*Suetonius, Augustus, l. 2. c. 17. s. 3. 1:173}

5733. Antony sent Alexas or Alexander, a Laodicean, to Herod. He had been introduced to him at Rome by Timagenes, who had more influence on Antony than any other Greek. Alexas was to prevent Herod from defecting to Caesar, but Alexas betrayed Antony and stayed with Herod. {*Plutarch, Antony, l. 1. c. 72. s. 2. 9:303}

5734. Alexandra hoped that Herod would be thoroughly punished by Caesar, who was his enemy. She solicited her father, Hyrcanus, not to allow this affliction of their family, but to hope for better things. She also counselled him to ask protection from Malchus, the king of Arabia. Hyrcanus first found these suggestions repulsive. Finally, her constant pleadings got the better of him and cherishing higher hopes, he contemplated the treachery of Herod. Through Dositheus, a friend of his, he sent letters to the Arabian, asking him to send cavalry who would escort him to the Dead Sea, which was about forty miles from Jerusalem. Dositheus was a relative of Joseph, who had been put to death by Herod. His brothers, along with others, had also been put to death, by Antony, at Tyre. Nevertheless, to curry favour with the king, Dositheus showed Herod the letter. Herod thanked him and asked for a favour. He wanted him to put a new seal on the letter, deliver it to Malchus and get his reply. The Arabian wrote back that he was ready to help Hyrcanus and his family, and all the Jews who belonged to that faction. He would send a band of soldiers, who would escort him in safety and would obey him in all matters. After Herod had received this letter also, he summoned Hyrcanus and asked him if he had any alliance with Malchus, which Hyrcanus denied. Herod showed the letters in the council of the Sanhedrin and ordered that he be put to death. This is how these matters are recorded in Herod's commentaries, but they are reported otherwise by others, who say that Hyrcanus was not put to death for this crime but for some other treasons against the king. {*Josephus, Antiq., l. 15. c. 6. s. 2. (165-173) 8:83}

5735. Antony and Cleopatra sent envoys to Caesar in Asia. Cleopatra asked for the kingdom of Egypt for her children and Antony asked that he be permitted to lead

a private life in Athens. If that was not granted, then he wished to live in Egypt. Because of the lack of friends and the distrust which they felt, due to defections, Antony sent Euphronius, the teacher of their children, as an envoy. {*Plutarch, Antony, l. 1. c. 72. s. 1,2. 9:303} Without Antony's knowledge, Cleopatra sent Caesar a gold sceptre, a gold crown and a golden chair, as if she were delivering her kingdom over to him. If he really hated Antony, she hoped he might have some pity on her. Caesar accepted the presents, considering them to be good omens, but gave Antony no answer. In actual fact, he publicly threatened Cleopatra and replied that if she would lay aside her arms and her kingdom, he would then advise what should appropriately be done with her; privately, he promised her impunity and her kingdom, if she would put Antony to death. {*Dio, l. 51. (6) 6:19,21} *[E755]*

5736. After Herod had executed Hyrcanus, he sent a message to Caesar, because he realised that the friendship he had shown to Antony would not help him. *[K480]* He suspected that Alexandra might use this opportunity to incite the people to rebel and fill the kingdom with domestic seditions, so he committed the care of the kingdom to his brother Pheroras and left his mother Cypros, his sister Salome, and all his family in the citadel of Masada. He ordered that, if anything untoward should happen, his brother Pheroras was to assume the government of the kingdom. He also placed his wife, Mariamme, in Alexandrion with her mother Alexandra, because she could not get along with his mother, and committed their custody to his steward, Joseph, and Soemus, an Iturian. These were men who had always been faithful to him and were now being appointed to this duty to honour them. However, he ordered that if they were to know for certain that any sinister mishap had befallen him, they were to kill both the ladies at once and to the utmost of their power, continue the kingdom for his children and his brother Pheroras. {*Josephus, Antiq., l. 15. c. 6. s. 5. (183-186) 8:87,89}

5737. After giving these commands, Herod sent to Rhodes, asking to meet with Caesar there. When Herod arrived, he only laid aside his crown, but retained his other princely attire. He was admitted into Caesar's presence and showed still more fully the greatness of his spirit by neither turning to supplication, as would have been natural in the circumstances, nor offering a petition as if in acknowledgment of transgression. Instead, he freely confessed the alliance he had with Antony, as well as the help by way of grain and money which he had sent Antony, because the Arabian war had prevented him from helping him in person. Then he added that he was ready to be a faithful friend of Caesar. Caesar exhorted him, restored his crown to him and honoured him exceedingly. So, beyond all expectations, Herod was again confirmed in his kingdom through the free gift of Caesar and by a decree of the Senate, which Caesar obtained for him. {*Josephus, Jewish War, l. 1. c. 20. s. 1-2. (387-392) 2:183,185} {*Josephus, Antiq., l. 15. c. 6. s. 6,7. (187-196) 8:89,95} Strabo also noted that: {*Strabo, l. 16. c. 2. s. 46. 7:299}

"He (Herod) surpassed his ancestors to such a degree, especially in friendship with the Romans, that he was declared king, first by Antony and later, when Caesar granted him the same authority."

5738. We also read that: {*Tacitus, Histories, l. 5. c. 9. 3:191}

"When Augustus was conqueror, he enlarged Herod's kingdom, which had been given to him by Antony."

5739. To show his generosity, Herod gave presents not only to Caesar, but his friends as well, and this beyond his capacity. He also endeavoured to secure a pardon for Alexas, or Alexander, the Laodicean, who had been sent to him from Antony. Herod was unable to do so, because Caesar had sworn that he would punish him, for he had been the strongest defender of Antony concerning all the machinations which Cleopatra had used against Octavia. Consequently, Alexas, taking heart from Herod's good reception, dared to come into Caesar's presence. He was promptly taken, put in bonds and carried into his own country, where he was executed on Caesar's orders. This was during the lifetime of Antony, whom he had betrayed. {*Josephus, Jewish War, l. 1. c. 20. s. 3. (393,394) 2:185} {*Josephus, Antiq., l. 15. c. 6. s. 7. (197,198) 8:95} {*Plutarch, Antony, l. 1. c. 72. s. 3. 9:303,305}

5740. Antony and Cleopatra sent other envoys to Caesar. Through them, Cleopatra promised Caesar an enormous amount of money, while Antony reminded him of the friendship and family ties existing between them and made excuses for the familiarity that he had with the Egyptian woman. Antony recalled the former alliance between them and the deeds they had done together in their youth. Furthermore, he turned Publius Turullius over to Caesar. He was a senator who had been one of Caesar's murderers and later Antony's friend. Antony also promised that he would kill himself if, by so doing, he might obtain security for Cleopatra. Caesar executed Turullius on the isle of Cos, where Turullius had felled trees from Aesculapius' Grove, for ship timber. Caesar sent no reply to Antony. {*Dio, l. 51. (8) 6:23} [K481]

5741. In the absence of Herod, his wife Mariamme and his mother-in-law Alexandra were very unhappy at being confined to the citadel as if in a prison, so that they could neither enjoy their own estate, nor avail themselves of other men's goods. They became very upset when Mariamme, using her feminine flatteries, fished out of Soemus what orders Herod had given him concerning them. She then began to wish that Herod would never return home, believing life with him would be intolerable. She did not hide her discontent, but openly said what it was that bothered her. Beyond all expectations, Herod had returned and now told Mariamme of the successes he had enjoyed. Not seeming to take any notice, she would sigh at all the caresses that he made, so that Herod plainly knew about the hatred his wife had against him and himself wavered between love and hatred toward her. {*Josephus, Antiq., l. 15. c. 7. s. 1. (202-208) 8:97-101}

5742. Before Caesar went into Egypt with his army, he went into Syria. {*Josephus, Antiq., l. 15. c. 6. s. 7. (198,19) 8:95} {*Suetonius, Augustus, l. 2. c. 17. s. 3. 1:173} {*Plutarch, Antony, l. 1. c. 74. s. 1. 9:307} {Orosius, l. 6. c. 19.}

5743. Phraates and Tiridates were fighting over the kingdom of Parthia and asked help from Caesar. He did not reply directly, but said he would consider it at another time, because of the problems in Egypt. [E756] In fact, he did nothing, in the hope that the civil war in Parthia would weaken both sides. {*Dio, l. 51. (18) 6:51}

5744. Gaius Merius was a centurion who had done outstanding exploits in the war against Antony. In an ambush by his enemies, he was surprised and surrounded, then brought before Antony in Alexandria. Antony asked him what he thought was an appropriate way to deal with him. The centurion replied:

"Order to have my throat cut, for I can neither be sufficiently persuaded by gifts nor by fear of death, to stop being Caesar's soldier or to start being yours."

5745. Antony pardoned him for his outstanding character. {*Valerius Maximus, l. 3. c. 8. s. 8. 1:327,329}

5746. Antony and Cleopatra thought it best that their children should be sent ahead to the Red Sea, with part of the queen's treasure. {Orosius, l. 6. c. 19.} They placed garrisons in the two corner coasts of Egypt, at Pelusium and Paraetonium, and prepared a fleet and forces, for the purpose of starting the war again. {Orosius, l. 6. c. 19.} {*Florus, l. 2. c. 21. s. 12. 1:327}

5747. Antony sent his son, Antyllus, to Caesar, with a third embassy and a large amount of gold. Caesar sent him back again, without either granting his embassy or giving any answer; he did, however, take his gold. For the third time, Caesar reiterated the same numerous threats and promises to Cleopatra. {*Dio, l. 51. (8) 6:23,25}

5748. Caesar sent Thyrsus, who was his freedman and very discreet, to Cleopatra, to win her over to him. {*Dio, l. 51. (8) 6:25} {*Plutarch, Antony, l. 1. c. 73. s. 1. 9:305} Caesar was afraid that Antony and Cleopatra would despair of a pardon and so persist in their intentions. They would either defeat him by their own strength, or else go into Spain or Gaul, or Cleopatra, as she had threatened to do, would burn all the treasures that she had stored in her tomb. He therefore sent Thyrsus, who conferred very courteously with Cleopatra and told her that Caesar was in love with her. He thereby hoped that she, who was greatly disposed toward having all men in love with her, would kill Antony to save herself and her money. {*Dio, l. 51. (8) 6:25}

5749. Caesar himself marched through Syria against Antony, and his generals through Libya. {*Plutarch, Antony, l. 1. c. 74. s. 1. 9:307} Caesar sent Cornelius Gallus ahead of him with four of Scarpus' legions, which had been stationed at Cyrene to guard that place. [K482] They made a surprise attack on Paraetonium, which was an important city of Egypt near the border of Libya, and captured it. {*Dio, l. 51. (9) 6:25} {Orosius, l. 6. c. 19.}

5750. When Antony found out about this defeat, he changed his plans of going into Syria to the gladiators. Instead, he marched toward Paraetonium, hopeful that he could easily draw those forces away from Gallus to himself, since he knew that they were favourably disposed toward him, because they had been soldiers together. If that failed, he would win them by force, for he had brought large naval and land forces with him. Antony was not even able to talk to these soldiers, because Gallus ordered all the trumpeters to sound, so that no one could hear anything. In addition, Antony sustained some losses through a sudden sally and his fleet was also defeated. At night, Gallus had laid a chain, which was hidden underwater, across the mouth of the harbour. He held the port with a concealed guard and allowed Antony's ships to sail boldly into the harbour in contempt of him. When the ships were in the harbour, he used certain engines to raise the chains up and prevent the ships from leaving. Then he either burnt or sank the ships, which were attacked on every side, by sea and land, and also from the houses. {*Dio, l. 51. (9) 6:25,27}

5751. At Ptolemais, Herod very royally entertained Caesar, as he was journeying through Syria into Egypt. He showed every hospitality toward his army and gave them plenty of supplies. By this, he became one of Caesar's best friends and was in the habit of riding about with him when he mustered his army. Herod also entertained Caesar and his friends with the service of a hundred and fifty men, who were clothed in very rich and sumptuous apparel. (Loeb text amended to read differently. Editor.) He did not allow them to want for anything on their march to Pelusium, although those places were barren and lacked water. Caesar's army lacked neither wine nor water, which the soldiers appreciated. He also gave Caesar eight hundred talents. Indeed, he gave such a good reception, everyone thought that it was more than the kingdom could afford. {*Josephus, Jewish War, l. 1. c. 20. s. 3. (394,395) 2:185,187} {*Josephus, Antiq., l. 15. c. 6. s. 7. (198-201) 8:95,97}

5752. Thyrsus convinced Cleopatra that Caesar was in love with her. She wanted it to be true, because she had enslaved both Caesar's father and Antony in the same way. Therefore, she not only hoped for a pardon and the kingdom of Egypt, but for the Roman Empire itself. {*Dio, l. 51. (9) 6:27} Antony took Thyrsus, who was being honoured very highly by her, and whipped him soundly, then sent him back to Caesar. He wrote that he had done this, because he had been provoked by his insulting pride. Antony, who was easily irritable because of his current bad fortune, said: [E757]

"If you (Caesar) do not like this, you have Hipparchus, my freedman. Hang him up and whip him and then we shall be even."

5753. To remove all jealousies and suspicions, Cleopatra marvellously honoured Antony. In the past, she had modestly celebrated her birthday, but now she celebrated his birthday with the greatest splendour and magnificence she was capable of. Many were invited to the feast—they came poor, and went away rich. {*Plutarch, Antony, l. 1. c. 73. s. 2,3. 9:305}

5754. It was reported that Caesar had taken Pelusium by force, but it was really through the treachery of Cleopatra. {*Dio, l. 51. (9) 6:27,29} There was a common report that this town had been given to Caesar by Seleucus, with her consent. To clear herself, she turned Seleucus' wife and children over to Antony, so he could execute his revenge on them. {*Plutarch, Antony, l. 1. c. 74. s. 1,2. 9:307} After Antony was defeated by Cornelius Gallus at Paraetonium and immediately after that, at Pharos, he returned to Alexandria. {Orosius, l. 6. c. 19.} [K483]

5755. Cleopatra had storehouses and monuments built, which were very exquisite and high. These were joined to the temple of Isis and there she stored the most precious things of all her royal treasures like: gold, silver, emeralds, pearls, ebony, ivory and cinnamon. She also stored a large supply of torch wood and tow (hemp fibre). Consequently, Caesar was afraid that he would lose such riches and that, in despair, she would burn them, so he daily gave her good reasons to hope while he marched with his army toward the city. {*Plutarch, Antony, l. 1. c. 74. s. 2. 9:307} She privately forbade the citizens of Alexandria to attack Caesar, while publicly she encouraged them to do battle with him. {*Dio, l. 51. (10) 6:27}

*5756.* Caesar took up his position near the hippodrome with his army and Antony sallied out, fought valiantly and routed Caesar's cavalry, driving them right up to their camp. Encouraged by this victory, he entered the palace, kissed Cleopatra while in his armour and recommended a man to her who had fought very courageously. Cleopatra rewarded the man with solid gold armour and headpiece, but that very night, after having received these, he defected to Caesar. {*Plutarch, Antony, l. 1. c. 74. s. 3. 9:307}

*5757.* Antony shot messages into Caesar's camp, in which he promised each soldier six thousand sesterces. Caesar voluntarily read these letters to the soldiers and by this means caused Antony to be hated more. Caesar tried to make them feel ashamed over the suggested treachery and generated enthusiasm for himself. After this, the soldiers became exceedingly angry that their fidelity had been questioned and behaved so valiantly, that when Antony fought in a battle using only his foot soldiers, he was soundly defeated. {*Dio, l. 51. (10) 6:29} Another historian also mentioned this: {*Strabo, l. 17. c. 1. s. 10. 8:43}

"As one goes through the hippodrome, one comes to Nicopolis, which is a settlement by the sea, no smaller than a city. It is about four miles from Alexandria. Caesar Augustus honoured this place, because he defeated Antony's troops there in a battle."

*5758.* After this, Antony, through his envoys, challenged Caesar to a single duel. Caesar replied that Antony had many ways to die. Therefore, Antony thought that he could die most honourably by being killed in battle and determined to attack Caesar by sea and land. At supper (as it was reported), he bade his servants drink and feast heartily, as it was uncertain what they would be doing tomorrow, or what master they would serve, if he was dead and gone. This made Antony's friends weep. Then Antony told them that he would not lead them out to battle, since he was seeking an honourable death for himself from it, rather than safety and victory. {*Plutarch, Antony, l. 1. c. 75. s. 1,2. 9:307,309}

*5759.* About the middle of that night, when the whole city was quiet and depressed in fear and expectation of what was coming, it was reported that, suddenly, sweet music from all types of instruments could be heard. There was the sound of a large number of people, as at the feasts of Bacchus, and satyr-like frisking and dancing, as if it had indeed been the feast of Bacchus himself, to whom Antony always most likened himself. The noise was so loud, that this very large gathering seemed to be located almost in the very middle of the city. It moved toward that gate which led to the enemy outside, then finally passed through this gate and so vanished. {*Plutarch, Antony, l. 1. c. 75. s. 3,4. 9:309} [K484]

*5760.* Dio reported that, besides this, many other prodigies foreshadowed the bondage of Egypt. He said it rained in those places which had never had rain before and it was not just water, but blood mixed with the drops. This was not the only sign—there were flashes of armour from the clouds as this rain fell; a dragon of an incredible size, which hissed horribly, was suddenly seen among the Egyptians; comets, and the ghosts of the dead, appeared also, while the statues seemed to frown and Apis made a mournful lowing and shed tears. {*Dio, l. 51. (17) 6:47,49} [E758]

*5761.* On the first of August, as soon as it was day, Antony went down to the harbour to organize his fleet. {Orosius, l. 6. c. 19.} But Cleopatra had caused the fleet to defect from him {*Dio, l. 51. (10) 6:29} and as soon as Antony's fleet had rowed near the other fleet, they greeted Caesar's soldiers and defected to them. Then, combining all the ships into one fleet, they came to attack the city. While Antony was watching this, his cavalry deserted him, as did his foot soldiers. He withdrew into the city and cried out that he had been betrayed by Cleopatra, for whom he had taken up arms. {*Plutarch, Antony, l. 1. c. 76. s. 1. 9:309,311}

*5762.* Cleopatra feared the anger and despair of Antony. She pretended that she had done this in fear of Caesar and that she would kill herself. She fled to her tomb with one eunuch and two maids and sent a message to Antony that she was dead. He believed her and therefore wanted his faithful servant, Eros, to kill him. Eros had long ago promised that he would kill him, if necessity required it. He drew out his naked sword as if to strike Antony, but turned his face from him and killed himself. When he fell at Antony's feet, Antony said:

"Noble Eros has shown me what must be done by myself, but could not endure to do it for me."

*5763.* He stabbed himself in the belly and fell on a bed. The wound did not bring a speedy death, for the blood stopped flowing after he laid down. When he had recovered a little, he asked those who stood around to thrust him through, but they all fled from the chamber and left him crying and writhing in pain. After this, a great tumult arose. When Cleopatra heard it, she looked out from the top of the tomb, for the door was so constructed, that, once it was shut, it could not be opened again. Only the upper parts of it had not yet been finished. She also sent Diomedes, her secretary, to bring Antony into the tomb to her. As soon as Antony knew that she was alive, he arose, because he thought he might live. However, he lost hope of living because of his excessive bleeding and with the help of his servants, was carried to the door of the tomb, as he requested. {*Plutarch, Antony, l. 1. c. 76,77. 9:311,313} {*Dio, l. 51. (10) 6:29,31}

{*Livy, l. 133. 14:163} {*Florus, l. 2. c. 21. s. 11. 1:327} {*Velleius Paterculus, l. 2. c. 87. s. 1,2. 1:233} {*Strabo, l. 17. c. 1. s. 11. 8:47} {*Suetonius, Augustus, l. 2. c. 17. s. 4. 1:175} {Eutropius, l. 7.} {Orosius, l. 6. c. 19.}

5764. While this was happening, Dercetaeus, one of his bodyguards, took Antony's sword and concealed it, then stole away and ran to Caesar. He was the first one to tell him of Antony's death, and showed him the blood-covered sword. When Caesar heard this news, he withdrew into the innermost room of his tent, where he greatly bewailed Antony as his relative and colleague, who had been his companion in many battles and in the government of the empire. Then he took his letters and called his friends together and read them to them, showing them how proudly and rudely Antony had replied to all his mild and just demands. [K485] Then he sent Proculeius with orders to take Cleopatra alive, if possible. Caesar was afraid to lose her treasure and also thought that she would be a magnificent trophy in his triumph, if he could take her alive. {*Plutarch, Antony, l. 1. c. 78. s. 1-3. 9:315}

5765. In the interim, Antony was drawn up into the tomb by ropes which were hung for pulling the stones up. {*Dio, l. 51. (10) 6:31} They said there was nothing more lamentable than this sight. Antony was all besmeared with blood and almost dead. He was tied to the ropes and drawn up by the great efforts of Cleopatra and the two servants who were with her, while those who were underneath him, helped lift him up. Antony stretched out his hands to Cleopatra and lifted himself up as well as he could. As soon as Cleopatra had taken him in, she laid him on a bed. Then she tore off her headpiece and beat her breasts and scratched her breasts and face with her own hands. She was all covered in gore and blood and called him, *Master, Husband* and *Imperator*. She almost forgot her own miseries, in compassion for him. After Antony had appeased her grief a little, he called for some wine, either because he was thirsty, or because he thought it would hasten his death. After he had drunk it, he advised her to take care of her own affairs and to save her life, if she could do so without dishonour. He said that, of all Caesar's friends, she could trust Proculeius the most. She should not lament the miserable change in his fortune, but rejoice at the great good fortune that had been his, because he had been the most famous and powerful prince of all men. He was a Roman and had not been ignobly conquered, a Roman by a Roman. He died just as Proculeius came from Caesar. {*Plutarch, Antony, l. 1. c. 77,78. 9:313,315}

5766. Caesar sent Gaius Proculeius, who was an equestrian, and Epaphroditus, his freedman. He told them both what they should say and do. However, Cleopatra

feared that they would deal harshly with her and stayed in the tomb. She thought there was no other way she could procure her safety, but that she might redeem her pardon and the kingdom of Egypt from Caesar, through his fear of losing her money. Caesar wished to get her money and to take Cleopatra alive, so that he could parade her in a triumph. In spite of this, he was unwilling to be seen to have tricked her. [E759] After he had given her a pledge, he wanted to treat her as a captive and to a certain extent, subdue her against her will. {*Dio, l. 51. (11) 6:33}

## The Empire of the Roman Caesars

## 3974c AM, 4684 JP, 30 BC

5767. Cleopatra would not entrust herself to Proculeius but she talked with him from the building as he stood on the outside at the door, which was at ground level. Although the door was barred, he could hear what she was saying. In this meeting, she asked for the kingdom for her children. Proculeius bade her to be of good cheer and refer everything to Caesar. When he had adequately surveyed the place, he reported everything to Caesar, who sent Gallus back to her, to ask her for an answer. When he arrived at the door, he deliberately kept her talking, while Proculeius and two servants set up ladders and got in at the window through which the women had taken in Antony. He immediately went down to the door where Cleopatra sat talking with Gallus. As soon as she saw Proculeius, she tried to kill herself with a dagger she had on her belt. Proculeius came running, restrained her with both his hands and took the dagger from her. He shook her clothes for fear that she had some poison hidden on her. This is how Plutarch related the story. {*Plutarch, Antony, l. 1. c. 78,79. 9:315,317} [K486]

5768. Dio related the events like this: Gaius Proculeius and Epaphroditus talked with Cleopatra and offered her very tolerable conditions. Suddenly, before she had agreed to them, they laid hands on her and removed anything she might be able to use to kill herself. They allowed her to stay there some days, until she had embalmed Antony's body. Then they brought her into the palace and gave her the customary train of servants and honour, so that thereby she would be led to hope that she would get what she wanted and not harm herself. {*Dio, l. 51. (11) 6:33} As soon as Cleopatra was captured, one of her eunuchs willingly put asps on himself and was bitten, then fell into a grave which he had previously prepared for himself. {*Dio, l. 51. (14) 6:39,41}

5769. At his first approach, Caesar conquered Alexandria, which was a very rich and large city. {*Livy, l. 133. 14:163} {*Strabo, l. 17. c. 1. s. 6. 8:23} {*Suetonius, Augustus, l. 2. c. 17.

*s. 3. 1:173}* *{Orosius, l. 6. c. 19.}* As he entered Alexandria, he talked with Areius, a philosopher of Alexandria. Caesar took him by the right hand, so his countrymen would honour him the more, when they saw him so honoured by Caesar. *{*Plutarch, Antony, l. 1. c. 80. s. 1. 9:317,319}* Caesar had been his student in philosophy and was very well acquainted with him and his two sons, Dionysius and Nicanor. *{*Seneca, On Mercy, l. 1. c. 10. s. 1. 1:387}* *{*Suetonius, Augustus, l. 2. c. 89. s. 1. 1:281}* *{*Plutarch, Precepts of Statecraft, l. 1. c. 18. 10:241}* *{*Dio, l. 51. (16) 6:45}* *{*Dio, l. 52. (36) 6:175}* *{Octavius, Julius Caesar}*

5770. Then he went into the gymnasium and ascended a tribunal, which had been set up especially for him. He ordered the citizens, who had fallen on their knees before him in fear, to rise. In a speech, he freely pardoned all the people for several reasons. (He spoke in Greek so everyone could understand him.) He pardoned them for their founder, Alexander, their god Serapis, for the greatness of the city and for the sake of his friend, Areius. He also pardoned all of the Egyptians, because he was unwilling that so many men, who had done good service for the Romans in many other things, should be put to death. *{*Plutarch, Antony, l. 1. c. 80. s. 1,2. 9:319}* *{*Dio, l. 51. (16) 6:45}* *{Julian, Ad Alexandria, Epistle 51.}*

5771. At the request of Areius, he pardoned many, including, among others, Philostratus, who was the ablest sophist of his time. However, when he incorrectly said that he belonged to the school of the Academy, Caesar hated his behaviour and rejected Philostratus' request. As a result, Philostratus let his beard grow long and followed Areius in mourning, always repeating this verse:

"A wise man will a wise man save, if wise he be."

5772. When Caesar heard of this, he pardoned him, more in order to free Areius from envy, than Philostratus from fear. *{*Plutarch, Antony, l. 1. c. 80. s. 2,3. 9:319}*

5773. Young Antony, or Antyllus, was the older of the two sons Antony had by Fulvia, and he was betrothed to Caesar's daughter, Julia. He fled into the shrine of the Deified Julius, which Cleopatra had made to honour Julius Caesar. Caesar took him from the image of Julius and killed him, after he had made many fruitless prayers. *{*Plutarch, Antony, l. 1. c. 81. s. 1. 9:319}* *{*Suetonius, Augustus, l. 2. c. 17. s. 5. 1:175}* *{*Dio, l. 51. (15) 6:43}* *{Orosius, l. 6. c. 19.}* As the soldiers beheaded him, Theodorus, his school teacher, who had betrayed him, took a most precious jewel from his neck and sewed it into his belt. Although he denied the deed, it was found on him and he was crucified. *{*Plutarch, Antony, l. 1. c. 81. s. 1. 9:319}* *[K487]* Caesar ordered that Jullus, the other son of Antony by Fulvia, should receive everything in the estate. Jullus' freedmen were ordered to give him all the things which dying men are commanded by the laws to leave to their heirs. *{*Dio, l. 51. (15) 6:45}* *[E760]*

5774. The children that Antony had by Cleopatra were very honourably taken care of with their governors and train of servants who waited on them. Caesar saved and nourished and cherished them, no less than if they had been linked in an alliance with him. *{*Suetonius, Augustus, l. 2. c. 17. s. 5. 1:175}* *{*Plutarch, Antony, l. 1. c. 81. s. 2. 9:319}*

5775. Of those who favoured Antony, Caesar executed some and pardoned others, either of his own good will or through the intercession of friends. *{*Dio, l. 51. (16) 6:45}* Among those put to death was Canidius, always a most bitter enemy to Caesar and unfaithful to Antony. *{Orosius, l. 6. c. 19.}* He died in a more cowardly fashion than seemed fitting for one who had bragged that he was not afraid of death. *{*Velleius Paterculus, l. 2. c. 87. s. 3. 1:235}* Quintus Orinius was also put to death at Caesar's own command, because he was a senator of the people of Rome, but very dishonourably, was not ashamed to be governor to the queen's spinners and weavers. *{Orosius, l. 6. c. 19.}*

5776. Antony had many children of kings and princes at Alexandria. Some were being kept as hostages and others on false accusations. Caesar sent some of them home, married others to one another and kept some with him. He returned Jotape to her father, the king of the Medes, who had found asylum with him after his defeat. He did not send Artaxes' brothers back, as he requested, because he had killed the Romans who had been left behind in Armenia. *{*Dio, l. 51. (16) 6:45}*

5777. When he viewed the tomb (which was of glass *{*Strabo, l. 17. c. 1. s. 8. 8:37}*) and the body of Alexander the Great, which had been taken out of the vault, Caesar put a crown upon it and scattered flowers over it and worshipped it. As he touched the body, he broke off a piece of his nose. He was asked if he wanted to see the bodies of the Ptolemys. The Alexandrians really wanted him to see them, but he refused and said that he wished to see a king, not corpses. *{*Suetonius, Augustus, l. 2. c. 18. s. 1,2. 1:175}* *{*Dio, l. 51. (16) 6:45,47}* For that very reason, he would not go to see Apis, because he said he usually worshipped gods, not cattle. *{*Dio, l. 51. (16) 6:47}*

5778. Many great kings and captains desired to bury Antony, but Caesar refused to take him from Cleopatra, who buried him in a splendid and magnificent manner. Caesar allowed her to take as much time as she required for his funeral. *{*Plutarch, Antony, l. 1. c. 82. s. 1. 9:321}*

5779. Due to all her deep sorrow and grief (for her breasts were covered with inflammations and ulcers from the blows she had given herself), Cleopatra developed a fever, which she gladly used as an excuse to stop eating, so that she would die without any more trouble. She had a physician whose name was Olympus, to whom she declared her real intentions and whom she used as a counsellor and assistant in her death. Olympus recorded this in his history of these events. When Caesar suspected this, he threatened both her and her children. She had allowed herself to become quite sick, but later she let herself be cured and ate properly. {*Plutarch, Antony, l. 1. c. 82. s. 2. 9:321}

5780. Caesar himself came to visit her shortly after, and comforted her. {*Plutarch, Antony, l. 1. c. 83. s. 1. 9:321} She fell down at his feet and tried in vain to seduce him, but her beauty was beneath the prince's dignity. [K488] Although he perceived that she intended to stir up affections in him, he concealed his feelings and fixing his eyes on the ground, said only this:

"Woman, be of good cheer, you shall have no harm done to you."

5781. She was not merely requesting life, which Caesar had promised her, but she really wanted his love and her kingdom. {*Florus, l. 2. c. 21. s. 10,11. 1:327} {*Dio, l. 51. (12) 6:35,37}

5782. Last of all, she handed over a list to Caesar of all the treasures she had. When Seleucus, one of her treasurers, accused her of having omitted some things and not having told all, she leaped up, took him by the hair and beat him soundly. When Caesar smilingly reproved her, she answered:

"It is not a great matter, oh Caesar, since you have come and visited me in this condition in which I am and have talked with me, that I should be accused by my own servants, as if I had kept back some jewels. These were not for myself, who am a poor wretch, but that I might present them to Octavia and your Livia. I hoped that by their intercession to you I might find more mercy and favour from you."

5783. Caesar was glad about this and hoped that she now wanted to live. He told her that he would do both this for her, and other things, beyond her expectations. He departed, supposing that he had deceived her, but he had, in fact, been more deceived by her. {*Plutarch, Antony, l. 1. c. 83. s. 3-5. 9:323,325}

5784. There was a young gentleman named Cornelius Dolabella, who was a close friend of Caesar. This man was in love with Cleopatra and at her request, he secretly told her, through a messenger, that Caesar was to journey by land through Syria and that he was determined to send her and her children into Italy within three days.

When she learned this, she begged Caesar to permit her to pay her last respects to Antony. Once she had done this, she put garlands on the tomb and kissed it. Then she ordered a bath to be made for her. After she had bathed, she feasted sumptuously. {*Plutarch, Antony, l. 1. c. 84,85. 9:325,327} [E761]

5785. After dinner, she gave Epaphroditus, into whose charge she had been committed, a letter to carry to Caesar and pretended it was about some other business. However, the letter really contained her request to be buried with Antony. She then excused herself and sent him on his way. {*Plutarch, Antony, l. 1. c. 84. s. 2. 9:325} {*Dio, l. 51. (13) 6:39}

5786. After Epaphroditus left, Cleopatra shut the doors and only kept with her two women-in-waiting, Iras, or Nairas, and Charmion, who usually dressed her. One of them could expertly do up her hair and the other pared her nails. Cleopatra adorned herself with the very best clothes she had. Then on her left arm she put an asp, which she had asked to have brought to her. The asp had been covered with figs, grapes and flowers, to deceive her guards. She died from its bite, as if she were in a slumber. {*Florus, l. 2. c. 21. s. 10.11. 1:327} {*Velleius Paterculus, l. 2. c. 87. s. 1,2. 1:233} {*Plutarch, Antony, l. 1. c. 85,86. s. 3,4. 9:327,329} {Galen, De Theriaca Ad Posinem} {*Dio, l. 51. (14) 6:39,41} {Eutropius, l. 7.} {Orosius, l. 6. c. 19.}

5787. Other historians commented on the deceptive nature of Cleopatra and doubted whether an asp would have been able to kill her so quickly. They questioned if she actually died from the bite of an asp. Some say that Cleopatra made a large, deep wound in her arm with her teeth, or some other object, and into this wound put poison, which she had previously prepared from an asp and which was brought to her in a bone. After the poison had entered her body, she peacefully ended her life without her guards even knowing it. {Galen, De Theriaca Ad Posinem} {*Strabo, l. 17. c. 1. s. 10. 8:43} {*Plutarch, Antony, l. 1. c. 86. s. 1-3. 9:329} {*Dio, l. 51. (14) 6:39,41} Only two little pricks were found in her arm. [K489] Caesar, who saw her dead body, carried a picture of her, with an asp attached to her arm, in his triumph. {*Plutarch, Antony, l. 1. c. 86. s. 3. 9:329} {*Dio, l. 51. (14) 6:39} Horace said this of her death: {*Horace, Odes, l. 1. c. 37. (25-32) 1:99}

> …So stout she could
> With cheerful countenance behold,
> Her ruined palace, asps receive,
> And of their poison them bereave:
>  By delay in death more keen;
> Envies the Liburnians they
> Should she, so great a queen,
> In triumph lead a secret prey.

*5788.* When Caesar opened Cleopatra's letters, he knew at once what had occurred. First, he thought to go there himself and sent some ahead quickly, to see what had happened. They ran there as quickly as they could and found the guards standing before the door, not knowing what had taken place. When they opened the door, they found Cleopatra dead, lying on a golden bed in all her royal robes. Iras, or Nairas, was lying dead at her feet, where she had fallen, and Charmion, half-dead and heavy-headed, was trimming the diadem that she wore. When someone asked her angrily:

"A fine deed, this, Charmion!"

*5789.* She answered:

"It is, indeed, most fine, and befitting the descendant of so many kings."

*5790.* She did not speak another word, but fell down there by the bedside. {*Plutarch, Antony, l. 1. c. 85. s. 3,4. 9:327,329} {*Dio, l. 51. (13,14) 6:39} When Caesar saw Cleopatra's body, he tried everything possible to see if she could be revived. He brought in the Psylli to suck out the venom and poison, but in vain. (These Psylli are males, for there are no women born in their tribe, and they have the power to suck out poison of any reptile, if use is made of them immediately, before the victim dies; and they are not harmed themselves when bitten by any such creature.) {*Dio, l. 51. (14) 6:41} {*Suetonius, Augustus, l. 2. c. 17. s. 4,5. 1:175} {Orosius, l. 6. c. 19.}

*5791.* Once he was certain that Cleopatra was dead, Caesar admired and pitied her. He was very grieved, because he thought that he had lost the main attraction for his triumph. He ordered that her body be sumptuously and royally buried and laid in the same tomb with Antony. {*Plutarch, Antony, l. 1. c. 86. s. 4. 9:329,331} {*Dio, l. 51. (15) 6:41} He performed this honour for them in that he had them buried in the same sepulchre and finished the tomb which they had begun. {*Suetonius, Augustus, l. 2. c. 17. s. 4,5. 1:175} Caesar also ordered that her women attendants be honourably buried. {*Plutarch, Antony, l. 1. c. 86. s. 4. 9:329,331}

*5792.* Plutarch wrote that Cleopatra lived thirty-nine years and reigned twenty-two, which was the number of years from the death of her father, Ptolemy Auletes. Some historians—Ptolemy, Clement, Porphyry, Eusebius and others—assign only twenty-one years and two or three months to her reign. *[E762]* Plutarch wrote that she reigned more than fourteen years with Antony. Tertullian stated that she reigned thirteen years under Octavius, calculating the start of the government of Antony from the death of Julius Caesar and of Octavius' government from his first consulship. The Macedonian Empire, according to both Ptolemy and Clement, lasted two hundred and ninety-four years from the death of Alexander the Great, who first founded it, to the death of Antony and Cleopatra, with whom it fell. We deduce the time as two hundred and ninety-three and a quarter years. {*Plutarch, Antony, l. 1. c. 86. s. 4. 9:331} {Ptolemy, Canon of Kings} {Ptolemy, Great Syntaxis, l. 1. c. 8. 3159} {Porphyry, Scaliger's Greek Eusebius, p. 226.} {*Tertullian, Answer to the Jews, l. 1. c. 8. 3:159} {*Eusebius, Chronicles, l. 1. 1:237} {*Clement, Stromateis, l. 1. c. 21. 2:329} [K490]

*5793.* At this time, Caesar put an end to the civil wars. {*Florus, l. 2. c. 21. s. 12. 1:327} {*Velleius Paterculus, l. 2. c. 87. s. 1. 1:233} Dionysius Halicarnassus also confirmed that he came into Italy as soon as Augustus Caesar had put an end to the civil wars, in the middle of the 187th Olympiad. {*Dionysius Halicarnassus, l. 1. c. 7. s. 2. 1:23} This was the beginning of the third year, in the month of August, after Egypt had been reduced under the power of the Romans and an end had been made to their civil wars. The words of the decree of the Senate are recorded by Macrobius. {Macrobius, Saturnalia, l. 1. c. 12.} Censorinus stated that the Egyptians calculated the years of the Augusti (not of the Θεων Σεβασων, as Scaliger thought, but of Caesar Augustus, who had the dominion over them), from the time in which they came under the power and government of the people of Rome. {Censorinus, De Die Natali, l. 1. c. 21.} He said that he wrote this book in the Philippic year of the Augusti, two hundred and sixty-eight (for thus the best copies have it, not two hundred and sixty-seven), and from the death of Alexander the Great, five hundred and sixty-two years, and from Nabonassar, nine hundred and eight-six years. (The beginnings of these years were taken from the first of the moveable month of Thoth of the Egyptians.) He agreed with Ptolemy, who said that four hundred and twenty-four Egyptian years elapsed from the beginning of the reign of Nabonassar to the death of Alexander, and then a further two hundred and ninety-four years to the empire of Augustus. {Ptolemy, Great Syntaxis, l. 3.}

*5794.* Therefore, that Egyptian epoch began on the first day of the moveable month of Thoth in the year of the Philippic account, beginning two hundred and ninety-three years from the death of Alexander the Great, which in turn was seven hundred and seventeen years from Nabonassar. It was, in fact, on the first day of the week, as is found in a writing of a certain Jew, recorded at Norimberge with Messahala. Namely, it was in the month of August in 30 BC, or 4684 JP, on the 31st day, which, according to the incorrect reckoning of leap years that was being used at Rome at the time, was called the 29th day of August. This was that epoch *of the years of Augustus*, which was accommodated by Ptolemy to the moveable year of the Egyptians. {Ptolemy, Great Syntaxis, l. 3. c. 8.} Vettius Valens, an Antiochian, in book 1 of Ανθολογων γενεθλιακων, used that epoch and stated that Augustus ruled Egypt forty-three years, as Philo also showed. We find, also, that there were many who calculated Caesar's empire to be that long. {*Philo, Gaius, l. 1. c. 22. (148) 10:75} {Ptolemy, Canon of Kings} {*Clement, Stromateis, l. 1. c. 21. 2:329}

5795. Cleopatra had sent her son Caesarion, whose father had been Julius Caesar, through Ethiopia into India, with a large sum of money. His tutor, Rhodon, persuaded him to return, as if Caesar had recalled him to his mother's kingdom. As Caesar was deciding what he should do with him, Areius, the philosopher, said to him:

> "It is not good that Caesar's name should be too common."

5796. Consequently, Caesar put him to death, following on the death of his mother. {*Plutarch, Antony, l. 1. c. 81,82. 9:321} {*Dio, l. 51. (6) 6:17,19} {*Dio, l. 51. (15) 6:43}

5797. The statues of Antony were thrown down, but Cleopatra's were not touched, because Caesar, for the sum of two thousand talents, had granted her friend, Archibilius, that they would not be thrown down, as Antony's were. {*Plutarch, Antony, l. 1. c. 86. s. 5. 9:331} [K491]

5798. In the palace, a large amount of money was found, which had been stored there by Cleopatra from the spoils of almost all the temples. She had also exacted much from those who had been found guilty of any crime, while two thirds of their goods had been demanded of anyone else who could not be accused of any crime. All the soldiers' arrears were paid and Caesar also gave a thousand sesterces to each of the soldiers he had with him, so they would not plunder the city. Caesar also paid all the debts he owed to anyone, and gave many gifts to the senators and equestrians who had accompanied him in the war. {*Dio, l. 51. (17) 6:49} [E763]

5799. For this part of the year, Caesar chose as his colleague in the consulship Marcus Tullius Cicero, who was the son of Cicero the orator, whom Antony had murdered. Cicero read out to the people the letters that Caesar had sent to Rome about the defeat of Antony in the Alexandrian War (not Actium, as Appian erroneously wrote). He read the copy of the letters in the rostrum where his father's head and hand had previously been publicly displayed. {*Plutarch, Cicero, l. 1. c. 49. s. 4. 7:209} {*Appian, Civil Wars, l. 4. c. 4. (20) 4:173} {*Appian, Civil Wars, l. 4. c. 6. (51) 4:229} {*Dio, l. 51. (19) 6:53}

5800. The Marble Table at Capua showed that this year, on the Ides of September (September 13), Marcus Tullius was chosen as the consul to replace Marcus Licinius, {Pighius, Annals of Rome, Tom. 3. p. 495.} and that on the same day: {*Pliny, l. 22. c. 6. 6:305}

> "When Augustus was consul with the son of Marcus Cicero, Augustus was presented with an obsidional (siege) crown by the Senate; so inadequate was the civic crown thought to be."

5801. Many crowns and processions were decreed for Caesar in Rome at that time. He also had another triumph granted him for subduing the Egyptians. The day when Alexandria was taken was declared a lucky day, and the inhabitants were to use that day as the starting point in their calculations of time. Caesar was given the tribunal power for the rest of his life. He would have the power to help anyone asking for it within the pomoerium or one mile beyond the walls, a privilege not possessed by any of the tribunes. {*Dio, l. 51. (19) 6:53,55}

5802. Herod wavered between love and hatred toward his wife Mariamme. He was continually being incensed against her by the false accusations of his sister Salome and his mother Cyros, who stirred him up to hatred and jealousy against her. He may have dealt more harshly with her, had not the news come, at just the right time, that Antony and Cleopatra were both dead and that Caesar had won Egypt. Herod hurried to meet Caesar and left his family as it was. When he left, he commended Mariamme to Soemus, and told him that he owed him a great deal of respect for the concern he had for her. He also gave him the government of a part of Judea. {*Josephus, Antiq., l. 15. c. 7. s. 3. (213-216) 8:103}

5803. Caesar built a city at the place where he had defeated Antony and called it Nicopolis. He held the same plays which he previously had held at Actium. {*Dio, l. 51. (18) 6:49} {*Dio, l. 51. (1) 6:5} {*Strabo, l. 17. c. 1. s. 10. 8:43}

5804. Caesar organized Egypt into a province, to make it more fruitful and suitable for producing grain for the city of Rome. His soldiers scoured all the canals into which the Nile River overflowed and which had been choked with mud for a long time. {*Suetonius, Augustus, l. 2. c. 18. s. 2. 1:175} He also constructed some new canals. {*Dio, l. 51. (18) 6:49} [K492]

### 3975a AM, 4684 JP, 30 BC

5805. Herod met with Caesar in Egypt and confident of his friendship, he spoke freely with him and was highly honoured by him. Caesar gave him the four hundred Gauls who had formerly been Cleopatra's bodyguard and added Gadara, Hippos and Samaria to his kingdom, as well as the cities of Gaza, Anthedon, Joppa and Straton's Tower. These additions increased the splendour of his kingdom. {*Josephus, Jewish War, l. 1. c. 20. s. 3. (396,397) 2:187} {*Josephus, Antiq., l. 15. c. 7. s. 3. (216,217) 8:103,105}

5806. Caesar did not commit the province of Egypt to the Senate because of Egypt's large and fickle population.

Egypt was too important because it was the source of grain for Rome and it had incredible wealth. He forbade any senators to live in Egypt and he so distrusted the Egyptians that he forbade any Egyptian to become a senator. Other cities were permitted to govern themselves after their own laws, but he ordered the Alexandrians to govern the city without senators. {*Dio, l. 51. (17) 6:47}

5807. Areius, the philosopher, refused the government of Egypt, although it was offered to him. {Julian, Ad Themistium} Therefore, Caesar made Cornelius Gallus, who was of lowly estate, the governor of the province of Egypt, thus making him the first Roman governor that Egypt ever had. {*Strabo, l. 17. c. 1. s. 53. 8:135} {*Suetonius, Augustus, l. 2. c. 66. s. 1. 1:249} {*Dio, l. 51. (17) 6:47} {Eutropius, l. 7.} {Sextus Rufus, Breviary} Gallus was from Forum Julium, which Virgil mentioned in his Eclogue. {*Virgil, Eclogue, l. 1. c. 10. 1:77} {*Ammianus Marcellinus, l. 17. c. 4. s. 5. 1:319} {*Eusebius, Chronicles, l. 1. 1:246} There are also Erotica (love verses) extant, which are attributed to him and which were dedicated by Parthenius of Nice. Virgil imitated his prose in his Latin verses, {*Aulus Gellius, Attic Nights, l. 13. c. 27. s. 3. 2:503} {Macrobius, Saturnalia, l. 5. c. 17.} while Tiberius also imitated him in his Greek poems. {*Suetonius, Tiberius, l. 3. c. 70. s. 2. 1:409}

5808. After Caesar had settled affairs in Egypt as he thought best, he went into Syria with his land forces. {*Dio, l. 51. (18) 6:49,51} {Orosius, l. 6. c. 19.} Herod escorted him as far as Antioch. {*Josephus, Antiq., l. 15. c. 7. s. 4. (218) 8:105}

5809. Tiridates fled into Syria after being defeated and Phraates, the conqueror, sent envoys to Caesar. [E764] Caesar gave them both a friendly answer and did not actually promise Tiridates any help, but gave him permission to tarry in Syria. Phraates sent his son to Caesar with the envoys. He kindly accepted Phraates' son and brought him to Rome, where he kept him as a hostage. {*Dio, l. 51. (18) 6:51} He was the youngest son of Phraates and through the negligence of those who guarded him, was captured and stolen away, according to Justin, {Justin, Trogus, l. 42. c. 5.} who, however, referred this event to a later time.

5810. Caesar departed from Syria. Messala Corvinus deceived the Cyzicenian gladiators, who had been allowed to live in Daphne, a suburb of Antioch. They were sent to various places on the pretext of being enlisted in the legions and then killed, as opportunities presented themselves. {*Dio, l. 51. (7,8) 6:23}

5811. Caesar appointed Athenodorus as governor over Tarsus in Cilicia. He was a citizen of that city and the son of Sandon, a Stoic philosopher, and had been Caesar's teacher. [K493] He restored the state, which had been corrupted by Boethus and his soldiers, who had domineered there right up to the death of Antony. Athenodorus was slandered with the following graffiti:

Work for the young men,
Counsels for the middle aged,
And flatulence for the old men.

5812. He took the inscription as a joke and ordered that *Thunder for the old men* be written beside it. Someone, who was contemptuous of all decency and afflicted with a loose bowel, profusely splattered the door and wall of Athenodorus' house. The next day, he said in an assembly: {*Strabo, l. 14. c. 5. s. 14. 6:351}

"One may see the sickly plight and the disaffection of the city in many ways, and in particular from its excrements."

5813. Caesar went into the province of Asia, where he organized his winter quarters and settled all the affairs of his subjects. {*Dio, l. 51. (18) 6:49,51} {Orosius, l. 6. c. 19.}

## 3975b AM, 4685 JP, 29 BC

5814. On the Calends of January (January 1), Caesar entered into his fifth consulship while on the island of Samos. {*Suetonius, Augustus, l. 2. c. 26. s. 3. 1:187} On the same day, all his ordinances were confirmed by oath. At the same time that he received letters about the Parthian affairs, the following four things were decreed. In the Parthians' songs he should be recognised among their gods. A tribe should be called *Julian* after him. The senators who had participated in his victory should take part in the triumph with him and be arrayed in purple-bordered togas. Lastly, the day on which he entered Rome should be solemnised with public sacrifices and always be considered sacred. {*Dio, l. 51. (20) 6:55}

5815. Caesar permitted temples to be built at Ephesus and Nicaea (for those were considered the most famous cities of Asia and Bithynia), and dedicated them to the city of Rome and to his father Julius. The Romans in these cities were to honour these deities. He also gave foreigners, whom he called Greeks, permission to build temples to him, which was then done by the Asians at Pergamum and the Bithynians at Nicomedia. He permitted Pergamum to dedicate the plays, which they called *Sacred*, in honour of his temple. {*Dio, l. 51. (20) 6:57} Tacitus stated: {*Tacitus, Annals, l. 4. c. 37. 4:65,67}

"Augustus, of most famous memory, did not forbid a temple to be built in Pergamum in honour of himself and the city of Rome."

5816. The next summer, Caesar crossed over into Greece on his way to his triumph for Actium. {*Dio, l. 51. (21) 6:59} While he was at Corinth, a fisherman was sent to him as an envoy from the island of Gyaros. He begged for the tribute to be reduced, for they were compelled to pay a hundred and fifty drachmas, when they were barely able to pay a hundred because the island was so poor. {*Strabo, l. 10. c. 5. s. 3. 5:165,167}

5817. When Caesar entered Rome, others offered sacrifices (as had been decreed), and the consul, Valerius Potitius (who replaced Sextus Apuleius), sacrificed publicly on behalf of the Senate and people of Rome for his coming. This had never been done for anyone before that time. {*Dio, l. 51. (21) 6:59} Caesar held three triumphs as he rode in his chariot: one was for the victory in Illyria, and one each for Actium and Alexandria. This lasted for three days, one triumph following another. {*Livy, l. 133. 14:163} {*Suetonius, Augustus, l. 2. c. 22. 1:181} Virgil wrote: {*Virgil, Aeneid, l. 8. (714-717) 2:109}

> But when thrice Rome with Caesar's triumphs now
> Had rung, to the Latin gods he made a vow,
> Three hundred temples all the city round
> With joy, with plays and with applauses found.

5818. Propertius wrote: {Propertius, Elegies, l. 2. c. 1.}

> Whether of Egypt or Nile, whose
> Stream into seven channels parted goes;
> Or of the golden chains kings' necks surround,
> Or how the Actian beaks sail on the ground. [E765]

5819. Caesar brought three triumphs into the city in the month of August, as the words of the decree of the Senate showed. {Macrobius, Saturnalia, l. 1. c. 12.} [K494] This did not occur on the 8th of the Ides of January (January 6), when he was in Asia, as Orosius wrote. {Orosius, l. 6. c. 20.} On the first day, he triumphed for the Pannonians, Dalmatians, Japydes and their neighbours, and for some people of Gaul and Germany. On the second, he triumphed for his victory at sea at Actium and on the third, for the conquest of Egypt. The last triumph was the most costly and magnificent and he made more preparation for it than all the rest. In it, the effigy of Cleopatra was carried in a bed, with an asp biting her arm, showing how she died. Her children by Antony were led among the captives. They were Alexander and Cleopatra, who were named the *Sun* and *Moon*. {*Dio, l. 51. (21) 6:61,63}

5820. Alexander, the brother of Jamblichus, the king of the Arabians, was captured in the Actian war and was led in triumph, then later put to death. {*Dio, l. 51. (2) 6:7} The Cleopatra who was called the *Moon* and was led in triumph, was given in marriage to Juba, who was himself led in triumph by Julius Caesar. Caesar gave this Juba, who was brought up in Italy and had followed his wars, both this Cleopatra and his father's kingdom of Maurusia. He gave the two sons of Antony and Cleopatra to them, also, namely Alexander and Ptolemy, but Juba later had another son by his wife Cleopatra, whom he called Ptolemy and who succeeded him in his kingdom. {*Dio, l. 51. (15) 6:43} {*Strabo, l. 17. c. 3. s. 7. 8:169} {*Plutarch, Caesar, l. 1. c. 55. s. 2. 7:571} {*Plutarch, Antony, l. 1. c. 87. s. 1. 9:331}

5821. On the 5th of the Calends of September (August 28), an altar was dedicated to *Victory* in the courthouse, as was noted in the old marble calendar. {Gruter, Inscriptions, p. 133.} It was placed in the Julian courthouse and decorated with the spoils of Egypt. Caesar demonstrated that he got the empire through the goddess *Victory*. In the temple of his father Julius, he hung the dedicated items which came from the Egyptian spoils. He also consecrated many things to Jupiter Capitoline, Juno and Minerva. By a decree of the Senate, all the ornaments which had previously been hung up there, were removed, as being defiled. {*Dio, l. 51. (22) 6:63} He restored sacred edifices which had gone to ruin though lapse of time or had been destroyed by fire, and adorned both these and other temples with most lavish gifts. Into the shrine of Jupiter Capitoline he brought one donation of sixteen thousand pounds of gold, besides pearls and precious stones, valued at fifty million sesterces. {*Suetonius, Augustus, l. 2. c. 30. s. 2. 1:197} Rome was so greatly enriched with the wealth of Alexandria that the price of goods and other valuables doubled and the interest rate fell from twelve to four per cent. {*Dio, l. 51. (21) 6:61} {Orosius, l. 6. c. 19.}

5822. In the fifth consulship, Caesar accepted the name of *Imperator*, but not, according to the old custom, for some military victory. He had often received this title before and also received it after this. It was now given to him because he had saved the whole government. This had previously been decreed to his father Julius and his descendants. {*Dio, l. 52. (42) 6:187,189} The following inscription was placed this year in honour of Caesar: {Gruter, Inscriptions, p. 126.}

> "*Senatus Populusque Romanus Imp. Caesari Divi Iuli F. Cos. Quinct. Col. Design. Sex. Imp. Sept. Republica conservata.*"

> "The Senate and people to the Imperator Caesar, the son of Julius of blessed memory, consul the fifth time, elected the sixth time Imperator the seventh for having saved the commonwealth."

5823. Diocles Phoenix, the son of Artemidorus, was among the captives. He was the scholar of Tyrannio Amisenus and had been captured by Lucullus. [K495] Diocles was called Tyrannio, after his teacher's name. Diocles was bought by Dimantis, a freedman of

Caesar's, and was given to Terentia, the wife of Cicero. Terentia lived more than a hundred and three years. {*Pliny, l. 7. c. 48. 2:613} {*Valerius Maximus, l. 8. c. 13. s. 6 2:265,267} Diocles was freed by her and taught at Rome, where he wrote sixty-eight books. {Suidas, in Voc. Τυραννιων.}

## 3976a AM, 4685 JP, 29 BC

5824. Caesar summoned Antiochus of Commagene before him, because he had treacherously killed an envoy who had been sent to Rome by his brother, who was at variance with him. Caesar brought him before the Senate and when judgment was passed, he was put to death. {*Dio, l. 52. (43) 6:191}

5825. For a whole year after Herod returned from Caesar, his suspicions of his wife Mariamme daily increased, as did the tensions between them. Apart from avoiding her husband's caresses, she constantly upbraided him for the death either of her grandfather Hyrcanus or her brother Aristobulus, so that Herod could barely restrain himself from striking her. When his sister Salome heard the noise, she was greatly disturbed and sent in the butler, who had been prepared by her a long time before, to tell the king that he had been solicited by Mariamme to deliver a love potion to him which, whatever it was, he had gotten from her. Thereupon, Herod examined the most faithful servant of Mariamme by torture, because he knew that she would do nothing without his knowledge. He could not endure the torments but confessed nothing except that she had been offended about some things that Soemus had told her. When the king heard this, he cried out that Soemus, who had always been completely faithful both to him and the kingdom, would never have spoken of these things, had there not been some more secret friendship between them. [E766] Consequently, he ordered Soemus to be apprehended and put to death, then called a council of his friends and accused his wife of planning to poison him. He used such sharp words, that those present easily understood that the king intended her to be condemned. So she was condemned by the common consent of everyone present. When they thought that she should not be executed hurriedly, but detained in one of the king's citadels, Salome urged the king insistently to have her killed at once, because she feared that there could be a revolt among the people if she were alive and in prison and so Mariamme was executed. {*Josephus, Antiq., l. 15. c. 7. s. 4. (218-231) 8:105-111}

5826. Her mother Alexandra saw this and realised she could expect the same treatment from Herod. To clear herself of involvement in the same crime, she upbraided her daughter before everyone and called her extremely wicked and ungrateful toward her husband, saying that she had deserved such a death, since she had dared to do such a heinous act. Even though she pretended these things and would pull her daughter by the hair, those present severely condemned her hypocrisy. Her daughter did not reply but endured the false accusation with resolute mental and physical composure, undergoing her death without fear. {*Josephus, Antiq., l. 15. c. 7. s. 5. (232-236) 8:111,113}

5827. After she was executed, Herod began to be more inflamed with love for her, often calling her name and lamenting her far beyond what was becoming. Although he tried to forget her by seeking pleasure in feasting and drinking, nothing worked. As a result, he forgot about the government of his kingdom and was so overcome with grief, that he would ask his servants to call for Mariamme as though she were still alive. {*Josephus, Antiq., l. 15. c. 7. s. 7. (240-242) 8:113,115}

## 3976b AM, 4686 JP, 28 BC

5828. While Herod was thus affected, a plague occurred, which killed a large number of the people and nobility. [K496] Everyone believed that this plague had been sent because of the unjust death of the queen, which merely increased the king's depression, until he finally hid himself in a solitary wilderness, on the pretext of hunting. He afflicted himself and succumbed to a serious and painful inflammation of the neck, so that he began to rave. None of the remedies relieved him, but rather made the disease more painful, so that they began to despair for his life. The physicians let him have whatever he wanted, because the disease was so serious and he was in so great a danger of dying, anyway. {*Josephus, Antiq., l. 15. c. 7. s. 7. (243-246) 8:115,117}

5829. While Herod was sick in Samaria, Alexandra tried to capture the two citadels at Jerusalem. One was joined to the temple and the other was located within the city. So she plied their governors with the request that they would surrender them to her and to Mariamme's children, lest they be seized by others, if Herod were to die. The men who had formerly been faithful, were now even more diligent in their office because they hated Alexandra and thought it a great offence to give up on the health of their prince. These men were the king's old friends and one of them, Achiabus, was the king's cousin, so they promptly sent messengers to Herod to tell him of Alexandra's actions and he soon ordered her to be killed. At length, he overcame his disease and was restored to his former strength, both of body and mind but he had grown so cruel, that he was ready to put anyone to death for the least cause. {*Josephus, Antiq., l. 15. c. 7. s. 8. (247-252) 8:117,119}

5830. Suetonius noted the three times that Octavius took a census of the people. {*Suetonius, Augustus, l. 2. c. 27. s. 5. 1:191} The first one was carried out in the lustrum, that is, the first year of the five years, or lustrum, when he and Marcus Agrippa were consuls. This is shown from the Marble Table of Capua. {*Pighius, Annals of Rome, Tom. 3. p. 495.*} {*Gruter, Inscriptions, p. 230.*}

"In my sixth consulship, with my colleague Marcus Agrippa, I numbered the people and I made another census after forty-one years."

5831. That is, from the censorships of Gnaeus Lentulus and Lucius Gellius, after whom the musters were laid abandoned.

"In the census, Rome had forty hundred thousand and sixty three thousand citizens."

5832. That is, 4,063,000 for which Eusebius had 4,164,000. {*Eusebius, Chronicles, l. 1. 1:245*}

5833. Together with Marcus Agrippa, Caesar held the festival that had been decreed for the victory at Actium. In this festival, he showed men and boys from the patricians, fighting on horseback. This festival was held every four years and was committed to the four orders of the priests to arrange, namely the chief priests, the augurs, the Septemviri and the Quindecimviri. {*Dio, l. 53. (1) 6:195*}

5834. In the 188th Olympiad, Thebes in Egypt was razed to the ground by Cornelius Gallus. {*Eusebius, Chronicles, l. 1. 1:246*} [E767] Georgius Syncellus, from the writings Julius Africanus, stated that Gallus defeated the cities of the rebellious Egyptians. {*Georgius Syncellus, Chronicles, p. 308.*} With a few men, he recovered Heroonpolis, which had revolted. He very suddenly put down a revolt that had been raised about taxes. {*Strabo, l. 17. c. 1. s. 53. 8:135,137*} He drained the city through extensive embezzlements {*Ammianus Marcellinus, l. 17. c. 4. s. 5. 1:319*} and erected statues for himself across almost all of Egypt and wrote his own acts on the pyramids. {*Dio, l. 53. (23) 6:255*}

## 3977 AM, 4687 JP, 27 BC

5835. When Caesar was consul for the seventh time, he read a speech in the Senate saying that he would resign his government and turn it over to the Senate and the people. [K497] When he had ended his speech, many spoke and expressed the desire that he alone should take the whole administration of the government upon himself. Finally, they convinced him to assume the whole government, though many believed that this was just a ruse on his part. {*Dio, l. 53. (2) 6:199*} {*Dio, l. 53. (11) 6:217,219*} He did this on the 7th of the Ides of January (January 7), as recorded on the Marble Tables of Narbon. {*Gruter, Inscriptions, p. 229.*}

5836. In this way, Caesar had the empire confirmed to him by the Senate and the people. To appear democratic, he took the empire upon himself, but said he would be very careful of the public affairs because they required the care of someone diligent. He said explicitly that he would not govern all the provinces. Also, he would not govern the ones that he was governing at present, if he could turn them over to the Senate sooner. As a result, he restored to the Senate the weaker provinces, because they were the more peaceable, while he retained the stronger provinces, where there was more danger, or that had enemies close by, or that were likely to have seditions. He did this under the pretence that the Senate might safely govern the best parts of the empire, while he would assume the harder, more dangerous provinces. This was merely a pretext to render them disarmed and unfit for war, and so allowing him to win both the arms and the soldiers to his side. For this reason, Africa, Numidia, Asia and Greece, with Epirus, Dalmatia, Macedonia, Sicily, Crete, Libya, Cyrene, Bithynia with the adjoining Pontus, Sardinia and Hispania Baetica were assigned to the Senate. Caesar governed the rest of Spain, all Gaul, Germany, Coelosyria, Cilicia, Cyprus and Egypt. He assumed this government over the provinces for a period of ten years, promising himself that within this time he would easily reduce them to order. He also added, in a bragging way, like a young man, that if he could subdue them in a shorter time, then he would hand them over sooner, as well, for the Senate to manage. He then appointed patricians as governors over all the provinces. However, over Egypt he appointed a man who was an equestrian, not a senator, for the reasons stated previously. {*See note on 3975a AM. <<5806>>*} He gave Africa and Asia to the ex-consuls on his own authority, and assigned all the rest of the provinces to those who had been praetors. He forbade that they receive any provinces by lot, until the fifth year after they had held an office in the city. {*Dio, l. 53. (12-14) 6:219-227*}

5837. On the Ides of January (January 13), the provinces were allocated, as Ovid noted, speaking thus about Caesar Germanicus: {*Ovid, Fasti, l. 1. (587-590) 5:45*}

On the Ides the half-man priest in Jove's great feign
    Offers the entrails of a sheep with flame,
Then all the provinces came to us, and then
    Thy grandsire was Augustus named among men.

5838. On the same day, Caesar received the title of Augustus. Censorinus {*Censorinus, De Die Natali, l. 1. c. 21.*} showed that this took place on the fourth day after the allocation of the provinces:

"On the 16th day before the Calends of February (January 17), the Emperor Caesar, the son of him of blessed memory, on the motion of Lucius Munacius Plancus, was greeted as Augustus by the Senate and the rest of the citizens. He was consul for the seventh time and Marcus Vipsanius Agrippa was the other consul, for the third time."

5839. When Caesar had settled everything and organized the provinces into a certain form, he was surnamed *Augustus*. {*Livy, l. 134. 14:163} [K498] This name was given to him in his seventh consulship and at the request of Plancus, with the consent of the whole Senate and the people of Rome. {*Dio, l. 53. (16) 6:235} {*Velleius Paterculus, l. 2. c. 91. s. 1. 1:243} Suetonius wrote: {*Suetonius, Augustus, l. 2. c. 7. s. 2. 1:159}

> "The motion of Munatius Plancus, that Caesar should be called *Augustus*, prevailed (though some were of the opinion that he should be called Romulus, as if he had also been a founder of the city), not only because it was a new, but also a more honourable, name. [E768] The sacred places and those in which anything is consecrated by augural rites, are called *Augusta*, from the increase in dignity, or from the movements or feeding of birds, as Ennius also indicated, when he wrote: *After by augury augustus illustrious Rome had been founded*."

5840. Florus stated: {*Florus, l. 2. c. 34. 1:351}

> "It was also debated in the Senate whether he should be called Romulus, because he had founded the empire. However, the name Augustus seemed to be the more holy and venerable, so that while he now lived on earth, he might be deified by the name and title itself."

5841. Dio said many similar things and noted that he was called *Augustus* by the Romans and the Greeks, because of the splendour of his dignity and the sanctity of the honour. The term *Augustus* signified that he was more than human for all the most precious and sacred objects were termed *augusta*. {*Dio, l. 53. (16) 6:235} cf. {Ac 25:21,25 27:24 2Th 2:4} Ovid added: {*Ovid, Fasti, l. 1. (607-614) 5:45}

> All common persons have their common fame,
> But he with Jove enjoys an equal name,
> Of old, most sacred things Augusta were:
> Temples that name, and hallowed things, do bear:
> Yea, augury depends upon this word,
> And whatever more Jove does afford:
> Let it enlarge his rule and live let all,
> Our coast, be guarded by a fenced wall.

5842. In this way, the whole power of the people and Senate was conferred upon Augustus. {*Dio, l. 53. (18) 6:235} This name had previously been held sacred and until now, no governor had dared assume it. He took so expansive a title for the usurped empire of the world, and from that day, its whole commonwealth and government

began to be and to remain in the possession of one man. The Greeks called this a monarchy. {Orosius, l. 6. c. 20.} The Romans began the epoch of their Augustus from the Calends of January (January 1). Censorinus compared the 265th year of this account with the 283rd year of the Julian account. He, in the next chapter, put the consulship of Marcius Censorinus and Asinius Gallus in the twentieth year of Augustus, which was the 38th year of the Julian account, from the time of Julius Caesar's calendar reform. {Censorinus, De Die Natali, l. 1. c. 21,22.}

5843. Tralles, a city in Asia, was destroyed by an earthquake. The gymnasium collapsed and was later rebuilt by Tiberius Caesar. {*Eusebius, Chronicles, l. 1. 1:246} {*Strabo, l. 12. c. 8. s. 18. 5:517} {*Tacitus, Annals, l. 2. c. 47. 3:459}

### 3978 AM, 4688 JP, 26 BC

5844. Costobarus, the Idumean, and his wife Salome, Herod's sister, had a disagreement. She, contrary to the custom of the Jews, sent him a bill of divorce and went to her brother Herod and told him that she preferred her brother's goodwill over her marriage. [K499] She said that Costobarus was plotting seditions with Lysimachus, Antipater and Dositheus. To make her story more credible, she said that he had now secretly kept and guarded Baba's children, within his country, for twelve years from the time of the taking of Jerusalem by Herod. All this had been done without the knowledge and goodwill of the king. As soon as Herod knew, he sent some men to their hiding places and killed them, along with all who were accomplices in the crime. He did this, so all of Hyrcanus' family would be killed thereby removing any threat to the throne, so there would be no one to resist him. {*Josephus, Antiq., l. 15. c. 7. s. 9,10. (253-266) 8:119-127}

5845. Herod became more secure and departed more and more from his country's customs, which he violated with new institutions. First of all, he instituted wrestling every fifth year, in honour of Caesar. To hold this, he began to build a theatre in Jerusalem and an amphitheatre in the plain. Both were of sumptuous workmanship, but in direct violation of Jewish customs. [E769] There was no Jewish tradition for these shows, but he wanted this observed and proclaimed to the countries around him, as well as to the foreign countries. He offered large prizes and invited athletes and other classes of contestants and musicians and actors. Nothing bothered the Jews as much as the trophies, which were covered with armour and which they thought to be images, since such were forbidden by their law. To appease them, Herod ordered the ornaments to be removed and showed them that the trophies were merely wooden poles. After this was done, their anger turned into laughter. {*Josephus, Antiq., l. 15. c. 8. s. 1,2. (267-279) 8:127-133}

5846. The Fifth Calippic Period began.

5847. Cornelius Gallus spoke many things against Augustus, with great vanity. {*Dio, l. 53. (23) 6:255} Ovid wrote the following with reference to Gallus: {*Ovid, Tristia, l. 2. (445,446) 6:87}

> To court Lycoris was not Gallus' shame,
> But he, when lisped by drink, defiled his name.

5848. Augustus noted Gallus' infamy and forbade him his house, as well as to live within any of the provinces, because he was so ungrateful and malevolent. Gallus was also accused of robbery, of pillaging the provinces and of many other crimes, at first by Valerius Largus, who was a very wicked man, as well as being his associate and friend. Later, many others, who had previously flattered Gallus, accused him. They left him, when they saw Largus become more powerful. It was decreed by the whole Senate that Gallus was guilty and should be banished. All his goods were to be confiscated for Augustus and because of this, the Senate would offer sacrifices. Gallus was not able to handle his grief, fearing that the nobility were highly incensed against him, to whom the care of this judgment had been committed. He fell upon his own sword and by his suicide prevented his condemnation. Gallus was forced, by the testimony of his accusers and by the decree of the Senate, to kill himself. Augustus actually praised their love toward himself, for being so displeased for his sake. In spite of this, Augustus wept and bewailed his own misfortune, that he alone could not be angry with his friends, as much as he was with himself. {*Suetonius, Augustus, l. 2. c. 66. s. 1,2. 1:249} {*Dio, l. 53. (23) 6:255} {*Ammianus Marcellinus, l. 17. c. 4. s. 5. 1:319,321} {*Eusebius, Chronicles, l. 1. 1:246} [K500]

5849. Petronius was appointed the new governor, to replace Gallus in Egypt. With only his bodyguards, he withstood the charge of a number of the Alexandrians, who threw stones at him. He killed some of them and subdued the rest. {*Strabo, l. 17. c. 1. s. 53. 8:137}

5850. Polemon, the king of Pontus, was included among the allies and confederates of the people of Rome. The senators were given the privilege of having the front seats in the theatres throughout his whole kingdom. {*Dio, l. 53. (25) 6:257} It seems that it was from him that Pontus took the name of Polemoniacus. {Justin, Novella, 8.}

## 3979 AM, 4689 JP, 25 BC

5851. Ten citizens of Jerusalem conspired against Herod, hiding their swords under their garments. One of them was blind and joined them to show that he was ready to suffer anything that would happen to the defenders of their country's rights. One of the men whom Herod had appointed to find out such things, discovered the plot and told Herod. When the conspirators were apprehended, they boldly drew out their swords and proclaimed that it was not for any personal gain, but for the public good, that they had undertaken this conspiracy. At this, they were led away by the king's officers and executed with all manner of tortures. Shortly after this, the spy who had exposed the plot and was hated by everyone, was killed by some men, cut in pieces and thrown to the dogs in the presence of many. The murderers were not caught until long and wearisome inquisitions had been undertaken by Herod. With the use of torture, it was wrung out of some silly women who had known of the act. Then the authors of that murder were punished, along with their whole families. {*Josephus, Antiq., l. 15. c. 8. s. 3-5. (281-291) 8:133-139}

5852. So that he would be more secure from the seditions of the tumultuous people, Herod began to fortify Samaria in the thirteenth year of his reign (to be reckoned from the death of Antigonus). Samaria was a day's journey from Jerusalem and he called the place Sebaste, which was Greek for the Latin name of Augusta. It had a circumference of two and a half miles, and in the very middle of a precinct three hundred yards in circumference he built an exquisitely adorned temple. He arranged for many of the soldiers who had always helped him, as well as people of the neighbouring countries, to come and live there. {*Josephus, Antiq., l. 15. c. 8. s. 5. (296-298) 8:141,143} [E770] Georgius Syncellus, quoting from Africanus, called it the city of the Gabinians, for Samaria was destroyed by John Hyrcanus, then rebuilt by Aulus Gabinius and repopulated with the name of Γαβινιυν or Γαβινειυν. {Georgius Syncellus, Chronicles, p. 308.} {See note on 3947b AM. <<4644>>} This can be understood only as the colony which Gabinius brought there. I am pleased that this was also noted by that man of learning and good breeding, James Goarus. The recent famous edition of the Georgian Chronicle was published due to his great industry.

5853. Herod also built another citadel, previously called Straton's Tower, to control the country. He named it Caesarea. He also built a citadel in the large plain and selected men from his cavalry by lot, to guard it. He built Gaba in Galilee and Hesebonitis in Peraea. All these citadels were strategically located in the country, so as to permit him quickly to put down any rebellion of the people. {*Josephus, Antiq., l. 15. c. 8. s. 5. (293,294) 8:139,141}

5854. Augustus began his ninth consulship in Tarraco (a city of the Nearer Spain), in the 3rd year of the 188th Olympiad. {*Suetonius, Augustus, l. 2. c. 26. s. 3. 1:187} The Indians asked for friendly relations with Augustus. {*Eusebius, Chronicles, l. 1. 1:246} [K501] King Pandion sent envoys, as we have also found noted on some Roman tables. {Georgius Syncellus, Chronicles, p. 311.}

*5855.* Publius Orosius stated that envoys from the Indians came to Augustus at Tarraco, who were from the most distant part of the east and from the Scythians from the north, with presents from both their nations. {*Orosius, l. 6. c. 21.*} Horace wrote these verses about this occasion: {*\*Horace, Carmen Saeculare, l. 1. (55,56) 1:355*}

The lofty Scythian and the Indians late,
Came for the answer of their future fate.

*5856.* Horace, in an ode to Augustus, wrote: {*\*Horace, Odes, l. 4. c. 14. (41,45) 1:341*}

The yet untamed Cantaber in thee,
Mede, Indian, Scythian do mirrors see:
Thou that preservest Italy from dread,
And Rome, her glory and exalted head.

*5857.* Florus wrote: {*\*Florus, l. 2. c. 34. 1:349,351*}

"The Scythians and Samatians sent their envoys and desired friendship. The Seres (Chinese) and the Indians, who live beneath the sun, brought presents which included precious stones, pearls and elephants. Nothing spoke so much for their sincerity as the length of the journey, which had lasted four years. The complexion of the men seemed as if they had come from another world."

*5858.* Suetonius wrote: {*\*Suetonius, Augustus, l. 2. c. 21. s. 3. 1:179*}

"He induced the Scythians and Indians (countries known only by name) to make suit of their own accord through envoys, for amity with him and the people of Rome."

*5859.* Eutropius also wrote: {*Eutropius, l. 7.*}

"The Scythians and Indians, to whom the Roman name was unknown, sent presents and envoys to him."

*5860.* To conclude, Aurelius Victor listed several other countries also:

"Indians, Scythians, Garamantians and Bactrians sent envoys to him, to desire a league with him."

*5861.* After Amyntas died, Augustus did not turn over the kingdom to his sons, but made it a Roman province. From that time on, Galatia and Lycaonia had a Roman governor. {*\*Dio, l. 53. (26) 6:261*} Marcus Lollius, the propraetor, governed that province. {*\*Eusebius, Chronicles, l. 1. 1:246*} {*Eutropius, l. 7.*} {*Sextus Rufus, Breviary*} The towns of Pamphylia, however, which had formerly been given to Amyntas, were restored to their own district. {*\*Dio, l. 53. (26) 6:261,263*}

*5862.* In the thirteenth year of Herod's reign, very grievous calamities befell the country of the Jews. First, there was a continual drought, followed by a famine. The change in diet necessitated by the famine, caused a pestilent disease in the land. Herod did not have sufficient means to supply the public needs, so he melted down everything in the palace that contained gold or silver. He spared nothing, no matter how exquisitely it was made, and even melted down his own dinner plates and cups. He made money from this and sent it to Egypt while Petronius was governor there. *[E771]* Even though Petronius was plagued by a number of people who had fled to him from the famine, because he was privately Herod's friend and desired the preservation of his subjects, he nonetheless gave permission to the Jews in particular to export grain. Petronius helped them in the buying and shipping of the grain, so that the greatest means of the preservation of the country was attributed to Petronius. {*\*Josephus, Antiq., l. 15. c. 9. s. 1,2. (299-316) 8:143-151*}

*5863.* As soon as Herod received the grain, he very carefully apportioned it to those who could not take care of themselves. *[K502]* Since there were many who, through old age or some other disability, could not prepare it for themselves, he assigned certain cooks to them, so that they might have their food prepared. Because of his diligence, the people changed their minds about him and he was praised as a bountiful and providential prince. {*\*Josephus, Antiq., l. 15. c. 9. s. 2. (309-316) 8:147-151*}

*5864.* From the 29th of August (that is, the 3rd day before the beginning of the Syrian month of Elul, or of our September), on the sixth day of the week, the Egyptian epoch started which Albatenius calls Al-Kept (that is, the epoch of the Coptitiae or Egyptians). {*Albatenius, Al-Kept, l. 1. c. 32.*} He said the account and order of the motions of the stars were determined from Theon's calculations. Albatenius said that from the epoch of Dilkarnain (or of the Seleucidae, which he began with the Syrians, from the beginning of Elul or September), two hundred and eighty-seven years had passed to this time. This is how it reads in the manuscript, not, as published, three hundred and eighty-seven years. For in this year, the first day of the month of Thoth—both in the moveable year of the Egyptians as in the fixed year of the Greeks and Alexandrians (as Theon wrote)—was found to fall upon the same day of August 29. This happens only after the full period of one thousand four hundred and sixty of the Alexandrian years and one thousand four hundred and sixty-one of the Egyptian years have passed, when their year lines up again with the solar year and the seasons fall on the correct dates. Theon stated:

"This renewing happened after one thousand and four hundred and sixty years from a certain beginning of time, namely, the fifth year of the reign of Augustus."

5865. This is according to Theon, in the explanation of μτ πεντε ετη, that ended at this time or five years after the beginning of the empire of Augustus. Both Theon and Ptolemy agreed that this renewing began two hundred and ninety-four years after the death of Alexander, or the Philippic account. From this Philippic account even to this renewing are two hundred and ninety-nine years, as correctly noted in the astronomical epitome of Theodorus Metochita. Panodorus, the Alexandrian monk, did not intend anything else in discussing this period and constitution of one thousand four hundred and sixty years which happened on August 29 from the epoch about which he wrote that account. The motions of the stars and the eclipses are to be ordered in the astronomical calculations. However Georgius Syncellus, who was very unskilled in these matters, clearly perverted the meaning because he did not understand it. {*Georgius Syncellus, Chronicles, p. 312,313.}*

## 3980a AM, 4689 JP, 25 BC

5866. Herod provided for his subjects against the harshness of the winter, so that everyone would have proper clothing, since their cattle were dead and there was a shortage of wool and other things. When he had provided for his own subjects, he also took care of the neighbouring cities of the Syrians. He also gave seed for sowing. All the citadels and cities, and the common people who had large families, came to Herod for help and he was able to help the foreigners, too. He gave ten thousand cors of grain to foreigners and eighty thousand cors to his own subjects. (One cor equals ten Athenian medimni, and one Athenian medimni equals six bushels.) {*Josephus, Antiq., l. 15. c. 9. s. 2. (310-314) 8:149,151}*

5867. Since Augustus was ill, he could not attend the marriage at Rome of his daughter and Marcellus, the son of his sister Octavia. He solemnised it with the help of Marcus Agrippa. {*Dio, l. 53. (27) 6:265} [K503]*

## 3980b AM, 4690 JP, 24 BC

5868. On the Calends of January (January 1), when Augustus entered his tenth consulship, the Senate confirmed with an oath that they approved of all his acts. He had promised every man in Rome four hundred sesterces.

5869. As he approached the city, from which he had been absent for a long time because of his illness, he said that before he would give the money, the Senate must give their assent. The Senate then freed him from legal constraints and declared that he should have absolute power and be sole emperor, with power to do as he wished. {*Dio, l. 53. (17) 6:235} {*Dio, l. 53. (28) 6:265,267}*

5870. As soon as the grain was ready to harvest, Herod sent fifty thousand men, whom he had fed during the famine, back to their own countries and to his neighbours, the Syrians. By his diligence, Herod restored the almost ruined circumstances of his own subjects and greatly helped his neighbours, who had been afflicted with the same calamities. {*Josephus, Antiq., l. 15. c. 9. s. 2. (312-313) 8:149}*

5871. At the same time, Herod sent five hundred select men to Caesar for his bodyguards. Aelius Gallus led these men to the wars with Arabia, where they performed valiantly. {*Josephus, Antiq., l. 15. c. 9. s. 3. (317) 8:151} [E772]*

5872. Aelius Gallus (incorrectly called Aelius Largus in the later editions of Dio) was of the equestrian order, according to Pliny. {*Pliny, l. 6. c. 32. 2:459}*

5873. He was the third governor of Egypt under Augustus. He was also the friend and companion of Strabo, {*Strabo, l. 2. c. 5. s. 12. 1:453,455}* who wrote that the two of them together saw the statue of Memnon at Thebes. {*Strabo, l. 17. c. 1. s. 46. 8:123}* Augustus sent him into Arabia with part of the Roman garrison stationed in Egypt, so that he might try to subdue those countries. {*Strabo, l. 2. c. 5. s. 12. 1:453,455} {*Strabo, l. 17. c. 1. s. 54. 8:137}* This was on the border which Egypt shared with the Ethiopians and Troglodytes, near the Arabian Gulf (Red Sea). The land was very narrow there and separated the Arabians from the Troglodytes. Augustus advised him to make peace with them if they were willing, otherwise, to subdue them by force. {*Strabo, l. 16. c. 4. s. 32. 7:353,355}*

5874. For this expedition into Arabia, Aelius built eighty ships of two and three tiers of oars and some light galleys at Cleopatris, which was near the old canal of the Nile River. When there was no chance of any naval battle with the Arabians, he corrected his mistake and built a hundred and thirty cargo ships. He sailed with ten thousand Roman foot soldiers and some allied forces, which included five hundred Jews and a thousand Nabateans under Syllaeus. {*Strabo, l. 16. c. 4. s. 23. 7:355,357}*

5875. At that time, Obadas was king of the Nabateans and was a slothful and lazy man, especially about military matters. This was a common vice of all the Arabian kings. He had committed the government of his affairs to Syllaeus, who was a young, crafty man. {*Strabo, l. 16. c. 4. s. 24. 7:357} {*Josephus, Antiq., l. 16. c. 7. s. 6. (220,221) 8:297}* Syllaeus had promised Aelius that he would be his guide and would help him with provisions and anything he should need, but he acted treacherously in all matters. He did not lead them safely, by land or sea, but through byways and circuitous, barren routes. He took them to shores that were unfit for harbour and had dangerous submerged rocks or miry bogs, because the sea never refreshed those places. {*Strabo, l. 16. c. 4. s. 23. 7:357}*

*5876.* After many miseries, Aelius Gallus reached the territory of Album (Leuce Come, that is, the White Village) in fourteen days. This was the largest trading place of all the Nabateans. *[K504]* He had lost many of his ships, along with some of his men, who died, not from war, but from the difficult trip. These difficulties were caused by the villainy of Syllaeus, who had said that no army could be brought into the territory of Album by land, when, in fact, merchants came and went there by land, with large numbers of camels and men. The way they took was both safe and well supplied with provisions from one end of Arabia Petra to the other. So many came and went in caravans, they seemed like an army in number. {*\*Strabo, l. 16. c. 4. s. 23. 7:357*}

*5877.* When the army of Aelius arrived there, it was stricken with the diseases of stomacaccis (scurvy) and scelotyrbe, both of which were diseases found in that country. One was, as it were, a palsy of the mouth and the other a lameness in the legs. These were caused by the bad water and the plants they ate. Because of this, Aelius was forced to stay there a whole summer and winter, to refresh his sick men. {*\*Strabo, l. 16. c. 1. s. 24. 7:357,359*}

*5878.* Zenodorus leased the land of Lysanias or the territory of Trachonitis, Batanea and Auranitis. Because he was not satisfied with its profits, he joined up with the Trachonites, who lived in caves like wild beasts. They were accustomed to rob and plunder the Damascenes. The people who lived in those countries were forced to complain to Varro, their governor of Syria. They asked if he would send letters to Caesar, telling of the wrongs done by Zenodorus. Caesar wrote back that he would take special care utterly to root out these thieves. Consequently, Varro attacked the suspected places with his soldiers, purged the land from the thieves and took away the country from Zenodorus. {*\*Josephus, Jewish War, l. 1. c. 20. s. 4. (398,399) 2:187,189*} {*\*Josephus, Antiq., l. 15. c. 10. s. 1. (343-348) 8:167,169*}

*5879.* Herod built a palace in Zion which contained two very large and stately houses, and with which the temple itself could in no way compare. He called one of them Caesarea, after Caesar, and the other Agrippium, after Agrippa. {*\*Josephus, Jewish War, l. 1. c. 21. s. 1. (402) 2:189,191*} {*\*Josephus, Antiq., l. 15. c. 9. s. 3. (318) 8:153*}

## 3981a AM, 4690 JP, 24 BC
*5880.* The 29th Jubilee.

## 3981b AM, 4691 JP, 23 BC
*5881.* Herod removed Jesus, the son of Phabes, from the priesthood and replaced him with Simon, a priest of Jerusalem, who was the son of Boethus of Alexandra and whose daughter, Mariamme, Herod married. She was the most beautiful woman of that time. {*\*Josephus, Antiq., l. 15. c. 9. s. 3. (320-322) 8:153,155*} {*\*Josephus, Antiq., l. 18. c. 5. s. 4. (136) 9:93*} *[E773]*

*5882.* After the marriage was over, Herod began to build a new palace, and next to it he made a town, called Herodion, after himself. This place was about seven and a half miles from Jerusalem toward Arabia, and was the spot where he had defeated the Jews when he was thrust out by the armies of Antigonus. {*\*Josephus, Antiq., l. 14. c. 16. s. 2. (481,482) 7:697,699*} {*\*Josephus, Antiq., l. 15. c. 9. s. 4. (323,324) 8:155*} {*\*Josephus, Jewish War, l. 1. c. 18. s. 2. (353) 2:165,167*} {*\*Josephus, Jewish War, l. 1. c. 13. s. 8. (266) 2:125*} Pliny mentioned Herodion with the celebrated town of the same name. {*\*Pliny, l. 5. c. 15. 2:275*}

*5883.* Gallus left the Nabatean village of Album with his army and went through places so dry, that he was compelled to carry his water on camels. This happened to him as a result of the hostility of the guides, which also meant that it was only after many days that he came into the land of Aretas, who was allied with Obadas, the king of the Nabateans. This country was hard to cross, because of the treachery of Syllaeus. He took thirty days to cross it, travelling on unbeaten paths, during which time his food was used up and he was left with very few dates and used butter instead of oil. Finally, he came to the country of the nomads, which was mainly a desert. It was called Ararene and was under Sabos, their king. {*\*Strabo, l. 16. c. 4. s. 24. 7:359,361*} *[K505]*

*5884.* Sabos was the king of Arabia Felix. No one came out to oppose Aelius, but he continued this difficult journey. It was a hot, sunny desert country and the waters, which were naturally infected, caused the death of most of his army. That disease was unlike any of ours: The head was affected and became parched, thus killing many. Those who escaped death, had the disease go through their whole body, into their legs, so that only their legs were affected. There was no other remedy than to drink oil mixed with wine and anoint oneself with it. Very few could do this, because neither was readily available where they were, nor had they brought much with them. During these misfortunes, the barbarians, who at first had lost every battle, as well as some towns, also used the disease as an opportunity to recover from their losses. They attacked the Romans, recovered their lost towns and drove the rest of the Romans from the country. {*\*Dio, l. 53. (29) 6:269,271*}

*5885.* These were the first and only Romans to carry the war so far into Arabia Felix, even to the famous city of Athlula, or Athrula. {*\*Dio, l. 53. (29) 6:271*} In that expedition, Gallus defeated these towns, named by previous writers: Negrana, Nestus, Nesca, Magusus, Caminacus,

Labaetia, Mariba (which was six miles in circumference) and Caripeta, which was the farthest place he went. {*Pliny, l. 6. c. 32. 2:459} Had Syllaeus not betrayed him, he would have conquered all of Arabia Felix. {*Strabo, l. 17. c. 1. s. 53. 8:137} We now give Strabo's account of this.

5886. Fifty days were spent in travelling across Ararene on impassable ways. When he reached the city of the Agrans (or rather, the Negranians) in a tranquil and fruitful country, King Sabos fled and the city was taken on the first assault. From there, on the sixth day, he reached the river, where the barbarians met him in battle array and ten thousand of their number fell, compared with only two of the Romans. The barbarians were very cowardly and used their weapons unskilfully. Some used the bow, the lance, the sword and the sling, but for the most part, they used a double-edged axe. Then Aelius took the city of Asca, which had been abandoned by the king. From there, he came to Athrula and easily took it, putting a garrison there. He took supplies of grain and dates for his journey and came to Marsiaba, a city of the Rhammanites, who were under Ilasarus. He attacked and besieged it for six days. Later, he abandoned the place because of lack of water. From the captives, he understood that he was only a journey of two days away from the area where the spices grow; but he spent six months in getting there, due to the deceit of his guides. {*Strabo, l. 16. c. 4. s. 24. 7:361}

5887. At last, when he discovered the treachery, he returned by another way and in nine days reached Negrana, where there was a battle. Then, on the eleventh day, he came to the place called Hepta Phreata, named after the seven wells there. He travelled through areas that were being farmed, to the village of Chaalla and later to Malotha, which was located by the riverside. After that, he went through deserts, where there was not much water, to the village of Egra (or Hygra), which was under Obadas and was beside the sea. In all, he spent only sixty days on his return journey, whereas his journey there had taken him six months. {*Strabo, l. 16. c. 4. s. 24. 7:361,363}

5888. While Aelius Gallus was waging war with part of the Egyptian army in Arabia, the Ethiopians, who lived beyond Egypt, were sent on a sudden invasion by their Queen Candace (a manly woman, and blind in one eye). [K506] At Syene, Elephantine and Philae, they surprised the garrisons of three cohorts and carried them away as captives. They overthrew Caesar's statues. Petronius, the governor of Egypt, with less than a thousand foot soldiers and eight hundred cavalry, marched out to fight the enemy of thirty thousand men. At first, he forced them to flee into Pselchis, a city of Ethiopia. Then he sent to them to demand back the things which they had

taken away and also to hear their reason for starting this war. [E774] When they said that they had been wronged by the Nomarchs, he replied that the Nomarchs were not lords of the country, but that Caesar was. They asked for a time of three days to deliberate and in the meantime did nothing to satisfy him, so he marched toward them and forced them to fight. He soon routed them, because they were poorly organized and badly armed. They had large shields made of raw oxhide and used weapons like axes and pikes, while some had swords. A number were forced into the city, while some fled into the deserts and others to the neighbouring island. Petronius, after he crossed the river in boats and ships, captured Queen Candace's captains and sent them to Alexandria. He went to Pselchis and captured it and when he numbered the captives and those who had died in battle, he concluded that very few had escaped. {*Strabo, l. 17. c. 1. s. 54. 8:137,139} {*Dio, l. 54. (5) 6:293,295}

5889. From Pselchis, Petronius went to Premnis, which was a naturally well-fortified city. To get there, he had to cross the same sand dunes which had overwhelmed Cambyses' army in a sandstorm. {See note on 3480 AM. <<989>>} He took it on the first assault, then went on to Napata (called Tanape by Dio), where Candace's palace was and her son lived. She was in a nearby citadel and sent envoys to negotiate for peace. She returned the statues and the captives who had been taken from Syene; but Petronius stormed Napata and took it, so that her son was forced to flee. Petronius could not go any farther because of the sand and the heat, nor easily stay there with the whole army, so he fortified Premnis with walls and stationed a garrison there, with enough food for four hundred men for two years. He returned to Alexandria and sold most of the captives. Some died of diseases and he sent a thousand captives to Caesar, who had recently returned from the Cantabrian war. {*Strabo, l. 17. c. 1. s. 54. 8:139,141} {*Dio, l. 54. (5) 6:295}

5890. Pliny also wrote: {*Pliny, l. 6. c. 35. 2:473}

"In the time of Augustus, the Romans entered the country of the Ethiopians under Publius Petronius, their general, who was an equestrian and the governor of Egypt. He overcame their towns which he found in the same order that we list them: Pselcis, Primi, Bocchis, Cambyses' Market, Attenia and Stadissis. At the last place, the inhabitants had lost their hearing because of the noise of the cataract in the Nile River. He also sacked Napata. The farthest that he went from Syene was eight hundred and seventy miles. It was not the Romans who destroyed the land, but the constant wars Ethiopia had with Egypt."

*5891.* Phraates III was restored to his kingdom with a lot of help from the Scythians. When Tiridates heard of their coming, he fled to Caesar with a large number of his friends. He wanted to be restored to that kingdom and promised that Parthia would be subject to Rome if Caesar would give him that kingdom. *[K507]* When Phraates heard this, he soon sent envoys to Caesar and asked him to send back his servant Tiridates and his own son, whom he had given to Caesar as a hostage. {*Justin, Trogus, l. 42. c. 5.*}

*5892.* When Tiridate's and Phraate's envoys arrived in Rome, Augustus brought them both into the Senate. When the Senate had apprised him of the matter, he heard the demands of each party. He then told them that he would not surrender Tiridates to the Parthians, nor would he help Tiridates against the Parthians. Lest they should seem to have gained nothing for their trouble, Augustus ordered a very generous allowance to be given to Phraates, as long as he stayed at Rome. He sent back Phraates' son, so that, in his stead, he might recover the captives and ensigns that had been lost in the defeat of Crassus and Antony. {*Justin, Trogus, l. 42. c. 5.*} {*Dio, l. 53. (33) 6:277,279*}

*5893.* There were mutual grudges between Marcus Agrippa and Marcus Marcellus, who was the nephew and son-in-law of Augustus. Each one thought that the other was more respected by Augustus than himself. Augustus, fearing that the contentions would get worse if they both stayed in the same place, promptly sent Agrippa away into Asia, to govern those provinces beyond the sea in his place. Agrippa left the city, but sent his lieutenants into Syria while he stayed at Mitylene, on the isle of Lesbos. {*Dio, l. 53. (31) 6:273,275*} {*Velleius Paterculus, l. 2. c. 93. s. 2. 1:247*} {*Josephus, Antiq., l. 15. c. 10. s. 2. (350,351) 8:169*} {*Suetonius, Augustus, l. 2. c. 66. s. 3. 1:249,251*}

*5894.* Augustus resigned his eleventh consulship and made Lucius Sestius, the great favourite of Brutus, consul in his place. The Senate decreed the following honours to Augustus—he would be the perpetual tribune of the common people; he could convene the Senate as often as he wished, even though he was not a consul; he could make whatever laws he pleased; he would always have proconsular power, even within the walls of the city; he would not need to renew this power; and he would always have greater power in the provinces than even the governors themselves. {*Dio, l. 53. (30) 6:271*} {*Dio, l. 53. (32) 6:275,277*}

### 3982a AM, 4691 JP, 23 BC

*5895.* Aelius Gallus returned from the Arabian expedition. He left the village of Egra in the kingdom of the Nabateans and in eleven days, marched his army across to the Myus Harbour. From there, he marched overland to Coptus and arrived at Alexandria with the forces that were still able to bear arms. *[E775]* He had lost the rest, not in war, which had claimed only seven men, but by famine, labour, diseases and the difficult route. {*Strabo, l. 16. c. 4. s. 24.7:363*} Some of his medicines were mentioned by Galen and among these was a formula which he had used to save many of his soldiers and which he gave to Caesar. {*Galen, de Antidotis, l. 2.*}

*5896.* Marcus Marcellus died, who was the son of Octavia, the sister of Augustus; he was the husband of Augustus' daughter, Julia. {*Velleius Paterculus, l. 2. c. 93. 1:247*} {*Dio, l. 53. (30) 6:273*} {*Dio, l. 53. (33) 6:279*}

### 3982b AM, 4692 JP, 22 BC

*5897.* Augustus restored the control of Cyprus and Gallia Narbonensis to the Roman people, because these provinces did not need any troops, while he himself took control of Dalmatia. {*Dio, l. 53. (12) 6:221*} {*Dio, l. 54. (4) 6:291*}

*5898.* Antic dancing and stage plays were first brought to Rome by Pylades Cilices and Bathyllus. Pylades was the first ever to have a choir to accompany him. {*Eusebius, Chronicles, l. 1. 1:247*} {*Eusebius, Scaliger's Greek Eusebius, p. 390.*} {*Eusebius, Scaliger's Greek Eusebius (Animadversions), p. 155,156.*}

*5899.* After Herod had built Sebaste, he began to build another very magnificent city in a place by the seaside, where Straton's Tower stood. *[K508]* He called it Caesarea and constructed a harbour of admirable work, equal in size to the harbour of Piraeus at Athens. He finished all this in twelve years, sparing neither labour nor cost. {*Josephus, Jewish War, l. 1. c. 21. s. 5. (408-410) 2:193*} {*Josephus, Antiq., l. 15. c. 9. s. 6. (331,332) 8:159*} Eutropius described it like this: {*Eutropius, l. 7.*}

> "The name of Caesar was so beloved by the barbarians that kings who were friends of the people of Rome built cities in honour of him and called them Caesarea. King Juba built a city in Mauritania, and in Palestine there was another most famous city by the same name."

*5900.* Herod sent his sons, Alexander and Aristobulus, whom he had by Mariamme the Asmonean, to Rome to Caesar, to be raised there. They stayed at the house of Pollio, who was a good friend of Herod. Caesar entertained the young men very courteously and gave Herod the power to select one of his sons as the heir to his kingdom. Caesar also gave him Trachonitis, Batanea and Auranitis. {*Josephus, Antiq., l. 15. c. 10. s. 1. (342,343) 8:165*}

### 3983a AM, 4692 JP, 22 BC

*5901.* After Herod had received Trachonitis, he took guides and went to the dens of the thieves, where he restrained their villainies and brought peace to the inhabitants. Zenodorus was angry from envy at having lost his possessions to Herod. He went to Rome to accuse Herod, but could do nothing. {*Josephus, Antiq., l. 15. c. 10. s. 1,2. (344-350) 8:167,169}

5902. After Herod had greeted his best friend Agrippa at Mitylene, he returned into Judea. {*Josephus, Antiq., l. 15. c. 10. s. 2. (350,351) 8:169}

5903. Some citizens of Gadara went to Agrippa to accuse Herod. Refusing even to hear their complaints, he bound them and sent them to Herod, but Herod spared them. Although he was inexorable toward his own people, yet he willingly overlooked and forgave injuries received from strangers. {*Josephus, Antiq., l. 15. c. 10. s. 2,3. (351,356) 8:169-173}

5904. Augustus went into Sicily to settle its affairs. He went to other provinces also, even as far as Syria. {*Dio, l. 54. (6) 6:295}

### 3983b AM, 4693 JP, 21 BC

5905. Augustus sent for Agrippa, wishing that the latter had more patience. (Because of some light suspicion of harshness on whose part, under the pretence that he could not become emperor, he had left everything and gone to Mitylene.) Augustus asked him to come to him from Asia to Sicily. He ordered him to divorce his wife, although she was the daughter of Octavia, Augustus' own sister, and to marry his daughter Julia, the widow of Marcellus. Soon after, he sent him to solemnise the marriage and to undertake the government of the city of Rome. {*Dio, l. 54. (6) 6:297} {*Velleius Paterculus, l. 2. c. 93. s. 2. 1:247} {*Suetonius, Augustus, l. 2. c. 63. 1:243} {*Suetonius, Augustus, l. 2. c. 66. s. 3. 1:249}

5906. Zenodorus, in desperation, had rented out Auranitis, a part of his country, to the Arabians for fifty talents yearly. Although this area was included in the grant that Caesar gave Herod, the Arabians, who hated Herod, would in no way allow it to be taken from them. Sometimes they laid claim to it by invasions and force; sometimes they contended for the right of possession before the judges. They won over some needy soldiers who, as is often the case with wretched men, hoped for better fortunes through seditions. Herod, however, wisely tried to settle the matter by reason rather than by force, so that he would not provide opportunity for new seditions. {*Josephus, Antiq., l. 15. c. 10. s. 2. (351-353) 8:171}

5907. After Augustus had ordered things in Sicily, he crossed over into Greece and at this point took Aegina and Eretria from the Athenians, because, as some reported, the Athenians had favoured Antony. {*Dio, l. 54. (7) 6:299} [K509]

5908. Petronius went with troops to strengthen Premnis against Candace, the queen of the Ethiopians, who had attacked the garrison of Premnis with many thousands. He entered the citadel and strengthened it with many provisions and compelled the queen to accept conditions of peace. {*Strabo, l. 17. c. 1. s. 54. 8:141} {*Dio, l. 54. (5) 6:295}

5909. Petronius ordered the envoys who were sent to him, to go to Caesar if they wanted to demand anything. [E776] When they denied any knowledge of Caesar or of where they might find him, he ordered that they be escorted to Caesar, who was at Samos. {*Strabo, l. 17. c. 1. s. 54. 8:141}

### 3984a AM, 4693 JP, 21 BC

5910. After Augustus had settled his affairs in Greece, he sailed to Samos and wintered there. {*Dio, l. 54. (7) 6:299}

5911. The people of Armenia brought accusations against Artabazes, or Artaxis, or Artaxias (the son of Artavasdes, who had been captured through the treachery of Antony), and requested that his brother Tigranes, who was then at Rome, be their king. Augustus sent Tiberius to drive out Artabazes and to make Tigranes king in his place. {*Dio, l. 54. (9) 6:303} {*Tacitus, Annals, l. 2. c. 3. 3:387}

5912. The envoys of Candace came to Samos, where they found Caesar preparing to go to Syria and to send Tiberius into Armenia. They easily obtained from him what they desired and he also remitted their tribute. {*Strabo, l. 17. c. 1. s. 54. 8:141}

### 3984b AM, 4694 JP, 20 BC

5913. In the spring, when Marcus Apuleius and Publius Silius were consuls, Augustus went into Asia and from there into Bithynia. Although these provinces belonged to the people of Rome, he handled them with as much care as he did the provinces for which he was directly responsible. He settled all affairs where it was suitable. To some he gave money, while he imposed new sums on others, over and above their regular tribute. He took away the freedom of the Cyzicenians because, in a certain sedition, they had put some Romans to death, after having scourged them. {*Dio, l. 54. (7) 6:299}

5914. Augustus went into Syria in the tenth year after his last visit to that province. {*Josephus, Jewish War, l. 1. c. 20. s. 4. (399) 2:189} This was the seventeenth year of the reign of Herod from the death of Antigonus. {*Josephus, Antiq., l. 15. c. 10. s. 3. (354) 8:171} He took their freedom away from Tyre and Sidon, because of their factions. {*Dio, l. 54. (7) 6:299,301}

5915. Zenodorus had solemnly sworn to the Gadarenes that he would never stop trying to free them from the jurisdiction of Herod and the condition of being annexed to Caesar's province. Thereafter, many of them began to complain against Herod, calling him cruel and tyrannical. They complained to Caesar of his violence and rapines, and accused him of violating and razing their temples. Herod was not frightened by this and was prepared to answer for himself, but Caesar treated him courteously and was not at all alienated from him by all this tumultuous multitude. The Gadarenes perceived the inclinations of Caesar and his friends and were afraid that they might be turned over to Herod. The night following the meeting, some of them cut their own throats; others, fearing torture, killed themselves by jumping from high places; some drowned themselves in the river. Thus, by these actions, they seemed to condemn themselves and Caesar immediately absolved Herod. {*Josephus, Antiq., l. 15. c. 10. s. 3. (355-358) 8:173}

5916. Zenodorus' bowels ruptured and he lost a great deal of blood. He died at Antioch in Syria. {*Josephus, l. 15. c. 10. s. 3. (359) 8:173,175}

5917. Augustus gave the tetrarchy of Zenodorus to Herod. {*Josephus, Antiq., l. 15. c. 10. s. 3. (360) 8:175} {*Dio, l. 54. (9) 6:303} [K510] This was a large tract of land located between Galilee and Trachonitis, containing Ulatha and Paneas and the neighbouring countries. He also made him one of the governors of Syria and ordered the governors of that province to do nothing without Herod's advice. {*Josephus, Jewish War, l. 1. c. 20. s. 4. (400) 2:189} {*Josephus, Antiq., l. 15. c. 10. s. 4. (360) 8:175}

5918. Herod successfully asked Caesar for a tetrarchy for his brother Pheroras. Herod gave Pheroras a hundred talents from the revenues of his own kingdom, with the intent that if he should happen to die, Pheroras' estate might be assured and not subject to Herod's children. {*Josephus, Antiq., l. 15. c. 10. s. 3. (362) 8:175}

5919. Claudius Tiberius Nero was sent with an army by Augustus, his father-in-law, to visit and settle the provinces which were in the east. He was an extremely well-educated youth who had many natural talents. He entered Armenia with the legions, subdued it and brought it under the power of the people of Rome. He turned the kingdom over to Artavasdes. At this, the king of the Parthians, terrified by the reputation of so great a man as Caesar, sent his sons as hostages to Caesar. (Velleius Paterculus tended to flatter Tiberius immensely.) {*Velleius Paterculus, l. 2. c. 94. s. 4. 1:249}

5920. All historians also mention that Tigranes, the son of Artavasdes, was made king of the Armenians at that time. Artavasdes had been led captive into Egypt by Cleopatra and Antony. His oldest son, Artaxias (whom Dio here called Artabazes, by his father's name), reigned in the kingdom of Armenia. {*Dio, l. 54. (9) 6:303} Archelaus and Nero expelled him by force from the kingdom and made his younger brother king instead. (Velleius calls him Artavasdes, after his father's name, but all the others call him Tigranes. {*Velleius Paterculus, l. 2. c. 94. s. 4. 1:249}) [E777] Thus, Josephus related the story using the name of Archelaus, the king of Cappadocia, and the name of Nero Caesar, although Tiberius Claudius Nero had not yet been adopted by Caesar. {*Josephus, Antiq., l. 15. c. 4. s. 3. (104,105) 8:51} The narration in Horace was about Nero: {*Horace, Epistles, l. 1. c. 12. (25-28) 2:331}

> Know further too what places do partake
> Roman affairs: Cantabrian to Agrippa falls,
> Armenia by Claudius Nero did take:
> The younger brother Phraates has all,
> Caesar's both right and rule imperial.

5921. Ovid agrees with it: {*Ovid, Tristia, l. 2. (227,228) 6:71}

> The Armenians sue for peace, the Parthian bow,
> Horse, arms, and ensigns are resigned now.

5922. However, Dio affirmed that Tiberius Claudius Nero did nothing worthy of the preparations he had engaged in. Artabazes, or Artaxias, was killed by the Armenians before his arrival. {*Dio, l. 54. (9) 6:303} Concerning this incident, Tiberius boasted that he had done everything in his own power, especially because sacrifices had been decreed for it at the time. Tacitus also seemed to favour his account: {*Tacitus, Annals, l. 2. c. 3. 3:387,389}

> "Artaxias was killed through the treachery of his closest friends. Tigranes was made the king of the Armenians and brought into the kingdom by Tiberius Nero."

5923. Tiberius led his army into the east and restored the kingdom of Armenia to Tigranes, putting the crown on his head in the tribunal. {*Suetonius, Tiberius, l. 3. c. 9. s. 1. 1:325}

5924. Suetonius further said that Tiberius received the ensigns that the Parthians had taken from Marcus Crassus. The Parthians, at Augustus' demand, also restored the military ensigns that they had taken from Marcus Crassus and Mark Antony. Beyond that, they also offered hostages when Augustus came into Syria to settle the affairs in the east. {*Suetonius, Augustus, l. 2. c. 21. s. 3. 1:179,181} [K511] Phraates, who had not carried out anything he had agreed to, feared that Augustus might make war on Parthia and sent him back the Roman ensigns which Orodes had taken at the defeat of Crassus and those which his son had taken when Antony was routed. He also handed over all the captives from the armies of Crassus and Antony, who were spread throughout Parthia. Only a few were not returned. These had either killed themselves out of shame or stayed privately in Parthia. Augustus received these things as if he had conquered the Parthians in war. {*Livy, l. 139. 14:165} {*Florus, l. 2. c. 34. 1:351} {*Strabo, l. 1. c. 1. s. 17. 1:37} {*Strabo, l. 16. c. 1. s. 28. 7:237} {*Velleius Paterculus, l. 2. c. 91. s. 1. 1:241,243} {Justin, Trogus, l. 42. c. fin.} {*Dio, l. 54. (8) 6:301} {Eutropius, l. 7.} {Orosius, l. 6. c. 21.} {Cassiodorus, Chronicle}

5925. Eutropius wrote that the Persians, or Parthians, gave hostages to Caesar, a thing they had never before done to anyone. By delivering the king's children with a solemn procession as hostages, they secured a firm league. {Orosius, l. 6. c. 21.} Strabo confirmed that Phraates entrusted his sons and his grandsons to Augustus Caesar and with the greatest possible reverence, desired to earn his friendship by delivering hostages to him. {*Strabo, l. 6. c. 4. s. 2. 3:147} Justin also confirmed that his sons and grandchildren were hostages to Augustus. {Justin, Trogus, l. 42, c. fin.} However, Tacitus gave his real reasons for doing this: {*Tacitus, Annals, l. 2. c. 1. 3:385}

> "He showed all duty and reverence to Augustus and sent some of his children to him for the strengthening of their friendship. He did this not so much for fear of him, as out of distrust of the loyalty of his own subjects."

5926. Thermusa, an Italian woman, was Phraates' concubine, whom he later made his wife. She intended to get the kingdom of the Parthians for her son Phraataces, whom she had borne to the king while she was still his concubine. She persuaded the king, who was now her husband and with whom she could do anything she wished, to send his lawfully begotten children to Rome as hostages. {*Josephus, Antiq., l. 18. c. 2. s. 4. (39-42) 9:33,35} Phraates called Titius, who was then the governor of Syria, to a conference. He turned his four lawfully begotten sons over to Titius for hostages. These were Seraspadanes, Cerospades, Phraates and Bonones, along with two of their wives and four sons. He feared a sedition and the possibility of some treachery being plotted against him by his enemies. [E778] So he sent his sons away, having persuaded himself that no one would be able to do anything against him, if he were to have none of the royal family of the Arsaces to take his place, since the Parthians were extremely fond of that royal family. {*Strabo, l. 16. c. 1. s. 28. 7:237} In an old Roman inscription, another son of Phraates was added with Seraspadanes (for so it was written), who was not mentioned by Strabo. He was Rhodaspes, a Parthian and the son of Phraates Arsaces, the king of kings. {Gruter, Inscriptions, p. 288.} (The Loeb text for Strabo writes *Rhodaspes* for *Cerospades*. Editor.)

5927. In the east, Augustus established his subjects according to the Roman laws, but allowed those who were in league with him to live according to the laws of their ancestors. He did not consider it desirable to take anything from his subjects, or extend the empire, but to be content with what they had. He consequently wrote this to the Senate and made no wars at this time. To Jamblichus, the son of Jamblichus, he gave his father's principality in Arabia. He also gave to Tarcondimotus, the son of Tarcondimotus, his father's principality in Cilicia, except for some coastal towns. These he gave to Archelaus, along with the kingdom of Lesser Armenia, because the Mede, who had held the kingdom previously, had died. He gave Commagene to Mithridates, who was only a child, because its king had killed the father of Mithridates. {*Dio, l. 54. (9) 6:303} [K512]

5928. After Herod had escorted Caesar to the coast, he returned into his kingdom and there built a beautiful temple of white marble in honour of Caesar. This was near Panium, at the foot of the hills where the springs of the Jordan River were. He also remitted a part of their tribute to his subjects, on the pretext that they should have some relief after the famine. In actual fact, however, he did it to put their minds at rest, because they were so offended at such vast building projects of the king, that tended toward the destruction of their religion and good customs. {*Josephus, Antiq., l. 15. c. 10. s. 3,4. (363-365) 8:175,177}

### 3985a AM, 4694 JP, 20 BC

5929. To prevent seditions, Herod forbade all private meetings in the city and too many feasts. He also had spies, who would mingle in companies and note what the people talked about. Indeed, he himself would go in the night, in the clothes of a common man, and mingle in the company of the people to learn what they thought of him. All those who obstinately disagreed with his actions, he punished without mercy. The rest of the multitude he bound to him with an oath in which they swore to be loyal to him. {*Josephus, Antiq., l. 15. c. 10. s. 4. (366-368) 8:177,179}

5930. Herod required this oath from many followers of the Pharisees, including Pollion and Samaias. Although he could not make these two take the oath, he did not punish them as he did the others, out of respect for the reverence he bore to Pollion. Nor did he impose this oath on the Essenes, whom he esteemed highly for Manaemus' sake, who was a prophet. When Herod as a boy had still been a private citizen, Manaemus had greeted him as king of the Jews and had foretold that he would reign as king for more than thirty years. {*Josephus, Antiq., l. 15. c. 10. s. 4,5. (370-379) 8:183}

5931. Gaius was born to Agrippa by his wife Julia. A yearly sacrifice was decreed on his birthday, along with some other things. {*Dio, l. 54. (8) 6:301}

*5932.* Augustus returned to Samos and again wintered there. To reward their hospitality, he granted the Samians liberty. A great many embassies came to him there. The Indians ratified the peace by a firm league which they had previously sought through their envoys. {*See note on 3979 AM. <<5854>>*} Among the presents that the Indians sent, were tigers, which had never before been seen by either the Romans or Greeks. They also gave him a certain young man who had no shoulders or arms (like the statues of Mercury or Hermes), who did everything with his feet instead of his hands. He was said to bend a bow and shoot an arrow and sound a trumpet. {*Dio, l. 54. (9) 6:305*}

*5933.* Nicolaus Damascene reported that he saw these Indian envoys at Antioch near Daphne. The letter they brought mentioned more envoys, but he said he only saw three alive, as the rest had died because the journey was so long. The letter, which indicated that it was sent by Porus, was written in Greek on parchment. Although Porus ruled six hundred kings, he esteemed Caesar's friendship so much, that he was ready to meet him wherever Caesar wished and said that he would help him in anything that was right. Nicolaus said that these things were contained in that letter. Moreover, they brought presents by eight naked servants, dressed only in breeches and covered with perfumes. Among the presents was the youth, Hermes, who had no arms, as well as large vipers, a snake fifteen feet long, a river tortoise about five feet long and a partridge larger than a vulture. {*Strabo, l. 15. c. 1. s. 73. 7:125,127*} [K513]

## 3985b AM, 4695 JP, 19 BC

*5934.* Also among the presents was Zarmarus, or Zarmanochegas, one of the wise men of the Indians. He killed himself according to the customs of his country, out of ostentatious pride or due to old age, or to make a display of himself before Augustus and the Athenians (for he had come into Athens). He was made a priest of the Greek gods and although this was done at an unlawful time (as they reported), it was done nonetheless, as a favour for Augustus. He believed that he had to die, lest some adversity should happen to him if he stayed any longer. *[E779]* He laughed as he leaped on the funeral fire, his body naked and anointed. The following inscription was written on his sepulchre: {*Strabo, l. 15. c. 1. s. 73. 7:127,129*} {*Dio, l. 54. (9) 6:305,307*}

> "Here lies Zarmanochegas, an Indian from Bargosa, who immortalised himself according to the ancestral customs of Indians."

*5935.* On his return to Rome, Augustus entered the city on horseback in a triumph. He was honoured with a triumphal arch that carried his trophies. {*Dio, l. 54. (8) 6:301*}

*5936.* Augustus considered it very praiseworthy that, without any fighting, he had recovered the things which had formerly been lost in war. Therefore, he ordered it to be decreed that sacrifices should be offered for this reason. A temple of *Mars Ultor* (The Revenger) should be built on the Capitol, in imitation of Jupiter Feretrius, where the ensigns were to be hung up. This was done. {*Dio, l. 54. (8) 6:301*}

*5937.* He had formerly vowed to build this temple to Mars, before the victory at Philippi. He now proclaimed that he had received another like benefit from Mars, and so he performed his vow at the end of his twenty-second year. In this he imitated Romulus, who had killed Acro, the king of the Coeninenses, and had hung up his arms in the temple he had dedicated to Jupiter Feretrius. Augustus built a temple to Mars, the Twice Revenger, and then placed in it the military ensigns that he had recovered from the Parthians. He also instituted the Circus Games, to be solemnised every year in memory of these things. Ovid wrote: {*Ovid, Fasti, l. 5. (579-598) 5:303,305*}

> It does not Mars suffice once named to have gained
> He prosecutes the Parthian Ensigns yet retained.
> A country guarded with store of horses, bows, plains,
> For rivers inaccessible remains.
> Other Crassus yet much spirited by the fall,
> At once of army, standard, general.
> The Roman ensigns did the Parthian bear,
> And, while an enemy, their eagle wear.
> This blemish still had stuck; But Caesar's might,
> Better defended Latium's ancient right:
> He took the ensigns, cancelled that disgrace,
> And made the eagle know her proper place.
> What profits shooting back, thine envious land,
> Thy swifter steed, oh Parthian? thy hand
> Delivers back thine ensigns, and thy bow:
> Thou canst no trophies of the Roman show.
> A temple duly vote Bis-ultor thy
> Honour receiveth most deservedly.
> More honourable Romans celebrate
> His plays: no scene supplies Bellona's state.

*5938.* [E780] [K514] Horace added: {*Horace, Odes, l. 4. c. 15. (4-8) 1:345*}

> …Caesar, thine age
> Affords plenteous fruits to the fields,
> And to Jove's Capitol our ensigns yields
> From Parthian pillars snatched.…

*5939.* Many of Augustus' coins carried the inscription, *SIGNIS RECEPTIS*, referring to the recovered ensigns.

*5940.* Herod, in the eighteenth year of his reign (as calculated from the death of Antigonus), told the Jews of his intention to build the temple at Jerusalem. When he saw that they were troubled, in case he could not finish the new one after he had demolished the old, he assured them that the old temple would remain intact until all materials necessary for the new building were ready. He did not deceive them. He provided a thousand wagons to carry stones and selected ten thousand of the most skilful craftsmen and also provided priestly robes for a thousand priests. At his own expense, he trained some of them as masons and carpenters and ordered them to start the work, since the materials were ready. {*Josephus, Antiq., l. 15. c. 11. s. 1,2. (380-381) 8:185,187}

### 3986 AM, 4696 JP, 18 BC

5941. When Augustus' first ten-year term had almost expired, he extended it for another five years. He also gave Marcus Agrippa another five years, along with some powers that were almost the same as his, such as the tribunal power. He said that so many years would then be sufficient, although, shortly after, he accepted more years of the imperial power, so that his Principality could be made decennial. {*Dio, l. 54. (12) 6:313}

5942. The Sibylline books had become worn out with age. Augustus ordered the priests to write them out with their own hands, so that no other person should see or read them. {*Dio, l. 54. (17) 6:325,327}

5943. Augustus restored Pylades, the Cilician dancer who had been exiled from Rome because of a sedition, and through this won the favour of the people. Once, when Augustus reproved him because he was always quarrelling with Bathyllus, a fellow artist and also a friend of Maecenas, Pylades cleverly rejoined: {*Dio, l. 54. (17) 6:327}

> "It is to your advantage, oh Caesar, that the people should devote their spare time to us."

### 3987b AM, 4697 JP, 17 BC

5944. All the materials necessary for starting the temple were assembled within the time of two years. Herod began to build the temple of Jerusalem, forty-six years before the first passover of the ministry of Christ. This was confirmed by the words of the Jews: {Joh 2:20}

> "This temple has been built forty and six years before this...."

5945. The aorist tense in that verse was correctly translated by our countryman, Tho. Lydiate.

5946. The building of the second temple under Zerubbabel had been started in the first year of the reign of Cyrus, and then the building programme had been interrupted for some time. It was finally finished after twenty years, in the sixth year of Darius, the son of Hystaspes. Now, at this time, the magnificent building of this new temple was begun by Herod and was finished in nine and a half years. [K515] When comparing the time spent in building this most magnificent structure, with the time it took to erect the previous temple, we must take into consideration not only the labour for these two temples, but their finished work also. When Herod's temple was completed: {*Josephus, Jewish War, l. 5. c. 5. s. 1. (187-188) 4:57,59}

> "many ages had been spent, and all the holy treasures which had been sent there to God from all the parts of the world."

5947. Herod did not only pay for this but for other projects as well. Much of his wealth was spent on generous gifts and on building so many palaces, temples and cities. He was building the city and port of Caesarea, which was his most costly building project, at the same time as he was building the temple. Tacitus called it: {*Tacitus, Histories, l. 5. c. 8. 3:189}

> "a temple of immense riches"

5948. The great building project of the temple, which was begun by Herod, was carried on right up to the beginning of the war of the Jews under Gessius Florus, through generous gifts which were consecrated to God. Josephus stated: {*Josephus, Antiq., l. 20. c. 9. s. 7. (219,220) 10:117,119}

> "When the temple was finished, the people realised that more than eighteen thousand workmen, who had made their living by building the temple, would be unemployed. They were unwilling that the holy treasure should be stored there, for fear it should become a prize for the Romans. They wanted to provide work for the workmen, because, if one had worked only one hour, he was immediately paid his wages. [E781] They persuaded King Agrippa (the younger) to build the eastern porch, which enclosed the outermost parts of the temple."

5949. In Italy, Marcus Agrippa had Lucius by his wife Julia, and Augustus immediately adopted both this boy and his brother Gaius, and appointed them as his heirs to his empire. {*Dio, l. 54. (18) 6:327}

5950. In Cyprus, many sections of its cities were destroyed by earthquakes. {*Eusebius, Chronicles, l. 1. 1:248}

### 3988 AM, 4698 JP, 16 BC

5951. After Marcus Agrippa had organized quinquennial games, which were held for the fourth time since the battle of Actium, Augustus sent him to Syria. {*Dio, l. 54. (19) 6:331}

*5952.* Herod sailed for Italy to greet Caesar and to see his children at Rome. {*Josephus, Antiq., l. 16. c. 1. s. 2. (6) 8:211*} On his way, he stopped over in Greece. He attended and was a judge at the Olympic games in the 191st Olympiad, in which Diodorus Tyaneus won the prize. When Herod saw that these games were too grand for the place where they were held, due to the poverty of the people of Elis, he gave them annual revenues, to enable them to make their sacrifices more splendid, and other things that might contribute to the gracing of such great games. For his generosity, he was declared a perpetual judge of these games. {*Josephus, Jewish War, l. 1. c. 21. s. 12. (426,427) 2:201,203*} {*Josephus, Antiq., l. 16. c. 5. s. 3. (149) 8:267*}

*5953.* When Caesar had courteously entertained Herod at Rome, he returned his sons, who had finished their instructions in the liberal sciences. {*Josephus, Antiq., l. 16. c. 1. s. 2. (6,7) 8:211*} Caesar went into Gaul. {*Dio, l. 54. (20) 6:333*}

*5954.* Aemilius Macer, a poet of Veron, died in Asia. {*Eusebius, Chronicles, l. 1. 1:248*} Albius Tibullus wrote of him: {*Tibullus, Corpus Tibullianum*}

> What shall poor Amor now do all alone,
> Since sweet-songed Macer to the camp is gone?

*5955.* At Jerusalem, the priests completed the building of the temple, properly so called, because it contained the Holy and the Holy of Holies. *[K516]* This took about eighteen months, during which time it was reported that it never rained in the day, but only at nights. In the following eight years, the porches, the ranges and the rest of the buildings around the temple were all completed. {*Josephus, Antiq., l. 15. c. 11. s. 6,7. (421-425) 8:205,207*}

*5956.* Two descriptions of this temple are extant: one was by Josephus, who himself was a priest in it; {*Josephus, Antiq., l. 15. c. 11. s. 5. (410-420) 8:199-205*} {*Josephus, Jewish War, l. 5. c. 5. s. 1-8. (184-247) 4:57-79*} the other was by R. Judas, almost a hundred and twenty years after the destruction of the temple, in a book of his Mishma, which was entitled מידרות. We have a description of the former from Ludovicus Capellus, at the end of his short history of the Jews. The latter we have from Constantine Lempereur, as a preface in his commentary on the book of *Middoth*. In the preface he showed that the prevailing opinion of the Jews was that the temple of Zerubbabel, and this one of Herod, were rightly considered to be the same building. Likewise, he showed that it was thought that the temple that was captured by Pompey was the same temple that was then besieged by Titus. {*Tacitus, Histories, l. 5. c. 9. 3:191*}

## 3989 AM, 4699 JP, 15 BC

*5957.* When Alexander and Aristobulus returned to Judea, they were highly favoured by all men. Salome, the sister of Herod, and her followers, fearing that they would at some time revenge their mother's death, spread gossip among the people that the sons hated their father because he had killed their mother. However, Herod did not yet suspect anything and treated them very honourably, as they deserved. Since they were mature young men, he selected wives for them. For Alexander, he selected Bernice, the daughter of Salome, and for Aristobulus, Glaphyra, the daughter of Archelaus, the king of the Cappadocians. {*Josephus, Antiq., l. 16. c. 1. s. 2. (7-11) 8:211,213*}

*5958.* Augustus restored liberty to the Cyzicenians and also gave money to the Paphians in Cyprus, who had been afflicted with an earthquake. He permitted, by a decree of the Senate, that their city should be called Augusta. {*Dio, l. 54. (23) 6:343*}

*5959.* When Herod heard that Marcus Agrippa had again come into Asia, he went to him. He begged him to come into his kingdom as his friend and guest. {*Josephus, Antiq., l. 16. c. 2. s. 1. (12,13) 8:213*}

## 3990a AM, 4699 JP, 15 BC

*5960.* Herod entertained Agrippa in all the cities he had recently built, and showed him the buildings. He provided the best food for Agrippa and his friends, as well as all kinds of other delights and magnificence. He showed him Sebaste, the port of Caesarea, and the citadels which he had built, such as Alexandrion, Herodion and Hyrcania. He brought him to the city of Jerusalem, where all the people met him in their best festive attire and with joyful acclamations. *[E782]* Agrippa made a large number of sacrifices to God and feasted the people. Although he would gladly have stayed there longer, he nonetheless hurried to sail into Ionia for fear of storms, since winter was now approaching. He and his friends were honoured with generous presents. {*Josephus, Antiq., l. 16. c. 2. s. 1. (13-15) 8:213,215*}

*5961.* After Asander, who was the king of Cimmerian Bosphorus, died, he left his kingdom to his wife Dynamis, the daughter of Pharnaces and grand-daughter of Mithridates. Scribonius, who claimed to be a great-grandson of Mithridates and to have received the kingdom from Augustus, married Dynamis and seized the kingdom. When Agrippa heard of this, he sent Polemon, the king of that Pontus which bordered Cappadocia, to make war on him. {*Dio, l. 54. (24) 6:345*}

## 3990b AM, 4700 JP, 14 BC

*5962.* As soon as the Bosphorans were aware of this deceit, they killed Scribonius and resisted Polemon, who came against them because they feared that he would be made their king. *[K517]* Polemon conquered them in battle, but yet did not subdue them. {*Dio, l. 54. (24) 6:345*}

*5963.* As soon as it was spring, Herod heard that Agrippa was going to Bosphorus with an army. He hurried to go to him and sailed by Rhodes and Chios. He expected to find him when he arrived at Lesbos, but he was detained by contrary north winds and stayed at Chios. Many came to greet him privately and he gave them many princely gifts. He saw the portico of the city, which had been thrown down in the war against Mithridates and was still lying in ruins. It had not been repaired to its former beauty and greatness, because they were so poor. Herod gave them more than enough money to finish restoring the gate and exhorted them to restore the city to its former beauty and greatness as soon as they could. {*Josephus, Antiq., l. 16. c. 2. s. 2. (16-19) 8:215,217}

*5964.* As soon as the wind changed, Herod sailed first to Mitylene and then to Byzantium. There he found out that Agrippa had already gone past the Cyanean Rocks, so he followed him as fast as possible and overtook him at Sinope, a city in Pontus, where he arrived with his ships, much to the surprise of Agrippa. He was very grateful for Herod's arrival and they embraced each other with singular affection, because it was an evident sign of Herod's fidelity and friendship that he had left his own affairs and come to him at so opportune a time. Therefore, Herod still stayed with him in the army and was his companion in his labours and partaker in his counsels. Herod was the only man who was consulted in difficult matters because of the affection Herod had for Agrippa and in pleasant times, for honour's sake. {*Josephus, Antiq., l. 16. c. 2. s. 2. (20-22) 8:217}

*5965.* Agrippa defeated the Bosphorans and recovered the Roman ensigns in war, which they had long ago captured under Mithridates. Agrippa forced them to give them back. {Orosius, l. 6. c. 21.}

*5966.* Julia, the daughter of Augustus and wife of Agrippa, went to Illium at night. It so happened that Julia and her servants who waited on the coach were in extreme danger while crossing the Scamander River, because it was greatly swollen by sudden floods and the people of Illium did not know she was coming. Agrippa was angry that they had not helped her and fined them a hundred thousand drachmas of silver. {Life of Nicolaus Damascene, Excerpts from Henric Valesius, p. 418.}

*5967.* The envoys from Illium did not dare to oppose Agrippa. They entreated Nicolaus Damascene, who happened to be there, to get King Herod to speak for them and to help them. Nicolaus did this because of the ancient renown of the city and told the king the whole story: that Agrippa was unjustly angry with the Illienses, since Julia had come without notice and they had not known of her coming because it was night.

Herod undertook the cause of the Illienses. He had their fine removed and reconciled Agrippa to them, who was angry with them. {Life of Nicolaus Damascene, Excerpts from Henric Valesius, p. 418.} {*Josephus, Antiq., l. 16. c. 2. s. 2. (26) 8:219}

*5968.* The Bosphorans finally laid down their arms and were put under the rule of Polemon, who then married Dynamis with the approval of Augustus. For this, there was a procession in Agrippa's name. However, he did not have a triumph, although it was decreed, nor did he write anything at all to the Senate about his affairs. *[K518]* In later times, others followed his example. They did not confirm their deeds by letters, nor did they accept a triumph, although it was offered to them. Instead, they were content with only the triumphal honours. {*Dio, l. 54. (24) 6:345,347}

*5969.* After the trouble of Pontus was over, Agrippa and Herod came by land to Ephesus through Paphlagonia, Cappadocia and Greater Phrygia. From there, they sailed to Samos. {*Josephus, Antiq., l. 16. c. 2. s. 2. (23) 8:217}

*5970.* The Illienses returned into their country, because they had lost all hope of obtaining a pardon. When Herod was about to go into Paphlagonia to Agrippa, he gave Nicolaus Damascene a letter concerning the remission of their fine. *[E783]* Then he carried on to Chios and Rhodes, where his sons waited for him, while Nicolaus sailed from Amisus and came to the port of Byzantium. From there, he sailed to Troas and came to Illium. After he had delivered his letter about the remission of their fine, both he, and especially Herod, received great honours from the Illienses. {Life of Nicolaus Damascene, Excerpts from Henric Valesius, p. 418.}

*5971.* Agrippa did Herod favours in many things on their entire journey through many cities. Through the intercession of Herod, the cities had many of their needs met. If anyone required an intercessor to Agrippa, he could not obtain his suit more easily through anyone else than through Herod. Herod also paid Caesar's praetors the money owed by the Chians and got them immunity, as well as assisting others in whatever they had need of. {*Josephus, Antiq., l. 16. c. 2. s. 2. (24-26) 8:217,219}

*5972.* When they came into Ionia, they came across a large number of Jews who lived in that country. When the Jews had an opportunity, they complained of the wrongs they received from those of their countrymen who would not permit them to live after their own laws. On the Jewish festival days, they hauled them before the tribunals and forbade them to send holy money to Jerusalem. They publicly compelled the Jews to give them the holy money intended for religious use contrary to the privileges granted them by the Romans. Herod made every effort to ensure that Agrippa should hear their complaints. He allowed their case to be pleaded by Nicolaus Damascene, who was one of Herod's friends and who had now returned from Troas. Nicolaus pleaded their case to Agrippa, who was accompanied by many of the most honourable Romans as well as some kings and princes. The Greeks did not deny anything, but only made the excuse that the Jews, who lived among them, were troublesome to them. The Jews proved that they were freeborn citizens and that they lived by their own laws, doing injury to no one. Therefore Agrippa answered that, for his friend Herod's sake, he was ready to grant them their request, and also because they seemed to be demanding what was just. He therefore ordered that the privileges which had formerly been granted them should not be revoked and that no one should molest them for living by their country's laws. Then Herod rose up and thanked Agrippa in the name of them all. After they mutually embraced each other, they said goodbye to each other and Herod sailed from Lesbos to Caesarea. {*Josephus, Antiq., l. 16. c. 2. s. 3-5. (27-62) 8:219-233}

5973. A few days later, Herod arrived at Caesarea, due to favourable winds. From there he went to Jerusalem, where he called all the people together and gave them a report of his journey and how he had procured an immunity for the Jews living in Asia. To further gratify them, he said he would remit the fourth part of their tribute to them. [K519] Very pleased, they wished the king every possible happiness and departed with great joy. {*Josephus, Antiq., l. 16. c. 2. s. 5. (62-65) 8:233}

### 3991 AM, 4701 JP, 13 BC

5974. Augustus assumed the Roman high priesthood after the death of Lepidus, who had previously been in the triumviri and been the priest. Augustus could not decide to take it from him while he was alive. {*Suetonius, Augustus, l. 2. c. 31. s. 1. 1:197} {*Dio, l. 54. (27) 6:355} This was done on the day before the Nones of March (March 6). {*Ovid, Fasti, l. 3. (419-421) 5:151}

5975. When Augustus was made high priest, he burned any books, in either Greek or Latin, that had no author's name or were not of substance, to a total of two thousand books, keeping only the Sibylline books. From these, he selected some and placed them in two golden cases at the base of the pillar where the image of Apollo stood, on the Palatine hill. {*Suetonius, Augustus, l. 2. c. 31. s. 1,2. 1:197}

5976. A colony was sent to Berytus. {*Eusebius, Chronicles, l. 1. 1:249} It was highly honoured with the favour of Augustus {Ulpian. C. Sciendum est D. de Censibus.} and received two legions, which were sent there by Agrippa. {*Strabo, l. 16. c. 2. s. 19. 7:263,265}

5977. Herod was incensed at the false accusations and machinations of his sister, Salome, and his brother, Pheroras, against his two sons by Mariamme, Alexander and Aristobulus. To bring down their ambitious spirits, he began publicly to promote his other son, Antipater, as his heir to the kingdom. He was his oldest son, who had been born to him when he was a private man, and his mother was also of lowly birth. Herod had banished him from the city in favour of his two other sons and only gave him freedom to come there on feast days. Herod often wrote to Caesar on his behalf and privately gave him very great commendations. Overcome by the entreaties of Antipater, Herod brought his mother, Doris, into the court, who was a woman of Jerusalem whom Herod had divorced when he had married Mariamme. {*Josephus, Jewish War, l. 1. c. 22. s. 1. (431-433) 2:205} {*Josephus, Antiq., l. 16. c. 3. s. 1-3. (66-80) 8:233-239}

### 3992a AM, 4701 JP, 13 BC

5978. Agrippa's ten years of government in Asia (to be calculated from the time when he was sent by Caesar to Asia and Syria and the time he stayed at Lesbos) were over and he was now ready to leave. Herod sailed to greet him and of all his sons, took only Antipater with him. Herod gave Agrippa many gifts and asked him to take Antipater to Rome, to be received into Caesar's favour. {*Josephus, Antiq., l. 16. c. 3. s. 3. (86) 8:241} [E784]

### 3992b AM, 4702 JP, 12 BC

5979. When Agrippa returned from Syria, Augustus sent him to make war in Pannonia and granted him the tribunal power for a further five years. When he arrived, the Pannonians were terrified and stopped their rebellion. On his return journey, Agrippa died in Campania. His body was brought into the forum at Rome and Augustus commended him in a funeral speech. {*Livy, l. 139. 14:165} {*Dio, l. 54. (28) 6:355,357}

5980. Antipater was highly honoured at Rome and was commended by his father's letters to all his friends. Although he was absent, he continued to stir up his father in letters against the sons of Mariamme. He pretended to be concerned for his father's safety, but was in fact promoting himself by his wicked practices, in the hope of getting the kingdom. {*Josephus, Antiq., l. 16. c. 4. s. 1. (87-89) 8:241,243}

5981. Against his will, Augustus made his son-in-law, Tiberius, his partner in the government to replace Agrippa, because his grandsons, Gaius and Lucius, were still children. Therefore, he betrothed his daughter Julia, the widow of Agrippa, to Tiberius. Augustus forced Tiberius to divorce his wife Agrippina, the daughter of Agrippa and the grand-daughter of Pomponius Atticus. [K520] Tiberius was upset by this, because his wife was nursing his son, Drusus, and was expecting another child. {*Suetonius, Augustus, l. 2. c. 63. s. 2. 1:243} {*Suetonius, Tiberius, l. 3. c. 7. 1:321} {*Dio, l. 54. (31) 6:363}

## 3993 AM, 4703 JP, 11 BC

5982. Herod had now become an enemy to his sons, Alexander and Aristobulus. He sailed to Rome with them to accuse them before Caesar. {*Josephus, Antiq., l. 16. c. 4. s. 1. (90) 8:243} In the same ship, he took Nicolaus Damascene with him, with whom he had studied philosophy. {Life of Nicolaus Damascene, Excerpts from Henric Valesius, p. 421.}

5983. Herod did not find Augustus at Rome and followed him all the way to Aquilia. Herod accused them of treachery against him, but the young men satisfied all who were present of their innocence. They were finally reconciled to their father, after many entreaties and tears. They thanked Caesar and departed together. Antipater also went, pretending that he was glad that they were reconciled. {*Josephus, Antiq., l. 16. c. 4. s. 1-4. (90-126) 8:243-257}

5984. A few days later, Herod gave three hundred talents to Caesar, who was holding spectacles and giving gifts to the people. In return, Caesar gave him half the revenues of the copper mines of Cyprus and committed the other half to his oversight. Caesar honoured him with other gifts of hospitality and gave him permission to choose which of his sons he wanted for his successor, or whether he would rather divide his kingdom among them. Herod was ready to divide his kingdom right then, but Caesar would not allow Herod to do this in Herod's lifetime. He would not deprive him of his kingdom or his authority over his sons. {*Josephus, Antiq., l. 16. c. 4. s. 5. (127-129) 8:257,259}

5985. In Herod's absence, a rumour was spread that he was dead. The men of Trachonitis revolted from him and started their old thievery, but the captains whom Herod had left in the kingdom were able to subdue them again. Forty of the leaders of these thieves, terrified by what happened to those who were captured, fled their country for Arabia Nabatea. They were welcomed by Syllaeus, who was an enemy to Herod, because Herod refused to give him his sister, Salome, for a wife. Syllaeus gave them a certain well-fortified place. {*Josephus, Antiq., l. 16. c. 4. s. 6. (130) 8:259} {*Josephus, Antiq., l. 16. c. 9. s. 1. (271-274) 8:319}

5986. Herod and his sons sailed home and on the way came to Eleusa (its name was changed to Sebaste), a city of Cilicia. There they met with Archelaus, the king of Cappadocia, who very courteously entertained Herod and rejoiced greatly that his sons were reconciled to him. He was glad that Alexander had honestly answered the charges made against him. They gave each other royal gifts and parted company. {*Josephus, Antiq., l. 16. c. 4. s. 6. (131,132) 8:259}

5987. When Herod returned into Judea, he called the people together and told them what he had done on his journey. He told them that his sons were to reign after him, first Antipater and then Alexander and Aristobulus. The last two were his sons by Mariamme. {*Josephus, Antiq., l. 16. c. 4. s. 6. (132-134) 8:259}

## 3994 AM, 4704 JP, 10 BC

5988. About this time, the lame man was born who was more than forty years old when he was healed by Peter at the gate called *Beautiful* at the temple. {Ac 4:22} Agrippa was born, who was the first king of the Jews by that name, and who died when struck by an angel when he was fifty-four years old. {Ac 12:23} {*Josephus, Antiq., l. 19. c. 8. s. 2. (350) 9:381}

5989. Augustus married his daughter Julia to Tiberius, after having previously betrothed her to him. {*Dio, l. 54. (31) 6:363} [K521]

5990. Caesarea Sebaste was finished in the 28th year of Herod's reign (beginning from the death of Antigonus), in the 3rd year of the 192nd Olympiad. It was dedicated with great solemnity and most sumptuous preparations. Musicians were brought together, to see who was the best. [E785] Naked wrestlers and a large number of sword players and wild beasts were also brought there to perform, together with whatever else was being done, either at Rome or in other countries. These sports were consecrated to Caesar and were to be held every fifth year. The king provided all the preparations to be brought there at his own expense, to show the greatness of his magnificence. Julia, the wife of Caesar (Josephus always called her Livia), contributed many things toward the sports. The total cost of the event was over five hundred talents and a large crowd came to see these sports. Herod entertained all the envoys who were sent to him from various countries, to thank him for the favours they had received from him. He lodged, feasted and entertained them, spending all the days in seeing the sports and the nights in banquets. {*Josephus, Antiq., l. 16. c. 5. s. 1. (136-141) 8:261,263}

## 3995a AM, 4704 JP, 10 BC

5991. After the dedication and feasts, Herod began to build another city in a place called Capharsalama (or Capharsuluma {Apc 1Ma 7:31}), which he named Antipatris, after his father Antipater. He built a citadel which he called Cypros, after his mother. In honour of his dead brother, he built a good tower in the city of Jerusalem, not inferior to Pharos at Alexandria, and called it Phasael. Later, he built a town by the same name in the valley of Jericho, from which the surrounding country is called Phasaelis. {*Josephus, Antiq., l. 16. c. 5. s. 2. (142-145) 8:263,265}

## 3995b AM, 4705 JP, 9 BC

*5992.* Through their envoys, the Jews of Asia and Cyrene complained to Augustus that the Greeks would not allow them to practise their religion and ignored the immunities which had been granted to them by the Romans. The envoys wanted to obtain letters confirming these privileges. {*Josephus, Antiq., l. 16. c. 6. s. 1. (160,161) 8:271}*

*5993.* Herod had depleted his wealth with his great expenses and now needed money. He followed the example of John Hyrcanus and went by night, without the knowledge of the people, and opened David's sepulchre. He found no money, but large amounts of costly attire and ornaments of gold, which he removed. To atone for this, he built a most sumptuous monument of white marble at the entrance of the sepulchre. Nicolaus Damascene, who recorded the acts of King Herod in his lifetime, mentioned this monument, but nothing of the king's breaking into the sepulchre. {*Josephus, Antiq., l. 16. c. 7. s. 1. (179-183) 8:281,283}*

*5994.* Antipater continued to implicate his brothers, Alexander and Aristobulus, by false accusations made through others. He often seemed to be the one defending them, so that he might more easily oppress them, by making a pretence of goodwill toward them. In this subtle way, he so achieved his way with his father, that Herod thought he was his only preserver. Therefore, the king commended his steward, Ptolemy, to Antipater and discussed all his plans with Antipater's mother, Doris. Everything was done according to their wishes and they made the king displeased with those whom it was to their advantage that he should be angry with. {*Josephus, Antiq., l. 16. c. 7. s. 2. (188-191) 8:285}*

*5995.* Pheroras fell so madly in love with his own servant, that he refused the marriage with Cypros, Herod's daughter, who was offered to him by Herod. He was persuaded by Ptolemy, the king's steward, to promise to divorce his servant and to marry Cypros within thirty days, which he failed to do. *[K522]* He also accused Herod to his son, Alexander, saying that he had heard from Salome, his sister (which she denied), that Herod was greatly in love with Alexander's wife, Glaphyra. This made the king highly displeased with both of them. {*Josephus, Antiq., l. 16. c. 7. s. 3,4. (194-208) 8:287-293}*

## 3996 AM, 4706 JP, 8 BC

*5996.* The man who was diseased started to lie by the pool of Bethesda. He was healed by Christ thirty-eight years later. {*Joh 5:5}*

*5997.* Alexander was driven to desperation by the wiles of his adversaries. He was reconciled to his father by Archelaus, the king of the Cappadocians, who came to Jerusalem. {*Josephus, Antiq., l. 16. c. 8. s. 6. (261-266) 8:313-317}*

*5998.* Archelaus was considered one of Herod's best friends. He received generous gifts from Herod and departed for Cappadocia, with Herod accompanying him as far as Antioch. Herod and Titus, the governor of Syria, reconciled their differences and Herod returned to Judea. {*Josephus, Antiq., l. 16. c. 8. s. 6. (269,270) 8:317}*

*5999.* Herod went a third time to Rome to Caesar. {*Josephus, Antiq., l. 16. c. 9. s. 1. (271) 8:319}*

*6000.* While Herod was away from his kingdom, the thieves of the Trachonites, who had fled to Syllaeus, the Arabian, molested all of Judea and Coelosyria with their robberies. Syllaeus granted them impunity and protection for their thievery. {*Josephus, Antiq., l. 16. c. 9. s. 1. (275) 8:319}*

*6001.* When Augustus was the high priest, he restored the incorrect intercalation of the year which had been decreed by Julius Caesar, but which had later, through negligence, been incorrectly intercalated. {*Suetonius, Augustus, l. 2. c. 31. s. 2. 1:197}* In thirty-six years, twelve days were intercalated where only nine days ought to have been intercalated. Therefore, Augustus commanded that twelve years should pass without any leap year at all, so that those extra three days, which had been added over thirty-six years by the over-zealous priests, would be eliminated in the following twelve years. {*Pliny, l. 2. c. 6. (36) 1:191}* {*Solinus, c. 3.*} {*Pliny, l. 18. c. 57. (211) 5:323,325}* {*Macrobius, Saturnalia, l. 1. c. 14.*} [E786]

*6002.* When he corrected the year, Augustus called the month of Sextilis August, after himself, rather than naming the month of September after himself, even though he was born in that month. He did this because he had first been consul in the month of Sextilis, and also had won many great victories in that month. {*Suetonius, Augustus, l. 2. c. 31. s. 3. 1:197}* {*Dio, l. 55. (6) 6:395}* Macrobius recorded the very words of the decree of the Senate. {*Macrobius, Saturnalia, l. 1. c. 12.*} He also mentioned the decree of the people concerning the same matter. Pacuritus, the tribune of the people, proposed the law. This occurred when Gaius Marcius Censorinus and Gaius Asinius Gallus were consuls. {*Censorinus, De Die Natali, l. 1. c. 22.*} {*Dio, l. 55. (5) 6:391}*

*6003.* In their consulship, a second census of the citizens was conducted at Rome. In the census, there were 4,233,000 Roman citizens, as was recorded in the fragments of the Ancyran Marble. {*Augustus, l. 1. c. 8. 1:357}* {*Gruter, Inscriptions, p. 230.*} In Suidas in Αυχουσθ, the number was 4,101,017. Suidas very ridiculously stated that this number was for the city, and not the whole world.

*6004.* When Herod returned from Rome, he celebrated the dedication of the temple built again by him, which had taken nine and a half years. He dedicated it on the very anniversary of his kingdom, on the day when he had first received it from the Senate. It was his custom to solemnise the day with great joy. The king sacrificed three hundred oxen to God and many others offered sacrifices according to their abilities. {*Josephus, Antiq., l. 15. c. 11. s. 6. (421-423) 8:205} [K523]

## 3997a AM, 4706 JP, 8 BC

6005. Herod had found that, in his absence, his people had been greatly harmed by those thieves from Trachonitis. He was unable to subdue them, because they were under the protection of the Arabians, but he could not tolerate their attacks either, so he entered Trachonitis and killed all their relatives. They were all the more incensed by this, because they had a law commanding them not to allow the slaughter of their families to go unrevenged. Therefore, they ignored all dangers and molested all of Herod's country with continual excursions, plundering and carrying away their goods. {*Josephus, Antiq., l. 16. c. 9. s. 1. (276,277) 8:321}

6006. When Augustus indicated his willingness to resign his principality, because another ten years had almost passed, he assumed it again, as though against his will. He made war on the Germans, sending Tiberius against them, but he himself stayed home. {*Dio, l. 55. (6) 6:393} He also gave money to the soldiers because they had Gaius along with them for the first time, taking part in their military exercises. {*Dio, l. 55. (6) 6:395}

## 3997b AM, 4707 JP, 7 BC

6007. Dionysius Halicarnassus began to write the books of the Roman history in the 193rd Olympiad, when Claudius Tiberius Nero and Gnaeus Calpurnius Piso were consuls. This he stated in the preface to these books. {*Dionysius Halicarnassus, Roman Antiquities, l. 1. c. 3. s. 4. 1:11} He was considered a historian by Clement and a rhetorician by Quintilian. {*Clement, Stromateis, l. 1. c. 21. 2:324} {Quintilian, l. 3. c. 1.}

6008. Herod sent to Saturninus and Volumnius, the governors of Syria who had been appointed by Caesar, demanding that he be allowed to punish those thieves from Trachonitis who were wasting his country with their invasions from Arabia and Nabatea. The governors were told that the robbers had increased to about a thousand and had begun to make sudden invasions and to waste both fields and villages and cut the throats of all who fell into their hands. Therefore, Herod demanded these thieves be turned over to him and asked for the sixty talents that he had lent Obadas under Syllaeus' security. Syllaeus had expelled Obadas from the government and was now ruling everything himself. He denied that the thieves were in Arabia and deferred to pay the money.

This was debated before Saturninus and Volumnius. Finally, it was determined by them that, within thirty days, the money was to be repaid and the runaways from both countries should be turned over to each other. {*Josephus, Antiq., l. 16. c. 9. s. 1. (277-281) 8:321,323} Syllaeus also swore, in the presence of these governors of Syria, by the fortune of Caesar, that he would pay the money within thirty days and turn the fugitives over to Herod. {*Josephus, Antiq., l. 16. c. 10. s. 8. (346) 8:349}

6009. When the appointed time arrived, Syllaeus was unwilling to live up to his agreement and went to Rome. With the permission of Saturninus and Volumnius, who had given him permission to prosecute these obstinate people, Herod entered Arabia with an army. In three days, he travelled as far as they usually did in seven. When he came to the citadel where the thieves lived, he took it at the first assault. He demolished this fortress called Rhaeptu without doing any harm to the inhabitants of the country. When a captain of the Arabians came to their defence, both sides joined the battle. A few of the Herodians were killed and about twenty-five Arabians, along with their captain. The rest of the Arabians fled. When Herod had avenged himself upon the thieves, he brought three thousand Idumeans into Trachonitis, to restrain the thieves who lived there. He sent letters to the Roman governors, who were in Phoenicia at the time, in which he told them that he had only used the power they had granted him against these obstinate Arabians, and nothing else. [E787] [K524] When they inquired into this, they found that what Herod had said, was true. {*Josephus, Antiq., l. 16. c. 9. s. 2. (282-285) 8:323,325}

## 3998a AM, 4707 JP, 7 BC

6010. At Rome, Syllaeus received letters about what had happened, but they grossly exaggerated everything. These lies so incensed Caesar against Herod, that he wrote threatening letters to him because he had marched out of his kingdom with an army. At first, Caesar would not even admit the envoys who had been sent to plead Herod's cause. They again petitioned to be heard, but he dismissed them without anything being done. {*Josephus, Antiq., l. 16. c. 9. s. 3. (286-291) 8:325,327}

6011. The Trachonites and the Arabians seized this opportunity and attacked the garrison of the Idumeans that Herod had sent to them. Herod was terrified by Caesar's anger and was forced to bear it. {*Josephus, Antiq., l. 16. c. 9. s. 3,4. (292,293) 8:327}

6012. After Obadas, the king of the Arabians (of Nabatea), had died, Aeneas, who changed his name and was called Aretas, succeeded him in the kingdom. While Syllaeus was at Rome, he used false accusations to try to have Aretas expelled from the kingdom and to get the kingdom for himself. He gave a great deal of money to the courtiers and promised Caesar many great things. He knew Caesar was offended with Aretas, because he had dared assume the kingdom without his consent. {*Josephus, Antiq., l. 16. c. 9. s. 4. (294,295) 8:327,329}

### 3998b AM, 4708 JP, 6 BC

6013. Gaius and Lucius, the sons of Augustus by adoption, were raised in the imperial house. They were quite insolent even when they were very young. Lucius, the younger of the two, entered the theatre unattended, where he was received with a general applause. This increased his boldness. Gaius ran for consul and was elected by the people before he was of military age! When Augustus heard this, he hoped that there would never be a time when, as in his own case, the consulship had to be given to one who was not yet twenty years old. When his son earnestly requested this of him, he then said that this office was to be undertaken by someone who could both avoid making mistakes and resist the wishes of the people. Finally, he gave Gaius the priesthood and permission to go into the Senate and sit with the senators, both at the spectacles and the feasts. {*Dio, l. 55. (9) 6:401} He also granted that, even though they were not yet seventeen, they should be called the *Princes of the Youth*, but Augustus declined the consulship for them, which they passionately wanted. {*Tacitus, Annals, l. 1. c. 3. 3:247}

6014. To make his sons behave more modestly, like private citizens, Augustus granted Tiberius the power of tribune for five years. He assigned him to Armenia, which had revolted after the death of Tigranes, who had been made king by Tiberius. This did not work out as Augustus planned and both the sons and Tiberius were offended. The sons felt ignored and Tiberius, fearing their anger, went to Rhodes instead of Armenia. He used the pretence that he wanted to study the arts, but his real reason was so that the sons would be relieved of the sight of him and his actions. {*Dio, l. 55. (9) 6:403} He feared that his own glory could dim the beginnings of the careers of two rising young men. {*Velleius Paterculus, l. 2. c. 99. s. 2. 1:257} Some thought that Tiberius left the place and the position of second highest in the empire, which he had held for so long, when Augustus' sons were young men, and that in this he followed the example of Marcus Agrippa, who went to Mitylene when Marcus Marcellus was admitted to public office. If Tiberius were present, he might conflict with them and detract from their glory. Tiberius gave this reason many years later. {*Suetonius, Tiberius, l. 3. c. 10. 1:327} [K525]

6015. Some think that he went away because of his wife, Julia, whom he dared not accuse or divorce, but whom

he could not endure any longer. {*Suetonius, Tiberius, l. 3. c. 10. s. 1. 1:327} {*Dio, l. 55. (9) 6:405} Others say that he was offended that he had not been adopted by Caesar. Still others claim that he was sent there by Augustus because he had acted treacherously against his sons. {*Dio, l. 55. (9) 6:405}

6016. Concealing his true reasons, Tiberius asked permission of Augustus, who was his father-in-law, to leave Rome and his wife. {*Velleius Paterculus, l. 2. c. 99. s. 1,2. 1:255,257} {*Suetonius, Tiberius, l. 3. c. 10. s. 1. 1:327} Nor did he yield to his mother, who humbly besought him, or his father-in-law, who complained that he, too, had been forsaken by the Senate. When they resolutely detained him, he ate nothing in four days until, finally, they granted him permission to go. He went down at once to Ostia and did not say a word to those who went with him. He kissed very few of them before he sailed. {*Suetonius, Tiberius, l. 3. c. 10. s. 2. 1:327} At his departure, he opened his will and read it before his mother and Augustus. {*Dio, l. 55. (9) 6:405}

6017. From Ostia he sailed along the coast of Campania, where he heard of the weakness of Augustus. He stayed there for a little while, but the rumour increased, as though he were tarrying for an opportunity for greater things; so he sailed to Rhodes, almost in foul weather. {*Suetonius, Tiberius, l. 3. c. 11. s. 1. 1:327} He undertook his journey like a private man, except that he compelled the Pharians to sell him a statue of Vesta, which he dedicated in the temple of Concord. {*Dio, l. 55. (9) 6:403,405} [E788]

6018. When he arrived in Rhodes, he was contented with a small house there and a slightly larger one in the country. He lived a very retired life, sometimes walking into their gymnasiums without either a lictor or a messenger. He gave and received courtesies from the Greeks on equal terms. {*Suetonius, Tiberius, l. 3. c. 11. s. 2. 1:329} Nevertheless, all the proconsuls and governors who were going into foreign provinces went out of their way to visit him and always submitted their fasces to him. He stated that as a private citizen in his retirement, he was more honoured than when he had been in the government. {*Velleius Paterculus, l. 2. c. 99. s. 4. 1:257} In his retirement, he diligently listened to Theodorus, the Gadarene, who was a rhetorician. Theodorus, however, wished to be called a Rhodian. {Quintilian, l. 3. c. 1.}

6019. There was a great conjunction of the planets, which only occurred once every eight hundred years.

6020. Aeneas, who was also called Aretas, the new king of the Arabians of Nabatea, sent letters and gifts to Caesar which included a crown worth many talents. In his letters, he accused Syllaeus of many crimes and of being a most wicked servant, who had poisoned Obadas. He claimed that while Obadas was alive, Syllaeus had done as he pleased. Caesar would not even hear his envoys and dismissed them without anything being done, and also despised his presents. {*Josephus, Antiq., l. 16. c. 9. s. 4. (296) 8:329}

6021. Herod was compelled by the wrongdoings and insolence of the Arabians to send Nicolaus Damascene to Rome, to see if he could get any justice from Caesar through his friend's mediation. {*Josephus, Antiq., l. 16. s. 4. (297-299) 8:329,331}

6022. The discord of Herod with his sons by Mariamme was significantly worsened through the wiles of Eurycles, a Lacedemonian. He was the same person (unless I am mistaken) who, twenty-five years earlier, had fled with Antony from the battle of Actium. He was now being entertained by Herod and was staying at Antipater's house. [K526] After he had ingratiated himself with Alexander, Herod gave him fifty talents for information against Alexander. Eurycles went to Archelaus, the king of Cappadocia, and bragged how he had reconciled Alexander to his father's favour again. He received money from Archelaus as well, and returned to Lacedemon. There he continued his wicked ways and was banished from Lacedemon. {*Josephus, Jewish War, l. 1. c. 25. s. 1-4. (513-531) 2:243-253} {*Josephus, Antiq., l. 16. c. 10. s. 1. (300-310) 8:331-335}

6023. Herod made diligent inquiry about his sons. He put to death, by extreme torture, many of his own friends and those of his sons; but he found nothing wrong, except that some were too free in what they said about these unfortunate young men. They had complained of their father's immoderate cruelty and of his willingness to listen to any gossip of wicked men. They had noted the impiety and wicked deceits of their brother Antipater and of the faction that was united against them, and they intended to escape further harm by fleeing to Archelaus. His two sons did not deny this, but Herod put them in prison, as if they had been guilty of treason against their father. He said that he would punish them depending on how his affairs went at Rome. On that matter, he sent letters to Caesar by Volumnius (the general of his army), as Josephus called him, and Olympius, his friend. {*Josephus, Jewish War, l. 1. c. 27. s. 1. (535) 2:255} Herod ordered that on their trip they should stop at Eleusa, a town of Cilicia, and give a letter to Archelaus. They were to expostulate with him, because he was a partner in his sons' plans. {*Josephus, Antiq., l. 16. c. 10. s. 7. (332) 8:343}

6024. At Rome, Nicolaus Damascene allied himself with the Arabians who had come to accuse Syllaeus. He claimed to be Herod's accuser before Augustus, and not Herod's defender, otherwise he would not likely have been allowed to speak, but would have been turned away

as others had been. When Nicolaus had publicly exposed many of Syllaeus' crimes, he also added that Caesar had been misled by his lies in the case of Herod. When he had publicly shown this and had confirmed it by certain and authentic records, Caesar condemned Syllaeus and remanded him to the province to be punished, after he had paid his debt. {*Josephus, Antiq., l. 16. c. 10. s. 8,9. (335-350) 8:345-350}

6025. From this time, Augustus was reconciled to Aretas and Herod. Augustus received Aretas' presents, which he had so often rejected before. By his authority, he confirmed the kingdom of the Arabians to him. He also advised Herod by letter that he should call a council at Berytus to meet with the governors of Syria, with Archelaus, the king of the Cappadocians, and others of his friends and noblemen, and that together they should settle the whole business. {*Josephus, Antiq., l. 16. c. 11. s. 1. (356-359) 8:353}

6026. On the isle of Cos, an earthquake destroyed much property. {*Eusebius, Chronicles, l. 1. 1:250}

6027. The angel Gabriel (who had, at an earlier time foretold to Daniel the coming of the Messiah {Da 9:24-27}) appeared at the right side of the altar of incense to Zacharias, the priest of the course of Abijah, as he was offering incense in the temple of the Lord, according to the custom of the priest's office. {Ex 30:7,8} [E789] He told him that he, who was now quite old, and his aged wife, Elizabeth, who was barren, would have a son. He would be called John, and would be a Nazarite and the forerunner of the Lord. He would minister in the spirit and power of Elijah. Zacharias did not believe the promise and was struck dumb. {Lu 1:5-22}

### 3999a AM, 4708 JP, 6 BC

6028. After the days of his ministry were finished, Zacharias returned home and his wife Elizabeth conceived a son by him and hid herself away for five months, saying: {Lu 1:23-25}

> "Thus hath the Lord dealt with me in the days in which he looked on me, to take away my reproach among men." [K527]

6029. When Herod received Augustus' letters, he was overjoyed because he had been restored into his favour and had been given the power to do what he wanted with his sons. Through messengers, he convened all those whom Caesar had appointed to meet at Berytus, except for Archelaus, who was holding his sons not far from the city of Platana, a city of the Sidonians. First of all, Saturninus, who had been a consul and was a man of great dignity, spoke his opinion. He was moderate and said that the sons of Herod were indeed to be condemned, but not to be put to death. After him, his three sons, who were their father's lieutenants, were of the same opinion. On the other side, Volumnius stated that they were to be punished with death, because they had been so impious toward their father. Most followed his opinion. Then the king took his sons with him to Tyre, where Nicolaus had arrived from Rome. After Herod had conferred with him about his sons, he ordered Nicolaus to sail with him to Caesarea. {*Josephus, Antiq., l. 16. c. 11. s. 2,3. (361-372) 8:353-359}

6030. At Caesarea a certain old soldier named Tiro smartly reprehended Herod for the wickedness he planned against his sons and told him that he and three hundred officers were of the same opinion. Herod ordered him to be cast into prison. Trypho, the king's barber, used this occasion to accuse Tiro and said that he had often been solicited by Tiro to cut the king's throat with his razor as he was trimming him. At once, both the barber and Tiro and his son were tortured. His son saw his father so cruelly treated and to free him from the tortures, was imprudently merciful and accused him of intending to murder the king. Then Herod brought those three hundred officers together, with Tiro and his son, and the barber. He accused them all before the people. The people threw anything and everything that was handy and killed every one of them. {*Josephus, Antiq., l. 16. c. 11. s. 5-7. (379-393) 8:361-365}

6031. Alexander and Aristobulus were led to Sebaste and strangled there at their father's command. Their bodies were buried in the citadel of Alexandrion, where Alexander, their maternal grandfather, and many of their family were buried. {*Josephus, Antiq., l. 16. c. 11. s. 7. (394) 8:365,367} {*Josephus, Jewish War, l. 1. c. 27. s. 6. (550,551) 2:261}

### 3999b AM, 4709 JP, 5 BC

6032. When Augustus had assumed the twelfth consulship, he brought Gaius, who was now of age, into the court and designated him *Prince of the Youth*, and made him a prefect of a tribe. {*Suetonius, Augustus, l. 2. c. 26. s. 2. 1:187} {*Dio, l. 55. (10) 6:405} Augustus also noted: {*Augustus, l. 2. c. 14. 1:367}

> "All the Roman equestrians gave them silver shields and spears."

6033. Augustus stated this in the breviary of his deeds and also mentioned the consulship that was decreed to both Gaius and Lucius at the time. {*Augustus, l. 2. c. 14. 1:365,367}

> "In respect of honouring me, the Senate and people of Rome designated them consuls when they were only fifteen years old, so that they might enter into that office after five years, to be calculated from that day when they were brought into the court."

6034. So it was written on the Ancyran Marble, {*Augustus, l. 2. c. 14. 1:365,367} {Gruter, Inscriptions, p. 231.} whereas on another Roman stone it is said that the people created Gaius consul when he was only fourteen years old. (By *created* it means *designated*, for at this time his fourteenth year was ended and he was entering into his fifteenth year.)

6035. After his brothers were dead, Antipater intended to remove his father also. Since Antipater knew he was hated by many in the kingdom, he endeavoured to get the goodwill of his friends at Rome and in Judea with bribes. He especially solicited Saturninus, the governor of Syria, and Pheroras and Salome, the brother and sister of Herod. {*Josephus, Antiq., l. 17. c. 1. s. 1. (1-7) 8:375} [K528]

6036. Herod sent Glaphyra, the widow of his son Alexander, home to her father Archelaus, the king of Cappadocia. He also gave her a dowry from the king's treasury, in case some controversy should arise about it. He took good care of the young children of Alexander and Aristobulus. Antipater was grieved at this and feared that when they were come of age, they would restrain his power. Hence, he plotted their destruction also, and so overcame Herod with his entreaties, that he allowed him to marry the daughter of Aristobulus and allowed Antipater's son to marry the daughter of his uncle, Pheroras. {*Josephus, Antiq., l. 17. c. 1. s. 1,2. (11-18) 8:377-381}

6037. Herod invited Zamaris, a Babylonian Jew, and gave him land in Trachonitis to inhabit, so that he would guard that country against thieves. He came with five hundred cavalry and a hundred of his relatives, and built various citadels in several places around Trachonitis and also at Bathyra. [E790] He gave safe passage to the Jews who travelled from Babylon to the feasts at Jerusalem, protecting them from the thievery of the Trachonites and others. {*Josephus, Antiq., l. 17. c. 2. s. 1-3. (23-29) 8:383-387}

6038. Antipater plotted treason against his father in which he involved his uncle Pheroras, along with some of the king's women, who belonged mainly to the Pharisees. Salome remained loyal to her brother Herod. The Pharisees were a crafty people, arrogant and enemies to kings. Subsequently, when the whole country was to swear loyalty to the king and Caesar, they alone, numbering more than six thousand, refused to swear. For this reason they were fined by the king, but the wife of Pheroras paid their fine for them. Since they were thought to be able to foresee the future, they in return foretold to her that it was decreed that the kingdom would be taken from Herod and his children and would be given to her and her husband and their children. Salome told Herod about this and that they had solicited and corrupted many of his courtiers with bribes. Herod killed the leading Pharisees who were involved, along with the eunuch Bagoas and his catamite, Karos, who had been commended to Herod for his handsomeness. Herod also killed whomever of his family he had found to have conspired with the Pharisees. {*Josephus, Antiq., l. 17. c. 2. s. 4. (32-45) 8:393}

6039. After Herod had convicted the Pharisees and punished them, he called a council of his friends. Before them, he began an accusation against Pheroras' wife. When Pheroras would not forsake her in favour of his brother, Herod forbade Antipater to associate with Pheroras. {*Josephus, Antiq., l. 17. c. 3. s. 1. (46-51) 8:393-397}

6040. To remove all suspicion of his father from himself, Antipater, through his friends who lived at Rome, requested that Herod should immediately send Antipater to Augustus. Herod sent many expensive presents and his will along with him. In it he stated that Antipater should be king, but that if he died, then Herod Philip, Herod's son by Mariamme, the daughter of Simon the high priest, would be the king. {*Josephus, Antiq., l. 17. c. 3. s. 2. (52,53) 8:397}

6041. In the sixth month after John was conceived, the angel Gabriel was sent by God to Nazareth in Galilee, to the most blessed virgin Mary, who was betrothed to Joseph. They were both of the tribe of Judah and of David's family. He greeted her and declared that she should bring forth the Son of God and should call his name Jesus. She was more fully instructed by the angel about the amazing manner of her conception to be performed by the power of the Holy Spirit, who would overshadow her. [K529] With great faith, she said that it should be done to her, the handmaid of the Lord, according to his word. {Lu 1:26-38}

6042. Christ was thus conceived and the mother of the Lord hurried into the hill country, to a city of Judah; that is, Hebron, a city of the priests located in the mountains of Judah. {Jos 21:10,11} When she had entered into the house of Zacharias, the priest, and had greeted her cousin Elizabeth, the latter felt the child leap in her womb. Elizabeth was filled with the Holy Spirit and declared that Mary was blessed. Mary believed this and affirmed that the things that had been told her by the Lord would come about. Mary imitated the song of Hannah, {1Sa 2:1-10} and spoke that divine hymn: My soul doth magnify the Lord.... Mary stayed with Elizabeth for about three months. {Lu 1:39-56}

6043. Syllaeus, the Arabian, went to Rome, but had done nothing of what Caesar had ordered him to do. Antipater accused him before Caesar of the same crimes of which Nicolaus Damascene had previously accused him. Also present was another accuser, Aretas, the king of the Nabateans, who accused him of the murder of

many honourable men without his consent. He especially complained about the murder of Soemus, a man most famous for every kind of virtue. He also complained about the murder of Fabatus, Caesar's slave. {*Josephus, Jewish War, l. 1. c. 29. s. 3. (574-577) 2:273,275} {*Josephus, Antiq., l. 17. c. 3. s. 2. (53-57) 8:397,399}

6044. Herod banished his brother Pheroras into his tetrarchy, because he so obstinately persisted in the love for his wife. He went willingly, swearing that he would never return until he heard of Herod's death. Soon after that, Pheroras became sick and Herod repeatedly sent for him to receive some private instructions from Pheroras as he lay on his death bed, but he refused to come, on account of his oath. {*Josephus, Jewish War, l. 1. c. 29. s. 4. (578,579) 2:275} {*Josephus, Antiq., l. 17. c. 3. s. 3. (58,59) 8:399}

6045. When Elizabeth's time had come, she gave birth to a son. When he was to be circumcised on the eighth day, the bystanders would have called him Zacharias, after his father, but his parents said that he would be called John. Zacharias had his speech restored, was filled with the Holy Spirit and prophesied, saying, Blessed be the Lord God of Israel.... {Lu 1:57-68} When Joseph found that Mary, his betrothed wife, was pregnant, he was willing to put her away quietly. [E791] He was told by God in a dream that she had conceived by the Holy Spirit and would bring forth a son, Jesus, who would save his people from their sins. He then took her as his wife. {Mt 1:18-24}

6046. When Pheroras became sick beyond all hope of getting well, his brother Herod came and visited him and very kindly sought help for him; but he died within a few days. Herod brought his body to Jerusalem, to bury it there, and honoured him with public mourning. {*Josephus, Jewish War, l. 1. c. 29. s. 4. (580,581) 2:275,277} {*Josephus, Antiq., l. 17. c. 3. s. 3. (60) 8:399}

6047. Two of Pheroras' freedmen, who were most dear to him (and who were Taphenites), told Herod how he had been killed with poison by Doris, the mother of Antipater. (This turned out not to be true and Pheroras actually died of a natural death.) Herod inquired into this alleged villainy and by luck he gradually uncovered even greater villainies and the obvious treasons of his son Antipater. On his journey to Rome, Antipater had given a deadly poison to Pheroras to use to poison Herod. [K530] Theudion, the brother of Doris, had sent it from Egypt by Antiphilus, one of Antipater's friends, to kill Antipater's father. Theudion had done this while Antipater was away, so that no one would suspect he had anything to do with his father's death. {*Josephus, Antiq., l. 17. c. 4. s. 1,2. (61-77) 8:401-407}

6048. Consequently, Herod expelled Doris, the mother of Antipater, from the palace and took her jewels from her, which were worth many talents. Herod divorced his wife, the second Mariamme, the daughter of the high priest, who was in on this plot. He removed her son, Herod Philip, from his will, in which he was appointed successor. He also deprived his father-in-law, Simon, of the high priesthood and substituted Matthias, the son of Theophilus, who was born at Jerusalem. {*Josephus, Antiq., l. 17. c. 4. s. 2. (78) 8:407,409}

## 4000a AM, 4709 JP, 5 BC

6049. On the day of atonement, when there was a solemn fast of the Jews, the new high priest, Matthias, could not perform the divine service because he had suffered from nocturnal pollution. So Joseph, the son of Ellemus, was appointed to be his assistant and substitute, since he was his relative. That same day he entered into the Holy of Holies. {*Josephus, Antiq., l. 17. c. 6. s. 4. (166,167) 8:447,448}

6050. Bathyllus, the freedman of Antipater, arrived from Rome. When he was tortured, he confessed that he had brought a poison which he had given to Antipater's mother Doris and to Pheroras to poison Herod. He had said that if the first poison was too weak, they could certainly kill Herod with this one. Antipater had his friends at Rome send letters to the king. These accused Archelaus and Philip, Herod's sons, of complaining about the murder of Alexander and Aristobulus and pitying the misfortune of their innocent brothers. At that time, these young men were at Rome to study, but now their father ordered them to return. After that, Antipater bribed his friends with large gifts, getting them to make his father suspect these two men, who stood in the way of Antipater's ambitions. Antipater himself wrote to his father about them, as if he were excusing them because they were young. {*Josephus, Antiq., l. 17. c. 4. s. 3. (79,80) 8:409} {*Josephus, Jewish War, l. 1. c. 30. s. 1. (582,583) 2:277}

6051. Augustus ordered that all the Roman world should be taxed. This taxing first happened when Cyrenius was governor of Syria. {Lu 2:1} From this, a little book was made by Augustus, containing all the public riches, as well as the number of Roman citizens and armed allies. It listed the navies, kingdoms and provinces, and it recorded what tribute and customs were required to be paid. {*Tacitus, Annals, l. 1. c. 11. 3:267} {*Suetonius, Augustus, l. 2. c. 101. s. 4. 1:309}

6052. Publius Sulpicius Quirinius was called Cyrenius in the Greek, Κυτιωιου or Κυρνινιου, and had been a consul at Rome for seven years prior to this. Strabo wrote about the Homonadensians, a people of Cilicia: {*Strabo, l. 12. c. 6. s. 5. 5:479}

> "Quirinius overcame them by famine and took four thousand men and distributed them into the neighbouring cities."

6053. Tacitus wrote: {*Tacitus, Annals, l. 3. c. 48. 3:597,599}

> "He was a valiant warrior and ambitious in all his duties. He had the consulship under Augustus. He was famous, for he won the citadels of the Homonadensians by assault and obtained the ensigns of triumph."

6054. Augustus himself had decreed that the magistrates should not be sent into the provinces as soon as they had left office. {*Suetonius, Augustus, l. 2. c. 36. 1:207} They should wait five years after their term of office expired. {*Dio, l. 53. (14) 6:227}

6055. After that, Quirinius obtained the proconsulate of Cilicia. He could be sent into nearby Syria, either as censor, with an extraordinary power, or as Caesar's governor, with ordinary power. [K531] He would still retain the proconsulship of Cilicia and Sextius Saturninus, the governor of Syria. We have often read in Josephus that Volumnius and Saturninus were both equally called governors of Syria, whereas only Volumnius, was the governor of Syria. {*Josephus, Jewish War, l. 1. c. 27. s. 2. (538) 2:255} [E792] A little later, Quintilius Varus was made successor to Saturninus, with the proconsular authority. So nothing is incorrect, in that Quirinius may be said to have succeeded to, or rather to have been added to, the office of administrating Caesar's affairs, as King Herod was. Josephus noted that Herod was to be the governor of all Syria. {*Josephus, Jewish War, l. 1. c. 20. s. 4. (400) 2:189} This was so constituted by Augustus, in order that Herod was added to the governors and so that all things would be done according to his wishes. {*Josephus, Antiq., l. 15. c. 10. s. 4. (360) 8:175} Hence both would govern together. Tertullian stated: {*Tertullian, Against Marcion, l. 4. c. 19. 3:378}

> "There was a tax raised under Augustus in Judea, by Sentius Saturninus."

6056. Luke stated, when this same taxing was made: {Lu 2:1,2}

> "when Cyrenius or Quirinius was governor of Syria."

6057. Luke would rather mention him than the governor Saturninus, because he would compare this taxing with another that was made ten years later by the same Quirinius, after Archelaus was sent into banishment. He stated that, of the two taxings, this was the first taxing and this was the time of the birth of Christ.

6058. When this first taxing was enacted, Joseph went up from Galilee, from the city of Nazareth into Judea, to the city of David, called Bethlehem. He was of the house and lineage of David and would be taxed there with his wife Mary, who was due to deliver. {Lu 2:4,5}

# The Seventh Age of the World

## 4000a AM, 4709 JP, 5 BC

*6059.* Jesus Christ, the Son of God, was born of the most blessed virgin Mary at Bethlehem in the fulness of time. *{Mt 1:25 2:1,5 Ga 4:4}* Mary wrapped him in swaddling clothes and laid him in a manger, because there was no room in the inn. *{Lu 2:7}*

*6060.* The birth of our Saviour was revealed by an angel of the Lord to shepherds who were watching their flocks by night in the neighbouring fields. They heard the words of a multitude of the heavenly host praising God and saying *Glory to God in the highest and on earth peace and goodwill to men.* The shepherds hurried to Bethlehem and found Mary and Joseph, and the child lying in the manger. They told everyone what they had heard concerning the child and came back praising and glorifying God. *{Lu 2:8-20}*

## 4000b AM, 4710 JP, 4 BC

*6061.* The child was circumcised on the eighth day after his birth and was given the name Jesus, as had been foretold by the angel before he was conceived in the womb. *{Lu 2:21}*

*6062.* The wise men from the east were guided by a star and came to Herod at Jerusalem. *[K532]* When they were told that the birthplace of Christ was in Bethlehem of Judea, they went there and entered the house which was shown to them by the star that stood over it. They found the little child with his mother, Mary. They fell down and worshipped him and gave him their treasures of gold, frankincense and myrrh. They were warned by God in a dream that they should not return to Herod, and so they departed into their own country by another way. *{Mt 2:1-12}*

*6063.* On the fortieth day after her delivery, Mary and Joseph went to Jerusalem to the temple, to present the child to the Lord according to the law of the firstborn. She offered a pair of turtle doves for herself, or two young pigeons, for she could not afford to offer a lamb. This was according to the Levitical law. *{Lu 2:22-24,27 Le 12:2-4,6,8}*

*6064.* When his parents brought the child Jesus into the temple to perform the requirements of the law, Simeon came into the temple, to whom it had been revealed by God that he would not die until he had seen the Anointed of the Lord. He took Jesus in his arms and praised the Lord and spoke prophecies about Christ and his mother. At the same time, Anna, a prophetess and the daughter of Phanuel, came up and publicly acknowledged the Lord, and spoke of him to all who looked for redemption in Jerusalem. *{Lu 2:25-38}*

*6065.* When Joseph and Mary had carried out all the things required by the law of the Lord, they returned into Galilee, to their own city of Nazareth. *{Lu 2:39} [E793]*

*6066.* The angel of the Lord appeared to Joseph in a dream and warned him to flee to Egypt, to save the life of the child and escape the machinations of Herod. When he awoke, he took the young child and his mother and went by night into Egypt, where he remained until the death of Herod. *{Mt 2:13-15}*

*6067.* Herod thought the young child was still at Bethlehem. He killed all the children who were in Bethlehem and in all the surrounding area, who were two years old or less. This was in accordance with the time when the star was first seen in the east and when the wise men enquired about the child. *{Mt 2:16}*

*6068.* Herod received letters from Antipater in Rome, in which he told him that he had settled all his business according to his wishes and would be returning home in a short time. When Herod wrote back to him, he concealed his anger. Herod said he should hurry home, in case anything should happen to him (Herod) while Antipater was away. Herod also mildly complained about his mother and promised that he would settle all differences after his return. *{\*Josephus, Antiq., l. 17. c. 5. s. 1. (83) 8:411}*

*6069.* Because he was hated by everyone, Antipater had heard no news all this time, either of the death of Pheroras, or of those things that had been brought against him, even though seven months had elapsed. *{\*Josephus, Jewish War, l. 1. c. 31. s. 2. (606,607) 2:289} {\*Josephus, Antiq., l. 17. c. 4. s. 3. (82) 8:409,411}* On his journey, he received a letter at Tarentum about Pheroras' death. In Cilicia, he got the letters from his father telling him to hurry home. When he came to Celenderis, a town of Cilicia, he began to have doubts about his return and was extremely sorrowful over the disgrace of his mother. *[K533]* However, he sailed on and came to Sebaste, the port of Caesarea. He was greeted by no one and went to Jerusalem. *{\*Josephus, Jewish War, l. 1. c. 31. s. 3,4. (608-616) 2:289-293} {\*Josephus, Antiq., l. 17. c. 5. s. 1. (83-88) 8:411,413}*

*6070.* It happened that Quintilius Varus, who had been sent as the successor to Saturninus in Syria and had been summoned by Herod, was at Jerusalem at the same time. Herod wanted Varus to help him with his council in his weighty affairs. As they were both sitting together,

Antipater came in, not suspecting anything. He entered the palace in his purple robe, which he usually wore. When he entered, the guards at the gates allowed none of his followers to come in with him. As he approached them, his father pushed him away from him and accused him of the murder of Pheroras, Herod's brother, and of intending to poison his father (Herod). He told him that on the following day Varus would both hear and decide on all matters between them. {*Josephus, Antiq., l. 17. c. 5. s. 2. (89-92) 8:413}

6071. The next day, Varus and the king sat in judgment. His father Herod first began the accusation. He left the prosecution and confirmation of it to Nicolaus Damascene, his dear and close friend, and one who knew the whole business. When Antipater could not clear himself of the crimes alleged against him, Varus ordered that the poison be brought out, which he had prepared for his father. It was given to another condemned man, who died immediately. After this, Varus arose from the council and went to Antioch on the following day, because this was the main palace of the Syrians. Herod soon put his son into prison and sent letters to Caesar indicating what he had done. He also sent messengers who might verify the cursed treason of Antipater to Caesar by word of mouth. {*Josephus, Antiq., l. 17. c. 5. s. 3-7. (93-133) 8:415-433}

6072. At the same time, letters were intercepted from Antiphilus in Egypt to Antipater, along with others from Rome which were sent to Antipater and Herod, the king, and written by Acme. She was a Jew and a chambermaid to Livia, Caesar's wife. She had been well-bribed by Antipater and sent a forged letter to Herod, as if it had been written from Salome to Livia against him, in which she expressed the desire to be given permission to marry Syllaeus. (This was the Nabatean who was Herod's sworn enemy. A little after this, Syllaeus was beheaded at Rome for having betrayed Aelius Gallus on the Arabian expedition and for other crimes. {*Strabo, l. 16. c. 4. s. 25. 7:363}) Herod sent his envoys to Caesar with a copy of these letters, together with letters of his own against his son. {*Josephus, Antiq., l. 17. c. 5. s. 7. (134-145) 8:433-439}

6073. While the envoys hurried to Rome, Herod fell sick and made his will. He left his kingdom to his youngest son, Herod Antipas, since he was now estranged from Archelaus and Philip because of the false accusations of Antipater. {*Josephus, Antiq., l. 17. c. 6. s. 1. (146-148) 8:439}

6074. Judas, the son of Sariphaeus, and Matthias, the son of Margalothus, were two of the most learned of the Jews and the best interpreters of the law. When they realised that the king's sickness was incurable, they persuaded some young men, who were their scholars, to pull down the golden eagle that Herod had erected over the large gate of the temple. They went at noonday and with their axes, pulled and hewed down the eagle, while a large number in the temple witnessed their actions. As soon as the captain was told about this, he came with a strong band of soldiers and seized about forty of the young men, together with their teachers, and brought them to Herod. [E794] [K534] These continually defended their actions and Herod ordered them to be bound and sent to Jericho. He convened the rulers of the Jews and was brought into the assembly in a litter, because he was so weak. He did not so much complain of the wrong done to himself, as that done to God. They denied that they had initiated it and Herod dealt more mildly with them. He took away the high priesthood from Matthias, since he had known of this affair, and replaced him with Joazar, the brother of his wife Mariamme, the daughter of Simon the high priest. He burned alive the other Matthias, who was a partner in this sedition, along with his companions. That night the moon was eclipsed on March 13, three hours after midnight, according to the astronomical tables. This was the only eclipse mentioned by Josephus in all his writings. {*Josephus, Antiq., l. 17. c. 6. s. 2-4. (149-167) 8:439-449}

6075. Herod's disease grew worse, for he was inflamed with a slow fire which could not be felt, but it burned up his very bowels. He also had the disease called bulimia, which was a continual desire for food. To satisfy this, he was always eating. He was also continually tortured with ulcers in his bowels and colic pains. His feet swelled with a moist liquid, while his thighs and his limbs rotted and were full of worms. He also had a filthy and no less troublesome priapism and a most terrible stench. In addition, he was troubled with convulsions and had difficulty in breathing. {*Josephus, Antiq., l. 17. c. 6. s. 5. (168-170) 8:449}

6076. Although he was so grievously tormented that everyone thought he would die from this, he himself still hoped he would get well. He very carefully sent for physicians and sought medicines from every place. He also went beyond the Jordan River into the hot baths at Callirrhoe, which drained into the Dead Sea. Besides their medicinal value, the water is pleasant to drink. On the advice of his physicians, he was placed in a bathing tub filled with oil. When he seemed to have died, his friends suddenly cried out and bewailed him. He came to himself and now realised there was no more hope for recovery. He ordered fifty drachmas to be given to every soldier and was generous to his captains and friends. Then he returned to Jericho. {*Josephus, Antiq., l. 17. c. 6. s. 5. (171,172) 8:451}

6077. Augustus heard of the edict of Herod, by which all the children who were two years old or under were ordered to be killed. When he heard that one of Herod's own sons was also killed because of this same edict, he said that: {*Macrobius, Saturnalia, l. 2. c. 4.*}

"It was better to be Herod's sow, than his son."

## 4001a AM, 4710 JP, 4 BC

*6078.* By an edict, Herod convened to Jericho the most noble of the Jews from every place and locked them up in a place called the hippodrome. He told his sister Salome and her husband Alexas that, as soon as he was dead, they were to order the soldiers to kill all those who were confined in the hippodrome, so that the people would have cause for sorrow. Otherwise, they would rejoice at the death of their king, whom they hated so much. {*Josephus, Antiq., l. 17. c. 6. s. 5. (173,174) 8:451,453*}

*6079.* Letters came from Rome from the envoys who had been sent to Caesar. They stated that Acme had been put to death by Caesar, who was angry over her involvement in Antipater's conspiracy, and that Antipater had been left to his father's pleasure, either to be banished or be put to death. When Herod heard these things, he was cheered a little, but presently he was in pain again. He was hungry and called for an apple and a knife to peel it. *[K535]* When he tried to stab himself, his nephew Achiabus prevented him and called for help as he held out Herod's right hand. A great sorrow, with fear and tumult, struck the whole palace, as if Herod had been dead. {*Josephus, Antiq., l. 17. c. 7. s. 1. (182,-184) 8:455,457*}

*6080.* When Antipater heard the noise, he thought for certain that his father was dead. He began to bargain with his keeper about letting him out, promising him many things, now and in the future, when it was within his power. The keeper told the king, who cried out in sheer anger. Although he was so near death, he still raised himself up in his bed and ordered one of his guard to go at once and execute Antipater. He was to be buried in the citadel of Hyrcania without any honour. {*Josephus, Antiq., l. 17. c. 7. s. 1. (185-187) 8:457,459*}

*6081.* Then Herod changed his mind and made a new will. He made Antipas, whom he had made his successor in the kingdom, tetrarch of Galilee and Peraea instead. He gave the kingdom to Archelaus and assigned the regions of Gaulanitis, Trachonitis, Batanea and Paneas to his son Philip in the name of a tetrarchy. To his sister Salome he gave Jamnia, Azotus and Phasaelis, with five hundred thousand drachmas. To the rest of his family he gave money and yearly pensions. To Caesar he gave ten million drachmas of silver and all his vessels, as well as gold, silver and a large quantity of precious clothes. To Livia, Caesar's wife, and to some certain friends, he gave five million drachmas. {*Josephus, Antiq., l. 17. c. 8. s. 1. (188-190) 8:459*}

*6082.* After Herod had ordered these things, he died on the fifth day after he had executed Antipater. *[E795]* He had held the kingdom for thirty-four years after having killed Antigonus, but thirty-seven years from the time that he was declared king by the Romans. {*Josephus, Antiq., l. 17. c. 8. s. 1. (191) 8:459*} He started to reign after the death of Antigonus in 37 BC because 31 BC was the seventh year of his reign in which the battle of Actium was fought. {*Josephus, Jewish War, l. 1. c. 19. s. 2. (370) 2:173,175*} Hence 4 BC would be the last year of his thirty-four year reign. He died about the 25th of November, that is, the 7th of the month of Chisleu, which was therefore accounted a joyful and a festival day, because on that day:

"Herod died, who hated all wise men."

*6083.* This was according to Edward Liveley, a most learned man, as noted in his chronology, in the תענית מגילת, or the Volume of the Fejunii.

*6084.* Before the king's death became known, Salome and Alexas sent home all those who had been locked up in the hippodrome. They said that Herod had so ordered, that they should leave for their homes and go about their own business. {*Josephus, Antiq., l. 17. c. 8. s. 2. (193,194) 8:461*}

*6085.* When the king's death was declared, all the soldiers were called into the amphitheatre of Jericho. They first read the king's letter to the soldiers, in which Herod thanked them for their fidelity and love to him. Herod asked that they would be faithful to his son Archelaus, whom he had appointed to be his successor in the kingdom. Then Ptolemy, the keeper of the king's seal, read his will, which he could not ratify without Caesar's consent. Then there was a shout for joy that Archelaus was king and the soldiers came flocking in with their captains around him. They promised that they would be just as faithful to him as they had been to his father and they prayed to God to prosper him in his reign. Archelaus prepared most royally for the king's funeral. {*Josephus, Antiq., l. 17. c. 8. s. 2. (194,195) 8:461*}

## 4001b AM, 4711 JP, 3 BC

*6086.* After Herod, who sought the life of the young child Jesus, had died, the angel of the Lord appeared to Joseph in Egypt in a dream and ordered that he should return with the young child and his mother to the land of Israel. *[K536]* When he awoke, he did what he had been commanded to do. {*Mt 2:19-21*}

*6087.* When Joseph came into the land of Israel, he heard that Archelaus reigned in Judea in the place of his father Herod and so he was afraid to go there. God warned him in a dream and he departed into the region of Galilee (the tetrarchy which Archelaus' father, Herod, had given to Antipas in his will). He settled in the city of

Nazareth from whence Jesus acquired the name of *Nazarene* and the Christians the name of *Nazarenes*. {*Mt 2:22,23 Ac 24:5*}

6088. Herod's body was carried twenty-five miles in a funeral procession, from Jericho to the citadel of Herodion, where he had arranged to be buried. {*Josephus, Jewish War, l. 1. c. 33. s. 9. (673) 2:319,321*} Each day they only travelled one mile. He was carried on a golden bier embroidered with precious jewels and covered with a purple cloth. His body was also dressed in purple. A diadem was put on his head, as well as a crown of gold above him and a sceptre in his right hand. His son and his relatives walked beside the bier and were followed by the soldiers, marshalled according to their countries. Then came five hundred servants who carried perfumes. {*Josephus, Jewish War, l. 1. c. 33. s. 9. (671-673) 2:319,321*} {*Josephus, Antiq., l. 1. c. 8. s. 3. (196-199) 8:463*}

6089. After the funeral ceremony was over, Archelaus came to Jerusalem and solemnised the mourning for his father for seven days, according to the traditions of the Jews. At the end of the mourning, he provided a funeral banquet for the people. He went up into the temple and was congratulated wherever he went. He went up to a higher place and sat on a golden throne. He spoke graciously and honestly to the people but he said that he would not take the name of king until Caesar had confirmed his father's will. After the sacrifices were over, he banqueted with his friends. {*Josephus, Antiq., l. 17. c. 8. s. 4. (200-202) 8:463,465*} {*Josephus, Jewish War, l. 2. c. 1. s. 1. (1-3) 2:323-325*}

6090. The friends of those whom Herod had put to death for tearing down the golden eagle, instigated a sedition. They reproached the dead king and also demanded that some of his friends be punished. Moreover, they wanted the high priest Joazar removed from the priesthood. Archelaus tried to appease them, but in vain. It so happened that, about the feast of the passover, Archelaus sent the whole army against them and three thousand men were killed by the cavalry around the temple. The rest fled to the adjoining mountains. {*Josephus, Antiq., l. 17. c. 9. s. 1-3. (206-218) 8:467-473*} {*Josephus, Jewish War, l. 2. c. 1. s. 2,3. (4-13) 2:325-329*}

6091. Archelaus went down to the sea with his mother Malthace, a Samaritan, to sail to Caesar. He took along Nicolaus Damascene, Ptolemy (Herod's agent) and his many other friends. He committed his family and kingdom to the trust of his brother Philip. Salome, the sister of Herod, also went with him and took all her children with her. Others of his relatives also went, on the pretext of helping him to get the kingdom, when in fact they planned to oppose him and accuse him of the deed which had been committed in the temple.

{*Josephus, Antiq., l. 17. c. 9. s. 3. (219,220) 8:473,475*} {*Josephus, Jewish War, l. 2. c. 2. s. 1. (14,15) 2:329*}

6092. As Archelaus was travelling with this group, Sabinus, Caesar's agent in Syria, met him and said he had been sent to Judea to take charge of Herod's property. [K537] Fortunately Varus, the governor of Syria, met him and restrained him, for Archelaus had sent Ptolemy to bring Varus. Sabinus yielded to the governor and did not seize the citadels of Judea nor seal up the king's treasures. [E796] He left all things in Archelaus' control until such time as Caesar determined something concerning them. After he had promised this, Sabinus stayed on at Caesarea, but after Archelaus had set sail for Rome and Varus had returned to Antioch, Sabinus went to Jerusalem and seized the palace. He convened the captains of the citadels and the king's agents, and then demanded the accounts from them and ordered that the citadels be handed over to him. The captains obeyed Archelaus and kept all things as they were until the king's return, but pretended that they were keeping them for Caesar. {*Josephus, Antiq., l. 17. c. 9. s. 3. (221-223) 8:475*} {*Josephus, Jewish War, l. 2. c. 2. s. 2. (16-19) 2:329,331*}

6093. At the same time, Antipas, the son of Herod, sailed to Rome with hopes of getting the kingdom for himself. Salome had instigated him to do this, since he was preferred over Archelaus, because he had been appointed the successor to the kingdom in Herod's first will, which should have had more validity than the second. He took his mother Cleopatra, who was born at Jerusalem, with him, and Ptolemy, the brother of Nicolaus Damascene. Ptolemy had been one of Herod's best friends and favoured Antipas being king. Antipas purposely included the orator Irenaeus, who was an eloquent man knowledgeable in the king's business, to help him secure the kingdom. After Antipas came to Rome, all the relatives sided with him, because they hated Archelaus. Sabinus, too, wrote letters to Caesar to accuse Archelaus. {*Josephus, Antiq., l. 17. c. 9. s. 4. (224-227) 8:475,477*} {*Josephus, Jewish War, l. 2. c. 2. s. 3,4. (20-24) 2:331*}

6094. Archelaus, through Ptolemy, showed a petition to Caesar containing his own right to the throne and the accounts of Herod's money, which was sealed up. When Caesar had read the petition, as well as Varus' and Sabinus' letters, he convened his friends. He gave the first place in the council to Gaius, the son of Agrippa and his daughter Julia, whom he had now adopted. Antipater, the son of Salome, who was a very eloquent man, spoke against Archelaus, who was being defended by Nicolaus Damascene. When he had finished his discourse, Archelaus fell down at the feet of Caesar, who courteously raised him up and pronounced that he was worthy of the kingdom. Caesar feigned that he would do nothing unless it was prescribed in his father's will, or would be profitable for Archelaus. When Caesar saw that the young man was made hopeful and encouraged by his promise, he decided nothing more at that time. {*Josephus, Antiq., l. 17. c. 9. s. 5-7. (228-249) 8:475-487} {*Josephus, Jewish War, l. 2. c. 2. s. 4-6. (24-38) 2:331-337}

6095. Varus came from Antioch to repress the seditions that had arisen in Judea after Archelaus' departure. He punished the instigators of the sedition and when it was mostly settled, he returned to Antioch and left one legion in Jerusalem to prevent any further seditions. As soon as he was gone, Sabinus, Caesar's agent, arrived there and took control of these troops. Believing he was more than a match for the people, he tried to seize the citadels and forcibly searched for the king's money, for his own private wealth and covetousness. {*Josephus, l. 17. c. 10. s. 1. (250-253) 8:489} {*Josephus, Jewish War, l. 2. c. 3. s. 1. (39-41) 2:337-339}

6096. Many tens of thousands came to the feast of Pentecost, not so much for religion's sake, but to revenge themselves upon Sabinus. They not only came from Judea, which had been more grievously afflicted, but from Galilee, Idumea, Jericho and the towns that were beyond the Jordan River. They attacked Sabinus fiercely, dividing their troops into three brigades. The Roman soldiers valiantly opposed them and killed many of them. [K538] The soldiers entered the treasure house containing the holy treasure and stole most of it. Four hundred talents of that money was publicly brought to Sabinus. A company of the most warlike Jews besieged the palace, but Rufus and Gratus, who had three thousand men of the best and most warlike of Herod's soldiers under their command, allied themselves with the Romans. In spite of this, the Jews zealously continued the assault and undermined the walls. They exhorted their adversaries to depart and promised them safe conduct but Sabinus did not trust them and would not withdraw his soldiers, since he was expecting help from Varus. {*Josephus, Antiq., l. 17. c. 10. s. 2,3. (254-268) 8:491-497} {*Josephus, Jewish War, l. 2. c. 3. s. 2-4. (45-54) 2:339-343}

6097. In this state of things, various other seditions were raised in Judea and in other places, because the country did not have a king of its own to restrain the multitude and compel obedience to the law. Two thousand men who had served under Herod were disbanded to live at home. They got together and attacked the king's faction, led by Archiab, Herod's cousin and general for the king. He dared not attack the old soldiers and so he defended himself and his side as well as he could, by retreating to the inaccessible mountainous regions. {*Josephus, Antiq., l. 17. c. 10. s. 4. (269,270) 8:497} {*Josephus, Jewish War, l. 2. c. 4. s. 1. (55) 2:343,345}

6098. Judas (the son of Ezekias, who headed a band of robbers and had, in previous times, tried to overthrow Herod) gathered a band of desperate men at Sepphoris, a city of Galilee, and made incursions into the king's dominion. He captured the king's armoury and armed all his soldiers, then seized the king's treasure in those places. After that, he began to terrorise the inhabitants and plundered all that fell into his hands. He also aspired to the kingdom, not by lawful means, of which he was wholly ignorant, but by force. {*Josephus, Antiq., l. 17. c. 10. s. 5. (271,272) 8:499} {*Josephus, Jewish War, l. 2. c. 4. s. 1. (56) 2:345} [E797] The Hebrew word יהודה is the same as the Syrian word תודה from which the names Judas and Thaddaeus are derived. {Lu 6:16 Mr 3:18} The correct name is Theudas, since this Judas seems to be none other than the Theudas of whom Gamaliel spoke: {Ac 5:36}

> "For before these days rose up Theudas, boasting himself to be somebody, to whom a number of men, about four hundred, joined themselves, who were killed; and all, as many as obeyed him, were scattered and brought to nought."

6099. In addition to these seditions, Simon, a servant of King Herod, and a wise man esteemed among all men for his handsomeness, height and strength, dared to assume the kingdom. He was attended by a large company, who proclaimed him king. These were an unbridled multitude that persuaded him that he was more fit to be the king than anyone else. He began his kingdom by plundering and burning the king's palace at Jericho. Then he burned other palaces and gave their plunder to his followers. He would also have done more licentious deeds, had he not been quickly stopped. Gratus, the captain of the king's soldiers, joined with the Roman forces and marched against Simon. There was a fierce conflict on the other side of the Jordan. Simon's men fought in disarray and more from courage than skill, and so were defeated. Gratus captured Simon as he was fleeing through a narrow valley, and cut off his head. {*Josephus, Antiq., l. 17. c. 10. s. 6. (273-276) 8:499,501} {*Josephus, Jewish War, l. 2. c. 4. s. 2. (57-59) 2:345,347} Tacitus attributed this to Quintilius Varus and wrote the following about Simon: {*Tacitus, Histories, l. 5. c. 9. 3:191} [K539]

> "After the death of Herod, Simon made himself king, without so much as looking for Caesar's consent, but he was punished by Varus, the governor of Syria."

6100. At Ammatha, also by the Jordan River, a royal palace of the king was burned by Simon's rabble of men. Athronges, who was an obscure shepherd and only famous for his great height and strength, made himself king. He had four brothers who were just as tall and strong, whom he made his captains over the multitude that came flocking to him in this time of unrest. He wore a crown and although he consulted others, he kept the sole command in his own hands. The power of this man lasted a long time, for he was not a king for nothing, until he was brought under the power of Archelaus when he returned from Rome. {*Josephus, Antiq., l. 17. c. 10. s. 6,7. (277-280) 8:501,503} {*Josephus, Jewish War, l. 2. c. 4. s. 3. (60-62) 2:347}

6101. Athronges' cruelty was directed especially at the Romans and the king's side, for he hated them both equally. His forces surprised a cohort near Emmaus, as it was carrying food and weapons to the army. Athronges and his men used their arrows against them and killed Arius, a centurion, along with forty of his best foot soldiers. The rest would also have been killed, had not Gratus arrived with the king's soldiers and rescued them but he left the dead bodies. {*Josephus, Antiq., l. 17. c. 10. s. 6,7. (281-283) 8:503,505} {*Josephus, Jewish War, l. 2. c. 4. s. 3. (63) 2:347}

6102. From his letters, Quintilius Varus knew the danger that Sabinus was in and feared the utter destruction of the third legion. He left with two other legions (for there were only three legions at the most in all Syria), four troops of cavalry and the auxiliaries of the king and the tetrarchs. He hurried into Judea to help the besieged, ordering those who were sent ahead to meet him at Ptolemais. On his way past the city of Berytus, he received fifteen hundred auxiliaries from them. Aretas of Petra, a friend to the Romans and an enemy of Herod, sent him a good number of cavalry and foot soldiers. {*Josephus, Antiq., l. 17. c. 10. s. 9. (286,287) 8:505,507} {*Josephus, Jewish War, l. 2. c. 5. s. 1. (66-68) 2:349}

6103. After all the army had come to Ptolemais, Varus turned part of it over to his son and one of his friends. They were to march against the Galileans who bordered on Ptolemais. When they entered the country, they put to flight all who dared oppose them. They took the city of Sepphoris and sold all the inhabitants and burned the city. {*Josephus, Antiq., l. 17. c. 10. s. 9. (288,289) 8:507} {*Josephus, Jewish War, l. 2. c. 5. s. 1. (68,69) 2:349}

6104. Varus went toward Samaria with the army, but did not harm the city because he knew it had not been involved in the sedition. He pitched his camp in a certain village called Arous, which was in the possession of Ptolemy. The Arabians had burned it, because they hated Herod, as well as anyone who was Herod's friend. He marched on and came to Sampho, which the Arabians first plundered and then burned, even though it was well fortified. On all that march, they burned everything and killed anyone they encountered. Emmaus was burned on the order of Varus, to avenge his soldiers who were killed there but the inhabitants had previously abandoned it.

{*Josephus, Antiq., l. 17. c. 10. s. 9. (289-291) 8:507,509} {*Josephus, Jewish War, l. 2. c. 5. s. 1. (69-71) 2:349,351}

6105. When they approached Jerusalem, the Jews who were besieging the Romans on that side were terrified as soon as they saw the army coming and abandoned the attack they had begun. Those in Jerusalem were grievously reproved by Varus. They excused themselves by saying that the people were in fact gathered together for the feast, but that the sedition had not been started with their consent. It had been caused by the boldness of the strangers who had come there. [E798] [K540] Varus was met by Joseph, a nephew of King Herod's, by Gratus and Rufus with their soldiers and by the Romans that had endured the siege. Sabinus would not come, but stole away secretly and hurried to the coast. {*Josephus, Antiq., l. 17. c. 10. s. 9. (292-294) 8:509} {*Josephus, Jewish War, l. 2. c. 5. s. 2. (72-74) 2:351}

6106. Then Varus sent part of his army throughout all the country to capture the instigators of this sedition. When he found them, he punished the most guilty, while some were allowed to go free. About two thousand were crucified for this sedition. After this, he dismissed his army, who were disorderly and disobedient, and committed many outrages simply for money's sake. When he heard that ten thousand Jews were gathered together, he hurried to apprehend them. They dared not withstand him and surrendered on the advice of Achiabus. Varus pardoned the common people for their sedition, but sent the ringleaders to Caesar. So everything was made peaceful again and he left the same legion in the garrison in Jerusalem, while he returned to Antioch. {*Josephus, Antiq., l. 17. c. 10. s. 10. (295-297) 8:509,511} {*Josephus, Jewish War, l. 2. c. 5. s. 2,3. (75-77) 2:351,353}

6107. Malthace, the mother of Archelaus, died of a sickness at Rome. {*Josephus, Antiq., l. 17. c. 10. s. 1. (250) 8:489}

6108. When Caesar had received Varus' letter about the revolt of the Jews, he pardoned the rest of the captains of the seditions and only punished some of King Herod's relatives, who had fought against their own relatives, with no regard for justice. {*Josephus, Antiq., l. 17. c. 10. s. 10. (298) 8:511} {*Josephus, Jewish War, l. 2. c. 5. s. 2,3. (78,79) 2:353}

6109. At the same time, with the permission of Varus, an embassy of the Jews arrived, who requested that they might live according to their own laws, without a king. There were about fifty envoys, who were joined by about eight thousand Jews who lived at Rome. Caesar had convened a council of his friends and chief citizens in the temple of Apollo, which he had built at great expense. The envoys, and a multitude of the Jews who followed them, also went there. Archelaus, too, came with his company. Philip was also there, who had come from Syria on Varus' advice to be an advocate for his brother, whom Varus wished well. Philip also wanted a share in the division of Herod's kingdom. The envoys were given permission to speak and began with accusations against Herod and Archelaus and then desired that they might have no more kings. They wanted the government to be annexed to Syria and said that they would obey the governors sent to them from Rome. When Nicolaus Damascene had answered the objections for Herod, who was dead, and for Archelaus, who was present, Caesar dismissed the council. {*Josephus, Antiq., l. 17. c. 11. s. 1-4. (299-317) 8:511-519} {*Josephus, Jewish War, l. 2. c. 6. s. 1-3. (80-93) 2:353-357}

6110. A few days later, Caesar declared that Archelaus was not king, but made him ethnarch of half of the dominion that had been left to him by his father Herod. He promised him a kingdom if he behaved himself in such a way as to merit a kingdom. A fourth part of their tribute was remitted, because they had not joined the seditions. These cities were included in his government: Straton's Tower, Sebaste, Joppa and Jerusalem. The cities of Gaza, Gadara and Hippos were cities which followed the laws of Greece and for this reason, Caesar annexed them to Syria. Six hundred talents annually accrued to Archelaus from his own dominion. (Josephus, in the *Jewish War*, stated it was four hundred talents. Editor.) {*Josephus, Antiq., l. 17. c. 11. s. 4. (317-320) 8:519,521} {*Josephus, Jewish War, l. 2. c. 6. s. 3. (94-97) 2:357,359}

6111. Caesar divided the other half of Herod's dominion into two parts, one for each of Herod's sons. Herod Antipas was given Galilee with the little country of Peraea. *[K541]* It was a most fertile country and was beyond Jordan, between the two lakes of Tiberias and the Dead Sea. This generated two hundred talents a year in revenue. Philip received Batanea with Trachonitis, as well as Auranitis, with a certain part of the palace of Zenodorus (as they called it), which paid a hundred talents annually. Salome, in addition to the cities which had been left to her by her brother, received Jamnia, Azotus and Phasaelis, and five hundred thousand drachmas of silver. Caesar gave her a palace in Askelon, and she also received sixty talents from those places which were subject to her. Her residence was within the dominion of Archelaus. The rest of Herod's relatives received what was bequeathed by his will. Also, two of Herod's daughters, who were virgins, in addition to what was bequeathed them, received a quarter million drachmas of silver from the bounty of Caesar and were married to the sons of Pheroras. Caesar gave his own portion of the king's estate, which amounted to the sum of fifteen hundred talents, to his sons. He kept only a few vessels, not so much for their value, but as keepsakes for the memory of his friend Herod. {*Josephus, Antiq., l. 17. c. 11. s. 4,5. (317-323) 8:519-523} {*Josephus, Jewish War, l. 2. c. 6. s. 3. (94-100) 2:357-361}

6112. Thus the children of Herod governed the country and were now restrained by a threefold division. {*Tacitus, Histories, l. 5. c. 9. 3:191} Strabo added this about Herod's children: {*Strabo, l. 16. c. 2. s. 46. 7:299}

> "Some of them Herod put to death himself under the charges of treachery, others he left as his successors at his death and assigned to everyone his portion. Caesar also highly honoured Herod's children and his sister Salome, and Berenice, the daughter of Salome."

6113. A certain young man, a Jew of lowly parentage, was brought up in Sidon with a Roman freedman. In his face he resembled Alexander, the son of Herod, and so, with the help of a certain friend of his guardian he pretended to be Alexander, who had been saved from death with his brother Aristobulus. *[E799]* This man took on an accomplice who was very well acquainted with Herod's palace and had been well instructed through this fellow's cunning and deceits. When he had sailed into Crete, he persuaded all the Jews who came to meet him, that this thing was so. He got money from them and sailed to the island of Melos, where he acquired a large sum of money under the pretence that he was of the king's family. He now hoped to recover his father's kingdom and hurried to Rome with his friends. When he had sailed to Puteoli, he was likewise well received there and deceived the Jews. As he was coming to Rome, all the Jews who lived there came out to meet him. When this news was brought to Caesar, he sent Celadus there, one of his freedmen, who had previously been very well acquainted with the young men. Caesar ordered that if he was Alexander, he should bring him to him. He, too, was deceived and brought him to Caesar. However, he did not deceive Caesar, who sent this false Alexander, when he had confessed his imposture, to the galleys as a rower, because he had a strong body. He executed the one that had put him up to this fraud. {*Josephus, Antiq., l. 17. c. 12. s. 1,2. (324-338) 8:523-529} {*Josephus, Jewish War, l. 2. c. 7. s. 1,2. (101-110) 2:361,363}

## 4002a AM, 4711 JP, 3 BC

6114. When Archelaus returned to his government in Judea, he removed the priesthood from Joazar, the son of Boethus (or Boethus' grandchild by his son Simon), accusing him of having favoured the seditions. He gave that office to Joazar's brother, Eleazar. {*Josephus, Antiq., l. 17. c. 13. s. 1. (339) 8:529}

## 4002b AM, 4712 JP, 2 BC

*6115.* In his thirteenth consulship, Augustus brought his son Lucius into the court. {*Suetonius, Augustus, l. 2. c. 26. s. 2. 1:187}* He conferred the same honours on him which three years earlier he had conferred on his brother Gaius, as shown by the inscriptions on the coins. They show ensigns of Gaius and Lucius with bucklers and spears, with this inscription: *C. L. Caesares, Augusti. F. Cos. Des. Principes. Juvent.* This means: *Gaius and Lucius Caesar, the sons of Augustus, consuls elect, Princes of Youth. [K542]*

*6116.* In the same thirteenth consulship, he wrote on the Ancyran Marble that he: {*Augustus, l. 3. c. 15. 1:369,371}*

"gave sixty denarii to the common people that received public grain. (welfare)"

*6117.* He added:

"there were more than two hundred thousand."

*6118.* This very thing is also found in Xyphiline, in his writings based on Dio, except that for sixty denarii, which the Greeks called drachmas, the Latin author wrote two hundred and forty denarii. We do not know the basis for the change. {*Dio, l. 55. (9,10) 6:405,407}*

*6119.* When Augustus and Gallus Coninius were consuls, they satisfied the desires of the Roman people with gladiatorial shows and a sham naval battle. {*Velleius Paterculus, l. 2. c. 100. s. 2. 1:257}* {*Eusebius, Chronicles, l. 1. 1:250}* For these shows, Augustus brought water into the Circus. Thirty-six crocodiles were killed. {*Dio, l. 55. (10) 6:409}*

*6120.* He also held a naval battle and hollowed out the ground around the Tiber River. That place was later called Caesar's Grove. {*Suetonius, Augustus, l. 2. c. 43. s. 1,2. 1:217}* The hollowed place was eighteen hundred feet long and two hundred feet wide. He had thirty warships and many galleys and smaller boats fight. This is recorded in the breviary of his doings, which was engraved on the Ancyran Marble. {*Augustus, l. 4. c. 23. 1:383}* Augustus wrote that this was a novelty in Rome. Ovid made mention of this: {*Ovid, Art of Love, l. 1. (171-174) 2:25}*

What Caesar, when, like a naval battle by land,
Made the Persian and Cecropian beaks the sand
To ride? He brought both men and maids from the
main,
And made the city all the world retain.

*6121.* When Augustus was preparing his games in Rome, there was trouble in Armenia. Only Pompey had exposed the Armenians to the government of Roman governors. They had expelled Artavasdes (or Artabazes), whom Augustus had set over them as governor, and had substituted Tigranes in his place. To support this revolt, they had called in the Parthians for help. So Armenia yielded to the Parthians and the Parthians broke their alliance with Rome and seized Armenia. {*Florus, l. 2. c. 32. 1:341,343}* {*Velleius Paterculus, l. 2. c. 100. s. 1. 1:257}* {*Tacitus, Annals, l. 2. c. 3. 3:387,389}* {*Dio, l. 55. (10) 6:413}* {*Sextus Rufus, Breviary}*

*6122.* Augustus brought Gaius and Lucius, who were still very young, into the government service. He sent them around the provinces and armies and they had the title of consuls elect. {*Suetonius, Augustus, l. 2. c. 64. s. 1,2. 1:245}* [E800] Hence, we read in Velleius Paterculus that Gaius went about the provinces to settle them. {*Velleius Paterculus, l. 2. c. 101. s. 1. 1:259}* Beatus Rhenanus thought it should read *to quiet them.* Lipsius thought it should read, *to visit them.* (The Loeb edition of Paterculus noted three variant readings for this passage. Editor.) This last is the best reading, as was also recorded by Dio: {*Dio, l. 55. (10) 6:413}*

"Gaius Caesar went about, as they usually do in peacetime, and viewed the legions which were encamped by the Ister River. He never had any command in the wars, even though wars were going on at that time. This was because he had learned the arts in peace and security, while the dangers of the war were committed to others to manage." [K543]

*6123.* At Rome in the very year that Augustus held the shows of the combatants on land and sea, there was a filthy and horrible disaster in his own house. His daughter Julia, who was altogether unmindful of the greatness of either her father or her husband, left no disgraceful deed, which it was possible for a woman to do or have happen to her, untried. She measured the greatness of her position by her liberty in sinning and considered everything lawful if it pleased her. {*Velleius Paterculus, l. 2. c. 100. s. 3. 1:259}* She reached such heights of lasciviousness that she held her excessive feasting and drinking bouts in the very courts of justice. She abused those very courts, in which her father had made the law against adultery, with lascivious acts. In consequence, her father was so enraged, that he could not contain his anger within his own house, but proclaimed these things publicly and notified the senators about them. {*Seneca, On Benefits, l. 6. c. 32. s. 1. 3:431}* {*Dio, l. 55. (10) 6:411}* He was not present, but he had a quaestor read a note to them, declaring everything that had happened. He also kept himself from any gathering of people for a very long time, out of very deep shame. He was also thinking of putting his daughter to death. {*Suetonius, Augustus, l. 2. c. 65. s. 1. 1:245}* At last, she was banished to Pandataria, an island of Campania, and her mother Scibonia voluntarily accompanied her into exile. {*Velleius Paterculus, l. 2. c. 100. s. 5. 1:259}* {*Dio, l. 55. (10) 6:411,413}* Her mother had been divorced from Caesar on the very day Julia had been born. Lucius Martius and Gaius Sabinus were consuls at that time, in 39 BC.

{*Dio, l. 48. (34) 5:291} Hence, Julia was thirty-eight years old at the time. Macrobius confirmed she was at least that old. {Macrobius, Saturnalia, l. 2. c. 5.}

6124. Tiberius was in Rhodes and heard that his wife Julia had been condemned for her lusts and adulteries and that a divorce had been sent to her in his name by the order of Augustus. Although he was glad, he still considered it his duty to write frequently to Augustus. He begged him to forgive his daughter and regardless of what she deserved, allow her to keep any gifts which he himself had made to her at any time. {*Suetonius, Tiberius, l. 3. c. 11. s. 4. 1:329,331}

## 4003a AM, 4712 JP, 2 BC

6125. When Augustus heard that the Armenians had revolted and had been helped by the Parthians, he was grieved and did not know what to do. He could not manage the war himself, because he was too old. Tiberius had withdrawn himself, and he dared not trust any of the more powerful citizens. Gaius and Lucius were too young and unfit for such matters, but of necessity, he sent Gaius and made him a proconsul. To give him more honour, he had him get married, as he would then have more friends to give him wise counsel. {*Dio, l. 55. (10) 6:413,415} He married Lollia Paulina, who was either the daughter or grand-daughter of Marcus Lollius. {*Suetonius, Claudius, l. 5. c. 26. s. 3. 2:53} {*Pliny, l. 9. c. 35. 3:243} {Solinus, c. 53.} Augustus wanted him to be an adviser for his young son. {*Velleius Paterculus, l. 2. c. 102. s. 1. 1:261} {*Suetonius, Tiberius, l. 3. c. 12. s. 2,3. 1:331}

6126. When Gaius was being prepared for this expedition, Ovid mentioned the recent naval battle which had ended. He also said: {*Ovid, Art of Love, l. 1. (177-184) 2:25}

> Caesar prepares with courage to subdue
> Of the whole world the only unconquered crew,
> Now must the Parthian, by him overcome,
> Receive chastisement and observe his doom.
> Rejoice yon buried Crassians, what you lost,
> Revengefully is taken, to their cost, *[K544]*
> By one, though captain young, yet shows the world,
> Such high achievements cannot be controll'd. *[E801]*

6127. He added a little later:

> With father's fate and gravity renowned,
> Thy fighting shalt with victory be crowned:
> Such expectation doth thy name obtain,
> Though now of young, a prince of old thou let reign.

6128. Ovid was a very good prophet in trying to predict the outcome of this expedition. He recorded Gaius' age correctly. His father Augustus was nineteen years old when he gathered his army, as was shown earlier from the Ancyran Marble. Gaius just turned nineteen when he prepared for the Armenian and Parthian war. He was a commander in war at the very same age as his father had been.

6129. Augustus sent Dionysius, who was a most excellent geographer, ahead into the east, to note the geography of the land for his older son, who was to go into Armenia. Pliny recorded information about Parthia and Arabia. {*Pliny, l. 6. c. 27-32. 2:421-459} We do not know whether it was that famous Dionysius whose records of geography are extant in Greek poetry, or Dionysius, the son of Diogenes, of whom Marcianus Heracleota, in his first book of journeys, said that he measured the circumference of the earth.

6130. Gaius Caesar was assigned Armenia for his province. {*Tacitus, Annals, l. 2. c. 3. 3:387,389} {*Tacitus, Annals, l. 3. c. 48. 3:599} He was sent into Syria. {*Velleius Paterculus, l. 2. c. 101. s. 1. 1:259} He was made the governor of the east. {*Suetonius, Tiberius, l. 3. c. 12. s. 2,3. 1:331} He was sent by Augustus to order the provinces of Egypt and Syria. {Orosius, l. 7. c. 3.} Pliny cited the letters of King Juba, written to the same Gaius, concerning the expedition into Arabia. {*Pliny, l. 6. c. 31. 2:445.} Gaius had only seen Arabia, but had never made any expedition there. {*Pliny, l. 6. c. 32. 2:459}

6131. As soon as Phraates, the king of the Parthians, heard of the preparations for war that Gaius was making against the barbarians, he sent an apology for the things that had been done and sought peace. Caesar replied by letters and ordered him to leave Armenia. At that time, Tigranes sent no embassy to him. {*Dio, l. 55. (10a) 6:415-419}

## 4003b AM, 4713 JP, 1 BC

6132. When the time of his tribuneship was over, Tiberius finally confessed that he had gone into his retirement only to avoid all suspicion of envy between himself and Gaius and Lucius. There was now no danger of that, because they were grown men and next in authority to Augustus. Tiberius requested that Augustus give him permission to see his relatives again, since he had a great desire to see them. This was not granted and he was warned that he should forget about those whom he had so willingly left. {*Suetonius, Tiberius, l. 3. c. 11. s. 5. 1:331}

6133. So Tiberius stayed at Rhodes against his will. At his mother's request, he succeeded in being allowed to remain there as an envoy to Augustus, to cover his ignominy. He lived only as a private citizen and was in danger and fear. He hid in the middle of the island, to avoid being seen by those who sailed there. {*Suetonius, Tiberius, l. 3. c. 12. s. 1,2. 1:331}

6134. When Gaius went to the Armenian war, Tiberius crossed over to Chios to offer his service to him. *[K545]*

He removed all suspicions about himself and was very humble to Gaius and to his followers. {*Dio, l. 55. (10a) 6:415} Velleius flattered Tiberius, as he always did, and wrote that Gaius gave all honour to Tiberius as his superior. {*Velleius Paterculus, l. 2. c. 101. s. 1. 1:259,261} Suetonius wrote that Tiberius went, not to Chios, but Samos, to see his son-in-law Gaius. He was not well received, because of the false accusations of Marcus Lollius. {*Suetonius, Tiberius, l. 3. c. 12. s. 2. 1:331}

6135. Tiberius also came under suspicion due to some centurions he had appointed. They went back to the camp again from meeting him and appeared to have given dubious commands to many, which might tempt them to a revolt. When Augustus heard of this suspicion, Tiberius persistently requested that Augustus send him someone, of any rank, to be a witness to his words and deeds. Tiberius stopped his usual riding and his other martial exercises. He went about in his coat and shoes and laid aside his country living. For the next two years, he lived at Rhodes in this fashion, and every day he was more despised and hated. {*Suetonius, Tiberius, l. 3. c. 12,13. 1:331,333} [E802]

6136. Gaius passed through Judea and scorned to worship at Jerusalem. As soon as Augustus learned of this, he highly commended him for it. {*Suetonius, Augustus, l. 2. c. 93. s. 1. 1:285} {Orosius, l. 7. c. 3.} Orosius added that Gaius came from Egypt and passed by the borders of Palestine.

6137. Dio stated that Gaius came from there into Syria and did nothing praiseworthy. {*Dio, l. 55. (10) 6:415} Velleius Paterculus stated that he behaved himself with such versatility, that there was much for which he could be praised, as well as criticised. {*Velleius Paterculus, l. 2. c. 101. s. 1. 1:261} By virtue of the greatness and majesty of the Roman name, he settled all things. {Sextus Rufus, Breviary}

6138. When Quirinius returned to Rome, he married that generous woman, Lepida, who had for some time been intended to be the wife for Lucius Caesar and to be the daughter-in-law to Augustus. After twenty years, when Gaius Marcus Valerius Messala and Marcus Aurelius Cotta were consuls in 20 AD, or 4733 JP, he divorced her and accused her of trying to poison him. {*Suetonius, Tiberius, l. 3. c. 49. 1:377,379} {*Tacitus, Annals, l. 3. c. 22,23. 3:557,559}

6139. When Augustus wrote the letters to Phraates, he did not call him king. Phraates was not intimidated, but proudly wrote back again, calling himself *king*, and calling Augustus nothing but *Caesar*. {*Dio, l. 55. (10) 6:415,417} When Phraates knew that Gaius had come into Syria, he suspected that his subjects would not be peaceful because they hated him. Hence, he made a peace with Gaius on the condition that he (Phraates) would lay aside all claims to Armenia. {*Dio, l. 55. (10a) 6:419} From this we read: {Eutropius, l. 7.}

"Augustus received Armenia from the Parthians."

6140. We read, also, that Gaius Caesar made peace with the Parthians. {*Eusebius, Chronicles, l. 1. 1:251}

6141. When Artabazes or Artavasdes had died of a disease, Tigranes sent presents to Augustus for joy that his enemy was gone. He did not address himself as king and begged Augustus for the kingdom. Augustus was troubled by these things and feared a Parthian war. He accepted his presents and offered him some hope if he went to Syria. {*Dio, l. 55. (10a) 6:415,417} Sextus Rufus said that: {Sextus Rufus, Brevariy} [K546]

"The Armenians, who were then stronger than the Parthians, have been subdued by Gaius. The Armenians allied themselves with the Parthians and were easily overcome by Gaius Augustus. The Armenians thought it better to be reconciled to the friendship of the Romans and to live in their own country than to join with the Parthians and lose their country and have the hostility of the Romans."

## 4004 AM, 4714 JP, 1 AD

6142. This was the first year of the common Christian era, of which we now calculate there to have been 1663 years (when Ussher wrote this paragraph). Gaius Caesar was now twenty years old, and this was five years after he had been brought into the forum. He was consul in the east, as Pighius showed from a marble table of Naples and Anagnia. {Pighius, Annals of Rome}

6143. Also this year, when Tiberius lived at Rhodes in ostensible retirement and actual exile, he studied nothing except anger, hypocrisy and secret lasciviousness. {*Tacitus, Annals, l. 1. c. 4. 3:249} Daily he became the object of contempt and aversion. For that reason, when his name was mentioned in a banquet, a man promised Gaius that he would sail at once to Rhodes if he would allow him, and bring him the head of that banished man. Tiberius was compelled, more from danger than fear, to seek his return through his own mother's most earnest requests. However, Augustus was determined to do nothing about this matter except what pleased Gaius. {*Suetonius, Tiberius, l. 3. c. 13. s. 1,2. 1:333}

6144. After his climactic year was past, Augustus celebrated his sixty-fourth birthday. On the 9th of the Calends of October (September 23), he wrote this letter to Gaius.

"All hail my Gaius, my best delight, whom I always sincerely long for when you are from me, but especially on such days as this is. My eyes always long for Gaius and wherever you are, I hope that you are merry and in health and celebrated my sixty-fourth birthday. For you have seen that I have passed the sixty-third, the common climactic year of all old men. I pray the gods that for the rest of my life that remains, I may lead it in happy circumstances for the government and that you are healthy and behaving yourself like a man and will succeed in my place."

*6145.* This was taken from a book of the letters of Augustus to Gaius, which Aulus Gellius had preserved. {*Aulus Gellius, Attic Nights, l. 15. c. 7. s. 3. 3:79}

### 4005a AM, 4714 JP, 1 AD

*6146.* Gaius went to a conference with the king of the Parthians on an island in the Euphrates River. Each side had a retinue of equal size. The Roman and the Parthian army faced each other on either side of the river. First, the Parthians were feasted by Gaius on the Roman side, and then Gaius by the Parthians, on the Parthian side. Velleius Paterculus witnessed this event. He was the paymaster for the troops, since he was a tribune for the soldiers. {*Velleius Paterculus, l. 2. c. 101. s. 1-3. 1:261}

*6147.* On that occasion, the Parthians told Gaius Caesar of the perfidious, subtle and cunning councils of Marcus Lollius. {*Velleius Paterculus, l. 2. c. 102. s. 1. 1:261} [E803] He was notorious for taking bribes from the kings and for robbing all the countries of the east. Gaius excluded him from his circle of friends, although his own wife, the daughter or grand-daughter of this Lollius, was said to have been given a gown by Lollius that was covered with pearls and valued at forty million sesterces. (Some say this was a third of a million pounds of gold!) {*Pliny, l. 9. c. 38. 3:243} {Solinus, c. 55.} The more Gaius was offended with Lollius, the more he showed himself gentle and kind to his father-in-law Tiberius. {*Suetonius, Tiberius, l. 3. c. 13. s. 2. 1:333}

*6148.* Velleius did not know if the death of Lollius, which happened a few days later, was accidental or a suicide. [K547] Pliny and Solinus stated that he died by taking poison. Velleius stated that everyone rejoiced as heartily over this man's death, as the city mourned the death of Censorinus, who died a little later in that province and was very well-liked by everyone. {*Pliny, l. 9. c. 38. 3:243} {Solinus, c. 55.} {*Velleius Paterculus, l. 2. c. 102. s. 1. 1:261,263} It seems that this Censorinus was Gaius Marcius, who represented the Jews of Cyrene and of Asia to Augustus. {*Josephus, Antiq., l. 16. c. 6. s. 2. (165) 8:273}

### 4005 AM, 4715 JP, 2 AD

*6149.* Quirinius was made adviser to Gaius Caesar, to replace Lollius. After his service to Gaius in Armenia, Quirinius was no less attentive to Tiberius, who was then staying at Rhodes. Tiberius acknowledged this in the Senate after the death of Quirinius, accusing Lollius of having been the author of the ill-will and differences between himself and Gaius Caesar. {*Tacitus, Annals, l. 3. c. 48. 3:599}

*6150.* With Gaius' consent, Tiberius was recalled, but on the condition that he would hold no office in the government. {*Suetonius, Tiberius, l. 3. c. 13. s. 2. 1:333}

*6151.* Tiberius was very skilful in astrology. He had Thrasyllus, an astrologer, with him, when the latter saw a ship sailing toward them in the distance, which he said was bringing the good news from Livia and Augustus of his permission to return from exile. Tiberius did not believe him and intended, at that very time as they walked together, to throw him headlong into the sea, since he believed he was a false prophet and that he had too hastily been made the confidant of Tiberius' secrets. Dio's account was different. He stated that at one time, as they walked by the walls, Tiberius intended to throw him into the sea, because he knew so many of Tiberius' thoughts. He did not carry out his intention, when he saw that Thrasyllus was gloomy. Tiberius asked him why and Thrasyllus said he had a premonition that some peril was in store for him. Tiberius was amazed that Thrasyllus could foresee the mere intent of the plot and so kept him on. {*Suetonius, Tiberius, l. 3. c. 14. s. 4. 1:335} {*Dio, l. 55. (11) 6:421,423}

*6152.* Tiberius had stayed at Rhodes for seven years. He returned home in the eighth year after his departure from his country, when Publius Vinicius was consul and Lucius and Gaius were still alive. {*Suetonius, Tiberius, l. 3. c. 14. s. 1. 1:333} {*Velleius Paterculus, l. 2. c. 99. s. 4. 1:257} {*Velleius Paterculus, l. 2. c. 103. s. 1-3. 1:263} When he returned to Rome, he introduced his son Drusus to public life. Tiberius soon moved from the Carinae and Pompey's house to the gardens of Maecenas on the Esquiline. He led a very retired life, merely attending to his personal affairs and performing no public functions. {*Suetonius, Tiberius, l. 3. c. 15. s. 1. 1:335,337}

*6153.* As Lucius was about to join the armies in Spain, he died suddenly of a disease at Massilia (which was Marseilles), before he could do anything of note. This was twenty-two months before his brother Gaius' death. {*Florus, l. 2. c. 32. 1:343} {*Velleius Paterculus, l. 2. c. 102. s. 4. 1:263} {*Tacitus, Annals, l. 1. c. 3. 3:247} {*Suetonius, Augustus, l. 2. c. 65. s. 2. 1:247} {*Dio, l. 55. (10) 6:421}

*6154.* After Lucius' death, Augustus would have liked to have adopted Tiberius, but he resolutely refused to do so, for he feared the envy of Gaius. {*Velleius Paterculus, l. 2. c. 103. s. 2. 1:263}

## 4006 AM, 4716 JP, 3 AD

*6155.* Gaius entered into Armenia and at first had good success. A little later, Addon, or Adduus (he was also called Ador by Strabo), the governor of Artagera, or Artagira, persuaded the citadel to revolt. He enticed Gaius to the wall, as though he wanted to tell him some secret business, and wounded him. Caesar's captains took the citadel by continual assault and destroyed it. {*Velleius Paterculus, l. 2. c. 103. 1:263} {*Strabo, l. 11. c. 14. s. 6. 5:327} {*Dio, l. 55. (10a) 6:419}

*6156.* Florus related this story in detail. Dones, or Domitus, whom the king had made governor of Artaxatis, or Artagera, pretended to betray the king. He wounded Gaius, as he was looking over a scroll he had given him, containing a record of the treasures. Gaius was indeed wounded, but in a short time recovered from his wound. *[K548]* The barbarians were attacked on every side by the army with their swords. Domitus was wounded and hurled himself upon a burning pyre. Thus he made atonement with his life to Caesar, who outlived him. {*Florus, l. 2. c. 32. 1:343} Sextus Rufus, in his breviary, also followed the account given by Florus. {Sextus Rufus, Breviary} However, he recounted this as if it related to the Parthians, and not to the Armenians. Without any reason, Rufus added:

> "The Parthians, to give satisfaction for such a bold attempt, first gave hostages to Octavius Caesar and restored the ensigns that were taken away under Crassus."

*6157.* The following is the account of all those things attributed to this history of Gaius (incorrectly called Claudius, both here and by Jornandes, and in that writing of the Latins which Georgius Syncellus transferred into his Greek Chronicle) which Suetonius had in fact written about the Parthians. {*Suetonius, Augustus, l. 2. c. 21. s. 3. 1:179,181} He confused the two accounts and combined them into one:

> "The Parthians easily yielded up Armenia to (Octavius) who claimed it. They restored the military ensigns to him that he demanded, which were taken from Marcus Crassus and Mark Antony. Moreover, they offered hostages."

*6158.* At their request, Gaius made Ariobarzanes the governor over the Armenians; he was a Mede and was very handsome and intelligent. {*Tacitus, Annals, l. 2. c. 4. 3:389} [E804]

*6159.* Gaius was less useful because of his wound and less energetic, and his mind was less profitable to the state. He never lacked the companionship of men who, by their flattery, encouraged his vices. In this way, it came about that he preferred to spend all his time in any corner of the world, rather than return to Rome. {*Velleius Paterculus, l. 2. c. 102. s. 2,3. 1:263} He became less astute through sickness and more retiring, and he desired to be allowed to live a private life. Augustus was grieved by this and advised him that he should return to Italy. He sailed to Lycia and died of a sickness in the city of Limyra. {*Velleius Paterculus, l. 2. c. 102. s. 3. 1:263} Tacitus noted that he died on his return from Armenia, while he was ill from his wound. {*Tacitus, Annals, l. 1. c. 3. 3:247} Sextus Rufus affirmed that he died from his wound after he returned to Syria. {Sextus Rufus, Breviary} Suetonius confirmed that he died in Lycia, as did Dio also, and Velleius (who was a tribune of soldiers and then served under Gaius). {*Suetonius, Augustus, l. 2. c. 65. s. 1. 1:245} {*Dio, l. 55. (10a) 6:419,421}

*6160.* Augustus was deeply grieved by the death of Gaius. In a letter (using the polite and even familiar tone customary in that most forbearing of men) that despite this great recent bereavement of his one of his dearest friends had had a full-dress supper party. Pollio wrote back:

> "I supped after the same fashion when I lost my son Herius."

*6161.* Who would ask for greater grief from a friend than from a father? So Marcus Seneca related this in the preface to his Controversies. {*Seneca the Elder, Controversiae, l. 4. c. 0. s. 4,5. 1:427}

*6162.* The bodies of Gaius and Lucius were brought to Rome escorted by the captains, armies and commanders of every city. The golden (or silver) shields and spears, which they had received from the equestrians when they had reached manhood, were hung up in the Senate house. {*Dio, l. 55. (12) 6:423} Bellonius related in the second book of his observations that the epitaph of Gaius Caesar may be seen at Hama, or Emesa, in Syria. Despite this claim, however, his bones were buried at Rome, as this epitaph showed, which was seen before the temple of the gods, behind the temple of Minerva: *OSSA C. CAESARIS AUGUSTI F. PRINCIPIS IUVENTUTIS.* This means the bones of Gaius Caesar, the son of Augustus, prince of youth. {Gruter, Inscriptions, p. 235.} [K549] There was a suspicion that both these brothers were taken out of the way by the deceit of their stepmother Livia, to allow her son Tiberius to succeed Augustus in the empire. {*Tacitus, Annals, l. 1. c. 3. 3:247} {*Dio, l. 55. (10a) 6:421}

*6163.* Augustus was made a god by the people. He did not approve and forbade it by an edict. {*Dio, l. 55. (12) 6:423} {*Suetonius, Augustus, l. 2. c. 53. s. 1. 1:231,233}

## 4007a AM, 4716 JP, 3 AD

*6164.* After the third ten-year term of his government had expired, he took the empire upon himself for another ten years. He did this as though it were on compulsion.

He had now become more mild and was reluctant to exasperate the senators and would no longer offend anyone. {*Dio, l. 55. (12) 6:423}

6165. Augustus made Tiberius Nero his partner in the tribuneship. Tiberius vehemently refused, both privately and in the Senate. {*Velleius Paterculus, l. 2. c. 103. s. 3. 1:263,265} Suetonius stated that the tribuneship was given to him for five years. {*Suetonius, Tiberius, l. 3. c. 16. s. 1. 1:337} Dio stated it was for ten years. {*Dio, l. 55. (13) 6:425} (The Loeb edition of Suetonius incorrectly translated Latin as "three," not "five." Editor.)

## 4007b AM, 4717 JP, 4 AD

6166. The Julian calendar was now correct. The third intercalary day, which was superfluous and had been added by the carelessness of the Roman priests, was omitted this year, in the month of February. Later Augustus, who was the high priest, ordered that, at the beginning of every fifth year, one day should be intercalated, according to the edict of Julius Caesar. To ensure the perpetual keeping of this order, he ordered that it should be engraved in a brass table. {Macrobius, Saturnalia, l. 1. c. 14. fin.} From this institution, the records of all subsequent times are calculated. {Solinus, c. 3.} It was no marvel, for it was constantly observed after this, until the change of the calendar made by Pope Gregory XIII in the year 1579 AD. Nevertheless, in case the market, which was held by the Romans at the beginning of every ninth day, should fall on the Calends of January (January 1), one day was often added at the end of the previous year and was removed again in the following year. This would keep the time in agreement with Julius Caesar's edicts. {*Dio, l. 48. (33) 5:289} {*Dio, l. 60. (25) 7:433}

6167. After five years, Augustus brought his daughter Julia from the island to the continent and gave her some milder conditions of exile. However, he could not bring himself to recall her altogether. When the Roman people entreated him for her and were very insistent with him, he used this curse publicly on them: that they should have such daughters and such wives. {*Suetonius, Augustus, l. 2. c. 65. s. 3. 1:247}

6168. When Aelius Catus and Sentius (Saturninus) were consuls, on the 5th of the Calends of July (June 27), Augustus adopted Tiberius Nero. {*Velleius Paterculus, l. 2. c. 103. s. 3. 1:265} He swore before the people that he was adopting him for the sake of the commonwealth. {*Velleius Paterculus, l. 2. c. 104. s. 1,2. 1:265} {*Suetonius, Tiberius, l. 3. c. 21. s. 3. 1:343} [E805] Marcus Agrippa, the brother of Gaius and Lucius, whom Julia bore after the death of Agrippa, was adopted on the same day. {*Velleius Paterculus, l. 2. c. 104. s. 1. 1:265} {*Suetonius, Tiberius, l. 3. c. 15. s. 2. 1:337} Augustus feared that Tiberius could grow proud and incite a rebellion.

Before he adopted him, he made Tiberius adopt Germanicus, the son of his brother Drusus, although Tiberius had a son of his own. {*Dio, l. 55. (13) 6:425} {*Suetonius, Tiberius, l. 3. c. 15. s. 2. 1:337} {*Tacitus, Annals, l. 1. c. 3. 1:247}

6169. Immediately after his adoption, Tiberius was sent into Germany, and Paterculus went with him and served as an officer in the cavalry. He was an eyewitness of all that Tiberius did for nine years. {*Velleius Paterculus, l. 2. c. 104,105. 1:265-269} [K550]

6170. When Tiberius had been sent into Germany, the envoys of the Parthians came to Rome with their embassy. They were also ordered to go into the province to Tiberius. {*Suetonius, Tiberius, l. 3. c. 16. s. 1. 1:337} There were many contending for the Parthian kingdom and the envoys came from the noblemen of Parthia and asked to have a king from one of the three sons of Phraates, who were still in Rome as hostages. Vonones was preferred ahead of his other brothers and was helped by Caesar. He was joyfully accepted by the Parthians for some time. {*Suetonius, Augustus, l. 2. c. 21. s. 3. 1:179,181} {*Josephus, Antiq., l. 18. c. 2. s. 4. (50-52) 9:41} {*Tacitus, Annals, l. 2. c. 2. 3:387,389}

6171. Augustus accepted the proconsular power, so that he could complete a census in Italy. {*Dio, l. 55. (13) 6:427}

## 4008 AM, 4718 JP, 5 AD

6172. The sun was partially eclipsed on March 28 about three o'clock in the afternoon, according to the astronomical tables. {*Dio, l. 55. (22) 6:451}

6173. The *toga virilis*, which was the gown that the Roman men wore at age eighteen, was given to Marcus Agrippa Postumus, who was born after the death of his father and had never had the honours that his brothers Gaius and Lucius had received. {*Dio, l. 55. (22) 6:451}

## 4009 AM, 4719 JP, 6 AD

6174. The rulers of the Jews, as well as those of the Samaritans, could no longer put up with the tyranny of Archelaus and accused him to Caesar. They knew that he had acted contrary to Caesar's command, since he had been commanded by him to govern his subjects with justice and equity. When Caesar heard this, he was very angry and sent for Archelaus' agent, who lived at Rome. He did not write anything to Archelaus, but ordered his agent to go to Judea and bring his master to him at once. {*Josephus, Jewish War, l. 2. c. 7. s. 3. (111) 2:365} {*Josephus, Antiq., l. 17. c. 13. s. 2. (342,343) 8:531}

6175. Archelaus claimed to have had a dream foretelling this misfortune. In it, he saw nine ears of grain which were eaten up by oxen. Simon, an Essene, interpreted these ears to be nine years of his kingdom and said that the end of his government was now at hand. Five days after this, the agent of Archelaus was said to have come to Judea. He found Archelaus banqueting with his friends and told him it was Caesar's pleasure that he must come and answer the accusations. {*Josephus, Jewish War, l. 2. c. 7. s. 3. (112,113) 2:365} {*Josephus, Antiq., l. 17. c. 13. s. 3. (345-348) 8:531,533}

### 4010a AM, 4719 JP, 6 AD

6176. About our November, on the 7th of the Jewish month of Chisleu, the tenth year of Archelaus' reign began. Augustus called it an ethnarchy and the Jews called it a kingdom. Joseph, the priest, had a son named Matthias in the tenth year of the reign of Archelaus, as recorded in the public registers. Flavius Josephus, the historian, was the son of Matthias. {*Josephus, Life, l. 1. c. 1. (5) 1:5} For this very reason, Josephus thought it best to change what he had earlier written in his books of the wars of the Jews, about the nine years of Archelaus. In his books of antiquities he substituted the ten years in his kingdom and ten ears in the dream, but no such amendment was needed. Archelaus only reigned a few days in this tenth year of his ethnarchy, or kingdom. He was sent into banishment at the end of that year, when Marcus Aemilius Lepidus and Lucius Aruntius were consuls. Under their consulship: {*Dio, l. 55. (27) 6:465,467}

> "Herod of Palestine, who was indeed none other than this Archelaus, was accused by his countrymen and was banished beyond the Alps and his government was confiscated."

6177. When Caesar heard the accusations and the defence of Archelaus, he banished him to Vienna in France and confiscated his country and his treasure. {*Josephus, Jewish War, l. 2. c. 7. s. 3. (111) 2:365} {*Josephus, Antiq., l. 17. c. 13. s. 2. (344) 8:531} [K551] This was that son of Herod, of whom Strabo noted that he had lived in exile among the Allobrogian Gauls. {*Strabo, l. 16. c. 2. s. 46. 7:299}

### 4010b AM, 4720 JP, 7 AD

6178. Augustus proscribed his only nephew, Marcus Agrippa, who was born after the death of his father. He could not be accused of being virtuous and relied on his brute-like physical strength. He had been convicted of no public scandal, but Augustus confiscated all his goods into the military treasury and banished him to Planasia, an island near Corsica. {*Tacitus, Annals, l. 1. c. 3. 3:247} {*Dio, l. 55. (32) 6:475}

6179. The government of Archelaus, which consisted of Judea (containing the tribe of Judah and Benjamin), Samaria and Idumea, was organized into a province and annexed to Syria. Quirinius was sent by Caesar to be the governor of Syria, so that he could tax both this province and all Syria. He was sent to evaluate the wealth of the Jewish estates and to sell Archelaus' property and bring its money into his own country. {*Josephus, Jewish War, l. 2. c. 8. s. 1. (117) 2:367} {*Josephus, Antiq., l. 17. c. 13. s. 5. (354,355) 8:535,537} {*Josephus, Antiq., l. 18. c. 1. s. 1. (1) 9:3} [E806]

6180. Although the Jews could barely tolerate even the mention of a tax, Joazar, the high priest and the son of Boethus, nonetheless convinced them. He had either been restored by Archelaus, or else had taken the priesthood back again in his absence. Without much opposition, they allowed themselves to be taxed. {*Josephus, Antiq., l. 18. c. 1. s. 1. (2,3) 9:5}

6181. At the time of this taxing, Judas, a Galilean, arose and drew away many people after him. After he died, all who had followed him were dispersed, according to Gamaliel. {Ac 5:37} Josephus called him a Gaulanite. {*Josephus, Antiq., l. 18. c. 1. s. 1. (3) 9:5} He was born in the town of Gamala, but in another place Josephus agreed with Gamaliel and called him a Galilean, writing that he had instigated the people to revolt from the Romans when Quirinius taxed Judea. {*Josephus, Antiq., l. 18. c. 1. s. 1. (3) 9:5} {*Josephus, Jewish War, l. 2. c. 8. s. 1. (118) 2:367,369} {*Josephus, Antiq., l. 20. c. 5. s. 2. (102) 10:55}

6182. Saddok, a Pharisee, was his associate and tried to stir up the people to rebel. He said that this taxing was nothing less than an obvious sign of their servitude and exhorted all the country to stand up for their liberty, thereby giving them the hope that through this they would enjoy better lives. They would be confirmed in the possession of their estates and would be considered valiant. They could not expect any help from God if they did not help themselves. The people readily received these speeches and were encouraged to do something. These men troubled the country, for they committed widespread murders and robberies. They plundered without any regard for friend or foe, and murdered many noble personages. All this was done under the pretext of defending the public liberty, but in actual fact it was for their private profit. Judas and Saddok were the instigators of all these calamities and became the example for all who wanted to encourage seditions. So this not only disturbed the country now, but became the seeds of all the future calamities. {*Josephus, Antiq., l. 18. c. 1. s. 1. (4-10) 9:5-9}

6183. To the three ancient sects of the Jews (that is the Pharisees, Sadducees and Essenes), Judas, the Galilean, added a fourth one, which he founded. Its followers agreed with the Pharisees and affirmed that God alone is to be accounted Lord and master of all. They would more readily endure the most horrible torture of any kind, together with their friends and children, than call any mortal man Lord. {*Josephus, Jewish War, l. 2. c. 8. s. 2-14. (119-166) 2:369-387} {*Josephus, Antiq., l. 18. c. 1. s. 2-6. (11-22) 9:9-21}

*6184.* Quirinius confiscated and sold Archelaus' goods and went through the land with the tax. This happened in the 37th year after the victory at Actium, beginning in September of the previous year. *[K552]* A sedition of the common people was made against Joazar, the high priest, so Quirinius removed him from his office and substituted Ananus, or Annas, the son of Seth, in his place. {*Josephus, Antiq., l. 18. c. 2. s. 2. (26) 9:23}*

*6185.* Quirinius was accompanied by Coponius, who was of the equestrian order. Coponius had been sent by Augustus to be the first governor of Judea, after it was organized into a province. {*Josephus, Antiq., l. 18. c. 1. s. 1. (2) 9:5}* {*Josephus, Jewish War, l. 2. c. 8. s. 1. (117) 2:367}* The term of the governors seems always to have expired after three years.

## 4011 AM, 4721 JP, 8 AD

*6186.* When Coponius was governor of Judea, in the passover of this or the following year, the priests had opened the gates of the temple about midnight (as was always the custom at this feast). Certain Samaritans secretly entered Jerusalem and scattered men's bones in the middle of the porch and throughout the temple. After this, the priests watched the temple much more diligently than before. {*Josephus, Antiq., l. 18. c. 2. s. 2. (29,30) 9:25,27}*

*6187.* At this year's passover, in the twelfth year of his age, Christ was brought to Jerusalem by Joseph and Mary. After the seven days of unleavened bread were over, his parents returned home and he stayed behind. They did not know where he was and looked for him for three days. They found him in the temple, sitting in the midst of the teachers. He was listening to them and asking them questions. All who heard him, were astonished at his understanding and answers. {*Lu 2:41-47}*

*6188.* Jesus went down to Nazareth with his parents and was obedient to them. {*Lu 2:51}* He followed his father's trade as a carpenter and ate his bread by the sweat of his brow. It was because of this that his fellow citizens of Nazareth stated: *Is not this the carpenter, the son of Mary?* {*Mr 6:3}*

## 4012 AM, 4722 JP, 9 AD

*6189.* Ovid was banished to Tomis in Pontus, because he saw some dishonest act of Augustus which the latter had not wanted to be seen. We read him complaining about this misfortune: {*Ovid, Tristia, l. 2. (103,104) 6:63}*

Why saw I ought? Why did I guilty make
My eyes? This sin, why did I, wretch, partake? *[E807]*

*6190.* He was also exiled for his love of books, as he himself confirmed and as was noted by Sidonius Apollinaris and other writers, as well. {*Ovid, Tristia, l. 2. (61-69) 6:61}*

We have earlier shown that he was born in the consulship of Hirtius and Pansa, and at this time he was fifty-one years old, but the current year had not ended. The poet records his age: {*Ovid, Tristia, l. 4. c. 10. (95-98) 6:205}*

When twice five times with olive girt the knight
Had borne away the prize (his virtue's right),
When by my prince's rage I had command
Of the Exine (Black Sea) Tomis to seek the land.

*6191.* That is, as it is more clearly expressed by him in the book which he wrote against his accusers when he first arrived at Tomis: {*Ovid, Ibis, l. 1. (1) 2:237}*

When to this time ten lustrals (fifty years) I had seen.

*6192.* He did not confuse the Olympiads, which were every four years, with the lustrals of the Romans, which were every five years. *[K553]*

## 4013 AM, 4723 JP, 10 AD

*6193.* Ovid signified that he had passed the first winter in Pontus and with that, the first year of his banishment, for he had spent the former winter on his journey: {*Ovid, Tristia, l. 3. c. 12. (1-4) 6:147}*

Now zephyr tames the cold; the years run round,
A longer winter the Maeotae found.
The sign in Aries, the night did make
Her equal hours with the day partake.

*6194.* He noted the second year of his banishment: {*Ovid, Tristia, l. 4. c. 6. (19,20) 6:187}*

Since I my country left, the barns twice filled
And presses, grain and wine did to them yield.

*6195.* Marcus Ambivius was sent into Judea by Augustus, as the second governor. During his stay, Salome, who was the sister of Herod, died. To Julia (or Livia, Augustus' wife), she bequeathed Jamnia, with its government, Phasaelis which was located in the plain, and Archelaus. This last was very well planted with date palms which bore excellent fruit. {*Josephus, Antiq., l. 18. c. 2. s. 2. (31) 9:27,29}*

## 4015 AM, 4725 JP, 12 AD

*6196.* Ovid recalled the beginning of his third winter spent in Pontus: {*Ovid, Tristia, l. 5. c. 10. (1,2) 6:245}*

Since I to Pontus came, thrice Ister stood
With frost, and thrice lay glazed
the Exine flood (Black Sea).

*6197.* The Senate and people of Rome, at Augustus' request, made a decree that Tiberius should have the same power in all the provinces and armies as he himself had. {*Velleius Paterculus, l. 2. c. 121. s. 1. 1:307}* *[E808]* Suetonius stated that the following law was proposed by the consuls: that Tiberius should govern the provinces in common with Augustus. {*Suetonius, Tiberius, l. 3. c. 21. s. 1. 1:343} Germanicus was consul all that year, whom the aged Augustus commended in writing to the Senate and the latter to Tiberius. {*Dio, l. 56. (26) 7:59} It was no wonder that the Senate should be commended by Augustus: {*Tacitus, Annals, l. 1. c. 3. 3:247}

> "to his son, his colleague of the empire and partner in the tribuneship."

6198. Tiberius was also made censor and committed the care of the city to Lucius Piso, because he had spent two days and two nights in drinking with him, since Tiberius had now been made a prince. {*Pliny, l. 14. c. 38. 4:281} Tacitus confirmed that Piso was the prefect of the city for twenty years and did his job well. He died when Domitius Ahenobarbus and Aulus Vitellius were consuls in 32 AD and was honoured with a public funeral. {*Tacitus, Annals, l. 6. c. 11. 4:173,175} From this can be concluded that Tiberius was now prince, or viceroy, in 12 AD, two whole years before Augustus' death. Therefore a distinction must be noted between the beginning of Tiberius' first being a prince, or viceroy, and his later becoming emperor.

## 4016 AM, 4726 JP, 13 AD

6199. In his eulogy to Maximus, Ovid noted his fourth winter lived in exile: {*Ovid, Pontus, l. 1. c. 2. (25,26) 6:273}

> Here the fourth winter wearied me doth hold,
> Resisting adverse fate, weapons, sharp cold. [K554]

6200. Annius Rufus was sent as the third governor to Judea by Augustus. {*Josephus, Antiq., l. 18. c. 2. s. 2. (32) 9:29}

## 4017a AM, 4726 JP, 13 AD

6201. When Lucius Munatius and Gaius Silius were consuls, the fourth ten-year term of Augustus' empire was about to expire. Against his will, he accepted the government of the state for another ten years and continued Tiberius' tribuneship. {*Dio, l. 56. (28) 7:63}

## 4017b AM, 4727 JP, 14 AD

6202. When Sextus Pompeius and Sextus Apuleius were consuls, Augustus, in a breviary of his acts which was engraved on the Ancyran Marble, wrote that he, with his colleague Tiberius, had numbered the people of Rome for the third time. In this census, the Roman citizens totalled 4,937,000. {*Augustus, l. 2. c. 8. 1:359} {Gruter, Inscriptions, p. 230.} Eusebius was incorrect when he said that 9,370,000 were numbered. {*Eusebius, Chronicles, l. 1. 1:253} Jornandes, in his book, followed Eusebius in this error and gave an even larger number. {Jornandes, De Regnorum ac Temporum Succession} He added that Augustus had:

> "commanded all the world to be numbered, since there was peace at the birth of Jesus Christ."

6203. Both he and Eusebius in that place conjecture that the birth of the Lord happened in the 42nd year of Augustus' empire.

6204. When Augustus was making the lustrum in Mars' field, there were a number of people present there. The lustrum was a sacrifice of purification made every five years by one of the censors when a census was completed. An eagle fluttered about Augustus numerous times and then went and sat on a nearby temple on the first letter of Agrippa's name. When Augustus saw this, he commanded his colleague Tiberius to make the vows that were usually made for the next year. For even though all things had already been prepared for the solemnities of these vows, yet he refused to make any vows which he thought he would not live to perform. {*Suetonius, Augustus, l. 2. c. 97. s. 1,2. 1:297}

6205. At about the same time, the first letter of his name fell down from the inscription of his statue in the Capitol, after it was struck by a flash of lightning. The soothsayers said that he would live only a hundred days after that, because the letter C denoted a hundred in Roman numerals. Also, he should be canonized as a god, because AESAR, which was the rest of his name, meant god in the Etruscan language. {*Dio, l. 56. (29) 7:67} {*Suetonius, Augustus, l. 2. c. 97. s. 2. 1:297}

6206. Meanwhile, Augustus wrote a summary of his doings, which he wanted to have engraved in tables of brass and placed over his tomb. {*Suetonius, Augustus, l. 2. c. 101. s. 4. 1:309} {*Dio, l. 56. (33) 7:73} An example of this, which was written on the Ancyran Marble so often mentioned by us, was the census described earlier, that he had recently taken. On his last day, he called his friends and asked them whether it seemed to them that he had played the comedy of life aptly. He added this remark: {*Suetonius, Augustus, l. 2. c. 99. s. 1. 1:303}

> Since well I played my part,
>   all clap your hands
> And from the stage
>   dismiss me with applause.

6207. He added that he had found Rome made of clay, but left it to them made of marble. He was not referring to the appearance of its buildings, but rather to the strength of the empire. {*Dio, l. 56. (30) 7:69} So Augustus ended his days at Nola in Campania when Pompeius Sextus and Appuleius Sextus were consuls and so were named on his tomb. {*Velleius Paterculus, l. 2. c. 123. s. 2. 1:311} {*Suetonius, Augustus, l. 2. c. 100. s. 1. 1:303} {*Tacitus, Annals, l. 1. c. 5. 3:251} {*Tacitus, Annals, l. 1. c. 7. 3:255} {*Dio, l. 56. (31) 7:71} He died in the same house and room where his father Octavius had died. {*Suetonius, Augustus, l. 2. c. 100. s. 1. 1:303} {*Tacitus, Annals, l. 1. c. 9. 3:259} He died on the 14th of the Calends of September (August 19), which was on the same day that he was first made consul. {*Suetonius, l. 2. c. 100. s. 1. 1:303} {*Dio, l. 56. (30) 7:69} [E809]

6208. Tiberius did not announce the death of Augustus before he had killed Agrippa Postumus. To the captain who killed him and brought back word that he had done as Tiberius had ordered, he replied that he had not ordered it and that the captain would have to give an account to the Senate. At that time, Tiberius tried to avoid this reproach, for later his silence consigned that matter to oblivion. {*Suetonius, Tiberius, l. 3. c. 22. 1:347} {*Tacitus, Annals, l. 1. c. 6. 3:251,253} {*Dio, l. 57. (3) 7:119,121} [K555] After all things that the circumstances required had been done, it was announced that Augustus was dead and that Tiberius Nero was emperor. {*Tacitus, Annals, l. 1. c. 5. 3:251}

6209. Although he had every intention of taking over the empire, yet for a long time he refused it most imprudently and held the Senate in suspense. They begged him and fell on their knees to him. He replied with doubtful and delaying answers, so that some upbraided him to his face for his indecision. {*Suetonius, Tiberius, l. 3. c. 24. s. 1,2. 1:349} {*Velleius Paterculus, l. 2. c. 124. s. 2. 1:311,313} {*Tacitus, Annals, l. 1. c. 7. 3:255} {*Dio, l. 57. (2) 7:117}

6210. Between this new principate, as Tacitus called it, and the former, which he had acquired two years before Augustus' death, was the following difference. {*Tacitus, Annals, l. 1. c. 6,7. 3:251-257} The former had extended only to the armies and provinces of the Roman Empire, but this to the head city itself, in which Tiberius had only had the authority of censorship and tribuneship. He now had the Augustal Principality, that is, of governing after his own will and being freed from all bonds of law. For Tiberius had not had equal power with Augustus, as Lucius Varus had with Antony, the philosopher, who governed the state with equal authority, according to Spartianus. {Spartianus, Hadrian} {Aelius Verus} {Marcus Aurelius} His power was like that which Antonius Pius had with Hadrian, who was adopted by him and made colleague with his father in the proconsular power (in respect of the other provinces) and in the tribuneship (at home), as Julius Capitoline stated. Consequently, Tiberius did not issue the edict by which he called the senators into the Senate by the authority of his new principate, but by the power of the tribuneship that he had under Augustus. However, he controlled the Praetorian cohorts as emperor. {*Tacitus, Annals, l. 1. c. 7. 3:255}

## 4018a AM, 4727 JP, 14 AD

6211. The legions of Pannonia rebelled, but were frightened by a sudden eclipse of the moon and so submitted themselves to Tiberius. {*Tacitus, Annals, l. 1. c. 28. 3:291,293} {*Dio, l. 57. (4) 7:121,123} This total eclipse happened on September 27 at five hours after midnight, so that the moon set even during the very eclipse.

6212. Ovid wrote to Sextus Pompeius, who was consul this year. {*Ovid, Pontus, l. 4. c. 5. 6:439} In the next poem, to Brutus, Ovid mentioned the death both of Augustus and of Fabius Maximus. {*Ovid, Pontus, l. 4. c. 6. (9-14) 6:441} (It was obvious from Tacitus, that Maximus died this year under Tiberius. {*Tacitus, Annals, l. 1. c. 5. 3:251}) Ovid showed in these verses that he was more than five years into his exile and that he was then entering the sixth (of the beginning of which we are certain): {*Ovid, Pontus, l. 4. c. 6. (5,6) 6:441}

> Now one quinquennial Olympiad's run,
> In Scythia I, and the second Lustral begun.

6213. In this sixth year he also remembered: {*Ovid, Pontus, l. 4. c. 10. (1,2) 6:463}

> This is the sixth summer on the Cymerian shores
> That I must spend amongst these Getic boors. [E810]

## 4018b AM, 4728 JP, 15 AD

6214. In his eulogy to Carus, Ovid made mention of his sixth winter (from which he counts the beginning of the seventh year of his banishment): {*Ovid, Pontus, l. 4. c. 13. (39,40) 6:477}

> This the sixth winter (my dear friend)
> Must I in this cold climate spend. [K556]

6215. He also told of a poem at this time, written by him in the language of the Getes, about the canonization of Augustus: {*Ovid, Pontus, l. 4. c. 13. (19-23) 6:477}

> Ah shame, in Getic language then did I
> Compile a book, fancy my poetry;
> Yea gloried in it, and soon began
> Among these barbarians to be the only man.

6216. A Hebrew woman who was later restored by Christ to health, was bound for eighteen years by Satan, starting from this date. {Lu 13:1-16}

6217. Valerius Gratus was sent by Tiberius to replace Annius Rufus as governor to Judea. Gratus held the government for eleven years. {*Josephus, Antiq., l. 18. c. 2. s. 2. (33-35) 9:29,31}

6218. When the governor of Crete died, the island was committed to the charge of the quaestor and his assessor for the rest of the governor's term. {*Dio, l. 57. (14) 7:147}

## 4019 AM, 4729 JP, 16 AD

6219. The Armenians received Vonones into their kingdom after he was expelled from his own by the threats of Artabanus, the king of the Parthians and Medes. Vonones solicited Tiberius in vain for help, through the envoys he sent to Rome. Since the most powerful of the Armenians followed the faction of Artabanus, Vonones gave up all hope of recovering the kingdom. With a large amount of treasure, he retired to Antioch and submitted himself to Creticus Silanus, the governor of Syria. Because Vonones was educated at Rome, the governor kept him with him in Syria and set a guard over him, but allowed him to maintain the pomp and name of a king. Artabanus made Orodes, one of his sons, king over the Armenians. {*Josephus, Antiq., l. 18. c. 2. s. 4. (39-52) 9:33-41} {*Tacitus, Annals, l. 2. c. 4. 3:389} {*Suetonius, Tiberius, l. 3. c. 49. s. 2. 1:379}

## 4020 AM, 4730 JP, 17 AD

6220. Ovid, the poet, died in exile and was buried near the city of Tomis. {*Eusebius, Chronicles, l. 1. 1:253}

6221. Through the letters of Livia, Tiberius had Archelaus, the king of Cappadocia, tricked into coming to Rome. Tiberius hated him, because he had not offered him any help in all the time he had lived at Rhodes. Livia did not hide her son's displeasure with him, but offered him mercy if he would come and ask for it. Archelaus did not know of the treachery or possible hostility and hurried to Rome. He was churlishly entertained and not long after was accused of fabricated crimes in the Senate. {*Tacitus, Annals, l. 2. c. 42. 3:447,449} He was accused of planning a sedition. The old king was worn out with extreme old age and gout and was believed to be demented. He defended himself in a letter in the Senate and pretended that he was not well in his mind at the time, and so escaped danger for the time being. {*Dio, l. 57. (17) 7:157,159} However, not long after this he died from other causes, because he was tired from grief and old age. Then Cappadocia was organized into a province and committed to the government of an equestrian. {*Dio, l. 57. (17) 7:159} {*Tacitus, Annals, l. 2. c. 42. 3:449} {*Suetonius, Tiberius, l. 3. c. 37. s. 4. 1:367}

6222. Tiberius stated that, with the profits from the kingdom of Cappadocia, their tribute of one per cent sales tax on auctioned goods could now be reduced to half that rate. {*Tacitus, Annals, l. 2. c. 42. 3:449} {*Tacitus, Annals, l. 1. c. 78. 3:377} He ordered that Cappadocia's chief city, a most noble city called Mazaca, should be called Caesarea. {*Eusebius, Chronicles, l. 1. 1:254}

6223. At the same time, following the death of Antiochus, the king of the Commagenes, a contention arose between the nobility and the common people. The nobility wanted the kingdom to be made into a province and the common people wanted another king. {*Tacitus, Annals, l. 2. c. 42. 3:449} {*Josephus, Antiq., l. 18. c. 2. s. 5. (53) 9:41} In similar manner, the country of the Cilicians was in a turmoil when their King Philopator died. Many wanted it to become a Roman province and many wanted a kingdom. [K557] The provinces of Syria and Judea were oppressed with taxes and made a petition that their tribute be lessened. {*Tacitus, Annals, l. 2. c. 42. 3:449,451}

6224. Tiberius discussed these things with the Senate and persuaded them that these problems in the east could only be settled by the wisdom of Germanicus. As a result, Germanicus was given charge of all the provinces east of Italy, by the decree of the Senate. This was a greater command than anyone before him had ever had. {*Tacitus, Annals, l. 2. c. 43. 3:451} Under the pretence of the problems in the east, Tiberius intended to take him from the legions which he usually commanded and give him charge over new provinces, which exposed him to greater treachery and hazards. {*Tacitus, Annals, l. 2. c. 5. 3:391} [E811]

6225. Because the governor of Syria, Creticus Silanus, was related to Germanicus, Tiberius appointed Gnaeus Piso as his successor. He was a headstrong and rebellious man and was well aware of the fact that he had been made governor of Syria to thwart Germanicus. Some believed that he had secret orders from Tiberius to do so. Without a doubt, his wife Plancina was advised by Augustus' widow to use female jealousy to start a quarrel with Agrippina (the daughter of Marcus Agrippa) and Julia, the wife of Germanicus {*Tacitus, Annals, l. 2. c. 43. 3:451,453}

6226. In the same year, twelve famous cities of Asia were destroyed by an earthquake in one night. These were Ephesus, Magnesia, Sardis, Mosthene, Aegea, Hiero-Caesarea, Philadelphia, Temnus, Cyme, Myrina, Apollonia, and Hyrcania. It was also recorded that large mountains were laid flat and plains raised up into hills, while fire flashed out of the ruins. The disaster was most serious at Sardis and created much sympathy for them. Tiberius promised them ten million sesterces and said he would release them, for a time of five years, of all that they were to have paid to the common treasury. Magnesia, near Mount Sipylus, was the next most damaged. They were given relief from taxes for five years, as well as the cities of Temnus, Philadelphia, Aegea, Apollonia, and the people who are called the Mosthenians, or Macedonians, of Hyrcania, and those who lived at Hiero-Caesarea, Myrina and Cyme. Tiberius sent some of the senators to them to assess the situation and help them. This charge was committed to Marcus Ateius, who had once been a praetor. If one who had been consul over Asia had been sent, there might have been some envy between equals, that is, between him and the governor of Asia, and the business would have been hindered. {*Tacitus, Annals, l. 2. c. 47. 3:459,461} {*Strabo, l. 12. c. 8. s. 18. 5:515,517} {*Strabo, l. 13. c. 4. s. 8. 6:179} {*Pliny, l. 2. c. 86. 1:331} {*Dio, l. 57. (17) 7:159} {*Eusebius, Chronicles, l. 1. 1:254} {Orosius, l. 7. c. 4.}

6227. For this magnificent generosity to the public, a large statue of Tiberius was erected in the forum at Rome, near the temple of Venus. Each of the cities which were rebuilt also erected a statue of Tiberius, according to Phlegon of Tralles in his book of wonders, recorded from Apollonius the Grammarian. Scaliger also added that silver medals were coined to commemorate these things. On one side of the coin was the face of Tiberius and on the reverse side was the picture of Asia in a woman's clothing, seated, with these words: *CIVITATIBUS ASIAE RESTITUTIS*, meaning *for the cities of Asia restored.*

## 4021 AM, 4731 JP, 18 AD

6228. Germanicus was sent out to settle the affairs of the east. {*Suetonius, Caligula, l. 4. c. 1. s. 1. 1:419} He sailed to the isle of Lesbos, where his wife Agrippina had previously given birth to Julia. He wanted to see the places of antiquity and fame, and went to the borders of Asia, to Perinthus and Byzantium, which were cities of Thrace. Then he entered the straits of Propontis and the mouth of the Pontic Sea. [K558] In addition, he relieved the provinces which were oppressed because of civil discord or by oppressive magistrates. He sailed to Colophon and consulted the oracle of Clarian Apollo, which told him in obscure wording, as was the manner of oracles, that his death was near. {*Tacitus, Annals, l. 2. c. 54. 3:469,471}

6229. Gnaeus Piso sailed as quickly as possible past the Cyclades Islands and using the shortest routes by sea, overtook Germanicus at Rhodes. Although Piso was saved from danger of shipwreck by Germanicus, he was still not kindly disposed toward Germanicus. He left Germanicus and went ahead of him to Syria, and when he came to the legions, he tried to win them over to him with gifts and bribes. He reached such a height of corruption, that among the common people he was called the father of the legions. Both he and his wife Plancina, as well, were involved in this. She incited some of the soldiers to obey her base commands and spoke disrespectfully against Agrippina and Germanicus. It was all the easier, because it was secretly whispered that this was being done with Tiberius' consent. {*Tacitus, Annals, l. 2. c. 55. 3:471,473}

6230. Although Germanicus knew about these things, the affairs of Armenia required his attention first. At that time, the Armenians had expelled Vonones and had no king. (This is if we can believe Tacitus, for Suetonius

stated that the king of Armenia was conquered by Germanicus. {*Suetonius, Caligula, l. 4. c. 1. s. 2. 1:419} This king was Orodes, the son of Artabanus, king of the Parthians, as it was recorded from Josephus. {*Josephus, Antiq., l. 18. c. 2. s. 4. (52) 9:41}) The goodwill of the country was more inclined toward Zeno, the son of Polemon, the king of Pontus. From his childhood, he had imitated the customs and clothing of the Armenians in hunting and feasting and other exercises which were greatly esteemed by the barbarians. He had won the goodwill of the nobles and common people to himself. Germanicus intended to make him king in the city of Artaxata and the noblemen approved of this. While the multitudes flocked around him, the rest reverenced him as their king and greeted him by the name of Artaxias, after the name of their city. {*Tacitus, Annals, l. 2. c. 56. 3:473,475} [E812]

6231. At that time, the Cappadocians were organized into a province and Quintus Veranius was made its governor. To give them the idea that the Roman government would be mild, some of the tributes which they used to pay to their kings, were reduced. Quintus Servaeus was made governor over Commagene and so this province was ruled by a praetor for the first time. {*Tacitus, Annals, l. 2. c. 56. 3:475}

## 4022a AM, 4731 JP, 18 AD

6232. After all the affairs of the allies had been successfully settled, Germanicus was still uneasy about Piso's arrogance. Germanicus had ordered that either Piso himself, or his son, should lead some of the legions into Armenia and neither had done anything. Finally, they both met at Cyrus, a city of Syria, where the tenth legion wintered. In the presence of a few families, Caesar had a heated discussion with Piso and Piso answered with a proud submission, which resulted in them departing with grudges against each other. After that, Piso was seldom at Caesar's tribunal, and if he assisted at any time, he presented as obstinate and made it obvious that he disagreed with him. This was also reported of him that at a banquet made by the king of the Nabateans, large crowns of gold were given to Germanicus and Agrippina, and small ones to Piso and the rest. The king stated that this feast was made for the son of a Roman prince and not for the son of the Parthian king. Piso threw away his crown and gave a diatribe on luxury. Although Germanicus found it difficult to handle this, he nonetheless endured it all patiently. {*Tacitus, Annals, l. 2. c. 57. 3:475,477}

6233. Envoys from Artabanus, the king of the Parthians, came to Germanicus to renew the friendship and league between them. [K559] The king said that he would yield to the honour of Germanicus to the extent that he was prepared to come to the banks of the Euphrates River. He requested in the meantime that Vonones should not stay in Syria, in case he might make a rebellion among the noblemen of the country around there using secret messengers. Germanicus answered by agreeing the alliance between the Romans and the Parthians. As far as the king's coming was concerned, and the honour done to himself, he answered politely and with modesty. Vonones was moved to Pompeiopolis, a coastal town of Cilicia, not so much as a result of Artabanus' request, as to spite Piso, who found Vonones most agreeable for the many services and gifts which he had given to Plancina, Piso's wife. {*Tacitus, Annals, l. 2. c. 58. 3:477,479}

## 4022b AM, 4732 JP, 19 AD

6234. When Marcus Silanus and Lucius Norbanus were consuls, Germanicus went into Egypt to view its antiquities, but feigned a concern for the province. He opened the granaries, brought down the price of grain and did other things to win the favour of the people. He went about without soldiers, wore open shoes and dressed like a Greek. Tiberius lightly reprimanded him for his behaviour and apparel and sharply rebuked him for having entered Alexandria without the permission of the prince, contrary to Augustus' order. However, Germanicus did not yet know that his journey was frowned upon and sailed up the Nile River, starting at the town of Canopus. Later, he visited the great ruins of Thebes, where the Egyptian letters could still be seen in the old buildings which contained their ancient wealth. He intended to see other marvels, of which the main attraction was the stone image of Memnon. When it was illuminated by the sun, it made a sound like a man's voice. He also saw the pyramids, as high as mountains, built by the former kings to show their riches. He saw the impassable sands and the handmade lake to hold the flooding of the Nile River. Elsewhere, he saw narrow gorges and deeps impervious to the plummet of the explorer. Then he came to Elephantine and Syene. This meant that Germanicus spent all that summer in seeing various provinces. {*Tacitus, Annals, l. 2. c. 59-61. 3:487-493}

6235. At the same time, Vonones bribed his guards and tried by every means to escape to the Armenians and from there to the Albanians and Heniochians and to his relative, the king of Scythia. Under the pretence of going hunting, he left the seacoasts and took the byways. His fast horse quickly brought him to the Pyramus River, but the inhabitants had broken down the bridges when they had heard of the king's escape and the river was too deep to ford. As a result, he was captured on the bank of the river and bound by Vibius Fronto, an officer in the cavalry. Remmius Evocatus ran him through

in anger, because Vonones had first been committed to him to be guarded. {*Tacitus, Annals, l. 2. c. 68. 3:493}

6236. The daughter of Jairus, the ruler of the synagogue, was born. She was his only child and died when she was twelve years old. Christ restored her to life. During this year, also, the woman became sick who had the issue of blood. Twelve years later, she was healed by touching the garment of Jesus. {Lu 8:42,43 Mr 5:25,42}

6237. There were many false oracles that circulated as though they had been the Sibylline oracles, concerning the destruction of Rome, which was to happen in the nine hundredth year from its founding. Tiberius reproved them and saw all the books which contained any prophecies. Some he rejected as of no importance and others he accepted into the number of those which were to be approved. {*Dio, l. 57. (18) 7:161,163} [E813]

6238. The Senate debated the issue of the elimination of the Egyptian and Jewish religions. An act was made that those who observed them had to depart from Italy, if they did not stop those practices by a certain day. {*Tacitus, Annals, l. 2. c. 85. 3:517} [K560] They were compelled to burn all their religious garments and everything associated with them. {*Suetonius, Tiberius, l. 3. c. 36. 1:363,365} This may also be what Seneca referred to: {*Seneca, Epistles, l. 1. c. 108. (22) 6:243}

> "When I was a young man in the government of Tiberius, some foreign rites of the countries were removed. It was thought incorrect to abstain from some foods and was used as a proof of one belonging to a strange cult."

6239. A horrible crime was committed against Paulina, a noble Roman woman, by the priests of the Egyptian religion. When it became known, Tiberius commanded the temple of Isis to be thrown down and Isis' statue to be drowned in the Tiber River. {*Josephus, Antiq., l. 18. c. 3. s. 4. (65-80) 9:51-59} A certain impostor was the reason for the expulsion of the Jews. He had fled his country, for fear of being punished according to their laws. He then lived at Rome and made himself out to be an interpreter of Moses' law. He also had three associates like himself. When the noblewoman Fulvia embraced the Jewish religion and became their scholar, they persuaded her that she should send purple and gold to the temple of Jerusalem, but when they had received this, they used it for themselves. Tiberius was informed of this by his friend Saturninus, Fulvia's husband, who complained of the wrong done to his wife. Tiberius ordered all the Jews to get out of the city. {*Josephus, Antiq., l. 18. c. 3. s. 5. (81-83) 9:59,61}

6240. From the Jews, the consuls enlisted as soldiers four thousand of the youth who were the sons of freedmen. These were sent into Sardinia to suppress the robbers.

The consuls considered it no great loss if they should perish to the pestilential climate. Many, who refused to be enlisted because of the religion of their country, were grievously punished. The rest of that nationality, or any who followed their religion, were turned out of the city under the penalty of perpetual slavery if they did not obey. {*Josephus, Antiq., l. 18. c. 3. s. 5. (84) 9:61} {*Suetonius, Tiberius, l. 3. c. 36. 1:363} {*Tacitus, Annals, l. 2. c. 85. 3:517}

6241. Rhascupolis, or Rhescoporis, the king of Thrace, killed Cotys, his brother's son, who was also his partner in the kingdom. Rhascupolis was betrayed by Pomponius Flaccus. (Ovid mentioned Flaccus as governor of Moesia. {*Ovid, Pontus, l. 4. c. 9. (75-77) 6:459}) He was brought to Rome, where he was condemned and taken to Alexandria. He was killed in a way that made it look as though he had made an attempt to flee from there. {*Tacitus, Annals, l. 2. c. 67. 3:487} {*Velleius Paterculus, l. 2. c. 129. s. 1,2. 1:323} {*Suetonius, Tiberius, l. 3. c. 37. s. 4. 1:367}

## 4023a AM, 4732 JP, 19 AD

6242. When Germanicus returned from Egypt, he found that everything he had ordered dealing with the legions or cities had not been done, or the exact opposite of what he had ordered had been done. Therefore, he had very harsh words with Piso, presenting it as if Piso had disobeyed the emperor himself. As a result, Piso decided to leave Syria, but was then detained due to Germanicus' sickness. When he heard he was getting better and that vows were to be made for his health, he, through his lictors, drove away the beasts brought to the altar and disturbed the preparation for the sacrifices and the solemn meeting of the people of Antioch, where Germanicus was. {*Tacitus, Annals, l. 2. c. 69. 3:493} While Germanicus was sick, Piso behaved very harshly toward him in words and deeds, without showing any restraint. {*Suetonius, Caligula, l. 4. c. 2. 1:421}

6243. Then, Piso went to Seleucia, expecting Germanicus to become sick again. {*Tacitus, Annals, l. 2. c. 69. 3:493} In the house where Germanicus lived, they exhumed human bodies, verses and charms, his name engraved on lead sheets, half-burned ashes mingled with corrupt blood and other sorceries. It was believed that in this way the souls were dedicated to the infernal powers. {*Tacitus, Annals, l. 2. c. 69. 3:495} {*Dio, l. 57. (18) 7:163} [K561]

6244. Germanicus was very angry and renounced Piso's friendship by letters, according to the ancient custom. Some add that he ordered him to leave the province. Piso did not stay, but weighed anchor. However, he sailed slowly, so that he could return sooner, if news of Germanicus' death should open a way for him to Syria. {*Tacitus, Annals, l. 2. c. 70. 3:495} {*Suetonius, Caligula, l. 4. c. 3. s. 3. 1:421,423}

6245. Germanicus was greatly weakened by his sickness and knew his end was near. He accused Piso and his wife, Plancina, and asked his friends to avenge it. He died, to the great regret of the province and the neighbouring people. {*Tacitus, Annals, l. 2. c. 71,72. 3:495-499} He died at Antioch, from an incessant disease when he was thirty-four years old. It was suspected that he had been poisoned and that the poison was given to him through the treachery of Tiberius and Piso. {*Suetonius, Caligula, l. 4. c. 1,2. 1:419,421}

6246. The day that Germanicus died, the temples were battered with a storm of stones, altars were overturned, the household gods were thrown into the streets by some and children were laid out to die. [E814] They reported also that the barbarians, with whom there was civil war, or war against the Romans, consented to a truce for public mourning. Some of their governors cut off their beards and shaved their wives' heads, as a sign of their deepest mourning. The king of kings did no hunting or feasting with the nobles on that day, even though it was a holiday among the Parthians. {*Suetonius, Caligula, l. 4. c. 5. 1:423,425}

6247. His funeral was without any images or pomp and was solemnised with the praises and memory of his virtues. Before his body was cremated, it lay naked in the forum of Antioch, the place destined for the final rites. It was uncertain whether he showed any signs of poison, for there was a difference of opinion. Those who favoured Germanicus thought he did, and those who favoured Piso did not think so. {*Tacitus, Annals, l. 2. c. 73. 3:499,501} In addition to the dark spots all over his body and the froth which came from his mouth, the heart did not burn with the rest of his body. It was thought that it would not be consumed by fire, if the man had died from poison. {*Suetonius, Caligula, l. 4. c. 1. 1:419,421} In a speech Vitellius later made, he tried to prove Piso guilty of this villainy by using this argument and publicly testified that the heart of Germanicus could not be burned because of the poison. Piso used the defence that the hearts of those who die of the disease called *Cardiaca Passio* cannot be burned. {*Pliny, l. 11. c. 71. 3:549}

6248. Gnaeus Sentius was chosen as the governor of Syria by the lieutenants and senators who were there. They sent Martina to Rome, a woman infamous in that province for poisoning, but very much liked by Piso's wife, Plancina. This was done at the request of Vitellius and Veranius, who alleged crimes and accusations against them as if they had already been found guilty. {*Tacitus, Annals, l. 2. c. 74. 3:501} Although Agrippina was worn out with grief and sickness, she was impatient with anything which might hinder her revenge. She sailed with Germanicus' ashes and took her children. {*Tacitus, Annals, l. 2. c. 75. 3:501}

6249. Piso received news of Germanicus' death at the isle of Cos and expressed his joy most immoderately. Plancina was more insolent, for she had been mourning for the death of her sister at the time, but stopped wearing mourning clothes when Germanicus died. {*Tacitus, Annals, l. 2. c. 75. 3:501,503} The centurions came flocking around Piso and told him that the legions were already at his command and that he should return to the province which had been wrongfully taken from him and now had no governor. {*Tacitus, Annals, l. 2. c. 76. 3:503} [K562] He sent letters to Tiberius and accused Germanicus of riotousness and pride, claiming that he himself had been driven out to make way for a revolt Germanicus was planning. Piso said that he had taken charge of the army again with the same fidelity with which he had governed it before. He had ordered Domitius Celer to sail to Syria with a warship across the open sea as quickly as possible, avoiding the longer coastal route. Piso then marshalled and armed renegades and his rascal companions. He sailed over to the continent and intercepted an ensign of new soldiers who were going to Syria, and he also wrote to the leaders of Cilicia to send him help. {*Tacitus, Annals, l. 2. c. 78. 3:505}

6250. Piso and his companions sailed along the coast of Lycia and Pamphylia and met with the ships which conveyed Agrippina. They each hated one another and prepared to fight. Equally afraid of each other, they only exchanged harsh words. Vibius Marsus summoned Piso to return to Rome, to defend himself. He scoffingly replied that he would come when the praetor, who knew about poisoning cases, would appoint a day for the plaintiff and defendant. {*Tacitus, Annals, l. 2. c. 79. 3:505,507}

6251. In the meantime, Domitius went to Laodicea, a city of Syria, and came to the winter quarters of the sixth legion. It was the best one to corrupt, but he was prevented from doing this by the commanding officer, Pacuvius Sentius. After warning Piso by letters that he should not set out to corrupt the army or raise any war in the province, he marched off at once with a strong force and was ready to fight against Piso. {*Tacitus, Annals, l. 2. c. 79. 3:507}

6252. Piso seized the strong citadel of Celenderis in Cilicia. He had intermixed the renegades and the new soldiers he had intercepted, with his own troops, Plancina's slaves and the forces which the leaders of the Cilicians had sent him. He marshalled them into the form of a legion and then he drew out his companies before the citadel walls on a steep and craggy hill. All the other sides were surrounded by the sea. When the Roman cohorts came, the Cilicians fled and barricaded themselves in the citadel. {*Tacitus, Annals, l. 2. c. 80. 3:507,509} [E815]

6253. In the meantime, Piso tried in vain to attack the navy that was not far off, after which he returned to the citadel. From the walls, he beat his breast and called every soldier by name. He offered bribes and tried to raise a rebellion. He succeeded so well, that the standard-bearer of the sixth legion defected to him with his ensign. Then Sentius commanded the cornets and trumpets to sound and made an assault on the rampart. He raised the ladders and ordered the ablest men to follow him and others to shoot arrows, stones and firebrands from the engines. In the end, Piso was overcome and entreated that since he had laid down his arms, he wanted to stay in the citadel until Caesar was consulted as to who should be the governor of Syria. These conditions were rejected and he was granted nothing except a naval escort and a safe conduct to Rome. {*Tacitus, Annals, l. 2. c. 81. 3:509}

6254. When the rumour of Germanicus' death spread, it was exaggerated by the time it had travelled the distance to Rome. The people were deeply grieved by his death. {*Tacitus, Annals, l. 2. c. 82. 3:511} However, nothing pleased Tiberius and Livia more. {*Dio, l. 57. (18) 7:163} No consolations or edicts could restrain the public mourning, which lasted all the festival days of the month of December. {*Suetonius, Caligula, l. 4. c. 6. s. 2. 1:425}

6255. Germanicus was decreed every honour which love or imagination could conceive. Arches were erected at Rome and on the bank of the Rhine River. On Mount Amanus in Syria, an inscription was placed, telling of what he had done and that he had died for the country. A sepulchre was made at Antioch for his burial, and a funeral monument erected at Epidaphne, where he died. {*Tacitus, Annals, l. 2. c. 83. 3:513} [K563]

6256. Although it was winter, Agrippina still continued her voyage by sea and arrived at the island of Corcyra, opposite the coast of Calabria. She rested a few days to settle her mind and then sailed to Brundisium. After she landed with her two children, holding the funeral urn in her hand, there was a general mourning among them all. {*Tacitus, Annals, l. 3. c. 1. 3:523}

## 4023b AM, 4733 JP, 20 AD

6257. Drusius, the son of Tiberius, along with Germanicus' brother, Claudius, and the children of Germanicus who had remained in the city, went as far as Tarracina to meet her. The new consuls, Marcus Valerius and Marcus Aurelius, the Senate and a large number of the people lined the way. {*Tacitus, Annals, l. 3. c. 2. 3:525}

6258. The day that the remains of Germanicus were placed in Augustus' tomb in Campus Martius, there was a desolate silence that was sometimes broken by their weeping. Everyone honoured Germanicus and had great sympathy for his widow Agrippina, while they railed against Tiberius. {*Tacitus, Annals, l. 3. c. 4,5. 3:527,529}

6259. When Piso came to Rome, he landed at the mausoleum of Caesar. That day the shore was full of people. Piso went ashore with a large company of followers after him, while Plancina had a number of women in her train. They both looked very cheerful and celebrated their happy return in a house which overlooked the forum and was decked out for feasts and banquets. {*Tacitus, Annals, l. 3. c. 9. 3:533,535} The next day, Fulcinius Trio accused Piso before the consuls. Tiberius referred the whole case to the Senate. {*Tacitus, Annals, l. 3. c. 10. 3:535} The day the Senate met Drusius, Tiberius made a prepared speech and tried to accommodate and moderate the defendant's offence. {*Tacitus, Annals, l. 3. c. 12. 3:537,539} The accusers were given two days to bring in their accusations and after a period of six days, the defendant had three days to answer for himself. {*Tacitus, Annals, l. 3. c. 13. 3:541}

6260. As the case was pleaded, the outcry of the people could be heard before the court. They said they would tear him to pieces if the Senate found him innocent. They had dragged Piso's effigies to the Gemonian Stairs and began to break them in pieces. These steps descended from the Capitol to the forum and were used to expose the bodies of executed criminals. However, on Tiberius' orders, they were restrained from their actions. {*Tacitus, Annals, l. 3. c. 14. 3:543} They showed the same hatred against Plancina, but she was protected by Tiberius, through the influence of his wife. Piso knew he was finished when his wife separated her defence from her husband's, whereupon he killed himself, by cutting his throat with his own sword. {*Tacitus, Annals, l. 3. c. 15. 3:543,545}

6261. Suetonius wrote that he was almost torn to pieces by the people and was condemned to death by the Senate. {*Suetonius, Caligula, l. 4. c. 2. 1:421} Dio related this account. For the death of Germanicus, Piso was brought into the Senate by Tiberius himself. Piso requested to be given time to defend himself and committed suicide. {*Dio, l. 57. (18) 7:165} Suetonius implicated Tiberius in the death of Germanicus, because of Tiberius' later actions toward Germanicus' family, and confirmed Tacitus' suspicions about a book Piso had. {*Suetonius, Tiberius, l. 3. c. 52. s. 3. 1:383} Cornelius Tacitus said that he had often heard from the old men that a little book was frequently seen in Piso's hand, which he kept to himself. His friends said it contained Tiberius' letters and his commission against Germanicus. Piso had planned to disclose it to the senators and to accuse Tiberius, had he not been deluded by Tiberius' vain promises. Piso did not kill himself, but someone was sent to murder him. Tacitus said: {*Tacitus, Annals, l. 3. c. 16. 3:545,547}

"I will not confirm either of these things, although I ought not to conceal that it was said by those who lived until I came to a man's age."

## 4025 AM, 4735 JP, 22 AD

6262. Licences for ordaining sanctuaries increased greatly throughout the cities of Greece. [E816] These places became havens for debtors against their creditors and for those who were suspected of capital crimes. In this way, the wickedness of men was protected by the ceremonies of the gods. Tiberius ordered that the cities should send their charters and envoys to the Senate at Rome for confirmation. [K564] The Ephesians were first heard concerning this business; then came the cities and places of Magnesia, Aphrodisia, Stratonicia, Hiero-Caesarea, Cyprus, Pergamum, Smyrna, Tenos, Sardis, Miletus, Crete and others. An honourable standard was prescribed. They were commanded to erect altars in the temples themselves as a solemn memorial, but they should not, under the pretence of religion, fall into rivalries in so doing. {*Tacitus, Annals, l. 3. c. 60-63. 3:617-623}

6263. Gaius Silvanus was accused of bribery by his companions and banished to the isle of Gyarus, but he was allowed to retire to the isle of Cythnus, since Gyarus was so bleak. {*Tacitus, Annals, l. 3. c. 66-69. 3:627-633} Caesius Cordus was also accused of bribery by the people of Cyrene and when convicted by Ancharius Priscus, was condemned. {*Tacitus, Annals, l. 3. c. 70. 3:633}

## 4026 AM, 4736 JP, 23 AD

6264. Aelius Sejanus killed Drusius with poison given him by Lygdus, a eunuch. (Drusius was the son of Tiberius, and was his partner in the tribuneship and was killed by Sejanus after Sejanus had committed adultery with Drusius' wife, Livia.) {*Tacitus, Annals, l. 4. c. 8-10. 4:17-21} As well, the Jews who lived at Rome were accused by Sejanus to Tiberius of fabricated crimes, in an effort, on his part, wholly to destroy that nationality. He knew they were the main ones who opposed his wicked practices, and so he said that they were conspiring against the life of the emperor. {*Philo, Gaius, l. 1. c. 24. (159) 10:81} {*Philo, Flaccus, l. 1. c. 1. (1) 9:303}

6265. After Drusius' funeral was over, Tiberius returned to his accustomed business and took no extra time off. He jeered the envoys from Illium, who came too late to comfort him, as though the memory of grief had been blotted out. He replied that he also was sorry when they had lost so gallant a citizen as Hector was. {*Suetonius, Tiberius, l. 3. c. 52. s. 2,3. 1:383}

6266. The Senate passed the decrees of Tiberius, that the cities of Cibyra in Asia and Aegina in Achaia, which were badly damaged by an earthquake, should not have to pay tribute for the next three years. {*Tacitus, Annals, l. 4. c. 13. 4:25} The Samians and the men of Cos sent their envoys to Rome and requested confirmation of their ancient right of sanctuaries—one temple was for Juno and the other for Aesculapius. {*Tacitus, Annals, l. 4. c. 14. 4:27}

6267. Lucilius Longus died, who had been the companion in the fortunes of Tiberius, whether good or bad, and who, alone of all the senators, had been Tiberius' companion when he had exiled himself to Rhodes. {*Tacitus, Annals, l. 4. c. 15. 4:29}

6268. Lucilius Capito, the governor of Asia, was condemned on the accusation of the province. In the previous year, they had brought Gaius Silanus to justice and the cities of Asia had decreed a temple dedicated to Tiberius, his mother and the Senate. They received permission to build it. {*Tacitus, Annals, l. 4. c. 15. 4:29}

6269. Valerius Gratus, the governor of Judea, removed Ananus, or Annas, from the high priesthood and made Ishmael, the son of Phabi, the high priest, but soon removed him, also. {*Josephus, Antiq., l. 18. c. 2. s. 2. (33,34) 9:29}

## 4027 AM, 4737 JP, 24 AD

6270. Ishmael was removed from the high priesthood and Eleazar, the son of Annas, or Ananus, who had previously been removed, was made high priest by Valerius. {*Josephus, Antiq., l. 18. c. 2. s. 2. (34,35) 9:29}

6271. Cassius Severus, the orator, had seventeen years earlier been banished to Crete for his vicious tongue, by the decree of the Senate. When he behaved just as poorly there, he had all his estate taken from him. He was forbidden both water and fire and was banished onto the stony island of Seriphos. Eight years later, he died in extreme poverty. {*Tacitus, Annals, l. 4. c. 21. 4:41} {*Eusebius, Chronicles, l. 1. 1:254}

6272. Publius Dolabella, the proconsul of Africa, summoned Ptolemy, the son of Juba, King of Mauritania, to help him and his countrymen. He killed Tacfarinas and put an end to the Numidian war. [K565] The king of the Garamantians had helped Tacfarinas with light cavalry, which he had sent from a long way off. When Tacfarinas was killed, the Garamantians sent envoys to give satisfaction to the people of Rome. {*Tacitus, Annals, l. 4. c. 23-26. 4:41-47}

6273. Vibius Serenus, a banished man, was falsely accused of treason by his son, and was condemned for an old grudge that Tiberius had against him. Asinius Gallus was of the opinion that he should be confined to either Gyarus or Donusa. Tiberius set aside his grudge and said that he disagreed with that sentence, because both those islands lacked water, and anyone to whom life was granted, was also to be granted the things necessary for life. As a result, Serenus was banished to Amorgus, one of the islands of the Sporades. {*Tacitus, Annals, l. 4. c. 28-30. 4:49-53}

6274. The ten-year term of Tiberius' empire had expired and he made no plans of resuming it by any decree for a further ten years, nor did he want to have it divided into ten-year periods, as Augustus had done. He just continued on by his own authority, but the decennial plays were nevertheless held. {*Dio, l. 57. (24) 7:181} [E817]

## 4028 AM, 4738 JP, 25 AD

6275. Valerius Gratus removed Eleazar from the high priesthood after one year and gave the office to Simon, the son of Camith. {*Josephus, Antiq., l. 18. c. 2. s. 2. (34) 9:29}

6276. The citizens of Cyzicum imprisoned some Roman citizens, and they had not completed the temple for Augustus, which they had started to build. For this, they had their liberty taken from them again, which they had earned by being besieged in the war of Mithridates. {*Tacitus, Annals, l. 4. c. 36. 4:65} {*Dio, l. 57. (24) 7:183}

6277. Fonteius Capito, who had governed Asia as proconsul, was acquitted, because it was found that he had been falsely accused by Vibius Serenus. {*Tacitus, Annals, l. 4. c. 36. 4:65}

## 4029a AM, 4738 JP, 25 AD

6278. Eleven cities in Asia vied with great rivalry to see which of them would build the temple that was appointed for Tiberius and the Senate. Tiberius heard their envoys disputing in the Senate for many days over this matter. The cities of Hypaepa and Tralles, as also Laodicea and Magnesia, were eliminated as not having enough resources to do this. The city of Illium related how Troy was the mother of Rome, and it had a good argument, but its glory of antiquity was doubted and it was eliminated. The city of Halicarnassus affirmed that it had not been shaken by an earthquake for twelve hundred years and that the foundation of their temple was upon a natural rock. The city of Pergamum was excluded, because it already had a temple to Augustus and the senators thought one temple was enough for them. The Ephesians and Milesians were excluded, because their cities were already involved with the ceremonies of Apollo and Diana. The decision was between the cities of Sardis and Smyrna, and they each presented their case. The Senate preferred Smyrna, and Vibius Marius was of the opinion that Manius Lepidus, who governed that province, should be placed in charge of the new temple, in addition to his other duties. When Lepidus refused through modesty, the Senate by lot selected Valerius Naso, who had been praetor, for the job. {*Tacitus, Annals, l. 4. c. 55,56. 4:97-101}

## 4029b AM, 4739 JP, 26 AD

*6279.* When Simon had held the high priesthood for one year, Valerius Gratus appointed Joseph as his successor in that office. He was surnamed Caiaphas, the son-in-law of Annas, or Ananus, who had formerly been removed from the priesthood. {*Joh 18:13*} After the annual changes of the high priest were completed, Gratus returned to Rome, after having been in Judea for eleven years. {*\*Josephus, Antiq., l. 18. c. 2. s. 2. (34,35) 9:29,31*} Due to this last mentioned fact, we are more inclined to connect these changes to the end of his government, than to the beginning.

*6280.* Pontius Pilate was sent out as the successor to Valerius Gratus. {*\*Josephus, Antiq., l. 18. c. 2. s. 2. (35) 9:31*} Philo documented Pilate's actions in his government. {*\*Philo, Gaius, l. 1. c. 38. 10:151*} [K566] Philo wrote that Pilate was afraid that the embassy, which had been sent by the Jews to confiscate the bucklers dedicated to him within the Holy City, would find out about his other crimes:

> "sale of justice, rapines, slaughters, rackings, condemning innocent men to death, savage cruelty...."

## 4030a AM, 4739 JP, 26 AD

*6281.* The thirtieth Jubilee happened in the thirtieth year of our Lord Jesus Christ, which marked the beginning of his gospel. It was now proclaimed by the voice of one crying in the wilderness:

> "Prepare ye the way of the Lord, make his paths straight." {*Mr 1:1-3*}

*6282.* He also proclaimed the start of the acceptable year of the Lord, or the time of his divine pleasure, in which the God showed the Great One to the world. {*Isa 61:2 Lu 4:19*}

*6283.* It was in the 15th year of the reign of Tiberius Caesar (being the 13th year of his empire, which began after the death of Augustus) when Pontius Pilate was governor of Judea, Herod Antipas was tetrarch of Galilee and his brother Philip tetrarch of Iturea and the region of Trachonitis, and Lysanias tetrarch of Abilene—under the priesthoods of Annas and Caiaphas, that the word of the Lord came to John, the son of Zacharias, in the desert. {*Lu 3:1,2*} By God's authority, he was a Nazarite who was both a priest and prophet of the Lord and baptized in the desert of Judea. (The area referred to is that mentioned in Joshua. {*Jos 15:1-6*}) He preached the baptism of repentance for the remission of sins. {*Mt 3:1,2 Mr 1:4 Lu 3:3*} By his ministry, he announced Christ, who would come after him, and made him known to Israel. {*Joh 1:7,8,13*} In order that John would know with certainty who he was, God gave him this sign. He would know that the one on whom he saw

the Holy Spirit descending and remaining, was the one who would baptize others with the Holy Spirit. {*Joh 1:33*}

*6284.* It is most probable that his ministry began on that most appropriate day, the tenth day of the seventh month (about the 9th day of our October); this was the solemn fast when whoever did not afflict his soul was to be cut off from his people. It was the day of atonement, on which the high priest went into the holy of holies with blood that was offered to expiate the sins of the people. On the same day, a trumpet was sounded, announcing the start of the year of Jubilee in the land. {*Le 25:9,10*}

*6285.* Hence, John the Baptist was the preacher of repentance and remission of sins, to be attained by the blood of Christ, who was to come. [E818] John went into every region around Jordan, lifting up his voice like a trumpet and proclaiming:

> "Repent, for the kingdom of heaven is at hand."

*6286.* Many came to him from Jerusalem, from all Judea and the regions around the Jordan River. This would be especially true of that large multitude who returned from Jerusalem after the feast of tabernacles was over, around the beginning of November. Many were baptized by him in the Jordan and confessed their sins. {*Mt 3:2,3,5,6 Mr 1:5*}

*6287.* John had a garment of camel's hair and a leather belt about his waist, like Elijah. {*2Ki 1:8*} He ate locusts, which was a clean, inexpensive food, {*Le 11:22*} and wild honey. {*Mt 3:4 Mr 1:6*} [K567]

*6288.* John sharply rebuked the Pharisees who came to his baptism. {*Mt 3.7 Lu 3:7*} The people asked John what they were to do and he instructed them. {*Lu 3:10-14*} When the people wondered if John was the Christ, John answered:

> "I indeed baptize you with water, but there cometh one who is more powerful than I, whose shoe latchet I am not worthy to unloose, he shall baptize you with the Holy Spirit and with fire, whose fan is in his hand, and he will thoroughly purge his floor and gather his wheat into his barn, and will burn up the chaff with unquenchable fire." {*Lu 3:15-17 Mt 3:11,12 Mr 1:7,8*}

## 4030b AM, 4740 JP, 27 AD

*6289.* When all the people were being baptized, Jesus came from Nazareth of Galilee to the Jordan, to be baptized by John. {*Lu 3:21 Mt 3:13 Mr 1:9*} John denied that Jesus needed any baptism from him, but the Lord urged him and said that it was necessary, so that all righteousness would be fulfilled. Then John baptized him. {*Mt 3:14,15*} Jesus was about thirty years old. {*Lu 3:23*}

*6290.* A most obvious manifestation of the trinity was given. The Son of God, in the human nature which he had assumed, ascended out of the water and was praying; the heavens were opened and the Spirit of God was seen in bodily form, like a dove, descending on him. The voice of the Father was heard from heaven, saying:

> "This is my beloved Son, in whom I am well pleased."
> {Mt 3:16,17 Mr 1:10,11 Lu 3:21,22}

6291. Jesus was full of the Holy Spirit and returned from the Jordan. He was driven by the Spirit into the desert, where he was tempted for forty days and nights by Satan, while he remained among wild beasts. He ate nothing and after this was over, he was hungry. {Lu 4:1,2 Mt 4:1,2 Mr 1:12,13}

6292. Satan then presented the Lord with a threefold temptation. When this was over, Satan left him for a time {Mt 4:3-11 Lu 4:3-13} and the angels came and ministered to him. {Mt 4:11 Mr 1:13} Jesus returned into Galilee in the power of the Spirit. {Lu 4:14}

6293. Herod Agrippa, the son of Aristobulus, had by Cypros, the daughter of Phasael Agrippa the younger, a son who was the last king of the Jews. This Herod the younger is mentioned in Acts. {Ac 25:1-26:32} He was seventeen years old when his father died. {*Josephus, Antiq., l. 18. c. 5. s. 4. (137) 9:93} {*Josephus, Antiq., l. 19. c. 9. s. 1. (354) 9:383}

## 4031 AM, 4741 JP, 28 AD

6294. Berenice, his sister, of whom mention is likewise made in Acts, was born. She was later married to Herod, the king of Chalcis, and was sixteen years old when her father died. {Ac 25:13} {*Josephus, Antiq., l. 18. c. 5. s. 4. (137) 9:93} {*Josephus, Antiq., l. 19. c. 9. s. 1. (354) 9:383}

## 4033a AM, 4742 JP, 29 AD

6295. The fourth year of John the Baptist's ministry started. His ministry of preparing the people for Christ was drawing to a close, for this was his primary purpose. The Lord himself, whose way John had prepared, now entered into his ministry. He executed his prophetic office and sealed his ministry with famous miracles, for John did no miracles. {Joh 10:41} John's ministry of preparation was celebrated by Isaiah and Malachi, so many ages before. [K568] It should not be surprising that we assigned so long a period of time to it, when one considers that for so great a work a shorter time would have been too short, especially without the help of miracles to accomplish all that the angel Gabriel confirmed to his father, Zacharias, that John would do:

> "Many of the children of Israel shall he turn to the Lord their God, and he shall go before him in the spirit and power of Elijah, that he may turn the hearts of the fathers to the children, and the disobedient to the wisdom of the just, and to prepare a people ready for the Lord." {Lu 1:16,17}

6296. The following words of Paul argue that not a short period of time, but a full course of preaching, was to be finished by John before the coming of the Lord:

> "When John had first preached before his coming the baptism of repentance to all the people of Israel. And as John fulfilled his course, he said, Whom think ye that I am? I am not he. But, behold there cometh one after me, whose shoes of his feet I am not worthy to loose." {Ac 13:24,25}

## 4033b AM, 4743 JP, 30 AD

6297. The day after Christ had come, the Jews from Jerusalem sent some priests and Levites of the sect of the Pharisees to John, as he was baptising at Bethabara by the Jordan. They asked him to tell them plainly if he was the Christ, or not. He denied that he was Elijah, or that prophet who had been foretold by Moses. [E819] That prophet was in fact the Christ, but the Jews thought him to be another. {De 18:15 Ac 3:22 7:37} John said he was: {Joh 1:23}

> "The voice of one crying in the wilderness, make straight the way of the Lord."

6298. Then he added that testimony about Christ which Paul so praised in Acts:

> "I baptize with water, but there standeth one among you, whom ye know not, he it is, who cometh after me, who is preferred before me, whose shoe latchet I am not worthy to unloose." {Joh 1:19-28; 5:33}

6299. The next day, John saw Jesus coming to him and said:

> "Behold the Lamb of God that taketh away the sins of the world. This is he of whom I spoke, there cometh one after me, that is preferred before me, for he was before me... and I saw him, and testify that this is the Son of God." {Joh 1:29-34}

6300. The next day, as John stood with two of his disciples, he saw Jesus walking by and said: *Behold the Lamb of God.* When his two disciples heard this, they followed Jesus and stayed with him that day, for it was about the tenth hour (four o'clock). Andrew was one of these two, and he brought his brother Simon to Jesus. When Jesus saw Simon, he said: *You are Simon, son of Jona, you shall be called Cephas.* {Joh 1:35-42}

6301. The next day, Jesus went into Galilee and asked Philip (who was from Bethsaida, the city of Andrew and Simon Peter) to follow him. Philip found Nathanael under a fig tree and brought him to Jesus. Jesus said that he was truly an Israelite in whom there was no guile. Jesus then intimated that he was that ladder of heaven (foreshadowed by Jacob's dream, {*Ge 28:12*}) upon which the angels of God were seen ascending and descending. {*Joh 1:43-51*}

*6302.* On the third day, there was a marriage in Cana of Galilee, to which Jesus was invited, along with his mother and his disciples. There he turned the water into wine, which was his first miracle. His glory was thus shown and his disciples believed in him. {*Joh 2:1-11*} After this, he went down into Capernaum, and stayed there not many days with his mother, brethren and the disciples. {*Joh 2:12*} *[K569]*

*6303.* Now we have arrived at the public ministry of Christ, whose acts we have recorded according to the four distinct passovers, which we can gather from the harmony of the four gospels, as written by that learned man who has laboured much in the studies of the Holy Scriptures, John Richardson, Doctor of Divinity and worthy Bishop of Ardah, in our province of Armagh. In this record, it is noteworthy that only Matthew neglected the order of time, which is constantly observed by the other three gospels (if you exclude the parenthesis when John was cast into prison by Herod). {*Lu 3:19,20*} *[E820]*

The
FIRST PASSOVER
of the
MINISTRY of CHRIST.
{*Joh 2:13*}

From which the first year of the
seventieth and last week of Daniel
begins, in which the covenant is
confirmed with many.
{*Da 9:27 cf. Mt 26:28*}

*6304.* Jesus went to Jerusalem for the passover. {*Joh 2:13*}

*6305.* Jesus went into the temple, where he scourged those who bought and sold there and drove them out. As a sign of his authority, he told them how the temple of his body would be destroyed by the Jews and be raised again by himself. This event took place forty-six years after Herod started to build the temple. {*See note on 3987 AM. <<5944>>*} {*Joh 2:14-22*}

*6306.* He performed miracles and many believed in him, but he did not commit himself to them, because he knew what was in man. {*Joh 2:23-25*}

*6307.* He instructed Nicodemus, the disciple who came to him by night, about the mystery of regeneration, about faith, about his death and about the condemnation of unbelievers. {*Joh 3:1-21*}

## 4034a AM, 4743 JP, 30 AD

*6308.* Jesus left Jerusalem and went into the land of Judea with his disciples. {*Joh 3:22*}

*6309.* Jesus stayed there and baptized people. (That is, his disciples baptized people who had been baptized before, either by himself or John.) John baptized in Aenon, for he had not yet been cast into prison. {*Joh 3:22-24*}

*6310.* John's disciples and the Jews had a discussion about purifying. {*Joh 3:25*} *[K570]*

*6311.* John instructed his disciples, who were envious of Jesus. John told them about Jesus and his office and of the excellency of Jesus Christ, the Son of God. He gave this notable and last testimony to him before his own imprisonment. {*Joh 3:26-36*}

*6312.* Herod, the tetrarch, cast John into prison for reprehending his incest with his brother Philip's wife, as well as his wickedness. {*Mr 6:17-20 Mt 14:3-5*}

*6313.* Jesus heard that John had been cast into prison and that the Pharisees had heard that Jesus had made and baptized many disciples, that is, at the hand of his disciples. He left Judea, after he had stayed there about eight months, and went into Galilee. {*Joh 4:1-3 Mt 4:12*}

*6314.* Jesus needed to go through Samaria, where he converted the Samaritan woman near the city of Sychar, as well as the citizens of Sychar. *[E821]* It was four months before the harvest (or the passover, about the middle of the ninth month, called Abib or Nisan). {*Joh 4:4-42*}

*6315.* After having stayed two days in Sychar, he continued on to Galilee. This was his second return from Judea to Galilee since his baptism. {*Joh 4:43,44*}

*6316.* Jesus was welcomed by the Galileans, who had seen what great things he had done at Jerusalem. He preached with great fame in their synagogues. {*Joh 4:45 Lu 4:14,15 Mr 1:14,15*}

*6317.* In Cana, Jesus healed the sick son of a nobleman. This was the second miracle that Jesus did, when he left Judea and came to Galilee. {*Joh 4:46-54*}

## 4034b AM, 4744 JP, 31 AD

*6318.* He did miracles in Capernaum and later came to Nazareth, where he had been raised, and there entered the synagogue. As his custom was, he expounded the prophecy of Isaiah about himself. The citizens first wondered at this, but later were filled with wrath. They threw him out of the city and tried to push him headlong down from a hill. However, he passed through the crowd and went on his way. {*Lu 4:16-30*}

6319. He left Nazareth and lived at Capernaum. He taught them on the Sabbath days and they were astonished at his doctrine. {Lu 4:31,32 Mr 1:21,22 Mt 4:13-17}

6320. In the synagogue of Capernaum, he cast out an unclean spirit and ordered the spirit not to tell who he was. {Lu 4:33-37 Mr 1:23-28} [K571]

6321. He left the synagogue and went into the house of Simon and Andrew, where he healed Simon's wife's mother, who lay sick with a fever. {Lu 4:38,39 Mr 1:29-31 Mt 8:14,15}

6322. About sunset, he healed all the sick who were brought to him and cast out demons. He ordered the demons not to speak. {Lu 4:40,41 Mr 1:32-34 Mt 8:16,17}

6323. In the morning, he went into a deserted place to pray. When Simon and others looked for him and tried to prevent him from leaving, he replied that he had to preach to other cities also. {Lu 4:42-44 Mr 1:35-39}

6324. He went throughout Galilee, teaching in their synagogues and casting out demons. {Lu 4:44 Mr 1:39}

6325. As he stood by the Lake of Gennesaret, a large multitude pressed upon him, so he entered into Simon's ship and taught the multitude from there. {Lu 5:1-4}

6326. When he had finished speaking, the disciples went fishing at his command and caught a large number of fish. Simon Peter, Andrew, James and John were astonished. Jesus commanded them to follow him and he would make them fishers of men. {Lu 5:4-11 Mr 1:16-20 Mt 4:18-22}

6327. Jesus went throughout Galilee and taught in their synagogues and healed every disease. His fame spread throughout all of Syria and a large multitude followed him. {Mt 4:23-25}

6328. In a certain city, he healed a leper. Jesus forbade the man to tell anyone, but he told everyone he met. People came to him from every place, to hear him and to be healed. So many came, that he could not publicly enter the city and he went into deserted places and prayed. {Lu 5:12-16 Mr 1:40-45 Mt 8:1-4}

6329. After some days, he again returned to his own city of Capernaum, where he taught them at home. In the presence of the scribes, the Pharisees and a large crowd, he forgave the sins of someone who was sick with the palsy. The sick man had been let down through the roof of the house and Jesus healed the disease, to the astonishment of them all. {Lu 5:17-26 Mr 2:1-12 Mt 9:1-8} [E822]

6330. Jesus went out again along the shore and all the multitude came to him and he taught them. As he passed by, he saw and called Levi, or Matthew, who was sitting at the tax collector's booth. {Lu 5:27,28 Mr 2:13,14 Mt 9:9} [K572]

6331. In the house of Levi, Jesus defended himself and his disciples, for they ate with tax collectors. He excused and vindicated them against the Pharisees, because his disciples did not fast. {Lu 5:29-39 Mr 2:15-22 Mt 9:10-13}

6332. It came to pass on the second Sabbath, after the first (that is, the first Sabbath of the new year, which had been instituted after the Jews left Egypt and which began from the month of Nisan, or Abib), that Jesus went through the grain fields. After clearing his disciples from the reproach of the Pharisees, because they had plucked the ears of grain, he explained the doctrine of the Sabbath. {Lu 6:1-5 Mr 2:23-28 Mt 12:1-8}

## The SECOND PASSOVER
## of the
## MINISTRY of CHRIST.
{Joh 5:1 cf. Joh 4:3,5,35}

From which begins the second year
of the 70th week of Daniel.

6333. After these things, the feast of the Jews was approaching and Jesus went up to Jerusalem. On the Sabbath day, he healed a man who lay at the pool of Bethesda and who had been crippled for thirty-eight years. He responded to the Jews, who were seeking to kill him for saying that God was his Father. {Joh 5:1-47}

6334. He went from there and again entered a synagogue and taught the people. He healed a man who had a withered hand. The Pharisees went out immediately and discussed with the Herodians how they could destroy him. {Lu 6:6-11 Mr 3:1-6 Mt 12:9-14}

6335. When Jesus knew this, he withdrew himself to the lake side and healed the multitudes who followed him, strictly charging them not to make him known. He told his disciples to have a small boat ready for him, because of the multitudes who thronged him. {Mr 3:7-12 Mt 12:15-21}

6336. It came to pass in those days, that he went into a mountain to pray and continued all night in prayer. When it was day, he chose the twelve whom he called apostles. {Lu 6:12-16 Mr 3:13-19} [K573]

6337. Jesus went down with them and stood in a plain, where a large multitude came to him and he healed all who were sick. {Lu 6:17-19}

6338. They went into a house and the multitude gathered again, so much so, that they could not even eat a meal. When his friends heard of all this, they went to seize Jesus, for they said that he was beside himself. {Mr 3:19-21}

*6339.* When he saw the multitude, he went up into a mountain and as he sat down, his disciples came to him. He then preached that long and excellent sermon, first to the apostles and later to all the people. {*Lu 6:20-49 Mt 5:1-7:29*} *[E823]*

*6340.* When he had finished speaking to the people, he went into Capernaum and healed the centurion's servant, who lay sick with the palsy and was almost dead. {*Lu 7:1-10 Mt 8:5-13*}

*6341.* The next day, he went into the city of Nain and raised a man who was dead and was being carried out for burial. He was the only son of a widow. After this, his fame spread abroad. {*Lu 7:11-17*}

*6342.* While John was in prison, he was told by his disciples about the fame and the deeds of Jesus. John sent two of them to Jesus to ask him if he was the one they should expect, or whether they should look for someone else. After they returned to John with Jesus' answer, Jesus gave a great testimony about John. Then he upbraided some cities for their ingratitude. He rested in the fact of the divine sovereignty of his Father, who hid these things from some and revealed them to others. {*Lu 7:18-35 Mt 11:2-30*}

*6343.* Simon, the Pharisee, wanted Jesus to dine with him. As they were eating, Simon criticised the actions of a woman, because she was a great sinner. Jesus defended the woman, who washed his feet with her tears and wiped them with the hairs of her head, kissing and anointing them. {*Lu 7:36-50*}

*6344.* It came about later, that he went out from the city and preached. His disciples were with him and certain women ministered to him. {*Lu 8:1-3*} *[K574]*

*6345.* They brought him someone who had a demon and who was blind and dumb. Jesus healed him and vigorously defended himself against the Pharisees and scribes, who came down from Jerusalem and blasphemed him by saying that he cast out demons through Beelzebub. {*Mr 3:22-30 Mt 12:22-37*} Some of the scribes and Pharisees asked for a sign, but after Jesus had sharply rebuked them, he gave them no other sign than that of Jonah. {*Mt 12:38-45*}

*6346.* While he spoke to the people, he was told that his mother and brethren stood outside and wanted to see and speak with him. Jesus replied by declaring to them whom he considered to be his mother, brothers and sisters. {*Lu 8:19-21 Mr 3:31-35 Mt 12:46-50*}

*6347.* That same day, Jesus left the house and sat by the shore. Large multitudes came to him, so that he got into a boat. He sat and taught them many things through the parable of the sower and many other parables. {*Lu 8:4-18 Mr 4:1-34 Mt 13:1-53*}

*6348.* That same day at evening, he told his disciples to sail across the lake. When he had given an answer to some who wanted to follow him, he sent away the multitudes. As they were sailing, a strong wind and storm came up. He rebuked the wind and calmed the sea and saved his disciples. {*Lu 8:22-26 Mr 4:35-41 Mt 8:18-27*}

*6349.* They reached the other side, which was the country of the Gadarenes, or Gergesenes, on the opposite shore from Galilee. When he came ashore, he was met by two fierce men who were possessed with demons. (Mark and Luke mention only one man.) He cast out the demons and allowed them to enter into a herd of swine. {*Lu 8:26-36 Mr 5:1-16 Mt 8:28-33*} The Gadarenes asked him to leave their country, while the previously possessed persons begged to be allowed to stay with Jesus. This request was denied and Jesus sent them back to proclaim around Decapolis what great things Jesus had done for them. *[E824]* Jesus sailed across the lake again to his own city of Capernaum. {*Lu 8:37-39 Mr 5:17-20 Mt 8:34*} *[K575]*

*6350.* It came to pass that when Jesus returned, the people gladly welcomed him, for they had been waiting for him. He was by the shore. {*Lu 8:40 Mr 5:21*}

*6351.* The disciples of John came to him and asked why they and the Pharisees fasted often, but Jesus' disciples did not fast? He answered their question. {*Mt 9:14-17*}

*6352.* While he was speaking, Jairus, one of the rulers of the synagogue, came and begged him to heal his only daughter. She was about twelve years old and lay at the point of death. As he was walking along and almost at Jairus' house, a woman who had had an issue of blood for twelve years was suddenly healed by touching the hem of Jesus' garment. The dead daughter of Jairus was restored to life by his word alone. He strictly ordered them to tell no one about it. {*Lu 8:41-56 Mr 5:22-42 Mt 9:18-26*}

*6353.* When he departed from there, two blind men followed him, whom he healed. He strictly ordered them to tell no one, but they told everyone they met. {*Mt 9:27-31*}

*6354.* As they went out, a dumb man who was possessed with a demon was brought to Jesus. When the demon was cast out, the dumb man spoke and the multitude marvelled, but the Pharisees blasphemed. {*Mt 9:32-34*}

*6355.* Jesus went all around their cities and villages, teaching them and healing their diseases. When he came into his own country with his disciples, he taught in their synagogue on the Sabbath day. He was once again despised by them and called the carpenter, even though they were astonished at his doctrine. {*Mr 6:1-6 Mt 13:54-58*}

6356. He went around their villages and taught them. {Mr 6:6}

6357. He was moved with compassion toward the multitude when he saw how large the harvest was and how few labourers there were. He told his disciples that they should pray to the Lord that he would send forth more labourers. {Mt 9:35-38}

6358. Jesus sent out the twelve apostles, two by two. He instructed them to preach and gave them power to heal diseases. {Lu 9:1-5 Mr 6:7-11 Mt 10:1-42}

6359. It came to pass that, after Jesus had finished instructing his disciples, he departed from there to teach and to preach in their cities. {Mt 11:1,12-16} [K576]

6360. After the twelve had departed, they went through the towns, preaching the gospel and healing everywhere. {Lu 9:6}

## 4035a AM, 4744 JP, 31 AD

6361. On the 17th of November, Sejanus was killed. {*Tacitus, Annals, l. 6. c. 25. 4:195} After his death, Tiberius knew immediately that all the crimes of which Sejanus had accused the Jews were imaginary. Therefore, Tiberius commanded the governments of all the provinces that in every town, this nationality was to be spared. Only a very few, who were guilty persons, should be punished. They should not alter their customs, but should take note that these men were lovers of peace and their customs were for the public peace. {*Philo, Gaius, l. 1. c. 24. (160) 10:81}

## 4035b AM, 4745 JP, 32 AD

6362. After Severus, the governor of Egypt, had died, Tiberius appointed Flaccus Avillius, one of his friends, as his successor for six years. He governed the province well for the first five years, as long as Tiberius was alive. {*Philo, Flaccus, l. 1. c. 1. (2) 9:303} [E825]

6363. John the Baptist was beheaded. {Mt 14:10}

6364. When his disciples heard this, they came and took up the body and buried it, and came and told Jesus. {Mr 6:27-29 Mt 14:6-12}

6365. Herod the tetrarch and others heard of the fame of Jesus and Herod wanted to see him. {Lu 9:7-9 Mt 14:1-4}

6366. When the apostles returned, they told Jesus the things they had done. {Lu 9:10 Mr 6:30}

6367. When Jesus had been told of the death of John and of the deeds of the apostles, he told them to go to a deserted place and rest for a while. The multitude had kept them so busy, they had not had time to eat. He set sail with the twelve and privately went into a deserted place near Bethesda. When the multitude heard about it, they followed him on foot from all the cities and came to him. So Jesus taught and healed them. {Lu 9:10,11 Mr 6:31-34 Mt 14:13,14}

6368. Jesus went up into a mountain and sat there with his disciples. [K577] The passover was close at hand. That evening, he fed more than five thousand men, in addition to women and children, with five barley loaves and two little fishes. There were twelve baskets full of the leftovers. When they wanted to make him a king, Jesus constrained his disciples to go ahead of him to the other side, opposite to Bethesda, toward Capernaum, while he went alone up into a mountain. When the disciples had gone about three or four miles, Jesus walked out to them on the sea in the fourth watch of the night. He told them not to be afraid. Peter asked to join him and walked out to Jesus. When Peter began to sink, Jesus rebuked him for having little faith. They were all amazed. They landed and came to the country of Gennesaret. When he left the boat, as soon as it became known, they brought their sick, so that they could touch the hem of his garment, and they were made whole. {Joh 6:1-21 Lu 9:12-17 Mr 6:35-56 Mt 14:15-36}

6369. The following day after Jesus had crossed over, the people who stood on the side of the lake Jesus had left, sailed to Capernaum to look for Jesus. He preached to them in the synagogue of Capernaum about the bread of life and affirmed to the Jews who murmured, that he was the bread of life. From that time, many of his disciples left him, but the apostles did not go away. However, he called one of them a devil. {Joh 6:22-71}

### The THIRD PASSOVER
### of the
### MINISTRY of CHRIST
{Joh 6:4}

From which began the third year
of the 70th week of Daniel.

6370. The scribes and Pharisees who came from Jerusalem, went to Jesus. When they saw some of his disciples eat with unwashed hands, they found fault with them for not following the traditions of the elders. [E826] [K578] Jesus answered them about their traditions; he told them that they frustrated the commands of God, in order to keep the traditions of men. He taught the people, and also told his disciples at home, that nothing which enters into a man defiles him, but that it is what comes from within that defiles a man. {Mr 7:1-23 Mt 15:1-20}

6371. Jesus left and went into the country of Tyre and Sidon, but he could not escape the crowds. A Canaanite woman, a Gentile of the Syrophoenician nationality, came to him and earnestly begged him for her daughter, who was possessed by a demon. Jesus praised her great faith and cast out the demon from her daughter. {Mr 7:24-30 Mt 15:21-28}

6372. After he left the country of Tyre and Sidon, he came to the Sea of Galilee through the middle of the country of Decapolis. They brought him a deaf man, who also had a speech impediment. Jesus healed him, ordering him in vain not to tell anyone. {Mr 7:31-37}

6373. When he went up into a mountain, he sat there and healed many, and the multitude wondered. {Mt 15:29-31}

6374. In those days, when a very large multitude had stayed with him in the desert for three days, he fed four thousand men, in addition to women and children, with only seven loaves and a few little fishes. They gathered seven baskets full of leftovers. {Mr 8:1-9 Mt 15:32-38}

6375. Immediately, Jesus dismissed the crowd and with his disciples sailed over to the country of Dalmanutha or Magdala. {Mr 8:10 Mt 15:39}

6376. The Pharisees came and required a sign from him from heaven. Jesus sighed deeply, then refused to give them any sign but that of Jonah. He called them hypocrites because they knew how to tell the weather from the appearance of the sky, but could not discern the times. He left them and sailed to the other side. {Mr 8:11-13 Mt 16:1-4}

6377. When he and his disciples reached the other side, they had forgotten to take food with them and had only one loaf of bread with them in the ship. When Jesus warned them to beware of the leaven of the Pharisees and Sadducees and the leaven of Herod, they reasoned among themselves that Jesus had said this, because they had forgotten to take bread. [K579] Jesus rebuked them for having forgotten the miraculous multiplication of the loaves and helped them understand that he was speaking, not of the leaven of bread, but of doctrine. {Mr 8:12-14 Mt 16:5-12}

6378. Then he came to Bethsaida and a blind man was brought to him. The blind man was led out of town, and Jesus anointed his eyes with spittle and his sight was restored. Jesus forbade him to tell anyone about it. {Mr 8:22-26}

6379. Jesus and his disciples went into the towns of Caesarea Philippi. It came to pass, as he was alone with his disciples, praying, and then as they were going along the way, he asked his disciples who the people thought he was. When they had answered, he asked them their opinion. When Peter answered that he was the Christ, Jesus declared him blessed and gave him promises. He

forbade his disciples to tell anyone that he was the Christ. He foretold his death and resurrection and called Peter *Satan*, because he rebuked Jesus for talking about his death. Then he preached to his disciples and the multitude about that cross which everyone must bear who will follow him. Finally, he foretold them of his second coming. {Lu 9:18-27 Mr 8:27-38 Mt 16:13-28} [E827]

6380. About eight days after these sayings (or six intermediate days), Jesus was transfigured on a high mountain. When they came down from the mountain, he commanded them not to tell anyone what they had seen, until he had risen from the dead. They kept this private and asked one another what the rising from the dead might mean. They asked him why the scribes were saying that Elijah must first come. From Jesus' reply they understood that Jesus was speaking of John the Baptist as being Elijah. {Lu 9:28-36 Mr 9:1-13 Mt 17:1-13}

6381. After this, on the next day, as they were coming down from the hill, Jesus came to his disciples. He saw a large multitude around them and the scribes asking questions. [K580] When all the multitude saw him, they were greatly amazed and ran at once to greet him. As he was asking about their questions, the father of a lunatic child told him that it was about his child, who had an unclean spirit and was deaf and dumb. His disciples had been unable to cast him out. Then Jesus cast out the spirit and restored the child, now well, to his father. When Jesus went home, he explained to his disciples the reason why they had been unable to cast out this demon. {Lu 9:37-42 Mr 9:14-29 Mt 17:14-21}

6382. They departed from there and passed through Galilee. Jesus did not want anyone to know, because he was teaching his disciples about his death and resurrection, but they did not understand this. They were deeply grieved, but were afraid to ask him. {Lu 9:43-45 Mr 9:30-32 Mt 17:22,23}

6383. When they came to Capernaum, Peter was asked about Jesus' tribute money. When Jesus came into the house, he anticipated Peter's question and told him that he would find a coin in a fish's mouth and he was to use it to pay the tribute for both of them. {Mt 17:24-27}

6384. At Capernaum, Jesus asked his disciples what they had been discussing on the way. At first they were silent, and then they said that it was about who would be greatest in the kingdom of heaven. Jesus took a child and placed him in their midst and taught that they should have just such childlike humility. He warned them that the world was full of stumbling blocks and that they must take heed that neither hand, nor foot, nor eye cause them to offend. Little children were not to be despised.

If our brother sinned against us, he was to be reproved. He told of the power of the church to bind and loose. They were to forgive someone who asked for forgiveness as much as seventy times seven times, as he illustrated in the parable of the two debtors and the king. {Lu 9:46-48 Mr 9:33-37 Mt 18:1-35}

6385. John replied and said that they had seen one casting out demons through Christ's name. Jesus taught that he was not to be forbidden and again warned them about not offending little ones and about seeing to it that neither hand, foot, nor eye caused them to offend. {Lu 9:49,50 Mr 9:38-50} [K581]

6386. Junius Gallio, who was trying to induce the soldiers to be loyal to the state rather than the emperor, proposed that, when their time of service had expired, Tiberius' Praetorian Guard should sit in the same benches with the equestrians to see the plays. Tiberius banished him, under the pretence that Gallio would seem to be persuading the soldiers to be loyal to the state rather than to Tiberius. [E828] When someone wrote that it would be easy for him to endure his banishment on so pleasant an island as Lesbos was, he was brought back to Rome and handed over to the custody of the magistrates. {*Tacitus, Annals, l. 6. c. 3. 4:157,159} {*Dio, l. 58. (18) 7:233}

6387. Cassius Severus, the orator, died in the twenty-fifth year of his banishment on the island of Seriphos. He had been reduced to such poverty, that he scarcely had a cloth to preserve his modesty. {*Eusebius, Chronicles, l. 1. 1:258}

6388. At Rome a proposal was made in the Senate by Quintilian, the tribune of the people, concerning a Sibylline book. Caninius Gallus, one of the Fifteen for Religious Ceremonies, had requested that it be included among other books by the same prophetess and passed a decree of the Senate to ratify it. When this was done by joint vote, Tiberius sent letters mildly rebuking the tribune as not being well-versed in the old customs, because he was young. He attacked Gallus very smartly, as he was a man with much experience in the ceremonies, who, in spite of this, had introduced the business into the Senate at a time when many of the senators had been absent. He pointed out that the author of the poem was uncertain and the college had not delivered their opinion on it. Also, the poem had not been revised and adjusted by the masters (of the priests), according to the usual custom. As a result, the book was referred to the cognizance of the Fifteen. {*Tacitus, Annals, l. 6. c. 12. 4:175}

## 4036a AM, 4745 JP, 32 AD

6389. After these things Jesus walked about in Galilee, for he would not walk about in Judea, because the Jews were seeking to kill him. The feast of tabernacles was approaching and Jesus did not go up to the feast at that time, as his brothers wished. As of yet, they did not believe in him. Jesus went up after them, not publicly but privately. {Joh 7:1-10}

6390. It came to pass, when the days were approaching for his ascension, he resolutely set out for Jerusalem. He sent messengers ahead into a village of the Samaritans to prepare a place for them to stay. [K582] That village would not accept him and they went into another village. He rebuked his disciples, who wanted fire to come down from heaven upon the people. {Lu 9:51-56}

6391. As they were walking along the way, Jesus answered some who wanted to follow him. {Lu 9:57-62}

6392. After this, Jesus sent seventy disciples, two by two, into every town and place where he was going to proclaim that the kingdom of God was at hand, and gave them power to authenticate their message. {Lu 10:1-16}

6393. The multitude asked after him and murmured about him. Midway through the feast, Jesus taught in the temple. When they wondered at his doctrine, he answered that his doctrine was not his own, but belonged to the one who had sent him. He said many things in reply to those who reproached him and objected to his words. Officers were sent to apprehend him. On the last and greatest day of the feast, Jesus spoke out loudly concerning faith in him. There was a division over him among the people, but the officers who had been sent, and Nicodemus, defended Jesus and his cause before the Pharisees, who spoke against Jesus. {Joh 7:11-53} [E829]

6394. Jesus went to the Mount of Olives and early in the morning he again sat and taught in the temple. He was not willing to condemn, in the manner of a judge, the woman taken in adultery, but warned her to sin no more. He taught in the treasury of the temple, affirming that he was the light of the world and defending the fact that he testified on his own behalf. He taught many things concerning the Father and himself, about where he was going, who he is, about their father Abraham, about the servitude of sin and the Devil. He denied that he had a demon, as the people thought. He said that whoever kept his sayings would not taste death. He finished by saying that he was before Abraham. At this, they took up stones to throw at him, but Jesus hid himself and went out of the temple, right through their midst, and so passed by. {Joh 8:1-59} [K583]

6395. As Jesus passed by, he saw a man begging, who had been blind from his youth, and healed him. When the beggar and his parents were examined by the authorities, he was expelled from the synagogue, after which he found and worshipped Jesus. {Joh 9:1-41}

6396. Jesus preached that he was the door of the sheepfold and the good shepherd. He taught about thieves and hirelings and once again there was a division among the Jews because of these sayings. {Joh 10:1-21}

6397. The seventy returned with joy, and he further warned and instructed them. He told them privately that they were blessed and should rejoice that their names were written in heaven. {Lu 10:17-24}

6398. A certain lawyer asked him what he must do to inherit eternal life. Jesus instructed him from the law, using the parable of the man who fell among thieves to teach him who his neighbour was. {Lu 10:25-37}

6399. As he went on his way, he came to a certain town and was invited into the house of Martha. She herself ministered to them, while Mary heard the words of Jesus. Jesus said that Mary had chosen the better part. {Lu 10:38-42}

## 4036b AM, 4746 JP, 33 AD

6400. One day, he was praying in a certain place. When he stopped, one of his disciples asked him to teach them to pray as John had taught his disciples. Therefore he, for the second time, prescribed to them the Lord's prayer. He also used arguments to stir them up to constancy in prayer and for obtaining the assurance of their faith. {Lu 11:1-13}

6401. Jesus cast out a demon from a man who was mute and the multitude marvelled. He rebuked some blasphemers and denied that he was casting out the demons through Beelzebub. {Lu 11:14-26}

6402. It came to pass as he spoke these things, that a certain woman in the crowd said to him that his mother was blessed. [K584] His reply to her was that those are blessed who hear the Word of God and keep it. {Lu 11:27,28}

6403. When the multitude had increased around him, he said that their generation was seeking a sign, but that they would have no sign except that of Jonah. He added that the queen of the south and the Ninevites would condemn that generation. They were to take heed that the light that was in them was not really darkness. {Lu 11:29-36}

6404. When he had spoken these things, a certain Pharisee invited him to dine with him. When he wondered that Jesus had not first washed, Jesus severely reprehended him, along with the rest of the Pharisees, for their apparent outward holiness with hypocrisy, while inwardly there was wickedness, covetousness and pride. He pronounced a woe on the lawyers, also. {Lu 11:37-54}

6405. In the meantime, when an innumerable company were gathered together, Jesus warned his disciples to beware of the leaven of the Pharisees, which was hypocrisy, and not to be afraid of those who kill the body. {Lu 12:1-12} [E830]

6406. One of the company asked Jesus to talk to his brother, so that he would divide the inheritance with him. Jesus asked him who had made him a judge. On this occasion he preached against covetousness, using the parable of the rich man who wanted to build larger barns. He warned them against an anxious, distrustful and unprofitable carping about the necessary things of this life and urged them rather to seek the kingdom of God. They should be like those who wait for the coming of their Lord, as befits a faithful and wise steward. Jesus said that he would send the fire of division on the earth and upbraided them for not recognising that this was the appointed time. {Lu 12:13-59}

6407. At that time, some people told him of the Galileans whose blood Pilate had mingled with their sacrifices. From this, Jesus preached about repentance and propounded the parable of the barren fig tree. {Lu 13:1-9}

6408. He taught in one of the synagogues on the Sabbath day. There was a woman who for eighteen years had suffered with a spirit of infirmity and was bent over. He healed her on the Sabbath and defended the deed against the indignation of the ruler of the synagogue. [K585] Then he likened the kingdom of heaven to a grain of mustard seed and to leaven. {Lu 13:10-21}

6409. He went through all the cities and villages, teaching as he was journeying toward Jerusalem for the feast of dedication. {Lu 13:22}

6410. Someone asked him if there would only be a few who would be saved. He replied that they must strive to enter in at the narrow gate. {Lu 13:23-30}

6411. On the same day, some of the Pharisees came to him and warned him to leave the area, for Herod wanted to kill him. He gave them a resolute answer. {Lu 13:31-35}

6412. One sabbath day, he was invited into the house of one of the chief Pharisees, to dine with him. There was a man there afflicted with the dropsy, whom he healed. He defended the deed, although done on the Sabbath. He spoke a parable to those who had been invited to the feast and also instructed the Pharisee who had invited him to dine. {Lu 14:1-14}

6413. When one of those who was dining with him heard these things, he said to him that he who will eat bread in the kingdom of God was blessed. Jesus answered him by propounding the parable of the great supper and of each excuse made by those who were invited. {Lu 14:15-24}

6414. There was a large multitude going with him and he turned and preached to them that life itself is to be surrendered for Christ. He told them the parables of the man who was about to build a tower and of the king going to war. {Lu 14:25-35}

6415. All the tax collectors and sinners came to him to hear him, but the scribes and Pharisees murmured. He spoke the parables to them about the lost sheep, the lost coin and the prodigal son. {Lu 15:1-32}

6416. He told the disciples the parable of the unjust steward who was accused to his master, and drew a practical application from it. The Pharisees heard all these things and were covetous and derided him. He then preached against them and taught many other things, also telling about the rich man who fared sumptuously and of Lazarus the beggar. {Lu 16:1-31} [E831] [K586]

6417. Jesus warned his disciples about those who cause offences. He taught that the brother who sinned against them was to be forgiven. {Lu 17:1-4}

6418. Then the apostles asked Jesus to increase their faith. He spoke about the power of faith and told the parable of the servant who came in after working and immediately ministered to his master. He showed them that they were unprofitable servants when they had done all that they had been commanded, for they had done no more than what was their duty. {Lu 17:5-10}

6419. As he was going to Jerusalem, he travelled through Samaria and Galilee. He entered a certain village, where he was met by ten lepers. After they had been healed and were going to the priest as Jesus had commanded, only one of them came back to Jesus to thank him, and he was a Samaritan. {Lu 17:11-19}

6420. The Pharisees asked Jesus when the kingdom of God would come. Jesus replied that the kingdom of God would not come with observation, but was within. He told his disciples that just as it had been in the days of Noah and Lot, so it will be on the day that the Son of Man will be revealed. However, he first had to suffer many things. {Lu 17:20-37}

6421. He spoke a parable to them to illustrate that they should pray continually. He used the example of a widow who interceded with an unjust judge, and contrasted this with God, who is a just avenger. {Lu 18:1-8}

6422. He also spoke to some who thought that they were righteous and despised others. He told the parable about the Pharisee and tax collector praying in the temple. {Lu 18:9-14}

6423. At Jerusalem, during the feast of dedication in the winter time, Jesus was walking in the temple in Solomon's porch. The Jews came around him and asked how long he would keep them in suspense as to who he really was. He pointed to his miracles and said that he and his Father are one. [K587] Again they took up stones to stone him. He defended himself, proving from the scriptures and by his works that he was God. They tried again to take him, but he escaped from their hands. {Joh 10:22-39}

6424. Again he went beyond the Jordan River, to the place where John had first baptized, and stayed there, and many came to him. As was his custom, he taught them and healed them and many there believed in him. {Joh 10:40-42 Mr 10:1 Mt 19:1,2}

6425. The Pharisees came to him and tested him, asking if it was lawful for a man to divorce his wife for any reason. Jesus denied it and said to the Pharisees who objected, that the bill of divorce had been commanded by Moses. Jesus taught them the true meaning of marriage. When his disciples heard this, they said it was better for a man not to marry. {Mr 10:2-12 Mt 19:3-12}

6426. They brought little children to him, that he should lay his hands on them and pray. His disciples tried to prevent it and Jesus rebuked them. After he had laid his hands on the children and blessed them, he departed from there. {Lu 18:15-17 Mr 10:13-16 Mt 19:13-15}

6427. As Jesus was leaving, a rich young ruler met him on the way and asked him what he had to do to inherit eternal life. He called Jesus *Good Master*. Jesus spoke about the title he had given him and pointed him to the commandments. He replied that he had observed and kept them from his youth, and Jesus loved him. [E832] However, when he told him to sell all that he had and give to the poor, he sent him away very sorrowful. Jesus vehemently spoke against covetous rich men. {Lu 18:18-30 Mr 10:17-31 Mt 19:16-30} Peter replied that they had left everything to follow him. Jesus made notable promises to all who followed him, especially to his twelve apostles. He added that many who were first would be last. He instructed them with a parable of labourers going into a vineyard. Many were indeed called, but few were chosen. {Mt 20:1-16}

6428. Lazarus of Bethany was sick, so his sisters sent to Jesus, to tell him of his sickness. [K588] From the time that he heard that Lazarus was sick, he stayed where he was for a further two days, but later he told his disciples to go into Judea again. They reminded him that the Jews had just recently tried to stone him there and asked him whether he really wanted to go back again. Jesus replied that Lazarus was asleep, speaking of his death, not of his sleep, and that they should go to him. Thomas added that they may die with him. {Joh 11:1-16}

6429. When Jesus came near Bethany, he found that Lazarus had been buried and in the grave four days. Martha came to meet him and they talked about the resurrection. Mary heard of his coming and quickly came to him. When Jesus saw her weep, he also wept and went to the grave. He asked them to remove the stone and thanked his Father for hearing him. Jesus called Lazarus from his grave. Thereupon, many believed on him and some went to the Pharisees and told them the things Jesus had done. {Joh 11:17-46}

6430. Therefore, the Pharisees convened a council in which Caiaphas prophesied about Jesus. From that day on, they consulted together about how they could put him to death. They ordered that anyone who knew where he was, should tell them, so they could take him. On account of this, Jesus did not walk publicly among the Jews, but went into a town called Ephraim and stayed there with his disciples. {Joh 11:47-54}

6431. As they were on the way up to Jerusalem, Jesus went ahead of them and they were afraid. He again took the twelve aside and began to tell them all that would happen to him, but they did not understand. {Lu 18:31-34 Mr 10:32-34 Mt 20:17-19}

6432. James and John, the sons of Zebedee, with their mother, came to him and asked that they might sit with him in the kingdom, one on the right hand and the other on the left of Jesus. Jesus rebuked them and the rest were upset with the two disciples. Jesus admonished them all by saying that he who wanted to be great and first among them, had to be the minister and servant of all. {Mr 10:35-45 Mt 20:20-28} [K589]

6433. It happened that when he came near Jericho, a certain blind man sat begging by the roadside. When he asked who it was that was passing by and was told it was Jesus of Nazareth, he earnestly implored his mercy, even though the crowd rebuked him. Jesus called out to him and he received his sight and followed him, glorifying God. {Lu 18:35-43}

6434. As Jesus entered and passed through Jericho, he saw Zacchaeus in a sycamore tree and told him he needed to stay at his house that day. {Lu 19:1-10}

6435. As they left the city of Jericho, a large crowd followed him. He restored the sight of two blind men (one of whom was Bartimaeus), and they followed him. {Mr 10:46-52 Mt 20:29-34} [E833]

6436. When they heard all these things, and because they were near Jerusalem, they thought that the kingdom of God would appear immediately. As they went along, Jesus told the parable of the nobleman who went into a far country and gave his ten servants ten pounds, to invest until he returned. When he returned, he determined who had gained the most through trading and rewarded each of them according to the proportion of their gain. {Lu 19:11-27}

6437. The passover was near and many from the country went up to Jerusalem before the passover, to purify themselves. {Joh 11:55-57}

6438. Six days before the passover, therefore, Jesus came to Bethany. They prepared a supper for him and Lazarus sat with him. Mary anointed his feet and wiped them with the hairs of her head. Jesus rebuked Judas' criticism of her. Many people gathered there, not only because of Jesus, but in order to see Lazarus. However, the chief priests consulted how they could put Lazarus to death, as well, since many of the Jews believed in Jesus because of him. {Joh 12:1-11}

6439. Jesus went ahead and ascended up toward Jerusalem. It transpired that when he was near Bethphage and Bethany, at the mount called the Mount of Olives (Sunday, March 29), he sent two of his disciples for the foal of an ass, that was tied up in the town ahead. (Matthew also makes mention of the she-ass.) {Lu 19:28-35 Mr 11:1-7 Mt 21:1-7} [K590]

6440. Therefore, they brought the colt to Jesus, put their garments on it and Jesus sat on the colt. Many people met him, who were coming to the feast. Many cast their garments in his path and others cut down branches of trees and spread them in the road. When he came to the descent of the Mount of Olives, the crowd who went ahead of him and those who followed behind, cried: "Hosanna to the son of David." Some of the Pharisees told him to rebuke his followers, but he replied that he would not. Because of this, the Pharisees said among themselves that the whole world was following him. {Joh 12:12-19 Lu 19:36-40 Mr 11:8-10 Mt 21:8,9}

6441. When he came near and overlooked the city, he wept over it. He predicted her utter destruction. When he entered into Jerusalem, all the city was stirred and asked who he was. {Joh 12:19 Lu 19:41-44 Mr 11:10,11}

6442. Jesus went into the temple of God and cast out those who were buying and selling in it and healed the blind and the lame who were there. He justified the children who were crying 'hosanna' in the temple, over the objections of the Pharisees and scribes. He taught daily in the temple and those who heard him were very attentive, but the chief priests and elders of the people tried to kill him. {Lu 19:45-48 Mr 11:11 Mt 21:12-16}

6443. Some Greeks, who had come to worship at the feast, wanted to see him. He told the men who told him about these Greeks, about his passion. He called on his Father and received an answer from heaven. Some thought it was thunder and others thought an angel had spoken to him. He again spoke of the lifting up of the Son of Man from the earth. He gave an answer to those who asked him who the Son of Man was. [K591] After he left there, he hid himself from them. When it was evening, he went with the twelve to Bethany. Although he had done so many miracles among them, they still did not believe in him, so that the word of Isaiah might be fulfilled. [E834] However, many of the rulers believed in him, but did not confess him publicly for fear of the Pharisees. Jesus preached about having faith in himself. {Joh 12:20-50 Mt 11:17}

6444. The next morning, when he came from Bethany, he was hungry and saw a fig tree which had only leaves on it. He cursed it and it withered at once. They came to Jerusalem and entered the temple. He again expelled those who were buying and selling, and did not want anyone to carry merchandise through the temple. He taught them about having faith in himself. However, the chief priests looked for ways to kill him, for they feared him, because all the people were astonished at his doctrine. When evening came, Jesus left the city. {Mr 11:12-19 Mt 21:18,19}

6445. The next morning, as they passed the fig tree, they saw that it was dried up from the roots, as Peter observed. Jesus preached to them about the power of faith, especially in prayer. They again came to Jerusalem and as he walked in the temple and taught the people, the chief priests, elders and scribes came to him. They asked by whose authority he did these things. Jesus replied by asking them about John's baptism. He told them the parable of the two sons and asked them, which of the two had done the will of their father, and then applied it to them. He further told the parable of the vineyard, that was rented out to vine-growers who killed the heir of the vineyard, and he also made an application of this. Therefore, from that hour, they sought to apprehend him, but they feared the people, for the people thought he was a prophet. [K592] Again, he propounded the parable of the king's son to them, and the refusals and excuses of some who were invited and the wickedness and punishments of others, especially of the one who was not wearing a proper wedding garment. Then the Pharisees went and discussed how they could possibly trip him up in his talk. Therefore, they sent their disciples out to him, together with the Herodians, and these men asked him if it was lawful to pay tribute to Caesar. Astonished at his answer, they left him and went their way. {Lu 20:1-26 Mr 11:13-12:37 Mt 21:19-22:46}

6446. The same day, the Sadducees came to him and asked about a woman who had seven brothers, in turn, as her husband. They wanted to know who would be her husband in the resurrection. When the multitude heard his answer to prove the resurrection, they were astonished at his doctrine. Then a Pharisee, a lawyer, tested him by asking, which was the greatest commandment in the law. After Jesus had replied, he asked the Pharisees whose son Christ was. No man was able to answer him, nor did anyone dare ask him any more questions after that. {Lu 20:27-44}

6447. Then Jesus spoke to the multitude and to his disciples about the scribes and Pharisees. Eight times he pronounced a woe against them and addressing the city of Jerusalem, he accused her of cruelty and obstinacy and foretold her desolation. {Lu 20:45-47 Mr 12:38-40 Mt 23:1-39}

6448. As Jesus sat opposite the treasury, he commended a widow, who had thrown in two mites, more than those who had tossed in much more. {Lu 21:1-4 Mr 12:41-44}

6449. As he went out of the temple, his disciples pointed out the magnificent buildings and stones of the temple, and he predicted its utter destruction in that generation. {Lu 21:5-36 Mr 13:1-37 Mt 24:1-51} [E835]

6450. As Jesus sat on the Mount of Olives opposite the temple, his disciples asked him when these things would happen and what would be the sign of his coming and the end of the age. He gave a lengthy reply concerning the sign of his coming. He warned them to watch and to be ready, for they did not know the hour when the Lord would come. {Mr 13:1-37 Lu 21:1:36 Mt 24:1-51}

6451. He taught the same things through the parable of the ten virgins and the parable of the talents given to the servants to invest. [K593] He described the coming judgment of those in this world using the illustration about setting the sheep on the right hand and the goats on the left and passing sentence on each of them. By day, he taught in the temple, but at night he went to the Mount of Olives. All the people came to him early in the morning and he taught them in the temple. {Lu 21:37,38 Mt 25:1-46}

6452. When Jesus had finished saying these things, he told his disciples that after two days it would be the passover, and that the Son of Man would be betrayed and crucified. In the palace of the high priest, the Jewish leaders consulted together about how they could kill Jesus. They agreed that it should not be done on the feast day, in case there should be a riot. {Mr 14:1,2 Mt 26:1-5}

*6453.* When he was in the house eating with Simon the Leper, Jesus defended a woman who poured an alabaster box of ointment on his head, because his disciples were murmuring about this. He used it to foretell his burial. {*Mr 14:3-9 Mt 26:6-13*}

*6454.* Then Satan entered into Judas, who was to betray Jesus to the Jewish leaders. {*Lu 22:1-13 Mr 14:10,11 Mt 26:14-16*}

### The FOURTH PASSOVER
in which CHRIST, our PASSOVER,
was sacrificed,
{*1Co 5:7*} and so
put an end to all the legal
sacrifices prefiguring this one.
The beginning of the fourth, or middle
year of the last week of Daniel.
{*Da 9:27*}

*6455.* On the first day of unleavened bread, when the passover was to be killed (Thursday, April 2), his disciples asked Jesus where they should prepare it. He sent Peter and John into the city, telling them that there they would meet a man carrying a pitcher of water. They were to follow him to a house and ask the owner of that house for the use of the guest chamber. They would find the guest chamber already furnished by the good man of the house. {*Mr 14:12-16 Mt 26:17-19*} [K594]

*6456.* In the evening, Jesus went there with the twelve disciples and ate supper. Jesus said that he had eagerly desired to eat this passover with them before his sufferings. Taking the cup, he asked them to divide it among themselves. He said that he would not eat of the passover or drink of the fruit of the vine again, until the kingdom of God would come. He also said that one of them would betray him. They became sorrowful and each individually asked if he was the one. [E836] Jesus replied that it was the man who was dipping his hand in the dish with him. When Judas asked if it was he, Jesus said it was. {*Lu 22:14-18 Mr 14:17-21 Mt 26:20-25*}

*6457.* While they were eating, Jesus instituted the sacrament of his body and blood, which were symbolised by the bread and the wine. After he had drunk the wine, he said that he would not drink of the fruit of the vine after this, until he would drink it anew with them in the kingdom of his Father. He stated that the one who would betray him was eating with them. Then they began to enquire among themselves if anyone among them would do this. {*Lu 22:19-23 Mr 14:22-25 Mt 26:26-29*}

*6458.* There was also a dispute among them over who would be the greatest. After supper, Jesus arose and laid aside his garments. He took a towel and tied it about his waist and began to wash and to dry his disciple's

feet. At first Peter refused to have this done to him, but later he consented. After this, Jesus sat down and said that he had given them an example. Just as he had done, they also should wash one another's feet. Whoever wanted to be the greatest among them, had to become the least. He added, moreover, that he was not speaking about everyone, for he knew whom he had chosen. When he had said these things, he was troubled in the spirit and said that one of them would betray him. [K595] Therefore, his disciples looked at each other and were uncertain as to whom he might be referring to. Peter beckoned to the beloved disciple that he should ask who it was. Jesus answered that it was the one to whom he would give the sop after dipping it. He gave it to Judas and told him to do quickly what he had to do. When Judas had received the sop, he went out immediately into the night. {*Joh 13:2-38 Lu 22:24-30*}

*6459.* After Judas left, Jesus said that the Son of Man was now glorified and God was glorified in him. He reminded them that he would be leaving them suddenly and admonished them to love one another. He also said to Simon that Satan had desired to sift him like wheat, but that he had prayed for him and that when he was converted, he was to strengthen his brethren. Peter, too, confidently replied that he would die for Jesus. Jesus answered that he would deny him three times before the cock had crowed. Then Jesus told them all that he who had a purse, was to take it and he who did not have a sword, was to go and buy one. They said they had two swords, to which Jesus replied that it was enough. {*Lu 22:31-38*}

*6460.* Jesus anticipated their sorrow over his death and comforted them, as he usually did. He answered the questions raised by Thomas, Philip and Judas (who was also Lebbaeus, surnamed Thaddaeus, another of the sons of Alphaeus and a brother of James). He promised them that the Holy Spirit would be their teacher and left them his peace. Again he reminded them of his approaching death and of its joyful fruit. Then he said that the time had come to leave. They sang a hymn and then left for the Mount of Olives. {*Joh 14:1-31 Mr 14:26 Mt 26:30*}

*6461.* On their way, he told them the parable of the vine and the branches and exhorted them to bring forth fruit and to remain in the love of God toward them. They should have mutual love one toward another and patiently endure the hatred of the world, since it also hated Christ himself. [E837] They should not be offended by persecution. [K596] Again he comforted them about the sorrow they felt over his approaching death, with the promise of sending them the Comforter, who was the Spirit of Truth and would be a witness against the world and help them. He warned them that in a little while, they would not see him. They did not understand what he meant. He explained it to them and said that their anticipated sorrow would be turned into joy, just as a woman rejoiced who had given birth to a son. He predicted his return to them and told them of the Father's love toward them and of his willingness to hear the petitions that they would make in his name. He said that he had come into the world from the Father and he would leave the world again to return to the Father. His disciples said they now understood what he meant and believed that he had come from God. Jesus replied that the time had now come when they would all be scattered and he would be left alone. At last, he concluded with a most divine prayer to the Father, seeking both his own and the Father's glory, as well as praying for the apostles and the whole company of believers. {Joh 15:1-17:26}

6462. When Jesus had spoken these things, he went with his disciples, as was his custom, and crossed over the brook Kidron to the Mount of Olives. Then Jesus told them that all of them would be offended because of him that night. However, after he had risen again, he would go ahead of them into Galilee. Peter replied that although everyone else might be offended, yet he would not be, so Jesus told Peter that before the cock would crow, he would deny him three times. Peter and all the disciples replied that although they would die with him, they would never deny him. {Joh 18:1 Lu 22:39 Mr 14:27-31 Mt 26:31-36}

6463. Then they came into a place called Gethsemane, where there was a garden. After Jesus had entered with his disciples, he told them to pray, lest they fall into temptation. They were to sit there while he went away to pray. [K597] He took Peter and the two sons of Zebedee with him and began to be very sorrowful. He told them to stay there and watch, while he went a little farther, about a stone's throw, and kneeled down and prayed that this cup might pass from him. An angel appeared from heaven and strengthened him, then he returned and found his disciples sleeping. He reprehended and admonished them and went a second time and prayed more earnestly. He was in an agony and began to sweat drops of blood, as it were. He came again and found them sleeping for sorrow, for their eyes were heavy. He admonished them again and they did not know what to say. He then left them and went away again and prayed the same words. Then, returning to his disciples, he noted that they were still sleeping and resting. He said that the Son of Man had been betrayed into the hands of sinners and he told them to get up and go, for the man who had betrayed him was close by. {Lu 22:40-46 Mr 14:32-42 Mt 26:36-46}

6464. While he was speaking, Judas arrived, who knew the place, because Jesus often went there with his disciples. He brought with him the chief priests, Pharisees, captains of the temple, elders of the people, officers and a band of men sent out from them. [E838] They came there with lanterns and torches and a large number had swords and staves. Judas had given a sign, saying that the one they were after would be the one he kissed. Judas immediately kissed Jesus. Jesus asked Judas why he had come and whether he would betray the Son of Man with a kiss. Jesus, who knew all that would happen to him, went out to them and asked whom they were after. When they said they wanted Jesus of Nazareth, Jesus told them he was the one. They drew back and fell to the ground. He asked them again and answered them as he had done the first time, adding that if they were only after him, to let the disciples go their way. They took him. [K598] When those who were around him saw what would happen, they asked him if they should fight for him and Peter struck off the right ear of Malchus, a servant of the high priest. Jesus told Peter to put away his sword, because if Jesus wanted to, he could call down more than twelve legions of angels. He said that it was right that he should drink of the cup that his Father had given him and they should allow it to happen. Jesus touched Malchus' ear and healed him, then asked the crowd why they had come to him with swords and staves, as if he were a thief. He told them that this was their hour, and that of the power of darkness. Then all his disciples left him and fled. A certain young man (of their company), who was seized, left his linen cloth behind and fled away from them, naked. {Joh 18:2-11 Lu 22:47-53 Mr 14:43-52 Mt 26:47-56}

6465. They bound Jesus and first brought him to Annas, the father-in-law of Caiaphas. Annas sent him bound to Caiaphas, the high priest, who had previously prophesied that it was expedient that one man should die for the people. All the chief priests, elders and scribes of the people were gathered together. Caiaphas asked Jesus about his disciples and his doctrine. Jesus said that he had spoken publicly and to ask those who had heard him. At that, one of the officers struck him with a staff. Jesus asked him why he had hit him, since he had answered properly. Then all the council looked for false witnesses against him, but could find none. Finally two false witnesses came, but their testimonies disagreed with each other. Caiaphas asked Jesus to reply to what these witnesses had said against him, but Jesus said nothing. Then Caiaphas adjured him that he should say whether he was the Christ. Jesus answered that he was and that they would see the Son of Man sitting at the right hand of the power of God and coming in the clouds of heaven. For this blasphemy, they judged him guilty of death. [K599] Then they mocked and spat on him and cruelly cuffed him and beat him with staves. They covered his eyes and asked him to prophesy who had hit him. They spoke reproachfully against him and did many other things and much more.

*6466.* Peter followed afar off, to observe the outcome of it. Another disciple accompanied him, who was known to the high priest. He went with Jesus into the palace, but Peter, whom that other disciple (who had spoken to the maid who kept the door) had brought in, stood outside at the door. As Peter was warming himself at the fire that burned in the courtyard, for it was cold, the maid who kept the door asked him and affirmed that he was one of Jesus' disciples. *[E839]* Peter denied it and claimed that he did not know him, or what the maid was speaking about. A little later, he went out into the porch and the cock crowed. As he was going out, another maid saw him and said to those present that Peter had been with Jesus of Nazareth. Another person said to him that he was one of the disciples. Then Peter again denied it with an oath. About an hour later, those who were standing around came and said to him that his accent gave him away. The cousin of Malchus, who was among their number, said that he had seen Peter in the garden. As Peter was denying this, the cock crowed the second time. Then Jesus turned around and looked at Peter. Peter remembered the words of Jesus and went out and wept bitterly. {Joh 18:12-27 Lu 22:54-65 Mr 14:53-72 Mt 26:57-75}

*6467.* As soon as it was day, the elders of the people, the chief priests and the scribes came together, led him into their council and asked Jesus if he was the Christ. He replied that they would not believe him nor answer his questions were he to ask them. Once Jesus said he was the Son of God, they replied that they did not need any more witnesses. {Lu 22:66-71} *[K600]*

*6468.* In the morning, the whole multitude promptly arose and led him, bound, from Caiaphas to the hall of judgment to appear before Pontius Pilate, the governor (Friday, April 3). They themselves, however, did not go into the judgment hall, in case they would be defiled and so be unable to eat the passover. When Jesus stood before the governor, Pilate asked the crowd what his crime was. They said that if he had not been a criminal, they would not have brought Jesus to him. They accused Jesus of perverting the country and forbidding anyone to pay tribute to Caesar. They also said that Jesus claimed to be Christ, a king. Jesus refused to answer them and Pilate asked him why he did not defend himself against their many accusations. Jesus did not even answer Pilate so much as a word, so that Pilate marvelled. When Pilate told the crowd to take him and judge him according to their law, they replied that they did not have the power to kill him. Then Pilate entered into the judgment hall again and called for Jesus. He asked Jesus if he was the king of the Jews. Jesus asked Pilate whether he was ask-

ing the question of his own accord, or if others had told him that. Pilate retorted that he was not a Jew and that Jesus' own people and the chief priests had brought him to him. He asked Jesus what he had done. Jesus stated that his kingdom was not an earthly kingdom. Pilate asked if he were a king, to which Jesus said that this was the reason he had come into the world, so that he might witness to the truth. Pilate asked him, what truth was, and then went out again to the Jews and said Jesus was innocent. The crowd became more hostile and said he had stirred up the people and taught throughout all the country of the Jews, starting from Galilee even to that place.

*6469.* When Pilate heard about Galilee, he asked Jesus if he were a Galilean. *[K601]* When he knew that he belonged to Herod's jurisdiction, he sent him to Herod, who was at Jerusalem in those days. Herod was exceedingly glad and hoped to see some miracle. *[E840]* Jesus would not answer Herod or the chief priests and scribes, who vehemently accused him. After Herod had defied Jesus and mocked him, he sent him back to Pilate, arrayed in a gorgeous robe. That same day, the two governors became friends.

*6470.* When Pilate had called together the chief priests, the rulers and the people, he told them that both he and Herod had found Jesus innocent, and so he would chastise Jesus and release him. It was the custom, on every feast day, for the governor to free any prisoner the people wanted. The crowd cried out loudly and began to demand that he do for them as he had always done. Therefore, Pilate addressed them and asked whether they wanted him to release the king of the Jews, or Barabbas. Pilate knew that the chief priests had delivered him up out of envy. However these men stirred up the people to demand that Pilate should release Barabbas to them, instead of Jesus. Barabbas was an infamous thief who had been imprisoned for insurrection and murder in the city. As Pilate sat in the judgment seat, his wife sent him a message saying that he should have nothing to do with that just man, because that day she had suffered many things in a dream because of him.

*6471.* Consequently, Pilate asked the crowd again whom they wanted to have released, because he really wanted to release Jesus. However, they all cried out and said they did not want Jesus, but Barabbas, and so Pilate asked them what he should do with the man they called the king of the Jews. *[K602]* They all cried out again and said he should be crucified. Pilate asked a third time what his crime was. He had found Jesus to be innocent and wanted to chastise him and let him go free. They cried out more earnestly and loudly, that he should be crucified. So Pilate took Jesus and scourged him. The soldiers made a crown of thorns and placed it on his head and clothed him with purple. They mocked him and greeted him as the king of the Jews and beat him with staves. Then, Pilate again went out to them and said that he was bringing Jesus, whom he had found to be innocent, out to them. Jesus was led out, wearing the crown of thorns and the robe. Pilate told them to look at Jesus. When the chief priests and officers saw him, they cried out that he should be crucified. Pilate told them to take and crucify him, but that he was innocent. The Jews replied that he should die, because he said he was the Son of God. When Pilate heard that, he was more afraid and went back into the judgment hall and asked Jesus where he had come from. Jesus did not reply. Pilate admonished him to answer, and bragged that he had the power to crucify him, but Jesus answered that he would have no power had it not been given to him from above.

6472. From that time on, Pilate tried to release him, but the Jews replied that if he did, he was not Caesar's friend. *[E841]* When Pilate heard this, he brought Jesus out and sat in the judgment seat in the place called *the Pavement*. It was the preparation for the passover and about the sixth hour. He told the Jews that this was their king. They cried out that he should be crucified. Pilate asked if he should crucify their king, but the chief priests said that they had no king but Caesar. *[K603]* When Pilate saw he was getting nowhere and that he had a potential riot on his hands, he took some water and washed his hands before the crowd. He said that he was innocent of the blood of this just person. All the people replied that his blood should be on them and their children. To placate the multitude, Pilate released Barabbas. After Pilate had scourged Jesus, he did as the crowd wanted and ordered Jesus to be crucified. {*Joh 19:1-40 Lu 23:1-25 Mr 15:1-37 Mt 27:11-31*}

6473. When the soldiers of the governor had led Jesus into the hall called the Praetorium, they called their whole band together. When they had stripped him, they put a purple robe on him. They made a crown of thorns and put it on his head and put a reed in his right hand. They bowed down and mocked him and greeted him as the king of the Jews. When they had spat on him, they took the reed and hit him on the head. After they had mocked him, they took the purple robe off again and put his own clothes on him and led him out to be crucified.

6474. When Judas, who had betrayed him, saw that he had been condemned, he repented and brought the thirty pieces of silver back to the chief priests. He confessed his sin to them, threw the silver pieces into the temple and went out and hanged himself. They used the money to buy the potter's field, in order that the prophecy might be fulfilled. {*Zec 11:13 Ps 69:25 109:8*}

6475. Jesus went out carrying his cross. As they were leading him, they found Simon of Cyrene, who had come from the country. They took him and compelled him to carry the cross after Jesus. Two thieves were also led out with him, to be crucified. A large multitude of people followed, which included women who were lamenting him. Turning to them, he foretold the terrible destruction of Jerusalem. *[K604]* When they came to the place called Calvary, which was called Golgotha in the Hebrew, they gave him vinegar to drink, which had been mixed with myrrh and gall. When he had tasted it, he refused to drink it. There, they crucified him and the two thieves, at about the third hour (nine a.m.). One thief was on each side of him. Jesus prayed to his Father to forgive the people, because they did not know what they were doing.

6476. Pilate wrote a superscription in Hebrew, Greek and Latin, and put it on the cross. The chief priests asked Pilate to change it, but he refused. After they had crucified him, the soldiers divided his garments into four parts, one for each soldier who had worked on the execution. However, they cast lots for his seamless coat, rather than divide it up, so that the scripture might be fulfilled. {*Ps 22:18*} They sat down and watched him there and the people stood and watched.

6477. Those who passed by, reviled him and shook their heads. *[E842]* They told him to come down from the cross, because he had said he could destroy the temple and raise it up again in three days. The chief priests, also, and the rulers, as well as the people, mocked and scoffed at him, along with the scribes and elders. They said that he could save others, but he could not save himself. If he really was the king of Israel and the Christ, the Chosen One of God, he should come down from the cross and then they would believe him. They said he trusted in God to save him, for Jesus claimed to be the Son of God. The soldiers also came up to him and mocked him. They offered him vinegar and said that if he was really the king of the Jews, he should save himself.

6478. The thieves, who were crucified with him, also threw the same in his face. While one of them continued railing against him, the other was converted and rebuked the first thief. *[K605]* He asked Jesus to remember him when he came into his kingdom. Jesus promised him that that very day he would be with him in paradise.

6479. His mother stood by his cross, as well as his mother's sister, Mary, the wife of Cleophas and Mary Magdalene. As Jesus' mother stood there, and the disciple whom he loved was standing beside her, he said to his mother to behold her son and to the disciple to behold his mother.

6480. When the sixth hour (noon) had come, there was darkness over all the land until the ninth hour (three p.m.). In the ninth hour, Jesus cried out with a loud voice, *Eli Eli*, or, *Eloi Eloi Lama Sabachthani.* Some who stood nearby said that he had called for Elijah. After this, when Jesus knew that all things had been accomplished so that the scripture might be fulfilled, he said he was thirsty. {*Ps 69:21*} Beside the cross there was a vessel full of vinegar. They filled a sponge with vinegar and put it upon hyssop, or a reed. They put it to his mouth and said with the rest that they would wait and see if Elijah would come and take him down from the cross. When Jesus had received the vinegar, he said that it was finished. Once again he cried out with a loud voice and commended his spirit to his Father. Then Jesus bowed his head and gave up the ghost. When the centurion saw that he had cried out in this way and died, he glorified God and testified that this was most certainly an innocent man and the Son of God. {*Lu 23:26-46 Mr 15:38-43 Mt 27:32-50*}

6481. The veil of the temple was ripped in two, from the top to the bottom, and there was an earthquake and the rocks were split. The graves were opened and many of the saints, who had died, arose and came out of the graves after his resurrection and went into Jerusalem and appeared to many. *[K606]* When the centurion and those who were standing around Jesus witnessed the earthquake and the things that had happened, they were terrified and testified that this was certainly the Son of God. Then all the people who had come to watch the crucifixion beat their chests and returned home. His acquaintances and the women who had followed him from Galilee, stood afar off and saw these things. Among them were Salome, Mary Magdalene and Mary, the mother of James the Less, and Joses. When Jesus had been in Galilee, these had followed him and ministered to him, along with many other women who had come up to Jerusalem with him. {*Lu 23:47-49 Mt 27:51-56*} *[E843]*

6482. Because it was the Preparation Day (for that Sabbath was a high day e.g., not only a Sabbath but the first day of the Feast of Unleavened Bread), and the Jews did not want the bodies to remain on the cross on the Sabbath, they asked Pilate that their legs might be broken and they be taken down. So the soldiers came and broke the legs of the two thieves, but not of Jesus, because he was already dead. One of the soldiers pierced his side with a spear and at once blood and water came out. These things took place so that the scripture might be fulfilled that not a bone of him would be broken. {*Joh 19:31-37 Ex 12:46 Nu 9:12*}

6483. When evening came, because it was the Preparation, that is, the day before the Sabbath, Joseph of Arimathea came to Pilate. Joseph was a rich man and an honourable councillor, who also looked forward to the kingdom of God. He was a good and just man and in the council had not consented to their plans. He was a secret disciple for fear of the Jews, but he came boldly to Pilate and asked to be given the body of Jesus. Pilate marvelled that Jesus was already dead and questioned a centurion about Jesus. When Pilate had it confirmed, he gave the body to Joseph. Nicodemus, who had first come to Jesus by night, brought a mixture of myrrh and aloes, about a hundred pounds in weight. *[K607]* Therefore, they took the body of Jesus and wound it in a linen cloth with the spices, as was the custom of the Jews when burying a body. When Joseph had wrapped it in a clean linen cloth, he laid it in his own new sepulchre, hewn from a rock, which had not been used previously. The sepulchre was in a garden near the place where Jesus was crucified. Joseph rolled a large stone to the door of the sepulchre. Mary Magdalene and Mary, the mother of Joses, who had come with Jesus from Galilee, saw where they had laid him and sat opposite the sepulchre. They went home and prepared spices and ointments and rested on the Sabbath day, according to the commandment.

6484. The next day (Saturday, April 4), the Pharisees asked Pilate to secure the sepulchre until the third day, because Jesus had said he would arise on the third day. When Pilate agreed, they went and secured the sepulchre. They sealed the stone and set a watch. {*Joh 19:38-42 Lu 23:50-56 Mr 15:42-47 Mt 27:57-61*}

6485. When the Sabbath was over (Sunday, April 5) and the first day of the week was dawning, very early in the morning, while it was still dark, Mary Magdalene and Mary, the mother of James, and Salome arrived with spices. They had come to see the sepulchre and anoint Jesus, and were wondering who would roll the stone away from the door for them. At sunrise, they came to the sepulchre and saw that the stone was rolled away. There was a large earthquake, for an angel of the Lord came down from heaven and rolled away the stone and sat upon it. The guards shook for fear and fell over as though dead. The women went in and did not find the body of the Lord Jesus. *[K608]* They were very perplexed by this, when two men in shining clothes came to them, their faces bright as lightning and their garments white as snow. *[E844]* Matthew and Mark mention only one angel. Afraid, the women bowed their faces to the earth, but the angels told them not to be afraid, for they were seeking Jesus, who had been crucified. They told them he was not dead, but alive, and invited the women to see the sepulchre for themselves. They reminded them that when Jesus was still in Galilee with them, he had told them that the Son of Man had to be delivered into the hands of sinful men, be crucified and rise again on the third day. The angels told them to go quickly and tell his disciples and Peter that he was risen again from the dead. They also said that Jesus had gone ahead of them to Galilee and that they would see him there. Then the women remembered the words of Jesus and quickly left the sepulchre in fear, wonder and great joy. They ran to tell his disciples, but said nothing to anyone along the way, for they were afraid. When the women had told these things to the eleven and to all the rest, their words seemed to them like idle tales. Mary Magdalene had told Peter and the other disciple whom Jesus loved that they had taken away the Lord and she did not know where they had laid him.

6486. Peter and that other disciple left for the sepulchre, but the other disciple outran Peter and reached the sepulchre first. When he stooped down, he saw the linen cloths lying there, but did not go in. *[K609]* Then Peter came and went into the sepulchre. He saw the linen cloths lying there and the napkin that had been about his head, not lying with the linen cloths, but wrapped together in a place by itself. Then the other disciple went in and saw and believed. Peter went to his own home, wondering about what had happened. As yet they did not know the scriptures that Jesus had to rise again from the dead. The disciples went to their own home.

6487. Mary Magdalene stood outside the sepulchre and wept. As she wept, she stooped down into the sepulchre and saw two angels in white sitting where the body of Jesus had been, the one at the head and the other at the feet. They asked her why she was weeping. She told them that they had taken away her Lord and she did not know where they had laid him. When she had said this, she turned around and saw Jesus standing there, but did not know that it was Jesus. Jesus asked her why she was weeping and whom she was looking for. Thinking the man was the gardener, she asked that if he had taken the body away, he would show her where he had put it. Jesus said *Mary* and she immediately recognised him. He told her not to touch him, for he had not yet ascended to his Father, but she was to go and tell his brethren. She went to his disciples and those that had been with him, and found them weeping and mourning. She told them that she had seen the Lord and that he had said these things to her, but they did not believe her. The women went from the sepulchre (perhaps Mary Magdalene was absent) to go and tell his disciples. *[E845] [K610]* Jesus met with the women and greeted them and they all came and held him by the feet and worshipped him. Jesus told them not to be afraid, but to tell his brethren to go into Galilee and meet him there.

6488. As they were going, some of the guard went into the city and told the chief priests everything that had happened. These then met with them and together they decided with the elders that they would give the soldiers a large amount of money, so that in return, the soldiers would say that his disciples had come by night and stolen the body away while they were asleep. They said they would protect the soldiers from any harm, should the governor hear about this. So the soldiers took their money and did as they were told. This story was commonly reported among the Jews, even to this day. {*Joh 20:1-18 Lu 24:1-12 Mr 16:1-11 Mt 27:62-28:15*}

6489. That same day, two of Jesus' followers happened to be going into the country to the village of Emmaus, which was about eight miles from Jerusalem. As they journeyed, an apparent stranger accompanied them and they told him the things that had happened in recent days about Jesus of Nazareth. He had been crucified and was supposed to rise again on the third day. Jesus, for this was the identity of the stranger, showed them from the scriptures that it was necessary for Christ to suffer in order to enter into his glory. In the village, as they were eating, he took bread, gave thanks, broke it and gave it to them. He revealed himself to them and their eyes were opened and they recognised him, at which he vanished from their sight. They left that same hour and returned to Jerusalem, to the eleven and those who were with them. The disciples told these two that the Lord had indeed risen and had appeared to Simon. Then the two told them what had happened to them on the way and how they had recognised him as he broke bread with them. The others did not believe the two men. {*Lu 24:13-35 Mr 16:12,13*}

6490. In the evening of this first day of the week, while they were still talking, they had the doors locked for fear of the Jews. Suddenly Jesus appeared in their midst and greeted them. *[K611]* They were frightened and terrified and thought they had seen a spirit, but he upbraided them for their unbelief and hardness of heart, because they had not believed those who had seen him since he had risen. He asked them why they were troubled and showing them his hands and his feet, said that a spirit does not have flesh and bones. He showed them the wounds in his hands, his feet and his side. As they were wondering and were unable to believe for joy, he asked them if there was anything to eat and then he ate a piece of broiled fish and a honeycomb. The disciples rejoiced that they had seen the Lord. Jesus told them that what had happened was exactly what he had told them would happen, so that everything would be fulfilled which was written about Christ in the law of

Moses, the prophets and the Psalms. Then he opened their understanding, so that they could understand the scriptures. He told them it had been necessary for Christ to suffer and to rise from the dead on the third day, so that repentance and remission of sins could be preached in his name in all countries. *[E846]* He told them that they were witnesses of these things and giving them the promise from his Father, he said they were to stay at Jerusalem until they would be endued with power from on high. Again he greeted them and said that, as his Father had sent him, so he would send them. They were to go into all the world and preach the gospel to everyone. He who believed and was baptized would be saved, but he who did not believe would be damned. He would give them signs to authenticate their message—In the name of Jesus, they would cast out demons and speak in new languages; they would take up serpents and if they drank any deadly thing, it would not harm them; they would lay their hands on the sick and these would recover. *[K612]* After he had said all these things, he breathed on them and told them to receive the Holy Spirit. Anyone, whose sins they forgave, would be forgiven and whose sins they retained, these would be retained. Thus Jesus appeared five times on the very first day of his resurrection. {Joh 20:19-23 Lu 24:36-49 Mr 14:14-18}

6491. Thomas, one of the twelve, who was called Didymus, had not been with the disciples when Jesus had first come. When the rest of the disciples told him that they had seen the Lord, he very confidently professed that he would not believe it without evidence. After eight days (Sunday, April 12), Thomas was present with the rest, when Jesus came again while the doors were locked. He stood in their midst and greeted them and abundantly satisfied Thomas' unbelief. {Joh 20:24-29 Lu 24:16-20}

6492. Then the eleven disciples went into Galilee, to the mountain where Jesus had told them to meet him. When they saw him, they worshiped him, but some doubted. When Jesus met with them, he said that he had all power and that they were to go and tell the gospel message to everyone. He promised to be with them to the end of the world. After that, Jesus was seen by more than five hundred brethren at once and subsequently, by James. {1Co 15:6,7 Mt 28:16-20}

6493. Later, Jesus again showed himself to his disciples at the sea of Tiberias, or at least to seven of them, as they were fishing. After they had fished all night and caught nothing, Jesus stood on the shore and they did not recognise him. He told them to cast their net out on the right side of the boat, where they then caught a hundred and fifty-three large fish. Jesus bade them to come and dine with him and no one dared ask him who he

was, for they knew it was the Lord. When they had dined, he warned Peter three times of his pastoral charge, and foretold how Peter would die. When Peter asked about John, Jesus replied, but his answer was incorrectly understood by the brethren. {Joh 21:1-24} [K613]

6494. Last of all, he appeared to his disciples in Jerusalem and led them out as far as Bethany. There he lifted up his hands and blessed them. It happened that as he was blessing them, he was taken from them and carried up into heaven. {Lu 24:50,51 Mr 16:19} [E847]

6495. Here ends the history of the acts of Christ recorded by the four evangelists, and which also includes his forerunner, John the Baptist. Josephus had a short note of honourable mention about John the Baptist: {*Josephus, Antiq., l. 18. c. 5. s. 2. (116-119) 9:81-85}

> "Herod, the tetrarch, killed John, surnamed the Baptist, who was a most excellent man. He motivated the Jews to the study of virtues, especially of piety and justice. He encouraged them to be baptized, which he said would be acceptable to God, if they made use of it, not for the remission of their sins only, but first having their minds purged through righteousness, then they would also purify the body. Many went out to him, especially the common people, who were pleased with his words. Herod feared lest the great authority of the man would cause some rebellion, because it seemed as though they would listen to nothing but which John advised them. Herod thought it safer to take him out of the way before there was any sedition, rather than act when it was too late. Therefore, he commanded him to be sent as a prisoner to Machaeras and then to be put to death."

6496. Josephus stated this about Christ, our Lord: {*Josephus, Antiq., l. 18. c. 3. s. 3. (6,64) 9:49,51}

> "At the same time there was a wise man named Jesus, if we may call him a man. He was a worker of miracles and a teacher of those who willingly received the truth. He had many Jews and Gentiles who followed him and was believed to be the Christ. When Pilate had crucified him because of the envy of our rulers, those who had first loved him nevertheless continued loyal in their love for him and he appeared to them alive the third day. The prophets in their prophecies foretold both these and many other powerful things concerning him. The Christians, who are named after him, continue to this very day."

6497. This is how Jerome, in his book of ecclesiastical writers, has translated this passage, and his rendering was:

> "He was believed to be the Christ."

6498. This rendering should be preferred to that of Eusebius or Rufinus, or as it is in our books: {*Eusebius, Ecclesiastical History, l. 1. c. 11. 1:83}

"This was the Christ."

6499. It is clear that Josephus came no nearer to our religion than King Agrippa, to whom he was most devoted and whose confession to Paul was: {Ac 26:28}

"Almost you have persuaded me to be a Christian."

6500. Cornelius Tacitus stated: {*Tacitus, Annals, l. 15. c. 44. 5:283}

"Christ was put to death by Pontius Pilate, the governor of Judea, in the reign of Tiberius."

6501. Eusebius also mentioned Lucian. {*Eusebius, Ecclesiastical History, l. 9. c. 6. 2:341} Lucian, the martyr, testified in Rufinus to the darkness at that time by appealing to the writings of the heathen themselves:

"Search your writings and you shall find that, in Pilate's time, when Christ suffered, the sun was suddenly withdrawn and a darkness followed."

6502. Before him, Tertullian had stated: {*Tertullian, Apology, l. 1. c. 21. 3:35}

"At the same moment, the day was withdrawn even when the sun was at the height. Those who never knew that this also had been spoken concerning Christ, judged it to be nothing but an eclipse. [K614] However, you shall find this event, that happened to the world, recorded even in your own archives."

6503. Thallus and Phlegon of Tralles both called it an eclipse. {Thallus, Histories, l. 3} {Phlegon, Chronicles, l. 13.} (Thallus lived at the time of these events and wrote a history starting from the Trojan War down to the death of Christ. Phlegon lived at the time of Hadrian and wrote a history starting from the first Olympiad down to 140 AD. Editor.) Thallus was quoted by Julius Africanus in his third chronography. {*Julius Africanus, Chronology, l. 1. c. 18. 6:136,137} Africanus was a contemporary of Origen. Phlegon was quoted in Origen's book and in his 35th tract. {Origen, Against Celsus, p. 83,99. Greek edition} Phlegon stated that in the 19th year of Tiberius (as Eustathius Antiochus noted in Hexaemeron) and the fourth year of the 202nd Olympiad (that is 33 AD), the following events took place. (Ussher has a large quote from the Greek from Origen. Editor.) Jerome translated this into Latin in Eusebius' Chronicle. (Ussher has a large quote in Latin from Jerome's translation of Eusebius. Editor.) The English translation is: {*Eusebius, Chronicles, l. 1. 1:256}

"There was the largest and most famous eclipse that had ever occurred. The day was so turned into night

at the sixth hour (noon), that the stars were seen. Also, an earthquake in Bithynia destroyed many houses in the city of Nicaea."

6504. (Sir Robert Anderson gave the dates for the passover from 22 AD to 37 AD. {*Anderson, The Coming Prince, 1:104} Note that the passover would start at sundown on the previous day and end at sundown for the date shown. The passover meal would be eaten the previous evening. These dates are:

| Year AD | Passover Day | Date |
|---|---|---|
| 22 | Sunday | April 22 |
| 23 | Thursday | March 25 |
| 24 | Wednesday | April 12 |
| 25 | Sunday | April 1 |
| 26 | Thursday | March 21 |
| 27 | Wednesday | April 9 |
| 28 | Monday | March 29 |
| 29 | Sunday | April 17 |
| 30 | Thursday | April 6 |
| 31 | Tuesday | March 27 |
| 32 | Monday | April 14 |
| 33 | Friday | April 3 |
| 34 | Tuesday | March 23 |
| 35 | Monday | April 11 |
| 36 | Friday | March 30 |
| 37 | Thursday | April 18 |

6505. Anderson independently confirmed the date that Ussher computed for the passover for 33 AD. Hence we assume his other calculations are equally accurate. In his book, he stated at length how these were done, so it appeared he did his homework well. The day of the week was calculated independently by the editor using the Online Bible Calendar program and was not included with the original material by Anderson. Ironically, Anderson selected 32 AD as the year that Christ died and goes to great pains to show why the Jews celebrated the passover on the wrong day, that is, on Friday, not Monday. The only plausible date from the list is 33 AD for Good Friday, as the only other date for Good Friday would be in 36 AD, which is too late. This independently confirms the writings of Phlegon. It is a common belief that Jesus was thirty-three years old when he died. This is based on the assumption that he started his ministry when he was thirty. {Lu 3:23} Luke was a very precise historian. If Jesus had been thirty years old, he would not have said about thirty. Based on that text, the only thing one can say for certain is that Jesus was not thirty years old at the start of his ministry. However, he was likely about thirty when he was baptized by John the Baptist in 27 AD. About three years elapsed between his baptism and the start of his public ministry in 29 AD. According to what we know about when he was born, he would have been thirty-six years old when he died. The 33 AD date is also confirmed by John {*Joh 2:20*} for this establishes the date of the first passover of Christ at 30 AD, forty-six full years after Herod started to rebuild the temple in 17 BC. {*See note on 4033b AM <<6305>>*} This synchronisation is overlooked by most modern historians. Editor.)

6506. From the historical accounts of the gospels about the sayings and acts of Christ, Luke made this transition to the Acts of the Apostles:

"The former treatise I have made, oh Theophilus, of all that Jesus began to do and teach, until the day (Thursday, May 14) on which he was taken up, after he, through the Holy Spirit, had given commandments to his apostles whom he had chosen: to whom he also showed himself alive after his passion by many infallible proofs, being seen by them for forty days and speaking of things pertaining to the kingdom of God." {*Ac 1:1-3*}

6507. When they were assembled together, the Lord commanded them that they should not leave Jerusalem, but should wait for the promise of the Father, which was the baptism of the Holy Spirit. {*Ac 1:4,5 11:16*} The apostles asked the Lord if it was at this time that he would restore the kingdom to Israel. He replied that it was not for them to know the times that the Father had put in his own power. However, they would receive the Holy Spirit and would bear witness to him, not only in Jerusalem, Judea and Samaria, but to the uttermost parts of the earth. After he had spoken these things, and while they were watching, he was taken up and a cloud received him from their sight. *[E848]* They were also instructed by two angels in white clothes, who suddenly appeared and told them that he would come again in the very same way as they had now seen him go up into heaven. {*Ac 1:6-11*}

6508. When they had worshipped him, they returned with great joy to Jerusalem {*Lu 24:52*} from the Mount of Olives, which was a Sabbath day's journey from there. {*Ac 1:12*} The Syrian version gave it as seven furlongs (almost 7/8 of a mile), as does the Theophylact, based on Josephus. However, our copies of Josephus read that the Mount of Olives was either five furlongs (5/8 of a mile) {*Josephus, Antiq., l. 20. c. 8. s. 6. (169,170) 10:93*} or six, as the Greek {*Josephus, Jewish War, l. 5. c. 2. s. 3. (70) 4:23*} or the Latin copy had it. {*Josephus, Antiq. - Latin Copy, l. 6. c. 3.*}

6509. The eleven apostles stayed in an upper room in Jerusalem, together with the women, Mary, the mother of Jesus, and his brothers, and they were of one mind as they continued in prayer. {*Ac 1:13,14*} *[K615]*

6510. In those days, Peter stood up in the midst of the disciples, who numbered about a hundred and twenty, and spoke to them about choosing a successor for the traitor Judas, who had fallen down headlong and his body had burst open in the middle. When they had prayed, they cast lots to decide between Joseph, called Barsabas, and Matthias. The lot fell to Matthias and he was chosen to be numbered with the apostles. {*Ac 1:15-26*}

6511. On the day of Pentecost (Sunday, May 24), when all the one hundred and twenty were assembled together with one accord, there suddenly came a sound from heaven like a mighty rushing wind and it filled the whole house where they sat. Divided tongues, as of fire, appeared to them and sat on each of them, and they were all filled with the Holy Spirit. They began to speak with other tongues, as the Spirit gave them utterance. At Jerusalem, there were devout Jews from every country under heaven. When these people heard them speaking in their own languages about the wonderful things of God, they were all amazed. Some, however, profanely derided the miracle, but Peter, in a most serious sermon, refuted their charge of drunkenness, as it was only the third hour of the day (nine a.m.). He then expounded to them about Christ from the law and the prophets and proved that he had risen. Through the power of the Spirit, three thousand were converted. Peter commanded them to repent and be baptized in the name of Jesus Christ for remission of sins. {*Ac 2:1-41*}

6512. They continued faithfully in the apostles' doctrine and fellowship. They broke bread together and prayed. Fear came upon every soul and the apostles performed many signs and wonders. All who believed were united and had all things in common and sold their possessions and goods, dividing them among all, according to their needs. They continued daily with one accord in the temple and breaking bread from house to house, they ate with gladness and singleness of heart. They praised God and were highly regarded by all the people and the Lord daily added to the church those who were being saved. {*Ac 2:42-47*}

6513. At about the hour of prayer, which was the ninth hour (three p.m.), Peter and John went up together into the temple. At the gate of the temple, which was called *Beautiful*, they healed a man in the name of Christ, who had been lame from his birth and was now about forty years old. Because of this, the people came running into Solomon's porch and then Peter expounded the mystery of salvation through Christ and upbraided their ingratitude and exhorted them to repentance. Many who heard him believed and the number of men was about five thousand. However, the priests and rulers of the temple came, with the Sadducees, and took Peter and John and put them in prison until the next day, because it was evening by then. The next day the council was convened (which included Annas, the high priest, who was the head of the council, along with Caiaphas, John and Alexander and many of the high priest's relatives). When the apostles were questioned about the miracles they had done, they boldly defended the cause of Christ and the council forbade them to speak any more in the name of Christ. The apostles replied that it was better to obey God than men, after which they were threatened and released. They returned to their own home, where, together with the whole church, they poured out fervent prayer to God for the propagation of the gospel. *[K616]* The Lord answered this prayer by causing an earthquake and they were filled with the Holy Spirit. {*Ac 3:1-4:31*}

6514. The multitude of those who believed were of one heart and one soul and they had all things in common. No one lacked anything, because as many as had lands or houses, went and sold them and brought the money and laid it down at the apostles' feet, to be distributed to the poor. Josephus, or Joses, a Levite from Cyprus, whom the apostles surnamed Barnabas (that is, the son of consolation), set the first example by selling his possessions. {*Ac 4:32-37*} *[E849]*

6515. Ananias and his wife Sapphira fraudulently conspired to keep back some of the money they had received for the land they sold. When they lied and said they had given the whole amount, they were struck dead at the word and rebuke of Peter, who exposed the fraud and avenged it by the power of the Holy Spirit, to whom they had lied. Great fear fell on all the church and on as many as heard of these things. {*Ac 5:1-11*}

6516. The apostles performed many miracles among the people and all of their number were gathered together in Solomon's Porch. None of the rest dared join them. However, the people esteemed them highly and the Lord added more believers to the church. They brought the sick into the streets, so that at least the shadow of Peter would fall on them as he passed by, and they would be healed. A large multitude came from the cities around Jerusalem and brought the sick and those who were vexed with unclean spirits, and they were all healed. {*Ac 5:12-16*}

6517. The high priest and the Sadducees who were with him were envious and cast the apostles into prison. In the night they were freed by an angel and told to teach the people boldly and without fear. When they were brought to the council, they escaped death, due to the advice given the council by Gamaliel, a Pharisee. {*See note on 4007b AM. <<6098>>*} He was a teacher of the law and held in high esteem among the people. After the

apostles had been scourged, they were freed and left the council, rejoicing that they had been counted worthy to suffer shame for the name of Jesus. They taught daily in the temple. {*Ac 5:17-42*}

## 4037a AM, 4746 JP, 33 AD

6518. The number of believers increased at Jerusalem and the money that came in helped support the poor of the church. There arose (as it commonly happens among a multitude) a murmuring of the Greeks against the Hebrews, because they thought their widows were being neglected in the daily distribution. The apostles did not have time to be involved in distributing the gifts from the rich of the church to the poor, or to manage the money that came in from the sale of property for the church. Seven men were chosen to be stewards of the church's goods and manage that service. These were Stephen, Philip, Prochorus, Nicanor, Timon, Parmenas and Nicolaus, a proselyte of Antioch. (It was evident, because they all had Greek names, that, in this selection, there was no way the Greeks could say they had been ignored.) The word of the Lord increased and the number of the disciples was multiplied at Jerusalem and many of the priests were obedient to the faith. {*Ac 6:1-7*} *[K617]*

6519. Stephen did many wonders and miracles among the people and stoutly defended the cause of Christ against the Jews of the synagogue of the Libertines (those freed by their masters), the Cyrenians, Alexandrians and of those from Cilicia and Asia. He disputed with them about Christ and when they could not resist the wisdom and spirit by which he spoke, they falsely accused him. They captured him and brought him before the council, where they had false witnesses who were prepared to swear that they had heard him speak blasphemous words against the temple and the law. {*Ac 6:8-15*}

6520. In a long speech before the high priest, Annas, and the council, Stephen showed that the true worship of God was observed by Abraham and his posterity before the temple was built by Solomon and even before Moses was born. He stated that Moses testified of Christ and that the outward ceremonies that were given to their fathers, were only to last for a time. Then, he sharply reprehended the Jews because they had always resisted the Holy Spirit and had wickedly put Christ to death, of whom the prophets had foretold that he would come into the world. At that, the council was furious with rage and they cast this holy man out of the city and stoned him to death as he was praying for them. {*Ac 7:1-60*}

6521. Before the witnesses, in accordance with the law, {*De 17:7*} were about to throw the first stones at Stephen, they laid their garments at the feet of a young man called Saul. He watched their clothes and consented to the death of Stephen. {Ac 7:58 8:1 22:20} Saul described himself as a Hebrew of the Hebrews, of the tribe of Benjamin, born at Tarsus in Cilicia, of which Strabo said that it was a city famous for the study of philosophy and the liberal sciences. {*Strabo, l. 14. c. 5. s. 13. 6:347} Saul was of the sect of the Pharisees and the son of a Pharisee. At that time, he was studying divinity in Jerusalem, in the synagogue of the Cilicians. He frequented the school of Gamaliel, who was that famous teacher among the Pharisees and an extremely strict observer of the law of Moses and of the traditions delivered to the fathers. {Ac 21:39 22:3 23:6,34 26:4,5 2Co 11:22 Ga 1:14 Php 3:5,6}

6522. Devout men carried Stephen to his burial and mourned deeply for him. {Ac 8:2}

6523. Aelius Lamia, who was the absentee governor of Syria, died at Rome. Flaccus Pomponius, the true governor of Syria, died in the province. {*Tacitus, Annals, l. 6. c. 27. 4:199} {*Suetonius, Tiberius, l. 3. c. 42. s. 1. 1:371}

## 4037b AM, 4747 JP, 34 AD

6524. Herod Agrippa had his daughter Mariamme by Cypros, ten years before his death. {*Josephus, Antiq., l. 18. c. 5. s. 4. (130) 9:89} {*Josephus, Antiq., l. 19. c. 9. s. 1. (354) 9:385}

6525. After the death of Stephen, a great persecution arose against the whole church which was at Jerusalem. {Ac 8:1 11:19} Saul, in an exceedingly great rage, made havoc of the church. [E850] He received authority from the chief priests and testified against the saints who were killed. He also entered into every house and took men and women captive. He bound and put them in prison and often beat them in every synagogue. He compelled some to deny Christ and to blaspheme, while others, who kept the faith, he persecuted to death. {Ac 8:1 9:13,21 22:4,5,19 26:9-11 Ga 1:13,23 Php 3:6 1Ti 1:13} [K618]

6526. This persecution dispersed the church into various countries, but was for the great advantage of the church. The apostles were left alone at Jerusalem, while the rest, of whom there were some thousands, {Ac 2:41 4:4} were dispersed into the regions of Judea and Samaria. They preached the gospel wherever they went. {Ac 8:1-4} Others went to Damascus, {Ac 9:19,25} among whom was Ananias, a devout man according to the law and one who had a good report among all the Jews who lived there. {Ac 22:12} It was very likely that others went even to Rome itself, and that among them were Junia and Andronicus, who were of note among the apostles and relatives of this persecutor, Paul. They had embraced the faith before him. {Ro 16:7} Others travelled as far as Phoenicia, Cyprus and Antioch and preached the word of God to the Jews only, {Ac 11:19} that is, to those who were dispersed among the Gentiles. {Jas 1:1 1Pe 1:1}

6527. Philip was among those who went to Samaria. After Stephen, the first martyr, he was the second in order among the seven who had been chosen. {Ac 8:5 21:8} Philip came into the city of Samaria and preached Christ there. The people with one accord listened to what he said. They saw the miracles which he did, for unclean spirits cried out with a loud voice and came out of many. He healed many who were stricken with palsies, or were lame. There was great joy in that city and many men and women believed and were baptized. Simon Magus also listened to Philip. For a long time, Simon had bewitched the people of Samaria with his sorceries. Everyone had said this was the great power of God. When Simon saw the great signs and wonders which Philip did, he believed and was baptized also. {Ac 8:5-13}

6528. When the apostles, who were at Jerusalem, heard that Samaria had received the word of the Lord, they sent Peter and John to them. They prayed and laid their hands on them, and the new converts received the Holy Spirit. When Simon Magus saw this, he offered them money so that he, too, might receive the gift of conferring the Holy Spirit. Peter sharply rebuked his mad impiety and warned him to repent of his wickedness and to ask pardon from God. Simon wanted the apostles to pray to the Lord for him. When they had completed their ministry in those regions, they returned to Jerusalem, preaching the gospel in the villages of Samaria as they went. {Ac 8:14-25}

6529. After many ages had passed since it had last been sighted, a bird called the Phoenix returned to Egypt and the learned Egyptians and the Greeks discussed many things about this miracle. {*Tacitus, Annals, l. 6. c. 28. 4:201} Dio stated that this bird appeared in Egypt two years later. {*Dio, l. 58. (27) 7:253}

6530. Philip, the tetrarch, who was always considered a modest man and a lover of ease and quietness, died in the twentieth year of Tiberius. He had governed Trachonitis, Gaulanitis and Batanea for thirty-seven years and died at Julias. He was put in a monument that he had previously built for himself, in which he was magnificently and lavishly interred. Since Philip had died without children, Tiberius annexed that principality to the province of Syria, but the tributes which were collected in this tetrarchy were to be kept within the borders of that country. {*Josephus, Antiq., l. 18. c. 4. s. 6. (106) 9:75} [K619]

6531. At Rome, in this twentieth year of Tiberius' reign, the consuls, Lucius Vitellius and Fabius Priscus, held the ten-year games, so that they might, as it were, extend the government for him, as it had previously been done repeatedly for Augustus. {*Dio, l. 58. (24) 7:247}

6532. In this year (as Dio wrote), or three years later (as Tacitus hinted at the end of the fifth book of his annals), this story was told. A certain young man said that he was Drusius, Germanicus' son. He was first seen in the isles of the Cyclades and soon after that on the continent of Greece and Ionia. He was attended by some of Caesar's freedmen and the ignorant were attracted by the fame of his name, because the minds of the Greeks were always ready for new and wonderful things. For they pretended and were convinced that if this Drusius could leave those who minded him, he would go to his father's armies and would invade Egypt or Syria. When Poppaeus Sabinus, who was in charge of Macedonia and Achaia, heard these things, he entered Nicopolis, which was a Roman colony. There he found out that the young man, when examined more closely, had said that he was Marcus Silanus' son. *[E851]* Many of his followers had sailed away and he sailed out as if he was going to Italy. Tacitus said he was never seen again and that this was the end of the matter. However, Dio added that this impostor was willingly received by the cities and strengthened with troops. He would, without doubt, have come into Syria and taken over the armies, had not someone recognised him and apprehended him and sent him to Tiberius. {*Tacitus, Annals, l. 5. c. 10. 4:151,153} {*Dio, l. 58. (25) 7:249} {*Dio, l. 58. (25) 7:249}

## 4038a AM, 4747 JP, 34 AD

6533. Philip, the Evangelist, was directed by an angel to go to Gaza, which was in a desert. {See note on 3672c AM. <<1818>>} There he met a eunuch, who had charge of the treasure of Candace, queen of the Ethiopians, in Meroe. He was returning in his chariot from Jerusalem, where he had been to worship. He was reading from Isaiah, when the Holy Spirit told Philip to go to him. Philip instructed him concerning faith in Christ and baptized him, after which Philip was immediately snatched away out of his sight by the Holy Spirit and found himself at Azotus. He passed through the country and preached the gospel in all the towns, until he came to Caesarea. {Ac 8:26-40}

## 4038b AM, 4748 JP, 35 AD

6534. Saul was still breathing out threatenings and slaughter against the disciples of the Lord and obtained letters from the high priest (Annas, {Ac 4:6} and the council of which he was then the head) for the synagogues of Damascus. They stated that if he found any who were Christians, he was to bring them bound to Jerusalem, to be punished. As he was approaching Damascus at noon, a light from heaven, brighter than the sun, shone around him and those with him. When they had all fallen to the ground, he heard a voice speaking to him in the Hebrew language:

"Saul, Saul, why persecutest thou me? It is hard for thee to kick against the pricks." {Ac 26:16}

6535. He asked who it was and was told:

"...I am Jesus, whom thou persecutest. But rise, and stand upon thy feet: for I have appeared unto thee for this purpose, to make thee a minister and a witness both of these things which thou hast seen, and of those things in the which I will appear unto thee; Delivering thee from the people, and *from* the Gentiles, unto whom I now send thee, to open their eyes, *and* to turn *them* from darkness to light, and *from* the power of Satan unto God, that they may receive forgiveness of sins, and an inheritance among them who are sanctified by faith that is in me." {Ac 26:15-18} [K620]

6536. Saul who was trembling and full of fear, asked what the Lord would have him do. He was told to go to Damascus and await further instructions. The men who were journeying with Saul were so amazed that they were speechless. They saw the light and heard a sound of words, but did not see Christ, who was speaking, nor understand anything that he said. {Ac 9:1-7 22:5-14 26:12-18}

6537. Saul got up from the earth, blinded by the glory of the light. They led him by the hand to Damascus, {Ac 9:8 22:11} where he stayed for three days without sight and did not eat or drink. There was a certain disciple named Ananias, to whom the Lord spoke in a vision. He was told to go to the street called *Straight* and enquire after Saul of Tarsus in the house of Judas. The Lord told him that Saul was praying. (Then Saul, in a vision, saw Ananias coming and laying his hands on him, that he might receive his sight.) Ananias objected that he had heard of this fellow and that he had authority from the religious leaders in Jerusalem to arrest all the Christians. The Lord told Ananias to go, for Saul would become a great missionary and witness for Christianity and would suffer much for it. Ananias went to the house and laid his hands on Saul. He told Saul that it was Jesus who had appeared to Saul on his way to Damascus and he, Ananias, had come to restore his sight and to anoint him with the Holy Spirit. At once, it was as if scales had fallen from his eyes and he received his sight. {Ac 9:9-18}

6538. Ananias told him:

"...The God of our fathers hath chosen thee, that thou shouldest know his will, and see that Just One, and shouldest hear the voice of his mouth. For thou shalt be his witness unto all men of what thou hast seen and heard. And now why tarriest thou? arise, and be baptized, and wash away thy sins, calling on the name of the Lord." {Ac 22:14-16}

*6539.* Saul got up and was baptized. He ate and was strengthened. {*Ac 9:18,19*}

*6540.* Luke, in Acts, did not mention what was revealed by the Lord to Saul at Damascus, concerning what he was to do. We learn from the book of Galatians what happened immediately after his conversion. He was told not to confer with men, nor go to Jerusalem to the apostles, but to spend some time in Arabia, or places near Damascus. There he would receive the knowledge of the gospel, not from men, but directly from Jesus Christ. {*Ga 1:12,16,17*} [*E852*]

*6541.* After this, Saul returned to Damascus and spent a few days with the disciples. {*Ga 1:17*} He immediately preached in the synagogues that Christ was the Son of God. All who heard these things were amazed. They asked each other whether this was not the man who had come from Jerusalem, to tie up the Christians and take them back to Jerusalem? Saul increased more and more in strength and confounded the Jews who lived at Damascus by teaching that Jesus was the Christ. {*Ac 9:19-22*} His first preaching of the gospel was to the Jews who lived at Damascus. {*Ac 26:20*}

*6542.* Tiberius was informed from Palestine, by Pilate, about the matters involving Christ. [*K621*] Tiberius proposed to the Senate that Christ should be considered one of the gods. The Senate opposed this, but Tiberius did not change his mind, and threatened that:

> "It would be dangerous for any to accuse a Christian."

*6543.* This is how it was related by Tertullian {*Tertullian, Apology, l. 1. c. 5,21. 3:22,35*} and others who followed him. {*Eusebius, Chronicles, l. 1. 1:258,259*} {*Eusebius, Ecclesiastical History, l. 2. c. 2. 1:111*} Our English writer, Gildas, stated this in a letter about the destruction of Britain: The first persecution, which arose in Judea after the murder of Stephen, ceased partly because of the conversion of Saul, who had greatly promoted it, and partly due to the fear of Tiberius.

*6544.* Lucius Vitellius, who had been consul at Rome the year before, was sent out by Tiberius as the proconsul for Syria. He arrived in Jerusalem, right at the feast of the passover, and received an honourable welcome. He remitted the whole tribute of the fruits put out for sale and allowed that the high priest's garments, with everything that belonged to them, be stored in the temple by the priests. These were formerly kept by the Roman governor in the citadel of Antonia. In this way, he satisfied the Jews. He appointed Jonathan, the son of Ananus (or Annas), as the high priest, instead of Joseph Caiaphas. He then went to Antioch. {*Josephus, Antiq.,*

*l. 15. c. 11. s. 4. (406-409) 8:197*} {*Josephus, Antiq., l. 18. c. 4. s. 3. (90,91) 9:65*}

*6545.* After Artaxias, the king of Armenia, had died, Artabanus, the king of Parthia, made Arsaces, the oldest of his children, king over the Armenians. Since Tiberius did not object or interfere, he made an attempt on Cappadocia and demanded the treasure left by Vonones in Syria and Cilicia, as well as asserting his right to the ancient boundaries of the Persians and Macedonians. He bragged and threatened that he would invade all the territory that was possessed by Cyrus or Alexander. Sinnaces was a rich nobleman who was supported by Abdus, a eunuch. They drew the leading men of the Parthians over to themselves, but they could find no suitable descendants of the royal family of the Arsacides, since most of them had been killed by Artabanus, or were too young to be king. So they sent secret messengers to Tiberius to make a request for their king, Phraates, the son of Phraates, who was being kept hostage at Rome. He was the son of Phraates III. {*Tacitus, Annals, l. 6. c. 31. 4:207,209*} {*Dio, l. 58. (26) 7:251,253*}

*6546.* Tiberius sent Phraates, sufficiently armed, into his father's kingdom and by astute diplomacy without warfare, manipulated foreign policy while he stayed quietly in Rome. In the meantime, these conspiracies became known. Artabanus, pretending friendship, invited Abdus to a banquet and gave him a slow poison. He also pretended friendship to Sinnaces with gifts, and kept him busy doing other things. Phraates, meanwhile, when he arrived in Syria, abandoned the Roman manner of life to which he had been accustomed, and resumed the Parthian customs but he was unable to handle his country's customs and fell sick and died. {*Tacitus, Annals, l. 6. c. 32. 4:209*}

*6547.* After the death of Phraates, Tiberius sent Tiridates III, who was from the same royal family and who was an enemy of Artabanus. To help him get the kingdom more quickly, Tiberius wrote to Mithridates, the Iberian, that he should invade Armenia. Tiberius hoped by this means to draw Artabanus from his own kingdom, as he would go to help his son. To this end, he reconciled Mithridates to his brother Pharasmanes, who had succeeded his father Mithridates in the kingdom of Iberia. With large gifts, he egged on Pharasmanes himself and the king of the Alanes to make a surprise attack on Artabanus. Tiberius made Lucius Vitellius the general over all these preparations in the east. {*Tacitus, Annals, l. 6. c. 32. 4:211*} {*Josephus, Antiq., l. 18. c. 4. s. 4. (96) 9:69,71*} {*Dio, l. 58. (26) 7:253*} [*K622*]

*6548.* Using both policy and force, Mithridates induced his brother Pharasmanes to advance his endeavours. Arsaces, the son of Artabanus, was killed by his servants, who were bribed with large sums of gold to do this. The

Iberians invaded Armenia and destroyed the city of Artaxata. When Artabanus heard these things, he equipped his son Orodes to avenge it. He gave him the Parthian troops and sent others to get mercenaries. On the opposing side, Pharasmanes allied himself to the Albanians and summoned the Sarmatians to his help, whose princes were called *Sceptruchi*, or *Wand-bearers*. Since the Sarmatians had received gifts, as the custom of that country was, from both sides, it supplied troops to both sides. The Iberians controlled all the passes and so had the Sarmatians enter Armenia by way of the Caspian passes. The Sarmatians who came from the Parthians were easily driven back, as there was only one pass available to them and it was between the farthest Albanian Mountains and the shore of the Caspian Sea. It was impassable in the summer because the Etesian gales flooded the seaboard. {*Tacitus, Annals, l. 6. c. 33. 4:211,213} {*Josephus, Antiq., l. 18. c. 4. s. 4. (98-100) 9:71,73} [E853]

6549. When Pharasmanes had received reinforcements, he forced Orodes, who was without his allies, to fight a battle, in which Pharasmanes then wounded Orodes through his helmet. He could not hit Orodes again, because he was carried away from him on his horse and the stoutest of his guard defended their wounded king. Nevertheless, a false rumour spread that he had been killed, and because the Parthians believed it and were dismayed, they lost the battle. {*Tacitus, Annals, l. 6. c. 34,35. 4:217} Hence, the Parthians lost Armenia again. {*Josephus, Antiq., l. 18. c. 4. s. 4. (98) 9:71} It was given to Mithridates of Iberia. {*Dio, l. 58. (26) 7:253}

## 4039a AM, 4748 JP, 35 AD

6550. Artabanus went at once, with the whole strength of his kingdom, to revenge this, but due to their better knowledge of the terrain, the Iberians were successful. Artabanus would not have given up, had Vitellius not gathered together his legions and spread a rumour, indicating he would invade Mesopotamia. Artabanus was afraid of the Roman forces. After this, Artabanus' fortune declined. He lost Armenia and Vitellius enticed his subjects to abandon their king, who was a tyrant in peace and unlucky in war. At this, Sinnaces had a secret conference with Abdagaeses and others and caused them to revolt. The way had already been prepared by the continual Parthian defeats. His subjects served through fear, not goodwill, and were encouraged when they had captains to follow. Vitellius bribed some friends and relatives of Artabanus, to try to kill him. When Artabanus learned of the conspiracy, he could find no way to thwart it. He was in danger from his nobility and he suspected even those who remained under his protection. He fled to the higher provinces and places near Scythia and hoped for help from the Carmanians and Hyrcanians, with whom he was related by marriage. {*Tacitus, Annals, l. 6. c. 36. 4:217,219} {*Josephus, Antiq., l. 18. c. 4. s. 4. (99,100) 9:71,73}

## 4039b AM, 4749 JP, 36 AD

6551. Agrippa, the son of Aristobulus, when he was in great financial need at Ptolemais, borrowed money at interest from Protus, a freedman, as he had previously done from his mother Bernice, who had since died. He used the help of Marsyas, his own freedman. Protus stated that Agrippa had defrauded him of some money and forced Marsyas to draw up a bond for twenty thousand Attic drachmas, but to accept twenty-five hundred less. Protus yielded, because he had no alternative. When Agrippa got this money, he went to Anthedon and prepared to sail to Italy. When Herennius Capito, the governor of Jamnia, heard that he was there, he sent soldiers there to exact from Agrippa the three hundred thousand drachmas of silver that he had owed to Caesar's treasury when he had lived at Rome. In this way, he was forced to stay, and so he made a pretence of obeying their commands, but as soon as it was night, he cut his cables and sailed to Alexandria. [K623] There, he offered to borrow two hundred thousand drachmas of silver from Alexander, the alabarch. He, however, said that he would lend him nothing, but would lend to his wife, Cypros, for in her he admired her love for her husband and her other virtues. When she had become his security, Alexander, the alabarch, advanced him five talents at Alexandria. He promised to deliver the rest to him at Puteoli, because he feared Agrippa would be a bad debt. {*Josephus, Antiq., l. 18. c. 6. s. 3. (155-160) 9:101-105}

6552. Philo, the Jew, mentioned the arrival of Agrippa at the city of Alexandria, when Flaccus was governor of Egypt at the time. {*Philo, Flaccus, l. 1. c. 5. (28,29) 9:319} Josephus stated that Philo was the brother of Alexander, the alabarch. {*Josephus, Antiq., l. 18. c. 8. s. 1. (259) 9:155} Jerome also stated, in his catalogue of ecclesiastical writers, that Philo was of the same family as the priests. Because of this, Baronius considered Philo to be none other than that Alexander who was said to be of the family of the priests. {Ac 4:6} {Baronius, 34 AD, num. 265.} However, this was that Alexander Lysimachus, who bore the office of alabarch (a governor of the Jews) at Alexandria. {Juvenal, Satire, 1.} Previously, he had been the steward of Antonia who was the mother of Emperor Claudius and he also was the father of Tiberius Alexander, the governor of Judea. Alexander was the richest of all the Jews of Alexandria. {*Josephus, Antiq., l. 19. c. 5. s. 1. (276) 9:343} {*Josephus, Antiq., l. 20. c. 5. s. 2. (100) 10:55} He melted gold and silver for the gates of the temple at Jerusalem (and not his father, as Baronius wrote in the place previously mentioned.) {*Josephus, Jewish War, l. 5. c. 5. s. 3. (205) 4:65}

6553. When Cypros had supplied her husband for his journey to Italy, she returned with her children to Judea by land. When Agrippa came to Puteoli, he wrote to Tiberius Caesar, who was then living at Capri. He told him that he had come so far to see him and asked permission to come to the island. Tiberius immediately wrote back a kind answer, to the effect that he would be glad to see him at Capri. Tiberius received him with great cheerfulness when he came and embraced him and offered him hospitality. {*Josephus, Antiq., l. 18. c. 6. s. 3,4. (160-162) 9:105}

6554. The next day, Caesar received letters from Herennius concerning the three hundred thousand drachmas Agrippa owed. Tiberius ordered the people of his household not to admit Agrippa until he had paid the debt. [E854] Agrippa was dismayed at Caesar's displeasure and begged Antonia, the mother of Germanicus and Claudius (later emperor), to lend him three hundred thousand drachmas, so that he would not lose Caesar's friendship. She recalled the friendship between herself and Bernice, Agrippa's mother, and that he had been brought up with her son Claudius, and so lent him the money. He paid his debt, regained Tiberius' favour and was so thoroughly reconciled to Caesar, that the latter commended his grandson Tiberius Gemellus, the son of Drusus, to Agrippa's charge. He ordered his grandson to accompany Agrippa wherever he went. Since Agrippa was deeply obliged to Antonia for this benefit, he began to revere Gaius Caligula, her grandson, who was considered gracious by everyone and was honoured for the memory of his father. By chance, Thallus, a Samaritan, was there at the same time, so he borrowed a million drachmas from him and repaid Antonia's debt. He kept the rest, to enable him to attend to Gaius more honourably. {*Josephus, Antiq., l. 18. c. 6. s. 4. (163-167) 9:105-109}

6555. Tigranes IV was the son of Alexander (who was killed by his father, Herod) and of Glaphyra, the daughter of Archelaus, king of the Cappadocians. He had turned from the Jews to the Greeks' religion and was the king of Armenia for a time. He was accused at Rome and punished there, dying without children. {*Tacitus, Annals, l. 6. c. 40. 4:225} {*Josephus, Antiq., l. 18. c. 5. s. 4. (139,141) 9:95} [K624]

6556. The Cietae, a tribe on the coast of Cilicia Trachea, were subject to Archelaus, the Cappadocian. They were compelled, after the Roman custom, to bring in the value of their annual revenues and to pay tribute. They migrated to the Taurus Mountains and there defended themselves, through the strong location of the place, against the weak forces of their king. Finally, Marcus Trebellius was sent by Vitellius, the governor of Syria, with four thousand legionary soldiers and some choice auxiliaries. They surrounded with works the two hills occupied by the barbarians. The smaller hill was called Cadra and the other one, Davara. They killed any who dared leave their strongholds and compelled the rest to surrender for lack of water. {*Tacitus, Annals, l. 6. c. 41. 4:225,227}

6557. After Artabanus had fled, the minds of the people turned to a new king. Vitellius persuaded Tiridates to seize the opportunity, and led his legions and auxiliaries to the bank of the Euphrates River. As they were sacrificing, some prepared the Suovetaurilia (a boar, a ram, and a bull offered to Mars), according to the custom of the Romans. Others prepared a horse to sacrifice, to pacify the river. The inhabitants around the Euphrates River told them that the river had risen greatly of its own accord, without any heavy rains. They also said that the white froth made circles in the form of a diadem, which was an omen of a prosperous journey. Others, however, interpreted it more astutely, saying that the beginnings of their expedition would be prosperous, but that this would not be long-lasting. They said this, because they gave more credit to the things which were portended by the earth and heaven, because the nature of rivers was not constant. If the rivers did show any good signs, they soon disappeared. Vitellius made a bridge from boats and crossed over the river with his army. Orospades came to his camp with several thousand cavalry and joined him. He had once been a banished man and had brought considerable aid to Tiberius when the latter had warred in Dalmatia. For that, Tiberius had made him a citizen of Rome. After this present service, he entered anew into the king's favour, and he made him governor of Mesopotamia. Not long after that, Sinnaces joined Tigranes, as also did Abdagaeses. They were the mainstay of his side and brought him the court treasure and royal regalia. Vitellius considered it sufficient to have shown the Roman forces and admonished Tiridates to remember his grandfather Phraates and his upbringing with Caesar. He should consider the nobles, so that they would be obedient to their king, and he should reverence the Romans. Everyone should keep their word. Then Vitellius returned to Syria with his legions. {*Tacitus, Annals, l. 6. c. 37. 4:219,221}

6558. From the Parthians, Tiridates received the cities of Nicephorium, Anthemusias and the other cities of Macedonia which spoke Greek. Halus and Artemita, cities of Parthia, also greatly rejoiced, for they had hated the cruelty of Artabanus, who had been brought up among the Scythians. They hoped that Tiridates would be gentle because he had been raised among the Romans. The Seleucians used a great deal of flattery and said their city was strong and surrounded by walls, not corrupted with barbarity, but keeping the laws of their founder, Seleucus. When Tiridates arrived there, they honoured him highly and reproached Artabanus as someone who was, indeed, of the family of the Arsacides on his mother's side, but who in all other things had degenerated. Tiridates committed the government of the country to the people, whereas Artabanus had given it over to the rule of three hundred of the nobility. {*Tacitus, Annals, l. 6. c. 41,42. 4:225-229}

6559. Tiridates then consulted what day he should be crowned. He received letters from Phraates and Hieron, two of the ruling nobility, who held the strongest governments, and who desired that he wait for a time. To satisfy these great men, he waited. In the meantime, he went to Ctesiphon, the seat of the kingdom, to await their arrival. When they delayed from one day to the next, Surenas, with the approval of many who were present, crowned Tiridates according to the custom of the country. [E855] [K625] If Tiridates had entered farther into the country and the other countries, all those who were wavering with doubts, would have been convinced and the Parthian empire would have been his. Instead, he stayed too long, besieging a citadel where Artabanus had stored his treasure and concubines. He gave them a breathing-space in which agreements could be repudiated. Phraates, Hieron and some others took no part in the celebration on the day appointed for his coronation. Some did this from fear and some out of envy of Abdagaeses who controlled the new king and was the only favourite at court. These defected to Artabanus. {*Tacitus, Annals, l. 6. c. 42,43. 4:229}

6560. Artabanus was discovered in Hyrcania, dressed in very humble attire and living by hunting with a bow. At first he was fearful, as if there were some treachery involved. When they had assured him that they had come to restore him to his kingdom again, he stayed only long enough to assemble the Scythian forces. (Josephus related that he got together a large army of the Dahae and Sacae.) He went with them at once, and did not change his poor clothes, to make the common people pity him more. Neither craftiness nor prayers were omitted, nor anything else by which he might draw the doubtful to him or make the willing more committed. {*Tacitus, Annals, l. 6. c. 43,44. 4:229,231} {*Josephus, Antiq., l. 18. c. 4. s. 4. (100) 9:73}

6561. He then approached Seleucia with a strong force. Tiridates was afraid of Artabanus and began to hesitate as to what action to take, whether he should encounter him immediately or delay the war. It was Abdagaeses' opinion that he should retire into Mesopotamia, with the river between them. In the meantime, he should raise forces from the Armenians and Elymeans and the rest of the countries beyond them. Then, after they had increased

their forces with the allies and any that the Roman captain would send, he should try his fortune. His advice was followed, because of Abdagaeses' authority and Tiridates' cowardliness. This retreat differed very little from a rout and the Arabians first led the way. The rest either went home or to Artabanus' camp. Tiridates returned to Syria with a small company and did not accuse them of the infamy of treason. {*Tacitus, Annals, l. 6. c. 44. 4:231}

6562. Artabanus easily overcame his enemies and was restored to his kingdom. {*Josephus, Antiq., l. 18. c. 4. s. 4. (100) 9:73} {*Dio, l. 58. (26) 7:253} He wrote letters to Tiberius, accusing him of parricides, murders, indolence and luxury. He also told Tiberius that he would swiftly appease the most righteous hatred of the citizens by his voluntary death. {*Suetonius, Tiberius, l. 3. c. 66. 1:403,405} Artabanus invaded Armenia and planned to attack Syria. {*Dio, l. 59. (27) 7:349}

6563. Gaius Caligula maintained a close friendship with Agrippa. On a certain day, as Agrippa was riding in the same coach with Gaius, Agrippa expressed the wish that Tiberius would shortly turn over the empire to Gaius, since he was a more deserving person. Eutychus, who was one of Agrippa's freedmen and his coach driver, overheard these words and said nothing. Later, Eutychus was accused of having stolen a garment from his patron. He had stolen it and fled. When he was brought back again, he was taken to Piso, the prefect of the city, and asked why he had fled. He replied that he had some secrets which he wanted to reveal to Caesar, that concerned Caesar's safety. At this, he was sent in bonds to Capri, where he was a prisoner for a long time before it pleased Caesar to give him any hearing. {*Josephus, Antiq., l. 18. c. 6. s. 5. (168-170) 9:109,111}

6564. A certain impostor persuaded the Samaritans that they should meet at Mount Gerizim, which was considered most holy by that people. He affirmed that he would then show them the holy vessels, buried where Moses had put them. Believing him, they took up arms and camped around a village called Tirathana, to await the arrival of the rest, so that they could ascend the hill with the larger company. [K626] Pilate took control of the top of the hill with his cavalry and foot soldiers and attacked those who were camped at the village. Some he killed, others fled and the rest were captured. He beheaded the ringleaders and those of their number with the most power. {*Josephus, Antiq., l. 18. c. 4. s. 1. (85-87) 9:61,63}

## 4040a AM, 4749 JP, 36 AD

6565. The leading men of Samaria appealed to Vitellius, the governor of Syria, and accused Pilate of this slaughter. They denied that this assembly at Tirathana had been in any way a revolt from the Romans, but simply a refuge from the tyranny of Pilate. As a result, Vitellius sent his friend, Marcellus, to take charge of Judea and ordered Pilate to go to Rome, to answer before Caesar for the crimes the Jews alleged he had done. He had lived ten years in that province, to which would be added the short time of four or five months, unless it was that he deferred his voyage through fear of storms. (The fast of the seventh month was past. {*Ac 27:9*}) He may have been detained by contrary winds or by some delay that made him prolong his journey. Before Pilate arrived in Rome, Tiberius had died. {*Josephus, Antiq., l. 18. c. 4. s. 2. (88,89) 9:63,65*}

6566. When Tiberius came from Capri to Tusculum, which was a region about twelve miles from Rome, he was persuaded, although much against his will, that he should hear Eutychus, so that they would know of what crime he was accusing his patron. When he looked into the matter, he found that Agrippa had neglected his commands to honour his grandson Tiberius, Drusus' son, and had wholly given himself over to Gaius. *[E856]* So he ordered Macro, who had succeeded Sejanus in the command of the praetorian guard, to bind Agrippa. Then Agrippa pleaded and begged for pardon for the sake of the memory of Tiberius' son, with whom he had been brought up in good friendship, and because of the services he had done for the young Tiberius. This was all in vain, and the praetorian soldiers carried him to prison, even in his purple robes. It was very hot weather at the time and he was very thirsty for want of wine. He saw a servant of Gaius carrying a pitcher of water and asked for a drink. When the servant willingly complied, Agrippa drank it and said to him:

> "Truly, lad, you have done me this service for your own good, for as soon as I shall be free from this bondage, I will beg Gaius for your freedom."

6567. Agrippa followed through on his promise. {*Josephus, Antiq., l. 18. c. 6. s. 6. (179-194) 9:115-123*}

6568. Agrippa stood bound among the other prisoners before the palace and leaned in a melancholy posture against a tree in which sat an owl. One of the prisoners, who was a German, saw the bird and asked a soldier who the prisoner in the purple robe was. When he heard that he was one of the chief nobility of the Jews, he was led to him and through an interpreter, told Agrippa that this bird signified that there would be a sudden change in his present fortune: He would be advanced to great dignity and power and would have a happy death. His death was most unhappy and showed that the German was a false prophet. He added that when he would see this bird again, he would die within five days. {*Josephus, Antiq., l. 18. c. 6. s. 7. (195-200) 9:123,125*}

6569. Antonia was grieved at the calamity of Agrippa, but thought it would be pointless to speak to Tiberius on his behalf. However, she obtained this much from Macro—that he might be committed to the custody of the soldiers who were kinder and that he would have a centurion who would provide him with his food. *[K627]* He was permitted the use of his daily things and his friends and freedmen, whose services might relieve him, were allowed to come to him. Then Silas, his friend, visited him, along with his freedmen Marsyas and Stechus. They brought him his favourite foods and also brought garments, as if they intended to sell them, on which he lay at night. The soldiers allowed this, having received orders to that end from Macro. In this way, he spent six months in prison, until the death of Tiberius. {*Josephus, Antiq., l. 18. c. 6. s. 7. (202-204) 9:127*}

6570. In the district of Gabalis, Herod, the tetrarch, and Aretas, the king of Arabia Petra, had a dispute over the boundaries. Aretas had not forgotten the wrong done to his daughter, whom Herod had married. Herod had despised her and had married Herodias, his brother's wife, in her place. Herod and Aretas waged war through their commanders. When the battle started, Herod's army was totally defeated, because they were betrayed by some refugees who had been driven from the tetrarchy of Philip and had served under Herod. Herod wrote letters to Tiberius, telling him what had happened. Tiberius was angry at Aretas for his bold attack, and wrote to Vitellius that he should make war on him. Tiberius wanted Vitellius either to bring him alive or, if dead, to send him his head. The Jews thought that Herod's defeat was the just judgment of God for the murder of John the Baptist. {*Josephus, Antiq., l. 18. c. 5. s. 1,2. (109-116) 9:77-81*}

## 4040b AM, 4750 JP, 37 AD

6571. When Gnaeus Acerronius and Gaius Pontius Nigrinus were consuls, Tiberius died on the 17th of the Calends of April (March 16). {*Suetonius, Tiberius, l. 3. c. 73. s. 1. 1:413*} {*Tacitus, Annals, l. 6. c. 50. 4:243*} It may have been on the 26th of March, when he had reigned twenty-two years, seven months and seven days from the death of Augustus. {*Dio, l. 58. (28) 7:257*} It was not five months and three days, as Josephus stated in the Antiquities; {*Josephus, Antiq., l. 18. c. 6. s. 10. (224) 9:137*} nor was it six months and three days, as he wrote in his Jewish War. {*Josephus, Jewish War, l. 2. c. 9. s. 5. (180) 2:393*}

6572. After the death of Tiberius was known, Marsyas ran to his patron Agrippa, whom he found bathing himself. He nodded his head and told him in Hebrew:

> "The lion is dead."

6573. When the centurion who was responsible for him, heard from them that Tiberius was dead, he took off Agrippa's bonds and wished them well. As they were merrily eating and drinking, someone came and said Tiberius was still alive and that he would shortly return to the city. The centurion was terrified by this and ordered Agrippa to be pushed away from the rabble and bound and to be more carefully guarded. The next day, Gaius sent two letters: One went to the Senate, stating that Gaius had succeeded Tiberius in the empire; the other went to Piso, the prefect of the city, and said the same thing, adding that he should set Agrippa free and restore him to the house where he had previously lived. Although he had been a prisoner, he had nevertheless lived at his own discretion. {*Josephus, Antiq., l. 18. c. 6. s. 10. (228-236) 9:139-143}

6574. Gaius returned to Rome, bringing the body of Tiberius. He held a very lavish funeral with great solemnity. He would have released Agrippa on the same day but on the advice of Antonia, he did not. She wished Agrippa well, but said he should not free him too quickly, in case he seemed to be doing this out of hatred for Tiberius, who had imprisoned Agrippa. [E857] Not many days later, however, he sent for him at his house and ordered his hair to be cut, changed his clothes and then put a crown on his head. [K628] He made him king of Philip's tetrarchy and also gave him the tetrarchy of Lysanias. He changed his chain of iron into a chain of gold of the same weight, and sent Marullus as cavalry commander to Judea. {*Josephus, Antiq., l. 18. c. 6. s. 10. (236,237) 9:143}

6575. Gaius Caligula freed Agrippa, the grandson of Herod, from bonds which Tiberius had put on him, and gave him his grandfather's principality. {*Dio, l. 59. (8) 7:283} Philo stated that he was honoured with the office of governor by the Roman Senate, and that Gaius gave him the kingdom and the third part of the old dominion that his uncle Philip had possessed. {*Philo, Flaccus, l. 1. c. 5. (25,26) 9:317} When Agrippa had received the kingdom, he asked Gaius for Thaumastus, who had given him a drink while he was a prisoner. Agrippa gave him his liberty and made him steward of his goods. When Agrippa died, he left him in the same office to his son Agrippa and daughter Bernice. Thaumastus was highly respected as long as he lived. {*Josephus, Antiq., l. 18. c. 6. s. 6. (194) 9:123}

6576. Caligula gave Antiochus, the son of Antiochus Commagene, his father's kingdom, as well as the coastal region of Cilicia. {*Dio, l. 59. (8) 7:283}

6577. Vitellius, the governor of Syria, took two legions of heavily armed foot soldiers, as well as the foot soldiers and cavalry that had been sent by the kings who were allies. He hurried toward Petra and came to

Ptolemais. He intended to lead his army through Judea, but the leaders of that country approached him and asked him not to pass that way, as the customs of their country would not permit any images to be carried there, and the Roman banners had many images. Yielding to their request, he sent his army through the large plain, while he himself came to Jerusalem with Herod, the tetrarch, and his friends, to offer sacrifices to God at the next feast, which was to happen soon. When he arrived, he was magnificently entertained by the people and stayed there three days. In the meantime, he transferred the high priesthood from Jonathan to his brother Theophilus. {*Josephus, Antiq., l. 18. c. 5. s. 3. (120-124) 9:85,87}

6578. Four days later, Vitellius received letters of Tiberius' death, after which he made the people take the oath of fidelity to the new emperor, Gaius. {*Josephus, Antiq., l. 18. c. 5. s. 3. (124) 9:87} Thereupon, Agrippa sent letters to Gaius and stated: {*Philo, Gaius, l. 1. c. 36. (288) 10:145}

"They greatly desired succession (Oh emperor), and it was first heard of at Jerusalem and the same news was diffused to the neighbouring provinces from the holy city. Since this city, of all the east, first greeted you as emperor, it is fitting that it should be treated more graciously by you."

6579. In the councils of the Jews, in their speech made some time later to Petronius, Agrippa said something very similar: {*Philo, Gaius, l. 1. c. 32. (231,233) 10:121}

"When Gaius had obtained the empire, we first, of all Syria, congratulated you with Vitellius (whose successor you are). He was in our city and had received letters concerning this business. We spread this joyful news to other cities and our temple was the first of all temples to sacrifice for the empire of Gaius."

6580. Vitellius recalled his forces and abandoned his intended war, because of the new emperor. Some reported that when Aretas had heard the news of this expedition, he had learned from auguries that it was impossible for Vitellius' army to come to Petra, because one of the leaders would die - either the one who had ordered the expedition against Aretas, or the one who was leading the expedition. {*Josephus, Antiq., l. 18. c. 5. s. 3. (124,125) 9:87}

6581. Josephus wrote that Vitellius went to Antioch and sent his army into their winter quarters. {*Josephus, Antiq., l. 18. c. 5. s. 3. (124) 9:87} [K629] This was not likely, since it was the beginning of summer. He should have said that he went with his forces to the Euphrates River to make a league with the king of the Parthians. It appears, from Suetonius and Dio, that this was done, not in Tiberius' reign (as Josephus thought), but under

Gaius, for Artabanus always hated and despised Tiberius, but willingly sought an alliance with Gaius. Vitellius, using all his diplomacy, not only had a conference with him, but also had him worship the Roman standards. As Artabanus was crossing the Euphrates River, he admired the Roman eagles and sacrificed to the images of Augustus and Gaius. He agreed to the conditions of peace, which were favourable to the Romans, and gave his children as hostages. {*Suetonius, Caligula, l. 4. c. 14. s. 3. 1:437} {*Suetonius, Vitellius, l. 7. c. 2. s. 4. 2:239} {*Dio, l. 59. (27) 7:349,351}

6582. The king and Vitellius met in the middle of a bridge, each with their guard. After they had agreed to the terms of a league, Herod invited them both to a banquet in a pavilion he had erected at great cost in the middle of the river. Then Vitellius returned to Antioch and Artabanus to Babylon. However, Herod sent this news to Caesar before Vitellius' envoys could inform Caesar. When he received his letters, Caesar wrote back to Vitellius that he had already known of all these things through Herod's messengers. This greatly angered Vitellius, but he did nothing about it at the time. {*Josephus, Antiq., l. 18. c. 4. s. 5. (101-105) 9:73,75} [E858]

6583. Not long after, Artabanus sent his son Darius as hostage, along with many gifts. These included Eleazar, a Jew who was ten and a half feet tall and was called the giant. {*Josephus, Antiq., l. 18. c. 4. s. 5. (104) 9:75}

6584. After the Jews of Alexandria had given Gaius all the honours that were lawful for them to decree, they came and offered the decree to Flaccus Avillius. They wanted him to send an embassy, since they were not permitted to do so. He said he would be pleased to send it by his messengers. He read the decree and allowed many of its points. He smilingly said:

> "Your piety highly pleases me, I will send it as you desire, I will be your envoy that Gaius may perceive your gratitude and I will be a witness of the peoples' modesty and obedience, well-known to me."

6585. However, he withheld this decree, in order to make it seem as though they were the only enemies of Gaius. {*Philo, Flaccus, l. 1. c. 12. (97,98) 9:357}

6586. In the first year of the reign of Gaius Caligula, Josephus, the writer of the history of the Jews, was born. He was the son of Mattathias, a priest, as Josephus stated in his autobiography. {*Josephus, Life, l. 1. c. 1. (5) 1:5}

## 4041a AM, 4750 JP, 37 AD

6587. When Saul had preached the gospel at Damascus for a long time, the Jews discussed how they might kill him and they were helped in this by the governor under

Aretas (who had recently defeated the army of Herod, the tetrarch). He held Damascus with a garrison and watched the gates day and night, so that they might take Saul and kill him. However, Saul was let down by a rope at night, in a basket, and escaped from them. {Ac 9:23-25 2Co 11:32,33}

6588. After the first three years of his apostleship were over, Saul returned to Jerusalem to see Peter and stayed with him for fifteen days. {Ga 1:18} [K630] He tried to join with the disciples, but they were all afraid of him and did not believe that he was a disciple. However, Barnabas took him and brought him to the apostles (that is, Peter and James, the brother of the Lord, for he saw no other apostles, {Ga 1:19}). Barnabas told them how Saul had seen the Lord on the road and that Jesus had spoken to him, and how Saul had preached boldly at Damascus in the name of Jesus. {Ac 9:26,27}

6589. Saul spoke boldly at Jerusalem in the name of Jesus and disputed with the Greeks, or the Jews who spoke Greek, as the Syriac version correctly translated this passage. The Jews planned to kill him. {Ac 9:29}

6590. When Saul was in the temple praying, he fell into a trance and saw the Lord speaking to him, to hurry and get out of Jerusalem, for the Jews would not hear his message. He replied that the Jews knew that he had imprisoned and beaten those in every synagogue who believed in Jesus. When the blood of the martyr Stephen was shed, Saul was also standing by, guarding the garments of those who killed him. The Lord told him to leave, and he would send him to the Gentiles. {Ac 22:17-21}

6591. The brethren at Jerusalem brought him to Caesarea and sent him into his own city of Tarsus. {Ac 9:30} He went into the countries of Syria and Cilicia. His face was unknown to the churches of Judea, who had only heard that he was preaching the faith which once he had destroyed, but they glorified God in him. {Ga 1:21-23}

6592. The churches had rest throughout all Judea, Galilee and Samaria. They were edified and walked in the fear of the Lord and the comfort of the Holy Spirit, and were multiplied. {Ac 9:31}

## 4041b AM, 4751 JP, 38 AD

6593. Herod Agrippa had a daughter by Cypros, whom he named Drusilla (and who later married Felix). {Ac 24:24} She was six years old when her father died. {*Josephus, Antiq., l. 18. c. 5. s. 4. (132,133) 9:91} {*Josephus, Antiq., l. 19. c. 9. s. 1. (354,355) 9:385}

6594. Gaius Caligula forced Macro, to whom Egypt had been committed (for the six years that were appointed by Tiberius for the government of Flaccus Avillius had expired), and his wife, Ennia, with whose help he had acquired the empire, to commit suicide. {*Philo, Gaius, l. 1. c. 8. (60,61) 10:31} {*Philo, Flaccus, l. 1. c. 4. (16) 9:311,313} {*Suetonius, Caligula, l. 4. c. 26. s. 1. 1:457} {*Dio, l. 59. (10) 7:291}

6595. After Macro was killed, Flaccus, who was the governor of Egypt and on whom Caligula most relied, was shrewdly afraid of Caligula. Dionysius, Lampo and Isidorus persuaded him to use that occasion to be generous to the people of Alexandria and befriend them. When these three said that nothing would please the people more than allowing them to plunder the Jews, Flaccus heeded their advice. {*Philo, Flaccus, l. 1. c. 4. (16-24) 9:311-317}

6596. Caligula, by a decree of the Senate, gave Sohaemus the kingdom of the Arabians of Iturea. To Cotys he gave Lesser Armenia and some parts of Arabia; to Rhoemetalces he gave the kingdom of Cotys, while the son of Polemon received his father's kingdom, that is, Pontus. {*Dio, l. 59. (12) 7:295,297}

6597. In the second year of Caligula's reign, Herod Agrippa asked permission to return home to settle the affairs of his kingdom, promising that when he had done that, he would return. {*Josephus, Antiq., l. 18. c. 6. s. 11. (238,239) 9:145} [E859] [K631] The emperor persuaded him that taking the fastest way was by sea, saying that the Etesian winds were expected any day. He therefore advised him to go directly to Alexandria and go home the rest of the way by land, which would be easier than sailing all the way. Agrippa followed his advice and went to Puteoli. There he found a ship ready to set sail for Alexandria, and a few days later he arrived in Alexandria. {*Philo, Flaccus, l. 1. c. 5. (25-27) 9:317}

6598. The Alexandrians naturally hated the Jews and did not like the fact that they had a king. In their gymnasium, they derided Agrippa with scurrilous speeches and mocking verses recited by jesters. They brought in a madman by the name of Carabas, who night and day went about naked in the streets. They put him in an elevated position, so everyone could see him, and gave him a paper crown and a mat for his body instead of a robe. For his sceptre, he had a piece of a reed taken from the ground. He was adorned with the trappings of a king, in the manner of actors, and the young men carried poles on their shoulders as a mock guard. Others came up to greet him while some asked for justice and others asked him for advice concerning the state. Then there was a general acclamation by all those surrounding him, and they called him *Marin*, which means *Lord* in the Syrian language. {*Philo, Flaccus, l. 1. c. 5,6. (33-39) 9:321-323} Thus the king of the Jews was derided by others in the same manner just as the Jews themselves, five years

earlier, had mocked the true majesty of their own king, Jesus Christ.

6599. The Jews of Alexandria informed Agrippa of the treachery that Flaccus, the governor, had plotted for their destruction. They also gave him the writing which they had given to Flaccus to be sent to Gaius at the beginning of his reign. Through malice, Flaccus had made it impossible for them to send it any sooner. {*Philo, Flaccus, l. 1. c. 12. (103) 9:359} {*Philo, Gaius, l. 1. c. 28. (178-180) 10:91,93}

6600. The apostle Peter visited the churches of Judea, Galilee and Samaria and called on the saints that lived at Lydda. There he healed Aeneas, who was sick with the palsy and had been confined to his bed for eight years. When all who lived at Lydda and Sharon saw this miracle, they turned to the Lord. {Ac 9:31-35} Lydda and Sharon are mentioned in the Old Testament. {1Ch 5:16 1Ch 27:29}

6601. A certain disciple, whose name was Tabitha in the Syriac language and Dorcas in the Greek, meaning a *she-goat*, and who did many good deeds of charity, died at Joppa. Because Lydda was close to Joppa, the disciples had heard that Peter was there, so they sent two men to him, to have him come to Joppa at once. When Peter arrived, he fell on his knees and prayed, and restored her to life. This became known throughout all Joppa and many believed in the Lord. Peter stayed there many days in the house of Simon, a tanner. {Ac 9:36-43}

6602. When the common people of Alexandria had regained the favour of Flaccus, the governor, they all agreed early one morning that the statues of Caesar were to be set up in the synagogues of the Jews. [K632] The governor allowed this to be done without any regard for the public security, even though he knew that there were more than a million Jews living in Alexandria and throughout all the vast country from the descent of Libya right to the border of Ethiopia. {*Philo, Flaccus, l. 1. c. 6. (42-43) 9:325,327} Then they assembled in large companies and either ravaged their synagogues by cutting down their groves, or razed them to the ground. In all the synagogues which they could not overthrow or burn, because of the large number of Jews who lived nearby, they set up the images of Gaius. In the greatest and most frequented synagogues they set up statues, in elevated positions, of chariots with four brass horses. In their zeal, they ran out of new chariots, so they took out the old rusty ones, whose horses lacked their ears, tails, and feet, and those that had been dedicated (as was reported) to that Cleopatra who was the great grandmother of the last queen by that name. Gaius believed that all these things were happening out of the love that the Alexandrians had for him. He heard about these events through the registers sent to him from Alexandria (for he read them more willingly than any poem or history) and from some domestic servants (of whom many were Egyptians). They were in the habit of praising these things and laughing at them with him. {*Philo, Gaius, l. 1. c. 18. (120-126) 10:61,63}

6603. When Drusilla, his sister, died, Gaius Caligula decreed a period of public mourning for her. Anyone who laughed, bathed or held a feast on that day would be killed. {*Suetonius, Caligula, l. 4. c. 24. s. 1. 1:453} {*Dio, l. 59. (13) 7:301}

6604. Flaccus, the governor of Egypt, made an edict in which he declared the Jews to be foreigners and did not give them the freedom to plead their cases, but condemned them outright. [E860] The city of Alexandria had five divisions named after the first five letters of the Greek alphabet. Two of them were called the Jewish quarters, because most of the Jews lived there, although many Jews had houses here and there throughout the other quarters. The common people of Alexandria obtained permission from Flaccus to plunder the Jews. They expelled them from four of the divisions and drove them into a small section of the remaining division. The area could not hold them all and the Jews fled out to the beaches, tombs and dung hills and were robbed of everything, as their enemies ran violently through their abandoned houses. They divided the spoils, just like a victorious army, and broke open the shops of the Jews, which were closed at the time, because of the mourning for Drusilla's death. They carried many things away from there and used them for themselves. The ransacking of four hundred houses did less harm to the Jews than their loss of trade, because once the creditors had lost their security, no husbandman, mariner, merchant or craftsman was allowed to practise his trade. {*Philo, Flaccus, l. 1. c. 8. (53-57) 9:333,335} {*Philo, Flaccus, l. 1. c. 11. (94) 9:355}

6605. Their enemies thought that in no time they would see them lie in heaps, since so many thousands of men, women and children had been pushed like beasts into a narrow corner of the city, that they would either be killed, or die from famine, or be stifled in that hot place. Even the neighbouring air was fouled by their breath. They watched diligently, in case any should secretly escape. As many as they intercepted, they first tormented and then killed, using all manner of cruelty. Another band of them lay in wait for the Jews who arrived at the ports. [K633] When they had taken away their merchandise, they burned the owners in a fire made from the rudders, oars and planks of the ships. In the middle of the city, others were burned to death in a most miserable manner. Lacking wood, the Alexandrians used green vines and made a fire with them, into which they cast these miserable men, who were killed from the

smoke rather than the fire. Others were dragged through the market place with cords tied to their ankles, while the common people mocked them. They mutilated their dead bodies and cut off their members, trampling on them with such cruelty, that they allowed no remains to be found for burial. {*Philo, Gaius, l. 1. c. 19. (127-131) 10:63-65} Any who mourned the misfortune of their friend or relative, were punished for their compassion. They were scourged and after they had endured every kind of torment that bodies were able to endure, they were crucified. {*Philo, Flaccus, l. 1. c. 9. (58-72) 9:335-341}

6606. Flaccus, the governor, ordered that thirty-eight of the senate, whom Augustus had appointed as a public council of the Jews, be arrested in their own houses and bound at once. They dragged these old men through the market place, with their hands tied behind them, some bound with cords, others with chains. They were brought into the theatre, where they were stripped and scourged as they stood before their enemies, who sat as judges. Among these men were Euodius Trypho and Andro, who were treated thus in the sight of those who had robbed them of their goods. It was a custom that no one should be condemned until the solemn celebrations and feast days of the births of the Augustans were past. However, on one of those very days (for the birthday of Gaius was on the last day of August), Flaccus afflicted these innocent men that day in the following way: From the morning to the third or fourth hour of the day (nine or ten a.m.), the Jews were scourged, hung, tied to wheels, condemned and led through the middle of the wrestling place for punishment. Then dancers were brought in, as well as jesters, trumpeters and other entertainments. The women were carried away as captives for any trifling matter, not only in the market place, but also in the open theatre. They were brought onto the stage amid distressing accusations. When the crowd discovered that any were not Jews, they were released, for in their haste, they mistakenly apprehended many as Jews before determining their place of origin. If they found any Jews among the spectators, the crowd became tyrannical and ordered the Jews to eat swine's flesh. All the Jewish women who ate it, for fear of further torture, were let go, but those who refused to eat it, were tortured most cruelly. {*Philo, Flaccus, l. 1. c. 10,11. (73-96) 9:343-357}

6607. Castus, who was the boldest of the centurions, was ordered by the governor to take the bravest of his band with him and break into the Jews' houses, to see if they had any hidden weapons. Castus immediately did as he was ordered. The Jews allowed the searchers into all the private areas of their homes. Their women, who never went abroad, and the fearful virgins, who out of modesty avoided the sight of being seen by their own kindred, were displayed to eyes, not merely unfamiliar, but terrorising, through the fear of military violence. However, after all this scrutiny, the arms which they were looking for were not found. For Bassus had, a short time before, taken all arms from the Egyptians, on the orders of Flaccus, *[K634]* since it was possible to observe a large number of ships arriving at the port, full of arms suitable for seditious men, who had often before tried to revolt. However, the Jews had never been involved in nor been suspected of being part of any revolt. They went about their business and behaved as good citizens of the city. {*Philo, Flaccus, l. 1. c. 11. (86-95) 9:349-355} [E861]*

### 4042a AM, 4751 JP, 38 AD

*6608.* Because of this persecution, the Jews did not observe the feast of tabernacles around the autumnal equinox. Flaccus, the governor, was suddenly arrested by Bassus, the centurion, while he was at a feast hosted by Stephanio, the freedman of Tiberius Caesar. Bassus had been sent from Italy with a band of soldiers, specifically to apprehend Flaccus. When he set sail on the return journey at the beginning of winter, he was storm-tossed and barely arrived in Italy after much toil. There, Flaccus was immediately welcomed by those two malicious accusers, Lampo and Isidorus, who had incited him against the Jews. Flaccus was condemned and stripped of all his inheritance and goods, which were very valuable. He would have been banished to the most barren island of Gyara, in the Aegean Sea, had Lepidus not begged that he be sent to live on Andros, which was close to Gyara. He was killed there, on the command of Gaius, who did the same to all the noblemen who were banished. {*Philo, Flaccus, l. 1. c. 13-21. (108-191) 9:361-403}*

### 4042b AM, 4752 JP, 39 AD

*6609.* Herodias, the sister of Agrippa and wife of Herod the tetrarch, was mad with envy to see Agrippa so glorious in his kingly majesty. She persuaded her husband, Herod, that they should go to Rome and beg Caesar for similar honours. Agrippa knew of their intention and preparation for the journey. As soon as he heard that they had sailed, he sent his freedman Fortunatus to Rome also, to go to Caesar with gifts and letters written against his uncle. Herod arrived at Baiae, a delightful town in Campania, where Caesar was staying. He was admitted into his presence, but before he could do anything, Caesar gave him the letters he had received from Agrippa. These letters accused Herod of having previously conspired with Sejanus against Tiberius and of currently favouring Artabanus, the Parthian, over the new government of Gaius. They claimed that he had prepared, for that purpose, enough arms to furnish seventy thousand heavily armed foot soldiers. When Gaius asked Herod if the things which were being said about the

number of arms were true, he acknowledged it, for he could not deny it. Gaius thought he had enough evidence of a planned revolt and took the tetrarchy of Galilee and Peraea from him, later adding it to Agrippa's kingdom, together with all of Herod's treasure. He sent Herod to Lyons in Gaul and condemned him to perpetual exile. When Gaius learned that Herodias was Agrippa's sister, he allowed her to keep her own wealth. He did not think that she would willingly be her husband's companion in exile and so promised to spare her as a favour to Agrippa. She thanked Gaius for this favour, but professed that she would not make use of it at this time, as she considered it a sin to forsake her husband in his calamity, when she had enjoyed prosperous times with him. Gaius took this as a reproach and ordered that she also be banished, with her husband, while he gave her goods to Agrippa. {*Josephus, Antiq., l. 18. c. 7. s. 1,2. (240-256) 9:145-153}* So they were punished for their incestuous marriage, eight years after John the Baptist had been beheaded by this Herod and six years after Christ our Saviour had been mocked by the same Herod. {*Lu 23:11} [K635]*

*6610.* Pontius Pilate was so continually vexed by Gaius, that he committed suicide. {*Eusebius, Chronicles, l. 1. 1:260} {*Eusebius, Ecclesiastical History, l. 2. c. 7. 1:125} {Orosius, l. 7. c. 5.} {Cassidorus, Chronicle}*

*6611.* Gaius spanned the gulf between Misenum and Puteoli with a pontoon bridge almost three and a half miles long. He crossed the bridge with his chariot, followed by a long train of his supposed spoils. Among the hostages in the train was the Parthian lad, Darius, who was the son of Artabanus. Gaius mocked Darius and Xerxes, because he claimed to have made a longer bridge across the sea than Xerxes had. {*Josephus, Antiq., l. 19. c. 1. s. 1. (5,6) 9:217} {*Suetonius, Caligula, l. 4. c. 19. 1:445} {*Dio, l. 59. (17) 7:311,313}*

*6612.* Under the pretence of the German war, Gaius also went a little beyond the Rhine River and then returned immediately, as though he intended to go into Britain. {*Dio, l. 59. (21) 7:325}*

*6613.* Gaius sent for Vitellius from Syria in order to execute him. He was accused of having allowed Tiridates, whom Tiberius had sent to the Parthians as king, to be kicked out of his kingdom by them. {*Dio, l. 59. (27) 7:351}*

*6614.* Gaius sent Petronius to Syria as the successor for Vitellius. {*Josephus, Antiq., l. 18. c. 8. s. 2. (261) 9:155}* His full name was Publius Petronius. {*Philo, Gaius, l. 1. c. 42. (333) 10:167} {*Josephus, Antiq., l. 19. c. 6. s. 3. (301) 9:357}* (Strabo also mentioned him.) {See note on 3983b AM. <<5908>>} He was not, as Baronius thought, the Lucius Petronius who died long before this time, about whom Valerius Maximus mentioned that he was born of low parentage and rose to the level of an equestrian. {*Valerius Maximus, l. 4. c. 7. s. 5. 1:421} {Baronius, 41 AD, num. 4.}

6615. Vitellius came to Gaius Caligula and escaped death. He conducted himself more humbly than was appropriate for his rank. [E862] Falling at Caesar's feet, he burst out crying and called him a god and worshipped him. He vowed that if he should escape this punishment, he would sacrifice to him. He so mollified and appeased Caesar, that Gaius not only allowed him to live, but counted him among his best friends. {*Dio, l. 59. (27) 7:351} He was the first who gave Gaius the idea of being worshipped as a god. Vitellius was quite good at flattery. When he returned from Syria, he did not dare come into Gaius' presence, but turning himself around fell prostrate on the ground with his face covered. {*Suetonius, Vitellius, l. 7. c. 2. s. 5. 2:239,241} Later, when Gaius affirmed that he was talking with the Moon goddess, he asked Vitellius if he had not seen him while he was accompanied by the goddess. Vitellius, with his eyes cast down as though astonished and trembling, replied in a low voice that the gods alone were permitted to see one another. {*Dio, l. 59. (27) 7:351} Thus Vitellius made this beginning. Although he had governed the provinces with the same virtues as his ancestors, he surpassed all men in flattery. {*Dio, l. 59. (27) 7:351} {*Tacitus, Annals, l. 6. c. 32. 4:211}

6616. Then Gaius appointed himself a priest and took his horse as colleague in his priesthood. {*Dio, l. 59. (28) 7:355} He ordered that a temple be built to him, at Miletus in Asia, having selected that city ahead of the others, because he said that Ephesus worshipped Diana and Pergamum and Smyrna were dedicated to Augustus and Tiberius. [K636] The real reason was, that he wanted to use for himself the large and beautiful temple which the people of Miletus had built to Apollo. {*Dio, l. 59. (28) 7:351-355} He also planned to finish the oracle, Apollo Didymeon, at Miletus. {*Suetonius, Caligula, l. 4. c. 21. 1:447}

## 4043a AM, 4752 JP, 39 AD

6617. Strangers from the neighbouring countries had crept into Jamnia, a city of Judea that was very populous. They always tried to do something which opposed the Jewish customs. When they heard how much Gaius wanted to be worshipped as a god and what a good friend he was to the country of the Jews, they promptly built an altar of clay bricks to vex the Jews. The Jews were scornful and destroyed the altar, whereupon their adversaries accused them before Capito, the quaestor, who had the oversight of the tributes in Judea. He wrote to Gaius and aggravated and embellished the matter.

Gaius ordered that in place of the destroyed brick altar in Jamnia, the Jews should erect a large image in honour of him, all in gold, in the temple of Jerusalem. In this, he was following the advice of Helicon, an Egyptian, and Apelles of Askelon, a tragic actor. Gaius sent letters to Petronius, the governor of Syria, detailing the dedication of the statue. He was to march from the Euphrates River against the Jews with half the army (appointed for defence against the seditions of the kings and countries of the east). He was to accompany the statue, not necessarily so that the dedication would be more majestic, but so that anyone who resisted could be executed at once. The statue was not sent from Italy, nor was Petronius commanded to take any troops from Syria, otherwise some sudden sedition would have occurred over the violation of the Jewish laws. Petronius ordered a statue to be made closer at hand and sent for the best craftsmen from Phoenicia, as well as locating the materials and a place where they could make it at Sidon. {*Philo, Gaius, l. 1. c. 30,31. (200-223) 10:103-117}

6618. In the meantime, he gathered as large an army as he could and wintered at Ptolemais with two legions. He intended to undertake the war at the beginning of the spring. He sent a letter to Gaius, who commended his industry and advised him to use every force necessary in the process and so subdue the stubbornness of that country. {*Josephus, Antiq., l. 18. c. 8. s. 2. (262) 9:155,157}

## 4043b AM, 4753 JP, 40 AD

6619. In a dispute that arose between the Jews and the Greeks who lived in Alexandria, three chosen envoys from each side were sent to Gaius. Philo, who the most famous of them, headed the embassy of the Jews. Apion headed the Greek embassy. {*Josephus, Antiq., l. 18. c. 8. s. 1. (257-260) 9:153,155} He was born at an oasis in Egypt and wished to be called an Alexandrian, because he had been made a citizen of that city. {*Josephus, Apion, l. 2. c. 3. (29) 1:303} Pliny stated that some had surnamed him *The Cantankerous.* {*Pliny, l. 37. c. 19. 10:225} Pliny added the following things about him, in the preface to his whole work to Titus Vespasian: {*Pliny, l. 1. c. 0. (26) 1:17}

> "Apion, the grammarian (the person whom Tiberius Caesar called the *world's cymbal,* whereas he might rather have been thought to be a drum, advertising his own renown), wrote that persons to whom he dedicated his compositions received from him the gift of immortality."

6620. He wrote a most untruthful book against the Jews, to which Josephus replied in his second book against Apion, as the first book was against other slanderers of the Jews.

6621. The envoys of the Jews (of whom Philo, at the end of the embassy written by himself, said there were five and not three, as Josephus stated) sailed to Gaius in the middle of winter, to entreat him to stop the wrongs which they were suffering. *[E863] [K637]* They gave him a record containing the list of all the calamities as well as the petition against them, taken from that larger petition which the Jews had sent him through their King Agrippa. However, their adversaries won the favour of Helicon, the Egyptian, who was the prefect of the emperor's chamber. They did this, not so much with money as with the hope of future honours, which they promised to give him when Gaius came to Alexandria. When the Jewish envoys wanted to pacify and appease Gaius, they were not allowed access to him. {*Philo, Gaius, l. 1. c. 27. (172-174) 10:89}

6622. At first, Gaius concealed his hatred against the Jews and received their envoys in Mars' field. As he came from his mother's gardens, he greeted them with a cheerful countenance and with his right hand, made a gesture which indicated that he would be kind to them. He sent Homilus to them, who was the master of the ceremonies, and through him promised that he would take care of their cause when he had time. {*Philo, Gaius, l. 1. c. 28. (181) 10:93} Later, when he came to visit the gardens of Mecenas and Lamia, which were near the other garden and the city, the envoys were brought in and humbly showed their reverence to Gaius. They greeted him by the name of Augustus and he smilingly asked them:

> "Are you the ones who are hated of the gods, who alone despise me, who am declared a god by the confession of all men, and had rather worship your unnamed thing?"

6623. Then he held up his hands to heaven and burst into a speech which was neither lawful to hear nor, much less, to repeat. The Jews' adversaries then greatly rejoiced and called him by all the names of the gods. When Isidorus, a bitter sycophant, saw how he was pleased with these titles, he said:

> "You would, oh my lord, detest them and all their country more, if you knew their impiety and malice against you. For all men kill sacrifices of vows for your health, while only they refrain to offer sacrifice."

6624. Then the envoys cried out with one voice:

> "Oh, my lord Gaius, we are falsely accused, we have sacrificed hecatombs. We have not, as is the custom of some, brought a little blood to the altar and then carried the flesh home to feast on. We have committed whole sacrifices to be burned with the holy fire, and that three times. First, when you became emperor,

again when you escaped a great sickness, at which all the world was sorrowful, and thirdly, as a vow for your victory over Germany."

6625. Gaius replied:

> "Well, say it were so, that you offered sacrifice, but to another, and to me you certainly did no sacrifices."

6626. Then horror seized the envoys, who were terrified at his last words. In the meantime, Gaius paced throughout the houses, the halls and parlours, both on the ground and upper floors. He specifically asked the envoys:

> "Why do you not eat swine's flesh?"

6627. Finally, setting aside his fierceness, he said:

> "These men seem to me not to be so much wicked, as miserable, in that they cannot persuade themselves that I am partaker of the divine nature."

6628. He promptly left and ordered the envoys to leave. {*Philo, Gaius, l. 1. c. 44. (349-367) 10:175-183}

6629. Gaius gave the tetrarchy of Agrippa's father-in-law, Herod (who had been banished to Lyons in Gaul), to Agrippa when he returned from his kingdom. For when he had reigned for three years in the tetrarchy of Philip, Herod's kingdom was given to him in the fourth year. {*Josephus, Antiq., l. 19. c. 8. s. 2. (351) 9:381,383} Philo quoted Agrippa as saying: {*Philo, Gaius, l. 1. c. 41. (326) 10:163}

> "No greater fortune could befall a mortal man than that you have given me the kingdom, which at first was merely one region, but you have enlarged by the addition of Trachonitis and Galilee." *[K638]*

6630. Petronius convened the leaders of the Jewish priests and magistrates, to pass on to them what Gaius had commanded. He was to erect Gaius' statue and dedicate it in their temple. He urged them, patiently to bear the decrees of his emperor, and cautioned them of the imminent danger that would ensue, were they to disobey. The whole power of the Syrian army was ready to make havoc of them and their country. At the first mention of these things they were so shocked, they had not a word to say, but poured out rivers of tears, tearing out their hair and pulling their beards in a most mournful way. However, the citizens of Jerusalem and all the surrounding country who heard this, came flocking together with one accord and mourned publicly. They left their houses, towns and citadels desolate and in one group, continued their march until they came to Phoenicia, where Petronius was. At first they made such a doleful and deep noise, that those who were nearby could not hear, or be heard, because of it. The calamitous times dictated what they had to do. They were organized into six ranks, or orders: of old men, young men and boys, of old women, wives and maidens. When they saw Petronius on a high place, all the ranks, as if at a general command, fell prostrate on the ground and wailed, as it were, in a mournful tone. When they were ordered to rise, they could barely be persuaded to do so. Finally, when they did, they cast dust on themselves and hung their hands behind them, like condemned persons. They came before him and made their pitiful complaint and supplication. Petronius and all those sitting with him were deeply moved. *[E864]* When he had consulted about the matter, he ordered letters to be sent to Gaius, telling him that the dedication of the statue had been deferred. The workmen needed more time to finish the colossus and time was needed to gather grain for such an expedition. It was reported that Gaius had intended to go to Egypt. The grain was fully ripe at the time and it was feared that the Jews would take the loss of their religion so badly, that they would not value their own lives and so waste and burn all the harvest throughout the fields and mountains, in their desperation. {*Philo, Gaius, l. 1. c. 32,33. (225-253) 10:117-131}*

*6631.* When Gaius received the letters, he concealed his anger against Petronius, for he greatly feared the governors, because they had the power to create seditions. This was especially true of those in large provinces with numerous armies, like the province of Syria, which extended to the Euphrates River. Thus Petronius, by his letters, appeased Gaius, who seemed to applaud his prudence and skill in anticipating future problems. Gaius ordered that once the harvest was over, he should dedicate the statue without delay. {*Philo, Gaius, l. 1. c. 34. (254-260) 10:131,133}*

*6632.* The envoys of the Alexandrian Jews received the message that Gaius had ordered his colossus to be erected at the innermost entrance of the temple and that it was to be dedicated to himself under the name of Jupiter. This news terrified them. Together, they all entered into the conclave and deplored their common, as well as their personal, calamity. They hoped that God, who had so often delivered their country from ruin, would not abandon them. {*Philo, Gaius, l. 1. c. 29. (184-189) 10:95,97}*

*6633.* When Agrippa came to greet Gaius in his usual manner, he looked at him sternly and said:

> "Your good and honest citizens, who alone of all mankind think it scornful to have Gaius for a god, are actually taking a course of action which is likely to bring destruction upon themselves because of their rebellious contempt for the law. *[K639]* When I ordered the statue of Jupiter to be dedicated in their temple, they fled as one body from the city—not,

indeed, like suppliants, but truly despisers of my commands."

*6634.* At these words, Agrippa was so struck with horror, that he trembled and his knees knocked together and would certainly have fallen to the ground, had not the bystanders supported him. They were ordered to carry him home in that condition. Due to the suddenness of the events, Agrippa had lost his memory and had grown quite stupid and senseless. Gaius, however, was all the more exasperated against the country of the Jews and said: {*Philo, Gaius, l. 1. c. 35. (261-268) 10:135,137}*

> "If Agrippa, who is my close friend and obliged to me by so many benefits, is so attached to his country's customs that he cannot endure that they be violated, even if only by my word, without fainting, what is to be expected from those who have no tie to restrain them?"

*6635.* When Agrippa was come to himself, he wrote a very long letter to Gaius on behalf of his country. {*Philo, Gaius, l. 1. c. 36-41. (276-329) 10:139-165}* (Philo placed a copy of it in his book.) He closed with this epilogue:

> "What will my countrymen or anyone else say of me? For either it will follow that I betrayed my country, or I must be blotted out from the list of your friends. Which of the two can be more unhappy? For before this, I was your close friend, and now I shall be considered a traitor if I do not keep my country from indemnity, nor the temple sacred. For you have the power for the protection of men. If I am offensive to you in anything, do me the favour not to bind me, as Tiberius did, but, lest I should live with the fear of bonds, kill me immediately. For what need do I then have of life, since the hope of my welfare rests wholly on your favour."

*6636.* Gaius seemed to be somewhat appeased by these letters and replied more mildly, granting Agrippa the great favour that the statue should not be dedicated. He wrote the same to Petronius, the governor of Syria, that he cause no sedition in the temple of the Jews. In case this favour should seem too generous, he added some terror and by writing:

> "If anyone in the other province, or anywhere outside the metropolis in any other city, shall be pleased to dedicate any temple or altar to me, let whoever shall oppose it either be executed immediately, or sent to me."

*6637.* Divine providence so ordained that no one in any of the other provinces planned to do this. {*Philo, Gaius, l. 1. c. 42. (330-333) 10:165,167}*

*6638.* When the persecution grew very severe at Babylon, a large number of the Jews left for Seleucia. More arrived five years later from Nearda, which is a city of Babylon, on an island in the Euphrates River, that has an academy of the Jews. In Syriac it is called נהר-דעא, as if one were to say:

"The river of knowledge."

*6639.* At Seleucia, the Greeks and Syrians were always at odds, but the Greek faction was too strong for the Syrians. With the arrival of the Jews, the Syrians made their friendship and became the stronger party. In addition, they still increased in warlike and resolute men. Therefore, when the Greeks saw they were becoming weaker and did not know how to change the situation, they did as much as they could to develop friendship, in an effort to have a peace mediated between them and the Syrians. *[E865]* This was easily achieved for the chief men on both sides were involved, and they concluded and confirmed a peace on the condition that both sides persecute the Jews. They made a surprise attack on them and killed fifty thousand men, so that no one escaped except those who were saved through the mercy of some friends or relatives. *[K640]* They escaped to Ctesiphon, a Greek city near Seleucia, where the king used to make his winter quarters and where he stored the majority of and the best part of his household belongings. They settled there and established themselves under the protection of the regal majesty. The terror of the Babylonians and Seleucians spread over all the regions where there were Jews. In these regions, wherever there were any Syrians together with Seleucians, they conspired the ruin of the Jews. Hence it came about that many fled to Nearda and Nisibis, where they had security because the cities were strongly fortified, although otherwise they were occupied by very warlike people. {*Josephus, Antiq., l. 18. c. 9. s. 9. (374-379) 9:209,211}*

*6640.* Gaius triumphantly entered Rome on his birthday (which was the last day of the month of August). {*Suetonius, Caligula, l. 4. c. 49. s. 2. 1:489}*

**4044a AM, 4753 JP, 40 AD**

*6641.* When the Alexandrian envoys appeared before Gaius, Apion accused the Jews of many things and claimed that they did not give Caesar the respect due to him. All the countries had built temples and altars to Gaius and were worshipping him, giving him equal honour with the rest of their deities. Only the Jews despised to build altars to him or swear by the name of Caesar. When Apion had alleged these and any other matters he thought would exasperate Gaius, Philo prepared to reply. Before he could do so, he was interrupted by Caesar, who ordered him to get out and who was so enraged, that Philo barely escaped without harm. After Philo was put out, he encouraged those who were with him. Although Gaius's words showed him to be very angry, they could nevertheless be assured that God would defend and provide for them, in spite of all that Gaius would do. {*Josephus, Antiq., l. 18. c. 8. s. 1. (259,260) 9:155}* {*Eusebius, Ecclesiastical History, l. 2. c. 5. 1:119,121}*

*6642.* Gaius regretted the favour he had given the Jews. He ordered another colossus, of brass covered with gold, to be built at Rome. The statue at Sidon was left alone, lest it should cause any sedition among the people. The new statue was to be transported secretly by ship and placed in the temple at Jerusalem before any were aware of it. This was to be done as they sailed to Egypt, for Gaius had a great desire to see Alexandria. He took great care in preparing for his journey, because he intended to stay for a long time. He was obsessed that his deification, of which he dreamed, would succeed in this city alone, because from there the religion would spread to smaller cities. All this was according to Philo, who was very well acquainted with these matters. {*Philo, Gaius, l. 1. c. 42,43. (337,338) 10:169}* Tacitus should be amended: {*Tacitus, Histories, l. 5. c. 9. 3:191}*

"They were ordered by Caesar to place his statue in their temple and they chose instead to take up arms. The death of Caesar ended the rebellion."

*6643.* Apelles from Askelon, who had incited Gaius against the Jews, was punished for some other crimes he committed. Gaius had him bound and racked in a most tormenting and drawn out manner, with some intermissions to make it more painful. {*Philo, Gaius, l. 1. c. 30. (206) 10:107}*

*6644.* Gaius was admonished, by an oracle of the goddess of Fortune at Antium, to beware of Cassius. Cassius Longinus, who was proconsul of Asia at the time, was suspected, because he was of the family of Cassius, one of the murderers of Caesar. Gaius ordered him to be bound and brought to him, and then condemned him to death. He forgot that Chaerea, who killed him a little later on, was also called Cassius. {*Suetonius, Caligula, l. 4. c. 57. s. 3,4. 1:503}* {*Dio, l. 59. (29) 7:359}*

**4044b AM, 4754 JP, 41 AD**

*6645.* Apollonius, the Egyptian, who had foretold the death of Gaius at home in Egypt, was dragged before Gaius at Rome, on the day before Gaius' death. Suetonius said this was on the 9th of the Calends of February (January 23). {*Suetonius, Caligula, l. 4. c. 58. s. 1. 1:503}*.) *[K641]* His punishment was postponed and he escaped death, when Gaius died first. {*Dio, l. 59. (29) 7:359}*

*6646.* Caligula reigned three years, ten months and eight days. {*Suetonius, Caligula, l. 4. c. 59. s. 1. 1:505}* {*Clement, Stromateis, l. 1. c. 21. 2:333}* Dio stated it was three years, nine months and twenty-eight days. {*\*Dio, l. 59. (30) 7:362}* His uncle, Claudius Caesar, the son of Drusius, was declared emperor by the praetorian guard.

6647. King Agrippa heard that the empire had been forced upon Claudius by the soldiers. Getting through the multitude with a great deal of difficulty, he reached Claudius and found him troubled and wanting to resign his place to the Senate. Agrippa dispelled his fears and encouraged him to go on courageously and assume the empire. When Agrippa was called by the Senate, he pretended that he knew nothing of the business and arrived as if ready to dine. He asked them what had been done about Claudius and they told him the truth and asked his advice. He said he would avoid no danger where the dignity of the Senate was at stake, and that he thought the best way forward was to send someone to Claudius who could persuade him to surrender his authority. He offered to be a part of that embassy. *[E866]* When Agrippa was sent with others to Claudius, he told him plainly the state of fear the Senate was in and advised him to answer like a prince. Agrippa was the reason that Claudius was more lenient with the Senate than he would otherwise have been. {*\*Josephus, Antiq., l. 19. c. 4. s. 1,2. (236-247) 9:325-329}*

6648. After Claudius was confirmed in the empire, he sent Mithridates of Iberia, whom Gaius had kept in bonds, home to receive his kingdom. To another Mithridates, who was descended from that great Mithridates, he gave the kingdom of Bosphorus, except for a region of Cilicia, which he gave to Polemon. {*\*Dio, l. 60. (8) 7:387}*

6649. Claudius enlarged Agrippa's kingdom, since he had helped him to get the empire and was at Rome at the time. Claudius also bestowed on him the honours of a consul. He gave his brother Herod praetorian honours, the principality of Chalcis, and permitted them to go into the Senate and to thank the senators. {*\*Dio, l. 60. (8) 7:387}*

6650. Claudius also proposed an edict whereby he confirmed Agrippa in the kingdom formerly granted to him by Gaius. He praised his endeavour and his industry and added Judea and Samaria to his kingdom. These had formerly belonged to the kingdom of his grandfather Herod, and so he restored them as due to the family. He also added to his kingdom Abila which had been ruled by Lysanias and the regions around Mount Libanus which belonged to the emperor. A league between the king and the people of Rome was engraved in brass and placed in the centre of the forum of the city. {*\*Josephus, Antiq., l. 19. c. 5. s. 1. (274,275) 9:341,343}*

6651. Claudius released Alexander Lysimachus, the alabarch, who was his old friend and had formerly been the guardian of his mother Antonia, and whom Gaius in his anger had committed to bonds. Bernice, the daughter of Agrippa, was betrothed to his son Marcus, who died while married to her as her first husband. {*Ac 25:13,23}* The king gave her to his brother Herod, after obtaining the kingdom of Chalcis for him from Claudius. {*\*Josephus, Antiq., l. 19. c. 5. s. 1. (276,277) 9:343}*

6652. Claudius restored Commagene and a larger part of Cilicia to Antiochus, whom Gaius had deprived of his kingdom. {*\*Dio, l. 60. (8) 7:387}* {*\*Josephus, Antiq., l. 19. c. 5. s. 1. (276) 9:343}* *[K642]*

6653. Claudius executed Helicon, the Egyptian, who had been master of the bedchamber to Gaius and the man who had most incited him against the Jews. {*\*Philo, Gaius, l. 1. c. 30. (206) 10:107}* Philo's book was ironically entitled *De Virtutibus*, for in it the wickedness of Gaius was clearly recounted. Philo was said to have read it before the whole Senate at the command of Claudius. Later, the Romans so liked this and his other works, that they thought them worthy of being granted a place in their libraries. {*\*Eusebius, Ecclesiastical History, l. 2. c. 17. 1:159}* Among his writings were five books about the miseries the Jews endured under the empire of Gaius, of which three books were lost. {*\*Eusebius, Ecclesiastical History, l. 2. c. 5. 1:117,119}* The books about Flaccus and Philo's embassy to Gaius still exist.

6654. After Gaius was murdered, the Jews, who under him had been severely oppressed by the Alexandrians, were encouraged and took up arms. Claudius ordered the governor of Egypt that he should appease this sedition. At the entreaty of Agrippa, the king of Judea, and Herod, the king of Chalcis, Claudius sent this edict to Alexandria: {*\*Josephus, Antiq., l. 19. c. 5. s. 1. (278-285) 9:343-351}*

> "It is my will that their rites not be infringed by the madness of Gaius and that they shall have full authority and liberty to persevere in their fathers' religion and worship. I order both parties, as much as in them lies, to live peaceably with one another and to endeavour to prevent all distractions or seditions of state between them."

6655. At the entreaty of these two kings, when he had been designated consul for the second time in the first year of his reign, Claudius permitted the Jews in Alexandria and in his whole empire to live according to their own laws and the customs of their ancestors. Along with this, he advised them that, under this grace, they should live the more modestly and circumspectly and not abuse the religions of other countries, but be content quietly to enjoy their own customs and traditions. {*Josephus, Antiq., l. 19. c. 5. s. 3. (286-291) 9:351,353} When the Jews grew so numerous at Rome that the city could scarcely hold them without tumults, he did not eject them, but forbade those who lived after their own laws to hold meetings. Also, he disbanded the clubs which Gaius had allowed and abolished the taverns where they met and drank. {*Dio, l. 60. (6) 7:383,385}

6656. Through his letters, Claudius commended Agrippa to all the governors of the provinces. He sent King Agrippa into his own kingdom to take care of it. Agrippa made a very large expedition and came to Jerusalem, where he paid his vows. He omitted nothing prescribed by the law. He ordered many Nazarites to be shaven. In the holy temple over the treasury, he hung up a gold chain which he had received from Gaius, as a memorial of his many miseries and happy deliverances by God. When he had duly performed his vows to God, he removed Theophilus, the son of Ananus, from the high priesthood and appointed Simon, surnamed Cantheras, in his place. [E867] Simon was the son of Boethus, whose daughter Herod the Great had married. Agrippa gained the goodwill and gratitude of the people at Jerusalem, by remitting a tribute to them which was paid annually by household. [K643] He made Silas, who was his constant companion in all his difficulties and plans, master over all the army. {*Josephus, Antiq., l. 19. c. 6. s. 1-3. (292-299) 9:353-357}

6657. A little after this, under the pretence of religion, certain rash young men from Dora erected a statue to Caesar in the temple at Jerusalem. Agrippa, the king of the Jews, was very angry and immediately went into Syria to Petronius to complain about their impudent boldness. Petronius was equally offended by this impious action, especially since it went directly against the laws of the empire. He wrote very sharply to the magistrates of the city of Dora, ordering them to bind and send to him those men, whoever they were, who had dared do such actions that were so contrary to the emperor's edicts. He ordered them never to let this happen again. {*Josephus, Antiq., l. 19. c. 6. s. 3,4. (299-316) 9:356-363}

6658. At Caesarea, Cornelius, who was a Roman centurion of a company belonging to the Italian band, favoured the Jewish religion and studied it. He was uncircumcised. (The Hebrews usually called such people *Proselytes of the Gate*, and the *Godly of the Nations*.) Around the ninth hour of the day (three p.m.), he was ordered by an angel who appeared to him, to send for Simon Peter. Simon Peter had spent a long time at the house of Simon, a tanner at Joppa. Cornelius obeyed the command and sent two of his household servants and a godly soldier, who was one of those who were constantly with him. {Ac 10:1-8 9:43}

6659. The next day, as they journeyed and came near the city, Peter ascended to the housetop to pray, at about the sixth hour (noon). While he was waiting for dinner to be prepared, he became hungry. He saw a large linen sheet coming down from heaven, full of all kinds of animals. He was ordered to eat freely, without regard to what he ate. By this object lesson, Peter was taught that the Gentiles were not to be considered unclean. The next day, Peter arrived at Caesarea with the men who had been sent by Cornelius and six brethren who accompanied them from Joppa. At Cornelius' house, Peter found the centurion's whole family assembled. They were converted to faith in Christ and the Spirit of God descended on them all of his own accord, without any laying on of hands by Peter. Then Peter baptized them into Christ. {Ac 10:9-48 11:5-17}

6660. The apostles and brethren at Judea heard that the Gentiles had also received the Word of God. When Peter arrived in Jerusalem, a contention arose between those who had been converted from Judaism to Christ and Peter, because Peter had associated with uncircumcised persons and eaten with them. Once Peter had told them everything that had happened and verified it by the testimony of the six men who were with him, they were satisfied. They glorified God, who had given repentance that leads to life to the Gentiles, also. {Ac 11:1-18}

## 4045 AM, 4755 JP, 42 AD

6661. King Agrippa removed Simon Cantheras from the high priesthood. He would have restored it to Jonathan, the son of Ananus, but he declined out of modesty and because he had held the office before. Jonathan recommended it be given to his brother, Matthias, since he thought his brother was more worthy than he. {*Josephus, Antiq., l. 19. c. 6. s. 4. (311-316) 9:361,363}

6662. Gaius Vibius Marsus succeeded Petronius as governor in the province of Syria. {*Josephus, Antiq., l. 19. c. 6. s. 4. (316) 9:363}

6663. Silas was the general of King Agrippa's cavalry. All along, he had been faithful to him and had shared every danger with him, so he was a very close friend of Agrippa. [K644] Silas began to desire equal honours with the king, because of his close friendship. Sometimes he praised himself beyond all modesty and recalled the hard times they had gone through together. He did this so often, that he severely exasperated the king against him. Agrippa was so disgusted, that he removed Silas from his command and sent him bound to his own country, to be held in custody. A little later, the king was to celebrate his birthday and sent for Silas to attend the kingly feast. Silas returned such a churlish answer, that the king left him with his keepers. {*Josephus, Antiq., l. 19. c. 7. s. 1. (317-325) 9:363-367}

*6664.* King Agrippa now turned his attention to Jerusalem. He fortified the walls of the section called the New City and made the gates wider and higher than they had been before, while doing all this at the public expense. He would have completed the walls to the point where they would have been impregnable by human force, had not Marsus, the governor of Syria, written letters to Claudius about this. The emperor, suspecting that the Jews were about to attempt some sedition, wrote earnestly to Agrippa that he should stop this work and he obeyed at once. {*Josephus, Antiq., l. 19. c. 7. s. 2. (326-328) 9:367,369}

*6665.* A door of faith was now opened to the Gentiles. The men of Cyprus and Cyrene were dispersed to Antioch after the martyrdom of Stephen and preached Christ to the Greeks. *[E868]* (It was Ελληνας, *Greeks* in the oldest book of Alexandria, not, as in the common edition, Ελληνισας.) A large number believed and turned to the Lord. When the church at Jerusalem heard this, they sent Barnabas there, who admonished them all to adhere steadfastly to the Lord. A large number were added to the Lord. {Ac 11:20-24}

*6666.* A severe famine raged at Rome. Claudius provided plenty of provisions for the immediate need and made provision for the future. Since most of the grain and other provisions came from foreign lands and the mouth of the Tiber River had no good ports, Claudius built the port of Ostia. {*Dio, l. 60. (11) 7:393,395} It was barely finished after eleven years, although he kept thirty thousand men working on it constantly. {*Suetonius, Claudius, l. 5. c. 20. s. 2. 2:37,39}

*6667.* This famine happened in the second year of Claudius. There was also a notable famine in his eleventh year, as mentioned by others. {*Tacitus, Annals, l. 12. c. 43. 4:377} {*Suetonius, Claudius, l. 5. c. 18. s. 2. 2:35,37} {Orosius, l. 7. c. 6.} This was not that world wide famine which was foretold by Agabus; that one began in the fourth year of Claudius, as evident from history. {*Eusebius, Chronicles, l. 1. 1:261} {Orosius, l. 7. c. 6.} This first famine happened at the same time as Herod Agrippa's death. {Ac 12:23-25}

## 4046 AM, 4756 JP, 43 AD

*6668.* Barnabas went to Tarsus to find Saul and when he had located him, he brought him to Antioch. For a whole year, they met together in the church and taught a large multitude. The disciples were first called Christians at Antioch. {Ac 11:25,26} This name was derived from the Latin form and not from the Greek form of the word for Christ. The term seems to have been coined by some Romans who were in Antioch at the time.

*6669.* At about this time, the prophets went down from Jerusalem to Antioch. One of these was Agabus, who declared by the Spirit that a severe famine would occur throughout the whole world. {Ac 11:27,28}

*6670.* Claudius brought the Lycians, who had revolted and killed many Romans, under his servitude again, adding their country to the prefecture of Pamphylia. *[K645]* While he was examining this business in court, he asked a certain envoy, who had been born at Rome of Lycian parents, a question in Latin. When the envoy did not understand Latin, Claudius deprived him of his Roman citizenship, saying it was not fitting that he should be a Roman when he could not speak Latin. {*Dio, l. 60. (17) 7:411}

*6671.* At Berytus, King Agrippa built a theatre, an amphitheatre, baths and porches, at enormous cost and celebrated their dedication most sumptuously. In the theatre, he staged shows consisting of musical performances of the greatest variety and in the amphitheatre, he held many gladiatorial games. Furthermore, because he wished to gratify and please the spectators, he had two troops of seven hundred criminals brought in to fight with each other. This staged war was a suitable punishment for the malefactors, as well as a delight to those who loved peace. So they were all killed by the wounds they inflicted on each other. {*Josephus, Antiq., l. 19. c. 7. s. 5. (335-337) 9:373}

*6672.* Finally, a number of kings from the surrounding regions came to Agrippa at Tiberius in Galilee: Antiochus of Commagene, Sampsiceramus of the Emesa, Cotys of Lesser Armenia, Polemon of Pontus and his own brother Herod, king of Chalcis. While they were all together, Marsus, the governor of Syria, also arrived. Therefore, Agrippa paid his due respects to the Romans and went out to meet him, as far as the seventh road marker (about a mile). Seeing Agrippa ride in the same chariot with his guests, Marsus distrusted the friendship of so many kings, so he sent his messengers to each one separately, telling them to depart without delay. Agrippa was most deeply offended by this, so that he hated Marsus, {*Josephus, Antiq., l. 19. c. 8. s. 1. (338-342) 9:373-377} and in his letters frequently solicited Claudius to remove Marsus from being governor of Syria. {*Josephus, Antiq., l. 20. c. 1. s. 1. (1) 10:3}

*6673.* Agrippa transferred the high priesthood from Matthias, the son of Ananus, to Elionaeus, the son of Cantheras. {*Josephus, Antiq., l. 19. c. 8. s. 1. (342) 9:377}

## 4047 AM, 4757 JP, 44 AD

*6674.* The famine foretold by Agabus increased, and the Christians of Antioch collected a gift for their friends living in Judea. They sent it by Barnabas and Saul, after these two had preached the word of the Lord to the people of Antioch for a whole year. {Ac 11:26,29,30}

6675. About this time, King Herod Agrippa (as the Syriac paraphrase correctly called him) apprehended those who belonged to the church, {*Ac 12:1*} because they opposed the institutions and rites of their country, of which Agrippa was a most religious observer. {*Josephus, Antiq., l. 19. c. 6. s. 3. (300) 9:357*}

6676. Agrippa killed James, the son of Zebedee and brother of John, with a sword. {*Ac 12:2*} Clement of Alexandria, from the tradition of his ancestors, added that the very same man who brought James to judgment became a Christian. [E869] He saw how freely James gave his testimony of Jesus and that he publicly confessed to being a Christian, in spite of having received most severe warnings. Therefore, when they were brought together for punishment, he asked James' forgiveness and James treated it as a small thing and said:

"Peace be to you."

6677. James kissed him and so they were both later beheaded. {*Clement, Hypotyposes, l. 7. 2:579*} {*Eusebius, Ecclesiastical History, l. 2. c. 9. 1:127*} [K646]

6678. When the king saw that the death of James pleased the people, he cast Peter into prison during the days of the feast of unleavened bread. He was guarded by sixteen soldiers. Agrippa intended to bring him out to the people after the passover. The church prayed daily for him and an angel of the Lord delivered him miraculously in the night. He went to the house of Mary, the mother of John Mark, where many had gathered and were praying. He told them of his deliverance, so that they could inform James, the son of Alphaeus and brother of our Lord, and the rest of the believers. Peter then went to another place. {*Ac 12:3-17*}

6679. Herod Agrippa was frustrated and in a rage, ordered the innocent keepers to be dragged to execution. He travelled down to Caesarea and stayed there. He was displeased with the people of Tyre and Sidon, whose land was not sufficient to maintain them, especially in that year of famine, and who were therefore forced to seek sustenance from Galilee and other places under Herod's jurisdiction. Consequently, they came to him unanimously through the mediation of Blastus, the king's chamberlain, whom they had befriended, wishing to make peace with him. A day was appointed and Herod sat before the tribunal in his royal attire and made a speech to them. With acclamations, the people kept shouting that this was the voice of a god, not a man. At once, an angel of the Lord smote him, because he had not given the glory to God. He was eaten up by worms and died. {*Ac 12:18-23*}

6680. The historian Josephus mentioned this, adding that an owl appeared to him, lest the prophecy of his German prophet should be invalid: {*Josephus, Antiq., l. 19. c. 8. s. 2. (343-350) 9:377-381*}

"When Agrippa had now finished the third year of his reign and was starting his fourth year, he went to Caesarea, which was formerly called Straton's Tower. There he solemnised some annual plays for Caesar's health, which were attended by a large number of noblemen and youngsters from all the province. On the second day of this celebration, he came all dressed up in his princely robes. These were richly and intricately woven with silver, which produced an angelic or extraordinary lustre by the reflection of the rising sun, and struck reverence into the spectators. Immediately some wicked men shouted from the distance and greeted him as a god and asked him to be propitious to them. Before this, they had only honoured him as a man, but now they saw there was something more in him than human. He neither refused nor repelled this impious adulation. A little later, he looked up and saw an owl over his head, sitting on a rope that was stretched out for some occasion. He knew at once that what had been a token of his good fortune, was now a sign of his ruin, and he was struck to the very heart. Later his belly began to torment him more and more grievously. Therefore, turning to his friends, he said: *Behold I, who by your greeting was called god, am now ordered from this life. My certain fate gives the lie to your flattery. I, whom you greeted as immortal, am forced to die. I must endure the wishes of providence, for I have not lived poorly, nor so happily, that all men may call me blessed.* When he had said those things, his pain grew worse and worse. These things were promptly told around the country and the rumour went out that he was dying. Immediately, therefore, all the people, including their wives and children, were in sackcloth, according to their country's custom, praying to God for the health of their king. They made all places resound with their lamentations and howling. As the king, who was lying on a high bed, looked down and saw the people prostrate on their faces, he could not stop weeping. His pain lasted, in the most intense degree and without interruption, for five days and then he died." [K647]

6681. Josephus stated that he reigned for seven years, four under Gaius (less three or four months, for Gaius himself did not rule four full years), and three under Claudius (adding, in like manner, three or four months). He stated that his yearly revenue came to twelve million drachmas and that, because he was so noble and generous, this was not enough and he had been forced to borrow money. {*Josephus, Antiq., l. 19. c. 8. s. 2. (351-352) 9:381,383*}

*6682.* Before the king's death became known, Herod, the king of Chalcis, and Helcias, the general of the cavalry, conferred together and sent Ariston to kill Silas, their common enemy, as if on Agrippa's orders. {*Josephus, Antiq., l. 19. c. 8. s. 3. (353) 9:383}

*6683.* Agrippa left only one son, Agrippa, who was seventeen and was being educated at Rome with Claudius. He left three daughters, of whom Bernice was married to her uncle Herod at the age of sixteen and the others were still virgins. Mariamme was ten years old and was betrothed by her father to Julius Archelaus, the son of Helcias. Drusilla was six years old and betrothed to Epiphanes, son of Antiochus, the king of Commagene. {*Josephus, Antiq., l. 19. c. 9. s. 1. (354,355) 9:383,385} [E870]

*6684.* When it was known for certain that Agrippa was dead, the people of Caesarea and Sebaste (two cities which were built by his father) acted like enemies of the dead prince. The common soldiers, with one accord, dragged his and his daughters' statues from the palace and brought them into the brothels. They abused them in such calumnious ways that it was a shame to recount. They made feasts and banquets in every public place. To express their great happiness, they adorned themselves with garlands and anointed their bodies. They sacrificed and made offerings to Charon and even worshipped one another, for the joy they felt over the death of the king. {*Josephus, Antiq., l. 19. c. 9. s. 1. (356-359) 9:385,387}

*6685.* The word of God was sown, increased and multiplied. Barnabas and Saul returned to Jerusalem. When they had finished their ministry there, they took John Mark along with them. {Ac 12:24,25}

*6686.* Claudius deprived the Rhodians of their liberty because they had crucified some Romans. {*Dio, l. 60. (24) 7:429}

*6687.* When Claudius wanted to send the young Agrippa into his kingdom to succeed his father, Claudius' freedmen and his friends, who had much influence with Claudius, dissuaded him. They said it was dangerous to commit so large a kingdom to so young a youth, who had barely reached manhood. He was very unqualified to rule there, since the kingdom required a large force of soldiers to keep it. Claudius could not deny that they spoke rationally and truly. {*Josephus, Antiq., l. 19. c. 9. s. 2. (360-362) 9:387} Although, in actual fact, their aim was the government of that kingdom, by which to make themselves rich. Tacitus stated: {*Tacitus, Histories, l. 5. c. 9. 3:191}

> "When the kings either had all died, or lost most of their territory, Claudius made Judah into a province to be governed by Roman equestrians or freedmen."

*6688.* Therefore, Claudius made Cuspius Fadus governor of Judea and the entire kingdom of Agrippa (which was much larger than the first kingdom of Herod, his grandfather). Claudius honoured the dead king in this, in that he would not bring Marsus, his enemy, into his kingdom. He ordered Fadus to chastise severely the cities of Caesarea and Sebaste for their ingratitude to their dead king and the contumely against his daughters, who were still alive. *[K648]* He wanted the troops from Caesarea and Sebaste, along with the five cohorts, to make war in Pontus. In their place, he would substitute soldiers chosen from the Roman legions who had been ordered to defend Syria. However, the soldiers sent an envoy to Claudius and obtained permission to stay in Judea. In later times, they were involved in the most grievous calamity to the Jews and sowed the seeds of the war which started when Florus was governor. {*Josephus, Antiq., l. 19. c. 9. s. 2. (363-366) 9:387,389}

*6689.* Josephus wrote that Claudius removed Marsus as a favour to his dead friend, Agrippa, and made Cassius Longinus the governor of Syria in his place. {*Josephus, Antiq., l. 20. c. 1. s. 1. (1) 10:3} Tacitus stated that this happened three years later.

## 4048a AM, 4757 JP, 44 AD

*6690.* The Jews living beyond the Jordan River had a dispute with the Philadelphians about the limits of the village of Zia, a place full of very warlike people. These same Jews had taken up arms without the knowledge or consent of their rulers and had killed many of the Philadelphians. When Cuspius heard this, he was greatly offended. The Jews should have let him decide the matter, if they believed that the Philadelphians had done them any wrong, rather than so rashly take up arms of their own accord against them. So he captured three of the ringleaders and had them bound. He executed Annibas and banished Amaramus and Eleazar. Not long after this, he captured and condemned Tholomaeus to death, because he was the leader of the robbers and had done many wrongs to Idumea and Arabia. He tried to eliminate all the robbers from the whole country of Judea. {*Josephus, Antiq., l. 20. c. 1. s. 1. (1-5) 10:3,5}

## 4048b AM, 4758 JP, 45 AD

*6691.* When Cassius Longinus (whom Tacitus believed to be Vibius Marsus) was governor of Syria, he went to Jerusalem with his army, together with Cuspius Fadus, the governor of the Jews. They convened the priests and the leaders of the Jews and clearly explained to them the full intent of the emperor's commands. They were to store the clothes of the high priest in the tower of Antonia, where the Romans would guard them, as had been done in the time of Vitellius. The Jews dared not oppose them in anything, but asked for time to send envoys to Caesar, to try to gain from him the favour that they would not be deprived of the privilege of keeping the holy clothes. They also wanted nothing to be done until Caesar had replied. Fadus and Longinus said they would allow this, if they would first give hostages while they waited for Caesar's reply. They readily turned over their children and sent off the envoys. {*Josephus, Antiq., l. 15. c. 11. s. 4. (405-407) 8:195,197} {*Josephus, Antiq., l. 20. c. 1. s. 1. (6-8) 10:5,7}

6692. At the church at Antioch there were prophets and teachers, such as Barnabas, Simeon, who was called Niger, Lucius of Cyrene, Menahem, who was educated together with Herod the Tetrarch, and Saul. All of them served God and fasted. [E871] The Holy Spirit told the church to separate Paul and Barnabas out from among their number for the task to which he had called them. These were commended to God by the church with fasting and praying and laying on of hands. Taking John Mark with them as a servant, they came to Seleucia. From there they sailed into Cyprus (Barnabas' country), where they first began to preach the word of God in the synagogues of the Jews at Salamis. {Ac 13:1-4}

6693. They travelled over that island as far as Paphos, where they came across a false Jewish prophet, Barjesus, surnamed Elymas, or Magus. [K649] He tried to turn away Sergius Paulus, the ruler of that country, who had a desire to hear Saul and Barnabas. Saul sharply reproved this man, who was immediately struck with blindness. The proconsul was stirred by this miracle and the gospel, and was converted to the faith. From this time on, Luke in his history always calls Saul by the name of Paul. He and those who had come with him to Paphos went on to Perga of Pamphylia, where John Mark left them and returned to Jerusalem. {Ac 13:6-13}

6694. Through the intercession of Agrippa, who was with Claudius at the time, the envoys from Jerusalem obtained confirmation of the privilege which had first been granted to them by Vitellius, of retaining the holy garments. They also received a written ruling about this matter from the emperor, in the fifth year of his tribunal power, to take to the magistrates at Jerusalem. This was dated on the 4th of the Calends of July (June 27), when Rufus and Pompeius Silvanus were consuls at Rome. Claudius did this to please his good friends, Herod, the king of Chalcis, and Aristobulus the younger. {*Josephus, Antiq., l. 15. c. 11. s. 4. (407) 8:197} {*Josephus, Antiq., l. 20. c. 1. s. 1,2. (9-14) 10:7,9}

6695. About the same time, Herod, the king of Chalcis, successfully petitioned Claudius for the authority over the temple and the holy treasury, as well as the right to choose the high priests. {*Josephus, Antiq., l. 20. c. 1. s. 3. (15,16) 10:9,11}

6696. Since there was to be an eclipse of the sun on his birthday and because of some other portents that had already taken place, Claudius was afraid that it could become an occasion for some sedition. Ahead of the due time, he wrote down and had it made known that there would be an eclipse. He noted the very time, place, and all its natural causes and showed that it was inevitable. {*Dio, l. 60. (26) 7:433,435} The birthday of Claudius was on the first of August, {*Dio, l. 60. (5) 7:379} on which day the sun was partially eclipsed about two hours before noon, to a fourth part of its diameter.

6697. Herod, the king of Chalcis, removed Simon Cantheras and placed Joseph, the son of Camei, in the high priesthood. {*Josephus, Antiq., l. 20. c. 1. s. 3. (16) 10:11}

6698. Theudas, a mere impostor, by pretending to be a prophet, persuaded a large number of the Jews to take their riches with them and follow him to the Jordan River. He promised them that he would divide the river and make an easy way for them to pass through. Fadus Cuspius, the governor of the Jews, sent out some cavalry troops who overtook the company by surprise. They killed a large number of them and took many alive. Theudas was beheaded and they took his head to Jerusalem. {*Josephus, Antiq., l. 20. c. 5. s. 1. (97-99) 10:53,55}

6699. Paul and Barnabas left Perga and came to Antioch in Pisidia. When they entered their synagogues on the Sabbath day, after the reading of the law and the prophets, they were invited by the rulers of the synagogue to teach. After Paul had preached an excellent sermon, the Jews left the synagogue, but the Gentiles asked that they would expound the same things to them on the next Sabbath day. After they had broken up, many devout Jews and religious proselytes followed Paul and Barnabas, who spoke to them and admonished them to continue in the grace and favour of God. {Ac 13:14-43}

6700. On the following Sabbath, almost all the city came flocking to hear the Word of God. When the Jews saw the multitude, they were filled with envy and with blasphemies opposed what Paul taught. [K650] Paul and Barnabas were deeply offended and leaving the Jews, preached only to the Gentiles. These joyfully embraced the gospel and all those who were ordained to eternal life, believed. The Word of God was spread over that entire country. The Jews were frustrated in their malicious designs and stirred up many honourable religious women (called Proselytes of the Gate by the Jews), and the chief men in the city. They raised a commotion and drove Paul and Barnabas from their region. Paul and

Barnabas shook the dust off their feet against them and travelled to Iconium. The disciples were filled with joy and the Holy Spirit. {*Ac 13:44-52*}

6701. At Iconium, Paul and Barnabas entered the synagogue of the Jews and spoke there. A large number of Jews and Greeks believed, but the unbelieving Jews exasperated and prejudiced the minds of the Greeks against the brethren. However, they stayed there a long time and spoke freely, as inspired by the Lord, who gave testimony to the word of his grace and by doing many miracles through them. {*Ac 14:1-3*} It was thought to have been at this time that Thecla, a noble maid of Iconium, was converted to Christ. Her acts are most deservedly recorded among the Apocrypha by the seventy, a synod of bishops who met under Gelasius. [*E872*]

6702. The multitude of Iconium was divided. Some were for the Jews and some for the apostles. When it came to pass that a number of Jews and Gentiles, together with their chief rulers, came to assault and stone them, they fled away into the cities of Lycaonia, Lystra, Derbe and the surrounding regions and preached the gospel there. {*Ac 14:4-7*}

6703. At Lystra, Paul healed a man who was born lame. When the men of Lystra would have sacrificed to Paul as Mercury, and Barnabas as Jupiter, the two men tore their clothes, refused the honour and had much trouble restraining the multitude from sacrificing to them. Soon after, the unbelieving Jews came there from Iconium and Antioch and raised a tumult in which they excited the people against them. The furious multitude stoned Paul and threw his body out of the city, for they thought he was dead. When his disciples gathered around him, he he got up and made his way into the city. {*Ac 14:8-20*}

6704. In this year, and maybe at this very time, Paul was taken into the third heaven, where he heard unspeakable words, fourteen years before the second letter to the Corinthians was written. {*2Co 12:2-4*} This may be the event that is thought to relate to that of Triephon in Lucian, or the more ancient author of that dialogue by Philopatris:

> "When I met that Jewish bald head, I justly laughed at him who was raptured into the very third heavens through the air. There he learned those things that were most excellent and glorious. He renewed us by water and caused us to walk in the steps of the blessed and redeemed us from the dominions of the wicked."

6705. So Triephon:

> "God reigned on high, great, heavenly and eternal, the Son of the Father, the Spirit, proceeding from the Father, one of three, and three of one."

6706. In a similar manner, the Christians used to preach.

6707. Paul and Barnabas left Lystra and came to Derbe. They preached the gospel there and led many converts to Christ. {*Ac 14:20,21*}

6708. Among many others who were converted to Christ at this time, was Timothy, with his holy mother Eunice and his grandmother Lois, who had taught him the Scriptures from his infancy. [*K651*] Timothy was there and although still a child, he was an eyewitness of the sufferings of his spiritual father, Paul, at Antioch (in Pisidia), Iconium and Lystra (in Lycaonia). {*Ac 16:1,2 2Ti 1:2-5 3:11-15*}

6709. Paul and Barnabas went no farther than Derbe and returned to Lystra, Iconium and Antioch. They confirmed the minds of the disciples and exhorted them to endure affliction for their faith's sake, without wavering. They appointed bishops over them in each of their churches and prayed for them with fasting, commending them to the God in whom they believed. Later, they travelled across Pisidia and came into Pamphylia. After they had declared and spread the word of the Lord at Perga, they crossed to Attalia and sailed to Antioch, from where they had set out. There they told the congregated churches what God had done through them and how he had opened the door of faith to the Gentiles. {*Ac 14:21-27*}

6710. Tiberius Alexander replaced Cuspius Fadus as the governor of the Jewish government. He was the son of Alexander, the alabarch of Alexandria (an old friend of Claudius), who had forsaken the Jewish religion. {*\*Josephus, Antiq., l. 20. c. 5. s. 2. (100,101) 10:55*}

6711. A little after this, when the news spread through all Judea, Helena, the queen of Adiabene (in the confines of Assyria and Mesopotamia), was converted by a certain Jew to the worship of the true God and came to visit the temple at Jerusalem. She wanted to worship the true God there and to pay her vows, and made ample provision for her journey. She was delayed for a few days by her son, Izates, who was king at the time and was later converted to the same religion by Ananias, a Jewish merchant. When she saw many of the Jews starving from famine, she sent some men to Alexandria for a large quantity of wheat, for which she herself paid. She sent others to Cyprus, to get a large quantity of figs for their relief. These quickly returned and she divided all the food to those who needed it. When her son Izates heard of the hardships caused by the famine, he sent money to the chief magistrates at Jerusalem. {*\*Josephus, Antiq., l. 20. c. 2. s. 1-5. (17-53) 10:11-31*}

6712. Izates, the king, sent his five sons to Jerusalem to learn their language and customs correctly. His mother

Helena also erected three pyramids, about six hundred yards from Jerusalem, in which the bones of her son Izates were entombed. {*Josephus, Antiq., l. 20. c. 3. s. 4. (71) 10:39} {*Josephus, Antiq., l. 20. c. 4. s. 3. (95,96) 10:51} The monuments of Helena were extant, not only in the time of Josephus, but in the time of Eusebius, also. {*Josephus, Jewish War, l. 5. c. 2. s. 2. (54-55) 4:19} {*Eusebius, Ecclesiastical History, l. 2. c. 12. 1:135,137} {Jerome, Epistle 27.}

## 4050a AM, 4759 JP, 46 AD

6713. Paul and Barnabas stayed at Antioch with the disciples for a long time. {Ac 14:28} After that, it appears as though Paul preached the gospel even as far as Illyria to those who never heard it before. {Ro 15:19,20} [E873] It was there that he suffered the things which he mentioned in his second letter to the Corinthians. {2Co 11:24-26} He mentioned that he had been whipped with rods at Philippi and twice elsewhere by the Gentiles. Five times he received thirty-nine stripes from the Jews. He had been shipwrecked three times and spent all night in the sea. [K652] We find that five years elapsed between the return of Paul and Barnabas to Antioch and their going to the council at Jerusalem. We cannot place the above events in a better place than here, where there is so large a gap of silence in the history of the church.

6714. When Valerius Asiaticus was consul again, the island of Therasia rose from the Aegean Sea on a night when the moon was eclipsed. {*Seneca, Natural Questions, l. 2. c. 26. 7:139,141} {*Seneca, Natural Questions, l. 6. c. 21. 8:189} {Aurelius Victor, De Viris Illustribus, Claudius} This eclipse was observed on the last night of December (which ended the year that Valerius Asiaticus was consul for the second time), and the first of January, which began the consulships of Claudius (fourth time) and Lucius Vitellius (third time). This little island appeared for the first time near Thera. {*Dio, l. 60. (29) 8:3,5}

## 4050b AM, 4760 JP, 47 AD

6715. James and Simon, the sons of Judas of Galilee, were crucified because they incited the Jews to revolt in Quirinius' time. {*Josephus, Antiq., l. 20. c. 5. s. 2. (102) 10:55,57}

6716. Herod, the king of Chalcis, removed Joseph, the son of Camei, and made Ananias, the son of Nebedaeus, the high priest in his place. {*Josephus, Antiq., l. 20. c. 5. s. 2. (103) 10:57}

6717. Gotarzes prepared to kill his father Artabanus, the king of the Parthians, along with his wife and son. {*Tacitus, Annals, l. 11. c. 8. 4:261} However, Artabanus died and left his kingdom to his son Vardanes. {*Josephus, Antiq., l. 20. c. 2. s. 4. (69) 10:37} Tacitus stated that Gotarzes and Vardanes were brothers, and Josephus believed them to be Artabanus' sons.

6718. The Parthians, fearing the cruelty of Gotarzes, invited Vardanes to be their king. He had always been an adventurous man and in two days he covered three hundred and fifty miles and invaded Gotarzes, who was terrified by his sudden coming. Without delay, Vardanes seized the adjacent provinces as well. Only the city of Seleucia refused to submit and since they had also revolted against his father, he was very angry with them. He unwisely wasted time by besieging their very strong city, which was fortified on the one side by a river and on the other with a very strong guard. In the interim, Gotarzes, with the help of the Dahae and the Hyrcanians, recruited his forces and renewed the war. As a result, Vardanes was forced to abandon the siege of Seleucia and withdraw to Bactria. {*Tacitus, Annals, l. 11. c. 8. 4:261}

6719. The news of the Parthian discord and of their fighting to appoint a new king, reached Rome. Mithridates, the king of Greater Armenia, was advised by Claudius Caesar to march into Armenia. He trusted in the power and wealth of his brother Pharasmanes, the king of the Iberians. In fact, the affairs of the east were in such a turmoil, that Mithridates took over Armenia. The Roman soldiers subdued the strong citadels, while the Iberian army held the field. The Armenians did not resist, for their general, Demonax, was killed in a battle. Immediately, Cotys, the king of Lesser Armenia, advanced there, but Caesar convinced him otherwise through letters he sent to him. All the countries rallied to Mithridates, who behaved more harshly than was appropriate for a new king. {*Tacitus, Annals, l. 11. c. 8,9. 4:261,263}

6720. Gotarzes and Vardanes were about to fight, when Gotarzes showed his brother the treachery of the people and they shook hands and swore at an altar to revenge themselves on each others' enemies. [K653] They made peace between themselves and as Vardanes appeared to be better able to hold the kingdom, Gotarzes retired into Hyrcania, to avoid all strife. {*Tacitus, Annals, l. 11. c. 9. 4:263}

6721. When Vardanes returned, Seleucia surrendered, in the seventh year after its defection. After this, he invaded the strongest provinces and then planned to recover Armenia. Vibius Marsus (or, according to Josephus, Cassius Longinus), who was the governor of Syria, threatened him with war through his envoy. {*Tacitus, Annals, l. 11. c. 9. 4:263}

## 4051 AM, 4761 JP, 48 AD

6722. Ventidius Cumanus replaced Tiberius Alexander as the governor of the Jews. Herod, the king of Chalcis, brother of that great Agrippa, died in the eighth year of Claudius' reign. He was survived by three sons, of whom Aristobulus had been born to his former wife, Mariamme; Berniciansus and Hyrcanus were sons of

Bernice, his brother's daughter. {*Josephus, Antiq., l. 20. c. 5. s. 3. (103,104) 10:57}

6723. As the feast of the passover was approaching, many people from all regions came to the feast. Cumanus followed the example of the previous governors and set one cohort as a guard on the porch of the temple to preclude any riots. On the fourth day of the feast, one of the soldiers obscenely exposed his private parts to the crowd, who cried out and were enraged by this action. They said that the one whom they honoured in that feast was affronted by it, while some of the boldest of them railed against Cumanus, saying this impudent soldier had been sent by him. [E874] When Cumanus heard this, he was quite troubled and wanted the people to raise no commotions during the time of the feast. When they continued to rail at him, he commanded the whole army to proceed to Antonia, a citadel that adjoined the temple. When the common people saw the soldiers coming, they were afraid. They began to flee in panic and stampeded into a narrow passage, thinking that the soldiers had pursued them. They crushed and trampled one another, so that twenty thousand of them ended up dead. {*Josephus, Antiq., l. 20. c. 5. s. 3. (105-112) 10:57-61} Josephus stated elsewhere that thirty thousand died. Other manuscripts of Josephus read only ten thousand. {*Josephus, Jewish War, l. 2. c. 12. s. 1. (227) 2:413} {*Eusebius, Ecclesiastical History, l. 2. c. 19. 1:161} Rufinus noted that more than thirty thousand perished. Eusebius and Orosius also confirmed Rufinus' figure. {*Eusebius, Chronicles, l. 1. 1:262} {Orosius, l. 7. c. 6.}

6724. Some, who had fled and escaped this tumult, robbed Caesar's servant, Steven, on the road near Bethhoron, about twelve miles from Jerusalem, taking all his baggage. When Cumanus heard this, he sent soldiers there with orders to destroy the surrounding villages. In this havock, one of the soldiers brought out the books of the Mosaic law, which he had found in one of these villages. He tore it up before them all and railed exceedingly against the law and the Jews. When the Jews heard this, they gathered a large company and went to Caesarea, where Cumanus lived. They entreated him to revenge this act, not just for their sakes, but because of the contempt for and wrong done to their God. Then the governor, who was afraid of a revolt among the people, acted on the advice of his friends and executed the soldier that had done this, thereby appeasing the people. {*Josephus, Antiq., l. 20. c. 5. s. 4. (113-117) 10:61,63} [K654]

## 4052 AM, 4762 JP, 49 AD

6725. Apollonius of Tyana, on his journey to the Indians, entered the city of Babylon in the second month of the third year of Vardanes and conferred with the king. {*Philostratus, Apollonius, l. 1. c. 28. 1:83} {*Philostratus, Apollonius, l. 1. c. 31. 1:87,89} {Eusebius, Treatise of Eusebius (Hierocles)}

6726. Gotarzes regretted having surrendered his kingdom and was recalled by his nobility, who were all the more enslaved by the peace. He gathered a large force and fought a fierce battle with Vardanes at the Erindes River. Vardanes won and proceeded with good success, subduing the mid countries as far as the Sindes River, which divided the Dahae and the Arii. There his success ended, for, although the Parthians were conquerors, they hated fighting a long way from home. Therefore, he erected monuments glorifying his power and the subjection of peoples that had never before been subject to the Parthians. Vardanes returned home with great glory and became even sterner and more intolerable toward his subjects. {*Tacitus, Annals, l. 11. c. 10. 4:265}

6727. Vardanes went to Izates, the king of Abilene, and tried to persuade him to join with him in a war against the Romans. Izates tried to change his mind by telling him of the Roman acts and their power. Vardanes was offended at this and promptly planned to make war against Izates, but his death prevented this war. {*Josephus, Antiq., l. 20. c. 3. s. 4. (69-73) 10:37,39} When the Parthians learned that he planned to make war with the Romans, they surprised and killed him while he was hunting. He died in his prime, being one of the most famous kings for one so young. If he had obtained the love of his subjects as he had the fear of his enemies, he might have been numbered among the old kings. {*Josephus, Antiq., l. 20. c. 3. s. 4. (73) 10:39} {*Tacitus, Annals, l. 11. c. 10. 4:265}

6728. The Parthian affairs were thrown into confusion by the death of Vardanes and they did not know who would be the next king. Many favoured Gotarzes and some wanted Meherdates (the son of Phraates III, who was the son of Zenones I); Meherdates was a hostage with the Romans at the time. At last Gotarzes prevailed and occupied the throne. Because of his luxurious lifestyle and cruelty, he forced the Parthians to send a secret request to Claudius, to send them Meherdates as their king. They complained of Gotarzes' cruelty to the nobility and the common people. First, Gotarzes had killed his brothers, then his close relatives, then his more distant relatives. He even killed pregnant women and their small children. Slothful and licentious at home and unlucky in war, he covered his foul deeds by his cruelty. {*Tacitus, Annals, l. 12. c. 10. 4:265}

6729. Didius, the Roman general, had deposed Mithridates from the kingdom of Bosphorus and made his son Cotys, a rash young fellow, king there. Didius led away the full power of the army and left the new king with only a few cohorts under the command of Julius Aquila, a Roman equestrian. After he had lost everything, Mithridates wandered about inciting the countries and gathering all the renegades from them.

He got together an army and ejected the king of the Dandarians and took over his kingdom. {*Tacitus, Annals, l. 12. c. 15. 4:337} [E875]

6730. After Claudius had heard the Parthian envoys, he sent Meherdates, or Mithridates, to be their king. He told him that he should not think of himself as an autocrat among slaves, but as a guide of free men and that he should show mercy and justice. He ordered Gaius Cassius, who was the governor of Syria, to escort the young man safely to the banks of the Euphrates River. {*Tacitus, Annals, l. 12. c. 11. 4:331} [K655]

6731. At this time, Cassius excelled all others in his legal skill but was inexperienced in martial affairs because there were no wars going on. He revived the ancient customs of exercising the legions with the same care, as if an enemy had been invading the country. He wanted to live up to the name of the Cassian family and his ancestors, who were held in high esteem in those countries. When he had pitched his tents at Zeugma, where the river could be crossed easily, he convened those who had voted to make Meherdates the king. When the Parthian nobles and the king of the Arabians, Acbarus (or Abgarus), had arrived, he admonished the young man, Meherdates, in their presence, not to delay, since this caused people to lose enthusiasm and instigate treachery. He therefore advised him to press on quickly with his plans. Meherdates despised this good advice, through the deceit of Acbarus. Meherdates was young and thought that all royalty consisted of unbridled luxury, so he stayed at the town of Edessa for many days. {*Tacitus, Annals, l. 12. c. 12. 4:331,333}

6732. Mithridates had captured the kingdom of the Dandarians and was thinking of invading the Bosphorus. Julius Aquila and Cotys did not think they could handle Mithridates with their own weak forces, because Zorsines, king of the Siracene (toward the Caucasus), had joined with Mithridates. So they sent for foreign troops and sent envoys to Eunones, who ruled over the country of the Aorsi (among the Scythians), and whose friendship they easily gained by showing how Mithridates had rebelled against the Romans. Therefore, they agreed that Eunones should fight the cavalry battles, while the Romans would handle the besieging of their cities. {*Tacitus, Annals, l. 12. c. 15. 4:337}

6733. They marshalled their forces and advanced, with the Romans and the Bosphorans defending each wing of the Aorsi from before and behind. After they had driven the enemy back, they came to Soza, a town of the Dandarians, which had been abandoned by Mithridates, because the loyalty of the people was suspect. The invading forces thought it best to take it and

leave a garrison there, after which they went on into the country of the Siracians. After they crossed the Panda River, they besieged Uspe, which was defended by walls and moats. The walls were not made of stone, but of wickerwork hurdles with earth between, and were weak. From the high siege towers, the Romans attacked the besieged with firebrands and spears. If night had not come and stopped the battle, the place would have been captured the same day. {*Tacitus, Annals, l. 12. c. 16. 4:339}

6734. The next day, envoys unsuccessfully asked that those who were freeborn might be allowed to go free, and offered ten thousand slaves. The conquerors despised this offer, because it would be cruel to kill those who had surrendered and dangerous to keep such a large company of prisoners. They decided to let the matter be settled in a battle. They ordered the soldiers who scaled the walls to kill everyone in the city. The rest of the country was terrified at the destruction of Uspe. They realised that eminent and fortified places were of no value, because the enemy broke through rivers and all. Zorsines thought hard about the future of his alliance with Mithridates and whether he should rather attend to his own distressed country. At last, he abandoned Mithridates and gave hostages to the Romans. He fell down before the image of Caesar, in respect to the great glory of the Roman army, who were victorious. The Romans were unscathed and triumphant and were only a three-day journey from the Tanais River. However, their return journey was not so successful. Some of their returning ships ran aground on the coasts of the Tuarians and the barbarians surrounded them, killing the captain of their cohort and many of the auxiliaries. {*Tacitus, Annals, l. 12. c. 17. 4:339,341}

6735. In the interim, Mithridates had no relief and tried to decide whose mercy he had best seek. His brother Cotys, who had earlier betrayed him, he now feared as his enemy. Among the Romans, there was no one of sufficient authority for his promises to carry much weight. So he fled to Eunones, entered his palace, fell at his feet and said: [K656]

> "Mithridates, hunted for by sea and land for so many years, behold, is now present of his own accord. Use as you please the son of great Achamenes, for my enemies have taken all other help from me."

6736. Eunones was moved by the honour of the person, the change of his fortune and his generous petition. He wrote to Claudius and sent envoys on behalf of Mithridates, who deserved sterner treatment. Mithridates asked for neither power nor royalty, but simply that he should not be led in triumph nor put to death for his faults. Claudius was undecided whether to punish or pardon him. At last, he decided to grant a more merciful sentence. {*Tacitus, Annals, l. 12. c. 18-20. 4:341-354}

## 4053a AM, 4762 JP, 49 AD

6737. Carenes sent for Meherdates to take over the kingdom and told him it would be very easy if he came without delay. Meherdates was given bad advice and did not go straight to Mesopotamia, but instead took a more roundabout way through Armenia, at the start of the winter season, which was a difficult time to travel. [E876] They were exhausted by the journey through the mountains when they finally arrived in the plain country. They joined forces with Carenes, crossed the Tigris River and marched across Adiabene in northern Assyria, whose King Izates was publicly friendly with Meherdates, but privately loyal to Gotarzes. In spite of their journey, they captured the ancient Assyrian capital city of Nineveh. {*Tacitus, Annals, l. 12. c. 12,13. 4:331-335}

6738. Mithridates of Bosphorus was brought to Rome by Junius Cilo, the governor of Pontus. He was said to have addressed Caesar somewhat more haughtily than his situation warranted and to have said these words:

> "I have not been sent back to you, but I have come back. If you do not believe me, let me go again— and then try to catch me."

6739. At the rostrum, when he was exposed to public view and hemmed in on all sides with guards, his expression remained undaunted. Consular ensigns were given to Cilo and the praetorian ensigns to Julius Aquila. {*Tacitus, Annals, l. 12. c. 21. 4:345}

6740. The Bithynians accused their governor, Junius Cilo, of taking many large bribes. They spoke before Claudius in such a riotous fashion, that Claudius did not understand what they were saying. He asked those who stood by, what they had said. Narcissus lied and replied that they thanked him for Junius Cilo. Claudius believed it and said: {*Dio, l. 60. (33) 8:25}

> "Let him therefore be their governor for two more years."

6741. At this time, the Bithynians accused their governor, Cadius Rufus, of extortion, and he was condemned. {*Tacitus, Annals, l. 12. c. 22. 4:347} {*Tacitus, Histories, l. 1. c. 77. 2:121,123} (Both Loeb and Ussher associate Cadius Rufus with this later reference in Tacitus. We did not see the reason for the relationship. Editor.)

6742. When King Sohaemus of Iturea and King Agrippa of Judea had died, their countries were added to the province of Syria. {*Tacitus, Annals, l. 12. c. 23. 4:347} Josephus calculated the length of the reign of Agrippa the Younger: He stated that the beginning of the Jewish war,

which started in May 66 AD, was in the seventeenth year of King Agrippa. {*Josephus, Jewish War, l. 2. c. 14. s. 4. (284,285) 2:435} It can also be calculated from the Greek money, which stated that when Judea was taken, around September 70 AD, it was the twenty-first year of Agrippa. Claudius did not give Agrippa the Younger his father's kingdom of Judea, but gave him the kingdom of his uncle, Herod of Chalcis. Agrippa also received authority over the temple and holy treasury and the right to choose the high priests, which had earlier been granted to his uncle Herod. {*Josephus, Jewish War, l. 2. c. 12. s. 1. (223) 2:411} His father's kingdom was added to Syria, so that it should have a governor there. [K657] However, by Caesar's choice, Ventidius Cumanus (as had previously been the case) retained the administration of Judea and Galilee at this time, while Felix was sent as governor of Samaria, which lay between them. Felix was a freedman of Claudius and his mother Antonia and he had his surname of Antonius from her and Claudius from him. He was the brother of another freedman, Pallas, of whom Tacitus noted that he was most affectionately beloved by his patron, Claudius. {*Tacitus, Annals, l. 12. c. 53,54. 4:393,395}

## 4053b AM, 4763 JP, 50 AD

6743. At Mount Sambulos, Gotarzes made vows to the local god; the chief cult of this place was Hercules. Gotarzes' army was not yet strong enough, so he used the Corma River for his defence. Although he was incited to battle by envoys who challenged him, he delayed and moved from place to place, while sending bribes to corrupt the loyalty of his enemies. The king of Adiabene and King Acbarus of the Arabians (of Edessa) defected to Gotarzes because they knew from experience that the barbarians would rather seek a king at Rome than keep Meherdates. Meherdates was stripped of his forces and did not trust those who remained, so he resolved to decide the matter in a battle. Gotarzes met him in battle, confident now that he could defeat Meherdates' weakened forces. They fought with a large slaughter and uncertain outcome. When Carenes routed his opponents and advanced too far, fresh troops cut off his return. Meherdates gave up all hope and relied on the promises of Parraces, his father's vassal. Meherdates was defeated by Parraces' treachery and turned over to the conqueror. Gotarzes sneered at Meherdates as being no relative of his and not of the royal family of the Arsaces, but one who was a Roman and a foreigner. He cut off his ears in contempt of the Romans and gave him his life to show his mercy. {*Tacitus, Annals, l. 12. c. 13,14. 4:333,335}

6744. At the age of fourteen, Josephus, the son of Matthias, was an accomplished scholar and was consulted about the fuller sense and meaning of the law, even by the high priests and leaders of Jerusalem. {*Josephus, Life, l. 1. c. 2. (7,8) 1:5}

6745. After Gotarzes died of a disease, Venones, the king of the Medes, was called to rule there. He had a short and most undistinguished reign among them. The Parthian kingdom was given to Vologeses, his son; his mother was a concubine and he attained the kingdom with the agreement of his brothers. {*Tacitus, Annals, l. 12. c. 14. 4:337} {*Tacitus, Annals, l. 12. c. 44. 4:377,379} Josephus wrote that Gotarzes was killed by treachery and his brother Vologeses succeeded him. He added that he divided the kingdom between his two brothers, by the same father but by different mothers. [E877] Pacorus, who was the oldest, received Media and to the younger, Tiridates, he gave Armenia. {*Josephus, Antiq., l. 20. c. 3. s. 4. (74) 10:39,41}

## 4054 AM, 4764 JP, 51 AD

6746. A war arose between the Armenians and Iberians, which was the cause of very serious troubles between the Romans and the Parthians. Pharasmanes had obtained Iberia by ancient possession and his brother, Mithridates, had gained Armenia with the help of the Romans. Pharasmanes had a son called Radamistus, who was very handsome, had proper composure, had a very strong body and was much admired by the whole country. When he began to desire his father's kingdom, the aged Pharasmanes was afraid and tried to divert him, by giving him the idea of taking over Armenia. He told his son that he had defeated the Parthians and had given the country to Mithridates. He added that it was better to use craft than force to get it and thereby take Mithridates by surprise. Then they would easily be able to oust him and do what they pleased. So Radamistus pretended to have fallen out with his father and said he could not endure his stepmother's hostility. [K658] He then defected to his uncle Mithridates and behaved himself well, but all the while, he was seducing the Armenian nobles and leaders to rebel. {*Tacitus, Annals, l. 12. c. 44. 4:377,379}

6747. Radamistus pretended to be reconciled and when he returned to his father, he told him how far he had gone using deceit and that the rest now had to be done by force. In the interim, Pharasmanes had trumped up some reasons for war. He alleged that his brother, during the war against the king of the Albanians, had opposed his appeal for Roman help and now had to pay for that wrong with his life. He gave his son a large army, with which the latter suddenly invaded Armenia. Mithridates, terrified and deprived of his country, was compelled to withdraw to the citadel of Gorneas. The place was very secure, because of its location and the strong guard under Caelius Pollio, whose centurion was Casperius. After he tried in vain and with great loss to capture the fortress, Radamistus then began to see if he could bribe Pollio with money. Casperius, however, opposed the overthrow of a king and ally, because Armenia had been given to Mithridates by the Romans and should not be sold for money. At last as Pollio continued to plead the numbers of the enemy and Radamistus pleaded his father's orders, Casperius stipulated a truce and left. He said that although he had frightened Pharasmanes with wars, he would make Titus Ummidius Quadratus, the governor of Syria, aware of the state of affairs in Armenia. {*Tacitus, Annals, l. 12. c. 45. 4:381}

6748. The sixth Calippic period began.

6749. After the departure of Casperius the centurion, Pollio the prefect was no longer under his supervision. He urged Mithridates to make a league with his older brother, Pharasmanes. Pollio argued that Mithridates had married Pharasmanes' daughter and was an uncle to Radamistus, as well as giving him many other reasons. Mithridates delayed the matter, because he did not trust Pollio, because he had seduced one of the royal concubines and had abandoned himself to all manner of lust and luxury. He was known to be available for any villainy, for a price. In the meantime, Casperius insisted that Pharasmanes withdraw the Iberians from the siege. Pharasmanes gave vague answers and seemed inclined to do it, while in the meantime he secretly sent to Radamistus, telling him to capture the citadel as quickly as possible and by any means he could. Radamistus secretly bribed the soldiers to demand peace and to threaten to stop fighting. This forced Mithridates to appoint a day for a conference, and so he left the citadel. At first, Radamistus feigned obedience, embracing him and calling him his father-in-law and parent. He swore an oath that he would not harm him with the sword or poison. He led him at once to a nearby grove and told Mithridates that he had made preparations to sacrifice there, so that their peace might be confirmed by the witness of the gods. But then Mithridates was thrown down and bound with chains. Finally, when Pharasmanes' orders were received, Radamistus, as if mindful of his oath, cast down his father-in-law (Radamistus' uncle), together with his wife (Radamistus' sister), and heaped heavy clothing on them, so that they were smothered to death. Mithridates' sons were all killed because they cried at their parents' death. {*Tacitus, Annals, l. 12. c. 46,47. 4:381-385}

6750. When Quadratus heard that Mithridates had been betrayed and killed and Armenia was being ruled by his murderers, he called a council to explain the business and avenge the matter. After they had debated the issue, many were of the opinion to do nothing. However, lest it should seem that they were giving assent to such wickedness and Caesar should order them otherwise, they sent messengers to Pharasmanes, ordering him to get out of Armenia and to recall his son. {*Tacitus, Annals, l. 12. c. 48. 4:385,387}

## 4055a AM, 4764 JP, 51 AD

*6751.* Julius Paelignus was the governor of Cappadocia and was as contemptible for his stupidity as for his appearance. [K659] While still a private man, he had been extremely intimate with Claudius and most amused with a life of ease and sloth. Paelignus gathered together the auxiliaries of the provinces as if planning to recover Armenia. He then preyed on his friends, rather than his enemies. His troops deserted him and he was left defenceless against the barbarian invasions. He went to Radamistus, who bribed him well. [E878] Paelignus urged him to assume the kingly ensigns and was, in fact, the one who authored the idea and abetted him in it. When this dishonourable conduct became known, in order that the rest of the Romans would not be branded with Paelignus' faults, Helvidius Priscus was sent as an envoy with a legion for a time, to take care of these unsettled affairs. He quickly crossed the Taurus Mountains and settled more things by diplomacy than by force. But then he was ordered to return into Syria for fear of a new Parthian war because Vologeses planned to invade Armenia, which was part of his ancient kingdom and was now ruled by a wicked foreign king. He gathered an army and prepared to give his brother, Tiridates, the kingdom, so that none of the family might be without a kingdom. When the Parthians came, the Iberians were overcome without a fight and the cities of Armenia, Artaxata and Tigranocerta came under their yoke. A very terrible winter followed and an epidemic broke out among the Parthians for lack of supplies, compelling Vologeses to evacuate the country for the time being. {*Tacitus, Annals, l. 12. c. 49,50. 4:387,389}

*6752.* Radamistus invaded Armenia now that there was no ruler there. He behaved more cruelly than before, as if he had come against rebels who, in time, would rebel again. Although the Armenians were accustomed to servitude, their patience ran out and they took up arms. They surrounded the palace and forced Radamistus and his wife Zenobia to flee on fast horses. His wife was great with child and tried at first to endure the flight, for she feared the enemy and loved her husband. Later with the continued haste, her womb was jarred too much and her system was tormented with pains. She begged that she might die honourably, rather than live in the disgrace of captivity. At first, he embraced her, cherished her and helped her. He admired her courage and was sick with fear that if he should have to leave her,

someone might find and harm her. At last, due to the vehemence of his love and being no stranger to wicked exploits, he drew his sabre. After having wounded her sufficiently, he dragged her body to the bank of the Araxes River and threw her into it, so that she would not fall into enemy hands. Then he immediately went through to Iberia, to his father's throne. In the meantime, some shepherds found Zenobia, obviously breathing and alive, and thought by her appearance that she was nobly born. They bound up her wounds and applied their country medicines. When they learned her name and story, they carried her to Artaxata. From there, she was officially brought to Tiridates, who accepted her courteously and took her as his queen. {*Tacitus, Annals, l. 12. c. 50,51. 4:389,391}

*6753.* Certain professors of the name of Christ, who belonged to the sect of the Pharisees, came down to Antioch from Judea. They said that the Gentile Christians ought to be circumcised and to keep the law of Moses in order to be saved. They upset many of the brethren in Syria and Cilicia with their perverse doctrine, and both Paul and Barnabas stiffly opposed them. {Ac 15:1,2,5,23,24} Paul called them *false brethren brought in unawares.* {Ga 2:4} Philastrius and Epiphanius said that Cerinthus, who was an arch heretic, was the first to hold these heresies. {Philastrius, De Heres., c. 87.} {Epiphanius, Heresy, l. 1. c. 28.}

## 4055b AM, 4765 JP, 52 AD

*6754.* Fourteen years after having gone to Jerusalem, which had been three years after his conversion, Paul again went to Jerusalem, together with Barnabas. {Ga 2:1} [K660] Both of them, with some others, had been sent by the church at Antioch to ask the verdict of the apostles and elders at Jerusalem (whose names those disturbers had misused to bolster their own opinion), concerning the recent controversy. {Ac 15:2,3,24}

*6755.* Paul went up in response to a revelation and Titus, a Greek, accompanied him. Paul would not compel him to be circumcised, lest it should seem as though he were giving in to the false brethren, even for a moment. {Ga 2:1-5}

*6756.* On their journey through Phoenicia and Samaria, Paul and Barnabas told of the conversion of the Gentiles, to the great joy of all the brethren. When they came to Jerusalem, they were received by the church and by the apostles and elders. Paul and Barnabas told of the things God had done through them. {Ac 15:3,4}

*6757.* Paul privately related the gospel that he had preached among the Gentiles to the leaders among the apostles, James, Peter and John (who were considered the pillars of the church). They saw that the preaching of the gospel among the Gentiles had been committed to Paul, just as the Jews had been to Peter. They observed the grace that had been given to Paul and gave him and Barnabas the right hand of fellowship, that they should perform the office of the apostleship among the Gentiles, while they themselves would do so among the Jews. They advised them only that they should be careful to relieve the poor at Jerusalem. {Ga 2:2,7,9,10} [E879]

6758. In a council of the apostles and elders, held at Jerusalem, a long dispute took place. After Peter had spoken his opinion, Barnabas and Paul told of the great miracles God had done through them among the Gentiles. Then James concluded that it seemed good to the apostles and elders that the Gentiles should abstain from things sacrificed to idols, fornication, strangled animals and eating blood. To this end, letters were written to those at Antioch and to the rest of the brethren in Syria and Cilicia. Paul and Barnabas along with Judas and Silas carried these letters to Antioch. After the letters had been delivered and read, the brethren rejoiced greatly. Judas and Silas, who were also prophets, said much to encourage and strengthen the brethren. {Ac 15:6-32}

6759. Later, Judas returned to the apostles and Silas thought it best to stay at Antioch, where Paul and Barnabas were preaching the gospel along with many others. {Ac 15:33-35}

6760. Josephus, the son of Matthias, when he was sixteen years old, began with much effort and diligence to learn as much as he could about all three sects of the Jews: the Pharisees, Sadducees and Essenes. {*Josephus, Life, l. 1. c. 2. (9) 1:5}

6761. Pallas, the freedman of Claudius, was given an honorary praetorship and fifteen million sesterces. {*Tacitus, Annals, l. 12. c. 53. 4:393}

6762. When the Galileans went up to the feast at Jerusalem, they had to travel through Samaria. {Joh 4:3,4} It happened that a Galilean was murdered in a Samaritan village called Gema, or Ginea, causing a fight between the travellers and the villagers, in which many of the Galileans were killed. [K661] The Jewish rulers took this very grievously and stirred up the Jews to arms, exhorting them to defend their liberty. They maintained slavery was bad enough, without having to suffer additional wrongs, as well. At Jerusalem, the common people left the feast, took up arms and invaded Samaria. They would not stop, nor did they heed the magistrates who tried to restrain them. The people also called for help from Eleazar, the son of Dinaeus, and Alexander, who were both captains of the thieves. They invaded the part of Samaria which bordered on the country of Acrabatene and carried out an indiscriminate slaughter.

They spared no one on account of their age or sex and also set fire to the towns. When Cumanus learned what had been done, he took with him one cavalry troop from Sebaste and four cohorts of foot soldiers, together with armed Samaritans, and set out in pursuit of the Jews. When he had overtaken them, he killed many of the men who followed Eleazar, but took even more prisoners. When the rulers of Jerusalem saw the magnitude of the calamity, they put on sackcloth and threw ashes on their heads, pleading with the rest of the multitude, who who were about to go and destroy the territories of Samaria, that they would change their minds. When they told them how their country would be destroyed, the temple burned and their wives and children taken captives, they begged them to put down their arms and go home. The Jews obeyed and went home; the thieves, however, retired to their strongholds again and from this time on, Judea was overrun by thieves. {*Josephus, Jewish War, l. 2. c. 12. s. 3-5. (232-239) 2:415,417} {*Josephus, Antiq., l. 20. c. 6. s. 1. (118-124) 10:63-67}

6763. The leading Samaritans resorted to Ummidius Quadratus, the governor of Syria, who was living at Tyre at the time. They begged him to take vengeance on the Jews who had plundered and burned their towns. Some of the Jewish nobility and Jonathan, the son of Ananus, the high priest, answered the charges. They stated that the Samaritans had started this sedition by murdering a Jew, and that Cumanus was the cause of all the calamities that followed, because he had been bribed and so would not revenge that murder. When Quadratus had heard them, he deferred his sentence, saying that he would decide the matter when he came to Judea and would there find out the truth of the affair with greater accuracy. So they departed and nothing was done. {*Josephus, Jewish War, l. 2. c. 12. s. 5,6. (239-241) 2:417} {*Josephus, Antiq., l. 20. c. 6. s. 2. (125-129) 10:67,69}

6764. In the meantime, Felix, by his injudicious disciplinary measures, provoked the Jews to offend all the more. Ventidius Cumanus, who controlled part of the province, rivalled him in all manner of wickedness. Cumanus administered the area of Galilee and Felix the Samaritans. Both countries were always at odds, but much more so at this time, due to the contempt of their governors. As a result, they invaded one another and sent thieves and robbers in to plunder. They laid ambushes and sometimes fought battles, from which they brought the plunder to the governors. At first the governors were pleased, but when the disorder grew intolerable, they sent soldiers to quell it, who were all killed. The whole province would have been in an uproar, had not Quadratus redressed the matter in time. {*Tacitus, Annals, l. 12. c. 54. 4:393,395} [E880]

*6765.* Quadratus acted immediately, by executing the Jews who had killed the Roman soldiers. Cumanus' and Felix's actions were reported to Claudius. When he heard the causes of the rebellion, he gave authority to Quadratus to deal with the matter, and even with the officials of the provinces. Quadratus appointed Felix among the judges (because he was the brother of Pallas, the great favourite at Rome) and received him into the tribunal, to intimidate his accusers. *[K662]* Cumanus alone was condemned for the faults that both had committed. By this means, Quadratus made peace in the province. {*\*Tacitus, Annals, l. 12. c. 54. 4:395*}

*6766.* The Cietae tribes of Cilicia made Troxobor their captain. They camped on rough mountains and from there ran down to the shores and cities, where they plundered the farmers and citizens, but most commonly the merchants and seamen. They also besieged the city of Anemurium, as well as routing the cavalry who had been sent from Syria under their captain, Curtius Severus. For the places around there were suited to fighting on foot, but poor for the cavalry. Then Antiochus Epiphanes IV, the king of that country, by using diplomacy toward the common people and craft toward their captain, divided their forces. He executed Troxobor and some of the ringleaders and appeased the rest through his clemency. {*\*Tacitus, Annals, l. 12. c. 55. 4:395,397*}

*6767.* When the apostle Peter came to Antioch, he ate with and enjoyed the fellowship of the believing Gentiles. However, when certain Jewish brethren came there from James, he withdrew himself from the Gentiles, and some of the Jews of the church at Antioch followed his example. Even Barnabas was led astray by their hypocrisy. This was plainly contrary to the gospel and Paul did not stand for it. He withstood Peter to the face and sharply reproved his fearfulness before them all. {*Ga 2:11-14*}

## 4056 AM, 4766 JP, 53 AD

*6768.* When Quadratus came to Samaria, he ordered those who stood accused to defend their actions and found that the tumult had been caused by the Samaritans. When he went to Caesarea, he learned that some Jews were trying to rebel, so he crucified those whom Cumanus had taken alive as prisoners. He went to Lydda, which was almost the size of a city, and held a tribunal, in order to hear the cause of the Samaritans once more. From a certain Samaritan he learned that Doetus, a ruler of the Jews, had persuaded the Jews to a revolt, so Quadratus had Doetus executed. He also beheaded eighteen Jews who had been in the fight. {*\*Josephus, Jewish War, l. 2. c. 12. s. 6. (241-243) 2:417,419*} {*\*Josephus, Antiq., l. 20. c. 6. s. 2. (129-131) 10:69,71*}

*6769.* Quadratus sent the high priests, Jonathan and Ananias, to Caesar, as well as Ananus, the son of Ananias, along with some of the nobility of the Jews and of the Samaritans. He also ordered Cumanus, the governor, and Celer, the tribune, to go to Rome, to give an account to Caesar of what they had done in the country. {*\*Josephus, Jewish War, l. 2. c. 12. s. 6. (243,244) 2:419*} {*\*Josephus, Antiq., l. 20. c. 6. s. 2. (131,132) 10:71*}

*6770.* After this had been done, Quadratus feared that the Jews might revolt. He went from Lydda to Jerusalem, where he found everything quiet and the people busy celebrating their feast of unleavened bread and offering sacrifices. So he thought that they would be quiet and left them busy at their feast, while he returned to Antioch. {*\*Josephus, Jewish War, l. 2. c. 12. s. 6. (244) 2:419*} {*\*Josephus, Antiq., l. 20. c. 6. s. 2. (132,133) 10:71*}

*6771.* Cumanus and the Samaritans were sent to Rome. On an appointed day, they were ordered to defend their actions. They obtained the favour of Caesar's freedmen and friends and would have won their case, but King Agrippa, the Younger, who was living at Rome, saw that the rulers of the Jews were being overpowered by the favour of the great ones. *[K663]* So, with persistent entreating, he convinced Agrippina, the wife of Claudius, to persuade her husband to hear the matter fully and execute justice on those he found to be the authors of the sedition. Claudius yielded to their requests and when he had heard both sides, he realised that the Samaritans had started the fighting. Claudius executed those who had come before him to plead their cause. He punished Cumanus with banishment and sent Celer, the tribune, to Jerusalem as a prisoner, to be turned over to the Jews to be punished; he was to be dragged through the city and then beheaded. {*\*Josephus, Jewish War, l. 2. c. 12. s. 7. (245,246) 2:419*} {*\*Josephus, Antiq., l. 20. c. 6. s. 3. (134-136) 10:71,73*}

*6772.* Claudius sent Claudius Felix, the brother of Pallas, to be the governor of Judea as well as Samaria and Galilee. {*\*Josephus, Jewish War, l. 2. c. 12. s. 8. (247-249) 2:419,421*} Jonathan, the high priest, had begged Caesar for him. {*\*Josephus, Antiq., l. 20. c. 8. s. 5. (162) 10:89*} Suetonius wrote: {*\*Suetonius, Claudius, l. 5. c. 28. 2:57*}

> "Claudius preferred Felix, one of his freedmen, to command the cavalry or foot soldiers and run the government of Judea. He became the husband of three queens."

*6773.* Tacitus wrote: {*\*Tacitus, Annals, l. 12. c. 54. 4:395*}

> "When Felix was the governor of Judea, he thought he could do any wickedness with impunity and behaved arrogantly."

6774. He added this about his tyrannical government in Judea: {*Tacitus, Histories, l. 5. c. 9. 3:191,193}

"Antonius Felix exercised regal power with the instincts of a slave, with all cruelty and lust. He married Drusilla, the grand-daughter of Cleopatra and Antony, and so was the grandson-in-law of Antony, while Claudius was Antony's grandson." [E881]

6775. King Agrippa, the Younger, had governed Chalcis for four years. After the twelfth year of ruling his empire, Claudius took Chalcis from Agrippa and gave him a larger jurisdiction. He received the tetrarchy of Philip, which contained Batanea, Gaulanitis and Trachonitis. He also added Abilene, or Abila, which was the tetrarchy of Lysanias, and which had been governed by Varus. {*Josephus, Jewish War, l. 2. c. 12. s. 8. (247,248) 2:421} {*Josephus, Antiq., l. 20. c. 7. s. 1. (138) 10:75}

6776. After Agrippa had been advanced through Caesar's gifts, he gave his sister Drusilla in marriage to Azizus, the king of the Emesa, who consented to be circumcised. Epiphanes, the son of Antiochus, king of the Commagenians, had refused her, because he had changed his mind and would not embrace the Jewish religion, as he had promised her father. Agrippa gave Mariamme in marriage to Julius Archelaus, the son of Helcias, to whom she had been betrothed by her father Agrippa. {*Josephus, Antiq., l. 20. c. 7. s. 1. (139,140) 10:75,77}

6777. Josephus, the son of Matthias, began to adopt the lifestyle of Bannus, who lived in the wilderness. He clothed himself with what the trees produced and for his food he used those things which grew in the wild. To keep himself chaste, he often washed himself in cold water and in this manner he lived for three years. {*Josephus, Life, l. 1. c. 2. (11,12) 1:7}

6778. Nero, the adopted son of Claudius, took up the cause of Illium in a speech. He said that the Romans were descended from Troy and that Aeneas was the father of the Julian family, as well as many ancient things, which were probably fables. The city of Illium was freed from tribute forever, because they were the founders of the Romans. {*Tacitus, Annals, l. 12. c. 58. 4:401} Nero read an ancient letter from the Senate and the people of Rome, written in Greek to King Seleucus, in which they promised him their friendship and alliance only on the condition that he should keep their relatives of Illium free from every burden. {*Suetonius, Claudius, l. 5. c. 25. s. 3. 2:51}

6779. The Rhodians repented of their old misdeeds and Claudius restored their liberty. [K664] It was frequently either taken away or confirmed, depending on what they had merited in foreign wars or how they had offended by having seditions at home. {*Suetonius, Claudius, l. 5. c. 25. s.

3. 2:51} {*Tacitus, Annals, l. 12. c. 58. 4:401} Suetonius wrote that Nero pleaded for the Rhodians and Illienses in Greek before his father Claudius, who had been in his last consulship two years earlier. {*Suetonius, Nero, l. 6. c. 7. s. 2. 2:93,95} Claudius remitted all tribute to the city of Apamea for five years, because their city was destroyed by an earthquake. {*Tacitus, Annals, l. 12. c. 58. 4:401}

6780. After that, Claudius spoke about freeing the island of Cos from tribute. He alleged many things about their antiquity, such as that the Argives, or perhaps Coeus, the father of the goddess Latona (after whom the island was named), were the ancient inhabitants. Aesculapius had brought the art of healing there and was famous among all his posterity. Claudius gave their names and in what epochs they had lived. Then he said that Xenophon, his own physician, was from Cos and was descended from that family. Claudius had yielded to his entreaty that they might henceforth be free from tribute and permitted to devote themselves to the service of that god. {*Tacitus, Annals, l. 12. c. 61. 4:405}

6781. Paul asked Barnabas to go with him again and visit the churches where they had preached the gospel. Barnabas was determined to take John Mark with him, but Paul did not think it good to take him since he had abandoned them in Pamphylia {Ac 13:13} and had not gone with them to the work. Barnabas took this badly that such dishonour should be attached to his sister's son. {Col 4:10} The contention was so sharp, that they parted company. Barnabas took Mark and sailed to his own country of Cyprus, but Paul, having been commended to the grace of God, chose Silas and went into Syria and Cilicia and confirmed the brethren. {Ac 15:36-41}

6782. Paul came to Derbe and Lystra and there, among the disciples, he found Timothy, who was born of a Greek, or Gentile, father, but his mother (Eunice) was a believing Jew, of whom all the brethren at Iconium and Lystra gave a good report. Paul wanted to take Timothy with him and so, to win over the Jews more easily, he had Timothy circumcised. {Ac 16:1-3}

6783. As Paul and Silas passed through the cities, they gave them the decrees they were to keep, which had been ordained by the apostles and elders at Jerusalem. The churches were established in the faith and daily increased in number. {Ac 16:4,5}

6784. When they had gone through Phrygia and the region of Galatia, they were forbidden by the Spirit to preach the word of God in Asia. When they arrived at Mysia, they planned to go into Bithynia, but the Spirit did not allow them. So they left Mysia and came down to Troas, where Paul had a vision of a man asking them to come into Macedonia to help them. {Ac 16:6-9}

6785. When he had seen this vision, they planned to go into Macedonia, certain that the Lord had called them there to preach the gospel. {Ac 16:10} [E882] Thus said Luke, who from then on spoke of Paul and his companions in the first person, whereas before he had always spoken in the third person. [K665] He thereby showed that from that time on, he was one of Paul's companions in the preaching of the Gospel.

## 4057a AM, 4766 JP, 53 AD

6786. Paul and Silas, together with Luke and Timothy, sailed from Troas and went straight to Samothracia. The next day, they arrived at Neapolis and from there went to Philippi, which was the main city of that part of Macedonia and a Roman colony. They stayed there for some days. {Ac 16:11,12}

6787. On the Sabbath day, they left the city to go to the riverside, where there was a house of prayer, and spoke to the women who came there. Among these was Lydia, who worshipped God and was a seller of purple in the city of Thyatira. She listened to the things which Paul said and the Lord opened her heart and she believed in Christ. When she and her household were baptized, she entertained Paul and his companions. {Ac 16:13-15}

6788. Later, at the place of prayer, they cast out an unclean spirit from a servant girl who had the spirit of divination. She had followed them for many days, crying out that these men were the servants of the most High God and telling the way of salvation. Paul was grieved and in the name of Jesus, ordered the spirit to come out of her. When the masters of the maid saw that the source of their financial gain was gone, they dragged Paul and Silas into the market place and caused a commotion before the rulers. The rulers had both Paul and Silas publicly scourged and cast into prison. At midnight, as they were praying and singing psalms, there was a violent earthquake and all the doors of the prison were opened and all the prisoners' bonds were released. Because of this, the jailor, in desperation, would have killed himself with his naked sword, but Paul and Silas preached to him and he was converted to the faith and baptized that same night, with all his family. When it was day, the magistrates sent them word that they were free to go. Paul and Silas objected about the shame and injury done to them because they had scourged them publicly and cast them into prison without a trial. At this, the magistrates came in person to set them at liberty with honour and asked them to depart from the city. They went to Lydia's house and comforted the brethren who came to them, and so left the city. {Ac 16:16-40}

6789. As they journeyed through Amphipolis and Apollonia, they came to Thessalonica, the main city of Macedonia, where there was a synagogue of the Jews. {Ac 17:1-3} Paul wrote that there, after having been shamefully mistreated at Philippi, he preached the gospel with much zeal. {1Th 2:2} As was his custom, Paul went into the synagogue of the Jews for three Sabbaths and reasoned with them from the scriptures concerning Christ. Some Jews believed, along with a large number of the religious Greeks and many of the chief women. {Ac 17:2-4}

6790. Paul taught the Thessalonians about faith in Christ and concerning the future apostasy surrounding the the man of lawlessness and his appearing. {2Th 2:5-12}

6791. During the long time that Paul stayed at Thessalonica, he time and time again received relief for his needs from the Philippians. {Php 4:16} The unbelieving Jews stirred up some ignorant ruffians and caused an uproar in the city. [K666] They dragged Jason, at whose house Paul and his companion were staying, and some of the brethren before the magistrates and accused them in riotous fashion. When the magistrates had taken a pledge from them, the brethren sent Paul and Silas away by night to Berea. {Ac 17:5-10}

6792. There they entered the synagogue of the Jews and diligently preached Christ from the scriptures. Those who heard the message, painstakingly compared it with the scriptures. When the scriptures confirmed what was being said, many of them believed, including many honourable Greek women and men. When the Jews of Thessalonica arrived there, they stirred up the masses against Paul. Immediately the brethren sent him away, as if he were going to the sea, but they brought him to Athens. Paul asked that Silas and Timothy, whom he had left at Berea, should join him quickly. {Ac 17:10-15}

## 4057b AM, 4767 JP, 54 AD

6793. The Jews, at the instigation of Chrestus, continually caused trouble, so that Claudius expelled them from Rome. {*Suetonius, Claudius, l. 5. c. 25. 2:51} Suetonius (if I am not mistaken) mentioned only Chrestus. I am not convinced that Christ, our Lord, is meant here, after whom the believers are called Christians in another place.

6794. While Paul waited for Silas and Timothy at Athens, he reasoned in the synagogue with the Jews and devout men, and daily in the market place with anyone who would listen. He also argued with the philosophers of the Epicurean and Stoic sects about Christ and the resurrection. He was brought to Mars Hill, so that people could hear him expound about these strange gods. Paul defended his cause in a most learned speech. He used the example of the altar dedicated to the *unknown God*, as well as quoting from the testimony of Aratus, the poet, and confirming that all were the *offspring of God*. It was that very God, whom they ignorantly worshipped, that Paul was speaking to them about. {*Ac 17:16-31*} *[E883]* The God of the Jews was known as the *unknown God* among the Gentiles. In the same sense, Lucan called him *the uncertain God*. {*Lucan, Phalaris, l. 2. (8) 1:27*} Trebellius Pollio called him the *God of uncertain power*. {*Pollio, Claudius*} Gaius Caligula called him the *unnamed God*. {*Philo, Gaius, l. 1. c. 44. (353) 10:177*} The inhabitants of Mount Carmel attributed neither image nor temple to him, but only an altar and reverence. {*Tacitus, Histories, l. 2. c. 78. 2:285,287*} Hence, the Athenians had made an *Altar to Mercy* in the middle of their city, without any image. Statius stated: {*Statius, Thebes, l. 12.*}

> God's form by pictures cannot be expressed,
> He loves to dwell within the heart and breast.

6795. Among Paul's converts were Dionysius, the Areopagite, and a woman called Damaris (who may have been his wife, as Ambrose, Chrysostom and Augustine believed) and some others. {*Ac 17:34*}

6796. When Felix, the governor of Judea, saw Drusilla, the sister of King Agrippa, he fell in love with her. He sent his friend, Simon, a Jew from Cyprus, who went pretending to be a soothsayer, to persuade the woman to leave her husband, Azizus king of Emesa, and marry Felix. *[K667]* Felix promised that she would be happy if she did not refuse him. Because she wanted to escape the malice of her sister Bernice—for she was exceedingly abused by Bernice because of her beauty—so she broke the laws of the Jewish religion and married Felix unadvisedly. However, Bernice, the widow of her uncle, persuaded Polemo to be circumcised and to marry her. She thought that by doing this she might prove the gossip false, which said that she was having illegal relations with Agrippa, the Younger. Polemo agreed because she was rich, but the marriage did not last long. Bernice left him (so it was reported) on account of her licentiousness. As soon as he was abandoned by his wife, he immediately left the Jewish religion. {*Josephus, Antiq., l. 20. c. 7. s. 2,3. (141-146) 10:77-81*}

6797. At the same time as well, King Agrippa's third sister, Mariamme, scorned Julius Archelaus, the son of Helcias. She went and married Demetrius, a chief man among the Jews of Alexandria, both on account of his birth and his wealth, and who was the alabarch at that time. {*Josephus, Antiq., l. 20. c. 7. s. 3. (147) 10:81*}

6798. Paul sent Silas and Timothy, who had come to him from Berea, back into Macedonia again and remained alone at Athens. He planned to return to Thessalonica, but Satan hindered his plans, so he sent Timothy there to strengthen and comfort the Thessalonians in the faith. {*Ac 18:5 1Th 2:17,18 3:1,2*}

6799. In the meantime, Paul left Athens and went to Corinth, where he found Aquila, a Jew, and his wife Priscilla, who had recently come from Italy, because Claudius had made a decree that all Jews had to leave Rome. Paul stayed with them, because they were both tentmakers. Paul reasoned in the synagogue every Sabbath and persuaded the Jews and the Greeks. {*Ac 18:1-5*}

6800. Paul personally baptized the family members of Stephanus, who were the firstfruits of Achaia and who had dedicated themselves to the ministry of the saints. {*1Co 1:16 16:15*}

6801. As Silas and Timothy arrived from Macedonia, the Jews withstood Paul's preaching of Christ with great zeal and blasphemed him. Paul shook his clothes in protest against them and turned to the Gentiles. He went into the house of one surnamed Justus, who lived near the synagogue and who worshipped God. {*Ac 18:6,7*}

6802. Crispus, the ruler of the synagogue, believed in the Lord with all his family and when many of the Corinthians heard the gospel, they too believed and were baptized. {*Ac 18:8*} Of these, Paul himself only baptized Crispus and Gaius with his own hand. {*1Co 1:14*}

6803. The Lord told Paul in a vision by night, not to be afraid and to speak boldly. He told him that no one would harm him, for the Lord had many people in that city. Paul stayed another eighteen months and taught the word of the Lord among them. {*Ac 18:9-11*} Silvanus, or Silas, and Timothy assisted him. {*2Co 1:19*}

6804. After the return of Timothy from Macedonia, Paul, together with these same two, Timothy and Silvanus, or Silas, wrote the first letter to the Thessalonians. {*1Th 3:6*} *[K668]* He wrote some difficult things about the day of judgment, since it was very imminent at that time. {*1Th 5:1-5*} He later wrote another letter to them, in which he expounded the subject more clearly. {*2Th 2:2,3*} *[E884]* This was written during the time when he had Silvanus and Timothy as his companions in the ministry of the gospel {*1Th 1:1*} and after he had been with the Thessalonians and they had embraced the faith of Christ. {*2Th 2:5*} Grotius was quite mistaken in thinking that it was written at the time of Gaius Caligula.

6805. The Parthians invaded Armenia after driving out Radamistus, who had often reigned there as king and often been ejected, and had finally given up the struggle. {*Tacitus, Annals, l. 13. c. 6. 5:11*} When Vologeses' son Vardanes revolted from the king of the Parthians, the Parthians abandoned Armenia, as if deferring the war. {*Tacitus, Annals, l. 13. c. 7. 5:13}

## 4058a AM, 4767 JP, 54 AD

6806. Claudius died on the 3rd of the Ides of October (October 13), when Asinius Marcellus and Asilius Aviola were consuls. Claudius' wife Agrippina poisoned him. {Seneca, Ludi de Morte Claudii, initio} {*Suetonius, Claudius, l. 5. c. 45. 2:79} {*Dio, l. 60. (34) 8:31} He had reigned thirteen years, eight months and twenty days. {*Dio, l. 60. (34) 8:31} {*Josephus, Antiq., l. 20. c. 8. s. 1. (148) 10:81} In the middle of the same day, the gates of the palace were suddenly thrown open and Nero, the son-in-law and adopted son, was declared emperor. {*Tacitus, Annals, l. 12. c. 69. 4:417}

6807. At the beginning of Nero's reign, Junius Silanus was the proconsul of Asia, a nobleman and descended from the Caesars. Nero, who had barely reached manhood, was not involved in his murder. Junius was murdered through the treachery of Nero's mother, Agrippina. Publius Celer, an equestrian of Rome, and Helius, a freedman, were his officers, who had the charge of the prince's revenues in Asia, and it was they who poisoned the proconsul at a feast. {*Tacitus, Annals, l. 13. c. 1. 5:3}

6808. The envoys of Armenia pleaded their cause before Nero. When his mother wanted to come up to the emperor's tribunal and sit with him, everyone was stupefied for this was not to be done. Seneca advised Nero to meet his mother and so, under pretence of doing his duty, he prevented a scandal. {*Tacitus, Annals, l. 13. c. 5. 5:9}

6809. The report was brought to Rome that the Parthians had occupied Armenia. Nero ordered that the youth of the neighbouring provinces be mustered to supply the eastern legions, which were to be stationed near Armenia. The two old kings, Agrippa of Judea and Antiochus IV of Commagene, were to prepare their forces to invade Parthia. Bridges were to be built over the Euphrates River. Nero gave Aristobulus the kingdom of Lesser Armenia and Sohaemus was given the kingdom of Sophene, and both had royal status. He sent Domitius Corbulo to hold Armenia and allocated the forces of the east. Some were to remain in the province of Syria with Ummidius Quadratus, its governor, while a similar number of citizens and allies should accompany Corbulo, with other cohorts and cavalry who had wintered in Cappadocia. Nero ordered the confederate kings to be ready for war if required. {*Tacitus, Annals, l. 13. c. 6-8. 5:11-15}

## 4058b AM, 4768 JP, 55 AD

6810. In the first year of Nero's empire, Azizus, the king of Emesa, died and his brother Sohaemus succeeded him in the kingdom. Aristobulus, the son of Herod, king of Chalcis, received the kingdom of Lesser Armenia

from Nero, as already mentioned from Tacitus. Nero added four cities to the kingdom of Agrippa, together with all the land belonging to them. [K669] In Galilee, he received the cities of Tiberias and Tarichea. In Iturea beyond Jordan, he was given Abila and Julias. He received the land that contained fourteen villages. {*Josephus, Antiq., l. 20. c. 8. s. 4. (158,159) 10:87,89} {*Josephus, Jewish War, l. 2. c. 13. s. 2. (252) 2:421}

6811. Domitius Corbulo hurried to Aegeae, a city of Cilicia, where he met Quadratus, who had deliberately gone there, because if Corbulo had entered Syria to receive the forces, it was likely that all men's eyes would have been on him to the detriment of Quadratus. They each sent messengers to Vologeses, the king of the Parthians, asking him to choose peace and send hostages to secure it. He was to continue to respect the people of Rome, as his ancestors had done. Either to buy time to better prepare for war, or else to remove all contenders for the throne, Vologeses turned over the most noble of the family of the Arsacides. Quadratus sent the centurion Insteius to receive them. When Corbulo learned this, he ordered Arrius Varus, the captain of a cohort of foot soldiers, to go and receive the hostages, whereupon there was a quarrel between the captain and the centurion. So as not to air their differences in front of foreigners, both men let the hostages decide with whom they wanted to go. They selected the captain to escort them, because Corbulo was famous even among Rome's enemies. Hence Corbulo and Quadratus had a falling-out: Quadratus complained that he had been robbed of the fruits of his negotiations, while Corbulo protested that the king had not offered hostages until Corbulo had been chosen as the general, and that the king was afraid of him. To settle the differences, Nero proclaimed the order that Quadratus and Corbulo, for their prosperous success, should have their imperial fasces wreathed with laurel. {*Tacitus, Annals, l. 13. c. 8,9. 5:15,17} [E885]

6812. At the beginning of Nero's reign, all Judea was filled with thieves, enchanters and seducers of the ignorant masses. Every day Felix put to death as many as he could capture. Eleazar, the son of Dinaeus, who led a large band of thieves, was persuaded by Felix to come to him. Felix had given him his word that Eleazar would suffer no harm from him, but when he came, Felix bound him and sent him to Rome. {*Josephus, Antiq., l. 20. c. 8. s. 5. (160,161) 10:89} {*Josephus, Jewish War, l. 2. c. 13. s. 2. (253) 2:423}

6813. Felix could no longer tolerate Jonathan, the high priest, who so often and so freely admonished him over his government of the Jews. By promising him a large sum of money, he persuaded Doras, a great friend of Jonathan, to kill Jonathan by using some assassins.

These entered the city under the pretence of religious worship, with daggers hidden secretly under their garments. They mingled among his family and killed Jonathan. Because that murder went unpunished, it became an invitation to more licentiousness. Others came at every feast and hid their daggers in the same way; mixing with the crowd, they freely killed some of their private enemies. Some were hired for money to murder in the city, and even in the temple. {*Josephus, Antiq., l. 20. c. 8. s. 5. (162-166) 10:89,91}

6814. In this way, the city became infested with thieves. The deceivers and magicians enticed and drew multitudes into the deserts, promising to show them signs and wonders done by the power of God. When the multitude had been persuaded in this manner, they suffered the penalty for their folly. They were brought back by Felix and put to death. {Mt 24:24-26} {*Josephus, Jewish War, l. 2. c. 13. s. 3,4. (254-260) 2:423,425} {*Josephus, Antiq., l. 20. c. 8. s. 6. (167,168) 10:91,93}

6815. At that time, there was a certain Egyptian who called himself a prophet. He gathered thirty thousand men, or four thousand, according to Luke, {Ac 21:38} [K670] and brought them from the wilderness to the Mount of Olives. He told them that from there they would see the walls of Jerusalem fall down, by which means they would then be able to enter the city. When Felix found out, he attacked this seduced multitude with his Roman cavalry and foot soldiers, as well as a large number of Jews. He killed four hundred and took two hundred prisoners alive. The rest of the multitude dispersed into their own countries. No one knew what became of the Egyptian and the few who escaped from that skirmish. {*Josephus, Antiq., l. 20. c. 8. s. 6. (169-172) 10:93} {*Josephus, Jewish War, l. 2. c. 13. s. 5. (261-263) 2:425} Lysias the captain mentioned him to Paul when he asked whether Paul was that Egyptian who, in earlier days had created an uproar and had led four thousand men, who were murderers, into the desert. {Ac 21:38}

6816. When Gallio was proconsul of Achaia, the Jews of Corinth brought Paul before his judgment seat. The Greeks took Sosthenes, the ruler of the synagogue, and beat him, and Gallio was not concerned about it. {Ac 18:12-17}

6817. Lucius Junius Gallio was the brother of Lucius Annaeus Seneca, who, together with Burrhus, commanded everything at Rome through his young student, Nero. Gallio derided the deifying of Claudius, who had died from poisoning and was claimed to have been taken up to heaven on a litter. He said Claudius had received *pumpkinfication* not deification! {*Dio, l. 60. (35) 8:33} There is a work extant, the Book of Controversies, by Marcus Annaeus Seneca, father of the three sons, Novatus, Sen-

eca and Mela. In the second volume of this work, Lucius Seneca, in his consolation to his mother Helvia, said that: {*Seneca the Elder, Controversies, l. 2. (3,4) 1:201}

"One of his brothers (Novatus) received honours by his industry, the other (Mela) despised them."

6818. The first one referred to, Novatus, who had been adopted by Junius Gallio, had been banished by Tiberius. {See note on 4035b AM. <<6386>>} He was also called Gallio, and the same Seneca called him *Lord*, because he was his older brother, as Lipsius noted: {Lipsius, Epistle 104.}

"This was the saying of my Lord Gallio, who began to have a fever in Achaia and immediately sailed away, crying that it was not the disease of the body, but of the place."

## 4059 AM, 4769 JP, 56 AD

6819. Paul stayed many days at Corinth. After the riot at Gallio's tribunal, Paul said goodbye to the brethren and sailed for Syria from the port of Cenchrea. He first arrived at Ephesus, where he entered a synagogue and reasoned with the Jews. When they wanted him to stay longer, he did not agree to it, saying that he wanted to keep the feast at Jerusalem. He promised that he would return to them again, if God willed. After bidding them farewell, he left Aquila and Priscilla behind and sailed from Ephesus with the rest of his companions. {Ac 18:18-22}

6820. Paul landed at Caesarea (Stratonis) and went to greet the church at Jerusalem. He went down to Antioch (of Syria) and after staying there for some time, he left and systematically crossed all the regions of Galatia and Phrygia, to strengthen all the disciples. {Ac 18:22,23} The Galatians received him as an angel of God, or as Jesus Christ himself. {Ga 4:14} [E886] Among other things, he arranged that the collections for the poor should be set aside every Lord's day. {1Co 16:1,2} [K671]

6821. After the three years which he spent living with Bannus in the wilderness, Josephus, the son of Matthias, returned to Jerusalem. Now nineteen years old, he began to dabble in public affairs and followed the sect of the Pharisees, which was the closest sect to the Greek Stoics. {*Josephus, Life, l. 1. c. 2. (12) 1:7}

6822. A certain Alexandrian Jew by the name of Apollos was an eloquent man and powerful in the scriptures. He came to Ephesus, where he was instructed in the way of the Lord because he was fervent in spirit, speaking and diligently teaching the things of the Lord, even though he knew only about the baptism of John. He began to speak freely in the synagogue. Aquila and Priscilla heard him and took him aside and expounded the way of the Lord to him more fully. When Apollos planned to go into Achaia, the brethren exhorted him and wrote to the disciples there to receive him. When he arrived, he helped those who had believed, because with great zeal he convinced the Jews publicly, showing from the scriptures that Jesus was the Christ. {*Ac 18:24-28*}

## 4060a AM, 4769 JP, 56 AD

*6823.* When Apollos was at Corinth, Paul passed through the upper regions of Galatia and Phrygia. At Ephesus, he came across twelve disciples who only knew of the baptism of John and had not yet received the Holy Spirit through the laying-on of hands. After Paul had further instructed them in the doctrine of Christ, he laid his hands on them and the Holy Spirit came upon them, at which they spoke in tongues and prophesied. Then he went into the synagogue and spoke freely, disputing and persuading them about the things concerning the kingdom of God. {*Ac 19:1-8*}

## 4060b AM, 4770 JP, 57 AD

*6824.* Some Jews, who were hardened and who refused to believe, spoke evil of the way of the Lord, so Paul left them, taking the disciples with him, and daily disputed in the school of Tyrannus for two whole years. All who lived in Asia, both Jews and Greeks, heard the word of the Lord Jesus. Paul performed many miracles. Handkerchiefs and aprons that had touched his body were brought to the sick and they were healed, and evil spirits came out of them. {*Ac 19:9-12*}

*6825.* The province of Asia accused Publius Celer of his crimes. Caesar could not absolve him, so he delayed his trial until Celer died from old age. Celer had killed Silanus, the proconsul, and the magnitude of this villainy only masked Celer's other wickednesses. {*Tacitus, Annals, l. 13. c. 33. 5:55*}

*6826.* The Cilicians accused Cossutianus Capito of being a man besotted and defiled with every conceivable vice. He thought that, in the province, he had the same authority to behave wickedly that he had exercised in the city of Rome. The prosecution was so determined, that he abandoned his defence and was condemned for extortion. {*Tacitus, Annals, l. 13. c. 33. 5:55*} It was he (according to Lipsius) who is referred to in the following lines from Juvenal: {*Juvenal, Satire, 8.*}

> …How the Senate's just thunderstruck
> Capito and Tutor for making prize,
> As pirates, of the Cilician merchandise."

*6827.* Quintilian mentioned: {*Quintilian, l. 6. c. 1.*} [K672]

> "The accuser of Cossutianus seemed to us young men to speak bravely, it was in Greek, but to this sense, *He was ashamed to be afraid of Caesar.*"

*6828.* Intrigue played out on behalf of Epirus Marcellus, from whom the Lycians were demanding restitution, was so effective, that a number of the accusers were banished, on the grounds that they had endangered an innocent man. {*Tacitus, Annals, l. 13. c. 33. 5:55*}

## 4061 AM, 4771 JP, 58 AD

*6829.* The war over who would control Armenia, which had started coolly enough between the Romans and Parthians, was now being hotly pursued. Vologeses would not allow his brother, Tiridates, to be removed from the kingdom that he had given him, or let him accept it as a gift from another. Corbulo thought it worthy of the greatness of the people of Rome to recover what had previously been captured by Lucullus and Pompey. So he prepared his army for this war in the old manner, according to the old severity and discipline of the Romans. Then Corbulo entered Armenia, where he destroyed some citadels and burned Artaxata, while Tiridates did not dare do battle with him. {*Tacitus, Annals, l. 13. c. 34-41. 5:57-73*} [E887]

*6830.* Seven exorcists of the Jews, the sons of Sceva, a chief priest, called upon those who had unclean spirits. They tried to cast out an unclean spirit in the name of the Lord Jesus, whom Paul preached but the man who had the unclean spirit leaped on them and forced them to flee the house, wounded and naked. When this became known to both the Jews and the Greeks who lived at Ephesus, they were all afraid and the name of the Lord Jesus was magnified. Many of those who believed, confessed and revealed their practices. Many who practised magic, brought their books together and burned them before everyone. These books were valued at fifty thousand pieces of silver. So the word grew mightily and prevailed. {*Ac 19:13-20*}

*6831.* As soon as Paul had left them, the Galatians {*Ac 18:23*} were seduced by false brethren into believing that they were to be justified by the works of the law. Paul sent a strongly worded letter to them, to correct this error. {*Ga 1:6,7*}

## 4062 AM, 4772 JP, 59 AD

*6832.* Paul planned to go to Jerusalem after he had passed through Macedonia and Achaia. He said that after he had been to Jerusalem, he wanted to go to Rome, as well. {*Ac 19:21*} He thought he would first go to Corinth, and from there to Macedonia, and then return to Corinth. From there, he would travel to Judea {*1Co 1:15,16*} to take the collections for the poor saints at Jerusalem. After that, he planned to go to Rome and then on to Spain. {*Ro 15:24-28*}

*6833.* While Paul thought about this, he sent Timothy and Erastus to Macedonia, but he remained in Asia for a while. {Ac 19:22} It is likely that he was in Lydia, where he seems to have preached the gospel for nine months to the cities which were near Ephesus. Since he spent two years teaching in the school of Tyrannus and three months teaching in the synagogue of Ephesus, he spent three years in total, labouring in Asia. {Ac 20:18,31} He said that a great door had been opened for him, although there were many adversaries. {1Co 16:9}

6834. On the 2nd of the Calends of May (April 30), when Vipsanius and Fonteius were consuls, there was an eclipse in Campania between one and two p.m. Corbulo, the general, who was in Armenia, wrote that it was visible between four and five p.m. {*Pliny, l. 2. c. 72. 1:313} {*Tacitus, Annals, l. 13. c. 41. 5:71,73} [K673] At Rome, this eclipse was observed at the very time of the sacrifices that were being made by the decree of the Senate, on behalf of Agrippina, who had been killed by her son, Nero. It was so dark, that the stars could be seen. {*Dio, l. 62. (16) 8:73} {*Tacitus, Annals, l. 14. c. 12. 5:127}

## 4063a AM, 4772 JP, 59 AD

6835. People from the family of Chloe told Paul that there was a schism in the church of Corinth—some said they followed Paul, some Apollos, some Cephas and some Christ. {1Co 1:11,12 3:3,4} Apollos and some other believers went from Corinth to Paul in Asia, {1Co 16:12} bringing with them the letter which the Corinthians had written to Paul, in which they asked his advice about the matter of marriage and the single life. {1Co 7:1}

6836. Paul, together with Sosthenes, the ruler of the synagogue at Corinth who had been converted to Christ, wrote the first letter to the Corinthians from Lydia. Timothy was not in Asia at the time, {1Co 16:10 Ac 19:22} so Paul sent it with Stephanas, Fortunatus and Achaicus, who had been sent from Corinth to visit the apostle. Apollos did not wish to return to the Corinthians at that time. {1Co 1:1 16:12,13,17,19}

6837. In this letter, Paul ordered the incestuous Corinthian, who was immorally living with his father's wife, to be handed over to Satan. {1Co 5} He also corrected other errors that had crept into the church; he corrected errors in conduct and refuted the error of the Sadducees, who said there was no resurrection. {1Co 15} He told them that when he arrived, he would set the rest of the church in order. {1Co 4:18,19 11:34} He intended to pass through Macedonia, but planned to stay at Ephesus until Pentecost, unless something came up that changed his plans. {1Co 16:5-8}

6838. Demetrius, a silversmith who made silver shrines for Diana, feared that he would lose his livelihood. He convened all the workmen of the same craft and raised an uproar against Paul, claiming that Paul had persuaded the Ephesians and almost the whole of Asia, that images made by men were not gods. They seized Gaius and Aristarchus, who were from Macedonia and were Paul's travelling companions, and rushed with them into the theatre. When Paul wanted to go there, some of the disciples and some of the chief men of Asia (who financed the plays shown in the theatre), as well as his friends, would not allow Paul to go to the people. When Alexander the Jew tried to make his defence before the people, a great cry went up from their midst, which lasted for almost two hours: *Great is Diana of the Ephesians.* [E888] At length the tumult was settled through the wisdom of the townclerk. After calling the brethren together, Paul took his leave and departed for Macedonia. {Ac 19:24-41 20:1}

6839. Aquila and Priscilla left Ephesus and returned to Rome, after having risked their lives to save Paul. {Ro 16:3,4 1Co 16:19} The Jews everywhere returned to Rome, since the edict of Claudius, which had ordered their expulsion, had expired after his death. {Ac 28:17-21}

6840. Paul went from Ephesus to Troas. Although he had opportunities to preach the gospel, he was troubled because he did not find Titus there, whom he had sent to the Corinthians with another brother. Paul sailed from there into Macedonia, {2Co 2:12,13 12:18} [K674] where, on his arrival, he earnestly exhorted the brethren. {Ac 20:2}

6841. Paul's afflictions continued. People opposed him and he was fearful. He was comforted by the arrival of Titus, who told him the good news about the Corinthian church. {2Co 7:5-16} Paul used the Corinthians as an example to stir up the Macedonians to provide collections to be sent to Jerusalem. He said that Achaia had been ready for this a year ago. {2Co 8:1-5 9:2}

## 4063b AM, 4773 JP, 60 AD

6842. When Titus told Paul how well his first letter had been received by the Corinthians, he sent them another letter with Timothy. He told of the great afflictions that he had suffered in Asia because of Demetrius. He said that he had not come to them, as he had intended to do, in order to spare them. {2Co 1:8,9 17-23} He wanted them to pardon the incestuous Corinthian upon his repentance. {2Co 6:5-11} Paul sent Titus to them again, along with another brother, who was famous among all the churches for his proclamation of the gospel. This man was thought to be Luke. These two were to prepare them, so that they would have their collections ready for sending to Jerusalem by the time Paul arrived. {2Co 8:16-19 9:3-5}

6843. Paul went from Macedonia into Greece and stayed there three months. {Ac 20:2,3} During that time, he went to Corinth and received the collections in Achaia for the relief of the believers at Jerusalem. {1Co 16:3-5 2Co 9:4}

6844. The famous letter to the Romans was written from Corinth at this time, as Origen confirmed, with many reasons, in his preface to the exposition of that letter. It was dictated by Paul, written by Tertius and sent through Phoebe, a servant of the church of Cenchrea, near Corinth. {Ro 16:1,2,22} This was at the time that Paul was about to make his journey to Jerusalem with the collections from Macedonia and Achaia. {Ro 15:25,26}

6845. When Paul planned to go directly from there to Syria to carry the collections to Jerusalem, the Jews planned to ambush him. At that, he thought it best to return to Macedonia, from where he had come, and from there he would pass into Asia. {Ac 20:3,4}

6846. From Philippi in Macedonia, Paul sent his travelling companions ahead to Asia. Sopater, or Sosipater, of Berea, {Ro 16:11} Aristarchus and Secundus of Thessalonica, Gaius of Derbe and Timothy, with Tychicus and Trophimus, of Asia, were to wait for him at Troas. Meanwhile, Paul, Luke and the rest sailed from Philippi after the days of unleavened bread and arrived at Troas in five days. They stayed there for seven days. {Ac 20:4-6}

6847. On the eighth day, which was the first day of the week, the disciples assembled together to break bread. Paul preached to them, as he was leaving the next day. He continued until midnight and restored Eutychus to life, a young man who fell down from the third loft in the room where they were assembled. {Ac 20:7-12}

6848. From here, Paul travelled on foot to Assos, to where Luke and his other companions had sailed. [K675] They took him on board and sailed to Mitylene. They left there and on the following day they sailed past Chios, arriving at Samos on the day after that. They stayed at Trogyllium and the next day they came to Miletus. {Ac 20:13-15}

6849. Paul hurried to be at Jerusalem in time for the feast of Pentecost. Therefore, to save time, he bypassed Ephesus and sent messengers from Miletus to Ephesus, to summon the elders of the church to meet with him. He delivered a very grave speech to them, warned them of their duty and seriously exhorted them to do it. He kneeled and prayed with them and they all wept, especially because Paul thought he would never see them again. {Ac 20:16-38} [E889]

6850. After they had launched from Troas, they sailed straight for Cos. The next day they came to Rhodes and from there to Patara, where they took a ship which was sailing for Phoenicia. They sailed north of Cyprus and arrived at Tyre. {Ac 21:1-3}

6851. They stayed with some disciples for seven days. These warned Paul through the Spirit that he should not go up to Jerusalem. However, he kneeled down on the shore and prayed with them. He sailed from Tyre to Ptolemais and there stayed many days with Philip, the evangelist, who was one of the seven deacons {Ac 6:5} and had four daughters who were virgins and prophesied. Paul was met by Agabus, a prophet from Judea, who bound his own hands and feet and foretold about the bonds that awaited Paul. However the brethren were unable to persuade Paul not to go to such a dangerous place, and he went to Jerusalem nonetheless. The disciples accompanied him from Caesarea and brought Mnason of Cyprus with them. He was an old disciple, with whom Paul would stay. {Ac 21:4-16}

6852. The church welcomed them with great joy. James and all the elders at Jerusalem advised Paul to remove the stigma that he carried. It was alleged that he taught the Jewish converts to Christianity to forsake the law of Moses. Paul went with four men who were believing Jews and had made the vow of the Nazarite. He purified himself with them according to the command of the law, but this proved to be of no avail. When some of the unbelieving and rebellious Jews of Asia, who had come to Jerusalem to the feast, saw him in the temple, they made a great clamour and noise, and stirred up the people about Paul's alleged crime. They said that Paul had brought Trophimus, a Gentile of Ephesus, into the temple and had profaned the temple. When they were about to kill him, Claudius Lysias, who was the chief captain, came with a band of men and took Paul away to the safety of the citadel. The chief captain allowed him to speak in Hebrew to the people. {Ac 21:17-40}

6853. The Jews were enraged and cried out more vehemently against him because of his speech, so the chief captain Lysias ordered him to be examined by scourging. [K676] He was spared this punishment because he was a Roman citizen. The chief captain wanted to know of what crime the Jews had accused him. The next day, he ordered the chief priests and all their council to come together and then he set Paul before them and released him from his bonds. {Ac 22}

6854. As Paul was beginning to plead his cause before the council, Ananias ordered him to be struck on the mouth. He was the high priest (the son of Nebidius, who, although he had been removed from the high priesthood, still seemed to be the head of the council. This was similar to what had happened before him with Annas, or Ananus, who was the father-in-law of Caiaphas). Therefore, Paul severely rebuked him and called him a whitewashed wall. Then Paul proclaimed openly that he was a Pharisee and that he was being queried because of the hope of the resurrection. At this, a dissension arose between the Sadducees, who accused him, and the Pharisees, who excused him. Then Lysias, the chief captain, was afraid that he would be torn to pieces by them in the course of their fighting. He removed Paul from them with his soldiers and brought him into the citadel. The next night, the Lord appeared to Paul and comforted him because he was downcast. The Lord encouraged Paul and told him that he must bear witness in Rome, also. {Ac 23:1-11}

6855. When it was day, more than forty of the zealous Jews bound themselves by an oath, neither to eat nor drink until they had killed Paul in an ambush. Paul's sister's son told the chief captain about the plot and so, in the third hour of the night, he sent Paul with a guard of soldiers to Felix, the governor of the province. Felix took Paul to Antipatris during the night and then, the next day, to Caesarea, where Felix had ordered that he be kept in Herod's judgment hall. {Ac 23:12-35} All these things happened within one week, as is evident when the two following verses are compared together. {Ac 24:1,11}

6856. Five days later, Paul was accused before the governor of Caesarea by Ananias and the elders, through Tertullus, an orator. Paul cleared himself of their false accusations. This was twelve days after he had been attacked in the temple. When Felix, who had governed the Jews many years (for this was now the tenth year of his government), had heard the accusations of the Jews, he deferred his sentence to another time. He ordered a centurion that Paul should be kept in custody, but that he be allowed to have some freedom. All his visitors could come and minister to him. {Ac 24:1-23} [E890]

6857. Some days later, Felix arrived with his wife Drusilla, who was Jewish (the sister of King Agrippa). There was another Drusilla, besides this Drusilla, the wife of Felix. She was the daughter of Juba, the king of Mauritania, and was the niece of Antony and Cleopatra. Felix called for Paul and heard him. He trembled as he heard Paul reason about faith in Christ, righteousness, temperance and the judgment to come. He spoke with Paul quite often and hoped to be able to redeem himself with money. He kept Paul in bonds for two whole years. {Ac 24:24-27}

6858. Tigranocerta surrendered to Corbulo, who had subdued all of Armenia. {*Tacitus, Annals, l. 14. c. 13-26. 5:127-151}

6859. Tigranes, the son of Alexander (the son of that Alexander who was executed by his father, Herod the Great) and of Glaphyra (the daughter of Archelaus, the King of Cappadocia), was kept hostage at Rome for a long time. He was sent by Nero to take the kingdom of Armenia, but was not accepted there by the general

agreement of the people. While some still loved the family of the Arsacides and the Persians, most hated the arrogance of the Parthians and wanted a king to be given them from Rome. [K677] He was given a guard of a thousand legionary soldiers, three cohorts of allies and two squadrons of cavalry, to help him defend his new kingdom more easily. The frontier regions of Armenia were allocated to them, to defend the new king. These regions bordered on the kingdoms of the neighbouring kings (Pharasmanes of Iberia, Polemo II of Pontus, Aristobulus of Lesser Armenia and Antiochus IV Epiphanes of Commagene). {*Tacitus, Annals, l. 14. c. 26. 5:151} {*Josephus, Antiq., l. 18. c. 5. s. 4. (139-142) 9:95}

6860. Corbulo went into Syria to be the governor, because Ventidius Ummidius Quadratus, who had been the governor there, had died, and so Syria had been committed to Corbulo's charge. {*Tacitus, Annals, l. 14. c. 26. 5:151}

6861. In the same year Laodicea, one of the most famous cities of Asia, was destroyed by an earthquake. They rebuilt the city themselves, using their own wealth. {*Tacitus, Annals, l. 14. c. 27. 5:151}

## 4064 AM, 4774 JP, 61 AD

6862. Tarquitius Priscus was condemned for extortion when the Bithynians brought a suit against him. The Senate remembered that he had once accused his proconsul, Titus Statilius Taurus (II), and was delighted. {*Tacitus, Annals, l. 14. c. 46. 5:181} {*Tacitus, Annals, l. 12. c. 59. 4:401}

6863. A contention arose at Caesarea between the Jews and the Syrians over the equal right to privileges in the city. The Jews, who were rich, reproached the poor Syrians. Although the Syrians were poorer, they thought they were better, because many of them had served the Romans in the wars fought in those territories and were natives of Caesarea and Sebaste; so they thought they were as good as the Jews. Eventually, they began to throw stones at one another, so that many were killed or hurt on both sides. The Jews, however, won the victory. When Felix demanded that the Jews stop this mini-war, they refused, so he sent soldiers among them, who killed many of them and took many prisoners. He also allowed his soldiers to plunder many of the rich houses. The more honourable and modest Jews feared that they would be next to suffer, so they begged Felix that he would call off his soldiers and spare what remained. They repented and asked Felix's pardon, which he granted. {*Josephus, Antiq., l. 20. c. 8. s. 7. (173-178) 10:95,97} {*Josephus, Jewish War, l. 2. c. 13. s. 7. (266-270) 2:427,429}

6864. At the same time, King Agrippa conferred the high priesthood on Ishmael, the son of Phabi. A dispute also arose between the chief priests and the rest of the priests and rulers of Jerusalem. Both factions were guarded by a company of very bold and seditious men, who decided their arguments with reproachful language and by throwing stones. No one curbed them, since the city had no magistrates. The impudence of the high priests grew to such heights, that they dared to send their servants to the very grain floors themselves, to take away the tithes that were the portion of the priests. So much did the violence of the seditious men prevail over justice, that many poor priests died from lack of food. {*Josephus, Antiq., l. 20. c. 8. s. 8. (179-181) 10:97,99}

## 4065a AM, 4774 JP, 61 AD

6865. Mark, the evangelist who had first preached Christ at Alexandria, died in the eighth year of Nero and was buried at Alexandria. {Jerome, Scriptor. Ecclesiastical Catalogue} The elders of Alexandria chose one of their number whom they placed in a higher position and called a bishop. They followed a pattern similar to an army choosing a general. Deacons, likewise, would choose one from among their number, whom they knew to be most industrious, to be the archdeacon. {Jerome, Scriptor. Ecclesiastical Catalogue, Epist. 85. ad Euagrium} They chose Annianus, who was a man dear to God for his piety and admirable in all aspects. He was the first bishop of the church of Alexandria after Mark and was there for twelve years, from the eighth year of Nero to the fourth year of Domitian. {Jerome, Scriptor. Ecclesiastical Catalogue} {*Eusebius, Chronicles, l. 1. 1:265} {*Eusebius, Ecclesiastical History, l. 2. c. 24. 1:179} {*Eusebius, Ecclesiastical History, l. 3. c. 14. 1:233} [K678]

## 4065b AM, 4775 JP, 62 AD

6866. Vologeses, the king of the Parthians, tried to restore to power his brother Tiridates, who had been driven out of Armenia. He sent one army into Armenia and another into Syria. Corbulo sent part of his army to Tigranes, the king of Armenia, while he himself not only drove the Parthians from Syria, but threatened to invade them. [E891] They stopped their war and sent envoys to sue for peace, but Nero dismissed them without granting their request. Caesennius Paetus was appointed general for the defence of Armenia. {*Tacitus, Annals, l. 15. c. 1-7. 5:217-227}

6867. When Felix observed that the sedition between the Jews and Syrians of Caesarea was still going on, he sent some of the nobility from both sides as envoys to Nero, to argue their cause before him. {*Josephus, Jewish War, l. 2. c. 13. s. 7. (270) 2:429} He also sent some priests as prisoners to Rome for a very minor fault. They were good and honest men and were to plead their own cause before Nero. {*Josephus, Life, l. 1. c. 3. (13) 1:7} As well as that, he left the apostle Paul confined, as a favour to the Jews, after having already kept him prisoner for two whole years at

Caesarea. Paul was still a prisoner there when Porcius Festus arrived from Nero as Felix's successor in the province. {Ac 24:27}

6868. Three days after Festus arrived in the province, he went up from Caesarea to Jerusalem. The high priest and the rulers of the Jews accused Paul and requested that he be brought from Caesarea to Jerusalem. They planned to ambush and kill him on the way. Festus refused and ordered Paul's accusers to come to Caesarea. He spent about ten more days in Jerusalem and then travelled back down to Caesarea. The next day he sat in his tribunal and listened to the Jews accusing Paul and Paul clearing himself of their accusations. Festus wanted to please the Jews and asked Paul if he was prepared to have the matter of which he was accused judged before him at Jerusalem. Paul knew the intent of the question and at whose instigation he had asked it, and feared some kind of treachery from the Jews. He refused to go there and appealed to Caesar. After Festus had conferred with his council, he agreed to send Paul to Caesar. {Ac 25:1-12}

6869. After some days, Agrippa, the king, and Bernice, his sister, came to Caesarea to greet the new governor. They stayed there for many days. Festus did not know what to write to Caesar about Paul and so consulted with Agrippa on the matter, who said he would be willing to hear him himself. The next day, Agrippa and Bernice, along with the captains and the principal men of the city, entered the place of the hearing with much pomp. Festus summoned Paul to be brought out to them, bound in chains. {Ac 25:13-27} Paul made an eloquent speech and demonstrated that he was innocent. The governor, who was ignorant of these things, thought he was mad. The king, however, who was well-versed in the scriptures, stated that Paul had almost persuaded him to become a Christian. The whole council decided that this man had done nothing worthy of death or bonds and furthermore, that he could have been set at liberty, had he not appealed to Caesar. {Ac 26}

6870. The rulers of the Jews living at Caesarea went to Rome to accuse Felix. He would have suffered punishment for the wrongs he had done to the Jews, had Nero not pardoned him upon the entreaties of his brother Pallas, who at that time was in great favour with Nero. {*Josephus, Antiq., l. 20. c. 8. s. 9. (182) 10:99} Later that year, Pallas was poisoned by Nero for keeping a large sum of money from Nero by living so long, instead of dying, so that Nero could get the estate. {*Tacitus, Annals, l. 14. c. 65. 5:213} [K679]

6871. Two principal men of the Syrians from Caesarea bribed Beryllus with a large sum of money. He had been

Nero's schoolteacher, but was at this time his secretary for the Greek language. He was to get the emperor to revoke the decree so the Jews could be deprived of all authority in the city, for they currently shared this authority with the Syrians. This he easily accomplished. When the Jews of Caesarea learned what had happened, they continued their seditions right up to the beginning of the wars of the Jews, which had their seeds in this sedition. {*Josephus, Antiq., l. 20. c. 8. s. 9. (183) 10:99,101}

6872. When Festus came into Judea, he found it most severely afflicted everywhere with thieves who plundered the villages. The most cruel of the thieves were called cut-throats and they were very numerous. They carried a short, crooked sword like the Persian scimitar. Thrusting themselves into the crowd of people who came to Jerusalem to celebrate the feast days as God had commanded, they could easily kill as many as they pleased. They also attacked the villages of their enemies, which they burned, after having plundered them. {*Josephus, Antiq., l. 20. c. 8. s. 10. (185-187) 10:103} Festus pursued and captured many of these thieves and executed a large number of them. {*Josephus, Jewish War, l. 2. c. 14. s. 1. (271) 2:429}

6873. When it was decreed that Paul would be sent to Caesar, he was turned over to Julius, a centurion of Augustus' band, along with some other prisoners. Julius put him onto a ship from Adramyttium, that was to sail to Asia. Aristarchus of Macedonia, besides Timothy and Luke, accompanied Paul. The next day, they landed at Sidon, where Julius treated Paul courteously, allowing him to go visit his friends and to refresh himself. They sailed past Cyprus because the winds were unfavourable. When they had sailed across the sea off Cilicia and Pamphylia, they came to Myra, a city of Lycia. [E892] When the centurion had found an Alexandrian ship, whose figurehead was Castor and Pollux, which was bound for Italy, he put the captives on board. After having sailed slowly for many days, they barely managed with difficulty to reach the sea off Cnidos and then they sailed south of Crete, off Salmone. After passing by it with difficulty, they came to a place called Fair Havens, on the isle of Crete. {Ac 27:1-8}

## 4066a AM, 4775 JP, 62 AD

6874. After the Jewish feast of the day of Atonement, in the seventh month, was past, sailing was dangerous. Paul foresaw the danger facing them and advised them to winter there. When that seemed to be an unsuitable port in which to winter, they planned to winter in another port of Crete, called Phenice. As they sailed out, they had a favourable south wind at first. A little later, a tempestuous wind arose, called Euroclydon, by which they were driven to the little island of Clauda. Because they were caught and tossed about by the violent storm, they lightened the ship. On the third day, they cast out the tackling of the ship with their own hands. They saw neither sun nor stars for many days. When all hope of safety was gone, an angel told Paul in the night that he had to be brought before Caesar and that God had given him all who were sailing with him in the ship. On the fourteenth day, as they were being driven up and down in the Adriatic Sea, the sailors thought that they were near some land, which they later learned was the island of Melita. [K680] As they tried to head there, the ship was broken up by the violence of the storm, but all on board made it safely to land. Some swam, while others floated in on some planks and boards from the ship. {Ac 27:9-44}

6874a. After they had survived the shipwreck, they were courteously taken in by the inhabitants of Melita. They made a fire to dry their clothes and to get warm. When Paul was bitten by a viper as he was putting some wood on the fire, he shook it off with no ill effects. The barbarians were amazed and said Paul must be a god. They stayed with Publius, a chief man of the island, for three days. It so happened that Publius' father was sick with a fever and a bloody flux. Paul healed him, as well as many others on the island. {Ac 28:1-9}

6875. Caesennius Paetus had not sufficiently fortified his winter camps nor made provision for grain, so he quickly marched over the Taurus Mountains and took a few citadels with some plunder. He made long marches and overran places which he could not hold. When the provisions he had taken had spoiled, he returned back to the place he had come from and wrote letters to Caesar in exalted words, as though the war had been finished. This, however, was far from the truth. {*Tacitus, Annals, l. 15. c. 8. 5:227,229}

6876. In the meantime, Corbulo took special care to fortify the bank of the Euphrates River with more garrisons and to frighten Vologeses against entering Syria. Therefore, Vologeses turned against Paetus and attacked him so severely, that he forced him into a dishonourable peace, which was witnessed by Monobazus, King of Adiabene. The fortresses that Corbulo had built on the other side of the Euphrates River were demolished. The Armenians were left to decide their own future. At Rome, trophies and triumphal arches were set up in the middle of the Capitoline Hill, as decreed by the Senate, in honour of the victory over the Parthians. However, the war resumed again and all this was done only for show and not in consideration of what had actually happened. {*Tacitus, Annals, l. 15. c. 9-18. 5:229-243}

## 4066b AM, 4776 JP, 63 AD

6877. Paul and his companions were highly honoured by the inhabitants of Melita and had all their needs supplied. After staying there three months, they travelled in a ship from Alexandria which had wintered at the island, and came to Syracuse. There they stayed for three days and then sailed on to Rhegium. After one day, a south wind blew and on the second day they came to Puteoli, where they found brethren who wanted them to stay with them for seven days. So they went toward Rome, in the ninth year of Nero's reign. {*Ac 28:10-14*}

6878. The brethren left Rome to meet Paul while he was as far away as Appii Forum and Three Taverns. When they came to Rome, the centurion delivered the prisoners to the captain of the guard. Paul was allowed to live by himself with a soldier who guarded him. After three days, he called together the leaders of the Jews who were at Rome and told them the reason why he had been sent to Rome as a prisoner and that he had been compelled to appeal to Caesar. They denied that they had received any letters about him from Judea and said that they had only heard that this heresy was being spoken against everywhere. When they had set a day, they came to him at his lodging. Paul expounded Christ from the law and the prophets from morning until evening. Some assented to the things that were said and others did not believe. Paul pronounced their judgment from Isaiah and they left him. After that, Paul turned to the Gentiles. *[K681]* He remained in his own hired house for two whole years and received all who came to him. He preached the kingdom of God and taught about the Lord Jesus Christ and no man hindered him. {*Ac 28:14-31*} *[E893]*

6879. Onesiphorus very diligently sought Paul out at Rome and when he found him, he encouraged him. {*2Ti 1:16,17*}

6880. At the beginning of spring, the envoys of the Parthians brought the messages and letters of King Vologeses to Rome. These requested that Armenia, which the Parthians had already taken, be given to them and that a peace be confirmed. Both these things were denied and the government of Syria was committed to Gaius Cestius as the governor, while Corbulo managed the war. The fifteenth legion was brought from Pannonia by Marius Celsus, while the tetrarchs, kings, prefects and governors, and those ruling in the neighbouring provinces, were ordered to obey Corbulo as the supreme commander. He received the same authority that Pompey had been given in fighting the pirate war. Paetus was sent back to Rome and feared the worst. Nero thought it enough to scoff at him, saying that he would pardon him at once, in case he should become sick with fear over the uncertainty surrounding Nero's actions. {*Tacitus, Annals, l. 15. c. 24,25. 5:253,255*}

6881. Having mustered his army, Corbulo went into Armenia, where the envoys of Vologeses met him and

requested peace. Tiridates was forced to come into the Roman camp. He took off his crown and laid it at Caesar's image, also agreeing to go to Rome to receive it back from Nero himself. His only condition was that he might first go visit his family and friends. In the meantime, he left his daughter as hostage and sent supplicatory letters to Nero. As he went away, he found Pacorus with the Medes and Vologeses at Ecbatana. {*Tacitus, Annals, l. 15. c. 26-31. 5:255-263*}

6882. In Judea, Festus sent foot soldiers and cavalry against a certain impostor, a magician, who drew men after him into the wilderness, deceiving them with promises that they would be freed from all their misfortunes. The soldiers killed both the seducer and his followers. {*Mt 24:24-26*} {*Josephus, Antiq., l. 20. c. 8. s. 10. (188) 10:103*}

6883. At the same time, King Agrippa built a stately house near the porch in the palace of Jerusalem. In previous times, this site had belonged to the Asmoneans and was located on a high place, from where one could get a good view of all Jerusalem. The chief men of Jerusalem were not pleased that the sacrifices and everything that was done in the temple could easily be seen from a private house. They therefore built a high wall, which blocked the king's view of the city, as well as of the western porch in the outer court of the temple, where the Roman soldiers stood guard on the feast days for the safekeeping of the temple. Both the king and Festus, the governor of the province, were offended by this and Festus ordered that it be pulled down. However (with his permission), ten chief men were sent as envoys to Nero about this matter, together with Ishmael, the high priest, and Helcias, the keeper of the holy treasure. After Nero had heard their embassy, he forgave the Jews and allowed the wall to remain. This was as a favour to his wife Poppaea, who favoured the Jewish religion and became their intercessor before Nero. She allowed the ten men to return, but kept Ishmael and Helcias with her as hostages. *[K682]* When Agrippa learned this, he took away the high priesthood from Ishmael and gave it to Joseph, surnamed Kabi, the son of Simon, who had formerly been a high priest. {*Josephus, Antiq., l. 20. c. 8. s. 11. (189-196) 10:103-107*}

6884. Josephus, the son of Matthias, heard that some priests, who had been his close friends, had been sent to Rome as prisoners by Felix. In this unfortunate circumstance, they still obeyed their religion and lived only on figs and nuts. He went to Rome at age twenty-six, to see if he could free them. He had a perilous sea voyage, as their ship sank in the middle of the Adriatic Sea. Of the six hundred who swam all night, about eighty of those swimming were more fortunate than the rest, because they were saved and picked up by a ship from Cyrene.

Among these was Josephus. After he was set ashore, he made his way to Dicaearchia (or Puteoli, as the Italians called it) where he became acquainted with Aliturus, a Jewish actor who was much liked by Nero. Through him, he was introduced to Poppaea, the empress, and by her intervention had those priests freed at once. {*Josephus, Life, l. 1. c. 3. (13-16) 1:7,9}

6885. After Festus died in the province, Nero sent Albinus to be his successor in Judea. King Agrippa took away the high priesthood from Joseph and gave it to Ananas, the son of Ananas, or that Ananus who had formerly had the high priesthood, a long time earlier. Ananus had five sons who had also been high priests, which had never happened to any of the high priests before. {*Josephus, Antiq., l. 20. c. 9. s. 1. (197,198) 10:107}

6886. Ananus, the new high priest, was of the sect of the Sadducees. He was a bold and headstrong man and thought it was a good time to convene the Sanhedrin of judges, since Festus was dead and the new governor, Albinus, had not yet arrived. They brought James, the brother of Jesus, before them, who was accused of transgressing the law. James was condemned and stoned. {*Josephus, Antiq., l. 20. c. 9. s. 1. (199,200) 10:107,109} [E894] At the time of the passover, James was thrown down from a pinnacle of the temple and stoned. One of them, who was a fuller, killed James by hitting him on the head with the club he used to press clothes. Eusebius related this from the fifth book of the history of Hegesippus. {*Eusebius, Ecclesiastical History, l. 2. c. 23. 1:169-175}

6887. The murder of James greatly displeased all the good men and those who kept the law. So they secretly sent a messenger to King Agrippa and requested from him that he would order Ananus to stop acts of this kind. Some also went to meet Albinus as he was coming from the city of Alexandria and informed him that Ananus had no power to call a council without his permission. He was persuaded by their words and wrote a sharp letter to Ananus, in which he threatened to punish him. For the same reason, Agrippa later took the high priesthood from him when he had only held it for three months and gave it to Jesus, the son of Damnaeus. {*Josephus, Antiq., l. 20. c. 9. s. 1. (201-203) 10:109} After the death of James, Simon, the son of Clophas, was appointed bishop of the church of Jerusalem. {*Eusebius, Ecclesiastical History, l. 3. c. 32. 1:273}

6888. As soon as Albinus came to Jerusalem, he diligently tried to restore order by executing all the thieves. The high priest Ananias, the son of Nebedaeus, increased more and more every day in the love and esteem of the people and was honoured by all men for his generosity. Albinus daily honoured the high priest for the gifts he sent to him. Ananias had some very wicked servants,

who attracted a company of headstrong men that went from farm to farm and took away the priests' tithes, beating those who refused to give it to them. [K683] Some of the priests also did the same, for no one was able to restrain them. Many of the priests, who lived on those tithes, perished from hunger. {*Josephus, Antiq., l. 20. c. 9. s. 2. (204-207) 10:109,111}

6889. At the feast of Pentecost, the thieves entered Jerusalem at night and captured the scribe Eleazar, who was the son of Ananias, the high priest. They held him hostage, then sent to Ananias to have Albinus free ten of the thieves in exchange for the freeing of the scribe. Ananias was forced to obtain this request from Albinus. This was the beginning of greater calamities, for the thieves always found some trick to intercept some of Ananias' family, whom they would then refuse to free until some of their own men had been freed. Consequently, they increased in boldness and number and plundered the whole country. {*Josephus, Antiq., l. 20. c. 9. s. 3. (208-210) 10:111,113}

6890. At this time, King Agrippa enlarged the walls of Caesarea Philippi and changed its name to Neronias, in honour of Nero. At Berytus, he built a theatre at great expense and annually held games which cost him large amounts of money. He also gave grain and oil to the people of Berytus. He decorated that city in various places with statues and with original images made many years earlier, transferring almost all that was ornamental in his kingdom to that city. Hence his own subjects began to hate him, because he had stripped them of their ornaments to adorn a foreign city. {*Josephus, Antiq., l. 20. c. 9. s. 4. (211,212) 10:113}

## 4067a AM, 4776 JP, 63 AD

6891. Four years before the Jewish war (that was carried out by Vespasian), at a time when the city of Jerusalem enjoyed both peace and plenty, Jesus, the son of Ananias, a countryman and one of the common people, arrived at the feast of tabernacles and suddenly began to cry out:

> "A voice from the east, a voice from the west, a voice from the four winds, a voice against Jerusalem and the temple, a voice against the bridegroom and the bride, a voice against all this people."

6892. He cried like this night and day, as he went through all the streets of the city. Some of the nobility, ignoring any sign of the impending trouble, took the fellow and scourged him with many stripes. However, he spoke nothing privately to himself or to them that scourged him, but continued on with the same cry. The magistrates thought he had a message from God and brought him to the Roman governor. He was beaten until his bones showed, yet he never made an entreaty nor shed a tear, but at every stroke replied, with as much composure as a weeping voice would permit:

"Woe, woe, to Jerusalem."

*6893.* Albinus then asked who he was, where he was born and why he persisted in crying after this manner? He gave no reply and continued ceaselessly to bewail the city, until Albinus thought he was mad and allowed him to leave. He cried like this most earnestly on the feast days, and continued in this for seven years (or rather six, as Photius has it) and five months, and yet he was never hoarse nor weary. In the end, he was killed by a stone shot from an engine at the time of the siege. {*Josephus, Jewish War, l. 6. c. 5. s. 3. (300-309) 4:265-269} {Photius, Bibliotheca, c. 47} [K684]

## 4067b AM, 4777 JP, 64 AD

*6894.* At the command of King Agrippa, Jesus, the son of Gamaliel, succeeded Jesus, the son of Damnaeus, in the high priesthood, with the latter very unwillingly relinquishing it. Consequently, a discord arose between them. They both had a following of resolute young fellows who started arguing and then throwing stones. Since Ananias was the wealthiest, he used his money to get most of them on his side. [E895] Costobar and Saul, who were of royal blood and received special favours because they were closely related to King Agrippa, each got together a band of rascals. Despite their royal connections, these two were violent and as eager as any to exploit anyone weaker than themselves. {*Josephus, Antiq., l. 20. c. 9. s. 4. (212-214) 10:113,115}

*6895.* From this time on, the civil state of the Jews degenerated on a daily basis. {*Josephus, Antiq., l. 20. c. 9. s. 4. (214) 10:115} The seeds of the future destruction were sown at this time through the number of leaders who led these bands. {*Josephus, Jewish War, l. 2. c. 14. s. 1. (275,276) 2:431}

*6896.* Albinus, the governor, robbed private citizens of their goods in the name of justice and greatly burdened the whole country with heavy taxes. For a price, he freed not only the thieves whom the soldiers of the city had captured, but also those whom the former governors had left in prison. Those who could not afford to bribe him, remained in prison as the most heinous offenders. {*Josephus, Jewish War, l. 2. c. 14. s. 1. (272-276) 2:429,431}

*6897.* At the same time, also, the insolence of those wanting a revolution in Jerusalem increased. The rich among them bribed Albinus to overlook their seditions, while those who delighted in disturbances, allied themselves with Albinus' side. Each of them had a troop of rascals and Albinus himself was over them all, as a tyrant and a prince of thieves. He used the help of his guard to rob the quieter sort. So it was that those whose houses were ransacked held their peace and those who escaped were glad to flatter those who they knew deserved death, in case they themselves should suffer the same things. {*Josephus, Jewish War, l. 2. c. 14. s. 1. (274-276) 2:431}

*6898.* When Rome was on fire, Nero watched it burn from Mecena's Tower and was very greatly delighted with the beauty of the flames. He sang of the destruction of Troy in his lyre-player's clothes, comparing the present evil to those old ruins. {*Tacitus, Annals, l. 15. c. 38-40. 5:271-277} {*Suetonius, Nero, l. 6. c. 38. 2:149,151} {*Dio, l. 62. (16-18) 8:111-115} Some noted that this fire began on the 14th of the Calends of August (July 19), on the same day on which the Senonian Gauls had set the city on fire, after they had taken it. Others, in their curiosity, went so far as to calculate the very days and months that were between the two fires. They said there were four hundred and eighteen years, four hundred and eighteen months and four hundred and eighteen days between the two fires. {*Tacitus, Annals, l. 15. c. 41. 5:277,279}

*6899.* To quell the rumour that he had started the fire, Nero falsely accused the Christians and punished them most grievously, with highly refined torments. Those who confessed to being Christians were the first to be apprehended; then, based on their information, a large multitude were convicted. They were hated, not so much for allegedly having set the city on fire, as for the general hatred that everyone bore against them. These people suffered and died most cruelly. Some were covered with beasts' skins, to be torn by dogs; some were crucified and some burned—when it was night, their bodies were turned into torches to give light by night. Nero made his garden fit for the spectacle and held shows in the circus. [K685] He mingled among the common people in the clothes of a charioteer, or stood in a ring. The Christians were pitied, since they were not suffering for any common good, but to satisfy one man's cruelty. {*Tacitus, Annals, l. 15. c. 44. 5:283,285} The words of an old scholiast were mentioned, as commenting on Juvenal's writings: {Juvenal, Satire, 1.}

> Thou shalt be made a torch by night to shine
> And burn impaled, name thou but Tigilline.

> "If you touch Tigillinus, you shall be burned alive, as it was in the shows of Nero, who commanded them to be made into torches, that they might give light to the spectators. They were fastened through their throat, so that they could not bend themselves. Nero clothed malefactors with pitch, paper and wax and set them on fire."

*6900.* This was the first persecution raised against the Christians by the Roman emperors. Suetonius, a heathen writer, mentioned: {*Suetonius, Nero, l. 6. c. 16. 2:107}

"The Christians were punished, who were men of a new and pernicious superstition."

6901. Tertullian, a Christian, stated: {*Tertullian, Apology, l. 1. c. 5. 3:22}

"Search your records, then you shall find that Nero was the first that used Caesar's sword against this sect, which at that time greatly increased at Rome. However, we glory in the author of our condemnation for he who understands, knows that Nero could only condemn that which is very good."

## 4068a AM, 4777 JP, 64 AD

6902. Nero appointed Cestius Gallus as governor of Syria and Gessius Florus of Judea. Florus had been born in the city of Clazomene and had married Cleopatra, a wicked woman and a friend of the Empress Poppaea, who got this appointment for him. {*Josephus, Antiq., l. 20. c. 11. s. 1. (252,253) 10:135} {*Josephus, Jewish War, l. 2. c. 14. s. 3. (280) 2:433} [E896]

6903. When Albinus heard that Florus was coming to succeed him, he wanted to gratify the citizens of Jerusalem, so he summoned all the prisoners. Those who were notoriously guilty of any capital crime were executed, while those who were in prison for smaller offences, he remanded to prison again and freed them on payment of a bribe. By this means, the prisons were emptied, but Judea was filled with thieves. {*Josephus, Antiq., l. 20. c. 9. s. 5. (215) 10:115}

6904. In the meantime, the Levites, whose office it was to sing hymns in the temple, went to King Agrippa and by their entreaty, persuaded him to call a council and permit them the use of the linen robe, which at the time was only granted to the priests. They said that this new custom would serve as a perpetual memorial to his reign. So the king, on the advice of his council, permitted those who sang the hymns to set aside their former clothes and wear a linen garment, as they desired. Also at their entreaty, he allowed another part of the same tribe, one that was allocated to the services of the temple, to learn to sing the sacred hymns. {*Josephus, Antiq., l. 20. c. 9. s. 6. (216-218) 10:115}

6905. The Philippians sent Epaphroditus to Rome with money, to visit Paul in prison and to minister to him in his needs. He became Paul's helper and fellow soldier for the work of Christ. He did not regard his life and risked it, for he fell seriously ill. {Php 2:25-30 4:10,14,18}

6906. Although Paul was old and in prison, he won Onesimus to Christ. He was a servant who had fled from Colosse, from his master, Philemon. {Phm 1:9,10,15 Col 4:9,18} [K686]

6907. Timothy, who was being kept as a prisoner with Paul, was set at liberty. {Heb 13:23}

6908. Paul wrote the letter to the Philippians through Epaphroditus, after the latter had recovered his health. He also hoped to be able to send Timothy to them in a little while and as soon as he would find out how they were, to be able to come to them himself soon. {Php 2:19-29} At that time, Paul's bonds for Christ were famous throughout the court, and even some of Caesar's palace staff were converted to the faith. {Php 1:12,13 4:22} Since he had been sent to prison by Caesar, he was more well known in Caesar's family and so turned the house of persecution into the church of Christ. {Jerome, Commentary on Philemon}

6909. Paul wrote a letter to Philemon and sent it to Colosse by his servant Onesimus. Paul reconciled and commended Onesimus to his master and indicated that he himself hoped to be freed from prison and wanted Philemon to prepare a guest room for Paul. Paul used Onesimus and Tychicus to deliver a letter to the Colossians, whom he had never seen, but who had been instructed in the doctrine of Christ by Epaphras. {Col 1:7,8 2:1 4:7-9,18} At that time, besides Timothy (whose name is prefixed to both of these letters), there were with Paul at Rome the following Jews, his companions in bonds, Aristarchus of Thessalonica and Mark, Barnabas' sister's son. {Ac 20:4} Paul instructed the Colossians to receive Mark, should he come to them. Also with Paul was Jesus, who was called Justus, as well as Luke, the beloved physician, and Demas and Epaphras. Paul told of Epaphras' great affection for the Colossians, and for those at Laodicea and Hierapolis (it was Epaphras who, together with Archippus, had supplied Paul's ministry, but now he was absent). {Col 4:10-14,17 Phm 1:23,24}

6910. Paul also sent that same Tychicus, who had been his companion in his travels from Asia, {Ac 20:4} back to them in Asia, so that the brethren might know his affairs. He carried with him Paul's letter to the Ephesians. {Eph 6:21,22} Tertullian and Epiphanius confirmed what was said by Marcion, the heretic, that this letter went by the name of the letter to the Laodiceans. {*Tertullian, Against Marcion, l. 5. c. 17. 3:465} {Epiphanius, Heresy, l. 1. c. 42.} Grotius thought it credible enough to have been done by Paul from the merit of the church of Laodicea. Affirming that there was no reason why he should tell a lie in this matter and he deduced from this that the letter to the Ephesians and the Laodiceans was written with the same words. It can be seen in some old books (as it appears from Basil {Basil, Against Eunomius, l. 2.} and from Jerome's commentary on this passage, relating to the apostle) that it was generally written as follows (as was the custom with the copies of letters that were to be sent to various places): *To the Saints who are at xxxxxxxx, and to the faithful in Christ Jesus.* This indicated that it had probably first been sent to Ephesus, as the metropolis of Asia, and from there sent on to the rest of the churches of that province (the name of each church would be inserted for the xxxxxxxx). Some of these churches had never seen Paul, which his words clearly bear out:

> "After I heard of your faith in Christ Jesus and love to all the saints," {*Eph 1:15*}

6911. Again Paul stated:

> "If you have heard of the dispensation of the grace of God which is given to me for you...." {*Eph 3:2-4*} [E897] [K687]

6912. Perhaps Marcion's idea might better relate to the Laodiceans, who had not seen the apostle {*Col 2:1*} than to the Ephesians, with whom he had spent so much time. {*Ac 19:8-10 20:31*}

6913. At about the same time, Paul wrote the letter to the Hebrews. Timothy had been set at liberty, but had left him for somewhere else for a time. He promised to visit them with Timothy, if the latter were to come shortly. In the meantime, he sent them greetings from the brethren in Italy. {*Heb 13:23,24*}

## 4068b AM, 4778 JP, 65 AD

6914. The building of the temple was now finished and the people realised that about eighteen thousand workmen, who had previously worked on the temple, would be idle. They did not want the holy treasure to fall prey to the Romans, as well as wanting to help the workmen. If they worked only one hour, they were promptly paid. So they tried to persuade King Agrippa to repair the eastern porch. This porch hung over a deep and narrow valley and was supported by a wall that was six hundred feet long, built from stones that were thirty feet square and nine feet high. Claudius Caesar had committed the charge of the temple to King Agrippa. Agrippa believed that any large building could easily be pulled down, but was hard to set up, and especially this porch. It would cost much time and money to do, hence he denied their request, but he allowed them to pave their city with white stone, if they so desired. {*Josephus, Antiq., l. 20. c. 9. s. 7. (219-223) 10:117,119*}

6915. After two years of having been detained, Paul was released. He had taught the gospel at Rome during this period. {*Ac 28:30*} He seems to have gone from there to Asia and to have lived with Philemon at Colosse. {*Phm 1:22*}

6916. During the feast of unleavened bread, on the 8th of Xanthikos (Niese: April 25, Capellus: April 8), around the ninth hour of the night (3 a.m.), a light shone for half an hour between the altar and the temple, so that it was as bright as noon. On the same feast day, a cow that was being led to sacrifice brought forth a lamb in the middle of the temple. The east gate of the temple was made of brass and was extremely heavy. In the evening it could barely be closed by twenty men and was locked with bars of iron and had bolts that were let down deep into a threshold that was made entirely from one stone. About the sixth hour of the night (midnight), the gate opened of its own accord. When the watchmen of the temple reported this to the captain as they went on their rounds, he went there and could barely shut it. {*Josephus, Jewish War, l. 6. c. 5. s. 3. (290-294) 4:263*} Tacitus also listed similar signs of the upcoming war. {*Tacitus, Histories, l. 5. c. 13. 3:197,199*} {*Lu 21:25,26*}

6917. Josephus relates the following and said many would be deemed as a fable but he had it on the good authority of many eyewitnesses. On the 21st day of Artemisios (Niese: June 8, Capellus: May 21), before sunset, all over the country, iron chariots were seen in the air and armies in battle array, passing along in the clouds and surrounding the cities. At the feast of Pentecost, the priests went into the inner temple by night, according to their custom, to perform the divine service. At first they found that the place was moving and making a noise, then later they heard a sudden voice, which said: {*Josephus, Jewish War, l. 6. c. 5. s. 3. (296-300) 4:265*} {*Lu 21:20*}

> "Let us depart hence."

6918. Paul preached the gospel on the isle of Crete, where he left Titus behind, so that Titus might set in order the things that were lacking and ordain elders in every city there. {*Tit 1:5*} [K688]

6919. King Agrippa took the priesthood from Jesus, the son of Gamaliel, and gave it to Matthias, the son of Theophilus. The Jewish war started when he was the high priest. {*Josephus, Antiq., l. 20. c. 9. s. 7. (223) 10:119*}

6920. After Josephus had received gifts of money from the Empress Poppaea, he returned to his own country. Observing many signs of sedition and rebellion among the people there, he endeavoured in vain to dissuade them from their unhappy enterprise. {*Josephus, Life, l. 1. c. 3,4. (16-19) 1:9*}

6921. Gessius Florus abused his authority so outrageously, that the Jews wanted Albinus again and considered Albinus their benefactor. Although privately Albinus was as wicked and injurious as he could possibly be, Florus openly perpetrated his villainies and bragged publicly of the wrongs he was doing to the country. He left nothing in the way of rapines and punishments undone, to the height of iniquity. He was inflexible to any mercy, insatiable in his quest for gain, equally greedy of small and great things, so much so, that he became a partner with the thieves. Many became thieves and paid part of the booty to him, to escape prosecution. There was no moderation in or end of their wrongs, so that the miserable Jews, unable to endure the savage insolence of the thieves, were constrained to abandon both their houses and religion and flee to foreign countries. They thought this was better, even if it meant living among the Gentiles. {*Josephus, Antiq., l. 20. c. 11. s. 1. (252-257) 10:135,137} {*Josephus, Jewish War, l. 2. c. 14. s. 2. (277-279) 2:431,433}

6922. Nero's wife Poppaea, who was great with child and sick, upbraided Nero as he returned late from driving his chariot. In his anger, he killed her with a kick of his foot. This was after the end of his Quinquennial Games, which had been held for the second time and Nero had won first prize. [E898] These games were instituted in 60 AD. {*Suetonius, Nero, l. 6. c. 35. s. 3. 2:143} {*Tacitus, Annals, l. 16. c. 2-6. 5:339-345}

6923. Paul stayed at Ephesus for some time and then left Timothy there while he went to Macedonia, so that Timothy would administer that church in his absence. {1Ti 1:3 3:14,15} In Macedonia, he stayed with the Philippians, as he had previously promised them. {Php 1:25,26 2:24}

## 4069a AM, 4778 JP, 65 AD

6924. Paul wrote his first letter to Timothy, in which he declared that he had delivered Hymenaeus and Alexander over to Satan, because they had made shipwreck of their faith. By being chastised, they would learn not to blaspheme. {1Ti 1:20} Hymenaeus denied the resurrection to come, as did Philetus, saying that it was already past. {2Ti 2:17,18} Alexander seemed to be that coppersmith who had greatly hindered Paul and had so vehemently withstood his preaching. {Ac 20:33,34 2Ti 4:14,15}

6925. Paul also wrote another letter, this one to Titus in Crete, asking that when Paul sent Artemas or Tychicus to him, Titus would come to Paul at Nicopolis (a place famous for the victory at Actium), where Paul planned to spend the winter. Paul also said that he should speedily send Zenas, the lawyer, and Apollos on their journey, so that they would lack nothing. {Tit 3:12,13}

## 4069b AM, 4779 JP, 66 AD

6926. After winter was over, Paul returned to Timothy at Ephesus and from there went to Troas, where he left his cloak behind. Erastus remained at Corinth, where he was the city treasurer. {Ro 16:23} Paul left Trophimus sick at Miletus. {1Ti 3:14 2Ti 4:13,20}

6927. Cestius Gallus came from Antioch to Jerusalem, to make a report for Nero on the strength and state of the city. [K689] Since he despised that country, he asked the high priests if it were possible for them to count the people. It was the day of the passover, when they killed sacrifices from the ninth hour to the eleventh. There were two hundred and fifty-five thousand and six hundred sacrifices made. Each lamb would be eaten by ten or twenty individuals. An estimated two million, seven hundred thousand people were present for the feast. {*Josephus, Jewish War, l. 6. c. 9. s. 3. (423-427) 4:301}

6928. When Cestius Gallus visited Jerusalem, more than three million Jews came to him and begged him to take pity on the calamities of their country. They asked him to remove Florus, who was plaguing their country. Although Florus was with Gallus and in full view of the people, he was unmoved and laughed at their cries against him. At that time, Gallus appeased the rage of the people and promised to make Florus gentler toward them. He returned to Antioch again and Florus brought him as far as Caesarea, deceiving him with lies while he planned to make war on the country of the Jews. This was the best way he could think of to hide his villainies, for, as long as the peace continued, he would always have the Jews accusing him to Caesar. If he could make them revolt, then his impieties would seem small, compared to the Jewish revolt. Every day he increased their calamities more strenuously to make that country revolt from the Roman Empire. {*Josephus, Jewish War, l. 2. c. 14. s. 3. (280-283) 2:433}

6929. Paul came to Rome for the second time and was heard and acquitted by Nero. He mentioned this: {2Ti 4:16,17}

"In my first answer, no man stood with me, but all forsook me: I pray God it be not laid to their charge. Notwithstanding, the Lord stood with me, and strengthened me; that by me the preaching might be fully known, and that all the Gentiles might hear: and I was delivered out of the mouth of the lion."

6930. So, as he had earlier done for two years, so now again for a whole year, he preached the gospel to the people of all countries, who came from every place and flocked to Rome, to make it their home country.

6931. Demas, loving this present world more, left Paul and went to Thessalonica, Crescens went into Galatia, and Titus to Dalmatia. Only Luke remained with Paul at Rome. {2Ti 4:10,11}

6932. There was an old saying that was commonly talked about right across all the east. There was a prophecy which said that from Judea should come those who would be masters of the world. It was later obvious, by what happened, that this had been foretold of the Roman emperor; but the Jews applied this prophesy to themselves and rebelled. {*Suetonius, Vespasian, l. 8. c. 4. s. 5. 2:273} The Jews patiently endured, until Gessius Florus was made governor. {*Tacitus, Histories, l. 5. c. 10. 3:193} Under him the war began, in the month of Artemisios, or our May, in the twelfth year of Nero's empire, the seventeenth year of the reign of Agrippa and the second year of the government of Gessius Florus. {*Josephus, Jewish War, l. 2. c. 14. s. 4. (284,285) 2:433,435} {*Josephus, Antiq., l. 20. c. 11. s. 1. (257,258) 10:137} This war was fully described by Josephus in the later part of the second book and the five following books of his *Jewish War*. We have taken a summary of this from the abridgement of the Jewish history of that most eminent man, Ludovicus Capellus. (The day and the month given by Josephus appear to conflict with the Loeb footnotes as computed by the modern writer, Niese, and with those given by Capellus, whom Ussher used. The Macedonian months given by Josephus appear to be those in common use in Syria. We listed Josephus' date, as well as the date by Niese and Capellus. However, Niese's dates for then fall of Jerusalem and the burning of the temple do not agree with other ancient writers. Worse he states that the final siege of Jerusalem began on May 1 which was a new moon. This siege happened at the beginning of the Passover, which occurred near the full moon, but never on a new moon. Further, if the Macedonian months referred to actual lunar months, then Niese's dates do not agree with the known lunar cycle. Capellus assumed that Josephus used the Macedonian month names to refer to the twelve Roman Julian months, as was the practice at Antioch. {See note on 3956a AM. <<4870>>} When this is done his dates for the fall of Jerusalem and the destruction of the temple agree with ancient writers. The sign in the heavens given by Josephus occurred during the feast of unleavened bread. {See note on 4068b AM. <<6916>>} This feast would occur after the full moon of April 3 for that month. If Niese's date of April 25 is correct, this feast would occur before the full moon which is impossible. We will leave it to the reader to decide who is correct. Editor.)

6933. Nero crossed into Greece and stayed there until winter. {*Dio, l. 62. (8) 8:149}

6934. In a long speech, King Agrippa vainly tried to dissuade the Jews from war. {*Josephus, Jewish War, l. 2. c. 16. s. 3,4. (344-405) 2:457-481} [E899] A little while after he left Jerusalem, some of the seditious men took the strong citadel of Masada by surprise and occupied it, killing all the Romans they found there. [K690] At Jerusalem, Eleazar, the son of Ananias the high priest, and commander of the soldiers of the temple, was a bold and factious young man. He persuaded the priests not to offer any sacrifices except for the Jews; none were to be offered for Caesar or the Romans. The chief priest and the nobles, who were peaceful men, judged this rash act to be intolerable, since they recognised it as an invitation to open rebellion. However, they could not make these seditious men change their minds, so they sent messengers to Caesarea, to Florus and to King Agrippa, asking them to send troops immediately to quash the rebellion in its very beginnings. Because Florus wanted a revolt, he did nothing. Agrippa sent two thousand cavalry who, together with the rulers and priests and the rest of the peace-loving multitude, captured and held the upper city from the seditious men, who held the temple and the lower city. There were continual skirmishes between them for the next seven days. On the feast day, as people carried wood into the temple, many murderers were admitted into the temple. These, with the rest of their party, attacked the king's soldiers and forced them from the upper part of the city. They drove them into Herod's palace and burned the place where the records were kept, as well as the palace of the Asmoneans (which was Agrippa's court at the time), and the house of Ananias, the high priest. The next day, which was the 15th of August, they captured the citadel of Antonia after a two-day siege, killed all the Roman soldiers there and burned the citadel. A little later, they attacked the king's palace. (Manahemus, the son of Judas Galilaeus, was their captain, and after he had taken the citadel of Masada and plundered Herod's armoury, he brought his armed murderers into Jerusalem.) After they had taken the palace and burned it, Manahemus seized the leadership of the revolt. Immediately after this, as he was praying in the temple, he was killed by Eleazar, the captain of the temple. Manahemus' men were driven out, and returned to Masada under the leadership of Eleazar, the son of Jairus, who was related to Manahemus. The seditious men, also of Jerusalem, had put the Romans to death on the Sabbath day itself. After the palace was won by assault, the Romans retired into the citadels of Hippicus, Phasael and Mariamme. When they were besieged, they surrendered and turned over their arms. They were promised safety, but the Jews broke their oath and put them to death. {*Josephus, Jewish War, l. 2. c. 17. s. 2-10. (408-456) 2:483-501}

6935. That same day, at Caesarea, Florus instigated the Gentiles to kill all the Jews who lived there, and so twenty thousand were killed. The Jews throughout the whole country were vexed in the same way. The Gentiles attacked the villages of the Syrians and the neighbouring cities of Philadelphia, Heshbon, Gerasa, Pella, Scythopolis, Gadara, Hippos, Gaulanitis, Kedasa, Ptolemais, Gaba, Caesarea, Sebaste, Askelon, Anthedon and Gaza. A general slaughter was also conducted by the Syrians of the Jews in the whole of Syria. This was done partly from the old hatred against the Jews and their religion, and partly for the love of plunder and desire for revenge. Only the people of Antioch, Apamea and Sidon spared the Jews who lived among them. At Alexandria, the metropolis of Egypt, during a sedition, fifty thousand Jews were killed in one day by two Roman legions that were sent to put down the sedition. {*Josephus, Jewish War, l. 2. c. 18. s. 1-8. (457-498) 2:501-517}

6936. Cestius Gallus, the governor of Syria, was very upset by these riotous actions. He left Antioch for Judea with the twelfth legion, as well as King Agrippa's soldiers and other forces. From Ptolemais, he invaded Joppa and burned it. He sent Caesennius Gallus into Galilee, which the latter pacified. After staying at Sepphoris, he came to Caesarea. {*Josephus, Jewish War, l. 2. c. 18. s. 9-11. (499-513) 2:517-523} [K691]

6937. Peter and Paul were warned, by revelation from the Lord, of their approaching death. {2Pe 1:14 2Ti 4:6,7}

6938. Peter wrote his second letter to the Hebrews, who were dispersed throughout Pontus, Galatia, Cappadocia, Asia and Bithynia. {2Pe 3:1 1Pe 1:1}

6939. Paul, by the hand of Tychicus, sent his second letter to Timothy at Ephesus, where the family of Onesiphorus lived. This was after Aquila and Priscilla had left Rome and returned to Ephesus. {2Ti 4:12,19} In this letter, he wanted Timothy to come to him before winter and bring Mark with him, who was very beneficial to him in the ministry. {2Ti 4:9,11,21} Paul sent greetings from Eubulus, Pudens, Linus and Claudia. {2Ti 4:21}

## 4070a AM, 4779 JP, 66 AD

6940. During the feast of tabernacles, after Cestius Gallus had burned Lydda, he marched toward Jerusalem. About seven or eight miles from there, the men of Jerusalem met him and fought a perilous battle near Bethhoron. When fresh troops arrived for Cestius, he forced the Jews into Jerusalem. On the 4th of the month of Hyperberetaios (Niese: October 17, Capellus: October 4), he broke in and captured the lower part of the city (also known as Bezetha, or the *New City* and the Timber Market). Then he attacked the temple and the upper city. He would easily have taken it, had he continued the attack more valiantly, for most of the people favoured the Romans and only the seditious men opposed them. {*Josephus, Jewish War, l. 2. c. 19. s. 1-4. (513-532) 2:521-529} [E900]

6941. When Cestius had almost captured the temple, he raised the siege for no good reason and retreated to Antipatris. Many of the Romans and auxiliary soldiers died on this march who were killed by the pursuing Jews.

In their flight, the Romans abandoned most of their baggage, ammunition, engines, slings and other arms. The Jews later made good use of this equipment in their own defence against the siege of Titus. This humiliating retreat happened on the 8th of the month of Dios (Niese: November 25, Capellus: November 8), in the twelfth year of Nero. (That is, the twelfth year was over.) The thirteenth year of Nero had begun on the 13th of the previous October. {*Josephus, Jewish War, l. 2. c. 19. s. 5-9. (533-555) 2:529-537}

6942. The Jews returned to Jerusalem, elated by this victory. They appointed Joseph, the son of Gorion, and Ananus, the high priest, as governors of the city and sent many commanders into each province to govern. As one of these, Josephus (the writer of this war of the Jews), was sent into Galilee. After he had fortified and walled many of the towns, he made all the preparations necessary to endure a war because he was expecting the invasion of the Romans. {*Josephus, Jewish War, l. 2. c. 20. s. 1-8. (556-584) 2:537-547}

6943. In the meantime, there were many riots and numerous and frequent rebellions of the cities against Josephus. These were due to the craftiness and fraud of John, the son of a certain Levite, and out of envy of some of the governors of Jerusalem, who wanted the government taken from Josephus. However, Josephus thwarted all their schemes with his prudence and patience. He forced John to flee with his forces to Jerusalem from Gischala, a town of Galilee, which John had fortified. {*Josephus, Jewish War, l. 2. c. 21. s. 1-10. (585-646) 2:547-571} At Jerusalem, Ananias, the governor of the city, made preparations for a real war by repairing the walls and ensuring that warlike instruments, arrows and arms, were made throughout the whole city. He endeavoured in vain to reconcile those who were called the Zealots. He tried to catch Simon, the son of Gioras, who was a thief, but when he sent soldiers against him, Simon fled with his followers to the thieves who held Masada. From there, they infested the whole country of Judea and Idumea plaguing it with their robberies. {*Josephus, Jewish War, l. 2. c. 22. s. 1,2. (647-654) 2:571,573} [K692]

6944. Cestius, meanwhile, sent messengers to Nero, who was in Achaia at the time, telling him of the troubled state of Judea. Disturbed by this news, Nero ordered Vespasian to go there. On receiving this command, Vespasian sent his son Titus to Alexandria, to bring the fifteenth legion from there into Judea. Meanwhile, Vespasian himself, with the fifth and the tenth legions under his command, went by land from Achaia into Asia and came from there into Syria and Antioch. {*Josephus, Jewish War, l. 3. c. 1. s. 1-3. (1-8) 3:3,5} {*Josephus, Jewish War, l. 3. c. 4. s. 2. (65) 3:23}

## 4070b AM, 4780 JP, 67 AD

*6945.* At Rome, Peter and Paul foretold that it would shortly come to pass, that God would send a king who would overcome the Jews and who would lay their city level with the ground. He would besiege them until they so pined with hunger and thirst, that they would start eating one another. Finally, they would fall into their enemies' hands and would see their wives most grievously tormented in their sight and their virgins violated and prostituted. Their sons would be torn asunder and their little ones dashed to pieces. Everything would be destroyed by fire and sword and they would forever be banished from their own lands. All this would happen, because they had exalted themselves above the most loving Son of God, who was approved by God himself. {*Lactantius, Divine Institutions, l. 4. c. 21. 7:123}

*6946.* At Antioch, Vespasian gathered together the Roman forces and the auxiliaries from the kings. Then, from there, he went to Ptolemais and recovered Sepphoris, which favoured the Romans. {*Josephus, Jewish War, l. 3. c. 2. s. 4. (29-34) 3:11,13}

*6947.* Titus came from Alexandria to join his father at Ptolemais sooner than could have been hoped for, because it was winter. Their combined forces, together with the auxiliaries, numbered sixty thousand cavalry and foot soldiers, besides their servants and the baggage. {*Josephus, Jewish War, l. 3. c. 4. s. 2. (64-69) 3:23,25}

*6948.* Vespasian invaded Galilee and burned and wasted the city of the Gadarenes, which he took at the first assault. From there, he went to Jotapata on the 21st day of Artemisios (Niese: June 8, Capellus: May 21) and fought against it. {*Josephus, Jewish War, l. 3. c. 6,7. (110-160) 3:37-53}

*6949.* On the 29th day of June (which was the last day of that month that happened within the reign of Nero for he died on June 9 of the following year), Paul was beheaded at Rome, as the records of both the eastern and western church confirm. Consequently, Chrysostom affirmed without doubt that the day of Paul's death was known with greater certainty than the death of Alexander the Great himself. {*Chrysostom, II Corinthians, Homily 26. c. 5. 12:402} Dionysius, the bishop of the Corinthians, in a letter to the Romans, affirmed that Peter also suffered martyrdom at the same time, together with him. {*Eusebius, Ecclesiastical History, l. 2. c. 25. 1:181} Origen stated that Peter was crucified at Rome, with his head downward, as he had desired. {Origen, Genesis, tome. 3.} {*Eusebius, Ecclesiastical History, l. 3. c. 1. 1:191} The prediction of Christ, which he had made to Peter, was fulfilled at that time:

"When thou art old, thou shalt stretch forth thine hands, and another shall gird thee, and carry thee whither thou wouldest not." {Joh 21:18,19} [E901]

*6950.* After a forty-seven day siege, Vespasian captured Jotapata by force and burned it. It was valiantly defended by Josephus, who was the governor at the time, on the Calends of July (July 1), in the thirteenth year of Nero. It was taken on the first of the month of Panemos (Niese: July 20, Capellus July 1). {*Josephus, Jewish War, l. 3. c. 7. s. 8-36. (161-339) 3:53-99} Vespasian captured Josephus as he lay hidden in a cave and gave him his life, but kept him prisoner. {*Josephus, Jewish War, l. 3. c. 8. s. 1-9. (340-408) 3:99-119}

*6951.* After Jotapata was destroyed, Vespasian retired to Caesarea with his army. There he stationed two legions, to refresh themselves after the siege, while he sent a third legion to Scythopolis, also to rest. {*Josephus, Jewish War, l. 3. c. 9. s. 1. (409-413) 3:119,121} He went to Caesarea Philippi, where he and his army were feasted by King Agrippa for twenty days. There he prepared for the siege of Tiberias and Tarichea. [K693] Tiberias surrendered immediately and at the entreaty of King Agrippa, the city was not razed. After Tarichea had endured a siege, it was taken by storm. {*Josephus, Jewish War, l. 3. c. 9. s. 7,8. (443-461) 3:129-133} {*Josephus, Jewish War, l. 3. c. 10. s. 1-10. (462-541) 3:133-158}

*6952.* Once these cities had been recovered or overthrown, almost all of Galilee was inclined to the Romans, with the exception of Gamala in Gaulanitis, Gischala and Mount Tabor. {*Josephus, Jewish War, l. 4. c. 1. s. 1. (1-2) 3:159}

## 4071a AM, 4780 JP, 67 AD

*6953.* After a whole month's siege, Gamala was taken and overthrown, on the 23rd day of the month of Hyperberetaios (Niese: Nov 10, Capellus: October 23). A little later, Mount Tabor was also taken by the Romans. {*Josephus, Jewish War, l. 4. c. 1. s. 1-10. (1-83) 3:159-183} Titus attacked Gischala, which was being held by John and his party, made up of the seditious men. John appeared to like the conditions of peace that were offered by Titus, but in the night he and his party fled from the city to Jerusalem. Titus spared the city, but placed a garrison there, and then went to Caesarea. {*Josephus, Jewish War, l. 4. c. 2. s. 1-5. (84-120) 3:183-193} Vespasian left Caesarea for Jamnia and Azotus and after he had conquered them both, he returned to Caesarea. {*Josephus, Jewish War, l. 4. c. 3. s. 2. (130) 3:195}

*6954.* Meanwhile there was a great dissension throughout all Judea. Some wanted to continue the war, while others wanted to remain under the protection of the Romans. As a result, whole troops of thieves were gathered together all over Judea, who plundered those wanting peace.

Laden with their plunder, they were received into Jerusalem, where they spread murders, dissensions, discords and rapines abroad. First, they imprisoned Antipas, together with a great many noblemen and the chief men of the city. Soon after that, they killed them without any trial, having falsely accused them of intending to surrender the city to the Romans. When the people attempted to rise up against them, they seized the temple and used it as a citadel against the people. For a high priest, they appointed Phanni by lot, who was not descended from the high priests, but was such a clown that he scarcely knew what the high priesthood meant. {*Josephus, Jewish War, l. 4. c. 3. s. 1-9. (121-161) 3:193-205}

6955. Ananus and the nobler priests stirred up and armed the people against those Zealots, as they called themselves, and attacked them in the temple itself, forcing them into the inner temple. The Zealots secretly sent letters to the captains of the Idumeans, accusing Ananus of treachery. They complained that they had been besieged in the temple while they were fighting for liberty, and asked the Idumeans to help them. The Idumeans arrived at once with twenty thousand men and were secretly let into the city and the temple by night, by the Zealots. They conducted a massive slaughter in Jerusalem, with large-scale destruction and rapines. For eighty-five hundred were killed that night and, during the days that followed, they killed Ananus and others of the nobility to a total of twelve thousand, besides an uncountable number of the common people. A little later, the Idumeans began to regret this action, when they saw the wickedness of the Zealots and saw no indication in the nobility of that treachery of which the Zealots had accused them; so they freed two thousand, whom they had held in prison, and then left Jerusalem and returned home. Once they had left, the Zealots began to use more cruelty against the nobility than before. They refused to allow any dead nobleman to be buried and killed anyone they suspected would flee to the Romans, without burying their bodies. They guarded all the exits and diligently watched for defectors. {*Josephus, Jewish War, l. 4. c. 3-6. (162-388) 3:205-271}

6956. In the meantime, a dissension arose among the Zealots. John, who had fled from Gischala to Jerusalem, was the leader in their tyranny, and others who before had considered him their equal, could not endure him as their superior. [K694] Thus, while they were unanimous in robbing the common people and all Judea, they disagreed among themselves. They followed the example of Jerusalem, which was teeming with thieves and desperately vexed. {*Josephus, Jewish War, l. 4. c. 7. s. 1,2. (389-409) 3:271-277}

6957. The Jews were destroying each other with these discords. Vespasian was roused to action by the cries of those who fled to him, entreating him to preserve and free their country from this sedition. As Vespasian was preparing for the siege of Jerusalem, he did not want anyone behind him who would be able to cause trouble while he was besieging Jerusalem; so he went with his army to Gadara to quench those remnants of the war. This was the country on the other side of the Jordan River and he had been summoned there by the moderate men of the city, who wanted peace rather than war. He promptly took the city and the seditious men fled, whereupon he sent Placidus to pursue them with his cavalry and put them all to the sword. So he possessed all the country beyond the river, as far as the Dead Sea, except for the citadel of Machaerus. {*Josephus, Jewish War, l. 4. c. 7. s. 3-6. (410-439) 3:277-285} [E902] He put garrisons throughout the towns and arranged the winter quarters for his soldiers, then went back to Caesarea and wintered there. {*Josephus, Jewish War, l. 4. c. 8. s. 1. (440-443) 3:285,286}

## 4071b AM, 4781 JP, 68 AD

6958. Vespasian received news of the rebellions in Gaul, led by their governor, Julius Vindex, who had armed the Gauls against the Romans. This made him more determined to finish the war against the Jews. So, at the beginning of the spring, he led his army out from Caesarea and overran all Judea and Idumea and wasted it. Bringing back his army, he led them through Samaria to Jericho. When the inhabitants fled to the mountain country opposite Jerusalem, he pursued them and drove them from the hills. He attacked the citadels at Jericho and other places and surrounded the Jews on every side. {*Josephus, Jewish War, l. 4. c. 8. s. 1-4. (440-485) 3:285-301}

6959. Nero now faced a revolt against him by Julius Vindex in Gaul. Should he be deposed, some astrologers promised him the government of the east, some the kingdom of Jerusalem and several the recovery of his previous fortunes. {*Suetonius, Nero, l. 6. c. 40. s. 2. 2:155}

6960. Nero knew he was doomed, when he heard that Galba and Spain had revolted from him. {*Suetonius, Nero, l. 6. c. 42. s. 1. 2:159} In the end, he killed himself, on the 9th of June, after he had reigned thirteen years and eight months. {*Dio, l. 63. (29) 8:193}

## 4072b AM, 4782 JP, 69 AD

6961. On the Calends of January (January 1), in Germany, the images of Galba were pulled down and on the third day, the army greeted Aulus Vitellius as the new emperor. On the 15th day of the same month, Galba was killed, seven months after the death of Nero. {*Tacitus, Histories, l. 1. c. 55-57. 2:95-99}

6962. After Galba was killed, Otho was created emperor by his soldiers, who did not know that Vitellius had assumed the empire. Dio stated that Otho was later killed on the ninetieth day of his reign and Suetonius added that Otho was buried on the ninety-fifth day. {*Dio, l. 63. (15) 8:219} {*Suetonius, Otho, l. 7. c. 11. s. 2. 2:233}

6963. Tiberius Alexander, the governor of Egypt, was the first to have the legions swear to support Vespasian on the Calends of July (July 1). This day was his first day as emperor and was later kept as a festival. Then, on the 5th of the Ides of July (July 11), his army in Judea swore their loyalty to him. {*Suetonius, Vespasian, l. 8. c. 6. s. 3. 2:279} {*Tacitus, Histories, l. 2. c. 79. 2:287} There was only one year and twenty-two days between the death of Nero and the beginning of the reign of Vespasian. {*Dio, l. 66. (17) 8:295}

6964. When Vespasian returned to Caesarea, he prepared to take his whole army to besiege Jerusalem. When he received news of Nero's death, he deferred the war against the Jews and sent his son, Titus, to Galba, who had succeeded Nero, wanting to know what he wished to do about the Jewish war. [K695] Titus sailed to Achaia and there heard that Galba had been killed, upon which he immediately returned to his father at Caesarea. They were both in suspense, while the empire seemed to be tottering, so they deferred the wars of Judea. They were afraid that some harm would come to their own country and did not consider it a convenient time to be invading a foreign country. {*Josephus, Jewish War, l. 4. c. 9. s. 2. (491-502) 3:303-307}

6965. In the meantime, Simon, the son of Gioras (about whom we wrote earlier), who was a bold and valiant young man, left Masada, where he had fled. He went into the mountain country of Judea to the murderers and promised liberty to the servants and rewards to the freemen. In a short time, he had gathered a band of thieves and gradually increased his forces. He not only wasted villages but invaded whole cities. In no time at all, he had conquered all Idumea and wasted Judea, until finally he arrived before Jerusalem, where he pitched his tents. He was a terror to the people of Jerusalem, as well as to the Zealots. In this way, the citizens of Jerusalem were sorely oppressed on both sides, from within, by the Zealots whom John commanded, and from without, by Simon, an extremely cruel man. {*Josephus, Jewish War, l. 4. c. 9. s. 3-8. (503-544) 3:307-317} In the meantime, the Idumeans who belonged to John's party and were among his forces, had a falling-out with him. They fought with him and killed many of the Zealots. They captured John's palace and burned it, so that he was forced to flee into the temple with his followers. The Idumeans also feared the citizens, in case John should make an excursion into the city by night and burn it. They discussed the matter and

sent for Simon, whom they admitted into the city, so that they could defend themselves against John. When Simon's forces came, they attacked the temple, but the Zealots fought valiantly. {*Josephus, Jewish War, l. 4. c. 9. s. 11. (566-576) 3:323-327}

6966. Vespasian left Caesarea and went to Berytus and Antioch. From there, he sent Mucianus with troops into Italy, but Vespasian went to Alexandria. {*Josephus, Jewish War, l. 4. c. 10. s. 6. (620,621) 3:341} {*Josephus, Jewish War, l. 4. c. 11. s. 1. (630-633) 3:343}

## 4073a AM, 4782 JP, 69 AD

6967. In Moesia, Antonius Primus, who followed Vespasian's party, led the third legion into Italy against the side of Vitellius. At Cremona, he fought a battle against Vitellius' forces and routed them. He then went to Rome, where he joined up with Mucianus in the middle of the city and then defeated Vitellius' army, whereupon the army dragged Vitellius himself through the forum and there cut his throat. [E903] Mucianus made Domitian, the son of Vespasian, prince of the empire while his father was coming from Syria. {*Josephus, Jewish War, l. 4. c. 11. s. 2-4. (633-655) 3:343-351}

## 4073b AM, 4783 JP, 70 AD

6968. When Vespasian heard these things at Alexandria, he sent his son Titus with forces into Judea, to conclude the Judean war, while he sailed to Italy. {*Josephus, Jewish War, l. 4. c. 11. s. 5. (656-658) 3:349,351}

6969. While Titus was still at Alexandria, the city of Jerusalem was divided into three factions. {Re 16:19} Simon, whom the citizens of Jerusalem had sent for against John and admitted into the city, held the higher city and a section of the tower. John with his Zealots had occupied the temple and the other part of the lower city. This latter faction was again divided into two. Eleazar, who had been the first commander and captain of the Zealots, was displeased that John, with his boldness and craftiness, was running things all by himself. So he left him and taking some followers with him, occupied the inner part of the temple from where he then fought against John. Eleazar had fewer men than John, but his position was more easily defended, because John held the outer parts of the temple and the porches. There was a battle on two fronts, one against Eleazar and the other against Simon. [K696] They burned many things around the temple and ruined the grain and much of the provisions which could have lasted them for many years of a siege. Because these things had been spoiled and consumed, they suffered a severe famine later, when they were besieged by the Romans. {*Josephus, Jewish War, l. 5. c. 1. s. 1-5. (1-38) 4:3-15}

*6970.* Titus came from Alexandria to Caesarea, where he gathered his forces together and then marched to Jerusalem with four legions and the auxiliaries of the neighbouring kings. {*Josephus, Jewish War, l. 5. c. 1. s. 6. (39-46) 4:15,17}* He pitched his camp about a mile or so from the city, a little before the Feast of Unleavened Bread. By this means, he enclosed within the city an enormous multitude of people (about three million) who had gone up to the feast, according to the custom. In a short time, an extremely cruel famine oppressed the city. All food and nourishment was quickly consumed, and a most horrid and memorable consequence of this happened at the time: A mother devoured her own child. {*Josephus, Jewish War, l. 6. c. 3. s. 4. (201-213) 4:237,239} {De 28:53-57}* On the feast day of Unleavened Bread, about the 14th of the month of Xanthikos (Capellus: April 14), Eleazar, who had seized the inner temple, had opened the gate of the temple so that the people could sacrifice. John used this opportunity and secretly sent in many from his side who were armed with swords hidden under their garments. When they were admitted into the temple with the rest of the multitude, they attacked Eleazar and seized the inner temple and slaughtered many Zealots. Hence, the faction that had been threefold had now become twofold. John had eighty-four hundred men on his side and Simon had about ten thousand men, in addition to five thousand Idumeans. {*Josephus, Jewish War, l. 5. c. 3. s. 3-5. (98-130) 4:31-41} {*Josephus, Jewish War, l. 5. c. 6. s. 1. (248-252) 4:79,81}*

*6971.* Titus approached the walls and pitching his camp near the tower of Psephinus, immediately raised a mount. He battered the wall with a ram and beat it down by force. {*Josephus, Jewish War, l. 5. c. 3. s. 4. (133) 4:41}* On the 7th of the month of Artemisios (Niese: May 25, Capellus: May 7), he broke into the city, after the first wall was beaten down. The Jews retreated to the inner city and Titus occupied the northern quarter of the city, up to the citadel of Antonia and the valley of Kidron. Five days later, a certain tower of the second wall was battered and broken down with the ram from the northern quarter, and Titus went into the new lower city. He was driven back by the Jews, but four days later he retook it and then prepared for the assault on the third wall. On the 12th of the month of Artemisios (Niese: May 30, Capellus: May 12), he ordered four mounts to be raised: two at the citadel of Antonia, with which he hoped to gain the temple, and two at John the high priest's tomb, by which he hoped to gain the upper city. John fought the Romans at Antonia, while Simon fought them at John's tomb. These mounts were completed in seventeen days, on the 29th of the month of Artemisios (Niese: June 16, Capellus: May 29), after which the Romans began to batter the wall. John, through a tunnel he made from Antonia, cast down one mount and

burned it. Two days later, Simon made a sally and burned the two mounts opposite him, along with the rams and other engines. The Jews attacked the Romans in their camp, but when Titus came from Antonia, they were forced back into the city. {*Josephus, Jewish War, l. 5. c. 6-11. (248-490) 4:79-155}*

*6972.* Because the previous mounts had been destroyed and burnt, Titus thought it best to raise new ones to assault the city. He also surrounded the city with a wall, so that no one could flee from it, nor could anything be brought into it. So, within three days, he built a wall, about five miles long, around the city. Around this wall he built thirteen citadels whose united circumferences amounted to two and a half miles. *[K697]* As a result, famine prevailed in the city to such an extent and raged so cruelly, that not only did the common people die of it, but the seditious men were severely oppressed by it. {*Josephus, Jewish War, l. 5. c. 12. s. 1-4. (491-526) 4:155-165}* So many perished from famine and pestilence that, from the 14th of the month of Xanthikos (Niese: May 1, Capellus: April 14) (on which day the siege began) to the 1st of the month of Panemos (Niese: July 20, Capellus: July 1), through only one gate (according to the account of Mennaeus, who had fled), *[E904]* were carried out a hundred and fifteen thousand eight hundred corpses from among the poor people, who were buried at the common expense. This did not include those who were buried by their relatives and friends. A little later, it was learned from those who had fled, that a total of six hundred thousand were carried out of the gates for burial. Later still, there were not enough people to bury the poor, so they piled them into great heaps in empty houses and shut the doors on them. The manner of their burial was nothing more than simply throwing them over the walls and filling up the ditches with them. {*Josephus, Jewish War, l. 5. c. 13. s. 7. (567-572) 4:177,179}*

*6973.* In the meantime inside the city, Simon had not refrained from murders and rapines. He killed Matthias, the high priest, whom he accused of treachery, making out that he had wanted to flee to the Romans. (It was ironic that it was Matthias who had let Simon into the city.) Simon also killed three of Matthias' sons and fifteen of the noblest of the people, all of them uncondemned. Moreover, he raged with such cruelty, that Judas, one of his captains, so abhorred his cruelty, that he planned to turn the part of the city under his control over to the Romans. Simon prevented him from doing so by killing him, along with the ten men who were in on the plot. {*Josephus, Jewish War, l. 5. c. 13. s. 1,2. (527-540) 4:165-169}* John was compelled, of necessity, to use the sacred things of the temple for his own use. Not only did he use the vessels of gold and silver and the money of the temple, but he was forced to distribute to his soldiers the very oil and wine which were set apart for the divine service. {*Josephus, Jewish War, l. 5. c. 13. s. 6. (562-566) 4:175,177}

6974. Titus, too, had to fetch materials from every place and cut down all the woods and trees, even as far as eleven miles away. With great toil, he raised new mounts in twenty-one days. He constructed four around Antonia, one on every side of the citadel. When John vainly and in a cowardly way attempted to overthrow these, he was repulsed by the Romans. On the 1st of the month of Panemos (Niese: July 20, Capellus: July 1), the Romans began to batter the wall of Antonia. On the 5th of the month of Panemos (Niese: July 24, Capellus: July 5), they made a breach and broke into Antonia, and then they pursued the fleeing Jews right into the temple. After a long skirmish, the Romans were held off for some time. On the 17th of the month of Panemos (Niese: August 5, Capellus: July 17), there were not enough men to offer the daily sacrifice. On that same day, Titus asked Josephus to urge the seditious men to surrender, but in vain. Seven days later, Titus brought his mounts nearer. He was now bringing the materials for the mounts from a distance of twelve to thirteen miles away. He overturned the foundations of Antonia and made an easy ascent to the temple. He broke through by way of Antonia and seized the northern and western porches of the outer temple court. A section of the porches, especially of those which adjoined Antonia, was burned and destroyed by the Jews. Two days later, on the 24th of the month of Panemos (Niese: August 12, Capellus: July 24), the other part was burned by the Romans. The Jews did not put out the fire, but let it burn, so that the porch would be clearly separated from Antonia. {*Josephus, Jewish War, l. 6. c. 1,2. (1-168) 4:181-227}

6975. On the 27th of the month of Panemos (Niese: August 15, Capellus: July 27), the Jews again burned the western porch, as far as the bridge that led to the gallery, and many Romans were burnt to death. The Jews withdrew from there, to draw the Romans into the trap. The next day, the Romans burned all the northern porch, right up to the eastern porch. {*Josephus, Jewish War, l. 6. c. 3. s. 1,2. (177-192) 4:229-235}

6976. By the 8th of the month of Loos (Niese: August 27, Capellus: August 8), Titus was getting nowhere by battering the wall of the inner temple with the ram, nor by undermining the foundations of the gates, because of their large size and the fact that the stones were so strongly cemented together. [K698] Nor could the Romans get up into the porches with ladders, for the Jews drove them back from above. Due to the reverence of the place, Titus had not burnt it, but necessity now com-

pelled him to do so. He ordered the gates of the inner temple to be set on fire and the fire caught onto the adjoining porches, until everything was aflame. The Jews watched and wondered at it, but did not try to stop and quench the fire, in sheer amazement. Hence, the porches burned all that day and the following night. Titus and his captains had determined to keep the temple from burning, but he was unable to do this. On the 10th of the month of Loos (Niese: August 29, Capellus: August 10), when the Romans who kept the guard in the outer range of the temple were provoked by the Jews, they made a charge on those who were quenching the fire on the inner range and when they had driven them into the temple itself, a Roman soldier took a flaming firebrand and getting up on his companion's shoulders, tossed the brand through the golden window into the houses and chambers built along the northern side of the temple. They caught fire immediately, also burning the temple which adjoined them. In vain, Titus ordered his soldiers to quench the fire. This happened in the second year of Vespasian, in the same month and on the very same day of the month that the first temple was burned by Nebuchadnezzar. {See note on 3416d AM. <<850>>} {*Josephus, Jewish War, l. 6. c. 4. s. 1-8. (220-270) 4:241-257}

6977. When the temple had been pillaged and burnt, the ensigns were set up on the eastern gate of the temple. After making sacrifices, Titus was proclaimed Imperator by the army. [E905] From the bridge which joined the temple to the city with a gallery, Titus, through an interpreter, exhorted the seditious men, who had fled into the upper city, to surrender. Although he offered them their lives, they refused his offer. They asked that they might have permission to leave the city with their wives and children and to go into the wilderness. Titus treated this contemptuously and threatened them with utter destruction. He ordered all the lower city to be set on fire, including the Palace Acra, which he had captured. Then he began to assault the upper city, which was located on a steep rock. On the 20th of the month of Loos (Niese: September 8, Capellus: August 20), he began to raise his mounts and completed them on the 7th of the month of Gorpiaios (Niese: September 25, Capellus: September 7). Then he brought his engines to the walls and after he had made a breach, the tyrants fled with their guards in fear and amazement. On the 8th of the month of Gorpiaios (Niese: September 26, Capellus: September 8), the Romans broke in and destroyed everything with fire and the sword. {*Josephus, Jewish War, l. 6. c. 6-8. (316-408) 4:271-297}

6978. Jerusalem was destroyed on a Saturday. {*Dio, l. 65. (7) 8:271} This was the day the Jews observe most religiously and that year the 8th of the month of Gorpiaios (Niese:

Wednesday, September 26, Capellus: Saturday, September 8) fell on a Saturday. The city was taken and destroyed. Titus commanded all the city and temple to be razed to its foundations and flattened, as well as being ploughed according to the custom. He spared only the west part of the wall and the three towers, Hippicus, Phasael and Mariamme. Because of their great beauty and strength, he left these to posterity, as a monument to the magnificence of that city. {*Josephus, Jewish War, l. 7. c. 1. s. 1. (1-4) 4:307}

6979. After Titus had thus taken the city and had filled every available place with dead bodies, the neighbouring countries wanted to crown him. [K699] However, he replied that he was unworthy of the honour, for it was not he who was the author of this work, but that he had given his hands to God, who had shown his anger against the Jews. {*Philostratus, Apollonius, l. 6. c. 29. 2:111} However, there are coins of Titus which are marked with a trophy and a triumphal chariot; and there are coins of Vespasian with the image of a woman sitting sorrowfully under a palm tree and bearing the inscription, *JUDEA CAPTA S.C.* Money was also coined around the end of the 21 year of the reign of King Agrippa, with an inscription in Greek (but here translated into English):

"Vespasian, Emperor and Caesar, Judea was taken in the year twenty-one of Agrippa."

## 4074a AM, 4783 JP, 70 AD

6980. When Titus had finished the war, he rewarded the soldiers and committed the custody of Jerusalem to the tenth legion. The twelfth legion, which had fought poorly under Cestius from Syria, was banished by Titus and sent to the Euphrates River into the region of Armenia and Cappadocia. He took the fifth and fifteenth legions to Caesarea on the coast, where he gathered together all the plunder and the captives. Since winter was coming, it was too dangerous to sail to Italy. {*Josephus, Jewish War, l. 7. c. 1. s. 2,3. (5-20) 4:307-313}

6981. The two tyrants, John and Simon, were captured as they were hiding in the vaults of Jerusalem. John was condemned to life-long imprisonment and Simon was reserved for the triumph. In those same vaults, two thousand men were discovered who had either perished from hunger or had killed each other, rather than surrender to the Romans. {*Josephus, Jewish War, l. 6. c. 9. s. 4. (428-434) 4:301,303} {*Josephus, Jewish War, l. 7. c. 2. s. 2. (26-36) 4:315,317}

6982. Titus stayed at Caesarea, where he celebrated the birthday of his brother Domitian, who was born on October 24. In the course of this celebration, more than twenty-five hundred Jews perished, either being forced to fight with wild beasts, being burned with fire or being killed in fighting each other. {*Josephus, Jewish War, l. 7. c. 3. s. 1. (37,38) 4:317}

## 4074b AM, 4784 JP, 71 AD

6983. Later, Titus came to Berytus in Phoenicia, where he stayed longer and with great magnificence celebrated the birthday of his father, who was born on November 17. (This was not the anniversary of his empire, which was celebrated on the first of July, according to Suetonius and Tacitus.) A multitude of captives also died, in a similar manner as before. {*Josephus, Jewish War, l. 7. c. 3. s. 1. (39) 4:319}

6984. Titus went to see Antioch and the other cities of Syria. He then travelled with the fifth and fifteenth legions through Judea and Jerusalem, to Alexandria in Egypt. From there, he sailed to Rome, where he was welcomed home by everyone. He and his father held a triumph for the conquest of Judea. {*Josephus, Jewish War, l. 7. c. 5. s. 1-7. (96-162) 4:337-355}

6985. The two captains of the sedition, John and Simon, were led in that triumph, along with seven hundred other Jews who were impressive in strength and beauty. Only Simon was killed. (He was also known as Bargiora. {*Dio, l. 65. (7) 8:269,271}) The book of the law of the Jews was carried in this triumph as the last of the spoils. It and the purple veil of the sanctuary were stored in the palace. {*Josephus, Jewish War, l. 7. c. 5. s. 3. (116-118) 4:341,343} {*Josephus, Jewish War, l. 7. c. 5. s. 5-7. (132-162) 4:347-355}

6986. From this victory, both father and son were given the name of *Imperator*. However, neither of them was called *Judaicus*, although many other things were decreed for them, especially triumphal arches. {*Dio, l. 65. (7) 8:271} There still remains, at the foot of the hill of Palatine, a marble triumphal arch erected to the honour of Titus. Taken from it, there is a copy, written by Villalpandus, of the instruments of the temple which were carried in the triumph. {Villalpandus, Ezekiel, Tom. 2. l. 5. c. 7. p. 587.} [E906]

## 4075a AM, 4784 JP, 71 AD

6987. Lucilius Bassus was sent as a deputy into Judea and received control of the army from Sextus Vettenlenus Cerialis. The citadel of Herodion and its garrison surrendered to Bassus, while a little later, he assaulted and captured the strong citadel of Machaerus beyond Jordan. {*Josephus, Jewish War, l. 7. c. 6. s. 1-4. (163-209) 4:355-367} [K700]

## 4075b AM, 4785 JP, 72 AD

6988. Some think the eclipses described by Pliny were foretold by our Saviour. {Mt 24:29} {*Pliny, l. 2. c. 10. 1:207}

"It happened even in our time, that there was an eclipse of the sun and moon within fifteen days of each other when the Vespasians were emperors, and both were consuls, the father for the third time (perhaps the fourth) and the son, the second time."

*6989.* Caesar wrote to Laberius Maximus, the governor of Judea, that he should sell all the land of the Jews. He imposed a tribute on all the Jews, wherever they lived, and ordered them annually to bring in to the Capitol the two drachmas which they had formerly paid to the temple of Jerusalem. {*Josephus, Jewish War, l. 7. c. 6. s. 6. (216-218) 4:369,371}

*6990.* In the fourth year of Vespasian, Caesennius Paetus, the governor of Syria, drove Antiochus, the king of Commagene, from his kingdom. Antiochus fled into Cilicia while his son fled to the Parthians. Later, both of them were reconciled to Vespasian and Antiochus was restored to his kingdom. {*Josephus, Jewish War, l. 7. c. 7. s. 1-3. (219-244) 4:371-377}

## 4076b AM, 4786 JP, 73 AD

*6991.* The Alani invaded Media and totally laid it waste, while King Pacorus fled before them. They later went into Armenia, where Tiridates, the king, himself opposed them and was almost captured in the battle itself. {*Josephus, Jewish War, l. 7. c. 7. s. 4. (245-251) 4:377,379}

## 4076c AM, 4786 JP, 73 AD

*6992.* When Bassus died, Flavius Silva replaced him in the government of Judea. On the 15th of the month of Xanthikos (Niese: May 2, Capellus: April 15), he used force to capture the impregnable citadel of Masada that was being held by Eleazar, the nephew of Judas Balitaeus, the captain of the thieves. Eleazar persuaded all the thieves in the citadel, numbering nine hundred and sixty with their wives and children, to kill each other. First they set fire to the citadel with all the household belongings, lest they should fall into Roman hands. In this way, the last remains of the Jewish wars were eliminated and all Judea was quiet. {*Josephus, Jewish War, l. 7. c. 8,9. (252-406) 4:379-421}

*6993.* Many of the thieves who escaped from Judea, fled into Egypt, to Alexandria, where they tried to solicit the Jews to revolt. However, persuaded by their rulers, the common people attacked these thieves; they captured six hundred of them, and handed them over to the Romans to be punished. The rest, who escaped into Egypt and Thebes, were also captured. In connection with this, Caesar ordered Lupus, the governor of Alexandria, to pull down the temple of the Jews. (This temple had been built a long time ago in Egypt, by Onias, the brother of the high priest.) Lupus, however, did no more than remove some furniture from the temple and then sealed it up. Paulinus, his successor in the government, removed all the furniture and sealed up the doors. He ordered that no one be permitted to come there, so that not even a trace of religion remained there. {*Josephus, Jewish War, l. 7. c. 10. s. 1-4. (407-436) 4:421-429}

*6994.* Jonathan, a certain Jewish weaver, escaped to Cyrene, where he raised a sedition and drew two thousand Jews into the wilderness. Catullus, the governor of the Pentapolis of Libya, sent his cavalry and foot soldiers out and easily defeated them. When Jonathan was brought before him, he falsely accused the most wealthy of the Jews of being the main instigators of this revolt. Catullus willingly listened to these accusations and immediately executed three thousand of them. He did this without fear of retribution, because he first confiscated their estates to Caesar's treasury. Catullus sent Jonathan with the other captives as a prisoner to Rome, to Vespasian, to enable him to accuse of sedition the most honest of those living at Rome and Alexandria. Among many other things, he affirmed that Josephus, the writer of the Jewish history, had sent him both arms and money. [K701] Vespasian knew that this accusation was not lawfully being brought against these men and acquitted them at Titus' entreaty, but deservedly punished Jonathan. First, he scourged him and then he had him burned alive. Catullus also, through the mercy of the emperor, was not punished. But not long after, he was overcome by a complicated and incurable disease and was tortured and tormented in his mind. He thought that he saw the ghosts of those he had killed ever before him. Finally, his bowels rotted and spilled out of him, and he died. {*Josephus, Jewish War, l. 7. c. 11. s. 1-4. (436-453) 4:429-435} {*Josephus, Life, l. 1. c. 76. (424,425) 1:155,157}

*6995.* Here Josephus ended the history of the destruction of Judea. After being captured in this war, he was made a freedman by Flavius Vespasian, the emperor, and assumed the name of Flavius from his patron. {*Josephus, Jewish War, l. 7. c. 11. s. 5. (454,455) 4:435}

*6996.* Cornelius Tacitus and Suetonius related that there were six hundred thousand Jews killed in this war. Josephus, a Jew, was a commander in that war and also deserved thanks and pardon from Vespasian, for foretelling him that he would be emperor. Josephus wrote that a million perished by the sword and through famine, and that the rest of the Jews that were dispersed all over the world and put to death in various ways, numbered ninety thousand. Orosius also stated the same. {Orosius, l. 7. c. 9.} I cannot find the number of six hundred thousand of those who were killed, in Suetonius' writings. [E907] In Josephus, the number of captives was ninety-seven thousand, while the other number of one million and one hundred thousand refers only to those who perished in the six-month siege of Jerusalem. {*Josephus, Jewish War, l. 6. c. 9. s. 3. (420) 4:299}

6997. Justus Lipsius made the following catalogue from Josephus of those who perished outside of Jerusalem during the whole seven years. {Lipsius, de Constantia, l. 2. c. 21.}

| | |
|---|---|
| At Jerusalem, first killed upon the command of Florus | 630 |
| By the inhabitants of Caesarea in hatred toward them and their religion | 20,000 |
| At Scythopolis (a city of Syria) | 30,000 |
| At Askelon in Palestine by the inhabitants | 2,500 |
| Likewise at Ptolemais | 2,000 |
| At Alexandria in Egypt under Tiberius Alexander the Governor | 50,000 |
| At Damascus | 10,000 |
| At the taking of Joppa by Gessius Florus | 8,400 |
| At a certain mountain called Cabulo | 2,000 |
| In a fight at Askelon | 10,000 |
| By an ambush | 8,000 |
| At Aphaca when it was taken | 15,000 |
| Killed at Mount Gerizim | 11,600 |
| At Jotapata, where Josephus was | 30,000 |
| At Joppa, when it was taken, were drowned | 4,200 |
| Killed at Tarichea | 6,500 |
| At Gamala, killed, as well as those who threw themselves down over a cliff | 9,000 |
| (The only survivors in the whole city were two women who were sisters.) | |
| When they forsook Gischala, [K702] killed in the flight | 2,000 |
| Killed of the Gadarenes, besides an infinite number that leaped into the river | 13,000 |
| Killed in the villages of Idumea | 10,000 |
| At Gerizim | 1,000 |
| At Machaerus | 1,700 |
| In the wood of Jardes | 3,000 |
| In the citadel of Masada, who killed themselves | 960 |
| In Cyrene by Catullus the Governor | 3,000 |
| Which number of the dead, being added to those who died at the siege of Jerusalem | 1,100,000 |
| Total | 1,337,490 |

6998. An innumerable company were omitted who perished through famine, banishment and other miseries.

(Josephus estimated that at the passover feast, a few years earlier, there had been about three million people in Jerusalem. {*Josephus, Jewish War, l. 6. c. 9. s. 3. (424-426) 4:301} {See note on 4069b AM. <<6927>>} There were probably this many there for the passover when Titus began the siege. Most were unaccounted for, which would make the official death toll low by at least two million. Current estimates place the number of people in Jerusalem at more than three million. Most perished! Editor.)

6999. Justus Tiberiensis, in his chronicle of the Kings of the Jews, showed that Agrippa, the last king of the family of Herod, had his kingdom augmented by Vespasian. {Photius, Bibliotheca, cod. 33.} Dio related that he had praetorian honours given to him. His sister Bernice, who came to Rome with him, lived in the palace. Titus was so in love with her, that he made her believe he would marry her and she behaved in every way as though she had been his wife. However, when Titus became aware that the people of Rome did not take this well, he put her away. {*Suetonius, Titus, l. 8. c. 7. s. 2. 2:311} {*Dio, l. 65. (15) 8:291} The observation of Josephus about the rest of Herod's progeny was very memorable, namely that they all, with few exceptions, perished within a hundred years of Herod's death, although they were very numerous. {*Josephus, Antiq., l. 18. c. 5. s. 3. (128) 9:89}

7000. This was the end of the Jewish affairs and happened as predicted by Jesus in the Gospels. We close this history with a quote from Bancroft: {*Klopsch, Many Thoughts of Many Minds, 1:130}

"It is the time when the hour of conflict is over that history comes to a right understanding of the strife and is ready to exclaim, *Lo, God is here and we knew him not!*"

**Soli Deo Gloria in aeternum.**

**FINIS**

# Bibliography

We would give our eye-teeth to have all the books Ussher referred to in preparing his history. Alas, some of the material is now lost forever and was destroyed in a fire in Dublin in 1922.

We have gone through and prepared a bibliography. We have used the history books published by the Loeb Classical Library as the basis for most of this work. These are serious history books written for dedicated scholars. They have the Greek or Latin of the original writer with an English translation. They also note all textual problems. Wherever possible, Ussher's footnotes were updated to reflect books published by Loeb.

All footnotes in the text are delimited by {...}. They follow this simple format:

{*Pliny, Natural History, l. 9. c. 23. (56) 3:201}

where:

* — reference verified. No "*" means we could not locate the reference because we did not have the book or we did not have time to track it down.

Pliny — name of author

Natural History — title of book

l. 9. — Book 9 in original author's series

c. 23. — chapter 23 in original author's series

(56) — Modern reference number in the original text. Not all writers are so indexed, e.g., Herodotus

3:201 — Loeb Series, book 3, page 201

Note that some of the original writers did not use chapter breaks, e.g., Dio Cassius. In that case the footnote would have no chapter reference.

The writings of Josephus deserve special mention. We have cross-indexed it with the Loeb edition and included the new indexing system for it so you can readily cross-index it with the Hendrickson reprint of Whiston's English version. For reasons unknown, the chapter and section numbers vary between these two publishers. We followed Loeb for the references.

{*Josephus, Jewish War, l. 6. c. 9. s. 3. (420) 4:299}

The number in (...) is the key to Hendrickson's edition and all other editions that follow the Greek text. Each of Josephus' books are numbered from the beginning with a reference number in the text. This reference in the above example is found in book 6 number 420. The Greek text also identifies this as chapter nine section 3. This scheme has the advantage of universality in that it is not tied to any page numbers for a given publisher.

In the bibliography, works published by Loeb are indicated by a *LCL* (Loeb Classical Library) and no further publisher information is noted. These are all published by Harvard University Press at Cambridge, Massachusetts. The Loeb reference numbers follow the the books by that author are listed after the reference.

Format of the bibliography is: author name, book title, publisher information. Note special abbreviations:

ANF — Anti-Nicene Fathers
NPNF1 — Nicene and Post-Nicene Fathers, Series 1
NPNF2 — Nicene and Post-Nicene Fathers, Series 2

This series of the early church writers was published by Hendrickson in 1994.

## Authors Cited

Books marked with a "*" refer to ones we did not have copies of and hence could not check the reference. This list is only partial. Ussher mentioned many authors in passing but did not give references to their works. Likewise, the counts represent a lower bound for the actual number of citations from a writer. Again, Ussher mentioned cited authors without giving the reference. Since the total work has over fourteen thousand quotes, we are not surprised Ussher did not document them all. Most modern history books only document a fraction of the authors they cite. These original writers account for more than 98 percent of the footnotes!

Aelian: 165–230 AD, OCD p. 18 [Count 40]
  History of Animals (LCL 446, 448, 449)
  Historical Miscellany (LCL 486)
Aeschylus: 525–456 BC?, OCD p. 26 [Count 2]
  Life in Persia* (LCL 145, 146)
Agathias: 532–580 AD, OCD p. 36 [Count 1]
  Histories*, J. D. Frendo, 1975
Alexander Polyhistor: 1st century BC, OCD p. 60 [Count 3]
  Chronography*
Ambrose: c. 340–397 AD, OCD p. 71 [Count 1]
  Commentary*
Ammianus Marcellinus: c. 330–390 AD, OCD p. 73 [Count 19]
  Roman History (LCL 300, 315, 331)
Apion: c. 1st century AD, OCD p. 121 [Count 1]
  Egyptian Affairs*, S. Neitzel, 1977 (Only fragments exist)
Appian of Alexandria: 2nd century AD, OCD p. 130 [Count 833]
  Roman History (LCL 2, 3, 4, 5)
  Parthian Wars* (Only fragments exist)
Aristeas: Letter of, OCD p. 160 [Count 8]
  Letter to Ptolemy Philadelphus*
  Septuagint Interpreters*
Aristides: 117–181 AD, OCD p. 160? [Count 2]
  Leuctia*
  Rhodiaca*
Aristotle: 384–322 BC, OCD p. 165 [Count 8]
  History of Animals (LCL 437, 438, 439)
  Metaphysics* (LCL 271, 287)
  Oeconomics* (LCL 287)
  Politics* (LCL 264)
  Rhetoric* (LCL 193)
Arrian: c. 86–160 AD, OCD p. 175 [Count 465]
  History of Alexander and Indica (LCL 236, 269)
  Affairs after Alexander*
Asconius Pedianus: 3–88 AD, OCD p. 188 [Count 26]
  Against Cecilius*
  Against Divinations*
  Against Verres*
  De Domo Sua*
  In Pison*
  Pro Cornelio*
  Pro Milone*
Athenaeus: c. 200 AD, OCD p. 202 [Count 99]
  Deipnosphistae (LCL 204, 208, 224, 235, 274, 327, 345)
Augustine: 354–430 AD, OCD p. 215 [Count 7]
  Against Gaudentius*
  City of God (NPNF1, Book 2) (LCL 411, 412, 413, 414, 415, 416, 417)
  Epistle to Dulcitius*
Augustus: 63 BC–14 AD, OCD p. 216–218 [Count 8]
  The Acts of Augustus (In Velleius Paterculus LCL 152)
Aulus Gellius: 125–180? AD, OCD p. 627 [Count 28]
  Attic Nights (LCL 195, 200, 212)
Aurelius Victor: 4th century AD, OCD p. 222 [Count 19]
  De Viris illustribus*, H. Bird, 1994
Ausonius: 4th century AD, OCD p. 223 [Count 2]
  Ordo Urbium Nobilium* (LCL 96, 115)
  Idyllion*
Basil the Great: c. 330–379 AD, OCD p. 234 [Count 2]
  Against Eunomius*
  Hexaemeron (NPNF2, Book 8)
Berosus: 3rd century BC, OCD p. 239 [Count 5]
  Chaldean History* (Only fragments exist)
Caesar, Julius: 100–44 BC, OCD p. 780 [Count 122]
  Alexandrian, African and Spanish Wars (LCL 402)
  Civil Wars (LCL 039)
  Gallic Wars (LCL 072)
Cassidorus: c. 490-585 AD, OCD p. 298 [Count 5]
  Chronicle*
Censorinus: 3rd century AD, OCD p. 308 [Count 11]
  De Die Natali (The Birthday)*, N. Sallmann, 1983

Chrysostom, John: c. AD 354–407, OCD p. 329 [Count 2]
  Commentaries*
  II Corinthians (NPNF1, Book 12)
Cicero, Tullius: 106–43 BC, OCD p. 1558–1564 [Count 633]
  Rhetorical Treatises
    Brutus (LCL 342)
    De Fato (LCL 349)
    De Oratore (LCL 348, 349)
  Orations
    Agrarian Law (LCL 240)
    De Domo Sua (LCL 158)
    De Haruspicum Responsis (LCL 158)
    De Provinciis Consularibus (LCL 447)
    In Catilinam &c (LCL 324)
    Philippics (LCL 189)
    Pro Archia Poeta (LCL 158)
    Pro Aulus Cluentio (LCL 198)
    Pro Bablo (LCL 447)
    Pro Caelio (LCL 447)
    Pro Dejotaro (LCL 252)
    Pro Flacco (LCL 324)
    Pro Lege Manilia (LCL 198)
    Pro Ligario (LCL 252)
    Pro Murena (LCL 324)
    Pro Plancio (LCL 158)
    Pro Rabirio Postumo (LCL 252)
    Pro Sestio (LCL 309)
    Verrine Orations (LCL 221, 293)
  Philosophical Treatises
    Academica (Lucullus) (LCL 268)
    De Amicita (LCL 154)
    De Divinatione (LCL 154)
    De Natura Decorum (LCL 268)
    De Finibus (LCL 040)
    De Officiis (LCL 30)
    De Senectute (LCL 154)
    Tusculan Disputations (LCL 141)
  Letters
    Letters to Brutus (LCL 462)
    Letters to Atticus (LCL 7, 8, 97)
    Letters to his Friends (LCL 205, 216, 230)
    Letters to his Brother Quintus (LCL 462)
Clement of Alexandra: c. 200 AD, OCD p. 344 [Count 33]
  Stromateis (ANF, Book 2) F. W. Sagnard, 1947
  Hypotyposes (ANF, Book 2)
Columella, Lucius Junius Moderatus: c. 50 AD., OCD p. 367 [Count 2]
  De Re Rustica* (LCL 361, 407, 408)
Cornelius Nepos: c. 124–65 BC, OCD p. 396 [Count 5]
  Life of Atticus (LCL 467)
Ctesias of Cnidos: late 5th century BC, OCD p. 411, 412 [Count 44]
  History of Persia* (The Greek Accounts of Eastern History) R. Drews, 1973
Curtius, Quintus: 1st or 2nd century AD, OCD p. 416 [Count 349]
  History of Alexander (LCL 368, 369)
Cyril of Alexandria: died AD 444, OCD p. 422 [Count 2]
  Against Julian*, Ed. Migne, PG 68–77
Demosthenes, 384–322 BC, OCD p. 456–458 [Count 4]
  Peace, Liberty of Rhodes* (LCL 238)
  Against Leptines* (LCL 238)
  Against Aristocrates* (LCL 299)
  For Ctesiphontem*
Dio Cassius: c. 164–229 AD, OCD p. 299, 300 [Count 914]
  Roman History (LCL 32, 37, 53, 66, 82, 83, 175, 176, 177)
Diodorus Siculus: 1st century BC, OCD p. 472, 473 [Count 835]
  Bibliotheca (LCL 279, 303, 340, 375, 384, 399, 389, 422, 377, 390, 409, 423)
Diogenes Laertius: 3rd century AD, OCD p. 474, 475 [Count 39]
  Lives of Eminent Philosophers (184, 185)
Dionysius of Halicarnassus: c. 1st century BC, OCD p. 478 [Count 20]
  Ammaeus (LCL 466)

Servius: 4th century AD, OCD p. 1395 [Count 3]
  Commentary on Virgil*, Thilo and Hagen 1881–1902
Simplicius: 6th century AD, OCD p. 1409,1410 [Count 1]
  De Caelo* (Latin for, *About the Heavens*), R. Sorabji, 1987, *The Ancient Commentators of Aristotle*
Solinus, Julius: c. 200 AD, OCD p. 786 [Count 14]
  Die Collectanea Rerum Memorabilium*, H. Walter, 1968
Strabo: 64 BC–21 AD, OCD p. 1447 [Count 405]
  Geography (LCL 49, 50, 182, 196, 211, 223, 241, 267)
Suetonius: c. 70–130 AD, OCD p. 1451,1452 [Count 217]
  De Viris Illustribus (LCL 031, 038)
Suidas: (name of a lexicon not an author), c. 980 AD, OCD p. 1451 [Count 27]
  English translation*, Byzantine Humanism, 1986
Sulpicius Severus: c. 360–420 AD, OCD p. 1398 [Count 22]
  Sacred History (NPNF, Book 11)
Tacitus: 56–118? AD, OCD p. 1469–1471 [Count 217]
  Dialogue on Oratory (LCL 35)
  Histories and Annals (LCL 111, 249, 312, 322)
Talmudists: OCD p. 1471,1472 [Count 1]
  Baba-bathra*
Tatian: c. 172 AD, OCD p. 1477 [Count 2]
  Oration to the Greeks (ANF Book 2)
Tertullian: c. 160–c. 240 AD, OCD p. 1487 [Count 11]
  Against Marcion (ANF Book 3)
  Answer to the Jews (ANF Book 3)
  Apology (ANF Book 3)
  De Anima (ANF Book 3)
  De Pallio (ANF Book 4)
Thallus: 1st century AD, OCD p. 1491 [Count 1]
  Chronology from Trojan War to 109 BC*
Theocritus: 3rd century BC, OCD p. 1498,1499 [Count 2]
  Poetry*, Gow, 1952
Theophilus: c. 180 AD, OCD p. 1504,1505 [Count 3]
  Ad Autolycum (ANF Book 2)
Theophrastus: 372–288 BC, OCD p. 1504 [Count 2]
  Enquiry Into Plants* (LCL 070, 079)
Thucydides: c. 455–c. 400 BC, OCD p. 1516,1517 [Count 100]
  History (LCL 108, 109, 110, 169)
Tibullius, Albius: 55-48–19 BC?, OCD p. 1524 [Count 2]
  Corpus Tibullianum*, Lee, 1982
  Elegies*, G. Lee, 1982
Valerius Maximus: 1st century AD, OCD p. 1579 [Count 94]
  History (LCL 492, 493)
Varro: 116-27 BC, OCD p. 1582 [Count 3]
  Human Antiquities* (De Re Rustica)
  De Lingua Latina (LCL 333, 334)
Vegetius Renatus: 5th century AD, OCD p. 1584 [Count 1]
  De Re Militaris*, N. P. Milner, 1993
Velleius Paterculus: 20 BC–31 AD?, OCD p. 1585 [Count 194]
  History (LCL 152)
Virgil: 70–19 BC, OCD p. 1602–1607 [Count 7]
  Aeneid (LCL 063, 064)
  Eclogue (LCL 063)
  Georgics (LCL 063)
Vitruvius: 1st century BC, OCD p. 1609,1610 [Count 6]
  De Architectura (LCL 251, 280)
Xenophon: 430–360?
BC, OCD p. 1628–1631 [Count 206]
  Agesilaus (LCL 183)
  Anabasis (LCL 090)
  Cyropaedia (LCL 051, 052)
  Hellenica (LCL 088, 089)
  Oeconomicus (LCL 168)
Zeno of Rhodes: 2nd century BC, p. 1635 [Count 1]
  History of Rhodes, G. Lehmann, 1988
Zonaras: c. 1120 AD, OCD p. 1639 [Count 1]
  History*
Zosimus: late 5th century AD, OCD p. 1640 [Count 2]
  History*, Mendelssohn 1887

The following authors are not listed in the Oxford Classical Dictionary, and we think they wrote after the classical period or lived about the time of Ussher.

Abulensis: [Count 1]
  Catechism*
Abydenus: [Count 5]
  Assyrian History*
Albatenius: [Count 1]
  Al-Kept* (Astronomical work)
Baronius: [Count 2]
  History*
Bellovacensis: [Count 1]
  History*
Bochartus: [Count 1]
  Sacred Geography*
Christophorus Helvicus, [Count 1]
  Genealogy of Christ*
Cunaeus: [Count 1]
  De Republic Hebra.*
David Paraeus* [Count 1]
Emilius Probus: [Count 64]
  Life of Agesilaus*
  Life of Alcibiades*
  Life of Aristides*
  Life of Chabrias*
  Life of Cimon*
  Life of Conon*
  Life of Datames*
  Life of Eumenes*
  Life of Hannibal*
  Life of Iphicrates*
  Life of Lysander*
  Life of Miltiades*
  Life of Pausanias*
  Life of Themistocles*
Eschines: [Count 2]
  Against Ctesiphontem*
  De False Legation*
Fortunius Licetus: [Count 1]
  de Spontanco Viventium ortu*
Gruter: [Count 30]
  Inscriptions*
Henric Valesius: [Count 4]
  Life of Nicolaus Damascene*
Hilduinus: [Count 1]
  Areopagatica*
Jornandes: [Count 5]
  De Regnorum ac Temporum Succession*
Julius Capitoline: [Count 1]
  Maximus and Balbinus
Justus Lipsius: [Count 4]
  De Constantia*
  Letters*
  Syntagma of Libraries*
Lipsius: [Count 4]
  De Constantia*
  Elector.*
  Epistle*
  Syntagma of Libraries*
Nicephorus Calistus: [Count 1]
  Ecclesiastical History*
Nicolaus Fullerus: [Count 1]
  Miscellany*
Phavorinus: [Count 1]
  Varia Historia*
Philastrius Brixiensis: [Count 1]
  De Heres*
Ribera: [Count 1]
  De Temple*

Ramusius: [Count 1]
    Navigations*
Rupert Tuitiensis: [Count 1]
    De Victoria Verbi*
Sextus Rufus: [Count 17]
    Breviary*
Stephanus Byzantinus: [Count 3]
    de Urbibus*
Thodores: [Count 1]
    Commentary on Deuteronomy*
Ussher: [Count 11]
    Egyptian Chronology*
    Macedonian and Asiatic Year*
Vossius: [Count 1]
    Greek Historians*

## Modern writers used in revising this work

Anderson, Sir Robert. *The Coming Prince*. Grand Rapids, MI: Kregal Publications, 1975 reprint.

*Apocrypha*. Oxford Edition, 1769 Edition; Revised Standard Version, 1957 Edition; Authorized Version. Cambridge, 1769 Edition.

Bone, Dorothy. *Chronology of the Hebrew Divided Kingdom*. London: Avon Books, 1997.

Bray, John. *Matthew 24 Fulfilled*. Lakeland, FL: John Bray Ministry, Inc., 1998 Edition.

Chilton, David. *The Days of Vengeance*. Tyler, TX: Dominion Press, 1987.

*Concise Bible Dictionary*. Addison, IL: Bible Truth Publishers.

Gill, John. *Gill's Expositor*. 1810. Republished on the Online Bible CD-ROM, 1995.

Grayson, A.W. *Assyrian and Babylonian Chronicles*. Winona Lake, IN: Eisenbrauns, 2000.

Jones, Floyd. *Chronology of the Old Testament*. The Woodlands, TX: KingsWood Press, 1999.

Klopsch, Louis. *Many Thoughts of Many Minds*. New York, NY: The Christian Herald, Bible House, 1896.

Mauro, Philip. *The Wonders of Bible Chronology*. Swengel, PA: Reiner Publications.

_____. *The Seventy Weeks and the Great Tribulation*. Sterling VA: Grace Abounding Ministries, 1988.

## Other works used by the editor in preparing this edition:

*Oxford English CD-ROM Dictionary* (OED). Second Edition, 1994.
*Oxford Classical Dictionary* (OCD). Third Edition, 1996.
*Oxford Latin Dictionary* (OLD). 1996 Edition.
Ussher. *Annals of the World*, 1654. Photocopy of Latin Edition.
Ussher. *Annals of the World*, 1658. Photocopy of English Edition.

Ussher referred to many other writers but did not give the exact reference. We usually omitted these writers from this bibliography.

## Biblical Book Name Abbreviations

| | | | |
|---|---|---|---|
| Genesis | Ge | Nahum | Na |
| Exodus | Ex | Habakkuk | Hab |
| Leviticus | Le | Zephaniah | Zep |
| Numbers | Nu | Haggai | Hag |
| Deuteronomy | De | Zechariah | Zec |
| Joshua | Jos | Malachi | Mal |
| Judges | Jud | Matthew | Mt |
| Ruth | Ru | Mark | Mr |
| 1 Samuel | 1Sa | Luke | Lu |
| 2 Samuel | 2Sa | John | Joh |
| 1 Kings | 1Ki | Acts | Ac |
| 2 Kings | 2Ki | Romans | Ro |
| 1 Chronicles | 1Ch | 1 Corinthians | 1Co |
| 2 Chronicles | 2Ch | 2 Corinthians | 2Co |
| Ezra | Ezr | Galatians | Ga |
| Nehemiah | Ne | Ephesians | Eph |
| Esther | Es | Philippians | Php |
| Job | Job | Colossians | Col |
| Psalms | Ps | 1 Thessalonians | 1Th |
| Proverbs | Pr | 2 Thessalonians | 2Th |
| Ecclesiastes | Ec | 1 Timothy | 1Ti |
| Song of Solomon | So 2 | Timothy | 2Ti |
| Isaiah | Isa | Titus | Tit |
| Jeremiah | Jer | Philemon | Phm |
| Lamentations | La | Hebrews | Heb |
| Ezekiel | Eze | James | Jas |
| Daniel | Da | 1 Peter | 1Pe |
| Hosea | Ho | 2 Peter | 2Pe |
| Joel | Joe | 1 John | 1Jo |
| Amos | Am | 2 John | 2Jo |
| Obadiah | Ob | 3 John | 3Jo |
| Jonah | Jon | Jude | Jude |
| Micah | Mic | Revelation | Re |

## Apocryphal Book Name Abbreviations

The following books are in the Oxford Authorized Version Apocrypha:

| | |
|---|---|
| 1 Esdras | 1Es |
| 2 Esdras | 2Es |
| Tobit | Tob |
| Judith | Jdt |
| Rest of Esther | Est |
| Wisdom of Solomon | Wis |
| Ecclesiasticus (Sirach) | Sir |
| Baruch | Bar |
| Prayer of Azariah | Aza |
| History of Susanna | Sus |
| Bel and the Dragon | Bel |
| Prayer of Manasses | Man |
| 1 Maccabees | 1Ma |
| 2 Maccabees | 2Ma |

From the 1957 RSV Apocrypha which was not in the Oxford text.

| | |
|---|---|
| 3 Maccabees | 3Ma |
| 4 Maccabees | 4Ma |
| Psalm 151 | 2Ps |

Citations from the Oxford Apocrypha noted as *Apc* and ones from the RSV Apocrypha noted as *RApc*.

# Appendix A: Roman Calendars

**Roman Republican Calendar to end of 46 BC**

| | Jan. | Feb. | March | April | May | June | July | Aug. | Sep. | Oct. | Nov. | Dec. |
|---|---|---|---|---|---|---|---|---|---|---|---|---|
| | 29 | 28 | 31 | 29 | 31 | 29 | 31 | 29 | 29 | 31 | 29 | 29 |
| 1 | Calends | Calends | Calends | Calends | Calends | Calends | Calends | Calends | Calends | Calends | Calends | Calends |
| 2 | 4 | 4 | 6 | 4 | 6 | 4 | 6 | 4 | 4 | 6 | 4 | 4 |
| 3 | 3 | 3 | 5 | 3 | 5 | 3 | 5 | 3 | 3 | 5 | 3 | 3 |
| 4 | 2 | 2 | 4 | 2 | 4 | 2 | 4 | 2 | 2 | 4 | 2 | 2 |
| 5 | Nones | Nones | 3 | Nones | 3 | Nones | 3 | Nones | Nones | 3 | Nones | Nones |
| 6 | 8 | 8 | 2 | 8 | 2 | 8 | 2 | 8 | 8 | 2 | 8 | 8 |
| 7 | 7 | 7 | Nones | 7 | Nones | 7 | Nones | 7 | 7 | Nones | 7 | 7 |
| 8 | 6 | 6 | 8 | 6 | 8 | 6 | 8 | 6 | 6 | 8 | 6 | 6 |
| 9 | 5 | 5 | 7 | 5 | 7 | 5 | 7 | 5 | 5 | 7 | 5 | 5 |
| 10 | 4 | 4 | 6 | 4 | 6 | 4 | 6 | 4 | 4 | 6 | 4 | 4 |
| 11 | 3 | 3 | 5 | 3 | 5 | 3 | 5 | 3 | 3 | 5 | 3 | 3 |
| 12 | 2 | 2 | 4 | 2 | 4 | 2 | 4 | 2 | 2 | 4 | 2 | 2 |
| 13 | Ides | Ides | 3 | Ides | 3 | Ides | 3 | Ides | Ides | 3 | Ides | Ides |
| 14 | 17 Feb. | 16 Mar. | 2 | 17 May | 2 | 17 Jul. | 2 | 17 Sep. | 17 Oct. | 2 | 17 Dec. | 17 Jan. |
| 15 | 16 | 15 | Ides | 16 | Ides | 16 | Ides | 16 | 16 | Ides | 16 | 16 |
| 16 | 15 | 14 | 17 April | 15 | 17 June | 15 | 17 Aug. | 15 | 15 | 17 Nov. | 15 | 15 |
| 17 | 14 | 13 | 16 | 14 | 16 | 14 | 16 | 14 | 14 | 16 | 14 | 14 |
| 18 | 13 | 12 | 15 | 13 | 15 | 13 | 15 | 13 | 13 | 15 | 13 | 13 |
| 19 | 12 | 11 | 14 | 12 | 14 | 12 | 14 | 12 | 12 | 14 | 12 | 12 |
| 20 | 11 | 10 | 13 | 11 | 13 | 11 | 13 | 11 | 11 | 13 | 11 | 11 |
| 21 | 10 | 9 | 12 | 10 | 12 | 10 | 12 | 10 | 10 | 12 | 10 | 10 |
| 22 | 9 | 8 | 11 | 9 | 11 | 9 | 11 | 9 | 9 | 11 | 9 | 9 |
| 23 | 8 | 7 | 10 | 8 | 10 | 8 | 10 | 8 | 8 | 10 | 8 | 8 |
| 24 | 7 | 6 | 9 | 7 | 9 | 7 | 9 | 7 | 7 | 9 | 7 | 7 |
| 25 | 6 | 5 | 8 | 6 | 8 | 6 | 8 | 6 | 6 | 8 | 6 | 6 |
| 26 | 5 | 4 | 7 | 5 | 7 | 5 | 7 | 5 | 5 | 7 | 5 | 5 |
| 27 | 4 | 3 | 6 | 4 | 6 | 4 | 6 | 4 | 4 | 6 | 4 | 4 |
| 28 | 3 | 2 | 5 | 3 | 5 | 3 | 5 | 3 | 3 | 5 | 3 | 3 |
| 29 | 2 | | 4 | 2 | 4 | 2 | 4 | 2 | 2 | 4 | 2 | 2 |
| 30 | | | 3 | | 3 | | 3 | | | 3 | | |
| 31 | | | 2 | | 2 | | 2 | | | 2 | | |

1) The Roman lunar year had 355 days.

2) Calends are given for previous month.

> e.g. 8th Calends of February is January 23

3) The months of January, April, June, August, September, November and December each have 29 days. March, May, July, and October have 31 days. February had 28 days.

4) To keep the calendar in line with the solar year, February was shortened to 23 or 24 days and followed by an intercalary month of 27 days. This intercalation was so poorly done that by the time of Caesar, the civic year was about three months ahead of the solar year.

**Roman Julian Calendar 45 BC**

| | Jan. | Feb. | Leap Feb. | March | April | May | June | July | Aug. | Sep. | Oct. | Nov. | Dec. |
|---|---|---|---|---|---|---|---|---|---|---|---|---|---|
| | 31 | 28 | 29 | 31 | 30 | 31 | 30 | 31 | 31 | 30 | 31 | 30 | 31 |
| 1 | Calends | Calends | Calends | Calends | Calends | Calends | Calends | Calends | Calends | Calends | Calends | Calends | Calends |
| 2 | 4 | 4 | 4 | 6 | 4 | 6 | 4 | 6 | 4 | 4 | 6 | 4 | 4 |
| 3 | 3 | 3 | 3 | 5 | 3 | 5 | 3 | 5 | 3 | 3 | 5 | 3 | 3 |
| 4 | 2 | 2 | 2 | 4 | 2 | 4 | 2 | 4 | 2 | 2 | 4 | 2 | 2 |
| 5 | Nones | Nones | Nones | 3 | Nones | 3 | Nones | 3 | Nones | Nones | 3 | Nones | Nones |
| 6 | 8 | 8 | 8 | 2 | 8 | 2 | 8 | 2 | 8 | 8 | 2 | 8 | 8 |
| 7 | 7 | 7 | 7 | Nones | 7 | Nones | 7 | Nones | 7 | 7 | Nones | 7 | 7 |
| 8 | 6 | 6 | 6 | 8 | 6 | 8 | 6 | 8 | 6 | 6 | 8 | 6 | 6 |
| 9 | 5 | 5 | 5 | 7 | 5 | 7 | 5 | 7 | 5 | 5 | 7 | 5 | 5 |
| 10 | 4 | 4 | 4 | 6 | 4 | 6 | 4 | 6 | 4 | 4 | 6 | 4 | 4 |
| 11 | 3 | 3 | 3 | 5 | 3 | 5 | 3 | 5 | 3 | 3 | 5 | 3 | 3 |
| 12 | 2 | 2 | 2 | 4 | 2 | 4 | 2 | 4 | 2 | 2 | 4 | 2 | 2 |
| 13 | Ides | Ides | Ides | 3 | Ides | 3 | Ides | 3 | Ides | Ides | 3 | Ides | Ides |
| 14 | 19 Feb. | 16 Mar. | 16 Mar. | 2 | 18 May | 2 | 18 Jul. | 2 | 19 Sep. | 18 Oct. | 2 | 18 Dec. | 19 Jan. |
| 15 | 18 | 15 | 15 | Ides | 17 | Ides | 17 | Ides | 18 | 17 | Ides | 17 | 18 |
| 16 | 17 | 14 | 14 | 17 Apr. | 16 | 17 June | 16 | 17 Aug. | 17 | 16 | 17 Nov. | 16 | 17 |
| 17 | 16 | 13 | 13 | 16 | 15 | 16 | 15 | 16 | 16 | 15 | 16 | 15 | 16 |
| 18 | 15 | 12 | 12 | 15 | 14 | 15 | 14 | 15 | 15 | 14 | 15 | 14 | 15 |
| 19 | 14 | 11 | 11 | 14 | 13 | 14 | 13 | 14 | 14 | 13 | 14 | 13 | 14 |
| 20 | 13 | 10 | 10 | 13 | 12 | 13 | 12 | 13 | 13 | 12 | 13 | 12 | 13 |
| 21 | 12 | 9 | 9 | 12 | 11 | 12 | 11 | 12 | 12 | 11 | 12 | 11 | 12 |
| 22 | 11 | 8 | 8 | 11 | 10 | 11 | 10 | 11 | 11 | 10 | 11 | 10 | 11 |
| 23 | 10 | 7 | 7 | 10 | 9 | 10 | 9 | 10 | 10 | 9 | 10 | 9 | 10 |
| 24 | 9 | 6 | 6 | 9 | 8 | 9 | 8 | 9 | 9 | 8 | 9 | 8 | 9 |
| 25 | 8 | 5 | **6 | 8 | 7 | 8 | 7 | 8 | 8 | 7 | 8 | 7 | 8 |
| 26 | 7 | 4 | 5 | 7 | 6 | 7 | 6 | 7 | 7 | 6 | 7 | 6 | 7 |
| 27 | 6 | 3 | 4 | 6 | 5 | 6 | 5 | 6 | 6 | 5 | 6 | 5 | 6 |
| 28 | 5 | 2 | 3 | 5 | 4 | 5 | 4 | 5 | 5 | 4 | 5 | 4 | 5 |
| 29 | 4 | | 2 | 4 | 3 | 4 | 3 | 4 | 4 | 3 | 4 | 3 | 4 |
| 30 | 3 | | | 3 | 2 | 3 | 2 | 3 | 3 | 2 | 3 | 2 | 3 |
| 31 | 2 | | | 2 | | 2 | | 2 | 2 | | 2 | 2 | 2 |

Note:

1) From 45 BC to 9 BC, the leap year was inserted every three years instead of every four years by mistake. This added three extra days into the calendar. Augustus corrected this by omitting the leap years from 8 BC to 1 AD. This dropped the three extra days.

2) In 8 BC, Augustus took one day from February to reduce it from 29 days to 28 days and added the extra day to the sixth month on the old Roman calendar and renamed the month August, after himself. For more details, see Ussher on 5072, 5280 and 6001.

3) In this work we give both the Julian date as well as the old Roman date that used Ides, Nones, and Calends.

4) The months of January, August, and December each have 31 days and the Ides on the 13th. March, May, July, and October have 31 days and the Ides on the 15th. April, June, September, and November have 30 days and have the Ides on the 13th. In a non-leap year, February has 28 days and the Ides are on the 13th. For leap years, an extra "6th of the Calends of March" (indicated above by "**") added to February.

# Appendix B: The Forgotten Archbishop

When it comes to suggesting a date for the creation of the earth, perhaps few people have been the butt of more ridicule on the subject from sceptics than Archbishop James Ussher. It was Ussher who in the 1650s put forward the idea that this occurred on October 23, 4004 BC, and this year appeared as a marginal note in many Bibles up until about the mid-20th century. So was Ussher a wise man, a charlatan, or just naive? And what should we think about his date?

## The Scholar of Honour and Repute

James Ussher was born in Dublin, Ireland, in 1581. As a young man he resolved to devote himself wholly to the work of the Church, and the Lord honoured him in his resolve. At 18, he entered Dublin University, which was then one of the major universities. At 20, he was ordained a deacon and priest in the Anglican Church at Dublin. At 26, he was appointed chairman of the Department of Divinity at Dublin, an honour accorded to very few who were that young. He was a professor from 1607 to 1621, and was twice appointed vice-chancellor of Trinity College, Dublin.

From his early school days he excelled in history, and from the time he was 20, for the next two decades, he read every history book he could get his hands on. He excelled in church history and prepared several large authoritative works dealing with the Irish and English churches from the times of the Apostles.

In 1625, he was appointed Archbishop of Armagh, which was the highest position in the Irish Anglican Church. An expert in Semitic languages, he argued for the reliability of the Hebrew text of the Old Testament and wrote widely on Christianity in Asia, and other Bible-related topics.

In 1628, King James appointed him to his Privy Council in Ireland. He was critical of the rebellion against Charles the First. However, Cromwell, who headed the rebellion, held him in great esteem. When Ussher died, Cromwell held a magnificent funeral for him and had him buried in Westminster Abbey.

## The Only Reliable Source Document

One of Ussher's many projects was the writing, in Latin, of a complete history of the world covering every major event from the time of creation to 70 AD. He published this 1,600-page tome in Latin in 1650. An English translation was published in 1658, two years after his death. This work is fascinating to read; however, very few of us had access to it until it was republished.

In preparing this work, Ussher first made the assumption that the Bible was the only reliable source document of chronological information for the time periods covered in the Bible. In fact, before the Persian Empire, very little is known about Greek, Roman, and Egyptian history, or the history of other nations. Much rests on speculation and myths. Dates in secular history become more certain with the founding of the Media-Persian Empire.

For events before this time, Ussher relied solely on the data from the Bible to erect his historical framework. He chose the death of Nebuchadnezzar as a reliable date to anchor all the earlier biblical dates to. Hence, working backward from that date, he ended up with his date for creation of October 23, 4004 BC.

## How Did He Arrive At This Date?

Nowhere in your Bible does it say that the day was October 23. Because the Jews and many other ancient peoples started their year in the autumn, Ussher assumed there must be a good reason for it. He therefore concluded that God created the world in the autumn. After consulting astronomical tables he picked the first Sunday after the autumnal equinox.

We all know that the equinox occurs around September 21, not October 23. Well, it does now, thanks to some juggling of the calendar. In his studies, Ussher found that the ancient Jews and the Egyptians did not use a year based on the moon. Instead they had a year made up of 12 months, each 30 days long. At the end of the year they tacked on 5 days. Every 4 years they added 6 days. However, a year of 365 days is too short, and one of exactly 365.25 days is too long. You have to drop days from it to keep the seasons from drifting.

When Julius Caesar reformed the calendar, he adopted the system we now use, with 12 months of various lengths. On September 2, 1752, 11 days were dropped from the English calendar to make the seasons start when they were supposed to. Another day was dropped in 1800 and again in 1900. These years would normally have been leap years, but were made normal years to keep the calendar in line. Today we use the Gregorian calendar which is a refinement of the Julian calendar.

Before Julius Caesar's reform, no correcting adjustments were made to the calendar. For the four thousand years from Caesar's time to the time of creation almost 32 days have to be dropped to make the seasons start when they should. Hence, by making these adjustments,

Ussher arrived at the date of October 23, not September 21.

Now you ask, how did he get the year 4004 BC?

Answer: He took the chronologies in Genesis 5 and 11, together with some other Bible passages which we will look at. To simplify the calculations, we will tie the chronology to the fall of Jerusalem in 588 BC. The detailed calculations cover over 100 pages in the original document!

From Genesis 5 we get the following:

### First Genealogy — Genesis 5

| Verse | Event | Age of the Earth |
|---|---|---|
| 1:1-31 | Creation | 0 |
| 5:3 | Seth born when Adam was 130 | 130 |
| 5:6 | Enos born when Seth was 105 | 235 |
| 5:9 | Cainan born when Enos was 90 | 325 |
| 5:12 | Mahalaleel born when Cainan was 70 | 395 |
| 5:15 | Jared born when Mahalaleel was 65 | 460 |
| 5:18 | Enoch born when Jared was 162 | 622 |
| 5:21 | Methuselah born when Enoch was 65 | 687 |
| 5:25 | Lamech born when Methuselah was 187 | 874 |
| 5:28 | Noah born when Lamech was 182 | 1056 |
| 11:10 | Shem born when Noah was 502 | 1558 |
| 7:6 | Flood when Noah was 600 | 1656 |

From Genesis 11 we get:

| 11:10 | Arphaxad born when Shem was 100 | 1658 |
|---|---|---|
| 11:12 | Salah born when Arphad was 35 | 1693 |
| 11:14 | Eber born when Salah was 30 | 1723 |
| 11:16 | Peleg born when Eber was 34 | 1757 |
| 11:18 | Reu born when Peleg was 30 | 1787 |
| 11:20 | Serug born when Reu was 32 | 1819 |
| 11:22 | Nahor born when Serug was 30 | 1849 |
| 11:24 | Terah born when Nahor was 29 | 1878 |
| 11:32, 12:4 | Abraham born when Terah was 130 | 2008 |
| 12:4 | Abraham enters Canaan was 75 | 2083 |

In the Bible there are some large time periods given. These enable us to do the same calculations as Ussher, without going into all the intermediate details as he did.

### Golden Arches of Time

| | |
|---|---|
| Abraham left Haran until the Exodus, exactly 430 years to the day. (Ge 12:10, Ex 12:40, Gal 3:17) | 2513 |
| Exodus to start of Temple, 479 years (1 Ki 6:1, in the 480th year or after 479 years) | 2992 |
| Start of Temple to division of the Kingdom, 37 (Solomon reigned 40 years, 1Ki 11:42, temple started in his 4th year) | 3029 |
| Division of the Kingdom to final deportation about four years after Jerusalem fell, 390 whole years plus part of one year (Eze 4:4-6) | 3421 |
| Final deportation in 584 BC | |

Hence date creation = 584 + 3421 - 1 = 4004 BC

Now you have a rough idea of how Ussher did his calculations.

Ussher started from the Bible and not from secular history. That is why he used a date of 588 BC for the fall of Jerusalem, and not 586 BC. He noted that the fourth year of King Jehoiakim's reign corresponded to the first year of Nebuchadnezzar's reign (Jeremiah 25:1). In working through the king lists of Judah, he determined that this was in 607 BC, two years before the death of Nebuchadnezzar's father. His father died in 605 BC and many historians concluded that this was the start of Nebuchadnezzar's reign, when in fact he was already ruling as viceroy for two years. It was the normal procedure to count as the first year of the reign of a king from the year he became a viceroy. Starting from the Bible, Ussher was able to correct this error in secular history.

### So Was Ussher Right?

Ussher was neither charlatan nor naive; in fact, he was one of the most learned men of his day. Understanding the assumptions with which he began his calculations (particularly the one we should all begin with, namely that God's Word is true and reliable), we can readily understand how he arrived at his date for creation. In fact, if one assumes that there are no deliberate "jumps" or gaps in the later genealogies (for which the evidence in my view is inadequate), then his date is a perfectly reasonable deduction based on his detailed knowledge of and reverence for the Word of God.

### Astronomy and Ussher

Astrogeophysicist Dr. John Eddy, who was at the time solar astronomer at the High Altitude Observatory at Boulder, Colorado, made some revealing comments at a symposium in 1978, as reported in *Geotimes*, Vol. 23, September 1978, p. 18.

> "There is no evidence based solely on solar observations, Eddy stated, that the sun is $4.5$-$5 \times 10^9$ years old. 'I suspect,' he said, 'that the Sun is 4.5-billion years old. However, given some new and unexpected results to the contrary, and some time for frantic recalculation and theoretical readjustment, I suspect that we could live with Bishop Ussher's value for the age of the earth and sun. I don't think we have much in the way of observational evidence in astronomy to conflict with that.' "

# Appendix C: Ussher's Time Line for the Divided Kingdom

The time line for the divided kingdom has caused many problems recently for those who do not take the Bible as their final authority. This article documents this time line and points out the difficulties with it. Archaeology seems to have caused the most grief, as well-meaning individuals try to harmonize man's conjectures with the infallible Word of God.

This work is based on the Old Testament Scriptures of the Bible. Any translation that accurately translates the current Hebrew texts into English can be used. The LXX is inaccurate in many places and is unsuitable for this. Likewise, any translation that is not based on the Hebrew text but uses the Greek LXX or the Latin Vulgate suffers from the same problems. Many foreign language versions are derived from the LXX, i.e., the Russian Synodal Bible. We used the 1769 English Authorized Version in preparing this work.

We have reconstructed the king lists for the divided kingdom based on the work of James Ussher's *The Annals of the World*. We have shown all chronological data for the period of the kings as we have gleaned it from Kings, Chronicles, Isaiah, Jeremiah, Ezekiel, and Daniel. We have not knowingly omitted any passages in those books that contain chronological information. We have also documented all the supposed contradictions people have found in the chronological data and have explained them in location. Most of these disappear with an accurate reconstruction of the king lists. Only twice does there appear to be a scribal error in transmission and even these do not affect the king list chronology. The list of contradictions was taken from John Halley. (p. 396-404)

Ussher did not always state how he arrived at his findings. It was not until we broke the years down into the seasons that we were able to reproduce his findings. His untranslated Latin work called the *Sacred Chronology* holds the detailed documentation of how Ussher arrived at his results. We plan to translate the relevant portions at some future date.

## 1.0 Abbreviations

| | |
|---|---|
| SK — | Southern Kingdom |
| NK — | Northern Kingdom |
| BB — | Babylonian Kingdom |
| YDK — | Year From Division of Kingdom |
| 1Ki — | 1 Kings |
| 2Ki — | 2 Kings |
| 1Ch — | 1 Chronicles |
| 2Ch — | 2 Chronicles |
| Isa — | Isaiah |
| Jer — | Jeremiah |
| Eze — | Ezekiel |
| Da — | Daniel |

The year is divided into four parts as follows in the same way Ussher divided up the year.

| | |
|---|---|
| b — | winter |
| c — | spring and approximate start of Jewish New Year |
| d — | summer |
| a — | fall |

Jubilee years are marked and will be explained in detail in the article for the time period after the exodus. This article is already rather long.

    * — Indicates king who was murdered by his successor or forced to commit suicide to avoid being murdered by his successor. (e.g., Zimri)

    X — Indicates king who was killed but not murdered by his successor

## 2.0 Terms

The first three terms are used in explaining objections to Ussher's system and we did not otherwise use them. The three terms came from Dr. McFall.

Accession Year — This was the year a king came to the throne and was not normally considered the first year of his reign.

Accession Year System — This computes the length of a king's reign based on the number of Jewish New Years that happened during his reign. If a king reigned only a week before and a week after the New Year, he would be said to reign one year because exactly one Jewish New Year occurred in his reign. Both the Talmud and the Mishnah specify this is the normal way to calculate the length of a king's reign. This system was the normal way kings counted their years of reign. If a king had no Jewish New years in his reign, the length of his reign was normally given in months. The *Accession Year System* is also called *Postdating* by some writers.

Non-accession Year System — The remainder of the previous king's year is counted as the first year of his successor and also counted as the last year of the previous king. If a king reigned only a week before and a week after the New Year, he would be said to reign two years when using this system. This system was not normally used, so think of it as non-standard. Only when you plot out the actual reigns, can you determine if this system was used. The *Non-Accession Year System* is also called *Antedating* by some writers.

Viceregent — This is like an assistant or co-king. The regular king was still on the throne. The only example of this was Jehoram who was made viceregent sometime in the 16th year of Jehoshaphat. Jehoshaphat was preparing to help Ahab fight with the Syrians and appointed his son as caretaker while he would be away. Jehoram numbered his years of reign from this point until he was made viceroy 6 years later.

Viceroy — This position is considered to be defacto king. The viceroy's father was still alive, but the viceroy was running the kingdom. There were two reasons why a king made his son viceroy. First, the father was going to war and wanted to make sure of a smooth transition in case he was killed. Secondly, the father was in ill health and not able to manage the kingdom any more. Most viceroyships were rather short and occurred a year or so before the death of the king. According to the Talmud and the Mishnah {*see Virtual Jerusalem website*}, the viceroy always counted his first year as king when he became viceroy, not the sole king. Ussher found no exceptions to this rule. Since appointing a viceroy was usually a planned choice, the logical time to do this would be at the start of the Jewish New Year in Nisan.

## 3.0 Assumptions

1) The biblical data, not archaeological data, is the final authority. You cannot use secular dates from archaeologists to overthrow the biblical data. The terminal date for biblical chronology is 562 BC with the release of Jehoiachin and is taken from Ptolemy's king lists. {*Thiele, p. 227*} {*Jer 52:28*} This date was the anchor Ussher used for his chronology before this time. The time from creation to the release of Jehoiachin forms a continuous chronology in the Bible. If you do not agree with this assumption of *scriptura sola*, you can justify almost any reconstruction of this period.

2) The king calculated his first year at the month of Nisan (first month of the Jewish New Year in the spring), even though he may have reigned for a few months in the previous year. That is, they all used the Accession Year system. This was the rule laid down in the Talmud and the Mishnah ({*J. Halley, p. 397*}, {*Virtual Jerusalem Website*} Anstey and other chronologers cite the same rule).

Every rule has its exceptions. It seems the NK started using the Non-Accession Year system with Jeroboam and switched to the Accession Year system after Ahaziah. That is, the eight kings from Jeroboam down to Ahaziah all used the Non-Accession Year system. The subsequent kings followed in his steps until Jehoram. He started using the Accession Year system of the SK. (There is a possibility that Amaziah also used the Accession Year system. The Scriptures would allow either method. Since he was made viceroy by his father Ahab, we assume this happened on the Jewish New Year and hence the Accession method would apply to his reign.) The Accession Year system was used throughout the entire time of the SK.

3) The king counted the first year of his reign from his viceroyship. Viceroy years were assumed to start at the beginning of the Jewish New Year. Ussher found no exceptions to this rule as laid down by the Talmud and the Mishnah. {*See Virtual Jerusalem website.*}

Ahaziah (SK) {*2Ki 8:25 2Ch 22:2*} presents an interesting case which conforms to this rule although at first glance it may not seem to. Jehoram (SK) in his 7th year as king was struck with a disease that lasted two years (part of the 7th year and part of his 8th year), which eventually killed him. Likely in the 7th year Ahaziah was made viceroy because Jehoram could no longer handle the kingdom because he was quite sick. This would be after the Jewish New Year so Ahaziah would not normally consider this his first year of the kingdom until the next Jewish New Year. {*2Ki 8:25*} We are told the he became king in the 11th year of Jehoram or Joram (NK) {*2Ki 9:29*} Joram was not killed by Jehu until his 12th year so this refers to the time when Jehoram (SK) made Ahaziah viceroy. The Bible said he reigned for one year {*2Ki 8:25*} and although he reigned in part of the 11th year of Joram (NK) his first new year did not occur until the 12th year of Joram (NK).

4) The Babylonian kings counted the start of their reign like the kings of Israel and Judah, only they used the starting period of Nabonassar. This epoch started on the Wednesday evening of February 26, 747 BC. (Thiele, in an appendix to his book *Mysterious Numbers of the Hebrew Kings*, states without giving his source, that this was based on a 365-day year and would regress one day every four years. If this was so, the Babylonian New Year would be in mid-January on the Julian calendar by the time of Nebuchadnezzar. We know the Babylonians used a lunar calendar so this may introduce further uncertainty into the exact date for any given year.) The fact that the Babylonian New Year started a few weeks or months before the Jewish New Year, helps

considerably in sorting out some supposed contradictions in the biblical chronology for the period of Nebuchadnezzar.

5) Part years may be counted as full years (see Virtual Jerusalem website). You cannot impose 20th century western ideas of time-keeping on the Orientals either of today or those of 3,000 years ago. This concept manifests itself in the Non-Accession Year dating method that was initially used by the NK and never used in the SK.

6) The phrase "in the nth year of A, B began to reign" can be understood in one of two ways.

a) The nth year of A was the first year of the reign of B starting from Nisan. B actually reigned a few months before Nisan but this is not counted.

This is the most frequent situation and should be followed unless there is a good reason not to.

b) In the nth year of A was the actual time B started to reign before the month of Nisan. The first year of the reign of B would start on the following Nisan or the year n + 1 of A.

This situation was relatively rare. Ussher found this case only occurred eight times.

Asa {1Ki 15:8-10}
Jehoshaphat {1Ki 22:41,42}
Jehoram {2Ki 1:17 3:1 9:29}
Jehoash {2Ki 13:10}
Amaziah {2Ki 14:1,2 17:17}
Ahaz {2Ki 16:1,2}
Hosea {2Ki 17:1}
Hezekiah {2Ki 18:1}

This situation is normally created by the Nisan to Nisan method of computing the 1st year of a king's reign. It becomes clear when you plot the kings' reigns how this is to be interpreted in each case. If you treat this case like the first case, you will not proceed very far before you encounter a logical contradiction in calculating the king lists. For the reasons why Ussher treated these kings like this, see the Latin copy of his *Sacred Chronology*. The author is now translating this into English.

The usual meaning for the phrase *began to reign* refers to the time the king first started to rule either as sole king (if he was not appointed viceroy previously) or to the time when he was appointed as viceroy. Occasionally, it refers to the time when a king began to reign as a sole king after reigning for some months or years as viceroy. Two examples of this are Omri in 925 BC and Jeroboam in 825 BC. In both these cases the *nth year of King X* refers from the time the king first reigned as viceroy not as sole king.

### Asa

From the charts for the period of 960–946 BC, we can see that if the first Jewish New Year of Asa was the 20th year of Jeroboam, then the reign of Asa would overlap by part of a year with his father Abijam. From the passage 1Ki 15:8-10, it most likely seems that Abijam died before Asa reigned. Also if Asa started his reign a year early then Nadab would overlap the last year of his father Jeroboam. It seems unlikely that both Abijam and Jeroboam would appoint there sons a viceroys. To avoid these unlikely scenarios, it seems best to have the first partial year of Asa correspond with the 20th year of Jeroboam.

### Jehoshaphat

From the charts for the period of 915–886 BC, we can see that if the first Jewish New Year of Jehoshaphat was the 4th year of Ahab then Ahab's son, Jehoram would start his reign a year earlier and would overlap both Ahab and Ahab's son, Amaziah by a year. It is highly unlikely Ahab would appoint two son's a viceroys. The passage 2Ki 1:17 states that Jehoram reigned after the death of Amaziah, not before. Therefore, the first partial year of Jehoshaphat's reign must be noted as the 4th year of Ahab at avoid this contradiction.

### Jehoram

From the chart for the period of 900–886 BC, we can see that if the case of Jehoram was treated normally than he would have been reigning in the 22nd year of Ahab and in the second year of Azariah. It is unlikely that Ahab would appoint two son as viceroy at the same time. The passage 2Ki 1:17 states that Jehoram reigned after the death of Amaziah, not before. Therefore, the first partial year of his reign must be noted as the second year of Jehoram of Judah to avoid this contradiction.

### Jehoash

Explanation awaits the completion of the translation of Ussher's *Sacred Chronology* from the Latin.

### Amaziah

Explanation awaits the completion of the translation of Ussher's *Sacred Chronology* from the Latin.

### Ahaz

Explanation awaits the completion of the translation of Ussher's *Sacred Chronology* from the Latin.

### Hosea

If you started the reign a year earlier, Hezekiah's reign would be a year earlier, too, and you would destroy the meaning of the sign the Lord gave to Hezekiah.

### Hezekiah

If you start the actual reign of Hezekiah a year earlier you destroy the meaning of the sign God gave him in the last year of the attack by Sennacherib. {2Ch 32:22 Isa 37:31,32} The Jubilee year would have been a year later in the reign of Hezekiah and the sign would be contradicted. Hence, you must start the first partial year of Hezekiah with the 3rd year of Hoshea. See Ussher's *Annals of the World*, paragraph 673ff for more details.

### 4.0 Constraints

1) The king lists synchronise themselves at 884 BC when Jehu killed the kings of both kingdoms and the late fall of 722 BC or the winter of 721 BC when Samaria fell.

2) The two intersection points with secular history are the fall of Samaria in early 721 BC, and the death of Nebuchadnezzar in early 562 BC. The text says *at the end of three years they took it,* {2Ki 18:10} which would most likely by late winter in 721 BC or very late in the fall of 722 BC. The biblical data would favour the late winter of 721 BC but could be harmonized with the 722 BC date if there was data to establish that date.

| Southern Kingdom 975–588 BC | | |
|---|---|---|
| **Monarch** | **Viceroy** | **Sole Monarch** |
| Rehoboam | | 975–959 |
| Abijam | | 959–956 |
| Asa | | 956–915 |
| Jehoshaphat | | 915–890 |
| Jehoram | 898–890 | 890–884 |
| Ahaziah | 885–884 | 884 |
| Athaliah | | 884–878 |
| Joash | | 878–839 |
| Amaziah | 840–839 | 839–811 |
| Uzziah | | 811–759 |
| Jotham | 759 | 759–743 |
| Ahaz | | 743–727 |
| Hezekiah | 728 | 727–699 |
| Manasseh | | 699–644 |
| Amnon | | 644–642 |
| Josiah | | 642–611 |
| Jehoahaz | | 610 |
| Jehoiakim | | 610–599 |
| Jehoiachin | | 599 |
| Zedekiah | | 599–588 |

| Northern Kingdom 975–721 BC | | |
|---|---|---|
| **Monarch** | **Viceroy** | **Sole Monarch** |
| Jeroboam I | | 975–954 |
| Nadab | | 954–953 |
| Baasha | | 953–930 |
| Elah | | 930–929 |
| Zimri | | 929 |
| Tibni | | 929–925 |
| Omri | | 929–918 |
| Ahab | | 918–897 |
| Ahaziah | 898–897 | 897 |
| Jehoram | | 897–884 |
| Jehu | | 884–857 |
| Jehoahaz | | 857–840 |
| Jehoash | 842–840 | 840–826 |
| Jeroboam II | 836–826 | 826–785 |
| Interregnum | 785–773 | |
| Zachariah | | 773–772 |
| Shallum | | 772 |
| Menahem | | 772–762 |
| Pekahiah | | 762–760 |
| Pekah | | 760–740 |
| Interregnum | 740–731 | |
| Hoshea | | 731–721 |

Since the old Jewish New Year does not follow our calendar year but started normally in April, there is some leeway of about one year in the preceding tables for the dates. For example, the Bible does not tell us the exact month Rehoboam died. If he died between January and the Jewish New Year of 958 BC, then the number of his years and that of his successor's reign would still be the same as if he had died after the Jewish New Year of 959 BC and before the end of 959 BC in December. Hence, all things being equal, there is a 75% chance he died in 959 BC and about a 25% chance it was early 958 BC. Therefore, you cannot produce an absolute date for the reigns of many of the preceding kings unless the month of the king's death is known. However, the tables are an excellent guide to the approximate time each king reigned and the opening and closing date for each table is accurate while the ending date for most kings and the starting date for the next king could be the following year with a probability of 25%.

### 5.0 Alias Names for Kings

The following kings went by more than one name. The date reflects the year they started to reign.

958 BC — Abijam or Abijah (SK)
896 BC — Jehoram or Joram (NK)
878 BC — Joash or Jehoash (SK)
841 BC — Joash or Jehoash (NK)
811 BC — Uzziah or Azariah (SK)
599 BC — Jehoiachin or Jeconiah or Coniah (SK)

## 6.0 The Chronology of the Divided Kingdom

```
            1   2   3   4   5   6   7   8   9 YDK
   975 974 973 972 971 970 969 968 967 966 BC
   bcdabcdabcdabcdabcdabcdabcdabcdabcda
SK .1...2...3...4...5...6...7...8...9..10.. Rehoboam
NK  1..2...3...4...5...6...7...8...9..10.. Jeroboam
    a b         c   d
```

a) Rehoboam, at age 41, reigned for 17 years {*1Ki 14:21 2Ch 12:13*}

b) Jeroboam reigned for 22 years. {*1Ki 14:20*} He used Non-Accession Year dating. He was crowned on the 23rd of the third Jewish month called Sivan and the Jews hold a fast in memorial of this sad event. {*\*Josephus, Antiq., l. 14. c. 4. s. 3. note (a) in Whiston's translation*}

c) Rehoboam forsook God in his 3rd year. {*2Ch 11:17*}

d) Shishak invaded Judah in the 5th year of Rehoboam. {*1Ki 14:25 2Ch 12:2*}

```
           10  11  12  13  14  15  16  17  18  19 YDK
   965 964 963 962 961 960 959 958 957 956 BC
   bcdabcdabcdabcdabcdabcdabcdabcdabcda
SK 11..12..13..14..15..16..17..       Rehoboam
                        ..1...2...3.. Abijam
                                  . Asa
NK 11..12..13..14..15..16..17..18..19..20.. Jeroboam
                        a         b
```

a) In the 18th year of Jeroboam, Abijam reigned for 3 years {*1Ki 15:1,2 2Ch 13:1,2*}

b) In the 20th (24th in the LXX) year of Jeroboam, Asa reigned for 41 years. {*1Ki 15:9,10*}

```
           20  21  22  23  24  25  26  27  28  29 YDK
   955 954 953 952 951 950 949 948 947 946 BC
   bcdabcdabcdabcdabcdabcdabcdabcdabcda
SK .1..2...3...4...5...6...7...8...9..10.. Asa
             .1...2...3...4...5...6.. Asa's Peace
NK .21.22..                          Jeroboam
        1.2*                         Nadab
             1..2...3...4...5...6...7...8.. Baasha
        a  b   c
```

a1) In the 2nd year of Asa, Nadab reigned 2 years, in the last part of the 2nd year of Asa and the first part of the 3rd year of Asa. He used Non-Accession Year dating. {*1Ki 15:25*}

a2) 10th Jubilee

b) In the 3rd year of Asa, Baasha murdered Nadab and reigned for 24 years. NK used Non-Accession dating. {*1Ki 15:28,33*}

c) This was the start of 10 years of peace for Asa. {*2Ch 14:1,6,9 15:10*} The origin was determined by counting backward from {*2Ch 15:10*} which was the 15th year, 3rd month of reign of Asa.

## Problem 1:

1) Asa had 10 years of peace.

   a) Asa had 10 years of peace. {*2Ch 14:1*}

   b) There was no war until the 35th year of Asa. {*2Ch 15:19*}

2) Asa had war with Baasha all his days. {*1Ki 15:16,32*}

Resolution:

1) He likely had 10 years of relative peace with no major wars before 941 BC.

```
           30  31  32  33  34  35  36  37  38  39 YDK
   945 944 943 942 941 940 939 938 937 936 BC
   bcdabcdabcdabcdabcdabcdabcdabcdabcda
SK 11..12..13..14..15..16..17..18..19..20.. Asa
   .7...8...9..10..                    Asa's Peace
NK .9..10..11..12..13..14..15..16..17..18.. Baasha
        a  b
```

a) The invasion of Ethiopians occurred shortly before this celebration which was in the 35th year from the start of the divided kingdom. {*2Ch 15:10 15:19*} The victory celebration was in the 15th year and the 3rd month of the reign of Asa. {*2Ch 15:10*}

b) Baasha reacted to defection of his subjects to Asa and started to build Ramah in the 36th (38th in the LXX) year from the start of the divided kingdom. {*2Ch 15:9,16:1*}

## Problem 2:

1) Baasha attacked Asa in the 36th year of his reign. {*2Ch 16:1*}

2) Baasha died in the 26th year of Asa's reign.

   a) In the 3rd year of Asa, Baasha murdered Nadab and reigned for 24 years. {*1Ki 15:28,33*}

   b) Therefore he died in the 26th year of Asa.

Resolution:

1) This was in the 36th year of the divided kingdom not the 36th year of the reign of Asa. The Hebrew could be rendered either way.

```
           40  41  42  43  44  45  46  47  48  49 YDK
   935 934 933 932 931 930 929 928 927 926 BC
   bcdabcdabcdabcdabcdabcdabcdabcdabcda
SK 21..22..23..24..25..26..27..28..29..30.. Asa
NK 19..20..21..22..23..24..                Baasha
                        1.2.*              Elah
                          1                Zimri
                        1.2...3....4.      Tibni
                          1.2...3....4.. Omri
                        a  b
```

a) In the 26th (omitted by the LXX) year of Asa, Elah reigned 2 years, part of one year and part of the next year. He used Non-Accession Year dating. {1Ki 16:8}

b1) In the 27th (omitted by the LXX) year of Asa, Zimri murdered Elah and reigned 7 days and committed suicide to avoid being killed by Omri. {1Ki 16:10,15}

b2) Some of the people made Tibni king who reigned for 5 years. He used Non-Accession Year dating. {1Ki 16:21}

b3) Some of the people made Omri king who reigned for 12 years. He used Non-Accession Year dating. {1Ki 16:22}

Problem 3:

1) Baasha died in the 27th year of Asa.

   a) In the 3rd year of Asa, Baasha murdered Nadab and reigns for 24 years. {1Ki 15:28,33}

2) Baasha died in the 26th year of Asa. {1Ki 16:8}

Resolution:

1) Baasha used the Non-Accession Year dating system for calculating the years of his reign and counted the year he murdered the previous king as the first year of his reign. Normally, he should have waited until the Jewish New Year to calculate his first year.

Problem 4:

1) In the 26th year of Asa, Elah reigned for 2 years. {1Ki 16:8}

2) a. In the 26th year of Asa, Elah reigned for 2 years. {1Ki 16:8}

   b. In the 27th year of Asa, Zimri reigned for 7 days. {1Ki 16:10}

   c. Therefore Elah only reigned for one year.

(Hint: 27 - 26 = 1)

Resolution:

1) The NK used the Non-Accession dating method at this time.

Problem 5:

1) Omri started to reign in the 27th year of Asa. {1Ki 16:15-21}

2) Omri started to reign in the 31st year of Asa. {1Ki 16:23}

Resolution:

1) The first case refers to the divided reign of Omri and Tibni and the second case refers to the start of Omri's sole reign after Tibni was killed. The text hints at this {1Ki 16:23} where it says he only reigned for 6 years in Tirzah. Likely, he took a year to build Samaria after defeating Tibni and then moved into his new capital city. A king started counting his years from the year he ascended to the throne. In this case Omri was king for about 5 years before the 31st year of Asa.

```
     50  51  52  53  54  55  56  57  58  59 YDK
    925 924 923 922 921 920 919 918 917 916 BC
    bcdabcdabcdabcdabcdabcdabcdabcdabcdabcda
SK 31..32..33..34..35..36..37..38..39..40.. Asa
                                      ..1.. Asa's Disease
NK .5.*                                     Tibni
   .5...6...7..8...9..10..11..12..           Omri
                            1.2...3.. Ahab
    a                       b   c
```

a) In the 31st year of Asa, Tibni was killed and Omri reigned for 12 years starting from the time of death of Zimri and he reigned 6 years in Tirzah. {1Ki 16:22,23}

b) In the 38th year of Asa, Ahab reigned for 22 years. {1Ki 16:29} He used Non-Accession Year dating. (The LXX has 2nd year of Jehoshaphat instead of 38th year of Asa.)

c) In the 39th year of Asa, he was diseased in his feet until he died in his 41st (40th the LXX) year. {1Ki 15:23,24 2Ch 16:12,13}

```
     60  61  62  63  64  65  66  67  68  69 YDK
    915 914 913 912 911 910 909 908 907 906 BC
    bcdabcdabcdabcdabcdabcdabcdabcdabcdabcd
SK 41..                                     Asa
   .2..                                     Asa's Disease
     ..1...2...3...4...5...6...7..8...9.. Jehoshaphat
NK .4...5...6...7..8...9..10..11..12..13.. Ahab
    a       b                       c
```

a) In the 4th year of Ahab, Jehoshaphat, at age 35, reigned for 25 years. {1Ki 22:41,42 2Ch 20:31}

b) In his 3rd year, Jehoshaphat sent Levites to instruct the people. {2Ch 17:7-9}

c) The 11th Jubilee.

```
     70  71  72  73  74  75  76  77  78  79 YDK
    905 904 903 902 901 900 899 898 897 896 BC
    bcdabcdabcdabcdabcdabcdabcdabcdabcdabcda
SK 10..11..12..13..14..15..16..17..18..19.. Jehoshaphat
                            1...2...3. Jehoram
                                       Viceregent
NK 14..15..16..17..18..19..20..21..22.X Ahab
               ...1...2...3.. Peace with
                                       Syria
                            1...2.. Ahaziah
                                       Viceroy/king
                                 ..1.. Jehoram
            a       b       c       d
```

a) First Syrian invasion of NK by Benhadad. {*1Ki 20:1-25 22:1,2*}

b1) Second invasion by Benhadad about a year later. {*1Ki 20:26*}

b2) There were 3 years of peace with Syria ending with Ahab's death. {*1Ki 22:1,2*}

c1) a. In the 18th year of Jehoshaphat, Jehoram (NK) reigned for 12 years. {*2Ki 3:1*}

b. In the 2nd year of Jehoram (SK), Jehoram (NK) started to reign. {*2Ki 1:17*} This was the 18th year of Jehoshaphat in the LXX where the verse is 18 not 17.

c. Therefore, Jehoram (SK), became viceregent in the 17th year of Jehoshaphat. Jehoshaphat was preparing for war with Ahab against Syria and appointed his son as viceregent for that time. (Hint: 18 - 2 + 1 = 17)

c2) In the 17th year of Jehoshaphat, Amaziah reigned as viceroy for 2 years. Amaziah reigned for part of one and part of the next year. If Ahab appointed him viceroy on the Jewish New Year then Amaziah used Accession Year dating. If he was made viceroy after the New Year then Amaziah used Non-Accession Year dating. Both possibilities exist and are agreeable to the Scriptures. Both Jehoshaphat and Ahab planned to fight with Syria and left their sons in charge lest any misfortune overtook them. This was a prudent precaution. {*1Ki 22:51 2Ki 3:1*}

d) a. In the 18th year of Jehoshaphat, Jehoram (NK) reigned for 12 years. {*2Ki 3:1*}

b. In the 2nd year of Jehoram's viceregency (SK), Jehoram (NK) started to reign. {*2Ki 1:17*} NK used Accession dating starting with this king until the fall of the NK.

Problem 6:

1) a. In the 17th year of Jehoshaphat, Amaziah (NK) reigned for 2 years. {*1Ki 22:51*}

b. Therefore Ahab must have died in the 17th year of Jehoshaphat.

2) a. Ahab became king in the 38th year of Asa and reigned for 22 years. {*1Ki 16:29*}

b. Jehoshaphat became king in the 4th year of Ahab. {*1Ki 22:41*}

c. Therefore Ahab died in 18th year of Jehoshaphat. (Hint: 22 - 4 = 18)

Resolution:

1) The first case refers to the time when Ahab made Amaziah viceroy before going to fight with the Syrians. Both the father and son died in the 18th year of Jehoshaphat, the father by the Syrians and the son by a disease.

Problem 7:

1) Jehoram (NK) began to reign in the 2nd year of Jehoram (SK). {*2Ki 1:17*}

2) Jehoram (SK) began to reign in the 5th year of Jehoram of Israel. {*2Ki 8:16,17*}

Resolution:

1) The first case refers from the time when Jehoram (SK) was made viceregent and the second case refers to the time when he was made viceroy by Jehoshaphat. It appears the years of the king's reign were counted either from the time he became viceregent or viceroy. See discussion for "Viceregent" under "Terms" as well as under point E in this section.

```
    80   81   82   83   84   85   86   87   88   89 YDK
   895  894  893  892  891  890  889  888  887  886 BC
   bcdabcdabcdabcdabcdabcdabcdabcdabcdabcda
SK 20..21..22..23..24..25..                        Jehoshaphat
   .4...5...6...                                    Jehoram
                                                    Viceregent
          1...2...3...4...5...6...7..               Jehoram
                                                    Viceroy/king
                                     .. Jehoram's
                                        Disease
                                     .. Ahaziah
                                        Viceroy
NK .2...3...4...5...6...7..8...9..10..11.. Jehoram
                 a                   b   c
```

a) In the 5th year of Jehoram (NK), Jehoram (SK) at age 32 reigned for 8 years. This was a unique case in the chronology and neither the Bible nor the Talmud shed any light on how to handle it. This was the only time when a viceregent became a viceroy. From the chart we see that Jehoshaphat made him viceroy at the beginning of his 23rd year of his reign and he was viceroy until Jehoshaphat died about 3 years later. {*2Ki 8:16,17 2Ch 21:2,3,5,20*}

b) Jehoram was diseased in his bowels for two years before he died after reigning for 8 years. {*2Ch 21:18-20*}

c) In the 11th year of Joram, Amaziah was made viceroy, likely because of Jehoram's disease which he contracted the previous year. {*See a1 under 885 BC.*} {*2Ki 9:29*}

```
     90  91  92  93  94  95  96  97  98  99 YDK
    885 884 883 882 881 880 879 878 877 876 BC
   bcdabcdabcdabcdabcdabcdabcdabcdabcdabcda
SK .8...                                    Jehoram
   .1...                                    Jehoram's Disease
   .1..X                                    Ahaziah
     .1..2...3...4...5...6...7*             Athaliah
                             1...2...3..    Joash
NK 12..*                                    Jehoram
   .1..2...3...4...5...6...7...8...9..      Jehu
      a                       b
```

```
    100 101 102 103 104 105 106 107 108 109 YDK
    875 874 873 872 871 870 869 868 867 866 BC
   bcdabcdabcdabcdabcdabcdabcdabcdabcdabcda
SK .4...5...6...7...8...9..10..11..12..13.. Joash
NK 10..11..12..13..14..15..16..17..18..19.. Jehu

    110 111 112 113 114 115 116 117 118 119 YDK
    865 864 863 862 861 860 859 858 857 856 BC
   bcdabcdabcdabcdabcdabcdabcdabcdabcdabcda
SK 14..15..16..17..18..19..20..21..22..23.. Joash
NK 20..21..22..23..24..25..26..27..28..     Jehu
                               .1.. Jehoahaz
                               ab c
```

a1) In the 12th year of Jehoram (NK), Ahaziah, at 22 years of age, reigned for part of a year. {2Ki 8:25,26 2Ch 22:2} He had already been viceroy so when the Jewish New Year came he started his first year of his reign. In {2Ch 22:2} his age is given as 42 and as 20 in the LXX.

a2) Jehu killed Jehoram (NK). {2Ki 9:24,25}

a3) Jehu killed Ahaziah (SK). {2Ki 9:27}

a4) Athaliah reigned over Judah for 6 years and was killed in her 7th year. (LXX — 8th year — {2Ch 23:1} and in {2Ki 11:4 2Ch 24:1} it is the 7th year!) {2Ki 11:3,4,16 2Ch 22:12 23:1,15}

a5) Jehu killed Joram (Jehoram (NK)) and reigned in Israel for 28 years. {2Ki 9:14,10:36}

b) Athaliah was murdered and Joash, at age 7, reigned for 40 years.

Problem 8:

1) Ahaziah was 22 years old when he became king. {2Ki 8:26}

2) Ahaziah was 42 years old when he became king. {2Ch 22:2}

Resolution:

1) The writer was referring to his age from when Omri became king.

2) There was a scribal error confusing Hebrew letter KAHF (number 20) for the letter MEM (number 40). This is the most likely explanation.

This does not alter the chronology.

Problem 9:

1) Ahaziah became king in the 11th year of Joram. {2Ki 9:29}

2) Ahaziah became king in the 12th year of Joram. {2Ki 8:25}

Resolution:

1) He became viceroy in the 11th year and king in the 12th year. Judah's King Jehoram was not a well man. See point 3 under assumptions for a fuller treatment of this case.

a) In the 23rd year of Joash, Jehoahaz reigned for 17 years over Israel. {2Ki 13:1}

b) The 12th Jubilee.

c) Joash repaired the temple in his 23rd year. {2Ki 12:6}

Problem 10:

1) Jehoahaz's reign started in the 23rd year of Joash. {2Ki 13:1}

2) Jehoahaz's reign started in the 22nd year of Joash.

a) Jehu reigned for 28 years. {2Ki 10:36}

b) In the 7th year of Jehu, Joash reigned for 40 years. {2Ki 12:1}

c) Jehu died in the 22nd year of Joash. (Hint: 28 - 7 + 1 = 22)

d) Therefore Jehoahaz's reign started in the 22nd year of Joash.

Resolution:

1) According to the rules for Accession dating, when Athaliah was executed on the Jewish New Year then she would have been reckoned to have reigned a whole year instead of just part of the first day of that new year. Likewise Joash would reckon this the first year of his reign since he also reigned on the first day of that Jewish New Year. Otherwise if Athaliah was killed after the Jewish New Year then Joash would have to use Non-Accession dating to remove this contradiction. This would have been the only time in the entire SK that Non-Accession dating was used which is most unlikely. What better time to put an end to Athaliah's wickedness and start fresh than on the Jewish New Year? Also, since that new year was on Friday, April 21, there would be a double cohort of priests available to better effect the coup, the outgoing cohort whose service would end the next day and the incoming cohort whose service would begin on the next day which was the sabbath. Hence this would make Jehoahaz start to rule in the 23rd not the 22nd year of Joash.

```
    120 121 122 123 124 125 126 127 128 129 YDK
    855 854 853 852 851 850 849 848 847 846 BC
    bcdabcdabcdabcdabcdabcdabcdabcdabcdabcda
SK 24..25..26..27..28..29..30..31..32..33.. Joash
NK .2...3...4...5...6...7...8...9..10..11.. Jehoahaz

    130 131 132 133 134 135 136 137 138 139 YDK
    845 844 843 842 841 840 839 838 837 836 BC
    bcdabcdabcdabcdabcdabcdabcdabcdabcdabcda
SK 34..35..36..37..38..39..40.X              Joash
                    ..1...2...3...4..         Amaziah
NK 12..13..14..15..16..17                    Jehoahaz
                    ..1...2...3..4...5...6..  Jehoash
                                        1..  Jeroboam II
                                             (Viceroy)
                a           b          c
```

a) In the 37th year of Joash, Jehoash was made vice-roy for 2 years, and reigned for 16 years. {2Ki 13:10}

b) In the 2nd year of Jehoash, Amaziah, at age 25, was made viceroy and then king for 29 years. {2Ki 14:1,2 2Ch 25:1}

c) In the 15th year of Amaziah, Jeroboam II began to reign as sole king for 41 years. {2Ki 14:23} However, in {2Ki 15:1} we find that Uzziah became the king in the 27th year of Jeroboam. To reconcile this we must assume that Jeroboam was made vice-roy for 12 years in the 4th year of Amaziah or in the 6th year of Jeroboam's father, Jehoash. (Josephus gave a similar explanation. {Josephus, Antiq., l. 9. c. 10. s. 3. (215,216) 6:113,115}) In {2Ki 13:25} we read that Jehoash fought and won three battles with the Syrians. We are not told when these battles were fought but it may be after the time Jeroboam was made viceroy. Jehoash likely appointed Jeroboam as viceroy before fighting these major battles with an enemy that had beaten Israel before, and had killed a king of Israel in a previous battle. This would explain the long overlap in the reigns be-tween the father and the son. In spite of Elisha's promises of victory {2Ki 13:19}, Jehoash wanted to be careful just in case Elisha was wrong. The his-tory of the Northern Kingdom was not noted for a smooth transition of power when a king died. Ahab appointed his son as viceroy before he went to fight with the Syrians, as did Jehoshaphat who accompanied Ahab in the battle with the Syrians.

Another explanation of this has been given by Lightfoot and others. They think Uzziah reigned in the 27th year of Jeroboam and Jeroboam was not a viceroy with his father. This would create an interregnum in the SK of 13 or so years, thus ex-tending the entire period of the divided kingdom by that much time to about 403 years. This is most unlikely, since the SK was politically very stable at this time, unlike the NK.

Problem 11:

1) Jehoash began to reign in the 37th year of Joash. {2Ki 13:10}

2) a. In the 23rd year of Joash (SK), Jehoahaz reigned for 17 years. {2Ki 13:1}

   b. Therefore Jehoash began to reign in the 39th or 40th year of Joash. (Hint: 23 + 17 = 40 or 23 + 17 - 1 = 39)

Resolution:

1) Jehoash was made viceroy in the 37th year of Joash. You cannot assume he started to reign after the death of Jehoahaz without creating a logical contradiction.

Problem 12:

1) In the 23rd year of Joash (SK), Jehoahaz's reign lasted 17 years. {2Ki 13:1}

2) a. In the 23rd year of Joash (SK), Jehoahaz reigned in the NK. {2Ki 13:1}

   b. In the 37th year of Joash (SK), Jehoash reigned in the NK. {2Ki 13:10}

   c. Therefore, Jehoahaz's reign lasted 15 years. (Hint: 37 - 23 + 1 = 15)

Resolution:

1) Jehoash was made viceroy for 2 years by Jehoahaz.

```
    140 141 142 143 144 145 146 147 148 149 YDK
    835 834 833 832 831 830 829 828 827 826 BC
    bcdabcdabcdabcdabcdabcdabcdabcdabcdabcda
SK .5...6...7...8...9..10..11..12..13..14.. Amaziah
NK .7...8...9..10..11..12..13..14..15..16.. Jehoash
    .2...3...4...5...6...7...8...9..10..11.. Jeroboam II
                                             (Viceroy)
                                          . Jeroboam II
                                             (Sole King)
                                          a
```

a) In the 15th year of Amaziah, Jeroboam II began to reign as sole king for 41 years. {2Ki 14:23} Uzziah's ascension date started from time Jeroboam became viceroy not when he became sole king.

Problem 13:

1) a. Jehu reigned for 28 years. {2Ki 10:36}

   b. In the 7th year of Jehu, Joash became king and reigned for 40 years. {2Ki 12:1}

   c. Therefore, Amaziah reigned in the 47th year from the start of Jehu's reign. (Hint: 40 + 7 = 47)

2) a. Jehu reigned for 28 years. {2Ki 10:36}

    b. In the 23rd year of Joash, Jehoahaz became king and reigned 17 years. {2Ki 13:10}

    c. Amaziah started to reign in the 2nd year of Jehoahaz. {2Ki 14:1}

    d. Therefore the start of Amaziah's reign in 49th year from the start of Jehu's reign which would be the 4th year of Jehoahaz. (Hint: 7 + 23 + 17 + 2 = 49)

Resolution:

1) a. Joash counted the year he became king as his first year since he was crowned on the first day of the Jewish New Year. This is in accord with the Accession System. This accounts for one year of the difference. This reduces both totals by one to 46 from 47 and 48 from 49.

    b. Jehoahaz made Jehoash viceroy for 2 years. This subtracts 2 years from the second total of 49, making it 47.

    c. Therefore, the correct total of years for this period when one considers the year a king became king and viceroy relationships is 47 years.

This supposed contradiction was most involved and we are surprised anyone found it!

```
     150 151 152 153 154 155 156 157 158 159 YDK
     825 824 823 820 819 818 817 816 BC
     bcdabcdabcdabcdabcdabcdabcdabcdabcdabcda
SK  15..16..17..18..19..20..21..22..23..24.. Amaziah
    .1...2...3...4...5...6...7...8...9..10.. To Death of
                                             Amaziah
NK  12..13..14..15..16..17..18..19..20..21.. Jeroboam II
                                             (Viceroy)
    .1...2...3...4...5...6...7...8...9..10.. Jeroboam II
                                             (Sole King)
a
```

a1) In the 15th year of Amaziah, Jeroboam II reigned as sole king for 41 years after the death of his father, Jehoash who died the same year. {2Ki 14:23}

a2) Amaziah lived for 15 years after the death of Jehoash. {2Ki 14:17,23 2Ch 25:25}

```
     160 161 162 163 164 165 166 167 168 169 YDK
     815 814 813 812 811 810 809 808 807 806 BC
     bcdabcdabcdabcdabcdabcdabcdabcdabcdabcda
SK  25..26..27..28..29..                     Amaziah
    11..12..13..14..15..                     To Death of
                                             Amaziah
                      ..1...2...3...4...5.. Uzziah
NK  22..23..24..25..26..27..28..29..30..31.. Jeroboam II
                                             (Viceroy)
    11..12..13..14..15..16..17..18..19..20.. Jeroboam II
                                             (Sole King)
              a              b
```

a) In the 27th year from the viceroyship of Jeroboam II, Uzziah, at age 16 began to reign for 52 years. This corresponds to the 15th year of Jeroboam II reigning as sole king. {2Ki 15:1,2 2Ch 26:3}

b) The 13th Jubilee.

```
     170 171 172 173 174 175 176 177 178 179 YDK
     805 804 803 802 801 790 799 798 797 796 BC
     bcdabcdabcdabcdabcdabcdabcdabcdabcdabcda
SK  .6...7...8...9..10..11..12..13..14..15.. Uzziah
NK  32..33..34..35..36..37..38..39..40..41.. Jeroboam II
                                             (Viceroy)
    21..22..23..24..25..26..27..28..29..30.. Jeroboam II
                                             (Sole king)
```

**Problem 14:**

1) The first year of Uzziah's reign was the 27th year of Jeroboam II. {2Ki 15:1}

2) a. Amaziah reigned for 29 years. {2Ki 14:2}

    b. Amaziah lived 15 years after the death of Jehoash (NK). {2Ki 14:17}

    c. In the 15th year of Amaziah, Jeroboam II became king. {2Ki 14:23}

    d. Therefore, Uzziah's first year of his reign was the 16th year of Jeroboam II. (Hint: 29 + 1 - 15 = 15)

Resolution:

1) Jeroboam became viceroy likely when his father went to fight the Syrians in 836 BC. The first case refers to the time from his viceroyship, whereas the second case is dated from the time he became sole king. The Talmudic rule is that a king's first year always began with his first year as viceroy not as sole king.

**Problem 15:**

1) a. In the 15th year of Amaziah, Jeroboam II became king and reigned for 41 years. {2Ki 14:23}

    b. In the 27th year of Jeroboam II, Uzziah became king. {2Ki 15:1}

    c. Therefore, Jeroboam was contemporary with Uzziah for 14 years. (Hint: 41 - 27 + 1 = 15)

2) a. Jeroboam II died in the 38th year of Uzziah when Zachariah became king. {2Ki 15:8}

    b. Therefore Jeroboam was contemporary with Uzziah for 38 years.

Resolution:

1) Same resolution as the previous problem. In case 2 it is incorrect to assume that Zachariah became king the same year as Jeroboam II's

death, for Jeroboam II died in the 26th year of Uzziah, about 12 years earlier. There was an interregnum of about 12 years before Zachariah came to the throne.

```
 180 181 182 183 184 185 186 187 188 189 YDK
 795 794 793 792 791 790 789 788 787 786 BC
 bcdabcdabcdabcdabcdabcdabcdabcdabcda
SK 16..17..18..19..20..21..22..23..24..25.. Uzziah
NK 42..43..44..45..46..47..48..49..50..51.. Jeroboam II
                                            (Viceroy)
   31..32..33..34..35..36..37..38..39..40.. Jeroboam II
                                            (Sole King)
```

```
 190 191 192 193 194 195 196 197 198 199 YDK
 785 784 783 782 781 780 779 778 777 776 BC
 bcdabcdabcdabcdabcdabcdabcdabcdabcda
SK 26..27..28..29..30..31..32..33..34..35.. Uzziah
NK 52..                                     Jeroboam II
                                            (Viceroy)
   41..                                     Jeroboam II
                                            (Sole King)
   ..1...2...3...4...5...6...7...8...9.. Interregnum
   a
```

a) There is no king mentioned who reigned in the Northern Kingdom during this period of about 12 years. {2Ki 14:23 15:8}

```
 200 201 202 203 204 205 206 207 208 209 YDK
 775 774 773 772 771 770 769 768 767 766 BC
 bcdabcdabcdabcdabcdabcdabcdabcdabcda
SK 36..37..38..39..40..41..42..43..44..45.. Uzziah
NK 10..11..12.                              Interregnum
          .*                                Zachariah
           *                                Shallum
           ...1...2...3...4...5...6.. Menahem
          a bc
```

a) In the last 6 months of Uzziah's 38th year, Zachariah reigned for 6 months. {2Ki 15:8} We assumed it was the last 6 months for sake of argument. Any 6 month period that started in Uzziah's 38th year and ended in Nisan or later in Uzziah's 39th year would also work.

b) In the 39th year of Uzziah, Shallum murdered Zachariah and reigned one month. {2Ki 15:13}

c) Menahem murdered Shallum and reigned 10 years. This illustrates the Nisan to Nisan rule. Although he started to rule in the 2nd month of the 39th year of Uzziah, his first year was not counted until the 40th year. He really reigned more than 10 whole years but using the Nisan to Nisan method, his reign is given as 10 years only and the months he reigned in the 39th year of Uzziah are not counted. {2Ki 15:13,17}

```
 210 211 212 213 214 215 216 217 218 219 YDK
 765 764 763 762 761 760 759 758 757 756 BC
 bcdabcdabcdabcdabcdabcdabcdabcdabcda
SK 46..47..48..49..50..51..52..              Uzziah
               ..1...2...3.. Jotham
NK .7...8...9...10..                         Menahem
          ..1...2.*                          Pekahiah
            ..1...2...3...4.. Pekah
          a       b c d
```

a) In the 50th year of Uzziah, Pekahiah reigned for 2 years. {2Ki 15:23}

b) In the 52nd year of Uzziah, Pekah murdered Pekahiah and reigned for 20 years. {2Ki 15:27}

c) The 14th Jubilee.

d) In the 2nd year of Pekah, Jotham, at age 25, reigned for 16 years. {2Ki 15:32, 2Ch 27:1,8} Jewish tradition stated that Uzziah was smitten with leprosy in the last few months of his life and Jotham reigned as viceroy during that time. They placed this event at the same time Isaiah {Isa 6:4} had his vision of the Lord. The text said the posts of the temple moved when the Lord spoke. Josephus stated that an earthquake occurred and the temple's holy of holies was rent allowing light to enter when Uzziah was in it offering his sacrifice. His account of the earthquake is a little hard to believe. He said that half the mountain near Eroge, was rolled half a mile by the earthquake. If this was the case, we think all of Jerusalem would have been flattened by the force of the quake. In Amos {Am 1:1} a memorable earthquake is mentioned. According to Ussher's chronology, this would have been about 25 years earlier when the kings that were mentioned in that verse were still alive. Earthquakes in Judea are quite common. {Josephus, Antiquities, l. 9. c. 10. s. 2. (225-227) 6:119,121} {Gill's Expositor, on Isaiah 6:4, Amos 1:1} The *Assyrian Eponym List* record two earthquakes (they were called plagues), one in 765 BC and one in 759 BC. The latter earthquake coincided with the death of Uzziah and was likely the earthquake mentioned by Josephus. {Dorothy Bone, p. 204,205}

```
 220 221 222 223 224 225 226 227 228 229 YDK
 755 754 753 752 751 750 749 748 747 746 BC
 bcdabcdabcdabcdabcdabcdabcdabcdabcda
SK .4...5...6...7...8...9..10..11..12..13.. Jotham
NK .5...6...7...8...9..10..11..12..13..14.. Pekah
```

```
 230 231 232 233 234 235 236 237 238 239 YDK
 745 744 743 742 741 740 739 738 737 736 BC
 bcdabcdabcdabcdabcdabcdabcdabcdabcda
SK 14..15..16..                             Jotham
          ..1...2...3...4...5...6...7.. Ahaz
          ..1...2...3...4...5...6.. Isaiah's
                                            Prophecy
NK 15..16..17..18..19..20.*                 Pekah
               ..1...2...3...4.. Interregnum
          a     b       c
```

a) In the 17th year of Pekah, Ahaz, at age 20, reigned for 16 years. {2Ki 16:1,2, 2Ch 28:1}

b) In the first year of Ahaz, Isaiah predicted the final and utter destruction of the Northern Kingdom in 65 years. {Isa 7:8,9}

c) There was no king mentioned in the Northern Kingdom who reigned during this period. Hoshea murdered Pekah but was unable to gain control of the kingdom. {2Ki 15:27,30 17:1}

Problem 16:

1) Hoshea started to reign in the 20th year of Jotham. {2Ki 15:30}

2) Jotham only reigned 16 years. {2Ki 15:33}

Resolution:

1) This was an unusual way of reckoning. For some reason, Ahaz was ignored in Judah's king list (maybe because he was so wicked), and the time was calculated from the start of Jotham's reign.

2) Jotham may have turned the kingdom entirely over to his son in the 16th year of his reign and retired from public affairs and lived 4 more years. He would have died in the 20th year from the time he became king.

Problem 17:

1) In the 20th year of Jotham (4th year of Ahaz), Hoshea killed Pekah and became king. {2Ki 15:30}

2) Hoshea started to reign in the 12th year of Ahaz. {2Ki 17:1}

Resolution:

1) Unless we had the text for the second point we would normally assume Hoshea reigned directly after the death of Pekah. This text said that Hoshea began to reign in the 12th year of Ahaz. Hence, we deduce that there was an interregnum of 9 years when there was no king. This interpretation does no violence to the Hebrew text. The text for the first point stated he "reigned in his stead." The text for the second case clarifies the first and stated that he "began...to reign" in the 12th year of Ahaz.

```
     240 241 242 243 244 245 246 247 248 249 YDK
     735 734 733 732 731 730 729 728 727 726 BC
     bcdabcdabcdabcdabcdabcdabcdabcdabcdabcda
SK   .8...9..10..11..12..13..14..15..16..    Ahaz
     .7...8...9..10..11..12..13..14..15..16  Isaiah's Prophecy
                               ..1...2..     Hezekiah
NK   .5...6...7...8...9..                     Interregnum
                     ..1...2...3...4...5.    Hoshea
                     a           b   c
```

a) In the 12th year of Ahaz, Hosea reigned for 9 years. {2Ki 17:1}

b) In the 3rd year of Hoshea, while Ahaz was still alive, Hezekiah, at age 25, was made viceroy then king after the death of Ahaz. He reigned for 29 years. {2Ki 18:1,2 2Ch 29:1}

c) Hezekiah repaired the temple in the first month of the first year of his reign. {2Ch 29:3}

Problem 18:

1) Hezekiah started to reign at age 25. {2Ki 18:2}

2) Ahaz, his father died at age 36. {2Ki 16:2}

Resolution:

1) It is not medically impossible for an eleven year old to sire a child. There are documented cases where ten-year-old children have done this.

2) There was an error in the age of his father.

```
     250 251 252 253 254 255 256 257 258 259 YDK
     725 724 723 722 721 720 719 718 717 716 BC
     bcdabcdabcdabcdabcdabcdabcdabcdabcdabcda
SK   17..18..19..20..21..22..23..24..25..26..  Isaiah's Prophecy
     .3...4...5...6...7...8...9..10..11..12..   Hezekiah
NK   .6...7...8...9...                          Hoshea
          a           b
```

a) In the 4th year of Hezekiah and in the 7th year of Hoshea, Assyria attacked the Northern Kingdom and besieged Samaria for 3 years. {2Ki 17:5 18:9}

b) In the 9th year of Hoshea and the 6th year of Hezekiah, the Assyrians captured the Northern Kingdom. This is toward the end of the 3rd year of the siege in early 721 BC. {2Ki 17:6 18:10}

```
     260 261 262 263 264 265 266 267 268 269 YDK
     715 714 713 712 711 710 709 708 707 706 BC
     bcdabcdabcdabcdabcdabcdabcdabcdabcdabcda
SK   27..28..29..30..31..32..33..34..35..36..  Isaiah's Prophecy
     13..14..15..16..17..18..19..20..21..22..   Hezekiah
         .1...2...3..                           Sennacherib's War
         a b         cde
```

a) In the 14th year of Hezekiah, Sennacherib attacked Hezekiah. {2Ki 18:13, Isa 36:1} This war on Egypt and Judea lasted three whole years. {Isa 20:3} It appears Sennacherib launched his initial attack on Hezekiah and then went and fought in Egypt for 3 years and then returned to finish off Hezekiah.

b) a. Hezekiah reigned for 29 years. {2Ki 18:1,2 2Ch 29:1}

b. 15 years were added to Hezekiah's life. {2Ki 20:6, Isa 38:5}

c. Therefore his life was extended in the 15th year of Hezekiah. (Hint: 29 + 1 - 15 = 15)

c) Sennacherib abandons attack on Hezekiah, returns to Assyria, and is killed by his sons. {2Ki 19:37} This was likely 55 days after his return to Assyria. {1APC Tob 1:21}

d) Manasseh born, 3 years after Hezekiah's life was lengthened and 12 years before his death. {2Ki 21:1}

e) The 15th Jubilee.

```
    270 271 272 273 274 275 276 277 278 279 YDK
    705 704 703 702 701 700 699 698 697 696 BC
    bcdabcdabcdabcdabcdabcdabcdabcdabcdabcda
SK 23..24..25..26..27..28..29.         Hezekiah
   37..38..39..40..41..42..43..44..45..46.. Isaiah's Prophecy
                                 ..1...2...3.. Manasseh
                                        a
```

a) Manasseh, at age 12, reigned for 55 years. {2Ki 21:1 2Ch 33:1}

```
    280 281 282 283 284 285 286 287 288 289 YDK
    695 694 693 692 691 690 689 688 687 686 BC
    bcdabcdabcdabcdabcdabcdabcdabcdabcdabcda
SK 47..48..49..50..51..52..53..54..55..56.. Isaiah's Prophecy
   .4...5...6...7...8...9..10..11..12..13.. Manasseh
```

```
    290 291 292 293 294 295 296 297 298 299 YDK
    685 684 683 682 681 680 679 678 677 676 BC
    bcdabcdabcdabcdabcdabcdabcdabcdabcdabcda
SK 57..58..59..60..61..62..63..64..65.     Isaiah's Prophecy
   14..15..16..17..18..19..20..21..22..23.. Manasseh
                                         a
```

a) In the 1st year of Ahaz's reign, Isaiah predicted that in 65 years, the Northern Kingdom would be completely destroyed. This final destruction of the Northern Kingdom happened 65 years later by Esarhaddon. {Isa 7:8,9 2Ki 17:24} Tradition states that this was the time Manasseh was deported to Babylon. His captivity must have been brief since the Scriptures take no notice of it. {2Ch 33:11} {See Gill's Expositor on "Isa 7:8"}

```
    300 301 302 303 304 305 306 307 308 309 YDK
    675 674 673 672 671 670 669 668 667 666 BC
    bcdabcdabcdabcdabcdabcdabcdabcdabcdabcda
SK 24..25..26..27..28..29..30..31..32..33.. Manasseh
```

```
    310 311 312 313 314 315 316 317 318 319 YDK
    665 664 663 662 661 660 659 658 657 656 BC
    bcdabcdabcdabcdabcdabcdabcdabcdabcdabcda
SK 34..35..36..37..38..39..40..41..42..43.. Manasseh
                                         a
```

a) The 16th Jubilee.

```
    320 321 322 323 324 325 326 327 328 329 YDK
    655 654 653 652 651 650 649 648 647 646 BC
    bcdabcdabcdabcdabcdabcdabcdabcdabcdabcda
SK 44..45..46..47..48..49..50..51..52..53.. Manasseh
```

```
    330 331 332 333 334 335 336 337 338 339 YDK
    645 644 643 642 641 640 639 638 637 636 BC
    bcdabcdabcdabcdabcdabcdabcdabcdabcdabcda
SK 54..55..                            Manasseh
   ..1...2.X                           Amnon
         ..1...2...3...4...5...6..      Josiah
     a      b
```

a) Amnon, at age 22, reigned 2 years and was murdered by his subjects. {2Ki 21:19 2Ch 33:21}

b) Josiah, at age 8, reigned 31 years, then died in a battle with Egyptians. {2Ki 22:1,23:29 2Ch 34:1}

```
    340 341 342 343 344 345 346 347 348 349 YDK
    635 634 633 632 631 630 629 628 627 626 BC
    bcdabcdabcdabcdabcdabcdabcdabcdabcdabcda
SK .7...8...9..10..11..12..13..14..15..16.. Josiah
                  1...2...3...4.. Jeremiah's
                                   Prophecy
     a            b c
```

a) In his 8th year, Josiah sought the Lord. {2Ch 34:3}

b) In his 12th year, Josiah started to clean up Judah of idols. {2Ch 34:3}

c) From the 13th year of Josiah until the 4th year of Jehoiakim was 23 years. This time period may have started with Josiah's great cleanup of the land. {Jer 1:2 25:1,3}

```
    350 351 352 353 354 355 356 357 358 359 YDK
    625 624 623 622 621 620 619 618 617 616 BC
    bcdabcdabcdabcdabcdabcdabcdabcdabcdabcda
SK 17..18..19..20..21..22..23..24..25..26.. Josiah
   .5...6...7...8...9..10..11..12..13..14.. Jeremiah's
                                            Prophecy
     1...2...3...4...5...6...7...8...9.. Ezekiel's Prophecy
       .1...2...3...4...5...6...7...8.. Judah's Apostasy
     a b
```

a1) In the 18th year of Josiah, the great passover was held. {2Ki 22:3 23:23 2Ch 34:8 35:19}

a2) From the great passover until the 5th year of Jehoiachin's captivity, was 30 years. {Eze 1:1}

b) This marks the beginning of the 40 years of Judah's apostasy. After the mountain top experience of the Great Passover, Judah's religious life went downhill for 40 years until the last of them were deported from the land. {Eze 4:6 Jer 52:30}

The 23-year time period given by Jeremiah and the 30-year time period given for Ezekiel spanned the reign of several kings. These served as an independent check on the procedure used to calculate this chronology. If Ussher had not followed the Talmudic rules, these two confirmations would not have occurred.

```
    360 361 362 363 364 365 366 367 368 369 YDK
    615 614 613 612 611 610 609 608 607 606 BC
    bcdabcdabcdabcdabcdabcdabcdabcdabcdabcda
SK 27..28..29..30..31..                  Josiah
   15..16..17..18..19..20..21..22..23     Jeremiah's
                                          Prophecy
   10..11..12..13..14..15..16..17..18..19.. Ezekiel's Prophecy
                          .                 Jehoahaz
                          1...2...3...4...5.. Jehoiakim
   .9..10..11..12..13..14..15..16..17..18.. Judah's Apostasy
                              ....1... Nebuchadnezzar
BB
                    a     bc     de
```

a) The 17th Jubilee.

b) Jehoahaz, at age 23, reigned three months. {2Ki 23:31 2Ch 36:2}

c) Jehoiakim at age 25, reigned for 11 years. {2Ki 23:36 2Ch 36:5}

d) Nebuchadnezzar was made viceroy in 607 BC just after the Babylonian New Year. He become sole king after the death of his father in 605 BC. If Nebuchadnezzar attacked Jerusalem in mid-February he would be in the third year of Jehoiakim's reign. If he captured it in the month Nisan a few weeks later, he would be in the fourth year of Jehoiakim's reign. {Jer 25:1 Da 1:1} This was the biblical evidence for the viceroyship of Nebuchadnezzar lasting for more than one year. Secular historians only allow a one-year viceroy period for Nebuchadnezzar. Christians who follow the secular historians, invariably reconstruct this period covering the entire reign of Nebuchadnezzar incorrectly. Eusebius stated that he was viceroy for 20 months and this agrees with the biblical reconstruction of that period.

e1) The time from the start of Jeremiah's prophecies in the 13th year of Josiah to the 4th year of Jehoiakim, was 23 years. {Jer 25:1,3}

e2) Jeremiah's prophecy in the 4th year of Jehoiakim. {Jer 36:1 45:1} Chapter 36 is chapter 43 in the LXX. Chapter 45 starts at 51:31 in the LXX.

e3) Nebuchadnezzar defeated Pharaohnecho in the 4th year of Jehoiakim. {Jer 46:2} Chapter 46 is chapter 26 in the LXX.

Problem 19:

1) The 4th year of Jehoiakim's reign was 1st year of Nebuchadnezzar's. {Jer 25:1 46:2}

2) In the 3rd year of Jehoiakim's reign, Nebuchadnezzar was king. {Da 1:1}

Resolution:

1) The regal years for the Babylonian kings follow the period of Nabonassar which occurs a few weeks before the Jewish New Year. Nebuchadnezzar's 1st year as viceroy would overlap the last few weeks of Jehoiakim's 3rd year and most of his 4th year.

```
370 371 372 373 374 375 376 377 378 379 YDK
605 604 603 602 601 600 599 598 597 596 BC
bcdabcdabcdabcdabcdabcdabcdabcdabcdabcda
SK  20..21..22..23..24..25..26..27..28..29.. Ezekiel's Prophecy
  .6...7...8..9..10..11...                    Jehoiakim
                                .              Jehoiachin
                        1...2...3...4.. Jehoiachin's
                                              Captivity
                           ...1...2...3.. Zedekiah
   19..20..21..22..23..24..25..26..27..28.. Judah's Apostasy
BB   2...3...4...5...6...7...8...9..10..11... Nebuchadnezzar
   a   bc                   d  e
```

a) Jeremiah's prophecy was made in the 5th year and the 9th month of Jehoiakim. {Jer 36:9} Chapter 36

is chapter 43 in the LXX. In the LXX it is the 8th year in the 9th month.

b) Nebuchadnezzar's dream occurred in the 2nd year of his kingdom after the death of his father. {Da 2:1}

c) Jehoiakim rebelled against Nebuchadnezzar after serving him for 3 years. {2Ki 24:1}

d1) Nebuchadnezzar at the beginning of his 8th year just before the Jewish New Year in Nisan, captured Jehoiakim. At the end of his 7th year, 3023 Jews were deported. Jehoiakim's captivity would start just before the Jewish New Year. {2Ki 24:12 Jer 52:28} Jer 52:28 is omitted in the LXX.

d2) Jehoiachin, at age 18, reigned for last part of Jewish Year and a short time into the next year for a total of 3 months and 10 days. Nebuchadnezzar removed him before the Jewish New Year after his short 3 months and 10 day reign. {2Ch 36:9,10} If he only reigned after the Jewish New Year then Jehoiakim would have reigned 12 years not 11 as the Bible stated. {2Ki 24:8 2Ch 36:9}

d3) This marked the beginning of Jehoiachin's 37 years of captivity. {2Ki 25:27 Jer 52:31}

e) Zedekiah, at age 21, reigned for 11 years, starting just after the Jewish New Year. {2Ki 24:18 2Ch 36:10,11 Jer 52:1}

Problem 20:

1) Nebuchadnezzar's dream occurred in his 2nd year. {Da 2:1}

2) a. Daniel and his friends were on probation for 3 years. {Da 1:1,5,18}

  b. 3rd and 4th year of Jehoiakim's reign overlapped the 1st year of Nebuchadnezzar's when Daniel and his company were carried away captive. {Jer 25:1 46:2 Da 1:1}

  c. Therefore, Nebuchadnezzar's dream was in his 3rd year.

Resolution:

1) The first case refers to the time from when he became sole ruler and the second case refers to the time from when he became viceroy. Foreign kings were not bound by Talmudic rules.

Problem 21:

1) Jehoiachin was 18 years old. {2Ki 24:8}

2) Jehoiachin was 8 years old. {2Ch 36:9}

Resolution:

1) There is likely a scribal error in {2Ch 36:9} where the Hebrew letter YODH (number 10) was dropped from the text.

Problem 22:

1) Jehoiachin was captured by Nebuchadnezzar in the 8th year of his reign. {2Ki 24:12}

2) Jehoiachin was captured by Nebuchadnezzar in the 7th year of his reign. {Jer 52:28}

Resolution:

1) This was likely toward the end of the 7th year of Nebuchadnezzar and the beginning of the 8th year. The process of deportation may have carried on for a few weeks and spanned two years of Nebuchadnezzar's reign. This is the traditional Jewish understanding of this verse.

```
   380 381 382 383 384 385 386 387 388 389 YDK
   595 594 593 592 591 590 589 588 587 586 BC
bcdabcdabcdabcdabcdabcdabcdabcdabcdabcdabcda
SK .5...6...7...8...9..10..11..12..13..14.. Jehoiachin's
                                            Captivity
   .4...5...6...7...8...9..10..11..          Zedekiah
   30..                                      Ezekiel's Prophecy
                               ..1...2..     Ezekiel's Vision
   29..30..31..32..33..34..35..36..37..38..  Judah's Apostasy
BB 2..13..14..15..16..17..18..19..20..21...  Nebuchadnezzar
     a   b   c   d   e fg   h i
```

a1) Hananiah's false prophecy was in the 4th year and 5th month of Zedekiah and his death was in the 7th month of the same year. {Jer 28:1,17} Chapter 28 is chapter 35 in the LXX.

a2) Ezekiel's first vision was in the 5th year of Jehoiachin's captivity. This was the 30th year, 4th month, and the 5th day from the time Ezekiel started to prophesy. {Eze 1:1,2}

b) Ezekiel's vision of Jerusalem, was in the 6th year, 6th month, and the 5th day of Jehoiachin's captivity. The LXX has 5th month. {Eze 8:1}

c) Ezekiel's vision of Israel was in the 7th year, 5th month, and the 10th day of Jehoiachin's captivity. The LXX omits the month and has the 15th day. {Eze 20:1}

d) Ezekiel's vision of various countries was in the 9th year, 10th month, and the 10th day of Jehoiachin's captivity. {Eze 24:1}

e) In the 9th year, 10th month, and the 10th day of Zedekiah's reign, Nebuchadnezzar besieged Jerusalem for 3 years. The first part of Jeremiah chapter 39 is chapter 46 in the LXX. The LXX omitted the month in this reference. In Jer 52:4, the LXX has the 9th month instead of the 10th month. {2Ki 25:1,2 Jer 39:1,2 52:4}

f) Ezekiel's vision of Pharaoh was in the 10th year, 10th month, and the 12th day of Jehoiachin's captivity. The LXX has 12th year, 10th month, and the 1st day. {Eze 29:1}

g1) The 10th year of Zedekiah was the 18th year of Nebuchadnezzar. {Jer 32:1} Chapter 32 is chapter 39 in the LXX.

g2) In the 18th year of his reign, Nebuchadnezzar deported 832 Jews. This is omitted in the LXX. {Jer 52:29}

g3) Ezekiel's vision of Egypt was in the 11th year, 1st month, and the 7th day of Jehoiachin's captivity. {Eze 30:20}

g4) Ezekiel's vision of Egypt was in the 11th year, 3rd month, and the 1st day of Jehoiachin's captivity. {Eze 31:1}

h1) In the 11th year, 4th month, and the 9th day of Zedekiah and the 19th year of Nebuchadnezzar, Jerusalem fell. The LXX omitted the reference to the 4th month in Jer. 52:6 and the 19th year in Jer. 52:12. {2Ki 25:3,8 Jer 39:2 52:5,6,12}

h2) In the 11th year, 5th month, and the 7th day of Zedekiah and the 19th year of Nebuchadnezzar, Jerusalem was burned. {2Ki 25:8 Jer 52:5,12}

i1) Ezekiel's vision of Israel was in the 12th year, 12th month, and the 1st day of Jehoiachin's captivity. The LXX has the 10th month. {Eze 32:1}

i2) Ezekiel's vision of Israel was in the 12th year, 12th month, and the 15th day of Jehoiachin's captivity. The 12th month was supplied from context. The LXX incorrectly had the 1st month. {Eze 32:1,17}

i3) Ezekiel was told of destruction of Jerusalem in the 12th year, 10th month, and the 5th day of Jehoiachin's captivity, about 6 months after the city was burned. The LXX had the 10 year and 12th month, which was an obvious transposition error. {Eze 33:21} Modern scholars who have incorrectly reconstructed the chronology, assume this would have been 18 months after the fall of Jerusalem and hence cite this as proof that the Nisan to Nisan calendar was not used.

```
     390 391 392 393 394 395 396 397 398 399  YDK
     585 584 583 582 581 580 579 578 577 576  BC
     bcdabcdabcdabcdabcdabcdabcdabcdabcdabcda
SK   15..16..17..18..19..20..21..22..23..24..  Jehoiachin's
                                               Captivity
     .3...4...5...6...7...8...9..10..11..12.   Ezekiel's Vision
     39..40.                                   Judah's Apostasy
BB   22.23..24..25..26..27..28..29..30..31..3  Nebuchadnezzar
           a
```

a1) In the 23rd year of Nebuchadnezzar, Nebuzaradan deported 730 of the remaining Jews. The LXX omitted this verse. {Jer 52:30}

a2) This completed the 40 years of the iniquity of Judah and the 390 years of iniquity for Israel. {1Ki 12:26-33 Eze 4:5,6}

```
     400 401 402 403 404 405 406 407 408 409  YDK
     575 574 573 572 571 570 569 568 567 566  BC
     bcdabcdabcdabcdabcdabcdabcdabcdabcdabcda
SK   25..26..27..28..29..30..31..32..33..34..  Jehoiachin's
                                               Captivity
     13                                        Ezekiel's Vision
BB   2..33..34..35..36..37..38..39..40..41..   Nebuchadnezzar
                       ...1...2...3...4         Nebuchadnezzar's
                                               Insanity
        a       b              c
```

a) Ezekiel's vision of the temple was in the 25th year, 1st month, and the 10th day of Jehoiachin's captivity, in the 14th year after Jerusalem fell. The chart shows 13 full years and about 7 months from the fall of Jerusalem, so this would be in the 14th year. The LXX correctly supplies the "1st month" which is not in the Hebrew text but is clearly implied. {Eze 40:1}

b) Ezekiel's vision about Egypt was in the 27th year, 1st month, and the 1st day of Jehoiachin's captivity {Eze 29:17}

c) This time marked the beginning of Nebuchadnezzar's insanity. This is a deduction based on history. Apparently he finished the conquest of Egypt in 571 BC. He had his dream as given in Daniel 4 in 570 BC. During that year he built up Babylon, including the famous hanging gardens. After this he was put out of his kingdom after he bragged to himself about what he had done.

```
     410 411 412 413 414 415 416 417 418 419  YDK
     565 564 563 562 561 560 559 558 557 556  BC
     bcdabcdabcdabcdabcdabcdabcdabcdabcdabcda
SK   35..36..37...                             Jehoiachin's
                                               Captivity
BB   42..43..44...                             Nebuchadnezzar
     ...5...6...7                              Nebuchadnezzar's
                                               Insanity
              ab
```

a1) The 18th Jubilee.

a2) Nebuchadnezzar was restored to his kingdom.

b1) Nebuchadnezzar died a few months after he was restored to his kingdom in the winter of this year. According to Eusebius Nebuchadnezzar reigned for 20 months as viceroy and 43 years as sole king. Just before his death, he predicted that Cyrus would capture Babylon. The date of 562 BC for his death is derived from Ptolemy's king lists. {Thiele, p. 227.}

b2) Jehoiachin was freed in a Jubilee year in the 37th year, 12th month and 27th day of his captivity. {2Ki 25:27 Jer 52:31}

Problem 23:

1) Jehoiachin was freed on the 27th day. {2Ki 25:27}

2) Jehoiachin was freed on the 25th day. {Jer 52:31}

Resolution:

1) The decree to free Jehoiachin was determined and ratified on the 25th and executed on the 27th day.

2) There was a scribal error.

This does not alter the chronology.

## 7.0 Differences Between Hebrew and the LXX Texts

1) In 20th (24th in the LXX) year of Jeroboam, Asa reigned for 41 years. {1Ki 15:9,10}

2) Baasha reacted to the defection of his subjects to Asa and started to build Ramah in the 36th (38th in the LXX) year from the start of the divided kingdom {2Ch 15:9,16:1}

3) In the 26th (omitted in the LXX) year of Asa, Elah reigned two years, part of one year, and part of another. {1Ki 16:8}

4) In the 27th (omitted by the LXX) year of Asa, Zimri murdered Elah, reigned 7 days, and committed suicide to avoid being killed by Omri. {1Ki 16:10,15}

5) In the 38th year of Asa, Ahab reigned for 22 years. {1Ki 16:29} (The LXX has 2nd year of Jehoshaphat instead of the 38th year of Asa.)

6) In his 39th year, Asa became diseased in his feet until he died in his 41st (40th in the LXX) year. {1Ki 15:23,24 2Ch 16:12,13}

7) In the 2nd year of Jehoram (SK), Jehoram (NK) started to reign. {2Ki 1:17} This was the 18th year of Jehoshaphat in the LXX and verse is 18 not 17.

8) In the 12th year of Jehoram (NK), Ahaziah at 22 years of age, reigned for part of a year. {2Ki 8:25,26 2Ch 22:2} In {2Ch 22:2} his age was given as 42 and it was 20 in the LXX.

9) Athaliah reigned over Judah for 6 years and was killed in her 7th year. (8th year {2Ch 23:1} and 7th year in {2Ki 11:4 2Ch 24:1} in the LXX.) {2Ki 11:3,4,16 2Ch 22:12 23:1,15}

10) Jeremiah's prophecy was in the 5th year of Jehoiakim. {Jer 36:9} In the LXX it was the 8th year in the 9th month.

11) Nebuchadnezzar at the beginning of his 8th year just before the Jewish New Year in Nisan, captured Jehoiakim. At the end of his 7th year, 3023 Jews were deported. {2Ki 24:12 Jer 52:28} Jer 52:28 was omitted in the LXX.

12) Ezekiel's vision of Jerusalem, was in the 6th year, 6th month and the 5th day of Jehoiachin's captivity. The LXX had 5th month. {Eze 8:1}

13) Ezekiel's vision of Israel was in the 7th year, 5th month, and the 10th day of Jehoiachin's captivity. The LXX omitted the month and had the 15th day. {Eze 20:1}

14) In the 9th year, 10th month, and the 10th day of Zedekiah's reign, Nebuchadnezzar besieged Jerusalem for 3 years. The LXX omitted the month in Jer 39:1,2. In Jer 52:4, the LXX had 9th month instead of 10th month. {2Ki 25:1,2 Jer 39:1,2 52:4}

15) In the 18th year of his reign, Nebuchadnezzar deported 832 Jews. This was omitted in the LXX. {Jer 52:29}

16) Ezekiel's vision of Pharaoh was in the 10th year, 10th month, and the 12th day of Jehoiachin's captivity; the LXX had the 12th year, 10th month, 1st day. {Eze 29:1}

17) In the 11th year, 4th month, and the 9th day of Zedekiah and the 19th year of Nebuchadnezzar, Jerusalem fell. The LXX omitted the reference to the 4th month in Jer. 52:6 and the 19th year in Jer. 52:12. {2Ki 25:3,8 Jer 39:2 52:5,6,12}

18) Ezekiel's vision of Israel was in the 12th year, 12th month, and the 1st day of Jehoiachin's captivity. The LXX had the 10th month. {Eze 32:1}

19) Ezekiel's vision of Israel was in the 12th year, 12th month, and the 15th day of Jehoiachin's captivity. The 12th month was supplied from the context. The LXX incorrectly had the 1st month. {Eze 32:1,17}

20) Ezekiel told of the destruction of Jerusalem in the 12th year, 10th month, and the 5th day of Jehoiachin's captivity. The LXX had the 10th year and 12th month, which is an obvious transposition error. {Eze 33:21}

21) In the 23rd year of Nebuchadnezzar, Nebuzaradan deported 730 of the remaining Jews. The LXX omitted this verse. {Jer 52:30}

22) Ezekiel's vision of the temple was in the 25th year, 1st month, and the 10th day of Jehoiachin's captivity, in the 14th year after Jerusalem fell. The LXX correctly supplies "1st month" which was not in the Hebrew text but was clearly implied. {Eze 40:1}

Of the 22 differences, seven are critical. 1, 3, 4, 5, 7, 8, and 9 would throw the chronology off if the LXX was used instead of the Hebrew text. Hence, our admonition is justified that the chronology must be based on the Hebrew text.

**8.0 Summary of the Viceroy Relationships**

1) In his 18th year, Jehoshaphat made Jehoram viceregent while he went off to war with Syria.

2) In his 23rd year, Jehoshaphat made Jehoram viceroy and died two years later.

3) In his 21st year, Ahab (NK) made Ahaziah (NK) viceroy and Ahab died the same year in a battle with Syria.

4) In his 7th year, Jehoram made Ahaziah viceroy and died the next year of a disease of his bowels.

5) In his 15th year, Jehoahaz (NK) made Jehoash viceroy and died two years later.

6) In his 39th year, Joash made Amaziah viceroy and died two years later.

7) In his 6th year, Jehoash (NK) made Jeroboam II (NK) viceroy before he went to fight with the Syrians. He won, much to his surprise, and lived for another 11 years.

8) In his 52nd year, Uzziah made Jotham viceroy and died of leprosy a few months later.

9) In his 15th year, Ahaz made Hezekiah viceroy and died the next year.

10) According to Eusebius, Nebuchadnezzar was made viceroy while his father went off to war and was killed 20 months later.

In every case there is a good reason for these viceroy relationships. A king was virtually abdicating the throne when he appointed his son as a viceroy. Kings did not make such serious decisions on a mere whim. In cases 1, 3, 7, and 10, the king was going to war and wanted to ensure a smooth transition of power in case he did not return. In the other cases, the viceroy relationship was toward the end of the king's life and did not last for very long. The king was likely in failing health and needed help with the administration of the kingdom.

Almost all viceroy periods were quite short, usually one or two years. The exception was Jeroboam II, whose period lasted over 11 years. His father, Jehoash, did not expect to defeat the Syrians even though Elisha said he would. He thought he would come back on his shield, not holding it!

## 9.0 Some Objections

Modern chronology for the divided kingdom appears to be quite different than the one developed by Ussher. In order to force fit the biblical data with the preconceived ideas of Assyrian history, those of the Assyrian Academy must eliminate two interregnums from the biblical data. The concept of interregnums is not new and was common in this period of history among foreign nations. Therefore, we should not be surprised, given the political turmoil in the Northern Kingdom, to find one or more interregnums during the death-throes of that kingdom. The Southern Kingdom was much more stable during this time and we should not expect to find interregnums there.

From history, we know of at least four interregnums in foreign countries.

1) In 704 BC, after Arkeanos, there was no king in Babylon for two years. {15}

2) In 688 BC, there was no king in Babylon for eight years. {15}

3) In 687 BC, civil disorder increased in Egypt, because there was no king for two years. {16}

4) In 637 BC, there was a one year interregnum in Babylon. {17}

All serious students of history know about these interregnums. We are not surprised that those advocating the use of the conjectured Assyrian Chronology to amend the Bible, conveniently forget about them, and recoil in horror at such a concept for they know that if the concept is allowed, it is fatal to their schemes of interpretation. Neither Dr. Thiele or Dr. McFall breathe a word about this and indeed it is one of the best-kept secrets of the Assyrian Academy. Indeed, Galil goes so far as to state in his basic assumptions (without proof) there were no interregnums in the biblical chronology! This begs the question — "How does he know?"

We shall discuss this and other the errors in the most popular modern chronology that was developed by Dr. Thiele and refined by Dr. McFall in another article.

## 10.0 Interesting Observations

There was no king in the Northern Kingdom on two separate occasions, one starting in 784 BC and the other starting in 740 or 739 BC.

Viceroy relationships are essential to the understanding of the king lists. These become apparent as you actually plot out the data in detail. In reading the Bible, you would not normally be aware of most of these relationships unless you did your homework.

Jehoshaphat and Ahab both had two sons. Both had sons by the same name, Ahaziah and Jehoram. All of them were made viceroys at one time or another. This period in the king list was the most confusing until Jehu simplified it in 884 BC by terminating the kings!

Some have claimed that a different dating method was used by the writer of Chronicles than the writer of Kings. We found no evidence of this. Except for the difference in the age when two kings started to reign, all the data is identical.

Some have claimed a different accession-year scheme was used at different times for either of the kingdoms. That is, the Nisan to Nisan rule was abandoned for considerable periods of time and they deliberately used a different accession month (i.e., month Tishri to Tishri). We found no evidence to justify this claim.

## 11.0 Conclusion

Ussher's results, based on the Bible alone, violate just about every "absolute date" in archaeology. Amen. All this shows is that we may not know as much about history as God does. This provides an excellent incentive for Christians to reevaluate the findings of archaeology to find their mistakes. This has been done before by Christians. Let us do the same for the rest of archaeology's so-called "absolute dates." We will never forget what Gordon Franz, who was guiding a tour to Israel in 1998, said on the mound of Jericho.

"Absolute *truth* in archaeology lasts about 20 years."

Maybe we should substitute "conjecture" for "truth!"

Archaeology is to history what evolution is to science. Evolutionists find a fossil and make up a story to go with it. Likewise, many archaeologists find a broken pot or a fragment of a scroll and spin a tale to explain it. If you are well respected in the field, your story becomes the gospel until something better comes along. This is not at all an exaggeration. The classic case was the time when Dr. Woods examined the dates for Jericho as determined by Kathleen Kenyon and found them too recent. She (Kenyon) excavated an eight meter square and dated the fall of Jericho based on the type of pottery she DID NOT find! (We are sure this had nothing at all to do with her anti-biblical bias!) This farce rode on the coat-tails of her reputation for decades until Dr. Woods exploded it. At the very best, archaeology can only confirm what the Bible says, never refute it. It may give us background information to help us understand the Bible better.

We have been able to recreate the background documentation to justify Ussher's reconstruction of the king lists for the divided kingdom. We have been careful to state all the assumptions we used and state all the known problems that people have found that relate to this chronological period. We have solely relied on the Bible for our information. We do not claim that this reconstruction is unique. There may be other ways to do it. However, we have shown that there exists at least one way it can be done without doing violence to the Scriptures. That is sufficient to overthrow a host of inaccurate reconstructions for this same time period which result in a much shorter time for this biblical period.

We are open to suggestions and amendments. However, we will only entertain corrections that are rooted in the Bible. Archaeological arguments that violate the Scriptures carry no weight with us.

## 11.0 Bibliography

*Authorized Version of the Bible, The.* Cambridge, England: University Printing House [Her Majesty's Printers], 1769.

Blaiklock, Edward (editor). *The New International Dictionary of Biblical Archaeology* (IBDA). Grand Rapids, MI: Zondervan Publishing House, 1984.

Bone, Dorothy M. *Chronology of the Hebrew Divided Kingdom.* London, England: Avon Books, 1997.

Diodorus, Siculus. *Loeb Classical Library*, Book 1, Chapter 66. Cambridge, MA: Harvard University Press, 1933, p. 227.

Galil, Gershon. *The Chronology of the Kings of Israel and Judah.* Leiden; New York: E. J. Brill, 1996, p. 120.

Gill, John. *Gill's Expositor.* Online Bible CD Rom, 1995; first published in 1760.

Halley Henry. *Halley's Bible Handbook.* Grand Rapids, MI: Zondervan, 1965, revised edition.

Halley, John W. *Alleged Discrepancies of the Bible.* Grand Rapids, MI: Baker Book House, 1976; first published in 1874.

*International Standard Bible Encyclopaedia* (ISBE). Peabody, MA: Hendrickson Publishers, 1929.

McFall, Dr. Leslie. "A Translation Guide to the Chronological Data in Kings and Chronicles." *Bibliotheca Sacra*, volume 148, number 589, January–March 1991.

*Septuagint Version of the Old Testament, The.* Grand Rapids, MI: Zondervan Publishing House, 1978.

Smith, William. *Smith's Bible Dictionary* (American edition). Cambridge: Riverside Press, 1869. This is the 4-volume set, not the one-volume abridged version.

Tadmor Hayim. *The Inscriptions of Tiglath-Pileser III King of Assyria.* Jerusalem: The Israel Academy of Sciences and Humanities, 1994.

Thiele, Edwin R. *The Mysterious Numbers of the Hebrew Kings.* Chicago, IL: University of Chicago Press, 1983.

———. *The Mysterious Numbers of the Hebrew Kings.* Grand Rapids, MI: Kregel Publications, 1994. Appendix C - Canon of Ptolemy, p. 227.

Ussher. *Annals of the World.* First published in 1654.

*Virtual Jerusalem*, Internet website: http://www.virtual.

co.il/torah/webshas/main.htm, Jerusalem. This has the whole Talmud and Mishnah in English. There are special subsections at that site that deal with Jewish time calculations.

# Appendix D: Evidentiallism — The Bible and Assyrian Chronology

In the last 100 years, various reconstructions of Assyrian chronology have been used to undermine the accepted chronology of the period of the divided kingdom. Edwin Thiele's work on Hebrew chronology—as reinterpreted in the light of Assyrian chronology—has become widely accepted by evangelicals and secular historians. We will show Assyrian chronology is not as simple as Thiele would have us believe and there is no reason to bend the Bible to fit the current reconstructions of Assyrian chronology.

———————

It is refreshing to see the creation movement maturing from the strictly evidential approach of the 1960s and 1970s to the biblically based, axiomatic approach of recent years. This represents a shift in emphasis from science to philosophy, from looking at theories to looking at how to build theories and interpret facts. The emphasis is on the authority of the Bible. Our understanding of the sciences pertaining to origins has been greatly enhanced as a result of using this *Bible first* approach.

One area, which has been almost totally untouched, is the area of biblical chronologies, especially for the period of the divided kingdom. Chronological problems are identical to the problems faced by the creation movement in dealing with the early chapters of Genesis. However, the arguments and logic are not nearly so simplistic and most people surrender when confronted by a wordy argument. Reduced to the simplest terms, we have the same problem we faced in Genesis stated in a more complex way: *What is your authority?* In this article, we will concentrate mainly on the latest accepted Assyrian chronology as popularized by Edwin Thiele. (There is little to be gained by examining previous reconstructions that have now been abandoned. These older abandoned reconstructions should make us very wary of accepting newer models that likewise conflict with the Bible.) We will show how Thiele has massaged the biblical data to make it fit with the current understanding of Assyrian chronology. You can guess very accurately which came out second best, the Bible or Assyrian chronology. Thiele stated:[1]

> "Between the absolute chronology of the Hebrews and that of their neighbours there can be no conflict. If the biblical chronology seems to be at variance with Assyrian chronology, it may be because of errors in the Hebrew records, but it may also be because the data preserved in these records are not correctly understood."

This statement sets the tone for Thiele's work. We were not aware that Assyrian chronology was inspired!

Thiele's book, *The Mysterious Numbers of the Hebrew Kings,* has been published three times, 1951,[2] 1965,[3] and 1983.[4] There are major revisions between each printing. We will be referring to material from all three printings but wherever possible use the latest printing. Also, we will refer to the work by Leslie McFall in 1991,[5] which has some minor refinements to Thiele's chronology.

## General Problems with Ancient History

Before we start, let's look at two well-documented examples from ancient history that illustrate some of the problems we face in trying to reconstruct an accurate history. Both of these deal with the life of Alexander the Great and have abundant documentation from the ancient writers.

1. On the west side of the Hyphasis River in India, Alexander had his troops construct an oversized camp containing extra large furnishings. He did this to give an exaggerated impression of his armies' stature and deeds to those who saw them in later times. If an Indian archaeologist discovered these a few hundred years later and did not have access to the historical accounts of Plutarch, Diodorus, Arrian, and Curtius, he may be misled and come to the wrong conclusions about the invading army of Alexander.

2. In attacking the citadel of the Mallians in India, Alexander was severely wounded. Depending on the accounts you read, even those who were present when this happened disagree among themselves in important details. The Latin historian Curtius wryly observed that so great was the carelessness of those old historians, it was hard to know what to believe!

These two items illustrate the problems faced when dealing with secular history. First, the accounts may have been deliberately misrepresented to glorify the doer of the deeds. Secondly, even eyewitness accounts may conflict. (Anyone who has sat on a jury will vouch for that.) Assyrian chronology suffers from all this and more as we shall see. Those who accept the authority of the Scriptures, know that only the records of the Bible are accurate when compared to secular accounts for the same historical period.

## The Problem

The problem with biblical chronology is that it does not fit with our current understanding of Assyrian chronology. The biblical chronology is too long by about 40 to 50 years, depending on who you read. The latest reconstruction by Thiele is but one of many attempts in the last 100 years to adjust the biblical account to match the current conjectured chronology of the Assyrians. Thiele very creatively manipulated the biblical data to eliminate about 40 years of history. He did this by constructing viceroy relationships to collapse the length of a king's reign by overlapping it with the king's predecessor. He was the first person we know of to make such a detailed reconstruction of the divided kingdom using this approach. (Variations on his scheme can be traced back at least 75 years before him.) By this, he gave his shortened chronology much credibility. Having it published by a well-known university press instead of by his church denomination considerably helped his cause.

Let us look at the three dates where Assyrian and biblical history are supposed to intersect. These three dates are the main reason for abridging the biblical chronology. These dates are 841 BC, 853 BC, and 701 BC.[6] There is no mention in the Bible of the events that supposedly happened in the years of the first two dates. Their intersection with biblical history rests entirely on secular interpretations of Assyrian records, not on biblical data.

## 841 BC

This date is documented on the Black Obelisk of Shalmaneser III. Thiele states:

> "The date of 841 is established by Jehu's payment of tribute to Shalmaneser III of Assyria in that year and, together with 853, becomes one of the basic dates in Hebrew history. Although the Bible makes no mention of Jehu's payment of tribute to Assyria, Shalmaneser III mentions that in the eighteenth year of his reign he went against 'Hazael of Aram,' shut him up in 'Damascus, his royal city,' and 'received tribute of the men of Tyre, Sidon and of Jehu, the son of Omri.' "

From the Bible, it is easy to deduce that Jehu started to reign about 12 years after the death of Ahab. This would fix the date for the death of Ahab at 853 BC and the first year of Jehu at 841 BC.

At first glance, this seems to be impeccable evidence for discarding the longer biblical chronology. According to it, Ahab died in 897 BC and Jehu started to reign about 885 BC. If this were so, obviously Jehu would be dead and gone long before Shalmaneser III started to reign. However, remember that very few archaeologists are Christians and most are hostile to the Word of God. Therefore, expect anything they find to be *interpreted* in

the worst possible way to confound Bible-believing Christians. Once these *interpretations* are published, they seem to get a life all of their own and many *Christian* authors echo them without bothering to check what was actually found. This was the very reason the Christian Church caved in on evolution and why many churches ignore the historical portions of the Old Testament as being unreliable. It is a slippery road to liberalism that is well greased with the opinions of scholars.

Fossils and radiometric dating seemed to provide the *absolute* truth as to the age of the world until someone took the time to see what assumptions are involved. Likewise, in this case it is extremely important to determine what was actually found and ignore the *just so stories* that became associated with the find. We had to search many sources before we found one that was honest enough to admit what was really found and what it meant.

The basis of what Thiele stated comes from the inscriptions found on the Black Obelisk of Shalmaneser III. We found the following in a Bible dictionary.

> "The text depicts Shalmaneser's triumphs over several kingdoms of Syria and the West. Of special interest to Bible students is one panel in the second row in which a bearded Semite bows before the king while his servants present gifts. The text refers to the humble suppliant as Jehu, son of Omri (a name by which all Israelite kings were identified, whether of the Omride dynasty or not), and describes the gifts he brought. The event, apparently from the year 841 BC, gives us the earliest surviving picture of an Israelite and shows how such a person might have appeared to an Assyrian sculptor. There is no evidence, however, that the obelisk was actually depicting the Israelite monarch Jehu."[7]

So, except for the fact we are not certain of the actual date of the obelisk and who is in the picture, we are in fine shape! Just as the Israelite kings were described as *sons of Omri*, when many were not, likewise many may have been identified with the name *Jehu*. We do not have enough evidence from secular history to determine this.

Much more damaging is the evidence uncovered by Faulstich. He documents that much of the information on the Black Obelisk that is attributed to Shalmaneser was taken from earlier monuments.[8] Are we so egocentric as to think historical revisionism is a recent phenomenon? This plagiarism was so common in Assyrian history that the father of Shalmaneser III pronounced a special curse on later kings who tried to steal his fame by ascribing deeds he had done to themselves. Faulstich goes on to document inconsistencies among the Black Obelisk, the Tigris Inscriptions, the Statue Inscriptions, and the Bull-Colossi.

This type of historical revisionism results in the collapsing of historical events into a shorter time frame. From the inspired biblical accounts, we know this has happened. Rarely do we find historians mentioning the problems with Assyrian chronology when they use Assyrian data to amend the biblical chronology. Thiele and McFall are very silent on this. As in the case of Alexander's wound, we will likely never know the correct story.

## 853 BC

This was the date of the famous battle of Qarqar that was fought between Shalmaneser III and an anti-Assyrian coalition. The Bible dictionary lists *A-ha-ab-bu Sir'-i-la-a-a* as supplying 2000 chariots and 10,000 men for this battle. *A-ha-ab-bu* is taken to mean *Ahab*. *Sir'-i-la-a-a* is taken to mean *Israel*.[9] This is given as proof positive that the Ahab of 1 Kings was present at this battle.

This word may be translated *Ahab* but that does not prove that it was the King Ahab of the Bible. Several possibilities exist. In ancient history, it is the rule, not the exception, that different writers gave the same person different names. Consider this example:

> "After Laborosoarchodus, who was disposed of by his subjects for his acts of villainy, Nebuchadnezzar's grandchild by his daughter succeeded him. The new king was his son by Evilmerodach and called by Berosus, *Nabonidus*, but by Herodotus, *Labynitus*, by Abydenus, *Nabannidochus* and by Daniel, *Belshazzar* or *Baltazar*."[10]

Nebuchadnezzar's grandson had at least four or five different names depending on who wrote the history! Just because you see a historian use a name that is the same as a name mentioned elsewhere by a different historian, you cannot assume both historians are referring to the same individual. You must study the context to be sure. This is the major failing of Assyrian history. Because the material is so scanty and fragmentary, we often do not have enough information to be absolutely sure of who we are reading about and if we are interpreting it correctly. However, that has never stopped a scholar from spinning a good story about what he thinks it says. If he has enough prestige, his story will soon become the gospel.

Another possibility is that the person in command of the force was a general of a king of Israel and not the king himself. Saul, David, Solomon, and Pekah had generals over their armies and the names are recorded in the Scriptures.

The story may be improbable given the events that happened during Ahab's reign. He suffered a three-year drought that destroyed most of the livestock in the kingdom. Just a few years before this alleged event at Qarqar took place, Ahab was invaded by Benhadad. In that battle, Ahab was scarcely able to muster 7,000 soldiers, much less any chariots or horsemen. However, the story is that he sent 10,000 troops and 2,000 chariots to this battle at Qarqar. This was no small force, especially considering the large number of chariots.

Another explanation was touched on previously—historical revisionism. The events described here likely happened, but at an earlier date, since the inscriptions were most likely doctored by a later king to enhance his glory.

No doubt some king from Israel sent an army to the battle of Qarqar. However, it was not likely King Ahab. We shall see later when we look at the biblical problems, how much the texts of the Bible were twisted to force Ahab into this later time period when the battle of Qarqar took place.

## 701 BC

We are not certain why this date is essential to Thiele's chronology. If Thiele had not made this synchronisation with Hezekiah, he would have had much less criticism of his scheme. Thiele conjectures that this was the date that Sennacherib invaded Hezekiah in the 14th year of his reign. By forcing this synchronisation, Thiele ignores several synchronisations of the biblical text. We shall discuss this under the heading of the "Third Biblical Example."

### Biblical Considerations

The main problem with all attempts to harmonize the Bible with Assyrian chronology is the violence it does to the Scriptures. To remove about 40 years from a chronology, as well defined as the one we have in the Bible, requires some very creative exegesis or worse, discarding numbers that do not fit our preconceived ideas. This is a classic case of starting with evidence outside the Bible and making the Bible say what we want to hear. In the preface to the third edition, Thiele stated:[11]

> "The only basis for a sound chronology of the period to be discussed is a completely unbiased use of biblical statements in the light of all other knowledge we can bring to bear on the problem, notably the history and chronology of the ancient Near East."

This statement indicates Thiele's approach to the Word of God and secular history. For Thiele used the supposed dates from Assyrian chronology, which allegedly intersect with the biblical chronology, to force-fit the biblical data into the mould of secular chronology. We will only deal with the most serious problems in his work.

**First Biblical Example**
To collapse the biblical history, you must create overlapping reigns of kings so that the total length of the period is significantly shortened. The fun really begins with Uzziah. Up until then, the dates on Thiele's and McFall's chronology are within a couple of years of the one derived from the longer biblical chronology.

As we said, there is very little disagreement with the longer reconstruction for the first 150 years even to the 12-year viceroyship of Jeroboam II with Jehoash. This is not only true for Thiele but for all reconstructions done in the last 100 years that we have seen published. However, at this point, all the chronologies diverge from the traditional chronology. Thiele stated that in the 27th year of Jeroboam, Uzziah became sole king and that he had a viceroy relationship with his father for 24 years. The only rationale for selecting a 24-year period is that Thiele can make it fit with current archaeological expectations. Again, Josephus and all the writers before 1850 never guessed that there was a viceroyship of any length, much less 24 years for Uzziah. The Bible says:

> "And *they* brought him [Amaziah, Uzziah's father] on horses, and he was buried at Jerusalem with his fathers in the city of David. And all the people of Judah took Azariah [Uzziah] which *was* sixteen years old and made him king instead of his father Amaziah." (2 Kings 14:20–21)

> "In the twenty and seventh year of Jeroboam king of Israel, began Azariah [Uzziah] the son of Amaziah king of Judah to reign. Sixteen years old was he when he began to reign and he reigned two and fifty years in Jerusalem...." (2 Kings 15:1–2)

By all rules of exegesis, one would conclude that Uzziah was made king when he was 16 years old, after the death of his father. This event happened in the 27th year of Jeroboam. Not so according to Thiele and others! A little arithmetic will show that it is rather difficult to be made king 8 years before you were born! For if you came to the throne when you were 16 but had been a viceroy with your father for 24 years already, you were made viceroy 8 years before you were born! According to Thiele, McFall, and others, the text is incorrect. It should read in the 3rd year of Jeroboam not the 27th.[12] By happy chance, by having Uzziah as viceroy for 24 years, Thiele can manipulate the rest of the numbers for Uzziah's reign without violating too many synchronisms. THERE IS ABSOLUTELY NO BIBLICAL OR SOUND LOGICAL REASON FOR THIS AMENDMENT.

Before we proceed to the next example, a little historical note is of interest. Thiele was not the first one to propose Uzziah's imaginary viceroy relationship. We found it in a very old Bible produced around 1900, and in the 1909 International Standard Bible Encyclopaedia (ISBE).[13] The latter also documents this non-existent viceroy relationship that Uzziah had with his father for exactly the same period of 24 years. However, it creates a 12-year viceroy relationship between Uzziah and his son, Jotham, and has Pekah becoming king in the 52nd year of Uzziah as one would expect. Unless one checked the Bible and found out that Pekah ruled for 20 years one would not notice a problem. However, the ISBE chart shows Pekah coming to the throne in 736 BC. This means his rule finished in 717 BC, four years after the fall of his kingdom of Samaria in 721 BC. This is a tad ridiculous. No doubt, some wag pointed out this piece of illogic to the theological "experts" and this view was quietly dropped.

This brings us to the next example and how Thiele found another place to delete these 12 years from the chronology.

**Second Biblical Example**
To delete the 12 years requires incredible ingenuity. Thiele worked on the reign of Pekah just as the ISBE had done many years earlier. Read the following Scripture texts carefully:

> "In the nine and thirtieth year of Azariah [Uzziah] king of Judah began Menahem the son of Gadi to reign over Israel, *and reigned* ten years in Samaria." (2 Kings 15:17)

> "And Menahem slept with his fathers; and Pekahiah his son began to reign in his stead. In the fiftieth year of Azariah [Uzziah] king of Judah Pekahiah the son of Menahem began to reign over Israel in Samaria, *and reigned* two years.... But Pekah the son of Remaliah, a captain of his, conspired against him and smote him in Samaria, in the palace of the king's house, with Argob and Arieh, and with him fifty men of the Gileadites: and he killed him and reigned in his room.... In the two and fiftieth year of Azariah [Uzziah] king of Judah Pekah the son of Remaliah began to reign over Israel in Samaria, *and reigned* twenty years." (2 Kings 15:22–27)

There are two views on how to understand this passage.

a) The traditional view to those who are not under the influence of modern scholarship is this. Menahem reigned for 10 years, followed by his son, Pekahiah, who reigned for two years. Pekahiah was murdered by his commander, Pekah, who in turn reigned for 20 years. By normal rules of exegesis, this would be the most normal way to understand the text. Accession dating[14] is used in all these examples.

| Uzziah Regal Year | Northern Kingdom King |
|---|---|
| 39 | Menahem, 10 years (2Ki 15:17) |
| 50 | Pekahiah, 2 years (2Ki 15:23) |
| 52 | Pekah, 20 years (2Ki 15:27) |

| 39 | 40 | 41 | 42 | 43 | 44 | 45 | 46 | 47 | 48 | 49 | 50 | 51 | 52 | - Years of Uzziah |
|---|---|---|---|---|---|---|---|---|---|---|---|---|---|---|
|  | 1 | 2 | 3 | 4 | 5 | 6 | 7 | 8 | 9 | 10 |  |  |  | - Reign of Menahem |
|  |  |  |  |  |  |  |  |  |  |  | 1 | 2 |  | - Reign of Pekahiah |
|  |  |  |  |  |  |  |  |  |  |  |  |  | 1 | - Reign of Pekah |

b) Both Thiele and McFall would have the diagram look like this:

| 39 | 40 | 41 | 42 | 43 | 44 | 45 | 46 | 47 | 48 | 49 | 50 | 51 | 52 | - Years of Uzziah |
|---|---|---|---|---|---|---|---|---|---|---|---|---|---|---|
|  | 1 | 2 | 3 | 4 | 5 | 6 | 7 | 8 | 9 | 10 |  |  |  | - Reign of Menahem |
|  |  |  |  |  |  |  |  |  |  |  | 1 | 2 |  | - Reign of Pekahiah |
|  | 1 | 2 | 3 | 4 | 5 | 6 | 7 | 8 | 9 | 10 | 11 | 12 | 13 | - Reign of Pekah |

Absolutely no biblical justification is given for starting the reign of Pekah in the 39th year of Uzziah. They say Pekah was a rival king in Gilead to both Menahem and Pekahiah, and Pekah really started his sole reign in the 52nd year of Uzziah. The Bible says that Pekah was the captain of Pekahiah, not a rival king reigning in Gilead. Further, the Bible says Pekah started to reign in the 52nd year, not the 39th year, of Uzziah.

Lets look at all the kings of the Northern Kingdom who were dated by the reign of Uzziah.

| Uzziah Regal Year | Northern Kingdom King |
|---|---|
| 38 | Zachariah, 6 months (2Ki 15:8) |
| 39 | Shallum, 1 month (2Ki 15:13) |
| 39 | Menahem, 10 years (2Ki 15:17) |
| 50 | Pekahiah, 2 years (2Ki 15:23) |
| 52 | Pekah, 20 years (2Ki 15:27) |

By all rules of exegesis, one would think these kings in the Northern Kingdom reigned sequentially. Not so if you have the guide of enlightened scholarship. It is obvious that Menahem's and Pekahiah's reigns overlap the first 12 years of Pekah's reign, or is it? Both Thiele and McFall wrest the obvious meaning of the Bible. {2Ki 15:25,27} THERE IS ABSOLUTELY NO BIBLICAL JUSTIFICATION FOR THIS. Indeed, they use different rules when it suits them. In the first example we

gave, they said the synchronisation date referred to the time when Uzziah was made viceroy. In this case, they say the synchronisation refers to the time when Pekah became sole king. You cannot have it both ways, and no matter which way Thiele and McFall go, they create logical inconsistencies in the text. Further the "just-so story" they created about Pekah is pure fiction and contradicts the Bible. {2Ki 15:25} Pekah was a commander of Pekahiah and not a rival king to him!

**Third Biblical Example**

Thiele holds to a synchronisation for the year 701 BC to make it the 14th year of the reign of Hezekiah when Sennacherib invaded Judah. Thiele is forced to discard three synchronisations to do this. According to the Bible:

a) Hezekiah started to reign in the 3rd year of Hoshea. {2Ki 18:1,2}

b) In the 6th year of Hezekiah and the 9th year of Hoshea, Israel was captured. {2Ki 18:10}

c) In the 12th year of Ahaz, Hoshea began to reign over Israel. {2Ki 17:1}

Thiele claims these are late amendments to the biblical text and is honest enough to admit he cannot make these verses fit his chronology. In forcing this synchronisation, Thiele has Hezekiah and his son, Manasseh, co-reigning for at least 11 years. THERE IS ABSOLUTELY NO BIBLICAL EVIDENCE to support this aside from this forced synchronisation.

Thiele also runs into problems with the secular chronology of Babylon. The Bible says that Hezekiah was visited by representatives from Merodachbaladan, the king of Babylon. According to our understanding of Ptolemy's canon, this king ruled in Babylon from 721–710 BC and then died. If Thiele had not tried to force this connection with Sennacherib for the year 701 BC, he would not have had this problem.

According to Assyrian chronology, this Sennacherib, whoever he was, went on and reigned for a number of years after this invasion. The Bible states he returned to his own land and was killed by his sons. {2Ki 19:36,37} No great time is implied between the unsuccessful invasion and his untimely death. According to Tobit in the Apocrypha, Sennacherib returned and conducted some ethnic cleansing to rid the land of Jews. About 55 days after his return, he was murdered by his two sons. {APC Tob 1:15-22} Verse 15 states that Sennacherib's *estate was troubled*. This may refer to the loss of the 185,000 men in the campaign against Hezekiah. {2Ki 19:35} If so, it would account for Sennacherib's fury against any Jews he found.

McFall tries to salvage the synchronisms that Thiele discards by saying Hezekiah reigned as viceroy with his father for the first 16 years of his reign. Then he commenced his sole reign after the death of his father in 715 BC. Thereby, the synchronisations Thiele could not make fit, McFall does. (This solution is not new and was proposed 40 years ago in the New Bible Dictionary. Thiele never accepted it.) This creates some real exegetical problems, for in the 6th year of Hezekiah, Israel fell and in the 14th year Hezekiah was invaded by Sennacherib. By all rules of logic, you would assume about 8 years elapsed between these events. Wrong! According to this "new math" over 22 years elapsed if you use Thiele's dates of 723 BC for the fall of Israel and 701 BC for the invasion by Sennacherib! McFall tries to wiggle out of this by claiming the first date (6th year) was from the time Hezekiah was made viceroy with his father and the second date (14th year) was dated from the time Hezekiah became sole king. How would anyone know this if he was reading just the Bible?

Earlier Bible dictionaries like the 1909 ISBE did not require this synchronisation and we really wonder if it is required either. The biblical record does not list all the invasions and battles that Israel and Judah fought. Nations generally avoid documenting their disastrous defeats so it should come as no surprise that the earlier ill-fated invasion is passed by in silence in the Assyrian records. Also, the name for a particular person may not resemble the name given to him in another country. Ancient history abounds with examples of this.

**Other Issues**

There are many more problems with Thiele's chronology (and McFall's amendments) which space does not permit us to deal with. How much time should be wasted refuting a defective system? Until we get good biblical answers for the 24-year vice-regency of Uzziah and the 12-year overlap of Pekah with the other kings of Israel, not to mention the many conflicts introduced by these changes, we should not surrender the older, longer chronology of the Bible.

Since most historians for the Egyptian period have blindly accepted Thiele's dates, they are labouring under a 40 to 50-year error when they try to align Egyptian history with biblical history. Egyptian history is challenging enough without being handicapped by the errors introduced by Thiele's dubious dating procedures! It is most amusing to see them conjecture who the pharaoh of the Exodus was in 1446 BC when the biblical date for the Exodus is closer to 1491 BC!

**Conclusion**

The arbitrary nature in which Thiele, McFall, and others handle the biblical text is obvious. Their methods are no different than the methods of those who came before them and amended the Bible based on what they thought the Assyrian records stated. All who do this create imaginary viceroy relationships when it suits them. Sometimes they count years from when a king became a viceroy, sometimes from when he became sole king. The only reason for this is to escape the logical contradictions they created by their incorrect initial assumptions. The longer chronology consistently measures time from when a king became viceroy. This procedure is in accord with the oldest Talmudic understanding of how this was done. Thiele, McFall, and others sweep aside methods of interpretation that are derived from the most ancient writers, in favour of a new capricious way of handling the text according to the external dictates of archaeology. Their work has indeed rendered the numbers of the Hebrew Kings most mysterious.

Christians have largely abdicated the fields of history and archaeology to those who are worldly wise. Many have been told, even in Bible colleges, that the historical portions of the Bible are unreliable. This is hardly faith-building! Fifty years ago, most Christians did not have ready access to the wealth of material we have today concerning science and evolution. We can thank Dr. Henry Morris and others who have followed in his steps for this. We do not have all the answers about Assyrian chronology and how it fits with the Bible. However, we must learn the same lesson about *history* as we learned about *science*. True science does not conflict with the Bible. Likewise, true history agrees with and does not refute the Scriptures. Pray that God will raise up Christians in the field of history to help us write a true history that honours the Bible.

Lewis Dabney was a *voice crying in the wilderness* 140 years ago. He recognized most clearly the problems and sounded a warning against the dangers of science, *falsely so called*, to the Church. No one listened and the Church madly pursued a course of compromise which would have destroyed her, but for the grace of God. At that time he said, concerning attacks made by geologists against the Bible:[15]

"The authority of the Bible, as our rule of faith, is demonstrated by its own separate and independent evidences, literary history, moral, internal, prophetical. It is found by the geologist in possession of the field, and he must assume the aggressive, and positively dislodge it from its position. The defender of the Bible need only stand on the defensive. That is, the geologist must not content himself with saying that his hypothesis, which is opposed to Bible teachings, is plausible, that it cannot be scientifically refuted, that it may adequately satisfy the requirements of all the physical phenomena to be accounted for. All this is naught, as a successful assault on us. We are not bound to retreat until he has constructed an absolutely exclusive demonstration of his hypothesis; until he has shown, by strict scientific proofs, not only that his hypothesis *may be* the true one, but that *it alone can be* the only true one; that it is impossible any other can exclude it."

What applies to attacks on the Bible from geology applies equally to attacks from historians and archaeologists. The Bible is the only book that provides a continuous history from creation down to the death of Nebuchadnezzar. More importantly, the Bible is the inspired Word of God and is without error. Assyrian chronology is not inspired and is fraught with errors. Both Thiele and McFall have too low a view of inspiration. If what they claim is true, why should we ever trust any historical portion in the Bible until it has been interpreted by the *sure word* of the archaeologist? If we cannot trust the numbers in the Bible, why should we trust the words between the numbers? Are we to trust the fallible word of sinful fallen men who have yet to get their first theory right? Or are we to trust the infallible Word written by God, who has yet to make his first mistake and never will?[16]

### Addendum:

The author strongly suggests to any critics that before responding to this item, they first download the work cited in footnote 16 and ensure that their arguments are derived from and based on the authority of the Bible.

### References

1. Edwin Thiele, *The Mysterious Numbers of the Hebrew Kings* (Chicago, IL: University of Chicago Press, 1951).

2. Ibid.

3. Edwin Thiele, *The Mysterious Numbers of the Hebrew Kings* (Grand Rapids, MI: William B. Eerdmans Publishing Co., 1965).

4. Edwin Thiele, *The Mysterious Numbers of the Hebrew Kings* (Grand Rapids, MI: Zondervan Corp., 1983).

5. Leslie McFall, "A Translation Guide to the Chronological Data in Kings and Chronicles," *Bibliotheca Sacra*, volume 148, number 589, January–March 1991. Guide is also available from: http://www.btinternet.com/~lmf12.

6. See footnote 3, p. 103 and 104; see footnote 1, p. 62 and 66.

7. *New International Dictionary of Biblical Archaeology* (Grand Rapids, MI: Zondervan Publishing House, 1983), entry: "Shalmaneser, Black Obelisk of," p. 409.

8. E.W. Faulstich, *History, Harmony & the Hebrew Kings* (Spencer, IA: Chronology Books, 1986), p. 143–157.

9. See footnote 7, entry: "Qarqar," p. 376.

10. James Ussher, *Annales Veteris Testamenti* (London, England: J. Flesher & L. Sadler, 1650), p. 139. (This work is in Latin. In this revised English edition, the paragraph number is 913 on page 113.)

11. See footnote 3, p. 16; see footnote 1, p. vi.

12. See footnote 3, p. 119; see footnote 1, p. 68–70 and 83. Each edition treats this matter in less detail than the previous edition.

13. *The International Bible Encyclopaedia*, article entitled "Chronology of the Old Testament" (Peabody, MA: Hendrickson Publishers, 1929), vol. 1, p. 640. (The original publication was published in 1909. Editor.)

14. Accession dating means that a king did not start counting his years of reign until the Jewish New Year was past. So the length of his reign is really given in the number of Jewish New Years he celebrated. According to the Bible this was in Nisan. (Exodus 12:2) According to Thiele and McFall, the godly Southern Kingdom used Tishri (about October), and the ungodly Northern Kingdom used Nisan (about April). No convincing proof is given except they say *it works*.

15. Robert Lewis Dabney, *Discussions of Robert Lewis Dabney* (Carlisle, PA: Banner of Truth Trust, 1982), vol. 3, p. 136.

16. A detailed outline of the longer chronology is available from the author and is available for download from Answers in Genesis website. In it, he considers all the numbers in not just Kings and Chronicles but from the prophets as well. All popular problems with the chronology are addressed in detail.

# Appendix E: Some Objections Considered

When we published the article "Evidentiallism — The Bible and Assyrian Chronology," Dr. Leslie McFall raised some issues in a letter that we will now deal with. It was quite satisfying to note that no one could point to any error in the divided kingdom article that would require one date to be altered. That alone is a necessary and sufficient condition to overthrow their defective systems of chronology.

Space will only permit us to reply to one of Dr. McFall's items dealing with 2 Kings 15:8. That should be sufficient to show the bankruptcy of the chronology based on Assyrian conjectures. We shall reply under the following heads:

a) Interregnum phobia is totally unjustified

b) Unwarranted biblical contradictions created by the Assyrian academy

c) Source of Assyrian academy conjectures — David Luckenbill's vivid imagination

d) Other problems — Sabbatic, Jubilee cycle

Dr. McFall noted two Scriptures that he claims would invalidate the concept of interregnums in the Northern Kingdom. We will deal with the concept of interregnums first.

**Interregnum Phobia**

The concept of interregnums in biblical history seems strange at first to those who are not aware of the history for that period. The fact that the Bible does not directly mention them should not be a concern if the information can be logically deduced from the biblical data. The Bible does not mention viceroy relationships or the Trinity either, but these can all be logically deduced from the Scriptures, and few Christians doubt these. If the logical reasoning is correct, such deductions are just as valid as the Scriptures themselves. (This may come as a shock to "modern evangelicals" who decry the use of logic. Those of the Reformed faith are quite familiar with this concept and have enshrined it in Article VI of Chapter I of the Westminster Confession of Faith.) Here is a trivial example to illustrate the point. Nowhere does the Bible say Absalom was the son of a king of Israel. This fact can be deduced from the Bible because we know that Absalom was the son of David and David was a king of Israel. Therefore, applying logic, Absalom was the son of a king of Israel.

The concept of interregnums is not new and was common in this period of history among foreign nations. Therefore, we should not be surprised, given the political turmoil in the Northern Kingdom, to find one or more interregnums during the death-throes of that kingdom. The Southern Kingdom was much more stable during this time and we should not expect to find interregnums there.

From history, we know of at least four interregnums in foreign countries.

1) In 704 BC, after Arkeanos, there was no king in Babylon for two years. {*Ptolemy, Canon of Kings*}

2) In 688 BC, there was no king in Babylon for eight years. {*Ptolemy, Canon of Kings*}

3) In 687 BC, civil disorder increased in Egypt, because there was no king for two years. {*Diodorus Siciculus, Book 1, Chapter 66 (page 227 in Loeb edition)*}

4) In 637 BC, there was a one year interregnum in Babylon. {*Gershon Galil, The Chronology of the Kings of Israel and Judah, p. 120.*}

All serious students of history know about these interregnums. We are not surprised that those advocating the use of the conjectured Assyrian chronology to amend the Bible, conveniently forget about them, and recoil in horror at such a concept, for they know that if the concept is allowed, it is fatal to their schemes of interpretation. Neither Dr. Thiele nor Dr. McFall breathe a word about this and indeed it is one of the best-kept secrets of the Assyrian Academy. Indeed, Galil goes so far as to state in his basic assumptions (without proof) there were no interregnums in the biblical chronology! This begs the question — "How does he know?"

Therefore, the problem is not with the concept of interregnums, but with trying to reconcile the alleged reconstructions of Assyrian history with the biblical chronology. In order to do so, it just so happens that two interregnums in the Northern Kingdom must be eliminated. This raises two questions.

1) Can this be done without compromising the biblical chronology? We have shown that this is impossible but will go over the same ground in more simple terms so you will be able to clearly see the problem.

2) How do we know the reconstruction of the Assyrian chronology is accurate?

Only Dr. McFall's letter mentions any biblical data, and we will deal with those issues first. All biblical quotations are from the Authorized Version unless otherwise noted.

1) **2 Kings 15:8** — This verse says that:

> "In the thirty and eighth year of Azariah [Uzziah] king of Judah did Zachariah the son of Jeroboam reign over Israel in Samaria six months."

Dr. Mcfall says that Jeroboam II died in the 38th year of Uzziah before Zachariah came to the throne. Although the actual verse mentions nothing of this (however, it may be inferred from 2 Kings 14:29), let's grant this conjecture and see if it is logically consistent with the statements of the Scripture. If Dr. McFall can prove his claim correct from the Bible, then the first interregnum is a fiction of Ussher. If he cannot, then the whole Assyrian-based reconstruction of the biblical chronology is incorrect and comes tumbling down like a house of cards.

**Required to Prove:** There was no interregnum after the death of Jeroboam II and his son Zachariah reigned immediately after his father.

**Proof:**

> "And Jeroboam slept with his fathers, even with the kings of Israel; and Zachariah his son reigned in his stead." {2Ki 14:28}

> "In the thirty and eighth year of Azariah king of Judah did Zachariah the son of Jeroboam reign over Israel in Samaria six months." {2Ki 15:8}

Before we proceed, we should note that the phrase "reigned in his stead" does not necessarily mean the son directly reigned after his father. If there are no other time statements relating to the transition, this may be a safe assumption to make. You can assume that if you are making a list of kings, the son ruled after his father in that order. This exact same Hebrew phrase occurs in 1 Kings 22:50, and even Dr. McFall admits that if you were to assume that Jehoram started to reign after the death of Jehoshaphat you would be incorrect. How do you know? There are other time statements that define the time when Jehoram began to reign. These MUST be used to qualify and interpret this verse.

In the case before us, there indeed are other Scriptures containing time statements to consider and we cannot take 2 Kings 14:28, 15:8 in isolation:

> "In the twenty and seventh year of Jeroboam king of Israel began Azariah [Uzziah] son of Amaziah king of Judah to reign." {2Ki 15:1}

Therefore, according to Dr. McFall, Uzziah must have been viceroy for 24 years because he was made sole king in the 27th year of Jeroboam and Jeroboam died in the 38th year of Uzziah when his son Zachariah ruled.

But the next verse states:

> "Sixteen years old was he [Uzziah] when he began to reign, and he reigned two and fifty years in Jerusalem." {2Ki 15:2}

We have arrived at a contradiction, for it is impossible to do anything eight years before you are born! (24 - 16 = 8 years) To avoid this problem, Dr. McFall says this refers to the first time Uzziah was made viceroy and the verses should now be read as follows:

> "In the twenty and seventh year of Jeroboam king of Israel began Azariah son of Amaziah king of Judah to reign *AS SOLE KING*. Sixteen years old was he when he began to reign *AS A VICEROY TWENTY FOUR YEARS EARLIER.*"

The text in capitals is Dr. McFall's amendment interpretation to the text. This is a neat dodge and no proof is given. Dr. McFall is forced to put forth this interpretation because of his premise that there are no interregnums. The problem now gets worse, for look at these verses:

> "[19] Now they made a conspiracy against him [Amaziah] in Jerusalem: and he fled to Lachish; but they sent after him to Lachish, and slew him there. [20] And they brought him on horses: and he was buried at Jerusalem with his fathers in the city of David. [21] And all the people of Judah took Azariah [Uzziah], which was sixteen years old, and made him king instead of his father Amaziah." {2Ki 14:19-21 with a parallel passage in 2Ch 25:27-26:1}

Ask a child what these verses mean and he will tell you without exception that the people killed Amaziah and made Uzziah king when he was 16 years old. Here we have a second contradiction!

Dr. McFall is aware of this and digs himself in still deeper and says the verses must be read as follows:

> "[21] And all the people of Judah took Azariah [Uzziah], which was sixteen years old, and made him king instead of his father Amaziah. [19] Now *TWENTY-FOUR YEARS LATER*, they made a conspiracy against him [Amaziah] in Jerusalem: and he fled to Lachish; but they sent after him to Lachish, and slew him there. [20] And they brought him on horses: and he was buried at Jerusalem with his fathers in the city of David." {2Ki 14:19-21}

"¹Then all the people of Judah took Uzziah, who [was] sixteen years old, and made him king in the room of his father Amaziah. ²⁷Now after the time *TWENTY-FOUR YEARS LATER* that Amaziah did turn away from following the LORD they made a conspiracy against him in Jerusalem; and he fled to Lachish: but they sent to Lachish after him, and slew him there. ²⁸And they brought him upon horses, and buried him with his fathers in the city of Judah."
{*2 Ch 25:27-26:1*}

The king — not the people — appointed his viceroy. Israel was not a democracy, at least not when there was a living king as there would have been in this case if Dr. McFall's conjecture is correct. The text in capitals is Dr. McFall's amendment to the text. Dr. McFall forces an unnatural order on the historical narrative by claiming that verse 21 should really come before verse 19 in the 2 Kings passage and likewise a similar transposition in the passage cited from 2 Chronicles as you can see in our reproduction. (This violates accepted rules of Hebrew grammar.) This begs the question, if the writer of Kings got the verses in the wrong order, why did not the later writer of the Chronicles fix it up? The only rationale for Dr. McFall's amendment is trying to eliminate this interregnum. It seems the Holy Spirit has gone to great pains to make such an amendment by Dr. McFall untenable.

No proof is given for this amendment either, except for Dr. McFall's commitment to Assyrian chronology. Stating something is so does not prove it so, at least when I went to university. Likewise, it is a "no-no" to use your premise as part of your proof. This logical fallacy has a cute Latin name — *petito principii* — and is known in English as *begging the question*. The only way you can prove there was no interregnum after the death of Jeroboam II is if you assume there are no interregnums and then read the Scripture in that light. Dr. McFall's rationale for this assumption is his commitment to Assyrian chronology which forces him to delete 40 or so years from the divided kingdom. If you honestly start from the Word of God and that alone, you will never arrive at a chronology remotely resembling what Dr. McFall promotes. The very fact that the best theologians down through the millennia never dreamed of this gloss Dr. McFall and Dr. Thiele force on these Scriptures, should make one very wary of their novel theories.

## Review of Pivotal Dates in Assyrian Chronology

### 1. Fall of Samaria 723 BC and the Assyrian Eponym List

Lets look at a section of the Assyrian eponym list so you can see for yourself how flimsy the evidence is for Assyrian history.

Dr. Thiele firmly declares that Samaria fell in 723 BC and adjusts the biblical chronology two years to shift the biblically deduced date of 721 BC to 723. (If the integrity of the Scriptures was not at stake, this is no big deal!) This he claims is supported by the eponym list and publishes a copy of the list in Appendix F of his work *The Mysterious Numbers of the Hebrew Kings*. Lets take a look at what was actually published. Dr. Jones has provided this information and I can do no better than quote him directly. {*Dr. Floyd Jones, Chronology of the Old Testament, p. 190, KingWord Press, The Woodlands, Texas, 1999*}

…Unfortunately, the register is badly mutilated for the years 725–720; nonetheless, Luckenbill has restored them to read: {*Luckenbill, Ancient Records of Assyria and Babylonia, Vol. II., p. 437. New York: Greenwood Press. 1968*}

| 726 | Marduk-bel-usur | (governor) of Amedi | in the land |
|---|---|---|---|
| 725 | Mahde | (governor) of Nineveh | against [Samaria] |
| 724 | Ash-ishmeani | (governor) of [Kakzi] | against [Samaria] |
| 723 | Shalmaneser | king of Assyria | against [Samaria] |
| 722 | Urt-ilia | [field-marshal] | [the foundation of the temple of Nabu was torn up (for repairs)] |
| 721 | Nabutaris | [high chamberlain] | [Natu entered the new temple] |

However, the fact is the eye/mind cannot properly appreciate the full significance of the fragmented nature of the above, even with the brackets and parenthesis present. The true extent of the mutilation can be seen below. Bear in mind that this is how the register actually appears, only without the years being listed.

| 726 | Marduk-bel-usur | of Amedi | in the land |
|---|---|---|---|
| 725 | Mahde | of Nineveh | against |
| 724 | Ash-ishmeani | of | against |
| 723 | Shalmaneser | king of Assyria | against |
| 722 | Urt-ilia | | |
| 722 | Nabutaris | | |

This then is the *only* Assyrian evidence which is uncontested. The rationale for using it to establish the date for the fall of Samaria is:

1. The biblical account states that the siege of Samaria lasted *three* years.

2. The eponym list has the word "against" *three* years in succession (725–723) with the name of enemy location completely missed.

3. The coincidence of both "three's" was deemed by Luckenbill (Olmstead also) as the "restoration" as shown in the first listing and subsequent "fixing" of the date of the fall of Samaria as being 723 BC.

This ends the quote from Dr. Jones. As one can see, the 723 BC date for the fall of Samaria rests firmly on scholarly conjecture and interpolation. There are better foundations to build a history on! There is absolutely no evidence from the actual eponym list to contradict the established date of 721 BC or any other date you wish for the fall of Samaria *BECAUSE* the translated list, when the scholarly interpolations are deleted, *NEVER MENTIONS SAMARIA!*

Even worse for Luckenbill is a later independent translation of the eponym list done in 1994 which has even less data and none of Luckenbill's interpolations. Consider this and note the text in [ ] is conjectured:

| 726 | Marduk-belu*-usur | [of Ame]di | i[      ] |
| 725 | Mahde | of Nineveh | to [     ] |
| 724 | Ashur*-ishmeani | [of Kili]zi | to [     ] |
| 723 | Shalmaneser (V) | king [of Assyria] | t[o     ] |
| 722 | Niurta-ilaya* | [       |         ] |
| 722 | Nabu-taris | [       | t]i |

I marked the name changes with an "*". Note the major change in the name for the entry for 722 BC. Luckenbill did not even mark the interpolated text correctly! What this does establish is that Luckenbill has a very vivid imagination and any translation he does should be carefully checked for accuracy to make sure nothing is read into the translations.

### 2. Jehu and the Black Obelisk in 841 BC

Dr. Thiele accepts as an established fact that Jehu paid tribute to Shalmaneser in 841. As we pointed out in the article, there is *NO EVIDENCE* that the obelisk was actually depicting the Israelite monarch Jehu. So much for this date! Are you surprised that the translation *scholars* use to justify this was done by Luckenbill? The only rationale for even thinking it was Jehu is the alleged presence of Ahab at the battle of Qarqar in 853 BC. Even that rests on much conjecture! Dr. Jones pointed out that the image of the individual in the picture shows

him with a rounded beard, something the Jewish law had forbidden. This casts further doubt that this was really Jehu.

### 3. Ahab and the battle of Qarqar. 853 BC

This is the most critical date, for if it can be established beyond a shadow of a doubt, then there are serious problems with the Hebrew Bible text we have. Again, we can do no better than quote Dr. Floyd Jones on this matter:

> "Simply stated, the problem begins with the fact that the 'Monolith Inscription' documents that in the sixth year of his reign, Shalmaneser II (III), son of Ashur-nasir-pal (II), fought against a twelve king alliance at the battle of Qarqar (Karkar) during the eponymous year of Daian-Assur. The inscription states that one of the kings against whom King Shalmaneser II (III) engaged was a certain 'A-ha-ab-bu Sir-i-la-a-a.'"

Before we continue with Dr. Jones's quote, note that Luckenbill translates this as *Ahab of Samaria,* and notes that he had 2,000 chariots and 10,000 men. Now the Hebrew and Assyrian language are quite closely related. In their consonantal form (as we would expect to see on inscriptions), we would expect the same names to share at least the same consonants. *IN BOTH OF THESE CASES THEY DIFFER FROM THE HEBREW CONSONANTAL FORM!* Hence, it would be reasonable to conclude that we are not talking about the same person as Ahab in the Bible. This is especially true when we look at the history of Ahab. His kingdom had a 42-month drought. Today, much shorter droughts in Africa virtually eliminated the livestock including horses, and no doubt this was true in Ahab's case, too. In spite of this, we are to believe that Ahab had more chariots than even Solomon who only had 1,400? About 70 years earlier, Israel could field an army of 800,000 men, whereas now Ahab is hard pressed to get even one percent of this total, yet we are to believe he had more chariots than Solomon! Where did all the horses come from to pull these? Also, when Ahab was attacked a few years before his death, he could only muster a force of 7,000 men. The ratio of chariots to men does not correspond to actual battles, for the number of chariots is much too high for the fighting force or the number for the men is low by at least an order of magnitude or more. Something is very wrong here.

Dr. Jones[1] notes further:

Most Assyriologists understand "A-ha-ab-bu Sir-i-la-a-a" to be Ahab, the Israelite. This may be true, but there are problems associated with this identification. First, the identification may be incorrect. "A-ha-ab-bu Sir-i-la-a-a" may be some other historically obscure ruler, perhaps of something no more than a city-state anywhere along the nearly three hundred mile seacoast area of the fertile crescent. Some researchers go so far as to accuse Shalmaneser II (III) of taking credit for this and other events which actually belonged to his father, Ashur-nasir-pal (II). Among them, Faulstich addresses several perceived inconsistencies or contradictions regarding military expeditions and warns:[2]

> "Some of the claims of Shalmaneser are preposterous, and it would be ill-advised to reconstruct the Hebrew chronology to satisfy his inaccurate boasting."

After advancing examples, he concludes:[3]

> "...that the inconsistencies in Shalmaneser's annals would make it impossible to accurately date the battle of Qarqar."

Whereas we do not concur with or endorse all of Faulstich's determinations, we cite him to expose the uncertain nature of much of the oft-cited Assyrian assertions. Nor is Faulstich alone. Daniel David Luckenbill cautions in his comments prior to Shalmaneser's royal annals that:

> "It is possible that the first of these, which contained a full account of the events of the year of accession, belongs to a much earlier period."[4]

Thus, says Dr. Jones. Space does not permit us to deal with the second verse mentioned by Dr. McFall. See Dr. Jones's work for a full treatment of that point.

## Sabbatical and Jubilee Cycles

These two cycles run like a checksum through biblical history. When one accurately reconstructs biblical history, he should expect the cycles to agree with secular history, for Josephus records a sabbatical year in 163 BC and 37 BC. This agrees with the start of the first sabbatical year as deduced from the Bible by Ussher of 1445 BC and the resulting cycles. If you start to delete years (unless they are a multiple of 7 for the sabbatical cycle) from the Divided Kingdom, you can no longer make the sabbatic cycle agree with the observations of Josephus. Ussher noted some very interesting Jubilee years in history:

a) When Solomon finished the temple in the eighth month (about November) of 1005 BC, he waited until the seventh month (about October) of the following year to dedicate this multi-billion dollar building — the seventh month of 1004 BC was the start of a Jubilee.

b) The seventh month of the same year of Hezekiah's deliverance from the Assyrians in 710 BC, was the start of a Jubilee.

c) The Jubilee year in 563/562 BC marked the year when Nebuchadnezzar was freed from his insanity and Jeconiah was freed from his imprisonment.

d) The last Jubilee in biblical history heralded the start of the ministry of John the Baptist in the fall of 26 AD.

The last three relationships are lost if one follows the Assyrian Academy's reconstruction of biblical history. Space does not permit me to go into greater detail on this, except to note that not one of the conjectured reconstructions of the Divided Kingdom by the Assyrian Academy, agrees with the sabbatic cycles and they do not even mention the subject! Ussher's reconstruction agrees perfectly.

## Conclusion:

Enough has been said to show the following:

a) Interregnums were relatively common during this period of history and to arbitrarily exclude them based on preconceived notions is unjustified.

b) In dealing with the first interregnum in Israel, we have shown that you cannot eliminate it without severely undermining the obvious meaning of the text in at least five places!

c) The Assyrian data used to eliminate the interregnums in Israel is in itself highly suspect.

d) No one could point to any error in my article on the Divided Kingdom that required one date to change. This is not surprising since the errors noted were mainly obscure spelling errors — blunders according to Dr. McFall! — and that in itself undermines their position.

This is a whole new area for creationists to explore and reclaim back from the secular *scholars*. Dr. Floyd Jones's ground-breaking work, *Chronology of the Old Testament,* has opened the way for further research. His work is available from AiG for those who are really serious about the farce some scholars have made of the biblical history by their Assyrian conjectures. Dr. Jones's work contains a much fuller treatment of the points raised in these letters plus many other issues dealing with biblical history.

## References:

1. Dr. Floyd Jones, *Chronology of the Old Testament* (The Woodlands, TX: KingsWord Press, 1999), p. 159–160.

2. E.W. Faulstich, *History, Harmony & the Hebrew Kings* (Spencer, IA: Chronology Books, 1986), p. 144. See p. 143–157 where he details his thesis.

3. David Luckenbill, *Ancient Records of Assyria and Babylonia,* Vol. 1, sec. 626 (New York, NY: Greenwood Press, 1968), p. 157.

4. Ibid., p. 232.

# Appendix F: MAPS
## Ionia and Western Asia Minor

MAP OF
**IONIA AND
WESTERN ASIA MINOR**

Scale

0  100  200  300  400 Stadia

0  10  20  30  40  50 Miles

# Thrace and the Euxine

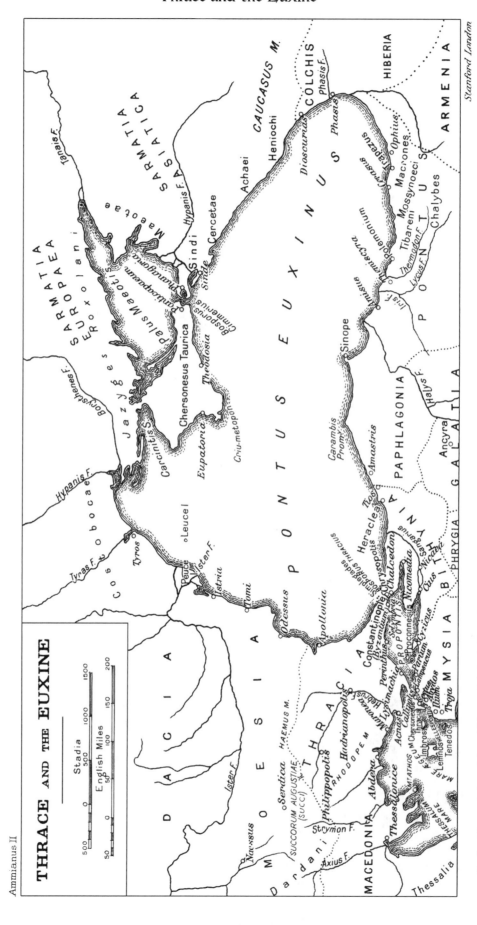

# Conquests of Alexander

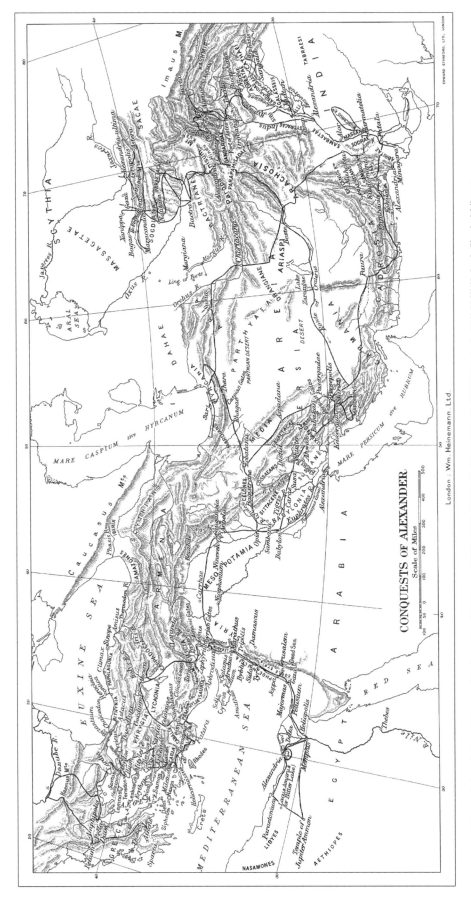

## CONQUESTS OF ALEXANDER
### Scale of Miles

London : Wm. Heinemann Ltd

# Sicily and Greece

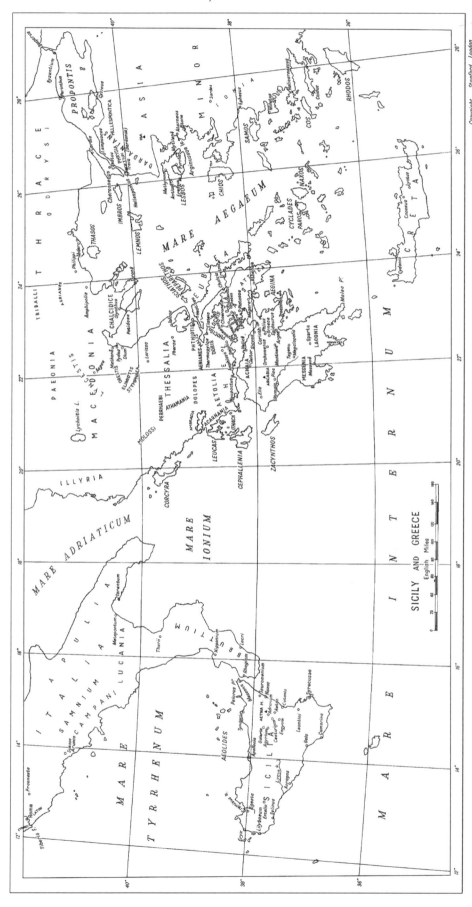

SICILY AND GREECE

Reprinted by permission of the publishers and the Loeb Classical Library, DIODORUS SICULUS: LIBRARY OF HISTORY, Books XVI.66-XVII, Loeb Classical Library Volume L422, Cambridge, Mass.: Harvard University Press, 1963. The Loeb Classical Library ® is a registered trademark of the President and Fellows of Harvard College.

# Appendix G: The *Seder Olam Rabbah* —Why Jewish Dating Is Different

The *Seder Olam Rabbah*[1] or the *Book of the Order of the World* was compiled by Rabbi Yose ben Halafta (died 160 AD), and is to this day the traditional Jewish chronology.[2] From this ancient work, the Jewish people reckon the current year (2003 AD) as 5763 and understand it to be the number of years since the creation.

At the time the *Seder Olam* was compiled, the Jews generally dated their years from 312 BC—the beginning of the Seleucid era. For the next few centuries, the *Seder Olam* was of interest exclusively to only students of the Talmud.[3]

When the centre of Jewish life moved from Babylonia to Europe during the 8th and 9th centuries AD, calculations from the Seleucid era became meaningless. Over those centuries, it was replaced by that of the *anno mundi* era (AM = "from the creation of the world") of the *Seder Olam*. From the 11th century, *anno mundi* dating became dominant throughout most of the world's Jewish communities.[4]

As Old Testament Scripture is the basis for *Seder Olam* dating, we would suppose the Jewish chronology to be similar to that of Ussher's and thus expect them to place the creation date around 6,000 years ago. Yet rather than 4004 BC, the *Seder Olam* places creation at 3761. The question thus becomes: On what basis do the Jews number their years such that a 243-year shortfall occurs?

**The Missing Years:**[5]

1. From the creation to the birth of Abraham

| Ussher | 2008 years | 4004–1996 BC |
|---|---|---|
| *Seder Olam* | 1948 years | 3761–1811 BC (exclusive reckoning) |
| | shortfall — 60 years | |

Terah was 130 years old rather than 70 when Abraham was born (Ge 11:26; but cf. Ge 11:32 12:4 where 205-75 = 130). Thus, the first deficit is about 60 years.

2. From the birth of Abraham to the Exodus

| Ussher | 505 years | 1996–1491 BC |
|---|---|---|
| *Seder Olam* | 500 years | 1811–1311 BC |
| | shortfall — 5 years | |

Abraham was 75 years old when the covenant was made; {*Ge 12:4*} the Exodus was 430 years later. {*Ga 3:17 Ex 12:40-41*} Without New Testament revelation for clarification, the *Seder Olam* reckons five fewer years. The shortfall now totals 65 years.

3. From the exodus to the laying of the temple foundation {*1Ki 6:1*}

| Ussher | 480 years | 1491–1012 BC (inclusive reckoning) |
|---|---|---|
| *Seder Olam* | 480 years | 1311–831 BC |
| | shortfall — 0 years | |

As there is no difference, the total shortfall remains at 65 years.

4. From the foundation of the first temple to the consecration of the second temple

| Ussher | 497 years | 1012–515 BC |
|---|---|---|
| *Seder Olam* | 480 years | 831–351 BC |
| | shortfall — 17 years | |

Differing decisions in placing the dates of the kings of Israel with respect to the kings of Judah during the period of the divided monarchy account for these 17 years.

Thus far, the *Seder Olam* reckons 82 (65 + 17) fewer years over a 3,489 year span (4004–515) from creation to the consecration of the second temple—of which the major part concerns the age of Terah at Abraham's birth.

5. From the consecration of the second temple to its destruction by Titus of Rome

| Ussher | 584 years | 515 BC–70 AD |
|---|---|---|
| *Seder Olam* | 420 years | 351 BC–70 AD |
| | shortfall — 164 years | |

Here we see the main source of the discrepancy found in the *Seder Olam*'s shorter chronology. Its 420 years are divided into spans of 34, 180, 103, and 103 years of successive foreign rule over Israel. As shown in that which follows, it is remarkable that the 164-year disparity is almost entirely from within (a; see below), the first or Persian period. The remaining three periods closely approximate that of the standard chronology.[6]

a) 34 years (351–317 BC) for the remainder of the Persian rule over Israel: from the dedication of the second temple to Ptolemy I Soter's invasion of Jerusalem (Ptolemy I was one of Alexander the Great's favourite generals—also called Soter or Saviour, 367?–283 BC. After Alexander's death in 323, he seized Egypt as his share of the divided Greek empire and assumed the title "King of Egypt").

b) 180 years (317–137 BC) for the Grecian rule: from Ptolemy's invasion to the times when Simon the Maccabean became ruler in Israel and Rome recognized the independence of the Jewish state.

c) 103 years (137–34 BC) for the rule of the Hasmonean (Maccabean) family in Israel: from Simon to the beginning of the reign of Herod the Great.

d) 103 years (34 BC–70 AD) for the Herodian rule until the destruction of the temple.

There is some discrepancy with the standard dates in the later three periods (b, c, & d). The standard date for Alexander's defeat of Darius is 331 BC rather than the *Seder Olam's* 321. It gives Simon's rule as beginning in 142 BC (not 137) and Herod's in 37 BC (not 34).[7]

But what are we to understand from (a) where the *Seder Olam* allows only 34 years for the remainder of the Persian period? Indeed, by *Seder Olam* reckoning there are only 30 years from the dedication of the second temple to Darius' defeat at the hands of Alexander in 321 BC and merely four years after that unto Jerusalem's capture by Ptolemy following Alexander's death.

Moreover, here the two systems exhibit a striking contrast. The Ptolemaic chronology lists eight Persian kings from Darius I Hystaspes to Darius III Codomannus, the king whom Alexander overcame. However, the *Seder Olam* identifies the Darius who was reigning during the dedication of the second temple as the same Darius that Alexander defeated.[8]

Recording only five Persian monarchs, the *Seder Olam* gives the following chronology for its 52/53-year depiction of Persian history:

1. Darius the Mede reigns 1 year
       3389–3390 AM (374–373 BC)
   Babylon conquered
   Daniel in the lions den

2. Cyrus reigns 3 years
       3390–3392 AM (373–371 BC, inclusive)
   The Jews return
   Second temple construction begins

3. Artaxerxes (Cambyses) reigns one-half year
       3393 AM (370 BC)
   Temple construction halted

4. Ahasuerus reigns 14 years
       3393–3407 AM (370–356 BC)
   Esther chosen Queen
   Esther bears Darius the Persian

5. Darius the Persian reigns 35 years
       3407–3442 AM (356 BC)
   Temple construction resumes — 3408 AM (355 BC)
   Second temple dedicated — 3412 AM (355 BC)
   Ezra comes to Jerusalem — 3413 AM (350 BC)
   Nehemiah comes to Jerusalem — 3426 AM (337 BC)
   Darius defeated by Alexander — 3442 AM (321 BC)

Thus, the *Seder Olam* depicts the Kingdom of Persia as lasting a mere 53 years from 374 to 321 BC, rather than about 207 years (538-331 BC).[9]

Over the centuries, orthodox rabbis have differed somewhat in their listing of the Persian kings, but they generally have not departed from the 52/53-year parameter established within the *Seder Olam*.[10]

The result of this shorting of the span of the Persian Empire is that the paramount prophecy and major foundation block of chronology—the Daniel 9:25 seventy weeks of years—has become dislodged. Furthermore, this shorting as perpetuated within the *Seder Olam* is deliberate!

While not openly admitting this, present day Jewish scholars acknowledge that there is something enigmatic about the *Seder Olam's* dating. For example, after stating that the commonly received dates in the Ptolemaic chronology "can hardly be doubted," Rabbi Simon Schwab nevertheless goes on to uphold his own tradition:[11]

"It should have been possible that our Sages—for some unknown reason—had 'covered up' a certain historic period and *purposely eliminated and suppressed all records and other material pertaining thereto.* If so, what might have been their compelling reason for so unusual a procedure? Nothing short of a *Divine command* could have prompted ...those saintly 'men of truth' to leave out completely from our annals a period of 165 years and to correct all data and historic tables in such a fashion that the subsequent chronological gap could escape being noticed by countless generations, known to a few initiates only who were duty-bound to keep the secret to themselves." (emphasis Schwab's)

This is an astonishing proposal! Schwab, along with other Jewish commentators, further suggests that the reason God directed the sages of the 2nd century AD to become involved in falsifying the data was to confuse anyone who might try to use the prophecies of Daniel to predict the time of the Messiah's coming.

This was supposedly done to honour Da 12:4: "shut up the words, and seal the book, even to the time of the end." He adds that the reason the sages had adopted the non-Jewish Seleucid Era calendar was part of the scheme to do just that—to close up the words and seal the book of Daniel.[12] Schwab also states that if the 165 years were included it would reveal, "we are much closer to the end of the 6th Millennium than we had surmised"[13] (Schwab mentions this date as the time when many rabbis expect Messiah to come.).

But can any sincere reader accept such a flimsy reason as justification for distorting history? It actually accuses God himself of perpetrating a dishonest deception.

Indeed, it is manifestly apparent that the real reasons for the deliberate altering of their own national chronology in the *Seder Olam* were: (1) to conceal the fact that the Da 9:25 prophecy clearly pointed to Jesus of Nazareth as its fulfilment and therefore the long awaited Messiah, and (2) to make that seventy week of years prophecy point instead to Simon Bar Kokhba!

Rabbis in the century immediately following Christ Jesus had a tremendous problem with so direct a prophecy as Da 9:24–27. This chapter speaks of Messiah's appearing 69 "weeks" (i.e., 69 sevens) or 483 years after the going forth of a commandment to restore and to build Jerusalem. This 538 BC prophecy {Da 9:1} unmistakably points to the start of the ministry of Jesus Christ in 29 AD.

Such must either be acknowledged and his person accepted or completely erased from Jewish consciousness. The latter could be accomplished if the 69 (or 70) weeks of years could somehow be made to apply to the century after the life of Christ. Then it would be possible for the rabbis to point to *another messiah* who, as circumstances would have it, was cut off in death some 100 years after the crucifixion of our Lord.[14]

The 10th day of the month Ab (c. mid-August) is a great day of sorrow to Israel. On this day in 588 BC, the Babylonians destroyed Solomon's Temple. Further, the second temple was laid waste by the Romans under Titus on the same day in 70 AD. And on this very day in 135 AD, at the conclusion of a 3½-year revolt, the Romans crushed the army of the "messianic" Simon Bar Kokhba (also spelled "Cocheba").

Bar Kokhba had been declared the long-awaited Messiah by the foremost Jewish scholar of that day, the highly venerated Rabbi Akiva (Akiba) ben Joseph. In 130 AD, Emperor Hadrian of Rome declared his intention to raise a shrine to Jupiter on the site of the temple,[15] and in 131 he issued a decree forbidding circumcision as well as public instruction in the Jewish law.[16] Having preached peace all his life, the 90-year-old Akiva gave his blessing to the revolution by proclaiming that Bar Kokhba was the "star out of Jacob" and the "sceptre out of Israel." {Nu 24:17}[17]

In his 98th year, Akiva was eventually imprisoned and condemned to death by the Romans.[18] Among the many accolades heaped upon Akiva, that which elevated him as a pre-eminent authority, was the acknowledging of him as "the father of the Mishnah."[19] Such prominence gave great weight to the messianic expectancy Akiva placed upon Bar Kokhba.

Akiva's students became some of the most prominent sages of the following generation. Among these was Yose (Josi) ben Halafta. Akiva's influence on Halafta is apparent from a statement made concerning his education; it was merely said that Rabbi Akiva had been his teacher.[20] As his mentor, Akiva's regard for Bar Kokhba would have been thoroughly imbedded in Yose.[21]

The preceding overview explains why the *Seder Olam* is held in such veneration and why the Jews still use it for their national dating. Yet the fact remains that it is a dishonest attempt to conceal the truth with regard to the Da 9:24–27 prophecy.

By removing the 164 (or 165) years from the duration of the Persian Empire, Rabbi Halafta was able to make the 483 year Da 9:24–27 prophecy fall reasonably close to the years prior to the 132 AD revolt during which Bar Kokhba rose to prominence as Israel's military and economic leader.[22] Then with Akiva proclaiming, "This is the King Messiah"[23] followed by "all the contemporary sages regarded him as the King Messiah,"[24] the Jewish populace united around this false hope.

Dio Cassius states that the whole of Judea was in revolt. To quell the rebellion, Hadrian dispatched Julius Severus, his ablest general, from Britain. The Romans destroyed 985 towns in Palestine and slew 580,000 men. A still larger number perished through starvation, disease, and fire. All Judah was laid waste, and Bar Kokhba himself fell while defending Bethar.[25]

Even more astonishing is that "even in later generations, despite the disappointment engendered by his defeat, his image persisted as the embodiment of messianic hopes."[26] Indeed, the consistent verdict of Jewish historians is: "The most important historical messianic figure was surely Bar Kokhba."[27]

Yose ben Halafta[28] and his fellow compilers of the *Seder Olam* sought to terminate the 69 "weeks of years" as close to the 132 AD revolt as possible, but they were limited as to where they could make the "cuts." As the chronology of the Seleucid era onward was firmly fixed among the Jews, years could not be pared from their history after 312 BC.

Since the Da 9:24–27 prophecy dealt with a decree that was biblically and historically issued by a Persian monarch, this left only the Persian period of history for them to exploit. The Persians had been so hated by the Greeks and later by the Moslems that these two conquerors destroyed nearly all of the Persian records. This has created great difficulty in recovering their sequence of kings, the length of their reigns, and thereby their chronology. Thus, the Persian period was readily vulnerable to manipulation.[29]

This author offers the conclusions given herein as the only reasonable, logical deductions that can be drawn from the historical and biblical facts.

Floyd Nolen Jones, Th. D., Ph. D., 2003 AD,
minor editing by Larry Pierce

**References:**

1. The *Seder Olam* is divided into three parts, each consisting of ten chapters (called tractates). Part One gives the dates of major events from the creation to the crossing of the Jordan River under Joshua's command. Part Two extends from the Jordan crossing to the murder of Zachariah, King of Israel. {2Ki 15:10} Chapters 21–27 of Part Three extend to Nebuchadnezzar's destruction of the temple, and chapter 28 to the conquest of Babylon by Cyrus. Chapter 29 and the first part of 30 cover the Persian period. The remainder of chapter 30 contains a summary of events from the conquest of Persia by Alexander to the 132 AD Bar Kokhba (also spelled "Cocheba") revolt during the reign of Hadrian (AD 76–138). *Encyclopedia Judaica* (Jerusalem, Israel: Keter Publishing House, Ltd., 1971), Vol. 14, "Seder Olam Rabbah," p. 1091–1092.

2. Jack Moorman, *Bible Chronology: The Two Great Divides* (Collingswood, NJ: Bible For Today Press, 1999), p. 10–15. Moorman's research was a primary source for this exposé.

3. *Encyclopedia Judaica*, "Seder Olam Rabbah." p. 1092.

4. *Ibid.*

5. Not having access to *Seder Olam* for this exposé, the numbers are those recorded by Moorman. As his source occasionally reckoned exclusively or inclusively, so did he. Most Jewish dates may be confirmed in Jack Finegan, *Handbook of Biblical Chronology* (Peabody MA: Hendrickson Publishers, 1998), p. 130.

6. Moorman, *Bible Chronology: The Two Great Divides,* p. 12.

7. *Ibid.*

8. Martin Anstey, *The Romance of Bible Chronology* (London: Marshall Bros., 1913), p. 23–24.

9. Moorman, *Bible Chronology: The Two Great Divides,* p. 12.

10. *Ibid.* p. 13.

11. Simon Schwab, *Dr. Joseph Breuer Jubilee Volume,* "Comparative Jewish Chronology" (New York, NY: Rabbi Samson Raphael Hirsch Publications Society, Philipp Felheim Inc., 1962), p. 188.

12. Shimon Schwab, *Selected Speeches: A Collection of Addresses and Essays on Hashkafah, Contemporary Issues and Jewish History,* "Comparative Jewish Chronology" (Lakewood, NJ: CIS Pub., 1991), p. 270–272.

13. Schwab, *Dr. Joseph Breuer Jubilee Volume,* p. 190–191.

14. Of course no such admission by any of the Jewish sages can be cited, but the facts are obvious.

15. Dio Cassius, *Roman History,* Vol. VIII, Loeb (2000), Bk. 69, p. 447.

16. Will Durant, *The Story of Civilization. Caesar and Christ,* Volume 3 (New York, NY: Simon and Schuster, 1944), p. 548.

17. *Encyclopedia Judaica,* Vol. 2, "Akiva," p. 489.

18. Durant, *The Story of Civilization. Caesar and Christ,* p. 548–549.

19. Akiva made a preliminary gathering and formulation of the material for the six orders (containing 63 chapters or tractates) of that religious code which was the heart of the Talmud. Near the end of the 2nd century, Judah ha-Nasi completed the work. Moorman, *Bible Chronology: The Two Great Divides,* p. 14.

20. *Encyclopedia Judaica,* Vol. 16, "Yose ben Halafta." p. 852.

21. *Ibid.* p. 853. Yose ben Halaft's own influence may be seen in that some of his writings were included in Judah ha-Nasi's final editing of the Mishnah, and his name is mentioned in 59 of its 63 tractates. Though referred to in the Mishnah and Talmud, Halafta's *Seder Olam* is not a formal part of that work. Nevertheless, it is a work of Talmudic authority, and to openly contradict it would be unthinkable to orthodox Jews. As Rabbi Schwab stated: "...our traditional chronology is based on *Seder Olam* because of the authority of its author. It is therefore quite inconceivable that any post-Talmudic teacher could possible 'reject' those chronological calculations which have been the subject of many a Talmudic discussion." (Schwab, *Dr. Joseph Breuer Jubilee Volume,* p. 186). Thus it is that the *Seder Olam* is held in such high esteem and is still used by the Jews for their national dating.

22. *Encyclopedia Judaica,* Vol. 4, "Bar Kokhba," p. 230.

23. *Ibid.*

24. *Ibid.*, p. 231.

25. Dio Cassius, *Roman History,* Vol. VIII, Bk. 69, p. 449–450; Durant, *Caesar and Christ,* p. 548.

26. *Encyclopedia Judaica,* Vol. 4, "Bar Kokhba," p. 231.

27. *Ibid.*, Vol. 11, "Messiah," p. 1410.

28. Not only do the Jews venerate Jose because the *Seder Olam* had its origin in his school, he is regarded with a near superstitious reverence. This may be seen in that it was said: "that he was worthy of having the prophet Elijah reveal himself to him regularly in order to teach him." *Encyclopedia Judaica,* Vol. 16, "Yose ben Halafta," p. 853.

29. Yet despite all that has been said concerning the Jews veneration for Jose, the *Encyclopedia Judaica* forthrightly admits: "The most significant confusion in Jose's calculation is the compression of the Persian period, from the rebuilding of the temple by Zerubbabel in 516 BC to the conquest of Persia by Alexander, to no more than 34 years" (*Encyclopedia Judaica,* Vol. 14, "Seder Olam Rabbah," p. 1092).

# Appendix H: Archaeology and the Bible
## by Phillip Climer

The December 18, 1995, issue of *Time* magazine had as its cover story, "Is the Bible Fact or Fiction? Archaeologists in the Holy Land are shedding new light on what did — and did not — occur in the greatest stories ever told." The article describes recent archaeological finds in Israel and surrounding areas, and then categorizes public and scholarly reaction to these finds into three main groupings: "Jewish and Christian ultraconservatives," who do not believe any part of the Bible is fiction; "atheists," who want to debunk the whole Bible; and "the moderate majority," who want to be sure that the Bible is scientifically "grounded in truth."

As Christians we fall into what *Time* calls the "ultraconservative" group. We believe that the Bible is infallible not only in spiritual matters, but also in accounts with historical and geographical content.

When archaeologists excavate biblical lands and, based on their findings, reach conclusions that differ with the historical account of Scripture, how should a Christian respond? To say that we accept the Word of God by faith, whatever the claims of archaeology or any other branch of science, is the correct reply. However, making that statement without any further explanation may sound as though we are pitting blind irrational faith against rational scientific research. This essay is intended to demonstrate that while the science of archaeology may be reasonable, it is not truthful; and *a faith that provides truth is much to be preferred over a research program that does not.*

Of the other two groups mentioned in the magazine article, we can easily understand the "atheists." We accept the Bible as true; they reject it. As *Time* points out, even when archaeology supports a biblical narrative, the atheists are likely to reject both Scripture and science. Their position is one of faith as much as is ours; it is just that the object of their faith is their own ideas. But what is one to make of the third category, the "moderate majority"?

Many Evangelicals fall into this category, for they are delighted whenever an archaeological find supports a part of Scripture, or as *Time* says, "strengthens the Bible's claim to historical accuracy." But if a supportive archaeologist enhances Scripture's claim to accuracy, does a scientific detractor weaken the Bible's claim to truth? And if Christians accept only those archaeological findings that they agree with, can they not be justly accused of being childish in their refusal to face up to disagreeable facts?

The whole unfortunate enterprise of trying to verify the claims of Scripture with the findings of archaeology rests on a conflict between the science of archaeology and the Christian faith on the question, "What is truth?" To focus on this dispute, let us confront the claims of archaeology with the simple question, "How do you know?" The answer to this one question reveals the principles upon which are based all claims to knowledge and truth by any science, philosophy, or religion.

To begin with, we must know what the science of archaeology is, and the type of claims it makes. Secondly, we must compare and contrast archaeological information and biblical truth. Finally, against this background, let us review the conflict that *Time* calls "fact vs. faith."

### Archaeological Information

Archaeology is "the scientific study of extinct peoples through skeletal remains, fossils, and objects of human workmanship (as implements, artifacts, monuments, or inscriptions) found in the earth" (*Webster's Third International Dictionary of the English Language*, 1981). Archaeologists excavate and sift through the remains of ancient civilizations and then try to piece together their findings into a coherent picture of how the people of that society lived, and how its institutions functioned.

Perhaps the most important artifact that any civilization leaves behind is its body of literature. Many societies in the ancient Middle East left their writings in stone (the hieroglyphs of Egypt) or on soft clay tablets that hardened into stone over time (the Babylonians and Assyrians). The ancient Hebrews apparently used paper or possibly animal skins. Since these materials decompose, documents written on them had to be recopied time and again. Archaeologists generally accept hieroglyphs and clay tablets as being more accurate than paper manuscripts, since the former are more likely to be the original writings. There is obviously much less room for error or editing in a document carved on stone than on a manuscript copy several times removed from the original.

The *Time* article gives several examples of archaeologists rejecting biblical manuscripts in favour of their own theories based on other artifacts. The Book of Joshua, chapter 6, records the destruction of the walls of Jericho, allowing the Israelites under the leadership of Joshua to conquer the city. *Time* tells us that after extensive excavations at the site of ancient Jericho, archaeologists have determined that the location was abandoned between about 1500–1100 BC. According to them, no walled cities existed during this time in this area of Canaan. Conservative biblical scholars and archaeologists also disagree on the date of the Israelite entrance into Canaan, but they both agree that it falls well within the time range mentioned above. Given this chronology, modern archaeology concludes that the Hebrews moved onto vacant or sparsely populated land. This thinking allows no walls to come tumbling down, and no city to conquer. The sceptics also doubt that Joshua even existed. Without a battle, who needs a general? Now let us ask the test question: How do they know that Jericho and its walls did not exist during this time period?

Just as our society paves over old streets and erects new buildings over the remains of old foundations, so ancient civilizations built towns and cities over the debris of earlier structures. When archaeologists excavate a site they divide it into different levels, each level or layer corresponding to a defined era of human habitation or abandonment. The methods by which a date for a particular level is determined are quite involved, and a detailed explanation of them is beyond the scope of this essay.

To gain some idea of what is involved, consider a future archaeologist excavating our civilization and finding only ceramic dishes up to a certain level. Above that level, he finds plastic and ceramic dishes. Suppose he also finds some sort of preserved calendar dated "1950" with the plastic dishes. He now has his dating "key": the calendar and the plastic dishes. This key tells him that at his initial site plastic dishes were not in use before 1950. If he encounters plastic dishes at any other site, he assumes that the level in which he finds them was inhabited in 1950 or later. At Jericho, the scientists found some sort of artifacts (probably pottery) at a certain level that allowed them to date that level at 1500–1100 BC, based upon their "key" with similar artifacts at other excavations. This particular level did not contain the foundations or remains of any city walls, buildings, or other structures that would indicate a city. How to explain this discrepancy with the biblical account? The earliest extant manuscript of the Book of Joshua dates from a period hundreds of years after the events described in the book. Sceptics theorize that such a manuscript, in being recopied from a decaying original, could have been altered by a zealous scribe, seeking to glorify his God and the history of his nation by inventing a battle that never occurred and a leader who never existed.

The archaeologists who excavated Jericho published their theory. These findings were debated and ultimately accepted by most of the archaeological community. Unless and until some new evidence comes along, the modern science of archaeology has determined that the Israelite conquest of Canaan as described in the Book of Joshua is not factual. Specifically, Joshua did not fight the battle of Jericho. This is an archaeological "truth," or more accurately, a testing by archaeological research methods of a biblical story, and the Bible fails the test.

Conservative biblical scholars disagree, but their objections are tainted, because they are trying to prove the Bible, instead of looking at it objectively — or so the scientists say. Now if religious bias is the problem, perhaps we could demonstrate the objectivity of archaeology in the reconstruction of ancient civilizations by examining a site that has no religious significance today, but one that has been widely excavated by numerous scientists. In such a case, there would be no believers to muddy the waters for the clear-thinking scientists. There are many such sites; perhaps the most famous is Troy.

**Searching for Troy**

In approximately 800 BC, a blind Greek poet named Homer composed the first (and arguably the greatest) poem of European literature: *The Iliad.* This epic work tells of a great war fought approximately 400 years earlier, between a number of Greek city-states and the rich and powerful city of Troy, on the coast of Asia Minor (modern-day Turkey). Perhaps the reader recalls some of the particulars of this story. Helen, queen of Sparta, was carried off to Troy by Paris, a prince of the Trojan royal family. Outraged, a number of Greek cities combined forces, sailed to Troy, and besieged the city for ten long years. They were not able to breach the massive walls of Troy, so finally they resorted to subterfuge. By means of a giant hollow wooden idol, the famed Trojan horse, the Greeks infiltrated Troy. The gates were thrown open, and the city was lost. Those Trojans not killed were enslaved, and Troy itself was burned and demolished. The victorious Greeks sailed home with the beautiful Helen, the cause of it all, "the face that launched a thousand ships."

Since Roman times scholars have debated *The Iliad*: Does it describe a real war, or is it just a myth? If there was such a war, how accurate is Homer's telling of it? In the 1850s, modern archaeology took up the debate. For the last 140 years, team after team of scientists has excavated a now-deserted site on the coast of Turkey. Their very impressive and voluminous findings were reviewed by a recent documentary series on public television, "In Search of the Trojan War." According to this program, the site suspected to contain the ruins of Troy was continuously occupied by humans for over 5,000 years. It contains 50 separate levels. Nine of these levels show the characteristics of true cities, that is, walls, palaces, etc. Nine of the levels also show signs of violent destruction, either by warfare or natural disaster, such as earthquakes.

What of Homer's Troy? Which level, if any, matches the magnificent city of *The Iliad*? Did the Trojan War really happen? Almost a century and a half of modern scientific investigation, without any religious interference or bias, has yielded a new answer for each new investigator. The archaeological "truth" about Troy changes with each generation of archaeologists. The original excavator "proved" that *The Iliad* was as accurate as Christians believe the Bible to be. A later archaeological team threw out most of his conclusions and "proved" that Homer exaggerated greatly, if he told the truth at all. A subsequent generation of diggers "proved" that an earthquake largely destroyed Troy, and that pirates finished the job. And so on. The only points on which all the experts agree are that the site was inhabited for thousands of years, and it is now abandoned. But what of the sophisticated techniques for dating artifacts and levels of occupation? Each artifact was precisely catalogued by the team that found it. Each highly trained archaeologist looked at those catalogued findings, possibly made some excavations of his own, and then came up with a different interpretation to explain how all those artifacts got there.

The narrator of the documentary series takes us through these diverse theories in six hours of analysis. At the end, he makes this startling observation on the archaeological search for truth about the Trojan war: *"There can never be a final word, only a new interpretation by each generation in terms of its own dreams and needs."* This is the "proof," the "knowledge," and the "truth" that modern archaeology gives us: *"never a final word, only a new interpretation...."*

### Ever Learning...Never Able...

Returning to archaeological excavations in the lands of the Bible, let us review the case of Joshua and the battle of Jericho. The current secular view is that no battle took place there, and no walls existed. The proof is in the pottery, so to speak. But the final archaeological word is not in, and it never will come in. This is not the conclusion of a religious fanatic defending Scripture; this is a limitation of the method of the science of archaeology, as demonstrated in the search for Troy.

The sceptic may think that we are playing with words in reaching this conclusion. Perhaps he would say that the present theory of "no walls at Jericho" is *substantially* true, and that later excavations in the area will "fine tune" it. The sceptic would be wrong. In archaeology, any theory, no matter how well established, can be turned

on its head by the next shovelful of dirt at the next dig. The *Time* article provides us with just such an example.

Many secular archaeologists questioned the existence of King David, because there are no records of him, dating from the time of his rule (traditional dates 1025–985 BC). As with Joshua and the conquest of Canaan, these scientists speculate that the legend of David may have been added by a scribe recopying documents at a much later date, trying to "improve" the history of Israel. But in modern Israel in 1993 an inscription in stone dating from about 900 BC was found containing the phrases "House of David," and "King of Israel." That one inscription was enough to turn sceptical opinion around: Now archaeologists generally accept that David really existed.

A monument and inscription from 1200 BC commemorating Joshua's victory at the mighty walls of Jericho would similarly turn the archaeological world's theory of the Hebrew conquest of Canaan on its head. Does such a monument exist? Who can say? But it is certainly true that the archaeological "truth" about Joshua and Jericho will not be the same 50 years from now as it is today, or as it was 50 years ago.

The reader may question the phrasing in saying that the truth of a past event is going to change every 50 years. How does the truth of the past change? Obviously, it never does. We have an account in writing of Joshua and the Israelites conquering the walled city of Jericho. Now that event either took place or it did not take place. The same can be said for any event for which we have record. The Greeks sailed to Troy to get Helen, or they did not. The theorizing of modern-day archaeologists does not change a jot or tittle of history, because it is already past; it is out of their grasp; they can never relive or recall those events. Even if an archaeologist constructed a hypothesis that was absolutely accurate in explaining the Trojan War or Joshua and the battle of Jericho, no one could ever know it was absolutely accurate, because no one can go back in time and test the hypothesis against reality.

This may all seem very basic, but it demonstrates that archaeological research fails to give us historical truth not just occasionally, but consistently. No hypothesis of history based upon archaeological research has ever or can ever be shown to be true. The theories will continue to pour out of the minds of archaeologists, but none of them will ever be proved, either. Naturally this conclusion includes written records, also. We do not know if those indestructible clay tablets of the Assyrians or Hittites are true or not, and we never will. The same can be said for the Egyptian hieroglyphs and even for our friend Homer. He tells a wonderful story, but we will *know* if Achilles and Hector fought outside the walls of golden Troy only when we get a word from God on the subject.

## Biblical Truth

Scientifically, we do not know if the Bible is true, and we never will. That, of course, does not derogate from the truth or authority of Scripture, for two reasons: Scripture is self-authenticating; and science cannot prove anything true.

Scripture teaches that from eternity past, God predetermined everything, everyone, every action, and every moment. By his Spirit and his Word he executed his eternal plan and brought the universe and time itself into existence. Since he is creator of all, including time, he stands outside of it and is therefore unchanging. When he inspired the prophets and apostles to write down that portion of his eternal plan which he chose to reveal to us, he directed them to write his *unchanging* Word describing his *unchanging* plan. When it comes to the past, how could anyone possibly imagine a more authoritative history than the Word of the one who determined that history and then brought it to pass?

Revisiting Joshua and Jericho one last time, let us pose the same question to the biblical narrative that we did to the archaeological theory. How do we know that the scriptural account of the battle of Jericho is true? Because the Bible says so. No hypotheses here, no guesses, just truth, from the God of truth, who not only infallibly knows the events at Jericho, but also predetermined them and brought them to pass. To doubt the veracity of any historical event in Scripture is to doubt the very nature of God himself.

The "moderate majority" will discount the previous argument as an evasion, circular reasoning, irrationalism, and double-talk. It is simply wrong, say they, to believe that the Bible speaks truthfully on historical matters because it says it does. The Bible itself must be checked, or "verified." But by what can Scripture be corrected? What is the standard the moderates use to judge the Bible? Archaeological methods of research can provide us with mountains of information about — or at least mountains of — pottery and spears used in ancient Israel, and we should respect that information, and the scientists who work so diligently to extract and study the artifacts they find. But any theory they devise concerning any part of biblical history is by the nature of their own inductive method tentative and inconclusive. One cannot verify any narrative with a worse theory. The "moderate majority" cannot legitimately test biblical history with scientific methodology, and since there

currently are no other possibilities with which to verify it, they must either receive the scriptural narrative in faith or reject it for no good reason.

The reader may wonder why this discussion of archaeology and the Bible has been limited to the Old Testament, and why the subject of miracles has not been considered more extensively. Aside from time and space constraints, there are two main reasons: The New Testament manuscripts are now generally accepted, even among sceptics. (A few generations ago they were not accepted as genuine, but someone came up with a new theory and now they are.) The sceptics do not believe what the manuscripts say, but they do, at least for the moment, accept them as dating from the apostolic age. Second, archaeological methods of research cannot give us a true theory of any event that is *not* a miracle. Given that failure, how can archaeologists even begin to comment with any credibility upon Bible history that contains many miracles, such as the Gospels?

## "Fact vs. Faith"

The notion of "fact vs. faith," as *Time* put it, now can be seen in all of its absurdity. *To test any scriptural historical account by means of any theory of archaeology is to test that which cannot be false by means of that which cannot be true.* It is the height of absurdity.

The Bible is the only means by which God reveals his plan of redemption to his people. As such, it is primarily concerned with spiritual matters, and when we read it we should also be primarily concerned with the spiritual knowledge it contains. But the great drama of redemption is being played out upon the stage of the visible universe and history. We cannot fully appreciate the scope and grandeur of God's plan of salvation if we neglect the platform upon which it is presented. We must not take lightly the denial of the accuracy of biblical history by modern archaeology. If we do not proclaim the truth about Joshua and Jericho and King David or any other historical narrative in Scripture, we are guilty of not proclaiming "the whole counsel of God." We are in a battle for truth, and we must look to God for patience and courage to see our way through it.

When the youthful David visited his brothers on the battlefield, he heard Goliath taunting Israel. He was outraged, asking, "Who is this uncircumcised Philistine that he should defy the armies of the living God?" {1Sa 17:26} David immediately volunteered to face Goliath in combat, and he slew that blasphemer.

David had to battle the enemies of Israel militarily. Our war with the enemies of Christ is spiritual and intellectual in nature, but it is just as real, and even more deadly.

As Christians, our posture should be one of righteous indignation against the giant of sceptical archaeology that slurs the truth of the Word of Almighty God. Who are these archaeologists who think they can disprove Scripture with a piece of broken pottery dug out of the mud? Who are the "moderate majority" who dare tell us what parts of the Bible are "reasonable" to believe? Let us be as eager to confront the giant of archaeology as David was to confront the Philistine champion. In the struggle between the eternal Word of God and secular theories, we know by revelation that God will crush all anti-Christian arguments and imaginations under our feet. *"Is not my word like fire?" says the Lord, and like a hammer that breaks the rock in pieces?* {Jer 23:29}

---

Phillip Climer is a free-lance writer living in California.

This article was first published by the *Trinity Review*, number 170, April 1999. Used by permission. Copyright (c) 1999, John W. Robbins, P. O. Box 68, Unicoi, Tennessee, 37692. Tel: (423) 743-0199.

# Index

(All references are to paragraph numbers)

Herod Antipas, 6073; very offended that a golden eagle he had placed over the largest gate of the temple was torn down, 6074; foresaw the joy the leaders would have at his death and planned to quash it, 6078; changed his will and left the kingdom to Archelaus, 6081; after enduring most grievous pains, ended a miserable life, 6082; his progeny died out within a hundred years, 6999

Herod: the tetrarch, lost his army, 6570; divorced the daughter of Aretas, king of Arabia, and married Herodias, 6570; became Gaius' enemy through Agrippa's letters and he and his wife Herodias were banished, 6609

Herod: king of Chalcis, received the command of the temple and right of choosing high priests from Claudius, 6695; died, 6722

Herod Agrippa: left Caligula and returned home, 6597; mocked by Alexandrians, 6598; received the tetrarchies of his uncle Herod, who was banished by Gaius, 6629; executed James the Apostle, 6677; died a miserable death, 6679

Herod Antipas received Galilee from Caesar Augustus, 6111

Herodotus: born, 1103; honoured at Athens for his history, 1260

Herod's, See Joseph, Herod's uncle

Hezekiah: born, 587; made viceroy in the kingdom with his father Ahaz, 618; purged the temple, 622; destroyed the brazen serpent, renewed the law of tithes, 626; healed from a deadly disease and his life extended, 644; healing confirmed by the long day, 647; boasted of his treasures to the Babylonians, 651; buried, 683

Hierax paid Ptolemy Physcon's soldiers to prevent a rebellion, 3706

Hillel, the Babylonian, lived at Jerusalem, 5654

Hipparchus: the Bithynian, most skilful in astronomy, 3515; his first observation of the autumnal equinox, 3515; his second observation, 3548; his third observation, 3554; his fourth observation, 3624; his fifth observation, 3635; his sixth observation, 3677; observed the vernal equinox and the summer solstice, 3730; observed the vernal equinox, 3793; observations of the sun and the moon, 3799

Hippias: married his daughter to Aeantides of Lampsacus, 1038; Athenian tyrant, fled to King Darius, 1046; guided Persians to Marathon and there defeated, 1093; died in the battle of Marathon, 1094

Hippocrates, the Lacedemonian general, killed by Alcibiades, 1380

Hirom reigned in Tyre, 918

Histiaeus: cast into prison and released, 1062; crossed over to Mitylene, 1070; captured and crucified, 1075

Holophernes beheaded by Judith, 712

Hosea foretold the invasion of the kingdom of Israel, 557

Hoshea: took possession of the kingdom, 615; refused the yearly tribute to Shalmaneser, 629

Hybreas ingeniously remarked to Antony, when he intended to burden the cities with a double tribute, 5358

Hydaspes: Alexander brought boats to the river, 2084; flooded its banks, 2127

Hyksos: took Memphis, 57; first king was Salatis, 57; expelled from Egypt, they journeyed toward Syria and built Jerusalem, 100

Hypsicratia, Mithridates' wife, accompanied him in his flight and was a great comfort to him in his troubles, 4411

Hyrcanus, Aristobulus' brother, was left king by Pompey, but without a diadem, 4553

Hyrcanus: received the government and priesthood from Caesar, 5019; desired to confirm his friendship with Caesar, 5064; when Malichus was killed, he was greatly distressed, 5242; his ears were cropped by Antigonus, so that he would be unfit for the priesthood, 5412; led bound to Parthia, 5413; when freed from bonds, he was permitted to live in Babylon, 5501; between his own desire, and the deceit of Herod, he desired to return to his own country, 5501; when dealing with Malchus, the king of the Arabians, to raise a rebellion, he was betrayed by the letter Dositheus gave to Herod, 5734; convicted and executed by Herod, 5734

Hyrcanus: son of Joseph, warred against the Arabians, 3173; committed suicide, 3208

Hyrcanus, See John Hyrcanus

Iberus, See Mithridates Iberus

Ibzan judged Israel, 374

Idrieus died, 1680

Illienses: assessed a large fine by Agrippa because they did not help Julia, 5967; at Herod's request, the fine was forgiven, 5967; greatly honoured Herod, 5970

Indians: various countries conquered by Alexander the Great, 2088; envoys came to Augustus at Tarraco, 5854; confirmed a peace with Augustus, 5932; gave rare presents to Augustus, 5933

indictions which were 15-year taxation cycles, began to be used, 4870

Indus River, 2223

interregnum: 12 years in NK, 564; 9 years in NK, 611; 2 years in Babylon, 680; 8 years in Babylon, 687; 2 years in Egypt, 690

Iphicrates: made general of the army of Artaxerxes, 1579; disagreed with Pharnabazus, 1586

Isaac: born at Beersheba, 86; weaned and Ishmael cast out, 87; married Rebekah, 94; promises made to Abraham, were now given to him, 104; died, 131

Isaiah: Isaiah and Joel were famous in Judea, and Jonah, Hosea, and Amos in Israel, 554; Onias misquotes Isaiah to justify building a temple in Egypt, 3599

Ishbosheth killed, 417

Ishmael: born, 80; died, 109

Ishmael, the son of Nethaniah, 856

Ismenias pretended to prostrate himself before King Artaxerxes, 1595

Isocrates: the grammarian, defended the death of Octavius, 3491; when he knew the trouble he was in, he went mad, 3540

Israelites: when they had wandered 40 years, were commanded to go straight to Canaan, 308; crossed the Jordan River under the leadership of Joshua, 309; celebrated the first passover in Canaan, 311; the manna ceased, 312; conquered Jericho, 314; punished for the sacrilege of Achan, 315; took Ai treacherously, 315; celebrated the feast of tabernacles, 335; placed the tabernacle at Shiloh, 336; delivered into the hands of Cushan, king of the Mesopotamians, for their idolatry and marriages with the Canaanites, 342; defeated by Eglon, 346; delivered into the hands of Jabin, king of Canaan, 350; delivered again into the hands of the Midianites, 355; worshipped Baalberith, 358; delivered into the hands of the Philistines and Ammonites, 368; oppressed again by the Philistines, 381; oppressed again, and lost the ark, 387; cast away their idols and drew water in Mizpah, 391; Philistines took away their smiths, 394; suffered from hunger, 448; the end of the kingdom of Israel, 634

Isthemus built, 713

Iturea and Judea were added to the province of Syria, 6810

Jacob: born, 99; took the blessing from his brother, 112; endured seven year's service for Rachel, 116; left Laban and returned to his own country, 124; made a covenant with Laban, 125; wrestled with the angel, 126; met his brother Esau, 127; went into Succoth, 127; sent ten of his sons into Egypt to buy grain, 135; sent Benjamin to Egypt, 136; he and his sons went down to Egypt, 139; blessed his sons and died, 146; his body was wrapped in spices, lamented, and placed in the cave of Machpelah, 147

Jair: judged Israel, 367; died, 371

Jamblichus, the Arabian king, was tortured to death by Antony, 5667

Jamblichus received his father's kingdom of Arabia from Augustus, 5927

Jambri's sons were killed, 3535

Jamnites' harbour and navy burned by Judas Maccabeus, 3453

Jannaeus, See Alexander Jannaeus

Jannas, king of Egypt, 70

Japheth born, 30

Jared: born, 17; died, 28

Jason: the son of Simon II, high priest, promised money to Antiochus, for the office of the high priesthood, 3209; removed his brother and assumed the priesthood, 3209; sent messengers to Tyre for Hercules, 3214; after three years, removed from the priesthood, 3221; expelled by Menelaus, 3222; attacked Jerusalem, 3256

Jeconiah: born, 749; reigned (also called Coniah and Jehoiachin), 795

Jehoahaz: succeeded his father Jehu, 542; died, 546

Jehoahaz: the son of Josiah, was born, 732; reigned, 760; deposed by Necho and led into Egypt the same year, 761

Jehoiakim: reigned, and in the same year was taken and bound in chains, 776; tore and burned part of the Scriptures, 779; rebelled, 785; taken prisoner, 794; cast out without burial, 794

Jehoram: born, 505; killed his brothers, 527; set up Baal worship, 528; plundered by the Philistines, 529; tormented with a disease in his bowels, 530; appointed his son Ahaziah as viceroy, 531; died most miserably, 532

Jehoshaphat: born, 494; reigned, 509; took away the high places, used the Levites to instruct the people, 510; appointed his son Jehoram as viceroy, 516; besieged Ramothgilead with Ahab, 518; lost his ships, 521; allocated cities to his sons, 526; died, 527

Jehu anointed the king of Israel, killed Jehoram and Jezebel and killed all of Ahab's family, 534

Jephthah subdued the Ammonites, sacrificed his daughter to God and killed the Ephraimites, 372

Jeremiah: called to prophesy, 738; preached and was imprisoned, 764; foretold the 70 years captivity and ruin of Babylon, 771; predicted Jehoiakim's ruin, 773; predicted the capture of Jerusalem, 834; beaten and cast into a dungeon, 843; freed and left in Judea, 854

Jeroboam: promoted the worship of calves, 481; rejected the lawful priests, 484

Jeroboam II: made viceroy by his father Joash, 547; succeeded his father who died, 551; after his death, the kingdom of Israel went to ruin, 564

Jerusalem: taken and burned, 844; Ptolemy Philometor judged that the temple at Jerusalem had been built according to Moses' law, 3604; a sedition arose, 5286; plundered by the Parthians, 5411; besieged by Gaius Sossius and Herod for five months, 5474; taken with a large slaughter of the citizens, 5477

Jesus, the son of Sirach, translated his grandfather's book from Hebrew into Greek, 3749

Jesus, the son of Gamaliel, succeeded the son of Jesus Damnaeus in the high priesthood, 6894

Jesus Christ: born, 6059; heard and questioned the teachers in the temple, 6187; made himself known to the world, 6282; baptized, 6293; tempted, 6295; turned water into wine, 6302; Pilate delivered him up to the will of the Jews, 6472; crucified, 6475; rose again, 6485; ascended into heaven, 6494

Jews: led captive by the Israelites of the NK, 603; carried away captive by the Edomites, 604; the best Jewish youth, including Daniel, taken for Nebuchadnezzar's service, 777; 3023 Jews were led captive by Nebuchadnezzar, 792; led captive by Nebuzaradan, 851; remainder of the Jews fled into Egypt, 859; Nebuzaradan carried away remaining Jews, 867; planned their return to their country, 952; laid the foundation of the second temple, 952; hindered by the Samaritans, 957; fasts of the fifth and seventh months irksome, 1031; celebrate the first Passover in the second temple, 1034; killed the ten sons of Haman and the rest of their foes, 1047; subject to Seleucus, 2728; two angels delivered Jews from death, 2936; some apostates built a school under the tower of Zion, 3213; killed more than 20,000 of their foes, 3434; afflicted by Bacchides, 3530; made an alliance with the Romans, 3531; sent by Jonathan and freed Demetrius from the people of Antioch, 3645; invaded Syria, 3774; different from the Idumeans, 3786; large company of Jews killed by Ptolemy Lathurus, 3865; sought relief from Alexandra, their queen, when they were oppressed by the Pharisees, 4207; made tributaries to the Romans, 4532; 12,000 killed by Pompey's soldiers, 4538; governed aristocratically, 4646; saved from a great famine by Herod the Great, 5862; petitioned Caesar to be permitted to live without a king, 6109; expelled from Rome, 6239; asked Vitellius that the Roman ensigns with images might not pass through their country, 6577; in Alexandria, told Herod Agrippa of the treason instigated by Flaccus Avillius, 6599; miserably treated by Avillius, 6602; cast down the altar for Gaius Caligula, 6617; Greeks and Syrians kill 50,000 at Caesarea, 6639; 20,000 killed in a riot when a soldier exposed himself, 6723; lost all rights in the city of Caesarea, 6871; fighting until the start of the Jewish war, 6871; final rebellion against the Romans, 6932; 20,000 killed at the instigation of Gessius Florus, 6935; the calamity of the Jews foretold by Peter and Paul, 6945; state degenerated to violence, 6954; had a severe famine when besieged by Titus, 6970; captured and made to fight with beasts, 6982; number of the Jews that died by famine and war, 6997

Joash: born, 533; anointed king at age seven, killed Athaliah, and destroyed Baal's temple, 537; repaired the temple, 539; the son reigned with his father Jehoahaz, 543; killed, 545

Joash: visited dying Elisha, 546; plundered Jerusalem, 550

John, the brother of Jonathan, was killed, 3535

John Hyrcanus: made high priest after his father, 3727; when Jerusalem was besieged, he expelled the weak and the infirm from the city, 3734; pitied those he expelled and allowed them in again, 3736; made peace with Antiochus, 3736; took 3,000 talents from the sepulchre of King David, 3737; accompanied Antiochus and overcame the Hyrcani, as a result of which he received the name Hyrcanus, 3757; took Sichem and Gerizim, 3778; subdued the Idumeans and compelled them to be circumcised, 3786; never allowed his son Alexander Jannaeus to see him, 3797; sent envoys to the Romans, 3798; died, 3844

John Richardson, Bishop of Ardah, author of the harmony of the Gospels, 6303

John the Baptist: born, 6045; preached the baptism of repentance, 6281; his ministry lasted for four years, 6291; sent disciples to Jesus, 6311; cast into prison, 6312; beheaded in prison, 6363

Jonathan, a certain Jew, was burned, 6994

Jonathan: succeeded Judas, his brother, 3535; leaped into the Jordan River and swam to the other side, 3536; found out about the enemy's treachery, 3552; restored the walls that were destroyed in Bethbasi, 3553; defeated Apollonius, 3617; sent 3,000 soldiers to Demetrius, 3645; advanced toward Damascus, 3653; in great danger, 3655; surrounded by the deceit of Tryphon and captured, 3661; killed by Tryphon, 3665; bones buried by his brother Simon, 3666

Jonathan, the son of Uzziel, author of the Chaldean Paraphrase, 5654

Joppa: burned in the night by Judas Maccabeus, 3453; surrendered to Jonathan, 3617

Joseph: born, 122; cast into a pit by his brothers and sold and led into Egypt, 129; in prison, interpreted Pharaoh's dream, 132; advanced to second in the kingdom and married Potiphar's daughter, 132; stored the money gathered in exchange for grain in the treasury, 142; Egyptians sold their flocks and herds to Joseph, 143; assigned lands to be tilled by the Egyptians, 144; died, 149

Joseph the Jew, the son of Tobias, 2946

Joseph, Herod's brother, lost six cohorts and was killed, 5457

Joseph, the husband of the blessed virgin, went up to Bethlehem to be enrolled, 6058

Joseph, the son of Camei, became high priest, 6697

Joseph, Herod's uncle: secretly ordered by Herod to kill his wife Mariamme, if his affairs with Antony went badly, 5599; told Mariamme of Herod's command as a sure token of Herod's love to her, 5601

Josephus: error in his history concerning Alcimus, 3533; contradiction in length of time that Alcimus was high priest, 3541; corrected, 3801; corrected, 3844;

corrected, 4373; incorrectly said Herod was the high priest, 4541; error in age of Herod the Great, 5027; error in length of Asmonean kingdom, 5486; made honourable mention of John the Baptist, 6495; made honourable mention of our Saviour, 6496; born, 6586; his fame in scholarship, 6744; studied zealously, 6760; shipwrecked and came into Italy, 6884; given gifts by Poppaea Augusta and returned into his country, 6920; went to Galilee to await the Roman force there, 6942; his life was spared by Vespasian, 6950

Joshua: when confirmed in his call, sent two spies to Jericho, 305; restored the interrupted use of circumcision, 310; hung the five kings, 320; took Medeba, Libnah, Lachish with other cities and conquered the Anakims, 328; died, 341

Josiah: born, 714; purged Judah from idolatry, 737; had the book of the law read, demolished the altar of Jeroboam, and restored the temple, 743; observed the Passover and removed all the diviners and other abominations, 744; killed in battle and bewailed by Jeremiah, 756

Jotapata captured by storm by Vespasian and burned to the ground, 6950

Jotape returned by Octavius to her father, the king of the Medes, 5776

Jotham: succeeded his father, who was a leper, 565; defeated the Ammonites, 586; Isaiah, Micah, and Hosea prophesied in his reign, 586

Juba: obtained from Caesar his father's kingdom of Maurusia, 5820; father of Ptolemy by Cleopatra Selene (Moon), 5820

Jubilees: the First Jubilee, 344; the Second, 345; the Third, 351; the Fourth, 356; the Fifth, 369; the Sixth, 382; the Seventh, 390; the Eighth, 413; the Ninth, famous for the feast of dedication of Solomon's temple, 469; the Tenth, 490; the Eleventh, 512; the Twelfth, 540; the Thirteenth Jubilee under two most prosperous kings, Uzziah and Jeroboam II, 554; the Fourteenth Jubilee and Isaiah's vision, 584; the Fifteenth, joyful time of celebration by Hezekiah for deliverance from Assyria, 673; the Sixteenth, 709; the Seventeenth, 752; the Eighteenth, in which Nebuchadnezzar restored and Jeconiah freed, 889; the Nineteenth, 1038; the Twentieth, 1213; Twenty-first Jubilee was the last seen by Old Testament prophets, 1304; the Twenty-second, 1602; the Twenty-third, 2482; the Twenty-fourth, 2817; the Twenty-fifth, 2894; the Twenty-sixth, 3245; the Twenty-seventh, 3826; the Twenty-eighth, 4146; the Twenty-ninth, 5880; the Thirtieth, start of John the Baptist's ministry, 6281

Judah born, 121

Judas: thought to be Theudas, headed rebel bands of men, 6098; killed with his followers, 6181; his new sect, 6183

Judas Aristobulus: succeeded his father, 3849; organized the government into a kingdom, 3849; starved his mother to death in prison, 3850; subdued a large part of Iturea, 3853; killed his brother Antigonus, his viceroy in the kingdom, 3854; acknowledged divine revenge upon him and died, 3855

Judas Maccabeus: spent his life in the wilderness, 3318; to avoid impurity, he lived on herbs, 3318; succeeded his father Matthias, 3387; valiantly carried on the war in Judea, 3395; overcame Nicanor, 3409; plundered the camp, 3411; dedicated a new altar, 3419; victoriously warred against the sons of Esau, 3434; defeated the Ammonites, 3436; defeated Timothy, killing 20,500 foot soldiers and 600 cavalry, 3437; killed about 30,000 of Timothy soldiers, 3457; killed 25,000 men at Carnaim, 3459; utterly demolished Ephron, a well-fortified city, 3460; routed Gorgias' soldiers, 3464; conquered Esau's sons, 3466; attacked Eupator's camp at night, 3471; took revenge upon the defectors, 3512; hid himself from Nicanor, 3521; encouraged his soldiers with his dream, 3525; defeated Nicanor and decapitated him, 3525; fought valiantly and was killed, 3529; buried in Modin, 3529

Jugaeus reigned over the Babylonians, 619

Julia: bore Gaius to Agrippa, 5931; bore Lucius, after having borne Gaius to Agrippa, 5949; in great danger of her life, 5966; after Agrippa died, she married Tiberius, 5989; gave herself over to luxury and filthiness, 6123; exiled to an island, 6123; more courteously treated, but not restored, 6167

Julius Caesar: stayed with Nicomedes and was thought to have homosexual relationship with him, 4059; when knew of Sulla's death, returned to Rome, 4084; captured by pirates, 4108; crucified the captive pirates, 4109; confirmed the wavering cities, 4113; saw the statue of Alexander the Great and grieved at his own lack of achievements, 4393; suspected of conspiracy, 4428; entered into friendship with Crassus and Pompey, 4613; did not dismiss his army and started the civil war, 4854; made dictator, 4869; resigned his dictatorship after 11 days, 4869; defeated Pompey at Pharsalia, 4885; burned Pompey's letters, 4889; pardoned those who aided Pompey, 4889; pursued Pompey, 4901; freed Asia from the tax collectors, 4915; pursued Pompey to Egypt, 4917; wept when he received Pompey's ring, 4944; commanded Pompey's head to be buried, 4947; gracious to Pompey's friends, 4948; all men strove to heap honours upon him, 4956; favoured Cleopatra over her brother, 4960; gave the kingdom of Egypt to Ptolemy and Cleopatra, 4962; after Pompey murdered, had battles in Alexandria, 4969; fought Achillas, 4969; conquered the Egyptians in a naval battle, 4986; jumped out of his ship and swam to another ship, 4986; most cities in Syria send troops to Caesar, 4989; sent away King Ptolemy, who was very young, 4990; rigged his navy to deceive the Egyptians, 4998; captured Alexandria, 5004; gave the kingdom of Egypt to Cleopatra, 5005; had engraved on a brass pillar the rights of the Alexandrian Jews, 5008; sent friendly letters to Cicero, 5012; went into Syria, 5016; re-

his navy defected to Caesar, 5761; wounded himself, 5763; drawn up by ropes to Cleopatra who had gone to her tomb, 5765; died, 5765; honourably interred by Cleopatra, 5778; his statues were thrown down, 5797

Marsus killed himself, 5240

Marsyas, the Alexandrian general, was captured in war, 3795

Marsyas told Herod Agrippa of the death of Tiberius by saying to Agrippa in Hebrew: *The Lion is dead*, 6572

Martha, a Syrian woman, a prophetess, 3877

Marullus sent as cavalry commander to Judea by Gaius, 6574

Mary: Gabriel appeared to her, 6041; came to the temple to present Jesus to the Lord, 6063; returned with Joseph into Galilee, 6065

Massagetae defeated, 2018

Mattathias: called the son of Asamonaeus, 3359; killed a Jew sacrificing to idols, 3360; died and buried in Modin, 3387

Matthias Curtus, the great-grandfather of Josephus, the historian, was born, 3738

Mausolus caused many cities to revolt from Artaxerxes, 1613

Mazaca, a city of Cappadocia, was renamed Caesarea, 6222

Mazaces, Darius' governor of Egypt, received Alexander, 1825

Mazares demanded Pactyes from the Cymeans and received him from the men of Chios, 928

Medeius caused the Asian Mysians to revolt from Antony, 5657

Medes: submitted themselves to the rule of Dejoces, 672; surrendered to Darius, 1368; Phraates and Artaxes conquered their king, 5645

Megabyzus: revolted from Artaxerxes, 1256; defeated the Persians, 1257; victorious again, 1258; reconciled to the king and alienated again the same year, 1259; reconciled again to the king and died of old age, 1265

Meherdates had his ears cut off when defeated by Gotarzes, 6743

Meles reigned in Lydia, 596

Memnon: betrayed Hermias, 1678; took the island of Chios by treachery, 1745; died, 1749

Memnon had a speaking statue, 6234

Memphites: son of Ptolemy Euergetes II by his sister and wife Cleopatra, 3652; killed by his father and ordered to be presented to his mother at a birthday feast, 3788

Menahem was confirmed in his kingdom by Pul, king of Assyria, 575

Menas, Prusias' envoy, incited rebellion of subjects against Prusias, 3609

Menelaus: made himself the high priest in the place of Jason, 3221; removed the golden vessels from the temple, 3249; convicted of the crime but escaped when he bribed Ptolemy to bribe the king, 3253; allied himself with Eupator's army, 3469; died a death befitting his wicked life, 3482

Menocharis, the envoy, came to Rome, 3545

Mentor: betrayed the Sidonians, 1654; conquered the enemies of the Persians, 1671

Mephibosheth: born, 397; became lame, 407

Mephramuthosis, king of Egypt, 128

Mephres, king of Egypt, 123

Merbalus reigned in Tyre, 915

Mesisimordakos reigned in Babylon, 686

Metella, the wife of Lucius Cornelius Sulla, fled from Rome to her husband, 4005

Metellus: captured many cities, 4310; took the city of Eleuthera by treachery, 4369; captured the island of Crete, 4388

Metellus, who remained loyal to Antony, was saved by the loyalty of his son, 5721

Metellus Scipio obtained the province of Syria, 4857

Methuselah: born, 19; died, 33

Meton observed the solstice and determined the lunar cycle, 1275

Metrodorus headed the embassy to Rhodes, 3304

Metrodorus Scepsis: sent as envoy from Mithridates to Tigranes the Armenian, 4174; betrayed and given honourable burial by Tigranes, 4175

Metrophanes sent Mithridates to overrun Euboea and was routed by Bruttius, 3952

Miamun, See Ramesses Miamun

Micah prophesied, 654

Milesians: revolted from the Athenians, 1314; besieged by land and sea by Cyrus, 1398; a Milesian woman was condemned for aborting her unborn child, 4082

Miltiades, Demetrius' envoy, came to Rome, 3555

Minor, See Cato Minor

Minucius Basillus, one of Caesar's murderers, was killed by his servants, 5264

Mithridates: after driven from his kingdom, went to Gabinius, 4679; killed by his brother Orodes, 4706

Mithridates: of Pergamum, gathered many supplies to bring to Caesar, who was in danger at Alexandria, 4974; killed Dioscorides, 4993; made use of the benevolent Jews, 4995; overcame the Alexandrians, 4997; made king of Bosphorus by Caesar, 5044

Mithridates: revealed the councils of the Parthians to Antony, 5546; received gold plates from Antony, 5549

Mithridates: made king of Parthia by Claudius, 6730; smothered to death and murdered by Radamistus, 6749

Mithridates I: killed, 2643; Antigonus' dream about him, 2644

Mithridates Iberus: Tiberius instigated him to invade Armenia, 6547; by deceit and force, he compelled his brother Pharasmanes to help in his plans, 6548; sent back by Claudius to receive his kingdom, 6648; invaded Armenia, 6719; when driven from his kingdom of Bosphorus by Didius the Romans, he ejected the king, 6729; asked Eunones to mediate with Caesar when his enemies had removed all other help from him, 6736; brought to Rome and addressed Claudius haughtily, 6738

Mithridates II waged war against Sinope, 2909

Mithridates of Pergamum ransacked the temple of Leucothea, 5071

Mithridates V Euergetes: king of Pontus and Lesser Armenia, entered into league with the Romans, 3606; killed by the treachery of his servants, 3817

Mithridates VI Eupator: born, 3721; succeeded his father Euergetes as king of Pontus, 3817; sent Gordius to Rome, 3908; captured Cappadocia, 3908; prepared for war against the Romans, 3918; spoke 22 languages, 3918; sent his son to govern the kingdom of Cappadocia, 3920; his generals routed Nicomedes, 3925; routed Aquilius, 3926; showed no clemency to Aquilius, 3934; received Magnesia, Mitylene and Ephesus, 3935; overran the Roman provinces in Asia, 3936; ordered massacre of over 80,000 Roman citizens in Asia, 3942; sailed to the Cos, where he found Cleopatra's treasure, 3945; returned from failed attempt to capture Rhodes, 3949; his dream, 3950; dejected when the crown was broken, 3954; suspected his friends of treachery when his men were defeated, 3973; driven from Galatia, 3973; raged against those that revolted from him, 3989; bestowed liberty on the Greek Cities, 3989; defeated by Fimbria and fled, 3996; made a league with Sulla by means of Archelaus, 4006; returned into Pontus and subdued the cities that had revolted from him, 4033; killed his son whom he had bound in golden chains, 4033; prepared an army against the Bosphorus, 4038; subdued Bosphorus, 4057; lost two divisions of his army, 4066; ordered by Sulla to get out of Cappadocia, 4067; restored Cappadocia to Ariobarzanes and sent an embassy to Rome, 4079; entered a league with Quintus Sertorius, 4093; again prepared for war against the Romans, 4107; gathered another army and routed Marcus Cotta, 4122; forced to lift the siege of Cyzicum and cross over into Bithynia, 4147; sailed for Pontus and was shipwrecked, 4165; sailed to Heraclea in Pontus with Selemus the pirate, 4169; fearful of fighting the Romans and journeyed on the Hypius River, 4170; used a large feast to capture Heraclea, 4171; his soldiers were defeated by the Romans, 4194; prepared for his flight, 4195; a horse was prepared by his eunuch for his flight, 4196; sent Bacchus, or Bacchides, to kill his sisters, wives, and concubines, 4200; his officers defect to Lucullus, 4204; his navy defeated by Triarius, 4240; conferred with his son-in-law, Tigranes, 4262; sent back into Pontus with 10,000 cavalry, 4262; fled in a cowardly manner, 4313; invaded Armenia, where he attacked the Romans scattering and killing them, 4326; defeated Marcus Fabius, 4327; defeated by Triarius, 4329; defeated Triarius, 4339; wounded, 4339; conquered Triarius with his Romans, killing over 7,000, 4340; lost courage and sent envoys to Pompey requesting peace, 4382; besieged by Pompey and escaped secretly, 4401; routed in a night battle, 4407; went to a citadel located between Greater and Lesser Armenia, 4412; gave deadly poison to his friends, 4413; rejected by Tigranes, 4414; travelled through the Scythian countries, 4443; his most esteemed concubine, Stratonice, was taken by Pompey, 4468; sent envoys to Pompey to promise him tribute if he would grant him his father's kingdom, 4485; considered an expedition into Italy, 4495; spared his son Pharnaces, who was guilty of treason against him, 4503; army refused to consider an expedition into Italy, 4504; went to his wives, concubines, and daughters and gave them all poison, 4507; unaffected by poison and the wound he gave himself, finally killed by a soldier of his bodyguard, 4508

Mithrobarzanes, Tigranes' general, was killed and his entire army fled, 4265

Mitylenian Exiles: captured Rhoetium and Antandros, 1294; defeated by the Athenians, 1295; killed by Lucullus, 4037; the city of the Mitylenians was demolished, 4064

Mizraim, the son of Ham, lead colonies into Egypt, 52

Mnemon, See Artaxerxes Mnemon

Molo, the rhetorician, was the first who spoke in the Senate without an interpreter, 4058

Molon controlled Antiochus' royal court, 2869

Monima, the Milesian, Mithridates' wife, had her throat slit, 4202

Mopsuestia was destroyed by Antiochus, Seleucus and Philip, 3906

Mordecai: honoured, 1043; instituted the feast of Purim, 1050

Moses: born, 164; Pharaoh's daughter found him in an ark of reeds, 166; killed an Egyptian, 170; God appeared to him on Mount Horeb, 174; God sent him to Pharaoh, 174; afflicted Pharaoh with ten plagues, 181; celebrated the first Passover, 189; led Israel across the Red Sea, 192; defeated the Amalekites with prayer, 193; received the law on Mount Sinai, 195; broke the golden calf into pieces (destroyed the golden calf), 201; erected the tabernacle, 213; celebrated the second Passover, 213; appointed the Levites for the ministry of the tabernacle, 219; finished the tabernacle and altar, 224; appointed 70 elders, 237; sent spies into the land of Canaan, 241; his offices and Aaron's priesthood confirmed in that the seditious were destroyed with fire and swallowed alive by the earth, 250; died, 299

Mosollamus showed folly of the seers, 2570
Mucius, See Quintus Mucius Scaevola
Mummius, See Lucius Mummius
Murcus and Ahenobarbus victorious in a naval battle, 5336
Murena, the son of Murena, praetor of Asia, was left by Lucullus to continue
    the siege, 4183
Murena, See Lucius Murena
Musicanus crucified by Alexander, 2193
Mylasians defeated by the Rhodians, 3375

Nabarzanes surrendered to Alexander, 1954
Nabuchodonosor defeated Arphaxad in battle, 710
Nachor: born, 54; died, 62
Nadab: king of Israel, 491; killed by Baasha, his successor, 492
Nadius reigned over the Babylonians, 613
Naphtha, its nature, 4268
Nebuchadnezzar: made viceroy in Babylon, 770; reigned and subdued the Jews,
    775; captured all Egyptian land between Egypt and the Euphrates River,
    782; besieged Jerusalem, 832; conquered Egypt, 881; returned to Babylon,
    882; his dream, 882; went mad for seven years, 886; restored to health and
    his kingdom, 890; died, 891
Nectanabis: king of Egypt, allied himself with Agesilaus, 1624; gave 230,000
    talents to Agesilaus, 1626; lost Egypt and fled, 1661
Nehemiah: mourned and fasted, 1227; received commission to rebuild Jerusa-
    lem, 1229; frustrated the plans of the enemy, 1233; lightened the taxes on the
    people, 1234; completed the wall in 52 days, 1235; returned to the king after
    12 years in Jerusalem, 1263
Nephereus, king of Egypt, helped the Lacedemonians, 1500
Neriglassaros reigned at Babylon, 901
Nero: ordered the city of Illium should be free from taxes, 6778; declared em-
    peror, 6806; received Caesennius Paetus scornfully for his poor handling of
    matters, 6880; favoured the Jews upon the intercession of his wife Poppaea,
    6883; watched Rome burn, 6898; raged against the Christians, 6899; kicked
    his pregnant wife, Poppaea, to death, 6922; crossed into Greece and stayed
    there till the approaching winter, 6933; sent Vespasian into Judea, 6944; com-
    mitted suicide, 6960
Nicanor, the leader of the Silver Shields, died, 1961
Nicanor: defeated by Seleucus, 2565; killed by Seleucus, 2618
Nicanor: routed by Judas Maccabeus, 3409; lived on friendly terms with Judas
    Maccabeus, 3517; King Demetrius criticised him for his kindness to Judas,
    3518; behaved treacherously to Judas, 3518; Judas withdrew from him, 3521;
    threatened the Jews that he would burn the house of God, unless they deliv-
    ered Judas to him, 3523; killed and pulled to pieces, 3525
Nicator, See Demetrius Nicator
Nicator, See Seleucus I Nicator
Nicias destroyed the Athenian army, 1310
Nicomedes became king of Bithynia, 2764
Nicomedes: son of Nicomedes Philopator, made king of Bithynia by the Senate,
    3916; driven out by his brother Socrates, 3916; restored to Bithynia and in-
    stigated by the Romans to invade Mithridates' kingdom, 3919; died without
    children and left his kingdom to the people of Rome, 4098
Nicomedes Philopator: too well-liked by the Bithynians and was sent to Rome
    by his father Prusias, 3574; invaded his father's kingdom, 3611; helped by
    Attalus against his father, 3611; died, 3916
Nicopolis: built by Pompey, 4416; the city built by Octavius Caesar, called
    Nicopolis, 5803
Nile canals are cleared, 5804
Nineveh defeated, 740
Ninus, the son of Belus, founded the Assyrian Empire, 353
Ninus, the younger, obtained the kingdom, 597
Nisibis captured by Lucullus, 4322
Noah: born, 24; sent to preach to the world, 29; died, 63
Nudus deprived of his riches by Mithridates, 4124
Numenius sent by the kings of Egypt to thank the Romans for their kindness,
    3338
Numenius, the son of Antiochus, was sent with others as envoys to Rome by the
    Jews, 3691
Nyssa, the sister of Mithridates, was captured and freed by Lucullus, 4203

Obadas, king of the Nabateans, 5883
Obadiah prophesied, 864
Ochus or Darius Ochus, became king, 1299
Ochus: the son of Artaxerxes, killed his brother Arsames, 1628; when his father
    was dead, made himself king and behaved cruelly toward his kindred, 1631;
    subdued Jericho, 1658; subjected Egypt, 1661; made Mentor the governor
    of the Asian coast, 1670; poisoned by Bagoas, 1684
Octavia: arbitrated between her husband Antony and her brother Octavius,
    5396; married Antony when pregnant from her previous husband, who
    died, 5399

Octavius: also called Octavian and Augustus, was born, 4554; heir to Julius Cae-
    sar, 5114; haughtily entertained by Antony, 5120; held games for Caesar's
    victory, 5127; raised an army, 5131; disagreed with Antony, 5137; gathered
    10,000 men who were not well-armed, 5145; met a large company coming
    from Rome to see him, 5156; marched into Etruria, 5157; rewarded the two
    Macedonian legions that defected to him, 5179; received extraordinary com-
    mand, 5181; relieved Decimus Brutus who was besieged at Mutina by Antony,
    5210; army favoured him more than the Senate, 5213; entered friendship with
    Lepidus and Antony, 5249; while consulting an augury, vultures appeared to
    him, 5253; chosen consul, 5253; received unlimited power from the Senate to
    act as he pleased and retained this power all his life for 56 years, 5258; as-
    sumed the name of Gaius Julius Caesar Octavius, 5259; an eagle sat on his
    tent and downed two ravens, 5266; defeated Brutus, 5340; divorced Claudia,
    Fulvia's daughter, 5372; entered the last league with Antony, 5396; trium-
    phal entry into Rome, 5552; made extensive preparations for war against
    Antony, 5629; when the consuls fled to Antony, he claimed they had been
    sent by him, 5633; after the consuls were gone, he did and said whatever he
    pleased, 5633; accused Antony to the common people, 5638; took Antony's
    will from the vestal virgins, 5638; publicly read Antony's will, 5638; went
    into Epirus, 5662; victory at Actium, 5692; distributed to the men and cities
    rewards and punishments according to their actions, 5703; sailed to Athens,
    5707; released the veteran army, 5716; many things decreed for his honour at
    Rome, 5719; twice shipwrecked by storms, 5729; came very speedily into Asia,
    5732; did not answer the embassy of Antony, 5735; promised Cleopatra im-
    punity if she would kill Antony, 5735; went to Syria, 5742; captured Pelusium
    when Cleopatra betrayed it, 5754; entered Alexandria, 5755; his speech in
    Greek promised a pardon to all the Egyptians, 5770; generously protected
    the children of Antony and Cleopatra, 5774; admired the size and beauty of
    Alexander the Great's tomb, 5777; did not go to Apis and said he would
    worship gods, not oxen, 5777; came to comfort Cleopatra, 5780; not taken
    with Cleopatra's enticements, 5780; sorrowed over Cleopatra's death because
    the glory of his triumph was lost, 5791; did not trust the Egyptians, 5806; did
    not place Egypt under the control of the Senate, 5806; made Gaius Cornelius
    Gallus governor of Egypt, 5807; came into Syria, 5808; went into the prov-
    ince of Asia and wintered there, 5813; showed that he obtained the empire
    by the goddess Victory, 5821; feigned abdication from the empire and was
    convinced to stay on, 5835; controlled the most dangerous provinces and the
    army, 5836; Senate controlled safe provinces, 5836; honours were decreed to
    him, 5841; Senate granted him immunity from all laws, 5869; separated
    Marcus Agrippa and Marcus Marcellus, who were at odds, 5893; marched
    into Sicilia, 5904; in Greece, he took Aegina and Eretria from the Athenians,
    5907; in Asia, he deprived the Cyzicenians of their liberty, 5913; revoked
    liberty of the Tyrians and Sidonians, 5914; returned to Rome, 5935; built a
    temple to Mars for the ensigns he regained from the Parthians, 5936; when
    the first quinquennial of his empire expired, he extended it for a further five
    years, 5941; restored liberty to the Cyzicenians, 5958; became the high priest,
    5974; burning the rest of the books of prophesy, he kept only the Sibylline
    Books, 5975; took Tiberius to replace Agrippa, 5981; amended the year in-
    stituted by Julius Caesar, 6001; called the month of Sextilis, August, 6002; as
    if unwilling, prolonged his empire, 6006; reconciled to Aretas and Herod,
    6025; staged a naval battle, 6119; grieved by the death of Gaius, 6160; would
    not abide being called a god, 6163; took the empire upon him, as if com-
    pelled, for the fourth ten-year term, 6164; restored the calendar to its perfec-
    tion, 6166; assumed the empire for another, the fifth, time, 6201; his death
    foretold, 6205; died at Nola, 6207
Octavius, See Gnaeus Octavius
Ogygian flood in Attica, 107
Olthacus: the prince of the Dandarians, promised Mithridates that he would kill
    Lucullus, 4182; courteously entertained by Lucullus, 4182; fled from Lucullus'
    camp, 4188
Olympiads, first Olympiad held, 566
Olympias: surrendered to Cassander, 2493; murdered by Cassander, 2509
omens presaging Augustus' victory, 5684
Omphis resigned to Alexander, 2068
Omri: reigned alone in Israel, 504; transferred the seat of the kingdom to Samaria,
    506; died, 507
Onesimus converted by Paul, 6906
Onesiphorus found Paul and encouraged him, 6879
Onias: the high priest, 2859; admonished and prayed for the healing of Heliodorus,
    3199
Onias: befriended Ptolemy Philometor and Cleopatra, 3484; obtained permis-
    sion to build a temple in the area of Heliopolis, 3598; took up the war on
    Cleopatra's behalf, 3639
Onias, a certain just man, was killed by the Jews for his pious prayers, 4438
Ophellas killed, 2599
Orobazus, the Parthian envoy, was heard by Sulla, 3912
Orobius, a Roman general, killed the Athenians at night, 3951
Orodes: the Parthian king, 4678; ordered Mithridates to be killed in his presence,
    4706; sent envoys to Crassus, 4746; solicited by Pompey for help in his civil

war, 4866; imprisoned envoy Lucius Hirtius against the laws of the countries, 4884; went mad when he heard about the defeat of his army, 5447; killed by his son Phraates, 5496

Orodes, one of the sons of Artabanus, was made king of Armenia, 6219

Oroeses defeated by Pompey, 4450

Oroetes, the Persian, was a tyrant, 1004

Orontes: falsely accused Tiribazus to the king, 1566; captured Tiribazus by deceit and sent him bound to the king, 1567; betrayed many cities and much treasure to Artaxerxes Mnemon, 1618

Orophernes: asked for help from Demetrius Soter against Ariarathes, 3546; expelled his brother Ariarathes and ruled tyrannically, 3549; introduced the refined debauchery of Ionia, 3550; plundered the temple of Zeus to pay his soldiers, 3557

Orosius: his record contained an error, 4861

Orus, king of Egypt, 148

Othniel conquered Cushan, 343

Otho: unaware of Vitellius' assumption of the empire, was made emperor by the soldiers, 6962; killed on the 90th day of his empire, 6962

Ovid: his birthday was the same day that both the consuls died together in battle, 5211; banished into Pontus, 6189; ended his days in Pontus, 6220

Pacorus: the son of Orodes, made war on the province of Syria, 4802; subdued all Syria, 5392; killed in battle, 5444

Paetus, See Caesennius Paetus

Pallas, Claudius' freedman, received 15 million sesterces, 6761

palms grew on Clearchus' tomb, 1534

Palmyra was about to be plundered by Antony's cavalry and the inhabitants moved across the Euphrates River, 5376

Pamphylia: envoys brought a golden crown to Rome, 3291; town of Pamphylia was restored to their former district, 5861

Pannonian legions revolted and submitted to Tiberius when terrified by a lunar eclipse, 6211

Pansa, the consul, died of a wound he received in the battle with Mark Antony, 5211

Pantomimian, antic dancing, first performed in Rome, 5898

Paphos, how their royal family was destroyed, 2585

Pappus killed by Herod for killing his brother Joseph, 5463

Parma, See Cassius of Parma

Parmenion: took Damascus by treachery, with the king's treasure and concubines, 1779; made governor of Syria, 1783; sent to be admiral of the Persian Navy, 1784

Parthians: defect from Macedonian rule, 2833; their empire, how it came to its height, 3683; their envoys desired peace with the Romans, 3912; defeated the Romans, 4758; killed Crassus, 4769; came to help Caecilius Bassus, 5087; routed by the Romans and the king of Media, 5627; beginning of the Parthians and Romans fight for control over Armenia, 6746

Parysatis: who was Cyrus' mother, buried the head of her son Cyrus, 1447; Cyrus' mother revenged his death, 1454; killed Queen Statira with poison and was banished to Babylon, 1455

Pasippidas of Sparta banished, 1365

Passover: the first that Jesus Christ celebrated, 6304; the second one that Jesus Christ celebrated, 6333; the third Passover that Jesus Christ celebrated, 6370; the fourth, wherein our Passover was killed, 6456

Paul: the Apostle, returned to Jerusalem after spending three years at Damascus, 6588; preached at Iconium with Barnabas, 6701; raptured into the third heaven, 6704; called into Macedonia by a vision, 6784; Philippians supply needs, 6791; disputed at Athens with the philosophers, 6794; came to Corinth, 6799; came to Ephesus, 6819; ended his third year in Asia, 6833; wrote his first letter to the Corinthians, 6836; sailed from Troas into Macedonia, 6840; wrote his second letter to the Corinthians, 6842; wrote his letter to the Romans, 6844; returned to Troas, 6846; came to Cos, 6850; hurried through many cities to Jerusalem, 6851; preached to the riotous Jews, 6854; appealed to Caesar, 6868; shipwrecked, 6874; came to Rome, 6878; wrote his letter to the Philippians, 6908; wrote his letter to the Hebrews, 6913; sailed into Asia and preached the gospel in Crete, 6918; wrote his first letter to Timothy, 6924; wrote to Titus, 6925; returned to Ephesus to Timothy, 6926; came to Rome for the second time and was absolved by Nero, 6929; warned of his death by revelation, 6937; wrote his second letter to Timothy, 6939; beheaded with a sword at Rome, 6949

Paulus, See Aemilius Paulus

Pausanias: freed many Greek cities, 1171; took Byzantium and sent the captives to Xerxes, 1173; his insolence, 1173; accused and dismissed, 1174; died from hunger, 1176

Pausistratus lost his navy, 3068

Pedius, See Quintus Pedius

Pekah: son of Remaliah, reigned, 583; killed 120,000 Jews, 603

Pekahiah succeeded his father Menaham, 581

Peleg: born, 47; died, 61

Peloponnesian War: began, 1277; ended, 1417

Peloponnesians: sacked the city of Iasus, 1320; murmured against Astyochus and Tissaphernes, 1335; defeated by the Athenians in a naval battle, 1399; defeated the Athenian navy at Caunus, 1501

Perdiccas: received Alexander's ring, 2358; allocated Alexander's empire, 2374; defeated Ariarathes, 2398; with Philip, destroyed two cities of Pisidia, 2400; married Nicaea, 2401; divorced Nicaea, 2406; fought with Ptolemy over Alexander's body, 2407; attacked Ptolemy in Egypt, 2417; killed, 2419

Pericles died, 1285

period, See Calippic Period

Perperna, See Marcus Perperna

Persepolis sacked and burned by Alexander, 1919

Perseus: ambushed Eumenes, 3225; after his dialogue with the Romans, wrote letter supporting his position, 3235; defeated the Romans but unable to obtain a peace treaty with Licinius, the consul, 3240; routed by Licinius and fled to Pella, 3246; worked through Prusias to obtain peace with Romans, 3292; he and Gentius, the king of the Illyrians, decreed to send envoys to the Romans, 3304; solicited Eumenes with three options, 3306; talked with Eumenes concerning the redemption of the captives, 3306; defeated, 3323; came to Amphipolis in Thrace with almost 500 Cretans, 3324; fled to the temple of Castor and Pollux in Samothracia, 3324; murdered Evander, his best friend, 3330; deceived by Oroandes, the Cretian, and fled to a corner of the temple, 3331; surrendered himself with his son to Octavius, 3332

Persians: routed the Ionians, 1066; twice defeated the Carians, but were finally defeated by treachery, 1068; defeated Ionians in a naval battle, 1073; destroyed Miletus, 1074; took Chios, Lesbos, and Tenedos, 1076; defeated by the Athenians, 1093; twice defeated under Xerxes, 1127; scattered by Pausanias, 1154; defeated by the Egyptians and Athenians on sea, 1218; defeated by the Egyptians and Athenians on land, 1219; many slaughtered, 1219; under Megabyzus, defeated the Egyptians and Greeks, 1226; made a league with the Athenians, 1250; helped Cyrus, 1440; large expedition against the Egyptians came to naught, 1586; many slaughtered at battle of Issus, 1771; 300,000 killed in battle at Issus, 1886; Alexander plundered the Persian riches, 1887; revolt against Antiochus Theos, 2834

Perusia captured by Octavius, 5389

pestilence infects the Jews severely, 5828

Peter: the Apostle healed Aeneas and Tabitha, 6601; warned of his death by revelation, 6937; wrote his second letter, 6938; crucified at Rome, 6949

Petronius: succeeded Cornelius Gallus as governor of Egypt, 5849; defeated the Ethiopians, 5888; took Premnis, a city of Ethiopia, 5889; compelled Candace to make peace, 5908; made governor of Syria by Gaius, 6614; prepared a statue for Gaius Caligula, 6617; Jewish petitions delay setting up Gaius' statue, 6630; praised by Gaius for his plans to subdue the Jews, 6631

Peucestes: added to Alexander's bodyguard, 2253; made governor of Persia, 2269; watched by all, 2489; disputed with Antigenes, 2490; sent troops to Persia, 2494

Pharaohnecho: reigned in Egypt, his loss and expeditions, 750; fought with the Assyrians, 754

Pharasmanes defeated Orodes, 6549

Pharisees: contended with the Sadducees, 3843; convicted of treason and killed by Herod, 6038

Pharnabazus: defeated the Greeks, 1515; made a friendship with Agesilaus, 1517; plundered the fields of Abydus, 1529

Pharnabazus conquered by Publius Canidius Crassus, 5499

Pharnaces: sent envoys about peace, 3172; scorned the Romans, 3176; sent envoys and broke his promises, 3178

Pharnaces: born to Mithridates Eupator, 3892; noted as a friend of the Romans, 4503; sent his father's corpse to Pompey, 4558; revolted from the Romans during Roman civil war, 4882; occupied Pontus, 5009; advanced to the Lesser Armenia, 5013; sent envoys to Caesar, 5029; ordered by Caesar to get out of Pontus, 5034; defeated by Caesar, 5036; fled again to Sinope, 5040; surrendered Sinope to Domitius Calvinus, 5049; killed by Asander, 5054

Pharos built, 2720

Phasael: made governor of Jerusalem by his father, Antipater, 5026; had a son also called Phasael, 5028; gained the friendship of the Jews, 5051; angry with Hyrcanus, 5286; killed himself, rather than be executed by Parthians, 5413

Phaselis built in Pamphylia, 696

Pheroras: obtained the tetrarchy from Caesar at the request of his brother Herod, 5918; fell madly in love with his maid, 5995; sent back by Herod into his tetrarchy, 6044; died, 6047

Philadelphians started their epoch of time, 4556

Philadelphus, See Attalus Philadelphus

Philadelphus, See Ptolemy II Philadelphus

Philetaerus, the first king of Pergamum, 2735

Philip: sent Nicanor to exterminate the Jews, 3404; prepared an expedition against Lysias, 3476; killed by Eupator, 3489

Philip: besieged Perinthus, 1683; made general of the war against the Persians, 1686; sent three commanders into Asia before him, 1687; murdered, 1699

Philip: the son of Herod, received part of his father's kingdom from Augustus, 6111; the tetrarch died, 6530

Ptolemy VIII Euergetes II: (also called Physcon) opposed the plans of Cleopatra, 3640; compelled Cleopatra to marry him, 3640; killed her son in his mother's arms on their very wedding day, as well as many others, 3640; executed certain Cyrenians for rebuking him for his courtesan, Irene, 3652; divorced Cleopatra, 3713; married her daughter after raping her, 3713; his subjects secretly fled to Cyprus, 3777; killed his oldest son, 3788; ordered his son Memphites, whom he had by Cleopatra, to be killed and presented to her at her birthday feast, 3788; commended a new king to the Syrians, 3804; died, 3828

Ptolemy X Alexander I: reigned over Cyprus, 3833; the brother of Ptolemy Lathurus, succeeded his brother in the kingdom of Egypt, 3852

Ptolemy XI Alexander II: killed his wife Cleopatra, 4065; common error in the length of his reign refuted, 4065; the king of Egypt, expelled by Alexandrians, 4435; appointed the people of Rome as his heirs in the kingdom, 4476

Ptolemy XII Auletes: started to reign in Egypt, 4435; came to Rome, 4635; killed and bribed the Alexandrian envoys, so that they would not hinder his cause in the Senate, 4651; journeyed to Ephesus, 4664; lost hope for his kingdom, 4664; restored to his kingdom by Gabinius, 4699; killed his daughter, Bernice, 4703; died, 4789

Ptolemy XIII: the youth, expelled Cleopatra (both his wife and his sister) from the kingdom, 4880; routed by Caesar, drowned when his ship sank, 5001

Ptolemy XIV the younger, was poisoned by his wife and sister, Cleopatra, 5174

Publius Canidius was executed by Octavius, 5775

Publius Celer was accused by the Asians, 6825

Publius Clodius: when accused, bought justice, 4586; despised the delegation given to him, 4623; took revenge on Ptolemy, king of Cyprus, by confiscating his kingdom, 4628; sent Tigranes away free, 4630; slandered Cato's administration of affairs, 4676

Publius Cornelius Dolabella: reproached Caesar after he had been murdered, 5105; when consul, he obtained the province of Syria and the management of the Parthian war, 5112; accused by Rhodians, 5188

Publius Cornelius Spinther: proconsul of Cilicia, was called imperator, 4739; triumphed at Rome, 4827

Publius Dolabella, proconsul of Africa, killed Tacfarinas and ended the Numidian war, 6272

Publius Lentulus unwillingly received by the Rhodians, 5229

Publius Licinius Crassus: high priest, made war against Aristonicus, 3752; skilful in the Greek language, 3758; his severity against a carpenter, 3759; died, 3761

Publius Rupilius ended the slave war in Sicily, 3750

Publius Rutilius, Marcus Cotta's general, was killed with most of the army, 4122

Publius Rutilius Rufus: unjustly convicted, 3900; went into voluntary banishment, 3902; happier in his banishment than when at Rome, 3903; disguised as a philosopher to avoid being killed, 3944

Publius Servilius: the proconsul, subdued Cilicia, 4083; tamed the Isaurians' pirates, 4092; rode in triumph, 4116

Publius Turullius was turned over to Caesar by Antony and executed, 5740

Publius Ventidius Bassus: made consul, 5268; routed Labienus, 5416; extorted money from the government of Palestine, 5427; deceived Pacorus with Channaeus' help, 5440; defeated the Parthians, 5444; carried Pacorus' head about Syria and easily subdued that country, 5446; compelled Antiochus Commagene to seek peace, 5450

Pylades Mimus expelled from Rome and was restored by Augustus, 5943

Pyrrhus: his exploits, 2675; after Neoptolemus was killed, took over the kingdom of Epirus, 2678; his exploits, 2697; defeated by Romans, 2800; returned to Epirus, 2801; his exploits, 2809

Pythagoras: stayed 22 years in Egypt, 925; knew the Magi at Babylon, 982

Quintilis, the month, was called July, in honour of Julius Caesar, 5091

Quintilius Varus: settled matters in Judea and returned to Antioch, 6092; his son destroyed Sepphoris, 6103

Quintus Marcius sent as proconsul into Asia, 4348

Quintus Metellus, the Numidian, studied philosophy when banished, 3884

Quintus Metellus had a triumph for Crete, 4571

Quintus Mucius Scaevola: sent as proconsul into Asia, 3896; won the people to the Romans by his fair dealings, 3896

Quintus Oppius, proconsul of Pamphylia, fell into the hands of Mithridates, 3932

Quintus Orinius executed by Octavius, 5775

Quintus Pedius: led the third triumph for Spain, 5086; introduced the Pedian Law, which banished all Caesar's murderers, 5260

Quintus Postumius, the senator, was killed at the command of Antony, 5667

Quintus Tullius Cicero: appointed praetor for Asia, 4584; freed the cities of Asia from the cost of outfitting a navy, 4589; a third year was added to his praetorship, 4616; left the province, 4626

Quirinius: and Cyrenius are the same among the Greeks, and are the same as Publius Sulpicius Quirinius with the Romans, 6052; married Lepida, 6138; made governor of Syria, 6179

Rabirius Postumus: at Alexandria, tried to recover the money he had lent Ptolemy, 4704; accused and defended by Cicero, 4744

Radamistus: enticed the leaders of the Armenians to revolt, 6746; killed Mithridates and his wife, 6749; flung his own wife, wounded, into a river, lest she should fall into enemy hands, 6752

Ramesses reigned in Egypt, 160

Ramesses Miamun: reigned in Egypt, 161; oppressed the Israelites, 161; his edict concerning the drowning of the Hebrew children, 163; died, 172

Rathotis reigned in Egypt, 154

Razis: exposed his body and life for Judaism, 3358; called the *Father of the Jews*, 3358; ripped out his bowels, flung them among the crowd and died, 3524

Rebekah conceived twins, 98

Rechabites left their tents and went to Jerusalem, 774

Regebelos reigned in Babylon, 685

Rehoboam: born, 456; ten tribes revolted against him, 477; forsook God's law, 485; plundered by Shishak, king of Egypt, 486

Reu: born, 51; died, 67

Reuben born, 118

Rhascupolis, king of Thrace, was killed, 6241

Rheomithras exposed to the king the ringleaders of those who revolted, 1620

Rhodians: captured Demetrius' ships, 2628; made Ptolemy a god, 2629; prepared for war with the Byzantines, 2904; prepared for war against Antiochus the Great, 3013; navy helped Romans against Antiochus the Great, 3067; embassy received from Rome about Lycia, 3197; received envoys from Perseus concerning pending war with Rome, 3235; envoys courteously entertained by Quintus Marcius, the consul, and Gaius, the admiral of the fleet, 3274; Senate treated envoys courteously, 3274; their arrogant embassy to the Romans, 3293; decreed to give a benign answer to Perseus and Gentius, 3314; entreated Popilius to help mediate a peace, 3320; made a decree that whoever favoured Perseus would be executed, 3328; Romans despise their embassy, 3369; an uncertain answer was given them, 3371; denied Roman friendship, 3380; sought their ancient right in Lycia and Caria from the Romans, 3496; those Italians who escaped from Asia, found sanctuary at Rhodes, 3948; renewed their league with the Romans, 4783; refused aid to Cassius and Brutus, 5290; crucified some Romans, 6686; had their liberty restored once more, 6779

Rhoemetalces received Cotys' former kingdom from Caligula, 6596

Rome: founded, 590; embassy to Philip, 2978; embassy to Antiochus, 2998; proclaimed freedom for Greece, 3015; proclaimed liberty for Greece, 3017; embassy to the Carthaginians about Hannibal, 3028; first worshipped as a goddess, 3033; envoys to Antiochus and Eumenes, 3044; Romans go to Ephesus, 3045; Roman navy strained resources of Phocaea, 3063; conquered Antiochus the Great, 3099; peace treaty with Antiochus the Great, 3111; subdued the Galatians, 3128; imposed law and order on the Galatians, 3146; changed the hostages of Antiochus, 3199; sent envoys to the kings in league with them, 3230; prepared for war against Perseus, 3232; temple dedicated to Rome as a goddess, 3265; sent envoys to Prusias, 3569; frustrated by Prusias' impertinence, renounced his friendship, 3570; honourably received Simon's envoys, 3691; 80,000 executed at Mithridates' command, 3944; offended that Antony led Artabazes in triumph at Alexandria, 5617

Roxane bore a son, 2362

Roxane, the sister of Mithridates, perished by poison, 4202

Rufinus received command of three legions from Julius Caesar, 5097

Rufus, See Publius Rutilius Rufus

Rutilius, See Publius Rutilius Rufus

Sabacon burned Boccaris alive, 617

Sabbath: Jews burned to death in cave because their law prohibited fighting on the Sabbath, 3361; the keeping of the Sabbath hindered the Jews from defending their temple, 4521

Sabinus, Caesar's governor, made violent search for the royal treasure in Judea, 6092

sacrifices were performed in the temple at Jerusalem, even when Pompey was attacking the temple, 4524

sacrilege: of Antiochus was punished, 3425; Cassius committed, 5317; Sextus Pompeius plundered Nicaea and Nicomedia, 5576

Saddok stirred up strife among the Jews, 6182

Sadyattes: king of Lydia, 733; invaded the Milesians, 742

Salah: born, 45; died, 89

Salome: Joseph's wife, accused her husband Joseph to Herod, 5604; divorced her husband Costobarus, 5844

Samaria was levelled to the ground by Hyrcanus, 3841

Samaritans: burned Andromachus alive, 1846; Alexander avenged the death of Andromachus, 1847; denied they were Jews and pretended they were originally Sidonians for fear of persecution, 3335; petitioned that their temple at Gerizim might be called the temple of Zeus of Greece, 3335; seduced by an impostor and punished by Pilate, 6564

Sambus fled to save himself, 2191

Samenians, the queen of the Samenians, warred with the Parthians, 3909

Samians: revolted from the Athenians, 1267; defeated in naval battle, 1268; surrendered, 1272

acknowledged God as the author of the Jewish calamity, 6979; celebrated the birthday of his brother Domitian at Caesarea, 6982; celebrated the birthday of his father at Berytus, 6983; triumphed with his father at Rome, 6984; obtained the name Imperator, 6986; did not marry Bernice lest he offend the Romans, 6999

Tobit (or Tibia) buried the dead, 670

Tola judged Israel, 361

Torquatus: persuaded Ptolemy the younger, that he should not go to Cyprus, 3513

Tower of Babel constructed, 49

Trachonites: 40 fled to Herod's enemy, Syllaeus, in Arabia Nabatea, 5985; in Herod's absence, resumed their plundering, 6000; invaded Judea and Coelosyria, 6000; became the more troublesome, 6005

Trebonius, See Gaius Trebonius

tribune power given by Senate to Octavius for as long as he lived, 5554

Triumvirs Octavius, Lepidus, and Antony appointed to run the government for five years, 5271

Trocmians, a tribe of the Galatians, were unable to capture Cappadocia, 3438

Troxobor, the captain of the Cilicians, was killed by Antiochus, 6766

Troy conquered by the Greeks, 373

Tryphena: killed her sister Cleopatra, 3832; a victim of her own wickedness, 3835

Tryphon: honourably received Jonathan and then deceived him, 3661; captured Jonathan and many of his soldiers by treachery, 3661; killed Jonathan, 3665; killed Antiochus Theos treacherously, 3669; sent a gold statue to Rome, 3670; his soldiers defected to Cleopatra, 3688; received into Adora and besieged by Antiochus, 3696; sailed for Orthosia, 3700; by scattering money slowed his pursuers, 3704; died, 3705

Tullius, See Quintus Tullius Cicero

Tullius Cimber: drunk, 5130; one of Caesar's murderers, 5237; hastened to help Cassius, 5237

Tyrannio: the grammarian, was taken and freed, 4213; organized Cicero's library, 4669

Tyre: besieged, 866; surrendered to Nebuchadnezzar, 878; Tyre ruled by judges, 894; obtained her liberty, 1053; sent a crown of gold and provisions to Alexander, whom they kept out of their city, 1788; besieged, 1788; bound the image of Apollo with chains, 1801; captured, and 2,000 citizens crucified, 1805; surrendered to Antigonus, 2551

Tyrians were admitted into the Senate, 4695

Ummidius Quadratus was informed against the Jews, 6763

Uriah prophesied, 765

Urim and Thummin and the other stones in the high priest's breastplate lost their lustre because of the sins of the people, 3848

Uxians country subdued by Alexander, 1905

Uzziah: born, 548; succeeded his father Amaziah, 553

Valerius, See Lucius Valerius Flaccus

Valerius Gratus appointed governor of Judea, 6217

Vardanes: invited by the Parthians to be their king, 6718; fought with his brother Gotarzes for the kingdom, 6718; reconciled with his brother, 6720; overcame Gotarzes later, while he was raising troops, 6726; while intending to make war on the Romans, was killed by the Parthians, 6727

Varus, See Quintilius Varus

Velleius Paterculus, a flatterer of Tiberius Caesar, 5919

Venator, See Prusias Venator

Ventidius, See Publius Ventidius Bassus

Ventidius Cumanus succeeded Tiberius Alexander as the governor of the Jews, 6722

Vespasian: sent by Nero into Judea, 6944; cut off Tarichea, 6951; plundered and burned the cities of the Gadarenes, 6957; heard of Nero's death and he and Titus deferred the Jewish war, 6964; sailed into Italy, sent his son Titus into Judea, to finish the Jewish war, 6968

Vibius Marsus succeeded Petronius in the province of Syria, 6662

Vibius Serenus, after he was banished, he was falsely accused by his son and condemned, 6273

Vitellius, See Aulus Vitellius

Vitellius, See Lucius Vitellius

Vologeses: succeeded his father Venones, 6745; sought to control Armenia through envoys, but failed, 6880

Vonones: one of the sons of Phraates III was made king of Parthia by Caesar, 6170; when deprived of his kingdom, sought Tiberius' help in vain, 6219; the king of the Medes was summoned into the Parthian Kingdom, but had a short reign, 6219; when captured in flight, he was returned and executed, 6235

war, See Peloponnesian War

wines made when Lucius Opimius was consul were still around in the time of Pliny, 3827

wonders, See Ancient Wonders

Xanthians defeated by Brutus and killed themselves, 5300

Xenoetas, Antiochus' general, killed with his men, 2886

Xenophon's generosity to the goddess Diana, 1522

Xerxes: declared king, 1099; subdued the Egyptians, 1102; gathered a large army and navy, 1104; dug through the isthmus and bridged the Hellespont with ships, 1107; his cruelty to the son of Pythius, the Lydian, 1108; saw citadel of King Priam, 1110; wept at the sight of his large army, 1111; cast a golden vial into the Hellespont, 1112; the number of his ships and army, 1114; Leonidas opposed Xerxes' army by land, 1121; Eurybiades opposed Xerxes' army by sea, 1123; captured Athens, 1124; twice defeated by the Greeks, 1127; army plagued with a pestilence, 1137; fled in a fishing boat, 1140; his incest and adulteries, 1170; celebrated the anniversary of his kingdom, 1172; had his throat cut in bed by Artabanus, 1178

Xerxes: succeeded his father, 1291; murdered by his brother, 1296

Xiphares, Mithridates' son by Stratonice was killed by his father while his mother looked on, 4469

Zachariah, the son of Jeroboam II; reigned, 564; killed, 568

Zacharias: with his wife, Elizabeth, lived in distressing times, 5484; saw the angel Gabriel, 6027

Zamaris, the Jew of Babylon, erected citadels through Trachonitis and defended those who travelled from Babylon to Jerusalem, 6037

Zarbienus: king of the Gordians killed by Tigranes, 4229; Lucullus held a funeral for him, 4302

Zarmarus, the Indian sophist, cast himself into a burning pyre, 5934

Zealots: of the Jews would not listen to reason, 6943; made Phanni, a common person, the high priest, 6954; disagreed among themselves, 6956

Zebinas recommended as king to the Syrians by Ptolemy Physcon, 3804

Zebinas, See Alexander Zebinas

Zechariah, the priest, stoned to death, 544

Zechariah: the prophet, 1018; his vision and consolation given, 1023

Zedekiah: born, 746; reigned, 806; admonished by Jeremiah, 807; rebelled, 828; captured, blinded, and carried into Babylon in bonds, 849

Zenobia, Radamistus' wife, was wounded, thrown into the waters, and saved by shepherds, 6752

Zenobius: captured the citadels of the Chians, 3974; put into prison by the Ephesians and was killed, 3976

Zenodorus: encouraged the thieves, 5878; persuaded the Gadarenes that he would free them from Herod's dominion, 5915; died, 5916

Zenodotian citizens perfidiously beheaded the Romans admitted into their city, 4726

Zeugma, a little town located on Euphrates, taken from the king of the Commagenians, 4694

Zipoetes died, 2764

Zober, the king of Albania, 5499